DISCOVERING LITERATURE

Fiction, Poetry, and Drama

HANS P. GUTH
GABRIELE L. RICO

San Jose State University

A BLAIR PRESS BOOK

PRENTICE HALL, ENGLEWOOD CLIFFS, NJ 07632

Library of Congress Cataloging-in-Publication Data

Guth, Hans Paul
    Discovering literature / Hans P. Guth and Gabriele L. Rico.
        p.   cm.
    "A Blair Press book."
    Includes index.
    ISBN 0-13-219734-0
    1. English language—Rhetoric.   2. Literature—Collections.
    3. College readers.   I. Rico, Gabriele L.   II. Title.
    PE1417.G866   1993
    808—dc20   92-30035
                                                                    CIP

Cover designer: Thomas Nery
Prepress buyer: Herb Klein
Manufacturing buyers: Robert Anderson and Patrice Fraccio
Photo researchers: Joelle Burrows and Lori Morris-Nantz
Cover art: Michelangelo, *The Creation of Adam* (detail), Vatican, Sistine Chapel, 1508–1512.
Scala/Art Resource. Diego Rivera, *The Flower Vendor* (detail), 1949. Museo Espaniol de Arte
Contemporaneo, Madrid.

Acknowledgments appear on pages 1613–1624, which constitute a continuation of the copyright
page.

Blair Press
The Statler Building
20 Park Plaza, Suite 1113
Boston, MA 02116-4399

 © 1993 by Prentice Hall, Inc.
A Simon & Schuster Company
Englewood Cliffs, NJ 07632

Printed in the United States of America
10 9 8 7 6 5 4 3 2 1

ISBN 0-13-219734-0

Prentice-Hall International (UK) Limited, *London*
Prentice-Hall of Australia Pty. Limited, *Sydney*
Prentice-Hall Canada Inc., *Toronto*
Prentice-Hall Hispanoamericana, S.A., *Mexico*
Prentice-Hall of India Private Limited, *New Delhi*
Prentice-Hall of Japan, Inc., *Tokyo*
Simon & Schuster Asia Pte. Ltd., *Singapore*
Editora Prentice-Hall do Brasil, Ltda., *Rio de Janerio*

PREFACE
To the Instructor

Everything is new under the sun.
CZESLAW MILOSZ

Silence is the real crime against humanity.
NADYEZHDA MANDELSHTAM

The purpose of *Discovering Literature* is to help today's students discover the life of the imagination and the power of literature. In this book we set out

✧ to help students (many of them non-readers) become active and responsive readers;

✧ to do justice to the emotional and imaginative as well as the intellectual dimensions of literature;

✧ to contribute to the task of redefining the canon, making works by women and by authors from culturally diverse backgrounds an integral part of the study of literature;

✧ to help students bring their own imagination and creativity into play;

✧ to talk to today's students in a lively, supportive, and accessible style designed to demystify traditional terms and categories;

✧ to provide more motivation, guidance, and student models for writing about literature than any comparable text.

REDEFINING THE CANON

Discovering Literature provides balanced coverage of the rich diversity of our literary culture. We have aimed at a fruitful interaction of classics and moderns (and we have included many modern classics). We have aimed at a balance of women and men—for example, more than half of the short stories are by women. We frequently juxtapose traditional or mainstream authors with writers from culturally diverse backgrounds.

Rediscovering the Heritage   Classics are works that speak to readers across distances in time or place. Our reward as teachers comes when classics are rediscovered by a new generation of students. *Discovering Literature* tries to make students sense the enduring freshness and power of classic stories (by Joyce, Welty, Steinbeck), of classic poems (by Donne, G. M. Hopkins, Millay), and of classic plays (by Sophocles, Shakespeare, Miller, Hansberry). The book features fresh readings of authors like Emily Dickinson, Robert Frost, and Flannery O'Connor.

Tomorrow's Classics We take special pride in recognizing contemporary writers who write with integrity and passion. The book highlights poems by poets like Sharon Olds, Denise Levertov, William Stafford, and Gwendolyn Brooks; short fiction by writers like Alice Walker and Bobbie Ann Mason; drama by Caryl Churchill, Wendy Wasserstein, and August Wilson.

Multicultural Literacy A central aim of teaching literature is the broadening of imaginative sympathy. This book is rich in selections by authors who offer new perspectives—Third World and non-Western writers like Yukio Mishima, Wole Soyinka, Gabriel García Márquez; writers who dramatize the meeting of cultures, like Barahti Mukherjee; or feminist writers and critics listening to the "unheard voices" of Ophelia, of Jocasta, of Linda Loman.

Juxtapositions Paired readings help students see the presence of the past or the continuity of perennial themes in works rooted in diverse cultural traditions. Often a classic is seen in a fresh light as it is juxtaposed with a modern story, poem, or play on the same theme—an abridged modern version of the medieval *Everyman* is juxtaposed with Luis Valdez' play about a modern Everyman sent as a G. I. to Vietnam. Often juxtapositions help students see the continuity between canonized traditional readings and newer voices—a short story by Sherwood Anderson juxtaposed with one by Jamaica Kincaid, a poem by John Donne juxtaposed with one by N. Scott Momaday.

Authors Covered in Depth Featured authors are covered in depth with a rich array of biographical and critical materials. The major author of fiction selected for close study is Flannery O'Connor. Major featured poets are Emily Dickinson (with focus on the poet's voice), Robert Frost (with focus on poet and persona), and Gwendolyn Brooks (with focus on commitment and universality).

THE ACTIVE READER

The questions and activities following literary selections promote the ideal of the active, involved, empathetic reader. Several strands intermesh in the after-selection apparatus: "The Receptive Reader"—promoting close, attentive reading; "The Personal Response"—validating the personal connection that makes the literature meaningful for readers; and "The Creative Dimension"—fostering the creative participation that brings the readers' own imaginations into play and helps them enter imaginatively into a writer's world.

DISCOVERING LITERATURE

The Receptive Reader This strand promotes close reading (and rereading) of story or poem or play, encouraging openness to the difficult and new. Questions and discussions focus on how details and formal elements serve the larger whole. (The questions encourage exploration not only of the what but also of the why and so what.)

The Personal Response Questions and activities under this heading validate the reader's personal response, doing justice to the imaginative and emotional as well as the intellectual appeal of literature. Students are encouraged to find the personal connection, to relate what they read to their own experience.

The Creative Dimension Creative activities following many selections bring the reader's imagination into play. Students are invited, for instance, to re-create a haunting image or dominant impression, to write a sequel to a classic story, to dramatize a key moment or scene, or to resee a story or play from the point of view of a different character.

A DYNAMIC CRITICAL PERSPECTIVE

This book owes a special debt to the dynamic variety of contemporary literary criticism and literary theory. We are indebted to provocative recent readings of authors like John Steinbeck, Emily Dickinson, and Flannery O'Connor; to probing readings of authors from Shakespeare and Ibsen to Gilman and Millay from a feminist perspective.

Updating the Critical Tradition For decades, literature texts in the tradition of the New Criticism taught the elements of literature as if they were ends in themselves (contrary to the spirit of the best New Critics). The best current criticism has moved beyond a formalistic preoccupation with the technical workings of literature—without abandoning the tradition of close, faithful attention to the text that is the major legacy of the twentieth-century critical tradition. Throughout this book we aim at the right balance of close reading, personal engagement, and creative participation.

Correlating Form and Meaning In teaching students to respond to the formal elements of literature, we focus on how setting, character, point of view, image, metaphor, or irony serves its larger human meaning. Setting, for instance, is more than a matter of physical location; when we study setting, we focus on the world a story or a play creates, which may bring with it a characteristic history, set of assumptions, or way of life. Point of view is more than a technical concern; when we study point of view, we become aware of the window a story or poem opens on the world.

The Range of Interpretation As Pablo Neruda has said, it takes two poets to make a poem: The poet who wrote it and the poet-reader who brings the letters on the page to life in the theater of the mind. This book explores the range of both critics' reactions and students' responses to key works. Major critical trends are shown in exceptionally accessible critical excerpts representing the range of interpretation for selected authors: Flannery O'Connor, Franz Kafka, Emily Dickinson, and Robert Frost. Shakespeare's *Hamlet* serves as a test case for how a great classic serves as a mirror in which different readers see their own preoccupations, their own concerns, their own faces. Samplings of varied student responses encourage students to give voice to their own individual readings of and reactions to the texts.

A TEXT FOR TEACHERS AND LEARNERS

Our aim is to help teachers find *a way into* literature for their students—regardless of the students' previous experiences or the preconceptions they bring to the reading. We have made it our special concern to help teachers overcome negative attitudes that students may bring with them from previous encounters with poetry or with Shakespeare.

A Lively, Accessible Style   To make key terms and categories come to life for today's students means initiating students who tend to be unschooled in mastering demanding concepts or new terms. We try not to give students technically correct "dictionary definitions" purporting to take care of key terms once and for all. Instead, we try to make students see the need for or the vital significance of a key term. We focus on essentials first, having students discover complications and finer points later. We provide the reinforcement needed if students are to make key concepts their own.

A Learning Sequence   The organization of the book often leads students from the more accessible to the more challenging. (Literal chronological sequence is one thing; the dynamics of learning and discovery are another.) For instance, Ibsen, who still speaks directly to contemporary audiences concerned with feminist themes, appears *before* Shakespeare and Molière as part of the students' introduction to drama. In the chapter on Greek drama, *Antigone* (Sophocles' earlier play) appears first, because of its immediate contemporary resonance among idealistic young readers. It is followed by *Oedipus Rex* as the touchstone for Aristotle's and subsequent definitions of tragedy.

Cross-References   "Cross-references" for discussion or writing invite students to explore connections between selections related in theme or form—helping them discover recurrent patterns and illuminating contrasts, helping them see a familiar selection from a fresh perspective.

Inviting Shakespeare Editions   This book includes two new glossed (rather than footnoted) student editions—*Hamlet* and *A Midsummer Night's Dream*. Specially prepared for this volume, marginal glosses, close at hand and available at a glance, illuminate difficult passages and provide the closest modern meaning in the context of a line. Our ambition has been to make our introduction to Shakespeare more inviting, more intelligible, and more motivating than that in any competing book.

WRITING ABOUT LITERATURE

We have tried to provide more guidance, encouragement, and recognition for student writing than any comparable text. Guidelines for writing about literature and sample student papers do not appear in a one-size-fits-all writing chapter or as an afterthought in an appendix. Instead, they come with *each* chapter.

Writing Workshops   The writing workshops following each chapter focus on the process that makes substantial, purposeful, live student writing take shape. Students repeatedly see sample assignments move from prewriting (journal writing, note-taking, clustering, brainstorming) to drafting and from there to instructor response and peer critique and then to revision and final editing.

The Imaginative Dimension   As part of both after-selection apparatus and the writing workshops, imaginative writing opportunities enable students to give voice to their own experience and bring their own creativity into play.

Model Student Papers   A wealth of motivated, well-developed student writing provides models for class discussion of writing strategies and for peer review. Emphasis is on the potential, the promise, of student writing. Peer editors are encouraged to help student writers build on their strengths as well as to correct their weaknesses.

Research and Documentation   *Discovering Literature* initiates students into library research and sets up an ample choice of research paper projects on literary topics. The text provides guidelines and models of documented papers for *each* genre—short story, poetry, and drama. Pointed instructions elucidate for the student the mysteries of the current MLA documentation style, clarifying the rationale while giving a wealth of sample entries.

ACKNOWLEDGMENTS

Working on this book has been a privilege and a joy. We owe special thanks to Kathleen Evans, who did first-rate work while helping us with many editing and writing tasks. Nancy Perry of Blair Press had the vision to make this book possible, and she and Denise Wydra accomplished the impossible, coordinating the work of perceptive, dedicated reviewers and shepherding a complex enterprise. We owe a special debt to the admirable patience and competence of Julie Sullivan, who saw the book through production.

We are indebted to students whose intelligence, curiosity, and imagination have kept alive our faith in the power of literature and in the human enterprise. Of the many students from whose writing we have learned and who have allowed us to use or adapt their papers, we want to thank especially Debbie Nishimura, Andrea Sandke, Olivia Nunez, Francia Stephens, Mike DeAngelis, Dea Nelson, Kam Chieu, Greg Grewell, Johanna Wright, Merritt Ireland, Linda Spencer, Elizabeth Kerns, Conard Mangrum, Joyce Halenar, Marilyn Johnson, Michael Guth, John Newman, Judith Gardner, Pamela Cox, Rita Farkas, Barbara Hill, Melody Brune, Paul Francois, Ruth Randall, Katheryn Crayton-Shay, Dorothy Overstreet, Bill Irwin, Ruth Veerkamp, Martha Kell, Kevin McCabe, Thomas Perez-Jewell, Janelle Ciraulo, Irina Raicu, Joyce Sandoval, Catherine Hooper, Gail Bowman, Todd Marvin, and Catherine Russell.

Among the colleagues who pored over the manuscript and shared with us their enthusiasms and apprehensions, we want to thank especially William E. Cain, Wellesley College; Patricia E. Connors, Memphis State University; John L. Davis, The University of Texas at San Antonio; Kitty Chen Dean, Nassau Community College; Ellen Dugan-Barrette, Brescia College; Carla Johnson, St. Mary's College; Bob Mayberry, University of Nevada at Las Vegas; Susan J. Miller, Santa Fe Community College; Patricia G. Morgan, Louisiana State University; Melita Schaum, University of Michigan, Dearborn; William E. Sheidley, University of Connecticut; and Brent Spencer, Creighton University.

Working with colleagues from around the country has renewed our faith in our common task. As members of our profession, in spite of the political and theoretical allegiances that divide us, we share the love of learning, the love of language, and the love of literature. May this book give pleasure to those who teach and learn from it.

HANS P. GUTH
GABRIELE L. RICO

BRIEF CONTENTS

CONTENTS

OTHER VOICES/OTHER VISIONS *Poems for Further Reading* 784

WRITING ABOUT LITERATURE
Writing Workshops at a Glance

some way or at some level with a character caught between conflicting role models or rival influences—whether father or mother, school as against church, or traditional gender roles versus the right of people to realize their own potential. Many young people reach a stage where they have to make choices, chart their own course. Many at some point try to break free—trying to be themselves rather than what the family, their religion, the school, the team, or the gang wants them to be.

Release Your Own Creativity   Creativity is part of everyone's birthright. There is a poet buried in every one of us. You will often make a story, poem, or play truly your own if you try an imaginative or creative response. You may choose to re-create in your own way a key image in a poem, following the train of associations it set in motion. Or you may want to re-create a haunting overall impression that a story imprinted on your mind. You are likely to get more fully into the spirit of a play if you look at its world through the eyes of a main character—perhaps starting an imaginary monologue with "I, Antigone, . . ." or "I, Hamlet, . . ." At other times, you may want to see the world of a play through the eyes of a supporting character, as when you look at Shakespeare's *Hamlet* through the eyes of Ophelia, the young woman he rejected and whose life ended in madness and suicide.

Write about What You Read   When you write about literature, you write to share your impressions with others—but you write first of all to find out what your own considered reactions *are*. You want to *learn* as much as to enlighten others. You will read more attentively when you know that you are going to write about a story, poem, or play. When you keep a reading log or journal, you have a chance to record revealing details, striking quotations, first impressions, tentative conclusions, or personal reactions. When you prepare for a formal paper, you reread, you take notes, you reconsider. You sort out and organize your responses. Just as people who read well become better writers, people who write about what they read become better readers.

Don't be discouraged when a challenging poem or story seems baffling at first reading. Think about it. Come back to it again. Listen to what others have to say about it. One definition of a classic is that is has rich meanings that unfold on second or third reading. Remember that the selections you read in this book are here because they have pleased and inspired readers before you—stimulating their imagination, making them think and feel, and giving them joy.

FICTION

*A story really isn't any good
unless it successfully hangs on
and expands in the mind.*
JOYCE CAROL OATES

1 PREVIEW
The World of Fiction

Fiction . . . is like a spider's web, attached ever so lightly perhaps, but still attached to life at all four corners.
VIRGINIA WOOLF

Truth may be stranger than fiction, but fiction is truer.
FREDERIC RAPHAEL

Catching the very note and trick, the strange irregular rhythm of life, that is the attempt whose strenuous force keeps Fiction upon her feet.
HENRY JAMES

FOCUS ON FICTION

Listeners have been enchanted with the storyteller's art from time immemorial. The people who painted bison and horses on cave walls fifty thousand years ago very likely gathered around the fire on long winter nights to listen to the storyteller of the clan or tribe. The gift of "storying," of weaving stories, enabled human beings to find the connecting thread in the events of the past. It helped them find continuity and meaning in their lives.

Through the centuries, people have told and listened to stories—on long winter evenings on an isolated farm, in a country retreat while waiting out an epidemic ravaging the city, on the dusty road while on a pilgrimage to a famous shrine. What is the perennial appeal of a good story? The Greek writer Nikos Kazantzakis tells a story that is very short but has in it essential elements of the storyteller's art:

> There was a smell of fig trees in the air. A little old woman who was walking past stopped next to me. She lifted up some leaves covering a basket she was carrying. She picked out two of the figs in the basket and offered them to me. "Do you know me from somewhere, granny?" I asked. She looked at me, surprised. "No, my lad. Do I have to know you to give you something? You are a human being. So am I. Isn't that enough?"

This very short story does for us in miniature what other stories take longer to do for their readers. The story takes us on a flight of the imagination to a setting; it takes us to a time and a place. We come to know two characters, who become real to us as human beings. Something happens that is worth remembering, worth telling. As we imagine ourselves in the traveler's place, we are likely to be moved by what the old woman said. The figs become a symbol—they represent the nourishment that sustains life, but they are also a token of human solidarity, of the fellow feeling or bonding that helps us survive. What happened here, what the woman did and said, is likely to make us think. (Is the woman unlike other people? Or does she represent something that is part of human nature? Would we have acted similarly or differently in the same situation?) In the hurry and worry of everyday life, this incident stands out. It is complete and self-contained, with a meaning of its own. It makes a good story.

In the last hundred years, the writing of short stories has become a craft. Many of the same authors also write novels, but they approach the shorter form as a special challenge, where they can make every detail count. The test for the classics of the modern short story is that they become richer on second and third reading. They become more rewarding as we reread. A good storyteller has a lively imagination—the ability to create an imaginary world, to widen our horizons by taking us to an imaginary setting and having us accept the assumptions on which it operates. A good storyteller is an alert observer, sharpening our gifts of observation, helping us use our eyes. Much good storytelling probes personality, giving us a glimpse of a character's real motives, making us reexamine and rethink stereotypes. Effective storytelling makes us take pleasure in language more rich and expressive than everyday talk, carrying graphic details and shades of feeling, leaving us with haunting images that stay with us.

GUIDELINES FOR THE RECEPTIVE READER

The process of reading is not a half-sleep, but, in the highest sense, a gymnast's struggle. . . . The reader is to do something for himself, must be on the alert, must himself or herself construct indeed the poem, the argument, the history—the text furnishing the hints, the clue, the start or framework.

WALT WHITMAN

Receptive readers meet the author halfway. Storytelling is a cooperative enterprise—the writer provides the script, but the readers bring it to life by using their imagination. What can you do to get out of a story what the writer put in? Remember guidelines like the following:

◇ *Read with an open mind:* A story takes you into a world of its own, with values that may be different from yours. Try to be a receptive, responsive reader. Some readers are too quick to find fault with what is new and unfamiliar. They are too quick to judge writing that looks at the world through lenses different from their own. If you are too quick to judge, to reject, you may cut yourself off from much that good reading has to offer.

✧ *Read a story more than once:* A story is not like a note with a message that we take in before we crumple up the paper and throw it away. The "message" of a story is in the way it takes shape, the way it creates its own reality. The stories in this book offer rewards for the reader who lingers over them, who goes back to them for a closer look. Look for significant details that may have passed by too quickly. Be alert for revealing words, telling gestures.

✧ *Take notes as you read:* Highlight key passages or dramatic moments. Do a running commentary. Jot down quotable quotes. (If nothing else, write a few exclamation marks and question marks in the margin!)

✧ *Try to get a sense of the story as a whole:* As you look back over your notes, try to see whether an overall pattern has taken shape. Try to see what role details play in the larger context of the story.

✧ *Use your imagination:* Try to visualize the scenes, the people, the events. Learn to hear the dialogue with the mind's ear as if it were being read aloud. Try to see the world from the vantage point of the narrator, the person telling the story.

✧ *Allow your emotions to come into play:* Respond with your feelings as well as your analytical faculties. A short story does not present a case history for your diagnosis. Try to relate to the characters as people. Develop your capacity for empathy—for entering imaginatively into what others think and feel.

✧ *Think about your reactions:* Were you puzzled? appalled? frustrated when the story took a turn you did not expect? What standards and expectations did you bring to the story?

✧ *Talk with other readers:* Learn from their reactions, questions, and confusions. Explore your reading with others—one on one or in small groups. What did they see that you missed? What triggered reactions different from yours?

✧ *Do some unrequired reading:* Branch out. Discover on your own authors that mean something to you personally or other stories by a favorite author.

THE ART OF THE STORY

We are story-telling animals. As our primitive ancestors sat around the fire carving spearheads and eating blackberries, they told stories which in time were woven into a tapestry of myth and legend. These tales were the first encyclopedia of human knowledge.

SAM KEEN

Writing a story is one way of discovering sequence in experience. Connections slowly emerge. Like distant landmarks you are approaching, cause and effect begin to align themselves.

EUDORA WELTY

*A writer out of loneliness is trying to communicate like a
distant star sending signals. . . . We are lonely animals.
We spend all life trying to be less lonesome. One of our
ancient methods is to tell a story, begging the listener to
say—and to feel—"Yes, that the way it is, or at least the
way I feel it. You're not as alone as you thought."*
JOHN STEINBECK

Every story is different. It makes its own rules; it creates its own world. Nevertheless, as readers, we become aware of questions that arise in our minds again and again. We expect the storyteller to answer them in one way or another—not in so many words; rather, we expect the story as a whole to provide the answers. Some of these questions loom larger in some stories than in others, and any one of them may seem beside the point in a given story. However, together they make us more responsive to the elements of a short story—to the dimensions that we need to respond to as readers, to the clues we need to read if we are to take in the writer's meaning.

A preview of key questions that readers and critics ask about a story might look like this:

SETTING: Where are we? Where is the story taking us? What kind of world, what kind of reality, does it create for us? What difference do the time and the place make to the story as a whole?

CHARACTER: Who are these people? What is their history or their current situation? What are their real motives, needs, or desires? What explains the way they act?

PLOT: What happens in the story and why? What pattern, or story line, gives shape to the story as a whole? Is there a central conflict or a central problem, and how is it going to be resolved? Do events build up to a high point? Is there a turning point, a turning of the tide?

POINT OF VIEW: Who is telling the story? Through whose eyes do you see the people and events? Through what window are you looking at the world?

SYMBOL: What in the story has a meaning beyond itself? Do objects, people, or incidents acquire a symbolic meaning— the way a handshake might symbolize brotherhood, or the way a new shoot on a tree might stand for rebirth or renewal?

THEME: Does the story make you think? What issues does it raise? What ideas does it explore? Does it imply or act out an idea about life or a point about human nature that you can try to spell out?

STYLE: How does the author use language? Is the language graphic, rich in striking images? Does the story play down or play up emotion? Is the tone mournful, bitter, happy, or ironic —making us look at events with a wry smile?

Look at *short* short stories (or "short shorts") in which one or the other of these elements plays a major role.

Setting

Where Are We? Whatever else storytellers do, they take us to a world of their creation. That world may share many features with our own, but it may also strike us as different or strange. The story takes us to a place, a time, a situation. Often the place becomes so vivid that we forget for the duration of a story that we are not in a real place but merely in an imagined setting, a country of the mind.

To become more aware of setting, you can ask yourself: Could this story be happening anywhere? You will be reading a different story depending on whether you watch white officials in a colonial situation in Africa, or tenant farmers scraping together a living in the backwoods, or a young woman growing up in an old-fashioned patriarchal family. Setting, in fiction as in reality, is a major player in the drama of life. It molds character; it helps make people what they are. It sets boundaries, limiting what people can strive for or aspire to. It sets up challenges. It limits or creates opportunities.

Sometimes a story is devoted almost entirely to creating a setting. Sandra Cisneros, a Mexican American writer, centers her story "The House on Mango Street" (1983) on the contrast between the dream house a family always wanted and the places in which they have to live. The house the parents talk about is a house of their own with a yard and trees, where the children could make noise without the landlord banging on the ceiling with a broom, where the water pipes would not break rusted through with age. It would be a house with a basement and several bathrooms, "so when we took a bath we wouldn't have to tell everybody."

But the house on Mango Street where the girl telling the story finds herself after one of the family's frequent moves is not the way the parents had described their ideal house at all:

> It's small and red with tight little steps in front and windows so small you'd think they were holding their breath. Bricks are crumbling in places, and the front door is so swollen you have to push hard to get in. There is no front yard . . . the house has only one washroom, very small. Everybody has to share a bedroom.

The story is in the contrast between how things should be and in how they are, and in the girl's determination not to settle for today's reality. She remembers when she pointed out another house where the family used to live to a nun from her school. The nun said, "You live *there?*" As the girl telling the story says at the end:

> I knew then I had to have a house. A real house. One I could point to. But this isn't it. The house on Mango Street isn't it. For the time being, Mama say. Temporary, says Papa. But I know how those things go.

Character

Who Are the People? In a traditional story, the storyteller places believable characters in a vividly imagined setting and then puts them in motion. How well do we get to know them? What is their history? What goes on behind the subdued public surface? What are their true needs, their true motives? Is what they do or say "in character"?

We come to know characters in fiction by reading a variety of clues. We may know them from what the author says about them (or, more exactly, from what the **narrator** says—the person telling the story). We may come to know them at least in part from what *other* characters in the story tell us. However, we also watch characters in action—reaching conclusions about their motives, their problems, their ambitions, their desires. Above all, we know them from listening to them. The following short short story by Grace Paley is in large part talk—it consists mostly of **dialogue.** The verbal exchange between the two people in the story is like a tennis match—except that instead of our eyes following the ball from one side of the net to the other, our ears turn alternately from one speaker to the other. At the same time, we listen in to the narrator mentally talking to herself, thinking to herself.

How much do you learn about the two people in this story? How much can you infer about these characters from listening to what one critic has called their "loud, energetic, quirky voices full of Paley's humor" (Kathleen A. Coppula)? For each, can you piece together a coherent person from the glimpses you get of their memories, regrets, resentments, apprehensions, or ambitions?

GRACE PALEY (born 1922)

Wants 1974

I saw my ex-husband in the street. I was sitting on the steps of the new library.

Hello, my life, I said. We had once been married for twenty-seven years, so I felt justified.

He said, What? What life? No life of mine.

I said, O.K. I don't argue when there's real disagreement. I got up and went into the library to see how much I owed them.

The librarian said $32 even and you've owed it for eighteen years. I didn't deny anything. Because I don't understand how time passes. I have had those books. I have often thought of them. The library is only two blocks away. 5

My ex-husband followed me to the Books Returned desk. He interrupted the librarian, who had more to tell. In many ways, he said, as I look back, I attribute the dissolution of our marriage to the fact that you never invited the Bertrams to dinner.

That's possible, I said. But really, if you remember: first, my father was sick that Friday, then the children were born, then I had those Tuesday-night meetings, then the war began. Then we didn't seem to know them any more. But you're right. I should have had them to dinner.

I gave the librarian a check for $32. Immediately she trusted me, put my past behind her, wiped the record clean, which is just what most other municipal and/or state bureaucracies will *not* do.

I checked out the two Edith Wharton books I had just returned because I'd read them so long ago and they are more apropos now than ever. They were *The House of Mirth* and *The Children,* which is about how life in the United States in New York changed in twenty-seven years fifty years ago.

A nice thing I do remember is breakfast, my ex-husband said. I was surprised. All we ever had was coffee. Then I remembered there was a hole in the back of the kitchen closet which opened into the apartment next door. There, they always ate sugar-cured smoked bacon. It gave us a very grand feeling about breakfast, but we never got stuffed and sluggish. 10

That was when we were poor, I said.

When were we ever rich? he asked.

Oh, as time went on, as our responsibilities increased, we didn't go in need. You took adequate financial care, I reminded him. The children went to camp four weeks a year and in decent ponchos with sleeping bags and boots, just like everyone else. They looked very nice. Our place was warm in winter, and we had nice red pillows and things.

I wanted a sailboat, he said. But you didn't want anything.

Don't be bitter, I said. It's never too late. 15

No, he said with a great deal of bitterness. I may get a sailboat. As a matter of fact I have money down on an eighteen-foot two-rigger. I'm doing well this year and can look forward to better. But as for you, it's too late. You'll always want nothing.

He had had a habit throughout the twenty-seven years of making a narrow remark which, like a plumber's snake, could work its way through the ear down the throat, halfway to my heart. He would then disappear, leaving me choking with equipment. What I mean is, I sat down on the library steps and he went away.

I looked through *The House of Mirth,* but lost interest. I felt extremely accused. Now, it's true, I'm short of requests and absolute requirements. But I do want *something.*

I want, for instance, to be a different person. I want to be the woman who brings these two books back in two weeks. I want to be the effective citizen who changes the school system and addresses the Board of Estimate on the troubles of this dear urban center.

I *had* promised my children to end the war before they grew up. 20

I wanted to have been married forever to one person, my ex-husband or my present one. Either has enough character for a whole life, which as it turns out is really not such a long time. You couldn't exhaust either man's qualities or get under the rock of his reasons in one short life.

Just this morning I looked out the window to watch the street for a while and saw that the little sycamores the city had dreamily planted a couple of years before the kids were born had come that day to the prime of their lives.

Well! I decided to bring those two books back to the library. Which proves that when a person or an event comes along to jolt or appraise me I *can* take some appropriate action, although I am better known for my hospitable remarks.

THE RECEPTIVE READER

1. What would you include in a brief *capsule portrait* of the narrator—the character doing most of the talking in this story? What do you think are her outstanding traits, and how are they shown? (Do they go together to make up a believable personality?)

2. What kind of person is the ex-husband? How does he serve as a *foil*—a character who brings out traits in the other character that otherwise might have lain dormant?

3. Do you think readers will care about these people one way or the other? Why or why not?

Plot

What Is Happening and Why?   What is the situation? What tensions simmer? What needs or wants create an unfinished agenda? What conflicts are coming to a head? What resentments are waiting to be acted out? Stories vary greatly in how much overt action they incorporate. Whatever development unfolds in a story may be taking place in a character's mind. (Note that the *failure* of something to happen, or the failure of a character to budge, can also make a story.)

The following African folktale shows the power of a good story line to create **suspense**, to hold the reader's attention. The tale is one of many retold by Chinua Achebe, a famous Nigerian novelist, in his *Things Fall Apart* (1958). His recreating of a traditional tale shows how a storyteller hooks us into a story. We need to know: How will it come out? In this story, as we see turtle best his friends, their—and our?—resentment builds. We are waiting for his comeuppance—and the story obliges; we are not disappointed. A good storyteller creates expectations and then fulfills them (or sometimes disappoints them on purpose).

CHINUA ACHEBE   (born 1930)
Why the Tortoise's Shell Is Not Smooth   1958

Low voices, broken now and again by singing, reached Okonkwo from his wives' huts as each woman and her children told folk stories. Ekwefi and her daughter, Ezinma, sat on a mat on the floor. It was Ekwefi's turn to tell a story.

"Once upon a time," she began, "all the birds were invited to a feast in the sky. They were very happy and began to prepare themselves for the great day. They painted their bodies with red cam wood and drew beautiful patterns on them with dye.

"Tortoise saw all these preparations and soon discovered what it all meant. Nothing that happened in the world of the animals ever escaped his notice; he was full of cunning. As soon as he heard of the great feast in the sky his throat began to itch at the very thought. There was a famine in those days and Tortoise had not eaten a good meal for two moons. His body rattled like a piece of dry stick in his empty shell. So he began to plan how he would go to the sky."

"But he had no wings," said Ezinma.

"Be patient," replied her mother. "That is the story. Tortoise had no wings, but he went to the birds and asked to be allowed to go with them.

"'We know you too well,' said the birds when they had heard him. 'You are full of cunning and you are ungrateful. If we allow you to come with us you will soon begin your mischief.'

" 'You do not know me,' said Tortoise. 'I am a changed man. I have learned that a man who makes trouble for others is also making it for himself.'

"Tortoise had a sweet tongue, and within a short time all the birds agreed that he was a changed man, and they each gave him a feather, with which he made two wings.

"At last the great day came and Tortoise was the first to arrive at the meeting place. When all the birds had gathered together, they set off in a body. Tortoise was very happy as he flew among the birds, and he was soon chosen as the man to speak for the party because he was a great orator.

" 'There is one important thing which we must not forget,' he said as they flew on their way. 'When people are invited to a great feast like this, they take new names for the occasion. Our hosts in the sky will expect us to honor this age-old custom.'

"None of the birds had heard of this custom but they knew that Tortoise, in spite of his failings in other directions, was a widely traveled man who knew the customs of different peoples. And so they each took a new name. When they had all taken, Tortoise also took one. He was to be called *All of you.*

"At last the party arrived in the sky and their hosts were very happy to see them. Tortoise stood up in his many-colored plumage and thanked them for their invitation. His speech was so eloquent that all the birds were glad they had brought him, and nodded their heads in approval of all he said. Their hosts took him as the king of the birds, especially as he looked somewhat different from the others.

"After kola nuts had been presented and eaten, the people of the sky set before their guests the most delectable dishes Tortoise had even seen or dreamed of. The soup was brought out hot from the fire and in the very pot in which it had been cooked. It was full of meat and fish. Tortoise began to sniff aloud. There was pounded yam and also yam pottage cooked with palm oil and fresh fish. There were also pots of palm wine. When everything had been set before the guests, one of the people of the sky came forward and tasted a little from each pot. He then invited the birds to eat. But Tortoise jumped to his feet and asked: 'For whom have you prepared this feast?'

" 'For all of you,' replied the man.

"Tortoise turned to the birds and said: 'You remember that my name is *All of you.* The custom here is to serve the spokesman first and the others later. They will serve you when I have eaten.'

"He began to eat and the birds grumbled angrily. The people of the sky thought it must be their custom to leave all the food for their king. And so Tortoise ate the best part of the food and then drank two pots of palm wine, so that he was full of food and drink and his body grew fat enough to fill out his shell.

"The birds gathered round to eat what was left and to peck at the bones he had thrown all about the floor. Some of them were too angry to eat. They chose to fly home on an empty stomach. But before they left each took back the feather he had lent to Tortoise. And there he stood in his hard shell full of food and wine but without any wings to fly home. He asked the birds to take a message for his wife, but they all refused. In the end Parrot, who had felt more angry than the others, suddenly changed his mind and agreed to take the message.

" 'Tell my wife,' said Tortoise, 'to bring out all the soft things in my house and cover the compound with them so that I can jump down from the sky without very great danger.'

"Parrot promised to deliver the message, and then flew away. But when he reached Tortoise's house he told his wife to bring out all the hard things in the house. And so she brought out her husband's hoes, machetes, spears, guns, and even his cannon. Tortoise looked down from the sky and saw his wife bringing things out, but it was too far to see what they were. When all seemed ready he let himself go. He fell and fell and fell until he began to fear that he would never stop falling. And then like the sound of his cannon he crashed on the compound."

"Did he die?" asked Ezinma.

20

"No," replied Ekwefi. "His shell broke into pieces. But there was a great medicine man in the neighborhood. Tortoise's wife sent for him and he gathered all the bits of shell and stuck them together. That is why Tortoise's shell is not smooth."

THE RECEPTIVE READER

1. What makes the characters and the story *believable*? (Do you think modern readers would be too sophisticated to be charmed by animals talking and acting like people?)

2. Do you feel a sneaking admiration for the cleverness of the turtle? Or do you mainly sympathize with his victims?

3. How did you expect the story to come out? When did you first guess what the ending would be?

4. Many traditional stories follow the pattern of a journey. How does this one?

5. Folklorists call this kind of tale a "tell-me-why" story (or *pourquoi* story, from the French word for *why*). Do you know any other stories of this type? (Tell it to your classmates.)

THE CREATIVE DIMENSION

Modern readers have often felt the urge to update proverbs or to rewrite folktales to bring them into harmony with the modern temper. Try your hand at a modern rewrite of this traditional tale or of a folktale likely to be familiar to your readers. (In rewriting this story, would you choose different and more familiar animals? Would you change the way the animals behave and the way readers—or listeners—are expected to react?)

Point of View

Through Whose Eyes Are We Looking at the World?   From what point of view? What is included, what left out? What special insights or privileged information are we able to share? What biases may cloud our vision? What blind spots do we need to take into account? The following story is told from the point of view of a white male. What difference does it make?

T O B I A S   W O L F F   (born 1945)

Say Yes

1985

They were doing the dishes, his wife washing while he dried. He'd washed the night before. Unlike most men he knew, he really pitched in on the housework. A few months earlier he'd overheard a friend of his wife's congratulate her on having such a considerate husband, and he thought, *I try*. Helping out with the dishes was a way he had of showing how considerate he was.

They talked about different things and somehow got on the subject of whether white people should marry black people. He said that all things considered, he thought it was a bad idea.

"Why?" she asked.

Sometimes his wife got this look where she pinched her brows together and bit her lower lip and stared down at something. When he saw her like this he knew he should keep his mouth shut, but he never did. Actually it made him talk more. She had that look now.

"Why?" she asked again, and stood there with her hand inside a bowl, not washing it but just holding it above the water.

"Listen," he said, "I went to school with blacks, and I've worked with blacks and lived on the same street with blacks, and we've always gotten along just fine. I don't need you coming along now and implying that I'm a racist."

"I didn't imply anything," she said, and began washing the bowl again, turning it around in her hand as though she were shaping it. "I just don't see what's wrong with a white person marrying a black person, that's all."

"They don't come from the same culture as we do. Listen to them sometime— they even have their own language. That's okay with me, I *like* hearing them talk"—he did; for some reason it always made him feel happy—"but it's different. A person from their culture and a person from our culture could never really *know* each other."

"Like you know me?" his wife asked.

"Yes. Like I know you."

"But if they love each other," she said. She was washing faster now, not looking at him.

Oh boy, he thought. He said, "Don't take my word for it. Look at the statistics. Most of those marriages break up."

"Statistics." She was piling dishes on the drainboard at a terrific rate, just swiping at them with the cloth. Many of them were greasy, and there were flecks of food between the tines of the forks. "All right," she said, "what about foreigners? I suppose you think the same thing about two foreigners getting married."

"Yes," he said, "as a matter of fact I do. How can you understand someone who comes from a completely different background?"

"Different," said his wife. "Not the same, like us."

"Yes, different," he snapped, angry with her for resorting to this trick of repeating his words so that they sounded crass, or hypocritical. "These are dirty," he said, and dumped all the silverware back into the sink.

The water had gone flat and gray. She stared down at it, her lips pressed tight together, then plunged her hands under the surface. "Oh!" she cried, and jumped back. She took her right hand by the wrist and held it up. Her thumb was bleeding.

"Ann, don't move," he said. "Stay right there." He ran upstairs to the bathroom and rummaged in the medicine chest for alcohol, cotton, and a Band-Aid. When he came back down she was leaning against the refrigerator with her eyes closed, still holding her hand. He took the hand and dabbed at her thumb with the cotton. The bleeding had stopped. He squeezed it to see how deep the wound was and a single drop of blood welled up, trembling and bright, and fell to the floor. Over the thumb she stared at him accusingly. "It's shallow," he said. "Tomorrow you won't even know it's there." He hoped that she appreciated how quickly he had come to her aid. He'd acted out of concern for her, with no thought of getting anything in return, but now the thought occurred to him that it would be a nice gesture on her part not to start up that conversation again, as he was tired of it. "I'll finish up here," he said. "You go and relax."

5

10

15

"That's okay," she said. "I'll dry."

He began to wash the silverware again, giving a lot of attention to the forks. 20

"So," she said, "you wouldn't have married me if I'd been black."

"For Christ's sake, Ann!"

"Well, that's what you said, didn't you?"

"No, I did not. The whole question is ridiculous. If you had been black we probably wouldn't even have met. You would have had your friends and I would have had mine. The only black girl I ever really knew was my partner in the debating club, and I was already going out with you by then."

"But if we had met, and I'd been black?" 25

"Then you probably would have been going out with a black guy." He picked up the rinsing nozzle and sprayed the silverware. The water was so hot that the metal darkened to pale blue, then turned silver again.

"Let's say I wasn't," she said. "Let's say I am black and unattached and we meet and fall in love."

He glanced over at her. She was watching him and her eyes were bright. "Look," he said, taking a reasonable tone, "this is stupid. If you were black you wouldn't be you." As he said this he realized it was absolutely true. There was no possible way of arguing with the fact that she would not be herself if she were black. So he said it again: "If you were black you wouldn't be you."

"I know," she said, "but let's just say."

He took a deep breath. He had won the argument but he still felt cornered. "Say 30
what?" he asked.

"That I'm black, but still me, and we fall in love. Will you marry me?"

He thought about it.

"Well?" she said, and stepped close to him. Her eyes were even brighter. "Will you marry me?"

"I'm thinking," he said.

"You won't, I can tell. You're going to say no." 35

"Let's not move too fast on this," he said. "There are lots of things to consider. We don't want to do something we would regret for the rest of our lives."

"No more considering. Yes or no."

"Since you put it that way–"

"Yes or no."

"Jesus, Ann. All right. No." 40

She said. "Thank you," and walked from the kitchen into the living room. A moment later he heard her turning the pages of a magazine. He knew that she was too angry to be actually reading it, but she didn't snap through the pages the way he would have done. She turned them slowly, as if she were studying every word. She was demonstrating her indifference to him, and it had the effect he knew she wanted it to have. It hurt him.

He had no choice but to demonstrate his indifference to her. Quietly, thoroughly, he washed the rest of the dishes. Then he dried them and put them away. He wiped the counters and the stove and scoured the linoleum where the drop of blood had fallen. While he was at it, he decided, he might as well mop the whole floor. When he was done the kitchen looked new, the way it looked when they were first shown the house, before they had ever lived here.

He picked up the garbage pail and went outside. The night was clear and he could see a few stars to the west, where the light of the town didn't blur them out. On El Camino the traffic was steady and light, peaceful as a river. He felt ashamed that he had let his wife get him into a fight. In another thirty years or so they would both be dead. What would all that stuff matter then? He thought of the years they had spent together, and how close they were, and how well they knew each other, and his throat tightened so that he could hardly breathe. His face and neck began to tingle. Warmth flooded his chest. He stood there for a while, enjoying these sensations, then picked up the pail and went out the back gate.

The two mutts from down the street had pulled over the garbage can again. One of them was rolling around on his back and the other had something in her mouth. Growling, she tossed it into the air, leaped up and caught it, growled again and whipped her head from side to side. When they saw him coming they trotted away with short, mincing steps. Normally he would heave rocks at them, but this time he let them go.

The house was dark when he came back inside. She was in the bathroom. He stood outside the door and called her name. He heard bottles clinking, but she didn't answer him. "Ann, I'm really sorry," he said. "I'll make it up to you, I promise." 45

"How?" she asked.

He wasn't expecting this. But from a sound in her voice, a level and definite note that was strange to him, he knew that he had come up with the right answer. He leaned against the door. "I'll marry you," he whispered.

"We'll see," she said. "Go on to bed. I'll be out in a minute."

He undressed and got under the covers. Finally he heard the bathroom door open and close.

"Turn off the light," she said from the hallway. 50

"What?"

"Turn off the light."

He reached over and pulled the chain on the bedside lamp. The room went dark. "All right," he said. He lay there, but nothing happened. "All right," he said again. Then he heard a movement across the room. He sat up, but he couldn't see a thing. The room was silent. His heart pounded the way it had on their first night together, the way it still did when he woke at a noise in the darkness and waited to hear it again—the sound of someone moving through the house, a stranger.

THE RECEPTIVE READER

1. How does the world look as we see it through the eyes of the white male narrator?

2. Do you find yourself taking sides in the argument between him and the woman? Would you call him a biased or prejudiced person? (How do you think he looks to readers who are not male or not white?)

3. How do you react to the way the story ends?

THE CREATIVE DIMENSION

How might the story read if it were retold from the point of view of the woman? Write a short alternative story as told by her; or write a part of her story.

Symbol

What in the Story Might Have a Meaning beyond Itself? What objects, people, or incidents seem to have a **symbolic** significance beyond their literal meaning? A river, for instance, might begin to suggest the steady, slow flow of time, which can never be stopped or reversed. How do such symbolic elements acquire a meaning beyond themselves?

In the following short short, we focus on a single significant day in the life of a couple. We learn something about the setting of their lives, about them as people, about their relationship. But details of setting, character, and plot are almost crowded out by something the wife has brought home from the store: Halloween pumpkins. They are the first and last things we see in the story. The people work on them and talk about them for most of the story. They loom large. What do they mean? What role do they play?

MARY ROBISON (born 1949)
Yours   1983

Allison struggled away from her white Renault, limping with the weight of the last of the pumpkins. She found Clark in the twilight on the twig-and-leaf-littered porch behind the house.

He wore a wool shawl. He was moving up and back in a padded glider, pushed by the ball of his slippered foot.

Allison lowered a big pumpkin, let it rest on the wide floorboards.

Clark was much older—seventy-eight to Allison's thirty-five. They were married. They were both quite tall and looked something alike in their facial features. Allison wore a natural-hair wig. It was a thick blond hood around her face. She was dressed in bright-dyed denims today. She wore durable clothes, usually, for she volunteered afternoons at a children's day-care center.

She put one of the smaller pumpkins on Clark's long lap. "Now, nothing surreal," she told him. "Carve just a *regular* face. These are for kids."   5

In the foyer, on the Hepplewhite desk, Allison found the maid's chore list with its cross-offs, which included Clark's supper. Allison went quickly through the day's mail: a garish coupon packet, a bill from Jamestown Liquors, November's pay-TV program guide, and the worst thing, the funniest, an already opened, extremely unkind letter from Clark's relations up North. "You're an old fool," Allison read, and, "You're being cruelly deceived." There was a gift check for Clark enclosed, but it was uncashable, signed, as it was, "Jesus H. Christ."

Late, late into this night, Allison and Clark gutted and carved the pumpkins together, at an old table set on the back porch, over newspaper after soggy newspaper, with paring knives and with spoons and with a Swiss Army knife Clark used for exact shaping of tooth and eye and nostril. Clark had been a doctor, an internist, but also a Sunday watercolorist. His four pumpkins were expressive and artful. Their carved features were suited to the sizes and shapes of the pumpkins. Two looked ferocious and jagged. One registered surprise. The last was serene and beaming.

Allison's four faces were less deftly drawn, with slits and areas of distortion. She had cut triangles for noses and eyes. The mouths she had made were just wedges—two turned up and two turned down.

By one in the morning they were finished. Clark, who had bent his long torso forward to work, moved back over to the glider and look out sleepily at nothing. All the lights were out across the ravine.

Clark stayed. For the season and time, the Virginia night was warm. Most leaves 10
had been blown away already, and the trees stood unbothered. The moon was round
above them.

Allison cleaned up the mess.

"Your jack-o'-lanterns are much, much better than mine," Clark said to her.

"Like hell," Allison said.

"Look at me," Clark said, and Allison did.

She was holding a squishy bundle of newspapers. The papers reeked sweetly with 15
the smell of pumpkin guts.

"Yours are *far* better," he said.

"You're wrong. You'll see when they're lit," Allison said.

She went inside, came back with yellow vigil candles. It took her a while to get
each candle settled, and then to line up the results in a row on the porch railing. She
went along and lit each candle and fixed the pumpkin lids over the little flames.

"See?" she said.

They sat together a moment and looked at the orange faces. 20

"We're exhausted. It's good night time," Allison said. "Don't blow out the candles. I'll put in new ones tomorrow."

That night, in their bedroom, a few weeks earlier in her life than had been predicted, Allison began to die. "Don't look at me if my wig comes off," she told Clark.
"Please."

Her pulse cords were fluttering under his fingers. She raised her knees and kicked
away the comforter. She said something to Clark about the garage being locked.

At the telephone, Clark had a clear view out back and down to the porch. He
wanted to get drunk with his wife once more. He wanted to tell her, from the
greater perspective he had, that to own only a little talent, like his, was an awful,
plaguing thing; that being only a little special meant you expected too much, most of
the time, and liked yourself too little. He wanted to assure her that she had missed
nothing.

He was speaking into the phone now. He watched the jack-o'-lanterns. The jack- 25
o'-lanterns watched him.

THE RECEPTIVE READER

1. How do you learn about the situation in which the two characters find themselves? What clues are especially important?

2. What role does the age difference between the two people play in the story? Is
it treated differently from what you might have expected? How?

3. When do you first suspect that the pumpkins have a special significance? (What
kind of fruit are they? What associations with them do you bring to the story?) What
role do they play in the story as a whole? Does it matter that they are carved differently?
What do you think they symbolize?

THE PERSONAL RESPONSE

This story deals with age, illness, and death. How does it treat these topics?
Do you think the story as a whole is affirmative toward life or disillusioned or depressing?

Theme

What Is the Meaning of the Story as a Whole? A good storyteller makes us think. Even a short and lighthearted story is likely to say something about human nature; it may offer some comment on life. It is likely to have a point, although that point may not be spelled out in so many words. We call the implied point, the implied comment, the theme of the story. Most writers in our century have been wary of spelling out the **theme** of a story too directly—afraid that it would sound like a ready-made secondhand sentiment, a cliché. They want us to live through the experience of the story to discover what it has to say. What we witness raises questions to which the story as a whole suggests possible answers. The ideas implied slowly come into focus as we think about what we have read.

Many twentieth-century writers refuse to preach, to editorialize. Old-fashioned storytelling was often less shy about pointing out the moral of the tale. A case in point is the traditional **fable,** going back thousands of years to ancient Greece (many of the familiar traditional fables are attributed to Aesop). Traditionally, the fable ends by spelling out the advice the story was written to drive home. Even so, many of the fables would make their point even if the moral had been lost. Often the story speaks for itself. The following is a modern rendering of a fable that William Caxton had included in the fifteenth century in one of the first books printed in England. In this retelling, the moral has been left out. What to you is the idea acted out in the story?

A E S O P   (sixth century B.C.)

The Wolf and the Lamb   about 570 B.C.

The wolf and the lamb were both thirsty and went to the river to drink. It happened that the wolf drank a ways up the river and the lamb drank farther down. And as the wolf saw and perceived the lamb, he said in a loud voice: "Hah, knave, why has thou troubled and befouled my water that I should now drink?" "Alas, My Lord, God save Your Grace," said the lamb, "the water flows down the river from you towards me!" Then said the wolf to the lamb: "Hast thou no shame or dread to curse me?" And the lamb said "My Lord, I am sorry." And the wolf said again: "It is only six months ago that thy father wronged me in the same manner." And the lamb answered: "I was then not even born." And the wolf said again to him: "Thou hast killed and devoured my father!" And the lamb said: "But I have no teeth to eat meat!" Then said the wolf: "Thou art like your father, and for that sin and misdeed thou shalt die!" The wolf then seized the lamb and devoured him.

THE RECEPTIVE READER

1. What is the *moral?* What statement does the fable seem to make about human nature? Is it out-of-date, obsolete—or does the fable have a meaning for you as a modern reader?

2. Does this fable give us a *realistic* view of human nature? Or would you call it pessimistic? Would you call it cynical?

Style

How Does the Author Use Language?   What is the relation between what is said and how it is said? What we mean, what we communicate to others, is not just in what we say but also in how we say it. Language is not just words—it is also the knowing wink, the twinkle in the eye, the bitter tone, the exasperated gesture. Similarly, the style of a writer can make a passage seem passionate or low-key, eloquent or halting, conciliatory or bitter, assertive or diffident. Style is more than a matter of style—it makes a statement of its own.

The following story is written in an understated early modern style. Hemingway set the directions for the style of much modern fiction with his suspicion of cheap words, emotional outbursts, or stylistic embellishments. Most of what is important in the story we have to read between the lines. (Many of Hemingway's stories are set in a foreign country, such as Italy or Spain. In the following story, the Ebro is a river in Spain, and *reales* are Spanish coins.)

ERNEST HEMINGWAY (1899–1961)
Hills like White Elephants 1927

The hills across the valley of the Ebro were long and white. On this side there was no shade and no trees and the station was between two lines of rails in the sun. Close against the side of the station there was the warm shadow of the building and a curtain, made of strings of bamboo beads, hung across the open door into the bar, to keep out flies. The American and the girl with him sat at a table in the shade, outside the building. It was very hot and the express from Barcelona would come in forty minutes. It stopped at this junction for two minutes and went on to Madrid.

"What should we drink?" the girl asked. She had taken off her hat and put it on the table.

"It's pretty hot," the man said.

"Let's drink beer."

"Dos cervezas," the man said into the curtain. 5

"Big ones?" a woman asked from the doorway.

"Yes. Two big ones."

The woman brought two glasses of beer and two felt pads. She put the felt pads and the beer glasses on the table and looked at the man and the girl. The girl was looking off at the line of hills. They were white in the sun and the country was brown and dry.

"They look like white elephants," she said.

"I've never seen one," the man drank his beer. 10

"No, you wouldn't have."

"I might have," the man said. "Just because you say I wouldn't have doesn't prove anything."

The girl looked at the bead curtain. "They've painted something on it," she said. "What does it say?"

"Anis del Toro. It's a drink."

"Could we try it?" 15

The man called "Listen" through the curtain. The woman came out from the bar.

"Four reales."

"We want two Anis del Toro."

"With water?"

"Do you want it with water?" 20

"I don't know," the girl said. "Is it good with water?"

"It's all right."

"You want them with water?" asked the woman.

"Yes, with water."

"It tastes like licorice," the girl said and put the glass down. 25

"That's the way with everything."

"Yes," said the girl. "Everything tastes of licorice. Especially all the things you've waited so long for, like absinthe."

"Oh, cut it out."

"You started it," the girl said. "I was being amused. I was having a fine time."

"Well, let's try and have a fine time." 30

"All right. I was trying. I said the mountains looked like white elephants. Wasn't that bright?"

"That was bright."

"I wanted to try this new drink. That's all we do, isn't it—look at things and try new drinks?"

"I guess so."

The girl looked across at the hills. 35

"They're lovely hills," she said. "They don't really look like white elephants. I just meant the coloring of their skin through the trees."

"Should we have another drink?"

"All right."

The warm wind blew the bead curtain against the table.

"The beer's nice and cool," the man said. 40

"It's lovely," the girl said.

"It's really an awfully simple operation, Jig," the man said. "It's not really an operation at all."

The girl looked at the ground the table legs rested on.

"I know you wouldn't mind it, Jig. It's really not anything. It's just to let the air in."

The girl did not say anything. 45

"I'll go with you and I'll stay with you all the time. They just let the air in and then it's all perfectly natural."

"Then what will we do afterward?"

"We'll be fine afterward. Just like we were before."

"What makes you think so?"

"That's the only thing that bothers us. It's the only thing that's made us unhappy." 50

The girl looked at the bead curtain, put her hand out and took hold of two of the strings of beads.

"And you think then we'll be all right and be happy."

"I know we will. You don't have to be afraid. I've known lots of people that have done it."

"So have I," said the girl. "And afterward they were all so happy."

"Well," the man said, "if you don't want to you don't have to. I wouldn't have you do it if you didn't want to. But I know it's perfectly simple." 55

"And you really want to?"

"I think it's the best thing to do. But I don't want you to do it if you don't really want to."

"And if I do it you'll be happy and things will be like they were and you'll love me?"

"I love you now. You know I love you."

"I know. But if I do it, then it will be nice again if I say things are like white elephants, and you'll like it?" 60

"I'll love it. I love it now but I just can't think about it. You know how I get when I worry."

"If I do it you won't ever worry?"

"I won't worry about that because it's perfectly simple."

"Then I'll do it. Because I don't care about me."

"What do you mean?" 65

"I don't care about me."

"Well, I care about you."

"Oh, yes. But I don't care about me. And I'll do it and then everything will be fine."

"I don't want you to do it if you feel that way."

The girl stood up and walked to the end of the station. Across on the other side, were fields of grain and trees along the banks of the Ebro. Far away, beyond the river, were mountains. The shadow of a cloud moved across the field of grain and she saw the river through the trees. 70

"And we could have all this," she said. "And we could have everything and every day we make it more impossible."

"What did you say?"

"I said we could have everything."

"We can have everything."

"No, we can't." 75

"We can have the whole world."

"No, we can't"

"We can go everywhere."

"No, we can't. It isn't ours any more."

"It's ours." 80

"No, it isn't. And once they take it away, you never get it back."

"But they haven't taken it away."

"We'll wait and see."

"Come on back in the shade," he said. "You mustn't feel that way."

"I don't feel any way," the girl said. "I just know things." 85

"I don't want you to do anything that you don't want to do—"

"Nor that isn't good for me," she said. "I know. Could we have another beer?"

"All right. But you've got to realize—"

"I realize," the girl said. "Can't we maybe stop talking?"

They sat down at the table and the girl looked across at the hills on the dry side of the valley and the man looked at her and at the table. 90

"You've got to realize," he said, "that I don't want you to do it if you don't want to. I'm perfectly willing to go through with it if it means anything to you."

"Doesn't it mean anything to you? We could get along."

"Of course it does. But I don't want anybody but you. I don't want any one else. And I know it's perfectly simple."

"Yes, you know it's perfectly simple."

"It's all right for you to say that, but I do know it." 95

"Would you do something for me now?"

"I'd do anything for you."

"Would you please please please please please please please stop talking?"

He did not say anything but looked at the bags against the wall of the station. There were labels on them from all the hotels where they had spent nights.

"But I don't want you to," he said, "I don't care anything about it." 100

"I'll scream," the girl said.

The woman came out through the curtains with two glasses of beer and put them down on the damp felt pads. "The train comes in five minutes," she said.

"What did she say?" asked the girl.

"That the train is coming in five minutes."

The girl smiled brightly at the woman, to thank her. 105

"I'd better take the bags over to the other side of the station," the man said. She smiled at him.

"All right. Then come back and we'll finish the beer."

He picked up the two heavy bags and carried them around the station to the other tracks. He looked up the tracks but could not see the train. Coming back, he walked through the barroom, where people waiting for the train were drinking. He drank an Anis at the bar and looked at the people. They were all waiting reasonably for the train. He went out through the bead curtain. She was sitting at the table and smiled at him.

"Do you feel better?" he asked.

"I feel fine," she said. "There's nothing wrong with me. I feel fine." 110

THE RECEPTIVE READER

1. As you first listen to the conversation of the two characters in this story, what makes the *dialogue* seem trivial or empty? (How does their style of talking echo their life-style?)

2. The woman's comparing the hills to white elephants is touched on several times in the story. (And it gave the story its title.) Do the hills or other elements of the story have a *symbolic* significance?

3. When do you first realize that these two people are talking about an important *choice*? How does the man talk about it? (What does it mean to him?) How does the woman talk about it? (What does it mean to her?) How does the woman react to the man's attitude?

4. Hemingway, as one of the first great moderns, was wary of emotionalism and melodrama. Where in the story are you most aware of the emotions and tensions beneath the understated, "cool" surface?

5. Does this story reach a *conclusion*? Has anything changed or been accomplished by the end? (Where do you think these two people are headed? What is ahead for them?)

THE PERSONAL RESPONSE

Eloquent pleas for sympathy are not part of the Hemingway style. Do you find yourself taking sides? If so, how and why?

EXPLORATIONS ━━━━━━━━

Setting Up Expectations

The following is the opening of a short story called "The Coming Triumph of the Free World" by Rick DeMarinis. What kind of setting do these opening paragraphs establish? What characters come into focus? What kind of story can you imagine taking place in this setting? Answer the questions that follow the excerpt. Then write a brief story that you can imagine as following these opening paragraphs.

The grizzled psychotic entered Safeway laughing. His laugh had the false heartiness of a department-store Santa Claus. He stood in front of the checkout lines, chuckling at some private observation that tickled him. He was full of expansive, arm-waving gestures. A young woman, on her way out, made the mistake of stopping near him to adjust the shoulder strap of her purse. He laughed out loud and opened his arms, inviting her to join his merry world. As his arm circled her neck, she pushed it deftly away, as if accustomed to handling the blunt familiarities of the insane. She was good-natured and not at all frightened. The man was at least six feet three and over two hundred pounds. His raggy clothes were stiff with grime.

I'd seen him before. He was not usually so happy. Most of the time he seemed stunned and bewildered. He'd stand, teetering on the balls of his feet, touching his face with trembling finger-tips as if trying to remember how it once looked. Or he would move, zombie-slow, through the aisles, perplexed by the rage of colors and shapes that gleamed like hallucinations from the shelves. Once I saw him marching fiercely to a Sousa piece on the Muzak, a large fresh salmon and a six-pack of toilet paper in his cart. I didn't know his name, but I called him Muni, after the 1930s movie actor, Paul Muni, whom the man resembled in some distorted way.

Muni followed the young woman out of the store and into the moonlit parking lot. A checkout clerk followed them to make sure Muni didn't try any rough stuff. I wheeled my cart after the clerk, thinking that neither one of us would be a match for Muni if he got it into his head to fight for love. Raquel, my wife, lagged at the checkout counter, squinting suspiciously at the receipt. "Are you coming?" I yelled. I was nervous and annoyed. Muni wasn't the only reason for getting out of Safeway quickly. They were out in droves that Monday night, even though the moon was not quite full . . . bag ladies, bikers, frayed winos fondling slim bottles of fortified Tokay.

THE RECEPTIVE READER

1. Does the setting seem strange or familiar to you? What striking details help bring it to life? What for you is the keynote or unifying prevailing mood?

2. How much do you learn about the characters? Do they become believable?

3. Is there a germ of a plot here? What do you think might happen in the rest of the story?

4. From whose point of view is the story told? What difference does it make?

5. Does anything here have possible symbolic significance?

6. What might be a possible theme? What statement might the story as a whole be making about the homeless mentally ill or about the cityscape in which many Americans live?

7. What is the *tone* of these paragraphs—what seems to be the attitude of the nar-

rator; what mood or what emotions seem to prevail? For instance, do these paragraphs sound angry, sentimental, humorous, or earnest? Does the style make the narrator seem passionate or detached? How does the writer steer our reactions toward Muni?

CLOSE READING AND THE PERSONAL RESPONSE

My writing expects, demands participatory reading, and that is what I think literature is supposed to do. It's not just about telling the story; it's about involving the reader. The reader supplies the emotions. The reader supplies even some of the color, some of the sound. My language has to have holes and spaces so that the reader can come into it.
TONI MORRISON

Reading imaginative literature is different from recording data or crunching numbers. It is more multidimensional. It brings not only our intelligence but also our imagination and our emotions into play. It involves us as complete human beings. When we respond fully to a story or a poem, we are living more alertly in the world. We are broadening our sympathies. We are educating the emotions.

You may want to think of your reading as involving three major dimensions:

The Receptive Reader   A receptive reader is on the writer's side. As a receptive reader, you make an extra effort of understanding; you give a difficult story the benefit of the doubt. You develop the habit of close, attentive reading (rather than skimming the page to get a "general idea"). In a well-crafted short story, details are not just there to fill the page. You are likely to notice striking details that make the author's world real for the reader. You should be alert to gestures or actions that provide a clue to a character's motives. You will need an eye for objects with symbolic overtones, an ear for revealing comments and shades of meaning. You will need to respond to patterns that give shape to the story as a whole.

The Personal Response   The stories and the writers we return to have some special personal meaning for us. The stories that move us powerfully do in some way touch our own lives, though the connection may not always be obvious. At some level, they engage with our own needs, desires, or apprehensions. The writer does not really expect us to read the story the way an electronic scanner would, retrieving data to be analyzed later. Our emotions as well as our intellect must be engaged if we are to understand what mattered to the author.

The following is one student's reaction to a short story classic. How did she make the personal connection? What mattered to her most in the story, and why?

"The Open Boat" by Stephen Crane is a story about men who were shipwrecked and forced to brave the open sea with very little protection and with little hope of survival. While I read this story, I felt much concern about the men who were trying to survive in a contest with nature that seemed bent on defeating them and had the power to destroy them. What struck me most in this story was the spirit of teamwork, of working together. They helped each other out in order to survive; they knew that was the only way to beat the sea. The cook bailed the water out of their tiny boat; the journalist and the engineer took turns rowing the boat ("Will you spell me for a little while?"), never complaining or saying they were dead tired when they were all on the brink of exhaustion. The captain, although he was injured and unable to do physical work, gave directions and moral support to the "crew." What if they had not been able to work as a team? What if they had started bickering, using abusive language, as many people would today? What if they had let the short fuse set off an explosion of stupid hostility and pride? They would all have drowned. At the end of the story, I found myself cheering them all on, and I was full of grief when one of the crew drowned. The surprising thing to me was that the one who drowned was the strongest of the four. It may not always be the "fittest" who survive.

The Creative Dimension   Fiction stimulates the reader's imagination. For instance, you may want to re-create an impression that lingered in your memory. You may want to evoke a haunting image that in some ways seems to sum up the story. Look at the following student-written response to Mary Robison's "Yours." Does it in any way add to or enhance your own reading of the story?

Pumpkins in orange October,
    their sweet soggy smell
    rises from carved insides
    on wet news
Their fierce pumpkin faces, lit by candles,
    glow till morning,
    the live flame softening their shells
Pumpkin, a child's toy,
    not for May or December,
    but for late October, ushering in
    November and a Thanksgiving of sorts
Pumpkins from the brittle vine
    the last sweet
    harvest

WRITING ABOUT LITERATURE

1. Keeping a Short Story Journal (Materials for Writing)

The Writing Workshop   Writing is more than a way of communicating what you already know. It is a way of learning, of understanding, of thinking through what you have learned. Writing about literature can make you a more attentive, a more thoughtful reader. When you keep a short story **journal**, you record your impressions and reactions as you read. You have a chance to register your questions, to record tentative conclusions, and to do some preliminary sorting out of your thinking. You try to formulate your personal responses, puzzling over contradictory or unexpected reactions on your part. You experiment with creative responses to what you have read, such as quickly sketched re-creations of a haunting image, a prevailing mood, a turning point in a story.

Writing weekly or biweekly entries in a reading journal or reading log gives you a chance to do some extensive prewriting for more structured papers, to accumulate a rich fund of materials for more formal writing tasks. Here are some possible kinds of entries for your journal:

Thinking about Previous Reading   In one of your first journal entries, you may want to look back over your previous experiences as a reader of fiction. What kind of reading has shaped your expectations as a reader? What kind of story made a lasting impression on you, and why? The story you write about may be a story you loved or admired, but it could also be a story that upset you or disturbed you. Perhaps you will choose a story that did not mean much at the time but that in retrospect has acquired a special meaning.

First Impressions   You will often find it helpful to record your initial impressions after your first reading of a story. Sort out and put into words your first reactions and your preliminary understanding of the story. Take time to gather your thoughts, to pull together what seems most significant. Include any questions the story may have raised in your mind. Here is one reader's first reaction to a story by the Canadian author Alice Munro:

> Alice Munro's "Boys and Girls" takes place in Canada where the head of a small family raises silver foxes for furs. Of the two children, the girl tells the story, making pertinent observations on life on the fox farm and on the other members of the family. Life is seen entirely through her eyes. Foxes are slaughtered and their skins prepared for sale. Old injured horses are killed for food for the foxes. What it means to be a boy and what it means to be a girl become major issues in the story. (Is it significant that both the foxes and the horses are given male and female names?) Gender roles flip-flop in the story as the narrator prides herself on doing "man's work" as her father's helper while her mother grumbles about not getting enough help from her in the kitchen. Stereotypes are constantly challenged, but in the end they seem to triumph as the girl realizes she is "only a girl."

Running Commentary   An excellent way to make the most of your reading is to prepare a running commentary. You jot down your observations, queries, and comments as you read along. You include striking details, quotable quotations, and puzzlers to be checked out later. What at first was a puzzling detail may acquire fuller meaning as the author sounds the same note again or follows up an earlier hint.

Your entry will be your record of how your understanding of a story took shape. Doing such a running commentary will alert you to the clues the author provides to the intention, overall pattern, or overall meaning of a story. However, it will also make sure you get involved in the detail of the story before you interpret, speculate, or editorialize. It will make you realize how much of the **texture** of a story—its web of revealing details, significant dialogue—can be missed in a quick reading.

The following running commentary traces one reader's growing understanding of Ernest Hemingway's "Hills like White Elephants." The story takes the reader into a world of thinking and feeling different from the macho world of bullfights, big-game hunting, and deep-sea fishing that for many readers is the stereotypical Hemingway setting.

A man and a woman (American) are at a railroad station somewhere in Spain. Everything is hot and dry. Very succinct and concrete images: "a curtain, made of strings of bamboo beads, hung across the open door into the bar, to keep out flies."

There seems to be some kind of communication problem, or a misunderstanding of some sort that is unresolved between them. The woman says the hills remind her of "white elephants" but later says that the man "wouldn't have" seen one, so he couldn't know what they look like. He doesn't have the spirit of adventure or the imagination?

Why does everything taste like licorice? The exotic drinks—Anis del Toro and absinthe—both taste like licorice to the woman: "the things you've waited so long for" taste like licorice. A note of bitterness, discontent?

There seems to be a pointlessness in their lives: "all we do" is "look at things and try new drinks."

They start talking about an operation. The man keeps saying it's "an awfully simple operation." The operation is "just to let the air in"—ha! The man pretends he wouldn't mind if the girl didn't go through with the abortion: "If you don't want to you don't have to." Actually, he sees it as very important: "the only thing that bothers us." She feels, "once they take it away, you never get it back." But she also knows that if she decides against the abortion he will not be happy.

The girl knows she really has no choice despite the man's words. He keeps saying, "I don't want you to, I don't care anything about it." But he is actually pushing her to have the abortion. She cannot listen to him anymore; she drives home the word PLEASE seven times when she tells him to stop talking. She says, "I'll scream."

She probably knows that either way they are at the end of their once carefree relationship. Nothing will be as before. "We could have everything and every day we make it more impossible." She sees the end of their lives, as they know them.

At the end, the woman says, "There's nothing wrong with me. I feel fine." But she is not fine. As in much of the story, we have to read her true feelings between the lines. The author doesn't waste words; as he shows in portraying the man in the story, words are cheap. The effect of the story emerges as much from what is not said in the story as from what is.

Possible symbolic overtones: The two lines of railroad track going in opposite directions may stand for the diverging lives of the two characters? The young woman's comparing the hills to elephants shows her affinity with living things—does it hint at her positive attitude toward the unborn child?

Is Hemingway passé? On the surface, the man acts concerned and reassuring: "I don't want anyone but you." But he is really selfish, deceiving, and pushy. This story is timely today. A young woman close to me and her boyfriend are going through the same thing now. He wants her to have an abortion, because that would be easy for him, but she doesn't want one. It is an age-old dilemma. Hemingway doesn't hit the reader over the head with it; there are no flowery descriptive phrases. He never mentions the word *abortion,* and he gives just barely enough facts. But the meaning emerges from the story cleanly, economically, and poignantly.

Clustering   Many writers use clustering to start and organize the flow of ideas. For a story to work, it has to engage with what we already know. What images and feeling does a story activate in the reader's mind? What associations with a central term does the reader bring to the story? **Clustering** is a prewriting technique that lets you explore a network of images, memories, or associations. With strands of ideas branching out from a central stimulus word, you can follow the different chains of associations the central idea brings into play. The idea is to sketch in freely, spontaneously, what a key word or key term brings to mind.

Clustering is a stimulus technique of double value to you if you are the kind of writer who might otherwise be staring at a blank sheet or screen. First, you call up from the memory bank of your mind much material that might potentially be relevant to a topic. You access thoughts and feelings; you map graphically what you are inclined to think and feel on a topic. At the same time, however, a pattern takes shape. You begin to see possible connections and relations. Some sorting, some shaping, is going on at the same time that you are taking stock of relevant memories, associations, and overtones.

In a story like Bernard Malamud's "The Magic Barrel" or Shirley Jackson's "The Lottery," tradition plays a central role—tradition and the way the characters in the story live up to it, or make it suit their purposes. A cluster like the one on the next page might map the network of associations that a reader brings to the story. Notice that in this cluster a pattern is taking shape: The cluster graphically shows thinking in progress. It shows the writer thinking about the two-sided nature of tradition, a force for good and evil.

The passage following the cluster lays out the material and traces the pattern that the cluster has generated.

SAMPLE CLUSTER

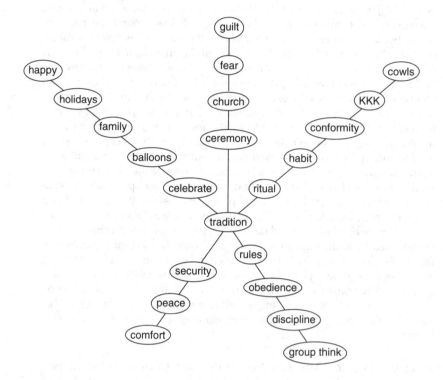

Tradition to many of us means first of all nostalgic memories of Christmas or Easter or Passover, happy hours spent with family and friends, birthday celebrations with balloons and ice cream cake and candles. In the traditional family, there is a sense of security—of knowing what to do, of relying on the tried and true. However, we also feel the weight of tradition— feeling guilty about not going to mass, feeling fear of retribution for our sins and backslidings. The inherent danger in tradition is the reliance on groupthink. Blind obedience to traditional rules and regulations can lead to unquestioned acceptance of cruel or idiotic practices. When we look at the dual nature of tradition, we see interlocking elements that can suddenly cover the face of love with a cowl of enmity and violence.

Focusing on Character In other journal entries, you may go beyond the note-taking stage to start to organize your thinking. For instance, in a **capsule portrait** of a character, you pull together traits illustrated in the incidents of the story. You integrate crucial hints about the character that may be scattered over quite a few pages. What kind of person does the author show you? What are key traits, and how are they related? Is there a trait that provides the clue to the character as a whole? Does the character change or grow in the course of the story? Here is a sample of such a character portrait:

The central character in Alice Munro's story "Boys and Girls" is struggling to adjust to the fact that she is slowly changing from a girl to a young woman. In the beginning, she is her Daddy's helper around the fox farm where her father raises foxes for their pelts. Oblivious to the stereotypical female gender role, she helps her father care for the animals, rakes up the grass or weeds he has cut, and does other traditional "male" chores. However, she begins to realize that as a female she is expected to do some things and not others; in particular, she is expected to help her mother in the kitchen, a place she detests. She rebels against her expected role, trying to stay out of the kitchen and close to the outdoors she loves. Her grandmother's comments, such as "Girls don't slam doors like that" or "Girls keep their knees together when they sit down," lead her to continue to slam doors and to sit as awkwardly as possible. Her rebellious behavior shows her strong will, stubbornness, and nonconformity, and, most of all, her spirit. Her spiritedness is mirrored in her daydreams of performing heroic rescues. She has a zest for constant excitement in life, and when her life doesn't supply it, she creates her own, as when she dares her three-year-old little brother to climb the barn ladder to the top beam. As she gets older, her old spirit carries over when she allows Flora, the horse scheduled to be shot for meat for the foxes, to escape through the gate. This scene shows her developing her own person, her own opinions, her own values. Despite the ending of the story, where she seems to be submitting herself to her expected gender roles, I believe that the strong spirit she has exhibited throughout the story will never leave her.

Focusing on Theme   You may frequently want to sum up for yourself the impact or meaning of a story as a whole. What idea or ideas stay with the reader at the end of the story? What seems to give the story its special quality or particular force? Here is a sample entry:

"The Open Boat," by Stephen Crane, is a late 19th to early 20th century story. Crew members and a newspaper correspondent in a lifeboat struggle for days in the stormy shark-infested sea, with their hopes for rescue or an easy landfall repeatedly dashed. In the end one of them drowns; the others make it to shore. This is an early modern view: There is no loving or benevolent nature. The shipwrecked sailors undergo a terrible ordeal, but they do not conclude that nature was out to punish them, nor do they feel that nature is loving or maternal. Birds were made to survive on the ocean; they are part of nature. The only way for human beings to survive is to work together—practice brotherhood. Since they are not at home in nature, they must make their home within it with the help of others. They need solidarity. Nature is alien and inhospitable; it couldn't care less.

For Class Interaction   You may want to share one or more early journal entries with your classmates. For instance, you might want to discuss with them what made a story especially meaningful to you, or what expectations you brought to it, or what made it difficult for you to read or enjoy.

2 SETTING
Landscapes of the Mind

Here I am, where I ought to be. A writer must have a place where he or she feels this, a place to love and be irritated with.

LOUISE ERDRICH

Once in their lives people ought to concentrate their minds upon the remembered earth. They ought to give themselves up to a particular landscape in their experience, looking at it from as many angles as they can, to wonder upon it, to dwell upon it.

N. SCOTT MOMADAY

FOCUS ON SETTING

A story creates its own world. It takes us to a **setting** in space and in time. In a successful story, that place becomes a small universe of its own, consistent in itself. The story creates a context whose assumptions we accept for the duration of the story. We enter into the world of the story the way we might honor customs, closing hours, and curfews when we spend time in another country. While a powerful story works its spell, we think and feel in the context of the story—somewhat the way organisms in a biosphere live on the terms of their self-contained environment.

Some writers sketch times and locations only in rough outline, leaving much to our imagination. But other writers painstakingly re-create or reenact a setting, a scene. They conjure up a place and take us there. They rely heavily on the setting to help them create the illusion of reality, so that we will accept characters and events as real also. Toward the beginning of his story "Araby," James Joyce takes us to the Dublin of his childhood, where the neighborhood boys played in a dead-end street during the short days of winter, when dusk fell early. What kind of world is beginning to take shape in the following passage?

When we met in the street the houses had grown somber. The space of sky above us was the color of ever-changing violet and toward it the lamps of

31

the street lifted their feeble lanterns. The cold air stung us and we played till our bodies glowed. Our shouts echoed in the silent street. The career of our play brought us through the dark muddy lanes behind the houses where we ran the gauntlet of the rough tribes from the cottages, to the back doors of the dark dripping gardens where odors arose from the ashpits, to the dark odorous stables where a coachman smoothed and combed the horse or shook music from the buckled harness.

In creating this setting for us, the imaginative writer is our scout and interpreter. He is more alert and sensitive than ordinary people, more responsive to experience, taking in more of its sights and sounds and odors. Joyce recreates for us the shade of light, the feeble streetlights "lifting" their lanterns toward the sky, the odors from the ashpits and the stables. He registers what there is for an alert observer to see and hear and smell. The reality he re-creates for us is down-to-earth, with dark muddy alleys, danger from rough kids from a low-income neighborhood close by, and the decaying odor of ashes from old-style hearths and stoves. But the world created for us here is also laced with strange beauty—"the ever-changing violet of the sky," the jangling metal of the horse's harness sounding like music that the coachman "shook" from the gear.

The setting created in the opening paragraphs of this story is not just a backdrop against which any optional drama might be played out. It projects a **mood**—a somber if not gloomy mood, contrasting with the intense vitality of the shouting children, who played till their bodies "glowed." Subliminally, this contrast creates expectations; it steers our attention. Whatever shape the story may take, we do not expect a story in which frivolous characters will tiptoe through tulips. Nor do we expect a story in which burnt-out individuals play variations on a theme of "I-don't-care." Instead, we will not be surprised if we see an imaginative, intense character (or characters) in a setting that offers obstacles or limitations to the life of the imagination.

Becoming sensitive to setting will help you meet a story on its own terms. Often the setting will not just be geographical or physical; it will bring with it ways of thinking or feeling that come with the territory. It is likely to come with customs, assumptions, or collective memories that will play a role in the story. The story may in fact be about how a character discovers these, is shaped by them, rebels against them, or leaves them behind. The setting of a story is not just an external landscape; it is more often a landscape of the mind.

THE SETTING AND THE STORY

There are deserts in every life, and the desert must be depicted if we are to give a fair and complete idea of the country.

ANDRÉ MAUROIS

One of the first questions we ask of a story is, "Where is the story taking us?" By establishing the setting, a writer lets us know where we are, makes us realize what time it is. The setting may create a pervasive mood, felt not only by the reader but also by the characters in the story—decay, constraint, splendor, guilt, liberation. The setting may be exotic, with the story placing us in strange circumstances, requiring of us a major effort of the imagination. But the setting may also be totally ordinary, reacquainting us with what Marian Evans (whose pen name was George Eliot) called "the beauty of the commonplace." It may ask us to look at familiar surroundings as if we were seeing them for the first time.

Often the setting plays a major role in shaping the characters, the action, or the theme of a story. A *New York Times* reviewer said about the stories in Bobbie Ann Mason's *Shiloh and Other Stories* (1982),

> Mason's setting was Kentucky—not the old Kentucky of small towns and gracious farms, but that proud territory of the new South speckled with shopping malls and subdivisions, fast-food franchises and drive-in movies, a shiny new place, vacuumed clean of history and tradition. Reeling from the swiftness of the transition, Mason's characters all seemed to wander about in a fog, either spacing out in front of the television or passively drifting away from their families and friends, aware, however dimly, that they had misplaced something important along the way. (Michiko Kakutani)

Here are some major ways the setting may help give shape to a story as a whole.

The Setting as Mirror   The setting may mirror a prevailing mood. It may signal or reinforce prevailing emotions. An arid landscape, for instance, may mirror despair, spiritual desolation. Barren hills, scrubby vegetation, and dusty dirt roads may provide a fitting setting for emotionally dried-up characters. On the other hand, sultry weather and thunderstorms, like the mood music in a movie, may prepare you for pent-up passions and emotional upheavals.

However, we cannot always expect an obvious connection between the setting and the people who play their roles in it. The setting may be ironic. Our sense of **irony** makes us respond with a grim smile when things do not turn out the way we would like or expect, while a little voice in the back of our minds says: "I should have known!" Modern writers often have a highly developed sense of irony. Their characters are just as likely to be depressed as happy in a springtime setting. A modern story may show us people who are lonely in a crowd.

The Setting as Mold   The setting of a story often shapes character. It helps make people what they are. Someone growing up on a farm, with its endless chores, dependence on rain and sun, and closeness to living things, is likely to have a different outlook, a different definition of life, than someone growing up in a city neighborhood where the only open spaces are parking lots.

A story may show its characters as creatures of the setting, reflecting its mood, living out its mores or approved ways of acting and thinking. A familiar theme in serious modern fiction is that of invisible walls: Characters find themselves trapped in a restrictive environment. The story may show them discovering its limitations, coming up against invisible barriers that hem them in. Characters may find themselves trapped in the spiritual wasteland of suburbia, or in a small decaying town that becomes for them the graveyard of hope. (On the other hand, a story may show a character rebelling against a stifling environment, struggling to break free, to break out.)

The Setting as Challenge   A story may take people out of their usual setting, their daily routine, and put them to the test. An unusual setting may become a major player in the drama acted out in a story. In Jack London's classic "To Light a Fire," the extreme numbing cold of the frozen north becomes the mortal enemy of the traveler who finds himself unable to light the life-saving fire.

The Setting as Escape   Escape literature takes us to imaginary settings where we act out daydreams to which ordinary reality is not hospitable. The story may take us to a mansion in the pre–Civil War South to make us witness scenes of flaming passion. It may take us to ancient Rome to appall us with scenes of treachery and depravity. However, a faraway setting may not necessarily provide an escape; it may really be the destination of a journey of discovery, where we may encounter facets of our own personality denied an outlet in our ordinary world.

The Alien Setting   Much modern literature circles back to the loss of roots, the loss of home. You may find yourself in a setting that is inhospitable, like an alien planet. You may identify with the exile, the undesirable, the refugee. In the short stories of Ernest Hemingway and other writers of the twenties and thirties, you encounter the eternal tourist, the expatriate—the person in exile from his or her own country. In much of the fiction of Franz Kafka, you find yourself in a nightmare setting. As in a bad dream, you may struggle with an environment that defies your best efforts at getting control of the situation, at understanding what is going on.

A CLASSIC SHORT STORY: JOYCE'S "ARABY"

"This race and this country and this life produced me," he said. "I shall express myself as I am."
JAMES JOYCE, *A PORTRAIT OF THE ARTIST AS A YOUNG MAN*

James Joyce (1882–1941), one of the towering innovators in modern fiction, was one of the Irish writers that have helped shape twentieth-century literature. Like other artists, writers, and intellectuals of his time, Joyce worked most of his life in self-imposed exile from his native country, becoming one of the great expatriate authors of the century. Joyce was born in a suburb of

Dublin; he left Dublin at the age of twenty-two, and he was to return only twice for brief visits. However, the city of his birth and its people are in almost everything he wrote.

Joyce was the son of an outgoing but spendthrift father and a devoutly Catholic mother. At the age of six, he entered a school run by Jesuit priests; he later enrolled at the Jesuit order's Belvedere College in Dublin. (His mother wanted him as the oldest of her ten children to become a priest in the Roman Catholic church.) His work is steeped in the vocabulary, and in the ways of thinking and feeling, of centuries of religious tradition. However, he decided against entering the priesthood, fighting the narrowing of vision that he saw as the price of committing to a traditional creed. He similarly distanced himself from the passionate and often intolerant nationalism that was the legacy of his country's struggle for liberation from British colonial rule. Family, church, and country came to seem to him like nets thrown to contain and restrain the free exercise of the creative spirit. He came to see his native city as "a place too pre-occupied with the past and too much in love with lost causes." As he said in his largely autobiographical first novel, *A Portrait of the Artist as a Young Man* (1916), "I will not serve that in which I no longer believe."

For almost a quarter of a century, Joyce barely survived by teaching Eng-lish and doing clerical work, first in Zurich (Switzerland) and later in Trieste (Italy) and Paris. He wrote constantly, developing the narrative technique known as **stream of consciousness** that was to revolutionize much of modern fiction. Human beings do not think in complete sentences, carry on coherent logical conversations with themselves, or make rational decisions after lining up the pro and con. Instead, their mental world is a shifting sequence of sensa-tions, thoughts, and feelings—a kaleidoscopic mix of fleeting images, bodily sensations, memories, half-finished trains of thought. To approximate the real-ity of what it feels like to be a feeling, thinking human being, a writer should transcribe this **interior monologue,** tracing the typical mixture of daydream and reality, pursuing chains of association. In Joyce's masterpiece, the novel *Ulysses* (1922), a thread of external events alternates with extended stretches of interior monologue immersing the readers in a stream of impressions, reminis-cences, and half-formulated thoughts.

Since the mind dwells on basic emotional concerns without polite dis-guise, the treatment of sex in *Ulysses* was too explicit for the guardians of pub-lic morality, and the novel for many years had to be smuggled into the United States. At the same time, it made wide use of complex allusions and symbolic parallels to Greek mythology, with the daily round of Leopold Bloom, a Dublin salesman, paralleling the mythical journey of Ulysses. In his *Finnegan's Wake* (1939), Joyce developed a rich private language exploiting multileveled puns, allusions, and associations.

We call a work of literature a classic when readers and critics return to it again and again, when it survives changes in fashion. The following classic short story is from an early collection, *Dubliners* (1914), intended by Joyce as "a chapter of the moral history of Ireland." Compared with Joyce's later work, these stories have a straightforward, conventional story line. However, they anticipate his later work by focusing on the private thoughts, emotions, and daydreams of his characters.

J A M E S   J O Y C E   (1882–1941)
Araby 1914

[A few references in this story might puzzle today's reader. One of the books mentioned early told the life story of Vidocq, a legendary French detective. The Freemasons, members of private fraternal organizations, were viewed with suspicion by people with traditional religious views. The florin was a British silver coin worth two shillings. A Café Chantant was a French coffeehouse with musical entertainment.]

North Richmond Street, being blind, was a quiet street except at the hour when the Christian Brothers' School set the boys free. An uninhabited house of two stories stood at the blind end, detached from its neighbors in a square ground. The other houses of the street, conscious of decent lives within them, gazed at one another with brown imperturbable faces.

The former tenant of our house, a priest, had died in the back drawing-room. Air, musty from having been long enclosed, hung in all the rooms, and the waste room behind the kitchen was littered with old useless papers. Among these I found a few paper-covered books, the pages of which were curled and damp: *The Abbot*, by Walter Scott, *The Devout Communicant* and *The Memoirs of Vidocq*. I liked the last best because its leaves were yellow. The wild garden behind the house contained a central apple-tree and a few straggling bushes under one of which I found the late tenant's rusty bicycle-pump. He had been a very charitable priest; in his will he had left all his money to institutions and the furniture of his house to his sister.

When the short days of winter came dusk fell before we had well eaten our dinners. When we met in the street the houses had grown somber. The space of sky above us was the color of ever-changing violet and toward it the lamps of the street lifted their feeble lanterns. The cold air stung us and we played till our bodies glowed. Our shouts echoed in the silent street. The career of our play brought us through the dark muddy lanes behind the houses where we ran the gauntlet of the rough tribes from the cottages, to the back doors of the dark dripping gardens where odors arose from the ash-pits, to the dark odorous stables where a coachman smoothed and combed the horse or shook music from the buckled harness. When we returned to the street light from the kitchen windows had filled the areas. If my uncle was seen turning the corner we hid in the shadow until we had seen him safely housed. Of if Mangan's sister came out on the doorstep to call her brother in to his tea we watched her from our shadow peer up and down the street. We waited to see whether she would remain or go in and, if she remained, we left our shadow and walked up to Mangan's steps resignedly. She was waiting for us, her figure defined by the light from the half-opened door. Her brother always teased her before he obeyed and I stood by the railings looking at her. Her dress swung as she moved her body, and the soft rope of her hair tossed from side to side.

Every morning I lay on the floor in the front parlor watching her door. The blind was pulled down to within an inch of the sash so that I could not be seen. When she came out on the doorstep my heart leaped. I ran to the hall, seized my books and followed her. I kept her brown figure always in my eye and, when we came near the point at which our ways diverged, I quickened my pace and passed her. This happened morning after morning. I had never spoken to her, except for a few casual words, and yet her name was like a summons to all my foolish blood.

Her image accompanied me even in places the most hostile to romance. On Saturday evenings when my aunt went marketing I had to go to carry some of the parcels. We walked through the flaring streets, jostled by drunken men and bargaining women, amid the curses of laborers, the shrill litanies of shop-boys who stood on guard by the barrels of pigs' cheeks, the nasal chanting of street-singers, who sang a *come-all-you* about O'Donovan Rossa, or a ballad about the troubles in our native land. These noises converged in a single sensation of life for me: I imagined that I bore my chalice safely through a throng of foes. Her name sprang to my lips at moments in strange prayers and praises which I myself did not understand. My eyes were often full of tears (I could not tell why) and at times a flood from my heart seemed to pour itself out into my bosom. I thought little of the future. I did not know whether I would ever speak to her or not or, if I spoke to her, how I could tell her of my confused adoration. But my body was like a harp and her words and gestures were like fingers running upon the wires.

One evening I went into the back drawing-room in which the priest had died. It was a dark rainy evening and there was no sound in the house. Through one of the broken panes I heard the rain impinge upon the earth, the fine incessant needles of water playing in the sodden beds. Some distant lamp or lighted window gleamed below me. I was thankful that I could see so little. All my senses seemed to desire to veil themselves and, feeling that I was about to slip from them, I pressed the palms of my hands together until they trembled, murmuring: *"O love! O love!"* many times.

At last she spoke to me. When she addressed the first words to me I was so confused that I did not know what to answer. She asked me was I going to *Araby*. I forgot whether I answered yes or no. It would be a splendid bazaar, she said she would love to go.

"And why can't you?" I asked.

While she spoke she turned a silver bracelet round and round her wrist. She could not go, she said, because there would be a retreat that week in her convent. Her brother and two other boys were fighting for their caps and I was alone at the railings. She held one of the spikes, bowing her head towards me. The light from the lamp opposite our door caught the white curve of her neck, lit up her hair that rested there and, falling, lit up the hand upon the railing. It fell over one side of her dress and caught the white border of a petticoat, just visible as she stood at ease.

"It's well for you," she said.

"If I go," I said, "I will bring you something."

What innumerable follies laid waste my waking and sleeping thoughts after that evening! I wished to annihilate the tedious intervening days. I chafed against the work of school. At night in my bedroom and by day in the classroom her image came between me and the page I strove to read. The syllables of the word *Araby* were called to me through the silence in which my soul luxuriated and cast an Eastern enchantment over me. I asked for leave to go to the bazaar on Saturday night. My aunt was surprised and hoped it was not some Freemason affair. I answered few questions in class. I watched my master's face pass from amiability to sternness; he hoped I was not beginning to idle. I could not call my wandering thoughts together. I had hardly any patience with the serious work of life which, now that it stood between me and my desire, seemed to me child's play, ugly monotonous child's play.

On Saturday morning I reminded my uncle that I wished to go to the bazaar in the evening. He was fussing at the hallstand, looking for the hat-brush, and answered me curtly:

"Yes, boy, I know."

As he was in the hall I could not go into the front parlor and lie at the window. I felt the house in bad humor and walked slowly toward the school. The air was pitilessly raw and already my heart misgave me. 15

When I came home to dinner my uncle had not yet been home. Still it was early. I sat staring at the clock for some time and, when its ticking began to irritate me, I left the room. I mounted the staircase and gained the upper part of the house. The high cold empty gloomy rooms liberated me and I went from room to room singing. From the front window I saw my companions playing below in the street. Their cries reached me weakened and indistinct and, leaning my forehead against the cool glass, I looked over at the dark house where she lived. I may have stood there for an hour, seeing nothing but the brown-clad figure cast by my imagination, touched discreetly by the lamplight at the curved neck, at the hand upon the railings and at the border below the dress.

When I came downstairs again I found Mrs. Mercer sitting at the fire. She was an old garrulous woman, a pawn-broker's widow, who collected used stamps for some pious purpose. I had to endure the gossip of the tea-table. The meal was prolonged beyond an hour and still my uncle did not come. Mrs. Mercer stood up to go: she was sorry she couldn't wait any longer, but it was after eight o'clock and she did not like to be out late, as the night air was bad for her. When she had gone I began to walk up and down the room, clenching my fists. My aunt said:

"I'm afraid you may put off your bazaar for this night of Our Lord."

At nine o'clock I heard my uncle's latchkey in the halldoor. I heard him talking to himself and heard the hallstand rocking when it had received the weight of his overcoat. I could interpret these signs. When he was midway through his dinner I asked him to give me the money to go to the bazaar. He had forgotten.

"The people are in bed and after their first sleep now," he said. 20

I did not smile. My aunt said to him energetically:

"Can't you give him the money and let him go? You've kept him late enough as it is."

My uncle said he was very sorry he had forgotten. He said he believed in the old saying: "All work and no play makes Jack a dull boy." He asked me where I was going and, when I had told him a second time he asked me did I know *The Arab's Farewell to his Steed*. When I left the kitchen he was about to recite the opening lines of the piece to my aunt.

I held a florin tightly in my hand as I strode down Buckingham Street toward the station. The sight of the streets thronged with buyers and glaring with gas recalled to me the purpose of my journey. I took my seat in a third-class carriage of a deserted train. After an intolerable delay the train moved out of the station slowly. It crept onward among ruinous houses and over the twinkling river. At Westland Row Station a crowd of people pressed to the carriage doors; but the porters moved them back, saying that it was a special train for the bazaar. I remained alone in the bare carriage. In a few minutes the train drew up beside an improvised wooden platform. I passed out on to the road and saw by the lighted dial of a clock that it was ten minutes to ten. In front of me was a large building which displayed the magical name.

I could not find any sixpenny entrance and, fearing that the bazaar would be 25 closed, I passed in quickly through a turnstile, handing a shilling to a weary-looking man. I found myself in a big hall girdled at half its height by a gallery. Nearly all the stalls were closed and the greater part of the hall was in darkness. I recognized a silence like that which pervades a church after a service. I walked into the center of the bazaar timidly. A few people were gathered about the stalls which were still open. Before a curtain, over which the words *Café Chantant* were written in colored lamps, two men were counting money on a salver. I listened to the fall of the coins.

Remembering with difficulty why I had come I went over to one of the stalls and examined porcelain vases and flowered tea-sets. At the door of the stall a young lady was talking and laughing with two young gentlemen. I remarked their English accents and listened vaguely to their conversation.

"O, I never said such a thing!"

"O, but you did!"

"O, but I didn't!"

"Didn't she say that?"

"Yes. I heard her."

"O, there's a . . . fib!"

Observing me the young lady came over and asked me did I wish to buy anything. The tone of her voice was not encouraging; she seemed to have spoken to me out of a sense of duty. I looked humbly at the great jars that stood like eastern guards at either side of the dark entrance to the stall and murmured:

"No, thank you."

The young lady changed the position of one of the vases and went back to the two young men. They began to talk of the same subject. Once or twice the young lady glanced at me over her shoulder.

I lingered before her stall, though I knew my stay was useless, to make my interest in her wares seem the more real. Then I turned away slowly and walked down the middle of the bazaar. I allowed the two pennies to fall against the sixpence in my pocket. I heard a voice call from one end of the gallery that the light was out. The upper part of the hall was now completely dark.

Gazing up into the darkness I saw myself as a creature driven and derided by vanity; and my eyes burned with anguish and anger.

What might a responsive reader get from this story? There are probably at least two ways to look at the role of the setting in this story. (Which is closer to your own response as a reader?)

✧ Love surfaces in unlikely places—in the ordinary settings of uninteresting people and their dull lives. When we see the ordinary boys play in the muddy street, we do not expect an emotional attachment that has the intensity of religious devotion. However, the power of the imagination transfigures the dull, everyday reality of people's lives. We are not doomed to be unimaginative clods.

✧ The setting sets invisible limits. We have a capacity for love, for worship, for imagination far beyond what the ordinary reality of our lives can accommodate or bring to fruition. We are doomed to disappointment. Our yearnings create a dream of fulfillment that cannot possibly come true. The setting, the real world we live in, is hostile to our dreams.

THE RECEPTIVE READER

1. What striking details help the setting come to life for you? Which seem to set the tone or point forward to the rest of the story?

2. What striking images help you understand the boy's feelings? What images give his devotion a quasi-religious quality? (What are the associations of the word *chalice*; what feelings does it bring into play?)

3. Is the boy able to share his feelings with anyone? If not, why not?

4. What is the role of the uncle in the story?

5. Is it a coincidence that the climactic high point of the story takes place in a bazaar—a special annual event?

6. As we watch crucial scenes in the story, we at times have to sense the boy's feelings rather than having them explained in so many words by the author. What are some examples?

THE PERSONAL RESPONSE

Is the boy merely infatuated? Should he have known better? Is he acting "immature"?

THE CREATIVE DIMENSION

Writers sometimes describe how a short story took shape from a striking, teasing image in the writer's mind. Sometimes after we finish reading, what stays with us is a haunting image that seems to sum up something essential in the story. The following student-written passages re-create a key moment in Joyce's "Araby." What do they capture in the story? Write your own re-creation of a haunting image or key moment in Joyce's story or in another story in this chapter.

1. We played in
   the cold, short winter evenings
   colored violet with dusk.
   We made a career
   of playing long in
   the streets
   and alleys with shadows
   our bodies small and cold
   and glowing.
   In the street the lamps
   lined up,
   illuminating
   a playmate's sister strolling
   towards us,
   soft smooth hair,
   swinging skirt.

2. When I was eight, I would play till the night came on, the dusk slipping over the world in the sky above our heads and between the buildings. As the violet glowed stronger, the world would suddenly, for a flash, have sharp outlines, shapes of heavy black cut out against the coming night. I would be running hard. There were the times after the shouts had flown past me down

the streets, when the echoes of my feet clacked underneath me, and then I would pull up breathless at the front steps, my throat raw. Mangan's sister there, in the dim light, three years older than I, with her long rich brown hair. I would watch from the shadows. I watched the night come on. I felt its chill; I felt its warmth.

SETTINGS: THE SENSE OF PLACE

Some writers are especially effective at creating a compelling environment —a world that we can imaginatively enter and reenter. In reading the following stories, pay special attention to the role the setting plays in the story as a whole.

EUDORA WELTY (born 1909)

What alone can instruct the heart is the experience of living, experience which can be vile; but what can never do it any good, what harms it more than vileness, are those tales, those legends . . . , those universal false dreams, the hopes, sentimental and ubiquitous, which are not on any account to be gone by.

EUDORA WELTY

Eudora Welty was born and has spent most of her life in Mississippi. Both as a writer and as a friendly critic of other writers' work, she helped make the modern short story a major contemporary literary form. Critics have identified as major themes in her work her love of the South, the pain of growing up, and the agony of loneliness. Her novels include *The Optimist's Daughter* (1972), for which she received the Pulitzer Prize in 1973.

Welty helped set the tone for much modern fiction by her refusal to indulge in "false dreams" and sentimental hopes. Katherine Anne Porter, another master of the modern short story, said of her that she had "an eye and an ear sharp, shrewd, and true as a tuning fork." Welty prided herself on what Porter called her "blistering humor" and "just cruelty." In the following story, Welty looks at both youth and age without sentimentality—without the rosy glow that comes from making reality more innocent, more heart-warming, or more reassuring than it is.

A Visit of Charity 1941

It was mid-morning—a very cold, bright day. Holding a potted plant before her, a girl of fourteen jumped off the bus in front of the Old Ladies' Home, on the outskirts of town. She wore a red coat, and her straight yellow hair was hanging down loose from the pointed white cap all the little girls were wearing that year. She stopped for a moment beside one of the prickly dark shrubs with which the city had beautified the Home, and then proceeded slowly toward the building, which was of whitewashed brick and reflected the winter sunlight like a block of ice. As she walked vaguely up the steps she shifted the small pot from hand to hand; then she had to set it down and remove her mittens before she could open the heavy door.

"I'm a Campfire girl. . . . I have to pay a visit to some old lady," she told the nurse at the desk. This was a woman in a white uniform who looked as if she were cold; she had close-cut hair which stood up on the very top of her head exactly like a sea wave. Marian, the little girl, did not tell her that this visit would give her a minimum of only three points in her score.

"Acquainted with any of our residents?" asked the nurse. She lifted one eyebrow and spoke like a man.

"With any old ladies? No—but—that is, any of them will do," Marian stammered. With her free hand she pushed her hair behind her ears, as she did when it was time to study Science.

The nurse shrugged and rose. "You have a nice *multiflora cineraria* there," she remarked as she walked ahead down the hall of closed doors to pick out an old lady.

There was loose, bulging linoleum on the floor. Marian felt as if she were walking on the waves, but the nurse paid no attention to it. There was a smell in the hall like the interior of a clock. Everything was silent until, behind one of the doors, an old lady of some kind cleared her throat like a sheep bleating. This decided the nurse. Stopping in her tracks, she first extended her arm, bent her elbow, and leaned forward from the hips—all to examine the watch strapped to her wrist; then she gave a loud double-rap on the door.

"There are two in each room," the nurse remarked over her shoulder.

"Two what?" asked Marian without thinking. The sound like a sheep's bleating almost made her turn around and run back.

One old woman was pulling the door open in short, gradual jerks, and when she saw the nurse a strange smile forced her old face dangerously awry. Marian, suddenly propelled by the strong, impatient arm of the nurse, saw next the side-face of another old woman, even older, who was lying flat in bed with a cap on and a counterpane drawn up to her chin.

"Visitor," said the nurse, and after one more shove she was off up the hall.

Marian stood tongue-tied; both hands held the potted plant. The old woman, still with that terrible, square smile (which was a smile of welcome) stamped on her bony face, was waiting. . . . Perhaps she said something. The old woman in bed said nothing at all, and she did not look around.

Suddenly Marian saw a hand, quick as a bird claw, reach up in the air and pluck the white cap off her head. At the same time, another claw to match drew her all the way into the room, and the next moment the door closed behind her.

"My, my, my," said the old lady at her side.

Marian stood enclosed by a bed, a washstand and a chair; the tiny room had altogether too much furniture. Everything smelled wet—even the bare floor. She held onto the back of the chair, which was wicker and felt soft and damp. Her heart beat more and more slowly, her hands got colder and colder, and she could not hear whether the old women were saying anything or not. She could not see them very clearly. How dark it was! The window shade was down, and the only door was shut. Marian looked at the ceiling. . . . It was like being caught in a robber's cave, just before one was murdered.

"Did you come to be our little girl for awhile?" the first robber asked.

Then something was snatched from Marian's hand—the little potted plant.

5

10

15

"Flowers!" screamed the old woman. She stood holding the pot in an undecided way. "Pretty flowers," she added.

Then the old woman in bed cleared her throat and spoke. "They are not pretty," she said, still without looking around, but very distinctly.

Marian suddenly pitched against the chair and sat down in it.

"Pretty flowers," the first old woman insisted. "Pretty—pretty. . . ." 20

Marian wished she had the little pot back for just a moment—she had forgotten to look at the plant herself before giving it away. What did it look like?

"Stinkweeds," said the other old woman sharply. She had a bunchy white forehead and red eyes like a sheep. Now she turned them toward Marian. The fogginess seemed to rise in her throat again, and she bleated, "Who—are—you?"

To her surprise, Marian could not remember her name. "I'm a Campfire Girl," she said finally.

"Watch out for the germs," said the old woman like a sheep, not addressing anyone.

"One came out last month to see us," said the first old woman. 25

A sheep or a germ? wondered Marian dreamily, holding onto the chair.

"Did not!" cried the other old woman.

"Did so! Read to us out of the Bible, and we enjoyed it!" screamed the first.

"Who enjoyed it!" said the woman in bed. Her mouth was unexpectedly small and sorrowful, like a pet's.

"We enjoyed it," insisted the other. "You enjoyed it—I enjoyed it." 30

"We all enjoyed it," said Marian, without realizing that she had said a word.

The first old woman had just finished putting the potted plant high, high on the top of the wardrobe, where it could hardly be seen from below. Marian wondered how she had ever succeeded in placing it there, how she could ever have reached so high.

"You mustn't pay any attention to old Addie," she now said to the little girl. "She's ailing today."

"Will you shut your mouth?" said the woman in bed. "I am not."

"You're a story." 35

"I can't stay but a minute—really, I can't," said Marian suddenly. She looked down at the wet floor and thought that if she were sick in here they would have to let her go.

With much to-do the first old woman sat down in a rocking chair—still another piece of furniture!—and began to rock. With the fingers on one hand she touched a very dirty cameo pin on her chest. "What do you do at school?" she asked.

"I don't know . . ." said Marian. She tried to think but she could not.

"Oh, but the flowers are beautiful," the old woman whispered. She seemed to rock faster and faster; Marian did not see how anyone could rock so fast.

"Ugly," said the woman in bed. 40

"If we bring flowers—" Marian began, and then fell silent. She had almost said that if Campfire Girls brought flowers to the Old Ladies' Home, the visit would count one extra point, and if they took a Bible with them on the bus and read it to the old ladies, it counted double. But the old woman had not listened, anyway; she was rocking and watching the other one, who watched back from the bed.

"Poor Addie is ailing. She has to take medicine—see?" she said, pointing a horny finger at a row of bottles on the table, and rocking so high that her black comfort shoes lifted off the floor like a little child's.

"I am no more sick than you are," said the woman in bed.

"Oh yes you are!"

"I just got more sense than you have, that's all," said the other old woman, nodding her head. 45

"That's only the contrary way she talks when *you all* come," said the first old lady with sudden intimacy. She stopped the rocker with a neat pat of her feet and leaned toward Marian. Her hand reached over—it felt like a petunia leaf, clinging and just a little sticky.

"Will you hush! Will you hush!" cried the other one.

Marian leaned back rigidly in her chair.

"When I was a little girl like you, I went to school and all," said the old woman in the same intimate, menacing voice. "Not here—another town. . . ."

"Hush!" said the sick woman. "You never went to school. You never came and 50 you never went. You never were anywhere—only here. You never were born! You don't know anything. Your head is empty, your heart and hands and your old black purse are all empty, even that little old box that you brought with you you brought empty—you showed it to me. And yet you talk, talk, talk, talk, talk all the time until I think I'm losing my mind. Who are you? You're a stranger—a perfect stranger! Don't you know you're a stranger? Is it possible that they have actually done a thing like this to anyone—sent them in a stranger to talk, and rock, and tell away her whole long rigmarole? Do they seriously suppose that I'll be able to keep it up, day in, day out, night in, night out, living in the same room with a terrible old woman—forever?"

Marian saw the old woman's eyes grow bright and turn toward her. This old woman was looking at her with despair and calculation in her face. Her small lips suddenly dropped apart, and exposed a half circle of false teeth with tan gums.

"Come here, I want to tell you something," she whispered. "Come here!"

Marian was trembling, and her heart nearly stopped beating altogether for a moment.

"Now, now, Addie," said the first old woman. "That's not polite. Do you know what's really the matter with old Addie today?" She, too, looked at Marian; one of her eyelids drooped low.

"The matter?" the child repeated stupidly. "What's the matter with her?" 55

"Why, she's mad because it's her birthday!" said the first old woman, beginning to rock again and giving a little crow as though she had answered her own riddle.

"It is not, it is not!" screamed the old woman in bed. "It is not my birthday, no one knows when that is but myself, and will you please be quiet and say nothing more, or I'll go straight out of my mind!" She turned her eyes toward Marian again, and presently she said in the soft, foggy voice, "When the worst comes to the worst, I ring this bell, and the nurse comes." One of her hands was drawn out from under the patched counterpane—a thin little hand with enormous black freckles. With a finger which would not hold still she pointed to a little bell on the table among the bottles.

"How old are you?" Marian breathed. Now she could see the old woman in bed very closely and plainly, and very abruptly, from all sides, as in dreams. She wondered about her—she wondered for a moment as though there was nothing else in the world to wonder about. It was the first time such a thing had happened to Marian.

"I won't tell!"

The old face on the pillow, where Marian was bending over it, slowly gathered and 60 collapsed. Soft whimpers came out of the small open mouth. It was a sheep that she sounded like—a little lamb. Marian's face drew very close, the yellow hair hung forward.

"She's crying!" She turned a bright, burning face up to the first old woman.

"That's Addie for you," the old woman said spitefully.

Marian jumped up and moved toward the door. For the second time, the claw almost touched her hair, but it was not quick enough. The little girl put her cap on.

"Well, it was a real visit," said the old woman, following Marian through the doorway and all the way out into the hall. Then from behind she suddenly clutched the child with her sharp little fingers. In an affected, high-pitched whine she cried, "Oh, little girl, have you a penny to spare for a poor old woman that's not got anything of her own? We don't have a thing in the world—not a penny for candy—not a thing! Little girl, just a nickel—a penny—"

Marian pulled violently against the old hands for a moment before she was free. 65
Then she ran down the hall, without looking behind her and without looking at the nurse, who was reading *Field & Stream* at her desk. The nurse, after another triple motion to consult her wrist watch, asked automatically the question put to visitors in all institutions: "Won't you stay and have dinner with *us?*"

Marian never replied. She pushed the heavy door open into the cold air and ran down the steps.

Under the prickly shrub she stooped and quickly, without being seen, retrieved a red apple she had hidden there.

Her yellow hair under the white cap, her scarlet coat, her bare knees all flashed in the sunlight as she ran to meet the big bus rocketing through the street.

"Wait for me!" she shouted. As though at an imperial command, the bus ground to stop.

She jumped on and took a big bite out of the apple. 70

THE RECEPTIVE READER

1. The *setting* of a story helps create expectations—it can precondition us to expect certain kinds of things (and not others) to happen there. What striking details early in the story help establish the mood? How do they make you feel about the institution? How do they guide your expectations?

2. What telling details shape your reaction to the nurse?

3. How does the author bring the two old women to life? (What are striking images?) How do the two women fit the setting in which they live?

4. What are the motives and feelings of the girl as the *major character?* Why is she there? How does she respond to finding herself transplanted to a strange new setting? How does she react to being "out of her element"?

5. Is the apple at the end of the story a *symbol?* What might it stand for or symbolize?

THE PERSONAL RESPONSE

How do you think the author expects you to feel toward the girl? toward the old women? How do *you* feel toward them? Do you think the girl should have acted more "mature"? Do you think the old women should be shown more compassion?

THE CREATIVE DIMENSION

How much of the way a setting strikes the reader is in the eye of the author? Do you think a more cheerful person (or, for that matter, an angrier person) would have seen the old folks' home and the staff there in a different light? Rewrite the opening paragraphs of the story as they might have been written by someone seeing the place and the personnel through different eyes.

BOBBIE ANN MASON (born 1940)

Mason was part of a group of writers (informally called the literary "brat pack") who became known in the eighties. Their trademark was studied understatement and a determination to be true to the trivial, undramatic realities of ordinary life. The stories in her collection *Shiloh and Other Stories* (1982) are set in Paducah, in rural Kentucky, where she grew up. She takes her readers to a New South where the struggles with the North are ancient history. Her characters are part of a new working class of truck drivers, retail clerks, and Tupperware sales representatives, who bake zucchini bread and make casseroles from potatoes and mushroom soup, and who pass their free time building model log cabins from Lincoln Logs or making wall hangings of an Arizona sunset. These characters are steeped in American popular culture—talk shows, shopping malls, made-for-TV movies.

Against this setting, Mason plays off plots where, "with no decisive snap of the thread, human relationships become unraveled" (Francis King); where "restless women strain again the confines of marriage" (Robert Towers); and where the men are sometimes "silent and transient" (Anatole Broyard). As David Quammen said in the *New York Times Book Review*, Mason "examines in her various truck drivers and sales clerks the dawning recognition—in some cases only a vague worry—of having missed something, something important, some alternate life more fruitful than the life that's been led." What has struck reviewers of her stories is that she does not treat these "unremarkable" people with condescension but with "complete respect." They are capable of moments of insight or self-understanding; they try "so hard, and with such optimism, to keep up with change" (Anne Tyler).

Shiloh　　　　　　　　　　　　　　　　　　　　　　　　　　　　　1982

Leroy Moffitt's wife, Norma Jean, is working on her pectorals. She lifts three-pound dumbbells to warm up, then progresses to a twenty-pound barbell. Standing with her legs apart, she reminds Leroy of Wonder Woman.

"I'd give anything if I could just get these muscles to where they're real hard," says Norma Jean. "Feel this arm. It's not as hard as the other one."

"That's 'cause you're right-handed," says Leroy, dodging as she swings the barbell in an arc.

"Do you think so?"

"Sure." 5

Leroy is a truckdriver. He injured his leg in a highway accident four months ago, and his physical therapy, which involves weights and a pulley, prompted Norma Jean to try building herself up. Now she is attending a body-building class. Leroy has been collecting temporary disability since his tractor-trailer jackknifed in Missouri, badly twisting his left leg in its socket. He has a steel pin in his hip. He will probably not be able to drive his rig again. It sits in the backyard, like a gigantic bird that has flown home to roost. Leroy has been home in Kentucky for three months, and his leg is almost healed, but the accident frightened him and he does not want to drive any more long hauls. He is not sure what to do next. In the meantime, he makes things from craft kits. He started by building a miniature log cabin from notched Popsicle sticks. He varnished it and placed it on the TV set, where it remains. It reminds him of a rustic Nativity scene. Then he tried string art (sailing ships on black velvet), a macramé owl kit, a snap-together B-17 Flying Fortress, and a lamp made out of a model truck, with a light fixture screwed in the top of the cab. At first the kits were diversions, something to kill time, but now he is thinking about building a full-scale log house from a kit. It would be considerably cheaper than building a regular house, and besides, Leroy has grown to appreciate how things are put together. He has begun to realize that in all the years he was on the road he never took time to examine anything. He was always flying past scenery.

"They won't let you build a log cabin in any of the new subdivisions," Norma Jean tells him.

"They will if I tell them it's for you," he says, teasing her. Ever since they were married, he has promised Norma Jean he would build her a new home one day. They have always rented, and the house they live in is small and nondescript. It does not even feel like a home, Leroy realizes now.

Norma Jean works at the Rexall drugstore, and she has acquired an amazing amount of information about cosmetics. When she explains to Leroy the three stages of complexion care, involving creams, toners, and moisturizers, he thinks happily of other petroleum products—axle grease, diesel fuel. This is a connection between him and Norma Jean. Since he has been home, he has felt unusually tender about his wife and guilty over his long absences. But he can't tell what she feels about him. Norma Jean has never complained about his traveling; she has never made hurt remarks, like calling his truck a "widow-maker." He is reasonably certain she has been faithful to him, but he wishes she would celebrate his permanent homecoming more happily. Norma Jean is often startled to find Leroy at home, and he thinks she seems a little disappointed about it. Perhaps he reminds her too much of the early days of their marriage, before he went on the road. They had a child who died as an infant, years ago. They never speak about their memories of Randy, which have almost faded, but now that Leroy is home all the time, they sometimes feel awkward around each other, and Leroy wonders if one of them should mention the child. He has the feeling that they are waking up out of a dream together—that they must create a new marriage, start afresh. They are lucky they are still married. Leroy has read that for most people losing a child destroys the marriage—or else he heard this on *Donahue*. He can't always remember where he learns things anymore.

At Christmas, Leroy bought an electric organ for Norma Jean. She used to play   10
the piano when she was in high school. "It don't leave you," she told him once. "It's like riding a bicycle."

The new instrument had so many keys and buttons that she was bewildered by it at first. She touched the keys tentatively, pushed some buttons, then pecked out "Chopsticks." It came out in an amplified fox-trot rhythm, with marimba sounds.

"It's an orchestra!" she cried.

The organ had a pecan-look finish and eighteen preset chords, with optional flute, violin, trumpet, clarinet, and banjo accompaniments. Norma Jean mastered the organ almost immediately. At first she played Christmas songs. Then she bought *The Sixties Songbook* and learned every tune in it, adding variations to each with the rows of brightly colored buttons.

"I didn't like these old songs back then," she said. "But I have this crazy feeling I missed something."

"You didn't miss a thing," said Leroy.   15

Leroy likes to lie on the couch and smoke a joint and listen to Norma Jean play "Can't Take My Eyes Off You" and "I'll Be Back." He is back again. After fifteen years on the road, he is finally settling down with the woman he loves. She is still pretty. Her skin is flawless. Her frosted curls resemble pencil trimmings.

Now that Leroy has come home to stay, he notices how much the town has changed. Subdivisions are spreading across western Kentucky like an oil slick. The sign at the edge of town says "Pop: 11,500"—only seven hundred more than it said twenty years before. Leroy can't figure out who is living in all the new houses. The farmers who used to gather around the courthouse square on Saturday afternoons to play checkers and spit tobacco juice have gone. It has been years since Leroy has thought about the farmers, and they have disappeared without his noticing.

Leroy meets a kid named Stevie Hamilton in the parking lot at the new shopping center. While they pretend to be strangers meeting over a stalled car, Stevie tosses an ounce of marijuana under the front seat of Leroy's car. Stevie is wearing orange jogging shoes and a T-shirt that says CHATTAHOOCHEE SUPER-RAT. His father is a prominent doctor who lives in one of the expensive subdivisions in a new white-columned brick house that looks like a funeral parlor. In the phone book under his name there is a separate number, with the listing "Teenagers."

"Where do you get this stuff?" asks Leroy. "From your pappy?"

"That's for me to know and you to find out," Stevie says. He is slit-eyed and skinny.   20

"What else you got?"

"What you interested in?"

"Nothing special. Just wondered."

Leroy used to take speed on the road. Now he has to go slowly. He needs to be mellow. He leans back against the car and says, "I'm aiming to build me a log house, soon as I get time. My wife, though, I don't think she likes the idea."

"Well, let me know when you want me again," Stevie says. He has a cigarette in   25
his cupped palm, as though sheltering it from the wind. He takes a long drag, then stomps it on the asphalt and slouches away.

Stevie's father was two years ahead of Leroy in high school. Leroy is thirty-four. He married Norma Jean when they were both eighteen, and their child Randy was born a few months later, but he died at the age of four months and three days. He would be about Stevie's age now. Norma Jean and Leroy were at the drive-in, watching a double feature (*Dr. Strangelove* and *Lover Come Back*), and the baby was sleeping in the back seat. When the first movie ended, the baby was dead. It was the sudden infant death syndrome. Leroy remembers handing Randy to a nurse at the emergency room, as though he were offering her a large doll as a present. A dead baby feels like a sack of flour. "It just happens sometimes," said the doctor, in what Leroy always recalls as a nonchalant tone. Leroy can hardly remember the child anymore, but he still sees vividly a scene from *Dr. Strangelove* in which the President of the United States was talking in a folksy voice on the hot line to the Soviet premier about the bomber accidentally headed toward Russia. He was in the War Room, and the world map was lit up. Leroy remembers Norma Jean standing catatonically beside him in the hospital and himself thinking: Who is this strange girl? He had forgotten who she was. Now scientists are saying that crib death is caused by a virus. Nobody knows anything, Leroy thinks. The answers are always changing.

When Leroy gets home from the shopping center, Norma Jean's mother, Mabel Beasley, is there. Until this year, Leroy has not realized how much time she spends with

Norma Jean. When she visits, she inspects the closets and then the plants, informing Norma Jean when a plant is droopy or yellow. Mabel calls the plants "flowers," although there are never any blooms. She always notices if Norma Jean's laundry is piling up. Mabel is a short, overweight woman whose tight, brown-dyed curls look more like a wig than the actual wig she sometimes wears. Today she has brought Norma Jean an off-white dust ruffle she made for the bed; Mabel works in a custom-upholstery shop.

"This is the tenth one I made this year," Mabel says. "I got started and couldn't stop."

"It's real pretty," says Norma Jean.

"Now we can hide things under the bed," says Leroy, who gets along with his mother-in-law primarily by joking with her. Mabel has never really forgiven him for disgracing her by getting Norma Jean pregnant. When the baby died, she said that fate was mocking her.

"What's that thing?" Mabel says to Leroy in a loud voice, pointing to a tangle of yarn on a piece of canvas.

Leroy holds it up for Mabel to see. "It's my needlepoint," he explains. "This is a *Star Trek* pillow cover."

"That's what a woman would do," says Mabel. "Great day in the morning!"

"All the big football players on TV do it," he says.

"Why, Leroy, you're always trying to fool me. I don't believe you for one minute. You don't know what to do with yourself—that's the whole trouble. Sewing!"

"I'm aiming to build a log house," says Leroy. "Soon as my plans come."

"Like *heck* you are," says Norma Jean. She takes Leroy's needlepoint and shoves it into a drawer. "You have to find a job first. Nobody can afford to build now anyway."

Mabel straightens her girdle and says, "I still think before you get tied down y'all ought to take a little run to Shiloh."

"One of these days, Mama," Norma Jean says impatiently.

Mabel is talking about Shiloh, Tennessee. For the past few years, she has been urging Leroy and Norma Jean to visit the Civil War battleground there. Mabel went there on her honeymoon—the only real trip she ever took. Her husband died of a perforated ulcer when Norma Jean was ten, but Mabel, who was accepted into the United Daughters of the Confederacy in 1975, is still preoccupied with going back to Shiloh.

"I've been to kingdom come and back in that truck out yonder," Leroy says to Mabel, "but we never yet set foot in that battleground. Ain't that something? How did I miss it?"

"It's not even that far," Mabel says.

After Mabel leaves, Norma Jean reads to Leroy from a list she has made. "Things you could do," she announces. "You could get a job as a guard at Union Carbide, where they'd let you set on a stool. You could get on at the lumberyard. You could do a little carpenter work, if you want to build so bad. You could—"

"I can't do something where I'd have to stand up all day."

"You ought to try standing up all day behind a cosmetics counter. It's amazing that I have strong feet, coming from two parents that never had strong feet at all." At the moment Norma Jean is holding on to the kitchen counter, raising her knees one at a time as she talks. She is wearing two-pound ankle weights.

"Don't worry," says Leroy. "I'll do something."

"You could truck calves to slaughter for somebody. You wouldn't have to drive any big old truck for that."

"I'm going to build you this house," says Leroy. "I want to make you a real home."

"I don't want to live in any log cabin."

"It's not a cabin. It's a house." 50

"I don't care. It looks like a cabin."

"You and me together could lift those logs. It's just like lifting weights."

Norma Jean doesn't answer. Under her breath, she is counting. Now she is marching through the kitchen. She is doing goose steps.

Before his accident, when Leroy came home he used to stay in the house with Norma Jean, watching TV in bed and playing cards. She would cook fried chicken, picnic ham, chocolate pie—all his favorites. Now he is home alone much of the time. In the mornings, Norma Jean disappears, leaving a cooling place in the bed. She eats a cereal called Body Buddies, and she leaves the bowl on the table, with the soggy tan balls floating in a milk puddle. He sees things about Norma Jean that he never realized before. When she chops onions, she stares off into a corner, as if she can't bear to look. She puts on her house slippers almost precisely at nine o'clock every evening and nudges her jogging shoes under the couch. She saves bread heels for the birds. Leroy watches the birds at the feeder. He notices the peculiar way goldfinches fly past the window. They close their wings, then fall, then spread their wings to catch and lift themselves. He wonders if they close their eyes when they fall. Norma Jean closes her eyes when they are in bed. She wants the lights turned out. Even then, he is sure she closes her eyes.

He goes for long drives around town. He tends to drive a car rather carelessly. 55 Power steering and an automatic shift make a car feel so small and inconsequential that his body is hardly involved in the driving process. His injured leg stretches out comfortably. Once or twice he has almost hit something, but even the prospect of an accident seems minor in a car. He cruises the new subdivisions, feeling like a criminal rehearsing for a robbery. Norma Jean is probably right about a log house being inappropriate here in the new subdivisions. All the houses look grand and complicated. They depress him.

One day when Leroy comes home from a drive he finds Norma Jean in tears. She is in the kitchen making a potato and mushroom-soup casserole, with grated-cheese topping. She is crying because her mother caught her smoking.

"I didn't hear her coming. I was standing here puffing away pretty as you please," Norma Jean says, wiping her eyes.

"I knew it would happen sooner or later," says Leroy, putting his arm around her.

"She don't know the meaning of the word 'knock,'" says Norma Jean. "It's a wonder she hadn't caught me years ago."

"Think of it this way," Leroy says. "What if she caught me with a joint?" 60

"You better not let her!" Norma Jean shrieks. "I'm warning you, Leroy Moffitt!"

"I'm just kidding. Here, play me a tune. That'll help you relax."

Norma Jean puts the casserole in the oven and sets the timer. Then she plays a ragtime tune, with horns and banjo, as Leroy lights up a joint and lies on the couch, laughing to himself about Mabel's catching him at it. He thinks of Stevie Hamilton—a doctor's son pushing grass. Everything is funny. The whole town seems crazy and small. He is reminded of Virgil Mathis, a boastful policeman Leroy used to shoot pool with. Virgil recently led a drug bust in a back room at a bowling alley, where he seized ten thousand dollars' worth of marijuana. The newspaper had a picture of him holding up the bags of grass and grinning widely. Right now, Leroy can imagine Virgil breaking down the door and arresting him with a lungful of smoke. Virgil would probably have been alerted to the scene because of all the racket Norma Jean is making. Now she sounds like a hard-rock band. Norma Jean is terrific. When she switches to a Latin-rhythm version of "Sunshine Superman," Leroy hums along. Norma Jean's foot goes up and down, up and down.

"Well, what do you think?" Leroy says, when Norma Jean pauses to search through her music.

"What do I think about what?" 65

His mind has gone blank. Then he says, "I'll sell my rig and build a house." That wasn't what he wanted to say. He wanted to know what she thought—what she *really* thought—about them.

"Don't start in on that again," says Norma Jean. She begins playing "Who'll Be the Next in Line?"

Leroy used to tell hitchhikers his whole life story—about his travels, his hometown, the baby. He would end with a question: "Well, what do you think?" It was just a rhetorical question. In time, he had the feeling that he'd been telling the same story over and over to the same hitchhikers. He quit talking to hitchhikers when he realized how his voice sounded—whining and self-pitying, like some teenage-tragedy song. Now Leroy has the sudden impulse to tell Norma Jean about himself, as if he had just met her. They have known each other so long they have forgotten a lot about each other. They could become reacquainted. But when the oven timer goes off and she runs to the kitchen, he forgets why he wants to do this.

The next day, Mabel drops by. It is Saturday and Norma Jean is cleaning. Leroy is studying the plans of his log house, which have finally come in the mail. He has them spread out on the table—big sheets of stiff blue paper, with diagrams and numbers printed in white. While Norma Jean runs the vacuum, Mabel drinks coffee. She sets her coffee cup on a blueprint.

"I'm just waiting for time to pass," she says to Leroy, drumming her fingers on the 70 table.

As soon as Norma Jean switches off the vacuum, Mabel says in a loud voice, "Did you hear about the datsun dog that killed the baby?"

Norma Jean says, "The word is 'dachshund.'"

"They put the dog on trial. It chewed the baby's legs off. The mother was in the next room all the time." She raises her voice. "They thought it was neglect."

Norma Jean is holding her ears. Leroy manages to open the refrigerator and get some Diet Pepsi to offer Mabel. Mabel still has some coffee and she waves away the Pepsi.

"Datsuns are like that," Mabel says. "They're jealous dogs. They'll tear a place to 75 pieces if you don't keep an eye on them."

"You better watch out what you're saying, Mabel," says Leroy.

"Well, facts is facts."

Leroy looks out the window at his rig. It is like a huge piece of furniture gathering dust in the backyard. Pretty soon it will be an antique. He hears the vacuum cleaner. Norma Jean seems to be cleaning the living room rug again.

Later, she says to Leroy, "She just said that about the baby because she caught me smoking. She's trying to pay me back."

"What are you talking about?" Leroy says, nervously shuffling blueprints. 80

"You know good and well," Norma Jean says. She is sitting in a kitchen chair with her feet up and her arms wrapped around her knees. She looks small and helpless. She says, "The very idea, her bringing up a subject like that! Saying it was neglect."

"She didn't mean that," Leroy says.

"She might not have *thought* she meant it. She always says things like that. You don't know how she goes on."

"But she didn't really mean it. She was just talking."

Leroy opens a king-sized bottle of beer and pours it into two glasses, dividing it   85
carefully. He hands a glass to Norma Jean and she takes it from him mechanically. For a
long time, they sit by the kitchen window watching the birds at the feeder.

Something is happening. Norma Jean is going to night school. She has graduated
from her six-week body-building course and now she is taking an adult-education
course in composition at Paducah Community College. She spends her evenings outlin-
ing paragraphs.

"First you have a topic sentence," she explains to Leroy. "Then you divide it up.
Your secondary topic has to be connected to your primary topic."

To Leroy, this sounds intimidating. "I never was any good in English," he says.

"It makes a lot of sense."

"What are you doing this for, anyhow?"   90

She shrugs. "It's something to do." She stands up and lifts her dumbbells a few
times.

"Driving a rig, nobody cared about my English."

"I'm not criticizing your English."

Norma Jean used to say, "If I lose ten minutes' sleep, I just drag all day." Now she
stays up late, writing compositions. She got a B on her first paper—a how-to theme on
soup-based casseroles. Recently Norma Jean has been cooking unusual foods—tacos,
lasagna, Bombay chicken. She doesn't play the organ anymore, though her second
paper was called "Why Music Is Important to Me." She sits at the kitchen table, concentrating on her outlines, while Leroy plays with his log house plans, practicing with a
set of Lincoln Logs. The thought of getting a truckload of notched, numbered logs
scares him, and he wants to be prepared. As he and Norma Jean work together at the
kitchen table, Leroy has the hopeful thought that they are sharing something, but he
knows he is a fool to think this. Norma Jean is miles away. He knows he is going to
lose her. Like Mabel, he is just waiting for time to pass.

One day, Mabel is there before Norma Jean gets home from work, and Leroy finds   95
himself confiding in her. Mabel, he realizes, must know Norma Jean better than he
does.

"I don't know what's got into that girl," Mabel says. "She used to go to bed with
the chickens. Now you say she's up all hours. Plus her a-smoking. I like to died."

"I want to make her this beautiful home," Leroy says, indicating the Lincoln Logs.
"I don't thinks she even wants it. Maybe she was happier with me gone."

"She don't know what to make of you, coming home like this."

"Is that it?"

Mabel takes the roof off his Lincoln Log cabin. "You couldn't get *me* in a log   100
cabin," she says. "I was raised in one. It's no picnic, let me tell you."

"They're different now," says Leroy.

"I tell you what," Mabel says, smiling oddly at Leroy.

"What?"

"Take her on down to Shiloh. Y'all need to get out together, stir a little. Her
brain's all balled up over them books."

Leroy can see traces of Norma Jean's features in her mother's face. Mabel's worn   105
face has the texture of crinkled cotton, but suddenly she looks pretty. It occurs to
Leroy that Mabel has been hinting all along that she wants them to take her with them
to Shiloh.

"Let's all go to Shiloh," he says. "You and me and her. Some Sunday."

Mabel throws up her hands in protest. "Oh, no, not me. Young folks want to be
by theirselves."

When Norma Jean comes in with groceries, Leroy says excitedly, "Your mama here's been dying to go to Shiloh for forty-five years. It's about time we went, don't you think?"

"I'm not going to butt in on anybody's second honeymoon," Mabel says.

"Who's going on a honeymoon, for Christ's sake?" Norma Jean says loudly. 110

"I never raised no daughter of mine to talk that-a-way," Mabel says.

"You ain't seen nothing yet," says Norma Jean. She starts putting away boxes and cans, slamming cabinet doors.

"There's a log cabin at Shiloh," Mabel says. "It was there during the battle. There's bullet holes in it."

"When are you going to *shut up* about Shiloh, Mama?" asks Norma Jean.

"I always thought Shiloh was the prettiest place, so full of history," Mabel goes on. 115
"I just hoped y'all could see it once before I die, so you could tell me about it." Later, she whispers to Leroy, "You do what I said. A little change is what she needs."

"Your name means 'the king,'" Norma Jean says to Leroy that evening. He is trying to get her to go to Shiloh, and she is reading a book about another century.

"Well, I reckon I ought to be right proud."

"I guess so."

"Am I still king around here?"

Norma Jean flexes her biceps and feels them for hardness. "I'm not fooling around 120
with anybody, if that's what you mean," she says.

"Would you tell me if you were?"

"I don't know."

"What does *your* name mean?"

"It was Marilyn Monroe's real name."

"No kidding!" 125

"Norma comes from the Normans. They were invaders," she says. She closes her book and looks hard at Leroy. "I'll go to Shiloh with you if you'll stop staring at me."

On Sunday, Norma Jean packs a picnic and they go to Shiloh. To Leroy's relief, Mabel says she does not want to come with them. Norma Jean drives, and Leroy, sitting beside her, feels like some boring hitchhiker she has picked up. He tries some conversation, but she answers him in monosyllables. At Shiloh, she drives aimlessly through the park, past bluffs and trails and steep ravines. Shiloh is an immense place, and Leroy cannot see it as a battleground. It is not what he expected. He thought it would look like a golf course. Monuments are everywhere, showing through the thick clusters of trees. Norma Jean passes the log cabin Mabel mentioned. It is surrounded by tourists looking for bullet holes.

"That's not the kind of log house I've got in mind," says Leroy apologetically.

"I know *that*."

"This is a pretty place. Your mama was right." 130

"It's O.K.," says Norma Jean. "Well, we've seen it. I hope she's satisfied."

They burst out laughing together.

At the park museum, a movie on Shiloh is shown every half hour, but they decide that they don't want to see it. They buy a souvenir Confederate flag for Mabel, and then they find a picnic spot near the cemetery. Norma Jean has brought a picnic cooler, with pimiento sandwiches, soft drinks, and Yodels. Leroy eats a sandwich and then smokes a joint, hiding it behind the picnic cooler. Norma Jean has quit smoking altogether. She is picking cake crumbs from the cellophane wrapper, like a fussy bird.

Leroy says, "So the boys in gray ended up in Corinth. The Union soldiers zapped 'em finally, April 7, 1862."

They both know that he doesn't know any history. He is just talking about some of the historical plaques they have read. He feels awkward, like a boy on a date with an older girl. They are still just making conversation. 135

"Corinth is where Mama eloped to," says Norma Jean.

They sit in silence and stare at the cemetery for the Union dead and, beyond, at a tall cluster of trees. Campers are parked nearby, bumper to bumper, and small children in bright clothing are cavorting and squealing. Norma Jean wads up the cake wrapper and squeezes it tightly in her hand. Without looking at Leroy, she says, "I want to leave you."

Leroy takes a bottle of Coke out of the cooler and flips off the cap. He holds the bottle poised near his mouth but cannot remember to take a drink. Finally he says, "No, you don't."

"Yes, I do."

"I won't let you." 140

"You can't stop me."

"Don't do me that way."

Leroy knows Norma Jean will have her own way. "Didn't I promise to be home from now on?" he says.

"In some ways, a woman prefers a man who wanders," says Norma Jean. "That sounds crazy, I know."

"You're not crazy." 145

Leroy remembers to drink from his Coke. Then he says, "Yes, you *are* crazy. You and me could start all over again. Right back at the beginning."

"We *have* started all over again," says Norma Jean. "And this is how it turned out."

"What did I do wrong?"

"Nothing."

"Is this one of those women's lib things?" Leroy asks. 150

"Don't be funny."

The cemetery, a green slope dotted with white markers, looks like a subdivision site. Leroy is trying to comprehend that his marriage is breaking up, but for some reason he is wondering about white slabs in a graveyard.

"Everything was fine till Mama caught me smoking," says Norma Jean, standing up. "That set something off."

"What are you talking about?"

"She won't leave me alone—*you* won't leave me alone." Norma Jean seems to be crying, but she is looking away from him. "I feel eighteen again. I can't face that all over again." She starts walking away. "No, it *wasn't* fine. I don't know what I'm saying. Forget it." 155

Leroy takes a lungful of smoke and closes his eyes as Norma Jean's words sink in. He tries to focus on the fact that thirty-five hundred soldiers died on the grounds around him. He can only think of that war as a board game with plastic soldiers. Leroy almost smiles, as he compares the Confederates' daring attack on the Union camps and Virgil Mathis's raid on the bowling alley. General Grant, drunk and furious, shoved the Southerners back to Corinth, where Mabel and Jet Beasley were married years later, when Mabel was still thin and good-looking. The next day, Mabel and Jet visited the battleground, and then Norma Jean was born, and then she married Leroy and they had a baby, which they lost, and now Leroy and Norma Jean are here at the same battleground. Leroy knows he is leaving out a lot. He is leaving out the insides of history.

History was always just names and dates to him. It occurs to him that building a house out of logs is similarly empty—too simple. And the real inner workings of a marriage, like most of history, have escaped him. Now he sees that building a log house is the dumbest idea he could have had. It was clumsy of him to think Norma Jean would want a log house. It was a crazy idea. He'll have to think of something else, quickly. He will wad the blueprints into tight balls and fling them into the lake. Then he'll get moving again. He opens his eyes. Norma Jean has moved away and is walking through the cemetery, following a serpentine brick path.

Leroy gets up to follow his wife, but his good leg is asleep and his bad leg still hurts him. Norma Jean is far away, walking rapidly toward the bluff by the river, and he tries to hobble toward her. Some children run past him, screaming noisily. Norma Jean has reached the bluff, and she is looking out over the Tennessee River. Now she turns toward Leroy and waves her arms. Is she beckoning to him? She seems to be doing an exercise for her chest muscles. The sky is unusually pale—the color of the dust ruffle Mabel made for their bed.

THE RECEPTIVE READER

1. This story takes us to a working-class *setting*, with such class markers as the characters' working-class language. Where does their language become most noticeable, or where does it become an issue, in the story? ✧ Attitudes toward the working class have traditionally ranged from snobbish contempt to solidarity for the aspirations of common people. What is the attitude of the author?

2. Some Southern readers feel particularly at home in this story. To you, what if anything is Southern about the setting and about this story as a whole?

3. Mason is a fanatic for apparently trivial *realistic detail*—about Leroy's job, his accident, his therapy; about Norma Jean's job at the drugstore, her body-building exercises, her classes at the college; about their trip to Shilo, and so forth. What to you are striking examples of these apparent trivia? What do they do for the story as a whole?

4. Mason makes the setting real with striking uses of *figurative language*—language using imaginative comparisons. What images and feelings does she bring into play when she says that Leroy's rig parked in the back was like a big bird come home to roost? What are other striking examples of imaginative comparisons?

5. How ordinary are the lives of these people? What are some of the ordinary everyday things that make their lives average? Do extraordinary things happen to them?

6. The *dialogue* in this story is very sparse. What are occasions in the story where you expect them to say more about their lives or their feelings than they do? Are their feelings "frozen," as one student reader said?

7. What role does Mabel, Leroy's mother-in-law, play as a *minor character* in the story? What is her relationship with Leroy? with her daughter? How does the author use her to develop or round out the setting of the story?

8. Readers are likely to detect *symbolic* meanings or overtones in details and incidents in this story. What are the possible symbolic meanings of the parked rig, the "nondescript" rented home, the electronic organ, the change in the cooking, Mabel's hair, the log cabin Leroy wants to build, the trip to the battlefield?

9. When did you first decide that the marriage was going to break up? For you, was the breakup a foregone conclusion? Who or what is to blame?

10. Both *major characters*, Leroy and Norma Jean, change or develop in the course of this story. How do they change or grow? Do they develop in the same direction or along parallel lines? Do they understand what is happening to them? (How much self-realization is there in this story?)

THE PERSONAL RESPONSE

Anne Tyler, a fellow writer reviewing Mason's stories for the *New Republic,* said that it was "heartening to find male characters portrayed sympathetically, with an appreciation for the fact that they can feel as confused and hurt and lonely as the female characters." What are your personal feelings toward the two major characters in "Shiloh?" Do you feel closer to Leroy or to Norma Jean? Why?

YUKIO MISHIMA (1925–1970)

Yukio Mishima (pen name of Kimitake Hiraoka) was a prolific writer of novels, plays, and stories. He was a flamboyant media personality who became a cult figure in Japan and a legend in the West. Alienated from Westernized, materialistic modern Japan, he became obsessed with Japanese history and traditional Japanese values. He set out to revive and reenact the code and ritual of the Samurai warriors of Japan's feudal, aristocratic past, with traditions akin to the code of chivalry of the European Middle Ages. He studied the martial arts—boxing, karate, and sword fighting; he created the Shield Society, a private army of a hundred dedicated followers. In a final spectacular rejection of the decadent present, he committed *seppuku,* or public ritual suicide, in 1970.

Translations of Mishima's best-known works include *Confessions of a Mask* (1958), *The Sailor Who Fell from Grace with the Sea* (1965), and *Sun and Steel* (1970). In *The Sailor Who Fell from Grace,* a boy who disapproves of the lover of his widowed mother joins with a band of his fellows in an effort to terminate the love affair and the lover. Mishima's short stories were collected in *Death and Midsummer and Other Stories* (1966). Some of his best-known stories celebrate the ecstasy of married love, loyalty to the empire, and ceremonial suicide. He once spoke of "my heart's leaning toward Death, Night, and Blood." The following story will take you to a different world—not merely a different geographical setting but a different world of thought and feeling.

Swaddling Clothes   1966

TRANSLATED BY IVAN MORRIS

He was always busy, Toshiko's husband. Even tonight he had to dash off to an appointment, leaving her to go home alone by taxi. But what else could a woman expect when she married an actor—an attractive one? No doubt she had been foolish to hope that he would spend the evening with her. And yet he must have known how she dreaded going back to their house, unhomely with its Western-style furniture and with the bloodstains still showing on the floor.

Toshiko had been oversensitive since girlhood: that was her nature. As the result of constant worrying she never put on weight, and now, an adult woman, she looked more like a transparent picture than a creature of flesh and blood. Her delicacy of spirit was evident to her most casual acquaintance.

Earlier that evening, when she had joined her husband at a night club, she had been shocked to find him entertaining friends with an account of "the incident." Sitting there in his American-style suit, puffing at a cigarette, he had seemed to her almost a stranger.

"It's a fantastic story," he was saying, gesturing flamboyantly as if in an attempt to outweigh the attractions of the dance band. "Here this new nurse for our baby arrives from the employment agency, and the very first thing I notice about her is her stomach. It's enormous—as if she had a pillow stuck under her kimono! No wonder, I thought, for I soon saw that she could eat more than the rest of us put together. She polished off the contents of our rice bin like that. . . ." He snapped his fingers. "'Gastric dilation'—that's how she explained her girth and her appetite. Well, the day before yesterday we heard groans and moans coming from the nursery. We rushed in and found her squatting on the floor, holding her stomach in her two hands, and moaning like a cow. Next to her our baby lay in his cot, scared out of his wits and crying at the top of his lungs. A pretty scene, I can tell you!"

"So the cat was out of the bag?" suggested one of their friends, a film actor like Toshiko's husband. 5

"Indeed it was! And it gave me the shock of my life. You see, I'd completely swallowed that story about 'gastric dilation.' Well, I didn't waste any time. I rescued our good rug from the floor and spread a blanket for her to lie on. The whole time the girl was yelling like a stuck pig. By the time the doctor from the maternity clinic arrived, the baby had already been born. But our sitting room was a pretty shambles!"

"Oh, that I'm sure of!" said another of their friends, and the whole company burst into laughter.

Toshiko was dumbfounded to hear her husband discussing the horrifying happening as though it were no more than an amusing incident which they chanced to have witnessed. She shut her eyes for a moment and all at once she saw the newborn baby lying before her: on the parquet floor the infant lay, and his frail body was wrapped in bloodstained newspapers.

Toshiko was sure that the doctor had done the whole thing out of spite. As if to emphasize his scorn for this mother who had given birth to a bastard under such sordid conditions, he had told his assistant to wrap the baby in some loose newspapers, rather than proper swaddling. This callous treatment of the newborn child had offended Toshiko. Overcoming her disgust at the entire scene, she had fetched a brand-new piece of flannel from her cupboard and, having swaddled the baby in it, had lain him carefully in an armchair.

This all had taken place in the evening after her husband had left the house. 10 Toshiko had told him nothing of it, fearing that he would think her oversoft, oversentimental; yet the scene had engraved itself deeply in her mind. Tonight she sat silently thinking back on it, while the jazz orchestra brayed and her husband chatted cheerfully with his friends. She knew that she would never forget the sight of the baby, wrapped in stained newspapers and lying on the floor—it was a scene fit for a butchershop. Toshiko, whose own life had been spent in solid comfort, poignantly felt the wretchedness of the illegitimate baby.

I am the only person to have witnessed its shame, the thought occurred to her. The mother never saw her child lying there in its newspaper wrappings, and the baby itself of course didn't know. I alone shall have to preserve that terrible scene in my memory. When the baby grows up and wants to find out about his birth, there will be no one to tell him, so long as I preserve silence. How strange that I should have this feeling of guilt! After all, it was I who took him up from the floor, swathed him properly in flannel, and laid him down to sleep in the armchair.

They left the night club and Toshiko stepped into the taxi that her husband had called for her. "Take this lady to Ushigomé," he told the driver and shut the door from the outside. Toshiko gazed through the window at her husband's smiling face and noticed his strong, white teeth. Then she leaned back in the seat, oppressed by the knowledge that their life together was in some way too easy, too painless. It would have been difficult for her to put her thoughts into words. Through the rear window of the taxi she took a last look at her husband. He was striding along the street toward his Nash car, and soon the back of his rather garish tweed coat had blended with the figures of the passers-by.

The taxi drove off, passed down a street dotted with bars and then by a theater, in front of which the throngs of people jostled each other on the pavement. Although the performance had only just ended, the lights had already been turned out and in the half dark outside it was depressingly obvious that the cherry blossoms decorating the front of the theater were merely scraps of white paper.

Even if that baby should grow up in ignorance of the secret of his birth, he can never become a respectable citizen, reflected Toshiko, pursuing the same train of thoughts. Those soiled newspaper swaddling clothes will be the symbol of his entire life. But why should I keep worrying about him so much? Is it because I feel uneasy about the future of my own child? Say twenty years from now, when our boy will have grown up into a fine, carefully educated young man, one day by a quirk of fate he meets the other boy, who then will also have turned twenty. And say that the other boy, who has been sinned against, savagely stabs him with a knife. . . .

It was a warm, overcast April night, but thoughts of the future made Toshiko feel cold and miserable. She shivered on the back seat of the car. 15

No, when the time comes I shall take my son's place, she told herself suddenly. Twenty years from now I shall be forty-three. I shall go to that young man and tell him straight out about everything—about his newspaper swaddling clothes, and about how I went and wrapped him in flannel.

The taxi ran along the dark wide road that was bordered by the park and by the Imperial Palace moat. In the distance Toshiko noticed the pinpricks of light which came from the blocks of tall office buildings.

Twenty years from now that wretched child will be in utter misery. He will be living a desolate, hopeless, poverty-stricken existence—a lonely rat. What else could happen to a baby who has had such a birth? He'll be wandering through the streets by himself, cursing his father, loathing his mother.

No doubt Toshiko derived a certain satisfaction from her somber thoughts: she tortured herself with them without cease. The taxi approached Hanzomon and drove past the compound of the British Embassy. At that point the famous rows of cherry trees were spread out before Toshiko in all their purity. On the spur of the moment she decided to go and view the blossoms by herself in the dark night. It was a strange decision for a timid and unadventurous young woman, but then she was in a strange state of mind and she dreaded the return home. That evening all sorts of unsettling fancies had burst open in her mind.

She crossed the wide street—a slim, solitary figure in the darkness. As a rule when she walked in the traffic Toshiko used to cling fearfully to her companion, but tonight she darted alone between the cars and a moment later had reached the long narrow park that borders the Palace moat. Chidorigafuchi, it is called—the Abyss of the Thousand Birds. 20

Tonight the whole park had become a grove of blossoming cherry trees. Under the calm cloudy sky the blossoms formed a mass of solid whiteness. The paper lanterns that hung from wires between the trees had been put out; in their place electric light bulbs, red, yellow, and green, shone dully beneath the blossoms. It was well past ten o'clock and most of the flower-viewers had gone home. As the occasional passers-by strolled through the park, they would automatically kick aside the empty bottles or crush the waste paper beneath their feet.

Newspapers, thought Toshiko, her mind going back once again to those happenings. Bloodstained newspapers. If a man were ever to hear of that piteous birth and know that it was he who had lain there, it would ruin his entire life. To think that I, a perfect stranger, should from now on have to keep such a secret—the secret of a man's whole existence. . . .

Lost in these thoughts, Toshiko walked on through the park. Most of the people still remaining there were quiet couples; no one paid her any attention. She noticed two people sitting on a stone bench beside the moat, not looking at the blossoms, but gazing silently at the water. Pitch black it was, and swathed in heavy shadows. Beyond the moat the somber forest of the Imperial Palace blocked her view. The trees reached up, to form a solid dark mass againt the night sky. Toshiko walked slowly along the path beneath the blossoms hanging heavily overhead.

On a stone bench, slightly apart from the others, she noticed a pale object—not, as she had at first imagined, a pile of cherry blossoms, nor a garment forgotten by one of the visitors to the park. Only when she came closer did she see that it was a human form lying on the bench. Was it, she wondered, one of those miserable drunks often to be seen sleeping in public places? Obviously not, for the body had been systematically covered with newspapers, and it was the whiteness of those papers that had attracted Toshiko's attention. Standing by the bench, she gazed down at the sleeping figure.

It was a man in a brown jersey who lay there, curled up on layers of newspapers, other newspapers covering him. No doubt this had become his normal night residence now that spring had arrived. Toshiko gazed down at the man's dirty, unkempt hair, which in places had become hopelessly matted. As she observed the sleeping figure wrapped in its newspapers, she was inevitably reminded of the baby who had lain on the floor in its wretched swaddling clothes. The shoulder of the man's jersey rose and fell in the darkness in time with his heavy breathing.

It seemed to Toshiko that all her fears and premonitions had suddenly taken concrete form. In the darkness the man's pale forehead stood out, and it was a young forehead, though carved with the wrinkles of long poverty and hardship. His khaki trousers had been slightly pulled up; on his sockless feet he wore a pair of battered gym shoes. She could not see his face and suddenly had an overmastering desire to get one glimpse of it.

She walked to the head of the bench and looked down. The man's head was half buried in his arms, but Toshiko could see that he was surprisingly young. She noticed the thick eyebrows and the fine bridge of his nose. His slightly open mouth was alive with youth.

But Toshiko had approached too close. In the silent night the newspaper bedding rustled, and abruptly the man opened his eyes. Seeing the young woman standing directly beside him, he raised himself with a jerk, and his eyes lit up. A second later a powerful hand reached out and seized Toshiko by her slender wrist.

She did not feel in the least afraid and made no effort to free herself. In a flash the thought had struck her. Ah, so the twenty years have already gone by! The forest of the Imperial Palace was pitch dark and utterly silent.

25

THE RECEPTIVE READER

1. What is strange and what is familiar about the *setting*? What expectations (or what stereotypes) do you bring to the Japanese setting of the story? How much of an effort of the imagination is necessary for you to get into the spirit of this story?

2. The author makes a point of the Westernized or Americanized ways of Toshiko's husband. What are revealing details? What contrast is Mishima setting up between the husband and the wife as *key characters*? What role does that contrast play in the story as a whole? ✧ What is the author's attitude toward the husband?

3. What are Toshiko's feelings about the illegitimate child? Does she reflect the expected attitudes of her culture? Are there parallels in American culture or social mores to the attitude toward unwed mothers and children born out of wedlock that play a strong role in this story? (Are our attitudes more enlightened or just different?)

4. Is the ending a *surprise ending*, or has the author prepared you for it? Does the story as a whole lead up to it? How? Do you react to it as something that really happened or as a dream, a nightmare?

5. Some of the details in this story are not just mentioned in passing. They come up again, providing a kind of link or a continuing strand. What is the role of recurrent details like the cherry blossoms or newspapers in this story?

6. One editor said that "this fiercely condensed" story, focused on a "single, overpowering incident," "explodes in a burst of revelation or illumination" (Irving Howe). For you, what is that revelation? Does this story have a point? Does it have a *theme*— some key idea acted out or implied in the story as a whole?

THE PERSONAL RESPONSE

Does the story as a whole remain strange or alien for you? How do you relate to Toshiko as the central character? How do you relate to the story as a whole?

THE RANGE OF INTERPRETATION

Mishima's story invites a wide range of reactions. In your judgment, which of the following student responses best gets into the spirit of the story? How or why does the student writer seem to do justice to the author's intention? How are these responses different from your own interpretation of the story?

1. Since Mishima's story takes place in Japan, we might expect a setting where the standards of a different culture prevail. Instead, the interaction of conflicting cultures plays a central role in this story. At the beginning, Mishima sets up a contrast between the Westernized husband and the traditional Japanese wife. While her loud, insensitive husband goes to his important appointments, the wife is put in a taxicab to her home. His flashy, flamboyant ways and Westernized suits seem a corruption of the traditional Japanese lifestyle. (I would guess that the author despises the husband.) Toshiko in the story seems to be most strongly aware of the traditional values of her society. While her blasé husband seems to look at the horrifying birth of the baby as an "amusing incident," Toshiko is acutely aware of the shame and prejudice that attend illegitimate birth in the traditional culture. While some Americans still hold similar views toward children born out of wedlock, as Americans we have generally become more liberal. (We don't have to worry about shaming 10,000 years of ancestors.) But paradoxically Toshiko is also the one who rebels against the traditional treatment of the illegitimate child. She is the only one who seems to care. While her husband only apes Western ways, Toshiko seems closest to our own ideal of compassion for the unfortunate. Actually, she seems to care more than most people would in either culture.

2. This story is very disturbing. Although it is set in Japan, the story reflects stereotypical sex roles reminding me of many couples I know. The husband

is domineering and shallow, and Toshiko is the stereotypically passive, dependent "oversensitive" wife. Under the quiet stereotypical surface, Toshiko is a warm, caring person. But whereas she is a keen observer of her culture (her gloomy prediction for the baby reveals this), she lives her whole life in her fears and feelings. While the husband is vain and self-absorbed, Toshiko spends her life alone in the private world of her fears. She feels great warmth toward the child, but she knows that it will suffer greatly as the result of its dishonorable beginnings. What we see in Toshiko is the constant battle waged between the traditional role and the emergence of the more modern woman. She is alienated from her callous, self-centered husband, and she assumes responsibility for the harsh treatment that society has in store for the newborn child.

3. This story is very fatalistic. The child, because of its illegitimate birth, is doomed to "utter misery." I expected Toshiko to come to a tragic end. I could empathize with Toshiko somewhat because of her culture and beliefs, but I wanted to stop her from feeling so guilty and destroying her life. It is as if Toshiko created the ending in the park. She is determined to sacrifice herself. At times I wanted to reach into the story and stop her from being so guilt-ridden and oversensitive. As a woman, it made me angry that she would destroy herself.

4. On the literal level, this story leaves many questions unresolved. The abrupt, surprising ending leaves me wondering whether it is real—is it a dream? a nightmare? If the derelict in the park literally attacked the woman, was the result death? rape? Symbolically, in the context of the story as a whole, Toshiko is taking the place of her own son. She is sacrificing herself in his stead, so that she rather than he will be the target of the dispossessed child's anger and resentment when it returns to exact vengeance. In spite of the difference in cultures, the story made me hear echoes of my own Catholic upbringing. The incident where Toshiko wrapped the child in swaddling clothes mirrored the birth of Christ in a manger where Mary wrapped him in swaddling clothes. The ending where Toshiko is willing to give up her life so that her son may live parallels Christ's willingness to give up his life so that his people may have eternal life.

WRITING ABOUT LITERATURE

2. Exploring the Setting (The Structured Paper)

It still comes as a shock to me to realize that I don't write about what I know: I write in order to find out what I know.

PATRICIA HAMPL

The Writing Workshop As you write about setting, explore the major dimensions that together give shape to the characteristic world of a story. Location in city or country, the past history of a region, the ways people make a living there, local customs or traditions—all of these may help you understand the characters, the ways they live and think and feel, or the situations in which they find themselves.

As you develop a paper focused on setting, you will go through many of the same basic steps as in writing papers focused on other facets of the storyteller's art. The first step toward real writing is to build up a rich backlog of material. No one can write a full paper from an empty mind. To write good papers about literary topics, try to operate on the computer principle of "good input makes for good output." Build the habit of scribbling comments in the margins of what you read (not in library copies!). Make it a habit to take ample reading notes. Compare notes and impressions with classmates or friends.

However, the second major step is to bring your material under control. Early in the process of gathering the material, you will start thinking through the issues it raises. You may begin to focus on a key question you will want to answer, a key issue that you may want to explore. You will start formulating a strategy for presenting your findings to your reader. You will think about laying out your evidence in a pattern that makes sense. Early in your reading, you will start pulling together quotations that bear on the same point; you will begin collating details that help you answer the same question. This process of sorting out, of pulling your material into shape, will provide the ground plan or working outline for your first draft. You then refine or adjust your plan as necessary as you revise your paper.

What are some basic requirements for the finished paper that will be the result of this process of focusing, shaping, and revising? Remember: Each paper is different. The following guidelines are meant to alert you to needs that arise again and again in student papers. In considering these guidelines, try not to look at them as a formula that fits all topics. Change or adapt what needs to be changed to suit your purpose.

✧ *Avoid generic titles.* Although you may not hit on the right title until late in the process of writing your paper, remember that the title will be the first thing to strike your reader. Titles should not be perfunctory and interchangeable—good perhaps for filing the paper under the author's name or the name of the story, but not enough to hook the reader into reading your essay. A good title is informative (it helps map the territory), but it should also be beckoning. Your title should be specific and attractive enough to invite the reader. It need not be a "grabber," but it should be alive: It should suggest a topic, a point of view, a program, a tone, a style.

TOO INTERCHANGEABLE: Joyce's "Araby"
INFORMAL (and perhaps too cute?):   A Boy and His Bubble
FORMAL: The Dark Infatuation of Joyce's "Araby"

✧ *Take your reader into the world of the story.* Help your reader get into the spirit by starting with a revealing quotation or a crucial incident:

"Your name means 'the king,'" Norma Jean informs her husband Leroy in Bobbie Ann Mason's "Shiloh," but Leroy, a disabled truck driver, model-kit hobbyist, and occasional joint smoker, is more like the palace grounds-keeper than the king.

✧ *Bring your paper into focus.* The first page is crucial. What is your central focus? What is your overall plan? After a brief pointed introduction, use your opening paragraphs to set directions. Try to provide a preview or program. Sketch out or hint at your overall scheme. Avoid a program that is too general—too open and interchangeable:

WEAK: In this story, certain elements of the setting underscore and highlight the problems of the main characters.

(What certain elements? This is too vague: No one is going to say, "I am all excited—I am going to be told about certain elements!")

Instead, for a short paper, try to sketch out a three-point or four-point program that provides a road map for your reader. Create expectations that your paper as a whole is going to fulfill. For instance, in writing about Mason's "Shiloh," you might plan to show how three main characters relate differently to their setting:

The characters in Mason's story relate differently to their Southern setting: Leroy, the husband, is stranded in the present; Mabel, the mother-in-law, is living in the past; Norma Jean, the wife, has a future.

This statement provides a **thesis,** summing up the central idea of the paper. However, it also implies an itinerary. It alerts the reader to how the thesis is going to be followed up as the writer looks at each of the major characters in turn.

✧ *Wean yourself from a mere plot summary.* Follow a logical rather than merely chronological order. Sometimes, especially for a story with a complicated plot, an initial tracing of the story line can help writer and reader get their bearings. But avoid a mere "read-along-with-me" effect—make sure your readers do not think your paper as a whole will merely retell the story. Show that you have tied things together, that you can bring together evidence from different parts of the story. Show that you can pull out relevant quotations or incidents that bear on a key question or key point. (If you follow the order of the story, look at each segment from the angle that is the issue. Use each stage in the story to make a point that is part of your overall argument.)

✧ *Weave in rich, authentic detail.* Remember that any point worth making is worth following up with examples and support. Provide ample telling detail and show its significance in the story. For instance, in "Shiloh," the organ is rich in electronic wizardry—and Norma Jean masters it "almost immediately" (a hint of her ability to adjust to what is new?). Early in your paper, start weaving in telling, revealing short quotations. For instance, you might use the following interchange between Leroy and Norma Jean when you try to show the reader how these two are "slowly drifting apart":

"We *have* started all over again," says Norma Jean. "And this is how it turned out."

"What did I do wrong?"

"Nothing."

Use specific details and apt quotations to show your command of the material. Build up a rich texture of supporting detail to counteract the thin, anemic, overgeneral effect of improvised, hastily written prose.

✧ *Strengthen logical connections.* Avoid lame **transitions** like *also* or *another*. When you find yourself writing "another important aspect of the setting is . . . , " ask yourself: How is this feature of the setting *related* to the others—how is it part of the whole picture?

Perhaps you have made a point of Leroy's inability to communicate. (He wants to talk about their marriage but instead lamely repeats that he will build his wife a house.) You now want to move on to a second point: "Leroy's anachronistic behavior is *another problem* in the Moffitt marriage." (His playing with the plans for model log houses points to the past, not the future.) What is the logical connection between the two points? What is the connection in the larger context of the story? Perhaps you could strengthen the connection by a transition like the following;

TRANSITION: Having no way to voice his feelings articulately with words, he builds model log houses because he has no other way to express himself. However, this preoccupation with symbols of the past only serves to widen the gap between him and his wife. . . .

✧ *Aim at a strong conclusion.* Revise a conclusion that is merely a lame recapitulation of points already clear. Try bringing your paper full circle by picking up an image, incident, or keynote from the beginning of the paper. Use the opportunity to drive home a key point. Or use the opportunity to branch out, showing larger implications, showing a personal connection. One student paper started: "'Shiloh' by Bobbie Ann Mason presents a dull yet strikingly real vision of America." The following conclusion drives home the central point and highlights the connection between the story and our own lives:

"Shiloh" is a perfect portrayal of life in the 1990s. It is realistic, poignant, and depressing. It is ordinary, sometimes dismal, but rarely extravagant. That is left for Oprah and Geraldo to display on television. We see ourselves in the couple—our drive to succeed and prosper in Norma Jean and our love of the couch in Leroy.

Study the following sample paper. What role does the setting of the story play in the paper? How well does the paper live up to the requirements sketched above?

SAMPLE STUDENT PAPER

Muscle Building in the New South

Bobbie Ann Mason's short story "Shiloh" is a bleak portrait of a marriage at the point of dissolution—a picture of two people poised at the brink of what for the woman is a new life of personal growth and freedom but what is for the man the loss of most in his life that he thought secure. Mason uses physical detail—the way the characters relate to their bodies and to their physical setting—to mirror the wife's upward spiral and the husband's decline. They both find themselves in a new world that is different from the old South represented by Leroy's mother-in-law. But for one of them this new world means disillusionment and stagnation; for the other it means opportunity.

Leroy Moffitt is a truck driver from Kentucky, who is at home recovering from an accident in which his leg was badly injured. It is the first time since the early days of his marriage that he has been at home for any length of time, and he begins to feel that he has missed much of his married life. He realizes "that in all the years he was on the road he never took time to examine anything. He was always flying past scenery." Now his years of flying past the scenery of his life are over, and he for the first time is experiencing what it is like to stay in one place. Having a chance to watch his wife for more than hurried intervals, he finds that she is a different person from the woman he married.

His injured leg symbolizes Leroy's new slowing down, his new lack of mobility. It was badly twisted in its socket when his truck jackknifed in the road, and he now has a steel pin in his hip. Although he is healing, he is scared to go back on the road; he has moved from an extremely fast-paced, always-moving lifestyle to one in which he can walk only with difficulty. His career and his marriage have shuddered painfully to a standstill. He finds himself in a setting where much of what he does merely helps to pass the time: building small-scale model log houses, expecting his wife to play old favorites on a state-of-the-art electronic piano.

Leroy's new immobility is reflected even in Leroy's drug of choice. Where before he took drugs that were suited to his fast, mobile lifestyle, he now uses drugs of a more mellow nature: "Leroy used to take speed on the road. Now he has to go slowly. He needs to be mellow." The weed he buys allows him to dull and slow down his perception of his surroundings. He buys his joints from a source who represents the downside of the New South—a son of a doctor, whose drug-dealing symbolizes the rejection of his goal-oriented doctor father.

While Leroy is slowing down, however, his wife Norma Jean is speeding up. After fifteen years of staying home while her husband traveled, she is physically and symbolically stepping out into a new world. She is trying to move beyond the drugstore job—beyond the feeling of going nowhere experienced by people who are trapped in an average existence. She is taking steps toward personal improvement and intellectual growth—steps which are reflected in her new attention to her body. Early in the story, we see her working out with dumbbells, improving her muscle tone and physical appearance: "I'd give anything if I could just get these muscles to where they're real hard," she says impatiently. Leroy, with some foreboding, sees the potential for improvement in her, thinking that as she stood with her legs apart she reminded him of "Wonder Woman." Norma Jean wears ankle weights, lifts barbells, and flexes her arm to test the size of her biceps—testing, symbolically, her emotional and intellectual strength as she nears the point of breaking away from Leroy.

As she is improving herself physically, she improves herself intellectually with night classes and reading. As Leroy notes, "she stays up late, writing compositions." Norma Jean breaks out of confining old habits: She quits smoking; she cooks unusual foods, walking around the kitchen with ankle weights attached. Although she is still living in their house, her mind and body are already in a different place.

The differences in Leroy's and Norma Jean's emotional and intellectual needs lead to the final breakup in a setting full of hints of forgotten conflicts, the Civil War battleground at Shiloh. When Norma Jean walks away from Leroy, he is physically unable to follow her, for "his good leg is asleep and his bad leg still hurts him." She moves quickly, widening the chasm where their marriage used to be. In our last glimpse of Leroy and Norma Jean, she is waving her arms in some sort of "exercise for her chest muscles," testing her wings, perhaps, before moving upward and away from her old life.

QUESTIONS

How well does the introduction get you into the spirit of the story? Where does the central idea or thesis come into focus? Where does the program or agenda for the paper as a whole become clear to the reader? Where does the writer do a good job of relating specific details to the concerns of the paper as a whole? What use does the paper make of quotations? What transitions effectively move the reader from point to point? How does the conclusion wrap up the paper? How does it hark back to earlier parts of the paper; what does it add that is new? Where do you agree and where would you take issue with the paper?

3 CHARACTER
The Buried Self

I don't invent characters because the Almighty has already invented millions, just as experts at fingerprints do not create fingerprints but learn how to read them.

ISAAC BASHEVIS SINGER

I am enormously interested in other people, other lives, and with the least provocation I could "go into" your personality and try to imagine it, try to find a way of dramatizing it. I am fascinated by people I meet, or don't meet, people I only correspond with, or read about. . . . It seems to me that there are so many people who are inarticulate but who suffer and doubt and love, nobly, who need to be explained.

JOYCE CAROL OATES

I live with the people I create, and it has always made my essential loneliness less keen.

CARSON McCULLERS

FOCUS ON CHARACTER

Storytellers strive to create believable characters and set them in motion. The writers appeal to an ancient curiosity: We are fascinated with the variety of people in our world. We are willing to hear about their quirks and ploys, their clever and dense ways, their ways of acting smart and outsmarting themselves. However, the more we learn about them, the harder it is for us to stay aloof. We begin to care; we take sides; we become involved.

In the following passage from Bobbie Ann Mason's "Shiloh," we begin to see character traits of the husband who was a truck driver but has been in a bad accident. What kind of a person is beginning to emerge?

. . . Leroy has been home in Kentucky for three months, and his leg is almost healed, but the accident frightened him and he does not want to drive any more long hauls. He is not sure what to do next. In the meantime, he makes things from craft kits. He started by building a miniature log cabin from notched Popsicle sticks. He varnished it and placed it on the TV set, where it remains. It reminds him of a rustic Nativity scene. Then he tried string art (sailing ships on black velvet), a macramé owl kit, a snap-together B-17 Flying Fortress, and a lamp made out of a model truck, with a light fixture screwed in the top of the cab. At first the kits were diversions, something to kill time, but now he is thinking about building a full-scale log house from a kit. It would be considerably cheaper than building a regular house, and besides, Leroy has grown to appreciate how things are put together.

What clues to the character does this description furnish the reader? The kind of person that emerges does not seem to feel the need to act macho, to prove something by going back to the dangerous job. Instead, he was spooked by the accident (as many ordinary people might have been). He does not seem to be making any grandiose plans but seems to have the patience for tasks that require careful plodding work—and not a great deal of imagination. He certainly has no high-flown tastes for avant-garde art; the projects he works on all seem in keeping with the most average popular taste. Like many average people, he seems to have a liking for tradition—the Nativity scene, the log cabin. He likes the idea of saving money and doing something with his hands by building an actual log cabin to live in. All in all, we seem to be looking at a quiet, unambitious, average person, with very average tastes. We probably do not expect him to initiate any upheavals or make angry speeches. Perhaps he is going to be more passive than active in the story that is about to take shape.

Notice that the author here does not take shortcuts but lets the character build as you read. The author does not put *labels* on Leroy but lets you reach your own conclusions about how average and basically dull he apparently is. At the same time, he does not fit a simple *stereotype*—whether of a grumbling, resentful, unemployed individual or of the couch potato with no initiative at all (he *is* thinking about building a log house). Finally, the character is not static, set in cement. He is changing or developing in response to what he experiences (he has come to appreciate how things are put together).

THE RANGE OF CHARACTERIZATION

You would have me, when I describe horse thieves, say:
"Stealing horses is evil." But that has been known for ages
without my saying so. Let the jury judge them; it's my job
simply to show what sort of people they are.
ANTON CHEKHOV

How do you come to understand the characters in a short story you read? An author may give you a capsule portrait as advance notice of what you may expect of a character. However, in much modern fiction, you read to see character *unfold*. You see people act out (and hear them talk out) who they are. The author may choose to make you watch a character from outside, letting you draw your own conclusions. Or the author may take you inside the character's mind, letting you overhear private thoughts and share in feelings masked to the outside world.

When you pay close attention to character, you try to anwer questions like the following:

Who are these people?
How do you get to know them?
How does what they say reveal character?
How does what they do reveal character?
What incidents or challenges put them to the test?
What motives do you recognize?
How do the characters look to other people in the story?
Does what others say about them tend to inform you or mislead you?
How do they interact with other people?
Do they live up to your estimate of them, or do they surprise you?
Does the author directly or indirectly steer your reactions?

As you explore such questions, bear in mind features that will keep you from giving oversimple answers:

Action and Motivation As you study character in fiction, you will find yourself going from the *what* to the *why*—from people's words and actions to their motives. Why do people talk and act the way they do? Be prepared to ponder the byways of **motivation.** Characters who act spiteful or hostile may not be by temperament spiteful or hostile people. They may be venting pent-up frustrations; they may have been driven to the edge of their endurance by a series of adverse events. Apparent hostility may be a way to fend off unwanted sympathy. Be prepared to look for clues to behavior that may seem puzzling on the surface. Be ready to look at the real motives behind the rationalizations or alibis offered by a character.

Flat and Round Characters **Flat characters** are people with a one-track personality: The miser is always a Scrooge, the braggart is always the blowhard, the whiner always finds fault. Such one-dimensional characters are common in popular fiction and make for easy recognition (and, sometimes, the easy laugh). **Round characters** have the combination of traits that make real people complicated (and at times infuriating). They may be loyal to a person or a cause—with their loyalty tempered by serious private doubts. They may have been raised in an atmosphere of rah-rah patriotism but discover unsuspected sympathies for a prisoner of war—the "enemy." In your study of characters in fiction, be prepared to recognize divided loyalties, mixed emotions.

Static and Growing Characters In serious fiction, characters may prove capable of growth, development. Stories like Alice Munro's "Boys and Girls" are stories of **initiation.** They reenact rites of passage—from childhood to adolescence, from the happy protected childhood world to a realization of the limitations of the adult world.

Person and Persona   Many writers of modern fiction delight in going beyond the surface, beyond the stereotype. They probe for the hidden personality, the buried self, beneath the public **persona.** They love to explore the contrast between the image, the face we present to the outside world (perfect hostess, Mr. Personality), and our private insecurities, doubts, hang-ups, or vendettas.

The Interplay of Characters   Sometimes only a single character emerges from the background—giving, as it were, a solo performance. More typically, a character's personality is revealed in the interaction with others. We see characters as part of a web of relationships. In the Alice Munro story, the girl who is at the center of the story is influenced by two conflicting role models, her father and her mother.

Guard against predictable ways of short-circuiting your understanding of a character. Let the character develop—instead of saying prematurely, "I know the type!" Similarly, try not to judge or reject prematurely: Once you turn angry or judgmental, you may not be able to muster the empathy needed to sense how the mind of a character works. Try to understand before you judge.

JUXTAPOSITIONS

Capsule Portraits

In both of the following short shorts, a character takes shape before our eyes in a brief space. The first story was written by a writer who for a time was one of the most authentic voices of heartland America. The second was written by an immigrant from the West Indies whose candor and commitment gained her a large audience in her adopted country. What would you include in a capsule portrait of the central character in each story? Do you recognize or understand these people?

SHERWOOD ANDERSON   (1876–1941)

Sherwood Anderson grew up in the small country towns and factory towns of Ohio. He worked on farms, in livery stables, and on racetracks; and he eventually left his family and a job as a factory manager to become a full-time writer in Chicago. His *Winesburg, Ohio* (1919) went beyond the polite social surface to probe the emotional drives and frustrations of his characters. Anderson influenced and inspired critics and writers searching for a more vigorous, more experimental, more modern American literature, including H. L. Mencken, Ernest Hemingway, and William Faulkner. A fellow writer said of him that in his fiction "the uneventful and imprisoned life he saw around him became moving and tragic as though another dimension had been added when it passed through his passionate survey—like the same river flowing between deeper walls."

Paper Pills 1919

He was an old man with a white beard and huge nose and hands. Long before the time during which we will know him, he was a doctor and drove a jaded white horse from house to house through the streets of Winesburg. Later he married a girl who had money. She had been left a large fertile farm when her father died. The girl was quiet, tall, and dark, and to many people she seemed very beautiful. Everyone in Winesburg wondered why she married the doctor. Within a year after the marriage she died.

The knuckles of the doctor's hands were extraordinarily large. When the hands were closed they looked like clusters of unpainted wooden balls as large as walnuts fastened together by steel rods. He smoked a cob pipe and after his wife's death sat all day in his empty office close by a window that was covered with cobwebs. He never opened the window. Once on a hot day in August he tried but found it stuck fast and after that he forgot all about it.

Winesburg had forgotten the old man, but in Doctor Reefy there were the seeds of something very fine. Alone in his musty office in the Heffner Block above the Paris Dry Goods Company's store, he worked ceaselessly, building up something that he himself destroyed. Little pyramids of truth he erected and after erecting knocked them down again that he might have the truths to erect other pyramids.

Doctor Reefy was a tall man who had worn one suit of clothes for ten years. It was frayed at the sleeves and little holes had appeared at the knees and elbows. In the office he wore also a linen duster with huge pockets into which he continually stuffed scraps of paper. After some weeks the scraps of paper became little hard round balls, and when the pockets were filled he dumped them out upon the floor. For ten years he had but one friend, another old man named John Spaniard who owned a tree nursery. Sometimes, in a playful mood, old Doctor Reefy took from his pockets a handful of the paper balls and threw them at the nursery man. "That is to confound you, you blithering old sentimentalist," he cried, shaking with laughter.

The story of Doctor Reefy and his courtship of the tall dark girl who became his wife and left her money to him was a very curious story. It is delicious, like the twisted little apples that grow in the orchards of Winesburg. In the fall one walks in the orchards and the ground is hard with frost underfoot. The apples have been taken from the trees by the pickers. They have been put in barrels and shipped to the cities where they will be eaten in apartments that are filled with books, magazines, furniture, and people. On the trees are only a few gnarled apples that the pickers have rejected. They look like the knuckles of Doctor Reefy's hands. One nibbles at them and they are delicious. Into a little round place at the side of the apple has been gathered all of its sweetness. One runs from tree to tree over the frosted ground picking the gnarled, twisted apples and filling his pockets with them. Only the few know the sweetness of the twisted apples.

The girl and Doctor Reefy began their courtship on a summer afternoon. He was forty-five then and already he had begun the practice of filling his pockets with the scraps of paper that became hard balls and were thrown away. The habit had been formed as he sat in his buggy behind the jaded white horse and went slowly along country roads. On the papers were written thoughts, ends of thoughts, beginnings of thoughts.

One by one the mind of Doctor Reefy had made the thoughts. Out of many of them he formed a truth that arose gigantic in his mind. The truth clouded the world. It became terrible and then faded away and the little thoughts began again.

The tall dark girl came to see Doctor Reefy because she was in the family way and had become frightened. She was in that condition because of a series of circumstances also curious.

The death of her father and mother and the rich acres of land that had come down to her had set a train of suitors on her heels. For two years she saw suitors almost every evening. Except two they were all alike. They talked to her of passion and there was a strained eager quality in their voices and in their eyes when they looked at her. The two who were different were much unlike each other. One of them, a slender young man with white hands, the son of a jeweler in Winesburg, talked continually of virginity. When he was with her he was never off the subject. The other, a black-haired boy with large ears, said nothing at all but always managed to get her into the darkness, where he began to kiss her.

For a time the tall dark girl thought she would marry the jeweler's son. For hours she sat in silence listening as he talked to her and then she began to be afraid of something. Beneath his talk of virginity she began to think there was a lust greater than in all the others. At times it seemed to her that as he talked he was holding her body in his hands. She imagined him turning it slowly about in the white hands and staring at it. At night she dreamed that he had bitten into her body and that his jaws were dripping. She had the dream three times, then she became in the family way to the one who said nothing at all but who in the moment of his passion actually did bite her shoulder so that for days the marks of his teeth showed. 10

After the tall dark girl came to know Doctor Reefy it seemed to her that she never wanted to leave him again. She went into his office one morning and without her saying anything he seemed to know what had happened to her.

In the office of the doctor there was a woman, the wife of the man who kept the bookstore in Winesburg. Like all old-fashioned country practitioners, Doctor Reefy pulled teeth, and the woman who waited held a handkerchief to her teeth and groaned. Her husband was with her and when the tooth was taken out they both screamed and blood ran down on the woman's white dress. The tall dark girl did not pay any attention. When the woman and the man had gone the doctor smiled. "I will take you driving into the country with me," he said.

For several weeks the tall dark girl and the doctor were together almost every day. The condition that had brought her to him passed in an illness, but she was like one who has discovered the sweetness of the twisted apples, she could not get her mind fixed again upon the round perfect fruit that is eaten in the city apartments. In the fall after the beginning of her acquaintanceship with him she married Doctor Reefy and in the following spring she died. During the winter he read to her all of the odds and ends of thoughts he had scribbled on the bits of paper. After he had read them he laughed and stuffed them away in his pockets to become round hard balls.

THE RECEPTIVE READER

1. Like other characters in Anderson's stories, the doctor as the *central character* is likely to seem an eccentric or outsider to the people around him. Do *you* think he is strange? What makes him seem strange or understandable to you? What is the author's attitude toward him, and how can you know?

2. What kind of person is the woman in the story? What picture do you form of the two men who are courting her? What determines her choices?

3. What might be the *symbolic* significance of the "twisted apples"?

THE PERSONAL RESPONSE

Would you call this story a love story? How is it different from what you might expect in a love story? How do you react to it?

JAMAICA KINCAID (born 1941)

When people say you're charming you are in deep trouble.
JAMAICA KINCAID

Jamaica Kincaid was born in Antigua in the West Indies and left home to come to the United States when she was sixteen. An interviewer said of her that she grew up "in the shadow of a loving but domineering mother while learning proper British etiquette at colonial schools" (Donna Perry). After she came to New York and shed her original name (Elaine Potter Richardson), she worked at odd jobs, took photography classes, and was eventually discovered by the *New Yorker*. Two novels, *Annie John* (1983) and *Lucy* (1990), grew out of her *New Yorker* stories. She says that she felt like an outsider even when she lived at home among people who were mostly black like her and many of whom were women like her. She has been praised for her honesty and criticized for her anger, which she directs both at the suffering brought by colonialism and at the shortsightedness of the new rulers of the Third World.

A few words in Kincaid's story go back to the local dialect of her childhood: *benna* is calypso-inspired popular music; *doukona* is a spicy pudding.

Girl 1978

Wash the white clothes on Monday and put them on the stone heap; wash the color clothes on Tuesday and put them on the clothesline to dry; don't walk barehead in the hot sun; cook pumpkin fritters in very hot sweet oil; soak your little cloths right after you take them off; when buying cotton to make yourself a nice blouse, be sure that it doesn't have gum on it, because that way it won't hold up well after a wash; soak salt fish overnight before you cook it; is it true that you sing benna in Sunday school?; always eat your food in such a way that it won't turn someone else's stomach; on Sundays try to walk like a lady and not like the slut you are so bent on becoming; don't sing benna in Sunday school; you mustn't speak to wharf-rat boys, not even to give directions; don't eat fruits on the street—flies will follow you; *but I don't sing benna on Sundays at all and never in Sunday school;* this is how to sew on a button; this is how to make a buttonhole for the button you have just sewed on; this is how to hem a dress when you see the hem coming down and so to prevent yourself from looking like the slut I know you are so bent on becoming; this is how you iron your father's khaki shirt so that it doesn't have a crease; this is how you iron your father's khaki pants so that they don't have a crease; this is how you grow okra—far from the house, because okra tree harbors red ants; when you are growing dasheen, make sure it gets plenty of water or else it makes your throat itch when you are eating it; this is how you sweep a corner;

this is how you sweep a whole house; this is how you sweep a yard; this is how you smile to someone you don't like too much; this is how you smile to someone you don't like at all; this is how you smile to someone you like completely; this is how you set a table for tea; this is how you set a table for dinner; this is how you set a table for dinner with an important guest; this is how you set a table for lunch; this is how you set a table for breakfast; this is how to behave in the presence of men who don't know you very well, and this way they won't recognize immediately the slut I have warned you against becoming; be sure to wash every day, even if it is with your own spit; don't squat down to play marbles—you are not a boy, you know; don't pick people's flowers—you might catch something; don't throw stones at blackbirds, because it might not be a blackbird at all; this is how to make a bread pudding; this is how to make doukona; this is how to make pepper pot; this is how to make a good medicine for a cold; this is how to make a good medicine to throw away a child before it even becomes a child; this is how to catch a fish; this is how to throw back a fish you don't like, and that way something bad won't fall on you; this is how to bully a man; this is how a man bullies you; this is how to love a man, and if this doesn't work there are other ways, and if they don't work don't feel too bad about giving up; this is how to spit up in the air if you feel like it, and this is how to move quick so that it doesn't fall on you; this is how to make ends meet; always squeeze bread to make sure it's fresh; *but what if the baker won't let me feel the bread?*; you mean to say that after all you are really going to be the kind of woman who the baker won't let near the bread?

THE RECEPTIVE READER

1. The central character in this short short takes shape entirely through *dialogue*. What kind of person do you hear talking? ✧ What is her range of favorite topics? (*Benna* in the story is a dialect word for popular music—calypso, rock and roll—that the speaker considers a bad influence.) ✧ What expressions or ways of talking do you recognize, and why?

2. As in many one-way conversations, the listener in this story does not have a chance to have her say. Do you nevertheless hear her thinking? What would she say if she had a chance?

THE PERSONAL RESPONSE

Do you find yourself siding with the girl? Does the older woman have a point?

THE CREATIVE DIMENSION

Write a last letter from Anderson's doctor to his wife, or from the wife to her husband. Or write a letter from the girl in Kincaid's story to the person lecturing her.

THE UNIQUENESS OF HUMAN BEINGS

Unlike social scientists, who make descriptive statements about the varying divorce rates between, say, middle-class blacks and blue-collar whites, short-story writers seek to strip away these labels and create characters whose lives are contradictory and unfinished and do not possess the coherence of a psychological theory. Writers reveal instead

*the unpredictability of human beings, caught between the
lack of consciousness or conviction or certainty and the
need to make decisions and get on with their lives.*
MICHAEL NAGLER AND WILLIAM SWANSON

In some stories, the characters stay pale. They may seem interchangeable with others of their time, their setting; they may be representative of their stage in life or of their class. In other stories, the mystery of personality seems at the center of the story. The story probes a character's motives, explores surface contradictions, or ponders a change of heart. To a large extent, the character is the story. In the stories that follow, character plays a central role.

RAYMOND CARVER (1939–1988)

*Carver has an acute sense of the singularity, the endearing
oddity, of each human being; to each person he grants a
measure of dignity because, if nothing else at all, this
person has the sure distinction that no one else is exactly
like him—no human life can be replicated; therefore each,
however flawed, is precious.*
JONATHAN YARDLEY

*No one's brevity is as rich, as complete, as Raymond
Carver's.*
PATRICIA HAMPL

Raymond Carver has been praised for his intentional "blue-collar realism and unsophistication" (John Barth). Carver had himself worked at blue-collar jobs in the towns of the Pacific Northwest that is the setting of many of his stories. He himself, like some of his characters, had done battle against alcoholism. His characters are often unskilled, unemployed, and unremarkable, yet of sufficient human interest to the author. He often gives a voice to the feelings or point of view of people of few words, "speaking the thoughts of those who cannot themselves speak" (John Clute). One reviewer thought of him as the kind of writer "who turned banality's pockets out and found all their contents beautiful" (Marilynne Robinson).

Carver is one of a group of contemporary writers tending toward a **minimalist** stance (though he himself disliked the fashionable label). Like other minimalist writers, he kept his stories to the essential minimum, writing on the theory that "less is more," being suspicious of all showy effects. He once said, "I cut my work to the marrow, not just the bone." Carver seems to enjoy teasing the reader with the puzzle of personality. His narrator, as in the following story, may be someone listening to another character, piecing together the pieces of the puzzle, wanting to say (as does Carver's reader) "Tell me more. "

The Third Thing That Killed My Father Off 1977

I'll tell you what did my father in. The third thing was Dummy, that Dummy died. The first thing was Pearl Harbor. And the second thing was moving to my grandfather's farm near Wenatchee. That's where my father finished out his days, except they were probably finished before that.

My father blamed Dummy's death on Dummy's wife. Then he blamed it on the fish. And finally he blamed himself—because he was the one that showed Dummy the ad in the back of *Field and Stream* for live black bass shipped anywhere in the U.S.

It was after he got the fish that Dummy started acting peculiar. The fish changed Dummy's whole personality. That's what my father said.

I never knew Dummy's real name. If anyone did, I never heard it. Dummy it was then, and it's Dummy I remember him by now. He was a little wrinkled man, bald-headed, short but very powerful in the arms and legs. If he grinned, which was seldom, his lips folded back over brown, broken teeth. It gave him a crafty expression. His watery eyes stayed fastened on your mouth when you were talking—and if you weren't, they'd go to someplace queer on your body.

I don't think he was really deaf. At least not as deaf as he made out. But he sure   5
couldn't talk. That was for certain.

Deaf or no, Dummy'd been on as a common laborer out at the sawmill since the 1920s. This was the Cascade Lumber Company in Yakima, Washington. The years I knew him, Dummy was working as a cleanup man. And all those years I never saw him with anything different on. Meaning a felt hat, a khaki workshirt, a denim jacket over a pair of coveralls. In his top pockets he carried rolls of toilet paper, as one of his jobs was to clean and supply the toilets. It kept him busy, seeing as how the men on nights used to walk off after their tours with a roll or two in their lunchboxes.

Dummy carried a flashlight, even though he worked days. He also carried wrenches, pliers, screwdrivers, friction tape, all the same things the millwrights carried. Well, it made them kid Dummy, the way he was, always carrying everything. Carl Lowe, Ted Slade, Johnny Wait, they were the worst kidders of the ones that kidded Dummy. But Dummy took it all in stride. I think he'd gotten used to it.

My father never kidded Dummy. Not to my knowledge, anyway. Dad was a big, heavy-shouldered man with a crew-haircut, double chin, and a belly of real size. Dummy was always staring at that belly. He'd come to the filing room where my father worked, and he'd sit on a stool and watch my dad's belly while he used the big emery wheels on the saws.

Dummy had a house as good as anyone's.

It was a tarpaper-covered affair near the river, five or six miles from town. Half a   10
mile behind the house, at the end of a pasture, there lay a big gravel pit that the state had dug when they were paving the roads around there. Three good-sized holes had been scooped out, and over the years they'd filled with water. By and by, the three ponds came together to make one.

It was deep. It had a darkish look to it.

Dummy had a wife as well as a house. She was a woman years younger and said to go around with Mexicans. Father said it was busybodies that said that, men like Lowe and Wait and Slade.

She was a small stout woman with glittery little eyes. The first time I saw her, I saw those eyes. It was when I was with Pete Jensen and we were on our bicycles and we stopped at Dummy's to get a glass of water.

When she opened the door, I told her I was Del Fraser's son. I said, "He works with—" And then I realized. "You know, your husband. We were on our bicycles and thought we could get a drink."

"Wait here," she said.

She came back with a little tin cup of water in each hand. I downed mine in a single gulp.

But she didn't offer us more. She watched us without saying anything. When we started to get on our bicycles, she came over to the edge of the porch.

"You little fellas had a car now, I might catch a ride with you."

She grinned. Her teeth looked too big for her mouth.

"Let's go," Pete said, and we went.

There weren't many places you could fish for bass in our part of the state. There was rainbow mostly, a few brook and Dolly Varden in some of the high mountain streams, and silvers in Blue Lake and Lake Rimrock. That was mostly it, except for the runs of steelhead and salmon in some of the freshwater rivers in late fall. But if you were a fisherman, it was enough to keep you busy. No one fished for bass. A lot of people I knew had never seen a bass except for pictures. But my father had seen plenty of them when he was growing up in Arkansas and Georgia, and he had high hopes to do with Dummy's bass, Dummy being a friend.

The day the fish arrived, I'd gone swimming at the city pool. I remember coming home and going out again to get them since Dad was going to give Dummy a hand—three tanks Parcel Post from Baton Rouge, Louisiana.

We went in Dummy's pickup, Dad and Dummy and me.

These tanks turned out to be barrels, really, the three of them crated in pine lath. They were standing in the shade out back of the train depot, and it took my dad and Dummy both to lift each crate into the truck.

Dummy drove very carefully through town and just as carefully all the way to his house. He went right through his yard without stopping. He went on down to within feet of the pond. By that time it was nearly dark, so he kept his headlights on and took out a hammer and a tire iron from under the seat, and then the two of them lugged the crates up close to the water and started tearing open the first one.

The barrel inside was wrapped in burlap, and there were these nickel-sized holes in the lid. They raised it off and Dummy aimed his flashlight in.

It looked like a million bass fingerlings were finning inside. It was the strangest sight, all those live things busy in there, like a little ocean that had come on the train.

Dummy scooted the barrel to the edge of the water and poured it out. He took his flashlight and shined it into the pond. But there was nothing to be seen anymore. You could hear the frogs going, but you could hear them going anytime it newly got dark.

"Let me get the other crates," my father said, and he reached over as if to take the hammer from Dummy's coveralls. But Dummy pulled back and shook his head.

He undid the other two crates himself, leaving dark drops of blood on the lath where he ripped his hand doing it.

From that night on, Dummy was different.

Dummy wouldn't let anyone come around now anymore. He put up fencing all around the pasture, and then he fenced off the pond with electrical barbed wire. They said it cost him all his savings for that fence.

Of course, my father wouldn't have anything to do with Dummy after that. Not since Dummy ran him off. Not from fishing, mind you, because the bass were just babies still. But even from trying to get a look.

One evening two years after, when Dad was working late and I took him his food and a jar of iced tea, I found him standing talking with Syd Glover, the millwright. Just as I came in, I heard Dad saying, "You'd reckon the fool was married to them fish, the way he acts."

"From what I hear," Syd said, "he'd do better to put that fence round his house."   35

My father saw me then, and I saw him signal Syd Glover with his eyes.

But a month later my dad finally made Dummy do it. What he did was, he told Dummy how you had to thin out the weak ones on account of keeping things fit for the rest of them. Dummy stood there pulling at his ear and staring at the floor. Dad said, Yeah, he'd be down to do it tomorrow because it had to be done. Dummy never said yes, actually. He just never said no, is all. All he did was pull on his ear some more.

When Dad got home that day, I was ready and waiting. I had his old bass plugs out and was testing the treble hooks with my finger.

"You set?" he called to me, jumping out of the car. "I'll go to the toilet, you put the stuff in. You can drive us out there if you want."

I'd stowed everything in the back seat and was trying out the wheel when he came   40
back out wearing his fishing hat and eating a wedge of cake with both hands.

Mother was standing in the door watching. She was a fair-skinned woman, her blonde hair pulled back in a tight bun and fastened down with a rhinestone clip. I wonder if she ever went around back in those happy days, or what she ever really did.

I let out the handbrake. Mother watched until I'd shifted gears, and then, still unsmiling, she went back inside.

It was a fine afternoon. We had all the windows down to let the air in. We crossed the Moxee Bridge and swung west onto Slater Road. Alfalfa fields stood off to either side, and farther on it was cornfields.

Dad had his hand out the window. He was letting the wind carry it back. He was restless, I could see.

It wasn't long before we pulled up at Dummy's. He came out of the house wear-   45
ing his hat. His wife was looking out the window.

"You got your frying pan ready?" Dad hollered out to Dummy, but Dummy just stood there eyeing the car. "Hey, Dummy!" Dad yelled. "Hey, Dummy, where's your pole, Dummy?"

Dummy jerked his head back and forth. He moved his weight from one leg to the other and looked at the ground and then at us. His tongue rested on his lower lip, and he began working his foot into the dirt.

I shouldered the creel. I handed Dad his pole and picked up my own.

"We set to go?" Dad said. "Hey, Dummy, we set to go?"

Dummy took off his hat and, with the same hand, he wiped his wrist over his head.   50
He turned abruptly, and we followed him across the spongy pasture. Every twenty feet or so a snipe sprang up from the clumps of grass at the edge of the old furrows.

At the end of the pasture, the ground sloped gently and became dry and rocky, nettle bushes and scrub oaks scattered here and there. We cut to the right, following an old set of car tracks, going through a field of milkweed that came up to our waists, the dry pods at the tops of the stalks rattling angrily as we pushed through. Presently, I saw the sheen of water over Dummy's shoulder, and I heard Dad shout, "Oh, Lord, look at that!"

But Dummy slowed down and kept bringing his hand up and moving his hat back and forth over his head, and then he just stopped flat.

Dad said, "Well, what do you think, Dummy? One place good as another? Where do you say we should come onto it?"

Dummy wet his lower lip.

"What's the matter with you, Dummy?" Dad said. "This your pond, ain't it?" 55

Dummy looked down and picked an ant off his coveralls.

"Well, hell," Dad said, letting out his breath. He took out his watch. "If it's all right with you, we'll get to it before it gets too dark."

Dummy stuck his hands in his pockets and turned back to the pond. He started walking again. We trailed along behind. We could see the whole pond now, the water dimpled with rising fish. Every so often a bass would leap clear and come down in a splash.

"Great God," I heard my father say.

We came up to the pond at an open place, a gravel beach kind of. 60

Dad motioned to me and dropped into a crouch. I dropped too. He was peering into the water in front of us, and when I looked, I saw what had taken him so.

"Honest to God," he whispered.

A school of bass was cruising, twenty, thirty, not one of them under two pounds. They veered off, and then they shifted and came back, so densely spaced they looked like they were bumping up against each other. I could see their big, heavy-lidded eyes watching us as they went by. They flashed away again, and again they came back.

They were asking for it. It didn't make any difference if we stayed squatted or stood up. The fish just didn't think a thing about us. I tell you, it was a sight to behold.

We sat there for quite a while, watching that school of bass go so innocently about 65 their business, Dummy the whole time pulling at his fingers and looking around as if he expected someone to show up. All over the pond the bass were coming up to nuzzle the water, or jumping clear and falling back, or coming up to the surface to swim along with their dorsals sticking out.

Dad signaled, and we got up to cast. I tell you, I was shaky with excitement. I could hardly get the plug loose from the cork handle of my pole. It was while I was try-ing to get the hooks out that I felt Dummy seize my shoulder with his big fingers. I looked, and in answer Dummy worked his chin in Dad's direction. What he wanted was clear enough, no more than one pole.

Dad took off his hat and then put it back on and then he moved over to where I stood.

"You go on, Jack" he said. "That's all right, son—you do it now."

I looked at Dummy just before I laid out my cast. His face had gone rigid, and there was a thin line of drool on his chin.

"Come back stout on the sucker when he strikes," Dad said. "Sons of bitches got 70 mouths hard as doorknobs."

I flipped off the drag lever and threw back my arm. I sent her out a good forty feet. The water was boiling even before I had time to take up the slack.

"Hit him!" Dad yelled. "Hit the son of a bitch! Hit him good!"

I came back hard, twice. I had him, all right. The rod bowed over and jerked back and forth. Dad kept yelling what to do.

"Let him go, let him go! Let him run! Give him more line! Now wind in! Wind in! No, let him run! Woo-ee! Will you look at that!"

The bass danced around the pond. Every time it came up out of the water, it shook its head so hard you could hear the plug rattle. And then he'd take off again. But by and by I wore him out and had him in up close. He looked enormous, six or seven pounds maybe. He lay on his side, whipped, mouth open, gills working. My knees felt so weak I could hardly stand. But I held the rod up, the line tight.

Dad waded out over his shoes. But when he reached for the fish, Dummy started sputtering, shaking his head, waving his arms.

"Now what the hell's the matter with you, Dummy? The boy's got hold of the biggest bass I ever seen, and he ain't going to throw him back, by God!"

Dummy kept carrying on and gesturing toward the pond.

"I ain't about to let this boy's fish go. You hear me, Dummy? You got another think coming if you think I'm going to do that."

Dummy reached for my line. Meanwhile, the bass had gained some strength back. He turned himself over and started swimming again. I yelled and then I lost my head and slammed down the brake on the reel and started winding. The bass made a last, furious run.

That was that. The line broke. I almost fell over on my back.

"Come on, Jack," Dad said, and I saw him grabbing up his pole. "Come on, god-damn the fool, before I knock the man down."

That February the river flooded.

It had snowed pretty heavy the first weeks of December, and turned real cold before Christmas. The ground froze. The snow stayed where it was. But toward the end of January, the Chinook wind struck. I woke up one morning to hear the house getting buffeted and the steady drizzle of water running off the roof.

It blew for five days, and on the third day the river began to rise.

"She's up to fifteen feet," my father said one evening, looking over his newspaper. "Which is three feet over what you need to flood. Old Dummy going to lose his darlings."

I wanted to go down to the Moxee Bridge to see how high the water was running. But my dad wouldn't let me. He said a flood was nothing to see.

Two days later the river crested, and after that the water began to subside.

Orin Marshall and Danny Owens and I bicycled out to Dummy's one morning a week after. We parked our bicycles and walked across the pasture that bordered Dummy's property.

It was a wet, blustery day, the clouds dark and broken, moving fast across the sky. The ground was soppy wet and we kept coming to puddles in the thick grass. Danny was just learning how to cuss, and he filled the air with the best he had every time he stepped in over his shoes. We could see the swollen river at the end of the pasture. The water was still high and out of its channel, surging around the trunks of trees and eating away at the edge of the land. Out toward the middle, the current moved heavy and swift, and now and then a bush floated by, or a tree with its branches sticking up.

We came to Dummy's fence and found a cow wedged in up against the wire. She was bloated and her skin was shiny-looking and gray. It was the first dead thing of any size I'd ever seen. I remember Orin took a stick and touched the open eyes.

We moved on down the fence, toward the river. We were afraid to go near the wire because we thought it might still have electricity in it. But at the edge of what looked like a deep canal, the fence came to an end. The ground had simply dropped into the water here, and the fence along with it.

We crossed over and followed the new channel that cut directly into Dummy's land and headed straight for his pond, going into it lengthwise and forcing an outlet for itself at the other end, then twisting off until it joined up with the river farther on.

You didn't doubt that most of Dummy's fish had been carried off. But those that hadn't been were free to come and go.

Then I caught sight of Dummy. It scared me, seeing him. I motioned to the other fellows, and we all got down.

Dummy was standing at the far side of the pond near where the water was rushing out. He was just standing there, the saddest man I ever saw.

"I sure do feel sorry for old Dummy, though," my father said at supper a few weeks after. "Mind, the poor devil brought it on himself. But you can't help but be troubled for him."

Dad went on to say George Laycock saw Dummy's wife sitting in the Sportsman's Club with a big Mexican fellow.

"And that ain't the half of it—"

Mother looked up at him sharply and then at me. But I just went on eating like I hadn't heard a thing.

Dad said, "Damn it to hell, Bea, the boy's old enough!"

He'd changed a lot, Dummy had. He was never around any of the men anymore, not if he could help it. No one felt like joking with him either, not since he'd chased Carl Lowe with a two-by-four stud after Carl tipped Dummy's hat off. But the worst of it was that Dummy was missing from work a day or two a week on the average now, and there was some talk of his being laid off.

"The man's going off the deep end," Dad said. "Clear crazy if he don't watch out."

Then on a Sunday afternoon just before my birthday, Dad and I were cleaning the garage. It was a warm, drifty day. You could see the dust hanging in the air. Mother came to the back door and said, "Del, it's for you. I think it's Vern."

I followed Dad in to wash up. When he was through talking, he put the phone down and turned to us.

"It's Dummy," he said. "Did in his wife with a hammer and drowned himself. Vern just heard it in town."

When we got out there, cars were parked all around. The gate to the pasture stood open, and I could see tire marks that led on to the pond.

The screen door was propped ajar with a box, and there was this lean, pock-faced man in slacks and sports shirt and wearing a shoulder holster. He watched Dad and me get out of the car.

"I was his friend," Dad said to the man.

The man shook his head. "Don't care who you are. Clear off unless you got business here."

"Did they find him?" Dad said.

"They're dragging," the man said, and adjusted the fit of his gun.

"All right if we walk down? I knew him pretty well."

The man said, "Take your chances. They chase you off, don't say you wasn't warned."

We went on across the pasture, taking pretty much the same route we had the day we tried fishing. There were motorboats going on the pond, dirty fluffs of exhaust hanging over it. You could see where the high water had cut away the ground and carried off trees and rocks. The two boats had uniformed men in them, and they were going back and forth, one man steering and the other man handling the rope and hooks.

An ambulance waited on the gravel beach where we'd set ourselves to cast for Dummy's bass. Two men in white lounged against the back, smoking cigarettes.

One of the motorboats cut off. We all looked up. The man in back stood up and started heaving on his rope. After a time, an arm came out of the water. It looked like the hooks had gotten Dummy in the side. The arm went back down and then it came out again, along with a bundle of something.

It's not him, I thought. It's something else that has been in there for years.

The man in the front of the boat moved to the back, and together the two men hauled the dripping thing over the side.

I looked at Dad. His face was funny the way it was set. 120

"Women," he said. He said, "That's what the wrong kind of woman can do to you, Jack."

But I don't think Dad really believed it. I think he just didn't know who to blame or what to say.

It seemed to me everything took a bad turn for my father after that. Just like Dummy, he wasn't the same man anymore. That arm coming up and going back down in the water, it was like so long to good times and hello to bad. Because it was nothing but that all the years after Dummy drowned himself in that dark water.

Is that what happens when a friend dies? Bad luck for the pals he left behind? 125

But as I said, Pearl Harbor and having to move back to his dad's place didn't do my dad one bit of good, either.

THE RECEPTIVE READER

1. How do we learn what we come to know about Dummy? Who is the *narrator*—what kind of person tells us the story? What is his role in the story? Is he a major or a minor character? What is his vantage point? What are his limitations?

2. How does the author make Dummy come to life in the early sections of the story? What is Dummy's problem? Can you visualize his physical appearance? How much and what kind of *descriptive detail* do we get?

3. How do Dummy's coworkers treat him, and how are we expected to feel about them?

4. What is the relationship between the narrator's father and Dummy? Who is the true *central character* in the story? Does the story have a hero?

5. As the story unfolds, how much insight do we get into Dummy's personality or character? Do you understand the way Dummy acts about the fish, the pond, the flood? (How important are the fish in the story as a whole?)

6. What role does Dummy's wife play in the story? Is she playing a bit part? Is she expendable?

7. A central *irony* in the story is that Dummy is the character who seems to have urgent things to say to the others, but he is unable to communicate through language. How *does* he communicate? What is he trying to tell the others?

8. What is the role of humor in the story? What is the tone of the references to the father's death in the title, at the beginning, and in the conclusion? Do they color the story as a whole?

9. Do you think the author should have given the reader less of an outsider's and more of an insider's view of Dummy as a major character in the story? Would you have liked more insight into the workings of Dummy's mind?

10. What is the pattern of the narrative as a whole? Do you think its leisurely pace and straightforward development are part of the author's larger intentions or overall conception of the story?

THE PERSONAL RESPONSE

For you, is Dummy an eccentric—an isolated individual, a person with special personal problems all of his own? Is he someone "acting peculiar"? Or does his story have a more general human meaning?

THE CREATIVE DIMENSION

Assume Dummy could have been a more articulate or eloquent character. Write an extended suicide note that he might have written to explain himself to his friends.

ALICE MUNRO   (born 1931)

Alice Munro is one of several Canadian writers who became widely known in the United States in the 1970s and 1980s. She grew up in southwestern Ontario, and many of her stories take us to rural settings—the countryside and small towns of eastern Canada, where during the harsh winters snowdrifts would curl around the houses "like sleeping whales." Her father was a farmer, and when she writes in the first person as a girl growing up on a farm, it is tempting to equate the "I" telling the story with the author. However, she also uses the "I" when she has a small-town boy tell the story of his experimenting with liquor and first love on a Saturday night and finding both wanting. The "I" of her stories is fictitious—it is part of a vividly imagined world that blends autobiographical materials and sharp-eyed observation of fellow humanity.

Munro's first collection of short stories, *Dance of the Happy Shades*, was published in 1968 and received the Canadian Governor General's Literary Award. She published her second collection of stories, *Something I've Been Meaning to Tell You*, in 1972. Her novel *Lives of Girls and Women* appeared in 1971.

Munro has a special gift for creating a sense of place. In her story "Thanks for the Ride," she takes us to a town where the signs in Pop's Cafe (between fly-speckled and slightly yellowed cutouts of strawberry sundaes and tomato sandwiches) say things like "Don't ask for information—if we knew anything, we wouldn't be here." One of the boys in the story has a habit of reading signs out loud—"Mission Creek. Population 1700. Gateway to the Bruce. We love our children." The houses are likely to have linoleum on the floor; there is likely to be a glossy sofa "with a Niagara Falls and 'To Mother' cushion on it"; a big vase of paper apple blossoms may round out the decor.

In such settings, created in faithful and totally believable detail, she places characters who are often undergoing a rite of passage. (One editor said about Munro's stories that her "characters' lives and landscapes are inextricably intertwined.") They may be at a turning point in their lives, moving from childhood to adolescence, or from the confused passions of adolescence to the world of adult responsibilities. Her characters are often people who are still spontaneous and innocent but who encounter people more knowing, more experienced, and perhaps more defeated than they are. Such a story may become a story of **initiation,** as the hero or heroine discovers the limitations, the invisible walls, that mark his or her world.

In the following story, there is much nostalgic recreation of the golden world of childhood. But at the center of the story is a young woman at the crossroads. Who is this young woman? What are the contradictory influences that help shape her identity? Viewed as a rite of passage, her story is a passage from what to what? Where is she headed at the end of the story?

Boys and Girls 1968

It is difficult to stand forth in one's growing if one is not permitted to live through the states of one's unripeness, clumsiness, unreadiness, as well as one's grace and aptitude.

M. C. RICHARDS

[The Ave referred to in a song mentioned early in the story is short for the Catholic prayer Ave Maria, or Hail Mary. Orangemen's Day (July 12) is a Protestant holiday dedicated to the memory of William of Orange, who replaced the Catholic James II as king of England in 1689. Judy Canova was a popular entertainer of the 1930s and 1940s.]

My father was a fox farmer. That is, he raised silver foxes, in pens; and in the fall and early winter, when their fur was prime, he killed them and skinned them and sold their pelts to the Hudson's Bay Company or the Montreal Fur Traders. These companies supplied us with heroic calendars to hang, one on each side of the kitchen door. Against a background of cold blue sky and black pine forests and treacherous northern rivers, plumed adventurers planted the flags of England or of France; magnificent savages bent their backs to the portage.

For several weeks before Christmas, my father worked after supper in the cellar of our house. The cellar was whitewashed, and lit by a hundred-watt bulb over the worktable. My brother Laird and I sat on the top step and watched. My father removed the pelt inside-out from the body of the fox, which looked surprisingly small, mean and ratlike, deprived of its arrogant weight of fur. The naked, slippery bodies were collected in a sack and buried at the dump. One time the hired man, Henry Bailey, had taken a swipe at me with this sack, saying, "Christmas present!" My mother thought that was not funny. In fact she disliked the whole pelting operation—that was what the killing, skinning, and preparation of the furs was called—and wished it did not have to take place in the house. There was the smell. After the pelt had been stretched inside-out on a long board my father scraped away delicately, removing the little clotted webs of blood vessels, the bubbles of fat; the smell of blood and animal fat, with the strong primitive odor of the fox itself, penetrated all parts of the house. I found it reassuringly seasonal, like the smell of oranges and pine needles.

Henry Bailey suffered from bronchial troubles. He would cough and cough until his narrow face turned scarlet, and his light blue, derisive eyes filled up with tears; then he took the lid off the stove, and, standing well back, shot out a great clot of phlegm—hsss—straight into the heart of the flames. We admired him for this performance and for his ability to make his stomach growl at will, and for his laughter, which was full of high whistlings and gurglings and involved the whole faulty machinery of his chest. It was sometimes hard to tell what he was laughing at, and always possible that it might be us.

After we had been sent to bed we could still smell fox and still hear Henry's laugh, but these things, reminders of the warm, safe, brightly lit downstairs world, seemed lost and diminished, floating on the stale cold air upstairs. We were afraid at night in the winter. We were not afraid of *outside* though this was the time of year when snowdrifts curled around our house like sleeping whales and the wind harassed us all night, coming up from the buried fields, the frozen swamp, with its old bugbear chorus of threats and misery. We were afraid of *inside*, the room where we slept. At this time the upstairs of our house was not finished. A brick chimney went up one wall. In the middle of the floor was a square hole, with a wooden railing around it; that was where the stairs came up. On the other side of the stairwell were the things that nobody had any use for any more—a soldiery roll of linoleum, standing on end, a wicker baby carriage, a fern basket, china jugs and basins with cracks in them, a picture of the Battle of Balaclava, very sad to look at. I had told Laird, as soon as he was old enough to understand such things, that bats and skeletons lived over there; whenever a man escaped from the county jail, twenty miles away, I imagined that he had somehow let himself in the window and was hiding behind the linoleum. But we had rules to keep us safe. When the light was on, we were safe as long as we did not step off the square of worn carpet which defined our bedroom-space; when the light was off no place was safe but the beds themselves. I had to turn out the light kneeling on the end of my bed, and stretching as far as I could to reach the cord.

In the dark we lay on our beds, our narrow life rafts, and fixed our eyes on the faint light coming up the stairwell, and sang songs. Laird sang "Jingle Bells," which he would sing any time, whether it was Christmas or not, and I sang "Danny Boy." I loved the sound of my own voice, frail and supplicating, rising in the dark. We could make out the tall frosted shapes of the windows now, gloomy and white. When I came to the part, *When I am dead, as dead I well may be*—a fit of shivering caused not by the cold sheets but by pleasurable emotion almost silenced me. *You'll kneel and say, and Ave there above me*—What was an Ave? Every day I forgot to find out.

Laird went straight from singing to sleep. I could hear his long, satisfied, bubbly breaths. Now for the time that remained to me, the most perfectly private and perhaps the best time of the whole day, I arranged myself tightly under the covers and went on with one of the stories I was telling myself from night to night. These stories were about myself, when I had grown a little older; they took place in a world that was recognizably mine, yet one that presented opportunities for courage, boldness and self-sacrifice, as mine never did. I rescued people from a bombed building (it discouraged me that the real war had gone on so far away from Jubilee). I shot two rabid wolves who were menacing the schoolyard (the teachers cowered terrified at my back). I rode a fine horse spiritedly down the main street of Jubilee, acknowledging the townspeople's gratitude for some yet-to-be-worked-out piece of heroism (nobody ever rode a horse there, except King Billy in the Orangemen's Day parade). There was always riding and shooting in these stories, though I had only been on a horse twice—bareback because we did not own a saddle—and the second time I had slid right around and dropped under the horse's feet; it had stepped placidly over me. I really was learning to shoot, but I could not hit anything yet, not even tin cans on fence posts.

5

Alive, the foxes inhabited a world my father made for them. It was surrounded by a high guard fence, like a medieval town, with a gate that was padlocked at night. Along the streets of this town were ranged large, sturdy pens. Each of them had a real door that a man could go through, a wooden ramp along the wire, for the foxes to run up and down on, and a kennel—something like a clothes chest with airholes—where they slept and stayed in winter and had their young. There were feeding and watering dishes attached to the wire in such a way that they could be emptied and cleaned from the outside. The dishes were made of old tin cans, and the ramps and kennels of odds and ends of old lumber. Everything was tidy and ingenious; my father was tirelessly inventive and his favorite book in the world was *Robinson Crusoe*. He had fitted a tin drum on a wheelbarrow, for bringing water down to the pens. This was my job in summer, when the foxes had to have water twice a day. Between nine and ten o'clock in the morning, and again after supper, I filled the drum at the pump and trundled it down through the barnyard to the pens, where I parked it, and filled my watering can and went along the streets. Laird came too, with his little cream and green gardening can, filled too full and knocking against his legs and slopping water on his canvas shoes. I had the real watering can, my father's, though I could only carry it three-quarters full.

The foxes all had names, which were printed on a tin plate and hung beside their doors. They were not named when they were born, but when they survived the first year's pelting and were added to the breeding stock. Those my father had named were called names like Prince, Bob, Wally and Betty. Those I had named were called Star or Turk, or Maureen or Diana. Laird named one Maud after a hired girl we had when he was little, one Harold after a boy at school, and one Mexico, he did not say why.

Naming them did not make pets out of them, or anything like it. Nobody but my father ever went into the pens, and he had twice had blood-poisoning from bites. When I was bringing them their water they prowled up and down on the paths they had made inside their pens, barking seldom—they saved that for nighttime, when they might get up a chorus of community frenzy—but always watching me, their eyes burning, clear gold, in their pointed, malevolent faces. They were beautiful for their delicate legs and heavy, aristocratic tails and the bright fur sprinkled on dark down their backs—which gave them their name—but especially for their faces, drawn exquisitely sharp in pure hostility, and their golden eyes.

Besides carrying water I helped my father when he cut the long grass, and the   10 lamb's quarter and flowering money-musk, that grew between the pens. He cut with the scythe and I raked into piles. Then he took a pitchfork and threw fresh-cut grass all over the top of the pens, to keep the foxes cooler and shade their coats, which were browned by too much sun. My father did not talk to me unless it was about the job we were doing. In this he was quite different from my mother, who, if she was feeling cheerful, would tell me all sorts of things—the name of a dog she had had when she was a little girl, the names of boys she had gone out with later on when she was grown up, and what certain dresses of hers had looked like—she could not imagine now what had become of them. Whatever thoughts and stories my father had were private, and I was shy of him and would never ask him questions. Nevertheless I worked willingly under his eyes, and with a feeling of pride. One time a feed salesman came down into the pens to talk to him and my father said, "Like to have you meet my new hired man." I turned away and raked furiously, red in the face with pleasure.

"Could of fooled me," said the salesman. "I thought it was only a girl."

After the grass was cut, it seemed suddenly much later in the year. I walked on stubble in the earlier evening, aware of the reddening skies, the entering silences, of fall. When I wheeled the tank out of the gate and put the padlock on, it was almost dark. One night at this time I saw my mother and father standing talking on the little rise of ground we called the gangway, in front of the barn. My father had just come from the meathouse; he had his stiff bloody apron on, and a pail of cut-up meat in his hand.

It was an odd thing to see my mother down at the barn. She did not often come out of the house unless it was to do something—hang out the wash or dig potatoes in the garden. She looked out of place, with her bare lumpy legs, not touched by the sun, her apron still on and damp across the stomach from the supper dishes. Her hair was tied up in a kerchief, wisps of it falling out. She would tie her hair up like this in the morning, saying she did not have time to do it properly, and it would stay tied up all day. It was true, too; she really did not have time. These days our back porch was piled with baskets of peaches and grapes and pears, bought in town, and onions and tomatoes and cucumbers grown at home, all waiting to be made into jelly and jam and preserves, pickles and chili sauce. In the kitchen there was a fire in the stove all day, jars clinked in boiling water, sometimes a cheesecloth bag was strung on a pole between two chairs straining blue-black grape pulp for jelly. I was given jobs to do and I would sit at the table peeling peaches that had been soaked in the hot water, or cutting up onions, my eyes smarting and streaming. As soon as I was done I ran out of the house, trying to get out of earshot before my mother thought of what she wanted me to do next. I hated the hot dark kitchen in summer, the green blinds and the flypapers, the same old oilcloth table and wavy mirror and bumpy linoleum. My mother was too tired and preoccupied to talk to me, she had no heart to tell about the Normal School Graduation Dance; sweat trickled over her face and she was always counting under her breath, pointing at jars, dumping cups of sugar. It seemed to me that work in the house was endless, dreary and peculiarly depressing; work done out of doors, and in my father's service, was ritualistically important.

I wheeled the tank up to the barn, where it was kept, and I heard my mother saying, "Wait till Laird gets a little bigger, then you'll have a real help."

What my father said I did not hear. I was pleased by the way he stood listening, politely as he would to a salesman or a stranger, but with an air of wanting to get on with his real work. I felt my mother had no business down here and I wanted him to feel the same way. What did she mean about Laird? He was no help to anybody. Where was he now? Swinging himself sick on the swing, going around in circles, or trying to catch caterpillars. He never once stayed with me till I was finished. 15

"And then I can use her more in the house," I heard my mother say. She had a dead-quiet, regretful way of talking about me that always made me uneasy. "I just get my back turned and she runs off. It's not like I had a girl in the family at all."

I went and sat on a feed bag in the corner of the barn, not wanting to appear when this conversation was going on. My mother, I felt, was not to be trusted. She was kinder than my father and more easily fooled, but you could not depend on her, and the real reasons for the things she said and did were not to be known. She loved me, and she sat up late at night making a dress of the difficult style I wanted, for me to wear when school started, but she was also my enemy. She was always plotting. She was plotting now to get me to stay in the house more, although she knew I hated it (*because* she knew I hated it) and keep me from working for my father. It seemed to me she would do this simply out of perversity, and to try her power. It did not occur to me that she could be lonely, or jealous. No grown-up could be; they were too fortunate. I sat and kicked my heels monotonously against a feed bag, raising dust, and did not come out till she was gone.

At any rate, I did not expect my father to pay any attention to what she said. Who could imagine Laird doing my work—Laird remembering the padlock and cleaning out the watering dishes with a leaf on the end of a stick, or even wheeling the tank without it tumbling over? It showed how little my mother knew about the way things really were.

I have forgotten to say what the foxes were fed. My father's bloody apron reminded me. They were fed horsemeat. At this time most farmers still kept horses, and when a horse got too old to work, or broke a leg or got down and would not get up, as they sometimes did, the owner would call my father, and he and Henry went out to the farm in the truck. Usually they shot and butchered the horse there, paying the farmer from five to twelve dollars. If they had already too much meat on hand, they would bring the horse back alive, and keep it for a few days or weeks in our stable, until the meat was needed. After the war the farmers were buying tractors and gradually getting rid of horses altogether, so it sometimes happened that we got a good healthy horse, that there was just no use for any more. If this happened in the winter we might keep the horse in our stable till spring, for we had plenty of hay and if there was a lot of snow— and the plow did not always get our road cleared—it was convenient to be able to go to town with a horse and cutter.

The winter I was eleven years old we had two horses in the stable. We did not know what names they had had before, so we called them Mack and Flora. Mack was an old black workhorse, sooty and indifferent. Flora was a sorrel mare, a driver. We took them both out in the cutter. Mack was slow and easy to handle. Flora was given to fits of violent alarm, veering at cars and even at other horses, but we loved her speed and high-stepping, her general air of gallantry and abandon. On Saturdays we went down to the stable and as soon as we opened the door on its cosy, animal-smelling darkness Flora threw up her head, rolled her eyes, whinnied despairingly and pulled herself through a crisis of nerves on the spot. It was not safe to go into her stall; she would kick.

This winter also I began to hear a great deal more on the theme my mother had sounded when she had been talking in front of the barn. I no longer felt safe. It seemed that in the minds of the people around me there was a steady undercurrent of thought, not to be deflected, on this one subject. The word *girl* had formerly seemed to be innocent and unburdened, like the word *child;* now it appeared that it was no such thing. A girl was not, as I had supposed, simply what I was; it was what I had to become. It was a definition, always touched with emphasis, with reproach and disappointment. Also it was a joke on me. Once Laird and I were fighting, and for the first time ever I had to use all my strength against him; even so, he caught and pinned my arm for a moment, really hurting me. Henry saw this, and laughed, saying, "Oh, that there Laird's gonna show you, one of these days!" Laird was getting a lot bigger. But I was getting bigger too.

My grandmother came to stay with us for a few weeks and I heard other things. "Girls don't slam doors like that." "Girls keep their knees together when they sit down." And worse still, when I asked some questions, "That's none of girls' business." I continued to slam the doors and sit as awkwardly as possible, thinking that by such measures I kept myself free.

When spring came, the horses were let out in the barnyard. Mack stood against the barn wall trying to scratch his neck and haunches, but Flora trotted up and down and reared at the fences, clattering her hooves against the rails. Snow drifts dwindled quickly, revealing the hard gray and brown earth, the familiar rise and fall of the ground, plain and bare after the fantastic landscape of winter. There was a great feeling of open-

20

ing-out, of release. We just wore rubbers now, over our shoes; our feet felt ridiculously light. One Saturday we went out to the stable and found all the doors open, letting in the unaccustomed sunlight and fresh air. Henry was there, just idling around looking at his collection of calendars which were tacked up behind the stalls in a part of the stable my mother had probably never seen.

"Come to say goodbye to your old friend Mack?" Henry said. "Here, you give him a taste of oats." He poured some oats into Laird's cupped hands and Laird went to feed Mack. Mack's teeth were in bad shape. He ate very slowly, patiently shifting the oats around in his mouth, trying to find a stump of a molar to grind it on. "Poor old Mack," said Henry mournfully. "When a horse's teeth's gone, he's gone. That's about the way."

"Are you going to shoot him today?" I said. Mack and Flora had been in the stable so long I had almost forgotten they were going to be shot. 25

Henry didn't answer me. Instead he started to sing in a high, trembly, mocking-sorrowful voice, *Oh, there's no more work, for poor Uncle Ned, he's gone where the good darkies go*. Mack's thick, blackish tongue worked diligently at Laird's hand. I went out before the song was ended and sat down on the gangway.

I had never seen them shoot a horse, but I knew where it was done. Last summer Laird and I had come upon a horse's entrails before they were buried. We had thought it was a big black snake, coiled up in the sun. That was around in the field that ran up beside the barn. I thought that if we went inside the barn, and found a wide crack or a knothole to look through, we would be able to see them do it. It was not something I wanted to see; just the same, if a thing really happened, it was better to see it, and know.

My father came down from the house, carrying the gun.

"What are you doing here?" he said.

"Nothing." 30

"Go on up and play around the house."

He sent Laird out of the stable. I said to Laird, "Do you want to see them shoot Mack?" and without waiting for an answer led him around to the front door of the barn, opened it carefully, and went in. "Be quiet or they'll hear us," I said. We could hear Henry and my father talking in the stable, then the heavy, shuffling steps of Mack being backed out of his stall.

In the loft it was cold and dark. Thin, crisscrossed beams of sunlight fell through the cracks. The hay was low. It was a rolling country, hills and hollows, slipping under our feet. About four feet up was a beam going around the walls. We piled hay up in one corner and I boosted Laird up and hoisted myself. The beam was not very wide; we crept along it with our hands flat on the barn walls. There were plenty of knotholes, and I found one that gave me the view I wanted—a corner of the barnyard, the gate, part of the field. Laird did not have a knothole and began to complain.

I showed him a widened crack between two boards. "Be quiet and wait. If they hear you you'll get us in trouble."

My father came in sight carrying the gun. Henry was leading Mack by the halter. 35 He dropped it and took out his cigarette papers and tobacco; he rolled cigarettes for my father and himself. While this was going on Mack nosed around in the old, dead grass along the fence. Then my father opened the gate and they took Mack through. Henry led Mack way from the path to a patch of ground and they talked together, not loud enough for us to hear. Mack again began searching for a mouthful of fresh grass, which was not to be found. My father walked away in a straight line, and stopped short at a distance which seemed to suit him. Henry was walking away from Mack too, but sideways, still negligently holding on to the halter. My father raised the gun and Mack looked up as if he had noticed something and my father shot him.

Mack did not collapse at once but swayed, lurched sideways and fell, first on his side; then he rolled over on his back and, amazingly, kicked his legs for a few seconds in the air. At this Henry laughed, as if Mack had done a trick for him. Laird, who had drawn a long, groaning breath of surprise when the shot was fired, said out loud, "He's not dead." And it seemed to me it might be true. But his legs stopped, he rolled on his side again, his muscles quivered and sank. The two men walked over and looked at him in a business-like way; they bent down and examined his forehead where the bullet had gone in, and now I saw his blood on the brown grass.

"Now they just skin him and cut him up," I said. "Let's go." My legs were a little shaky and I jumped gratefully down into the hay. "Now you've seen how they shoot a horse," I said in a congratulatory way, as if I had seen it many times before. "Let's see if any barn cat's had kittens in the hay." Laird jumped. He seemed young and obedient again. Suddenly I remembered how, when he was little, I had brought him into the barn and told him to climb the ladder to the top beam. That was in the spring, too, when the hay was low. I had done it out of a need for excitement, a desire for something to happen so that I could tell about it. He was wearing a little bulky brown and white checked coat, made down from one of mine. He went all the way up just as I told him, and sat down on the top beam with the hay far below him on one side, and the barn floor and some old machinery on the other. Then I ran screaming to my father, "Laird's up on the top beam!" My father came, my mother came, my father went up the ladder talking very quietly and brought Laird down under his arm, at which my mother leaned against the ladder and began to cry. They said to me, "Why weren't you watching him?" but nobody ever knew the truth. Laird did not know enough to tell. But whenever I saw the brown and white checked coat hanging in the closet, or at the bottom of the rag bag, which was where it ended up, I felt a weight in my stomach, the sadness of unexorcised guilt.

I looked at Laird, who did not even remember this, and I did not like the look on this thin, winter-pale face. His expression was not frightened or upset, but remote, concentrating. "Listen," I said, in an unusually bright and friendly voice, "you aren't going to tell, are you?"

"No," he said absently.

"Promise."

40

"Promise," he said. I grabbed the hand behind his back to make sure he was not crossing his fingers. Even so, he might have a nightmare; it might come out that way. I decided I had better work hard to get all thoughts of what he had seen out of his mind—which, it seemed to me, could not hold very many things at a time. I got some money I had saved and that afternoon we went into Jubilee and saw a show, with Judy Canova, at which we both laughed a great deal. After that I thought it would be all right.

Two weeks later I knew they were going to shoot Flora. I knew from the night before, when I heard my mother ask if the hay was holding out all right, and my father said, "Well, after tomorrow there'll just be the cow, and we should be able to put her out to grass in another week." So I knew it was Flora's turn in the morning.

This time I didn't think of watching it. That was something to see just one time. I had not thought about it very often since, but sometimes when I was busy, working at school, or standing in front of the mirror combing my hair and wondering if I would be pretty when I grew up, the whole scene would flash into my mind: I would see the easy, practiced way my father raised the gun, and hear Henry laughing when Mack kicked his legs in the air. I did not have any great feeling of horror and opposition, such as a city child might have had; I was too used to seeing the death of animals as a necessity by which we lived. Yet I felt a little ashamed, and there was a new wariness, a sense of holding-off, in my attitude to my father and his work.

It was a fine day, and we were going around the yard picking up tree branches that had been torn off in winter storms. This was something we had been told to do, and also we wanted to use them to make a teepee. We heard Flora whinny, and then my father's voice and Henry's shouting, and we ran down to the barnyard to see what was going on.

The stable door was open. Henry had just brought Flora out, and she had broken away from him. She was running free in the barnyard, from one end to the other. We climbed up on the fence. It was exciting to see her running, whinnying, going up on her hind legs, prancing and threatening like a horse in a Western movie, and unbroken ranch horse, though she was just an old driver, an old sorrel mare. My father and Henry ran after her and tried to grab the dangling halter. They tried to work her into a corner, and they had almost succeeded when she made a run between them, wild-eyed, and disappeared around the corner of the barn. We heard the rails clatter down as she got over the fence, and Henry yelled, "She's into the field now!" 45

That meant she was in the long L-shaped field that ran up by the house. If she got around the center, heading towards the lane, the gate was open; the truck had been driven into the field this morning. My father shouted to me, because I was on the other side of the fence, nearest the lane, "Go shut the gate!"

I could run very fast. I ran across the garden, past the tree where our swing was hung, and jumped across a ditch into the lane. There was the open gate. She had not got out, I could not see her up on the road; she must have run to the other end of the field. The gate was heavy. I lifted it out of the gravel and carried it across the roadway. I had it halfway across when she came in sight, galloping straight toward me. There was just time to get the chain on. Laird came scrambling through the ditch to help me.

Instead of shutting the gate, I opened it as wide as I could. I did not make any decision to do this, it was just what I did. Flora never slowed down; she galloped straight past me, and Laird jumped up and down, yelling, "Shut it, shut it!" even after it was too late. My father and Henry appeared in the field a moment too late to see what I had done. They only saw Flora heading for the township road. They would think I had not got there in time.

They did not waste any time asking about it. They went back to the barn and got the gun and the knives they used, and put these in the truck; then they turned the truck around and came bouncing up the field toward us. Laird called to them, "Let me go too, let me go too!" and Henry stopped the truck and they took him in. I shut the gate after they were all gone.

I supposed Laird would tell. I wondered what would happen to me. I had never disobeyed my father before, and I could not understand why I had done it. Flora would not really get away. They would catch up with her in the truck. Or if they did not catch her this morning somebody would see her and telephone us this afternoon or tomorrow. There was no wild country here for her to run to, only farms. What was more, my father had paid for her, we needed the meat to feed the foxes, we needed the foxes to make our living. All I had done was make more work for my father who worked hard enough already. And when my father found out about it he was not going to trust me any more; he would know that I was not entirely on his side. I was on Flora's side, and that made me no use to anybody, not even to her. Just the same, I did not regret it; when she came running at me and I held the gate open, that was the only thing I could do. 50

I went back to the house, and my mother said, "What's all the commotion?" I told her that Flora had kicked down the fence and got away. "Your poor father," she said, "now he'll have to go chasing over the countryside. Well, there isn't any use planning dinner before one." She put up the ironing board. I wanted to tell her, but thought better of it and went upstairs and sat on my bed.

Lately I had been trying to make my part of the room fancy, spreading the bed with old lace curtains, and fixing myself a dressing table with some leftovers of cretonne for a skirt. I planned to put up some kind of barricade between my bed and Laird's, to keep my section separate from his. In the sunlight, the lace curtains were just dusty rags. We did not sing at night any more. One night when I was singing Laird said, "You sound silly," and I went right on but the next night I did not start. There was not so much need to anyway, we were no longer afraid. We knew it was just old furniture over there, old jumble and confusion. We did not keep to the rules. I still stayed awake after Laird was asleep and told myself stories, but even in these stories something different was happening, mysterious alterations took place. A story might start off in the old way, with a spectacular danger, a fire or wild animals, and for a while I might rescue people; then things would change around, and instead, somebody would be rescuing me. It might be a boy from our class at school, or even Mr. Campbell, our teacher, who tickled girls under the arms. And at this point the story concerned itself at great length with what I looked like—how long my hair was, and what kind of dress I had on; by the time I had these details worked out the real excitement of the story was lost.

It was later than one o'clock when the truck came back. The tarpaulin was over the back, which meant there was meat in it. My mother had to heat dinner up all over again. Henry and my father had changed from their bloody overalls into ordinary working overalls in the barn, and they washed their arms and necks and faces at the sink, and splashed water on their hair and combed it. Laird lifted his arm to show off a streak of blood. "We shot old Flora," he said, "and cut her up in fifty pieces."

"Well I don't want to hear about it," my mother said. "And don't come to my table like that."

My father made him go and wash the blood off.   55

We sat down and my father said grace and Henry pasted his chewing gum on the end of his fork, the way he always did; when he took it off he would have us admire the pattern. We began to pass the bowls of steaming, overcooked vegetables. Laird looked across the table at me and said proudly, distinctly, "Anyway it was her fault Flora got away."

"What?" my father said.

"She could of shut the gate and she didn't. She just open' it up and Flora run out."

"Is that right?" my father said.

Everybody at the table was looking at me. I nodded, swallowing food with great   60
difficulty. To my shame, tears flooded my eyes.

My father made a curt sound of disgust. "What did you do that for?"

I did not answer. I put down my fork and waited to be sent from the table, still not looking up.

But this did not happen. For some time nobody said anything, then Laird said matter-of-factly, "She's crying."

"Never mind," my father said. He spoke with resignation, even good humor, the words which absolved and dismissed me for good. "She's only a girl," he said.

I didn't protest that, even in my heart. Maybe it was true.

THE RECEPTIVE READER

1. What about the physical *setting* of this story is most real? What striking images or imaginative comparisons help bring the setting to life? How would you expect the physical world of the story to influence a person's character? How do you think watching the work with the foxes and horses would affect a person's outlook?

2. Like many adolescents, the girl in this story faces a *conflict* between different models that she might choose to follow. What kind of role model is her father? How would you describe his kind of person or temperament? How does she feel about his work? What scenes or incidents do most to illuminate her relationship with her father?

3. What kind of role model is the mother? What is the girl's relationship with the mother and what she stands for? What makes the father and the mother in this story *polar opposites*? What details for you most strikingly bring the opposition between the father's and the mother's influence into focus?

4. The setting in which people grow up often set limits to what they can be or become. What are these limits in this story? How do we become aware of them? Can you point to a key phrase or to a *thematic passage*—spelling out a key idea acted out in the story as a whole?

5. The story reaches its *climax,* or high point, when Flora, the horse about to be shot, gets away. Why does the girl relate to Flora differently than she did to Mack, the other horse in the story? What is the girl's role in the climactic episode? Why does she do what she does? How does her behavior here change the way she thinks of her father and of herself?

6. What is the role of the *minor characters* in this story? What are the roles of Henry and of the grandmother? In this story of growing up, how does the role of Laird, the girl's younger brother, change? What facets of the girl's character are shown in her relationship with her brother?

7. If you read this story as a story of *initiation,* of passing from one stage to another, how would you sum up the girl's starting point and the stage she reaches at the end of the story?

THE PERSONAL RESPONSE

Do you think of the girl as defeated by the end of the story? What do you think are her prospects for the future? What facets of her character would you consider in making a prediction?

THE CREATIVE DIMENSION

Write a *monologue* (one person talking without interruption by others) in which you imagine yourself in the place of one of the characters in the story. From that person's point of view, look at one of the *other* characters in the story. For instance, look at

- ◇ the younger brother as seen through the eyes of the girl (or vice versa);
- ◇ the father as seen through the eyes of the girl;
- ◇ the girl as seen through the eyes of her mother;
- ◇ the mother as seen through the eyes of her daughter.

CROSS-REFERENCES—For Discussion or Writing

Compare and contrast Joyce's "Araby" and Munro's "Boys and Girls" as stories of initiation, or growing up.

ANN BEATTIE (born 1947)

I don't think my characters are what they are because of interesting psychological complexities. They're not clinical studies to me. . . . I just seem to react to what is right in front of me. So that's usually the way I write.

ANN BEATTIE

Ann Beattie is often heard as a voice of the post-Vietnam generation. Her characters are often people who grew up with the love-ins and teach-ins and antiwar demonstrations of the sixties, who experienced the euphoria of the rock festivals and of the counterculture. As the passions and euphoria of the hippie era faded, many of her generation were left with a vague sense of betrayal; no energy seemed to remain for great enthusiasms or commitments. She often writes about no-longer-young urban malcontents who feel they have compromised their youthful ideals but who have no sense of where to go from here. As Beattie said about her novel *Chilly Scenes of Winter* (1976), she writes about people who feel let down—either "by not having involved themselves more" or by "having involved themselves to no avail."

Beattie, like other currently fashionable authors, writes in a **minimalist** mode, staying close to the boring surface of everyday life, avoiding flights of imagination or bursts of emotion. Some critics have faulted her for failing to live up to more conventional expectations: She seems to have an obsession with petty, disjointed detail—the lyrics of popular songs, recipes for junky food, reading matter like the *National Enquirer.* Her characters do not seem to have "an emotional core" or vital center; they do not seem to have "meaningful connections" with others; they do not seem to develop or grow. Her stories do not seem to work toward a resolution or conclusion. However, her admirers see in what she calls her "flat simple sentences" an "uncanny fidelity" to the ordinary and familiar (John Updike), a concern for "the integrity of things and people in themselves" (John Romano).

Of the two presidential candidates alluded to in the following story, Nixon talked about peace with honor and McGovern talked about peace, period.

Shifting   1979

The woman's name was Natalie, and the man's name was Larry. They had been childhood sweethearts; he had first kissed her at an ice-skating party when they were ten. She had been unlacing her skates and had not expected the kiss. He had not expected to do it, either—he had some notion of getting his face out of the wind that was blowing across the iced-over lake, and he found himself ducking his head toward her. Kissing her seemed the natural thing to do. When they graduated from high school he was named "class clown" in the yearbook, but Natalie didn't think of him as being particularly funny. He spent more time than she thought he needed to studying chemistry, and he never laughed when she joked. She really did not think of him as funny. They went to the same college, in their hometown, but he left after a year to go to a larger, more impressive university. She took the train to be with him on weekends, or he took the train to see her. When he graduated, his parents gave him a car. If they had given it to him when he was still in college, it would have made things much easier. They waited to give it to him until graduation day, forcing him into attending the graduation exercises. He thought his parents were wonderful people, and Natalie liked them in a way, too, but she resented their perfect timing, their careful smiles. They were afraid that he would marry her. Eventually, he did. He had gone on to graduate school after college, and he set a date six months ahead for their wedding so that it would take place after his first-semester final exams. That way he could devote his time to studying for the chemistry exams.

When she married him he had had the car for eight months. It still smelled like a brand-new car. There was never any clutter in the car. Even the ice scraper was kept in the glove compartment. There was not even a sweater or a lost glove in the back seat. He vacuumed the car every weekend, after washing it at the car wash. On Friday nights, on their way to some cheap restaurant and a dollar movie, he would stop at the car wash, and she would get out so he could vacuum all over the inside of the car. She would lean against the metal wall of the car wash and watch him clean it.

It was expected that she would not become pregnant. She did not. It had also been expected that she would keep their apartment clean, and keep out of the way as much as possible in such close quarters while he was studying. The apartment was messy, though, and when he was studying late at night she would interrupt him and try to talk him into going to sleep. He gave a chemistry-class lecture once a week, and she would often tell him that overpreparing was as bad as underpreparing. She did not know if she believed this, but it was a favorite line of hers. Sometimes he listened to her.

On Tuesdays, when he gave the lecture, she would drop him off at school and then drive to a supermarket to do the week's shopping. Usually she did not make a list before she went shopping, but when she got to the parking lot she would take a tablet out of her purse and write a few items on it, sitting in the car in the cold. Even having a few things written down would stop her from wandering aimlessly in the store and buying things that she would never use. Before this, she had bought several pans and cans of food that she had not used, or that she could have done without. She felt better when she had a list.

She would drop him at school again on Wednesdays, when he had two seminars that together took up all the afternoon. Sometimes she would drive out of town then, to the suburbs, and shop there if any shopping needed to be done. Otherwise, she would go to the art museum, which was not far away but hard to get to by bus. There was one piece of sculpture in there that she wanted very much to touch, but the guard was always nearby. She came so often that in time the guard began to nod hello. She wondered if she could ever persuade the man to turn his head for a few seconds—only that long—so she could stroke the sculpture. Of course she would never dare ask. After wandering through the museum and looking at least twice at the sculpture, she would go to the gift shop and buy a few postcards and then sit on one of the museum benches, padded with black vinyl, with a Calder mobile hanging overhead, and write notes to friends. (She never wrote letters.) She would tuck the postcards in her purse and mail them when she left the museum. But before she left, she often had coffee in the restaurant: she saw mothers and children struggling there, and women dressed in fancy clothes talking with their faces close together, as quietly as lovers.

On Thursdays he took the car. After his class he would drive to visit his parents and his friend Andy, who had been wounded in Vietnam. About once a month she would go with him, but she had to feel up to it. Being with Andy embarrassed her. She had told him not to go to Vietnam—told him that he could prove his patriotism in some other way—and finally, after she and Larry had made a visit together and she had seen Andy in the motorized bed in his parents' house, Larry had agreed that she need not go again. Andy had apologized to her. It embarrassed her that this man, who had been blown sky-high by a land mine and had lost a leg and lost the full use of his arms, would smile up at her ironically and say, "You were right." She also felt as though he wanted to hear what she would say now, and that now he would listen. Now she had nothing to say. Andy would pull himself up, relying on his right arm, which was the stronger, gripping the rails at the side of the bed, and sometimes he would take her hand. His arms were still weak, but the doctors said he would regain complete use of his right arm with time. She had to make an effort not to squeeze his hand when he held hers because she found herself wanting to squeeze energy back into him. She had a morbid curiosity about what it felt like to be blown from the ground—and go up, and to come crashing down. During their visit Larry put on the class-clown act for Andy, telling funny stories and laughing uproariously.

Once or twice Larry had talked Andy into getting in his wheelchair and had loaded him into the car and taken him to a bar. Larry called her once, late, pretty drunk, to say that he would not be home that night—that he would sleep at his parents' house. "My God," she said. "Are you going to drive Andy home when you're drunk?" "What the hell else can happen to him?" he said.

Larry's parents blamed her for Larry's not being happy. His mother could only be pleasant with her for a short while, and then she would veil her criticisms by putting them as questions. "I know that one thing that helps enormously is good nutrition," his mother said. "He works so hard that he probably needs quite a few vitamins as well, don't you think?" Larry's father was the sort of man who found hobbies in order to avoid his wife. His hobbies were building model boats, repairing clocks, and photography. He took pictures of himself building the boats and fixing the clocks, and gave the pictures, in cardboard frames, to Natalie and Larry for Christmas and birthday presents. Larry's mother was very anxious to stay on close terms with her son, and she knew that Natalie did not like her very much. Once she had visited them during the week, and Natalie, not knowing what to do with her, had taken her to the museum. She had pointed out the sculpture, and his mother had glanced at it and then ignored it. Natalie hated her for her bad taste. She had bad taste in the sweaters she gave Larry, too, but he wore them. They made him look collegiate. That whole world made her sick.

When Natalie's uncle died and left her his 1965 Volvo, they immediately decided to sell it and use the money for a vacation. They put an ad in the paper, and there were several callers. There were some calls on Tuesday, when Larry was in class, and Natalie found herself putting the people off. She told one woman that the car had too much mileage on it, and mentioned body rust, which it did not have; she told another caller, who was very persistent, that the car was already sold. When Larry returned from school she explained that the phone was off the hook because so many people were calling about the car and she had decided not to sell it after all. They could take a little money from their savings account and go on the trip if he wanted. But she did not want to sell the car. "It's not an automatic shift," he said. "You don't know how to drive it." She told him that she could learn. "It will cost money to insure it," he said, "and it's old and probably not even dependable." She wanted to keep the car. "I know," he said, "but it doesn't make sense. When we have more money, you can have a car. You can have a newer, better car."

The next day she went out to the car, which was parked in the driveway of an old lady next door. Her name was Mrs. Larsen and she no longer drove a car, and she told

10

Natalie she could park their second car there. Natalie opened the car door and got behind the wheel and put her hands on it. The wheel was covered with a flaky yellow-and-black plastic cover. She eased it off. A few pieces of foam rubber stuck to the wheel. She picked them off. Underneath the cover, the wheel was a dull red. She ran her fingers around and around the circle of the wheel. Her cousin Burt had delivered the car—a young opportunist, sixteen years old, who said he would drive it the hundred miles from his house to theirs for twenty dollars and a bus ticket home. She had not even invited him to stay for dinner, and Larry had driven him to the bus station. She wondered if it was Burt's cigarette in the ashtray or her dead uncle's. She could not even remember if her uncle smoked. She was surprised that he had left her his car. The car was much more comfortable than Larry's, and it had a nice smell inside. It smelled a little the way a field smells after a spring rain. She rubbed the side of her head back and forth against the window and then got out of the car and went in to see Mrs. Larsen. The night before, she had suddenly thought of the boy who brought the old lady the evening newspaper every night; he looked old enough to drive, and he would probably know how to shift. Mrs. Larsen agreed with her—she was sure that he could teach her. "Of course, everything has its price," the old lady said.

"I know that. I meant to offer him money," Natalie said, and was surprised, listening to her voice, that she sounded old too.

She took an inventory and made a list of things in their apartment. Larry had met an insurance man one evening while playing basketball at the gym who told him that they should have a list of their possessions, in case of theft. "What's worth anything?" she said when he told her. It was their first argument in almost a year—the first time in a year, anyway, that their voices were raised. He told her that several of the pieces of furniture his grandparents gave them when they got married were antiques, and the man at the gym said that if they weren't going to get them appraised every year, at least they should take snapshots of them and keep the pictures in a safe-deposit box. Larry told her to photograph the pie safe (which she used to store linen), the piano with an inlaid mother-of-pearl decoration on the music rack (neither of them knew how to play), and the table with hand-carved wooden handles and a marble top. He bought her an Instamatic camera at the drugstore, with film and flash bulbs. "Why can't you do it?" she said, and an argument began. He said that she had no respect for his profession and no understanding of the amount of study that went into getting a master's degree in chemistry.

That night he went out to meet two friends at the gym, to shoot baskets. She put the little flashcube into the top of the camera, dropped in the film and closed the back. She went first to the piano. She leaned forward so that she was close enough to see the inlay clearly, but she found that when she was that close the whole piano wouldn't fit into the picture. She decided to take two pictures. Then she photographed the pie safe, with one door open, showing the towels and sheets stacked inside. She did not have a reason for opening the door, except that she remembered a *Perry Mason* show in which detectives photographed everything with the doors hanging open. She photographed the table, lifting the lamp off it first. There were still eight pictures left. She went to the mirror in their bedroom and held the camera above her head, pointing down at an angle, and photographed her image in the mirror. She took off her slacks and sat on the floor and leaned back, aiming the camera down at her legs. Then she stood up and took a picture of her feet, leaning over and aiming down. She put on her favorite record: Stevie Wonder singing "For Once in My Life." She found herself wondering what it would be like to be blind, to have to feel things to see them. She thought about the piece of sculpture in the museum—the two elongated mounds, intertwined, the smooth gray stone as shiny as sea pebbles. She photographed the kitchen, bathroom, bedroom and living room. There was one picture left. She put her left hand on her thigh, palm up, and with some difficulty—with the camera nestled into her neck like a violin—snapped a picture of it with her right hand. The next day would be her first driving lesson.

He came to her door at noon, as he had said he would. He had on a long maroon scarf, which made his deep-blue eyes very striking. She had only seen him from her window when he carried the paper in to the old lady. He was a little nervous. She hoped that it was just the anxiety of any teen-ager confronting an adult. She needed to have him like her. She did not learn about mechanical things easily (Larry had told her that he would have invested in a "real" camera, except that he did not have the time to teach her about it), so she wanted him to be patient. He sat on the footstool in her living room, still in coat and scarf, and told her how a stick shift operated. He moved his hand through the air. The motion he made reminded her of the salute spacemen gave to earthlings in a science-fiction picture she had recently watched on late-night television. She nodded. "How much—" she began, but he interrupted and said, "You can decide what it was worth when you've learned." She was surprised and wondered if he meant to charge a great deal. Would it be her fault and would she have to pay him if he named his price when the lessons were over? But he had an honest face. Perhaps he was just embarrassed to talk about money.

He drove for a few blocks, making her watch his hand on the stick shift. "Feel how the car is going?" he said. "Now you shift." He shifted. The car jumped a little, hummed, moved into gear. It was an old car and didn't shift too easily, he said. She had been sitting forward, so that when he shifted she rocked back hard against the seat—harder than she needed to. Almost unconsciously, she wanted to show him what a good teacher he was. When her turn came to drive, the car stalled. "Take it easy," he said. "Ease up on the clutch. Don't just raise your foot off of it like that." She tried it again. "That's it," he said. She looked at him when the car was in third. He sat in the seat, looking out the window. Snow was expected. It was Thursday. Although Larry was going to visit his parents and would not be back until late Friday afternoon, she decided she would wait until Tuesday for her next lesson. If he came home early, he would find out that she was taking lessons, and she didn't want him to know. She asked the boy, whose name was Michael, whether he thought she would forget all he had taught her in the time between lessons. "You'll remember," he said.

15

When they returned to the old lady's driveway, the car stalled going up the incline. She had trouble shifting. The boy put his hand over hers and kicked the heel of his hand forward. "You'll have to treat this car a little roughly, I'm afraid," he said. That afternoon, after he left, she made spaghetti sauce, chopping little pieces of pepper and onion and mushroom. When the sauce had cooked down, she called Mrs. Larsen and said that she would bring over dinner. She usually ate with the old lady once a week. The old lady often added a pinch of cinnamon to her food, saying that it brought out the flavor better than salt, and that since she was losing her sense of smell, food had to be strongly flavored for her to taste it. Once she had sprinkled cinnamon on a knockwurst. This time, as they ate, Natalie asked the old lady how much she paid the boy to bring the paper.

"I give him a dollar a week," the old lady said.

"Did he set the price, or did you?"

"He set the price. He told me he wouldn't take much because he has to walk this street to get to his apartment anyway."

"He taught me a lot about the car today," Natalie said. 20
"He's very handsome, isn't he?" the old lady said.

She asked Larry, "How were your parents?"

"Fine," he said. "But I spent almost all the time with Andy. It's almost his birthday, and he's depressed. We went to see Mose Allison."

"I think it stinks that hardly anyone else ever visits Andy," she said.

"He doesn't make it easy. He tells you everything that's on his mind, and there's 25 no way you can pretend that his troubles don't amount to much. You just have to sit there and nod."

She remembered that Andy's room looked like a gymnasium. There were handgrips and weights scattered on the floor. There was even a psychedelic pink hula hoop that he was to put inside his elbow and then move his arm in circles wide enough to make the hoop spin. He couldn't do it. He would lie in bed with the hoop in back of his neck, and holding the sides, lift his neck off the pillow. His arms were barely strong enough to do that, really, but he could raise his neck with no trouble, so he just pretended that his arms pulling the loop were raising it. His parents thought that it was a special exercise that he had mastered.

"What did you do today?" Larry said now.

"I made spaghetti," she said. She had made it the day before, but she thought that since he was mysterious about the time he spent away from her ("in the lab" and "at the gym" became interchangeable), she did not owe him a straight answer. That day she had dropped off the film and then she had sat at the drugstore counter to have a cup of coffee. She bought some cigarettes, though she had not smoked since high school. She smoked one mentholated cigarette and then threw the pack away in a garbage container outside the drugstore. Her mouth still felt cool inside.

He asked if she had planned anything for the weekend.

"No," she said. 30

"Let's do something you'd like to do. I'm a little ahead of myself in the lab right now."

That night they ate spaghetti and made plans, and the next day they went for a ride in the country, to a factory where wooden toys were made. In the showroom he made a bear marionette shake and twist. She examined a small rocking horse, rhythmically pushing her finger up and down on the back rung of the rocker to make it rock. When they left they took with them a catalogue of toys they could order. She knew that they would never look at the catalogue again. On their way to the museum he stopped to wash the car. Because it was the weekend there were quite a few cars lined up waiting to go in. They were behind a blue Cadillac that seemed to inch forward of its own accord, without a driver. When the Cadillac moved into the washing area, a tiny man hopped out. He stood on tiptoe to reach the coin box to start the washing machine. She doubted if he was five feet tall.

"Look at that poor son of a bitch," he said.

The little man was washing his car.

"If Andy could get out more," Larry said. "If he could get rid of that feeling he 35 has that he's the only freak . . . I wonder if it wouldn't do him good to come spend a week with us."

"Are you going to take him in the wheelchair to the lab with you?" she said. "I'm not taking care of Andy all day."

His face changed. "Just for a week was all I meant," he said.

"I'm not doing it," she said. She was thinking of the boy, and of the car. She had almost learned how to drive the car.

"Maybe in the warm weather," she said. "When we could go to the park or something."

He said nothing. The little man was rinsing his car. She sat inside when their turn came. She thought that Larry had no right to ask her to take care of Andy. Water flew out of the hose and battered the car. She thought of Andy, in the woods at night, stepping on the land mine, being blown into the air. She wondered if it threw him in an arc, so he ended up somewhere away from where he had been walking, or if it just blasted him straight up, if he went up the way an umbrella opens. Andy had been a wonderful ice skater. They all envied him his long sweeping turns, with his legs somehow neatly together and his body at the perfect angle. She never saw him have an accident on the ice. Never once. She had known Andy, and they had skated at Parker's pond, for eight years before he was drafted.

The night before, as she and Larry were finishing dinner, he had asked her if she intended to vote for Nixon or McGovern in the election. "McGovern," she said. How could he not have known that? She knew then that they were farther apart than she had thought. She hoped that on Election Day she could drive herself to the polls—not go with him and not walk. She planned not to ask the old lady if she wanted to come along because that would be one vote she could keep Nixon from getting.

At the museum she hesitated by the sculpture but did not point it out to him. He didn't look at it. He gazed to the side, above it, at a Francis Bacon painting. He could have shifted his eyes just a little and seen the sculpture, and her, standing and staring.

After three more lessons she could drive the car. The last two times, which were later in the afternoon than her first lesson, they stopped at the drugstore to get the old lady's paper, to save him from having to make the same trip back on foot. When he came out of the drugstore with the paper, after the final lesson, she asked him if he'd like to have a beer to celebrate.

"Sure," he said.

They walked down the street to a bar that was filled with college students. She wondered if Larry ever came to this bar. He had never said that he did.

She and Michael talked. She asked why he wasn't in high school. He told her that he had quit. He was living with his brother, and his brother was teaching him carpentry, which he had been interested in all along. On his napkin he drew a picture of the cabinets and bookshelves he and his brother had spent the last week constructing and installing in the house of two wealthy old sisters. He drummed the side of his thumb against the edge of the table in time with the music. They each drank beer, from heavy glass mugs.

"Mrs. Larsen said your husband was in school," the boy said. "What's he studying?"

She looked up, surprised. Michael had never mentioned her husband before. "Chemistry," she said.

"I liked chemistry pretty well," he said. "Some of it."

"My husband doesn't know you've been giving me lessons. I'm just going to tell him that I can drive the stick shift, and surprise him."

"Yeah?" the boy said. "What will he think about that?"

"I don't know," she said. "I don't think he'll like it."

"Why?" the boy said.

His question made her remember that he was sixteen. What she had said would never have provoked another question from an adult. The adult would have nodded or said, "I know."

She shrugged. The boy took a long drink of beer. "I thought it was funny that he 55
didn't teach you himself, when Mrs. Larsen told me you were married," he said.

They had discussed her. She wondered why Mrs. Larsen wouldn't have told her
that, because the night she ate dinner with her she had talked to Mrs. Larsen about
whan an extraordinarily patient teacher Michael was. Had Mrs. Larsen told him that
Natalie talked about him?

On the way back to the car she remembered the photographs and went back to the
drugstore and picked up the prints. As she took money out of her wallet she remembered that today was the day she would have to pay him. She looked around at him, at
the front of the store, where he was flipping through magazines. He was tall and he was
wearing a very old black jacket. One end of his long thick maroon scarf was hanging
down his back.

"What did you take pictures of?" he said when they were back in the car.

"Furniture. My husband wanted pictures of our furniture, in case it was stolen."

"Why?" he said. 60

"They say if you have proof that you had valuable things, the insurance company
won't hassle you about reimbursing you."

"You have a lot of valuable stuff?" he said.

"My husband thinks so," she said.

A block from the driveway she said, "What do I owe you?"

"Four dollars," he said. 65

"That's nowhere near enough," she said and looked over at him. He had opened
the envelope with the pictures in it while she was driving. He was staring at the picture
of her legs. "What's this?" he said.

She turned into the driveway and shut off the engine. She looked at the picture.
She could not think of what to tell him it was. Her hands and heart felt heavy.

"Wow," the boy said. He laughed. "Never mind. Sorry. I'm not looking at any
more of them."

He put the pack of pictures back in the envelope and dropped it on the seat between them.

She tried to think what to say, of some way she could turn the pictures into a joke. 70
She wanted to get out of the car and run. She wanted to stay, not to give him the
money, so he would sit there with her. She reached into her purse and took out her
wallet and removed four one-dollar bills.

"How many years have you been married?" he asked.

"One," she said. She held the money out to him. He said "Thank you" and leaned
across the seat and put his right arm over her shoulder and kissed her. She felt his
scarf bunched up against their cheeks. She was amazed at how warm his lips were in the
cold car.

He moved his head away and said, "I didn't think you'd mind if I did that." She
shook her head no. He unlocked the door and got out.

"I could drive you to your brother's apartment," she said. Her voice sounded hollow. She was extremely embarrassed, but she couldn't let him go.

He got back in the car. "You could drive me and come in for a drink," he said. 75
"My brother's working."

When she got back to the car two hours later she saw a white parking ticket
clamped under the windshield wiper, flapping in the wind. When she opened the car
door and sank into the seat, she saw that he had left the money, neatly folded, on
the floor mat on his side of the car. She did not pick up the money. In a while she

started the car. She stalled it twice on the way home. When she had pulled into the driveway she looked at the money for a long time, then left it lying there. She left the car unlocked, hoping the money would be stolen. If it disappeared, she could tell herself that she had paid him. Otherwise she would not know how to deal with the situation.

When she got into the apartment, the phone rang. "I'm at the gym to play basketball," Larry said. "Be home in an hour."

"I was at the drugstore," she said. "See you then."

She examined the pictures. She sat on the sofa and laid them out, the twelve of them, in three rows on the cushion next to her. The picture of the piano was between the picture of her feet and the picture of herself that she had shot by aiming into the mirror. She picked up the four pictures of their furniture and put them on the table. She picked up the others and examined them closely. She began to understand why she had taken them. She had photographed parts of her body, fragments of it, to study the pieces. She had probably done it because she thought so much about Andy's body and the piece that was gone—the leg, below the knee, on his left side. She had had two bourbon-and-waters at the boy's apartment, and drinking always depressed her. She felt very depressed looking at the pictures, so she put them down and went into the bedroom. She undressed. She looked at her body—whole, not a bad figure—in the mirror. It was an automatic reaction with her to close the curtains when she was naked, so she turned quickly and went to the window and did that. She went back to the mirror; the room was darker now and her body looked better. She ran her hands down her sides, wondering if the feel of her skin was anything like the way the sculpture would feel. She was sure that the sculpture would be smoother—her hands would move more quickly down the slopes of it than she wanted—that it would be cool, and that somehow she could feel the grayness of it. Those things seemed preferable to her hands lingering on her body, the imperfection of her skin, the overheated apartment. If she were the piece of sculpture and if she could feel, she would like her sense of isolation.

This was in 1972, in Philadelphia.   80

THE RECEPTIVE READER

1. Beattie is a writer who patiently chronicles the uneventful events of the ordinary day. Which of the thoughts going through the main character's mind seem trivial? Which seem more significant, more likely to help you understand her character?

2. How does her relationship with her husband help define her as a person? What kind of person is he? How does he serve as a *foil*? How does she react to his attitude toward his studies? How does she interact with his parents? How does she relate to his car?

3. The Vietnam War and the disabled war veteran return in this story like a refrain. What is Natalie's involvement with or reaction to both? How has the experience with both helped shape her character?

4. To what in her makeup as a person does the dead uncle's car appeal? What are her dealings with the boy who teaches her to drive it? What side (or sides) of her character does the relationship reveal or bring into play?

THE PERSONAL RESPONSE

As a writer of the minimalist school, Beattie does not go out of her way to burden the reader with explanations, psychological theories, or background. How well do you come to know Natalie? What unanswered questions about the main character remain in your mind? How do you relate to her as a person? (Is it true, as one critic claimed, that Beattie is "unable to make us feel any empathy for most of the characters—perhaps because they are too self-absorbed to feel anything for each other"?)

WRITING ABOUT LITERATURE

3. Tracing Character (Focus on Prewriting)

The Writing Workshop   Our interest in a story often centers on a main character, or on the interaction of two or more main characters, in a story. A paper focused on a central character may show how a key trait, an overriding ambition, or a basic fear or trauma serves as the key unlocking the character's personality. Or a paper may trace the vital contradictions that make a character a complex human being rather than a cardboard cutout with simple predictable motives. Or a paper may trace the growth of a character in flux, still malleable, still subject to formative influences.

In working on this and on other papers, imagine yourself in a writing workshop situation. In a workshop format, no one expects a full-blown paper to materialize overnight. Instead, there is time for preliminaries, for tentative first attempts, for feedback, for revision and fine-tuning. In writing your paper on characterization, your basic task will be the same as in writing papers on other dimensions of fiction. You will need to immerse yourself in the story first—and then push toward general conclusions that you can present and support in a well-developed paper. You will need to take your paper through major (overlapping) stages in the writing process.

In particular, make time for three important **prewriting** activities that should precede your writing of your first draft: note taking, pushing toward a thesis, and structuring your paper.

Running Commentary   The following is part of a running commentary—on the Munro story—prepared by a reader with open eyes and alert ears, who is keeping an open mind about the possible general drift of the story. These reading notes seize on possibly meaningful striking details; they record verbatim quotations that could be useful in helping get a reader into the prevailing mood of the story. These notes already include much material related to the girl narrator's search for identity:

> Senses predominate. Penetrating smell of foxes, dead flesh, blood. Beauty of live foxes contrasts with scraping particles of fat and blood from the inside of the dead skin. Naked slippery dead carcasses look "surprisingly small, mean and rat-like." When alive, foxes have faces "drawn exquisitely sharp in pure hostility" and "golden eyes."

> Death and blood are taken rather casually by the men. There is something alarming about the coldness of the term "fox farm." There is a hierarchy of value? Horses are killed to feed foxes, who provide furs and money.

Children's unfinished bedroom in the loft is a place of childhood fears. Brother and sister sing "Jingle Bells" and "Danny Boy" to ward off fear of the dark.

Life is seen entirely through the eyes of the young girl telling the story, who is naturally inclined toward "male activities." The work done "in her father's service" was important like a ritual. Her little brother tags timidly along, obeying her.

The narrator is treated like a boy and acts like one, and she is introduced by her father as "my new hired man." The salesman responds that he thought it was "only a girl." The girl wants to possess the characteristic masculine strengths and virtues.

The mother is constantly invoking the female stereotype, implying that when her daughter helps the father with "male" duties, the help is not real. She is eager to get her daughter into the house to help with girl work. ("It's not like I had a girl in the family at all.") The girl "hated the hot dark kitchen in summer"; "work in the house was endless, dreary and peculiarly depressing."

The horses give an interesting twist to the gender issue, because there is a male and a female. The male, Mack, is slow and docile, while the female, Flora, is spirited, temperamental and rebellious . . .

Pushing toward a Thesis   Early in your note taking, the central question is likely to emerge: In the world of Munro's story, what does it mean to be a girl? What does it mean to be a boy? In your paper, you may want to focus on the key issue: Some people easily take to the role society has sketched out for them. They fit the mold. But the girl in this story is an independent, adventurous, imaginative spirit.

In the following paragraph, the student who prepared the reading notes sums up what might become the unifying overall idea of a paper:

> Children search for their identities and constantly run up against the wall of gender stereotypes to which they are made to conform. *The girl in the story reluctantly conforms to the stereotypes that will deny a part of her personality.* In her innocence, the girl in the story identifies with the outdoor work of her father, "red in the face with pleasure" when her father seems to praise and accept her as a co-worker. Her daydreams are about heroic rescues in which she plays the hero's part. However, her mother and grandmother conspire to drive home what is expected of a girl. It seems that after a last act of futile rebellion the invisible walls of the predestined gender roles will close in on her.

Structuring the Paper   How will your paper be laid out? Since this is a story of initiation, your paper as a whole might follow the pattern of a spiritual journey. In addition, a contrast of polar opposites (light/dark, male/female) may help structure the paper. For instance, in writing about the Munro story, you may move from the girl's innocent identification with the father's work and *male* values to the weight of traditional stereotypes about the *female* role. Early in your work with the paper, prepare a **scratch outline** like the one that guided the author of the reading notes in her first draft:

—spirited imaginative character—the prank played on kid brother, leadership etc. daydreams: "courage, boldness, and self-sacrifice"
—the lure of the father's job
—the mother and grandmother as voices of the stereotype
—the climactic rebellion
—pivotal role of younger brother—he will overtake her by virtue of the mere fact of being born male; he has the advantage

Look at the way the student's prewriting fed into a first draft of a paper. What use did the student make of her prewriting? How nearly finished is this paper? What suggestions or advice would you give the student writer when she is ready to prepare a final draft?

SAMPLE FIRST DRAFT

A Story of Initiation

Alice Munro's story "Boys and Girls" introduces us to a spirited, imaginative young girl. She plays scary pranks on her kid brother, making him climb to the top beam of the barn. She also experiences the fears of childhood, as she and the brother try to mark off a "safe" zone among the scary shadows of the unfinished loft where they sleep, singing "Jingle Bells" and "Danny Boy" to ward off fear of the dark. Above all, she admires her father, who runs a fox farm for the pelts of the animals. As her father's helper and Girl Friday, she is used to the penetrating smell of the foxes. She responds to the beauty of the live foxes who have faces "drawn exquisitely sharp in pure hostility" and "golden eyes." She is just as used to the naked slippery dead carcasses that look "surprisingly small, mean and rat-like." However, in the course of the story, the girl has to leave this world of her childhood behind, growing up to discover her true destined role in a "man's world."

Children search for their identities and constantly run up against the wall of gender stereotypes to which they are made to conform. The girl in the story reluctantly conforms to the stereotypes that will deny a part of her personality. In her innocence, the girl in the story identifies with the outdoor work of her father, "red in the face with pleasure" when her father seems to praise and accept her as a co-worker. Her daydreams are about heroic rescues in which she plays the hero's part. However, her mother and grandmother conspire to drive home what is expected of a girl. It seems that after a last act of futile rebellion the invisible walls of the predestined gender roles will close in on her.

Life is seen entirely through the eyes of the young girl telling the story. As a child, she seems naturally inclined toward "male activities." The work done "in her father's service" is important to her like a ritual. (Her little brother tags timidly along, obeying her.) The narrator is treated like a boy and acts like one, and she is introduced by her father as "my new hired man." The salesman he is talking to responds that he thought it was "only a girl," a hint of the disillusionment that lies ahead. In her innocence, the narrator values and espouses those traditionally male qualities admired by the world, and she strives to cultivate those strengths within herself, as yet unburdened by the weight of stereotypes.

However, the mother increasingly represents the weight of the adult world, invoking the female stereotype, implying that when her daughter helps the father with "male" duties, the help is not real. The mother is eager to get her daughter into the house to help with girl work. ("It's not like I had a girl in the family at all.") The girl "hated the hot dark kitchen in summer"; "work in the house was endless, dreary and peculiarly depressing."

The horses that are kept to provide meat for the foxes give an interesting twist to the gender issue, because there are a male and a female. The male, Mack, is slow and docile, while the female, Flora, is spirited, temperamental and rebellious. When Flora's turn comes to be killed and butchered to feed the foxes, the narrator, in a dramatic act of rebellion against the way things are, lets her escape through the open gate that her father asks her to close. In trying to free the horse, she is making a last symbolic attempt to free herself. But she fails, both literally and symbolically. Flora is free for only a few hours longer. And the narrator, who is "only a girl," cannot free herself from the stereotype society has imposed on her, except for a few brief childhood years.

QUESTIONS

What, to you, are the strengths and possible weaknesses of this paper? How clear is the overall pattern of the paper? In her final draft, what details or what features do you think the student should add to round out the character?

4 PLOT
The Chain of Events

There has to be a tension, a sense that something is imminent, that certain things are in relentless motion, or else, most often, there simply won't be a story.

RAYMOND CARVER

A narrative line is in its deeper sense the tracing out of a meaning, and the real continuity of a story lies in this probing forward.

EUDORA WELTY

Writing prose is like laying a mosaic.

KURT TUCHOLSKY

FOCUS ON PLOT

A traditional short story puts believable characters in a setting that becomes real and then sets them in motion. We focus on **plot** when we trace what happens as a result. The plot is the story line, the sequence of actions or events that gives direction to the story as a whole. When we study plot, we focus on what drives, motivates, shapes the story. Plot sets up the scaffolding that supports the rest of the narrative; it maps out the itinerary that takes the reader to the conclusion.

An effective plot pulls us into the story. It does not just activate our curiosity; it stirs our emotions. True, some stories leave us cold, or lukewarm at best; we read them to pass the time or to satisfy an assignment. But stories that come to mean something have a way of drawing us in; they make us live through rather than merely watch an experience.

Frank O'Connor's short story classic "Guests of the Nation" takes us to the Irish side in the war between the Irish and the English that led to the establishment of the Irish Free State in 1922, after centuries of English rule. We spend our time with two young soldiers in the Irish Republican Army. They are guarding two English prisoners—although security is lax, since with their English accents and khaki tunics the prisoners would not get very far, even if they had a mind to escape. The foursome pass the time playing cards, arguing about capitalism and communism, about priests and love of country. The Englishmen join in the occasional dances with the local young women; one of the Englishmen becomes a mainstay and helpmate to the lady of the house, doing chores and running errands for her. Inevitably, however, the grim realities of the war catch up with us: The English have executed Irish rebels, and the two English hostages will be shot in retaliation.

Where are we as readers in this story? Maybe we can keep cool and refuse to become involved. It's not *our* war; the hostages have long been dead and buried. More likely, however, we will be drawn into the story. We will be saying when word comes down from headquarters to execute the hostages: "No, you cannot do that!" We are likely to argue and agonize and prevaricate. The chances are we will finally do as told; we will feel sick about it afterwards; and, like the narrator in the story, we will never again be quite the same. We will not know what to say when the lady of the house asks: "What did ye do with them?"

PLOTTING THE STORY

Storytellers, in their speaking, allow us to see the narrative character of our lives. The stories they tell touch us. What we thought was an accidental sequence of experience suddenly takes the dramatic shape of an unresolved story.
                                                              J. P. CARSE

Order and form no more spring out of order and form than they come riding in to us upon seashells through the spray. In fiction they have to be made out of their very antithesis, life.
                                                              EUDORA WELTY

When you think about plot, you ask yourself: "How does the story take shape? What sets it in motion? What keeps it going? What brings it to a satisfying close?"

A well-plotted tale establishes a **situation** that has in it the seeds of a story. As you start reading a story, you need to be alert for signs of something unstable, some agenda to be attended to, some score to be settled. This initial setting up or **exposition** creates a situation that has the seed of further developments in it. You need to pay special attention here to see where the story might be headed. Perhaps a new element disturbs the status quo: A stranger arrives; an outsider marries into the family; a distant relative comes close.

The **characters** of a story are by definition capable of engaging in action, of precipitating events. Their motives—their motivation—is their potential for action: "what sets them in motion." An accident-prone character is, as we say, "an accident waiting to happen." A character with seething resentment is a time bomb waiting to go off. A desperately lonely character may take desperate steps to make human contact. As an attentive reader, you will be sizing up characters for what they might do.

As the lives of several characters intersect, there is a potential for **conflict.** Rivals in love or ambition may face off like the **protagonist** (the first or chief contender) and the **antagonist** (the worthy or formidable opponent) in ancient Greek drama. However, the conflict need not be dramatic but may be low-key. People may find themselves at cross-purposes without the will or ability to articulate loud grievances. Mason's "Shiloh" develops a conflict between the opposed, diverging needs of a couple; the conflict plays itself out without fireworks or fanfare.

The story line may involve **external** physical action—quarrels, journeys, acts of defiance, suicides. The characters may have mountains to scale or adversaries to confront. But much of the action may be **internal,** psychological. A character may experience a change in perspective, learning something about others. A character may reach a moment of self-realization, facing up to something important about himself or herself. Then again, characters may merely act out who they are.

The actual story line—the central action or progression of events—will vary greatly from story to story:

✧ There may be a **loose** narrative structure, with events coming to pass in leisurely, apparently artless fashion, in chronological order. Things just seem to happen—"and then" this, "and then" that. In Carver's "The Third Thing That Killed My Father Off," we see the central character develop an interest in a hobby that interferes with his performance at work. An apparent misunderstanding leads to the alienation of old friends. Unexpected natural events intervene. In other stories, there may be a **tight** narrative structure, with events marching on relentlessly from cause to effect. In John Steinbeck's story "Flight," a proud young boy is provoked into a fatal brawl and then is hunted down methodically by the friends of the man he killed. Some writers much prefer this kind of compact, tightly plotted story. They start close to a crisis, focusing on what Frank O'Connor has called "some glowing center of action."

✧ Many stories build to a **climax,** or high point. In Malamud's "The Magic Barrel," you are going to see a pattern of deliberate, purposeful repetition. You will find a repeated pattern of marriage prospects touted by the matchmaker and found to be disappointing—till the plot takes a turn that brings the search to a climactic conclusion.

✧ A more experimental narrative structure may break up the chronological sequence of events. **Flashbacks** may gradually fill in the missing pieces of a puzzle. In a Faulkner story like "A Rose for Emily" (included in this chapter), you may have to reconstruct the actual chain of events from partial clues, gradually letting the puzzle take shape.

Traditional stories tend to have a strong plot line that you can chart from beginning through middle to end. They may move from cause to effect, or from motive to action and reaction. At the other end of the spectrum, much modern fiction plays down plot, with little happening that would appear on a police blotter or make the evening news. However, whether played up or played down, plot serves a number of functions basic to the storyteller's art:

✧ *The plot of a story engages and holds our attention.* For the story to succeed, we have to keep turning the page to see how things will come out. Much traditional fiction concentrated on this function of plot (and much popular fiction still does). Many a well-plotted story aims at creating and maintaining **suspense.** We feel that we *have* to know whether an enterprise will prosper or falter, whether an escape will succeed or fail, whether or not a secret meant to be buried with the dead will be revealed.

A classic kind of science fiction story might show us a young man seated at a lifeline predictor machine. It is a little after nine o'clock. The man inserts a coin and pushes the predictor button. The message screen lights up, with the message reading: "You will die of a heart attack today at 10:05 A.M." Taken aback, the young man pushes a button for "death averted." The screen lights up with a clip showing him finishing his college education, getting a degree, taking a job. A year later he is killed by a hit-and-run car. Again the young man pushes "death averted." The next clip shows him getting a promotion to manager, getting married, having a child. He is killed in a plane accident as an airliner collides with a commuter plane. Again the young man pushes "death averted." He is watching his first grandchild being born when the wall clock shows 10:05 A.M. He drops dead of a heart attack.

This story sets up a pattern that keeps us moving in accordance with accepted premises: It repeats several times the pattern of a threat surfacing and the threat removed. It keeps us turning the pages leading up to the surprise ending—which, however, is not a total surprise. It was prepared for early, and it pulls all the pieces of the story together in a satisfying overall pattern.

⬦ *The plot gives shape to the story as a whole.* A story like Bobbie Ann Mason's "Shiloh" is rich in leisurely surface detail, from Norma Jean's three-pound dumbbells to Leroy's "lamp made out of a model truck, with a light fixture screwed in the top of the cab." However, the story moves by slow stages to its final destination. The plot takes us from first signs of estrangement, through the husband's ineffectual yearning for a return to their happier past, to a last doomed try at picking up the pieces during the trip to the battlefield at Shiloh. At the end of the story, something has been settled; a chapter in their lives has been written. Although their lives will go on, their marriage seems to be over. The story leaves us with a satisfying sense of completion. It achieves **closure**—a satisfying wrapping up or pulling together.

Note: Writers of the serious modern short story became suspicious of the plot devices of **popular fiction.** Audiences used to love a story that ends with a twist: A husband sells his gold watch to buy an expensive comb for his wife's rich, full hair; the wife has her hair cut short and sells it to buy an expensive attachment for the husband's watch. Popular audiences now as always love a happy end: A last-minute rescue heads off disaster. A rich uncle leaves an inheritance. A miracle drug restores eyesight. Much serious modern fiction refuses to rely on such strokes of good luck (although an occasional story still does!). Much modern fiction appeals to our sense of **irony:** With a wry smile, we see good intentions defeated by naive bumbling. We see evil resulting not from fiendish malice but from well-meant efforts by people who do not know what they do.

EXPLORATIONS

Short Short

The following short short is by a novelist who was born in Persia (now Iran), grew up in a British colony in Africa (now Zimbabwe), and went to live in England. What happens in the story? What is the unifying thread? How do its characters interact? What leaves the reader with a gratifying sense of completion? (Isaac Babel was a Jewish writer who wrote about Jewish life in Russia. Do we need to know who he is or how he writes for the story to work?)

DORIS LESSING (born 1919)

Homage for Isaac Babel 1958

The day I had promised to take Catherine down to visit my young friend Philip at his school in the country, we were to leave at eleven, but she arrived at nine. Her blue dress was new, and so were her fashionable shoes. Her hair had just been done. She looked more than ever like a pink-and-gold Renoir girl who expects everything from life.

Catherine lives in a white house overlooking the sweeping brown tides of the river. She helped me clean up my flat with a devotion which said that she felt small flats were altogether more romantic than large houses. We drank tea, and talked mainly about Philip, who, being fifteen, has pure stern tastes in everything from food to music. Catherine looked at the books lying around his room, and asked if she might borrow the stories of Isaac Babel to read on the train. Catherine is thirteen. I suggested she might find them difficult, but she said: "Philip reads them, doesn't he?"

During the journey I read newspapers and watched her pretty frowning face as she turned the pages of Babel, for she was determined to let nothing get between her and her ambition to be worthy of Philip.

At the school, which is charming, civilized, and expensive, the two children walked together across green fields, and I followed, seeing how the sun gilded their bright friendly heads turned toward each other as they talked. In Catherine's left hand she carried the stories of Isaac Babel.

After lunch we went to the pictures. Philip allowed it to be seen that he thought going to the pictures just for the fun of it was not worthy of intelligent people, but he made the concession, for our sakes. For his sake we chose the more serious of the two films that were showing in the little town. It was about a good priest who helped criminals in New York. His goodness, however, was not enough to prevent one of them from being sent to the gas chamber; and Philip and I waited with Catherine in the dark until she had stopped crying and could face the light of a golden evening. 5

At the entrance of the cinema the doorman was lying in wait for anyone who had red eyes. Grasping Catherine by her suffering arm, he said bitterly: "Yes, why are you crying? He had to be punished for his crime, didn't he?" Catherine stared at him, incredulous. Philip rescued her by saying with disdain: "Some people don't know right from wrong even when it's *demonstrated* to them." The doorman turned his attention to the next red-eyed emerger from the dark; and we went on together to the station, the children silent because of the cruelty of the world.

Finally Catherine said, her eyes wet again: "I think it's all absolutely beastly, and I can't bear to think about it." And Philip said: "But we've got to think about it, don't you see, because if we don't it'll just go on and *on,* don't you see?"

In the train going back to London I sat beside Catherine. She had the stories open in front of her, but she said: "Philip's awfully lucky. I wish I went to that school. Did you notice that girl who said hullo to him in the garden? They must be great friends. I wish my mother would let me have a dress like that, it's *not* fair."

"I thought it was too old for her."

"Oh, *did* you?"

Soon she bent her head again over the book, but almost at once lifted it to say: "Is he a very famous writer?"

"He's a marvellous writer, brilliant, one of the very best."

"Why?"

"Well, for one thing he's so simple. Look how few words he uses, and how strong his stories are."

"I see. Do you know him? Does he live in London?"

"Oh no, he's dead."

"Oh. Then why did you—I thought he was alive, the way you talked."

"I'm sorry, I suppose I wasn't thinking of him as dead."

"When did he die?"

"He was murdered. About twenty years ago, I suppose."

"Twenty years." Her hands began the movement of pushing the book over to me, but then relaxed. "I'll be fourteen in November," she stated, sounding threatened, while her eyes challenged me.

I found it hard to express my need to apologize, but before I could speak, she said, patiently attentive again: "You said he was murdered?"

"Yes."

"I expect the person who murdered him felt sorry when he discovered he had murdered a famous writer."

"Yes, I expect so."

"Was he old when he was murdered?"

"No, quite young really."

"Well, that was bad luck, wasn't it?"

"Yes, I suppose it was bad luck."

"Which do you think is the very best story here? I mean, in your honest opinion, the very very best one."

I chose the story about killing the goose. She read it slowly, while I sat waiting, wishing to take it from her, wishing to protect this charming little person from Isaac Babel.

When she had finished, she said: "Well, some of it I don't understand. He's got a funny way of looking at things. Why should a man's legs in boots look like *girls?*" She finally pushed the book over at me, and said: "I think it's all morbid."

"But you have to understand the kind of life he had. First, he was a Jew in Russia. That was bad enough. Then his experience was all revolution and civil war and. . . ."

But I could see these words bounding off the clear glass of her fiercely denying gaze; and I said: "Look, Catherine, why don't you try again when you're older? Perhaps you'll like him better then?"

She said gratefully: "Yes, perhaps that would be best. After all, Philip is two years older than me, isn't he?"

A week later I got a letter from Catherine.

Thank you very much for being kind enough to take me to visit Philip at his school. It was the most lovely day in my whole life. I am extremely grateful to you for taking me. I have been thinking about the Hoodlum Priest. That was a film which demonstrated to me beyond any shadow of doubt that Capital Punishment is a Wicked Thing, and I shall never forget what I learned that afternoon, and the lessons of it will be with me all my life. I have been meditating about what you said about Isaac Babel, the famed Russian short story writer, and I now see that the conscious simplicity of his style is what makes him, beyond the shadow of a doubt, the great writer that he is, and now in my school compositions I am endeavoring to emulate him so as to learn a conscious simplicity which is the only basis for a really brilliant writing style. Love, Catherine. P.S. Has Philip said anything about my party? I wrote but he hasn't answered. Please find out if he is coming or if he just forgot to answer my letter. I hope he comes, because sometimes I feel I shall die if he doesn't. P.P.S. Please don't tell him I said anything, because I should die if he knew. Love, Catherine.

THREE MASTER STORYTELLERS

A plot is a narrative of events, the emphasis falling on
causality. "The king died and then the queen died" is a
story. "The king died, and then the queen died of grief" is
a plot.

E. M. FORSTER

The following three selections are by writers who know how to write gripping stories. They know how to entice readers into a story and then lock in their interest until the story reaches its satisfying conclusion. However, the three writers use very different techniques, ranging from the more traditional to the more modern. Try to chart the plot, the story line, as you read.

BERNARD MALAMUD (1914–1986)

A bad reading of my work would indicate that I'm
writing about losers. That would be a very bad reading.
One of my most important themes is a man's hidden
strength.

BERNARD MALAMUD

Bernard Malamud was born and went to school in Brooklyn; he continued his education at the College of the City of New York and Columbia University. He taught high school evening classes for years before he could make a living as a writer and university teacher. He knew the cultural heritage of the American Jewish community from close by, and he wrote about Jewish everyday life and Jewish history in novels like *The Assistant* (1956), about a struggling neighborhood grocer and the down-and-out stranger he befriends. *The Fixer* (1966) tells the story of a Jew accused of ritual murder in czarist Russia. Malamud's fiction is colored by the tragic view of life of a people who underwent centuries of persecution. (In the depths of loneliness and bitterness, Leo Finkle, the rabbinical student in Malamud's story "The Magic Barrel," reminds himself "that he was yet a Jew and that a Jew suffered.") However, intermeshing with this mournful strand is a zany sense of humor, as likely to target one's own shortcomings as those of others. Finally, even in defeat, Malamud's characters often seem to project a love of life and a solidarity with suffering humanity that defy adversity.

Malamud's "The Magic Barrel" has the kind of straightforward surface plot that delights lovers of unspoilt spontaneous storytelling. A young rabbinical student, shy and lonely, enlists the services of a traditional matchmaker or marriage broker in his search for a suitable wife. The young man's quest for happiness leads him through a series of tragicomic adventures that seem to doom him to disappointment. However, the story shows him overcoming the obstacles in his path and leads to a surprise ending that is a happy ending or not depending on the beholder's point of view.

What makes the story rich and complex is that it moves on more than one level. While the official plot is played out toward its conclusion, much of what the characters publicly say and do plays to a counterpoint of private thoughts and feelings. These are often betrayed by revealing gestures, hesitations, or slips of the tongue. The role each character plays—the matchmaker, the serious theology student, the teacher looking for a spouse—is a public **persona**; it is the personality they exhibit to the outside world, the face they wear in public. Much of the comedy is in the sad and funny contrast between their deliberate public pronouncements and their unacknowledged real selves.

Once you focus on the private feelings of the characters, you are likely to observe that parallel to the overt action—the search for a mate—a spiritual journey takes place. The main plot with its quest for happiness is the occasion for a parallel story line—a journey toward self-discovery. Leo learns things about himself that before he did not know or care to admit. He reexamines his life, his history, his vocation. What does he learn? How does his character develop or grow in the course of the story?

The Magic Barrel   1958

Not long ago there lived in uptown New York, in a small, almost meager room, though crowded with books, Leon Finkle, a rabbinical student in the Yeshivah University. Finkle, after six years of study, was to be ordained in June and had been advised by an acquaintance that he might find it easier to win himself a congregation if he were married. Since he had no present prospects of marriage, after two tormented days of turning it over in his mind, he called in Pinye Salzman, a marriage broker, whose two-line advertisement he had read in the *Forward*.

The matchmaker appeared one night out of the dark fourth-floor hallway of the graystone rooming house, grasping a black, strapped portfolio that had been worn thin with use. Salzman, who had been long in the business, was of slight but dignified build, wearing an old hat and an overcoat too short and tight for him. He smelled frankly of fish, which he loved to eat, and although he was missing a few teeth, his presence was not displeasing, because of an amiable manner curiously contrasted by mournful eyes. His voice, his lips, his wisp of beard, his bony fingers were animated, but give him a moment of repose, and his mild blue eyes soon revealed a depth of sadness, a characteristic that put Leo a little at ease although the situation, for him, was inherently tense.

He at once informed Salzman why he had asked him to come, explaining that his home was in Cleveland, and that but for his parents, who had married comparatively late in life, he was alone in the world. He had for six years devoted himself entirely to his studies, as a result of which, quite understandably, he had found himself without time for a social life and the company of young women. Therefore he thought it the better part of trial and error—of embarrassing fumbling—to call in an experienced person to advise him in these matters. He remarked in passing that the function of the marriage broker was ancient and honorable, highly approved in the Jewish community, because it made practical the necessary without hindering joy. Moreover, his own parents had been brought together by a matchmaker. They had made, if not a financially profitable marriage—since neither had possessed any worldly goods to speak of—at least a successful one in the sense of their everlasting devotion to one another. Salzman listened in embarrassed surprise, sensing a sort of apology. Later, however, he experienced a glow of pride in his work, an emotion that had left him years ago, and he heartily approved of Finkle.

The two men went to their business. Leo had led Salzman to the only clear place in the room, a table near a window that overlooked the lamplit city. He seated himself at the matchmaker's side but facing him, attempting by an act of will to suppress the unpleasant tickle in his throat. Salzman eagerly unstrapped his portfolio and removed a loose rubber band from a thin packet of much-handled cards. As he flipped through them, a gesture and sound that physically hurt Leo, the student pretended not to see and gazed steadfastly out the window. Although it was still February, winter was on its last legs, signs of which he had for the first time in years begun to notice. He now observed the round white moon, moving high in the sky through a cloud-menagerie, and watched with half-open mouth as it penetrated a huge hen and dropped out of her like an egg laying itself. Salzman, though pretending through eyeglasses he had just slipped on, to be engaged in scanning the writing on the cards, stole occasional glances at the young man's distinguished face, noting with pleasure the long, severe scholar's nose, brown eyes heavy with learning, sensitive yet ascetic lips, and a certain almost hollow quality of the dark cheeks. He gazed around at shelves upon shelves of books and let out a soft but happy sigh.

When Leo's eyes fell upon the cards, he counted six spread out in Salzman's hand.   5

"So few?" he said in disappointment.

"You wouldn't believe me how much cards I got in my office," Salzman replied. "The drawers are already filled to the top, so I keep them now in a barrel, but is every girl good for a new rabbi?"

Leo blushed at this, regretting all he had revealed of himself in a curriculum vitae he had sent to Salzman. He had thought it best to acquaint him with his strict standards and specifications, but in having done so now felt he had told the marriage broker more than was absolutely necessary.

He hesitantly inquired, "Do you keep photographs of your clients on file?"

"First comes family, amount of dowry, also what kind promises," Salzman replied,   10 unbuttoning his tight coat and settling himself in the chair. "After comes pictures, rabbi."

"Call me Mr. Finkle. I'm not a rabbi yet."

Salzman said he would, but instead called him doctor, which he changed to rabbi when Leo was not listening too attentively.

Salzman adjusted his horn-rimmed spectacles, gently cleared his throat and read in an eager voice the contents on the top card:

"Sophie P. Twenty-four years. Widow for one year. No children. Educated high school and two years college. Father promises eight thousand dollars. Has a wonderful wholesale business. Also real estate. On mother's side comes teachers, also one actor. Well known on Second Avenue."

Leo gazed up in surprise. "Did you say a widow?"   15

"A widow don't mean spoiled, rabbi. She lived with her husband maybe four months. He was a sick boy, she made a mistake to marry him."

"Marrying a widow has never entered my mind."

"This is because you have no experience. A widow, specially if she is young and healthy like this girl, is a wonderful person to marry. She will be thankful to you the rest of her life. Believe me, if I was looking now for a bride, I would marry a widow."

Leo reflected, then shook his head.

Salzman hunched his shoulders in an almost imperceptible gesture of disappoint-   20
ment. He placed the card down on the wooden table and began to read another:

"Lily H. High-school teacher. Regular. Not a substitute. Has savings and new Dodge car. Lived in Paris one year. Father is successful dentist thiry-five years. Interested in professional man. Well Americanized family. Wonderful opportunity."

"I know her personally," said Salzman. "I wish you could see this girl. She is a doll. Also very intelligent. All day you could talk to her about books and theater and what not. She also knows current events."

"I don't believe you mentioned her age?"

"Her age?" Salzman said, raising his brows in surprise. "Her age is thirty-two years."

Leo said after a while, "I'm afraid that seems a little too old."   25

Salzman let out a laugh. "So how old are you, rabbi?"

"Twenty-seven."

"So what is the difference, tell me, between twenty-seven and thirty-two? My own wife is seven years older than me. So what did I suffer?—Nothing. If Rothschild's daughter wants to marry you, would you say on account of her age, no?"

"Yes," Leo said dryly.

Salzman shook off the no in the yes. "Five years don't mean a thing. I give you my   30
word that when you will live with her for one week, you will forget her age. What does it mean five years—that she lived more and knows more than somebody who is younger? On this girl, God bless her, years are not wasted. Each one that it comes makes better the bargain."

"What subject does she teach in high school?"

"Languages. If you heard the way she reads French, you will think it is music. I am in the business twenty-five years, and I recommend her with my whole heart. Believe me, I know what I'm talking, rabbi."

"What's on the next card?" Leo said abruptly.

Salzman reluctantly turned up the third card:

"Ruth K. Nineteen years. Honor student. Father offers thirteen thousand dollars   35
cash to the right bridegroom. He is a medical doctor. Stomach specialist with marvelous practice. Brother-in-law owns own garment business. Particular people."

Salzman looked up as if he had read his trump card.

"Did you say nineteen?" Leo asked with interest.

"On the dot."

"Is she attractive?" He blushed. "Pretty?"

Salzman kissed his fingertips. "A little doll. On this I give you my word. Let me call the father tonight and you will see what means pretty." 40

But Leo was troubled. "You're sure she's that young?"

"This I am positive. The father will show you the birth certificate."

"Are you positive there isn't something wrong with her?" Leo insisted.

"Who says there is wrong?"

"I don't understand why an American girl her age should go to a marriage broker." 45

A smile spread over Salzman's face.

"So for the same reason you went, she comes."

Leo flushed. "I am pressed for time."

Salzman, realizing he had been tactless, quickly explained. "The father came, not her. He wants she should have the best, so he looks around himself. When we will locate the right boy, he will introduce him and encourage. This makes a better marriage than if a young girl without experience takes for herself. I don't have to tell you this."

"But don't you think this young girl believes in love?" Leo spoke uneasily. 50

Salzman was about to guffaw, but caught himself and said soberly, "Love comes with the right person, not before."

Leo parted dry lips but did not speak. Noticing that Salzman had snatched a quick glance at the next card, he cleverly asked, "How is her health?"

"Perfect," Salzman said, breathing with difficulty. "Of course, she is a little lame on her right foot from an auto accident that it happened to her when she was twelve years, but nobody notices on account she is so brilliant and also beautiful."

Leo got up heavily and went to the window. He felt curiously bitter and upbraided himself for having called in the marriage broker. Finally, he shook his head.

"Why not?" Salzman persisted, the pitch of his voice rising. 55

"Because I hate stomach specialists."

"So what do you care what is his business? After you marry her, do you need him? Who says he must come every Friday night to your house?"

Ashamed of the way the talk was going, Leo dismissed Salzman, who went home with melancholy eyes.

Though he had felt only relief at the marriage broker's departure, Leo was in low spirits the next day. He explained it as arising from Salzman's failure to produce a suitable bride for him. He did not care for his type of clientele. But when Leo found himself hesitating over whether to seek out another matchmaker, one more polished than Pinye, he wondered if it could be—his protestations to the contrary, and although he honored his father and mother—that he did not, in essence, care for the matchmaking institution? This thought he quickly put out of his mind yet found himself still upset. All day he ran around in a fog—missed an important appointment, forgot to give out his laundry, walked out of a Broadway cafeteria without paying and had to run back with the ticket in his hand; had even not recognized his landlady in the street when she passed with a friend and courteously called out, "A good evening to you, Doctor Finkle." By nightfall, however, he had regained sufficient calm to sink his nose into a book and there found peace from his thoughts.

Almost at once there came a knock on the door. Before Leo could say enter, Salzman, commercial cupid, was standing in the room. His face was gray and meager, his 60 expression hungry, and he looked as if he would expire on his feet. Yet the marriage broker managed, by some trick of the muscles, to display a broad smile.

"So good evening. I am invited?"

Leo nodded, disturbed to see him again, yet unwilling to ask him to leave.

Beaming still, Salzman laid his portfolio on the table. "Rabbi, I got for you tonight good news."

"I've asked you not to call me rabbi. I'm still a student."

"Your worries are finished. I have for you a first-class bride."   65

"Leave me in peace concerning this subject." Leo pretended lack of interest.

"The world will dance at your wedding."

"Please, Mr. Salzman, no more."

"But first must come back my strength," Salzman said weakly. He fumbled with the portfolio straps and took out of the leather case an oily paper bag, from which he extracted a hard seeded roll and a small smoked whitefish. With one motion of his hand he stripped the fish out of its skin and began ravenously to chew. "All day in a rush," he muttered.

Leo watched him eat.   70

"A sliced tomato you have maybe?" Salzman hesitantly inquired.

"No."

The marriage broker shut his eyes and ate. When he had finished, he carefully cleaned up the crumbs and rolled up the remains of the fish in the paper bag. His spectacled eyes roamed the room until he discovered, amid some piles of books, a one-burner gas stove. Lifting his hat, he humbly asked, "A glass of tea you got, rabbi?"

Conscience-stricken, Leo rose and brewed the tea. He served it with a chunk of lemon and two cubes of lump sugar, delighting Salzman.

After he had drunk his tea, Salzman's strength and good spirits were restored.   75

"So tell me, rabbi," he said amiably, "you considered any more the three clients I mentioned yesterday?"

"There was no need to consider."

"Why not?"

"None of them suits me."

"What, then, suits you?"   80

Leo let it pass because he could give only a confused answer.

Without waiting for a reply, Salzman asked, "You remember this girl I talked to you—the high-school teacher?"

"Age thirty-two?"

But, surprisingly, Salzman's face lit in a smile. "Age twenty-nine."

Leo shot him a look. "Reduced from thirty-two?"   85

"A mistake," Salzman avowed. "I talked today with the dentist. He took me to his safety deposit box and showed me the birth certificate. She was twenty-nine last August. They made her a party in the mountains where she went for her vacation. When her father spoke to me the first time, I forgot to write the age and I told you thirty-two, but now I remember this was a different client, a widow."

"The same one you told me about? I thought she was twenty-four?"

"A different. Am I responsible that the world is filled with widows?"

"No, but I'm not interested in them, nor for that matter, in schoolteachers."

Salzman passionately pulled his clasped hands to his breast. Looking at the ceiling   90
he exclaimed, "Jewish children, what can I say to somebody that he is not interested in high-school teachers? So what then you are interested?"

Leo flushed but controlled himself.

"In who else you will be interested," Salzman went on, "if you not interested in this fine girl that she speaks four languages and has personally in the bank ten thousand dollars? Also her father guarantees further twelve thousand. Also she has a new car, wonderful clothes, talks on all subjects, and she will give you a first-class home and children. How near do we come in our life to paradise?"

"If she's so wonderful, why wasn't she married ten years ago?"

"Why," said Salzman with a heavy laugh. "—Why? Because she is *partikler*. This is why. She wants only the *best*."

Leo was silent, amused at how he had trapped himself. But Salzman had aroused his interest in Lily H., and he began seriously to consider calling on her. When the marriage broker observed how intently Leo's mind was at work on the facts he had supplied, he felt positive they would soon come to an agreement.

Late Saturday afternoon, conscious of Salzman, Leo Finkle walked with Lily Hirschorn along Riverside Drive. He walked briskly and erectly, wearing with distinction the black fedora he had that morning taken with trepidation out of the dusty hatbox on his closet shelf, and the heavy black Saturday coat he had thoroughly whisked clean. Leo also owned a walking stick, a present from a distant relative, but had decided not to use it. Lily, petite and not unpretty, had on something signifying the approach of spring. She was *au courant*, animatedly, with all subjects, and he weighed her words and found her surprisingly sound—score another for Salzman, whom he uneasily sensed to be somewhere around, hiding perhaps high in a tree along the street, flashing the lady signals; or perhaps a cloven-hoofed Pan, piping nuptial ditties as he danced his invisible way before them, strewing wild buds on the walk and purple summer grapes in their path, symbolizing fruit of a union, of which there was yet none.

Lily startled Leo by remarking, "I was thinking of Mr. Salzman, a curious figure, wouldn't you say?"

Not certain what to answer, he nodded.

She bravely went on, blushing, "I for one am grateful for his introducing us. Aren't you?"

He courteously replied, "I am."

"I mean," she said with a little laugh—and it was all in good taste, or at least gave the effect of being not in bad—"do you mind that we came together so?"

He was not afraid of her honesty, recognizing that she meant to set the relationship aright, and understanding that it took a certain amount of experience in life, and courage, to want to do it quite that way. One had to have some sort of past to make that kind of beginning.

He said that he did not mind. Salzman's function was traditional and honorable—valuable for what it might achieve, which, he pointed out, was frequently nothing.

Lily agreed with a sigh. They walked on for a while, and she said after a long silence, again with a nervous laugh, "Would you mind if I asked you something a little bit personal? Frankly, I find the subject fascinating." Although Leo shrugged, she went on half embarrassedly, "How was it that you came to your calling? I mean, was it a sudden passionate inspiration?"

Leo, after a time, slowly replied, "I was always interested in the Law."

"You saw revealed in it the presence of the Highest?"

He nodded and changed the subject. "I understand you spent a little time in Paris, Miss Hirschorn?" ↓ something wrong - doesn't really care about a calling

"Oh, did Mr. Salzman tell you, Rabbi Finkle?" Leo winced, but she went on, "It was ages and ages ago and almost forgotten. I remember I had to return for my sister's wedding."

But Lily would not be put off. "When," she asked in a trembly voice, "did you become enamored of God?"

He stared at her. Then it came to him that she was talking not about Leo Finkle, but a total stranger, some mystical figure, perhaps even passionate prophet that Salzman had conjured up for her—no relation to the living or dead. Leo trembled with rage and weakness. The trickster had obviously sold her a bill of goods, just as he had him, who'd expected to become acquainted with a young lady of twenty-nine, only to behold, the moment he laid eyes upon her strained and anxious face, a woman past thirty-five and aging very rapidly. Only his self-control, he thought, had kept him this long in her presence.

"I am not," he said gravely, "a talented religious person," and in seeking words to go on, found himself possessed by fear and shame. "I think," he said in a strained manner, "that I came to God not because I love Him, but because I did not."

This confession he spoke harshly because its unexpectedness shook him.

Lily wilted. Leo saw a profusion of loaves of bread sailing like ducks high over his head, not unlike the loaves by which he had counted himself to sleep last night. Mercifully, then, it snowed, which he would not put past Salzman's machinations.

He was infuriated with the marriage broker and swore he would throw him out of the room the moment he reappeared. But Salzman did not come that night, and when Leo's anger had subsided, an unaccountable despair grew in its place. At first he thought this was caused by his disappointment in Lily, but before long it became evident that he had involved himself with Salzman without a true knowledge of his own intent. He gradually realized—with an emptiness that seized him with six hands—that he had called in the broker to find him a bride because he was incapable of doing it himself. This terrifying insight he had derived as a result of his meeting and conversation with Lily Hirschorn. Her probing questions had somehow irritated him into revealing—to himself more than her—the true nature of his relationship with God, and from that it had come upon him, with shocking force, that apart from his parents, he had never loved anyone. Or perhaps it went the other way, that he did not love God so well as he might, because he had not loved man. It seemed to Leo that his whole life stood starkly revealed and he saw himself, for the first time, as he truly was—unloved and loveless. This bitter but somehow not fully unexpected revelation brought him to a point of panic controlled only by extraordinary effort. He covered his face with his hands and wept.

The week that followed was the worst of his life. He did not eat, and lost weight. His beard darkened and grew ragged. He stopped attending lectures and seminars and almost never opened a book. He seriously considered leaving the Yeshivah, although he was deeply troubled at the thought of the loss of all his years of study—saw them like pages from a book strewn over the city—and at the devastating effect of this decision upon his parents. But he had lived without knowledge of himself, and never in the Five Books and all the Commentaries—*mea culpa*—had the truth been revealed to him. He did not know where to turn, and in all this desolating loneliness there was no *to whom*, although he often thought of Lily but not once could bring himself to go downstairs and make the call. He became touchy and irritable, especially with his landlady, who asked him all manner of questions; on the other hand, sensing his own disagreeableness, he waylaid her on the stairs and apologized abjectly, until mortified, she ran from him. Out of this, however, he drew the consolation that he was yet a Jew and that a

110

115

Jew suffered. But gradually, as the long and terrible week drew to a close, he regained his composure and some idea of purpose in life: to go on as planned. Although he was imperfect, the ideal was not. As for his quest of a bride, the thought of continuing afflicted him with anxiety and heartburn, yet perhaps with this new knowledge of himself he would be more successful than in the past. Perhaps love would now come to him and a bride to that love. And for this sanctified seeking who needed a Salzman?

The marriage broker, a skeleton with haunted eyes, returned that very night. He looked, withal, the picture of frustrated expectancy—as if he had steadfastly waited the week at Miss Lily Hirschorn's side for a telephone call that never came.

Casually coughing, Salzman came immediately to the point: "So how did you like her?"

Leo's anger rose and he could not refrain from chiding the matchmaker: "Why did you lie to me, Salzman?"

Salzman's pale face went dead white, as if the world had snowed on him.

"Did you not state that she was twenty-nine?" Leo insisted. 120

"I give you my word—"

"She was thirty-five. At *least* thirty-five."

"Of this I would not be too sure. Her father told me—"

"Never mind. The worst of it was that you lied to her."

"How did I lie to her, tell me?" 125

"You told her things about me that weren't true. You made me out to be more, consequently less than I am. She had in mind a totally different person, a sort of semi-mystical Wonder Rabbi."

"All I said, you was a religious man."

"I can imagine."

Salzman sighed. "This is my weakness that I have," he confessed. "My wife says to me I shouldn't be a salesman, but when I have two fine people that they would be wonderful to be married, I am so happy that I talk too much." He smiled wanly. "This is why Salzman is a poor man."

Leo's anger went. "Well, Salzman, I'm afraid that's all." 130

The marriage broker fastened hungry eyes on him.

"You don't want any more a bride?"

"I do," said Leo, "but I have decided to seek her in a different way. I am no longer interested in an arranged marriage. To be frank, I now admit the necessity of premarital love. That is, I want to be in love with the one I marry."

"Love?" said Salzman, astounded. After a moment he said, "For us, our love is our life, not for the ladies. In the ghetto they—"

"I know, I know," said Leo. "I've thought of it often. Love, I have said to myself, 135 should be a by-product of living and worship rather than its own end. Yet for myself I find it necessary to establish the level of my need and to fulfill it."

Salzman shrugged but answered, "Listen, rabbi, if you want love, this I can find for you also. I have such beautiful clients that you will love them the minute your eyes will see them."

Leo smiled unhappily. "I'm afraid you don't understand."

But Salzman hastily unstrapped his portfolio and withdrew a manila packet from it.

"Pictures," he said, quickly laying the envelope on the table.

Leo called after him to take the pictures away, but as if on the wings of the wind, 140 Salzman had disapeared.

March came. Leo had returned to his regular routine. Although he felt not quite himself yet—lacked energy—he was making plans for a more active social life. Of course it would cost something, but he was an expert in cutting corners; and when there were no corners left he could make circles rounder. All the while Salzman's pictures had lain on the table, gathering dust. Occasionally as Leo sat studying, or enjoying a cup of tea, his eyes fell on the manila envelope, but he never opened it.

The days went by, and no social life to speak of developed with a member of the opposite sex—it was difficult, given the circumstances of his situation. One morning Leo toiled up the stairs to his room and stared out the window at the city. Although the day was bright, his view of it was dark. For some time he watched the people in the street below hurrying along and then turned with a heavy heart to his little room. On the table was the packet. With a sudden relentless gesture he tore it open. For a half-hour he stood there, in a state of excitement, examining the photographs of the ladies Salzman had included. Finally, with a deep sigh he put them down. There were six, of varying degrees of attractiveness, but look at them long enough and they all became Lily Hirschorn: all past their prime, all starved behind bright smiles, not a true person-ality in the lot. Life, despite their anguished struggles and frantic yoohooings, had passed them by; they were photographs in a brief case that stank of fish. After a while, however, as Leo attempted to return the pictures into the envelope, he found another in it, a small snapshot of the type taken by a machine for a quarter. He gazed at it a moment and let out a cry.

Her face deeply moved him. Why, he could at first not say. It gave him the impres-sion of youth—all spring flowers—yet age—a sense of having been used to the bone, wasted; this all came from the eyes, which were hauntingly familiar, yet absolutely strange. He had a strong impression that he had met her before, but try as he might he could not place her, although he could almost recall her name, as if he had read it writ-ten in her own handwriting. No, this couldn't be; he would have remembered her. It was not, he affirmed, that she had an extraordinary beauty—no, although her face was attractive enough; it was that *something* about her moved him. Feature for feature, even some of the ladies of the photographs could do better; but she leaped forth to the heart—had lived, or wanted to—more than just wanted, perhaps regretted it—had somehow deeply suffered: it could be seen in the depths of those reluctant eyes, and from the way the light enclosed and shone from her, and within her, opening whole realms of possibility: this was her own. Her he desired. His head ached and eyes nar-rowed with the intensity of his gazing, then, as if a black fog had blown up in the mind, he experienced fear of her and was aware that he had received an impression, somehow, of filth. He shuddered, saying softly, it is thus with us all. Leo brewed some tea in a small pot and sat sipping it, without sugar, to calm himself. But before he had finished drinking, again with excitement he examined the face and found it good: good for him. Only such a one could truly understand Leo Finkle and help him to seek whatever he was seeking. How she had come to be among the discards in Salzman's barrel he could never guess, but he knew he must urgently go find her.

Leo rushed downstairs, grabbed up the Bronx telephone book, and searched for Salzman's home address. He was not listed, nor was his office. Neither was he in the Manhattan book. But Leo remembered having written down the address on a slip of paper after he had read Salzman's advertisement in the "personals" column of the *For-ward*. He ran up to his room and tore through his papers, without luck. It was exasper-ating. Just when he needed the matchmaker he was nowhere to be found. Fortunately Leo remembered to look in his wallet. There on a card he found his name written and a Bronx address. No phone number was listed, which, Leo now recalled, was the reason he had originally communicated with Salzman by letter. He got on his coat, put a hat on over his skull cap and hurried to the subway station. All the way to the far end of the

Bronx he sat on the edge of his seat. He was more than once tempted to take out the picture and see if the girl's face was as he remembered it, but he refrained, allowing the snapshot to remain in his inside coat pocket, content to have her so close. When the train pulled into the station, he was waiting at the door and bolted out. He quickly located the street Salzman had advertised.

The building he sought was less than a block from the subway, but it was not an office building, nor even a loft, nor a store in which one could rent office space. It was an old and grimy tenement. Leo found Salzman's name in pencil on a soiled tag under the bell and climbed three dark flights to his apartment. When he knocked, the door was opened by a thin, asthmatic, gray-haired woman, in felt slippers. 145

"Yes?" she said, expecting nothing. She listened without listening. He could have sworn he had seen her somewhere before but knew it was illusion.

"Salzman—does he live here? Pinye Salzman," he said, "the matchmaker?"

She stared at him a long time. "Of course."

He felt embarrassed. "Is he in?"

"No." Her mouth was open, but she offered nothing more. 150

"This is urgent. Can you tell me where his office is?"

"In the air." She pointed upward.

"You mean he has no office?" Leo said.

"In his socks."

He peered into the apartment. It was sunless and dingy, one large room divided by a half-open curtain, beyond which he could see a sagging metal bed. The nearer side of the room was crowded with rickety chairs, old bureaus, a three-legged table, racks of cooking utensils, and all the apparatus of a kitchen. But there was no sign of Salzman or his magic barrel, probably also a figment of his imagination. An odor of frying fish made Leo weak to the knees. 155

"Where is he?" he insisted, "I've got to see your husband."

At length she answered, "So who knows where he is? Every time he thinks a new thought he runs to a different place. Go home, he will find you."

"Tell him Leo Finkle."

She gave no sign that she had heard.

He went downstairs, deeply depressed. 160

But Salzman, breathless, stood waiting at his door.

Leo was overjoyed and astounded. "How did you get here before me?"

"I rushed."

"Come inside."

They entered. Leo fixed tea and a sardine sandwich for Salzman. 165

As they were drinking, he reached behind him for the packet of pictures and handed them to the marriage broker.

Salzman put down his glass and said expectantly, "You found maybe somebody you like?"

"Not among these."

The marriage broker turned sad eyes away.

"Here's the one I like." Leo held forth the snapshot. 170

Salzman slipped on his glasses and took the picture into his trembling hand. He turned ghastly and let out a miserable groan.

"What's the matter?" cried Leo.

"Excuse me. Was an accident this picture. She is not for you."

Salzman frantically shoved the manila packet into his portfolio. He thrust the snapshot into his pocket and fled down the stairs.

Leo, after momentary paralysis, gave chase and cornered the marriage broker in the vestibule. The landlady made hysterical outcries, but neither of them listened. [175]

"Give me back the picture, Salzman."

"No." The pain in his eyes was terrible.

"Tell me where she is then."

"This I can't tell you. Excuse me."

He made to depart, but Leo, forgetting himself, seized the matchmaker by his tight coat and shook him frenziedly. [180]

"Please," sighed Salzman. *"Please."*

Leo ashamedly let him go. "Tell me who she is," he begged. "It's very important for me to know."

"She is not for you. She is a wild one—wild, without shame. This is not a bride for a rabbi."

"What do you mean wild?"

"Like an animal. Like a dog. For her to be poor was a sin. This is why she is dead now." [185]

"In God's name, what do you mean?"

"Her I can't introduce to you," Salzman cried.

"Why are you so excited?"

"Why he asks," Salzman said, bursting into tears. "This is my baby, my Stella, she should burn in hell."

Leo hurried up to bed and hid under the covers. Under the covers he thought his whole life through. Although he soon fell asleep he could not sleep her out of his mind. He woke, beating his breast. Though he prayed to be rid of her, his prayers went unanswered. Through days of torment he struggled endlessly not to love her; fearing success, he escaped it. He then concluded to convert her to goodness, himself to God. The idea alternately nauseated and exalted him. [190]

He perhaps did not know that he had come to a final decision until he encountered Salzman in a Broadway cafeteria. He was sitting alone at a rear table sucking the bony remains of a fish. The marriage broker appeared haggard, and transparent to the point of vanishing.

Salzman looked up at first without recognizing him. Leo had grown a pointed beard, and his eyes were weighted with wisdom.

"Salzman," he said, "love has at last come to my heart."

"Who can love from a picture?" mocked the marriage broker.

"It is not impossible." [195]

"If you can love her, then you can love anybody. Let me show you some new clients that they just sent me their photographs. One is a little doll."

"Just her I want," Leo murmured.

"Don't be a fool, doctor. Don't bother with her."

"Put me in touch with her, Salzman," Leo said humbly. "Perhaps I can do her a service."

Salzman had stopped chewing, and Leo understood with emotion that it was now arranged. [200]

Leaving the cafeteria, he was, however, afflicted by a tormenting suspicion that Salzman had planned it all to happen this way.

Leo was informed by letter that she would meet him on a certain corner, and she was there one spring night, waiting under a street lamp. He appeared, carrying a small bouquet of violets and rosebuds. Stella stood by the lamppost, smoking. She wore white with red shoes, which fitted his expectations, although in a troubled moment he had imagined the dress red, and only the shoes white. She waited uneasily and shyly. From afar he saw that her eyes—clearly her father's—were filled with desperate innocence. He pictured, in hers, his own redemption. Violins and lit candles revolved in the sky. Leo ran forward with the flowers outthrust.

Around the corner, Salzman, leaning against a wall, chanted prayers for the dead.

THE RECEPTIVE READER

1. What kind of story is this? What kind of story do the title and the *beginning* lead you to expect? Are your expectations fulfilled or disappointed by the rest of the story?

2. What is the *conflict* between the traditional view of love and romantic love in this story? How central is this conflict to the plot? How is the conflict resolved?

3. What are hints or touches that require you to read between the lines? Where are you most aware of the comic contrast between what the characters say and what they really think or know? What are striking examples of the contrast between make-believe and reality?

4. What role does Salzman play in the story as a whole? How essential is he to the plot? What are Finkle's mixed feelings about the "commercial cupid"?

5. What makes Salzman a *comic* figure? (What features do you recognize in his use of English?) How would you describe the kind of humor that pervades this story? What are striking examples?

6. Where in this story does Finkle experience *self-discovery* or self-revelation? What does he discover about himself? What role does this self-examination play in the story as a whole?

7. How believable is the *ending*?

THE PERSONAL RESPONSE

How essential is an understanding of Jewish culture or tradition to the reader's appreciation of this story? For you, does the author's ethnic background limit or enhance the appeal of the story? Why (or why not)?

CROSS-REFERENCES—For Discussion or Writing

Compare and contrast the plot of Malamud's story with the plot or narrative line of one or more of the stories by Joyce, Welty, or Mason printed earlier in this volume.

SHIRLEY JACKSON   (1919–1965)

This story is about you—de te fabula.
                    FRANK O'CONNOR

*I hoped, by setting a particularly brutal ancient rite in the
present and in my own village, to shock the story's readers
with a graphic dramatization of the pointless violence and
general inhumanity in their own lives.*
                    SHIRLEY JACKSON

Shirley Jackson was a native of San Francisco who attended Syracuse University and settled in Vermont. She is a master of the modern horror story in which evil surfaces in ordinary everyday surroundings. Her story "The Lottery" is one of the great controversial stories of modern times. When first published in the *New Yorker* on June 28, 1948, it raised a tempest of protest. The story takes us to a village where we watch the preparations for a traditional ritual—in which one of the villagers is going to meet a terrible fate. The proceedings might remind us of accounts of ceremonial sacrifices to a vegetation god to ensure a rich harvest. ("Lottery in June, corn be heavy soon" is a folk saying in the village.)

Apparently two facets of the story were particularly disturbing to its original readers: First, the people in the story were not a prehistoric tribe whose primitive rituals they could have watched with detachment. This was a village that had a post office, a bank, and a school; the villagers talked about tractors and taxes. (Jackson once said she had in mind North Bennington, the town where she lived with her husband, who taught at Bennington College.) Second, the people selected to play the central role in the ritual were selected by lot—without the benefit of due process or trial by jury. They were chosen more simply and cheaply by a lottery.

Many of its original readers hated this story with a passion. The story generated "great batches" of mail, most of it critical and much of it abusive, making the author feel grateful that many in her own town did not know she was a writer. She said about the experience, "One of the most terrifying aspects of publishing stories is the realization they are going to be read, and read by strangers. . . . I had begun to perceive that I was very lucky indeed to be safely in Vermont, where no one in our small town had ever heard of the *New Yorker*, much less read my story. Millions of people, and my mother, had taken a pronounced dislike to me." Columnists in Chicago and New York reported gleefully that *New Yorker* subscriptions were being canceled left and right.

What explains the climate of fear in Jackson's story? We might try to see the story against the backdrop of its historical setting: Totalitarian regimes in Hitler's Germany and in Stalin's Russia had been persecuting artists, intellectuals, dissidents—a whole range of supposed "antisocial elements" and "enemies of the people." People whose families had lived in Germany for centuries, discovered—because their grandparents had been of the Jewish faith—that they were denied the right to live. In Stalinist Russia, young people whose family had owned a farm or a store found they were of the wrong social class—they had no right to go to school, to join the army, to make a living. Closer to home, during the Great Depression, families had been losing their farms or businesses and turned into hoboes. They were the random victims of an economic tailspin that threw millions out of work.

Here is the power of Jackson's story: What happens is irrational, but it seems inevitable. We see it coming but find it impossible to stop, like a freight train. The story has a concentrated impact created by a tightly crafted, linear plot. The author does not allow our attention to be distracted from her agenda. She once said about the writing of short stories, "no scene and no character can be allowed to wander off by itself; there must be some furthering of the story in every sentence."

At the same time, the characters remain fairly anonymous. They are part of the group, and they do what the community expects them to do. Perhaps this is what makes our identification with them possible—whether we identify with the victims or with the other townspeople, be they instigators or bystanders. As the Irish writer Frank O'Connor said about the secret of a powerful story, *"De te fabula"*—this fable, this story, is not about somebody else; it is about you.

The Lottery 1948

The morning of June 27th was clear and sunny, with the fresh warmth of a full-summer day; the flowers were blossoming profusely and the grass was richly green. The people of the village began to gather in the square, between the post office and the bank, around ten o'clock; in some towns there were so many people that the lottery took two days and had to be started on June 26th, but in this village, where there were only about three hundred people, the whole lottery took less than two hours, so it could begin at ten o'clock in the morning and still be through in time to allow the villagers to get home for noon dinner.

The children assembled first, of course. School was recently over for the summer, and the feeling of liberty sat uneasily on most of them; they tended to gather together quietly for a while before they broke into boisterous play, and their talk was still of the classroom and the teacher, of books and reprimands. Bobby Martin had already stuffed his pockets full of stones, and the other boys soon followed his example, selecting the smoothest and roundest stones; Bobby and Harry Jones and Dickie Delacroix—the villagers pronounced this name "Dellacroy"—eventually made a great pile of stones in one corner of the square and guarded it against the raids of the other boys. The girls stood aside, talking among themselves, looking over their shoulders at the boys, and the very small children rolled in the dust or clung to the hands of their older brothers or sisters.

Soon the men began to gather, surveying their own children, speaking of planting and rain, tractors and taxes. They stood together, away from the pile of stones in the corner, and their jokes were quiet and they smiled rather than laughed. The women, wearing faded house dresses and sweaters, came shortly after their menfolk. They greeted one another and exchanged bits of gossip as they went to join their husbands. Soon the women, standing by their husbands, began to call to their children, and the children came reluctantly, having to be called four or five times. Bobby Martin ducked under his mother's grasping hand and ran, laughing, back to the pile of stones. His father spoke up sharply, and Bobby came quickly and took his place between his father and his oldest brother.

The lottery was conducted—as were the square dances, the teenage club, the Halloween program—by Mr. Summers, who had time and energy to devote to civic activities. He was a round-faced, jovial man and he ran the coal business, and people were sorry for him, because he had no children and his wife was a scold. When he arrived in the square, carrying the black wooden box, there was a murmur of conversation among the villagers, and he waved and called, "Little late today, folks." The postmaster, Mr. Graves, followed him, carrying a three-legged stool, and the stool was put in the center of the square and Mr. Summers set the black box down on it. The villagers kept their distance, leaving a space between themselves and the stool, and when Mr. Summers said, "Some of you fellows want to give me a hand?" there was a hesitation before two men, Mr. Martin and his oldest son, Baxter, came forward to hold the box steady on the stool while Mr. Summers stirred up the papers inside it.

The original paraphernalia for the lottery had been lost long ago, and the black box now resting on the stool had been put into use even before Old Man Warner, the oldest man in town, was born. Mr. Summers spoke frequently to the villagers about making a new box, but no one liked to upset even as much tradition as was represented by the black box. There was a story that the present box had been made with some pieces of the box that had preceded it, the one that had been constructed when the first people settled down to make a village here. Every year, after the lottery, Mr. Summers began talking again about a new box, but every year the subject was allowed to fade off without anything's being done. The black box grew shabbier each year; by now it was no longer completely black but splintered badly along one side to show the original wood color, and in some places faded or stained.

Mr. Martin and his oldest son, Baxter, held the black box securely on the stool until Mr. Summers had stirred the papers thoroughly with his hand. Because so much of the ritual had been forgotten or discarded, Mr. Summers had been successful in having slips of paper substituted for the chips of wood that had been used for generations. Chips of wood, Mr. Summers had argued, had been all very well when the village was tiny, but now that the population was more than three hundred and likely to keep on growing, it was necessary to use something that would fit more easily into the black box. The night before the lottery, Mr. Summers and Mr. Graves made up the slips of paper and put them in the box, and it was then taken to the safe of Mr. Summers' coal company and locked up until Mr. Summers was ready to take it to the square next morning. The rest of the year, the box was put away, sometimes one place, sometimes another; it had spent one year in Mr. Graves's barn and another year underfoot in the post office, and sometimes it was set on a shelf in the Martin grocery and left there.

There was a great deal of fussing to be done before Mr. Summers declared the lottery open. There were the lists to make up—of heads of families, heads of households in each family, members of each household in each family. There was the proper swearing-in of Mr. Summers by the postmaster, as the official of the lottery; at one time, some people remembered, there had been a recital of some sort, performed by the official of the lottery, a perfunctory, tuneless chant that had been rattled off duly each year; some people believed that the official of the lottery used to stand just so when he said or sang it, others believed that he was supposed to walk among the people, but years and years ago this part of the ritual had been allowed to lapse. There had been, also, a ritual salute, which the official of the lottery had had to use in addressing each person who came up to draw from the box, but this also had changed with time, until now it was felt necessary only for the official to speak to each person approaching. Mr. Summers was very good at all this; in his clean white shirt and blue jeans, with one hand resting carelessly on the black box, he seemed very proper and important as he talked interminably to Mr. Graves and the Martins.

Just as Mr. Summers finally left off talking and turned to the assembled villagers, Mrs. Hutchinson came hurriedly along the path to the square, her sweater thrown over her shoulders, and slid into place in the back of the crowd. "Clean forgot what day it was," she said to Mrs. Delacroix, who stood next to her, and they both laughed softly. "Thought my old man was out back stacking wood," Mrs. Hutchinson went on, "and then I looked out the window and the kids was gone, and then I remembered it was the twenty-seventh and came a-running." She dried her hands on her apron, and Mrs. Delacroix said, "You're in time, though. They're still talking away up there."

Mrs. Hutchinson craned her neck to see through the crowd and found her husband and children standing near the front. She tapped Mrs. Delacroix on the arm as a farewell and began to make her way through the crowd. The people separated good-humoredly to let her through; two or three people said, in voices just loud enough to be heard across the crowd, "Here comes your Missus, Hutchinson," and "Bill, she made it after all." Mrs. Hutchinson reached her husband, and Mr. Summers, who had been waiting, said cheerfully, "Thought we were going to have to get on without you, Tessie." Mrs. Hutchinson said, grinning, "Wouldn't have me leave m'dishes in the sink, now, would you, Joe?" and soft laughter ran through the crowd as the people stirred back into position after Mrs. Hutchinson's arrival.

"Well, now," Mr. Summers said soberly, "guess we better get started, get this over with, so's we can go back to work. Anybody ain't here?"   10

"Dunbar," several people said, "Dunbar, Dunbar."

Mr. Summers consulted his list. "Clyde Dunbar." he said. "That's right. He's broke his leg, hasn't he? Who's drawing for him?"

"Me, I guess," a woman said, and Mr. Summers turned to look at her. "Wife draws for her husband," Mr. Summers said. "Don't you have a grown boy to do it for you, Janey?" Although Mr. Summers and everyone else in the village knew the answer perfectly well, it was the business of the official of the lottery to ask such questions formally. Mr. Summers waited with an expression of polite interest while Mrs. Dunbar answered.

"Horace's not but sixteen yet," Mrs. Dunbar said regretfully. "Guess I gotta fill in for the old man this year."

"Right," Mr. Summers said. He made a note on the list he was holding. Then he asked, "Watson boy drawing this year?"   15

A tall boy in the crowd raised his hand. "Here," he said. "I'm drawing for m'mother and me." He blinked his eyes nervously and ducked his head as several voices in the crowd said things like "Good fellow, Jack," and "Glad to see your mother's got a man to do it."

"Well," Mr. Summers said, "guess that's everyone. Old Man Warner make it?"

"Here," a voice said, and Mr. Summers nodded.

A sudden hush fell on the crowd as Mr. Summers cleared his throat and looked at the list. "All ready?" he called. "Now, I'll read the names—heads of families first—and the men come up and take a paper out of the box. Keep the paper folded in your hand without looking at it until everyone has had a turn. Everything clear?"

The people had done it so many times that they only half listened to the directions; most of them were quiet, wetting their lips, not looking around. Then Mr. Summers raised one hand high and said, "Adams." A man disengaged himself from the crowd and came forward. "Hi, Steve," Mr. Summers said, and Mr. Adams said, "Hi, Joe." They grinned at one another humorlessly and nervously. Then Mr. Adams reached into the black box and took out a folded paper. He held it firmly by one corner as he turned and went hastily back to his place in the crowd, where he stood a little apart from his family, not looking down at his hand.   20

"Allen," Mr. Summers said. "Anderson. . . . Bentham."

"Seems like there's no time at all between lotteries any more," Mrs. Delacroix said to Mrs. Graves in the back row. "Seems like we got through with the last one only last week."

"Time sure goes fast," Mrs. Graves said.

"Clark. . . . Delacroix."

"There goes my old man," Mrs. Delacroix said. She held her breath while her hus- 25
band went forward.

"Dunbar," Mr. Summers said, and Mrs. Dunbar went steadily to the box while one of the women said, "Go on, Janey," and another said, "There she goes."

"We're next," Mrs. Graves said. She watched while Mr. Graves came around from the side of the box, greeted Mr. Summers gravely, and selected a slip of paper from the box. By now, all through the crowd there were men holding the small folded papers in their large hands, turning them over and over nervously. Mrs. Dunbar and her two sons stood together, Mrs. Dunbar holding the slip of paper.

"Harburt. . . . Hutchinson."

"Get up there, Bill," Mrs. Hutchinson said, and the people near her laughed.

"Jones." 30

"They do say," Mrs. Adams said to Old Man Warner, who stood next to him, "that over in the north village they're talking of giving up the lottery."

Old Man Warner snorted. "Pack of crazy fools," he said. "Listening to the young folks, nothing's good enough for *them*. Next thing you know, they'll be wanted to go back to living in caves, nobody work any more, live *that* way for a while. Used to be a saying about 'Lottery in June, corn be heavy soon.' First thing you know, we'd all be eating stewed chickweed and acorns. There's *always* been a lottery," he added petulantly. "Bad enough to see young Joe Summers up there joking with everybody."

"Some places have already quit lotteries," Mrs. Adams said.

"Nothing but trouble in *that*," Old Man Warner said stoutly. "Pack of young fools."

"Martin." And Bobby Martin watched his father go forward. "Overdyke. . . . 35
Percy."

"I wish they'd hurry," Mrs. Dunbar said to her older son. "I wish they'd hurry."

"They're almost through," her son said.

"You get ready to run tell Dad," Mrs. Dunbar said.

Mr. Summers called his own name and then stepped forward precisely and selected a slip from the box. Then he called, "Warner."

"Seventy-seventh year I been in the lottery," Old Man Warner said as he went 40
through the crowd. "Seventy-seventh time."

"Watson." The tall boy came awkwardly through the crowd. Someone said, "Don't be nervous, Jack," and Mr. Summers said, "Take your time, son."

"Zanini."

After that, there was a long pause, a breathless pause, until Mr. Summers, holding his slip of paper in the air, said, "All right, fellows." For a minute, no one moved, and then all the slips of paper were opened. Suddenly, all the women began to speak at once, saying, "Who is it?," "Who's got it?," "Is it the Dunbars?," "Is it the Watsons?" Then the voices began to say, "It's Hutchinson. It's Bill," "Bill Hutchinson's got it."

"Go tell your father," Mrs. Dunbar said to her older son.

People began to look around to see the Hutchinsons. Bill Hutchinson was stand- 45
ing quiet staring down at the paper in his hand. Suddenly, Tessie Hutchinson shouted to Mr. Summers, "You didn't give him time enough to take any paper he wanted. I saw you. It wasn't fair."

"Be a good sport, Tessie," Mrs. Delacroix called, and Mrs. Graves said, "All of us took the same chance."

"Shut up, Tessie," Bill Hutchinson said.

"Well, everyone," Mr. Summers said, "that was done pretty fast, and now we've got to be hurrying a little more to get done in time." He consulted his next list. "Bill," he said, "you draw for the Hutchinson family. You got any other households in the Hutchinsons?"

"There's Don and Eva," Mrs. Hutchinson yelled. "Make *them* take their chance!"

"Daughters draw for their husbands' families, Tessie," Mr. Summers said gently. "You know that as well as anyone else."

"It wasn't *fair*," Tessie said.

"I guess not, Joe," Bill Hutchinson said regretfully. "My daughter draws with her husband's family, that's only fair. And I've got no other family except the kids."

"Then, as far as drawing for families is concerned, it's you." Mr. Summers said in explanation, "and as far as drawing for households is concerned, that's you, too. Right?"

"Right," Bill Hutchinson said.

"How many kids, Bill?" Mr. Summers asked formally.

"Three," Bill Hutchinson said. "There's Bill, Jr., and Nancy, and little Dave. And Tessie and me."

"All right, then," Mr. Summers said. "Harry, you got their tickets back?"

Mr. Graves nodded and held up the slips of paper. "Put them in the box, then," Mr. Summers directed. "Take Bill's and put it in."

"I think we ought to start over," Mrs. Hutchinson said, as quietly as she could, "I tell you it wasn't *fair*. You didn't give him time enough to choose. *Every*body saw that."

Mr. Graves had selected the five slips and put them in the box, and he dropped all the papers but those onto the ground, where the breeze caught them and lifted them off.

"Listen, everybody," Mrs. Hutchinson was saying to the people around her.

"Ready, Bill?" Mr. Summers asked, and Bill Hutchinson, with one quick glance around at his wife and children, nodded.

"Remember," Mr. Summers said, "take the slips and keep them folded until each person has taken one. Harry, you help little Dave." Mr. Graves took the hand of the little boy, who came willingly with him up to the box. "Take a paper out of the box, Davy," Mr. Summers said. Davy put his hand into the box and laughed. "Take just *one* paper," Mr. Summers said. "Harry, you hold it for him." Mr. Graves took the child's hand and removed the folded paper from the tight fist and held it while little Dave stood next to him and looked up at him wonderingly.

"Nancy next," Mr. Summers said. Nancy was twelve, and her school friends breathed heavily as she went forward, switching her skirt, and took a slip daintily from the box. "Bill, Jr.," Mr. Summers said, and Billy, his face red and his feet over-large, nearly knocked the box over as he got a paper out. "Tessie," Mr. Summers said. She hesitated for a minute, looking around defiantly, and then set her lips and went up to the box. She snatched a paper out and held it behind her.

"Bill," Mr. Summers said, and Bill Hutchinson reached into the box and felt around, bringing his hand out at last with the slip of paper in it.

The crowd was quiet. A girl whispered, "I hope it's not Nancy," and the sound of the whisper reached the edges of the crowd.

"It's not the way it used to be," Old Man Warner said clearly. "People ain't the way they used to be."

"All right," Mr. Summers said. "Open the papers. Harry, you open little Dave's."

Mr. Graves opened the slip of paper and there was a general sigh through the crowd as he held it up and everyone could see that it was blank. Nancy and Bill, Jr.

opened theirs at the same time, and both beamed and laughed, turning around to the crowd and holding their slips of paper above their heads.

"Tessie," Mr. Summers said. There was a pause, and then Mr. Summers looked at Bill Hutchinson, and Bill unfolded his paper and showed it. It was blank. 70

"It's Tessie," Mr. Summers said, and his voice was hushed. "Show us her paper, Bill."

Bill Hutchinson went over to his wife and forced the slip of paper out of her hand. It had a black spot on it, the black spot Mr. Summers had made the night before with the heavy pencil in the coal-company office. Bill Hutchinson held it up, and there was a stir in the crowd.

"All right, folks," Mr. Summers said. "Let's finish quickly."

Although the villagers had forgotten the ritual and lost the original black box, they still remembered to use stones. The pile of stones the boys had made earlier was ready; there were stones on the ground with the blowing scraps of paper that had come out of the box. Mrs. Delacroix selected a stone so large she had to pick it up with both hands and turned to Mrs. Dunbar. "Come on," she said. "Hurry up."

Mrs. Dunbar had small stones in both hands, and she said, gasping for breath, "I can't run at all. You'll have to go ahead and I'll catch up with you." 75

The children had stones already, and someone gave little Davy Hutchinson a few pebbles.

Tessie Hutchinson was in the center of a cleared space by now, and she held her hands out desperately as the villagers moved in on her. "It isn't fair," she said. A stone hit her on the side of the head.

Old Man Warner was saying, "Come on, come on, everyone." Steve Adams was in the front of the crowd of villagers, with Mrs. Graves beside him.

"It isn't fair, it isn't right," Mrs. Hutchinson screamed, and then they were upon her.

THE RECEPTIVE READER

1. The story is told in apparently straightforward *chronological* fashion. As you read along, do you feel nevertheless that essential information is missing? What is being withheld and why? Why does the author tell the story the way she does?

2. Why do you think the author goes into such detail about the procedure, the preparations, the box used and its history? What possibly significant details stand out?

3. How did you expect the story to come out? When were you sure of the outcome? Does the author provide any *foreshadowing* or early hints of what is to come?

4. *Tradition* becomes a key force in this story. What role does it play in the story as a whole? What is its influence, its power? Who speaks up for it? Does anyone question it?

5. Jackson is a master of *irony*—of contradictions between what we might innocently expect and what happens in grim reality. What is ironic about the organizer, Mr. Summers—his other activities, his behavior during the ritual? Is there any humor in the way the author portrays him, and if so, what kind?

6. How does the author lead up the *climactic* event? How does she first introduce the victim and why? Why do you think the author puts in a second drawing—somewhat like a runoff election?

7. This story is often read as a study in mass psychology. What are the reactions of the crowd as the story approaches its climactic ending? Do they provide a comment on or insights into mob psychology?

8. How does the victim react? Is she right when she says the drawing was not fair? What are your feelings as you watch her reaction?

9. Where are you in this story? Do you identify with the victims? the instigators? the bystanders? Or do you stay aloof, like an observer from a distant planet? (How do your reactions compare with those of your classmates?)

10. Is there any division in the story along gender lines? Is it a coincidence that the lottery is run by men but that the victim in the story is a woman? Does the story show us a society in which the supporters of the lottery are male and potential resistance is female?

11. Do you object to or resent the story? How do you explain the reactions of hostile readers?

THE PERSONAL RESPONSE

What do you know about societies that used stoning as punishment? (What biblical reference comes to mind?) Can you think of any parallel situation from your own observation, experience, reading, or viewing? Does our society today have similar rituals? Are any of the psychological dynamics Jackson traces in this story at work in our society today?

THE CREATIVE DIMENSION

Have you ever felt unsatisfied at the end of a story? Have you felt unwilling to let the matter rest where the author concluded the story? Use your imagination—write a sequel to a story that left you wondering or unsatisfied. Study the following sequel as an example. How well does it get into the spirit of the original?

The Lottery, Part II

It is now twenty years later—June 27, 1968. It's the morning of the annual lottery. For a while, the lottery had taken two days to complete because there were so many townspeople, but in the last few years many of them moved out of the area and, too, there weren't many new people resettling there.

Bob and Harry Jones, Dave Hutchinson, Dick Delacroix, and their wives and children are the first villagers to arrive. In a short time, all the villagers are there, even Really Old Man Warner, who has just turned 97 but gets around in his wheelchair.

Suddenly a hush falls over the crowd as Mr. Summers, scoutmaster and conductor of the lottery, comes forward carrying a grey box (at one time it was black) and pronounces the lottery open. One by one, the head of each household comes up and draws a slip of paper from the grey box—Adams, Bowman, Carter, and so forth until Really Old Man Warner draws the last slip of paper.

After that, there's a sort of pause and then everyone opens up his or her slip of paper. Everyone begins talking at once. "Who is it?" Who's got the dot?" Then the people begin to say, "It's Warner. It's Really Old Man Warner."

Everyone looks at Really Old Man Warner, who seems to be backpedalling in his wheelchair. "You know," he croaks, "some villages are talking about giving up the lottery."

CROSS-REFERENCES—For Discussion or Writing

Some years later, Shirley Jackson wrote *The Witchcraft of Salem Village,* a book for adolescents on the trial and execution of the Salem witches in seventeenth-century Massachusetts. (She had a private collection of over five hundred books on witchcraft and demonology from many countries.) This history of persecution and mass hysteria may already have been in Jackson's mind when she wrote "The Lottery." Research the Salem witchcraft trials. What are important parallels and differences between them and the events of this story?

EXPLORATIONS

The Critic's Voice

Lenemaja Friedman says in her book *Shirley Jackson* (1975),

Jackson views man's nature as basically evil, and she indicates that, in his relationship with his fellow beings, man does not hesitate to lie, cheat, and steal—even to kill when it suits his purposes to do so. As in "The Lottery," he may be persuaded that the evil committed is for the common good; but he nevertheless has the herd instinct and does not oppose the harmful mores of his community. And, sadly enough, man does not improve with age; the grandmothers are as guilty of hypocrisy and wrongdoing as the younger members of society. (p. 76)

What evidence from the story would you cite when supporting or taking issue with this view?

WILLIAM FAULKNER (1897–1962)

INTERVIEWER: Some people say they can't understand your writing, even after they read it two or three times. What approach would you suggest to them?
FAULKNER: Read it four times.

Faulkner was one of the great experimenters and innovators in early-twentieth-century fiction. In spite of his difficult, challenging prose (with many-layered sentences that may sprawl across paragraph breaks) and in spite of the broken-mirror effects of his narrative technique, he became one of the most widely read, translated, and discussed writers of modern times. His best-known novels—*As I Lay Dying* (1930), *Sanctuary* (1931), *Absalom, Absalom!* (1936), *Intruder in the Dust* (1948), *Requiem for a Nun* (1951)—have been read around the world. His first major critical success, *The Sound and the Fury* (1929), told the story of the same events as seen in turn by four different characters. He made readers look at characters and events as though seen through the different facets of a prism, with his readers left to form their own perception of the underlying story. All or part of a Faulkner story may use the technique of the **interior monologue,** transcribing the thoughts and feelings racing through a character's mind.

Faulkner's novels and short stories take us to a setting rich in the memories and traumas of the Old South. Many of his stories and novels were part of an ongoing saga of the people of his fictitious Yoknapatawpha County, modeled on Lafayette County in northern Mississippi, where he lived in Oxford, home of the University of Mississippi. As a child, Faulkner lived with a kindly but determined Scottish great-grandfather who made each child in the house recite a memorized Bible verse before breakfast (or else no breakfast). Faulkner served briefly in the Royal Canadian Flying Corps in World War I and lived in New Orleans for a time, working for a newspaper and trying to make a living as a writer. He returned to Mississippi in 1926 and eventually became a writer in residence at the university. He received the Nobel Prize for literature in 1950 and gave a much-reprinted acceptance speech in which he spoke of "the writer's duty" to champion personal values in an age of mass culture. As he once said in a interview, he believed in an individual code through which an individual "makes himself a better human being than his nature wants to be, if he followed his nature only."

Two sources of conflict tend to set events in motion in Faulkner's fiction:

⋄ The first source of conflict is the meeting of the old world and the new. His characters are often embittered by seeing their values threatened in an uprooted modern world. They are often country people trying to live "off here to themselves"—to keep their distance from a new world of neon lights, easy quick money, and shiny automobiles traded in for a new model before the old one is paid for. Often the characters in his stories are fiercely, stubbornly independent—a thorn in the side to state officials, tax collectors, and government agents trying to "interfere with how a man farmed his own land, raised his own cotton."

⋄ The second source of conflict derives from the traditional class structure of the South. Faulkner's own great-grandfather had become wealthy and famous in the Mississippi of before the Civil War. He became a colonel in the Confederate Army and was killed years later in a duel. Many of Faulkner's characters belong to clans—the Sartorises, the Compsons, the Sutpens, the McCaslins, the de Spains—that represent the old social aristocracy of the South. They belong to families that trace their origins back to the original settlers and that often still live in the antebellum, prewar mansions with their columned porticoes.

However, often the offspring of the old families are beset by debts and social upstarts—such as Flem Snopes, one of the "litter" of a family of poor white tenant farmers who never stay long in one place. In a story like "Spotted Horses" (1931), we see Flem at work—pushy, unscrupulous, dishonest, advancing his fortunes with dubious money-making schemes. In "Barn Burning" (1939), we look through the eyes of a boy named Colonel Sartoris Snopes at a vindictive, abusive father. The elder Snopes is a man with "wolflike independence" and "a ferocious conviction in the rightness of his own action." He spent years during or after the war hiding out with a string of captured (stolen) horses; he burnt down a neighbor's barn after a quarrel over a runaway hog; he first smears with his dirty boots and then ruins for good a precious white rug in the mansion of his new landlord, a Major de Spain. And always there are the black people of the Old South—often as servants, as observers, but at other times, as in the story "Dry September" (1931), caught up in the whirlpool of racial hatred and bigotry.

Faulkner broke up traditional plot structure. He told his stories in indirect, or oblique, ways, forcing us as readers to wonder at and puzzle out what is happening (the way we are often forced to in real life). Tense antagonisms, destructive passion, and raw violence erupt in the stories, but we tend to see the violent events only from a partial angle or in a confused rush, as we might in real life. The stories often lead up to a **climax**—a climactic event or revelation. However, they do so in a nonlinear way, through partial testimonies or through provocative details that yet seem to carry only incomplete information. Faulkner frequently uses **flashbacks**, in which glimpses of the past slowly begin to explain or illuminate the present. In the following famous Faulkner story, how does the truth, at first only hinted at, come slowly into focus? What makes a Faulkner story such as this one more haunting than straightforward storytelling?

A Rose for Emily   1931

When Miss Emily Grierson died, our whole town went to her funeral: the men through a sort of respectful affection for a fallen monument, the women mostly out of curiosity to see the inside of her house, which no one save an old manservant—a combined gardener and cook—had seen in at least ten years.

It was a big, squarish frame house that had once been white, decorated with cupolas and spires and scrolled balconies in the heavily lightsome style of the seventies, set on what had once been our most select street. But garages and cotton gins had encroached and obliterated even the august names of that neighborhood; only Miss Emily's house was left, lifting its stubborn and coquettish decay above the cotton wagons and the gasoline pumps—an eyesore among eyesores. And now Miss Emily had gone to join the representatives of those august names where they lay in the cedar-bemused cemetery among the ranked and anonymous graves of Union and Confederate soldiers who fell at the battle of Jefferson.

Alive, Miss Emily had been a tradition, a duty, and a care; a sort of hereditary obligation upon the town, dating from that day in 1894 when Colonel Sartoris, the mayor—he who fathered the edict that no Negro woman should appear on the streets without an apron—remitted her taxes, the dispensation dating from the death of her father on into perpetuity. Not that Miss Emily would have accepted charity. Colonel Sartoris invented an involved tale to the effect that Miss Emily's father had loaned money to the town, which the town, as a matter of business, preferred this way of repaying. Only a man of Colonel Sartoris' generation and thought could have invented it, and only a woman could have believed it.

When the next generation, with its more modern ideas, became mayors and aldermen, this arrangement created some little dissatisfaction. On the first of the year they mailed her a tax notice. February came, and there was no reply. They wrote her a formal letter, asking her to call at the sheriff's office at her convenience. A week later the mayor wrote her himself, offering to call or to send his car for her, and received in reply a note on paper of an archaic shape, in a thin, flowing calligraphy in faded ink, to the effect that she no longer went out at all. The tax notice was also enclosed, without comment.

They called a special meeting of the Board of Aldermen. A deputation waited upon her, knocked at the door through which no visitor had passed since she ceased giving china-painting lessons eight or ten years earlier. They were admitted by the old Negro into a dim hall from which a stairway mounted into still more shadow. It smelled of dust and disuse—a close, dank smell. The Negro led them into the parlor. It was furnished in heavy, leather-covered furniture. When the Negro opened the blinds of one window, they could see that the leather was cracked; and when they sat down, a faint dust rose sluggishly about their thighs, spinning with slow motes in the single sun-ray. On a tarnished gilt easel before the fireplace stood a crayon portrait of Miss Emily's father. 5

They rose when she entered—a small, fat woman in black, with a thin gold chain descending to her waist and vanishing into her belt, leaning on an ebony cane with a tarnished gold head. Her skeleton was small and spare; perhaps that was why what would have been merely plumpness in another was obesity in her. She looked bloated, like a body long submerged in motionless water, and of that pallid hue. Her eyes, lost in the fatty ridges of her face, looked like two small pieces of coal pressed into a lump of dough as they moved from one face to another while the visitors stated their errand.

She did not ask them to sit. She just stood in the door and listened quietly until the spokesman came to a stumbling halt. Then they could hear the invisible watch ticking at the end of the gold chain.

Her voice was dry and cold. "I have no taxes in Jefferson. Colonel Sartoris explained it to me. Perhaps one of you can gain access to the city records and satisfy yourselves."

"But we have. We are the city authorities, Miss Emily. Didn't you get a notice from the sheriff, signed by him?"

"I received a paper, yes," Miss Emily said. "Perhaps he considers himself the sheriff. . . . I have no taxes in Jefferson." 10

"But there is nothing on the books to show that, you see. We must go by the—"

"See Colonel Sartoris. I have no taxes in Jefferson."

"But, Miss Emily—"

"See Colonel Sartoris." (Colonel Sartoris had been dead almost ten years.) "I have no taxes in Jefferson. Tobe!" The Negro appeared. "Show these gentlemen out."

II

So she vanquished them, horse and foot, just as she had vanquished their fathers thirty years before about the smell. That was two years after her father's death and a short time after her sweetheart—the one we believed would marry her—had deserted her. After her father's death she went out very little; after her sweetheart went away, people hardly saw her at all. A few of the ladies had the temerity to call, but were not received, and the only sign of life about the place was the Negro man—a young man then—going in and out with a market basket. 15

"Just as if a man—any man—could keep a kitchen properly," the ladies said; so they were not surprised when the smell developed. It was another link between the gross, teeming world and the high and mighty Griersons.

A neighbor, a woman, complained to the mayor, Judge Stevens, eighty years old.

"But what will you have me do about it, madam?" he said.

"Why, send her word to stop it," the woman said. "Isn't there a law?"

"I'm sure that won't be necessary," Judge Stevens said. "It's probably just a snake or a rat that nigger of hers killed in the yard. I'll speak to him about it." 20

The next day he received two more complaints, one from a man who came in diffident deprecation. "We really must do something about it, Judge. I'd be the last one in the world to bother Miss Emily, but we've got to do something." That night the Board of Aldermen met—three graybeards and one younger man, a member of the rising generation.

"It's simple enough," he said. "Send her word to have her place cleaned up. Give her a certain time to do it in, and if she don't . . ."

"Dammit, sir," Judge Stevens said, "will you accuse a lady to her face of smelling bad?"

So the next night, after midnight, four men crossed Miss Emily's lawn and slunk about the house like burglars, sniffing along the base of the brickwork and at the cellar openings while one of them performed a regular sowing motion with his hand out of a sack slung from his shoulder. They broke open the cellar door and sprinkled lime there, and in all the outbuildings. As they recrossed the lawn, a window that had been dark was lighted and Miss Emily sat in it, the light behind her, and her upright torso motionless as that of an idol. They crept quietly across the lawn and into the shadow of the locusts that lined the street. After a week or two the smell went away.

That was when people had begun to feel really sorry for her. People in our town, remembering how old lady Wyatt, her great-aunt, had gone completely crazy at last, believed that the Griersons held themselves a little too high for what they really were. None of the young men were quite good enough for Miss Emily and such. We had long thought of them as a tableau, Miss Emily a slender figure in white in the background, her father a spraddled silhouette in the foreground, his back to her and clutching a horsewhip, the two of them framed by the back-flung front door. So when she got to be thirty and was still single, we were not pleased exactly, but vindicated; even with insanity in the family she wouldn't have turned down all of her chances if they had really materialized.

When her father died, it got about that the house was all that was left to her; and in a way, people were glad. At last they could pity Miss Emily. Being left alone, and a pauper, she had become humanized. Now she too would know the old thrill and the old despair of a penny more or less.

The day after his death all the ladies prepared to call at the house and offer condolence and aid, as is our custom. Miss Emily met them at the door, dressed as usual and with no trace of grief on her face. She told them that her father was not dead. She did that for three days, with the ministers calling on her, and the doctors, trying to persuade her to let them dispose of the body. Just as they were about to resort to law and force, she broke down, and they buried her father quickly.

We did not say she was crazy then. We believed she had to do that. We remembered all the young men her father had driven away, and we knew that with nothing left, she would have to cling to that which had robbed her, as people will.

III

She was sick for a long time. When we saw her again, her hair was cut short, making her look like a girl, with a vague resemblance to those angels in colored church windows—sort of tragic and serene.

The town had just let the contracts for paving the sidewalks, and in the summer after her father's death they began the work. The construction company came with niggers and mules and machinery, and a foreman named Homer Barron, a Yankee—a big, dark, ready man, with a big voice and eyes lighter than his face. The little boys would follow in groups to hear him cuss the niggers, and the niggers singing in time to the rise and fall of picks. Pretty soon he knew everybody in town. Whenever you heard a lot of laughing anywhere about the square, Homer Barron would be in the center of the group. Presently we began to see him and Miss Emily on Sunday afternoons driving in the yellow-wheeled buggy and the matched team of bays from the livery stable.

At first we were glad that Miss Emily would have an interest, because the ladies all said, "Of course a Grierson would not think seriously of a Northerner, a day laborer." But there were still others, older people, who said that even grief could not cause a real lady to forget *noblesse oblige*—without calling it *noblesse oblige*. They just said, "Poor Emily. Her kinsfolk should come to her." She had some kin in Alabama; but years ago her father had fallen out with them over the estate of old lady Wyatt, the crazy woman, and there was no communication between the two families. They had not even been represented at the funeral.

And as soon as the old people said, "Poor Emily," the whispering began. "Do you suppose it's really so?" they said to one another. "Of course it is. What else could . . ." This behind their hands; rustling of craned silk and satin behind jalousies closed upon the sun of Sunday afternoon as the thin, swift clop-clop-clop of the matched team passed: "Poor Emily."

She carried her head high enough—even when we believed that she was fallen. It was as if she demanded more than ever the recognition of her dignity as the last Grierson; as if it had wanted that touch of earthiness to reaffirm her imperviousness. Like when she bought the rat poison, the arsenic. That was over a year after they had begun to say "Poor Emily," and while the two female cousins were visiting her.

"I want some poison," she said to the druggist. She was over thirty then, still a slight woman, though thinner than usual, with cold, haughty black eyes in a face the flesh of which was strained across the temples and about the eyesockets as you imagine a lighthouse-keeper's face ought to look. "I want some poison," she said.

"Yes, Miss Emily. What kind? For rats and such? I'd recom—"   35

"I want the best you have. I don't care what kind."

The druggist named several. "They'll kill anything up to an elephant. But what you want is—"

"Arsenic," Miss Emily said. "Is that a good one?"

"Is . . . arsenic? Yes, ma'am. But what you want—"

"I want arsenic."   40

The druggist looked down at her. She looked back at him, erect, her face like a strained flag. "Why, of course," the druggist said. "If that's what you want. But the law requires you to tell what you are going to use it for."

Miss Emily just stared at him, her head tilted back in order to look him eye for eye, until he looked away and went and got the arsenic and wrapped it up. The Negro delivery boy brought her the package; the druggist didn't come back. When she opened the package at home there was written on the box, under the skull and bones: "For rats."

IV

So the next day we all said, "She will kill herself"; and we said it would be the best thing. When she had first begun to be seen with Homer Barron, we had said, "She will marry him." Then we said, "She will persuade him yet," because Homer himself had remarked—he liked men, and it was known that he drank with the younger men in the Elks' Club—that he was not a marrying man. Later we said, "Poor Emily" behind the jalousies as they passed on Sunday afternoon in the glittering buggy, Miss Emily with her head high and Homer Barron with his hat cocked and a cigar in this teeth, reins and whip in a yellow glove.

Then some of the ladies began to say that it was a disgrace to the town and a bad example to the young peple. The men did not want to interfere, but at last the ladies forced the Baptist minister—Miss Emily's people were Episcopal—to call upon her. He would never divulge what happened during that interview, but he refused to go back again. The next Sunday they again drove about the streets, and the following day the minister's wife wrote to Miss Emily's relations in Alabama.

So she had blood-kin under her roof again and we sat back to watch develop- 45
ments. At first nothing happened. Then we were sure that they were to be married. We learned that Miss Emily had been to the jeweler's and ordered a man's toilet set in silver, with the letters H.B. on each piece. Two days later we learned that she had bought a complete outfit of men's clothing, including a nightshirt, and we said, "They are married." We were really glad. We were glad because the two female cousins were even more Grierson than Miss Emily had ever been.

So we were not surprised when Homer Barron—the streets had been finished some time since—was gone. We were a little disappointed that there was not a public blowing-off, but we believed that he had gone on to prepare for Miss Emily's coming, or to give her a chance to get rid of the cousins. (By that time it was a cabal, and we were all Miss Emily's allies to help circumvent the cousins.) Sure enough, after another week they departed. And, as we had expected all along, within three days Homer Barron was back in town. A neighbor saw the Negro man admit him at the kitchen door at dusk one evening.

And that was the last we saw of Homer Barron. And of Miss Emily for some time. The Negro man went in and out with the market basket, but the front door remained closed. Now and then we would see her at a window for a moment, as the men did that night when they sprinkled the lime, but for almost six months she did not appear on the streets. Then we knew that this was to be expected too; as if that quality of her father which had thwarted her woman's life so many times had been too virulent and too furious to die.

When we next saw Miss Emily, she had grown fat and her hair was turning gray. During the next few years it grew grayer and grayer until it attained an even pepper-and-salt iron-gray, when it ceased turning. Up to the day of her death at seventy-four it was still that vigorous iron-gray, like the hair of an active man.

From that time on her front door remained closed, save for a period of six or seven years, when she was about forty, during which she gave lessons in china-painting. She fitted up a studio in one of the downstairs rooms, where the daughters and grand-daughters of Colonel Sartoris' contemporaries were sent to her with the same regularity and in the same spirit that they were sent on Sundays with a twenty-five cent piece for the collection plate. Meanwhile her taxes had been remitted.

The newer generation became the backbone and the spirit of the town, and the 50
painting pupils grew up and fell away and did not send their children to her with boxes of color and tedious brushes and pictures cut from the ladies' magazines. The front door closed upon the last one and remained closed for good. When the town got free postal delivery, Miss Emily alone refused to let them fasten the metal numbers above her door and attach a mailbox to it. She would not listen to them.

Daily, monthly, yearly we watched the Negro grow grayer and more stooped, going in and out with the market basket. Each December we sent her a tax notice, which would be returned by the post office a week later, unclaimed. Now and then we would see her in one of the downstairs windows—she had evidently shut up the top floor of the house—like the carven torso of an idol in a niche, looking or not looking at us, we could never tell which. Thus she passed from generation to generation—dear, inescapable, impervious, tranquil, and perverse.

And so she died. Fell ill in the house filled with dust and shadows, with only a doddering Negro man to wait on her. We did not even know she was sick; we had long since given up trying to get any information from the Negro. He talked to no one, probably not even to her, for his voice had grown harsh and rusty, as if from disuse.

She died in one of the downstairs rooms, in a heavy walnut bed with a curtain, her gray head propped on a pillow yellow and moldy with age and lack of sunlight.

V

The Negro met the first of the ladies at the front door and let them in, with their hushed, sibilant voices and their quick, curious glances, and then he disappeared. He walked right through the house and out the back and was not seen again.

The two female cousins came at once. They held the funeral on the second day, with the town coming to look at Miss Emily beneath a mass of bought flowers, with the crayon face of her father musing profoundly above the bier and the ladies sibilant and macabre; and the very old men—some in their brushed Confederate uniforms—on the porch and the lawn, talking of Miss Emily as if she had been a contemporary of theirs, believing that they had danced with her and courted her perhaps, confusing time with its mathematical progression, as the old do, to whom all the past is not a diminishing road, but, instead, a huge meadow which no winter ever quite touches, divided from them now by the narrow bottleneck of the most recent decade of years. 55

Already we knew that there was one room in that region above stairs which no one had seen in forty years, and which would have to be forced. They waited until Miss Emily was decently in the ground before they opened it.

The violence of breaking down the door seemed to fill this room with pervading dust. A thin, acrid pall as of the tomb seemed to lie everywhere upon this room decked and furnished as for a bridal: upon the valance curtains of faded rose color, upon the rose-shaded lights, upon the dressing table, upon the delicate array of crystal and the man's toilet things backed with tarnished silver, silver so tarnished that the monogram was obscured. Among them lay a collar and tie, as if they had just been removed, which, lifted, left upon the surface a pale crescent in the dust. Upon the chair hung the suit, carefully folded; beneath it the two mute shoes and the discarded socks.

The man himself lay in the bed.

For a long while we just stood there, looking down at the profound and fleshless grin. The body had apparently once lain in the attitude of an embrace, but now the long sleep that outlasts love, that conquers even the grimace of love, had cuckolded him. What was left of him, rotted beneath what was left of the nightshirt, had become inextricable from the bed in which he lay; and upon him and upon the pillow beside him lay that even coating of the patient and biding dust.

Then we noticed that in the second pillow was the indentation of a head. One of us lifted something from it, and leaning forward, that faint and invisible dust dry and acrid in the nostrils, we saw a long strand of iron-gray hair. 60

THE RECEPTIVE READER

1. Faulkner said that the seed of this story was a picture in his mind "of the strand of hair on the pillow. . . . Simply a picture of a strand of hair on the pillow in the abandoned house." How does the strand of hair sum up what happened in this story or what is important in this story?

2. How and why does Faulkner's story depart from straightforward chronological storytelling? Where and how does Faulkner introduce the plot elements most essential to your understanding of the story? Can you reconstruct from the author's *flashbacks* a chronological sequence of events?

3. What is the keynote in Faulkner's treatment of the *setting*—Miss Emily's house, her street, the town?

4. How essential to the story is Faulkner's treatment of tradition and the Old South? What is Faulkner's attitude toward Colonel Sartoris' generation and the "next generation, with its more modern ideas"? What is the meaning of *noblesse oblige,* and what is the role of this concept in the story?

5. What picture emerges of Miss Emily as the *main character?* Is there a central clue to her personality? Is she a creature of her environment? What explains the attitude of the townspeople toward her?

6. Poetic justice is meted out to a character in poetry or fiction when he or she is justly punished for an offense, whether or not it was punishable according to law. Is Homer Barron the victim of poetic justice?

7. Faulkner is known for a *style* rich in unusual words, provocative images, and emotional overtones. What is the meaning of *coquettish, macabre, impervious, perverse?* How are these words related to the prevailing mood of the story? What is the effect on the reader of comparing Emily to a "carven torso of an idol in a niche"? What other striking imaginative comparisons play a role in the story?

8. The word *grotesque* describes literature or art that produces mixed reactions— emotions of terror or disgust mingling with dark or shuddery humor. Where do such mixed effects play a role in this story?

9. One student wrote : "Time does not pass in linear chronological fashion in this story; the plot does not move forward through the traditional build-up of tension to climax and denouement. However, in its indirect and apparently meandering way, the story leads to a much more startling climax than could have been possible in a classic short-story format." Can you show whether the student was right?

THE PERSONAL RESPONSE

As you read the story, do you feel you are expected to admire Miss Emily, condemn her, write her off as an eccentric? In what ways does the author steer your reactions about her? What are your feelings about her? Do you think you would feel different about her if Faulkner had told her story in a more traditional fashion? How or why?

CROSS-REFERENCES—For Discussion or Writing

✧ Compare and contrast the Old South of Faulkner's "A Rose for Emily" with the New South of Mason's "Shiloh." What is the relationship between the setting and the characters in each story?

✧ Compare and contrast plot structure in this story and in a more traditional story like Welty's "A Visit of Charity" or Malamud's "The Magic Barrel." How do differences in the story line affect the overall impact of each story?

✧ Compare and contrast Jackson's "The Lottery" and Faulkner's "A Rose for Emily" as modern horror stories. How does their use of horror differ from its use in popular entertainment? What use do the two authors make of the grotesque—a mixture of terror and dark humor?

WRITING ABOUT LITERATURE
4. Charting the Plot (Focus on Revision)

The Writing Workshop   In writing about plot, try to focus on the key question: How does the plot serve the story as a whole? Is it a mere scaffolding—a mere opportunity for characters to talk and act, to show who they are? Or does something important develop, take shape? Is the story perhaps headed toward some climactic event—some goal? Does it move toward a recognition or *epiphany*—some insight that strikes us forcibly, illuminating in a flash something that was previously obscure?

Do not just retell the story. Ask yourself: What am I going to do with this story? In the sequence of miscellaneous events, try to find a ground plan. Look for the pattern—the design in the carpet. (When you start writing in the "and-then," "and-then" mode, your paper is likely to be in trouble.) Consider guidelines like the following:

❖ *Avoid mere plot summaries.* Use them only if they are needed to help the readers find their bearings. (Summaries can be useful for giving an initial overview—they can make the reader see the overall line of development in a complex or multilayered story.)

❖ *Look at what sets a story in motion.* Look at key characters and their unmet needs, unfulfilled desires, or hidden agendas. Look at a situation that has in it potential sources of conflict: festering resentments, fatal misunderstandings.

❖ *Identify major stages.* Make sure your readers get a sense of the overall development of the story. Highlight turning points. Show how a story builds to a climactic event. Show how a conflict plays itself out and reaches a resolution.

❖ *Disentangle major threads.* Look for **polarities**—the possible play of polar opposites, such as the romantic and the realistic strands in Malamud's "The Magic Barrel."

❖ *Look for features that reinforce the overall pattern.* Look for examples of **foreshadowing**—for early hints of what is to come. Look for **recurrence** of key elements, for passages that echo earlier issues or concerns.

❖ *Take a second look at apparent detours or digressions.* See if you can relate apparently minor details to the larger pattern.

Instructor's Comments and Revision   Much revision of student writing used to be little more than retyping with a few cosmetic touches. With the coming of computers, changes in a previous draft have become much easier to make. Whether you use a typewriter or a word processor, take seriously editorial suggestions that ask you to do some real rewriting, some real rethinking.

Learn to respond to feedback from an instructor or editor as you revise a first draft. Study the samples of instructors' comments in the material that follows. Look at rewrites of passages in response to an instructor's comments.

✧ *Pay special attention to comments on your opening paragraphs.* Does the focus of your paper become clear enough? Does your reader get a preview of your overall approach? Should you spell out your main point or **thesis** more fully or more clearly early in your paper? (Remember that in real life many readers don't go on beyond the opening of an essay if they find it unfocused, murky, or confusing.)

✧ *Respond to suggestions for strengthening your overall plan.* Consider if reshuffling material might make for a stronger progression—for instance, from the fairly obvious to the controversial or new.

✧ *Respond to advice for improving the flow of material.* Respond to suggestions for building up a rich texture of comment, quotation, and interpretation.

ORIGINAL: After his first meeting with Salzman, the strange little matchmaker, Leo expresses doubts about the wisdom of having a bride chosen by someone else. Malamud writes,

> Leo was low in spirits. . . . He explained it as arising from Salzman's failure to produce a suitable bride for him. He did not care for his type of clientele. But when Leo found himself hesitating over whether to seek out another matchmaker, one more polished than Pinye, he wondered if it could be—his protestations to the contrary, and although he honored his father and mother—that he did not, in essence, care for the matchmaking institution? This thought he quickly put out of his mind.

COMMENT: You are probably using too many block quotations ("chunk quotations"—because they can make your paper seem chunky or lumpy). Save them to clinch an argument or highlight a major turning point. Try to work short, apt quotations into the flow of your argument.

REVISED: The first meeting with Salzman, the strange little matchmaker, does not go well. Leo is disheartened and expresses doubts about the wisdom of having a bride chosen by someone else. He entertains notions of hiring another matchmaker, someone "more polished than Pinye." But when Leo examines his deeper feelings, he wonders "if it could be—his protestations to the contrary, and although he honored his father and mother—that he did not, in essence, care for the matchmaking institution?" Although Leo has not yet realized it, this question is the beginning of the conflict between his traditional upbringing and his romantic nature. Although he "quickly put [this thought] out of his mind," it has planted a niggling suspicion that reaches full bloom as the story progresses.

✧ *Pay special attention to comments on weak transitions.* Where did the reader fail to see a logical connection that you thought was there? Be sure to respond to questions like "Why is this in here at this point? How are these two sections of your paper *related*? How does this fit into your overall plan?"

❖ *Respond to suggestions for strengthening your conclusion.*

ORIGINAL: Jackson's "The Lottery" showed how people will do all kinds of crazy things, even things they don't really want to do, in the name of tradition.

COMMENT: Perfunctory or lame conclusion? What *is* the force of tradition? Why does it seem to carry such weight?

REVISED: Jackson's "The Lottery" shows how tradition is like a subliminal force—because of it, people will do all kinds of crazy things, even things they don't really want to. We witness the peer pressure involved in tradition, forcing people to do something just because everyone else is doing it, and no one else is questioning it. As the story shows, human beings have a strong need to belong and be accepted by their society. This need causes them to want to conform, blindly and almost unconsciously, to the rules that their society has set up. Even stronger than tradition itself are the peer pressure and the human need for acceptance that fuel it.

Study the following sample student paper. Does it make you more conscious of the role of plot in giving shape to a story as a whole?

SAMPLE STUDENT PAPER

Magic and Reality

"The Magic Barrel." In its very title, Bernard Malamud hints at the paradoxical nature of his short story. "The Magic Barrel" prepares us, the readers, to expect a fairy tale; it asks us to enter imaginatively into a world where miracles are possible. On the other hand, "The Magic Barrel" also gives us pause. "The Magic Barrel?" A rounded wooden vessel used to store wine or fish, magical? Had Malamud chosen "The Magic Well" or "The Magic Chalice" as his title, we would have been less puzzled, less intrigued. Adept at creating dualities and contrasts, Malamud invests his plot with "magic" elements as well as with sobering, realistic ones, just as he does his title. Malamud's plot introduces us to the lonely young scholar and the eccentric, enigmatic matchmaker, both likely inhabitants of a fairy-tale world. However, it also reveals conditions all too familiar to many in their everyday reality: the desperate lovelessness of the scholar and the harsh poverty of the matchmaker. As the plot is unveiled, Bernard Malamud's story is both like and unlike a fairy tale, ultimately a story in which fantasy and reality blend.

As "The Magic Barrel" begins, we are introduced to a person who is well suited to the world of the fairy tale: Leo Finkle, a rabbinical student, lives in a room which is "small, almost meager . . . though crowded with books." Leo has been studying for six years and is about to be ordained. From the first words of the story, Leo appears to be the stereotypical poor, lonely scholar, possessing little in the way of worldly goods but rich in spirituality, a kind of inner prosperity. We would wish a devoted companion for such a worthy, lonely fellow, and we are not disappointed. Leo, the author tells us, has decided to enlist the services of Pinye Salzman, a professional matchmaker, or "commercial cupid" as Malamud calls him . Malamud prepares the reader for a traditional romantic story, and he does not disappoint. The plot follows Leo as he listens without satisfaction to the descriptions of Salzman's clients, and as he meets, without enthusiasm, one of the eligible women. It follows Leo after he decides he must have romantic love before marriage, and after he finds a small, displaced photograph in an envelope of snapshots loaned to him by Salzman to help him in his quest. In true romantic style, Leo chases around the city attempting to locate the matchmaker (and so the woman) as frantically as Prince Charming's courtiers tried to locate the owner of the lone glass slipper. In true romantic style, Leo finds he has fallen for the one woman he should not have, Stella, the "shameless" daughter Salzman considers dead, a woman whose picture found its way into the matchmaker's envelope only by mistake (a marvelous, unlikely coincidence). In true romantic style, Leo pursues her anyway, and, with the power of wishful thinking triumphing over probability fairy-tale style, he finds her. Leo's discovery of his need for romantic love and the actions he takes to fulfill that need are suited to the world of fairy tales.

However, Malamud's plot not only explores the romantic occurrences in Leo's life, it also explores the more mundane, realistic ones. If Leo is not Prince Charming, he is at least a close relative. He is, however, also very human. The plot takes him through experiences that belong in the potentially painful real world rather than in the fairy-tale world. Leo has been studying diligently to become a rabbi for six years, but we also learn that his motives were not particularly admirable. "I think," Leo confesses to Lily Hirschorn, startling himself as much as the reader, "that I came to God not because I love Him, but because I did not." After this revelation, Leo experiences the worst week of his life. "With shocking force," he realizes that apart from his parents, he had never loved anyone. "It seemed to Leo that his whole life stood starkly revealed and he saw himself, for the first time, as he truly was—unloved and loveless." This young student stops eating and begins to lose weight. As his health suffers, he stops attending class. Malamud eventually allows Leo to "regain his composure," but this section of the plot takes the student about as far down as a human can go. The romantic events in Leo's life may predominate in the story, but they do not create an unrealistic story. Leo earns his romance the hardest way possible.

Malamud's most ambiguous scene occurs at the end of "The Magic Barrel." On one hand, it is the most romantic moment. On the other, it is curious and ambiguous. In this scene, after he has extracted some cooperation from Salzman, Leo succeeds in meeting Stella, the love of his life. She seems a bit wild, but not in an incorrigible way. She stands by a lamppost, smoking, but she waits "uneasily and shyly," her eyes filled with "desperate innocence." Experiencing "violins and lit candles" revolving in the sky, Leo rushes toward her, a bouquet of flowers outstretched in his hands. This moment, the most romantic in the story, is love found. However, its ambiguity lies in Salzman's presence and actions. The matchmaker stands "around the corner . . . leaning against a wall," chanting "prayers for the dead." Salzman could be blessing the union in the only way he knows how while steadfastly opposing Stella's earlier lifestyle, thus contributing to a romantic ending. Conversely, he could be offering his last prayers to a daughter whom he is deserting. He could be saying a farewell to one who he thinks is making her biggest and final error in an already "wicked" life, contributing to a modern, realistic ending. Malamud's plot follows the fairy-tale romantic events in Leo's life as well as the soberingly realistic ones. In his ambiguous ending, the author illustrates both views in one stroke.

Bernard Malamud's "The Magic Barrel" navigates between fantasy and reality. Some of Leo's acts, such as finding the woman of his dreams in a displaced photograph, desperately searching for her, then finding her, are very romantic, befitting a fairy tale. Other events in Leo's life, such as his realization that he is "unloved and loveless" and his ensuing crisis, belong in the realm of reality, not the fairy tale. In choosing to craft his plot to encompass both realms, Malamud creates a story that satisfies both the romantic and the pragmatist in us, the readers. He reminds us that fairy tales were created by real people; they are based on real life, not separate from it. Romantic happenings and happy endings can be and should be a part of everyday reality.

QUESTIONS

Does this paper add something to your own reading and understanding of the story? What is the overall thesis of this paper? How well do you think it fits the story? How well does the student writer use evidence to support it? Where do you want to disagree or take issue? How do you react to the ending of the paper?

5 POINT OF VIEW
Windows on the World

*The deepest quality of a work of art will always be the
quality of the mind of the producer.*

HENRY JAMES

*The author is the central intelligence through whose eyes
and mind we see the story.*

MARTHA COX

FOCUS ON POINT OF VIEW

Whatever reality a story creates for us is always a selection. We look at the world through the eyes of the writer. We attend to what the author has brought into focus; we look at it from his or her angle of vision. No objective reality exists "out there" that is the same for everyone. What we call reality is our *perception* of reality, a picture we have constructed from input that is necessarily fragmentary, biased, incomplete. We read a story in part to share imaginatively in a writer's perception of reality, a writer's vision of the world. Often that vision, that perception, is as unmistakable as a signature.

Much modern fiction, like much critical discussion of fiction, takes this awareness of the angle of vision in a story an important step further. Quite apart from the author who is writing the story, who is telling the story *in the story?* Who is the **narrator** observing the events—observing them from what angle? In much nineteenth-century fiction, the **omniscient** author could pretend to be God—to know everything, to read the minds of all the different characters in a story, to be in several places at once to observe dispersed events. But this all-knowingness is unlike the way we take in reality in our own lives. We perceive reality according to our limited lights. We try to piece together the truth from partial and contradictory information.

Much modern fiction opts for a **limited** point of view. In Faulkner's "A Rose for Emily," we know of Miss Emily only through what the townspeople had a chance to observe. We share in what they had the opportunity to hear, to suspect, and to speculate. In a modern story, we are often aware of the **reflector**—a person inside or outside the story through whose eyes and ears we

148

register details and events. We may take in only what a bystander or an observer at the scene would actually have witnessed. Or we may share in the private thoughts and feelings of only one of the characters, seeing the world through his or her eyes. We then become more conscious of the window that a story opens on the world.

THE LIMITED POINT OF VIEW

The effect of compactness and instantaneity sought in the short story is attained mainly by the observance of two "unities"—the old traditional one of time, and that other, more modern and complex, which requires that any rapidly enacted episode shall be seen through only one pair of eyes.

EDITH WHARTON

A short story condenses a particular vision of life. Much modern discussion of fiction is concerned with examining the angle of vision. From what vantage point does the person telling the story look at the world? Modern writers tend to be self-conscious, self-aware of the *how* as well of the *what* of their writing. They have generally moved away from traditional ways of envisioning the events of a story in order to limit the narrator's point of view. Here are some possible variations of narrative point of view. (At times, these may blend or overlap.)

The Omniscient Author   The traditional **omniscient,** all-knowing author had access to the private thoughts and feelings of everyone in a novel or a story. A nineteenth-century novelist like George Eliot (pen name of Marian Evans) knew what went on in the minds and hearts of her several characters. Of course, what the so-called omniscient author chose to tell the readers was a limited selection—the author merely acted as if she "knew all." The typical objection of her twentieth-century successors was that in our own reality we see the world from our particular window. A story should limit itself to what can be taken in by "one pair of eyes."

The Intruding Author   Some authors serve the reader as guides to their fictional world. The **intruding** author feels free to comment, to chat with us as the readers, to take us into his or her confidence. We are very much aware of the author's presence as the narrator. It is as if every so often the author stepped into the story from the outside, interrupting it to turn to us and offer asides, philosophical reflections, a personal view of life.

Third Person Objective   In many stories, there is no "I, the author" (or "I, the narrator") and no "You, the reader." The story talks about its characters in the "third person": *She* did so-and-so; *he* did such-and-such. What the characters think and feel is seen from the outside. In much early modern fiction, the stance of the author was: We are not mind readers; we can never enter totally into someone else's world of thinking and feeling. We *can* try to be impartial observers, faithful to what we see and hear. In a Hemingway story, for instance, the author often assumes the stance of the honest witness, the incorruptible reporter. It is as if the author were saying to us, "I tell you what I see—you draw your own conclusions." In such an **objective** narrative, there is little or no comment—a minimum of editorializing, judging, preaching. Our gain as readers is a sense of integrity—no one is trying to sell us a subjective interpretation. The limitation is that much of what we see and hear we can only speculate about; we never enter fully into the thoughts and emotions of the people in the story.

First Person Autobiographical   Much writing is at the opposite pole from the objective-observer stance of the Hemingway school. In many stories that seem deeply felt, we sense that the authors are speaking in thinly disguised form about their own childhood, their own families, their own conflicts or alienation. They are deeply involved, and their involvement, their commitment, shows. The "I" speaking in the story is talking about scenes and people from personal experience—perhaps with names and dates altered. Such writing may have a confessional tone; the writer may be unburdening his or her heart. Writing the story or novel may have been a way of coming to terms with traumatic happenings, with feelings of guilt. The act of writing may have been therapy or catharsis—a cleansing, a clearing of the slate. First-person narratives often have a special fascination; they create a special effect of intimacy. Someone is taking us into his or her confidence. We have a chance to look beyond the public façade.

However, even then, the **autobiographical** material is shaped by the creative imagination. Autobiographical fact shades over into fiction. The "I" speaking to us in the story then becomes a **persona**—an assumed identity. (A persona was originally the mask actors wore on the classical Greek stage; through it the sound of their voices came forth to reach the spectator—it "sounded through.") The distance between person and persona varies greatly from story to story, or from writer to writer. The persona of the narrator may have much in common with the author. Or else it may represent the author in disguise, as if wearing a mask. Finally, it may be a freely created imaginary identity, incorporating some elements or traits from the author's personality or experience.

First Person Observer   The fictionalized "I" will play different roles in different stories. We may see the story through the eyes of someone who is on the sidelines, who is not a major player. This person then becomes our scout, our reliable source, our "chosen interpreter." The person becomes our **reflector**—anything that happens in the story will reach us by way of his or her perceptions. Edith Wharton, in *The Writing of Fiction* (1925), spelled out a modern credo when she said that to create the "effect of probability" it was necessary never to let the character who serves as a reflector record anything not naturally within his register. It should be the storyteller's first care to choose this reflecting mind deliberately, as one would choose a building site, or decide upon the orientation of one's house, and when this is done, to live inside the mind chosen, trying to feel, see, and react exactly as the latter would, no more, no less, and, above all, no otherwise.

First Person Protagonist The **protagonist**—the main character, the hero or heroine—in a story may tell his or her story in the first person. This perspective places us at the center of the action. It is likely to draw us into the conflicts at the heart of the story; it may force us to take sides. In Alice Munro's "Boys and Girls," told in the first-person-protagonist mode, it is hard for us to look at the events from the point of view of the mother or of the younger brother. The feelings of the young girl telling the story are too strong, inevitably coloring our reactions.

The Naive Narrator A special kind of **irony** may make us react to the perspective of the narrator with a wry smile. We smile at the **naive narrator** who seems to know and understand less than an alert reader. Mark Twain's Huckleberry Finn in the classic of the same name watches the world with wide-open innocent eyes—recognizing human duplicity or vindictiveness long after the more knowing reader. Huck may be foolish to be more trusting than we are, but at the same time we may envy him the youthful innocence that makes him less bitter or cynical than we are.

Interior Monologue James Joyce and other early moderns experimented with the **stream-of-consciousness** technique. We enter into the mind of the narrator, sharing in a flow of thought and feeling. We listen in on the **interior monologue.** The narrative is not linear or logical but moves by leaps and bounds of association. We may be distracted by bodily sensations (like the feel of a wet bar of soap in a trouser pocket). We may be sent off on a tangent by a scent, or by a remark that rekindles a long-forgotten memory. However, like our own private thoughts and feelings, the narrator's flow of thought—trivial or pathetic much of the time—is likely to circle back sooner or later to the hopes, anxieties, or traumas that really matter.

However, many stories that take us into the mind of the narrator make us follow a more focused, more continuous interior monologue. We might call it an *edited* interior monologue. In Tillie Olsen's "I Stand Here Ironing," we share in the private thoughts of the narrator. However, her memories, thoughts, and feelings are focused on the hardships, struggles, and regrets related to the bringing up of her oldest child. No current distractions—thoughts of the next meal, worries about an appointment—interfere with the stock taking, the weighing of responsibilities, at the heart of the story.

When you look at how point of view shapes what you experience in a story, remember that critical categories tend to be neater than the realities of creative work. Different perspectives may blend or alternate. In Katherine Anne Porter's "The Jilting of Granny Weatherall," you follow an interior monologue in which the central character's blurred observations of events in the sickroom and her memories and regrets intersect. But this strand alternates with objectively recorded conversations that the central character no longer hears or understands.

JUXTAPOSITIONS

The Perspective of Youth

Stories of youth and adolescence often adopt a distinctive, limited point of view. They see the world through the eyes of people less experienced, less knowing than we are. Children and adolescents have an incomplete, unfinished view of the world. Much of what happens to them they experience for the first time. Both of the following stories, written a century apart, look at the world from the perspective of youth. How and how well does the author control the point of view in each story? What does the reader gain, and what does the reader lose, by looking at the world from a limited perspective?

ANTON CHEKHOV   (1860–1904)

The first story is by Anton Chekhov, a nineteenth-century Russian writer from a lower-class family who became famous as a playwright and as a writer of short stories. He helped chart the directions for much short fiction in the twentieth century; his well-focused, tightly unified narratives departed from earlier, more leisurely forms of storytelling. His stories are self-contained— seizing on a pregnant moment and making it the center of a well-focused narrative.

Chekhov's family had only recently risen from the status of peasants and serfs, the lowest rung of nineteenth-century czarist Russia. After a rigidly religious upbringing, he tried to escape from poverty through work as a hack writer and journalist. He studied and practiced medicine but eventually devoted more and more of his time to writing. His plays—*Three Sisters, The Cherry Orchard*—are still part of the modern theatrical repertory. What features of the following story remind you that it takes its readers back to the prerevolutionary czarist past? What do you think might account for the appeal the story has for modern readers?

Vanka   1886

Vanka Zhukov, a nine-year-old boy, who had been apprenticed to Alyahin the shoemaker these three months, did not go to bed on Christmas Eve. After his master and mistress and the journeymen had gone to midnight Mass, he got an inkpot and a penholder with a rusty nib out of the master's cupboard and, having spread out a crumpled sheet of paper, began writing. Before he formed the first letter he looked fearfully at the doors and windows several times, shot a glance at the dark icon, at either side of which stretched shelves filled with lasts, and heaved a broken sigh. He was kneeling before a bench on which his paper lay.

"Dear Granddaddy, Konstantin Makarych," he wrote. "And I am writing you a letter. I wish you a merry Christmas and everything good from the Lord God. I have neither father nor mother, you alone are left me."

Vanka shifted his glance to the dark window on which flickered the reflection of his candle and vividly pictured his grandfather to himself. Employed as a watchman by the Zhivaryovs, he was a short, thin, but extraordinarily lively and nimble old man of about sixty-five whose face was always crinkled with laughter and who had a toper's eyes. By day he slept in the servants' kitchen or cracked jokes with the cook; at night, wrapped in an ample sheepskin coat, he made the rounds of the estate, shaking his clapper. The old bitch, Brownie, and the dog called Wriggles, who had a black coat and a long body like a weasel's, followed him with hanging heads. This Wriggles was extraordinarily deferential and demonstrative, looked with equally friendly eyes both at his masters and at strangers, but did not enjoy a good reputation. His deference and meekness concealed the most Jesuitical spite. No one knew better than he how to creep up behind you and suddenly snap at your leg, how to slip into the icehouse, or how to steal a hen from a peasant. More than once his hind legs had been all but broken, twice he had been hanged, every week he was whipped till he was half dead, but he always managed to revive.

At the moment Grandfather was sure to be standing at the gates, screwing up his eyes at the bright-red windows of the church stamping his felt boots, and cracking jokes with the servants. His clapper was tied to his belt. He was clapping his hands, shrugging with the cold, and, with a senile titter, pinching now the housemaid, now the cook.

"Shall we have a pinch of snuff?" he was saying, offering the women his snuffbox.   5

They each took a pinch and sneezed. Grandfather, indescribably delighted, went off into merry peals of laughter and shouted:

"Peel it off, it has frozen on!"

The dogs too are given a pinch of snuff. Brownie sneezes, wags her head, and walks away offended. Wriggles is too polite to sneeze and only wags his tail. And the weather is glorious. The air is still, clear, and fresh. The night is dark, but one can see the whole village with its white roofs and smoke streaming out of the chimneys, the trees silvery with hoarfrost, the snowdrifts. The entire sky is studded with gaily twinkling stars and the Milky Way is as distinctly visible as though it had been washed and rubbed with snow for the holiday. . . .

Vanka sighed, dipped his pen into the ink and went on writing:

"And yesterday I got it hot. The master pulled me out into the courtyard by the   10 hair and gave me a hiding with a knee-strap because I was rocking the baby in its cradle and happened to fall asleep. And last week the mistress ordered me to clean a herring and I began with the tail, and she took the herring and jabbed me in the mug with it. The helpers make fun of me, send me to the pothouse for vodka and tell me to steal pickles for them from the master, and the master hits me with anything that comes handy. And there is nothing to eat. In the morning they give me bread, for dinner porridge, and in the evening bread again. As for tea or cabbage soup, the master and mistress bolt it all themselves. And they tell me to sleep in the entry, and when the baby cries I don't sleep at all, but rock the cradle. Dear Granddaddy, for God's sake have pity on me, take me away from here, take me home to the village, it's more than I can bear. I bow down at your feet and I will pray to God for you forever, take me away from here or I'll die."

Vanka puckered his mouth, rubbed his eyes with his black fist, and gave a sob.

"I will grind your snuff for you," he continued, "I will pray to God for you, and if anything happens, you may thrash me all you like. And if you think there's no situation for me, I will beg the manager for Christ's sake to let me clean boots, or I will take Fedka's place as a shepherd boy. Dear Granddaddy, it's more than I can bear, it will simply be the death of me. I thought of running away to the village, but I have no boots and I am afraid of the frost. And in return for this when I grow big, I will feed you and won't let anybody do you any harm, and when you die I will pray for the repose of your soul, just as for my Mom's.

"Moscow is a big city. The houses are all the kind the gentry live in, and there are lots of horses, but no sheep, and the dogs are not fierce. The boys here don't go caroling, carrying the star at Christmas, and they don't let anyone sing in the choir, and once in a shop window I saw fishing-hooks for sale all fitted up with a line, for every kind of fish, very fine ones, there was even one hook that will hold a forty-pound sheatfish. And I saw shops where there are all sorts of guns, like the master's at home, so maybe each one of them is a hundred rubles. And in butchers' shops there are woodcocks and partridge and hares, but where they shoot them the clerks won't tell.

"Dear Granddaddy, when they have a Christmas tree with presents at the master's, do get a gilt walnut and put it away in the little green chest. Ask the young lady, Olga Ignatyevna, for it, say it's for Vanka."

Vanka heaved a broken sigh and again stared at the window. He recalled that it was his grandfather who always went to the forest to get the Christmas tree for the master's family and that he would take his grandson with him. It was a jolly time! Grandfather grunted, the frost crackled, and, not to be outdone, Vanka too made a cheerful noise in his throat. Before chopping down the Christmas tree, Grandfather would smoke a pipe, slowly take a pinch of snuff, and poke fun at Vanka who looked chilled to the bone. The young firs draped in hoarfrost stood still, waiting to see which of them was to die. Suddenly, coming out of nowhere, a hare would dart across the snowdrifts like an arrow. Grandfather could not keep from shouting: "Hold him, hold him, hold him! Ah, the bob-tailed devil!"

15

When he had cut down the fir tree, Grandfather would drag it to the master's house, and there they would set to work decorating it. The young lady, Olga Ignatyevna, Vanka's favorite, was the busiest of all. When Vanka's mother, Pelageya, was alive and a chambermaid in the master's house, the young lady used to give him goodies, and, having nothing with which to occupy herself, taught him to read and write, to count up to a hundred, and even to dance the quadrille. When Pelageya died, Vanka had been relegated to the servants' kitchen to stay with his grandfather, and from the kitchen to the shoemaker's.

"Do come, dear Granddaddy," Vanka went on. "For Christ's sake, I beg you, take me away from here. Have pity on me, an unhappy orphan, here everyone beats me, and I am terribly hungry, and I am so blue, I can't tell you how, I keep crying. And the other day the master hit me on the head with a last, so that I fell down and it was a long time before I came to. My life is miserable, worse than a dog's—I also send greetings to Alyona, one-eyed Yegorka and the coachman, and don't give my harmonica to anyone. I remain, your grandson, Ivan Zhukov, dear Granddaddy, do come."

Vanka twice folded the sheet covered with writing and put it into an envelope he had bought for a kopeck the previous day. He reflected a while, then dipped the pen into the ink and wrote the address:

To Grandfather in the village

Then he scratched himself, thought a little, and added: *Konstantin Makarych*. Glad that no one had interrupted him at his writing, he put on his cap and, without slipping on his coat, ran out into the street with nothing over his shirt.

The clerks at the butchers' whom he had questioned the day before had told him that letters were dropped into letter boxes and from the boxes they were carried all over the world in troikas with ringing bells and drunken drivers. Vanka ran to the nearest letter box and thrust the precious letter into the slit.

An hour later, lulled by sweet hopes, he was fast asleep. In his dream he saw the stove. On the stove sat grandfather, his bare legs hanging down, and read the letter to the cooks. Near the stove was Wriggles, wagging his tail.

20

THE RECEPTIVE READER

1. What would you include in a *capsule portrait* of Vanka?

2. Why do you think Chekhov does not include any specific reference to the boy's mistreatment until we have read one-third of the story?

3. What details in the story keep reminding us of Vanka's limited *point of view*? (Does anything get into the story that should really be beyond the central character's ken?)

4. Where is the author in this story, and why does he adopt this limited perspective? What is the appeal for the reader—what do you gain (or lose) from looking at the world through Vanka's eyes?

THE PERSONAL RESPONSE

For you, does this story capture essential elements in a child's view of the world? (Does its picture of childhood seem dated or slanted in some way?)

THE CREATIVE DIMENSION

Write a letter that you might have written when you were nearer Vanka's age. Write about a topic that seemed important at the time; address your letter to someone who was then important in your life.

JOYCE CAROL OATES (born 1938)

Writers are always under attack, usually for not being "moral" enough. . . . There is insufficient recognition of the fact that one of the traditional roles of the writer is to bear witness—not simply to the presumably good things in life, the uplifting, life-enhancing, happy things, but to their polar opposites as well.

JOYCE CAROL OATES

The second story in this pairing is by Joyce Carol Oates, whose disturbing stories often make the reader look at familiar reality from a startling new perspective. Oates was thirty-one and one of the youngest writers so honored when she received the National Book Award for fiction in 1970. In the course of her career, she has published over twenty novels and over fifteen collections of short stories, not counting books of poems, essays, and literary criticism as well as plays and countless articles and reviews. Her best-known novel, *Them* (1961), is set in Detroit, where she taught. It takes place in a violent urban landscape that many Americans would prefer to ignore or block out. Her method is to activate a "brimming" memory not merely of images but also of the emotions connected with them—and to combine the results with systematic research of a topic (like boxing) or a period in history.

Oates has a gift for taking us into a reality that at first we may accept only reluctantly as part of our world. Her characters are often defined by what they are not; they often upset or annoy the reader by their failure to fit the reader's assumptions about what is normal, comforting, reassuring. Her characters tend to be "opaque, ungiving, uncharming; they have the taciturn qualities that come with the kind of people they are—heavy, hallucinated, outside the chatty middle class" (Alfred Kazin).

Oates' stories often call for a change in our usual perspective, making us try out a new and different point of view. Her story "Stalking" focuses on Gretchen, the central character, and takes us into her own private world. For the duration of the story, like it or not, we live in Gretchen's universe. We see what is in her field of vision. (What do we see?) We are tuned in to her ongoing daydream or fantasy. (What is it about? What role does it play in the story?) We return with her to her suburban home. (What is her connection with home and family?)

Stalking   1972

The Invisible Adversary is fleeing across a field.

Gretchen, walking slowly, deliberately, watches with her keen unblinking eyes the figure of the Invisible Adversary some distance ahead. The Adversary has run boldly in front of all the traffic—on long spiky legs brisk as colts' legs—and jumped up onto a curb of new concrete, and now is running across a vacant field. The Adversary glances over his shoulder at Gretchen.

Saturday afternoon. November. A cold gritty day. Gretchen is out stalking. She has hours for her game. Hours. She is dressed for the hunt, her solid legs crammed into old blue jeans, her big, square, strong feet jammed into white leather boots that cost her mother forty dollars not long ago, but are now scuffed and filthy with mud. Hopeless to get them clean again, Gretchen doesn't care. She is wearing a dark-green corduroy jacket that is worn out at the elbows and the rear, with a zipper that can be zipped up or down, attached to a fringed leather strip. On her head nothing, though it is windy today.

She has hours ahead.

Cars and trucks and buses from the city and enormous interstate trucks hauling automobiles pass by on the highway; Gretchen waits until the way is nearly clear, then starts out. A single car is approaching. *Slow down,* Gretchen thinks; and like magic he does.

Following the footprints of the Invisible Adversary. There is no sidewalk here yet, so she might as well cut right across the field. A gigantic sign announces the site of the new Pace & Fischbach Building, an office building of fifteen floors to be completed the

5

following year. The land around here is all dug up and muddy; she can see the Adversary's footsteps leading right past the gouged-up area . . . and there he is, smirking back at her, pretending panic.

I'll get you. Don't worry. Gretchen thinks carefully.

Because the Adversary is so light-footed and invisible, Gretchen doesn't make any effort to be that way. She plods along as she does at school, passing from classroom to classroom, unhurried and not even sullen, just unhurried. She knows she is very visible. She is thirteen years old and weighs one hundred and thirty-five pounds. She's only five feet three—stocky, muscular, squat in the torso and shoulders, with good strong legs and thighs. She could be good at gym, if she bothered; instead, she just stands around, her face empty, her arms crossed and her shoulders a little slumped. If forced, she takes part in the games of volleyball and basketball, but she runs heavily, without spirit, and sometimes bumps into other girls, hurting them. *Out of my way,* she thinks; at such times her face shows no expression.

And now? . . . The Adversary is peeking out at her from around the corner of a gas station. Something flickers in her brain. *I see you,* she thinks, with quiet excitement. The Adversary ducks back out of sight. Gretchen heads in the direction, plodding through a jumbled, bulldozed field of mud and thistles and debris that is mainly rocks and chunks of glass. The gas station is brand-new and not yet opened for business. It is all white tile, white concrete, perfect plate-glass windows with whitewashed X's on them, a large driveway and eight gasoline pumps, all proudly erect and ready for business. But the gas station has not opened since Gretchen and her family moved here— about six months ago. Something must have gone wrong. Gretchen fixes her eyes on the corner where the Adversary was last seen. He can't escape.

One wall of the gas station's white tile has been smeared with something like tar. Dreamy, snakelike, thick twistings of black. Black tar. Several windows have been broken. Gretchen stands in the empty driveway, her hands jammed into her pockets. Traffic is moving slowly over here. A barricade has been set up that directs traffic out onto the shoulder of the highway, on a narrow, bumpy, muddy lane that loops out and back again onto the pavement. Cars move slowly, carefully. Their bottoms scrape against the road. The detour signs are great rectangular things, bright yellow with black zigzag lines. SLOW DETOUR. In the two center lanes of the highway are bulldozers not being used today, and gigantic concrete pipes to be used for storm sewers. Eight pipes. They are really enormous; Gretchen's eyes crinkle with awe, just to see them.

She remembers the Adversary.

There he is—headed for the shopping plaza. *He won't get away in the crowds,* Gretchen promises herself. She follows. Now she is approaching an area that is more completed, though there are still no sidewalks and some of the buildings are brand-new and yet unoccupied, vacant. She jumps over a concrete ditch that is stained with rust-colored water and heads up a slight incline to the service drive of the Federal Savings Bank. The drive-in tellers' windows are all dark today, behind their green-tinted glass. The whole bank is dark, closed. Is this the bank her parents go to now? It takes Gretchen a minute to recognize it.

Now a steady line of traffic, a single lane, turns onto the service drive that leads to the shopping plaza. BUCKINGHAM MALL. 101 STORES. Gretchen notices a few kids her own age, boys or girls, trudging in jeans and jackets ahead of her, through the mud. They might be classmates of hers. Her attention is captured again by the Invisible Adversary, who has run all the way up to the Mall and is hanging around the entrance of the Cunningham Drug Store, teasing her.

You'll be sorry for that, Gretchen thinks with a smile.

10

Automobiles pass her slowly. The parking lot for the Mall is enormous, many 15
acres. A city of cars on a Saturday afternoon. Gretchen sees a car that might be her
mother's, but she isn't sure. Cars are parked slanted here, in lanes marked LOT K, LANE
15; LOT K, LANE 16. The signs are spheres, bubbles, perched up on long slender poles.
At night they are illuminated.

Ten or twelve older kids are hanging around the drugstore entrance. One of them
is sitting on top of a mailbox, rocking it back and forth. Gretchen pushes past them—
they are kidding around, trying to block people—and inside the store her eye darts
rapidly up and down the aisles, looking for the Invisible Adversary.

Hiding here? Hiding?

She strolls along, cunning and patient. At the cosmetics counter a girl is showing
an older woman some liquid makeup. She smears a small oval onto the back of the
woman's hand, rubs it in gently. "That's Peach Pride," the girl says. She has shimmering blond hair and eyes that are penciled to show a permanent exclamatory interest. She
does not notice Gretchen, who lets a hand drift idly over a display of marked-down lip-
sticks, each only $1.59.

Gretchen slips the tube of lipstick into her pocket. Neatly. Nimbly. Ignoring the
Invisible Adversary, who is shaking a finger at her, she drifts over to the newsstand,
looks at the magazine covers without reading them, and edges over to another display.
Packages in a cardboard barrel, out in the aisle. Big bargains. Gretchen doesn't even
glance in the barrel to see what is being offered . . . she just slips one of the packages
in her pocket. No trouble.

She leaves by the other door, the side exit. A small smile tugs at her mouth.

The Adversary is trotting ahead of her. The Mall is divided into geometric 20
areas, each colored differently; the Adversary leaves the blue pavement and is now on
the green. Gretchen follows. She notices the Adversary going into a Franklin Joseph
store.

Gretchen enters the store, sniffs in the perfumy, overheated smell, sees nothing
that interests her on the counters or at the dress racks, and so walks right to the back of
the store, to the ladies' room. No one inside. She takes the tube of lipstick out of her
pocket, opens it, examines the lipstick. It has a tart, sweet smell. A very light pink:
Spring Blossom. Gretchen goes to the mirror and smears the lipstick onto it, at first
lightly, then coarsely; part of the lipstick breaks and falls into a sink littered with hair.
Gretchen goes into one of the toilet stalls and tosses the tube into the toilet bowl. She
takes handfuls of toilet paper and crumbles them into a ball and throws them into the
toilet. Remembering the package from the drugstore, she takes it out of her pocket—
just toothpaste. She throws it, cardboard package and all, into the toilet bowl, then, her
mind glimmering with an idea, she goes to the apparatus that holds the towel—a single
cloth towel on a roll—and tugs at it until it comes loose, then pulls it out hand over
hand, patiently, until the entire towel is out. She scoops it up and carries it to the toilet.
She pushes it in and flushes the toilet.

The stuff doesn't go down, so she tries again. This time it goes partway down before it gets stuck.

Gretchen leaves the rest room and strolls unhurried through the store. The Adversary is waiting for her outside—peeking through the window—wagging a finger at her.
Don't you wag no finger at me, she thinks, with a small tight smile. Outside, she follows
him at a distance. Loud music is blaring around her head. It is rock music, piped out
onto the colored squares and rectangles of the Mall, blown everywhere by the November wind, but Gretchen hardly hears it.

Some boys are fooling around in front of the record store. One of them bumps into Gretchen and they all laugh as she is pushed against a trash can. "Watch it, babe!" the boy sings out. Her leg hurts. Gretchen doesn't look at them but, with a cold, swift anger, her face averted, she knocks the trash can over onto the sidewalk. Junk falls out. The can rolls. Some women shoppers scurry to get out of the way and the boys laugh.

Gretchen walks away without looking back. 25

She wanders through Sampson Furniture, which has two entrances. In one door and out the other, as always, it is a ritual with her. Again she notices the sofa that is like the sofa in their family room at home—covered with black and white fur, real goatskin. All over the store there are sofas, chairs, tables, beds. A jumble of furnishings. People stroll around them, in and out of little displays, displays meant to be living rooms, dining rooms, bedrooms, family rooms. . . . It makes Gretchen's eyes squint to see so many displays: like seeing the inside of a hundred houses. She slows down, almost comes to a stop. Gazing at a living-room display on a raised platform. Only after a moment does she remember why she is here—whom she is following—and she turns to see the Adversary beckoning to her.

She follows him outside again. He goes into Dodi's Boutique and, with her head lowered so that her eyes seem to move to the bottom of her eyebrows, pressing up against her forehead, Gretchen follows him. *You'll regret this,* she thinks. Dodi's Boutique is decorated in silver and black. Metallic strips hang down from a dark ceiling, quivering. Salesgirls dressed in pants suits stand around with nothing to do except giggle with one another and nod their head in time to the music amplified throughout the store. It is music from a local radio station. Gretchen wanders over to the dress rack, for the hell of it. Size 14. "The time is now 2:35," a radio announcer says cheerfully. "The weather is 32 degrees with a chance of showers and possible sleet tonight. You're listening to WCKK, Radio Wonderful. . . ." Gretchen selects several dresses and a salesgirl shows her to a dressing room.

"Need any help?" the girl asks. She has long swinging hair and a high-shouldered, indifferent, bright manner.

"No," Gretchen mutters.

Alone, Gretchen takes off her jacket. She is wearing a navy blue sweater. She zips 30 one of the dresses open and it falls off the flimsy plastic hanger before she can catch it. She steps on it, smearing mud onto the white wool. She lets it lie there and holds up another dress, gazing at herself in the mirror.

She has untidy, curly hair that looks like a wig set loosely on her head. Light brown curls spill out everywhere, bouncy, a little frizzy, a cascade, a tumbling of curls. Her eyes are deep set, her eyebrows heavy and dark. She has a stern, staring look, like an adult man. Her nose is perfectly formed, neat and noble. Her upper lip is long, as if it were stretched to close with difficulty over the front teeth. She wears no makeup, her lips are perfectly colorless, pale, a little chapped, and they are usually held tight, pursed tightly shut. She has a firm, rounded chin. Her facial structure is strong, pensive, its features stern and symmetrical as a statue's, blank, neutral, withdrawn. Her face is attractive. But there is a blunt, neutral stillness to it, as if she were detached from it and somewhere else, uninterested.

She holds the dress up to her body, smooths it down over her chest, staring at herself.

After a moment she hangs the dress up again, and runs down the zipper so roughly that it breaks. The other dress she doesn't bother with. She leaves the dressing room, putting on her jacket.

At the front of the store the salesgirl glances at her . . ."—Didn't fit?—"

"No," says Gretchen. 35

She wanders around for a while, in and out of Carmichael's, the Mall's big famous store, where she catches sight of her mother on an escalator going up. Her mother doesn't notice her. She pauses by a display of "winter homes." Her family owns a home like this, in the Upper Peninsula, except theirs is larger. This one comes complete for only $5330: PACKAGE ERECTED ON YOUR LOT—YEAR-ROUND HOME FIBER GLASS INSULA-TION—BEAUTIFUL ROUGH-SAWN VERTICAL B. C. CEDAR SIDING WITH DEEP SIMULATED SHADOW LINES FOR A RUGGED EXTERIOR.

Only 3:15. Gretchen goes into the Big Boy restaurant and orders a ground-round hamburger with French fries. Also a Coke. She sits at the crowded counter and eats slowly, her jaws grinding slowly, as she glances at her reflection in the mirror directly in front of her—her mop of hair moving almost imperceptibly with the grinding of her jaws—and occasionally she sees the Adversary waiting outside, coyly. *You'll get yours,* she thinks.

She leaves the Big Boy and wanders out into the parking lot, eating from a bag of potato chips. She wipes her greasy hands on her thighs. The afternoon has turned dark and cold. Shivering a little, she scans the maze of cars for the Adversary—yes, there he is—and starts after him. He runs ahead of her. He runs through the parking lot, waits teasingly at the edge of a field, and as she approaches he runs across the field, trotting along with a noisy crowd of four or five loose dogs that don't seem to notice him.

Gretchen follows him through that field, trudging in the mud, and through anoth-er muddy field, her eyes fixed on him. Now he is at the highway—hesitating there—now he is about to run across in front of traffic—now, now—now he darts out—

Now! He is struck by a car. His body knocked backward, spinning backward. Ah, now, *now how does it feel?* Gretchen asks. 40

He picks himself up. Gets to his feet. Is he bleeding? Yes, bleeding! He stumbles across the highway to the other side, where there is a sidewalk. Gretchen follows him as soon as the traffic lets up. He is staggering now, like a drunken man. *How does it feel? Do you like it now?*

The Adversary staggers along the sidewalk. He turns onto a side street, beneath an archway, *Piney Woods.* He is leading Gretchen into the Piney Woods subdivision. Here the homes are quite large, on artificial hills that show them to good advantage. Most of the homes are white colonials with attached garages. There are no sidewalks here, so the Adversary has to walk in the street, limping like an old man, and Gretchen follows him in the street, with her eyes fixed on him.

Are you happy now? Does it hurt? Does it?

She giggles at the way he walks. He looks like a drunken man. He glances back at her, white-faced, and turns up a flagstone walk . . . goes right up to a big white colo-nial house. . . .

Gretchen follows him inside. She inspects the simulated brick of the foyer: yes, 45 there are blood spots. He is dripping blood. Entranced, she follows the splashes of blood into the hall, to the stairs . . . forgets her own boots, which are muddy . . . but she doesn't feel like going back to wipe her feet.

Nobody seems to be home. Her mother is probably still shopping, her father is out of town for the weekend. The house empty. Gretchen goes into the kitchen, opens the refrigerator, takes out a Coke, and wanders to the rear of the house, to the family room. It is two steps down from the rest of the house. She takes off her jacket and toss-es it somewhere. Turns on the television set. Sits on the goatskin sofa and stares at the screen: a return of a Shotgun Steve show, which she has already seen.

If the Adversary comes crawling behind her, groaning in pain, weeping, she won't even bother to glance at him.

THE RECEPTIVE READER

1. Oates is a master at noting in passing apparently random, mindless *detail* that we later suspect was planted deliberately in the story. What is the point of telling us about Gretchen's white leather boots—or about the car approaching when she crosses the highway? (What other details early in the story stuck in your mind?)

2. Gretchen is the kind of person who is popularly said to have an "attitude." What is her attitude toward school and gym? What is her attitude toward the schoolmates she meets at the mall?

3. What are striking details about the suburban landscape through which Gretchen wanders? As you follow her through this *setting*, do you notice any connecting thread? Is there a keynote—a recurrent note struck more than once?

4. What kind of shoplifter is Gretchen? How does she do it? What are her *motives*—why does she do it? Do you feel you are getting an inside look at teenage vandalism in this story? How does she operate, and why?

5. Late in the story, Oates furnishes a fairly complete physical description of Gretchen. Do you learn anything from it? Does it include any clues to her character?

6. At a few points earlier in the story, we are reminded that Gretchen has a mother, a family, a home. What impression do these hints create? What kind of home, what kind of family, awaits Gretchen at the end of her excursion?

7. What is the role of the imaginary adversary in the story?

THE PERSONAL RESPONSE

The story presents Gretchen strictly on her own terms—with no comment. There is no editorializing, moralizing, or preaching by the author. For you, what is the point of the story? Is there a key to the central character—a unifying thread to her behavior and attitudes? How do you relate to her?

THE RANGE OF INTERPRETATION

How much depends on what you as a reader bring to Gretchen's story? Which of the following student-written responses is closest to your own? Why? Which to you seems least responsive to the story, and why?

1. Gretchen seems to me to be a very angry adolescent. Her anger is directed against her absent parents, her schoolmates who probably don't even notice her, but mostly against herself. Gretchen is an overweight, unattractive, thirteen-year-old. She is a loner. She can only express her anger through her game of stalking "the adversary." This make-believe character represents to Gretchen all the anger she hides inside herself. These stalking games are ritualistic to Gretchen; through them she can release her anger and best her adversary for a period of time.

2. I was able to feel empathy toward the character of Gretchen in Oates' story, despite her unpleasant personality. I thought both she and her surroundings epitomized the sterility and alienation of much modern suburban life; there is a rootlessness inherent in the setting that manifests itself in Gretchen's utter lack of interest or engagement. This lack of engagement with the world around her is central to explaining many of the things she does, such as her aimless shoplifting and careless muddying of her parents' home. She was not raised in an environment that would give her any cause for en-

thusiasm for anything. It is perhaps because Gretchen had no positive interests to draw her attention and enthusiasm outward that she became so carelessly destructive of herself and her environment.

3. Gretchen is pure isolation. She is an imaginative, creative person trapped in a suburban theater where the only stimuli are shopping malls and television. Her mother and father are not shown as bad people; they are just kept out of the picture. Her companion instead is the invisible adversary—playmate, lover, villain, whipping boy who never says no to any adventure she devises. Her relentless pursuit of him gives her day a purpose and a victory. In her conventional reality, the frustration and pain of failure in a social arena where only pretty girls are admitted would be too much to bear. Her destructive behavior is an acting out of her frustrated need to belong. If a lipstick or dress is not going to improve the problem, then they should be destroyed. And if there is no place to go, why hurry?

THE CREATIVE DIMENSION

What do you think you would see if you could be a mind reader looking into Gretchen's mind? Write a passage in which you change the point of view of the story. Imagine you can share in Gretchen's private thoughts and feelings instead of watching her much of the time from the outside. Write in the first person, as if she were talking confidentially to the reader.

WORLDS OF THOUGHT AND FEELING

Both of the following stories take us into a central character's personal world. They make us look at the world as seen through one character's eyes. Since the central characters in these stories are very different people, each takes us into a different universe of thought and feeling. However, in addition, the point of view from which the author chooses to tell the story varies, with the second story taking us a step closer to sharing fully in the character's most personal, most private thoughts and emotions.

TILLIE OLSEN   (born 1912)

*The power and the need to create, over and beyond
reproduction, is native in both women and men. Where
the gifted among women (and men) have remained mute,
or have never attained full capacity, it is because of
circumstances, inner or outer, which oppose the needs of
creation.*

TILLIE OLSEN

Tillie Olsen has come to be widely admired for giving voice to the story of the unheard, the silenced, in American society. Writing about the Great Depression of the thirties, she wrote with bitter eloquence about the working-class experience—poverty, illness, hunger, unemployment, soul-deadening jobs. Her novel *Yonnondio: From the Thirties* (1974) paid tribute to people thwarted, deprived of their chance to develop into full human beings "so that a few may languidly lie on couches and trill 'how exquisite' to paid dreamers." A native of Omaha, Nebraska, with only a high school education, she herself lived through grey poverty to write powerful stories shaking up our complacency, our euphemisms and alibis. Her story "Tell Me a Riddle" won the O. Henry Award as the best short story of the year in 1961. She has since received prestigious grants and honors and lectured at universities including Amherst and Stanford.

Women readers and women writers made her a revered figure in the women's movement. They identified with the heroic struggle of a "family wage earner at dull and time-sapping menial jobs" (Nolan Miller)—a woman who "held down a job, raised four children, and still somehow managed to become and remain a writer," surviving a "grueling obstacle race" that cost her "twenty years of her writing life" (Margaret Atwood). In her collection *Silences* (1978), Olsen collected and reprinted the testimony of writers, and especially women from Virginia Woolf to Katherine Mansfield, about the social and psychological forces that hobble the creative spirit, forcing many who are not white, male, or affluent into silence.

The following story is the kind of personally committed writing that stays close to personal experience but turns it into art by focusing it and interpreting it. We look through the eyes of a mother at a daughter who was "the child of anxious, not proud love." What world do we see through the narrator's eyes? (The WPA referred to in the story is the Works Progress Administration, begun in 1935 to provide federally funded jobs for the unemployed during the Great Depression.)

I Stand Here Ironing 1961

I stand here ironing, and what you asked me moves tormented back and forth with the iron.

"I wish you would manage the time to come in and talk with me about your daughter. I'm sure you can help me understand her. She's a youngster who needs help and whom I'm deeply interested in helping."

"Who needs help." . . . Even if I came, what good would it do? You think because I am her mother I have a key, or that in some way you could use me as a key? She has lived for nineteen years. There is all that life that has happened outside of me, beyond me.

And when is there time to remember, to sift, to weigh, to estimate, to total? I will start and there will be an interruption and I will have to gather it all together again. Or I will become engulfed with all I did or did not do, with what should have been and what cannot be helped.

She was a beautiful baby. The first and only one of our five that was beautiful at 5 birth. You do not guess how new and uneasy her tenancy in her now-loveliness. You did not know her all those years she was thought homely, or see her poring over her baby pictures, making me tell her over and over how beautiful she had been—and would be, I would tell her—and was now, to the seeing eye. But the seeing eyes were few or nonexistent. Including mine.

I nursed her. They feel that's important nowadays. I nursed all the children, but with her, with all the fierce rigidity of first motherhood, I did like the books then said. Though her cries battered me to trembling and my breasts ached with swollenness, I waited till the clock decreed.

Why do I put that first? I do not even know if it matters, or if it explains anything.

She was a beautiful baby. She blew shining bubbles of sound. She loved motion, loved light, loved color and music and textures. She would lie on the floor in her blue overalls patting the surface so hard in ecstasy her hands and feet would blur. She was a miracle to me, but when she was eight months old I had to leave her daytimes with the woman downstairs to whom she was no miracle at all, for I worked or looked for work and for Emily's father, who "could no longer endure" (he wrote in his good-bye note) "sharing want with us."

I was nineteen. It was the pre-relief, pre-WPA world of the depression. I would start running as soon as I got off the streetcar, running up the stairs, the place smelling sour, and awake or asleep to startle awake, when she saw me she would break into a clogged weeping that could not be comforted, a weeping I can hear yet.

After a while I found a job hashing at night so I could be with her days, and it was better. But it came to where I had to bring her to his family and leave her.   10

It took a long time to raise the money for her fare back. Then she got chicken pox and I had to wait longer. When she finally came, I hardly knew her, walking quick and nervous like her father, looking like her father, thin, and dressed in a shoddy red that yellowed her skin and glared at the pockmarks. All the baby loveliness gone.

She was two. Old enough for nursery school they said, and I did not know then what I know now—the fatigue of the long day, and the lacerations of group life in the kinds of nurseries that are only parking places for children.

Except that it would have made no difference if I had known. It was the only place there was. It was the only way we could be together, the only way I could hold a job.

And even without knowing, I knew. I knew the teacher that was evil because all these years it has curdled into my memory, the little boy hunched in the corner, her rasp, "why aren't you outside, because Alvin hits you? that's no reason, go out, scaredy." I knew Emily hated it even if she did not clutch and implore "don't go Mommy" like the other children, mornings.

She always had a reason why we should stay home. Momma, you look sick.   15
Momma, I feel sick. Momma, the teachers aren't there today, they're sick. Momma, we can't go, there was a fire there last night. Momma, it's a holiday today, no school, they told me.

But never a direct protest, never rebellion. I think of our others in their three-, four-year-oldness—the explosions, the tempers, the denunciations, the demands—and I feel suddenly ill. I put the iron down. What in me demanded that goodness in her? And what was the cost, the cost to her of such goodness?

The old man living in the back once said in his gentle way: "You should smile at Emily more when you look at her." What *was* in my face when I looked at her? I loved her. There were all the acts of love.

It was only with the others I remembered what he said, and it was the face of joy, and not of care or tightness or worry I turned to them—too late for Emily. She does not smile easily, let alone almost always as her brothers and sisters do. Her face is closed and sombre, but when she wants, how fluid. You must have seen it in her pantomimes, you spoke of her rare gift for comedy on the stage that rouses laughter out of the audience so dear they applaud and applaud and do not want to let her go.

Where does it come from, that comedy? There was none of it in her when she came back to me that second time, after I had had to send her away again. She had a new daddy now to learn to love, and I think perhaps it was a better time.

Except when we left her alone nights, telling ourselves she was old enough. 20

"Can't you go some other time, Mommy, like tomorrow?" she would ask. "Will it be just a little while you'll be gone? Do you promise?"

The time we came back, the front door open, the clock on the floor in the hall. She rigid awake. "It wasn't just a little while. I didn't cry. Three times I called you, just three times, and then I ran downstairs to open the door so you could come faster. The clock talked loud. I threw it away, it scared me what it talked."

She said the clock talked loud again that night I went to the hospital to have Susan. She was delirious with the fever that comes before red measles, but she was fully conscious all the week I was gone and the week after we were home when she could not come near the new baby or me.

She did not get well. She stayed skeleton thin, not wanting to eat, and night after night she had nightmares. She would call for me, and I would rouse from exhaustion to sleepily call back: "You're all right, darling, go to sleep, it's just a dream," and if she still called, in a sterner voice, "now go to sleep, Emily, there's nothing to hurt you." Twice, only twice, when I had to get up for Susan anyhow, I went in to sit with her.

Now when it is too late (as if she would let me hold and comfort her like I do the 25 others) I get up and go to her at once at her moan or restless stirring. "Are you awake, Emily? Can I get you something?" And the answer is always the same: "No, I'm all right, go back to sleep, Mother."

They persuaded me at the clinic to send her away to a convalescent home in the country where "she can have the kind of food and care you can't manage for her, and you'll be free to concentrate on the new baby." They still send children to that place. I see pictures on the society page of sleek young women planning affairs to raise money for it, or dancing at the affairs, or decorating Easter eggs or filling Christmas stockings for the children.

They never have a picture of the children so I do not know if the girls still wear those gigantic red bows and the ravaged looks on the every other Sunday when parents can come to visit "unless otherwise notified"—as we were notified the first six weeks.

Oh it is a handsome place, green lawns and tall trees and fluted flower beds. High up on the balconies of each cottage the children stand, the girls in their red bows and white dresses, the boys in white suits and giant red ties. The parents stand below shrieking up to be heard and the children shriek down to be heard, and between them the invisible wall: "Not to Be Contaminated by Parental Germs or Physical Affection."

There was a tiny girl who always stood hand in hand with Emily. Her parents never came. One visit she was gone. "They moved her to Rose Cottage," Emily shouted in explanation. "They don't like you to love anybody here."

She wrote once a week, the labored writing of a seven-year-old. "I am fine. How is 30 the baby. If I write my leter nicly I will have a star. Love." There never was a star. We wrote every other day, letters she could never hold or keep but only hear read—once. "We simply do not have room for children to keep any personal possessions," they patiently explained when we pieced one Sunday's shrieking together to plead how much it would mean to Emily, who loved so to keep things, to be allowed to keep her letters and cards.

Each visit she looked frailer. "She isn't eating," they told us.

(They had runny eggs for breakfast or mush with lumps, Emily said later, I'd hold it in my mouth and not swallow. Nothing ever tasted good, just when they had chicken.)

It took us eight months to get her released home, and only the fact that she gained back so little of her seven lost pounds convinced the social worker.

I used to try to hold and love her after she came back, but her body would stay stiff, and after a while she'd push away. She ate little. Food sickened her, and I think much of life too. Oh she had physical lightness and brightness, twinkling by on skates, bouncing like a ball up and down up and down over the jump rope, skimming over the hill; but these were momentary.

She fretted about her appearance, thin and dark and foreign-looking at a time   35
when every little girl was supposed to look or thought she should look a chubby blonde replica of Shirley Temple. The doorbell sometimes rang for her, but no one seemed to come and play in the house or be a best friend. Maybe because we moved so much.

There was a boy she loved painfully through two school semesters. Months later she told me how she had taken pennies from my purse to buy him candy. "Licorice was his favorite and I brought him some every day, but he still liked Jennifer better'n me. Why, Mommy?" The kind of question for which there is no answer.

School was a worry to her. She was not glib or quick in a world where glibness and quickness were easily confused with ability to learn. To her overworked and exasperated teachers she was an overconscientious "slow learner" who kept trying to catch up and was absent entirely too often.

I let her be absent, though sometimes the illness was imaginary. How different from my now-strictness about attendance with the others. I wasn't working. We had a new baby, I was home anyhow. Sometimes, after Susan grew old enough, I would keep her home from school, too, to have them all together.

Mostly Emily had asthma, and her breathing, harsh and labored, would fill the house with a curiously tranquil sound. I would bring the two old dresser mirrors and her boxes of collections to her bed. She would select beads and single earrings, bottle tops and shells, dried flowers and pebbles, old postcards and scraps, all sorts of oddments; then she and Susan would play Kingdom, setting up landscapes and furniture, peopling them with action.

Those were the only times of peaceful companionship between her and Susan. I   40
have edged away from it, that poisonous feeling between them, that terrible balancing of hurts and needs I had to do between the two, and did so badly, those earlier years.

Oh there are conflicts between the others too, each one human, needing, demanding, hurting, taking—but only between Emily and Susan, no, Emily toward Susan that corroding resentment. It seems so obvious on the surface, yet it is not obvious. Susan, the second child, Susan, golden- and curly-haired and chubby, quick and articulate and assured, everything in appearance and manner Emily was not; Susan, not able to resist Emily's precious things, losing or sometimes clumsily breaking them; Susan telling jokes and riddles to company for applause while Emily sat silent (to say to me later: that was *my* riddle, Mother, I told it to Susan); Susan, who for all the five years' difference in age was just a year behind Emily in developing physically.

I am glad for that slow physical development that widened the difference between her and her contemporaries, though she suffered over it. She was too vulnerable for that terrible world of youthful competition, of preening and parading, of constant measuring of yourself against every other, of envy, "If I had that copper hair," "If I had that skin. . . ." She tormented herself enough about not looking like the others, there was enough of the unsureness, the having to be conscious of words before you speak, the constant caring—what are they thinking of me? without having it all magnified by the merciless physical drives.

Ronnie is calling. He is wet and I change him. It is rare there is such a cry now. That time of motherhood is almost behind me when the ear is not one's own but must always be racked and listening for the child cry, the child call. We sit for a while and I hold him, looking out over the city spread in charcoal with its soft aisles of light. "*Shoogily,*" he breathes and curls closer. I carry him back to bed, asleep. *Shoogily.* A funny word, a family word, inherited from Emily, invented by her to say: *comfort.*

In this and other ways she leaves her seal, I say aloud. And startle at my saying it. What do I mean? What did I start to gather together, to try and make coherent? I was at the terrible, growing years. War years. I do not remember them well. I was working, there were four smaller ones now, there was not time for her. She had to help be a mother, and housekeeper, and shopper. She had to set her seal. Mornings of crisis and near hysteria trying to get lunches packed, hair combed, coats and shoes found, everyone to school or Child Care on time, the baby ready for transportation. And always the paper scribbled on by a smaller one, the book looked at by Susan then mislaid, the homework not done. Running out to that huge school where she was one, she was lost, she was a drop; suffering over the unpreparedness, stammering and unsure in her classes.

There was so little time left at night after the kids were bedded down. She would struggle over books, always eating (it was in those years she developed her enormous appetite that is legendary in our family) and I would be ironing, or preparing food for the next day, or writing V-mail to Bill, or tending the baby. Sometimes, to make me laugh, or out of her despair, she would imitate happenings or types at school. 45

I think I said once: "Why don't you do something like this in the school amateur show?" One morning she phoned me at work, hardly understandable through the weeping: "Mother, I did it. I won, I won; they gave me first prize; they clapped and clapped and wouldn't let me go."

Now suddenly she was Somebody, and as imprisoned in her difference as she had been in anonymity.

She began to be asked to perform at other high schools, even in colleges, than at city and statewide affairs. The first one we went to, I only recognized her that first moment when thin, shy, she almost drowned herself into the curtains. Then: Was this Emily? The control, the command, the convulsing and deadly clowning, the spell, then the roaring, stamping audience, unwilling to let this rare and precious laughter out of their lives.

Afterwards: You ought to do something about her with a gift like that—but without money or knowing how, what does one do? We have left it all to her, and the gift has as often eddied inside, clogged and clotted, as been used and growing.

She is coming. She runs up the stairs two at a time with her light graceful step, and I know she is happy tonight. Whatever it was that occasioned your call did not happen today. 50

"Aren't you ever going to finish the ironing, Mother? Whistler painted his mother in a rocker. I'd have to paint mine standing over an ironing board." This is one of her communicative nights and she tells me everything and nothing as she fixes herself a plate of food out of the icebox.

She is so lovely. Why did you want me to come in at all? Why were you concerned? She will find her way.

She starts up the stairs to bed. "Don't get me up with the rest in the morning." "But I thought you were having midterms." "Oh, those," she comes back in, kisses me, and says quite lightly, "in a couple of years when we'll all be atom-dead they won't matter a bit."

She has said it before. She *believes* it. But because I have been dredging the past, and all that compounds a human being is so heavy and meaningful in me, I cannot endure it tonight.

I will never total it all. I will never come in to say: She was a child seldom smiled at. Her father left me before she was a year old. I had to work her first six years when there was work, or I sent her home and to his relatives. There were years she had care she hated. She was dark and thin and foreign-looking in a world where the prestige went to blondeness and curly hair and dimples, she was slow where glibness was prized. She was a child of anxious, not proud, love. We were poor and could not afford for her the soil of easy growth. I was a young mother, I was a distracted mother. There were other children pushing up, demanding. Her younger sister seemed all that she was not. There were years she did not want me to touch her. She kept too much in herself, her life was such she had to keep too much in herself. My wisdom came too late. She has much to her and probably little will come of it. She is a child of her age, of depression, of war, of fear. 55

Let her be. So all that is in her will not bloom—but in how many does it? There is still enough left to live by. Only help her to know—help make it so there is cause for her to know—that she is more than this dress on the ironing board, helpless before the iron.

THE RECEPTIVE READER

1. Who is the *you* addressed in the story?

2. How do the physical conditions, the circumstances of her life, shape the narrator's outlook? What physical details are especially telling or have a possible symbolic meaning?

3. Early in the story, we catch glimpes of the teacher, of Emily's father, and of the old man who lives in the back. What role do these people on the periphery of the story play in the narrator's world and her view of the world?

4. What is the narrator's attitude toward *institutions*? Why do they loom so large in the story? What are striking details? Is the narrator's attitude one-sided?

5. What picture of Emily as the oldest child emerges in this story? What are key points the narrator wants us to see or understand about Emily as a person? What makes the child—and the mother's relationship with her—*complex* rather than simple?

6. Although it is told in a low key, without melodrama or eloquent indictments, there are powerful undercurrents of *emotion* running in this story. What are they? Where are they harshest—or most frankly described?

7. What kind of summing up does the *ending* of the story provide? What attitude toward life or view of the world emerges here? Is it of one piece with the story as a whole?

8. Why do you think the author wrote this story? What do you think the act of writing did for her as the writer?

9. How do you think the situation or the child might have looked when seen from a *different* point of view? For instance, what might have been the perspective of a teacher or social worker? Does the narrator acknowledge different points of view?

THE PERSONAL RESPONSE

How do you relate to the narrator in the story? Do you think of her as a bitter person? an angry person? a defeated person? How do you relate to the daughter in the story? What do you think the future holds for her?

KATHERINE ANNE PORTER (1890–1980)

*The truth is, I have never written a story in my life that
didn't have a very firm foundation in actual human
experience—somebody else's experience quite often, but an
experience that became my own by hearing the story, by
witnessing the thing, by hearing just a word perhaps. It
doesn't matter, it just takes a little—a tiny seed. Then it
takes root, and it grows.*

KATHERINE ANNE PORTER

*In Katherine Anne Porter's stories, the effect has surely
been never to diminish life but always to intensify life in
the part significant to her story.*

EUDORA WELTY

*What her work celebrates is the toughness and integrity of
the individual.*

ROBERT PENN WARREN

Katherine Anne Porter became known as a writer more interested in a
character's state of mind than in external action. She published *Flowering
Judas,* her first collection of short stories, in 1930. Born in Texas, she drew on
her experiences as a young girl growing up in the South and as an observer of
revolutionary turmoil in Mexico. She is best known for her novellas (long
short stories or short novels) "Noon Wine" (1937) and "Pale Horse, Pale
Rider" (1939). She traveled widely, and she drew on her observations of Europe in the thirties and forties in her novel *Ship of Fools* (1962). This novel,
made into a movie with José Ferrer, Oskar Werner, and Simone Signoret, followed a group of travelers on a voyage to Germany in 1931, when the Nazi
movement was gathering strength, anti-Semitism was on the rise, and ominous
signs pointed toward the Nazi takeover in 1933.

"The Jilting of Granny Weatherall" is a short story that takes us inside the
consciousness of the main character, making us follow the stream of observations, memories, and rationalizations as they pass through the character's
mind. Instead of following external action from cause to effect, or from action
to reaction, we follow the **stream of consciousness.** In most of the story, we
hear the main character thinking to herself; we listen to the **interior monologue.** Eudora Welty has said in *The Eye of the Story* (1965) that Porter is contemplating "the inner, secret faces" of her characters:

> Often the revelation that pierces a character's mind and heart and shows him
> his life or his death comes in a dream, in retrospect, in illness or in utter de-
> feat, the moment of vanishing hope, the moment of dying. What Porter makes
> us see are those subjective worlds of hallucination, obsession, fever, guilt. The
> presence of death hovering about Granny Weatherall she makes as real and
> brings as near as Granny's own familiar room that stands about her bed.

In this story, we move on two levels: We get glimpses of the outer, or surface, reality of the sickroom. But we also participate in the inner reality of the
central character's observations, thoughts, and feelings. As often with the

stream-of-consciousness technique, some of the stream of thoughts and emotions seems trivial or routine. But eventually the character's thinking circles back to what really matters.

The Jilting of Granny Weatherall   1929

She flicked her wrist neatly out of Doctor Harry's pudgy careful fingers and pulled the sheet up to her chin. The brat ought to be in knee breeches. Doctoring around the country with spectacles on his nose! "Get along now, take your schoolbooks and go. There's nothing wrong with me."

Doctor Harry spread a warm paw like a cushion on her forehead where the forked green vein danced and made her eyelids twitch. "Now, now, be a good girl, and we'll have you up in no time."

"That's no way to speak to a woman nearly eighty years old just because she's down. I'd have you respect your elders, young man."

"Well, Missy, excuse me." Doctor Harry patted her cheek. "But I've got to warn you, haven't I? You're a marvel, but you must be careful or you're going to be good and sorry."

"Don't tell me what I'm going to be. I'm on my feet now, morally speaking. It's   5
Cornelia. I had to go to bed to get rid of her."

Her bones felt loose, and floated around in her skin, and Doctor Harry floated like a balloon around the foot of the bed. He floated and pulled down his waistcoat and swung his glasses on a cord. "Well, stay where you are, it certainly can't hurt you."

"Get along and doctor your sick," said Granny Weatherall. "Leave a well woman alone. I'll call for you when I want you. . . . Where were you forty years ago when I pulled through milk-leg and double pneumonia? You weren't even born. Don't let Cornelia lead you on," she shouted, because Doctor Harry appeared to float up to the ceiling and out. "I pay my own bills, and I don't throw my money away on nonsense!"

She meant to wave good-by, but it was too much trouble. Her eyes closed of themselves, it was like a dark curtain drawn around the bed. The pillow rose and floated under her, pleasant as a hammock in a light wind. She listened to the leaves rustling outside the window. No, somebody was swishing newspapers: no, Cornelia and Doctor Harry were whispering together. She leaped broad awake, thinking they whispered in her ear.

"She was never like this, *never* like this!" "Well, what can we expect?" "Yes, eighty years old. . . ."

Well, and what if she was? She still had ears. It was like Cornelia to whisper around   10
doors. She always kept things secret in such a public way. She was always being tactful and kind. Cornelia was dutiful; that was the trouble with her. Dutiful and good: "So good and dutiful," said Granny, "that I'd like to spank her." She saw herself spanking Cornelia and making a fine job of it.

"What'd you say, Mother?"

Granny felt her face tying up in hard knots.

"Can't a body think, I'd like to know?"

"I thought you might want something."

"I do. I want a lot of things. First off, go away and don't whisper."   15

She lay and drowsed, hoping in her sleep that the children would keep out and let her rest a minute. It had been a long day. Not that she was tired. It was always pleasant to snatch a minute now and then. There was always so much to be done, let me see: to-morrow.

Tomorrow was far away and there was nothing to trouble about. Things were fin-ished somehow when the time came; thank God there was always a little margin over for peace: then a person could spread out the plan of life and tuck in the edges orderly. It was good to have everything clean and folded away, with the hair brushes and tonic bottles sitting straight on the white embroidered linen: the day started without fuss and the pantry shelves laid out with rows of jelly glasses and brown jugs and white stone-china jars with blue whirligigs and words painted on them: coffee, tea, sugar, ginger, cinnamon, allspice: and the bronze clock with the lion on top nicely dusted off. The dust that lion could collect in twenty-four hours! The box in the attic with all those let-ters tied up, well, she'd have to go through that tomorrow. All those letters—George's letters and John's letters and her letters to them both—lying around for the children to find afterwards made her uneasy. Yes, that would be tomorrow's business. No use to let them know how silly she had been once.

While she was rummaging around she found death in her mind and it felt clammy and unfamiliar. She had spent so much time preparing for death there was no need for bringing it up again. Let it take care of itself now. When she was sixty she had felt very old, finished, and went around making farewell trips to see her children and grandchil-dren, with a secret in her mind: This is the very last of your mother, children! Then she made her will and came down with a long fever. That was all just a notion like a lot of other things, but it was lucky too, for she had once for all got over the idea of dying for a long time. Now she couldn't be worried. She hoped she had better sense now. Her father had lived to be one hundred and two years old and had drunk a noggin of strong hot toddy on his last birthday. He told reporters it was his daily habit, and he owed his long life to that. He had made quite a scandal and was very pleased about it. She be-lieved she'd just plague Cornelia a little.

"Cornelia! Cornelia!" No footsteps, but a sudden hand on her cheek. "Bless you, where have you been?"

"Here, Mother."

"Well, Cornelia, I want a noggin of hot toddy."

"Are you cold, darling?"

"I'm chilly, Cornelia. Lying in bed stops the circulation. I must have told you that a thousand times."

Well, she could just hear Cornelia telling her husband that Mother was getting a little childish and they'd have to humor her. The thing that most annoyed her was that Cornelia thought she was deaf, dumb, and blind. Little hasty glances and tiny gestures tossed around her and over her head saying, "Don't cross her, let her have her way, she's eighty years old," and she sitting there as if she lived in a thin glass cage. Some-times Granny almost made up her mind to pack up and move back to her own house where nobody could remind her every minute that she was old. Wait, wait, Cornelia, till your own children whisper behind your back!

In her day she had kept a better house and had got more work done. She wasn't too old yet for Lydia to be driving eighty miles for advice when one of the children jumped the track, and Jimmy still dropped in and talked things over: "Now, Mammy, you've a good business head, I want to know what you think of this? . . ." Old. Cor-nelia couldn't change the furniture around without asking. Little things, little things! They had been so sweet when they were little. Granny wished the old days were back again with the children young and everything to be done over. It had been a hard pull, but not too much for her. When she thought of all the food she had cooked, and all

20

25

the clothes she had cut and sewed, and all the gardens she had made—well, the children showed it. There they were, made out of her, and they couldn't get away from that. Sometimes she wanted to see John again and point to them and say, Well, I didn't do so badly, did I? But that would have to wait. That was for tomorrow. She used to think of him as a man, but now all the children were older than their father, and he would be a child beside her if she saw him now. It seemed strange and there was something wrong in the idea. Why, he couldn't possibly recognize her. She had fenced in a hundred acres once, digging the post holes herself and clamping the wires with just a negro boy to help. That changed a woman. John would be looking for a young woman with the peaked Spanish comb in her hair and the painted fan. Digging post holes changed a woman. Riding country roads in the winter when women had their babies was another thing: sitting up nights with sick horses and sick negroes and sick children and hardly ever losing one. John, I hardly ever lost one of them! John would see that in a minute, that would be something he could understand, she wouldn't have to explain anything!

It made her feel like rolling up her sleeves and putting the whole place to rights again. No matter if Cornelia was determined to be everywhere at once, there were a great many things left undone on this place. She would start tomorrow and do them. It was good to be strong enough for everything, even if all you made melted and changed and slipped under your hands, so that by the time you finished you almost forgot what you were working for. What was it I set out to do? she asked herself intently, but she could not remember. A fog rose over the valley, she saw it marching across the creek swallowing the trees and moving up the hill like an army of ghosts. Soon it would be at the near edge of the orchard, and then it was time to go in and light the lamps. Come in, children, don't stay out in the night air.

Lighting the lamps had been beautiful. The children huddled up to her and breathed like little calves waiting at the bars in the twilight. Their eyes followed the match and watched the flame rise and settle in a blue curve, then they moved away from her. The lamp was lit, they didn't have to be scared and hang on to mother any more. Never, never, never more. God, for all my life I thank Thee. Without Thee, my God, I could never have done it. Hail, Mary, full of grace.

I want you to pick all the fruit this year and see that nothing is wasted. There's always someone who can use it. Don't let good things rot for want of using. You waste life when you waste good food. Don't let things get lost. It's bitter to lose things. Now, don't let me get to thinking, not when I am tired and taking a little nap before supper. . . .

The pillow rose about her shoulders and pressed against her heart and the memory was being squeezed out of it: oh, push down the pillow, somebody: it would smother her if she tried to hold it. Such a fresh breeze blowing and such a green day with no threats in it. But he had not come, just the same. What does a woman do when she has put on the white veil and set out the white cake for a man and he doesn't come? She tried to remember. No, I swear he never harmed me but in that. He never harmed me but in that . . . . and what if he did? There was the day, the day, but a whirl of dark smoke rose and covered it, crept up and over into the bright field where everything was planted so carefully in orderly rows. That was hell, she knew hell when she saw it. For sixty years she had prayed against remembering him and against losing her soul in the deep pit of hell, and now the two things were mingled in one and the thought of him was a smoky cloud from hell that moved and crept in her head when she had just got rid of Doctor Harry and was trying to rest a minute. Wounded vanity. Ellen, said a sharp voice in the top of her mind. Don't let your wounded vanity get the upper hand of you. Plenty of girls get jilted. You were jilted, weren't you? Then stand up to it. Her eyelids wavered and let in streamers of blue-gray light like tissue paper over her eyes. She must get up and pull the shades down or she'd never sleep. She was in bed again and the shades were not down. How could that happen? Better turn over, hide from the light, sleeping in the light gave you nightmares. "Mother, how do you feel now?" and a stinging wetness on her forehead. But I don't like having my face washed in cold water!

Hapsy? George? Lydia? Jimmy? No, Cornelia, and her features were swollen and full of little puddles. "They're coming, darling, they'll all be here soon." Go wash your face, child, you look funny.

Instead of obeying, Cornelia knelt down and put her head on the pillow. She seemed to be talking but there was no sound. "Well, are you tongue-tied? Whose birthday is it? Are you going to give a party?"

Cornelia's mouth moved urgently in strange shapes. "Don't do that, you bother me, daughter."

"Oh, no, Mother. Oh, no. . . ."

Nonsense. It was strange about children. They disputed your every word. "No what, Cornelia?"

"Here's Doctor Harry."

"I won't see that boy again. He just left five minutes ago."

"That was this morning, Mother. It's night now. Here's the nurse."

"This is Doctor Harry, Mrs. Weatherall. I never saw you look so young and happy!"

"Ah, I'll never be young again—but I'd be happy if they'd let me lie in peace and get rested."

She thought she spoke up loudly, but no one answered. A warm weight on her forehead, a warm bracelet on her wrist, and a breeze went on whispering, trying to tell her something. A shuffle of leaves in the everlasting hand of God, He blew on them and they danced and rattled. "Mother, don't mind, we're going to give you a little hypodermic." "Look here, daughter, how do ants get in this bed? I saw sugar ants yesterday." Did you send for Hapsy too?

It was Hapsy she really wanted. She had to go a long way back through a great many rooms to find Hapsy standing with a baby on her arm. She seemed to herself to be Hapsy also, and the baby on Hapsy's arm was Hapsy and himself and herself, all at once, and there was no surprise in the meeting. Then Hapsy melted from within and turned flimsy as gray gauze and the baby was a gauzy shadow, and Hapsy came up close and said, "I thought you'd never come," and looked at her very searchingly and said, "You haven't changed a bit!" They leaned forward to kiss, when Cornelia began whispering from a long way off, "Oh, is there anything you want to tell me? Is there anything I can do for you?"

Yes, she had changed her mind after sixty years and she would like to see George. I want you to find George. Find him and be sure to tell him I forgot him. I want him to know I had my husband just the same and my children and my house like any other woman. A good house too and a good husband that I loved and fine children out of him. Better than I hoped for even. Tell him I was given back everything he took away and more. Oh, no, oh, God, no, there was something else besides the house and the man and the children. Oh, surely they were not all? What was it? Something not given back. . . . Her breath crowded down under her ribs and grew into a monstrous frightening shape with cutting edges; it bored up into her head, and the agony was unbelievable: Yes, John, get the doctor now, no more talk, my time has come.

30

35

40

When this one was born it should be the last. The last. It should have been born first, for it was the one she had truly wanted. Everything came in good time. Nothing left out, left over. She was strong, in three days she would be as well as ever. Better. A woman needed milk in her to have her full health.

"Mother, do you hear me?"

"I've been telling you—"

"Mother, Father Connolly's here."

"I went to Holy Communion only last week. Tell him I'm not so sinful as all that."

"Father just wants to speak to you."

He could speak as much as he pleased. It was like him to drop in and inquire about her soul as if it were a teething baby, and then stay on for a cup of tea and a round of cards and gossip. He always had a funny story of some sort, usually about an Irishman who made his little mistakes and confessed them, and the point lay in some absurd thing he would blurt out in the confessional showing his struggles between native piety and original sin. Granny felt easy about her soul. Cornelia, where are your manners? Give Father Connolly a chair. She had her secret comfortable understanding with a few favorite saints who cleared a straight road to God for her. All as surely signed and sealed as the papers for the new Forty Acres. Forever . . . heirs and assigns forever. Since the day the wedding cake was not cut, but thrown out and wasted. The whole bottom dropped out of the world, and there she was blind and sweating with nothing under her feet and the walls falling away. His hand had caught her under the breast, she had not fallen, there was the freshly polished floor with the green rug on it, just as before. He had cursed like a sailor's parrot and said, "I'll kill him for you." Don't lay a hand on him, for my sake leave something to God. "Now, Ellen, you must believe what I tell you. . . ."

So there was nothing, nothing to worry about any more, except sometimes in the night one of the children screamed in a nightmare, and they both hustled out shaking and hunting for the matches and calling, "There, wait a minute, here we are!" John, get the doctor now, Hapsy's time has come. But there was Hapsy standing by the bed in a white cap. "Cornelia, tell Hapsy to take off her cap. I can't see her plain."

Her eyes opened very wide and the room stood out like a picture she had seen somewhere. Dark colors with the shadows rising toward the ceiling in long angles. The tall black dresser gleamed with nothing on it but John's picture, enlarged from a little one, with John's eyes very black when they should have been blue. You never saw him, so how do you know how he looked? But the man insisted the copy was perfect, it was very rich and handsome. For a picture, yes, but it's not my husband. The table by the bed had a linen cover and a candle and a crucifix. The light was blue from Cornelia's silk lampshades. No sort of light at all, just frippery. You had to live forty years with kerosene lamps to appreciate honest electricity. She felt very strong and she saw Doctor Harry with a rosy nimbus around him.

"You look like a saint, Doctor Harry, and I vow that's as near as you'll ever come to it."

"She's saying something."

"I heard you, Cornelia. What's all this carrying-on?"

"Father Connolly's saying—"

Cornelia's voice staggered and bumped like a cart in a bad road. It rounded corners and turned back again and arrived nowhere. Granny stepped up in the cart very lightly and reached for the reins, but a man sat beside her and she knew him by his hands, driving the cart. She did not look in his face, for she knew without seeing, but looked instead down the road where the trees leaned over and bowed to each other and a thousand birds were singing a Mass. She felt like singing too, but she put her hand in the bosom of her dress and pulled out a rosary, and Father Connolly murmured Latin in a very solemn voice and tickled her feet. My God, will you stop that nonsense? I'm a married woman. What if he did run away and leave me to face the priest by myself? I found another a whole world better. I wouldn't have exchanged my husband for anybody except Saint Michael himself, and you may tell him that for me with a thank you in the bargain.

Light flashed on her closed eyelids, and a deep roaring shook her. Cornelia, is that lightning? I hear thunder. There's going to be a storm. Close all the windows. Call the children in. . . . "Mother, here we are, all of us." "Is that you, Hapsy?" "Oh, no, I'm Lydia. We drove as fast as we could." Their faces drifted above her, drifted away. The rosary fell out of her hands and Lydia put it back. Jimmy tried to help, their hands fumbled together, and Granny closed two fingers around Jimmy's thumb. Beads wouldn't do, it must be something alive. She was so amazed her thoughts ran round and round. So, my dear Lord, this is my death and I wasn't even thinking about it. My children have come to see me die. But I can't, it's not time. Oh, I always hated surprises. I wanted to give Cornelia the amethyst set—Cornelia, you're to have the amethyst set, but Hapsy's to wear it when she wants, and, Doctor Harry, do shut up. Nobody sent for you. Oh, my dear Lord, do wait a minute. I meant to do something about the Forty Acres, Jimmy doesn't need it and Lydia will later on, with that worthless husband of hers. I meant to finish the altar cloth and send six bottles of wine to Sister Borgia for her dyspepsia. I want to send six bottles of wine to Sister Borgia, Father Connolly, now don't let me forget.

Cornelia's voice made short turns and tilted over and crashed. "Oh, Mother, oh, Mother, oh, Mother. . . ."

"I'm not going, Cornelia. I'm taken by surprise. I can't go."

You'll see Hapsy again. What about her? "I thought you'd never come." Granny made a long journey outward, looking for Hapsy. What if I don't find her? What then? Her heart sank down and down, there was no bottom to death, she couldn't come to the end of it. The blue light from Cornelia's lampshade drew into a tiny point in the center of her brain, it flickered and winked like an eye, quietly it fluttered and dwindled. Granny lay curled down within herself, amazed and watchful, staring at the point of light that was herself; her body was now only a deeper mass of shadow in an endless darkness and this darkness would curl around the light and swallow it up. God, give a sign! 60

For the second time there was no sign. Again no bridegroom and the priest in the house. She could not remember any other sorrow because this grief wiped them all away. Oh, no, there's nothing more cruel than this—I'll never forgive it. She stretched herself with a deep breath and blew out the light.

THE RECEPTIVE READER

1. In how much of this story do we look at the world from Granny Weatherall's *point of view?* How much is inner reality, or stream of consciousness? ✧ What is the alternative strand of things happening that the main character does not fully take in? How much of the story is the outer reality of the sickroom? ✧ What kind of rhythm does the alternation of the two points of view set up for the story as a whole?

2. What kinds of memories and concerns take up the early pages of the story? What are striking examples of the blending of present and past?

3. When does the narrative begin to close in on the events alluded to in the title? How are you able to piece together the story of what happened sixty years earlier? ✧ What is the central character's attitude toward those events from the distant past? What are her memories, emotions, thoughts, defenses? Is there a keynote—a recurrent thought or dominant feeling? What role did the jilting play in her life as a whole? ✧ Why do you think the author approaches this central topic in such a roundabout way?

4. What role does Cornelia play in the story? What role do Granny's husband and family play in the story as a whole? What role does Hapsy play in Granny's thoughts and feelings as the end approaches?

5. Does this story have a *plot*? Does any action or development take place parallel to the physical events of the sickroom? How does the ending tie major concerns of the story together?

6. How would you sum up in one sentence the attitude toward life implied in this story?

THE PERSONAL RESPONSE

How would you describe the central character in the story? What kind of person emerges from the story as a whole? What kind of life has she had? How do you relate to her as the reader? How do you think the author *expected* you to feel toward the central character? (Does she seem to steer the reader's feelings or reactions?)

CROSS-REFERENCES—For Discussion or Writing

✧ The technique of the interior monologue is designed to give you an intimate inside view of a character's thoughts and feelings. Does this story give you a fuller understanding of its central character than other stories you have read so far? Compare what and how you learn about the central character in this story and in a story like Alice Munro's "Boys and Girls."

✧ Feminist critics have praised in Porter's writing "the splendid portraits of women which fill her work"; her sympathy with "frustrated, maligned, unvalued, struggling, emotionally blocked, and intellectually undernourished women"; and her exasperation with "conventional social patterns, especially male-dominated marriage and the creed of domesticity" (Jane Flanders). How much of this description fits "The Jilting of Granny Weatherall"?

WRITING ABOUT LITERATURE

5. Sharing a Point of View (Focus on Peer Response)

The Writing Workshop How does point of view shape a story as a whole? What window does the story open on the world? Through whose eyes do we see the people and events, and what difference does it make? In writing a paper about point of view, ask yourself questions like the following:

✧ What is the narrator's relation to the events of the story? Are we listening to a casual observer? to a reliable impartial witness? to a person with an axe to grind? Does the story read like self-justification? like nostalgic reenactment of the past?

✧ How does the point of view limit your vision as the reader? (What is left out that you might want to know?) How does it steer your reactions? (Do you anywhere resist what the narrator apparently expects you to think or feel?)

✧ How might the events of the story look if seen from a different point of view? Try to imagine what the story would be like if told from the perspective of someone else in the story.

✧ Does the narrator take in more of what happens than someone else might—or less? Do you at times feel that you know (or suspect) more than the narrator does? Are you expected to question the perceptions of the narrator?

✧ Are there deliberate shifts in perspective or changes in point of view? Is part of the story seen through one pair of eyes, and another part through another? Does a more comprehensive overall view emerge from such a double perspective?

Focus on Peer Response

When you work on papers about the stories you read, bringing the topic into focus, gathering material, and pulling it into shape will absorb much of your attention. But sooner or later, you will begin to focus on what happens when your writing reaches the reader. In many writing classes, student writers have a chance to learn from **peer response.** When your writing is critiqued by your peers, you become more audience-conscious. You become more aware of how readers react. You become more conscious of what will help and what may hinder your reader.

When you in turn participate in peer response, you formulate your reactions to the writing of fellow students, trying to help them revise and strengthen their papers. Remember the golden rule of peer criticism: Respond unto others as you would have them respond unto you. Try to avoid mere faultfinding. Respond to both strengths and weaknesses, showing that you are basically on the writer's side. In responding to the paper of a fellow student, try to see details in the context of the paper as a whole. How do they affect the overall effectiveness of the paper? What can the writer do to make the paper more effective? Try to answer questions like the following:

✧ *What is the writer trying to do?* What seems to be the general purpose? How well has it been achieved?

✧ *Does the paper get off to a good start?* Do the title and the opening lines capture the attention of the reader? Do they channel it in the right direction?

✧ *Does the paper have a strong central idea or thesis?* Is it spelled out clearly enough—at the beginning or, sometimes, toward the end of the paper? Does the writer keep it in view or lose sight of it as the paper develops?

✧ *What is the general strategy or master plan?* Does it become clear enough to the reader? Or does the reader need more of a preview or program early in the paper? Does the reader run into apparent detours or digressions? Should the organization be streamlined? Should major sections of the paper be reshuffled?

✧ *Are key points well developed?* Is there a rich supporting texture of short quotable quotes and striking authentic detail? Where do you feel a lack of support or follow-through? Are any points merely mentioned in passing and then dropped?

✧ *How effective are the transitions from one point to the next?* Does the paper show the connection between major parts? Does it signal turning points or steps in an argument? Does the paper need stronger logical links?

✧ *Does the conclusion merely rehash points already made?* Or does it do a needed job of pulling together different parts of an argument? Does it add anything to show the larger meaning or implications of the author's points? Does it leave readers with a striking quotation or telling incident to remember?

✧ *How well does the paper communicate its points?* Where would you put in the margin "well put" or "well said" or "good touch"? Where are readers likely to stumble over garbled or incomplete sentences or over missing commas? Where are they likely to be confused by words that are near misses or just plain wrong? Where are big words or shifting, confusing terms used without definition? Where is the wording too disrespectful or slangy—and where too stiff or pretentious? Where do you hear clichés rather than the writer's own voice?

✧ *Does the paper show any personal involvement or commitment?* Does it sound too much like an "assignment"? Is there a personal connection?

Peer Responses to a Draft

Study the following sample student paper and the excerpts from peer responses that follow it. How carefully have the authors of the peer responses read the paper? How do these readers compare with your own vision of an ideal responsive reader for your own writing?

SAMPLE STUDENT PAPER

Creating an Empathetic Audience: A Skillful Use of Point of View

Point of view is a useful author's tool. If used skillfully, it can allow the reader to learn much about a character from a few carefully placed clues. This type of storytelling avoids preachy didacticism and allows the reader to form personal opinions about the character that are not influenced by other characters' thoughts or actions. Tillie Olsen's "I Stand Here Ironing" is an example of a first-person narrative in which the main character is speaking mostly about her nineteen-year-old daughter Emily, but the reader still learns much about the narrator herself. Also, by telling the story from the mother's point of view, Olsen allows the reader to feel empathy for a character who might otherwise inspire anger or disgust.

If this story were told from the troubled Emily's point of view, one can only imagine the vision of the mother that would emerge. A fly on the wall in the counselor's office who confronts Emily's mother at the beginning of the story might have heard Emily describe her mother in a negative light. Emily might tell the counselor, "My mother never smiled at me; she only smiled at my younger sister, Susan, who was prettier. She sent me away all the time—first to my father's family, then to a day school, then to an awful convalescent hospital. She never had time for me; she always worked. She was never there when I needed her." And so on, until all the mother's evils were categorized and the reader feels nothing but anger at the seemingly heartless mother and sympathy for Emily. But by telling the story from the mother's point of view, Olsen uncovers the flip side of the situation, allowing the woman to respond to her daughter's allegations and explain her actions, thus letting the reader empathize with her and gain a better understanding of her. In this way, Olsen also makes a point about the difficulties a single woman can face raising a child and how, oftentimes, innocent lives can be sacrificed and lost in the daily struggle to survive.

The narrator begins the story by describing how difficult it was for her in the early years after her husband left her, describing the hectic pace of her life as she tried to scrape up the daily necessities. "I would start running as soon as I got off the streetcar, running up the stairs, . . ." She describes how she had to send her daughter away to her husband's family, and then later, once she was finally able to bring her back, how she had to send her to nursery school during the day. The narrator guiltily admits that she knew the nursery was evil, but "it was the only place there was." It was the only way we could be together, the only way I could hold a job." The first-person narrative of the story allows her readers this insight into the woman's actions. It allows them to learn that such actions, although they may seem cruel, were the only alternative the woman had as she desperately tried to support herself and her child.

Later in the story, the narrator explains how she had to send Emily away again—this time because she did not get well after a bout with the red measles. "They persuaded me at the clinic to send her away to a convalescent home in the country," she says. They told her Emily would receive "the kind of food and care you can't manage for her." The narrator discusses with heartwrenching guilt the "ravaged looks" of the girls in the home and how she desperately tried to get Emily back. If her readers did not have this insight into the woman's feelings, they might believe she was a careless or apathetic mother who found it easier to stick her child into a gruesome home rather than take proper care of her.

The narrator does admit, however, that she made many mistakes with Emily. She rarely smiled at Emily when she was a child, she never held and loved Emily as she did the other children, and she denied Emily the affection she showered on Susan, the second child. She knows these and other things made life harder on Emily than it was on the other children. The narrator admits her error, but knows in her heart that sometimes such happenings are inevitable. "I was at the terrible, growing years. War years. I do not remember them well. I was working, there were four smaller ones now, there was not time for her. She had to help be a mother, and housekeeper, and shopper." Through comments such as these, the reader learns that the narrator, very young herself, was also having a rough time making ends meet. And although it does seem a heavy burden to fall on Emily's small shoulders, placed in the context of an impoverished woman struggling to feed six mouths with one paycheck, Emily's burden becomes one of necessity, not of cruelty. The story's first-person point of view allows the reader the indulgence of pity for Emily and her difficult youth, yet also allows empathy for the mother. Because the reader is privy to the narrator's side of the situation, Emily's hardship is lessened in the face of the family's fierce struggle to survive.

Tillie Olsen's use of first-person narrative in "I Stand Here Ironing" permits the reader to step into the shoes of a poor working-class mother and her daily fight for survival. It permits those of us who have never experienced such hardship to ask ourselves "What would I do if . . . ?" The answer might shock us: we might do the exact thing the narrator was forced to do, which was to rely on a child to perform chores beyond her, in essence robbing that child of the playtime essential to healthy growth. The narrator Olsen creates is universal: a character struggling to survive despite overwhelming odds. And, although that character makes mistakes, these are forgiven in the face of the struggle. The situation Olsen creates is also universal, telling the often unavoidable fate of the children born into such conditions, whose own personalities are lost in the cycle of poverty and the fight for survival.

PEER RESPONSES

1. While reading this essay, I started on a very negative slant, but the author won me over. The paper starts slowly and actually somewhat awkwardly. To begin with, the title, for me, is too long and general. It gives no hint of what the major focus of the story is. Then the first three sentences are solely generalizations about point of view in general. Then, finally, the writer introduces the story that will be the major subject of the essay. So I stop to wonder—is the author writing about point of view, using this story as a convenient example, or is she writing about how point of view makes this story what it is? It is a subtle difference, but it significantly affects how one approaches the story. Both the title and the beginning talk about point of view in very general terms, and that hardly draws the reader in. However, once the author starts writing about Tillie Olsen and her story, she does an excellent job of following up and using quotes effectively to support her thesis: In this story, point of view creates a receptive, empathetic reader. She keeps this central idea in focus well throughout her essay.

2. The writer hints at her thesis in the title and then spells it out at the end of her first paragraph. The main point is that the first-person narrative—the point of view used in "I Stand Here Ironing"—lets the reader get inside the skin of the character and helps readers understand and empathize with her. The paper shows good use of counterpoint in the second paragraph: One key element that works well in this paper is that the writer balances the narrator's point of view with the projected point of view of the daughter. The reader is made to see how the story might have been completely different if told from the perspective of the daughter. The paper leads up effectively to an awareness of the universal nature of the narrator's predicament and her guilt. The ending shows great strength, making up for some of the mechanical quality of the beginning. As for the title, something more imaginative, perhaps drawn from the inner core of the story, would be better.

3. We get a good idea of the importance of point of view in this paper. The author gets right to the point and stays there. The purpose of the paper is to justify the mother's actions and decisions. I feel more attention could have been paid to how the mother actually felt about Emily. She may have resented ever having her. Often a parent will like one child and dislike another. Some phrases slip into clichés: "making ends meet"; "despite overwhelming odds."

QUESTIONS

1. Where are the student responses in substantial *agreement* on the strengths and weaknesses of this paper?

2. How do the responses *differ*? If you were the author of the paper, whose judgment would you be inclined to trust, and why?

3. What revised or improved *title* would you suggest that would be snappier and more informative at the same time?

4. What *opening quotation* chosen from the story might get the reader's attention and lead up effectively to the writer's thesis?

6 SYMBOL
The Eloquent Image

A symbol assumes two planes, two worlds of ideas and sensations, and a dictionary of correspondences between them.

ALBERT CAMUS

Symbolism adds a new value to an object or an act, without thereby violating its immediate or "historical" validity. . . . seen in this light the universe is no longer sealed off, nothing is isolated inside its own existence: everything is linked by a system of correspondences and assimilations.

MIRCEA ELIADE

FOCUS ON SYMBOLS

Symbols are images that have a meaning beyond themselves. In a short story, a symbol is a detail, a character, or an incident that has a meaning beyond its literal role in the narrative. When a flower, the moon, or a fountain is used as a symbol, it comes to mean more than the bloom of a plant, a source of light at night, or a device that recycles water. It is pregnant with a larger significance; it means something beyond itself. The "inconstant moon," for instance, may stand for change, uncertainty, lack of continuity. Or the pale moon may stand for the night side of our existence, for the hidden part of our character that shuns daylight.

Symbolic language gives expression to "the art of thinking in images" (Ananda Coomaraswamy). A symbol is an image that is not presented for its own sake. Imaginative literature involves us in sensory, sensuous experience that often seems richer than what our blunted senses take in from day to day. As we read, the mind's eye takes in images—vividly imagined details, shapes, textures. But often we sense that there is more there than meets the eye. Something tells us: "The sun in this story is not just a physical fact. It becomes overpowering, threatening. It leaves the landscape parched; it dries up the sources of life-giving water. It means something—it tells us something, if only we knew how to read between the lines."

182

When we reach the climactic incidents in Alice Munro's "Boys and Girls," we can read them on a literal level: On the fox farm where the story takes place, useless, discarded horses are needed as meat for the foxes. The young girl impulsively helps one of the horses escape—though only for a time. However, as we are watching her open the gate, we already sense that this is no routine incident. It is not just part of the day's work. This is the first time she has gone directly against the order of the father she admires. When we think about the girl and the horse, we discover strange parallels. They are both spirited. They are both rebelling against what seems to be their fate. The horse becomes a symbol: It is symbolic of the girl's rebellion, of her high-spiritedness that is doomed to be denied and defeated.

Symbols are concrete and tangible first. The literal-minded reader therefore may see only their physical surface. Not all readers may sense a larger symbolic significance, and different readers may read the same symbol differently. However, to respond fully to a story, you have to become sensitive to possible symbolic overtones and implications.

THE LANGUAGE OF SYMBOLS

In the short story the action is usually small, while the meanings are large.

THOMAS A. GULLERSON

Much of what imaginative literature tells you it does not say in so many words. Although symbols in fiction come to you through the medium of language, they are in a way a **nonverbal** language. Like the gestures of the actor, or the drumbeats of a Beethoven symphony, they do not put verbal labels on what they communicate. You as the reader have to decode, interpret, put into words what the images seem to tell you. Responding to symbols is a way of reading between (or behind) the lines.

As you interpret the language of symbols, keep points like the following in mind:

✧ Some symbols come into a story from *a shared language* of symbols. Much in human experience has traditional symbolic associations: the dawn with hope, the dark forest with evil, clay with death, water with fertility. Light is often the symbol for knowledge, for "enlightenment"—*fiat lux* ("let there be light") is the rallying cry of those fighting the darkness of ignorance.

✧ Some symbols have a *special personal meaning* for the writer, and their meaning may come into focus as they return again and again in the writer's work. Speaking of the Irish poet Seamus Heaney, a critic said that the source of his imaginative power lay in his rural childhood experience "that is centered and staked in the image of the pump. The pump, like his poetry, taps hidden springs to conduct what is sustaining and life-giving. The pump is a symbol of the nourishment which comes from knowing and belonging to a certain place and a certain mode of life" (Elmer Andrews).

✧ Literary symbols are *rich in associations*. They have more resonance, more reverberations than simple signs. The skull and bones that say "poison" have a clear, unequivocal message. But literary symbols do not simply signal "Danger" or "All Clear." One of the oldest symbols in the literature of Western culture is the garden. It brings with it a wealth of associations: The Garden of Eden was a scene of innocence and happiness, before the fall of Adam. The garden is a symbol of nature fruitful and life-sustaining. Like the Garden of Eden, it may be the cultivated spot in the surrounding wilderness. It may suggest the oasis in the desert. It may suggest a retreat from the intrigues of office or business—we retreat there to "cultivate our own garden." (It may also be a place where we struggle against pests and weeds.)

✧ Symbols *may be ambiguous*. In Melville's great American classic *Moby Dick,* the great mythic white whale seems paradoxically double-faced. To the obsessed Captain Ahab, the whale stands for everything that is destructive in nature—and the whale does in the end send his ship and his crew to the bottom of the sea. But at other times, the whale seems to stand for everything that is most serenely beautiful in nature—as it floats through the becalmed sea shedding "enticings."

✧ Symbols acquire their full meaning *in the context of a story*. In Nathaniel Hawthorne's novel *The Scarlet Letter,* the letter *A* for adultery, embroidered on the sinner's gown, may at first seem a matter of historical interest. We can say, "This is how the Puritans identified an adulteress; this is how it was done." But as we watch her and her innocent child, the scarlet letter begins to haunt us; it makes us think. The author used it as the title of the whole novel: *The Scarlet Letter*. As we finish the novel, that scarlet letter is likely to have been burned into our consciousness. It becomes a symbol of our consciousness of guilt, of our doubts about who is truly guilty. We begin to imagine it carried by others (like the Puritan minister Dimmesdale), who are implicated but not literally stigmatized.

✧ When symbols work together to act out a story, the result is **allegory.** In Le Guin's "The Ones Who Walk Away from Omelas," everything seems potentially symbolic. We are not in any place we could find on a map. The people who are happy in Le Guin's strange Utopia (Greek for "no-place" or neverland), the prisoner who is the dark secret of this beautiful place, and the people who "walk away"—all these play their role in a web of symbolic meaning.

The Range of Interpretation

Readers vary greatly in how responsive they are to symbolic overtones. The following excerpt is from an article by Danielle Schaub titled "Shirley Jackson's Use of Symbols in 'The Lottery.'" Her thesis: The story as a whole centers on the duality of a harmless-seeming everyday surface and the "horrendous" evil that will erupt. Similarly, much in the setting of the story has "ambivalent" symbolic overtones—benign when looked at from one point of view, ominous when looked at from another. Look at the polarities the critic traces in the story. Which to you seem well within the range of a shared language of symbols to which readers are likely to respond? Which to you seem most likely to be at work in the story?

DANIELLE SCHAUB
Symbols in "The Lottery" 1990

The author's recurrent use of symbols stresses the duality of things and beings, which paves the way for the final horrendous revelation. . . . Their ambivalence corroborates the message of the story, namely that first-hand impressions may well be deceptive; on the surface, things are smooth; deep down, reality is cruder. The usually positive value of any symbol needs to be counterbalanced by its hidden or less well-known negative value for us to have a clearer picture of the text. Its richness and quality result from the mixture of opposite values. Instead of a straightforward account of small-town life, the reader gets a fuller picture of Life with its inescapable conjunction of opposites.

Tension is already present in the description of the setting and in the atmosphere. Like a Janus figure [the two-faced god of Roman mythology], the sun is felt throughout as an ambiguous presence. Its generative heat, associated with youth, vitality, and fertility, heals and restores, but come midsummer and its scorching heat leads to the poisoning, burning madness of the solstice rite. The sun will provide better crops but only at the cost of the ritual murder of an innocent villager. Besides, the ambivalent character of the rite is stressed by the profusely blossoming flowers. By their very nature they symbolize beauty as well as point to the transitory stages of the vegetal cycle. They suggest not only virtue, goodness, and purity but also temptation and deceit. As such they are part of pleasant occasions but also of distressing functions—as a last tribute paid at a funeral, Tessie's for example. The green grass too reveals the discrepancy between the characters' appearance and deeds. Indeed, on the one hand, green suggests fertility, peace, balance, harmony, freshness, youth: these qualities, at first sight, seem to fit the description of the population. But, on the other hand, green implies ignorance, unripeness, inexperience—the very characteristics attributed to pagan sacrifices. Significantly too, prior to the insane murder of Tessie Hutchinson, the villagers gather in the square. As the square stands for firmness and stability, organization and construction, it is the source of order. No wonder then that traditions are perpetuated in the square.

From *Journal of the Short Story in English,* Spring 1990

A SHORT STORY CLASSIC: STEINBECK'S "CHRYSANTHEMUMS"

Literary classics, like public monuments in a park, become familiar. We have taken in whatever they have to offer; we feel that it is time to pass on to something new. However, the test of a true classic is that it surprises us by refusing to be passé. A new generation reads it from a fresh perspective, and rediscovers its power and its appeal.

JOHN STEINBECK (1902–1968)

Much of Steinbeck's fiction takes us to "Steinbeck Country"—California's agricultural Salinas Valley and scenic Monterey Bay, stretching south to the rugged coast of Big Sur. This area, where Steinbeck grew up and went to school, sets the scene for books like *Tortilla Flat* (1935), *Of Mice and Men* (1937), *Cannery Row* (1945), and *East of Eden* (1952). Many characters he places in this setting are social outcasts, poor people, derelicts, migrant workers—and the people who befriend them.

Steinbeck's work was part of the tradition of naturalistic fiction, represented earlier by Americans like Stephen Crane and Jack London. After decades of Victorian high-mindedness, **naturalism** (late in the nineteenth century) set out to correct the balance—to recognize the physical and instinctual nature of people. It tried to be more honest about their suppressed (or repressed) physical and emotional needs. Writers tried to strip life of its genteel pretenses, to look at it, if necessary, in the raw. Steinbeck represents the native tradition of naturalistic fiction in several ways: He has a special sympathy for unglamorous, unfashionable characters. He affectionately renders the coarse texture of common life. He chooses a few strong but simple symbols to carry his central themes.

Some of Steinbeck's best-known work was part of the literature of **social protest** of the thirties and forties. In the depths of the Great Depression, Steinbeck became famous with his novel *The Grapes of Wrath* (1939). Made into a movie starring Henry Fonda, Steinbeck's mythical novel proved to have a powerful hold on the imagination of millions around the world—more haunting and persuasive than the analyses and excuses prepared by historians and sociologists. Steinbeck told the story of the "Okies" (rural Americans from Oklahoma and other parts of the Dust Bowl of the thirties) who were driven from their farms by dust storms and *laissez-faire* (let-market-forces-do-their-work) economics. They were transformed from God-fearing, family-oriented, self-reliant Americans into homeless nomads looking desperately for work and a place to live. They were driven from migrant camp to migrant camp by sheriffs and politicians who were in the pay of those with power and money.

Feminist critics have in recent years taken a fresh look at the "strong women" in Steinbeck's fiction. These range from Ma Joad and Rose of Sharon, the "earth mother" figures in *The Grapes of Wrath,* to women like Elisa Allen in his short story "The Chrysanthemums." They may be women who have a strength of will missing in their husbands; they seem to have more energy and vitality than is needed for their tasks. They "must somehow express themselves meaningfully within the narrow possibilities open to women in a man's world" (Marilyn H. Mitchell).

Steinbeck wrote more than fifty short stories, including such classics as "Flight" and the stories that make up *The Red Pony* (1938). "The Chrysanthemums" has been called "Steinbeck's ultimate masterpiece in short fiction" (R. S. Hughes). Steinbeck said that this story was "designed to strike without the reader's knowledge." He meant that we may read the story casually but will feel after it is finished "that something profound has happened"—although we may "not know what nor how." Perhaps this is a key feature of fiction rich in symbolism—we finish reading with a sense that there is more to the story than meets the eye.

The Chrysanthemums   1937

The high grey-flannel fog of winter closed off the Salinas Valley from the sky and from all the rest of the world. On every side it sat like a lid on the mountains and made of the great valley a closed pot. On the broad, level land floor the gang plows bit deep and left the black earth shining like metal where the shares had cut. On the foothill ranches across the Salinas River, the yellow stubble fields seemed to be bathed in pale cold sunshine, but there was no sunshine in the valley now in December. The thick willow scrub along the river flamed with sharp and positive yellow leaves.

It was a time of quiet and of waiting. The air was cold and tender. A light wind blew up from the southwest so that the farmers were mildly hopeful of a good rain before long; but fog and rain do not go together.

Across the river, on Henry Allen's foothill ranch there was little work to be done, for the hay was cut and stored and the orchards were plowed up to receive the rain deeply when it should come. The cattle on the higher slopes were becoming shaggy and rough-coated.

Elisa Allen, working in her flower garden, looked down across the yard and saw Henry, her husband, talking to two men in business suits. The three of them stood by the tractor shed, each man with one foot on the side of the little Fordson. They smoked cigarettes and studied the machine as they talked.

Elisa watched them for a moment and then went back to her work. She was thirty-five. Her face was lean and strong and her eyes were as clear as water. Her figure looked blocked and heavy in her gardening costume, a man's black hat pulled low down over her eyes, clodhopper shoes, a figured print dress almost completely covered by a big corduroy apron with four big pockets to hold the snips, the trowel and scratcher, the seeds and the knife she worked with. She wore heavy leather gloves to protect her hands while she worked.

She was cutting down the old year's chrysanthemum stalks with a pair of short and powerful scissors. She looked down toward the men by the tractor shed now and then. Her face was eager and mature and handsome; even her work with the scissors was over-eager, over-powerful. The chrysanthemum stems seemed too small and easy for her energy.

She brushed a cloud of hair out of her eyes with the back of her glove, and left a smudge of earth on her cheek in doing it. Behind her stood the neat white farm house with red geraniums close-banked around it as high as the windows. It was a hard-swept looking little house, with hard-polished windows, and a clean mud-mat on the front steps.

Elisa cast another glance toward the tractor shed. The strangers were getting into their Ford coupe. She took off a glove and put her strong fingers down into the forest of new green chrysanthemum sprouts that were growing around the old roots. She spread the leaves and looked down among the close-growing stems. No aphids were there, no sowbugs or snails or cutworms. Her terrier fingers destroyed such pests before they could get started.

Elisa started at the sound of her husband's voice. He had come near quietly, and he leaned over the wire fence that protected her flower garden from cattle and dogs and chickens.

"At it again," he said. "You've got a strong new crop coming." 10

Elisa straightened her back and pulled on the gardening glove again. "Yes. They'll be strong this coming year." In her tone and on her face there was a little smugness.

"You've got a gift with things," Henry observed. "Some of those yellow chrysanthemums you had this year were ten inches across. I wish you'd work out in the orchard and raise some apples that big."

Her eyes sharpened. "Maybe I could do it, too. I've a gift with things, all right. My mother had it. She could stick anything in the ground and make it grow. She said it was having planters' hands that knew how to do it."

"Well, it sure works with flowers," he said.

"Henry, who were those men you were talking to?" 15

"Why, sure, that's what I came to tell you. They were from the Western Meat Company. I sold those thirty head of three-year-old steers. Got nearly my own price, too."

"Good," she said. "Good for you."

"And I thought," he continued, "I thought how it's Saturday afternoon, and we might go into Salinas for dinner at a restaurant, and then to a picture show—to celebrate, you see."

"Good," she repeated. "Oh, yes. That will be good."

Henry put on his joking tone. "There's fights tonight. How'd you like to go to 20
the fights?"

"Oh, no," she said breathlessly. "No, I wouldn't like fights."

"Just fooling, Elisa. We'll go to a movie. Let's see. It's two now. I'm going to take Scotty and bring down those steers from the hill. It'll take us maybe two hours. We'll go in town about five and have dinner at the Cominos Hotel. Like that?"

"Of course I'll like it. It's good to eat away from home."

"All right, then. I'll go get up a couple of horses."

She said, "I'll have plenty of time to transplant some of these sets, I guess." 25

She heard her husband calling Scotty down by the barn. And a little later she saw the two men ride up the pale yellow hillside in search of the steers.

There was a little square sandy bed kept for rooting the chrysanthemums. With her trowel she turned the soil over and over, and smoothed it and patted it firm. Then she dug ten parallel trenches to receive the sets. Back at the chrysanthemum bed she pulled out the little crisp shoots, trimmed off the leaves of each one with her scissors and laid it on a small orderly pile.

A squeak of wheels and plod of hoofs came from the road. Elisa looked up. The country road ran along the dense bank of willows and cottonwoods that bordered the river, and up this road came a curious vehicle, curiously drawn. It was an old spring-wagon, with a round canvas top on it like the cover of a prairie schooner. It was drawn by an old bay horse and a little grey-and-white burro. A big stubble-bearded man sat between the cover flaps and drove the crawling team. Underneath the wagon, between the hind wheels, a lean and rangy mongrel dog walked sedately. Words were painted on the canvas, in clumsy, crooked letters. "Pots, pans, knives, sisors, lawn mores, Fixed." Two rows of articles, and the triumphantly definitive "Fixed" below. The black paint had run down in little sharp points beneath each letter.

Elisa, squatting on the ground, watched to see the crazy, loose-jointed wagon pass by. But it didn't pass. It turned into the farm road in front of her house, crooked old wheels skirling and squeaking. The rangy dog darted from between the wheels and ran ahead. Instantly the two ranch shepherds flew out at him. Then all three stopped, and with stiff and quivering tails, with taut straight legs, with ambassadorial dignity, they slowly circled, sniffing daintily. The caravan pulled up to Elisa's wire fence and stopped. Now the newcomer dog, feeling out-numbered, lowered his tail and retired under the wagon with raised hackles and bared teeth.

The man on the wagon seat called out, "That's a bad dog in a fight when he gets started." 30

Elisa laughed. "I see he is. How soon does he generally get started?"

The man caught up her laughter and echoed it heartily. "Sometimes not for weeks and weeks," he said. He climbly stiffly down, over the wheel. The horse and the donkey drooped like unwatered flowers.

Elisa saw that he was a very big man. Although his hair and beard were greying, he did not look old. His worn black suit was wrinkled and spotted with grease. The laughter had disappeared from his face and eyes the moment his laughing voice ceased. His eyes were dark, and they were full of the brooding that gets in the eyes of teamsters and of sailors. The calloused hands he rested on the wire fence were cracked, and every crack was a black line. He took off his battered hat.

"I'm off my general road, ma'am," he said. "Does this dirt road cut over across the river to the Los Angeles highway?"

Elisa stood up and shoved the thick scissors in her apron pocket. "Well, yes, it does, but it winds around and then fords the river. I don't think your team could pull through the sand." 35

He replied with some asperity, "It might surprise you what them beasts can pull through."

"When they get started?" she asked.

He smiled for a second. "Yes. When they get started."

"Well," said Elisa, "I think you'll save time if you go back to the Salinas road and pick up the highway there."

He drew a big finger down the chicken wire and made it sing. "I ain't in any hurry, ma'am. I go from Seattle to San Diego and back every year. Takes all my time. About six months each way. I aim to follow nice weather." 40

Elisa took off her gloves and stuffed them in the apron pocket with the scissors. She touched the under edge of her man's hat, searching for fugitive hairs. "That sounds like a nice kind of a way to live," she said.

He leaned confidentially over the fence. "Maybe you noticed the writing on my wagon. I mend pots and sharpen knives and scissors. You got any of them things to do?"

"Oh, no," she said quickly. "Nothing like that." Her eyes hardened with resistance.

"Scissors is the worst thing," he explained. "Most people just ruin scissors trying to sharpen 'em, but I know how. I got a special tool. It's a little bobbit kind of thing, and patented. But it sure does the trick."

"No. My scissors are all sharp." 45

"All right, then. Take a pot," he continued earnestly, "a bent pot, or a pot with a hole. I can make it like new so you don't have to buy no new ones. That's a saving for you."

"No," she said shortly. "I tell you I have nothing like that for you to do."

His face fell to an exaggerated sadness. His voice took on a whining undertone. "I ain't had a thing to do today. Maybe I won't have no supper tonight. You see I'm off my regular road. I know folks on the highway clear from Seattle to San Diego. They save their things for me to sharpen up because they know I do it so good and save them money."

"I'm sorry," Elisa said irritably. "I haven't anything for you to do."

His eyes left her face and fell to searching the ground. They roamed about until they came to the chrysanthemum bed where she had been working. "What's them plants, ma'am?" 50

The irritation and resistance melted from Elisa's face. "Oh, those are chrysanthemums, giant whites and yellows. I raise them every year, bigger than anybody around here."

"Kind of a long-stemmed flower? Looks like a quick puff of colored smoke?" he asked.

"That's it. What a nice way to describe them."

"They smell kind of nasty till you get used to them," he said.

"It's a good bitter smell," she retorted, "not nasty at all." 55

He changed his tone quickly. "I like the smell myself."

"I had ten-inch blooms this year," she said.

The man leaned farther over the fence. "Look. I know a lady down the road a piece, has got the nicest garden you ever seen. Got nearly every kind of flower but no chrysantheums. Last time I was mending a copper-bottom washtub for her (that's a hard job but I do it good), she said to me, 'If you ever run acrost some nice chrysantheums I wish you'd try to get me a few seeds.' That's what she told me."

Elisa's eyes grew alert and eager. "She couldn't have known much about chrysanthemums. You *can* raise them from seed, but it's much easier to root the little sprouts you see there."

"Oh," he said. "I s'pose I can't take none to her, then." 60

"Why yes you can," Elisa cried. "I can put some in damp sand, and you can carry them right along with you. They'll take root in the pot if you keep them damp. And then she can transplant them."

"She'd sure like to have some, ma'am. You say they're nice ones?"

"Beautiful," she said. "Oh, beautiful." Her eyes shone. She tore off the battered hat and shook out her dark pretty hair. "I'll put them in a flower pot, and you can take them right with you. Come into the yard."

While the man came through the picket gate Elisa ran excitedly along the geranium-bordered path to the back of the house. And she returned carrying a big red flower pot. The gloves were forgotten now. She kneeled on the ground by the starting bed and dug up the sandy soil with her fingers and scooped it into the bright new flower pot. Then she picked up the little pile of shoots she had prepared. With her strong fingers she pressed them into the sand and tamped around them with her knuckles. The man stood over her. "I'll tell you what to do," she said. "You remember so you can tell the lady."

"Yes, I'll try to remember." 65

"Well, look. These will take root in about a month. Then she must set them out, about a foot apart in good rich earth like this, see?" She lifted a handful of dark soil for him to look at. "They'll grow fast and tall. Now remember this: In July tell her to cut them down, about eight inches from the ground."

"Before they bloom?" he asked.

"Yes, before they bloom." Her face was tight with eagerness. "They'll grow right up again. About the last of September the buds will start."

She stopped and seemed perplexed. "It's the budding that takes the most care," she said hesitantly. "I don't know how to tell you." She looked deep into his eyes, searchingly. Her mouth opened a little, and she seemed to be listening. "I'll try to tell you," she said. "Did you ever hear of planting hands?"

"Can't say I have, ma'am." 70

"Well, I can only tell you what it feels like. It's when you're picking off the buds you don't want. Everything goes right down into your fingertips. You watch your fingers work. They do it themselves. You can feel how it is. They pick and pick the buds. They never make a mistake. They're with the plant. Do you see? Your fingers and the plant. You can feel that, right up your arm. They know. They never make a mistake. You can feel it. When you're like that you can't do anything wrong. Do you see that? Can you understand that?"

She was kneeling on the ground looking up at him. Her breast swelled passionately.

The man's eyes narrowed. He looked away self-consciously. "Maybe I know," he said. "Sometimes in the night in the wagon there——"

Elisa's voice grew husky. She broke in on him, "I've never lived as you do, but I know what you mean. When the night is dark—why, the stars are sharp-pointed, and there's quiet. Why, you rise up and up! Every pointed star gets driven into your body. It's like that. Hot and sharp and—lovely."

Kneeling there, her hand went out toward his legs in the greasy black trousers. Her hesitant fingers almost touched the cloth. Then her hand dropped to the ground. She crouched low like a fawning dog.   75

He said, "It's nice, just like you say. Only when you don't have no dinner, it ain't."

She stood up then, very straight, and her face was ashamed. She held the flower pot out to him and placed it gently in his arms. "Here. Put it in your wagon, on the seat, where you can watch it. Maybe I can find something for you to do."

At the back of the house she dug in the can pile and found two old and battered aluminum saucepans. She carried them back and gave them to him. "Here, maybe you can fix these."

His manner changed. He became professional. "Good as new I can fix them." At the back of his wagon he set a little anvil, and out of an oily tool box dug a small machine hammer. Elisa came through the gate to watch him while he pounded out the dents in the kettles. His mouth grew sure and knowing. At a difficult part of the work he sucked his under-lip.

"You sleep right in the wagon?" Elisa asked.   80

"Right in the wagon, ma'am. Rain or shine I'm dry as a cow in there."

"It must be nice," she said. "It must be very nice. I wish women could do such things."

"It ain't the right kind of a life for a woman."

Her upper lip raised a little, showing her teeth. "How do you know? How can you tell?" she said.

"I don't know, ma'am," he protested. "Of course I don't know. Now here's your kettles, done. You don't have to buy no new ones."   85

"How much?"

"Oh, fifty cents'll do. I keep my prices down and my work good. That's why I have all them satisfied customers up and down the highway."

Elisa brought him a fifty-cent piece from the house and dropped it in his hand. "You might be surprised to have a rival some time. I can sharpen scissors, too. And I can beat the dents out of little pots. I could show you what a woman might do."

He put his hammer back in the oily box and shoved the little anvil out of sight. "It would be a lonely life for a woman, ma'am, and a scarey life, too, with animals creeping under the wagon all night." He climbed over the singletree, steadying himself with a hand on the burro's white rump. He settled himself in the seat, picked up the lines. "Thank you kindly, ma'am," he said. "I'll do like you told me; I'll go back and catch the Salinas road."

"Mind," she called, "if you're long in getting there, keep the sand damp."   90

"Sand, ma'am? . . . Sand? Oh, sure. You mean around the chrysantheums. Sure

I will." He clucked his tongue. The beasts leaned luxuriously into their collars. The mongrel dog took his place between the back wheels. The wagon turned and crawled out the entrance road and back the way it had come, along the river.

Elisa stood in front of her wire fence watching the slow progress of the caravan. Her shoulders were straight, her head thrown back, her eyes half-closed, so that the scene came vaguely into them. Her lips moved silently, forming the words "Good-bye—good-bye." Then she whispered, "That's a bright direction. There's a glowing there." The sound of her whisper startled her. She shook herself free and looked about to see whether anyone had been listening. Only the dogs had heard. They lifted their heads toward her from their sleeping in the dust, and then stretched out their chins and settled asleep again. Elisa turned and ran hurriedly into the house.

In the kitchen she reached behind the stove and felt the water tank. It was full of hot water from the noonday cooking. In the bathroom she tore off her soiled clothes and flung them into the corner. And then she scrubbed herself with a little block of pumice, legs and thighs, loins and chest and arms, until her skin was scratched and red. When she had dried herself she stood in front of a mirror in her bedroom and looked at her body. She tightened her stomach and threw out her chest. She turned and looked over her shoulder at her back.

After a while she began to dress, slowly. She put on her newest underclothing and her nicest stockings and the dress which was the symbol of her prettiness. She worked carefully on her hair, penciled her eyebrows and rouged her lips.

Before she was finished she heard the little thunder of hoofs and the shouts of 95
Henry and his helper as they drove the red steers into the corral. She heard the gate bang shut and set herself for Henry's arrival.

His step sounded on the porch. He entered the house calling, "Elisa, where are you?"

"In my room, dressing. I'm not ready. There's hot water for your bath. Hurry up. It's getting late."

When she heard him splashing in the tub, Elisa laid his dark suit on the bed, and shirt and socks and tie beside it. She stood his polished shoes on the floor beside the bed. Then she went to the porch and sat primly and stiffly down. She looked toward the river road where the willow-line was still yellow with frosted leaves so that under the high grey fog they seemed a thin band of sunshine. This was the only color in the grey afternoon. She sat unmoving for a long time. Her eyes blinked rarely.

Henry came banging out of the door, shoving his tie inside his vest as he came. Elisa stiffened and her face grew tight. Henry stopped short and looked at her. "Why—why, Elisa. You look so nice!"

"Nice? You think I look nice? What do you mean by 'nice'?" 100

Henry blundered on. "I don't know. I mean you look different, strong and happy."

"I am strong? Yes, strong. What do you mean 'strong'?"

He looked bewildered. "You're playing some kind of a game," he said helplessly. "It's a kind of a play. You look strong enough to break a calf over your knee, happy enough to eat it like a watermelon."

For a second she lost her rigidity. "Henry! Don't talk like that. You didn't know what you said." She grew complete again. "I'm strong," she boasted. "I never knew before how strong."

Henry looked down toward the tractor shed, and when he brought his eyes back 105
to her, they were his own again. "I'll get out the car. You can put on your coat while I'm starting."

Elisa went into the house. She heard him drive to the gate and idle down his motor, and then she took a long time to put on her hat. She pulled it here and pressed it there. When Henry turned the motor off she slipped into her coat and went out.

The little roadster bounced along on the dirt road by the river, raising the birds and driving the rabbits into the brush. Two cranes flapped heavily over the willow-line and dropped into the river-bed.

Far ahead on the road Elisa saw a dark speck. She knew.

She tried not to look as they passed it, but her eyes would not obey. She whispered to herself sadly, "He might have thrown them off the road. That wouldn't have been much trouble, not very much. But he kept the pot," she explained. "He had to keep the pot. That's why he couldn't get them off the road."

The roadster turned a bend and she saw the caravan ahead. She swung full around toward her husband so she could not see the little covered wagon and the mismatched team as the car passed them. 110

In a moment it was over. The thing was done. She did not look back.

She said loudly, to be heard above the motor, "It will be good, tonight, a good dinner."

"Now you're changed again," Henry complained. He took one hand from the wheel and patted her knee. "I ought to take you in to dinner oftener. It would be good for both of us. We get so heavy out on the ranch."

"Henry," she asked, "could we have wine at dinner?"

"Sure we could. Say! That will be fine." 115

She was silent for a while; then she said, "Henry, those prize fights, do the men hurt each other very much?"

"Sometimes a little, not often. Why?"

"Well, I've read how they break noses, and blood runs down their chests. I've read how the fighting gloves get heavy and soggy with blood."

He looked around at her. "What's the matter, Elisa? I didn't know you read things like that." He brought the car to a stop, then turned to the right over the Salinas River bridge.

"Do any women ever go to the fights?" she asked. 120

"Oh, sure, some. What's the matter, Elisa? Do you want to go? I don't think you'd like it, but I'll take you if you really want to go."

She relaxed limply in the seat. "Oh, no. No. I don't want to go. I'm sure I don't." Her face was turned away from him. "It will be enough if we can have wine. It will be plenty." She turned up her coat collar so he could not see that she was crying weakly—like an old woman.

THE RECEPTIVE READER

1. What is the meaning of the chrysanthemums as the central, gradually evolving *symbol* in the story? How much of a continuing thread do they provide for the story as a whole? What role do they play at the high point of the story? Were you surprised when you saw the flowers in the road?

2. When flowers are used as symbols, they activate a whole range of memories, associations, *connotations*. Cluster the word *flower*. What chains of association and patterns of thought does it bring to mind? Which of these do you think are especially relevant to this story?

3. What telling or revealing *details*—dress, the weather, features of the physical setting, the boxing, the wine—might be charged with symbolic significance?

4. Critics have found much sexual imagery, symbolism, or allusion in the encounter between Elisa and the tinker. What are striking examples? What is significant in the description of his arrival? What is strange or paradoxical about their relationship?

5. What is the role of the husband in this story? What kind of person is he? What kind of marriage do he and Elisa have? What are striking details or images that bring the nature of their relationship into focus?

6. What is the role of traditional assumptions about men's work and women's work, or about men's interests and women's interests, in this story? Do you see in the heroine an "ambiguous combination of feminine and masculine traits" (Marilyn H. Mitchell)?

7. Would you call the sight of the discarded flowers in the road the *climax*, or high point, of the story? Where does the story go afterwards? What impact have the developments of the story had on Elisa? How does the story end?

8. Critics have singled out Steinbeck as one of the few male authors of his time who went beyond stereotypical portraits of women. Do you think they are right? How might this story have been different if it had been written by a woman?

THE PERSONAL RESPONSE

How do you relate to Elisa as the *central character*? Do you find her sympathetic? strong? weak? strange? (Support your answer in detail.)

THE RANGE OF INTERPRETATION

In the following two critical excerpts, compare a traditional reading of the story by a male critic with a rereading of this and another story from a feminist point of view. Stanley Renner, in "The Real Woman inside the Fence in 'The Chrysanthemums,'" claims that "the story's evidence does not support the view that Elisa is a woman kept from fulfillment by male domination." For him, the story is shaped by traditional male complaints "against the sexual unresponsiveness of the female, against an ambivalent female sexuality that both invites and repels male admiration, against the sexual delicacy of the female, who, repelled by sexual reality, holds out for indulgences of her emotional and spiritual yearnings":

> Unlike men, women incline more toward romantic fantasies of sex than the act of love itself. Clearly Elisa romanticizes the tinker. In ironic mockery of Elisa's great and perverse capacity for romanticizing reality, Steinbeck makes everything about the tinker the utter antithesis of her fastidious tidiness, which symbolizes her delicate sexual sensibility. Unshaven, unwashed, his clothes "wrinkled and spotted with grease," he represents everything she furiously purges from her garden and scrubs out of her house. Yet she fantasizes sexual intercourse with him when he gratifies her hunger for romance because it is only a fantasy: he will presently climb back into his slovenly wagon and ride away into the romantic sunset. Henry, clean and reliable if a bit stodgy and clumsy, is reality pressing against Elisa's fence seeking an actual sexual relationship. But in rejecting reality, albeit unideal, as reality always is, for a patently falsified romantic fantasy, she defeats her own impulses toward a fuller life.
>
> From *Modern Fiction Studies*, Summer 1985

Contrasting with Renner's perspective focusing on male dissatisfaction and complaints, Marilyn H. Mitchell, in "Steinbeck's Strong Women: Feminine Identity in the Short Stories," claims that Steinbeck shows women who "are trapped between society's definition of the masculine and the feminine and are struggling against the limitations of the feminine." Steinbeck is using them "to refute outmoded conceptions of what a woman should be" and aims to show "the real human beauty beneath Elisa's rough and somewhat masculine exterior":

Two of John Steinbeck's more intricate and memorable stories are "The Chrysanthemums" and "The White Quail." Both examine the psychology and sexuality of strong women who must somehow express themselves meaningfully within the narrow possibilities open to women in a man's world. In each case the woman chooses a traditional feminine activity, gardening, as a creative outlet. . . . Steinbeck reveals fundamental differences between the way women see themselves and the way they are viewed by men. For example, both husbands relate primarily to the physical attributes of their wives, making only meager attempts to comprehend their personalities. Consequently, a gulf of misunderstanding exists between the marriage partners, which creates verbal as well as sexual blocks to communication. In each marriage, at least one of the spouses is aware of some degree of sexual frustration, although dissatisfaction is never overtly articulated. Furthermore, the propensity of the men to see their wives as dependent inferiors, while the women perceive themselves as being equal if not superior partners, creates a strain within the marriage which is partially responsible for the isolation of each of the characters.

Both Elisa Allen of "The Chrysanthemums" and Mary Teller in "The White Quail" display a strength of will usually identified with the male but which, in these cases, the husbands are not shown to have. . . . Elisa Allen demonstrates a very earthly sensuality in "The Chrysanthemums," though not in the presence of her husband, indicating that their failure as a couple may be as much his fault as hers.

From R. S. Hughes, *Steinbeck: A Study of the Short Fiction*

Is there any common basis for these two approaches to the story? How and why do they disagree? Who do you think is more nearly right, and why?

CROSS-REFERENCES—For Discussion or Writing

Compare and contrast the treatment of unfulfilled desire in Katherine Anne Porter's "The Jilting of Granny Weatherall" and in John Steinbeck's "The Chrysanthemums." (Does it make a difference that one of the stories is by a female author and the other by a male author?)

THE CENTRAL SYMBOL

Often a **central symbol** becomes the focal point of a story. A central symbol focuses our attention. It provides a tangible object for our emotions— since many of us find it hard to anchor our feelings to disembodied ideas. A central symbol becomes the hub for meanings and associations. It may slowly evolve, acquiring its full meaning only as the story as a whole takes shape. In each of the following stories, a rich central symbol helps give shape to the story as a whole.

CHARLOTTE PERKINS GILMAN (1860–1935)

Gilman was a leading feminist and social activist at the turn of the century. She grew up in a family that included prominent suffragists (advocates of a woman's right to vote); one of her great-aunts was the abolitionist Harriet Beecher Stowe, author of *Uncle Tom's Cabin*. In her *Women and Economics* (1898) and other nonfiction works, Gilman argued that the traditional conception of women's roles was the result of social custom; it was culturally conditioned rather than anchored in biology. She proposed revolutionary rearrangements of domestic life to free women for work outside the home.

Born and raised in Connecticut, Gilman moved to California after separating from her first husband, and she edited and published feminist publications there. She helped organize the California Women's Congresses of 1894 and 1895 and was one of the founders of the Women's Peace Party. Besides writing nonfiction, she wrote novels and short stories that dramatized her belief in women's capacity for independence and self-realization.

Gilman's much-anthologized "The Yellow Wallpaper" chronicles a young woman's descent into insanity. The story has been read as a clinical study of the escalation of mental illness—as if we were watching the patient from the *outside,* somewhat the way the husband-physician does in the story. But the author makes us see everything in her story from the *inside.* We see everything from the point of view of the patient—including the limitations and condescending attitude of the doctor-husband. Gilman herself had suffered from severe postpartum depression after the birth of a daughter in 1884. She was treated by a specialist who prescribed a "rest cure"—bed rest and no physical exertion or intellectual stimulation. (This is the Weir Mitchell mentioned by the patient's husband in the story.) The treatment, Gilman said later, drove her "so near the borderline of mental ruin" that she "could see over."

The Yellow Wallpaper   1892

It is very seldom that mere ordinary people like John and myself secure ancestral halls for the summer.

A colonial mansion, a hereditary estate, I would say a haunted house, and reach the height of romantic felicity—but that would be asking too much of fate!

Still I will proudly declare that there is something queer about it.

Else, why should it be let so cheaply? And why have stood so long untenanted?

John laughs at me, of course, but one expects that in marriage.   5

John is practical in the extreme. He has no patience with faith, an intense horror of superstition, and he scoffs openly at any talk of things not to be felt and seen and put down in figures.

John is a physician, and *perhaps*—(I would not say it to a living soul, of course, but this is dead paper and a great relief to my mind—) *perhaps* that is one reason I do not get well faster.

You see he does not believe I am sick!

And what can one do?

If a physician of high standing, and one's own husband, assures friends and rela- 10
tives that there is really nothing the matter with one but temporary nervous depression—a slight hysterical tendency—what is one to do?

My brother is also a physician, and also of high standing, and he says the same
thing.

So I take phosphates or phosphites—whichever it is, and tonics, and journeys, and
air, and exercise, and am absolutely forbidden to "work" until I am well again.

Personally, I disagree with their ideas.

Personally, I believe that congenial work, with excitement and change, would do
me good.

But what is one to do? 15

I did write for a while in spite of them; but it *does* exhaust me a good deal—having
to be so sly about it, or else meet with heavy opposition.

I sometimes fancy that in my condition if I had less opposition and more society
and stimulus—but John says the very worst thing I can do is to think about my condition, and I confess it always makes me feel bad.

So I will let it alone and talk about the house.

The most beautiful place! It is quite alone, standing well back from the road, quite
three miles from the village. It makes me think of English places that you read about,
for there are hedges and walls and gates that lock, and lots of separate little houses for
the gardeners and people.

There is a *delicious* garden! I never saw such a garden—large and shady, full of 20
box-bordered paths, and lined with long grape-covered arbors with seats under them.

There were greenhouses, too, but they are all broken now.

There was some legal trouble, I believe, something about the heirs and coheirs;
anyhow, the place has been empty for years.

That spoils my ghostliness, I am afraid, but I don't care—there is something
strange about the house—I can feel it.

I even said so to John one moonlight evening, but he said what I felt was a
draught, and shut the window.

I get unreasonably angry with John sometimes. I'm sure I never used to be so sen- 25
sitive. I think it is due to this nervous condition.

But John says if I feel so, I shall neglect proper self-control; so I take pains to control myself—before him, at least, and that makes me very tired.

I don't like our room a bit. I wanted one downstairs that opened on the piazza
and had roses all over the window, and such pretty old-fashioned chintz hangings! but
John would not hear of it.

He said there was only one window and not room for two beds, and no near room
for him if he took another.

He is very careful and loving, and hardly lets me stir without special direction.

I have a schedule prescription for each hour in the day; he takes all care from me, 30
and so I feel basely ungrateful not to value it more.

He said we came here solely on my account, that I was to have perfect rest and all
the air I could get. "Your exercise depends on your strength, my dear," said he, "and
your food somewhat on your appetite; but air you can absorb all the time." So we took
the nursery at the top of the house.

It is a big, airy room, the whole floor nearly, with windows that look all ways, and
air and sunshine galore. It was nursery first and then playroom and gymnasium, I
should judge; for the windows are barred for little children, and there are rings and
things in the walls.

The paint and paper look as if a boys' school had used it. It is stripped off—the paper—in great patches all around the head of my bed, about as far as I can reach, and in a great place on the other side of the room low down. I never saw a worse paper in my life.

One of those sprawling flamboyant patterns committing every artistic sin.

It is dull enough to confuse the eye in following, pronounced enough to constant- 35 ly irritate and provoke study, and when you follow the lame uncertain curves for a little distance they suddenly commit suicide—plunge off at outrageous angles, destroy themselves in unheard of contradictions.

The color is repellent, almost revolting; a smouldering unclean yellow, strangely faded by the slow-turning sunlight.

It is a dull yet lurid orange in some places, a sickly sulphur tint in others.

No wonder the children hated it! I should hate it myself if I had to live in this room long.

There comes John, and I must put this away,—he hates to have me write a word.

I

We have been here two weeks, and I haven't felt like writing before, since that 40 first day.

I am sitting by the window now, up in this atrocious nursery, and there is nothing to hinder my writing as much as I please, save lack of strength.

John is away all day, and even some nights when his cases are serious.

I am glad my case is not serious!

But these nervous troubles are dreadfully depressing.

John does not know how much I really suffer. He knows there is no *reason* to suf- 45 fer, and that satisfies him.

Of course it is only nervousness. It does weigh on me so not to do my duty in any way!

I meant to be such a help to John, such a real rest and comfort, and here I am a comparative burden already!

Nobody would believe what an effort it is to do what little I am able,—to dress and entertain, and order things.

It is fortunate Mary is so good with the baby. Such a dear baby!

And yet I *cannot* be with him, it makes me so nervous. 50

I suppose John never was nervous in his life. He laughs at me so about this wallpaper!

At first he meant to repaper the room, but afterwards he said that I was letting it get the better of me, and that nothing was worse for a nervous patient than to give way to such fancies.

He said that after the wallpaper was changed it would be the heavy bedstead, and then the barred windows, and then that gate at the head of the stairs, and so on.

"You know the place is doing you good," he said, "and really, dear, I don't care to renovate the house just for a three months' rental."

"Then do let us go downstairs," I said, "there are such pretty rooms there." 55

Then he took me in his arms and called me a blessed little goose, and said he would go down cellar, if I wished, and have it whitewashed into the bargain.

But he is right enough about the beds and windows and things.

It is as airy and comfortable room as any one need wish, and, of course, I would not be so silly as to make him uncomfortable just for a whim.

I'm really getting quite fond of the big room, all but that horrid paper.

Out of one window I can see the garden, those mysterious deep-shaded arbors, the 60 riotous old-fashioned flowers, and bushes and gnarly trees.

Out of another I get a lovely view of the bay and a little private wharf belonging to the estate. There is a beautiful shaded lane that runs down there from the house. I always fancy I see people walking in these numerous paths and arbors, but John has cautioned me not to give way to fancy in the least. He says that with my imaginative power and habit of story-making, a nervous weakness like mine is sure to lead to all manner of excited fancies, and that I ought to use my will and good sense to check the tendency. So I try.

I think sometimes that if I were only well enough to write a little it would relieve the press of ideas and rest me.

But I find I get pretty tired when I try.

It is so discouraging not to have any advice and companionship about my work. When I get really well, John says we will ask Cousin Henry and Julia down for a long visit; but he says he would as soon put fireworks in my pillow-case as to let me have those stimulating people about now.

I wish I could get well faster. 65

But I must not think about that. This paper looks to me as if it *knew* what a vicious influence it had!

There is a recurrent spot where the pattern lolls like a broken neck and two bulbous eyes stare at you upside down.

I get positively angry with the impertinence of it and the everlastingness. Up and down and sideways they crawl, and those absurd, unblinking eyes are everywhere. There is one place where two breadths didn't match, and the eyes go all up and down the line, one a little higher than the other.

I never saw so much expression in an inanimate thing before, and we all know how much expression they have! I used to lie awake as a child and get more entertainment and terror out of blank walls and plain furniture than most children could find in a toy-store.

I remember what a kindly wink the knobs of our big, old bureau used to have, and 70 there was one chair that always seemed like a strong friend.

I used to feel that if any of the other things looked too fierce I could always hop into that chair and be safe.

The furniture in this room is no worse than inharmonious, however, for we had to bring it all from downstairs. I suppose when this was used as a playroom they had to take the nursery things out, and no wonder! I never saw such ravages as the children have made here.

The wallpaper, as I said before, is torn off in spots, and it sticketh closer than a brother—they must have had perseverance as well as hatred.

Then the floor is scratched and gouged and splintered, the plaster itself is dug out here and there, and this great heavy bed which is all we found in the room, looks as if it had been through the wars.

But I don't mind it a bit—only the paper. 75

There comes John's sister. Such a dear girl as she is, and so careful of me! I must not let her find me writing.

She is a perfect and enthusiastic housekeeper, and hopes for no better profession. I verily believe she thinks it is the writing which made me sick!

But I can write when she is out, and see her a long way off from these windows.

There is one that commands the road, a lovely shaded winding road, and one that just looks off over the country. A lovely country, too, full of great elms and velvet meadows.

This wallpaper has a kind of subpattern in a different shade, a particularly irritating 80 one, for you can only see it in certain lights, and not clearly then.

But in the places where it isn't faded and where the sun is just so—I can see a strange, provoking, formless sort of figure, that seems to skulk about behind that silly and conspicuous front design.

There's sister on the stairs!

II

Well, the Fourth of July is over! The people are all gone and I am tired out. John thought it might do me good to see a little company, so we just had mother and Nellie and the children down for a week.

Of course I didn't do a thing. Jennie sees to everything now.

But it tired me all the same.

John says if I don't pick up faster he shall send me to Weir Mitchell in the fall.

But I don't want to go there at all. I had a friend who was in his hands once, and she says he is just like John and my brother, only more so!

Besides, it is such an undertaking to go so far.

I don't feel as if it was worth while to turn my hand over for anything, and I'm getting dreadfully fretful and querulous.

I cry at nothing, and cry most of the time.

Of course I don't when John is here, or anybody else, but when I am alone.

And I am alone a good deal just now. John is kept in town very often by serious cases, and Jennie is good and lets me alone when I want her to.

So I walk a little in the garden or down that lovely lane, sit on the porch under the roses, and lie down up here a good deal.

I'm getting really fond of the room in spite of the wallpaper. Perhaps *because* of the wallpaper.

It dwells in my mind so!

I lie here on this great immovable bed—it is nailed down, I believe—and follow that pattern about by the hour. It is as good as gymnastics, I assure you. I start, we'll say, at the bottom, down in the corner over there where it has not been touched, and I determine for the thousandth time that I *will* follow that pointless pattern to some sort of a conclusion.

I know a little of the principle of design, and I know this thing was not arranged on any laws of radiation, or alternation, or repetition, or symmetry, or anything else that I ever heard of.

It is repeated, of course, by the breadths, but not otherwise.

Looked at in one way each breadth stands alone, the bloated curves and flourishes—a kind of "debased Romanesque" with *delirium tremens* go waddling up and down in isolated columns of fatuity.

But, on the other hand, they connect diagonally, and the sprawling outlines run off in great slanting waves of optic horror, like a lot of wallowing seaweeds in full chase.

The whole thing goes horizontally, too, at least it seems so, and I exhaust myself in trying to distinguish the order of its going in that direction.

They have used a horizontal breadth for a frieze, and that adds wonderfully to the confusion.

There is one end of the room where it is almost intact, and there, when the crosslights fade and the low sun shines directly upon it, I can almost fancy radiation after all,—the interminable grotesques seem to form around a common center and rush off in headlong plunges of equal distraction.

It makes me tired to follow it. I will take a nap I guess.

III

I don't know why I should write this. 105

I don't want to.

I don't feel able.

And I know John would think it absurd. But I *must* say what I feel and think in some way—it is such a relief!

But the effort is getting to be greater than the relief. [contradicts herself]

Half the time now I am awfully lazy, and lie down ever so much. 110

John says I mustn't lose my strength, and has me take cod liver oil and lots of tonics and things, to say nothing of ale and wine and rare meat.

Dear John! He loves me very dearly, and hates to have me sick. I tried to have a real earnest reasonable talk with him the other day, and tell him how I wish he would let me go and make a visit to Cousin Henry and Julia.

But he said I wasn't able to go, nor able to stand it after I got there; and I did not make out a very good case for myself, for I was crying before I had finished. [hysterical woman]

It is getting to be a great effort for me to think straight. Just this nervous weakness I suppose.

And dear John gathered me up in his arms, and just carried me upstairs and laid 115 me on the bed, and sat by me and read to me till it tired my head.

He said I was his darling and his comfort and all he had, and that I must take care of myself for his sake, and keep well.

He says no one but myself can help me out of it, that I must use my will and self-control and not let any silly fancies run away with me.

There's one comfort, the baby is well and happy, and does not have to occupy this nursery with the horrid wallpaper.

If we had not used it, that blessed child would have! What a fortunate escape! Why, I wouldn't have a child of mine, an impressionable little thing, live in such a room for worlds.

I never thought of it before, but it is lucky that John kept me here after all, I can 120 stand it so much easier than a baby, you see.

Of course I never mention it to them any more—I am too wise,—but I keep watch of it all the same.

There are things in that paper that nobody knows but me, or ever will.

Behind that outside pattern the dim shapes get clearer every day.

It is always the same shape, only very numerous.

And it is like a woman stooping down and creeping about behind that pattern. I 125 don't like it a bit. I wonder—I begin to think—I wish John would take me away from here! [first mention of the lady]

IV

It is so hard to talk with John about my case, because he is so wise, and because he loves me so.

But I tried it last night.

It was moonlight. The moon shines in all around just as the sun does.

I hate to see it sometimes, it creeps so slowly, and always comes in by one window or another.

John was asleep and I hated to waken him, so I kept still and watched the moon- 130 light on that undulating wallpaper till I felt creepy.

The faint figure behind seemed to shake the pattern, just as if she wanted to get out.

I got up softly and went to feel and see if the paper *did* move, and when I came back John was awake.

"What is it, little girl?" he said. "Don't go walking about like that—you'll get cold."

I thought it was a good time to talk, so I told him that I really was not gaining here, and that I wished he would take me away.

"Why, darling!" said he, "our lease will be up in three weeks, and I can't see how to leave before. 135

"The repairs are not done at home, and I cannot possibly leave town just now. Of course if you were in any danger, I could and would, but you really are better, dear, whether you can see it or not. I am a doctor, dear, and I know. You are gaining flesh and color, your appetite is better, I feel really much easier about you."

"I don't weigh a bit more," said I, "nor as much; and my appetite may be better in the evening when you are here, but it is worse in the morning when you are away!"

"Bless her little heart!" said he with a big hug, "she shall be as sick as she pleases! But now let's improve the shining hours by going to sleep, and talk about it in the morning!"

"And you won't go away?" I asked gloomily.

"Why, how can I, dear? It is only three weeks more and then we will take a nice lit- 140 tle trip of a few days while Jennie is getting the house ready. Really dear you are better!"

"Better in body perhaps—" I began, and stopped short, for he sat up straight and looked at me with such a stern, reproachful look that I could not say another word.

"My darling," said he, "I beg of you, for my sake and for our child's sake, as well as for your own, that you will never for one instant let that idea enter your mind! There is nothing so dangerous, so fascinating, to a temperament like yours. It is a false and foolish fancy. Can you not trust me as a physician when I tell you so?"

So of course I said no more on that score, and we went to sleep before long. He thought I was asleep first, but I wasn't, and lay there for hours trying to decide whether that front pattern and the back pattern really did move together or separately.

V *decided she wouldn't tell him anything else; it is hidden.*

On a pattern like this, by daylight, there is a lack of sequence, a defiance of law, that is a constant irritant to a normal mind.

The color is hideous enough, and unreliable enough, and infuriating enough, but 145 the pattern is torturing.

You think you have mastered it, but just as you get well underway in following, it turns a back-somersault and there you are. It slaps you in the face, knocks you down, and tramples upon you. It is like a bad dream.

The outside pattern is a florid arabesque, reminding one of a fungus. If you can imagine a toadstool in joints, an interminable string of toadstools, budding and sprouting in endless convolutions—why, that is something like it.

That is, sometimes!

There is one marked peculiarity about this paper, a thing nobody seems to notice but myself, and that is that it changes as the light changes.

When the sun shoots in through the east window—I always watch for that first 150 long, straight ray—it changes so quickly that I never can quite believe it.

That is why I watch it always.

By moonlight—the moon shines in all night when there is a moon—I wouldn't know it was the same paper.

At night in any kind of light, in twilight, candlelight, lamplight, and worst of all by moonlight, it becomes bars! The outside pattern I mean, and the woman behind it is as plain as can be.

I didn't realize for a long time what the thing was that showed behind, that dim subpattern, but now I am quite sure it is a woman.

By daylight she is subdued, quiet. I fancy it is the pattern that keeps her so still. It is so puzzling. It keeps me quiet by the hour. 155

I lie down ever so much now. John says it is good for me, and to sleep all I can.

Indeed he started the habit by making me lie down for an hour after each meal.

It is a very bad habit I am convinced, for you see I don't sleep.

And that cultivates deceit, for I don't tell them I'm awake—O no!

The fact is I am getting a little afraid of John. 160

He seems very queer sometimes, and even Jennie has an inexplicable look.

It strikes me occasionally, just as a scientific hypothesis,—that perhaps it is the paper!

I have watched John when he did not know I was looking, and come into the room suddenly on the most innocent excuses, and I've caught him several times *looking at the paper!* And Jennie too. I caught Jennie with her hand on it once.

She didn't know I was in the room, and when I asked her in a quiet, a very quiet voice, with the most restrained manner possible, what she was doing with the paper— she turned around as if she had been caught stealing, and looked quite angry—asked me why I should frighten her so!

Then she said that the paper stained everything it touched, that she had found yellow smooches on all my clothes and John's, and she wished we would be more careful! 165

Did not that sound innocent? But I know she was studying that pattern, and I am determined that nobody shall find it out but myself!

VI

Life is very much more exciting now than it used to be. You see I have something more to expect, to look forward to, to watch. I really do eat better, and am more quiet than I was.

John is so pleased to see me improve! He laughed a little the other day, and said I seemed to be flourishing in spite of my wallpaper.

I turned it off with a laugh. I had no intention of telling him it was *because* of the wallpaper—he would make fun of me. He might even want to take me away.

I don't want to leave now until I have found it out. There is a week more, and I think that will be enough. 170

VII

I'm feeling ever so much better! I don't sleep much at night, for it is so interesting to watch developments; but I sleep a good deal in the daytime.

In the daytime it is tiresome and perplexing.

There are always new shoots on the fungus, and new shades of yellow all over it. I cannot keep count of them, though I have tried conscientiously.

It is the strangest yellow, that wallpaper! It makes me think of all the yellow things I ever saw—not beautiful ones like buttercups, but old foul, bad yellow things.

But there is something else about that paper—the smell! I noticed it the moment we came into the room, but with so much air and sun it was not bad. Now we have had a week of fog and rain, and whether the windows are open or not, the smell is here. 175

It creeps all over the house.

I find it hovering in the dining-room, skulking in the parlor, hiding in the hall, lying in wait for me on the stairs.

It gets into my hair.

Even when I go to ride, if I turn my head suddenly and surprise it—there is that smell! *It's everywhere!*

Such a peculiar odor, too! I have spent hours in trying to analyze it, to find what it smelled like. 180

It is not bad—at first, and very gentle, but quite the subtlest, most enduring odor I ever met.

In this damp weather it is awful, I wake up in the night and find it hanging over me.

It used to disturb me at first. I thought seriously of burning the house—to reach the smell. *Very disturbed person*

But now I am used to it. The only thing I can think of that it is like is the *color* of the paper! A yellow smell. *(a sulfur smell – makes you think of yellow)*

There is a very funny mark on this wall, low down, near the mopboard. A streak 185 that runs round the room. It goes behind every piece of furniture, except the bed, a long, straight, even *smooch*, as if it had been rubbed over and over.

I wonder how it was done and who did it, and what they did it for. Round and round and round—round and round and round!—it makes me *dizzy!*

smooch → she was creeping for a long time shoulder up against the wall so you don't get lost

Jennie complains about the yellow stain

VIII

I really have discovered something at last.

Through watching so much at night, when it changes so, I have finally found out.

The front pattern *does* move—and no wonder! The woman behind shakes it!

Sometimes I think there are a great many women behind, and sometimes only one, 190 and she crawls around fast, and her crawling shakes it all over.

Then in the very bright spots she keeps still, and in the very shady spots she just takes hold of the bars and shakes them hard.

And she is all the time trying to climb through. But nobody could climb through that pattern—it strangles so; I think that is why it has so many heads.

They get through, and then the pattern strangles them off and turns them upside down, and makes their eyes white!

If those heads were covered or taken off it would not be half so bad.

IX

I think that woman gets out in the daytime! 195

And I'll tell you why—privately—I've seen her!

I can see her out of every one of my windows!

It is the same woman, I know, for she is always creeping, and most women do not creep by daylight.

I see her in that long shaded lane, creeping up and down. I see her in those dark grape arbors, creeping all around the garden.

I see her on that long road under the trees, creeping along, and when a carriage 200 comes she hides under the blackberry vines.

I don't blame her a bit. It must be very humiliating to be caught creeping by daylight! *That woman creeps, she creeps*

I always lock the door when I creep by daylight. I can't do it at night, for I know John would suspect something at once. *she's the one who is queen*

And John is so queer now, that I don't want to irritate him. I wish he would take another room! Besides, I don't want anybody to get that woman out at night but myself.

I often wonder if I could see her out of all the windows at once. 205

[handwritten: gets away from the original person, herself the one who agrees with her husband always]

But, turn as fast as I can, I can only see out of one at one time.

And though I always see her, she *may* be able to creep faster than I can turn! *[handwritten: She's gone in the Mind]*

I have watched her sometimes away off in the open country, creeping as fast as a cloud shadow in a high wind.

X

If only that top pattern could be gotten off from the under one! I mean to try it, little by little.

I have found out another funny thing, but I shan't tell it this time! It does not do to trust people too much.

There are only two more days to get this paper off, and I believe John is beginning to notice. I don't like the look in his eyes. 210

And I heard him ask Jennie a lot of professional questions about me. She had a very good report to give.

She said I slept a good deal in the daytime.

John knows I don't sleep very well at night, for all I'm so quiet!

He asked me all sorts of questions, too, and pretended to be very loving and kind.

As if I couldn't see through him! *[handwritten: his pretending (she says this)]* 215

Still, I don't wonder he acts so, sleeping under this paper for three months.

It only interests me, but I feel sure John and Jennie are secretly affected by it.

XI

Hurrah! This is the last day, but it is enough. John to stay in town over night, and won't be out until this evening.

Jennie wanted to sleep with me—the sly thing! but I told her I should undoubtedly rest better for a night all alone.

That was clever, for really I wasn't alone a bit! As soon as it was moonlight and that poor thing began to crawl and shake the pattern, I got up and ran to help her. 220

I pulled and she shook, I shook and she pulled, and before morning we had peeled off yards of that paper.

A strip about as high as my head and half around the room.

And then when the sun came and that awful pattern began to laugh at me, I declared I would finish it today!

We go away tomorrow, and they are moving all my furniture down again to leave things as they were before.

Jennie looked at the wall in amazement, but I told her merrily that I did it out of pure spite at the vicious thing. 225

She laughed and said she wouldn't mind doing it herself, but I must not get tired.

How she betrayed herself that time!

But I am here, and no person touches this paper but me,—not *alive!* *[handwritten: It's a threat]*

She tried to get me out of the room—it was too patent! But I said it was so quiet and empty and clean now that I believed I would lie down again and sleep all I could; and not to wake me even for dinner—I would call when I woke.

So now she is gone, and the servants are gone, and the things are gone, and there is nothing left but that great bedstead nailed down, with the canvas mattress we found on it. 230

We shall sleep downstairs tonight, and take the boat home tomorrow.

I quite enjoy the room, now it is bare again.

How those children did tear about here!

This bedstead is fairly gnawed! 235

But I must get to work.

I have locked the door and thrown the key down into the front path.

I don't want to go out, and I don't want to have anybody come in, till John comes.

I want to astonish him.

I've got a rope up here that even Jennie did not find. If that woman does get out, and tries to get away, I can tie her!

But I forgot I could not reach far without anything to stand on!   240

This bed will *not* move!

I tried to lift and push it until I was lame, and then I got so angry I bit off a little piece at one corner—but it hurt my teeth.

Then I peeled off all the paper I could reach standing on the floor. It sticks horribly and the pattern just enjoys it! All those strangled heads and bulbous eyes and waddling fungus growths just shriek with derision!

I am getting angry enough to do something desperate. To jump out of the window would be admirable exercise, but the bars are too strong even to try.

Besides I wouldn't do it. Of course not. I know well enough that a step like that is   245
improper and might be misconstrued.

I don't like to *look* out of the windows even—there are so many of those creeping women, and they creep so fast.

I wonder if they all come out of that wallpaper as I did?

But I am securely fastened now by my well-hidden rope—you don't get *me* out in the road there!

I suppose I shall have to get back behind the pattern when it comes night, and that is hard!

It is so pleasant to be out in this great room and creep around as I please!   250

I don't want to go outside. I won't, even if Jennie asks me to.

For outside you have to creep on the ground, and everything is green instead of yellow.

But here I can creep smoothly on the floor, and my shoulder just fits in that long smooch around the wall, so I cannot lose my way.

Why there's John at the door!

It is no use, young man, you can't open it!   255

How he does call and pound!

Now he's crying for an axe.

It would be a shame to break down that beautiful door!

"John dear!" said I in the gentlest voice, "the key is down by the front steps, under a plaintain leaf!"

That silenced him for a few moments.   260

Then he said—very quietly indeed, "Open the door, my darling!"

"I can't," said I. "The key is down by the front door under a plaintain leaf!"

And then I said it again, several times, very gently and slowly, and said it so often that he had to go and see, and he got it of course, and came in. He stopped short by the door.

"What is the matter?" he cried. "For God's sake, what are you doing!"

I kept on creeping just the same, but I looked at him over my shoulder.   265

"I've got out at last," said I, "in spite of you and Jane! And I've pulled off most of the paper, so you can't put me back!"

Now why should that man have fainted? But he did, and right across my path by the wall, so that I had to creep over him every time!

[handwritten margin note: 2nd narrator, escapes / John; control, marriage / laid]

THE RECEPTIVE READER

1. At the beginning, the narrator refers to her husband John and herself as "ordinary people." What makes the setting and the people at the beginning of the story seem ordinary? What kind of ordinary person does the narrator seem to be? When do you notice the first hints of something extraordinary?

2. What and how do you learn about the narrator's illness? What and how do you learn about the treatment proposed by the doctor-husband?

3. What is the husband-physician's attitude toward his wife? What is her attitude toward him? How does it change in the course of the story? (How is your attitude toward him different from hers?)

4. How does the wallpaper become an obsessive preoccupation in this story? How does its appearance slowly change and shift? How does its meaning change or evolve as the *central symbol* in the story? What are some major stages?

5. Who is the woman behind the wallpaper? How does your perception of her change and evolve? What is the significance of the smudge (running the length of the wallpaper) that the woman begins to perceive?

6. What is the symbolic contrast between the garden and the enclosed, confined room? (Why does the woman herself throw the key away?)

7. What, for you, is the symbolic meaning of the way the story ends? (Can the ending be read as a kind of liberation?)

8. Feminist critics have found a special significance in the fact that the narrator has to do her writing secretly, against the wishes of her husband. What symbolic significance do you think they find in his prohibition?

THE PERSONAL RESPONSE

For you, what does the story as a whole say about the author's view of mental illness and her view of the relation between women and male physicians? Is the story still thought-provoking to current readers, or have changes in the modern world made the questions it raises obsolete?

G A B R I E L   G A R C Í A   M Á R Q U E Z   (born 1928)

In García Márquez's world, love is the primordial power that reigns as an obscure, impersonal, and all-powerful presence.

OCTAVIO PAZ

It always amuses me that the biggest praise for my work comes for the imagination, while the truth is that there's not a single line in all my work that does not have a basis in reality. The problem is that Caribbean reality resembles the wildest imagination.

GABRIEL GARCÍA MÁRQUEZ

García Márquez is a Colombian writer who became internationally famous with his novel *One Hundred Years of Solitude* (1967). His work became part of a Latin American renaissance that made the writings of Octavio Paz, Pablo Neruda, Jorge Luis Borges, and Carlos Fuentes known around the world.

García Márquez' stories are often marked by a mixture of grim reality and the surreal that has been called "magic realism." His "A Very Old Man with Enormous Wings" (1968) is about a very old, moth-eaten angel—"a dirty, muttering, helpless old man with bedraggled wings" (John Updike)—who falls out of the sky and confounds the inhabitants of the town. García Márquez is a master at evoking mixed emotions. His tales mix wit and horror; his voice is "able to praise and curse, laugh and cry, fabulate and sing" (Thomas Pynchon).

García Márquez moved from Colombia to Mexico in 1954 and later went to live in Spain. He has written plays and film scripts as well as novels and stories; he was awarded the Nobel Prize in literature in 1982. He became famous when he was almost forty after years of struggle that made him feel "like an extra," thinking that "I did not count anywhere." In an interview, he said that he sees both his books and his work with films as helping "to create a Latin American identity," helping "Latin Americans to become more aware of their own culture." His novel *Love in the Time of Cholera*—about a man who maintains his unanswered, unfulfilled passion for the love of his youth for fifty-one years—appeared in 1987.

(Esteban is Spanish for Stephen. The Sir Walter Raleigh alluded to in the story lived from 1552 to 1618 and was an English explorer and pirate of the Elizabethan Age.)

The Handsomest Drowned Man in the World   1970
A Tale for Children
TRANSLATED BY GREGORY RABASSA

The first children who saw the dark and slinky bulge approaching through the sea let themselves think it was an empty ship. Then they saw it had no flags or masts and they thought it was a whale. But when it washed up on the beach, they removed the clumps of seaweed, the jellyfish tentacles, and the remains of fish and flotsam, and only then did they see that it was a drowned man.

They had been playing with him all afternoon, burying him in the sand and digging him up again, when someone chanced to see them and spread the alarm in the village. The men who carried him to the nearest house noticed that he weighed more than any dead man they had ever known, almost as much as a horse, and they said to each other that maybe he'd been floating too long and the water had got into his bones. When they laid him on the floor they said he'd been taller than all other men because there was barely enough room for him in the house, but they thought that maybe the ability to keep on growing after death was part of the nature of certain drowned men. He had the smell of the sea about him and only his shape gave one to suppose that it was the corpse of a human being, because the skin was covered with a crust of mud and scales.

They did not even have to clean off his face to know that the dead man was a stranger. The village was made up of only twenty-odd wooden houses that had stone courtyards with no flowers and which were spread about on the end of a desertlike cape. There was so little land that mothers always went about with the fear that the wind would carry off their children and the few dead that the years had caused among them had to be thrown off the cliffs. But the sea was calm and bountiful and all the men fit into seven boats. So when they found the drowned man they simply had to look at one another to see that they were all there. That night they did not go out to work at sea. While the men went to find out if anyone was missing in neighboring villages, the women stayed behind to care for the drowned man. They took the mud off with grass swabs, they removed the underwater stones entangled in his hair, and they scraped the crust off with tools used for scaling fish. As they were doing that they noticed that the vegetation on him came from faraway oceans and deep water and that his clothes were in tatters, as if he had sailed through labyrinths of coral. They noticed too that he bore his death with pride, for he did not have the lonely look of other drowned men who came out of the sea or that haggard, needy look of men who drowned in rivers. But only when they finished cleaning him off did they become aware of the kind of man he was and it left them breathless. Not only was he the tallest, strongest, most virile, and best built man they had ever seen, but even though they were looking at him there was no room for him in their imagination.

They could not find a bed in the village large enough to lay him on nor was there a table solid enough to use for his wake. The tallest men's holiday pants would not fit him, nor the fattest ones' Sunday shirts, nor the shoes of the one with the biggest feet. Fascinated by his huge size and his beauty, the women then decided to make him some pants from a large piece of sail and a shirt from some bridal brabant linen so that he could continue through his death with dignity. As they sewed, sitting in a circle and gazing at the corpse between stitches, it seemed to them that the wind had never been so steady nor the sea so restless as on that night and they supposed that the change had something to do with the dead man. They thought that if that magnificent man had lived in the village, his house would have had the widest doors, the highest ceiling, and the strongest floor, his bedstead would have been made from a midship frame held together by iron bolts, and his wife would have been the happiest woman. They thought that he would have had so much authority that he could have drawn fish out of the sea simply by calling their names and that he would have put so much work into his land that springs would have burst forth from among the rocks so that he would have been able to plant flowers on the cliffs. They secretly compared him to their own men, thinking that for all their lives theirs were incapable of doing what he could do in one night, and they ended up dismissing them deep in their hearts as the weakest, meanest, and most useless creatures on earth. They were wandering through that maze of fantasy when the oldest woman, who as the oldest had looked upon the drowned man with more compassion than passion, sighed:

"He has the face of someone called Esteban." 5

It was true. Most of them had only to take another look at him to see that he could not have any other name. The more stubborn among them, who were the youngest, still lived for a few hours with the illusion that when they put his clothes on and he lay among the flowers in patent leather shoes his name might be Lautaro. But it was a vain illusion. There had not been enough canvas, the poorly cut and worse sewn pants were too tight, and the hidden strength of his heart popped the buttons on his shirt. After midnight the whistling of the wind died down and the sea fell into its Wednesday drowsiness. The silence put an end to any last doubts: he was Esteban. The women who had dressed him, who had combed his hair, had cut his nails and shaved him were unable to hold back a shudder of pity when they had to resign themselves to his being dragged along the ground. It was then that they understood how unhappy he must have been with that huge body since it bothered him even after death. They could see him in life, condemned to going through doors sideways, cracking his head on cross-beams, remaining on his feet during visits, not knowing what to do with his soft, pink, sea lion hands while the lady of the house looked for her most resistant chair and begged him, frightened to death, sit here, Esteban, please, and he, leaning against the wall, smiling, don't bother, ma'am, I'm fine where I am, his heels raw and his back roasted from having done the same thing so many times whenever he paid a visit, don't bother, ma'am, I'm fine where I am, just to avoid the embarrassment of breaking up the chair, and never knowing perhaps that the ones who said don't go, Esteban, at least wait till the coffee's ready, were the ones who later on would whisper the big boob finally left, how nice, the handsome fool has gone. That was what the women were thinking beside the body a little before dawn. Later, when they covered his face with a handkerchief so that the light would not bother him, he looked so forever dead, so defenseless, so much like their men that the first furrows of tears opened in their hearts. It was one of the younger ones who began the weeping. The others, coming to, went from sighs to wails, and the more they sobbed the more they felt like weeping, because the drowned man was becoming all the more Esteban for them, and so they wept so much, for he was the most destitute, most peaceful, and most obliging man on earth, poor Esteban. So when the men returned with the news that the drowned man was not from the neighboring villages either, the women felt an opening of jubilation in the midst of their tears.

"Praise the Lord," they sighed, "he's ours!"

The men thought the fuss was only womanish frivolity. Fatigued because of the difficult nighttime inquiries, all they wanted was to get rid of the bother of the newcomer once and for all before the sun grew strong on that arid, windless day. They improvised a litter with the remains of foremasts and gaffs, tying it together with rigging so that it would bear the weight of the body until they reached the cliffs. They wanted to tie the anchor from a cargo ship to him so that he would sink easily into the deepest waves, where fish are blind and divers die of nostalgia, and bad currents would not bring him back to shore, as had happened with other bodies. But the more they hurried, the more the women thought of ways to waste time. They walked about like startled hens, pecking with the sea charms on their breasts, some interfering on one side to put a scapular of the good wind on the drowned man, some on the other side to put a wrist compass on him, and after a great deal of *get away from there, woman, stay out of the way, look, you almost made me fall on top of the dead man*, the men began to feel mistrust in their livers and started grumbling about why so many main-altar decorations for a stranger, because no matter how many nails and holy-water jars he had on him, the sharks would chew him all the same, but the women kept piling on their junk relics, running back and forth, stumbling, while they released in sighs what they did not in tears, so that the men finally exploded with *since when has there ever been such a fuss over a drifting corpse, a drowned nobody, a piece of cold Wednesday meat*. One of the women, mortified by so much lack of care, then removed the handkerchief from the dead man's face and the men were left breathless too.

He was Esteban. It was not necessary to repeat it for them to recognize him. If they had been told Sir Walter Raleigh, even they might have been impressed with his gringo accent, the macaw on his shoulder, his cannibal-killing blunderbuss, but there could be only one Esteban in the world and there he was, stretched out like a sperm whale, shoeless, wearing the pants of an undersized child, and with those stony nails that had to be cut with a knife. They only had to take the handkerchief off his face to see that he was ashamed, that it was not his fault that he was so big or so heavy or so handsome, and if he had known that this was going to happen, he would have looked for a more discreet place to drown in, seriously, I even would have tied the anchor off a galleon around my neck and staggered off a cliff like someone who doesn't like things in order not to be upsetting people now with this Wednesday dead body, as you people say, in order not to be bothering anyone with this filthy piece of cold meat that doesn't have anything to do with me. There was so much truth in his manner that even the most mistrustful men, the ones who felt the bitterness of endless nights at sea fearing that their women would tire of dreaming about them and begin to dream of drowned men, even they and others who were harder still shuddered in the marrow of their bones at Esteban's sincerity.

That was how they came to hold the most splendid funeral they could conceive of for an abandoned drowned man. Some women who had gone to get flowers in the neighboring villages returned with other women who could not believe what they had been told, and those women went back for more flowers when they saw the dead man, and they brought more and more until there were so many flowers and so many people that it was hard to walk about. At the final moment it pained them to return him to the waters as an orphan and they chose a father and mother from among the best people, and aunts and uncles and cousins, so that through him all the inhabitants of the village became kinsmen. Some sailors who heard weeping from a distance went off course and people heard of one who had himself tied to the mainmast, remembering ancient fables about sirens. While they fought for the privilege of carrying him on their shoulders along the steep escarpment by the cliffs, men and women became aware for the first time of the desolation of their streets, the dryness of their courtyards, the narrowness of their dreams as they faced the splendor and beauty of their drowned man. They let him go without an anchor so that he could come back if he wished and whenever he wished, and they all held their breath for the fraction of centuries the body took to fall into the abyss. They did not need to look at one another to realize that they were no longer all present, that they would never be. But they also knew that everything would be different from then on, that their houses would have wider doors, higher ceilings, and stronger floors so that Esteban's memory could go everywhere without bumping into beams and so that no one in the future would dare whisper the big boob finally died, too bad, the handsome fool has finally died, because they were going to paint their house fronts gay colors to make Esteban's memory eternal and they were going to break their backs digging for springs among the stones and planting flowers on the cliffs so that in future years at dawn the passengers on great liners would awaken, suffocated by the smell of gardens on the high seas, and the captain would have to come down from the bridge in his dress uniform, with his astrolabe, his pole star, and his row of war medals and, pointing to the promontory of roses on the horizon, he would say in fourteen languages, look there, where the wind is so peaceful now that it's gone to sleep beneath the beds, over there, where the sun's so bright that the sunflowers don't know which way to turn, yes, that's Esteban's village.

10

THE RECEPTIVE READER

1. What are your reactions as the story develops in the opening paragraphs? What are striking or puzzling details that linger in the reader's mind?

2. Is it a coincidence that the corpse washed up on the beach is discovered by children? (What is it about children that makes them the right—or the wrong—audience for this tale?)

3. A reviewer said of Márquez' stories that the "arid, unyielding rock" on which the tales are built is a reality of "poverty, hopelessness, exploitation, despotic and demonic rulers" from which the tales "are an escape" (Charles Champlin). What harsh realities provide the "rock" on which this story is built?

4. The same reviewer said that the wellsprings of García's stories "are in the legends, folk tales, superstition, and indeed in the prevalence of miracles in the orthodox

faith of Latin America." What miracle happens in this story? Does the reader have to believe in miracles to respond to the story?

5. What does the corpse of the drowned man symbolize? Do other supporting *symbols* play a role in this story?

6. What is the significance of the way the story ends?

7. What is paradoxical about the role death plays in this story?

THE PERSONAL RESPONSE

The following is the conclusion of a student paper titled "The Most Vibrant Corpse in the World." How do you react to this reader's search for a real-life application of the symbolism in the story? What real-life parallel or application would *you* suggest? How would you explain it or defend it?

All that is beautiful, enriching, animating, and ultimately effective in life is symbolized—with no lack of strangeness or irony—by a corpse in "The Handsomest Drowned Man in the World." Márquez' attractive cadaver is dead, yet he is far from lifeless. This corpse named Esteban is so full of life, he transmits it to anyone who looks upon him. After finishing the story, Márquez' slightly startled reader may wonder, what in real life is inanimate and yet so stimulating? Márquez may be suggesting that the answer is his own medium, literature. A story is alive and vibrant when it is being written down, fresh from the imagination of the writer, but it is only a dead thing when lying between the covers of a book; it is only flat, black print on a page. When it finds its way into the hands of an inhabitant of the village of Earth, however, and is gazed upon and absorbed by this inhabitant, it lives again, in a completely new way. No reader is exactly the same after such an encounter. She too may be inspired to paint her "house front gay colors"; she too may be inspired to break her back "digging for springs among the stones and planting flowers on the cliffs."

CROSS-REFERENCES—For Discussion or Writing

Examine the role of the imagination in the stories by Steinbeck, Gilman, and Márquez. How does it mirror or reflect reality? How does it change or transform it?

URSULA K. LE GUIN (born 1929)

Ursula K. Le Guin once described herself as an "aging, angry woman laying mightily about me with my handbag, fighting hoodlums off." She was born in Berkeley and educated at Radcliffe and Columbia. She has written eloquently in defense of the environment, passenger trains, abortion rights, and the cultural traditions of native Americans. She is widely admired as an author of travel literature, essays on feminist and other social topics, and science fiction. Her essays about the real America—away from the trendmongers and media events of the big cities—bear witness to her love of the land, her ear for the way people talk, her quick sympathetic eye for their weaknesses and strengths. Her science fiction does not focus on space-age gadgets and monstrous aliens but instead raises questions about human nature and human destiny. The novels of her *Earthsea Trilogy* (1968–1972) and her later novels made her a favorite of thoughtful readers.

The basic question underlying much science fiction is "What if?" The writer assumes something far removed from ordinary reality—talking apes have evolved and taken over the planet, or colonists from earth discover on Mars haunting memories of a lost civilization. The author then rewrites our familiar reality in accordance with this premise. Much early science fiction sketched out a future utopia in which age-old human dreams—of unlimited power, of perpetual happiness—were coming true. But gradually the vision of an ideal future darkened and many wrote the opposite—*dystopias,* or future worlds that made our nightmares come true. Where on the spectrum ranging from utopia to dystopia would you place the following story? (The William James alluded to in the subtitle of the story lived from 1842 to 1910 and was a pioneering American psychologist who wrote a famous book on the range of religious experience.)

The Ones Who Walk Away from Omelas   1973
Variations on a Theme by William James

With a clamor of bells that set the swallows soaring, the Festival of Summer came to the city Omelas, bright-towered by the sea. The rigging of the boats in harbor sparkled with flags. In the streets between houses with red roofs and painted walls, between old moss-grown gardens and under avenues of trees, past great parks and public buildings, processions moved. Some were decorous: old people in long stiff robes of mauve and grey, grave master workmen, quiet, merry women carrying their babies and chatting as they walked. In other streets the music beat faster, a shimmering of gong and tambourine, and the people went dancing, the procession was a dance. Children dodged in and out, their high calls rising like the swallows' crossing flights over the music and the singing. All the processions wound toward the north side of the city, where on the great water-meadow called the Green Fields boys and girls, naked in the bright air, with mud-stained feet and ankles and long, lithe arms, exercised their restive horses before the race. The horses wore no gear at all but a halter without bit. Their manes were braided with streamers of silver, gold, and green. They flared their nostrils and pranced and boasted to one another; they were vastly excited, the horse being the only animal who has adopted our ceremonies as his own. Far off to the north and west the mountains stood up half encircling Omelas on her bay. The air of morning was so clear that the snow still crowning the Eighteen Peaks burned with white-gold fire across the miles of sunlit air, under the dark blue of the sky. There was just enough wind to make the banners that marked the racecourse snap and flutter now and then. In the silence of the broad green meadows one could hear the music winding through the city streets, farther and nearer and ever approaching, a cheerful faint sweetness of the air that from time to time trembled and gathered together and broke out into the great joyous clanging of the bells.

Joyous! How is one to tell about joy? How describe the citizens of Omelas?

They were not simple folk, you see, though they were happy. But we do not say the words of cheer much any more. All smiles have become archaic. Given a description such as this one tends to make certain assumptions. Given a description such as this one tends to look next for the King, mounted on a splendid stallion and surrounded by his noble knights, or perhaps in a golden litter borne by great-muscled slaves. But there was no king. They did not use swords, or keep slaves. They were not barbarians. I do not know the rules and laws of their society, but I suspect that they were singularly few. As they did without monarchy and slavery, so they also got on without the stock exchange, the advertisement, the secret police, and the bomb. Yet I repeat that these were not simple folk, not dulcet shepherds, noble savages, bland utopians. They were not less complex than us. The trouble is that we have a bad habit, encouraged by pedants and sophisticates, of considering happiness as something rather stupid. Only pain is intellectual, only evil interesting. This is the treason of the artist: a refusal to admit the banality of evil and the terrible boredom of pain. If you can't lick 'em, join 'em. If it hurts, repeat it. But to praise despair is to condemn delight, to embrace violence is to lose hold of everything else. We have almost lost hold, we can no longer describe a happy man, nor make any celebration of joy. How can I tell you about the people of Omelas? They were not naïve and happy children—though their children were, in fact, happy. They were mature, intelligent, passionate adults whose lives were not wretched. O miracle! but I wish I could describe it better. I wish I could convince you. Omelas sounds in my words like a city in a fairy tale, long ago and far away, once upon a time. Perhaps it would be best if you imagined it as your own fancy bids, assuming it will rise to the occasion, for certainly I cannot suit you all. For instance, how about technology? I think that there would be no cars or helicopters in and above the streets; this follows from the fact that the people of Omelas are happy people. Happiness is based on a just discrimination of what is necessary, what is neither necessary nor destructive, and what is destructive. In the middle category, however—that of the unnecessary but undestructive, that of comfort, luxury, exuberance, etc.—they could perfectly well have central heating, subway trains, washing machines, and all kinds of marvelous devices not yet invented here, floating light-sources, fuelless power, a cure for the common cold. Or they could have none of that: it doesn't matter. As you like it. I incline to think that people from towns up and down the coast have been coming in to Omelas during the last days before the Festival on very fast little trains and double-decked trams, and that the train station of Omelas is actually the handsomest building in town, though plainer than the magnificent Farmers' Market. But even granted trains, I fear that Omelas so far strikes some of you as goody-goody. Smiles, bells, parades, horses, bleh. If so, please add an orgy. If an orgy would help, don't hesitate. Let us not, however, have temples from which issue beautiful nude priests and priestesses already half in ecstasy and ready to copulate with any man or woman, lover or stranger, who desires union with the deep godhead of the blood, although that was my first idea. But really it would be better not to have any temples in Omelas—at least, not manned temples. Religion yes, clergy no. Surely the beautiful nudes can just wander about, offering themselves like divine soufflés to the hunger of the needy and the rapture of the flesh. Let them join the processions. Let tambourines be struck above the copulations, and the glory of desire be proclaimed upon the gongs, and (a not unimportant point) let the offspring of these delightful rituals be beloved and looked after by all. One thing I know there is none of in Omelas is guilt. But what else should there be? I thought at first there were no drugs, but that is puritanical. For those who like it, the faint insistent sweetness of *drooz* may perfume the ways of the city, *drooz* which first brings a great lightness and brilliance to the mind and limbs, and then after some hours a dreamy languor, and wonderful visions at last of the very arcana and inmost secrets of the Universe, as well as exciting the pleasure of sex beyond all belief; and it is not habit-forming. For more modest tastes I think there ought to be beer. What else, what else belongs in the joyous city? The sense of victory, surely, the celebration of courage. But as we did without clergy, let us do without soldiers. The joy built upon successful slaughter is not the right kind of joy; it will not do; it is fearful and it is trivial. A boundless and generous contentment, a magnanimous triumph felt not against some outer enemy but in communion with the finest and fairest in the souls of all men everywhere and the splendor of the world's summer: this is what swells the hearts of the people of Omelas, and the victory they celebrate is that of life. I really don't think many of them need to take *drooz*.

Most of the procession have reached the Green Fields by now. A marvelous smell of cooking goes forth from the red and blue tents of the provisioners. The faces of small children are amiably sticky; in the benign grey beard of a man a couple of crumbs of rich pastry are entangled. The youths and girls have mounted their horses and are beginning to group around the starting line of the course. An old woman, small, fat, and laughing, is passing out flowers from a basket, and tall young men wear her flowers in their shining hair. A child of nine or ten sits at the edge of the crowd, alone, playing on a wooden flute. People pause to listen, and they smile, but they do not speak to him, for he never ceases playing and never sees them, his dark eyes wholly rapt in the sweet, thin magic of the tune.

He finishes, and slowly lowers his hands holding the wooden flute. 5

As if that little private silence were the signal, all at once a trumpet sounds from the pavilion near the starting line: imperious, melancholy, piercing. The horses rear on their slender legs, and some of them neigh in answer. Sober-faced, the young riders stroke the horses' necks and soothe them, whispering, "Quiet, quiet, there my beauty, my hope. . . ." They begin to form in rank along the starting line. The crowds along the racecourse are like a field of grass and flowers in the wind. The Festival of Summer has begun.

Do you believe? Do you accept the festival, the city, the joy? No? Then let me describe one more thing.

In a basement under one of the beautiful public buildings of Omelas, or perhaps in the cellar of one of its more spacious private homes, there is a room. It has one locked door, and no window. A little light seeps in dustily between cracks in the boards, secondhand from a cobwebbed window somewhere across the cellar. In one corner of the little room a couple of mops, with stiff, clotted, foul-smelling heads, stand near a rusty bucket. The floor is dirt, a little damp to the touch, as cellar dirt usually is. The room is about three paces long and two wide: a mere broom closet or disused tool room. In the room a child is sitting. It could be a boy or a girl. It looks about six, but actually is nearly ten. It is feeble-minded. Perhaps it was born defective, or perhaps it has become imbecile through fear, malnutrition, and neglect. It picks its nose and occasionally fumbles vaguely with its toes or genitals, as it sits hunched in the corner farthest from the bucket and the two mops. It is afraid of the mops. It finds them horrible. It shuts its eyes, but it knows the mops are still standing there; and the door is locked; and nobody will come. The door is always locked; and nobody ever comes, except that sometimes— the child has no understanding of time or interval—sometimes the door rattles terribly and opens, and a person, or several people, are there. One of them may come in and kick the child to make it stand up. The others never come close, but peer in at it with frightened, disgusted eyes. The food bowl and the water jug are hastily filled, the door is locked, the eyes disappear. The people at the door never say anything, but the child, who has not always lived in the tool room, and can remember sunlight and its mother's voice, sometimes speaks. "I will be good," it says. "Please let me out. I will be good!" They never answer. The child used to scream for help at night, and cry a good deal, but now it only makes a kind of whining, "eh-haa, eh-haa," and it speaks less and less often.

It is so thin there are no calves to its legs; its belly protrudes; it lives on a half-bowl of corn meal and grease a day. It is naked. Its buttocks and thighs are a mass of festered sores, as it sits in its own excrement continually.

They all know it is there, all the people of Omelas. Some of them have come to see it, others are content merely to know it is there. They all know that it has to be there. Some of them understand why, and some do not, but they all understand that their happiness, the beauty of their city, the tenderness of their friendships, the health of their children, the wisdom of their scholars, the skill of their makers, even the abundance of their harvest and the kindly weathers of their skies, depend wholly on this child's abominable misery.

This is usually explained to children when they are between eight and twelve,   10
whenever they seem capable of understanding; and most of those who come to see the child are young people, though often enough an adult comes, or comes back, to see the child. No matter how well the matter has been explained to them, these young spectators are always shocked and sickened at the sight. They feel disgust, which they had thought themselves superior to. They feel anger, outrage, impotence, despite all the explanations. They would like to do something for the child. But there is nothing they can do. If the child were brought up into the sunlight out of the vile place, if it were cleaned and fed and comforted, that would be a good thing, indeed; but if it were done, in that day and hour all the prosperity and beauty and delight of Omelas would wither and be destroyed. Those are the terms. To exchange all the goodness and grace of every life in Omelas for that single, small improvement: to throw away the happiness of thousands for the chance of the happiness of one: that would be to let guilt within the walls indeed.

The terms are strict and absolute; there may not even be a kind word spoken to the child.

Often the young people go home in tears, or in a tearless rage, when they have seen the child and faced this terrible paradox. They may brood over it for weeks or years. But as time goes on they begin to realize that even if the child could be released, it would not get much good of its freedom: a little vague pleasure of warmth and food, no doubt, but little more. It is too degraded and imbecile to know any real joy. It has been afraid too long ever to be free of fear. Its habits are too uncouth for it to respond to humane treatment. Indeed, after so long it would probably be wretched without walls about it to protect it, and darkness for its eyes, and its own excrement to sit in. Their tears at the bitter injustice dry when they begin to perceive the terrible justice of reality, and to accept it. Yet it is their tears and anger, the trying of their generosity and the acceptance of their helplessness, which are perhaps the true source of the splendor of their lives. Theirs is no vapid, irresponsible happiness. They know that they, like the child, are not free. They know compassion. It is the existence of the child, and their knowledge of its existence, that makes possible the nobility of their architecture, the poignancy of their music, the profundity of their science. It is because of the child that they are so gentle with children. They know that if the wretched one were not there snivelling in the dark, the other one, the flute-player, could make no joyful music as the young riders line up in their beauty for the race in the sunlight of the first morning of summer.

Now do you believe in them? Are they not more credible? But there is one more thing to tell, and this is quite incredible.

At times one of the adolescent girls or boys who go to see the child does not go home to weep or rage, does not, in fact, go home at all. Sometimes also a man or woman much older falls silent for a day or two, and then leaves home. These people go out into the street, and walk down the street alone. They keep walking, and walk straight out of the city of Omelas, through the beautiful gates. They keep walking across the farmlands of Omelas. Each one goes alone, youth or girl, man or woman. Night falls; the traveler must pass down village streets, between the houses with yellow-lit windows, and on out into the darkness of the fields. Each alone, they go west or north, toward the mountains. They go on. They leave Omelas, they walk ahead into the darkness, and they do not come back. The place they go toward is a place even less imaginable to most of us than the city of happiness. I cannot describe it at all. It is possible that it does not exist. But they seem to know where they are going, the ones who walk away from Omelas.

THE RECEPTIVE READER

1. How does the author create the "joyous" setting of the opening paragraphs? What striking details help create a beckoning world? What words are especially rich in positive *connotations*—overtones and associations that convey pleasurable or pleasing emotions and attitudes?

2. Why do you think the author lets each reader fill in his or her own details to complete the description of Omelas?

3. In her own specifications, what does the author explicitly exclude from her imaginary world and why? (For instance, how much or how little technology is there?) What do you make of her discussion of pros and cons, or of her warding off of possible misunderstandings?

4. What is the relationship between the author's science fiction world and your own? How is the world she creates similar to and different from your own ordinary reality?

5. When do you first suspect that the joyous, happy surface of Omelas might be deceptive?

6. What is the role of the imprisoned child in the world of the people of Omelas? For what in their world or yours is the child a *symbol*? Are there parallels in your world for what the child represents?

7. Do you think the author meant to suggest that the world of Omelas was fatally flawed—or that it was nearly perfect except for one serious flaw?

THE PERSONAL RESPONSE

Do you think you would have been among those who "walked away from Omelas"? Or would you have been one of those who stayed behind? Justify your choice.

THE CREATIVE DIMENSION

Science fiction has a special way of stimulating the imagination. Does it stimulate yours? Write down what your *first impressions* would be if you suddenly found yourself walking the streets of Omelas (or the streets of another imaginary location in a story you have read). Would your impressions be similar to or different from those in the following student-written sample?

Walking in Omelas

I am walking down the crowded streets of Omelas. It would be a lovely day except that the sunlight is too bright, the weather is too warm, and the noise of the crowd is too loud. It is not easy walking down the street; people bump into me, and sometimes I have to disentangle myself from their welcoming embraces. This celebration of which I am a part reminds me of Mardi Gras in New Orleans, which suggests that I do have memories of a time before Omelas. The people of Omelas are all smiling, but their smiles are only on their lips and do not reach their eyes. Those smiling faces are too perfect, and they remind me of masks. I wonder what is behind those smiling faces. The people all talk to me, but although I understand their words, I do not understand their meaning. As the crowd presses against me, I feel as though I might suffocate. Will I ever be able to walk away from Omelas?

WRITING ABOUT LITERATURE

6. Decoding Symbols (Two Readings of a Story)

The Writing Workshop   Writing about symbols tests your ability to be a responsive reader—to respond fully to the way imaginative literature acts out or embodies meanings. You cannot be too literal-minded, since you may miss much of the meaning a symbol suggests or implies. You cannot be too clinical or detached if strong, richly charged symbols are to bring into play the emotions and attitudes they are likely to carry. Here is the kind of advice a writing teacher might give you after studying several sets of papers focused on the role symbols play in short fiction:

⋄ *Explore the full range of possible associations of a symbol.* Literary symbols tend not to be one-track, one-dimensional signals that simply say "danger" or "evil lurks here." A serpent may symbolize danger. It may symbolize guile (the snake in the grass). It may stand for the alien or otherness (since reptiles represent a very different life from our own mammalian existence). It may represent danger that has a strange paradoxical attraction or beauty.

The cluster on the next page traces some of the possible associations of flowers as familiar recurrent symbols carrying rich traditional freight. Many of these associations may be activated by a story like Steinbeck's "The Chrysanthemums," where flowers play a central role at turning points in the story. (Which of these associations do you think are relevant to Steinbeck's story?)

⋄ *Trace the full meaning of a gradually evolving central symbol.* A symbol is not likely to come into a story with its symbolic value ready-made, like the monetary value of a dollar bill. In Gilman's "The Yellow Wallpaper," we at first look at the twisted pattern of the paper the way an interior designer might wonder at its strange design. But gradually we—or rather the narrator through whose eyes we see everything in the story—read more and more human meaning into its strange shapes. They come to life, making the narrator participate in the struggle of whatever seems imprisoned behind its bars. It is as if each time we look at the paper we discover a new and frightening dimension, leading to an escalation of apprehension and terror. We have to read and ponder the story as a whole to sense what the wallpaper comes to stand for as the story heads for its frightening conclusion.

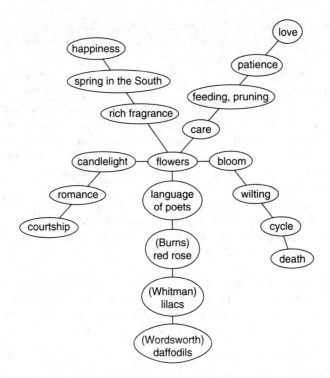

❖ *Look for secondary symbols that echo the major theme of a story.* In addition to the chrysanthemums in Steinbeck's story, readers have scrutinized the pots and pans in need of mending as a possible symbol; they have wondered about the symbolic meaning of the fog that closes off the valley:

> "The high grey-flannel fog of winter closed off the Salinas Valley from the sky and from all the rest of the world," Steinbeck begins. This introductory sentence points to one of the basic themes of the story. Something (in this case, the fog) is keeping something or someone "closed off"—held in, cut off. The fog covers the valley. Similarly, Elisa's situation closes in on her, keeps her trapped, holds her back. Neither her husband nor the itinerant tinker understands the energy and care she puts into the chrysanthemums, and her ability and potential go unrecognized and unappreciated; they are kept under wraps, "closed off." The fog is the lid that keeps the sun from penetrating; Elisa's circumstances put the "lid" on her vital energy and desires.

❖ *Look for contrasts or polarities.* Often the play of opposites helps organize a story. In Steinbeck's "Chrysanthemums," a key contrast juxtaposes the farm family that stays fogbound and the tinker who follows "the nice weather." The conventional cattle-tending chores of the predictable, unimaginative husband contrast with the mismatched team pulling the strange wagon of the unconventional traveler. In Gilman's "The Yellow Wallpaper," the central symbol is the wallpaper, but a major polarity that helps organize the narrative plays off the colors green and yellow and what they symbolize in the story.

✧ *Relate key terms* (as in other kinds of papers) *specifically to the story.* If you bring in a term from the outside, show how it applies to the story. For instance, if you say that the García Márquez story "is simply a fantasy," *what kind* of fantasy is acted out in the story? What are its workings or dynamics? (In the story, the corpse of the drowned man seems to become a kind of catalyst for the villagers' imagination. Fantasy here is not divorced from reality or an escape from it; it seems to be the kind of active imagination that makes the villagers *transform* their reality.)

✧ *Look for the personal connection.* How does the use of symbols in a story touch your own life, your own experience? What symbols have a special personal meaning for you—as the way Elisa dresses in the chrysanthemums story had for the student writer of the following passage?

> Steinbeck's story dealt with feminine emotions that can be very hard to understand. I was struck by the contrast between Elisa's mannish "working clothes" (her shapeless outfit, her heavy gloves) and the makeup and dress she puts on after her encounter with the tinker. Much of her thinking revolves around whether the men in her world would respect her work and desire her at the same time. Her change of clothes symbolizes the fact that in the male world the woman has to play a dual role. She has to be a man's equal to survive in the world of work, yet on the other hand she is expected to be feminine and seductive. Today a woman has to look more like a man by wearing a dark "power" suit and practically no makeup to compete with men, or she may not be taken seriously. In a recent sitcom episode, I watched a sterile-looking businesswoman teaching a fashionable female how to dress for business success. Her pupil donned a blue suit, a buttoned white shirt, and a bandage-type thing to hide her breasts. Steinbeck's story points up this unresolved conflict: It is a sad but honest account of how women are taken advantage of when they expose their feminine selves.

Two Readings of a Story

The language of symbols may be universal, but it also by its very nature fosters a range of interpretation. Writers relying heavily on symbols are the least likely to spell out the meaning or the moral of a story in so many words. Where do the two following readings of "The Yellow Wallpaper" seem to agree? Where do they differ in emphasis or interpretation? Which is closer to your own reading of the story? Which do you learn from the most?

SAMPLE STUDENT PAPER 1

"The Yellow Wallpaper": A Woman's Struggle with Madness

"I've got out at last. . . . And I've pulled off most of the paper, so you can't put me back!" declares the narrator of "The Yellow Wallpaper" at the end of her futile struggle with madness. By peeling off the yellow wallpaper and releasing the woman the narrator sees trapped behind its "conspicuous front design," the narrator peels off the façade of normalcy she is trapped behind and releases her own madness. This façade is created by a "very careful and loving" husband, who refuses to believe his wife is ill, and is perpetuated by the medical conventions of the time that dismiss her mental illness as "a slight hysterical tendency."

In his effort to help his wife get over her "temporary nervous depression," John takes her to a house in the country which is "quite alone, standing well back from the road, quite three miles from the village." He feels that this quiet atmosphere along with "perfect rest" is just what she needs. In fact, she is "absolutely forbidden to 'work'" and has "a scheduled prescription for each hour of the day." The narrator, on the other hand, feels "that congenial work, with excitement and change, would do me good." However, because her husband is "a physician of high standing," she feels he must know what is best for her. When they first move into the house, she wants a room "downstairs that opened on the piazza and had roses all over the window, and such pretty old-fashioned chintz hangings" but "John would not hear of it." He insists they take "the nursery at the top of the house" even though "the windows are barred." The floor "is scratched and gouged and splintered, the plaster itself is dug out here and there," and the room is covered in a "horrid paper"—"one of those sprawling flamboyant patterns committing every artistic sin" and colored "repellent, almost revolting . . . unclean yellow." He also insists that she stop writing, which she feels "would relieve the press of ideas and rest me." She does manage to write a bit "in spite of them," but it is too exhausting "having to be so sly about it."

Consequently, with no outlet for her "imaginative power and habit of story-making," she develops a grotesque fascination with the yellow wallpaper. At first the paper is just irritating, "dull enough to confuse the eye in following, pronounced enough to constantly irritate and provoke study." But, as the narrator studies the wallpaper more and more, she begins to see hideous images in the pattern. "The pattern lolls like a broken neck and two bulbous eyes. . . . those absurd, unblinking eyes are everywhere." She dwells on this pattern and soon sees "a kind of subpattern in a different shade . . . that seems to skulk about behind" the front design. The wallpaper so disturbs the narrator that she tries to have "a real earnest reasonable talk" with her husband about her condition. He tells her that she is getting better, but she replies, "Better in body perhaps." He dismisses her concern for her mental state as "a false and foolish fancy." He tells her that she must not give in to her feelings, and that only she can help herself get better. She must use her "will and self-control and not let any silly fancies run away with [her]."

It is at this point in the story, after the narrator tries, unsuccessfully, to share her fears for her sanity, that she can no longer control the madness she has been struggling to contain. This madness takes the form of the woman behind the wallpaper. "I didn't realize for a long time what the thing was that showed behind, that dim subpattern, but now I am quite sure it is a woman." The narrator describes the woman as "subdued, quiet," and the narrator believes "it is the pattern that keeps her so still." The narrator is, in fact, describing herself, so quiet and subdued, and the pattern keeping her that way is her life.

As the narrator's illness progresses, she begins to identify more and more with the woman behind the wallpaper. She sees the woman creeping around everywhere: "in that long shaded lane. . . . in those dark grape arbors. . . . on that long road under the trees, creeping along, and when a carriage comes she hides." The narrator sympathizes with this woman for she, too, is creeping around. "I always lock the door when I creep by daylight," the narrator writes.

Ultimately, her madness takes complete control and her one purpose in life is to help the woman escape from the wallpaper. Piece by piece, the narrator peels off the wallpaper as she peels away at her own sanity, until the woman is able to escape from behind the paper, and the narrator is able to escape into her own madness. The narrator wonders "if they all come out of the wallpaper as I did?"

No less obvious than the symbolism of the yellow wallpaper is the irony of the story. A loving husband, a physician no less, prescribes a treatment of rest and relaxation he feels will improve his wife's slightly depressed condition; however, instead of helping her, he unwittingly drives her to insanity. His mistake was in not taking her condition seriously, not accepting that she was, indeed, very ill. We want to say, "Poor woman, if she existed today, she could have been helped." Maybe, and maybe not. Situations similar to the narrator's do exist today. The modern term for John is "enabler." Just as John, by pretending nothing was seriously wrong, enabled his wife to succumb to her illness, many spouses and families of alcoholics enable them to continue being alcoholics by not admitting they have a problem. They, too, are trapped behind the facades of normalcy they create. This is only one example. We are all "enablers" in one way or another. By ignoring the problems that exist all around us, and refusing to admit they are real problems, we perpetuate those problems. Only by admitting a problem exists, whether in the family or in society, can we truly begin to find a solution.

SAMPLE STUDENT PAPER 2

Yellow Women

Gilman's "The Yellow Wallpaper" is a tragic story of a woman's attempt to recover from post-partum depression. This story represents through symbolism the characteristic attitude toward woman and of women during the late 1800's and early 1900's. Gilman writes honestly of the isolated and confused feelings women were feeling. The woman in "The Yellow Wallpaper" goes through three periods of change throughout the story. The story begins with the description of the woman as being sick, but there are no signs of mental illness, and she is aware of her environment and even believes she is not really sick. Then there is a curious change in her character, and she appears to be disillusioned and on the verge of becoming mentally insane. And in the end she does go over the edge, and her character is literally lost. There are factors which cause these changes; I will explore these three major changes in her life as well as the use of powerful symbolism.

The woman in this story is taken to a summer house to rest and recuperate. Her husband, John, who is also her doctor, treats her as a child, and she says that "perhaps that is one reason I do not get well faster." She is apparently suffering from the baby blues, which is a depression some women experience after giving birth to a child. However, her husband sticks her in an atrocious nursery with barred windows and a wallpaper that she describes as

> dull enough to confuse the eye in following, pronounced enough to constantly irritate and provoke study, and when you follow the lame uncertain curves for a little distance they suddenly commit suicide—plunge off at outrageous angles, destroy themselves in unheard of contradictions.

Her description of the wallpaper represents her feelings about the paper, but it also symbolizes the feelings she has about herself. This confusing pattern could be a typical categorization of women, whereas a typical pattern for men might be straight and neat lines that meet at edges and appear to have an overall meaning. I say this because, in the story, John apparently knows all and has prescribed his wife's life as he sees fit. In a description of John's sister, the woman says she is "a perfect and enthusiastic housekeeper, and hopes for no better profession." This heartless description lacks praise for her sister-in-law's profession; it also symbolizes the status of women in the time the story was written.

Her husband, who calls her "his little girl" and his "blessed goose," forbids her to work until she is well; she disagrees, believing "congenial work, with excitement and change," would do her good. She believes she could recover from her baby blues if only she were able to keep active and do other things than sit alone in a nursery and stare at the wallpaper. She even asks her husband to have company for companionship, but he tells her "he would as soon put fireworks in my pillow-case as to let me have those stimulating people about now." She might not even have progressed to her second stage if it were not for her husband, brother, and sister-in-law constantly reminding her of how tired and sick she is.

Her second stage begins when she becomes "fond" of the wallpaper. She is losing contact with the outside world, instead spending her time trying, in a painstaking effort, to understand the overall pattern of the wallpaper. She sees a figure that looks like a "woman stooping down and creeping about behind that pattern." She also goes on to say, "I don't like it a bit. . . . I wish John would take me away from here." She is herself the woman "creeping" through the wallpaper. The woman creeping symbolizes women who are not allowed to stand tall and free and speak their minds. She "creeps" at night when her husband is asleep and, when she is caught "creeping," her husband tells her to get back in bed. Her husband, who has good intentions, keeps on assuring her that she is getting better, and when she disagrees with him by saying, "Better in body perhaps," he looks at her with such a "stern, reproachful" stare that she does not dare say another word.

She is alone in her own little world with no real support from anyone. She cannot be blamed for her condition and eventually insanity takes over her body. Here is another example of how the wallpaper symbolizes women:

> The front pattern *does* move—and no wonder! The woman behind shakes it!
> Sometimes I think there are a great many women behind. . . . And she is all the time trying to climb through. But nobody could climb through that pattern—it strangles so; I think that is why it has so many heads.

She realizes she is not the only woman who is lost but also many other women. This realization pushes her to her mental limit, and she tries to peel all of the wallpaper off so that the "strangled heads" can be free. She feels secure and safe in the room "creeping" and she says, "I don't want to go outside. . . . For outside you have to creep on the ground, and everything is green instead of yellow." She has no desire to live in the "green" world, and she chooses the "yellow" familiar world instead. She even locks herself in the room and throws away the key. This act symbolizes an instance of control over her own life. Comfortable in her "creeping" role, she does not want anyone to bother her. She is now mentally insane.

The woman in "The Yellow Wallpaper" represents many women, even today, in the late 20th century. There are many women who do not take advantage of their freedom, many who are also servants in life. I have seen this to be so in my grandmother's as well as in my mother's marriage. However, the wallpaper women are hiding behind is slowly being peeled off by both men and women.

QUESTIONS

1. Do these two papers agree in their estimate of the relation between the woman and her physician-husband?

2. How do the two papers compare in their interpretation of key symbolic elements: the wallpaper pattern, the woman behind the paper, the creeping, the peeling off of the paper?

3. Do both papers interpret the symbolism of the colors green and yellow, and do they agree in their interpretation?

4. How do the two papers compare in their view of what the story means to today's women?

THE PERSONAL RESPONSE

After reading the second paper, one student reader wrote the following comment. Where do you agree or disagree with it, and why?

> I remember that when first reading the story I was totally overpowered by it. This is a fascinating, disturbing paper that has made me see this terrible story in a new way. The "yellow women" designated by this student writer are not just victims to her; they are also "yellow," i.e. chicken, afraid, able only to escape via insanity. There's a strange implication—and judgment of—learned helplessness. Without quite saying it, this writer attempts to say that the flight into insanity is as much a cop-out as it is the oppressor's unknowing way of forcing insanity on the female. I get an ambiguous picture: the male isn't being deliberately patronizing; he is just as much a victim of the cultural norm as the female is. Conversely, the female plays as big a part in her insanity as the male. She could "choose" the green way—partly because she knows where the "green way" is: downstairs, near the roses and the entrance to the garden—and in her writing. A key word in this paper is "choose." The implication is that she can't buck convention enough to stand up for herself, so she retreats into the "yellow" room on the second floor, giving up the organic living greenness and groundedness in earth and reality of the first floor where she could heal naturally from a natural disequilibrium. If this writer does what I think she's doing, she has become aware of a double tragedy often missed: the pathetic ignorance of men as well as women in roles they wear because they know no other.

7 THEME
The Search for Meaning

*Invention, not preaching, enchants the modern reader
and sustains the illusion of reality.*
ANN CHARTERS

*Instead of placing one body of knowledge against another,
storytellers invite us to return from knowledge to thinking,
from a bounded way of looking to an unbounded way of
seeing.*
JAMES P. CARSE

*If I never contradict myself, then I'm either not thinking
or I'm conciliating positions and, therefore, not growing.*
NIKKI GIOVANNI

FOCUS ON THEME

Imaginative literature has the power to make you think about life, about yourself and other human beings. It is true that at times you will read mainly for entertainment or in order to escape from the daily routine. Even when you read imaginative literature for its human meaning, it may speak as much to your feelings as to your intellect. A story may make you vividly imagine scenes and events; it may stir your emotions—sometimes making you discover a capacity for feeling that you didn't know was there. However, a story that has a strong impact on you is also likely to make you think. It is likely to raise questions to which the story as a whole suggests possible answers. It is likely to make you reexamine or rethink some facet of human life. When you try to put the human meaning of a story into your own words, you formulate its **theme.** You try to state the idea or ideas that the story as a whole seems to act out.

Writers of earlier generations felt free to spell out the meaning of a story in **thematic passages.** They might put these in the mouth (or in the mind) of an observer or of a key character. In "The Blue Hotel" (1898), a story set in Nebraska in the Old West, Stephen Crane traces the events leading up to a barroom brawl in which a man is killed. From the beginning, our attention centers on the strange behavior of a recent arrival, the Swede. He is subject to

225

neurotic fears, he covers up his apprehensions with bluster and bravado, and he is a source of irritation to the small group of men spending the night in the hotel. A long evening of drinking and random quarreling comes to a head when the Swede accuses a callous, loudmouthed local boy of cheating at poker and batters him in a bloody fight. Flushed with liquor and his sense of victory, the Swede checks out of the hotel (to the great relief of the innkeeper) and stumbles on to a saloon. He there picks a fight with a gambler who refuses to drink with him, and the trouble-making Swede is killed in the ensuing brawl.

> There was a great tumult, and then was seen a long blade in the hand of the gambler. It shot forward, and a human body, this citadel of virtue, wisdom, power, was pierced as easily as if it had been a melon. The Swede fell with a cry of supreme astonishment.

There are different ways to read this story. First, Crane has a grim sense of **irony.** He dramatizes the laughable lack of fit between our expectations or explanations on the one hand and reality on the other. The Swede's paranoid fears were unjustified. No one was out to destroy him. The irony is that he was destroyed anyway. Secondly, the more callous and dense among the locals feel that the Swede only got what he deserved; he had it coming. But Crane wants us to learn something else from this story, and in case we missed it, he puts it in the mouth of one of his characters. The "Easterner" has been mostly a silent observer and at times a calming, moderating influence in the story. He finally says to a local cowboy who accuses the Swede of acting like a jackass:

> You're a bigger jackass than the Swede by a million majority. Now let me tell you one thing. . . . Johnnie *was* cheating. I saw him. . . . And I refused to stand up and be a man. I let the Swede fight it out alone. And you—you were simply puffing around the place and wanting to fight. . . . We are all in it! . . . Every sin is the result of collaboration. We, five of us, have collaborated in the murder of this Swede. . . . that fool of an unfortunate gambler came merely as the culmination . . . and gets all the punishment.

Evil is the result of collaboration. Crane's theme in this story is a generalization, but it is not a glib or secondhand generalization. It is an earned generalization—not brought into the story ready-made from the outside. It is fully anchored in the lived experience of the story.

Most twentieth-century writers have gone a step beyond Crane. Rather than have the gambler sum up the theme in so many words, they probably would have preferred to have the reader *think* about the role collaboration plays in causing evil. Even more so than Crane, later writers have harbored a suspicion of glib words—big words not anchored to lived realities, uplifting messages delivered with no attempt to make their promise come true. Katherine Anne Porter echoed a prevailing modern creed when she praised Katherine Mansfield, another short story writer, for her "fine objectivity." Porter said about her fellow writer that "she bares a moment of experience, real experience, in the life of some one human being; she states no belief, gives no motives, airs no theories, but simply presents to the reader a situation, a place, and a character, and there it is."

Because of the modern writer's reluctance to editorialize, the themes of modern fiction tend to be implied rather than spelled out. They are ideas organically embedded in image, action, and emotion. Although they have something to tell us about life or human nature or society, what they say comes to us in a language different from that of official guidelines, advice columns in the newspapers, or sayings that can be printed in an almanac.

Short Short: A Story with a Twist

The following short short is by a writer whose stories are known for their surreal quality and dark humor. Luisa Valenzuela was born in Argentina and worked with Jorge Luis Borges at the National Library in Buenos Aires before she was twenty. She went to live in Paris for a time, working for Argentine publications, writing for French television and radio, and becoming part of a circle of avant-garde writers and critics. She later came to the United States, where she has participated in programs for writers at Iowa and Columbia. Her collection titled *Strange Things Happen Here* was published in 1975; *The Lizard's Tail,* a later volume, in 1983.

The story that follows creates suspense and ends with a shuddery surprise twist. Does it have a larger meaning? What is its theme?

LUISA VALENZUELA (born 1938)
The Censors 1988

TRANSLATED BY DAVID UNGER

Poor Juan! One day they caught him with his guard down before he could even realize that what he had taken as a stroke of luck was really one of fate's dirty tricks. These things happen the minute you're careless and you let down your guard, as one often does. Juancito let happiness—a feeling you can't trust—get the better of him when he received from a confidential source Mariana's new address in Paris and he knew that she hadn't forgotten him. Without thinking twice, he sat down at his table and wrote her a letter. *The* letter that keeps his mind off his job during the day and won't let him sleep at night (what had he scrawled, what had he put on that sheet of paper he sent to Mariana?).

Juan knows there won't be a problem with the letter's contents, that it's irreproachable, harmless. But what about the rest? He knows that they examine, sniff, feel, and read between the lines of each and every letter, and check its tiniest comma and most accidental stain. He knows that all letters pass from hand to hand and go through all sorts of tests in the huge censorship offices and that, in the end, very few continue on their way. Usually it takes months, even years, if there aren't any snags; all this time the freedom, maybe even the life, of both sender and receiver is in jeopardy. And that's why Juan's so down in the dumps: thinking that something might happen to Mariana because of his letters. Of all people, Mariana, who must finally feel safe there where she always dreamed she'd live. But he knows that the *Censor's Secret Command* operates all over the world and cashes in on the discount in air rates; there's nothing to stop them from going as far as that hidden Paris neighborhood, kidnapping Mariana, and returning to their cozy homes, certain of having fulfilled their noble mission.

Well, you've got to beat them to the punch, do what everyone tries to do: sabotage the machinery, throw sand in its gears, get to the bottom of the problem so as to stop it.

This was Juan's sound plan when he, like many others, applied for a censor's job—not because he had a calling or needed a job: no, he applied simply to intercept his own letter, a consoling but unoriginal idea. He was hired immediately, for each day more and more censors are needed and no one would bother to check on his references.

Ulterior motives couldn't be overlooked by the *Censorship Division,* but they needn't be too strict with those who applied. They knew how hard it would be for those poor guys to find the letter they wanted and even if they did, what's a letter or two when the new censor would snap up so many others? That's how Juan managed to join the *Post Office's Censorship Division,* with a certain goal in mind. 5

The building had a festive air on the outside which contrasted with its inner staidness. Little by little, Juan was absorbed by his job and he felt at peace since he was doing everything he could to get his letter for Mariana. He didn't even worry when, in his first month, he was sent to *Section K* where envelopes are very carefully screened for explosives.

It's true that on the third day, a fellow worker had his right hand blown off by a letter, but the division chief claimed it was sheer negligence on the victim's part. Juan and the other employees were allowed to go back to their work, albeit feeling less secure. After work, one of them tried to organize a strike to demand higher wages for unhealthy work, but Juan didn't join in; after thinking it over, he reported him to his superiors and thus got promoted.

You don't form a habit by doing something once, he told himself as he left his boss's office. And when he was transferred to *Section J,* where letters are carefully checked for poison dust, he felt he had climbed a rung in the ladder.

By working hard, he quickly reached *Section E* where the work was more interesting, for he could now read and analyze the letters' contents. Here he could even hope to get hold of his letter which, judging by the time that had elapsed, had gone through the other sections and was probably floating around in this one.

Soon his work became so absorbing that his noble mission blurred in his mind. Day after day he crossed out whole paragraphs in red ink, pitilessly chucking many letters into the censored basket. These were horrible days when he was shocked by the subtle and conniving ways employed by people to pass on subversive messages; his instincts were so sharp that he found behind a simple "the weather's unsettled" or "prices continue to soar" the wavering hand of someone secretly scheming to overthrow the Government. 10

His zeal brought him swift promotion. We don't know if this made him happy. Very few letters reached him in *Section B*—only a handful passed the other hurdles—so he read them over and over again, passed them under a magnifying glass, searched for microprint with an electronic microscope, and tuned his sense of smell so that he was beat by the time he made it home. He'd barely manage to warm up his soup, eat some fruit, and fall into bed, satisfied with having done his duty. Only his darling mother worried, but she couldn't get him back on the right road. She'd say, though it wasn't always true: Lola called, she's at the bar with the girls, they miss you, they're waiting for you. Or else she'd leave a bottle of red wine on the table. But Juan wouldn't overdo it: any distraction could make him lose his edge and the perfect censor had to be alert, keen, attentive, and sharp to nab cheats. He had a truly patriotic task, both self-denying and uplifting.

His basket for censored letters became the best fed as well as the most cunning basket in the whole *Censorship Division*. He was about to congratulate himself for having finally discovered his true mission, when his letter to Mariana reached his hands. Naturally, he censored it without regret. And just as naturally, he couldn't stop them from executing him the following morning, another victim of his devotion to his work.

THE RECEPTIVE READER

Does this story make a statement about censorship? about human nature? What does it say? Does it act out ideas about life? about society? How?

THE MAKING OF MEANING

Art shrinks from . . . every abstract thing, from all that is of the brain only, from all that is not a fountain jetting from the entire hopes, memories, and sensations of the body.
WILLIAM BUTLER YEATS

The truth about any subject only comes when all the sides of the story are put together, and all their different meanings make one new one.
ALICE WALKER

As you encounter references to literary themes, you may note two slightly different uses. Often *theme* simply means a focus of attention, an area of concern. In this sense, one great modern theme is alienation—the feeling of uprootedness, the loss of the sense of home. A related theme is loneliness—our inability to communicate truly with others, our difficulty in forging lasting bonds. Another modern theme is a runaway technology that has put us at odds with nature. In much of our modern world, these "are in the air"; we encounter them again and again, like the strain of a popular song that we hear over and over—on the radio, in the supermarket, in the elevator.

This meaning of *theme* shades over into its more specific meaning, which makes us go a step or two beyond identifying an issue or an area of concern. It makes us ask what a story as a whole might be saying *about* an issue or area of attention. In this sense, the theme of a story is not alienation but what the story as a whole says about alienation. The story as a whole may be making a statement about the roots of alienation, or about our ways of coping with it, or about how alienation explains the kind of people we are. It is this kind of implied statement that you will usually be exploring when talking or writing about theme.

When reading for theme or when trying to formulate the theme of a story, remember cautions like the following:

✧ *Beware of large abstractions.* Part of the modern temper has been a suspicion of big words, hasty generalizations, and premature abstractions. **Abstractions** (from a Latin word meaning "pulling away") draw us away from the nitty gritty of unsorted detail to the larger labels and categories that we need to find our way in a complex, multilayered world. But because they cover much (they are "umbrella" terms), abstract terms easily become foggy or misleading. Be prepared to ask: "freedom"—to do what? "discovery of the self"—focusing on what? "love of humanity"—what part or what features of it?

✧ *Beware of oversimplification.* Often the meaning of a story takes shape in the interplay of conflicting human commitments and emotions. If you were to look for a common denominator for stories by Faulkner, Jackson, and Hawthorne in this volume, you might start by saying their authors agree that "evil lurks in the human heart." But this much most readers probably are ready to grant *before* they read one of these stories. The questions each story raises and the possible answers it leads us to explore are more complex than that. Like other writers who have wrestled with the problem of how to explain evil, how to think of evil, in our world, each of these authors has arrived at a somewhat different answer.

✧ *Beware of clichés.* "All you need is love" makes a marvelous Beatles song. But it is too sweeping and inspirational (and too obviously untrue) to serve as a lasting insight that we carry away from a gripping story. If you bring a ready-made phrase to a story from outside, it is not going to carry the authentic stamp of honest feeling, of lived experience. Be wary of greeting-card phrases—phrases we take down ready-made from the rack when we find it hard to put our own honest feeling and thinking into words.

THE THINKING READER

The concepts of beauty and ugliness are mysterious to me. Many people write about them. In mulling over them, I try to get underneath them and see what they mean, understand the impact they have on what people do. I also write about love and death. The problem I face as a writer is to make my stories mean something. You can have wonderful, interesting people, a fascinating story, but it's not about anything. It has no real substance.

TONI MORRISON

Serious readers have always turned to literature as not just entertainment but as an interpretation of life. They listen attentively to writers who help them make sense of experience. They remember writers who served them as guideposts or beacons in times of bewilderment and confusion. Each of the following three stories puts its characters into situations that make them ask themselves searching questions. What are these questions in each story? What answers does the story as a whole suggest? What ideas—about people, about human nature, about good and evil—are acted out or fleshed out in each story?

ALICE WALKER (born 1944)

*Her deepest concern is with individuals and how their
relationships are affected by their confrontations with
wider political and moral issues.*

CAROL RUMENS

Alice Walker's novel *The Color Purple* (1982) was a major publishing event that established her as a dominant voice in the quest for a new black identity and black pride. In her Pulitzer Prize–winning novel, as in some of her short stories, her heroines are women in the black community struggling to emerge from a history of oppression and abuse. They find strength in bonding with other women, and they turn to the African past in the search for alternatives to our rapacious technological civilization. A recurrent feature in her fiction are black males representing a generation of men who "had failed women—and themselves." Walker's more recent novel, *The Temple of My Familiar* (1989), has been called a book of "amazing, overwhelming" richness, with characters "pushing one another toward self-knowledge, honesty, engagement" (Ursula K. Le Guin).

Born in Eatonton, Georgia, Walker knew poverty and racism at close quarters as the child of sharecroppers in the Deep South. While a student at Spelman College in Atlanta, she joined in the rallies, sit-ins, and freedom marches of the civil rights movement, which, she said later, "broke the pattern of black servitude in this country." She worked as a caseworker for the New York City Welfare Department and as an editor for *Ms.* magazine. She has written and lectured widely on the relationship between black men and women, between black and white women, and between her writing and the work of African American writers—Jean Toomer, Zora Neale Hurston—who were her inspiration. She has taught creative writing and black literature at colleges including Jackson State College, Wellesley, and Yale.

Many of Walker's essays, articles, and reviews were collected in her *In Search of Our Mothers' Gardens* (1983). In the title essay, she paid tribute to women of her mother's and grandmother's generations, who channeled the creative and spiritual energies that were denied other outlets into their rich gardens and into the "fanciful, inspired, and yet simple" quilts they fashioned from "bits and pieces of worthless rags." In the following story, the older generation tries to hold on to its hard-won pride, while members of a younger generation assert their independence from the past by adopting Muslim names and African greetings.

Everyday Use
For Your Grandmamma

1973

I will wait for her in the yard that Maggie and I made so clean and wavy yesterday afternoon. A yard like this is more comfortable than most people know. It is not just a yard. It is like an extended living room. When the hard clay is swept clean as a floor and the fine sand around the edges lined with tiny, irregular grooves, anyone can come and sit and look up into the elm tree and wait for the breezes that never come inside the house. _ashamed of her looks_

Maggie will be nervous until after her sister goes: she will stand hopelessly in corners, homely and ashamed of the burn scars down her arms and legs, eying her sister with a mixture of envy and awe. She thinks her sister has held life always in the palm of one hand, that "no" is a word the world never learned to say to her.

You've no doubt seen those TV shows where the child who has "made it" is confronted, as a surprise, by her own mother and father, tottering in weakly from backstage. (A pleasant surprise, of course: What would they do if parent and child came on the show only to curse out and insult each other?) On TV mother and child embrace and smile into each other's faces. Sometimes the mother and father weep, the child wraps them in her arms and leans across the table to tell how she would not have made it without their help. I have seen these programs.

Sometimes I dream a dream in which Dee and I are suddenly brought together on a TV program of this sort. Out of a dark and soft-seated limousine I am ushered into a bright room filled with many people. There I meet a smiling, gray, sporty man like Johnny Carson who shakes my hand and tells me what a fine girl I have. Then we are on the stage and Dee is embracing me with tears in her eyes. She pins on my dress a large orchid, even though she has told me once that she thinks orchids are tacky flowers.

In real life I am a large, big-boned woman with rough, man-working hands. In the winter I wear flannel nightgowns to bed and overalls during the day. I can kill and clean a hog as mercilessly as a man. My fat keeps me hot in zero weather. I can work outside all day, breaking ice to get water for washing; I can eat pork liver cooked over the open fire minutes after it comes steaming from the hog. One winter I knocked a bull calf straight in the brain between the eyes with a sledge hammer and had the meat hung up to chill before nightfall. But of course all this does not show on television. I am the way my daughter would want me to be: a hundred pounds lighter, my skin like an uncooked barley pancake. My hair glistens in the hot bright lights. Johnny Carson has much to do to keep up with my quick and witty tongue.

But that is a mistake. I know even before I wake up. Who ever knew a Johnson with a quick tongue? Who can even imagine me looking a strange white man in the eye? It seems to me I have talked to them always with one foot raised in flight, with my head turned in whichever way is farthest from them. Dee, though. She would always look anyone in the eye. Hesitation was no part of her nature.

"How do I look, Mama?" Maggie says, showing just enough of her thin body enveloped in pink skirt and red blouse for me to know she's there, almost hidden by the door.

"Come out into the yard," I say.

Have you ever seen a lame animal, perhaps a dog run over by some careless person rich enough to own a car, sidle up to someone who is ignorant enough to be kind to them? That is the way my Maggie walks. She has been like this, chin on chest, eyes on ground, feet in shuffle, ever since the fire that burned the other house to the ground.

Dee is lighter than Maggie, with nicer hair and a fuller figure. She's a woman now, though sometimes I forget. How long ago was it that the other house burned? Ten, twelve years? Sometimes I can still hear the flames and feel Maggie's arms sticking to me, her hair smoking and her dress falling off her in little black papery flakes. Her eyes seemed stretched open, blazed open by the flames reflected in them. And Dee. I see her standing off under the sweet gum tree she used to dig gum out of; a look of concentration on her face as she watched the last dingy gray board of the house fall in toward the red-hot brick chimney. Why don't you do a dance around the ashes? I'd wanted to ask her. She had hated the house that much.

I used to think she hated Maggie, too. But that was before we raised the money, the church and me, to send her to Augusta to school. She used to read to us without pity; forcing words, lies, other folks' habits, whole lives upon us two, sitting trapped and ignorant underneath her voice. She washed us in a river of make-believe, burned us with a lot of knowledge we didn't necessarily need to know. Pressed us to her with the serious way she read, to shove us away at just the moment, like dimwits, we seemed about to understand.

Dee wanted nice things. A yellow organdy dress to wear to her graduation from high school; black pumps to match a green suit she'd made from an old suit somebody gave me. She was determined to stare down any disaster in her efforts. Her eyelids would not flicker for minutes at a time. Often I fought off the temptation to shake her. At sixteen she had a style of her own: and knew what style was.

I never had an education myself. After second grade the school was closed down. Don't ask me why: in 1927 colored asked fewer questions than they do now. Sometimes Maggie reads to me. She stumbles along good naturedly but can't see well. She knows she is not bright. Like good looks and money, quickness passed her by. She will marry John Thomas (who has mossy teeth in an earnest face) and then I'll be free to sit here and I guess just sing church songs to myself. Although I never was a good singer. Never could carry a tune. I was always better at a man's job. I used to love to milk till I was hooked in the side in '49. Cows are soothing and slow and don't bother you, unless you try to milk them the wrong way.

I have deliberately turned my back on the house. It is three rooms, just like the one that burned, except the roof is tin; they don't make shingle roofs any more. There are no real windows, just some holes cut in the sides, like the portholes in a ship, but not round and not square, with rawhide holding the shutters up on the outside. This house is in a pasture, too, like the other one. No doubt when Dee sees it she will want to tear it down. She wrote me once that no matter where we "choose" to live, she will manage to come see us. But she will never bring her friends. Maggie and I thought about this and Maggie asked me, "Mama, when did Dee ever *have* any friends?"

She had a few. Furtive boys in pink shirts hanging about on washday after school. Nervous girls who never laughed. Impressed with her they worshiped the well-turned phrase, the cute shape, the scalding humor that erupted like bubbles in lye. She read to them. 15

When she was courting Jimmy T she didn't have much time to pay to us, but turned all her faultfinding power on him. He *flew* to marry a cheap city girl from a family of ignorant flashy people. She hardly had time to recompose herself.

When she comes I will meet—but there they are!

Maggie attempts to make a dash for the house, in her shuffling way, but I stay her with my hand. "Come back here," I say. And she stops and tries to dig a well in the sand with her toe.

It is hard to see them clearly through the strong sun. But even the first glimpse of leg out of the car tells me it is Dee. Her feet were always neat-looking, as if God himself had shaped them with a certain style. From the other side of the car comes a short, stocky man. Hair is all over his head a foot long and hanging from his chin like a kinky mule tail. I hear Maggie suck in her breath. "Uhnnnh," is what it sounds like. Like when you see the wriggling end of a snake just in front of your foot on the road. "Uhnnnh."

Dee next. A dress down to the ground, in this hot weather. A dress so loud it hurts 20
my eyes. There are yellows and oranges enough to throw back the light of the sun. I
feel my whole face warming from the heat waves it throws out. Earrings gold, too, and
hanging down to her shoulders. Bracelets dangling and making noises when she moves
her arm up to shake the folds of the dress out of her armpits. The dress is loose and
flows, and as she walks closer, I like it. I hear Maggie go "Uhnnnh" again. It is her sister's hair. It stands straight up like the wool on a sheep. It is black as night and around
the edges are two long pigtails that rope about like small lizards disappearing behind
her ears.

"Wa-su-zo-Tean-o!" she says, coming on in that gliding way the dress makes her
move. The short stocky fellow with the hair to his navel is all grinning and he follows
up with "Asalamalakim, my mother and sister!" He moves to hug Maggie but she falls
back, right up against the back of my chair. I feel her trembling there and when I look
up I see the perspiration falling off her chin.

"Don't get up," says Dee. Since I am stout it takes something of a push. You can
see me trying to move a second or two before I make it. She turns, showing white heels
through her sandals, and goes back to the car. Out she peeks next with a Polaroid. She
stoops down quickly and lines up picture after picture of me sitting there in front of the
house with Maggie cowering behind me. She never takes a shot without making sure
the house is included. When a cow comes nibbling around the edge of the yard she
snaps it and me and Maggie *and* the house. Then she puts the Polaroid in the back seat
of the car, and comes up and kisses me on the forehead.

Meanwhile Asalamalakim is going through motions with Maggie's hand. Maggie's
hand is as limp as a fish, and probably as cold, despite the sweat, and she keeps trying to pull it back. It looks like Asalamalakim wants to shake hands but wants to do it
fancy. Or maybe he don't know how people shake hands. Anyhow, he soon gives up on
Maggie.

"Well," I say. "Dee."

"No, Mama," she says. "Not 'Dee,' Wangero Leewanika Kemanjo!" 25

"What happened to 'Dee'?" I wanted to know.

"She's dead," Wangero said. "I couldn't bear it any longer, being named after the
people who oppress me."

"You know as well as me you was named after your aunt Dicie," I said. Dicie is my
sister. She named Dee. We called her "Big Dee" after Dee was born.

"But who was *she* named after?" asked Wangero.

"I guess after Grandma Dee," I said. 30

"And who was she named after?" asked Wangero.

"Her mother," I said, and saw Wangero was getting tired. "That's about as far
back as I can trace it," I said. Though, in fact, I probably could have carried it back beyond the Civil War through the branches.

"Well," said Asalamalakim, "there you are."

"Uhnnnh," I heard Maggie say.

"There I was not," I said, "before 'Dicie' cropped up in our family, so why should 35
I try to trace it that far back?"

He just stood there grinning, looking down on me like somebody inspecting a
Model A car. Every once in a while he and Wangero sent eye signals over my head.

"How do you pronounce this name?" I asked.

"You don't have to call me by it if you don't want to," said Wangero.

"Why shouldn't I?" I asked. "If that's what you want us to call you, we'll call
you."

"I know it might sound awkward at first," said Wangero.

"I'll get used to it," I said. "Ream it out again." 40

Well, soon we got the name out of the way. Asalamalakim had a name twice as long and three times as hard. After I tripped over it two or three times he told me to just call him Hakim-a-barber. I wanted to ask him was he a barber, but I didn't really think he was, so I didn't ask.

"You must belong to those beef-cattle peoples down the road," I said. They said "Asalamalakim" when they met you, too, but they didn't shake hands. Always too busy: feeding the cattle, fixing the fences, putting up salt-lick shelters, throwing down hay. When the white folks poisoned some of the herd the men stayed up all night with rifles in their hands. I walked a mile and a half just to see the sight.

Hakim-a-barber said, "I accept some of their doctrines, but farming and raising cattle is not my style." (They didn't tell me, and I didn't ask, whether Wangero (Dee) had really gone and married him.)

We sat down to eat and right away he said he didn't eat collards and pork was un- 45 clean. Wangero, though, went on through the chitlins and corn bread, the greens and everything else. She talked a blue streak over the sweet potatoes. Everything delighted her. Even the fact that we still used the benches her daddy made for the table when we couldn't afford to buy chairs.

"Oh, Mama!" she cried. Then turned to Hakim-a-barber. "I never knew how lovely these benches are. You can feel the rump prints," she said, running her hands underneath her and along the bench. Then she gave a sigh and her hand closed over Grandma Dee's butter dish. "That's it!" she said. "I knew there was something I wanted to ask you if I could have." She jumped up from the table and went over in the corner where the churn stood, the milk in it clabber by now. She looked at the churn and looked at it.

"This churn top is what I need," she said. "Didn't Uncle Buddy whittle it out of a tree you all used to have?"

"Yes," I said.

"Uh huh," she said happily. "And I want the dasher, too."

"Uncle Buddy whittle that, too?" asked the barber. 50

Dee (Wangero) looked up at me.

"Aunt Dee's first husband whittled the dash," said Maggie so low you almost couldn't hear her. "His name was Henry, but they called him Stash."

"Maggie's brain is like an elephant's," Wangero said, laughing. "I can use the churn top as a centerpiece for the alcove table," she said, sliding a plate over the churn, "and I'll think of something artistic to do with the dasher."

When she finished wrapping the dasher the handle stuck out. I took it for a moment in my hands. You didn't even have to look close to see where hands pushing the dasher up and down to make butter had left a kind of sink in the wood. In fact, there were a lot of small sinks; you could see where thumbs and fingers had sunk into the wood. It was beautiful light yellow wood, from a tree that grew in the yard where Big Dee and Stash had lived.

After dinner Dee (Wangero) went to the trunk at the foot of my bed and started 55 rifling through it. Maggie hung back in the kitchen over the dishpan. Out came Wangero with two quilts. They had been pieced by Grandma Dee and then Big Dee and me had hung them on the quilt frames on the front porch and quilted them. One was in the Lone Star pattern. The other was Walk Around the Mountain. In both of them were scraps of dresses Grandma Dee had worn fifty and more years ago. Bits and pieces of Grandpa Jarrell's Paisley shirts. And one teeny faded blue piece, about the size of a penny matchbox, that was from Great Grandpa Ezra's uniform that he wore in the Civil War.

"Mama," Wangero said sweet as a bird. "Can I have these old quilts?"

I heard something fall in the kitchen, and a minute later the kitchen door slammed.

"Why don't you take one or two of the others?" I asked. "These old things was just done by me and Big Dee from some tops your grandma pieced before she died."

"No," said Wangero. "I don't want those. They are stitched around the borders by machine."

"That'll make them last better," I said.

60

"That's not the point," said Wangero. "These are all pieces of dresses Grandma used to wear. She did all this stitching by hand. Imagine!" She held the quilts securely in her arms, stroking them.

"Some of the pieces, like those lavender ones, come from old clothes her mother handed down to her," I said, moving up to touch the quilts. Dee (Wangero) moved back just enough so that I couldn't reach the quilts. They already belonged to her.

"Imagine!" she breathed again, clutching them closely to her bosom.

"The truth is," I said, "I promised to give them quilts to Maggie, for when she marries John Thomas."

She gasped like a bee had stung her.

65

"Maggie can't appreciate these quilts!" she said. "She'd probably be backward enough to put them to everyday use."

"I reckon she would," I said. "God knows I been saving 'em for long enough with nobody using 'em. I hope she will!" I didn't want to bring up how I had offered Dee (Wangero) a quilt when she went away to college. Then she had told me they were old-fashioned, out of style.

"But they're *priceless!*" she was saying now, furiously; for she has a temper. "Maggie would put them on the bed and in five years they'd be in rags. Less than that!"

"She can always make some more," I said. "Maggie knows how to quilt."

Dee (Wangero) looked at me with hatred. "You just will not understand. The point is these quilts, *these* quilts!"

70

"Well," I said, stumped. "What would *you* do with them?"

"Hang them," she said. As if that was the only thing you *could* do with quilts.

Maggie by now was standing in the door. I could almost hear the sound her feet made as they scraped over each other.

"She can have them, Mama," she said, like somebody used to never winning anything, or having anything reserved for her. "I can 'member Grandma Dee without the quilts."

I looked at her hard. She had filled her bottom lip with checkerberry snuff and it gave her face a kind of dopey, hangdog look. It was Grandma Dee and Big Dee who taught her how to quilt herself. She stood there with her scarred hands hidden in the folds of her skirt. She looked at her sister with something like fear but she wasn't mad at her. This was Maggie's portion. This was the way she knew God to work.

75

When I looked at her like that something hit me in the top of my head and ran down to the soles of my feet. Just like when I'm in church and the spirit of God touches me and I get happy and shout. I did something I never had done before: hugged Maggie to me, then dragged her on into the room, snatched the quilts out of Miss Wangero's hands and dumped them into Maggie's lap. Maggie just sat there on my bed with her mouth open.

"Take one or two of the others," I said to Dee.

But she turned without a word and went out to Hakim-a-barber.

"You just don't understand," she said, as Maggie and I came out to the car.

"What don't I understand?" I wanted to know. 80

"Your heritage," she said. And then she turned to Maggie, kissed her, and said, "You ought to try to make something of yourself, too, Maggie. It's really a new day for us. But from the way you and Mama still live you'd never know it."

She put on some sunglasses that hid everything above the tip of her nose and her chin.

Maggie smiled; maybe at the sunglasses. But a real smile, not scared. After we watched the car dust settle I asked Maggie to bring me a dip of snuff. And then the two of us sat there just enjoying, until it was time to go in the house and go to bed.

THE RECEPTIVE READER

1. What is the self-image of the mother? How does her sense of her real self contrast with her daydreams? ◇ How does her initial self-portrait as the *narrator* and central character point forward to what happens later in the story?

2. What is the contrasting history of the two siblings? How does one serve as a *foil* to the other? What is most significant in their earlier history?

3. What is the mother's view of Dee and her companion? How would you spell out the mother's attitude implied at various points in the story? What touches seem satirical and why? ◇ Is everything in the story seen from the mother's *point of view*?

4. How does the confrontation over the quilts bring things to a head? What do the quilts symbolize? How does the climactic ending resolve the central conflict in this story? How does it turn the tables on Dee's use of terms like *backward* and *heritage*?

5. How would you spell out in so many words the *theme* of this story? (How does the title hint at the central theme?)

6. What in the story helps especially to bring the theme to life for you and keep it from becoming an abstract idea?

THE PERSONAL RESPONSE

Do you identify with the narrator in this story? Is there another side to the story? Could you say something in defense of Dee?

THE CREATIVE DIMENSION

Write a passage in which one or the other of the daughters tells her side of the story. Or rewrite the ending the way you would have preferred the story to come out.

STEPHEN CRANE (1871–1900)

Stephen Crane is an outstanding early representative of **naturalism** in American fiction. Naturalist writers did not shirk the task of looking at nature in the raw or of confronting unembellished human nature. Like other writers in that tradition, Crane preferred not to preach or editorialize but to let the grim facts speak for themselves. He was born in Newark, New Jersey, as the fourteenth child in the home of a Methodist minister. After his college year Lafayette and Syracuse, he scraped together a living as a free-lance journ and much of his fiction looks at harsh realities with the impartial honest the reporter. His first novel, *Maggie: A Girl of the Streets* (1893), took an uncompromising look at a subject then not considered a fit topic for polite conversation. He became famous with *The Red Badge of Courage* (1895), a novel about the Civil War. Anticipating modern war novels, Crane went beyond the flag-waving and heroic oratory of stay-at-home patriots to probe the psychological realities of war: the fear of death, the horror of mass destruction, the sense of solidarity with one's doomed comrades.

Crane had the strongly developed sense of irony that was to become the hallmark of much twentieth-century literature. His stories and poems highlight the sad and laughable contrast between our naive hopes or rosy daydreams and the world in which we actually live. Driven into exile by gossip about his irregular personal life, enmeshed in what one editor has called "a malignant tangle of debts," he died of tuberculosis after publishing fourteen books in his short lifetime.

The following short story classic, which he called a tale "after the fact," is based on his personal experience as the survivor of the shipwreck of the steamer *Commodore*. He had earlier written a factual account of the experience for the New York *Press*, published on January 7, 1887. What is the theme (or are the themes) of this story? What does it say about the relationship between human beings and nature? What does it say about male bonding? What does it say about the survival of the fittest—or, for that matter, about the survival of the unfit?

The Open Boat   1897

I

None of them knew the color of the sky. Their eyes glanced level, and were fastened upon the waves that swept toward them. These waves were of the hue of slate, save for the tops, which were of foaming white, and all of the men knew the colors of the sea. The horizon narrowed and widened, and dipped and rose, and at all times its edge was jagged with waves that seemed thrust up in points like rocks.

Many a man ought to have a bathtub larger than the boat which here rode upon the sea. These waves were most wrongfully and barbarously abrupt and tall, and each froth-top was a problem in small-boat navigation.

The cook squatted in the bottom, and looked with both eyes at the six inches of gunwale which separated him from the ocean. His sleeves were rolled over his fat forearms, and the two flaps of his unbuttoned vest dangled as he bent to bail out the boat. Often he said, "Gawd! that was a narrow clip." As he remarked it he invariably gazed eastward over the broken sea.

The oiler, steering with one of the two oars in the boat, sometimes raised himself suddenly to keep clear of water that swirled in over the stern. It was a thin little oar, and it seemed often ready to snap.

The correspondent, pulling at the other oar, watched the waves and wondered why he was there.

The injured captain, lying in the bow, was at this time buried in that profound dejection and indifference which comes, temporarily at least, to even the bravest and most enduring when, willy-nilly, the firm fails, the army loses, the ship goes down. The mind of the master of a vessel is rooted deep in the timbers of her, though he command for a day or a decade; and this captain had on him the stern impression of a scene in the

5

greys of dawn of seven turned faces, and later a stump of a topmast with a white ball on it, that slashed to and fro at the waves, went low and lower, and down. Thereafter there was something strange in his voice. Although steady, it was deep with mourning, and of a quality beyond oration or tears.

"Keep 'er a little more south, Billie," said he.

"A little more south, sir," said the oiler in the stern.

A seat in his boat was not unlike a seat upon a bucking broncho, and by the same token a broncho is not much smaller. The craft pranced and reared and plunged like an animal. As each wave came, and she rose for it, she seemed like a horse making at a fence outrageously high. The manner of her scramble over these walls of water is a mystic thing, and, moreover, at the top of them were ordinarily these problems in white water, the foam racing down from the summit of each wave requiring a new leap, and a leap from the air. Then, after scornfully bumping a crest, she would slide and race and splash down a long incline, and arrive bobbing and nodding in front of the next menace.

A singular disadvantage of the sea lies in the fact that after successfully surmount- 10 ing one wave you discover that there is another behind it just as important and just as nervously anxious to do something effective in the way of swamping boats. In a ten-foot dinghy one can get an idea of the resources of the sea in the line of waves that is not probable to the average experience which is never at sea in a dinghy. As each slaty wall of water approached, it shut all else from the view of the men in the boat, and it was not difficult to imagine that this particular wave was the final outburst of the ocean, the last effort of the grim water. There was a terrible grace in the move of the waves, and they came in silence, save for the snarling of the crests.

In the wan light the faces of the men must have been grey. Their eyes must have glinted in strange ways as they gazed steadily astern. Viewed from a balcony, the whole thing would doubtless have been weirdly picturesque. But the men in the boat had no time to see it, and if they had had leisure, there were other things to occupy their minds. The sun swung steadily up the sky, and they knew it was broad day because the color of the sea changed from slate to emerald green streaked with amber lights, and the foam was like tumbling snow. The process of the breaking day was unknown to them. They were aware only of this effect upon the color of the waves that rolled to-ward them.

In disjointed sentences the cook and the correspondent argued as to the difference between a life-saving station and a house of refuge. The cook had said: "There's a house of refuge just north of the Mosquito Inlet Light, and as soon as they see us they'll come off in their boat and pick us up."

"As soon as who see us?" said the correspondent.

"The crew," said the cook.

"Houses of refuge don't have crews," said the correspondent. "As I understand 15 them, they are only places where clothes and grub are stored for the benefit of ship-wrecked people. They don't carry crews."

"Oh, yes, they do," said the cook.

"No, they don't," said the correspondent.

"Well, we're not there yet, anyhow," said the oiler, in the stern.

"Well," said the cook, "perhaps it's not a house of refuge that I'm thinking of as being near Mosquito Inlet Light; perhaps it's a life-saving station."

"We're not there yet," said the oiler in the stern. 20

II

As the boat bounced from the top of each wave the wind tore through the hair of the hatless men, and as the craft plopped her stern down again the spray slashed past them. The crest of each of these waves was a hill, from the top of which the men surveyed for a moment a broad tumultuous expanse, shining and wind-riven. It was probably splendid, it was probably glorious, this play of the free sea, wild with lights of emerald and white and amber.

"Bully good thing it's an on-shore wind," said the cook. "If not, where would we be? Wouldn't have a show."

"That's right," said the correspondent.

The busy oiler nodded his assent.

Then the captain, in the bow, chuckled in a way that expressed humor, contempt, tragedy, all in one. "Do you think we've got much of a show now, boys?" said he.

Whereupon the three were silent, save for a trifle of hemming and hawing. To express any particular optimism at this time they felt to be childish and stupid, but they all doubtless possessed this sense of the situation in their minds. A young man thinks doggedly at such times. On the other hand, the ethics of their condition was decidedly against any open suggestion of hopelessness. So they were silent.

"Oh, well," said the captain, soothing his children, "we'll get ashore all right."

But there was that in his tone which made them think; so the oiler quoth, "Yes! if this wind holds."

The cook was bailing. "Yes! if we don't catch hell in the surf."

Canton-flannel gulls flew near and far. Sometimes they sat down on the sea, near patches of brown seaweed that rolled over the waves with a movement like carpets on a line in a gale. The birds sat comfortably in groups, and they were envied by some in the dinghy, for the wrath of the sea was no more to them than it was to a covey of prairie chickens a thousand miles inland. Often they came very close and stared at the men with black bead-like eyes. At these times they were uncanny and sinister in their unblinking scrutiny, and the men hooted angrily at them, telling them to be gone. One came, and evidently decided to alight on the top of the captain's head. The bird flew parallel to the boat and did not circle, but made short sidelong jumps in the air in chicken-fashion. His black eyes were wistfully fixed upon the captain's head. "Ugly brute," said the oiler to the bird. "You look as if you were made with a jackknife." The cook and the correspondent swore darkly at the creature. The captain naturally wished to knock it away with the end of the heavy painter, but he did not dare do it, because anything resembling an emphatic gesture would have capsized this freighted boat; and so, with his open hand, the captain gently and carefully waved the gull away. After it had been discouraged from the pursuit the captain breathed easier on account of his hair, and others breathed easier because the bird struck their minds at this time as being somehow gruesome and ominous.

In the meantime the oiler and the correspondent rowed. And also they rowed. They sat together in the same seat, and each rowed an oar. Then the oiler took both oars; then the correspondent took both oars; then the oiler; then the correspondent. They rowed and they rowed. The very ticklish part of the business was when the time came for the reclining one in the stern to take his turn at the oars. By the very last star of truth, it is easier to steal eggs from under a hen than it was to change seats in the dinghy. First the man in the stern slid his hand along the thwart and moved with care, as if he were of Sèvres. Then the man in the rowing-seat slid his hand along the other thwart. It was all done with the most extraordinary care. As the two sidled past each other, the whole party kept watchful eyes on the coming wave, and the captain cried: "Look out, now! Steady, there!"

The brown mats of seaweed that appeared from time to time were like islands, bits of earth. They were travelling, apparently, neither one way nor the other. They were, to all intents, stationary. They informed the men in the boat that it was making progress slowly toward the land.

The captain, rearing cautiously in the bow after the dinghy soared on a great swell, said that he had seen the lighthouse at Mosquito Inlet. Presently the cook remarked that he had seen it. The correspondent was at the oars then, and for some reason he too wished to look at the lighthouse; but his back was toward the far shore, and the waves were important, and for some time he could not seize an opportunity to turn his head. But at last there came a wave more gentle than the others, and when at the crest of it he swiftly scoured the western horizon.

"See it?" said the captain.

"No," said the correspondent, slowly; "I didn't see anything."　　35

"Look again," said the captain. He pointed. "It's exactly in that direction."

At the top of another wave the correspondent did as he was bid, and this time his eyes chanced on a small, still thing on the edge of the swaying horizon. It was precisely like the point of a pin. It took an anxious eye to find a lighthouse so tiny.

"Think we'll make it, Captain?"

"If this wind holds and the boat don't swamp, we can't do much else," said the captain.

The little boat, lifted by each towering sea and splashed viciously by the crests,　　40 made progress that in the absence of seaweed was not apparent to those in her. She seemed just a wee thing wallowing, miraculously top up, at the mercy of five oceans. Occasionally a great spread of water, like white flames, swarmed into her.

"Bail her, cook," said the captain, serenely.

"All right, Captain," said the cheerful cook.

III

It would be difficult to describe the subtle brotherhood of men that was here established on the seas. No one said that it was so. No one mentioned it. But it dwelt in the boat, and each man felt it warm him. They were a captain, an oiler, a cook, and a correspondent, and they were friends—friends in a more curiously iron-bound degree than may be common. The hurt captain, lying against the water-jar in the bow, spoke always in a low voice and calmly; but he could never command a more ready and swiftly obedient crew than the motley three of the dinghy. It was more than a mere recognition of what was best for the common safety. There was surely in it a quality that was personal and heart-felt. And after this devotion to the commander of the boat, there was this comradeship, that the correspondent, for instance, who had been taught to be cynical of men, knew even at the time was the best experience of his life. But no one said that it was so. No one mentioned it.

"I wish we had a sail," remarked the captain. "We might try my overcoat on the end of an oar, and give you two boys a chance to rest." So the cook and the correspondent held the mast and spread wide the overcoat; the oiler steered; and the little boat made good way with her new rig. Sometimes the oiler had to scull sharply to keep a sea from breaking into the boat, but otherwise sailing was a success.

Meanwhile the lighthouse had been growing slowly larger. It had now almost as-　　45 sumed color, and appeared like a little grey shadow on the sky. The man at the oars could not be prevented from turning his head rather often to try for a glimpse of this little grey shadow.

At last, from the top of each wave, the men in the tossing boat could see land. Even as the lighthouse was an upright shadow on the sky, this land seemed but a long black shadow on the sea. It certainly was thinner than paper. "We must be about opposite

New Smyrna," said the cook, who had coasted this shore often in schooners. "Captain, by the way, I believe they abandoned that life-saving station there about a year ago."

"Did they?" said the captain.

The wind slowly died away. The cook and the correspondent were not now obliged to slave in order to hold high the oar. But the waves continued their old impetuous swooping at the dinghy, and the little craft, no longer under way, struggled woundily over them. The oiler or the correspondent took the oars again.

Shipwrecks are apropos of nothing. If men could only train for them and have them occur when the men had reached pink condition, there would be less drowning at sea. Of the four in the dinghy none had slept any time worth mentioning for two days and two nights previous to embarking in the dinghy, and in the excitement of clambering about the deck of a foundering ship they had also forgotten to eat heartily.

For these reasons, and for others, neither the oiler nor the correspondent was fond of rowing at this time. The correspondent wondered ingenuously how in the name of all that was sane could there be people who thought it amusing to row a boat. It was not an amusement; it was a diabolical punishment, and even a genius of mental aberrations could never conclude that it was anything but a horror to the muscles and a crime against the back. He mentioned to the boat in general how the amusement of rowing struck him, and the weary-faced oiler smiled in full sympathy. Previously to the foundering, by the way, the oiler had worked a double watch in the engine-room of the ship. 50

"Take her easy now, boys," said the captain. "Don't spend yourselves. If we have to run a surf you'll need all your strength, because we'll sure have to swim for it. Take your time."

Slowly the land arose from the sea. From a black line it became a line of black and a line of white—trees and sand. Finally the captain said that he could make out a house on the shore. "That's the house of refuge, sure," said the cook. "They'll see us before long, and come out after us."

The distant lighthouse reared high. "The keeper ought to be able to make us out now, if he's looking through a glass," said the captain. "He'll notify the life-saving people."

"None of those other boats could have got ashore to give word of this wreck," said the oiler, in a low voice, "else the life-boat would be out hunting us."

Slowly and beautifully the land loomed out of the sea. The wind came again. It had veered from the north-east to the south-east. Finally a new sound struck the ears of the men in the boat. It was the low thunder of the surf on the shore. "We'll never be able to make the lighthouse now," said the captain. "Swing her head a little more north, Billie." 55

"A little more north, sir," said the oiler.

Whereupon the little boat turned her nose once more down the wind, and all but the oarsman watched the shore grow. Under the influence of this expansion doubt and direful apprehension were leaving the minds of the men. The management of the boat was still most absorbing, but it could not prevent a quiet cheerfulness. In an hour, perhaps, they would be ashore.

Their backbones had become thoroughly used to balancing in the boat, and they now rode this wild colt of a dinghy like circus men. The correspondent thought that he had been drenched to the skin, but happening to feel in the top pocket of his coat, he found therein eight cigars. Four of them were soaked with sea-water; four were perfectly scatheless. After a search, somebody produced three dry matches; and thereupon the four waifs rode impudently in their little boat and, with an assurance of an impending rescue shining in their eyes, puffed at the big cigars, and judged well and ill of all men. Everybody took a drink of water.

IV

"Cook," remarked the captain, "there don't seem to be any signs of life about your house of refuge."

"No," replied the cook. "Funny they don't see us!" 60

A broad stretch of lowly coast lay before the eyes of the men. It was of low dunes topped with dark vegetation. The roar of the surf was plain, and sometimes they could see the white lip of a wave as it spun up the beach. A tiny house was blocked out black upon the sky. Southward, the slim lighthouse lifted its little grey length.

Tide, wind, and waves were swinging the dinghy northward. "Funny they don't see us," said the men.

The surf's roar was here dulled, but its tone was nevertheless thunderous and mighty. As the boat swam over the great rollers the men sat listening to this roar. "We'll swamp sure," said everybody.

It is fair to say here that there was not a life-saving station within twenty miles in either direction; but the men did not know this fact, and in consequence they made dark and opprobrious remarks concerning the eyesight of the nation's life-savers. Four scowling men sat in the dinghy and surpassed records in the invention of epithets.

"Funny they don't see us." 65

The light-heartedness of a former time had completely faded. To their sharpened minds it was easy to conjure pictures of all kinds of incompetency and blindness and, indeed, cowardice. There was the shore of the populous land, and it was bitter and bitter to them that from it came no sign.

"Well," said the captain, ultimately, "I suppose we'll have to make a try for ourselves. If we stay out here too long, we'll none of us have strength left to swim after the boat swamps."

And so the oiler, who was at the oars, turned the boat straight for the shore. There was a sudden tightening of muscles. There was some thinking.

"If we don't all get ashore," said the captain—"if we don't all get ashore, I suppose you fellows know where to send news of my finish?"

They then briefly exchanged some addresses and admonitions. As for the reflec- 70
tions of the men, there was a great deal of rage in them. Perchance they might be formulated thus: "If I am going to be drowned—if I am going to be drowned—if I am going to be drowned, why, in the name of the seven mad gods who rule the sea, was I allowed to come thus far and contemplate sand and trees? Was I brought here merely to have my nose dragged away as I was about to nibble the sacred cheese of life? It is preposterous. If this old ninny-woman, Fate, cannot do better than this, she should be deprived of the management of men's fortunes. She is an old hen who knows not her intention. If she has decided to drown me, why did she not do it in the beginning and save me all this trouble? The whole affair is absurd.—But no; she cannot mean to drown me. She dare not drown me. She cannot drown me. Not after all this work." Afterward the man might have had an impulse to shake his fist at the clouds. "Just you drown me, now, and then hear what I call you!"

The billows that came at this time were more formidable. They seemed always just about to break and roll over the little boat in a turmoil of foam. There was a preparatory and long growl in the speech of them. No mind unused to the sea would have concluded that the dinghy could ascend these sheer heights in time. The shore was still afar. The oiler was a wily surfman. "Boys," he said swiftly, "she won't live three minutes more, and we're too far out to swim. Shall I take her to sea again, Captain?"

"Yes; go ahead!" said the captain.

This oiler, by a series of quick miracles and fast and steady oarsmanship, turned the boat in the middle of the surf and took her safely to sea again.

There was a considerable silence as the boat bumped over the furrowed sea to deeper water. Then somebody in gloom spoke: "Well, anyhow, they must have seen us from the shore by now."

The gulls went in slanting flight up the wind toward the grey, desolate east. A squall, marked by dingy clouds and clouds brick-red like smoke from a burning building, appeared from the southeast. 75

"What do you think of those life-saving people? Ain't they peaches?"

"Funny they haven't seen us."

"Maybe they think we're out here for sport! Maybe they think we're fishin'. Maybe they think we're damned fools."

It was a long afternoon. A changed tide tried to force them southward, but wind and wave said northward. Far ahead, where coast-line, sea, and sky formed their mighty angle, there were little dots which seemed to indicate a city on the shore.

"St. Augustine?" 80

The captain shook his head. "Too near Mosquito Inlet."

And the oiler rowed, and then the correspondent rowed; then the oiler rowed. It was a weary business. The human back can become the seat of more aches and pains than are registered in books for the composite anatomy of a regiment. It is a limited area, but it can become the theatre of innumerable muscular conflicts, tangles, wrenches, knots, and other comforts.

"Did you ever like to row, Billie?" asked the correspondent.

"No," said the oiler; "hang it!"

When one exchanged the rowing-seat for a place in the bottom of the boat, he suffered a bodily depression that caused him to be careless of everything save an obligation to wiggle one finger. There was cold sea-water swashing to and fro in the boat, and he lay in it. His head, pillowed on a thwart, was within an inch of the swirl of a wave-crest, and sometimes a particularly obstreperous sea came inboard and drenched him once more. But these matters did not annoy him. It is almost certain that if the boat had capsized he would have tumbled comfortably out upon the ocean as if he felt sure that it was a great soft mattress. 85

"Look! There's a man on the shore!"

"Where?"

"There! See 'im? See 'im?"

"Yes, sure! He's walking along."

"Now he's stopped. Look! He's facing us!" 90

"He's waving at us!"

"So he is! By thunder!"

"Ah, now we're all right! Now we're all right! There'll be a boat out here for us in half an hour."

"He's going on. He's running. He's going up to that house there."

The remote beach seemed lower than the sea, and it required a searching glance to discern the little black figure. The captain saw a floating stick, and they rowed to it. A bath towel was by some weird chance in the boat, and, tying this on the stick, the captain waved it. The oarsman did not dare turn his head, so he was obliged to ask questions. 95

"What's he doing now?"

"He's standing still again. He's looking, I think.—There he goes again—toward the house.—Now he's stopped again."

"Is he waving at us?"

"No, not now; he was, though."

"Look! There comes another man!" 100

"He's running."

"Look at him go, would you!"

"Why, he's on a bicycle. Now he's met the other man. They're both waving at us. Look!"

"There comes something up the beach."

"What the devil is that thing?" 105

"Why, it looks like a boat."

"Why, certainly, it's a boat."

"No; it's on wheels."

"Yes, so it is. Well, that must be the life-boat. They drag them along shore on a wagon."

"That's the life-boat, sure." 110

"No, by God, it's—it's an omnibus."

"I tell you it's a life-boat."

"It is not! It's an omnibus. I can see it plain. See? One of these big hotel omnibuses."

"By thunder, you're right. It's an omnibus, sure as fate. What do you suppose they are doing with an omnibus? Maybe they are going around collecting the life-crew, hey?"

"That's it, likely. Look! There's a fellow waving a little black flag. He's standing on 115 the steps of the omnibus. There come those other two fellows. Now they're all talking together. Look at the fellow with the flag. Maybe he ain't waving it!"

"That ain't a flag, is it? That's his coat. Why, certainly, that's his coat."

"So it is; it's his coat. He's taken it off and is waving it around his head. But would you look at him swing it!"

"Oh, say, there isn't any life-saving station there. That's just a winter-resort hotel omnibus that has brought over some of the boarders to see us drown."

"What's that idiot with the coat mean? What's he signalling, anyhow?"

"It looks as if he were trying to tell us to go north. There must be a life-saving sta- 120 tion up there."

"No; he thinks we're fishing. Just giving us a merry hand. See? Ah, there, Willie!"

"Well, I wish I could make something out of those signals. What do you suppose he means?"

"He don't mean anything; he's just playing."

"Well, if he'd just signal us to try the surf again, or to go to sea and wait, or go north, or go south, or go to hell, there would be some reason in it. But look at him! He just stands there and keeps his coat revolving like a wheel. The ass!"

"There come more people." 125

"Now there's quite a mob. Look! Isn't that a boat?"

"Where? Oh, I see where you mean. No, that's no boat."

"That fellow is still waving his coat."

"He must think we like to see him do that. Why don't he quit it? It don't mean anything."

"I don't know. I think he is trying to make us go north. It must be that there's a 130 life-saving station there somewhere."

"Say, he ain't tired yet. Look at 'im wave!"

"Wonder how long he can keep that up. He's been revolving his coat ever since he caught sight of us. He's an idiot. Why aren't they getting men to bring a boat out? A fishing-boat—one of those big yawls—could come out here all right. Why don't he do something?"

"Oh, it's all right now."

"They'll have a boat out here for us in less than no time, now that they've seen us."

A faint yellow tone came into the sky over the low land. The shadows on the sea slowly deepened. The wind bore coldness with it, and the men began to shiver. 135

"Holy smoke!" said one, allowing his voice to express his impious mood, "if we keep on monkeying out here! If we've got to flounder out here all night!"

"Oh, we'll never have to stay here all night! Don't you worry. They've seen us now, and it won't be long before they'll come chasing out after us."

The shore grew dusky. The man waving a coat blended gradually into this gloom, and it swallowed in the same manner the omnibus and the group of people. The spray, when it dashed uproariously over the side, made the voyagers shrink and swear like men who were being branded.

"I'd like to catch the chump who waved the coat. I feel like socking him one, just for luck."

"Why? What did he do?" 140

"Oh, nothing, but then he seemed so damned cheerful."

In the meantime the oiler rowed, and then the correspondent rowed, and then the oiler rowed. Grey-faced and bowed forward, they mechanically, turn by turn, plied the leaden oars. The form of the lighthouse had vanished from the southern horizon, but finally a pale star appeared, just lifting from the sea. The streaked saffron in the west passed before the all-merging darkness, and the sea to the east was black. The land had vanished, and was expressed only by the low and drear thunder of the surf.

"If I am going to be drowned—if I am going to be drowned—if I am going to be drowned, why, in the name of the seven mad gods who rule the sea, was I allowed to come thus far and contemplate sand and trees? Was I brought here merely to have my nose dragged away as I was about to nibble the sacred cheese of life?"

The patient captain, drooped over the water-jar, was sometimes obliged to speak to the oarsman.

"Keep her head up! Keep her head up!" 145

"Keep her head up, sir." The voices were weary and low.

This was surely a quiet evening. All save the oarsman lay heavily and listlessly in the boat's bottom. As for him, his eyes were just capable of noting the tall black waves that swept forward in a most sinister silence, save for an occasional subdued growl of a crest.

The cook's head was on a thwart, and he looked without interest at the water under his nose. He was deep in other scenes. Finally he spoke. "Billie," he murmured, dreamfully, "what kind of pie do you like best?"

V

"Pie!" said the oiler and the correspondent, agitatedly. "Don't talk about those things, blast you!"

"Well," said the cook, "I was just thinking about ham sandwiches and—" 150

A night on the sea in an open boat is a long night. As darkness settled finally, the shine of the light, lifting from the sea in the south, changed to full gold. On the northern horizon a new light appeared, a small bluish gleam on the edge of the waters. These two lights were the furniture of the world. Otherwise there was nothing but waves.

Two men huddled in the stern, and distances were so magnificent in the dinghy that the rower was enabled to keep his feet partly warm by thrusting them under his companions. Their legs indeed extended far under the rowing-seat until they touched the feet of the captain forward. Sometimes, despite the efforts of the tired oarsman, a wave came piling into the boat, an icy wave of the night, and the chilling water soaked them anew. They would twist their bodies for a moment and groan, and sleep the dead sleep once more, while the water in the boat gurgled about them as the craft rocked.

The plan of the oiler and the correspondent was for one to row until he lost the ability, and then arouse the other from his sea-water couch in the bottom of the boat.

The oiler plied the oars until his head drooped forward and the overpowering sleep blinded him; and he rowed yet afterward. Then he touched a man in the bottom of the boat, and called his name. "Will you spell me for a little while?" he said, meekly.

"Sure, Billie," said the correspondent, awaking and dragging himself to a sitting position. They exchanged places carefully, and the oiler, cuddling down in the sea-water at the cook's side, seemed to go to sleep instantly. 155

The particular violence of the sea had ceased. The waves came without snarling. The obligation of the man at the oars was to keep the boat headed so that the tilt of the rollers would not capsize her, and to preserve her from filling when the crests rushed past. The black waves were silent and hard to be seen in the darkness. Often one was almost upon the boat before the oarsman was aware.

In a low voice the correspondent addressed the captain. He was not sure that the captain was awake, although this iron man seemed to be always awake. "Captain, shall I keep her making for that light north, sir?"

The same steady voice answered him. "Yes. Keep it about two points off the port bow."

The cook had tied a life-belt around himself in order to get even the warmth which this clumsy cork contrivance could donate, and he seemed almost stove-like when a rower, whose teeth invariably chattered wildly as soon as he ceased his labor, dropped down to sleep.

The correspondent, as he rowed, looked down at the two men sleeping underfoot. The cook's arm was around the oiler's shoulders, and, with their fragmentary clothing and haggard faces, they were the babes of the sea—a grotesque rendering of the old babes in the wood. 160

Later he must have grown stupid at his work, for suddenly there was a growling of water, and a crest came with a roar and a swash into the boat, and it was a wonder that it did not set the cook afloat in his life-belt. The cook continued to sleep, but the oiler sat up, blinking his eyes and shaking with the new cold.

"Oh, I'm awful sorry, Billie," said the correspondent, contritely.

"That's all right, old boy," said the oiler, and lay down again and was asleep.

Presently it seemed that even the captain dozed, and the correspondent thought that he was the one man afloat on all the oceans. The wind had a voice as it came over the waves, and it was sadder than the end.

There was a long, loud swishing astern of the boat, and a gleaming trail of phosphorescence, like blue flame, was furrowed on the black waters. It might have been made by a monstrous knife. 165

Then there came a stillness, while the correspondent breathed with open mouth and looked at the sea.

Suddenly there was another swish and another long flash of bluish light, and this time it was alongside the boat, and might almost been reached with an oar. The correspondent saw an enormous fin speed like a shadow through the water, hurling the crystalline spray and leaving the long glowing trail.

The correspondent looked over his shoulder at the captain. His face was hidden, and he seemed to be asleep. He looked at the babes of the sea. They certainly were asleep. So, being bereft of sympathy, he leaned a little way to one side and swore softly into the sea.

But the thing did not then leave the vicinity of the boat. Ahead or astern, on one side or the other, at intervals long or short, fled the long sparkling streak, and there was to be heard the *whirroo* of the dark fin. The speed and power of the thing was greatly to be admired. It cut the water like a gigantic and keen projectile.

The presence of this biding thing did not affect the man with the same horror that it would if he had been a picnicker. He simply looked at the sea dully and swore in an undertone. 170

Nevertheless, it is true that he did not wish to be alone with the thing. He wished one of his companions to awake by chance and keep him company with it. But the captain hung motionless over the water-jar, and the oiler and the cook in the bottom of the boat were plunged in slumber.

VI

"If I am going to be drowned—if I am going to be drowned—if I am going to be drowned, why, in the name of the seven mad gods who rule the sea, was I allowed to come thus far and contemplate sand and trees?"

During this dismal night, it may be remarked that a man would conclude that it was really the intention of the seven mad gods to drown him, despite the abominable injustice of it. For it was certainly an abominable injustice to drown a man who had worked so hard, so hard. The man felt it would be a crime most unnatural. Other people had drowned at sea since galleys swarmed with painted sails, but still—

When it occurs to a man that nature does not regard him as important, and that she feels she would not maim the universe by disposing of him, he at first wishes to throw bricks at the temple, and he hates deeply the fact that there are no bricks and no temples. Any visible expression of nature would surely be pelleted with his jeers.

Then, if there be no tangible thing to hoot, he feels, perhaps, the desire to confront a personification and indulge in pleas, bowed to one knee, and with hands supplicant, saying, "Yes, but I love myself." 175

A high cold star on a winter's night is the word he feels that she says to him. Thereafter he knows the pathos of his situation.

The men in the dinghy had not discussed these matters, but each had, no doubt, reflected upon them in silence and according to his mind. There was seldom any expression upon their faces save the general one of complete weariness. Speech was devoted to the business of the boat.

To chime the notes of his emotion, a verse mysteriously entered the correspondent's head. He had even forgotten that he had forgotten this verse, but it suddenly was in his mind.

> *A soldier of the Legion lay dying in Algiers;*
> *There was lack of woman's nursing, there was dearth of woman's tears;*
> *But a comrade stood beside him, and he took that comrade's hand,*
> *And he said, "I never more shall see my own, my native land."*

In his childhood the correspondent had been made acquainted with the fact that a soldier of the Legion lay dying in Algiers, but he had never regarded the fact as important. Myriads of his schoolfellows had informed him of the soldier's plight, but the dinning had naturally ended by making him perfectly indifferent. He had never considered it his affair that a soldier of the Legion lay dying in Algiers, nor had it appeared to him as a matter for sorrow. It was less to him than the breaking of a pencil's point.

Now, however, it quaintly came to him as a human, living thing. It was no longer 180
merely a picture of a few throes in the breast of a poet, meanwhile drinking tea and
warming his feet at the grate; it was an actuality—stern, mournful, and fine.

The correspondent plainly saw the soldier. He lay on the sand with his feet out
straight and still. While his pale left hand was upon his chest in an attempt to thwart the
going of his life, the blood came between his fingers. In the far Algerian distance, a city
of low square forms was set against a sky that was faint with the last sunset hues. The
correspondent, plying the oars and dreaming of the slow and slower movements of the
lips of the soldier, was moved by a profound and perfectly impersonal comprehension.
He was sorry for the soldier of the Legion who lay dying in Algiers.

The thing which had followed the boat and waited had evidently grown bored at
the delay. There was no longer to be heard the slash of the cutwater, and there was no
longer the flame of the long trail. The light in the north still glimmered, but it was apparently no nearer to the boat. Sometimes the boom of the surf rang in the correspondent's ears, and he turned the craft seaward then and rowed harder. Southward, some
one had evidently built a watch-fire on the beach. It was too low and too far to be seen,
but it made a shimmering, roseate reflection upon the bluff in back of it, and this could
be discerned from the boat. The wind came stronger, and sometimes a wave suddenly
raged out like a mountain cat, and there was to be seen the sheen and sparkle of a broken crest.

The captain, in the bow, moved on his water-jar and sat erect. "Pretty long night,"
he observed to the correspondent. He looked at the shore. "Those life-saving people
take their time."

"Did you see that shark playing around?"

"Yes, I saw him. He was a big fellow, all right." 185

"Wish I had known you were awake."

Later the correspondent spoke into the bottom of the boat. "Billie!" There was a
slow and gradual disentanglement. "Billie, will you spell me?"

"Sure," said the oiler.

As soon as the correspondent touched the cold, comfortable sea-water in the bottom of the boat and had huddled close to the cook's life-belt he was deep in sleep, despite the fact that his teeth played all the popular airs. This sleep was so good to him
that it was but a moment before he heard a voice call his name in a tone that demonstrated the last stages of exhaustion. "Will you spell me?"

"Sure, Billie." 190

The light in the north had mysteriously vanished, but the correspondent took his
course from the wide-awake captain.

Later in the night they took the boat farther out to sea, and the captain directed
the cook to take one oar at the stern and keep the boat facing the seas. He was to call
out if he should hear the thunder of the surf. This plan enabled the oiler and the correspondent to get respite together. "We'll give those boys a chance to get into shape
again," said the captain. They curled down and, after a few preliminary chatterings and
trembles, slept once more the dead sleep. Neither knew they had bequeathed to the
cook the company of another shark, or perhaps the same shark.

As the boat caroused on the waves, spray occasionally bumped over the side and
gave them a fresh soaking, but this had no power to break their repose. The ominous
slash of the wind and the water affected them as it would have affected mummies.

"Boys," said the cook, with the notes of every reluctance in his voice, "she's drifted in pretty close. I guess one of you had better take her to sea again." The correspondent, aroused, heard the crash of the toppled crests.

As he was rowing, the captain gave him some whisky-and-water, and this steadied 195
the chills out of him. "If I ever get ashore and anybody shows me even a photograph of
an oar—"

At last there was a short conversation.

"Billie!—Billie, will you spell me?"

"Sure," said the oiler.

VII

When the correspondent again opened his eyes, the sea and the sky were each of
the grey hue of the dawning. Later, carmine and gold was painted upon the waters.
The morning appeared finally, in its splendor, with a sky of pure blue, and the sunlight
flamed on the tips of the waves.

On the distant dunes were set many little black cottages, and a tall white windmill 200
reared above them. No man, nor dog, nor bicycle appeared on the beach. The cottages
might have formed a deserted village.

The voyagers scanned the shore. A conference was held in the boat. "Well," said
the captain, "if no help is coming, we might better try a run through the surf right
away. If we stay out here much longer we will be too weak to do anything for ourselves
at all." The others silently acquiesced in this reasoning. The boat was headed for the
beach. The correspondent wondered if none ever ascended the tall wind-tower, and if
then they never looked seaward. This tower was a giant, standing with its back to the
plight of the ants. It represented in a degree, to the correspondent, the serenity of nature amid the struggles of the individual—nature in the wind, and nature in the vision
of men. She did not seem cruel to him then, nor beneficent, nor treacherous, nor wise.
But she was indifferent, flatly indifferent. It is, perhaps, plausible that a man in this situation, impressed with the unconcern of the universe, should see the innumerable flaws
of his life, and have them taste wickedly in his mind, and wish for another chance. A
distinction between right and wrong seems absurdly clear to him, then, in this new ignorance of the grave-edge, and he understands that if he were given another opportunity he would mend his conduct and his words, and be better and brighter during an
introduction or at a tea.

"Now, boys," said the captain, "she is going to swamp sure. All we can do is to
work her in as far as possible, and then when she swamps, pile out and scramble for the
beach. Keep cool now, and don't jump until she swamps sure."

The oiler took the oars. Over his shoulders he scanned the surf. "Captain," he said,
"I think I'd better bring her about and keep her head-on to the seas and back her in."

"All right, Billie," said the captain. "Back her in." The oiler swung the boat then,
and, seated in the stern, the cook and the correspondent were obliged to look over
their shoulders to contemplate the lonely and indifferent shore.

The monstrous inshore rollers heaved the boat high until the men were again en- 205
abled to see the white sheets of water scudding up the slanted beach. "We won't get in
very close," said the captain. Each time a man could wrest his attention from the
rollers, he turned his glance toward the shore, and in the expression of the eyes during
this contemplation there was a singular quality. The correspondent, observing the
others, knew that they were not afraid, but the full meaning of their glances were
shrouded.

As for himself, he was too tired to grapple fundamentally with the fact. He tried to
coerce his mind into thinking of it, but the mind was dominated at this time by the
muscles, and the muscles said they did not care. It merely occurred to him that if he
should drown it would be a shame.

There were no hurried words, no pallor, no plain agitation. The men simply looked at the shore. "Now, remember to get well clear of the boat when you jump," said the captain.

Seaward the crest of a roller suddenly fell with a thunderous crash, and the long white comber came roaring down upon the boat.

"Steady now," said the captain. The men were silent. They turned their eyes from the shore to the comber and waited. The boat slid up the incline, leaped at the furious top, bounced over it, and swung down the long back of the wave. Some water had been shipped, and the cook bailed it out.

But the next crest crashed also. The tumbling, boiling flood of white water caught   210
the boat and whirled it almost perpendicular. Water swarmed in from all sides. The correspondent had his hands on the gunwale at this time, and when the water entered at that place he swiftly withdrew his fingers, as if he objected to wetting them.

The little boat, drunken with this weight of water, reeled and snuggled deeper into the sea.

"Bail her out, cook! Bail her out!" said the captain.

"All right, Captain," said the cook.

"Now, boys, the next one will do for us sure," said the oiler. "Mind to jump clear of the boat."

The third wave moved forward, huge, furious, implacable. It fairly swallowed the   215
dinghy, and almost simultaneously the men tumbled into the sea. A piece of life-belt had lain in the bottom of the boat, and as the correspondent went overboard he held this to his chest with his left hand.

The January water was icy, and he reflected immediately that it was colder than he had expected to find it off the coast of Florida. This appeared to his dazed mind as a fact important enough to be noted at the time. The coldness of the water was sad; it was tragic. This fact was somehow mixed and confused with his opinion of his own situation, so that it seemed almost a proper reason for tears. The water was cold.

When he came to the surface he was conscious of little but the noisy water. Afterward he saw his companions in the sea. The oiler was ahead in the race. He was swimming strongly and rapidly. Off to the correspondent's left, the cook's great white and corked back bulged out of the water; and in the rear the captain was hanging with his one good hand to the keel of the overturned dinghy.

There is a certain immovable quality to a shore, and the correspondent wondered at it amid the confusion of the sea.

It seemed also very attractive; but the correspondent knew that it was a long journey, and he paddled leisurely. The piece of life-preserver lay under him, and sometimes he whirled down the incline of a wave as if he were on a hand-sled.

But finally he arrived at a place in the sea where travel was beset with difficulty. He   220
did not pause swimming to inquire what manner of current had caught him, but there his progress ceased. The shore was set before him like a bit of scenery on a stage, and he looked at it and understood with his eyes each detail of it.

As the cook passed, much farther to the left, the captain was calling to him, "Turn over on your back, cook! Turn over on your back and use the oar."

"All right, sir." The cook turned on his back, and, paddling with an oar, went ahead as if he were a canoe.

Presently the boat also passed to the left of the correspondent, with the captain clinging with one hand to the keel. He would have appeared like a man raising himself to look over a board fence if it were not for the extraordinary gymnastics of the boat. The correspondent marvelled that the captain could still hold to it.

They passed on nearer to shore—the oiler, the cook, the captain—and following them went the water-jar, bouncing gaily over the seas.

The correspondent remained in the grip of this strange new enemy—a current. The shore, with its white slope of sand and its green bluff topped with little silent cottages, was spread like a picture before him. It was very near to him then, but he was impressed as one who, in a gallery, looks at a scene from Brittany or Algiers.

He thought: "I am going to drown? Can it be possible? Can it be possible? Can it be possible?" Perhaps an individual must consider his own death to be the final phenomenon of nature.

But later a wave perhaps whirled him out of this small deadly current, for he found suddenly that he could again make progress toward the shore. Later still he was aware that the captain, clinging with one hand to the keel of the dinghy, had his face turned away from the shore and toward him, and was calling his name. "Come to the boat! Come to the boat!"

In his struggle to reach the captain and the boat, he reflected that when one gets properly wearied drowning must really be a comfortable arrangement—a cessation of hostilities accompanied by a large degree of relief; and he was glad of it, for the main thing in his mind for some moments had been horror of the temporary agony. He did not wish to be hurt.

Presently he saw a man running along the shore. He was undressing with most remarkable speed. Coat, trousers, shirt, everything flew magically off him.

"Come to the boat!" called the captain.

"All right, Captain." As the correspondent paddled, he saw the captain let himself down to bottom and leave the boat. Then the correspondent performed his one little marvel of the voyage. A large wave caught him and flung him with ease and supreme speed completely over the boat and far beyond it. It struck him even then as an event in gymnastics and a true miracle of the sea. An overturned boat in the surf is not a plaything to a swimming man.

The correspondent arrived in water that reached only to his waist, but his condition did not enable him to stand for more than a moment. Each wave knocked him into a heap, and the undertow pulled at him.

Then he saw the man who had been running and undressing, and undressing and running, come bounding into the water. He dragged ashore the cook, and then waded toward the captain; but the captain waved him away and sent him to the correspondent. He was naked—naked as a tree in winter; but a halo was about his head, and he shone like a saint. He gave a strong pull, and a long drag, and a bully heave at the correspondent's hand. The correspondent, schooled in the minor formulae, said "Thanks, old man." But suddenly the man cried, "What's that?" He pointed a swift finger. The correspondent said, "Go."

In the shallows, face downward, lay the oiler. His forehead touched sand that was periodically, between each wave, clear of the sea.

The correspondent did not know all that transpired afterward. When he achieved safe ground he fell, striking the sand with each particular part of his body. It was as if he had dropped from a roof, but the thud was grateful to him.

It seemed that instantly the beach was populated with men with blankets, clothes, and flasks, and women with coffee-pots and all the remedies sacred to their minds. The welcome of the land to the men from the sea was warm and generous; but a still and dripping shape was carried slowly up the beach; and the land's welcome for it could only be the different and sinister hospitality of the grave.

When it came night, the white waves paced to and fro in the moonlight, and the wind brought the sound of the great sea's voice to the men on the shore, and they felt that they could then be interpreters.

THE RECEPTIVE READER

1. In the naturalistic manner, Crane traces in patient *detail* the physical dimension of the men's ordeal. How does he make the grueling experience real for the reader? What are striking details? What are recurrent notes, struck again and again?

2. The *dialogue* of the men in the boat may at first seem trivial or inane (like many other conversations). Does it nevertheless circle back to major issues or concerns? What is the subject matter of these conversations? What is their tone?

3. When do you first conclude that there is something representative and symbolic about the men's experience? What *symbols* do you recognize? What do you think might be the symbolic meaning of the sea? of the boat? of the seabirds? of the shark? of the unmanned life-saving station? of the lighthouse? of the tourists on the beach?

4. How much commentary is there by the *intruding author*? What does Crane have to say about the captain of the ship? about the relationship developing among the men in the boat?

5. Much of the story centers on the men's reactions to their fate. Are there different *stages*? Do individuals react differently?

6. How did you expect the story to *end*? Does the ending seem unexpected? Does it make you think?

7. What is the *theme* of the story? What does the story as a whole say about human beings and nature? about male bonding? about survival? How are these three topics related in the story as a whole?

8. What are striking examples of *irony* in the story—of the sad and comical discrepancy between what should be and what is? What are some striking examples of the author's ironic tone?

THE PERSONAL RESPONSE

Much literature through the centuries has celebrated the beauty of nature. What role does the beauty of nature play in this story? What is your own personal view of the relationship between nature and humankind? How is it different from the view that seems to be dominant in this story?

NATHANIEL HAWTHORNE (1804–1864)

A dreamer may dwell so long among fantasies that the things without him will seem as real as those within.
                                              NATHANIEL HAWTHORNE

The mere doubt of the existence of good and the thought that other human beings are evil can become such a corrosive force that it can eat out the life of the heart.
                                              STUDENT PAPER

Nathaniel Hawthorne was born in Salem in Massachusetts and lived there for many years at his mother's house after finishing college. One of his ancestors had been a member of the court that sentenced the witches at the Salem witch trials in 1692. As a student and at first little-read writer, Hawthorne immersed himself in the history of colonial New England. When he married after a brief stint at a socialistic commune (Brook Farm), he settled at Concord, in the heart of historical New England.

Until Hawthorne went abroad to serve as an American consul in Liverpool in England, he spent most of his life in a setting where Puritan ministers like Cotton Mather and Jonathan Edwards had preached the depravity of mankind, the ever-powerful temptation of sin, the fear and trembling of sinners in the hands of an angry God, and the ever-lurking presence of the devil. Having left England to escape persecution as dissenters from the established Anglican church, Hawthorne's Puritanical ancestors set up a religious commonwealth where prayer and attendance at church services were rigidly enforced and where Quakers and other independent spirits were persecuted in turn.

Much of Hawthorne's fiction made his readers rethink and reexamine their assumptions about the Puritan past. His novel *The Scarlet Letter* (1850) has left readers around the world with unforgettable images of Hester Prynne, wearing the scarlet A branding her as an adulteress; her child Pearl at play in the forest; and the Puritan minister Dimmesdale, who had fathered the child, in the spiritual agonies of guilt. (As feminist critics have pointed out, Hester Prynne was for a long time the only central female character in a tradition of American fiction whose protagonists were more likely to be scouts, whaling captains, or runaway boys.)

The following much-discussed story is set in Puritan New England at the time of King William III, who ruled in England from 1689 to 1702. Salem Village, established only forty years before, was on the edge of the wilderness, with heathen natives in the forests. (The King Philip mentioned in the story was Metacomet, leader of the last organized Indian resistance in southern New England.) The people in the story, too humble to be called gentlemen and ladies, are called Goodman Brown and Goody (short for Goodwife) Cloyse or Goody Cory. (These women were among the victims of the Salem witchhunt that took the lives of twenty men and women.) Much of the learning of the Puritan divines had been concerned with witchcraft, and especially with the devil's power to create delusions and apparitions. At a Witches' Sabbath, according to the lore of the times, the devil himself would often preside at rituals that were a blasphemous perversion of the rites of the church.

Young Goodman Brown   1835

Young Goodman Brown came forth at sunset into the street at Salem village; but put his head back, after crossing the threshold, to exchange a parting kiss with his young wife. And Faith, as the wife was aptly named, thrust her own pretty head into the street, letting the wind play with the pink ribbons of her cap while she called to Goodman Brown.

"Dearest heart," whispered she, softly and rather sadly, when her lips were close to his ear, "prithee put off your journey until sunrise and sleep in your own bed tonight. A lone woman is troubled with such dreams and such thoughts that she's afeard of herself sometimes. Pray tarry with me this night, dear husband, of all nights in the year."

"My love and my Faith," replied Goodman Brown, "of all nights in the year, this one night must I tarry away from thee. My journey, as thou callest it, forth and back again, must needs be done 'twixt now and sunrise. What, my sweet, pretty wife, dost thou doubt me already, and we but three months married?"

"Then God bless you!" said Faith, with the pink ribbons; "and may you find all well when you come back."

"Amen!" cried Goodman Brown. "Say thy prayers, dear Faith, and go to bed at dusk, and no harm will come to thee." 5

So they parted; and the young man pursued his way until, being about to turn the corner by the meeting-house, he looked back and saw the head of Faith still peeping after him with a melancholy air, in spite of her pink ribbons.

"Poor little Faith!" thought he, for his heart smote him. "What a wretch am I to leave her on such an errand! She talks of dreams, too. Methought as she spoke there was trouble in her face, as if a dream had warned her what work is to be done tonight. But no, no; 'twould kill her to think it. Well, she's a blessed angel on earth; and after this one night I'll cling to her skirts and follow her to heaven."

With this excellent resolve for the future, Goodman Brown felt himself justified in making more haste on his present evil purpose. He had taken a dreary road, darkened by all the gloomiest trees of the forest, which barely stood aside to let the narrow path creep through, and closed immediately behind. It was all as lonely as could be; and there is this peculiarity in such a solitude, that the traveller knows not who may be concealed by the innumerable trunks and the thick boughs overhead; so that with lonely footsteps he may yet be passing through an unseen multitude.

"There may be a devilish Indian behind every tree," said Goodman Brown to himself; and he glanced fearfully behind him as he added, "What if the devil himself should be at my very elbow!"

His head being turned back, he passed a crook of the road, and, looking forward again, beheld the figure of a man, in grave and decent attire, seated at the foot of an old tree. He arose at Goodman Brown's approach and walked onward side by side with him. 10

"You are late, Goodman Brown," said he. "The clock of the Old South was striking as I came through Boston, and that is full fifteen minutes agone."

"Faith kept me back a while," replied the young man, with a tremor in his voice, caused by the sudden appearance of his companion, though not wholly unexpected.

It was now deep dusk in the forest, and deepest in that part of it where these two were journeying. As nearly as could be discerned, the second traveller was about fifty years old, apparently in the same rank of life as Goodman Brown, and bearing a considerable resemblance to him, though perhaps more in expression than features. Still they might have been taken for father and son. And yet, though the elder person was as simply clad as the younger, and as simple in manner too, he had an indescribable air of one who knew the world, and who would not have felt abashed at the governor's dinner table or in King William's court, were it possible that his affairs should call him thither. But the only thing about him that could be fixed upon as remarkable was his staff, which bore the likeness of a great black snake, so curiously wrought that it might almost be seen to twist and wriggle itself like a living serpent. This, of course, must have been an ocular deception, assisted by the uncertain light.

"Come, Goodman Brown," cried his fellow-traveller, "this is a dull place for the beginning of a journey. Take my staff, if you are so soon weary."

"Friend," said the other, exchanging his slow pace for a full stop, "having kept covenant by meeting thee here, it is my purpose now to return whence I came. I have scruples touching the matter thou wot'st of." 15

"Sayest thou so?" replied he of the serpent, smiling apart. "Let us walk on, nevertheless, reasoning as we go; and if I convince thee not thou shalt turn back. We are but a little way in the forest yet."

"Too far! too far!" exclaimed the goodman, unconsciously resuming his walk. "My father never went into the woods on such an errand, nor his father before him. We have been a race of honest men and good Christians since the days of the martyrs; and shall I be the first of the name of Brown that ever took this path and kept—"

"Such company, thou wouldst say," observed the elder person, interpreting his pause. "Well said, Goodman Brown! I have been as well acquainted with your family as with ever a one among the Puritans; and that's no trifle to say. I helped your grandfather, the constable, when he lashed the Quaker woman so smartly through the streets of Salem; and it was I that brought your father a pitch-pine knot, kindled at my own hearth, to set fire to an Indian village, in King Philip's war. They were my good friends, both; and many a pleasant walk have we had along this path, and returned merrily after midnight. I would fain be friends with you for their sake."

"If it be as thou sayest," replied Goodman Brown, "I marvel they never spoke of these matters; or, verily, I marvel not, seeing that the least rumor of the sort would have driven them from New England. We are a people of prayer, and good works to boot, and abide no such wickedness."

"Wickedness or not," said the traveller with the twisted staff, "I have a very general acquaintance here in New England. The deacons of many a church have drunk the communion wine with me; the selectmen of divers towns make me their chairman; and a majority of the Great and General Court are firm supporters of my interest. The governor and I, too—But these are state secrets." 20

"Can this be so?" cried Goodman Brown, with a stare of amazement at his undisturbed companion. "Howbeit, I have nothing to do with the governor and council; they have their own ways, and are no rule for a simple husbandman like me. But, were I to go on with thee, how should I meet the eye of that good old man, our minister, at Salem village? Oh, his voice would make me tremble both Sabbath day and lecture day."

Thus far the elder traveller had listened with due gravity; but now burst into a fit of irrepressible mirth, shaking himself so violently that his snake-like staff actually seemed to wriggle in sympathy.

"Ha! ha! ha!" shouted he again and again; then composing himself, "Well, go on, Goodman Brown, go on; but, prithee, don't kill me with laughing."

"Well, then, to end the matter at once," said Goodman Brown, considerably nettled, "there is my wife, Faith. It would break her dear little heart; and I'd rather break my own."

"Nay, if that be the case," answered the other, "e'en go thy ways, Goodman Brown. I would not for twenty old women like the one hobbling before us that Faith should come to any harm." 25

As he spoke he pointed his staff at a female figure on the path, in whom Goodman Brown recognized a very pious and exemplary dame, who had taught him his catechism in youth, and was still his moral and spiritual adviser, jointly with the minister and Deacon Gookin.

"A marvel, truly, that Goody Cloyse should be so far in the wilderness at nightfall," said he. "But with your leave, friend, I shall take a cut through the woods until we have left this Christian woman behind. Being a stranger to you, she might ask whom I was consorting with and whither I was going."

"Be it so," said his fellow-traveller. "Betake you to the woods, and let me keep the path."

Accordingly the young man turned aside, but took care to watch his companion, who advanced softly along the road until he had come within a staff's length of the old dame. She, meanwhile, was making the best of her way, with singular speed for so aged a woman, and mumbling some indistinct words—a prayer, doubtless—as she went. The traveller put forth his staff and touched her withered neck with what seemed the serpent's tail.

"The devil!" screamed the pious old lady. 30

"Then Goody Cloyse knows her old friend?" observed the traveller, confronting her and leaning on his writhing stick.

"Ah, forsooth, and is it your worship indeed?" cried the good dame. "Yea, truly it is, and in the very image of my old gossip, Goodman Brown, the grandfather of the silly fellow that now is. But—would your worship believe it?—my broomstick hath strangely disappeared, stolen, as I suspect, by that unhanged witch, Goody Cory, and that, too, when I was all anointed with the juice of smallage, and cinquefoil, and wolf's bane—"

"Mingled with fine wheat and the fat of a new-born babe," said the shape of old Goodman Brown.

"Ah, your worship knows the recipe," cried the old lady, cackling aloud. "So, as I was saying, being all ready for the meeting, and no horse to ride on, I made up my mind to foot it; for they tell me there is a nice young man to be taken into communion tonight. But now your good worship will lend me your arm, and we shall be there in a twinkling."

"That can hardly be," answered her friend. "I may not spare you my arm, Goody Cloyse; but here is my staff, if you will." 35

So saying, he threw it down at her feet, where, perhaps, it assumed life, being one of the rods which its owner had formerly lent to the Egyptian magi. Of this fact, however, Goodman Brown could not take cognizance. He had cast up his eyes in astonishment, and, looking down again, beheld neither Goody Cloyse nor the serpentine staff, but his fellow-traveller alone, who waited for him as calmly as if nothing had happened.

"That old woman taught me my catechism," said the young man; and there was a world of meaning in this simple comment.

They continued to walk onward, while the elder traveller exhorted his companion to make good speed and persevere in the path, discoursing so aptly that his arguments seemed rather to spring up in the bosom of his auditor than to be suggested by himself. As they went, he plucked a branch of maple to serve for a walking stick, and began to strip it of the twigs and little boughs, which were wet with evening dew. The moment his fingers touched them they became strangely withered and dried up as with a week's sunshine. Thus the pair proceeded, at a good free pace, until suddenly, in a gloomy hollow of the road, Goodman Brown sat himself down on the stump of a tree and refused to go any farther.

"Friend," said he, stubbornly, "my mind is made up. Not another step will I budge on this errand. What if a wretched old woman do choose to go to the devil when I thought she was going to heaven: is that any reason why I should quit my dear Faith and go after her?"

"You will think better of this by and by," said his acquaintance, composedly. "Sit here and rest yourself a while; and when you feel like moving again, there is my staff to help you along." 40

Without more words, he threw his companion the maple stick, and was as speedily out of sight as if he had vanished into the deepening gloom. The young man sat a few moments by the roadside, applauding himself greatly, and thinking with how clear a conscience he should meet the minister in his morning walk, nor shrink from the eye of good old Deacon Gookin. And what calm sleep would be his that very night, which was to have been spent so wickedly, but so purely and sweetly now, in the arms of Faith! Amidst these pleasant and praiseworthy meditations, Goodman Brown heard the tramp of horses along the road, and deemed it advisable to conceal himself within the verge of the forest, conscious of the guilty purpose that had brought him thither, though now so happily turned from it.

On came the hoof tramps and the voices of the riders, two grave old voices, conversing soberly as they drew near. These mingled sounds appeared to pass along the road, within a few yards of the young man's hiding-place; but, owing doubtless to the depth of the gloom at that particular spot, neither the travellers nor their steeds were visible. Though their figures brushed the small boughs by the wayside, it could not be seen that they intercepted, even for a moment, the faint gleam from the strip of bright sky athwart which they must have passed. Goodman Brown alternately crouched and stood on tiptoe, pulling aside the branches and thrusting forth his head as far as he durst without discerning so much as a shadow. It vexed him the more, because he could have sworn, were such a thing possible, that he recognized the voices of the minister and Deacon Gookin, jogging along quietly, as they were wont to do, when bound to some ordination or ecclesiastical council. While yet within hearing, one of the riders stopped to pluck a switch.

"Of the two, reverend sir," said the voice like the deacon's, "I had rather miss an ordination dinner than tonight's meeting. They tell me that some of our community are to be here from Falmouth and beyond, and others from Connecticut and Rhode Island, besides several of the Indian powwows, who, after their fashion, know almost as much deviltry as the best of us. Moreover, there is a goodly young woman to be taken into communion."

"Mighty well, Deacon Gookin!" replied the solemn old tones of the minister. "Spur up, or we shall be late. Nothing can be done, you know, until I get on the ground."

The hoofs clattered again; and the voices, talking so strangely in the empty air, passed on through the forest, where no church had ever been gathered or solitary Christian prayed. Whither, then, could these holy men be journeying so deep into the heathen wilderness? Young Goodman Brown caught hold of a tree for support, being ready to sink down on the ground, faint and overburdened with the heavy sickness of his heart. He looked up to the sky, doubting whether there really was a heaven above him. Yet there was the blue arch, and the stars brightening in it. 45

"With heaven above and Faith below, I will yet stand firm against the devil!" cried Goodman Brown.

While he still gazed upward into the deep arch of the firmament and had lifted his hands to pray, a cloud, though no wind was stirring, hurried across the zenith and hid the brightening stars. The blue sky was still visible, except directly overhead, where this black mass of cloud was sweeping swiftly northward. Aloft in the air, as if from the depths of the cloud, came a confused and doubtful sound of voices. Once the listener fancied that he could distinguish the accents of townspeople of his own, men, and women, both pious and ungodly, many of whom he had met at the communion table, and had seen others rioting at the tavern. The next moment, so indistinct were the sounds, he doubted whether he had heard aught but the murmur of the old forest, whispering without a wind. Then came a stronger swell of those familiar tones, heard daily in the sunshine at Salem village, but never until now from a cloud of night. There was one voice, of a young woman, uttering lamentations, yet with an uncertain sorrow, and entreating for some favor, which, perhaps, it would grieve her to obtain; and all the unseen multitude, both saints and sinners, seemed to encourage her onward.

"Faith!" shouted Goodman Brown, in a voice of agony and desperation; and the echoes of the forest mocked him, crying, "Faith! Faith!" as if bewildered wretches were seeking her all through the wilderness.

The cry of grief, rage, and terror was yet piercing the night, when the unhappy husband held his breath for a response. There was a scream, drowned immediately in a louder murmur of voices, fading into far-off laughter, as the dark cloud swept away, leaving the clear and silent sky above Goodman Brown. But something fluttered lightly down through the air and caught on the branch of a tree. The young man seized it, and beheld a pink ribbon.

"My Faith is gone!" cried he, after one stupefied moment. "There is no good on earth; and sin is but a name. Come, devil; for to thee is this world given." 50

And, maddened with despair, so that he laughed loud and long, did Goodman Brown grasp his staff and set forth again, at such a rate that he seemed to fly along the forest path rather than to walk or run. The road grew wilder and drearier and more faintly traced, and vanished at length, leaving him in the heart of the dark wilderness, still rushing onward with the instinct that guides mortal man to evil. The whole forest was peopled with frightful sounds—the creaking of the trees, the howling of wild beasts, and the yell of Indians; while sometimes the wind tolled like a distant church bell, and sometimes gave a broad roar around the traveller, as if all Nature were laughing him to scorn. But he was himself the chief horror of the scene, and shrank not from its other horrors.

"Ha! ha! ha!" roared Goodman Brown when the wind laughed at him. "Let us hear which will laugh loudest. Think not to frighten me with your deviltry. Come witch, come wizard, come Indian powwow, come devil himself, and here comes Goodman Brown. You may as well fear him as he fear you."

In truth, all through the haunted forest there could be nothing more frightful than the figure of Goodman Brown. On he flew among the black pines, brandishing his staff with frenzied gestures, now giving vent to an inspiration of horrid blasphemy, and now shouting forth such laughter as set all the echoes of the forest laughing like demons around him. The fiend in his own shape is less hideous than when he rages in the breast of man. Thus sped the demoniac on his course, until, quivering among the trees, he saw a red light before him, as when the felled trunks and branches of a clearing have been set on fire, and throw up their lurid blaze against the sky, at the hour of midnight. He paused, in a lull of the tempest that had driven him onward, and heard the swell of what seemed a hymn, rolling solemnly from a distance with the weight of many voices. He knew the tune; it was a familiar one in the choir of the village meeting-house. The verse died heavily away, and was lengthened by a chorus, not of human voices, but of all the sounds of the benighted wilderness pealing in awful harmony together. Goodman Brown cried out, and his cry was lost to his own ear by its unison with the cry of the desert.

In the interval of silence he stole forward until the light glared full upon his eyes. At one extremity of an open space, hemmed in by the dark wall of the forest, arose a rock, bearing some rude, natural resemblance either to an altar or a pulpit, and surrounded by four blazing pines, their tops aflame, their stems untouched, like candles at an evening meeting. The mass of foliage that had overgrown the summit of the rock was all on fire, blazing high into the night and fitfully illuminating the whole field. Each pendent twig and leafy festoon was in a blaze. As the red light arose and fell, a numerous congregation alternately shone forth, then disappeared in shadow, and again grew, as it were, out of the darkness, peopling the heart of the solitary woods at once.

"A grave and dark-clad company," quoth Goodman Brown. 55

In truth they were such. Among them, quivering to and fro between gloom and splendor, appeared faces that would be seen next day at the council board of the province, and others which, Sabbath after Sabbath, looked devoutly heavenward, and benignantly over the crowded pews, from the holiest pulpits in the land. Some affirm that the lady of the governor was there. At least there were high dames well known to her, and wives of honored husbands, and widows, a great multitude, and ancient maidens, all of excellent repute, and fair young girls, who trembled lest their mothers should espy them. Either the sudden gleams of light flashing over the obscure field bedazzled Goodman Brown, or he recognized a score of the church members of Salem village famous for their especial sanctity. Good old Deacon Gookin had arrived, and waited at the skirts of that venerable saint, his revered pastor. But, irreverently consorting with these grave, reputable, and pious people, these elders of the church, these chaste dames and dewy virgins, there were men of dissolute lives and women of spotted fame, wretches given over to all mean and filthy vice, and suspected even of horrid crimes. It was strange to see that the good shrank not from the wicked, nor were the sinners abashed by the saints. Scattered also among their pale-faced enemies were the Indian priests, or powwows, who had often scared their native forest with more hideous incantations than any known to English witchcraft.

"But where is Faith?" thought Goodman Brown; and, as hope came into his heart, he trembled.

Another verse of the hymn arose, a slow and mournful strain, such as the pious love, but joined to words which expressed all that our nature can conceive of sin, and darkly hinted at far more. Unfathomable to mere mortals is the lore of fiends. Verse after verse was sung; and still the chorus of the desert swelled between like the deepest tone of a mighty organ; and with the final peal of that dreadful anthem there came a sound, as if the roaring wind, the rushing streams, the howling beasts, and every other voice of the unconverted wilderness were mingling and according with the voice of guilty man in homage to the prince of all. The four blazing pines threw up a loftier flame, and obscurely discovered shapes and visages of horror on the smoke wreaths above the impious assembly. At the same moment the fire on the rock shot redly forth and formed a glowing arch above its base, where now appeared a figure. With reverence be it spoken, the figure bore no slight similitude, both in garb and manner, to some grave divine of the New England churches.

"Bring forth the converts!" cried a voice that echoed through the field and rolled into the forest.

At the word, Goodman Brown stepped forth from the shadow of the trees and approached the congregation, with whom he felt a loathful brotherhood by the sympathy of all that was wicked in his heart. He could have well-nigh sworn that the shape of his own dead father beckoned him to advance, looking downward from a smoke wreath, while a woman, with dim features of despair, threw out her hand to warn him back. Was it his mother? But he had no power to retreat one step, nor to resist, even in thought, when the minister and good old Deacon Gookin seized his arms and led him to the blazing rock. Thither came also the slender form of a veiled female, led between Goody Cloyse, that pious teacher of the catechism, and Martha Carrier, who had received the devil's promise to be queen of hell. A rampant hag was she. And there stood the proselytes beneath the canopy of fire. 60

"Welcome, my children," said the dark figure, "to the communion of your race. Ye have found thus young your nature and your destiny. My children, look behind you!"

They turned; and flashing forth, as it were, in a sheet of flame, the fiend worshippers were seen; the smile of welcome gleamed darkly on every visage.

"There," resumed the sable form, "are all whom ye have reverenced from youth. Ye deemed them holier than yourselves, and shrank from your own sin, contrasting it with their lives of righteousness and prayerful aspirations heavenward. Yet here are they all in my worshipping assembly. This night it shall be granted you to know their secret deeds: how hoary-bearded elders of the church have whispered wanton words to the young maids of their households; how many a woman, eager for widows' weeds, has given her husband a drink at bedtime and let him sleep his last sleep in her bosom; how beardless youths have made haste to inherit their fathers' wealth; and how fair damsels—blush not, sweet ones—have dug little graves in the garden, and bidden me, the sole guest, to an infant's funeral. By the sympathy of your human hearts for sin ye shall scent out all the places—whether in church, bedchamber, street, field, or forest—where crime has been committed, and shall exult to behold the whole earth one stain of guilt, one mighty blood spot. Far more than this. It shall be yours to penetrate, in every bosom, the deep mystery of sin, the fountain of all wicked arts, and which inexhaustibly supplies more evil impulses than human power—than my power at its utmost—can make manifest in deeds. And now, my children, look upon each other."

They did so; and, by the blaze of the hell-kindled torches, the wretched man beheld his Faith, and the wife her husband, trembling before that unhallowed altar.

"Lo, there ye stand, my children," said the figure, in a deep and solemn tone, almost sad with its despairing awfulness, as if his once angelic nature could yet mourn for our miserable race. "Depending upon one another's hearts, ye had still hoped that virtue were not all a dream. Now are ye undeceived. Evil is the nature of mankind. Evil must be your only happiness. Welcome again, my children, to the communion of your race." 65

"Welcome," repeated the fiend worshippers, in one cry of despair and triumph.

And there they stood, the only pair, as it seemed, who were yet hesitating on the verge of wickedness in this dark world. A basin was hollowed, naturally, in the rock. Did it contain water, reddened by the lurid light? or was it blood? or, perchance, a liquid flame? Herein did the shape of evil dip his hand and prepare to lay the mark of baptism upon their foreheads, that they might be partakers of the mystery of sin, more conscious of the secret guilt of others, both in deed and thought, than they could now be of their own. The husband cast one look at his pale wife, and Faith at him. What polluted wretches would the next glance show them to each other, shuddering alike at what they disclosed and what they saw!

"Faith! Faith!" cried the husband, "look up to heaven, and resist the wicked one."

Whether Faith obeyed he knew not. Hardly had he spoken when he found himself amid calm night and solitude, listening to a roar of the wind which died heavily away through the forest. He staggered against the rock, and felt it chill and damp; while a hanging twig, that had been all on fire, besprinkled his cheek with the coldest dew.

The next morning young Goodman Brown came slowly into the street of Salem 70 village, staring around him like a bewildered man. The good old minister was taking a walk along the graveyard to get an appetite for breakfast and meditate his sermon, and bestowed a blessing, as he passed, on Goodman Brown. He shrank from the venerable saint as if to avoid an anathema. Old Deacon Gookin was at domestic worship, and the holy words of his prayer were heard through the open window. "What God doth the wizard pray to?" quoth Goodman Brown. Goody Cloyse, that excellent old Christian, stood in the early sunshine at her own lattice, catechizing a little girl who had brought her a pint of morning's milk. Goodman Brown snatched away the child as from the grasp of the fiend himself. Turning the corner by the meeting-house, he spied the head of Faith, with the pink ribbons, gazing anxiously forth, and bursting into such joy at the sight of him that she skipped along the street and almost kissed her husband before the whole village. But Goodman Brown looked sternly and sadly into her face, and passed on without a greeting.

Had Goodman Brown fallen asleep in the forest and only dreamed a wild dream of a witch-meeting?

Be it so if you will; but, alas! it was a dream of evil omen for young Goodman Brown. A stern, a sad, a darkly meditative, a distrustful, if not a desperate man did he become from the night of that fearful dream. On the Sabbath day, when the congregation were singing a holy psalm, he could not listen because an anthem of sin rushed loudly upon his ear and drowned all the blessed strain. When the minister spoke from the pulpit with power and fervid eloquence, and, with his hand on the open Bible, of the sacred truths of our religion, and of saint-like lives and triumphant deaths, and of future bliss or misery unutterable, then did Goodman Brown turn pale, dreading lest the roof should thunder down upon the gray blasphemer and his hearers. Often, waking suddenly at midnight, he shrank from the bosom of Faith; and at morning or eventide, when the family knelt down at prayer, he scowled and muttered to himself, and gazed sternly at his wife, and turned away. And when he had lived long, and was borne to his grave a hoary corpse, followed by Faith, an aged woman, and children and grandchildren, a goodly procession, besides neighbors not a few, they carved no hopeful verse upon his tombstone, for his dying hour was gloom.

THE RECEPTIVE READER

1. As the story opens, what are major steps and key details in young Goodman Brown's journey into the forest? What is strange, what is frightening, and what is funny about the journey? Where does it go counter to our naive expectations, creating the effect of *irony*?

2. Much critical discussion of this much-discussed story has focused on the exact role of Brown's "aptly named" wife, Faith. What is her role in the story? When is she real; when is she a *symbol*? Could she be both? (What is the role of the pink ribbon?)

3. What exactly happens at the Witches' Sabbath? How does it end? What question or questions does it leave open?

4. How are we as readers expected to react to Brown's transformation after his experience in the forest?

5. How would you sum up in a sentence or two what the story as a whole says about sin or about evil? How does your statement of the *theme* compare with statements of the theme by your classmates?

THE RANGE OF INTERPRETATION

Hawthorne has a reputation for *ambiguity,* intentionally leaving his stories ambiguous and open-ended. Which of the following interpretations is to you most convincing? What evidence from the story would support it?

◇ Is young Goodman Brown's journey into the forest an evil dream (perhaps inspired by the devil)?

◇ Is his journey a dream vision telling him the truth about human nature?

◇ Is his journey a symbolic acting out of his own paranoid fears and suspicions about others?

✧ Is his journey a symbolic acting out of his own sinful nature, his secret inclination toward evil?

✧ Is Hawthorne's vision of evil in this story a recreation of a historical cycle that his generation had left behind? Or is it his own view?

CROSS-REFERENCES—For Discussion or Writing

Two other stories about evil lurking behind a genteel or reassuring surface are Shirley Jackson's "The Lottery" and William Faulkner's "A Rose for Emily." What is similar, or what is different, about the vision of evil in these three stories? Which do you find most persuasive, which least?

WRITING ABOUT LITERATURE
7. Tracing a Recurrent Theme (Comparing and Contrasting)

The Writing Workshop   A crucial part of your task as a writer is to make connections. When you compare the treatment of the same theme by two different writers, you become more aware of each author's distinct way of looking at the world. Try your hand at tracing the same or a similar theme in two stories by different authors. See what you can learn from such a paper about comparison and contrast as a major organizational strategy.

When you try to show the connections between several stories, the overall plan of your paper will be more complex than usual. (You won't be able to follow the developments of a single story from beginning to end.) How will you make your readers' eyes travel between the two stories to make them see the connections you want them to see? How will you go about highlighting similarities and differences? How are you going to lay out your material?

However you proceed, try not to let your paper break up into two mini-essays (one on each story)—with your readers left to establish the cross-references themselves.

Let us assume you are writing about the vision of evil in Hawthorne's "Young Goodman Brown" and Jackson's "The Lottery." You have tentatively mapped out three areas where the stories seem to converge in their vision of how evil enters our world. Both stories take us into a world that is superficially benign—people seem superficially dignified, harmless, friendly, or virtuous. But these apparently harmless or well-meaning people are observed to engage in strange rituals—puzzling, disturbing observances that seem like part of an ancient tribal religion. Finally, the community as a whole seems implicated—all seem in some way involved in evil.

What plan of organization will allow you to show these three features in both of the stories? Here are organizing strategies you might consider:

✧ You might try a **point-by-point** comparison. The first third of your paper might show that in both stories there is a reassuring façade of normalcy that hides evil from the casual observer (point A). Then the second third of your paper might show that in both stories we witness strange quasi-religious rituals—as if evil were not something that happens casually or almost by accident. It is built into the traditions of the community (point B). Finally, the last third of your paper might show that evil does not seem the work of isolated individuals—a "criminal element." The whole community seems implicated in one way or another (point C). With a point-by-point comparison there is little danger that your readers will miss the connections.

✧ You might feel that in a point-by-point comparison your readers would not get enough of a sense of the characteristic atmosphere of each story as a whole. You might then try a **parallel-order** comparison. You discuss each story separately, but each time you run through the three key points in the same order: first the reassuring benign surface, then the strange traditional rituals, and finally the involvement in evil of the whole community. As you go through the second story, you might nudge your reader into realizing that you are in fact lining up the major points in the same order for easy cross-reference.

✧ You might decide to start by showing *similarities* between the two stories first—especially if they are likely to be readily noticed by the reader. You might then go on to show a crucial *difference* your readers might have overlooked. (Conversely, you might point out differences first but then go on to important features that two superficially very different stories have in common.)

The following student paper compares and contrasts two short stories treating a similar or related theme. What is the writer's organizing strategy? Does it become clear to the reader? How successful is the writer in carrying it out?

SAMPLE STUDENT PAPER

Two Women's Passions

John Steinbeck's "The Chrysanthemums" and Alice Walker's "Everyday Use" explore obstacles that women, both white and black, have had to face. Women often find that they are taken for granted; their intelligence, creative abilities, even the hard labor that they do often go unappreciated. Facing this reality, women find themselves pulled in conflicting directions. On the one hand, there is the strong desire to be attractive to men. Yet by pursuing the traditional ideal of femininity, they may be stifling their true being: their true passions about independence and their struggle toward their own reality.

Elisa in "The Chrysanthemums" is a housewife who has a particular talent in working with flowers. Because this is normally considered "women's work," there is no one restricting her from becoming passionate about it, so she does. Perhaps she puts her energy into her garden only because of her discontent with the rest of her life, where there is little outlet for her energy and strength. Like Elisa's chrysanthemums, the handmade quilts in "Everyday Use" also represent a passion in a woman's life. These quilts were pieced together by the woman and other women in her family from scraps of old dresses, shirts, and even a "teeny faded blue piece . . . that was from Great Grandpa Ezra's uniform that he wore in the Civil War." More than Elisa's flowers, however, these quilts were objects of everyday life, in "everyday use" as bed covers and sources of warmth. They represent a tradition of making do with limited resources, making the best of what you have, in a setting where there is little room for waste or extravagance.

In both stories, the women struggle with the desire to be attractive to men and the harsh realities these longings produce. Elisa finds herself spilling her passions to an old, dirty tinker who shows some false interest in her flowers. She begins by telling him of the budding process and of how to plant the seeds, and his encouraging nods and grunts lead her to continue. She talks passionately of night-time and the stars—"driven into your body. . . . Hot and sharp and—lovely." Apparently even this poor excuse for a man holds her attention enough for Elisa to reach out to him, hoping to find some connection to make her less isolated and trapped in her restricted existence. Unfortunately, the encounter turns into a humbling experience for her, as in the end the tinker is only looking for some pots to mend and cares little for the passions of a sexually frustrated housewife.

The black woman in "Everyday Use" wishes to be attractive as well, although for her this attractiveness would be a way of gaining her daughter's approval. Ideally, she would be "the way my daughter would want me to be: a hundred pounds lighter, my skin like an uncooked barley pancake," giving the quick-witted Johnny Carson "much to do to keep up with my quick and witty tongue." She realizes, however, that this image is far from reality:

> In real life I am a large, big-boned woman with rough, man-working hands.
> In the winter I wear flannel nightgowns to bed and overalls during the day. I
> can kill and clean a hog as mercilessly as a man.

She knows too that in reality she has trouble looking white men (let alone a famous white comedian) in the eye; instead she has "talked to them always with one foot raised in flight." This fear or lack or confidence is part of her nature even though this woman is surviving on her own, feeding and educating her children with no help from a man.

Both women are patronized by others who care little for their passions and want to use them only for their own ends. The tinker in Steinbeck's story seems to listen with strong interest when Elisa goes on about the stars while he is actually waiting for the appropriate moment to ask for work. The mother in Walker's story is patronized by her daughter Dee, who goes through her mother's house looking for black artifacts that would be interesting objects to exhibit in her own home.

Today's reader is waiting for these women to leave their humiliation behind or to express their anger, to turn on those who condescend to them. Elisa's rebellion is weak and indirect at best. After seeing the chrysanthemums the tinker has discarded lying in the road, Elisa turns to her husband and asks him about some boxing matches, imagining them bloody and gory. Her interest in going to one surprises her husband, but he invites her to go. But she almost immediately draws back:

> She relaxed limply in the seat. "Oh, no. No. I don't want to go. I'm sure I
> don't. " Her face was turned away from him. "It will be enough if we can
> have wine. It will be plenty." She turned up her coat collar so he could not
> see that she was crying weakly—like an old woman.

The mother in "Everyday Use" is more assertive in regaining her pride. Despite her daughter Dee's claim that the mother knew nothing of her heritage, she did not give in to her daughter's request for the quilts. The mother had promised the quilts to Maggie, Dee's younger sister, and despite Dee's protest that Maggie would ruin them by using them every day, their mother "dragged" Maggie into the room, "snatched the quilts" out of Dee's hand, and "dumped them into Maggie's lap." In this seemingly insignificant incident, the mother stood up for what she believed in.

In these stories, we get glimpses of women's needs and passions but also of the strength and wisdom women have. Perhaps in the future they will be able to channel their passion into science, politics, art, and our changing world rather than into 10-inch chrysanthemums and patchwork quilts.

QUESTIONS

How does the writer set up an overall perspective for comparing the two stories? What is the organizing strategy? Does this paper tend to break up into two separate mini-essays? What does the writer do to make the reader see the connections between the two stories? How successful is the paper in tracing similarities? Does it do justice to how the stories are different?

8 STYLE
A Manner of Speaking

*The language must be careful and must appear effortless.
It must not sweat. It must suggest and be provocative at
the same time.*

TONI MORRISON

*Technique alone is never enough. You have to have
passion. Technique alone is just an embroidered potholder.*

RAYMOND CHANDLER

Writing is a struggle against silence.

CARLOS FUENTES

FOCUS ON STYLE

What is style? **Style** is the manner in which a writer uses language to create his or her reality. It is the writer's personal way of using words and sentences to help create a distinctive voice that we come to recognize. The following two passages come from short stories at opposite poles of the spectrum of prose style. The first is from Ernest Hemingway's "Big Two-Hearted River," a story about a camping trip to the Upper Peninsula in Michigan (a trout fisher's paradise).

He came down a hillside covered with stumps into a meadow. At the edge of the meadow flowed the river. Nick was glad to get to the river. He walked upstream through the meadow. His trousers were soaked with the dew as he walked. After the hot day, the dew had come quickly and heavily. The river made no sound. It was too fast and too smooth. At the edge of the meadow, before he mounted to a piece of high ground to make camp, Nick looked down the river at the trout rising. They were rising to insects come from the swamp on the other side of the stream when the sun went down. The trout jumped out of the water to take them. While Nick walked through the little stretch of meadow along the stream, trout had jumped high out of the water. Now as he looked down the river, the insects must be settling on the surface, for the trout were feeding steadily all down the stream. As far down the long stretch as he could see, the trout were rising, making circles all down the surface of the water, as though it were starting to rain.

This passage shows an unadorned modern style that aims at doing justice to reality. It does without embellishment, without fanfare, without grand gestures, without excessive emoting. There are several examples of the bare-fact sentences that for many readers became the hallmark of the stripped-down Hemingway style: "At the edge of the meadow flowed the river. . . . The river made no sound. It was too fast and too smooth." The words are simple, direct—and exactly adequate to their task of making the scene real for us: *soaked, dew, jumped, feeding, stream.* We know there is a feeling and thinking observer of the scene, but he does not come between us and the outdoor setting. The sentences that tell us about his state of mind—averaging in the story about one sentence for every paragraph full of patiently observed firsthand detail—are like minimal bulletins: "Nick was glad to get to the river."

However, this style of deliberate **understatement** does not keep us as readers from responding to the fresh, startling beauty of the unspoilt natural scene. Perhaps it makes us more rather than less ready to respond to the lovely image of the trout rising from below to feed on the insects settled on the surface of the water and making circles everywhere "as though it were starting to rain."

Fifty or a hundred years before Hemingway, the dominant style was to express emotion much more freely. A master at arousing the emotions of the audience was Edgar Allan Poe, who wrote the following passage in his short story "The Black Cat":

> With my aversion to this cat, however, its partiality for myself seemed to increase. It followed my footsteps with a pertinacity which it would be difficult to make the reader comprehend. Whenever I sat, it would crouch beneath my chair or spring upon my knees, covering me with its loathsome caresses. If I arose to walk, it would get between my feet and thus nearly throw me down, or, fastening its long and sharp claws in my dress, clamber in this manner to my breast. At such time, although I longed to destroy it with a blow, I was yet withheld from so doing, partly by a memory of my former crime, but chiefly—let me confess it at once—by absolute *dread* of the beast.

There are no bare-bones sentences here. Several sentences start with preambles like "If I . . ." or "Whenever I . . ." and then work their way through layers of mixed or complicated emotions. (The narrator would love to strangle the cat but is held back by his guilt feelings about having done the same to an earlier specimen.) The language is elevated, **formal**—deliberately above the trivial talk of everyday: *partiality* for *kindness, pertinacity* for *stubbornness, comprehend* for *understand.* Does the language signal that the events of this story are more important, more momentous, more ominous than what ordinary cat fanciers are likely to experience? The whole passage builds up to a climax of "absolute *dread.*" No reluctance here to use superlatives! (or to italicize for emphasis). Poe's style is one of **hyperbole**—he is willing to exaggerate, to enhance, to pull the stops. If Poe continues to be read, it may because the modern reader has a capacity for strong feelings that a dry understated modern style tends to leave unused.

THE ELEMENTS OF STYLE

Great writers leave their mark by the originality of their style, stamping it with an imprint that imposes a new face on the coins of language.

JEAN-JOSEPH GOUX

We are what we imagine.

N. SCOTT MOMADAY

Style is more than a matter of style. It makes a statement of its own. That statement, however, may not be simple but complex. When American colleges built quads and dorms in the Gothic style of medieval Oxford or Cambridge, they showed their desire to tread in the footsteps of these revered institutions. When modern architects built office towers of glass and steel, they asserted that the beauty of a building was in its basic design, not in embellishments stuck on to mask an ugly surface. When postmodern architects put frills and curlicues back on office towers, they suggested that the modern style had become too stark, too mechanical, too inhuman.

How can you become more sensitive to style in what you read? One way of becoming more aware of prose style is to place elements of a writer's style on a spectrum, or on a scale ranging from one extreme to the other. (The two poles do not necessarily represent good and bad, although writers and critics often have strong preferences one way or the other.)

Abstract and Concrete   Some prose remains general or **abstract,** whereas other prose becomes **concrete:** It engages in rich specific detail with the sensory surface of life—with what we can see, hear, smell, touch, feel. Hemingway, for instance, was a stickler for detail (like many of his characters, who are often perfectionists, sticklers for doing something exactly the right way). In the following pair, compare the thin passage that a writer in a hurry might have written with the texture of concrete detail in a Hemingway story:

GENERAL: He went down to the stream and got water for his coffee.

SPECIFIC: He had forgotten to get water for the coffee. Out of the pack he got a folding canvas bucket and walked down the hill, across the edge of the meadow, to the stream. The other bank was in the white mist. The grass was wet and cold as he knelt on the bank and dipped the canvas bucket into the stream. It bellied and pulled hard in the current. The water was ice cold. Nick rinsed the bucket and carried it full up to the camp. Up away from the stream it was not so cold.

From "Big Two-Hearted River"

Often Hemingway will choose words especially suited to do justice to the rich sensory texture of firsthand experience. Concrete words are graphic words that conjure up a more vivid image than common, averaged-out words might. Concrete words speak more vividly to our senses than more colorless substitutes. What does each of the following concrete words add that might be missing from a near synonym, a near equivalent? In the story about the camping trip, Hemingway makes us see the water *swirl* (rather than wash) around the logs of the bridge; he makes us see and hear the wings of grasshoppers *whirr*. The camper breaks off *sprigs* of the heathery fern; with his ax he cuts off a *slab* of pine; the current raises a mist of sand in *spurts* from the bottom of the creek.

Denotation and Connotation   Some words point and identify. The word *glass* simply points to an object that holds liquid for drinking. The word in itself says nothing about whether the person who used it was thirsty, or likes to drink, or prefers a glass to a mug or a stein. Other words, however, bring into play attitudes or emotions. When James Joyce, in his story "Araby," uses the word *chalice*, it calls up a range of feelings associated with religious ritual: otherworldliness, devotion, religious exaltation.

The objective, emotionally neutral meaning of a word is its **denotation;** the denotation of *knife* is simply an instrument for cutting. The range of attitudes or emotions a word brings into play is its **connotation.** The word *knife* may suggest menace, threat, treachery. Connotative words, words charged with emotion, help set the tone. Angry words, sweet words, wistful words, or judgmental words help shape the emotional coloring of a story.

Literal and Figurative   Figurative language uses imaginative comparisons to carry meanings that otherwise might be hard to put into words. **Metaphors** are imaginative comparisons that do not come with a sign that says: "This is a comparison!" There is no word such as *like* or *as if* to alert us that someone is speaking on an as-if basis. (**Similes** are figurative expressions that *do* provide the *like* or *as if* that signals the comparison. In Bobbie Ann Mason's "Shiloh," Norma Jean picks up "cake crumbs from the cellophane wrapper, *like a fussy bird*.")

In the work of an imaginative writer, metaphors are likely to be rich and provocative. They may reveal new dimensions as they develop their full implications. Patricia Hampl, talking about her own writing, said, "Our most ancient metaphor says life is a journey." Writing about her experience, she "is the traveler who goes on foot, living the journey, taking in mountains, enduring deserts, marveling at the lush green places." As she writes, she moves "through it all faithfully, not so much a survivor with a harrowing tale to tell as a pilgrim, seeking, wondering." The journey metaphor here is rich in meaning and visual content: It makes us think of life as something that is not disjointed but has continuity, a purpose, a destination. Specifying that the journey will be on foot slows us down: We will have a chance to take things in, responding to sights and sounds missed by the traveler in a speeding car or on a plane. The journey will be prolonged enough to take us through both deserts and green valleys. It will be not a hurried, absentminded kind of trip but a journey like a pilgrimage, undertaken in a serious mood, with a solemn purpose.

Formal and Informal Formal language can make events seem important and characters dignified. (When overdone, it can make characters seem pompous.) Informal language can put the reader at ease, but when it shades over into slang it can easily become disrespectful or insulting. (There is a world of difference between "Will you *please* leave now" and "Beat it, bozo.") *Who uses* distinctly formal or informal language in a story makes considerable difference to the narrative voice. If the formal or informal way of talking appears in **dialogue,** it helps create character—dignified, stodgy, laid-back, tough, or whatever. If it is used by the narrator, it will color the tone of the story as a whole. ("Ain't nobody gonna beat me at nuthin" says the tough city-kid narrator at the end of Toni Cade Bambara's "The Lesson.")

Simple and Complex Bare-bones sentences sound matter-of-fact. They often do in Hemingway's prose. However, varied sentence length (the short and the long of it) is a major source of sentence variety: An arresting short sentence after a series of long and involved sentences, full of ifs and buts, may focus our attention and highlight an important thought or detail. It catches us up short. Sentences with elaborate **parallelism**—repetition of grammatically similar elements—can create a strong rhythm, building up emotion, hammering home a point, leading up to a climactic finale. The following is the climactic final sentence of a story written in a florid nineteenth-century style, ending the story with a last rhetorical flourish:

> And pulseless and cold, with a Derringer by his side and a bullet in his heart, though still calm as in life, beneath the snow lay he who was at once the strongest and yet the weakest of the outcasts of Poker Flat. (Bret Harte)

Earnest and Ironic Some writers, like Bret Harte, have a saving sense of humor; others take life and literature *very* seriously. A pervasive feature of style in much modern fiction is a lively sense of **irony**—of the sad and comic contrast between expectation and event, between ideal and reality. The ironic tone may range from amused tolerance and indulgence of human foibles to cutting, sardonic exposure of stupidity and greed.

JUXTAPOSITIONS

Playing the Role

Each of the two stories that follow was written by a writer with a sharp eye for how people act and a quick ear for how people talk. (Both authors are alert observers of someone's personal *style.*) Dorothy Parker, who got her start in the publishing world by working for *Vogue* and *Vanity Fair,* became legendary in the twenties and thirties for her devastating wit. One interviewer said about her, "Her sentences are punctuated with observations phrased with lethal force." Parker said about her stories that they "made themselves stories by telling themselves through what people say. I haven't got a visual mind. I hear things." Toni Cade Bambara became known in the seventies for making her readers listen to the language of tough, scrappy kids from the poor part of town.

In both stories, young people without money come downtown to the pricey avenues of Manhattan. They come into stores that they know are not for them. The focus is on their manner: their style of behavior, their style of talking. What is similar, what is different, about the point of view from which we see the events of each story? What do the young people in the stories have in common? What is similar or different about the way they act and talk? Is there any connection between the roles the two sets of characters play in public? Do the stories differ in theme—in what each story as a whole has to say?

DOROTHY PARKER (1893–1967)
The Standard of Living   1926

Annabel and Midge came out of the tea room with the arrogant slow gait of the leisured, for their Saturday afternoon stretched ahead of them. They had lunched, as was their wont, on sugar, starches, oils, and butter-fats. Usually they ate sandwiches of spongy new white bread greased with butter and mayonnaise; they ate thick wedges of cake lying wet beneath ice cream and whipped cream and melted chocolate gritty with nuts. As alternates, they ate patties, sweating beads of inferior oil, containing bits of bland meat bogged in pale, stiffening sauce; they ate pastries, limber under rigid icing, filled with an indeterminate yellow sweet stuff, not still solid, not yet liquid, like salve that has been left in the sun. They chose no other sort of food, nor did they consider it. And their skin was like the petals of wood anemones, and their bellies were as flat and their flanks as lean as those of young Indian braves.

Annabel and Midge had been best friends almost from the day that Midge had found a job as stenographer with the firm that employed Annabel. By now, Annabel, two years longer in the stenographic department, had worked up to the wages of eighteen dollars and fifty cents a week; Midge was still at sixteen dollars. Each girl lived at home with her family and paid half her salary to its support.

The girls sat side by side at their desks, they lunched together every noon, together they set out for home at the end of the day's work. Many of their evenings and most of their Sundays were passed in each other's company. Often they were joined by two young men, but there was no steadiness to any such quartet; the two young men would give place, unlamented, to two other young men, and lament would have been inappropriate, really, since the newcomers were scarcely distinguishable from their predecessors. Invariably the girls spent the fine idle hours of their hot-weather Saturday afternoons together. Constant use had not worn ragged the fabric of their friendship.

They looked alike, though the resemblance did not lie in their features. It was in the shape of their bodies, their movements, their style, and their adornments. Annabel and Midge did, and completely, all that young office workers are besought not to do. They painted their lips and their nails, they darkened their lashes and lightened their hair, and scent seemed to shimmer from them. They wore thin, bright dresses, tight over their breasts and high on their legs, and tilted slippers, fancifully strapped. They looked conspicuous and cheap and charming.

Now, as they walked across to Fifth Avenue with their skirts swirled by the hot   5 wind, they received audible admiration. Young men grouped lethargically about news-stands awarded them murmurs, exclamations, even—the ultimate tribute—whistles. Annabel and Midge passed without the condescension of hurrying their pace; they held their heads higher and set their feet with exquisite precision, as if they stepped over the necks of peasants.

Always the girls went to walk on Fifth Avenue on their free afternoons, for it was the ideal ground for their favorite game. The game could be played anywhere, and, indeed, was, but the great shop windows stimulated the two players to their best form.

Annabel had invented the game; or rather she had evolved it from an old one. Basically, it was no more than the ancient sport of what-would-you-do-if-you-had-a-million dollars? But Annabel had drawn a new set of rules for it, had narrowed it, pointed it, made it stricter. Like all games, it was the more absorbing for being more difficult.

Annabel's version went like this: You must suppose that somebody dies and leaves you a million dollars, cool. But there is a condition to the bequest. It is stated in the will that you must spend every nickel of the money on yourself.

There lay the hazard of the game. If, when playing it, you forgot, and listed among your expenditures the rental of a new apartment for your family, for example, you lost your turn to the other player. It was astonishing how many—and some of them among the experts, too—would forfeit all their innings by such slips.

It was essential, of course, that it be played in passionate seriousness. Each purchase must be carefully considered and, if necessary, supported by argument. There was no zest to playing wildly. Once Annabel had introduced the game to Sylvia, another girl who worked in the office. She explained the rules to Sylvia and then offered her the gambit "What would be the first thing you'd do?" Sylvia had not shown the decency of even a second of hesitation. "Well," she said, "the first thing I'd do, I'd go out and hire somebody to shoot Mrs. Gary Cooper, and then . . ." So it is to be seen that she was no fun.

10

But Annabel and Midge were surely born to be comrades, for Midge played the game like a master from the moment she learned it. It was she who added the touches that made the whole thing cozier. According to Midge's innovations, the eccentric who died and left you the money was not anybody you loved, or, for the matter of that, anybody you even knew. It was somebody who had seen you somewhere and had thought, "That girl ought to have lots of nice things. I'm going to leave her a million dollars when I die." And the death was to be neither untimely nor painful. Your benefactor, full of years and comfortably ready to depart, was to slip softly away during sleep and go right to heaven. These embroideries permitted Annabel and Midge to play their game in the luxury of peaceful consciences.

Midge played with a seriousness that was not only proper but extreme. The single strain on the girls' friendship had followed an announcement once made by Annabel that the first thing she would buy with her million dollars would be a silver-fox coat. It was as if she had struck Midge across the mouth. When Midge recovered her breath, she cried that she couldn't imagine how Annabel could do such a thing—silver-fox coats were common! Annabel defended her taste with the retort that they were not common, either. Midge then said that they were so. She added that everybody had a silver-fox coat. She went on, with perhaps a slight loss of head, to declare that she herself wouldn't be caught dead in silver fox.

For the next few days, though the girls saw each other as constantly, their conversation was careful and infrequent, and they did not once play their game. Then one morning, as soon as Annabel entered the office, she came to Midge and said that she had changed her mind. She would not buy a silver-fox coat with any part of her million dollars. Immediately on receiving the legacy, she would select a coat of mink.

Midge smiled and her eyes shone. "I think," she said, "you're doing absolutely the right thing."

Now, as they walked along Fifth Avenue, they played the game anew. It was one of those days with which September is repeatedly cursed; hot and glaring, with slivers of dust in the wind. People drooped and shambled, but the girls carried themselves tall and walked a straight line, as befitted young heiresses on their afternoon promenade. There was no longer need for them to start the game at its formal opening. Annabel went direct to the heart of it.

"All right," she said. "So you've got this million dollars. So what would be the first thing you'd do?"

"Well, the first thing I'd do," Midge said, "I'd get a mink coat." But she said it mechanically, as if she were giving the memorized answer to an expected question.

"Yes," Annabel said, "I think you ought to. The terribly dark kind of mink." But she, too, spoke as if by rote. It was too hot; fur, no matter how dark and sleek and supple, was horrid to the thoughts.

They stepped along in silence for a while. Then Midge's eye was caught by a shop window. Cool, lovely gleamings were there set off by chaste and elegant darkness.

"No," Midge said, "I take it back. I wouldn't get a mink coat the first thing. Know what I'd do? I'd get a string of pearls. Real pearls."

Annabel's eyes turned to follow Midge's.

"Yes," she said, slowly. "I think that's kind of a good idea. And it would make sense, too. Because you can wear pearls with anything."

Together they went over to the shop window and stood pressed against it. It contained but one object—a double row of great, even pearls clasped by a deep emerald around a little pink velvet throat.

"What do you suppose they cost?" Annabel said.

"Gee, I don't know." Midge said. "Plenty, I guess."

"Like a thousand dollars?" Annabel said.

"Oh, I guess like more," Midge said. "On account of the emerald."

"Well, like ten thousand dollars?" Annabel said.

"Gee, I wouldn't even know," Midge said.

The devil nudged Annabel in the ribs. "Dare you to go in and price them," she said.

"Like fun!" Midge said.

"Dare you," Annabel said.

"Why, a store like this wouldn't even be open this afternoon," Midge said.

"Yes, it is so, too," Annabel said. "People just came out. And there's a doorman on. Dare you."

"Well," Midge said. "But you've got to come too."

They tendered thanks, icily, to the doorman for ushering them into the shop. It was cool and quiet, a broad, gracious room with paneled walls and soft carpet. But the girls wore expressions of bitter disdain, as if they stood in a sty.

A slim, immaculate clerk came to them and bowed. His neat face showed no astonishment at their appearance.

"Good afternoon," he said. He implied that he would never forget it if they would grant him the favor of accepting his soft-spoken greeting.

"Good afternoon," Annabel and Midge said together, and in like freezing accents.

"Is there something—?" the clerk said.

"Oh, we're just looking," Annabel said. It was as if she flung the words down from a dais.

The clerk bowed.

"My friend and myself merely happened to be passing," Midge said, and stopped, seeming to listen to the phrase. "My friend here and myself," she went on, "merely happened to be wondering how much are those pearls you've got in your window."

"Ah, yes," the clerk said. "The double rope. That is two hundred and fifty thousand dollars, Madam."

"I see," Midge said. 45

The clerk bowed. "An exceptionally beautiful necklace," he said. "Would you care to look at it?"

"No, thank you," Annabel said.

"My friend and myself merely happened to be passing," Midge said.

They turned to go; to go, from their manner, where the tumbrel awaited them. The clerk sprang ahead and opened the door. He bowed as they swept by him.

The girls went on along the Avenue and disdain was still on their faces. 50

"Honestly!" Annabel said. "Can you imagine a thing like that?"

"Two hundred and fifty thousand dollars!" Midge said. "That's a quarter of a million dollars right there!"

"He's got his nerve!" Annabel said.

They walked on. Slowly the disdain went, slowly and completely as if drained from them, and with it went the regal carriage and tread. Their shoulders dropped and they dragged their feet; they bumped against each other, without notice or apology, and caromed away again. They were silent and their eyes were cloudy.

Suddenly Midge straightened her back, flung her head high, and spoke, clear and 55 strong.

"Listen, Annabel," she said. "Look. Suppose there was this terribly rich person, see? You don't know this person, but this person has seen you somewhere and wants to do something for you. Well, it's a terribly old person, see? And so this person dies, just like going to sleep, and leaves you ten million dollars. Now, what would be the first thing you'd do?"

THE RECEPTIVE READER

1. How well do you come to know the young women? What is their style? How do they dress, act, and talk?

2. What does the game the two young women play tell you about them?

3. Parker was known for her sharp tongue and malicious *wit*. Do these show in the style of this story?

4. What is the author's attitude toward the two young women? How do you think she expects you to react to them?

THE PERSONAL RESPONSE

Does this story strike you as being based on real life? Do you think this story is out of date?

T O N I   C A D E   B A M B A R A   (born 1939)
The Lesson 1972

Back in the days when everyone was old and stupid or young and foolish and me and Sugar were the only ones just right, this lady moved on our block with nappy hair and proper speech and no makeup. And quite naturally we laughed at her, laughed the way we did at the junk man who went about his business like he was some big-time president and his sorry-ass horse his secretary. And we kinda hated her too, hated the way we did the winos who cluttered up our parks and pissed on our handball walls and stank up our hallways and stairs so you couldn't halfway play hide-and-seek without a goddamn gas mask. Miss Moore was her name. The only woman on the block with no first name. And she was black as hell, cept for her feet, which were fish-white and spooky. And she was always planning these boring-ass things for us to do, us being my cousin, mostly, who lived on the block cause we all moved North the same time and to the same apartment then spread out gradual to breathe. And our parents would yank our heads into some kinda shape and crisp up our clothes so we'd be presentable for travel with Miss Moore, who always looked like she was going to church, though she never did. Which is just one of the things the grownups talked about when they talked behind her back like a dog. But when she came calling with some sachet she'd sewed up or some gingerbread she'd made or some book, why then they'd all be too embarrassed to turn her down and we'd get handed over all spruced up. She'd been to college and said it was only right that she should take responsibility for the young ones' education, and she not even related by marriage or blood. So they'd go for it. Specially Aunt Gretchen. She was the main gofer in the family. You got some ole dumb shit foolishness you want somebody to go for, you send for Aunt Gretchen. She been screwed into the go-along for so long, it's a blood-deep natural thing with her. Which is how she got saddled with me and Sugar and Junior in the first place while our mothers were in a la-de-da apartment up the block having a good ole time.

So this one day Miss Moore rounds us all up at the mailbox and it's puredee hot and she's knockin herself out about arithmetic. And school suppose to let up in summer I heard, but she don't never let up. And the starch in my pinafore scratching the shit outta me and I'm really hating this nappy-head bitch and her goddamn college degree. I'd much rather go to the pool or to the show where it's cool. So me and Sugar leaning on the mailbox being surly, which is a Miss Moore word. And Flyboy checking out what everybody brought for lunch. And Fat Butt already wasting his peanut-butter-and-jelly sandwich like the pig he is. And Junebug punchin on Q.T.'s arm for potato chips. And Rosie Giraffe shifting from one hip to the other waiting for somebody to step on her foot or ask her if she from Georgia so she can kick ass, preferably Mercedes'. And Miss Moore asking us do we know what money is, like we a bunch of retards. I mean real money, she say, like it's only poker chips or monopoly papers we lay on the grocer. So right away I'm tired of this and say so. And would much rather snatch Sugar and go to the Sunset and terrorize the West Indian kids and take their hair ribbons and their money too. And Miss Moore files that remark away for next week's lesson on brotherhood, I can tell. And finally I say we oughta get to the subway cause it's cooler and besides we might meet some cute boys. Sugar done swiped her mama's lipstick, so we ready.

So we heading down the street and she's boring us silly about what things cost and what our parents make and how much goes for rent and how money ain't divided up right in this country. And then she gets to the part about we all poor and live in the slums, which I don't feature. And I'm ready to speak on that, but she steps out in the street and hails two cabs just like that. Then she hustles half the crew in with her and hands me a five-dollar bill and tells me to calculate 10 percent tip for the driver. And we're off. Me and Sugar and Junebug and Flyboy hangin out the window and hollering to everybody, putting lipstick on each other cause Flyboy a faggot anyway, and making farts with our sweaty armpits. But I'm mostly trying to figure how to spend this money. But they all fascinated with the meter ticking and Junebug starts laying bets as to how much it'll read when Flyboy can't hold his breath no more. Then Sugar lays bets as to how much it'll be when we get there. So I'm stuck. Don't nobody want to go for my plan, which is to jump out at the next light and run off to the first bar-b-que we can find. Then the driver tells us to get the hell out cause we there already. And the meter reads eighty-five cents. And I'm stalling to figure out the tip and Sugar say give him a dime. And I decide he don't need it bad as I do, so later for him. But then he tries to take off with Junebug foot still in the door so we talk about his mama something ferocious. Then we check out that we on Fifth Avenue and everybody dressed up in stockings. One lady in a fur coat, hot as it is. White folks crazy. ← Point of view

"This is the place," Miss Moore say, presenting it to us in the voice she uses at the museum. "Let's look in the windows before we go in."

"Can we steal?" Sugar asks very serious like she's getting the ground rules squared away before she plays. "I beg your pardon," say Miss Moore, and we fall out. So she leads us around the windows of the toy store and me and Sugar screamin, "This is mine, that's mine, I gotta have that, that was made for me, I was born for that," till Big Butt drowns us out.

"Hey, I'm goin to buy that there."

"That there? You don't even know what it is, stupid."

"I do so," he say punchin on Rosie Giraffe. "It's a microscope."

"Whatcha gonna do with a microscope, fool?"

"Look at things."

"Like what, Ronald?" ask Miss Moore. And Big Butt ain't got the first notion. So here go Miss Moore gabbing about the thousands of bacteria in a drop of water and the somethinorother in a speck of blood and the million and one living things in the air around us is invisible to the naked eye. And what she say that for? Junebug go to town on that "naked" and we rolling. Then Miss Moore ask what it cost. So we all jam into the window smudgin it up and the price tag say $300. So then she ask how long'd take for Big Butt and Junebug to save up their allowances. "Too long," I say. "Yeh," adds Sugar, "outgrown it by that time." And Miss Moore say no, you never outgrow learning instruments. "Why, even medical students and interns and," blah, blah, blah. And we ready to choke Big Butt for bringing it up in the first damn place.

"This here costs four hundred eighty dollars," says Rosie Giraffe. So we pile up all over her to see what she pointin out. My eyes tell me it's a chunk of glass cracked with something heavy, and different-color inks dripped into the splits, then the whole thing put into a oven or something. But for $480 it don't make sense.

"That's a paperweight made of semi-precious stones fused together under tremendous pressure," she explains slowly, with her hands doing the mining and all the factory work.

"So what's a paperweight?" asks Rosie Giraffe.

"To weigh paper with, dumbbell," say Flyboy, the wise man from the East.

"Not exactly," say Miss Moore, which is what she say when you warm or way off too. "It's to weigh paper down so it won't scatter and make your desk untidy." So right away me and Sugar curtsy to each other and then to Mercedes who is more the tidy type.

"We don't keep paper on top of the desk in my class," say Junebug, figuring Miss Moore crazy or lyin one.

"At home, then," she say. "Don't you have a calendar and pencil case and a blotter and a letter-opener on your desk at home where you do your homework?" And she know damn well what our homes look like cause she nosys around in them every chance she gets.

"I don't even have a desk," say Junebug. "Do we?"

"No. And I don't get no homework neither," says Big Butt.

"And I don't even have a home," say Flyboy like he do at school to keep the white folks off his back and sorry for him. Send this poor kid to camp posters, is his specialty.

"I do," says Mercedes. "I have a box of stationery on my desk and a picture of my cat. My godmother bought the stationery and the desk. There's a big rose on each sheet and the envelopes smell like roses."

"Who wants to know about your smelly-ass stationery," say Rosie Giraffe fore I can get my two cents in.

"It's important to have a work area all your own so that . . ."

"Will you look at this sailboat, please," say Flyboy, cuttin her off and pointin to the thing like it was his. So once again we tumble all over each other to gaze at this magnificent thing in the toy store which is just big enough to maybe sail two kittens across the pond if you strap them to the posts tight. We all start reciting the price tag like we in assembly. "Handcrafted sailboat of fiberglass at one thousand one hundred ninety-five dollars."

"Unbelievable," I hear myself say and am really stunned. I read it again for myself just in case the group recitation put me in a trance. Same thing. For some reason this pisses me off. We look at Miss Moore and she lookin at us, waiting for I dunno what.

"Who'd pay all that when you can buy a sailboat set for a quarter at Pop's, a tube of glue for a dime, and a ball of string for eight cents? It must have a motor and a whole lot else besides," I say. "My sailboat cost me about fifty cents."

"But will it take water?" say Mercedes with her smart ass.

"Took mine to Alley Pond Park once," say Flyboy. "String broke. Lost it. Pity."

"Sailed mine in Central Park and it keeled over and sank. Had to ask my father for another dollar."

"And you got the strap," laugh Big Butt. "The jerk didn't even have a string on it. My old man wailed on his behind."

Little Q.T. was staring hard at the sailboat and you could see he wanted it bad. But he too little and somebody'd just take it from him. So what the hell. "This boat for kids, Miss Moore?"

"Parents silly to buy something like that just to get all broke up," say Rosie Giraffe.

"That much money it should last forever," I figure.

"My father'd buy it for me if I wanted it."

"Your father, my ass," say Rosie Giraffe getting a chance to finally push Mercedes.

"Must be rich people shop here," say Q.T.

"You are a very bright boy," say Flyboy. "What was your first clue?" And he rap him on the head with the back of his knuckles, since Q.T. the only one he could get away with. Though Q.T. liable to come up behind you years later and get his licks in when you half expect it.

"What I want to know is," I says to Miss Moore though I never talk to her, I wouldn't give the bitch that satisfaction, "is how much a real boat costs? I figure a thousand'd get you a yacht any day."

"Why don't you check that out," she says, "and report back to the group?" Which really pains my ass. If you gonna mess up a perfectly good swim day least you could do is have some answers. "Let's go in," she say like she got something up her sleeve. Only she don't lead the way. So me and Sugar turn the corner to where the entrance is, but when we get there I kinda hang back. Not that I'm scared, what's there to be afraid of, just a toy store. But I feel funny, shame. But what I got to be shamed about? Got as much right to go in as anybody. But somehow I can't seem to get hold of the door, so

I step away from Sugar to lead. But she hangs back too. And I look at her and she looks at me and this is ridiculous. I mean, damn, I have never ever been shy about doing nothing or going nowhere. But then Mercedes steps up and then Rosie Giraffe and Big Butt crowd in behind and shove, and next thing we all stuffed into the door-way with only Mercedes squeezing past us, smoothing out her jumper and walking right down the aisle. Then the rest of us tumble in like a glued-together jigsaw done all wrong. And people lookin at us. And it's like the time me and Sugar crashed into the Catholic church on a dare. But once we got in there and everything so hushed and holy and the candles and the bowin and the handkerchiefs on all the drooping heads, I just couldn't go through with the plan. Which was for me to run up to the altar and do a tap dance while Sugar played the nose flute and messed around in the holy water. And Sugar kept givin me the elbow. Then later teased me so bad I tied her up in the shower and turned it on and locked her in. And she'd be there till this day if Aunt Gretchen hadn't finally figured I was lyin about the boarder takin a shower.

Same thing in the store. We all walkin on tiptoe and hardly touchin the games and puzzles and things. And I watched Miss Moore who is steady watchin us like she waitin for a sign. Like Mama Drewery watches the sky and sniffs the air and takes note of just how much slant is in the bird formation. Then me and Sugar bump smack into each other, so busy gazing at the toys, specially the sailboat. But we don't laugh and go into our fat-lady bump-stomach routine. We just stare at that price tag. Then Sugar run a finger over the whole boat. And I'm jealous and want to hit her. Maybe not her, but I sure want to punch somebody in the mouth. — the lesson about the value of money / the difference in people—getting to h[?]

"Watcha bring us here for, Miss Moore?"

"You sound angry, Sylvia. Are you mad about something?" Givin me one of them grins like she tellin a grown-up joke that never turns out to be funny. And she's lookin very closely at me like maybe she planning to do my portrait from memory. I'm mad, but I won't give her that satisfaction. So I slouch around the store bein very bored and say, "Let's go." — again she resists

Me and Sugar at the back of the train watchin the tracks whizzin by large then small then getting gobbled up in the dark. I'm thinkin about this tricky toy I saw in the store. A clown that somersaults on a bar then does chin-ups just cause you yank lightly at his leg. Cost $35. I could see me askin my mother for a $35 birthday clown. "You wanna who that costs what?" she'd say, cocking her head to the side to get a better view of the hole in my head. Thirty-five dollars could buy new bunk beds for Junior and Gretchen's boy. Thirty-five dollars and the whole household could go visit Grand-daddy Nelson in the country. Thirty-five dollars would pay for the rent and the piano bill too. Who are these people that spend that much for performing clowns and $1000 for toy sailboats? What kinda work they do and how they live and how come we ain't in on it? Where we are is who we are, Miss Moore always pointin out. But it don't neces-sarily have to be that way, she always adds then waits for somebody to say that poor people have to wake up and demand their share of the pie and don't none of us know what kind of pie she talking about in the first damn place. But she ain't so smart cause I still got her four dollars from the taxi and she sure ain't gettin it. Messin up my day with this shit. Sugar nudges me in my pocket and winks. R little girl level

Miss Moore lines us up in front of the mailbox where we started from, seem like years ago, and I got a headache for thinkin so hard. And we lean all over each other so we can hold up under the draggy-ass lecture she always finishes us off with at the end before we thank her for borin us to tears. But she just looks at us like she readin tea leaves. Finally she say, "Well, what did you think of F.A.O. Schwarz?"

Rosie Giraffe mumbles, "White folks crazy."

45

"I'd like to go there again when I get my birthday money," says Mercedes, and we shove her out the pack so she has to lean on the mailbox by herself.

"I'd like a shower. Tiring day," say Flyboy.

Then Sugar surprises me by sayin, "You know, Miss Moore, I don't think all of us here put together eat in a year what that sailboat costs." And Miss Moore lights up like somebody goosed her. "And?" she say, urging Sugar on. Only I'm standin on her foot so she don't continue.

"Imagine for a minute what kind of society it is in which some people can spend   50
on a toy what it would cost to feed a family of six or seven. What do you think?"

"I think," say Sugar pushing me off her feet like she never done before, cause I whip her ass in a minute, "that this is not much of a democracy if you ask me. Equal chance to pursue happiness means an equal crack at the dough, don't it?" Miss Moore is besides herself and I am disgusted with Sugar's treachery. So I stand on her foot one more time to see if she'll shove me. She shuts up, and Miss Moore looks at me, sorrow-fully I'm thinkin. And somethin weird is goin on, I can feel it in my chest.

"Anybody else learn anything today?" lookin dead at me. I walk away and Sugar has to run to catch up and don't even seem to notice when I shrug her arm off my shoulder.

"Well, we got four dollars anyway," she says.

"Uh hunh."

"We could go to Hascombs and get half a chocolate layer and then go to the Sun-   55
set and still have plenty money for potato chips and ice cream sodas."

"Un hunh."

"Race you to Hascombs," she say.

We start down the block and she gets ahead which is O.K. by me cause I'm going to the West End and then over to the Drive to think this day through. She can run if she want to and even run faster. But ain't nobody gonna beat me at nuthin.

THE RECEPTIVE READER

1. In this story we see the children from uptown through the eyes of one of their own. How does this *point of view* shape the story as a whole? What do we take in of their behavior, their thinking, their sense of humor? Do you recognize a pattern or a type?

2. How does the tough street language the narrator and her friends speak differ from the genteel middle-class language used by other authors? What distinctive features do you recognize? Do you find the language offensive? Why or why not?

3. How is Miss Moore introduced to the reader? How do you feel about her at the beginning? How does her role change in the story? Does your estimate of her change?

4. The story reaches a *turning point* when the group comes to the store. What theme becomes overt at this point? (What is "the lesson" promised in the title?) Does the story get too preachy for you?

5. Where does the story go after the climactic episode in the toy store? How does it *end*? What does the ending do for the story as a whole?

6. What do you think is the relationship between the author and the first-person narrator in the story? (What do you think is the distance between the author as a person and the *persona* speaking in the story?)

THE PERSONAL RESPONSE

People who talk tough may be playing a role. Do you think there is a different per-sonality behind the narrator's public persona?

THE CREATIVE DIMENSION

Write about a situation, real or imagined, in which a central character plays a public role—different from what he or she is when not observed by strangers or outsiders. The central character could be an imaginary third party (as in the Parker story), or *you* could be speaking in the first person as the narrator (as in the Bambara story). Recreate for your readers a manner of behaving, a style of talking. (You may want to try your hand at an episode or vignette in which the punch line is "Ain't nobody gonna beat me at nuthin.")

THE WRITER'S VOICE

When a writer has a distinctive style, we may recognize a passage regardless of the setting, plot, or theme of a particular story. Each writer in this section has a distinctive personal voice. Bret Harte writes in a popular nineteenth-century style, old-fashioned and ornate like a grandfather clock, with grand rhetorical flourishes and frank appeals to emotion. John Cheever writes in an ironic recent "postmodern" style—allusive, detached, wryly amused.

BRET HARTE (1836–1902)

Bret Harte, a native of Albany, New York, was a journalist who had come to California in time for the gold rush and who became nationally famous for his stories about the West. The short story that follows is a classic of American popular literature, and it preserves features of a long-popular nineteenth-century style. Harte is a shrewd observer of human nature, and his humor makes readers chuckle at the shenanigans of both the sober townspeople and a drunkard like Uncle Billy. At the same time, the story caters to the readers' love of **sentimentality,** making them cry both at the undeserved sufferings of the innocent and at unsuspected evidence of goodness in the guilty. Harte's prose is replete with fancy, flowery language (which is, however, often facetiously used). Both the author and his main character love rhetorical flourishes in keeping with a tradition of speech making that often verged on windbag oratory. At times, the author indulges in historical or literary allusions: a "Parthian volley" is like a hail of arrows launched by legendary enemies of the Romans; the English poet Alexander Pope translated the *Iliad,* Homer's epic about the Trojan War, in the eighteenth-century style.

The Outcasts of Poker Flat   1869

As Mr. John Oakhurst, gambler, stepped into the main street of Poker Flat on the morning of the twenty-third of November, 1850, he was conscious of a change in its moral atmosphere since the preceding night. Two or three men, conversing earnestly together, ceased as he approached and exchanged significant glances. There was a Sabbath lull in the air, which, in a settlement unused to Sabbath influences, looked ominous.

Mr. Oakhurst's calm, handsome face betrayed small concern in these indications. Whether he was conscious of any predisposing cause was another question. "I reckon they're after somebody," he reflected; "likely it's me." He returned to his pocket the handkerchief with which he had been whipping away the red dust of Poker Flat from his neat boots, and quietly discharged his mind of any further conjecture.

In point of fact, Poker Flat was "after somebody." It had lately suffered the loss of several thousand dollars, two valuable horses, and a prominent citizen. It was experiencing a spasm of virtuous reactions, quite as lawless and ungovernable as any of the acts that had provoked it. A secret committee had determined to rid the town of all improper persons. This was done permanently in regard to two men who were then hanging from the boughs of a sycamore in the gulch, and temporarily in the banishment of certain other objectionable characters. I regret to say that some of these were ladies. It is but due to the sex, however, to state that their impropriety was professional, and it was only in such easily established standards of evil that Poker Flat ventured to sit in judgment.

Mr. Oakhurst was right in supposing that he was included in this category. A few of the committee had urged hanging him as a possible example and a sure method of reimbursing themselves from his pockets of the sums he had won from them. "It's agin justice," said Jim Wheeler, "to let this yer young man from Roaring Camp—an entire stranger—carry away our money." But a crude sentiment of equity residing in the breasts of those who had been fortunate enough to win from Mr. Oakhurst overruled this narrower local prejudice.

Mr. Oakhurst received his sentence with philosophic calmness, none the less coolly that he was aware of the hesitation of his judges. He was too much of a gambler not to accept fate. With him life was at best an uncertain game, and he recognized the usual percentage in favor of the dealer.

A body of armed men accompanied the deported wickedness of Poker Flat to the outskirts of the settlement. Besides Mr. Oakhurst, who was known to be a coolly desperate man, and for whose intimidation the armed escort was intended, the expatriated party consisted of a young woman familiarly known as "The Duchess"; another who had won the title of "Mother Shipton"; and "Uncle Billy," a suspected sluice robber and confirmed drunkard. The cavalcade provoked no comments from the spectators, nor was any word uttered by the escort. Only when the gulch which marked the uttermost limit of Poker Flat was reached, the leader spoke briefly and to the point. The exiles were forbidden to return at the peril of their lives.

As the escort disappeared, their pent-up feelings found vent in a few hysterical tears from the Duchess, some bad language from Mother Shipton, and a Parthian volley of expletives from Uncle Billy. The philosophic Oakhurst alone remained silent. He listened calmly to Mother Shipton's desire to cut somebody's heart out, to the repeated statements of the Duchess that she would die in the road, and to the alarming oaths that seemed to be bumped out of Uncle Billy as he rode forward. With the easy good humor characteristic of his class, he insisted upon exchanging his own riding horse, "Five-Spot," for the sorry mule which the Duchess rode. But even this act did not draw the party into any closer sympathy. The young woman adjusted her somewhat draggled plumes with a feeble, faded coquetry; Mother Shipton eyed the possessor of Five-Spot with malevolence, and Uncle Billy included the whole party in one sweeping anathema.

The road to Sandy Bar—a camp that, not having as yet experienced the regenerating influences of Poker Flat, consequently seemed to offer some invitation to the emigrants—lay over a steep mountain range. It was distant a day's severe travel. In that advanced season the party soon passed out of the moist, temperate regions of the foothills into the dry, cold, bracing air of the Sierras. The trail was narrow and difficult.

5

At noon the Duchess, rolling out of her saddle upon the ground, declared her intention of going no farther, and the party halted.

The spot was singularly wild and impressive. A wooded amphitheater, surrounded on three sides by precipitous cliffs of naked granite, sloped gently toward the crest of another precipice that overlooked the valley. It was, undoubtedly, the most suitable spot for a camp, had camping been advisable. But Mr. Oakhurst knew that scarcely half the journey to Sandy Bar was accomplished, and the party were not equipped or provisioned for delay. This fact he pointed out to his companions curtly, with a philosophic commentary on the folly of "throwing up their hand before the game was played out." But they were furnished with liquor, which in this emergency stood them in place of food, fuel, rest, and prescience. In spite of his remonstrances, it was not long before they were more or less under its influence. Uncle Billy passed rapidly from a bellicose state into one of stupor, the Duchess became maudlin, and Mother Shipton snored. Mr. Oakhurst alone remained erect, leaning against a rock, calmly surveying them.

Mr. Oakhurst did not drink. It interfered with a profession which required coolness, impassiveness, and presence of mind, and, in his own language, he "couldn't afford it." As he gazed at his recumbent fellow exiles, the loneliness begotten of his pariah trade, his habits of life, his very vices, for the first time seriously oppressed him. He bestirred himself in dusting his black clothes, washing his hands and face, and other acts characteristic of his studiously neat habits, and for a moment forgot his annoyance. The thought of deserting his weaker and more pitiable companions never perhaps occurred to him. Yet he could not help feeling the want of that excitement which, singularly enough, was most conducive to that calm equanimity for which he was notorious. He looked at the gloomy walls that rose a thousand feet sheer above the circling pines around him, at the sky ominously clouded, at the valley below, already deepening into shadow; and, doing so, suddenly he heard his own name called.

A horseman slowly ascended the trail. In the fresh, open face of the newcomer Mr. Oakhurst recognized Tom Simson, otherwise known as "The Innocent," of Sandy Bar. He had met him sometime before over a "little game" and had, with perfect equanimity, won the entire fortune—amounting to some forty dollars—of that guileless youth. After the game was finished, Mr. Oakhurst drew the youthful speculator behind the door and thus addressed him: "Tommy, you're a good little man, but you can't gamble worth a cent. Don't try it over again." He then handed him his money back, pushed him gently from the room, and so made a devoted slave of Tom Simson.

There was a remembrance of this in his boyish and enthusiastic greeting of Mr. Oakhurst. He had started, he said, to go to Poker Flat to seek his fortune. "Alone?" No, not exactly alone; in fact (a giggle), he had run away with Piney Woods. Didn't Mr. Oakhurst remember Piney? She that used to wait on the table at the Temperance House? They had been engaged a long time, but old Jake Woods had objected, and so they had run away, and were going to Poker Flat to be married, and here they were. And they were tired out, and how lucky it was they had found a place to camp, and company. All this the Innocent delivered rapidly, while Piney, a stout, comely damsel of fifteen, emerged from behind the pine tree, where she had been blushing unseen, and rode to the side of her lover.

Mr. Oakhurst seldom troubled himself with sentiment, still less with propriety; but he had a vague idea that the situation was not fortunate. He retained, however, his presence of mind sufficiently to kick Uncle Billy, who was about to say something, and Uncle Billy was sober enough to recognize in Mr. Oakhurst's kick a superior power that would not bear trifling. He then endeavored to dissuade Tom Simson from delaying further, but in vain. He even pointed out the fact that there was no provision, nor

10

means of making a camp. But, unluckily, the Innocent met this objection by assuring the party that he was provided with an extra mule loaded with provisions, and by the discovery of a rude attempt at a log house near the trail. "Piney can stay with Mrs. Oakhurst," said the Innocent, pointing to the Duchess, "and I can shift for myself."

Nothing but Mr. Oakhurst's admonishing foot saved Uncle Billy from bursting into a roar of laughter. As it was, he felt compelled to retire up the canyon until he could recover his gravity. There he confided the joke to the tall pine trees, with many slaps of his leg, contortions of his face, and the usual profanity. But when he returned to the party, he found them seated by a fire—for the air had grown strangely chill and the sky overcast—in apparently amicable conversation. Piney was actually talking in an impulsive girlish fashion to the Duchess, who was listening with an interest and animation she had not shown for many days. The Innocent was holding forth, apparently with equal effect, to Mr. Oakhurst and Mother Shipton, who was actually relaxing into amiability. "Is this yer a d——d picnic?" said Uncle Billy, with inward scorn, as he surveyed the sylvan group, the glancing firelight, and the tethered animals in the foreground. Suddenly an idea mingled with the alcoholic fumes that disturbed his brain. It was apparently of a jocular nature, for he felt impelled to slap his leg again and cram his fist into his mouth.

As the shadows crept slowly up the mountain, a slight breeze rocked the tops of the pine trees and moaned through their long and gloomy aisles. The ruined cabin, patched and covered with pine boughs, was set apart for the ladies. As the lovers parted, they unaffectedly exchanged a kiss, so honest and sincere that it might have been heard above the swaying pines. The frail Duchess and the malevolent Mother Shipton were probably too stunned to remark upon this last evidence of simplicity, and so turned without a word to the hut. The fire was replenished, the men lay down before the door, and in a few minutes were asleep. 15

Mr. Oakhurst was a light sleeper. Toward morning he awoke benumbed and cold. As he stirred the dying fire, the wind, which was now blowing strongly, brought to his cheek that which caused the blood to leave it—snow!

He started to his feet with the intention of awakening the sleepers, for there was no time to lose. But, turning to where Uncle Billy had been lying, he found him gone. A suspicion leaped to his brain, and a curse to his lips. He ran to the spot where the mules had been tethered—they were no longer there. The tracks were already rapidly disappearing in the snow.

The momentary excitement brought Mr. Oakhurst back to the fire with his usual calm. He did not waken the sleepers. The Innocent slumbered peacefully, with a smile on his good-humored, freckled face; the virgin Piney slept beside her frailer sisters as sweetly as though attended by celestial guardians; and Mr. Oakhurst, drawing his blanket over his shoulders, stroked his mustaches and waited for the dawn. It came slowly in a whirly mist of snowflakes that dazzled and confused the eye. What could be seen of the landscape appeared magically changed. He looked over the valley and summed up the present and future in two words, "Snowed in!"

A careful inventory of the provisions, which, fortunately for the party, had been stored within the hut, and so escaped the felonious fingers of Uncle Billy, disclosed the fact that with care and prudence, they might last ten days longer. "That is," said Mr. Oakhurst *sotto voce* to the Innocent, "if you're willing to board us. If you ain't—and perhaps you'd better not—you can wait till Uncle Billy gets back with provisions." For some occult reason, Mr. Oakhurst could not bring himself to disclose Uncle Billy's rascality, and so offered the hypothesis that he had wandered from the camp and had accidentally stampeded the animals. He dropped a warning to the Duchess and Mother Shipton, who of course knew the facts of their associate's defection. "They'll find out the truth about us *all* when they find out anything," he added significantly, "and there's no good frightening them now."

Tom Simson not only put all his worldly store at the disposal of Mr. Oakhurst, but seemed to enjoy the prospect of their enforced seclusion. "We'll have a good camp for a week, and then the snow'll melt, and we'll all go back together." The cheerful gaiety of the young man and Mr. Oakhurst's calm infected the others. The Innocent, with the aid of pine boughs, extemporized a thatch for the roofless cabin, and the Duchess directed Piney in the rearrangement of the interior with a taste and tact that opened the blue eyes of that provincial maiden to their fullest extent. "I reckon now you're used to fine things at Poker Flat," said Piney. The Duchess turned away sharply to conceal something that reddened her cheeks through their professional tint, and Mother Shipton requested Piney not to "chatter." But when Mr. Oakhurst returned from a weary search for the trail, he heard the sound of happy laughter echoed from the rocks. He stopped in some alarm, and his thoughts first naturally reverted to the whisky, which he had prudently cached. "And yet it don't somehow sound like whisky," said the gambler. It was not until he caught sight of the blazing fire through the still blind storm, and the group around it, that he settled to the conviction that it was "square fun."

Whether Mr. Oakhurst had cached his cards with the whisky as something debarred the free access of the community, I cannot say. It was certain that, in Mother Shipton's words, he "didn't say 'cards' once" during that evening. Haply the time was beguiled by an accordion, produced somewhat ostentatiously by Tom Simson from his pack. Notwithstanding some difficulties attending the manipulation of this instrument, Piney Woods managed to pluck several reluctant melodies from its keys, to an accompaniment by the Innocent on a pair of bone castanets. But the crowning festivity of the evening was reached in a rude camp-meeting hymn, which the lovers, joining hands, sang with great earnestness and vociferation. I fear that a certain defiant tone and Covenanters' swing to its chorus, rather than any devotional quality, caused it speedily to infect the others, who at last joined in the refrain:

> "I'm proud to live in the service of the Lord,
> And I'm bound to die in His army."

The pines rocked, the storm eddied and whirled above the miserable group, and the flames of their altar leaped heavenward, as if in token of the vow.

At midnight the storm abated, the rolling clouds parted, and the stars glittered keenly above the sleeping camp. Mr. Oakhurst, whose professional habits had enabled him to live on the smallest possible amount of sleep, in dividing the watch with Tom Simson, somehow managed to take upon himself the greater part of that duty. He excused himself to the Innocent by saying that he had "often been a week without sleep." "Doing what?" asked Tom. "Poker!" replied Oakhurst sententiously. "When a man gets a streak of luck, he don't get tired. The luck gives in first. Luck," continued the gambler reflectively, "is a mighty queer thing. All you know about it for certain is that it's bound to change. And it's finding out when it's going to change that makes you. We've had a streak of bad luck since we left Poker Flat—you come along, and slap, you get into it, too. If you can hold your cards right along, you're all right. For," added the gambler, with cheerful irrelevance,

20

"I'm proud to live in the service of the Lord,
And I'm bound to die in His army."

The third day came, and the sun, looking through the white-curtained valley, saw the outcasts dividing their slowly decreasing store of provisions for the morning meal. It was one of the peculiarities of that mountain climate that its rays diffused a kindly warmth over the wintry landscape, as if in regretful commiseration of the past. But it revealed drift on drift of snow piled high around the hut—a hopeless, uncharted, trackless sea of white lying below the rocky shores to which the castaways still clung. Through the marvelously clear air the smoke of the pastoral village of Poker Flat rose miles away. Mother Shipton saw it and, from a remote pinnacle of her rocky fastness, hurled in that direction a final malediction. It was her last vituperative attempt and, perhaps for that reason, was invested with a certain degree of sublimity. It did her good, she privately informed the Duchess. "Just you go out there and cuss, and see." She then set herself to the task of amusing "the child," as she and the Duchess were pleased to call Piney. Piney was no chicken, but it was a soothing and original theory of the pair thus to account for the fact that she didn't swear and wasn't improper.

When night crept up again through the gorges, the reedy notes of the accordion rose and fell in fitful spasms and long-drawn gasps by the flickering campfire. But music failed to fill entirely the aching void left by insufficient food, and a new diversion was proposed by Piney—storytelling. Neither Mr. Oakhurst nor his female companions caring to relate their personal experiences, this plan would have failed too, but for the Innocent. Some months before he had chanced upon a stray copy of Mr. Pope's ingenious translation of the *Iliad*. He now proposed to narrate the principal incidents of that poem— having thoroughly mastered the argument and fairly forgotten the words—in the current vernacular of Sandy Bar. And so, for the rest of that night, the Homeric demigods again walked the earth. Trojan bully and wily Greek wrestled in the winds, and the great pines in the canyon seemed to bow to the wrath of the son of Peleus. Mr. Oakhurst listened with great satisfaction. Most especially was he interested in the fate of "Ashheels," as the Innocent persisted in denominating the "swift-footed Achilles."

So, with small food and much of Homer and the accordion, a week passed over the heads of the outcasts. The sun again forsook them, and again from leaden skies the snowflakes were sifted over the land. Day by day closer around them drew the snowy circle, until at last they looked from their prison over drifted walls of dazzling white that towered twenty feet above their heads. It became more and more difficult to replenish their fires, even from the fallen trees beside them, now half-hidden in the drifts. And yet no one complained. The lovers turned from the dreary prospect and looked into each other's eyes, and were happy. Mr. Oakhurst settled himself coolly to the losing game before him. The Duchess, more cheerful than she had been, assumed the care of Piney. Only Mother Shipton—once the strongest of the party—seemed to sicken and fade. At midnight on the tenth day, she called Oakhurst to her side. "I'm going," she said, in a voice of querulous weakness, "but don't say anything about it. Don't waken the kids. Take the bundle from under my head, and open it." Mr. Oakhurst did so. It contained Mother Shipton's rations for the last week, untouched. "Give 'em to the child," she said, pointing to the sleeping Piney. "You've starved yourself," said the gambler. "That's what they call it," said the woman querulously, as she lay down again and, turning her face to the wall, passed quietly away.

The accordion and the bones were put aside that day, and Homer was forgotten. When the body of Mother Shipton had been committed to the snow, Mr. Oakhurst took the Innocent aside and showed him a pair of snowshoes, which he had fashioned from the old packsaddle. "There's one chance in a hundred to save her yet," he said, pointing to Piney: "but it's there," he added, pointing toward Poker Flat. "If you can reach there in two days, she's safe." "And you?" asked Tom Simson. "I'll stay here," was the curt reply.

The lovers parted with a long embrace. "You are not going, too?" said the Duchess, as she saw Mr. Oakhurst apparently waiting to accompany him. "As far as the canyon," he replied. He turned suddenly and kissed the Duchess, leaving her pallid face aflame and her trembling limbs rigid with amazement.

Night came, but not Mr. Oakhurst. It brought the storm again and the whirling snow. Then the Duchess, feeding the fire, found someone had quietly piled beside the hut enough fuel to last a few days longer. The tears rose to her eyes, but she hid them from Piney.

The women slept but little. In the morning, looking into each other's faces, they read their fate. Neither spoke, but Piney, accepting the position of the stronger, drew near and placed her arm around the Duchess's waist. They kept this attitude for the rest of the day. That night the storm reached its greatest fury and, rending asunder the protecting vines, invaded the very hut.

Toward morning they found themselves unable to feed the fire, which gradually died away. As the embers slowly blackened, the Duchess crept closer to Piney and broke the silence of many hours: "Piney, can you pray?" "No, dear," said Piney simply. The Duchess, without knowing exactly why, felt relieved and, putting her head upon Piney's shoulder, spoke no more. And so reclining, the younger and purer pillowing the head of her soiled sister upon her virgin breast, they fell asleep. 30

The wind lulled as if it feared to waken them. Feathery drifts of snow, shaken from the long pine boughs, flew like white-winged birds and settled about them as they slept. The moon through the rifted clouds looked down upon what had been the camp. But all human stain, all trace of earthly travail, was hidden beneath the spotless mantle mercifully flung from above.

They slept all that day and the next, nor did they waken when voices and footsteps broke the silence of the camp. And when pitying fingers brushed the snow from their wan faces, you could scarcely have told from the equal peace that dwelt upon them which was she that had sinned. Even the law of Poker Flat recognized this and turned away, leaving them still locked in each other's arms.

But at the head of the gulch, on one of the largest pine trees, they found the deuce of clubs pinned to the bark with a bowie knife. It bore the following, written in pencil in a firm hand:

BENEATH THIS TREE
LIES THE BODY
OF
JOHN OAKHURST,
WHO STRUCK A STREAK OF BAD LUCK
ON THE 23D OF NOVEMBER, 1850,
AND
HANDED IN HIS CHECKS
ON THE 7TH DECEMBER, 1850.

And pulseless and cold, with a Derringer by his side and a bullet in his heart, though still calm as in life, beneath the snow lay he who was at once the strongest and yet the weakest of the outcasts of Poker Flat.

THE RECEPTIVE READER

1. Study examples of *formal* word choice, or diction, in the first three paragraphs of the story. What makes Harte's vocabulary more elevated, more dignified, than ordinary informal speech? What would be informal equivalents of some striking formal expressions? ✧ Why does some of the elevated, dignified diction here have a humorous effect? What are striking examples of *euphemisms*—roundabout innocuous-sounding phrases that disguise harsh realities?

2. Bret Harte was one of the writers creating the mystique of the American West that gave people cooped up in cities a larger scope for their imagination. What features of the setting and of the plot do you recognize as part of the Western *genre*?

3. What are telling touches in Harte's *satirical portrait* of the moral majority in Poker Flat? How and how successfully does Harte steer your reactions?

4. What types do you recognize among Harte's ill-assorted cast of characters? How does Mother Shipton fit the *stereotype* of the prostitute with a heart of gold? What stereotype does the young couple live up to? What other examples are there of the sentimental stereotype that there is some good in everyone? ✧ What is the role of Uncle Billy in the story?

5. What is the gambler's style? What is his role in the story? Do you find his actions surprising or predictable?

6. What is distinctive about the final sentence of the story? How would it read if you were to break it up into Hemingway sentences?

THE PERSONAL RESPONSE

How obsolete is Harte's brand of sentimentality? Do any features of it survive in current popular entertainment? Why do you think modern critics have made sentimentality a prime target? Do you agree with them? Or can something be said in its defense?

JOHN CHEEVER (1912–1982)

Fiction is art and art is the triumph over chaos (no less) and we can accomplish this only by the most vigilant exercise of choice, but in a world that changes more swiftly than we can perceive there is always the danger that our powers of selection will be mistaken and that the vision we serve will come to nothing.

JOHN CHEEVER

John Cheever was born in Quincy, Massachusetts, and was expelled from a private New England academy at seventeen. He returned to academic life only for brief stints teaching at Barnard and in the prestigious creative writing program at the University of Iowa. (He also received an honorary doctorate from Harvard in 1978.) He was much honored—receiving a Guggenheim, a National Book Award, a Pulitzer Prize.

Cheever is among the outstanding practitioners of the modern short story for whom the *New Yorker* provided an ideal outlet. (The magazine published more than two hundred of his stories.) His fiction seemed well attuned to the self-image of the mythical sophisticated *New Yorker* reader—who has a taste for the uncommon and a tolerance for human eccentricity, who has the appropriate liberal political sympathies but has a horror of sensationalism and popular enthusiasm. A key to Cheever's style is irony—the witty exposure of the discrepancy between what people should be and what they are. His stories often reach a turning point where the sunny, reassuring surface wears thin and a chilling note is heard, similar to "that hour of a spring day. . . when the dark of the woods and the cold and damp from any nearby pond or brook are suddenly felt, when you realize that the world was lighted, until a minute ago . . . and that your clothes are thin" ("Just Tell Me Who It Was").

Cheever often seems to look at his characters with wry amusement from without—rather than getting embroiled in their inner turmoil, sharing in their confusions and frustrations. His own journals, published after his death, and a book by his daughter probing her parents' unhappy marriage (*Home before Dark*, 1984) have given readers a glimpse of the writer's own traumas, which he masked by the defensive armor of his witty, ironic style. His son, Benjamin Cheever, said about him, "He showed the world what he thought it wanted to see. The picture he presented was sharp, witty, cogent, and often false." Many of Cheever's journal entries focus on his gay life-style (which he calls his "contested sexuality") and his struggles with alcoholism. He wrote early in his journal, "I come back again and again to the image of a naked prisoner in an unlocked cell, and to tell the truth I don't know how he will escape."

Cheever's "The Enormous Radio" revolves around strange fragmentary messages heard on a radio. The story is thus an ideal vehicle for the kind of **allusion** and name-dropping that became fashionable as part of a late-twentieth-century (postmodern) style. An allusion is a brief mention that activates our memory. It brings to mind a range of associations; it makes us recall a story. When we first read about the upwardly mobile couple in this story, we are expected to recognize that Andover is a tony private boarding school on the New England preppie circuit (the husband is an alumnus). Westchester (where the couple eventually hope to live) is a suburban sanctuary for well-shod commuters to New York City. The couple love classical composers like Mozart, Schubert, and Chopin—great composers, but part of a safe repertory (often too much with us?) that avoids the challenges of a Bach or a Stravinsky.

The Enormous Radio 1947

Jim and Irene Westcott were the kind of people who seem to strike that satisfactory average of income, endeavor, and respectability that is reached by the statistical reports in college alumni bulletins. They were the parents of two young children, they had been married nine years, they lived on the twelfth floor of an apartment house near Sutton Place, they went to the theatre on an average of 10.3 times a year, and they hoped someday to live in Westchester. Irene Westcott was a pleasant, rather plain girl with soft brown hair and a wide, fine forehead upon which nothing at all had been written, and in the cold weather she wore a coat of fitch skins dyed to resemble mink. You could not say that Jim Westcott looked younger than he was, but you could at least say of him that he seemed to feel younger. He wore his graying hair cut very short, he dressed in the kind of clothes his class had worn at Andover, and his manner was earnest, vehement, and intentionally naïve. The Westcotts differed from their friends, their classmates, and their neighbors only in an interest they shared in serious music. They went to a great many concerts—although they seldom mentioned this to anyone—and they spent a good deal of time listening to music on the radio.

Their radio was an old instrument, sensitive, unpredictable, and beyond repair. Neither of them understood the mechanics of radio—or of any of the other appliances that surrounded them—and when the instrument faltered, Jim would strike the side of the cabinet with his hand. This sometimes helped. One Sunday afternoon, in the middle of a Schubert quartet, the music faded away altogether. Jim struck the cabinet repeatedly, but there was no response; the Schubert was lost to them forever. He promised to buy Irene a new radio, and on Monday when he came home from work he told her that he had got one. He refused to describe it, and said it would be a surprise for her when it came.

The radio was delivered at the kitchen door the following afternoon, and with the assistance of her maid and the handyman Irene uncrated it and brought it into the living room. She was struck at once with the physical ugliness of the large gumwood cabinet. Irene was proud of her living room, she had chosen its furnishings and colors as carefully as she chose her clothes, and now it seemed to her that the new radio stood among her intimate possessions like an aggressive intruder. She was confounded by the number of dials and switches on the instrument panel, and she studied them thoroughly before she put the plug into a wall socket and turned the radio on. The dials flooded with a malevolent green light, and in the distance she heard the music of a piano quintet. The quintet was in the distance for only an instant; it bore down upon her with a speed greater than light and filled the apartment with the noise of music amplified so mightily that it knocked a china ornament from a table to the floor. She rushed to the instrument and reduced the volume. The violent forces that were snared in the ugly gumwood cabinet made her uneasy. Her children came home from school then, and she took them to the Park. It was not until later in the afternoon that she was able to return to the radio.

The maid had given the children their suppers and was supervising their baths when Irene turned on the radio, reduced the volume, and sat down to listen to a Mozart quintet that she knew and enjoyed. The music came through clearly. The new instrument had a much purer tone, she thought, than the old one. She decided that tone was most important and that she could conceal the cabinet behind a sofa. But as soon as she had made her peace with the radio, the interference began. A crackling sound like the noise of a burning powder fuse began to accompany the singing of the strings. Beyond the music, there was a rustling that reminded Irene unpleasantly of the sea, and as the quintet progressed, these noises were joined by many others. She tried all the dials and switches but nothing dimmed the interference, and she sat down, disappointed and bewildered, and tried to trace the flight of the melody. The elevator shaft in her building ran beside the living-room wall, and it was the noise of the elevator that gave her a clue to the character of the static. The rattling of the elevator cables and the opening and closing of the elevator doors were reproduced in her loudspeaker, and, realizing that the radio was sensitive to electrical currents of all sorts, she began to discern through the Mozart the ringing of telephone bells, the dialing of phones, and the lamentation of a vacuum cleaner. By listening more carefully, she was able to distinguish doorbells, elevator bells, electric razors, and Waring mixers, whose sounds had been picked up from the apartments that surrounded hers and transmitted through her loudspeaker. The powerful and ugly instrument, with its mistaken sensitivity to discord, was more than she could hope to master, so she turned the thing off and went into the nursery to see her children.

When Jim Westcott came home that night, he went to the radio confidently and worked the controls. He had the same sort of experience Irene had had. A man was speaking on the station Jim had chosen, and his voice swung instantly from the distance into a force so powerful that it shook the apartment. Jim turned the volume control and reduced the voice. Then, a minute or two later, the interference began. The ringing of telephones and doorbells set in, joined by the rasp of the elevator doors and the whir of cooking appliances. The character of the noise had changed since Irene had tried the radio earlier; the last of the electric razors was being unplugged, the vacuum cleaners had all been returned to their closets, and the static reflected that change in pace that overtakes the city after the sun goes down. He fiddled with the knobs but couldn't get rid of the noises, so he turned the radio off and told Irene that in the morning he'd call the people who had sold it to him and give them hell.

The following afternoon, when Irene returned to the apartment from a luncheon date, the maid told her that a man had come and fixed the radio. Irene went into the living room before she took off her hat or her furs and tried the instrument. From the loudspeaker came a recording of the "Missouri Waltz." It reminded her of the thin, scratchy music from an old-fashioned phonograph that she sometimes heard across the lake where she spent her summers. She waited until the waltz had finished, expecting an explanation of the recording, but there was none. The music was followed by silence, and then the plaintive and scratchy record was repeated. She turned the dial and got a satisfactory burst of Caucasian music—the thump of bare feet in the dust and the rattle of coin jewelry—but in the background she could hear the ringing of bells and a confusion of voices. Her children came home from school then, and she turned off the radio and went to the nursery.

When Jim came home that night, he was tired, and he took a bath and changed his clothes. Then he joined Irene in the living room. He had just turned on the radio when the maid announced dinner, so he left it on, and he and Irene went to the table.

Jim was too tired to make even pretense of sociability, and there was nothing about the dinner to hold Irene's interest, so her attention wandered from the food to the deposits of silver polish on the candlesticks and from there to the music in the other room. She listened for a few minutes to a Chopin prelude and then was surprised to hear a man's voice break in. "For Christ's sake, Kathy," he said, "do you always have to play the piano when I get home?" The music stopped abruptly. "It's the only chance I have," a woman said. "I'm at the office all day." "So am I," the man said. He added something obscene about an upright piano, and slammed a door. The passionate and melancholy music began again.

"Did you hear that?" Irene asked.

"What?" Jim was eating his dessert.

"The radio. A man said something while the music was still going on—something dirty."

"It's probably a play."

"I don't think it *is* a play," Irene said.

They left the table and took their coffee into the living room. Irene asked Jim to try another station. He turned the knob. "Have you seen my garters?" a man asked. "Button me up," a woman said. "Have you seen my garters?" the man said again. "Just button me up and I'll find your garters," the woman said. Jim shifted to another station. "I wish you wouldn't leave apple cores in the ashtrays," a man said. "I hate the smell."

"This is strange," Jim said.

"Isn't it?" Irene said.

Jim turned the knob again. "'On the coast of Coromandel where the early pumpkins blow,'" a woman with a pronounced English accent said, "'in the middle of the woods lived the Yonghy-Bonghy-Bò. Two old chairs, and half a candle, one old jug without a handle . . .'"

"My God!" Irene cried. "That's the Sweeneys' nurse."

"'These were all his worldly goods,'" the British voice continued.

"Turn that thing off," Irene said. "Maybe they can hear *us*." Jim switched the radio off. "That was Miss Armstrong, the Sweeneys' nurse," Irene said. "She must be reading to the little girl. They live in 17-B. I've talked with Miss Armstrong in the Park. I know her voice very well. We must be getting other people's apartments." 20

"That's impossible," Jim said.

"Well, that was the Sweeneys' nurse," Irene said hotly. "I know her voice. I know it very well. I'm wondering if they can hear us."

Jim turned the switch. First from a distance and then nearer, nearer, as if borne on the wind, came the pure accents of the Sweeneys' nurse again: "*Lady Jingly! Lady Jingly!*" she said, "*sitting where the pumpkins blow, will you come and be my wife? said the* Yonghy-Bonghy-Bò . . .'"

Jim went over to the radio and said "Hello" loudly into the speaker.

"*'I am tired of living singly,'*" the nurse went on, "*'on this coast so wild and shingly, I'm a-weary of my life; if you'll come and be my wife, quite serene would be my life . . .'*" 25

"I guess she can't hear us," Irene said. "Try something else."

Jim turned to another station, and the living room was filled with the uproar of a cocktail party that had overshot its mark. Someone was playing the piano and singing the "Whiffenpoof Song," and the voices that surrounded the piano were vehement and happy. "Eat some more sandwiches," a woman shrieked. There were screams of laughter and a dish of some sort crashed to the floor.

"Those must be the Fullers, in 11-E," Irene said. "I knew they were giving a party this afternoon. I saw her in the liquor store. Isn't this too divine? Try something else. See if you can get those people in 18-C."

The Westcotts overheard that evening a monologue on salmon fishing in Canada, a bridge game, running comments on home movies of what had apparently been a fortnight at Sea Island, and a bitter family quarrel about an overdraft at the bank. They turned off their radio at midnight and went to bed, weak with laughter. Sometime in the night, their son began to call for a glass of water and Irene got one and took it to his room. It was very early. All the lights in the neighborhood were extinguished, and from the boy's window she could see the empty street. She went into the living room and tried the radio. There was some faint coughing, a moan, and then a man spoke. "Are you all right, darling?" he asked. "Yes," a woman said wearily. "Yes, I'm all right, I guess," and then she added with great feeling, "But, you know, Charlie, I don't feel like myself anymore. Sometimes there are about fifteen or twenty minutes in the week when I feel like myself. I don't like to go to another doctor, because the doctor's bills are so awful already, but I just don't feel like myself, Charlie. I just never feel like myself." They were not young, Irene thought. She guessed from the timbre of their voices that they were middle-aged. The restrained melancholy of the dialogue and the draft from the bedroom window made her shiver, and she went back to bed.

The following morning, Irene cooked breakfast for the family—the maid didn't come up from her room in the basement until ten—braided her daughter's hair, and waited at the door until her children and her husband had been carried away in the elevator. Then she went into the living room and tried the radio. "I don't want to go to school," a child screamed. "I hate school. I won't go to school. I hate school." "You will 30 go to school," an enraged woman said. "We paid eight hundred dollars to get you into that school and you'll go if it kills you." The next number on the dial produced the worn record of the "Missouri Waltz." Irene shifted the control and invaded the privacy of several breakfast tables. She overheard demonstrations of indigestion, carnal love, abysmal vanity, faith, and despair. Irene's life was nearly as simple and sheltered as it appeared to be, and the forthright and sometimes brutal language that came from the loudspeaker that morning astonished and troubled her. She continued to listen until her maid came in. Then she turned off the radio quickly, since this insight, she realized, was a furtive one.

Irene had a luncheon date with a friend that day, and she left her apartment at a little after twelve. There were a number of women in the elevator when it stopped at her floor. She stared at their handsome and impassive faces, their furs, and the cloth flowers in their hats. Which one of them had been to Sea Island? she wondered. Which one had overdrawn her bank account. The elevator stopped at the tenth floor and a woman with a pair of Skye terriers joined them. Her hair was rigged high on her head and she wore a mink cape. She was humming the "Missouri Waltz."

Irene had two Martinis at lunch, and she looked searchingly at her friend and wondered what her secrets were. They had intended to go shopping after lunch, but Irene excused herself and went home. She told the maid that she was not to be disturbed; then she went into the living room, closed the doors, and switched on the radio. She heard, in the course of the afternoon, the halting conversation of a woman entertaining her aunt, the hysterical conclusion of a luncheon party, and a hostess briefing her maid about some cocktail guests. "Don't give the best Scotch to anyone who hasn't white hair," the hostess said. "See if you can get rid of that liver paste before you pass those hot things, and could you lend me five dollars? I want to tip the elevator man."

As the afternoon waned, the conversations increased in intensity. From where Irene sat, she could see the open sky above the East River. There were hundreds of clouds in the sky, as though the south wind had broken the winter into pieces and were blowing it north, and on her radio she could hear the arrival of cocktail guests and the return of children and businessmen from their schools and offices. "I found a good-sized diamond on the bathroom floor this morning," a woman said. "It must have fallen out of that bracelet Mrs. Dunston was wearing last night." "We'll sell it," a man said. "Take it down to the jeweler on Madison Avenue and sell it. Mrs. Dunston won't know the difference, and we could use a couple of hundred bucks . . ." "'Oranges and lemons, say the bells of St. Clement's,'" the Sweeneys' nurse sang. "'Halfpence and farthings, say the bells of St. Martin's. When will you pay me? say the bells at old Bailey . . .'" "It's not a hat," a woman cried, and at her back roared a cocktail party. "It's not a hat, it's a love affair. That's what Walter Florell said. He said it's not a hat, it's a love affair," and then, in a lower voice, the same woman added, "Talk to somebody, for Christ's sake, honey, talk to somebody. If she catches you standing here not talking to anybody, she'll take us off her invitation list, and I love these parties."

The Westcotts were going out for dinner that night, and when Jim came home, Irene was dressing. She seemed sad and vague, and he brought her a drink. They were dining with friends in the neighborhood, and they walked to where they were going. The sky was broad and filled with light. It was one of those splendid spring evenings that excite memory and desire, and the air that touched their hands and faces felt very soft. A Salvation Army band was on the corner playing "Jesus Is Sweeter." Irene drew on her husband's arm and held him there for a minute, to hear the music. "They're really such nice people, aren't they?" she said. "They have such nice faces. Actually, they're so much nicer than a lot of the people we know." She took a bill from her purse and walked over and dropped it into the tambourine. There was in her face, when she returned to her husband, a look of radiant melancholy that he was not familiar with. And her conduct at the dinner party that night seemed strange to him, too. She interrupted her hostess rudely and stared at the people across the table from her with an intensity for which she would have punished her children.

It was still mild when they walked home from the party, and Irene looked up at the spring stars. "'How far that little candle throws its beams,'" she exclaimed. "'So shines a good deed in a naughty world.'" She waited that night until Jim had fallen asleep, and then went into the living room and turned on the radio. 35

Jim came home at about six the next night. Emma, the maid, let him in, and he had taken off his hat and was taking off his coat when Irene ran into the hall. Her face was shining with tears and her hair was disordered. "Go up to 16-C, Jim!" she screamed. "Don't take off your coat. Go up to 16-C. Mr. Osborn's beating his wife. They've been quarreling since four o'clock, and now he's hitting her. Go up there and stop him."

From the radio in the living room, Jim heards screams, obscenities, and thuds. "You know you don't have to listen to this sort of thing," he said. He strode into the living room and turned the switch. "It's indecent," he said. "It's like looking in windows. You know you don't have to listen to this sort of thing. You can turn it off."

"Oh, it's so horrible, it's so dreadful," Irene was sobbing. "I've been listening all day, and it's so depressing."

"Well, if it's so depressing, why do you listen to it? I bought this damned radio to give you some pleasure," he said. "I paid a great deal of money for it. I thought it might make you happy. I wanted to make you happy."

"Don't, don't, don't, don't quarrel with me," she moaned, and laid her head on his shoulder. "All the others have been quarreling all day. Everybody's been quarreling. They're all worried about money. Mrs. Hutchinson's mother is dying of cancer in Florida and they don't have enough money to send her to the Mayo Clinic. At least, Mr. Hutchinson says they don't have enough money. And some woman in this building is having an affair with the handyman—with that hideous handyman. It's too disgusting. And Mrs. Melville has heart trouble, and Mr. Hendricks is going to lose his job in April and Mrs. Hendricks is horrid about the whole thing and that girl who plays the 'Missouri Waltz' is a whore, a common whore, and the elevator man has tuberculosis and Mr. Osborn has been beating Mrs. Osborn." She wailed, she trembled with grief and checked the stream of tears down her face with the heel of her palm. 40

"Well, why do you have to listen?" Jim asked again. "Why do you have to listen to this stuff if it makes you so miserable?"

"Oh, don't, don't, don't," she cried. "Life is too terrible, too sordid and awful. But we've never been like that, have we, darling? Have we? I mean, we've always been good and decent and loving to one another, haven't we? And we have two children, two beautiful children. Our lives aren't sordid, are they, darling? Are they?" She flung her arms around his neck and drew his face down to hers. "We're happy, aren't we, darling? We are happy, aren't we?"

"Of course we're happy," he said tiredly. He began to surrender his resentment. "Of course we're happy. I'll have that damned radio fixed or taken away tomorrow." He stroked her soft hair. "My poor girl," he said.

"You love me, don't you?" she asked. "And we're not hypercritical or worried about money or dishonest, are we?"

"No, darling," he said.

A man came in the morning and fixed the radio. Irene turned it on cautiously and was happy to hear a California-wine commercial and a recording of Beethoven's Ninth 45

Symphony, including Schiller's "Ode to Joy." She kept the radio on all day and nothing untoward came from the speaker.

A Spanish suite was being played when Jim came home. "Is everything all right?" he asked. His face was pale, she thought. They had some cocktails and went in to dinner to the "Anvil Chorus" from *Il Trovatore*. This was followed by Debussy's "La Mer."

"I paid the bill for the radio today," Jim said. "It cost four hundred dollars. I hope you'll get some enjoyment out of it."

"Oh, I'm sure I will," Irene said.

"Four hundred dollars is a good deal more than I can afford," he went on. "I wanted to get something that you'd enjoy. It's the last extravagance we'll be able to indulge in this year. I see that you haven't paid your clothing bills yet. I saw them on your dressing table." He looked directly at her. "Why did you tell me you'd paid them? Why did you lie to me?" 50

"I just didn't want you to worry, Jim," she said. She drank some water. "I'll be able to pay my bills out of this month's allowance. There were the slipcovers last month, and that party."

"You've got to learn to handle the money I give you a little more intelligently, Irene," he said. "You've got to understand that we don't have as much money this year as we had last. I had a very sobering talk with Mitchell today. No one is buying anything. We're spending all our time promoting new issues, and you know how long that takes. I'm not getting any younger, you know. I'm thirty-seven. My hair will be gray next year. I haven't done as well as I'd hoped to do. And I don't suppose things will get any better."

"Yes, dear," she said.

"We've got to start cutting down," Jim said. "We've got to think of the children. To be perfectly frank with you, I worry about money a great deal. I'm not at all sure of the future. No one is. If anything should happen to me, there's the insurance, but that wouldn't go very far today. I've worked awfully hard to give you and the children a comfortable life," he said bitterly. "I don't like to see all my energies, all of my youth, wasted in fur coats and radios and slipcovers and—"

"Please, Jim," she said. "Please. They'll hear us." 55

"*Who'll hear us?* Emma can't hear us."

"The radio."

"Oh, I'm sick!" he shouted. "I'm sick to death of your apprehensiveness. The radio can't hear us. Nobody can hear us. And what if they can hear us? Who cares?"

Irene got up from the table and went into the living room. Jim went to the door and shouted at her from there. "Why are you so Christly all of a sudden? What's turned you overnight into a convent girl? You stole your mother's jewelry before they probated her will. You never gave your sister a cent of that money that was intended for her— not even when she needed it. You made Grace Howland's life miserable, and where was all your piety and your virtue when you went to that abortionist? I'll never forget how cool you were. You packed your bag and went off to have that child murdered as if you were going to Nassau. If you'd had any reasons, if you'd had any good reasons—"

Irene stood for a minute before the hideous cabinet, disgraced and sickened, but she held her hand on the switch before she extinguished the music and the voices, hoping that the instrument might speak to her kindly, that she might hear the Sweeneys' nurse. Jim continued to shout at her from the door. The voice on the radio was suave and noncommital. "An early-morning railroad disaster in Tokyo," the loudspeaker said, "killed twenty-nine people. A fire in a Catholic hospital near Buffalo for the care of 60 blind children was extinguished early this morning by nuns. The temperature is forty-seven. The humidity is eighty-nine."

THE RECEPTIVE READER

1. What is the *keynote* in Cheever's description of his suburban couple? What are telling details? What is his attitude toward these people—how does it show?

2. Is there a *pattern*—a thread that connects the snatches of conversation or the fragments of people's lives that are heard on the strange radio?

3. On the subject of *allusions:* What is funny about the Whiffenpoof Song picked up by the radio being a college drinking song, or about the Missouri Waltz being a sentimental favorite that President Truman used to play on the piano? ✦ The snatches of humorous verse read by the "woman with the pronounced English accent" are from the work of Edward Lear, a cherished author of nonsense verse and a contemporary and kindred spirit of Lewis Carroll, the author of *Alice in Wonderland*. What touch do they lend to the story?

4. What has happened to the couple at the end? Why is what has happened to them *ironic* in the light of how the author described them at the beginning?

THE PERSONAL RESPONSE

For you, is the story as a whole amusing or serious, or both?

WRITING ABOUT LITERATURE

8. Responding to Style (Prewriting to Finished Paper)

The Writing Workshop   Writing about an author's style requires you to pay close attention to word choice, sentence rhythms, key images, ways of expressing (or suppressing) emotion. However, as you read closely for detail, try to see how features of style serve the larger purposes of a story. When you write about style, you confront in especially urgent and hard-to-miss form a need that you also face with many other writing tasks: You need to start with close attention to detail—and to stay close to detail—but you have to go on to sort out and lay out your material in a pattern that makes sense.

From Prewriting to First Draft

Do you ever suffer from writer's block? Do you find yourself staring at a blank screen or blank sheet of paper? Go through some of the steps that other writers use to start the flow. Draw on the different prewriting techniques that help a substantial, purposeful paper take shape.

Brainstorming   Brainstorming allows you to bring up from hidden corners of your memory material that might prove relevant to your topic. Let us assume you are going to write about Bret Harte's "The Outcasts of Poker Flat" as an example of the sentimentality that is a staple of American popular culture. Try to call up and jot down any phrases, catchwords, quotations, images, or incidents connected with your key word. Leave sifting and editing for later. Sample:

> Sentimentality: The word brings to mind true love and romance, life lovingly and beautifully portrayed, with death only a momentary transition to a better place. Every cloud has a silver lining. Life may be harsh and cruel, but redemption and salvation are the eventual outcome. Everything is loaded with sympathy, empathy, compassion, caring. There is some good in everyone. "Life is real; life is earnest." Live is invigorating, challenging.
>
> Death is softened, described almost tenderly. Mother holds the hand of darling child dying of tuberculosis. Dying soldier props himself up on elbow to remember loved ones. The gentle easing from sleep to death. Nothing gory, bloody, sickening.
>
> Hearts, flowers, sunsets, baby shoes. Make the reader feel good. Life may be cruel, but there is justice and beauty. Hallmark greeting cards.

Reading Notes   Focus your reading notes on questions of tone or style. Look for possible connections; try to be open to a possible pattern that might emerge. Sample notes:

> appeal to our sympathy: the heartless, self-righteous townspeople turn out the band of sinners in the dead of winter
>
> (Holman and Harmon on sentimentality in *A Handbook of Literature*: "an optimistic overemphasis on the goodness of humanity")
>
> finding goodness in unexpected places: Oakhurst, the gambler, gives up his horse to the Duchess, trading for her "sorry mule"; later, Oakhurst decides to stay with his "weaker and more pitiable companions"
>
> the naive young "innocents": "they unaffectedly exchanged a kiss, so honest and sincere that it might have been heard above the swaying pines"; note: the naive purity of the innocents softens the hardened sinners
>
> Mother Shipton, notorious for her coarse language and violent oaths, becomes the hooker with the heart of gold who starves herself so that the virginal Piney may eat an additional portion of the rations and so have a chance to live
>
> final good deed: Oakhurst piles firewood by the cabin before he dies with a flourish, "handing in his checks"
>
> softening of death: the Duchess and Piney (sin and innocence) die "locked in each other's arms," with the "younger and purer pillowing the head of her soiled sister upon her virgin breast"; they "fell asleep"; the fatal

blizzard becomes a flurry of soft flakes—"feathery drifts of snow" cover the dead

saving touches of grim realism: Uncle Billy is a true rascal and hard-bitten cynic (and he survives when the others die); the hypocritical citizens of Poker Flat are satirized for their self-righteousness

Structuring Your Paper   Look at the way the following excerpted paper plays off two different facets of an author's style in an "on-the-one-hand" and "on-the-other-hand" pattern:

The Sentimental Sinners of Poker Flat

(introduction: defining the key term)

Driven out of town by the moral majority, "The Outcasts of Poker Flat" perish (with one exception) in an early snowstorm that traps them in the mountains. Two prostitutes, a gambler, and a drunk—these, along with two innocents, are the main characters of Bret Harte's sentimental tale. In sentimental writing, the tender emotions, such as love and pity, are superabundant, and evil exists mainly to stimulate our pity for the victims and our moral indignation. We feel tender pity for the innocent victims and we feel a warm glow of emotion when evildoers repent or show an unexpected noble side.

(thesis: a sentimental story saved from mawkishness)

Bret Harte's characters do indeed act their parts in a story that has most of the elements of nineteenth-century sentimentality. Nevertheless, somehow the story does not leave us with that sickeningly sweet, cloying sensation that a truly sentimental narrative often produces. Harte's skillful use of humor rescues "The Outcasts" from complete mawkishness.

(first major point: the sentimental side of the story)

The story is indeed sentimental. A group of characters who are extremely unlikely candidates for sainthood nevertheless exhibit heroic virtue and selflessness. Their ordeal, rather than demonstrating the baseness of human nature, shows humanity's basic goodness. The only appearance of anything less than virtuous is in Uncle Billy, the drunk. He steals away in the night with the mules, stranding the others in the snowstorm. The rest of the group are inspired to attain a saintly goodness. There is no fighting over food or shelter; each individual is concerned only for the others. . . .

(further follow-up of first point: clinching examples)

The real heroics, though, come from the greatest "sinners," in true sentimental fashion. The gambler, Oakhurst, although he is known to be "a coolly desperate man," never "thought of deserting his weaker and more pitiable companions." Mother Shipton, the legendary prostitute with a heart of gold, starves herself to save the young virgin. . . .

(turning point of the essay: Harte's saving humor)

However, Harte's story as a whole is more successful and more enjoyable than this description would suggest. Humor is the key to Harte's success. Harte's wry humor—a Western, often ironic brand—runs throughout the story, setting it apart from other sentimental writing and allowing a modern reader to appreciate it. The beginning of the story sets the tone: The community of Poker Flat, having lately suffered the loss of "several thousand dollars, two valuable horses," and (almost as an afterthought)" a prominent citizen," is experiencing "a spasm of virtuous reactions." The real reason the townspeople are after Oakhurst is not simply that he is a gambler but that he is a better one than they are—and they want their money back. Oakhurst himself is presented as a worldly-wise character who looks at life with dry ironic humor: "With him life was at best an uncertain game, and he recognized the usual percentage in favor of the dealer."

(conclusion: sentimental ending with a final humorous touch)

The ending of the story is the closest approach to cloying sentimentality. The virgin and the prostitute huddle together in the snow and freeze to death in each other's arms. However, the story does not end there but with a final touch of humor. Oakhurst has left his own epitaph, scribbled on the deuce of clubs and pinned to a tree with a knife. In keeping with his character, it reads: "Beneath this tree lies the body of John Oakhurst, who struck a streak of bad luck . . . and handed in his checks on the 7th December, 1850."

QUESTIONS

Where or how is the initial definition of sentimentality echoed later in the paper? How would you state the central thesis in your own words? How and how well is the program it implies implemented in the paper? Where do you agree and where do you disagree with the student author?

9 THE WRITER'S VOICE
Flannery O'Connor

[handwritten annotation: Catholic - close to the church / major characters come to some realization, guilt, grace etc. / Her stories a reflection of this creation]

No writer is a pessimist; the very act of writing is an optimistic act.

FLANNERY O'CONNOR

FOCUS ON THE WRITER'S VOICE

Critics admonish us to read a story on its own terms: We should read it without preconceptions. We should let it create its own world, its own context, its own version of reality. In practice, however, we often do not read an anonymous story; we read Joyce or Faulkner or O'Connor. As we come to know the author, we anticipate certain kinds of pleasures and rewards. When we start reading an unfamiliar story by a familiar writer, we may feel like a traveler recognizing landmarks: We find our bearings more easily than in reading a new and unknown author. We begin to recognize the writer's voice: a familiar solemn or ironic tone, a familiar mood of foreboding or expectation, a way of looking at places and people. We bring expectations to the story, and we take pleasure in seeing them fulfilled. At the same time, we need to expect the unexpected. We need to remain flexible enough to see a side of the author that we did not notice before.

FLANNERY O'CONNOR: AUTHOR AND WORK

The creator of our nature has also imparted to us the character of love. . . . If love is absent, all the elements of the image are deformed.

GREGORY OF NYSSA

With the serious writer, violence is never an end in itself. It is the extreme situation that best reveals what we are essentially, and I believe these are the times when writers are more interested in what we are essentially than in the tenor of our daily lives.

FLANNERY O'CONNOR

300

When Flannery O'Connor (1924–1964) was asked to name the most important influences on her life, she replied they were probably "being a Catholic and a Southerner and a writer." O'Connor was a devout Catholic in the Baptist South; she attended Catholic schools before she went to Georgia Women's College. Readers of her fiction encounter two sides of a central paradox: Her characters live in a violent world in which evil seems to triumph. But her stories are written by an author who believes in redemption, in divine grace, in the supremacy of God's mercy. She once said that a writer of fiction is "concerned with ultimate mystery as we find it embodied in the concrete world of sense experience."

O'Connor grew up in Savannah and Milledgeville, Georgia, in the segregated South, in a landscape dotted with sharecroppers' shacks. When a Southern novelist was asked why the South had produced so many of America's best writers, he pointed to the lost war that made the Southern experience different from that of the North. O'Connor commented on his reply that he

> didn't mean by that simply that a lost war makes good subject matter. What he was saying was that we had our Fall. We have gone into the modern world with an inburnt knowledge of human limitations and with a sense of mystery which could not have developed in our first state of innocence—as it has not sufficiently developed in the rest of the country.

O'Connor was a master of the grotesque—the freakish mixture of the frightening and the comic. She had a sharp eye for the laughable, for the absurd. ("It is not surprising that she first wanted to be a cartoonist, and sent off cartoons, week after week, to the *New Yorker,* where they were invariably rejected"—Joyce Carol Oates). But in her fiction, horror and comedy mingle, and laughter is muted by our sense of unease, fear, and puzzlement as we watch her strange parables of antagonism and violence unfold. It is as if she had some implied vision of humankind in harmony with God's purposes by which our imperfect, sinful human reality is judged and found wanting—and laughable. She said: "Whenever I am asked why Southern writers particularly have a penchant for writing about freaks, I say it is because we are still able to recognize one. To be able to recognize a freak, you have to have some conception of the whole man, and in the South the general conception of man is still, in the main, theological." Even the good, in O'Connor's view, had traits of the freakish, the grotesque, because "in us the good is something under construction."

O'Connor suffered from a debilitating hereditary illness (lupus), and she was on crutches during most of her writing life. Some of her best work was not published until after her early death at age thirty-nine. Joyce Carol Oates said of her, "We measure an artist by the quality and depth of interior vision, and by the magnitude of achievement, and by these standards Flannery O'Connor is one of our finest writers." Her work "is a deeply moving, deeply disturbing, and ultimately a very beautiful record of a highly complex woman artist whose art was, perhaps, too profound for even the critic in her to grasp."

A Good Man Is Hard to Find   1955

The grandmother didn't want to go to Florida. She wanted to visit some of her connections in east Tennessee and she was seizing every chance to change Bailey's mind. Bailey was the son she lived with, her only boy. He was sitting on the edge of his chair at the table, bent over the orange sports section of the *Journal*. "Now look here, Bailey," she said, "see here, read this," and she stood with one hand on her thin hip and the other rattling the newspaper at his bald head. "Here this fellow that calls himself The Misfit is aloose from the Federal Pen and headed toward Florida and you read here what it says he did to these people. Just you read it. I wouldn't take my children in any direction with a criminal like that aloose in it. I couldn't answer to my conscience if I did."

Bailey didn't look up from his reading so she wheeled around then and faced the children's mother; a young woman in slacks, whose face was as broad and innocent as a cabbage and was tied around with a green headkerchief that had two points on the top like rabbit's ears. She was sitting on the sofa, feeding the baby his apricots out of a jar. "The children have been to Florida before," the old lady said. "You all ought to take them somewhere else for a change so they would see different parts of the world and be broad. They never have been to east Tennessee."

The children's mother didn't seem to hear her, but the eight-year-old boy, John Wesley, a stocky child with glasses, said, "If you don't want to go to Florida, why dontcha stay at home?" He and the little girl, June Star, were reading the funny papers on the floor.

"She wouldn't stay at home to be queen for a day," June Star said without raising her yellow head.

"Yes, and what would you do if this fellow, The Misfit, caught you?" the grandmother asked.

"I'd smack his face," John Wesley said.

"She wouldn't stay at home for a million bucks," June Star said. "Afraid she'd miss something. She has to go everywhere we go."

"All right, Miss," the grandmother said. "Just remember that the next time you want me to curl your hair."

June Star said her hair was naturally curly.

The next morning the grandmother was the first one in the car, ready to go. She had her big black valise that looked like the head of a hippopotamus in one corner, and underneath it she was hiding a basket with Pitty Sing, the cat, in it. She didn't intend for the cat to be left alone in the house for three days because he would miss her too much and she was afraid he might brush against one of the gas burners and accidentally asphyxiate himself. Her son, Bailey, didn't like to arrive at a motel with a cat.

She sat in the middle of the back seat with John Wesley and June Star on either side of her. Bailey and the children's mother and the baby sat in the front and they left Atlanta at eight forty-five with the mileage on the car at 55890. The grandmother wrote this down because she thought it would be interesting to say how many miles they had been when they got back. It took them twenty minutes to reach the outskirts of the city.

The old lady settled herself comfortably, removing her white cotton gloves and putting them up with her purse on the shelf in front of the back window. The children's mother still had on slacks and still had her head tied up in a green kerchief, but the grandmother had on a navy blue straw sailor hat with a bunch of white violets on the brim and a navy blue dress with a small white dot in the print. Her collar and cuffs were white organdy trimmed with lace and at her neckline she had pinned a purple spray of cloth violets containing a sachet. In case of an accident, anyone seeing her dead on the highway would know at once that she was a lady.

She said she thought it was going to be a good day for driving, neither too hot nor too cold, and she cautioned Bailey that the speed limit was fifty-five miles an hour and that the patrolmen hid themselves behind billboards and small clumps of trees and sped out after you before you had a chance to slow down. She pointed out interesting details of the scenery: Stone Mountain; the blue granite that in some places came up to both sides of the highway; the brilliant red clay banks slightly streaked with purple; and the various crops that made rows of green lace-work on the ground. The trees were full of silver-white sunlights and the meanest of them sparkled. The children were reading comic magazines and their mother had gone back to sleep.

"Let's go through Georgia fast so we won't have to look at it much," John Wesley said.

"If I were a little boy," said the grandmother, "I wouldn't talk about my native   15
state that way. Tennessee has the mountains and Georgia has the hills."

"Tennessee is just a hillbilly dumping ground," John Wesley said, "and Georgia is a lousy state too."

"You said it," June Star said.

"In my time," said the grandmother, folding her thin veined fingers, "children were more respectful of their native states and their parents and everything else. People did right then. Oh look at the cute little pickaninny!" she said and pointed to a Negro child standing in the door of a shack. "Wouldn't that make a picture, now?" she asked and they all turned and looked at the little Negro out of the back window. He waved.

"He didn't have any britches on," June Star said.

"He probably didn't have any," the grandmother explained. "Little niggers in the   20
country don't have things like we do. If I could paint, I'd paint that picture," she said.

The children exchanged comic books.

The grandmother offered to hold the baby and the children's mother passed him over the front seat to her. She set him on her knee and bounced him and told him about the things they were passing. She rolled her eyes and screwed up her mouth and stuck her leathery thin face into his smooth bland one. Occasionally he gave her a far-away smile. They passed a large cotton field with five or six graves fenced in the middle of it, like a small island. "Look at the graveyard!" the grandmother said, pointing it out. "That was the old family burying ground. That belonged to the plantation."

"Where's the plantation?" John Wesley asked.

"Gone With the Wind," said the grandmother. "Ha. Ha."

When the children finished all the comic books they had brought, they opened the   25
lunch and ate it. The grandmother ate a peanut butter sandwich and an olive and would not let the children throw the box and the paper napkins out the window. When there was nothing else to do they played a game by choosing a cloud and making the other two guess what shape it suggested. John Wesley took one the shape of a cow and June Star guessed a cow and John Wesley said, no, an automobile, and June Star said he didn't play fair, and they began to slap each other over the grandmother.

The grandmother said she would tell them a story if they would keep quiet. When she told a story, she rolled her eyes and waved her head and was very dramatic. She said once when she was a maiden lady she had been courted by a Mr. Edgar Atkins Teagarden from Jasper, Georgia. She said he was a very good-looking man and a gentleman and that he brought her a watermelon every Saturday afternoon with his initials cut in it, E.A.T. Well, one Saturday, she said, Mr. Teagarden brought the watermelon and there was nobody at home and he left it on the front porch and returned in his buggy to Jasper, but she never got the watermelon, she said, because a nigger boy ate it when he saw the initials, E.A.T.! This story tickled John Wesley's funny bone and he giggled and giggled but June Star didn't think it was any good. She said she wouldn't marry a man that just brought her a watermelon on Saturday. The grandmother said she would have done well to marry Mr. Teagarden because he was a gentleman and had bought Coca-Cola stock when it first came out and that he had died only a few years ago, a very wealthy man.

They stopped at The Tower for barbecued sandwiches. The Tower was a part-stucco and part-wood filling station and dance hall set in a clearing outside of Timothy. A fat man named Red Sammy Butts ran it and there were signs stuck here and there on the building and for miles up and down the highway saying, TRY RED SAMMY'S FAMOUS BARBECUE. NONE LIKE FAMOUS RED SAMMY'S! RED SAM! THE FAT BOY WITH THE HAPPY LAUGH. A VETERAN! RED SAMMY'S YOUR MAN!

Red Sammy was lying on the bare ground outside The Tower with his head under a truck while a gray monkey about a foot high, chained to a small chinaberry tree, chattered nearby. The monkey sprang back into the tree and got on the highest limb as soon as he saw the children jump out of the car and run toward him.

Inside, The Tower was a long dark room with a counter at one end and tables at the other and dancing space in the middle. They all sat down at a broad table next to the nickelodeon and Red Sam's wife, a tall burnt-brown woman with hair and eyes lighter than her skin, came and took their order. The children's mother put a dime in the machine and played "The Tennessee Waltz," and the grandmother said that tune always made her want to dance. She asked Bailey if he would like to dance but he only glared at her. He didn't have a naturally sunny disposition like she did and trips made him nervous. The grandmother's brown eyes were very bright. She swayed her head from side to side and pretended she was dancing in her chair. June Star said play something she could tap to so the children's mother put in another dime and played a fast number and June Star stepped out onto the dance floor and did her tap routine.

"Ain't she cute?" Red Sam's wife said, leaning over the counter. "Would you like to come be my little girl?" 30

"No, I certainly wouldn't," June Star said. "I wouldn't live in a broken-down place like this for a million bucks!" and she ran back to the table.

"Ain't she cute?" the woman repeated, stretching her mouth politely.

"Aren't you ashamed?" hissed the grandmother.

Red Sam came in and told his wife to quit lounging on the counter and hurry up with these people's order. His khaki trousers reached just to his hip bones and his stomach hung over them like a sack of meal swaying under his shirt. He came over and sat down at a table nearby and let out a combination sigh and yodel. "You can't win," he said. "You can't win," and he wiped his sweating red face off with a gray handkerchief. "These days you don't know who to trust," he said. "Ain't that the truth?"

"People are certainly not nice like they used to be," said the grandmother. 35

"Two fellers come in here last week," Red Sammy said, "driving a Chrysler. It was an old beat-up car but it was a good one and these boys looked all right to me. Said they worked at the mill and you know I let them fellers charge the gas they bought? Now why did I do that?"

"Because you're a good man!" the grandmother said at once.

"Yes'm, I suppose so," Red Sam said as if he were struck with this answer.

His wife brought the orders, carrying the five plates all at once without a tray, two in each hand and one balanced on her arm. "It isn't a soul in this green world of God's that you can trust," she said. "And I don't count nobody out of that, not nobody," she repeated, looking at Red Sammy.

"Did you read about that criminal, The Misfit, that's escaped?" asked the grand- 40 mother.

"I wouldn't be a bit surprised if he didn't attack this place right here," said the woman. "If he hears about it being here, I wouldn't be none surprised to see him. If he hears it's two cent in the cash register, I wouldn't be a tall surprised if he . . ."

"That'll do," Red Sam said. "Go bring these people their Co'-Colas," and the woman went off to get the rest of the order.

"A good man is hard to find," Red Sammy said. "Everything is getting terrible. I remember the day you could go off and leave your screen door unlatched. Not no more."

He and the grandmother discussed better times. The old lady said that in her opinion Europe was entirely to blame for the way things were now. She said the way Europe acted you would think we were made of money and Red Sam said it was no use talking about it, she was exactly right. The children ran outside into the white sunlight and looked at the monkey in the lacy chinaberry tree. He was busy catching fleas on himself and biting each one carefully between his teeth as if it were a delicacy.

They drove off again into the hot afternoon. The grandmother took cat naps and 45 woke up every few minutes with her own snoring. Outside of Toombsboro she woke up and recalled an old plantation that she had visited in this neighborhood once when she was a young lady. She said the house had six white columns across the front and that there was an avenue of oaks leading up to it and two little wooden trellis arbors on either side in front where you sat down with your suitor after a stroll in the garden. She recalled exactly which road to turn off to get to it. She knew that Bailey would not be willing to lose any time looking at an old house, but the more she talked about it, the more she wanted to see it once again and find out if the little twin arbors were still standing. "There was a secret panel in this house," she said craftily, not telling the truth but wishing that she were, "and the story went that all the family silver was hidden in it when Sherman came through but it was never found . . ."

"Hey!" John Wesley said. "Let's go see it! We'll find it! We'll poke all the woodwork and find it! Who lives there? Where do you turn off at? Hey Pop, can't we turn off there?"

"We never have seen a house with a secret panel!" June Star shrieked. "Let's go to the house with the secret panel! Hey, Pop, can't we go see the house with the secret panel!"

"It's not far from here, I know," the grandmother said. "It wouldn't take over twenty minutes."

Bailey was looking straight ahead. His jaw was as rigid as a horseshoe. "No," he said.

The children began to yell and scream that they wanted to see the house with the 50 secret panel. John Wesley kicked the back of the front seat and June Star hung over her mother's shoulder and whined desperately into her ear that they never had any fun even on their vacation, that they could never do what THEY wanted to do. The baby began to scream and John Wesley kicked the back of the seat so hard that his father could feel the blows in his kidney.

"All right!" he shouted and drew the car to a stop at the side of the road. "Will you all shut up? Will you all just shut up for one second? If you don't shut up, we won't go anywhere."

"It would be very educational for them," the grandmother murmured.

"All right," Bailey said, "but get this. This is the only time we're going to stop for anything like this. This is the one and only time."

"The dirt road that you have to turn down is about a mile back," the grandmother directed. "I marked it when we passed."

"A dirt road," Bailey groaned. 55

After they had turned around and were headed toward the dirt road, the grandmother recalled other points about the house, the beautiful glass over the front doorway and the candle lamp in the hall. John Wesley said that the secret panel was probably in the fireplace.

"You can't go inside this house," Bailey said. "You don't know who lives there."

"While you all talk to the people in front, I'll run around behind and get in a window," John Wesley suggested.

"We'll all stay in the car," his mother said.

They turned onto the dirt road and the car raced roughly along in a swirl of pink 60 dust. The grandmother recalled the times when there were no paved roads and thirty miles was a day's journey. The dirt road was hilly and there were sudden washes in it and sharp curves on dangerous embankments. All at once they would be on a hill, looking down over the blue tops of trees for miles around, then the next minute, they would be in a red depression with the dust-coated trees looking down on them.

"This place had better turn up in a minute," Bailey said, "or I'm going to turn around."

The road looked as if no one had traveled on it in months.

"It's not much farther," the grandmother said and just as she said it, a horrible thought came to her. The thought was so embarrassing that she turned red in the face and her eyes dilated and her feet jumped up, upsetting her valise in the corner. The instant the valise moved, the newspaper top she had over the basket under it rose with a snarl and Pitty Sing, the cat, sprang onto Bailey's shoulder.

The children were thrown to the floor and their mother, clutching the baby, was thrown out the door onto the ground; the old lady was thrown into the front seat. The car turned over once and landed right-side-up in a gulch on the side of the road. Bailey remained in the driver's seat with the cat—gray-striped with a broad white face and an orange nose—clinging to his neck like a caterpillar.

As soon as the children saw they could move their arms and legs, they scrambled 65 out of the car, shouting, "We've had an ACCIDENT!" The grandmother was curled up under the dashboard, hoping she was injured so that Bailey's wrath would not come down on her all at once. The horrible thought she had had before the accident was that the house she had remembered so vividly was not in Georgia but in Tennessee.

Bailey removed the cat from his neck with both hands and flung it out the window against the side of a pine tree. Then he got out of the car and started looking for the children's mother. She was sitting against the side of the red gutted ditch, holding the screaming baby, but she only had a cut down her face and a broken shoulder. "We've had an ACCIDENT!" the children screamed in a frenzy of delight.

"But nobody's killed," June Star said with disappointment as the grandmother limped out of the car, her hat still pinned to her head but the broken front brim standing up at a jaunty angle and the violet spray hanging off the side. They all sat down in the ditch, except the children, to recover from the shock. They were all shaking.

"Maybe a car will come along," said the children's mother hoarsely.

"I believe I have injured an organ," said the grandmother, pressing her side, but no one answered her. Bailey's teeth were clattering. He had on a yellow sport shirt with bright blue parrots designed in it and his face was as yellow as the shirt. The grandmother decided that she would not mention that the house was in Tennessee.

The road was about ten feet above and they could see only the tops of the trees on the other side of it. Behind the ditch they were sitting in there were more woods, tall and dark and deep. In a few minutes they saw a car some distance away on top of a hill, coming slowly as if the occupants were watching them. The grandmother stood up and waved both arms dramatically to attract their attention. The car continued to come on slowly, disappeared around a bend and appeared again, moving even slower, on top of the hill they had gone over. It was a big black battered hearselike automobile. There were three men in it.

It came to a stop over them and for some minutes, the driver looked down with a steady expressionless gaze to where they were sitting, and didn't speak. Then he turned his head and muttered something to the other two and they got out. One was a fat boy in black trousers and a red sweat shirt with a silver stallion embossed on the front of it. He moved around on the right side of them and stood staring, his mouth partly open in a kind of loose grin. The other had on khaki pants and a blue striped coat and a gray hat pulled down very low, hiding most of his face. He came around slowly on the left side. Neither spoke.

The driver got out of the car and stood by the side of it, looking down at them. He was an older man than the other two. His hair was just beginning to gray and he wore silver-rimmed spectacles that gave him a scholarly look. He had a long creased face and didn't have on any shirt or undershirt. He had on blue jeans that were too tight for him and was holding a black hat and a gun. The two boys also had guns.

"We've had an ACCIDENT!" the children screamed.

The grandmother had the peculiar feeling that the bespectacled man was someone she knew. His face was as familiar to her as if she had known him all her life but she could not recall who he was. He moved away from the car and began to come down the embankment, placing his feet carefully so that he wouldn't slip. He had on tan and white shoes and no socks, and his ankles were red and thin. "Good afternoon," he said. "I see you all had you a little spill."

"We turned over twice!" said the grandmother.

"Oncet," he corrected. "We seen it happen. Try their car and see will it run, Hiram," he said quietly to the boy with the gray hat.

"What you got that gun for?" John Wesley asked. "Whatcha gonna do with that gun?"

"Lady," the man said to the children's mother, "would you mind calling them children to sit down by you? Children make me nervous. I want all you all to sit down right together there were you're at."

"What are you telling us what to do for?" June Star asked.

Behind them the line of woods gaped like a dark open mouth. "Come here," said their mother.

"Look here now," Bailey began suddenly, "we're in a predicament! We're in . . ."

The grandmother shrieked. She scrambled to her feet and stood staring.

"You're The Misfit!" she said. "I recognized you at once!"

"Yes'm," the man said, smiling slightly as if he were pleased in spite of himself to be known, "but it would have been better for all of you, lady, if you hadn't of reckernized me."

Bailey turned his head sharply and said something to his mother that shocked even the children. The old lady began to cry and The Misfit reddened.

"Lady," he said, "don't you get upset. Sometimes a man says things he don't mean. I don't reckon he meant to talk to you thataway."

"You wouldn't shoot a lady, would you?" the grandmother said and removed a clean handkerchief from her cuff and began to slap at her eyes with it.

The Misfit pointed the toe of his shoe into the ground and made a little hole and then covered it up again. "I would hate to have to," he said.

"Listen," the grandmother almost screamed, "I know you're a good man. You don't look a bit like you have common blood. I know you must come from nice people!"

"Yes mam," he said, "finest people in the world." When he smiled he showed a row of strong white teeth. "God never made a finer woman than my mother and my daddy's heart was pure gold," he said. The boy with the red sweat shirt had come around behind them and was standing with his gun at his hip. The Misfit squatted down on the ground. "Watch them children, Bobby Lee," he said. "You know they make me nervous." He looked at the six of them huddled together in front of him and he seemed to be embarrassed as if he couldn't think of anything to say. "Ain't a cloud in the sky," he remarked, looking up at it. "Don't see no sun but don't see no cloud neither."

"Yes, it's a beautiful day," said the grandmother. "Listen," she said, "you shouldn't call yourself The Misfit because I know you're a good man at heart. I can just look at you and tell."

"Hush!" Bailey yelled. "Hush! Everybody shut up and let me handle this!" He was squatting in the position of a runner about to spring forward but he didn't move.

"I pre-chate that, lady," The Misfit said and drew a little circle in the ground with the butt of his gun.

"It'll take a half a hour to fix this here car," Hiram called, looking over the raised hood of it.

"Well, first you and Bobby Lee get him and that little boy to step over yonder with you," The Misfit said, pointing to Bailey and John Wesley. "The boys want to ask you something," he said to Bailey. "Would you mind stepping back in them woods there with them?"

"Listen," Bailey began, "we're in a terrible predicament! Nobody realizes what this is," and his voice cracked. His eyes were as blue and intense as the parrots in his shirt and he remained perfectly still.

The grandmother reached up to adjust her hat brim as if she were going to the woods with him but it came off in her hand. She stood staring at it and after a second she let it fall on the ground. Hiram pulled Bailey up by the arm as if he were assisting an old man. John Wesley caught hold of his father's hand and Bobby Lee followed. They went off toward the woods and just as they reached the dark edge, Bailey turned and supporting himself against a gray naked pine trunk, he shouted, "I'll be back in a minute, Mamma, wait on me!"

"Come back this instant!" his mother shrilled but they all disappeared into the woods.

"Bailey Boy!" the grandmother called in a tragic voice but she found she was looking at The Misfit squatting on the ground in front of her. "I just know you're a good man," she said desperately. "You're not a bit common!"

"Nome, I ain't a good man," The Misfit said after a second as if he had considered her statement carefully, "but I ain't the worst in the world neither. My daddy said I was a different breed of dog from my brothers and sisters. 'You know,' Daddy said, 'it's some that can live their whole life out without asking about it and it's others has to know why it is, and this boy is one of the latters. He's going to be into everything!" He put on his black hat and looked up suddenly and then away deep into the woods as if he were embarrassed again. "I'm sorry I don't have on a shirt before you ladies," he said, hunching his shoulders slightly. "We buried our clothes that we had on when we escaped and we're just making do until we can get better. We borrowed these from some folks we met," he explained.

"That's perfectly all right," the grandmother said. "Maybe Bailey has an extra shirt in his suitcase."

"I'll look and see terrectly," The Misfit said.

"Where are they taking him?" the children's mother screamed.

"Daddy was a card himself," The Misfit said. "You couldn't put anything over on him. He never got in trouble with the Authorities though. Just had the knack of handling them."

"You could be honest too if you'd only try," said the grandmother. "Think how wonderful it would be to settle down and live a comfortable life and not have to think about somebody chasing you all the time."

The Misfit kept scratching in the ground with the butt of his gun as if he were thinking about it. "Yes'm, somebody is always after you," he murmured.

The grandmother noticed how thin his shoulder blades were just behind his hat because she was standing up looking down on him. "Do you ever pray?" she asked.

He shook his head. All she saw was the black hat wiggle between his shoulder blades. "Nome," he said.

There was a pistol shot from the woods, followed closely by another. Then silence. The old lady's head jerked around. She could hear the wind move through the tree tops like a long satisfied insuck of breath. "Bailey Boy!" she called.

"I was a gospel singer for a while," The Misfit said. "I been most everything. Been in the arm service, both land and sea, at home and abroad, been twict married, been an undertaker, been with the railroads, plowed Mother Earth, been in a tornado, seen a man burnt alive oncet," and he looked up at the children's mother and the little girl who were sitting close together, their faces white and their eyes glassy; "I even seen a woman flogged," he said.

"Pray, pray," the grandmother began, "pray, pray . . . ."

"I never was a bad boy that I remember of," The Misfit said in an almost dreamy voice, "but somewheres along the line I done something wrong and got sent to the penitentiary. I was buried alive," and he looked up and held her attention to him by a steady stare.

"That's when you should have started to pray," she said. "What did you do to get sent to the penitentiary that first time?"

"Turn to the right, it was a wall," The Misfit said, looking up again at the cloudless sky. "Turn to the left, it was a wall. Look up it was a ceiling, look down it was a floor. I forget what I done, lady. I set there and set there, trying to remember what it was I done and I ain't recalled it to this day. Oncet in a while, I would think it was coming to me, but it never come."

"Maybe they put you in by mistake," the old lady said vaguely.

"Nome," he said. "It wasn't no mistake. They had the papers on me."

"You must have stolen something," she said.

The Misfit sneered slightly. "Nobody had nothing I wanted," he said. "It was a head-doctor at the penitentiary said what I had done was kill my daddy but I known that for a lie. My daddy died in nineteen ought nineteen of the epidemic flu and I never had a thing to do with it. He was buried in the Mount Hopewell Baptist churchyard and you can go there and see for yourself."

"If you would pray," the old lady said, "Jesus would help you."

"That's right," The Misfit said. 120

"Well then, why don't you pray?" she asked trembling with delight suddenly.

"I don't want no hep," he said. "I'm doing all right by myself."

Bobby Lee and Hiram came ambling back from the woods. Bobby Lee was dragging a yellow shirt with bright blue parrots in it.

"Throw me that shirt, Bobby Lee," The Misfit said. The shirt came flying at him and landed on his shoulder and he put it on. The grandmother couldn't name what the shirt reminded her of. "No, lady," The Misfit said while he was buttoning up, "I found out the crime don't matter. You can do one thing or you can do another, kill a man or take a tire off his car, because sooner or later you're going to forget what it was you done and just be punished for it."

The children's mother had begun to make heaving noises as if she couldn't get her 125 breath. "Lady," he asked, "would you and that little girl like to step off yonder with Bobby Lee and Hiram and join your husband?"

"Yes, thank you," the mother said faintly. Her left arm dangled helplessly and she was holding the baby, who had gone to sleep, in the other. "Hep that lady up, Hiram," The Misfit said as she struggled to climb out of the ditch, "and Bobby Lee, you hold onto that little girl's hand."

"I don't want to hold hands with him," June Star said. "He reminds me of a pig."

The fat boy blushed and laughed and caught her by the arm and pulled her off into the woods after Hiram and her mother.

Alone with The Misfit, the grandmother found that she had lost her voice. There was not a cloud in the sky nor any sun. There was nothing around her but woods. She wanted to tell him that he must pray. She opened and closed her mouth several times before anything came out. Finally she found herself saying, "Jesus, Jesus," meaning, Jesus will help you, but the way she was saying it, it sounded as if she might be cursing.

"Yes'm," The Misfit said as if he agreed. "Jesus thrown everything off balance. It 130 was the same case with Him as with me except He hadn't committed any crime and they could prove I had committed one because they had the papers on me. Of course," he said, "they never shown me my papers. That's why I sign myself now. I said long ago, you get you a signature and sign everything you do and keep a copy of it. Then you'll know what you done and you can hold up the crime to the punishment and see do they match and in the end you'll have something to prove you ain't been treated right. I call myself The Misfit," he said, "because I can't make what all I done wrong fit what all I gone through in punishment."

There was a piercing scream from the woods, followed closely by a pistol report. "Does it seem right to you, lady, that one is punished a heap and another ain't punished at all?"

"Jesus!" the old lady cried. "You've got good blood! I know you wouldn't shoot a lady! I know you come from nice people! Pray! Jesus, you ought not to shoot a lady. I'll give you all the money I've got!"

"Lady," The Misfit said, looking beyond her far into the woods, "there never was a body that give the undertaker a tip."

There were two more pistol reports and the grandmother raised her head like a parched old turkey hen crying for water and called, "Bailey Boy, Bailey Boy!" as if her heart would break.

"Jesus was the only One that ever raised the dead," The Misfit continued, "and 135 He shouldn't have done it. He thrown everything off balance. If He did what He said, then it's nothing for you to do but throw away everything and follow Him, and if He didn't then it's nothing for you to do but enjoy the few minutes you got left the best way you can—by killing somebody or burning down his house or doing some other mean-ness to him. No pleasure but meanness," he said and his voice had become almost a snarl.

"Maybe He didn't raise the dead," the old lady mumbled, not knowing what she was saying and feeling so dizzy that she sank down in the ditch with her legs twisted under her.

"I wasn't there so I can't say He didn't," The Misfit said. "I wisht I had of been there," he said, hitting the ground with his fist. "It ain't right I wasn't there because if I had of been there I would of known. Listen lady," he said in a high voice, "if I had of been there I would of known and I wouldn't be like I am now." His voice seemed about to crack and the grandmother's head cleared for an instant. She saw the man's face twisted close to her own as if he were going to cry and she murmured, "Why, you're one of my babies. You're one of my own children!" She reached out and touched him on the shoulder. The Misfit sprang back as if a snake had bitten him and shot her three times through the chest. Then he put his gun down on the ground and took off his glasses and began to clean them.

Hiram and Bobby Lee returned from the woods and stood over the ditch, looking down at the grandmother who half sat and half lay in a puddle of blood with her legs crossed under her like a child's and her face smiling up at the cloudless sky.

Without his glasses, The Misfit's eyes were red-rimmed and pale and defenseless-looking. "Take her off and throw her where you thrown the others," he said, picking up the cat that was rubbing itself against his leg.

"She was a talker, wasn't she?" Bobby Lee said, sliding down the ditch with a yodel.

"She would of been a good woman," The Misfit said, "if it had been somebody there to shoot her every minute of her life."

"Some fun!" Bobby Lee said.

"Shut up, Bobby Lee," The Misfit said. "It's no real pleasure in life."

THE RECEPTIVE READER

1. What kind of person is the grandmother? What roles (or how many roles) does she play as a *central character* in the development of the story? At how many points in the story does she play a major or minor part? ✦ Does she symbolically represent the past—the "old South"? Is there a conflict between the generations?

2. What is your reaction to the other members of the family as *minor characters* in the story? Are they comical? strange? ordinary? repellent?

3. What role does the *episode*, or interlude, at the "fat man's" barbecue play in the story?

4. How or why did these characters meet their fate? (How would you summarize the *plot* or story line?)

5. Is there anything representative or *symbolic* about what happens to these people?

6. What is the Misfit's story (and how much of it do you believe)? ✦ What are his manners? (Do you find them surprising or *ironic?*) ✦ What is the gist of the climactic conversation between the Misfit and the grandmother? Does it suggest a *theme*; does it have thematic implications?

7. Where would you draw the line between the comic and the tragic in this story? How does it illustrate the mixed genre critics call the *grotesque*?

8. Does this story change your idea about "senseless violence"? How?

THE PERSONAL RESPONSE

How true to the spirit of the story, or how far off, is the personal reaction in the following journal entry?

> Maybe the Misfit was like Lucifer, the misfit Angel. Lucifer didn't see things God's way, so God cast him out of heaven and punished him. Did Lucifer become evil because of the punishment not fitting the crime? Or was Lucifer just inherently evil? If he was inherently evil, he wouldn't have been an angel in the first place. I think those who jailed the Misfit turned him from just different to bad. I wasn't terribly sorry to see that family go, especially those rancid children. The mother was harmless, but I had real sympathy only for the Misfit, the baby, and the cat, Pitty Sing. Maybe O'Connor made the family so nasty and annoying to act as a foil for the Misfit, who really was a pitiful man.

THE CREATIVE DIMENSION

O'Connor's stories leave readers with haunting images or the memory of striking incidents. Critics puzzle over key phrases ("good country people"), provocative sentences ("a good man is hard to find"), symbolic gestures, climactic exchanges, violent confrontations. Focus on a haunting image, incident, gesture, or saying in O'Connor's stories. Re-create it, following the train of ideas, images, or associations it calls up in your mind.

As you start reading the following story by the same author, do you find yourself in familiar territory? Do its characters seem in some way akin to those in the preceding story? Does this second story raise issues or explore questions that seem related to those in the first?

Theme – Eyes

Everything That Rises Must Converge 1965

Her doctor had told Julian's mother that she must lose twenty pounds on account of her blood pressure, so on Wednesday nights Julian had to take her downtown on the bus for a reducing class at the Y. The reducing class was designed for working girls over fifty, who weighed from 165 to 200 pounds. His mother was one of the slimmer ones, but she said ladies did not tell their age or weight. She would not ride the buses by herself at night since they had been integrated, and because the reducing class was one of her few pleasures, necessary for her health, and *free*, she said Julian could at least put himself out to take her, considering all she did for him. Julian did not like to consider all she did for him, but every Wednesday night he braced himself and took her.

She was almost ready to go, standing before the hall mirror, putting on her hat, while he, his hands behind him, appeared pinned to the door frame, waiting like Saint Sebastian for the arrows to begin piercing him. The hat was new and had cost her seven dollars and a half. She kept saying, "Maybe I shouldn't have paid that for it. No, I shouldn't have. I'll take it off and return it tomorrow. I shouldn't have bought it."

Julian raised his eyes to heaven. "Yes, you should have bought it," he said. "Put it on and let's go." It was a hideous hat. A purple velvet flap came down on one side of it and stood up on the other; the rest of it was green and looked like a cushion with the stuffing out. He decided it was less comical than jaunty and pathetic. Everything that gave her pleasure was small and depressed him.

She lifted the hat one more time and set it down slowly on top of her head. Two wings of gray hair protruded on either side of her florid face, but her eyes, sky-blue, were as innocent and untouched by experience as they must have been when she was ten. Were it not that she was a widow who had struggled fiercely to feed and clothe and put him through school and who was supporting him still, "until he got on his feet," she might have been a little girl that he had to take to town.

"It's all right, it's all right," he said. "Let's go." He opened the door himself and started down the walk to get her going. The sky was a dying violet and the houses stood out darkly against it, bulbous liver-colored monstrosities of a uniform ugliness though no two were alike. Since this had been a fashionable neighborhood forty years ago, his mother persisted in thinking they did well to have an apartment in it. Each house had a narrow collar of dirt around it in which sat, usually, a grubby child. Julian walked with his hands in his pockets, his head down and thrust forward and his eyes glazed with the determination to make himself completely numb during the time he would be sacrificed to her pleasure.

The door closed and he turned to find the dumpy figure, surmounted by the atrocious hat, coming toward him. "Well," she said, "you only live once and paying a little more for it, I at least won't meet myself coming and going."

"Some day I'll start making money," Julian said gloomily—he knew he never would—"and you can have one of those jokes whenever you take the fit." But first they would move. He visualized a place where the nearest neighbors would be three miles away on either side.

"I think you're doing fine," she said, drawing on her gloves. "You've only been out of school a year. Rome wasn't built in a day."

She was one of the few members of the Y reducing class who arrived in hat and gloves and who had a son who had been to college. "It takes time," she said, "and the world is in such a mess. This hat looked better on me than any of the others, though when she brought it out I said, 'Take that thing back. I wouldn't have it on my head,' and she said, 'Now wait till you see it on,' and when she put it on me, I said, 'We-ull,' and she said, 'If you ask me, that hat does something for you and you do something for the hat, and besides,' she said, 'with that hat, you won't meet yourself coming and going.'"

Julian thought he could have stood his lot better if she had been selfish, if she had been an old hag who drank and screamed at him. He walked along, saturated in depression, as if in the midst of his martyrdom he had lost his faith. Catching sight of his long, hopeless, irritated face, she stopped suddenly with a grief-stricken look, and pulled back on his arm. "Wait on me," she said. "I'm going back to the house and take this thing off and tomorrow I'm going to return it. I was out of my head. I can pay the gas bill with that seven-fifty."

He caught her arm in a vicious grip. "You are not going to take it back," he said. "I like it."

"Well," she said, "I don't think I ought . . ."

"Shut up and enjoy it," he muttered, more depressed than ever.

"With the world in the mess it's in," she said, "it's a wonder we can enjoy anything. I tell you, the bottom rail is on the top."

Julian sighed.

"Of course," she said, "if you know who you are, you can go anywhere." She said this every time he took her to the reducing class. "Most of them in it are not our kind of people," she said, "but I can be gracious to anybody. I know who I am."

"They don't give a damn for your graciousness," Julian said savagely. "Knowing who you are is good for one generation only. You haven't the foggiest idea where you stand now or who you are."

She stopped and allowed her eyes to flash at him. "I most certainly do know who I am," she said, "and if you don't know who you are, I'm ashamed of you."

"Oh hell," Julian said.

"Your great-grandfather was a former governor of this state," she said. "Your grandfather was a prosperous land-owner. Your grandmother was a Godhigh." 20

"Will you look around you," he said tensely, "and see where you are now?" and he swept his arm jerkily out to indicate the neighborhood, which the growing darkness at least made less dingy.

"You remain what you are," she said. "Your great-grandfather had a plantation and two hundred slaves."

"There are no more slaves," he said irritably.

"They were better off when they were," she said. He groaned to see that she was off on that topic. She rolled onto it every few days like a train on an open track. He knew every stop, every junction, every swamp along the way, and knew the exact point at which her conclusion would roll majestically into the station: "It's ridiculous. It's simply not realistic. They should rise, yes, but on their own side of the fence."

"Let's skip it," Julian said. 25

"The ones I feel sorry for," she said, "are the ones that are half white. They're tragic."

"Will you skip it?"

"Suppose we were half white. We would certainly have mixed feelings."

"I have mixed feelings now," he groaned.

"Well let's talk about something pleasant," she said. "I remember going to Grand- 30 pa's when I was a little girl. Then the house had double stairways that went up to what was really the second floor—all the cooking was done on the first. I used to like to stay down in the kitchen on account of the way the walls smelled. I would sit with my nose pressed against the plaster and take deep breaths. Actually the place belonged to the Godhighs but your grandfather Chestny paid the mortgage and saved it for them. They were in reduced circumstances," she said, "but reduced or not, they never forgot who they were."

"Doubtless that decayed mansion reminded them," Julian muttered. He never spoke of it without contempt or thought of it without longing. He had seen it once when he was a child before it had been sold. The double stairways had rotted and been torn down. Negroes were living in it. But it remained in his mind as his mother had known it. It appeared in his dreams regularly. He would stand on the wide porch, listening to the rustle of oak leaves, then wander through the high-ceilinged hall into the parlor that opened onto it and gaze at the worn rugs and faded draperies. It occurred to him that it was he, not she, who could have appreciated it. He preferred its threadbare elegance to anything he could name and it was because of it that all the neighborhoods they had lived in had been a torment to him—whereas she had hardly known the difference. She called her insensitivity "being adjustable."

"And I remember the old darky who was my nurse, Caroline. There was no better person in the world. I've always had a great respect for my colored friends," she said. "I'd do anything in the world for them and they'd . . ."

"Will you for God's sake get off that subject?" Julian said. When he got on a bus by himself, he made it a point to sit down beside a Negro, in reparation as it were for his mother's sins.

"You're mighty touchy tonight," she said. "Do you feel all right?"

"Yes I feel all right," he said. "Now lay off." 35

She pursed her lips. "Well, you certainly are in a vile humor," she observed. "I just won't speak to you at all."

They had reached the bus stop. There was no bus in sight and Julian, his hands still jammed in his pockets and his head thrust forward, scowled down the empty street. The frustration of having to wait on the bus as well as ride on it began to creep up his neck like a hot hand. The presence of his mother was borne in upon him as she gave a pained sigh. He looked at her bleakly. She was holding herself very erect under the preposterous hat, wearing it like a banner of her imaginary dignity. There was in him an evil urge to break her spirit. He suddenly unloosened his tie and pulled it off and put it in his pocket.

She stiffened. "Why must you look like *that* when you take me to town?" she said. "Why must you deliberately embarrass me?"

"If you'll never learn where you are," he said, "you can at least learn where I am."

"You look like a—thug," she said. 40

"Then I must be one," he murmured.

"I'll just go home," she said. "I will not bother you. If you can't do a little thing like that for me . . ."

Rolling his eyes upward, he put his tie back on. "Restored to my class," he muttered. He thrust his face toward her and hissed, "True culture is in the mind, the *mind*," he said, and tapped his head, "the mind."

"It's in the heart," she said, "and in how you do things and how you do things is because of who you *are*."

"Nobody in the damn bus cares who you are." 45

"I care who I am," she said icily.

The lighted bus appeared on top of the next hill and as it approached, they moved out into the street to meet it. He put his hand under her elbow and hoisted her up on the creaking step. She entered with a little smile, as if she were going into a drawing room where everyone had been waiting for her. While he put in the tokens, she sat down on one of the broad front seats for three which faced the aisle. A thin woman with protruding teeth and long yellow hair was sitting on the end of it. His mother moved up beside her and left room for Julian beside herself. He sat down and looked at the floor across the aisle where a pair of thin feet in red and white canvas sandals were planted.

His mother immediately began a general conversation meant to attract anyone who felt like talking. "Can it get any hotter?" she said and removed from her purse a folding fan, black with a Japanese scene on it, which she began to flutter before her.

"I reckon it might could," the woman with the protruding teeth said, "but I know for a fact my apartment couldn't get no hotter."

"It must get the afternoon sun," his mother said. She sat forward and looked up 50 and down the bus. It was half filled. Everybody was white. "I see we have the bus to ourselves," she said. Julian cringed.

"For a change," said the woman across the aisle, the owner of the red and white canvas sandals. "I come on one the other day and they were thick as fleas—up front and all through."

"The world is in a mess everywhere," his mother said. "I don't know how we've let it get in this fix."

"What gets my goat is all those boys from good families stealing automobile tires," the woman with the protruding teeth said. "I told my boy, I said you may not be rich but you been raised right and if I ever catch you in any such mess, they can send you on to the reformatory. Be exactly where you belong."

"Training tells," his mother said. "Is your boy in high school?"

"Ninth grade," the woman said.

"My son just finished college last year. He wants to write but he's selling typewriters until he gets started," his mother said.

The woman leaned forward and peered at Julian. He threw her such a malevolent look that she subsided against the seat. On the floor across the aisle there was an abandoned newspaper. He got up and got it and opened it out in front of him. His mother discreetly continued the conversation in a lower tone but the woman across the aisle said in a loud voice, "Well that's nice. Selling typewriters is close to writing. He can go right from one to the other."

"I tell him," his mother said, "that Rome wasn't built in a day."

Behind the newspaper Julian was withdrawing into the inner compartment of his mind where he spent most of his time. This was a kind of mental bubble in which he established himself when he could not bear to be a part of what was going on around him. From it he could see out and judge but in it he was safe from any kind of penetration from without. It was the only place where he felt free of the general idiocy of his fellows. His mother had never entered it but from it he could see her with absolute clarity.

The old lady was clever enough and he thought that if she had started from any of the right premises, more might have been expected of her. She lived according to the laws of her own fantasy world, outside of which he had never seen her set foot. The law of it was to sacrifice herself for him after she had first created the necessity to do so by making a mess of things. If he had permitted her sacrifices, it was only because her lack of foresight had made them necessary. All of her life had been a struggle to act like a Chestny without the Chestny goods, and to give him everything she thought a Chestny ought to have; but since, said she, it was fun to struggle, why complain? And when you had won, as she had won, what fun to look back on the hard times! He could not forgive her that she had enjoyed the struggle and that she thought *she* had won.

What she meant when she said she had won was that she had brought him up successfully and had sent him to college and that he had turned out so well—good looking (her teeth had gone unfilled so that his could be straightened), intelligent (he realized he was too intelligent to be a success), and with a future ahead of him (there was of course no future ahead of him). She excused his gloominess on the grounds that he was still growing up and his radical ideas on his lack of practical experience. She said he didn't yet know a thing about "life," that he hadn't even entered the real world—when already he was as disenchanted with it as a man of fifty.

The further irony of all this was that in spite of her, he had turned out so well. In spite of going to only a third-rate college, he had, on his own initiative, come out with a first-rate education; in spite of growing up dominated by a small mind, he had ended up with a large one; in spite of all her foolish views, he was free of prejudice and unafraid to face facts. Most miraculous of all, instead of being blinded by love for her as she was for him, he had cut himself emotionally free of her and could see her with complete objectivity. He was not dominated by his mother.

The bus stopped with a sudden jerk and shook him from his meditation. A woman from the back lurched forward with little steps and barely escaped falling in his newspaper as she righted herself. She got off and a large Negro got on. Julian kept his paper

55

60

lowered to watch. It gave him a certain satisfaction to see injustice in daily operation. It confirmed his view that with a few exceptions there was no one worth knowing within a radius of three hundred miles. The Negro was well dressed and carried a briefcase. He looked around and then sat down on the other end of the seat where the woman with the red and white canvas sandals was sitting. He immediately unfolded a newspaper and obscured himself behind it. Julian's mother's elbow at once prodded insistently into his ribs. "Now you see why I won't ride on these buses by myself," she whispered.

The woman with the red and white canvas sandals had risen at the same time the Negro sat down and had gone further back in the bus and taken the seat of the woman who had got off. His mother leaned forward and cast her an approving look.

Julian rose, crossed the aisle, and sat down in the place of the woman with the canvas sandals. From this position, he looked serenely across at his mother. Her face had turned an angry red. He stared at her, making his eyes the eyes of a stranger. He felt his tension suddenly lift as if he had openly declared war on her. 65

He would have liked to get in conversation with the Negro and to talk with him about art or politics or any subject that would be above the comprehension of those around them, but the man remained entrenched behind his paper. He was either ignoring the change of seating or had never noticed it. There was no way for Julian to convey his sympathy.

His mother kept her eyes fixed reproachfully on his face. The woman with the protruding teeth was looking at him avidly as if he were a type of monster new to her.

"Do you have a light?" he asked the Negro.

Without looking away from his paper, the man reached in his pocket and handed him a packet of matches.

"Thanks," Julian said. For a moment he held the matches foolishly. A NO SMOKING sign looked down upon him from over the door. This alone would not have deterred him; he had no cigarettes. He had quit smoking some months before because he could not afford it. "Sorry," he muttered and handed back the matches. The Negro lowered the paper and gave him an annoyed look. He took the matches and raised the paper again. 70

His mother continued to gaze at him but she did not take advantage of his momentary discomfort. Her eyes retained their battered look. Her face seemed to be unnaturally red, as if her blood pressure had risen. Julian allowed no glimmer of sympathy to show on his face. Having got the advantage, he wanted desperately to keep it and carry it through. He would have liked to teach her a lesson that would last her a while, but there seemed no way to continue the point. The Negro refused to come out from behind his paper.

Julian folded his arms and looked stolidly before him, facing her but as if he did not see her, as if he had ceased to recognize her existence. He visualized a scene in which, the bus having reached their stop, he would remain in his seat and when she said, "Aren't you going to get off?" he would look at her as a stranger who had rashly addressed him. The corner they got off on was usually deserted, but it was well lighted and it would not hurt her to walk by herself the four blocks to the Y. He decided to wait until the time came and then decide whether or not he would let her get off by herself. He would have to be at the Y at ten to bring her back, but he could leave her wondering if he was going to show up. There was no reason for her to think she could always depend on him.

He retired again into the high-ceilinged room sparsely settled with large pieces of antique furniture. His soul expanded momentarily but then he became aware of his mother across from him and the vision shriveled. He studied her coldly. Her feet in little pumps dangled like a child's and did not quite reach the floor. She was training on him an exaggerated look of reproach. He felt completely detached from her. At that moment he could with pleasure have slapped her as he would have slapped a particularly obnoxious child in his charge.

He began to imagine various unlikely ways by which he could teach her a lesson. He might make friends with some distinguished Negro professor or lawyer and bring him home to spend the evening. He would be entirely justified but her blood pressure would rise to 300. He could not push her to the extent of making her have a stroke, and moreover, he had never been successful at making any Negro friends. He had tried to strike up an acquaintance on the bus with some of the better types, with ones that looked like professors or ministers or lawyers. One morning he had sat down next to a distinguished-looking dark brown man who had answered his questions with a sonorous solemnity but who had turned out to be an undertaker. Another day he had sat down beside a cigar-smoking Negro with a diamond ring on his finger, but after a few stilted pleasantries, the Negro had rung the buzzer and risen, slipping two lottery tickets into Julian's hand as he climbed over him to leave.

He imagined his mother lying desperately ill and his being able to secure only a Negro doctor for her. He toyed with that idea for a few minutes and then dropped it for a momentary vision of himself participating as a sympathizer in a sit-in demonstration. This was possible but he did not linger with it. Instead, he approached the ultimate horror. He brought home a beautiful suspiciously Negroid woman. Prepare yourself, he said. There is nothing you can do about it. This is the woman I've chosen. She's intelligent, dignified, even good, and she's suffered and she hasn't thought it *fun*. Now persecute us, go ahead and persecute us. Drive her out of here, but remember, you're driving me too. His eyes were narrowed and through the indignation he had generated, he saw his mother across the aisle, purple-faced, shrunken to the dwarf-like proportions of her moral nature, sitting like a mummy beneath the ridiculous banner of her hat. 75

He was tilted out of his fantasy again as the bus stopped. The door opened with a sucking hiss and out of the dark a large, gaily dressed, sullen-looking colored woman got on with a little boy. The child, who might have been four, had on a short plaid suit and a Tyrolean hat with a blue feather in it. Julian hoped that he would sit down beside him and that the woman would push in beside his mother. He could think of no better arrangement.

As she waited for her tokens, the woman was surveying the seating possibilities— he hoped with the idea of sitting where she was least wanted. There was something familiar-looking about her but Julian could not place what it was. She was a giant of a woman. Her face was set not only to meet opposition but to seek it out. The downward tilt of her large lower lip was like a warning sign: DON'T TAMPER WITH ME. Her bulging figure was encased in a green crepe dress and her feet overflowed in red shoes. She had on a hideous hat. A purple velvet flap came down on one side of it and stood up on the other; the rest of it was green and looked like a cushion with the stuffing out. She carried a mammoth red pocketbook that bulged throughout as if it were stuffed with rocks.

To Julian's disappointment, the little boy climbed up on the empty seat beside his mother. His mother lumped all children, black and white, into the common category, "cute," and she thought little Negroes were on the whole cuter than little white children. She smiled at the little boy as he climbed on the seat.

Meanwhile the woman was bearing down upon the empty seat beside Julian. To his annoyance, she squeezed herself into it. He saw his mother's face change as the woman settled herself next to him and he realized with satisfaction that this was more objectionable to her than it was to him. Her face seemed almost gray and there was a look of dull recognition in her eyes, as if suddenly she had sickened at some awful confrontation. Julian saw that it was because she and the woman had, in a sense, swapped sons. Though his mother would not realize the symbolic significance of this, she would feel it. His amusement showed plainly on his face.

The woman next to him muttered something unintelligible to herself. He was conscious of a kind of bristling next to him, a muted growling like that of an angry cat. He could not see anything but the red pocketbook upright on the bulging green thighs. He visualized the woman as she had stood waiting for her tokens—the ponderous figure, rising from the red shoes upward over the solid hips, the mammoth bosom, the haughty face, to the green and purple hat.

His eyes widened.

The vision of the two hats, identical, broke upon him with the radiance of a brilliant sunrise. His face was suddenly lit with joy. He could not believe that Fate had thrust upon his mother such a lesson. He gave a loud chuckle so that she would look at him and see that he saw. She turned her eyes on him slowly. The blue in them seemed to have turned a bruised purple. For a moment he had an uncomfortable sense of her innocence, but it lasted only a second before principle rescued him. Justice entitled him to laugh. His grin hardened until it said to her as plainly as if he were saying aloud: Your punishment exactly fits your pettiness. This should teach you a permanent lesson.

Her eyes shifted to the woman. She seemed unable to bear looking at him and to find the woman preferable. He became conscious again of the bristling presence at his side. The woman was rumbling like a volcano about to become active. His mother's mouth began to twitch slightly at one corner. With a sinking heart, he saw incipient signs of recovery on her face and realized that this was going to strike her suddenly as funny and was going to be no lesson at all. She kept her eyes on the woman and an amused smile came over her face. The little Negro was looking up at her with large fascinated eyes. He had been trying to attract her attention for some time.

"Carver!" the woman said suddenly. "Come heah!"

When he saw that the spotlight was on him at last, Carver drew his feet up and turned himself toward Julian's mother and giggled.

"Carver!" the woman said. "You heah me? Come heah!"

Carver slid down from the seat but remained squatting with his back against the base of it, his head turned slyly around toward Julian's mother, who was smiling at him. The woman reached a hand across the aisle and snatched him to her. He righted himself and hung backwards on her knees, grinning at Julian's mother. "Isn't he cute?" Julian's mother said to the woman with the protruding teeth.

"I reckon he is," the woman said without conviction.

His mother yanked him upright but he eased out of her grip and shot across the aisle and scrambled, giggling wildly, onto the seat beside his love.

"I think he likes me," Julian's mother said, and smiled at the woman. It was the smile she used when she was being particularly gracious to an inferior. Julian saw everything lost. The lesson had rolled off her like rain on a roof.

The woman stood up and yanked the little boy off the seat as if she were snatching him from contagion. Julian could feel the rage in her at having no weapon like his mother's smile. She gave the child a sharp slap across his leg. He howled once and then thrust his head into her stomach and kicked his feet against her shins. "Behave," she said vehemently.

The bus stopped and the Negro who had been reading the newspaper got off. The woman moved over and set the little boy down with a thump between herself and Julian. She held him firmly by the knee. In a moment he put his hands in front of his face and peeped at Julian's mother through his fingers.

"I see yoooooooo!" she said and put her hand in front of her face and peeped at him.

The woman slapped his hand down. "Quit yo' foolishness," she said, "before I knock the living Jesus out of you!"

Julian was thankful that the next stop was theirs. He reached up and pulled the cord. The woman reached up and pulled it at the same time. Oh my God, he thought. He had the terrible intuition that when they got off the bus together, his mother would open her purse and give the little boy a nickel. The gesture would be as natural to her as breathing. The bus stopped and the woman got up and lunged to the front, dragging the child, who wished to stay on, after her. Julian and his mother got up and followed. As they neared the door, Julian tried to relieve her of her pocketbook. 95

"No," she murmured, "I want to give the little boy a nickel."

"No!" Julian hissed. "No!"

She smiled down at the child and opened her bag. The bus door opened and the woman picked him up by the arm and descended with him, hanging at her hip. Once in the street she set him down and shook him.

Julian's mother had to close her purse while she got down the bus step but as soon as her feet were on the ground, she opened it again and began to rummage inside. "I can't find but a penny," she whispered, "but it looks like a new one."

"Don't do it!" Julian said fiercely between his teeth. There was a streetlight on the corner and she hurried to get under it so that she could better see into her pocketbook. The woman was heading off rapidly down the street with the child still hanging backward on her hand. 100

"Oh little boy!" Julian's mother called and took a few quick steps and caught up with them just beyond the lamppost. "Here's a bright new penny for you," and she held out the coin, which shone bronze in the dim light.

The huge woman turned and for a moment stood, her shoulders lifted and her face frozen with frustrated rage, and stared at Julian's mother. Then all at once she seemed to explode like a piece of machinery that had been given one ounce of pressure too much. Julian saw the black fist swing out with the red pocketbook. He shut his eyes and cringed as he heard the woman shout, "He don't take nobody's pennies!" When he opened his eyes, the woman was disappearing down the street with the little boy staring wide-eyed over her shoulder. Julian's mother was sitting on the sidewalk.

"I told you not to do that," Julian said angrily. "I told you not to do that!"

He stood over her for a minute, gritting his teeth. Her legs were stretched out in front of her and her hat was on her lap. He squatted down and looked her in the face. It was totally expressionless. "You got exactly what you deserved," he said. "Now get up."

He picked up her pocketbook and put what had fallen out back in it. He picked the hat up off her lap. The penny caught his eye on the sidewalk and he picked that up and let it drop before her eyes into the purse. Then he stood up and leaned over and held his hands out to pull her up. She remained immobile. He sighed. Rising above them on either side were black apartment buildings, marked with irregular rectangles of light. At the end of the block a man came out of a door and walked off in the opposite direction. "All right," he said, "suppose somebody happens by and wants to know why you're sitting on the sidewalk?" 105

She took the hand and, breathing hard, pulled heavily up on it and then stood for a moment, swaying slightly as if the spots of light in the darkness were circling around her. Her eyes, shadowed and confused, finally settled on his face. He did not try to conceal his irritation. "I hope this teaches you a lesson," he said. She leaned forward and her eyes raked his face. She seemed trying to determine his identity. Then, as if she found nothing familiar about him, she started off with a headlong movement in the wrong direction.

"Aren't you going on to the Y?" he asked.

"Home," she muttered.

"Well, are we walking?"

For answer she kept going. Julian followed along, his hands behind him. He saw no reason to let the lesson she had had go without backing it up with an explanation of its meaning. She might as well be made to understand what had happened to her. "Don't think that was just an uppity Negro woman," he said. "That was the whole colored race which will no longer take your condescending pennies. That was your black double. She can wear the same hat as you, and to be sure," he added gratuitously (because he thought it was funny), "it looked better on her than it did on you. What all this means," he said, "is that the old world is gone. The old manners are obsolete and your graciousness is not worth a damn." He thought bitterly of the house that had been lost for him. "You aren't who you think you are," he said. 110

She continued to plow ahead, paying no attention to him. Her hair had come undone on one side. She dropped her pocketbook and took no notice. He stooped and picked it up and handed it to her but she did not take it.

"You needn't act as if the world had come to an end," he said, "because it hasn't. From now on you've got to live in a new world and face a few realities for a change. Buck up," he said, "it won't kill you."

She was breathing fast.

"Let's wait on the bus," he said.

"Home," she said thickly. 115

"I hate to see you behave like this," he said. "Just like a child. I should be able to expect more of you." He decided to stop where he was and make her stop and wait for a bus. "I'm not going any farther," he said, stopping. "We're going on the bus."

She continued to go on as if she had not heard him. He took a few steps and caught her arm and stopped her. He looked into her face and caught his breath. He was looking into a face he had never seen before. "Tell Grandpa to come get me," she said.

He stared, stricken.

"Tell Caroline to come get me," she said.

Stunned, he let her go and she lurched forward again, walking as if one leg were shorter than the other. A tide of darkness seemed to be sweeping her from him. "Mother!" he cried. "Darling, sweetheart, wait!" Crumpling, she fell to the pavement. He dashed forward and fell at her side, crying, "Mamma, Mamma!" He turned her over. Her face was fiercely distorted. One eye, large and staring, moved slightly to the left as if it had become unmoored. The other remained fixed on him, raked his face again, found nothing and closed. 120

"Wait here, wait here!" he cried and jumped up and began to run for help toward a cluster of lights he saw in the distance ahead of him. "Help, help!" he shouted, but his voice was thin, scarcely a thread of sound. The lights drifted farther away the faster he ran and his feet moved numbly as if they carried him nowhere. The tide of darkness seemed to sweep him back to her, postponing from moment to moment his entry into the world of guilt and sorrow.

THE RECEPTIVE READER

1. What kind of person is Julian's mother? What kind of attitudes and mental habits shape her personality? (How are they revealed in such telling details as the hat, the to-do about the seating in the bus, the coin for the black child?) ✧ What is her view of her son? What are her true feelings about him? ✧ Is there any one dominant trait that provides a clue to her character?

2. O'Connor is a master of mixed feelings and contradictory emotions. What kind of person is Julian? What is his basic conflict with his mother? What are the central themes of his mental monologues? Which incidents are most revealing of his character? ✧ What would you identify as his most characteristic trait or problem? Are there any contradictions in his personality? (Are we supposed to like him or identify with his point of view?)

3. This story takes us to the South in a period of *transition*. Blacks or African Americans are still called Negroes (or, more politely, "colored"). Buses have recently been integrated, with no more relegation of colored people to the back of the bus. What is the role of black people in this story? What kind of person is the mother of the little boy? Is the author's portrait of her unflattering or favorable?

4. Can you find any passages that would serve as *capsule portraits* of the major characters?

5. What is the significance of the *ending*?

6. Does this story reinforce or does it counteract stereotypes about Southerners and blacks?

THE PERSONAL RESPONSE

In this story, do you find yourself taking sides between Julian's mother and her son? What side are you on, and why? Do you think the author expects you to like Julian or identify with his point of view?

THE CREATIVE DIMENSION

Flannery O'Connor is a writer who keeps very tight control over her characters, with every detail meaningful and very little left to chance. Suppose one of the characters—Julian's mother, Julian, or the black woman (or maybe the child)—had a chance to have a last word, talking freely about what he or she felt deep down. Choose one of these, and write what you think he or she might say.

The following is a lesser-known story by O'Connor. Do you recognize in it her characteristic way of looking at the world? Do you recognize features of the O'Connor style?

Enoch and the Gorilla 1952

Enoch Emery had borrowed his landlady's umbrella and he discovered as he stood in the entrance of the drugstore, trying to open it, that it was at least as old as she was. When he finally got it hoisted, he pushed his dark glasses back on his eyes and reentered the downpour.

The umbrella was one his landlady had stopped using fifteen years before (which was the only reason she had lent it to him) and as soon as the rain touched the top of it, it came down with a shriek and stabbed him in the back of the neck. He ran a few feet with it over his head and then backed into another store entrance and removed it. Then to get it up again, he had to place the tip of it on the ground and ram it open with his foot. He ran out again, holding his hand up near the spokes to keep them open and this allowed the handle, which was carved to represent the head of a fox terrier, to jab him every few seconds in the stomach. He proceeded for another quarter of a block this way before the back half of the silk stood up off the spokes and allowed the storm to sweep down his collar. Then he ducked under the marquee of a movie house. It was Saturday and a lot of children were standing more or less in a line in front of the ticket box.

Enoch was not very fond of children, but children always seemed to like to look at him. The line turned and twenty or thirty eyes began to observe him with a steady interest. The umbrella had assumed an ugly position, half up and half down, and the half that was up was about to come down and spill more water under his collar. When this happened the children laughed and jumped up and down. Enoch glared at them and turned his back and lowered his dark glasses. He found himself facing a life-size four-color picture of a gorilla. Over the gorilla's head, written in red letters was "GONGA! Giant Jungle Monarch and a Great Star! HERE IN PERSON!!!" At the level of the gorilla's knee, there was more that said, "Gonga will appear in person in front of this theater at 12 A.M. *TODAY!* A free pass to the first ten brave enough to step up and shake his hand!"

Enoch was usually thinking of something else at the moment that Fate began drawing back her leg to kick him. When he was four years old, his father had brought him home a tin box from the penitentiary. It was orange and had a picture of some peanut brittle on the outside of it and green letters that said, "A NUTTY SURPRISE!" When Enoch had opened it, a coiled piece of steel had sprung out at him and broken off the ends of his two front teeth. His life was full of so many happenings like that that it would seem he should have been more sensitive to his times of danger. He stood there and read the poster twice through carefully. To his mind, an opportunity to insult a successful ape came from the hand of Providence.

He turned around and asked the nearest child what time it was. The child said it was twelve-ten and that Gonga was already ten minutes late. Another child said that maybe the rain had delayed him. Another said, no, not the rain, his director was taking a plane from Hollywood. Enoch gritted his teeth. The first child said that if he wanted to shake the star's hand, he would have to get in line like the rest of them and wait his turn. Enoch got into line. A child asked him how old he was. Another observed that he had funny-looking teeth. He ignored all this as best he could and began to straighten out the umbrella.

In a few minutes a black truck turned around the corner and came slowly up the street in the heavy rain. Enoch pushed the umbrella under his arm and began to squint through his dark glasses. As the truck approached, a phonograph inside it began to play "Tarara Boom Di Aye," but the music was almost drowned out by the rain. There was a large illustration of a blonde on the outside of the truck, advertising some picture other than the one with the gorilla.

The children held their line carefully as the truck stopped in front of the movie house. The back door of it was constructed like a paddy wagon, with a grate, but the ape was not at it. Two men in raincoats got out of the cab part, cursing, and ran around to the back and opened the door. One of them stuck his head in and said, "Okay, make it snappy, willya?" The other jerked his thumb at the children and said, "Get back willya, willya get back?"

5

A voice on the record inside the truck said, "Here's Gonga, folks, Roaring Gonga and a Great Star! Give Gonga a big hand, folks!" The voice was barely a mumble in the rain.

The man who was waiting by the door of the truck stuck his head in again. "Okay, willya get out?" he said.

There was a faint thump somewhere inside the van. After a second a dark furry arm   10 emerged just enough for the rain to touch it and then drew back inside.

The man who was under the marquee took off his raincoat and threw it to the man by the door, who threw it into the wagon. After two or three minutes more, the gorilla appeared at the door, with the raincoat buttoned up to his chin and the collar turned up. There was an iron chain hanging from around his neck; the man grabbed it and pulled him down and the two of them bounded under the marquee together. A motherly-looking woman was in the glass ticket box, getting the passes ready for the first ten children brave enough to step up and shake hands.

The gorilla ignored the children entirely and followed the man over to the other side of the entrance where there was a small platform raised about a foot off the ground. He stepped up on it and turned facing the children and began to growl. His growls were not so much loud as poisonous; they appeared to issue from a black heart. Enoch was terrified and if he had not been surrounded by the children, he would have run away.

"Who'll step up first?" the man said. "Come on, come on, who'll step up first? A free pass to the first kid stepping up."

There was no movement from the group of children. The man glared at them. "What's the matter with you kids?" he barked. "You yellow? He won't hurt you as long as I got him by this chain." He tightened his grip on the chain and jangled it at them to show he was holding it securely.

After a minute a little girl separated herself from the group. She had long wood-   15 shaving curls and a fierce triangular face. She moved up to within four feet of the star.

"Okay okay," the man said, rattling the chain, "make it snappy."

The ape reached out and gave her hand a quick shake. By this time there was another little girl ready and then two boys. The line re-formed and began to move up.

The gorilla kept his hand extended and turned his head away with a bored look at the rain. Enoch had got over his fear and was trying frantically to think of a remark that would be suitable to insult him with. Usually he didn't have any trouble with this kind of composition but nothing came to him now. His brain, both parts, was completely empty. He couldn't think even of the insulting phrase he used every day.

There were only two children in front of him by now. The first one shook hands and stepped aside. Enoch's heart was beating violently. The child in front of him finished and stepped aside and left him facing the ape, who took his hand with an automatic motion.

It was the first hand that had been extended to Enoch since he had come to the   20 city. It was warm and soft.

For a second he only stood there, clasping it. Then he began to stammer. "My name is Enoch Emery," he mumbled. "I attended the Rodemill Boys' Bible Academy. I work at the city zoo. I seen two of your pictures. I'm only eighteen years old but I already work for the city. My daddy made me come . . ." and his voice cracked.

The star leaned slightly forward and a change came in his eyes: an ugly pair of human ones moved closer and squinted at Enoch from behind the celluloid pair. "You go take a jump," a surly voice inside the ape-suit said, low but distinctly, and the hand was jerked away.

Enoch's humiliation was so sharp and painful that he turned around three times before he realized which direction he wanted to go in. Then he ran off into the rain as fast as he could.

In spite of himself, Enoch couldn't get over the expectation that something was going to happen to him. The virtue of hope, in Enoch, was made up of two parts suspicion and one part desire. It operated on him all the rest of the day. He had only a vague idea what he wanted, but he was not a boy without ambition: he wanted to become something. He wanted to better his condition. He wanted, some day, to see a line of people waiting to shake his hand.

All afternoon he fidgeted and fooled in his room, biting his nails and shredding what was left of the silk off the landlady's umbrella. Finally he denuded it entirely and broke off the spokes. What was left was a black stick with a sharp steel point at one end and a dog's head at the other. It might have been an instrument for some specialized kind of torture that had gone out of fashion. Enoch walked up and down his room with it under his arm and realized that it would distinguish him on the sidewalk.

About seven o'clock in the evening he put on his coat and took the stick and headed for a little restaurant two blocks away. He had the sense that he was setting off to get some honor, but he was very nervous, as if he were afraid he might have to snatch it instead of receive it.

He never set out for anything without eating first. The restaurant was called the Paris Diner; it was a tunnel about six feet wide, located between a shoeshine parlor and a dry-cleaning establishment. Enoch slid in and climbed up on the far stool at the counter and said he would have a bowl of split-pea soup and a chocolate malted milkshake.

The waitress was a tall woman with a big yellow dental plate and the same color hair done up in a black hairnet. One hand never left her hip; she filled orders with the other one. Although Enoch came in nightly, she had never learned to like him.

Instead of filling his order, she began to fry bacon; there was only one other customer in the place and he had finished his meal and was reading a newspaper; there was no one to eat the bacon but her. Enoch reached over the counter and prodded her hip with the stick. "Listen here," he said, "I got to go. I'm in a hurry."

"Go then," she said. Her jaw began to work and she stared into the skillet with a fixed attention.

"Lemme just have a piece of theter cake yonder," he said, pointing to a half of pink and yellow cake on a round glass stand. "I think I got something to do. I got to be going. Set it up there next to him," he said, indicating the customer reading the newspaper. He slid over the stools and began reading the outside sheet of the man's paper.

The man lowered the paper and looked at him. Enoch smiled. The man raised the paper again. "Could I borrow some part of your paper that you ain't studying?" Enoch asked. The man lowered it again and stared at him; he had muddy unflinching eyes. He leafed deliberately through the paper and shook out the sheet with the comic strips and handed it to Enoch. It was Enoch's favorite part. He read it every evening like an office. While he ate the cake that the waitress had torpedoed down the counter at him, he read and felt himself surge with kindness and courage and strength.

When he finished one side, he turned the sheet over and began to scan the advertisements for movies that filled the other side. His eye went over three columns without stopping; then it came to a box that advertised Gonga, Giant Jungle Monarch, and listed the theaters he would visit on his tour and the hours he would be at each one. In thirty minutes he would arrive at the Victory on 57th Street and that would be his last appearance in the city.

25

30

If anyone had watched Enoch read this, he would have seen a certain transformation in his countenance. It still shone with the inspiration he had absorbed from the comic strips, but something else had come over it: a look of awakening.

The waitress happened to turn around to see if he hadn't gone. "What's the matter with you?" she said. "Did you swallow a seed?" 35

"I know what I want," Enoch murmured.

"I know what I want too," she said with a dark look.

Enoch felt for his stick and laid his change on the counter. "I got to be going now."

"Don't let me keep you," she said.

"You may not see me again," he said, "—the way I am." 40

"Any way I don't see you will be all right with me," she said.

Enoch left. It was a pleasant damp evening. The puddles on the sidewalk shone and the store windows were steamy and bright with junk. He disappeared down a side street and made his way rapidly along the darker passages of the city, pausing only once or twice at the end of an alley to dart a glance in each direction before he ran on. The Victory was a small theater, suited to the needs of the family, in one of the closer subdivisions; he passed through a succession of lighted areas and then on through more alleys and back streets until he came to the business section that surrounded it. Then he slowed up. He saw it about a block away, glittering in its darker setting. He didn't cross the street to the side it was on but kept on the far side, moving forward with his squint fixed on the glary spot. He stopped when he was directly across from it and hid himself in a narrow stair cavity dividing a building.

The truck that carried Gonga was parked across the street and the star was standing under the marquee, shaking hands with an elderly woman. She moved aside and a gentleman in a polo shirt stepped up and shook hands vigorously, like a sportsman. He was followed by a boy of about three who wore a tall Western hat that nearly covered his face; he had to be pushed ahead by the line. Enoch watched for some time, his face working with envy. The small boy was followed by a lady in shorts, she by an old man who tried to draw extra attention to himself by dancing up instead of walking in a dignified way. Enoch suddenly darted across the street and slipped noiselessly into the open back door of the truck.

The handshaking went on until the feature picture was ready to begin. Then the star got back in the van and the people filed into the theater. The driver and the man who was master of ceremonies climbed in the cab part and the truck rumbled off. It crossed the city rapidly and continued on the highway, going very fast.

There came from the van certain thumping noises, not those of the normal gorilla, but they were drowned out by the drone of the motor and the steady sound of wheels against the road. The night was pale and quiet, with nothing to stir it but an occasional complaint from a hoot owl and the distant muted jarring of a freight train. The truck sped on until it slowed for a crossing, and as the van rattled over the tracks, a figure slipped from the door and almost fell, and then limped hurriedly off toward the woods. 45

Once in the darkness of a pine thicket, he laid down a pointed stick he had been clutching and something bulky and loose that he had been carrying under his arm, and began to undress. He folded each garment neatly after he had taken it off and then stacked it on top of the last thing he had removed. When all his clothes were in the pile, he took up the stick and carefully began making a hole in the ground with it.

The darkness of the pine grove was broken by paler moonlit spots that moved over him now and again and showed him to be Enoch. His natural appearance was marred by a gash that ran from the corner of his lip to his collarbone and by a lump under his eye that gave him a dulled insensitive look. Nothing could have been more deceptive for he was burning with the intensest kind of happiness.

He dug rapidly until he had made a trench about a foot long and a foot deep. Then he placed the stack of clothes in it and stood aside to rest a second. Burying his clothes was not a symbol to him of burying his former self; he only knew he wouldn't need them any more. As soon as he got his breath, he pushed the displaced dirt over the hole and stamped it down with his foot. He discovered while he did this that he still had his shoes on, and when he finished, he removed them and threw them from him. Then he picked up the loose bulky object and shook it vigorously.

In the uncertain light, one of his lean white legs could be seen to disappear and then the other, one arm and then the other: a black heavier shaggier figure replaced his. For an instant, it had two heads, one light and one dark, but after a second, it pulled the dark black head over the other and corrected this. It busied itself with certain hidden fastenings and what appeared to be minor adjustments of its hide.

For a time after this, it stood very still and didn't do anything. Then it began to growl and beat its chest; it jumped up and down and flung its arms and thrust its head forward. The growls were thin and uncertain at first but they grew louder after a second. They became low and poisonous, louder again, low and poisonous again; they stopped altogether. The figure extended its hand, clutched nothing, and shook its arm vigorously; it withdrew the arm, extended it again, clutched nothing, and shook. It repeated this four or five times. Then it picked up the pointed stick and placed it at a cocky angle under its arm and left the woods for the highway. No gorilla anywhere, Africa or California or New York, was happier than he.

A man and woman sitting close together on a rock just off the highway were looking across an open stretch of valley at a view of the city in the distance and they didn't see the shaggy figure approaching. The smokestacks and square tops of buildings made a black uneven wall against the lighter sky and here and there a steeple cut a sharp wedge out of a cloud. The young man turned his neck just in time to see the gorilla standing a few feet away, hideous and black, with its hand extended. He eased his arm from around the woman and disappeared silently into the woods. She, as soon as she turned her eyes, fled screaming down the highway. The gorilla stood as though surprised and presently its arm fell to its side. It sat down on the rock where they had been sitting and stared over the valley at the uneven skyline of the city.

50

THE RECEPTIVE READER

1. What features of this story might make a reader recognize it as the work of Flannery O'Connor? For instance, what makes Enoch an outsider or misfit?

2. What details introduce *grotesque* overtones—or undertones? (What, for instance, makes the umbrella a very nonordinary umbrella?) Where does the author's wicked sense of humor show, and what is its relation to the more serious aspects of the story?

3. What is the role of *violence*? Is it similar to or different from its role in other O'Connor stories?

4. What is the meaning or *theme* of Enoch's story? Does the story as a whole have a redeeming or humanizing quality?

THE PERSONAL RESPONSE

How do you personally react to the story? Does it seem too far removed from your own concerns or from the concerns of ordinary people?

JUXTAPOSITIONS

A Range of Sources

With a puzzling, provocative author like Flannery O'Connor, readers may turn for help to a range of **secondary sources.** They may look for guidance in the author's own comments in conversations, lectures, or letters. They may look for helpful hints in tributes by fellow writers or in expert testimony by literary critics.

Author Testimony

O'Connor herself lectured and wrote extensively about the writing and teaching of literature. (She did, however, once say, "Asking me to lecture about story-writing is like asking a fish to lecture on swimming.") The following is her interpretation of one of her stories from a reading she presented to a college audience.

FLANNERY O'CONNOR
On "A Good Man Is Hard to Find"   1963

This is the story of a family of six which, on its way driving to Florida, gets wiped out by an escaped convict who calls himself the Misfit. The family is made up of the Grandmother and her son, Bailey, and his children, John Wesley and June Star and the baby, and there is also the cat and the children's mother. The cat is named Pitty Sing, and the Grandmother is taking him with them, hidden in a basket.

Now I think it behooves me to try to establish with you the basis on which reason operates in this story. Much of my fiction takes its character from a reasonable use of the unreasonable, though the reasonableness of my use of it may not always be apparent. The assumptions that underlie this use of it, however, are those of the central Christian mysteries. These are assumptions to which a large part of the modern audience takes exception. About this I can only say that there are perhaps other ways than my own in which this story could be read, but none other by which it could have been written. Belief, in my own case anyway, is the engine that makes perception operate.

The heroine of this story, the Grandmother, is in the most significant position life offers the Christian. She is facing death. And to all appearances she, like the rest of us, is not too well prepared for it. She would like to see the event postponed. Indefinitely.

I've talked to a number of teachers who use this story in class and who tell their students that the Grandmother is evil, that in fact, she's a witch, even down to the cat. One of these teachers told me that his students, and particularly his Southern students, resisted this interpretation with a certain bemused vigor, and he didn't understand why. I had to tell him that they resisted it because they all had grandmothers or great-aunts just like her at home, and they knew, from personal experience, that the old lady lacked comprehension, but that she had a good heart. The Southerner is usually tolerant of those weaknesses that proceed from innocence, and he knows that a taste for self-preservation can be readily combined with the missionary spirit.

This same teacher was telling his students that morally the Misfit was several cuts above the Grandmother. He had a really sentimental attachment to the Misfit. But then a prophet gone wrong is almost always more interesting than your grandmother, and you have to let people take their pleasures where they find them.

It is true that the old lady is a hypocritical old soul; her wits are no match for the Misfit's, nor is her capacity for grace equal to his; yet I think the unprejudiced reader will feel that the Grandmother has a special kind of triumph in this story which instinctively we do not allow to someone altogether bad.

I often ask myself what makes a story work, and what makes it hold up as a story, and I have decided that it is probably some action, some gesture of a character that is unlike any other in the story, one which indicates where the real heart of the story lies. This would have to be an action or a gesture which was both totally right and totally unexpected; it would have to be one that was both in character and beyond character; it would have to suggest both the world and eternity. The action or gesture I'm talking about would have to be on . . . the level which has to do with the Divine life and our participation in it. It would be a gesture that transcended any neat allegory that might have been intended or any pat moral categories a reader could make. It would be a gesture which somehow made contact with mystery.

There is a point in this story where such a gesture occurs. The Grandmother is at last alone, facing the Misfit. Her head clears for an instant and she realizes, even in her limited way, that she is responsible for the man before her and joined to him by ties of kinship which have their roots deep in the mystery she has been merely prattling about so far. And at this point, she does the right thing, she makes the right gesture. . . .

I don't want to equate the Misfit with the devil. I prefer to think that, however unlikely this may seem, the old lady's gesture, like the mustard seed, will grow to be a great crow-filled tree in the Misfit's heart, and will be enough of a pain to him there to turn him into the prophet he was meant to become. But that's another story.

From *Mystery and Manners*, edited by Sally and Robert Fitzgerald

QUESTION

Does this account by the author change your understanding of the story?

Author Correspondence

Readers often turn to an author's published **letters** for insights into the writer's personality and work. The following is an excerpt from a review by Joyce Carol Oates of a volume of O'Connor's letters. Oates said, "It will be no surprise to admirers of Flannery O'Connor's enigmatic, troubling, and highly idiosyncratic fiction to learn that there were, behind the near-perfect little rituals of violence and redemption she created, not one but several Flannery O'Connors."

JOYCE CAROL OATES
A Self-Portrait in Letters   1987

It must be said of the letters that they give life to a wonderfully warm, witty, generous, and complex personality, surely one of the most gifted of contemporary writers. At the same time they reveal a curiously girlish, childlike, touchingly timid personality. . . . The letters give voice, on one side, to a hilariously witty observer of the grotesque, the vulgar, and the merely silly in this society, and in the rather limited world of the Catholic imagination; and then they reveal a Catholic intellectual so conservative and docile that she will write to a priest-friend for permission to read Gide and Sartre (at that time on the Church's Index of forbidden writers). . . .

The first letter in the collection was written in 1948, when Flannery was "up north" at Yaddo, the writers' colony in Saratoga Springs. The last letter, a heartbreaking one, was written just before her death on August 3, 1964, when she knew she was dying of complications following an operation for the removal of a tumor. The years between 1948 and 1964 were rich, full ones, despite the fact that Flannery's debilitating condition (lupus) kept her at home, and frequently bedridden, for long periods of time. She was not at all a solitary, reclusive person; she had a wide circle of friends, and clearly loved seeing them, and writing to them often. . . .

She always knew that the process of creation was subjected to no rules, and that, as an artist, she "discovered" the truth of her stories in the writing of them. She enjoyed writing—perhaps it is not an exaggeration to say that she lived for it, and in it. Easily exhausted, she forced herself to work two or three hours every day, in the morning, and managed by this discipline to write about one story a year during the worst periods. During the final year of her life, 1964, when everything seemed to go wrong, she was completing the volume that would be her finest achievement, "Everything That Rises Must Converge," which would be published, to wide critical acclaim, after her death. One cannot imagine an ailing person less given to self-pity. When, as a fairly young woman, she learned she would probably be on crutches the rest of her life, she says merely, "So, so much for that. I will henceforth be a structure with flying buttresses. . . ." Writing to a friend in 1964, she says she must submit to an operation because "I have a large tumor and if they don't make haste and get rid of it, they will have to remove me and leave it." It is only near the very end of her life that she says, briefly, to the same friend: "Prayers requested. I am sick of being sick."

From "Flannery O'Connor: A Self-Portrait in Letters," in *Antaeus*, Autumn 1987

QUESTIONS

Which details or comments in this review do most to round out your mental picture of O'Connor? Which are most enlightening or thought provoking?

Tribute by a Fellow Writer

Alice Walker, author of *The Color Purple,* grew up in a sharecropper's shack a few miles from where O'Connor lived for a time in a house built by slaves. Walker discovered the "dazzling perfection" of O'Connor's writing while taking a course on Southern writers up North. Walker appreciated O'Connor's work because she wrote about Southern white women with "not a whiff of magnolia" hovering in the air and about "black folks without melons and superior racial patience." Walker says, "As a college student in the sixties I read her books endlessly, scarcely conscious of the difference between her racial and economic background and my own, but put them away in anger when I discovered that, while I was reading O'Connor—Southern, Catholic, and white—there were other women writers—some Southern, some religious, all black—I had not been allowed to know." Later, after discovering black writers like Zora Neale Hurston and Jean Toomer, Walker came to look at O'Connor's fiction from a new perspective.

ALICE WALKER
Beyond the Peacock 1975

Whether one "understands" her stories or not, one knows her characters are new and wondrous creations in the world and that none of her stories—not even the earliest ones in which her consciousness of racial matters had not evolved sufficiently to be interesting or to differ much from the insulting and ignorant racial stereotyping that preceded it—could have been written by anyone else. As one can tell . . . a Picasso from a Hallmark card, one can tell an O'Connor story from any story laid next to it. Her Catholicism did not in any way limit (by defining it) her art. After her great stories of sin, damnation, prophecy and revelation, the stories one reads casually in the average magazine seem to be about love and roast beef. . . .

She destroyed the last vestiges of sentimentality in white Southern writing; she caused white women to look ridiculous on pedestals, and she approached her black characters—as a mature artist—with unusual humility and restraint. She also cast spells and worked magic with the written word.

From *In Search of Our Mothers' Gardens*

QUESTIONS

How did you react to the references to black people in O'Connor's stories? Can you relate Walker's comments to the stories you have read?

The Critic's Voice

Many critics take their clue from O'Connor's Catholicism in looking in her "startling dramas" for hints of divine love or redemption—for religious overtones that are implied rather than spelled out. The critic who wrote the following excerpt said that love is "at the very core of Flannery O'Connor's fiction."

RICHARD GIANNONE
The Mystery of Love 1989

There is no reason to contest the fact that human dereliction sets O'Connor's narratives in motion and directs their course and outcome. What we need to look for is the gift of grace, the exultant salute to the eternal that she avows in her lectures and correspondence and that brings her anguished conflicts to a higher resolution. "It is a sign of maturity not to be scandalized and to try to find explanations in charity." O'Connor candidly challenges us to take a charitable view of her work, and scarcely anyone has met that challenge.

A shift in the locus of inquiry will bring about a change in our perception of O'Connor. She will emerge as more than an astute recorder of casual disasters. A quiet, patient smile of controlled abandonment to love shines through all of her fictional violence. And an unexpected contour will emerge from her art. . . . To the undiscerning or the psychologically oriented, O'Connor's unrelenting exposure of human fault might seem like obsession or preacherly harangue; for O'Connor, however, the sight of inner wretchedness precedes the experience of love. . . . The guilt and punishment that her characters bring upon themselves have no independent reality of their own, but are the dark shadows of the grace and life that O'Connor finds in existence. . . .

Her strange choices for heroes—nihilists, petty tyrants, and killers—turn out to be wanderers in love. Their encounter with the mystery of their existence, the adventurer of love whom O'Connor calls God, brings the quest to a close. All the endings take both protagonist and reader by surprise. O'Connor believes, and in powerful action shows, unfathomable reality to suggest the overwhelming boldness of divine love invading human life. Her fundamental understanding of this mysterious incursion is that love is not a human right or a mental deduction but a divine revelation, a gift of plenitude found within the human heart. "I believe love to be efficacious in the loooong run" she writes to a friend. O'Connor's fiction enacts her belief.

From *Flannery O'Connor and the Mystery of Love*

QUESTION

Does this critic make you reexamine the role of the author's religious convictions in her stories? How?

WRITING ABOUT LITERATURE

9. One Author in Depth (Integrating Sources)

The role autobiography plays in fiction is precisely the role that reality plays in a dream.

JOHN CHEEVER

The Writing Workshop When you are puzzled, intrigued, or provoked by a story, you may turn to other stories by the same author to see if you can find a pattern. You try to see if you can detect clues to familiar preoccupations or a recurrent theme. In addition, you may want to turn to personal testimony by the author—in letters, in lectures, in conversations with friends. You may be able to get ideas or help from biographers and critics who focus on the relationship between the author and the work. Choose an author for the subject of a paper in which you look for the common thread or a recurrent issue in several stories. Draw on background materials that help you bring a common theme or central issue into focus.

Your task will be to write a unified paper while integrating diverse materials. It will be especially important to develop an agenda—an overall purpose or direction. Ask yourself: "What am I trying to do in this paper?" Here are accounts of what gave purpose and direction to some sample projects:

✧ A student writer was intrigued by the fact that both the talkative grandmother in "A Good Man Is Hard to Find" and the mother in "Everything That Rises Must Converge" seem to live in the past, holding on to genteel traditions and to concepts of good breeding that no longer fit the realities of the South. The student found a third O'Connor story that spells out the same underlying theme even more directly: In "A Late Encounter with the Enemy," a teacher has been taking summer classes for years to earn a belated teaching credential. She plans to have her grandfather present at her graduation. He is a Confederate general, 104 years old, and she wants him to shame the upstarts by having him there to represent the "old traditions! Dignity! Honor! Courage! My kin!" The irony of the story is that the supposed general was actually a foot soldier in the war, who was given his general's uniform by a movie company promoting *Gone with the Wind.*

✧ One student wrote about a recurrent pattern in three stories by John Cheever: We start out with people in a comfortable middle-class or upper-middle-class existence, but something happens to show that these people "are not quite who they appear to be at first, and by the end of the story, their true natures are revealed." The "fragile veneer of the characters' happy lives begins to crack." Their weaknesses, disguised by a smug façade, are shown. By the end of the story, they may, like the main character in "The Swimmer," find themselves "miserable, cold, tired, and bewildered," exposed to the ridicule of passing motorists. Drawing on revealing comments by both Cheever himself and by his son, the student writer showed that this fear of exposure was a haunting preoccupation in Cheever's own private life.

✧ In a paper discussing several stories by Flannery O'Connor, a student writer focused on the "moment of revelation" (the *epiphany*) when a character "suddenly accepts into his or her consciousness key facts or conditions of his or her life." For instance, at the end of "A Good Man Is Hard to Find," the Misfit rejects the grandmother's last frantic appeal to spare her life as she tells him, "I know you come from nice people." She urges him to pray and reaches out to touch him: "Why, you're one of my babies. You're one of my own children!" The student writer quoted O'Connor as explaining the ending to an audience to whom she was reading this story: The grandmother realizes, "even in her limited way, that she is responsible for the man before her and joined to him by ties of kinship which have their roots deep in the mystery she has been merely prattling about so far." The paper found a similar pattern of a climactic final insight or realization in two other stories.

Writing an Integrated Paper

A paper tracing a common thread in several stories by the same author tests your ability to integrate material. Keep your paper from seeming stitched together—with too many of the seams showing. Consider guidelines like the following:

✧ *Push toward a unifying thesis.* Note the weak *also* in the following opening paragraph of a first draft. (How are the two points raised there related?)

FIRST DRAFT: O'Connor's stories shock the reader because, as she herself says, "No matter how well we are able to soften the
grotesque by humor or compassion, there is always an intensity about it that creates a general discomfort." O'Connor writes about the mixture of the frightening and the
comical that we call the grotesque. The conflict between
good and evil is also central to O'Connor's themes. These
themes are evident in several of her stories . . .

A more integrated trial thesis might read like this:

SECOND DRAFT: O'Connor's stories shock the reader because, as she herself says, "No matter how well we are able to soften the
grotesque by humor or compassion, there is always an intensity about it that creates a general discomfort." O'Connor's preoccupation with the grotesque is rooted in one
of her most basic themes: the struggle between good and
evil. *When evil erupts into our ordinary world, it is frightening, but it is also comical because it is so different from
what we expect or what should be.*

✧ *Chart your overall strategy.* For instance, you may decide to explore the
role of violence in each of three stories, tracing important continuities and key
differences as you examine *each story* in turn. You then have to make sure to
keep important connections in view as you leave one story behind and move
on to the next. Instead, you might plot your essay to move not from story to
story but from point to point. You might set up three or four key features of
the archetypal Southern lady found in many of O'Connor's stories and take up
each feature in turn. You might identify such common character traits as nostalgia for a more genteel past, outdated condescending views on race, and unrealistic expectations of the current crop of white people merely because they
are white. You would then take each of these up in turn and show that each
can be found in all three or four major characters you are examining.

✧ *Use brief characteristic quotations to take your reader into the author's
world.* Suppose you are trying to show in a lesser-known story by O'Connor
the familiar blend of the threatening and strange with the zany and comical. A
web of specific references and short apt quotations will create the familiar atmosphere:

Enoch in "Enoch and the Gorilla" is isolated from others. When he had
opened "a nutty surprise" that his father had brought for him from the penitentiary, a "coiled piece of steel had sprung out at him and broken off the
ends of his two front teeth." The waitress who instead of filling his order begins to fry bacon for herself bids him farewell by saying "Any way I don't see
you will be all right with me." When Enoch lines up with the children waiting to shake hands with a man in a gorilla suit promoting a gorilla movie, the
gorilla's hand is "the first hand that had been extended to Enoch since he had
come to the city." This handshake changes Enoch's life; he attacks the hapless gorilla to take over the suit so that he can "see people . . . waiting to
shake his hand."

✧ *Test a critic's opinion against your own firsthand reading.* Do not just accept the critic's say-so as gospel. Show why the critic's comment is helpful; show why you agree or disagree. The following passage does a good job of working a critical quotation into the student writer's own text:

> Susanne M. Paulson, in *Flannery O'Connor: A Study of the Short Fiction*, says, "Both the Misfit and the grandmother derive from the same human family tainted by sin and suffering in the material world." O'Connor is indeed showing the reader that the Misfit is not an alien being but might be one of our neighbors or our own family. The Misfit himself says, "I been most everything. Been in the arm service . . . twict married, been an undertaker, been with the railroads." He says, "I was a gospel singer for a while." We could have encountered him anywhere in familiar everyday reality.

✧ *Pay special attention to transitions.* You will need strong ties and cross-references between the several different stories you are discussing. Suppose you are moving on from the story about the Misfit to the story about Enoch and the gorilla. Avoid a lame transition like "We see similar themes in another O'Connor story." Provide the missing link between the two sections of your paper. Show a strong thematic connection by highlighting a major shared element:

TRANSITION: Like the Misfit in "A Good Man Is Hard to Find," Enoch in "Enoch and the Gorilla" is also a "misfit" in his world.

What is the focus of the following student paper? How successful is it in integrating material from several different stories? How successful is it in defining and making meaningful a key term in critical discussions of O'Connor's work?

SAMPLE STUDENT PAPER

Flannery O'Connor's Grotesques

> The grotesque: absurdly incongruous; departing markedly from the natural, the expected, or the typical . . . a combination of horror and humor.

This definition of the word *grotesque* perfectly describes the life of Flannery O'Connor. After all, isn't it absurd and unexpected that, as a young woman of twenty-five, her bones were so weak from lupus that she was forced to hobble around on crutches like a woman of eighty? Or ironic that she would eventually die from complications of an abdominal operation that was supposed to help improve her condition? And despite the horror O'Connor undoubtedly had to deal with during her illness, she still held a positive outlook on life, writing shortly before her relapse and death in 1964, "I intend to survive this." This absurdity, this incongruity, this grotesqueness that seemed to dominate the path of her life has carried over into O'Connor's writing, as can be seen in the short stories "A Good Man Is Hard to Find," "Everything That Rises Must Converge," and "Enoch and the Gorilla." In each of these stories lurk characteristics of the grotesque—descriptions and comparisons that seem unnatural or incongruous, ideas that are absurd or unexpected, and that same ironic combination of horror and positive humor that haunted O'Connor throughout her illness.

Perhaps it was her own physical illness that caused O'Connor's fascination with physical deformity. Many brief descriptions in her stories reflect this fascination, such as in "Everything That Rises Must Converge," when Julian turned his stricken mother over and saw that "her face was fiercely distorted. One eye, large and staring, moved slightly to the left as if it had become unmoored." This sense of grotesque distortion is also evident in the description of Enoch putting on the gorilla suit in "Enoch and the Gorilla." O'Connor portrays the act as a weird metamorphosis, as if the boy were actually turning into a gorilla:

> In the uncertain light, one of his lean white legs could be seen to disappear and then the other, one arm and then the other: a black heavier shaggier figure replaced his. For an instant, it had two heads, one light and one dark. . . .

Likewise, the comparisons O'Connor draws between two objects often seem unnatural or incongruous. In "A Good Man Is Hard to Find," the mother's face is described as "broad and innocent as a cabbage," which I found to be a peculiar comparison. Similarly, in "Enoch and the Gorilla," Enoch's broken umbrella is compared to "an instrument for some specialized kind of torture that had gone out of fashion," which I thought was a warped, distorted way of viewing a common household object.

The descriptions and comparisons were not the only hints of distortion or unnaturalness. In fact, some of O'Connor's main story ideas contain elements of the unnatural or the unexpected, sometimes to the point of absurdity. In "A Good Man Is Hard to Find," the whole idea of the grandmother trying to talk a hardened criminal out of killing her on the basis that she is "a good lady" and of "good blood" is absurd. The situation becomes even more ridiculous when the grandmother and the Misfit begin very nonchalantly to discuss the weather, or when the grandmother, showing her good breeding and southern hospitality, kindly offers him one of her own son's shirts to wear, despite the fact that he is just about to have her son killed and is planning to own the shirt the son had been wearing.

Also unexpected and absurd is the Misfit's exceedingly calm and polite manner. In fact, when he notices that the mother is getting very uneasy and anxious, he politely asks her, "Lady, would you and that little girl like to step off yonder with Bobby Lee and Hiram and join your husband?" to which the mother answers in obvious relief, "'Yes, thank you.'" Ever the gentleman, he orders his men to "hep that lady up."

Although the Misfit's gentlemanly mannerisms are very surprising, perhaps the most unexpected part of the story occurs when the grandmother has been talking to the Misfit for a while. Suddenly feeling as if she were beginning to understand him, she declares, "Why, you're one of my babies. You're one of my own children!" Ironically it is at this moment of understanding and intimacy that the Misfit chooses to kill her.

Despite the grim ending of this and the other two stories, there is evidence of an ironic blending of humor with horror. In "A Good Man Is Hard to Find," the images of the cat jumping onto Bailey's shoulder, "clinging . . . like a caterpillar," and the children scrambling out of the overturned car shouting, "'We've had an ACCIDENT!'" are humorous. In fact, even after we realize the mother has suffered serious injury, the accident still seems funny in a sick sort of way.

Similarly, in "Enoch and the Gorilla," Enoch's nervous introduction to Gonga the Gorilla is hilarious, although we know how hurt and humiliated Enoch must have felt afterwards:

> "My name is Enoch Emery," he mumbled. "I attended the Rodemill Boys' Bible Academy. I work at the city zoo. I seen two of your pictures. I'm only eighteen years old but I already work for the city. My daddy made me come. . . ." and his voice cracked. . . ."You go take a jump," a surly voice inside the ape-suit said.

In "Everything That Rises Must Converge," the humor found in Julian's rebellious fantasies in which he "brought home a beautiful suspiciously Negroid woman" or "imagined his mother lying desperately ill and his being able to secure only a Negro doctor for her" lies on the surface of a pain that lurks underneath, the pain of his and his mother's strained relationship. The humor is there, but the underlying pain and horror make it feel warped and distorted.

This warping of reality, this distortion of common things, this grotesqueness, is something O'Connor shows an affinity for and a talent in using. Through her manipulation of unnatural comparisons, unexpected and absurd ideas, and humor laced with horror, she shows how even her most self-righteous characters are not clean of the grotesque. Despite the grandmother's "good blood," she too was grotesque in her absurd conversation with the Misfit. Even bright, young, non-prejudiced, socially-aware Julian was tainted with the grotesque because of the delight he took in destroying his mother's comfortable little dreamworld in which she and her ancestors had a special identity. O'Connor has a knack for using distortion to create a confusing environment for her characters in which the line between the "good" and "evil" characters is very finely drawn. As one critic put it, "The real grotesques are the self-justified, the apparent grotesques may be the blessed."

QUESTIONS

How would you sum up the student writer's definition of the key term? What is the writer's strategy for structuring the paper? How adequate or convincing are the examples? What questions does the paper leave unanswered?

10 PERSPECTIVES
The Range of Interpretation

Writing disappears unless there is a response to it.
BARBARA CHRISTIAN

FOCUS ON CRITICISM

Critics are attracted to writers that present a challenge, that test their powers of interpretation. James Joyce, William Faulkner, and Flannery O'Connor are among writers whose fiction has drawn the attention of many commentators. Checking your college library for critical discussions of Nathaniel Hawthorne's "Young Goodman Brown," a richly symbolic and ambiguous story, you might find a hundred or more articles.

What accounts for differences in interpretation? For one thing, readers may focus on different corners of the familiar communication triangle: sender—message—receiver. An *author* (sender) writes a *text* (message) that will be read by a *reader* (receiver). Critics may focus attention on the author, on the internal workings of a story, or on what happens in the mind of the reader.

✧ Much traditional literary criticism focused on *the author*. **Author biography** aimed at a full accounting on the author's life and times. It studied the setting or *milieu* of the artist's work. It would place John Steinbeck, for instance, in the context of the California coastal and agricultural region that was his home. It would see his sympathy with the down-and-out against the background of the Great Depression. It would examine his ties with the Communist party, "in dubious battle" (the title of one of his books) against the capitalist system. It would probe his family life (marriages and children) for clues to what shaped his views of men and women. Modern biographers continue to look in depth at an author and his or her background. On the whole, they tend to be less genteel and discreet than their predecessors. Many modern biographers seem determined to go beyond an author's public image—the warmhearted storyteller, the loving parent—to probe the personal problems behind the public persona.

✧ In a reaction against the traditional focus on the author's life and times, the **New Criticism** (originally new in the forties and fifties) focused on *the*

338

work itself. It focused on a story or poem as a finished artifact—self-contained, complete in itself. Rather than studying the background, the author, or the times, critics let the work speak for itself. The emphasis shifted to the close reading of the text itself. Instead of bringing preconceptions to a story from the outside, readers read *out of* the story what it had to say about contemporary politics, contemporary religion, or whatever. In practice, the newer approach often meant close study of matters of form and technique, which could be studied directly in the text. Critics paid detailed attention to image, symbol, irony, point of view. Critics paying close attention to form and technique are often called **formalists,** a label implying that *too much* attention is being paid to form (rather than to the larger meanings).

❖ In recent years, many critics have put renewed emphasis on *the reader*. The experience of literature is not complete until the reader responds as a thinking and feeling being. A story is just dead letters on a page until the reader's imagination brings it to life in the theater of the mind. Major schools of criticism stress the importance of what happens in the reader's mind:

Psychoanalytic critics, or critics influenced by psychoanalysis, early claimed that a story grips the readers' imagination when it engages with deep-seated concerns, agendas, or traumas in their own personal experience. The symbolic action of the story takes them through a process of recognizing their own psychological burdens and trying to cope with them. Often these prove to be rooted in traumatic early childhood experiences or family conflicts—repressed or thwarted love for the mother, rebellion against a domineering father, or sibling rivalry.

Myth critics looked for the echoes of myths and archetypes anchored in the collective racial memory of the human species. Stories that have a powerful hold on the reader activate unconscious memories of basic patterns of human life. Archetypes are "the psychic residue" of numberless experiences "deeply implanted in the memory of the race"; although they may seem strange on the surface, there is "that within us which leaps at the sight of them, a cry of the blood which tells us we have known them always" (Gilbert Murray). Patterns of initiation into adulthood, rituals of death and rebirth, find a profound echo in our "racial memory."

Critics stressing **reader response** focus on how the experience, expectations, and needs that readers bring to a story shape their reading of the text. Readers are not empty vessels into which the author's meanings are poured. They experience and reconstruct a story or a poem in accordance with their own vital concerns and interests. They provide the "missing bridges" between the world of the story and their own personal experience (Wolfgang Iser).

❖ Among recent critical approaches are other strong countertrends to the tendency to see a story or a poem as a finished, self-contained masterpiece that could be displayed like an ancient Greek vase:

Deconstructionists probe beyond the finished surface of a story. Having been written by a human being with unresolved conflicts and contradictory emotions, a story may disguise rather than reveal the underlying anxieties or perplexities of the author. Below the surface, unresolved tensions or contradictions may account for the true dynamics of the story. A story may have one message for the ordinary unsophisticated reader and another for a reader who responds to its subtext, its subsurface ironies. Readers who deconstruct a text will be "resistant" readers. They will not be taken in by what a story says on the surface but will try "to penetrate the disguises" of the text.

Marxist critics focus on how literature mirrors, distorts, or tries to change social and economic reality. They look at the way a writer's assumptions and loyalties are shaped by social class and economic status. They study the way the power structure of a society tries to use (and at times to suppress) literature for its own purposes.

Feminist critics focus on how literature reflects, and at times challenges, traditional gender roles. They have a special interest in female authors and their neglect or recognition in a male-dominated culture. They make us more conscious of the way male authors have traditionally shaped our assumptions about men and women. In the work of many current critics, these major trends and countertrends meet or interact in fascinating ways.

KAFKA AND HIS READERS

We need the books that affect us like a disaster, that grieve us deeply, like the death of someone we loved more than ourselves, like being banished into forests far from everyone, like a suicide. A book must be the axe for the frozen sea within.
FRANZ KAFKA

Kafka's fictions all seem to be awakenings into an incomprehensible world, which he truly wants to understand.
FREDERICK R. KARL

Franz Kafka, whose enigmatic, disturbing stories have intrigued readers around the world, provides a vivid demonstration of the range of critical interpretation. How critics read his work is strongly influenced by the assumptions and interests they bring to his stories. Using one of his best-known stories as a test case, you will be able to test your own reading of the text against critical approaches that have shaped the expectations of many readers.

FRANZ KAFKA (1883–1924)

The only thing for me to do now . . . is to keep my intelligence calm and discriminating to the end.
FRANZ KAFKA, *THE TRIAL*

Kafka is one of the great prophetic voices of modern literature. His strange dreamlike stories and novels are parables that make us ponder the great twentieth-century themes. He was the prophet of alienation—homelessness, rootlessness—and the anxiety it generates. He foresaw a totalitarian future in which the individual is helpless when struggling against a faceless all-pervading bureaucratic authority. Kafka made *angst*—a feverish, all-pervading anxiety—a household world.

Kafka was born as the son of wealthy Jewish parents in Prague when Czechoslovakia was still part of the Austrian empire. Though surrounded by people speaking Czech, Kafka and his friends spoke German; he studied first German literature and then law at the German university in Prague. He wrote his best-known works—"The Judgment," "Metamorphosis," *The Trial, The Castle, Amerika*—between 1912 and his death from tuberculosis in 1924. He worked in an insurance office, dealing with workmen's compensation. However, he was channeling his vital energies into writing, which he pursued with intense seriousness and bouts of paralyzing self-doubt. Kafka published only his short stories during his lifetime, and even these only reluctantly. He instructed his friend Max Brod to burn all unpublished work (including the great novels) in case of Kafka's death. These instructions Brod decided he could not in good conscience carry out, thus saving for posterity what Thomas Mann called some of the "great mysterious fictions" of the twentieth century.

Kafka's narratives have been called "anti–fairy tales." In a fairy tale, the hero often sets out alone on a quest and overcomes obstacles in his search for good fortune. In a Kafka story, the hero is likely to get bogged down in the struggle. In his great mysterious novel *The Castle,* a homeless, nameless stranger—called K.—arrives in the village, claiming that he has been promised a job as a land surveyor. K. engages in an exhausting struggle to secure the most basic human needs: a place to live, a job to do, a minimum of privacy, some human contact and human warmth. K. moves among people who are cowed by a nameless fear of a faceless bureaucratic power, and he musters all his energy and ingenuity to make the bureaucracy recognize him as a human being. K.'s untiring efforts to accomplish his impossible mission are both sad and comical, reminding later readers of the sad clowns—Charles Chaplin, Buster Keaton—of the silent screen.

Kafka's blessing and bane were a tremendous hypersensitivity. The American novelist (and writer of short fiction) John Updike said of him, "He had a sensation of anxiety and shame, a sensitivity acute beyond usefulness, as if the nervous system, flayed of its old hide of social usage, must record every touch of pain." Kafka had a kinesthetic imagination, with ideas instantly translated not merely into feelings but into intense bodily sensations.

Kafka once called his fiction "rays of light into an infinite confusion." Readers have found his stories gripping and perturbing—without being able to agree on the source of their fascination. Critics have differed widely on what these stories say about the human condition. Like Shakespeare's *Hamlet,* Kafka's enigmatic tales have been for critics more like a mirror than a window. Critics look into the mirror of these tales and see reflected there their own preoccupations and perplexities.

The Country Doctor   1919

TRANSLATED BY WILLA MUIR AND EDWIN MUIR

I was in great perplexity; I had to start on an urgent journey; a seriously ill patient was waiting for me in a village ten miles off; a thick blizzard of snow filled all the wide spaces between him and me; I had a gig, a light gig with big wheels, exactly right for our country roads; muffled in furs, my bag of instruments in my hand, I was in the courtyard all ready for the journey; but there was no horse to be had, no horse. My own horse had died in the night, worn out by the fatigues of this icy winter; my servant girl was now running round the village trying to borrow a horse; but it was hopeless, I knew it, and I stood there forlornly, with the snow gathering more and more thickly upon me, more and more unable to move. In the gateway the girl appeared, alone, and waved the lantern; of course, who would lend a horse at this time for such a journey? I strode through the courtway once more; I could see no way out; in my confused distress I kicked at the dilapidated door of the yearlong uninhabited pigsty. It flew open and flapped to and fro on its hinges. A steam and smell as of horses came out of it. A dim stable lantern was swinging inside from a rope. A man, crouching on his hams in that low space, showed an open blue-eyed face. "Shall I yoke up?" he asked, crawling out on all fours. I did not know what to say and merely stooped down to see what else was in the sty. The servant girl was standing beside me. "You never know what you're going to find in your own house," she said, and we both laughed. "Hey there, Brother, hey there, Sister!" called the groom, and two horses, enormous creatures with powerful flanks, one after the other, their legs tucked close to their bodies, each well-shaped head lowered like a camel's, by sheer strength of buttocking squeezed out through the door hole which they filled entirely. But at once they were standing up, their legs long and their bodies steaming thickly. "Give him a hand," I said, and the willing girl hurried to help the groom with the harnessing. Yet hardly was she beside him when the groom clipped hold of her and pushed his face against hers. She screamed and fled back to me; on her cheek stood out in red the marks of two rows of teeth. "You brute," I yelled in fury, "do you want a whipping?" but in the same moment reflected that the man was a stranger; that I did not know where he came from, and that of his own free will he was helping me out when everyone else had failed me. As if he knew my thoughts he took no offense at my threat but, still busied with the horses, only turned round once toward me. "Get in," he said then, and indeed everything was ready. A magnificent pair of horses, I observed, such as I had never sat behind, and I climbed in happily. "But I'll drive, you don't know the way," I said. "Of course," said he, "I'm not coming with you anyway, I'm staying with Rose." "No," shrieked Rose, fleeing into the house with a justified presentiment that her fate was inescapable; I heard the door chain rattle as she put it up; I heard the key turn in the lock; I could see, moreover, how she put out the lights in the entrance hall and in further flight all through the rooms to keep herself from being discovered. "You're coming with me," I said to the groom, "or I won't go, urgent as my journey is. I'm not thinking of paying for it by handing the girl over to you." "Gee up!" he said; clapped his hands; the gig whirled off like a log in a freshet; I could just hear the door of my house splitting and bursting as the groom charged at it and then I was deafened and blinded by a storming rush that steadily buffeted all my senses. But this only for a moment, since, as if my patient's farmyard had opened out just before my courtyard gate, I was already there; the horses had come quietly to a standstill; the blizzard had stopped; moonlight all around; my patient's parents hurried out of the house, his sister behind them; I was almost lifted out of the gig; from their confused ejaculations I gathered not a word; in the sickroom the air was almost unbreathable; the neglected stove was smoking; I wanted to push open a window; but first I had to look at my patient. Gaunt, without any fever, not cold, not warm, with vacant eyes, without a shirt, the youngster heaved himself up from under the feather bedding, threw his arms around my neck, and whispered in my ear: "Doctor, let me die." I glanced round the room; no one had heard it; the parents were leaning forward in silence waiting for my verdict; the sister had set a chair for my hand-bag; I opened the bag and hunted among my instruments; the boy kept clutching at me from his bed to remind me of his entreaty; I picked up a pair of tweezers, examined them in the candlelight and laid them down again. "Yes," I thought blasphemously, "in cases like this the gods are helpful, send the missing horse, add to it a second because of the urgency, and to crown everything bestow even a groom—" And only now did I remember Rose again; what was I to do, how could I rescue her, how could I pull her away from under that groom at ten miles' distance, with a team of horses I couldn't control. These horses, now, they had somehow slipped the reins loose, pushed the windows open from outside, I did not know how; each of them had stuck a head in at a window and, quite unmoved by the startled cries of the family, stood eyeing the patient. "Better go back at once," I thought, as if the horses were summoning me to the return journey, yet I permitted the patient's sister, who fancied that I was dazed by the heat, to take my fur coat from me. A glass of rum was poured out for me, the old man clapped me on the shoulder, a familiarity justified by this offer of his treasure. I shook my head; in the narrow confines of the old man's thoughts I felt ill; that was my only reason for refusing the drink. The mother stood by the bedside and cajoled me toward it; I yielded, and, while one of the horses whinnied loudly to the ceiling, laid my head to the boy's breast, which shivered under my wet beard. I confirmed what I already knew; the boy was quite sound, something a little wrong with his circulation, saturated with coffee by his solicitous mother, but sound and best turned out of bed with one shove. I am no world reformer and so I let him lie. I was the district doctor and did my duty to the uttermost, to the point where it became almost too much. I was badly paid and yet generous and helpful to the poor. I had still to see that Rose was all right, and then the boy might have his way and I wanted to die too. What was I doing there in that endless winter! My horse was dead, and not a single person in the village would lend me another. I had to get my team out of the pigsty; if they hadn't chanced to be horses I should have had to travel with swine. That was how it was. And I nodded to the family. They knew nothing about it, and, had they known, would not have believed it. To write prescriptions is easy, but to come to an understanding with people is hard. Well, this should be the end of my visit, I had once more been called out needlessly, I was used to that, the whole district made my life a torment with my night bell, but that I should have to sacrifice Rose this time as well, the pretty girl who had lived in my house for years almost without my noticing her—that sacrifice was too much to ask, and I had somehow to get it reasoned out in my head with the help of what craft I could muster, in order not to let fly at this family, which with the best will in the world could not restore Rose to me. But as I shut my bag and put an arm out for my fur coat, the family meanwhile standing together, the father sniffing at the glass of rum in his hand, the mother, apparently disappointed in me—why, what do people expect?—biting her lips with tears in her eyes, the sister fluttering a blood-soaked towel, I was somehow ready to admit conditionally that the boy might be ill after all. I went toward him, he welcomed me smiling as if I were bringing him the most nourishing invalid broth—ah, now both horses were whinnying together; the noise, I suppose, was ordained by heaven to assist my examination of the patient—and this time I discovered that the boy was indeed ill. In his right side, near the hip, was an open wound as big as the palm of my hand. Rose-red, in many variations of shade, dark in the hollows, lighter at the edges, softly granulated, with irregular clots of blood, open as a surface mine to the daylight. That was how it looked from a distance. But on a closer inspection there was another complication. I could not help a low whistle of surprise. Worms, as thick and as long as my little finger, themselves rose-red and blood-spotted as well, were wriggling from their fastness in the interior of the wound toward the light, with small white heads and many little legs. Poor boy, you were past helping. I had discovered your great wound; this blossom in your side was destroying you. The family was pleased; they saw me busying myself; the sister told the mother, the mother the father, the father told several guests who were coming in, through the moonlight at the open door, walking on tiptoe, keeping their balance with outstretched arms. "Will you save me?" whispered the boy with a sob, quite blinded by the life within his wound. That is what people are like in my district. Always expecting the impossible from the doctor. They have lost their ancient beliefs; the parson sits at home and unravels his vestments, one after another; but the doctor is supposed to be omnipotent with his merciful surgeon's hand. Well, as it pleases them; I have not thrust my services on them; if they misuse me for sacred ends, I let that happen to me too; what better do I want, old country doctor that I am, bereft of my servant girl! And so they came, the family and the village elders, and stripped my clothes off me; a school choir with the teacher at the head of it stood before the house and sang these words to an utterly simple tune:

> Strip his clothes off, then he'll heal us,
> If he doesn't, kill him dead!
> Only a doctor, only a doctor.

Then my clothes were off and I looked at the people quietly, my fingers in my beard and my head cocked to one side. I was altogether composed and equal to the situation and remained so, although it was no help to me, since they now took me by the head and feet and carried me to the bed. They laid me down in it next to the wall, on the side of the wound. Then they all left the room; the door was shut; the singing stopped; clouds covered the moon; the bedding was warm around me; the horses' heads in the opened windows wavered like shadows. "Do you know," said a voice in my ear, "I have very little confidence in you. Why, you were only blown in here, you didn't come on your own feet. Instead of helping me, you're cramping me on my deathbed. What I'd like best is to scratch your eyes out." "Right," I said, "it is a shame. And yet I am a doctor. What am I to do? Believe me, it is not too easy for me either." "Am I supposed to be content with this apology? Oh, I must be, I can't help it. I always have to put up with things. A fine wound is all I brought into the world; that was my sole endowment." "My young friend," said I, "your mistake is: you have not a wide enough view. I have been in all the sickrooms, far and wide, and I tell you: your wound is not so bad. Done in a tight corner with two strokes of the ax. Many a one proffers his side and can hardly hear the ax in the forest, far less that it is coming nearer to him." "Is that really so, or are you deluding me in my fever?" "It is really so, take the word of honor of an official doctor." And he took it and lay still. But now it was time for me to think of escaping. The horses were still standing faithfully in their places. My clothes, my fur coat, my bag were quickly collected; I didn't want to waste time dressing; if the horses raced home as they had come, I should only be springing, as it were, out of this bed into my own. Obediently a horse backed away from the window; I threw my bundle into the gig; the fur coat missed its mark and was caught on a hook only by the sleeve. Good enough. I swung myself onto the horse. With the reins loosely trailing, one horse barely fastened to the other, the gig swaying behind, my fur coat last of all in the snow. "Gee up!" I said, but there was no galloping; slowly, like old men, we crawled through the snowy wastes; a long time echoed behind us the new but faulty song of the children:

> O be joyful, all you patients,
> The doctor's laid in bed beside you!

Never shall I reach home at this rate; my flourishing practice is done for; my successor is robbing me, but in vain, for he cannot take my place; in my house the disgusting groom is raging; Rose is the victim; I do not want to think about it any more. Naked, exposed to the frost of this most unhappy of ages, with an earthly vehicle, unearthly horses, old man that I am, I wander astray. My fur coat is hanging from the back of the gig, but I cannot reach it, and none of my limber pack of patients lifts a finger. Betrayed! Betrayed! A false alarm on the night bell once answered—it cannot be made good, not ever.

THE RECEPTIVE READER

As you read and reread the story, pay special attention to questions that come up again and again in critical interpretations:

1. How far into the story can you read while assuming it to be a realistic narrative of events? What are your first clues that this story is going to be *surreal*, like a dream?

2. What is the role of the *groom*? How is he different from the doctor, who is supposedly his employer? What is the doctor's attitude toward him?

3. What is the possible *symbolism* of the horses? the pigsty?

4. What is the role of *Rose*? (Could she be a "mother figure"? Could she be for the doctor an object of unacknowledged sexual desire?)

5. What do you make of the doctor's first declaring the patient healthy and then finding the incurable wound? (Could the wound be the wound in the side of Christ on the cross?)

6. What is the doctor's interaction with the patient's family? How do they treat him?

7. The doctor seems very inadequate as the modern physician-healer who is supposed to perform the miracles of modern medicine. Could he be a *satirical* portrait of the overreaching pride—or hubris—of modern science?

8. Why is the *parson* sitting at home unraveling his vestments?

9. Although the events of the story are surreal, the doctor often uses *trite sayings* that sound as if things were normal. Why? What are striking examples?

THE PERSONAL RESPONSE

Although many critics approach Kafka with deadly earnestness, other readers have marveled at the mixture of the sad and comic in his fiction. (Kafka read some of his stories to his friends with tears of laughter streaming down his face.) Does anything about this story strike you as comical?

CROSS-REFERENCES—For Discussion or Writing

Look at one or more stories that have been called Kafkaesque, such as Luisa Valenzuela's "The Censors" (included in this volume) or John Cheever's "The Swimmer" (not included). What is "Kafkaesque" about these stories?

THE RANGE OF INTERPRETATION

Reading about Kafka, one is usually struck by the chaotic variety of interpretations, in which each reader makes his own associations.

RONALD GRAY

Kafka is often so obscure, his imagery so vague . . . and his situations capable of being interpreted so variously, that his work lends itself to endless speculation.

H. S. REISS

The following discussions and excerpts sample major directions in Kafka criticism. What assumptions, what expectations, does each school of critics bring to a reading of his stories? Which of these approaches seem to you most directly applicable to "The Country Doctor"? Which shed light on the story in a more indirect way?

The Prophetic Kafka

Art is a mirror that, like a clock running too fast, foretells the future.

FRANZ KAFKA

Many readers have seen Kafka's fiction, and especially his novels, as a prophecy of modern totalitarian societies where the nameless, anonymous individual is at the mercy of an all-powerful bureaucratic authority. Innocent people find themselves hounded and judged, till they finally start to believe in their guilt themselves. The Czech writer Milan Kundera, who lived in Kafka's Prague under communist rule, found himself in a society like the one Kafka had predicted: "a world," in Kundera's words, "that is nothing but a single huge, labyrinthine institution" that Kafka's characters could not escape and could not understand. This Kafkaesque society provides the context for Kundera's novel *The Incredible Lightness of Being*, which became a best-seller in the West and was made into a movie centered on the suppression of the stirrings of political and cultural independence called the "Prague Spring."

The following excerpt from an article by Kundera probes the psychological roots of the modern totalitarian state. Kundera said, "Kafka made no prophecies. All he did was see what was 'behind.' He did not know that his seeing was also a fore-seeing. He did not intend to unmask a social system. He shed light on the mechanisms he knew from private and microsocial human practice, not suspecting that later developments would put those mechanisms into action on the great stage of History."

MILAN KUNDERA
Kafka and Modern History 1988

There are tendencies in modern history that produce the Kafkaesque quality in the broad social dimension: the progressive concentration of power, tending to deify itself [make itself godlike]; the bureaucratization of social activity that turns all institutions into boundless labyrinths; and the resulting depersonalization of the individual.

Totalitarian states, as extreme concentrations of these tendencies, have brought out the close relationship between Kafka's novels and real life. But . . . in fact, the society we call democratic is also familiar with the process that bureaucratizes and depersonalizes; the entire planet has become a theater of this process. . . .

Why was Kafka the first novelist to grasp these tendencies, which appeared on History's stage so clearly and brutally only after his death? Mystifications and legends aside, there is no significant trace anywhere of Franz Kafka's political interests; in that sense, he is different from all his Prague friends, from Max Brod, Franz Werfel, Egon Erwin Kisch, and from all the avantgardes that, claiming to know the direction of History, indulged in conjuring up the face of the future.

So how is it that not their works but those of their solitary, introverted companion, immersed in his own life and his art, are recognized today as a sociopolitical prophecy, and are for that very reason banned in a large part of the world?

I pondered this mystery one day after witnessing a little scene in the home of an old friend of mine. The woman in question had been arrested in 1951 during the Stalinist trials in Prague, and convicted of crimes she hadn't committed. Hundreds of Communists were in the same situation at the time. All their lives they had entirely identified themselves with their Party. When it suddenly became their prosecutor, they agreed, like Joseph K., "to examine their whole lives, their entire past, down to the smallest details" to find the hidden offense and, in the end, to confess to imaginary crimes. My friend managed to save her own life because she had the extraordinary courage to refuse to undertake—as her comrades did, as the poet A. did—the "search for her offense." Refusing to assist her persecutors, she became unusable for the final show trial. So instead of being hanged she got away with life imprisonment. After fourteen years, she was completely rehabilitated and released.

The woman had a one-year-old child when she was arrested. On release from prison, she thus rejoined her fifteen-year-old son and had the joy of sharing her humble solitude with him from then on. That she became passionately attached to the boy is entirely comprehensible. One day I went to see them—by then her son was twenty-five. The mother, hurt and angry, was crying. The cause was utterly trivial: the son had overslept or something like that. I asked the mother: "Why get so upset over such a trifle? Is it worth crying about? Aren't you overdoing it?"

It was the son who answered for his mother: "No, my mother's not overdoing it. My mother is a splendid, brave woman. She resisted when everyone else cracked. She wants me to become a real man. It's true, all I did was oversleep, but what my mother reproached me for is something much deeper. It's my attitude. My selfish attitude. I want to become what my mother wants me to be. And with you as a witness, I promise her I will."

What the party never managed to do to the mother, the mother had managed to do to her son. She had forced him to identify with an absurd accusation, to "seek his offense," to make a public confession. I looked on, dumbfounded, at this Stalinist minitrial, and I understood all at once that the psychological mechanisms that function in great (apparently incredible and inhuman) historical events are the same as those that regulate private (quite ordinary and very human) situations.

From *The Art of the Novel*

QUESTIONS

How is modern society like a labyrinth? Does it make sense to you that modern mass societies act out on a large scale patterns and motives that we can observe from close up in the family unit?

The Psychoanalytic Kafka

Psychoanalytic critics assume a basic similarity between the world of dreams and the world created by the imagination of a great artist. In both, according to Freud, repressed material beyond the grasp of the censorious conscious intellect rises from the unconscious to let us know things about ourselves that we did not suspect. With a writer like Kafka, the psychoanalytic critic has a head start: Many of Kafka's stories have the feverish, oppressive quality of a dream—of an anxiety dream, a nightmare that we find hard to shake off. For this psychoanalytic critic, "the Country Doctor's fantastic adventure points to an unrecognized, unadmitted sexual crisis on the part of a middle-aged bachelor professional."

JAMES M. MCGLATHERY
The Challenges of Desire   1981

The Country Doctor's experiences in answering a sick call in the middle of the night are best read as fantasy on the central figure's part. Also, just because it happens first, one should not assume that the night call brings on the crisis in the physician's relationship with his maid Rosa. On the contrary, the imaginary call to duty likely is the product of a developing crisis in his feelings about the live-in maid. And most important, his experiences with his patient cannot be divorced from his feelings—conscious and unconscious—regarding Rosa.

To some extent, at least, the physician must identify in his fantasy with the demonic figure of the stable boy, Rosa's would-be and presumably successful ravisher. Yet, on the conscious level, the doctor sees himself as quite the opposite, as Rosa's angel of rescue, as her only hope of escape from the rape attempt. This state of affairs suggests that his emotional crisis stems from unadmitted, unconscious sexual guilt. . . . Thus he blames his professional calling for the loss of his maid and of the opportunity to prove himself a hero in her eyes. Up to this time, however, he has not allowed himself to notice Rosa, much less to think of possessing her—a thought which even in his fantasy he cannot attribute to himself, and thus projects onto the stable boy.

The young man to whom the doctor is called to minister likely represents the latter's image of himself as a youth, when he was first reaching an age to marry. The patient's wish to die would then be a projection of the doctor's middle-aged bachelor guilt over his having fled as a young man from marriage into devotion to his calling. The doctor's failure at first to discover the wound may project his guilt over having suppressed awareness regarding the motivation for his complete dedication to his calling. And his subsequent discovery of the wound may reflect his dawning awareness of this guilt, even though he still cannot admit these feelings to himself.

The doctor's unadmitted shame and remorse over having escaped from the challenges of Desire into a career of healing may likewise express itself in the conclusion of his nightmarish fantasy, where he has given up the patient—that is, himself as a youth—for dead, and then finds himself condemned to be carried endlessly through the snowy wastes by an uncontrollable horse, bereft of his maid, his clothing, and likely also his practice.

From "Desire's Persecutions in Kafka's 'Judgement,' 'Metamorphosis,' and 'A Country Doctor,'" In *Perspectives on Contemporary Literature*, vol. 7

QUESTIONS

How much direct evidence is there in the story on the relations between the doctor, Rosa, and the groom? What details in the story suggest sexual overtones? What mechanisms of projection does the author of this excerpt describe? How believable are they?

The Marxist Kafka

Marxist critics look for the social and political implications of a writer's work. To what social class does the author belong? How does he relate to its political and economic interests? Does he accept or attack the existing class structure? Works of literature do not exist outside of society in an idyllic value-less sphere; they have inevitable social and political relevance. Some writers show their political commitments openly, others by implication. A writer who keeps quiet about the injustices of his society endorses and supports them by implication; artists and writers often allow themselves to be used to lend the prestige of "culture" to unjust social systems.

Marxist critics claimed early that the pervasive fear, the paralyzing anxiety, of Kafka's fiction was the result of living among the insecurities and injustices of a capitalistic, bourgeois society. Kafka's work found a tremendous echo among twentieth-century readers because of the all-pervasive sense of fear generated by political factors that were, to the Marxist, the logical outgrowth of the traditional capitalistic society: the rise of fascism and Hitlerism, the ever-present threat of nuclear war.

ERNST FISHER
"The Country Doctor" and Ideology   1981

Kafka's hero, always the same . . . is not a romantic hero, but a desperate petty bourgeois in the world of late capitalism. He would like to conform to society and applaud its everyday phenomena such as family, marriage, and job—but it doesn't work. The breach is unbridgeable: business success and private happiness, social career and humane personality have become irreconcilable. . . . In contrast to most writers of his generation, Kafka constantly dealt with the problem of work and profession, that is, with the great problems of the mechanized, industrialized, commercialized world. Horrified by the specialization, Taylorization [dehumanizing and speedup of labor], and fragmentation of work, Kafka senses the growing divergence between occupation and personality.

His heroes fail because of this division: they are not satisfied with an occupation they feel to be senseless; they are alienated by it; they are overwhelmed by the vanity of their efforts.

The country doctor, by nature an isolated person, is vulnerable to the tragicomic contradiction between the idea of being the helper in a wide area and the poverty of his means. He clings to the idea of being a helper, wards off resignation, is ready to sacrifice his private life for his professional ethics, and is forced in the most cruel way to recognize the vanity of his efforts. . . . one can recognize in the "unearthly horses" which emerge from the pigpen a fantastic and melancholy satire on ideals which have become ghosts, which are no longer appropriate to social conditions: . . . the bourgeois sense of duty, unconditional obedience when the signal sounds. Everything begins with a "false ringing of the night bell." . . . Not one word says: "Defend yourself, country doctor! You need a living horse, not ideological ghosts!" But when the ghost horses . . . so unwillingly drag themselves through the infinite snow after the death of the patient, we hear the lament, the protest:

> Naked, prey to the frost of this most unfortunate age, I, an old man, am driven around with an earthly coach and unearthly horses. My fur coat is hanging in the back of the coach; I can't reach it, and not one of the active churls among the patients lifts his finger. Deceived! Deceived!

It is the lament, the protest of him who has been cheated out of the dignity of his occupation; the sense of his life, the echo of a false alarm from the very beginning—not a call to revolution, but also not a recognition of the historically determined as an eternal *condition humaine* [human condition]; rather, a rebellion against the coldness, the frost of "this most unfortunate age."

From Kenneth Hughes, *Franz Kafka: An Anthology of Marxist Criticism*

QUESTIONS

How much direct evidence is there in the story of the doctor's view of his vocation or profession? How crucial is his inadequacy as a healer to the story as a whole?

The Feminist Kafka

A radical critique of literature, feminist in its impulse,
would take the work first of all as a clue to how we live,
how we have been living, how we have been led to imagine
ourselves . . . how we can begin to see—and therefore
live—afresh.

ADRIENNE RICH

Feminist critics have asked readers to reread and rethink literary classics from the perspective of the woman reader. How have traditional assumptions about what it means to be male or female shaped the literature of the past? How have these assumptions shaped the way scholars or critics have interpreted the classics of our literary heritage? The author of the following excerpt said that a feminist reading of Kafka must start by questioning his alleged "universality." Male critics finding universal themes in Kafka's prose were not necessarily speaking for women. "Kafka's fictional world is male." Where woman is not obscured, "she is seen as purely instrumental"; she is a pawn in the power struggles of a male world.

EVELYN TORTON BECK
Gender and Power in Kafka   1987

The essential power struggles in Kafka's texts are between the males. . . . Nowhere in Kafka does woman speak for herself. . . . Because it is his male heroes who organize the text's way of seeing, the angle of vision in Kafka's texts is necessarily androcentric—i.e., male centered. . . .

Throughout, Kafka's male characters think of women in the language of ownership. "I'm not thinking of handing the girl over to you," says the country doctor to his groom. . . . Woman exists only on the margins, entrapped in a power system in which she is never an actor, only acted upon. . . .

For women have been taught to see through an androcentric lens, it is a way of seeing we all have to un-learn. Such a paradigm shift is both exhilarating and disorienting, since it forces us to rethink our received truths about literary study and about the world. It challenges our codified values, especially about "old masters" and "eternal truths." It forces us to rethink and reconceptualize the values systems by which we live. Such disruptions are never comfortable, but to paraphrase a Kafka aphorism, a book should act on us like a sharp blow—it should serve as an ax for "frozen sea within us." Though I would prefer less violent language, this perception well describes the kind of awakening a feminist analysis of literature can catalyze. We ought to welcome it.

From "Kafka's Traffic in Women: Gender, Power, and Sexuality," in *The Dove and the Mole: Kafka's Journey into Darkness and Creativity,* edited by Moshe Lazar and Ronald Gottesman

QUESTIONS

How stereotypical is the treatment of Rose in the story? Do you think female readers can identify with the anxieties of the doctor? How or why?

CROSS-REFERENCE—For Discussion or Writing

Do you think there are "universals" that cut across gender divisions in the short stories by Flannery O'Connor and Franz Kafka? Or are there major differences in her female and his male perspective?

WRITING ABOUT LITERATURE
10. Quoting the Critics (Documented Paper)

The Writing Workshop   For a paper based on library research, you may be asked to study in depth one important critical approach to a much-discussed story. Or, instead of studying one critical perspective in depth, you may be asked to compare two or more different critical approaches. Some sample projects:

❖ Hundreds of critical articles (and chapters in books) have been written on Nathaniel Hawthorne's richly symbolic and ambiguous "Young Goodman Brown." You might want to focus on critics' differing views of the relationship between Hawthorne's story and the role of sin and guilt in the Puritan tradition of New England. Was Hawthorne himself profoundly influenced by that tradition? Or was he critical of it, distancing himself from it?

❖ A classic short story like John Steinbeck's "The Chrysanthemums" or Charlotte Gilman's "The Yellow Wallpaper" will reveal new or unexpected depth when a new generation of critics looks at it from a fresh perspective. You might want to contrast a more traditional approach to such a story with a recent rereading from a feminist perspective.

❖ You may want to choose a Kafka story—like "A Country Doctor," "Metamorphosis," or "The Judgment." Your paper might focus on the definition of a key term. For example, you might focus on the "Jewish" Kafka, or on Kafka as the prophet of totalitarianism, or on the Freudian Kafka.

Finding Promising Leads   To work up material for your paper, you are likely to begin by checking in electronic or printed indexes for books, collections of critical articles, and individual articles in periodicals. For a writer like Kafka, Hawthorne, or O'Connor, most college libraries will have a wide range of critical and scholarly sources.

For instance, although Kafka's work was banned in Nazi Germany after 1935 and by the communists in his native Prague after 1945, he became one of the most widely known and discussed authors of the twentieth century. (In the words of the critic Susan Sontag, he attracted "armies of interpreters.") Books on Kafka by his friend Max Brod (who stressed the influence on Kafka of Jewish tradition), by Wilhelm Emrich (who examined Kafka's relation to existentialist thought), and by Heinz Politzer (who focused on Kafka's use of paradox and irony) are only the major milestones in a vast amount of critical explication and argument. Beginning with Angel Flores' *The Kafka Problem* (1946), there have been over fifty collections of critical articles on Kafka, including critical anthologies like the following:

> Ronald Gray, *Kafka: A Collection of Critical Essays*
> Heinz Politzer, *Franz Kafka*
> Angel Flores, *The Kafka Debate*
> J.P. Stern, *The World of Franz Kafka*
> Kenneth Hughes, *Kafka: An Anthology of Marxist Criticism*
> Ruth V. Gross, *Critical Essays on Franz Kafka*

In addition, by searching for sources with Kafka's name in the title, you might be able to locate books like Anthony Northey's *Kafka's Relatives* (with background material for a biographical perspective on Kafka's fiction) or recent articles like John Felstiner's "Looking for Kafka" (in *Stanford* for December 1991).

Taking Notes   During your exploratory reading, you need to look sources over quickly, deciding whether they will be helpful. But you also have to slow down and close in when you hit upon promising materials. Remember:

✧ *Be a stickler for accuracy.* Copy direct quotations accurately, word for word. Enclose all quoted material in quotation marks to show material copied verbatim. (Include the *closing* quotation mark to show where the quotation ends.)

✧ *Tag your notes.* Start your notes with a tag or **descriptor.** (Indicate the subtopic or section of your paper where a quotation or piece of information will be useful.)

✧ *Look ahead.* Include all the publishing information you will need later when you identify your sources in a documented paper. Include exact page numbers for your quotations. (Also note *inclusive* page numbers for a whole article or story.) Sample notes might look like this:

self-contained quotation

KAFKA THE WRITER

"'A Country Doctor' reveals much about Kafka's attitude toward being a writer . . . what qualifies him to be a writer, what people expected of him as a writer, what he could accomplish, what would be his ultimate fate."

Peter Mailloux, *A Hesitation Before Birth: The Life of Franz Kafka* (Newark: U of Delaware P, 1989) 392.

partial quotation

SYMBOLS—horses

Critic John Hibberd believes Kafka's "unearthly" horses "represent the power of inspiration that promised Kafka fulfillment but carried him away to a devastating reminder of his helplessness."

John Hibberd, *Kafka in Context* (New York: Studio Vista, 1975) 84.

Distinguish clearly between **paraphrase** and direct firsthand quotation. When you paraphrase, you put someone else's ideas in your own words. You can thus highlight what seems most important to you and condense other parts. Even when you paraphrase, be sure to use quotation marks for striking phrases that you keep in the exact wording of the author. (For instance, in summing up briefly a critic's view of Kafka's doctor, put in quotation marks a striking reference to the doctor himself as "the patient, the smitten victim.")

Note finer points: Use **single quotation marks** for a phrase that appears as a quote-within-a-quote: "Freudian critics are fascinated by Kafka's 'unearthly horses.'" Use the **ellipsis**—three spaced periods—to show an omission (see Mailloux quotation above). Use four periods when the periods include the period at the end of a sentence. **Square brackets** show that you have inserted material into the original quotation: "He became engaged [to Felice Bauer], broke off the engagement, became engaged again."

Pushing toward a Thesis   Your note taking becomes truly productive when you begin to follow up tentative patterns and promising connections that you discover in your reading. Even during your preliminary reading and note taking, you will be looking for a unifying thread, for a figure in the carpet. Avoid a stitched-together pattern that goes from "one critic said this" to "another critic said that." Look for recurrent issues; look for a note that in your materials is struck again and again. The following might be a tentative thesis:

TRIAL THESIS: Critics again and again find a connection between the hesitations and ineffectualness of the country doctor and Kafka's own hesitations and doubts as a writer.

Using a Working Outline   To give direction to your reading and writing, sketch out a **working outline** as soon as you have a rough idea how your material is shaping up. At first, your plan might be very tentative. A working outline is not a final blueprint; its purpose is to help you visualize a possible pattern and to help you refine it as you go along. Suppose you are moving toward a paper showing how different critical approaches make the reader notice and concentrate on different key images in a story. At an intermediate stage, your working outline might look like this:

WORKING OUTLINE: —Freudian emphasis on sexual overtones
    the buttocking horses
    the animalistic groom
    Rose as victim
—Marxist emphasis on the doctor's social role
    ineffectualness of the doctor
    doctor vs. priest
    immobilized doctor at the end
—religious critic's emphasis on religious symbols
    wound in the side of the boy (allusion to Christ on
      the cross?)
    jeering, hostile patients (Christ reviled?)

Drafting and Revising   In your first draft, you are likely to concentrate on feeding into your paper the evidence you have collected. As always, feel free to work on later sections of the paper first—perhaps concentrating on key segments and filling in the connecting threads later. In your first draft, quotations are likely to be chunky, to be woven into the paper more tightly or more smoothly during revision. Often you will need to read a first draft back to yourself to see where major changes in strategy would be advisable. A reordering of major sections might be necessary to correct awkward backtrackings.

You might need to strengthen the evidence for major points and play down material that tends to distract from your major arguments.

Documenting the Paper   When you draw on a range of sources—for instance, a range of critical interpretations of a story—you may be asked to provide **documentation.** In a documented paper, you fully identify your sources, furnishing complete publishing information and exact page numbers. Accurate documentation shows that your readers are welcome to go to the sources you have drawn on—to check your use of them and to get further information from them if they wish. Unless instructed otherwise, follow the current style of documentation of the Modern Language Association (MLA). This current style has done away with footnotes (though it still provides for **explanatory notes** at the end of a paper).

The current MLA style requires you to remember three simple principles:

❖ *Identify your sources briefly in your text.* Generally, introduce a quotation by saying something like "Lucy M. Freibert says in her article on Margaret Atwood's *The Handmaid's Tale.* . . ."

❖ *Give page references in parentheses in your text.* For instance, type (89) or (280–82). If you have not mentioned the author, this is the place to give his or her last name: (Freibert 280–82). If you are using more than one source by the same author, you may also have to specify briefly which one (Freibert, "Control" 280–82). Remember to tag author or title in parentheses only if you have not already given the information in your running text.

❖ *Describe each source fully in a final alphabetical listing of Works Cited.* This used to be the bibliography (literally the "book list"), but it now often includes *non*print sources—interviews, lectures, PBS broadcasts, videotapes, computer software. Here is a typical entry for an article in a critical journal. This entry includes volume number (a volume usually covers all issues for one year), date, and the complete page numbers for the whole article (not just the material you have quoted):

Shumaker, Conrad. "'Too Terribly Good to Be Printed': Charlotte Gilman's 'The Yellow Wallpaper.'" *American Literature* 57 (1985): 588–99.

Study sample entries for your alphabetical listing of Works Cited. Remember a few pointers:

❖ Use *italics* (or <u>underlining</u> on a typewriter) for the title of a *whole* publication—whether a book-length study, a collection or anthology of stories or essays, a periodical that prints critical articles, or a newspaper that prints reviews. However, use quotation marks for titles of short stories or critical articles that are *part* of a collection.

❖ Leave two spaces after periods marking off chunks of information in the entry. Indent the second and following lines of each entry five spaces.

❖ Use *ed.* for editor, *trans.* for a translator.

❖ Abbreviate the names of publishing houses (Prentice for Prentice-Hall, Inc.; Southern Illinois UP for Southern Illinois University Press). Abbreviate the names of the months: Dec., Apr., Mar.

Primary sources: listing of short stories, letters, or interviews

Cheever, John. *The Stories of John Cheever.* New York: Knopf, 1978.
[Collected stories of the author. The publisher's name is short for Alfred A. Knopf.]

O'Connor, Flannery. *Everything That Rises Must Converge.* New York: Farrar, 1965.
[A selection of the author's stories, named after the title story. Name of publisher is short for Farrar, Straus and Giroux.]

Achebe, Chinua. "Dead Men's Path." *The Story and Its Writer: An Introduction to Short Fiction.* Ed. Ann Charters. 3rd ed. Boston: Bedford, 1991. 10–12.
[A story reprinted in an anthology, with editor's name and number of edition and with inclusive page numbers for the story.]

Cheever, Benjamin, ed. *The Letters of John Cheever.* New York: Simon, 1988.
[Author's correspondence, edited by his son.]

Faulkner, William. Interview. *Writers at Work: The* Paris Review *Interviews.* Ed. Malcolm Cowley. New York: Viking-Compass, 1959. 122–41.
[Compass was an imprint, or special line of books, of Viking Press. The title of the *Paris Review* is roman—straight type—to set it off from italicized book title.]

Tan, Amy. Lecture. Visiting Author Series. Santa Clara, 12 Jan. 1992.
[Talk by an author as part of a lecture series.]

Secondary sources: listing of critical studies, articles, or reviews

Abel, Darrel. *The Moral Picturesque: Studies in Hawthorne's Fiction.* West Lafayette, IN: Purdue UP, 1988.
[Book with subtitle, published by a university press.]

Emrich, Wilhelm. *Franz Kafka: A Critical Study of His Writings.* Trans. Sheema Zeben Buehne. New York: Ungar, 1968.
[Book with translator's name.]

Cady, Edwin H., and Louis J. Budd, eds. Introduction. *On Hawthorne: The Best from* American Literature. Durham: Duke UP, 1990. vi–x.
[Introduction to a collection with two editors—only the first typed with last name first. Page numbers for prefaces and the like are given in small roman numerals. Use roman type (not italics) for title within title.]

Freibert, Lucy M. "Control and Creativity: The Politics of Risk in Margaret Atwood's *The Handmaid's Tale.*" *Critical Essays on Margaret Atwood.* Ed. Judith McCombs. Boston: Hall, 1988. 280–91.
[Article in a collection, with inclusive page numbers. Note "Ed." for the editor who assembled the collection.]

Davenport, Mary. "Today's Minimalist Fiction." *New York Times* 15 May 1991, late ed., sec. 2: 1+.
[Newspaper article, with edition and section specified. Article starts on page 1 and continues later in the newspaper.]

Shumaker, Conrad. "'Too Terribly Good to Be Printed': Charlotte Gilman's 'The Yellow Wallpaper.'" *American Literature* 57 (1985): 588–99.
[Journal article, with volume number and inclusive page numbers. Note quotation in title—single quotation marks; note that title of story is

quoted in title of article—single quotation marks. Sometimes number of volume *and* issue may be needed when pages are not numbered consecutively throughout a single volume: *Fiction Review* 14.3 (1992): 17–21.]

The Art of the Story. Narr. Pat Evans. Writ. and prod. Jeremiah Phelps. KCBM, San Benito. 17 Nov. 1991.
[A television program with names of narrator and writer-producer. Should be listed alphabetically under "Art."]

Study the following example of a documented paper. How successful was the student author in finding contemporary sources? How well does the paper support its main points? How clear or adequate are parenthetical documentation and the entries in the Works Cited? Are there unusual situations or entries?

SAMPLE DOCUMENTED PAPER

The Psychoanalytic Kafka: Dream and Reality

Once, when Kafka was visiting his good friend Max Brod, he accidentally woke up Brod's father, who was sleeping on the couch. Instead of just simply apologizing, Kafka slowly tiptoed out of the room, whispering, "Please consider me a dream" (Baumer 2). When we look at Kafka the writer, this incident acquires symbolic meaning. Dreams fascinated Kafka, and he was obsessed with chronicling his "dreamlike inner existence," which threatened to crowd out ordinary daylight reality. He said in a diary entry for August 6, 1914:

> The taste for describing my dreamlike inner existence has pushed everything else in the background, where it has atrophied in a terrifying way and does not cease to atrophy. Nothing else can satisfy me. (qtd. in Baumer 3)

In a letter to Max Brod in 1922, Kafka called this exploration of the inner self "this descent to the dark powers, this unleashing . . . of dubious embraces and everything else that may be happening below." He said that a writer who "writes stories in the sunlight" above "no longer knows anything" about this hidden subconscious reality (qtd. in Baumer 7). For Kafka, "the dream reveals the reality" while "conception"— our ability to understand—"lags behind" (qtd. in Hamalian 12). It is this search for a deeper truth buried in our subconscious and revealed in dreams that made Franz Kafka, in the words of Peter Dow Webster, "the psychologist's perfect dreamer" (118). The psychoanalytical theory concerning dreams, first introduced by Freud, assumes that dreams tell us the real truth about ourselves, especially about our subconscious fears and desires. Our dreams keep coming back to our innermost preoccupations and dilemmas. In Kafka's case, in the words of Ruth Gross, these include "power and impotence," "marriage versus bachelorhood," and "success versus failure" (577).

Kafka's "A Country Doctor" has a typical dreamlike sequence of events, with time and space distorted in such a way that the events cannot be literally happening. The story reveals Kafka's innermost struggle with a choice he made in his own life and the subconscious feelings surrounding that choice. In a letter to Brod, Kafka wrote that "in order to devote himself to literature, the writer must sacrifice fulfillment in life" (qtd. in Sokel 1158). Kafka had a strong desire for marriage and family, but because of his fears and hesitancies—and because of his exclusive devotion to his mission as a writer—his various engagements and romantic involvements ended in failure. In his own words, "The price to pay for this 'life as a writer' is rigid, uncompromising aloneness, a radical isolation from the outside world, from other people and—most painfully—from his beloved" (qtd. in Beug 125).

The dreamlike images and plot of "A Country Doctor" encourage us to see the story as an exploration of Kafka's own ambivalent feelings toward major choices in his own life. As suggested in one critical interpretation, when the country doctor heeds "the call of the 'nightbell' summoning him to the bedside of a patient," the call of the bell "can be understood as a translation into sensory terms of Kafka's call to literature, which he understood as an art of healing and self-preservation, a 'doctor's' art" (Sokel 1158).

However, when the doctor tries to respond to the call, he finds out his horse has died from overexertion. Rose, the servant girl he has just begun to notice, is unable to borrow a horse—"no horse to be had, no horse." In his dilemma, the doctor turns "absentmindedly" to his forgotten pigsty and in doing so releases the animal-like groom and a team of unearthly horses (Kafka 137). He allows the groom to take Rose; contrary to what the doctor says, he does in fact leave Rose behind. She is the price for the groom's aid. "The 'unearthly horses' transport the doctor away from life, woman, and home" (Sokel 1158). This scene seems to mirror Kafka's continual withdrawal from the various women in his life when they would press him for a commitment. Whenever a relationship became too serious, he would back away, claiming that his fanatical dedication to his writing "would condemn his spouse to monastic loneliness" (Sokel 1153).

As Kafka writes about the journey between the two houses, the doctor's and the patient's, he mirrors his own ambivalence toward his writer's art and the sacrifices he has made on behalf of that art. In the story, the two houses graphically represent the two poles of the doctor's existence. In his own house, the doctor abandons the possibility of fulfillment through love; in the other house, the house of the patient, he dedicates himself to his art, exploring "the congenital wound of mortality"—the wound in the young patient's side (Sokel 1158).

The doctor's ambivalence is such that he cannot be content at either pole. At home, he sacrifices the young woman to his mission, but at his destination he regrets the price he has paid and wants to return. Thoughts of Rose begin to haunt him: "And only now did I remember Rose again: what was I to do, how could I rescue her, how could I pull her away from under that groom at ten miles distance, with a team of horses I couldn't control?" (Kafka 139). This pull in contradictory directions mirrors Kafka's own problem. He would make every effort to discourage a woman's hope for the future. However, in the case of Felice Bauer, for instance, the moment she showed signs of heeding his warning, he would return to the role of ardent wooer. As much as Kafka desired marriage and family, he was also fearful and would become "oppressed by the actual prospect of marriage" (Sokel 1154).

At the end of the story, the doctor is seen escaping the patient's house. While it took the doctor only seconds to arrive at the house of the sick boy, now it is taking him forever to get home: "Never shall I reach home at this rate; my flourishing practice is done for; my successor is robbing me . . ." (Kafka 143). The doctor is shown riding aimlessly between the houses—the distance between them has become immeasurable, and he cannot stay at either place.

Kafka's tendency to explore the subconscious in a dreamlike fashion is strongly evident in "The Country Doctor." As readers, we cannot be quite sure whether, in fact, his story is an actual dream (where the subconscious is revealed and dominates) or whether it is based on actual events with subconcious thoughts quickly intruding on the conscious mind. Kafka has chosen a country doctor to portray his own inner struggles as an author who must deal with the choices he has made. In this sense, we are all country doctors and have to deal with our own internal voices speaking to our consciousness. Kafka is not alone. What career mother leaving home and a sick child does not experience a twinge of guilt as her guilt feelings about her choices rise to the surface? What student working late into the night does not have visions of responsibilities denied or postponed—the dinner not cooked, the phone calls not returned?

Works Cited

Baumer, Franz. *Franz Kafka.* New York: Unger, 1971.

Beug, Joachim. "The Cunning of a Writer." *The World of Franz Kafka.* Ed. J. P. Stern. New York: Holt, 1980. 122–33.

Gross, Ruth V. "Fallen Bridge, Fallen Women, Fallen Text." *The Literary Review* 26.4 (1983): 577–87.

Hamalian, Leo. Introduction. *Franz Kafka: A Collection of Criticism.* Ed. Leo Hamalian. New York: McGraw, 1981. 1–17.

Kafka, Franz. *The Metamorphosis, the Penal Colony, and Other Stories.* Trans. Willa and Edwin Muir. New York: Schocken, 1975.

Sokel, Walter H. "Franz Kafka." *European Writers: The Twentieth Century.* Ed. George Stade. Vol. 9. New York: Scribner's, 1989. 1151–77.

Webster, Peter Dow. "'Dies Irae' in the Unconscious, or the Significance of Franz Kafka." *Franz Kafka: A Collection of Criticism.* Ed. Leo Hamalian. New York: McGraw, 1981. 118–25.

QUESTIONS

How convincing is the parallel between the doctor as healer and the writer who provides spiritual comfort and healing? In addition to the lines quoted in this paper, are there other references to Rose while the doctor is in the patient's house?

OTHER VOICES/OTHER VISIONS
Stories for Further Reading

D O N A L D   B A R T H E L M E   (1931–1989)
The Balloon   1967

The balloon, beginning at a point on Fourteenth Street, the exact location of which I cannot reveal, expanded northward all one night, while people were sleeping, until it reached the Park. There, I stopped it; at dawn the northernmost edges lay over the Plaza; the free-hanging motion was frivolous and gentle. But experiencing a faint irritation at stopping, even to protect the trees, and seeing no reason the balloon should not be allowed to expand upward, over the parts of the city it was already covering, into the "air space" to be found there, I asked the engineers to see to it. This expansion took place throughout the morning, soft imperceptible sighing of gas through the valves. The balloon then covered forty-five blocks north-south on either side of the Avenue in some places. That was the situation, then.

But it is wrong to speak of "situations," implying sets of circumstances leading to some resolution, some escape of tension; there were no situations, simply the balloon hanging there—muted heavy grays and browns for the most part, contrasting with walnut and soft yellows. A deliberate lack of finish, enhanced by skillful installation, gave the surface a rough, forgotten quality; sliding weights on the inside, carefully adjusted, anchored the great, vari-shaped mass at a number of points. Now we have had a flood of original ideas in all media, works of singular beauty as well as significant milestones in the history of inflation, but at that moment there was only *this balloon,* concrete particular, hanging there.

There were reactions. Some people found the balloon "interesting." As a response this seemed inadequate to the immensity of the balloon, the suddenness of its appearance over the city; on the other hand, in the absence of hysteria or other societally induced anxiety, it must be judged a calm, "mature" one. There was a certain amount of initial argumentation about the "meaning" of the balloon; this subsided, because we have learned not to insist on meanings, and they are rarely even looked for now, except in cases involving the simplest, safest phenomena. It was agreed that since the meaning of the balloon could never be known absolutely, extended discussion was pointless, or at least less purposeful than the activities of those who, for example, hung green and blue paper lanterns from the warm gray underside, in certain streets, or seized the occasion to write messages on the surface, announcing their availability for the performance of unnatural acts, or the availability of acquaintances.

360

Daring children jumped, especially at those points where the balloon hovered close to a building, so that the gap between balloon and building was a matter of a few inches, or points where the balloon actually made contact, exerting an ever-so-slight pressure against the side of a building, so that balloon and building seemed a unity. The upper surface was so structured that a "landscape" was presented, small valleys as well as slight knolls, or mounds; once atop the balloon, a stroll was possible, or even a trip, from one place to another. There was pleasure in being able to run down an incline, then up the opposing slope, both gently graded, or in making a leap from one side to the other. Bouncing was possible, because of the pneumaticity of the surface, and even falling, if that was your wish. That all these varied motions, as well as others, were within one's possibilities, in experiencing the "up" side of the balloon, was extremely exciting for children, accustomed to the city's flat, hard skin. But the purpose of the balloon was not to amuse children.

Too, the number of people, children and adults, who took advantage of the opportunities described was not so large as it might have been: a certain timidity, lack of trust in the balloon, was seen. There was, furthermore, some hostility. Because we had hidden the pumps, which fed helium to the interior, and because the surface was so vast that the authorities could not determine the point of entry—that is, the point at which the gas was injected—a degree of frustration was evidenced by those city officers into whose province such manifestations normally fell. The apparent purposelessness of the balloon was vexing (as was the fact that it was "there" at all). Had we painted, in great letters, "LABORATORY TESTS PROVE" or "18% MORE EFFECTIVE!" on the sides of the balloon, this difficulty would have been circumvented. But I could not bear to do so. On the whole, these officers were remarkably tolerant, considering the dimensions of the anomaly, this tolerance being the result of, first, secret tests conducted by night that convinced them that little or nothing could be done in the way of removing or destroying the balloon, and, secondly, a public warmth that arose (not uncolored by touches of the aforementioned hostility) toward the balloon, from ordinary citizens.

As a single balloon must stand for a lifetime of thinking about balloons, so each citizen expressed, in the attitude he chose, a complex of attitudes. One man might consider that the balloon had to do with the notion *sullied,* as in the sentence *The big balloon sullied the otherwise clear and radiant Manhattan sky.* That is, the balloon was, in this man's view, an imposture, something inferior to the sky that had formerly been there, something interposed between the people and their "sky." But in fact it was January, the sky was dark and ugly; it was not a sky you could look up into, lying on your back in the street, with pleasure, unless pleasure, for you, proceeded from having been threatened, from having been misused. And the underside of the balloon was a pleasure to look up into, we had seen to that, muted grays and browns for the most part, contrasted with walnut and soft, forgotten yellows. And so, while this man was thinking *sullied,* still there was an admixture of pleasurable cognition in his thinking, struggling with the original perception.

Another man, on the other hand, might view the balloon as if it were part of a system of unanticipated rewards, as when one's employer walks in and says, "Here, Henry, take this package of money I have wrapped for you, because we have been doing so well in the business here, and I admire the way you bruise the tulips, without which bruising your department would not be a success, or at least not the success that it is." For this man the balloon might be a brilliantly heroic "muscle and pluck" experience, even if an experience poorly understood.

Another man might say, "Without the example of——, it is doubtful that——

5

would exist today in its present form," and find many to agree with him, or to argue with him. Ideas of "bloat" and "float" were introduced, as well as concepts of dream and responsibility. Others engaged in remarkably detailed fantasies having to do with a wish either to lose themselves in the balloon, or to engorge it. The private character of these wishes, of their origins, deeply buried and unknown, was such that they were not much spoken of; yet there is evidence that they were widespread. It was also argued that what was important was what you felt when you stood under the balloon; some people claimed that they felt sheltered, warmed, as never before, while enemies of the balloon felt, or reported feeling, constrained, a "heavy" feeling.

Critical opinion was divided:

"monstrous pourings"

"harp"

XXXXXXX *"certain contrasts with darker portions"*
"inner joy"

"large, square corners"
"conservative eclecticism that has so far governed modern balloon design"
:::::: *"abnormal vigor"*
"warm, soft, lazy passages"

The Balloon

"Has unity been sacrificed for a sprawling quality?"
"Quelle catastrophe!"
"munching"

People began, in a curious way, to locate themselves in relation to aspects of the balloon: "I'll be at that place where it dips down into Forty-seventh Street almost to the sidewalk, near the Alamo Chile House," or, "Why don't we go stand on top, and take the air, and maybe walk about a bit, where it forms a tight, curving line with the façade of the Gallery of Modern Art—" Marginal intersections offered entrances with a given time duration, as well as "warm, soft, lazy passages" in which . . . But it is wrong to speak of "marginal intersections," each intersection was crucial, none could be ignored (as if, walking there, you might not find someone capable of turning your attention, in a flash, from old exercises to new exercises, risks and escalations). Each intersection was crucial, meeting of balloon and building, meeting of balloon and man, meeting of balloon and balloon.

It was suggested that what was admired about the balloon was finally this: that it was not limited, or defined. Sometimes a bulge, blister, or sub-section would carry all the way east to the river on its own initiative, in the manner of an army's movements on a map, as seen in a headquarters remote from the fighting. Then that part would be, as it were, thrown back again, or would withdraw into new dispositions; the next morning, that part would have made another sortie, or disappeared altogether. This ability of the balloon to shift its shape, to change, was very pleasing, especially to people whose lives were rather rigidly patterned, persons to whom change, although desired, was not available. The balloon, for the twenty-two days of its existence, offered the possibility, in its randomness, of mislocation of the self, in contradistinction to the grid of precise, rectangular pathways under our feet. The amount of specialized training currently needed, and the consequent desirability of long-term commitments, has been occasioned by the steadily growing importance of complex machinery, in virtually all kinds

10

of operations; as this tendency increases, more and more people will turn, in bewildered inadequacy, to solutions for which the balloon may stand as a prototype, or "rough draft."

I met you under the balloon, on the occasion of your return from Norway; you asked if it was mine; I said it was. The balloon, I said, is a spontaneous autobiographical disclosure, having to do with the unease I felt at your absence, and with sexual deprivation, but now that your visit to Bergen has been terminated, it is no longer necessary or appropriate. Removal of the balloon was easy; trailer trucks carried away the depleted fabric, which is now stored in West Virginia, awaiting some other time of unhappiness, sometime, perhaps, when we are angry with one another.

RAY BRADBURY (born 1920)
There Will Come Soft Rains 1948

[The incinerator in this story is compared to the biblical Baal, or Beelzebub, one of the false gods of idol-worshipers. The title of the story is borrowed from a poem the American poet Sara Teasdale wrote after the end of the carnage of World War I. The artworks consumed by the fire in this story are priceless paintings by the Spanish Pablo Picasso and the French Henri Matisse, two of the great early moderns.]

In the living room the voice-clock sang, *Tick-tock, seven o'clock, time to get up, time to get up, seven o'clock!* as if it were afraid that nobody would. The morning house lay empty. The clock ticked on, repeating and repeating its sounds into the emptiness. *Seven-nine, breakfast time, seven-nine!*

In the kitchen the breakfast stove gave a hissing sigh and ejected from its warm interior eight pieces of perfectly browned toast, eight eggs sunnyside up, sixteen slices of bacon, two coffees, and two cool glasses of milk.

"Today is August 4, 2026," said a second voice from the kitchen ceiling, "in the city of Allendale, California." It repeated the date three times for memory's sake. "Today is Mr. Featherstone's birthday. Today is the anniversary of Tilita's marriage. Insurance is payable, as are the water, gas, and light bills."

Somewhere in the walls, relays clicked, memory tapes glided under electric eyes.

Eight-one, tick-tock, eight-one o'clock, off to school, off to work, run, run, eight-one! But no doors slammed, no carpets took the soft tread of rubber heels. It was raining outside. The weather box on the front door sang quietly: "Rain, rain, go away; rubbers, raincoats for today . . ." And the rain tapped on the empty house, echoing. 5

Outside, the garage chimed and lifted its door to reveal the waiting car. After a long wait the door swung down again.

At eight-thirty the eggs were shriveled and the toast was like stone. An aluminum wedge scraped them into the sink, where hot water whirled them down a metal throat which digested and flushed them away to the distant sea. The dirty dishes were dropped into a hot washer and emerged twinkling dry.

Nine-fifteen, sang the clock, *time to clean.*

Out of warrens in the wall, tiny robot mice darted. The rooms were acrawl with the small cleaning animals, all rubber and metal. They thudded against chairs, whirling their mustached runners, kneading the rug nap, sucking gently at hidden dust. Then, like mysterious invaders, they popped into their burrows. Their pink electric eyes faded. The house was clean.

Ten o'clock. The sun came out from behind the rain. The house stood alone in a city of rubble and ashes. This was the one house left standing. At night the ruined city gave off a radioactive glow which could be seen for miles. 10

Ten-fifteen. The garden sprinklers whirled up in golden founts, filling the soft morning air with scatterings of brightness. The water pelted windowpanes, running down the charred west side where the house had been burned evenly free of its white paint. The entire west face of the house was black, save for five places. Here the silhouette in paint of a man mowing a lawn. Here, as in a photograph, a woman bent to pick flowers. Still farther over, their images burned on wood in one titanic instant, a small boy, hands flung into the air; higher up, the image of a thrown ball, and opposite him a girl, hands raised to catch a ball which never came down.

The five spots of paint—the man, the woman, the children, the ball—remained. The rest was a thin charcoaled layer.

The gentle sprinkler rain filled the garden with falling light.

Until this day, how well the house had kept its peace. How carefully it had inquired, "Who goes there? What's the password?" and, getting no answer from lonely foxes and whining cats, it had shut up its windows and drawn shades in an old-maidenly preoccupation with self-protection which bordered on a mechanical paranoia.

It quivered at each sound, the house did. If a sparrow brushed a window, the shade snapped up. The bird, startled, flew off! No, not even a bird must touch the house! 15

The house was an altar with ten thousand attendants, big, small, servicing, attending, in choirs. But the gods had gone away, and the ritual of the religion continued senselessly, uselessly.

Twelve noon.

A dog whined, shivering, on the front porch.

The front door recognized the dog voice and opened. The dog, once huge and fleshy, but now gone to bone and covered with sores, moved in and through the house, tracking mud. Behind it whirred angry mice, angry at having to pick up mud, angry at inconvenience.

For not a leaf fragment blew under the door but what the wall panels flipped open and the copper scrap rats flashed swiftly out. The offending dust, hair, or paper, seized in miniature steel jaws, was raced back to the burrows. There, down tubes which fed into the cellar, it was dropped into the sighing vent of an incinerator which sat like evil Baal in a dark corner. 20

The dog ran upstairs, hysterically yelping to each door, at last realizing, as the house realized, that only silence was here.

It sniffed the air and scratched the kitchen door. Behind the door, the stove was making pancakes which filled the house with a rich baked odor and the scent of maple syrup.

The dog frothed at the mouth, lying at the door, sniffing, its eyes turned to fire. It ran wildly in circles, biting at its tail, spun in a frenzy, and died. It lay in the parlor for an hour.

Two o'clock, sang a voice.

Delicately sensing decay at last, the regiments of mice hummed out as softly as blown gray leaves in an electrical wind. 25

Two-fifteen.

The dog was gone.

In the cellar, the incinerator glowed suddenly and a whirl of sparks leaped up the chimney.

Two thirty-five.

Bridge tables sprouted from patio walls. Playing cards fluttered onto pads in a shower of pips. Martinis manifested on an oaken bench with egg-salad sandwiches. Music played.

But the tables were silent and the cards untouched.

At four o'clock the tables folded like great butterflies back through the paneled walls.

Four-thirty.

The nursery walls glowed.

Animals took shape: yellow giraffes, blue lions, pink antelopes, lilac panthers cavorting in crystal substance. The walls were glass. They looked out upon color and fantasy. Hidden films clocked through well-oiled sprockets, and the walls lived. The nursery floor was woven to resemble a crisp, cereal meadow. Over this ran aluminum roaches and iron crickets, and in the hot still air butterflies of delicate red tissue wavered among the sharp aroma of animal spoors! There was the sound like a great matted yellow hive of bees within a dark bellows, the lazy bumble of a purring lion. And there was the patter of okapi feet and the murmur of a fresh jungle rain, like other hoofs, falling upon the summer-starched grass. Now the walls dissolved into distances of parched weed, mile on mile, and warm endless sky. The animals drew away into thorn brakes and water holes.

It was the children's hour.

Five o'clock. The bath filled with clear hot water.

Six, seven, eight o'clock. The dinner dishes manipulated like magic tricks, and in the study a *click*. In the metal stand opposite the hearth where a fire now blazed up warmly, a cigar popped out, half an inch of soft gray ash on it, smoking, waiting.

Nine o'clock. The beds warmed their hidden circuits, for nights were cool here.

Nine-five. A voice spoke from the study ceiling:

"Mrs. McClellan, which poem would you like this evening?"

The house was silent.

The voice said at last, "Since you express no preference, I shall select a poem at random." Quiet music rose to back the voice. "Sara Teasdale. As I recall, your favorite. . . .

"There will come soft rains and the smell of the ground,
And swallows circling with their shimmering sound;

And frogs in the pools singing at night,
And wild plum-trees in tremulous white;

Robins will wear their feathery fire
Whistling their whims on a low fence-wire;

And not one will know of the war, not one
Will care at last when it is done.

Not one would mind, either bird nor tree
If mankind perished utterly;

And Spring herself, when she woke at dawn,
Would scarcely know that we were gone."

The fire burned on the stone hearth and the cigar fell away into a mound of quiet ash on its tray. The empty chairs faced each other between the silent walls, and the music played.

At ten o'clock the house began to die.

The wind blew. A falling tree bough crashed through the kitchen window. Cleaning solvent, bottled, shattered over the stove. The room was ablaze in an instant!

"Fire!" screamed a voice. The house lights flashed, water pumps shot water from the ceilings. But the solvent spread on the linoleum, licking, eating under the kitchen door, while the voices took it up in chorus: "Fire, fire, fire!"

The house tried to save itself. Doors sprang tightly shut, but the windows were broken by the heat and the wind blew and sucked upon the fire.

The house gave ground as the fire in ten billion angry sparks moved with flaming ease from room to room and then up the stairs. While scurrying water rats squeaked from the walls, pistoled their water, and ran for more. And the wall sprays let down showers of mechanical rain.

But too late. Somewhere, sighing, a pump shrugged to a stop. The quenching rain ceased. The reserve water supply which had filled baths and washed dishes for many quiet days was gone.

The fire crackled up the stairs. It fed upon Picassos and Matisses in the upper halls, like delicacies, baking off the oily flesh, tenderly crisping the canvases into black shavings.

Now the fire lay in beds, stood in windows, changed the colors of drapes!

And then, reinforcements.

From attic trapdoors, blind robot faces peered down with faucet mouths gushing green chemical.

The fire backed off, as even an elephant must at the sight of a dead snake. Now there were twenty snakes whipping over the floor, killing the fire with a clear cold venom of green froth.

But the fire was clever. It had sent flame outside the house, up through the attic to the pumps there. An explosion! The attic brain which directed the pumps was shattered into bronze shrapnel on the beams.

The fire rushed back into every closet and felt of the clothes hung there.

The house shuddered, oak bone on bone, its bared skeleton cringing from the heat, its wire, its nerves revealed as if a surgeon had torn the skin off to let the red veins and capillaries quiver in the scalded air. Help, help! Fire! Run, run! Heat snapped mirrors like the first brittle winter ice. And the voices wailed Fire, fire, run, run, like a tragic nursery rhyme, a dozen voices, high, low, like children dying in a forest, alone, alone. And the voices fading as the wires popped their sheathings like hot chestnuts. One, two, three, four, five voices died.

In the nursery the jungle burned. Blue lions roared, purple giraffes bounded off. The panthers ran in circles, changing color, and ten million animals, running before the fire, vanished off toward a distant steaming river. . . .

Ten more voices died. In the last instant under the fire avalanche, other choruses, oblivious, could be heard announcing the time, playing music, cutting the lawn by remote-control mower, or setting an umbrella frantically out and in the slamming and opening front door, a thousand things happening, like a clock shop when each clock strikes the hour insanely before or after the other, a scene of maniac confusion, yet unity; singing, screaming, a few last cleaning mice darting bravely out to carry the horrid ashes away! And one voice, with sublime disregard for the situation, read poetry aloud in the fiery study, until all the film spools burned, until all the wires withered and the circuits cracked.

The fire burst the house and let it slam flat down, puffing out skirts of spark and smoke.

In the kitchen, an instant before the rain of fire and timber, the stove could be seen making breakfasts at a psychopathic rate, ten dozen eggs, six loaves of toast, twenty dozen bacon strips, which, eaten by fire, started the stove working again, hysterically hissing!

The crash. The attic smashing into kitchen and parlor. The parlor into cellar, cellar into sub-cellar. Deep freeze, armchair, film tapes, circuits, beds, and all like skeletons thrown in a cluttered mound deep under.

Smoke and silence. A great quantity of smoke.

Dawn showed faintly in the east. Among the ruins, one wall stood alone. Within   65
the wall, a last voice said, over and over again and again, even as the sun rose to shine upon the heaped rubble and steam:

"Today is August 5, 2026, today is August 5, 2026, today is . . . ."

KATE CHOPIN   (1851–1904)

The Story of an Hour   1891

Knowing that Mrs. Mallard was afflicted with a heart trouble, great care was taken to break to her as gently as possible the news of her husband's death.

It was her sister Josephine who told her, in broken sentences, veiled hints that revealed in half concealing. Her husband's friend Richards was there, too, near her. It was he who had been in the newspaper office when intelligence of the railroad disaster was received, with Brently Mallard's name leading the list of "killed." He had only taken the time to assure himself of its truth by a second telegram, and had hastened to forestall any less careful, less tender friend in bearing the sad message.

She did not hear the story as many women have heard the same, with a paralyzed inability to accept its significance. She wept at once, with sudden, wild abandonment, in her sister's arms. When the storm of grief had spent itself she went away to her room alone. She would have no one follow her.

There stood, facing the open window, a comfortable, roomy armchair. Into this she sank, pressed down by a physical exhaustion that haunted her body and seemed to reach into her soul.

She could see in the open square before her house the tops of trees that were all   5
aquiver with the new spring life. The delicious breath of rain was in the air. In the street below a peddler was crying his wares. The notes of a distant song which some one was singing reached her faintly, and countless sparrows were twittering in the eaves.

There were patches of blue sky showing here and there through the clouds that had met and piled above the other in the west facing her window.

She sat with her head thrown back upon the cushion of the chair quite motionless, except when a sob came up into her throat and shook her, as a child who has cried itself to sleep continues to sob in its dreams.

She was young, with a fair, calm face, whose lines bespoke repression and even a certain strength. But now there was a dull stare in her eyes, whose gaze was fixed away off yonder on one of those patches of blue sky. It was not a glance of reflection, but rather indicated a suspension of intelligent thought.

There was something coming to her and she was waiting for it, fearfully. What was it? She did not know; it was too subtle and elusive to name. But she felt it, creeping out of the sky, reaching toward her through the sounds, the scents, the color that filled the air.

Now her bosom rose and fell tumultuously. She was beginning to recognize this thing that was approaching to possess her, and she was striving to beat it back with her will—as powerless as her two white slender hands would have been.

When she abandoned herself a little whispered word escaped her slightly parted lips. She said it over and over under her breath: "Free, free, free!" The vacant stare and the look of terror that had followed it went from her eyes. They stayed keen and bright. Her pulses beat fast, and the coursing blood warmed and relaxed every inch of her body.

She did not stop to ask if it were not a monstrous joy that held her. A clear and exalted perception enabled her to dismiss the suggestion as trivial.

She knew that she would weep again when she saw the kind, tender hands folded in death; the face that had never looked save with love upon her, fixed and gray and dead. But she saw beyond that bitter moment a long procession of years to come that would belong to her absolutely. And she opened and spread her arms out to them in welcome.

There would be no one to live for during those coming years; she would live for herself. There would be no powerful will bending her in that blind persistence with which men and women believe they have a right to impose a private will upon a fellow creature. A kind intention or a cruel intention made the act seem no less a crime as she looked upon it in that brief moment of illumination.

And yet she had loved him—sometimes. Often she had not. What did it matter! What could love, the unsolved mystery, count for in face of this possession of self-assertion which she suddenly recognized as the strongest impulse of her being.

"Free! Body and soul free!" she kept whispering.

Josephine was kneeling before the closed door with her lips to the keyhole, imploring for admission. "Louise, open the door! I beg; open the door—you will make yourself ill. What are you doing, Louise? For heaven's sake open the door."

"Go away. I am not making myself ill." No; she was drinking in a very elixir of life through that open window.

Her fancy was running riot along those days ahead of her. Spring days, and summer days, and all sorts of days that would be her own. She breathed a quick prayer that life might be long. It was only yesterday she had thought with a shudder that life might be long.

She arose at length and opened the door to her sister's importunities. There was a feverish triumph in her eyes, and she carried herself unwittingly like a goddess of Victory. She clasped her sister's waist, and together they descended the stairs. Richards stood waiting for them at the bottom.

Some one was opening the front door with a latchkey. It was Brently Mallard who entered, a little travel-stained, composedly carrying his grip-sack and umbrella. He had been far from the scene of accident, and did not even know there had been one. He stood amazed at Josephine's piercing cry; at Richards' quick motion to screen him from the view of his wife.

But Richards was too late.

When the doctors came they said she had died of heart disease—of joy that kills.

RALPH ELLISON   (born 1914)

Mister Toussan   1941

Once upon a time
The goose drink wine
Monkey chew tobacco
And he spit white lime.
   RHYME USED AS A PROLOGUE TO NEGRO SLAVE STORIES

"I hope they all gits rotten and the worms git in 'em," the first boy said.

"I hopes a big windstorm comes and blows down all the trees," said the second boy.

"Me too," the first boy said. "And when old Rogan comes out to see what happened I hope a tree falls on his head and kills him."

"Now jus' look a-yonder at them birds," the second boy said, "they eating all they want and when we asked him to let us git some off the ground he had to come calling us names and chasing us home!"

"Doggonit," said the second boy, "I hope them birds got poison in they feet!"   5

The two small boys, Riley and Buster, sat on the floor of the porch, their bare feet resting upon the cool earth as they stared past the line on the paving where the sun consumed the shade, to a yard directly across the street. The grass in the yard was very green and a house stood against it, neat and white in the morning sun. A double row of trees stood alongside the house, heavy with cherries that showed deep red against the dark green of the leaves and dull dark brown of the branches. They were watching an old man who rocked himself in a chair as he stared back at them across the street.

"Just look at him," said Buster. "Ole Rogan's so scared we gonna git some of his ole cherries he ain't even got sense enough to go in outa the sun!"

"Well, them birds is gitting theirs," said Riley.

"They mockingbirds."

"I don't care what kinda birds they is, they sho in them trees."   10

"Yeah, old Rogan don't see *them*. Man, white folks ain't got no sense."

They were silent now, watching the darting flight of the birds into the trees. Behind them they could hear the clatter of a sewing machine: Riley's mother was sewing for the white folks. It was quiet and, as the woman worked, her voice rose above the whirring machine in song.

"Your mamma sho can sing, man," said Buster.

"She sings in the choir," said Riley, "and she sings all the leads in church."

"Shucks, I know it," said Buster. "You tryin' to brag?"   15

As they listened they heard the voice rise clear and liquid to float upon the morning air:

I got wings, you got wings,
All God's chillun got a-wings
When I git to heaven gonna put on my wings
Gonna shout all ovah God's heaven.
Heab'n, heab'n
Everybody talkin' bout heab'n ain't going there
Heab'n, heab'n, Ah'm gonna fly all ovah God's heab'n. . . .

She sang as though the words possessed a deep and throbbing meaning for her, and the boys stared blankly at the earth, feeling the somber, mysterious calm of church. The street was quiet and even old Rogan had stopped rocking to listen. Finally the voice trailed off to a hum and became lost in the clatter of the busy machine.

"Sure wish I could sing like that," said Buster.

Riley was silent, looking down to the end of the porch where the sun had eaten a bright square into the shade, fixing a flitting butterfly in its brilliance.

"What would you do if you had wings?" he said.   20

"Shucks, I'd outfly an eagle, I wouldn't stop flying till I was a million, billion, trillion, zillion miles away from this ole town."

"Where'd you go, man?"

"Up north, maybe to Chicago."

"Man, if I had wings I wouldn't never settle down."

"Me, neither. With wings you could go anywhere, even up to the sun if it wasn't   25
too hot. . . ."

". . . I'd go to New York. . . ."

"Even around the stars. . ."

"Or Dee-troit, Michigan. . ."

"You could git some cheese off the moon and some milk from the Milky Way. . . ."

"Or anywhere else colored is free. . . ."   30

"I bet I'd loop-the-loop. . . ."

"And parachute. . . ."

"I'd land in Africa and git me some diamonds. . . ."

"Yeah, and them cannibals would eat you too," said Riley.

"The heck they would, not fast as I'd fly away. . . ."   35

"Man, they'd catch you and stick soma them long spears in you!" said Riley.

Buster laughed as Riley shook his head gravely: "Boy, you'd look like a black pincushion when they got through with you," said Riley.

"Shucks, man, they couldn't catch me, them suckers is too lazy. The geography book says they 'bout the most lazy folks in the whole world," said Buster with disgust, "just black and lazy!"

"Aw naw, they ain't neither," exploded Riley.

"They is too! The geography book says they is!"   40

"Well, my ole man says they ain't!"

"How come they ain't then?"

"'Cause my ole man says that over there they got kings and diamonds and gold and ivory, and if they got all them things, all of 'em cain't be lazy," said Riley. "Ain't many colored folks over here got them things."

"Sho ain't, man. The white folks won't let 'em," said Buster.

It was good to think that all the Africans were not lazy. He tried to remember   45
all he had heard of Africa as he watched a purple pigeon sail down into the street and scratch where a horse had passed. Then, as he remembered a story his teacher had told him, he saw a car rolling swiftly up the street and the pigeon stretching its wings and lifting easily into the air, skimming the top of the car in its slow, rocking flight. He watched it rise and disappear where the taut telephone wires cut the sky above the curb. Buster felt good. Riley scratched his initials in the soft earth with his big toe.

"Riley, you know all them African guys ain't really that lazy," he said.

"I know they ain't," said Riley, "I just tole you so."

"Yeah, but my teacher tole me, too. She tole us 'bout one of them African guys named Toussan what she said whipped Napoleon!"

Riley stopped scratching the earth and looked up, his eyes rolling in disgust:

"Now how come you have to start lying?" 50

"Thass what she said."

"Boy, you oughta quit telling them things."

"I hope God may kill me."

"She said he was a *African?*"

"Cross my heart, man. . . ." 55

"Really?"

"Really, man. She said he come from a place named Hayti."

Riley looked hard at Buster and seeing the seriousness of the face felt the excitement of a story rise up within him.

"Buster, I'll bet a fat man you lyin'. What'd that teacher say?"

"Really, man, she said that Toussan and his men got up on one of them 60 African mountains and shot down them peckerwood soldiers fass as they'd try to come up. . . ."

"Why good-a-mighty!" yelled Riley.

"Oh boy, they shot 'em down!" chanted Buster.

"Tell me about it, man!"

"And they throwed 'em all off the mountain. . . ."

". . . Goool-leee! . . ." 65

". . . And Toussan drove 'em cross the sand. . . ."

". . . Yeah! And what was they wearing, Buster? . . ."

"Man, they had on red uniforms and blue hats all trimmed with gold, and they had some swords, all shining what they called sweet blades of Damascus. . . ."

"Sweet blades of Damascus! . . ."

". . . They really had 'em," chanted Buster. 70

"And what kinda guns?"

"Big, black cannon!"

"And where did ole what-you-call-'im run them guys? . . ."

"His name was Toussan."

"Toussan! Just like Tarzan. . ." 75

"Not *Taar*-zan, dummy, *Toou*-zan!"

"Toussan! And where'd ole Toussan run 'em?"

"Down to the water, man. . ."

". . . To the river water. . ."

". . . Where some great big ole boats was waiting for 'em. . ." 80

". . . Go on, Buster!"

"An' Toussan shot into them boats. . . ."

". . . He shot into 'em. . . ."

"With his great big cannons. . ."

". . . Yeah! . . ." 85

". . . Made a-brass. . ."

". . . Brass. . ."

". . . An' his big black cannonballs started killin' them peckerwoods. . . ."

". . . Lawd, Lawd. . ."

". . . Boy, till them peckerwoods hollered *Please, please, Mister Toussan, we'll be* 90 *good!*'"

"An' what'd Toussan tell 'em, Buster?"

"'Boy,' he said in his big deep voice, *'I oughta drown all a-you.'*"

"An' what'd the peckerwoods say?"

"They said, 'Please, Please, *Please, Mister Toussan*. . .'"

". . . 'We'll be good,'" broke in Riley. 95

"Thass right, man," said Buster excitedly. He clapped his hands and kicked his heels against the earth, his black face glowing in a burst of rhythmic joy.

"Boy!"

"And what'd ole Toussan say then?"

"He said in his big deep voice: 'You all peckerwoods better be good, *'cause this is sweet Papa Toussan talking and my men is crazy 'bout white meat!'*"

"Ho, ho, ho!" Riley bent double with laughter. The rhythm still throbbed within 100 him and he wanted the story to go on and on. . . .

"Buster, you know didn't no teacher tell you that lie," he said.

"Yes she did, man."

"That teacher said there was really a guy like that what called hisself Sweet Papa Toussan?"

Riley's voice was unbelieving and there was a wistful expression in his eyes which Buster could not understand. Finally he dropped his head and grinned.

"Well," he said, "I bet thass what ole Toussan said. You know how grown folks is, 105 they cain't tell a story right, 'cepting real old folks like grandma."

"They sho cain't," said Riley. "They don't know how to put the right stuff to it."

Riley stood, his legs spread wide, and stuck his thumbs in the top of his trousers, swaggering sinisterly.

"Come on, watch me do it now, Buster. Now I bet ole Toussan looked down at them white folks standing just about like this and said in a soft easy voice: 'Ain't I done begged you white folks to quit messin' with me? . . .'"

"Thass right, quit messing with 'im," chanted Buster.

"'But naw, you-all had to come on anyway. . . .'" 110

". . . Jus' 'cause they was black. . ."

"Thass right," said Riley. "Then ole Toussan felt so bad and mad the tears come a-trickling down. . . ."

". . . He was really mad."

"And then, man, he said in his big bass voice: 'white folks, how come you-all cain't let us colored alone?'"

". . . An' he was crying. . . ." 115

". . . An' Toussan tole them peckerwoods: 'I been beggin' you-all to quit bothering us. . . .'"

". . . Beggin' on his bended knees! . . ."

"Then, man, Toussan got real mad and snatched off his hat and started stompin' up and down on it and the tears was tricklin' down and he said: 'You-all come tellin' me about Napoleon. . . .'"

"They was tryin' to make him scared, man. . . ."

"Toussan said: 'I don't care about no Napoleon. . . .'" 120

". . . Wasn't studyin' 'bout him. . . ."

". . . Toussan said: 'Napoleon ain't nothing but a man!' Then Toussan pulled back his shining sword like this, and twirled it at them peckerwoods' throats so hard it z-z-z-zinged in the air!"

"Now keep on, finish it, man," said Buster. "What'd Toussan do then?"

"Then you know what he did, he said: 'I oughta beat you peckerwoods!'"

"Thass right, and he did it too," said Buster. He jumped to his feet and fenced vi- 125 olently with five desperate imaginary soldiers, running each through with his imaginary sword. Buster watched from the porch, grinning.

"Toussan musta scared them white folks almost to death!"

"Yeah, thass 'bout the way it was," said Buster. The rhythm was dying now and he sat back upon the porch, breathing tiredly.

"It sho is a good story," said Riley.

"Hecks, man, all the stories my teacher tells us is good. She's a good ole teacher— but you know one thing?"

"Naw; what?" 130

"Ain't none of them stories in the books! Wonder why?"

"You know why, ole Toussan was too hard on them white folks, thass why."

"Oh, he was a hard man!"

"He was mean. . . ."

"But a good mean!" 135

"Toussan was clean. . . ."

". . . He was a good, clean mean," said Riley.

"Aw, man, he was sooo-preme," said Buster.

"Riiiley!!"

The boys stopped short in their word play, their mouths wide. 140

"Riley I say!" It was Riley's mother's voice.

"Ma'am?"

"She musta heard us cussin'," whispered Buster.

"Shut up, man. . . . What you want, Ma?"

"I says I wants you-all to go around in the backyard and play, you keeping up too 145 much fuss out there. White folks says we tear up a neighborhood when we move in it and you-all out there jus' provin' them out true. Now git on round in the back."

"Aw, ma, we was jus' playing, ma. . . ."

"Boy, I said for you-all to go on."

"But, ma. . ."

"You hear me, boy!"

"Yessum, we going," said Riley. "Come on, Buster." 150

Buster followed slowly behind, feeling the dew upon his feet as he walked upon the shaded grass.

"What else did he do, man?" Buster said.

"Huh? Rogan?"

"Heck, naw! I mean Toussan."

"Doggone if I know, man—but I'm gonna ask that teacher." 155

"He was a fightin' son-of-a-gun, wasn't he, man?"

"He didn't stand for no foolishness," said Riley reservedly. He thought of other things now, and as he moved along he slid his feet easily over the short-cut grass, dancing as he chanted

Iron is iron,
And tin is tin,
And that's the way
The story . . .

"Aw come on man," interrupted Buster. "Let's go play in the alley. . . ."

And that's the way . . .

"Maybe we can slip around and git some cherries," Buster went on.

". . . the story ends," chanted Riley.

BHARATI MUKHERJEE (born 1940)
A Wife's Story   1987

Imre says forget it, but I'm going to write David Mamet. So Patels are hard to sell real estate to. You buy them a beer, whisper Glengarry Glen Ross, and they smell swamp instead of sun and surf. They work hard, eat cheap, live ten to a room, stash their savings under futons in Queens, and before you know it they own half of Hoboken. You say, where's the sweet gullibility that made this nation great?

Polish jokes, Patel jokes: that's not why I want to write Mamet:

Seen their women?

Everybody laughs. Imre laughs. The dozing fat man with the Barnes & Noble sack between his legs, the woman next to him, the usher, everybody. The theater isn't so dark that they can't see me. In my red silk sari I'm conspicuous. Plump, gold paisleys sparkle on my chest.

The actor is just warming up. *Seen their women?* He plays a salesman, he's had a bad day and now he's in a Chinese restaurant trying to loosen up. His face is pink. His wool-blend slacks are creased at the crotch. We bought our tickets at half-price, we're sitting in the front row, but at the edge, and we see things we shouldn't be seeing. At least I do, or think I do. Spittle, actors goosing each other, little winks, streaks of makeup.   5

Maybe they're improvising dialogue too. Maybe Mamet's provided them with insult kits, Thursdays for Chinese, Wednesdays for Hispanics, today for Indians. Maybe they get together before curtain time, see an Indian woman settling in the front row off to the side, and say to each other: "Hey, forget Friday. Let's get *her* today. See if she cries. See if she walks out." Maybe, like the salesmen they play, they have a little bet on.

Maybe I shouldn't feel betrayed.

Their women, he goes again. *They look like they've just been fucked by a dead cat.*

The fat man hoots so hard he nudges my elbow off our shared armrest.

"Imre. I'm going home." But Imre's hunched so far forward he doesn't hear. English isn't his best language. A refugee from Budapest, he has to listen hard. "I didn't pay eighteen dollars to be insulted."   10

I don't hate Mamet. It's the tyranny of the American dream that scares me. First, you don't exist. Then you're invisible. Then you're funny. Then you're disgusting. Insult, my American friends will tell me, is a kind of acceptance. No instant dignity here. A play like this, back home, would cause riots. Communal, racist, and antisocial. The actors wouldn't make it off stage. This play, and all these awful feelings, would be safely locked up.

I long, at times, for clear-cut answers. Offer me instant dignity, today, and I'll take it.

"What?" Imre moves toward me without taking his eyes off the actor. "Come again?"

Tears come. I want to stand, scream, make an awful scene. I long for ugly, nasty rage.

The actor is ranting, flinging spittle. *Give me a chance. I'm not finished, I can get back on the board. I tell that asshole, give me a real lead. And what does that asshole give me? Patels. Nothing but Patels.*   15

This time Imre works an arm around my shoulders. "Panna, what is Patel? Why are you taking it all so personally?"

I shrink from his touch, but I don't walk out. Expensive girls' schools in Lausanne and Bombay have trained me to behave well. My manners are exquisite, my feelings are delicate, my gestures refined, my moods undetectable. They have seen me through riots, uprootings, separation, my son's death.

"I'm not taking it personally."

The fat man looks at us. The woman looks too, and shushes.

I stare back at the two of them. Then I stare, mean and cool, at the man's elbow. Under the bright blue polyester Hawaiian shirt sleeve, the elbow looks soft and runny. "Excuse me," I say. My voice has the effortless meanness of well-bred displaced Third World women, though my rhetoric has been learned elsewhere. "You're exploiting my space."

Startled, the man snatches his arm away from me. He cradles it against his breast. By the time he's ready with comebacks, I've turned my back on him. I've probably ruined the first act for him. I know I've ruined it for Imre.

It's not my fault; it's the *situation*. Old colonies wear down. Patels—the new pioneers—have to be suspicious. Idi Amin's lesson is permanent. AT&T wires move good advice from continent to continent. Keep all assets liquid. Get into 7-11s, get out of condos and motels. I know how both sides feel, that's the trouble. The Patel sniffing out scams, the sad salesmen on the stage: postcolonialism has made me their referee. It's hate I long for; simple, brutish, partisan hate.

After the show Imre and I make our way toward Broadway. Sometimes he holds my hand; it doesn't mean anything more than that crazies and drunks are crouched in doorways. Imre's been here over two years, but he's stayed very old-world, very courtly, openly protective of women. I met him in a seminar on special ed. last semester. His wife is a nurse somewhere in the Hungarian countryside. There are two sons, and miles of petitions for their emigration. My husband manages a mill two hundred miles north of Bombay. There are no children.

"You make things tough on yourself," Imre says. He assumed Patel was a Jewish name or maybe Hispanic; everything makes equal sense to him. He found the play tasteless, he worried about the effect of vulgar language on my sensitive ears. "You have to let go a bit." And as though to show me how to let go, he breaks away from me, bounds ahead with his head ducked tight, then dances on amazingly jerky legs. He's a Magyar, he often tells me, and deep down, he's an Asian too. I catch glimpses of it, knife-blade Attila cheekbones, despite the blondish hair. In his faded jeans and leather jacket, he's a rock video star. I watch MTV for hours in the apartment when Charity's working the evening shift at Macy's. I listen to WPLJ on Charity's earphones. Why should I be ashamed? Television in India is so uplifting.

Imre stops as suddenly as he'd started. People walk around us. The summer sidewalk is full of theatergoers in seersucker suits; Imre's year-round jacket is out of place. European. Cops in twos and threes huddle, lightly tap their thighs with night sticks and smile at me with benevolence. I want to wink at them, get us all in trouble, tell them the crazy dancing man is from the Warsaw Pact. I'm too shy to break into dance on Broadway. So I hug Imre instead.

The hug takes him by surprise. He wants me to let go, but he doesn't really expect me to let go. He staggers, though I weigh no more than 104 pounds, and with him, I pitch forward slightly. Then he catches me, and we walk arm in arm to the bus stop. My husband would never dance or hug a woman on Broadway. Nor would my brothers. They aren't stuffy people, but they went to Anglican boarding schools and they have a well-developed sense of what's silly.

"Imre." I squeeze his big, rough hand. "I'm sorry I ruined the evening for you."

"You did nothing of the kind." He sounds tired. "Let's not wait for the bus. Let's splurge and take a cab instead."

Imre always has unexpected funds. The Network, he calls it, Class of '56.

In the back of the cab, without even trying, I feel light, almost free. Memories of Indian destitutes mix with the hordes of New York street people, and they float free, like astronauts, inside my head. I've made it. I'm making something of my life. I've left home, my husband, to get a Ph.D. in special ed. I have a multiple-entry visa and a small scholarship for two years. After that, we'll see. My mother was beaten by her mother-in-law, my grandmother, when she'd registered for French lessons at the Alliance Française. My grandmother, the eldest daughter of a rich zamindar, was illiterate. 30

Imre and the cabdriver talk away in Russian. I keep my eyes closed. That way I can feel the floaters better. I'll write Mamet tonight. I feel strong, reckless. Maybe I'll write Steven Spielberg too; tell him that Indians don't eat monkey brains.

We've made it. Patels must have made it. Mamet, Spielberg: they're not condescending to us. Maybe they're a little bit afraid.

Charity Chin, my roommate, is sitting on the floor drinking Chablis out of a plastic wineglass. She is five foot six, three inches taller than me, but weighs a kilo and a half less than I do. She is a "hands" model. Orientals are supposed to have a monopoly in the hands-modelling business, she says. She had her eyes fixed eight or nine months ago and out of gratitude sleeps with her plastic surgeon every third Wednesday.

"Oh, good," Charity says. "I'm glad you're back early. I need to talk."

She's been writing checks. MCI, Con Ed, Bonwit Teller. Envelopes, already stamped and sealed, form a pyramid between her shapely, knee-socked legs. The checkbook's cover is brown plastic, grained to look like cowhide. Each time Charity flips back the cover, white geese fly over sky-colored checks. She makes good money, but she's extravagant. The difference adds up to this shared, rent-controlled Chelsea one-bedroom. 35

"All right. Talk."

When I first moved in, she was seeing an analyst. Now she sees a nutritionist.

"Eric called. From Oregon."

"What did he want?"

"He wants me to pay half the rent on his loft for last spring. He asked me to move back, remember? He *begged* me." 40

Eric is Charity's estranged husband.

"What does your nutritionist say?" Eric now wears a red jumpsuit and tills the soil in Rajneeshpuram.

"You think Phil's a creep too, don't you? What else can he be when creeps are all I attract?"

Phil is a flutist with thinning hair. He's very touchy on the subject of *flautists* versus *flutists*. He's touchy on every subject, from music to books to foods to clothes. He teaches at a small college upstate, and Charity bought a used blue Datsun ("Nissan," Phil insists) last month so she could spend weekends with him. She returns every Sunday night, exhausted and exasperated. Phil and I don't have much to say to each other—he's the only musician I know; the men in my family are lawyers, engineers, or in business—but I like him. Around me, he loosens up. When he visits, he bakes us loaves of pumpernickel bread. He waxes our kitchen floor. Like many men in this country, he seems to me a displaced child, or even a woman, looking for something that passed him by, or for something that he can never have. If he thinks I'm not looking, he sneaks his hands under Charity's sweater, but there isn't too much there. Here, she's a model with high ambitions. In India, she'd be a flat-chested old maid.

I'm shy in front of the lovers. A darkness comes over me when I see them horsing around. 45

"It isn't the money," Charity says. Oh? I think. "He says he still loves me. Then he turns around and asks me for five hundred."

What's so strange about that, I want to ask. She still loves Eric, and Eric, red jump suit and all, is smart enough to know it. Love is a commodity, hoarded like any other. Mamet knows. But I say, "I'm not the person to ask about love." Charity knows that mine was a traditional Hindu marriage. My parents, with the help of a marriage broker, who was my mother's cousin, picked out a groom. All I had to do was get to know his taste in food.

It'll be a long evening, I'm afraid. Charity likes to confess. I unpleat my silk sari— it no longer looks too showy—wrap it in muslin cloth and put it away in a dresser drawer. Saris are hard to have laundered in Manhattan, though there's a good man in Jackson Heights. My next step will be to brew us a pot of chrysanthemum tea. It's a very special tea from the mainland. Charity's uncle gave it to us. I like him. He's a humpbacked, awkward, terrified man. He runs a gift store on Mott Street, and though he doesn't speak much English, he seems to have done well. Once upon a time he worked for the railways in Chengdu, Szechwan Province, and during the Wuchang Uprising, he was shot at. When I'm down, when I'm lonely for my husband, when I think of our son, or when I need to be held, I think of Charity's uncle. If I hadn't left home, I'd never have heard of the Wuchang Uprising. I've broadened my horizons.

Very late that night my husband calls me from Ahmadabad, a town of textile mills north of Bombay. My husband is a vice president at Lakshmi Cotton Mills. Lakshmi is the goddess of wealth, but LCM (Priv.), Ltd., is doing poorly. Lockouts, strikes, rock-throwings. My husband lives on digitalis, which he calls the food for our *yuga* of discontent.

"We had a bad mishap at the mill today." Then he says nothing for seconds. 50

The operator comes on. "Do you have the right party, sir? We're trying to reach Mrs. Butt."

"Bhatt," I insist. "*B* for Bombay, *H* for Haryana, *A* for Ahmadabad, double *T* for Tamil Nadu." It's a litany. "This is she."

"One of our lorries was firebombed today. Resulting in three deaths. The driver, old Karamchand, and his two children."

I know how my husband's eyes look this minute, how the eye rims sag and the yellow corneas shine and bulge with pain. He is not an emotional man—the Ahmadabad Institute of Management has trained him to cut losses, to look on the bright side of economic catastrophes—but tonight he's feeling low. I try to remember a driver named Karamchand, but can't. That part of my life is over, the way *trucks* have replaced *lorries* in my vocabulary, the way Charity Chin and her lurid love life have replaced inherited notions of marital duty. Tomorrow he'll come out of it. Soon he'll be eating again. He'll sleep like a baby. He's been trained to believe in turnovers. Every morning he rubs his scalp with cantharidine oil so his hair will grow back again.

"It could be your car next." Affection, love. Who can tell the difference in a traditional marriage in which a wife still doesn't call her husband by his first name? 55

"No. They know I'm a flunky, just like them. Well paid, maybe. No need for undue anxiety, please."

Then his voice breaks. He says he needs me, he misses me, he wants me to come to him damp from my evening shower, smelling of sandalwood soap, my braid decorated with jasmines.

"I need you too."

"Not to worry, please," he says. "I am coming in a fortnight's time. I have already made arrangements."

Outside my window, fire trucks whine, up Eighth Avenue. I wonder if he can hear   60
them, what he thinks of a life like mine, led amid disorder.

"I am thinking it'll be like a honeymoon. More or less."

When I was in college, waiting to be married, I imagined honeymoons were only
for the more fashionable girls, the girls who came from slightly racy families, smoked
Sobranies in the dorm lavatories and put up posters of Kabir Bedi, who was supposed
to have made it as a big star in the West. My husband wants us to go to Niagara. I'm
not to worry about foreign exchange. He's arranged for extra dollars through the Gu-
jarati Network, with a cousin in San Jose. And he's bought four hundred more on the
black market. "Tell me you need me. Panna, please tell me again."

I change out of the cotton pants and shirt I've been wearing all day and put on a
sari to meet my husband at JFK. I don't forget the jewelry; the marriage necklace of
mangalsutra, gold drop earrings, heavy gold bangles. I don't wear them every day. In
this borough of vice and greed, who knows when, or whom, desire will overwhelm.

My husband spots me in the crowd and waves. He has lost weight, and changed
his glasses. The arm, uplifted in a cheery wave, is bony, frail, almost opalescent.

In the Carey Coach, we hold hands. He strokes my fingers one by one. "How   65
come you aren't wearing my mother's ring?"

"Because muggers know about Indian women," I say. They know with us it's 24-
karat. His mother's ring is showy, in ghastly taste anywhere but India: a blood-red
Burma ruby set in a gold frame of floral sprays. My mother-in-law got her guru to bless
the ring before I left for the States.

He looks disconcerted. He's used to a different role. He's the knowing, suspicious
one in the family. He seems to be sulking, and finally he comes out with it. "You've
said nothing about my new glasses." I compliment him on the glasses, how chic and
Western-executive they make him look. But I can't help the other things, necessities
until he learns the ropes. I handle the money, buy the tickets. I don't know if this
makes me unhappy.

Charity drives her Nissan upstate, so for two weeks we are to have the apartment
to ourselves. This is more privacy than we ever had in India. No parents, no servants, to
keep us modest. We play at housekeeping. Imre has lent us a hibachi, and I grill saffron
chicken breasts. My husband marvels at the size of the Perdue hens. "They're big like
peacocks, no? These Americans, they're really something!" He tries out pizzas, burgers,
McNuggets. He chews. He explores. He judges. He loves it all, fears nothing, feels at
home in the summer odors, the clutter of Manhattan streets. Since he thinks that the
American palate is bland, he carries a bottle of red peppers in his pocket. I wheel a
shopping cart down the aisles of the neighborhood Grand Union, and he follows, swiftly, greedily. He picks up hair rinses and high-protein diet powders. There's so much I
already take for granted.

One night, Imre stops by. He wants us to go with him to a movie. In his work
shirt and red leather tie, he looks arty or strung out. It's only been a week, but I feel as
though I am really seeing him for the first time. The yellow hair worn very short at the
sides, the wide, narrow lips. He's a good-looking man, but self-conscious, almost arrogant.
He's picked the movie we should see. He always tells me what to see, what to read. He
buys the *Voice.* He's a natural avant-gardist. For tonight he's chosen *Numéro Deux.*

"Is it a musical?" my husband asks. The Radio City Music Hall is on his list of   70
sights to see. He's read up on the history of the Rockettes. He doesn't catch Imre's
sympathetic wink.

Guilt, shame, loyalty. I long to be ungracious, not ingratiate myself with both men.

That night my husband calculates in rupees the money we've wasted on Godard. "That refugee fellow, Nagy, must have a screw loose in his head. I paid very steep price for dollars on the black market."

Some afternoons we go shopping. Back home we hated shopping; but now it is a lovers' project. My husband's shopping list startles me. I feel I am just getting to know him. Maybe, like Imre, freed from the dignities of old-world culture, he too could get drunk and squirt Cheez Whiz on a guest. I watch him dart into stores in his gleaming leather shoes. Jockey shorts on sale in outdoor bins on Broadway entrance him. White tube socks with different bands of color delight him. He looks for microcassettes, for anything small and electronic and smuggleable. He needs a garment bag. He calls it a "wardrobe," and I have to translate.

"All of New York is having sales, no?"

My heart speeds watching him this happy. It's the third week in August, almost the end of summer, and the city smells ripe, it cannot bear more heat, more money, more energy. 75

"This is so smashing! The prices are so excellent!" Recklessly, my prudent husband signs away traveller's checks. How he intends to smuggle it all back I don't dare ask. With a microwave, he calculates, we could get rid of our cook.

This has to be love, I think. Charity, Eric, Phil: they may be experts on sex. My husband doesn't chase me around the sofa, but he pushes me down on Charity's battered cushions, and the man who has never entered the kitchen of our Ahmadabad house now comes toward me with a dish tub of steamy water to massage away the pavement heat.

Ten days into his vacation my husband checks out brochures for sightseeing tours. Shortline, Grayline, Crossroads: his new vinyl briefcase is full of schedules and pamphlets. While I make pancakes out of a mix, he comparison-shops. Tour number one costs $10.95 and will give us the World Trade Center, Chinatown, and the United Nations. Tour number three would take us both uptown *and* downtown for $14.95, but my husband is absolutely sure he doesn't want to see Harlem. We settle for tour number four: Downtown and the Dame. It's offered by a new tour company with a small, dirty office at Eighth and Forty-eighth.

The sidewalk outside the office is colorful with tourists. My husband sends me in to buy the tickets because he has come to feel Americans don't understand his accent.

The dark man, Lebanese probably, behind the counter comes on too friendly. 80 "Come on, doll, make my day!" He won't say which tour is his. "Number four? Honey, no! Look, you've wrecked me! Say you'll change your mind." He takes two twenties and gives back change. He holds the tickets, forcing me to pull. He leans closer. "I'm off after lunch."

My husband must have been watching me from the sidewalk. "What was the chap saying?" he demands. "I told you not to wear pants. He thinks you are Puerto Rican. He thinks he can treat you with disrespect."

The bus is crowded and we have to sit across the aisle from each other. The tour guide begins his patter on Forty-sixth. He looks like an actor, his hair bleached and blow-dried. Up close he must look middle-aged, but from where I sit his skin is smooth and his cheeks faintly red.

"Welcome to the Big Apple, folks." The guide uses a microphone. "Big Apple. That's what we native Manhattan degenerates call our city. Today we have guests from fifteen foreign countries and six states from this U. S. of A. That makes the Tourist Bureau real happy. And let me assure you that while we may be the richest city in the richest country in the world, it's okay to tip your charming and talented attendant." He laughs. Then he swings his hip out into the aisle and sings a song.

"And it's mighty fancy on old Delancey Street, you know. . . ."

My husband looks irritable. The guide is, as expected, a good singer. "The bloody man should be giving us histories of buildings we are passing, no?" I pat his hand, the mood passes. He cranes his neck. Our window seats have both gone to Japanese. It's the tour of his life. Next to this, the quick business trips to Manchester and Glasgow pale. 85

"And tell me what street compares to Mott Street, in July. . . ."

The guide wants applause. He manages a derisive laugh from the Americans up front. He's working the aisles now. "I coulda been somebody, right? I coulda been a star!" Two or three of us smile, those of us who recognize the parody. He catches my smile. The sun is on his harsh, bleached hair. "Right, your highness? Look, we gotta maharani with us! Couldn't I have been a star?"

"Right!" I say, my voice coming out a squeal. I've been trained to adapt; what else can I say?

We drive through traffic past landmark office buildings and churches. The guide flips his hands. "Art deco," he keeps saying. I hear him confide to one of the Americans: "Beats me. I went to a cheap guide's school." My husband wants to know more about this Art Deco, but the guide sings another song.

"We made a foolish choice," my husband grumbles. "We are sitting in the bus only. We're not going into famous buildings." He scrutinizes the pamphlets in his jacket pocket. I think, at least it's air-conditioned in here. I could sit here in the cool shadows of the city forever. 90

Only five of us appear to have opted for the "Downtown and the Dame" tour. The others will ride back uptown past the United Nations after we've been dropped off at the pier for the ferry to the Statue of Liberty.

An elderly European pulls a camera out of his wife's designer tote bag. He takes pictures of the boats in the harbor, the Japanese in kimonos eating popcorn, scavenging pigeons, me. Then, pushing his wife ahead of him, he climbs back on the bus and waves to us. For a second I feel terribly lost. I wish we were on the bus going back to the apartment. I know I'll not be able to describe any of this to Charity, or to Imre. I'm too proud to admit I went on a guided tour.

The view of the city from the Circle Line ferry is seductive, unreal. The skyline wavers out of reach, but never quite vanishes. The summer sun pushes through fluffy clouds and dapples the glass of office towers. My husband looks thrilled, even more than he had on the shopping trips down Broadway. Tourists and dreamers, we have spent our life's savings to see this skyline, this statue.

"Quick, take a picture of me!" my husband yells as he moves toward a gap of railings. A Japanese matron has given up her position in order to change film. "Before the Twin Towers disappear!"

I focus, I wait for a large Oriental family to walk out of my range. My husband holds his pose tight against the railing. He wants to look relaxed, an international businessman at home in all the financial markets. 95

A bearded man slides across the bench toward me. "Like this," he says and helps me get my husband in focus. "You want me to take the photo for you?" His name, he says, is Goran. He is Goran from Yugoslavia, as though that were enough for tracking him down. Imre from Hungary. Panna from India. He pulls the old Leica out of my hand, signaling the Orientals to beat it, and clicks away. "I'm a photographer," he says. He could have been a camera thief. That's what my husband would have assumed. Somehow, I trusted. "Get you a beer?" he asks.

"I don't. Drink, I mean. Thank you very much." I say those last words very loud, for everyone's benefit. The odd bottles of Soave with Imre don't count.

"Too bad." Goran gives back the camera.

"Take one more!" my husband shouts from the railing. "Just to be sure!"

The island itself disappoints. The Lady has brutal scaffolding holding her in. The museum is closed. The snack bar is dirty and expensive. My husband reads out the prices to me. He orders two french fries and two Cokes. We sit at picnic tables and wait for the ferry to take us back. 100

"What was that hippie chap saying?"

As if I could say. A day-care center has brought its kids, at least forty of them, to the island for the day. The kids, all wearing name tags, run around us. I can't help noticing how many are Indian. Even a Patel, probably a Bhatt if I looked hard enough. They toss hamburger bits at pigeons. They kick styrofoam cups. The pigeons are slow, greedy, persistent. I have to shoo one off the table top. I don't think my husband thinks about our son.

"What hippie?"

"The one on the boat. With the beard and the hair."

My husband doesn't look at me. He shakes out his paper napkin and tries to protect his french fries from pigeon feathers. 105

"Oh, him. He said he was from Dubrovnik." It isn't true, but I don't want trouble.

"What did he say about Dubrovnik?"

I know enough about Dubrovnik to get by. Imre's told me about it. And about Mostar and Zagreb. In Mostar white Muslims sing the call to prayer. I would like to see that before I die: white Muslims. Whole peoples have moved before me; they've adapted. The night Imre told me about Mostar was also the night I saw my first snow in Manhattan. We'd walked down to Chelsea from Columbia. We'd walked and talked and I hadn't felt tired at all.

"You're too innocent," my husband says. He reaches for my hand. "Panna," he cries with pain in his voice, and I am brought back from perfect, floating memories of snow, "I've come to take you back. I have seen how men watch you."

"What?" 110

"Come back, now. I have tickets. We have all the things we will ever need. I can't live without you."

A little girl with wiry braids kicks a bottle cap at his shoes. The pigeons wheel and scuttle around us. My husband covers his fries with spread-out fingers. "No kicking," he tells the girl. Her name, Beulah, is printed in green ink on a heart-shaped name tag. He forces a smile, and Beulah smiles back. Then she starts to flap her arms. She flaps, she hops. The pigeons go crazy for fries and scraps.

"Special ed. course is two years," I remind him. "I can't go back."

My husband picks up our trays and throws them into the garbage before I can stop him. He's carried disposability a little too far. "We've been taken," he says, moving toward the dock, though the ferry will not arrive for another twenty minutes. "The ferry costs only two dollars round-trip per person. We should have chosen tour number one for $10.95 instead of tour number four for $14.95."

With my Lebanese friend, I think. "But this way we don't have to worry about 115 cabs. The bus will pick us up at the pier and take us back to midtown. Then we can walk home."

"New York is full of cheats and whatnot. Just like Bombay." He is not accusing me of infidelity. I feel dread all the same.

That night, after we've gone to bed, the phone rings. My husband listens, then hands the phone to me. "What is this woman saying?" He turns on the pink Macy's lamp by the bed. "I am not understanding these Negro people's accents."

The operator repeats the message. It's a cable from one of the directors of Lakshmi Cotton Mills. "Massive violent labor confrontation anticipated. Stop. Return posthaste. Stop. Cable flight details. Signed Kantilal Shah."

"It's not your factory," I say. "You're supposed to be on vacation."

"So, you are worrying about me? Yes? You reject my heartfelt wishes but you   120
worry about me?" He pulls me close, slips the straps of my nightdress off my shoulder. "Wait a minute."

I wait, unclothed, for my husband to come back to me. The water is running in the bathroom. In the ten days he has been here he has learned American rites: deodorants, fragrances. Tomorrow morning he'll call Air India; tomorrow evening he'll be on his way back to Bombay. Tonight I should make up to him for my years away, the gutted trucks, the degree I'll never use in India. I want to pretend with him that nothing has changed.

In the mirror that hangs on the bathroom door, I watch my naked body turn, the breasts, the thighs glow. The body's beauty amazes. I stand here shameless, in ways he has never seen me. I am free, afloat, watching somebody else.

CARMEN NARANJO   (born 1931)
Walls

TRANSLATED BY BARBARA PASCHKE

I wonder why I was given this assignment? A response is a response, he says to himself as he watches the flight of a dark bird against the background of the clear blue sky, as they say in national anthems.

The meeting's to be here. He found it a natural place. A little town on hills of eucalyptus and pine, spread out to where the plains begin, with five blocks crowded with houses and the rest scattered among the streams and the lazy river bordered by stones and huge rocks where ferns grew and where lizards lay almost immobile.

In the hotel, a large old house with hallways all going toward the cobbled patio in the center full of tangled vines with meaty leaves and reddish flowers, they ask him how many days he's planning to stay. He says three. "Are you sure?" "Very sure, because I have other plans."

The room is dark and he finds it narrow and oppressive, the walls humid and spotted with mushrooms, which appear to be moving around on a badly drawn map. He leaves his small suitcase and goes out to look for the plaza and the church.

Bells are tolling for a funeral. Would this make it difficult to find the man? Fifth   5
row on the side aisle, counting from the pulpit. White shirt, gray pants, and a black hat on his knees.

Old women in mourning are hurrying toward the plaza. A package tomorrow. Another on Tuesday in front of the altar. The last on Wednesday near the Chapel of the Poor Souls. Some children holding flowers are waiting at the corner. A family, all in black, crosses the street.

The Church is neglected but beautiful, with thick columns on which vines and grape branches climb and which on one side have images of the Holy Family, St. Joseph, the Virgin Mary, Baby Jesus, and on the other side, a fat and smiling saint, completely unknown but obviously the town's patron.

The bells toll, lacking the seriousness of the occasion, having instead a cheerful ring. Or else the bell ringer doesn't know what he's doing or suffers in happiness for other people's sorrow.

Over on a hill a tall pine is going up in flames, collapsing with crackling and hissing and frightening the neighbors. Perhaps it was struck by unexpected lightning.

When he goes up the stairway, a dead bird falls near his feet. Perhaps it died in flight. 10

In the vestibule near the door, one of the beggars shows him a bloody empty hole that looks as though he had just pulled out his eye.

The church smells of incense and freshly cut lilies. It's full. From the back he counts the pews and in the fifth one there are six men wearing white shirts.

He waits while he listens to the lapidary requiem for the pine coffin. At the end four men carry it off. Solemn faces, carved in sadness. Further back a group walking arm in arm weep with their faces hidden. The funeral procession is a mix of peasants and workers.

When he sees the empty pew, the fifth, he sinks down in the middle of it and waits. He hears footsteps behind him and waits for the tap on his shoulder. He remembers the password. During the night the walls walk.

An hour goes by. Nothing, no one. Another hour goes by. Nothing, no one, not 15 even a devout old woman. Another hour. Better to come back tomorrow.

Lonely streets that seem even narrower lead him back to the hotel, and a lonely hallway takes him to his room. There he's surprised by how narrow it is. It looks like a cell. Moreover, he remembers that he left his suitcase in the middle of the room and now it's up against the wall, which, under careful inspection, looks as if it's become even blacker with mushrooms and feels as if it's grown thicker.

He sleeps badly because he thinks he feels the walls closing in and the mushrooms growing. It's hot in the room. It occurs to him to note the distance between the walls: eight feet wide by twelve feet long. More than a room, it's a niche, he says to himself, while he notices there are other spots of mushrooms, and maybe there's no mystery— maybe it's just that the paint is peeling because of the heat and the humidity. Several times he steps out the door in search of some open space to find out if it's dawn; his watch stopped when he arrived in town. But dawn is still a long way off, and each time he looks the darkness deepens. A heavy sleep envelops him in the early morning, and noon catches him in bed sweating, with bad breath. "Damn! I missed the nine o'clock appointment this morning and if he's not there at four, I'm taking the first flight out tomorrow."

At exactly four o'clock, passing through streets that are now really alleys, he finds the church empty, and empty he leaves it at seven, when the sacristan tells him he has to close up. What's going on, he wonders, maybe he didn't get the package, but he could have let me know, losing time like this and going back with nothing; the clients are really going to raise a stink.

In the hotel he's told that there won't be a plane until the airport is repaired; his flight was the last to land. And by road? Yes, that will be possible when the washed-out bridge is rebuilt. This can't be happening.

He walks through streets that seem like hallways. What am I going to do? Return to that room? Never! The night's getting cold. Returning to the hotel, he asks if there isn't another room; his is too small. They're all the same, sir, and they're all occupied.

The room seems even smaller and the walls are almost completely black with mushrooms. He measures seven feet wide by twelve feet long. It could be that during the night, half asleep, he didn't count correctly. Besides, he has to figure out how to get out, how the hell to get out of this damned town.

He puts his suitcase in order, without knowing why. He tries to remember and remembers only yesterday's funeral, the sound of the bells, the pine tree writhing amidst the flames, the dead bird falling at his feet, the beggar's bloody empty eye socket, the men's faces, the coffin, the procession. Yesterday's corpse, could that have been who he's waiting for?

Luck had always accompanied him. Always. In the worst times, when everything was against him, luck was there, on his side, saving him time and again. It wasn't fair to think it had left him now; that would be challenging luck. But they say luck gives out, changes, and things become different. He whistles and looks for a deck of cards to play a game of solitaire on the bed. If he wins, luck is with him, and if he loses, well, it's gone. The room shakes, yes, shakes. Violently! He opens the door and runs. In the hallway, no one, in the alley, no one. Those alleys, more and more shrunken, labyrinthine, almost mere passageways. A dead bird falls between his feet.

He returns to his room, and as he goes through the door he senses that the walls have moved. He counts again: five feet wide by ten feet long. It seems like a nightmare. It could have been the tremor. The best thing would be for the sun to come up soon. He gathers up the cards, feels it's better not to challenge luck. He tries to sleep and forget.

He hears a storm approaching; the distant thunder comes closer and a torrent of water falls on the roof. The roar inundates the room. It rains hard. The storm moves further away. It's time to rest, and the lullaby of the rain brings sleep. He moves the bed to get it away from the walls so he'll be able to know if this rare phenomenon is real, that here the walls walk, as the password says. Really, what a strange coincidence! Everything in this town is strange, even its name, Walls. Sleep closes his eyes as he debates with himself about staying awake, because strange things happen here, and sleeping, because the road will be long; he had planned to walk to the nearest town and there look for a way to get to the capital.

Around midnight, perhaps (time is so imprecise when one's watch doesn't work and the only reference point is darkness with no window), he wakes up, startled. Using his hands he confirms that there's no distance between his bed and the walls, both at the sides of the mattress, and at the ends of the bed. He looks for the door and doesn't find it; he's locked in, he's in prison. Yes, the kind of punishment he deserves has now been discovered and he knows it. It's all been a trap. The message to come to Walls, the transfer of the package, the hotel, the last plane flight, the destroyed bridge, the rain of dead birds, the funeral. What a subtle form of entrapment! Too subtle for him, an ordinary anonymous dealer. Why so elaborate and so complicated? Without a doubt, it would have been easier to detain him, interrogate him, and put him in some prison, just as he deserved. He did things with care, but there are always loose ends which only luck succeeds in tying up in favor of innocence, his innocence of appearing to be an anonymous being, a peaceful good citizen, an insignificant person no one pays any attention to. But underneath, an undesirable, and no one likes undesirables; they always want to capture them, torture them, and leave them to rot as they deserve.

The bed cracks, the walls are advancing. Another tremor, strong. The tremor hurls him down on the bed, which collapses on the floor.

A piece of plaster, hostile and sharp, falls on top of him. The end of the world. Yes, the end of the world, just as his grandmother said it would happen, December 31 at twelve midnight.

And the walls come together over the consciousness of someone who has been abandoned by luck for the first time.

He was found several days later. By then, swollen and foul smelling, his eyes open in terror. Indolence and bad service prevailed in the hotel. The cashier said the guy in room 21 had already been there a week and he figured he'd probably run out because there were no signs of life. There on top of the bed, half naked, he completely lost all sense of time and obligation to pay his debts. Later, the police searched thoroughly and found nothing to confirm the name and information he gave when he registered at the hotel. They called the number he'd given as his home phone, but a laundry answered and didn't know him. The town nurse, the only one who, along with the pharmacist, officially gave vaccinations and prescribed medicine, said it was a heart attack, judging from the terror on his face, as if something sudden and unexpected had come over him.

With nothing to do, no one to notify, they buried him in a corner of some public land, with no more formality than wrapping him in a sheet and putting him in a box that was inexpensive because the lid was made of a different wood and didn't fit very well.

The beggar with the bloody empty socket, master of all the dead birds, said to the other beggar, "Have you noticed that death is carrying away all the visitors to Walls?" "Really," answered the other, "I wonder why . . . ?"

EDGAR ALLAN POE (1809–1849)
The Cask of Amontillado
1846

The thousand injuries of Fortunato I had borne as I best could, but when he ventured upon insult I vowed revenge. You, who so well know the nature of my soul, will not suppose, however, that I gave utterance to a threat. *At length* I would be avenged; this was a point definitely settled—but the very definitiveness with which it was resolved precluded the idea of risk. I must not only punish but punish with impunity. A wrong is unredressed when retribution overtakes its redresser. It is equally unredressed when the avenger fails to make himself felt as such to him who has done the wrong.

It must be understood that neither by word nor deed had I given Fortunato cause to doubt my good will. I continued, as was my wont, to smile in his face, and he did not perceive that my smile *now* was at the thought of his immolation.

He had a weak point—this Fortunato—although in other regards he was a man to be respected and even feared. He prided himself on his connoisseurship in wine. Few Italians have the true virtuoso spirit. For the most part their enthusiasm is adopted to suit the time and opportunity, to practise imposture upon the British and Austrian *millionaires*. In painting and gemmary, Fortunato, like his countrymen, was a quack, but in the matter of old wines he was sincere. In this respect I did not differ from him materially;—I was skillful in the Italian vintages myself, and bought largely whenever I could.

It was about dusk, one evening during the supreme madness of the carnival season, that I encountered my friend. He accosted me with excessive warmth, for he had been drinking much. The man wore motley. He had on a tight-fitting parti-striped dress, and his head was surmounted by the conical cap and bells. I was so pleased to see him that I thought I should never have done wringing his hand.

I said to him—"My dear Fortunato, you are luckily met. How remarkably well you are looking to-day. But I have received a pipe of what passes for Amontillado, and I have my doubts."

"How?" said he. "Amontillado? A pipe? Impossible! And in the middle of the carnival!"

"I have my doubts," I replied; "and I was silly enough to pay the full Amontillado price without consulting you in the matter. You were not to be found, and I was fearful of losing a bargain."

"Amontillado!"

"I have my doubts."

"Amontillado!"

"And I must satisfy them."

"Amontillado!"

"As you are engaged, I am on my way to Luchresi. If any one has a critical turn it is he. He will tell me—"

"Luchresi cannot tell Amontillado from Sherry."

"And yet some fools will have it that his taste is a match for your own."

"Come, let us go."

"Whither?"

"To your vaults."

"My friend, no; I will not impose upon your good nature. I perceive you have an engagement. Luchresi—"

"I have no engagement;—come."

"My friend, no. It is not the engagement, but the severe cold with which I perceive you are afflicted. The vaults are insufferably damp. They are encrusted with nitre."

"Let us go, nevertheless. The cold is merely nothing. Amontillado! You have been imposed upon. And as for Luchresi, he cannot distinguish Sherry from Amontillado."

Thus speaking, Fortunato possessed himself of my arm; and putting on a mask of black silk and drawing a *roquelaire* closely about my person, I suffered him to hurry me to my palazzo.

There were no attendants at home; they had absconded to make merry in honor of the time. I had told them that I should not return until the morning, and had given them explicit orders not to stir from the house. These orders were sufficient, I well knew, to insure their immediate disappearance, one and all, as soon as my back was turned.

I took from their sconces two flambeaux, and giving one to Fortunato, bowed him through several suites of rooms to the archway that led into the vaults. I passed down a long and winding staircase, requesting him to be cautious as he followed. We came at length to the foot of the descent, and stood together upon the damp ground of the catacombs of the Montresors.

The gait of my friend was unsteady, and the bells upon his cap jingled as he strode.

"The pipe," he said.

"It is farther on," said I; "but observe the white web-work which gleams from these cavern walls."

He turned toward me, and looked into my eyes with two filmy orbs that distilled the rheum of intoxication.

"Nitre?" he asked at length.

"Nitre," I replied. "How long have you had that cough?"

"Ugh! ugh! ugh!—ugh! ugh! ugh!—ugh! ugh! ugh!—ugh! ugh! ugh!—ugh! ugh! ugh!"

My poor friend found it impossible to reply for many minutes.

"It is nothing," he said at last.

"Come," I said, with decision, "we will go back; your health is precious. You are rich, respected, admired, beloved; you are happy, as once I was. You are a man to be missed. For me it is no matter. We will go back; you will be ill, and I cannot be responsible. Besides, there is Luchresi—"

"Enough," he said; "the cough is a mere nothing; it will not kill me. I shall not die of a cough."

"True—true," I replied; "and, indeed, I had no intention of alarming you unnecessarily—but you should use all proper caution. A draught of this Medoc will defend us from the damps."

Here I knocked off the neck of a bottle which I drew from a long row of its fellows that lay upon the mould.

"Drink," I said, presenting him the wine.

He raised it to his lips with a leer. He paused and nodded to me familiarly, while his bells jingled.

"I drink," he said, "to the buried that repose around us."

"And I to your long life."

He again took my arm, and we proceeded.

"These vaults," he said, "are extensive."

"The Montresors," I replied, "were a great and numerous family."

"I forget your arms."

"A huge human foot d'or, in a field azure; the foot crushes a serpent rampant whose fangs are imbedded in the heel."

"And the motto?"

"*Nemo me impune lacessit.*"

"Good!" he said.

The wine sparkled in his eyes and the bells jingled. My own fancy grew warm with the Medoc. We had passed through long walls of piled skeletons, with casks and puncheons intermingling, into the inmost recesses of the catacombs. I paused again, and this time I made bold to seize Fortunato by an arm above the elbow.

"The nitre!" I said; "see, it increases. It hangs like moss upon the vaults. We are below the river's bed. The drops of moisture trickle among the bones. Come, we will go back ere it is too late. Your cough—"

"It is nothing," he said; "let us go on. But first, another draught of the Medoc."

I broke and reached him a flagon of De Grâve. He emptied it at a breath. His eyes flashed with a fierce light. He laughed and threw the bottle upwards with a gesticulation I did not understand.

I looked at him in surprise. He repeated the movement—a grotesque one.

"You do not comprehend?" he said.

"Not I," I replied.

"Then you are not of the brotherhood."

"How?"

"You are not of the masons."

"Yes, yes," I said; "yes, yes."

"You? Impossible! A mason?"

"A mason," I replied.

"A sign," he said, "a sign."

"It is this," I answered, producing from beneath the folds of my *roquelaire* a trowel.

"You jest," he exclaimed, recoiling a few paces. "But let us proceed to the Amontillado."

"Be it so," I said, replacing the tool beneath the cloak and again offering him my arm. He leaned upon it heavily. We continued our route in search of the Amontillado. We passed through a range of low arches, descended, passed on, and descending again, arrived at a deep crypt, in which the foulness of the air caused our flambeaux rather to glow than flame.

At the most remote end of the crypt there appeared another less spacious. Its walls had been lined with human remains, piled to the vault overhead, in the fashion of the great catacombs of Paris. Three sides of this interior crypt were still ornamented in this manner. From the fourth side the bones had been thrown down, and lay promiscuously upon the earth, forming at one point a mound of some size. Within the wall thus exposed by the displacing of the bones, we perceived a still interior crypt or recess, in depth about four feet, in width three, in height six or seven. It seemed to have been constructed for no especial use within itself, but formed merely the interval between two of the colossal supports of the roof of the catacombs, and was backed by one of their circumscribing walls of solid granite.

It was in vain that Fortunato, uplifting his dull torch, endeavored to pry into the depth of the recess. Its termination the feeble light did not enable us to see.

"Proceed," I said; "herein is the Amontillado. As for Luchresi—"

"He is an ignoramus," interrupted my friend, as he stepped unsteadily forward, while I followed immediately at his heels. In an instant he had reached the extremity of the niche, and finding his progress arrested by the rock, stood stupidly bewildered. A moment more and I had fettered him to the granite. In its surface were two iron staples, distant from each other about two feet, horizontally. From one of these depended a short chain, from the other a padlock. Throwing the links about his waist, it was but the work of a few seconds to secure it. He was too much astounded to resist. Withdrawing the key I stepped back from the recess.

"Pass your hand," I said, "over the wall; you cannot help feeling the nitre. Indeed, it is *very* damp. Once more let me *implore* you to return. No? Then I must positively leave you. But I must first render you all the little attentions in my power."

"The Amontillado!" ejaculated my friend, not yet recovered from his astonishment.

"True," I replied; "the Amontillado."

As I said these words I busied myself among the pile of bones of which I have before spoken. Throwing them aside, I soon uncovered a quantity of building stone and mortar. With these materials and with the aid of my trowel, I began vigorously to wall up the entrance of the niche.

I had scarcely laid the first tier of the masonry when I discovered that the intoxication of Fortunato had in a great measure worn off. The earliest indication I had of this was a low moaning cry from the depth of the recess. It was *not* the cry of a drunken man. There was a long and obstinate silence. I laid the second tier, and the third, and the fourth; and then I heard the furious vibrations of the chain. The noise lasted for several minutes, during which, that I might hearken to it with the more satisfaction, I ceased my labors and sat down upon the bones. When at last the clanking subsided, I resumed the trowel, and finished without interruption the fifth, the sixth, and the seventh tier. The wall was now nearly upon a level with my breast. I again paused, and holding the flambeaux over the mason-work, threw a few feeble rays upon the figure within.

65

70

75

A succession of loud and shrill screams, bursting suddenly from the throat of the chained form, seemed to thrust me violently back. For a brief moment I hesitated, I trembled. Unsheathing my rapier, I began to grope with it about the recess; but the thought of an instant reassured me. I placed my hand upon the solid fabric of the catacombs, and felt satisfied. I reapproached the wall; I replied to the yells of him who clamored. I re-echoed, I aided, I surpassed them in volume and in strength. I did this, and the clamorer grew still.

It was now midnight, and my task was drawing to a close. I had completed the eighth, the ninth and the tenth tier. I had finished a portion of the last and the eleventh; there remained but a single stone to be fitted and plastered in. I struggled with its weight; I placed it partially in its destined position. But now there came from out the niche a low laugh that erected the hairs upon my head. It was succeeded by a sad voice, which I had difficulty in recognizing as that of the noble Fortunato. The voice said—

"Ha! ha! ha!—he! he! he!—a very good joke, indeed—an excellent jest. We will have many a rich laugh about it at the palazzo—he! he! he!—over our wine—he! he! he!"

"The Amontillado!" I said.   80

"He! he! he!—he! he! he!—yes, the Amontillado. But is it not getting late? Will not they be awaiting us at the palazzo, the Lady Fortunato and the rest? Let us be gone."

"Yes," I said, "let us be gone."

"*For the love of God, Montresor!*"

"Yes," I said, "for the love of God."

But to these words I hearkened in vain for a reply. I grew impatient. I called   85
aloud—

"Fortunato!"

No answer. I called again—

"Fortunato!"

No answer still. I thrust a torch through the remaining aperture and let it fall within. There came forth in return only a jingling of the bells. My heart grew sick; it was the dampness of the catacombs that made it so. I hastened to make an end of my labor. I forced the last stone into its position; I plastered it up. Against the new masonry I re-erected the old rampart of bones. For the half of a century no mortal has disturbed them. *In pace requiescat!*

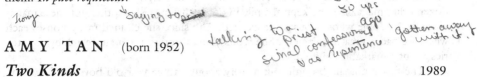

AMY TAN (born 1952)

Two Kinds   1989

My mother believed you could be anything you wanted to be in America. You could open a restaurant. You could work for the government and get good retirement. You could buy a house with almost no money down. You could become rich. You could become instantly famous.

"Of course you can be prodigy, too," my mother told me when I was nine. "You can be best anything. What does Auntie Lindo know? Her daughter, she is only best tricky."

America was where all my mother's hopes lay. She had come here in 1949 after losing everything in China: her mother and father, her family home, her first husband, and two daughters, twin baby girls. But she never looked back with regret. There were so many ways for things to get better.

We didn't immediately pick the right kind of prodigy. At first my mother thought I could be a Chinese Shirley Temple. We'd watch Shirley's old movies on TV as though they were training films. My mother would poke my arm and say, *"Ni kan"*—You watch. And I would see Shirley tapping her feet, or singing a sailor song, or pursing her lips into a very round O while saying, "Oh my goodness."

"*Ni kan*," said my mother as Shirley's eyes flooded with tears. "You already know how. Don't need talent for crying!"   5

Soon after my mother got this idea about Shirley Temple, she took me to a beauty training school in the Mission district and put me in the hands of a student who could barely hold the scissors without shaking. Instead of getting big fat curls, I emerged with an uneven mass of crinkly black fuzz. My mother dragged me off to the bathroom and tried to wet down my hair.

"You look like Negro Chinese," she lamented, as if I had done this on purpose.

The instructor of the beauty training school had to lop off these soggy clumps to make my hair even again. "Peter Pan is very popular these days," the instructor assured my mother. I now had hair the length of a boy's, with straight-across bangs that hung at a slant two inches above my eyebrows. I liked the haircut and it made me actually look forward to my future fame.

In fact, in the beginning, I was just as excited as my mother, maybe even more so. I pictured this prodigy part of me as many different images, trying each one on for size. I was a dainty ballerina girl standing by the curtains, waiting to hear the right music that would send me floating on my tiptoes. I was like the Christ child lifted out of the straw manger, crying with holy indignity. I was Cinderella stepping from her pumpkin carriage with sparkly cartoon music filling the air.

In all of my imaginings, I was filled with a sense that I would soon become *perfect*.   10
My mother and father would adore me. I would be beyond reproach. I would never feel the need to sulk for anything.

But sometimes the prodigy in me became impatient. "If you don't hurry up and get me out of here, I'm disappearing for good," it warned. "And then you'll always be nothing."

Every night after dinner, my mother and I would sit at the Formica kitchen table. She would present new tests, taking her examples from stories of amazing children she had read in *Ripley's Believe It or Not,* or *Good Housekeeping, Reader's Digest,* and a dozen other magazines she kept in a pile in our bathroom. My mother got these magazines from people whose houses she cleaned. And since she cleaned many houses each week, we had a great assortment. She would look through them all, searching for stories about remarkable children.

The first night she brought out a story about a three-year-old boy who knew the capitals of all the states and even most of the European countries. A teacher was quoted as saying the little boy could also pronounce the names of the foreign cities correctly.

"What's the capital of Finland?" my mother asked me, looking at the magazine story.

All I knew was the capital of California, because Sacramento was the name of the   15
street we lived on in Chinatown. "Nairobi!" I guessed, saying the most foreign word I could think of. She checked to see if that was possibly one way to pronounce "Helsinki" before showing me the answer.

The tests got harder—multiplying numbers in my head, finding the queen of hearts in a deck of cards, trying to stand on my head without using my hands, predicting the daily temperatures in Los Angeles, New York, and London.

One night I had to look at a page from the Bible for three minutes and then report everything I could remember. "Now Jehoshaphat had riches and honor in abundance and . . . that's all I remember, Ma," I said.

And after seeing my mother's disappointed face once again, something inside of me began to die. I hated the tests, the raised hopes and failed expectations. Before going to bed that night, I looked in the mirror above the bathroom sink and when I saw only my face staring back—and that it would always be this ordinary face—I began to cry. Such a sad, ugly girl! I made high-pitched noises like a crazed animal, trying to scratch out the face in the mirror.

And then I saw what seemed to be the prodigy side of me—because I had never seen that face before. I looked at my reflection, blinking so I could see more clearly. The girl staring back at me was angry, powerful. This girl and I were the same. I had new thoughts, willful thoughts, or rather thoughts filled with lots of won'ts. I won't let her change me, I promised myself. I won't be what I'm not.

So now on nights when my mother presented her tests, I performed listlessly, my head propped on one arm. I pretended to be bored. And I was. I got so bored I started counting the bellows of the foghorns out on the bay while my mother drilled me in other areas. The sound was comforting and reminded me of the cow jumping over the moon. And the next day, I played a game with myself, seeing if my mother would give up on me before eight bellows. After a while I usually counted only one, maybe two bellows at most. At last she was beginning to give up hope. 20

Two or three months had gone by without any mention of my being a prodigy again. And then one day my mother was watching *The Ed Sullivan Show* on TV. The TV was old and the sound kept shorting out. Every time my mother got halfway up from the sofa to adjust the set, the sound would go back on and Ed would be talking. As soon as she sat down, Ed would go silent again. She got up, the TV broke into loud piano music. She sat down. Silence. Up and down, back and forth, quiet and loud. It was like a stiff embraceless dance between her and the TV set. Finally she stood by the set with her hand on the sound dial.

She seemed entranced by the music, a little frenzied piano piece with this mesmerizing quality, sort of quick passages and then teasing lilting ones before it returned to the quick playful parts.

"*Ni kan*," my mother said, calling me over with hurried hand gestures. "Look here."

I could see why my mother was fascinated by the music. It was being pounded out by a little Chinese girl, about nine years old, with a Peter Pan haircut. The girl had the sauciness of a Shirley Temple. She was proudly modest like a proper Chinese child. And she also did this fancy sweep of a curtsy, so that the fluffy skirt of her white dress cascaded slowly to the floor like the petals of a large carnation.

In spite of these warning signs, I wasn't worried. Our family had no piano and we couldn't afford to buy one, let alone reams of sheet music and piano lessons. So I could be generous in my comments when my mother bad-mouthed the little girl on TV. 25

"Play note right, but doesn't sound good! No singing sound," complained my mother.

"What are you picking on her for?" I said carelessly.

"She's pretty good. Maybe she's not the best, but she's trying hard." I knew almost immediately I would be sorry I said that.

"Just like you," she said. "Not the best. Because you not trying." She gave a little huff as she let go of the sound dial and sat down on the sofa.

The little Chinese girl sat down also to play an encore of "Anitra's Dance" by 30
Grieg. I remember the song, because later on I had to learn how to play it.

Three days after watching *The Ed Sullivan Show,* my mother told me what my
schedule would be for piano lessons and piano practice. She had talked to Mr. Chong,
who lived on the first floor of our apartment building. Mr. Chong was a retired piano
teacher and my mother had traded housecleaning services for weekly lessons and a
piano for me to practice on every day, two hours a day, from four until six.

When my mother told me this, I felt as though I had been sent to hell. I whined
and then kicked my foot a little when I couldn't stand it anymore.

"Why don't you like me the way I am? I'm *not* a genius! I can't play the piano.
And even if I could, I wouldn't go on TV if you paid me a million dollars!" I cried.

My mother slapped me. "Who ask you be genius?" she shouted. "Only ask you be
your best. For you sake. You think I want you be genius? Hnnh! What for! Who ask
you!"

"So ungrateful," I heard her mutter in Chinese. "If she had as much talent as she 35
has temper, she would be famous now."

Mr. Chong, whom I secretly nicknamed Old Chong, was very strange, always tapping his fingers to the silent music of an invisible orchestra. He looked ancient in my
eyes. He had lost most of the hair on top of his head and he wore thick glasses and had
eyes that always looked tired and sleepy. But he must have been younger than I
thought, since he lived with his mother and was not yet married.

I met Old Lady Chong once and that was enough. She had this peculiar smell like
a baby that had done something in its pants. And her fingers felt like a dead person's,
like an old peach I once found in the back of the refrigerator; the skin just slid off the
meat when I picked it up.

I soon found out why Old Chong had retired from teaching piano. He was deaf.
"Like Beethoven!" he shouted to me. "We're both listening only in our head!" And he
would start to conduct his frantic silent sonatas.

Our lessons went like this. He would open the book and point to different things,
explaining their purpose: "Key! Treble! Bass! No sharps or flats! So this is C major! Listen now and play after me!"

And then he would play the C scale a few times, a simple chord, and then, as if in- 40
spired by an old, unreachable itch, he gradually added more notes and running trills
and a pounding bass until the music was really something quite grand.

I would play after him, the simple scale, the simple chord, and then I just played
some nonsense that sounded like a cat running up and down on top of garbage cans.
Old Chong smiled and applauded and then said, "Very good! But now you must learn
to keep time!"

So that's how I discovered that Old Chong's eyes were too slow to keep up with
the wrong notes I was playing. He went through the motions in half-time. To help me
keep rhythm, he stood behind me, pushing down on my right shoulder for every beat.
He balanced pennies on top of my wrists so I would keep them still as I slowly played
scales and arpeggios. He had me curve my hand around an apple and keep that shape
when playing chords. He marched stiffly to show me how to make each finger dance up
and down, staccato like an obedient little soldier.

He taught me all these things, and that was how I also learned I could be lazy and
get away with mistakes, lots of mistakes. If I hit the wrong notes because I hadn't practiced enough, I never corrected myself. I just kept playing in rhythm. And Old Chong
kept conducting his own private reverie.

So maybe I never really gave myself a fair chance. I did pick up the basics pretty quickly, and I might have become a good pianist at that young age. But I was so determined not to try, not to be anybody different that I learned to play only the most ear-splitting preludes, the most discordant hymns.

Over the next year, I practiced like this, dutifully in my own way. And then one day I heard my mother and her friend Lindo Jong both talking in a loud bragging tone of voice so others could hear. It was after church, and I was leaning against the brick wall wearing a dress with stiff white petticoats. Auntie Lindo's daughter, Waverly, who was about my age, was standing farther down the wall about five feet away. We had grown up together and shared all the closeness of two sisters squabbling over crayons and dolls. In other words, for the most part, we hated each other. I thought she was snotty. Waverly Jong had gained a certain amount of fame as "Chinatown's Littlest Chinese Chess Champion."

"She bring home too many trophy," lamented Auntie Lindo that Sunday. "All day she play chess. All day I have no time do nothing but dust off her winnings." She threw a scolding look at Waverly, who pretended not to see her.

"You lucky you don't have this problem," said Auntie Lindo with a sigh to my mother.

And my mother squared her shoulders and bragged: "Our problem worser than yours. If we ask Jing-mei wash dish, she hear nothing but music. It's like you can't stop this natural talent."

And right then, I was determined to put a stop to her foolish pride.

A few weeks later, Old Chong and my mother conspired to have me play in a talent show which would be held in the church hall. By then, my parents had saved up enough to buy me a secondhand piano, a black Wurlitzer spinet with a scarred bench. It was the showpiece of our living room.

For the talent show, I was to play a piece called "Pleading Child" from Schumann's *Scenes from Childhood.* It was a simple, moody piece that sounded more difficult than it was. I was supposed to memorize the whole thing, playing the repeat parts twice to make the piece sound longer. But I dawdled over it, playing a few bars and then cheating, looking up to see what notes followed, I never really listened to what I was playing. I daydreamed about being somewhere else, about being someone else.

The part I liked to practice best was the fancy curtsy: right foot out, touch the rose on the carpet with a pointed foot, sweep to the side, left leg bends, look up and smile.

My parents invited all the couples from the Joy Luck Club to witness my debut. Auntie Lindo and Uncle Tin were there. Waverly and her two older brothers had also come. The first two rows were filled with children both younger and older than I was. The littlest ones got to go first. They recited simple nursery rhymes, squawked out tunes on miniature violins, twirled Hula Hoops, pranced in pink ballet tutus, and when they bowed or curtsied, the audience would sigh in unison, "Awww," and then clap enthusiastically.

When my turn came, I was very confident. I remember my childish excitement. It was as if I knew, without a doubt, that the prodigy side of me really did exist. I had no fear whatsoever, no nervousness. I remember thinking to myself, This is it! This is it! I looked out over the audience, at my mother's blank face, my father's yawn, Auntie Lindo's stiff-lipped smile, Waverly's sulky expression. I had on a white dress layered with sheets of lace, and a pink bow in my Peter Pan haircut. As I sat down I envisioned people jumping to their feet and Ed Sullivan rushing up to introduce me to everyone on TV.

And I started to play. It was so beautiful. I was so caught up in how lovely I looked that at first I didn't worry how I would sound: So it was a surprise to me when I hit the first wrong note and I realized something didn't sound quite right. And then I hit another and another followed that. A chill started at the top of my head and began to trickle down. Yet I couldn't stop playing, as though my hands were bewitched. I kept thinking my fingers would adjust themselves back, like a train switching to the right track. I played this strange jumble through two repeats, the sour notes staying with me all the way to the end.

When I stood up, I discovered my legs were shaking. Maybe I had just been nervous and the audience, like Old Chong, had seen me go through the right motions and had not heard anything wrong at all. I swept my right foot out, went down on my knee, looked up and smiled. The room was quiet, except for Old Chong, who was beaming and shouting, "Bravo! Bravo! Well done!" But then I saw my mother's face, her stricken face. The audience clapped weakly, and as I walked back to my chair, with my whole face quivering as I tried not to cry, I heard a little boy whisper loudly to his mother, "That was awful," and the mother whispered back, "Well, she certainly tried."

And now I realized how many people were in the audience, the whole world it seemed. I was aware of eyes burning into my back. I felt the shame of my mother and father as they sat stiffly throughout the rest of the show.

We could have escaped during intermission. Pride and some strange sense of honor must have anchored my parents to their chairs. And so we watched it all: the eighteen-year-old boy with a fake mustache who did a magic show and juggled flaming hoops while riding a unicycle. The breasted girl with white makeup who sang from *Madama Butterfly* and got honorable mention. And the eleven-year-old boy who won first prize playing a tricky violin song that sounded like a busy bee.

After the show, the Hsus, the Jongs, and the St. Clairs from the Joy Luck Club came up to my mother and father.

"Lots of talented kids," Auntie Lindo said vaguely, smiling broadly.

"That was somethin' else," said my father, and I wondered if he was referring to me in a humorous way, or whether he even remembered what I had done.

Waverly looked at me and shrugged her shoulders. "You aren't a genius like me," she said matter-of-factly. And if I hadn't felt so bad, I would have pulled her braids and punched her stomach.

But my mother's expression was what devastated me: a quiet, blank look that said she had lost everything. I felt the same way, and it seemed as if everybody were now coming up, like gawkers at the scene of an accident, to see what parts were actually missing. When we got on the bus to go home, my father was humming the busy-bee tune and my mother was silent. I kept thinking she wanted to wait until we got home before shouting at me. But when my father unlocked the door to our apartment, my mother walked in and then went to the back, into the bedroom. No accusations. No blame. And in a way, I felt disappointed. I had been waiting for her to start shouting, so I could shout back and cry and blame her for all my misery.

I assumed my talent-show fiasco meant I never had to play the piano again. But two days later, after school, my mother came out of the kitchen and saw me watching TV.

"Four clock," she reminded me as if it were any other day. I was stunned, as though she were asking me to go through the talent-show torture again. I wedged myself more tightly in front of the TV.

"Turn off TV," she called from the kitchen five minutes later.

I didn't budge. And then I decided. I didn't have to do what my mother said anymore. I wasn't her slave. This wasn't China. I had listened to her before and look what happened. She was the stupid one.

She came out from the kitchen and stood in the arched entryway of the living room. "Four clock," she said once again, louder.

"I'm not going to play anymore," I said nonchalantly. "Why should I? I'm not a genius."

She walked over and stood in front of the TV. I saw her chest was heaving up and down in an angry way. 70

"No!" I said, and I now felt stronger, as if my true self had finally emerged. So this was what had been inside me all along.

"No! I won't!" I screamed.

She yanked me by the arm, pulled me off the floor, snapped off the TV. She was frighteningly strong, half pulling, half carrying me toward the piano as I kicked the throw rugs under my feet. She lifted me up and onto the hard bench. I was sobbing by now, looking at her bitterly. Her chest was heaving even more and her mouth was open, smiling crazily as if she were pleased I was crying.

"You want me to be someone that I'm not!" I sobbed. "I'll never be the kind of daughter you want me to be!"

"Only two kinds of daughters," she shouted in Chinese. "Those who are obedient 75 and those who follow their own mind! Only one kind of daughter can live in this house. Obedient daughter!"

"Then I wish I wasn't your daughter. I wish you weren't my mother," I shouted. As I said these things I got scared. I felt like worms and toads and slimy things were crawling out of my chest, but it also felt good, as if this awful side of me had surfaced, at last.

"Too late change this," said my mother shrilly.

And I could sense her anger rising to its breaking point. I wanted to see it spill over. And that's when I remembered the babies she had lost in China, the ones we never talked about. "Then I wish I'd never been born!" I shouted. "I wish I were dead! Like them."

It was as if I had said the magic words. Alakazam!—and her face went blank, her mouth closed, her arms went slack, and she backed out of the room, stunned, as if she were blowing away like a small brown leaf, thin, brittle, lifeless.

It was not the only disappointment my mother felt in me. In the years that followed, I failed her so many times, each time asserting my own will, my right to fall 80 short of expectations. I didn't get straight As. I didn't become class president. I didn't get into Stanford. I dropped out of college.

For unlike my mother, I did not believe I could be anything I wanted to be. I could only be me.

And for all those years, we never talked about the disaster at the recital or my terrible accusations afterward at the piano bench. All that remained unchecked, like a betrayal that was now unspeakable. So I never found a way to ask her why she had hoped for something so large that failure was inevitable.

And even worse, I never asked her what frightened me the most: Why had she given up hope?

For after our struggle at the piano, she never mentioned my playing again. The lessons stopped. The lid to the piano was closed, shutting out the dust, my misery, and her dreams.

So she surprised me. A few years ago, she offered to give me the piano, for my thirtieth birthday. I had not played in all those years. I saw the offer as a sign of forgiveness, a tremendous burden removed. 85

"Are you sure?" I asked shyly. "I mean, won't you and Dad miss it?"

"No, this your piano," she said firmly. "Always your piano. You only one can play."

"Well, I probably can't play anymore," I said. "It's been years."

"You pick up fast," said my mother, as if she knew this was certain. "You have natural talent. You could been genius if you want to."

"No I couldn't." 90

"You just not trying," said my mother. And she was neither angry nor sad. She said it as if to announce a fact that could never be disproved. "Take it," she said.

But I didn't at first. It was enough that she had offered it to me. And after that, every time I saw it in my parents' living room, standing in front of the bay windows, it made me feel proud, as if it were a shiny trophy I had won back.

Last week I sent a tuner over to my parents' apartment and had the piano reconditioned, for purely sentimental reasons. My mother had died a few months before and I had been getting things in order for my father, a little bit at a time. I put the jewelry in special silk pouches. The sweaters she had knitted in yellow, pink, bright orange—all the colors I hated—I put those in moth-proof boxes. I found some old Chinese silk dresses, the kind with little slits up the sides. I rubbed the old silk against my skin, then wrapped them in tissue and decided to take them home with me.

After I had the piano tuned, I opened the lid and touched the keys. It sounded even richer than I remembered. Really, it was a very good piano. Inside the bench were the same exercise notes with handwritten scales, the same secondhand music books with their covers held together with yellow tape.

I opened up the Schumann book to the dark little piece I had played at the recital. 95 It was on the left-hand side of the page, "Pleading Child." It looked more difficult than I remembered. I played a few bars, surprised at how easily the notes came back to me.

And for the first time, or so it seemed, I noticed the piece on the right-hand side. It was called "Perfectly Contented." I tried to play this one as well. It had a lighter melody but the same flowing rhythm and turned out to be quite easy. "Pleading Child" was shorter but slower; "Perfectly Contented" was longer but faster. And after I played them both a few times, I realized they were two halves of the same song.

POETRY

When I began to read nursery rhymes for myself, and, later, to read other verses and ballads, I knew I had discovered the most important things that could be ever. There they were, seemingly lifeless, made only of black and white, but out of them, out of their own being, came love and terror and pity and pain and wonder and all the other vague abstractions that made our ephemeral lives dangerous, great, and bearable.

DYLAN THOMAS

11 PREVIEW
What Is Poetry?

The poet, lacking the impediment of speech with which the rest of us are afflicted, gazes, records, diagnoses, and prophecies.

RICHARD SELZER

I dwell in Possibility—
A fairer House than Prose—
More numerous of Windows—
Superior—for Doors—

EMILY DICKINSON

Sei que canto. E a canção é tudo.
Tem sangue eterno e asa ritmada.
E um dia sei que estarei mudo:
—mais nada.

I know that I sing. And song is all for me.
Its heart beats forever as it flies on rhythmic wing.
And I also know that one day my voice will fall silent—
Never to be heard again.

CECÍLIA MEIRELES

FOCUS ON POETRY

What is poetry? Cautious readers might start by saying that poems are surrounded by more white space on the page than prose. (Poems are usually made up of lines that stop short of the margin.) Obviously, such a definition does not do justice to the pleasure poetry gives its readers, to its power to move, or to its power to take readers beyond what they already think and feel. The gift of language is what makes us human, and poets make the fullest use of it. They often seem to write with a heightened sense of awareness, with a special intensity—"in a fine frenzy," in Shakespeare's words.

Poets are in love with words. One way to define poetry is to call it language at its best: Poets use its full potential, using more of it and using it to

399

better advantage than we usually do. Poets mobilize to the fullest the image-making capacity of language. ("This morning," Javier Gálvez says, "the sun broke/my window/and came in laughing.") Poetry has the ability to delight the ear and the power to stir our emotions. It has the potential, if we let it, of making us more responsive and thoughtful human beings.

Read a short poem first of all as a communication from one fellow human being to another. Listen to the human voice speaking in the poem. That voice may be speaking about anything within the realm of human experience, real or imagined. Here is a modern American poet speaking to us about the pain of separation.

W. S. MERWIN (born 1927)

Separation 1963

Your absence has gone through me
Like thread through a needle.
Everything I do is stitched with its color.

What helps make this a poem rather than ordinary prose?

⬦ First of all, out of the confusing flow of experience, the poet has brought something into *focus*. For a moment, we stop hurrying to whatever we were doing next. We stop to pay attention. We linger for a while—to contemplate, to take something in.

⬦ Secondly, what we take in is not just talk. We are helped to *imagine* what separation is like. The poem gives us something to visualize, to take in with the mind's eye. It is as if our days, like a piece of embroidery, were stitched through with a continuing thread—of missing the other person. A sewing needle does not jab the fabric once and then think about something else. It does its work by making one stitch after the other, stitching in the thread that will hold the fabric together or that will shape a pattern in a piece of embroidered material.

⬦ Thirdly, the poem does not just give us information to feed into a data bank. We are not expected to record the message with no more emotion than a fax machine. Writing poetry is an act of faith: The poet assumes that we are capable of caring one way or the other. We are capable of entering imaginatively into the poet's *feelings*, of sharing his sense of loss.

⬦ Finally, the poem is printed as lines of verse. These measure out or mark off units of thought, laying out the message in a satisfying *pattern* (that we can take in at a glance). When we finish reading, we have the satisfying sense of having taken in a complete whole.

Poetry comes to us as one of our oldest heirlooms as human beings. Civilization began when the first artists painted bison on the walls of caves and the first poets chanted songs about the exploits of the tribe or the creation of all living things. In many early cultures, a dominant form, or genre, was the **epic,** a long poem that spoke to its listeners in an elevated style and embodied their values, aspirations, and traumas. Often, the traditional epic focused on a high point in the history of a people, the way Homer in the *Iliad* sang the Greek expedition to besiege and destroy the fabled city of Troy:

> As the many tribes of winged birds—
> The geese, the cranes, and the long-throated swans—
> Make their flight this way and that
> And then settle in fluttering swarms
> While a vast field echoes with their cries,
> So these many tribes poured out from their ships
> Onto the plain of Troy.

When we talk about poetry today, we usually think of a more personal kind of writing. We think of a fairly short poem that communicates personal observations, feelings, and thoughts. We call such a short poem the **lyric,** named after the lyre, or small harp, that the poets of ancient Greece played as they recited their verses.

USING THE IMAGINATION

Memory does not retain all, but only what strikes the spirit.
ÉMILE BERNARD

To find the raw material for poems, you don't need to backpack to Katmandu. No doubt some have done so and returned knowing less than Emily Dickinson knew from watching hummingbirds and garter snakes in the meadow across the road past her home.
X. J. KENNEDY

A real poet can make everything into poetry, including his or her own life.
DIANE WAKOSKI

Poets ask us to use our imagination. Although they make us think, they first of all ask us to imagine. They make us see, they make us feel, and they make us think. A dictionary definition of the word *presentiment* would tell us that it is a sudden fleeting feeling of anxiety—a sudden, passing sense of foreboding, a premonition that something hurtful is going to happen. Unlike a dictionary definition, the following poem does not *state* this idea; it brings it to life.

EMILY DICKINSON (1830–1886)
Presentiment 1863

Presentiment—is that long shadow—on the lawn—
Indicative that Suns go down—
The notice to the startled Grass
That Darkness—is about to pass—

This poem makes us *see*. The poem starts with a striking **image:** On a sunny day, we all of a sudden notice the dark shadow on the lawn that announces (or is an indication of) the coming of evening. The poem makes us *feel:* Like the grass, we may be startled, afraid of darkness. We may share in a shuddery feeling. The poem makes us *think:* We are reminded that "suns go down." We may reflect that, like them, sunny parts of our lives must sooner or later alternate with darkness.

The following poem is one of the best loved (and most often discussed) in the English language. What experience does it ask you to share? What does the poem invite you to see, feel, and think?

ROBERT FROST (1874–1963)
Stopping by Woods on a Snowy Evening 1923

Whose woods these are I think I know.
His house is in the village though;
He will not see me stopping here
To watch his woods fill up with snow.

My little horse must think it queer 5
To stop without a farmhouse near
Between the woods and frozen lake
The darkest evening of the year.

He gives his harness bells a shake
To ask if there is some mistake. 10
The only other sound's the sweep
Of easy wind and downy flake.

The woods are lovely, dark and deep.
But I have promises to keep,
And miles to go before I sleep, 15
And miles to go before I sleep.

In this poem, we find ourselves on a deserted rural road in the wintertime, away from the nearest village or farmhouse, with the driver of the horse-drawn vehicle stopping to look at the woods filling up with snow. It is cold enough for the lake to have frozen over, and the evening is getting very dark, so the normal thing would be to hurry on home. (The horse certainly seems to think so, wondering "if there is some mistake.")

But something strange happens in this poem: It is very quiet, the wind is an "easy wind," and the snowflakes are "downy," like a down-filled pillow beckoning us toward rest. The snow-covered woods look "lovely." It would be tempting not to go on—to go to sleep in the soft snow. It would be restful to push out of mind whatever cares, responsibilities, or pressures are waiting in the village. In the end, tempting as the thought may be of dropping out, of going to "sleep," the speaker in the poem is kept going by the thought of "promises to keep." There are still "miles to go," as the speaker says twice, "miles to go."

Perhaps the secret of this poem's appeal is its apparent simplicity. It sets up a situation that many different readers can in their own way find mirrored in their experience: It is likely to make them share the longing for rest, but at the same time it is likely to make them sense the need to go on. Some readers of this poem will remember the word *promises* especially: What "promises" does the speaker have to keep? Different readers might think of responsibilities to family, obligations to friends, debts to be repaid. Some readers will be haunted by the beckoning dark woods. One student said: "The horse does not know we are going to die, but the poet does."

THE RECEPTIVE READER

What kind of "promises" do you think the speaker had in mind? ✧ Critics have argued whether or not the dark woods in this poem are a symbol of death. What would be your answer to this question, and how would you support it? ✧ What is the effect of the poet's repeating the last line?

The images in a poem bring an experience to life for us by appealing to our senses—by making us see, hear, smell, taste, and touch. Vivid, graphic images re-create for us the **concrete** texture of experience, that is, the visible, tangible quality of the world we take in through our senses. At the same time, the images in a poem often carry meanings beyond their literal surface impact. They become a language of speaking and moving images, suggesting meanings that would remain pale or incomplete when spelled out in more literal terms. The most basic device poets use to convey meanings beyond those of ordinary literal speech is the **metaphor.** It "carries us beyond" ordinary literal meanings to something else. One of Shakespeare's best-known sonnets begins,

Let me not to the marriage of true minds
Admit impediments.

The poet is saying that no obstacles should be allowed to interfere with (to "impede") the marriage of minds sincerely meaning to be faithful to one another. Metaphorically, marriage here evokes a true meeting of minds, a perfect union of the kind we envision an ideal marriage to be. The marriage metaphor here carries a richer meaning than the literal word *union:* Traditionally, marriage has been a solemn occasion, surrounded by pomp and circumstance, sanctified by religion, and carrying with it the promise of lifelong devotion.

As you read and study poems, you will again and again encounter other features of the poet's language that make it richer and more imaginative than language for everyday use:

✧ If we read the woods in Frost's poem not as a place for a temporary rest but as a beckoning toward the final long rest of death, we are reading them as a **symbol.** The marriage in the Shakespeare sonnet need not literally take place; the poet very likely brought it into the poem as a metaphor. However, the woods in the Frost poem are literally there; we may choose to give them a larger symbolic significance.

✧ Poets use words rich in **connotation** and shades of meaning. They use words that carry the right overtones or emotional associations. In the Dickinson poem, *startled* says more than *surprised,* since we can be mildly surprised, whereas we find it hard to be mildly startled.

✧ Modern poets especially are likely to be sensitive to **irony;** they are likely to explore the puzzles posed by **paradox.** Irony goes counter to expectation, leaving us in varying degrees bemused and amused. It is ironic that in the Frost poem the horse, and not its human owner, thinks it's time to go on home. Paradox confronts us with contradictions that may make sense on second thought. It is paradoxical that in Frost's poem the snow, hostile to life, comes down in "downy" flakes (soft like the feathers used in pillows) and that the woods (which may be a symbol of death) are "lovely." On second thought, we may realize that to a harried person death could begin to seem restful and beautiful.

✧ Poets may call up a whole range of memories by way of **allusion.** A modern feminist poet referring to Helen may trust the brief mention to call up a whole range of associations with the legendary Helen of Troy—celebrated for her beauty, reviled for leaving her Greek husband for a Trojan prince, blamed for the war that destroyed Troy.

EXPLORATIONS

A Fresh Look

The following poems invite you to take a fresh look at something familiar—the human body, the rain, the moon. What do you look at in each poem, and how is the poet's angle of vision different or new? What new or unexpected connections does the poem establish? What new meanings does the poet find in familiar sights or familiar facts? What does the poet make you see and feel that a less imaginative observer might have missed?

AUDRE LORDE   (born 1934)

Coping   1968

It has rained for five days
running
the world is
a round puddle
of sunless water   5
where small islands
are only beginning
to cope
a young boy
in my garden   10
is bailing out water
from his flower patch
when I ask him why
he tells me
young seeds that have not seen sun   15
forget
and drown easily.

THE RECEPTIVE READER

1. What is *ordinary* about the situation described in this poem? What is *imaginative* about the way this poet looks at the rain? What gives the seeds a significance beyond their ordinary literal meaning?

2. What is the central word in this poem? How does the poet highlight it? What is its full meaning?

FEDERICO GARCÍA LORCA   (1898–1936)

Half Moon   1928

TRANSLATED BY W. S. MERWIN

The moon goes over the water.
How tranquil the sky is!
She goes scything slowly
the old shimmer from the river;
meanwhile a young frog   5
takes her for a little mirror.

THE RECEPTIVE READER

What does this poem by a well-known Spanish poet ask you to visualize, to imagine? What makes the imaginative comparisons in the poem new or unexpected? What makes them fitting?

L YOUNG (born 1939)

Chemistry

1968

What connects me to this moon
is legendary, and what connects
the moon to me is as
momentary as the night is
long before it burns away like   5
that fire in the eyes of lovers
when, spent, they turn
from one another and fall against
the dark sides of their pillows
to let their blood color cool.   10

You too know well the nature of
our chemistry: 65% oxygen,
18% carbon, 10% hydrogen,
3% nitrogen, a touch of calcium,
phosphorus and other elements.   15
But largely (by 70%) we're water:
2 parts hydrogen to 1 part oxygen,
and mostly we're still all wet—
9 parts fear chained to 1 part joy.
Is this why we're given to drowning   20
ourselves in pools of tears,
long on sorrow and shallow on laughter;
drowning ourselves in sugar and salt
as it were, as we are, as the treasured
substance of a former fish's life   25
can never be technically measured?

This chemistry we swim and skim
is what connects all light with me
olympically,° for real life   *in a godlike way*
science will forever be proving   30
this radiant suspension to be love
in but one of its bubbling mutations.

THE RECEPTIVE READER

1. In this poem, what is the connection between the moon and the lovers?

2. What knowledge of biology, or "life science," does the poet expect of his readers? What new and imaginative use does he make of biological facts? What is the connection he establishes between our body chemistry and our feelings? How would you sum up what he means by "real life science"?

THE PERSONAL RESPONSE

Audre Lorde and Al Young are among the best-known African American poets. Does knowing this biographical fact make a difference to the way you respond to the poems?

RHYMED OR UNRHYMED POETRY?

Talking becomes poetry as walking becomes dancing.
JOSEPHINE MILES

Does a poem have to rhyme? For the uninitiated reader, rhyme and meter are often the external signals that a writer is writing poetry. They are noticeable formal features of much traditional poetry, but they became more and more optional during the twentieth century. **Rhyme** is an echo effect produced when a poet repeats the same sounds at the end of the final syllables (sometimes whole final words) of two or more lines:

> The grizzly bear whose potent HUG
> Was feared by all is now a RUG.
>   Arthur Guiterman

Rhyme keeps alive the delight in repetition, in finding recurrent patterns, that children first experience when they recite "Hickory-dickory-DOCK / The mouse ran up the CLOCK." At the same time, rhyme helps a poet create patterns by marking off regular intervals, by measuring off lines of verse. At the end of a set of lines, rhyme gives us a sense of **closure,** of having arrived at a satisfying conclusion. This sense of a pleasing completeness is especially strong in a **closed couplet** (rhymed set of two lines), like the one Alexander Pope (1688–1744) wrote about Sir Isaac Newton, master physicist of the eighteenth century and pioneer of the modern theory of light:

> Nature and Nature's laws lay hid in NIGHT.
> God said, "Let Newton be!" and all was LIGHT.

Rhyme can help a poet give shape to a **stanza,** a set of related lines with a pattern that may be repeated in other such stanzas in the same poem. In the following opening stanza of a song from a Shakespeare play, we see an interlaced rhyme scheme: The first and third lines rhyme (SUN/DONE). So do the second and fourth, as well as the fifth and sixth (giving us a pattern of ababcc):

Fear no more the heat of the SUN,	a
Nor the furious winter's RAGES.	b
Thou thy worldly task hast DONE,	a
Home art gone, and taken thy WAGES.	b
Golden lads and girls all MUST,	c
As chimney-sweepers, come do DUST.	c

Serious students of poetry take stock of different kinds of rhyme and trace in detail the role they play in determining the texture and shape of poems. (See Chapter 17 for a closer, more technical look.) However, most poets of our century (and some earlier ones) have done *without* rhyme. They have moved from traditional form, with consistent use of rhyme and an underlying regular beat, or meter, toward **open form** (earlier also called **free verse**). They lay out their poems and give shape to them by other means.

In the following unrhymed modern poem, the layout of the lines on the page guides us in setting up the pauses that shape the rhythm of the poem as a whole.

WILLIAM CARLOS WILLIAMS (1883–1963)

This Is Just to Say
1934

I have eaten
the plums
that were in
the icebox

and which   5
you were probably
saving
for breakfast

Forgive me
they were delicious   10
so sweet
and so cold.

THE CREATIVE DIMENSION

Have you ever felt like leaving a message that might begin "This is just to say"? Look at the following student-written response to the Williams poem. How or how well did the student reader get into the spirit of the original poem? Then write a "This-is-just-to-say" message of your own.

This is just to say

I used
the last of
the gas
in your car

you will probably be in
a rush tomorrow
and won't have
time
to refill the
tank

I'm sorry
but I had
no money
and I so

detest the
smell of gas
on my
hands

JUXTAPOSITIONS ═══════════════════════════

To Rhyme or Not to Rhyme

The two poems that follow deal with a similar topic but are different in form. The first poem is by an eighteenth-century English poet who uses rhyme extensively. Lines and stanzas are neatly marked off and packaged. The second poem is by a twentieth-century poet who does without regular rhyme and whose lines move freely in an irregular pattern. How does the difference in form affect your response as a reader?

WILLIAM COWPER (1731–1800)

The Snail
before 1800

Give but his horns the slightest touch,
His self-collective power is such,
He shrinks into his house with much
    Displeasure.

Wherever he dwells, he dwells alone,   5
Except himself, has chattels° none,   *goods*
Well satisfied to be his own
    Whole treasure.

Thus hermit-like his life he leads,
Nor partner of his banquet needs,°   *nor does he need*   10
And if he meets one, only feeds
    The faster.

Who seeks him must be worse than blind
—He and his house are so combined—
If finding it, he fails to find   15
    Its master.

THE RECEPTIVE READER

1. What in the outward form of this poem mirrors the shrinking of the snail as it withdraws into the shell?

2. How does this poet go beyond the simplest use of rhyme—two consecutive lines that rhyme? Can you read this poem out loud so as to do justice to the echo effect of rhyme and to the spilling over of the sense (or the sentence) from the third into the fourth line of each stanza?

3. In how many ways does this poem compare the snail to a human being? With what effect? How are we reminded in the poem that the animal is *different* from a human being?

4. What is witty about this poem? Does it have a serious point?

MAY SWENSON   (born 1919)

Living Tenderly   1963

My body a rounded stone
with a pattern of smooth seams.
My head a short snake
retractive, projective.°   *able to pull in and jut out*
My legs come out of their sleeves   5
or shrink within,
and so does my chin.
My eyelids are quick clamps.
My back is my roof.
I am always at home.   10
I travel where my house walks.
It is a smooth stone.
It floats within the lake,
or rests in the dust.
My flesh lives tenderly   15
inside its bone.

THE RECEPTIVE READER

1. Modern poems doing without a regular rhyme scheme may nevertheless use *occasional* rhyme and echo effects similar to rhyme. How does this poet use rhyme and other repetition or echoing of sound?

2. What *other* kinds of repetition, and of lining up of opposites, help give shape to this poem?

3. What makes the last two lines a high point or fitting *conclusion* of the poem?

THE PERSONAL RESPONSE

Which of the two poems do you like better and why? (Are you inclined to favor the traditional or the modern?)

THE CREATIVE DIMENSION

Try your hand at writing a riddle poem similar to May Swenson's "Living Tenderly." Make sure to furnish your reader with vivid, revealing clues.

METER AND FREE VERSE

Poetry withers and dries out when it leaves music, or at least imagined music, too far behind.

EZRA POUND

The poem exists in the whole body of the person absorbing it, and particularly in the mouth that holds the intimate sounds touching each other, and in the leg that dances the rhythm.

DONALD HALL

Anyone who breathes is in the rhythm business.

WILLIAM STAFFORD

Does poetry have to have a strong regular rhythm, or meter? In traditional kinds of poetry, rhyme and meter go hand in hand in helping to shape the poem. **Meter** regulates the free-flowing irregular rhythms of ordinary speech. It sets up a regular underlying beat of the kind that in music we could accentuate by a drumbeat (or by tapping our toes and clapping our hands). Much modern poetry has moved toward freer, more irregular rhythms—hard to chart, or scan, as a regular beat. Many modern poets, like the poet Donald Hall, tend to think of meter not as a constraint but as "a loose set of probabilities."

Meter has an enticing (and sometimes hypnotic) effect because it mirrors basic rhythms of life: the lub-DUB, lub-DUB, lub-DUB of the heart; the one-two, one-two of walking or running; the in-and-out of deep breathing. The following lines from the poem by Robert Frost that you read earlier have an exceptionally regular beat. Each second syllable has a stronger stress than the first—with the exception of the fourth word in the first and second lines and the second word in the third line. However, since the basic underlying beat goes on, we sense these words as a departure from, or a variation on, the basic meter. These variations keep the basic four-beat line from becoming monotonous, like the tick-tack of a metronome:

Whose WOODS these <u>are</u> I THINK I KNOW
His HOUSE is <u>in</u> the VILLage, THOUGH.
He <u>will</u> not SEE me STOPping HERE.
To WATCH his WOODS fill UP with SNOW.

The fourth and last line shows the underlying four-beat rhythm most clearly. (The return to the basic regular meter often signals a return to the basic theme or point, or an answer after questions or doubts.) To chart the basic meter, we can cut up the line into four pairs of syllables, each with an *unstressed* or weak syllable first and a *stressed* or emphasized syllable second:

To WATCH | his WOODS | fill UP | with SNOW.

Each of these four segments (one stressed syllable each) is called a **foot.** A foot with only two syllables and the stress last is still called by its original Greek name. It is an **iambic** foot, and the "DeTROIT—DeTROIT—DeTROIT" meter it sets up (rather than "BOSton—BOSton—BOSton") is called iambic meter. Over the centuries, iambic meter with four or five beats to the line has become the dominant or most common meter in poetry written in English. (See Chapter 17 for a closer and more technical look at meter.)

Strongly metrical poetry, rhymed or unrhymed, was the norm till well into the nineteenth century. However, in true poetry meter is never merely mechanical. It provides only the underlying beat, not the music. The following poem is by Alfred, Lord Tennyson, in his time perhaps the most widely read poet of the Victorian Age (roughly the mid-nineteenth century). Read the poem out loud or hear it read out loud. Which lines come closest to a regular four-beat iambic meter? What makes the second and third lines different?

ALFRED, LORD TENNYSON (1809–1892)

The Eagle 1851

He clasps the crag with crooked hands;
Close to the sun in lonely lands,
Ringed with the azure° world, he stands.   *deep sky-blue*

The wrinkled sea beneath him crawls;
He watches from his mountain walls,   5
And like a thunderbolt he falls.

The first line of the poem (like the fourth) has a very regular beat:

He CLASPS | the CRAG | with CROOK | ed HANDS

But in the second line (as in the third), the stress pattern is reversed at the beginning of the line. This reversal, or inversion, sets up the kind of counter-rhythm that keeps meter from becoming too mechanical. (See Chapter 17 for more on this common **trochaic** inversion.)

CLOSE to | the SUN | in LONE | ly LANDS

In each stanza, there is a slowing down at the end as we rest momentarily on a final word that is crucial to the meaning and at the same time accentuated by rhyme: ". . . he STANDS"; ". . . he FALLS."

THE RECEPTIVE READER

1. How should this poem sound when read aloud? Listen as several classmates read the poem. Which of them comes closest to the right balance—making the reader sense the underlying rhythm without making it mechanical or obtrusive?

2. The eagle, although almost extinct, is everywhere in traditional lore and public symbols. What images, ideas, or associations does the eagle bring to mind? Are any of them echoed in Tennyson's poem? Is there anything new or different about the way Tennyson asks us to imagine the eagle in this poem?

Even in Tennyson's time, poets were experimenting with less regular rhythms. Here is an example of **free verse** by the American poet Walt Whitman (the "poet of democracy"). Whitman's free verse has a strong rhythm, but it does not have an easily charted regular beat. The lines vary greatly in length. (Some lines are short, but others go on and on.) There is nothing tidy or measured about Whitman's verse. He saw himself as the prophet of a new national consciousness and a new spirituality, and his lines have the flow and sweep of a prophet's inspirations.

Try to read the poem first with exaggerated stress on strongly stressed or accentuated syllables. Although there is no strong regular beat or meter, an irregular rhythmic pattern emerges. We can imagine that we are hearing the poet chant these lines. In the words of one student reader, "The almost chanting, yet not mesmerizingly regular rhythm elevates the tone of the poem and gives it almost oracular power."

WALT WHITMAN   (1819–1892)
A Noiseless Patient Spider   1881

A noiseless patient spider
I marked where on a little promontory° it stood isolated,   *outcropping*
Marked how to explore the vacant vast surrounding
It launched forth filament, filament, filament out of itself,
Ever unreeling them, ever tirelessly speeding them.   5
And you O my soul where you stand,
Surrounded, detached, in measureless oceans of space,
Ceaselessly musing, venturing, throwing, seeking the
    spheres to connect them,
Till the bridge you will need be formed, till the
    ductile° anchor hold,   *easily bent*
Till the gossamer thread you fling catch somewhere,
    O my soul.   10

This poem revolves around the parallel between "the noiseless patient spider" and the human soul. The spider stands "isolated" as if on a cliff jutting out into the sea, encircled by what is, for the spider, the "vacant vast surrounding." Similarly, the soul finds itself "detached, in measureless oceans of space"—in the vast spaces our thoughts can travel without finding a firm support or rest. The spider with tireless repetition spins and launches forth "filament, filament, filament," hoping they will catch at points beyond the empty space to allow it to anchor its net. (The word *launch* implies exploration, as when we launch a space probe into the reaches of outer space.) Similarly, the human soul, "ceaselessly musing, venturing, throwing, seeking," launches forth the thoughts that will allow it to find a firm point of rest or to connect with what gives meaning to our lives.

The slow, solemn rhythm of the lines suits the elevated subject: our search for spiritual fulfillment, our faith in our ability to find a spiritual anchor in what at first seems a vast meaningless universe. Here is how you might mark the stresses that account for the rhythm of the first three lines:

A NOISEless PATient SPIDer
I MARKed where on a LITTle PROMontory it STOOD ISolated,
MARKed how to exPLORE the VACant VAST surROUNDing

THE RECEPTIVE READER

1. How well do you respond to the *rhythm* of Whitman's verse? Can you chart the major stressed syllables in the rest of the poem? Do you and your classmates agree on the rhythmic patterns of the lines?

2. What ideas or associations do spiders usually bring to mind? What is *different* about the way Whitman looks at the spider in this poem?

3. What is the connection between the spider and the poet's *soul*? What is the "bridge" the soul will need? What is the "gossamer thread" the soul flings in this poem?

4. Why does the poet start with the *image* of the patient spider—rather than with the central idea of the poem? What does the poet lose or gain by not letting us know till halfway through the poem that it is addressed to his soul?

Much later free verse has a less strong, less chanting rhythm than Whitman's poems. The following lines are from a poem by Daniela Gioseffi, an American poet and playwright writing a century later. Her lines illustrate the irregular length of line and the underplayed, almost conversational rhythm of much current poetry. The poet is not speaking from a podium or preaching from a pulpit; she is talking with us easily and confidentially. (Try to identify stressed or accented syllables as you read.)

A silver watch you've worn for years
is suddenly gone
leaving a pale white stripe
blazing on your wrist.

JUXTAPOSITIONS ⌐━━━━━━━━━━━━━

Meter and Free Verse

The following two poems are by poets who choose to use traditional rhyme and meter in some of their poems and modern free verse in others. Most readers know Edna St. Vincent Millay for poems on traditional themes, mourning lost happiness and the passing of love. However, she also wrote intensely personal poems in a less traditional mold and passionate indictments of war and oppression. Her poem, the first of the two reprinted here, is a sonnet, a traditional fourteen-line poem, elaborately crafted, and often addressed to a lover. (You will be able to take a closer look at the sonnet form in Chapter 17.) Gwendolyn Brooks is best known for eloquent poems about the injustices suffered by black Americans, although many of her poems are loving portraits of people she cherished. In the first poem, look closely at the workings of traditional rhyme and meter. In the second poem, look at the workings of modern free verse.

EDNA ST. VINCENT MILLAY (1892–1950)

Pity me not because the light of day 1917

Pity me not because the light of day
At close of day no longer walks the sky;
Pity me not for beauties passed away
From field and thicket as the years go by;
Pity me not the waning of the moon,   5
Nor that the ebbing tide goes out to sea,
Nor that man's desire is hushed so soon,
And you no longer look with love on me.
This have I known always: Love is no more
Than the wide blossom which the wind assails,   10
Than the great tide that treads the shifting shore,
Strewing fresh wreckage gathered in the gales:
Pity me that the heart is slow to learn
What the swift mind beholds at every turn.

THE RECEPTIVE READER

1. A key feature of the sonnet is its interlaced *rhyme scheme*. Which lines rhyme in this sonnet?

2. Another traditional feature is the five-beat iambic meter (called *iambic pentameter,* after the Greek word for five). Which lines have the most regular iambic beat, on the "DeTROIT-DeTROIT-DeTROIT" model? Which lines vary the beat by starting with a strongly accented first syllable?

3. The rhyme scheme and the traditional meter help make a sonnet a unified, finished whole. In this poem, how do the *repetition* of phrases and the use of parallel, similar sentence structure contribute to the same effect?

4. What *images* does the poet draw on to help you imagine the nature of love? What do these images have in common?

5. As in many other sonnets, the final *couplet* provides a turning point, an answer to a question raised earlier. Here, we go on from the "Pity me not . . ." pattern of the earlier lines to what *does* deserve our pity. What is the difference between the slow heart and the swift mind?

PERSONAL RESPONSE

illay was out of fashion for a time but is being rediscovered by a new generation of readers. Can you relate to the mood or the predominant feeling of this sonnet? Why or why not?

GWENDOLYN BROOKS   (born 1917)

Truth   1949

equality

And if sun comes
How shall we greet him?
Shall we not dread him,
Shall we not fear him
After so lengthy a   5
Session with shade?

Though we have wept for him,
Though we have prayed
All through the night-years—
What if we wake one shimmering morning to   10
Hear the fierce hammering
Of his firm knuckles
Hard on the door?

Shall we not shudder?—
Shall we not flee   15
Into the shelter, the dear thick shelter
Of the familiar
Propitious° haze?   *promising good fortune*

Sweet is it, sweet is it
To sleep in the coolness   20
Of snug unawareness.

The dark hangs heavily
Over the eyes.

THE RECEPTIVE READER

1. This poem does not use traditional rhyme and meter. It nevertheless has a stronger rhythm than much modern free verse. What guides you in reading the poem with the *right rhythm?* Point out examples of the poet's repeating phrases or sentence frames. Can you show how this repetition sets up patterns that help make the poem a unified whole? What is the effect of the frequent repetition or echoing on you as the reader?

2. Traditional guidelines for rhyme ruled out the repetition of identical words at the end of lines. Modern critics know it occurs in contemporary poetry; they sometimes call it *para-rhyme* (a rhyme that is not really a rhyme but something like it). Where does it occur in this poem? They also call pairs of words that do not rhyme but more distantly sound alike *half-rhymes* or *slant rhymes*. Where do you find these in the poem?

3. How are the images and feelings associated with the sun in this poem different from more familiar or predictable ones? How are the images and feelings associated with the dark, its opposite, different from what we might expect?

4. What "fierce" and feared or dreaded truths do you think the poet had in mind? What kind of "night-years" may the poet have been thinking about?

THE PERSONAL RESPONSE

Many readers read Brooks' poetry in the context of the civil rights struggle of the sixties and seventies. Does this poem's perspective on truth apply to other contexts, other situations? (Is the poem both timely and timeless at the same time?)

THE CREATIVE DIMENSION

Suppose you were asked to draw up five questions designed to test your respondents' loyalty to the truth. What would your questions be?

CLOSE READING AND THE PERSONAL RESPONSE

The poem must provoke its readers: force them to hear—to hear themselves.
                                        OCTAVIO PAZ

The purpose of poetry is to remind us how difficult it is to remain just one person, for our house is open, there are no keys in the doors, and invisible guests come in and out at will.
        CZESLAW MILOSZ, "THE POETIC VOICE IN US"

May God us keep / From single vision.
        WILLIAM BLAKE

What is your role as the reader? A poem is not like an art object in a glass case in a museum, with a sign that says "Do not touch the artifacts." A successful poem does something for you as the reader: It may open a new perspective. It may shake you up; it may move you to laughter or to tears. The poem ceases to be just words on a page when it triggers this kind of interaction between the poet and you as the reader.

Some readers get much out of even a fairly short or simple poem. It is as if their antennas were especially well equipped to pick up the signals the poem sends. To make the most of your reading, consider guidelines like the following:

✧ *Give the poem a close reading.* Take in as much as you can; be open to whatever the poem has to offer. Many readers start with a fairly quick reading of the whole poem to get an overall impression. But then they go back to take in important details. They linger over a key line. They weigh the impact of a key image. They puzzle over apparent contradictions.

✧ *Get your bearings.* Who is speaking in the poem? What is the situation or occasion? What seems to be the agenda? For instance, are we looking at a scene from the world of nature? Are we witnessing a confrontation between parent and child? Is a lover talking to the beloved?

✧ *Respond to the poem as a whole.* Try to get a sense of its overall pattern. Look for key words or phrases that echo in the poem. Look at how the poem as a whole takes shape. For instance, does it move from now to then (and then perhaps back again to now)? Does it play off two different ways of looking at our world? Does it set up polarities—for instance, does it move from innocence to experience? Does it travel between city life and nature?

✧ *Get into the spirit of the poem.* We are disappointed when someone reading a poem aloud reads without expression, without feeling. We want the reader's face, gestures, and body language to act out the mood, the rhythm, or the overall shape of the poem. Even when reading silently, a receptive reader may betray by nods and frowns and gestures that the poem is being experienced, acted out, in the reader's mind.

✧ *Be ready for a personal response.* We do not read poetry in order to analyze poems that leave us cold. Writing poetry is an act of faith assuming that the poet's observations and experiences will find an echo in the experience of the reader. A poem that is reprinted and reread time and again has touched a chord in many different readers. To be moved by a poem about the loss of a father, we need not have lost a father ourselves, but the poem may remind us of the loss of somebody or something dear to us.

Give the following short poem a careful, patient, line-by-line reading. Then look at one student reader's close reading of the poem. What did you miss that the student reader noticed? What in turn did you notice that she apparently missed?

LINDA PASTAN   (born 1932)

Sometimes in Winter   1991

when I look into
the fragile faces
of those I love,

I long to be
one of those people who skate   5
over the surface

of their lives, scoring
the ice with patterns
of their own making,

people who have   10
no children.
who are attached

to earth only by
silver blades moving
at high speed,   15

who have learned to use
the medium of the cold
to dance in.

Compare the reading in the following sample student paper with your own reading of the poem.

SAMPLE STUDENT PAPER

Dancing in the Medium of the Cold

In the poem "Sometimes in Winter," we are asked to explore the relationship between life and ice-skating. Taken out of context, the metaphor of life as skating over ice might not appear to be entirely serious. But the images that are used in this poem make us think seriously about the comparison. The comparison is followed up in a chain of related words and images: winter, cold, a surface that can be scored but not penetrated, patterns sketched in the ice, silver blades speeding across the ice.

On the surface, the sight of the "silver blades moving / at high speed" across the ice is very appealing. The skaters score "the ice with patterns / of their own making." They seem in charge, in control, deciding for themselves whether they want to score in the ice a figure 8 or some other kind of graceful loop. What a relief it would be to be a free-floating skater and not to have to worry about the needs and demands of others who depend on us.

However, the person speaking to us in the poem cannot be like an ice-skater skimming over the surface of life. For her, love means attachment. Looking into the "fragile" faces of those she loves, she sees how vulnerable they are. The speaker implies that love for children holds her to the earth when she says that people who have no children are attached to the earth only by "silver blades moving / at high speed." Is this connection enough to hold a person to the earth for very long? What happens to the ice-skater when this tenuous connection is severed? Does she fly off the earth? Does she cease to exist? That is what the metaphor implies. People who are not attached to loved ones are not fully participating in life; they only glide over the surface. They dance on top of life, but they do not enter into it.

The speaker in the poem says that she longs to be one of the people who skate over the surface of life, but the metaphor she uses belies or contradicts that claim. She may be attracted to the speed and flash of the ice-skater, but the images we see make us realize that the flash is all on the surface. The skaters are adapting to the medium in which they live; they are surrounded by the cold, so they have learned to dance (live) in it. If they were allowed to choose all over again, might they not say that they long to be attached to the earth by something more than silver blades moving at high speed?

Bickering, emergency phone calls, and disrupted schedules make life in close contact with others very different from skating gracefully over the ice. But could we stand "the medium of the cold" if we severed our ties?

QUESTIONS

Does this reading explain why there is so much ice and cold in this poem? What do the "silver blades" make you see or feel? Were you surprised by the use of the word *fragile* at the beginning of the poem? (Does the student writer do enough to explain how it makes us feel?) How do you explain that the skaters are "dancing"?

To judge from this student paper, our personal response to this poem will depend at least in part on how we feel about living in a close web of personal relationships as against the free-floating loneliness of the skater. But the student writer's own personal answer is only implied. (One reader started a more personal response to this poem by saying, "Not just sometimes in winter but several times a day I muse how I might be better off on my own.")

The two responses that follow the next poem (by an Irish poet) are by one reader. The first response is again the kind of close reading that tries to do justice to the poem in front of us on the page. The second response, however, goes a step further. The reader asked: What does this poem mean to me personally? Is there any personal connection between this poem and something in my own life? Study the two different dimensions of this reader's response. How are they different? How are they related?

SEAMUS HEANEY (born 1939)
Valediction 1966

Lady with the frilled blouse
And simple tartan skirt,
Since you have left the house
Its emptiness has hurt
All thought. In your presence   5
Time rode easy, anchored
On a smile; but absence
Rocked love's balance, unmoored
The days. They buck and bound
Across the calendar   10
Pitched from the quiet sound
Of your flower-tender
Voice. Need breaks on my strand;°   *beach, shore*
You've gone, I am at sea.
Until you resume command   15
Self is in mutiny.

Look at the way the following reading pulls out and interprets significant details in the poem:

CLOSE READING: The poem "Valediction" describes the emotional experience of a man whose female companion (probably his wife) has left him. The poet uses a central metaphor to explain the speaker's emotional state, a metaphor he develops in a variety of ways, to describe exactly how the man in the poem is affected by her absence.

The metaphor in the poem is that of a boat on a lake or an ocean. When the "lady with the frilled blouse / And simple tartan skirt" was present, the boat was "anchored" secure in its mooring. "Time rode easy," suggesting the placid setting and the speaker's previously peaceful state of mind. With her absence, however, the calmness is lost: "love's balance," which existed in her presence, is "rocked," and the days "unmoored." Time is no longer safe at anchor but cast off, wild. The days now "buck" and "bound" as the boat pitches in the water; there is nothing smooth about the man's existence anymore.

Meanwhile, the waves have started to break on the beach. The waves are the man's "need," the beach his "strand." With the lady gone, the speaker is truly "at sea." He can only visualize calm in his life once more if she will return to "command" the boat that is the speaker himself. Until that time the boat is doomed to be "in mutiny," that is, beyond his control, at the mercy of time and the waves.

THE RECEPTIVE READER

What details in the poem follow up the contrast between the calm before and the turmoil after the woman's departure? Were you surprised by the phrase "resume command"? What do you think it shows about the relationship between the two people? Did this reader miss any significant details in this poem?

Look at the way the following response by the same reader relates the poem to the reader's own experience. A paper anchored in close reading but going on to the personal connection would answer both basic questions: What does this poem mean—to perhaps a majority of perceptive readers? And what does the poem mean to me?

PERSONAL RESPONSE: It is easy to identify with a poem that carries such an obvious central metaphor. It uses the boat rocked by waves as the metaphor for an event disturbing the equilibrium of someone's life. While I have never experienced what it is like to have the most important person in my life walk out on me, curiously enough, I dreamed about this happening to me just a few nights ago. In my dream I was in college, and J. had just left me. (As is common with dreams, there was no obvious reason for this occurrence.)

I experienced total and utter despair. Although several close friends and family were with me, they were unable, even unwilling, to help me through the experience. I was truly "at sea." I started out into the streets, attempting to find my way "home" to J. A wind started to roar toward me, hindering my steps, and the flat road suddenly became a hill. My last impression before awaking involved a clear realization that I never would succeed in reaching the crest of the hill and passing over to the other side.

Thinking about this dream, I have become aware that I fear greatly this absence that Heaney describes in his poem. I find myself believing that I would act like the man he describes and like the person I appeared to be in my dream. Fortunately for me, I have the warning ahead of time—never to take your loved ones for granted.

ECEPTIVE READER

w do you explain this reader's dream? What is the connection between the
nd the poem? Did this poem bring any personal associations or memories to
your mind? How did you personally react to the poem?

EXPLORATIONS

The Personal Response

Of the following poems, choose the one that speaks to you most directly
or that means most to you personally. First, read the poem carefully, paying
special attention to details that might seem difficult or unexpected on first
reading. Present your own close reading of the poem in such a way that it could
lead a fellow reader to a fuller understanding and appreciation of the poem.
Then present your personal response to the poem, explaining your personal reaction or showing why the poem has a special meaning for you as a reader.

ALICE WALKER (born 1944)

New Face   1972

I have learned not to worry about love;
but to honor its coming
with all my heart.
To examine the dark mysteries
of the blood   5
with headless heed and
swirl,
to know the rush of feelings
swift and flowing
as water.   10
The source appears to be
some inexhaustible
spring
within our twin and triple
selves;   15
the new face I turn up
to you
no one else on earth
has ever
seen.   20

THE RECEPTIVE READER

1. What is the focus of this poem? What sets it in motion?
2. Although this poem addresses a large recurrent question in our lives, it translates the poet's feelings and ideas into strong graphic images. What are striking examples? What gives them special force?
3. This poem comes to a close with a beautiful fresh image. What is its meaning?

WALLACE STEVENS (1879–1955)
Disillusionment of Ten O'Clock 1923

The houses are haunted
By white nightgowns.
None are green,
Or purple with green rings,
Or green with yellow rings,   5
Or yellow with blue rings.
None of them are strange,
With socks of lace
And beaded ceintures.°   *fancy sashes*
People are not going   10
To dream of baboons and periwinkles.°   *cone-shaped snails*
Only, here and there, an old sailor,
Drunk and asleep in his boots,
Catches tigers
In red weather.   15

THE RECEPTIVE READER

1. Why is this poet "disillusioned"? About what?

2. What is funny about the idea of these houses being "haunted"? Why does the color of people's nightgowns matter in this poem? The critic Irving Howe said that the nightgowns are the "uniform of ordinariness and sober nights." What did he mean?

3. Why do *dreams* matter in this poem? What do the people's dreams and their nightgowns have in common?

4. Does the poet share the conventional attitude toward *drunks*? Howe said that the sailor is the one person in this poem who "stands outside the perimeter of busy dullness." What did he mean?

THE CREATIVE DIMENSION

Most poets would be content if their readers were to give a poem a close, careful reading and allow it to activate a personal reaction. Their readers would thus already be moving beyond the stage of mere passive, uninvolved reading. However, a third way of "getting into" a poem is to allow it to trigger a creative response, to bring your own creativity into play. One way to get into the spirit of a poem is to write a similar poem of your own or a passage of your own triggered in some way by the poem. This way you get to know the poem "from the inside"—the way a person playing an instrument or acting a part in amateur performance ceases to be a passive spectator.

For instance, we know that a student has understood and appreciated the Wallace Stevens poem when we see the following student-written re-creation. How or how well does the student poem capture the mood and intention of the original? How close is it to the original in pattern or form?

Disenchantment at the Dance

The dance is crowded
With blue denim.
There are no dresses
Of shiny, red satin
Or shimmering silk.
No bright feathered hats
No rhinestone buttons.
People aren't dancing
The foxtrot or cha cha.
Only, once in a while,
A few underclassmen
In T-shirts and jeans
Clap their hands
Shuffle their feet.

When a poem moves you in a special way, it may trigger a creative effort of your own—a poem, a prose passage, a drawing, a photograph. Such a creative response or re-creation may sum up a personal impression, or it may pursue a train of thought set in motion by something in the original poem. It may focus on a haunting image or take off from a provocative phrase. It may talk back to the original poem. One basic function of poetry is to keep alive the poet in each of us. We are not likely to become good readers of poetry if we seldom use our own imagination.

EXPLORATIONS

Reading and Writing Haiku

As we know from the Japanese experience of the haiku, as well as the experience of many brief poems in the Western tradition, poetry can be present in fifteen words, or in ten words. Length or meter or rhyme have nothing to do with it.
ROBERT BLY

Boy with dollar cries
Sign in poetry shop reads:
"No haiku today"
STUDENT HAIKU

Several traditional kinds of Japanese poetry work on the principle of "much in little." They give you snapshots (or **vignettes**) of three lines or five lines each—very short poems that focus your attention on something that is worth looking at but that busy, harried people might overlook. Reading and re-creating these short poems can help you move from passive to more active and appreciative reading.

The best known of these centuries-old short forms is the three-liner, or **haiku**. It fixes a sight or observation in a beautifully crafted form, the way amber encases and preserves an insect caught in the sap of a tree. (One early translator said that haiku about dragonflies are almost as numerous as the dragonflies themselves in the early autumn.)

A giant firefly
that way, this way, that way, this—
and it passes by.

In its strict traditional form, the haiku arranges exactly seventeen syllables in three lines of five, seven, and five syllables each. Count the syllables in the following example. (The m in the last line counts as a separate syllable.)

Kumonosu no	5	Ah! Unsuspecting	5
Atari ni asobu	7	the whir of the dragonfly	7
To-m-bo kana!	5	Near the spider's net	5

The most famous of haiku poets is Basho, and his most famous haiku, often translated, is the following.

BASHO (1644–1694)

Furuike ya	5	An old quiet pond—	5
kawazu tobikomu	7	Frog splashes into water,	7
mizu no oto	5	Breaking the silence	5

Most modern re-creations keep the basic three-line format but do not observe the strict syllable count. The following translations preserve the short-long-short of the haiku without the strict five-seven-five pattern. Both originals were written by women, who "dominated the early years of the literary tradition in Japan not only in numbers, but in formal, aesthetic terms as well" (Rob Swigart).

UKIHASHI (17th century)

TRANSLATED BY KENNETH REXROTH AND IKUKO ATSUMI

Whether I sit or lie
My empty mosquito net
Is too large.

KAWAI CHIGETSU-NI (1632–1736)

TRANSLATED BY KENNETH REXROTH AND IKUKO ATSUMI

Grasshoppers
Chirping in the sleeves
Of a scarecrow.

Study the following student-written examples of modernized haiku. Then try your hand at some of your own. Note that the focus in the poems themselves is on what we see—although we as readers may take the poem as a starting point for thoughts and feelings. Note the focus on thought-provoking specifics—the absence of blank-check words like *beautiful, sweet, innocent.* The first two examples are formal haiku observing the 5-7-5 pattern:

FORMAL: A seed yearning for
the dark warm earth to moisten
must practice patience.

Husband's warm body,
Comforting hum of furnace—
I drift back to sleep.

INFORMAL: An old woman
looking at granddaughter
reminisces

Bright yellow cranes,
Old building standing
Condemned to die.

Tranquil is the garden of Eden
before the inevitable intrusion
Of the stealthy reptile

A related Japanese form, fixing a moment in time, is the five-liner (or **tanka**). In the strict traditional form, it adds two seven-syllable lines, giving the poet a little more elbowroom. (Historically, the haiku is actually an abbreviated tanka, first written by poets who considered the five-liner too wordy.) The following translation does not observe the strict syllable count.

LADY HORIKAWA (12th century)

TRANSLATED BY KENNETH REXROTH AND IKUKO ATSUMI

How long will it last?
I do not know
his heart.
This morning my thoughts are tangled
as my black hair.

The following student-written tanka does rise to the challenge of the traditional 5-7-5-7-7 pattern:

On the bottom shelf	5
the cheese from three months ago	7
has grown pale-blue fur	5
and I think I heard it growl	7
I'm pretty sure it was cheese.	7

The following student-written five-liners vary the traditional pattern. Try writing some five-line poems of your own.

Batman	Honey
flits across my rooftop,	Comb, the Queen Bee,
sits on my TV antenna	Reigns with trifling, stoic
and pretends	Elegance, keeping her left eye
he's a 200-pound pigeon.	Droneward.

WRITING ABOUT LITERATURE

11. Keeping a Poetry Journal (Suggestions for Writing)

Cover done by MAC
Inside done by IBM
Each word is a joy
"WORD PROCESSING HAIKU," STUDENT JOURNAL

The Writing Workshop   Keeping a poetry journal helps you become a more responsive, more thoughtful reader. Your journal can also be the place where you do much of the **prewriting** for more structured formal papers. In writing a paper, you will be able to turn to your journal for tentative ideas, relevant evidence, and background information.

◇ Your journal gives you a chance to formulate your *overall impression* of a poem. You may start with first impressions, trying to organize them into some preliminary pattern. You may try to get down and organize some of the free-floating associations and reactions that the poem activates on first reading. Keeping a journal will get you into the habit of thinking about the significance, shape, and tone of a poem as a whole.

◇ Your journal enables you to keep a rough record of what you take in as you read. You may want to use part of your journal for a *running commentary,* highlighting striking passages, key images, or notes struck more than once in a poem. In your journal, you can focus on a question that bothers you or on puzzling details. Your journal then serves as the record of your close reading of a poem, as you get involved in the way it takes shape and as you try to do justice to nuances and shades of meaning.

◇ Your journal gives you a chance to formulate your *personal response.* Some poems move us strongly. They strike a powerful chord. We seem to be listening to a kindred spirit. Other poems are impressive or thought provoking, but we read them from a respectful distance. Still other poems we fight, because they seem to be looking at our world through the wrong end of the telescope. Or they may make us confront topics or issues we have been trying to avoid. In your journal, you can begin to explain and justify to yourself your own personal interaction with a poem.

The following sample entries from student journals illustrate possible topics and formats for your own journal. Note that the entries show evidence of careful firsthand reading—weaving into the text quoted words and phrases, half lines and whole lines, from the poems being discussed.

Focus on Words   A large part of careful close reading is trying to decode fully the shades of meaning, the overtones, and the associations of the poet's words. In a short poem, each word counts. (It has been estimated that the weight per word is five to ten times in a poem what it would be in ordinary casual prose.) The author of the following journal entry "read out" of the poet's choice of words considerably more than their bare dictionary meaning:

> William Carlos Williams in "The Dance" makes us see the peasants making merry in a painting by Breughel, a sixteenth-century Flemish painter of peasant life. Right away we see that the people in the painting are big, beefy, corpulent, solid peasant types. The poet uses the word *round* several times ("the dancers go round, they go round and / around"). The poet compares their bellies to the "thick- / sided glasses whose wash they impound."
>
> Williams uses words like *squeal* and *blare* and *tweedle* to describe the music of the bagpipes. These words are not normally used to describe music; in fact, they have connotations of being really annoying sounds. *Squeal* brings to mind pictures of stuck pigs, angry children, or the air being let out of tires. *Blare* makes us hear the horns of frustrated drivers, the sound a donkey makes, unwelcome stereos at 3 a.m., or a charging elephant. *Tweedle* to me is an annoying, monotonous sound that alternates between two high-pitched notes, back and forth, back and forth. The choice of these words gives us an idea that the dancers are not a noble bunch. These are people whose children probably don't wear shoes; these dancers dance to loud music and drink and belch and don't give a second thought. Just from these word choices, I see big bellies that shirts don't quite cover. I see women with enormous hips. Food in enormous quantities is being eaten, perhaps without utensils or even plates. Faces are being wiped on sleeves, not napkins or towels. These people are hard workers, and they celebrate hard, with great happiness.

Focus on Metaphor   Often a poem comes into focus for us as we begin to see the full meaning of a central metaphor or organizing symbol. The following journal entry traces in detail the possible ramifications of a haunting central image:

> Spiders usually bring associations of haunted, spooky places inhabited by ghosts, witches, and skeletons. Spiders are often thought of as cruel beings who suck the blood out of poor trapped helpless bugs. On the other hand,

spiders also bring visions of beautiful, sparkling, intricate webs. In his poem "A Noiseless Patient Spider," Walt Whitman takes us way beyond the ordinary associations. He sees the spider sympathetically as it noiselessly and patiently performs the simple life-supporting function of sending out its web in search of its needs. So Whitman can easily slip into the parallel search of each person (not just poets!). "Ceaselessly musing, venturing, throwing," we search for the ideas, beliefs, values, or mission that can be the anchor of our lives. The "gossamer threads" that the soul flings are the searching thoughts, the trial and error, the seeking that each person performs to find a happy or at least bearable environment in which the mind and heart can live. The bridge each soul seeks to build will take it to a meaning that imposes order on the universe, which without it remains an incomprehensible, dangerous place.

The Reader's Background   A poem is a transaction between the poet and the reader. A poem is not sufficient unto itself. It activates and shapes what the reader brings to the poem—in the way of memories, associations, overtones of words, shared values, or cultural heritage. The student author of the following entry was able to get into the spirit of a poem because it stimulated a range of relevant associations. She was able to make the right connections:

In his poem "Pied Beauty," G. M. Hopkins writes about beauty that is not smooth and boring but instead dappled, freckled, "counter, original, spare, strange." The poem cites as an example different occupations or trades with their "gear and tackle and trim." I thought right away of a friend who was a rock climber—he had a fascinating variety of ropes, clips, wedges, "helpers," with the ropes and slings in bright, varied colors. I also thought of painters or roofers, with their trucks loaded down with various gear—ladders, paint cans with paint dripping down the sides, plastic coverings, drop cloths spattered with paint. Hopkins looked with wonder and delight at asymmetrical things that to him became a symbol of the color and variety of God's creation.

The student who wrote the following entry felt he had a special way into a poem because of his regional background:

An image is the picture that is worth a thousand words. But do images communicate equally effectively with different readers? If the reader does not have the background that a poet assumes, does the significance of the poem suffer? I cannot help feeling that something is lost if people are not aware of what it takes to rise on a bitter cold winter morning as "imaged" in Robert Hayden's poem "Those Winter Sundays." In the "blueblack cold," the father, with cracked hands that ached from his weekday labor, made the "banked fires blaze"—but "no one ever thanked him" for this labor of love. As an Easterner transplanted to Southern California, I know it is difficult to explain bitter cold, or the glory of thunderstorms, or the bite of the air on a crisp autumn day. Here there is no weather. Spirits cannot be brought down by yearning for a weekend that is then rained out—two months in a row. Spirits cannot be raised by the first sight of buds on the trees, the first call of spring birds. There are no major mood swings.

The Personal Response   How we as readers experience a poem depends on our private agendas, emotional needs, and moral values. A poem can have a powerful impact on us if it gives voice and direction to what we already strongly feel:

> In his poem "London," William Blake takes us to an eighteenth-century city where we hear the "infant's cry of fear," "the hapless soldier's sigh," and the "youthful harlot's curse" among soot-blackened churches and castles whose walls are figuratively covered with blood. Every day my own point of view toward today's cities comes closer to Blake's. Cities today are filled with poverty, violence, and hunger. I cannot walk to school without seeing the lines of people in the naturalization offices, the children waiting in line at the rescue mission, or the homeless and mentally challenged sleeping on the grass outside Grace Baptist Church. I honestly don't know why I get so upset about all the poverty in the city. I guess I feel so guilty because of all the advantages I have had. And when I see the children lining up to get at least one real meal, the guilt sets in.

The Creative Dimension   A poem may serve as a stimulus or catalyst for a creative effort of your own that spins off from the original. The student author of the following entry had read Thomas Hardy's end-of-the-century poem "The Darkling Thrush"—the century being the nineteenth century (p. 438). She wrote the following farewell poem for the twentieth century:

An Epitaph for the Twentieth Century by 438-11-7322

Nine digits we're linked to
from birth
A number that stays with us
till our last day on earth

Without a number
You can have no card
Without a card
All business retards

Whether you're a king, queen, or jack
Hinges on where your card fits into the stack

In the future they'll remark:
Humankind gave the digit a high place
and did much to erase
Fingerprint and face.

How to Cite Poetry   In writing your journal entries, practice the conventions that you will have to observe in more formal papers.

✧ Put the title of the poem in quotation marks; *italicize* (<u>underscore</u> on an old-fashioned typewriter) the book or collection in which it appears.

Judy Grahn's poem "Paris and Helen" appears in her collection *The Queen of Wands.*

✧ When you run in lines of poetry as part of your own text, use a **slash** (with a space on either side) to show line breaks in the original poem:

Asked to let anger out of its cage, the speaker in the poem says that anger, once loose, "may / turn on me, maul / my face, draw blood."

✧ Normally set off three or more lines of verse as a **block quotation**—indent and center on page, *no* quotation marks. (You may choose to set off even a single line or two lines to make them stand out.)

The rose plays a somewhat unusual role in the opening lines of Gwendolyn Brooks' poem "A Song in the Front Yard":

I've stayed in the front yard all my life.
I want to peek at the back
Where it's rough and untended and hungry weeds grow.
A girl gets sick of a rose.

✧ Use double quotation marks for ordinary quotations; use **single quotation marks** for a quote-within-a-quote:

In her introduction to Janet Lewis' *Poems Old and New: 1918–1978,* Helen Trimpi says that Lewis' poetry has a drive "toward balance—to 'bind despair and joy / into a stable whole'—in life as well as in music and art."

12 PATTERN
The Whole Poem

The person who writes out of an inner need is trying to order his corner of the universe; very often the meaning of an experience or an emotion becomes clear only in this way.

MAXINE KUMIN

When I was young, to make something in language, a poem that was all of a piece, a poem that could stand for what I was at the time—that seemed to be the most miraculous thing in the world.

THEODORE ROETHKE

FOCUS ON PATTERN

Poetry, like its sister arts, springs from the human impulse to give shape to experience. A poem opens, moves forward, and comes to a close. It has an overall pattern; it has a design. When we read attentively, we sense how the poem takes shape. As we read and reread, we begin to see how details work in **context**—as part of a web of meanings. Parts that seemed puzzling at first may slowly fall into place. They become part of the whole—they help make up the poem's overall shape, or configuration. A configuration is a fitting together of parts in a distinctive pattern. When we see the New York City skyline with the twin towers of the World Trade Center and the tapered tip of the Empire State Building, we are not likely to say: "Chicago!" We recognize a distinct silhouette, unmistakable like a signature.

The following is a poem that many readers have found beautifully finished, complete in itself. When they finish reading it, the poem has satisfied the expectations it has created. It has accomplished its agenda, unlike a conversation that has lost its thread.

432

WENDELL BERRY (born 1934)
The Peace of Wild Things   1968

When the despair of the world grows in me
and I wake in the night at the least sound
in fear of what my life and my children's life may be,
I go and lie down where the wood drake°   *male duck with brilliant plumage*
rests in his beauty on the water, and the great heron feeds.   5
I come into the peace of wild things
who do not tax their lives with forethought
of grief. I come into the presence of still water.
And I feel above me the day-blind stars
waiting with their light. For a time   10
I rest in the grace of the world, and am free.

What gives this poem its satisfying shape? The poet takes us on a journey of the mind—a journey from one state of mind to another. The poem focuses on a need—the need for an antidote to anxiety and despair. This is the need the speaker in the poem feels while lying awake in the dark of night, worrying about a threatening future. The poem as a whole then fills that need, leaving the speaker ("for a time") at peace and at rest, feeling "free."

Each detail in this poem is part of this larger pattern. The speaker in the poem wakes up at night from an uneasy, fearful sleep "at the least sound" that might suggest threat or danger. The unknown, nameless threats that the future holds for him and his children fill him with anxiety and despair. He then seeks and finds in nature images that inspire a healing sense of calm—the wood drake that "rests in his beauty on the water," the great heron feeding, the "still water." The "wild things" of nature (although perhaps themselves living in a threatening world) are not troubled by "forethought / of grief." The starlight, entirely above the turmoil of knotted human emotions, calms and lifts the spirit. The keynote—the central term that sums up much of the meaning or goal of the poem—is the word *peace*. It appears first in the title, and it appears again at a pivotal point in the poem when we "come into the peace of wild things."

The poet raises a question and gives an answer. That answer may not be the last word on the issue (it may work only "for a time"). It will not suit everyone. However, the poem gives us a strong sense that the poet finished what he had started. The poet has done his part. When a poem gives us this satisfying sense of completeness, we say that it has achieved **closure.** Something worthwhile has been accomplished or completed.

THE RECEPTIVE READER

1. What associations with or reactions to *nature* do you bring to this poem? (How do you usually think and feel about nature?) Does the poet's relation to nature (or, more precisely, that of the speaker in the poem) seem strange or understandable to you?

2. How are the stars "day-blind," and how are they nevertheless a consoling presence in this poem?

3. The word *grace* has several possible meanings, from "gracefulness" to "divine grace." What does the word mean in the context of the last line?

4. In this poem, how is *sound* related to sense? Does this poem sound neatly packaged—or does it sound free-flowing to you? Does it have a soothing effect on the reader? When read out loud, should it sound challenging, desperate, quiet, angry, defiant, passionate?

THE PERSONAL RESPONSE

What do you think are the fears that keep the speaker in the poem awake at night? Do you think people can find ways to escape from "forethought" or worry about the future?

As a potter takes formless clay and shapes it into a lovely lasting pitcher or jar, so the poet uses words to give a satisfying shape to the miscellaneous flow of experience. Something previously blurred comes into focus; something that might have gone unnoticed receives attention. Things that were disjointed fit together. They become part of a shape or configuration; they become part of a pattern.

THE POWER OF ATTENTION

A poem is a momentary stay against confusion.
ROBERT FROST

How do poems organize the miscellaneous flow of experience? How do they give shape to what is often shapeless, unsorted? First of all, poems focus our attention. Too often we are hurried, unable to pay undivided attention to any one thing. The poet asks us to slow down, to stop for a closer look. The poem, for a time, brings part of our human reality into **focus.** For instance, it may ask us to focus on a place, a person, or an event in order to fix a moment in time. The following poem is like a freeze frame capturing a picture that, though mute, has something to say to us. What does the poem make you see? What does it make you feel? What does it make you think?

WILLIAM CARLOS WILLIAMS (1883–1963)

Between Walls   1934

the back wings
of the

hospital where
nothing

will grow lie   5
cinders

in which shine
the broken

pieces of a green bottle

THE RECEPTIVE READER

1. Why do you think the poet bypassed the rest of the building and of the hospital grounds to focus your attention where he does?

2. Some of the key words in this poem are *hospital, nothing,* and *cinders.* Why are they key words? How does the poem make them stand out?

3. What is the lone touch of *color* in these lines? What does it make you feel or think?

4. This poem uses bare-minimum lines, with no chance for lush rhythms to develop. Why?

The following poem is by a poet who became well known in the eighties. What do you see in the frame the poet sets up in the poem? Is there a movement or a mental journey to give a pattern to the poem as a whole?

S H A R O N   O L D S   (born 1942)

The Possessive   1980

My daughter—as if I
owned her—that girl with the
hair wispy as a frayed bellpull

has been to the barber, that knife grinder,
and had the edge of her hair sharpened.   5

Each strand now cuts
both ways. The blade of new bangs
hangs over her red-brown eyes
like carbon steel.

        All the little   10
spliced ropes are sliced. The curtain of
dark paper-cuts veils the face that
started from next to nothing in my body—

My body. My daughter. I'll have to find
another word. In her bright helmet   15
she looks at me as if across a
great distance. Distant fires can be
glimpsed in the resin light of her eyes:

the watch fires of an enemy, a while before
the war starts.   20

This poem focuses on a crucial stage in the relationship between mother and daughter: The distance seems to be growing between mother and child. We come in at a turning point when the daughter is moving from a non-threatening wispy-hair or curly-hair stage to a new helmetlike hairdo, with bangs that remind the mother of sharpened blades, hinting at future hostility and aggressiveness. The poem leaves us with the uneasy sense of a coming confrontation. Parent and child are headed for a future where they will be like two armies, each waiting around its campfires on the evening before battle.

THE RECEPTIVE READER

1. How does hair become an issue in this poem? (What exactly did the barber do to the girl's hair?)

2. How many words in the poem remind you of *weapons* used to fend off or hurt an enemy?

3. Possessive pronouns show where or to whom something belongs: *my* daughter, *your* son, *her* briefcase. Where and how does a possessive pronoun become an issue in this poem?

THE PERSONAL RESPONSE

A sixties musical celebrating the spirit of protest of a new generation was called *Hair*. Why or how does hair become an issue in the confrontation between the generations? Do adults overreact to the hairstyles of the young?

THE CREATIVE DIMENSION

Often what lingers in the mind after we read a poem is something that appeals strongly to the visual imagination—a central image or a key metaphor (or a web of related metaphors). What did the student author of the following re-creation carry away from the poem? Do a similar brief re-creation of a central image or metaphor in this or in an earlier poem in this chapter.

> My daughter has pulled on a helmet
> as protection from sharp words.
> She hears nothing but feels
>   all.
> Her eyes look out from behind the blades
> of her new bangs.
> Behind their curtain
> she prepares for battle.

The following poem again focuses on a significant moment. A poet from the Southwest, who published a book of poems called *Hijo del Pueblo*—Son of the Pueblo, remembers an encounter that acquires a new meaning in retrospect. What is that meaning?

LEROY V. QUINTANA   (born 1944)

Legacy II   1976

Grandfather never went to school
spoke only a few words of English,
a quiet man; when he talked
talked about simple things
planting corn or about the weather   5
sometimes about herding sheep as a child.
One day pointed to the four directions
taught me their names

         El Norte
Poniente   Oriente   10
         El Sur

He spoke their names as if they were
one of only a handful of things
a man needed to know

Now I look back   15
only two generations removed
realize I am nothing but a poor fool
who went to college

trying to find my way back
to the center of the world   20
where Grandfather stood
that day

THE RECEPTIVE READER

1. *El Norte* and *El Sur* are Spanish for north and south; *Poniente* means west ("where the sun sets") and *Oriente* means east ("where the sun rises"). Poems that use the physical arrangement of words on a page to mirror meaning are often called *concrete poetry*. How does the arrangement of the Spanish names on the page help the poet make the main point of the poem?

2. How are we supposed to feel about or toward the grandfather who is at the center of this poem?

3. How does the treatment of the grandfather-grandson relationship compare with the treatment of the mother-daughter relationship in the poem by Sharon Olds?

THE PERSONAL RESPONSE

A central issue in our growing up is how we accept or reject the heritage of family tradition, regional ties, or ethnic roots. Write about your relation to one major part of your own "legacy."

JUXTAPOSITIONS ═══════════════════

To Look on Nature

The two following poems observe a similar pattern: Both focus on a scene from the natural world. This scene then inspires feelings and reflections. Both poems project human feelings and thoughts into nature's creatures, as if to break down the barrier that usually separates us from the creatures of the animal kingdom. Thomas Hardy, an English poet and novelist who had become well known by the 1880s and 1890s, wrote the first of the two following poems on the last day of the nineteenth century. During the preceding decades, there had been much questioning of traditional religious faith. What was the poet's end-of-century mood? (The thrush is a small bird known as an excellent singer.)

THOMAS HARDY (1840–1928)

The Darkling Thrush   1900

I leant upon a coppice° gate   *grove of small trees*
   When Frost was specter-gray,
And Winter's dregs made desolate
   The weakening eye of day.
The tangled bine-stems° scored the sky   *shoots of climbers*   5
   Like strings of broken lyres,°   *small (poet's) harps*
And all mankind that haunted nigh°   *near*
   Had sought their household fires.

The land's sharp features seemed to be
   The Century's corpse outleant,   10
His crypt the cloudy canopy,°   *raised cloth covering*
   The wind his death-lament.
The ancient pulse of germ and birth
   Was shrunken hard and dry,
And every spirit upon earth   15
   Seemed fervorless° as I.   *without passion*

At once a voice arose among
   The bleak twigs overhead
In a full-hearted evensong°   *sung evening prayer*
   Of joy illimited;°   *unlimited*   20
An aged thrush, frail, gaunt, and small,
   In blast-beruffled plume,°   *feathers, plumage*
Had chosen thus to fling his soul
   Upon the growing gloom.

So little cause for carolings   25
   Of such ecstatic sounds
Was written on terrestrial° things   *earthly*
   Afar or nigh around,

That I could think there trembled through
 His happy good-night air   30
Some blessed Hope, whereof he knew
 And I was unaware.

THE RECEPTIVE READER

1. Take a close look at the poet's *language:* What is "the weakening eye of day"? What is the "cloudy canopy"? What is the "ancient pulse of germ and birth"? How was the bird's plumage "blast-beruffled"?

2. Where did you expect this poem to lead you as the reader? What details help make the *setting* unpromising for what happens later in the poem?

3. Where does this poem leave you? What makes the thrush in this poem a good *symbol* for hope?

4. Which words in the poem have religious overtones or *connotations*? Do you think the poet is religious?

THE CREATIVE DIMENSION

Assume today is the last day of another century, a hundred years after Hardy wrote his poem. Write your own epitaph for the *twentieth* century.

Compare the following poem with the poem by Hardy. Compare and contrast the natural scenes the two poets bring into focus, the emotions they invite you to share, and the thoughts they inspire.

SYLVIA PLATH (1932–1963)

Frog Autumn   1959

Summer grows old, cold-blooded mother.
The insects are scant, skinny.
In these palustral° homes we only   *swampy*
Croak and wither.

Mornings dissipate in somnolence.°   *sleepiness* 5
The sun brightens tardily
Among the pithless° reeds. Flies fail us.   *weak-stemmed*
The fen° sickens.   *bog, swamp*

Frost drops even the spider. Clearly
The genius of plenitude°   *bountifulness* 10
Houses himself elsewhere. Our folk thin
Lamentably.

THE RECEPTIVE READER

1. Who is speaking in this poem? To whom? How does the choice of speaker change our usual *perspective* on life in the bog? What details make us imagine real creatures of the fen or swamp?

2. Some of the sentences in this poem are very sparse yet charged with meaning. What are some striking examples? (Why is a sparse, bare-bones sentence style appropriate to this poem?)

3. The word *lamentably* points to something to be lamented, to be mourned and deplored. How does the poet make the word stand out? How does the rest of the poem lead up to it?

THE PERSONAL RESPONSE

Do you consider the poem complete? Do you want it to go on—for instance, to find out what happens to the bog dwellers? Why or why not?

CROSS-REFERENCES—For Discussion or Writing

Many poets have turned to nature as an oracle, listening intently for its message. In this chapter, three poets—Berry, Hardy, and Plath—look in the mirror of nature and each see a different face. Compare and contrast the poets' relationship to nature in these three poems.

THE SHAPE OF THE POEM

To know one thing, you must know its opposite just as much; else you don't know that one thing.
HENRY MOORE

Each poem has its own unique shape. There is no standard formula to guide the poet's creative imagination. Nevertheless, when we look at a finished poem, we often see shaping forces at work that we recognize. The ability to focus, to concentrate, takes us a first big step toward bringing order into the bewildering flow of experience. A second organizing strategy that poets employ is intentional, purposeful **repetition**. Repetition can be thoughtless or mechanical; it then grates on our ears. Repetition is purposeful when the poet uses it to highlight, to emphasize. It is illuminating when it lines up like and like, when it confronts like and unlike.

By merely looking at the following poem from a distance, you can see that the poet repeats exactly the way each set of lines, or stanza, is laid out on the page. What are the uses of repetition in the poem?

DOROTHY PARKER (1893–1967)
Solace 1931

There was a rose that faded young;
I saw its shattered beauty hung
    Upon a broken stem.

I heard them say, "What need to care
With roses budding everywhere?"   5
     I did not answer them.

There was a bird, brought down to die;
They said, "A hundred fill the sky—
     What reason to be sad?"
There was a girl, whose lover fled;   10
I did not wait, the while they said:
     "There's many another lad."

This poem, like much poetry traditional in form, uses repetition at the most basic level to create sound patterns pleasing to the ear. End rhymes, in an interlaced rhyme scheme, mark off lines of similar length and help punctuate the poet's words. Lines with a recurrent underlying iambic meter (there WAS a ROSE that FADed YOUNG) alternate with a three-beat line (uPON a BROKen STEM). These formal features serve to reinforce a pattern of repetition that helps guide our thoughts and feelings in the poem as a whole. The same sentence frame—"*There was a* rose"; "*There was a* bird"; "*There was a* girl"—introduces each of the three parts of the poem. These sentences are **parallel** in grammatical form—a signal to the reader that the three scenarios they introduce might also be parallel in content or in meaning. And so they are—they each tell different versions of the same basic story.

THE RECEPTIVE READER

1. What is the same basic story that is repeated in the three parts of the poem? What is the reaction of the speaker in the poem?

2. Can you trace the close similarity in the way each parallel mini-event is patterned beyond the first half of the opening lines?

THE PERSONAL RESPONSE

Are you inclined to side with the "I" or the "they" of the poem?

Repetition sets up the routine of our lives. It helps us identify the constants that enable us to chart our course. Other basic patternings are similarly rooted in common human experience. For instance, our minds are prepared to see a sequence of events build up to a **climax**. We are geared to see a series of preparatory steps lead up to a high point. Clouds slowly darken the sky until a climactic thunderstorm releases crashing thunder and pouring rain. Tensions in a marriage slowly build up until they explode in a divorce. Much of what we plan and do is **cumulative**—we build on what has gone before till we reach a destination.

Look at the way the following poem builds up to a climax. (Sleepers in rural communities used to be awakened by the bugling, blaring cockadoodle-doo of the rooster stretching its neck and throwing back its head to greet the morning.)

ARCHIBALD MACLEISH (1892–1982)

The Genius 1933

Waked by the pale pink
Intimation° to the eastward, *first hint*
Cock, the prey of every beast,
Takes breath upon the hen-house rafter,
Leans above the fiery brink 5
And shrieks in brazen obscene burst
On burst of uncontrollable derisive° laughter: *contemptuous*
Cock has seen the sun! He first! He first!

THE RECEPTIVE READER

1. To build up to a *climax,* we often start slowly and in a low key. Then we gradually pile up strong and stronger details until we reach the high point. How does the poem follow this pattern? How does the poet give extra force to the high point?

2. Like earlier poems in this chapter, this poem is a striking example of *personification*—of treating objects or animals as if they were persons. The poet reads human attitudes and feelings into our cousins of the animal world. What human feelings and attitudes does he dramatize in this poem?

3. What do you think the poet meant by the *title?*

In the following poem, repetition and climactic order combine with a third organizing strategy: The poem hinges on a pivotal *but* that provides the turning point. We go from point to **counterpoint,** from statement to counterstatement.

WILLIAM MEREDITH (born 1919)

A Major Work 1958

Poems are hard to read
Pictures are hard to see
Music is hard to hear
And people are hard to love

But whether from brute need 5
Or divine energy
At last mind eye and ear
And the great sloth heart will move.

In the first four lines, the basic sentence frame ("_____ are hard to _____") is repeated four times. We sense that all four grammatically **parallel** statements are part of the same pattern. They are parallel not only in structure but also in *meaning:* Our minds are slow to grapple with a serious poem. Our eyes only slowly take in the rich texture in the painting of an old master (or puzzle over the strange shapes in the work of a modern). The untrained ear resists Beethoven. And finally, people—no less complicated than a sonnet or a sonata—are also hard to read and love.

Here, however, we come to the reversal or counterpoint: As we again look at mind, eye, ear, and heart in the same parallel order, we see them overcome resistance or inertia. When we come to the inertia-ridden and slothful "great sloth heart," we realize that the order of the four test cases was not accidental but *cumulative*. It is the slowness of the human heart to be moved to love that most concerns the poet. The last line is climactic; the poem as a whole has led up to this weighty, emphatically stressed line: "And the GREAT | SLOTH | HEART | WILL | MOVE."

THE RECEPTIVE READER

1. What does the phrase "from brute need / Or divine energy" mean?
2. If the poet were asked to spell out how, why, where, or when the "great sloth heart will move," what do you think he would say?

In much of our living and thinking, we see the play of opposites. When we can line them up as clearly defined polar opposites, we call them **polarities.** Polarities help us organize our thoughts; they help us draw our mental maps. They are built into the basic texture of our lives: man and woman, night and day, land and sea, arrival and departure, storm and calm, then and now. We chart our course between opposite poles: work and play, success and failure, dependence and independence, freedom and commitment. The following passage from the King James Bible rehearses age-old polarities that are constants in human experience.

ECCLESIASTES (3:1-8)

To every thing there is a season

To every thing there is a season, and a time to every purpose under the heaven:
A time to be born, and a time to die; a time to plant, and a time to pluck up that which
    is planted;
A time to kill, and a time to heal; a time to break down, and a time to build up;
A time to weep, and a time to laugh; a time to mourn, and a time to dance;
A time to cast away stones, and a time to gather stones together; a time to embrace,
    and a time to refrain from embracing;   5
A time to get, and a time to lose; a time to keep, and a time to cast away;
A time to rend, and a time to sew; a time to keep silence, and a time to speak;
A time to love, and a time to hate; a time of war, and a time of peace.

THE RECEPTIVE READER

Which of these opposed pairs from biblical times still play a major role in our lives? For those that seem dated or obsolete, what would be a modern counterpart?

THE CREATIVE DIMENSION

How would *you* fill in the frame "A time to . . . a time to . . ."? Write your own updated catalog of modern polarities.

The following poem lines up polar opposites in an exactly parallel pattern. Which opposing details are exceptionally neatly balanced?

JON SWAN
The Opening   1959

Seed said to flower:
    You are too rich and wide.
    You spend too soon and loosely
    That grave and spacious beauty
    I keep secret, inside.   5
    You will die of your pride.

Flower said to seed:
    Each opens, gladly
    Or in defeat. Clenched, close,
    You hold a hidden rose   10
    That will break you to be
    Free of your dark modesty.

In this poem, we listen to a dialogue between two opposed points of view. The poet allots nearly equal time to the two sides. The parallel openings ("Seed said to flower" / "Flower said to seed") are a signal that the poet's exploration of the same issue is continuing.

THE RECEPTIVE READER

As the poet presents both sides of the dialogue, which details are for you most telling or significant? In this confrontation, is there something to be said on both sides? What side is the poet on, and how can you tell? What side are you on, and why?

JUXTAPOSITIONS ═══════════════

Point and Counterpoint

Look for the uses of repetition and the play of point and counterpoint in the following poems. First, study the uses of repetition in the following lines from a longer poem by New England's first poet.

ANNE BRADSTREET   (about 1612–1672)
From *The Vanity of All Worldly Things*   1650

As he said "vanity!" so "vain!" say I,
"Oh! vanity, O vain all under sky."

Where is the man can say,° "Lo, I have found   *who can say*
On brittle earth a consolation sound"?
What is't in honor to be set on high?°   *raised to high station*   5
No, they like beasts and sons of men shall die,
And whilst they live, how oft doth turn their fate;
He's now a captive that was king of late.°   *only recently*
What is't in wealth great treasures to obtain?
No, that's but labor, anxious care, and pain.   10
He heaps up riches, and he heaps up sorrow,
It's his today, but who's his heir tomorrow?
What then? Content in pleasure canst thou find?
More vain than all, that's but to grasp the wind.
The sensual senses for a time they please,   15
Meanwhile the conscience rage, who shall appease?
What is't in beauty? No, that's but a snare,
They're foul° enough today that once were fair.   *ugly*
What is't in flowering youth or manly age?
The first is prone to vice, the last to rage.   20
Where is it then, in wisdom, learning, arts?
Sure, if on earth, it must be in those parts;
Yet these the wisest man of men did find
But vanity, vexation of mind.

THE RECEPTIVE READER

1. The poet's first line takes up the words of the preacher who repeated the biblical "Vanity of vanities; all is vanity." Can you show that the parts making up this excerpt are *parallel* both in wording and in meaning?

2. What examples of *point and counterpoint* can you find in these lines?

3. Religion in Bradstreet's time was often more demanding than in ours. How much of her outlook is strange and how much is familiar to you as a modern reader?

The second poem was written by a poet who was a collector and editor of black American poetry. What is the role of repetition and of point and counterpoint in this poem?

ARNA BONTEMPS   (1902–1973)

A Black Man Talks of Reaping   1940

I have sown beside all waters in my day.
I planted deep, within my heart the fear
That wind or fowl would take the grain away.
I planted safe against this stark, lean year.

I scattered seed enough to plant the land   5
In rows from Canada to Mexico,
But for my reaping only what the hand
Can hold at once is all that I can show.

Yet what I sowed and what the orchard yields
My brother's sons are gathering stalk and root,
Small wonder then my children glean in fields
They have not sown, and feed on bitter fruit.

10

THE RECEPTIVE READER

1. How is the central claim the speaker in this poem makes reinforced or reiterated by sentences *parallel* in form and meaning?

2. Where does the countermovement start in this poem, and how is it sustained or reinforced? (How is "gleaning" different from "reaping"?)

3. A rhyme word at the end of a line, a group of lines, or the whole poem can highlight a crucial idea and make us pause and ponder its significance. How does the poem as a whole lead up to the phrase "bitter fruit"?

4. The imaginative comparisons around which the poem is built are the harvest metaphor and the family metaphor. What gives them special force? (Do you remember any traditional lore or biblical quotations that involve sowing and reaping?)

THE CREATIVE DIMENSION

We call a heightened and compressed playing off of opposites an *antithesis*. (*Thesis* and *antithesis* are the original Greek words for statement and counterstatement.) Study the following examples of antithesis. For each, write one or more imitations (close or approximate) of your own.

1. To err is human; to forgive, divine. (Alexander Pope)
   SAMPLE IMITATION: To whine is childish; to ask, adult.

2. There are a thousand hacking at the branches of evil to one who is striking at the root. (Henry David Thoreau)
   SAMPLE IMITATION: There are a thousand correcting with red ink to one who writes an encouraging word.

3. It is a miserable state of mind to have few things to desire and many things to fear. (Sir Francis Bacon)

A SENSE OF PATTERN

The mysteries remain,
I keep the same
cycle of seed-time
and of sun and rain.
H. D. (HILDA DOOLITTLE), "THE MYSTERIES REMAIN"

A sense of pattern is in our bones. At times, the patterning that gives shape to a poem seems to be directly inspired by the patterns of nature or of ordinary human life. Sometimes the patterns that organize a poem seem to echo lived rhythms from afar. And sometimes the poet seems to play variations on, or intentionally go counter to, patterns built into common human experience. One of the constants in human experience is the daily cycle from night to dawn to noon to dusk and back to night. The title of the following poem means "dawn." In early medieval poetry, night was the friend and dawn the enemy of lovers. (In a medieval castle, a *bower* was the private room of a lady.) Ezra Pound, one of the great early moderns, often re-created the poetic styles of earlier periods in his poems.

E Z R A P O U N D (1885–1972)

Alba 1926

When the nightingale to his mate
Sings day-long and night late
My love and I keep state
In bower
In flower 5
Till the watchman on tower
Cry:
    "Up! Thou rascal, Rise,
    I see the white
      Light 10
      And the night
        Flies."

THE RECEPTIVE READER

1. How does rhyme in this poem highlight the alternation between night and day? How does it emphasize the watchman's (and the poem's) message?

2. Pound often turned to the literature of distant places and distant centuries for inspiration. In the setting of this poem, do you find yourself a total stranger?

The following poem reminds us of the cycle of the seasons, but it uses thoughts about the falling leaves of October as a springboard for reflections on the similar cycle of youth and age. Autumn with the falling of leaves is a major way station of the passing year, just as the realization of approaching age is a major way station in human life. The sumac mentioned in the poem is a shrub whose leaves turn a brilliant dark red in the fall.

K A Y B O Y L E (born 1903)

October 1954 1954

Now the time of year has come for the leaves to be burning.
October, and the months fill me with grief
For the girl who used to run with the black dogs through them,

Singing, before they burned. Light as a leaf
Her heart, and her mouth red as the sumac turning.   5

Oh, girl, come back to tell them with your bell-like singing
That you are this figure who stands alone, watching
                              the dead leaves burn.
(The wind is high in the trees, and the clang of bluejay
                              voices ringing   10
Turns the air to metal. This is not a month for anyone
                              who grieves.)
For they would say that a witch had passed in fury if
                              I should turn,
Gray-haired and brooding, and run now as once I ran   15
                              through the leaves.

THE RECEPTIVE READER

1. How does the poet focus our attention on the burning leaves? What do they stand for as a central symbol in the poem? How does the poet use *repetition* to make the key words echo through the poem?

2. How many details help develop the *polarity* of youth and age?

3. Why is October "not a month for anyone who grieves"?

THE PERSONAL RESPONSE

To some people, the cycle of the changing seasons has come to mean very little. What does it mean in your own life?

The following poem is by e. e. cummings, a poet who often seems to march to a different drummer. But he then often turns out to be exceptionally attuned to basic rhythms that shape our lives. This poem focuses on two entirely anonymous and representative people: "anyone" (somebody who could be *anyone*) and "noone" (somebody who was *no one* in particular). Noone loved anyone while other someones married those who were everybody or everything to them. (Are you keeping up with the games cummings plays with pronouns?) How does the poem trace the life cycle of "anyone" and "noone"?

E. E. CUMMINGS   (1894–1963)

anyone lived in a pretty how town   1940

anyone lived in a pretty how town
(with up so many floating bells down)
spring summer autumn winter
he sang his didn't he danced his did.

Women and men (both little and small)   5
cared for anyone not at all

they sowed their isn't they reaped their same
sun moon stars rain

children guessed (but only a few
and down they forgot as up they grew   10
autumn winter spring summer)
that noone loved him more by more

when by now and tree by leaf
she laughed his joy she cried his grief
bird by snow and stir by still   15
anyone's any was all to her

someones married their everyones
laughed their cryings and did their dance
(sleep wake hope and then) they
said their nevers they slept their dream   20

stars rain sun moon
(and only the snow can begin to explain
how children are apt to forget to remember
with up so floating many bells down)

one day anyone died i guess   25
(and noone stooped to kiss his face)
busy folk buried them side by side
little by little and was by was

all by all and deep by deep
and more by more they dream their sleep   30
noone and anyone earth by april
wish by spirit and if by yes.

Women and men (both dong and ding)
summer autumn winter spring
reaped their sowing and went their came   35
sun moon stars rain

cummings (the lower case is the original author's) is a favorite of readers
who delight in **word play.** He syncopates the English language the way a jazz
musician syncopates a melody. We hear echoes of the original melody, but they
are broken up and come back in snatches, played back against the grain. The
fourth line, for instance, might read in ordinary peoplespeak as follows: "He
sang (talked about?) what he didn't do and danced (acted out?) what he did."

The poet delights in the play of opposites, as when in the third stanza people who grow "up" forget "down." We might say in ordinary language that
women and men reaped what they had sown and that they first came into this
world but finally went from it again like everybody else. The poet (at the end
of the poem) says that they "reaped their sowing and went their came."

Embedded in the word play and repetitions like those of a nursery rhyme
are the way stations in the uneventful ordinary lives of the anonymous "anyone" and "noone." Apparently the latter loved the former, and they shared joy

and grief. "Anyone" eventually died, mourned by "noone" (who kissed his face), and they were finally buried side by side, while around them the cycles of sowing and reaping, symbolic of our life cycles, continue.

THE RECEPTIVE READER

1. The names of the four seasons echo through this poem like a *refrain* (or like a bell). Why? Why do they appear in changing, rotating order? What other set of four terms serves a similar function in the poem? How?

2. This poet delights in playing off *polarities* that make up the web of anyone's experience, such as joy and grief. What other such polarities can you find in the poem?

3. The *form* of the poem—with its simple four-line stanzas, its occasional simple or predictable rhymes, the poet's fondness for repetition—has some of the simple child-like quality of a nursery rhyme or childhood jingle. Do form and meaning go together in this poem? How?

THE PERSONAL RESPONSE

For you, is this a sad poem? a funny poem? What would you say to readers who want to dismiss it as a nonsense poem?

THE CREATIVE DIMENSION

In a Quaker reading, members of a group each take turns reading part of a text. With your classmates, do a Quaker reading of cummings' poem, perhaps changing readers at each stanza break.

JUXTAPOSITIONS

The Daily Cycle

Both of the following poems follow the ever-recurring daily cycle from dawn through noon to dusk and night. One makes us trace it in wonder and awe, as if we were the first people on earth. The other plays variations on it that are part serious, part tongue in cheek. The first poem is by a poet of Kiowa ancestry who grew up in Oklahoma; his poems often draw on the legends and ways of the tribal life of the past.

N. SCOTT MOMADAY (born 1934)

New World 1976

1.
First Man,
behold:
the earth
glitters
with leaves;   5
the sky
glistens
with rain.   2.
Pollen   At dawn   10
is borne   eagles
on winds   hie and
that low   hover
and lean   above   3.
upon   the plain   At noon   15
mountains.   where light   turtles
Cedars   gathers   enter
blacken   in pools.   slowly
the slopes—   Grasses   into   4.
and pines.   shimmer   the warm   At dusk   20
and shine.   dark loam.   the gray
Shadows   Bees hold   foxes
withdraw   the swarm.   stiffen
and lie   Meadows   in cold;
away   recede   blackbirds   25
like smoke.   through planes   are fixed
of heat   in the
and pure   branches.
distance.   Rivers
follow   30
the moon,
the long
white track
of the
full moon.   35

THE RECEPTIVE READER

    1. For people living closer to nature than we do, each stage of the day (like each stage in the cycle of the seasons) had its own characteristic feel or atmosphere. What is the morning feeling in this poem? How do the details selected by the poet conjure up the feeling of high noon? What is striking about the visual images that bring up dusk?

    2. How does the sense of an immemorial cycle that gives shape to this poem affect you as a reader? What feelings are you left with as you finish the poem?

THE CREATIVE DIMENSION

    What are the three (four? five?) stages of the day in your own present-day world? Bring them to life for your reader in a poem or prose passage.

The second poem is by an English poet of the early seventeenth century who rewrote conventions and crossed established boundaries. He was one of the **metaphysical** poets of his time, passionate, but at the same forever analyzing and rationalizing their emotions. What use does the poet make of the familiar stages of the daily cycle? How does he impose his own perspective and priorities?

JOHN DONNE (1572–1631)

A Lecture upon the Shadow

1635

Stand still, and I will read to thee
A lecture, love, in Love's philosophy.
   These three hours that we have spent
   Walking here, two shadows went
Along with us, which we ourselves produced;   5
   But, now° the sun is just above our head,   *now that*
   We do those shadows° tread,   *on those shadows*
And to brave clearness all things are reduced.
   So, whilst° our infant loves did grow,   *while*
   Disguises did and shadows flow   10
   From us and our cares,° but now 'tis not so.   *our fears*

That love hath not attained the highest degree
Which is still diligent lest others° see.   *so others won't*

Except° our loves at this noon stay,   *unless*
We shall new shadows make the other way.   15
   As the first were made to blind
   Others, these which come behind
Will work upon ourselves, and blind our eyes.
   If our loves faint and westwardly decline,
   To me thou° falsely thine,   *you . . . your* 20
And I to thee mine, actions shall disguise.
   The morning shadows wear away,
   But these grow longer all the day;
But oh, love's day is short, if love decay.

Love is a growing or full constant light,   25
And his first minute after noon is night.

THE RECEPTIVE READER

1. The shadow cast by the sun becomes the central *metaphor* in this poem. What were the shadows in the morning? (What were the "cares" and "disguises" of the morning?) What happens to the shadows at high noon? What is the crucial difference between the morning shadows and the shadows after noon?

2. How does this poem ask you to revise your usual sense of the daily cycle? What familiar associations of dawn, noon, and night does the poem preserve? How does it depart from them?

THE PERSONAL RESPONSE

How do you react to the three student-written responses that follow? Which comes closest to your own response to the poem and why? Which do you disagree with and why?

1. John Donne did not write flowery, sickening-sweet love poetry but instead took his images from areas like philosophy, botany, or astronomy. The link between the shadow and love is not a worn-out comparison like spring or a rough road. What could be less permanent or more fleeting and transitory than a shadow? Just as a day ages and changes, so do the lovers age and change, and so does their love. Naturally the sun will not obey the lovers' wants and commands. It follows a cyclical pattern: Love grows, reaches a high point, and then declines and dies. This poem leaves me unsettled. I keep getting the idea that as soon as I fall in love I better steel myself so that I will not be disappointed when the shadows reappear.

2. I like the beginning of this poem much more than the end. As the sun moves through the sky, the shadows cast according to the position of the sun change, just as love in a relationship is different when it is young and when it is tried and true. At first, we hide behind shadows or façades instead of showing our true selves, but after a while we can put our disguises away just as at noon we can walk on our shadows. However, in the afternoon, love might grow weary and turn false, with the afternoon shadows pointing forward to the night and the end of love. The reason I would rather focus on the first half of the poem is that I think love should continue to grow and build on itself. If love grows weary, making "new shadows" the other way, I don't think it was love in the first place. I have never heard a parent say: "I have fallen out of love with my children; I think I will find a more suitable child elsewhere." Would that be true love?

3. This poem takes a very intellectual approach. It fuses "reason" and "love" to create an intellectual's love poetry. The very first sentence commands his lover to "stand still" so that the speaker can give a lecture on "love's philosophy." This is an unusual way to begin a poem, since the word *lecture* makes us expect to be preached to and given a lesson. Donne seems to say that the sun can be held in check, not physically in the actual universe around us, but spiritually by an effort of our minds that preserves love's full noon. But his philosophy is an "all-or-nothing" philosophy, since the "first minute after noon" is already night. As we see the lengthening shadows and observe deceit creeping into our love, we realize our vulnerability. The lecturer sounded very cool and intellectual at the beginning, but he ends by being naked and vulnerable. Having chosen the sun as a symbol of love, what can he do to avoid the evening and night?

CROSS-REFERENCES—For Discussion or Writing

John Donne's "A Lecture upon the Shadow" and Marge Piercy's "Simple Song" (p. 455), though separated by three centuries, focus on our yearning for full and complete communication with another human being and the obstacles that defeat or thwart us in our quest. Compare and contrast the two poems.

EXPLORATIONS

Concrete Poetry

In **concrete poetry,** the external shape of the poem mirrors its meaning. The external layout—otherwise usually a simple series of lines of equal or varying length—speaks to us and makes a statement. A poem about a bell is bell-shaped; a poem about the wings of angels is printed in the shape of wings. The following poem, by a native Alaskan whose native language is Tlingit, uses many repetitions of the Tlingit word for apple (*x'aax'*) to make up the shape of an apple. At the top of the apple, we see a little squiggle making up the stem—it's the Tlingit word for stem (*akat'ani*). The poem also uses the native word for worm (*tl'ukwx̠*). Where is the worm?

NORA DAUENHAUER   (born 1927)

Tlingit Concrete Poem   1984

POEMS FOR FURTHER STUDY

In reading the following poems, pay special attention to features that give shape to the poem as a whole. For instance, where does the poem focus your attention? Is there a playing off of opposites? Is there a movement from then to now, or from question to answer? What makes the poem a complete, finished whole?

MARGE PIERCY (born 1936)

Simple Song   1968

When we are going toward someone we say
You are just like me
your thoughts are my brothers
word matches word
how easy to be together.   5

When we are leaving someone we say:
how strange you are
we cannot communicate
we can never agree
how hard, hard and weary to be together.   10

We are not different nor alike
But each strange in his leather body
sealed in skin and reaching out clumsy hands
and loving is an act
that cannot outlive   15
the open hand
the open eye
the door in the chest standing open.

THE RECEPTIVE READER

1. What is simple about this "simple song"?

2. What does the poet mean by "your thoughts are my brothers"? (Or by "word matches word"?) What are we supposed to think or feel when we are told that we are in a "leather body" and "sealed in skin"? What is the role or significance of the open hand, the open eye, the open door?

3. How does this poem use *parallelism* to line up opposites and to bond things that are similar?

4. How would you chart the overall *development* or shape of this poem?

THE CREATIVE DIMENSION

Some poems leave an exceptionally clear or compelling pattern imprinted on our minds. Choose one such poem. Can you sum up the pattern as briefly as the student author did in the following response to the Piercy poem? (Can you do so without oversimplifying?)

When we agree
I like you
we are one.
When we disagree
I don't like you
we are separate.
You are my enemy.

GARY SOTO   (born 1952)

We are beginning to see the work of **bilingual** poets—American poets who speak English as a second language or who are part of the first generation in their family to speak mainly English while another language is still the language of the home. The following poem is by a Chicano poet who grew up in a Mexican-American neighborhood in Fresno, California. One listener at one of Soto's poetry readings said that he "was funny, and humble, and touching, and completely terrific."

Oranges   1985

The first time I talked
With a girl, I was twelve,
Cold, and weighted down
With two oranges in my jacket.
December. Frost cracking   5
Beneath my steps, my breath
Before me, then gone,
As I walked toward
Her house, the one whose
Porch light burned yellow   10
Night and day, in any weather.
A dog barked at me, until
She came out pulling
At her gloves, face bright
With rouge. I smiled,   15
Touched her shoulder, and led
Her down the street, across
A used car lot and a line
Of newly planted trees,
Until we were breathing   20
Before a drugstore. We
Entered, the tiny bell
Bringing a saleslady
Down a narrow aisle of goods.
I turned to the candies   25
Tiered like bleachers
And asked what she wanted—
Light in her eyes, a smile

Starting at the corners
Of her mouth. I fingered   30
A nickel in my pocket,
And when she lifted a chocolate
That cost a dime,
I didn't say anything.
I took the nickel from   35
My pocket, then an orange,
And set them quietly on
The counter. When I looked up,
The lady's eyes met mine,
And held them, knowing   40
Very well what it was all
About.

      Outside,
A few cars hissing past,
Fog hanging like old   45
Coats between the trees.
I took my girl's hand
In mine for two blocks,
Then released it to let
Her unwrap the chocolate   50
That was so bright against
The grey of December
That, from some distance,
Someone might have thought
I was making a fire in my hands.   55

THE RECEPTIVE READER

1. This poet has an uncanny gift for recalling the small revealing details that conjure up scenes from the past. What are striking examples in this poem?

2. How does this poem develop and take shape? What is the overall pattern? What are major stages or high points? What helps the reader experience a sense of completion?

3. Gary Soto is known for poems presenting candid and bittersweet childhood memories in understated and wryly humorous fashion. How does this poem show these qualities?

JAMES LAUGHLIN   (born 1914)
Junk Mail   1986

is a pleasure to at least
one person a dear old man

in our town who is drift-
ing into irreality he

walks each morning to the   5
post office to dig the

treasure from his box he
spreads it out on the lob-

by counter and goes through
it with care and delight.   10

THE RECEPTIVE READER

1. A *vignette* is a snapshot (using words or a picture) that captures a moment in time. It makes us focus briefly on something worth attention, or it makes us look at something from a fresh perspective. Does the above vignette fit this definition?

2. Is there any movement or development in this poem? From what to what?

ROBERT FROST   (1874–1963)

Fire and Ice   1923

Some say the world will end in fire,
Some say in ice.
From what I've tasted of desire
I hold with those who favor fire.
But if I had to perish twice   5
I think I know enough of hate
To say that for destruction ice
Is also great
And would suffice.

THE RECEPTIVE READER

1. How is Frost playing off opposites in this poem? How well do fire and ice fit the emotions for which they serve as symbols in this poem?

2. How does the rhyme scheme in this poem serve to highlight the polar opposites?

THE PERSONAL RESPONSE

Where have you encountered the destructiveness of desire as a theme in your reading or viewing?

ADRIENNE RICH   (born 1929)

Novella   1967

Two people in a room, speaking harshly.
One gets up, goes out to walk.
(That is the man.)

The other goes out into the next room
and washes the dishes, cracking one.   5
(That is the woman.)
It gets dark outside.
The children quarrel in the attic.
She has no blood left in her heart.
The man comes back to a dark house.   10
The only light is in the attic.
He has forgotten his key.
He rings at his own door
and hears sobbing on the stairs.
The lights go on in the house.   15
The door closes behind him.
Outside, separate as minds,
the stars too come alight.

THE RECEPTIVE READER

1. From what perspective or vantage point are we watching the scene unfolding in this poem?

2. Many of the sentences in this poem are spare and factual. What are striking examples? Where and how do the powerful emotions involved in what we observe shine through?

3. A *novella* is a story that is shorter and more pointed than a full-length novel. Does the poet expect us to read this poem as the story of two specific individuals? Or are the people in this poem representative or even archetypal—standing for an age-old, often-repeated pattern?

4. The final two lines bring the poem to a close by serving as a summing up and last word. How?

WRITING ABOUT LITERATURE

12. The Whole Paper (From Notes to Revision)

The Writing Workshop   How does a successful paper about a poem take shape? A well-worked-out paper will not arrive on your desk ready-made. Think of your writing as a process that starts with your first reading of a poem and ends with a revised final draft. Be prepared to take a paper through overlapping stages: careful reading, note taking, thinking about the poem, planning your strategy, preparing a rough first draft, working on a more polished revision, final editing and proofreading.

Remember that false starts and blind alleys are part of a writer's day. Be prepared to change direction as necessary. Always go back to the poem itself as your main source of ideas and evidence.

Reading Notes   Suppose you are working on a paper about Marge Piercy's "Simple Song" (p. 455). Allow time for the preliminary note-taking stage. Many readers find it useful to jot down a running commentary as they work their way through a poem. Here they note key phrases and striking images, questions that arise in the reader's mind, or possible clues to the poet's intention or the larger meaning of the poem. Your **reading notes** for the poem might look like this:

> title: why "Simple Song"? Words in the poem are very simple (none need to be looked up in a dictionary)
>
> (line 5) it's "easy to be together" because they don't really see who's there
>
> second stanza is exactly parallel in layout to the first—but now we exit from the relationship
>
> (line 7) "how strange you are"—the other person was not really known to begin with
>
> (line 10) last lines in first and second stanzas are parallel: "how easy . . ."; "how hard . . ." But the same line in second stanza is longer, more drawn-out ("how hard, hard and weary . . .") to make the point of how hard and weary it is to stay together when love is gone
>
> (line 12) "leather body"—leather used as a protection since early times; it's tough, more impenetrable than human skin
>
> (line 17) the "open eye"—we really see others for what they are?
>
> (line 18) "door in the chest standing open"—willingness to let someone in

Reading Journal   A journal entry will often record your interpretation of a poem—the way you make sense of it—and your more personal reaction. It may also note your queries—your attempts to puzzle out difficult passages, your tentative answers to unsolved questions. In your paper, you will then be able to draw on some of the more unstructured and informal material in your journal. A journal entry for the Piercy poem might look as follows:

> I felt in reading this poem that most people operate exactly the way the first ten lines of this poem describe. In the early stages of courtship, all is euphoria. People focus on everything they can share and agree on. They say, "how easy to be together." Then they slowly let down their guard. They let their differences come to the surface; they become impatient with each other. They start calling each other weird and "strange." Getting along becomes "hard, hard and weary." Although this poem seems to talk mainly about romantic or sexual relationships, I believe the pattern applies to friendships as well.

Planning the Paper   Even while taking notes and recording tentative reactions, you will be thinking about how to lay out your material in a paper. You will be pushing toward an overall impression or keynote—a key idea or ideas that will make your details add up. You will be sketching out a master plan—the major stages through which you will take your reader. Give special thought to the following way stations in the itinerary to be traveled by your reader:

✧ *Introduction, or lead*   How are you going to attract and focus the attention of your reader? You may want to lead your readers into the poem from a biographical fact, such as a revealing detail about the poet's war experience or family history that could serve to illuminate the poem. You may want to start with a striking quote from the poet, illuminating his or her intention. You may want to dramatize the setting or the time, vividly re-creating the context of the poem.

✧ *Overview*   What is going to be your central focus? If possible, let a graphic, vivid introduction lead your readers directly to your main point. State it as your **thesis** and then devote your paper to developing and supporting it. A thesis sums up in a short, memorable statement what the paper as a whole is trying to prove. (Sometimes, however, you will prefer to raise a question to be pondered by the reader and to be answered by the paper as a whole. Or you may want to state a tentative claim or working hypothesis to be tested or modified by your paper.)

Give the kind of preview or overview here that will point your readers in the right direction. Help them find their bearings. Often a thesis statement already broadly hints at the major stages in the writer's master plan. It furnishes the reader with a capsule itinerary for the journey ahead.

✧ *Plan*   How are you going to follow up your thesis? For the body of a short paper, try to sketch out a three-step or four-point plan to serve as your grand design. Make sure that you arrive at a clear agenda: first this, next this, then that. Highlight the transitions from one major point or stage to the next, so your readers will not get lost in detail. Signal turning points, crucial objections, clinching arguments: "on the other hand"; "readers hostile to easy answers may object . . ."; "however, such objections will carry much less weight when we realize. . . ."

Often the way the poem itself takes shape will provide a tentative blueprint for all or part of your paper. The "Simple Song" poem swings from the extreme of euphoria, of being blissfully and uncritically in love, to the opposite extreme of sour disappointment and failure to communicate. We may well look to the third and last part of the poem for some middle ground, or for some lesson to be learned, or for some sort of answer. The paper, like the poem, could go from point to counterpoint and then toward some kind of resolution.

✧ *Follow-up*   Whatever your claims or generalizations, remember that each general statement you make is a promise to your readers: "This is what I claim, and here is the evidence to support it." Much of your text should show a rich texture of quotation, explication (close, careful explanation), and interpretation. Choose brief revealing quotations (but don't rip them out of context, omitting essential ifs and buts). Explain what your quotations say and how they say it; explore their overtones and implications. Relate them to the larger context of the poem: What role do they play in the poem as a whole?

✧ *Conclusion* End on a strong note. Pull together essentials of your argument. Put them in the perspective of today, or of your own experience, or of the readers' lives. Or relate the individual poem to the larger patterns of the poet's work. Aim for a wrap-up or a clincher sentence that your readers will remember.

✧ *Title* Writers are often content with a dull working title while drafting a paper ("Structure in Marge Piercy's 'Simple Song'"). Then, first things last, they hit on the title that is both informative and provocative. An effective title is serious enough to do justice to the topic but also interesting enough to beckon to the reader. A thought-provoking quote can attract the reader's attention. A play on a key word or an allusion to a figure from myth or legend can make a title stand out from the mass of unread material that harried readers pass by each day.

Read the following student paper to see how it lives up to the criteria sketched in these guidelines.

SAMPLE STUDENT PAPER

The Real Act of Love

In her introduction to *Circle on the Water,* a book of her selected poems, Marge Piercy writes that a poem should "function for us in the ordinary chaos of our lives." Her intention in writing her poems is to "give voice to something in the experience of life. . . . To find ourselves spoken for in art gives dignity to our pain, our anger, our lust, our losses."

Her poem "Simple Song" achieves these goals for me. The poem asks us to face the most terrifying and difficult of human activities: loving another person and opening ourselves to love in return. The title promises us a "simple song." The simplicity promised in the title is carried out in the three-part structure of the poem and conveyed in its simple language. By focusing on the essentials of a very complex issue, the poem helps us see first the lacking sense of reality and second the inevitable alienation that defeats us when we "reach out" to others. It then takes us to a third stage that explains the dilemma and may offer a way out.

The poem filters out all intermediate stages to focus on the two phases that are like turning points in our lives: "going toward" and "leaving." The first group of five lines makes us feel the sweetness and newness of someone we have just met. This is the state of falling in love when we feel totally in harmony with the other person. We say, "You are just like me / your thoughts are my brothers / word matches word / how easy to be together." We feel we have found the perfect soulmate, who thinks and speaks like us.

However, anyone with experience can already forecast the exact opposite stage. In the next set of five lines, we are leaving. The other person has become "strange": "we cannot communicate / we can never agree / how hard, hard and weary to be together." Here we have a feeling of loss, a feeling of confusion and defeat as for some reason we stop loving. The lines in this second stanza are arranged in parallel fashion to those in the first; they serve as a mirror image to those in the first. "You are just like me" turns into "how strange you are." "Word matches word" turns into "we cannot communicate." These contrasting lines give us a clue that maybe our "going toward" was not a clear-eyed move but at least in part self-deception. It did not make allowance for hard times or unexpected problems. Did we know the person whom we told "your thoughts are my brothers" in any real sense?

The last stanza moves beyond the dilemma that confronts us in the first two stanzas and points toward a possible solution to our confusion and pain. The first three lines of the stanza say, "We are not different nor alike / But each strange in his leather body / sealed in skin and reaching out clumsy hands." Our problem is not that we are different from each other. We are all "strange." We are each in a leather body, which sounds tough, isolated from human touch like an animal. To be "sealed in skin" sounds sterile, like being put in a vacuum plastic pouch. We are impenetrable, isolated human beings, groping for contact with "clumsy hands." But we are too thick-skinned to let in another in order to know the soft-skinned person inside the leather covering.

The last five lines may be pointing to a course between the polar opposites of uncritical acceptance and resentful rejection. The poem says, "loving is an act / that cannot outlive / the open hand / the open eye / the door in the chest standing open." The image of the open hand may imply an opening up of our fist to show what's there and let the other person see who we really are. But it may also imply the willingness to accept what the other person has to offer, without illusions that we create about the other person in our minds. The "open eye" implies willingness to see others as they really are, to see that rarely does "word match word" and that it not "easy to be together" on a continuous basis. We have to risk the open door if we do not want to be satisfied with the less fearful business of having someone fill a temporary need for companionship.

The type of love in the first stanza cannot last because it makes us imagine a perfect merging of people who are really unique and strange. When we exaggerate everything we have in common, we already program ourselves for the disappointment acted out in the second stanza. I read a book recently that talks about a "matching game"—trying to build a relationship on everything that makes two people alike. The real key is to teach our "clumsy hands" to be more accepting of what makes us different. This way we can be in love with a real person rather than with a creation of our own minds.

QUESTIONS

How effectively do title and introduction lead toward the main point of the paper? What overview or preview does the paper provide—how effectively does it prepare you for what is to come? How clear does the structure or shape of the poem become to the reader? What important details stand out, and how well does the writer explain them? What does the conclusion do that the rest of the paper has not already done? Where do you agree and where do you part company with the student writer?

A Checklist for Revision   It is usually ill-advised to complete a first draft and act as if it were a finished paper. If at all possible, let your draft lie on your desk or sit in your computer. To revise and polish your paper, you will need some distance, some perspective. For a day or two, enjoy the relief of having pulled your material into preliminary shape. Then reread your first draft. Look at it through the reader's eye. Ask yourself questions like the following:

1. Is the introduction too colorless and dutiful? Does it say things like "In this paper, I will examine important similarities and differences between two poems"? When revising, dramatize and highlight one key difference or similarity to give your readers a foretaste of what your paper will cover.

2. Does your paper have a clear enough focus? Can you point to a sentence that spells out in so many words your main point or your overall perspective? Does it stand out as a **thesis statement** early in your paper or as a well-earned conclusion at the end?

3. Does your preview or overview give your readers enough of a sense of direction? For instance, does it alert your readers that your paper will be built around a contrast of then and now, or around a turning from dejection to a renewal of hope?

4. As your paper develops, is your master plan clear enough to your readers? Revision is your chance to smooth out apparent detours, backtrackings, or leads that lead nowhere. Can you sum up your strategy in a three-point or four-point (maybe a five-point) outline? If not, try to streamline your overall plan of organization.

5. Do you signal major way stations in your paper clearly enough? (Try not to make your readers slog through an unmarked, uncharted line-by-line reading.) Check for lame **transitions** like "also" or "another point we might mention." Spell out why the next point is the logical next step in your paper. For instance, does it introduce clinching evidence for a claim you made earlier? Does it raise an important objection? Does it defuse charges by others who disagree with you?

6. Do you make enough use of striking, revealing quotations? Do you use striking short quotations early enough in the paper to get the reader into the spirit of the poem (or poems)? For example, in writing about Gwendolyn Brooks' poem "Truth," do you early in the paper make your readers hear "the fierce hammering" of the knuckles of Truth on the door, awakening the people sheltered in the "propitious haze" of unawareness?

7. Do you tie your personal reactions closely enough to a detailed reading of the text? Or are you using isolated phrases and images as a launching pad to spin you out on mental journeys of your own? When you make much of a key word or a key line of the poem, make sure you pay attention to how it works in the context of the poem as a whole.

8. Have you found the happy medium between a hyperformal and a supercasual use of words? Make sure the language of a poem, alive with image and rhythm, does not clash with your own stodgy, overwritten impersonal style. ("A deep look at the whole poem gives overwhelming reference to the plight of alienation and illuminates the poet's transcendent purpose.") Skirt the opposite extreme of discussing a poem about humanity's spiritual quest in the language in which you would ask for pretzels in the pub. ("Wait a minute! I thought this was a poem about a spider!")

9. Does your conclusion bring your paper to a satisfying close? Does it leave your readers with a point, an image, or a question to remember? Revise a conclusion that will seem too interchangeable—saying things that could be said about many different poems. ("This poem asks readers to be more aware of their environment and to be more critical of themselves.") Make sure your conclusion sounds as if it were custom-made for your subject today, for a specific poem or poems.

13 IMAGE
The Open Eye

Great literature, if we read it well, opens us up to the world. It makes us more sensitive to it, as if we acquired eyes that could see through things and ears that could hear smaller sounds.

DONALD HALL

FOCUS ON IMAGE

Poets take you into a world of images. An **image** is a vividly imagined detail that speaks to your sense of sight, hearing, smell, taste, or touch. Poets expect you to read their poems with open eyes and willing ears. They write with a heightened awareness, making you take in more of the world around you than people do who see only the stretch of asphalt in front of their cars. Poets ask you to look, to marvel at what you see. It is as if the poet were clearing a fogged-over windshield to help you take a closer look at your world—to take in the texture and shape of clouds, the look on faces in the crowd, the dartings and peckings of birds.

The following poem centers on a memorable image. It asks you focus on and take in a striking sight. If you let it, the central image in this poem will etch itself on your memory. It will start a chain of associations activating disturbing thoughts and feelings. It may come back to haunt you at unexpected moments.

WILLIAM STAFFORD (born 1914)
At the Bomb Testing Site   1960

member of United Brethren
Conscientious objector during WW II

At noon in the desert a panting lizard
waited for history, its elbows tense,
watching the curve of a particular road
as if something might happen.

465

It was looking for something farther off *— looking at life*   5
than people could see, an important scene
acted in stone for little selves
at the flute end of consequences.

There was just a continent without much on it
under a sky that never cared less.   10
Ready for a change, the elbows waited.
The hands gripped hard on the desert.

This poem begins and ends with the sight the poet calls up before our eyes: the panting watchful lizard, its elbows tense, gripping the desert floor hard with its hands, surrounded by the empty desert (like a "continent without much on it"), under the empty uncaring cloudless sky. This is a striking image, and the poet takes the time to let it sink in.

At the same time, as often with poetic images, there is more to the lizard than meets the eye. Our first hint is that the panting lizard "waited for history." We *are* at a bomb testing site. Something disastrous might happen to the desert life at any moment. The lizard, part of life that has existed on this earth for untold millions of years, might presently perish in the blinding flash of a nuclear holocaust.

From there the chain of associations and forebodings will take each of us to our own personal version of the distant "important scene" at the "flute end of consequences"—where our common history will be channeled as toward the end of a flute toward its final destination. We each will have our own version of the journey to the time when both the lizard and we ourselves will be history, destroyed by the self-important machinations of our busybody johnny-come-lately species. However, whatever our fears or speculations, we are left to ponder the image of the lizard, survivor from the dim prehistoric past, now endangered. The poem does not preach; the image of the lizard is mute and eloquent at the same time.

THE RECEPTIVE READER

1. Does it make any difference to the poem as a whole that the time is noon? that the lizard is watching a curve in the road? Why is the "important scene" in the future acted out for "little selves"?

2. For many people, lizards, like other reptiles, seem alien, remote from human beings in the chain of evolution. For you, does the lizard make a good central image for this poem? Why or not? (What for you would have been a better choice?)

VISUAL AND OTHER IMAGES

*Images in verse are not mere decoration, but the very
essence of an intuitive language.*
                                        T. E. HULME

*It is better to present one image in a lifetime than to
produce voluminous works.*
                                        EZRA POUND

*I am an instrument in the shape
of a woman trying to translate pulsations
into images*
                        ADRIENNE RICH, "PLANETARIUM"

Vivid and thought-provoking imagery satisfies what for many modern readers is the test of true poetry: A poem should not merely verbalize ideas but translate ideas and feelings into graphic images. It should not tell us about an experience but act it out for us. It should not take inventory of feelings but make us share in them. Look for the striking visual images in the following poem. What does the poem make you see? What does it make you feel? What does it make you think?

MARY OLIVER (born 1935)

The Black Snake   1979

When the black snake
flashed onto the morning road,
and the truck could not swerve—
death, that is how it happens.

Now he lies looped and useless   5
as an old bicycle tire.
I stop the car
and carry him into the bushes.

He is as cool and gleaming
as a braided whip, he is as beautiful and quiet   10
as a dead brother.
I leave him under the leaves

and drive on, thinking,
about *death:* its suddenness,
its terrible weight,   15
its certain coming. Yet under

reason burns a brighter fire, which the bones
have always preferred.
It is the story of endless good fortune.
It says to oblivion: not me!   20

It is the light at the center of every cell.
It is what sent the snake coiling and flowing forward
happily all spring through the green leaves before
he came to the road.

The speaker in this poem is thinking about what keeps us going in face of the knowledge that disaster may strike. Death may lurk at any turn in the road. (The one thing sure about death is its "certain coming.") However, the person speaking does her thinking in vivid images. The poem focuses on the black snake—which has to become real for us if the poem is to carry its true weight. We need to imagine the snake as it moves "happily . . . through the green leaves" until it meets sudden death in the road. Perhaps then we will be ready to say with the poet: "That is how it happens." The snake apparently is not some alien creature "out there." *We* are like the snake, moving through life merrily until of a sudden something terrible overtakes us. We feel the "terrible weight" of that knowledge.

Paradoxically, however, the poem will leave many readers not with the image of the dead snake but with the image of the live snake moving "happily all spring through the green leaves." The poem does not move from life to death but from the experience of death to an affirmation of life. To keep going, we have to believe that we are special and therefore deserving of survival. When oblivion threatens to erase the memory of our existence, we feel deep down: "not me!" Deep down we believe in "endless good fortune." This faith in our own invulnerability enables us to say no to "oblivion"—to the inevitable future when we will be forgotten.

THE RECEPTIVE READER

1. What graphic images make you see the way the snake moved when it was alive? What images help you see the way it looked after it had been hit?

2. How is what "reason" says in this poem different from what people know (or prefer to believe) in their "bones"? What striking image helps you visualize the intense vital energy of that knowledge?

3. What is "the light at the center of every cell"? What do you know about cells that can help you understand this phrase and its role in the poem?

THE PERSONAL RESPONSE

Does it strike you as strange that both Stafford and Oliver choose a reptilian for the central image in a poem raising questions about life and death?

By *image*, we usually mean a picture we see with the mind's eye. However, we also use the word more generally for any detail that speaks to our senses, whether of sight, hearing, smell, taste, or touch. Most poetic images are visual images—something we can see the way we look in a mirror and see an image of ourselves. However, others are sound images, like the rustling of leaves or the pounding of the surf. Still others are taste images—like the sourness of a lemon that makes the mouth pucker. Still others might be touch images, like the sensation we feel when we run our fingers over the rough bark of a tree.

The images we grasp with our senses make poetry **concrete**—they bring our eyes and ears and nerve ends into play. Concrete, sensory details take us into a world of sights, sounds, smells, tastes, and sensations. Concrete details are at the opposite end of the spectrum from **abstract** ideas. Abstract ideas like happiness, freedom, and honor "draw us away" from concrete experience toward large categories and general labels. The American poet Theodore Roethke had a special gift for using the image-making language of poetry to re-create the rich texture of sensory experience. In the following poem, Roethke uses visual images, but he also uses images that speak strongly to other senses. What does the poem make you see? And how does the poet go *beyond* visual images to include other kinds of sensory detail? What sensations and feelings does the boy experience?

THEODORE ROETHKE (1908–1963)

My Papa's Waltz

1948

The whiskey on your breath
Could make a small boy dizzy;
But I hung on like death:
Such waltzing was not easy.

We romped until the pans   5
Slid from the kitchen shelf;
My mother's countenance
Could not unfrown itself.

The hand that held my wrist   10
Was battered on one knuckle;
At every step you missed
My right ear scraped a buckle.

You beat time on my head
With a palm caked hard by dirt,
Then waltzed me off to bed   15
Still clinging to your shirt.

THE RECEPTIVE READER

1. What does this poem make you see? What details in the poem bring senses *other* than sight into play?

2. What helps you put yourself in the boy's place? Where and how do *you* share in what the boy sensed and felt?

THE RANGE OF INTERPRETATION

Many readers find that this poem makes them relive the experience but does not really tell them what to make of it. Critics have read the poem different ways. *Romp* is usually an approving word; it makes us think of a happy, boisterous, energetic kind of running or dancing. Do you think the boy liked the romp in this poem? As he looks back, how does the speaker in the poem feel about his father? Is he critical of the father? Or is he expressing feelings of love for him?

EXPLORATIONS

The Range of Imagery

The following poem starts out to give general advice but almost immediately begins translating it into striking imagery. Which images are visual, and which represent other kinds?

ANN DARR (born 1920) - writer/actress

Advice I Wish Someone Had Given Me

1971

Be strange if it is necessary, be
quiet, kindly as you can without
feeling the heel marks on your head.
Be expert in some way that pleasures
you, story-telling, baking, bed;   5
marvel at the marvelous
in leaves, stones, intercepted light;   narrator has been hurt
put truth and people in their right-   stepped on
full angle in the sun . . . find the shadow,
what it falls upon.   10
Trust everyone a little, no one much.
Care carefully.   - be cautious
Thicken your skin to hints and hurts, be
allergic to the soul scrapers.
            ← big hurt — confessional poem
                        giving advice

THE RECEPTIVE READER

1. Explain the striking *visual* images in this poem. How would we put "truth and people in their right- / full angle in the sun"? What is the "shadow" that we are asked to find?

2. Which images are visual while at the same time bringing bodily *sensations* into play? What sensations are we made to experience by the "heel marks" (and what caused them)? Who are the "soul scrapers"? What sensations or feelings does the phrase bring into play?

3. What is contradictory or paradoxical about the *play on words* in "Care carefully"? Does this piece of advice make sense to you? Does any of the advice in this poem have a special meaning for you?

4. This poet makes minimal and somewhat unusual use of *rhyme*. How?

IMAGES AND FEELINGS

*If. . . it makes my whole body so cold no fire can ever
warm me, I know* that *is poetry. If I feel physically as if the
top of my head were taken off, I know* that *is poetry.*
                                            EMILY DICKINSON

Poetic images have the power to stir our emotions. At times, the poet may
seem to adopt the stance of the neutral, unemotional reporter. The poet's eye
then is the objective camera eye, recording dispassionately what it sees. However, many poems travel without warning from what the poet saw to what the
poet felt and thought. The scene we find ourselves reenacting in the following
poem has the hallucinatory intensity of a dream. What feeling or feelings does
it invite you to share?

URSULA K. LE GUIN (born 1929)

The Old Falling Down   1988

In the old falling-down
house of my childhood
I go down-
stairs to sleep out-
side on the porch   5
under stars and dream
of trying to go up-
stairs but there are no
stairs so I climb
hand over hand clambering   10
scared and when I get there
to my high room, find
no bed, no chair, bare floor.

THE RECEPTIVE READER

1. What for you is the dominant *emotion* in this poem? (Does it make you share in
mixed or contradictory emotions?) What haunting images create the emotional effect?

2. What is the difference between "climbing" and "clambering"?

3. Several split or *divided words* in this poem make us move on from the end of a
line to the next without the break or rest we would normally expect. Do you see any connection between this extra effort required of the reader and the subject of the poem?

THE CREATIVE DIMENSION

Do you recognize the feeling or feelings pervading this poem? Have you ever had a
similar dream? Write a passage (or poem) about a haunting and perhaps recurrent
dream.

Poets vary greatly in how fully they signal their emotions. Often, like Theodore Roethke in "My Papa's Waltz," they let the experience speak for itself. Whether the boy in the poem felt a sickening fear or a mad dizzy joy is for our own emotional antennas to pick up. Contrast the Roethke poem with another father-son poem by Robert Hayden, who in other poems has written eloquently about the heritage of African-Americans. What feelings does the poet express in response to the scenes he dramatizes in this poem?

ROBERT HAYDEN (1913–1980)

Those Winter Sundays   1962

Sundays too my father got up early,
and put his clothes on in the blueblack cold,
then with cracked hands that ached
from labor in the weekday weather made
banked fires blaze. No one ever thanked him.   5

I'd wake and hear the cold splintering, breaking.
When the rooms were warm, he'd call,
and slowly I would rise and dress,
fearing the chronic angers of that house.

Speaking indifferently to him,   10
who had driven out the cold
and polished my good shoes as well.
What did I know, what did I know
of love's austere and lonely offices?

held back – self denying

In this poem, the poet makes us suffer the bitter cold by appealing to our senses of sight and touch. We can visualize the "blueblack cold" and feel the "cracked hands that ached." When the blazing fire drives out the icy cold, our sense of hearing is brought into play: As the blazing wood shifts and splits, we seem to "hear the cold splintering, breaking." Speaking of his father, the poet early sounds a note of regret: "No one ever thanked him." Frightened by the constant angry quarrels in his parents' house, the boy acted indifferent, retreating into a shell. He never responded to the love the father showed by the "lonely offices" or services of every day.

THE RECEPTIVE READER

1. As the poet steers your emotions in this poem, what are your feelings toward the lonely father?

2. The word *austere* means being self-denying but at the same time being proud to be so, holding aloof. How does this key word fit into the poem?

3. Why does the poet repeat the question "What did I know?" in the next to the last line of the poem?

THE CREATIVE DIMENSION

Most of us can think of an occasion or person that we did not appreciate properly. We remember lost opportunities, occasions for regret. Write a passage or poem on the theme of "What did I know, what did I know."

JUXTAPOSITIONS

The Sense of Place

Both of the following poems take you to a place to which the poet has strong emotional ties. What images make the setting real for you? How do the poets communicate their feelings? Can you share in the feelings expressed in these poems?

WILLIAM STAFFORD (born 1914)

One Home   1963

Mine was a Midwest home—you can keep your world.
Plain black hats rode the thoughts that made our code.
We sang hymns in the house; the roof was near God.

The light bulb that hung in the pantry made a wan light,
but we could read by it the names of preserves—   5
outside, the buffalo grass, and the wind in the night.

A wildcat sprang at Grandpa on the Fourth of July
when he was cutting plum bushes for fuel,
before Indians pulled the West over the edge of the sky.

To anyone who looked at us we said, "My friend";   10
liking the cut of a thought, we could say, "Hello."
(But plain black hats rode the thoughts that made our code.)

The sun was over our town; it was like a blade.
Kicking cottonwood leaves we ran toward storms.
Wherever we looked the land would hold us up.   15

THE RECEPTIVE READER

1. What striking images put us in the Midwest that was the poet's home? Where do the poet's feelings about the land show? Where do his feelings about the people show? How?

2. Like much earlier traditional poetry, this twentieth-century poem is divided into *stanzas*, or sets of lines that each follow a similar pattern, like the verses of a song. Can you show that each stanza (or almost each stanza) focuses on one dimension or aspect of the midwestern tradition or mentality that is the subject of this poem?

3. In some songlike poems, the same line (or group of lines) comes back in each stanza as a *refrain*. In this poem, a key line is repeated only once. Why is it important enough for the poet to repeat it?

4. This poem makes some limited, low-key use of rhyme. Where and how? The poem also uses lines of roughly similar length, with a steady underlying beat. Can you find some lines that have a clear five-beat rhythm? (Note that usually *more than one* unstressed syllable comes between beats.) Why is it not surprising that this poet would like a style that is low-key but has a steady underlying beat?

The second poem about a favorite place takes us to the now-empty and fenced-in lots under a raised freeway in California, with the small houses gone and the fruit trees and vegetable patches running wild. The Hispanic poet talking here about childhood scenes slides from English into Spanish (the language of her childhood) and back, moving easily between two languages like other bilingual Americans.

LORNA DEE CERVANTES   (born 1954)
Freeway 280   1981

Las casitas° near the gray cannery	*the little houses*
nestled amid wild abrazos° of climbing roses	*hugs*
and man-high red geraniums	
are gone now. The freeway conceals it	
all beneath a raised scar.	5
But under the fake windsounds of the open lanes,	
in the abandoned lots below, new grasses sprout,	
wild mustard remembers, old gardens	
come back stronger than they were,	
trees have been left standing in their yards.	10
Albaricoqueros, cerezos, nogales° . . .	*apricot, cherry, walnut*
Viejitas° come here with paper bags to gather greens.	*little old women*
Espinaca, verdolagas, yerbabuena° . . .	*spinach, purslane, mint*
I scramble over the wire fence	
that would have kept me out.	15
Once, I wanted out, wanted the rigid lanes	
to take me to a place without sun,	
without the smell of tomatoes burning	
on swing shift in the greasy summer air.	
Maybe it's here	20
en los campos extranos de esta ciudad°	*in the strange fields of this city*
where I'll find it, that part of me	
mown under	
like a corpse	
or a loose seed.	25

THE RECEPTIVE READER

1. What is the "raised scar"? What are the "windsounds," and why are they "fake"? How does the poet feel about the freeway?

2. How did the poet feel about this setting when she grew up there? What role

did the cannery play in her childhood or adolescence?

3. What are her feelings as she returns to this setting? What does she mean when she says that "wild mustard remembers"?

4. Students of language use the term *code-switching* for shifting from one language, or linguistic code, to the other. At what points in the poem does the poet shift back to the Spanish of her childhood? What might have been lost if she had used the literal English translations here printed in the margin?

THE PERSONAL RESPONSE

Do you think the part of the poet (or of her past) that was "mown under" will prove a "corpse" or a "seed"? What images of continuing growth earlier in this poem might help you answer this question?

THE CREATIVE DIMENSION

Most people have intense personal associations—positive or negative—with a childhood setting that may haunt them in their dreams. Write a poem or prose passage about a childhood setting or favorite place recalled in vivid memories or revisited in a dream.

POETRY AND PARAPHRASE

I think that the one thing that's been consistently true about my poetry is this determination to get authenticity of detail.

MAXINE KUMIN

For many modern poets, insisting on concrete images, anchored in authentic firsthand observation, has been a safeguard against secondhand ideas. They are likely to speak in vivid images even when making a general point about life or about people. They are likely to remind us that the poem and a prose translation, or **paraphrase,** are not the same. Look at the relation between idea and image in the following example.

KENNETH REXROTH (born 1905)

Trout

[handwritten margin note: - nature poems, lived in the mountains of California, self educated 1956]

The trout is taken when he
Bites an artificial fly.
Confronted with fraud, keep your
Mouth shut, and don't volunteer.

How is fraud like fishing for trout? What would be lost if this poet had given us only the last two lines? The trout is totally without guile, going about its legitimate business as nature prompts it. People producing the artificial fly used in trout fishing invest great ingenuity and resourcefulness in producing something to fool an unsuspecting victim that has done them no harm. By dramatizing the relationship between the perpetrator and the victim of fraud, the poet makes us "see it feelingly"; we know how it feels to be hooked.

In a paraphrase, we put someone else's ideas into our own words, thus making sure we understand the plain literal meaning. But we must try not to reduce something that was alive with human feelings and purposes to a residue of inert ideas. We can often paraphrase a poem to extract its prose meaning, but in the process much of what the poem does to involve our senses, our hearts, and our minds is likely to be lost. In reading the following poem, pay special attention to the images that make the speaker's thoughts and feelings real for us. What makes the poem different from the paraphrase that follows it?

EDNA ST. VINCENT MILLAY (1892–1950)

Childhood Is the Kingdom Where Nobody Dies   1937

Childhood is not from birth to a certain age and at a certain age
The child is grown, and puts away childish things.
Childhood is the kingdom where nobody dies.

Nobody that matters, that is. Distant relatives of course
Die, whom one never has seen or has seen for an hour,   5
And they gave one candy in a pink-and-green striped bag, or a jack-knife,
And went away, and cannot really be said to have lived at all.

And cats die. They lie on the floor and lash their tails,
And their reticent fur is suddenly all in motion
With fleas that one never knew were there,   10
Polished and brown, knowing all there is to know,
Trekking off into the living world.
You fetch a shoe-box, but it's much too small, because she won't curl up now:
So you find a bigger box, and bury her in the yard, and weep.

But you do not wake up a month from then, two months,   15
A year from then, two years, in the middle of the night
And weep, with your knuckles in your mouth, and say Oh, God! Oh, God!
Childhood is the kingdom where nobody dies that matters,—mothers and fathers
    don't die.

And if you have said, "For heaven's sake, must you always be kissing a person?"
Or, "I do wish to gracious you'd stop tapping on the window with your thimble!"   20
Tomorrow, or even the day after tomorrow if you're busy having fun,
Is plenty of time to say, "I'm sorry, mother."

To be grown up is to sit at the table with people who have died, who neither listen nor
    speak;
Who do not drink their tea, though they always said
Tea was such a comfort.   25

Run down into the cellar and bring up the last jar of raspberries;
    they are not tempted.
Flatter them, ask them what was it they said exactly
That time, to the bishop, or to the overseer, or to Mrs. Mason;
They are not taken in.
Shout at them, get red in the face, rise,   30
Drag them up out of their chairs by their stiff shoulders and shake them and yell
    at them;
They are not startled, they are not even embarrassed;
    they slide back into their chairs.

Your tea is cold now.
You drink it standing up,
And leave the house.   35

A short prose paraphrase of the flow of thought in this poem might read like this:

> Childhood is not a matter of chronology; we leave it behind when we become aware of the reality of death. During childhood, death is not real. Death is not real when distant relatives die whom we have known only from short visits. Childhood pets die and are buried, but they do not cause wild passionate grief that lasts for months and years. Our childhood continues as long as our parents are spared and there is plenty of time to apologize and make amends after a temporary estrangement. We know that we have passed from childhood to adulthood when we are forced to accept the fact that people who were close to us and part of our lives are gone forever. They and their familiar mannerisms may be so vivid in our memories that they may seem to be in the room with us, but we are forever cut off from communicating with them. We find ourselves alone in an empty house; we have no reason to linger there to be with someone close to us.

This paraphrase can serve as a chart to the poet's thoughts, but we must remember that it is different from the real poem, just as a map of a river is different from the river. In the paraphrase, the relatives, the pets, the parents, and grief for their loss all remain abstractions, as different from the living currency of thought and feeling as the figures in a checkbook are from the actual currency we spend.

THE RECEPTIVE READER

What striking images make the relatives and childhood perceptions of them real for the reader? What graphic, unexpected images dramatize the death of childhood pets? What images make the speaker's grief real when people die who "matter"? How does the poet dramatize the feeling of being cut off from human contact with the dead?

THE PERSONAL RESPONSE

Millay was widely admired in her day but fell from favor when critical trends encouraged distance and control in the expression of personal emotions. Feminist critics today praise her as women writers increasingly use poetry as a medium for coming to terms with intensely felt personal experience. How do you respond to the emotions expressed in this poem?

POEMS FOR FURTHER STUDY

In reading the following poems, pay special attention to imagery that brings a scene or a natural setting to life for the reader. How does it appeal to the senses? What does it do for the reader?

PETER MEINKE   (born 1932)

Sunday at the Apple Market   1977

Apple-smell everywhere!
Haralson   McIntosh   Fireside   Rome
old ciderpresses weathering in the shed
old ladders tilting at empty branches
boxes and bins of apples by the cartload   5
yellow and green and red
piled crazy in the storehouse barn
miraculous profusion, the crowd
around the testing table laughing rolling
the cool applechunks in their mouths   10
dogs barking at children in the appletrees
couples holding hands, so many people

out in the country carrying bushels
and baskets and bags and boxes of apples
to their cars, the smell of apples   15
making us for one Sunday afternoon free
and happy as people must have been meant to be.

THE RECEPTIVE READER

1. What are striking realistic details that only an observer who knows the scene well could have noticed? What senses *other* than sight does the poem bring into play? Which images in this poem stay with you after you finish reading?

2. Some poems early strike a *keynote* that sets the tone and recurs through the poem like the tolling of a bell. What is the keynote in this poem, and how does it echo through the poem?

THE PERSONAL RESPONSE

Why does the apple market become a symbol of happiness for the poet? Are you the kind of person who would have shared in the happy feeling? Why or why not?

JOHN KEATS (1795–1821)

To Autumn

1819

Season of mists and mellow fruitfulness,
    Close bosom-friend of the maturing sun;
Conspiring with him how to load and bless
    With fruit the vines that round the thatch-eaves° run;   *of thatched roofs*
To bend with apples the mossed cottage-trees,   5
    And fill all fruit with ripeness to the core;
        To swell the gourd, and plump the hazel shells
With a sweet kernel; to set budding more,
    And still more, later flowers for the bees,
    Until they think warm days will never cease,   10
        For summer has o'er-brimmed their clammy cells.

Who hath not seen thee oft amid thy store?
    Sometimes whoever seeks abroad may find
Thee sitting careless on a granary floor,
    Thy hair soft-lifted by the winnowing wind;   15
Or on a half-reaped furrow half asleep,
    Drowsed with the fume of poppies, while thy hook
        Spares the next swath and all its twinèd flowers:
And sometimes like a gleaner thou dost keep
    Steady thy laden head across a brook;   20
    Or by a cider-press with patient look
        Thou watchest the last oozings hours by hours.

Where are the songs of Spring? Aye, where are they?
    Think not of them, thou hast thy music too—
While barrèd° clouds bloom the soft-dying day,   *streaked* 25
    And touch the stubble-plains with rosy hue;
Then in a wailful choir the small gnats mourn
    Among the river sallows,° borne aloft   *low willow trees*
        Or sinking as the light wind lives or dies;
And full-grown lambs loud bleat from hilly bourn;°   *field* 30
    Hedge crickets sing; and now with treble soft
    The redbreast whistles from a garden-croft;°   *small plot*
        And gathering swallows twitter in the skies.

THE RECEPTIVE READER

1. Readers have long turned to Keats' poetry for its rich sensuous imagery. How much of Keats' *harvest imagery* does the modern reader still recognize? (Can you visualize the reaper cutting a swath through the wheat interspersed with flowers? Can you visualize the wind winnowing the grain—by blowing the lighter chaff away as the grain is thrown into the air?)

2. What words and images in this poem help create the prevailing *mood*—the rich harvest mood of things coming to fruition, offering a feast to the senses? (Which images are visual images? Which are sound images? Which involve sensations—touch,

taste?) What does Keats' way of looking at the nuts, the bees, or the cider press contribute to the characteristic feeling that pervades the poem?

3. Why are the swallows gathering? Is it a mere coincidence that Keats mentions them last in the poem?

THE PERSONAL RESPONSE

Keats, like other Romantic poets of the early nineteenth century, saw the healing influence of nature as an antidote to the ills of city civilization. Can you get into the spirit of his nature poetry? Is your own relationship with nature similar or different?

T. S. ELIOT   (1888–1965)
Preludes   1917

1
The winter evening settles down
With smell of steaks in passageways.
Six o'clock.
The burnt-out ends of smoky days.
And now a gusty shower wraps   5
The grimy scraps
Of withered leaves about your feet
And newspapers from vacant lots;
The showers beat
On broken blinds and chimney-pots,   10
At the corner of the street
A lonely cab-horse steams and stamps.
And then the lighting of the lamps.

2
The morning comes to consciousness
Of faint stale smells of beer   15
From the sawdust-trampled street
With all its muddy feet that press
To early coffee-stands.
With the other masquerades
That time resumes,   20
One thinks of all the hands
That are raising dingy shades
In a thousand furnished rooms.

3
You tossed a blanket from the bed,
You lay upon your back, and waited;   25
You dozed, and watched the night revealing
The thousand sordid images
Of which your soul was constituted;
They flickered against the ceiling.
And when all the world came back   30

And the light crept up between the shutters
And you heard the sparrows in the gutters,
You had such a vision of the street
As the street hardly understands;
Sitting along the bed's edge, where   35
You curled the papers from your hair,
Or clasped the yellow soles of feet
In the palms of both soiled hands.

4
His soul stretched tight across the skies
That fade behind a city block,   40
Or trampled by insistent feet
At four and five and six o'clock;
And short square fingers stuffing pipes,
And evening newspapers, and eyes
Assured of certain certainties,   45
The conscience of a blackened street
Impatient to assume the world.

I am moved by fancies that are curled
Around these images, and cling:
The notion of some infinitely gentle   50
Infinitely suffering thing.

Wipe your hand across your mouth, and laugh;
The worlds revolve like ancient women
Gathering fuel in vacant lots.

THE RECEPTIVE READER

1. T. S. Eliot was one of the leaders in the early modern rebellion against the conventionally beautiful or superficially pretty in poetry. How many of the images make this poem head in the opposite direction? Which are most striking or memorable for you, and why?

2. How does the "you" addressed in the poem relate to the "sordid" images shown in this poem? How does the "I" that is speaking? How do you?

THE CREATIVE DIMENSION

Much modern poetry explores negative or mixed emotions about the urban landscape or cityscape in which most of us live. Write a passage or poem packed with images that project your own feelings about the city or about the American small town. How do you react to the following example?

After the first rain, the city's smells only reek louder and damper: damp wool, wet newspapers, the oily dirty street. The smell of yesterday's meatloaf wafts from the neighboring apartment when I open the window to smell the wet cement. Today will be like yesterday. I open a thousand locks on the front door and lock a thousand behind me.

DANA GIOIA   (born 1950)

California Hills in August   1982

I can imagine someone who found
these fields unbearable, who climbed
the hillside in the heat, cursing the dust,
cracking the brittle weeds underfoot,
wishing a few more trees for shade.   5

An Easterner especially, who would scorn
the meagreness of summer, the dry
twisted shapes of black elm,
scrub oak, and chaparral—a landscape
August has already drained of green.   10

One who would hurry over the clinging
thistle, foxtail, golden poppy,
knowing everything was just a weed,
unable to conceive that these trees
And sparse brown bushes were alive.   15

And hate the bright stillness of the noon,
without wind, without motion,
the only other living thing
a hawk, hungry for prey, suspended
in the blinding, sunlit blue.   20

And yet how gentle it seems to someone
raised in a landscape short of rain—
the skyline of a hill broken by no more
trees than one can count, the grass,
the empty sky, the wish for water.   25

THE RECEPTIVE READER

1. What is the task the poet set herself in this poem? Why does she make us look
at the landscape familiar to her through the eyes of the *outsider*?

2. What images or details make the landscape real for you? Were you surprised
when the poem reached its turning point at the beginning of the last stanza?

3. What phrase or phrases would you nominate as the key to the characteristic
quality of the landscape in this poem?

4. Do your sympathies lie with the Easterner or the Westerner in this poem?

THE CREATIVE DIMENSION

Have you ever felt defensive about a place dear to your heart? Write about it, first
from the point of view of the outsider and then from your own point of view. For a
possible model, look at the following re-creation of the Gioia poem.

To the outsider, the August hills are dry, barren,
brittle, devoid of life.
But in those dusty landscapes I see the

promise of emerald hills sparkling with dew
orange and yellow poppies
lupine and mustard.
I imagine warm and humid days alive
with the hum of insects.
I know beauty is just a rain away.

WRITING ABOUT LITERATURE

13. Looking at Imagery (Using Detail)

The Writing Workshop   You need to read a poem with an open eye and a willing ear. One of your first questions will be: "What does the poet want me to see and hear? What does the poet want me to visualize, to imagine?" You have to be receptive to the signals that are designed to call up vivid images on your mental screen. If you are a reader with a technical bent, you will have to shift from a number-crunching or data-collecting mode to a mode of recording images and decoding their meanings.

In preparing a paper on the imagery of a poem, ask yourself questions like the following:

✧ How does the poet make the *setting* real for you? Where is the poem taking you? What revealing details bring the place, the people, or the situation to life for you?

✧ What *key images* are particularly striking or revealing? What sights seem to stand out? Why are they important in the poem as a whole? Quote phrases, half-lines, or lines to make your reader see key images and how they come back or find an echo at other points in the poem.

✧ Does the poem appeal to more than your sense of sight? Does it bring *other senses* into play—your hearing, your sense of smell, or your sense of touch? One way to organize your paper might be to sort out the different kinds of imagery.

✧ What *emotions* do the images in the poem stir in the reader? What attitudes do they bring into play? Do they in any way trigger contradictory feelings or mixed emotions? One way to organize your paper might be to look first at images that steer the reader's reactions one way and to look later at images that point in a different direction.

✧ Is the poem unified by a prevailing *mood*? Or does it move through stages as images shift or as the associations and implications of key images change? One way to organize your paper might be to mark off major stages in the way the poem shapes the reader's thoughts and feelings.

✧ In reading the poem, do you remain caught up in the surface texture of vivid graphic imagery? Or does the poem raise issues that go beyond a particular scene? Does the poem imply more *general meanings*? (Does the poem make you think?)

Study the following student paper focused on a poem's imagery. How does the writer set her paper in motion? Is there a preview or hint of her general strategy? Does the paper follow up what you took to be the writer's overall plan? What use does she make of short, apt quotations? How does she wind up her paper?

SAMPLE STUDENT PAPER

At Peter Meinke's Apple Market

"Apple-smell everywhere!" So starts Peter Meinke's poem, "Sunday at the Apple Market." Apples of all kinds (Haralson, McIntosh, Fireside, Rome), apple smells, and the paraphernalia of the apple harvest are everywhere in this poem—in "miraculous profusion." The poet could simply have said, "The apple market was busy Sunday afternoon with lots of people buying tons of apples of different colors and kinds." Instead, Peter Meinke assaults our senses with a feast of concrete imagery. We can choose to let this poem simply "be," as Archibald MacLeish says—to let it simply exist and speak for itself. Or we can choose to look behind the images to find a larger meaning. Either way, we cannot help relishing the rich sensuous quality of its "being."

Poems often display vivid visual and auditory imagery, and this poem does so in exceptional profusion. We see yellow, green, and red apples "piled crazy in the storehouse barn (7), apples in "bushels / and baskets and bags and boxes" (13–14), "apples by the cartload" (5). We hear "the crowd / around the testing table laughing" (8–9) and the "dogs barking at children in the appletrees (11)."

However, this poem appeals to all the senses; indeed, apple smell is everywhere, from the beginning to the "smell of apples" at the end (l5). We experience taste along with smell as the people around the testing table roll "the cool applechunks in their mouths" (10) or as we recall the juice made by the "old ciderpresses weathering in the shed" (3). We can imagine ourselves holding hands as the couples do in the poem; we carry the weight of bushels, baskets, bags, and boxes.

Why is the crowd laughing; why are the people happy? We see them at the apple market at the time of harvest, of ripeness and fruition. All the previous stages, from winter and pruning of the trees through blossom time, have led up to this stage of fullness and culmination. We can imagine the harvest cycle as parallel to our own journey through life, since all the stages of our own growth are represented: We see the children in the apple trees; we see the couples holding hands; we see the children's parents carrying apples back to their cars. We can enjoy a sense of cycle that leads up to this moment when we enjoy the fruits of our journey through life.

However, the poem does not stop there. Contrasting with the dominating concrete images of the ample harvest are hints of a further stage in the cycle. The "old ciderpresses weathering in the shed" (3) suggest fermentation and aging. The "old ladders tilting at empty branches" (4) foreshadow the end of fertility, with the coming of barrenness and decay—the inevitable continuation of the process we experience at the high point of the cycle in this poem. We see "so many people / out in the country" (13) on this Sunday to capture and carry back with them this happy moment of fulfillment that cannot last. For "one Sunday afternoon" these people are "free / and happy as people must have been meant to be" (16–17).

Reading the poem, I was struck by the image of the dogs barking at the children in the apple trees. It brought to mind a time when my grandparents' orchard was for me a "free and happy" world of its own. I remember a Sunday when I was hiding from my cousins in my grandmother's apple tree, stifling giggles on a high branch, my Sunday dress torn on the rough bark. I wrote a brief poem recalling the experience; it ends as follows:

In Sunday black and white like spotted puppies
they sniff and search under apple carts
and behind the stacked up empty wooden crates.
Behind heavy leaves red apples hide.
I hide, too.

QUESTIONS

1. How does the student writer set the scene or the tone? How well does she get into the spirit of the poem?

2. Does she provide the evidence needed to support her conclusions?

3. How do you react to the way she winds up her paper?

4. Is your response to the poem different from that of the student writer? Do you disagree with any of her conclusions?

14 METAPHOR
Making Connections

When we attempt to express living experience with words, logical speech quickly becomes permeated with symbols and metaphors.

CHARLES M. JOHNSTON

To a wholly new experience, one can give sufficient organization only by relating it to the already known, by perceiving a relation between this experience and another experience already ordered, placed, and incorporated.

JAMES OLNEY

Metaphor, in the small sense and the large, is the main property of poetry.

RICHARD WILBUR

FOCUS ON METAPHOR

Poets use striking imaginative comparisons to go beyond the resources of literal speech. They take us into a world of vivid visual images, but often there is more to the image than meets the eye. When a poet says, "The bird of love is on the wing," the line is meant to call up a vivid visual image before the mind's eye. But the poem is not literally talking about a bird. Instead, it *compares* the feeling of falling in love to the exhilaration a bird might experience in flight.

The bird here is an example of **metaphor,** language used imaginatively to carry ideas and feelings that otherwise might be hard to put into words. A metaphor is a brief, compressed comparison that talks about one thing as if it were another. The comparison is implied and not spelled out. It comes into the poem unannounced, without the words *like* or *as* to signal that something is not literally a bird but only in some way like a bird. (A close cousin of metaphor, which signals the comparison by words such as *like* or *as if,* is called a **simile.**)

486

The following poem shows the way metaphors come into a poem.

EMILY DICKINSON   (1830–1886)

Apparently with no surprise   1884

Apparently with no surprise
to any happy Flower
The Frost beheads it at its play—
In accidental power—
The blonde Assassin passes on—   5
The Sun proceeds unmoved
To measure off another Day
For an approving God.

As we read this poem, our first hint that the poet is speaking metaphorically is the word *happy* applied to the flower. Flowers are not literally happy or
unhappy. They have no feelings, just as they do not "play" (any more than
they go about serious business). These metaphors are each built on an implied
as if: It is *as if* the flower had been happily and innocently at play when it was
attacked by the frost. It is *as if* the killer frost were an executioner who "beheads" the condemned victim. It is *as if* the frost were an "assassin," thus
adding the idea of treachery to the brutality of the victim's execution.

The metaphors in this poem make us think of both the frost and the
flower as if they were human beings, acting out a grim minidrama that stirs our
sympathies and raises troubling questions in our minds. (This kind of
metaphor, which treats things or plants as if they were persons, is called **personification.**) Metaphor here serves functions that make it a vital part of the
poet's language:

❖ First, metaphor has the power to call up striking visual *images*. We see
with the mind's eye the flower at play, the murderous frost beheading it, the
"blonde" assassin (not a stereotypical beetle-browed villain) passing on nonchalantly. We see (or imagine) the sun proceeding on its course as if nothing
special had occurred. Metaphor is one of the poet's chief means of living up
to the ideal that "a poem does not talk about ideas; it *enacts them*" (John
Ciardi).

❖ Second, metaphor has the power to stir our *feelings*: We are likely to
shudder at the swift destruction of the helpless, harmless flower. We should
feel at least a twinge of terror at seeing it destroyed. The ability of metaphor to
engage our emotions makes for a key difference between poetic language on
the one hand and scientific or other kinds of emotionally neutral language on
the other. The English Romantic poet Samuel Taylor Coleridge voiced a requirement echoed by many moderns when he said that poetry should "be sensuous, and by its imagery elicit truth at a flash, and be able to move our
feelings and awaken our affections."

✧ Third, metaphor has the power to make us *think*. Since we are thinking beings, it is hard for us to watch the spectacle of the killer frost without asking ourselves uneasy questions. Is it true that only we, sentimental humans, care? Do only we feel forebodings of sudden death as the frost does its killer job? The poem gives us pause. It raises questions to which it does not provide easy answers.

What is the difference between image and metaphor? The poet's *images* can make us feel more fully alive, more alert to our surroundings. The poet's image making invites us to respond to the rich sensuous or sensory surface of the world. In Peter Meinke's "Sunday at the Apple Market," we visualize apples, we smell apples, we roll apple chunks around in our mouths. There are apples literally everywhere in the poem. Whatever associations they bring into play, they are first of all literal apples.

By contrast, in Emily Dickinson's poem there are no literal beheadings or assassins; the sun does not literally measure off a day the way a tailor measures off cloth. These are *metaphors*. The images they make us see have their meaning beyond what meets the eye. We have to decode the metaphors in order to understand what they stand for in the world of real flowers, real frost, and the real sun.

THE RECEPTIVE READER

Dickinson's poems often have puzzling, provocative phrases tucked away in them that become more meaningful on second thought and on second reading. Why "accidental power"? Why "blonde assassin"? Is the scene being watched by an "approving God"?

READING FOR METAPHOR

Without metaphor, language would lose its lifeblood and stiffen into a conventional system of signs.
ERNST CASSIRER

I love metaphor. It provides two loaves where there seems to be one. Sometimes it throws in a load of fish.
BERNARD MALAMUD

The English eighteenth-century poet William Blake says, "The tigers of wrath are wiser than the horses of instruction." We need no nudging to make us realize that these animals are not literally there. They are brought in by way of comparison. Reading such metaphors, we mentally fill in the possible connections: Righteous anger is fiery *like* a tiger and moves us to swift action. Compared with the powerful welling-up of passion, instruction is more plodding, like the horses pulling a brewery wagon. It makes us do what we are told, as horses do what pleases their masters. It is not likely to move us to generous or passionate endeavor.

Both an image on the literal level and a metaphor may appeal strongly to our visual imagination. The difference is that the metaphor makes us visualize something that we could not literally interact with or see. When the poet Adrien Stoutenburg says, "The strawberry's leaves / Are a green hand spread open," we are looking at real leaves but not at a real hand. We are looking at small leaves that together form a kind of hand holding up the ripening strawberry. The psalm says, "The Lord is my shepherd; / I shall not want. / He maketh me to lie down in green pastures: / He leadeth me beside the still waters." When we recite the psalm, the sheep and the caring, protecting shepherd are not literally there as part of our lives. *We* are there, and the psalm is about our relationship to the Lord.

Metaphor (from a Greek word meaning "to carry over") carries us over from the normal surface meaning of a word to something else. It exploits similarities and makes connections between things we might otherwise keep apart. A metaphor may be a single word: Blake uses the single word *tiger* to set up the metaphorical connection between righteous wrath and the fiery, ferocious, threatening animal. The richer the metaphor, the more it challenges our imagination to call up a full range of similarities. For instance, righteous anger is fiery and passionate. It is threatening to evildoers, and it would probably be futile to try to control.

Often, however, the poet will develop a metaphor beyond a single word. Such an **extended metaphor** traces the ramifications of the implied comparison, following up related similarities. Look at the extended (or **sustained**) metaphor in the following poem by a leading figure of the "Harlem Renaissance" of the thirties and forties.

COUNTEE CULLEN (1903–1946) — *major moving force in the Harlem Renaisance*

For My Grandmother
1927

This lovely flower fell to seed;
Work gently sun and rain;
She held it as her dying creed
That she would grow again.

The central metaphor in this poem compares the grandmother to a flower. But the poet extends the metaphor beyond the flower in bloom to its whole life cycle: The flower grows from a seed, helped by sun and rain; it then decays and in turn leaves a seed. We cherish it because of its loveliness, but it is also subject to death and decay. However, the seed the flower leaves behind carries the promise of renewed growth—of rebirth and new life.

THE RECEPTIVE READER

Are the sun and the rain in this poem literal or metaphorical or both? When speaking of renewed growth, was the poet thinking of resurrection and eternal life? Or was he thinking of the grandchildren that were the "seed" representing continued life?

When a single extended metaphor gives shape to a poem as a whole, it becomes an **organizing metaphor** (it is also called a **controlling metaphor**). More often, however, a poem moves through several related, interacting metaphors. The following poem is built around three related metaphors: the house, the horse, and the dog. Look at the way these metaphors work together. What do they make you see? What do they make you feel? How do they challenge more familiar ways of looking at our bodies?

M A Y   S W E N S O N   (born 1919)

Question 1954

Body my house
my horse my hound
What will I do
When you are fallen

Where will I sleep 5
How will I ride
What will I hunt

Where can I go without my mount
all eager and quick
How will I know 10
in thicket ahead
is danger or treasure
When Body my good
bright dog is dead

How will it be 15
to lie in the sky
without roof or door
and wind for an eye

with cloud for shift°
                                    woman's shirt or chemise
how will I hide? 20

In this poem, three interlocking, meshing metaphors make us reexamine the way we feel about our bodies. To judge from the way the poet develops or follows them up in the poem, these metaphors mean something like the following:

✧ The poet calls the body "my house," reminding us that it puts up the roof and walls giving us shelter and the doors barring intruders. It offers us a place to sleep, to hide. The word *house* is likely to make us think of a place that offers refuge and protection.

✧ The poet calls the body "my horse." Apparently we are asked to imagine not a tired nag but a spirited mount—"all eager and quick"—ready to carry us to adventure. We are not rooted like a tree. Life is movement, motion, activity—but only if we can depend on the body to carry us into action.

✧ The poet calls the body "my hound"—a "good bright dog" that like a hunting dog serves its master well. It alerts us to danger (lurking "in thicket ahead") or hunts down "treasure." We depend on our bodies to keep us alert, prepared to deal with the threats and promises of every day.

THE RECEPTIVE READER

1. How is the way this poem looks at the body different from other, more familiar ways of looking at our bodies? Do you share the feelings or sympathize with the attitudes that the metaphors in this poem suggest?

2. For you, what is the connecting *thread* that links the three metaphors? What do they have in common?

3. What tone does the *title* set for the poem? What is the poet's "question"? Does the poem suggest an answer?

THE CREATIVE DIMENSION

Explore your own possible metaphors for the body. Complete the line "My body my . . ." in your own way, writing your own body poem or passage about the body. How well does the central metaphor work in the following example?

Body

You ship of a fool!
Why do I worry about
   sprung planks
   leaky decks
   spent rigging
   peeling paint?
The rats left a long time ago,
and you're still afloat!

EXPLORATIONS

Understanding Metaphor

How do you explain the metaphors in the following lines? What do they make you see? What do they make you feel? What do they make you think? Compare your own responses with those of other readers.

1. We drive the same highways
  in the dark, not seeing each other,
            only the lights.
      Diane Wakoski, "Meeting an Astronomer"

[handwritten: — hiding in the body / who was in the car?]

2. Like any other man
  I was born with a knife
  in one hand
  and a wound in the other.
      Gregory Orr, "Like Any Other Man"

[handwritten: we hurt ourselves / the things that we do / come back on us.]

3. The heart has need of some deceit
   To make its pistons rise and fall;
   For less than this it would not beat,
   Nor flush the sluggish veins at all.
   Countee Cullen, "Only the Polished Skeleton"

4.   One morning last March,
   I pressed against the new barbed and galvanized

   fence on the Boston Common. Behind their cage,
   yellow dinosaur steamshovels were grunting
   as they cropped up tons of mush and grass
   to gouge their underworld garage.
   Robert Lowell, "For the Union Dead"

EXPLORATIONS

The Extended Metaphor

What is the central metaphor in the following poem? How does the poet develop it into an extended metaphor? Which of the similarities between hope and "the thing with feathers" seem most fitting? Which seem most strange? Which to you are most thought provoking or revealing?

EMILY DICKINSON (1830–1886)

"Hope" is the thing with feathers   1861

"Hope" is the thing with feathers—
That perches in the soul—
And sings the tune without the words—
And never stops—at all—

And sweetest—in the Gale—is heard—   5
And sore must be the storm—
That could abash° the little Bird – hope   *subdue and silence*
That kept so many warm—

birds like to be fed – we don't have to do anything for hope.

I've heard it in the chillest land—
And on the strangest Sea—   10
Yet, never, in Extremity,°   *in extreme danger or adversity*
It asked a crumb—of Me.

THE RECEPTIVE READER

1. What, to the poet, makes a bird a good metaphor for hope? What related details or ramifications make this *extended metaphor* vivid or real for you?

2. Why would the song be heard "sweetest in the gale"? How does the song keep "so many warm"? What does it say about hope that the bird never "asked a crumb"?

THE CREATIVE DIMENSION

Cluster the word *hope*. What images, memories, or associations does the word call up? In your cluster, how do they branch out from the central stimulus word? What kind of pattern takes shape? Write a passage that pulls together the ideas and associations. How do your own associations with the word compare with those in Dickinson's poem?

CROSS-REFERENCES—For Discussion or Writing

Dickinson's "'Hope' is the thing with feathers" and Hardy's "The Darkling Thrush" (Chapter 12) are both poems about hope. Explore how one poet uses a bird as an image and the other uses a bird as a metaphor.

FIGURATIVE LANGUAGE: METAPHOR, SIMILE, PERSONIFICATION

Metaphor is one kind of nonliteral language under the larger umbrella heading of **figurative** language. Like a metaphor, a **simile** is a brief, compressed imaginative comparison. Unlike a metaphor, a simile uses the words *as* or *like* or *as if* to advertise that a comparison will follow. These signals alert us to look for the similarities that the poet had in mind: "My love is like a red, red rose"; "My love is like a silken tent." A simile says outright that something is like something else. Sometimes simile is considered merely a special kind of metaphor—a metaphor announced rather than implied.

Love poems through the centuries have used metaphor and simile to express feelings that might otherwise be hard to put into words. A famous simile opens the following poem by the Scottish poet Robert Burns. Look at what the two similes in the opening stanza (group of four related lines) do for the poem as a whole. Note that *fair* in this poem means "beautiful"—as in much early love poetry.

ROBERT BURNS   (1759–1796)

A Red, Red Rose   1796

O my luve's like a red, red rose
That's newly sprung in June;
O my luve's like the melodie
That's sweetly played in tune.

As fair art thou, my bonny lass,°   *my dear girl*   5
So deep in luve am I;
And I will luve thee still, my dear,
Till a'° the seas gang dry°—   *all / run (go) dry*

Till a' the seas gang dry, my dear,
And the rocks melt wi' the sun: 10

O I will luve thee still, my dear,
While the sands o' life shall run.

And fare thee weel, my only luve,
And fare thee weel awhile!
And I will come again, my luve,   15
Though it were a thousand mile.

The opening simile here draws on the rich traditional associations of the rose: For instance, its rich red color is pleasing to the eye (and it is often associated with passion). People who love roses treasure the delicate petals and the fresh scent on a June morning. The second simile likens the poet's love to a "melody sweetly played in tune"—soothing the nerves frazzled by the jangling noises of every day. The poet then tells his readers what many of them want to hear: A love like the poet's is not a casual, passing encounter. It will last forever, longer than the rocks and the sea. Any separation will be only for "awhile."

THE RECEPTIVE READER

1. How, or how well, do the two opening *similes* work together?
2. What explains the "sands of life" *metaphor?* Sand (on beaches) does not usually "run." What traditional device used sand to measure time?
3. Much traditional love poetry used *hyperbole,* or extreme exaggeration—for instance, to praise the beauty of the beloved to the skies. What instances of hyberbole can you find in this poem?

THE PERSONAL RESPONSE

To you, does Burns' love poem seem timeless or out of date? Would you consider sending it to someone? If someone sent it to you, what might be your response?

The bolder and the more original a poet's similes, the more they are likely to stimulate our imagination. The following poem focuses on the big bird— "the great gull"—that came from the sea. What images and feelings are brought into the poem by two key similes: "like a high priest" and "like a merchant prince"?

HOWARD NEMEROV   (born 1920)

The Great Gull

[handwritten: Man may feel insignificant to the gull. bird can fly. land where it chooses. Bird has control]   1951

Restless, rising at dawn
I saw the great gull come from the mist
To stand upon the lawn.
And there he shook his savage wing
To quiet, and stood like a high priest *[handwritten: — simile]*   5
Bird-masked, mantled in gray.
Before his fierce austerity

My thought bowed down, imagining
The wild sea-lanes he wandered by
And the wild waters where he slept,   10
Still as a candle in the crypt.
Noble, and not courteous,
He stared upon my green concerns.
Then, like a merchant prince
Come to some poor province,   15
Who, looking all about, discerns
No spice, no treasure house,
Nothing that can be made
Delightful to his haughty trade,
And so spreads out his sail,   20
Leaving to savage men
Their miserable regimen;°   *rigidly ordered life*
So did he rise, making a gale
About him with his wings,
And fought his huge freight into air   25
And vanished seaward with a cry—
A strange tongue but the tone clear.

This poem focuses on the large seabird that came out of the ocean fog to
stand on the lawn. The speaker in the poem is fascinated by the sight of the
bird, from the time it lands and stashes its large wings for an at-rest position
until it finally unfolds them again for takeoff. Concrete visual images help us
imagine this fascinating bird: First, the bird "shook his savage wing / To
quiet"; later, it spread out its wings like a sail, creating a miniature storm like a
gale at sea, "fighting" its way into the air to lift the "huge freight" of its body.
The poet's carefully trimmed lawn (his "green concerns") must seem petty and
tame to this "savage," "fierce," and "haughty" bird from the "wild sea-lanes"
and "wild waters."

The poet uses several similes to help us share his feelings about this majestic wild bird. For instance, he compares the bird to a high priest, wearing a
bird mask and mantle of gray (like its coat of gray feathers), expecting us to
bow down to it as to a priest in a strange pagan ritual. This simile should help
us sense the bird's "fierce austerity": The bird is aloof, not wasting time on
frivolous diversions; it is "not courteous"—not folksy like someone trying to
sell us a used car.

THE RECEPTIVE READER

1. The second simile compares the bird to a "merchant prince." How would such
a person be different from an ordinary merchant? What would such a merchant prince
be looking for and where? What would be disappointing about the "poor province" the
gull actually found? What does this second simile have in common with the first?

2. A third simile makes us imagine the bird sleeping on the waters "still as a candle
in the crypt." What images and feelings does this simile bring into the poem? How is it
related to the other two similes?

3. For you, what is the connecting thread that links the three similes? How do they work together; how are they related?

THE PERSONAL RESPONSE

What animal would *you* choose to represent untamed savage nature? Do you think a sea animal would be a better choice than a land animal? Why?

Personification is a metaphor or a simile that treats something nonhuman as if it were human. It is figurative language that makes things or animals behave as if they were human. The heavens are personified in the line "The heavens declare the glory of God" (as if they were preachers or apostles). Talking about a bird from the sea as if it were a high priest or a merchant prince exemplifies personification. Personification often serves to project personal human feelings onto a larger screen. It can make the world around us mirror our own state of mind. When a blues singer sings, "The sky is crying / Look at the tears roll down the street," the whole world seems to share the singer's sadness and loneliness.

Note: Students of poetry have often set up additional subcategories for figurative language. **Metonymy,** for instance, is a metaphor that does not rove far afield but lights on something closely related. It uses *Pentagon* for the Defense Department, *crown* for the monarchy, *laurels* (from the practice of honoring people with laurel wreaths) for fame. *Gown* (academic gown) comes to stand for university in the expression "town and gown." **Synecdoche** uses the part to stand for the whole: "give us a *hand*" (when we actually need the assistance of the whole person). Or it may use the whole to stand for the part: "Outraged *womanhood* called for his resignation" (actually only a group of outraged women). It may use the individual to stand for the species (or vice versa), as when we call every miser a Scrooge.

EXPLORATIONS

Understanding Similes

How do you explain each of the following similes?

1. I had even forgotten how married love
   is a territory more mysterious
   the more it is explored, like one of those terrains
   you read about, a garden in the desert
   where you stoop to drink, never knowing
   if your mouth will fill with water or sand.
                    Linda Pastan, "After an Absence"

2. A sentence starts out like a lone traveler
   Heading into a blizzard at midnight.
                    Billy Collins, "Winter Syntax"

3. If we have quarreled our bodies wait
   patient as horses for their owners' huffy
   departure. Those masters gone they turn,
   nuzzle, and flank to flank speak
   to each other all night long
   the eloquent touching language of the dumb.
                                    Nils Peterson, "Bedtime"

EXPLORATIONS

A Dream Deferred

In the thirties and forties, Langston Hughes came to be considered the "poet laureate" or unofficial voice of black America. Each simile in the following poem sets up a different scenario for what might happen if a dream is deferred or hope denied. Which similes fit exceptionally well? Which scenario can you most vividly imagine? Which seems to you most likely?

LANGSTON HUGHES   (1902–1967)

Dream Deferred   1951

What happens to a dream deferred?
Does it dry up
Like a raisin in the sun?
Or fester like a sore—
And then run?   5
Does it stink like rotten meat?
Or crust and sugar over—
like a syrupy sweet?

Maybe it just sags
like a heavy load.   10

Or does it explode?

THE RANGE OF METAPHOR

When I put myself out on a saucer
in the sun
or moonlight
of the back stoop
cats
in
the form of
images
come feeding
DIANA CHANG, "CANNIBALISM"

Poetic metaphors range from the easily accessible to the more challenging. Many of the metaphors of ordinary speech are well established and familiar. We turn to a dog-eared page, watch tempers boil, or give someone a fish-eyed stare. When they have become overused, losing their tread like a bald tire, such metaphors turn into **clichés:** the tip of the iceberg, the bottom of the barrel, the window of opportunity. By contrast, poetic metaphors are often fresh and thought provoking. They forge new connections; they discover unexpected, revealing similarities. When the American poet Carl Sandburg asks us to

Remember all paydays of lilacs and songbirds

no familiar connection between paydays and songbirds guides us. We have to work out the implied equation ourselves. It sounds as if the poet had in mind the sense of reward and elation that workers might feel on payday. That elation corresponds to the joy brought by the rich blooms of the lilac and the song of birds.

Poets—and major styles in the history of poetry—vary in how boldly they explore new metaphorical connections. Love poems of earlier centuries featured fanciful extended metaphors called **conceits.** Although elaborately developed, they often moved along conventional or fairly predictable lines. A conceit sets up an analogy between what we are literally talking about (the beloved person, say) and what we are metaphorically calling it (the sun of our universe, for example). It then traces the analogy in careful detail. Such conceits were an expected ornament of the love sonnets written by the Italian fourteenth-century poet Petrarch and the many translators and followers he inspired. The **sonnet** is an elaborately crafted fourteen-line poem with an interlaced rhyme scheme and iambic meter. (See Chapter 17 for more on the formal features of the traditional sonnet.)

In the following sonnet by one of Petrarch's English translators, the lover's "enemy" steering the ship is also called "my lord." Both of these terms early love poets applied to the haughty, disdainful, "cruel" lady to whom they addressed their "plaints." (Note: Wyatt's editors are not sure whether he intended us to read as two syllables words like *charged* and *forced*—chargèd? forcèd?—which would then make for a more regular iambic beat.)

What is the central conceit or extended metaphor in the poem? How is it developed?

THOMAS WYATT (1503–1542)

My galley charged with forgetfulness

before 1540

My galley charged with forgetfulness
Thorough° sharp seas in winter nights doth pass   *through*
'Tween rock and rock; and eke° mine enemy, alas,   *also*
That is my lord, steereth with cruelness;
And every oar a thought in readiness,   5
As though that death were light in such a case.
An endless wind doth tear the sail apace
Of forced sighs and trusty fearfulness
A rain of tears, a cloud of dark disdain,
Hath done the wearied cords great hinderance;   10
Wreathed with error and eke with ignorance,
The stars be hid° that led me to this pain;   *are hidden*
Drowned is reason that should me consort,°   *stay with me*
And I remain despairing of the port.

THE RECEPTIVE READER

1. A conceit often follows the basic metaphor into every conceivable detail. (In this poem, once we are on the ship, we stay on the ship.) Why is it winter and night? What are the oars, the wind, the rain, the cloud, the harbor? Who or what drowned? What are the rocks?

2. What is the *keynote* of this poem? What are the prevailing emotions? Why do you think generations of readers related to this kind of love poetry (and still do)?

When conceits become too predictable, they may seem to hem in rather than stimulate the imagination. (The poet has to stay on the track prescribed by the dominating metaphor.) By contrast, the metaphors in a Shakespearean sonnet more often keep developing and shifting. They may start as elaborate conceits, but then they escalate, following up new and unexpected associations. What are the three key metaphors in the following sonnet? How do they develop; how do they mesh? (Note that the word *choir* in the fourth line stands for the part of a church reserved for the choir.)

WILLIAM SHAKESPEARE (1564–1616)

Sonnet 73

before 1598

That time of year thou mayst in me behold
When yellow leaves, or none, or few, do hang
Upon those boughs which shake against the cold,
Bare ruined choirs, where late the sweet birds sang.
In me thou seest the twilight of such day   5
As after sunset fadeth in the west;
Which by and by° black night doth take away,   *gradually*
Death's second self, that seals up all in rest.
In me thou seest the glowing of such fire
That on the ashes of his youth doth lie,   10
As the deathbed whereon it must expire,
Consumed with that which it was nourished by.
This thou perceivest, which makes thy love more strong,
To love that well which thou must leave ere long.°   *before long*

The much-analyzed first metaphor in this sonnet makes us think of approaching age as the late autumn of the speaker's life, when we see the bare branches of the tree shaken by cold winds, with only a few last withered yellow leaves clinging to the boughs. But the metaphor shifts and develops: The bare wood of the branches apparently makes the poet think of the wooden pews where the choirboys or choristers used to sit in church (where they sang the way the "sweet birds" sang in the tree). Now the church is in ruins (like many of the great abbey churches of England after the Protestant reformation had shut down the monasteries). Both the tree and the church used to be filled with sweet song, but they are now fitting metaphors for the approaching decay and loneliness of age. They are likely to make us long for the rich growth and sweet bird song of summers past.

THE RECEPTIVE READER

1. What is the *second* major metaphor, developed in the second set of four lines (or quatrain) in the sonnet? What parallels or connections make it especially fitting or expressive? How does it shift to acquire a further dimension? (How is night "Death's second self"?)

2. What is the metaphor in the *third* set of four lines? (What was "consumed with that which it was nourished by," and how?) Can you see more than one parallel or connection between this third major metaphor and the other two?

3. Many Shakespearean sonnets provide a "turning" in the final couplet, or set of two lines—an answer to a central question, or a *counterpoint* to an earlier assertion. How does this sonnet fit this pattern?

POEMS FOR FURTHER STUDY

Pay special attention to the workings of metaphor, simile, and personification in the following poems.

ROSEMARY CATACALOS   (born 1944)

La Casa   1984

The house by the acequia,°   *irrigation canal*
its front porch dark and
cool with begonias,
an old house, always there,
always of the same adobe,   5
always full of the same lessons.
We would like to stop.
We know we belonged there once.
Our mothers are inside.
All the mothers are inside,   10
lighting candles, swaying
back and forth on their knees,
begging The Virgin's forgiveness
for having reeled us out
on such very weak string.   15
They are afraid for us.
They know we will not stop.
We will only wave as we pass by.
They will go on praying
that we might be simple again.   20

THE RECEPTIVE READER

In this poem by a bilingual Mexican American poet, what is the key metaphor for
parents' sending children into the outside world? What are the implications and ramifications of the metaphor? Is the speaker in the poem thinking of a literal house—a real
house she remembers from her childhood? How would you sum up the speaker's attitude toward the past?

WILLIAM SHAKESPEARE   (1564–1616)

Sonnet 29   before 1598

When, in disgrace with Fortune and men's eyes,
I all alone beweep my outcast state,
And trouble deaf heaven with my bootless° cries,   *useless*
And look upon myself and curse my fate,
Wishing me like to one more rich in hope,   5
Featured like him, like him with friends possessed,
Desiring this man's art and that man's scope,
With what I most enjoy contented least;
Yet in these thoughts myself almost despising,
Haply I think on thee, and then my state°   *condition*   10
(Like to the lark at break of day arising

From sullen earth) sings hymns at heaven's gate;
For thy sweet love remembered such wealth brings
That then I scorn to change my state with kings.

THE RECEPTIVE READER

1. In the first eight lines, or *octave,* of this sonnet, what is literal statement? What is metaphor? (What image or associations does the reference to Fortune bring to mind?)

2. Lines 11 and 12 combine simile, metaphor, and personification. How? As Shakespeare's use of figurative language often does, the lark simile seems to escalate, shifting to a further and bolder metaphor in midflight. How, and with what effect on the reader?

3. Sonnets often reach a turning point at the end of the octave; Shakespeare's sonnets especially often lead up to a concluding couplet that leaves us with a thought to remember. How does this sonnet illustrate both of these features?

LINDA PASTAN　(born 1932)

Anger　　　　　　　　　　　　　　　　　　　　　　1985

You tell me
that it's all right
to let it out of its cage,
though it may claw someone,
even bite.　　　　　　　　　　　　　　　　　　　　　　　5
You say that letting it out
may tame it somehow.
But loose it may
turn on me, maul
my face, draw blood.　　　　　　　　　　　　　　　　　　10
Ah, you think you know so much,
you whose anger is a pet dog,
its canines dull with disuse.
But mine is a rabid thing, sharpening its teeth
on my very bones,　　　　　　　　　　　　　　　　　　　15
and I will never let it go.

THE RECEPTIVE READER

1. What is the *central metaphor* in this poem? Into how many details can you trace this central organizing metaphor? Which details are especially graphic or concrete? Where and how does the metaphor branch out into two opposite variations?

2. Prepare a *paraphrase,* translating the poet's metaphorical language into plain literal prose. What is lost in the translation?

THE PERSONAL RESPONSE

Where do you stand on the question raised by this poem?

THE CREATIVE DIMENSION

Write an imaginative response to this poem, using your own central metaphor instead of the one used by the poet. Or do the same for another poem with a striking central metaphor. How do you react to the following student-written sample?

> I watch you,
> you who say,
> "Be emotional; it's all right."
> But you sit with the emotion
> clamped to your leg
> like a steel trap on a rabbit.
> You struggle to get free
> without chance of success.
> I watch you
> trying to gnaw it loose
> as the rabbit would.

NIKKI GIOVANNI (born 1943)

The Drum 1983

daddy says the world is
a drum tight and hard
and i told him
i'm gonna beat
out my own rhythm 5

THE RECEPTIVE READER

1. How does the central metaphor change its meaning or implications in this poem?

2. How would it change the poem if instead of "i'm gonna" the poet had written "I am going to" or "I shall"?

SYLVIA PLATH (1932–1963)

Metaphors 1960

I'm a riddle in nine syllables,
An elephant, a ponderous° house, — pregnant *very weighty*
A melon strolling on two tendrils.
O red fruit, ivory, fine timbers!
This loaf's big with its yeasty rising. 5
Money's new-minted in this fat purse.
I'm a means, a stage, a cow in calf.
I've eaten a bag of green apples,
Boarded the train there's no getting off.

THE RECEPTIVE READER

1. Where in your reading of the poem did you first guess at the answer to the riddle? What in the poem did most to confirm your guess?

2. Why "nine syllables"? Why a poem of nine lines of nine syllables each? (The title has nine letters, but this may be just a coincidence.)

3. Why green apples? Which metaphors in the poem seem to be most expressive or to fit the speaker's condition best?

4. What are the speaker's feelings? Which of the metaphors do most to reveal her attitude? Is there humor in the poem, and what kind?

THE PERSONAL RESPONSE

The situation in which the speaker in this poem finds herself has often inspired mixed emotions or contradictory feelings. Have you observed or perhaps personally shared these? Write about the mixed emotions.

LAURA ST. MARTIN   (born 1957)

The Ocean   1977

the ocean is a strange
midnight lover
skinny dipping when the beach patrol has left
she is a cool seduction
wrapping blue thunder around slick brown shoulders   5
raising great foam-fringed arms to a steel sky
rushing over us
sometimes tumbling us to the shore
licking the rocks passionately
only to retreat into swirling   10
indecision
tense always prancing
and the moon casts a furious gleam on the many-knuckled sea

THE RECEPTIVE READER

How does this poem go beyond routine and limited personification? What striking human qualities does this poem read into the ocean and the moon? Does the poet's use of personification make the ocean less or more real?

THE PERSONAL RESPONSE

How do you react to this poem? What does it do for you as the reader?

JOHN DONNE (1572–1631)

A Valediction: Forbidding Mourning 1611

As virtuous men pass mildly away,
And whisper to their souls to go,
Whilst some of their sad friends do say
The breath goes now, and some say no:

So let us melt, and make no noise, 5
No tear floods, nor sigh-tempests move;
'Twere profanation° of our joys   *it would make something sacred common*
To tell the laity our love.

Moving of the earth° brings harms and fears;   *earthquakes*
Men reckon what it did and meant; 10
But trepidation of the spheres,°   *trembling of the heavenly spheres*
Though greater far, is innocent.

Dull sublunary° lovers' love   *below the moon, earthbound*
(Whose soul is sense) cannot admit
Absence, because it doth remove 15
Those things which elemented° it.   *gave it substance*

But we, by a love so much refined
That ourselves know not what it is,
Inter-assurèd° of the mind,   *mutually sure*
Care less eyes, lips, and hands to miss. 20

Our two souls, therefore, which are one,
Though I must go, endure not yet
A breach, but an expansion,
Like gold° to airy thinness beat.   *like gold leaf*

If they be two, they are two so 25
As stiff twin compasses are two:
Thy soul, the fixed foot, makes no show
To move, but doth if the other do.

And though it in the center sit,
Yet when the other far doth roam, 30
It leans and harkens after it,
And grows erect as that comes home.

Such wilt thou be to me, who must,
Like the other foot, obliquely° run;   *at a wide angle*
Thy firmness makes my circle just,°   *makes it perfect* 35
And makes me end where I begun.

THE RECEPTIVE READER

1. According to Izaak Walton, a contemporary biographer, Donne wrote this farewell poem for his wife before leaving on a journey to France. What is the connection

between the parting of the spouses and the death scene described in the first stanza? (Why do you think Donne's contemporaries believed that good, virtuous people would have a "mild" or gentle death?)

2. If outsiders are the "laity," what does the implied comparison make the two people in love?

3. Donne's contemporaries believed that the heavens were perfect (reflecting the perfection of God). Everything "sublunary"—below the moon, on this earth—was *imperfect*, subject to decay and death. Furthermore, the planets moving in orbit around the earth in the geocentric, earth-centered Ptolemaic view of the universe were attached to spheres of crystal. At times these moved or shook, accounting for apparent irregularities in the astronomers' calculations. How does Donne draw on these contemporary beliefs in this poem?

4. Probably the best-known example of figurative language in English literature is the comparison of the two people in love to the pair of "twin compasses" used in geometry classes to draw a circle. What does this device look like? How does it work? How does Donne put it to work in this poem?

THE PERSONAL RESPONSE

Critics (and presumably lovers) have been divided on whether to welcome into love poetry comparisons drawn from areas like astronomy, geometry, and medicine. How would you vote on this issue, and why?

WRITING ABOUT LITERATURE

14. Interpreting Metaphor (Organizing the Paper)

The Writing Workshop Reading a poem is different from scanning unemployment statistics. One key difference is that in reading a poem we have to be alert to metaphor and simile. We have to respond to imaginative comparisons that make us see one thing while making us think of another.

For instance, in John Donne's "A Valediction: Forbidding Mourning," we are asked to visualize "gold to airy thinness beat"—gold hammered incredibly thin by the goldsmith's art, so that an ounce or less of the metal will yield enough gold leaf to gild a whole column or an altar in a church. But in reading the poem, we are expected to make the connection between the gold leaf we see and the love uniting the speaker in the poem and his wife. Their love (precious like gold) also is infinitely malleable or "stretchable," so that instead of the journey causing a "breach" or break, their love will merely expand (enduring an "expansion") to bridge the distance.

When you prepare a paper that focuses on the workings of metaphor, consider the following guidelines:

✧ Look for imaginative comparisons *spelled out or implied*. Similes are easy to recognize because the *as* or *like* or *as if* is part of the text ("*As* virtuous men pass mildly away . . ."). Metaphors do not carry such a label; the *as if* is merely implied. They are easiest to recognize when something is clearly not literally true. "Tear-floods" and "sigh-tempests" are not literally floods and tempests.

✧ Look for *sustained or extended metaphors* that the poet traces into their ramifications. The poet comparing his love to a ship lost at sea is likely to show more than one way in which being in love is like being on a drifting ship.

✧ Look for *organizing metaphors* that play a central role in the poem as a whole. A poem may be built around the metaphor of the ice skaters, who are like people moving quickly across the surface of their lives, dancing on the ice. (Often a poem builds up to a culminating metaphor that stays with us after we finish reading.)

✧ Respond to the *range of associations* of key metaphors. With most poetic metaphors, there is no simple one-to-one relationship between figurative and literal meaning. Try to do justice to what is left out in a simple prose paraphrase of a metaphorical line. Explore the images it conjures up; respond to the emotions it brings into play.

✧ Look for the *connections* between the metaphors in a poem. For instance, they may be variations on a theme, reinforcing or driving home a central concern of the poet. Or they may reflect polarities that set up the basic tension or challenge in a poem. Or they may be part of an escalating series of metaphors that lead up to a new way of seeing or feeling.

Reading Notes   When writing a paper about a poem rich in metaphor and simile, you may want to start with reading notes that take stock of the imaginative comparisons in the poem. Here are sample reading notes for John Donne's "A Valediction: Forbidding Mourning":

The parting of the lovers is compared to a death: "As virtuous men pass mildly away / . . . So let us melt, and make no noise." Virtuous people who are dying have nothing to fear in the afterlife and therefore die in peace. A journey separating the lovers is in some ways like the separation caused by death, but it should be like a virtuous person's death—without fear and emotional upheaval.

The noisy mourning of others is compared to floods ("tear-floods") and tempests ("sigh-tempests").

Telling others of the speaker's intimate, private love (through loud display of grief) would be like priests revealing the mysteries of their faith to "the laity," that is, to lay people—to unappreciative, unprepared outsiders. The lovers would then "profane" the mysteries of their love—desecrating something sacred by taking it down to the level of ordinary reality.

The upheavals in the lives of ordinary lovers are earthquakes ("moving of the earth"). But any disturbance in the more refined loves of the two people in this poem is "a trepidation of the spheres"—it is like the far-off trembling in the crystal spheres of the heavens, which is "innocent" or harmless as far as actual damage in the world around us is concerned.

The "souls" of ordinary clods are not really soul but sense—they stay on the level of sense perception and sensual feeling; they don't really have a "soul."

True love is like gold—it can be stretched incredibly thin like gold leaf without breaking.

The souls of the two lovers are joined like twin compasses. One leg, "the fixed foot," is planted firmly in the center. The other "travels," describing a perfect circle, returning to its point of origin. The farther the moving leg extends from the fixed center, the more the stationary leg needs to incline or lean toward it (it "harkens after it"). But at the same time the stationary leg keeps the moving leg from roaming too far, from going off on a tangent. In fact the firmness of the "fixed foot" (the person who stayed home) makes sure the absent lover comes full circle.

Organizing the Paper How would you organize this material? The metaphors and similes in Donne's poem are each bold and original in their own right. You often need to make the required mental leap from what you see to what it means. At the same time, the metaphors shift rapidly, and you need to be alert if you are not to be left behind. To write a unified paper, you will have to aim at working out an overall framework or perspective. You will have to try to fit the rapidly shifting individual metaphors into an overall pattern.

The student author of the following paper uses the idea of the journey—which is the subject of the poem—as the organizing principle for the paper.

SAMPLE STUDENT PAPER

Thou Shalt Not Cry When I Am Gone

In a favorite scene in yesterday's romantic movies, someone is boarding a train, going off to war or to some far-off assignment or tour of duty. The person left behind is fighting back tears as the train slowly pulls out of the station. The traveler is trying to stay calm, forestalling the "tear-floods" and "sigh-tempests" that John Donne dreads in his farewell poem, "A Valediction: Forbidding Mourning." Scheduled to leave on a journey to France, Donne pleads with his wife Anne More to accept his departure in a spirit of calm acceptance, confident that the strength of their love will triumph over their physical separation.

In arguing against mourning and emotional upheaval, Donne takes us on a journey through a sequence of bold unexpected images, each one a metaphor or a simile for the love between him and his wife. Finally we reach the circle drawn by the twin compasses in the final stanzas as the metaphor for a perfect love that will bring him back to the starting point of his journey, making "me end where I begun." The structure of the poem, a progression from one striking metaphor or simile to another, is the more appropriate when we consider that the poem was presented to his wife before he departed on a journey.

The journey begins with an unexpected analogy between the impending separation of the lovers and death. The poet says, "So let us melt"—go quietly, like snow that melts in the March sun, making "no noise" (5). The startling comparison is between their parting and the death of "virtuous men," who "pass mildly away / And whisper to their souls to go" (1–2). Virtuous men and their friends have no need to mourn unduly at their passing—after all, their virtue in this life has assured them of glory and reward in the life to come. Similarly, the poet and his love have no need for noise at their separation—"no tear-floods, nor sigh-tempests" (6). There is no need to weep and sigh, since the beauty and strength of their love will survive their separation.

Their love is in fact almost sacred. It would be profaned if it should be made known to others, who could not comprehend love on such a high spiritual plane. Since it is almost holy, the lovers should not cheapen or defile it through such ordinary demonstration of grief as weeping or lamenting. Like priests, they should guard their sacred mysteries from "profanation" by the laity (7–8).

We next move to a larger circle than the temple where love is protected from the uninitiated. Even the earth is not adequate to contain true love. For more common lovers, the earthquake of separation would bring "harms and fears" (9). But the love between the poet and his wife is above the reach of such earthly upheavals. It is as if their love resided in the heavens, among the crystal spheres of the Ptolemaic universe. Even when there is "trepidation" or trembling of the spheres, it is "innocent"—it will cause no harm here below. Donne remains in the Ptolemaic universe for another verse or two: Ordinary earth-bound lovers are caught up in the physical presence of the other person, which like all material things in this "sublunary" sphere below the moon is subject to change and decay. Their "soul is sense"; the only outlet for what soul they have is through the five senses. Their love hinges on the physical act of love, which cannot be consummated in the absence of the beloved. More refined lovers don't need the presence of the physical body; they "care less" if they have to miss "eyes, lips, and hands" (13–20).

The love of these two exceptional lovers is like gold—not just because it is precious, but because gold can be beaten into a layer of the thinnest gold leaf that stretches incredibly far—perhaps even from England to France without a "breach" or breaking. However, the culminating metaphor is that of the twin compasses, which "are two" only in the sense that there are two legs joined permanently at the top. The "fixed foot" of the stay-at-home "leans and harkens" after the other that "far doth roam" (25–30). As the foot that actually draws the circle travels around the stationary part, that part must incline at the right angle. (It cannot just forget about the "roaming" part.)

Together, the twin compasses create a circle, to Donne's contemporaries the most perfect shape in the universe. The firmness of the "other foot" enables the poet to come full circle; it makes his journey "end where I begun" (36).

QUESTIONS

1. How well does this paper read the metaphors in the poem? (In the poem, which are metaphors, and which are similes?) Where or how does the paper help you understand Donne's figurative language? Do you disagree with any of the interpretations? Did the student writer miss anything important?

2. Which of the metaphors or similes in this poem seem to you particularly unexpected or strange? Which make the most sense after the reader has a chance to think about them?

3. One reader thought the poem "terribly romantic," since the poet wants the love between him and his wife to be perfect, better than anyone else's. At the opposite end of the spectrum, another reader found the poet to be romantic on the surface but really insensitive, lecturing a silent, passive partner about what she should feel and think. Where do you stand? How do you respond to the poem?

15 SYMBOL
A World of Meanings

Symbols are the bridging language between the visible and the invisible world.

ANGELIS ARRIEN

FOCUS ON SYMBOLS

A **symbol** is something that we can see but that has acquired a meaning beyond itself. A plow was literally the peasant's most basic tool—needed to break the sod and start the planting cycle that would lead to the bounty of the harvest. Through the ages, the plow became a symbol for the steady anonymous toil required to feed humankind. Like other powerful symbols, the plow activates a rich network of associations. It reminds us to honor the labor that staves off famine. It serves as an admonition to the privileged who squander in thoughtless luxury what the workers in the fields gain toiling from sunup to sundown.

We all know the language of symbols: The dove of peace prevails when nations sheathe the sword of war. The red cross protects volunteers on missions of mercy. The daily bread stands for what we need to sustain life; it becomes "the staff of life." Posters used in political campaigns often speak a symbolic language: The raised fist calls to armed struggle. Hands joined in a handshake proclaim human brotherhood. Chains were used to shackle a prisoner; they became a symbol of slavery and oppression. A broken chain, in turn, became a powerful symbol of freedom.

Many such symbols are well established. We read them the way we read familiar gestures: the raised palm that says "Stop!" or the outstretched palm that says "Please give." Poets use or adapt traditional symbols, but they will also often give new symbolic significance to objects and events. Rather than bring the meaning of a symbol *into* the poem from the outside, we have to read the meaning of the symbol *out of* the poem.

The following poem focuses our attention on the rose and on water, which are both rich in symbolic overtones and associations. The rose, often a deep red or blood red, has long stood for passion or for beauty. The more arid

511

the country, the more water is likely to be worshiped as the source of life, making the desert bloom, creating an oasis in a wasteland of rock or sand. What is the symbolic meaning of the rose and of water in this poem?

DENISE LEVERTOV   (born 1923)

To One Steeped in Bitterness   1964

Nail the rose
     to your mind's door
like a rat, a thwarted chickenhawk.
Yes, it has had its day.

And the water   5
    poured for you
which you disdain to drink,
yes, throw it away.

Yet the fierce rose
    stole nothing   10
from your cooped heart,
nor plucked your timid eye;
and from inviolate rock
    the liquid light
was drawn, that's dusty now   15
and your lips dry.

[handwritten annotations: Symbolism / the rose / the water; giving her love — wouldn't take it; fierce love; Treated it like a rat, nailed it to your mind's door; his heart like a rock; dead; No actual rose]

In this poem, we see a number of symbolic objects and symbolic gestures. We can imagine someone being offered a rose or a drink of water. We can also imagine the person turning these down. In the poem, as in real life, both of these gestures invite symbolic interpretation. Both the water and the disdainful gesture that throws it out are likely to mean something beyond themselves. They reveal an attitude, a state of mind. The gesture of pouring the water may mean friendship or hospitality. The gesture of refusing it may symbolize bitterness and hostility.

What is likely to be the symbolic meaning of the rose? We are asked to imagine it nailed to the "mind's door" by the bitter, hostile person being addressed in the poem. The person "steeped in bitterness," with a "cooped heart," would nail the rose to the barn door the way ranchers nail varmint they consider their natural enemies. The bitter person has become hostile to what would bring rich beauty like that of the rose into his or her starved life. The rose is "fierce"; its beauty is not meek (like that of a shrinking violet) but assertive, calling passionately for our attention. But it would take or steal nothing for offering its intense, challenging beauty to the beholder.

THE RECEPTIVE READER

What is likely to be the symbolic meaning of the water? The person steeped in bitterness disdainfully rejects the offered water, which is like "liquid light," and which would bring much-needed liquid to dry, parched lips. What would the parched soul be thirsting for? Love? Human contact?

What is the difference between symbol and metaphor?

✧ The water being offered a person is *literally* there. It could be provided impersonally the way a glass of water is routinely set down in front of a restaurant guest. But it can also become part of a symbolic gesture, the way we offer a drink to show hospitality, human interest. The water then becomes a symbol. It is literally there, but it has a meaning beyond itself.

✧ When in the poem the rose is nailed to the "mind's door," the mind does not literally have any doors. The mind resides in the gray matter of the brain, where there are no hinges or knobs, no doors. The door is not literally there; it is a metaphor. It is *as if* the mind had a door like a barn door, to which the embittered person could nail the offering like a trophy, the way a vengeful farmer might display there the pelt of a coyote. The metaphor acts out the rejecting person's anger and hostility, enabling us to visualize and share these emotions.

THE LANGUAGE OF SYMBOLS

What the bee knows
Tastes in the honey
Sweet and sunny.
JOHN FANDEL, "TRIBUTE"

Symbols, like metaphors, are close to the heart of the poet's language. Metaphor and symbol both connect what we see to something else, but they work differently. We use a metaphor when we call our planet "spaceship earth." We focus on the planet and compare it to a spaceship (which has limited resources and an uncertain destination). The spaceship is not literally there. We speak symbolically when we make the ill-fated *Titanic* a symbol of human pride. In this case, the ship was literally there and sank to the bottom of the sea. There was a real ship, which now makes us think of something beyond itself—shortsighted human pride brought low by a catastrophic event.

A poet will often center a poem on a unifying symbol. Often these symbols are rooted in age-old human experience, drawing on a community of shared meanings. They are often rich in overtones and associations. For instance, since the dawn of human history, the first budding green life of April, after the barrenness and ice of winter, has served as a symbol of the triumph of life over death. The earliest poets and storytellers told stories of the return of spring; Easter rites celebrated the faith of the tribe in rebirth and renewal. Green is a potently symbolic color: In the depth of winter, a sprig of evergreen (or a whole tree) can symbolize our defiant faith that burgeoning life will return to the barren, frozen land.

Poets draw on this common fund of symbolic meanings, shaping them to their own creative purposes. In reading the following poem, we soon realize that the frogs in the basement of the abandoned house are more than a strange footnote in the speaker's childhood memories. They make us wonder: Where do they come from? How can they survive in the wrecked ruin of the abandoned house? We are likely to conclude that they have a larger meaning: They become symbols of surviving and renewing life. The "green chorus" of the green frogs, who had "slept in an icy bed" all winter, comes back to life in the spring, "pouring / Out of their green throats."

DAVID WAGONER   (born 1926)

The Other House   1983

As a boy, I haunted an abandoned house
Whose basement was always full of dark-green water
Or dark-green ice in winter,
Where frogs came back to life and sang each spring.

On broken concrete under the skeleton   5
Of a roof, inside ribbed walls, I listened alone
Where the basement stairs went down
Under the water, down into their music.

During storms, our proper house would be flooded too.
The water would spout from drains, through the foundation   10
And climb the basement stairs
But silently, and would go away silently,
As silent as my father and mother were
All day and during dinner and after
And after the radio   15
With hardly a murmur all the way into sleep.   *go silent into sleep and stay silent*

All winter, the frogs slept in an icy bed,   *— even when they go silent they sing*
Remembering how to sing when it melted.   *again*
If I made a sound, they stopped
And listened to me sing nothing, singing nothing.   20

But gradually, finally April would come pouring
Out of their green throats in a green chorus
To chorus me home toward silence.
Theirs was the only home that sang all night.

THE RECEPTIVE READER

1. Would you call the sound the frogs make "music"? What makes the "other house" an unlikely or unpromising setting for songs celebrating the return of spring? Do the frogs and the setting undercut the symbolism of spring and renewal for you?

2. The poet does not take us to the boy's own "proper house" till the third stan-

za. Why? What is the key to the polar opposition of what the two houses stand for? How is this polarity central to the poem as a whole?

3. Is there anything symbolic about the frogs' falling silent when they heard the boy?

4. Do you think the boy has been permanently influenced by his parents? Do you agree with the following student reaction to the poem?

> There is no renewal in spring-green trees if it does not resonate on the inside. A soul that cannot sing at the melting of the snows is winter-cold, ice-hard, regardless of the sun's warmth. A dark mysterious center that sings without sunlight breathes more life than this proper emptiness. The coldness of the silent parent is visited upon the son, perhaps for always, so his soul can never vibrate with mysterious yearnings, never feel the spring-green trees.

THE PERSONAL RESPONSE

In your own growing up, how much "silence" has there been and how much "song"?

THE CREATIVE DIMENSION

When we read a poem that has a strong impact on us, a haunting image or central symbol may linger in our minds. Look at the way the following student-written passage re-creates the lasting impression the poem left in the student's mind. Then do your own re-creation of a lasting impression left in your mind by this poem, by the Levertov poem, or by a poem later in this chapter.

> In spring,
> after the ice melts
> and the drains fill
> the concrete cracks
> of the basement floor
> with green water,
> the frogs are born
> to keep me company
> and fill my silent nights
> with songs.

When the language of symbols threatens to become too conventional, poets—like painters, photographers, or journalists—help it evolve and refresh itself. In our modern world, the bulldozer and the oil-drenched seabird have become symbols in the confrontation between technological progress and ecological survival. In a newspaper photograph printed after an oil spill, we do not just see an individual bird, its plumage clotted with black goo. We see a symbol of both wildlife and human life endangered by a technology spinning out of control.

In the following poem, the poet seizes on a symbolic incident in order to enlist the readers' sympathies. How does the chain saw become a symbol for the machine age in the poem?

DONALD FINKEL (born 1929)

They   1975

are at the end of our street now cutting down trees
a scream like a seven foot locust
they have cut off another
neatly at the pavement
never again will the pin-oak threaten a taxi   5
will the ash lie in wait to fall on a child   *— bad angle dead tree*

it is a good time for this
the sun is bright
the plane° has only just begun   *sycamore*
to sprout little shoots from under her fingernails *— personification*   10
never again will she dance
her terrible saraband° in the tornado   *stately court dance*
the sweet gum trembles
bristling with tiny mines like brown sea urchins
never again will he drop them on the walk   15
to menace the sensible shoes of mailmen

they have brought a machine that eats trees
and shits sawdust
they cut off limbs to feed it
snarling it chews the pale green fingers of the plane   20
the pin-oak's wrinkled elbows and knees
they fill truck after truck with the dust   *— must be cutting down alot of trees*
in the schoolyard now they are cutting down the children
I hear their screams
first at the ankles   25
it is nothing then to sever
their soles from the asphalt
there is no danger their falling
on the school and crushing it

I have invented a machine that shoots words *they can cut faster than he*   30
I type faster and faster   *can write*
I cannot keep up with them
in front of the house now they are cutting the rosebush
vainly she scratches their hands like a drowning kitten
they are cutting the grass   35
scythes in their wheels they race over our lawn
flashing in the sun like the chariots of the barbarians
the grass blades huddle whimpering
there is no place to go
it is spring and the street is alive   40
with the clamor of motors
the laughter of saws

THE RECEPTIVE READER

1. Where in the poem do we hear the voices approving of the tree-cutting operation? With what effect does the poet cite them?

2. How many examples can you find of pervasive *personification* in this poem—ascribing quasi-human features to the vegetation? What is the effect on the readers? How does it prepare them for what happens in the school yard? (Why is there no stanza break or transition before the school yard massacre?) What makes the cutting of the rose bush especially traumatic?

3. How does the chariot *simile* reinforce the prevailing perspective of the poem? Why does the poet keep reminding us that it is spring?

THE PERSONAL RESPONSE

What makes the machines in this poem frightening symbols of human technology? What side do you take in the confrontation conjured up by this poet?

The following poem is by a Chinese immigrant who came with his parents from Indonesia. Central to the poem is the meeting of two worlds: One of these worlds is symbolized by the scroll paintings that link the father to millennia of old-country tradition and by the fruit (the persimmon) that is a touch of home to the poet but a curiosity to his classmates. The other world is represented by the monolingual teacher questioning the intelligence of students learning to learn in a new language, learning to live in a new culture.

LI-YOUNG LEE   (born 1957) *born in Indonesia. Believes that the King James Bible contains the greatest poetry.*

Persimmons

1986

In sixth grade Mrs. Walker
slapped the back of my head
and made me stand in the corner
for not knowing the difference
between *persimmon* and precision.   5
How to choose

how to eat a persimmon

persimmons. This is precision.
Ripe ones are soft and brown-spotted.
Sniff the bottoms. The sweet one
will be fragrant. How to eat: 10
put the knife away, lay down newspaper.
Peel the skin tenderly, not to tear the meat.
Chew on the skin, suck it,
and swallow. Now, eat
the meat of the fruit,   15
so sweet
all of it, to the heart.

Dona undresses, her stomach is white.
In the yard, dewy and shivering
with crickets, we lie naked,   20
face-up, face-down.
I teach her Chinese. Crickets: *chiu chiu*. Dew: I've forgotten.
Naked: I've forgotten.
Ni, wo: you and me.
I part her legs,   25
remember to tell her
she is beautiful as the moon.

Other words
that got me into trouble were
fight and *fright, wren* and *yarn*.   30
Fight was what I did when I was frightened,
fright was what I felt when I was fighting.
Wrens are small, plain birds,
yarn is what one knits with.
Wrens are soft as yarn.   35
My mother made birds out of yarn.
I loved to watch her tie the stuff;
a bird, a rabbit, a wee man.

Mrs. Walker brought a persimmon to class
and cut it up   40
so everyone could taste
a *Chinese apple*. Knowing
it wasn't ripe or sweet, I didn't eat
but watched the other faces.

My mother said every persimmon has a sun   blindness - see & not see   45
inside, something golden, glowing,
warm as my face.

Once, in the cellar, I found two wrapped in newspaper
forgotten and not yet ripe.
I took them and set them both on my bedroom windowsill,   50
where each morning a cardinal
sang. *The sun, the sun.*

Finally understanding
he was going blind,
my father would stay up all one night   55
waiting for a song, a ghost.
I gave him the persimmons,
swelled, heavy as sadness,
and sweet as love.

This year, in the muddy lighting   60
of my parents' cellar, I rummage, looking
for something I lost.
My father sits on the tired, wooden stairs,

black cane between his knees,
hand over hand, gripping the handle. 65

He's so happy that I've come home.
I ask how his eyes are, a stupid question.
All gone, he answers.

Under some blankets, I find a box.
Inside the box I find three scrolls. 70
I sit beside him and untie
three paintings by my father:
Hibiscus leaf and a white flower.
Two cats preening.
Two persimmons, so full they want to drop from the cloth.

He raises both hands to touch the cloth,
asks, *Which is this?*

This is persimmons, Father.

Oh, the feel of the wolftail on the silk,
the strength, the tense 80
precision in the wrist.
I painted them hundreds of times
eyes closed. These I painted blind.
Some things never leave a person:
scent of the hair of one you love, 85
the texture of persimmons,
in your palm, the ripe weight.

THE RECEPTIVE READER

1. From what angle are you looking at the bilingual student's learning in this poem? How is it different from what you might have expected? (How does the poem turn the tables on the teacher?)

2. The persimmon is first introduced in a casual or humorous way. (How and why?) It becomes a *central symbol,* providing a common strand for the poem as a whole. What different associations and memories cluster around the fruit? What role does it play in the poem as a whole?

3. What other details in this poem have a symbolic significance?

4. How close to or distant from the family's cultural roots is the speaker in the poem?

THE PERSONAL RESPONSE

What experience have you had with different cultural traditions or bilingual Americans? What have you learned about barriers to communication? Does this poem help you cross the barriers separating different cultures?

THE CREATIVE DIMENSION

Write about a symbolic object or incident that for you calls up memories of home, family, or the older generation. Choose a symbol that best sums up deep-seated feelings or vivid memories.

EXPLORATIONS ⟩———

Understanding Symbols

The following poem was written by a famous English poet of the Romantic Age, an era of both revolution and reaction. The title of the poem names an Egyptian pharaoh who, like other early Egyptian rulers, commissioned colossal statues of himself. According to the poem, what did he want the statue he commissioned to symbolize? What does the statue symbolize for the poet? Shelley, like other Romantics, was a rebel against tyrannical authority. How does this commitment show in the poem?

PERCY BYSSHE SHELLEY (1792–1822)

Ozymandias   1818

I met a traveler from an antique land
Who said: "Two vast and trunkless legs of stone
Stand in the desert . . . Near them on the sand,
Half-sunk, a shattered visage° lies, whose frown,   *face*
And wrinkled lip, and sneer of cold command,   5
Tell that its sculptor well those passsions read
Which yet survive, stamped on these lifeless things,
The hand that mocked them, and the heart that fed:
And on the pedestal these words appear:
'My name is Ozymandias, king of kings: 10
Look on my works, ye Mighty, and despair!'
Nothing beside remains. Round the decay
Of that colossal wreck, boundless and bare
The lone and level sands stretch far away."

PUBLIC AND PRIVATE SYMBOLS

Some poets develop a symbolic language of their own that may at first seem private or obscure. However, it gradually becomes more meaningful to us as we learn more about the poet or read several poems by the same poet. We learn the poet's symbolic language; we gradually feel less like strangers in the poet's world of meanings. The English poet William Blake was a precursor of the Romantic movement. For him, all experience was shot through with symbolic meanings—he was able "to see a world in a grain of sand / And a heaven in a wild flower." Breaking with eighteenth-century standards of rationality and restraint, he used bold, unusual symbols to celebrate the divine energies at work in the universe. He glorified exuberance and excess, using the lion, the tiger, and the eagle as symbols of the fierce, terrifying divine energy animating creation.

The following is Blake's most famous poem. What do you think would be the poet's answers to the questions he asks in this poem?

WILLIAM BLAKE   (1757–1827)

The Tyger 1794

Tyger! Tyger! burning bright
In the forests of the night,
What immortal hand or eye
Could frame thy fearful symmetry?

In what distant deeps or skies 5
Burnt the fire of thine eyes?
On what wings dare he aspire?
What the hand, dare° seize the fire? *hand that dares*

And what shoulder, & what art,
Could twist the sinews of thy heart? 10
And when thy heart began to beat,
What dread hand? & what dread feet?

What the hammer? what the chain?
In what furnace was thy brain?
What the anvil? what dread grasp 15
Dare its deadly terrors clasp?

When the stars threw down their spears,
And water'd heaven with their tears,
Did he smile his work to see?
Did he who made the lamb make thee? 20

Tyger! Tyger! burning bright
In the forests of the night,
What immortal hand or eye
Dare frame thy fearful symmetry?

THE RECEPTIVE READER

1. How does Blake make us see the tiger as beautiful and terrifying at the same time?

2. How does Blake make us imagine the process of creation? (What associations do the images in the fourth stanza—the anvil, the furnace, the forge—bring into play?) How is his vision of the process different from what we might conventionally expect?

3. How has the lamb traditionally been used as a symbol of goodness? How has the tiger traditionally been used as a symbol of evil? How is Blake's use of these symbols different? Is the tiger evil or sinister in this poem?

4. What is the answer to the questions the poet asks in this poem?

In the twentieth century, the Irish poet William Butler Yeats stands out among poets using a highly individual symbolic language. In his earlier poetry, he had often drawn inspiration from the folklore and history of his native Ireland. In his later years, he repeatedly used symbols from the rich religious art of Byzantium (later Constantinople and now Istanbul), the fabled capital of the eastern part of the Roman Empire during the early Christian era. Byzantine art was famous for precious materials and finely crafted artifice. It was legendary for the ornamental patterns of its mosaics, for its carved ivory, its enamel work, and the work of its goldsmiths. Shortly before he wrote the following poem, Yeats had seen spectacular examples of Byzantine mosaics depicting saints and prophets (the "sages" mentioned in the third stanza) in a church at Ravenna in northern Italy.

In the poem, the poet takes us on a symbolic voyage. We travel from a country of the young that is "no country for old men" to a country of the mind more attuned to the spiritual needs of the aging speaker in the poem— "the holy city of Byzantium." What special fascination does the "artifice" of the Greek artists of Byzantium hold for the poet?

WILLIAM BUTLER YEATS (1865–1939)
Sailing to Byzantium 1927

1
That is no country for old men. The young
In one another's arms, birds in the trees
—Those dying generations—at their song,
The salmon-falls, the mackerel-crowded seas,
Fish, flesh, or fowl, commend all summer long 5
Whatever is begotten, born, and dies.
Caught in that sensual music all neglect
Monuments of unaging intellect.

2
An aged man is but a paltry thing,
A tattered coat upon a stick, unless 10
Soul clap its hands and sing, and louder sing
For every tatter in its mortal dress,
Nor is there singing school but studying
Monuments of its own magnificence;
And therefore I have sailed the seas and come 15
To the holy city of Byzantium.

3
O sages standing in God's holy fire
As in the gold mosaic of a wall,
Come from the holy fire, perne in a gyre,° *turn with a spiral motion*
And be the singing masters of my soul. 20
Consume my heart away, sick with desire
And fastened to a dying animal
It knows not what it is; and gather me
Into the artifice of eternity.

4
Once out of nature, I shall never take   25
My bodily form from any natural thing,
But such a form as Grecian° goldsmiths make   *Greek*
Of hammered gold and gold enameling
To keep a drowsy Emperor awake;
Or set upon a golden bough to sing   30
To lords and ladies of Byzantium
Of what is past, or passing, or to come.

Much of the early part of the poem revolves around a polar opposition of youth and age. The speaker in the poem finds himself out of place in a country of the young that is full of "sensual music." Conditioned to think positively of youth and burgeoning nature, we have to read out of the poem what turns the speaker away from them: Paradoxically, the very fact that the lovers are young reminds us that they are part of the inevitable cycle of begetting, growth, and decay. Like the birds in the trees, they are "dying generations"—the script that dooms them to aging, decay, and death is already written.

To the aging speaker in the poem, fastened to his decaying body as "to a dying animal" (line 22), there is no comfort in the surface vitality of a life caught up in the world of the senses. The second stanza focuses on the central paradox of the poem: The body decays, leaving the physical person little more than a scarecrow, "a tattered coat upon a stick." However, the intellect survives; the soul is still capable of song and artistic creation. Here is the answer to the decay of the body: The soul can metaphorically "clap its hands" and create immortal music. The "singing school" for the soul, teaching it to triumph over decay, is the work of artists that have gone before. In them, the human spirit has created "monuments of its own magnificence."

It is the search for a "singing school" for the human spirit that makes us embark on the voyage to the mythical "holy city of Byzantium." In the third stanza, we get a glimpse of the art that flourishes there. It does not aim at imitating nature. Instead, it creates an alternative to nature—a world of art that will defy age, decay, and death. We prize precious metals because they do not turn to rust like common iron. The hammered gold leaf and the finely crafted products of the goldsmith's art triumph over corrosion. Mosaics and enamel inlays resist the ravages of time. For us today, the word *artifice* often carries negative connotations, suggesting artwork that is *too* artificial, too far removed from nature. But here the creation of "artifice" is the whole point of the artist's work. The art of Byzantium shows sages and prophets purged of mortality in "God's holy fire." The incorruptible gold of the Byzantine goldsmith's work becomes a symbol of eternity.

In the fourth stanza, the speaker projects a state "out of nature," after death. Given a chance to assume a new shape, he would choose to be a bird made of hammered gold and gold enameling, set on a golden bough, singing "to lords and ladies of Byzantium." Art would leave nature behind. The creative spirit would triumph over the imperfections of the body. The conflict of youth and age would be resolved in the ageless permanence of art.

THE RECEPTIVE READER

1. Much of this poem revolves around related *polarities:* the opposition of youth and age, of intellect and the body, and of nature and art. What striking details help flesh out each of these polarities?

2. Why do the salmon fighting their way up the "salmon-falls" provide the poet with an especially appropriate *symbol* for life in the natural world?

3. In your own words, what vision of art or "artifice" is developed in the final two stanzas? How will "artifice" provide the answer to age and decay? What makes the artifacts of Byzantine art apt symbols for the poet's way of transcending or overcoming age?

4. In this poem, Yeats uses a finely crafted interlaced rhyme scheme called *ottava rima* (or "set of eight"). Why is it more appropriate to this poem than free-flowing free verse would be?

THE PERSONAL RESPONSE

Do you know or believe in a different view of the relationship between nature and art? How does it compare with the view developed in this poem?

CROSS-REFERENCES —For Discussion or Writing

Another famous exploration of the relation between life and art is John Keats' "Ode on a Grecian Urn" (p. 699). Compare and contrast the way the two poems deal with such central themes as youth and age, change and permanence, nature and art.

EXPLORATIONS

Crossing the Boundaries

The Russian poet Yevgeny Yevtushenko said, "Poetry is like a bird. It ignores all frontiers." How true is this statement of the language of symbols? How universal are they? Look at the use of a central but multifaceted symbol in the following poem by a Latin American poet. Gabriela Mistral grew up in poverty in Chile and left school at age eleven, but she became a teacher and was for many years the best-known woman writing in Latin America. She was the first Latin American to win the Nobel Prize (1945). She worked on educational reform in Mexico and later taught at Barnard, Vassar, Middlebury, and the University of Puerto Rico.

GABRIELA MISTRAL   (1889–1957)

To Drink   1938

TRANSLATED BY GUNDA KAISER

I remember gestures of infants
and they were gestures of giving me water.

In the valley of Rio Blanco
where the Aconcagua has its beginning,
I came to drink, I rushed to drink   5
in the fountain of a cascade,
which fell long and hard
and broke up rigid and white.
I held my mouth to the boiling spring
and the blessed water burned me,   10
and my mouth bled three days
from that sip from the valley of Aconcagua.

In the fields of Mitla, a day
of harvest flies, of sun, of motion,
I bent down to a well and a native came   15
to hold me over the water,
and my head, like a fruit,
was within his palms.
I drank what he drank,
for his face was with my face,   20
and in a lightning flash I realized
I, too, was of the race of Mitla.

On the Island of Puerto Rico,
During the slumber of full blue,
my body calm, the waves wild,   25
and the palms like a hundred mothers,
a child broke through skill
close to my mouth a coconut for water,
and I drank, like a daughter,
water from a mother, water from a palm.   30
And I have not partaken greater sweetness
with my body nor with my soul.

At the house of my childhood
my mother brought me water.
From one sip to another sip   35
I saw her over the jug.
The more her head rose up
the more the jug was lowered.
I still have my valley,
I have my thirst and her vision.   40
This will be eternity
for we still are as we were.

I remember gestures of infants
and they were gestures of giving me water.

THE RECEPTIVE READER

How does water serve as the central symbol in this poem? What are its widening circles of association and symbolic meaning? Which of the symbolic meanings and associations seem universal? Which seem specific to this poem or to this poet's experience?

THE CREATIVE DIMENSION

Water—like sun, earth, light, birth, or death—is one of the great constants of human experience. Cluster one of these. Then write a passage tracing the web of meanings that the term has for you.

SYMBOL AND ALLEGORY

In an **allegory,** symbols work together in a set pattern. Symbolic figures or objects play their roles like actors in a drama. In the following poem, the road, the hill, the inn, the darkness at end of day, the traveler, and the other wayfarers all play their assigned roles in the poet's allegorical vision of our journey through life. Each detail in the literal journey has its parallel in our spiritual journey to our final destination. The poet belonged to a group of painters and writers (the Pre-Raphaelites) who turned to medieval art and religion for inspiration, and her poem has the earnest, solemn tone of much English Victorian (mid-nineteenth-century) poetry.

CHRISTINA ROSSETTI (1830–1894)

Uphill   1858

Does the road wind uphill all the way?
    Yes, to the very end.
Will the day's journey take the whole long day?
    From morn to night, my friend.   — life

But is there for the night a resting place?   5
    A roof for when the slow dark hours begin. — death eternity
May not the darkness hide it from my face?
    You cannot miss that inn.   can't miss death

Shall I meet other wayfarers at night?
    Those who have gone before.   10
Then must I knock, or call when just in sight?
    They will not keep you standing at that door.

Shall I find comfort, travel-sore and weak?
    Of labor you shall find the sum.
Will there be beds for me and all who seek?   15
    Yea, beds for all who come.

THE RECEPTIVE READER

Who are the two speakers in this poem? What is the meaning of each of the symbolic details in this allegory? What makes this poem earnest and uplifting in the Victorian nineteenth-century manner?

EXPLORATIONS

Understanding Allegory

In the following short allegorical poem, what is the meaning of the symbolic details? What role does each play in the allegory?

WILLIAM BLAKE   (1757–1827)

A Poison Tree   1794

I was angry with my friend:
I told my wrath, my wrath did end.
I was angry with my foe:
I told it not, my wrath did grow.

And I watered it in fears,   5
Night and morning with my tears:
And I sunnèd° it with smiles,   *gave it sunlight*
And with soft deceitful wiles.

And it grew both day and night,
Till it bore an apple bright.   10
And my foe beheld it shine,
And he knew that it was mine.

And into my garden stole
When the night had veiled the pole:
In the morning glad I see   15
My foe outstretched beneath the tree.

THE RECEPTIVE READER

1. Much medieval poetry preached against wrath as one of the seven deadly sins. Is this poem a warning against wrath?

2. What makes this poem simple and almost childlike in its form and its symbolism? Does the simple form undercut the serious question the poem raises?

THE PERSONAL RESPONSE

Are you aware of any trends in pop psychology that relate to the issue of whether to hold in or release negative emotions?

EXPLORATIONS

Interacting Symbols

What is the relationship between the three key symbols in the following poem by Mexico's best-known poet? Octavio Paz, who won a Nobel Prize for literature in 1991, has lectured to large audiences in the United States. He served as Mexico's ambassador to India but resigned in 1968 in protest over the bloody repression of student demonstrators before the Olympic Games in Mexico City. He has thought and written much about the dialogue between the North American and Latin American cultures. He has said, "The vision of Latin America as part of the Third World is oversimple. . . . It's enough to reflect that we are Christians, we are Spanish and Portuguese and gained our independence with the tools of French and English ideas."

OCTAVIO PAZ   (born 1914)
Wind and Water and Stone   1979

TRANSLATED BY MARK STRAND

The water hollowed the stone,
the wind dispersed the water,
the stone stopped the wind.
Water and wind and stone.

The wind sculpted the stone.   5
the stone is a cup of water,
the water runs off and is wind.
Stone and wind and water.

The wind sings in its turnings,
the water murmurs as it goes,   10
the motionless stone is quiet.
Wind and water and stone.

One is the other, and is neither:
among their empty names
they pass and disappear,   15
water and stone and wind.

THE RECEPTIVE READER

In this poem, what is the relationship of water, wind, and stone? What is their possible symbolic significance? Why does the order of the three vary in the last line of each stanza?

POEMS FOR FURTHER STUDY

In reading the following poems, pay special attention to objects or figures that may have symbolic significance. How does the poet use or change familiar symbols? What images, emotions, or ideas does the symbol bring into play? What role does a symbol play in the poem as a whole?

LORNA DEE CERVANTES   (born 1954)

Refugee Ship   1981

Like wet cornstarch, I slide
past my grandmother's eyes. Bible
at her side, she removes her glasses.
The pudding thickens.
Mama raised me without language,   5

I'm orphaned from my Spanish name.
The words are foreign, stumbling
on my tongue. I see in the mirror
My reflection: bronzed skin, black hair.

I feel I am a captive   10
aboard the refugee ship.
The ship that will never dock.
El barco que nunca atraca.

THE RECEPTIVE READER

1. Do the cornstarch and the Bible in this poem have possible *symbolic* meanings?
2. How could the speaker in the poem have been raised "without language" and be "orphaned" from her Spanish name?
3. What did the mirror tell her?
4. The last line repeats in Spanish the previous line about the refugee ship "that will never dock." Why are some refugee ships not allowed to dock or their passengers not allowed to reach land? What makes the refugee ship a symbol of the speaker's own journey? What makes it a symbol of the experience of untold millions of refugees in the modern world?

THE CREATIVE DIMENSION

Sometimes a poem is for us like a mirror in which we see our own faces. Look at what one student saw in the mirror of the Cervantes poem. Then write your own response to a poem that seems like a mirror for a part of yourself.

> The refugee ship reminds me of the girl I see in the mirror every day. The speaker feels left out of the culture in which she grew up. In the Hispanic culture, there is a certain pressure from the family to retain one's culture. Maybe the poet is a refugee because she forgot all her tradition. Now she sees the Hispanic only in her appearance, not in her head.

MATTHEW ARNOLD   (1822–1888)

Dover Beach   1867

The sea is calm tonight.
The tide is full, the moon lies fair
Upon the straits; on the French coast the light

Gleams and is gone; the cliffs of England stand,
Glimmering and vast, out in the tranquil bay.   5
Come to the window, sweet is the night-air!
Only, from the long line of spray
Where the sea meets the moon-blanched° land,   *pale under the moon*
Listen! you hear the grating roar
Of pebbles which the waves draw back, and fling,   10
At their return, up the high strand,
Begin, and cease, and then again begin,
With tremulous cadence° slow, and bring   *regular rhythm*
The eternal note of sadness in.

Sophocles° long ago   *Greek playwright* 15
Heard it on the Aegean,° and it brought   *sea circling Greece*
Into his mind the turbid° ebb and flow   *murky*
Of human misery; we
Find also in the sound a thought,
Hearing it by this distant northern sea.   20

The Sea of Faith
Was once, too, at the full, and round° earth's shore   *around*
Lay like the folds of a bright girdle° furled.   *sash circling waist*
But now I only hear
Its melancholy, long, withdrawing roar,   25
Retreating, to the breath
Of the night-wind, down the vast edges drear
And naked shingles° of the world.   *pebble-strewn beaches*

Ah, love, let us be true
To one another! for the world, which seems   30
To lie before us like a land of dreams,
So various, so beautiful, so new,
Hath really neither joy, nor love, nor light,
Nor certitude, nor peace, nor help for pain;
And we are here as on a darkling plain   35
Swept with confused alarms of struggle and flight,
Where ignorant armies clash by night.

THE RECEPTIVE READER

Matthew Arnold, influential Victorian lecturer and critic, was part of an idealistic generation beset by religious doubts. What is the *central symbol* in this poem? What gives it its special power or hold on the imagination? How is it followed up or reinforced in the poem? What is the poet's answer to the religious soul-searching of his time?

JOHN KEATS (1795–1821)

Bright Star   1819

Bright star, would I° were steadfast as thou art—   *I wish*
   Not in lone splendor hung aloft the night°   *high in night sky*

And watching, with eternal lids apart,
    Like nature's patient, sleepless Eremite,°   *religious hermit*
The moving waters at their priestlike task   5
    Of pure ablution° round earth's human shores,   *cleansing*
Or gazing on the new soft fallen mask
    Of snow upon the mountains and the moors—
No—yet still steadfast, still unchangeable,
    Pillowed upon my fair love's ripening breast,   10
To feel forever its soft fall and swell.
    Awake forever in a sweet unrest,
Still, still to hear her tender-taken breath,
And so live ever—or else swoon to death.

THE RECEPTIVE READER

1. Like the other Romantic poets of his generation, Keats intuitively and naturally imbued the physical universe around us with quasi-human life and feeling, at the same time endowing it with divine qualities inspiring religious awe. How does *personification* help Keats achieve these ends in this poem? (What is striking about images like the "eternal lids apart" or ebb and tide attending to their task of "pure ablution"?)

2. The first eight lines (or octave) of this sonnet develop one set of symbolic associations for the star, and then the next six lines (sestet) *reject* these. Why? What is the basic symbolic meaning of the star in this poem? Why is it strange or unexpected when applied to human love?

LUCILLE CLIFTON (born 1936)

My Mama Moved among the Days   1969

My Mama moved among the days
like a dreamwalker in a field;
seemed like what she touched was hers
seemed like what touched her couldn't hold,
she got us almost through the high grass   5
then seemed like she turned around and ran
right back in
right back on in

THE RECEPTIVE READER

What is the symbolic meaning of the high grass? Why does the poet repeat the last line?

ADRIENNE RICH (born 1929)

Aunt Jennifer's Tigers   1951

Aunt Jennifer's tigers prance across a screen,
Bright topaz denizens of a world of green.

They do not fear the men beneath the tree;
They pace in sleek chivalric certainty.

Aunt Jennifer's fingers fluttering through her wool   5
Find even the ivory needle hard to pull.
The massive weight of Uncle's wedding band
Sits heavily upon Aunt Jennifer's hand.

When Aunt is dead, her terrified hands will lie
Still ringed with ordeals she was mastered by.   10
The tigers in the panel that she made
Will go on prancing, proud and unafraid.

THE RECEPTIVE READER

1. What do the tigers represent in Aunt Jennifer's world? What does the wedding band represent? How do these two symbols function as *polar opposites* in this poem?

2. What is the range of meaning your dictionary gives for words like *topaz, denizen, chivalric, ordeal*? What do these words mean in the context of this poem?

3. In a later reprinting of this poem, the poet changed the words *prance* (line 1) and *prancing* (line 12) to *stride* and *striding*. What difference does the change make? Why do you think the poet might have wanted to change the words?

WRITING ABOUT LITERATURE

15. Seeing Symbols in Context (Focus on Prewriting)

> *A short poem is like a cricket; it rubs parts of its small body together to produce a sound that is magnified far above that of larger bodies and leaves a loud, chirping sound reverberating in the ears of a listener, saying, "I am small, but I am alive."*
>
> STUDENT PAPER

The Writing Workshop   When you write about symbolic meanings, you soon learn to steer your course between two extremes. Some readers are too *literal-minded* to respond to symbolic overtones and associations. To them, water is always just water. They need to become more perceptive, more alert to possible symbolic overtones. Water, for instance, may become the symbol of spiritual regeneration in a wasteland of dried-up feeling, where a poet might say: "In the desert of the heart / Let the healing fountain start" (W. H. Auden).

At the other extreme, some readers free-associate *too freely*, stopping only briefly to take a partial clue from the poem and leaving it behind too soon. If you do not keep an eye on how a symbol works in the poem, the danger is that anything may come to mean anything else. Look for reinforcement of possible symbolic meanings in the **context** of the poem as a whole. Green, a color that in one poem may symbolize envy, may in another poem be a symbol of growth, standing for the bright untamed vitality of nature. Ask yourself:

❖ Does a poem focus on *recurrent* elements with symbolic meanings? In Adrienne Rich's poem "Aunt Jennifer's Tigers," the proud, unafraid tigers keep prancing and pacing throughout the poem.

❖ Does the poem play off symbolic elements against their *opposites,* the way Rich plays off the untamed tigers against the restraining heavy wedding band symbolizing an oppressive marriage?

❖ Does the poem *build up* to the poet's introduction of a central symbol?

Focus on Prewriting

The following might be part of your prewriting as you work up a paper on Adrienne Rich's "Aunt Jennifer's Tigers."

Reading Notes   Here is a partial record of one student's close attention to key words and phrases:

> "Aunt Jennifer's *tigers* prance across a screen"
> Rich uses the tigers to represent Aunt Jennifer's free and true spirit, that part of her which is suppressed by her marriage to Uncle. This symbol is close to Blake's "Tyger," which represents divine energy that animates all creation. In Rich, the tiger represents that same energy within Aunt Jennifer, and ultimately in all women. The tiger is feared but not despised. Its ferocity is tempered because of its feline, catlike grace that makes it seem both beautiful and terrible at the same time.

> "Bright *topaz* denizens of a world of green. . .
> They pace in sleek *chivalric* certainty."
> The word *topaz* stands for a jewel, implying that the tigers are precious to the aunt. *Denizen* means "native inhabitant." These tigers are in their natural element, just as Aunt Jennifer wishes to be her true self. *Chivalric* seems to imply that like knights in armor the tigers are proud and sure in their role, not afraid of the men in their native territory.

> "The *massive* weight of Uncle's *wedding band*
> Sits *heavily* upon Aunt Jennifer's hand."
> The wedding ring, traditionally a symbol of love, honor, and protection, is transformed by words like *massive* and *heavily.* We get a mental picture of shackles and chains, not of wedding bells and love tokens.

Clustering   **Clustering** is a way of exploring the associations and connections of key words or concepts. In the more linear kind of free association, you jot ideas down more or less in the order in which they come to mind. Clustering instead allows you to branch out from a common core, pursuing different lines of association that soon form a web of meaning. Clustering is more suited to sketching possible *connections* than other kinds of brainstorming and prewriting.

Since many related associations tend to cluster around a central symbol, clustering may prove a good way to map the possible range of associations of a symbol that you mean to focus on in a paper. Here is one student's cluster of the key word *green:*

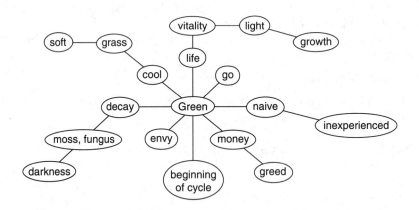

Here is the student writing up the results of the cluster:

> The word *green* has many positive associations; in fact, I listed all of my positive ones before the negative ones. Green makes us think of grass, rich in color, soft to the touch. Green vegetation signifies life—a plant thriving with water and sunlight. Plants are green at the beginning of their life cycle. (They fall into the "sear and yellow leaf" at the end—see *Macbeth*.) With this comes vitality. On the possibly negative side, green represents envy, as well as the greed associated with money. Green can be found in moss and fungus, a note of contrast with the green grass. Green, because of its use with unripe early vegetation, also represents inexperience (one who "just fell off the turnip truck," one who is not street-smart).

Background Notes   The tiger poem is one of the poet's earlier poems (Rich wrote it while she was a student). She wrote about Aunt Jennifer "with deliberate detachment" as a woman of a different generation, keeping a "cool" distance. In hindsight, she realized that she was weaving into this poem a part of herself she did not yet fully understand or recognize—her own role as a woman in a man's world. One student writer found the following illuminating statement by the poet in a collection of her essays:

> In writing this poem, composed and apparently cool as it is, I thought I was creating a portrait of an imaginary woman. But this woman suffers from the opposition of her imagination, worked out in

tapestry, and her life-style, "ringed with ordeals she was mastered by." It was important to me that Aunt Jennifer was a person as distinct from myself as possible—distanced by the formalism of the poem, by its objective, observant tone—even by putting the woman in a different generation.

From *On Lies, Secrets, and Silence*

A paper has a good chance of success when the writer at the beginning of the process of shaping and organizing has this kind of prewriting material at hand—a rich array of notes and tentative ideas to sort out and pull into shape.

SAMPLE STUDENT PAPER

Tigers and Terrified Hands

"When Aunt is dead, her terrified hands will lie / Still ringed with ordeals she was mastered by. / The tigers in the panel that she made / Will go on prancing, proud and unafraid." So ends the lush and very focused poem "Aunt Jennifer's Tigers" by Adrienne Rich. With memorable symbolism, the poet illuminates the tragedy of a woman who has lived the greater part of her life as the subordinate member in an unbalanced marriage.

The tiger has been symbolically used many times, and readers may assume that the presence of a tiger represents evil or darkness. In this poem, however, the tigers have an entirely different symbolic meaning. Aunt Jennifer's tigers, those "topaz denizens of a world of green" (2), are the brilliant jewel-like embodiments of the faded shadows hiding in their creator's spirit. Their world of green, bursting with life, vitality, regeneration, receives its life-force from the crushed stirrings in Aunt Jennifer's defeated soul. Any shred of hope or victory or joy that somehow remains within her flows unconsciously through her fluttering fingers into the tapestry she so painfully sews. These wonderful tigers do not sidle or sneak or skulk; they stride "proud and unafraid" (12). With the natural confidence of knighthood, they "pace in sleek chivalric certainty" (4). And, perhaps most importantly, they "do not fear the men beneath the tree" (3). Aunt Jennifer stitches her defiance the only way she can, unconscious of her own vision.

Aunt Jennifer is the perfect foil for her creations, the gorgeous tigers. She is so fraught with anxiety, nervous confusion, exhausted resignation, fear, and defeat, that her fingers, which can only "flutter" through her wool (5), "find even the ivory needle hard to pull" (6). This shade of woman is still weighed down by the "massive weight of Uncle's wedding band," which has doubtlessly drained her of any capacity for joy, celebration of life, or even peace. She is feeble, afraid, and "mastered." Even in death her "terrified hands will lie / Still ringed with ordeals she was mastered by" (9–10). She cannot escape the "ordeals" that were thrust upon her by her partner in marriage; the dominance and oppression that were her lot in marriage will always be part of who she was.

However, she has left a legacy. She has stitched a panel of glittering tigers that will "go on prancing, proud and unafraid" (12). Other women will come after Aunt Jennifer, and they may be inspired by her tigers to hold their heads up proudly and assume their rightful places as equals, rejecting any subordinate or humiliating roles. The tigers, often symbols of vitality, power, pride, fearlessness, here are those and more: They are the irrepressible human spirit and symbols of hope for woman's future.

The readers are not told of the particular ordeals in her marriage that defeated Aunt Jennifer. But they can make guesses and poke around for possibilities. The word *mastered* itself, used to describe Aunt Jennifer's situation, implies a "master." It is not a wild or unlikely conjecture that Aunt Jennifer's husband resembled other males who played the role of "master of the house," such as the poet's own father. Rich has said about her father: "After your death I met you again as the face of patriarchy, could name at last precisely the principle you embodied; there was an ideology at last which let me dispose of you, identify the suffering you caused, hate you righteously as part of a system, the kingdom of the fathers." Aunt Jennifer's husband, in the poet's mind, represents the traditional power of the male. And as one who has stated that "the search for justice and compassion is the great wellspring for poetry in our time," Rich is drawing from that wellspring in her poem "Aunt Jennifer's Tigers."

QUESTIONS

1. How does the initial quotation bring the two central interacting symbols in the poem into focus? What sentence in the introduction serves as the *thesis* spelling out the aunt's role in her marriage?

2. The body of the paper has a clear *plan;* it is laid out in accordance with a simple design. We look first at the tigers and their symbolic implications: What, according to this paper, do they symbolize? We then look at the symbolic meaning of the wedding ring: For what does it serve as a symbol? We then *return* to the tigers and look at them as the aunt's legacy: How does it point forward to the life of a future generation?

3. The flow of the paper owes much to *transitions* that point up an organic or dynamic rather than mechanical sequence. (The writer does not start major sections by saying, "The first symbol means . . ." and "The second symbol means. . . .") What major links highlight logical connections between key sections of the paper?

4. Major paragraphs of this paper have a rich *texture* of brief quotations interwoven with explanation and interpretation. For instance, how does the writer spell out shades of meanings or overtones and associations when looking at the role key words like *prance* or *chivalric* play in the poem?

5. Having finished the close reading of the poem, the writer addresses a question in the minds of many readers: "What is the connection between this poem and the poet's own life?" How does the *conclusion* of the paper answer this question?

6. Where do you agree and where do you want to take issue with this writer?

16 WORDS
The Web of Language

*Humans are animals suspended in webs of significance
they themselves have spun.*

CLIFFORD GEERTZ

*After many years as a writer, I find myself falling in love
with words. Maybe this is strange, like a carpenter
suddenly discovering how much he likes wood.*

J. RUTH GENDLER

*Stripped
day by day of all my garments,
dry naked tree,
in my solitary withered mouth
fresh words
will still blossom*

ALAÍDE FOPPA, "WORDS"

FOCUS ON WORDS

Poets are in love with words. Language is their tool, but it is a tool that fascinates and challenges them. They wrestle with words and meanings. They are sticklers for the right word. They may spend hours and days fine-tuning a poem—trading an almost-right word for a word with the exact shade of meaning. As readers, we have to be prepared to slow down and respond fully to a single word, taking in its full meaning, savoring its overtones and associations. We have to see how an important word echoes or interacts with other words in a poem. A key word may have widening circles of associations that spread from a center like the ripples when a rock has been dropped in a pond.

The following poem is by a nineteenth-century Catholic priest. His intense and difficult poetry remained unpublished in his lifetime, but he delighted twentieth-century readers with his bold, unconventional use of language. How does the poet's diction go beyond ordinary language?

537

GERARD MANLEY HOPKINS   (1844–1889)
Pied Beauty   1877

Glory be to God for dappled things—
    For skies of couple-color as a brinded° cow;   *streaked, flecked*
        For rose-moles all in stipple upon trout that swim;
Fresh firecoal chestnut-falls; finches' wings;
    Landscape plotted and pieced—fold,° fallow, and plow;   *pasture*   5
        And áll trádes, their gear and tackle and trim.
All things counter, original, spare, strange;
    Whatever is fickle, freckled (who knows how?)
        With swift, slow; sweet, sour; adazzle, dim;
He fathers-forth whose beauty is past change: 10
              Praise him.

This poem, in the words of one reader, is about "all the lovely dappled, alternating, changing and shifting things in the world" that come from God (J. R. Watson). Several points about the use of language in this poem stand out:

✦ First, the poet draws on a *range* of words for the "pied beauty" that he loves—and that he prefers to whatever is too smooth, too simple, too much of one piece. The word *pied* itself means showing two or more colors in blotches or splotches, like the hide of a horse. Then we have *dappled, stipple, plotted* (for land laid out in small strips and plots that alternate pasture, land lying fallow, and land under the plow). We have *pieced* (together), *freckled*. All these words work together to show the poet's preference for what goes "counter" to boring smoothness and simplicity—the same preference that makes the poet value sweet-and-sour over either cloying sweet or mouth-puckering sour.

✦ Second, the wording is often *compressed,* with much meaning packed into a compact phrase. For instance, "Fresh firecoal chestnut-falls" asks us to visualize chestnuts that have freshly fallen from the tree. They have split open their thick green covering on hitting the ground, revealing the intense reddish-brown of their skins. These seem to glow like coals on fire.

✦ Third, the poet's vocabulary is rooted in common speech. A cow is a cow, and a finch a finch. *Plow, trade, gear,* and *tackle* are all part of our everyday vocabulary. However, the poet's language easily moves *beyond* common speech: With "swift, slow," we might expect "bright, dim" as a parallel pairing of opposites. However, the poet uses "*adazzle,* dim" instead—heightening the contrast, making it more dazzling.

THE RECEPTIVE READER

1. What in the *wording* of this poem is most difficult for you? What are skies of "couple-color"? What do you make of the compressed phrase "fathers-forth"?

2. How would the gear and tackle of different trades meet Hopkins' criteria of beauty? Can you give examples of what he might have had in mind? What, for you, would be examples of things "counter, original, spare, strange"?

3. Is it strange that an unchanging God would create beauty that is variable and made up of contradictory elements?

4. How does the language of this poem live up to the poet's own standard of what is beautiful?

THE PERSONAL RESPONSE

The poet Richard Wilbur called this poem a "celebration of the rich and quirky particularity of all things whatever." Can you relate to this taste for the "quirky" and irregular, or do you prefer beauty that is smooth and harmonious?

When we concentrate on a poet's choice of words, we focus on the poet's **diction.** At times, prevailing fashion made poets adopt a special **poetic diction,** more elevated and more refined than ordinary speech. Poets went out of their way to widen the distance between common language and the language of poetry. The deer being hunted in the forest became the "beasts of chase" and the antlered trophies in the hunter's lodge became the "horny spoils that grace the walls." A phrase that takes the long way around, like *primary residence* for home, is called a **circumlocution.** In the eighteenth century, a fashionable poet might have called the finches in Hopkins' poem "members of the feathered tribe" or the plow "the plowman's humble tool." Modern poets have generally thought of common language and poetic language as a continuum. The poet uses our common mother tongue, making us hear in poetry the echo of the natural human voice. But the poet makes fuller and better use of it, going beyond the limited register of everyday talk. The poet uses *more* of language than we ordinarily do.

THE WILLING EAR

I wanted to write poetry in the beginning because I had fallen in love with words. The first poems I knew were nursery rhymes, and before I could read them for myself I had come to love them just for the words of them, the words alone.

DYLAN THOMAS

Although poems speak to the heart and the mind, they first of all please the ear. Words have a shape and texture of their own, and they combine in patterns that please (or grate upon) our ears. Children first fall in love with poetry not because of its meaning but because of its sound. (What is the meaning of "Hickory-dickory-dock / The mouse ran up the clock"?) The following poem makes us see the nighttime setting and share in night thoughts. However, it asks us first of all to relish the words and revel in the way they echo and play off one another in the poem. (How should the poem sound when read aloud?)

REUEL DENNEY (born 1913)

Fixer of Midnight 1961

He went to fix the awning,
Fix the roping,
In the middle of the night,
On the porch;
He went to fix the awning, 5
In pajamas went to fix it,
Fix the awning,
In the middle of the moonlight,
On the porch;
He went to fix it yawning; 10
The yawning of this awning
In the moonlight
Was his problem of the night;
It was knocking,
And he went to fix its flight. 15
He went to meet the moonlight
In the porch-night
Where the awning was up dreaming
Dark and light.
It was shadowy and seeming; 20
In the night the unfixed awning,
In his nightmare,
Had been knocking dark and bright.
It seemed late
To stop it in its deep careening. 25
The yawner went to meet it,
Meet the awning,
By the moon of middle night,
On his porch;
And he went to fix it right. 30

The sounds in this poem echo and run together without a full stop till the end. We can listen to the sound the way we can listen to the comings and goings of the surf as it washes over rocks by the shore. However, even with this poem, we do not just let the sounds wash over us. We delight in the interplay of sound and meaning. We can imagine the wide-open mouth of the sleepy "yawner" as the words *y-A-A-W-W-n-i-n-g* and *A-A-W-W-ning* echo through the poem. We can almost hear the "fixer" tiptoeing "in the middle of the night." We seem to hear the repeated KNOCK-KNOCK-KNOCKing of the careening awning echoing through the nightmare of the sleeper by the moon of middle night.

THE RECEPTIVE READER

Listen to more than one classmate read this poem aloud. How close do they come to how you think the poem is meant to sound?

When sound and sense intertwine as they do in "Fixer of Midnight," the sound seems to dance out the meaning. Sound echoes sense just as strongly in the following poem, inspired by a painting by the sixteenth-century Flemish painter Pieter Breughel. Breughel delighted in painting down-to-earth scenes of rural life, showing the peasants cavorting at weddings or at a country fair (the traditional Kermess). Look for the words that help you hear the sounds of the peasant music. Look for the words that help you see the peasants dance.

WILLIAM CARLOS WILLIAMS (1883–1963)
The Dance   1944

In Breughel's great picture, The Kermess,
the dancers go round, they go round and
around, the squeal and the blare and the
tweedle of bagpipes, a bugle and fiddles
tipping their bellies (round as the thick-   5
sided glasses whose wash they impound)
their hips and their bellies off balance
to turn them. Kicking and rolling about
The Fair Grounds, swinging their butts, those
shanks must be sound to bear up under such   10
rollicking measures, prance as they dance
in Breughel's great picture, The Kermess.

Many of the words here seem exactly right for what they stand for. Blunt words like *bellies* (thick as the thick-sided glasses) and *butts* and *shanks* seem more right than would squeamish words when applied to the anatomy of these very physical, unpolished merrymakers. *Squeal* and *blare* and *tweedle* make us hear the rustic instruments (it's not the New York Philharmonic!). The word *squeal* seems to sound out the penetrating, high-pitched sound that pigs make when in distress; *blare* blares forth like a trumpet; *tweedle* seems to tootle like a bagpipe that forever runs over the same limited range of sounds. The words for movements seem to roll and rollick just as the peasants do. *Prance* is indeed a prancing word, quite different from *slink* or *shuffle* or *slouch*. (To prance, we need room to high-step and half-lift our arms, proud of ourselves, feeling our oats.)

THE RECEPTIVE READER

1. Can you read this poem with the right rolling, rollicking rhythm? Can you read it so that your listeners can hear the underlying drumbeat of the peasant music? (Your class may want to audition several readings of this poem and vote for the best rendition.)

2. What is the difference between violins and fiddles, between belly and abdomen? (Where does the poet show that he is not *limited* to blunt down-to-earth language?)

THE PERSONAL RESPONSE

What kind of readers would love this poem? What kind of readers might get little out of it?

When words seem to sound out the sounds they describe, we call them **onomatopoeic,** or sound-mirroring, words. The *pop* in "Pop! goes the weasel" is onomatopoeic, as are the meow of the cat, the cockadoodledo of the rooster, and the ta-ra-ra-boom-diay of the marching band. We hear the same sound-mirroring effect in the hisssing of snakes, the buzzzing of bees, the rUMBLing of thunder, and the C-R-A-C-K of a whip. Although sound seldom echoes sense this closely, the right word in a poem is often a word that sounds right. When G. M. Hopkins says that "generations have TROD, have TROD," we seem to hear the heavy, slow, monotonous tread of successive generations. The same poet asks us to imagine a plowshare being made shiny by the friction of the plowed-up earth as the plodding horse pulls the plow through the furrow: "sheer PLOD makes PLOW down sillion [furrow] / Shine." The repeated initial *pl-* sound (which seems to offer more resistance than a simple *l*), together with the sequence of single syllables that each seem to require almost equal stress, seems to slow down the reader. It attunes the reader's ear to the slow plodding movement the passage describes. In a successful poem, there seems to be a wedding of words and meaning, of sound and sense.

EXPLORATIONS ⟨══════════════════════⟩

The Sound of the Poem

What makes the following poem appeal to the ear as much as to the eye and the mind?

A L   Y O U N G   (born 1939)

For Poets   1968

Stay beautiful
but don't stay down underground too long
Dont turn into a mole
or a worm
or a root   5
or a stone

Come on out into the sunlight
Breathe in trees
Knock out mountains
Commune with snakes   10
& be the very hero of birds

Dont forget to poke your head up
& blink
think
Walk all around   15
Swim upstream

Dont forget to fly

THE RECEPTIVE READER

1. How should this poem sound when read aloud? How does this poet use rhyme, repetition, and parallel phrasing? How do you think they should guide the reader?

2. Where does this poem go counter to what is conventional or expected? Where does a counterrhythm seem to mirror the poet's determination to "swim upstream"?

THE RIGHT WORD

A poet is, before anything else, a person who is passionately in love with language.

W. H. AUDEN

I try to make each and every word carry its full measure and not just its meaning defined.

LUCILLE CLIFTON

*I have a lot to say,
but no words to use.
I have problems to release,
but no release valve.
HELP ME!*

STUDENT POEM

Poets wrestle with both the sounds of words and their meanings. A short poem is a message that says much in little. In the days before direct long-distance dialing, fax, and Federal Express, people sent important messages by telegram. The hitch was that the telegraph office charged by the word, so the sender had to make every word count. Poets are not charged by the word, but they feel a similar need to make every word count. Instead of three words that blur the point, poets try to find the one word that has the right shade of meaning. The following poem, though very short, has long been a favorite of readers.

WILLIAM CARLOS WILLIAMS (1883–1963)

The Red Wheelbarrow   1923

so much depends
upon

a red wheel
barrow

glazed with rain   5
water

beside the white
chickens.

In a poem addressed to Williams and titled "So Much Depends," William Coles, psychiatrist and writer, talked about "so many things / the rest of us would never / have seen except for you." How does rainwater look on a surface like that of the wheelbarrow? If we said the water "coated" the surface, the objection might be that often a coat covers up what is underneath. "*Glazed* with rain / water" is right because it means coated with a shiny, transparent cover not hiding what is underneath. When another poet refers to the "distant glitter / of the January sun," *glitter* is a better word than *blaze* or *glare* because it is colder, more frigid, less blinding, though bright.

THE CREATIVE DIMENSION

Write your own "So much depends" passage or poem.

Poets have a *range* of vocabulary that enables them to make the right choices. The following poem stays especially close to the tangible details that make up firsthand experience. In much of this poem, the poet's language serves as a mirror of "what was there." Many of the words are specific, accurate words that give a faithful accounting of sights and events. (Others bring in striking imaginative comparisons, like the simile that compares the pink swim bladder of the fish to a big peony.)

ELIZABETH BISHOP (1911–1979)

The Fish   1946

I caught a tremendous fish
and held him beside the boat
half out of water, with my hook
fast in a corner of his mouth.
He didn't fight.   5
He hadn't fought at all.
He hung a grunting weight,

battered and venerable
and homely. Here and there
his brown skin hung in strips   10
like ancient wall-paper,
and its pattern of darker brown
was like wall-paper:
shapes like full-blown roses
stained and lost through age.   15
He was speckled with barnacles,
fine rosettes of lime,
and infested
with tiny white sea-lice,
and underneath two or three   20
rags of green weed hung down.
While his gills were breathing in
the terrible oxygen
—the frightening gills,
fresh and crisp with blood,   25
that can cut so badly—
I thought of the coarse white flesh
packed in like feathers,
the big bones and the little bones,
the dramatic reds and blacks   30
of his shiny entrails,
and the pink swim-bladder
like a big peony.
I looked into his eyes
which were far larger than mine   35
but shallower, and yellowed,
the irises backed and packed
with tarnished tinfoil
seen through the lenses
of old scratched isinglass.°   *fish gelatin*   40
They shifted a little, but not
to return my stare.
—It was more like the tipping
of an object toward the light.
I admired his sullen face,   45
the mechanism of his jaw,
and then I saw
that from his lower lip
—if you would call it a lip—
grim, wet, and weapon-like,   50
hung five old pieces of fish-line,
or four and a wire leader
with the swivel still attached,
with all their five big hooks
grown firmly in his mouth.   55
A green line, frayed at the end
where he broke it, two heavier lines,

and a fine black thread
still crimped from the strain and snap
when it broke and he got away. 60
Like medals with their ribbons
frayed and wavering,
a five-haired beard of wisdom
trailing from his aching jaw.
I stared and stared 65
and victory filled up the little rented boat,
from the pool of bilge
where oil had spread a rainbow
around the rusted engine
to the bailer rusted orange, 70
the sun-cracked thwarts,
the oarlocks on their strings,
the gunnels—until everything
was rainbow, rainbow, rainbow!
And I let the fish go. 75

The poet has the language resources to give us not just a distant, blurry picture of the fish and the boat but to close in on the specifics that call the scene up before our eyes in vivid detail. Many of the words in this poem are *specific* words—*barnacles, gills*—that the poet uses to call things by their right names. Many are **concrete** words that bring our senses into play, calling up for us things we can see, hear, or touch. We can almost see the fish "speckled with barnacles" and "infested / with tiny white sea-lice." We get a vivid picture of the brown skin that "hung in strips." We feel its "grunting weight" as the fish hangs half out of water with a "hook / fast in the corner of his mouth."

Without words like *speckled, barnacles, strips, gills, bilge,* or *bailer,* the poem could not make us share as completely in the experience the speaker in the poem relives here. Without these and the striking similes—the wall-paper, the "tarnished tinfoil" of the irises, the "beard of wisdom"—we could not put ourselves as completely in her shoes when at the end she makes the decision that otherwise might seem strange or irrational. The fish, with its yellowed eyes and its "beard" of broken fish lines, becomes overpoweringly real—indeed a "tremendous fish."

THE RECEPTIVE READER

1. How familiar are you with the *special language* of boaters and anglers? What are thwarts, oarlocks, gunnels?

2. How and where does the speaker in the poem show her *feelings* about the fish? Which details make the fish seem near-human? Which remind you that it is a fish?

3. What was the *rainbow* that the speaker saw spreading in the bilge at the bottom of the boat?

4. Were you ready for the *ending*? Were you prepared for what happened in the last line of the poem? Why or why not?

DENOTATION AND CONNOTATION

*[Poets] must learn to strum that colossal and resonant
harp, the English language, a temperamental instrument
that calls for practiced fingering.*
                              X. J. KENNEDY

*You may as well think of pushing a brick out of a wall
with your forefinger as attempt to remove a word out of
any of their finished passages.*
SAMUEL TAYLOR COLERIDGE ABOUT SHAKESPEARE AND MILTON

Poets have a keen ear for the emotional quality of words. Language does
not just describe or report; it is alive with threat, warning, pleading, rejection,
and regret. Words do not simply point—they point with pride; they point the
finger. A demagogue was once literally a "leader of the people," but today we
use the word to point the finger at a leader who leads the people by the nose.
A paramour (a word using the French word for love) is more than a bedmate;
medieval poets used the word for a lover cherished in defiance of a censorious
society. Language is not like the Morse code, where a dot and a dash and two
dots always stand for the letter *l*—no more and no less. Language is more like
the icons on road signs that say "Slippery" (so look out!) or "Vista Point"
(good place to stop and rest!).

Fews words are void of preference or emotion; many carry built-in attitudes, preferences, and feelings. We call the emotional overtones and attitudes
that words carry the **connotations** of a word. In plain fact, the word *candle*
stands for an old-fashioned lighting device that gives a limited, flickering light.
But the word has romantic connotations, since candles light tender moments
(or expensive meals in elegant restaurants). We call the stripped-down, bare-
fact meaning of a word its **denotation.** The denotation of *hound* is dog, but
there may be more to a hound than nondescript ordinary doggishness. Traditionally, *hound* has often stood for a special kind of dog, more sleek or alert, a
valuable hunting dog or the like.

The following lines glow with the magic of words that have favorable,
pleasing connotations—*slender, roses, music, blooms, flares, candle*—the more so
since they are played off against the drab "grey streets":

> When I with you so wholly disappear
> into the mirror of your slender hand
> grey streets of the city grow roses
> and daisies, the music of flowers
> blooms in our voices, the eye of
> the grocer flares like a candle
>   Peter Meinke, "When I with You"

Connotations range over the whole spectrum from the most positive or
flattering to the most negative and condemning. The word *sword* often has

connotations of valor and chivalry, but the word *dagger* connotes treachery, making us expect to be stabbed in the back. Poets use words with the right connotations to steer our reactions, to guide our emotions. The following short poem makes us feel the contradictory emotions of first getting up in the morning.

CHARLES SIMIC (born 1938)

Poem   1971

Every morning I forget how it is.
I watch the smoke mount
In great strides above the city.
I belong to no one.

Then, I remember my shoes, 5
How I have to put them on,
How, bending over to tie them up,
I will look into the earth.

As many readers read this poem, the central polarity in it opposes the sensation of looking up into the morning sky and feeling free ("I belong to no one") to the feeling of bending over to put on shoes, a move that brings us down to earth. The two key words at the opposite poles of this poem are *strides* and *earth*. *Stride* is a very different word from *slink, trudge,* or *shuffle* (let alone *crawl* or *creep*). When we stride, we walk with fresh energy and a sense of purpose, as if certain of our destination. The connotations of *stride* are just right to help us share the early-morning feeling of being ready to meet the opportunities of the new day.

Earth has the right connotations to convey the opposite feeling. The poet could have said *floor,* because that is literally what people look at when putting on shoes. But much of the emotional impact of the poem would have been lost, since the floor is simply the part of the building that keeps us from falling through the ceiling of the apartment below. Earth represents what is heavy, tied down, and grubby about our existence. It keeps us from soaring.

THE RECEPTIVE READER

1. *Earth* is a richly *connotative* word that has different associations in different contexts. What other connotations could the word have in other contexts? (Cluster the word to explore the personal meanings and associations it has for you.)

2. Some readers see the *polarity* in this poem differently. The first stanza to them has negative connotations. It makes them feel disconnected and lost, like the smoke that rises and dissipates, dooming them "to belong to no one." Could you argue in favor of this alternative reading? And do you think there is a way to read the second stanza positively—finding security and safety in our bonds to the earth?

THE PERSONAL RESPONSE

How well did the student who wrote the following response get into the spirit of the poem? How do *you* respond to the poem?

> Every morning I wake up like Charles Simic and forget how the city is. I watch the smoke mount in vaporous strides over city roof tops. In the morning, the smoke and I belong to no one. Then I remember that the hard lines of schedules wait for me to put my shoes on and walk those lines. How I hate putting them on; the bending stiffens me. I tie the leather on the stumps of my feet, locking myself to the earth.

JUXTAPOSITIONS

Cityscapes

In the following poems (written within ten years of each other), two English poets look at the city of London. However, they use language to steer the reader's reactions in very different directions. In reading these poems, explore especially the connotations of words—their emotional impact, overtones, and associations.

WILLIAM WORDSWORTH (1770–1850)

Composed upon Westminster Bridge, September 3, 1802   1802

Earth has not anything to show more fair:°   *more beautiful*
Dull would he be of soul who could pass by
A sight so touching in its majesty;
This City now doth, like a garment, wear
The beauty of the morning; silent, bare,   5
Ships, towers, domes, theaters, and temples lie
Open unto the fields, and to the sky;
All bright and glittering in the smokeless air.
Never did sun more beautifully steep
In his first splendor, valley, rock, or hill;   10
Never saw I, never felt, a calm so deep!
The river glideth at his own sweet will:
Dear God! the very houses seem asleep;
And all that mighty heart is lying still!

THE RECEPTIVE READER

Explore the associations and overtones of the many connotative words in this poem. What would be missing from the poem if the poet had said, "Dull would he be of brain" rather than "of soul"? What if he had said, "doth, like a coat, wear" instead of "like a garment" wear? What makes the words *domes* and *temples* different from the word *churches*? What if the poet had said, "With his first rays" rather than "In his first splendor"? What would be different if the poet had said at the end, "that mighty nerve center" rather than "that mighty heart"?

WILLIAM BLAKE (1757–1827)

London 1794

I wander through each chartered° street,   *legally set up*
Near where the chartered Thames does flow,
And mark in every face I meet
Marks of weakness, marks of woe.

In every cry of every man,   5
In every Infant's cry of fear,
In every voice, in every ban,°   *announcement*
The mind-forged manacles I hear.

How the chimney-sweeper's cry
Every blackening church appalls;   10
And the hapless soldier's sigh
Runs in blood down Palace walls.

But most through midnight streets I hear
How the youthful Harlot's curse
Blasts the new-born Infant's tear,   15
And blights with plagues the Marriage hearse.

[Handwritten annotations: "handcuffs"; "what people are doing to other people"; "little kids"; "pregnant, unwanted child"; "Death of what should be a marriage."]

THE RECEPTIVE READER

1. What words most directly describe the speaker's *emotions* when contemplating a city with maimed or penniless veterans, young prostitutes, and soot-covered churches? What would be different if the poet had used "mind-made bonds" rather than "mind-forged manacles"? What would be missing in the last line if he had said "damages" rather than "blights"? What gives metaphors like "Runs in blood down Palace walls" and the "Marriage hearse" their special force?

2. How would you pinpoint the difference in *perspective* between this and Wordsworth's poem?

THE PERSONAL RESPONSE

If you were to write out your feelings about one of today's cities, would your point of view be closer to Wordsworth's or to Blake's?

THE CREATIVE DIMENSION

Try your hand at a modern *rewrite* or update of one of these poems. How might a modern poet looking at the identical sights describe them—in what language?

THE LIMITS OF LANGUAGE

*The reader must not sit back and expect the poet to do all
the work.*

EDITH SITWELL

*Everything which opens out to us a new world is bound to
appear strange at first.*

EDITH SITWELL

Poets vary greatly in how far they will stretch the limits of language. Difficult but rewarding poets use language in original or intensely personal ways. First of all, the poet's vocabulary may include exotic gleanings brought back from excursions into ancient history, legend, or fabled places. The following poem delights readers who cherish words that, like rare coins, seldom see the light of common day.

JOHN MASEFIELD (1878–1967)

Cargoes   1902

Quinquereme of Nineveh from distant Ophir,
Rowing home to haven in sunny Palestine,
With a cargo of ivory,
And apes and peacocks,
Sandalwood, cedarwood, and sweet white wine.   5

Stately Spanish galleon coming from the Isthmus,
Dipping through the Tropics by the palm-green shores,
With a cargo of diamonds,
Emeralds, amethysts,
Topazes, and cinnamon, and gold moidores.   10

Dirty British coaster with a salt-caked smoke-stack,
Butting through the Channel in the mad March days,
With a cargo of Tyne coal,
Road-rails, pig-lead,
Firewood, iron-ware, and cheap tin trays.   15

What is a quinquereme? The context of the poem tells us that it is an ancient ship being rowed to its home harbor, carrying rich exotic cargo. (Some readers may remember the triremes of ancient Rome, with three banks of galley slaves plying *three* levels of oars. The legendary ship in this poem then would have *five* levels of oars.) Nineveh is clearly a city in ancient Palestine, wealthy enough to outfit magnificent trading ships. (It is mentioned in the Bible as a great city.) Ophir sounds like a legendary faraway city of great wealth. (Poets mention it: "More than all of Ophir's gold / does the fleeting second hold.")

The second of the three ships in this poem—the elaborately ornamented Spanish galleon carrying rich loot from tropical Central America back to the Old World—takes us closer to what we know about history and geography. The "Isthmus" is likely to be the isthmus of Panama—a thin strip of land that kept ships from reaching the Pacific from the Atlantic until the Panama Canal saved them the trouble of going around the southernmost tip of South America.

Although not likely to be able to afford emeralds, amethysts, and topazes, we can at least revel in the marvelous exotic names of these priceless gems. If *quinquereme* has not sent us to the dictionary, *moidores* will—although our knowledge that the Spanish conquistadores melted down the golden artifacts of the Aztecs and Incas in their greed for gold might make us conclude that these would be gold coins (actually "money of gold" minted in Portugal and Brazil).

By the third stanza, finally, we are within range of a more everyday vocabulary: The coal is from Newcastle-upon-Tyne ("carrying coals to Newcastle" was for a long time the equivalent of shipping hogs to Missouri).

THE RECEPTIVE READER

1. One student reader called this poem a "three-sided prism," with each stanza reflecting a different view of the cargo ships that since time immemorial have plied the seas. How would you label the three different cargoes?

2. Which words in this poem are rich in *connotation*—in overtones or personal association—for you? For instance, what ideas or feelings do words like *Palestine, ivory, peacock, galleon,* or *emerald* bring to mind?

THE RANGE OF INTERPRETATION

Where do you stand on the issue raised in the following excerpt from a student paper about this poem? What in the poem helps you make up your mind one way or the other?

> The last stanza is particularly intriguing in its contrast with the other two. The "dirty British coaster" brings us forward in time to the grimy industrial age. The sooty words and leaden cargo describe a harshly realistic working vessel, whereas the other two ships were romanticized, idealized, and seen through a nostalgic haze. We could easily argue that the harshness of the final stanza gives us a negative view of the modern world. We get a glimpse here of the sordid materialism of our age.
>
> However, we might easily argue the opposite as well. If the poet had cast the same realistic eye on the past as he did on the present, he might have picked slave ships or cattle boats, quite common in the ancient days, or he might have shown us the chained galley slaves rowing the splendid ancient ship. The dirty British coaster then would not come off so badly after all. In any case, Masefield suggests strength and power and working muscle in his description of the coaster "butting" stubbornly through the English Channel in ugly weather. This ship carries no glittering booty from "palm-green shores." It is a workaday mule of the seas. Its cargo represents the

everyday needs served by the economy of an industrial nation. We should not look down on it but accept it as part of living everyday reality.

Poets whose work is especially challenging may not only extend the reaches of language but also use language resources in provocative creative ways. They may use words that combine familiar building blocks in strange new patterns. They may yoke words together that do not usually work together. They may employ strange telescopings or foreshortenings. They may use reversals or transposings that pull words out of their usual order for special attention.

Some of the poet's creative innovations may take us only one step beyond ordinary language. In a poem about a lonely dark winter setting, the poet may not use the familiar word *absent-minded* but *absent-spirited* instead. Apparently the word *absent-minded* was not strong enough, because the speaker was not just temporarily thinking about something else. Instead, the speaker's *spirit* was too heavy with wintery thoughts and feelings to attend to trivial tasks at hand.

Some of the poetry most admired by modern readers goes farther in testing the boundaries of language. The following poem shows the word play and wrenchings of normal word order that we expect to find in the tense religious poetry of Gerard Manley Hopkins. The poem centers on the dove as a familiar symbol of peace. But here the bird is a "wild wooddove," shyly "roaming" around the poet. As a wild bird of the forest, it is hard to entice it to settle down with the speaker in the poem, who would, like a tree, spread for it protective "boughs."

GERARD MANLEY HOPKINS   (1844–1889)

Peace   1887

When will you ever, Peace, wild wooddove, shy wings shut,
Your round me roaming end, and under be my boughs?
When, when, Peace, will you, Peace? I'll not play hypocrite
To own my heart: I yield° you do come sometimes; but   *I admit*
That piecemeal peace is poor peace. What pure peace allows   5
Alarms of wars, the daunting wars, the death of it?

O surely, reaving° Peace, my Lord should leave in lieu   *taking away*
Some good! And so he does leave Patience exquisite,
That plumes° to Peace thereafter. And when Peace does here house   *spreads plumage*
He comes with work to do, he does not come to coo,   10
    He comes to brood and sit.

Where does the text of the poem run counter to what you are prepared to read? What changes does the poet ring on the central word *peace*?

The phrase "Your round me roaming end" would normally be "end your roaming around me." The poet's reordering of the words pulls the key word out for emphasis: "Your ROUND me roaming end" (the bird keeps away, roaming *around* the speaker). At the same time, the reshuffling sets up a strong counterpull or counterrhythm (part of what the poet called **sprung rhythm**). The result is a jostling effect in keeping with the restless, "peaceless" feelings of someone whose strong faith has yet left him strangely restless, with only "sometimes" a feeling of inner peace.

That word—*peace*—echoes through the poem like a plea for something intensely desired. The poet uses two **puns** to keep the word ringing in our ears. We use a pun when we play on the different meanings of words that sound or look alike. We want *peace* that is all of a *piece*. Instead, we get *piecemeal* peace that comes in small unsatisfactory pieces. That makes the peace we obtain poor peace when what we desire is *pure* peace. As one student reader said, "Hopkins must make his own peace with the piecemeal bits of faith that come to him."

THE RECEPTIVE READER

1. Could you argue that the changed *word order* in "under be my boughs" and "to own my heart" also pulls a key word to the front of a phrase?

2. What does the *metaphor* make you visualize when the poet says that patience "plumes to Peace thereafter"?

3. What kind of *work* does the poet seem to have in mind at the end? (What kind of brooding is productive rather than counterproductive?)

Less dramatic or experimental departures from the kind of language we expect may nevertheless seriously change the **tone** of a poem—the attitude it suggests (toward the subject or toward the reader) or its emotional coloring. A poet may branch out beyond current standard English in one of several directions:

✧ Language that is no longer in common use is **archaic.** Examples are *brethren* for brothers, *fain* or *lief* for gladly, and *ere* for before. (When words have gone out of use altogether, they are **obsolete.**) *Thou , thy,* and *thine*—and the special verb forms that go with *thou* ("thou liest")—were still current in Shakespeare's time, used in exchanges between people who, as we would say today, were on a first-name basis. "Hamlet, thou hast thy father much offended," says Queen Gertrude to her son. As these forms became archaic, poets used them to strike a special solemn, elevated note: "Dust thou art, to dust returnest, / Was not spoken of the soul" (Henry Wadsworth Longfellow).

✧ A poet may move beyond the standard English of office, school, and media to echo the **folk speech** of factory, pool hall, or down-home neighborhood. "We real cool" begins a famous poem by Gwendolyn Brooks. Shifts from formal to informal English or **slang** can make for brash, humorous effects: "My telephone rang in the middle of the night, / but I didn't answer it. It rang and rang / and rang and SHUT UP! and rang as if it were possessed" (Richard Brautigan).

✧ For a time, observers of language habits assumed that radio, television, and cheap paperbacks would average out regional differences. However, recent years have seen a renewed pride in traditional **dialects,** which help their speakers assert a regional identity separate from that promoted by a central government, synchronized school system, and official national language. Dialects are regional variations of a common language that are still mutually intelligible—but some are actually on the borderline of becoming separate languages. How much do you understand of the Scots, or Scottish dialect, in the following lines?

HUGH MACDIARMID (1892–1978)
Weep and Wail No More
1948

Stop killin' the deid. Gi'e owre
Your weepin' and wailin'.
    You maun keep quiet
If you want to hear them still
And no' blur their image in your mind.   5

For they've only a faint wee whisperin' voice
Makin' nae mair noise ava'
Than the growin' of the grass
That flourishes whaur naebody walks.

EXPLORATIONS
The Range of Reference

In the following poem, the English Romantic poet John Keats moves beyond everyday language to create a rich overlay of associations taking us beyond the ordinary. He compares his awe and excitement at discovering Chapman's sixteenth-century translation of Homer's *Iliad* with the excitement the Spanish conquerors of Mexico must have felt when they first saw the Pacific Ocean from Darien in Panama. Which words are unfamiliar or difficult for you? Which would you have to check in a dictionary?

JOHN KEATS (1795–1821)
On First Looking into Chapman's Homer
1816

Much have I traveled in the realms of gold,
    And many goodly states and kingdoms seen;
    Round many western islands have I been
Which bards in fealty to Apollo hold.
Oft of one wide expanse had I been told   5
    That deep-browed Homer ruled as his demesne;
    Yet did I never breathe its pure serene
Till I heard Chapman speak out loud and bold:

Then felt I like some watcher of the skies
   When a new planet swims into his ken; 10
Or like stout Cortez when with eagle eyes
   He stared at the Pacific—and all his men
Looked at each other with a wild surmise—
   Silent, upon a peak in Darien.

THE RECEPTIVE READER

1. Each of the following is a simpler or more familiar word for a richer, *more connotative* word used by the poet. Parentheses enclose the overtones or associations added by the word Keats actually chose in the poem. Which word in the poem matches each of the following: (ancient, venerable) kingdom; (ancient, honored) poets; loyalty (to a feudal medieval overlord); (brilliant, divine) patron of poetry; (a lord's) lands; expanse (of calm, pure sky or sea); (sharply perceived) field of vision?

2. What features make you recognize this poem as a *sonnet*? Where is its turning point? Can you argue that the poem follows a cumulative or climactic order?

EXPLORATIONS

Testing the Boundaries

When we call a poem difficult, it is often because the poet has trusted us to read the right meanings out of apparent shortcuts and shifts. Dylan Thomas, a Welsh poet, often seems impatient with plodding ordinary language, leaping ahead instead to make new connections. One reader said of him that he "strips from words their old, dull, used sleepiness, and gives them a refreshed and awakened meaning."

Read the following poem the first time without puzzling over difficult phrases. Allow yourself to be carried along by the chanting rhythm. Then go back over the poem, trying to see connections and meanings in Thomas' plays on words and in his strange telescopings or juxtapositions. (Fern Hill is the name of a farm that Thomas' uncle and aunt rented as tenant farmers.)

DYLAN THOMAS (1914–1953)
Fern Hill 1946

Now as I was young and easy under the apple boughs
About the lilting house and happy as the grass was green,
   The night above the dingle° starry, *wooded valley*
      Time let me hail and climb
   Golden in the heydays of his eyes, 5
And honored among wagons I was prince of the apple towns
And once below a time I lordly had the trees and leaves

Trail with daisies and barley
Down the rivers of the windfall light.

And as I was green and carefree, famous among the barns   10
About the happy yard and singing as the farm was home,
    In the sun that is young once only,
        Time let me play and be
    Golden in the mercy of his means,
And green and golden I was huntsman and herdsman, the calves   15
Sang to my horn, the foxes on the hills barked clear and cold,
        And the sabbath rang slowly
    In the pebbles of the holy streams.

All the sun long it was running, it was lovely, the hay
Fields high as the house, the tunes from the chimneys, it was air   20
    And playing, lovely and watery
        And fire green as grass.
    And nightly under the simple stars
As I rode to sleep the owls were bearing the farm away,
All the moon long I heard, blessed among stables, the night-jars°   *night birds*   25
Flying with the ricks,° and the horses   *haystacks*
        Flashing into the dark.

And then to awake, and the farm, like a wanderer white
With the dew, come back, the cock on his shoulder: it was all
    Shining, it was Adam and maiden,   30
        The sky gathered again
    And the sun grew round that very day.
So it must have been after the birth of the simple light
In the first, spinning place, the spellbound horses walking warm
        Out of the whinnying green stable   35
        On to the fields of praise.

And honored among foxes and pheasants by the gay house
Under the new made clouds and happy as the heart was long,
    In the sun born over and over,
        I ran my heedless ways,   40
    My wishes raced through the house high hay
And nothing I cared, at my sky blue trades, that time allows
In all his tuneful turning so few and such morning songs
    Before the children green and golden
        Follow him out of grace,   45

Nothing I cared, in the lamb white days, that time would take me
Up to the swallow thronged loft by the shadow of my hand,
    In the moon that is always rising,
        Nor that riding to sleep
    I should hear him fly with the high fields   50
And wake to the farm forever fled from the childless land.
Oh as I was young and easy in the mercy of his means,
        Time held me green and dying
    Though I sang in my chains like the sea.

THE RECEPTIVE READER

1. Try to puzzle out possible connections that explain telescoped phrases or strange juxtapositions in the early stanzas. For instance, what could have been "lilting" about the house? How did the child "hail and climb / Golden" in the heydays of Time? How was he "prince of the apple towns"? What is the connection between light and "rivers" and a "windfall"? Why in this poem is the sun "young once only"?

2. What is the *symbolic* meaning of the colors "green and golden," whose names echo through this poem?

3. What are key *images* and prevailing feelings in the poet's account of the first days after Creation? What is borrowed from and what is different from the account in Genesis?

4. What are the "chains" at the conclusion of the poem? Assuming the words are not meant literally, in what sense did Time hold the child "green and dying"?

POEMS FOR FURTHER STUDY

In reading the following poems, pay special attention to the poet's word choice, or diction. Where does the sound of words seem to mirror sense? Which words seem particularly accurate or fitting? Which seem to have just the right connotations, overtones, or associations? Where does the poet seem to stretch the limits of ordinary language?

MARGARET ATWOOD (born 1939)

Dreams of the Animals   1970

Mostly the animals dream
of other animals   each
according to its kind

      (though certain mice and small rodents
      have nightmares of a huge pink   5
      shape with five claws descending)

: moles dream of darkness and delicate
mole smells

frogs dream of green and golden
frogs   10
sparkling like wet suns
among the lilies

red and black
striped fish, their eyes open
have red and black striped   15
dreams   defense, attack, meaningful
patterns

birds dream of territories
enclosed by singing.

Sometimes the animals dream of evil   20
in the form of soap and metal
but mostly the animals dream
of other animals.

There are exceptions:

>   the silver fox in the roadside zoo   25
>   dreams of digging out
>   and of baby foxes, their necks bitten
>
>   the caged armadillo
>   near the train
>   station, which runs   30
>   all day in figure eights
>   its piglet feet pattering,
>   no longer dreams
>   but is insane when waking;
>
>   the iguana   35
>   in the petshop window on St. Catherine Street
>   crested, royal-eyed, ruling
>   its kingdom of water-dish and sawdust
>
>   dreams of sawdust

THE RECEPTIVE READER

1. What are the usual associations of the animals in this poem? How does the poem transform these associations or leave them behind? Look at the words that cluster around the names of the animals here. Which of the words have positive connotations, showing the poet's empathy or fellow feeling? (Which of these words are especially *unusual* or unexpected?)

2. In this poem, what is the difference between the animals in the wild and those in captivity? What words especially drive home the contrast between the animals in the wild and their caged cousins?

THE PERSONAL RESPONSE

Disney cartoons have often made animals seem cute, harmless, and lovable. Disney wildlife films, however, have often taken an uncompromisingly honest look at life in the wild. Does Atwood make animals seem too lovable and human?

GERARD MANLEY HOPKINS (1844–1889)

The Windhover   1877

To Christ Our Lord

I caught this morning morning's minion,° king-   *beloved*
    dom of daylight's dauphin,° dapple-dawn-drawn Falcon, in his riding   *crown prince*
    Of the rolling level underneath him steady air, and striding

High there, how he rung upon the rein of a wimpling° wing   *rippling*
In his ecstasy! then off, off forth on swing,   5
     As a skate's heel sweeps smooth on a bow-bend: the hurl and gliding
     Rebuffed the big wind. My heart in hiding
Stirred for a bird,— the achieve of, the mastery of the thing!

Brute beauty and valor and act, oh, air, pride, plume, here
     Buckle! AND the fire that breaks from thee then, a billion   10
Times told lovelier, more dangerous, O my chevalier!°   *knight*

     No wonder of it: shéer plód makes plow down sillion°   *furrow*
Shine, and black-blue embers, ah my dear,
     Fall, gall themselves, and gash gold-vermilion.

THE RECEPTIVE READER

1. Several of the words Hopkins applies to the falcon and to Christ suggest the glamor and pageantry of chivalry: a *minion* is a cherished, beloved court favorite; the *dauphin* was the crown prince of medieval France; a *chevalier* is a knight who represents the chivalric virtues (*chevalier* and *chivalry* come from the same root). Where in the poem does Hopkins spell out the *connotations* that these words suggest?

2. When the poet celebrates the masterful, ecstatic flight of the falcon, what do *concrete* words like *riding, striding, sweep, hurl,* and *gliding* add to the meaning of the generic term *fly?* (What does each make you visualize? What associations or feelings does it carry with it?) What makes *rebuff* different from *resist?*

3. In the pivotal word *buckle,* not only do the inspiring qualities of the falcon "come together" or are welded together (as the two ends of a belt are buckled or fastened). The two parts of the poem also meet: the splendor of God's creation and the billionfold "lovelier, more dangerous" splendor of "Our Lord." How do the two concluding images in the last three lines of the poem mirror the relationship between the "brute" creature and its creator?

4. In addition to the end rhyme that is traditional in a sonnet like this one, Hopkins uses *alliteration*—the repetition of the same sound at the beginning of several words in the same line ("this MORNing MORNing's MINion"). The telescoped phrase "dapple-dawn-drawn" allows the poet to complete the alliteration started by "DAYlight's DAUPHin." How would you spell out the meaning of the telescoped phrase in more ordinary language?

THE RANGE OF INTERPRETATION

According to a recent introduction to Hopkins' poetry, some critics "have seen the poem as one of frustration and sadness." The poem is "concerned with the unbridgeable distance between the hawk, flying so freely and beautifully, and the poet, whose heart is 'in hiding'; the heart is hidden away as if afraid, locked up by the severe discipline of the priesthood and the demands of self-sacrifice which it makes." To other readers, the poem "does not seem to be a poem of frustration so much as a poem of enthusiasm and exultation. . . . The excitement is conveyed in the way in which the heart, while it may have been 'in hiding,' that is, inactive, now 'Stirred for a bird'; as if the heart moved and leaped at the sight of the hawk" (J. R. Watson, *The Poetry of Gerard Manley Hopkins*). Which of these two interpretations would you be inclined to support? (What do *you* make of the phrase "my heart in hiding"?)

WOLE SOYINKA (born 1934)

Nobel Prize winner Wole Soyinka—playwright, poet, and novelist—is one of the African writers best known in the West. After the end of British colonial rule, his native Nigeria went through a phase of tribal conflict, with an unsuccessful war of secession fought by the Ibo. Soyinka, a Yoruba, wrote some of his poems while imprisoned during the civil war. He has written with biting satire about discrimination based on color and about the political maneuverings of leaders, whether in the Western imperialist, the Eastern socialist, or the Third World camp.

Lost Tribe   1988

Ants disturbed by every passing tread,
The wandering tribe still scurries round
In search of lost community. Love by rote,
Care by inscription. Incantations without magic.
Straws outstretched to suck at every passing broth,   5
Incessant tongues pretend to a way of thought—
Where language mints are private franchise,
The coins prove counterfeit on open markets.

Hard-sell pharmacies dispense all social pills:
"Have a nice day now." "Touch someone."   10
There's premium on the verb imperative—some
Instant fame psychologist pronounced it on TV—
He's now forgotten like tomorrow's guru,
Instant cult, disposable as paper diaper—
Firm commands denote sincerity;   15
The wish is wishy-washy, lacks "contact
Positive." The waiter barks: "Enjoy your meal,"
Or crisper still "Enjoy!" You feel you'd better!
Buses, subway, park seats push the gospel,
Slogans like tickertapes emblazon foreheads—   20
"Talk it over with someone—now, not later!"
"Take down fences, not mend them."
"Give a nice smile to someone." But, a tear-duct
Variant: "Have you hugged your child today?"

THE RECEPTIVE READER

1. Soyinka has a marvelous quick ear for how language reveals (or betrays) who we are. How does this poem show him to be a good listener?

2. What has happened to the magic of language according to this poem? Who or what is to blame?

3. This poem is rich in provocative metaphor. What are the figurative meanings of the ants, the straws, the coins, the pharmacies, the paper diaper? Look at the lines referring to the tickertapes and to the tear ducts. Can you translate what they say into more ordinary language? What is the difference between the ordinary-language version and the poet's use of language?

4. To judge from the poet's examples, what is the imperative form of a verb? What kind of question concludes the poem?

5. In what sense were the original lost tribes of Israel lost, and what use does the poem make of this biblical allusion?

THE PERSONAL RESPONSE

Do you share the poet's allergy to the kind of language he focuses on in this poem? Can you think of other examples? Is there something to be said in defense of this kind of language?

JOHN HEAVISIDE
A Gathering of Deafs   1989

By the turnstiles
in the station
where the L train greets
the downtown six there was
a congregation of deafs   5
passing forth
a jive wild
and purely physical
in a world dislocated
from the subway howling   10
hard sole shoe stampede
punk rock blasted radio
screaming, pounding, honking
they gather in community
lively and serene, engaging   15
in a dexterous conversation

An old woman
of her dead husband tells
caressing the air
with wrinkled fingers that demonstrate the story with   20
delicate, mellifluous motion
she places gentle configurations before the faces of the group

A young Puerto Rican
describes a fight with his mother emphasizing each word
with abrupt, staccato movements jerking his elbows   25
and twisting his wrists
teeth clenched and lips pressed
he concluded the story
by pounding his fist
into his palm   30

By the newsstand
two lovers express emotion

caressing the air
with syllables
graceful and slow   35
joining their thoughts
by the flow of fingertips

THE RECEPTIVE READER

1. In this student-written poem, what is right about words like *congregation, jive, community, dexterous, configuration?* How effective or expressive are the words setting up the contrast between the punk rock and the silent conversation of the deaf?

2. What is the difference between *mellifluous* and *staccato?* What words clustering around each of these help a reader unfamiliar with them?

3. What statement is the student poet making about the sign language of the deaf?

WRITING ABOUT LITERATURE

16. Responding to Connotation (Interpreting the Evidence)

The Writing Workshop   When studying a poem rich in connotative language, you will be paying special attention to emotional overtones and implied attitudes. How do emotionally charged words steer the reactions of the reader? (Remember that dictionaries tend to concentrate on the denotations of words, though they may include hints on possible connotations.)

⋄ You may want to start your paper by defining your *key term.* You may want to get the subject of connotative language clearly into focus, using brief striking illustrations.

⋄ Show evidence of close, careful reading. Show that you have read carefully for *implications*—you have gone through the poem line by line, paying special attention to key words or to recurrent words that echo in the poem.

⋄ Do not take words out of *context.* Is a word part of a network of similar or related terms? Are its associations or implications reinforced by what goes with it in the poem? Or are unusual associations negated or overruled by other words that strongly affect the tone or emotional quality of the poem?

⋄ Work out a clear overall *plan.* For instance, you may want to follow the overall pattern of the poem. (Is there perhaps an initial set of words with very similar connotations but then a turning, with the poem moving in a different or opposed direction?) Or you may sort out different kinds of connotative language or different effects of connotative language on the reader.

Study the model student paper examining connotative language in the following poem. How carefully has the writer read the poem? What use does she make of evidence from the poem? Are any of the connotations she traces private or personal rather than widely shared associations? How convincing are her conclusions?

JEFFREY HARRISON
Bathtubs, Three Varieties 1975

First the old-fashioned kind, standing on paws,
like a domesticated animal—
I once had a whole flock of these
(seven—for good luck? I never asked
the landlord) under a walnut tree 5
in my backyard, like sheep in shade.
They collected walnuts in the fall then filled up with snow, like thickening wool.

Modern tubs are more like ancient tombs.
And it is a kind of death we ask for
in the bath. Nothing theatrical 10
like Marat with his arm hanging out—
just that the boundary between the body
and the world dissolve, that we forget
ourselves, and that the tub become
the sarcophagus of dreams. 15

My bathtub in Japan was square, and deep.
You sat cross-legged like a Zen
monk in meditation, up to your neck
in water always a little too hot,
relaxed and yet attentive to the moment 20
(relaxation as a discipline)—
staring through a rising cloud of steam
at the blank wall in front of you.

SAMPLE STUDENT PAPER

Connotative Language: Harrison's Three Bathtubs

Dictionary meanings are usually denotative meanings; they give us exact, objective, limited definitions. When words take us beyond objective labeling to expand our associations, when they carry an overlay of emotional association, they have connotative meaning. For example, the word *house* denotes a structure with walls, floors, ceilings, and doors, and including bedrooms and a kitchen; *house* does not have the emotional overlay that the word *home* suggests. *Home* may recall the warmth of a featherbed in winter or the smell of newly-mown grass in summer. It suggests a place that provides security and protection, an anchor in an uncertain world.

Connotative meanings may be personal and private. Abigail may be a beautiful name to many, but if we have known an Abigail who was cross and domineering, the word will have unpleasant associations for us. To work for the poet, a word must usually have more broadly shared layers of meaning. When Romeo calls Juliet's balcony the east and Juliet the sun, we know he is suggesting that, like the rising sun, Juliet is new, fresh, bright, warm, and central in his life.

In Jeffrey Harrison's "Bathtubs, Three Varieties," the poet relies on both the denotative and connotative meanings of words. In three stanzas, he describes three kinds of bathtubs: "an old-fashioned kind," "modern tubs," and his "bathtub in Japan." He does not flatly state his preference for one kind of bathtub over another, but if we focus on his word choices and the connotations of certain words, we may conclude that he does indeed have a preference.

In the first stanza, the speaker in the poem surprises us with not one but seven old-fashioned tubs under a walnut tree in his backyard. Parenthetically, he adds that he has not asked his landlord why they are there, but he associates seven with "good luck." Interior decorators call old-fashioned tubs claw-footed or lion-footed, but the speaker chooses to see this kind of tub as standing on "paws, / like a domesticated animal." Unlike lions' claws, paws are non-threatening and connote the softness of a cat's paws. Another reference to a domesticated animal, tame and trusting, reinforces this kind of feeling: Seven of these tubs make a "whole flock" of "sheep in shade"; the connotation here is of a gathering of domesticated animals in a pleasant, pastoral scene. When cold weather comes, the tubs fill with snow—normally cold and forbidding, but here compared to the thickening wool of the sheep; thus the snow sounds paradoxically warm and protecting. Earlier, the tubs were collecting walnuts, reminding us of the rich bounty of harvest time.

The second stanza, on modern tubs, presents a startling contrast. Here we have tubs "like ancient tombs," a bath that is a "kind of death," and a tub that becomes a "sarcophagus," or massive stone coffin. Our tub death is not even "theatrical," like the dramatic death in the French painter David's portrait of Marat, the French revolutionary hero stabbed in his bath.

In the third stanza, we find ourselves in a Japanese tub described as "square"— without the welcoming comfort of a circular or oval shape. We do not stretch out in this tub but sit "cross-legged like a Zen / monk in meditation." We sit up to our necks in deep water "always a little too hot." We hear an echo here of the expressions "up to our necks in something" and "being in hot water," both of which have negative implications. This is a strange mixture of relaxation with "discipline," as we find ourselves staring "at the blank wall." This tub sounds uninviting for any but those stoic people who like a strenuous life.

For me, at least, the tubs in the first stanza suggest memories of peaceful contentment. There is something bleak and forbidding about the modern tomblike tub. And it would probably take special training in Zen to maintain the proper half-relaxed, half-disciplined attitude proper to the over-hot, steamy Japanese variety.

QUESTIONS

Do you agree with this student's reading of the poem? Why or why not? Did she overlook any significant details? Does she bring in personal associations that you would question? What parts of the paper are for you especially instructive or convincing?

17 FORM
Rhyme, Meter, and Stanza

*Remember: Our deepest perceptions are a waste if we have
no sense of form.*

THEODORE ROETHKE

*Let chaos storm!
Let cloud shapes swarm!
I wait for form.*
ROBERT FROST, "PERTINAX"

FOCUS ON FORM

Poetry today moves between the two poles of traditional form and the **open form** that is second nature to many modern poets. Traditional form is shaped by such features as rhyme, meter, and stanza. Open form in varying degrees modifies or abandons these, allowing the poet to give each poem its own unique pattern and rhythm.

For centuries, strongly metrical lines of verse ("With HOW | sad STEPS, | O MOON, | thou CLIMB'ST | the SKIES") were often marked off by rhyme (SKIES / TRIES). They were often arranged in stanzas of similar shape. These traditional formal features long helped make the difference between poetry and prose. When handled too mechanically, they make a poem jingle, lulling us to sleep rather than sharpening our attention. However, for first-rate poets traditional form has been (and is) a challenge, stimulating their imagination and creative abilities.

The following poem is a traditional sonnet, written by a leading poet of the English Romantic movement. As sonnets have for over five hundred years, the poem has fourteen lines. Like many other sonnets, it has an interlaced rhyme scheme: "free—Nun—sun—(tranquili)ty; Sea—(a)wake—make—(everlasting)ly" (abbaabba). It has the traditional underlying five-beat meter (iambic pentameter): "The HO | ly TIME | is QUI | et AS | a NUN." However, its pattern, rhythm, and tone make it memorable and unique. It is different from any other sonnet. Look at the interplay of traditional form and creative freedom in this poem. Like several other Wordsworth poems, this poem addresses a younger sister, who lived with him and shared his love of nature.

566

WILLIAM WORDSWORTH   (1770–1850)

It Is a Beauteous Evening   1807

It is a beauteous° evening, calm and free,   *beautiful*
The holy time is quiet as a Nun
Breathless with adoration; the broad sun
Is sinking down in its tranquility;
The gentleness of heaven broods o'er the Sea: 5
Listen! the Mighty Being is awake,
And doth with his eternal motion make
A sound like thunder—everlastingly.
Dear Child! dear Girl! that walkest with me here,
If thou appear untouched by solemn thought,   10
Thy nature is not therefore less divine:
Thou liest in Abraham's bosom all the year,
And worship'st at the Temple's inner shrine,
God being with thee when we know it not.

What keeps this poem from being predictable in its use of traditional form?

⋄ First, the poem has a strong metrical pattern, but it is not monotonous: At several key points, the poem reverses the iambic (DeTROIT—DeTROIT) pattern to stress the first rather than the second syllable of a line: "BREATHless with adoration"; "LIsten! the Mighty Being is awake"; "GOD being with thee." This variation does more than introduce variety. It emphasizes key words; it sets off key stages in how the poem as a whole takes shape. Sound and sense, form and meaning, blend.

⋄ Second, rhyme words do not neatly mark off sentences or clauses. At the end of the second line, we are pulled over into the third with only a minor pause. But then we come to a major break *within* the line, setting up a strong counterrhythm: "The holy time is quiet as a Nun / Breathless with adoration; || the broad sun. . . ." Strong breaks vary the rhythm when the speaker turns to the person addressed: "Listen! || the Mighty Being . . ."; "Dear Child! || dear Girl! || that walkest with me here. . . ." Again, these breaks are not just pleasing variations of a pattern. They at the same time make us stop and listen; they help make the listener pay solemn attention to the words of the speaker.

THE RECEPTIVE READER

1. How should this poem *sound* when read aloud? How much should the reading make the listener aware of the meter—and of the line breaks following the rhyme words? At what point would overemphasis on these formal features begin to make the poem sound mechanical?

2. What is the *rhyme* scheme in the concluding six lines (sestet) of this sonnet? Which of the lines in the sestet are closest to illustrating regular iambic *meter*?

3. How many *images* in this poem help the poet create and maintain a feeling of religious awe?

4. What is the attitude of the speaker in the poem toward the person listening?

Form, traditional or modern, is a large umbrella heading for features that determine the texture and shape of a poem. Form is what makes a poem more deliberate, more crafted, than the effortless flow of ordinary language. Poetic form intertwines in fascinating ways with meaning. When a poem is truly of one piece, formal features do not seem imposed on meaning from without, like the ornaments hung on a Christmas tree. A successful poem does not have a prior prose meaning that could have been separately expressed by other means. We expect form to be organic. We expect the texture and shape of a poem to evolve from within. *What* the poem means and *how* the poem means blend and become one.

RHYME, ALLITERATION, FREE VERSE

Like meter, rhyme is a highly formal device. It is a signal that language is going to be used in an unusual, often a serious and memorable, way. . . . Because it is out of the ordinary, rhyme attracts our attention and prepares us for a completely organized and unusually expressive language.

KARL SHAPIRO

Why **rhyme?** Rhyme bonds two or more lines by final syllables that start out differently but end alike. Children—and adults who have kept children's gift for finding inexpensive, wholehearted pleasures—delight in the echo effects of rhyme: "Celery, RAW, / Develops the JAW, / But celery, STEWED, / Is more quietly CHEWED" (Ogden Nash). Beyond this simple pleasure, as elementary as the pleasure of hopping and skipping, rhyme can serve as the most visible external sign that the poem we are reading is going to have a shape, a pattern. It is going to be more patterned, more ordered, than ordinary fragmented and disjointed life, not to mention life at its chaotic, nerve-jarring worst.

Rhyme helps the poet measure off lengths of verse; it sets up recurrent points of rest. It thus helps the poet set up a basic rhythm, as different from disjointed chatter as purposeful walking is from scurrying hither and yon. We can see this measuring-off effect of rhyme well in song lyrics like the following.

AMERICAN FOLK SONG (Anonymous)

Black Is the Color

traditional

Black, black, black is the color of my true love's hair.   a
His lips are something wond'rous fair,   a
The purest eyes and the bravest hands,   b
I love the ground whereon he stands.   b
Black, black, black is the color of my true love's hair.   a

5

I love my love and well he knows	c
I love the ground whereon he goes.	c
And if my love no more I see,	d
My life would quickly fade away.	d
Black, black, black is the color of my true love's hair.	a 10

Lines like "I love the ground whereon he stands," marked off by the rhyme word *stands,* stand out from the stream of audio input that reaches our ears and linger in the memory. At the same time, rhyme has a bonding effect, giving a sense of continuity, of meaningful forward movement. This effect of pulling things together or keeping them headed in the same direction is especially strong with **multiple** rhymes—more than two lines rhyming—as in the following opening lines of a Bob Dylan song:

Darkness at the break of noon	a
Shadows even the silver spoon	a
The hand made blade, the child's balloon	a
Eclipses both the sun and moon	a 5
To understand you know too soon,	a
There is no sense in trying.	b

Bob Dylan, "It's Alright Ma (I'm Only Bleeding)"

Rhymes that are too predictable (*love/dove*) make a poem sound slight and pat. At the opposite extreme, farfetched or forced rhymes can have a humorous effect—sometimes unintentional but often, as in the last two lines of the following excerpt, intentional:

I shall be sweet and crafty, soft and sly;
You will not catch me reading any more:
I shall be called a wife to pattern by;
And some day when you knock and push the door,
Some sane day, not too bright and not too stormy,
I shall be gone, and you may whistle for me.

Edna St. Vincent Millay, "Oh, oh, you will be sorry for that word"

Some poets have relied more strongly on the segmenting effect of rhyme than others. In the eighteenth century, when prevailing fashion encouraged the tidy packaging of ideas, rhyme helped seal off sets of two rhyming lines in self-contained **closed couplets.** In the following eighteenth-century poem, rhyme helps the poet frame snapshots of city sights in two neatly boxed lines. Most of the couplets give us a capsule portrait of one of the city people—from the apprentice cleaning up the employer's premises to the prison "turnkey" letting out his jailbirds at night for apparently most irregular purposes.

JONATHAN SWIFT (1667–1745)
A Description of the Morning 1709

Now hardly here and there a hackney-coach	a	
Appearing, showed the ruddy morn's approach.	a	
Now Betty from her master's bed had flown,	b	
And softly stole to discompose her own;	b	
The slip-shod 'prentice from his master's door	c	5
Had pared the dirt and sprinkled round the floor.	c	
Now Moll had whirled her mop with dexterous airs,	d	
Prepared to scrub the entry and the stairs.	d	
The youth with broomy stumps began to trace	e	
The kennel-edge, where wheels had worn the place.	e	10
The small-coal man was heard with cadence deep,	f	
Till drowned in shriller notes of chimney-sweep:	f	
Duns at his lordship's gate began to meet;	g	
And brickdust Moll had screamed through half the street.	g	
The turnkey now his flock returning sees,	h	15
Duly let out a-nights to steal for fees:	h	
The watchful bailiffs take their silent stand,	i	
And schoolboys lag with satchels in their hands.	i	

THE RECEPTIVE READER

1. Which of the *couplets* strike you as exceptionally neatly packaged?

2. Swift had a sharp *satirical* eye. What are some of the seedier sights you see in this poem? (What are duns, and why is their appearance at the lord's gate one of Swift's satirical touches?) Do the more positive elements in this "description of the morning" counterbalance the negative ones?

Later poets moved away from neatly packaged rhymed couplets. We see fewer boxed-in lines where rhyme routinely signals both the end of a sentence and the end of a line. Instead, we see more of the fluid spillover effect that results when the unfinished sense pulls us beyond what might have been a full stop into the next line. Then the sentence may come to an end halfway through the next line, causing a strong break that works counter to the prevailing pattern of strong breaks *between* rather than *within* lines:

> We are as clouds that veil the midnight moon; ‖
> How restlessly they speed, and gleam, and quiver, →
> Streaking the darkness radiantly! ‖ Yet soon →
> Night closes round, and they are lost forever.
>   Percy Bysshe Shelley, "Mutability"

We call the spillover from one line to the next **enjambment,** with the same sentence straddling two lines. We call the strong break that comes *within* a line—contrary to the prevailing pattern—a **caesura** (literally, a "cut" that divides the line). The straddling effect of enjambment partly counteracts the segmenting effect of rhyme. It sometimes helps weave a long series of lines into a kind of verse paragraph.

Like songbirds, rhymes are easier to listen to and enjoy than to classify. Rhyme watchers note many variations from the simple *love/dove, moon/soon* pattern:

✧ Most rhymes are **end rhymes,** marking off a line of verse. **Internal rhymes** multiply the echo effect of rhyme *within* a line:

> All is SEARED with trade; BLEARED, SMEARED with toil.
>   Gerard Manley Hopkins, "God's Grandeur"

✧ **Single** (or **masculine**) **rhymes** are the prevailing single-syllable rhymes. Only the opening consonant (or consonant cluster) varies, while the rest of the syllable stays the same: *high/sky, leave/grieve, stone/own.* **Double** (or **feminine**) **rhymes** match two-syllable words (or parts of words) with the first syllable stressed and the second unstressed: *ocean/motion, started/parted, (re)peated/(de)feated.* **Triple rhymes** are three-syllable rhymes, with stress on the first of the three (*beautiful/dutiful*). The following stanza uses all three kinds of rhyme:

Now Donna Inez had, with all her merit,	a	double
A great opinion of her own good qualities;	b	triple
Neglect, indeed, requires a saint to bear it,	a	double
And such, indeed, she was in her moralities;	b	triple
But then she had a devil of a spirit,	a	double
And sometimes mixed up fancies with realities,	b	triple
And let few opportunities escape	c	single
Of getting her liege lord into a scrape.	c	single

Lord Byron, "Don Juan"

✧ In the stanza from "Don Juan," the double rhymes are actually only **half-rhymes,** since the vowel sounds in the first syllables of *merit/bear it/spirit* are only similar, not alike. Byron here uses them tongue-in-cheek. However, for poets who came to consider traditional rhyme too conventional and predictable, such **slant rhymes** were a step toward a greater range of choice. (Words that coincide in spelling but not in sound, like *come* and *home,* are called **sight rhymes.**)

In the following poem, which rhymes are slant rhymes?

EMILY DICKINSON   (1830–1886)
The Soul selects her own Society
about 1862

The Soul selects her own Society—
Then—shuts the Door—

To her divine Majority—
Present no more—

Unmoved—she notes the Chariots—pausing   5
At her low Gate—
Unmoved—an Emperor be kneeling
Upon her Mat—

I've known her—from an ample nation—
Choose One—   10
Then—close the Valves of her attention—
Like Stone—

THE RECEPTIVE READER

1. Which are conventional *full* rhymes? Which are slant rhymes?
2. A literal *paraphrase* of this poem might run like this:

> The human soul chooses friends or soulmates carefully and then shuts
> out any others, allowing no one else to join in. It will not be moved by others
> humbly asking to be admitted. I have known her to select only one from a
> large group and then pay absolutely no attention to anyone else.

How do the metaphors in the poem go beyond this bare-bones paraphrase? What
do they make you see? What do they make you feel? What do they make you think?

✧ When only the internal vowel sounds of final syllables are similar or
alike, the result is **assonance,** again a more distant echo than full rhyme. Assonance is a partial sound echo, as in *break/fade* or *mice/fight.*

✧ Occasionally, a poet goes back to a very different kind of rhyme. **Alliteration** is an echo effect that was once a key feature of poetry and that is still
active in popular speech: "safe and sound," "spick and span," "kit and caboo-
dle." Alliteration was the precursor and the opposite of end rhyme. Traditionally, three or more stressed syllables in a line *started* with the same sound: "A
wonder on the wave—water turned bone" (from a riddle whose answer is
"ice"). The words that alliterated started either with the same consonant or
else with any vowel. The earliest recorded poems in English used an alliterating four-beat line, approximated in the following modernized passage:

Leave sorrow aside | for it seems more wise
To fight for a friend | than to fret and mourn.
We all in the end | go out of this world.
Let us do great deeds | before death takes us.
That is best for the brave | who are born to die.

From Beowulf

In later times, partial alliteration, not following a regular pattern and
sometimes stretching over more than one line, has served to enrich the texture
of both rhymed and unrhymed verse. Shakespeare at times uses alliteration to
accentuate the often highly individualized rhythm of his sonnets. Look for the
repetition of initial consonants in the following example.

WILLIAM SHAKESPEARE   (1564–1616)

Sonnet 30

before 1598

When to the sessions of sweet silent thought
I summon up remembrance of things past,
I sigh the lack of many a thing I sought,
And with old woes new wail° my dear time's waste: *newly mourn*
Then can I drown an eye (unused to flow)   5
For precious friends hid in death's dateless° night,   *endless*
And weep afresh love's long since canceled woe,
And moan the expense° of many a vanished sight.   *the loss*
Then can I grieve at grievances foregone,°   *griefs long past*
And heavily from woe to woe tell o'er   10
The sad account of fore-bemoanèd moan,
Which I new pay as if not paid before.
But if the while I think on thee, dear friend,
All losses are restored and sorrows end.

THE RECEPTIVE READER

1. Look at the repetition of the initial *s* in the first three lines. In reading the poem aloud, how much would you make the alliterating syllables stand out?

WHEN to | the SESS | ions of | SWEET SI | lent THOUGHT
I SUMM | on UP | ReMEM | brance of | things PAST,
I SIGH | the LACK | of MAN | y a THING | I SOUGHT.

2. How many other examples of repeated initial consonants can you find? How important are the alliterating words in the poem?
3. Where is the *turning point* in this sonnet? How does the poem lead up to it?

As part of the changing outward shape of poetry during the last century, rhyme became increasingly optional. Today, some poets rely on rhyme; many more don't; and some use it when it suits their purpose. Instead of making every line, or every second line, rhyme, they may use rhyme, if at all, at irregular intervals. The decline of rhyme, together with the appeal of rhythms freer and more variable than traditional meter, made possible the rise of **free verse**—poetry less governed by formal conventions—as the dominant mode of poetry.

EXPLORATIONS

Understanding Rhyme

Point out any examples of full rhyme, single and double rhyme, half-rhyme, internal rhyme, assonance, or alliteration.

1. Durable bird pulls interminable worm,
   Coiled in subterranean caverns;
   Feeds on fossils of ferns and monsters.
                    Beatrice Janosco, "To a Tidelands Oil Pump"

2. My last defense
   Is the present tense.

   It little hurts me to know
   I shall not go

   Cathedral-hunting in Spain
   Nor cherrying in Michigan or Maine.
                    Gwendolyn Brooks, "Old Mary"

3. Last night I saw the savage world
   And heard the blood beat up the stair;
   The fox's bark, the owl's shrewd pounce,
   The crying creatures—all were there,
   And men in bed with love and fear.
                    Elizabeth Jennings, "Song for a Birth or a Death"

4. I bring fresh showers for the thirsting flowers,
   From the seas and the streams;
   I bear light shade for the leaves when laid
   In their noonday dreams.
   From my wings are shaken the dews that waken
   The sweet buds every one,
   When rocked to rest on their mother's breast,
   As she dances about the sun.
                    Percy Bysshe Shelley, "The Cloud"

RHYTHM AND METER

*Poetry is oral; it is not words, but words performed. . . .
the "real" poem is not the scratches on the paper, but the
sounds those scratches stand for.*

                    JUDSON JEROME

*In a poem, the words charm the ear as much as what is
said charms the mind.*

                    WILLIAM J. MARTZ

*The line will have the more charm for not being
mechanically straight. We enjoy the straight crookedness of
a good walking stick.*

                    ROBERT FROST

Meter regularizes the natural rhythms of speech. Poetry is rhythmic, like breathing, walking, dancing. When the rhythm of successive lines is regular enough to become predictable, we call it meter. The poet enters into a metrical contract with the reader, setting up an underlying recurring beat over which the actual poem plays variations. The meter is the steadying beat of the metronome over which longer and shorter notes dance out the actual music of the verse. The metrical pattern creates expectations that please us when they are satisfied and that keep us from being lulled to sleep when they are denied.

Meter regularizes the natural ups and downs that make live language different from the drone of computerized speech. In natural speech, **stress,** or accent, makes us raise our voices slightly and makes us seem to linger briefly over the accented syllable or word. Stress makes one syllable stand out from the others in words like reMAIN and dePART; or LIsten and SUMmon; or PEDigree and destiNAtion. In a sentence as a whole, stressed words (or stressed parts of words) stand out in phrases like "in the WOODS," "under the SUN," or "have to aGREE." Meter results when we lay words and phrases end to end in such a way that the stressed syllables set up a regular beat, as in the opening lines of the Beatles song:

> PICture yourSELF on a BOAT in a RIVer,
> With TANgerine TREES and MARmalade SKIES,
> SOMEbody CALLS you, you ANswer quite SLOWly,
> A GIRL with kaLEIdoscope EYES.
>   "Lucy in the Skies with Diamonds"

Meter is rhythm regular enough to be measured, or scanned. **Scansion** charts the underlying beat and its variations, the way a cardiogram charts the heartbeat and any irregularities. In the actual poem, of course, meter is not noted or transcribed as part of the written text; we need to listen for it with the inner ear. We have to sense it as the eye moves over successive lines. To make meter visible, we can use a special notation for stressed and unstressed syllables: a sharp accent (´) for strong stress; a flat accent (`) for weaker stress; no mark (or often a small half-circle resting on its curved side) for an unstressed syllable.

Read the following short poem first with exaggerated emphasis on the underlying beat ("The WAY a CROW / Shook DOWN on ME"). Then try to read it with enough variation in the *degree* of stress to bring your reading closer to the natural rhythms of speech. Note weaker or secondary stress alternating with strong stress in the first two lines.

R O B E R T   F R O S T   (1874–1963)
Dust of Snow   1923

The wày a crów
Shook dówn on mè
The dúst of snów
From a hémlock trée

Has gíven my héart   5
A chánge of móod
And sáved some párt
Of a dáy I had rúed.°   *viewed with regret*

The basic unit of our metrical currency is the **foot**—one stressed syllable with one or more unstressed ones. Several feet together make up a line of verse. The Frost poem uses an unusually short line with only two feet: "The dúst | of snów." The traditional line of verse most commonly used is a four-beat or five-beat line; in other words, it is made up of four or five feet:

> Wórds are | like léaves; | and whére | they móst | abóund,
> Much frúit | of sénse | benéath | is ráre | ly fóund.
> Alexander Pope, "Essay on Criticism"

❖ The most common meter of English poetry has for centuries been **iambic**—a basic "one-TWO | one-TWO | one-TWO" rhythm akin to the rhythm of walking. The iamb is a foot made up of two syllables, with the stressed one last: DETROIT—DETROIT—DETROIT—DETROIT. (The Greek name originally labeled a lame-footed person, whose gimpy gait made one foot come down harder than the other.) The following lines set up a prevailing iambic beat. Notice that words spill over from one foot to the next, preventing the meter from cutting the lines mechanically like slices of cheese:

> I képt | my án | swers smáll | and képt | them néar;
> Big qués | tions brúised | my mínd | but stíll | I lét
> Small án | swers bé | a búl | wark tò | my féar.
> Elizabeth Jennings, "Answers"

❖ The first line in the Pope couplet shows a common reversal (or **inversion**): "WORDS are | like leaves. . . ." The stress has shifted to the first syllable; the result is a **trochaic** foot, or trochee, on the "BOSton—BOSton—BOSton" model. A line of trochaic feet changes the metrical pattern from "clip-CLOP | clip-CLOP | clip-CLOP" to "CLIP-clop | CLIP-clop | CLIP-clop." Poems with an underlying trochaic beat throughout are rare. The most common assignment of the trochaic foot is to bring variation into a prevailing iambic pattern. A trochaic foot, starting out strong, can serve as an attention getter. (Is it only an accident that in Pope's couplet the most important word—namely, *Words*—is pulled to the front of the first line by trochaic inversion?)

Here is an example of a predominantly trochaic poem. The seventh and eighth lines fall back on the more common iambic pattern. (In reading this poem aloud, can you make the listener aware of the trochaic pattern—without making it sound mechanical?)

PERCY BYSSHE SHELLEY (1792–1822)

To ——— 1824

Músic, | whèn soft | vóices | díe,	trochaic
Víbrates | ìn the | mémo | r`y.	trochaic
Odors, | whèn sweet | víolets | sícken,	trochaic
Líve with | ín the | sénse they | quícken.	trochaic
Róse leaves, | whèn the | róse is | déad,	trochaic
Are héaped | for the | belóv | ed's béd.	iambic
And só | thy thóughts, | when thóu | are góne,	iambic
Lóve it | sélf shall | slúmber | ón.	trochaic

❖ A third kind of foot also serves mainly as a bit player introducing variation into an iambic line. The **anapest** doubles up two unstressed syllables to lead up to the third and stressed syllable, on the "New ROCHELLE—New ROCHELLE—New ROCHELLE" model. The added unstressed syllable can have a "hurry UP \| hurry UP \| hurry UP" effect. A predominantly anapestic line would look like this:

> *But his* wíngs \| *will not* rést \| *and his* féet \| *will not* stáy \| for us.
> Algernon Charles Swinburne, "At Parting"

More common is anapestic variation in an otherwise iambic line:

> The wóods \| *are pre*pár \| *ing to* wáit \| out wínter.
> Gusts blów \| *with an* éarn \| *est of* áll \| there ís \| *to be* dóne
> Charles Tomlinson, "The View"

❖ A fourth kind of foot, reversing the pattern of the anapest, was familiar to readers of classical Greek but is nearly extinct in English. The **dactyl** doubles up two unstressed syllables after a stressed one, on the "BALtimore—BALtimore—BALtimore" model. A hundred years ago, there was a large popular audience for dactylic verse like the following. Listen for the doubling up of the unstressed syllables in Longfellow's six-beat line:

> Thís *is the* \| fórest *prim* \| éval; *but* \| whére *are the* \| héarts *that be* \| néath it,
> Léaped *like the* \| róe, *when he* \| héars *in the* \| wóodland *the* \| vóice *of the* \|
> húntsman?
> Henry Wadsworth Longfellow, "Evangeline"

In discussions of meter, one further term labels a variation that can strongly emphasize part of a line. The **spondee** is *all* emphasis—it juxtaposes *two* stressed syllables, slowing down the reader and calling special attention. (This is the way many people pronounce HONG KONG.) A spondee often follows or comes before a set of two *un*stressed syllables, so that the total number of beats in a line need not change. The following are the opening lines of a sonnet John Milton wrote in 1655 about his blindness. The spondee in the second line propels us into the world of darkness in which he already lived when he dictated his most ambitious poems:

When I | consíd | er hòw | my líght | is spént
Ere hálf | my dáys | *in this* | DARK WORLD | and wíde . . .

Even in verse that is alive with variations and pauses, exceptionally regular lines are likely to help establish or maintain the basic underlying beat. Meter is the combined product of the chosen kind of foot multiplied by the *number* of feet per line. To label different kinds of meter, we identify the kind of foot (iambic or trochaic, for instance) and then show the number of feet (for instance, pentameter—a five-beat line). Meters with four or five feet to the line are by far the most common.

◇ Three-beat or four-beat lines make up many songs and songlike poems. As a trilogy is a set of three books (or plays), so **trimeter** is meter with three stressed syllables to the line. **Tetrameter** is meter with four stressed syllables to the line. In folk song and ballad, tetrameter and trimeter often alternate in a four-line stanza:

They líghted dówn to táke a drínk	tetrameter
Of the spríng that rán so cléar,	trimeter
And dówn the spríng ran his góod heart's blóod,	tetrameter
And sóre she begán to féar.	trimeter
"Hold úp, hold úp, Lord Wílliam," she sáys,	tetrameter
"For I féar that yòu are sláin."	trimeter
"Tis nóthing but the shádow of my scárlet clóak,	tetrameter
That shínes in the wáter so pláin."	trimeter

(Anonymous) "The Douglas Tragedy"

◇ The five-beat line is by far the most common in English poetry, whether rhymed as in the sonnet, or unrhymed as in the **blank verse** of Shakespeare's plays. As the pentagon is a building with five sides, so **pentameter** is a meter with five stressed syllables to the line. A five-foot line using predominantly iambic feet is in iambic pentameter. The iambic pentameter line often sounds natural and unforced; it seems to stay especially close to the natural speech patterns of English. ("By dáy the bát is cóusin tò the móuse. / He líkes the áttic òf an áging hóuse"—Theodore Roethke.)

◇ A six-beat line, or **hexameter,** was the line of Homer's epics. Later, English poets who knew Greek sometimes slowed down their verse by following the usual pentameter lines with a hexameter line "thát, like a wóunded snáke, drágs its slow léngth alóng" (Alexander Pope). In the following lines, as often with hexameter, a slight break, marked here by a slash, divides the long lines into half-lines. (A noticeable break *within* a line is called a **caesura.**) How would you read these lines?

I would that we were, my beloved, / white birds on the foam of the sea!
We tire of the flame of the meteor, / before it can fade and flee;

And the flame of the blue star of twilight, / hung low on the rim of the sky,
Has awaked in our hearts, my beloved, / a sadness that may not die.
William Butler Yeats, "The White Birds"

When poetry started to break loose from traditional meter, poets like Walt Whitman for a time wrote poems with irregular length of line and with a harder-to-chart but nevertheless strongly felt rhythm. In most of the free-flowing, metrically irregular **free verse** of the twentieth century, the rhythmic beat has been less pronounced—more understated and "cool." Commenting on long-prevailing critical trends, one recent observer said, "The cooler the voice, the warmer the reception" (Alicia Ostriker).

The following poem is in its own way insistent and cumulative, but its beat does not become chanting. (The opening lines allude to the beginning of a sonnet by William Wordsworth: "The world is too much with us.")

DENISE LEVERTOV   (born 1923)

O Taste and See   1962

The world is
not with us enough.
O taste and see

the subway Bible poster said,
meaning The Lord, meaning   5
if anything all that lives
to the imagination's tongue,

grief, mercy, language,
tangerine, weather, to
breathe them, bite,   10
savor, chew, swallow, transform

into our flesh our
deaths, crossing the street, plum, quince,
living in the orchard and being

                                                                   15
hungry, and plucking
the fruit.

THE RECEPTIVE READER

1. How noticeable should the *line breaks* be when the poem is read aloud?

2. This poem owes its insistent rhythm in part to its repeated use of a *series*—several items of the same kind, separated by commas and juxtaposed in a sequence that allows us to dwell briefly on each. Which series can you identify? Which string together items that are clearly related? Which contain items that seem oddly matched?

3. How is what the speaker in the poem says about the imagination analogous to what the Bible poster said about God?

4. How does the poem as a whole lead up to the last few lines?

EXPLORATIONS

Understanding Meter

What is the dominant meter in each of the following passages as a whole or in individual lines? What variations are there? Which are lines of free verse, difficult or impossible to scan along traditional lines?

1. Double, double, toil and trouble;
   Fire burn and caldron bubble.
                  Shakespeare, *Macbeth*

2. My wife and I lived all alone,
   contention was our only bone.
   I fought with her, she fought with me,
   and things went on right merrily.
                  Robert Creeley, "Ballad of the Despairing Husband"

3. It was many and many a year ago,
   In a kingdom by the sea,
   That a maiden there lived whom you may know
   By the name of Annabel Lee.
                  Edgar Allan Poe, "Annabel Lee"

4. But yesterday the word of Caesar might
   Have stood against the world. Now lies he here,
   And none so poor to do him reverence.
                  Shakespeare, *Julius Caesar*

5. Poplars are standing there still as death.
                  Arna Bontemps, "Southern Mansion"

6. last week
   my mother died/
   & the most often asked question
   at the funeral
   was not of her death
   or of her life before death
                                but
   why was i present
   with/out
   a
   tie on.
                  Don L. Lee, "Last Week"

THE CREATIVE DIMENSION

Eighteenth-century writers delighted in using the *closed couplet* (two self-contained rhymed lines, usually in iambic pentameter) to sum up a striking thought in pointed, quotable form. You are likely to appreciate the polish and sparkle of these couplets more if you have tried your hand at a few of them. See how close you can come to the form and spirit of the original couplets.

ORIGINAL: Good nature and good sense must ever join;
       To err is human; to forgive, divine.
              Alexander Pope, "Essay on Criticism"

SAMPLE IMITATION: Use witty sayings once, and then no more—
              First time, it's wit; the second time, a bore.

TRADITIONAL STANZA FORM

Scorn not the sonnet: Critic, you have frowned
Mindless of its just honors; with this key
Shakespeare unlocked his heart.
                        WILLIAM WORDSWORTH

Much traditional poetry is laid out in **stanzas.** It is fashioned into sets of lines similar in shape. Traditional stanzas may repeat the same rhyme scheme, as if programed to make lines rhyme according to the same formula. They may show the same alternation of longer and shorter lines, making lines expand or contract in the same sequence. As each stanza leads us through the familiar established pattern, we experience the pleasure of recognition.

Familiar stanza form harks back to a time when the history of song and poem was still one. We expect a songlike poem to have stanzas the way we expect a song to have successive verses, all sung to the same melody. Some of the golden moments in Shakespeare's comedies come when the jester and assorted revelers take time out to sing haunting, bittersweet songs of innocent young love, simple country life, or cruel death. Look at the rhyme scheme that is shared by both stanzas in each of the following songs. Look at how the final lines of the stanza come back in the second song.

WILLIAM SHAKESPEARE   (1564–1616)
O Mistress Mine   1602

O mistress mine, where are you roaming?   a
O, stay and hear; your true love's coming   a
That can sing both high and low.   b
Trip no further, pretty sweeting,   c
Journeys end in lovers meeting,   c   5
Every wise man's son doth know.   b

What is love? 'Tis not hereafter;
Present mirth hath present laughter;
What's to come is still unsure.
In delay there lies no plenty;   10
Then come kiss me, sweet and twenty,
Youth's a stuff will not endure.

Under the Greenwood Tree 1599

Under the greenwood tree	a	
Who loves to lie with me,	a	
And turn his merry note	b	
Unto the sweet bird's throat,	b	
Come hither, come hither, come hither!	c	5
Here shall he see	a	
No enemy	a	
But winter and rough weather.	c	

Who doth ambition shun,
And loves to live i' the sun, 10
Seeking the food he eats,
And pleased with what he gets,
Come hither, come hither, come hither!
Here shall he see
No enemy 15
But winter and rough weather.
From *As You Like It*

The interlaced, intertwining rhyme schemes (such as aabccb) help knit each stanza together. They help give it a distinctive shape, or configuration, that imprints itself easily on our memory. (A configuration is a pattern with a distinctive outline—like the New York City skyline—that human minds, and computers, can easily pick up and recognize.) In the second song, the configuration of the stanza is especially distinctive: the line length contracts from a three-beat line to a two-beat line (in the sixth and seventh lines of each stanza) and then expands again in the last line. The second poem has a **refrain**—a line, or set of lines, that comes back in each stanza—usually at the end. A refrain sounds a keynote that comes back like the tolling of a bell.

CROSS-REFERENCES—For Discussion or Writing

Do you know any current popular songs that are in form and content in some way similar to these Shakespearean songs? Do you know any that are strikingly different? Compare or contrast the lyrics of one or several current favorites with these Shakespeare lyrics.

Refrains that come back and drive home a prevailing mood or idea are also a feature of another kind of songlike poem—the **popular ballads.** These anonymous folk ballads (many of them going back to the Middle Ages) were originally sung as the record of a notable exploit or calamity, often presented in stark outline, hitting home without frivolous embellishment.

Some of the best-known early ballads repeat a question-and-answer format in a pattern of **cumulative** repetition. The questioner persists in asking questions until the horrible truth is revealed. "Why does your brand (sword) so drip with blood?" asks the mother of her son in one of the best-known Scottish ballads. "I have killed my hawk," answers the son at the end of the first stanza; and then, "I have killed my steed" at the end of the second stanza; and finally, "I have killed my father" at the end of the third.

Poets of later ages have often re-created the ballad style. The following **literary ballad** picks up the question-and-answer style of many earlier ballads. Here, the question-and-answer pattern is repeated three times. Once we become attuned to the pattern, we wait for the next question—and the next answer, as the poem builds up to its grim conclusion. (Make sure you read this poem—or hear the poem read—aloud.)

MELVIN WALKER LA FOLLETTE   (born 1930)

The Ballad of Red Fox

1959

Yellow sun yellow
Sun yellow sun,
When, oh, when
Will red fox run?

When the hollow horn shall sound,   5
When the hunter lifts his gun
And liberates the wicked hound,
Then, oh, then shall red fox run.

Yellow sun yellow
Sun yellow sun,   10
Where, oh, where
Will red fox run?

Through meadows hot as sulphur,
Through forests cool as clay,
Through hedges crisp as morning   15
And grasses limp as day.

Yellow sky yellow
Sky yellow sky,
How, oh, how
Will red fox die?   20

With a bullet in his belly,
A dagger in his eye,
And blood upon his red red brush
Shall red fox die.

THE RECEPTIVE READER

1. The questions in this poem provide a variable rather than completely identical *refrain*. How does it change?

2. To what extent do the answers in this poem follow the *rhyme* scheme of the traditional ballad stanza—a four-liner (or quatrain) rhyming abcb? A rhyming pattern can place special emphasis on key words in a poem. What rhymes make key words echo throughout this poem?

3. What do you think accounts for the continuing appeal of the old ballad style?

THE PERSONAL RESPONSE

In the battle between the hunter and the hunted, on which side is the poet? On which side are you?

Many of the more elaborately crafted traditional stanza patterns go back to the love poetry of the Middle Ages and the Renaissance. The word *artificial* then did not yet mean unnatural or insincere. Rather, it meant artfully done, finely crafted, pleasing to the eye and ear. An example of such an artfully crafted form is the **villanelle** (originally a song in a country setting). Intermeshing rhymes link the three-line stanzas (or **tercets**) until the poem slows down and comes to a stop in the final four-line stanza (or **quatrain**). Rhymes and whole lines keep coming back. What is the pattern?

ELIZABETH BISHOP (1911–1979)
One Art   1976

The art of losing isn't hard to master;
so many things seem filled with the intent
to be lost that their loss is no disaster.

Lose something every day. Accept the fluster
of lost door keys, the hour badly spent.   5
The art of losing isn't hard to master.

Then practice losing farther, losing faster:
places, and names, and where it was you meant
to travel. None of these will bring disaster.

I lost my mother's watch. And look! my last, or   10
next-to-last, of three loved houses went.
The art of losing isn't hard to master.

I lost two cities, lovely ones. And, vaster,
some realms I owned, two rivers, a continent.
I miss them, but it wasn't a disaster.   15

—Even losing you (the joking voice, a gesture
I love) I shan't have lied. It's evident
the art of losing's not too hard to master
though it may look like (Write it!) like disaster.

THE RECEPTIVE READER

1. What is the *rhyme* scheme of this typical villanelle? Where does the poet stretch it by slant rhyme or by a playful forced rhyme?
2. The villanelle uses a double *refrain*. How does it work?
3. The highly-patterned villanelle, like other highly patterned traditional forms, can be half playful and half serious. What are the serious and the playful parts in this poem?

The best known and most widely practiced of traditional stanza forms is the **sonnet.** The sonnet is a single, self-contained stanza of fourteen lines (although the best known of the early sonneteers repeated the same form again and again in sonnet sequences of over a hundred poems). During the height of the sonneteering vogue in the sixteenth century, sonnets were poems of unrequited love, with the mournful, humble lover forever replaying his "plaint" to the conventionally cruel, disdainful lady-on-the-pedestal. Soon, however, poets extended the form to other personal, political, and religious subjects.

Traditionally, the sonnet works with a five-beat iambic line; it therefore often has ten or eleven syllables to the line. Sonneteers following the model of the Italian poet Petrarch rhyme the first eight lines (the **octave**) in an interlaced pattern: abbaabba. The remaining six lines (the **sestet**) may rhyme cdcdee or cdecde. Sonneteers imitating the Shakespearean sonnet group the fourteen lines somewhat differently: They generally have alternating rhymes in the first three **quatrains,** or groups of four (abab/cdcd/efef), followed by a concluding couplet (gg).

In a Petrarchan sonnet, a turning in the flow of thought may start at or near the break after the first eight lines. The remaining six lines then represent a kind of countertide. (Robert Frost said that "a true sonnet goes eight lines and then takes a turn for better or worse.") Where is the turn in the flow of ideas in John Milton's poem on his blindness?

JOHN MILTON   (1608–1674)

When I consider how my light is spent   1655

When I consider how my light is spent	
Ere° half my days, in this dark world and wide,	*before*
And that one talent which is death to hide	
Lodged with me useless, though my soul more bent	
To serve therewith my Maker, and present	5
My true account, lest he° returning chide;	*so he won't*
"Doth God exact day-labor, light denied?"°	*with sight denied*
I fondly° ask; but Patience to prevent	*foolishly*
That murmur, soon replies, "God doth not need	
Either man's work or his own gifts; who best	10
Bear his mild yoke, they serve him best. His state	
Is kingly. Thousands at his bidding speed	
And post° o'er land and ocean without rest:	*carry messages*
They also serve who only stand and wait."	

Milton's sonnet illustrates the tremendous variety of rhythm and effect possible with traditional form when sentences are not neatly packaged into lines or couplets. In Milton's sonnet, the magnificent long first sentence runs through all but the last three lines of the fourteen-line poem. It elaborates on a train of thought whose underlying pattern is "When I think about my blindness . . . I ask a foolish rebellious question (does God expect a blind poet to continue his work?) . . . but Patience replies that God does not depend on any one person's labor or gifts." This long elaborate sentence puts the poet's whole situation—both the question it raises and the answer the poet has reached—before us. But after the first period, which comes almost at the end of the eleventh line, we stop short at a terse sentence that goes to the opposite extreme. It has four words. It makes us take in and ponder the essence of the lesson the poet has learned: the majesty of God. "His state / Is kingly." His glory does not depend on our praise or service, however dedicated.

THE RECEPTIVE READER

1. What *rhyme* words fill in the typical Petrarchan rhyme scheme?
2. What lines come closest to perfect *iambic pentameter*? Where do you see clear examples of trochaic inversion at the beginning of a line?
3. What are some striking examples of *enjambment*, with the sense spilling over into the next line to give the poem a characteristically Miltonic sense of flow—of long, rich sentences moving forward regardless of line boundaries? (Where does a subsequent *caesura*, or cut within a line, help to set up a syncopating counterrhythm?)
4. How does the poem as a whole lead up to its famous last line?

EXPLORATIONS

An Unconventional Sonnet

Conventionally, sonnets looked at love from the perspective of the lover yearning for a love that often seemed unattainable. How does the author of the following sonnet depart from this convention?

EDNA ST. VINCENT MILLAY (1892–1950)
I, being born a woman and distressed   1923

I, being born a woman and distressed
By all the needs and notions of my kind,
Am urged by your propinquity° to find   *nearness*
Your person fair, and feel a certain zest
To bear your body's weight upon my breast: 5
So subtle is the fume of life designed
To clarify the pulse and cloud the mind,
And leave me once again undone, possessed.
Think not for this, however, the poor treason
Of my stout blood against my staggering brain,   10
I shall remember you with love, or season
My scorn with pity,—let me make it plain:
I find this frenzy insufficient reason
For conversation when we meet again.

THE RECEPTIVE READER

1. What *formal* features of the traditional sonnet does this poem illustrate? (What is the rhyme scheme?)

2. What basic *polarities* help organize this poem? Where in this sonnet is there a turning or countertide, and what makes it central to the poem as a whole?

THE PERSONAL RESPONSE

Millay has been called "very much a revolutionary in all her sympathies, and a whole-hearted Feminist" (Floyd Dell). In most of the sonnet tradition, the woman was the silent audience and the silent partner in the love relationship. How do you react as the woman in this poem speaks up and talks back?

CROSS-REFERENCES—For Discussion or Writing

Compare and contrast the perspective on love in this sonnet with the perspective on love in sonnets in the Petrarchan tradition—sonnets by Wyatt (p. 499), Petrarch (p. 656), and Shakespeare (p. 573).

TRADITIONAL FORM AND OPEN FORM

Of all the possible distinctions between verse and prose, the simplest, and most objective, is that verse uses the line as a unit. Prose goes right on. . . . Verse turns.
JUDSON JEROME

As rhyme, meter, and stanza become optional, a more basic definition of poetic form remains: Poetry is lines of verse, laid out in a pattern on a page. The individual lines slow down the hasty reader; they encourage full attention to the individual image and to each phase in the flow of thought. This laying out of the text is a signal that even modern **open form** is not formless. It is merely less obvious, harder to chart and to schematize. However, like traditional form, open form (or free verse) makes for a richer, denser texture than that of ordinary language. It still uses patterns of repetition, the echoing of sounds and of words, the playing off of opposites, the interplay of sound and meaning.

For a time, champions of modernism did battle with defenders of tradition, who scorned poets playing "tennis with the net down" (Robert Frost). However, widely admired twentieth-century poets have written poems in either vein—some poems with a stricter traditional pattern, and some in a more open modern style. Study the following two examples, both by poets who move easily between traditional formal discipline and modern creative freedom. What can traditional form do that might be hard to achieve in a more open modern format? What is possible with open form that traditional form might make it hard for the poet to do?

ANNE SEXTON   (1928–1974)

Her Kind   1960

I have gone out, a possessed witch,
haunting the black air, braver at night;
dreaming evil, I have done my hitch
over the plain houses, light by light:
lonely thing, twelve-fingered, out of mind.   5
A woman like that is not a woman, quite.
I have been her kind.

I have found the warm caves in the woods,
filled them with skillets, carvings, shelves,
closets, silks, innumerable goods;   10
fixed the suppers for the worms and the elves:
whining, rearranging the disaligned.
A woman like that is misunderstood.
I have been her kind.

I have ridden in your cart, driver,   15
waved my nude arms at villages going by,
learning the last bright routes, survivor
where your flames still bite my thigh
and my ribs crack where your wheels wind.
A woman like that is not ashamed to die.   20
I have been her kind.

   How do the formal features of this poem serve the poet's purpose? The
poem is intense, concentrated, deliberate. The patterns of repetition and the
refrains give it a ritualistic quality. It is like an incantation—the poem, as it
were, puts a spell (or a hex, if you wish) on the reader. The poem is elaborately
crafted, using major features of traditional form:

   ✧ The poem is divided into three stanzas of identical shape, each following the same rhyme scheme, each laid out according to the same plan. This
poet deals with a disturbing subject—which she has brought fully under *control.* The poem has a finished, definitive quality—as if the poet had earlier
worked through her horror and anguish and is now ready to give us, for the
time being, her final word on the subject.

   ✧ Each stanza, clearly marked off in the traditional fashion, frames a striking, haunting picture. The stanza brings that picture into sharp *focus,* allowing
us to ponder it as the stanza is brought to a close and the picture becomes
etched into memory. Within each stanza, the interlacing rhyme scheme knits
the material together, as if all distracting detail had been left out.

   ✧ The threefold repetition of the elaborately crafted stanza form makes us
expect that each of the three will indeed be part of the same story. This expectation is strongly reinforced by **parallelism,** that is, closely similar sentence
structure or wording. The opening lines are parallel in sentence pattern: "I
have gone . . ."; "I have found . . ."; "I have ridden. . . ." So is the last-but-

one line in each stanza ("A woman like that is . . ."). The poem has the impact that comes from exceptional *unity* and concentration. We sense that the perspective will remain the same: The speaker will continue to look at the witch not from the point of view of her persecutors but of someone who identifies with the outcast: "I have been her kind."

⬦ The last line, affirming the speaker's human solidarity with "her kind," returns at the end of each stanza and thus serves as a refrain. But this refrain does more than repeat. Each time it comes back, it gains in force, until the *cumulative* pattern of the poem reaches its climax in martyrdom and final defiance.

THE RECEPTIVE READER

1. How does the *rhyme scheme* bond the two weighty final lines of each stanza to the earlier lines? How does the rhyme scheme link stanza to stanza?

2. What *details* give this poem the intensity of a nightmare?

3. Women accused of being witches were for centuries the target of persecution and lynch justice. How does the poet want you to think of the women behind the caricatures and stereotypes?

THE CREATIVE DIMENSION

Have you ever identified with the outcast, the outsider, the underdog? Write a poem or passage in which the refrain might be "I have been her (his) kind."

In the following poem, what gives shape to the poem as a whole—in the absence of such traditional features as rhyme, meter, and stanza?

S H A R O N   O L D S   (born 1942)

I Go Back to May 1937   1987

I see them standing at the formal gates of their colleges,
I see my father strolling out
under the ochre sandstone arch, the
red tiles glinting like bent
plates of blood behind his head, I   5
see my mother with a few light books at her hip
standing at the pillar made of tiny bricks with the
wrought-iron gate still open behind her, its
sword-tips black in the May air,
they are about to graduate, they are about to get married,   10
they are kids, they are dumb, all they know is they are
innocent, they would never hurt anybody.
I want to go up to them and say Stop,
don't do it—she's the wrong woman,
he's the wrong man, you are going to do things   15
you cannot imagine you would ever do,

you are going to do bad things to children,
you are going to suffer in ways you never heard of,
you are going to want to die. I want to go
up to them there in the late May sunlight and say it,   20
her hungry pretty blank face turning to me,
her pitiful beautiful untouched body,
his arrogant handsome blind face turning to me,
his pitiful beautiful untouched body,
but I don't do it. I   25
want to live. I take them up like the male and female
paper dolls and bang them together
at the hips like chips of flint as if to
strike sparks from them. I say
Do what you are going to do, and I will tell about it.   30

What makes this second poem an example of open form?

Some differences meet the eye (and ear): There is no rhyme (although there are some echo effects like "at the *hips* like *chips*"). The lines are of irregular, unpredictable length, and the line breaks often come at strange points in the middle of a phrase (the / red tiles), making it hard for the poet to rhyme lines even if she had wanted to. There is no steady underlying drumbeat of meter. No stanzas segment the poem, pleasing us with the recurrence of a characteristic pattern. These differences in the formal features of the two poems prepare us for differences in the way they affect the reader:

✧ Compared with the Sexton poem, this poem seems more *open-ended*. We have the sense that the story of the speaker's parents, and her attempt to come to terms with it, are still in progress. As the flashback to a time before the speaker's birth continues, we can still share in the impulse to tell her parents No! but then resolve to let human nature take its course. Key phrases like "I want to live" are not pulled out, set off, and dramatized. Instead, they appear as natural stages in the flow of thought.

✧ **Parallelism** in this poem sets up open frames allowing the poet *free scope* to multiply the striking lifelike details that well up from her active imagination. Open-ended parallel structure ("I see . . .."; "I see . . .."; "I see . . ..") allows the poet to build up the details that make the imagined campus scene come hauntingly to life, from the sandstone arch and glinting red tiles to the "few light books" at the mother's hip and the black "sword-tips" of the wrought-iron gate. The same kind of open frame allows her to keep sounding the note of urgent warning that builds up in intensity in the middle of the poem ("you are going to . . .."; "you are going to . . .."; "you are going to . . ..").

THE RECEPTIVE READER

1. What *line breaks* come at an unexpected place in a sentence or in the middle of a phrase, partly counteracting the pause traditionally signaled by the end of a line?

2. How does *parallel structure* serve for emphasis in the lines, making us look at the faces and bodies of the parents? How do these lines sum up the mixed emotions of the speaker?

3. How does this poem achieve *closure,* leaving us with a satisfying sense of completeness?

THE PERSONAL RESPONSE

In recent years, the concern of (grown) children with the quality of the parenting they received has become a major focus in the media and in popular psychology. How would you sum up the attitude of the speaker in this poem toward her parents? How does it compare with your own attitudes?

JUXTAPOSITIONS

Close and Free Translation

Translators of poetry have to decide how far they will go to reproduce features of form, such as meter and rhyme. It is often very difficult to approximate the origanic blend of form and meaning in the original, so that many translations use a more open form than the original poet did.

The two following translations are different versions of a much-translated poem by a widely translated German poet. The first translation hews close to the regular iambic pentameter and the end rhymes of the original stanzas. (In the original, the first and third lines of each stanza also rhyme.) The second translation aims at getting close to the spirit of the original while abandoning the more traditional formal features of the original. How does the difference in form affect your response to the poem?

RAINER MARIA RILKE   (1875–1926)

The Panther   1927

TRANSLATED BY HANS P. GUTH

Jardin des Plantes, Paris

From pacing past the barriers of his cage
His tired gaze no longer seems to see.
All that exists: a thousand iron bars.
The world beyond the bars has ceased to be.

The supple tread of sinuous steps revolves   5
In circles of benumbing narrowness,
Like power dancing round a pedestal
Where a majestic will stands powerless.

And yet, at times, the veil that blunts his eye
Moves stealthily aside—an image enters,   10
Glides through the silence of his tautened limbs—
And ceases where his being centers.

Many translators of poetry are poets in their own right. They bring to the translator's task a special empathy, a special ability to get into the spirit of a fellow poet. This affinity shows when Robert Bly translates and comments on the same Rilke poem.

The Panther   1927

TRANSLATED BY ROBERT BLY

From seeing and seeing the seeing has become so exhausted
it no longer sees anything anymore.
The world is made of bars, a hundred thousand
bars, and behind the bars, nothing.

The lithe swinging of that rhythmical easy stride   5
that slowly circles down to a single point
is like a dance of energy around a hub,
in which a great will stands stunned and numbed.

At times the curtains of the eye lift
without a sound—then a shape enters,   10
slips through the tightened silence of the shoulders,
reaches the heart and dies.

The poet translator said about this much-reprinted poem:

Rilke . . . watched a panther at the zoo, and his German lines, in rhythm and sound, embody movingly the repetitive, desperate walk of the panther. By the end of the poem he is somehow inside the panther's body. Each time the panther glimpses a shape, say a dog or a child, the image goes to the body's center, the place from which a leap begins; but no leap can take place. A leap can't take place, and so the image "reaches the heart, and dies."

THE RECEPTIVE READER

Where do the two translations seem very close, reflecting the common original? Where do they diverge and with what effect? What difference does the difference in form make to your response? What do you think is the key to the fascination this poem has had for readers and translators around the world?

POEMS FOR FURTHER STUDY

In reading the following poems, pay special attention to the way they use or modify traditional formal features, such as rhyme, meter, and stanza form.

POPULAR BALLAD   (Anonymous)

Lord Randal   traditional

"O where have you been, Lord Randal, my son?
And where have you been, my handsome young man?"
"I have been at the greenwood; mother, make my bed soon,
For I'm wearied with hunting, and fain° would lie down."   *gladly*

"And who met you there, Lord Randal, my son?   5
And who met you there, my handsome young man?"
"O I met with my true-love; mother, make my bed soon,
For I'm wearied with hunting, and fain would lie down."

"And what did she give you, Lord Randal, my son?
And what did she give you, my handsome young man?"   10
"Eels fried in a pan; mother, make my bed soon,
For I'm wearied with hunting, and fain would like down."

"And who got your leavings, Lord Randal, my son?
And what became of them, my handsome young man?"
"My hawks and my hounds; mother, make my bed soon,   15
For I'm wearied with hunting, and fain would lie down."

"And what became of them, Lord Randal, my son?
And what became of them, my handsome young man?"
"They stretched their legs out and died; mother, make my bed soon,
For I'm wearied with hunting, and fain would lie down."   20

"O I fear you are poisoned, Lord Randal, my son!
I fear you are poisoned, my handsome young man!"
"O yes, I am poisoned; mother, make my bed soon,
For I'm sick at heart, and fain would lie down."

"What d' you leave to your mother, Lord Randal, my son?
What d' you leave to your mother, my handsome young man?"   25
"Four and twenty milk kine;° mother, make my bed soon,   *cattle*
For I'm sick at heart, and fain would lie down."

"What d' you leave to your sister, Lord Randal, my son?
What d' you leave to your sister, my handsome young man?"   30
"My gold and my silver; mother, make my bed soon,
For I'm sick at heart, and fain would lie down."

"What d' you leave to your brother, Lord Randal, my son?
What d' you leave to your brother, my handsome young man?"
"My houses and my lands; mother, make my bed soon,   35
For I'm sick at heart, and fain would lie down."

"What d' you leave to your true-love, Lord Randal, my son?
What d' you leave to your true-love, my handsome young man?"
"I leave her hell and fire; mother, make my bed soon,
For I'm sick at heart, and fain would lie down."   40

THE RECEPTIVE READER

When does the often-repeated *refrain* first turn ominous? How does this ballad use the pattern of *cumulative repetition* twice? How does the ballad strip the story down to *essentials*? What do you think made this story survive through the centuries?

CHRISTINE DE PISAN (1363–1430)

Marriage Is a Lovely Thing   before 1400

TRANSLATED BY JOANNA BANKIER

Marriage is a lovely thing
—my own example proves it—
for her whose husband is as kind
as he whom God has found for me.
Since day by day he has sustained me,   5
praised be He who guards his life
and keeps him safe for me,
       and surely my gentle one loves me well.

On the night of our union,
the first time we slept together   10
I could see how kind he was.
Nothing did that could have hurt me
and before the rising sun
had kissed me, oh a hundred times
but never urged against my will,   15
       and surely my gentle one loves me well.

And how sweet the words he spoke;
"Dearest Friend, God led me to you
to serve you courteously and well
as if he wished to raise me up."   20
Thus he mused all through the night
and his manner never faltered
but stayed the same, unwaveringly,
       and surely my gentle one loves me well.

O Prince, his love can drive me to distraction   25
when he assures me he's all mine
and of sweetness makes me burst.

THE RECEPTIVE READER

1. Like many other love poems of the Middle Ages, this poem has a *refrain* and a "send-off" (or *envoi*) of three lines. (The modern translator has not attempted to reproduce the rhymes of the original French poem.) What gives the refrain in this poem its special appeal or special force? How does the poem as a whole lead up to the send-off?

2. Christine de Pisan, a native of Italy living in France, was happily married for a few short years. After her husband's death, she became one of the first women in Eu-

rope to support herself by her writing. How is the treatment of love in this poem different from that in other early love lyrics you have read?

WILLIAM WORDSWORTH (1770–1850)

I Wandered Lonely as a Cloud   1807

I wandered lonely as a cloud
    That floats on high o'er vales and hills,
When all at once I saw a crowd,
    A host,° of golden daffodils;   *massed ranks*
Beside the lake, beneath the trees,   5
Fluttering and dancing in the breeze.

Continuous as the stars that shine
    And twinkle on the milky way,
They stretched in never-ending line
    Along the margin of a bay: 10
Ten thousand saw I at a glance,
Tossing their heads in sprightly dance.

The waves beside them danced; but they
    Outdid the sparkling waves in glee;
A poet could not but be gay,   15
    In such a jocund° company;   *joyful*
I gazed—and gazed—but little thought
What wealth the show to me had brought:

For oft, when on my couch I lie
    In vacant or in pensive° mood,   *thoughtful*   20
They flash upon that inward eye
    Which is the bliss of solitude;
And then my heart with pleasure fills,
And dances with the daffodils.

THE RECEPTIVE READER

How does the poet use rhyme, meter, and stanza form? Does the poet make the experience reenacted in this poem come to life for you as the reader? Can you follow, and sympathize with, the train of thought in the last stanza?

CROSS-REFERENCES—For Discussion or Writing

During the years when Wordsworth wrote much of his best-known nature poetry, his sister Dorothy kept her *Journals,* in which she recorded many of the activities they shared: their long nature walks, their observation of the rapidly changing moods of nature, their observation of the country people at work in the fields or on the road in search of work or a place to live. The following is Dorothy Wordsworth's journal account of the same (or same kind of) experience that inspired her brother's poem. What are the major differences in the way the prose and the poem affect the reader? What does the poem do that the prose journal does not? What does the journal have that the poem does not?

The wind seized our breath; the lake was rough. There was a boat by itself floating in the middle of the bay below Water Millock. . . . When we were in the woods beyond Gowbarrow park we saw a few daffodils close to the waterside. We fancied that the lake had floated the seeds ashore and that a little colony had sprung up. But as we went along, there were more and yet more; and at last under the boughs of the trees, we saw that there was a long belt of them along the shore, about the breadth of a country turnpike road. I never saw daffodils so beautiful. They grew among the mossy stones and about them, some rested their heads upon these stones as on a pillow for weariness, and the rest tossed and reeled and danced and seemed as if they verily laughed. The wind blew upon them over the lake; they looked so gay ever glancing ever changing.

THOMAS NASHE (1567–1601)

A Litany in Time of Plague   1592

Adieu, farewell, earth's bliss;
This world uncertain is;
Fond° are life's lustful joys;   *foolish*
Death proves them all but toys;
None from his darts can fly;   5
I am sick, I must die.
          Lord, have mercy on us!

Rich men, trust not in wealth,
Gold cannot buy you health:
Physic° himself must fade;   *the physician's art*   10
All things to end are made;
The plague full swift goes by.
I am sick, I must die.
          Lord, have mercy on us!

Beauty is but a flower   15
Which wrinkles will devour;
Brightness falls from the air;
Queens have died young and fair;
Dust hath closed Helen's° eye.   *Helen of Troy*
I am sick, I must die.   20
          Lord, have mercy on us!

Strength stoops unto the grave,
Worms feed on Hector° brave;   *Trojan prince*
Swords may not fight with fate;
Earth still holds ope° her gate;   *open*   25
Come, come, the bells do cry.
I am sick, I must die.
          Lord, have mercy on us!

Wit with his wantonness
Tastes death's bitterness;   30
Hell's executioner

Hath no ears for to hear
What vain art can reply.
I am sick, I must die.
        Lord, have mercy on us!   35

Haste, therefore, each degree,°   *rank*
To welcome destiny;
Heaven is our heritage,
Earth but a player's stage;
Mount we° unto the sky;   *let us mount* 40
I am sick, I must die.
        Lord, have mercy on us!

THE RECEPTIVE READER

1. A litany is a chantlike prayer with much *repetition*. What use does this prayer make of outright repetition? What use does it make of parallel structure?

2. What is the *rhyme scheme*? How does rhyme carry over from one stanza to the next? What is the central word to which the carryover rhyme directs attention?

3. What is the underlying *meter* in the first five lines of each stanza? In what lines does it show most clearly? What is the major recurrent variation on this metrical pattern? How does the meter change in the refrain? How does the change in meter affect your reading of the poem?

THE PERSONAL RESPONSE

How remote or how understandable are the sentiments expressed in this poem for you as a modern reader?

THEODORE ROETHKE (1908–1963)

The Waking   1953

I wake to sleep, and take my waking slow.
I feel my fate in what I cannot fear.
I learn by going where I have to go.

We think by feeling. What is there to know?
I hear my being dance from ear to ear.   5
I wake to sleep, and take my waking slow.

Of those so close beside me, which are you?
God bless the ground! I shall walk softly there,
And learn by going where I have to go.

Light takes the Tree; but who can tell us how?   10
The lowly worm climbs up a winding stair;
I wake to sleep, and take my waking slow.

Great Nature has another thing to do
To you and me; so take the lively air,
And, lovely, learn by going where to go.   15

This shaking keeps me steady. I should know
What falls away is always. And is near.
I wake to sleep, and take my waking slow.
I learn by going where I have to go.

THE RECEPTIVE READER

1. How does this poem illustrate the traditional formal features of the *villanelle*? Where does it modify the traditional rhyme scheme by the use of half-rhymes?

2. What is the meaning of some of the *recurrent phrases* to which the circular pattern of the villanelle keeps returning? How does the poem as a whole lead up to the two concluding lines?

WRITING ABOUT LITERATURE

17. Relating Form to Meaning (First and Second Draft)

The Writing Workshop   Much writing about poetry aims at showing the connection between form and meaning. It tries to trace the relationship between technical formal features and what the poem as a whole does for the reader. Writing about form and meaning is an ambitious undertaking. In the first place, you obviously need to be able to recognize traditional formal features. You then need to look at how they work in a poem. You need to study the interplay between what is said and how is it said. Furthermore, you need to recognize how formal features are modified or replaced in much modern poetry.

Remember the following guidelines:

✧ See what use the poem makes of *rhyme*. Does it use traditional full rhymes throughout? part of the time? in strategic places? Is there an alternating rhyme scheme or other pattern that bonds a series of lines? Does the poem make use of half-rhymes or internal rhymes? Does rhyme serve to highlight important words? Does it help to segment the poem neatly into lines, or does the sense of a line frequently spill over into the next line (enjambment)?

✧ Check if the poem sets up a strong underlying beat, or *meter*. (Be sure to read lines aloud.) Does it use the common iambic pentameter line? How regular are the lines? Is there much variation—with what effect? Is variation used for emphasis, or to speed up or slow down a line? If the poem uses free verse, is it strongly rhythmic—and does the rhythm give the lines an eloquent or hypnotic effect? Or is the rhythm of the lines closer to the casual pattern of ordinary speech? Is the poet's treatment of the subject or attitude toward the reader also casual?

✧ Check whether the poem is divided into *stanzas*. Does the poet use a traditional stanza such as the four-line ballad stanza or the fourteen-line sonnet? If the first, does the poem have a songlike quality? Does it keep commentary out, ballad-style? Does it use a refrain—with what effect? If the second, does the poem have the ceremonial, carefully crafted quality of the traditional sonnet?

✧ If the poem uses modern *open form,* check for features that help organize or structure the poem. Look for deliberate repetition for emphasis, parallel sentence structure tying together closely related parts of the poem, the echoing of words or phrases, the playing off of opposites.

The following are key sections from the first draft of a student paper that focuses on form and meaning. The comments are feedback from an instructor; they are designed to guide the writer in revising and strengthening the paper. Study the comments, and then see how the student writer has responded to them in the second draft of the paper.

FIRST DRAFT

New England Discipline

COMMENT: Title too dry or uninformative? Use a title that conveys the spirit of the poem in more dramatic fashion?

In his sonnet "New England," Edwin Arlington Robinson skillfully employs the powers of form and sound to intensify the meaning of the poem. Robinson fittingly uses the most demanding of poetic forms, the Petrarchan or Italian sonnet, to frame his objection to the New England tradition of emphasizing discipline and self-denial at the expense of love and joy. Robinson himself observes the strict discipline of the traditional fourteen lines, subdivided into octet (first eight lines) and sestet (remaining six lines). . . .

COMMENT: Excellent focus on the central concern of the poem and on its overall intention. To introduce your thesis more effectively, replace the somewhat interchangeable first sentence (it could fit many different poems)? Perhaps start with a striking quotation instead?

The first word of the poem appropriately forms an inversion of the iambic rhythm, a trochee: "Here where the wind is always north-north-east," focusing the reader's attention quite forcibly on cold New England. The "always north-north-east" wind, and the children in the next line who "learn to walk on frozen toes," start out the poem on a distinctly chilly note. New England is cold in more ways than one. Here it is so cold that "joy shivers in the corner where she knits." Note that in this line the word *joy* forms a spondee with the following word, *shivers,* adding emphasis. . . .

COMMENT: Good here and later on how formal features emphasize or highlight meaning. Try to explain more—and demonstrate the workings of the technical features a little more graphically?

Lines three to eight introduce a major contrast. They are like a simmering stew of lush, hothouse words that describe the opposite of traditional New England values—"those / Who boil elsewhere with such a lyric yeast / Of love that you will hear them at a feast / Where demons would appeal for some repose, / Still clamoring where the chalice overflows / And crying wildest who have drunk the least." Here all the bars are down—the words rush by and knock down the structure that contained them. The reader is flooded with a rush of passionate warmth and feeling, which the New Englander can only regard with "wonder [that] begets . . . envy." Robinson has used enjambment to create this effect. . . .

COMMENT: A good paragraph. Set off the group of five lines as a block quotation for easier reading (and for added emphasis). Use partial quotes to avoid awkward use of square brackets?

At the end of line eight, the sonnet takes its traditional turn in direction. The excursion into passion ends. The sestet, or concluding six lines, sums up the poet's rebellion against the traditional New England attitude toward life: "Passion here is a soilure of the wits, / We're told, and Love a cross for them to bear," it begins. . . .

Edwin Arlington Robinson, himself a New Englander with deep roots in the Puritan tradition, has written a memorable poem that utilized traditional form very effectively to deepen its message.

COMMENT: Your conclusion, like your introduction, seems too perfunctory and interchangeable. Develop the key point about the poet's own New England roots?

SECOND DRAFT

Shivering Joy, Comfortable Conscience

"Joy shivers in the corner where she knits / And Conscience always has the rocking-chair" (11–12). With such vivid images, Edwin Arlington Robinson in his sonnet "New England" explores the New England values of hard work, moral uprightness, and distrust of emotion. Robinson skillfully employs form and sound to enhance the meaning of the poem.

Fittingly, he uses the most highly disciplined and demanding of poetic forms, the sonnet, to explore and question the New England tradition of rigorous discipline and self-denial at the expense of such human passions as love and joy. Robinson's sonnet observes the traditional discipline of fourteen lines; a variation of the traditional Petrarchan rhyme scheme (abba/abba/cdcdcd); and the traditional iambic pentameter. Ironically, however, the traditional sonnet form here becomes a vehicle for questioning traditional attitudes that restrict the free development of the human spirit.

The very first word of the poem causes an inversion of the iambic rhythm, shifting the stress from the second syllable of the line to the first (a trochee). The first line reads: "*Here* where I the wind I is al I ways north- I north-east," focusing the reader's attention forcibly on cold New England. The "always north-north-east" wind and the children in the next line who "learn to walk on frozen toes" start out the poem on a distinctly chilly note. The poet's native New England is cold in more ways than one, we are soon to learn. Here it is so cold that "Joy shivers in the corner where she knits" (11). In this line, the word *Joy,* stressed at the beginning of the line, forms a spondee with what would normally be the second and accented syllable of the first iambic foot: "*Joy shiv* I ers in I the cor I ner where I she knits." Several words in that line—*shivers, in, knits*—have the short *i* sound, suggesting smallness or diminution, which is apparently what the strict New Englanders, apprehensive that joy might get out of hand, would desire. And even joy must not sit idly wasting time—she sits in her designated cold corner, knitting, probably warm mittens or woollen socks needed for survival in the chill outdoors.

And now for the polar opposite: Lines three to eight are a simmering stew of lush, hothouse words, describing those

> Who boil elsewhere with such a lyric yeast
> Of love that you will hear them at a feast
> Where demons would appeal for some repose,
> Still clamoring where the chalice overflows
> And crying wildest who have drunk the least. (4–8)

Here all the bars are down: The words rush unrestrainedly, seemingly of their own volition, and knock down the structure that has been carefully erected to contain them. The lines spill over (enjambment), as in "a lyric yeast / Of love" (4–5). The reader is flooded with a rush of passionate warmth and feeling, which the New Englander can only regard with wonder that "begets an envy" (3).

At the end of line eight, however, the sonnet takes the traditional turn in direction. The excursion into passion ends. The sestet, or concluding six lines, reaffirms the dominance of a more restrictive view of life. "Passion here is a soilure of the wits, / We're told, and Love a cross for them to bear" (9–10). The key word at the beginning of these lines again is emphasized by trochaic inversion: "*Passion* I here is." In these final six lines, everything is again under control, with the thoughts arranged in neat rhyming couplets. Here we see Joy shivering in her corner, while the mistress of the house, Conscience, "always has the rocking-chair." Conscience is perversely "cheerful"—note again the emphasis on this unexpected word through trochaic inversion: "*Cheer*ful I as when . . ." (13). She was apparently equally cheerful when she caused the death of the first cat to be killed not, as in the familiar saying, by curiosity but, New England style, by too much worry and care.

Edward Arlington Robinson was himself a New Englander with deep roots in the Puritan tradition. He was related through his mother to Anne Bradstreet, Puritan New England's first poet. In this poem, he uses the traditional sonnet form effectively to explore the New England tradition of stressing discipline and distrusting emotion.

QUESTIONS

1. Where and how does this student writer show examples of outward form serving as "a mirror to the sense"? How convincing are the examples in this paper?

2. Does this paper seem to capture Robinson's attitude toward the New England tradition? Does the paper seem prejudiced or too negative?

3. Why does the poet's use of traditional form seem ironic to the student writer?

4. When confronted with the polarity explored in this paper, where would you take your stand?

18 PERSONA
Masks and Faces

All writing is the assumption of a mask, a persona,
an implied author.

DAVID W. SMIT

*I write in the first person because I have always
wanted to make my life more interesting than it was.*

DIANE WAKOSKI

*This is my daily mask
daughter, sister
wife, mother
poet, teacher
grandmother.*

*My mask is control
concealment
endurance
my mask is escape
from my
self.*

MITSUYE YAMADA, "MASKS OF WOMAN"

FOCUS ON PERSONA

The **persona** is the voice speaking to us in a poem. This voice may be different from that of the poet as a person. In reading a poem, we often need to ask: "Who is speaking? And to whom?" We may need to distinguish between the poet as a biographical person (whom we could interview and question about the poem) and the "I" addressing us in the poem—the persona.

The distance between the poet and the persona speaking in the poem varies greatly from poem to poem. A poet may share with us real-life experiences and personal feelings. We then hear the voice of the poet speaking to us as a person, taking us into his or her confidence, the way someone might speak to us in a frank personal letter. However, the poet may be revealing to us only one part of his or her personality—perhaps a side that is often hidden from view. Or else the voice speaking in the poem may be an idealized version of the actual poet-as-a-person. The poet may then be speaking to us in a public role, living up to a public image or speaking to us as the voice of a group or a movement. Finally, the persona speaking in the poem may be a disguise, a mask—designed to shield the real poet from prying eyes.

Sometimes the persona is a historical personage or an imaginary character very different from the poet. Listen to the voice you hear in the following poem. Who is speaking? To whom?

C. K. WILLIAMS   (born 1936)
Hood   1969

Remember me? I was the one
In high school you were always afraid of.
I kept cigarettes in my sleeve, wore
engineer's boots, long hair, my collar
up in back and there were always   5
girls with me in the hallways.
You were nothing. I had it in for you—
when I peeled rubber at the lights
you cringed like a teacher.
And when I crashed and broke both lungs   10
on the wheel, you were so relieved
that you stroked the hard Ford paint
And your hands shook.

In this poem, we are exceptionally aware of the speaker. We are listening to the "hood" of the title, who is speaking to a third person. If we remember being bullied ourselves, we are likely to sympathize with the victim. We are likely to share the cringing—and the guilty feeling of relief when the bully crashed. Where is the poet in this poem? Maybe the poet is somewhat of a bully, but more likely the bully's role is an assumed identity.

THE RECEPTIVE READER

1. Does the "hood" of this poem become a believable bully? Why or why not? Can you identify with the listener? What details help make the situation real for you?

2. In this brief confrontation, where is the poet? As a person, is the poet likely to resemble the speaker or the listener? What do you think made the poet write this poem?

THE CREATIVE DIMENSION

Write a passage or poem in which you re-create the persona of a childhood bully or other person who teased or tormented you in earlier years.

THE AUTOBIOGRAPHICAL "I"

All poetry is confession.
JOHANN WOLFGANG VON GOETHE

I hadn't found the courage yet to do without authorities,
or even to use the pronoun "I."
ADRIENNE RICH

I am not a metaphor or symbol.
This you hear is not the wind in the trees,
Nor a cat being maimed in the street.
It is I being maimed in the street.
CALVIN C. HERNTON, "THE DISTANT DRUM"

Poems using the **autobiographical "I"** share with us their personal experiences and feelings. Such poetry is sometimes called **confessional poetry,** as if the poet were sharing secrets never before revealed. The poet takes us into his or her confidence, revealing part of the self that may normally be hidden behind a noncommittal façade. We are privileged to look beyond the outer shell that shields people from prying or ridicule. The more autobiographical the poem, the more the person speaking in the poem and the poet who wrote the poem become identical in the reader's mind.

Some poems are occasioned by actual events in the poet's life. A poet-playwright and contemporary of Shakespeare wrote the following poem about an actual son who was named Benjamin (literally "child of the right hand") and who died at age seven.

BEN JONSON   (1572–1637)

On My First Son   1616

Farewell, thou child of my right hand, and joy;
My sin was too much hope of thee, loved boy:
Seven years thou wert lent to me, and thee I pay,°   *pay back*
Exacted° by thy fate, on the just day.   *when billed*
O could I lose all father° now! For why   *fatherly thoughts*   5
Will man lament the state he should envy—
To have so soon escaped world's and flesh's rage
And, if no other misery, yet age?
Rest in soft peace and, asked,° say, "Here doth lie   *when asked*
Ben Jonson his° best piece of poetry."   *Jonson's*   10
For whose sake henceforth all° his vows be such   *may all*
As what he loves may never° like too much.   *may he never*

THE RECEPTIVE READER

1. The father's feelings in this poem are in keeping with traditional religious attitudes toward death. How? Are these attitudes still meaningful to the modern reader? Why or why not?

2. Where in the poem do you think the father's personal feelings show most strongly? Where do his thoughts and feelings seem different or unexpected to you?

Poets take a risk when they remove the mask that usually hides private feelings from the outside world. However, they also set up a special human contact with the sympathetic, responsive reader. Poetry in the "I" mode often records a part of the poet's spiritual history. We embark with the poet on an exploration of inner space, which may take us to childhood scenes or to way stations in the poet's later life. We watch a fellow human being fitting together the pieces of the puzzle that together make up a person.

How well do you come to know or understand the persons behind the two following poems?

MAXINE KUMIN   (born 1925)

Nurture   1976

From a documentary on marsupials I learn
that a pillowcase makes a fine
substitute pouch for an orphaned kangaroo.

I am drawn to such dramas of animal rescue.
They are warm in the throat. I suffer, the critic proclaims,   5
from an overabundance of maternal genes.

Bring me your fallen fledgling, your bummer lamb,
lead the abused, the starvelings, into my barn.
Advise the hunted deer to leap into my corn.

And had there been a wild child—   10
filthy and fierce as a ferret, he is called
in one nineteenth-century account—

a wild child to love, it is safe to assume,
given my fireside inked with paw prints,
there would have been room.   15

Think of the language we two, same and not-same,
Might have constructed from sign,
scratch, grimace, grunt, vowel:

Laughter our first noun, and our long verb, howl.

THE RECEPTIVE READER

1. What *tone* does the poet set by her opening reference to kangaroos and other marsupials?

2. What in this poem strikes you as autobiographical fact and what as imaginative *what if*?

3. What is the special fascination of stories about abandoned children growing up wild without human nurture or language? What is the special fascination of such stories for the poet?

4. What is the perspective on *language* in this poem? What poet's-eye view does the poem give you of the origin or basic functions of language?

5. What kind of *person* would you expect the poet to be? Where would you expect to encounter her? What would you expect her to do?

THE PERSONAL RESPONSE

Is a nurturing, caring attitude toward life a gender-specific quality? Is nurturing the special province of women? What are some practical or political implications of the debate—what difference does it make? What side would you take?

In classical Greece, the Nine Muses were quasi-divine beings who inspired poets, musicians, historians, and followers of the other arts and sciences. The philosopher Plato called Sappho "the tenth Muse," and many Greeks considered her their most outstanding lyric poet. She lived on the island of Lesbos and is thought to have run a school for women there. Book burners of a later age destroyed most of her poems (but not her legendary reputation). A few whole poems and fragments of others survive. Gay women still call themselves lesbians in her honor.

SAPPHO (about 620–550 B.C.)

Letter to Anaktoria sixth century B.C.

TRANSLATED BY RICHMOND LATTIMORE

Like the very gods in my sight is he who
sits where he can look in your eyes, who listens
close to you, to hear the soft voice, its sweetness
    murmur in love and

laughter, all for him. But it breaks my spirit;   5
underneath my breath all the heart is shaken.
Let me only glance where you are, the voice dies,
    I can say nothing,

but my lips are stricken to silence, underneath my skin the tenuous flame suffuses;   10
nothing shows in front of my eyes, my ears are
    muted in thunder.

And the sweat running upon me, fever
shakes my body, paler I turn than grass is;
I can feel that I have been changed, I feel that   15
    death has come near me.

THE RECEPTIVE READER

What kind of person is speaking in this poem? What is the situation? What are the mixed emotions the speaker feels toward the two people in this poem? Do her feelings seem strange or familiar? How would you expect to react to a poem written 2,500 years ago? How *do* you react to this poem?

THE CREATIVE DIMENSION

Write a poem or prose passage that re-creates what for you is the dominant emotion in this poem.

Intensely personal poetry often seems like a catharsis—a cleansing or purifying of painful memories or passionate grievances. In recent decades, minority authors have made the majority listen to the voices of those that Martin Luther King, Jr., called the "unheard." The following poem speaks for young native Americans taken from their families to be made over in the white man's image. Of German and Chippewa heritage, the poet relives her experience with the forced assimilation of young people denied pride in their own past.

LOUISE ERDRICH   (born 1954)

Indian Boarding School: The Runaways   1984

Home's the place we head for in our sleep.
Boxcars stumbling north in dreams
don't wait for us. We catch them on the run.
The rails, old lacerations that we love,
soot parallel across the face and break   5
just under Turtle Mountains. Riding scars
you can't get lost. Home is the place they cross.

The lame guard strikes a match and makes the dark
less tolerant. We watch through cracks in boards
as the land starts rolling, rolling till it hurts   10
to be here, cold in regulation clothes.
We know the sheriff's waiting at midrun
to take us back. His car is dumb and warm.
The highway doesn't rock, it only hums
like a wing of long insults. The worn-down welts   15
of ancient punishments lead back and forth.

All runaways wear dresses, long green ones,
the color you would think shame was. We scrub
the sidewalks down because it's shameful work.
Our brushes cut the stone in watered arcs   20
and in the soak frail outlines shiver clear
a moment, things us kids pressed on the dark
face before it hardened, pale, remembering
delicate old injuries, the spines of names and leaves.

THE RECEPTIVE READER

1. To you, does the poem seem like intensely felt *personal experience* or like an imaginary situation vividly imagined? If pressed to explain your answer, what would you say?

2. What *assumptions* about reservation life and Indian schools do you bring to this poem? How does this poem change or challenge them?

3. What is the *situation* of the runaways? What do they think, feel, and remember?

4. In this poem, much of what you see—the railroad tracks, the highway, work, a color—takes on *symbolic* significance. Where and how?

THE PERSONAL RESPONSE

When you read this poem, are you looking at the young runaways from the outside? Do you identify with the "we" speaking in the poem? Why or why not?

JUXTAPOSITIONS

Variations of "I"

Even when using the autobiographical "I," poets differ widely in how completely they bare their souls. (Mitsuye Yamada has said that to discover our real selves we have to peel away our masks "like the used skin / of a growing reptile.") In much nineteenth-century poetry, even personal emotions went dressed in a high-minded vocabulary, with anything low or disturbing locked away in the private recesses of the mind. In the twentieth century, candor gradually drove out Victorian uplift and decorum. Compare the two following examples. The first is one of a series of sonnets that Elizabeth Barrett addressed to the poet Robert Browning when they were about to be married. The second was written more than a hundred years later in a more modern vein.

ELIZABETH BARRETT BROWNING (1806–1861)

How do I love thee? Let me count the ways 1845

How do I love thee? Let me count the ways.
I love thee to the depth and breadth and height
My soul can reach, when feeling out of sight
For the ends of Being and ideal Grace.
I love thee to the level of every day's 5
Most quiet need, by sun and candle-light.
I love thee freely, as men strive for right;
I love thee purely, as they turn from Praise.
I love thee with the passion put to use
In my old griefs, and with my childhood's faith. 10
I love thee with a love I seemed to lose
With my lost saints—I love thee with the breath,
Smiles, tears, of all my life!—and, if God choose,
I shall but love thee better after death.

THE RECEPTIVE READER

1. What kind of person is speaking in this poem? What kind of voice do you hear? Do you think of the person speaking as the poet herself or as a public *persona*?

2. What feelings voiced in this sonnet seem *old-fashioned* to you? How do you explain that this poem still appears in almost every major collection of favorite poems? What about it might still speak strongly to a modern reader?

3. How does the poet use a pattern of insistent *repetition* building up to a climactic ending?

What part of the poet's personality is uppermost in the following poem?

GWENDOLYN BROOKS   (born 1917)

A Song in the Front Yard   1945

I've stayed in the front yard all my life.
I want to peek at the back
Where it's rough and untended and hungry weeds grow.
A girl gets sick of a rose.

I want to go in the back yard now   5
And maybe down the alley,
To where the charity children play.
I want a good time today.

They do some wonderful things.
They have some wonderful fun.   10
My mother sneers, but I say it's fine
How they don't have to go in at quarter to nine.
My mother, she tells me that Johnnie Mae
Will grow up to be a bad woman.
That George will be taken to Jail soon or late   15
(On account of last winter he sold our back gate).

But I say it's fine. Honest, I do.
And I'd like to be a bad woman, too,
And wear the black stockings of night-black lace
And strut down the street with paint on my face.   20

THE RECEPTIVE READER

1. What is the *symbolic* meaning of the front yard, the back yard, the alley, and the street? Does it matter that the song is about the back yard but is sung in the front yard?

2. Brooks published this poem when she was an adult. What *identity* is she assuming in this poem? (What is the persona?) What kind of voice are you hearing? What kind of person does it make you imagine? (How is the person talking?)

3. Often a single *metaphor* carries much meaning, with various implications and associations. What is the full meaning of the line "A girl gets sick of a rose"? (Does it make a difference that this is one of the shortest lines in a poem of longer lines?)

THE PERSONAL RESPONSE

How well do the following student reactions get into the spirit of the poem? Write your own personal response to the poem.

1. I've always been a good boy. I've done what my parents say. I want to see how the others live. I want to throw a rock through a window and get chased by the cops. I want to knock on a door and run and hide. I want to be bad, just for a day.

2. How can a girl get sick of a rose? A rose has everything. It has beauty and ugliness; it grows and dies. A rose is well-balanced: If you are sick of a rose, try its thorns.

CROSS-REFERENCES—For Discussion or Writing

Which of the two poets do you think you come to know better as a person, and why? Which style of voicing personal emotions appeals to you more, and why?

THE PUBLIC PERSONA

The age
requires this task:
create
a different image;
re-animate
the mask.
    DUDLEY RANDALL

The "I" we hear in a poem may be speaking to us as the voice of a group, a commitment, or a cause. The plural *we* (like the editorial *we* or the royal *we*) may replace the singular *I*. It is as if the poet were speaking to us in an official capacity, assuming a public persona. Dylan Thomas was a Welsh poet whose chanting voice and powerful cryptic poems converted a generation of listeners and readers to the cause of poetry. In the following poem, he speaks of his mission as a poet with a grand sweep, without diffidence or self-doubt. The persona he assumes in the poem is that of the charismatic bard, mesmerizing his audience with his hypnotic voice, dramatizing and glorifying the poet's calling.

DYLAN THOMAS   (1914–1953)

In My Craft or Sullen Art   1946

In my craft or sullen art
Exercised in the still night
When only the moon rages
And the lovers lie abed
With all their griefs in their arms,   5
I labor by singing light
Not for ambition or bread
Or the strut and trade of charms
On the ivory stages
But for the common wages   10
Of their most secret heart.

Not for the proud man apart
From the raging moon I write
On these spindrift° pages   *sea spray*
Nor for the towering dead   15
With their nightingales and psalms
But for the lovers, their arms
Round the griefs of the ages,
Who pay no praise or wages
Nor heed my craft or art.   20

THE RECEPTIVE READER

1. Dylan Thomas' poetry was shot through with bold, provocative *metaphors.*
Why or how could his art be "sullen," and what could he mean by "singing light"?
How does he use metaphorically *bread, strut, ivory, common wages, spindrift pages, towering dead?*
2. Where and how often does the central word *art* appear in the poem, and with
what effect? What other key word rhymes with it, and where in the poem? Why is *wages*
also a key word in the poem? Where does it appear, and how many rhymes help it echo
through the poem?
3. What is the *symbolic* role of the moon in this poem?
4. With what *tone* should this poem be read? What kind of person do you imagine
the poet to be?

Among poets who have seen themselves as the conscience of their time,
Walt Whitman created for himself a persona as the voice of a new continent
and a new nation. In many of his poems, he is speaking to us as the prophet of
the new American democracy. The following poem, a part of his *Song of Myself,* shows the kind of **empathy**—sharing the feelings of others—that could
make him say, "I am the hounded slave," and, "I do not ask the wounded person how he feels, I myself become the wounded person."

WALT WHITMAN   (1819–1892)

I Understand the Large Hearts of Heroes   1855

I understand the large hearts of heroes.
The courage of present times and all times,
How the skipper saw the crowded and rudderless wreck of the steamship, and Death
    chasing it up and down the storm,
How he knuckled tight and gave not back an inch, and was faithful of days and faithful
    of nights,
And chalked in large letters on a board, "Be of good cheer, we will not desert you";   5
How he followed with them and tacked with them three days and would not give it up,
How he saved the drifting company at last,
How the lank loose-gowned women looked when boated from the side of their
    prepared graves,
How the silent old-faced infants and the lifted sick, and the sharp-lipped unshaved men;
All this I swallow, it tastes good, I like it well, it becomes mine,   10
I am the man, I suffered, I was there.

THE RECEPTIVE READER

1. Whitman was fascinated with *people*—how they looked and talked and moved, whether in developing the continent or in the agonies of civil war. What striking, revealing details make this account of shipwreck and rescue come to life for the reader?

2. What kind of *person* is speaking to you in this poem? Whitman has at times been accused of striking heroic poses. Do you think he is sincere in this poem? Why or why not?

THE PERSONAL RESPONSE

How do you react to the following *journal entry* by a fellow student?

"All this I swallow, it tastes good, I like it well, it becomes mine, / I am the man, I suffered, I was there." Whitman here boldy proclaims the glorious things that common people only sense in a confused, ambiguous way while thinking to themselves. At achieving this grand persona, few have matched the grandeur of Whitman. In this poem, Whitman rises to the level of a great and heroic event. The sea captain is the kind of person who will not deviate from a cause once the course is set. With absolute determination, "he knuckled tight and gave not back an inch, and was faithful of days and . . . nights." Whitman makes himself the spokesperson that commemorates and celebrates this courage and heroism: "I understand the large heart of heroes / The courage of present times and all times." Today, a poet might view the state of our nation as slipping into chaos one notch at a time. Every time an oil tanker spills its load or someone is gunned down in the streets, America loses another piece of its soul. In Whitman's time, this country was taking gigantic leaps forward. He had ample subject-matter for such heart-swelling subjects as this.

Today, some of the most eloquent voices we hear speak to us in the name of a larger group. They help formulate a changed consciousness, a new sense of group identity. They may speak for women in search of a new self-image. They may speak for minority groups proud of their heritage. The following poem is by an American poet of West Indian descent who has said that she speaks not only for the woman who inhabits her physical self but "for all those feisty incorrigible black women who insist on standing up and saying, 'I *am* and you cannot wipe me out, no matter how irritating I am, how much you fear what I might represent.' "

AUDRE LORDE   (born 1934)
Coal   1976

I
is the total black, being spoken
from the earth's inside.
There are many kinds of open
how a diamond comes into a knot of flame
how sound comes into a word, colored
by who pays what for speaking.

5

Some words are open like a diamond
on glass windows
singing out within the passing crash of sun. 10
Then there are words like stapled wagers
in a perforated book,—buy and sign and tear apart—
and come whatever wills all chances
the stub remains
an ill-pulled tooth with a ragged edge. 15
Some words live in my throat
breeding like adders. Others know sun
seeking like gypsies over my tongue
to explode through my lips
like young sparrows bursting from shell. 20
Some words
bedevil me.

Love is a word, another kind of open.
As the diamond comes into a knot of flame
I am Black because I come from the earth's inside 25
now take my word for jewel in the open light.

THE RECEPTIVE READER

1. Look at the bold provocative *metaphors* and *similes* in this poem. What is their meaning? What role do they play in the poem?

2. The word *open* becomes a key word in this poem. What role does it play? What meanings and associations cluster around it?

3. Some earlier black poets used a formal literary language, avoiding all echoes of *Black English*. How is this poem different? What is the effect on the reader?

4. Who is the collective *I* speaking in this poem? What kind of collective self-image takes shape in this poem?

CROSS-REFERENCES—For Discussion or Writing

Compare and contrast the two poems by Whitman and Lorde. How do the two poets compare as voices of social awareness? How do they shape our self-image as members of society, as socially responsible beings?

IMAGINED SELVES

Aye! I am a poet and upon my tomb
Shall maidens scatter rose leaves
And men myrtles, ere the night
Slays day with her dark sword.
EZRA POUND

Sometimes the voice speaking in a poem is clearly distant or separate from the poet's autobiographical self. The "I" speaking may be an imaginary or historical character to whom both we and the poet are listening. Poems by the author of the following poem have appeared in collections of science fiction poetry. What is the fictitious identity of the person speaking in the poem?

EDWARD LUCIE-SMITH (born 1933)

Afterwards

1964

Inhospitable.
        Another bald
Barren lump spinning in a thin shawl
Of unbreathable gas. I see it
From my narrow window, from what these
Hovering needles tell me in their   5
Too truthful gauges. I might descend,
Opening the airlock, adjusting my
Cumbersome helmet, hands gloved thick
Against the cold, or heat, or acid,   10
Strapping upon my back the light slim
Canister of my own atmosphere—
And each breath links me again with what,
The further I travel seems stranger:
Greenness, water, movement, a sphere not   15
Sufficient unto itself, but once
Happy to feed and lodge an itchy
Parasite.
        Now inhospitable.

THE RECEPTIVE READER

1. Where are we in this poem, and when? Who is speaking? What is the *persona*?
2. What is the *key word* in what the speaker says, and what is its effect on the reader? What details in the poem follow it up or make it come to life? What changes the impact of the word when it is repeated at the end of the poem?
3. What is the poet's attitude toward the human species and its prospects?
4. How is this poem different from other previews of a catastrophic future?

The speaker in a first-person poem is often a character from history or legend who has a special fascination for the poet. We may sense a special affinity or attraction, as we do in the following poem about Cassandra, the mad Trojan princess and priestess, who in the ancient Greek poems and plays about the siege of Troy speaks as the voice of impending doom. In her prophetic visions, Cassandra saw her native city in flames, with its towers crashing down. She also prophesied that Agamemnon, the Greek commander who carried her off as part of the spoils of war, would be murdered on his return to Greece by his wife and her lover.

LOUISE BOGAN (1897–1970)

Cassandra

1968

To me, one silly task is like another.
I bare the shambling tricks of lust and pride.
This flesh will never give a child its mother—

Song, like a wing, tears through my breast, my side,
And madness chooses out my voice again, 5
Again. I am the chosen no hand saves:
The shrieking heaven lifted over men,
Not the dumb earth, wherein they set their graves.

THE RECEPTIVE READER

1. What do you think is the special attraction the character of Cassandra had for the author as a woman and as a poet? What might make the legendary character a kind of *alter ego* for her—a "second self" or counterpart?

2. Why is it strange or contradictory that this poem should have a neat regular rhyme scheme and underlying iambic meter? Is it a coincidence that the word *again*, repeated at the beginning of the sixth line, breaks up the pattern of neatly marked off lines as it pulls us over into the new line?

What is the role the poet imagines for herself in the following poem? When Hitler drove many German artists and writers into exile, others, including this poet, went through a period of "emigration to the interior"—staying in Germany while trying to live intellectually and spiritually outside the mentality of the Nazi era. She was much honored by the West German literary establishment after the war. The following poem shows her affinity with an active women's movement in Germany.

MARIE LUISE KASCHNITZ (1901–1974)

Women's Program 1972

TRANSLATED BY LISEL MÜLLER

I give a talk on the radio
Toward morning when no one is listening
I offer my recipes

Pour milk into the telephone
Let your cats sleep 5
In the dishwashers
Smash the clocks in your washing machines
Leave your shoes behind

Season your peaches with paprika
And your soup meat with honey 10

Teach your children the alphabet of foxes
Turn the leaves in your gardens silver side up
Take the advice of the owl

When summer arrives put on your furs
Go meet the ones with the bagpipes 15
Who come from inside the mountains
Leave your shoes behind

Don't be too sure
Evening will come
Don't be too sure 20
That God loves you.

THE RECEPTIVE READER

1. What kind of person is speaking in this poem? (How close do you think the poet's personality is to the *persona* in the poem?)

2. What is the point and the motivation of the subversive advice given in this poem? (Does any of it seem particularly strange or particularly sensible?)

3. Where and how does the poet *allude* to the story of the Pied Piper of Hamlin? How does her use of the story depart from what you might expect?

EXPLORATIONS

The Dramatic Monologue

In some poems, we listen to a **dramatic monologue,** or lengthy first-person speech, as it might be delivered by a character in a play. The best-known author of dramatic monologues is the English nineteenth-century poet Robert Browning, who lived for a time in Italy after eloping with his fellow poet Elizabeth Barrett, the semi-invalid daughter of a domineering father. In many of his monologues, we listen as artists, scholars, church dignitaries, or aristocrats of the Italian Renaissance reveal to us their ambitions and aspirations—or, as in the following poem, their passions and hidden motives. In the poem that follows, we listen to a sixteenth-century Duke of Ferrara whose last duchess died young and who is now talking to a representative of another aristocratic family about a second marriage.

ROBERT BROWNING (1812–1889)

My Last Duchess 1842

Ferrara

That's my last duchess painted on the wall,
Looking as if she were alive. I call
That piece a wonder, now: Frà Pandolf's° hands   *Brother Pandolf (a monk or friar)*
Worked busily a day, and there she stands.
Will 't please you sit and look at her? I said   5
"Frà Pandolf" by design,° for never read   *on purpose*
Strangers like you that pictured countenance,°   *face*
The depth and passion of its earnest glance,
But to myself they turned (since none puts by
The curtain I have drawn for you, but I)   10
And seemed as they would ask me, if they durst,°   *dared*
How such a glance came there; so, not the first

Are you to turn and ask thus. Sir, 't was not
Her husband's presence only, called° that spot   *that called*
Of joy into the Duchess' cheek: perhaps   15
Frà Pandolf chanced to say "Her mantle laps
Over my lady's wrist too much," or "Paint
Must never hope to reproduce the faint
Half-flush that dies along her throat": such stuff
Was courtesy, she thought, and cause enough   20
For calling up that spot of joy. She had
A heart—how shall I say?—too soon made glad,
Too easily impressed; she liked whate'er
She looked on, and her looks went everywhere.
Sir, 't was all one! My favor° at her breast,   *love token*   25
The dropping of the daylight in the west,
The bough of cherries some officious° fool   *eager to serve*
Broke in the orchard for her, the white mule
She rode with round the terrace—all and each
Would draw from her alike the approving speech,   30
Or blush, at least. She thanked men—good! but thanked
Somehow—I know not how—as if she ranked
My gift of a nine-hundred-years-old name
With anybody's gift. Who'd stoop to blame
This sort of trifling? Even had you° skill   *if you had*   35
In speech—which I have not—to make your will
Quite clear to such an one, and say, "Just this
Or that in you disgusts me; here you miss,
Or there exceed the mark"—and if she let
Herself be lessoned so, nor plainly set   40
Her wit to yours, forsooth,° and made excuse   *in truth*
—E'en then would be some stooping; and I choose
Never to stoop. Oh sir, she smiled, no doubt,
Whene'er I passed her, but who passed without
Much the same smile? This grew; I gave commands;   45
Then all smiles stopped together. There she stands
As if alive. Will 't please you rise? We'll meet
The company below, then. I repeat,
The Count your master's known munificence°   *generosity*
Is ample warrant° that no just pretense   *guarantee, demand*   50
Of mine for dowry will be disallowed;
Though his fair daughter's self, as I avowed
At starting, is my object. Nay, we'll go
Together down, sir. Notice Neptune, though,
Taming a sea-horse, thought a rarity,   55
Which Claus of Innsbruck cast in bronze for me.

THE RECEPTIVE READER

1. What is the *situation*? Where in the poem did you first suspect what happened
to the duchess? When were you sure?

2. To judge from this monologue by her husband, what was the duchess like as a
person? What was her offense? Do you consider her a frivolous or superficial person?

3. What is the key to the *persona* created by Browning in this poem? What is the duke's problem? Why didn't he explain how he felt to the duchess?

4. What is strange about the duke's speaking in a relaxed, polite conversational *tone*? Is it in keeping with his character? Many of his sentences start in the middle of a line and spill over into the next. (The technical term for this effect is *enjambment*— from the French word for "straddling.") How does the straddling effect contribute to the conversational tone?

5. What public persona has the duke created for himself—what *image* does he present to the world? (The Italian Renaissance was a golden age of the creative arts. What is the role of art in this poem?)

THE PERSONAL RESPONSE

Has the duke's mentality become extinct with the passing of the aristocratic society of his time? Do you think there could be any modern parallels to his mind set and behavior?

POEMS FOR FURTHER STUDY

In reading the following poems, pay special attention to questions like the following: Who is speaking? What kind of voice do you hear in the poem? What is the persona or assumed identity? How much distance do you think there is between the persona and the person behind the poem?

COUNTEE CULLEN (1903–1946)

Saturday's Child

1925

Some are teethed on a silver spoon,
With the stars strung for a rattle;
I cut my teeth as the black raccoon—
For implements of battle.

Some are swaddled in silk and down,   5
And heralded by a star;
They swathed my limbs in a sackcloth gown
On a night that was black as tar.

For some godfather and goddame°   *godmother*
The opulent° fairies be;   *living richly*   10
Dame Poverty gave me my name,
And Pain godfathered me.

For I was born on Saturday—
"Bad time for planting a seed,"
Was all my father had to say,   15
And, "One more mouth to feed."

Death cut the strings that gave me life,
And handed me to Sorrow,
The only kind of middle wife
My folks could beg or borrow.   20

THE RECEPTIVE READER

1. How do the stanza form and rhyme scheme help the poet line up the *opposites* that give shape to the poem as a whole?

2. What is the role of *personified abstractions* in this poem? (How did "Death cut the strings that gave me life"?)

3. What is the *persona* the poet creates for himself in this poem? How close do you think it is to the poet's real-life personality?

DENISE LEVERTOV   (born 1923)

In Mind   1964

There's in my mind a woman
of innocence, unadorned but

fair-featured, and smelling of
apples or grass. She wears

a utopian smock or shift, her hair   5
is light brown and smooth, and she
is kind and very clean without
ostentation—
              but she has
no imagination.   10
              And there's a
turbulent moon-ridden girl

or old woman or both
dressed in opals and rags, feathers

and torn taffeta.   15
and who knows strange songs—

but she is not kind.

THE RECEPTIVE READER

Do you recognize the two different personalities in this poem? What are their virtues and shortcomings? (Are they polar opposites?) Do you think two such different personalities could dwell in the same mind?

CROSS-REFERENCES—For Discussion or Writing

Compare the treatment of two sides of the same personality in this poem and in Gwendolyn Brooks' "A Song in the Front Yard" earlier in this chapter.

NIKKI GIOVANNI   (born 1943)

Legacies

1972

her grandmother called her from the playground
    "yes, ma'am"
    "i want chu to learn how to make rolls," said the old
woman proudly
but the little girl didn't want   5
to learn how because she knew
even if she couldn't say it that
that would mean when the old one died she would be less
dependent on her spirit so
she said   10
    "i don't want to know how to make no rolls" with her lips poked out
and the old woman wiped her hands on
her apron saying "lord
    these children"
and neither of them ever   15
said what they meant
and i guess nobody ever does

THE RECEPTIVE READER

1. The poet says that both the grandmother and the girl in this poem never said what they really meant. What did the grandmother mean—what did she really think and feel? What did the girl mean—what did she really "know" without being able to put it into words?

2. Which of the two persons in this poem is closer to the poet as a person? Does she identify or sympathize more with the one or the other? (With which of the two do *you* identify or sympathize?)

SYLVIA PLATH   (1932–1963)

Mirror

1961

I am silver and exact. I have no preconceptions.
Whatever I see I swallow immediately
Just as it is, unmisted by love or dislike.
I am not cruel, only truthful—
The eye of a little god, four-cornered.   5
Most of the time I meditate on the opposite wall.
It is pink, with speckles. I have looked at it so long
I think it is a part of my heart. But it flickers.
Faces and darkness separate us over and over.

Now I am a lake. A woman bends over me,   10
Searching my reaches for what she really is.
Then she turns to those liars, the candles or the moon.

I see her back, and reflect it faithfully.
She rewards me with tears and an agitation of hands.
I am important to her. She comes and goes.
Each morning it is her face that replaces the darkness.
In me she has drowned a young girl, and in me an old woman
Rises toward her like a terrible fish.

15

THE RECEPTIVE READER

1. What touches early in the poem might make the mirror sound like a curious observer—with a limited or even naive perspective and no evil intentions? (How is the mirror like the eye of a god—and why of "a little god"?)

2. How does the lake metaphor make the mirror seem more knowing and more threatening? Why or how would "candles or the moon" be more likely to prove liars than the mirror?

3. Do you think the mirror is cruel? Do you think the poet is being cruel? Where is the poet in this poem?

THE CREATIVE DIMENSION

What story would your own mirror tell if it could speak?

CROSS-REFERENCES—For Discussion or Writing

Several poems in this chapter (as well as in other parts of this book) are the record of a poet exploring her identity as a woman or embarked in the search of self. Study several such poems, looking for shared themes, recurrent issues, or similar perspectives.

WRITING ABOUT LITERATURE
18. Playing the Role (Imitation and Parody)

The Writing Workshop We like to think that creative spirits burst upon the scene with the clear marks of genius. However, many poets passed through phases where they idolized a mentor or role model, and often the experience strongly influenced their attempts to find a style of their own. They often learned their craft by conscious *imitation* of what was famous, fashionable, or new. Adrienne Rich has said that at age sixteen she spent months memorizing and writing imitations of the sonnets of Edna St. Vincent Millay ("in notebooks of that period I find what are obviously attempts to imitate Dickinson's metrics and verbal compression").

As readers, we can learn as much from creative imitation as practicing poets do. Imitation or re-creation (like translation from another language) makes us enter into a poet's world of imagination more fully than a passive reading can. It alerts us to distinctive features of the poet's style, making us look at them from the performer's rather than the spectator's point of view.

Study the following attempts to re-create the persona of a poem in this chapter, and then try your hand at a similar imitation or re-creation of a poem of your choice. The first poem in this chapter is C. K. Williams' "Hood." The student who wrote the following personal re-creation of the "Hood" poem tried to create a similar persona. Compare the original and this student's response. How successful was the student poet?

Bully

Remember me?
I'm the one who calls you Chinaman.
I laugh at you all the time
and throw balls at you
when you don't know how to play.
I play jokes around you with my friends.
I took your lunch money in the restroom.
I'm the one you hate and fear the most.
When Teacher yelled at me,
you felt good.
When I am absent,
You feel safe.

Poets with an especially unmistakable style seem to invite imitation. Their poems seem to cry out for **parody**—an imitation that lovingly or mockingly exaggerates characteristic traits. The poetry of Robert Browning has been much imitated and much parodied. What features of the original did the student capture who wrote the following dramatic monologue?

My Last Essay

That's my last essay pinned up on the wall,
Looking as if it's not survived. I call
That piece a wonder, now! Jim Bello's hand
Worked busily an hour, and thus its state.
Will 't please you stay and read of it? I said
"Jim Bello" by design, for never saw
Strangers like you such tattered manuscript
But to myself they turned in stunned surprise
And seemed as they would ask me, if they durst,
How such red marks came there; so not the first
Are you to turn and ask thus. Nay, 't was not
Just split infinitives that roused his ire—
"Support unclear," he muttered through his teeth
In reference to my cherished prose. He had
A mind—how shall I say?—too soon made mad,
Too easily overcome; he slashed what words
He looked on, and his looks went everywhere!
Yes, 't was all one. My pronoun reference fault,
Verb disagreement, too—and "Comma splice!"

So, friend you see my tattered work displayed,
Defiled with red disgracefully, I know.
But I retyped it, and the ms sold
To Murdoch's tabloid for an even thou'.
You caught that issue? Thanks!

A parody is a close imitation with a humorous twist, achieving comic effects by exaggerating characteristic features of the original. A parody may be affectionate, gently spoofing mannerisms that are like quirks of someone we love. But a parody may also be cruel, holding up to ridicule what is overdone or outdated in its target.

To parody something well takes time and careful attention. Poets who write successful parody need a quick ear and a gift for patient observation. The following stanza is from a flip poem (written in 1601) by a would-be lover eager to dispense with the tedious preliminaries of courtship. The next stanza is from a student-written parody written almost four hundred years later.

I care not for these ladies,
That must be wooed and prayed:
Give me kind Amaryllis,
The wanton country maid.
   Her when we court and kiss,
   She cries, "Forsooth, let go!"
   But when we come where comfort is,
   She never will say no.
           Thomas Campion

The student who wrote the following rejoinder had a good ear, and she gets well into the spirit of the original poem:

They care not for us ladies
That want to be loved and pursued.
They care for Amaryllis
Who is impure and crude.
   'Cause when men seek a kiss,
   Her cries have just begun.
   No longer can she resist;
   She pleads for more than one.
           Sharee Pearson, "Ladies"

19 TONE
The Human Voice

Poetry is the revelation of a feeling that the poet believes to be interior and personal but which the readers recognize as their own.

SALVATORE QUASIMODO

The poet sheds his blood in the ring and calls the pools poems.

GEORGE BARKER

this is important enough:
to get your feelings down.
it is better than shaving
or cooking beans with garlic.
CHARLES BUKOWSKI, "COOKING BEANS WITH GARLIC"

FOCUS ON TONE

In the poet's language, as in ordinary language, much of the message is in the **tone.** Live language has a human coloring that conveys the feelings, attitudes, and intentions of the speaker. Live language does not pass on neutral information; it tells us much about the likes, dislikes, private agendas, and ulterior motives of a breathing human being. "It's you again!" may be said in a tone of welcome—but also in a tone of barely concealed disappointment. "Thanks!" may be said in a tone of warm gratitude or of a cold "thank-you-for-nothing."

Facing a speaker, we read the speaker's body language; we respond to the knowing wink or defiant gesture. We respond to the sweet or harsh music of the voice; we flinch at the raised volume; we perk up our ears at a whispered aside. When looking at a poem on the printed page, we have to read for tone the way an actor reads a script for clues to gesture and movement. The poet's words convey tone without the raised eyebrows, the shrug of the shoulders, or the raised decibels. To respond to tone, we need to become sensitive to tender or harsh and angry words. We need to respond to how a poet lets passion

624

build up—or plays down an emotion-charged situation. We need to sense when the poet is being serious and when speaking tongue-in-cheek.

Tone in poetry runs the gamut of human attitudes and emotions. The poet may set a *mournful* tone, as Walt Whitman does in the opening lines of his elegy on the death of President Lincoln:

> When lilacs last in the dooryard bloomed,
> And the great star early drooped in the western sky in the night,
> I mourned, and yet shall mourn with ever-returning spring.

The poet may speak in a tone of *religious awe,* as the seventeenth-century poet Henry Vaughan does in the opening lines of his poem "The World":

> I saw eternity the other night
> Like a great ring of pure and endless light,
>   All calm as it was bright;
> And round beneath it, Time, in hours, days, years,
>   Driven by the spheres,
> Like a vast shadow moved, in which the world
>   And all her train were hurled.

Toward the other end of the religious spectrum, the tone of a poem may be *irreverent,* as in these rebellious lines from Maxine Kumin's "Address to the Angels":

> Angels, where were you when
> my best friend did herself in?
> Were you lunching beside us
> that final noon, did you catch
> some nuance that went past my ear?
> Did you ease my father out
> of his cardiac arrest that wet
> fall day I sat at the high crib bed
> holding his hand? And when
> my black-eyed susan-child ran
> off with her European lover
> and has been ever since an unbelonger,
> were you whirligiging over
> the suitcases?

A poem may be playful in tone or gently spoofing, or it may be scornful, bitter, charged with contempt. To become sensitive to tone, remember that in reading a poem you are listening to a human voice. The printed poem on the page is to the heard and felt poem as the sheet music is to Beethoven's Moonlight Sonata. Reading aloud and hearing others read aloud is your best insurance against proving tone deaf to the human voice speaking to you in a poem.

THE REGISTER OF EMOTIONS

Forgive me that I pitch your praise too low.
Such reticence my reverence demands.
For silence falls with laying on of hands.
Forgive me that my words come thin and slow.
JOHN WAIN, "APOLOGY FOR UNDERSTATEMENT"

the voice of your eyes is deeper than all roses
nobody, not even the rain, has such small hands
E. E. CUMMINGS, "SOMEWHERE I HAVE NEVER TRAVELLED"

Poems vary greatly in emotional intensity. Traditionally, poetry has been the voice of passion: the joy of mutual love and the sorrow of separation, the fear of death and the joyful certainty of resurrection. Homer's warriors wept for their dead comrades; religious poetry through the ages has sung the grandeur of God. Much twentieth-century poetry has been more sparing in its expression of emotions. Modern poets have often been wary of anything that might seem gushy or maudlin. They have tended to understate rather than to overstate their feelings.

In much traditional love poetry, the poet's emotional thermostat is set high, with the poem giving voice to yearning, ecstasy, or despair. Romantic love celebrates love as an overwhelming passion, giving meaning to otherwise meaningless lives, promising fulfillment to frustrated, anxiety-ridden people. Poets in this tradition were given to **hyperbole**—frank overstatement praising the angelic beauty of the beloved, idealizing the devotion of the lover. "O she doth teach the torches to burn bright!" says Shakespeare's Romeo when discovering the loveliness of Juliet—"Beauty too rich for use, for earth too dear!" Shakespeare, like other poets of his time, occasionally rebelled against the convention of hyperbolical praise. ("My mistress' eyes are nothing like the sun; / Coral is far more red than her lips' red; / If snow be white, why then her breasts are dun.") But many of his sonnets use the traditional heightened, exalted language of idealized love.

WILLIAM SHAKESPEARE   (1564–1616)
Sonnet 18

before 1598

Shall I compare thee to a summer's day?	
Thou art more lovely and more temperate:	
Rough winds do shake the darling buds of May,	
And summer's lease° hath all too short a date:	*time span*
Sometimes too hot the eye of heaven shines,	5
And often is his gold complexion dimmed;	
And every fair° from fair sometimes declines,	*everything lovely*
By chance or nature's changing course untrimmed;°	*undone*

But thy eternal summer shall not fade,
Nor lose possession of that fair thou ow'st;°   *you own*   10
Nor shall death brag thou wander'st in his shade,
When in eternal lines° to time thou grow'st: *lines of verse*
So long as men can breathe, or eyes can see,
So long lives this, and this gives life to thee.

THE RECEPTIVE READER

1. How does this sonnet employ *hyperbole*? (How, in fact, does it go hyperbole one better?) Normally, to compare the beloved to the days of early summer or to the dazzling beauty of the glorious sun would be considered high praise. Why does the poet consider these comparisons inadequate?

2. Sometimes the final six lines (the *sestet*) and sometimes the final couplet provide a major "turning" in a sonnet. Which is it here? What answer does this poem give to the questions raised earlier?

Early in the twentieth century, the prevailing tone of poetry began to change from the richer chords of much traditional poetry to the sparer, understated tone that became the modern idiom. **Understatement** makes the poet play down personal feelings, letting the images of a poem speak for themselves. This does not mean that the poem is devoid of feeling. It often means that the poet trusts images and incidents faithfully rendered to call up the emotions and attitudes in the reader.

In many a modern poem, the emotional thermostat seems set lower than it might have been in an earlier day. The following is an understated modern poem that lets a thought-provoking, disturbing incident speak for itself.

WILLIAM STAFFORD   (born 1914)

Traveling through the Dark   1960

Traveling through the dark I found a deer
dead on the edge of the Wilson River road.
It is usually best to roll them into the canyon:
that road is narrow; to swerve might make more dead.

By glow of the tail-light I stumbled back of the car   5
and stood by the heap, a doe, a recent killing;
she had stiffened already, almost cold.
I dragged her off; she was large in the belly.

My fingers touching the side brought me the reason—
her side was warm; her fawn lay there waiting,   10
alive, still, never to be born.
Beside that mountain road I hesitated.

The car aimed ahead its lowered parking lights;
under the hood purred the steady engine.
I stood in the glare of the warm exhaust turning red;   15
around our group I could hear the wilderness listen.

I thought hard for us all—my only swerving—
then pushed her over the edge into the river.

The poem starts on a dry, matter-of-fact note: The deer is dead; the road is narrow; best "to roll them into the canyon" to prevent further accidents. The speaker in the poem unceremoniously calls the dead deer a "heap"; he notes that it is "a recent killing." But he soon makes it hard for us as readers to maintain a matter-of-fact attitude: The side of the killed deer is still warm; she is large with a fawn, "alive, still, never to be born." The speaker in the poem hesitates, but only for a time. Then he does the right thing.

What are the poet's feelings? Maybe the poet is sick at heart at the thought of a mindless machine barreling down the highway to destroy one of God's creatures. Maybe the poet is sickened at the thought of the budding life in the doe's belly dumped into the river like garbage. However, the poem does not say. We can "hear the wilderness listen," and we also listen. But we hear no expressions of protest or grief; the only sound we hear is the motor of the automobile "purring" steadily in the background. Whatever he may feel, the speaker in the poem does the practical and necessary thing. He does not wave his arms or shout "I hate you!" at the universe. We know he "thought hard for us all." As one student reader said, "for a brief moment, he makes us think of the impossible task of saving the fawn." He hesitates for a time—that was his "only swerving" from acting businesslike and sensible. We as readers are left to wrestle with the traumatic event.

THE RECEPTIVE READER

1. Some readers have found the title of the poem to have more than a simple descriptive or factual significance. What could be its *symbolic* meaning?

2. What details or phrases for you do most to *set the tone* of the poem?

3. Do you think the poet felt emotions that the poem does not express? Do you think he *should have* expressed them?

THE PERSONAL RESPONSE

Do you think different readers would react differently to this poem? How much depends on the reader's experience with similar situations and on the reader's mind set or personality?

Rather than emote for the reader, most modern poets re-create for the reader's eyes emotion-charged images. Such is the practice of the Latino poet (North American of Puerto Rican ancestry) who wrote the following poem. One of his readers said of him that he "brings to life his love for his people while etching haunting pictures that create lasting images" for his readers.

MARTIN ESPADA   (born 1957)

Latin Night at the Pawnshop   1987

Chelsea, Massachusetts
Christmas, 1987

The apparition of a salsa band
gleaming in the Liberty Loan
pawnshop window:

Golden trumpet.
silver trombone,   5
congas, maracas, tambourine,
all with price tags dangling
like the city morgue ticket
on a dead man's toe.

THE RECEPTIVE READER

What thoughts and feelings do you think were in the poet's mind in front of the pawnshop window? (What is sad about the name of the pawnshop? What are the emotions created by the concluding simile?)

Some poems build up emotional intensity by concentrating on a single overwhelming passion. Others, however, do justice to mixed feelings or contradictory emotions. Modern poets especially have often been fascinated by the crosscurrents and subtexts that complicate conventionally expected feelings. The following is a modern poem of mourning that does not focus on the sadness of the bereaved. What are the memories and emotions in the mourners' minds?

JOHN CROWE RANSOM   (1888–1974)

Bells for John Whiteside's Daughter   1924

There was such speed in her little body,
And such lightness in her footfall,
It is no wonder her brown study
Astonishes us all.

Her wars were bruited° in our high window,   *were heard of*   5
We looked among orchard trees and beyond
Where she took arms against her shadow,
Or harried unto the pond

The lazy geese like a snow cloud
Dripping their snow on the green grass,   10
Tricking and stopping, sleepy and proud,
Who cried in goose, Alas,

For the tireless heart within the little
Lady with rod that made them rise
From their noon apple-dreams and scuttle 15
Goose-fashion under the skies!

But now go the bells, and we are ready,
In one house we are sternly stopped
To say we are vexed at her brown study,
Lying so primly propped. 20

In this understated modern poem, the speaker does not pour forth his grief at the untimely death of a child. Instead, much of the poem helps us relive the speaker's delight in the remembered quickness and light footfall of the young girl. We flash back to the girl who used to play tirelessly in the orchard, conducting shadow wars with her own shadow or harrying the lazy, sleepy geese, driving them toward the pond. Now, as the bells call the mourners to pay their last respects to the body, they are "astonished" to see the child, who used to be so full of life, at rest as if in a "brown study"—as if she were absorbed in deciphering a difficult passage in a book. They are "vexed" or annoyed to see her once so speedy little body "lying so primly propped."

THE RECEPTIVE READER

1. Is there any hint of the mourners' emotions beyond their being "vexed"?
2. What is witty about the geese crying out "in goose"?
3. Do you feel mixed emotions in reading this poem?

THE RANGE OF INTERPRETATION

Critics have interpreted this poem in very different ways. Which of the two following ways of reading this poem seems more persuasive to you?

1. In this poem, the remembered delight in a child full of innocent life and the bitter disappointment at her death make us experience mixed emotions. The poet's feelings are ambivalent (from a Latin word meaning "marching in two directions at once"). For a parent or friend of the family, the loss of a young innocent child, full of life, is a shattering blow. But it is as if the vivid memory of the "tireless" child, carrying on her mock "wars" with the geese, and our "astonishment" at her transformation could for a time fend off the bitter irony of her death. We protect ourselves against the harsh, merciless reality of death by dwelling on our memory of the living child and by pretending to be "astonished" and not fully understand what has happened to her.

2. The speakers in the poem (the "we" in the poem) can recall the child's vitality in astonishment because it is not their child; it is "John Whiteside's Daughter." The speakers have watched the girl from their "high window," suggesting that the girl without a name of her own is a servant's child. (Ransom was a Southern poet.) The poem is not one of grief or bereavement as much as it is a poem of shock, of vexation. The speakers are not weeping or mourning; they are "sternly stopped." They are troubled more by the unpredictability of death's indifference to youth and vitality than they are grieving, as parents would.

EXPLORATIONS

The Poet's Voice

What is the prevailing tone in each of the following poems? How do they compare in emotional intensity? How overt is each poem in expressing the poet's attitudes and emotions? What kind of voice do you hear in each poem?

ROBERT HASS (born 1941)

Song   1973

Afternoon cooking in the fall sun—
who is more naked
                  than the man
yelling, "Hey, I'm home!"
                  to an empty house?   5
thinking because the bay is clear,
the hills in yellow heat,
& scrub oak red in gullies
            that great crowds of family
should tumble from the rooms   10
                  to throw their bodies on the Papa-body,
                        I-am-loved.

Cat sleeps in the windowgleam,
                  dust motes.
            On the oak table   15
      filets of sole
stewing in the juice of tangerines,
      slices of green pepper
            on a bone-white dish.

THE RECEPTIVE READER

1. What is the *underlying emotion* in this poem? For you, what images or phrases come closest to bringing it to the surface?

2. Would you call the poem as a whole *understated*? (Are the filets of sole and the bone-white dish in the poem by accident? How do the many short lines or half-lines affect the tone of the poem?)

LOUISE BOGAN (1897–1970)

The Dream   1941

O God, in the dream the terrible horse began
To paw at the air, and make for me with his blows.
Fear kept for thirty-five years poured through his mane,
And retribution equally old, or nearly, breathed through his nose.

Coward complete, I lay and wept on the ground   5
When some strong creature appeared, and leapt for the rein.
Another woman, as I lay half in a swound°   *fainting fit*
Leapt in the air, and clutched at the leather and chain.

Give him, she said, something of yours as a charm.
Throw him, she said, some poor thing you alone claim.   10
No, no, I cried, he hates me; he's out for harm,
And whether I yield or not, it is all the same.

But, like a lion in a legend, when I flung the glove
Pulled from my sweating, my cold right hand,
The terrible beast, that no one may understand,   15
Came to my side, and put down his head in love.

THE RECEPTIVE READER

1. What is the *prevailing tone* in this poem? What kind of a dream are we asked to
share? What words and phrases openly label emotion? What images help project it?
How many words refer to violent motion?

2. How is this poem like a legend or *fairy tale*?

3. How did you expect the poem to *end*? How did you react to the ending?

4. Why are the *long, flowing* lines of this poem more appropriate here than the
short, choppy lines of the preceding poem?

THE PERSONAL RESPONSE

What nightmares, if any, do you have? Have they changed over the years?

COUNTEE CULLEN   (1903–1946)

Incident   1925

Once riding in old Baltimore,
    Heart-filled, head-filled with glee,
I saw a Baltimorean
    Keep looking straight at me.

Now I was eight and very small,   5
    And he was no whit° bigger,   *not a bit*
And so I smiled, but he poked out
    His tongue and called me "Nigger."

I saw the whole of Baltimore
    From May until December;   10
Of all the things that happened there
    That's all that I remember.

THE RECEPTIVE READER

1. What is the prevailing tone of this poem? Is it hostile, angry, outraged, aggressive, militant? How would you have reacted to this "incident"?

2. What makes the poem an example of *understatement?*

3. Why do you think many readers remember this poem—even though they may have forgotten other, more emotional indictments of racial prejudice?

THE PERSONAL RESPONSE

What has been your own experience with racial or ethnic slurs or with other kinds of prejudiced language? How do you react to them?

DYLAN THOMAS (1914–1953)

Do Not Go Gentle into That Good Night 1952

Do not go gentle into that good night,
Old age should burn and rave at close of day;
Rage, rage against the dying of the light.

Though wise men at their end know dark is right,
Because their words had forked no lightning they   5
Do not go gentle into that good night.

Good men, the last wave by, crying how bright
Their frail deeds might have danced in a green bay,
Rage, rage against the dying of the light.

    10
Wild men who caught and sang the sun in flight,
And learn too late, they grieved it on its way,
Do not go gentle into that good night.

Grave men, near death, who see with blinding sight
Blind eyes could blaze like meteors and be gay,
Rage, rage against the dying of the light.   15

And you, my father, there on the sad height,
Curse, bless, me now with your fierce tears, I pray.
Do not go gentle into that good night.
Rage, rage against the dying of the light.

THE RECEPTIVE READER

1. What is the prevailing tone in this poem by the Welsh poet Dylan Thomas? How is the tone different from what you might expect in a poem about death?

2. The speaker in the poem does not address his own father directly till the *last stanza* of the poem. How does this last stanza affect your response to the poem? (How do you think your response to the poem might have been different if the father had been brought into the poem at the beginning?)

3. Thomas attracted a large following in the thirties and forties by writing with passionate intensity about the experiences of *ordinary people*. In this poem, what are striking examples of his writing about ordinary experience in heightened, intensely emotional language? How much of the heightened, passionate quality of his verse results from the playing off of extreme *opposites?*

4. This poem uses the traditional form of the *villanelle*, a set of three-line stanzas repeating the same rhyme scheme (aba), which is further reinforced by a fourth line added to the concluding stanza (rhyming abaa). What are the two opposed key words in the poem that the rhyme scheme keeps driving home? Two final lines alternate in the stanzas till they are juxtaposed in the concluding couplet. Why is this kind of insistent *repetition* more appropriate to Thomas' poem than it would be to a poem written in a more understated style?

THE PERSONAL RESPONSE

If wise men know that in the end "dark is right," is the "rage" the poet calls up futile? (Is it impious?)

JUXTAPOSITIONS

Poems of Mourning

Poems cover the emotional spectrum; they sensitize us to the feelings of others and educate the emotions. Some of the earliest known poems are **elegies,** or poems of mourning and lamentation. Compare the following more recent poems striking a mournful, elegiac note. The speaker in the first poem is "rueful"—filled with sadness and regret.

A . E . H O U S M A N   (1859–1936)

With Rue My Heart Is Laden   1896

With rue my heart is laden
   For golden friends I had,
For many a rose-lipped maiden
   And many a lightfoot lad.

By brooks too broad for leaping
   The lightfoot boys are laid;
The rose-lipped girls are sleeping
   In fields where roses fade.

5

THE RECEPTIVE READER

Why does the poet say that the "lightfoot lads" are laid "by brooks too broad for leaping"? Housman's sad poems were for a time immensely popular. Why do readers enjoy sad poems such as this one?

Traditional elegies do not always maintain the same note of bitterness to the end. They often work their way through bitter grief to calm acceptance or to the joyful certainty of resurrection. How does the following poem come to terms with loss?

THE GALLERY
Juxtaposing Word and Image

Marc Chagall, *The Descent of the Angel* (1923–47). Loan of Ida Chagall. Kunstmuseum Basel.

LAWRENCE FERLINGHETTI   (born 1919)

Don't let that horse

Don't let that horse
            eat that violin
        cried Chagall's mother
                    But he
            kept right on
                        painting
And became famous
And kept on painting
                The Horse With Violin In Mouth
And when he finally finished it
he jumped up upon the horse
                    and rode away
            waving the violin
And then with a low bow gave it
to the first naked nude he ran across
And there were no strings
                    attached

Vincent van Gogh, *The Starry Night* (1889). Oil on canvas. 29″ × 36¼″. Collection, the Museum of Modern Art, New York. Acquired through the Lillie P. Bliss Bequest.

ANNE SEXTON (1928–1974)

The Starry Night

*That does not keep me from having a terrible need of—shall
I say the word—religion. Then I go out at night to paint
the stars.*
    VINCENT VAN GOGH, IN A LETTER TO HIS BROTHER

The town does not exist
except where one black-haired tree slips
up like a drowned woman into the hot sky.
The town is silent. The night boils with eleven stars.
Oh starry starry night! This is how
I want to die.

It moves. They are all alive.
Even the moon bulges in its orange irons
to push children, like a god, from its eye.
The old unseen serpent swallows up the stars.
Oh starry starry night! This is how
I want to die:

into that rushing beast of the night,
sucked up by that great dragon, to split
from my life with no flag,
no belly,
no cry.

Sacrifice of Isaac in the Four Gospels, Armenian illuminated manuscript.
The Walters Art Gallery, Baltimore.

WILFRED OWEN   (1893–1918)

The Parable of the Old Men and the Young

So Abram rose, and clave the wood, and went,
And took the fire with him, and a knife.
And as they journeyed both of them together,
Isaac the first-born spake and said, My Father,
Behold the preparations, fire and iron,
But where the lamb for this burnt-offering?
Then Abram bound the youth with belts and straps,
And builded parapets and trenches there,
And stretched forth the knife to slay his son.
When lo! an angel called him out of heaven,
Saying, Lay not thy hand upon the lad,
Neither do anything to him. Behold,
A ram caught in a thicket by its horns;
Offer the Ram of Pride instead of him.
But the old man would not so, but slew his son—
And half the seed of Europe, one by one.

Robert Gwathmey, *Lullaby* (1947).
Private collection. Superstock, New York.

AUDRE LORDE   (born 1934)

Now That I Am Forever with Child

How the days went while you
                    were blooming within me
I remember each upon each—
the swelling changed planes of
                    my body
and how you first fluttered,
                    then jumped
and I thought it was my heart.

How the days wound down
and the turning of winter
I recall, with you growing heavy
against the wind. I thought
now her hands
are formed, and her hair
has started to curl
now her teeth are done
now she sneezes.
Then the seed opened
I bore you one morning just
                    before spring
My head rang like a fiery piston
my legs were towers
                    between which
A new world was passing.

Since then
I can only distinguish
one thread within running hours
You, flowing through selves
toward You.

CATHY SONG

Girl Powdering Her Neck

The light is the inside
sheen of an oyster shell,
sponged with talc and vapor,
moisture from a bath.

A pair of slippers
are placed outside
the rice paper doors.
She kneels at a low table
in the room,
her legs folded beneath her
as she sits on a buckwheat pillow.

Her hair is black
with hints of red,
the color of seaweed
spread over rocks.

Morning begins the ritual
wheel of the body,
the application of translucent skins.
She practices pleasure:
the pressure of three fingertips
applying powder.
Fingertips of pollen
some other hand will trace.

Kitagawa Utamaro, *Woman Making Up Herself.* Color woodblock
print. Musée Guimet, Paris. Lauros-Giraudon/Art Resource,
New York.

The peach-dyed kimono
pattered with maple leaves
drifting across the silk,
falls from right to left
in a diagonal, revealing
the nape of her neck
and the curve of a shoulder
like the slope of a hill
set deep in snow in a country of huge
    white solemn birds.
Her face appears in the mirror,
a reflection in a winter pond,
rising to meet itself.

She dips a corner of her sleeve
Like a brush into water
to wipe mirrors;
she is about to paint herself.

The eyes narrow
in a moment of self-scrutiny.
The mouth parts
as if desiring to disturb
the placid plum face:
Break the symmetry of silence.
But the berry-stained lips,
stenciled into the mask of beauty,
do not speak.
Two chrysanthemums
touch in the middle of the lake and drift apart.

Francisco Goya, *Third of May, 1808* (detail, 1814). Oil on canvas. 8'9" × 13'4". Museo del Prado Madrid. Scala/Art Resource, New York.

ANDREY VOZNESENSKY   (born 1933)

I Am Goya

TRANSLATED BY STANLEY KUNITZ

I am Goya
of the bare field, by the enemy's beak gouged
till the craters of my eyes gape
I am grief

I am the tongue
of war, the embers of cities
on the snows of the year 1941
I am hunger

I am the gullet
of a woman hanged whose body like a bell
tolled over a blank square
I am Goya

O grapes of wrath!
I have hurled westward
                    the ashes of the uninvited guest!
and hammered stars into the unforgetting sky—like nails
I am Goya

Pieter Breughel the Elder, *Landscape with the Fall of Icarus.* (detail, c.1558) Musées royaux des Beaux-Arts, Brussels. Scala/Art Resource, New York.

W. H. AUDEN   (1907–1973)

Musée des Beaux Arts

About suffering they were never wrong,
The Old Masters: how well they understood
Its human position; how it takes place
While someone else is eating or opening a window or just walking dully along;
How, when the aged are reverently, passionately waiting
For the miraculous birth, there always must be
Children who did not specially want it to happen, skating
On a pond at the edge of the wood:
They never forgot
That even the dreadful martyrdom must run its course
Anyhow in a corner, some untidy spot
Where the dogs go on with their doggy life and the torturer's horse
Scratches its innocent behind on a tree.

In Brueghel's *Icarus,* for instance: how everything turns away
Quite leisurely from the disaster; the plowman may
Have heard the splash, the forsaken cry,
But for him it was not an important failure; the sun shone
As it had to on the white legs disappearing into the green
Water; and the expensive delicate ship that must have seen
Something amazing, a boy falling out of the sky,
Had somewhere to get to and sailed calmly on.

Charles Demuth, *I Saw the Figure 5 in Gold* (1928). Oil on composition board. 36″ × 29¾″. The Metropolitan Museum of Art, New York. The Alfred Stieglitz Collection.

WILLIAM CARLOS WILLIAMS   (1883–1963)
The Great Figure

Among the rain
and lights
I saw the figure 5
in gold
on a red
firetruck
moving
tense
unheeded
to gong clangs
siren howls
and wheels rumbling
through the dark city.

N. SCOTT MOMADAY   (born 1934)

Earth and I Gave You Turquoise   1974

Earth and I gave you turquoise
    when you walked singing
We lived laughing in my house
    and told old stories
You grew ill when the owl cried   5
We will meet on Black Mountain

I will bring corn for planting
    and we will make fire
Children will come to your breast
    You will heal my heart   10
I speak your name many times
The wild cane remembers you

My young brother's house is filled
    I go there to sing
We have not spoken of you   15
    but our songs are sad
When Moon Woman goes to you
I will follow her white way

Tonight they dance near Chinle
    by the seven elms   20
There your loom whispered beauty
    They will eat mutton
and drink coffee till morning
You and I will not be there

I saw a crow by Red Rock   25
    standing on one leg
It was the black of your hair
    The years are heavy
I will ride the swiftest horse
You will hear the drumming hooves   30

THE RECEPTIVE READER

Although Momaday places his poem in the setting of the tribal past, it speaks a language that transcends time and place. Which of the images and statements in the poem do most to help you share the speaker's emotions? Which do most to help you place yourself in the speaker's place? How does the speaker deal with his grief?

THE PERSONAL RESPONSE

As you look back over these two poems, which of the two ways of dealing with loss and mourning appeals to you more? Why?

THE CREATIVE DIMENSION

The following re-creation captures the elegiac tone of Momaday's poem. For this or another poem in this chapter, do a similar re-creation that captures the tone of the original.

> We walked the earth together
> In my house we danced and drank coffee till morning
> I planted corn
> You wanted children
> But you became ill
> I thought love could heal you
> The years drag
> I'll dance no more
> But one day I'll speak your name
> And you'll come on a swift horse

THE USES OF WIT

> *Tsars,*
>   *Kings,*
>   *Emperors,*
> *sovereigns of all the earth,*
> *have commanded many a parade,*
> *but they could not command*
>   *humor.*
>   YEVGENY YEVTUSHENKO

> *The human mind is kind of like a piñata. When it breaks*
> *open, there's a lot of surprises inside.*
>   LILY TOMLIN

In our psychological armory, humor is a prize weapon for survival. It ranges from the inspired clowning that deflates pompousness to the dark humor that makes the unbearable bearable. When other means of attack seem unavailing, humor becomes the weapon of the satirist, using ridicule to cut an opponent down to size. Much humor deflates; we laugh when it punctures the balloon (while we may regret the loss of the balloon). What familiar daydreams are the target of the poet's wit in the following poem?

ISHMAEL REED (born 1938)
.05
                                                          1973

> If i had a nickel
> For all the women who've
> Rejected me in my life

I would be the head of the
World Bank with a flunkie   5
To hold my derby as i
Prepare to fly chartered
Jet to sign a check
Giving India a new lease
On life   10

If i had a nickel for
All the women who've loved
Me in my life i would be
The World Bank's assistant
Janitor and wouldn't need   15
To wear a derby
All i'd think about would
Be going home

In this poem, the soul of wit is **incongruity:** Things are mismatched, the way Charlie Chaplin's bowler hat and bow tie were mismatched with the king of silent screen comedy's baggy pants. A person thinking in terms of nickels is not likely to realize the impossible daydream of being a World Bank executive in a chartered jet—even if his money-raising scheme were based on something less pitiable than his failures in love. And if he did indeed achieve such status, he would likely call the person assisting him something more dignified than a "flunkie." We are likely to smile again when the neatly parallel second stanza juxtaposes our need for love, glorified by generations of poets, with an achievement record comparable to that of an assistant janitor.

THE RECEPTIVE READER

1. What details or phrases in this poem strike you as funny?
2. What is the connection between the daydream in this poem and current versions of the "American Dream"?

THE CREATIVE DIMENSION

Write your own "If-I-had-a-nickel" poem or prose passage.

Poems become more aggressive or bitter in tone when **satire** wields humor as a weapon. Satire employs ridicule to jab at callousness, pomposity, hypocrisy, false prophets, rip-off artists, and the law's delay. Some satirists flail out at miscellaneous abuses, but much effective satire takes clear aim at its target. It measures offenders against an implied standard of righteous or humane behavior and finds them wanting. What is the target in the following satirical poem?

EVE MERRIAM   (born 1916)
Robin Hood   1970

has returned
to Sherwood Forest
as
Secretary of the Interior

And the greenery   5
is to be preserved
for the public good

directly alongside
the parts reserved
for Hood enterprises   10

for Sherwood Homesites
Shop-and-Sher Parking Plaza
and
Sherburger Franchises.

THE RECEPTIVE READER

What accounts for the mocking tone of this poem? What is the target of the poet's *satire?* Where and how does the poem show the poet's wicked sense of humor?

What does the following poem imitate? What satirical points does it score?

DAVID WAGONER   (born 1927)
Breath Test   1983

He isn't going to stand for it sitting down
As far as he can from the unshaded glare
And the TV camera where he isn't breathing
In no machine no thanks because no way
Being sober as a matter of fact his body   5
Without a warrant is nobody's damn business
And to a republic for which he isn't
Putting that thing in his mouth as a citizen
Who voted he has a right to disobey
The Laws of Supply and Demand by running short   10
Of supplies and they can all go take a walk
On their own straight line all night if they feel like it.

THE RECEPTIVE READER

What garbled sayings and mixed clichés do you recognize in this monologue? What kind of person is talking? What is the *target* of the poet's satire?

EXPLORATIONS
Parodies Regained

Modern writers have often felt the urge to update traditional stories with comic effect. Often their retellings make us think both about the traditional story and the writer's modern slant on it.

A. D. HOPE   (born 1907)
Coup de Grâce   1970

Just at the moment the Wolf,
Shag jaws and slavering grin,
Steps from the property wood,
Oh, what a gorge, what a gulf
Opens to gobble her in,   5
Little Red Riding Hood!

O, what a face full of fangs!
Eyes like saucers at least
Roll to seduce and beguile.
Miss, with her dimples and bangs,   10
Thinks him a handsome beast;
Flashes the Riding Hood Smile;

Stands her ground like a queen,
Velvet red of the rose
Framing each little milk-tooth   15
Pink tongue peeping between.
Then, wider than anyone knows,
Opens her minikin mouth

Swallows up Wolf in a trice;
Tail going down gives a flick,   20
Caught as she closes her jaws.
Bows, all sugar and spice.
O, what a lady-like trick!
O, what a round of applause!

THE RECEPTIVE READER

1. What do you think moved the poet to retell this familiar classic? What about the old story needed updating and why?

2. What twists to the retelling seem to you particularly *modern*? What touches seem particularly comic and why? (What makes this poet a good storyteller?)

THE CREATIVE DIMENSION

Do your own modern retelling (in verse or prose) of a fairy tale that seems in need of updating.

POEMS FOR FURTHER STUDY

When reading the following poems, pay special attention to tone. What is the prevailing tone in each poem? What kind of voice is speaking to you in the poem?

SIR JOHN SUCKLING (1609–1642)
Song   1638

Why so pale and wan, fond° lover?   *foolish*
   Prithee,° why so pale?   *please*
Will, when looking well can't move her,
   Looking ill prevail?
   Prithee, why so pale?   5

Why so dull and mute, young sinner?
   Prithee, why so mute?
Will, when speaking well can't win her,
   Saying nothing do 't?

Quit, quit, for shame; this will not move,°   *persuade*   10
   This cannot take her.
If of herself she will not love,
   Nothing can make her:
   The devil take her!

RICHARD LOVELACE (1618–1658)
To Lucasta, Going to the Wars   1649

Tell me not, sweet, I am unkind
That from the nunnery
Of thy chaste breast and quiet mind,
To war and arms I fly.°   *hurry*

True, a new mistress now I chase,   5
The first foe in the field;
And with a stronger faith embrace
A sword, a horse, a shield.

Yet this inconstancy is such
As you too shall adore;   10
I could not love thee, dear, so much,
Loved I not° honor more.   *if I did not*

THE RECEPTIVE READER

What is the central metaphor the poet chooses for going away to war? What makes it playful or humorous? How does the poet play on words in the final two lines?

SHARON OLDS   (born 1942)

Quake Theory   1980

When two plates of earth scrape along each other
like a mother and daughter
it is called a fault.

There are faults that slip smoothly past each other
an inch a year, with just a faint rasp   5
like a man running his hand over his chin,
that man between us,

and there are faults that get stuck at a bend for twenty years.
The ridge bulges up like a father's sarcastic forehead
and the whole thing freezes in place, the man between us.   10

When this happens, there will be heavy damage
to industrial areas and leisure residences
when the deep plates
finally jerk past
the terrible pressure of their contact.   15
                            The earth cracks
and innocent people slip gently in like swimmers.

THE RECEPTIVE READER

How does the earthquake metaphor affect the tone of this poem? In developing
the implications of this central metaphor, how does the poet start in a low key and
build up to a climax? (Where is the high point? How does the poet make it stand out?)
What is the speaker's attitude toward the daughter? What is the speaker's attitude toward the father? Who are the "innocent people"?

CLAUDE MCKAY   (1890–1948)

If We Must Die   1919

If we must die, let it not be like hogs
Hunted and penned in an inglorious spot,
While round us bark the mad and hungry dogs,
Making their mock at our accursèd lot.
If we must die, O let us nobly die,   5
So that our precious blood may not be shed
In vain; then even the monsters we defy
Shall be constrained to honor us though dead!
O kinsmen we must meet the common foe!
Though far outnumbered let us show us brave,   10
And for their thousand blows deal one deathblow!
What though before us lies the open grave?
Like men we'll face the murderous, cowardly pack
Pressed to the wall, dying, but fighting back!

THE RECEPTIVE READER

1. How should this poem be read? What is the *stance* of the speaker in the poem? What words and images most strongly convey his feelings?

2. The language of protest and of race relations has changed since McKay's day. If you had been a contemporary of the poet, do you think you would have been moved by McKay's defiant rhetoric? Why or why not?

WRITING ABOUT LITERATURE

19. Responding to Tone (Reading the Clues)

The Writing Workshop   When you write about tone, you need to read between the lines. You need to have your antenna out for the emotional quality of a poem. Modern poets are not likely to establish the tone of a poem by announcement ("Ah, how I suffer!"). Neither can you simply infer the tone of a poem from its apparent subject matter. For instance, you might expect a poem about a funeral to be sad and solemn. However, you cannot take the tone for granted. The poem may have been written in a tone of stern moralizing about the shortcomings of the deceased. Or it may dwell on bittersweet memories of happier hours.

Make your paper show that you have read for clues to the attitudes and feelings that seem built into a poem:

◇ Pay special attention to the *connotations* of words. *Vexed, angry,* and *furious* are different points on a continuing scale. They go from a low-key state of annoyance and perplexity (or "vexation") through ordinary anger to furious uncontrolled rage. Look for a network of related words that might help set the tone of a poem. A poet might create a careless, joyful mood by the repeated use of synonyms or near-synonyms like *mirth, merry, jocund, revelry, good cheer, fiesta, frolic, joyous.* (A poem in which words like these echo is not likely to be a solemn ode in praise of the Puritan work ethic.)

◇ Listen to the *rhythm* of the poem as it is read out loud. Is the poem slow-moving, deliberate, earnest? Is it skipping and cheerful? Is it urgent, insistent, driven by passionate indignation?

◇ Take into account the attitude the poem adopts toward the *reader* or listener: Is the tone defiant, challenging? Does the poem take you into the speaker's confidence as if in a conspiratorial whisper? Does it treat you like a boon companion?

◇ Try to become sensitive to *nuances.* Unconditional love or hate or admiration is rare. A poet may admire something "this side idolatry" (as Ben Jonson did his fellow poet and playwright William Shakespeare).

◇ Look for signs of humorous intention or irreverent *wit.* When Lord Byron says about the high-toned philosophical speculations of a fellow poet, "I wish he would explain his explanations," we know that Byron's attitude will be less than worshipful. Watch especially for irreverent slangy expressions that undercut serious pretensions ("thus Milton's universe *went to smash*"). Read for revealing metaphors or similes ("Thus in his head / science and ignorance were kneaded like a sticky dough together").

⟡ Look for *shifts* in tone that may help shape a poem as a whole. A poem may move from a tone of bitterness and indignation to a more understanding and forgiving tone. A Christian elegy may start with notes of deep mourning but is likely to work its way to the joyful certainty of resurrection. It will not just project grief but try to come to terms with it, leaving us at the end cleansed and calm, ready to move on "to fresh woods, and pastures new."

How does the following student paper read the clues that help the poet set the tone?

SAMPLE STUDENT PAPER

"Quake Theory," or Whose Fault Is It?

There is nothing quite as much fun as a punning wit. To utilize one word to mean two different things creates an effect like those optical illusions where we can see an old woman or a young girl . . . or again an old woman—this tickles the brain. And, tickled, we smile until, as in Sharon Olds' poem "Quake Theory," the serious message sinks in, and we realize this isn't fun anymore.

An initial metaphor is developed in the first stanza; it also sets up the pun: "When two plates of earth scrape along each other / like a mother and daughter / it is called a fault." The word *fault* does double-time here as a description of a fracture in the earth and as a key word to alert us to the distance between a mother and her daughter. That distance can best be summed up in the question: "Whose fault is it?" What is the *it* that isn't working?

The poem does not enlighten us immediately. Instead it sounds for a moment as though it might drone along in a professorial manner, informing us of two different kinds of fault in two stanzas. ("There are faults that slip smoothly past each other / an inch a year.") We read along, smiling in anticipation of further developments in what may prove an extended joke. The tone is dry, almost too dry, but we have been trained by generations of deadpan comedians to expect lurking underneath the surface dryness the levity of a joke. Sharon Olds lures us in but then abruptly shifts gears to refer to "that man between us."

Just who is this man? The man, as Sharon Olds intended, is a discordant note in this poem. Not only does his introduction into the poem upset the flow of the poem, but he himself is an upsetting influence in the relationship between mother and daughter.

We read in the second stanza that a fault can be trouble-free with only a bit of friction—friction likened to what results when a man rubs his five-o'clock shadow (not just any man, but "that man between us"). However, in the third stanza, we read that a fault may also be blocked and build up tension "like a father's sarcastic forehead," and "the whole thing freezes in place, the man between us." With this ominous note, the poem no longer seems to point toward a humorous conclusion. The repeated references to "that man," ending each of the two stanzas, remind us that the central metaphor in this poem is the earthquake.

The point of view is that of the mother speaking to the daughter (or perhaps vice-versa). The speaker is trying to describe their relationship, which remains in constant motion, "scraping" at times, building up tension at others. But there is also a third dynamic, "that man," the father. He is there benignly or as an active threat, but he is certainly there.

What is the result when the tension builds up between the two locked bodies? "There will be heavy damage / . . . when the deep plates / finally jerk past / the terrible pressure of their contact." In keeping with the metaphor of the earthquake, the poem itself fractures at this point, skips a line, and then resumes:

> The earth cracks
> and innocent people slip gently in like swimmers.

What an odd analogy! We may assume that in a clash of wills or land masses, some who are bystanders will suffer, perhaps even be swallowed, but this image seems both deadly and harmless at the same time. To "slip gently in like swimmers" seems to belie the violence just described. But this is perhaps as it should be: In any family upset there are not necessarily bleeding victims left lying around afterwards. People are sucked under without a surface struggle or disturbance.

In this poem, we are carried along at first amused, then puzzled or disturbed, and then saddened at the end. We sense that things might have been different; there is regret here. But whose "fault" is it? It is neither the mother's nor the daughter's but, as in plate tectonics, the fault of the rift between them, the father.

QUESTIONS

1. How does this paper trace the shifts in tone in this poem? Does it discover nuances that you might have missed?

2. This student writer was especially sensitive to the relation between form and meaning, sound and sense. Where and how does the paper show the connection between meaning and outward shape or form?

3. How close is this writer's reaction to the poem to your own reaction?

20 IRONY AND PARADOX
Marrying Contraries

Although life is an affair of light and shadow, we never accept it as such. We are always reaching toward the light. From childhood we are given values which correspond only to an ideal world. The shadowy side of real life is ignored. Thus, we are unable to deal with the mixture of light and shadow of which life really consists.

MIGUEL SERRAN

Life is bounded by wonder on one side and terror on the other.

SAM KEEN

FOCUS ON IRONY AND PARADOX

Some art and poetry filter out what is ugly or disappointing in life. Their patrons adorn living room walls with paintings of sunsets or of stags posed in forest clearings. They like poems about children playing in a garden or about offspring honoring their elders. Filtered poetry is like a portrait photographer who airbrushes blemishes, frowns, and signs of age. We are flattered by the re-touched picture, but we know it tells only part of the truth. Most modern poets (like many poets of earlier ages) resist the temptation to make the world unconvincingly beautiful. They resist the impulse to oversimplify. They take naturally to irony and paradox as ways of doing justice to the undercurrents and countercurrents of life.

Irony and paradox are the poet's way of bringing in a neglected or ignored part of the story:

❖ **Irony** produces a wry humorous effect by bringing in a part of the truth that we might have preferred to hide. Irony knows that the idol has feet of clay, and may tell us so with glee. It often has the last word, undercutting the more flattering or idealizing hypothesis. The truth irony discovers may be unexpected or unwelcome, but it may be true nevertheless.

❖ A **paradox** is an apparent contradiction that begins to make sense on second thought. Something at first does not seem true, but when we think about it we see how it might be. Like irony, paradox is aware of the discrepancy between the rest of the idol and its feet, but it is more likely to make us try to resolve the contradiction. We may begin to see the point of it: Life itself is neither all clay or all gold. What is beautiful in our world is ultimately rooted in common clay.

Many observers have noted a special affinity between irony and the modern temper. Much of the best-known modern poetry has an ironic tone. Whenever something seems too beautiful to be true, we seem prepared for the ironic counterpoint. We seem ready for the kind of irony that is the revenge of reality on rosy projections. The following concluding stanza from a poem by Sylvia Plath is attuned to the modern temper.

SYLVIA PLATH   (1932–1963)

From *Watercolor of Grantchester Meadows*   1959

Droll, vegetarian, the water rat
Saws down a reed and swims from his limber grove,
While the students stroll or sit,
Hands laced, in a moony indolence° of love—   *carefree laziness*
Black-gowned, but unaware   5
How in such mild air
The owl shall stoop from his turret,° the rat cry out.   *small tower jutting from a castle*

The first few words of this stanza hint at an unusual perspective: The water rat (which we might expect to be repulsive) is described as "droll"— amusing in a harmless eccentric way—and "vegetarian," as if watching its health like a fellow human. The rat provides an ironic underside to the idyllic collegiate setting where students stroll lazily in the "mild air," absorbed in moony thoughts of young love. They are ironically unaware of the life-and-death drama played out as the owl swoops down on the harmless-seeming amusing rat.

Ironically, the students' sense of security is only an illusion. When we least suspect it, evil lurks, ready to strike and make us "cry out." The poet's sense of irony makes her bring into the poem the kind of knowledge we like to push to the back of our minds.

THE RECEPTIVE READER

1. Why did the poet make this minidrama take place in "mild air" rather than in threatening weather? Is there any point in her mentioning the black academic gowns? (Why are they being worn?)

2. Do you identify with the students? the rat? the owl?

3. In this excerpt, does irony have the *last word*? Why or why not?

THE PERSONAL RESPONSE

Does your own campus have an idyllic atmosphere? Is it ever threatened or disrupted?

THE USES OF IRONY

Neatness, madam has
nothing to do
with the Truth.
The Truth
is quite messy
like
a wind blown room.
WILLIAM J. HARRIS

Snowy egrets stand
graceful, majestic, serene
among the beer cans
STUDENT HAIKU

Irony makes us smile, but with a wry rather than a happy smile. It may leave us with a bitter aftertaste as we say to ourselves: "I should have known." It is ironic when a crusader for family values gets divorced. Such ironies may make us smile with a knowing smile, but they do not make us glad. What is the irony in the following poem by a master ironist among American poets?

STEPHEN CRANE (1871–1900)
A Man Saw a Ball of Gold 1895

A man saw a ball of gold in the sky;
He climbed for it,
And eventually he achieved it—
It was clay.
Now this is the strange part: 5
When the man went to earth
And looked again,
Lo, there was the ball of gold.
Now this is the strange part:
It was a ball of gold. 10
Ay, by heavens, it was a ball of gold.

There is a double irony in this poem: Something golden we worship from afar may turn out to be made of common clay when we come closer. (An admired leader may turn out to be corrupt. A person we adore may turn out to be petty or totally unresponsive to our love.) This sad and funny defeat of our human expectations is the essence of irony. But such disillusionment may not destroy our capacity for illusion: When we have barely returned to reality, our capacity for being fooled is already activated again. The larger irony is that we are protected against facing the truth as by an armored vest. We stubbornly refuse to learn from experience.

THE RECEPTIVE READER

1. What is the effect of the poet's abrupt, very brief presentation of the ironic counterpoint in line 4?

2. Why is there so much repetition in this poem? (Why do you think the poet considered it necessary? What effect does it have on the reader?)

THE PERSONAL RESPONSE

Have you had any experience with a "ball of gold" turning into common clay?

Irony ranges in tone from playful to bitter or desperate. It ranges from gently teasing to aggressive and slashing, turning into **sarcasm.** In the following poem, a master of the more playful and indulgent kind of irony points to the ironic discrepancy between our dignified, self-important self-image and our odd behavior.

OGDEN NASH (1902–1971)

The Hunter   1949

The hunter crouches in his blind
'Neath camouflage of every kind,
And conjures up a quacking noise
To lend allure to his decoys.
This grown-up man, with pluck and luck,   5
Is hoping to outwit a duck.

THE RECEPTIVE READER

In how many ways does Nash heighten the ironic contrast between the hunter and the target?

Ogden Nash delighted in the spectacle of a grown man pretending to be a duck. As the heavyweight of light verse, his mission was to help us take ourselves less seriously. Much modern poetry has gravitated to the opposite end of the spectrum, asking us to be more serious when we might be thoughtless or uncaring. The following bitterly ironic poem looks at the exploitation of the Indian past as a tourist attraction from the point of view of a native American poet. nila northSun was born in Nevada and is of Shoshoni-Chippewa heritage. What is the irony in this poem?

NILA NORTHSUN (born 1951)

Moving Camp Too Far 1984

i can't speak of
    many moons
    moving camp on travois
i can't tell of
    the last great battle   5
    counting coup or
    taking scalp
i don't know what it
    was to hunt buffalo
    or do the ghost dance   10
but
i can see an eagle
    almost extinct
    on slurpee plastic cups
i can travel to powwows   15
    in campers & winnebagos
i can eat buffalo meat
    at the tourist burger stand
i can dance to indian music
    rock-n-roll hey-a-hey-o   20
i can
    & unfortunately
    i do

THE RECEPTIVE READER

1. What's the meaning of *travois* and *counting coup*? What does the title mean?

2. An editor reprinting this poem said, "This poem is a mourning song, as it is one of a stunted and trivialized vision made to fit a pop-culture conception of the Indian. . . . it highlights some of the more enraging aspects of American culture" as they can appear only to native Americans. What did she mean?

THE PERSONAL RESPONSE

Have you ever experienced feelings similar to those expressed in this poem?

We use the term *irony* in at least two major ways. A contrast between what we expect and what really happens makes for **irony of situation.** When the ocean liner *Titanic,* touted as unsinkable, went down on her maiden voyage with a terrible loss of life, the English poet Thomas Hardy pondered the ironic contrast between human "vaingloriousness" and the ship's inglorious end. A deliberate contrast between what we say and what we really mean makes for **verbal irony**—intentional irony in our use of language. The following poem, by a British-born poet who became an American citizen, is an extended exercise in verbal irony, starting with the title. Monuments to the Unknown Soldier were meant to commemorate the heroic war dead by honoring the remains of an unidentified soldier killed in action. As we read the following poem, we find that there is nothing heroic about the "unknown citizen," and it is not the poet's intention to honor him. (What *is* the poet's intention?)

W. H. AUDEN (1907–1973)

The Unknown Citizen 1940

(To JS/O7/M/378
This Marble Monument
Is Erected by the State)

He was found by the Bureau of Statistics to be
One against whom there was no official complaint,
And all the reports of his conduct agree
That in the modern sense of an old-fashioned word, he was a saint,
For in everything he did he served the Greater Community.   5
Except for the War till the day he retired
He worked in a factory and never got fired,
But satisfied his employers, Fudge Motors Inc.
Yet he wasn't a scab° or odd in his views,   *strikebreaker*
For his Union reports that he paid his dues,   10
(Our report on his Union shows it was sound)
And our Social Psychology workers found
That he was popular with his mates° and liked a drink.   *his friends*
The Press are convinced that he bought a paper every day
And that his reactions to advertisements were normal in every way.   15
Policies taken out in his name prove that he was fully insured,
And his Health-card shows he was once in a hospital but left it cured.
Both Producers Research and High-Grade Living declare
He was fully sensible to the advantages of the Installment Plan
And had everything necessary to the Modern Man,   20
A phonograph, a radio, a car and a frigidaire.
Our researchers into Public Opinion are content
That he held the proper opinions for the time of year;
When there was peace, he was for peace; when there was war he went.
He was married and added five children to the population,   25
Which our Eugenist° says was the right number for a parent of his generation,   *population*
And our teachers report that he never interfered with their education.   *planner*
Was he free? Was he happy? The question is absurd:
Had anything been wrong, we should certainly have heard.

THE RECEPTIVE READER

1. The Unknown Soldier was anonymous because the remains could not be identified. Why does Auden give his Unknown Citizen no name but only a number?

2. What clues in the poem remind us that the poet is speaking ironically? For instance, what is wrong with holding "the proper opinions for the time of year"? What is ironic about the citizen's attitude toward war? Why is what the teachers say about him a

left-handed compliment? (Can you find other examples of mock compliments that are examples of verbal irony?)

3. Many of the institutions keeping tab on the citizenry apparently regarded JS/07/M/378 as a model citizen, if not a "saint." What is the poet's basic criticism of him? (What is the poet's basic criticism of the state?)

THE CREATIVE DIMENSION

Auden wrote this poem in 1940. What would you include in an updated portrait of the Unknown Citizen or the Unknown Consumer? Write your own ironic portrait of today's Unknown Citizen.

Much twentieth-century poetry has focused on the ironic contrast between official war propaganda and the horrible realities of war. The following poem is by Wilfred Owen, a British officer who wrote about the "sorrowful dark hell" of the Great War—World War I—and who was killed on the western front a week before the armistice ended the war in 1918. The motto he quotes in the title of the poem (and again at the end) is a quotation from the Roman poet Horace. It was known to every British schoolboy of Owen's generation: *Dulce et decorum est pro patria mori*—"How sweet and fitting it is to die for one's country." Owen once said, "My subject is war and the pity of war. The poetry is in the pity."

WILFRED OWEN (1893–1918)

Dulce et Decorum Est   1918

Bent double, like old beggars under sacks,
Knock-kneed, coughing like hags, we cursed through sludge,
Till on the haunting flares we turned our backs
And toward our distant rest began to trudge.
Men marched asleep. Many had lost their boots   5
But limped on, blood-shod. All went lame; all blind;
Drunk with fatigue; deaf even to the hoots
Of tired, outstripped Five-Nines° that dropped behind.   *gas shells*

Gas! Gas! Quick, boys!—An ecstasy of fumbling,
Fitting the clumsy helmets just in time;   10
But someone still was yelling out and stumbling,
And floundering like a man in fire or lime . . .
Dim, through the misty panes and thick green light,
As under a green sea, I saw him drowning.
In all my dreams, before my helpless sight,   15
He plunges at me, guttering, choking, drowning.

If in some smothering dreams you too could pace
Behind the wagon that we flung him in,
And watch the white eyes writhing in his face,
His hanging face, like a devil's sick of sin;   20

If you could hear, at every jolt, the blood
Come gargling from his froth-corrupted lungs,
Obscene as cancer, bitter as the cud
Of vile, incurable sores on innocent tongues,—
My friend, you would not tell with such high zest   25
To children ardent for some desperate glory,
The old Lie: Dulce et decorum est
Pro patria mori.

THE RECEPTIVE READER

1. How does the picture the first stanza paints of the troops being withdrawn from the front lines for "rest" differ from the one you would expect to encounter on propaganda posters or in patriotic speeches? Why is there a bitter irony in the *timing* of the gas attack in this poem?

2. Many people have read about the use of poison gas by the belligerents in World War I. How does Owen drive the realities of chemical warfare home? From what *perspectives*—when and how—do you see the victim? What is the effect on you as the reader?

3. How and with what effect is the word *drowning* repeated in this poem? What gives the word *innocent* toward the end of the poem its special power? Who is guilty in this poem?

4. This poem owes its eloquence in part to the insistent piling on of related words and similar, *parallel* structures. Where and how?

5. What is the basic irony in this poem?

THE PERSONAL RESPONSE

Are we today too removed from the realities of war to share feelings like those expressed in this poem? Are our feelings too blunted from overexposure? How does the treatment of war in the media affect our feelings about war?

JUXTAPOSITIONS ⟨━━━━━━━━━━━

Modern Parables

> *A man said to the universe:*
> *"Sir, I exist!"*
> *"However," replied the universe,*
> *"The fact has not created in me*
> *A sense of obligation."*
>   STEPHEN CRANE

A **parable** is a brief story with a weighty meaning, which the listeners or readers are left to ponder and make out for themselves. Study the workings of irony in the following short monologues and dialogues. Is there a common thread or a shared underlying attitude?

STEPHEN CRANE   (1871–1900)

The Wayfarer   1895

The wayfarer,
Perceiving the pathway to truth,
Was struck with astonishment.
It was thickly grown with weeds.
"Ha," he said,   5
"I see that none has passed here
In a long time."
Later he saw that each weed was a singular knife.
"Well," he mumbled at last,
"Doubtless there are other roads."   10

There Was Crimson Clash of War   1895

There was crimson clash of war.
Lands turned black and bare;
Women wept;
Babes ran, wondering.
There came one who understood not these things.   5
He said: "Why is this?"
Whereupon a million strove to answer him.
There was such intricate clamor° of tongues,   *confused outcry*
That still the reason was not.

THE RECEPTIVE READER

What is Crane's ironic comment on the pursuit of truth? What is his ironic comment on the causes of war?

BRUCE BENNETT   (born 1940)

Leader   1984

        A man shot himself
in the foot.

        "OW!" he howled,
hopping this way and
that. "Do something!   5
Do something!"

        "We are! We are!"
shouted those around
him. "We're hopping!
We're hopping!"   10

THE RECEPTIVE READER

How closely does this poem follow the pattern of Stephen Crane's "A-man-did-such-and-such" poems? What is the poet's ironic comment on leaders and followers?

THE CREATIVE DIMENSION

Write your own updated "A-person-did-such-and-such" poem.

THE USES OF PARADOX

Whatever it is, it must have
A stomach that can digest
Rubber, coal, uranium, moons, poems.
Like the shark, it contains a shoe.
It must swim for miles through the desert
Uttering cries that are almost human.
LOUIS SIMPSON ON AMERICAN POETRY

One must live in the middle of contradiction because if all
contradiction were eliminated at once life would collapse.
There are simply no answers to some of the great pressing
questions. You continue to live them out, making your life
a worthy expression of leaning into the light.
BARRY LOPEZ

Be patient with all that is unsolved in your heart.
RAINER MARIA RILKE

A **paradox** is a seeming contradiction that begins to make sense on second thought. Like irony, a paradox challenges us to keep more than one idea in mind at the same time. We are confronted with a paradox when we realize that many feel lonely in a crowd, that many are alone in the midst of our crowded, congested cities. When we think about it, however, this apparent contradiction begins to make sense: The physical presence of others is not enough; we need to be with people who understand and who care.

Poets have found love a paradoxical emotion, fraught with attraction and rejection, joy and pain, hope and despair. What makes the following poem about love paradoxical?

NELLE FERTIG   (born 1919)
I Have Come to the Conclusion   1974

I have come to the conclusion
       she said
that when we fall in love

we really fall in love with ourselves—
that we choose particular people   5
because they provide
the particular mirrors
in which we wish to see.

And when did you discover
this surprising bit of knowledge?   10
        he asked.

After I had broken a few
very fine mirrors
        she said.

What the woman in this poem says is paradoxical because at first glance it doesn't seem to be true. Supposedly, when we fall in love, we go beyond our usual self-love to make someone else more important than we are to ourselves. Isn't the beauty of love that it lifts us out of our petty needs and complaints? It makes us care for somebody else. But, on second thought, we may begin to see the point: We may well be prone to fall in love with people who think that we are in some way special or wonderful. We are moved when we ask the mirror on the wall, "Who's the fairest of them all?" and the mirror replies, "You are." We may get angry when the mirror replies, "Someone else is." (To judge from the poem, some "very fine mirrors" are broken this way.)

What then is the difference between irony and paradox? Both bring in a part of the truth that simpleminded people tend to ignore. But irony tends to have the last word. When we discover that the idol has feet of clay, we may cease to worship the idol. A paradox asks us to puzzle over the apparent contradiction and to balance off the conflicting points of view. We may have to live with both parts of the paradox. When we look for someone to admire, we may have to settle for someone who has human imperfections.

THE CREATIVE DIMENSION

Cluster the word *mirror*. What images, associations, or memories does the word bring to mind? Are any of them related to the role mirrors play in Fertig's poem?

Love poetry in the Western world long followed the lead of the Italian fourteenth-century poet Petrarch. In the Petrarchan tradition, love was a paradoxical mixture of joy and sorrow. Love was a source of much joy, but it was often disappointed and therefore also the cause of much suffering. The following is a modern translation of a sonnet by Petrarch. (Trace the interlaced rhyme scheme of the traditional fourteen-line poem, and listen for the underlying iambic meter.) What makes this poem paradoxical? How much of it makes sense on second thought?

FRANCESCO PETRARCA   (1304–1374)

Or Che 'l Ciel e la Terra e 'l Vento Tace   1369

TRANSLATED BY HANS P. GUTH

Calm now are heaven and earth, and the winds asleep.
No birds now stir; wild beasts in slumber lie.
Night guides her chariot across the starry sky.
No wave now moves the waters of the deep.
I only keep vigil—I think, I burn, I weep.   5
She who destroys me dazzles my mind's eye.
At war with myself, raging and grieving , I
Long for the peace that's hers to give or keep.
From the same single fountain of life
Rise the bitter and sweet that feed my soul.   10
I am caressed and slashed by the same hand.
A martyr in a world of ceaseless strife,
I have died and risen a thousandfold.
So far am I from reaching the promised land.

THE RECEPTIVE READER

1. What is fitting, and what is *paradoxical,* about the nighttime setting?

2. What examples can you find of *opposed* concepts, clashing images, and mixed emotions?

3. Poets who made love into a religion often used the vocabulary of religious devotion. Where and how does this poem use *religious imagery?* What makes the religious images paradoxical?

In the following Shakespeare sonnet, a central paradox sets up many of the apparent contradictions in the poem. At first, the time of year seems to be winter—freezing, bare, and barren. A loved person is away, and everything seems dark and empty. But here is the paradox: It's actually summer, the season of bird song and abundance. Why then is the speaker in the poem shivering and freezing? The answer is that it is summer outside but winter in the poet's soul. Our true mental climate is not determined by the outside temperature but by the built-in thermostats in our minds.

WILLIAM SHAKESPEARE   (1564–1616)

Sonnet 97   before 1598

How like a winter hath my absence been
From thee, the pleasure of the fleeting° year!   *quickly passing*
What freezings have I felt, what dark days seen!
What old December's bareness everywhere!

And yet this time removed° was summer's time   *with you absent*   5
The teeming autumn, big with rich increase,°   *full of new life*
Bearing the wanton burthen of the prime,°   *giving birth to spring's luxurious offspring*
Like widowed wombs after their lords' decease:
Yet this abundant issue seemed to me
But hope of orphans and unfathered fruit;   10
For summer and his pleasures wait on thee,
And, thou away,° the very birds are mute.   *with you away*
Or, if they sing, 'tis with so dull a cheer
That leaves look pale, dreading the winter's near.

THE RECEPTIVE READER

1. As one student reader said, "In this poem, summer comes only when the loved person is there." In how many different ways is this *central paradox* followed up or echoed in this poem?

2. Where and how does the central metaphor shift from autumn to widowhood? What is the connection? What paradoxical emotions does the orphan metaphor bring into the poem?

3. How do the leaves in the last line illustrate *personification*—reading human qualities into the inanimate world? Where else does the poem show the power of personification to turn the world around us into a mirror of our emotions?

EXPLORATIONS

Understanding Paradox

Explain the paradoxes in the following lines. What makes them strange or contradictory? How do they make sense on second thought?

1. I am the dove
   Whose wings are murder.
   My name is love.
                     Charles Causley, "Envoi"

2. The reverse side also has a reverse side.
                     Japanese proverb

3. Sprayed with strong poison
   my roses are crisp this year
   In the crystal vase
                     Paul Goodman, "Haiku"

4. All poems say the same thing, and each poem is unique.
                     Octavio Paz

EXPLORATIONS

Paradoxes of Faith

> *This, in its essence, is a description of the metaphysical poet who thinks with his body: an idea for him can be as real as the smell of a flower or a blow on the head. And those so lucky as to bring their whole sensory equipment to bear on the process of thought grow faster, jump more frequently from one plateau to another more often.*
>
> THEODORE ROETHKE

The **metaphysical** poets of the early seventeenth century are known for their love of paradox. They are fond of yoking together things from widely different areas of experience. In their religious poetry, they translate the mysteries of faith into language borrowed from science, medicine, mechanics, or war. They deal with the central paradoxes of religious doctrine: the certainty of death but yet the belief in life after death; our yearning for God's love and yet our stubborn attachment to sin.

The title of the following religious poem refers not to altars or incense but to a mechanical device made of wheels, blocks, and rope. A pulley was used to multiply human strength and lift heavy weights in the days before steam-powered or electricity-driven winches. One of Herbert's editors has said that the secret of Herbert's poetry is "the recovery of fresh feeling" from old formulas. What is different or unexpected about the relationship between God and humanity in the poem? What is the central paradox in this poem?

GEORGE HERBERT (1593–1633)

The Pulley

1633

When God at first made man,
Having a glass of blessings standing by,
"Let us," he said, "pour on him all we can:
Let the world's riches, which dispersèd° lie,   *lie scattered*
    Contract into a span."°   *short space*   5

    So strength first made a way;
Then beauty flowed, then wisdom, honor, pleasure.
When almost all was out, God made a stay,°   *paused*
Perceiving that, alone of all his treasure,
    Rest in the bottom lay.   10

    "For if I should," said he,
"Bestow° this jewel also on my creature,   *pass on*
He would adore my gifts instead of me,
And rest in Nature, not the God of Nature;
    So both should losers be.   15

"Yet let him keep the rest,
But keep them with repining° restlessness: *yearning*
Let him be rich and weary, that at least,
If goodness lead him not, yet weariness
　　May toss him to my breast."   20

THE RECEPTIVE READER

1. Admirers have praised Herbert and the other metaphysical poets for their *wit*, in the more general sense of a quick mind or intellectual alertness. Part of this mental quickness is their willingness to use a play on words, or *pun*, even when writing about solemn subjects. What does the word *rest* mean when "*Rest* in the bottom lay"? (*Restlessness* later appears as its opposite.) What does the word mean when God's creature is likely to "*rest* in Nature, not the God of Nature"? How does the poet pun, or play on the word, when God decides to let us "keep the *rest*"—everything except *rest*? (How does the poet make this key word stand out in the poem?)

2. What is paradoxical about richly blessed creatures suffering from "repining restlessness"? Do you think it is true?

3. One student wrote that in this poem humanity is "deprived rather than depraved." What did she mean?

The second metaphysical poem in this group focuses on a key paradox of Christian doctrine: Central to the believer's religious awakening is the realization of mortality, the fear of death. But ultimately the hope of resurrection makes death lose its sting. In the words of the poem, death has no reason to "swell" with pride. We are afraid of death, and yet we are not afraid of death.

JOHN DONNE (1572–1631)
Holy Sonnet 10   about 1609

Death, be not proud, though some have callèd thee
Mighty and dreadful, for thou are not so;
For those whom thou thinkst thou dost overthrow
Die not, poor Death, nor yet canst thou kill me.
From rest and sleep, which but thy pictures be,°   *are your lookalikes*   5
Much pleasure—then from thee much more must flow,
And soonest our best men with thee do go,
Rest of their bones, and soul's delivery.°   *release of their souls*
Thou art slave to fate, chance, kings, and desperate men,
And dost with poison, war, and sickness dwell,   10
And poppy or charm can make us sleep as well
And better than thy stroke; why swellst thou then?
One short sleep past, we wake eternally
And death shall be no more; Death, thou shalt die.

THE RECEPTIVE READER

1. In his religious poems, as in his earlier love poetry, Donne projects his personal feelings onto a large screen. He acts out his personal soul-searching on a large cosmic stage. What makes this poem a striking example?

2. How is death a "slave" to "fate, chance, kings, and desperate men"? How would he do their bidding? The poet refers to sleep once literally and once figuratively—where and how?

3. Donne often structures his poem like a set of arguments—the *rhetoric* of a lawyer pleading a case in front of a jury, for instance. Can you outline the arguments he uses to devalue "poor Death"?

4. What is the meaning of the *play on words* in the last half of the last line? How has the poem as a whole led up to it?

JUXTAPOSITIONS

Convention and Originality

> *No surprise for the writer, no surprise for the reader; we*
> *want the poem to change our way of seeing.*
> MICHAEL RYAN

The following two early-seventeenth-century poems are among the ten most widely reprinted poems in the English language. Both echo the familiar plea of the lover to a reluctant (or "coy") partner: "Seize the day; make use of the passing day" (**carpe diem** in the original Latin). The first poem follows a well-established convention: The too-soon-fading rose "smiles today," but if we do not enjoy it now, it will have wilted by tomorrow. Therefore, "gather ye rosebuds while ye may." The second poem, this one in the metaphysical vein, is Andrew Marvell's "To His Coy Mistress" (meaning "To His Reluctant Lady," without the current negative connotations of *mistress*). This poem has no rosebuds, no songbirds, and no conventional springtime setting in the English countryside. As you read these two poems, compare Herrick's pleasing conventional metaphors with the bold and jostling metaphors in Marvell's poem. Then read a poem by the Countess of Dia, a French poet of the twelfth century, who looks at love and courtship from a female rather than the conventional male perspective.

ROBERT HERRICK (1591–1674)
To the Virgins, to Make Much of Time 1648

Gather ye rosebuds while ye may,
    Old time is still a-flying,
And this same flower that smiles today
    Tomorrow will be dying.

The glorious lamp of heaven, the sun,   5
    The higher he's a-getting,
The sooner will his race be run,
    And nearer he's to setting.

That age is best which is the first,
    When youth and blood are warmer;   10
But being spent, the worse, and worst
    Times still succeed the former.

Then be not coy, but use your time,
    And while ye may go marry,
For, having lost but once your prime,°   *best season*   15
    You may forever tarry.°   *stay behind*

THE RECEPTIVE READER

    How much in this poem merely confirmed what you already knew? Did any part of it surprise you?

Marvell's poem goes beyond the convention. Its bold and paradoxical images roam from the Humber River in northern England to the river Ganges in India (then famous for its jewels and spices) and from there to "deserts of vast eternity." The poem ranges over vast stretches of time, from Noah's flood to the "conversion of the Jews," then not expected till the end of time. Paradoxically, the metaphors and similes in this poem are drawn from geography, biblical history, and botany—areas not conventionally associated with love.

ANDREW MARVELL   (1621–1678)

To His Coy Mistress   before 1678

    Had we but world enough, and time,
This coyness, lady, were° no crime.   *would be*
We would sit down and think which way
To walk and pass our long love's day.
Thou by the Indian Ganges' side   5
Shouldst rubies find; I by the tide
Of Humber would complain.° I would   *write plaintive love songs*
Love you ten years before the flood,
And you should, if you please, refuse
Till the conversion of the Jews.   10
My vegetable love should grow
Vaster than empires and more slow;
An hundred years should go to praise
Thine eyes and on thy forehead gaze,
Two hundred to adore each breast,   15
But thirty thousand to the rest,
An age at least to every part,

And the last age should show your heart.
For, lady, you deserve this state,°   *this high station*
Nor would I love at lower rate.   20
     But at my back I always hear
Time's wingèd chariot hurrying near,
And yonder all before us lie
Deserts of vast eternity.
Thy beauty shall no more be found,   25
Nor, in thy marble vault, shall sound
My echoing song; then worms shall try
That long-preserved virginity,
And your quaint honor° turn to dust,   *deliberate virtue*
And into ashes all my lust.   30
The grave's a fine and private place,
But none, I think, do there embrace.
     Now therefore, while the youthful hue
Sits on thy skin like morning dew,
And while thy willing soul transpires°   *breathes forth*   35
At every pore with instant fires,
Now let us sport us while we may,
And now, like amorous birds of prey,
Rather at once our time devour
Than languish in his slow-chapped° power.   *chewing with slow-moving jaws*   40
Let us roll all our strength and all
Our sweetness up into one ball,
And tear our pleasures with rough strife
Thorough° the iron gates of life.   *through*
Thus, though we cannot make our sun   45
Stand still, yet we will make him run.

THE RECEPTIVE READER

1. Where and how does Marvell carry *hyperbole,* or poetic exaggeration, to new extremes?

2. What is paradoxical about a "vegetable love" growing slowly to vast size like a giant cabbage? On second thought, what might be desirable or welcome about the idea?

3. What images and associations do time and eternity usually bring to your mind? How are the metaphors Marvell uses different? (What were the original uses of a chariot?)

4. What is the effect of the poet's bringing graveyard imagery into a love poem? (Can you find a good example of *verbal irony* in this passage?)

5. When Marvell replaces the conventional songbirds with birds of prey, what is the effect on the way we think about love and lovers? How do these birds help him turn the tables on all-devouring time? Why does he make us imagine "the iron gates of life" rather than a meadow with spring flowers?

6. How does Marvell's use of the sun differ from Herrick's? (Why would lovers want to make the sun "stand still"? How would they make the sun "run" to keep up with them?)

THE CREATIVE DIMENSION

A student poet wrote in her "Reply of Your Coy Mistress":

We have the world, and we have the time;
To wait a while longer would be no crime.

Write your own personal reply or response to either Herrick or Marvell.

We tend to think of the early love poets, or troubadours, of southern France as male. However, the poems of several women troubadours have come down to us. How does the following poem depart from the conventions of much male-oriented love poetry?

COUNTESS OF DIA (born about 1140)
I Sing of That Which I Would Rather Hide before 1200

TRANSLATED BY HANS P. GUTH

I sing of that which I would rather hide:
Where is the one who should be at my side
And whom I dearly love, come ebb or tide?
My kindness and sweet grace he has denied,
My beauty and good sense and goodly show. 5
I am betrayed, deceived, my love defied,
As if I were the lowest of the low.

Yet I take heart: I never brought you shame
Nor ever did the least to hurt your name.
My love surpasses loves of greater fame, 10
And I am pleased I beat you at love's game—
Outscored you when devotion was the test.
Your cold words and your slights all speak the same—
And yet you play the charmer with the rest.

THE RECEPTIVE READER

1. How is the *perspective* of the speaker in this poem different from that in traditional male-oriented poems of love and courtship? How much of this poem seems to belong to a different time, a different world? How much seems relevant or intelligible in our own time?

2. Modern translators of the southern French, or Provençal, poetry of the early Middle Ages often do not attempt to reproduce the finely crafted *stanza forms* and the intricate rhyme schemes of the originals. How do you think the rhyme scheme and the stanza form re-created here affect the reader's reactions to the poem?

CROSS-REFERENCES—For Discussion or Writing

In traditional *carpe diem* poetry, the woman who is admonished to make the most of time remains silent. What she thinks while the speaker in the poem makes his plea is not recorded. For an indication of possible unconventional responses, look at a modern poem like Edna St. Vincent Millay's "I, being born a woman and distressed" (p. 586).

POEMS FOR FURTHER STUDY

Pay special attention to the role of irony or paradox in the following poems. What is different, strange, or unexpected in each poem? If the poem uses irony, is it gentle and teasing or bitter and sarcastic? Does it have the last word? If the poem uses paradox, what is the basic contradiction? How does it begin to make sense on second thought?

ANNE SEXTON (1928–1975)

Ringing the Bells 1960

And this is the way they ring
the bells in Bedlam
and this is the bell-lady
who comes each Tuesday morning
to give us a music lesson 5
and because the attendants make you go
and because we mind by instinct,
like bees caught in the wrong hive,
we are the circle of the crazy ladies
who sit in the lounge of the mental house 10
and smile at the smiling woman
who passes us each a bell,
who points at my hand
that holds my bell, E flat,
and this is the gray dress next to me 15
who grumbles as if it were special
to be old, to be old,
and this is the small hunched squirrel girl
on the other side of me
who picks at the hair over her lip, 20
who picks at the hairs over her lip all day,
and this is how the bells really sound,
as untroubled and clean
as a workable kitchen,
and this is always my bell responding 25
to my hand that responds to the lady
who points at me, E flat;
and although we are no better for it,
they tell you to go. And you do.

THE RECEPTIVE READER

Bedlam was the name of a notorious London insane asylum. In the dark ages of mental health care, people came there to gawk at the antics of the inmates. What is the irony in the poet's use of this name? What is ironic about the music therapy she describes? What is ironic about the smiles in this poem? What is ironic about the sound of the bells? (How are the patients like "bees caught in the wrong hive"?) Why is there so much repetition, with everything running together without proper punctuation?

WILLIAM SHAKESPEARE (1564–1616)

Sonnet 130

before 1598

My mistress' eyes are nothing like the sun;		
Coral is far more red than her lips' red;		
If snow be white, why then her breasts are dun;°	*grayish brown*	
If hairs be wires, black wires grow on her head.		
I have seen roses damasked,° red and white,	*multicolored*	5
But no such roses see I in her cheeks;		
And in some perfumes there is more delight		
Than in the breath that from my mistress reeks.		
I love to hear her speak, yet well I know		
That music hath a far more pleasing sound;		10
I grant I never saw a goddess go;		
My mistress, when she walks, treads on the ground.		
And yet, by heaven, I think my love as rare°	*marvelous*	
As any she belied° with false compare.	*any woman misrepresented*	

THE RECEPTIVE READER

1. How does this poem illustrate the idea that irony is the revenge of reality on poetic exaggeration?

2. Readers hostile to irony accuse it of undercutting our capacity for sincere emotion. Do you think it does so in this sonnet?

PABLO NERUDA (1904–1973)

The Fickle One

1972

TRANSLATED BY DONALD D. WALSH

My eyes went away from me	
Following a dark girl	
who went by.	
She was made of black mother-of-pearl,	
Made of dark-purple grapes,	5
and she lashed my blood	
with her tail of fire.	

After them all
I go.

A pale blonde went by   10
like a golden plant
swaying her gifts.
And my mouth went
like a wave
discharging on her breast   15
lightningbolts of blood.

After them all
I go.

But to you, without my moving,
without seeing you, distant you,   20
go my blood and my kisses,
my dark one and my fair one,
my tall one and my little one,
my broad one and my slender one,
my ugly one, my beauty,   25
made of all the gold
and of all the silver,
made of all the wheat
and of all the earth,
made of all the water   30
of the sea waves,
made for my arms,
made for my kisses,
made for my soul.

THE RECEPTIVE READER

What is strange or paradoxical about the imagery in the early parts of the poem? How do you explain the yoking of contraries in the last part of the poem? Do you think the speaker in the poem can be sincere in the last part of the poem after what he said in the earlier parts? What is your personal reaction to the poem?

WRITING ABOUT LITERATURE

20. Exploring Irony and Paradox (Using Quotations)

The Writing Workshop Writing a paper focused on irony and paradox will remind you of the need to pay close attention to the poet's language. Poets are more aware than others of shades of meaning and the range of associations that connotative words activate. (To respond fully to the language of a poem, you have to be sensitive to the connotations of words like *prance, stride, pace*— they are very different from *slink, trudge, traipse*.) Poets are especially sensitive to the way words interact or form a web of meaning. We know, for instance, that a poet has a lively sense of paradox if we encounter contradictory, apparently self-canceling phrases like *aching joys, living death, sweet foe, angelic fiend.* (Such pairings are **oxymorons**—phrases that at the same time run hot and cold.)

Study the way the following sample paper pays close attention to the poet's language. Notice how close the paper stays to the actual text of the poem. Study the way the student writer weaves quotations into the texture of the paper.

SAMPLE STUDENT PAPER

Herbert's Pulley

"When God at first made man," begins George Herbert's original contribution to the creation myth. The poem, twenty lines divided neatly into four stanzas, is called "The Pulley." This is the first puzzle. The poet uses the name of a mechanical device, similar to a winch or other such mechanism, to title a poem that, on the surface and indeed on second and maybe even on third reading, does not appear to ever mention or explain a pulley.

In this very personal reinterpretation of Genesis, there is no mention of the creation of Eve or of original sin. Instead, the poem focuses on our paradoxical human reluctance to come to God. That reluctance is strange because Herbert's God speaks royally, like a magnanimous, loving sovereign bestowing gifts on his subject. "'Let us,' he said, 'pour on him all we can: / Let the world's riches, which dispersed lie, / Contract into a span.'" Herbert's God anticipates the magnanimous bearing of the Sun King, Louis XIV of France, surrounded by courtiers who depend on his liberality. But at the same time, paradoxically, this divine sovereign is very human—a being who craves adoration, who needs others to admire and worship him.

Looking at the last blessing in the "glass of blessings," God says that if he should "bestow this jewel also on my creature, / He would adore my gifts instead of me." This "jewel" is another puzzle, a pun. The word *rest* refers at the same time to the "rest" or remainder of God's gifts that we will be allowed to keep—and to the "rest" that God is going to deny his human subjects. This second punning use of the word *rest* refers not so much to restful sleep as to the concept of peace, of contentment (setting our minds at rest). God did desire all good things for His creature. Starting with strength, then "beauty flowed, then wisdom, honor, pleasure." Yet God felt that if everything was given to his human creation, they would want for nothing and would "rest in Nature, not the God of Nature; / So both should losers be."

Into such a short poem, Herbert packs ambiguous and punful words requiring the reader to do doubletakes. *Rest* can be the remainder ("let him keep the rest"); it can be serenity or peace ("alone of all his treasure, / Rest in the bottom lay"); and *rest* can mean to stay in place ("rest in Nature"). If we as human beings were too content to stay in our place in the natural world, we would never feel the need to come to God.

To prevent both himself and us from losing out, God has decided to keep the gift of rest or contentment from us. He reasons about his creature, "Let him be rich and weary, that at least / If goodness lead him not, yet weariness / May toss him to my breast." God appears to need a plan or device to prevent human beings from being caught up in this world. And so we sense the logic of calling the poem "The Pulley." A pulley is a device used in hoisting heavy objects that are hard to move. Our human restlessness is what God sees as his pulley, which will "toss" us to his breast.

And this is the ultimate paradox—that although God has given us many blessings and riches, yet he denies us the capacity to enjoy them and find lasting happiness in them. This is the way it had to be to keep us from turning away and forgetting our debt to our Maker.

QUESTIONS

How sensitive is the student writer to overtones or implications and to double meanings? Where does this paper clarify or illuminate parts of the poem that you found difficult or confusing? Do you anywhere part company with the writer's interpretation?

21 THEME
The Making of Meaning

For me the real issues of our time are the issues of
every time—the hurt and wonder of loving; making
in all its forms, children, loaves of bread, paintings,
building; and the conservation of life of all people and
all places, the jeopardizing of which no abstract
doubletalk of "peace" or "implacable foes" can excuse.
SYLVIA PLATH

A goal I think you can find in all my poems is to plead
with the world, with the reader, with the person the poem is
addressed to, to be kinder, more compassionate, more
understanding, more intelligent. My poems are often
about the pain I feel and they are a plea to the world to
relieve it.
DIANE WAKOSKI

When I landed in the republic of conscience
it was so noiseless when the engines stopped
I could hear a curlew high above the runway.
SEAMUS HEANEY, "FROM THE REPUBLIC OF CONSCIENCE"

FOCUS ON THEME

Poetry helps us find meanings in the bewildering flow of experience. Poems make us think: Often a poem asks us to look at familiar ideas in a new light. It may challenge familiar rutted ways of thinking. It may nudge us into trying a new route to the solution of a familiar problem. When we focus on the **theme** of a poem, we try to sum up its meaning. We try to put into words what makes the poem thought provoking: We look at the issues a poem seems to raise and the possible answers it suggests. We try to formulate the idea or insights that the poem as a whole seems to leave us with, for us to ponder and remember.

How close do poets come to spelling out in so many words the theme or central idea of a poem? Some poets leave larger meanings implied, hinted at, suggested only. Most twentieth-century poets have been wary of large abstrac-

669

tions: happiness, alienation, growth, patriotism, love. **Abstractions** are labels for large areas of human experience. In themselves, they are neither good nor bad. However, they do "abstract"—they draw us away, from specifics and individuals. They extrapolate the larger patterns that help us chart our way. Many modern poets have steered clear of them, afraid they might become *mere* abstractions, mere labels that remove us from flesh-and-blood realities.

Other poets are less shy about spelling out key ideas in so many words. Poets of earlier ages, and some in our own time, draw explicit conclusions; they formulate their insights. Even so, you have to remember an important caution: Ideas in poetry are live ideas—anchored to what you can see and hear and feel. You cannot take them out of a poem the way you take candy out of a wrapper. The poet's ideas take shape before your eyes—embedded in graphic images, acted out in scenes and events that stir your emotions.

The Polish poet Czeslaw Milosz, who resigned from the post–World War II Communist Polish government in protest against political repression, is an eloquent voice of human solidarity, of shared values crossing the borders of race, sex, and creed. What is the central idea or dominant theme in the following poem? How does the interplay of large abstractions and striking images give shape to the poem?

CZESLAW MILOSZ (born 1911)

Incantation   1968

TRANSLATED BY ROBERT PINSKY AND CZESLAW MILOSZ

Human reason is beautiful and invincible.
No bars, no barbed wire, no pulping of books,
No sentence of banishment can prevail against it.
It establishes the universal ideas in language,
And guides our hand so we write Truth and Justice   5
With capital letters, lie and oppression with small.
It puts what should be above things as they are,
Is an enemy of despair and a friend of hope.
It does not know Jew from Greek or slave from master,
Giving us the estate of the world to manage.   10
It saves austere and transparent phrases
From the filthy discord of tortured words.
It says that everything is new under the sun,
Opens the congealed fist of the past.
Beautiful and very young are Philo-Sophia   15
And poetry, her ally in the service of the good.
As late as yesterday Nature celebrated their birth,
The news was brought to the mountains by a unicorn and an echo.
Their friendship will be glorious; their time has no limit.
Their enemies have delivered themselves to destruction.   20

By modern standards, this poem has a high abstraction count. It invokes (with capital letters) ideas like Truth, Justice, and Nature. These abstractions are easy to abuse, and they have often been on poets' mental checklists of words to handle with care. ("Go in fear of abstractions," said the American poet Ezra Pound.) But the concern with the abuse of abstractions turns out to be exactly the impetus behind this poem. The poet's agenda is to cleanse "austere and transparent" words like *reason* and *justice* of the verbal pollution they have suffered. The agenda is to rescue them from dishonest use by timeservers, party hacks, and oppressors.

This work of verbal renewal and reconstruction Milosz accomplishes with the tools of the poet. He employs the eloquent image: the undesirable books being pulled off the shelves to be shredded and reduced to pulp. He uses the potent metaphor: Reason is "guiding our hand" as we write Truth and Justice; reason is helping us "open the congealed fist of the past." He uses words with a witty twist, as when he starts *oppression* with a lowercase letter, while capitalizing *Truth* and *Justice*. Finally, he restores jaded words to their full meaning (such as *philosophy*—"Philo-Sophia"—the "love of wisdom"). The unicorn bringing the good news to the mountains is a lovely symbol for the triumph of the imagination over its literal-minded enemies.

The theme or central idea that animates this poem is spelled out, stated explicitly in the first line: "Human reason is beautiful and invincible." The rest of the poem acts it out, translates it into memorable images, traces its ramifications and implications.

THE RECEPTIVE READER

1. Why is it witty that the poem starts *oppression* with a lowercase letter? What familiar saying does the poet play on when he says "everything is new under the sun"? What does he mean?

2. In your own words, what does this poem say about the large abstractions— Reason, Truth, and Justice? What does it say about the abuse of language? What is this poet's perspective on oppression?

3. When a poet's political agenda becomes overt, poetry shades over into political advocacy and finally into political propaganda. How overt is the poet's political agenda in this poem? Where would you place this poem on a spectrum ranging from disinterested poetry cutting across party lines through strong political commitment to political propaganda?

THE PERSONAL RESPONSE

Are any lines or phrases especially eloquent for you? Do any of them raise questions in your mind? In what ways does this poem connect with your own experience?

IDEA AND IMAGE

Poems are like dreams; in them you put what you don't know you know.

ADRIENNE RICH

*Poetry doesn't just come from the mind. Art is not just a
thing of the intellect, but of the spirit.*
LUCILLE CLIFTON

Poets and critics use the word *theme* in two different but related ways:
Sometimes the term simply points to the general **subject,** to a general area of
concern. A collection may sort poems out under such large thematic headings
as Love, Family, Identity, Alienation, and Dissent. Such themes are large umbrella headings, under which individual poems will offer different perspectives.
Under the heading of Family, one poem might be mourning the lost golden
world of childhood. Another poem might focus on the need for breaking the
fetters the family clamps on the individual.

However, often the term *theme* (as in this chapter) stands for the statement that a poem as a whole makes *about* a subject. The theme then is what
the poem as a whole says about identity, alienation, or dissent. The theme is
the recurrent message, insistent plea, or fresh insight that stays with us as we
leave the poem behind. To use an analogy from the fine arts, the Spanish
painter Francisco José de Goya (1746–1828) did a series of etchings about
Spanish resistance fighters being hunted down by Napoleon's armies. His general subject he summed up in his title for the series: "The Disasters of War."
But his theme in the sense of a central idea he summed up in the legend that
appears with his stark visions of repression and executions. This recurrent
statement, or indictment, reads "There is no remedy." Whereas other results
of human callousness and folly can be corrected or remedied, the carnage of
war cannot be made good.

Poets vary greatly in how explicitly they verbalize the ideas implied in or
acted out in their poems. Some poets largely let their images speak for themselves. (These are the poets who tell readers looking for a message to call
Western Union.) Other poets speak for their images, serving as guides or interpreters, spelling out more or less fully the message embedded in metaphor or
symbol.

The following is a famous poetic manifesto embodying the modern distrust of mere words. Its title, meaning "A Guide to the Art of Poetry," is borrowed from a work by the Roman poet Horace, who lived from 65 to 8 B.C.
(One of the familiar catchphrases from Horace's treatise is the admonition that
poetry should both "teach and delight.")

ARCHIBALD MACLEISH   (1892–1982)

Ars Poetica   1926

A poem should be palpable and mute
As a globed fruit,

Dumb
As old medallions to the thumb

Silent as the sleeve-worn stone   5
Of casement ledges where the moss has grown—

A poem should be wordless
As the flight of birds.

＊

A poem should be motionless in time
As the moon climbs,   10

Leaving, as the moon releases
Twig by twig the night-entangled trees,

Leaving, as the moon behind the winter leaves,
Memory by memory the mind—

A poem should be motionless in time   15
As the moon climbs.

＊

A poem should be equal to:
Not true.

For all the history of grief
An empty doorway and a maple leaf.   20

For love,
The leaning grasses and two lights above the sea—

A poem should not mean
But be.

The subtext, or implied message, of this poem is that poets should not use words lightly. There should be no showy displays of grief, no gushing about love. Since language is the poet's medium, what explains MacLeish's paradoxical preference for silence? In part, the answer lies in the historical context of the poem. The poet wrote it when the horrors of World War I had alienated many poets and artists from the oratory of flag-waving politicians. To MacLeish's generation, speeches eulogizing the "grateful dead" who had died in the trenches seemed impious. What was real was the grass growing over the graves in the military cemeteries, the bones in the sandy soil, and the wind and rain. Better to remain silent than to use words dishonestly.

But of course poems, including this one, are not literally silent. They are not literally "mute," "dumb," or "wordless." They use words, but, according to the speaker in this poem, they should use words to create images that speak for themselves. They should create for us something we can touch (something that is "palpable"), like the "globed fruit," over whose curved outline we can run our fingers, reading its texture and shape. Poems should give us something concrete to see and contemplate, like the "flight of birds" or the "empty doorway."

A central paradox of the poem is that "silent" sights can be more eloquent than preachings or editorializings. The grief of separation sinks in as we contemplate the "empty doorway" where friends or lovers used to linger while bidding each other good night. In the context of a poem, the deserted doorway becomes "equal to" our experience of grief; it becomes its concrete embodiment. The central idea of the poem is summed up in the often-quoted final lines: "A poem should not mean / But be." We should first of all let a poem exist, we should let it speak to our senses and emotions, before we interrogate it about what it means.

THE RECEPTIVE READER

1. Why do people finger (or thumb) "old medallions"? What emotions do you think you would feel when contemplating a "casement ledge" or windowsill worn smooth by people's sleeves resting on it but now overgrown with moss?

2. Why does the moon seem "motionless" while it is climbing at the same time? If we prefer poems without much overt motion (apparently preferring the still frames capturing the moon rising slowly behind the bare twigs of the wintery trees), what kinds of poetry would we seem to rule out?

3. Is it paradoxical that MacLeish himself spelled out the central idea of his poem in his concluding lines?

THE PERSONAL RESPONSE

Are you resistant or allergic to preaching, editorializing, lecturing?

Poets before and after MacLeish have often opted intuitively for concrete images over theory and explicit assertion. The following poem by the American poet Walt Whitman clearly "makes a statement" about the speaker's alienation from coldly analytical science, but it does so without verbalizing the poet's implied attitude.

WALT WHITMAN   (1819–1892)

When I Heard the Learn'd Astronomer   1865

When I heard the learn'd astronomer,
When the proofs, the figures, were ranged in columns before me,
When I was shown the charts and diagrams, to add, divide, and measure them,
When I sitting heard the astronomer where he lectured with much applause in the
    lecture room,
How soon unaccountable I became tired and sick,   5
Till rising and gliding out I wandered off by myself,
In the mystical moist night air, and from time to time,
Looked up in perfect silence at the stars.

What is the theme of Whitman's poem? The poem does not make an explicit assertion about the scientific as against the poetic temperament. But we can infer the poet's attitude from the brief scenario we see acted out. The speaker in the poem attended an astronomy lecture that showed modern science at its most methodical and analytical, with its toolbox of charts, diagrams, logical proofs, and mathematical calculations. Feeling "tired and sick," the speaker wandered off by himself. Once outside the lecture room, he found the antidote: Instead of feeling oppressed or stifled by figures and charts and columns, he could commune "in perfect silence" with the stars, soothed by the "mystical moist night air." The poem as a whole implies or points to a unifying central idea: Paradoxically, astronomy, when taught in a drily analytical mode, does not help us find wonder and inspiration in the stars.

THE PERSONAL RESPONSE

Do you sympathize with the poet's reponse to the astronomy lecture? Do you feel there is something to be said on the other side?

In the following poem, what is the relation between idea and image? How does the poet take a large abstraction to the level of firsthand experience?

WILLIAM STAFFORD (born 1914)

Freedom 1969

Freedom is not following a river.
Freedom is following a river
   though, if you want to.
It is deciding now by what happens now.
It is knowing that luck makes a difference.   5

No leader is free; no follower is free—
   the rest of us can often be free.
Most of the world are living by
creeds too odd, chancy, and habit-forming
   to be worth arguing about by reason.   10

If you are oppressed, wake up about
four in the morning; most places
you can usually be free some of the time
   if you wake up before other people.

Several recurrent notes are struck in this poem that together may help us formulate an overall perspective on freedom. First, much in our lives restricts our freedom. Apparently, being a leader and being a follower are both incompatible with making free choices. (Both leader and follower march with the main body of troops.) To be caught up in habitual creeds, to make today's decisions bound by yesterday's precedents, to be oppressed—all these limit the sphere of free choice. (The guardians of religious and legal doctrine do not encourage bold departures from received truth.) Nevertheless, there is a margin of freedom—if only in the margins of our existence—such as in the early morning hours, before the mechanisms that constrain us kick in.

THE RECEPTIVE READER

1. What do you make of the concrete *images* in this poem? When or how would someone want to follow a river? What does freedom have to do with following or not following it? What does freedom have to do with getting up early?

2. Why do you think the speaker claims that part of freedom is "deciding now by what happens now"? What makes the speaker in the poem say that neither a "leader" nor a "follower" can be free? What is "habit-forming" about "creeds" (and how do they limit your freedom)?

3. Does the poem provide any hints or guidelines on how to enlarge your margin of freedom?

4. How would you sum up in a sentence or two the *theme* of this poem—the statement the poem as a whole makes about freedom?

THE PERSONAL RESPONSE

How does the statement about freedom that the poem makes as a whole compare with the ideas you yourself associate with the word?

EXPLORATIONS

Religion and Poetry

John Donne's *Holy Sonnets*, like the religious poetry of some of his contemporaries, centered on the basic doctrines of traditional faith. However, Donne, like the other metaphysical poets, did not simply restate traditional beliefs. His poems are not **didactic** in the sense of teaching ideas already accepted and approved. Instead, the poet asks basic questions and then works his way toward the answers. How does the following poem reveal the poet's own religious temperament and the workings of the poet's imagination?

JOHN DONNE (1573–1631)

Holy Sonnet 5

1635

I am a little world made cunningly°	*skillfully*	
Of elements and an angelic sprite,°	*angel-like spirit*	
But black sin hath betrayed to endless night		
My world's both parts, and O, both parts must die.		
You which° beyond that heaven which was most high	*you who*	5
Have found new spheres and of new lands can write,		
Pour new seas in mine eyes, that so I might		
Drown my world with my weeping earnestly,		
Or wash it if it must be drowned no more.°	*(God's promise to Noah)*	
But O, it must be burnt! Alas, the fire		10
Of lust and envy have burnt it heretofore,		
And made it fouler; let their flames retire,		
And burn me, O Lord, with a fiery zeal		
Of Thee and Thy house, which doth in eating heal.		

THE RECEPTIVE READER

1. The poet starts from a basic shared assumption: the duality of body and soul. Where and how does this idea enter into the poem? What other *polarities* help organize this poem?

2. One familiar feature of Donne's poetry is the *paradoxical* intermingling of scientific and biblical lore. Where or how do science and faith meet in this poem?

3. Donne's *metaphors*, like Shakespeare's, are not static; they develop and shift in unexpected ways as the poem takes shape. How do both water and fire change their significance in the course of the poem?

THE PERSONAL RESPONSE

The following is one student's record of a close reading of the poem. How familiar or strange are Donne's religious ideas to a reader of your generation?

Water and Fire

Donne's Holy Sonnet 5 deals with the basic theme of sin and redemption. However, this poem is not a dry lecture on the subject of salvation. The poet is "weeping earnestly" for his sins and looking forward to redemption with "fiery zeal." In his search for his soul's salvation, he ranges from the waters that drowned the earth during Noah's flood to the reaches of outer space discovered by the new astronomy. His tears of repentance must be like oceans; or, alternatively, his repentance must be like a fire that cleanses and heals as it consumes the sins it feeds on.

What are the basic doctrines assumed by the poem? The poet tells us that he is a world cunningly, skillfully made of two parts: body and soul. This "little world" or microcosm, like the larger universe that it mirrors, houses both matter and spirit. The body is made up of the elements of the world of matter (such as earth and water). The soul is the "angelic sprite," a spirit made of the same substance as the angels.

The crucial "But" comes at the beginning of the third line of the sonnet: As the serpent entered the Garden of Eden, so sin has entered "my world's both parts" and "betrayed" them. As a result, both parts must die and face the "endless night" of damnation.

What is the answer? Donne, ranging far beyond our everyday world, turns to the astronomers who in his time were beginning to find new worlds beyond our own solar system. (These are the "new spheres" beyond the traditional heaven.) He invokes the explorers who, traveling across the uncharted oceans, were finding "new lands" or new continents. Between them, can the stargazers and navigators find new oceans to replenish his tears, so that his weeping can drown out his sinful world with a flood of tears? Or, since God promised after Noah's flood that he would drown humanity no more, the poet's tears could wash him clean of sin.

He feels that if he repents for his sins, he will be saved. Actually, however, the world will end not by water but by fire, as flames consume the world on the Day of Judgment. Before then, the flames of lust and envy (which turn the world foul) have to die out, and the flames of a "fiery" religious zeal have to cleanse the sinner. The poet knows he has to repent in time, because he knows what will happen if his heart is not with God at the point of death.

THE COMMITTED POET

The galleries are full of music, the pianist is storming the keys,
the great cellist is crucified over his instrument,
That none may hear the ejaculations of the sentinels,
Nor the sighs of the most numerous and the most poor;
the thud of their falling bodies.

W. H. AUDEN

I am a poet
who yearns to dance on rooftops,
to whisper delicate lines about joy
and the blessings of human understanding.
I try. I go to my land, my tower of words and
bolt the door, but the typewriter doesn't fade out
the sounds of blasting and muffled outrage.
                    LORNA DEE CERVANTES,
              "POEM FOR THE YOUNG WHITE MAN"

Bear in mind
that after the great destruction
one and all will prove
they were innocent.
              GÜNTER EICH

Should poems take sides? When we explore the ideas embedded in poems, we face the question of the poet's engagement or commitment. Should poets take a stand on the social and political issues of their time? Can they afford to testify on behalf of causes? Can poets serve party, ideology, or country?

Poets have often been warned to speak for neither their class nor their kind nor their trade: "Wrap the bard in a flag or a school and they'll jimmy his / door down and be thick in his bed—for a month" (Archibald MacLeish). When art becomes propaganda, when poets write poems "for daily political use," their art becomes disposable, fading like the campaign posters of yesteryear. When poets follow a party line, they may seem to cease speaking to us in their own right as one human being to another. Nevertheless, in practice, poets from William Shakespeare and John Milton to Gwendolyn Brooks and Adrienne Rich have found it hard to stay aloof from the political and ideological struggles of their time. When the British suppressed the Easter Rebellion in Ireland in 1916 and executed the leading rebels, William Butler Yeats, who was to become a leading poet of the Irish Renaissance, wrote:

We know their dream; enough
To know they dreamed and are dead . . .

I write it out in a verse—
MacDonagh and MacBride
And Connolly and Pearse
Now and in time to be,
Wherever green is worn,
Are changed, changed utterly:
A terrible beauty is born.
                    "Easter 1916"

Two world wars, the rise of fascism and communism, the struggle against colonialism, the Vietnam War—these made it hard for poets to stay on the fence. Many found they could not remain Rapunzel in the tower, never letting her hair down to ground level to help the real world climb in. Much modern poetry has been poetry of protest and of warning. At the same time, a poet's keeping *silent* about the political issues of the time has also often been seen as a political statement. By not confronting the issues, a poem might seem to be signaling acceptance of, or at least resignation to, oppression or abuses.

The German playwright Bertolt Brecht wrote the following poem when the rising tide of Nazism was driving writers and artists into exile.

BERTOLT BRECHT   (1898–1956)
On the Burning of Books   1936
TRANSLATED BY HANS P. GUTH

When the new masters announced that books full of harmful knowledge
Were to be publicly burned and when here and yonder
Oxen were made to draw carts full of books
To the stake, a poet, hunted from home (he was one of the best)
Discovered aghast, when reading the list of those burned,   5
His own books had been forgotten. He rushed to his desk,
Furious, and wrote to the rulers:

Burn me at once! he wrote with a frantic pen.
You cannot do this to me! How can you spare me?
Have I not always   10
Recorded the truth in my books? And now
you class me with liars!

                    This is an order:
Burn me!

Our response to the work of a committed poet like Brecht is shaped at least in part by our own commitments. Readers used to be told that their personal like or dislike of lobsters should not affect their reading of a poem about lobsters. But this detached stance is hard to maintain when, as Brecht would say, the lobsters wear helmets and boots. Readers will rejoice in the satirical barbs of Brecht's poem if they are inclined to share the poet's contempt for censors of "harmful knowledge." (Apparently censors do not tend to persecute harmful ignorance.) As often in his poetry and plays, Brecht strips a situation to its essentials. The ox-drawn carts probably make us imagine a simpler world than Hitler's Germany in the thirties. In such a world, books would be more rare and precious than they were later. The poet speaking in the poem also is a somewhat simpler and less complicated person than his modern counterparts: He rushes to defy the powers-that-be without a second thought. He turns the enemies' list of the "new masters" into an honor roll, from which he is "aghast" and "furious" to be excluded. We can relish his mimicking of people married not to the language of dialogue but to the language of command: "This is an order!" We can be proud to takes sides with those who have "always / Recorded the truth" against timeserving liars.

THE PERSONAL RESPONSE

What experiences with censorship have shaped your own attitudes toward censorship and censors? Do you find Brecht's poem eloquent or effective? Why or why not?

Poetry can be timely and timeless at the same time if readers sense that the poet's long-range solidarity with suffering and deluded humanity is as strong as the commitment to the current struggle. Does the following poem take sides? Whose?

DENISE LEVERTOV (born 1923)

What Were They Like? 1966

1) Did the people of Vietnam
   use lanterns of stone?
2) Did they hold ceremonies
   to reverence the opening of buds?
3) Were they inclined to quiet laughter? 5
4) Did they use bone and ivory,
   jade and silver, for ornament?
5) Had they an epic poem?
6) Did they distinguish between speech and singing?

1) Sir, their light hearts turned to stone. 10
   It is not remembered whether in gardens
   stone lanterns illumined pleasant ways.
2) Perhaps they gathered once to delight in blossom,
   but after the children were killed
   there were no more buds. 15
3) Sir, laughter is bitter to the burned mouth.
4) A dream ago, perhaps. Ornament is for joy.
   All the bones were charred.
5) It is not remembered. Remember,
   most were peasants; their life 20
   was in rice and bamboo.
   When peaceful clouds were reflected in the paddies
   and the water buffalo stepped surely along terraces,
   maybe fathers told their sons old tales.
   When bombs smashed those mirrors 25
   there was time only to scream.
6) There is an echo yet
   of their speech which was like a song.
   It was reported their singing resembled
   the flight of moths in moonlight. 30
   Who can say? It is silent now.

THE RECEPTIVE READER

1. Who are the two speakers in this poem? What is the difference in their *points of view*? What kind of person is asking the questions? What kind of person is giving the answers?

2. Why do you think the poet used a *question-and-answer* format? What effect does it have on the reader?

3. The poem shifts easily from the factual questionnaire mode to the metaphorical language of the poet. What are memorable *metaphors,* and what role do they play in the poem?

THE PERSONAL RESPONSE

What for you is the message of this poem? What is your personal response to this poem?

The following poem by a twentieth-century black writer is a tribute to Frederick Douglass, who in his autobiography told the story of his rebellion against and escape from slavery. As a journalist and public speaker, Douglass became a leader of the antislavery movement in the United States. What makes the following poem in his honor eloquent?

R O B E R T   H A Y D E N   (1913–1980)

Frederick Douglass   1966

When it is finally ours, this freedom, this liberty, this beautiful
and terrible thing, needful to man as air,
usable as earth; when it belongs at last to all,
when it is truly instinct, brain matter, diastole, systole,°   *phases of the heartbeat*
reflex action; when it is finally won, when it is more   5
than the gaudy mumbo jumbo of politicians:
this man, this Douglass, this former slave, this Negro
beaten to his knees, exiled, visioning a world
where none is lonely, none hunted, alien,
this man, superb in love and logic, this man   10
shall be remembered. Oh, not with statues' rhetoric,
nor with legends and poems and wreaths of bronze alone,
but with the lives grown out of his life, the lives
fleshing his dream of the beautiful, needful thing.

THE RECEPTIVE READER

1. What in this poem is different from the "gaudy mumbo jumbo of politicians" and conventional rhetoric in praise of liberty? What is strange or unexpected in the poet's description of freedom?

2. Is the poet speaking for a limited group? Is he speaking to a limited group? Do you think the poem would speak eloquently to a white audience? Why or why not?

THE PERSONAL RESPONSE

We are often told that modern audiences have few heroes. Write a tribute (poem or prose passage) to someone you admire, trying to make it convincing for the skeptical modern reader.

JUXTAPOSITIONS �⟩

Poems of War

Much modern poetry has dealt with the subject of war. From what point of view are you asked to look at war in each of the following poems? Does the poet spell out the ideas or attitudes implied or embedded in the poem? What does the poem as a whole say about war?

HENRY REED   (born 1914)

Naming of Parts   1946

Today we have naming of parts. Yesterday,
We had daily cleaning. And tomorrow morning,
We shall have what to do after firing. But today,
Today we have naming of parts. Japonica
Glistens like coral in all of the neighboring gardens,   5
    And today we have naming of parts.

This is the lower sling swivel. And this
Is the upper sling swivel, whose use you will see,
When you are given your slings. And this is the piling swivel,
Which in your case you have not got. The branches   10
Hold in the gardens their silent, eloquent gestures,
    Which in our case we have not got.

This is the safety-catch, which is always released
With an easy flick of the thumb. And please do not let me
See anyone using his finger. You can do it quite easy   15
If you have any strength in your thumb. The blossoms
Are fragile and motionless, never letting anyone see
    Any of them using their finger.

And this you can see is the bolt. The purpose of this
Is to open the breech, as you see. We can slide it   20
Rapidly backwards and forwards: we call this
Easing the spring. And rapidly backwards and forwards
The early bees are assaulting and fumbling the flowers:
    They call it easing the Spring.

They call it easing the Spring: it is perfectly easy   25
If you have any strength in your thumb: like the bolt,
And the breech, and the cocking-piece, and the point of balance,
Which in our case we have not got; and the almond-blossom
Silent in all of the gardens and the bees going backwards and forwards,
    For today we have naming of parts.   30

THE RECEPTIVE READER

1. Much of the talking in this poem is done by the drill instructor. Is what he says a *caricature*—a comic distortion exaggerating key traits to make them ridiculous? Or does it sound to you like a fairly accurate rendering of what an instructor might say?

2. The technology of war and the world of nature provide a steady play of *point and counterpoint* in this poem. How? With what effect? What does the poem as a whole say about technology and nature?

3. What is this poet's attitude toward war?

RICHARD EBERHART   (born 1904)

The Fury of Aerial Bombardment   1947

You would think the fury of aerial bombardment
Would rouse God to relent; the infinite spaces
Are still silent. He looks on shock-pried faces.
History, even, does not know what is meant.

You would feel that after so many centuries   5
God would give man to repent; yet he can kill
As Cain could, but with multitudinous will,
No farther advanced than in his ancient furies.

Was man made stupid to see his own stupidity?
Is God by definition indifferent, beyond us all?   10
Is the eternal truth man's fighting soul
Wherein the Beast ravens° in its own avidity?   *prowls*

Of Van Wettering I speak, and Averill,
Names on a list, whose faces I do not recall
But they are gone to early death, who late in school   15
Distinguished the belt feed lever from the belt holding pawl.

THE RECEPTIVE READER

1. What questions does this poem raise about God's intentions? What questions does it raise about our human responsibilities? Why does the poet bring the *allusion* to Cain into the poem?

2. Like Reed's poem, this poem takes us to the schoolrooms of military training. (Eberhart himself was for a time an aerial gunnery instructor in World War II.) How is Eberhart's use of the training experience similar to or different from Reed's?

3. Does this poem answer the questions it raises?

POEMS FOR FURTHER STUDY

In reading the following poems, pay special attention to theme. What ideas or attitudes are expressed or implied in the poem? What statement does the poem as a whole have for the reader? Does the poem spell it out in so many words? How does the poem as a whole carry its message?

DENISE LEVERTOV (born 1923)

The Mutes   1966

Those groans men use
passing a woman on the street
or on the steps of the subway
to tell her she is a female
and their flesh knows it,   5

are they a sort of tune,
an ugly enough song, sung
by a bird with a slit tongue

but meant for music?

Or are they the muffled roaring   10
of deafmutes trapped in a building that is
slowly filling with smoke?

Perhaps both.

Such men most often
look as if groan were all they could do,   15
yet a woman, in spite of herself,

knows it's a tribute:
if she were lacking all grace
they'd pass her in silence:

so it's not only to say she's   20
a warm hole. It's a word

in grief-language, nothing to do with
primitive, not an ur-language;°   *earliest human language*
language stricken, sickened, cast down

in decrepitude.° She wants to   *deterioration*   25
throw the tribute away, dis-
gusted, and can't,

it goes on buzzing in her ear,
it changes the pace of her walk,
the torn posters in echoing corridors   30

spell it out, it
quakes and gnashes as the train comes in.
Her pulse sullenly

had picked up speed,
but the cars slow down and   35
jar to a stop while her understanding

keeps on translating:
"Life after life after life goes by
without poetry
without seemliness   40
without love."

THE RECEPTIVE READER

1. What is the role in the poem of the bird metaphor? Why is the deaf-mute metaphor central to the poem? What kind of counterpoint does the subway provide in the poem?

2. What, in your own words, is the theme the poet spells out in the last stanza? How does the poem as a whole lead up to it?

3. Does this poem express hostility toward men?

THE PERSONAL RESPONSE

What attitudes about sexual harassment are widespread among women? What reactions to current concerns about sexual harassment are widespread among men? How does the poem relate to either?

PHILIP LARKIN (1922–1985)

Born Yesterday   1955

Tightly folded bud,
I have wished you something
None of the others would:
Not the usual stuff
About being beautiful,   5
Or running off a spring
Of innocence or love—
They all wish you that.
And should it prove possible,
Well, you're a lucky girl.   10

But if it shouldn't, then
May you be ordinary;
Have like other women
An average of talents:
Not ugly, not good-looking,   15
Nothing uncustomary
To pull you off your balance,
That, unworkable in itself,
Stops all the rest from working.
In fact, may you be dull—   20
If that is what a skilled,
Vigilant, flexible,
Unemphasized, enthralled
Catching of happiness is called.

THE RECEPTIVE READER

1. What is the meaning and effect of the *metaphor* in the first line?

2. One of the oldest temptations is for the older generation to make wishes or chart directions for the next. How does this poet try to steer clear of the "usual stuff"? What are his best wishes for the child's future?

THE PERSONAL RESPONSE

How would you react if someone told you, "May you be ordinary" and "May you be dull"?

A L I C E   W A L K E R   (born 1944)

Women   1970

They were women then
My mamma's generation
Husky of voice—Stout of
Step
With fists as well as   5
Hands
How they battered down
Doors
And ironed
Starched white   10
Shirts
How they led
Armies
Headragged Generals
Across mined   15
Fields
Booby-trapped
Ditches
To discover books
Desks   20
A place for us
How they knew what we
Must know
Without knowing a page
Of it   25
Themselves.

THE RECEPTIVE READER

1. What is the role of the *military metaphor* in this poem? (Why "headragged" generals?) What was the campaign in which the women of the mother's generation participated? (What clue is provided by the shirts?)

2. What is the paradox that concludes the poem?

3. What, for you, is the prevailing *mood* or emotion in this poem?

WRITING ABOUT LITERATURE

21. Tracing a Common Theme (Comparing and Contrasting)

The Writing Workshop   Comparison is a good teacher. It can alert us to what otherwise might go unnoticed; it can make us take a fresh look at what we took for granted. We value what we have when we look at what might take its place. We question what we have come to accept when someone shows us a viable alternative.

A **comparison-and-contrast** paper presents a special challenge to your ability to organize material. You will have to develop a strategy for laying out your material in such a way that your reader can see the points of comparison. The reader has to see important connections—whether unsuspected similarities or striking differences setting apart things that seem similar on the surface. Consider some familiar strategies for organizing a comparison and contrast of two poems:

✧ *You may want to develop a* **point-by-point** *comparison.* For instance, you may want to begin by showing how two poets share a distrust of "big words." This idea then provides the starting point both for your paper and for their poetic technique. You may go on to show how both poets rely on startling, thought-provoking images. Here you come to the heart of both your paper and of their way of writing poetry. You may conclude by showing how both nevertheless in the end spell out the kind of thought that serves as an *earned* conclusion, a generalization that the poem as a whole has worked out. Simplified, the scheme for such a point-by-point comparison might look like this:

> Point 1—poem A and then B
> Point 2—poem A and then B
> Point 3—poem A and then B

✧ *You may want to develop a* **parallel-order** *comparison.* You show first the distrust of abstractions, then the bold, provocative images, and finally the poet's spelling out of the theme in poem A. You then take these three points up again in the same, or parallel, order for poem B. This way you may be able to give your reader a better sense of how each poem works on its own terms, as a self-contained whole. However, you will have to make a special effort to remind your readers of what in the second poem is parallel to or different from what you showed in the first.

✧ *You may want to start from a common base.* You may want to emphasize similarities first. You may then want to go on to the significant differences. You might vary this strategy by starting with surface similarities that might deceive the casual observer. You then go on to essential distinctions.

How does the following student paper use or adapt these organizing strategies?

SAMPLE STUDENT PAPER

Today We Have Naming of Parts

Disillusioned by the experience of World War II, Henry Reed in "Naming of Parts" and Richard Eberhart in "The Fury of Aerial Bombardment" condemn and reject the horror of war. Both poems condemn our failure to see war as it is, attack our indifference, and reflect postwar antiwar feeling. We shall see that Eberhart's poem takes the attack on indifference one step further than Reed's poem does.

Henry Reed's "Naming of Parts" satirically attacks the callousness of the military. By using impersonal, neutral words and phrases ("Today we have naming of parts. Yesterday / We had daily cleaning"), the speaker satirizes how precise and impersonal these lessons are. The trainee learns a process, without being taught or made aware how terrible and ugly practicing that process is. References to "the lower sling swivel," "the upper sling swivel," and the "slings" describe machinery. Such references to mechanical parts evoke neutral or even positive feelings, since most machines are used for the good of humanity. This technical language conceals the horror of using this particular machinery. Saying that "you can do it quite easy / If you have any strength in your thumb" obscures the possibility that it might be difficult emotionally to gun down a fellow human being.

Reed uses a comparison to nature at the end of each stanza. Jumping from the mechanics of the gun to the beauty of the garden in consecutive sentences presents a contrast between the gun and the flower, the one a symbol of death and the other a symbol of life. The references in the first two stanzas stress the innocence of nature. The line "Japonica / Glistens like coral in all of the neighboring gardens" evokes an image of serenity and peace. The branches with "their silent, eloquent gestures" paint another image of bliss. The sterile descriptions of the gun and the beautiful descriptions of nature proceed in a point-counterpoint fashion.

Richard Eberhart's "The Fury of Aerial Bombardment" shares the theme of "Naming of Parts" in that both poems attack indifference to violence and suffering. By saying that "history, even, does not know what is meant," the poet seems to lament that even painful experience does not teach us to prevent the senselessness of war. We are "no farther advanced," making the poet ask: "Was man made stupid?" Here again, as in Reed's poem, technical, impersonal references to the "belt feed lever" and the "belt holding pawl" imply a criticism of the callousness with which people handle the subject of war. A lesson about a belt feed lever might be more instructive if the part were named the genocide lever, for instance.

However, "The Fury of Aerial Bombardment" contrasts with "Naming of Parts" because Eberhart goes beyond attacking human indifference by attacking divine indifference to the horrors of war. The poet questions why God has not intervened to stop the aerial bombardment. The answer, that "the infinite spaces / Are still silent," is a criticism of God's looking passively upon "shock-pried faces." These are the faces of the people who have witnessed the horror of the bombing but to whom God offers no respite. The poet seems to expect a thinking, feeling entity to intervene, but no such intervention takes place. Men still kill with "multitudinous will." In the third stanza, the poet asks: "Is God by definition indifferent, beyond us all?"

Both of these poems were written half a century ago, yet their relevance remains undiminished today. In an age when we read daily of war and death, indifference is commonplace. The way in which a news reporter casually reads death tolls from current conflicts is reminiscent of the cold, sterile wording of "Naming of Parts." The casual and callous projections of the cost in human lives of "winning" a nuclear war are another example of what is under attack in these poems. And people who ponder such atrocities as Auschwitz and Hiroshima have cause to question divine indifference, for the earth is long on suffering.

QUESTIONS

How convincing do the parallels between the two poems become in this paper? What are striking examples? How, according to this student writer, does the second poem go beyond the first? For you, do the two poems seem dated, or do they seem still relevant today?

22 MYTH AND ALLUSION
Twice-Told Tales

*The capacity to personify, mythologize, imagine,
harmonize, improvise, is one of the great mercies granted
in human life.*

STEPHEN NACHMANOVITCH

*Myths are public dreams; dreams are private myths. Myths
are vehicles of communication between the conscious and
the unconscious just as dreams are.*

JOSEPH CAMPBELL

The mythic journey is as ancient as the human race itself.

JOHN A. ALLEN

FOCUS ON MYTH

Myths (from *mythos,* the Greek word for tale) are stories about gods, monsters, and heroes. Myths are rooted in prehistoric oral tradition. People heard them in a spirit of religious awe, listening for clues to the nature of the mysterious universe in which they lived. Creation myths celebrated genesis— the creation of the earth, of man and woman, or of the alternation of sun and moon. In the dark of winter, myths of rebirth kept alive the faith in renewal, in the return of spring. In the prehistoric past, our ancestors listened to stories about how death entered the world or about the titanic struggle between good and evil. Often myths were embedded in **rituals** that acted out a mythical story or celebrated a godlike champion or redeemer.

In literal-minded times, the word *myth* has meant "superstition," to be swept away by the march of science. (In the language of politics, *myth* is a fancy word for a lie concocted by a self-serving opponent.) However, our modern world has seen a resurgence of interest in myth as a mirror—often obscure and tantalizing—of deep-seated human needs and feelings. What fascinates modern scholars is that many ancient myths have parallels in diverse cultures. It is as if recurrent mythical patterns were part of our collective consciousness, wired into the collective memory of the human race.

The American poet Stanley Kunitz said, "Old myths, old gods, old heroes have never died. They are only sleeping at the bottom of our minds, waiting for our call." Some of the myths "sleeping at the bottom of our minds" have had a special fascination for moderns. For instance, in traditions from many sources, we see a mythical god-king undergo a ritual of death and mourning, followed by rebirth or resurrection. We witness a cycle of defeat, death, and triumphant return. In the words of Joseph Campbell, we see different incarnations of "a hero with a thousand faces." Students of myth, from nineteenth-century anthropologists to today's feminist scholars, have reconstructed myths about the earth goddess that echo in the earliest lore of the Middle East, cradle of Western civilization. These myths give a voice to the need for bonding and nurturing essential for human survival. The Babylonian Ishtar and the Greek Demeter, goddess of the harvest, may hark back to a phase of human culture centered on the worship of a life-giving and life-preserving feminine principle.

Myth detects the long, slow rhythms of human experience that drum beneath the short staccato beats of short-range events. Many myths focus on **archetypal** experiences and needs that are constants in the lives of people from different cultures. Many cultures, for instance, have myths about the fire bringer—who brings the fire that symbolizes warmth, the hearth, survival, permanence, the light of knowledge. The fire bringer in Greek mythology was Prometheus, who defied the king of the gods by returning to humanity the fire that Zeus had meant to deny them. To poets and artists of later generations, Prometheus became a symbol of aspiration, of rebellion, of determination "to defy power, which seems omnipotent" (Percy Bysshe Shelley, *Prometheus Unbound*). We still call people Promethean who are willing to test the boundaries, to reach for what was thought unattainable.

Poets and artists discovered in myth and legend rich sources of symbol and allusion. An **allusion** is a brief mention that calls up a whole story, rich in overtones and associations. A single word, a single name, may activate a whole network of memories. When a poet alludes to Cassandra, we see with the mind's eye the Trojan princess to whom the god Apollo had given the gift of foreseeing the future—and the curse of not being believed. In her mad ravings, she foresaw the death of Hector, the Trojan champion; she saw Troy in flames, the towers falling down, the men killed, the women sold into slavery. But no one believed her. As Robinson Jeffers says in his poem "Cassandra," people truly "hate the truth"; they would sooner

Meet a tiger on the road.
Therefore the poets honey their truth with lying.

The following example shows the central role allusion can play in a poem. The central figure in the poem is a balloon vendor who is literally lame. But the poet calls him "goat-footed"—a hint that we may be watching a half-human, half-animal mythic creature.

E. E. CUMMINGS (1894–1963) 1923

in Just-

in Just-
spring   when the world is mud-
luscious the little
lame balloonman

whistles   far   and wee 5

and eddieandbill come
running from marbles and
piracies and it's
spring

when the world is puddle-wonderful 10

the queer
old balloonman whistles
far   and   wee
and bettyandisbel come dancing

from hop-scotch and jump-rope and 15

it's
spring
and
　　the

　　　　goat-footed 20

balloonMan   whistles
far
and
wee

Who has goat's feet and whistles? Pan, Greek god of flocks and shepherds, often appears in works of art as a sensual being with horns, a snub nose, and goat's feet. He is often shown dancing or playing the shepherd's flute, which he had invented. Often, he is leading the dances of the nymphs, or female woodland creatures. In later times, he is often shown as one of a group of goat-footed satyrs, fond of wine and sensual pleasures.

In short, Pan is one of the many lesser semidivine beings who, in Greek mythology, populate nature. They turn it from an alien, savage place into a world full of breathing, sensitive life. For cummings, Pan became a fitting symbol of spring—of the spirit of joy, mirth, frolic, holiday, or fiesta. It is a time of children dancing and skipping—as the poem itself skips over the printed page. The goat-footed balloonman (Pan in a modern disguise) becomes a symbol of innocent pleasure that children enjoy but that grownups seem to lose as they become neurotic, frustrated adults.

THE RECEPTIVE READER

1. What is "luscious" about mud or "wonderful" about puddles?

2. How should the poem *sound* when read aloud? How does it "dance out" the dancing and skipping it describes?

3. How does the poet use *repetition* and pauses to highlight, to focus our attention?

4. Do you think this poem would work for readers who have never heard of Pan? Why or why not?

THE RANGE OF ALLUSION

People do gossip
And they say about
Leda, that she
Once found an egg
hidden under
wild hyacinths
SAPPHO

Allusion is a kind of shorthand. What, in so many words, does a writer mean when saying, "We are all Custer"? The short, cryptic statement encloses layers of meaning that we can peel away like the layers of an onion. Some of the meaning is close to the surface: George Armstrong Custer was an American general in command of the U.S. Seventh Cavalry. He attacked a large encampment of the Sioux or Lakota on the Little Big Horn in 1876. He was killed with most of his men in the last desperate battle the Lakota fought against the invaders. The allusion here, however, says more: As Americans, it suggests, we are all implicated in a history that pitted the U.S. Cavalry against the native American tribes, ravaged by the starvation and disease the white settlers had brought. We share the guilt for the massacre at Wounded Knee, where men, women, and children were gunned down.

Richly allusive poetry assumes a shared cultural tradition that allows the poet to play on a common knowledge of myth, legend, and history. The language of allusion is as much a shared language as the language of the computer age—and it similarly challenges the uninitiated. One large source of allusion is **Greek mythology**—the body of myths and legends poets inherited from the civilization of ancient, classical Greece. What kind of cultural literacy does the poet assume in the following poem? What is the poet's range of allusion?

WILLIAM BUTLER YEATS   (1865–1939)
Leda and the Swan   1923

A sudden blow: the great wings beating still
Above the staggering girl, her thighs caressed
By the dark webs, her nape caught in his bill,
He holds her helpless breast upon his breast.

How can those terrified vague fingers push   5
The feathered glory from her loosening thighs?
And how can body, laid in that white rush,
But feel the strange heart beating where it lies?

A shudder in the loins engenders there
The broken wall, the burning roof and tower   10
And Agamemnon dead.

                        Being so caught up,
So mastered by the brute blood of the air,
Did she put on his knowledge with his power
Before the indifferent beak could let her drop?   15

The terrifying swan is a mythic creature: Zeus, the king of the Olympian gods (the Greek gods, residing on Mount Olympus) has assumed the shape of an animal. The offspring of his union with Leda is going to be Helen, whose abduction by the Trojan prince Paris will launch the "thousand ships" of the Greek war against Troy. The "broken wall, the burning roof and tower" call up before our eyes the city of Troy being reduced to rubble and ashes in defeat. In the aftermath of the war, Agamemnon, the leader of the Greek forces, will return home after years of absence, to be murdered by his wife Clytemnestra and her lover Aegisthus.

THE RECEPTIVE READER

Through the centuries, the world of Greek myth has offered artists and poets an alternative universe, where imaginings repressed in ordinary society could be enacted and explored. In the world of Greek myth, animals often do not have derogatory connotations. What are the connotations of the animal in Yeats' poem? Is the swan mostly beast? human? divine?

Helen of Troy—the daughter of Zeus, who had made love to Leda in the shape of a swan—was often blamed for the bloody conflict between Greece and Troy. Helen had married Menelaus, king of Sparta, and she incurred the hatred of her fellow Greeks when she allowed the "firebrand" Trojan prince Paris to carry her away to Troy, thus causing the bloody Trojan war. What two different ways of viewing Helen contend in the following poem?

H. D. (HILDA DOOLITTLE) (1886–1961)
Helen   1924

All Greece hates
the still eyes in the white face,
the luster as of olives
where she stands,
And the white hands.   5

All Greece reviles
the wan face when she smiles,
hating it deeper still
when it grows wan and white,
remembering past enchantments   10
And past ills.

Greece sees unmoved,
God's daughter, born of love,
the beauty of cool feet
and slenderest knees,   15
could love indeed the maid,
only if she were laid,
white ash amid funereal cypresses.

THE RECEPTIVE READER

1. How does the poet emphasize and drive home the unrelenting hate felt for
Helen by her countrymen and countrywomen?

2. What labels that the poet applies to Helen and what descriptive details *counteract*
these powerful negative feelings, and how? Explore as fully as you can the connotations—
associations, implications—of words like *luster, enchantments, maid,* and of phrases like
"God's daughter, born of love" and "beauty of cool feet / and slenderest knees."

3. Is the poet herself taking sides? As you read the poem, are you?

EXPLORATIONS

Understanding Allusions

In a dictionary or other reference work, look up the allusions in the following lines. What does a reader have to know to catch the allusion? What network of meanings and associations is the allusion supposed to activate? How
might these associations vary for different readers?

1. Janus writes books for women's liberation;
   His wife types up the scripts from his dictation.
   Laurence Perrine, "Janus"

2. But Ariadne's eyes are lakes
   Beside the maze's starwhite wall:
   For in the Caribbean midnight
   Of her wild and gentle wisdom, she foreknows
   And solves the maze's cruel algebra.
   Thomas Merton, "Ariadne"

3. Something is always approaching; every day
   Till then we say,
   Watching from a bluff the tiny, clear,
   Sparkling armada of promises draw near,
   How slow they are! And how much time they waste,
   Refusing to make haste!
   Philip Larkin, "Next, Please"

JUXTAPOSITIONS

The Sacrifice of Isaac

For many centuries, allusions to the Bible have been woven into the language of poets and artists. Old Testament themes like Cain's fratricide, Noah's flood, or David slaying Goliath are part of our collective memory bank of archetypes and symbols. New Testament parables like those of the Good Samaritan help shape our thinking on subjects like charity. The sacrifice of Isaac as the Lord's test of Abraham's obedience has long been a favorite subject for artists. Compare the Old Testament story with its use by a twentieth-century poet.

GENESIS (22:1–13)

And it came to pass after these things that God did tempt Abraham and said unto him, Abraham: and he said, Behold, here I am.

And he said, Take now thy son, thine only son Isaac, whom thou lovest, and get thee into the land of Moriah; and offer him there for a burnt offering upon one of the mountains which I will tell thee of.

And Abraham rose up early in the morning, and saddled his ass, and took two of his young men with him, and Isaac his son, and clave the wood for the burnt offering, and rose up, and went unto the place of which God had told him.

Then on the third day Abraham lifted up his eyes, and saw the place afar off.

And Abraham said unto his young men, Abide ye here with the ass; and I and the lad will go yonder and worship, and come again to you.

And Abraham took the wood of the burnt offering, and laid it upon Isaac his son; and he took the fire in his hand, and a knife; and they went both of them together.

And Isaac spake unto Abraham his father, and said, My father: and he said, Here am I, my son. And he said, Behold the fire and the wood: but where is the lamb for a burnt offering?

And Abraham said, My son, God will provide himself a lamb for a burnt offering: so they went both of them together.

And they came to the place which God had told him of; and Abraham built an altar there, and laid the wood in order, and bound Isaac his son, and laid him on the altar upon the wood.

And Abraham stretched forth his hand, and took the knife to slay his son.

And the angel of the Lord called unto him out of heaven, and said, Abraham, Abraham: and he said, Here am I.

And he said, Lay not thine hand upon the lad, neither do thou anything unto him: for now I know that thou fearest God, seeing thou hast not withheld thy son, thine only son from me.

And Abraham lifted up his eyes, and looked, and behold behind him a ram caught in a thicket by his horns: and Abraham went and took the ram, and offered him up for a burnt offering in the stead of his son.

Wilfred Owen wrote his adaptation of the biblical story during the years of trench warfare in World War I, when Britain, France, and Germany were sacrificing the lives of hundreds of thousands of young men. How far and how closely does the poet follow the biblical story? When do you first realize that Owen has transposed the story from its ancient setting? How does he change the climactic ending of the story?

WILFRED OWEN (1893–1918)
The Parable of the Old Men and the Young   1918

So Abram rose, and clave the wood, and went,
And took the fire with him, and a knife.
And as they journeyed both of them together,
Isaac the first-born spake and said, My Father,
Behold the preparations, fire and iron,   5
But where the lamb for this burnt-offering?
Then Abram bound the youth with belts and straps,
And builded parapets and trenches there,
And stretched forth the knife to slay his son.
When lo! an angel called him out of heaven,   10
Saying, Lay not thy hand upon the lad,
Neither do anything to him. Behold,
A ram caught in a thicket by its horns;
Offer the Ram of Pride instead of him.
But the old man would not so, but slew his son—   15
And half the seed of Europe, one by one.

THE RECEPTIVE READER

1. What are the *common* elements in both versions of the story?

2. How has the poet *changed* the meaning of the test undergone by Abraham? What does the "Ram of Pride" stand for? Who or what is the target of Owen's indictment?

3. What biblical *parables* do you know? How is this poem like a parable? Why does the poet's use of the biblical story give his indictment special force?

THE LANGUAGE OF MYTH

> . . . *still the heart doth need a language, still
> Doth the old instinct bring back the old names.*
> SAMUEL TAYLOR COLERIDGE

> *Man today, stripped of myth, stands famished among all
> his pasts and must dig frantically for roots, even if among
> the most remote antiquities.*
> FRIEDRICH NIETZSCHE

Often a myth seems to find an echo deep in our minds and feelings. It seems to act out for us deep-rooted patterns in human experience. To many modern readers, myths have seemed, in the words of the psychoanalyst Carl Jung, "still fresh and living" in the hidden recesses of their minds. Anthropologists and psychoanalysts have probed recurrent **archetypes**—symbolic embodiments of vital forces and life cycles that we encounter in many disguises and variations. The earliest religions may have centered on mother goddesses associated with the development of agriculture and worshiped in fertility cults. Such earth goddesses were Ishtar of Mesopotamia (now Iraq) or Cybele of Asia Minor (now Turkey). To some contemporary feminist poets, they symbolize the human need for bonding and for living in harmony with the generative forces in nature.

JUDY GRAHN (born 1940)
They Say She Is Veiled   1982

They say she is veiled
and a mystery. That is
one way of looking.
Another
is that she is where   5
she has always been,
exactly in place,
and it is we,
we who are mystified,
we who are veiled   10
and without faces.

THE RECEPTIVE READER

How does the poet play on the words *mystery* and *mystified*? What are the two ways "of looking" in this poem?

In Greek myth, the earth mother or "grain mother" is Demeter, the goddess of the harvest, who sustains and nourishes all that lives on land, in the sea, and in the air. When her daughter Persephone was abducted by Hades, the king of the netherworld, the distraught mother wandered in search of her, and warmth and light left the earth, ice and snow covered the land, and the fields turned barren. (Roman poets later called mother and daughter by their Latin names, Ceres and Proserpina.)

When Demeter finally found her daughter, she appealed to Zeus, the king of the gods, to let Persephone return to the light. However, once visitors to the world below had shared food with the dead, they were doomed to stay. Persephone had eaten only four of the juicy red seeds that make up the rich meaty center of the pomegranate fruit. So Zeus ruled that she would be able to rejoin her mother for part of the year but that she would have to spend four months each year with Hades in the regions of hell. When she returns to earth in the spring, grass sprouts on the hills, and flowers break through the earth's crust. To celebrate her daughter's return, Demeter causes the wheat to turn rich and golden on its stalks; clusters of grapes swell on the vines. Sheep and cattle turn plump and sleek, ready for sacrifice. The people raise their voices in thanksgiving to the

> Sacred Goddess, Mother Earth,
> Thou from whose immortal bosom
> Gods, and men, and beasts have birth.
> > Percy Bysshe Shelley, "Song of Proserpine"

At times, poets have immersed themselves in Greek myth as a world more attuned than grey reality to their needs as imaginative, passionate human beings. English Romantic poets like John Keats and Percy Bysshe Shelley take us to classical Greece (of the sixth or fifth century B.C.) as the ideal homeland of the artistic imagination. In his "Ode on a Grecian Urn," Keats calls up before our eyes mythological scenes of the kind he may have seen sculpted in marble or as vase paintings on ancient Greek amphoras (literally vases with two handles).

The **ode** is a Greek form with elaborately crafted stanzas fit for solemn subjects. As we read the stanzas of the ode, Keats makes us see the scenes we would see pictured on the urn as we slowly turn it. In the first three stanzas, we see young men (or gods?) pursuing young women in a forest setting. In the third stanza, we see a musician playing a shepherd's flute in a springtime setting of fresh leaves and flowers. In the fourth stanza, we see a religious procession leading an animal to the altar for sacrifice. Contemplating these scenes, Keats re-creates for us a mythical world closer to the heart's desire than inadequate reality. Here, gods and mortals intermingle, the music of flutes and drums resounds in forest glades, and the rich ceremonial of a religious holiday satisfies our yearning for dignity, grace, and beauty.

Like other poems taking us to the world of Greek mythology, the poem assumes a reader steeped in classical tradition. The setting is Greek: *Tempe* is a beautiful valley in Greece; *Arcady* (or Arcadia) is a Greek mountain region symbolic of idyllic, carefree country life. An *Attic* shape is from Attica, the region around Athens. Keats calls the urn a cold (that is, not moving or breathing) *pastoral* because, like traditional pastoral poetry, it takes us to fields and meadows, where *pastors,* or shepherds, tend their sheep. The *pipes* and *timbrels* are the simple flutes and small drums of early Greek times.

JOHN KEATS   (1795–1821)

Ode on a Grecian Urn   1819

1
Thou still unravished bride of quietness,
    Thou foster-child of silence and slow time,
Sylvan° historian, who canst thus express   *of the woods*
    A flowery tale more sweetly than our rhyme:
What leaf-fringed legend haunts about thy shape   5

Of deities or mortals, or of both,
    In Tempe or the dales° of Arcady?   *valleys*
    What men or gods are these? What maidens loth?°   *unwilling*
What mad pursuit? What struggle to escape?
      What pipes and timbrels? What wild ecstasy?   10

2

Heard melodies are sweet, but those unheard
    Are sweeter; therefore, ye soft pipes, play on;
Not to the sensual ear, but, more endeared,
    Pipe to the spirit ditties° of no tone: *songs*
Fair youth, beneath the trees, thou canst not leave   15
    Thy song, nor ever can those trees be bare;
      Bold Lover, never, never canst thou kiss,
Though winning near the goal—yet, do not grieve;
      She cannot fade, though thou hast not thy bliss,
    For ever wilt thou love, and she be fair!   20

3

Ah, happy, happy boughs! that cannot shed
    Your leaves, nor ever bid the Spring adieu;°   *farewell*
And, happy melodist,° unwearièd,   *musician*
    For ever piping songs for ever new;
More happy love! more happy, happy love!   25
    For ever warm and still to be enjoyed,
      For ever panting, and for ever young;
All breathing human passion far above,
    That leaves a heart high-sorrowful and cloyed,
      A burning forehead, and a parching tongue.   30

4

Who are these coming to the sacrifice?
    To what green altar, O mysterious priest,
Lead'st thou that heifer° lowing at the skies,   *young cow*
    And all her silken flanks with garlands dressed?
What little town by river or sea shore,   35
    Or mountain-built with peaceful citadel,°   *fortress*
      Is emptied of this folk, this pious morn?
And, little town, thy streets for evermore
    Will silent be; and not a soul to tell
      Why thou art desolate, can e'er° return.   *ever*   40

5

O Attic shape! Fair attitude! with brede°   *interwoven pattern*
    Of marble men and maidens overwrought,
With forest branches and the trodden weed;
    Thou, silent form, dost tease us out of thought
As doth eternity: Cold Pastoral!   45
    When old age shall this generation waste,
      Thou shalt remain, in midst of other woe
    Than ours, a friend to man, to whom thou say'st,
"Beauty is truth, truth beauty,"— that is all
    Ye know on earth, and all ye need to know.   50

In this poem, the language of myth provides the medium for the Romantic rebellion against the ordinary. The silent shape of the urn is able to "tease us out of" our ordinary dejected thoughts. The time travel of the poetic imagination takes us from the grimy city to a forest setting where lovers experience passion and "wild ecstasy." Later, instead of going about our dull routine chores, we participate with the priest and pious worshipers in the procession that takes the heifer bedecked with garlands to the sacrifice.

Paradoxically, however, we see nature here not face to face but in the mirror of art. The lovers are not flesh and blood; the music ("the spirit ditties of no tone") remains "unheard." The urn freezes a moment in time and preserves it for future generations. We may think these cold, frozen images inferior to warm breathing life, but they are really superior, because they are not corruptible, not subject to corruption and change. Living and "breathing human passion" leaves the heart "high-sorrowful and cloyed." Therefore, the unheard melodies are "sweeter." In the context of timeless art, beauty cannot fade, and love cannot fade, into the light of common day. The lovers in the poem, stopped in mid-course, will never attain the object of their quest—but they will therefore never lose it either. Art—whether the poet's, the sculptor's, or the potter's art—triumphs over decay and outlasts the ravages of time.

The poem culminates in the credo of the poet starved for beauty and passion in an unimaginative society: "Beauty is truth, truth beauty." That is all we need to know. This conclusion gives trouble to skeptical readers: Beauty is only skin deep, they say. Surface beauty may be a thin varnish covering ugly truths. But the speaker in the poem seems certain of the beauty of truth and the truth of beauty. This, for him, is the message of the urn. As Keats said in one of his letters, "I am certain of the heart's affection and the truth of imagination—What the imagination seizes as beauty must be truth." Art and poetry celebrate not surface prettiness but an indwelling unity and harmony that make life meaningful and the world livable.

THE RECEPTIVE READER

1. In your own words, how or why is the vase the "still unravished bride of quietness"?

2. What is the poet's view of "breathing human passion" in the real world?

3. Why are the "unheard" melodies of the vase sweeter than heard ones? What is the advantage that art has over nature?

THE PERSONAL RESPONSE

As you see it, is the truth ever beautiful? Or is it more likely to be ugly? Does the phrase "Beauty is truth" in some way have meaning for you?

THE CREATIVE DIMENSION

Museum-goers and gallery-goers (and readers of art books) experience thoughts and feelings that they often do not put into words. Verbalize the thoughts and feelings passing through your mind as you look at a work of art (or architecture) that your readers might recognize. For instance, write about the Mona Lisa, a Chagall painting, Michelangelo's "Creation of Adam" from the Sistine Chapel, the Lincoln Memorial, or the New York World Trade Center.

JUXTAPOSITIONS

The Icarus Myth

A universally known Greek myth is the story of Daedalus and Icarus. Daedalus fashioned wings for himself and his son Icarus, but as Icarus flew too close to the sun, the wax gluing the feathers in his wings melted and he perished in the sea. We know the Icarus story best in the version of the Roman poet Ovid (43 B.C.–A.D. 18), who in his *Metamorphoses* rewrote many of the ancient stories. The myth is part of a web of stories taking place on the island of Crete, where Pasiphaë, the queen of King Minos, had been consumed by tormented longing for a beautiful white bull and given birth to monstrous offspring, half man, half bull—the Minotaur. Daedalus was the Athenian inventor employed by King Minos to build the maze, or labyrinth, designed to pen in the Minotaur. Afterwards, when Minos refused Daedalus' request to let him and his son return to Athens, Daedalus constructed wings from feathers and wax so that father and son could make their escape through the air. Ovid concludes his retelling of the myth as follows:

> When the boy, too bold, too young, too ambitious in daring,
> Forced his way too high, leaving his father below,
> So the bonds of the wings were loosened, the fastenings melted,
> Nor could the moving arms hold in the desert of air.
> Panic seized him: he stared from heaven's height at the water;
> In the rush of his fear, darkness brimmed in his eyes.
> All of the wax was gone: his arms were bare as he struggled
> Beating the void of the air, unsupported, unstayed.
> "Father!" he cried as he fell, "Oh, father, father, I'm falling!"
> Till the green of the wave closed on the agonized cry,
> While the father, alas, a father no longer, was calling,
> "Icarus, where do you fly, Icarus, where in the sky?
> Icarus!" he would call—and saw the wings on the water.
> Now earth covers his bones; now that sea has his name.
> Translated by Rolfe Humphries

Different readers have used the traditional story as a prompt to construct their own private myths. Here are some of the readings:

✧ The myth acts out the age-old archetypes of impetuous, headstrong, ambitious youth and cautious, prudent, shell-shocked age.

✧ The myth focuses on the theme of overreaching, of overambitious, heedless pride that goes before a fall. In the words of a student reader, "Each time we dare, we taunt the gods a little." The Greeks called arrogant human pride *hubris*, and they expected it to provoke the wrath of the gods.

✧ The myth glorifies the human capacity for aspiration, for "testing the boundaries." Flight has long been a symbol for our human capacity to struggle up from the mud and clay, even at the risk of failure.

✧ The myth drives home the tragic irony of gallant effort coming to grief. It focuses on the agony of "almost-was"—we come close to triumph; we can see success within reach, yet it eludes our grasp.

✧ The myth focuses on the strongest kind of human love—the love of a parent for a child.

Look at the treatment of the Icarus myth in the following modern poems. What is the meaning of the myth for each poet?

A N N E   S E X T O N   (1928–1974)

To a Friend Whose Work Has Come to Triumph   1962

Consider Icarus, pasting those sticky wings on,
testing that strange little tug at his shoulder blade,
and think of that first flawless moment over the lawn
of the labyrinth. Think of the difference it made!
There below are the trees, as awkward as camels;   5
and here are the shocked starlings pumping past
and think of innocent Icarus who is doing quite well;
larger than a sail, over the fog and blast
of the plushy ocean he goes. Admire his wings!
Feel the fire at his neck and see how casually   10
he glances up and is caught, wondrously tunneling
into that hot eye. Who cares that he fell back into the sea?
See him acclaiming the sun and come plunging down
while his sensible daddy goes straight into town.

THE RECEPTIVE READER

1. Traditionally, people have listened to myths with grave attention. What details and imaginative comparisons give this poem a more irreverent or *ironic* modern twist?

2. What in the poem could lead a reader to conclude that nevertheless the myth has a serious meaning for the modern poet? What is the *theme* of this poem?

3. Both form and content of this poem play modern variations on traditional patterns. How does this fourteen-line poem live up to the requirements of the traditional *sonnet*? How does it depart from them?

The poem that follows gives us a retelling that takes us "down to earth" in its search for the reality behind the mythical tradition. The poem thus becomes a modern countermyth in which the ancient story becomes demythologized and the original heroes become modern antiheroes. The tone is irreverent toward both gods and human beings. How much does the poem preserve of the spirit or appeal of the original myth?

DAVID WAGONER   (born 1926)

The Return of Icarus   1958

He showed up decades later, crook-necked and hip-sprung,
Not looking for work but cadging food and wine as artfully
As a king, while our dogs barked themselves inside out
At the sight of his hump and a whiff of his goatskin.

We told him Daedalus was dead, worn out with honors   5
(Some of them fabulous), but especially for making
Wings for the two of them and getting them off the ground.
He said he remembered that time, but being too young a mooncalf,

He hadn't cared about those labyrinthine double-dealings
Except for the scary parts, the snorting and bellowing.   10
He'd simply let the wax be smeared over his arms
And suffered handfuls of half-stuck second-hand chicken feathers

And flapped and flapped, getting the heft of them, and taken
Off (to both their amazements), listening for his father's
Endless, garbled, and finally inaudible instructions   15
From further and further below, and then swooping

And banking and trying to hover without a tail and stalling
While the old man, a slow learner, got the hang of it.
At last, with the weight of his years and his genius,
Daedalus thrashed aloft and was gawkily airborne.   20

And they went zigzagging crosswing and downwind over the water,
Half-baked by the sirocco,° with Daedalus explaining   *hot wind*
Everything now: which way was up, how to keep your mouth
Shut for the purpose of breathing and listening,

How to fly low (having no choice himself) in case of Harpies,°   *monstrous birds* 25
And how to keep Helios° beaming at a comfortable distance   *the sun*
By going no higher than the absolute dangling minimum
To avoid kicking Poseidon,° the old salt, square in the froth.   *god of the sea*

But Icarus saw the wax at his skinny quill-tips sagging,
And he couldn't get a word in edgewise or otherwise,   30
So he strained even higher, searching for ships or landfalls
While he still had time to enjoy his share of the view,

And in the bright, high-spirited silence, he took comfort
From his father's lack of advice, and Helios turned
Cool, not hot as Icarus rose, joining a wedge of geese   35
For an embarrassing, exhilarating moment northward,

And then he grew cold till the wax turned brittle as marble,
Stiffening his elbows and suddenly breaking
Away, leaving him wingless, clawing at nothing, then falling
Headfirst with a panoramic, panchromatic vista   40

Of the indifferent sun, the indifferent ocean, and a blurred
Father passing sideways, still chugging and flailing away

With rows of eagle feathers. When Icarus hit the water,
He took its salt as deeply as his own.

He didn't tell us how he'd paddled ashore or where 45
He'd been keeping himself or what in the world he'd been doing
For a living, yet he didn't seem bitter. "Too bad
You weren't around," we said, "there'd have been something in it

For you, probably—an apartment straddling an aqueduct,
Orchards, invitations, hecatombs° of women."   *crowds (as in communal tombs)* 50
"No hard feelings," he said. "Wings weren't my idea."
And he told odd crooked stories to children for hours

About what lived under water, what lived under the earth,
And what still lived in the air, and why. A few days later
He slouched off on his game leg and didn't come back. 55
He didn't steal any chickens or girls' hearts

Or ask after his father's grave or his father's money
Or even kick the dogs. But he showed us calluses
Thicker than hooves on his soles and palms, and told us
That's how he'd stay in touch, keeping his feet on the ground. 60

THE RECEPTIVE READER

1. How does the first stanza signal that the ancient story is again being retold with a modern twist? How does it realign your perspective?

2. How does this retelling redraw the portrait of the father? How does it change your image of the father and your image of the young son? How does it reinterpret or refashion the relationship between father and son?

3. In the retelling of the flight, which parts of it are *humorous;* which seem serious?

4. For you, does the last line of the poem spell out the *theme* of the poem? Does it point a moral? Does it strike the keynote for the poem as a whole?

5. What is witty about the *allusion* in the father's "labyrinthine double-dealings" and the "snorting and bellowing"? What other references remind you that we are in the world of Greek mythology?

THE PERSONAL RESPONSE

Do this poet's changes in the story make the myth more believable or less?

The following modern sonnet strips the Icarus myth of many of its traditional trappings. There is no literal flight in this poem—no flying with false feathers like the original Icarus, nor flying in a metal bird that shears the clouds and becomes a menace to real birds. Perhaps we thus get to the mythic core of the ancient story. The flight of Icarus here becomes a central extended metaphor: The flights here are "imaged" flights, journeys of the mind. Although our bodies are earthbound, our minds are capable of tremendous flights of the imagination, making us outsoar the highest reaches of heaven and making us plummet to deepest hell.

VASSAR MILLER (born 1924)

The New Icarus   1956

Slip off the husk of gravity to lie
Bedded with wind; float on a whimsy, lift
Upon a wish: your bow's own arrow, rift
Newton's decorum—only when you fly.
But naked. No false-feathered fool, you try   5
Dalliance with heights, nor, plumed with metal, shift
And shear the clouds, imperiling lark and swift
And all birds bridal-bowered in the sky.
Your wreck of bone, barred their delight's dominions,   ←
Lacking their formula for flight, holds imaged   10
Those alps of air no eagle's wing can quell.
With arms flung crosswise, pinioned to wooden pinions,
You in one motion, plucked and crimson-plumaged,
Outsoar all Heaven, plummeting all Hell.

THE RECEPTIVE READER

1. Examine the poet's graphic *metaphors*. What is exceptionally appropriate or fitting about the image she creates by the phrase "Slip off the husk of gravity"?

2. Look at the *paradoxical* metaphors—metaphors that at first glance seem contradictory or physically impossible: How could the person addressed be told to be "your bow's own arrow"? (We propel our imaginary selves on the imagined voyage with the force of our own will and desire; these serve as the bow shooting forth ourselves as the arrow.) What do you make of the paradoxical "plumed with metal" or "alps of air"? What sense do they make on second thought?

3. The *allusion* to Newton, master physicist and mathematician of the eighteenth century, makes us think of Newtonian science. We are expected to think of a mechanistic model of the universe, where everything behaves according to the strict laws of physics—as if in accordance with strict etiquette or "decorum." How would the new Icarus "rift / Newton's decorum"?

4. The *pun* in the phrase "pinioned [fastened, shackled] to wooden pinions [wings]" makes us imagine a person with arms flung wide and fastened to the wooden wings as to a cross. Are you prepared to agree with the student who wrote the following passage about the possible religious implications of the poem?

> The new Icarus is Christ, whose "wreck of bone" finds salvation through suffering. Christ "pinioned to wooden pinions" and "crimson-plumaged" reaches heights of love that ancient humanity (Icarus) or modern humanity, "plumed with metal" of modern airplanes, will never outsoar. Living the life of the spirit incurs a great risk, since it can bring suffering , a "plummeting" to "all Hell." However, although Christ lacks the birds' "formula for flight," he can go the eagle one better. He can rise from his "plucked" "wreck of bone" to "those alps of air no eagle's wing can quell." Despite being nailed to the cross, "pinioned to wooden pinions," he can "in one motion . . . Outsoar all Heaven."

The following poem is one of several commenting on the painting "The Fall of Icarus" by the Flemish painter Pieter Breughel (about 1525–1569). How does the poem put the mythical story in perspective?

WILLIAM CARLOS WILLIAMS (1883–1963)
Landscape with the Fall of Icarus   1960

According to Breughel
when Icarus fell
it was spring

a farmer was plowing
his field   5
the whole pageantry

of the year was
awake tingling
near

the edge of the sea   10
concerned with itself
sweating in the sun
that melted the wings' wax

unsignificantly
off the coast   15
there was

a splash quite unnoticed
this was
Icarus drowning

CROSS-REFERENCES—For Discussion or Writing

Explore the versions of the Icarus myth found in these poems. What do they show about the perennial or universal appeal of the myth? What do they show about the difference between more traditional and more modern perspectives? Which of the poems do you find most congenial or personally appealing and why?

THE CREATIVE DIMENSION

Write your own personal version of the Icarus myth or of another myth that you have known for some time.

MODERN MYTHS

goddess of the silver screen
the only original American queen
JUDY GRAHN, "HELEN IN HOLLYWOOD"

Although many myths are age-old, we can see the mythmaking faculty at work in our own time. The lone rider of the American frontier assumed mythical proportions in the cowboy myth that is at the heart of our popular culture. Its central figure, like the mythical heroes of the past, appears in countless permutations, from Buffalo Bill to space-age cowboys like Captain Kirk. To city-dwellers hemmed in by the restrictions and annoyances of city life, the cowboy seems to stimulate a collective memory of wide-open spaces, of depending on oneself, of being able to move on.

The Hollywood dream factory created mythical sex goddesses. Norma Jean Baker was turned into Marilyn Monroe, who became the daydream of every immature male: "Marilyn, who was every man's love affair . . . who was blonde and beautiful and had a little rinky-dink of a voice . . . which carried such ripe overtones of erotic excitement and yet was the voice of a little child" (Norman Mailer, *Marilyn*). After her death, admirers and defenders created the countermyth of the actress rebelling against the stereotype of the dumb screen blonde that denied her her own humanity—Marilyn "who tried, I believe, to help us see that beauty has a mind of its own" (Judy Grahn).

SHARON OLDS   (born 1942)
The Death of Marilyn Monroe   1983

The ambulance men touched her cold
body, lifted it, heavy as iron,
onto the stretcher, tried to close the
mouth, closed the eyes, tied the
arms to the sides, moved a caught   5
strand of hair, as if it mattered,
saw the shape of her breasts, flattened by
gravity, under the sheet,
carried her, as if it were she,
down the steps.   10

These men were never the same. They went out
afterwards, as they always did,
for a drink or two, but they could not meet
each other's eyes.

        Their lives took   15
a turn—one had nightmares, strange
pains, impotence, depression. One did not
like his work, his wife looked
different, his kids. Even death
seemed different to him—a place where she   20
would be waiting,

And one found himself standing at night
in the doorway to a room of sleep, listening to
a woman breathing, just an ordinary
woman   25
breathing.

THE RECEPTIVE READER

1. What was the cause of Marilyn Monroe's death?
2. Why were the men in the poem "never the same"? What is the *mythic* or symbolic significance of Monroe in this poem?
3. Has popular entertainment left the *stereotype* of the Hollywood blonde behind?
4. Is the Marilyn Monroe myth alive?

THE CREATIVE DIMENSION

What is the keynote of this poem for you? What lasting impression does it leave in your mind? Look at the following re-creation by a fellow student, and then write your own.

Those ambulance men
shocked into recognition of death and tenuous life
shifted the body
prepared her for the journey
The body wasn't going anywhere special
they were
One to nightmares, strangeness
Another to dislike, to fear
The last to listening.

How does the following poem rewrite the cowboy myth?

E. E. CUMMINGS (1894–1963)

Portrait   1923

Buffalo Bill's
defunct
        who used to
        ride a watersmooth-silver
                                    stallion   5
and break onetwothreefourfive pigeonsjustlikethat
                        Jesus
he was a handsome man
                    and what i want to know is
how do you like your blueeyed boy   10
Mister Death

THE RECEPTIVE READER

Who was Buffalo Bill? What was his claim to fame? In what ways is he a symbol of his period in American history? What is the attitude toward him in this poem?

THE CREATIVE DIMENSION

A student wrote the following tribute shortly after e. e. cummings had died. How well did the student writer get into the spirit of the original? Try your hand at a similar portrait of someone more recently defunct.

Portrait II

```
e. e. someone
buried by busy ones,
                    used to
              wish yes aprils with a you
                              and a me
and write onetwothreefourfive poemsjustlikethat
                                  by dong and ding
he was a perceptive man
                    and what i want to know is
where is he now when we need him
Mister Death
```

POEMS FOR FURTHER STUDY

In reading the following poems, pay special attention to the poet's use of myth and allusion. What knowledge of myth, legend, or history does the poet assume? What is the role of an allusion in a poem as a whole?

WILLIAM WORDSWORTH (1770–1850)

The World Is Too Much with Us   1807

The world is too much with us; late and soon,
Getting and spending, we lay waste our powers;
Little we see in Nature that is ours;
We have given our hearts away, a sordid boon.
This Sea that bares her bosom to the moon,   5
The winds that will be howling at all hours,
And are up-gathered now like sleeping flowers,
For this, for everything, we are out of tune;
It moves us not.—Great God! I'd rather be
A Pagan suckled in a creed outworn;   10
So might I, standing on this pleasant lea,°   *grassland*
Have glimpses that would make me less forlorn;
Have sight of Proteus rising from the sea;
Or hear old Triton blow his wreathèd horn.

THE RECEPTIVE READER

From a dictionary or other reference work, what can you find out about Proteus and Triton? What role do they play in the poem? What does the world of Greek myth mean to the speaker in this sonnet?

EDNA ST. VINCENT MILLAY   (1892–1950)

An Ancient Gesture   1931

I thought, as I wiped my eyes on the corner of my apron:
Penelope did this too.
And more than once: you can't keep weaving all day
And undoing it all through the night;
Your arms get tired, and the back of your neck gets tight;   5
And along towards morning, when you think it will never be light,
And your husband has been gone, and you don't know where, for years,
Suddenly you burst into tears;
There is simply nothing else to do.

And I thought, as I wiped my eyes on the corner of my apron: 10
This is an ancient gesture, authentic, antique,
In the very best tradition, classic, Greek;
Ulysses did this too.
But only as a gesture,—a gesture which implied
To the assembled throng that he was much too moved to speak.   15
He learned it from Penelope . . .
Penelope, who really cried.

THE RECEPTIVE READER

1. What is the story of Penelope and Ulysses?
2. In Homer, men weep over their slain comrades. What makes this poet suspicious of Ulysses' tears?

WILLIAM DICKEY   (born 1928)

Exploration over the Rim   1959

Beyond that sandbar is the river's turning.
There a new country opens up to sight,
Safe from the fond researches of our learning.
Here it is day; there it is always night.

Around this corner is a certain danger.   5
The streets are streets of hell from here on in.
The Anthropophagi° and beings stranger   *man-eaters*
Roast in the fire and meditate on sin.

After this kiss will I know who I'm kissing?
Will I have reached the point of no return? 10
What happened to those others who are missing?
Oh, well, to hell with it. If we burn, we burn.

THE RECEPTIVE READER

What echoes of mythic voyages do you hear in this poem? Does the irreverent ending undercut the rest of the poem?

DONALD FINKEL (born 1929)

The Sirens 1959

The news lapped at us out of all
Horizons: the ticking night full
Of gods; sensed, heard the tactile

Sea turn in his bed, prickling
Among derelicts. When the song
Was clear enough, we spread our hair, 5

Caught it. Under the comb the strands
Whipped into fresh harmonies, untangled
Again. The wind took it, and he heard.

The droll ship swung leeward; 10
Caught sight of him (rather, could
Have seen, busy with the fugue)

Yanking his bonds, the strings of his wide
Neck drawn like shrouds, his scream
Caught in the sail. 15
                    Now in a sea

Of wheat he rows, reconstructing.
In his ridiculous, lovely mouth the strains
Tumble into place. Do you think
Wax could have stopped us, or chains? 20

THE RECEPTIVE READER

The sirens were mythical women whose song was so irresistible that mariners would steer their ships into the rocks of the sirens' island and perish. This poem alludes to the story of a famous traveler who passed by the island during his far-flung voyages. What is the story of Ulysses and the sirens? How does this poem reverse the usual perspective from which we see this story—and with what effect?

WRITING ABOUT LITERATURE

22. Reinterpreting Myth (Focus on Peer Review)

The Writing Workshop   Writers don't write in a vacuum. They live with feedback from friends, family, colleagues, editors, reviewers—or just plain readers. In a classroom, you can simulate such input by having your peers react to your writing as individuals or in a group. Such feedback helps make you more audience conscious; it strengthens your sense of what happens when your writing reaches the reader.

In turn, when you act as a peer reviewer for others, you help alert other writers to the reader's needs. You help them see their writing through the reader's eyes. Remember that critics and reviewers easily lapse into a faultfinding mode. Although it is important to identify weaknesses and mistakes, it is just as important to help writers develop what is promising and to help them build on their strengths. Try to balance negative criticism with constructive suggestions. The key question in your mind should be: What can the writer do to improve, to make the writing more instructive, more effective?

Here are sample passages with comments that might help a writer develop the full potential of a paper:

> Ovid, David Wagoner, and Vassar Miller offer vastly different interpretations of the classic myth. However, we are also able to see a few similarities.

COMMENT: What *are* these differences and similarities? Give us a hint to keep us interested? Give us more of a preview?

> In the biblical account, Abraham "bound Isaak his son, and laid him on the altar upon the wood." Owen's poem says that "Abram bound the youth with belts and straps, / And builded parapets and trenches." Belts and straps, parapets and trenches are surely alien to people of biblical times who herded sheep for a living. These words denote the military.

COMMENT: Follow up and explain? Why does the poet use these "military" references? What kind of warfare and what war does he have in mind?

> The first thing that must be taken into consideration about this poem is its basis in the traditional biblical story. . . . Once the element of war and sacrifice has been introduced, the whole concept of sacrifice is looked at in respect to the ones that do the sacrificing as well as the ones being sacrificed. . . . Owen has successfully conveyed the personalities and situations involved with war and sacrifice.

COMMENT: Rewrite to avoid the wooden, impersonal passive? "The element of war and sacrifice *has been introduced*"—by whom? Try "Once the poet *has introduced* . . . he *looks* at this theme . . ."? Cut down on jargony words like *basis, element, concept, situation?* Rewrite chunky passages like "looked at in respect to the ones that"?

STUDENT PAPER FOR PEER REVIEW

Monroe: Quest of Beauty

Marilyn Monroe became something more than human even before her suicide in the early 60s. Her image—celluloid clips, photo stills—keeps appearing in sometimes unlikely places. Sometimes her image reappears in another embodiment, such as Madonna, and the casual observer will still think "Monroe" before recognition sets in. We know who she is, or was. Or at least we think we do.

Norman Mailer in *Marilyn,* one of a never-ending stream of books about the "goddess of the silver screen," said, "She was not the dark contract of the passionate brunette depths that speak of blood, vows taken for life, and the furies of vengeance. . . . no, Marilyn suggested sex might be difficult or dangerous with others, but ice cream with her." Mailer said, "We think of Marilyn, who was every man's love affair" and whose "little rinky-dink voice" carried "ripe overtones of erotic excitement and yet was the voice of a little child."

In her poem "The Death of Marilyn Monroe," Sharon Olds describes the impact that Marilyn's death had on the ambulance attendants who carried "her cold / body" to the ambulance. "These men were never the same." One had nightmares, became impotent, suffered depression. One did not "like his work, his wife looked / different, his kids." Death became a place "where she / would be waiting." Another

> found himself standing at night
> in the doorway to a room of sleep, listening to
> a woman breathing, just an ordinary
> woman
> breathing.

For these men, and all men and women, the death of Marilyn meant far more than the tragedy of an individual; it was the death of a modern goddess, of a mythical being.

To Judy Grahn, a feminist poet, Monroe, like Harlowe, Holiday, or Taylor, represents an older myth, that of Helen of Troy. In her poem "Helen in Hollywood," she says, "'That's the one,' we say in instant recognition, / because our breath is taken away by her beauty, / or what we call her beauty." Helen herself, to Judy Grahn, is merely the human incarnation of a deity humanity has almost forgotten. This deity goes by many names and lives in many cultures and is represented in our world by the Hollywood star who

> writes in red red lipstick
> on the window of her body,
> long for me, oh need me!

We, her fans, crowd around her to share in her "luminescent glow," and we may destroy her in the process:

> We adore her. we imitate and rob her
> adulate   envy
> admire   neglect
> scorn.   leave alone
> invade, fill
> ourselves with her.
> we love her, we say
> and if she isn't careful
> we may even kill her.

She is our "leaping, laughing leading lady," who "sweeps eternally / down the steps / in her long round gown." But it is also she "who lies strangled / in the belltower"; it is she "who is monumentally drunk and suicidal." It is she who when "locked waiting in the hightower . . . leaps from her blue window."

For years after Marilyn's death, men would say (and women, too): "If only she had met me, I could have saved her!" Something in her flawed beauty, in her vulnerability, made her personal to millions of people. She became the best celluloid representation of the goddess of beauty, approachable and accepting of everyone's gifts. She taught us the power of sexual awareness, the power of our sexual selves. Everyone was welcome at her well. To Sharon Olds, not to have Marilyn as a symbol in our lives is the price the ambulance crew paid. It is not to have connection; it is not to have sexual, social, or family bonds. It is to stand alone in the dark, doubting and seeking reaffirmation of the reality of a loved person in our lives, "listening to / a woman breathing, just an ordinary / woman / breathing."

QUESTIONS

1. Should the writer have brought out her *thesis* earlier or more clearly in the paper? What would you suggest as a possible thesis statement early in the paper? Compare your suggestions with those of your classmates.

2. Could the relation between Mailer, Olds, and Grahn have been clarified more to make the overall *pattern* or drift of the paper clearer to the reader? What is the connection? What is the overall pattern?

3. Do you feel anywhere in the essay a need for additional *explanation* or discussion of the quoted passages?

4. Do you need additional *quotations*? Do you need more of a sense of the overall *intention* and pattern of a source? Where or why?

5. Do you have suggestions for strengthening *beginning and end*—title, introduction, conclusion?

6. What is your personal *reaction* to this writer's interpretation of the Monroe myth? Does it need more explanation or justification? How do you think other readers will react?

7. "Helen in Hollywood" appears in Judy Grahn's *Queen of Wands,* along with other Helen poems. Does this paper make you want to read the whole poem by Judy Grahn or more of her poetry? Why or why not?

23 THREE POETS IN DEPTH
Dickinson, Frost, Brooks

In our age, and typically in a large, mobile industrial society . . . people tend to become indifferent about their ability to think or feel for themselves. . . . the poet's voice is needed now more than ever before—that voice which celebrates the difficult, joyous, imaginative process by which the individual discovers and enacts selfhood.

EDWIN HONIG

Experiment escorts us last—
His pungent company
Will not allow an Axiom
An Opportunity

EMILY DICKINSON

FOCUS ON THE POET

When reading a poet like Emily Dickinson, Robert Frost, or Gwendolyn Brooks, we treasure the poet's personal voice. We recognize it with pleasure, the way we welcome a cherished face or honor a signature. For a time, the New Critics (originally "new" in the forties and fifties) asked that we treat each individual poem as a self-contained whole. We were to read each poem on its own terms, regardless of what we might know about the poet or the setting. This way, we could attend to what the poem actually said rather than what we *expected* it to say—because we knew the author, the time, or the party line. In practice, however, we do not read an anonymous poem and then discover with surprise that it is by Walt Whitman. There is name recognition in poets as there is in singers or composers. The memory of past pleasure attracts us. As we read, we are already attuned to the poet's way of looking at the world. Our previous acquaintance with the poet shapes our expectations—although of course a poem by a favorite poet may surprise us, taking a turn we find puzzling or strange.

In the poet's work, the individual poem is part of a larger whole. (We call the accumulated work of a poet the **canon** when it is formidable enough to be

716

inventoried by critics and scholars.) Moving from one poem to the next, we recognize themes, preoccupations, obsessions. One poem helps us understand another. We interpret a difficult passage by way of cross-reference to a similar passage elsewhere. In addition, we may test our interpretation against statements made by the poet or by people in the poet's confidence.

Looking at the work of three poets in depth, this chapter will ask you to focus in turn on three kinds of investigation that can enhance your understanding of an individual poem.

The Personal Voice The best-loved poets have an unmistakable personal idiom or **style.** They have an inimitable, personal way of looking at the world and sharing with us what they see. We do not mistake Emily Dickinson for e. e. cummings. (Beginning poets, by contrast, often find it difficult not to sound like clones of their fashionable predecessors.)

The Poet as a Person Ever since Samuel Johnson wrote his *Lives of the Poets* (1779–1781), **author biography** has been a thriving branch of literary scholarship. It is fueled by investigators who agree with Johnson that "the biographical part of literature is what I love most." Who is the biographical person behind the persona speaking in a poem? Who is the person behind the masks and disguises particular poems may create? How does a poem become more meaningful when we see it in the context of the poet's life?

The Poet's Commitment In the work of an **engaged,** that is, politically committed, poet, individual poems may be bulletins from an ongoing struggle. To relate to recurrent themes, we may have to understand the poet's sense of mission. We may have to understand the poet's social conscience, class consciousness, or solidarity with the oppressed.

EMILY DICKINSON: THE POET'S VOICE

In Amherst Emily lived on
though the world forgot
moving with calm coiled hair through tidy days.
Her face shrank to a locket. She explored
miniaturized worlds known only to moths and angels
walked to the far side of a raindrop—
trespassed
on Infinity.

OLGA CABRAL

Maybe that is one of the most valuable things about the
poetry of Emily Dickinson: to teach that there is something
in poetry that cannot be handled, cannot be studied
scientifically.

LINDA GREGG

Surgeons must be very careful
When they take the knife!
Underneath their fine incisions
Stirs the culprit,—Life!
                    EMILY DICKINSON

Emily Dickinson (1830–1886) is the supreme example of a poet with a distinctive voice—a voice that seemed willfully strange to her contemporaries but that gradually came to be recognized and cherished by lovers of poetry everywhere. She led a withdrawn life and found practically no recognition in her day. She thought about success and fame ("Fame is a bee. / It has a song— / It has a sting— / Ah, too it has a wing"), but she ultimately had to settle for "fame of my mind"—recognition in her own mind. It was for posterity to discover her

                    sheer sanity
     of vision, the serious mischief
     language, the economy of pain.
               Linda Pastan, "Emily Dickinson"

Although she sent over a hundred poems to editors and corresponded with an editor of the *Atlantic Monthly* for years, only a handful of her poems found their way into print in her lifetime. Magazines then published much conventionally uplifting poetry in dutifully regular meter and rhyme. To the editors, the bold experimental features of her poetry seemed "technical imperfections"; her work, like the work of other great innovators, was considered uncontrolled and eccentric. When they did publish her poems, editors conventionalized them. They changed bold metaphorical words to uninteresting ones; they changed her dashes to commas and periods; they made her off-rhymes and half-rhymes rhyme.

A collection of over a hundred poems published shortly after Dickinson's death astonished her publishers by running through eleven editions in two years. Almost two thousand of her poems have since been found and published. (Several times that number may have been lost.) Twentieth-century readers discovered in her a great precursor of the modern temper. They cherished her for her gift for provocative metaphor, her searching paradoxical intelligence, and her intensely personal point of view. Today, with her poems everywhere known and anthologized, and "with feminist considerations of her work abounding" (Leslie Camhi), she is widely recognized as America's greatest poet.

Much ink has flowed to create, embroider, and question the legend of Emily Dickinson as the mysterious lady dressed in white and living secluded in her father's house, embarked on her own private "journey into the interior." Who was the biographical person behind the persona—which she called the "supposed person"—that speaks to us in her poetry?

Dickinson "was born into a family that did everything for her but understand her" (Richard B. Sewall). Her grandfather had been a founder of

Amherst College. Her father—a lawyer, judge, and member of Congress—practiced a stern Puritanical religion in the New England tradition. He led morning prayers for family and servants, reading scripture in what his daughter Emily called a "militant accent." At a time when questioning even minor points of doctrine was scandalous, Dickinson developed serious doubts about original sin. She stopped going to church by the time she was thirty. She decided to keep the Sabbath at home, where, in her words, a "noted clergyman" (namely God) preached better and shorter sermons.

Her father was suspicious of books that "joggle the mind"; he banned novels, which young Emily and her brother Austin had to smuggle into the house while the father was "too busy with his briefs to notice what we do." She read and admired the great woman writers of her day, from the Brontë sisters to Elizabeth Barrett Browning. In addition to the Bible, Shakespeare, and theological works, her reading included Charlotte Brontë's *Jane Eyre* and George Eliot's *Middlemarch,* each the record of the spiritual pilgrimage of a woman in search of an identity other than the roles presented ready-made by society. In a poem she wrote a few years after the death of Charlotte Brontë, the poet said:

> Soft fall the sounds of Eden
> Upon her puzzled ear—
> Oh what an afternoon for Heaven,
> When "Brontë " entered there!

Dickinson attended Amherst Academy and for a year Mount Holyoke Female Seminary, one of the first women's colleges. Letters she wrote as a student show a young woman in love with exuberant word play and fired by youthful enthusiasm. Her quick wit and lively sense of irony never deserted her—in a poem written many years later, she said about a pompous fraud that "he preached upon 'Breadth' till it argued him narrow." However, she gradually withdrew from the outside world. One of her best-known poems begins "The Soul selects her own Society— / Then—shuts the door— / To her divine Majority— / Present no more."

She stayed in touch by letter with the few people who provided her with feedback for her poetry, including her sister-in-law Susan Gilbert Dickinson and Thomas Wentworth Higginson, the *Atlantic Monthly* editor whom she addressed as her mentor or "preceptor." Although Higginson had advanced ideas for his time, he was unable to come to terms with the strange and "wayward" poems she sent him. She in turn could not conform to the demands of the literary marketplace—to auction off "the Mind of Man" and to merchandise "Heavenly Grace" and the "Human Spirit."

As friends of earlier days drifted away, Dickinson, in the words of a biographer, increasingly withdrew to "her garden, her conservatory, the kitchen (where she baked bread for her father), but especially her room where, often far into the night, . . . she could explore her own 'real life' and write her poems in peace" (Richard B. Sewall).

Much detective work has probed possible psychological, social, or medical reasons for her increasing isolation. In poems and letters, she hints at intense emotional attachments that ended in anguish and disappointment. Passionate, yearning letters to an unknown recipient survive, possibly addressed to a married minister. Women writers today stress the fact that outlets for the creative energies of a fiercely independent woman were limited if not nonexistent in Dickinson's day. Thwarted in her early visions of fame, she was forced into resignation. Alternatively, psychoanalysts have searched her relationship with an authoritarian father, an invalid mother, or an uncomprehending brother and sister for clues to the intense, disturbed emotions in some of her poems. She may have suffered from agoraphobia, a debilitating fear of public places.

What is certain is that she found in the everyday routines of the household and in the enclosed natural life of her garden plot the food for far-flung questionings and explorations. In the words of one of her recent editors,

> From a life narrow by conventional standards, and from the household tasks that women have performed silently for generations, Dickinson drew the material for metaphysical speculation. Baking, sweeping, caring for the ill, mourning the dead, and observing the quiet nature of a garden were the occasions for sudden mysteries. . . . Ambivalent religious attitudes, together with the themes of death, immortality, and eternity, permeate her work. The Puritan sense of spiritual mystery inhabiting the circumstances of everyday life informs her minute observations of nature. Her meter is adapted from eighteenth-century hymns. But hers was "that religion / That doubts as fervently as it believes" (poem 1144).
>
> Leslie Camhi, "Emily Dickinson," in Marian Arkin and Barbara Shollar, eds., *Longman Anthology of World Literature by Women, 1875–1975*

What is the distinctive voice that makes her poems unmistakably hers? First of all, her poems remain fresh because of their intensely personal, often startling *perspective*. Her poems typically make us look at the world from an unexpected angle, thus forcing us to see something anew as if for the first time. She summed up her poetic credo in the following poem. (Numbers of poems refer to the numbering in Thomas H. Johnson's *The Collected Poems of Emily Dickinson*.)

Tell all the Truth but tell it slant

about 1868

J. 1129

Tell all the Truth but tell it slant—
Success in circuit lies
Too bright for our infirm Delight
The Truth's superb surprise

As Lightning to the Children eased
With explanation kind
The truth must dazzle gradually
Or every man be blind—

5

The truth is a "superb surprise," and it is too bright and dazzling for our infirm and weak capacity to absorb it. It must be presented "in circuit"—in a roundabout way. It must be allowed to dazzle and delight us "gradually." The way to tell the truth, therefore, is to tell it "slant"—not directly but aslant, so that it can approach us not head-on but from a slanted, nonthreatening angle. (We do not tell children straight-on about the awesome power of lightning to kill in a flash. Instead, we make the truth easy on them with "kind" explanation.)

CROSS-REFERENCES—For Discussion or Writing

What is the connection between this poem and Gwendolyn Brooks' poem "Truth" (p. 416)?

The way Dickinson tells the truth "slant" is not to preach at us but to speak to us through startling graphic *images* and eye-opening metaphors. She looks at the world with a special alertness, marveling at what she finds, keeping alive in us the art of wondering. For people who notice birds only in passing, the following poem presents a series of striking visual images designed to surprise them into paying attention.

A Bird came down the Walk

about 1862

J. 328

A Bird came down the Walk—
He did not know I saw—
He bit an Angleworm in halves
And ate the fellow, raw,

And then he drank a Dew   5
From a convenient Grass—
And then hopped sidewise to the Wall
To let a Beetle pass—

He glanced with rapid eyes
That hurried all around—   10
They looked like frightened Beads, I thought—
He stirred his Velvet Head

Like one in danger. Cautious,
I offered him a Crumb
And he unrolled his feathers   15
And rowed him softer home—

Than Oars divide the Ocean,
Too silver for a seam—
Or Butterflies, off Banks of Noon
Leap, plashless° as they swim.   *without a splash*   20

The opening lines zero in on the bird without much ado. They give us a startling close-up view of the visitor that has come down from its natural element the air to go about essential bird business: We see the angleworm being bitten "in halves," then eaten raw, and washed down with dew drunk from a conveniently close blade of grass. We keep watching as the bird hops sidewise to get out of the way of a beetle. We get a glimpse of the beadlike eyes that are forever hurriedly glancing and shifting, looking for lurking danger.

At the approach of the human observer (who means no harm and offers a crumb), the bird returns to its natural airborne habitat, where he "rowed him softer home" than an oar-propelled boat does in the ocean. We watch the striking transition from the comically hopping, restless, and anxious earthbound bird to the bird at home and at ease in the seamless air where it effortlessly glides. Indeed, the flight of the bird seems smoother, less slowed down by resistance, than the fluttering of butterflies as they "leap" into the air from their noontime resting place without making a splash and then "swim" in it.

Does the transformation (or metamorphosis) of the bird from its awkwardly hopping, frightened grounded state to its serenely floating skyborne state have a symbolic meaning? Are our bodies stumbling awkwardly through life in our present earthbound existence? Will our souls float serenely upward, returning to their spiritual home, during a future state? The poem does not say. If this is the larger truth hinted at in the poem, the poet tells it "slant."

THE RECEPTIVE READER

1. Dickinson's *wording* is often cryptic—compressing or telescoping meaning into short, puzzling phrases. When she talks about the "ocean" of air, what is the meaning of "too silver for a seam"? What is it about silver that keeps us from expecting to see seams? How would butterflies leap "off Banks of Noon"?

2. Many people lay out money for photographs, paintings, or figurines of pretty birds. Is the bird in this poem pretty? Why or why not?

3. What words and images in this poem make the natural creatures seem almost human? Which remind us that they are not? One student said after reading this poem, "We like to humanize animals, but we cannot communicate with them. Sometimes we feel kinship with animals, and at other times we don't." How would you sum up the poet's perspective on the animal world in this poem?

Dickinson's *metaphors* are often startling and thought provoking because they connect mundane details of every day with the most troubling questions about life, death, and immortality. In the following poem, household chores become a solemn metaphor for the housekeeping of the heart.

The Bustle in a House
J. 1078

about 1866

The Bustle in a House
The Morning after Death
Is solemnest of industries
Enacted upon Earth—

The Sweeping up the Heart 5
And putting Love away
We shall not want to use again
Until Eternity.

The solid ground floor of the metaphorical structure of this poem is the bustling of activity in the house after someone beloved has died. Literally, the diligent or industrious activity (the "solemnest of industries") involves tidying up—sweeping the house and putting things away that with the deceased gone may not be used again for a long time, if ever. But metaphorically these commonplace activities come to stand for the wrenching adjustments we have to make in our hearts. We try to purge our hearts of cluttered, destructive emotions; we try to put everything in order. We realize we can no longer put our love to its accustomed daily uses; we can only keep it on a back shelf until the distant day of resurrection.

A third feature of Dickinson's poetry is the deceptive *simplicity* of her style. There are no lush rhythms and elaborate rhymes to call attention to themselves. Her basic line is a sparse, irregular three-beat or four-beat line. Lines are usually held loosely together by slant rhyme or half-rhyme in a four-line stanza, reminding us of simple popular forms like hymns and ballads. No outward ornament comes between the poet and the reader. This very absence of extraneous adornment highlights the importance of the individual word, the individual metaphor. In one of her last letters, she wrote, "I hesitate which word to take, as I can take but a few and each must be the chiefest."

EXPLORATIONS

The Poet's Voice

What features of the following poem seem to illustrate the distinctive Dickinson style? For instance, does it show her way of looking at the world from a startling new perspective? Does it show her way of giving concrete shape to abstract ideas? Does it seem simple on the surface?

Because I could not stop for Death
J. 712

about 1863

Because I could not stop for Death—
He kindly stopped for me—
The Carriage held but just Ourselves—
And Immortality.

We slowly drove—He knew no haste 5
And I had put away
My labor and my leisure too,
For His Civility—

We passed the School, where Children strove
At Recess—in the Ring— 10
We passed the Fields of Gazing Grain—
We passed the Setting Sun—

Or rather—He passed Us—
The Dews drew quivering and chill—
For only Gossamer, my Gown— 15
My Tippet°—only Tulle—   *scarf (of lacelike material)*

We paused before a House that seemed
A Swelling of the Ground—
The Roof was scarcely visible—
The Cornice—in the Ground— 20

Since then—'tis Centuries—and yet
Feels shorter than the Day
I first surmised the Horses' Heads
Were toward Eternity—

THE RECEPTIVE READER

1. What is strange or different about the attitude toward *death* reflected in this poem? Can you sympathize with or relate to the feelings that seem to be mirrored in this poem?

2. What is the *symbolism* of the school, the fields, the setting sun, the house "that seemed / A Swelling of the Ground"?

EXPLORATIONS

The Range of Interpretation

Dickinson was an intensely personal poet, looking at the world from a highly individual perspective. In turn, critics have looked at her poetry from distinct, highly individual points of view. Study the following poem and the quotations that follow it. How do you react to them? Which do you tend to agree with and why?

I heard a Fly buzz—when I died   about 1862
J. 465

I heard a Fly buzz—when I died—
The Stillness in the Room
Was like the Stillness in the Air—
Between the Heaves of Storm—

The Eyes around—had wrung them dry— 5
And Breaths were gathering firm
For that last Onset—when the King
Be witnessed—in the Room—

I willed my Keepsakes—Signed away
What portion of me be   10
Assignable—and then it was
There interposed a Fly—

With Blue—uncertain stumbling Buzz—
Between the light—and me—
And then the Windows failed—and then   15
I could not see to see—

    1. The buzzing fly, so familiar a part of the natural order of persistent household discomfort, is brought in at the last to give the touch of petty irritabilities that are concomitant with living—and indeed with dying. (Thomas Johnson)

    2. The dying person does in fact not merely suffer an unwelcome external interruption of an otherwise resolute expectancy but falls from a higher consciousness, from liberating insight, from faith, into an intensely skeptical mood. . . . To the dying person, the buzzing fly would thus become a timely, untimely reminder of man's final, cadaverous condition and putrefaction. (Gerhard Friedrich)

    3. I understand that fly to be the last kiss of the world . . . think of the fly not as a distraction taking Emily's thoughts from glory and blocking the divine light . . . but a last dear sound from the world as the light of consciousness sank from her. (John Ciardi)

    4. The only sound of heavenly music, or of wings taking flight, was the "Blue— uncertain stumbling buzz" of a fly that filled her dying ear. Instead of a final vision of the hereafter, this world simply faded from her eyes. (Ruth Miller)

    5. And what kind of fly? A fly "With Blue—uncertain stumbling Buzz"—a blowfly. . . . She was a practical housewife, and every housewife abhors a blowfly. It pollutes everything it touches. Its eggs are maggots. . . . What we know of Emily Dickinson gives us assurance that just as she would abhor the blowfly she would abhor the deathbed scene. (Caroline Hogue)

CROSS-REFERENCES—For Discussion or Writing

    Other poems by Emily Dickinson included earlier in this volume are "Apparently with no surprise" (p. 487), "'Hope' is the thing with feathers" (p. 492), and "The Soul selects her own Society" (p. 571). Do these poems illustrate such characteristic features as a startling different perspective, bold metaphors, or a deceptive simplicity?

POEMS FOR FURTHER STUDY

    The following selection includes many of the most widely read of Dickinson's poems. What in each poem helps you recognize her unmistakable personal voice? What are themes she returns to again and again? What is her characteristic way of treating them?

J. 67   about 1859

Success is counted sweetest
By those who ne'er succeed
To comprehend a nectar

Requires sorest need.

Not one of all the purple Host 5
Who took the Flag today
Can tell the definition
So clear of Victory

As he defeated—dying—
On whose forbidden ear 10
The distant strains of triumph
Burst agonized and clear!

J. 214 about 1860

I taste a liquor never brewed—
From Tankards scooped in Pearl—
Not all the Vats upon the Rhine
Yield such an Alcohol!

Inebriate of Air—am I— 5
And Debauchee of Dew—
Reeling—thro endless summer days—
From inns of Molten Blue—

When "Landlords" turn the drunken Bee
Out of the Foxglove's door— 10
When Butterflies—renounce their "drams"—
I shall but drink the more!

Till Seraphs swing their snowy Hats—
And Saints—to windows run—
To see the little Tippler 15
Leaning against the—Sun—

J. 249 about 1861

Wild Nights—Wild Nights!
Were I with thee
Wild Nights should be
Our luxury!

Futile—the Winds— 5
To a Heart in port—
Done with the Compass—
Done with the Chart!

Rowing in Eden—
Ah, the Sea! 10
Might I but moor—Tonight—
In Thee!

J. 258   about 1861

There's a certain Slant of light,
Winter Afternoons—
That oppresses, like the Heft
Of Cathedral Tunes—

Heavenly Hurt, it gives us—   5
We can find no scar,
But internal difference,
Where the Meanings, are—

None may teach it—Any—
'Tis the Seal Despair—   10
An imperial affliction
Sent us of the Air—

When it comes, the Landscape listens—
Shadows—hold their breath—
When it goes, 'tis like the Distance   15
On the look of Death—

J. 288   about 1861

I'm Nobody! Who are you?
Are you—Nobody—Too?
Then there's a pair of us?
Don't tell! They'd advertise—you know!

How dreary—to be—Somebody!   5
How public—like a Frog—
To tell one's name—the livelong June—
To an admiring Bog!

J. 341   about 1862

After great pain, a formal feeling comes—
The Nerves sit ceremonious, like Tombs—
The stiff Heart questions was it He, that bore,
And Yesterday, or Centuries before?

The Feet, mechanical, go round—   5
Of Ground, or Air, or Ought—
A Wooden way
Regardless grown,
A Quartz contentment, like a stone—

This is the Hour of Lead—   10
Remembered, if outlived,
As Freezing persons, recollect the Snow—
First—Chill—then Stupor—then the letting go—

J. 435

about 1862

Much Madness is divinest Sense—
To a discerning Eye—
Much Sense—the starkest Madness—
'Tis the Majority
In this, as All, prevail—
Assent—and you are sane—
Demur—you're straightway dangerous—
And handled with a Chain—

5

Facsimile of Emily Dickinson's original manuscript. Courtesy The Houghton Library, Harvard University, Cambridge.

J. 449

about 1862

I died for Beauty—but was scarce
Adjusted in the Tomb
When One who died for Truth, was lain
In an adjoining Room—

He questioned softly "Why I failed"?
"For Beauty," I replied—
"And I—for Truth—Themself Are One—
We Brethren, are," He said—

And so, as Kinsmen, met a Night— 5
We talked between the Rooms—
Until the Moss had reached our lips—
And covered up—our names— 10

J. 526

about 1862

To hear an Oriole sing
May be a common thing—
Or only a divine.

It is not of the Bird
Who sings the same, unheard,
As unto Crowd— 5

The Fashion of the Ear
Attireth that it hear
In Dun, or fair—

So whether it be Rune, 10
Or whether it be none
Is of within.

The "Tune is in the Tree—"
The Skeptic—showeth me—
"No Sir! In Thee!" 15

J. 579

about 1862

I had been hungry, all the Years—
My Noon had Come—to dine—
I trembling drew the Table near—
And touched the Curious Wine—

'Twas this on Tables I had seen— 5
When turning, hungry, Home
I looked in Windows, for the Wealth
I could not hope—for Mine—

I did not know the ample Bread—
'Twas so unlike the Crumb 10
The Birds and I, had often shared
In Nature's—Dining Room—

The Plenty hurt me—'twas so new—
Myself felt ill—and odd—

15

As Berry—of a Mountain Bush—
Transplanted—to the Road—

Nor was I hungry—so I found
That Hunger—was a way
Of Persons outside Windows—
The Entering—takes away— 20

J. 986 about 1865

A narrow fellow in the Grass
Occasionally rides—
You may have met Him—did you not
His notice sudden is—

The grass divides as with a Comb— 5
A spotted shaft is seen—
And then it closes at your feet
And opens further on—

He likes a Boggy Acre° swampy ground
A Floor too cool for Corn—
Yet when a Boy, and Barefoot— 10
I more than once at Noon

Have passed, I thought, a Whiplash
Unbraiding in the Sun
When stooping to secure it 15
It wrinkled, and was gone—

Several of Nature's People
I know, and they know me—
I feel for them a transport° sudden impulsive feeling
Of cordiality— 20

But never met this Fellow
Attended, or alone
Without a tighter breathing
And Zero at the Bone—

J. 1052 about 1865

I never saw a Moor—
I never saw the Sea—
Yet know I how the Heather looks
And what a Billow be.

I never spoke with God 5
Nor visited in Heaven—
Yet certain am I of the spot
As if the Checks were given—

J. 1263

about 1873

There is no Frigate like a Book
To take us Lands away
Nor any Coursers like a Page
Of prancing Poetry—
This Traverse may the poorest take   5
Without oppress of Toll—
How frugal is the Chariot
That bears the Human soul.

J. 1732

about 1896

My life closed twice before its close—
It yet remains to see
If Immortality unveil
A third event to me
So huge, so hopeless to conceive   5
As these that twice befell
Parting is all we know of heaven,
And all we need of hell.

THE CREATIVE DIMENSION

From the poems by Dickinson you have read, choose a haunting image or a striking, puzzling detail that left a lasting impression. Write a passage in which you re-create the image or impression and follow the train of associations—of images, thoughts, or feelings—that it sets in motion in your mind.

CROSS-REFERENCES—For Discussion or Writing

For a library research project, search for books and articles that would provide material for a treatment of one of the following topics:

✧ A range of critical interpretations of the same Dickinson poem. How does the same poem look when read by different readers? Are there major areas of agreement? What are major differences in interpretation, and what might explain them?

✧ Several critics' treatment of a recurrent theme in Dickinson's poetry. What do different critics say about the poet's treatment of a central recurrent theme like death, nature, love, faith, or immortality?

✧ Several critics' discussion of a key feature of her style or personal voice.

Book-length sources you may be able to consult may include the following:

Charles R. Anderson, *Emily Dickinson's Poetry: Stairway to Surprise* (1960)
Richard B. Sewall, ed., *Emily Dickinson: A Collection of Critical Essays* (1963)
Albert Gelpi, *Emily Dickinson: The Mind of the Poet* (1965)
Ruth Miller, *The Poetry of Emily Dickinson* (1974)
Richard B. Sewall, *The Life of Emily Dickinson* (1974)
Robert Weisbuch, *Emily Dickinson's Poetry* (1975)

Sharon Cameron, *Lyric Time: Dickinson and the Limits of Genre* (1980)
David Porter, *Dickinson: The Modern Idiom* (1981)
Joanne F. Diehl, *Dickinson and the Romantic Imagination* (1981)
Antonina Clarke Mossberg, *Emily Dickinson: When a Writer Is a Daughter* (1982)
Susan Juhasz, *The Undiscovered Continent: Emily Dickinson and the Space of the Mind* (1983)
Susan Juhasz, ed., *Feminist Critics Read Emily Dickinson* (1983)
Jerome Loving, *Emily Dickinson: The Poet on the Second Story* (1986)
Helen McNeil, *Emily Dickinson* (1986)
Cynthia Griffin Wolff, *Emily Dickinson* (1986)
Christanne Miller, *Emily Dickinson: A Poet's Grammar* (1987)

Numberless discussions of Dickinson's poetry have appeared in periodicals ranging from the *Explicator* to *New Literary History*.

ROBERT FROST: POET AND PERSONA

We are all toadies to the fashionable metaphor of the hour.
Great is he who imposes the metaphor.
                                        ROBERT FROST

If Robert Frost was much honored in his lifetime, it was
because a good many preferred to ignore his darker truths.
                                        JOHN F. KENNEDY

The figure a poem makes . . . begins in delight and ends
in wisdom.
                                        ROBERT FROST

Robert Frost (1874–1963) became a living legend. He is the closest that twentieth-century America came to having a national poet who meant to the popular imagination what Whitman had meant to the new American nation in the nineteenth century. As with other legendary literary figures, biographers and critics have vested much effort in searching for the real-life person behind the legend. They have probed the paradoxical relationship between the public persona of the adored poet-sage and the personal difficulties and private demons of the poet's life.

In the early years, Frost struggled to make a living for himself and his family—as a farmer, a part-time teacher, a poet. Although he is commonly associated with the New England setting, he was born in San Francisco and spent his boyhood years in California. Frost's father, a Southerner who had named the boy Robert Lee, died when Frost was eleven years old. His Scottish mother then took him to New England, where she had relatives. Frost attended Lawrence High School in Massachusetts, where the curriculum was heavy on Greek and Roman history and literature. He later married Elinor White, who had been his covaledictorian there. He attended first Dartmouth and then

Harvard, but, as he put it later, he walked out of both of them, deciding to learn not from teachers but from "writers who had written before me."

With help from his grandfather, Frost bought a farm in New Hampshire, the setting of many of his early poems. Unable to make a living as a farmer and part-time teacher, unable to get more than a few poems accepted for publication, Frost and his wife took their growing family to England, where he made friends with other aspiring young poets. He was first recognized as a poet while in England, where he published two volumes: *A Boy's Will* (1913) and *North of Boston* (1914). When he returned to the United States, he was almost forty years old. Magazines started to print his poems, and he gradually became widely known as a poet and lecturer. His reading tours attracted large audiences. He helped found the Bread Loaf School of English at Middlebury College in Vermont. Honors multiplied: four Pulitzer Prizes, honorary degrees from Oxford and Cambridge, travel abroad as a government-sponsored ambassador of good will. Prestigious teaching appointments included stints as "poet in residence" at Amherst College and later at the University of Michigan in Ann Arbor. (He returned to Ann Arbor late in his life for the kind of poetry reading where he was adored and lionized by thousands of students.)

In his eighty-eighth year, Frost was asked to read one of his poems at the inauguration of President Kennedy. Eleven million television viewers saw the aged, white-maned poet struggle with his notes as the wind (or, in a different version of the story, the glaring sun) kept him from reading his prepared comments. He finally recited from memory "The Gift Outright," leaving his many admirers with the unforgettable memory of the poet's voice rising above the din and the hype of the nation's capital.

As a poet, performer, and public figure, Frost played the role of the New England sage. He appeared "wide-shouldered, craggy, tough in texture, solid as New Hampshire granite" (Louis Untermeyer). He spoke as the voice of homely truths, distrusting science, progress, and professors. He maintained the image of someone staying close to the grass roots, keeping in touch with the simple realities of rural living, distancing himself from movements and trends. ("I never dared be radical when young / For fear it would make me conservative when old.") He was wary of large abstractions and sweeping historical generalizations. He was impatient with talk that our period was particularly bad or the worst in the world's history. He said in a famous letter to the *Amherst Student,*

> Ages may vary a little. One may be a little worse than another. But it's not possible to get outside the age you are in to judge it exactly. Indeed it is as dangerous to try to get outside of anything as large as an age as it would be to try to engorge a donkey. Witness the many who in the attempt have suffered a dilation from which the tissues and muscles of the mind have never been able to recover natural shape. They can't pick up anything delicate or small anymore.

In the following poem, Frost assumes the characteristic stance of the country sage: Something ordinary happens, related to the familiar chores of the country dweller. Some small happening raises a question in the poet's mind. Two different ways of looking at the issue suggest themselves. The speaker in the poem weighs simple alternatives, honestly thinking the matter through. On reflection, what seemed a simple matter turns out to have a serious significance for how we think of ourselves or shape our lives. There is no waving of arms, no getting up on a soapbox to make a speech. The tone is one of New England understatement. There is something here worth thinking about, without getting all bothered and excited.

The Tuft of Flowers   1906

I went to turn the grass once after one
Who mowed it in the dew before the sun.

The dew was gone that made his blade so keen
Before I came to view the leveled scene.

I looked for him behind an isle of trees;   5
I listened for his whetstone on the breeze.

But he had gone his way, the grass all mown,
And I must be, as he had been—alone.

"As all must be," I said within my heart,
"Whether they work together or apart."   10

But as I said it, swift there passed me by
On noiseless wing a bewildered butterfly,

Seeking with memories grown dim o'er night
Some resting flower of yesterday's delight.

And once I marked his flight go round and round,   15
As where some flower lay withering on the ground.

And then he flew as far as eye could see,
And then on tremulous wing came back to me.

I thought of questions that have no reply,
And would have turned to toss the grass to dry;   20

But he turned first, and led my eye to look
At a tall tuft of flowers beside a brook,

A leaping tongue of bloom the scythe had spared
Beside a reedy brook the scythe had bared.

The mower in the dew had loved them thus,   25
By leaving them to flourish, not for us,

Nor yet to draw one thought of ours to him,
But from sheer morning gladness at the brim.

The butterfly and I had lit upon,
Nevertheless, a message from the dawn,   30

That made me hear the wakening birds around,
And hear his long scythe whispering to the ground,

And feel a spirit kindred to my own;
So that henceforth I worked no more alone,

But glad with him, I worked as with his aid,
And weary, sought at noon with him the shade;   35

And dreaming, as it were, held brotherly speech
With one whose thought I had not hoped to reach.

"Men work together," I told him from the heart,
"Whether they work together or apart."   40

In form, this poem has an almost childlike simplicity. Most of the stanzas are self-contained couplets in iambic pentameter, with little metrical variation. The most noticeable variation occurs early and is repeated in the last stanza. Initial trochaic inversion ("WHETHer | they WORK") serves to alerts us to the key issue and then accentuates the pronouncement to which the poem as a whole has built up. The stanzas tell the story step by step in simple "and-then" fashion, with no poetic frills. The speaker in the poem sees the grass that had been mown before and that is to be turned so it will dry in the sun. The mower is nowhere to be seen. The speaker in the poem thinks about the lonely fellow worker's morning labor. Later he notices first the butterfly, then the flowers by the brook that had been spared by the blade of the mower's scythe.

Yet in spite of this simple natural progression, the poem is not artless. Looking in vain for the mower who had worked early in the morning but is already gone, we are ready for the tentative initial thought about how all workers work essentially alone, doing their jobs whether recognized and supported by others or not. But the fluttering butterfly appears at the right time to guide us to the counterevidence: the tall tuft of flowers, the "leaping tongue of bloom," that the mower has left standing. The mower apparently did not intentionally spare the flowers for the sake of other human observers. Nevertheless, we become aware of a kindred spirit, who also took a special pleasure in the tuft of flowers and decided not to turn them into hay. The speaker in the poem neatly reverses his earlier conclusion: He "worked no more alone." The two contrasting points of view on whether we work alone or together are stated in exactly parallel form, with the last lines of the two related couplets serving as an identical refrain: "Whether they work together or apart" (lines 10 and 40).

Although many of Frost's best-loved poems are simple on the surface, they may turn out to be puzzlers; they remain open-ended. Frost once said that his poems "are set to trip the reader head foremost into the boundless." They trip us up, disturbing our smug set ways of thinking, making us ponder first one way of looking at things, then another. On another occasion, he said that he liked to write poems that seem "altogether obvious" to the casual reader but that turn out to be subtle in unexpected ways. We may want to reduce them to a simple formula, but we don't quite succeed.

Some of Frost's most famous poems have been interpreted in radically different ways. For instance, different readers have read diametrically opposed meanings into the poem "Mending Wall." Is it true that "Good fences make good neighbors"? Or is this kind of territorial thinking the product of an obsolete Stone Age mentality?

Mending Wall   1914

Something there is that doesn't love a wall,
That sends the frozen-ground-swell under it
And spills the upper boulders in the sun,
And makes gaps even two can pass abreast.
The work of hunters is another thing: 5
I have come after them and made repair
Where they have left not one stone on a stone,
But they would have the rabbit out of hiding,
To please the yelping dogs. The gaps I mean,
No one has seen them made or heard them made,   10
But at spring mending-time we find them there.
I let my neighbor know beyond the hill;
And on a day we meet to walk the line
And set the wall between us once again.
We keep the wall between us as we go.   15
To each the boulders that have fallen to each.
And some are loaves and some so nearly balls
We have to use a spell to make them balance:
"Stay where you are until our backs are turned!"
We wear our fingers rough with handling them.   20
Oh, just another kind of outdoor game,
One on a side. It comes to little more:
There where it is we do not need the wall:
He is all pine and I am apple orchard.
My apple trees will never get across   25
And eat the cones under his pines, I tell him.
He only says, "Good fences make good neighbors."
Spring is the michief in me, and I wonder
If I could put a notion in his head:
"Why do they make good neighbors? Isn't it   30
Where there are cows? But here there are no cows.
Before I built a wall I'd ask to know
What I was walling in or walling out,
And to whom I was like to give offense.
Something there is that doesn't love a wall,   35
That wants it down." I could say "Elves" to him,
But it's not elves exactly, and I'd rather
He said it for himself. I see him there,
Bringing a stone grasped firmly by the top
In each hand, like an old-stone savage armed.   40
He moves in darkness as it seems to me,

Not of woods only and the shade of trees.
He will not go behind his father's saying,
And he likes having thought of it so well
He says again, "Good fences make good neighbors."   45

The two critical excerpts that follow continue the dialogue between the speaker in the poem and his neighbor. The first reader, reading the poet's meanings out of the poem, agrees with the speaker: "Something there is that doesn't love a wall." (Even the first reader, however, reserves an escape clause, well aware that the poet might be up to "mischief.")

> Much of the public knows Frost by the phrase "Good fences make good neighbors." But the speaker in "Mending Wall" is saying just the opposite: that there is some mysterious force at work to break down barriers between human beings. "Elves," he calls it, in contrast to the matter-of-fact damage done by hunters (lines 5–11). But this is only a hint of what each person must discover for himself—companionship, respect, love, or the mystical togetherness of men who work.
>
> The speaker's description of his neighbor makes the point even clearer (lines 38–42). The man and his ideas still belong to stone-age savagery. The darkness which surrounds him is not simply the natural darkness of the woods, but the primordial destructiveness in the heart of man. There is darkness also in the conventional mentality that makes a man repeat "Good fences make good neighbors" simply because his father said it (lines 43–44), when it does not fit the new situation at all (lines 30–31).
>
> The poem, however, illustrates the difficulty of making a definite statement about any of Frost's ideas. The speaker does not agree with his neighbor in theory (lines 23–36); but, in the fact of his labor, he is doing the same thing his neighbor is doing.
>
> From David A. Sohn and Richard H. Tyre, *Frost: The Poet and His Poetry*

The second reader reaches the opposite conclusion. He brings into the poem **external evidence,** drawing on his previous knowledge of the poet's characteristic attitudes and themes. He thus illustrates to what extent the reader's reponse is often shaped by what the reader *brings to* the poem. Here, we are not reading the poem in isolation. We bring to bear our assumptions about the poet as the voice of traditional "Yankee individualist" values.

> Many general readers—and doubtless some stray sophisticated ones too—still see the poem as an argument against walls of all sorts, be they literal or metaphorical. To them walls are the divisive creations of selfish or shortsighted men who erect barriers to keep other people away. If only you will do away with useless, outmoded walls, they say, you will bring about a closer bond of fellowship—a deeper sense of community—among neighbors, in society at large, even among nations.
>
> Generally, however, careful readers regard such views as hostile to the themes and attitudes they characteristically find in Frost. To them "Mending Wall" is Frost's finest expression of concern that in a world which doesn't seem to love a wall the individual may somehow get lost. To them the Yankee farmer, despite the scoffing questions that he puts to his neighbor, is the symbol of all those who love their privacy and their independence, and are resentful

of those people—individuals or social planners—who would intrude upon that privacy. Or he is any individual who resents the levelers who would destroy walls and thus let others, even if friend or neighbor, infringe upon his right to be alone and to think his own thoughts after his own fashion. In short, despite the obvious warm appeal of the good neighborliness that wants walls down—even for the Yankee individualist resentful of intrusions—walls are nonetheless the essential barriers that must exist between man and man if the individual is to preserve his own soul, and mutual understanding and respect are to survive and flourish. . . .

A wall is something more than the means for walling something visible in or out. If apple trees and pine cones were the only concern, then good fences would scarcely be worth the trouble it takes to keep them repaired. But in spite of all his scoffing the narrator knows that this is the least of the purposes that are served by good fences. This is why each spring it is he who takes the initiative and lets his neighbor know beyond the hill that once again it's time for mending wall. Good fences make good neighbors.

From William S. Ward, "Lifted Pot Lids and Unmended Walls," *College English*, February 1966

THE RECEPTIVE READER

1. Cluster or free-associate the word *wall*. What images, associations, or memories does it bring to mind?

2. Which of the two readings do you agree with and why? Which of the two competing attitudes toward walls do you sympathize with and why?

3. Pressed in an interview to say where he stood on the issue of fences, Frost once said: "Maybe I was *both* fellows in the poem." What do you think he meant?

Honoring a poetic tradition that goes back to ancient Greece and Rome, Frost took his readers from the neuroses of city living to a simpler rural world. In the words of Babette Deutsch in *Poetry in Our Time,* he wrote about the commonplace subjects of country life: "the steady caring for crops and creatures"; the "homely details of barn and farmhouse, orchard, pasture and wood lot"; apple-picking, haymaking, repairing orchard walls of loosely piled stones. He celebrated "the jeweled vision of blueberries in rain-wet leaves"; no one wrote "more tenderly of the young life on and about the farm, be it a runaway colt, a young orchard threatened by false spring, a nestful of fledglings exposed by the cultivator."

Frost did not ignore the harsher or bleaker side of farm life: the "drudgery and isolation," ghastly accidents caused by machinery. However, only rarely do his best-known poems show the poet's darker and more pessimistic side. Donald Hall adored the older man when Hall himself was an aspiring young poet, and he befriended the aging poet toward the end of his career. Hall wrote about the anguish and sense of guilt that lay behind the public image of the "twinkling Yankee" of the Frost legend:

To him—I learned over the years—his family background seemed precarious, dangerous; and his adult life cursed with tragedy, for which he took responsibility. His father was a sometime drunk, dead at an early age; his mother endured a bad marriage, was widowed young, and failed as a schoolteacher when she returned to her native Massachusetts; yet she was a fond mother, kind to her children—and she wrote poems. Her son felt dangerously close to her, and followed that fondness into devotion to one young woman, Elinor White, whom he courted extravagantly, romantically, and doggedly. Apparently losing her, he considered suicide; at least, he later dropped hints to friends that he had considered suicide. When Elinor and Robert finally married, they settled in Derry, New Hampshire, and lived in poverty, enduring an extraordinary series of family misfortunes: their firstborn child, a son named Elliott, died of cholera infantum at the age of three; in later years, warning or bragging about his "badness," Frost said that the doctor who attended Elliott blamed him for the death, for not having called a doctor sooner. The next child was Lesley, daughter and eldest survivor, celebrator and denouncer of her father. Then there was Irma, mad in middle life and institutionalized; Frost's only sister had been insane, he himself frequently fearful of madness; he blamed himself and his genes for his daughter's insanity. Then came Carroll, his son, who killed himself at the age of thirty-eight. Youngest was Marjorie, dead after childbirth at twenty-nine.

The following late sonnet is the best known of the poems in which Frost confronted "the anguish of existence and the presence of the malign" (Babette Deutsch).

Design   1922

I found a dimpled spider, fat and white,
On a white heal-all, holding up a moth
Like a white piece of rigid satin cloth—
Assorted characters of death and blight
Mixed ready to begin the morning right,   5
Like the ingredients of a witches' broth—
A snow-drop spider, a flower like a froth,
And dead wings carried like a paper kite.

What had that flower to do with being white,
The wayside blue and innocent heal-all?   10
What brought the kindred spider to that height,
Then steered the white moth thither in the night?
What but design of darkness to appall?—
If design govern in a thing so small.

This poem is a finely crafted sonnet, with an underlying iambic pentameter beat, and with the interlaced rhyme scheme in the Petrarchan manner. The almost casual and at times playful tone sets up an ironic contrast with the miniature scene of death and blight:

Frost achieves utter horror in this poem, which many consider his most terrifying work, by juxtaposing pleasant images with disgusting ones: the fat spider is "dimpled" and "white" like a baby; "dead wings" become a "paper kite": "death and blight" are cheerfully "mixed ready to begin the morning right," as in an ad for breakfast food. An air of abnormality pervades the entire poem. The flower, ironically called the "heal-all," is usually blue, but this is a mutant. The spider is at a height where it would not normally be found. Moths are ordinarily attracted by light, but this one has been "steered" to its death in the night. And all the "characters of death" share the same ghastly whiteness.

Can we escape the conclusion that a dark design in nature plotted against the moth? The last line may not offer the ray of light its tone suggests. What would be better—that darkness terrorize by design, or that all the little evils in the world operate without design?

Consider also the game Frost plays with the reader by calling this sonnet "Design." A sonnet is a very small, yet intricately designed, poetic form of 14 lines; yet the speaker asks at the end if design really governs in very small things.

From David A. Sohn and Richard H. Tyre, *Frost: The Poet and His Poetry*

THE RECEPTIVE READER

Do you agree with these two editors on the "utter horror" and on the "air of abnormality" that they say pervades the poem? Do you tend to answer the final question raised by the poem the same way they do?

Robert Frost achieved the difficult feat of being admired (sometimes grudgingly) by critics and his poetic peers while at the same time reaching a large popular audience. Critics and fellow poets acclaimed him even though he was at odds with poetic fashions in the first half of the twentieth century. The most influential and most widely imitated poets of his time were poets like T. S. Eliot and Ezra Pound. They wrote difficult poems, filled with shifting images and obscure allusions, that to some readers made Frost's more accessible, simple-on-the-surface poems seem unsophisticated by comparison. Furthermore, Frost made himself the advocate of traditional form when the modern tendency was to reject traditional meter and rhyme as artificial, confining, or extraneous. He said on the role of form in our lives and in the world,

> Any psychiatrist will tell you that making a basket, or making a horseshoe, or giving anything form gives you a confidence in the universe. . . that it has form, see. When you talk about your troubles and go to somebody about them, you're just a fool. The best way to settle them is to make something that has form, because all you want to do is get a sense of form.

CROSS-REFERENCES—For Discussion or Writing

✧ Other poems by Robert Frost printed earlier in this volume include "Stopping by Woods" (p. 402) and "Fire and Ice" (p. 458). Do they illustrate some of the features characteristic of the poems you have just read?

✧ Compare and contrast Frost's "Design" with Whitman's "A Noiseless Patient Spider"—another poem in which a spider serves as the central symbol (p. 413).

POEMS FOR FURTHER STUDY

In reading these poems by Robert Frost, keep in mind questions like the following: Does the poem conform to the pattern of making a natural scene or an event real for you and then making you share in the reflections it inspires?

Does the poem play off two different ways of looking at things? Which prevails and how? Is the poem in the "cool" New England voice? Or do you hear a more bitter, passionate, or questioning voice?

After Apple-Picking   1914

My long two-pointed ladder's sticking through a tree
Toward heaven still,
And there's a barrel that I didn't fill
Beside it, and there may be two or three
Apples I didn't pick upon some bough.   5
But I am done with apple-picking now.
Essence of winter sleep is on the night,
The scent of apples: I am drowsing off.
I cannot rub the strangeness from my sight
I got from looking through a pane of glass   10
I skimmed this morning from the drinking trough
And held against the world of hoary grass.
It melted, and I let it fall and break.
But I was well
Upon my way to sleep before it fell,   15
And I could tell
What form my dreaming was about to take.
Magnified apples appear and disappear,
Stem end and blossom end,
And every fleck of russet showing clear.   20
My instep arch not only keeps the ache,
It keeps the pressure of a ladder-round.
I feel the ladder sway as the boughs bend.
And I keep hearing from the cellar bin
The rumbling sound   25
Of load on load of apples coming in.
For I have had too much
Of apple-picking: I am overtired
Of the great harvest I myself desired.
There were ten thousand thousand fruit to touch,   30
Cherish in hand, lift down, and not let fall.
For all
That struck the earth,
No matter if not bruised or spiked with stubble,
Went surely to the cider-apple heap   35
As of no worth.
One can see what will trouble
This sleep of mine, whatever sleep it is.
Were he not gone,
The woodchuck could say whether it's like his   40
Long sleep, as I describe its coming on,
Or just some human sleep.

The Road Not Taken 1915

Two roads diverged in a yellow wood,
And sorry I could not travel both
And be one traveler, long I stood
And looked down one as far as I could
To where it bent in the undergrowth; 5

Then took the other, as just as fair,
And having perhaps the better claim,
Because it was grassy and wanted wear;
Though as for that the passing there
Had worn them really about the same, 10

And both that morning equally lay
In leaves no step had trodden black.
Oh, I kept the first for another day!
Yet knowing how way leads on to way,
I doubted if I should ever come back. 15

I shall be telling this with a sigh
Somewhere ages and ages hence:
Two roads diverged in a wood, and I—
I took the one less traveled by,
And that has made all the difference. 20

The Oven Bird 1916

There is a singer everyone has heard,
Loud, a mid-summer and a mid-wood bird,
Who makes the solid tree trunks sound again.
He says that leaves are old and that for flowers
Mid-summer is to spring as one to ten. 5
He says the early petal-fall is past,
When pear and cherry bloom went down in showers
On sunny days a moment overcast;
And comes that other fall we name the fall.
He says the highway dust is over all. 10
The bird would cease and be as other birds
But that he knows in singing not to sing.
The question that he frames in all but words
Is what to make of a diminished thing.

Acquainted with the Night 1928

I have been one acquainted with the night.
I have walked out in rain—and back in rain.
I have outwalked the furthest city light.

I have looked down the saddest city lane.
I have passed by the watchman on his beat 5

And dropped my eyes, unwilling to explain.

I have stood still and stopped the sound of feet
When far away an interrupted cry
Came over houses from another street,

But not to call me back or say good-by;   10
And further still at an unearthly height,
One luminary clock against the sky

Proclaimed the time was neither wrong nor right.
I have been one acquainted with the night.

Neither Out Far Nor In Deep   1936

The people along the sand
All turn and look one way.
They turn their back on the land.
They look at the sea all day.

As long as it takes to pass   5
A ship keeps raising its hull;
The wetter ground like glass
Reflects a standing gull.

The land may vary more;
But wherever the truth may be—   10
The water comes ashore,
And the people look at the sea.

They cannot look out far.
They cannot look in deep.
But when was that ever a bar   15
To any watch they keep?

The Silken Tent   1939

She is as in a field a silken tent
At midday when a sunny summer breeze
Has dried the dew and all its ropes relent,
So that in guys it gently sways at ease,
And its supporting central cedar pole,   5
That is its pinnacle to heavenward
And signifies the sureness of the soul,
Seems to owe naught to any single cord,
But strictly held by none, is loosely bound
By countless silken ties of love and thought   10
To everything on earth the compass round,
And only by one's going slightly taut
In the capriciousness of summer air
Is of the slightest bondage made aware.

Once by the Pacific   1928

The shattered water made a misty din.
Great waves looked over others coming in,
And thought of doing something to the shore
That water never did to land before.
The clouds were low and hairy in the skies,   5
Like locks blown forward in the gleam of eyes.
You could not tell, and yet it looked as if
The shore was lucky in being backed by cliff,
The cliff in being backed by continent;
It looked as if a night of dark intent   10
Was coming, and not only a night, an age.
Someone had better be prepared for rage.
There would be more than ocean-water broken
Before God's last *Put out the Light* was spoken.

Facsimile of Robert Frost's original manuscript. Courtesy Robert Frost Collection, Clifton Waller Barrett Library, Special Collections Department, Manuscripts, University of Virginia Library.

The Night Light

1947

She always had to burn a light
Beside her attic bed at night.
It gave bad dreams and broken sleep,
But helped the Lord her soul to keep.
Good gloom on her was thrown away.   5
It is on me by night or day,
Who have, as I suppose, ahead
The darkest of it still to dread.

On Being Idolized

1947

The wave sucks back and with the last of water
It wraps a wisp of seaweed round my legs,
And with the swift rush of its sandy dregs
So undermines my barefoot stand I totter
And did I not take steps would be tipped over   5
Like the ideal of some mistaken lover.

Nothing Gold Can Stay

1923

Nature's first green is gold,
Her hardest hue to hold.
Her early leaf's a flower;
But only so an hour.
Then leaf subsides to leaf.   5
So Eden sank to grief,
So dawn goes down to day.
Nothing gold can stay.

CROSS-REFERENCES—For Discussion or Writing

For a library research project, search for books and articles that would provide material for the treatment of one of the following topics:

◇ Several critical discussions of the same poem by Robert Frost. How does the poem look from different critical perspectives? How much common ground is there? What are significant differences, and how do you explain them?

◇ Several different perspectives on the private person behind the public legend. Books and articles have been written to defend Frost against what friends and biographers considered unjustified attacks on the poet. What was involved in these controversies?

Books you may be able to consult may include the following:

Reuben Brower, *The Poetry of Robert Frost* (1963)
Radcliffe Squires, *The Major Themes of Robert Frost* (1963)
J. F. Lynan, *The Pastoral Art of Robert Frost* (1964)

Philip L. Gerber, *Robert Frost* (1966)
Reginald L. Cook, *Robert Frost: A Living Voice* (1975)
Richard Poirier, *Robert Frost: The Work of Knowing* (1977)
John C. Kemp, *Robert Frost and New England: The Poet as Regionalist* (1979)
James L. Potter, *The Robert Frost Handbook* (1980)
William Pritchard, *Frost: A Literary Life Reconsidered* (1984)
John Evangelist Walsh, *Into My Own: The English Years of Robert Frost* (1988)

GWENDOLYN BROOKS: COMMITMENT AND UNIVERSALITY

*Gwendolyn Brooks has never denied her engagement in the
contemporary situation or been over-obsessed by it.*
HARVEY CURTIS WEBSTER

*Art hurts. Art urges voyages—
and it is easier to stay at home,
the nice beer ready.*
GWENDOLYN BROOKS, "THE CHICAGO PICASSO"

*I am absolutely free of what any white critic might say
because I feel that it's going to be amazing if any of them
understand the true significance of the struggle that's
going on.*
GWENDOLYN BROOKS

Gwendolyn Brooks (born 1917) is the most powerful and most widely respected of contemporary African-American poets. Many of her poems deal uncompromisingly with the bleak realities of poverty and racism. At the same time, they often bring tremendous empathy to representative lives and people in the black community, especially the old and the very young. (She has written many poems for or about children.) In the late sixties and early seventies, she became part of the movement that explored sources of strength in the black heritage and in solidarity with fellow artists exploring the African past. During an age of passionate but often short-lived rhetoric, she has written poems of understated eloquence and harsh beauty.

Gwendolyn Brooks was born in Topeka, Kansas, but she lived most of her life in Chicago, and she became poet laureate of the state of Illinois. She grew up in a closely knit, loving, traditional family ("no child abuse, no prostitution, no Mafia membership," she said in a 1984 self-interview). The Brooks' house was filled with poetry, story, music, and song; she grew up in a "family-oriented" world with much visiting by and of relatives, traditional holiday feasts, family and church picnics. Her parents, she says, "subscribed to duty, decency, dignity, industry—*kindness.*" Her first poem was published in a children's magazine when she was ten; when in high school, she published several poems in the *Defender,* a black newspaper in Chicago. She received a Pulitzer Prize for poetry in 1950, the first and only African-American woman to receive the award until Alice Walker won a Pulitzer for *The Color Purple* in 1983. In 1987, Brooks was the first black woman to be elected an honorary fellow of the Modern Language Association. She has spent much of her time working with young people in colleges and schools and promoting workshops and awards for young poets.

The constant in Brooks' poetry has been her loyalty to characters who find themselves trapped in an environment scarred by racial discrimination, poverty, and violence. She populated the imaginary community of Bronzeville with a haunting array of the living human beings behind the stereotypes and government statistics. She chronicled their grey daily lives, their disillusionment and self-doubts, their defiance and futile rebellions. She observed with icy scorn the charitable rich who, from winters in Palm Beach and their world of "hostess gowns, and sunburst clocks, / Turtle soup, Chippendale," venture forth in search of the "worthy poor," only to be appalled by the squalor of the slums. Her most famous poem is a poem of doomed youth—jaunty, defiant, lost.

We Real Cool   1960

The Pool Players.
Seven at the Golden Shovel.

We real cool. We
Left school. We

Lurk late. We
Strike straight. We

Sing sin. We   5
Thin gin. We

Jazz June. We
Die soon.

This poem, with its broken, syncopated, beboppy counterrhythm ("We real cool. We / Left school"), is an anthem for doomed youth who act "cool" as a defensive armor. They have dropped out and find themselves in the slow lane to a dead end. They jazz up, or live up, June and will be dead soon after.

THE RECEPTIVE READER

Do you think you recognize the young people in the poem? What do you think is the poet's attitude toward them? How does she relate to them? How do you?

Brooks writes with special affection of young people who rebel against the narrow boundaries of their lives, adopting a stance of defiance or escaping into an intensely imagined fantasy world. The sense of being trapped and intensely imagined dreams of escape become recurrent themes in poems like "Hunchback Girl."

Hunchback Girl: She Thinks of Heaven 1945

My Father, it is surely a blue place
And straight. Right. Regular. Where I shall find
No need for scholarly nonchalance or looks
A little to the left or guards upon the
Heart to halt love that runs without crookedness 5
Along its crooked corridors. My Father,
It is a planned place surely. Out of coils,
Unscrewed, released, no more to be marvelous,
I shall walk straightly through most proper halls
Proper myself, princess of properness. 10

The poem is in the form of a passionate prayer, with the girl addressing "My Father" twice. The hunchbacked girl thinks of a future state where her burden will be lifted. In heaven ("surely a blue place / And straight"), she will no longer be stared or marveled at ("no more to be marvelous"). Everything that is crooked or coiled will there be straightened out, made right and regular and proper. She will walk "straightly through most proper halls," a very "princess of properness." She will no longer have to try hard to look nonchalant when being stared at; she will no longer have to avoid people's eyes. So desperately needed is this release, so insistently wished for and imagined, so firmly believed in, that no one, inside the poem or out, could have the heart to call it merely a dream.

THE RECEPTIVE READER

1. To judge from the poem, what is the girl's usual way of coping with her disability?

2. Some critics have noted the *ambiguity* of the words *marvel* and *marvelous*. These words may refer to something to be stared at in fear but also to something arousing wonder or to be contemplated in awe. Does the poem bring into play either or both of these meanings?

3. Is it *paradoxical* that in the girl's heart love runs "without crookedness"—but that the corridors of the heart (hers? ours?) are themselves crooked? What did the poet have in mind? How do you explain the paradox?

4. One reader said that the irony underlying this poem is that "nothing in life is without its crookedness." What did she mean?

THE PERSONAL RESPONSE

Would you call the feelings expressed in this poem a mere dream? Have you or has someone you know well ever experienced similar feelings?

Brooks seems to speak most directly in her personal voice in poems of buried emotion, of humanity defeated by harsh reality. In the following sonnet, the "glory" of the pianist's music and the feeling of "proud delight" it calls up prevail for a time until they are drowned out by the unheard phantom cries of bitter men killed in war.

Piano after War   1945

On a snug evening I shall watch her fingers,
Cleverly ringed, declining to clever pink,
Beg glory from the willing keys. Old hungers
Will break their coffins, rise to eat and thank.
And music, warily, like the golden rose   5
That sometimes after sunset warms the west,
Will warm that room, persuasively suffuse
That room and me, rejuvenate a past.
But suddenly, across my climbing fever
Of proud delight—a multiplying cry.   10
A cry of bitter dead men who will never
Attend a gentle maker of musical joy.
Then my thawed eye will go again to ice.
And stone will shove the softness from my face.

The music in this poem unfolds like a "golden rose," wakening long-since-buried capacities for joy. "Old hungers" break their coffins. The glow thaws the icy heart—but only for a time. Suddenly, the memory of the dead undercuts the feeling of gentleness and joy; their fate makes the glories of culture an unkept promise. However tempting, the blessings of traditional culture cannot really soften the bitterness left behind by disappointed hopes.

THE RECEPTIVE READER

1. What do you think are the "old hungers" aroused from "their coffins" in this poem?
2. How does this sonnet follow the traditional pattern of a *turning point* in the middle of a poem and of a concluding *couplet* that leaves the reader with a strong final impression?
3. Were you *surprised* by the turn the poem takes? Does the poem early strike a note of wariness, of ironic detachment?

Brooks writes with special empathy and understated tenderness about children, like the two girls in the following poem from *Bronzeville Boys and Girls*.

Mexie and Bridie 1945

A tiny tea-party
Is happening today.
Pink cakes, and nuts and bon-bons on
A tiny, shiny tray.

It's out within the weather, 5
Beneath the clouds and sun.
And pausing ants have peeked upon,
As birds and gods have done.

Mexie's in her white dress,
And Bridie's in her brown. 10
There are no finer ladies
Tea-ing in the town.

In the words of Gary Smith, the children in Brooks' poems confront the essential dilemma of "how to find meaning and purpose in a world that denies their very existence." They live in a world of enclosed space—"alleyways, front and back yards, vacant lots, and back rooms"—symbolizing the restrictions that prevent their physical and mental growth. "Although trees, flowers, and grass poke through the concrete blocks of the urban environment, they are only reminders of a forbidden Eden." Not surprisingly,

> the overwhelming desire for many of her children is the need to escape, to flee, the various forms of socioeconomic and psychological oppression that thwart self-fulfillment and threaten to destroy their lives. Because it is to a world free of adults where most of her children wish to escape, their unique ability to imagine this world—albeit on the wings of fantasy—distinguishes them from adults and creates some sense of hope.
> From Gary Smith, "Paradise Regained: The Children of Gwendolyn Brooks' *Bronzeville*," in Marie Mootry and Gary Smith, eds., *A Life Distilled: Gwendolyn Brooks, Her Poetry and Fiction*

Many of Brooks' poems were milestones in the spiritual journey of the black community from the goal of assimilation to the defiant acceptance of one's own identity. For her, as for many other black artists and writers, the years from 1967 to 1972 were years of awakening as the movement toward black pride and self-respect, in her words, "italicized black identity, solidarity, self-possession" and "vitally acknowledged African roots." In these years of "hot-breathing hope," when "the air was heavy with logic, illogic, zeal, construction," she read books about the black experience from W. E. Burghardt Du Bois' *The Souls of Black Folk* to the novels of Zora Neale Hurston. She exchanged views with black writers from James Baldwin to Don L. Lee. As she said later, "We talked, we walked, we read our work in taverns and churches and jail." She started to organize workshops for young poets and future teachers.

During these years, Brooks found her way to the self-affirmation and positive self-image needed to break the hold of negative stereotypes on one's own mind. She said,

Black woman . . . must remember that her personhood precedes her femalehood; that sweet as sex may be, she cannot endlessly brood on Black man's blondes, blues, blunders. She is a person in the world—with wrongs to right, stupidities to outwit, with her man if possible, on her own when not. And she is also here to enjoy. She will be here, like any other, once only. Therefore she must, in the midst of tragedy and hatred and neglect, in the midst of her own efforts to purify, mightily enjoy the readily available: sunshine and pets and children and conversation and games and travel (tiny or large) and books and walks and chocolate cake.

During the years of the civil rights movement, Brooks' work, like the work of many African-American writers and artists, became more committed and more political. In her poems on major events in the struggle, she speaks both as a "seer and sayer" for the black experience and as the voice of conscience for the larger community. One of her best-known poems takes stock of a reporter's foray to Little Rock, Arkansas, during the desegregation battle fought over the admission of the first nine black students to Central High. Backed by the Supreme Court's *Brown* decision outlawing segregated public schools, protected by federal troops called in by President Eisenhower, the students prevailed against the governor of the state, spitting and jeering mobs, and harassment and abuse from fellow students. (For a year, in a last-ditch stand, the governor closed all public schools.)

The Chicago Defender *Sends a Man to Little Rock*　　　　1960
Fall, 1957

In Little Rock the people bear
Babes, and comb and part their hair
And watch the want ads, put repair
To roof and latch. While wheat toast burns
A woman waters multiferns.　　　　　　　　　　　　　　　5

Time upholds or overturns
The many, tight, and small concerns.

In Little Rock the people sing
Sunday hymns like anything,
Through Sunday pomp and polishing.　　　　　　　　　　10

And after testament and tunes,
Some soften Sunday afternoons
With lemon tea and Lorna Doones.

I forecast
And I believe　　　　　　　　　　　　　　　　　　　15

Come Christmas Little Rock will cleave
To Christmas tree and trifle, weave,
From laugh and tinsel, texture fast.

In Little Rock is baseball; Barcarolle.
That hotness in July . . . the uniformed figures raw and implacable   20
And not intellectual,
Batting the hotness or clawing the suffering dust.
The Open Air Concert, on the special twilight green. . . .
When Beethoven is brutal or whispers to lady-like air.
Blanket-sitters are solemn, as Johann troubles to lean   25
To tell them what to mean. . . .

There is love, too, in Little Rock. Soft women softly
Opening themselves in kindness,
Or, pitying one's blindness,
Awaiting one's pleasure   30
In azure
Glory with anguished rose at the root. . . .
To wash away old semi-discomfitures.
They re-teach purple and unsullen blue.
The wispy soils go. And uncertain   35
Half-havings have they clarified to sures.

In Little Rock they know
Not answering the telephone is a way of rejecting life,
That it is our business to be bothered, is our business
To cherish bores or boredom, be polite   40
To lies and love and many-faceted fuzziness.

I scratch my head, massage the hate-I-had.
I blink across my prim and pencilled pad.
The saga I was sent for is not down.
Because there is a puzzle in this town.   45
The biggest News I do not dare
Telegraph to the Editor's chair:
"They are like people everywhere."

The angry Editor would reply
In hundred harryings of Why.   50

And true, they are hurling spittle, rock,
Garbage and fruit in Little Rock.
And I saw coiling storm a-writhe
On bright madonnas. And a scythe
Of men harassing brownish girls.   55
(The bows and barrettes in the curls
And braids declined away from joy.)

I saw a bleeding brownish boy. . . .

The lariat lynch-wish I deplored.

The loveliest lynchee was our Lord.   60

The people in this poem attend to their many large and small concerns—giving birth, baking, grooming, watering, tinkering, answering the telephone. They listen to operatic favorites (Offenbach's "Barcarolle") and Beethoven; sitting on blankets, they solemnly listen at the open-air concert to Johann (Sebastian Bach). They sing Sunday hymns "like anything," and come Christmas they will do it justice, tree and tinsel and all. They are capable of love, politeness, and boredom. The problem is that all this ordinariness is not what the editor of the *Defender* sent the reporter to Little Rock to find.

The dramatic discovery in this poem is what the German-Jewish writer Hannah Arendt has called the "banality of evil." The reporter from the *Chicago Defender* was ready to hate and revile melodramatic villains. But the "biggest news" is: Evil here is committed in a city of everyday people. The rock-throwing, spittle-hurling mob disperses to return to everyday homes. This discovery makes us rethink our usual assumption that people who do evil are monstrous creatures very different from ourselves. The people throwing the rocks and spitting on the "bright madonnas" are someone's Uncle Joe or Cousin Roy. Jesus was crucified in a city full of ordinary people. The poet encourages us to look for the sources of evil not outside among alien intruders but inside the human heart.

THE RECEPTIVE READER

1. How do you think the people trying to block desegregation were seen by the civil rights workers at the time? How do you think the segregationists saw themselves? How is the poet's perspective different from either?

2. What use does she make of *religious references* at the end of the poem? With what effect?

3. Do you think the stand the poet takes on the events of the time is too strong or not strong enough?

CROSS-REFERENCES—For Discusssion or Writing

Other poems by Gwendolyn Brooks included earlier in this volume are "Truth" (p. 416) and "A Song in the Front Yard" (p. 609). Do you recognize in them the poet's characteristic voice or a characteristic way of looking at the world?

POEMS FOR FURTHER STUDY

An editor and fellow poet said about Gwendolyn Brooks that she is "a woman who cannot live without her art, but who has never put her art above or before the people she writes about." In reading the following poems, pay special attention to the relation between content and form, between the poet's subject matter and her use of language.

When You Have Forgotten Sunday: The Love Story   1945

——And when you have forgotten the bright bedclothes on a Wednesday and a
    Saturday,
And most especially when you have forgotten Sunday—
When you have forgotten Sunday halves in bed,
Or me sitting on the front-room radiator in the limping afternoon
Looking off down the long street   5
To nowhere,
Hugged by my plain old wrapper of no-expectation
And nothing-I-have-to-do and I'm-happy-why?
And if-Monday-never-had-to-come—
When you have forgotten that, I say,   10
And how you swore, if somebody beeped the bell,
And how my heart played hopscotch if the telephone rang;
And how we finally went in to Sunday dinner,
That is to say, went across the front-room floor to the ink-spotted table in the
    southwest corner
To Sunday dinner, which was always chicken and noodles   15
Or chicken and rice
And salad and rye bread and tea
And chocolate chip cookies—
I say, when you have forgotten that,
When you have forgotten my little presentiment   20
That the war would be over before they got to you;
And how we finally undressed and whipped out the light and flowed into bed,
And lay loose-limbed for a moment in the week-end
Bright bedclothes,
Then gently folded into each other—   25
When you have, I say, forgotten all that,
Then you may tell,
Then I may believe
You have forgotten me well.

The Chicago Picasso, August 15, 1967   1967

*Mayor Daley tugged a white ribon, loosing the blue percale
wrap. A hearty cheer went up as the covering slipped off
the big steel sculpture that looks at once like a bird and a
woman.*

                                        CHICAGO *SUN-TIMES*

(Seiji Ozawa leads the Symphony.
The Mayor smiles.
And 50,000 See.)

Does man love Art? Man visits Art, but squirms.
Art hurts. Art urges voyages—
and it is easier to stay at home,

the nice beer ready.
        In commonrooms
we belch, or sniff, or scratch.
Are raw.

But we must cook ourselves and style ourselves for Art, who
is a requiring courtesan.
We squirm.
We do not hug the Mona Lisa.
We
may touch or tolerate
an astounding fountain, or a horse-and-rider.
At most, another Lion.

Observe the tall cold of a Flower
which is as innocent and as guilty,
as meaningful and as meaningless as any
other flower in the western field.

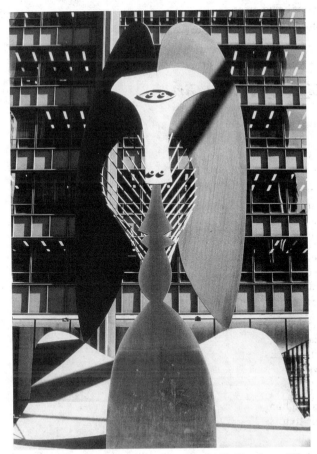

Pablo Picasso, "Chicago Civic Center." David H. Hamilton / The
Image Bank.

The Preacher Ruminates behind the Sermon 1945

I think it must be lonely to be God.
Nobody loves a master. No. Despite
the bright hosannas, bright dear-Lords, and bright
Determined reverence of Sunday eyes.

Picture Jehovah striding through the hall 5
Of His importance, creatures running out
From servant-corners to acclaim, to shout
Appreciation of his merit's glare.

But who walks with Him?—dares to take His arm,
To slap him on the shoulder, tweak His ear, 10
Buy Him a Coca-Cola or a beer,
Pooh-pooh his politics, call Him a fool?

Perhaps—who knows?—He tires of looking down.
Those eyes are never lifted. Never straight.
Perhaps sometimes he tires of being great 15
In solitude. Without a hand to hold.

The Ballad of the Light-Eyed Little Girl 1949

Sweet Sally took a cardboard box,
And in went pigeon poor.
Whom she had starved to death but not
For lack of love, be sure.

The wind it harped as twenty men. 5
The wind it harped like hate.
It whipped our light-eyed little girl,
It made her wince and wait.

It screeched a hundred elegies
As it punished her light eyes 10
(Though only kindness covered these)
And it made her eyebrows rise.

"Now bury your bird," the wind it bawled,
"And bury him down and down
Who had to put his trust in one 15
So light-eyed and so brown.

"So light-eyed and so villainous,
Who whooped and who could hum
But could not find the time to toss
Confederate his crumb." 20

She has taken her passive pigeon poor,
She has buried him down and down.

He never shall sally to Sally
Nor soil any roofs of the town.

She has sprinkled nail polish on dead dandelions. 25
And children have gathered around
Funeral for him whose epitaph
Is "PIGEON—Under the ground."

The Bean Eaters 1960

They eat beans mostly, this old yellow pair.
Dinner is a casual affair.
Plain chipware on a plain and creaking wood,
Tin flatware.
Two who are Mostly Good. 5
Two who have lived their day,
But keep on putting on their clothes
And putting things away.

And remembering . . .
Remembering, with twinklings and twinges, 10
As they lean over the beans in their rented back room that is full of beads and receipts
    and dolls and cloths, tobacco crumbs, vases and fringes.

The Boy Died in My Alley 1975

Without my having known.
Policeman said, next morning,
"Apparently died Alone."
"You heard a shot?" Policeman said.
Shots I hear and Shots I hear. 5
I never see the dead.

The Shot that killed him yes I heard
as I heard the Thousand shots before;
careening tinnily down the nights
across my years and arteries. 10

Policeman pounded on my door.
"Who is it?" "POLICE!" Policeman yelled.
"A boy was dying in your alley.
A boy is dead, and in your alley.
And have you known this Boy before?" 15

I have known this Boy before.
I have known this Boy before, who

ornaments my alley.
I never saw his face at all.
I never saw his futurefall.
But I have known this Boy. 20

I have always heard him deal with death.
I have always heard the shout, the volley.
I have closed my heart-ears late and early.
And I have killed him ever. 25
I joined the Wild and killed him
with knowledgeable unknowing.
I saw where he was going.
I saw him Crossed. And seeing,
I did not take him down. 30

He cried not only "Father!"
but "Mother!
Sister!
Brother!"
The cry climbed up the alley. 35
It went up to the wind.
It hung upon the heaven
for a long
stretch-strain of Moment.

The red floor of my alley
is a special speech to me. 40

CROSS-REFERENCES—For Discussion or Writing

For a library research project, search for books and articles that would provide material on one of the following topics:

✧ Gwendolyn Brooks' view of the social responsibility of the writer. What is the relationship between protest and poetry in her work? What are her views on the political responsibilities of the poet?

✧ Gwendolyn Brooks' relationship with or influence on other black writers. What black writer or writers did most to help shape her poetry or her views? What has been her influence on other black poets?

✧ What has been the treatment of black men in her poetry? Has it changed over the years?

Books you may be able to consult may include the following:

Harry B. Shaw, *Gwendolyn Brooks* (1980)
Claudia Tate, *Black Women Writers at Work* (1983)
Mari Evans, ed., *Black Women Writers (1950–80): A Critical Evaluation* (1984)
R. Baxter Miller, ed., *Black American Poets between Worlds, 1940–60* (1986)
Marie Mootry and Gary Smith, eds., *A Life Distilled: Gwendolyn Brooks, Her Poetry and Fiction* (1987)
Haki Madhubuti (Don L. Lee), *Say That the River Turns: The Impact of Gwendolyn Brooks* (1987)
D. H. Melhem, *Gwendolyn Brooks: Poetry and the Heroic Voice* (1987)
George E. Kent, *A Life of Gwendolyn Brooks* (1990)

WRITING ABOUT LITERATURE

23. The Poet and the Critics (Documented Paper)

The Writing Workshop   For the projects outlined earlier in this chapter, you will have to develop your own efficient, productive way of using library resources. Your finished paper will differ from other papers you have written in two major ways: First, you will be *integrating* material from a range of different sources. (Make sure that your paper will not appear to be made up of large chunks of undigested quotation.) Second, you will be *documenting* your sources, giving full information about the books and articles you have used.

Finding Promising Leads   To work up material for your paper, begin by checking in electronic or printed indexes for books, collections of critical articles, and individual articles in periodicals. For a writer like Dickinson, Frost, or Brooks, most college libraries will have a wide range of critical and scholarly sources. Often critical studies will include bibliographies alerting you to other promising leads.

Taking Notes   During your exploratory reading, you need to look sources over quickly, deciding whether they will be helpful. But you also have to slow down and close in when you hit upon promising materials. Remember:

✧ *Be a stickler for accuracy.* Copy direct quotations accurately, word for word. Enclose all quoted material in quotation marks to show material copied verbatim. (Include the *closing* quotation mark to show where the quotation ends.)

✧ *Tag your notes.* Start your notes with a tag or descriptor. (Indicate the subtopic or section of your paper where a quotation or piece of information will be useful.)

✧ *Record publishing information.* On your first entry for any one source (or in a separate bibliography entry), record all data you will need later when you identify your source in a documented paper. Include exact page numbers for your quotations. (Also note inclusive page numbers for a whole article or story.) Sample notes might look like this:

self-contained quotation

DICKINSON—SEXUAL IMAGERY

"Like her nature poetry, her use of female sexual imagery suggests . . . not the 'subversion' of an existing male tradition, nor the 'theft' of male power—but rather the assertion of a concept of female sexuality and female creativity."

Paula Bennett, *Emily Dickinson: Woman Poet* (Iowa City: U of Iowa P, 1990) 180.

paraphrase with partial direct quotation

DICKINSON—FREUDIAN PERSPECTIVE

The prime motive in D.'s life and poetry was fear created by a "bad child-parent relationship," specifically with her "cold and forbidding father." This relationship shaped her view of men, love, marriage, and religion. She viewed God as a forbidding father-figure who spurned her.

Clark Griffith, *The Long Shadow: Emily Dickinson's Tragic Poetry* (Princeton: Princeton UP, 1964) 78.

Distinguish clearly between **paraphrase** and direct quotation. When you paraphrase, you put someone else's ideas in your own words, highlighting what seems most important and condensing other parts. Even when you paraphrase, be sure to use quotation marks for striking phrases that you keep in the exact wording of the author.

Note finer points: Use **single quotation marks** for a phrase that appears as a quote-within-a-quote. Use the **ellipsis**—three spaced periods—to show an omission (see Bennett quotation above). Use four periods when the periods include the period at the end of a sentence. **Square brackets** show that you have inserted material into the original quotation: "In this poem, based on the Emmett Till murder [1955], Brooks creates a surreal aura of hysteria and violence underlying an ostensibly calm domestic scene."

Pushing toward a Thesis   Your note taking becomes productive when you begin to follow up tentative patterns and promising connections that you discover in your reading. Even during your preliminary reading and note taking, you will be looking for a unifying thread. Avoid a stitched-together pattern that goes from "one critic said this" to "another critic said that." Look for recurrent issues; look for a note that in your materials is struck again and again.

Suppose you are moving toward a paper showing how different critics have answered the question of Emily Dickinson's religious faith. The following might be a tentative thesis:

TRIAL THESIS: Emily Dickinson was not a believer or a skeptic but a poet always in search of the truth.

Using a Working Outline   To give direction to your reading and writing, sketch out a **working outline** as soon as you have a rough idea how your material is shaping up. At first, your plan might be very tentative. A working outline is not a final blueprint; its purpose is to help you visualize a possible pattern and to help you refine it as you go along. At an early stage, your working outline for the paper about Dickinson's faith might look like this:

WORKING OUTLINE: —poems of faith
                                    —poems of despair
                                    —poems of alienation
                                    —poems of rebellion

Drafting and Revising In your first draft, you are likely to concentrate on feeding into your paper the evidence you have collected. As always, feel free to work on later sections of the paper first—perhaps concentrating on key segments and filling in the connecting threads later. In your first draft, quotations are likely to be chunky, to be woven into the paper more tightly or more smoothly during revision. Often you will need to read a first draft back to yourself to see where major changes in strategy would be advisable. A reordering of major sections might be necessary to correct awkward backtrackings. You might need to strengthen the evidence for major points and play down material that tends to distract from your major arguments.

Documenting the Paper When you draw on a range of sources—for instance, a range of critical interpretations of a poem—you may be asked to provide **documentation.** Remember that in a documented paper you fully identify your sources, furnishing complete publishing information and exact page numbers. Accurate documentation shows that your readers are welcome to go to the sources you have drawn on—to check your use of them and to get further information from them if they wish. As with other documented papers, follow the current style of the Modern Language Association (MLA) unless instructed otherwise. This current style no longer uses footnotes (though it still allows for **explanatory notes** at the end of a paper).

Remember three key features of the current MLA style:

❖ *Identify your sources briefly in your text.* Generally, introduce a quotation by saying something like the following:

> Mary Jo Salter says in her article "Puns and Accordions: Emily Dickinson and the Unsaid" that Dickinson "has inspired a massive critical industry rivaling that devoted to Shakespeare and Milton."

❖ *Give page references in parentheses in your text.* Usually, they will go at the end of the sentence and before the final period, for instance (89) or (89–90). If you have not mentioned the author, give his or her last name (Salter 192–93). If you are using more than one source by the same author, you may also have to specify briefly which one (Salter, "Puns" 192–93). Remember to tag author or title in parentheses only if you have *not* already given the information in your running text.

❖ *Describe each source fully in a final alphabetical listing of Works Cited.* Originally a bibliography (literally the "book list"), it now often includes nonprint sources—interviews, lectures, PBS broadcasts, videotapes, computer software. Here is a typical entry for an article in a critical journal. This entry includes volume number (a volume usually covers all issues for one year), year, and the complete page numbers for the whole article (not just the material you have quoted):

> Morris, Timothy. "The Development of Dickinson's Style." American Literature 60 (1988): 26–42.

Study sample entries for your alphabetical listing of Works Cited. Remember a few pointers:

✧ Use *italics* (or <u>underlining</u> on a typewriter) for the title of a whole publication—whether a book-length study, a collection or anthology of stories or essays, a periodical that prints critical articles, or a newspaper that prints reviews. However, use quotation marks for titles of poems or critical articles that are *part* of a collection.

✧ Leave *two* spaces after periods marking off chunks of information in the entry. Indent the second and following lines of each entry *five* spaces.

✧ Use *ed.* for editor; *trans.* for translator.

✧ Abbreviate the names of publishing houses (Prentice for Prentice-Hall, Inc; Southern Illinois UP for Southern Illinois University Press). Abbreviate the names of the months: Dec., Apr., Mar. Abbreviate the names of states when needed to locate a little-known place of publication: CA, NY, NJ.

Primary sources: listing of poems, lectures, or interviews

Brooks, Gwendolyn. *The World of Gwendolyn Brooks.* New York: Harper, 1971.
    [Collected poems of the author. The publisher's name is short for Harper & Row.]

Colman, Cathy. "After Swimming in the Pacific." *New Poets: Women.* Ed. Terri Whetherby. Millbrae, CA: Les Femmes, 1976. 13.
    [A poem printed in an anthology, with editor's name and with page number for the poem.]

Johnson, Thomas H., ed. *The Complete Poems of Emily Dickinson.* Boston: Little, Brown, 1960.
    [Editor's name first when editor's work of compiling or establishing texts is important.]

Lorde, Audre. Interview. *Black Women Writers at Work.* Ed. Claudia Tate. Harpenden, Herts.: Oldcastle, 1985. 100–16.
    [An interview with the poet, published in a collection of interviews.]

Clifton, Lucille. Lecture. Visiting Poets Series. Tucson, 23 Feb. 1992.
    [Talk by a poet as part of a lecture series.]

Olsen, Tillie. Foreword. *Black Women Writers at Work.* Ed. Claudia Tate. Harpenden, Herts.: Oldcastle, 1985. ix–xxvi.
    [Foreword by other than editor, with page numbers in small roman numerals for introductory material.]

Secondary sources: listing of critical studies, articles, or reviews

Johnson, Thomas H. *Emily Dickinson: An Interpretive Biography.* Cambridge: Harvard UP, 1966.
    [Biography with subtitle, published by a university press.]

Rich, Adrienne. *On Lies, Secrets, and Silence: Selected Prose 1966–1978.* New York: Norton, 1975.
    [Book with subtitle, with critical essays by the author.]

Spillers, Hortense J. "Gwendolyn the Terrible: Propositions on Eleven Poems." *A Life Distilled: Gwendolyn Brooks, Her Poetry and Fiction.* Ed. Maria K. Mootry and Gary Smith. Urbana: U of Illinois P, 1987. 224–35.
    [Article in a collection, with inclusive page numbers. Note "Ed." for the editors who assembled the collection.]

Morris, Timothy. "The Development of Dickinson's Style." *American Litera-ture* 60 (1988): 26–42.
[Journal article, with volume number and inclusive page numbers. Note quotation marks for title of article; italics for title of publication.]

Monteiro, George. "Dickinson's 'We Thirst at First.'" *The Explicator* 48 (1990): 193–94.
[Title of poem (with single quotation marks) is cited in title of article (with double quotation marks).]

Jones, Rowena Revis. "'A Royal Seal': Emily Dickinson's Rite of Baptism." *Religion and Literature* 18.3 (1986): 29–51.
[Periodical with number of volume *and* issue. Number of issue may be needed when pages are not numbered consecutively throughout a single volume.]

Montgomery, Karen. "Today's Minimalist Poets." *New York Times* 22 Feb. 1992, late ed. , sec. 2: 1+.
[Newspaper article, with edition and section specified. Article starts on page 1 and continues not on the next page but later in the newspaper.]

Rev. of *The Penguin Book of Women Poets,* ed. Carol Cosman, Joan Keefe, and Kathleen Weaver. *Arts and Books Forum* May 1990: 17–19.
[Untitled, unsigned review.]

Poets of Protest. Narr. Joan Moreno. Writ. and prod. Lorna Herold. KSBM, Los Angeles. 8 Feb. 1992.
[A television program with names of narrator and writer-producer. To be listed alphabetically under "Poets."]

Study the following example of a documented paper. How well does the paper bring its subject into focus? How well does it support its main points? How clear and effective is its use of quotations from the poet and from the critics? Study the use of parenthetical documentation and the entries in the Works Cited; pay special attention to unusual situations or entries.

SAMPLE DOCUMENTED PAPER

Emily Dickinson's Strange Irreverence

Religion in one guise or another pervades many of Dickinson's poems. It appears in the form of tender and not so tender prayers, skeptical questionings, and bitter con-frontations. Critics have constructed a whole range of interpretations designed to pro-vide a key to her changing, ambivalent religious attitudes. Some have cast her in the role of the rebel, rescuing her readers from the harshness of a rigid, constricted reli-gious tradition, erecting for them a "citadel of art" and cultivating "the ego or con-sciousness" (Burbick 62). Others, however, see her as a "lone pilgrim" in the tradition of Puritan austerity and asceticism. She could not "allow herself the long luxury" of the evangelical movement of her own day, which was turning away from earlier, harsher versions of the Christian faith and promoting a sentimental attitude toward God as a "creature of caring, even motherly generosity" (Wolff 260). Still others at-tribute Dickinson's ambivalent, shifting religious attitudes to her need to keep her friends, to her "preoccupation with attachment" (Burbick 65). Some of Dickinson's dearest friends, to whom she wrote about her cherished hope for "one unbroken com-pany in heaven," had experienced a religious conversion at Mt. Holyoke Seminary, and she felt she had to follow their example so that the bonds of friendship that were so precious to her would not be dissolved.

Perhaps the closest to a connecting thread is Denis Donoghue's discussion of her as a truth-seeker, who in life as in poetry was *looking for* the truth. As Donoghue says, "In a blunt paraphrase, many of her peoms would contradict one another; but her answers are always provisional." Her answers are tentative; "only her questions are definitive" (13). Although there are in her poems many references to the Old and New Testaments, "nothing is necessarily believed" but may be entertained only as a poetic or symbolic truth (17).

Because of the elusive, ambivalent nature of Dickinson's relation to religion, each poem must be interpreted individually in the quest to plumb her heart. Several of her poems are direct affirmations of her faith in Christ. In poem 698 in the Johnson edition ("Life—is what we make it"), she calls Christ a "tender pioneer," who blazed the trail of life and death for his "little Fellowmen":

> He—would trust no stranger—
> Others—could betray—
> Just his own endorsement—
> That—sufficeth me.
>
> All the other Distance
> He hath traversed first—
> No new mile remaineth—
> Far as Paradise—
>
> His sure foot preceding—
> Tender Pioneer—
> Base must be the Coward—
> Dare not venture—now—   (333–34)

In other poems, however, the faith that is supposed to provide a bridge to the hereafter proves a bridge with "mouldering" or "brittle" piers. In a famous poem, "I heard a Funeral in my Brain" (280 in the Johnson edition), the promise of faith seems unable to counteract the sense of the nothingness at the end of life. The Christian teachings of resurrection and an afterlife here do not seem to avail against the "plunge" into despair:

> And then I heard them lift a Box
> And creak across my Soul
> With those same Boots of Lead, again,
> Then Space—began to toll,
>
> As all the Heavens were a Bell,
> And Being, but an Ear,
> And I, and Silence, some strange Race
> Wrecked, solitary, here—
>
> And then a Plank in Reason, broke,
> And I dropped down, and down—
> And hit a World, at every plunge,
> And Finished knowing—then   (128–29)

Other poems seem to protest against the "ambiguous silence maintained by God" (Griffith 273). The following are the opening lines of poem 376 in Johnson's edition:

> Of course—I prayed—
> And did God Care?

He cared as much as on the Air
A Bird—had stamped her foot—
And cried "Give Me"—   (179)

Many of her poems seem to mourn the absence of God, as does the following stanza from poem 502 in Johnson:

Thou settest Earthquake in the South—
And Maelstrom, In the Sea—
Say, Jesus Christ of Nazareth—
Hast thou no Arm for Me?   (244)

In her most rebellious poems, she openly expresses defiance. She protests against the "tyranny" of God that forced Abraham to consent to offer his own son Isaac in sacrifice (Johnson 571). She rebels against commandments that keep us within a "magic prison," a limited and "constricted life," while we are within sight of the feast of happiness that is earthly pleasure—as if God were jealous of "the heaven on earth that is human happiness" (McNeil 60).

To read Emily Dickinson's poems is to see a poet's struggle for finding a meaning in her existence, rebelling at times against blind faith but also shrinking from complete doubt. She looked for evidence of the divine not in traditional revealed faith but in our earthly human existence. In a letter written several years before her death, she wrote: "To be human is more than to be divine . . . when Christ was divine he was uncontented until he had been human" (qtd. in Wolff 519).

Works Cited

Burbick, Joan. "'One Unbroken Company': Religion and Emily Dickinson." *New England Quarterly* 53 (1980): 62–75.

Donoghue, Denis. *Emily Dickinson.* U of Minnesota Pamphlets on American Writers No. 81. 1969.

Griffith, Clark. *The Long Shadow: Emily Dickinson's Tragic Poetry.* Princeton: Princeton UP, 1964.

Johnson, Thomas H., ed. *The Complete Poems of Emily Dickinson.* Boston: Little, Brown, 1960.

McNeil, Helen. *Emily Dickinson.* New York: Pantheon, 1986.

Wolff, Cynthia Griffin. *Emily Dickinson.* Menlo Park, CA: Addison, 1988.

QUESTIONS

1. How does the writer succeed or fail in bringing the topic to life for you? Does she spell out her *thesis* early in the paper? Does a key term or key concept help sum up her point of view?

2. What are the major way stations in her overall *plan*? How convincing are the major points the writer makes? At what points in the paper would you have liked more explanation or support?

3. Does the *conclusion* merely recapitulate points already made?

4. Does the writer use a *range* of sources? Do her parenthentical documentation and her list of works cited show any major variations from routine identification or standard entries?

24 PERSPECTIVES
Poets and Critics

*Scholars and artists thrown together are often annoyed
at the puzzle of where they differ. Both work from
knowledge, but I suspect they differ most importantly in
the way their knowledge is come by. Scholars get theirs with
conscientious thoroughness along projected lines of logic;
poets theirs cavalierly and as it happens in and out of
books. They stick to nothing deliberately , but let what will
stick to them like burrs where they walk in the fields.*

ROBERT FROST

FOCUS ON CRITICISM

The critic is often the third party at the interaction between poet and audience. Critics help explain and defend difficult new work. They sit in judgment, making and breaking reputations. As trend makers, they help shape movements and countermovements. On the one hand, they help establish critical orthodoxies—approved or right ways of thinking. On the other hand, they foment rebellions against current fashion. For us as readers of poetry, those critics are most relevant and valuable who circle back to questions that arise in our minds as we read:

✧ What is the link between the poet's personal *experience* and the poet's art? How much of a poem is personal revelation? How much is impersonal art?

✧ What is the relationship between intellect and the poetic *imagination*? How much in poetic creation is conscious control; how much is intuitive or subconscious?

✧ What kind of shaping or *control* is needed to keep poetry from being a mere "turning loose of emotion" (T. S. Eliot)?

✧ How much of the *reader's response* is shaped by the poem? How much depends on what we as readers bring to the poem?

✧ What is the difference between *good and bad* poetry? Who decides, and on what grounds?

766

POETS ON POETRY

*A poet writes always of his personal life, in his finest work
out of its tragedy, whatever it be, remorse, lost love, or mere
loneliness.*
WILLIAM BUTLER YEATS

*I was early in life sick to my very pit with order that cuts
off the crab's feelers to make it fit into the box.*
WILLIAM CARLOS WILLIAMS

*I have never been one to write by rule, even by my own
rules.*
T. S. ELIOT

Today we see everywhere poets writing and lecturing about poetry—defending their art, explaining their work, or reminiscing about way stations in their poetic careers. Poetry, like other kinds of imaginative literature, has become very much self-aware, self-conscious, "self-reflective."

Some of the most influential poets have been poet-critics, publishing critical manifestos that chart new directions. One of the earliest of such poet-critics was Alexander Pope, who published his verse-essay on criticism in 1711 at the age of twenty-three. The following excerpts touch on some of the major tenets of the **neoclassical** thinking of his time: Sound *judgment* should guide and restrain the poetic imagination. The poet's language should observe *decorum*—it should be suitable to the purpose. Poetic language and form are the vehicle for the poet's ideas (frequently ideas already often thought "but ne'er so well expressed").

ALEXANDER POPE (1688–1744)

From *An Essay on Criticism*   1711

First follow nature, and your judgment frame
By her just standard, which is still the same.
Unerring nature, still divinely bright—
One clear, unchanged, and universal light—
Life, force, and beauty, must to all impart,°   *must give life . . . to all*   5
At once the source, and end, and test of art.

. . . .

Some, to whom Heaven in wit has been profuse,
Want° as much more, to turn it to its use;   *need*
For wit and judgment often are at strife,
Though meant each other's aid, like man and wife.   10
'Tis more to guide than spur the Muse's steed;
Restrain his fury, than provoke his speed;
The wingèd courser, like a generous horse,
Shows most true mettle when you check° his course.   *restrain*

. . . .

True wit is nature to advantage dressed,   15
What oft was thought, but ne'er so well expressed;
Something, whose truth convinced at sight we find,
That gives us back the image of our mind.

. . . .

Expression is the dress of thought, and still
Appears more decent, as more suitable.   20
A vile conceit° in pompous words expressed   *concept*
Is like a clown in regal purple dressed;
For different styles with different subjects sort°   *agree with*
As several garbs with country, town, and court.

QUESTIONS

1. A favorite topic of neoclassical writers was the relationship between *art and nature*. How is this relationship viewed in these excerpts?

2. *Wit* here does not just mean a capacity for witty remarks but more generally a quick, fertile intelligence. How would it be different from judgment?

3. What role does *Pegasus,* the winged horse that symbolizes poetic creation, play here?

4. What is the *recurrent metaphor* Pope uses for ideas and the way they are expressed?

5. How is the *closed couplet* "suitable" for the ideas Pope expresses here?

Much **Romantic** writing about poetry was part of a rebellion against the eighteenth-century overemphasis on reason and judgment. Like other Romantic poets, John Keats believed in the supremacy of the creative imagination over the reasoning intellect. He placed spontaneous feeling over deliberate control, believing, with his fellow Romantics, that what we feel deeply and sincerely cannot be wrong. In the following excerpt from a famous letter, he champions the passions and sensation, or sense experience, as against "consecutive reasoning."

JOHN KEATS (1795–1821)
Letter to John Bailey   1817

. . . I am certain of nothing but of the holiness of the Heart's affections and the truth of Imagination—What the Imagination seizes as Beauty must be truth—whether it existed before or not—for I have the same Idea of all our Passions as of Love: they are all in their sublime creative of essential Beauty. . . . I am the more zealous in this affair because I have never yet been able to perceive how anything can be known for truth by consecutive reasoning—and yet it must be—Can it be that even the greatest Philosopher ever arrived at his goal without putting aside numerous objections—However it may be, O for a Life of Sensations rather than of Thoughts!

QUESTIONS

In this excerpt, what is the relation between beauty, passion, and truth? What is the relation between the words *beautiful* and *sublime*?

CROSS-REFERENCES—For Discussion or Writing

How is the point of view expressed in this letter related to Keats' "Ode on a Grecian Urn" (p. 699)?

Poets vary greatly in their writing habits and in how they explain their motives and procedures in writing poetry. Dylan Thomas is a Welsh poet who did more than other poets to make his readers sense some of the sheer inspired exuberance of the creative act. The following excerpt is from "Notes on the Art of Poetry," which he wrote in response to a student's questions. A crowd-pleasing performer, he insisted that "a poem on a page is only half a poem," with the actual shared reading of a poem serving as the culminating acting out and interpretation of the written text.

DYLAN THOMAS   (1914–1953)
Notes on the Art of Poetry   1951

I wanted to write poetry in the beginning because I had fallen in love with words. The first poems I knew were nursery rhymes, and before I could read them for myself I had come to love just the words of them, the words alone. What the words stand for, symbolized, or meant was of very secondary importance. What mattered was the sound of them as I heard them for the first time on the lips of the remote and incomprehensible grown-ups who seemed, for some reason, to be living in my world. And these words were, to me, as the notes of bells, the sounds of musical instruments, the noises of wind, sea, and rain, the rattle of milkcarts, the clopping of hooves on cobbles, the fingering of branches on a window pane, might be to someone, deaf from birth, who has miraculously found his hearing. I did not care what the words said, overmuch, nor what happened to Jack and Jill and the Mother Goose rest of them; I cared for the shapes of sound that their names, and the words describing their actions, made in my ears; I cared for the colors the words cast on my eyes. I realize that I may be, as I think all that way, romanticizing my reactions to the simple and beautiful words of those pure poems; but that is all I can honestly remember, however much time might have falsified my memory. I fell in love—that is the only expression I can think of—at once, and am still at the mercy of words, though sometimes now, knowing a little of their behavior very well, I think I can influence them slightly and have even learned to beat them now and then, which they appear to enjoy. I tumbled for words at once. And, when I began to read the nursery rhymes for myself, and, later, to read other verses and ballads, I knew that I had discovered the most important thing to me, that could be ever. There they were, seemingly lifeless, made only of black and white, but out of them, out of their own being, came love and terror and pity and pain and wonder and all the other vague abstractions that make our ephemeral lives dangerous, great, and bearable. Out of them came the gusts and grunts and hiccups and heehaws of common fun on the earth; and though what the words meant was, in its own way, often deliciously funny enough, so much funnier seemed to me, at that almost forgotten time, the shape and shade and size and noise of the words as they hummed, strummed, jugged and galloped along.

From *Modern Poetics,* edited by James Scully

QUESTIONS

How would you describe this poet's relationship with words? In this selection, what are striking examples of Thomas' own wildly imaginative use of words?

CROSS-REFERENCES—For Discussion or Writing

Poems by Dylan Thomas reprinted in this volume include "In My Craft or Sullen Art" (p. 610), "Do Not Go Gentle into That Good Night" (p. 633), and "Fern Hill" (p. 556). How do they show the poet's love of language?

For many women who are part of the women's movement, poetry has become a means of self-definition and self-assertion. Audre Lorde is a black American poet of West Indian heritage. What does she mean when she says that "poems are not luxuries"?

A U D R E   L O R D E   (born 1934)

A new generation of women poets is already working out of the psychic energy released when women begin to move out toward what the feminist philosopher Mary Daly has described as the "new space" in the boundaries of patriarchy. Women are speaking to and of women in these poems, out of a newly released courage to name, to love each other, to share risk and grief and celebration.

ADRIENNE RICH

Poems Are Not Luxuries   1977

For each of us as women, there is a dark place within where hidden and growing our true spirit rises, "Beautiful and tough as chestnut / Stanchions against our nightmare of weakness" and of impotence. These places of possibility within ourselves are dark because they are ancient and hidden; they have survived and grown strong through darkness. Within these deep places, each one of us holds an incredible reserve of creativity and power, storehouse of unexamined and unrecorded emotion and feeling. The woman's place of power within each of us is neither white nor surface; it is dark, it is ancient, and it is deep.

When we view living, in the european mode, only as a problem to be solved, we rely solely upon our ideas to make us free, for these were what the white fathers told us were precious. But as we become more in touch with our own ancient, black, noneuropean view of living as a situation to be experienced and interacted with, we learn more and more to cherish our feelings, to respect those hidden sources of our power from where true knowledge and therefore lasting action comes. At this point in time, I believe that women carry within ourselves the possibility for fusion of these two approaches as a keystone for survival, and we come closest to this combination in our poetry. I speak here of poetry as the revelation or distillation of experience, not the sterile word play that, too often, the white fathers distorted the word *poetry* to mean—in order to cover their desperate wish for imagination without insight.

For women, then, poetry is not a luxury. It is a vital necessity of our existence. It forms the quality of the light within which we predicate our hopes and dreams toward survival and change, first made into language, then into idea, then into more tangible action. Poetry is the way we help give name to the nameless so it can be thought. The farthest external horizons of our hopes and fears are cobbled by our poems, carved from the rock experiences of our daily lives.

As they become known and accepted to ourselves, our feelings, and the honest exploration of them, become sanctuaries and fortresses and spawning ground for the most radical and daring of ideas, the house of difference so necessary to change and the conceptualization of any meaningful action. Right now, I could name at least ten ideas I would once have found intolerable or incomprehensible and frightening, except as they came after dreams and poems. This is not idle fantasy, but the true meaning of "It feels right to me." We can train ourselves to respect our feelings and to discipline (transpose) them into a language that catches those feelings so they can be shared.

From *Claims for Poetry*, edited by Donald Hall

QUESTIONS

According to this poet, what is the role of poetry in women's struggle for change and survival? What is the difference between the European and the non-European mode?

CROSS-REFERENCES—For Discussion or Writing

Audre Lorde's poem "Coal" appears on page 612 of this volume. How does it live up to the program sketched out in this selection?

JUXTAPOSITIONS

The Poet's Motives

In the following selections, two poets speak with exceptional candor about what makes them write. What inspired or motivated them as poets?

DIANE WAKOSKI (born 1937)

On Experience and Imagination 1974

It has always been a premise of mine in writing poetry that the poet has the same experiences everybody else does, but the technical challenge is to invent some imaginative way of talking about these problems, these realities so that they can be taken seriously. It does not really seem like a big deal to anyone else when you say a man or woman you loved betrayed you. So what? Everyone sometimes feels betrayed. However, that's precisely why it is so important for the poet to find a way to say it. I believe in the use of extravagant surrealist imagery, like the girl riding naked on a zebra wearing only diamonds, as a way of making the reader accept the specialness of the feelings of the speaker in the poem.

I write in the first person because I have always wanted to make my life more interesting than it was. So I created a Diane whose real experiences were dramatized and exaggerated, were presented as surrealist experiences or metaphysical ones, who involved herself with imaginary people who often had the characteristics of real people but were more interesting and mysterious. Perhaps I have always been the isolated lonely person living around dull or sad people, and the poems were a way of inventing myself into a new life. I do feel a strange connection with the worlds I have created and the people in them, though I do not feel they are me or my world. It had been my obsession to try to see and understand the world truly, but that means seeing it over and over again, with all its changes, its attendant contradictions. I am never satisfied with anything I see but must keep inventing and reinventing ways to understand it.

From "Introduction" to *Trilogy*

QUESTIONS

What, for Wakoski, is the relationship between common shared experience and imaginative creation? What, for her, is the relationship between "realism" and "surrealism"? What do you learn about the persona in those of her poems she likes best?

PABLO NERUDA (1904–1973)
Childhood and Poetry 1954

One time, investigating in the backyard of our house in Temuco the tiny objects and miniscule beings of my world, I came upon a hole in one of the boards of the fence. I looked through the hole and saw a landscape like that behind our house, uncared for, and wild. I moved back a few steps, because I sensed vaguely that something was about to happen. All of a sudden a hand appeared—a tiny hand of a boy about my own age. By the time I came close again, the hand was gone, and in its place there was a marvelous white sheep.

The sheep's wool was faded. Its wheels had escaped. All of this only made it more authentic. I had never seen such a wonderful sheep. I looked back through the hole but the boy had disappeared. I went into the house and brought out a treasure of my own: a pinecone, opened, full of odor and resin, which I adored. I set it down in the same spot and went off with the sheep.

I never saw either the hand or the boy again. And I have never again seen a sheep like that either. The toy I lost finally in a fire. But even now, in 1954, almost fifty years old, whenever I pass a toy shop, I look furtively into the window, but it's no use. They don't make sheep like that anymore.

I have been a lucky man. To feel the intimacy of brothers is a marvelous thing in life. To feel the love of people whom we love is a fire that feeds our life. But to feel the affection that comes from those whom we do not know, from those unknown to us, who are watching over our sleep and solitude, over our dangers and our weaknesses— that is something still greater and more beautiful because it widens out the boundaries of our being, and unites all living things.

That exchange brought home to me for the first time a precious idea: that all of humanity is somehow together. That experience came to me again much later; this time it stood out strikingly against a background of trouble and persecution.

It won't surprise you then that I attempted to give something resiny, earthlike, and fragrant in exchange for human brotherhood. Just as I once left the pinecone by the fence, I have since left my words on the door of so many people who were unknown to me, people in prison, or hunted, or alone.

From *Neruda and Vallejo: Selected Poems,* edited by Robert Bly

QUESTIONS

What was the significance of the childhood incident for the poet? In what way did it become a motivating force for his poetry?

EXPLICATION: SOUND AND SENSE

'Tis not enough no harshness gives offense;
The sound must seem an echo to the sense.
ALEXANDER POPE

Some poems are simple, but many are rich in concentrated meaning. Critics can help meanings reach the reader. A good critic can serve as a guide, explaining and interpreting, taking us step by step through a close reading of the poem. We call such patient line-by-line explanation **explication.** The critic who explicates a poem for us becomes our senior partner in the business of reading. The critic's function then is to make us pay attention, to defog our windshield, to alert us to missed clues, to fill in missed links.

The critic can be our guide to unsuspected shades and layers of meaning, our interpreter of metaphorical and symbolical significance. In particular, critics can alert us to the interplay of sound and sense, of form and meaning, that may escape the literal-minded reader. Critics in the modern tradition tend to ask not just *what* a poem means but *how* it means. In the following poem by G. M. Hopkins, sound and rhythm blend with the assertions made and questions asked by the poet in one of the great poems of English literature. The line-by-line explication by an experienced reader helps us clear up difficulties and helps us respond more fully to the richness of the poem.

GERARD MANLEY HOPKINS   (1844–1889)

God's Grandeur   1877

The world is charged with the grandeur of God.
    It will flame out, like shining from shook foil;
    It gathers to a greatness, like the ooze of oil
Crushed. Why do men then now not reck his rod?
Generations have trod, have trod, have trod;   5

And all is seared with trade; bleared, smeared with toil;
And wears man's smudge and shares man's smell: the soil
Is bare now, nor can foot feel, being shod.

And for all this, nature is never spent;
There lives the dearest freshness deep down things;
And though the last lights off the black West went   10
Oh, morning, at the brown brink eastward, springs—
Because the Holy Ghost over the bent
World broods with warm breast and with ah! bright wings.

J. R. WATSON

"God's Grandeur"   1987

The world is charged with the grandeur of God.

As a first line this is uncompromising. Its rhythm is confident and assured, and the full stop at the end of the line seems to emphasize the completeness and finality of the statement. The world is charged with God's grandeur, and that is that. Hopkins was so careful with line-endings and rhythms that this sentence within a line is evidently there for a purpose, to make the claim as strongly as possible. It does so especially because of the emphatic word "charged," which usefully has two meanings: "loaded," and "full of electricity" as a battery is when it has been charged. The world is therefore electric with God's grandeur, and loaded with it (which suggests that the grandeur is heavy and sub-stantial): the image of electricity is carried on in the second line, when he senses that the grandeur of God will "flame out, like shining from shook foil." As foil, when shak-en, gives off shining light, so the world, when looked at carefully, is full of the shining light of God Himself, leaping out like flames or sparks. Hopkins described it to Bridges as "I mean foil in its sense of leaf or tinsel. . . . Shaken gold foil gives off broad glares like sheet lightning, and this is true of nothing else, owing to its zigzag dints and creas-ings and network of small many cornered facets, a sort of fork lightning too"(L B 169). Its fullness is indicated by the next image

It gathers to a greatness, like the ooze of oil
Crushed.

Hopkins is here thinking of an olive press, with the oil oozing from the pressed fruit. It oozes from every part of the press, in a fine film, and then the trickles gather to-gether to form a jar of oil. In the same way the grandeur of God is found everywhere, trickling from every simple thing in the created universe and accumulating to form a greatness, a grandeur that is perceived by the discerning mind of the Christian and poet. This is made clear in the lines that follow, which are a lament for the neglect and indifference shown by mankind. Once again the poetry is dense with metaphors: in-stead of saying "why do men take no notice?" Hopkins writes

Why do men then now not reck his rod?

The rhythms and sounds are themselves awkward, like the question: "men then," "now not" and "reck his rod" (care for his rule: "reck"means "heed," occurring in ordinary speech in the word "reckless"). And these sounds continue, as if Hopkins is using the vocabulary and rhythms of his verse to act out, as well as describe, the situation:

> Generations have trod, have trod, have trod;
>   And all is seared with trade; bleared, smeared with toil;
>   And wears man's smudge and shares man's smell: the soil
> Is bare now, nor can foot feel, being shod.

Here the mechanical forces are captured in verse by the heavy accents. What is sometimes called the "daily grind" is a repetitive thump in which the feet of generations march on; and the "trod . . . trod . . . trod" sets up the three-beat rhythm of the next line: "seared . . . bleared . . . smeared." The verbs themselves sprawl across the line, preventing any delicacy of feeling or perception. "Seared," for instance, means "dried up" or it can mean "rendered incapable of feeling": it is accomplished by "bleared" (blurred inflammation of the eyes) and "smeared" (rubbed over with dirt). When we think of the minute attention to detail of Hopkins' drawings, these adjectives take on yet more force: they are part of the process of treading down, smudging, and generally spoiling nature. Because of this the soil is barren, and feet, being both shod with boots, cannot feel it. For Hopkins, the "foot feel" is but a part of the whole process of insensitivity: as a man's feet are encased in boots, so his whole soul is bound up, unfree. . . .

It is then that the sestet throws into the equation another mysterious force, the feeling of freshness and growth of nature that causes it to live on, to survive against all the neglect and exploitation of man. Its nature is in this way to be itself: to go on growing each year with its own process of generation and renewed life, so that against the unfeeling energies of man there is placed something greater, the inexhaustible forces of nature. Its spirit of growth is everywhere: it is as natural and inevitable as the coming of morning after nightfall. It is the "dearest freshness" deep down in things which ensures that "nature is never spent"; and in the final lines this inexhaustible quality is associated with the working of the Holy Ghost, the spirit of God who created all things and sustains them:

> Because the Holy Ghost over the bent
>   World broods with warm breast and with ah! bright wings.

From J. R. Watson, *The Poetry of Gerard Manley Hopkins*

QUESTIONS

How does the critic show that the word *charged* is charged with meaning? What inside information does he use from the poet himself? Where and how does the critic show the meshing of content and form? What difficulties did this reading clear up for you? How did this explication change your understanding of and response to the poem?

EVALUATION: POEMS GOOD AND BAD

There is something wrong
with this poem. Can you
find it?
RICHARD BRAUTIGAN, "CRITICAL CAN OPENER"

A poem on cabbages, if we like cabbages, may seem better
than a poem on kings, if we dislike kings.
JOSEPHINE MILES

Critics are not content to explain and interpret. They judge. They set standards; they rank the first-rate and the second-rate. In our time, however, movements and countermovements have made it difficult to set up generally binding standards for what makes good contemporary poetry. Nevertheless, some basic requirements underlie many of the critical judgments you may encounter:

✧ Critics look in good poetry for *freshness* of language. They look for phrases that make us pay attention, that recharge our power of vision, that startle us into taking a new look.

✧ Critics look in good poetry for more than raw experience. They look for some kind of *control*. They look for evidence of the sifting and shaping that take a poem beyond the expression of raw emotion. They expect poets to put some distance between themselves and whatever pain or grievance or joy might have been the original impetus of a poem. In more traditional terms, the poet needs to transform the raw stuff of life into art.

✧ Critics look in good poetry for a challenge. They look for some degree of *complexity*. Poetry that is too regular, too smooth, too uncomplicated, will seem to them undemanding and simpleminded. They expect the poet to do more than to indulge in a single mood, however pleasing. Whatever ordering or shaping takes place should make us sense that jostling reality has been brought under control. Modern critics look for the tensions, the paradoxes, or the ironies that enable poets to do justice to mixed emotions and divided loyalties. They look for attempts to face and resolve ambiguities. They delight in the play of polarities. They look for the inversions and breaks or counter-rhythms that break up the tedúm-tedúm-tedúm patterns of "jingle-poets." Complexity of form became for the modern critic one manifestation of a poem's "maturity or sophistication or richness or depth, and hence its value" (W. K. Wimsatt).

✧ Critics look for an *organic* relation between substance and form. They stress the interconnectedness of a poem's parts. Meter, rhyme, pleasing sounds—these should not be embellishments, added like ornaments on a Christmas tree. Stanza form should not be like an empty container, to be filled by interchangeable content. A rhymed stanza should not be like "a jug into which the syrup of verse is poured." Instead, modern critics have looked for the "interaction of every element—image, statement, rhythm, rhyme—every element that goes to make up the whole poem" (Louis Martz).

❖ Critics insist that emotion be appropriate to the subject or justified by the context. Modern critics have been wary of overindulgence in emotion. They disapprove of **sentimentality.** Sentimentality allows readers to bask in a glow of self-approving emotions. It does not challenge them to examine their thoughts and actions. The following poem is often criticized as an example of sentimentality or excessive emotion.

ROD MCKUEN   (born 1933)

Thoughts on Capital Punishment   1954

There ought to be capital punishment for cars
that run over rabbits and drive into dogs
and commit the unspeakable, unpardonable crime
of killing a kitty cat still in his prime.

Purgatory, at the very least   5
                should await the driver
        driving over a beast.

Those hurrying headlights coming out of the dark
that scatter the scampering squirrels in the park
should await the best jury that one might compose   10
of fatherless chipmunks and husbandless does

And then found guilty, after too fair a trial
should be caged in a cage with a hyena's smile
or maybe an elephant with an elephant gun
should shoot out his eyes when the verdict is done.   15

There ought to be something, something that's fair
to avenge Mrs. Badger as she waits in her lair
for her husband who lies with his guts spilling out
cause he didn't know what automobiles are about.

Hell on the highway, at the very least   20
should await the driver
driving over a beast.

The following is a short sample from one representative discussion of this poem:

> Sentimentality is the evocation of a greater amount of feeling or emotion than is justified by the subject. . . . The poet who adopts a sentimental tone becomes more tearful or more ecstatic over his subject than it deserves. The sentimentalist is addicted to worn-out baby shoes, gray-haired mothers, and small animals—subjects certain to evoke an automatic response in a particular kind of reader. But sentimentality is not so much a matter of subject as it is a matter of treatment. . . .
> The chief defect of this poem is its sentimentality; the feelings it expresses are wholly disproportionate to the subject matter. No person with decent feel-

ings, of course, takes pleasure in the deaths of animals on the road; and if it is our own pet that is killed we may be genuinely grieved. But to call such accidents unspeakable, unpardonable crimes seems rather excessive. Unfortunately there is no evidence that the speaker's maudlin language is redeemed by irony. "Kitty cat" is baby talk; and chipmunks with fathers, does with husbands, and Mrs. Badger and her husband belong to the world of children's animal stories. (Such sentimentality also yields failures in logic. Would the crime be more pardonable if the kitty cat were not in its prime? Are the cars or the drivers who steer them to be punished?) A little reflection leads us to the conclusion that there are worse evils in this world than the accidental deaths of animals on the road.

From C. F. Main and Peter J. Seng, *Poems,* 4th ed.

QUESTIONS

What is the key to the definition of sentimentality in this passage? How do the authors apply it to the poem? Do you agree with them? Can you give your own examples of "excessive" emotion? (Is there more to this poem than these critics seem to acknowledge?)

CROSS-REFERENCES—For Discussion or Writing

Compare and contrast McKuen's poem with two other road-kill poems: William Stafford's "Traveling through the Dark" (p. 627) and Mary Oliver's "The Black Snake" (p. 467).

To some readers, the term *criticism* implies negative criticism. However, if critics castigate clichés, glib abstractions, and jingling verse, they also praise with equal fervor what they consider authentic and challenging. The following is a modern poem in a style valued by many contemporary critics. Much modern criticism modeled its standards on the practice of the seventeenth-century **metaphysical** poets: John Donne, Andrew Marvell, and George Herbert in England; Edward Taylor in America. Modern critics prized in the metaphysicals their yoking of intellect and passion, their love of paradox and irony, their use of complex, demanding form.

A N N E   H A L L E Y   (born 1928)
Dear God, the Day Is Grey   1960

Dear God, the day is grey. My house
is not in order. Lord, the dust
sifts through my rooms and with my fear,
I sweep mortality, outwear
my brooms, but not this leaning floor
which lasts and groans. I, walking here,   5
still loathe the labors I would love
and hate the self I cannot move,
And God, I know the unshined boards,

the flaking ceiling, various stains   10
that mottle these distempered goods,
the greasy cloths, the jagged tins,
the dog that paws the garbage cans.
I know what laborings, love, and pains,
my blood would will, yet will not give: 15
the knot of hair that clogs the drains
clots in my throat. My dyings thrive.

The refuse, Lord, that I put out
burns in vast pits incessantly.
All piecemeal deaths, trash, undevout   20
and sullen sacrifice, to thee.

LAURENCE PERRINE
On "Dear God, the Day Is Grey"   1966

Three aspects of this poem strike one immediately. First, the quality of the religious devotion. The self-questioning, the struggling with the infirm will, the fear of unworthiness, the desire to be worthy—all express an intensity of religious feeling that takes us back to the seventeenth century. We can find counterparts of the feeling, to be sure, in T. S. Eliot and Gerard Manley Hopkins in more recent times, but the spirit of the poem finds its real reflection in Edward Taylor, George Herbert, and John Donne. Here, as in them, are expressed the burning desire to be found worthy in God's sight, full consciousness of the difficulty of performing the tasks imposed on one not only faithfully but with love, distress at the enormous impossibility of fulfilling the commandment "Be ye therefore perfect, even as your Father which is in heaven is perfect."

Then, secondly, the boldness with which the devotional feeling is coupled with the commonest, most daily domestic imagery. The sifting dust in a house, the brooms, "the flaking ceiling," the stains, "the knot of hair that clogs the drains"—these images bespeak a boldness of imagination that literary scholars have named "metaphysical"— denoting, in the words of Dr. Johnson, "a kind of *discordia concors,* a combination of dissimilar images, or discovery of occult resemblances in things apparently unlike." And yet the linking of love, sin, contrition, and the glory of God in this poem with greasy cloths, trash, and garbage cans does not strike us as bizarre or sacrilegious, but natural and devout. The tone of the poem is established early. When the poet says, "My house / is not in order," we know at once that she is speaking metaphorically and refers not to a house built of bricks and boards but to a life filled with strivings and failures, devout wishes, struggle with temptation, broken resolutions—in short, the problems of mortality.

Third, its modernity. In its religious devotion and in its bold domestic imagery, the poem reminds us of the seventeenth century. But it is not a seventeenth-century poem, as the imagery tells us. The jagged tins, the garbage cans, and the drains are part of the modern scene and could not have been found in a poem before this century. With all its seventeenth-century quality of subject and imagination, what gives the poem quality is its originality. That flaking ceiling and the knot of hair clogging the drain, we feel, have not been found in poetry before. The religious feeling of the poem is not faked, or imitated, but felt.

QUESTIONS

What qualities does this reader value in Halley's poem? Which of them do you consider most valuable (or least valuable) yourself?

CROSS-REFERENCES—For Discussion or Writing

Compare and contrast Halley's modern "metaphysical" poem with a poem by one of the seventeenth-century metaphysical poets printed earlier in this volume. Choose a religious poem by John Donne or George Herbert. What features of style and perspective do the two poems share?

EXPLORATIONS

Judging the Poem

Study the following poem and the two critical reactions that were published in *Poet and Critics*. Do you share the critics' reactions? Are they too harsh? Or too lenient? Write a short critical reaction of your own. Feel free to express your likes and dislikes, but support them by pointing to specific things in the poem.

DANIEL ORT

Can a Merry-Go-Round Horse Gallop in a Straight Line?   1966

As a kid on a merry-go-round
you could point at the whole
world by sticking one finger
out. Rings must have been
on rich kids' merry-go-rounds,   5
but there was lots of sky,
and mom's wave of new courage
always followed the popcorn
stand. The blind man would
squeeze your last ticket   10
into his brown hand while
Sousa's "Stars and Stripes
Forever" would come around
again like a red and white
goose after a blue elk and   15
you came to expect things.
Like the popcorn stand and mom.
Will a policeman who is used
to waving stop and go at anonymous
cars let a green and blue horse   20
on a yellow pole run a red light
on its way to the rainbow?

1. No: this doesn't work for me at all. . . . this is labored and heavy: cotton-candy stuffed with lead. For me, it never gets past cuteness, never gets past prose. And it's filled with sloganized nonsense: the "brown hand" of the ticket-taker (God: the thing might just as well be "weather-beaten"); the Sousa-music (for Colorful Nostalgia); and —egh—Mom, mom. Stuffed down a tuba, I hope.

No. My sympathies are all with the cop, who ought to take that green and blue little teensy horse and break both its legs. (Stanley Cooperman)

2. A poem is nothing for me unless it purges my sensitivities. Once it accomplishes this I give it an automatic ear-notch for having quality. Then I go back to the work and single out finer aspects, but keeping in mind that the poem has already done its job.

"Can a Merry-Go-Round Horse Gallop in a Straight Line?" has the ear-notch. It brings back a sensitivity of my youth. It is the excitement and wonder and mouth-gaping curiosity found at a carnival. It is wild imagination bounded by mother's pessimism and the authority of the traffic cop.

The poem is lacking in craft. A close examination reveals mulberry stains on the quilt. The sentence beginning "The blind man would . . ." is very awkward. "Would" is a vague verb and using it twice in the same sentence to show simultaneous actions weakens the structure. Going from the blind man's squeeze through the "Stars and Stripes Forever" and "like a red and white goose after a blue elk" is too much to swallow in one gulp.

Just one more thing. I can understand why a kid who has spent his last nickel for a ride on the merry-go-round is jealous of the rich kids, but where can I see one of these "rich kids' merry-go-rounds"? (Tom E. Knowlton)

WRITING ABOUT LITERATURE

24. Writing the Essay (Preparing for Tests)

The Writing Workshop   When you write about poetry as part of an essay exam, you need to be a quick, alert reader, and you need to think on your feet (metaphorically speaking). Common types of essay questions will ask you to

⬦ interpret a poem without detailed questions to guide you. You are on your own, applying the critical skills you have learned.

⬦ do a close reading of a poem, responding to detailed questions focused on the formal features of the poem.

⬦ compare and contrast two poems, mapping similarities but also striking differences in such areas as form, theme, or point of view.

⬦ respond to the thematic implications of a poem. You may, for instance, be asked to compare the way a common theme is treated in a poem and in a related prose passage.

Study the following sample exam. How would you answer the questions? Compare your answers with the student responses that follow the questions.

INSTRUCTIONS

Study the following poem, one of John Donne's *Holy Sonnets* (Number 5). Then answer the questions that follow it.

I am a little world made cunningly°	*skillfully*
Of elements and an angelic sprite;°	*spirit*
But black sin hath betrayed to endless night	
My world's both parts, and O, both parts must die.	
You which° beyond that heaven which was most high	*you who* 5
Have found new spheres and of new lands can write,	
Pour new seas in mine eyes, that so I might	
Drown my world with my weeping earnestly,	
Or wash it if it must be drowned no more.	
But O, it must be burned! Alas, the fire	10
Of lust and envy have burnt it heretofore	
And made it fouler; let their flames retire,	
And burn me, O Lord, with a fiery zeal	
Of thee and thy house, which doth in eating heal.	

QUESTIONS

1. What is the sustained or organizing metaphor in the first four lines?

2. By Donne's time, the new science of astronomy had made people think of new reaches of space beyond the traditional heavenly spheres. Explorers and navigators like Columbus had discovered new worlds. What use does Donne make of these developments in this poem?

3. After Noah's flood, God had promised not ever to send floods again to drown sinful humanity. Where and how does the poet allude to this promise?

4. Sonnets often reach a turning point at or near the division between the opening octet and the concluding sestet. Does this sonnet follow this pattern?

5. The final lines of the poem make us imagine three different kinds of fire or flame. What are they?

6. What is paradoxical about the concluding couplet?

7. What is the prevailing tone of this sonnet? What are the dominant emotions? What kind of speaker does it make you imagine?

8. How does the poem as a whole develop or take shape? What is the overall movement or pattern that gives shape to the poem as a whole?

Compare your own answers with the following sample student responses:

SAMPLE STUDENT RESPONSES

1. The sustained opening metaphor compares the speaker in the poem to the larger universe in which we live. A human being is a "little world" (a microcosm) made by the same creator that created the larger world outside. A human being is composed of earthly elements and an angelic, heavenly soul, just as the universe is composed of the earth and the heavens, inhabited by spirits or angels. Both the "little world" of the individual and the larger world (the macrocosm) will eventually be destroyed—the one at the end of our natural lives, the other on the eve of eternity.

2. Donne seems fascinated with geography, astronomy, and the other sciences. The opening up of new vistas in geography and astronomy gave his hyperbolical mind new areas in which to wander. In lines 5 and 6, he is turning to the new astronomers (who "have found new spheres") and to the discoverers of new continents (who can write "of new lands"). He asks them hyperbolically about newly discovered oceans that might replenish the reservoir of tears he has shed in weeping for his sins.

3. The speaker in the poem wants to "drown" his sinful "little world" with weeping, submerging it in tears. But God had promised Noah that He would not again allow humanity to be drowned; therefore, the speaker will use his tears merely to "wash" and cleanse rather than to drown (line 9).

4. There is a turning signaled by the word *but,* not exactly at the end of the octave but at the beginning of line 10. The tears of repentance alone will not be enough; the whole world will have to be destroyed by fire before we can enter into communion with God (no more floods—"the fire next time").

5. The first kind of fire is the physical fire that will destroy the world at the end. The second is the "fire of lust and envy" that leaves everything "foul" or scorched and besmirched. The third is the "fiery zeal" that cleanses us of sin.

6. It is paradoxical that Donne asks to be destroyed in order to be saved. The idea of a healing fire is paradoxical because the fire eats or devours what it consumes. But this fire "heals" by consuming only the infected part—it burns out sin.

7. The tone is paradoxical. The poem is somber and full of passionate remorse and despair, but it ends on a note of reaffirming the poet's faith . The speaker is a very intense person, passionately introspective, constantly dramatizing his own emotions.

8. The poem develops beautifully by first making us admire God's handiwork (the little world of the human body, "made cunningly" by God). But the poet almost immediately mourns its desperate condition after it has been "betrayed" by sin. The poet then asks for cleansing by water, then corrects himself in a rush of passion by asking for all-consuming fire. The poem proceeds by playing off polar opposites: the angelic spirit and the dark night of sin, water and fire.

OTHER VOICES/OTHER VISIONS
Poems for Further Reading

A N O N Y M O U S

Edward (traditional Scottish ballad)

1
"Why does your brand sae drap wi' bluid,°   *sword so drip with blood*
    Edward, Edward,
Why does your brand sae drap wi' bluid,
    And why sae sad gang° ye, O?"   *so sad go*
"O I ha'e killed my hawk sae guid,°   *good*   5
    Mither, mither,
O I ha'e killed my hawk sae guid,
    And I had nae mair but he, O."

2
"Your hawke's bluid was never sae reid,°   *red*
    Edward, Edward,   10
Your hawke's bluid was never sae reid,
    My dear son I tell thee, O."
"O I ha'e killed my reid-roan steed,
    Mither, mither,
O I ha'e killed my reid-roan steed,   15
    That erst was° sae fair and free, O."   *that once was*

3
"Your steed was auld, and ye ha'e gat mair,°   *more*
    Edward, Edward,
Your steed was auld, and ye ha'e gat mair,
    Some other dule ye drie,° O."   *other grief you suffer*   20
"O I ha'e killed my fader dear,
    Mither, mither,
O I ha'e killed my fader dear,
    Alas, and wae° is me, O!"   *woe*

4
"And whatten° penance wul ye drie for that,   *what sort of*   25
    Edward, Edward?
And whatten penance wul ye drie for that,

784

My dear son, now tell me, O?"
"I'll set my feet in yonder boat,
      Mither, mither,   30
I'll set my feet in yonder boat,
      And I'll fare over the sea, O."

5
"And what wul ye do wi' your towers and your ha',°   *hall*
      Edward, Edward?
And what wul ye do wi' your towers and your ha',   35
      That were sae fair to see, O?"
"I'll let them stand tul they down fa',°   *fall*
      Mither, mither,
I'll let them stand tul they down fa',
      For here never mair maun° I be, O."   *never more must*   40

6
"And what wul ye leave to your bairns° and your wife,   *children*
      Edward, Edward?
And what wul ye leave to your bairns and your wife,
      Whan ye gang over the sea, O?"
"The warlde's° room, let them beg thrae° life,   *world's/through* 45
      Mither, mither,
The warlde's room, let them beg thrae life,
      For them never mair wul I see, O."

7
"And what wul ye leave to your ain mither dear,
      Edward, Edward?   50
And what wul ye leave to your ain mither dear,
      My dear son, now tell me, O?"
"The curse of hell frae me sall° ye bear,   *from me shall*
      Mither, mither,
The curse of hell frae me sall ye bear,   55
      Sic° counsels ye gave to me, O."   *such*

ANONYMOUS

Sir Patrick Spens   thirteenth century

1
The king sits in Dumferling town,
      Drinking the blude-reid° wine: *blood-red*
"O whar will I get guid° sailor,   *good*
      To sail this ship of mine?"

2
Up and spak an eldern knicht,°   *spoke an elderly knight* 5
      Sat at the king's richt° knee: *right*
"Sir Patrick Spens is the best sailor
      That sails upon the sea."

3
The king has written a braid° letter   *broad*
    And signed it wi' his hand,   10
And sent it to Sir Patrick Spens,
    Was walking on the sand.

4
The first line that Sir Patrick read,
    A loud lauch° lauched he;   *laugh*
The next line that Sir Patrick read,   15
    The tear blinded his ee.°   *eye*

5
"O wha is this has done this deed,
    This ill deed done to me,
To send me out this time o' the year,
    To sail upon the sea?   20

6
"Mak haste, mak haste, my mirry men all,
    Our guid ship sails the morn."
"O say na sae,° my master dear,   *not so*
    For I fear a deadly storm.

7
"Late, late yestre'en I saw the new moon   25
    Wi' the auld moon in hir arm,
And I fear, I fear, my dear master,
    That we will come to harm."

8
O our Scots nobles were richt laith°   *loath*
    To weet their cork-heeled shoon,°   *wet their cork-heeled shoes*   30
But lang or° a' the play were played   *before*
    Their hats they swam aboon.°   *above*

9
O lang, lang may their ladies sit,
    Wi' their fans into their hand,
Or ere they see Sir Patrick Spens   35
    Come sailing to the land.

10
O lang, lang may the ladies stand
    Wi' their gold kems° in their hair,   *combs*
Waiting for their ain° dear lords,   *own*
    For they'll see them na mair.   40

11
Half o'er, half o'er to Aberdour
    It's fifty fadom deep,
And there lies guid Sir Patrick Spens
    Wi' the Scots lords at his feet.

APHRA BEHN   (1640–1689)

Song   1676

Love in fantastic triumph° sat,   *celebration of victory*
Whilst bleeding hearts around him flowed,
For whom fresh pains he did create,
And strange tyrannic power he showed.
From thy bright eyes he took his fire,   5
Which round about, in sport he hurled;
But 't was from mine he took desire,
Enough to undo the amorous° world.   *filled with love*

From me he took his sighs and tears,
From thee his pride and cruelty;   10
From me his languishments and fears,
And every killing dart from thee.
Thus thou and I, the god have armed,
And set him up a deity;°   *as a deity*
But my poor heart alone is harmed,   15
Whilst thine the victor is, and free.

JOHN BERRYMAN   (1914–1972)

Dream Song 14   1964

Life, friends, is boring. We must not say so.
After all, the sky flashes, the great sea yearns,
we ourselves flash and yearn,
and moreover my mother told me as a boy
(repeatingly) "Ever to confess you're bored   5
means you have no

Inner Resources." I conclude now I have no
inner resources, because I am heavy bored.
Peoples bore me,
literature bores me, especially great literature,   10
Henry bores me, with his plights & gripes
as bad as achilles,°   *mythical Greek warrior*
                                          invulnerable except in the heel

who loves people and valiant art, which bores me.
And the tranquil hills, & gin, look like a drag
and somehow a dog   15
has taken itself & its tail considerably away
into mountains or sea or sky, leaving
behind: me, wag.

W I L L I A M   B L A K E   (1757–1827)

The Chimney Sweeper   1789

When my mother died I was very young,
And my father sold me while yet my tongue
Could scarcely cry weep weep weep weep.°   *child's pronunciation of "sweep sweep"?*
So your chimneys I sweep & in soot I sleep.

Theres little Tom Dacre, who cried when his head   5
That curl'd like a lambs back, was shav'd, so I said
Hush Tom never mind it, for when your head's bare,
You know that the soot cannot spoil your white hair.

And so he was quiet, & that very night,
As Tom was a sleeping he had such a sight,   10
That thousands of sweepers Dick, Joe Ned & Jack
Were all of them lock'd up in coffins of black°   *due to lung diseases*

And by came an Angel who had a bright key,
And he open'd the coffins & set them all free.
Then down a green plain leaping laughing they run   15
And wash in a river and shine in the Sun.

Then naked & white, all their bags left behind,
They rise upon clouds, and sport in the wind.
And the Angel told Tom if he'd be a good boy,
He'd have God for his father & never want° joy.   *lack*   20

And so Tom awoke and we rose in the dark
And got with our bags & our brushes to work.
Tho' the morning was cold, Tom was happy & warm,
So if all do their duty, they need not fear harm.

W I L L I A M   B L A K E   (1757–1827)

The Lamb   1789

    Little Lamb, who made thee?
    Dost thou know who made thee?
Gave thee life & bid thee feed,
By the stream & o'er the mead;
Gave thee clothing of delight,   5
Softest clothing wooly bright;
Gave thee such a tender voice,
Making all the vales° rejoice!   *valleys*
    Little Lamb who made thee?
    Dost thou know who made thee?   10

    Little Lamb I'll tell thee,
    Little Lamb I'll tell thee!
He is callèd by thy name,

For he calls himself a Lamb:
He is meek & he is mild, 15
He became a little child:
I a child & thou a lamb,
We are callèd by his name.
    Little Lamb God bless thee.
    Little Lamb God bless thee. 20

LOUISE BOGAN   (1897–1970)

Women 1923

Women have no wilderness in them,
They are provident° instead, *frugal*
Content in the tight hot cell of their hearts
To eat dusty bread.

They do not see cattle cropping red winter grass, 5
They do not hear
Snow water going down under culverts
Shallow and clear.

They wait, when they should turn to journeys,
They stiffen, when they should bend. 10
They use against themselves that benevolence° *good will*
To which no man is friend.

They cannot think of so many crops to a field
Or of clean wood cleft by° an axe. *split by*
Their love is an eager meaninglessness 15
Too tense, or too lax.

They hear in every whisper that speaks to them
A shout and a cry.
As like as not, when they take life over their door-sills
They should let it go by. 20

SAMUEL TAYLOR COLERIDGE   (1772–1834)

Kubla Khan 1798

or a vision in a dream, a fragment

In Xanadu did Kubla Khan° *13th-century Chinese ruler*
A stately pleasure dome decree:
Where Alph, the sacred river, ran
Through caverns measureless to man
    Down to a sunless sea. 5
So twice five miles of fertile ground
With walls and towers were girdled round:

And there were gardens bright with sinuous rills,°   *winding brooks*
Where blossomed many an incense-bearing tree;
And here were forests ancient as the hills,   10
Enfolding sunny spots of greenery.

But oh! that deep romantic chasm which slanted
Down the green hill athwart a cedarn cover!
A savage place! as holy and enchanted
As e'er beneath a waning moon was haunted   15
By woman wailing for her demon lover!
And from this chasm, with ceaseless turmoil seething,
As if this earth in fast thick pants were breathing,
A mighty fountain momently° was forced: *moment by moment*
Amid whose swift half-intermitted burst   20
Huge fragments vaulted like rebounding hail,
Or chaffy grain beneath the thresher's flail:
And 'mid these dancing rocks at once and ever
It flung up momently the sacred river.
Five miles meandering with a mazy motion   25
Through wood and dale the sacred river ran,
Then reached the caverns measureless to man,
And sank in tumult to a lifeless ocean:
And 'mid this tumult Kubla heard from far
Ancestral voices prophesying war!   30
        The shadow of the dome of pleasure
        Floated midway on the waves;
        Where was heard the mingled measure
        From the fountain and the caves.
It was a miracle of rare device,   35
A sunny pleasure dome with caves of ice!

        A damsel with a dulcimer°   *a stringed musical instrument*
        In a vision once I saw:
        It was an Abyssinian° maid,   *Ethiopian*
        And on her dulcimer she played,   40
        Singing of Mount Abora.
        Could I revive within me
        Her symphony and song,
        To such a deep delight 'twould win me,
That with music loud and long,   45
I would build that dome in air,
That sunny dome! those caves of ice!
And all who heard should see them there,
And all should cry, Beware! Beware!
His flashing eyes, his floating hair!   50
Weave a circle round him thrice,
And close your eyes with holy dread,
For he on honey-dew hath fed,
And drunk the milk of Paradise.

ROBERT CREELEY (born 1926)

Fathers   1986

Scattered, aslant
faded faces a column
a rise of the packed
peculiar place to a
modest height makes   5
a view of common lots
in winter then, a ground
of battered snow crusted
at the edges under
it all, there under   10
my fathers their
faded women, friends,
the family all echoed,
names trees more tangible
physical place more tangible   15
the air of this place the road
going past to Watertown
or down to my mother's
grave, my father's grave, not
now this resonance of   20
each other one was his, his
survival only, his curious
reticence, his dead state,
his emptiness, his acerbic
edge cuts the hands to   25
hold him, hold on, wants
the ground, *wants* this frozen ground.

ROBERT CREELEY (born 1926)

Four   1973

This number for me
is comfort, a secure
fact of things. The

table stands on
all fours. The dog   5
walks comfortably,

and two by two
is not an army
but friends who love

one another. Four   10
is a square,
or peaceful circle,

celebrating return,
reunion,
love's triumph.   15

E. E. CUMMINGS   (1894–1963)

my sweet old etcetera   1926

my sweet old etcetera
aunt lucy during the recent

war could and what
is more did tell you just
what everybody was fighting   5

for,
my sister

isabel created hundreds
(and
hundreds) of socks not to   10
mention shirts fleaproof earwarmers

etcetera wristers etcetera, my
mother hoped that

i would die etcetera
bravely of course my father used   15
to become hoarse talking about how it was
a privilege and if only he
could meanwhile my

self etcetera lay quietly
in the deep mud et   20

cetera
(dreaming,
et

    cetera, of
Your smile   25
eyes knees and of your Etcetera)

JOHN DONNE   (1572–1631)

The Good-Morrow   1633

I wonder, by my troth, what thou and I
Did, till we loved? were we not weaned till then?
But sucked on country pleasures, childishly?
Or snorted° we in the Seven Sleepers'° den?   *snored/they slept 230 years in a cave*

'Twas so; but this,° all pleasures fancies be. *except for this*   5
If ever any beauty I did see,
Which I desired, and got, 'twas but a dream of thee.

And now good-morrow to our waking souls,
Which watch not one another out of fear;
For love, all love of other sights controls,   10
And makes one little room an everywhere.
Let sea-discoverers to new worlds have gone,
Let maps° to others, worlds on worlds have shown, *maps of the heavens*
Let us possess our world, each hath one, and is one.

My face in thine eye, thine in mine appears,   15
And true plain hearts do in the faces rest;
Where can we find two better hemispheres,
Without sharp north, without declining west?
Whatever dies was not mixed equally;° *dies as a result of bodily imbalance*
If our two loves be one, or, thou and I   20
Love so alike that none do slacken, none can die.

JOHN DONNE   (1572–1631)
Holy Sonnet 14   1633

Batter my heart, three-personed God; for You
As yet but knock, breathe, shine, and seek to mend;
That I may rise and stand, o'erthrow me, and bend
Your force to break, blow, burn, and make me new.
I, like an usurped town, to another due,   5
Labor to admit You, but Oh, to no end.
Reason, Your viceroy in me, me should defend,
But is captived, and proves weak or untrue.
Yet dearly I love You, and would be loved fain,° *gladly*
But am betrothed unto Your enemy: 10
Divorce me, untie or break that knot again,
Take me to You, imprison me, for I,
Except You enthrall me, never shall be free,
Nor ever chaste, except You ravish me.

RITA DOVE   (born 1952)
Daystar   1986

She wanted a little room for thinking:
but she saw diapers steaming on the line,
a doll slumped behind the door.
So she lugged a chair behind the garage
to sit out the children's naps.   5

Sometimes there were things to watch—
the pinched armor of a vanished cricket,
a floating maple leaf. Other days
she stared until she was assured
when she closed her eyes   10
she'd see only her own vivid blood.

She had an hour, at best, before Liza appeared
pouting from the top of the stairs.
And just *what* was mother doing
out back with the field mice? Why,   15

building a palace. Later
that night when Thomas rolled over and
lurched into her, she would open her eyes
and think of the place that was hers
for an hour—where   20
she was nothing,
pure nothing, in the middle of the day.

T. S. E L I O T   (1888–1965)

The Love Song of J. Alfred Prufrock   1917

> *S'io credesse che mia risposta fosse*
> *A persona che mai tornasse al mondo,*
> *Questa fiamma staria senza piu scosse.*
> *Ma perciocche giammai di questo fondo*
> *Non torno vivo alcun, s'i'odo il vero,*
> *Senza tema d'infamia ti rispondo.*

[From Dante's *Inferno*: "If I thought my answer were given / to anyone who
would ever return to the world, / this flame would stand still without moving
any further. / But since never from this abyss has anyone ever returned alive,
if what I hear is true, / without fear of infamy I answer thee."]

Let us go then, you and I,
When the evening is spread out against the sky
Like a patient etherized upon a table;
Let us go, through certain half-deserted streets,
The muttering retreats   5
Of restless nights in one-night cheap hotels
And sawdust restaurants with oyster-shells:
Streets that follow like a tedious argument
Of insidious intent
To lead you to an overwhelming question . . .   10
Oh, do not ask, "What is it?"
Let us go and make our visit.

In the room the women come and go
Talking of Michelangelo.

The yellow fog that rubs its back upon the window-panes   15
The yellow smoke that rubs its muzzle on the window-panes
Licked its tongue into the corners of the evening,
Lingered upon the pools that stand in drains,
Let fall upon its back the soot that falls from chimneys,
Slipped by the terrace, made a sudden leap,   20
And seeing that it was a soft October night,
Curled once about the house, and fell asleep.

And indeed there will be time
For the yellow smoke that slides along the street,
Rubbing its back upon the window-panes;   25
There will be time, there will be time
To prepare a face to meet the faces that you meet;
There will be time to murder and create,
And time for all the works and days of hands
That lift and drop a question on your plate;   30
Time for you and time for me,
And time yet for a hundred indecisions,
And for a hundred visions and revisions,
Before the taking of a toast and tea.

In the room the women come and go   35
Talking of Michelangelo.

And indeed there will be time
To wonder, "Do I dare?" and, "Do I dare?"
Time to turn back and descend the stair,
With a bald spot in the middle of my hair—   40
[They will say: "How his hair is growing thin!"]
My morning coat, my collar mounting firmly to the chin,
My necktie rich and modest, but asserted by a simple pin—
[They will say: "But how his arms and legs are thin!"]
Do I dare   45
Disturb the universe?
In a minute there is time
For decisions and revisions which a minute will reverse.

For I have known them all already, known them all:
Have known the evenings, mornings, afternoons,   50
I have measured out my life with coffee spoons;
I know the voices dying with a dying fall
Beneath the music from a farther room.
      So how should I presume?

And I have known the eyes already, known them all—   55
The eyes that fix you in a formulated phrase,
And when I am formulated, sprawling on a pin,
When I am pinned and wriggling on the wall,
Then how should I begin
To spit out all the butt-ends of my days and ways?   60
      And how should I presume?

And I have known the arms already, known them all—
Arms that are braceleted and white and bare
[But in the lamplight, downed with light brown hair!]
Is it perfume from a dress   65
That makes me so digress?
Arms that lie along a table, or wrap about a shawl.
        And should I then presume?
        And how should I begin?

                        . . . . .

Shall I say, I have gone at dusk through narrow streets   70
And watched the smoke that rises from the pipes
Of lonely men in shirt-sleeves, leaning out of windows? . . .

I should have been a pair of ragged claws
Scuttling across the floors of silent seas.

                        . . . . .

And the afternoon, the evening, sleeps so peacefully!   75
Smoothed by long fingers,
Asleep . . . tired . . . or it malingers,
Stretched on the floor, here beside you and me.
Should I, after tea and cakes and ices,
Have the strength to force the moment to its crisis?   80
But though I have wept and fasted, wept and prayed,
Though I have seen my head [grown slightly bald] brought in upon a platter,
I am no prophet—and here's no great matter;
I have seen the moment of my greatness flicker,
And I have seen the eternal Footman hold my coat, and snicker,   85
And in short, I was afraid.

And would it have been worth it, after all,
After the cups, the marmalade, the tea,
Among the porcelain, among some talk of you and me,
Would it have been worth while,   90
To have bitten off the matter with a smile,
To have squeezed the universe into a ball
To roll it toward some overwhelming question,
To say: "I am Lazarus,° come from the dead,   *whom Jesus raised from the dead*
Come back to tell you all, I shall tell you all"—   95
If one, settling a pillow by her head,
        Should say: "That is not what I meant at all.
        That is not it, at all."

And would it have been worth it, after all,
Would it have been worth while,   100
After the sunsets and the dooryards and the sprinkled streets,
After the novels, after the teacups, after the skirts that trail along the floor—
And this, and so much more?—
It is impossible to say just what I mean!
But as if a magic lantern threw the nerves in patterns on a screen: 105
Would it have been worth while
If one, settling a pillow or throwing off a shawl,
And turning toward the window, should say:

"That is not it at all,
That is not what I meant, at all."   110

. . . . .

No! I am not Prince Hamlet, nor was meant to be;
Am an attendant lord, one that will do
To swell a progress, start a scene or two,
Advise the prince; no doubt, an easy tool,
Deferential, glad to be of use,   115
Politic, cautious, and meticulous;
Full of high sentence, but a bit obtuse;
At times, indeed, almost ridiculous—
Almost, at times, the Fool.

I grow old . . . I grow old . . .   120
I shall wear the bottoms of my trousers rolled.

Shall I part my hair behind? Do I dare to eat a peach?
I shall wear white flannel trousers, and walk upon the beach.
I have heard the mermaids singing, each to each.

I do not think that they will sing to me.   125

I have seen them riding seaward on the waves
Combing the white hair of the waves blown back
When the wind blows the water white and black.

We have lingered in the chambers of the sea
By sea-girls wreathed with seaweed red and brown   130
Till human voices wake us, and we drown.

LAWRENCE FERLINGHETTI   (born 1919)

Constantly risking absurdity   1958

Constantly risking absurdity
                    and death
        whenever he performs
                above the heads
                    of his audience   5
    the poet like an acrobat
                climbs on rime
                    to a high wire of his own making
and balancing on eyebeams
                    above a sea of faces   10
            paces his way
                        to the other side of day
        performing *entrechats*°   *ballet leaps*
                    and sleight-of-foot tricks
and other high theatrics   15
                    and all without mistaking
        any thing
                for what it may not be

For he's the super realist
                    who must perforce perceive   20
        taut truth
                    before the taking of each stance or step
    in his supposed advance
                    toward that still higher perch
where Beauty stands and waits   25
                    with gravity
                            to start her death-defying leap
    And he
        a little charleychaplin man
                            who may or may not catch   30
            her fair eternal form
                    spreadeagled in the empty air
            of existence

ALLEN GINSBERG   (born 1926)

A Supermarket in California   1956

What thoughts I have of you tonight, Walt Whitman,
for I walked down the sidestreets under the trees with a
headache self-conscious looking at the full moon.

In my hungry fatigue, and shopping for images, I went
into the neon fruit supermarket, dreaming of your enumera-
tions!°   *cataloging of data*

What peaches and what penumbras!° Whole families   *partial shadows*
shopping at night! Aisles full of husbands! Wives in the avo-
cados, babies in the tomatoes—and you, Garcia Lorca,° what   *Spanish poet*
were you doing down by the watermelons?

I saw you, Walt Whitman, childless, lonely old grubber,
poking among the meats in the refrigerator and eyeing the
grocery boys.

I heard you asking questions of each: Who killed the
pork chops? What price bananas? Are you my Angel?   5

I wandered in and out of the brilliant stacks of cans following you, and followed in my imagination by the store detective.

We strode down the open corridors together in our solitary fancy tasting artichokes, possessing every frozen delicacy, and never passing the cashier.

Where are we going, Walt Whitman? The doors close in
an hour. Which way does your beard point tonight?

(I touch your book and dream of our odyssey in the supermarket and feel absurd.)

Will we walk all night through solitary streets? The trees
add shade to shade, lights out in the houses, we'll both be
lonely.   10

Will we stroll dreaming of the lost America of love past
blue automobiles in driveways, home to our silent cottage?

Ah, dear father, graybeard, lonely old courage-teacher,
what America did you have when Charon° quit poling his   *mythical ferryman conveying*
ferry and you got out on a smoking bank and stood watch-   *souls across River Styx to Hades*
ing the boat disappear on the black waters of Lethe?°   *mythical underworld river of*
                                                                forgetfulness

N I K K I   G I O V A N N I   (born 1943)

Nikki-Rosa   1968

childhood remembrances are always a drag
if you're Black
you always remember things like living in Woodlawn
with no inside toilet
and if you become famous or something   5
they never talk about how happy you were to have your mother
all to yourself and
how good the water felt when you got your bath from one of those
big tubs that folk in chicago barbecue in
and somehow when you talk about home   10
it never gets across how much you
understood their feelings
as the whole family attended meetings about Hollydale
and even though you remember
your biographers never understand   15
your father's pain as he sells his stock
and another dream goes
and though you're poor it isn't poverty that
concerns you
and though they fought a lot   20
it isn't your father's drinking that makes any difference
but only that everybody is together and you
and your sister have happy birthdays and very good christmasses
and I really hope no white person ever has cause to write about me
because they never understand Black love is Black wealth and they'll   25
probably talk about my hard childhood and never understand that
all the while I was quite happy

D O N A L D   H A L L   (born 1928)

My Son, My Executioner   1955

My son, my executioner,
    I take you in my arms,
Quiet and small and just astir,
    And whom my body warms.

Sweet death, small son, our instrument   5
    Of immortality,
Your cries and hungers document
    Our bodily decay.

We twenty-five and twenty-two,
    Who seemed to live forever,   10
Observe enduring life in you
    And start to die together.

THOMAS HARDY   (1840–1928)

In Time of "The Breaking of Nations"   1915

Only a man harrowing clods°   *breaking up lumps (thrown up*
    In a slow silent walk   *by the plow)*
With an old horse that stumbles and nods
    Half asleep as they stalk.

Only thin smoke without flame   5
    From the heaps of couch-grass;°   *creeping grassy weed*
Yet this will go onward the same
    Though dynasties pass.

Yonder a maid and her wight°   *young male*
    Come whispering by: 10
War's annals will cloud into night
    Ere° their story die.   *before*

SEAMUS HEANEY   (born 1939)

The Forge   1969

All I know is a door into the dark.
Outside, old axles and iron hoops rusting;
Inside, the hammered anvil's short-pitched ring,
The unpredictable fantail of sparks
Or hiss when a new shoe toughens in water.   5
The anvil must be somewhere in the center.
Horned as a unicorn, at one end square,
Set there immovable: an altar
Where he expends himself in shape and music.
Sometimes, leather-aproned, hairs in his nose,   10
He leans out on the jamb, recalls a clatter
Of hoofs where traffic is flashing in rows;
Then grunts and goes in, with a slam and flick
To beat real iron out, to work the bellows.

GEORGE HERBERT   (1593–1633)

The Collar   1633

I struck the board° and cried, "No more;   *table*
   I will abroad!
What? shall I ever sigh and pine?
My lines and life are free, free as the road,
  Loose as the wind, as large as store.°   *abundance*   5
    Shall I be still in suit?°   *begging favors*
  Have I no harvest but a thorn
  To let me blood, and not restore
What I have lost with cordial° fruit?   *life-giving*
    Sure there was wine   10
  Before my sighs did dry it; there was corn
  Before my tears did drown it.
Is the year only lost to me?
  Have I no bays° to crown it,   *laurel wreaths symbolizing honor*
No flowers, no garlands gay? All blasted?   15
    All wasted?
  Not so, my heart; but there is fruit,
    And thou hast hands.
  Recover all thy sigh-blown age
On double pleasures: leave thy cold dispute   20
Of what is fit and not. Forsake thy cage,
    Thy rope of sands,
Which petty thoughts have made, and made to thee
  Good cable, to enforce and draw,
    And be thy law,   25
  While thou didst wink and wouldst not see.
    Away! take heed;
    I will abroad.
Call in thy death's-head° there; tie up thy fears.   *skull*
    He that forbears   30
   To suit and serve his need,
    Deserves his load."
But as I raved and grew more fierce and wild
    At every word,
Methought I heard one calling, *Child!*   35
    And I replied, *My Lord*.

GEORGE HERBERT   (1593–1633)

Easter Wings   1633

Lord, who createdst man in wealth and store,°   abundance
    Though foolishly he lost the same,
        Decaying more and more
            Till he became
                Most poor.   5
                With thee
            O let me rise
        As larks, harmoniously,
    And sing this day thy victories:
Then shall the fall further the flight in me.   10

    My tender age in sorrow did begin:
    And still with sicknesses and shame
        Thou didst so punish sin,
            That I became
                Most thin.   15
                With thee
            Let me combine,
        And feel this day thy victory;
    For, if I imp° my wing on thine,   graft
Affliction shall advance the flight in me.   20

A. E. HOUSMAN   (1859–1936)

To an Athlete Dying Young   1896

The time you won your town the race
We chaired you through the market-place;
Man and boy stood cheering by,
And home we brought you shoulder-high.

Today, the road all runners come,   5
Shoulder-high we bring you home,
And set you at your threshold down,
Townsman of a stiller town.

Smart lad, to slip betimes away
From fields where glory does not stay   10
And early though the laurel grows
It withers quicker than the rose.

Eyes the shady night has shut
Cannot see the record cut,
And silence sounds no worse than cheers   15
After earth has stopped the ears:

Now you will not swell the rout
Of lads that wore their honors out,
Runners whom renown outran
And the name died before the man.   20

So set, before its echoes fade,
The fleet foot on the sill of shade,
And hold to the low lintel° up   *low beam*
The still-defended challenge-cup.

And round that early-laureled head   25
Will flock to gaze the strengthless dead,
And find unwithered on its curls
The garland briefer than a girl's.

LANGSTON HUGHES   (1902–1967)

End   1959

There are
No clocks on the wall,
And no time,
No shadows that move
From dawn to dusk   5
Across the floor.

There is neither light
Nor dark
Outside the door.

There is no door!   10

TED HUGHES   (born 1930)

Hawk Roosting   1959

I sit in the top of the wood, my eyes closed.
Inaction, no falsifying dream
Between my hooked head and hooked feet:
Or in sleep rehearse perfect kills and eat.

The convenience of the high trees!   5
The air's buoyancy and the sun's ray
Are of advantage to me;
And the earth's face upward for my inspection.

My feet are locked upon the rough bark.
It took the whole of Creation   10
To produce my foot, my each feather:
Now I hold Creation in my foot

Or fly up, and revolve it all slowly—
I kill where I please because it is all mine.

There is no sophistry° in my body: *plausible but fallacious argument*   15
My manners are tearing off heads—

The allotment of death.
For the one path of my flight is direct
Through the bones of the living.
No arguments assert my right: 20

The sun is behind me.
Nothing has changed since I began.
My eye has permitted no change.
I am going to keep things like this.

VICENTE HUIDOBRO (1892–1948)

Ars Poetica

TRANSLATED BY DAVID M. GUSS

Let poetry be like a key
Opening a thousand doors.
A leaf falls; something flies by;
Let all the eye sees be created
And the soul of the listener tremble.   5

Invent new worlds and watch your word;
The adjective, when it doesn't give life, kills it.

We are in the age of nerves.
The muscle hangs,
Like a memory, in museums;   10
But we are not the weaker for it:
True vigor
Resides in the head.

Oh Poets, why sing of roses!
Let them flower in your poems;   15

For us alone
Do all things live beneath the Sun.

The poet is a little God.

BEN JONSON (1572–1637)

Song: To Celia   1616

Drink to me only with thine eyes,
And I will pledge with mine;

Or leave a kiss but in the cup,
And I'll not look for wine.
The thirst that from the soul doth rise,   5
Doth ask a drink divine:
But might I of Jove's° nectar sup,   *Roman name of Zeus*
I would not change for thine.

I sent thee late a rosy wreath,
Not so much honoring thee,   10
As giving it a hope, that there
It could not withered be.
But thou thereon did'st only breathe,
And sent'st it back to me;
Since when it grows and smells, I swear,   15
Not of itself, but thee.

JUNE JORDAN   (born 1936)

Lullaby   1973

as suddenly as love

the evening burns a low
red
line occasional with golden glass
across the sky   5

i celebrate the color of the heat
you fill me with
the bloodbeat
you instill me with

as suddenly as love   10

DONALD JUSTICE   (born 1925)

Time and the Weather   1967

Time and the weather wear away
The houses that our fathers built.
Their ghostly furniture remains—
All the sad sofas we have stained
With tears of boredom and of guilt,   5

The fraying mottoes, the stopped clocks . . .
And still sometimes these tired shapes
Haunt the damp parlors of the heart.
What Sunday prisons they recall!
And what miraculous escapes!   10

JOHN KEATS (1795–1821)

Ode to a Nightingale 1820

1

My heart aches, and a drowsy numbness pains
  My sense, as though of hemlock° I had drunk, *poison*
Or emptied some dull opiate to the drains
  One minute past, and Lethe-wards° had sunk: *toward Lethe, mythical underworld*
'Tis not through envy of thy happy lot, *river of forgetfulness* 5
  But being too happy in thine happiness—
    That thou, light-wingèd Dryad° of the trees, *wood nymph*
      In some melodious plot
Of beechen green, and shadows numberless,
  Singest of summer in full-throated ease. 10

2

O, for a draught of vintage!° that hath been *drink of wine*
  Cooled a long age in the deep-delvèd earth,
Tasting of Flora° and the country green, *Roman goddess of flowers*
  Dance, and Provençal song,° and sunburnt mirth! *songs of Provence, in southern France*
O for a beaker full of the warm South, 15
  Full of the true, the blushful Hippocrene,° *fountain of the Muses in Greece*
    With beaded bubbles winking at the brim,
      And purple-stainèd mouth;
That I might drink, and leave the world unseen,
  And with thee fade away into the forest dim: 20

3

Fade far away, dissolve, and quite forget
  What thou among the leaves hast never known,
The weariness, the fever, and the fret
  Here, where men sit and hear each other groan;
Where palsy shakes a few, sad, last gray hairs, 25
  Where youth grows pale, and specter-thin, and dies,
    Where but to think is to be full of sorrow
      And leaden-eyed despairs,
Where Beauty cannot keep her lustrous eyes,
  Or new Love pine at them beyond tomorrow. 30

4

Away! away! for I will fly to thee,
  Not charioted by Bacchus and his pards,° *god of wine and his leopards*
But on the viewless° wings of Poesy, *invisible*
  Though the dull brain perplexes and retards:
Already with thee! tender is the night, 35
  And haply the Queen-Moon is on her throne,
    Clustered around by all her starry Fays;° *fairies*
      But here there is no light,
Save what from heaven is with the breezes blown
  Through verdurous glooms and winding mossy ways. 40

5
I cannot see what flowers are at my feet,
    Nor what soft incense hangs upon the boughs,
But, in embalmèd° darkness, guess each sweet   *perfumed*
    Wherewith the seasonable month endows
The grass, the thicket, and the fruit tree wild;   45
    White hawthorn, and the pastoral eglantine;°   *wood roses*
        Fast fading violets covered up in leaves;
                And mid-May's eldest child,
    The coming musk-rose, full of dewy wine,
        The murmurous haunt of flies on summer eves.   50

6
Darkling° I listen; and for many a time   *in darkness*
    I have been half in love with easeful Death,
Called him soft names in many a musèd rhyme,
    To take into the air my quiet breath;
Now more than ever seems it rich to die,   55
    To cease upon the midnight with no pain,
        While thou art pouring forth thy soul abroad
                In such an ecstasy!
    Still wouldst thou sing, and I have ears in vain—
        To thy high requiem become a sod.   60

7
Thou wast not born for death, immortal Bird!
    No hungry generations tread thee down;
The voice I hear this passing night was heard
    In ancient days by emperor and clown:
Perhaps the selfsame song that found a path   65
    Through the sad heart of Ruth,° when, sick for home,   *of the biblical Book of Ruth*
        She stood in tears amid the alien corn;
                The same that ofttimes hath
    Charmed magic casements, opening on the foam
        Of perilous seas, in faery lands forlorn.   70

8
Forlorn! the very word is like a bell
    To toll me back from thee to my sole self!
Adieu! the fancy cannot cheat so well
    As she is famed to do, deceiving elf.
Adieu! adieu! thy plaintive anthem fades   75
    Past the near meadows, over the still stream,
        Up the hill side; and now 'tis buried deep
                In the next valley-glades:
    Was it a vision, or a waking dream?
        Fled is that music:—Do I wake or sleep?   80

JOHN KEATS   (1795–1821)
When I Have Fears   1818

When I have fears that I may cease to be
    Before my pen has gleaned my teeming brain,
Before high-pilèd books, in charact'ry,°   *written symbols*
    Hold like rich garners the full-ripened grain;
When I behold, upon the night's starred face,   5
    Huge cloudy symbols of a high romance,
And think that I may never live to trace
    Their shadows, with the magic hand of chance;
And when I feel, fair creature of an hour,
    That I shall never look upon thee more,   10
Never have relish in the faery° power   *magical*
    Of unreflecting love!—then on the shore
Of the wide world I stand alone, and think
Till Love and Fame to nothingness do sink.

GALWAY KINNELL   (born 1927)
Blackberry Eating   1980

I love to go out in late September
among the fat, overripe, icy, black blackberries
to eat blackberries for breakfast,
the stalks very prickly, a penalty
they earn for knowing the black art   5
of blackberry-making; and as I stand among them
lifting the stalks to my mouth, the ripest berries
fall almost unbidden to my tongue,
as words sometimes do, certain peculiar words
like *strengths* or *squinched*,   10
many-lettered, one-syllabled lumps,
which I squeeze, squinch open, and splurge well
in the silent, startled, icy, black language
of blackberry-eating in late September.

ETHRIDGE KNIGHT   (born 1933)
He Sees through Stone   1968

He sees through stone
he has the secret
eyes this old black one
who under prison skies
sits pressed by the sun   5
against the western wall
his pipe between purple gums

the years fall
like overripe plums
bursting red flesh   10
on the dark earth

his time is not my time
but I have known him
in a time gone

he led me trembling cold   15
into the dark forest
taught me the secret rites
to take a woman
to be true to my brothers
to make my spear drink   20
the blood
of my enemies

now black cats circle him
flash white teeth
snarl at the air   25
mashing green grass beneath
shining muscles
ears peeling his words
he smiles
he knows   30
the hunt the enemy
he has the secret eyes
he sees through stone

AUDRE LORDE   (born 1934)

Sister Outsider   1978

We were born in a poor time
never touching
each other's hunger
never
sharing our crusts   5
in fear
the bread became enemy.

Now we raise our children
to respect themselves
as well as each other.   10

Now you have made loneliness
holy and useful
and no longer needed
now
your light shines very brightly   15
but I want you

to know
your darkness also
rich
and beyond fear.   20

ROBERT LOWELL   (1917–1977)

Skunk Hour   1959
(for Elizabeth Bishop)

Nautilus Island's° hermit   *in Castine, Maine*
heiress still lives through winter in her Spartan cottage;
her sheep still graze above the sea.
Her son's a bishop. Her farmer
is first selectman° in our village;   *elected official*   5
she's in her dotage.°   *second childhood*

Thirsting for
the hierarchic privacy
of Queen Victoria's century,
she buys up all   10
the eyesores facing her shore,
and lets them fall.

The season's ill—
we've lost our summer millionaire,
who seemed to leap from an L. L. Bean°   *sporting goods company*   15
catalogue. His nine-knot yawl°   *boat*
was auctioned off to lobstermen.
A red fox stain covers Blue Hill.

And now our fairy
decorator brightens his shop for fall;   20
his fishnet's filled with orange cork,
orange, his cobbler's bench and awl;
there is no money in his work,
he'd rather marry.

One dark night,   25
my Tudor Ford climbed the hill's skull;
I watched for love-cars. Lights turned down,
they lay together, hull to hull,
where the graveyard shelves on the town. . . .
My mind's not right.   30

A car radio bleats,
"Love, O careless Love. . . ." I hear
my ill-spirit sob in each blood cell,
as if my hand were at its throat. . . .
I myself am hell;   35
nobody's here—

only skunks, that search
in the moonlight for a bite to eat.
They march on their soles up Main Street:
white stripes, moonstruck eyes' red fire   40
under the chalk-dry and spar spire°   *pole used as a mast*
of the Trinitarian Church.

I stand on top
of our back steps and breathe the rich air—
a mother skunk with her column of kittens swills the garbage pail.   45
She jabs her wedge-head in a cup
of sour cream, drops her ostrich tail,
and will not scare.

CHRISTOPHER MARLOWE   (1564–1593)

The Passionate Shepherd to His Love   1600

Come live with me and be my love,
And we will all the pleasures prove°   *try*
That valleys, groves, hills, and fields,
Woods, or steepy mountain yields.

And we will sit upon the rocks,   5
Seeing the shepherds feed their flocks,
By shallow rivers to whose falls
Melodious birds sing madrigals.°   *harmonic songs*

And I will make thee beds of roses
And a thousand fragrant posies,   10
A cap of flowers, and a kirtle°   *skirt*
Embroidered all with leaves of myrtle;

A gown made of the finest wool
Which from our pretty lambs we pull;
Fair lined slippers for the cold,   15
With buckles of the purest gold;

A belt of straw and ivy buds,
With coral clasps and amber studs:
And if these pleasures may thee move,
Come live with me, and be my love.   20

The shepherds' swains° shall dance and sing   *lovers*
For thy delight each May morning:
If these delights thy mind may move,
Then live with me and be my love.

ANDREW MARVELL   (1621–1678)

The Definition of Love

before 1678

My Love is of a birth as rare
As 'tis, for object, strange and high;
It was begotten by Despair
Upon Impossibility.

Magnanimous Despair alone   5
Could show me so divine a thing,
Where feeble Hope could ne'er have flown
But vainly flapped its tinsel wing.

And yet I quickly might arrive
Where my extended soul is fixed;   10
But Fate does iron wedges drive,
And always crowds itself betwixt.

For Fate with jealous eye does see
Two perfect loves, nor lets them close;°   *unite*
Their union would her ruin be,   15
And her tyrannic power depose.

And therefore her decrees of steel
Us as the distant poles have placed
(Though Love's whole world on us doth wheel),
Not by themselves to be embraced,   20

Unless the giddy heaven fall,
And earth some new convulsion tear,
And, us to join, the world should all
Be cramped into a planisphere.°   *sphere projected on a plane surface*

As lines, so loves oblique may well   25
Themselves in every angle greet;°   *may converge*
But ours, so truly parallel,
Though infinite, can never meet.

Therefore the love which us doth bind,
But Fate so enviously debars,°   *prevents*   30
Is the conjunction of the mind,
And opposition of the stars.

W. S. MERWIN   (born 1927)

For the Anniversary of My Death

1967

Every year without knowing it I have passed the day
When the last fires will wave to me
And the silence will set out
Tireless traveler
Like the beam of a lightless star   5

Then I will no longer
Find myself in life as in a strange garment
Surprised at the earth
And the love of one woman
And the shamelessness of men   10
As today writing after three days of rain
Hearing the wren sing and the falling cease
And bowing not knowing to what

JOHN MILTON   (1608–1674)

How Soon Hath Time   1631

How soon hath Time, the subtle thief of youth,
 Stoln on his wing my three and twentieth year!
 My hasting days fly on with full career,
 But my late spring no bud or blossom shew'th.°   *shows*
Perhaps my semblance might deceive the truth,   5
 That I to manhood am arrived so near,
 And inward ripeness doth much less appear,
 That some more timely-happy spirits endu'th.°   *endow*
Yet be it less or more, or soon or slow,
 It shall be still in strictest measure even   10
 To that same lot, however mean or high,
Toward which Time leads me, and the will of Heaven;
 All is, if I have grace to use it so,
 As ever in my great Taskmaster's eye.

WILFRED OWEN   (1893–1918)

Anthem for Doomed Youth   1920

What passing-bells for these who die as cattle?
 Only the monstrous anger of the guns.
 Only the stuttering rifles' rapid rattle
Can patter out their hasty orisons.°   *prayers*
No mockeries now for them; no prayers nor bells,   5
 Nor any voice of mourning save the choirs—
The shrill, demented choirs of wailing shells;
 And bugles calling for them from sad shires.°   *shire horses*

What candles may be held to speed them all?
 Not in the hands of boys, but in their eyes   10
Shall shine the holy glimmers of good-byes.
 The pallor of girls' brows shall be their pall;
Their flowers the tenderness of patient minds,
And each slow dusk a drawing-down of blinds.

LINDA PASTAN　(born 1932)
1932–　　　　　　　　　　　　　　　　　　　1991

I saw my name in print the other day
with 1932 and then a blank
and knew that even now some grassy bank
just waited for my grave. And somewhere a gray

slab of marble existed already　　　　　　　　　　　　　　5
on which the final number would be carved—
as if the stone itself were somehow starved
for definition. When I went steady

in high school years ago, my boyfriend's name
was what I tried out, hearing how it fit　　　　　　　　10
with mine; then names of film stars in some hit.
My husband was anonymous as rain.

There is a number out there, odd or even
that will become familiar to my sons
and daughter. (They are the living ones　　　　　　　15
I think of now: Peter, Rachel, Stephen.)

I picture it, four integers in a row
5 or 7, 6 or 2 or 9:
a period; silence; an end-stopped line;
a hammer poised . . . delivering its blow.　　　　　20

LINDA PASTAN　(born 1932)
Posterity　　　　　　　　　　　　　　　　　　1991

For every newborn child
We planted one live tree,
A green posterity,°　　　　　　　　　　　　　*future generation*
So death could be beguiled°　　　　　　　*deluded or diverted*
By root and branch and flower　　　　　　　　　　　　5
To abdicate° some power.　　　　　　　　　　　*relinquish*
And we were reconciled.

Now we must move away
Leaving the trees behind
For anyone to climb.　　　　　　　　　　　　　　　10
The gold-rimmed sky goes gray.
Snow, as we turn our backs,
Obliterates our tracks.
Not even leaves can stay.

SYLVIA PLATH   (1932–1963)

Daddy   1965

You do not do, you do not do
Any more, black shoe
In which I have lived like a foot
For thirty years, poor and white,
Barely daring to breathe or Achoo.   5

Daddy, I have had to kill you.
You died before I had time—
Marble-heavy, a bag full of God,
Ghastly statue with one gray toe
Big as a Frisco seal   10

And a head in the freakish Atlantic
Where it pours bean green over blue
In the waters off beautiful Nauset.
I used to pray to recover you.
Ach, du.°   *O, you (German)*   15

In the German tongue, in the Polish town°   *Granbow, Otto Plath's birthplace*
Scraped flat by the roller
Of wars, wars, wars.
But the name of the town is common.
My Polack friend   20

Says there are a dozen or two.
So I never could tell where you
Put your foot, your root,
I never could talk to you.
The tongue stuck in my jaw.   25

It stuck in a barb wire snare.
Ich, ich, ich, ich,°   *I, I, I, I (German)*
I could hardly speak.
I thought every German was you.
And the language obscene   30

An engine, an engine
Chuffing me off like a Jew.
A Jew to Dachau, Auschwitz, Belsen.
I began to talk like a Jew.
I think I may well be a Jew.   35

The snows of the Tyrol, the clear beer of Vienna
Are not very pure or true.
With my gipsy ancestress and my weird luck
And my Taroc pack and my Taroc pack°   *Tarot cards used to tell the future*
I may be a bit of a Jew.   40

I have always been scared of *you*,
With your Luftwaffe,° your gobbledygoo.   *German air force*

And your neat mustache
And your Aryan eye, bright blue.
Panzer-man,° panzer-man, O You—   *member of tank crew*   45

Not God but a swastika
So black no sky could squeak through.
Every woman adores a Fascist,
The boot in the face, the brute
Brute heart of a brute like you.   50

You stand at the blackboard, daddy,
In the picture I have of you,
A cleft in your chin instead of your foot
But no less a devil for that, no not
Any less the black man who   55

Bit my pretty red heart in two.
I was ten when they buried you.
At twenty I tried to die
And get back, back, back to you.
I thought even the bones would do.   60

But they pulled me out of the sack,
And they stuck me together with glue.
And then I knew what to do.
I made a model of you,
A man in black with a Meinkampf° look   My Battle, *Adolf Hitler's autobiography*   65

And a love of the rack and the screw.
And I said I do, I do.
So daddy, I'm finally through.
The black telephone's off at the root,
The voices just can't worm through.   70

If I've killed one man, I've killed two—
The vampire who said he was you
And drank my blood for a year,
Seven years, if you want to know.
Daddy, you can lie back now.   75

There's a stake in your fat black heart
And the villagers never liked you.
They are dancing and stamping on you.
They always *knew* it was you.
Daddy, daddy, you bastard, I'm through.   80

EZRA POUND (1885–1972)

In a Station of the Metro   1916

The apparition of these faces in the crowd;
Petals on a wet, black bough.

EZRA POUND   (1885–1972)

The River-Merchant's Wife: A Letter   1915

(after Rihaku)°   *Japanese name for Li Po,*
an 8th-century Chinese poet

While my hair was still cut straight across my forehead
I played about the front gate, pulling flowers.
You came by on bamboo stilts, playing horse,
You walked about my seat, playing with blue plums.
And we went on living in the village of Chokan: 5
Two small people, without dislike or suspicion.

At fourteen I married My Lord you.
I never laughed, being bashful.
Lowering my head, I looked at the wall.
Called to, a thousand times, I never looked back.   10

At fifteen I stopped scowling,
I desired my dust to be mingled with yours
For ever and for ever and for ever.
Why should I climb the look out?

At sixteen you departed,   15
You went into far Ku-to-yen, by river of swirling eddies,
And you have been gone five months.
The monkeys make sorrowful noise overhead.

You dragged your feet when you went out.
By the gate now, the moss is grown, the different mosses,   20
Too deep to clear them away!
The leaves fall early this autumn, in wind.
The paired butterflies are already yellow with August
Over the grass in the West garden;
They hurt me. I grow older,   25
If you are coming down through the narrows of the river Kiang,
Please let me know beforehand,
And I will come out to meet you
        As far as Cho-fu-Sa.

SIR WALTER RALEIGH   (1552–1618)

The Nymph's Reply to the Shepherd   1600

(A reply to Marlowe's "The Passionate Shepherd to His Love")

If all the world and love were young,
And truth in every shepherd's tongue,
These pretty pleasures might me move
To live with thee and be thy love.

Time drives the flocks from field to fold   5
When rivers rage and rocks grow cold,

And Philomel° becometh dumb;   *the nightingale*
The rest complains of cares to come.

The flowers do fade, and wanton fields
To wayward winter reckoning yields;   10
A honey tongue, a heart of gall,°   *bitter heart*
Is fancy's spring, but sorrow's fall.

Thy gowns, thy shoes, thy beds of roses,
Thy cap, thy kirtle,° and thy posies   *dress*
Soon break, soon wither, soon forgotten—   15
In folly ripe, in reason rotten.

Thy belt of straw and ivy buds,
Thy coral clasps and amber studs,
All these in me no means can move
To come to thee and be thy love.   20

But could youth last and love still breed,
Had joys no date° nor age no need,   *no end*
Then these delights my mind might move
To live with thee and be thy love.

DUDLEY RANDALL   (born 1914)

Ballad of Birmingham   1969

(On the bombing of a church in Birmingham, Alabama, 1963)

"Mother dear, may I go downtown
Instead of out to play,
And march the streets of Birmingham
In a Freedom March today?"

"No, baby, no, you may not go,   5
For the dogs are fierce and wild,
And clubs and hoses, guns and jails
Aren't good for a little child."

"But, mother, I won't be alone.
Other children will go with me,   10
And march the streets of Birmingham
To make our country free."

"No, baby, no, you may not go,
For I fear those guns will fire.
But you may go to church instead   15
And sing in the children's choir."

She has combed and brushed her night-dark hair,
And bathed rose petal sweet.
And drawn white gloves on her small brown hands,
And white shoes on her feet.   20

The mother smiled to know her child
Was in the sacred place,
But that smile was the last smile
To come upon her face.

For when she heard the explosion,   25
Her eyes grew wet and wild.
She raced through the streets of Birmingham
Calling for her child.

She clawed through bits of glass and brick,
Then lifted out a shoe.   30
"Oh, here's the shoe my baby wore,
But, baby, where are you?"

JOHN CROWE RANSOM   (1888–1974)

Janet Waking   1927

Beautifully Janet slept
Till it was deeply morning. She woke then
And thought about her dainty-feathered hen,
To see how it had kept.

One kiss she gave her mother.   5
Only a small one gave she to her daddy
Who would have kissed each curl of his shining baby;
No kiss at all for her brother.

"Old Chucky, old Chucky!" she cried,
Running across the world upon the grass   10
To Chucky's house, and listening. But alas,
Her Chucky had died.

It was a transmogrifying° bee   *transforming*
Came droning down on Chucky's old bald head
And sat and put the poison. It scarcely bled,   15
But how exceedingly

And purply did the knot
Swell with the venom and communicate
Its rigor! Now the poor comb stood up straight
But Chucky did not.   20

So there was Janet
Kneeling on the wet grass, crying her brown hen
(Translated far beyond the daughters of men)
To rise and walk upon it.

And weeping fast as she had breath   25
Janet implored us, "Wake her from her sleep!"
And would not be instructed in how deep
Was the forgetful kingdom of death.

ADRIENNE RICH (born 1929)

Diving into the Wreck 1973

First having read the book of myths,
and loaded the camera,
and checked the edge of the knife-blade,
I put on
the body-armor of black rubber 5
the absurd flippers
the grave and awkward mask.
I am having to do this
not like Cousteau with his
assiduous° team *diligent* 10
aboard the sun-flooded schooner
but here alone.

There is a ladder.
The ladder is always there
hanging innocently 15
close to the side of the schooner.
We know what it is for,
we who have used it.
otherwise
it is a piece of maritime floss 20
some sundry° equipment. *miscellaneous*

I go down.
Rung after rung and still
the oxygen immerses me
the blue light 25
the clear atoms
of our human air.
I go down.
My flippers cripple me,
I crawl like an insect down the ladder 30
and there is no one
to tell me when the ocean
will begin.

First the air is blue and then
it is bluer and then green and then 35
black I am blacking out and yet
my mask is powerful
it pumps my blood with power
the sea is another story
the sea is not a question of power 40
I have to learn alone
to turn my body without force
in the deep element.

And now: it is easy to forget
what I came for 45

among so many who have always
lived here
swaying their crenellated° fans   indented, scalloped
between the reefs
and besides   50
you breathe differently down here.

I came to explore the wreck.
The words are purposes.
The words are maps.
I came to see the damage that was done   55
and the treasures that prevail.
I stroke the beam of my lamp
slowly along the flank
of something more permanent
than fish or weed   60

the thing I came for:
the wreck and not the story of the wreck
the thing itself and not the myth
the drowned face always staring
toward the sun   65
the evidence of damage
worn by salt and sway into this threadbare beauty
the ribs of the disaster
curving their assertion
among the tentative haunters.   70

This is the place.
And I am here, the mermaid whose dark hair
streams black, the merman in his armored body.
We circle silently
about the wreck   75
we dive into the hold.
I am she: I am he

whose drowned face sleeps with open eyes
whose breasts still bear the stress
whose silver, copper, vermeil° cargo lies   red   80
obscurely inside barrels
half-wedged and left to rot
we are the half-destroyed instruments
that once held to a course
the water-eaten log   85
the fouled compass

We are, I am, you are
by cowardice or courage
the one who find our way
back to this scene   90
carrying a knife, a camera
a book of myths
in which
our names do not appear.

EDWIN ARLINGTON ROBINSON　(1869–1935)
Richard Cory 1897

Whenever Richard Cory went down town,
We people on the pavement looked at him:
He was a gentleman from sole to crown,
Clean favored, and imperially slim.

And he was always quietly arrayed, 5
And he was always human when he talked;
But still he fluttered pulses when he said,
"Good-morning," and he glittered when he walked.

And he was rich—yes, richer than a king—
And admirably schooled in every grace: 10
In fine, we thought that he was everything
To make us wish that we were in his place.

So on we worked, and waited for the light,
And went without the meat, and cursed the bread;
And Richard Cory, one calm summer night, 15
Went home and put a bullet through his head.

THEODORE ROETHKE　(1908–1963)
I Knew a Woman 1958

I knew a woman, lovely in her bones,
When small birds sighed, she would sigh back at them;
Ah, when she moved, she moved more ways than one:
The shapes a bright container can contain!
Of her choice virtues only gods should speak, 5
Or English poets who grew up on Greek
(I'd have them sing in chorus, cheek to cheek).

How well her wishes went! She stroked my chin,
She taught me Turn, and Counter-turn, and Stand;° *dance moves of chorus in Greek plays*
She taught me Touch, that undulant white skin; 10
I nibbled meekly from her proffered hand;
She was the sickle; I, poor I, the rake,
Coming behind her for her pretty sake
(But what prodigious mowing we did make).

Love likes a gander, and adores a goose: 15
Her full lips pursed, the errant° note to seize; *straying*
She played it quick, she played it light and loose,
My eyes, they dazzled at her flowing knees;
Her several parts could keep a pure repose,
Or one hip quiver with a mobile nose 20
(She moved in circles, and those circles moved).

Let seed be grass, and grass turn into hay:
I'm martyr to a motion not my own;
What's freedom for? To know eternity.
I swear she cast a shadow white as stone. 25
But who would count eternity in days?
These old bones live to learn her wanton ways:
(I measure time by how a body sways).

ANNE SEXTON   (1928–1974)

The Truth the Dead Know   1961

For my mother, born March 1902, died March 1959
and my father, born February 1900, died June 1959

Gone, I say and walk from church,
refusing the stiff procession to the grave,
letting the dead ride alone in the hearse.
It is June. I am tired of being brave.

We drive to the Cape. I cultivate 5
myself where the sun gutters from the sky,
where the sea swings in like an iron gate
and we touch. In another country people die.

My darling, the wind falls in like stones
from the whitehearted water and when we touch 10
we enter touch entirely. No one's alone.
Men kill for this, or for as much.

And what of the dead? They lie without shoes
in their stone boats. They are more like stone
than the sea would be if it stopped. They refuse 15
to be blessed, throat, eye and knucklebone.

WILLIAM SHAKESPEARE   (1564–1616)

Sonnet 116   1609

Let me not to the marriage of true minds
Admit impediments. Love is not love
Which alters when it alteration finds,
Or bends with the remover to remove:°   *responds to inconstancy with inconstancy*
Oh, no! it is an ever-fixèd mark, 5
That looks on tempests and is never shaken;
It is the star to every wandering bark,°   *boat*
Whose worth's unknown, although his height be taken.°   *although its elevation can be measured*
Love's not Time's fool, though rosy lips and cheeks
Within his bending sickle's compass come; 10

Love alters not with his brief hours and weeks,
But bears it out even to the edge of doom.°   *Day of Judgment*
If this be error and upon me proved,
I never writ, nor no man ever loved.

PERCY BYSSHE SHELLEY (1792–1822)

To a Skylark   1820

Hail to thee, blithe Spirit!
   Bird thou never wert,
That from Heaven, or near it,
   Pourest thy full heart
In profuse strains of unpremeditated art.   5

Higher still and higher
   From the earth thou springest
Like a cloud of fire;
   The blue deep thou wingest,
And singing still dost soar, and soaring ever singest.   10

In the golden lightning
   Of the sunken sun,
O'er which clouds are bright'ning,
   Thou dost float and run;
Like an unbodied joy whose race is just begun.   15

The pale purple even
   Melts around thy flight;
Like a star of Heaven,
   In the broad daylight
Thou art unseen, but yet I hear thy shrill delight,   20

Keen as are the arrows
   Of that silver sphere,°   *star*
Whose intense lamp narrows
   In the white dawn clear
Until we hardly see—we feel that it is there.   25

All the earth and air
   With thy voice is loud,
As, when night is bare,
   From one lonely cloud
The moon rains out her beams, and Heaven is overflowed.   30

What thou art we know not;
   What is most like thee?
From rainbow clouds there flow not
   Drops so bright to see
As from thy presence showers a rain of melody.   35

Like a Poet hidden
   In the light of thought,

Singing hymns unbidden,
    Till the world is wrought
To sympathy with hopes and fears it heeded not: 40

Like a high-born maiden
    In a palace tower,
Soothing her love-laden
    Soul in secret hour
With music sweet as love, which overflows her bower:°   *private chamber* 45

Like a glowworm golden
    In a dell of dew,
Scattering unbeholden
    Its aërial hue
Among the flowers and grass, which screen it from the view!   50

Like a rose embowered
    In its own green leaves,
By warm winds deflowered,
    Till the scent it gives
Makes faint with too much sweet those heavy-wingèd thieves: 55

Sound of vernal° showers   *spring*
    On the twinkling grass,
Rain-awakened flowers,
    All that ever was
Joyous, and clear, and fresh, thy music doth surpass: 60

Teach us, Sprite° or Bird,   *spirit*
    What sweet thoughts are thine:
I have never heard
    Praise of love or wine
That panted forth a flood of rapture so divine.   65

Chorus Hymeneal°   *as for a wedding*
    Or triumphal chant,
Matched with thine would be all
    But an empty vaunt,°   *boast*
A thing wherein we feel there is some hidden want.   70

What objects are the fountains
    Of thy happy strain?
What fields, or waves, or mountains?
    What shapes of sky or plain?
What love of thine own kind? what ignorance of pain?   75

With thy clear keen joyance
    Languor° cannot be: *sluggishness*
Shadow of annoyance
    Never came near thee:
Thou lovest—but ne'er knew love's sad satiety.   80

Waking or asleep,
    Thou of death must deem
Things more true and deep

Than we mortals dream,
Or how could thy notes flow in such a crystal stream? 85

We look before and after,
And pine for what is not:
Our sincerest laughter
With some pain is fraught;
Our sweetest songs are those that tell of saddest thought. 90

Yet if we could scorn
Hate, and pride, and fear;
If we were things born
Not to shed a tear,
I know not how thy joy we ever should come near. 95

Better than all measures
Of delightful sound,
Better than all treasures
That in books are found,
Thy skill to poet were, thou scorner of the ground! 100

Teach me half the gladness
That thy brain must know,
Such harmonious madness
From my lips would flow
The world should listen then—as I am listening now. 105

GARY SNYDER   (born 1930)

After Work   1959

The shack and a few trees
float in the blowing fog

I pull out your blouse,
warm my cold hands
    on your breasts. 5
you laugh and shudder
peeling garlic by the
    hot iron stove.
bring in the axe, the rake,
the wood 10

we'll lean on the wall
against each other
stew simmering on the fire
as it grows dark
        drinking wine. 15

GARY SNYDER   (born 1930)

Hay for the Horses   1966

He had driven half the night
From far down San Joaquin
Through Mariposa, up the
Dangerous mountain roads,
And pulled in at eight a.m.   5
With his big truckload of hay
       behind the barn.
With winch and ropes and hooks
We stacked the bales up clean
To splintery redwood rafters   10
High in the dark, flecks of alfalfa
Whirling through shingle-cracks of light,
Itch of haydust in the
      sweaty shirt and shoes.
At lunchtime under black oak   15
Out in the hot corral,
—The old mare nosing lunchpails,
Grasshoppers crackling in the weeds—
"I'm sixty-eight" he said,
"I first bucked hay when I was seventeen.   20
I thought, that day I started,
I sure would hate to do this all my life.
And dammit, that's just what
I've gone and done."

CATHY SONG   (born 1955)

Lost Sister   1983

1
In China,
even the peasants
named their first daughters
Jade—
the stone that in the far fields   5
could moisten the dry season,
could make men move mountains
for the healing green of the inner hills
glistening like slices of winter melon.

And the daughters were grateful: 10
They never left home.
To move freely was a luxury
stolen from them at birth.
Instead, they gathered patience;
learning to walk in shoes   15

the size of teacups,
without breaking—
the arc of their movements
as dormant as the rooted willow,
as redundant as the farmyard hens.   20
But they traveled far
in surviving,
learning to stretch the family rice,
to quiet the demons,
the noisy stomachs.   25

2
There is a sister
across the ocean,
who relinquished her name,
diluting jade green
with the blue of the Pacific.   30
Rising with a tide of locusts,
she swarmed with others
to inundate another shore.
In America,
there are many roads   35
and women can stride along with men.

But in another wilderness,
the possibilities,
the loneliness,
can strangulate like jungle vines.   40
The meager provisions and sentiments
of once belonging—
fermented roots, Mah-Jong° tiles and firecrackers—set but   *Oriental game*
a flimsy household
in a forest of nightless cities.   45
A giant snake rattles above,
spewing black clouds into your kitchen.
Dough-faced landlords
slip in and out of your keyholes,
making claims you don't understand,   50
tapping into your communication systems
of laundry lines and restaurant chains.

You find you need China:
your one fragile identification,
a jade link   55
handcuffed to your wrist.
You remember your mother
who walked for centuries,
footless—
and like her,   60
you have left no footprints,
but only because
there is an ocean in between,
the unremitting space of your rebellion.

WALLACE STEVENS   (1879–1955)

Anecdote of the Jar   1923

I placed a jar in Tennessee,
And round it was, upon a hill.
It made the slovenly wilderness
Surround that hill.

The wilderness rose up to it,   5
And sprawled around, no longer wild.
The jar was round upon the ground
And tall and of a port in air.

It took dominion everywhere.
The jar was gray and bare.   10
It did not give of bird or bush,
Like nothing else in Tennessee.

WALLACE STEVENS   (1879–1955)

Thirteen Ways of Looking at a Blackbird   1923

1
Among twenty snowy mountains,
The only moving thing
Was the eye of the blackbird.

2
I was of three minds,
Like a tree   5
In which there are three blackbirds.

3
The blackbird whirled in the autumn winds.
It was a small part of the pantomime.

4
A man and a woman
Are one.   10
A man and a woman and a blackbird
Are one.

5
I do not know which to prefer,
The beauty of inflections
Or the beauty of innuendoes,   15
The blackbird whistling
Or just after.

6
Icicles filled the long window
With barbaric glass.

The shadow of the blackbird   20
Crossed it, to and fro.
The mood
Traced in the shadow
An indecipherable cause.

7
O thin men of Haddam,°   *an industrial Connecticut town*   25
Why do you imagine golden birds?
Do you not see how the blackbird
Walks around the feet
Of the women about you?

8
I know noble accents   30
And lucid,° inescapable rhythms;   *clear*
But I know, too,
That the blackbird is involved
In what I know.

9
When the blackbird flew out of sight,   35
It marked the edge
Of one of many circles.

10
At the sight of blackbirds
Flying in a green light,
Even the bawds of euphony°   *those who prostitute themselves to beautiful sounds*   40
Would cry out sharply.

11
He rode over Connecticut
In a glass coach.
Once, a fear pierced him,
In that he mistook   45
The shadow of his equipage
For blackbirds.

12
The river is moving.
The blackbird must be flying.

13
It was evening all afternoon.   50
It was snowing.
And it was going to snow.
The blackbird sat
In the cedar-limbs.

MARK STRAND (born 1934)

Eating Poetry 1967

Ink runs from the corners of my mouth.
There is no happiness like mine.
I have been eating poetry.

The librarian does not believe what she sees.
Her eyes are sad 5
and she walks with her hands in her dress.

The poems are gone.
The light is dim.
The dogs are on the basement stairs and coming up.

Their eyeballs roll, 10
their blond legs burn like brush.
The poor librarian begins to stamp her feet and weep.

She does not understand.
When I get on my knees and lick her hand,
she screams. 15

I am a new man.
I snarl at her and bark.
I romp with joy in the bookish dark.

ALFRED, LORD TENNYSON (1809–1892)

Ulysses 1833

It little profits that an idle king,
By this still hearth, among these barren crags,
Matched with an agèd wife, I mete and dole
Unequal laws unto a savage race,
That hoard, and sleep, and feed, and know not me. 5
I cannot rest from travel; I will drain
Life to the lees. All times I have enjoy'd
Greatly, have suffer'd greatly, both with those
That love me, and alone; on shore, and when
Thro' scudding drifts the rainy Hyades 10
Vexed the dim sea. I am become a name;
For always roaming with a hungry heart
Much have I seen and known,—cities of men
And manners, climates, councils, governments,
Myself not least, but honored of them all,— 15
And drunk delight of battle with my peers,
Far on the ringing plains of windy Troy.
I am a part of all that I have met;
Yet all experience is an arch wherethrough
Gleams that untravelled world whose margin fades 20

For ever and for ever when I move.
How dull it is to pause, to make an end,
To rust unburnished, not to shine in use!
As though to breathe were life! Life piled on life
Were all too little, and of one to me   25
Little remains; but every hour is saved
From that eternal silence, something more,
A bringer of new things; and vile it were
For some three suns to store and hoard myself,
And this gray spirit yearning in desire   30
To follow knowledge like a sinking star,
Beyond the utmost bound of human thought.
    This is my son, mine own Telemachus,
To whom I leave the scepter and the isle,—
Well-loved of me, discerning to fulfill   35
This labor, by slow prudence to make mild
A rugged people, and through soft degrees
Subdue them to the useful and the good.
Most blameless is he, centered in the sphere
Of common duties, decent not to fail   40
In offices of tenderness, and pay
Meet adoration to my household gods,
When I am gone. He works his work, I mine.
    There lies the port; the vessel puffs her sail;
There gloom the dark, broad seas. My mariners,   45
Souls that have toiled, and wrought, and thought with me,—
That ever with a frolic° welcome took   *cheerful*
The thunder and the sunshine, and opposed
Free hearts, free foreheads,—you and I are old;
Old age hath yet his honor and his toil.   50
Death closes all; but something ere the end,
Some work of noble note, may yet be done,
Not unbecoming men that strove with Gods.
The lights begin to twinkle from the rocks;
The long day wanes; the slow moon climbs; the deep   55
Moans round with many voices. Come, friends,
'Tis not too late to seek a newer world.
Push off, and sitting well in order smite
The sounding furrows; for my purpose holds
To sail beyond the sunset, and the baths   60
Of all the western stars, until I die.
It may be that the gulfs will wash us down;
It may be we shall touch the Happy Isles,
And see the great Achilles, whom we knew.
Though much is taken, much abides;° and though   *remains*   65
We are not now that strength which in old days
Moved earth and heaven, that which we are, we are,—
One equal temper of heroic hearts,
Made weak by time and fate, but strong in will
To strive, to seek, to find, and not to yield.   70

DYLAN THOMAS   (1914–1953)

The Force That through the Green Fuse Drives the Flower   1934

The force that through the green fuse drives the flower
Drives my green age; that blasts the roots of trees
Is my destroyer.
And I am dumb to tell the crooked rose°   *I have no way of telling the rose*
My youth is bent by the same wintry fever.   5

The force that drives the water through the rocks
Drives my red blood; that dries the mouthing streams
Turns mine to wax.
And I am dumb to mouth unto my veins
How at the mountain spring the same mouth sucks.   10

The hand that whirls the water in the pool
Stirs the quicksand; that ropes the blowing wind
Hauls my shroud sail.
And I am dumb to tell the hanging man
How of my clay is made the hangman's lime.°   *hangman's tree*   15

The lips of time leech to the fountain head;
Love drips and gathers, but the fallen blood
Shall calm her sores.
And I am dumb to tell a weather's wind
How time has ticked a heaven round the stars.   20

And I am dumb to tell the lover's tomb
How at my sheet goes the same crooked worm.

EDMUND WALLER   (1606–1687)

Go, Lovely Rose   1645

Go, lovely rose,
Tell her that wastes her time and me
   That now she knows,
When I resemble° her to thee,   *compare*
   How sweet and fair she seems to be.   5

   Tell her that's young,
And shuns to have her graces spied,
   That hadst thou sprung
In deserts, where no men abide,
   Thou must have uncommended died.   10

   Small is the worth
Of beauty from the light retired;
   Bid her come forth,
Suffer herself to be desired,
   And not blush so to be admired.   15

Then die, that she
The common fate of all things rare
      May read in thee:
How small a part of time they share,
      That are so wondrous sweet and fair.   20

WALT WHITMAN   (1819–1892)

There Was a Child Went Forth   1855

There was a child went forth every day,
And the first object he looked upon, that object he became,
And that object became part of him for the day or a certain
      part of the day,
Or for many years or stretching cycles of years.

The early lilacs became part of this child,   5
And grass and white and red morning-glories, and white and
      red clover, and the song of the phoebe-bird,
And the Third-month° lambs and the sow's pink-faint litter,   *March*
      and the mare's foal and the cow's calf,
And the noisy brood of the barnyard or by the mire of the
      pond-side,
And the fish suspending themselves so curiously below there,
      and the beautiful curious liquid,
And the water-plants with their graceful flat heads, all be-
      came part of him.   10

The field-sprouts of Fourth-month and Fifth-month became
      part of him,
Winter-grain sprouts and those of the light-yellow corn, and   *edible*
      the esculent° roots of the garden,
And the apple-trees covered with blossoms and the fruit af-
      terward, and wood-berries, and the commonest weeds
      by the road,
And the old drunkard staggering home from the outhouse
      of the tavern whence he had lately risen,
And the schoolmistress that passed on her way to the school,   15
And the friendly boys that passed, and the quarrelsome boys,
And the tidy and fresh-cheeked girls, and the barefoot negro
      boy and girl,
And all the changes of city and country wherever he went.

His own parents, he that had fathered him and she that had
      conceived him in her womb and birthed him,
They gave this child more of themselves than that,   20
They gave him afterward every day, they became part of him.

The mother at home quietly placing the dishes on the sup-
      per-table,
The mother with mild words, clean her cap and gown, a
      wholesome odor falling off her person and clothes as
      she walks by,

The father, strong, self-sufficient, manly, mean, angered, un-
    just,
The blow, the quick loud word, the tight bargain, the crafty
    lure,   25
The family usages, the language, the company, the furniture,
    the yearning and swelling heart,
Affection that will not be gainsayed,° the sense of what is   *denied*
    real, the thought if after all it should prove unreal,
The doubts of day-time and the doubts of night-time, the
    curious whether and how,
Whether that which appears so is so, or is it all flashes and
    specks?
Men and women crowding fast in the streets, if they are not
    flashes and specks what are they?   30
The streets themselves and the façades of houses, and goods
    in the windows,
Vehicles, teams, the heavy-planked wharves, the huge cross-
    ing at the ferries,
The village on the highland seen from afar at sunset, the
    river between,
Shadows, aureola° and mist, the light falling on roofs and   *bands of light*
    gables of white or brown two miles off,
The schooner near by sleepily dropping down the tide, the
    little boat slack-towed astern,   35
The hurrying tumbling waves, quick-broken crests, slapping,
The strata of colored clouds, the long bar of maroon-tint
    away solitary by itself, the spread of purity it lies mo-
    tionless in,
The horizon's edge, the flying sea-crow, the fragrance of salt
    marsh and shore mud,
These became part of that child who went forth every day,
    and who now goes, and will always go forth every day.

RICHARD WILBUR   (born 1921)

The Writer   1976

In her room at the prow of the house
Where light breaks, and the windows are tossed with linden,°   *shade trees with*
My daughter is writing a story.   *heart-shaped leaves*

I pause in the stairwell, hearing
From her shut door a commotion of typewriter-keys   5
Like a chain hauled over a gunwale.°   *boat's rail*

Young as she is, the stuff
Of her life is a great cargo, and some of it heavy:
I wish her a lucky passage.

But now it is she who pauses,   10
As if to reject my thought and its easy figure.
A stillness greatens, in which

The whole house seems to be thinking,
And then she is at it again with a bunched clamor
Of strokes, and again is silent.   15

I remember the dazed starling°   *bird*
Which was trapped in that very room, two years ago,
How we stole in, lifted a sash

And retreated, not to affright it;
And how for a helpless hour, through the crack of the door,   20
We watched the sleek, wild, dark

And iridescent creature
Batter against the brilliance, drop like a glove
To the hard floor, or the desk-top,

And wait then, humped and bloody,   25
For the wits to try it again; and how our spirits
Rose when, suddenly sure,

It lifted off from a chair-back,
Beating a smooth course for the right window
And clearing the sill of the world.   30

It is always a matter, my darling,
Of life or death, as I had forgotten. I wish
What I wished you before, but harder.

WILLIAM CARLOS WILLIAMS (1883–1963)
Spring and All   1923

By the road to the contagious hospital
under the surge of the blue
mottled clouds driven from the
northeast—a cold wind. Beyond, the
waste of broad, muddy fields   5
brown with dried weeds, standing and fallen

patches of standing water
the scattering of tall trees

All along the road the reddish
purplish, forked, upstanding, twiggy   10
stuff of bushes and small trees
with dead, brown leaves under them
leafless vines—

Lifeless in appearance, sluggish
dazed spring approaches—   15

They enter the new world naked,
cold, uncertain of all

save that they enter. All about them
the cold, familiar wind—

Now the grass, tomorrow   20
the stiff curl of wildcarrot leaf
One by one objects are defined—
It quickens: clarity, outline of leaf

But now the stark dignity of
entrance—Still, the profound change   25
has come upon them: rooted, they
grip down and begin to awaken

WILLIAM WORDSWORTH   (1770–1850)

A Slumber Did My Spirit Seal   1800

A slumber did my spirit seal;
    I had no human fears:
She seemed a thing that could not feel
    The touch of earthly years.

No motion has she now, no force;   5
    She neither hears nor sees;
Rolled round in earth's diurnal° course,   *daily*
    With rocks, and stones, and trees.

WILLIAM WORDSWORTH   (1770–1850)

The Solitary Reaper   1807

Behold her, single in the field,
    Yon solitary Highland lass!
Reaping and singing by herself;
    Stop here, or gently pass!
Alone she cuts and binds the grain,   5
And sings a melancholy strain;
O listen! for the Vale profound
Is overflowing with the sound.

No Nightingale did ever chant
    More welcome notes to weary bands   10
Of travelers in some shady haunt,
    Among Arabian sands:
A voice so thrilling ne'er was heard
In spring-time from the Cuckoo-bird,
Breaking the silence of the seas   15
Among the farthest Hebrides.°   *distant northern islands*

Will no one tell me what she sings?—
    Perhaps the plaintive numbers° flow   *mournful verses*
For old, unhappy, far-off things,
    And battles long ago: 20
Or is it some more humble lay,°   *song*
Familiar matter of to-day?
Some natural sorrow, loss, or pain,
That has been, and may be again?

Whate'er the theme, the Maiden sang   25
    As if her song could have no ending;
I saw her singing at her work,
    And o'er the sickle bending;—
I listened, motionless and still;
And, as I mounted up the hill,   30
The music in my heart I bore,
Long after it was heard no more.

SIR THOMAS WYATT   (1503–1542)

They Flee from Me   1557

They flee from me, that sometime did me seek,
With naked foot stalking in my chamber.
I have seen them, gentle, tame, and meek,
That now are wild, and do not remember
That sometime they put themselves in danger   5
To take bread at my hand; and now they range,
Busily seeking with a continual change.

Thanked be Fortune it hath been otherwise,
Twenty times better; but once in special,
In thin array, after a pleasant guise,°   *in a pleasing way*   10
When her loose gown from her shoulders did fall,
And she me caught in her arms long and small,°   *slender*
And therewith all sweetly did me kiss
And softly said, "Dear heart, how like you this?"

It was no dream, I lay broad waking.   15
But all is turned, thorough° my gentleness,   *through*
Into a strange fashion of forsaking;
And I have leave to go, of her goodness,
And she also to use newfangleness.°   *try something new*
But since that I so kindely° am served,   *according to her nature*   20
I fain° would know what she hath deserved.   *gladly*

MITSUYE YAMADA   (born 1923)

A Bedtime Story   1976

Once upon a time,
an old Japanese legend
goes as told
by Papa,
an old woman traveled through   5
many small villages
seeking refuge
for the night.
Each door opened
a sliver   10
in answer to her knock
then closed.
Unable to walk
any further
she wearily climbed a hill   15
found a clearing
and there lay down to rest
a few moments to catch
her breath.

The village town below   20
lay asleep except
for a few starlike lights.
Suddenly the clouds opened
and a full moon came into view
over the town.   25

The old woman sat up
turned toward
the village town
and in supplication
called out   30
Thank you people
of the village,
If it had not been for your
kindness
in refusing me a bed   35
for the night
these humble eyes would never
have seen this
memorable sight.

Papa paused, I waited.   40
In the comfort of our
hilltop home in Seattle
overlooking the valley,
I shouted
"That's the *end?*"   45

WILLIAM BUTLER YEATS (1865–1939)

The Second Coming 1921

Turning and turning in the widening gyre°   *spiral*
The falcon cannot hear the falconer;
Things fall apart; the center cannot hold;
Mere anarchy is loosed upon the world,
The blood-dimmed tide is loosed, and everywhere   5
The ceremony of innocence is drowned;
The best lack all conviction, while the worst
Are full of passionate intensity.

Surely some revelation is at hand;
Surely the Second Coming is at hand;   10
The Second Coming! Hardly are those words out
When a vast image out of *Spiritus Mundi*°   *Spirit of the World*
Troubles my sight: somewhere in sands of the desert
A shape with lion body and the head of a man,°   *sphinx*
A gaze blank and pitiless as the sun,   15
Is moving its slow thighs, while all about it
Reel shadows of the indignant desert birds.
The darkness drops again; but now I know
That twenty centuries of stony sleep
Were vexed to nightmare by a rocking cradle,   20
And what rough beast, its hour come round at last,
Slouches towards Bethlehem to be born?

DRAMA

There is a hunger to see the human presence acted out. As long as that need remains, people will find a way to do theater.
ZELDA FICHANDLER

25 PREVIEW
The Heart of Drama

The job is to ask questions—it always was—and to ask them as inexorably as I can. And to face the absence of precise answers with a certain humility.

ARTHUR MILLER

On the stage is always now; *the personages are standing on that razor edge between the past and the future that is the essential character of conscious beings.*

ANATOLE BROYARD

A dramatist is one who from his earliest years has found that sheer gazing at the shocks and countershocks among people is quite sufficiently engrossing without having to encase it in comment.

THORNTON WILDER

FOCUS ON CONFLICT

Dramatists create characters and set them in motion. They create human beings whose motives and agendas may bring them into conflict. As theatergoers, we witness the interaction of the people on the stage. We form our impressions of what commitments unite them or what issues divide them. We may see a situation develop that carries the seeds of conflict. Conflicting interests may lead to a fateful confrontation. A clash of values may put major characters on a collision course. Characters playing for high stakes may be in contention, with minor characters finding themselves caught between what Shakespeare's Hamlet calls the "incensed points of mighty opposites."

Conflict is the heart of drama. In Shakespeare's *Romeo and Juliet,* the ardor and impetuous passion of the two young lovers enchant the audience. However, their passion brings them into conflict with the stubborn hatreds of their feuding elders (and of the brawling young hotheads who perpetuate the quarrel between their two families). In the *Antigone* of Sophocles, Antigone's loyalty to her dead brother brings her into conflict with King Creon. He has declared her brother a traitor, to be left unburied and devoured by birds and

843

dogs. We as the spectators wait to see how the conflict is resolved; we become absorbed in how the conflict is played out.

Often the central conflict in a play takes shape between strong-willed individuals. However, the central conflict of a play may be staged in the mind of a single character. Shakespeare's *Macbeth* is a play with much external action: Macbeth, prodded by his wife, murders his king, destroys people who are in his way or their families, and is finally defeated by an army raised by the dead king's son. However, much of the time we as the audience focus on the **internal conflict** within the central figure. Macbeth is a character with a mind divided against itself. With one part of his mind, he yields to the siren song of ambition that makes him plot the assassination of King Duncan. Although he will start his ascent to the throne with bloody hands, in the words of Lady Macbeth, "a little water will clear us of this deed." But in another part of his mind, Macbeth is deeply troubled by his violated loyalty to his king, who is also a kinsman. Macbeth has a conscience; his religion teaches the abhorrence of murder. This inner conflict makes him a reluctant murderer, a hesitant assassin. He is a rebel who, in the words of his wife, has "too much of the milk of human kindness" to "catch the nearest way."

THE MAGIC OF THE STAGE

Any theater's special limitations are part of what gives it its special intensity. The curtain rising behind the proscenium arch says, "Fix your whole attention on this little space: Everything will happen here. For these three hours, there is nothing outside it."

AMLIN GRAY

What is the magic of live theater? The magic of the stage makes us witness a live performance. The actors, who are handed the play as words on a page, bring it to life. We see their faces, hear their voices. We respond to the language of gestures, to the actors' "body language." (A **pantomime** is a special kind of theater that uses the language of gestures *without* words; a mime acts out a story without speaking.) A successful performance draws us in; it carries us along. We participate in other lives. These may be more magnificent or drearier than our own. Or they may be so close to our own world that we experience the shock of recognition, making us say: "That is exactly the way it is."

A stage production is a collaboration. The playwright furnishes the script—often the result of much revision and of trial and error. (Contemporary dramatists may revise their plays after tryouts and initial reviews.) A director (or perhaps a directorial committee) charts directions or develops a general concept. For instance, a director might highlight the *youthfulness* of Shakespeare's Romeo and Juliet—their eagerness, their refusal to wait, their moving from heavenly joy to deadly despair in the course of a day. As strong conductors do with music, strong directors reinterpret traditional plays for their time and audience. A controversial experimental director might teleport Shakespeare's *Hamlet* from its original setting in Denmark to the antebellum mansion of a Southern senator (named Claudius), whose wife is a Southern belle (named Gertrude) and whose financial advisor is a talkative old man (named Polonius). To no one's surprise, Claudius' stepson (Hamlet) will be a young man alienated from his corrupt elders.

The performers, in turn, take their cue (and sometimes dictatorial instructions) from the director. However, they may be as stubbornly independent as directors can be, and at any rate they bring a part to life in their own way. In a BBC production available on videotape in many college libraries, Ron Cook plays Shakespeare's evil Richard III less as the traditional sniggering and gloating hunchback and more like a conniving, corrupt bank vice president. This change makes the character more deadly and the threat more real, since audiences cannot simply laugh at him as a stage villain. The actor's conception of the character takes murderous intent and brilliant deceit out of the world of stage melodrama and puts it into the real world.

Not all the action in the theater is on the stage. A major silent participant in the performance is you—the spectator. Without your collaboration the stage will not work its magic. In the theater, you become part of a community embarked on a common venture. There is something contagious about the enthusiasm or laughter of a live audience. As a group, the members of the audience "act out" their reactions to the play: They sigh and gasp; they may watch in stunned silence; they express relief in a burst of happy laughter. When the chemistry is right, there is a special interaction between performers and spectators. Performers respond to a receptive audience, creating for the performance the heightened mood of a festive event.

As a reader, you have to be receptive to the means a dramatist uses to create a play—not so much in order to label them as to respond to them. As a reader of a printed play, you have to translate the words on the page into action and dialogue the way directors and actors do. The difference is that you are enacting the drama in the theater of the mind. You have to be alert to how the elements of a play—setting, situation, characters, plot, style—work together to make the play come to life for you as a spectator or reader.

Exposition   The early scenes of a play take you to the setting and establish a situation. (Sometimes, **flashbacks** to earlier days help you understand the characters' current predicaments.) The early scenes of a play will usually answer basic questions in the spectators' minds: Where are we? Who are these people? What is the issue or the problem? What past history explains the current situation? This initial "setting up" is traditionally called the **exposition.**

Characters   Much of a playwright's task early in the play is **characterization**—feeding you the information that makes the characters come to life. You will learn much about the characters from what they say and do themselves. They may take you into their confidence in brief **asides** shared only with the audience. Or they might confide in you in lengthy solo speeches—soliloquies. (Sometimes a **confidant**—a close friend or trusted servant—may serve as a substitute or surrogate for the audience.) Obviously, you cannot take everything the characters say about themselves at face value. You will often do well to listen to what *others* say about a central figure; this is often a major function of minor characters. Often a supporting character serves as a **foil** who highlights by contrast a key quality in a major figure.

Dialogue   The dramatist's basic tool is the spoken word. Shakespeare's plays were acted on a wooden stage with little scenery and few props. He relied on the power of words to conjure up throne rooms, fields of battle, the queen's bedroom, or a fog-shrouded heath. He asked of his audiences, "Think when we talk of horses that you see them / Printing their proud hooves in the receiving earth." However, **dialogue** mainly serves as the medium of human interaction in a play. Dialogue becomes **monologue** when one person for a time does all or most of the talking. When there is not even a silent listener serving as captive audience, a monologue becomes a **soliloquy**—a character's extended conversation with himself or herself. Soliloquies give the audience a chance to listen in on thoughts and feelings usually hidden behind the polite social façade.

Plot   The **plot** of a play is the thread that leads us from initial tensions or problems, through complications, to climactic confrontations or turning points, and to the windup or final resolution of a conflict. The plot is more than a simple unsorted tracing of events in chronological order. However, there is no general formula for a successful plot. In some of Shakespeare's plays, the tide metaphor well describes the overall movement of the plot. In *Macbeth,* the rebel and usurper at first hesitates but then becomes hardened in his evil purpose as he eliminates potential threats to his power. For several acts, we see the rising tide of tyranny drive out upright individuals. The tyrant eliminates people threatening his power or thwarting his will; he becomes bloodier, more isolated, and more desperate as he moves on. But slowly the tide turns, and the forces of justice and retribution gather strength. In the end, the avenging armies corner the despot in his lair.

Some plays fit the traditional **pyramid** metaphor: The "rising action" leads to a peak or high point. Then the "declining action" takes us (often swiftly) to the conclusion. (In some plays, parallel conflicts or **subplots** reinforce the central theme.)

Plays differ greatly, depending on what drives the plot and leads to the final **resolution.** That resolution may be happy (as in comedy), unhappy (as in tragedy), or open-ended (as in many modern plays). The playwright may respond to the spectators' deep-seated yearning for good news. Perhaps the audience most of the time secretly hopes for a happy end, if only as the result of a lucky coincidence. (The ancient Greek theater had a contraption for lowering a god or goddess—the **deus ex machina**—onto the stage to work last-minute surprises.) In a more serious or realistic mood, audiences and critics are likely to look for action derived from character. In a play honoring this requirement, actions have consequences, although often unintended. Actions start a chain of events that it may be too late to stop. Often, in a gripping drama, we see what happens when people make fateful choices. We watch the tangled web they weave as they act on their impulses and passions.

Style Many successful playwrights have an uncanny ear for how people talk. The characters in a play speak in a characteristic **idiom**—a register of language, a way of talking. In Arthur Miller's *Death of a Salesman,* Willy Loman is a master of the trite folksy shirtsleeve English of the white lower middle class, peppered with small-town Chamber-of-Commerce clichés ("Well, I figure, what the hell, life is short, a couple of jokes"). A playwright may use a contrast in speaking styles to distinguish characters. In Tennessee Williams' *The Glass Menagerie,* the mother speaks in a refined, genteel "Southern lady" style that serves her well to hide harsh realities behind euphemistic talk: "You just have a little defect . . . when people have some slight disadvantage like that, they cultivate other things to make up for it." Her alienated son, when he gets angry enough, talks back to her in the rough language of his street buddies: "Every time you come in yelling that God damn 'Rise and Shine!' 'Rise and Shine!' I say to myself, 'How lucky dead people are!'"

Much traditional drama is in verse—sometimes in **rhymed couplets,** as in Molière's *Misanthrope.* The couplet—two self-contained lines—is a perfect medium for the neatly packaged, emphatic pronouncements Molière's characters love:

> To accept wholesale friendship I firmly decline;
> Who befriends one and all is no friend of mine.

Much modern drama is in prose. It approximates the freely moving rhythms of everyday speech—if only to mock them, as the British playwright Harold Pinter does in the following passage from *The Homecoming:*

> She's a great help to me over there. She's a wonderful wife and mother. She's a very popular woman. She's got lots of friends. It's a great life, at the University . . . you know . . . it's a very good life. We've got a lovely house . . . we've got all . . . we've got everything we want. It's a very stimulating environment.

The language of the people in a play may be as empty of poetry as the emotional lives of Pinter's characters. Or it may be alive with the soaring poetry of Shakespeare's Hamlet, to whom the star-spangled heavens are alternately "this majestical roof fretted with golden fire" and "a foul and pestilent congregation of vapors."

GLASPELL: READING FOR CLUES

*Glaspell was among the first writers to realize that it was
not enough to present women at the center of the stage. If
there were to be a radical break with plays of the past,
women would have to exist in a world tailored to their
persons and speak a language not borrowed from men.*

ENOCH BRATER

Susan Glaspell (1882–1948) devoted much of her life to the theater. Educated at Drake University in Des Moines, Iowa, she worked for a time as a newspaper reporter and drew on her experiences as a journalist in her short stories, novels, and plays. She was a cofounder of the Provincetown Players, who performed many of the American playwright Eugene O'Neill's one-act plays and who performed her own one-act play *Trifles*. She acted and directed; she wrote a dozen plays; and she won the Pulitzer Prize for drama in 1931. As head of the Chicago bureau of a federal theater project, she reviewed hundreds of plays and helped in the production of important works by black playwrights. Although she did much of her work in the East, she said, "Almost everything I write has its roots in the Middle West; I suppose because my own are there." She was a spiritual descendant of her pioneer ancestors who left "comfortable homes for unknown places." Many of her characters struggle against "fixity and stagnation," trying to move, as their pioneer forebears did, "into a new sphere, if not of place then of spirit" (Enoch Brater).

Glaspell's work was rediscovered by feminist critics who found in her plays a "woman's version" of events, created at a time when the theater was heavily dominated by male dramatists. Like her British contemporary Virginia Woolf, she has become an inspiration to women whose goal is "control over their own bodies and a voice with which to speak about it" (Susan Rubin Suleiman).

Although Glaspell's play *Trifles* involves violent death, it is not a drama of violence or of physical action. Instead, it focuses on the unraveling of motives and on the loyalties of the survivors. As in Greek tragedy, we witness none of the violent events directly—we merely hear about them. The real drama is in what goes on in the minds of the characters as they *react* to the events—as they think through their responsibilities, bring their memories to bear, come to understand what happened, and take sides.

As a reader of the play or as a theatergoer, your price of admission (figuratively speaking) is the need for paying attention. You need to read the clues Glaspell furnishes the audience to help them grasp the situation and to help them understand the characters. You need to be an attentive spectator as a central conflict slowly comes into focus.

SUSAN GLASPELL (1882–1948)
Trifles 1916

CHARACTERS

GEORGE HENDERSON, county attorney
HENRY PETERS, sheriff
LEWIS HALE, a neighboring farmer
MRS. PETERS
MRS. HALE

THE SETTING: *The kitchen in the now abandoned farmhouse of* JOHN WRIGHT.

SCENE: *The kitchen in the now abandoned farmhouse of* JOHN WRIGHT, *a gloomy kitchen, and left without having been put in order —unwashed pans under the sink, a loaf of bread outside the breadbox, a dish towel on the table—other signs of incompleted work. At the rear the outer door opens and the* SHERIFF *comes in followed by the* COUNTY ATTORNEY *and* HALE. *The* SHERIFF *and* HALE *are men in middle life, the* COUNTY ATTORNEY *is a young man; all are much bundled up and go at once to the stove. They are followed by the two women—the* SHERIFF'S *wife first; she is a slight wiry woman, a thin nervous face.* MRS. HALE *is larger and would ordinarily be called more comfortable looking, but she is disturbed now and looks fearfully about as she enters. The women have come in slowly, and stand close together near the door.*

COUNTY ATTORNEY (*rubbing his hands*): This feels good. Come up to the fire, ladies.
MRS. PETERS (*after taking a step forward*): I'm not—cold.
SHERIFF (*unbuttoning his overcoat and stepping away from the stove as if to mark the beginning of official business*): Now, Mr. Hale, before we move things about, you explain to Mr. Henderson just what you saw when you came here yesterday morning.
COUNTY ATTORNEY: By the way, has anything been moved? Are things just as you left them yesterday?
SHERIFF (*looking about*): It's just the same. When it dropped below zero last night I thought I'd better send Frank out this morning to make a fire for us—no use getting pneumonia with a big case on, but I told him not to touch anything except the stove—and you know Frank.
COUNTY ATTORNEY: Somebody should have been left here yesterday.
SHERIFF: Oh—yesterday. When I had to send Frank to Morris Center for that man who went crazy—I want you to know I had my hands full yesterday, I knew you could get back from Omaha by today and as long as I went over everything here myself—
COUNTY ATTORNEY: Well, Mr. Hale, tell just what happened when you came here yesterday morning.
HALE: Harry and I had started to town with a load of potatoes. We came along the road from my place and as I got here I said, "I'm going to see if I can't get John Wright to go in with me on a party telephone." I spoke to Wright about it once before and he put me off, saying folks talked too much anyway, and all he asked was peace and quiet—I guess you know about how much he talked himself; but I thought maybe if I went to the house and talked about it before his wife, though I

said to Harry that I didn't know as what his wife wanted made much difference to John—

COUNTY ATTORNEY: Let's talk about that later, Mr. Hale. I do want to talk about that, but tell now just what happened when you got to the house.

HALE: I didn't hear or see anything; I knocked at the door, and still it was all quiet inside. I knew they must be up, it was past eight o'clock. So I knocked again, and I thought I heard somebody say, "Come in." I wasn't sure, I'm not sure yet, but I opened the door—this door (*indicating the door by which the two women are still standing*) and there in that rocker—(*pointing to it*) sat Mrs. Wright.

They all look at the rocker.

COUNTY ATTORNEY: What—was she doing?

HALE: She was rockin' back and forth. She had her apron in her hand and was kind of—pleating it.

COUNTY ATTORNEY: And how did she—look?

HALE: Well, she looked queer.

COUNTY ATTORNEY: How do you mean—queer?

HALE: Well, as if she didn't know what she was going to do next. And kind of done up.

COUNTY ATTORNEY: How did she seem to feel about your coming?

HALE: Why, I don't think she minded—one way or other. She didn't pay much attention. I said, "How do, Mrs. Wright, it's cold, ain't it?" And she said, "Is it?"—and went on kind of pleating at her apron. Well, I was surprised; she didn't ask me to come up to the stove, or to set down, but just sat there, not even looking at me, so I said, "I want to see John." And then she—laughed. I guess you would call it a laugh. I thought of Harry and the team outside, so I said a little sharp: "Can't I see John?" "No," she says, kind o' dull like. "Ain't he home?" says I. "Yes," says she, "he's home." "Then why can't I see him?" I asked her, out of patience. "'Cause he's dead," says she. "*Dead?*" says I. She just nodded her head, not getting a bit excited, but rockin' back and forth. "Why—where is he?" says I, not knowing what to say. She just pointed upstairs—like that (*himself pointing to the room above*). I got up, with the idea of going up there. I walked from there to here—then I says, "Why, what did he die of?" "He died of a rope round his neck," says she, and just went on pleatin' at her apron. Well, I went out and called Harry. I thought I might—need help. We went upstairs and there he was lyin'—

COUNTY ATTORNEY: I think I'd rather have you go into that upstairs, where you can point it all out. Just go on now with the rest of the story.

HALE: Well, my first thought was to get that rope off. It looked . . . (*stops, his face twitches*) . . . but Harry, he went up to him, and he said, "No, he's dead all right, and we'd better not touch anything." So we went back down stairs. She was still sitting that same way. "Has anybody been notified?" I asked. "No," says she, unconcerned. "Who did this, Mrs. Wright?" said Harry. He said it businesslike— and she stopped pleatin' of her apron. "I don't know," she says. "You don't *know?*" says Harry. "No," says she. "Weren't you sleepin' in the bed with him?" says Harry. "Yes," says she, "but I was on the inside." "Somebody slipped a rope round his neck and strangled him and you didn't wake up?" says Harry. "I didn't wake up," she said after him. We must 'a looked as if we didn't see how that could be, for after a minute she said, "I sleep sound." Harry was going to ask her more questions but I said maybe we ought to let her tell her story first to the coroner, or the sheriff, so Harry went fast as he could to Rivers' place, where there's a telephone.

COUNTY ATTORNEY: And what did Mrs. Wright do when she knew that you had gone for the coroner?

HALE: She moved from that chair to this one over here (*pointing to a small chair in the corner*) and just sat there with her hands held together and looking down. I got a feeling that I ought to make some conversation, so I said I had come in to see if John wanted to put in a telephone, and at that she started to laugh, and then she stopped and looked at me—scared. (*The* COUNTY ATTORNEY, *who has had his notebook out, makes a note.*) I dunno, maybe it wasn't scared. I wouldn't like to say it was. Soon Harry got back, and then Dr. Lloyd came, and you, Mr. Peters, and so I guess that's all I know that you don't.

COUNTY ATTORNEY (*looking around*): I guess we'll go upstairs first—and then out to the barn and around there. (*to the* SHERIFF) You're convinced that there was nothing important here—nothing that would point to any motive.

SHERIFF: Nothing here but kitchen things.

The COUNTY ATTORNEY, *after again looking around the kitchen, opens the door of a cupboard closet. He gets up on a chair and looks on a shelf. Pulls his hand away, sticky.*

COUNTY ATTORNEY: Here's a nice mess.

The women draw nearer.

MRS. PETERS (*to the other woman*): Oh, her fruit; it did freeze. (*to the* COUNTY ATTORNEY) She worried about that when it turned so cold. She said the fire'd go out and her jars would break.

SHERIFF: Well, can you beat the women! Held for murder and worryin' about her preserves.

COUNTY ATTORNEY: I guess before we're through she may have something more serious than preserves to worry about.

HALE: Well, women are used to worrying over trifles.

The two women move a little closer together.

COUNTY ATTORNEY (*with the gallantry of a young politician*): And yet, for all their worries, what would we do without the ladies? (*The women do not unbend. He goes to the sink, takes a dipperful of water from the pail and pouring it into a basin, washes his hands. Starts to wipe them on the roller towel, turns it for a cleaner place.*) Dirty towels! (*kicks his foot against the pans under the sink*) Not much of a housekeeper, would you say, ladies?

MRS. HALE (*stiffly*): There's a great deal of work to be done on a farm.

COUNTY ATTORNEY: To be sure. And yet (*with a little bow to her*) I know there are some Dickson county farmhouses which do not have such roller towels.

He gives it a pull to expose its full length again.

MRS. HALE: Those towels get dirty awful quick. Men's hands aren't always as clean as they might be.

COUNTY ATTORNEY: Ah, loyal to your sex, I see. But you and Mrs. Wright were neighbors. I suppose you were friends, too.

MRS. HALE (*shaking her head*): I've not seen much of her of late years. I've not been in this house—it's more than a year.

COUNTY ATTORNEY: And why was that? You didn't like her?

MRS. HALE: I liked her all well enough. Farmers' wives have their hands full, Mr. Henderson. And then—

COUNTY ATTORNEY: Yes—?

MRS. HALE (*looking about*): It never seemed a very cheerful place.

COUNTY ATTORNEY: No—it's not cheerful. I shouldn't say she had the homemaking instinct.

MRS. HALE: Well, I don't know as Wright had, either.

COUNTY ATTORNEY: You mean that they didn't get on very well?

MRS. HALE: No, I don't mean anything. But I don't think a place'd be any cheerfuller for John Wright's being in it.

COUNTY ATTORNEY: I'd like to talk more of that a little later. I want to get the lay of things upstairs now.

He goes to the left, where three steps lead to a stair door.

SHERIFF: I suppose anything Mrs. Peters does'll be all right. She was to take in some clothes for her, you know, and a few little things. We left in such a hurry yesterday.

COUNTY ATTORNEY: Yes, but I would like to see what you take, Mrs. Peters, and keep an eye out for anything that might be of use to us.

MRS. PETERS: Yes, Mr. Henderson.

The women listen to the men's steps on the stairs, then look about the kitchen.

MRS. HALE: I'd hate to have men coming into my kitchen, snooping around and criticizing.

She arranges the pans under sink which the COUNTY ATTORNEY *had shoved out of place.*

MRS. PETERS: Of course it's no more than their duty.

MRS. HALE: Duty's all right, but I guess that deputy sheriff that came out to make the fire might have got a little of this on. (*gives the roller towel a pull*) Wish I'd thought of that sooner. Seems mean to talk about her for not having things slicked up when she had to come away in such a hurry.

MRS. PETERS (*who has gone to a small table in the left rear corner of the room, and lifted one end of a towel that covers a pan*): She had bread set.

Stands still.

MRS. HALE (*Eyes fixed on a loaf of bread beside the breadbox, which is on a low shelf at the other side of the room. Moves slowly toward it.*): She was going to put this in there. (*Picks up loaf, then abruptly drops it. In a manner of returning to familiar things.*) It's a shame about her fruit. I wonder if it's all gone. (*gets up on the chair and looks*) I think there's some here that's all right, Mrs. Peters. Yes—here; (*holding it toward the window*) this is cherries, too. (*looking again*) I declare I believe that's the only one. (*Gets down, bottle in her hand. Goes to the sink and wipes it off on the outside.*) She'll feel awful bad after all her hard work in the hot weather. I remember the afternoon I put my cherries last summer.

She puts the bottle on the big kitchen table, center of the room. With a sigh, is about to sit down in the rocking-chair. Before she is seated realizes what chair it is; with a slow look at it, steps back. The chair which she has touched rocks back and forth.

MRS. PETERS: Well, I must get those things from the front room closet. (*She goes to the door at the right, but after looking into the other room, steps back.*) You coming with me, Mrs. Hale? You could help me carry them.

They go in the other room; reappear, MRS. PETERS *carrying a dress and skirt,* MRS. HALE *following with a pair of shoes.*

MRS. PETERS: My, it's cold in there.

She puts the clothes on the big table, and hurries to the stove.

MRS. HALE (*examining the skirt*): Wright was close. I think maybe that's why she kept so much to herself. She didn't even belong to the Ladies Aid. I suppose she felt she couldn't do her part, and then you don't enjoy things when you feel shabby. She used to wear pretty clothes and be lively, when she was Minnie Foster, one of the town girls singing in the choir. But that—oh, that was thirty years ago. This all you was to take in?

MRS. PETERS: She said she wanted an apron. Funny thing to want, for there isn't much to get you dirty in jail, goodness knows. But I suppose just to make her feel more natural. She said they was in the top drawer in this cupboard. Yes, here. And then her little shawl that always hung behind the door. (*opens stair door and looks*) Yes, here it is.

Quickly shuts door leading upstairs.

MRS. HALE (*abruptly moving toward her*): Mrs. Peters?
MRS. PETERS: Yes, Mrs. Hale?
MRS. HALE: Do you think she did it?
MRS. PETERS (*in a frightened voice*): Oh, I don't know.
MRS. HALE: Well, I don't think she did. Asking for an apron and her little shawl. Worrying about her fruit.
MRS. PETERS (*Starts to speak, glances up, where footsteps are heard in the room above. In a low voice.*): Mr. Peters says it looks bad for her. Mr. Henderson is awful sarcastic in a speech and he'll make fun of her sayin' she didn't wake up.
MRS. HALE: Well, I guess John Wright didn't wake when they was slipping that rope under his neck.
MRS. PETERS: No, it's strange. It must have been done awful crafty and still. They say it was such a—funny way to kill a man, rigging it all up like that.
MRS. HALE: That's just what Mr. Hale said. There was a gun in the house. He says that's what he can't understand.
MRS. PETERS: Mr. Henderson said coming out that what was needed for the case was a motive; something to show anger, or—sudden feeling.
MRS. HALE (*who is standing by the table*): Well, I don't see any signs of anger around here. (*She puts her hand on the dish towel which lies on the table, stands looking down at table, one half of which is clean, the other half messy.*) It's wiped to here. (*Makes a move as if to finish work, then turns and looks at loaf of bread outside the breadbox. Drops towel. In that voice of coming back to familiar things.*) Wonder how they are finding things upstairs. I hope she had it a little more red-up up there. You know, it seems kind of *sneaking*. Locking her up in town and then coming out here and trying to get her own house to turn against her!
MRS. PETERS: But Mrs. Hale, the law is the law.
MRS. HALE: I s'pose 'tis. (*unbuttoning her coat*) Better loosen up your things, Mrs. Peters. You won't feel them when you go out.

MRS. PETERS *takes off her fur tippet, goes to hang it on hook at back of room, stands looking at the under part of the small corner table.*

MRS. PETERS: She was piecing a quilt.

She brings the large sewing basket and they look at the bright pieces.

MRS. HALE: It's log cabin pattern. Pretty, isn't it? I wonder if she was goin' to quilt it or just knot it?

Footsteps have been heard coming down the stairs. The SHERIFF *enters followed by* HALE *and the* COUNTY ATTORNEY.

SHERIFF: They wonder if she was going to quilt it or just knot it!

The men laugh; the women look abashed.

COUNTY ATTORNEY (*rubbing his hands over the stove*): Frank's fire didn't do much up there, did it? Well, let's go out to the barn and get that cleared up.

The men go outside.

MRS. HALE (*resentfully*): I don't know as there's anything so strange, our takin' up our time with little things while we're waiting for them to get the evidence. (*She sits down at the big table smoothing out a block with decision.*) I don't see as it's anything to laugh about.

MRS. PETERS (*apologetically*): Of course they've got awful important things on their minds.

Pulls up a chair and joins MRS. HALE *at the table.*

MRS. HALE (*examining another block*): Mrs. Peters, look at this one. Here, this is the one she was working on, and look at the sewing! All the rest of it has been so nice and even. And look at this! It's all over the place! Why, it looks as if she didn't know what she was about! (*After she has said this they look at each other, then start to glance back at the door. After an instant* MRS. HALE *has pulled at a knot and ripped the sewing.*)

MRS. PETERS: Oh, what are you doing, Mrs. Hale?

MRS. HALE (*mildly*): Just pulling out a stitch or two that's not sewed very good. (*threading a needle*) Bad sewing always made me fidgety.

MRS. PETERS (*nervously*): I don't think we ought to touch things.

MRS. HALE: I'll just finish up this end. (*suddenly stopping and leaning forward*) Mrs. Peters?

MRS. PETERS: Yes, Mrs. Hale?

MRS. HALE: What do you suppose she was so nervous about?

MRS. PETERS: Oh—I don't know. I don't know as she was nervous. I sometimes sew awful queer when I'm just tired. (MRS. HALE *starts to say something, looks at* MRS. PETERS, *then goes on sewing.*) Well, I must get these things wrapped up. They may be through sooner than we think. (*putting apron and other things together*) I wonder where I can find a piece of paper, and string.

MRS. HALE: In that cupboard, maybe.

MRS. PETERS (*looking in cupboard*): Why, here's a birdcage. (*holds it up*) Did she have a bird, Mrs. Hale?

MRS. HALE: Why, I don't know whether she did or not—I've not been here for so long. There was a man around last year selling canaries cheap, but I don't know as she took one; maybe she did. She used to sing real pretty herself.

MRS. PETERS (*glancing around*): Seems funny to think of a bird here. But she must have had one, or why would she have a cage? I wonder what happened to it.

MRS. HALE: I s'pose maybe the cat got it.

MRS. PETERS: No, she didn't have a cat. She's got that feeling some people have about cats—being afraid of them. My cat got in her room and she was real upset and asked me to take it out.

MRS. HALE: My sister Bessie was like that. Queer, ain't it?

MRS. PETERS (*examining the cage*): Why, look at this door. It's broke. One hinge is pulled apart.

MRS. HALE (*looking too*): Looks as if someone must have been rough with it.

MRS. PETERS: Why, yes.

She brings the cage forward and puts it on the table.

MRS. HALE: I wish if they're going to find any evidence they'd be about it. I don't like this place.

MRS. PETERS: But I'm awful glad you came with me, Mrs. Hale. It would be lonesome for me sitting here alone.

MRS. HALE: It would, wouldn't it? (*dropping her sewing*) But I tell you what I do wish, Mrs. Peters. I wish I had come over sometimes when *she* was here. I—(*looking around the room*)—wish I had.

MRS. PETERS: But of course you were awful busy, Mrs. Hale—your house and your children.

MRS. HALE: I could've come. I stayed away because it weren't cheerful—and that's why I ought to have come. I—I've never liked this place. Maybe because it's down in a hollow and you don't see the road. I dunno what it is, but it's a lonesome place and always was. I wish I had come over to see Minnie Foster sometimes. I can see now—

Shakes her head.

MRS. PETERS: Well, you mustn't reproach yourself, Mrs. Hale. Somehow we just don't see how it is with other folks until—something comes up.

MRS. HALE: Not having children makes less work—but it makes a quiet house, and Wright out to work all day, and no company when he did come in. Did you know John Wright, Mrs. Peters?

MRS. PETERS: Not to know him; I've seen him in town. They say he was a good man.

MRS. HALE: Yes—good; he didn't drink, and kept his word as well as most, I guess, and paid his debts. But he was a hard man, Mrs. Peters. Just to pass the time of day with him—(*shivers*) Like a raw wind that gets to the bone. (*pauses, her eye falling on the cage*) I should think she would 'a wanted a bird. But what do you suppose went with it?

MRS. PETERS: I don't know, unless it got sick and died.

She reaches over and swings the broken door, swings it again. Both women watch it.

MRS. HALE: You weren't raised 'round here, were you? (MRS. PETERS *shakes her head.*) You didn't know—her?

MRS. PETERS: Not till they brought her yesterday.

MRS. HALE: She—come to think of it, she was kind of like a bird herself—real sweet and pretty, but kind of timid and—fluttery. How—she—did—change. (*silence; then as if struck by a happy thought and relieved to get back to everyday things*) Tell you what, Mrs. Peters, why don't you take the quilt in with you? It might take up her mind.

MRS. PETERS: Why, I think that's a real nice idea, Mrs. Hale. There couldn't possibly be any objection to it, could there? Now, just what would I take? I wonder if her patches are in here—and her things.

They look in the sewing basket.

MRS. HALE: Here's some red. I expect this has got sewing things in it. (*brings out a fancy box*) What a pretty box. Looks like something somebody would give you. Maybe her scissors are in here. (*Opens box. Suddenly puts her hand to her nose.*) Why—(MRS. PETERS *bends nearer, then turns her face away.*) There's something wrapped up in this piece of silk.

MRS. PETERS: Why, this isn't her scissors.

MRS. HALE (*lifting the silk*): Oh, Mrs. Peters—it's—

MRS. PETERS *bends closer.*

MRS. PETERS: It's the bird.

MRS. HALE (*jumping up*): But, Mrs. Peters—look at it! Its neck! Look at its neck! It's all—other side *to.*

MRS. PETERS: Somebody—wrung—its—neck.

Their eyes meet. A look of growing comprehension, of horror. Steps are heard outside.
MRS. HALE *slips box under quilt pieces, and sinks into her chair. Enter* SHERIFF *and* COUNTY ATTORNEY. MRS. PETERS *rises.*

COUNTY ATTORNEY (*as one turning from serious things to little pleasantries*): Well, ladies, have you decided whether she was going to quilt it or knot it?

MRS. PETERS: We think she was going to—knot it.

COUNTY ATTORNEY: Well, that's interesting, I'm sure. (*seeing the birdcage*) Has the bird flown?

MRS. HALE (*putting more quilt pieces over the box*): We think the—cat got it.

COUNTY ATTORNEY (*preoccupied*): Is there a cat?

MRS. HALE *glances in a quick covert way at* MRS. PETERS.

MRS. PETERS: Well, not *now.* They're superstitious, you know. They leave.

COUNTY ATTORNEY (*to* SHERIFF PETERS, *continuing an interrupted conversation*): No sign at all of anyone having come from the outside. Their own rope. Now let's go up again and go over it piece by piece. (*They start upstairs.*) It would have to have been someone who knew just the—

MRS. PETERS *sits down. The two women sit there not looking at one another, but as if peering into something and at the same time holding back. When they talk now it is in the manner of feeling their way over strange ground, as if afraid of what they are saying, but as if they cannot help saying it.*

MRS. HALE: She liked the bird. She was going to bury it in that pretty box.

MRS. PETERS (*in a whisper*): When I was a girl—my kitten—there was a boy took a hatchet, and before my eyes—and before I could get there—(*covers her face an in-*

stant) If they hadn't held me back I would have—(*catches herself, looks upstairs where steps are heard, falters weakly*)—hurt him.

MRS. HALE (*with a slow look around her*): I wonder how it would seem never to have had any children around. (*pause*) No, Wright wouldn't like the bird—a thing that sang. She used to sing. He killed that, too.

MRS. PETERS (*moving uneasily*): We don't know who killed the bird.

MRS. HALE: I knew John Wright.

MRS. PETERS: It was an awful thing was done in this house that night, Mrs. Hale. Killing a man while he slept, slipping a rope around his neck that choked the life out of him.

MRS. HALE: His neck. Choked the life out of him.

Her hand goes out and rests on the birdcage.

MRS. PETERS (*with rising voice*): We don't know who killed him. We don't *know*.

MRS. HALE (*her own feeling not interrupted*): If there'd been years and years of nothing, then a bird to sing to you, it would be awful—still, after the bird was still.

MRS. PETERS (*something within her speaking*): I know what stillness is. When we homesteaded in Dakota, and my first baby died—after he was two years old, and me with no other then—

MRS. HALE (*moving*): How soon do you suppose they'll be through, looking for the evidence?

MRS. PETERS: I know what stillness is. (*pulling herself back*) The law has got to punish crime, Mrs. Hale.

MRS. HALE (*not as if answering that*): I wish you'd seen Minnie Foster when she wore a white dress with blue ribbons and stood up there in the choir and sang. (*a look around the room*) Oh, I *wish* I'd come over here once in a while! That was a crime! That was a crime! Who's going to punish that?

MRS. PETERS (*looking upstairs*): We mustn't—take on.

MRS. HALE I might have known she needed help! I know how things can be—for women. I tell you, it's queer, Mrs. Peters. We live close together and we live far apart. We all go through the same things—it's all just a different kind of the same thing. (*brushes her eyes; noticing the bottle of fruit, reaches out for it*) If I was you I wouldn't tell her her fruit was gone. Tell her it *ain't*. Tell her it's all right. Take this in to prove it to her. She—she may never know whether it was broke or not.

MRS. PETERS (*Takes the bottle, looks about for something to wrap it in; takes petticoat from the clothes brought from the other room, very nervously begins winding this around the bottle. In a false voice.*): My, it's a good thing the men couldn't hear us. Wouldn't they just laugh! Getting all stirred up over a little thing like a—dead canary. As if that could have anything to do with—with—wouldn't they *laugh*!

The men are heard coming down stairs.

MRS. HALE (*under her breath*): Maybe they would—maybe they wouldn't.

COUNTY ATTORNEY: No, Peters, it's all perfectly clear except a reason for doing it. But you know juries when it comes to women. If there was some definite thing. Something to show—something to make a story about—a thing that would connect up with this strange way of doing it—

The women's eyes meet for an instant. Enter HALE *from outer door.*

HALE: Well, I've got the team around. Pretty cold out there.

COUNTY ATTORNEY: I'm going to stay here a while by myself. (*to the* SHERIFF) You can send Frank out for me, can't you? I want to go over everything. I'm not satisfied that we can't do better.

SHERIFF: Do you want to see what Mrs. Peters is going to take in?

The COUNTY ATTORNEY *goes to the table, picks up the apron, laughs.*

COUNTY ATTORNEY: Oh, I guess they're not very dangerous things the ladies have picked out. (*Moves a few things about, disturbing the quilt pieces which cover the box. Steps back.*) No, Mrs. Peters doesn't need supervising. For that matter, a sheriff's wife is married to the law. Ever think of it that way, Mrs. Peters?

MRS. PETERS: Not—just that way.

SHERIFF (*chuckling*): Married to the law. (*moves toward the other room*) I just want you to come in here a minute, George. We ought to take a look at these windows.

COUNTY ATTORNEY (*scoffingly*): Oh, windows!

SHERIFF: We'll be right out, Mr. Hale.

HALE *goes outside. The* SHERIFF *follows the* COUNTY ATTORNEY *into the other room. Then* MRS. HALE *rises, hands tight together, looking intensely at* MRS. PETERS, *whose eyes make a slow turn, finally meeting* MRS. HALE'S. *A moment* MRS. HALE *holds her, then her own eyes point the way to where the box is concealed. Suddenly* MRS. PETERS *throws back quilt pieces and tries to put the box in the bag she is wearing. It is too big. She opens box, starts to take bird out, cannot touch it, goes to pieces, stands there helpless. Sound of a knob turning in the other room.* MRS. HALE *snatches the box and puts it in the pocket of her big coat. Enter* COUNTY ATTORNEY *and* SHERIFF.

COUNTY ATTORNEY (*facetiously*): Well, Henry, at least we found out that she was not going to quilt it. She was going to—what is it you call it, ladies?

MRS. HALE (*her hand against her pocket*): We call it—knot it, Mr. Henderson.

Curtain.

THE RECEPTIVE READER

1. Very early in the first scene, Hale, the neighbor, says in passing, "I didn't know as what his wife wanted made much difference to John." How does this statement give you a first hint of the major *conflict* underlying the play?

2. Why does the playwright have the characters talk about the preserves? To wind up this discussion, Hale says, "Well, women are used to worrying over trifles." How does this statement point forward to a major *theme* of the play? What makes the use of the word here and in the title of the play ironic? ✧ How is the theme of the "little things" that matter to women taken up again in the discussion of the quilt?

3. How do you first gather that Mrs. Hale does not share the men's views but instead has a feeling of solidarity with Mrs. Wright? How do you begin to realize that in much of this you will be looking at events and issues from the women's *point of view?*

4. The men representing the law are asking about a *motive*—"something to show anger, or—sudden feeling." What are some of the first clues that point toward the answer the play gives to this question?

5. What clues and comments help you piece together your view of John Wright's *character* as the women talk mostly about other things? What is ironic about his being described as "a good man"?

6. What makes the bird a central *symbol* in this play? What makes you first realize that the women are going to close ranks behind Mrs. Wright? What are some of the things the playwright does to help you understand and sympathize with their decision?

7. What is the *irony* in Mrs. Peters' being "married to the law"?

8. The events of this play might have provided the material for a traditional detective story or an episode in a crime show. How are the perspective on the story and its treatment in this play different from what you might expect in such a more conventional format?

THE CREATIVE DIMENSION

A major player in the events leading up to the events of the play—John, the husband—is no longer present to testify. What do you think he might say if, like Hamlet's father's ghost, he could come back among the living for a time to tell his side of the story? Or, what do you think he might have said in a letter he left for a friend to be read after an untimely death?

IBSEN: THE CLASH OF VALUES

Ibsen brings to the test of his ideal the society of his own times, observing it pitilessly, exactly, and at close range, studying the immediate and the particular in terms of the universal and the continuing.

UNA ELLIS-FERMOR

Everything I have written is intimately connected with what I have lived through, even if I have not lived it myself. Every new work has served me as emancipation and catharsis; for none of us can escape the guilt of the society to which we belong.

HENRIK IBSEN

Ibsen has been described as "in love with a future that will redeem the past." The test of his genius is the continuing vitality of his plays when the drama of most of his contemporaries is forgotten. Whenever he is pronounced outdated, a new production of *A Doll's House, The Wild Duck,* or *Ghosts* reminds theatergoers of his gift for asking questions to which they are still seeking the answers.

The Norwegian playwright Henrik Ibsen became one of the first great moderns by challenging the dominant middle-class morality of his time. He knew too well the prosperous middle class of shopkeepers, industrialists, bank managers, and doctors who in the cities and small towns were *The Pillars of the Community* (the title of an Ibsen play). He provoked them by attacking their self-righteousness: their belief that they stood for morality and law and order. In play after play, he insisted on dragging the skeletons from the middle-class closet. On Ibsen's stage, the obsession with respectability and propriety is often exposed as a façade: Present prosperity more often than not had its roots in shady business deals or the betrayal of friends. For all its genteel trappings,

Claire Bloom and Anthony Hopkins as Nora and Torvald Helmer in *A Doll's House*. Courtesy of Photofest.

the bourgeois society of the time was shown as ruthlessly competitive, with the strong prospering and the weak going under. On the fringe of proper, well-to-do society were poor relations, business failures, and misfits who lived in genteel poverty, embittered by their lot.

Ibsen was one of the first great truth tellers in the modern vein. He put on the stage businessmen who were unable to relate emotionally to their families, alienated from their wives and children. They compensated for the sexual inhibitions of their time by furtive affairs with maids and prostitutes. In a world without modern birth control, these often left in their wake a legacy of disowned illegitimate children, venereal disease, and dysfunctional marriages. In *Ghosts* (1881), the sins of the father are visited on a son whose life is being destroyed by the syphilis he has inherited from his father.

Ibsen's most memorable characters were women—Nora Helmer in *A Doll's House* (1879), Hedda in *Hedda Gabler* (1892)—who were in rebellion against the role reserved for them in this late-nineteenth-century Scandinavian version of a man's world. They dared talk back to the domineering men in their lives; they rebelled against the stereotype of the woman whose duty was to husband and family. They refused to be the "little woman" who was humored and condescended to and never entrusted with real responsibility. It has been said that the door that banged shut as Nora walked out of the doll's house was heard around the world.

The truths that Ibsen told and that often outraged his early audiences were rooted in his own experience. His father, a lavish spender, went bankrupt when Henrik was six. Ibsen was at odds with his brothers and alienated from his father, and in later years he had contacts only with his sister Hedwig. Instead of studying to be a physician, as he had hoped, he spent miserable years as a pharmacist's apprentice. He had a child out of wedlock with an older servant and paid child support for many years. Determined to be a playwright, Ibsen eventually found a small job with a theater. He managed to have plays printed and performed, but none were commercial successes, and he lived in what one of his translators calls "wretched poverty" for many years with his wife and son. (He recalled eating well for a few days when unsold copies of an early play were sold to a grocer for wrapping paper.) Assisted by a government grant, Ibsen eventually left Norway to live for many years in self-imposed exile, writing many of his best-known plays abroad in Germany and Italy.

Many of Ibsen's early plays dealt with the fantasy world of Scandinavian folklore and legend, as did his *Peer Gynt* (1867), a play in verse that was one of his first successes. However, he became famous with a series of realistic plays written in prose and mirroring contemporary Norwegian middle-class life. Among these plays, which later became known as **problem plays,** *A Doll's House* (1879) was the most spectacular and provocative. The play questioned the institution of marriage during an age when, with scandalous exceptions, marriage was for life. Outraged moralists saw the play as an attack on the foundations of morality and Christian civilization. It was eventually performed in Germany, and in an adaptation in England, creating much scandal and controversy, and it made Ibsen's reputation. He once said, "My enemies have been a great help to me—their attacks have been so vicious that people come flocking to see what all the shouting is about."

Ibsen was a master at setting up and playing out the conflicts that are the heart of drama. In his *The Wild Duck* (1882), the central conflict pits the powerful but compromised father against the bitter, alienated idealistic son. *A Doll's House* pits the stereotypical domineering husband against a wife who rebels against the ideal of self-denial, of the "angel in the house," imposed on her by her culture.

Ibsen's characters do not have road maps to a promised utopian future. As modern feminists point out, Nora knows that in leaving her doll's house "she can take nothing with her, neither her children nor anything that is rightfully her own." George Bernard Shaw, a fellow playwright, defined the spirit of Ibsenism as the human spirit outgrowing the ideals of the past and striking out in search of new ideas and a new vocabulary. In the words of a recent critic, we watch as "a new groping language pushes out the rehearsed phrasings" of the past (Naomi Lebowitz).

HENRIK IBSEN   (1828–1906)

A Doll's House   1879

TRANSLATED BY PETER WATTS

> *The legal subordination of one sex to the other is wrong in itself and now one of the chief hindrances to human improvement.*
>
> JOHN STUART MILL

> *I thought the time had come when a few boundaries ought to be moved.*
>
> HENRIK IBSEN

CHARACTERS

TORVALD HELMER, a lawyer
NORA, his wife
DR. RANK
NILS KROGSTAD, a barrister
MRS. LINDE
HELMER'S three small children
ANNA-MARIA, the nurse
A HOUSEMAID
A PORTER

The action takes place in HELMER'S *flat.*

ACT ONE

A comfortable room, furnished inexpensively, but with taste. In the back wall there are two doors; that to the right leads out to a hall, the other, to the left, leads to HELMER'S *study. Between them stands a piano.*

In the middle of the left-hand wall is a door, with a window on its nearer side. Near the window is a round table with armchairs and a small sofa.

In the wall on the right-hand side, rather to the back, is a door, and farther forward on this wall there is a tiled stove with a couple of easy chairs and a rocking-chair in front of it. Between the door and the stove stands a little table.

There are etchings on the walls, and there is a cabinet with china ornaments and other bric-à-brac, and a small bookcase with handsomely bound books. There is a carpet on the floor, and the stove is lit. It is a winter day.

A bell rings in the hall outside, and a moment later the door is heard to open. NORA *comes into the room, humming happily. She is in outdoor clothes, and is carrying an armful of parcels which she puts down on the table to the right. Through the hall door, which she has left open, can be seen a* PORTER; *he is holding a Christmas tree and a hamper, and he gives them to the* MAID *who has opened the front door.*

NORA: Hide the Christmas tree properly, Helena. The children mustn't see it till this evening, when it's been decorated. (*to the* PORTER, *taking out her purse*) How much is that?

PORTER: Fifty cents.

NORA: There's a crown. No, keep the change.

The PORTER *thanks her and goes.* NORA *shuts the door, and takes off her outdoor clothes, laughing quietly and happily to herself. Taking a bag of macaroons from her pocket, she eats one or two, then goes cautiously to her husband's door and listens.*

Yes, he's in. (*She starts humming again as she goes over to the table on the right.*)

HELMER (*from his study*): Is that my little skylark twittering out there?

NORA (*busy opening the parcels*): It is.

HELMER: Scampering about like a little squirrel?

NORA: Yes.

HELMER: When did the squirrel get home?

NORA: Just this minute. (*She slips the bag of macaroons in her pocket and wipes her mouth.*) Come in here, Torvald, and you can see what I've bought.

HELMER: I'm busy! (*A moment later he opens the door and looks out, pen in hand.*) Did you say "bought"? What, all that? Has my little featherbrain been out wasting money again?

NORA: But, Torvald, surely this year we can let ourselves go just a little bit? It's the first Christmas that we haven't had to economize.

HELMER: Still, we mustn't waste money, you know.

NORA: Oh, Torvald, surely we can waste a little now—just the teeniest bit? Now that you're going to earn a big salary, you'll have lots and lots of money.

HELMER: After New Year's Day, yes—but there'll be a whole quarter before I get paid.

NORA: Pooh, we can always borrow till then.

HELMER: Nora! (*He goes to her and takes her playfully by the ear.*) The same little scatterbrain. Just suppose I borrowed a thousand crowns today and you went and spent it all by Christmas, and then on New Year's Eve a tile fell on my head, and there I lay—

NORA (*putting a hand over his mouth*): Sh! Don't say such horrid things!

HELMER: But suppose something of the sort were to happen. . . .

NORA: If anything as horrid as that were to happen, I don't expect I should care whether I owed money or not.

HELMER: But what about the people I'd borrowed from?

NORA: Them? Who bothers about them? They're just strangers.

HELMER: Nora, Nora! Just like a woman! But seriously, Nora, you know what I think about that sort of thing. No debts, no borrowing. There's something constrained, something ugly even, about a home that's founded on borrowing and debt. You and I have managed to keep clear up till now, and we shall still do so for the little time that is left.

NORA (*going over to the stove*): Very well, Torvald, if you say so.

HELMER (*following her*): Now, now, my little songbird mustn't be so crestfallen. Well? Is the squirrel sulking? (*taking out his wallet*) Nora . . . guess what I have here!

NORA (*turning quickly*): Money!

HELMER: There! (*He hands her some notes.*) Good heavens, I know what a lot has to go on housekeeping at Christmas time.

NORA (*counting*): Ten—twenty—thirty—forty! Oh, thank you, Torvald, thank you! This'll keep me going for a long time!

HELMER: Well, you must see that it does.

NORA: Oh yes, of course I will. But now come and see all the things I've bought—so cheaply, too. Look, here's a new suit for Ivar, and a sword too. Here's a horse and a trumpet for Bob; and here's a doll and a doll's bed for Emmy. They're rather plain, but she'll soon smash them to bits anyway. And these are dress-lengths and handkerchiefs for the maids. . . . Old Nanny really ought to have something more. . . .

HELMER: And what's in *that* parcel?

NORA (*squealing*): No, Torvald! You're not to see that till this evening!

HELMER: Aha! And now, little prodigal, what do you think you want for yourself?

NORA: Oh, me? I don't want anything at all.

HELMER: Ah, but you must. Now tell me anything—within reason—that you feel you'd like.

NORA: No . . . I really can't think of anything. Unless . . . Torvald . . .

HELMER: Well?

NORA (*not looking at him—playing with his waistcoat buttons*): If you *really* want to give me something, you could—well, you could . . .

HELMER: Come along—out with it!

NORA (*in a rush*): You could give me money, Torvald. Only what you think you could spare—and then one of these days I'll buy something with it.

HELMER: But, Nora—

NORA: Oh, *do*, Torvald . . . please, please do! Then I'll wrap it in pretty gold paper and hang it on the Christmas tree. Wouldn't that be fun?

HELMER: What do they call little birds who are always making money fly?

NORA: Yes, I know—ducks-and-drakes! But let's do what I said, Torvald, and then I'll have time to think of something that I really want. Now, that's very sensible, isn't it?

HELMER (*smiling*): Oh, very. That is, it would be if you really kept the money I give you, and actually bought something for yourself with it. But if it goes in with the housekeeping, and gets spent on all sorts of useless things, then I only have to pay out again.

NORA: Oh, but, Torvald—

HELMER: You can't deny it, little Nora, now can you? (*putting an arm round her waist*) It's a sweet little bird, but it gets through a terrible amount of money. You wouldn't believe how much it costs a man when he's got a little songbird like you!

NORA: Oh, how *can* you say that? I really do save all I can.

HELMER (*laughing*): Yes, that's very true—"all you can." But the thing is, you *can't!*

NORA (*nodding and smiling happily*): Ah, if you only knew what expenses we skylarks and squirrels have, Torvald.

HELMER: What a funny little one you are! Just like your father—always on the look-out for all the money you can get, but the moment you have it, it seems to slip through your fingers and you never know what becomes of it. Well, I must take you as you are—it's in your blood. Oh yes, Nora, these things are hereditary.

NORA: I wish I'd inherited more of papa's good qualities.

HELMER: And I wouldn't want you to be any different from what you are—just my sweet little songbird. But now I come to think of it, you look rather—rather—how shall I put it?—rather as if you've been up to mischief today.

NORA: Do I?

HELMER: Yes, you certainly do. Look me straight in the face.

NORA (*looking at him*): Well?

HELMER (*wagging a finger at her*): Surely your sweet tooth didn't get the better of you in town today?

NORA: No . . . how could you think that?

HELMER: Didn't Little Sweet-Tooth just look in at the confectioner's?

NORA: No, honestly, Torvald.

HELMER: Not to taste one little sweet?

NORA: No, of course not.

HELMER: Not even to nibble a macaroon or two?

NORA: No, Torvald, really; I promise you.

HELMER: There, there, of course I was only joking.

NORA (*going to the table on the right*): I wouldn't do anything that you don't like.

HELMER: No, I know you wouldn't—besides, you've given me your word. (*going over to her*) Well, you keep your little Christmas secrets to yourself, Nora darling; I daresay I shall know them all this evening when the Christmas tree's lighted up.

NORA: Did you remember to invite Dr. Rank?

HELMER: No, but there's no need to—it's an understood thing that he dines with us. Still, I'll ask him when he looks in before lunch. I've ordered an excellent wine. . . . Oh, Nora, you can't imagine how much I'm looking forward to this evening.

NORA: So am I, Torvald—and how the children will love it.

HELMER: Oh, it's certainly wonderful to think that one has a good safe post and ample means. It's a very comforting thought, isn't it?

NORA: Oh, it's wonderful!

HELMER: Do you remember last Christmas? For three whole weeks beforehand you shut yourself up every evening till long after midnight, making flowers for the Christmas tree, and all the other wonderful surprises for us. Ugh, those were the most boring three weeks I've ever had to live through.

NORA: It wasn't the least bit boring for me.

HELMER (*smiling*): But there was so little to show for it, Nora!

NORA: Now, you mustn't tease me about that again. How could I help it if the cat got in and tore everything to bits?

HELMER: Poor little Nora—of course you couldn't. You did your best to please us— that's the main thing. But it's certainly good that the hard times are over.

NORA: Oh, it's really wonderful!

HELMER: Now I needn't sit here by myself and be bored, and you needn't tire your pretty eyes or your sweet little fingers—

NORA (*clapping her hands*): No, I needn't, need I? Not any more. Oh, it's really wonderful to know that. (*taking his arm*) Now I'll tell you how I've been thinking we ought to arrange things, Torvald. As soon as Christmas is over—

A bell rings in the hall.

Oh, that's the door! (*She tidies the room a little.*) It must be someone to see us— oh, that *is* tiresome!

HELMER: I'm not at home to callers, remember.

MAID (*at the door*): There's a lady to see you, madam.

NORA: Well, show her in.

MAID (*to* HELMER): And the Doctor's here as well, sir.

HELMER: Has he gone straight to my study?

MAID: Yes, sir.

HELMER *goes to his study. The* MAID *shows in* MRS. LINDE, *who is in travelling clothes, and shuts the door after her.*

MRS. LINDE (*subdued and rather hesitant*): How do you do, Nora?

NORA (*doubtfully*): How do you do . . .

MRS. LINDE: You don't remember me.

NORA: No, I'm afraid I—Wait a minute . . . surely it's—(*impulsively*) Kristina! Is it really you?

MRS. LINDE: Yes, it really is.

NORA: Kristina! And to think I didn't know you! But how could *I*? (*more gently*) You *have* changed, Kristina.

MRS. LINDE: Yes, I have . . . nine years—nearly ten—it's a long time.

NORA: Is it really as long as that since we saw each other? Yes, I suppose it is. But you know, I've been so happy these last eight years! And now you've come to town too? How brave of you to travel all that way in the middle of winter.

MRS. LINDE: I arrived by steamer this morning.

NORA: In time to have a lovely Christmas. Oh, this is wonderful! We'll have a splendid time. But do take your things off—aren't you absolutely frozen? (*helping her*) There! Now come and sit by the stove where it's cosy. No, you have the armchair, I'll sit in the rocking-chair. (*taking her hands*) Yes, now you look like your old self again—it was just the first moment. . . . But you're paler, Kristina, and a little thinner, perhaps. . . .

MRS. LINDE: And a lot older, Nora.

NORA: A little older, perhaps—just a teeny bit—but certainly not a lot. (*suddenly checking herself and speaking seriously*) Oh, how thoughtless of me! Here I am, chattering away . . . dear sweet Kristina, can you ever forgive me?

MRS. LINDE: What do you mean, Nora?

NORA: Poor Kristina, you're a widow now.

MRS. LINDE: Yes . . . three years ago.

NORA: Yes, I know; I saw it in the papers. Oh, Kristina, I kept meaning to write to you, honestly I did, but something always cropped up and I put it off . . .

MRS. LINDE: Dear Nora, I do understand.

NORA: No, it was horrid of me. Oh, poor Kristina, what you must have gone through! And he didn't leave you anything to live on?

MRS. LINDE: No.

NORA: And no children?

MRS. LINDE: No.

NORA: Nothing at all?

MRS. LINDE: Not even any regrets to break my heart over.

NORA (*looking at her incredulously*): Oh, but Kristina, that can't be true.

MRS. LINDE (*stroking* NORA'S *hair with a sad smile*): It happens like that sometimes, Nora.

NORA: But to be so completely alone—that must be terribly sad for you. *I* have three lovely children; you can't see them just now, they're out with their Nanny. . . . But now you must tell me all about it.

MRS. LINDE: No, no, I want to hear about you.

NORA: No, you first—I mustn't be selfish today—I'm not going to think about anything but your troubles. I must just tell you one thing, though. Do you know, we've just had the most wonderful stroke of luck—only the other day.

MRS. LINDE: Oh? What was it?

NORA: Just think—my husband's been made Manager of the Savings Bank.

MRS. LINDE: Your husband? But that's wonderful.

NORA: Yes, it's magnificent! A barrister's life is such an uncertain one—especially when he won't touch any case that isn't absolutely respectable. Of course Torvald never would—and I quite agree with him. Well, you can imagine how delighted we are.

He's to start at the Bank on New Year's Day, and he'll have a big salary and lots of commission. Oh, we shall be able to live quite differently from now on—to live as we'd like to. Oh, Kristina, I'm so happy! It'll be really wonderful to have lots of money, and never need to worry, won't it?

MRS. LINDE: Yes, it must be pleasant to have everything you need.

NORA: Oh, not just what we need! Heaps and heaps of money!

MRS. LINDE (*with a smile*): Nora, Nora! Haven't you learned sense yet? Even at school you were a terrible spendthrift.

NORA (*laughing quietly*): Yes, Torvald says I still am. (*wagging her finger*) But "Nora, Nora" isn't as silly as you think. We simply hadn't the money for me to waste; we both had to work.

MRS. LINDE: You as well?

NORA: Yes, with odds and ends of needlework—crochet and embroidery and so on. (*casually*) And in other ways too. You see, when we married, Torvald gave up his government post—there wasn't any hope of promotion in his department, and of course he had to earn more money than before. But he overworked dreadfully that first year; you see, he had to take on all sorts of extra jobs, and he worked from morning till night. He couldn't stand it; he was dreadfully ill, and the doctors said he'd simply *have* to go to the south.

MRS. LINDE: Oh yes, you went to Italy for a whole year, didn't you?

NORA: Yes, we did. It wasn't easy to manage, I can tell you. It was just after Ivar was born, but of course we had to go. Oh, it was a wonderful trip—beautiful! And it saved Torvald's life. But it cost a terrible lot of money, Kristina!

MRS. LINDE: I'm sure it did.

NORA: Twelve hundred dollars—four thousand eight hundred crowns. That's a lot of money.

MRS. LINDE: Yes, at times like that, it's very lucky to have money.

NORA: Well, you see, we got it from Papa.

MRS. LINDE: Oh? Yes, I remember, your father died just about then.

NORA: Yes, just then. And just think, Kristina, I couldn't go and nurse him. I was expecting Ivar to arrive any day, and there was my poor Torvald, dreadfully ill, to look after. Dear, kind Papa—I never saw him again—that was the hardest thing I've had to bear in all my married life, Kristina.

MRS. LINDE: I know how fond of him you were. . . . And so you went to Italy?

NORA: Yes, we left a month later. We had the money then, and the doctors said there was no time to lose.

MRS. LINDE: And when you came back your husband was cured?

NORA: Fit as a fiddle!

MRS. LINDE: But the doctor . . . ?

NORA: What doctor?

MRS. LINDE: That man who arrived at the same time as I did—I thought your maid said he was the doctor?

NORA: Ah, that was Dr. Rank—but he doesn't come here professionally, he's our best friend, he always looks in at least once a day. No, Torvald's never had a day's illness since. And the children are well and strong, and so am I. (*jumping up and clapping her hands*) Oh Lord, Kristina, it's wonderful to be alive and happy! Oh, but how awful of me, I've just gone on talking about myself! (*She sits on a footstool beside* KRISTINA *and puts her arms on her knees.*) Now, you mustn't be angry with me. Tell me, is it really true that you didn't love your husband? Why did you marry him, then?

MRS. LINDE: My mother was still alive; she was bedridden and helpless, and I had my two younger brothers to look after—I didn't feel I *could* refuse his offer.

NORA: No, no, I suppose you couldn't. And he was rich in those days?

MRS. LINDE: I believe he was quite well off; but his business wasn't sound, and when he died it went to pieces and there wasn't anything left.

NORA: And you . . . ?

MRS. LINDE: Well, I just had to struggle along—I ran a little shop, then a small school, and anything else I could turn my hand to. These last three years I never seem to have stopped working. Still, that's all over now, Nora—poor Mother's gone, she doesn't need me any longer. Nor do the boys—they're working, and they can look after themselves.

NORA: How relieved you must feel.

MRS. LINDE: No . . . just unspeakably empty—I've no one to live for any more. (*She gets up restlessly.*) That's why I couldn't bear to stay in that little backwater any longer. It must be easier to find some sort of work here that'll keep me busy and take my mind off things. If only I could be lucky enough to find some office work . . .

NORA: But, Kristina, that's terribly tiring, and you look worn out already. It'd be much better for you to go for a holiday.

MRS. LINDE (*going over to the window*): I haven't a father to pay my fare, Nora.

NORA (*rising*): Oh, don't be angry with me.

MRS. LINDE (*going to her*): No, Nora, it's you who mustn't be angry with me. That's the worst of my sort of life—it makes you so bitter. There's no one to work for, yet you can never relax. You must live, so you become self-centered. Why, do you know, when you told me the news of your good fortune, I wasn't nearly so glad for your sake as for my own!

NORA: But . . . Oh, I see what you mean—you think perhaps Torvald might be able to do something for you.

MRS. LINDE: Yes, I thought he might.

NORA: Oh, he will, Kristina; just leave it to me. I'll bring the subject up very cleverly. . . . I'll think of some wonderful way to put him in a good mood. . . . Oh, I should so like to help you.

MRS. LINDE: It *is* kind of you, Nora, to want to do this for me . . . especially when *you* know so little about the troubles and hardships of life.

NORA: I? So little?

MRS. LINDE (*smiling*): Well, good heavens, a little bit of sewing and that sort of thing! You're only a baby, Nora!

NORA (*crossing the room with a toss of her head*): Don't be so superior.

MRS. LINDE: No?

NORA: You're like all the others—you none of you think I could do anything worth while. . . .

MRS. LINDE: Well?

NORA: And you think I've had an easy life, with nothing to contend with.

MRS. LINDE: But, Nora dear, you've just told me all your troubles.

NORA: Pooh, they were nothing. (*dropping her voice*) I haven't told you the really important thing.

MRS. LINDE: The important thing? What was that?

NORA: I expect you look down on me, Kristina, but you've no right to. You're proud because you worked so hard for your mother all those years.

MRS. LINDE: I don't look down on anyone; but of course I'm proud—and glad—to know that I was able to make Mother's last days a little easier.

NORA: And you're proud of what you did for your brothers.

MRS. LINDE: I think I have every right to be.

NORA: I quite agree. But now let me tell you something, Kristina; I've got something to be proud of, too.

MRS. LINDE: I'm sure you have; what is it?

NORA: Not so loud—suppose Torvald were to hear! I wouldn't have him find out for the world. No one must know about it—no one but you, Kristina.

MRS. LINDE: But what is it?

NORA: Come over here. (*pulling her down on the sofa beside her*) Oh yes, I've something to be proud of. It was I who saved Torvald's life.

MRS. LINDE: Saved his life? But how?

NORA: I told you about our trip to Italy. Torvald would never have got better if we hadn't gone there.

MRS. LINDE: Yes, but your father gave you the money you needed.

NORA (*smiling*): That's what Torvald thinks—and so does everyone else—but . . .

MRS. LINDE: Well?

NORA: Papa never gave us a penny. It was I who raised the money.

MRS. LINDE: You? All that money?

NORA: Twelve hundred dollars—four thousand eight hundred crowns. What do you think of that?

MRS. LINDE: But how could you, Nora? Did you win it in a lottery?

NORA (*contemptuously*): A lottery! (*with a snort*) Pooh—where would be the glory in *that*?

MRS. LINDE: Where did you get it then?

NORA (*with an enigmatic smile*): Aha! (*humming*) Tra-la-la!

MRS. LINDE: Because you certainly couldn't have borrowed it.

NORA: Oh? Why not?

MRS. LINDE: Because a wife can't borrow without her husband's consent.

NORA (*with a toss of her head*): Ah, yes she can—when it's a wife with a little flair for business—a wife who knows how to set about it . . .

MRS. LINDE: But, Nora, I don't see how—

NORA: There's no reason why you should. Besides, I never said anything about *borrowing* the money. There are all sorts of ways I might have got it. (*lying back on the sofa*) I might have got it from some admirer or other—after all, I'm quite attractive . . .

MRS. LINDE: Don't be so silly!

NORA: You know, you're simply dying of curiosity, Kristina!

MRS. LINDE: Now, Nora dear, listen to me—you haven't done anything rash, have you?

NORA (*sitting up*): Is it rash to save your husband's life?

MRS. LINDE: I think it's rash to do something without his knowing . . .

NORA: But I couldn't possibly let him know. Good heavens, don't you see?—it would never have done for him to realize how ill he was. It was to *me* that the doctors came; they said that his life was in danger and that the only way to save him was to take him to the south. Do you think I didn't try to wheedle him into it first? I told him how nice it would be for me to have a holiday abroad like all the other young wives. I tried tears and entreaties—I told him that he really ought to think about my condition—that he must be a dear and do what I asked. I hinted that he could easily borrow the money. But then, Kristina, he nearly lost his temper, he told me I was frivolous, and that it was his duty as a husband not to give in to what I believe he called my "whims and fancies." "All right," I thought, "but your life must be saved somehow." And then I thought of a way . . .

MRS. LINDE: But surely your father must have told him that the money didn't come from *him*?

NORA: No—it was just then that Papa died. I'd always meant to tell him about it and ask him not to give me away, but he was so ill . . . and I'm afraid in the end there was no need.

MRS. LINDE: And *you've* never told your husband?

NORA: Good heavens no, how could I? When he's so strict about that sort of thing. . . . Besides, Torvald has his pride—most men have—he'd be terribly hurt and humiliated if he thought he owed anything to me. It'd spoil everything between us, and our lovely happy home would never be the same again.

MRS. LINDE: Aren't you ever going to tell him?

NORA (*thoughtfully, with a little smile*): Well—one day, perhaps. But not for a long time. When I'm not pretty any more. No, you mustn't laugh. What I mean, of course, is when Torvald isn't as fond of me as he is now—when my dancing and dressing up and reciting don't amuse him any longer. It might be a good thing, then, to have something up my sleeve . . . (*breaking off*). But that's nonsense—that time'll never come. Well, Kristina, what do you think of my great secret? Am I still no use? What's more, you can take my word for it that it's all been a great worry to me—it hasn't been at all easy to meet all my obligations punctually. In business, you know, there are things called "quarterly payments" and "installments," and they're always dreadfully hard to meet, so you see, I've had to scrape together a little bit here and a little bit there, whenever I could. I couldn't save much out of the housekeeping money, because Torvald has to live properly, and I couldn't have the children looking shabby. I didn't feel I could touch the money that I had for my little darlings.

MRS. LINDE: So it all had to come out of your own pocket-money? Poor Nora.

NORA: Of course. After all, it was my own doing. So whenever Torvald gave me money for new dresses and things, I never spent more than half of it—I always bought the simplest, cheapest things. Thank goodness anything looks well on me, so Torvald never noticed. But, oh Kristina, it hasn't been at all easy, because it's so nice to be beautifully dressed, isn't it?

MRS. LINDE: It certainly is.

NORA: Then I've found other ways of earning money too. Last winter I was lucky enough to get a lot of copying to do, so I locked myself in and sat writing—often till after midnight. Oh, I was so tired sometimes . . . so tired. Still, it was really tremendous fun sitting there working and earning money. It was almost like being a man.

MRS. LINDE: But how much have you been able to pay off?

NORA: Well, I don't really know exactly. You see, with a thing like that, it's very difficult to keep accounts. All I know is that I've paid out every penny that I've been able to scrape together. Often I've been at my wits' end. . . . (*smiling*) Then I used to sit here and imagine that a rich old gentleman had fallen in love with me—

MRS. LINDE: Oh? Who was it?

NORA: Wait a minute—and that he died, and when they read his will, there it was, as large as life: "All my money is to go to the lovely Mrs. Nora Helmer—cash down."

MRS. LINDE: But, Nora dear, who was he?

NORA: Oh, good heavens, don't you see? There wasn't really any old gentleman, it was just something that I used to sit here and imagine—often and often—when I simply didn't know which way to turn for the money. But that's all over now; the silly old gentleman can stay where he is for all I care—I've finished with him and his will, my troubles are all over! (*jumping up*) Oh, goodness, Kristina, just think of it! No more worries! To be able to have no more worries at all! To be able to romp with the children, and to have all the lovely up-to-date things about the house that Torvald likes so much. . . . And then it'll soon be spring, and the sky'll be so blue, and perhaps we'll be able to go away for a bit. Perhaps I shall see the sea again. Oh, isn't it wonderful to be alive and happy?

The doorbell is heard from the hall.

MRS. LINDE (*getting up*): There's someone at the door—perhaps I'd better go.
NORA: No, stay. It'll be someone for Torvald, they won't come in here.
MAID (*at the hall door*): Excuse me, Madam, there's a gentleman to see the Lawyer—
NORA: The Bank Manager, you mean.
MAID: Yes, the Bank Manger. But I didn't know—seeing the Doctor's with him—
NORA: Who is it?
KROGSTAD (*in the doorway*): It's me, Mrs. Helmer.

MRS. LINDE *gives a start, then, collecting herself, turns away to the window.*

NORA (*tensely and in a low voice, taking a step toward him*): You? What is it? Why do you want to see my husband?
KROGSTAD: Bank business—in a way. I have a small post at the Savings Bank, and I hear your husband is to be our new Manager—
NORA: So it's only—
KROGSTAD: Only dull official business, Mrs. Helmer; nothing else whatever.
NORA: Well, you'll find him in his study. (*She bows perfunctorily and shuts the hall door. Then she goes over and attends to the stove.*)
MRS. LINDE: Nora . . . who was that man?
NORA: He's a lawyer named Krogstad.
MRS. LINDE: So it was really he. . . .
NORA: Do you know him?
MRS. LINDE: I used to know him—years ago. He was once in a lawyer's office back at home.
NORA: Yes, so he was.
MRS. LINDE: How he's changed!
NORA: He's had a very unhappy married life.
MRS. LINDE: And now he's a widower?
NORA: With lots of children. There, that should burn up now.

She shuts the door of the stove and pushes the rocking-chair a little to one side.

MRS. LINDE: He has a finger in all sorts of business, they say.
NORA: Really? Well, they may be right, I don't know anything about. . . . But don't let's talk about business—it's so boring.

DR. RANK *comes out of* HELMER'S *room.*

RANK (*in the doorway*): No no, my dear fellow, I don't want to be in the way. Besides, I'd like to see your wife for a bit. (*As he shuts the door he notices* MRS. LINDE.) Oh, I'm sorry—I'm in the way here, too.
NORA: Not in the least. (*introducing them*) This is Dr. Rank—Mrs. Linde.
RANK: Ah, now that's a name that I'm constantly hearing in this house. I think I passed you on the stairs as I came up.

MRS. LINDE: Yes, I don't like stairs—I have to take them very slowly.

RANK: Ah, some little internal weakness?

MRS. LINDE: Only overwork, I think.

RANK: Is that all? So you've come to town for a rest—at all the parties?

MRS. LINDE: I've come here to look for work.

RANK: Is that a wise remedy for overwork?

MRS. LINDE: One must live, Doctor.

RANK: Yes, there seems to be a general impression that it's necessary.

NORA: Now, Dr. Rank, you know you want to live, too.

RANK: Yes, indeed I do. However wretched I may be, I always want to prolong the agony as long as possible. All my patients have the same idea. And it's the same with people whose sickness is moral, too. At this very moment there's a moral invalid in there with Helmer, and—

MRS. LINDE (*softly*): Ah.

NORA: Whom do you mean?

RANK: Oh, you wouldn't know him—it's a lawyer named Krogstad. He's rotten to the core, but the first thing he said—as if it were something really important—was that he must live.

NORA: Oh. What did he want to see Torvald about?

RANK: I don't really know; all I heard was that it was something to do with the Bank.

NORA: I didn't know that Krog—that this lawyer had anything to do with the Bank.

RANK: Yes, he has some sort of post there. (*to* MRS. LINDE) I don't know if it's the same where you live, but here there are people who grub around sniffing out moral corruption, and when they've found it they put it in a good job somewhere where they can keep an eye on it. The honest man probably finds himself left out in the cold.

MRS. LINDE: Well, I suppose the sick need looking after.

RANK (*shrugging his shoulders*): There you are! That's the sort of theory that's turning the community into a regular hospital!

NORA, *deep in her own thoughts, suddenly gives a quiet laugh and claps her hands.*

RANK: Why do you laugh at that? Do you really know what the community is?

NORA: What do I care for your dreary old community? I was laughing at something quite different—something frightfully funny. Tell me, Dr. Rank, do all the people who work at the Bank depend on Torvald now?

RANK: Is that what you found so "frightfully funny"?

NORA (*smiling and humming*): Ah, that's my business—that's my business! (*pacing around the room*) Yes, it really is frightfully funny to think that we—that Torvald has all that power over so many people. (*taking a bag from her pocket*) Won't you have a macaroon, Dr. Rank?

RANK: Macaroons? Now, now! I thought they were forbidden here!

NORA: Yes, but these are some that Kristina gave me.

MRS. LINDE: What? But I . . . ?

NORA: No, no, don't be frightened; you weren't to know that Torvald had forbidden them. The thing is, he's afraid I shall spoil my teeth with them. But pooh—just this once! That's right, isn't it, Dr. Rank? Here! (*She pops a macaroon into his mouth.*) And now you, Kristina. And I'll have one as well—just a little one. Or two at the most. (*pacing about again*) Oh, I'm really terribly happy! Now there's just one thing in the world that I want terribly badly.

RANK: Oh? What is it?

NORA: It's something that I've been wanting terribly to say in front of Torvald.

RANK: Then why can't you say it?

NORA: Oh, I daren't—it's very bad.

MRS. LINDE: Bad?

RANK: Then you'd better not say it. Though surely to *us* . . . What is it that you want so much to say in front of Torvald?

NORA: I terribly want to say—"Well I'm damned!"

RANK: You must be mad!

MRS. LINDE: But, good gracious, Nora—

RANK: Well, here he comes. Say it.

NORA (*hiding the macaroons*): Sh! Sh!

HELMER *comes out of his room with a coat over his arm and a hat in his hand.*

NORA (*going to him*): Well, so you got rid of him, Torvald dear?

HELMER: Yes, he's just gone.

NORA: Let me introduce you: this is Kristina—she's come to town.

HELMER: Kristina . . . ? I'm sorry, I'm afraid I don't—

NORA: Mrs. Linde, Torvald dear! Kristina Linde.

HELMER: Oh yes—surely you and my wife were girls together?

MRS. LINDE: Yes, we knew each other in the old days.

NORA: And just think, she's come all this way to see you!

HELMER: To see *me*?

NORA: Kristina's frightfully clever at office work, and she wants terribly to work under a really able man so that she can learn more still. . . .

HELMER: That's very wise of you, Mrs. Linde.

NORA: So when she heard that you'd been made a Bank Manager—they had a telegram about it—she came down here as quickly as she could. You'll be able to do something for her, Torvald, won't you? Just to please me?

HELMER: Well, it's not impossible. . . . I take it that you're a widow, Mrs. Linde?

MRS. LINDE: Yes.

HELMER: And you've had commercial experience?

MRS. LINDE: A certain amount, yes.

HELMER: Ah, then it's highly probable that I shall be able to find a post for you.

NORA (*clapping her hands*): There you are! You see!

HELMER: You've come at just the right moment, Mrs. Linde . . .

MRS. LINDE: I can't tell you how grateful I am.

HELMER: Oh, there's no need . . . (*putting on his overcoat*) But now you must excuse me. . . .

RANK: Wait, I'll come with you. (*He gets his fur coat from the hall and warms it at the stove.*)

NORA: Don't be long, Torvald dear.

HELMER: I shan't be more than about an hour.

NORA: Are you going too, Kristina?

MRS. LINDE (*putting on her outdoor things*): Yes, I must go and look for a room.

HELMER: Then perhaps we can all go down the street together.

NORA (*helping her*): How tiresome that we're so short of room here—we couldn't possibly—

MRS. LINDE: Oh no, you mustn't think of it. Good-bye, Nora dear—and thank you.

NORA: Good-bye for the present—you'll come back this evening, won't you? And you, too, Dr. Rank. What? "If you feel up to it"? Of course you will. Wrap up well, now!

They go out into the hall still talking: the CHILDREN'S *voices are heard on the stairs.*

NORA: Here they are! Here they are!

She runs out and opens the door; the nurse, ANNA-MARIA, *comes in with the* CHILDREN.

Come in, come in! (*She stoop down and kisses them.*) Oh, my little darlings! Look at them, Kristina, aren't they sweet?

RANK: Don't stand there chattering in the draught!

HELMER: Come along, Mrs. Linde, this is no place for anyone but a mother!

He and DR. RANK *and* MRS. LINDE *go down the stairs. The* NURSE *comes into the room with the* CHILDREN, *and* NORA *follows, shutting the hall door.*

NORA: How nice and healthy you look! Oh, what pink cheeks—like apples and roses!

The CHILDREN *keep chattering to her during the following:*

Did you enjoy yourselves? That's good. And so you gave Emmy and Bob a ride on your sledge? Both together? Well, fancy that! What a big boy you are, Ivar. Oh, let me take her for a minute, Nanny—my little baby dolly! (*She takes the youngest from the* NURSE *and dances with her.*) Yes, yes, Mummy'll dance with Bob too! What? You've been snowballing? Oh, I wish I'd been there. No, leave them, Nanny, I'll take their things off. Yes, let me do it, it's such fun. You look frozen—there's some hot coffee for you on the stove in the next room.

The NURSE *goes into the room on the left.* NORA *takes off the* CHILDREN'S *outdoor things, throwing them down anywhere, while the* CHILDREN *all talk at once.*

NORA: Well! So a great big dog ran after you? But he didn't bite you? No, dogs don't bite dear little baby dollies! No, don't look inside those parcels, Ivar. What's in them? Ah, wouldn't you like to know? No, no, it isn't anything nice at all! What, you want a game? What shall we play? Hide and seek? Yes, let's play hide and seek. Bob, you hide first. Me? All right, I'll hide first.

She and the CHILDREN *play, laughing and shouting, both in this room and the room on the right. At last,* NORA *hides under the table. The* CHILDREN *come rushing in to look for her but they can't find her. Then, hearing her smothered laughter, they run to the table, lift the cloth, and see her. Loud shouts. She comes out on all fours as if to frighten them. Fresh shouts. Meanwhile there has been knocking on the front door, but no one has noticed it. Now the door half opens, revealing* KROGSTAD. *He waits a little as the game continues.*

KROGSTAD: Excuse me, Mrs. Helmer . . .

NORA (*with a stifled cry she turns and half rises*): Oh! What do you what?

KROGSTAD: I'm sorry; the front door was open. Somebody must have forgotten to shut it.

NORA (*getting up*): My husband is out, Mr. Krogstad.

KROGSTAD: Yes, I know.

NORA: Then . . . what do you want here?

KROGSTAD: A word with you.

NORA: With . . . ? (*quietly, to the* CHILDREN) Go to Nanny. What? No, the strange man isn't going to hurt Mummy—directly he's gone, we'll go on with our game. (*She takes the* CHILDREN *out to the room on the left, shutting the door after them. Then, tense and wary.*) You want to see me?

KROGSTAD: Yes, I do.

NORA: Today? But it isn't the first of the month yet. . . .

KROGSTAD: No, it's Christmas Eve. It all depends on you whether you have a happy Christmas or not.

NORA: What do you want? I can't manage any today—

KROGSTAD: We'll talk about that later; this is something different. Can you spare a moment?

NORA: Well, yes . . . I can, but—

KROGSTAD: Good. I was sitting in Olsen's restaurant, and I saw your husband go down the street—

NORA: Well?

KROGSTAD: —with a lady.

NORA: What of it?

KROGSTAD: May I be so bold as to ask if the lady was a Mrs. Linde?

NORA: She was.

KROGSTAD: She's just arrived in town?

NORA: Today, yes.

KROGSTAD: She's a great friend of yours?

NORA: Yes, she is. But I don't see—

KROGSTAD: I knew her once, too.

NORA: Yes, I know.

KROGSTAD: Oh? So you know about it? I thought so. All right, then I can ask you straight out: is Mrs. Linde to have a post at the Bank?

NORA: How dare you question me, Mr. Krogstad—one of my husband's subordinates. But since you ask, I'll tell you. Yes, Mrs. Linde is to have a post, and it was I who recommended her, Mr. Krogstad. So now you know.

KROGSTAD: Yes, I guessed as much.

NORA (*walking up and down*): So it looks as if one has a *little* influence—just because one's a woman, it doesn't necessarily mean that—and people in subordinate positions, Mr. Krogstad, should be careful not to offend anyone who—well—

KROGSTAD: . . . who has influence?

NORA: Exactly.

KROGSTAD (*changing his tone*): Mrs. Helmer . . . would you please be good enough to use your influence on my behalf?

NORA: How? What do you mean?

KROGSTAD: Would you be so kind as to see that I keep my subordinate position at the Bank?

NORA: What do you mean? Who's trying to take it away?

KROGSTAD: Oh, you needn't pretend to *me* that you don't know. I can quite see that it wouldn't be pleasant for your friend to have to keep running into me. What's more, I know now whom I shall have to thank for getting me dismissed.

NORA: But I assure you—

KROGSTAD: Oh, of course, of course. But don't let's beat about the bush—I advise you, while there's still time, to use your influence to prevent it.

NORA: But, Mr. Krogstad, I haven't any influence.

KROGSTAD: No? I though you said just now—

NORA: I didn't mean it like that, of course. I? How do you think I could influence my husband in that sort of thing?

KROGSTAD: Well . . . I've known your husband since his student days—I don't think our noble Bank Manager is more inflexible than any other husband.

NORA: If you speak disrespectfully of my husband I shall show you the door!

KROGSTAD: How brave of you!

NORA: I'm not afraid of you any more. After the New Year I shall very quickly be free of the whole thing.

KROGSTAD (*controlling himself*): Listen to me, Mrs. Helmer. If need be, I shall fight to keep my little post at the Bank as I'd fight for my life.

NORA: So it seems.

KROGSTAD: It's not just for the money—that's the least important thing about it. No, there's something else . . . Well, I might as well tell you—it's this: of course you know—everyone does—that I got into trouble a few years ago.

NORA: I believe I heard something of the sort.

KROGSTAD: It never came to court, but since then it's been as if every way was closed to me—that's why I took to the business that you know about. I had to live somehow, and I think I can claim that I haven't been as bad as some. But now I want to give up all that sort of thing. My sons are growing up, and in fairness to them I must try to win back as much respect as I can in the town. This post at the Bank was the first step for me—and now your husband's going to kick me off the ladder again, back into the mud.

NORA: But honestly, Mr. Krogstad, there's nothing that I can do to help you.

KROGSTAD: That's because you don't want to. But I have ways of making you.

NORA: You won't tell my husband that I owe you money?

KROGSTAD: Ah . . . suppose I did?

NORA: That would be a vile thing to do. (*with tears in her voice*) I've been so proud of my secret; I couldn't bear to have him hear it like that—brutally and clumsily—and from *you*. It would put me in a most unpleasant position.

KROGSTAD: Only unpleasant?

NORA (*impetuously*): All right, then—tell him! But it'll be the worse for you, because my husband will see what a brute you are, and then you'll certainly lose your post.

KROGSTAD: I asked you if it was only domestic unpleasantness that you were afraid of?

NORA: If my husband finds out, naturally he'll pay you whatever I still owe, and then we'll have nothing more to do with you.

KROGSTAD (*taking a step toward her*): Listen, Mrs. Helmer; either my memory isn't very good, or you don't know much about business. I shall have to make things a little clearer to you.

NORA: How?

KROGSTAD: When your husband was ill you came to me to borrow twelve hundred dollars.

NORA: I didn't know where else to go.

KROGSTAD: I promised to find you the money—

NORA: And you did find it.

KROGSTAD: I promised to find you the money on certain conditions. At the time you were so worried about your husband's illness, and so anxious to get the money for your journey, that I don't think you paid much attention to the details—so it won't be out of place if I remind you of them. Well . . . I promised to find you the money against a note of hand which I drew up.

NORA: Yes, and which I signed.

KROGSTAD: Exactly. But below that I'd added a few lines making your father surety for the money. Your father was to sign this clause.

NORA: Was to? But he did sign.

KROGSTAD: I'd left the date blank—that's to say, your father was to fill in the date when he signed the paper. Do you remember?

NORA: Yes, I think so . . . .

KROGSTAD: Then I gave you the document so that you could post it to your father. Is that correct?

NORA: Yes.

KROGSTAD: And of course you sent it at once, because only five or six days later you brought it back to me with your father's signature . . . and I handed over the money.

NORA: Well? Haven't I paid it off regularly?

KROGSTAD: Yes, fairly regularly. But—to get back to the point—you were going through a trying time just then, Mrs. Helmer?

NORA: I certainly was.

KROGSTAD: Your father was ill, I believe?

NORA: He was dying.

KROGSTAD: He died soon afterwards?

NORA: Yes.

KROGSTAD: Tell me, Mrs. Helmer, do you happen to remember the day he died? The day of the month, I mean?

NORA: Papa died on the twenty-ninth of September.

KROGSTAD: That is correct—I've confirmed that for myself. And that brings us to a curious thing (*producing a paper*) which I'm quite unable to explain.

NORA: What curious thing? I don't know of any—

KROGSTAD: The curious thing, Mrs. Helmer, is that your father signed this note of hand three days after his death.

NORA: How? I don't understand.

KROGSTAD: Your father died on the twenty-ninth of September. But look at this—your father has dated his signature the second of October. Isn't that a curious thing, Mrs. Helmer?

NORA *is silent.*

Can you explain it?

NORA *is still silent.*

It's odd, too, that the words October the second and the year aren't in your father's handwriting, but in a writing that I think I know. Well, of course, that could be explained—your father might have forgotten to date his signature, and someone else might have guessed at the date before they knew of his death. There's nothing wrong in that. It's the signature that really matters. That *is* genuine, isn't it, Mrs. Helmer? It really was your father himself who wrote his name there?

NORA (*after a moment's pause, throwing her head back and looking defiantly at him*): No, it was not. *I* wrote Papa's name.

KROGSTAD: Look, Mrs. Helmer, you know that that's a very dangerous admission?

NORA: Why? You'll soon get your money.

KROGSTAD: May I ask you something? Why didn't you send the paper to your father?

NORA: I couldn't; he was far too ill. If I'd asked him for his signature, I should have had to tell him what the money was for—and when he was so ill himself, I couldn't tell him that my husband's life was in danger—I couldn't possibly.

KROGSTAD: Then it would have been better for you if you'd given up your trip abroad.

NORA: I couldn't do that. The journey was to save my husband's life—how could I give it up?

KROGSTAD: But didn't it occur to you that you were tricking me?

NORA: I couldn't worry about that—I wasn't thinking about you at all. I couldn't bear the way you were so cold-blooded—the way you made difficulties although you knew how desperately ill my husband was.

KROGSTAD: Mrs. Helmer, you obviously don't realize what you've been guilty of; but let me tell you that the thing that I once did that ruined my reputation was nothing more—and nothing worse—than that.

NORA: You? Are you trying to tell me that you would have done a brave deed to save your wife's life?

KROGSTAD: The law is not concerned with motives.

NORA: Then it must be a very stupid law.

KROGSTAD: Stupid or not, it's the law that you'll be judged by if I produce this paper in court.

NORA: I simply don't believe that. Hasn't a daughter the right to protect her dying father from worry and anxiety? Hasn't a wife the right to save her husband's life? I don't know much about the law, but I'm quite certain that it must say somewhere that things like that are allowed. Don't you, a lawyer, know that? You must be a very stupid lawyer, Mr. Krogstad.

KROGSTAD: Possibly. But you'll admit that I do understand business—the sort of business that you and I have been engaged in? Very well, you do as you please. But I tell you this—if I'm to be flung out for the second time, you'll keep me company! (*He bows and goes out through the hall.*)

NORA (*after a moment's thought, with a toss of her head*): What nonsense! Trying to frighten me like that! I'm not as silly as all that. (*She starts to busy herself by tidying the children's clothes, but soon stops.*) But . . . No, it isn't possible . . . I did it for love!

CHILDREN (*at the door to the left*): Mamma, the strange man's just gone out of the front door.

NORA: Yes . . . yes, I know. Now, you're not to tell anyone about the strange man, do you hear? Not even Papa.

CHILDREN: No, Mamma. Will you come and play with us again now?

NORA: No—not just now.

CHILDREN: But, Mamma, you promised!

NORA: Yes, but now I can't. Run along. I'm busy—run along, there's good children. (*She pushes them gently into the other room and shuts the door after them. She sits on the sofa and, picking up her needlework, she does a stitch or two but soon stops.*) No! (*She throws down the work and, rising, goes to the hall door and calls.*) Helena—bring me the tree, please. (*Going to the table on the left, she opens the drawer, then pauses again.*) No! It's simply not possible!

MAID (*with the Christmas tree*): Where shall I put it, Madam?

NORA: Here, in the middle of the room.

MAID: Is there anything else you want?

NORA: No, thank you, I've got all I want.

The MAID, *having put the tree down, goes out.*

NORA (*busily decorating the tree*): A candle here . . . and flowers here. . . . That horrible man! It's all nonsense . . . nonsense, there's nothing in it! We shall have a lovely tree—I'll do all the things you like, Torvald, I'll sing and dance—

HELMER *comes in with a bundle of papers under his arm.*

NORA: Oh, are you back already?

HELMER: Yes. Has there been anyone here?

NORA: Here? No.

HELMER: That's odd; I saw Krogstad coming out of the gate.

NORA: Did you? Oh yes, that's right; Krogstad *was* here for a moment.

HELMER: Nora, I can see by your face that he's been here begging you to put in a good word for him.

NORA: Yes.

HELMER: And you were to make it look as if it was your own idea. You weren't to let me know that he'd been here. That was what he asked, wasn't it?

NORA: Yes, Torvald, but—

HELMER: Nora, Nora, would you lend yourself to that sort of thing? Talking to a man like that—making him promises? And, worst of all, telling me a lie!

NORA: A lie?

HELMER: Didn't you say that no one had been here? (*shaking a finger at her*) My little songbird mustn't ever do that again. A songbird must have a clear voice to sing with—no false notes. (*putting his arm around her*) That's true, isn't it? Yes, I knew it was. (*letting her go*) Now we won't say any more about it. (*sitting by the stove*) Ah, this is nice and comfortable! (*He glances through his papers.*)

NORA (*after working at the Christmas tree for a little*): Torvald?

HELMER: Yes?

NORA: I'm terribly looking forward to the day after tomorrow—the fancy-dress party at the Stenborgs.

HELMER: And I'm "terribly" curious to see what surprise you're planning for me.

NORA: Oh, it's so silly . . .

HELMER: What is?

NORA: I can't think of anything that'll do. Everything seems so stupid and point-less.

HELMER: So little Nora's realized that?

NORA (*behind his chair, with her arms on the chair-back*): Are you very busy, Torvald?

HELMER: Well . . .

NORA: What are all those papers?

HELMER: Bank business.

NORA: Already?

HELMER: I've asked the retiring Manager to give me full authority to make some neces-sary changes in the staff, and the working arrangements—that'll take me all Christ-mas week. I want to have everything ready by New Year's Day.

NORA: So that was why poor Krogstad—

HELMER: Hm!

NORA (*still leaning over the chair-back, and gently stroking his hair*): If you hadn't been so busy, Torvald, I'd have asked you a terribly great favor. . . .

HELMER: Well, what is it? Tell me.

NORA: No one has such good taste as you have, and I do so want to look nice at the fancy-dress party. Torvald, couldn't you take me in hand and decide what I'm to go as—what my costume's to be?

HELMER: Aha! So my little obstinate one's out of her depth, and wants someone to res-cue her?

NORA: Yes, Torvald, I can't do anything without you to help me.

HELMER: Well, well . . . I'll think about it. We'll find something.

NORA: Oh, that *is* nice of you! (*She goes to the Christmas tree again. Pause.*) How pretty these red flowers look. . . . Tell me about this Krogstad—was it really so bad, what he did?

HELMER: He forged a signature. Have you any idea what that means?

NORA: Mightn't he have done it from dire necessity?

HELMER: Possibly—or, like so many others, from sheer foolhardiness. Oh, I'm not so hard-hearted that I'd condemn a man outright for just a single slip.

NORA: No, you wouldn't, would you, Torvald?

HELMER: Many a man can redeem his character if he freely confesses his guilt and takes his punishment.

NORA: Punishment . . . ?

HELMER: But Krogstad did nothing of the sort—he tried to wriggle out of it with tricks and subterfuges. That's what has corrupted him.

NORA: Do you think that would . . . ?

HELMER: Just think how a guilty man like that must have to lie and cheat and play the hypocrite with everyone. How he must wear a mask even with those nearest and dearest to him—yes, even with his own wife and children. Yes, even with his children—that's the most dreadful thing, Nora.

NORA: Why?

HELMER: Because an atmosphere of lies like that infects and poisons the whole life of a home. In a house like that, every breath that the children take is filled with the germs of evil.

NORA (*closer behind him*): Are you certain of that?

HELMER: Oh, my dear, as a lawyer I've seen it so often; nearly all young men who go to the bad have had lying mothers.

NORA: Why only mothers?

HELMER: It's generally the fault of the mother, though of course a father can have the same effect—as every lawyer very well knows. And certainly for years this fellow Krogstad has been going home and poisoning his own children with lies and deceit. That's why I call him a moral outcast. (*holding out his hands to her*) So my darling little Nora must promise me not to plead his cause. Let's shake hands on that. Now then, what's this? Give me your hand. . . . That's better; now it's a bargain. I tell you, it'd be quite impossible for me to work with him; when I'm near people like that, I actually feel physically ill.

NORA (*withdrawing her hand and going over to the far side of the Christmas tree*): How hot it is in here! And I have so much to see to.

HELMER (*rising and collecting his papers*): Yes, and I must try to look through a few of these before dinner. And I'll think about your fancy-dress, too. And perhaps I'll have something in gold paper to hang on the Christmas tree. (*taking her head in his hands*) My darling little songbird! (*He goes to his room, shutting the door behind him.*)

NORA (*in a hushed voice, after a moment*): Oh no! It can't be true . . . . no, it's not possible. It *can't* be possible!

NURSE (*at the door on the left*): The children want to come in to Mamma—they're asking so prettily.

NORA: No! No! Don't let them come near me! Keep them with you, Nanny.

NURSE: Yes Ma'am. (*She shuts the door.*)

NORA (*white with fear*): Corrupt my little children—poison my home? (*She pauses, then throws up her head.*) That's not true! It could never, never be true.

ACT TWO

The same room. In the corner by the piano stands the Christmas tree; it is stripped and dishevelled, with the stumps of burnt-out candles. NORA'S *outdoor clothes are on the sofa.*
NORA, alone in the room, walks about restlessly. Eventually she stops by the sofa and picks up her cloak.

NORA (*letting the cloak fall again*): Someone's coming! (*She goes to the door to listen.*) No—there's no one there. Of course no one would come today—not on Christmas Day. Nor tomorrow either. But perhaps . . . (*She opens the door and looks out.*) No, there's nothing in the letter-box—it's quite empty. (*coming back into the room*) What nonsense—he can't really have meant it. A thing like that *couldn't* happen. It isn't possible—I have three little children!

The NURSE *comes in from the room on the left, with a huge cardboard box.*

NURSE: I've found the box with the fancy-dress at last.
NORA: Thank you; put it on the table.
NURSE (*doing so*): But it's in a terrible state.
NORA: I should like to tear it all to pieces.
NURSE: Heaven forbid! It can soon be put right—it only needs a little patience.
NORA: Yes, I'll go and get Mrs. Linde to help me.
NURSE: You're never going out again—in this awful weather? You'll catch your death of cold, Miss Nora, Ma'am!
NORA: Well, there are worse things than that. How are the children?
NURSE: The poor little mites are playing with their presents, but—
NORA: Do they ask for me much?
NURSE: You see, they're so used to having their Mamma with them.
NORA: But, Nanny, I *can't* be with them like I used to.
NURSE: Oh well, young children'll get used to anything.
NORA: Do you think so? Do you think they'd forget their Mamma if she went away altogether?
NURSE: Went away altogether? But bless my soul . . . !
NORA: Tell me, Nanny . . . I've often wondered, how did you ever have the heart to hand over your child to strangers?
NURSE: But I had to, so that I could come and be Nanny to my little Nora.
NORA: Yes, but how could you *want* to?
NURSE: When I had the chance of such a good place? Any poor girl who'd got into trouble would be glad to. And that blackguard of a man never did a thing for me.
NORA: I suppose your daughter's quite forgotten you?
NURSE: No, indeed she hasn't. She wrote to me when she was confirmed, and again when she got married.
NORA (*putting her arms round her*): Dear old Nanny, you were a wonderful mother to me when I was little.
NURSE: Poor little Nora—she hadn't any other mother but me.
NORA: And if *my* babies hadn't any other mother, I know you'd . . . Oh, I'm talking nonsense. (*opening the box*) Go to them now; I must just—You'll see how fine I shall look tomorrow.

NURSE: I'm sure there won't be anyone in all the party as fine as you, Miss Nora, Ma'am. (*She goes out to the room on the left.*)

NORA (*starting to unpack the box, but soon pushing it away*): Oh, if only I dared go out! If I could be sure that no one would come—that nothing would happen here in the meantime. . . . Don't be so silly—no one will come. I just mustn't think about it. I'll brush the muff. Pretty, pretty gloves! Don't think about it—don't think! One . . . two . . . three . . . four . . . five . . . six—(*She screams.*) Ah, they're coming!

She starts for the door, but stands irresolute. MRS. LINDE *comes in from the hall, where she has left her street clothes.*

NORA: Oh, it's you, Kristina! There isn't anyone else out there? Oh, it was good of you to come!

MRS. LINDE: They told me you'd been over to ask for me.

NORA: Yes, I was just passing. Actually, there's something you could help me with. Come and sit on the sofa. Look, the people upstairs, the Stenborgs, are having a fancy-dress party tomorrow night, and Torvald wants me to go as a Neopolitan fisher-girl and dance the tarantella that I learned in Capri.

MRS. LINDE: I see, you're going to give a real performance?

NORA: Yes, Torvald says I ought to. Look, here's the costume—Torvald had it made for me when we were out there, but it's so torn now—I really don't know—

MRS. LINDE: Oh, we can easily put that right—it's just that some of the trimming's come undone in places. Have you got a needle and cotton? There, that's all we want.

NORA: Oh, this *is* kind of you.

MRS. LINDE (*as she sews*): So tomorrow you'll be all dressed up? I tell you what, Nora, I'll drop in for a moment and see you in all your finery. But I'm quite forgetting to thank you for a lovely evening yesterday.

NORA (*getting up and crossing the room*): Oh, yesterday . . . I didn't think it was as nice as usual. I wish you'd come up to town earlier, Kristina. Yes, Torvald certainly knows how to make a house attractive and comfortable.

MRS. LINDE: And so do you, if you ask *me,* or you wouldn't be your father's daughter. But tell me, is Dr. Rank always as depressed as he was last night?

NORA: No, it was worse than usual last night. But he's really very ill, poor man, he has consumption of the spine. The fact is, his father was a horrible man who had mistresses and that sort of thing, so, you see, the son's been delicate all his life.

MRS. LINDE (*putting down her sewing*): But, dearest Nora, how do you come to know about things like that?

NORA (*walking about*): Pooh—when you've had three children, you get visits from— from women with a certain amount of medical knowledge—and they gossip about these things.

MRS. LINDE (*after a short silence—sewing again*): Does Dr. Rank come here every day?

NORA: Oh yes, he and Torvald have been friends all their lives, and he's a great friend of mine too. Why, Dr. Rank's almost one of the family.

MRS. LINDE: But tell me, is he quite sincere? I mean doesn't he rather like saying things to please people?

NORA: Not in the least. Whatever makes you think that?

MRS. LINDE: Well, when you introduced us yesterday, he said he'd often heard my name in this house, but I noticed later that your husband had no idea who I was. So how could Dr. Rank . . . ?

NORA: Yes, that's quite right, Kristina. You see, Torvald's so incredibly fond of me that he wants to keep me all to himself, as he says. In the early days he used to get quite jealous if I even mentioned people I'd liked back at home, so of course I gave it up. But I often talk to Dr. Rank, because, you see, he likes to hear about them.

MRS. LINDE: Look, Nora, in lots of things you're still a child. I'm older than you in many ways and I've had a little more experience. There's something I'd like to say to you: you ought to stop all this with Dr. Rank.

NORA: What ought I to stop?

MRS. LINDE: Well . . . two things, I think. Yesterday you were talking about a rich admirer who was going to bring you money—

NORA: Yes, but he doesn't exist—unfortunately. But what about it?

MRS. LINDE: Is Dr. Rank rich?

NORA: Oh yes.

MRS. LINDE: And has no one to provide for?

NORA: No one; but—

MRS. LINDE: And he comes to the house every day?

NORA: Yes, I just said so.

MRS. LINDE: How can a man of his breeding be so tactless?

NORA: I simply don't know what you mean.

MRS. LINDE: Don't pretend, Nora. Do you think I don't know whom you borrowed that twelve hundred dollars from?

NORA: Have you gone completely mad? How could you think a thing like that? From a friend who comes here every single day? That would have been an absolutely impossible situation.

MRS. LINDE: It really wasn't him?

NORA: No, I promise you. Why, it would never have entered my head for a moment. Besides, in those days he hadn't the money to lend—he came into it later.

MRS. LINDE: Well, Nora dear, I think that was lucky for you.

NORA: No, it would never have entered my head to ask Dr. Rank. Though I'm quite sure that if I *were* to ask him . . .

MRS. LINDE: But of course you wouldn't.

NORA: Of course not. I can't imagine that there'd ever be any need. But I'm quite sure that if I told Dr. Rank—

MRS. LINDE: Behind your husband's back?

NORA: I must get clear of this other thing—that's behind his back too. I must get clear of that.

MRS. LINDE: Yes, that's what I was saying yesterday, but—

NORA (*pacing up and down*): A man can straighten out these things so much better than a woman . . .

MRS. LINDE: Her husband, yes.

NORA: Nonsense. (*coming to a halt*) When you've paid off everything you owe, you do get your bond back, don't you?

MRS. LINDE: Of course.

NORA: And you can tear it into little pieces and burn it—the horrid filthy thing?

MRS. LINDE (*giving her a penetrating look, she puts down her sewing and rises slowly*): Nora, you're hiding something from me.

NORA: Is it as obvious as all that?

MRS. LINDE: Something's happened to you since yesterday morning. Nora, what is it?

NORA (*going to her*): Kristina—(*listening*) Sh! Here's Torvald coming back. Look, go in and sit with the children for a bit—Torvald can't bear to see dressmaking. Let Nanny help you.

MRS. LINDE (*picking up a pile of things*): All right then; but I'm not going away till we've talked the whole thing over.

She goes out to the left as HELMER *comes in from the hall.*

NORA (*going to him*): Oh, Torvald dear, I've been so longing for you to come back.

HELMER: Was that the dressmaker?

NORA: No, it was Kristina—she's helping me to mend my costume. You know, I'm going to look so nice. . . .

HELMER: Now wasn't that a good idea of mine?

NORA: Splendid. But wasn't it nice of me to do as you said?

HELMER (*lifting her chin*): Nice? To do what your husband says? All right, little scatter-brain, I know you didn't mean it like that. But don't let me interrupt you—I know you'll be wanting to try it on.

NORA: I suppose you've got work to do?

HELMER: Yes (*showing her a bundle of papers*); look, I've been down to the Bank. (*He starts to go to his study.*)

NORA: Torvald . . .

HELMER (*stopping*): Yes?

NORA: If your little squirrel were to ask you very prettily for something . . .

HELMER: Well?

NORA: Would you do it?

HELMER: Well, naturally I should have to know what it is, first.

NORA: Your squirrel will scamper about and do all her tricks, if you'll be nice and do what she asks.

HELMER: Out with it, then.

NORA: Your skylark'll sing all over the house—up and down the scale . . .

HELMER: Oh well, my skylark does that anyhow!

NORA: I'll be a fairy and dance on a moonbeam for you, Torvald.

HELMER: Nora, you surely don't mean that matter you mentioned this morning?

NORA (*nearer*): Yes, Torvald, I really do beg you—

HELMER: I'm surprised at your bringing that up again.

NORA: Oh, but you must do as I ask—you must let Krogstad keep his place at the Bank.

HELMER: My dear Nora, it's his place that I'm giving to Mrs. Linde.

NORA: Yes, that's terribly nice of you. But you could dismiss some other clerk instead of Krogstad.

HELMER: Now, you're just being extremely obstinate. Because you're irresponsible enough to go and promise to put in a word for him, you expect me to—

NORA: No, it isn't that, Torvald—it's for your own sake. The man writes for the most scurrilous newspapers—you told me so yourself—there's no knowing what harm he could do you. I'm simply frightened to death of him. . . .

HELMER: Ah, now I understand; you remember what happened before, and that frightens you.

NORA: What do you mean?

HELMER: You're obviously thinking of your father.

NORA: Yes—yes, that's it. Just remember the wicked things they put in the papers about Papa—how cruelly they slandered him. I believe they'd have had him dismissed if the Ministry hadn't sent you to look into it, and if you hadn't been so kind and helpful to him.

HELMER: Dear little Nora, there's a considerable difference between your father and me. Your father's reputation as an official was not above suspicion—mine is, and I hope it will continue to be as long as I hold this position.

NORA: But you never know what harm people can do. We could live so happily and peacefully now, you and I and the children, Torvald, without a care in the world in our comfortable home. That's why I do implore you—

HELMER: But it's precisely by pleading for him that you make it impossible for me to keep him. They know already at the Bank that I mean to dismiss Krogstad; suppose it were to get about that the new Manager had let himself be influenced by his wife. . . .

NORA: Well, would that matter?

HELMER: No, of course not! So long as an obstinate little woman got her own way! So I'm to make a laughingstock of myself before the whole staff—with everybody saying that I can be swayed by all sorts of outside influences? I should soon have to face the consequences, I can tell you. Besides, there's one thing which makes it quite impossible for Krogstad to stay at the Bank so long as I'm Manager.

NORA: What?

HELMER: Perhaps at a pinch I might have overlooked his moral failings—

NORA: Yes, Torvald, couldn't you?

HELMER: And I hear that he's quite a good worker, too. But he was at school with me—it was one of those unfortunate friendships that one so often comes to regret later in life. I may as well tell you frankly that we were on Christian-name terms, and he's tactless enough to keep it up still—in front of everyone! In fact, he seems to think he has a *right* to be familiar with me, and out he comes with "Torvald this" and "Torvald that" all the time. I tell you, it's most unpleasant for me—he'll make my position in the Bank quite intolerable.

NORA: You surely can't mean that, Torvald!

HELMER: Oh? Why not?

NORA: Well—that's such a petty reason.

HELMER: What do you mean? Petty? Do you think I'm petty?

NORA: No, Torvald dear—far from it; that's just why—

HELMER: Never mind! You said my motives were petty, so I must be petty too. Petty! Very well, we'll settle this matter once and for all. (*He goes to the hall door and calls.*) Helena!

NORA: What are you going to do?

HELMER (*searching among his papers*): Settle things.

The MAID *comes in.*

Here, take this letter downstairs at once, find a messenger, and get him to deliver it. Immediately, mind. The address is on it. Wait—here's the money.

MAID: Yes, sir. (*She goes with the letter.*)

HELMER (*collecting his papers*): There, little Miss Stubborn!

NORA (*breathless*): Torvald . . . what was in that letter?

HELMER: Krogstad's notice.

NORA: Call it back, Torvald—there's still time. Oh Torvald, call it back, for my sake— for your own sake—for the children's sake. Listen, Torvald, you don't know what that letter can do to us all.

HELMER: It's too late.

NORA: Yes . . . it's too late.

HELMER: My dear Nora, I can forgive your anxiety—though actually it's rather insulting to me. Oh yes, it is. Isn't it insulting to believe that I could be afraid of some wretched scribbler's revenge? Still, it's a very touching proof of your love for me, so I forgive you. (*He takes her in his arms.*) Now, my own darling Nora, that's all settled. Whatever happens, when it comes to the point you can be quite sure that I shall have the necessary courage and strength. You'll see that I'm man enough to take it all on myself.

NORA (*horror-struck*): What do you mean?

HELMER: Exactly what I say.

NORA (*recovering*): You shall never never have to do that.

HELMER: Very well, Nora, then we shall share it as man and wife; that's what we'll do. (*caressing her*) Are you happy now? There—there—there—don't look like a little frightened dove—the whole thing's just sheer imagination. Now you must rehearse your tarantella—with the tambourine. I'll go and sit in the inner room and shut the doors, so you can make all the noise you like—I shan't hear a thing. (*turning in the doorway*) And when Dr. Rank comes, tell him where I am. (*Taking his papers, he gives her a nod and goes into his room, shutting the door behind him.*)

NORA (*half crazy with fear, she stands as if rooted to the spot and whispers*): He'd really do it—he'd do it! He'd do it in spite of everything. No—never in the world! Anything rather than that! There must be some way out—some help.

There is a ring at the door.

Dr. Rank! Yes, anything rather than that—anything—whatever it is.

Passing her hands over her face, she pulls herself together and goes and opens the hall door. DR. RANK *is standing there hanging up his fur coat. During the following scene it begins to grow dark.*

NORA: Good afternoon, Dr. Rank—I recognized your ring. But you mustn't go in to Torvald now, I think he's got some work to finish.

RANK: What about you?

NORA (*shutting the door after him as he comes into the room*): Oh, I always have time for you—you know that.

RANK: Thank you. I shall take advantage of that for as long as I'm able.

NORA: What do you mean by that? As long as you're able?

RANK: Yes . . . does that alarm you?

NORA: It seemed such an odd way to put it. Is anything going to happen?

RANK: Yes . . . something that I've been expecting for a long time—though I never really thought it'd come quite so soon.

NORA (*clutching his arm*): What have you just learned? Dr. Rank, you must tell me!

RANK (*sitting by the stove*): The sands are running out for me. . . . There's nothing to be done about it.

NORA (*with a sigh of relief*): Then it's *you* . . . !

RANK: Who else? There's no point in deceiving myself—I'm the most wretched of all my patients, Mrs. Helmer. These last few days I've been holding an audit of my internal economy. Bankrupt! In less than a month, perhaps, I shall lie rotting in the churchyard.

NORA: Oh no—that's a horrible thing to say.

RANK: The thing itself is damnably horrible. But worst of all is the horror that must be gone through first. There's still one more test to make, and when I've finished *that* I shall know pretty well when the final disintegration will begin. But there's something I want to say to you; Helmer's too sensitive to be able to face anything ugly—I won't have him in my sick-room.

NORA: But, Dr. Rank—

RANK: I won't have him there—not on any account. I shall lock the door against him.

As soon as I'm quite certain that the worst has come, I shall send you my card with a black cross on it and then you'll know that my disgusting end has begun.

NORA: No, you're really being absurd today—and just when I so wanted you to be in a particularly good mood.

RANK: What, with death just round the corner? And when it's to pay for someone else's sins! Where's the justice in that? Yet in one way or another there isn't a single family where some such inexorable retribution isn't being exacted.

NORA (*stopping her ears*): Nonsense! Cheer up—cheer up!

RANK: Yes, indeed, the whole thing's nothing but a joke! My poor innocent spine must pay for my father's amusements as a gay young subaltern.

NORA (*by the table on the left*): He was too fond of asparagus and *foie gras*—isn't that it?

RANK: Yes, and truffles.

NORA: Truffles, yes. And oysters, too, I suppose?

RANK: Oysters? Oh yes, certainly oysters.

NORA: And then all that port and champagne. What a shame that all those nice things should attack the bones.

RANK: Especially when the unfortunate bones that they attack never had the least enjoyment out of them.

NORA: Yes, that's the saddest part of all.

RANK (*with a searching look at her*): Hm! . . .

NORA (*after a moment*): Why did you smile?

RANK: No, it's you who were laughing.

NORA: No, you smiled, Dr. Rank.

RANK (*getting up*): You're more of a rascal than I thought.

NORA: I'm in a ridiculous mood today.

RANK: So it seems.

NORA (*putting both hands on his shoulders*): Dear, dear Dr. Rank, you mustn't die and leave Torvald and me.

RANK: Oh, you'd soon get over it—those who go away are quickly forgotten.

NORA (*looking at him anxiously*): Do you believe that?

RANK: People make new friends, and then . . .

NORA: Who makes new friends?

RANK: You and Torvald will, when I'm gone. It looks to me as if *you're* starting already. What was that Mrs. Linde doing here last night?

NORA: Oh, surely you're not jealous of poor Kristina.

RANK: Yes, I am. She'll take my place in this house. After I've gone, I expect that woman will—

NORA: Sh! Not so loud—she's in there!

RANK: There you are! She's here again today.

NORA: Only to mend my dress. Good gracious, you *are* being absurd. (*sitting on the sofa*) Now be nice, Dr. Rank, and tomorrow you'll see how beautifully I shall dance, and you can tell yourself that it's all for you—and for Torvald too, of course. (*taking various things out of the box*) Come and sit here, Dr. Rank, and I'll show you something.

RANK: What is it?

NORA: Look here. Look.

RANK: Silk stockings.

NORA: Flesh colored—aren't they lovely? The light's bad in here now, but tomorrow . . . No, no, no, you must only look at the feet. Oh well, you may see the rest, too.

RANK: Hm . . .

NORA: Why are you looking so critical? Don't you think they'll fit?

RANK: I can't possibly give you an opinion on that.

NORA (*looking at him for a moment*): You ought to be ashamed of yourself! (*She flips him lightly on the cheek with the stockings.*) Take that! (*She rolls them up again.*)

RANK: What other pretty things have you to show me?

NORA: You shan't see another thing—you've been very naughty. (*She hums a little as she rummages among her things.*)

RANK (*after a short pause*): When I sit here like this talking to you so intimately, I can't imagine—no, I really can't—what would have become of me if I hadn't had this house to come to.

NORA (*smiling*): I believe you really do feel at home with us.

RANK (*more quietly, looking straight in front of him*): And to have to leave it all!

NORA: Nonsense, you're not going to leave us.

RANK (*as before*): Not to be able to leave behind even the smallest token of gratitude— hardly even a passing regret. Nothing but an empty place that the next person to come along will fill just as well.

NORA: Suppose I were to ask you for a . . . No . . .

RANK: For a what?

NORA: For a great proof of your friendship.

RANK: Yes.

NORA: No, I mean a terribly great favor.

RANK: I should be very happy if—just for once—you'd give me the chance.

NORA: Ah, but you don't know what it is.

RANK: Tell me, then.

NORA: No, Dr. Rank, I can't. It's something really enormous—not just advice or help, but a really great favor.

RANK: The greater the better. I can't think what it can be, so tell me. Don't you trust me?

NORA: There's no one else I'd trust more than you. I know you're my best, most faith- ful friend, so I'll tell you. . . . Well, Dr. Rank—it's something you must help me to stave off. You know how much—how incredibly deeply—Torvald loves me. He wouldn't hesitate for a moment to give his life for me.

RANK (*leaning nearer to her*): Nora . . . Do you think he's the only one?

NORA (*with a slight start*): The only one . . . ?

RANK: Who'd gladly give his life for you?

NORA (*sadly*): Ah . . .

RANK: I promised myself that I'd tell you before I went away, and I could never have a better opportunity. Well, Nora, now you know. And you know, too, that you can trust me—more than anyone else.

NORA (*calmly and evenly; rising*): I must go.

RANK (*making way for her, but still sitting*): Nora . . .

NORA (*in the hall doorway*): Helena, bring the lamp. (*going to the stove*) Oh, dear Dr. Rank, that was really horrid of you.

RANK (*rising*): To have loved you as deeply as anyone else—was that horrid?

NORA: No . . . but to go and tell me so. There was really no need to do that.

RANK: What do you mean? Did you know?

The MAID *brings in the lamp, puts it on the table, and goes again.*

RANK: Nora—Mrs. Helmer—I ask you: did you know?

NORA: Oh, how can I say if I knew or didn't know? I've really no idea. How could you be so clumsy, Dr. Rank? When everything was going so well. . . .

RANK: Well, at any rate you know that I'm at your service—body and soul. So won't you say what it is?

NORA (*looking at him*): After what's happened?

RANK: Please—please tell me what it is.

NORA: I can never tell you now.

RANK: Please. You mustn't punish me like this. If you'll let me, I promise to do anything for you that a man can.

NORA: There's nothing you can do for me now. Besides, I certainly don't need any help—it was all my imagination, really it was. Honestly. (*smiling*) You're a fine one, Dr. Rank! Aren't you ashamed of yourself, now that the lamp's come in?

RANK: No . . . not really. But perhaps I ought to go—for good.

NORA: No. You certainly mustn't do that—of course you must come here just as usual. You know Torvald couldn't get on without you.

RANK: But what about you?

NORA: Oh, I'm always tremendously glad to see you.

RANK: That's just what misled me. You're a mystery to me. . . . I've sometimes thought you'd as soon be with me as with Helmer.

NORA: You see, there are some people that one loves, and others that perhaps one would rather be with.

RANK: Yes, there's something in that.

NORA: When I lived at home, naturally I loved Papa best, but I always found it terribly amusing to slip into the servants' hall, because they always talked about such interesting things, and they never lectured me at all.

RANK: Ah, and now I've taken their place?

NORA (*jumping up and going over to him*): Oh, dear kind Dr. Rank, that isn't what I meant at all. But I'm sure you can see that being with Torvald is very like being with Papa.

The MAID *comes in from the hall.*

MAID: Excuse me, Madam. . . . (*She whispers to* NORA *as she hands her a card.*)

NORA (*glancing at the card*): Oh! (*She puts it in her pocket.*)

RANK: Is there anything wrong?

NORA: No, no, not in the least. It's only something . . . it's my new dress.

RANK: But. . . ? Surely your dress is out there?

NORA: Ah, that one, yes. But this is another one that I've ordered—I don't want Torvald to know. . . .

RANK: Aha! So *that's* your great secret?

NORA: Yes, of course. Go in to Torvald—he's in the inner room—keep him there till . . .

RANK: Don't worry, I shan't let him escape. (*He goes into* HELMER'S *room.*)

NORA (*to the* MAID): Is he waiting in the kitchen?

MAID: Yes, Madam, he came up the back stairs.

NORA: But didn't you tell him there was someone here?

MAID: Yes, but it wasn't any good.

NORA: He wouldn't go away?

MAID: No, he won't go till he's seen you, Madam.

NORA: Oh, all right, let him come in. Quietly, though. Helena, you mustn't mention this to anyone—it's a surprise for my husband.

MAID: Yes, I understand. (*She goes.*)

NORA: Oh, this is dreadful—it's going to happen after all. No, no, no, it *can't*—I won't let it!

She goes and pushes the bolt home on HELMER'S *door. The* MAID *opens the hall door to let* KROGSTAD *in, and shuts it after him. He is wearing travelling clothes, high boots, and a fur cap.*

NORA (*going to him*): Keep your voice down—my husband's at home.

KROGSTAD: What of it?

NORA: What do you want?

KROGSTAD: To find out something.

NORA: Be quick, then; what is it?

KROGSTAD: You know that I've been dismissed?

NORA: I couldn't stop it, Mr. Krogstad. I did absolutely everything I could for you, but it was no good.

KROGSTAD: Your husband can't love you very much, can he? He knows that I can expose you, and yet he dares to—

NORA: You surely don't imagine that he knows about it?

KROGSTAD: Well, no—I didn't really think so; it wouldn't be at all like our worthy Torvald Helmer to have so much courage.

NORA: Kindly show some respect for my husband, Mr. Krogstad.

KROGSTAD: But of course—all the respect he deserves. As you seem so anxious to keep things secret, I presume that you have a rather clearer idea than you had yesterday of what it is that you've actually done.

NORA: Clearer than you could ever make it.

KROGSTAD: Oh yes, I'm such a stupid lawyer!

NORA: What do you want?

KROGSTAD: Only to see how things stood with you, Mrs. Helmer. I've been thinking about you all day. Even a mere cashier, a scribbler, a—well, a man like me, has a certain amount of what is called "feeling," you know.

NORA: Then show it. Think of my little children.

KROGSTAD: Have you or your husband ever thought of mine? But never mind that; I only wanted to tell you that you needn't take all this too seriously—I shan't make any accusation for the present.

NORA: No, of course not—I didn't think you would.

KROGSTAD: It can all be settled quite amicably. Nothing need come out—it can just be arranged between us three.

NORA: My husband must never know anything about it.

KROGSTAD: How can you stop it? Unless, perhaps, you can pay off the rest of the debt.

NORA: Well, not at the moment.

KROGSTAD: Then perhaps you've found some way to raise the money within the next day or two.

NORA: No way that I'd use.

KROGSTAD: Well, it wouldn't have helped you, anyhow. Even if you were to stand there with a mint of money in your hand, you wouldn't get your bond back from me.

NORA: What are you going to do with it? Tell me.

KROGSTAD: Just keep it—have it in my possession. No one who isn't concerned need know anything about it. So if you have any desperate plan—

NORA: I have.

KROGSTAD: —if you've thought of running away from your home—

NORA: I have.

KROGSTAD: —or of anything worse—

NORA: How did you know?

KROGSTAD: —you'd better give up the idea.

NORA: How did you know that I'd thought of *that*?

KROGSTAD: Most of us think of that at first. I thought of it, too—only I hadn't the courage.

NORA (*dully*): Nor had I.

KROGSTAD (*relieved*): No, you haven't the courage either, have you?

NORA: No, I haven't—I haven't.

KROGSTAD: Besides, it would have been a very stupid thing to do. You've only got just one domestic storm to go through, then . . . I have a letter to your husband in my pocket.

NORA: Telling him everything?

KROGSTAD: In the gentlest possible way.

NORA (*quickly*): He must never see it. Tear it up. I'll get the money somehow.

KROGSTAD: Excuse me, Mrs. Helmer, but I believe I told you just now—

NORA: Oh, I don't mean the money I owe you. Tell me how much you're asking from my husband, and I'll get it.

KROGSTAD: I'm not asking your husband for any money.

NORA: What are you asking, then?

KROGSTAD: I'll tell you. I want to get back my standing in the world, Mrs. Helmer; I want to get on, and that's where your husband's going to help me. For the last eighteen months I haven't touched anything dishonest, and all that time I've been struggling against the most difficult conditions. I was prepared to work my way up step by step. Now I'm being thrown down again, and it's not going to be good enough for me to be taken back as a favor. I want to get on, I tell you; I want to get back into the Bank—and in a better job. Your husband must make one for me.

NORA: He'll never do that.

KROGSTAD: I know him—he'll do it! He daren't so much as murmur. And once I'm in there with him, then you'll see! Inside a year, I shall be the Manager's right-hand man. It'll be Nils Krogstad who runs the Bank, not Torvald Helmer.

NORA: That'll never happen as long as you live.

KROGSTAD: Do you mean that you'll—

NORA: Yes, I have the courage now.

KROGSTAD: Oh, you can't frighten me! A fine pampered lady like you—

NORA: You'll see—you'll see!

KROGSTAD: Under the ice, perhaps? Down into the cold black water? And then in the spring you'd float up to the top, ugly, hairless, unrecognizable—

NORA: You can't frighten me.

KROGSTAD: Nor can you frighten me. People don't do such things, Mrs. Helmer. And what good would it be, anyhow? I'd still have the letter in my pocket!

NORA: Still? Even if I weren't . . .

KROGSTAD: You forget that *then* your reputation would be in my hands.

NORA *stands speechless, looking at him.*

KROGSTAD: Yes, now you've been warned, so don't do anything stupid. I shall expect to hear from Helmer as soon as he gets my letter. And remember, it's your husband who's forced me to do this sort of thing again. I shall never forgive him for that. Good-bye, Mrs. Helmer. (*He goes out into the hall.*)

NORA (*going to the hall door and opening it a little to listen*): He's going! He hasn't left the letter. No, no, it couldn't happen! (*She opens the door inch by inch.*) Listen—he's standing just outside—he's not going down the stairs. . . . Has he changed his mind? Is he . . . ?

A letter falls into the box. KROGSTAD'S *footsteps are heard fading away down the staircase.*

NORA (*With a stifled cry, runs over to the sofa table. A short pause.*): It's in the letter-box! (*creeping stealthily back to the hall door*) Yes, it's there. Oh, Torvald . . . Torvald—there's no hope for us now!

MRS. LINDE (*coming in from the left with the dress*): There—I don't think there's anything else that wants mending. Let's try it on.

NORA (*in a hoarse whisper*): Kristina, come here.

MRS. LINDE (*throwing the dress on the sofa*): What's the matter? What's upset you so?

NORA: Come here. Do you see that letter? There, look—through the glass of the letter-box.

MRS. LINDE: I can see it—Well?

NORA: That letter's from Krogstad.

MRS. LINDE: Nora . . . it was Krogstad who lent you the money!

NORA: Yes. And now Torvald'll find out everything.

MRS. LINDE: But, Nora, believe me, that'll be best for both of you.

NORA: There's something that you don't know. I forged a signature.

MRS. LINDE: Good heavens . . . !

NORA: There's just one thing I want to say, Kristina, and you shall be my witness.

MRS. LINDE: Witness? But what am I to—

NORA: If I were to go mad—as I easily might—

MRS. LINDE: Nora!

NORA: Or if anything else were to happen to me, so that I shouldn't be here—

MRS. LINDE: Nora, Nora, you must be out of your senses!

NORA: And in case there was someone else who tried to take it all on himself—all the blame, you understand—

MRS. LINDE: Yes . . . but how can you think . . . ?

NORA: —then, Kristina, you must bear witness that it isn't true. I'm perfectly sane, and I know exactly what I'm doing now, and I tell you this: no one else knew anything about it—I did it all by myself. Remember that.

MRS. LINDE: Of course I will. But I don't understand.

NORA: How could you understand this? We're going to see—a miracle.

MRS. LINDE: A miracle?

NORA: Yes, a miracle. But it's so dreadful. Kristina, it *mustn't* happen—not for anything in the world.

MRS. LINDE: I'm going straight round to talk to Krogstad.

NORA: No, don't go to him, he might do you some harm.

MRS. LINDE: There was a time when he would gladly have done anything for me.

NORA: Krogstad?

MRS. LINDE: Where does he live?

NORA: How should I know? Wait—(*feeling in her pocket*)—here's his card. But the letter—the letter . . . !

HELMER (*from inside his room, knocking on the door*): Nora!

NORA (*with a frightened cry*): What is it? What do you want?

HELMER (*off*): All right, there's nothing to be frightened of; we're not coming in. You've locked the door—are you trying on your dress?

NORA: Yes, I'm trying it on. I look so nice in it, Helmer.

MRS. LINDE (*having read the card*): He lives only just round the corner.

NORA: Yes, but it's no good; there's no hope for us now—the letter's in the box.

MRS. LINDE: And your husband has the key!

NORA: He always keeps it.

MRS. LINDE: Krogstad must ask for his letter back—unopened. He must find some excuse.

NORA: But this is just the time when Torvald always—

MRS. LINDE: Put him off. I'll be back as soon as I can. Go in to him now. (*She hurries out through the hall.*)

NORA (*going to* HELMER'S *door, unlocking it, and peeping in*): Torvald.

HELMER (*from the inner room*): Well, am I allowed in my own room again? Come along, Rank, now we're going to see—(*at the door*) But what's all this?

NORA: What, Torvald dear?

HELMER: Rank led me to expect a great transformation scene.

RANK (*at the door*): I certainly thought so—I must have been wrong.

NORA: No one's allowed to admire me in all my finery till tomorrow.

HELMER: But, Nora dear, you look tired out—have you been rehearsing too much?

NORA: No, I haven't rehearsed at all.

HELMER: Oh, but you should have.

NORA: Yes, I know I should have, but I can't do anything unless you help me, Torvald. I've forgotten absolutely everything.

HELMER: Oh, we'll soon polish it up again.

NORA: Yes, do take me in hand, Torvald—promise you will. I'm so nervous—all those people . . . You must give up the whole evening to me; you mustn't do a scrap of business—not even pick up a pen! You'll do that, won't you, dear Torvald?

HELMER: I promise. This evening I'll be wholly and entirely at your service—you poor helpless little creature! Ah, but first, while I think of it, I must just—(*going toward the hall door*).

NORA: What do you want out there?

HELMER: I'm just seeing if the post's come.

NORA: No, no, Torvald—don't do that.

HELMER: Why not?

NORA: Please don't Torvald—there's nothing there.

HELMER: I'll just look. (*He starts to go.*)

NORA, *at the piano, plays the opening bars of the tarantella.*

HELMER (*stopping in the doorway*): Aha!

NORA: I shan't be able to dance tomorrow if I don't go over it with you.

HELMER (*going to her*): Nora dear, are you really so worried about it?

NORA: Yes, terribly worried. Let me rehearse it now—there's still time before dinner. Sit down and play for me, Torvald dear; criticize me, and show me where I'm wrong, the way you always do.

HELMER: I'd like to, if that's what you want. (*He sits at the piano.*)

NORA *pulls a tambourine out of the box, then a long particolored shawl which she quickly drapes round herself. Then, with a bound, she takes up her position in the middle of the floor, and calls:*

NORA: Now play for me, and I'll dance!

HELMER *plays and* NORA *dances.* DR. RANK *stands behind* HELMER *at the piano and looks on.*

HELMER (*as he plays*): Slower—slower!

NORA: I can only do it this way.

HELMER: Not so violently, Nora!

NORA: This is how it should go.

HELMER (*stops playing*): No, no, that's all wrong.

NORA (*laughing and brandishing her tambourine*): There! Didn't I tell you?

RANK: Let me play for her.

HELMER (*rising*): Yes, do; then I can show her better.

RANK *sits at the piano and plays.* NORA *dances more and more wildly.* HELMER, *taking up a position by the stove, gives her frequent directions as she dances. She seems not to hear them, her hair comes down and falls over her shoulders, but she goes on dancing without taking any notice.* MRS. LINDE *comes in.*

MRS. LINDE (*stopping spellbound in the doorway*): Ah!

NORA (*as she dances*): Oh, this is fun, Kristina!

HELMER: But, Nora darling, you're dancing as if your life depended on it!

NORA: So it does.

HELMER: Stop, Rank. This is sheer madness—stop, I tell you!

RANK *stops playing, and* NORA *comes to an abrupt halt.*

HELMER (*going to her*): I'd never have believed it—you've forgotten everything I taught you.

NORA (*throwing the tambourine aside*): There! You see.

HELMER: Well, you'll certainly need a lot of coaching.

NORA: Yes, you see how much I need. You must coach me up to the last minute—promise me you will, Torvald?

HELMER: You can rely on me.

NORA: All today and all tomorrow, you mustn't think of anything else but me. You mustn't open any letters—you mustn't even open the letter-box.

HELMER: Ah, you're still afraid of that man.

NORA: Oh yes, that as well.

HELMER: Nora, I can see by your face that there's a letter from him already.

NORA: There may be—I don't know. But you mustn't read anything like that now; we won't let anything horrid come between us till this is all over.

RANK (*quietly to* HELMER): You'd better not upset her.

HELMER (*putting his arm round her*): My baby shall have her own way. But tomorrow night, after you've danced—

NORA: Then you'll be free.

MAID (*at the door on the right*): Dinner is served, Madam.

NORA: We'll have champagne, Helena.

MAID: Very good, Madam. (*She goes.*)

HELMER: Well, well—so we're having a banquet!

NORA: A champagne supper—lasting till dawn. (*calling*) And some macaroons, Helena—lots and lots, just for once.

HELMER (*taking her hands*): Now, now, now! You mustn't be so wild and excitable. Be my own little skylark again.

NORA: Oh yes, I will. But go into the dining-room now—and you too, Dr. Rank.

Kristina, you must help me put my hair straight.

RANK (*quietly as they go*): There isn't anything . . . ? I mean, she's not expecting . . . ?

HELMER: Oh no, my dear fellow. I've told you—she gets over-excited, like a child.

They go out to the right.

NORA: Well?

MRS. LINDE: He's gone out of town.

NORA: I saw it in your face.

MRS. LINDE: He'll be back tomorrow night; I left a note for him.

NORA: You should have let things alone—not tried to stop them. After all, it's a wonderful thing to be waiting for a miracle.

MRS. LINDE: What is it you're expecting?

NORA: You wouldn't understand. Go in and join the others—I'll come in a minute.

MRS. LINDE goes into the dining-room.

NORA (*standing for a moment as if to collect herself, then looking at her watch*): Seven hours till midnight. Then twenty-four hours till midnight tomorrow. Then the tarantella will be over. Twenty-four and seven . . . thirty-one hours to live.

HELMER (*at the door on the right*): But where's my little skylark?

NORA (*going to him with arms outstretched*): Here she is!

ACT THREE

The same scene. The table and chairs round it have been moved to the middle of the room; a lamp is alight on the table. The hall door is open and music for dancing can be heard from the flat above.

MRS. LINDE is sitting at the table, idly turning the pages of a book. She tries to read, but seems unable to concentrate. Once or twice she listens anxiously for the outer door.

MRS. LINDE (*looking at her watch*): Not here yet! There's not much more time—I do hope he hasn't—(*listening again*) Ah, here he is.

She goes out to the hall and carefully opens the front door. Soft footsteps are heard on the stairs. She whispers:

Come in—there's no one here.

KROGSTAD (*in the doorway*): I found a note from you at home. What's this about?

MRS. LINDE: I had to have a talk with you.

KROGSTAD: Oh? And did you have to have it in this house?

MRS. LINDE: I couldn't see you at the place where I'm staying—there's no separate entrance to my room. Come in, we're quite alone; the maid's asleep, and the Helmers are upstairs at the dance.

KROGSTAD (*coming into the room*): What? The Helmers at a dance tonight? Really?

MRS. LINDE: Yes. Why not?

KROGSTAD: True—why not?

MRS. LINDE: Well, Nils, let us have a talk.

KROGSTAD: Have you and I got anything more to talk about?

MRS. LINDE: A great deal.

KROGSTAD: I shouldn't have thought so.

MRS. LINDE: Well, you never really understood me.

KROGSTAD: Was there anything to understand—except what was so obvious to the whole world: a heartless woman throwing a man over when someone richer turns up?

MRS. LINDE: Do you really think I'm as heartless as all that? And do you think it was easy to break with you?

KROGSTAD: Wasn't it?

MRS. LINDE: Nils, did you really think that?

KROGSTAD: If it wasn't true, why did you write to me as you did at the time?

MRS. LINDE: What else could I do? I had to break with you, so it was up to me to kill any feeling that you might have had for me.

KROGSTAD (*clenching his hands*): So that was it? You did it—all of it—for the sake of the money?

MRS. LINDE: You mustn't forget that my mother was quite helpless, and that I had two small brothers. We couldn't wait for you, Nils—especially as you had no prospects in those days.

KROGSTAD: Even so, you had no right to throw me over for someone else.

MRS. LINDE: I've often asked myself if I had the right . . . I really don't know.

KROGSTAD (*softly*): When I lost you, it was just as if the very ground had given way under my feet. Look at me now—a shipwrecked man clinging to a spar.

MRS. LINDE: Help could be near.

KROGSTAD: It *was* near—until you came and got in the way.

MRS. LINDE: Without knowing it, Nils. I only found out today that it's *your* place that I'm to have at the Bank.

KROGSTAD: I'll believe you if you say so. But now that you do know, aren't you going to give it up?

MRS. LINDE: No. You see, that wouldn't benefit you in the least.

KROGSTAD: "Benefit—benefit!" *I* would have done it.

MRS. LINDE: I've learned to think before I act. Life and bitter necessity have taught me that.

KROGSTAD: Life has taught me not to believe in fine speeches.

MRS. LINDE: Then life has taught you something valuable. But you must believe in deeds?

KROGSTAD: What do you mean by that?

MRS. LINDE: You said you were like a shipwrecked man clinging to a spar.

KROGSTAD: I had good reason to say so.

MRS. LINDE: I'm like a shipwrecked woman clinging to a spar—no one to cry over, and no one to care for.

KROGSTAD: It was your own choice.

MRS. LINDE: There was no other choice at the time.

KROGSTAD: Well?

MRS. LINDE: Nils . . . suppose we two shipwrecked people could join forces?

KROGSTAD: What do you mean?

MRS. LINDE: Two on one spar would be better off than each of us alone.

KROGSTAD: Kristina!

MRS. LINDE: Why do you suppose I came to town?

KROGSTAD: Were you really thinking of me?

MRS. LINDE: I must work or life isn't bearable. All my life, as long as I can remember, I've worked—that's been my one great joy. But now that I'm alone in the world I feel completely lost and empty. There's no joy in working for oneself. Nils . . . let me have something—and someone—to work for.

KROGSTAD: I don't trust that. It's nothing but a woman's exaggerated sense of nobility prompting her to sacrifice herself.

MRS. LINDE: Have you ever noticed anything exaggerated in me?

KROGSTAD: Could you really do it? Tell me, do you know all about my past?

MRS. LINDE: Yes.

KROGSTAD: And do you know my reputation here?

MRS. LINDE: You suggested just now that with me you might have been a different man.

KROGSTAD: I'm certain of it.

MRS. LINDE: Couldn't that still happen?

KROGSTAD: Kristina—have you really thought about what you're saying? Yes, you have—I see it in your face. And you really have the courage?

MRS. LINDE: I need someone to be a mother to, and your children need a mother. You and I need each other. I have faith in you—the real you—Nils, with you I could dare anything.

KROGSTAD (*grasping her hands*): Thank you—thank you, Kristina. Now I shall be able to set myself right in the eyes of the world too. Oh, but I'm forgetting—

MRS. LINDE (*listening*): Sh! The tarantella! Go—quickly.

KROGSTAD: Why? What is it?

MRS. LINDE: Don't you hear the dancing up there? As soon as this is over, they'll be coming back.

KROGSTAD: Yes—I'll go. But all this will come to nothing . . . you see, you don't know what I've done against the Helmers.

MRS. LINDE: Yes, Nils, I know about it.

KROGSTAD: And you still have the courage . . . ?

MRS. LINDE: I know only too well how far despair can drive a man like you.

KROGSTAD: Oh, if only I could undo it!

MRS. LINDE: You can—your letter's still in the box.

KROGSTAD: Are you sure?

MRS. LINDE: Quite sure—but . . .

KROGSTAD (*with a searching look at her*): You want to save your friend at any price—is that it? Tell me frankly—is it?

MRS. LINDE: Nils, when you've sold yourself once for the sake of others, you don't do it a second time.

KROGSTAD: I shall ask for my letter back.

MRS. LINDE: No, no!

KROGSTAD: But of course. I'll wait here till Helmer comes down, and I'll tell him that he must give me my letter back—that it's only about my dismissal, and that he's not to read it.

MRS. LINDE: No, Nils, you mustn't ask for your letter back.

KROGSTAD: But surely that was the very reason why you asked me to come here?

MRS. LINDE: Yes—in my first moment of panic. But now, a whole day's gone by and I've witnessed things in this house that I could hardly believe. Helmer must know the whole story. This wretched secret must be brought into the open so that there's complete understanding between them. That'd be impossible while there's so much concealment and subterfuge.

KROGSTAD: Very well—if you'll take the risk. . . . But there's one thing I can do—and it shall be done at once—

MRS. LINDE (*listening*): Go—quickly! The dance is over—we can't stay here a moment longer.

KROGSTAD: I'll wait for you downstairs.

MRS. LINDE: Yes, do. You must see me home.

KROGSTAD: Kristina, this is the most marvellous thing that's ever happened to me.

He goes out by the front door. The door between the room and the hall remains open.

MRS. LINDE (*tidying the room a little, and putting her hat and cape ready*): What a difference—what a difference! Someone to work for—and live for. A home to look after—and oh, I'll make it so comfortable. Oh, if they'd only hurry up and come! (*listening*) Ah, here they are—I'll put my things on.

She picks up her hat and cape. HELMER's *and* NORA's *voices are heard outside. A key turns, and* HELMER *pulls* NORA *almost forcibly into the room. She is in Italian costume with a great black shawl round herself; he is in a black domino which opens to show his evening dress underneath.*

NORA (*still in the doorway, struggling with him*): No, no, I don't want to go in—I want to go back upstairs. It's far too early to leave.

HELMER: But, my darling Nora—

NORA: Oh, please, Torvald—I do beg you. . . . Just one more hour!

HELMER: Not a single minute, Nora dear—you know what we agreed. Now come along in, you'll catch cold out here.

In spite of her resistance he brings her gently into the room.

MRS. LINDE: Good evening.

NORA: Kristina!

HELMER: Why, Mrs. Linde—here so late?

MRS. LINDE: Yes, forgive me, but I did want to see Nora in her costume.

NORA: Have you been sitting here waiting for me?

MRS. LINDE: Yes, I'm afraid I didn't get here in time—you'd already gone upstairs— and I felt I really couldn't go away without seeing you.

HELMER (*taking* NORA's *shawl off*): Yes, just look at her! She's worth seeing, if you ask *me!* Isn't she lovely, Mrs. Linde?

MRS. LINDE: She certainly is.

HELMER: Remarkably lovely, isn't she? And that's what everybody at the dance thought, too. But this sweet little thing's dreadfully obstinate. What are we to do with her? You'd hardly believe it, but I practically had to use force to get her away.

NORA: You'll be very sorry you didn't let me stay, Torvald—even for just half an hour longer.

HELMER: Just listen to her, Mrs. Linde! She danced her tarantella; it was a huge success—and rightly so, even if it *was,* perhaps, a trifle too realistic—I mean, a little more so than was, strictly speaking, artistically necessary. . . . But never mind, it was a success—a huge success. Could I let her stay after that, and spoil the effect? No thank you; I put my arm round my lovely little Capri girl—I might almost say my *capricious* little Capri girl—we made a quick turn of the room, a bow all round, and then, as they say in the novels, the beautiful vision was gone! An exit should always be well-timed, Mrs. Linde; but that's something I simply cannot get Nora to see! Phew, it's warm in here. (*He throws his domino on a chair and opens the door to his room.*) Hullo, it's all dark! Oh yes, of course. . . . Excuse me—(*He goes in and lights the candles.*)

NORA (*in a rapid and breathless whisper*): Well?

MRS. LINDE (*softly*): I've had a talk with him.

NORA: Yes?

MRS. LINDE: Nora, you must tell your husband everything.

NORA (*dully*): I knew it.

MRS. LINDE: You've nothing to fear from Krogstad. But you *must* tell your husband.

NORA: I'll never tell him.

MRS. LINDE: Then the letter will.

NORA: Thank you, Kristina; now I know what I must do. . . . Sh!

HELMER (*coming in again*): Well, Mrs. Linde, have you been admiring her?

MRS. LINDE: Yes, indeed . . . and now I must say good night.

HELMER: What, already? Is this yours, this knitting?

MRS. LINDE (*taking it*): Oh yes, thank you—I nearly forgot it.

HELMER: So you knit?

MRS. LINDE: Oh yes.

HELMER: You know, it'd be much better if you did embroidery.

MRS. LINDE: Oh? Why?

HELMER: It's so much more graceful. I'll show you. You hold embroidery like this, in your left hand, and you work the needle with your right—in long easy sweeps. Isn't that so?

MRS. LINDE: Yes, I suppose so.

HELMER: But knitting's quite another matter—it can't help being ungraceful. Look here—arms held tightly in, needles going up and down—it has an almost Chinese effect. . . . That really was an excellent champagne they gave us tonight. . . .

MRS. LINDE: Well, good night. And Nora—don't be obstinate any longer.

HELMER: That's quite right, Mrs. Linde.

MRS. LINDE: Good night, Mr. Helmer.

HELMER (*seeing her to the door*): Good night—good night. I hope you get home safely. I'd be very glad to . . . but then you haven't far to go, have you? Good night— good night.

She goes. He shuts the door after her and comes back.

Well, I thought she'd never go—she's a terrible bore, that woman.

NORA: Aren't you tired out, Torvald?

HELMER: No, not in the least.

NORA: Not sleepy?

HELMER: Not a bit—in fact, I feel particularly lively. What about you? Yes, you do look tired out—why, you're half asleep.

NORA: Yes, I'm very tired—I could fall asleep here and now.

HELMER: There you are—there you are! You see how right I was not to let you stay any longer.

NORA: You're always right, Torvald, whatever you do.

HELMER (*kissing her on the forehead*): Now my little skylark's talking like a reasonable being. Did you notice how cheerful Rank was this evening?

NORA: Oh, was he? I didn't get a chance to talk to him.

HELMER: I hardly did; but I haven't seen him in such good spirits for a long time. (*He looks at* NORA *for a moment, then goes to her.*) Ah, it's wonderful to be back home again, all alone with you. . . . How fascinating you are, you lovely little thing.

NORA: Don't look at me like that, Torvald.

HELMER: Mayn't I look at my dearest treasure? At all the beauty that belongs to no one but me—that's all my very own?

NORA (*going round to the other side of the table*): You mustn't say things like that tonight.

HELMER (*following her*): I see you still have the tarantella in your blood—it makes you more enchanting than ever. Listen—the party's beginning to break up. (*softly*) Nora—soon the whole house'll be quiet . . .

NORA: Yes, I hope so.

HELMER: Yes, you do, don't you, my own darling Nora? I'll tell you something: when I'm out with you at a party, do you know why I hardly talk to you—don't come near you—and only steal a glance at you every now and then . . . do you know why? It's because I pretend that we're secretly in love—engaged in secret—and that no one dreams that there's anything between us.

NORA: Oh yes, yes, I know that you're always thinking of me.

HELMER: And when it's time to go, and I'm putting your shawl over your lovely young shoulders—round your exquisite neck—then I imagine that you're my little bride, that we've just come from the wedding, and that I'm bringing you back to my home for the first time—that for the first time I shall be alone with you—all alone with your young trembling loveliness. All the evening I've been longing for nothing but you. When I watched you swaying and beckoning in the tarantella, it set my blood on fire till I couldn't bear it any longer. That's why I brought you home so early—

NORA: No, Torvald, go away. Leave me alone—I don't want—

HELMER: What's all this? So my little Nora's playing with me! "Don't want"? I'm your husband, aren't I?

There is a knock on the front door.

NORA (*startled*): Listen!

HELMER (*going to the hall*): Who is it?

RANK (*outside*): It's I—may I come in for a moment?

HELMER (*angrily, under his breath*): Oh, what does he want now? (*aloud*) Wait a minute. (*He goes and opens the door.*) Ah, it's nice of you not to pass our door without looking in.

RANK: I thought I heard you talking, and I felt I'd like to see you. (*He lets his eye roam quickly round the room.*) Ah yes, this dear familiar place; you two must be very happy and comfortable here.

HELMER: It looked as if you were pretty happy upstairs, too.

RANK: Wonderfully—why not? Why shouldn't one enjoy everything the world has to offer—at any rate, as much as one can—and for as long as one can? The wine was superb!

HELMER: Especially the champagne.

RANK: You thought so too, did you? It's quite incredible the amount I managed to put away!

NORA: Torvald drank a good deal of champagne tonight, too.

RANK: Oh?

NORA: Yes, and that always puts him in high spirits.

RANK: Well, why shouldn't a man have a pleasant evening after a good day's work?

HELMER: A good day's work? I'm afraid I can't claim that.

RANK (*slapping him on the back*): Ah, but *I* can!

NORA: Dr. Rank . . . then you must have been working on a scientific test today?

RANK: Exactly.

HELMER: Well, well! Little Nora talking about scientific tests!

NORA: And am I to congratulate you on the result?

RANK: You may indeed.

NORA: It was good, then?

RANK: The best possible result—for doctor *and* patient. . . . Certainty.

NORA (*quickly, probing*): Certainty?

RANK: Complete certainty. So why shouldn't I give myself a jolly evening after that?

NORA: Yes, of course you must, Dr. Rank.

HELMER: I quite agree—as long as you don't have to pay for it the next morning.

RANK: Ah well, you don't get anything for nothing in this life.

NORA: Dr. Rank—you like fancy-dress parties, don't you?

RANK: Yes, when there are lots of pretty costumes.

NORA: Then tell me—what are you and I going to wear at our next?

HELMER: Little scatterbrain—thinking about the next dance already!

RANK: You and I? Yes, I can tell you—you shall be a mascot.

HELMER: Ah, but what costume would suggest *that*?

RANK: Your wife could go in what she wears every day . . .

HELMER: Very charmingly put. But don't you know what you'll wear?

RANK: Oh yes, my dear fellow, I'm quite certain about *that*.

HELMER: Well?

RANK: At the next fancy-dress party, I shall be invisible.

HELMER: What an odd idea!

RANK: There's a big black hat—you've heard of the Invisible Hat?—you put it on, and then no one can see you.

HELMER (*hiding a smile*): Well, perhaps you're right.

RANK: But I'm quite forgetting what I came for. Give me a cigar, Helmer—one of the black Havanas.

HELMER: With the greatest pleasure (*offering him the case*).

RANK (*taking one and cutting the end*): Thanks.

NORA (*striking a match*): Let me give you a light.

RANK: Thank you.

   She holds the match while he lights the cigar.

   And now—good-bye.

HELMER: Good-bye—good-bye, my dear fellow.

NORA: Sleep well, Dr. Rank.

RANK: Thank you for that wish.

NORA: Wish me the same.

RANK: You? Well, if you want me to. . . . Sleep well. And—thank you for the light. . . . (*With a nod to them both, he goes.*)

HELMER (*subdued*): He's had too much to drink.

NORA (*absently*): Perhaps.

   HELMER, *taking his keys from his pocket, goes out to the hall.*

NORA: Torvald—what do you want out there?

HELMER: I must empty the letter-box, it's almost full; there won't be room for tomorrow's paper.

NORA: Are you going to work tonight?

HELMER: You know perfectly well I'm not. Here, what's this? Someone's been at the lock!

NORA: At the lock?

HELMER: Yes, they certainly have. What can this mean? I shouldn't have thought that the maid—Here's a broken hairpin—Nora, it's one of yours!

NORA (*quickly*): Perhaps the children . . .

HELMER: Then you must break them of that sort of thing. Ugh—ugh—There, I've got it open all the same. (*emptying the letter-box and calling into the kitchen*) Helena? Helena, put out the lamp at the front door. (*He shuts the front door and comes into the room with the letters in his hand.*) Look—just look what a lot there are! (*looking through them*) Whatever's this?

NORA (*at the window*): The letter! No, Torvald, no!

HELMER: Two visiting-cards—from Rank.

NORA: From Dr. Rank?

HELMER (*looking at them*): "S. Rank, M.D." They were on top—he must have put them in as he left.

NORA: Is there anything on them?

HELMER: There's a black cross over the name . . . look. What a gruesome idea—it's just as if he were announcing his own death.

NORA: That's what he's doing.

HELMER: What? Do you know about it? Has he told you something?

NORA: Yes, when these cards came, it would be to say good-bye to us; he's going to shut himself up to die.

HELMER: My poor old friend. Of course I knew that he wouldn't be with me much longer—but so soon . . . ! And to go away and hide, like a wounded animal . . .

NORA: If it *must* be, then it's best to go without a word, isn't it, Torvald?

HELMER (*pacing up and down*): He'd come to be so much a part of our lives. I can't realize that he's gone. With all his loneliness and suffering, he seemed like a background of clouds that set off the sunshine of our happiness. Well, perhaps it's all for the best—for him, at any rate. (*coming to a halt*) And maybe for us too, Nora, now that you and I have no one but each other. (*putting an arm round her*) Oh, my darling, I feel as if I can't hold you close enough. You know, Nora, I've often wished that you could be threatened by some imminent danger so that I could risk everything I had—even my life itself—to save you.

NORA (*freeing herself, and speaking firmly and purposefully*): Now you must read your letters, Torvald.

HELMER: No, no, not tonight. I want to be with my darling wife.

NORA: When your friend's dying . . . ?

HELMER: Yes, you're right—it's upset us both. Something ugly has come between us— the thought of death and decay. We must try to shake it off. . . . And until we do, let us keep apart.

NORA (*putting her arms round his neck*): Good night, Torvald—good night.

HELMER (*kissing her on the forehead*): Good night, Nora—sleep well, my little songbird. Now I'll go and read my letters. (*He takes the bundle into his room, shutting the door behind him.*)

NORA (*Wild-eyed, groping round her she seizes* HELMER'S *domino and pulls it round herself. She speaks in hoarse, rapid, broken whispers.*): I shall never see him again! Never—never—never! (*She throws the shawl over her head.*) And never see the children again either—never, never again. The water's black, and cold as ice—and deep . . . so deep. . . . Oh, if only it were all over! He has it now—he's reading it. . . . Oh no, no—not yet! Good-bye, Torvald—good-bye, my children—

She is about to rush out through the hall, when HELMER *flings his door open and stands there with the open letter in his hand.*

HELMER: Nora!

NORA (*with a loud cry*): Ah . . . !

HELMER: What is all this? Do you know what's in this letter?

NORA: Yes, I know. Let me go—let me out!

HELMER (*holding her back*): Where are you going?

NORA (*struggling to free herself*): You shan't save me, Torvald!

HELMER (*taken aback*): It's true! So what it says here is true? How terrible! No, no, it's not possible—it *can't* be true.

NORA: It *is* true. I've loved you more than anything in the world.

HELMER: Now don't let's have any silly excuses.

NORA (*taking a step toward him*): Torvald . . . !

HELMER: You wretched woman—what have you done?

NORA: Let me go. You *shan't* take the blame—I won't let you suffer for me.

HELMER: We won't have any melodrama. (*locking the front door*) Here you shall stay until you've explained yourself. Do you realize what you've done? Answer me—do you realize?

NORA (*looking fixedly at him, her expression hardening as she speaks*): Yes, now I'm beginning to realize everything.

HELMER (*pacing about the room*): What a terrible awakening! For these last eight years you've been my joy and my pride—and now I find that you're a liar, a hypocrite—even worse—a criminal! Oh, the unspeakable ugliness of it all! Ugh!

NORA *looks fixedly at him without speaking. He stops in front of her.*

I might have known that something of this sort would happen—I should have foreseen it. All your father's shiftless character—Be quiet!—all your father's shiftless character has come out in you. No religion, no morality, no sense of duty . . . So this is what I get for condoning his fault! I did it for your sake, and this is how you repay me!

NORA: Yes—like this.

HELMER: You've completely wrecked my happiness, you've ruined my whole future! Oh, it doesn't bear thinking of. I'm in the power of a man without scruples; he can do what he likes with me—ask what he wants of me—order me about as he pleases, and I dare not refuse. And I'm brought so pitifully low all because of a shiftless woman!

NORA: Once I'm out of the way, you'll be free.

HELMER: No rhetoric, please! Your father was always ready with fine phrases too. How would it help me if you were "out of the way," as you call it? Not in the least! He can still see that the thing gets about, and once he does, I may very well be suspected of having been involved in your crooked dealings. They may well think that I was behind it—that I put you up to it. And it's you that I have to thank for all this—and after I've cherished you all through our married life. *Now* do you realize what you've done to me?

NORA (*calm and cold*): Yes.

HELMER: It's so incredible that I can't grasp it. But we must try to come to some understanding. Take off that shawl—take it off, I tell you. Somehow or other I must try to appease him—the thing must be hushed up at all costs. As for ourselves—we must seem to go on just as before . . . but only in the eyes of the world of course. You will remain here in my house—that goes without saying—but

I shall not allow you to bring up the children . . . I shouldn't dare trust you with them. Oh, to think that I should have to say this to someone I've loved so much—someone I still . . . Well, that's all over—it must be; from now on, there'll be no question of happiness, but only of saving the ruin of it—the fragments—the mere façade . . .

There is a ring at the front door.

HELMER (*collecting himself*): What's that—at this hour? Can the worst have—Could he . . . ? Keep out of sight, Nora—say that you're ill.

NORA *remains motionless.* HELMER *goes and opens the hall door.*

MAID (*at the door, half-dressed*): There's a letter for the Mistress.
HELMER: Give it to me. (*He takes the letter and shuts the door.*) Yes, it's from him. You're not to have it—I shall read it myself.
NORA: Yes, read it.
HELMER (*by the lamp*): I hardly dare—it may mean ruin for both of us. No, I *must* know! (*Tearing open the letter, he runs his eye over a few lines, looks at a paper that is enclosed, then gives a shout of joy.*) Nora!

She looks at him inquiringly.

Nora! Wait, I must just read it again. . . . Yes, it's true; I'm saved! Nora, I'm saved!
NORA: And I?
HELMER: You too, of course. We're both saved—both you and I. Look, he's sent you back your bond. He says that he regrets . . . and apologizes . . . a fortunate change in his life. . . . Oh, never mind what he says—we're saved, Nora, no one can touch you now. Oh Nora, Nora—Wait, first let me destroy the whole detestable business. (*casting his eye over the bond*) No, I won't even look at it—I shall treat the whole thing as nothing but a bad dream. (*Tearing the bond and the two letters in pieces, he throws them on the stove, and watches them burn.*) There! Now it's all gone. He said in his letter that since Christmas Eve you'd . . . Oh, Nora, these three days must have been terrible for you.
NORA: They've been a hard struggle, these three days.
HELMER: How you must have suffered—seeing no way out except . . . No, we'll put all those hateful things out of our minds. Now we can shout for joy, again and again: "It's all over—it's all over!" Listen, Nora—you don't seem to realize—it's all over. What's the matter? Such a grim face? Poor little Nora, I see what it is: you simply can't believe that I've forgiven you. But I have, Nora, I swear it—I've forgiven you everything. I know now that what you did was all for love of me.
NORA: That is true.
HELMER: You loved me as a wife *should* love her husband. It was just that you hadn't the experience to realize what you were doing. But do you imagine that you're any less dear to me for not knowing how to act on your own? No, no, you must simply rely on me—I shall advise you and guide you. I shouldn't be a proper man if your feminine helplessness didn't make you twice as attractive to me. You must forget all the hard things that I said to you in that first dreadful moment when it seemed as if the whole world was falling about my ears. I've forgiven you, Nora, I swear it—I've forgiven you.
NORA: Thank you for your forgiveness. (*She goes out through the door to the right.*)

HELMER: No, don't go. (*He looks in.*) What are you doing out there?

NORA (*off*): Taking off my fancy-dress.

HELMER (*at the open door*): Yes, do. Try to calm down and set your mind at peace, my frightened little songbird. You can rest safely, and my great wings will protect you. (*He paces up and down by the door.*) Oh, Nora, how warm and cosy our home is; it's your refuge, where I shall protect you like a hunted dove that I've saved from the talons of a hawk. Little by little, I shall calm your poor fluttering heart, Nora, take my word for it. In the morning you'll look on all this quite differently, and soon everything will be just as it used to be. There'll be no more need for me to tell you that I've forgiven you—you'll feel in your heart that I have. How can you imagine that I could ever think of rejecting—or even reproaching—you? Ah, you don't know what a real man's heart is like, Nora. There's something indescribably sweet and satisfying for a man to know deep down that he has forgiven his wife— completely forgiven her, with all his heart. It's as if that made her doubly his—as if he had brought her into the world afresh! In a sense, she has become both his wife and his child. So from now on, that's what you shall be to me, you poor, frightened, helpless, little darling. You mustn't worry about anything, Nora—only be absolutely frank with me, and I'll be both your will and your conscience. . . . Why, what's this? Not in bed? You've changed your clothes!

NORA (*in her everyday things*): Yes, Torvald, I've changed my clothes.

HELMER: But why? At *this* hour!

NORA: I shan't sleep tonight.

HELMER: But, my dear Nora—

NORA (*looking at her watch*): It's not so very late. Sit down here, Torvald—you and I have a lot to talk over. (*She sits down at one side of the table.*)

HELMER: Nora—what is all this? Why do you look so stern?

NORA: Sit down—this'll take some time. I have a lot to talk to you about.

HELMER (*sitting across the table from her*): Nora, you frighten me—I don't understand you.

NORA: No, that's just it—you don't understand me. And I've never understood you— until tonight. No, you mustn't interrupt—just listen to what I have to say. Torvald, this is a reckoning.

HELMER: What do you mean by that?

NORA (*after a short pause*): Doesn't it strike you that there's something strange about the way we're sitting here?

HELMER: No . . . what?

NORA: We've been married for eight years now. Don't you realize that this is the first time that we two—you and I, man and wife—have had a serious talk together?

HELMER: Serious? What do you mean by that?

NORA: For eight whole years—no, longer than that—ever since we first met, we've never exchanged a serious word on any serious subject.

HELMER: Was I to keep forever involving you in worries that you couldn't possibly help me with?

NORA: I'm not talking about worries; what I'm saying is that we've never sat down in earnest together to get to the bottom of a single thing.

HELMER: But, Nora dearest, what good would that have been to you?

NORA: That's just the point—you've never understood me. I've been dreadfully wronged, Torvald—first by Papa, and then by you.

HELMER: What? By your father and me? The two people who loved you more than anyone else in the world.

NORA (*shaking her head*): You've never loved me, you've only found it pleasant to be in love with me.

HELMER: Nora—what are you saying?

NORA: It's true, Torvald. When I lived at home with Papa, he used to tell me his opinion about everything, and so I had the same opinion. If I thought differently, I had to hide it from him, or he wouldn't have liked it. He called me his little doll, and he used to play with me just as I played with my dolls. Then I came to live in your house—

HELMER: That's no way to talk about our marriage!

NORA (*undisturbed*): I mean when I passed out of Papa's hands into yours. You arranged everything to suit your own tastes, and so I came to have the same tastes as yours . . . or I pretended to. I'm not quite sure which . . . perhaps it was a bit of both—sometimes one and sometimes the other. Now that I come to look at it, I've lived here like a pauper—simply from hand to mouth. I've lived by performing tricks for you, Torvald. That was how you wanted it. You and Papa have committed a grievous sin against me: it's your fault that I've made nothing of my life.

HELMER: That's unreasonable, Nora—and ungrateful. Haven't you been happy here?

NORA: No, that's something I've never been. I thought I had, but really I've never been happy.

HELMER: Never . . . happy?

NORA: No, only gay. And you've always been so kind to me. But our home has been nothing but a play-room. I've been your doll-wife here, just as at home I was Papa's doll-child. And the children have been my dolls in their turn. I liked it when you came and played with me, just as they liked it when I came and played with them. That's what our marriage has been, Torvald.

HELMER: There is some truth in what you say, though you've exaggerated and overstated it. But from now on, things will be different. Play-time's over, now comes lesson-time.

NORA: Whose lessons? Mine or the children's?

HELMER: Both yours and the children's, Nora darling.

NORA: Ah, Torvald, you're not the man to teach me to be a real wife to you—

HELMER: How can you say that?

NORA: —and how am I fitted to bring up the children?

HELMER: Nora!

NORA: Didn't you say yourself, a little while ago, that you daren't trust them to me?

HELMER: That was in a moment of anger—you mustn't pay any attention to that.

NORA: But you were perfectly right—I'm not fit for it. There's another task that I must finish first—I must try to educate myself. And you're not the man to help me with that; I must do it alone. That's why I'm leaving you.

HELMER (*leaping to his feet*): What's that you say?

NORA: I must stand on my own feet if I'm to get to know myself and the world outside. That's why I can't stay here with you any longer.

HELMER: Nora—Nora . . . !

NORA: I want to go at once. I'm sure Kristina will take me in for the night.

HELMER: You're out of your mind. I won't let you—I forbid it.

NORA: It's no good your forbidding me anything any longer. I shall take the things that belong to me, but I'll take nothing from you—now or later.

HELMER: But this is madness . . .

NORA: Tomorrow I shall go home—to my old home, I mean—it'll be easier for me to find something to do there.

HELMER: Oh, you blind, inexperienced creature . . . !

NORA: I must try to *get* some experience, Torvald.

HELMER: But to leave your home—your husband and your children. . . . You haven't thought of what people will say.

NORA: I can't consider that. All I know is that this is necessary for me.

HELMER: But this is disgraceful. Is this the way you neglect your most sacred duties?

NORA: What do you consider is my most sacred duty?

HELMER: Do I have to tell you that? Isn't it your duty to your husband and children?

NORA: I have another duty, just as sacred.

HELMER: You can't have. What duty do you mean?

NORA: My duty to myself.

HELMER: Before everything else, you're a wife and a mother.

NORA: I don't believe that any longer. I believe that before everything else I'm a human being—just as much as you are . . . or at any rate I shall try to become one. I know quite well that most people would agree with you, Torvald, and that you have warrant for it in books; but I can't be satisfied any longer with what most people say, and with what's in books. I must think things out for myself and try to understand them.

HELMER: Shouldn't you first understand your place in your own home? Haven't you an infallible guide in such matters—your religion?

NORA: Ah, Torvald, I don't really know what religion is.

HELMER: What's that you say?

NORA: I only know what Pastor Hansen taught me when I was confirmed. He told me that religion was this, that, and the other. When I get away from all this, and am on my own, I want to look into that too. I want to see if what Pastor Hansen told me was right—or at least, if it is right for me.

HELMER: This is unheard-of from a young girl like you. But if religion can't guide you, then let me rouse your conscience. You must have *some* moral sense. Or am I wrong? Perhaps you haven't.

NORA: Well, Torvald, it's hard to say; I don't really know—I'm so bewildered about it all. All I know is that I think quite differently from you about things; and now I find that the law is quite different from what I thought, and I simply can't convince myself that the law is right. That a woman shouldn't have the right to spare her old father on his deathbed, or to save her husband's life! I can't believe things like that.

HELMER: You're talking like a child; you don't understand the world you live in.

NORA: No, I don't. But now I mean to go into that, too. I must find out which is right—the world or I.

HELMER: You're ill, Nora—you're feverish. I almost believe you're out of your senses.

NORA: I've never seen things so clearly and certainly as I do tonight.

HELMER: Clearly and certainly enough to forsake your husband and your children?

NORA: Yes.

HELMER: Then there's only one possible explanation . . .

NORA: What?

HELMER: You don't love me any more.

NORA: No, that's just it.

HELMER: Nora! How can you say that?

NORA: I can hardly bear to, Torvald, because you've always been so kind to me—but I can't help it. I don't love you any more.

HELMER (*with forced self-control*): And are you clear and certain about that, too?

NORA: Yes, absolutely clear and certain. That's why I won't stay here any longer.

HELMER: And will you also be able to explain how I've forfeited your love?

NORA: Yes, I can indeed. It was this evening, when the miracle didn't happen—because then I saw that you weren't the man I'd always thought you.

HELMER: I don't understand that. Explain it.

NORA: For eight years I'd waited so patiently—for, goodness knows, I realized that miracles don't happen every day. Then this disaster overtook me, and I was completely certain that now the miracle would happen. When Krogstad's letter was lying out there, I never imagined for a moment that you would submit to his conditions. I was completely certain that you would say to him "Go and publish it to the whole world!" And when that was done . . .

HELMER: Well, what then? When I'd exposed my own wife to shame and disgrace?

NORA: When that was done, I thought—I was completely certain—that you would come forward and take all the blame—that you'd say "*I*'m the guilty one."

HELMER: Nora!

NORA: You think that I should never have accepted a sacrifice like that from you? No, of course I shouldn't. But who would have taken my word against yours? That was the miracle I hoped for . . . and dreaded. It was to prevent *that* that I was ready to kill myself.

HELMER: Nora, I'd gladly work night and day for you, and endure poverty and sorrow for your sake. But no man would sacrifice his *honor* for the one he loves.

NORA: Thousands of women have.

HELMER: Oh, you're talking and thinking like a stupid child.

NORA: Perhaps . . . But you don't talk or think like the man I could bind myself to. When your first panic was over—not about what threatened me, but about what might happen to *you*—and when there was no more danger, then, as far as you were concerned, it was just as if nothing had happened at all. I was simply your little songbird, your doll, and from now on you would handle it more gently than ever because it was so delicate and fragile. (*rising*) At that moment, Torvald, I realized that for eight years I'd been living here with a strange man, and that I'd borne him three children. Oh, I can't bear to think of it—I could tear myself to little pieces!

HELMER (*sadly*): Yes. I see—I see. There truly is a gulf between us. . . . Oh, but Nora, couldn't we somehow bridge it?

NORA: As I am now, I'm not the wife for you.

HELMER: I could change . . .

NORA: Perhaps—if your doll is taken away from you.

HELMER: But to lose you—to lose you, Nora! No, no, I can't even imagine it . . .

NORA (*going out to the right*): That's just why it *must* happen.

She returns with her outdoor clothes, and a little bag which she puts on a chair by the table.

HELMER: Nora! Not now, Nora—wait till morning.

NORA (*putting on her coat*): I couldn't spend the night in a strange man's house.

HELMER: But couldn't we live here as brother and sister?

NORA (*putting her hat on*): You know quite well that that wouldn't last. (*She pulls her shawl round her.*) Good-bye, Torvald. I won't see my children—I'm sure they're in better hands than mine. As I am now, I'm no good to them.

HELMER: But some day, Nora—some day . . . ?

NORA: How can I say? I've no idea what will become of me.

HELMER: But you're my wife—now, and whatever becomes of you.

NORA: Listen, Torvald: I've heard that when a wife leaves her husband's house as I'm doing now, he's legally freed from all his obligations to her. Anyhow, *I* set you free from them. You're not to feel yourself bound in any way, and nor shall I. We must both be perfectly free. Look, here's your ring back—give me mine.

HELMER: Even that?

NORA: Even that.

HELMER: Here it is.

NORA: There. Now it's all over. Here are your keys. The servants know all about running the house—better than I did. Tomorrow, when I've gone, Kristina will come and pack my things that I brought from home; I'll have them sent after me.

HELMER: Over! All over! Nora, won't you ever think of me again?

NORA: I know I shall often think of you—and the children, and this house.

HELMER: May I write to you, Nora?

NORA: No . . . you must never do that.

HELMER: But surely I can send you—

NORA: Nothing—nothing.

HELMER: —or help you, if ever you need it?

NORA: No, I tell you, I couldn't take anything from a stranger.

HELMER: Nora—can't I ever be anything more than a stranger to you?

NORA (*picking up her bag*): Oh, Torvald—there would have to be the greatest miracle of all . . .

HELMER: What would that be—the greatest miracle of all?

NORA: Both of us would have to be so changed that—Oh, Torvald, I don't believe in miracles any longer.

HELMER: But I'll believe. Tell me: "so changed that . . ."?

NORA: That our life together could be a real marriage. Good-bye. (*She goes out through the hall.*)

HELMER (*sinking down on a chair by the door and burying his face in his hands*): Nora! Nora! (*He rises and looks round.*) Empty! She's not here any more! (*with a glimmer of hope*) "The greatest miracle of all . . ."?

From below comes the noise of a door slamming.

THE RECEPTIVE READER

1. In the early acts, Torvald Helmer holds forth on the role of the husband and on standards of honesty or probity for dealing with money. Above all, in his talk and in many little ways, he demonstrates the role he has assigned to Nora in their household. What are some of the most revealing things he says and does? What portrait of him as a *major character* emerges in Acts 1 and 2? How do you react to him?

2. In what ways does Nora live up to the stereotype of the "little woman"? How does she conform or live up to her husband's conception of her? What are telling details or patterns of behavior that make her the weaker partner in their marriage? What are some of the more revealing things she says or does in the early acts of the play? ✧

When do you see the first signs that there might be another side to Nora's personality? When do you see signs that she might be a complex rather than a simple character? ◇ What are the first hints that Torvald and Nora are going to come into conflict?

3. In Acts 1 and 2, how does Mrs. Linde serves as a *foil* to Nora? How does Ibsen use her to remind the audience of the harsh economic realities facing women on the fringes of middle-class society? ◇ What light do the comments of the Nurse throw on the role of lower-class women?

4. Among the other *supporting characters*, what is the role of Dr. Rank, the physician? What role does he play in Nora's life? ◇ From what perspective does Rank see the major characters? How does Ibsen use him to throw added light on Nora and Torvald and their society?

5. What is Krogstad's central role in the *plot* of the play? How does he bring out into the open Helmer's (and his society's) standards about money, credit, and respectability? Why is the fact that at one time the two men were schoolmates an embarrassment to Helmer? ◇ What is the role of the relationship between Krogstad and Mrs. Linde in the play as a whole? ◇ Krogstad at one point tells Nora that even "a man like me has a certain amount of what is called feeling." How do you react to him? Is he a stage villain—someone all bad, whom the audience can hiss and despise?

6. What is the nature of Nora's dealings with Krogstad? How do they test her character and her view of the world? How do they make her change or grow? How do the revelations about the hushed-up events of the past change your view of Nora?

7. Torvald at the *climax*, or high point, of the play fails Nora—he fails to live up to her expectations. Why and how? What does she expect of him? How and why does she judge him? Do you concur in her judgment? ◇ In these climactic scenes in Act 3, what does Ibsen try to show about the workings of Torvald's kind of bourgeois morality? about Torvald's kind of person?

8. What questions does Nora raise about the nature of marriage in the final scenes? What answers does the play suggest? What is the meaning of Nora's concept of the "duty to myself"? What is her idea of a "real marriage"?

9. As in other Ibsen plays, the conflict between truth and lies becomes a central *theme* in *A Doll's House*. At other times, however, Ibsen seemed fascinated by the destructive potential of total honesty. What perspective on "truth" emerges from the play as a whole?

THE RANGE OF INTERPRETATION

One school of critics has seen Nora's search for her own true self as transcending sex roles. The play is "a metaphor for individual freedom" generally (Robert Brustein). Nora is Everyman trying to find himself or herself. However, recent feminist critics have stressed Nora's identity as a "nineteenth-century married woman." *A Doll's House* "is not about Everybody's struggle to find himself or herself" but "about Everywoman's struggle against Everyman" (Joan Templeton). Which of these two views is closer to your own reading of the play?

THE CREATIVE DIMENSION

To get his play performed in Germany, with opportunities for fame and fortune far beyond those of his native Norway, Ibsen rewrote the ending to make it more acceptable to the outraged forces of middle-class respectability. Gritting his teeth, he wrote a final scene in which Torvald makes Nora take a last look at her sleeping children:

TORVALD: Tomorrow, when they wake up and call for their mother, they will be . . . motherless!
NORA (*trembling*): Motherless!
TORVALD: As you once were.
NORA: Motherless! (*After an inner struggle, she lets her bag fall, and says*) Ah, though it is a sin against myself, I cannot leave them!

Choose one: Pretend you are a drama critic in Ibsen's time. Attack or defend the changed ending. Or do your own rewrite of the final page or pages for a current adaptation of the play—for instance, for a Hollywood movie or for an avant-garde production.

JUXTAPOSITIONS

A Modern Everyman

It is always ourselves that we see upon the stage.
WILLIAM BUTLER YEATS

Central to the religious teachings of the Middle Ages was that all were equal in the sight of God and that Death was no respecter of persons. Whether peasant, beggar, merchant, emperor, or pope, all would be summoned to a final reckoning. ("People, in the beginning / Look well ahead to the ending" says the Messenger at the beginning of the *Everyman* play.) The struggle in the soul of Everyman and Everywoman mirrored the struggle between the forces of good and the forces of evil in the larger world. The basic conflict in each individual was the battle between sin and righteousness, with the outcome determining salvation or perdition. The two selections that follow will enable you to compare the medieval conception of Everyman with a more modern Everyman—a Chicano G.I. being sent to Vietnam in a play by the Mexican American playwright Luis Valdez.

Medieval drama had its origins in scenes from Bible stories staged on movable platforms or wagons. Later, **morality plays** acted out basic teachings of the church, putting on the stage personified virtues and vices as part of a religious **allegory.** The best known (and in its time most widely acted) is the anonymous *Everyman* play, written about 1485. It survives also in a modern adaptation by the Austrian playwright Hugo von Hoffmansthal, which is still performed each year in front of Salzburg Cathedral. Like much of the **didactic** or teaching literature of the Middle Ages, *Everyman* drives home points of doctrine by insistent repetition, and the way it translates the theology of the church into simple teachings for the uneducated may seem naive to modern sophisticates. But even in an improvised classroom reading or in a miniproduction, the play can still make the modern audience feel the shudder at the sudden summons of incorruptible Death experienced by medieval Christians.

Everyman 1485

A Modern Abridgement

TRANSLATED BY HANS P. GUTH

SCENE 1

MESSENGER: I ask you all in the audience
    To hear our play with reverence:
    The Summoning of Everyman it is called
    It shows our lives and how they end,
    And how quickly our time passes on this earth.   5
    The topic of our play is most serious,
    But the lesson is more precious
    And sweet to carry away.
    The story says: People, in the beginning
    Look well ahead to the ending—   10
    No matter how carefree you are.
    Sin in the beginning seems most sweet,
    But in the end it causes the soul to weep,
    When the body has returned to dust.
    Here you shall see how Fellowship and Jollity,   15
    And Strength, Pleasure, and Beauty,
    Will fade away like a flower in May.
    And you will hear how our heavenly King
    Will call Everyman to a general reckoning.
    Now listen to what he will say.   20

    The MESSENGER *leaves and* GOD *speaks to the audience.*

GOD: I see here in my majesty
    How people forget the love they owe me.
    They live without fear in worldly prosperity
    And worldly riches is all they think about.
    They do not fear the sharp rod of my righteousness.   25
    Pride, greed, and every other deadly sin
    Have become acceptable in the world.
    People only think of their own pleasure.
    The more I show them kindness,
    The more they live in wickedness.   30
    They have forgotten the meaning of charity.
    Therefore, I will in all haste
    Have a reckoning of Everyman's conduct.
    I offered the people great riches of mercy,
    But there are few who sincerely seek it.   35
    The time has come to pronounce justice
    On Everyman living without fear.
    Where are you, Death, my mighty messenger?

    DEATH *enters.*

DEATH: Almighty God, I am here at your bidding

To fulfill your every commandment.   40
GOD: Go now to Everyman,
And tell him, in my name,
That he must go on a pilgrimage
Which he may in no way avoid,
And tell him to bring a sure accounting   45
Without excuse or any delay.
DEATH: Lord, I will go forth into the world
And search out cruelly both great and small.

GOD *leaves.*

SCENE 2

DEATH: I will find Everyman who lives like a beast,
        Ignoring God's laws, and sunk in folly.
        I will strike down those who love riches,
        To dwell in hell for time without end,
        Unless Good Deeds prove their friend.   5
        Lo, yonder I see Everyman walking—
        No way does he expect my coming!
        His mind is on the joys of the flesh and treasure,
        And great pain it shall cause him to endure
        Before the Lord, Heaven's king.   10

        EVERYMAN *enters.*

        Everyman, stand still! Where are you going
        So merrily? Have you forgotten your Maker?
EVERYMAN: Why do you ask?
        Who wants to know?
DEATH: That I will tell you: 15
        In great haste I am sent
        From God in His Majesty.
EVERYMAN: What! Sent to me?
DEATH: Most certainly.
        Though you have forgotten Him here,   20
        He thinks of you in His heavenly sphere,
        As, before we depart, you shall know.
EVERYMAN: What does God want from me?
DEATH: That I will tell you:
        He must have a speedy reckoning   25
        Without any delay.
EVERYMAN: To make a reckoning, I'll need more time.
        This sudden summons catches me unprepared.
DEATH: The time has come to take a long journey.
        And be sure to bring your book of accounts,   30
        For there is no way you could go back for it.
        And be sure your reckoning is straight and true—
        Showing much bad, and good deeds but a few;

How you have spent your life, in what wise
Before the Chief Lord of Paradise. 35
Make yourself ready to take that road,
For you can send none in your place.
EVERYMAN: Who are you to ask me for this accounting?
DEATH: I am Death, and I fear no one.
I summon all and spare no creature, 40
For God has decreed
That all must obey my call.
EVERYMAN: O Death, you come when I least expected you.
You have the power to save me—
If you spare me, I will give you great reward; 45
Yea, a thousand pounds will be yours
If you put off this matter till another day!
DEATH: Everyman, it cannot be.
I care nothing for gold, silver, or riches,
Or for Pope, emperor, king, duke, or princes, 50
For if I were to accept gifts,
I could have all the treasure of this world.
But such is quite contrary to my custom.
I brook no delay. Make ready to depart!
EVERYMAN: Alas! Is there no escape? 55
I may say Death gives no warning.
To think about you makes me sick at the heart,
For my book of accounts is not ready at all.
If I could have just a dozen more years,
I would clear my accounts in such a way 60
That a reckoning would not frighten me.
DEATH: In vain it is to cry, weep, or pray—
In all haste you must go on your journey.
Now you can put your friends to the test!
For, know well, time waits for no one, 65
And every living creature in the world
Must pay the price of death for the sin of Adam.
EVERYMAN: O gracious God, have mercy on me in my need!
And may I have any company as I leave this earth,
And have my acquaintance lead the way? 70
DEATH: Yes—if any be so bold
To go with you and share your voyage.
Too long you have thought your life and treasure were yours.
EVERYMAN: I thought so indeed!
DEATH: No, no—these were merely lent for a time! 75
For as soon as you are gone,
Another will have them for awhile, and then
Leave them behind, even as you have done.
Everyman, how foolish you are! You have your five wits,
But you did not use them to better your life— 80
For suddenly I come.
EVERYMAN: O wretch that I am! How can I flee
And escape from endless sorrow?
Now, kind Death, spare me till tomorrow,

And give me time to think. 85
DEATH: No, I cannot agree,
    Nor grant a delay to any.
    But I strike suddenly to the heart
    Without warning.
    And now I will leave you for a time— 90
    See that you be ready shortly,
    For this is the appointed day
    That no living person can escape.

    DEATH *leaves.*

SCENE 3

EVERYMAN: Alas! I may well weep with deep sighs:
    Now I have no kind of company
    To help me and comfort me in my journey.
    And also my reckoning is quite unready.
    What shall I say to excuse me? 5
    The time passes—God help me, that made all!
    It does me no good to grieve,
    For the day passes and is almost gone.
    To whom can I tell my troubles?
    What if I talked to Fellowship 10
    And told him this sudden news?
    For he is quite in my confidence.
    We have in the world on many a day
    Been good friends in sport and play.
    I see him yonder, certainly. 15
    I trust that he will keep me company.
    Therefore I will speak to him to ease my sorrow.

    FELLOWSHIP *enters.*

    Well met, good Fellowship, and good morrow!
FELLOWSHIP: Everyman, good morrow, and good day!
    Why, friend, do you look so distraught? 20
    If anything is amiss, you will let me know
    So that I may help bring the remedy.
EVERYMAN: Good Fellowship, I am in great danger.
FELLOWSHIP: My true friend, tell me what is on your mind.
    I will not forsake you to my life's end 25
    And provide you good company.
EVERYMAN: That was well spoken, and lovingly!
FELLOWSHIP: Sir, I must know the cause of your sorrow.
    I feel pity to see you in any distress.
    If any have wronged you, we shall have revenge, 30
    Though it should cost me my life.
EVERYMAN: I thank you most sincerely, Fellowship!
FELLOWSHIP: Ah—do not worry about thanking me:
    Tell me what is wrong and say no more.

EVERYMAN: But if I should open my heart to you,   35
  And you then turn away from my grief
  And offer me no comfort when I speak,
  Then should I be ten times more sorry.
FELLOWSHIP: Sir, I will do as I say, indeed.
EVERYMAN: Then you are a good friend in time of need,   40
  As I have found you a true friend before.
FELLOWSHIP: And so we shall be forevermore.
  For truly, if you were headed for hell,
  I would not let you go alone on your way.
EVERYMAN: You speak like a good friend, and I believe you.   45
  I will prove worthy of your friendship, you may be sure.
FELLOWSHIP: No need to prove anything between us two!
  For those who will promise and not keep their word
  Do not deserve to live in good company.
  Therefore tell me the sorrow in your mind   50
  As to a friend most loving and kind.
EVERYMAN: I shall show you how it is:
  I am commanded to go on a journey—
  A long way, hard and dangerous—
  And to render strict accounts, without delay,   55
  Before the highest judge of all.
  Therefore I beg of you to keep me company,
  As you have promised, on this journey.
FELLOWSHIP: Here is trouble indeed! A promise is a promise,
  But if I should set out on such a voyage,   60
  I know well it would cause me great grief,
  And I feel fear in my heart.
  Let us consider this matter most carefully,
  For your words would frighten the strongest man.
EVERYMAN: But you said that in my need   65
  You would never forsake me, dead or alive—
  Yes, even on the road to hell!
FELLOWSHIP: So I said, certainly.
  But this is no time for pleasant talk!
  If we took such a journey,   70
  When would we come back again?
EVERYMAN: Truly, never again, till the day of doom!
FELLOWSHIP: By my faith, then I will not go there.
  Who brought you this evil news?
EVERYMAN: It was Death, indeed, who came to see me.   75
FELLOWSHIP: Now by God that redeemed us all,
  If Death was the messenger,
  I will not go on that hated journey
  For any man living today—
  Not for the father that raised me from a child!   80
EVERYMAN: You promised otherwise, that's certain.
FELLOWSHIP: Of that I am well aware.
  And yet, if you wanted to eat, drink, and be merry,
  Or spend the pleasant hours in women's company,

I would stay with you the livelong day— 85
    For that you may trust me!
EVERYMAN: Yes indeed—then you would be ready!
    Your mind is set on mirth, pleasure, and play,
    And you would sooner attend to such folly
    Than keep me company in my long journey. 90
FELLOWSHIP: I cannot go—that is the truth.
EVERYMAN: Dear Friend, help me in my hour of need.
    Loyal love has long linked us—
    And now, sweet Fellowship, remember me!
FELLOWSHIP: Love or no love, I cannot go! 95
EVERYMAN: But at least do this much for me:
    In the name of charity, see me off at the city gate
    As I set out on the highway!
FELLOWSHIP: For love or money, I will not budge!
    If you could stay—then I would be your friend! 100
    But as it is, good luck in your journey!
    And now I must take my leave.
EVERYMAN: Don't leave me, Fellowship! Will you abandon me?
FELLOWSHIP: I must go. And may God look after you!

    FELLOWSHIP *leaves.*

EVERYMAN: Farewell, sweet Fellowship! Is this the end, 105
    Never to meet again?
    And not a word of comfort at the parting?
    Now where can I turn?
    Friends crowd around us in prosperity
    That will prove faithless in adversity. 110
    Now I must turn to family and kin,
    Asking them for help in my dire need.
    For your kin will befriend you when others shut their door.
    Yonder I see them walking—
    Now I will try their loyalty. 115

    KINSHIP *and* COUSIN *come in.*

SCENE 4

KINSHIP: Here we are, at your service.
    Tell us everything that is on your mind,
    And hold nothing back.
COUSIN: Yes, Everyman, and let us know
    What your errand is or your goal, 5
    For, as you know, we will live and die together.
KINSHIP: We will be with you in good luck and bad,
    For no one may turn down his kinfolk in need.
EVERYMAN: Many thanks, my kind friends.
    Now I shall tell you what grieves me. 10
    I received orders from a messenger

That is the chief officer of a high king:
He bade me start out on a pilgrimage, without fail,
From which I know I shall never return.
I must bring a strict accounting. 15
And along the way, the great enemy of our souls
Lies in wait to do me fatal harm.
Therefore I ask you to be by my side
And help me in the name of holy charity.
COUSIN: We should be by your side—is that what you ask? 20
No, Everyman, I would rather fast
And live on bread and water for five years!
KINSHIP: I hope you do not take it amiss,
But as for me, you shall go alone!
EVERYMAN: Alas, that ever I was born! 25
Cousin, will you not come with me?
COUSIN: No, by our Lady! I have a cramp in my toe.
Do not rely on me, for, so help me,
You are deceived!
KINSHIP: There is no way you can sway us— 30
But I have a maid who loves to travel,
To dance and go to feasts and gad about:
I will give her leave to go with you on that journey,
If you and she can agree.
EVERYMAN: Now tell me truly: 35
Will you go with me or stay behind?
KINSHIP: Stay behind? Yes, that I will and shall!
Therefore farewell until another day.

KINSHIP *leaves.*

EVERYMAN: This makes me sad:
People flatter me with fair promises, 40
But they forsake me when I need them most.
COUSIN: Cousin Everyman, I bid you farewell,
For truly I will not go with you.
It troubles me to think of my own accounting—
Therefore I will stay and make ready my own reckoning. 45

COUSIN *leaves.*

SCENE 5

EVERYMAN: Is this what I have come to?
Those who trust fair words are fools.
Kinship like Fellowship flees from me,
And all their promises were empty words.
Where now do I turn for a helping hand? 5
One thing I do remember:
All my life I have loved riches.
If my Worldly Goods could now help me,
It would set my mind at ease.

Where are you, my Worldly Goods and riches of this world? 10

The voice of WORLDLY GOODS *is heard from inside.*

WORLDLY GOODS: Who calls me? Everyman? What is your hurry?
    I lie here inside, trussed and piled so high,
    And locked securely in strong chests,
    Or packed into bags—I cannot stir,
    As you may see with your own eye. 15
EVERYMAN: Come here, Worldly Goods, and make haste,
    For I need your advice.

    WORLDLY GOODS *enters.*

WORLDLY GOODS: Sir, for any sorrow or adversity in this world,
    I can provide a speedy remedy.
EVERYMAN: My troubles are not of this world. 20
    I must go quite another way
    And give a strict reckoning
    Before the highest judge of all.
    All my life, you have been my pleasure and my joy.
    Therefore, I ask you to come with me, 25
    For it might be that before God Almighty
    You could help me balance my accounts.
    Certainly you have heard it said
    That money can set right many a wrong.
WORLDLY GOODS: No, Everyman—I sing a different song: 30
    I never follow anyone on such an errand.
    For, if I went along,
    You would fare much the worse for my presence.
    Because you always had me in mind,
    Your account is weighed down with many debts 35
    That will count heavily in the balance.
    For your love of me you will have to pay dearly.
EVERYMAN: Alas, I have loved you truly and had great pleasure
    All my life in worldly goods and treasure.
WORLDLY GOODS: That was your downfall—I tell no lie. 40
    For the love of me is contrary to Love Everlasting.
    But if you had loved me with moderation
    And given part of me to the poor,
    Then you would not be in this sorrowful state.
EVERYMAN: False friend that you are, 45
    And traitor to God, you have deceived me
    And caught me in a deadly snare!
WORLDLY GOODS: You have only yourself to blame.
    Your sorrows make me laugh—
    Why should I be sad? 50
EVERYMAN: I gave you all that should have been the Lord's.
    Now will you not come with me, indeed?
    Tell me the truth!
WORLDLY GOODS: I will not follow you, by God!
    Therefore farewell. 55

    WORLDLY GOODS *leaves.*

SCENE 6

EVERYMAN: Oh, whom now can I trust
  To go with me on that fearful journey?
  First, Fellowship promised to go with me;
  His words were pleasing and sweet,
  But afterward he deserted me.   5
  Then I turned to my Kin in despair;
  They also answered with words most fair—
  But they too forsook me in the end.
  Then I turned to my Worldly Goods that I loved,
  Hoping to find comfort; but it was not to be—   10
  He told me in sharp words
  That he has delivered many unto hell.
  Now do I feel remorse and shame;
  I know I am worthy of blame.
  Who is left to counsel me?   15
  I think I shall fare badly
  Unless I visit my Good Deeds—
  But alas! she is most weak;
  She can neither walk nor speak.
  And yet I must ask her for help.   20
  My Good Deeds, where are you?

  GOOD DEEDS *speaks, huddled on the ground.*

GOOD DEEDS: Here I lie, on the cold ground.
  Your sins have left me so weak
  That I cannot stir.
EVERYMAN: O Good Deeds, I am sore afraid.   25
  You must counsel me,
  For now help would be most welcome.
GOOD DEEDS: Everyman, I understand
  You have been summoned to a reckoning
  Before the King of the Heavenly Jerusalem.   30
  If you heed my words, I will share in your journey.
EVERYMAN: That indeed was my hope—
  That you would keep me company.
GOOD DEEDS: I most gladly would go, though I can hardly stand.
EVERYMAN: Why, has anything hurt you?   35
GOOD DEEDS: Yes—your heedless neglect!
  Here look at the record of your deeds.

  She shows him a book of accounts.

  Here is a sorry reckoning, all blotted and defaced,
  That spells eternal danger to your soul!
EVERYMAN: Good Deeds, I pray for your help,   40
  Or else I am damned forever!
  Therefore help me with my reckoning
  Before the King that is and was and ever will be.

GOOD DEEDS: Everyman, I pity you in your plight,
    And will help you as much as I can. 45
    And though my feet might not carry me farther,
    I have a sister who will also go with you:
    True Knowledge she is called, to keep with you
    And help you face that dreaded judgment.

    TRUE KNOWLEDGE *enters.*

TRUE KNOWLEDGE: Everyman, I will go with you and be your guide, 50
    In your hour of need to stay by your side.
EVERYMAN: Now do my fortunes mend,
    For which I thank my Creator.
GOOD DEEDS: She will bring you to the place
    Where you will be healed of your grief. 55
EVERYMAN: I thank you from my heart, Good Deeds!
    Your sweet words make me glad.
TRUE KNOWLEDGE: Now let us go together lovingly
    To Confession, that cleansing river.

    TRUE KNOWLEDGE *leads* EVERYMAN *to* CONFESSION.

SCENE 7

TRUE KNOWLEDGE: Here, this is Confession: kneel down and ask for mercy.
    For his counsel is well esteemed by God Almighty.

    EVERYMAN *kneels.*

EVERYMAN: O glorious fountain that washes away all uncleanness,
    Clear me of the spots of unclean vices.
    I come with True Knowledge for my redemption, 5
    Sorry from the heart for my sins.
CONFESSION: I know your sorrow well, Everyman.
    Because you have come to me with True Knowledge,
    I will comfort you as well as I can.
    And I will give you a precious jewel 10
    Called Penance, that wards off misfortune.
    Through it, your body will be chastised
    With abstinence and perseverance in God's service.
    Here you shall receive this scourge from me,
    As a sign of harsh penance that you must endure, 15
    To remind you that your Savior was lashed for your sake
    With sharp scourges, and suffered patiently.
    So in turn you must suffer patiently to save your soul.
    And if you stay on the right road,
    Your Good Deeds will be with you, 20
    And you will be sure of mercy.

    [In a section of the play left out in this adaptation, EVERYMAN
    punishes his body for the sins of the flesh and puts on the garment of

sorrow. He then takes leave of BEAUTY, STRENGTH, DISCRETION, *and* THE FIVE WITS *as he readies himself for the final stage of his journey.* GOOD DEEDS *stays with him to the end.]*

SCENE 8

EVERYMAN: Alas! I must be on my way
　　To present my reckoning and pay my debts,
　　For all the time that I had is now spent.
　　Remember well, all you who followed my story,
　　How they that I loved best abandoned me,　　　　　　　　　5
　　And only Good Deeds stayed with me to the end.
GOOD DEEDS: All the things of this earth are mere vanity.
　　Beauty, Strength, and Discretion fade away.
　　Foolish friends and heedless next of kin—
　　All flee from you, except Good Deeds.　　　　　　　　　　10
EVERYMAN: Have mercy on me, Almighty God!
GOOD DEEDS: Do not fear, I will speak for you.

　　EVERYMAN *and* GOOD DEEDS *descend into the grave.*

TRUE KNOWLEDGE: Now he has suffered what we must all endure.
　　Good Deeds will offer him safe conduct.
　　Now that the end has come　　　　　　　　　　　　　　15
　　I hear angels singing with great joy
　　Bidding welcome to the soul of Everyman.
　　Remember: After death no one can make amends,
　　And mercy and pity then do not avail.
　　If the final reckoning is faulty,　　　　　　　　　　　20
　　The sinner will burn in everlasting fire.
　　But if your accounting is whole and sound,
　　You will be crowned high in heaven.

THE RECEPTIVE READER

1. How does this play make audiences think of or feel about death? How does the perspective on death compare with more modern perspectives?

2. Purposeful insistent repetition, or *reiteration,* was a favorite teaching technique in medieval didactic literature. Is there a recurrent pattern in Everyman's encounters with the different allegorical characters? Are there other examples of repetition?

3. *Allegory* is sometimes described as lifeless or mechanical. Do the characters become human for you? Did the author have a sense of humor?

4. A familiar problem with didactic literature is that the good characters sometimes seem relatively lifeless compared with the bad. Is that true in this play?

THE PERSONAL RESPONSE

Does the spectator have to be religious to respond to this play? What, to you, is the central message of the play? How do you relate to it as a modern reader?

THE CREATIVE DIMENSION

This translation and abridgement of the play is suitable for a *readers' theater* presentation (where different readers read their parts) or other kind of classroom adaptation. One group of students rewrote the play for a miniproduction with *Everywoman* as the updated title. Work with a group of fellow students to prepare a miniproduction or adaptation of the play.

LUIS VALDEZ (born 1940)

*If you can sing, dance, walk, march, hold a picket sign,
play a guitar or harmonica or any other instrument, you
can participate! No acting experience required.*

FROM A RECRUITING LEAFLET
FOR THE ORIGINAL TEATRO CAMPESINO

Luis Valdez is the founder of the Teatro Campesino, which has performed and been honored throughout the United States and in Europe. He is a prolific writer, organizer, director, teacher, and promoter of Chicano drama. The dialogue in his plays, like the speech of many Mexican Americans, shifts easily from English to Spanish and back. The Teatro he founded in 1965 began by performing *actos*—short, one-act plays—in community centers, in church halls, and in the fields in California. The plays were designed to raise the political consciousness of agricultural workers struggling to make a living and preserve their dignity in a system rigged against them. (A *campesino* is someone who works in the fields.) Valdez has a lively sense of the tragedy and comedy of the lives of ordinary people. He also has a gift for cutting satire: At the beginning of his play *Los Vendidos* (*The Sellouts*, 1967) a secretary from the governor's office comes to Honest Sancho's Used Mexican Lot to look for a suave, not-too-dark Chicano to become a token Mexican American at social functions in the state capital.

Valdez himself started to work in the fields at age six, with the much-interrupted schooling (if any) of the children of America's migrant workers. He eventually accepted a scholarship at San Jose State University and graduated with a B.A. in English in 1964. Much of his early experience in the theater was with the San Francisco Mime Troupe, which practiced improvisational theater. Under his leadership, the Teatro Campesino explored the lives of urban Chicano youth, Mexican Indian legend and mythology, and materials from Third World sources. In 1987, Valdez wrote and directed the movie *La Bamba,* a biography of the Chicano rock 'n' roll singer Ritchie Valens. His PBS production of *Corridos: Tales of Passion and Revolution,* with Linda Ronstadt, won the Peabody Award.

Soldado razo, or *The Buck Private,* was first performed by the Teatro Campesino in 1971. What makes the private a modern Everyman? How is he similar to and how different from the medieval Everyman?

The Buck Private   1971

From *Soldado razo*

CHARACTERS

JOHNNY
THE FATHER
DEATH
THE MOTHER
CECILIA
THE BROTHER

DEATH (*enters singing*): I'm taking off as a private, I'm going to join the ranks . . . along with the courageous young men who leave behind beloved mothers, who leave their girlfriends crying, crying, crying their farewell. Yeah! How lucky for me that there's a war. How goes it, bro? I am death. What else is new? Well, don't get paranoid because I didn't come to take anybody away. I came to tell you a story. Sure, the story of the Buck Private. Maybe you knew him, eh? He was killed not too long ago in Vietnam.

JOHNNY *enters, adjusting his uniform.*

DEATH: This is Johnny, The Buck Private. He's leaving for Vietnam in the morning, but tonight—well, tonight he's going to enjoy himself, right? Look at his face. Know what he's thinking? He's thinking (JOHNNY *moves his lips.*) "Now, I'm a man!"

THE MOTHER *enters.*

DEATH: This is his mother. Poor thing. She's worried about her son, like all mothers. "Blessed be God," she's thinking; (THE MOTHER *moves her mouth.*) "I hope nothing happens to my son." (THE MOTHER *touches* JOHNNY *on the shoulder.*)

JOHNNY: Is dinner ready, mom?

MOTHER: Yes, son, almost. Why did you dress like that? You're not leaving until tomorrow.

JOHNNY: Well, you know. Cecilia's coming and everything.

MOTHER: Oh, my son. You're always bringing girlfriends to the house but you never think about settling down.

JOHNNY: One of these days I'll give you a surprise, ma. (*He kisses her forehead. Embraces her.*)

DEATH: Oh, my! What a picture of tenderness, no? But, watch the old lady. Listen to what she's thinking. "Now, my son is a man. He looks so handsome in that uniform."

JOHNNY: Well, mom, it's getting late. I'll be back shortly with Cecilia, okay?

MOTHER: Yes, son, hurry back. (*He leaves.*) May God take care of you, mom's pride and joy.

JOHNNY *reenters and begins to talk.*

DEATH: Out in the street, Johnny begins to think about his family, his girl, his neighborhood, his life.

JOHNNY: Poor mom. Tomorrow it will be very difficult for her. For me as well. It was pretty hard when I went to boot camp, but now? Vietnam! It's a killer, man. The old man, too. I'm not going to be here to help him out. I wasn't getting rich doing fieldwork, but it was something. A little help, at least. My little brother can't work yet because he's still in school. I just hope he stays there. And finishes. I never liked that school stuff, but I know my little brother digs it. He's smart too— maybe he'll even go to college. One of us has got to make it in this life. Me—I guess I'll just get married to Cecilia and have a bunch of kids. I remember when I first saw her at the Rainbow Ballroom. I couldn't even dance with her because I had had a few beers. The next week was pretty good, though. Since then. How long ago was that? June . . . no, July. Four months. Now I want to get hitched. Her parents don't like me, I know. They think I'm a good for nothing. Maybe they'll feel different when I come back from Nam. Sure, the War Veteran! Maybe I'll get wounded and come back with tons of medals. I wonder how the dudes around here are going to think about that? Damn neighborhood—I've lived here all my life. Now I'm going to Vietnam. (*taps and drum*) It's going to be a drag, man. I might even get killed. If I do, they'll bring me back here in a box, covered with a flag . . . military funeral like they gave Pete Gomez . . . everybody crying . . . the old lady—(*stops*) What the hell am I thinking, man? Damn fool! (*He freezes.*)

DEATH *powders* JOHNNY'S *face white during the next speech.*

DEATH: Foolish, but not stupid, eh? He knew the kind of funeral he wanted and he got it. Military coffin, lots of flowers, American flag, women crying, and a trumpet playing taps with a rifle salute at the end. Or was it goodbye? It doesn't matter, you know what I mean. It was first class all the way. Oh, by the way, don't get upset about the makeup I'm putting on him, eh? I'm just getting him ready for what's coming. I don't always do things in a hurry, you know. Okay, then, next scene. (JOHNNY *exits.*)

JOHNNY *goes on to* CECILIA'S *and exits.*

DEATH: Back at the house, his old man is just getting home.

THE FATHER *enters.*

FATHER: Hey, old lady, I'm home. Is dinner ready?

THE MOTHER *enters.*

MOTHER: Yes, dear. Just wait till Juan gets home. What did you buy?
FATHER: A sixpack of Coors.
MOTHER: Beer?
FATHER: Well, why not? Look—This is my son's last night.
MOTHER: What do you mean, his last night? Don't speak like that.
FATHER: I mean his last night at home, woman. You understand—hic.
MOTHER: You're drunk, aren't you?
FATHER: And if I am, what's it to you? I just had a few beers with my buddy and that's it. Well, what is this, anyway . . . ? It's all I need, man. My son's going to war and you don't want me to drink. I've got to celebrate, woman!
MOTHER: Celebrate what?

FATHER: That my son is now a man! And quite a man, the twerp. So don't pester me. Bring me some supper.

MOTHER: Wait for Juan to come home.

FATHER: Where is he? He's not here? Is that so-and-so loafing around again? Juan? Juan?

MOTHER: I'm telling you he went to get Cecilia, who's going to have dinner with us. And please don't use any foul language. What will the girl say if she hears you talking like that?

FATHER: To hell with it! Who owns this damn house, anyway? Aren't I the one who pays the rent? The one who buys the food? Don't make me get angry, huh? Or you'll get it. It doesn't matter if you already have a son who's a soldier.

MOTHER: Please. I ask you in your son's name, eh? Calm down. (*She exits.*)

FATHER: Calm down! Just like that she wants me to calm down. And who's going to shut my trap? My son the soldier? My son . . .

DEATH: The old man's thoughts are racing back a dozen years to a warm afternoon in July. Johnny, eight years old, is running toward him between the vines, shouting: "Paaa, I already picked 20 trays, paaapá!"

FATHER: Huh. Twenty trays. Little bugger.

THE BROTHER *enters.*

BROTHER: Pa, is Johnny here?

DEATH: This is Johnny's little brother.

FATHER: And where are you coming from?

BROTHER: I was over at Polo's house. He has a new motor scooter.

FATHER: You just spend all your time playing, don't you?

BROTHER: I didn't do anything.

FATHER: Don't talk back to your father.

BROTHER (*shrugs*): Are we going to eat soon?

FATHER: I don't know. Go ask your mother.

THE BROTHER *exits.*

DEATH: Looking at his younger son, the old man starts thinking about him. His thoughts spin around in the usual hopeless cycle of defeat, undercut by more defeat.

FATHER: That boy should be working. He's already fourteen years old. I don't know why the law forces them to go to school till they're sixteen. He won't amount to anything, anyway. It's better if he starts working with me so that he can help the family.

DEATH: Sure, he gets out of school and in three or four years, I take him the way I took Johnny. Crazy, huh?

JOHNNY *returns with* CECILIA.

JOHNNY: Good evening, pa.

FATHER: Son! Good evening. What's this? You're dressed as a soldier?

JOHNNY: I brought Cecilia over to have dinner with us.

FATHER: Well, have her come in, come in.

CECILIA: Thank you very much.

FATHER: My son looks good, doesn't he?

CECILIA: Yes, sir.

FATHER: Damn right. He's off to be a buck private. (*pause*) Well, let's see . . . uh, son, would you like a beer?!

JOHNNY: Yes, sir, but couldn't we get a chair first? For Cecilia?

FATHER: But, of course. We have all the modern conveniences. Let me bring one. Sweetheart? The company's here! (*He exits.*)

JOHNNY: How you doing?

CECILIA: Okay. I love you.

DEATH: This, of course, is Johnny's girlfriend. Fine, ha? Too bad he'll never get to marry her. Oh, he proposed tonight and everything—and she accepted, but she doesn't know what's ahead. Listen to what she's thinking. (CECILIA *moves her mouth.*) "When we get married I hope Johnny still has his uniform. We'd look so good together. Me in a wedding gown and him like that. I wish we were getting married tomorrow!"

JOHNNY: What are you thinking?

CECILIA: Nothing.

JOHNNY: Come on.

CECILIA: Really.

JOHNNY: Come on, I saw your eyes. Now come on, tell me what you were thinking.

CECILIA: It was nothing.

JOHNNY: Are you scared?

CECILIA: About what?

JOHNNY: My going to Vietnam.

CECILIA: No! I mean . . . yes, in a way, but I wasn't thinking that.

JOHNNY: What was it?

CECILIA (*pause*): I was thinking I wish the wedding was tomorrow.

JOHNNY: Really?

CECILIA: Yes.

JOHNNY: You know what? I wish it was too. (*He embraces her.*)

DEATH: And, of course, now he's thinking too. But it's not what she was thinking. What a world!

THE FATHER *and* THE BROTHER *enter with four chairs.*

FATHER: Here are the chairs. What did I tell you? (*to* THE BROTHER) Hey, you, help me move the table, come on.

JOHNNY: Do you need help, pa?

FATHER: No, son, your brother and I'll move it. (*He and* THE BROTHER *move imaginary table into place.*) There it is. And your mom says you should start sitting down because dinner's ready. She made tamales, can you believe that!

JOHNNY: Tamales?

BROTHER: They're Colonel Sanders, eeehh.

FATHER: You shut your trap! Look . . . don't pay attention to him, Cecilia; this little bugger, uh, this kid is always saying stupid things, uh, silly things. Sit down.

MOTHER (*entering with imaginary bowl*): Here come the tamales! Watch out because the pot's hot, okay? Oh, Cecilia, good evening.

CECILIA: Good evening, ma'am. Can I help you with anything?

MOTHER: No, no, everything's ready. Sit down, please.

JOHNNY: Ma, how come you made tamales? (DEATH *begins to put some more makeup on* JOHNNY's *face.*)

MOTHER: Well, because I know you like them so much, son.

DEATH: A thought flashes across Johnny's mind: "Too much, man. I should go to war every day." Over on this side of the table, the little brother is thinking: "What's so hot about going to war—tamales?"

BROTHER: I like tamales.

FATHER: Who told you to open your mouth? Would you like a beer, son?

JOHNNY (*nods*): Thanks, dad.

FATHER: And you, Cecilia?

CECILIA (*surprised*): No, sir, uh, thanks.

MOTHER: Juan, don't be so thoughtless. Cecilia's not old enough to drink. What are her parents going to say? I made some Kool-Aid, sweetheart; I'll bring the pitcher right out. (*She exits.*)

DEATH: You know what's going through the little brother's mind? He is thinking: "He offered her a beer! She was barely in the eighth grade three years ago. When I'm 17 I'm going to join the service and get really drunk."

FATHER: How old are you, Cecilia?

CECILIA: Eighteen.

DEATH: She lied, of course.

FATHER: Oh, well, what the heck, you're already a woman! Come on son, don't let her get away.

JOHNNY: I'm not.

MOTHER (*reentering*): Here's the Kool-Aid and the beans.

JOHNNY: Ma, I got an announcement to make. Will you please sit down?

MOTHER: What is it?

FATHER (*to* THE BROTHER): Give your chair to your mother.

BROTHER: What about my tamale?

MOTHER: Let him eat his dinner.

FATHER (*to* THE BROTHER): Get up!

JOHNNY: Sit down, Mom.

MOTHER: What is it, son? (*She sits down.*)

DEATH: Funny little games people play, ha? The mother asks, but she already knows what her son is going to say. So does the father. And even little brother. They are all thinking: "He is going to say: Cecilia and I are getting married!"

JOHNNY: Cecilia and I are getting married!

MOTHER: Oh, son!

FATHER: You don't say!

BROTHER: Really?

MOTHER: When, son?

JOHNNY: When I get back from Vietnam.

DEATH: Suddenly a thought is crossing everybody's mind: "What if he doesn't come back?" But they shove it aside.

MOTHER: Oh, darling! (*She hugs* CECILIA.)

FATHER: Congratulations, son. (*He hugs* JOHNNY.)

MOTHER (*hugging* JOHNNY): My boy! (*She cries.*)

JOHNNY: Hey, mom, wait a minute. Save that for tomorrow. That's enough, ma.

FATHER: Daughter. (*He hugs* CECILIA *properly.*)

BROTHER: Heh, Johnny, why don't I go to Vietnam and you stay here for the wedding? I'm not afraid to die.

MOTHER: What makes you say that, child?

BROTHER: It just came out.

FATHER: You've let out too much already, don't you think?

BROTHER: I didn't mean it! (THE BROTHER *exits.*)

JOHNNY: It was an accident, pa.

MOTHER: You're right; it was an accident. Please, sweetheart, let's eat in peace, ha? Juan leaves tomorrow.

DEATH: The rest of the meal goes by without any incidents. They discuss the wedding, the tamales, and the weather. Then it's time to go to the party.

FATHER: Is it true there's going to be a party?

JOHNNY: Just a small dance, over at Sapo's house.

MOTHER: Which Sapo, son?

JOHNNY: Sapo, my friend.

FATHER: Don't get drunk, okay?

JOHNNY: Oh, come on, dad, Cecilia will be with me.

FATHER: Did you ask her parents for permission?

JOHNNY: Yes, sir. She's got to be home by eleven.

FATHER: Okay. (JOHNNY *and* CECILIA *rise*.)

CECILIA: Thank you for the dinner, ma'am.

MOTHER: You're very welcome.

CECILIA: The tamales were really good.

JOHNNY: Yes, ma, they were terrific.

MOTHER: Is that right, son? You liked them?

JOHNNY: They were great. (*He hugs her*.) Thanks, eh?

MOTHER: What do you mean thanks? You're my son. Go then, it's getting late.

FATHER: Do you want to take the truck, son?

JOHNNY: No thanks, pa. I already have Cecilia's car.

CECILIA: Not mine. My parents' car. They loaned it to us for the dance.

FATHER: It seems like you made a good impression, eh?

CECILIA: He sure did. They say he's more responsible now that he's in the service.

DEATH (*to audience*): Did you hear that? Listen to her again.

CECILIA (*repeats sentence, exactly as before*): They say he's more responsible now that he's in the service.

DEATH: That's what I like to hear!

FATHER: That's good. Then all you have to do is go ask for Cecilia's hand, right, sweetheart?

MOTHER: God willing.

JOHNNY: We're going, then.

CECILIA: Good night.

FATHER: Good night.

MOTHER: Be careful on the road, children.

JOHNNY: Don't worry, mom. Be back later.

CECILIA: Bye!

JOHNNY *and* CECILIA *exit*. THE MOTHER *stands at the door*.

FATHER (*sitting down again*): Well, old lady, little Johnny has become a man. The years fly by, don't they?

DEATH: The old man is thinking about the Korean War. Johnny was born about that time. He wishes he had some advice, some hints, to pass on to him about war. But he never went to Korea. The draft skipped him, and somehow, he never got around to enlisting. (THE MOTHER *turns around*.)

MOTHER (*she sees* DEATH): Oh, my God! (*exit*)

DEATH (*ducking down*): Damn, I think she saw me.

FATHER: What's wrong with you? (THE MOTHER *is standing frozen, looking toward the spot where* DEATH *was standing.*) Answer me, what's up? (*pause*) Speak to me! What am I, invisible?

MOTHER (*solemnly*): I just saw Death.

FATHER: Death? You're crazy.

MOTHER: It's true. As soon as Juan left, I turned around and there was Death, standing—smiling! (THE FATHER *moves away from the spot inadvertently.*) Oh, Blessed Virgin Mary, what if something happens to Juan.

FATHER: Don't say that! Don't you know it's bad luck?

They exit. DEATH *reenters.*

The Greyhound Bus Depot.

DEATH: The next day, Johnny goes to the Greyhound Bus Depot. His mother, his father, and his girlfriend go with him to say goodbye. The Bus Depot is full of soldiers and sailors and old men. Here and there, a drunkard is passed out on the benches. Then there's the announcements: THE LOS ANGELES BUS IS NOW RECEIVING PASSENGERS AT GATE TWO, FOR KINGSBURG, TULARE, DELANO, BAKERSFIELD AND LOS ANGELES, CONNECTIONS IN L.A. FOR POINTS EAST AND SOUTH.

JOHNNY, FATHER, MOTHER, *and* CECILIA *enter.* CECILIA *clings to* JOHNNY.

FATHER: It's been several years since I last set foot at the station.

MOTHER: Do you have your ticket, son?

JOHNNY: Oh, no, I have to buy it.

CECILIA: I'll go with you.

FATHER: Do you have money, son?

JOHNNY: Yes, pa, I have it.

JOHNNY *and* CECILIA *walk over to* DEATH.

JOHNNY: One ticket, please.

DEATH: Where to?

JOHNNY: Vietnam. I mean, Oakland.

DEATH: Round trip or one way?

JOHNNY: One way.

DEATH: Right. One way. (*applies more makeup*)

JOHNNY *gets his ticket and he and* CECILIA *start back toward his parents.* JOHNNY *stops abruptly and glances back at* DEATH, *who has already shifted positions.*

CECILIA: What's wrong?

JOHNNY: Nothing. (*They join the parents.*)

DEATH: For half an hour then, they exchange small talk and trivialities, repeating some of the things that have been said several times before. Cecilia promises Johnny she will be true to him and wait until he returns. Then it's time to go: THE OAKLAND-VIETNAM EXPRESS IS NOW RECEIVING PASSENGERS AT GATE NUMBER FOUR. ALL ABOARD PLEASE.

JOHNNY: That's my bus.

MOTHER: Oh, son.

FATHER: Take good care of yourself then, okay, son?

CECILIA: I love you, Johnny. (*She embraces him.*)

DEATH: THE OAKLAND-VIETNAM EXPRESS IS IN THE FINAL BOARDING STAGES. PASSENGERS WITH TICKETS ALL ABOARD PLEASE. AND THANKS FOR GOING GREYHOUND.

JOHNNY: I'm leaving, now.

Embraces all around, weeping, last goodbyes, etc. JOHNNY *exits. Then parents exit.*
THE MOTHER *and* CECILIA *are crying.*

DEATH (*sings*): *Goodbye, Goodbye*
     Star of my nights
     A soldier said in front of a window
     I'm leaving, I'm leaving
     But don't cry, my angel
     For tomorrow I'll be back . . .

So Johnny left for Vietnam, never to return. He didn't want to go and yet he did. It never crossed his mind to refuse. How can he refuse the government of the United States? How could he refuse his family? Besides, who wants to go to prison? And there was the chance he'd come back alive . . . wounded maybe, but alive. So he took a chance—and lost. But before he died he saw many things in Vietnam; he had his eyes opened. He wrote his mother about them.

JOHNNY *and* THE MOTHER *enter at opposite sides of the stage.* JOHNNY *is in full battle gear. His face is now a skull.*

JOHNNY: Dear mom.
MOTHER: Dear son.
JOHNNY: I am writing this letter.
MOTHER: I received your letter.
JOHNNY: To tell you I'm okay.
MOTHER: And I thank the heavens you're all right.
JOHNNY: How's everybody over there?
MOTHER: Here, we're all doing fine, thank God.
JOHNNY: Ma, there's a lot happening here that I didn't know about before. I don't know if I'm allowed to write about it, but I'm going to try. Yesterday we attacked a small village near some rice paddies. We had orders to kill everybody because they were supposed to be V-C's, communists. We entered the small village and my buddies started shooting. I saw one of them kill an old man and an old lady. My sergeant killed a small boy about seven years old, then he shot his mother or some woman that came running up crying. Blood was everywhere. I don't remember what happened after that but my sergeant ordered me to start shooting. I think I did. May God forgive me for what I did, but I never wanted to come over here. They say we have to do it to defend our country.
MOTHER: Son what you are writing to us makes me sad. I talked to your father and he also got very worried, but he says that's what war is like. He reminds you that you're fighting communists. I have a candle lit and every day I ask God to take good care of you wherever you are and that he return you to our arms healthy and in one piece.
JOHNNY: Ma, I had a dream the other night. I dreamed I was breaking into one of the hooches, that's what we call the Vietnamese's houses. I went in firing my M-16 because I knew that the village was controlled by the gooks. I killed three of them right away, but when I looked down it was my pa, my little brother and you, mother. I don't know how much more I can stand. Please tell Sapo and all the dudes how it's like over here. Don't let them . . .

DEATH *fires a gun, shooting* JOHNNY *in the head. He falls.* THE MOTHER *screams without looking at* JOHNNY.

DEATH: Johnny was killed in action November 1965 at Chu Lai. His body lay in the field for two days and then it was taken to the beach and placed in a freezer, a converted portable food locker. Two weeks later he was shipped home for burial.

DEATH *straightens out* JOHNNY'S *body. Takes his helmet, rifle, etc.* THE FATHER, THE MOTHER, THE BROTHER, *and* CECILIA *file past and gather around the body. Taps plays.*

THE RECEPTIVE READER

1. The central conflict in the medieval *Everyman* was between sin and virtue. What is the central conflict in *The Buck Private?*

2. To judge from this excerpt, does this play have a universal appeal transcending the appeal to a particular ethnic group? In what ways is the buck private a modern Everyman?

3. How does the role of Death compare in the two plays? How does the role of Kinship compare in the two plays?

THE PERSONAL RESPONSE

For you, what is the central statement this selection makes about the war in Vietnam?

THE CREATIVE DIMENSION

Like the traditional *Everyman,* Valdez' modern Everyman play lends itself well to adaptation for a miniproduction designed to help an audience get into the spirit of the play. (One class production changed the G.I. in the Valdez play to a young woman and the war to the "Desert Storm" war against Iraq.) You and your classmates may want to organize a group project to stage your own reenactment of the Valdez play.

WRITING ABOUT LITERATURE

25. Keeping a Drama Journal (Formats for Writing)

The Writing Workshop In reading or watching a play, you will ideally be carried along by the action that develops. Later, as you sort out your impressions, you will find it useful to keep a drama journal that allows you to record both your scene-by-scene reactions and your first thoughts about the play as a whole. Different journal entries might explore topics like the following: Where does the play take us—what setting or context does it create? How do the characters come into focus? How do major issues shape up? Does a central conflict begin to give shape to the play as a whole? Does a major theme begin to echo in key passages? What means does the dramatist use to steer the reactions of the audience or to create dramatic effects?

In form, your journal entries may vary greatly, ranging from reading notes (or viewing notes) to finished paragraphs and mini-essays. Study the following sample entries:

Running Commentary   Many readers find it useful to keep a **running commentary** on key developments and key passages in a play. Look at the way the following sample entries start recording queries and important evidence on key points in the opening scenes of Ibsen's *A Doll's House*. Note the amount of direct quotation for possible later use in a more formal paper:

> Torvald constantly uses what he thinks are terms of endearment that actually belittle Nora: "Is that my little skylark twittering out there?" "Scampering about like a little squirrel?" "Has my little featherbrain been out wasting money again?" "My little songbird mustn't be so crestfallen."
>
> Torvald gives lectures on not getting into debt: "No debts, no borrowing. There's something constrained, something ugly even, about a home that's founded on borrowing and debt."
>
> He calls Nora a "prodigal" who spends money "on all sorts of useless things."
>
> Nora's "sweet tooth" becomes an issue. She is treated like a child?

Focusing on Character   You may want to devote an entry to a major character, pulling together impressions that at first might have seemed contradictory or inconclusive. The following sample entry is a **character portrait** of a major character in *The Women of Troy* by the ancient Greek playwright Euripides. He wrote the play toward the end of the fifth century B.C., when his native Athens was reaching the end of a disastrous long drawn-out war. In the words of one student reader, the play "draws portraits of strong, independent, capable individuals, gathered together in the hours after the fall of Troy to the Greeks to mourn their dead and say goodbye to their homeland and to one another." Although the women are about to be taken into slavery, they speak up with great dignity and passion. A major source of strength to the other women is Hecabe, the newly widowed wife of King Priam, who with many of his sons and warriors has been killed in the fall of Troy.

> Euripides' women each have a unique personality, each dealing with her terrible fate as best she can. Hecabe, former wife of King Priam of Troy, is a truly pitiable tragic character of impressive stature. Early in the play, she says, "Lift your neck from the dust; up with your head! This is not Troy." She maintains this royal bearing and pride throughout the play, even when, "maddened and sick with horror," she awaits her fate. She bemoans aloud her fate of having to be a slave in Greece where she is likely to be a keeper of keys and answerer of doors, sleeping on the floor and wearing rags. The audience can share in her anguish when she finds that her daughter Polyxena has been offered as a human sacrifice at the grave of the Greek champion Achilles. She is also an extremely sympathetic character when she buries her little grandson Astyanax, killed by the Greeks to keep the boy from growing up to seek vengeance for the death of his father, Hector. However, Hecabe shows a vengeful or vindictive streak when she denounces Helen, whom she blames for much of what has befallen her city, in front of Helen's husband Menelaus. At a time when Helen is trying to save her life in the presence of the husband she had betrayed, Hecabe shows her thirst for vengeance and her unforgiving hatred of her enemies.

Focusing on Plot Preparing a **plot summary** (of the play as a whole or perhaps of one climactic act) can give you a better sense of the flow of a play. When debating the larger questions about a play, you will often find it useful to go back to exactly what happens in an act or a scene. A caution to observe: You may not learn much if your summary turns into a perfunctory stocktaking of events on the "and-then" model ("And then Willy's sons take him to a restaurant"). Instead, ask yourself: Why are these plot developments important? For instance, your summary might trace major developments building up to a major turning point or to the final catastrophe. The following sample entry summarizes the action in the final scenes of Arthur Miller's *Death of a Salesman*. Willy Loman is losing his already weak grip on reality; his relationship with his alienated son Biff is coming to a head; Willy is hatching the scheme that will make up for his and Biff's lifetimes of failures:

> After leaving Willy "babbling in a toilet" at the restaurant, the boys go out on the town with their dates only to come home to be thoroughly castigated by their mother: "There isn't a stranger you would do that to!" Linda shouts. Meanwhile, Willy, retreating into his world of illusion, is planting vegetable seeds in the garden—in the middle of the night—while carrying on a conversation with the legendary Uncle Ben (who walked into the jungle and came back rich). At this point, we learn of Willy's plan to commit suicide, leaving the proceeds of his life insurance to Biff. "God, he'll be great yet," Willy explains to Ben. "And now with twenty-five thousand behind him." "It sounds like an interesting proposition, William," Ben concurs.
>
> After Linda's bitter lecture to the boys, Biff tells his mother that he is no good and that he is leaving, never to return. He goes into the garden to bring his father into the kitchen, where the climactic scene occurs. When Willy learns Biff is leaving, he is furious and denounces Biff for wasting his life. "Spite!" Willy screams. "Spite is the word of your undoing!" Ultimately, Biff breaks down, crying, "Let me go. Can't you see that I'm just no good? There's no spite in it anymore! I'm just what I am." Willy, too, is overcome, although he still cannot let go of his illusion: "God, he'll be great yet."
>
> Once everyone retires—Biff is to leave the following morning—Willy proceeds with his plan. But this is not the end of the play. We are in for yet another sad irony. The final scene is the funeral. Throughout the play, Willy had prided himself on his popularity gained during all his years of selling; he had believed he was "well-liked." No one comes to his funeral—a bitter and tragic ending for one consumed by the "American Dream."

Focusing on Technique The dramatist's means—the tools of the playwright's trade—are most effective when we are not aware of them. They help the playwright create the illusion of reality. It may not be until we try to understand the effect or the workings of a play that we become consciously aware of the means. The following journal entry focuses on a device Arthur Miller uses repeatedly to alert the audience to the sad and laughable mixture of daydream and reality in Willy Loman's talk:

> Already in the first scene we become acutely aware of Willy's tendency to drift in and out of reality. His words are filled with contradictions as he

evades the truth only to face it a moment later full of self-pity. His sales estimates change in the same breath from boasting ("I'm vital in New England!") to pitiful excuses (three of the stores were half-closed). He says "Biff is a lazy bum!" and a few lines later resolutely talks himself into believing the opposite: "And such a hard worker. There's one thing about Biff—he's not lazy." The rapid shifting from sad recognition of the truth—that, for Willy, it is all over—to sudden outbursts of illusion and false hope characterizes Willy throughout the play. Miller does a superlative job with dialogue as Willy contradicts himself continuously, particularly in scenes with Linda. For example, when Linda is explaining what they owe for the month, she mentions the payment due on the refrigerator. Willy remarks, "I hope we didn't get stuck on that machine." Linda replies that it has the best advertisements. Willy responds, "I know, it's a fine machine."

Focusing on an Issue An entry may explore a major theme or issue in a play. It may look at pros and cons, presenting a **trial thesis** that could be argued more fully in a formal paper. The following entry takes on a key question raised by Ibsen's *A Doll's House:* Did Nora make the right decision at the end of the play?

"I must find out which is right—the world or I," Nora Helmer says near the end of Act III of *A Doll's House.* I know my reaction is based on hindsight, but a woman today might well urge Nora to be cautious in pitting herself against the world. In leaving her husband and children, she violates a social order larger and more powerful than herself. People like Torvald more often than not close ranks against the rebel who threatens the status quo and jealously guard their advantage. Women will not befriend her except for those who are themselves outside the order. Christine, who is respectable as a widow, may or may not stand by her.

As it happens, the world is bigger, meaner, colder, and more ruthless than a single, isolated person such as Nora is likely to be. She should not refuse Torvald's help, nor should she walk out taking only what she brought as a bride. Nora is likely to find that the world is manned by Torvalds. She is likely to be drawn to them and they to her, for it has been a lifetime pattern already deeply instilled. She has the natural gift to delight and charm men, and she has worked this gift down to a science, as Ibsen shows us in the first two acts. It has been her vocation to be the perfect wife—charming and diverting on the surface and ruthlessly practical behind the scenes in arranging the loan and paying it back all these years.

Torvald's self-preoccupation, rage, and condemnation of her when he learns about the loan shatter Nora's illusion of him. Nora moves very quickly from focusing on what has happened in her relationship with Torvald—his selfishness and knee-jerk condemnation of her worth as a human being—to going into the world to find out who is right or wrong. The risks and variables of surviving in the world alone are large. She will need money and friends, and she may have neither because of her defiance of conventional, accepted behavior for women. She may not want to live a celibate life, either. Permanent relationships may offer the same kind of trap she is in with Torvald—maybe worse, temporary ones are fraught with danger, disease, unwanted pregnancy, further loss of status in the community.

In today's terms, Nora has no job skills, no money, no connections other than Christine and Krogstad. Today's feminists might urge her to see an attorney and get as much information as she can before she departs. Life may be rough at home, but it can be even worse alone and friendless in the cold, hard world.

The Personal Connection   A play will move us most strongly if it strikes a chord somewhere in our own experience, if at some level it relates to something we have strongly felt. In reading or watching a play, have you ever felt the kind of personal connection that is the subject of the following journal entry?

Shakespeare has a way of making the agony of a play intensely personal. Hamlet's anguish, I feel, is caused mainly by external difficulties, by people other than himself. He finds himself in a situation not of his own making, a situation over which he has no control. He says, "The world is out of joint. O cursed spite that I was born to set it right." Perhaps I relate to him strongly because I have had a traumatic experience of being at the mercy of other people's initiatives, with my own role being that of experiencing reactions rather than taking action. My parents each remarried shortly after their divorce ("O, most wicked speed"). I know what it feels like to be avoided, to be in the way. My father did not tell me that he got married until three weeks after the wedding. Of course, Hamlet's grievance was much stronger because he was a prince who had expected to follow his father to the crown. He struggled with the obligation to avenge his father. Today, instead of striking back, we are expected to work our way through the psychological upheaval. We are expected to "cope."

A final suggestion: Write about any play readings, showings of videotaped plays, or live performances. You may want to discuss impact, audience appeal, audience reactions. You may want to talk about technical features that impressed or puzzled you: costuming, staging, performers' authentic or fake British or Southern accents. Make your drama log or drama journal a rich record of your growing interest in the theater.

26 GREEK TRAGEDY
The Embattled Protagonist

Many awesome things walk the earth,
but nothing more awesome than man.
SOPHOCLES, *ANTIGONE*

The structure of a play is always the story of how the birds
come home to roost.
ARTHUR MILLER

Everyone is alone on the core of the earth
pierced by a ray of sunlight;
and suddenly it's evening.
QUASIMODO UNGARETTI

FOCUS ON GREEK TRAGEDY

The golden age of ancient Greek drama takes us back 2,500 years to the Athens of the fifth century B.C. Greek drama was "formed at the center of the culture of its time, and at the center of the life and awareness of the community" (Francis Fergusson). But the great plays—*Antigone, Oedipus Rex, The Women of Troy*—are still gripping drama today. In a play like Sophocles' *Antigone,* the characters speak to us across the gulf of time in terms we understand. We can relate to their dilemmas, decisions, and mistakes.

In the very first scene, Antigone speaks to an issue that has confronted many in our time: The powers that be command her to act in a way that goes against her conscience. What the law requires offends her sense of what is right. The question is: Is there a higher law that the individual should obey? Can the individual defy the state? Or should a reasonable, sensible person skirt the confrontation that will make power show its true ugly face? If the individual chooses to defy authority, will friends and family desert the rebel in order to save themselves?

Here is a key to the Greek influence on the tradition of Western culture: We witness the appearance of recognizable human beings that give voice to the hopes and fears, the dreams and nightmares, of our common humanity. True, the characters that occupy center stage are members of a privileged class:

937

tribal chieftains or warlords and their spouses and the clans they represent. But their thoughts and feelings, their ambitions and disappointments, as well as the calamities that overtake them, often mirror our own, although projected onto a larger screen. When they talk about their gods and myths and taboos, we may need the scholar to annotate references that have lost their meaning for us. But when they talk about their loyalties and jealousies, their loves and hatreds, we often do not need an interpreter. We see a strong individual—man or woman—center stage, embattled, engaged in a fateful conflict with other human beings or with the gods.

THE ROOTS OF GREEK DRAMA

Drama is prior to the arts, the sciences, and the philosophies of modern civilization.
FRANCIS FERGUSSON

Greek drama is part of the legacy of classical Greek civilization that reached its high point in the sixth and fifth centuries B.C. Its temples have through the centuries inspired monumental public *architecture* (a Greek word); its tradition of public debate and citizen involvement was the beginning of Western *democracy* (a Greek word); its statues helped shape the traditional Western ideal of beauty. Its *drama* (from the Greek for "doings" or "things done") to this day helps shape the expectations we bring to the theater as one of the great performance arts.

Greek drama grew out of springtime festivals in honor of the god Dionysus. (To the Romans, he was known by another of his many names: Bacchus, the god of wine and revelry.) A statue of the god was close to the stage; a priest of Dionysus had a special front-row seat. The word *tragedy* originally meant "goat song," from the goat that was offered to the god as a ritual sacrifice. Like the earlier religious rituals, the theater (from a Greek word meaning "something to see") was a community affair, with as many as fifteen thousand people in attendance. Multitudes of spectators crowded a large semicircular outdoor theater, carved into the side of a hill, with steeply rising tiered stone seats.

Actors spoke through masks with exaggerated features—so that spectators on the periphery could see who was king, queen, servant, or priest. With the spectators unable to read emotions in the human face, the actors are likely to have used large sweeping gestures to express fear, apprehension, hostility, defiance, and rage. (In a famous *Oedipus* production by the Canadian director Tyrone Guthrie, exaggerated stylized movements and gestures of the actors were choreographed for powerful emotional impact.) In later periods, the actors wore high-soled boots (a kind of elevator shoe) that amplified their stature. As on Shakespeare's stage and in the Japanese Kabuki theater, male actors, it is assumed, played the female roles.

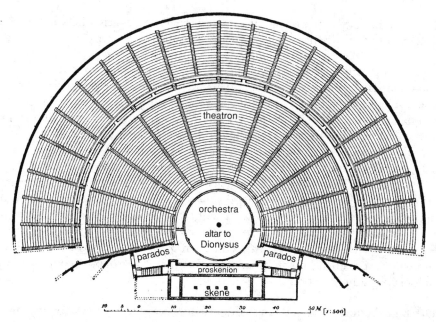

The Theater of Epidaurus in Athens, dating from the fourth century B.C. From A. E. Haigh, *The Attic Theater.*

Plays were chosen as part of elaborately organized drama contests that were major civic events. The plays were usually performed in groups of three, with the three playwrights competing for first prize. The major plays were **tragedies,** focused on famous calamities that had befallen the mighty. These plays dramatized traditional stories about lethal conflicts and fateful choices. The basic fare of three serious plays was spiced with a satyr play (named after the goat-footed, oversexed satyrs of Greek mythology). This early kind of **comedy** featured coarse, suggestive humor and satirical jabs at greedy contemporaries and obtuse leaders.

Greek drama evolved in the interplay of tradition and innovation. An early play, the *Prometheus Bound* of Aeschylus (525–456 B.C.), featured long static monologues by a single main actor. Sophocles took an important step toward the dramatic interplay of several characters by having more than two actors interacting on the stage at one time. A late play, *The Women of Troy* by Euripides (480–406 B.C.), put on stage the victims of the Greek conquest of Troy— women about to be taken to Greece as slaves, their men killed, their city in flames. We listen to a *range* of strong-minded individuals: the indomitable queen, Hecuba; the mad seer, Cassandra; Hector's virtuous wife, Andromache; and Helen, reviled as the cause of their calamity but determined to be a survivor.

To follow what happens on the Greek stage, you need to be comfortable with the **conventions,** the customary ways of doing things, that make classical

Greek drama different from what came after. (True classicists believe that the stagecraft of the ancient Greek dramatists has never been surpassed.)

Actors and the Chorus   Greek drama evolved from religious rituals using song and dance. As in the earlier rituals, the **chorus,** a group of performers, made solemn ceremonial entrances and exits. Led by the *choragos,* the chorus chanted and danced at regular intervals in the dramatic action. (The **orchestra,** a word we now use for a group of musicians, or for the seating area closest to the stage, was originally the circular "dancing area" in front of the stage.)

Before there were individual actors, the chorus, in song and dance, told the whole story. Gradually, individual actors (or soloists, you might say) began to act out the high points. (The word *episode* originally meant a dramatic scene between chants by the chorus.) As a result, the role of the chorus changed: In the plays that have come down to us, the chorus reacts to and comments on the action. The chorus in a way becomes an audience surrogate, or audience substitute, verbalizing for us what the reactions of a group of contemporary onlookers might have been.

Offstage Action   Greek drama stays in one place, such as the steps and open area in front of the king's palace. The play does not follow the action to different locations; instead, news of key events comes to the central location through messages or eyewitness reports. (A familiar walk-on part in Greek tragedy is that of the **messenger.**) A major effect: There is little *external action.* The plays do not act out the violence found in the ancient stories. Assassinations, suicides, parricides (slayings of parents), fatal quarrels, the abandonment or exposure of infants—these are reported, told, rather than enacted on the stage. The result is that the plays focus on *psychological* action—the characters' motives, loyalties, decisions, uncertainties—rather than on sensational physical violence.

Unity of Impact   Greek drama owes its impact to its single-minded concentration on the main action. There are no subplots, no comic interludes, no detours or distractions. At the height of classical drama, three actors at the most interacted on the stage at one time. In the great plays, a crisis or fateful conflict comes into focus; we are absorbed in how it came about and what will come of it. This gives the best of the Greek plays their concentrated power. They keep us spellbound, and they take us to their destination with single-minded determination. The concentrated effect comes from the celebrated three unities: unity of place, unity of time (a single day or at most a day and a half), unity of action.

THE DEFINITION OF TRAGEDY

The plot should be framed in such a way that
even without seeing the events take place someone
simply hearing the story should be moved to fear and pity.
ARISTOTLE, *POETICS*

The best-known Greek tragedies were traditional stories of terrible deeds among persons linked by close kinship. Later generations have brought to the tragedies expectations shaped by centuries of discussion of tragedy as a **genre,** or literary form. To this day, our definition of tragedy harks back to the Greek philosopher Aristotle, who included guidelines for the ideal tragedy in his more general discussion of imaginative literature, the *Poetics* (330 B.C.). For Aristotle, tragedy had attained its "true natural form" in a play like the *Oedipus Rex* of Sophocles (496–406 B.C.), the best known of the great Greek dramatists.

Plot   To Aristotle, the "life and soul" of tragedy was the plot, which had to be more than simply a sequence of disjointed episodes. Aristotle distinguished two major phases: setting up a problem or **complication,** and setting in motion the **denouement** (or unraveling) that resolves the issue. To Aristotle, the most powerful part of the plot was a sudden turn in the fortunes of the main character. This reversal (or **peripety**) was often brought on by an unexpected discovery. The turning point of the play might be the discovery of the true identity of the hero, or it might be the revelation of a long-forgotten incident from the past.

Character   Aristotle said that it was in the nature of tragedy to "arouse pity and fear." (He added, in passing, that the purpose was to bring about a cleansing or purging, or **catharsis,** of these feelings.) To arouse these tragic emotions, the playwright needed to create a tragic hero who was neither totally good nor totally bad. To see an outstandingly good person overtaken by undeserved calamity would arouse not fear but indignation—rebellion against unjust punishment. To see a villain come to a well-deserved end would arouse not pity but satisfaction. The ideal character would be an "intermediate" kind of person—great or admirable in some way but in other ways more like us. The character's misfortune would be brought on by an "error of judgment" or an imbalance in the character's personality.

Taking their clue from Aristotle, critics have looked in the personality of the hero for the **tragic flaw**—for instance, anger, self-righteousness, or indecision. Looking for a tragic flaw helps us make sense of the calamity we witness—we can see a connection between the characters' actions and their fate. In ancient Greek religion, the tragic flaw of arrogant humans was **hubris**—the overreaching pride that makes them forget their human limitations and makes them challenge the gods. In Sophocles' *Antigone,* the chorus, having the last word, ends the play by saying:

> The mighty words of the proud are paid in full
> with mighty blows of fate, and at long last
> those blows will teach us wisdom.

Self-Realization   In our time, critics have looked in true tragedy for evidence of growth in the tragic hero. They look for some kind of maturing or spiritual development. If we accept this requirement, we can think of the experience of tragedy as a spiritual journey. We come in at one point in the character's moral or spiritual development and come out at another. The central heroic figure should not just be a victim who is ground into the dust and learns nothing from the experience. The mere passive experience of pain and misery would represent not tragedy but **pathos** (from the Greek word for "suffering"). We look in the tragic figure for signs of the stature that comes from insight, from understanding.

THE *ANTIGONE* OF SOPHOCLES

*Come out of the twilight
and walk before us a while,
friendly, with the light step
of one whose mind is fully made up.*
BERTOLT BRECHT, *ANTIGONE*

*All human happiness or misery takes the form of action;
the end for which we live is a certain kind of activity, not
a quality. Character gives us qualities, but it is in our
actions—what we do—that we are happy or the reverse.*
ARISTOTLE

Sophocles wrote over a hundred plays for the drama festivals of ancient Athens. His *Antigone* (about 441 B.C.) is the first of three plays he based on the traditional story of Oedipus, king of Thebes, and his family. The doomed king had tried in vain to escape the fate marked out for him by the oracle of Apollo—

that I should lie with my own mother, breed
Children from whom all men would turn their eyes;
And that I should be my father's murderer.

Forewarned by the oracle, the parents of Oedipus—King Laius and Queen Jocasta of Thebes—had their newborn son exposed on a mountain to die, but the child was rescued by a shepherd and raised by the king of Corinth as his own son. When Oedipus was a young man, the oracle again sounded its prophecy of incest and parricide; in a vain attempt to thwart the oracle, Oedipus left his foster parents (whom he assumed to be his real parents). On a mountain highway, he became involved in a fatal quarrel and killed another traveler—unknown to him, this traveler was Laius, his real father. He cleared the Theban countryside of the rule of the monstrous Sphinx by solving her deadly riddle, and the grateful citizens of Thebes made him their king. He married their widowed queen Jocasta (unknown to him, his real mother).

In Sophocles' *Oedipus Rex,* Oedipus discovers his true identity and comes face to face with the unspeakable horror of incest. In the earlier *Antigone* play, Sophocles tells the story of the four children from Oedipus' incestuous union

A modern production of *Antigone.* © 1987 Martha Swope.

with Jocasta. Their father has died in exile, and their uncle Creon is now king of Thebes. Antigone is the more strong-willed and Ismene the more cautious of the two sisters. Of the two sons, one, Eteocles, has died fighting on the side of his native city in a war with neighboring Argos. But Polynices, the other brother, had turned traitor and fought on the side of Argos. He also has been killed in battle. Creon decrees that the corpse of the traitor be denied burial and be left to be devoured by dogs.

Creon's decree sets up the basic **conflict** of the play. On the one hand, loyalty to country—to the city-state (or *polis*)—was then as strong a force as patriotism, with the demands of the state for allegiance, is today. However, as in other early civilizations, burial customs and funeral rites were a cornerstone of Greek religion. Honoring its dead was a central duty of every family. Antigone is caught between these two conflicting loyalties. Should she obey the law of the gods and perform at least a symbolic burial for her dishonored brother? Her central role makes her the tragic **protagonist** in the play. Originally, *protagonist* merely meant the "first competitor," or first actor, initiating the action. However, today the term stands for a major force or principle of action in the play. Antigone is a powerfully motivated character who sets a fateful chain of events in motion. She is pitted against a worthy opponent, Creon, who is the **antagonist.** He is the counterforce that makes for a clash of powerful opposites.

In reading the play, you should try to visualize the clash between protagonist and antagonist as they act out their fateful confrontation. (If you can, try to view all or part of the play on videotape.) Antigone and Creon are often face to face, trading pointed scornful remarks in the quick-fire exchanges the Greeks called *stichomythy.* You should also listen carefully to the supporting characters who are caught between the two mighty opposites. Ismene, Antigone's sister, provides a **foil** to Antigone by voicing the more cautious view. Haemon, Antigone's fiancé, is caught between his headstrong father and his strong-willed intended bride. As in the later *Oedipus* play, Tiresias, the blind priest and prophet, is a voice of warning heeded too late.

S O P H O C L E S (496–406/5 B.C.)

Fate leads the willing, drags the unwilling.
CLEANTHES

Sophocles was an honored public servant and military officer during the height of the power of Athens. As a popular and handsome young man, he danced in the victory celebration after the Greeks defeated the Persians in the sea battle of Salamis (480 B.C.). He wrote over a hundred plays, seven of which have survived. He took first prize in the drama contests at Athens twenty-four times. He died shortly before Athens lost its disastrous long drawn-out war against its chief rival, Sparta.

Antigone   about 441 B.C.

TRANSLATED BY ROBERT FAGLES

[The characters in this play, and especially the chorus, use **allusions** to myths and legends familiar to Sophocles' audience. The chorus honors Dionysus, "god of many names" (Bacchus, Iacchus). He was the offspring of Zeus' union with a mortal (Semele). Other gods are mentioned: Aphrodite, goddess of love; Ares, god of war; and Demeter, goddess of the harvest. Antigone alludes to Niobe, who wept after losing all her numerous children (and in the end was turned to stone). The chorus compares Antigone's fate to that of Danaë, another mortal lover of Zeus, and to the fate of Lycurgus, a king who was punished for trying to suppress the cult of Dionysus.]

CHARACTERS

ANTIGONE, daughter of OEDIPUS and JOCASTA
ISMENE, sister of ANTIGONE
A CHORUS of old Theban citizens and their LEADER
CREON, king of Thebes, uncle of ANTIGONE and ISMENE
A SENTRY
HAEMON, son of CREON and EURYDICE
TIRESIAS, a blind prophet
A MESSENGER
EURYDICE, wife of CREON
Guards, attendants, and a boy

PROLOGUE

TIME AND SCENE: *The royal house of Thebes. It is still night, and the invading armies of Argos have just been driven from the city. Fighting on opposite sides, the sons of Oedipus, Eteocles and Polynices, have killed each other in combat. Their uncle,* CREON, *is now king of Thebes.*

　　Enter ANTIGONE, *slipping through the central doors of the palace. She motions to her sister,* ISMENE, *who follows her cautiously toward an altar at the center of the stage.*

ANTIGONE: My own flesh and blood—dear sister, dear Ismene,
　　how many griefs our father Oedipus handed down!
　　Do you know one, I ask you, one grief
　　that Zeus will not perfect for the two of us
　　while we still live and breathe? There's nothing,   5
　　no pain—our lives are pain—no private shame,
　　no public disgrace, nothing I haven't seen
　　in your griefs and mine. And now this:
　　an emergency decree, they say, the Commander
　　has just now declared for all of Thebes.   10
　　What, haven't you heard? Don't you see?
　　The doom reserved for enemies
　　marches on the ones we love the most.
ISMENE: Not I, I haven't heard a word, Antigone.
　　Nothing of loved ones,   15
　　no joy or pain has come my way, not since
　　the two of us were robbed of our two brothers,
　　both gone in a day, a double blow—
　　not since the armies of Argos vanished,
　　just this very night. I know nothing more,   20
　　whether our luck's improved or ruin's still to come.

ANTIGONE: I thought so. That's why I brought you out here,
    past the gates, so you could hear in private.
ISMENE: What's the matter? Trouble, clearly . . .
    you sound so dark, so grim. 25
ANTIGONE: Why not? Our own brothers' burial!
    Hasn't Creon graced one with all the rites,
    disgraced the other? Eteocles, they say,
    has been given full military honors,
    rightly so—Creon has laid him in the earth 30
    and he goes with glory down among the dead.
    But the body of Polynices, who died miserably—
    why, a city-wide proclamation, rumor has it,
    forbids anyone to bury him, even mourn him.
    He's to be left unwept, unburied, a lovely treasure 35
    for birds that scan the field and feast to their heart's content.

    Such, I hear, is the martial law our good Creon
    lays down for you and me—yes, me, I tell you—
    and he's coming here to alert the uninformed
    in no uncertain terms, 40
    and he won't treat the matter lightly. Whoever
    disobeys in the least will die, his doom is sealed:
    stoning to death inside the city walls!

    There you have it. You'll soon show what you are,
    worth your breeding, Ismene, or a coward— 45
    for all your royal blood.
ISMENE: My poor sister, if things have come to this,
    who am I to make or mend them, tell me,
    what good am I to you?
ANTIGONE: Decide.
    Will you share the labor, share the work? 50
ISMENE: What work, what's the risk? What do you mean?
ANTIGONE:

    [*Raising her hands.*]

    Will you lift up his body with these bare hands
    and lower it with me?
ISMENE: What? You'd bury him—
    when a law forbids the city?
ANTIGONE: Yes!
    He is my brother and—deny it as you will— 55
    your brother too.
    No one will ever convict me for a traitor.
ISMENE: So desperate, and Creon has expressly—
ANTIGONE: No,
    he has no right to keep me from my own.
ISMENE: Oh my sister, think— 60
    think how our own father died, hated,
    his reputation in ruins, driven on
    by the crimes he brought to light himself

to gouge out his eyes with his own hands—
then mother . . . his mother and wife, both in one,   65
mutilating her life in the twisted noose—
and last, our two brothers dead in a single day,
both shedding their own blood, poor suffering boys,
battling out their common destiny hand-to-hand.

Now look at the two of us, left so alone . . .   70
think what a death we'll die, the worst of all
if we violate the laws and override
the fixed decree of the throne, its power—
we must be sensible. Remember we are women,
we're not born to contend with men. Then too,   75
we're underlings, ruled by much stronger hands,
so we must submit in this, and things still worse.

I, for one, I'll beg the dead to forgive me—
I'm forced, I have no choice—I must obey
the ones who stand in power. Why rush to extremes?   80
It's madness, madness.

ANTIGONE: I won't insist,
no, even if you should have a change of heart,
I'd never welcome you in the labor, not with me.
So, do as you like, whatever suits you best—
I will bury him myself.   85
And even if I die in the act, that death will be a glory.
I will lie with the one I love and loved by him—
an outrage sacred to the gods! I have longer
to please the dead than please the living here: *Dead for eternity*
in the kingdom down below I'll lie forever.   90
Do as you like, dishonor the laws
the gods hold in honor.

ISMENE: I'd do them no dishonor . . .
but defy the city? I have no strength for that.

ANTIGONE: You have your excuses. I am on my way,
I will raise a mound for him, for my dear brother.   95

ISMENE: Oh Antigone, you're so rash—I'm so afraid for you!

ANTIGONE: Don't fear for me. Set your own life in order.

ISMENE: Then don't, at least, blurt this out to anyone.
Keep it a secret. I'll join you in that, I promise.

ANTIGONE: Dear god, shout it from the rooftops. I'll hate you   100
all the more for silence—tell the world!

ISMENE: So fiery—and it ought to chill your heart.

ANTIGONE: I know I please where I must please the most.

ISMENE: Yes, if you can, but you're in love with impossibility.

ANTIGONE: Very well then, once my strength gives out   105
I will be done at last.

ISMENE: You're wrong from the start,
you're off on a hopeless quest.

ANTIGONE: If you say so, you will make me hate you,
and the hatred of the dead, by all rights,
will haunt you night and day.   110

But leave me to my own absurdity, leave me
to suffer this—dreadful thing. I will suffer
nothing as great as death without glory.

[*Exit to the side.*]

ISMENE: Then go if you must, but rest assured,
　　　wild, irrational as you are, my sister,　　　　　　　　　　　　115
　　　you are truly dear to the ones who love you.

[*Withdrawing to the palace.*]

[*Enter a* CHORUS, *the old citizens of Thebes, chanting as the sun begins to rise.*]

CHORUS: Glory!—great beam of the sun, brightest of all
　　　that ever rose on the seven gates of Thebes,
　　　　　　you burn through night at last!
　　　　　　　　　Great eye of the golden day,　　　　　　　　120
　　　mounting the Dirce's banks you throw him back—
　　　the enemy out of Argos, the white shield, the man of bronze—
　　　he's flying headlong now
　　　　　　　　the bridle of fate stampeding him with pain!

　　　　　And he had driven against our borders,　　　　　　　　125
　　　　　launched by the warring claims of Polynices—
　　　　　like an eagle screaming, winging havoc
　　　　　over the land, wings of armor
　　　　　shielded white as snow,
　　　　　a huge army massing,　　　　　　　　　　　　　　130
　　　　　crested helmets bristling for assault.

He hovered above our roofs, his vast maw gaping
closing down around our seven gates,
　　　his spears thirsting for the kill
　　　　　　but now he's gone, look,　　　　　　　　　　135
　　　before he could glut his jaws with Theban blood
　　　or the god of fire put our crown of towers to the torch.
　　　He grappled the Dragon none can master—Thebes—
　　　　　　the clang of our arms like thunder at his back!

　　　　　Zeus hates with a vengeance all bravado,　　　　　　140
　　　　　the mighty boasts of men. He watched them
　　　　　coming on in a rising flood, the pride
　　　　　of their golden armor ringing shrill—
　　　　　and brandishing his lightning
　　　　　blasted the fighter just at the goal,　　　　　　　　145
　　　　　rushing to shout his triumph from our walls.
Down from the heights he crashed, pounding down on the earth!
And a moment ago, blazing torch in hand—
　　　　　　mad for attack, ecstatic
he breathed his rage, the storm　　　　　　　　　　　　150
　　　of his fury hurling at our heads!
But now his high hopes have laid him low
and down the enemy ranks the iron god of war

deals his rewards, his stunning blows—Ares
rapture of battle, our right arm in the crisis. 155

Seven captains marshaled at seven gates
seven against their equals, gave
their brazen trophies up to Zeus,
god of the breaking rout of battle,
all but two: those blood brothers, 160
one father, one mother—matched in rage,
spears matched for the twin conquest—
clashed and won the common prize of death.

But now for Victory! Glorious in the morning,
joy in her eyes to meet our joy 165
    she is winging down to Thebes,
our fleets of chariots wheeling in her wake—
    Now let us win oblivion from the wars,
thronging the temples of the gods
in singing, dancing choirs through the night! 170
    Lord Dionysus, god of the dance
    that shakes the land of Thebes, now lead the way!

SCENE 1

[*Enter* CREON *from the palace, attended by his guard.*]

CHORUS: But look, the king of the realm is coming,
Creon, the new man for the new day,
whatever the gods are sending now . . .
what new plan will he launch?
Why this, this special session? 5
Why this sudden call to the old men
summoned at one command?
CREON: My countrymen,
the ship of state is safe. The gods who rocked her,
after a long, merciless pounding in the storm,
have righted her once more.
                Out of the whole city 10
I have called you here alone. Well I know,
first, your undeviating respect
for the throne and royal power of King Laius.
Next, while Oedipus steered the land of Thebes,
and even after he died, your loyalty was unshakable, 15
you still stood by their children. Now then,
since the two sons are dead—two blows of fate
in the same day, cut down by each other's hands,
both killers, both brothers stained with blood—
as I am next in kin to the dead, 20
I now possess the throne and all its powers.

Of course you cannot know a man completely,
his character, his principles, sense of judgment,

not till he's shown his colors, ruling the people,
making laws. Experience, there's the test.   25
As I see it, whoever assumes the task,
the awesome task of setting the city's course,
and refuses to adopt the soundest policies
but fearing someone, keeps his lips locked tight,
he's utterly worthless. So I rate him now,   30
I always have. And whoever places a friend
above the good of his own country, he is nothing:
I have no use for him. Zeus my witness,
Zeus who sees all things, always—
I could never stand by silent, watching destruction   35
march against our city, putting safety to rout,
nor could I ever make that man a friend of mine
who menaces our country. Remember this:
our country *is* our safety.
Only while she voyages true on course   40
can we establish friendships, truer than blood itself.
Such are my standards. They make our city great.

Closely akin to them I have proclaimed,
just now, the following decree to our people
concerning the two sons of Oedipus.   45
Eteocles, who died fighting for Thebes,
excelling all in arms: he shall be buried,
crowned with a hero's honors, the cups we pour
to soak the earth and reach the famous dead.

But as for his blood brother, Polynices,   50
who returned from exile, home to his father-city
and the gods of his race, consumed with one desire—
to burn them roof to roots—who thirsted to drink
his kinsmen's blood and sell the rest to slavery:
that man—a proclamation has forbidden the city   55
to dignify him with burial, mourn him at all.
No, he must be left unburied, his corpse
carrion for the birds and dogs to tear,
an obscenity for the citizens to behold!

These are my principles. Never at my hands   60
will the traitor be honored above the patriot.
But whoever proves his loyalty to the state—
I'll prize that man in death as well as life.
LEADER: If this is your pleasure, Creon, treating
our city's enemy and our friend this way . . .   65
The power is yours, I suppose, to enforce it
with the laws, both for the dead and all of us,
the living.
CREON: Follow my orders closely then,
be on your guard.
LEADER: We are too old.
Lay that burden on younger shoulders.

CREON: No, no,   70
    I don't mean the body—I've posted guards already.
LEADER: What commands for us then? What other service?
CREON: See that you never side with those who break my orders.
LEADER: Never. Only a fool could be in love with death.
CREON: Death is the price—you're right. But all too often   *Oedipus wanted Creon [?]*
    the mere hope of money has ruined many men.   *accused him of wanting money*
                                                                    and power from his message.

    [*A* SENTRY *enters from the side.*]

SENTRY: My lord,
    I can't say I'm winded from running, or set out
    with any spring in my legs either—no sir,
    I was lost in thought, and it made me stop, often,
    dead in my tracks, wheeling, turning back,   80
    and all the time a voice inside me muttering,
    "Idiot, why? You're going straight to your death."
    Then muttering, "Stopped again, poor fool?
    If somebody gets the news to Creon first,
    what's to save your neck?"
                    And so,   85
    mulling it over, on I trudged, dragging my feet,
    you can make a short road take forever . . .
    but at last, look, common sense won out,
    I'm here, and I'm all yours,
    and even though I come empty-handed   90
    I'll tell my story just the same, because
    I've come with a good grip on one hope,
    what will come will come, whatever fate—
CREON: Come to the point!
    What's wrong—why so afraid?   95
SENTRY: First, myself, I've got to tell you,
    I didn't do it, didn't see who did—
    Be fair, don't take it out on me.
CREON: You're playing it safe, soldier,
    barricading yourself from any trouble.   100
    It's obvious, you've something strange to tell.
SENTRY: Dangerous too, and danger makes you delay
    for all you're worth.
CREON: Out with it—then dismiss!
SENTRY: All right, here it comes. The body—   105
    someone's just buried it, then run off . . .   *→ symbolically bury*
    sprinkled some dry dust on the flesh,   *[?]*
    given it proper rites.
CREON: What?
    What man alive would dare—
SENTRY: I've no idea, I swear it.
    There was no mark of a spade, no pickaxe there,   110
    no earth turned up, the ground packed hard and dry,
    unbroken, no tracks, no wheelruts, nothing,
    the workman left no trace. Just at sunup

the first watch of the day points it out—
it was a wonder! We were stunned . . .   115
a terrific burden too, for all of us, listen:
you can't see the corpse, not that it's buried,
really, just a light cover of road-dust on it,
as if someone meant to lay the dead to rest
and keep from getting cursed.   120
Not a sign in sight that dogs or wild beasts
had worried the body, even torn the skin.

But what came next! Rough talk flew thick and fast,
guard grilling guard—we'd have come to blows
at last, nothing to stop it; each man for himself   125
and each the culprit, no one caught red-handed,
all of us pleading ignorance, dodging the charges,
ready to take up red-hot iron in our fists,
go through fire, swear oaths to the gods—
"I didn't do it, I had no hand in it either,   130
not in the plotting, not the work itself!"

Finally, after all this wrangling came to nothing,
one man spoke out and made us stare at the ground,
hanging our heads in fear. No way to counter him,
no way to take his advice and come through   135
safe and sound. Here's what he said:
"Look, we've got to report the facts to Creon,
we can't keep this hidden." Well, that won out,
and the lot fell to me, condemned me,
unlucky as ever, I got the prize. So here I am,   140
against my will and yours too, well I know—
no one wants the man who brings bad news.
LEADER: My king,
        ever since he began I've been debating in my mind,
        could this possibly be the work of the gods?
CREON: Stop—
        before you make me choke with anger—the gods!   145
        You, you're senile, must you be insane?
        You say—why it's intolerable—say the gods
        could have the slightest concern for that corpse?
        Tell me, was it for meritorious service
        they proceeded to bury him, prized him so? The hero   150
        who came to burn their temples ringed with pillars,
        their golden treasures—scorch their hallowed earth
        and fling their laws to the winds.
        Exactly when did you last see the gods
        celebrating traitors? Inconceivable!   155

        No, from the first there were certain citizens
        who could hardly stand the spirit of my regime,
        grumbling against me in the dark, heads together,
        tossing wildly, never keeping their necks beneath
        the yoke, loyally submitting to their king.   160

These are the instigators, I'm convinced—
they've perverted my own guard, bribed them
to do their work.
    Money! Nothing worse
in our lives, so current, rampant, so corrupting.
Money—you demolish cities, root men from their homes,   165
you train and twist good minds and set them on
to the most atrocious schemes. No limit,
you make them adept at every kind of outrage,
every godless crime—money!
      Everyone—
the whole crew bribed to commit this crime,   170
they've made one thing sure at least;
sooner or later they will pay the price.

[*Wheeling on the* SENTRY.]

      You—
I swear to Zeus as I still believe in Zeus,
if you don't find the man who buried that corpse,
the very man, and produce him before my eyes,   175
simple death won't be enough for you,
not till we string you up alive
and wring the immorality out of you.
Then you can steal the rest of your days,
better informed about where to make a killing.   180
You'll have learned, at last, it doesn't pay
to itch for rewards from every hand that beckons.
Filthy profits wreck most men, you'll see—
they'll never save your life.
SENTRY: Please,
   may I say a word or two, or just turn and go?   185
CREON: Can't you tell? Everything you say offends me.
SENTRY: Where does it hurt you, in the ears or in the heart?
CREON: And who are you to pinpoint my displeasure?
SENTRY: The culprit grates on your feelings,
   I just annoy your ears.
CREON: Still talking?   190
   You talk too much! A born nuisance—
SENTRY: Maybe so,
   but I never did this thing, so help me!
CREON: Yes you did—
   what's more, you squandered your life for silver!
SENTRY: Oh it's terrible when the one who does the judging
   judges things all wrong.
CREON: Well now,   195
   you just be clever about your judgments—
   if you fail to produce the criminals for me,
   you'll swear your dirty money brought you pain.

       [*Turning sharply, reentering the palace.*]

SENTRY: I hope he's found. Best thing by far.
    But caught or not, that's in the lap of fortune: 200
    I'll never come back, you've seen the last of me.
    I'm saved, even now, and I never thought,
    I never hoped—
    dear gods, I owe you all my thanks!

about man & his place in the world.   [*Rushing out.*]

CHORUS: Numberless wonders
    terrible wonders walk the world but none the match for man—   205
    that great wonder crossing the heaving gray sea,
            driven on by the blasts of winter
    on through breakers crashing left and right,
        holds his steady course
    and the oldest of the gods he wears away—   210
    the Earth, the immortal, the inexhaustible—
    as his plows go back and forth, year in, year out
        with the breed of stallions turning up the furrows.

    And the blithe, lightheaded race of birds he snares,
    the tribes of savage beasts, the life that swarms the depths—   215
        with one fling of his nets
    woven and coiled tight, he takes them all,
        man the skilled, the brilliant!
    He conquers all, taming with his techniques
    the prey that roams the cliffs and wild lairs,   220
    training the stallion, clamping the yoke across
        his shaggy neck, and the tireless mountain bull.

    And speech and thought, quick as the wind
    and the mood and mind for law that rules the city—
        all these he has taught himself   225
    and shelter from the arrows of the frost
    when there's rough lodging under the cold clear sky
    and the shafts of lashing rain—
        ready, resourceful man!
            Never without resources   230
    never an impasse as he marches on the future—
    only Death, from Death alone he will find no rescue
    but from desperate plagues he has plotted his escapes.

    Man the master, ingenious past all measure
    past all dreams, the skills within his grasp—   235
        he forges on, now to destruction
    now again to greatness. When he weaves in
    the laws of the land, and the justice of the gods
    that binds his oaths together
        he and his city rise high—   240
        but the city casts out
    that man who weds himself to inhumanity
    thanks to the reckless daring. Never share my hearth
    never think my thoughts, whoever does such things.

SCENE 2

[*Enter* ANTIGONE *from the side, accompanied by the* SENTRY.]

CHORUS: Here is a dark sign from the gods—
    what to make of this? I know her,
    how can I deny it? That young girl's Antigone!
    Wretched, child of a wretched father,
    Oedipus. Look, is it possible?   5
    They bring you in like a prisoner—
    why? did you break the king's laws?
    Did they take you in some act of mad defiance?
SENTRY: She's the one, she did it single-handed—
    we caught her burying the body. Where's Creon?   10

[*Enter* CREON *from the palace.*]

LEADER: Back again, just in time when you need him.
CREON: In time for what? What is it?
SENTRY: My king,
    there's nothing you can swear you'll never do—
    second thoughts make liars of us all.
    I could have sworn I wouldn't hurry back   15
    (what with your threats, the buffeting I just took),
    but a stroke of luck beyond our wildest hopes,
    what a joy, there's nothing like it. So,
    back I've come, breaking my oath, who cares?
    I'm bringing in our prisoner—this young girl—   20
    we took her giving the dead the last rites.
    But no casting lots this time; this is *my* luck,
    my prize, no one else's.
                Now, my lord,
    here she is. Take her, question her,
    cross-examine her to your heart's content.   25
    But set me free, it's only right—
    I'm rid of this dreadful business once for all.
CREON: Prisoner! Her? You took her—where, doing what?
SENTRY: Burying the man. That's the whole story.
CREON: What?   30
    You mean what you say, you're telling me the truth?
SENTRY: She's the one. With my own eyes I saw her
    bury the body, just what you've forbidden.
    There. Is that plain and clear?
CREON: What did you see? Did you catch her in the act?
SENTRY: Here's what happened. We went back to our post,   35
    those threats of yours breathing down our necks—
    we brushed the corpse clean of the dust that covered it,
    stripped it bare . . . it was slimy, going soft,
    and we took to high ground, backs to the wind
    so the stink of him couldn't hit us;   40
    jostling, baiting each other to keep awake,

shouting back and forth—no napping on the job,
not this time. And so the hours dragged by
until the sun stood dead above our heads,
a huge white ball in the noon sky, beating,   45
blazing down, and then it happened—
suddenly, a whirlwind!
Twisting a great dust-storm up from the earth,
a black plague of the heavens, filling the plain,
ripping the leaves off every tree in sight,   50
choking the air and sky. We squinted hard
and took our whipping from the gods.

And after the storm passed—it seemed endless—
there, we saw the girl!
And she cried out a sharp, piercing cry,   55
like a bird come back to an empty nest,
peering into its bed, and all the babies gone . . .
Just so, when she sees the corpse bare
she bursts into a long, shattering wail
and calls down withering curses on the heads   60
of all who did the work. And she scoops up dry dust,
handfuls, quickly, and lifting a fine bronze urn,
lifting it high and pouring, she crowns the dead
with three full libations.
     Soon as we saw
we rushed her, closed on the kill like hunters,   65
and she, she didn't flinch. We interrogated her,
charging her with offenses past and present—
she stood up to it all, denied nothing. I tell you,
it made me ache and laugh in the same breath.
It's pure joy to escape the worst yourself,   70
it hurts a man to bring down his friends.
But all that, I'm afraid, means less to me
than my own skin. That's the way I'm made.
CREON:

[*Wheeling on* ANTIGONE.]

          You,
with your eyes fixed on the ground—speak up.
Do you deny you did this, yes or no?   75
ANTIGONE: I did it. I don't deny a thing.
CREON:

[*To the* SENTRY.]

You, get out, wherever you please—
you're clear of a very heavy charge.

[*He leaves;* CREON *turns back to* ANTIGONE.]

You, tell me briefly, no long speeches—
were you aware a decree had forbidden this?   80

ANTIGONE: Well aware. How could I avoid it? It was public.
CREON: And still you had the gall to break this law?
ANTIGONE: Of course I did. It wasn't Zeus, not in the least,
   who made this proclamation—not to me.
   Nor did that Justice, dwelling with the gods   85
   beneath the earth, ordain such laws for men.
   Nor did I think your edict had such force
   that you, a mere mortal, could override the gods,   *when man's law contradicts God's*
   the great unwritten, unshakable traditions.   *law – seen throughout history*
   They are alive, not just today or yesterday: 90
   they live forever, from the first of time,
   and no one knows when they first saw the light.

   These laws—I was not about to break them,
   not out of fear of some man's wounded pride,
   and face the retribution of the gods.   95
   Die I must, I've known it all my life—
   how could I keep from knowing?—even without
   your death-sentence ringing in my ears.
   And if I am to die before my time
   I consider that a gain. Who on earth,   100
   alive in the midst of so much grief as I,
   could fail to find his death a rich reward?
   So for me, at least, to meet this doom of yours
   is precious little pain. But if I had allowed
   my own mother's son to rot, an unburied corpse—   105
   that would have been an agony! This is nothing.
   And if my present actions strike you as foolish,
   let's just say I've been accused of folly
   by a fool.
LEADER: Like father like daughter,
   passionate, wild . . .   110
   she hasn't learned to bend before adversity.
CREON: No? Believe me, the stiffest stubborn wills
   fall the hardest; the toughest iron,
   tempered strong in the white-hot fire,
   you'll see it crack and shatter first of all.   115
   And I've known spirited horses you can break
   with a light bit—proud, rebellious horses.
   There's no room for pride, not in a slave,
   not with the lord and master standing by.

   This girl was an old hand at insolence   120
   when she overrode the edicts we made public.
   But once she had done it—the insolence,
   twice over—to glory in it, laughing,
   mocking us to our face with what she'd done.
   I am not the man, not now: she is the man   125
   if this victory goes to her and she goes free.

   Never! Sister's child or closer in blood
   than all my family clustered at my altar

worshiping Guardian Zeus—she'll never escape,
she and her blood sister, the most barbaric death.
Yes, I accuse her sister of an equal part   130
in scheming this, this burial.

[*To his attendants.*]

                              Bring her here!
I just saw her inside, hysterical, gone to pieces.
It never fails: the mind convicts itself
in advance, when scoundrels are up to no good,   135
plotting in the dark. Oh but I hate it more
when a traitor, caught red-handed,
tries to glorify his crimes.
ANTIGONE: Creon, what more do you want
    than my arrest and execution?   140
CREON: Nothing. Then I have it all.
ANTIGONE: Then why delay? Your moralizing repels me,
    every word you say—pray god it always will.
    So naturally all I say repels you too.
                              Enough.
    Give me glory! What greater glory could I win   145
    than to give my own brother decent burial?
    These citizens here would all agree,

[*To the* CHORUS.]

    they would praise me too
    if their lips weren't locked in fear.

[*Pointing to* CREON.]

    Lucky tyrants—the perquisites of power!   150
    Ruthless power to do and say whatever pleases *them*.
CREON: You alone, of all the people in Thebes,
    see things that way.
ANTIGONE: They see it just that way
    but defer to you and keep their tongues in leash.
CREON: And you, aren't you ashamed to differ so from them?   155
    So disloyal!
ANTIGONE: Not ashamed for a moment,
    not to honor my brother, my own flesh and blood.
CREON: Wasn't Eteocles a brother too—cut down, facing him?
ANTIGONE: Brother, yes, by the same mother, the same father.
CREON: Then how can you render his enemy such honors,   160
    such impieties in his eyes?
ANTIGONE: He will never testify to that,
    Eteocles dead and buried.
CREON: He will—
    if you honor the traitor just as much as him.
ANTIGONE: But it was his brother, not some slave that died—   165
CREON: Ravaging our country!—
    but Eteocles died fighting in our behalf.

ANTIGONE: No matter—Death longs for the same rites for all.

CREON: Never the same for the patriot and the traitor.

ANTIGONE: Who, Creon, who on earth can say the ones below   170
    don't find this pure and uncorrupt?

CREON: Never. Once an enemy, never a friend,
    not even after death.

ANTIGONE: I was born to join in love, not hate—
    that is my nature.

CREON: Go down below and love,   175
    if love you must—love the dead! While I'm alive,
    no woman is going to lord it over me.   *— has a problem w/ women too*

[*Enter* ISMENE *from the palace, under guard.*]

CHORUS: Look,
    Ismene's coming, weeping a sister's tears,
    loving sister, under a cloud . . .
    her face is flushed, her cheeks streaming.   180
    Sorrow puts her lovely radiance in the dark.

CREON: You—
    in my own house, you viper, slinking undetected,
    sucking my life-blood! I never knew
    I was breeding twin disasters, the two of you
    rising up against my throne. Come, tell me,   185
    will you confess your part in the crime or not?
    Answer me. Swear to me.

ISMENE: I did it, yes—
    if only she consents—I share the guilt,
    the consequences too.

ANTIGONE: No,   *— Justice personified*
    Justice will never suffer that—not you,   190
    you were unwilling. I never brought you in.

ISMENE: But now you face such dangers . . . I'm not ashamed
    to sail through trouble with you,
    make your troubles mine.

ANTIGONE: Who did the work?
    Let the dead and the god of death bear witness!
    I have no love for a friend who loves in words alone. *— friend in deed not just   195
in words*

ISMENE: Oh no, my sister, don't reject me, please,
    let me die beside you, consecrating
    the dead together.

ANTIGONE: Never share my dying,
    don't lay claim to what you never touched.   200
    My death will be enough.

ISMENE: What do I care for life, cut off from you?

ANTIGONE: Ask Creon. Your concern is all for him.

ISMENE: Why abuse me so? It doesn't help you now.

ANTIGONE: You're right—
    if I mock you, I get no pleasure from it,   205
    only pain.

ISMENE: Tell me, dear one,
    what can I do to help you, even now?
ANTIGONE: Save yourself. I don't grudge you your survival.
ISMENE: Oh no, no, denied my portion in your death?
ANTIGONE: You chose to live, I chose to die.
ISMENE: Not, at least,   210
    without every kind of caution I could voice.
ANTIGONE: Your wisdom appealed to one world—mine, another.
ISMENE: But look, we're both guilty, both condemned to death.
ANTIGONE: Courage! Live your life. I gave myself to death,
    long ago, so I might serve the dead.   215
CREON: They're both mad, I tell you, the two of them.
    One's just shown it, the other's been that way
    since she was born.
ISMENE: True, my king,
    the sense we were born with cannot last forever. . .
    commit cruelty on a person long enough   220
    and the mind begins to go.
CREON: Yours did,
    when you chose to commit your crimes with her.
ISMENE: How can I live alone, without her?
CREON: Her?
    Don't even mention her—she no longer exists.
ISMENE: What? You'd kill your own son's bride?
CREON: Absolutely: → *his attitude toward women*   225
    there are other fields for him to plow.
ISMENE: Perhaps,
    but never as true, as close a bond as theirs.
CREON: A worthless woman for my son? It repels me.
ISMENE: Dearest Haemon, your father wrongs you so!
CREON: Enough, enough—you and your talk of marriage!   230
ISMENE: Creon—you're really going to rob your son of Antigone?
CREON: Death will do it for me—break their marriage off.
LEADER: So, it's settled then? Antigone must die?
CREON: Settled, yes—we both know that.

    [*To the guards.*]

Stop wasting time. Take them in.   235
From now on they'll act like women.
Tie them up, no more running loose;
even the bravest will cut and run,
once they see Death coming for their lives.

    [*The guards escort* ANTIGONE *and* ISMENE *into the palace.* CREON *remains while the
    old citizens form their* CHORUS.]

CHORUS: Blest, they are the truly blest who all their lives   240
    have never tasted devastation. For others, once
    the gods have rocked a house to its foundations
        the ruin will never cease, cresting on and on

from one generation on throughout the race—
like a great mounting tide   245
driven on by savage northern gales,
        surging over the dead black depths
roiling up from the bottom dark heaves of sand
and the headlands, taking the storm's onslaught full-force,
roar, and the low moaning
           echoes on and on
                and now   250
as in ancient times I see the sorrows of the house,
the living heirs of the old ancestral kings,
piling on the sorrows of the dead
       and one generation cannot free the next—
some god will bring them crashing down,   255
the race finds no release.
And now the light, the hope
       springing up from the late last root
in the house of Oedipus, that hope's cut down in turn
by the long, bloody knife swung by the gods of death   260
by a senseless word
       by fury at the heart.
           Zeus,
yours is the power, Zeus, what man on earth
can override it, who can hold it back?
Power that neither Sleep, the all-ensnaring
       no, nor the tireless months of heaven   265
can ever overmaster—young through all time,
mighty lord of power, you hold fast
       the dazzling crystal mansions of Olympus.
And throughout the future, late and soon
as through the past, your law prevails: 270
no towering form of greatness
       enters into the lives of mortals
           free and clear of ruin.
             True,
our dreams, our high hopes voyaging far and wide
bring sheer delight to many, to many others   275
       delusion, blithe, mindless lusts
and the fraud steals on one slowly . . . unaware
till he trips and puts his foot into the fire.
       He was a wise old man who coined
the famous saying: "Sooner or later   280
foul is fair, fair is foul
to the man the gods will ruin"—
       He goes his way for a moment only
           free of blinding ruin.

SCENE 3

[*Enter* HAEMON *from the palace.*]

CHORUS: Here's Haemon now, the last of all your sons.
Does he come in tears for his bride,
his doomed bride, Antigone—
bitter at being cheated of their marriage?

CREON: We'll soon know, better than seers could tell us.   5

[*Turning to* HAEMON.]

Son, you've heard the final verdict on your bride?
Are you coming now, raving against your father?
Or do you love me, no matter what I do?

HAEMON: Father, I'm your *son* . . . you in your wisdom
set my bearings for me—I obey you.   10
No marriage could ever mean more to me than you,
whatever good direction you may offer.

CREON: Fine, Haemon.
That's how you ought to feel within your heart,
subordinate to your father's will in every way.
That's what a man prays for: to produce good sons—   15
a household full of them, dutiful and attentive,
so they can pay his enemy back with interest
and match the respect their father shows his friend.
But the man who rears a brood of useless children,
what has he brought into the world, I ask you?   20
Nothing but trouble for himself, and mockery
from his enemies laughing in his face.
                                        Oh Haemon,
never lose your sense of judgment over a woman.
The warmth, the rush of pleasure, it all goes cold
in your arms, I warn you . . . a worthless woman   25
in your house, a misery in your bed.
What wound cuts deeper than a loved one
turned against you? Spit her out,
like a mortal enemy—let the girl go.
Let her find a husband down among the dead.   30

Imagine it: I caught her in naked rebellion,
the traitor, the only one in the whole city.
I'm not about to prove myself a liar,
not to my people, no, I'm going to kill her!
That's right—so let her cry for mercy, sing her hymns   35
to Zeus who defends all bonds of kindred blood.
Why, if I bring up my own kin to be rebels,
think what I'd suffer from the world at large.
Show me the man who rules his household well:
I'll show you someone fit to rule the state.   40
That good man, my son,
I have every confidence he and he alone

can give commands and take them too. Staunch
in the storm of spears he'll stand his ground,
a loyal, unflinching comrade at your side.   45

But whoever steps out of line, violates the laws   → hubris again
or presumes to hand out orders to his superiors,
he'll win no praise from me. But that man
the city places in authority, his orders
must be obeyed, large and small,   even if it's wrong you do it   50
right and wrong.   ←————————   if the king says it.
                Anarchy—
show me a greater crime in all the earth!
She, she destroys cities, rips up houses,
breaks the ranks of spearmen into headlong rout.
But the ones who last it out, the great mass of them   55
owe their lives to discipline. Therefore
we must defend the men who live by law,
never let some woman triumph over us.
Better to fall from power, if fall we must,
at the hands of a man—never be rated   —   Anti-fem: attitude against woman 60
inferior to a woman, never.

LEADER: To us,
    unless old age has robbed us of our wits,
    you seem to say what you have to say with sense.
HAEMON: Father, only the gods endow a man with reason, —
    the finest of all their gifts, a treasure.   65
    Far be it from me—I haven't the skill,
    and certainly no desire, to tell you when,
    if ever, you make a slip in speech . . . though
    someone else might have a good suggestion.

    Of course, it's not for you,   70
    in the normal run of things, to watch
    whatever men say or do, or find to criticize.
    The man in the street, you know, dreads your glance,
    he'd never say anything displeasing to your face.
    But it's for me to catch the murmurs in the dark,   75
    the way the city mourns for this young girl.
    "No woman," they say, "ever deserved death less,
    and such a brutal death for such a glorious action.
    She, with her own dear brother lying in his blood—
    she couldn't bear to leave him dead, unburied,   80
    food for the wild dogs or wheeling vultures.
    Death? She deserves a glowing crown of gold!"
    So they say, and the rumor spreads in secret,
    darkly . . .
                I rejoice in your success, father—
    nothing more precious to me in the world.   85
    What medal of honor brighter to his children
    than a father's growing glory? Or a child's
    to his proud father? Now don't, please,
    be quite so single-minded, self-involved,

or assume the world is wrong and you are right.   90
Whoever thinks that he alone possesses intelligence,
the gift of eloquence, he and no one else,
and character too . . . such men, I tell you,
spread them open—you will find them empty.

                              No,

it's no disgrace for a man, even a wise man,   95
to learn many things and not to be too rigid.
You've seen trees by a raging winter torrent,
how many sway with the flood and salvage every twig,
but not the stubborn—they're ripped out, roots and all.
Bend or break. The same when a man is sailing: 100
haul your sheets too taut, never give an inch,
you'll capsize, and go the rest of the voyage
keel up and the rowing-benches under.

Oh give way. Relax your anger—change!
I'm young, I know, but let me offer this: 105
it would be best by far, I admit,
if a man were born infallible, right by nature.
If not—and things don't often go that way,
it's best to learn from those with good advice.

LEADER: You'd do well, my lord, if he's speaking to the point,   110
    to learn from him,

    [*Turning to* HAEMON.]

                              and you, my boy, from him.
    You both are talking sense.
CREON: So,
    men our age, we're to be lectured, are we?—
    schooled by a boy his age?
HAEMON: Only in what is right. But if I seem young,   115
    look less to my years and more to what I do.
CREON: Do? Is admiring rebels an achievement?
HAEMON: I'd never suggest that you admire treason.
CREON: Oh?—
    isn't that just the sickness that's attacked her?
HAEMON: The whole city of Thebes denies it, to a man.   120
CREON: And is Thebes about to tell me how to rule?
HAEMON: Now, you see? Who's talking like a child?
CREON: Am I to rule this land for others—or myself?
HAEMON: It's no city at all, owned by one man alone.
CREON: What? The city *is* the king's—that's the law!   125
HAEMON: What a splendid king you'd make of a desert island—
    you and you alone.
CREON:

    [*To the* CHORUS.]

                    This boy, I do believe,
    is fighting on her side, the woman's side.
HAEMON: If you are a woman, yes—

my concern is all for you.   130
CREON: Why, you degenerate—bandying accusations,
    threatening me with justice, your own father!
HAEMON: I see my father offending justice—wrong.
CREON: Wrong?
    To protect my royal rights?
HAEMON: Protect your rights?
    When you trample down the honors of the gods? — Hubris   135
CREON: You, you soul of corruption, rotten through—
    woman's accomplice!
HAEMON: That may be,
    but you will never find me accomplice to a criminal. — Creon the criminal for breaking
CREON: That's what *she* is,   God + law.
    and every word you say is a blatant appeal for her—   140
HAEMON: And you, and me, and the gods beneath the earth.
CREON: You will never marry her, not while she's alive.
HAEMON: Then she will die . . . but her death will kill another. — himself
CREON: What, brazen threats? You go too far!
HAEMON: What threat?
    Combating your empty, mindless judgments with a word?   145
CREON: You'll suffer for your sermons, you and your empty wisdom!
HAEMON: If you weren't my father, I'd say you were insane.
CREON: Don't flatter me with Father—you woman's slave! — insult
HAEMON: You really expect to fling abuse at me
    and not receive the same?
CREON: Is that so!   150
    Now, by heaven, I promise you, you'll pay—
    taunting, insulting me! Bring her out,
    that hateful—she'll die now, here,
    in front of his eyes, beside her groom!
HAEMON: No, no, she will never die beside me—   → City would suffer retribution
    don't delude yourself. And you will never   from the gods
    see me, never set eyes on my face again.   — usual death — seale up in a
    Rage your heart out, rage with friends   cave w/ a little food and   155
    who can stand the sight of you.   water, when it runs out
                                                       you starve — but the persons
                                                       blood not on the city.

                                                    [*Rushing out.*]

LEADER: Gone, my king, in a burst of anger.   160
    A temper young as his . . . hurt him once,
    he may do something violent.
CREON: Let him do—
    dream up something desperate, past all human limit!
    Good riddance. Rest assured,
    he'll never save those two young girls from death.   165
LEADER: Both of them, you really intend to kill them both?
CREON: No, not her, the one whose hands are clean—
    you're quite right.
LEADER: But Antigone—
    what sort of death do you have in mind for her?
CREON: I will take her down some wild, desolate path   170
    never trod by men, and wall her up alive

in a rocky vault, and set out short rations,
just the measure piety demands
to keep the entire city free of defilement.
There let her pray to the one god she worships: 175
Death—who knows?—may just reprieve her from death.
Or she may learn at last, better late than never,
what a waste of breath it is to worship Death.

[*Exit to the palace.*]

CHORUS: Love, never conquered in battle
    Love the plunderer laying waste the rich!   180
    Love standing the night-watch
                    guarding a girl's soft cheek,
    you range the seas, the shepherds' steadings off in the wilds—
    not even the deathless gods can flee your onset,
    nothing human born for a day—   185
    whoever feels your grip is driven mad.
                        Love!—
    you wrench the minds of the righteous into outrage,
    swerve them to their ruin—you have ignited this,
    this kindred strife, father and son at war
                        and Love alone the victor—   190
    warm glance of the bride triumphant, burning with desire!
    Throned in power, side-by-side with the mighty laws!
    Irresistible Aphrodite, never conquered—
    Love, you mock us for your sport.
            But now, even I would rebel against the king,   195
            I would break all bounds when I see this—
            I fill with tears, I cannot hold them back,
            not any more . . . I see Antigone make her way
            to the bridal vault where all are laid to rest.

SCENE 4

[ANTIGONE *is brought from the palace under guard.*]

ANTIGONE: Look at me, men of my fatherland,
            setting out on the last road
    looking into the last light of day
    the last I will ever see . . .
    the god of death who puts us all to bed   5
    takes me down to the banks of Acheron alive—
            denied my part in the wedding-songs,
    no wedding-song in the dusk has crowned my marriage—
    I go to wed the lord of the dark waters.
CHORUS: Not crowned with glory or with a dirge,   10
            you leave for the deep pit of the dead.
        No withering illness laid you low,
            no strokes of the sword—a law to yourself,
        alone, no mortal like you, ever, you go down
        to the halls of Death alive and breathing.   15

ANTIGONE: But think of Niobe—well I know her story—
  think what a living death she died,
Tantalus' daughter, stranger queen from the east:
there on the mountain heights, growing stone
binding as ivy, slowly walled her round   20
and the rains will never cease, the legends say
the snows will never leave her . . .
  wasting away, under her brows the tears
showering down her breasting ridge and slopes—
a rocky death like hers puts me to sleep.   25
CHORUS: But she was a god, born of gods,
  and we are only mortals born to die.
  And yet, of course, it's a great thing
  for a dying girl to hear, even to hear
  she shares a destiny equal to the gods,   30
  during life and later, once she's dead.
ANTIGONE: O you mock me!
Why, in the name of all my fathers' gods
why can't you wait till I am gone—
  must you abuse me to my face?
O my city, all your fine rich sons!   35
And you, you springs of the Dirce,
holy grove of Thebes where the chariots gather,
  you at least, you'll bear me witness, look,
unmourned by friends and forced by such crude laws
I go to my rockbound prison, strange new tomb—   40
  always a stranger, O dear god,
  I have no home on earth and none below,
  not with the living, not with the breathless dead.
CHORUS: You went too far, the last limits of daring—
  smashing against the high throne of Justice!   45
  Your life's in ruins, child—I wonder . . .
  do you pay for your father's terrible ordeal?
ANTIGONE: There—at last you've touched it, the worst pain
the worst anguish! Raking up the grief for father
  three times over, for all the doom   50
that's struck us down, the brilliant house of Laius.
O mother, your marriage-bed
the coiling horrors, the coupling there—
  you with your own son, my father—doomstruck mother!
Such, such were my parents, and I their wretched child.   55
I go to them now, cursed, unwed, to share their home—
  I am a stranger! O dear brother, doomed
  in your marriage—your marriage murders mine,
  your dying drags me down to death alive!

[*Enter* CREON.]

CHORUS: Reverence asks some reverence in return—
  but attacks on power never go unchecked,   60
  not by the man who holds the reins of power.
  Your own blind will, your passion has destroyed you.

ANTIGONE: No one to weep for me, my friends,
        no wedding-song—they take me away   65
        in all my pain . . . the road lies open, waiting.
        Never again, the law forbids me to see
        the sacred eye of day. I am agony!
        No tears for the destiny that's mine,
        no loved one mourns my death.
CREON: Can't you see?   70
    If a man could wail his own dirge *before* he dies,
    he'd never finish.

    [*To the guards.*]

                Take her away, quickly!
    Wall her up in the tomb, you have your orders.
    Abandon her there, alone, and let her choose—
    death or a buried life with a good roof for shelter.
    As for myself, my hands are clean. This young girl—   75
    dead or alive, she will be stripped of her rights,
    her stranger's rights, here in the world above.
ANTIGONE: O tomb, my bridal-bed—my house, my prison
        cut in the hollow rock, my everlasting watch!   80
        I'll soon be there, soon embrace my own,
        the great growing family of our dead
        Persephone has received among her ghosts.
                           I,
    the last of them all, the most reviled by far,
    go down before my destined time's run out.   85
    But still I go, cherishing one good hope:
    my arrival may be dear to father,
    dear to you, my mother,
    dear to you, my loving brother, Eteocles—
    When you died I washed you with my hands,
    I dressed you all, I poured the sacred cups   90
    across your tombs. But now, Polynices,
    because I laid your body out as well,
    this, this is my reward. Nevertheless
    I honored you—the decent will admit it—   95
    well and wisely too.
                Never, I tell you,
    if I had been the mother of children
    or if my husband had died, exposed and rotting—
    I'd never have taken this ordeal upon myself,
    never defied our people's will. What law,   100
    you ask, do I satisfy with what I say?
    A husband dead, there might have been another.
    A child by another too, if I had lost the first.
    But mother and father both lost in the halls of Death,
    no brother could ever spring to light again.   105
    For this law alone I held you first in honor.
    For this, Creon, the king, judges me a criminal
    guilty of dreadful outrage, my dear brother!

And now he leads me off, a captive in his hands,
with no part in the bridal-song, the bridal-bed,
denied all joy of marriage, raising children—
deserted so by loved ones, struck by fate,
I descend alive to the caverns of the dead.   110

What law of the mighty gods have I transgressed?
Why look to the heavens any more, tormented as I am?   115
Whom to call, what comrades now? Just think,
my reverence only brands me for irreverence!
Very well: if this is the pleasure of the gods,
once I suffer I will know that I was wrong.
But if these men are wrong, let them suffer   120
nothing worse than they mete out to me—
these masters of injustice!
LEADER: Still the same rough winds, the wild passion
    raging through the girl.
CREON:

[*To the guards.*]

                                  Take her away.
    You're wasting time—you'll pay for it too.
ANTIGONE: Oh god, the voice of death. It's come, it's here.
CREON: True. Not a word of hope—your doom is sealed.
ANTIGONE: Land of Thebes, city of all my fathers—
            O you gods, the first gods of the race!
            They drag me away, now, no more delay.
            Look on me, you noble sons of Thebes—   130
            the last of a great line of kings,
            I alone, see what I suffer now
            at the hands of what breed of men—
            all for reverence, my reverence for the gods!   135

[*She leaves under guard; the* CHORUS *gathers.*]

CHORUS: Danaë, Danaë—
        even she endured a fate like yours,
            in all her lovely strength she traded
        the light of day for the bolted brazen vault—
        buried within her tomb, her bridal-chamber,   140
        wed to the yoke and broken.
                But she was of glorious birth
                        my child, my child
        and treasured the seed of Zeus within her womb,
        the cloudburst streaming gold!   145
                The power of fate is a wonder,
                dark, terrible wonder—
                neither wealth nor armies
                towered walls nor ships
                black hulls lashed by the salt   150
                can save us from that force.

        The yoke tamed him too

young Lycurgus flaming in anger
king of Edonia, all for his mad taunts
Dionysus clamped him down, encased 155
in the chain-mail of rock
    and there his rage
        his terrible flowering rage burst—
sobbing, dying away . . . at last that madman
came to know his god— 160
        the power he mocked, the power
        he taunted in all his frenzy
        trying to stamp out
        the women strong with the god—
        the torch, the raving sacred cries— 165
        enraging the Muses who adore the flute.

And far north where the Black Rocks
    cut the sea in half
and murderous straits
split the coast of Thrace 170
    a forbidding city stands
where once, hard by the walls
the savage Ares thrilled to watch
a king's new queen, a Fury rearing in rage
        against his two royal sons— 175
        her bloody hands, her dagger-shuttle
stabbing out their eyes—cursed, blinding wounds—
their eyes blind sockets screaming for revenge!

They wailed in agony, cries echoing cries
        the princes doomed at birth . . . 180
and their mother doomed to chains,
walled up in a tomb of stone—
        but she traced her own birth back
to a proud Athenian line and the high gods
and off in caverns half the world away, 185
born of the wild North Wind
        she sprang on her father's gales,
        racing stallions up the leaping cliffs—
child of the heavens. But even on her the Fates
the gray everlasting Fates rode hard 190
my child, my child.

SCENE 5

[*Enter* TIRESIAS, *the blind prophet, led by a boy.*]

TIRESIAS: Lords of Thebes,
    I and the boy have come together,
        hand in hand. Two see with the eyes of one . . .
        so the blind must go, with a guide to lead the way.
CREON: What is it, old Tiresias? What news now? 5
TIRESIAS: I will teach you. And you obey the seer.

CREON: I will,
    I've never wavered from your advice before.
TIRESIAS: And so you kept the city straight on course.
CREON: I owe you a great deal, I swear to that.
TIRESIAS: Then reflect, my son: you are poised,   10
    once more, on the razor-edge of fate.   *— doesn't take much to go the other way*
CREON: What is it? I shudder to hear you.
TIRESIAS: You will learn
    when you listen to the warnings of my craft.
    As I sat on the ancient seat of augury,
    in the sanctuary where every bird I know   15
    will hover at my hands—suddenly I heard it,
    a strange voice in the wingbeats, unintelligible,
    barbaric, a mad scream! Talons flashing, ripping,
    they were killing each other—that much I knew—
    the murderous fury whirring in those wings   20
    made that much clear!
              I was afraid,
    I turned quickly, tested the burnt-sacrifice,
    ignited the altar at all points—but no fire,
    the god in the fire never blazed.
    Not from those offerings . . . over the embers   25
    slid a heavy ooze from the long thighbones,
    smoking, sputtering out, and the bladder
    puffed and burst—spraying gall into the air—
    and the fat wrapping the bones slithered off
    and left them glistening white. No fire!   30
    The rites failed that might have blazed the future
    with a sign. So I learned from the boy here:
    he is my guide, as I am guide to others.
              And it is you—
    your high resolve that sets this plague on Thebes.
    The public altars and sacred hearths are fouled,   35
    one and all, by the birds and dogs with carrion   *— spreading all over the city*
    torn from the corpse, the doomstruck son of Oedipus!
    And so the gods are deaf to our prayers, they spurn
    the offerings in our hands, the flame of holy flesh.
    No birds cry out an omen clear and true—   40
    they're gorged with the murdered victim's blood and fat.
    Take these things to heart, my son, I warn you.
    All men make mistakes, it is only human.
    But once the wrong is done, a man
    can turn his back on folly, misfortune too,   45
    if he tries to make amends, however low he's fallen,
    and stops his bullnecked ways. Stubbornness
    brands you for stupidity—pride is a crime.   *— hubris*
    No, yield to the dead!
    Never stab the fighter when he's down.   50
    Where's the glory, killing the dead twice over?

    I mean you well. I give you sound advice.
    It's best to learn from a good adviser

when he speaks for your own good:
it's pure gain.
CREON: Old man—all of you! So,   55
you shoot your arrows at my head like archers at the target—
I even have *him* loosed on me, this fortune-teller.
Oh his ilk has tried to sell me short
and ship me off for years. Well,
drive your bargains, traffic—much as you like—   60
in the gold of India, silver-gold of Sardis.
You'll never bury that body in the grave,   — Because he said so
not even if Zeus's eagles rip the corpse
and wing their rotten pickings off to the throne of god!
Never, not even in fear of such defilement   65
will I tolerate his burial, that traitor.
Well I know, we can't defile the gods—
no mortal has the power.
                              No,
reverend old Tiresias, all men fall,
it's only human, but the wisest fall obscenely   70
when they glorify obscene advice with rhetoric—
all for their own gain.
TIRESIAS: Oh god, is there a man alive
who knows, who actually believes . . .
CREON: What now?
What earth-shattering truth are you about to utter?   75
TIRESIAS: . . . just how much a sense of judgment, wisdom
is the greatest gift we have?
CREON: Just as much, I'd say
as a twisted mind is the worst affliction known.
TIRESIAS: You are the one who's sick, Creon, sick to death.
CREON: I am in no mood to trade insults with a seer.   80
TIRESIAS: You have already, calling my prophecies a lie.
CREON: Why not?
You and the whole breed of seers are mad for money!
TIRESIAS: And the whole race of tyrants lusts for filthy gain.
CREON: This slander of yours—
are you aware you're speaking to the king?   85
TIRESIAS: Well aware. Who helped you save the city?
CREON: You—
you have your skills, old seer, but you lust for injustice!
TIRESIAS: You will drive me to utter the dreadful secret in my heart.
CREON: Spit it out! Just don't speak it out for profit.
TIRESIAS: Profit? No, not a bit of profit, not for you.   90
CREON: Know full well, you'll never buy off my resolve.
TIRESIAS: Then know this too, learn this by heart!
The chariot of the sun will not race through
so many circuits more, before you have surrendered
one born of your own loins, your own flesh and blood,   — Haemon   95
a corpse for corpses given in return, since you have thrust
to the world below a child sprung for the world above,
ruthlessly lodged a living soul within the grave—

then you've robbed the gods below the earth,
keeping a dead body here in the bright air, 100
unburied, unsung, unhallowed by the rites.

You, you have no business with the dead,
nor do the gods above—this is violence
you have forced upon the heavens.
And so the avengers, the dark destroyers late 105
but true to the mark, now lie in wait for you,
the Furies sent by the gods and the god of death — Gods are pursuing you
to strike you down with the pains that you perfected! Avengers

There. Reflect on that, tell me I've been bribed.
The day comes soon, no long test of time, not now, 110
when the mourning cries for men and women break
throughout your halls. Great hatred rises against you—
cities in tumult, all whose mutilated sons
the dogs have graced with burial, or the wild beasts
or a wheeling crow that wings the ungodly stench of carrion 115
back to each city, each warrior's hearth and home.

These arrows for your heart! Since you've raked me
I loose them like an archer in my anger,
arrows deadly true. You'll never escape
their burning, searing force. 120

[*Motioning to his escort.*]

Come, boy, take me home.
So he can vent his rage on younger men,
and learn to keep a gentler tongue in his head
and better sense than what he carries now.

[*Exit to the side.*]

LEADER: The old man's gone, my king— 125
terrible prophecies. Well I know,
since the hair on this old head went gray,
he's never lied to Thebes.
CREON: I know it myself—I'm shaken, torn. Hubris
It's a dreadful thing to yield . . . but resist now? 130
Lay my pride bare to the blows of ruin?
That's dreadful too.
LEADER: But good advice, Doesn't matter how old or who
Creon, take it now, you must. good advice is good advice
CREON: What should I do? Tell me . . . I'll obey.
LEADER: Go! Free the girl from the rocky vault 135
and raise a mound for the body you exposed.
CREON: That's your advice? You think I should give in? ← still not quite convinced
LEADER: Yes, my king, quickly. Disasters sent by the gods
cut short our follies in a flash.
CREON: Oh it's hard,
giving up the heart's desire . . . but I will do it— 140
no more fighting a losing battle with necessity.

LEADER: Do it now, go, don't leave it to others.
CREON: Now—I'm on my way! Come, each of you,
   take up axes, make for the high ground,
   over there, quickly! I and my better judgment   145
   have come round to this—I shackled her,
   I'll set her free myself. I am afraid . . .
   it's best to keep the established laws
   to the very day we die.

[*Rushing out, followed by his entourage.*]

[*The* CHORUS *clusters around the altar.*]

CHORUS: God of a hundred names!
                    Great Dionysus—   150
             Son and glory of Semele! Pride of Thebes—
   Child of Zeus whose thunder rocks the clouds—
   Lord of the famous lands of evening—
   King of the Mysteries!
                    King of Eleusis, Demeter's plain
   her breasting hills that welcome in the world—   155
   Great Dionysus!
                    Bacchus, living in Thebes
   the mother-city of all your frenzied women—
                                     Bacchus
             living along the Ismenus' rippling waters
   standing over the field sown with the Dragon's teeth!

You—we have seen you through the flaring smoky fires,   160
             your torches blazing over the twin peaks
   where nymphs of the hallowed cave climb onward
                             fired with you, your sacred rage—
   we have seen you at Castalia's running spring
   and down from the heights of Nysa crowned with ivy   165
   the greening shore rioting vines and grapes
             down you come in your storm of wild women
                    ecstatic, mystic cries—
                                     Dionysus—
   down to watch and ward the roads of Thebes!

First of all cities, Thebes you honor first   170
you and your mother, bride of the lightning—
come Dionysus! now your people lie
in the iron grip of plague
come, in your racing, healing stride
                    down Parnassus' slopes   175
or across the moaning straits.
                    Lord of the dancing—
dance, dance the constellations breathing fire!
Great master of the voices of the night!
Child of Zeus, God's offspring, come, come forth!
Lord, king, dance with your nymphs, swirling, raving   180
arm-in-arm in frenzy through the night
      they dance you, Iacchus—

Dance, Dionysus
giver of all good things!

SCENE 6

[*Enter a* MESSENGER *from the side.*]

MESSENGER: Neighbors,
friends of the house of Cadmus and the kings,
there's not a thing in this mortal life of ours
I'd praise or blame as settled once for all.
Fortune lifts and Fortune fells the lucky   5
and unlucky every day. No prophet on earth
can tell a man his fate. Take Creon:
there was a man to rouse your envy once,
as I see it. He saved the realm from enemies,
taking power, he alone, the lord of the fatherland,   10
he set us true on course—he flourished like a tree
with the noble line of sons he bred and reared . . .
and now it's lost, all gone.
                                Believe me,
when a man has squandered his true joys,
he's good as dead, I tell you, a living corpse.   15
Pile up riches in your house, as much as you like—
live like a king with a huge show of pomp,
but if real delight is missing from the lot,
I wouldn't give you a wisp of smoke for it,
not compared with joy.
LEADER: What now?   20
What new grief do you bring the house of kings?
MESSENGER: Dead, dead—and the living are guilty of their death!
LEADER: Who's the murderer? Who is dead? Tell us.
MESSENGER: Haemon's gone, his blood spilled by the very hand—
LEADER: His father's or his own?
MESSENGER: His own . . .   25
raging mad with his father for the death—
LEADER: Oh great seer,
you saw it all, you brought your word to birth!
MESSENGER: Those are the facts. Deal with them as you will.

[*As he turns to go,* EURYDICE *enters from the palace.*]

LEADER: Look, Eurydice. Poor woman, Creon's wife,
so close at hand. By chance perhaps,   30
unless she's heard the news about her son.
EURYDICE: My countrymen,
all of you—I caught the sound of your words
as I was leaving to do my part,
to appeal to queen Athena with my prayers.
I was just loosing the bolts, opening the doors,   35
when a voice filled with sorrow, family sorrow,
struck my ears, and I fell back, terrified,

into the women's arms—everything went black.
Tell me the news, again, whatever it is . . .
sorrow and I are hardly strangers.   40
I can bear the worst.

MESSENGER: I—dear, lady,
I'll speak as an eye-witness. I was there.
And I won't pass over one word of the truth.
Why should I try to soothe you with a story,
only to prove a liar in a moment?   45
Truth is always best.
                    So,
I escorted your lord, I guided him
to the edge of the plain where the body lay,
Polynices, torn by the dogs and still unmourned.
And saying a prayer to Hecate of the Crossroads,   50
Pluto too, to hold their anger and be kind,
we washed the dead in a bath of holy water
and plucking some fresh branches, gathering . . .
what was left of him, we burned them all together
and raised a high mound of native earth, and then   55
we turned and made for that rocky vault of hers,
the hollow, empty bed of the bride of Death.
And far off, one of us heard a voice,
a long wail rising, echoing
out of that unhallowed wedding-chamber,   60
he ran to alert the master and Creon pressed on,
closer—the strange, inscrutable cry came sharper,
throbbing around him now, and he let loose
a cry of his own, enough to wrench the heart,
"Oh god, am I the prophet now? going down   65
the darkest road I've ever gone? My son—
it's *his* dear voice, he greets me! Go, men,
closer, quickly! Go through the gap,
the rocks are dragged back—
right to the tomb's very mouth—and look,   70
see if it's Haemon's voice I think I hear,
or the gods have robbed me of my senses."

The king was shattered. We took his orders,
went and searched, and there in the deepest,
dark recesses of the tomb we found her . . .   75
hanged by the neck in a fine linen noose,
strangled in her veils—and the boy,
his arms flung around her waist,
clinging to her, wailing for his bride,
dead and down below, for his father's crimes   80
and the bed of his marriage blighted by misfortune.
When Creon saw him, he gave a deep sob,
he ran in, shouting, crying out to him,
"Oh my child—what have you done? what seized you,
what insanity? what disaster drove you mad?   85
Come out, my son! I beg you on my knees!"

But the boy gave him a wild burning glance,
spat in his face, not a word in reply,
he drew his sword—his father rushed out,
running as Haemon lunged and missed!—   *Swinging at his father*   90
and then, doomed, desperate with himself,
suddenly leaning his full weight on the blade,
he buried it in his body, halfway to the hilt.
And still in his senses, pouring his arms around her,
he embraced the girl and breathing hard,   95
released a quick rush of blood,
bright red on her cheek glistening white.
And there he lies, body enfolding body . . .
he has won his bride at last, poor boy,   *early version of*
not here but in the houses of the dead.   *Romeo & Juliet*   100

Creon shows the world that of all the ills
afflicting men the worst is lack of judgment.

[EURYDICE *turns and reenters the palace.*]

LEADER: What do you make of that? The lady's gone,
    without a word, good or bad.
MESSENGER: I'm alarmed too
    but here's my hope—faced with her son's death   105
    she finds it unbecoming to mourn in public.
    Inside, under her roof, she'll set her women
    to the task and wail the sorrow of the house.
    She's too discreet. She won't do something rash. *—(kill herself)*
LEADER: I'm not so sure. To me, at least,   110
    a long heavy silence promises danger,
    just as much as a lot of empty outcries.
MESSENGER: We'll see if she's holding something back,
    hiding some passion in her heart.
    I'm going in. You may be right—who knows?   115
    Even too much silence has its dangers.

[*Exit to the palace.*]

[*Enter* CREON *from the side, escorted by attendants carrying* HAEMON'S *body on a bier.*]

LEADER: The king himself! Coming toward us,
        look, holding the boy's head in his hands.
        Clear, damning proof, if it's right to say so—
        proof of his own madness, no one else's,   120
            no, his own blind wrongs.
CREON: Ohhh,
        so senseless, so insane . . . my crimes,
        my stubborn, deadly—
        Look at us, the killer, the killed,   *— saying he killed his son*
        father and son, the same blood—the misery!   125
        My plans, my mad fanatic heart,
        my son, cut off so young!
        Ai, dead, lost to the world,
        not through your stupidity, no, my own. *takes the blame*
                                                  admits he was wrong

LEADER: Too late,
    too late, you see what justice means.
CREON: Oh I've learned   130
    through blood and tears! Then, it was then,
    when the god came down and struck me—a great weight
    shattering, driving me down that wild savage path,
    ruining, trampling down my joy. Oh the agony,
        the heartbreaking agonies of our lives.

[*Enter the* MESSENGER *from the palace.*]

MESSENGER: Master,   135
    what a hoard of grief you have, and you'll have more.
    The grief that lies to hand you've brought yourself—

[*Pointing to* HAEMON'S *body.*]

    the rest, in the house, you'll see it all too soon.
CREON: What now? What's worse than this?
MESSENGER: The queen is dead.
    The mother of this dead boy . . . mother to the end—   140
    poor thing, her wounds are fresh.
CREON: No, no,
    harbor of Death, so choked, so hard to cleanse!—
    why me? why are you killing me?
    Herald of pain, more words, more grief?
    I died once, you kill me again and again!   145
    What's the report, boy . . . some news for me?
    My wife dead? O dear god!
    Slaughter heaped on slaughter?

[*The doors open; the body of* EURYDICE *is brought out on her bier.*]

MESSENGER: See for yourself:
    now they bring her body from the palace.
CREON: Oh no,
    another, a second loss to break the heart.   150
    What next, what fate still waits for me?
    I just held my son in my arms and now,
    look, a new corpse rising before my eyes—
        wretched, helpless mother—O my son!
MESSENGER: She stabbed herself at the altar,   155
    then her eyes went dark, after she'd raised
    a cry for the noble fate of Megareus, the hero
    killed in the first assault, then for Haemon
    then with her dying breath she called down
    torments on your head—you killed her sons.   160
CREON: Oh the dread,
    I shudder with dread! Why not kill me too?—
    run me through with a good sharp sword?
    Oh god, the misery, anguish—
    I, I'm churning with it, going under.
MESSENGER: Yes, and the dead, the woman lying there,   165
    piles the guilt of all their deaths on you.

CREON: How did she end her life, what bloody stroke?

MESSENGER: She drove home to the heart with her own hand,
    once she learned her son was dead . . . that agony.

CREON: And the guilt is all mine— *[admits]*   170
      can never be fixed on another man,
      no escape for me. I killed you,
      I, god help me, I admit it all!

    [*To his attendants.*]

      Take me away, quickly, out of sight.
      I don't even exist—I'm no one. Nothing.   175

LEADER: Good advice, if there's any good in suffering.
    Quickest is best when troubles block the way.

CREON:

    [*Kneeling in prayer.*]

      Come, let it come!—that best of fates for me
      that brings the final day, best fate of all.
      Oh quickly, now—   180
      so I never have to see another sunrise. *[Asking them to kill him now]*

LEADER: That will come when it comes; *[God's haven't said to do it. Same thing as the end of Oedipus]*
    we must deal with all that lies before us.
    The future rests with the ones who tend the future.

CREON: That prayer—I poured my heart into that prayer!   185

LEADER: No more prayers now. For mortal men
    there is no escape from the doom we must endure. *[— fate]*

CREON: Take me away, I beg you, out of sight.
      A rash, indiscriminate fool!
      I murdered you, my son, against my will—   190
      you too, my wife . . . *[feels strongly]*
                    Wailing wreck of a man,
      whom to look to? where to lean for support?

    [*Desperately turning from* HAEMON *to* EURYDICE *on their biers.*]

      Whatever I touch goes wrong—once more
      a crushing fate's come down upon my head!

        [listening to the Gods, having good judgment] [*The* MESSENGER *and attendants lead* CREON *into the palace.*]

CHORUS: Wisdom is by far the greatest part of joy, *[shame to find out what the God's wanted]*   195
    and reverence toward the gods must be safeguarded.
    The mighty words of the proud are paid in full
    with mighty blows of fate, and at long last
    those blows will teach us wisdom.

                      [*The old citizens exit to the side.*]

[Shows the results if you don't have the wisdom to listen to the Gods.]

THE RECEPTIVE READER

    Greek drama had continuous action with no formal division into acts and scenes.
(Scenes have been marked off and numbered in this reprinting of the play for the

convenience of the reader.) The rhythm of the play is set up by the alternation of the dramatic episodes with the chants (or *odes*) of the chorus. The following questions should help you respond to the flow of the play as the central conflict works itself out and proceeds to its seemingly inevitable conclusion.

1. (Prologue) What makes the prologue an outstanding example of dramatic *exposition*? How does the playwright set up the situation? How does he fill you in on the necessary background? How does he initiate the central conflict? ✧ What is your first impression of Antigone? Where does she most forcefully state her convictions? ✧ What is the relationship between the two sisters? Can you understand Ismene's position? ✧ What subject does the chorus talk about, and what is its stance in its first appearance?

2. (Scene 1) What is your first impression of Creon? Does he seem an effective ruler? Or does he seem stubborn and wrongheaded to you? How does he deal with defiance or dissent? ✧ What stand does the chorus take as the challenge to Creon's authority unfolds?

3. (Scene 2) How does the contest of wills between protagonist and antagonist take shape in this scene? For you, where are the two polar opposites most clearly defined? (Is there any common ground?) Are you surprised by the stand Ismene takes in this scene? ✧ For a journal entry or a brief oral presentation, you may want to prepare a speech in which you enter into the *point of view* of the character whose motives and arguments you can most easily sympathize with or understand. Use the first person, on the "I, Creon, king of Thebes . . . " model.

4. (Scene 3) How would you describe Haemon's initial stance toward his father? Is he hostile to or angry with Creon? What is his strategy in trying to deal with his father? How does it work out and why? ✧ For you, which are the strongest arguments used by Creon and Haemon in this scene? (What are striking examples of the rapid-fire trading of one-liners, or *stichomythy*?) Does this scene change or confirm your estimate of Creon's character?

5. (Scene 4) What is the final impression you retain of Antigone in this last scene in which you see her? ✧ Antigone said about the chorus in Scene 2 that "these citizens" would all agree with her, that "they would praise me too / if their lips weren't locked in fear." Is she right? In Scene 3, what side does the chorus seem to take in the confrontation between Creon and his son? What is the role and position of the chorus in Scene 4?

6. (Scene 5) The appearance of Tiresias, the blind priest and prophet, signals the turning point, or *peripety,* of the play. What is the blind seer's intention and message? How does Creon receive it? What causes Tiresias to reveal his horrible prophecy? What is Creon's reaction? How does the playwright guide the reactions of the audience to the seer's prediction?

7. (Scene 6) Greek tragedy often appeals to the spectators' sense of *irony* as they witness with a bitter smile the contrast between people's hopes or expectations and their actual fate. In what ways is Creon the victim or target of this kind of irony? ✧ The play concludes with orthodox warnings against *hubris,* the sin of arrogant pride. How does the play as a whole lead up to this conclusion?

THE WHOLE PLAY—For Discussion or Writing

1. In Greek tragedy, we are often told that a person's *fate* was decreed by the gods. But we also see strong-willed individuals making fateful choices. To become great or admirable, the characters must not be mere pawns of fate but show evidence of strength of will. To what extent do both the major and the supporting characters in this

play exercise free will—showing evidence of deliberate choice or independent judgment? To what extent do they seem to you victims of fate?

2. What attitude toward *women* does Creon reveal in his denunciation of Antigone? Is that attitude shared by others in the play? Is it shared by the playwright?

3. George Steiner, in a book on the influence of *Antigone* on Western culture, says that the drama brings into play all five major sources of *conflict* inherent in the human condition: the confrontation of men and women, of age and youth, of society and the individual, of the living and the dead, and of human beings and gods. Can you show what role each plays and how important it is in the play as a whole?

THE RANGE OF INTERPRETATION

Creon says at the end, "The guilt is all mine." Do you agree? What is your final judgment of Antigone as the tragic heroine? The translator of this play questioned Antigone's "total indifference to the rights of the city" to protect itself against treason. He claimed that no one in the play really praises her, with the exception of her fiancé. She herself says that if the gods allowed her to suffer death for her stand she would know that she was wrong. Was she wrong? In your opinion, what in this play could or should have been done differently, and by whom?

THE CREATIVE DIMENSION

In a true dramatic conflict, something is to be said for both sides. As the audience, we may first take one side and then the other. This play of divided loyalties makes the difference between drama and melodrama. *Melodrama* makes the choice easier for the audience. The good are innocent, pure, vulnerable, and incredibly unselfish. The villains are sniggering, shifty-eyed, and ill-shaven. In melodrama, we know that in the end evil will get its comeuppance. (Sometimes the villain will repent and reform.) Modern directors have at times pushed Sophocles' play toward melodrama, casting Creon, for instance, as a dictator with a German accent.

Try your hand at rewriting a scene (or part) in a more melodramatic mode. For instance, recast one of the confrontations with Creon to make him sound more like a modern dictator. Or rewrite the ending so that the innocent will be saved and triumph over evil.

CROSS-REFERENCES—For Discussion or Writing

❖ In Sophocles' *Antigone*, rival loyalties compete for the characters' allegiance: loyalty to family, loyalty to country or state, loyalty to the laws of religion. Compare and contrast Sophocles' tragic heroine with Ibsen's Nora as heroines faced with divided loyalties. What is the nature of the conflict in each case? How does the heroine resolve it? What are important parallels or key differences?

❖ Compare and contrast Sophocles' *Antigone* and Ibsen's *A Doll's House* as plays centered on a conflict between a man and a woman.

JUXTAPOSITIONS

A Modern Antigone

In a tragedy, nothing is in doubt and everyone's destiny is known. That makes for tranquility.
JEAN ANOUILH, *ANTIGONE*

Through the centuries, numerous rewrites and adaptations have testified to the vitality of Sophocles' play. The French playwright Jean Anouilh, in his *Antigone,* retells the story in a much more informal modern idiom. The following excerpt is the concluding comment by the chorus in Anouilh's play. Compare it with the last words of the chorus in Sophocles' original. What are major differences between the ancient Greek and the modern perspective?

> CHORUS: And there we are. It is quite true that if it had not been for Antigone they would all have been at peace. But that is over now. And they are all at peace. All those who were meant to die have died: those who believed one thing, those who believed the contrary thing, and even those who believed nothing at all, yet were caught up in the web without knowing why. All dead: stiff, useless, rotting. And those who have survived will begin quietly to forget the dead: they won't remember who was who or which was which. It is all over. Antigone is calm tonight and we shall never know the name of the fever that consumed her. She has played her part.
>
> A great melancholy wave of peace now settles down upon Thebes, upon the empty palace, upon Creon, who can now begin to wait for his own death.
>
> Only the guards are left, and none of this matters to them. It's no skin off their noses. They go on playing cards.

SOPHOCLES' *OEDIPUS REX*

> *People of Thebes: look upon Oedipus.*
> *This is the king who solved the riddle of the sphinx*
> *And towered, powerful, above the crowd.*
> *The eyes of mortals looked on him with envy.*
> *Yet ruin overtook him in the end.*
> SOPHOCLES, *OEDIPUS REX*

> *The tragedies of Sophocles concern resolute, intelligent,*
> *civilized people, determined to understand everything; they*
> *never do, because there is a dark nonsensical element in*
> *things, which eludes their comprehension and, often,*
> *destroys them; but which has its own wild beauty.*
> RICHMOND LATTIMORE

> Quisque suos patimur.
> *We each suffer our own destinies.*
> VERGIL

Over ten years after he wrote *Antigone,* Sophocles returned to the story of the house of Oedipus. His *Oedipus Rex* (Oedipus the King) dramatized the story of Antigone's father, who had tried in vain to thwart Apollo's oracle predicting that he would kill his father and marry his own mother. Aristotle used this play as the example of a perfect tragedy. He saw in the fate that overtakes Oedipus the perfect example of a sudden **reversal**—the unexpected change from good fortune to bad fortune of a great personage.

In Oedipus as king of Thebes, this play again has a powerful **protagonist**—a great leader who saved the city from the ravages of the monstrous Sphinx, "that chanting Fury." He solved her riddle, which asked what spoke with one voice but had at various times two feet, four feet, or three feet—moving then on most feet when its strength was weakest. (Answer: a human being, walking on two feet when at full strength, but crawling on all fours when a helpless baby, and using a walking stick as a third leg when old.)

However, although Oedipus quarrels with his brother-in-law Creon and the blind seer Tiresias, his real **antagonist** is the god Apollo. Oedipus' natural parents were King Laius of Thebes and his wife Jocasta. The oracle of Apollo at Delphi had warned them before the birth of Oedipus that this child would slay his father, committing the unspeakable crime of parricide, and marry his mother, breaking the most powerful taboo of Greek culture. Laius and Jocasta had tried to thwart the oracle by having the child exposed, its feet bound, on a mountainside, but the compassion of shepherds saved him from death. (The injury to his feet earned him his name: Oedipus, or "Swellfoot.") Oedipus is raised by a royal couple in Corinth whom he takes to be his real parents. The oracle of Apollo speaks again: He will commit the unspeakable horrors of parricide and incest. He flees Corinth to forestall the oracle, unknowingly setting in motion the chain of events that will make it come true.

Oedipus Rex takes us closer than the *Antigone* play to the roots of Greek tragedy in myth and ritual. At the beginning of the play, the crops are blighted. A plague, like the epidemics that ravaged the population of Athens during the war with Sparta, infects the city. Women are barren. As in other early societies, the priests to whom the people turn in their despair identify the cause of the people's misery: The gods are offended, and they must be appeased. Something has polluted the city, and the city must undergo a ritual of cleansing, of purgation. Students of Greek myth have seen in the downfall of Oedipus a sacrifice to Apollo, a ritual cleansing of the infected community.

In the play, Oedipus is determined to track down the source of pollution and cleanse the city. Oedipus' struggle to escape the oracle, and his stubborn pursuit of the truth that will be his undoing, make the play a powerful example of **dramatic irony**. The audience knows the terrible truth before Oedipus does; it watches with a grim knowing smile as the characters on the stage, in their terrible ignorance, head for the abyss. As L.R. Lind said in introducing a new translation of the play,

> There is the abundant, almost constant, irony of the play, its lines filled with the double meaning which critics call dramatic irony: the awesome gap between the one meaning known to the audience and the other known to the players, into which flows a stream of emotion so strong it chokes the very heart. Oedipus calls Tiresias blind, when he himself is blinder . . . ; Oedipus curses Laius' murderer and thus curses himself; Oedipus answers the Sphinx but finds no answer for his own dilemma.

On the stage, the play seems to move with terrible simplicity to its foreordained conclusion. However, we as the spectators are each left to solve the cosmic riddle posed by the play on our own terms. Is human fate immovably fixed, and is free will an illusion? Are we expected to admire Oedipus and take his side, or are we expected to condemn him for hubris, for overreaching pride?

Oedipus the King   about 430 B.C.

TRANSLATED BY ROBERT FAGLES

[Although politically splintered and often at war among themselves, the Greeks had common traditions like the Olympic games, and they shared many religious beliefs and institutions. One such institution was the *oracle* of Apollo at Delphi. Its priests passed on the god's widely heeded predictions concerning, for instance, victory and defeat in war. Local priests, like Tiresias in this play, practiced various other kinds of prophecy, including *augury*—reading the future in the flight and intestines of birds.]

CHARACTERS

OEDIPUS, king of Thebes
A PRIEST of Zeus
CREON, brother of JOCASTA
A CHORUS of Theban citizens and their LEADER
TIRESIAS, a blind prophet
JOCASTA, the queen, wife of OEDIPUS
A MESSENGER from Corinth
A SHEPHERD
A MESSENGER from inside the palace
ANTIGONE, ISMENE, daughters of OEDIPUS and JOCASTA
Guards and attendants
Priests of Thebes

PROLOGUE

TIME AND SCENE: *The royal house of Thebes. Double doors dominate the façade; a stone altar stands at the center of the stage.*

Many years have passed since OEDIPUS *solved the riddle of the Sphinx and ascended the throne of Thebes, and now a plague has struck the city. A procession of priests enters; suppliants, broken and despondent, they carry branches wound in wool and lay them on the altar.*

The doors open. Guards assemble. OEDIPUS *comes forward, majestic but for a telltale limp, and slowly views the condition of his people.*

OEDIPUS: Oh my children, the new blood of ancient Thebes,
    why are you here? Huddling at my altar,
    praying before me, your branches wound in wool.
    Our city reeks with the smoke of burning incense,
    rings with cries for the Healer and wailing for the dead.   5
    I thought it wrong, my children, to hear the truth
    from others, messengers. Here I am myself—
    you all know me, the world knows my fame:
    I am Oedipus.

    [*Helping a priest to his feet.*]

Speak up, old man. Your years,
your dignity—you should speak for the others.   10
Why here and kneeling, what preys upon you so?
Some sudden fear? some strong desire?
You can trust me. I am ready to help,
I'll do anything. I would be blind to misery
not to pity my people kneeling at my feet.   15

PRIEST: Oh Oedipus, king of the land, our greatest power!
You see us before you now, men of all ages
clinging to your altars. Here are boys,
still too weak to fly from the nest,
and here the old, bowed down with the years,   20
the holy ones—a priest of Zeus myself—and here
the picked, unmarried men, the young hope of Thebes.
And all the rest, your great family gathers now,
branches wreathed, massing in the squares,
kneeling before the two temples of queen Athena   25
or the river-shrine where the embers glow and die
and Apollo sees the future in the ashes.
                         Our city—
look around you, see with your own eyes—
our ship pitches wildly, cannot lift her head
from the depths, the red waves of death . . .   30
Thebes is dying. A blight on the fresh crops
and the rich pastures, cattle sicken and die,
and the women die in labor, children stillborn,
and the plague, the fiery god of fever hurls down
on the city, his lightning slashing through us—   35
raging plague in all its vengeance, devastating
the house of Cadmus! And black Death luxuriates
in the raw, wailing miseries of Thebes.

Now we pray to you. You cannot equal the gods,
your children know that, bending at your altar.   40
But we do rate you first of men,
both in the common crises of our lives
and face-to-face encounters with the gods.
You freed us from the Sphinx, you came to Thebes
and cut us loose from the bloody tribute we had paid   45
that harsh, brutal singer. We taught you nothing,
no skill, no extra knowledge, still you triumphed.
A god was with you, so they say, and we believe it—
you lifted up our lives.
                 So now again,
Oedipus, king, we bend to you, your power—   50
we implore you, all of us on our knees:
find us strength, rescue! Perhaps you've heard
the voice of a god or something from other men,
Oedipus . . . what do you know?
The man of experience—you see it every day—   55
his plans will work in a crisis, his first of all.

Act now—we beg you, best of men, raise up our city!
Act, defend yourself, your former glory!
Your country calls you savior now
for your zeal, your action years ago. 60
Never let us remember of your reign:
you helped us stand, only to fall once more.
Oh raise up our city, set us on our feet.
The omens were good that day you brought us joy—
be the same man today! 65
Rule our land, you know you have the power,
but rule a land of the living, not a wasteland.
Ship and towered city are nothing, stripped of men
alive within it, living all as one.
OEDIPUS: My children,
I pity you. I see—how could I fail to see 70
what longings bring you here? Well I know
you are sick to death, all of you,
but sick as you are, not one is sick as I.
Your pain strikes each of you alone, each
in the confines of himself, no other. But my spirit 75
grieves for the city, for myself and all of you.
I wasn't asleep, dreaming. You haven't wakened me—
I have wept through the nights, you must know that,
groping, laboring over many paths of thought.
After a painful search I found one cure: 80
I acted at once. I sent Creon,
my wife's own brother, to Delphi—
Apollo the Prophet's oracle—to learn
what I might do or say to save our city.

Today's the day. When I count the days gone by 85
it torments me . . . what is he doing?
Strange, he's late, he's gone too long.
But once he returns, then, then I'll be a traitor
if I do not do all the god makes clear.
PRIEST: Timely words. The men over there 90
are signaling—Creon's just arriving.
OEDIPUS:

[*Sighting* CREON, *then turning to the altar.*]

                                    Lord Apollo,
let him come with a lucky word of rescue,
shining like his eyes!
PRIEST: Welcome news, I think—he's crowned, look,
and the laurel wreath is bright with berries. 95
OEDIPUS: We'll soon see. He's close enough to hear—

[*Enter* CREON *from the side; his face is shaded with a wreath.*]

Creon, prince, my kinsman, what do you bring us?
What message from the god?
CREON: Good news.

I tell you even the hardest things to bear,
   if they should turn out well, all would be well. 100
OEDIPUS: Of course, but what were the god's *words*? There's no hope
   and nothing to fear in what you've said so far.
CREON: If you want my report in the presence of these people . . .

[*Pointing to the priests while drawing* OEDIPUS *toward the palace.*]

   I'm ready now, or we might go inside.
OEDIPUS: Speak out,
   speak to us all. I grieve for these, my people, 105
   far more than I fear for my own life.
CREON: Very well,
   I will tell you what I heard from the god.
   Apollo commands us—he was quite clear—
   "Drive the corruption from the land,
   don't harbor it any longer, past all cure, 110
   don't nurse it in your soil—root it out!"
OEDIPUS: How can we cleanse ourselves—what rites?
   What's the source of the trouble?
CREON: Banish the man, or pay back blood with blood.
   Murder sets the plague-storm on the city.
OEDIPUS: Whose murder? 115
   Whose fate does Apollo bring to light?
CREON: Our leader,
   my lord, was once a man named Laius,
   before you came and put us straight on course.
OEDIPUS: I know—
   or so I've heard. I never saw the man myself.
CREON: Well, he was killed, and Apollo commands us now— 120
   he could not be more clear,
   "Pay the killers back—whoever is responsible."
OEDIPUS: Where on earth are they? Where to find it now,
   the trail of the ancient guilt so hard to trace?
CREON: "Here in Thebes," he said. 125
   Whatever is sought for can be caught, you know,
   whatever is neglected slips away.
OEDIPUS: But where,
   in the palace, the fields or foreign soil,
   where did Laius meet his bloody death?
CREON: He went to consult an oracle, Apollo said, 130
   and he set out and never came home again.
OEDIPUS: No messenger, no fellow-traveler saw what happened?
   Someone to cross-examine?
CREON: No,
   they were all killed but one. He escaped,
   terrified, he could tell us nothing clearly, 135
   nothing of what he saw—just one thing.
OEDIPUS: What's that?
   One thing could hold the key to it all,
   a small beginning give us grounds for hope.

CREON: He said thieves attacked them—a whole band,
　　　not single-handed, cut King Laius down.
OEDIPUS: 　　　　　　　　　　　　　　　　　　A thief, 　　　　　　　　　140
　　　so daring, so wild, he'd kill a king? Impossible,
　　　unless conspirators paid him off in Thebes.
CREON: We suspected as much. But with Laius dead
　　　no leader appeared to help us in our troubles.
OEDIPUS: Trouble? Your *king* was murdered—royal blood! 　　　145
　　　What stopped you from tracking down the killer
　　　then and there?
CREON: 　　　　　　　　The singing, riddling Sphinx.
　　　She . . . persuaded us to let the mystery go
　　　and concentrate on what lay at our feet.
OEDIPUS: 　　　　　　　　　　　　　　　　　　No,
　　　I'll start again—I'll bring it all to light myself! 　　　　150
　　　Apollo is right, and so are you, Creon,
　　　to turn our attention back to the murdered man.
　　　Now you have *me* to fight for you, you'll see:
　　　I am the land's avenger by all rights,
　　　and Apollo's champion too. 　　　　　　　　　　　　155
　　　But not to assist some distant kinsman, no,
　　　for my own sake I'll rid us of this corruption.
　　　Whoever killed the king may decide to kill me too,
　　　with the same violent hand—by avenging Laius
　　　I defend myself.

　　　[*To the priests.*]

　　　　　　　　　　　　Quickly, my children. 　　　　　　　160
　　　Up from the steps, take up your branches now.

　　　[*To the guards.*]

　　　One of you summon the city here before us,
　　　tell them I'll do everything. God help us,
　　　we will see our triumph—or our fall.

　　　　　　　　[OEDIPUS *and* CREON *enter the palace, followed by the guards.*]

PRIEST: Rise, my sons. The kindness we came for 　　　　　165
　　　Oedipus volunteers himself.
　　　Apollo has sent his word, his oracle—
　　　Come down, Apollo, save us, stop the plague.

　　　　　　　　[*The priests rise, remove their branches and exit to the side.*]

[*Enter a* CHORUS, *the citizens of Thebes, who have not heard the news that* CREON
brings. They march around the altar, chanting.]

CHORUS: 　　　　　　　　　　　　　　　　　　Zeus!
　　　Great welcome voice of Zeus, what do you bring?
　　　What word from the gold vaults of Delphi 　　　　　170
　　　comes to brilliant Thebes? Racked with terror—
　　　　　　　　　　　　terror shakes my heart

and I cry your wild cries, Apollo, Healer of Delos
I worship you in dread . . . what now, what is your price?
some new sacrifice? some ancient rite from the past   175
come round again each spring?—
     what will you bring to birth?
Tell me, child of golden Hope
    warm voice that never dies!

You are the first I call, daughter of Zeus   180
deathless Athena—I call your sister Artemis,
heart of the market place enthroned in glory,
          guardian of our earth—
I call Apollo, Archer astride the thunderheads of heaven—
O triple shield against death, shine before me now!   185
If ever, once in the past, you stopped some ruin
launched against our walls
     you hurled the flame of pain
far, far from Thebes—you gods
    come now, come down once more!
               No, no   190
the miseries numberless, grief on grief, no end—
too much to bear, we are all dying
O my people . . .
    Thebes like a great army dying
and there is no sword of thought to save us, no   195
and the fruits of our famous earth, they will not ripen
no and the women cannot scream their pangs to birth—
screams for the Healer, children dead in the womb
     and life on life goes down
           you can watch them go   200
   like seabirds winging west, outracing the day's fire
down the horizon, irresistibly
     streaking on to the shores of Evening
               Death
so many deaths, numberless deaths on deaths, no end—
Thebes is dying, look, her children   205
stripped of pity . . .
    generations strewn on the ground
unburied, unwept, the dead spreading death
and the young wives and gray-haired mothers with them
cling to the altars, trailing in from all over the city—   210
Thebes, city of death, one long cortege
      and the suffering rises
        wails for mercy rise
   and the wild hymn for the Healer blazes out
clashing with our sobs our cries of mourning—   215
    O golden daughter of god, send rescue
    radiant as the kindness in your eyes!

Drive him back—the fever, the god of death
       that raging god of war

not armored in bronze, not shielded now, he burns me, 220
battle cries in the onslaught burning on—
O rout him from our borders!
Sail him, blast him out to the Sea-queen's chamber
         the black Atlantic gulfs
    or the northern harbor, death to all 225
where the Thracian surf comes crashing.
Now what the night spares he comes by day and kills—
the god of death.

      O lord of the stormcloud,
you who twirl the lightning, Zeus, Father,
thunder Death to nothing! 230

Apollo, lord of the light, I beg you—
    whip your longbow's golden cord
showering arrows on our enemies—shafts of power
champions strong before us rushing on!

Artemis, Huntress, 235
torches flaring over the eastern ridges—
      ride Death down in pain!

God of the headdress gleaming gold, I cry to you—
your name and ours are one, Dionysus—
   come with your face aflame with wine 240
       your raving women's cries
   your army on the march! Come with the lightning
come with torches blazing, eyes ablaze with glory!
Burn that god of death that all gods hate!

SCENE 1

[OEDIPUS *enters from the palace to address the* CHORUS, *as if addressing the entire city
of Thebes.*]

OEDIPUS: You pray to the gods? Let me grant your prayers.
 Come, listen to me—do what the plague demands:
 you'll find relief and lift your head from the depths.

 I will speak out now as a stranger to the story,
 a stranger to the crime. If I'd been present then, 5
 there would have been no mystery, no long hunt
 without a clue in hand. So now, counted
 a native Theban years after the murder,
 to all of Thebes I make this proclamation:
 if any one of you knows who murdered Laius, 10
 the son of Labdacus, I order him to reveal
 the whole truth to me. Nothing to fear,
 even if he must denounce himself,
 let him speak up
 and so escape the brunt of the charge— 15

he will suffer no unbearable punishment,
nothing worse than exile, totally unharmed.

[OEDIPUS *pauses, waiting for a reply.*]

Next,
if anyone knows the murderer is a stranger,
a man from alien soil, come, speak up.
I will give him a handsome reward, and lay up   20
gratitude in my heart for him besides.

[*Silence again, no reply.*]

But if you keep silent, if anyone panicking,
trying to shield himself or friend or kin,
rejects my offer, then hear what I will do.
I order you, every citizen of the state   25
where I hold throne and power: banish this man—
whoever he may be—never shelter him, never
speak a word to him, never make him partner
to your prayers, your victims burned to the gods.
Never let the holy water touch his hands.   30
Drive him out, each of you, from every home.
He is the plague, the heart of our corruption,
as Apollo's oracle has just revealed to me.
So I honor my obligations:
I fight for the god and for the murdered man.   35

Now my curse on the murderer. Whoever he is,
a lone man unknown in his crime
or one among many, let that man drag out
his life in agony, step by painful step—
I curse myself as well . . . if by any chance   40
he proves to be an intimate of our house,
here at my hearth, with my full knowledge,
may the curse I just called down on him strike me!

These are your orders: perform them to the last.
I command you, for my sake, for Apollo's, for this country   45
blasted root and branch by the angry heavens.
Even if god had never urged you on to act,
how could you leave the crime uncleansed so long?
A man so noble—your king, brought down in blood—
you should have searched. But I am the king now,   50
I hold the throne that he held then, possess his bed
and a wife who shares our seed . . . why, our seed
might be the same, children born of the same mother
might have created blood-bonds between us
if his hope of offspring had not met disaster—   55
but fate swooped at his head and cut him short.
So I will fight for him as if he were my father,
stop at nothing, search the world
to lay my hands on the man who shed his blood,

the son of Labdacus descended of Polydorus,   60
Cadmus of old and Agenor, founder of the line:
their power and mine are one.
                             Oh dear gods,
my curse on those who disobey these orders!
Let no crops grow out of the earth for them—
shrivel their women, kill their sons,   65
burn them to nothing in this plague
that hits us now, or something even worse.
But you, loyal men of Thebes who approve my actions,
may our champion, Justice, may all the gods
be with us, fight beside us to the end!   70
LEADER: In the grip of your curse, my king, I swear
    I'm not the murderer, I cannot point him out.
    As for the search, Apollo pressed it on us—
    he should name the killer.
OEDIPUS: Quite right,
    but to force the gods to act against their will—   75
    no man has the power.
LEADER: Then if I might mention
    the next best thing . . .
OEDIPUS: The third best too—
    don't hold back, say it.
LEADER: I still believe . . .
    Lord Tiresias sees with the eyes of Lord Apollo.
    Anyone searching for the truth, my king,   80
    might learn it from the prophet, clear as day.
OEDIPUS: I've not been slow with that. On Creon's cue
    I sent the escorts, twice, within the hour.
    I'm surprised he isn't here.
LEADER: We need him—
    without him we have nothing but old, useless rumors.   85
OEDIPUS: Which rumors? I'll search out every word.
LEADER: Laius was killed, they say, by certain travelers.
OEDIPUS: I know—but no one can find the murderer.
LEADER: If the man has a trace of fear in him
    he won't stay silent long,   90
    not with your curses ringing in his ears.
OEDIPUS: He didn't flinch at murder,
    he'll never flinch at words.

[*Enter* TIRESIAS, *the blind prophet, led by a boy with escorts in attendance. He remains
at a distance.*]

LEADER: Here is the one who will convict him, look,
    they bring him on at last, the seer, the man of god.
    The truth lives inside him, him alone.   95
OEDIPUS: O Tiresias,
    master of all the mysteries of our life,
    all you teach and all you dare not tell,
    signs in the heavens, signs that walk the earth!

Blind as you are, you can feel all the more   100
what sickness haunts our city. You, my lord,
are the one shield, the one savior we can find.

We asked Apollo—perhaps the messengers
haven't told you—he sent his answer back:
"Relief from the plague can only come one way.   105
Uncover the murderers of Laius,
put them to death or drive them into exile."
So I beg you, grudge us nothing now, no voice,
no message plucked from the birds, the embers
or the other mantic ways within your grasp.   110
Rescue yourself, your city, rescue me—
rescue everything infected by the dead.
We are in your hands. For a man to help others
with all his gifts and native strength:
that is the noblest work.

TIRESIAS: How terrible—to see the truth   115
   when the truth is only pain to him who sees!
   I knew it well, but I put it from my mind,
   else I never would have come.

OEDIPUS: What's this? Why so grim, so dire?

TIRESIAS: Just send me home. You bear your burdens,   120
   I'll bear mine. It's better that way,
   please believe me.

OEDIPUS: Strange response . . . unlawful,
   unfriendly too to the state that bred and reared you—
   you withhold the word of god.

TIRESIAS: I fail to see
   that your own words are so well-timed.   125
   I'd rather not have the same thing said of me . . .

OEDIPUS: For the love of god, don't turn away,
   not if you know something. We beg you,
   all of us on our knees.

TIRESIAS: None of you knows—
   and I will never reveal my dreadful secrets,   130
   not to say your own.

OEDIPUS: What? You know and you won't tell?
   You're bent on betraying us, destroying Thebes?

TIRESIAS: I'd rather not cause pain for you or me.
   So why this . . . useless interrogation?   135
   You'll get nothing from me.

OEDIPUS: Nothing! You,
   you scum of the earth, you'd enrage a heart of stone!
   You won't talk? Nothing moves you?
   Out with it, once and for all!

TIRESIAS: You criticize my temper . . . unaware   140
   of the one *you* live with, you revile me.

OEDIPUS: Who could restrain his anger hearing you?
   What outrage—you spurn the city!

TIRESIAS: What will come will come.

Even if I shroud it all in silence.   145
OEDIPUS: What will come? You're bound to *tell* me that.
TIRESIAS: I will say no more. Do as you like, build your anger
    to whatever pitch you please, rage your worst—
OEDIPUS: Oh I'll let loose, I have such fury in me—
    now I see it all. You helped hatch the plot,   150
    you did the work, yes, short of killing him
    with your own hands—and given eyes I'd say
    you did the killing single-handed!
TIRESIAS: Is that so!
    I charge you, then, submit to that decree
    you just laid down: from this day onward   155
    speak to no one, not these citizens, not myself.
    You are the curse, the corruption of the land!
OEDIPUS: You, shameless—
    aren't you appalled to start up such a story?
    You think you can get away with this?
TIRESIAS: I have already.   160
    The truth with all its power lives inside me.
OEDIPUS: Who primed you for this? Not your prophet's trade.
TIRESIAS: You did, you forced me, twisted it out of me.
OEDIPUS: What? Say it again—I'll understand it better.
TIRESIAS: Didn't you understand, just now?   165
    Or are you tempting me to talk?
OEDIPUS: No, I can't say I grasped your meaning.
    Out with it, again!
TIRESIAS: I say you are the murderer you hunt.
OEDIPUS: That obscenity, twice—by god, you'll pay.   170
TIRESIAS: Shall I say more, so you can really rage?
OEDIPUS: Much as you want. Your words are nothing—
    futile.
TIRESIAS: You cannot imagine . . . I tell you,
    you and your loved ones live together in infamy,
    you cannot see how far you've gone in guilt.   175
OEDIPUS: You think you can keep this up and never suffer?
TIRESIAS: Indeed, if the truth has any power.
OEDIPUS: It does
    but not for you, old man. You've lost your power,
    stone-blind, stone-deaf—senses, eyes blind as stone!
TIRESIAS: I pity you, flinging at me the very insults   180
    each man here will fling at you so soon.
OEDIPUS: Blind,
    lost in the night, endless night that nursed you!
    You can't hurt me or anyone else who sees the light—
    you can never touch me.
TIRESIAS: True, it is not your fate
    to fall at my hands. Apollo is quite enough,   185
    and he will take some pains to work this out.
OEDIPUS: Creon! Is this conspiracy his or yours?
TIRESIAS: Creon is not your downfall, no, you are your own.

OEDIPUS: O power—
    wealth and empire, skill outstripping skill
    in the heady rivalries of life,   190
    what envy lurks inside you! Just for this,
    the crown the city gave me—I never sought it,
    they laid it in my hands—for this alone, Creon,
    the soul of trust, my loyal friend from the start
    steals against me . . . so hungry to overthrow me   195
    he sets this wizard on me, this scheming quack,
    this fortune-teller peddling lies, eyes peeled
    for his own profit—seer blind in his craft!

    Come here, you pious fraud. Tell me,
    when did you ever prove yourself a prophet?   200
    When the Sphinx, that chanting Fury kept her deathwatch here,
    why silent then, not a word to set our people free?
    There was a riddle, not for some passer-by to solve—
    it cried out for a prophet. Where were you?
    Did you rise to the crisis? Not a word,   205
    you and your birds, your gods—nothing.
    No, but I came by, Oedipus the ignorant,
    I stopped the Sphinx! With no help from the birds,
    the flight of my own intelligence hit the mark.

    And this is the man you'd try to overthrow?   210
    You think you'll stand by Creon when he's king?
    You and the great mastermind—
    you'll pay in tears, I promise you, for this,
    this witch-hunt. If you didn't look so senile
    the lash would teach you what your scheming means!   215
LEADER: I would suggest his words were spoken in anger,
    Oedipus . . . yours too, and it isn't what we need.
    The best solution to the oracle, the riddle
    posed by god—we should look for that.
TIRESIAS: You are the king no doubt, but in one respect,   220
    at least, I am your equal: the right to reply.
    I claim that privilege too.
    I am not your slave. I serve Apollo.
    I don't need Creon to speak for me in public.
                            So,
    you mock my blindness? Let me tell you this.   225
    You with your precious eyes,
    you're blind to the corruption of your life,
    to the house you live in, those you live with—
    who *are* your parents? Do you know? All unknowing
    you are the scourge of your own flesh and blood,   230
    the dead below the earth and the living here above,
    and the double lash of your mother and your father's curse
    will whip you from this land one day, their footfall
    treading you down in terror, darkness shrouding
    your eyes that now can see the light!
                    Soon, soon   235

[handwritten margin notes: "Shown pride + need that he doesn't need the Gods - very bad to the Greek audience"; "Hubris - Bad pride one of the main themes"]

you'll scream aloud—what haven won't reverberate?
What rock of Cithaeron won't scream back in echo?
That day you learn the truth about your marriage,
the wedding-march that sang you into your halls,
the lusty voyage home to the fatal harbor!   240
And a crowd of other horrors you'd never dream
will level you with yourself and all your children.

There. Now smear us with insults—Creon, myself
and every word I've said. No man will ever
be rooted from the earth as brutally as you.   245
OEDIPUS: Enough! Such filth from him? Insufferable—
what, still alive? Get out—
faster, back where you came from—vanish!
TIRESIAS: I would never have come if you hadn't called me here.
OEDIPUS: If I thought you would blurt out such absurdities,   250
you'd have died waiting before I'd had you summoned.
TIRESIAS: Absurd, am I! To you, not to your parents:
the ones who bore you found me sane enough.
OEDIPUS: Parents—who? Wait . . . who is my father?
TIRESIAS: This day will bring your birth and your destruction. 255
OEDIPUS: Riddles—all you can say are riddles, murk and darkness.
TIRESIAS: Ah, but aren't you the best man alive at solving riddles?
OEDIPUS: Mock me for that, go on, and you'll reveal my greatness.
TIRESIAS: Your great good fortune, true, it was your ruin.
OEDIPUS: Not if I saved the city—what do I care?   260
TIRESIAS: Well then, I'll be going.

[*To his attendant.*]

                              Take me home, boy.
OEDIPUS: Yes, take him away. You're a nuisance here.
Out of the way, the irritation's gone.

[*Turning his back on* TIRESIAS, *moving toward the palace.*]

TIRESIAS: I will go,
once I have said what I came here to say.
I will never shrink from the anger in your eyes—
you can't destroy me. Listen to me closely: 265
the man you've sought so long, proclaiming,
cursing up and down, the murderer of Laius—
he is here. A stranger,
you may think, who lives among you,   270
he soon will be revealed a native Theban
but he will take no joy in the revelation.
Blind who now has eyes, beggar who now is rich,
he will grope his way toward a foreign soil,
a stick tapping before him step by step.   275

[OEDIPUS *enters the palace.*]

Revealed at last, brother and father both
to the children he embraces, to his mother

son and husband both—he sowed the loins
his father sowed, he spilled his father's blood!

Go in and reflect on that, solve that.   280
And if you find I've lied
from this day onward call the prophet blind.

                                    [TIRESIAS *and the boy exit to the side.*]

CHORUS: Who—
    who is the man the voice of god denounces
    resounding out of the rocky gorge of Delphi?
            The horror too dark to tell,   285
    whose ruthless bloody hands have done the work?
    His time has come to fly
            to outrace the stallions of the storm
                        his feet a streak of speed—
    Cased in armor, Apollo son of the Father   290
    lunges on him, lightning-bolts afire!
    And the grim unerring Furies
                closing for the kill.
                        Look,
    the word of god has just come blazing
    flashing off Parnassus' snowy heights!   295
            That man who left no trace—
    after him, hunt him down with all our strength!
    Now under bristling timber
            up through rocks and caves he stalks
                        like the wild mountain bull—   300
    cut off from men, each step an agony, frenzied, racing blind
    but he cannot outrace the dread voices of Delphi
    ringing out of the heart of Earth,
            the dark wings beating around him shrieking doom
                        the doom that never dies, the terror—   305

The skilled prophet scans the birds and shatters me with terror!
I can't accept him, can't deny him, don't know what to say,
I'm lost, and the wings of dark foreboding beating—
I cannot see what's come, what's still to come . . .
and what could breed a blood feud between   310
        Laius' house and the son of Polybus?
I know of nothing, not in the past and not now,
no charge to bring against our king, no cause
to attack his fame that rings throughout Thebes—
        not without proof—not for the ghost of Laius,   315
        not to avenge a murder gone without a trace.

Zeus and Apollo know, they know, the great masters
                of all the dark and depth of human life.
But whether a mere man can know the truth,
whether a seer can fathom more than I—   320
there is no test, no certain proof
        though matching skill for skill
a man can outstrip a rival. No, not till I see

these charges proved will I side with his accusers.
We saw him then, when the she-hawk swept against him,   325
saw with our own eyes his skill, his brilliant triumph—
    there was the test—he was the joy of Thebes!
    Never will I convict my king, never in my heart.

SCENE 2

[*Enter* CREON *from the side.*]

CREON: My fellow-citizens, I hear King Oedipus
levels terrible charges at me. I had to come.
I resent it deeply. If, in the present crisis,
he thinks he suffers any abuse from me,
anything I've done or said that offers him   5
the slightest injury, why, I've no desire
to linger out this life, my reputation in ruins.
The damage I'd face from such an accusation
is nothing simple. No, there's nothing worse:
branded a traitor in the city, a traitor   10
to all of you and my good friends.
LEADER: True,
    but a slur might have been forced out of him,
    by anger perhaps, not any firm conviction.
CREON: The charge was made in public, wasn't it?
    I put the prophet up to spreading lies?   15
LEADER: Such things were said . . .
    I don't know with what intent, if any.
CREON: Was his glance steady, his mind right
    when the charge was brought against me?
LEADER: I really couldn't say. I never look   20
    to judge the ones in power.

[*The doors open.* OEDIPUS *enters.*]

               Wait,
    here's Oedipus now.
OEDIPUS: You—here? You have the gall
to show your face before the palace gates?
You, plotting to kill me, kill the king—
I see it all, the marauding thief himself   25
scheming to steal my crown and power!
                   Tell me,
in god's name, what did you take me for,
coward or fool, when you spun out your plot?
Your treachery—you think I'd never detect it
creeping against me in the dark? Or sensing it,   30
not defend myself? Aren't you the fool,
you and your high adventure. Lacking numbers,
powerful friends, out for the big game of empire—
you need riches, armies to bring that quarry down!

CREON: Are you quite finished? It's your turn to listen 35
　　for just as long as you've . . . instructed me.
　　Hear me out, then judge me on the facts.
OEDIPUS: You've a wicked way with words, Creon,
　　but I'll be slow to learn—from you.
　　I find you a menace, a great burden to me. 40
CREON: Just one thing, hear me out in this.
OEDIPUS: 　　　　　　　　　　　　Just one thing,
　　don't tell *me* you're not the enemy, the traitor.
CREON: Look, if you think crude, mindless stubbornness
　　such a gift, you've lost your sense of balance.
OEDIPUS: If you think you can abuse a kinsman, 45
　　then escape the penalty, you're insane.
CREON: Fair enough, I grant you. But this injury
　　you say I've done you, what is it?
OEDIPUS: Did you induce me, yes or no,
　　to send for that sanctimonious prophet? 50
CREON: I did. And I'd do the same again.
OEDIPUS: All right then, tell me, how long is it now
　　since Laius . . .
CREON: 　　　　　　Laius—what did *he* do?
OEDIPUS: 　　　　　　　　　　　　　Vanished,
　　swept from sight, murdered in his tracks.
CREON: The count of the years would run you far back . . . 55
OEDIPUS: And that far back, was the prophet at his trade?
CREON: Skilled as he is today, and just as honored.
OEDIPUS: Did he ever refer to me then, at that time?
CREON: 　　　　　　　　　　　　　　　No,
　　never, at least, when I was in his presence.
OEDIPUS: But you did investigate the murder, didn't you? 60
CREON: We did our best, of course, discovered nothing.
OEDIPUS: But the great seer never accused me then—why not?
CREON: I don't know. And when I don't, *I* keep quiet.
OEDIPUS: You do know this, you'd tell it too—
　　if you had a shred of decency.
CREON: 　　　　　　　　　What? 65
　　If I know, I won't hold back.
OEDIPUS: 　　　　　　　　　Simply this:
　　if the two of you had never put heads together,
　　we would never have heard about *my* killing Laius.
CREON: If that's what he says . . . well, you know best.
　　But now I have a right to learn from you 70
　　as you just learned from me.
OEDIPUS: 　　　　　　　　　Learn your fill,
　　you never will convict me of the murder.
CREON: Tell me, you're married to my sister, aren't you?
OEDIPUS: A genuine discovery—there's no denying that.
CREON: And you rule the land with her, with equal power? 75
OEDIPUS: She receives from me whatever she desires.
CREON: And I am the third, all of us are equals?

OEDIPUS: Yes, and it's there you show your stripes—
    you betray a kinsman.
CREON: Not at all.
    Not if you see things calmly, rationally,   80
    as I do. Look at it this way first:
    who in his right mind would rather rule
    and live in anxiety than sleep in peace?
    Particularly if he enjoys the same authority.
    Not I, I'm not the man to yearn for kingship,   85
    not with a king's power in my hands. Who would?
    No one with any sense of self-control.
    Now, as it is, you offer me all I need,
    not a fear in the world. But if I wore the crown . . . .
    there'd be many painful duties to perform,   90
    hardly to my taste.
                  How could kingship
    please me more than influence, power
    without a qualm? I'm not that deluded yet,
    to reach for anything but privilege outright,
    profit free and clear.   95
    Now all men sing my praises, all salute me,
    now all who request your favors curry mine.
    I am their best hope: success rests in me.
    Why give up that, I ask you, and borrow trouble?
    A man of sense, someone who sees things clearly   100
    would never resort to treason.
    No, I have no lust for conspiracy in me,
    nor could I ever suffer one who does.

    Do you want proof? Go to Delphi yourself,
    examine the oracle and see if I've reported   105
    the message word-for-word. This too:
    if you detect that I and the clairvoyant
    have plotted anything in common, arrest me,
    execute me. Not on the strength of one vote,
    two in this case, mine as well as yours.   110
    But don't convict me on sheer unverified surmise.

    How wrong it is to take the good for bad,
    purely at random, or take the bad for good.
    But reject a friend, a kinsman? I would as soon
    tear out the life within us, priceless life itself.   115
    You'll learn this well, without fail in time.
    Time alone can bring the just man to light—
    the criminal you can spot in one short day.
LEADER: Good advice,
    my lord, for anyone who wants to avoid disaster.
    Those who jump to conclusions may go wrong.   120
OEDIPUS: When my enemy moves against me quickly,
    plots in secret, I move quickly too, I must,
    I plot and pay him back. Relax my guard a moment,

waiting his next move—he wins his objective,
   I lose mine.
CREON: What do you want?   125
   You want me banished?
OEDIPUS: No, I want you dead.
CREON: Just to show how ugly a grudge can . . .
OEDIPUS: So,
   still stubborn? you don't think I'm serious?
CREON: I think you're insane.
OEDIPUS: Quite sane—in my behalf.
CREON: Not just as much in mine?
OEDIPUS: You—my mortal enemy?   130
CREON: What if you're wholly wrong?
OEDIPUS: No matter—I must rule.
CREON: Not if you rule unjustly.
OEDIPUS: Hear him, Thebes, my city!
CREON: My city too, not yours alone!
LEADER: Please, my lords.

[*Enter* JOCASTA *from the palace.*]

                    Look, Jocasta's coming,
   and just in time too. With her help   135
   you must put this fighting of yours to rest.
JOCASTA: Have you no sense? Poor misguided men,
   such shouting—why this public outburst?
   Aren't you ashamed, with the land so sick,
   to stir up private quarrels?   140

[*To* OEDIPUS.]

   Into the palace now. And Creon, you go home.
   Why make such a furor over nothing?
CREON: My sister, it's dreadful . . . Oedipus, your husband,
   he's bent on a choice of punishments for me,
   banishment from the fatherland or death.   145
OEDIPUS: Precisely. I caught him in the act, Jocasta,
   plotting, about to stab me in the back.
CREON: Never—curse me, let me die and be damned
   if I've done you any wrong you charge me with.
JOCASTA: Oh god, believe it, Oedipus,   150
   honor the solemn oath he swears to heaven.
   Do it for me, for the sake of all your people.

[*The* CHORUS *begins to chant.*]

CHORUS: Believe it, be sensible
       give way, my king, I beg you!
OEDIPUS: What do you want from me, concessions?   155
CHORUS: Respect him—he's been no fool in the past
   and now he's strong with the oath he swears to god.
OEDIPUS: You know what you're asking?

CHORUS: I do.

OEDIPUS: Then out with it!

CHORUS: The man's your friend, your kin, he's under oath—
        don't cast him out, disgraced   160
        branded with guilt on the strength of hearsay only.

OEDIPUS: Know full well, if that is what you want
        you want me dead or banished from the land.

CHORUS: Never—
        no, by the blazing Sun, first god of the heavens!
            Stripped of the gods, stripped of loved ones,   165
        let me die by inches if that ever crossed my mind.
        But the heart inside me sickens, dies as the land dies
        and now on top of the old griefs you pile this,
        your fury—both of you!

OEDIPUS: Then let him go,
        even if it does lead to my ruin, my death   170
        or my disgrace, driven from Thebes for life.
        It's you, not him I pity—your words move me.
        He, wherever he goes, my hate goes with him.

CREON: Look at you, sullen in yielding, brutal in your rage—
        you will go too far. It's perfect justice: 175
        natures like yours are hardest on themselves.

OEDIPUS: Then leave me alone—get out!

CREON: I'm going.
        You're wrong, so wrong. These men know I'm right.

                                            [*Exit to the side.*]

    [*The* CHORUS *turns to* JOCASTA.]

CHORUS: Why do you hesitate, my lady
            why not help him in?   180

JOCASTA: Tell me what's happened first.

CHORUS: Loose, ignorant talk started dark suspicions
        and a sense of injustice cut deeply too.

JOCASTA: On both sides?

CHORUS: Oh yes.

JOCASTA: What did they say?

CHORUS: Enough, please, enough! The land's so racked already   185
        or so it seems to me . . .
        End the trouble here, just where they left it.

OEDIPUS: You see what comes of your good intentions now?
        And all because you tried to blunt my anger.

CHORUS: My king,
        I've said it once, I'll say it time and again—   190
            I'd be insane, you know it,
        senseless, ever to turn my back on you.
        You who set our beloved land—storm-tossed, shattered—
        straight on course. Now again, good helmsman,
        steer us through the storm!

    [*The* CHORUS *draws away, leaving* OEDIPUS *and* JOCASTA *side by side.*]

JOCASTA: For the love of god,   195

Oedipus, tell me too, what is it?
Why this rage? You're so unbending.
OEDIPUS: I will tell you. I respect you, Jocasta,
much more than these men here . . .

[*Glancing at the* CHORUS.]

Creon's to blame, Creon schemes against me.   200
JOCASTA: Tell me clearly, how did the quarrel start?
OEDIPUS: He says *I* murdered Laius—I am guilty.
JOCASTA: How does he know? Some secret knowledge
or simple hearsay?
OEDIPUS: Oh, he sent his prophet in
to do his dirty work. You know Creon,   205
Creon keeps his own lips clean.
JOCASTA: A prophet?
Well then, free yourself of every charge!
Listen to me and learn some peace of mind:
no skill in the world,
nothing human can penetrate the future.   210
Here is proof, quick and to the point.

An oracle came to Laius one fine day
(I won't say from Apollo himself
but his underlings, his priests) and it declared
that doom would strike him down at the hands of a son,   215
our son, to be born of our own flesh and blood. But Laius,
so the report goes at least, was killed by strangers,
thieves, at a place where three roads meet . . . my son—
he wasn't three days old and the boy's father
fastened his ankles, had a henchman fling him away   220
on a barren, trackless mountain.
                                    There, you see?
Apollo brought neither thing to pass. My baby
no more murdered his father than Laius suffered—
his wildest fear—death at his own son's hands.
That's how the seers and all their revelations   225
mapped out the future. Brush them from your mind.
Whatever the god needs and seeks
he'll bring to light himself, with ease.
OEDIPUS: Strange,
hearing you just now . . . my mind wandered,
my thoughts racing back and forth.   230
JOCASTA: What do you mean? Why so anxious, startled?
OEDIPUS: I thought I heard you say that Laius
was cut down at a place where three roads meet.
JOCASTA: That was the story. It hasn't died out yet.
OEDIPUS: Where did this thing happen? Be precise.   235
JOCASTA: A place called Phocis, where two branching roads,
one from Daulia, one from Delphi,
come together—a crossroads.
OEDIPUS: When? How long ago?

JOCASTA: The heralds no sooner reported Laius dead   240
     than you appeared and they hailed you king of Thebes.
OEDIPUS: My god, my god—what have you planned to do to me?
JOCASTA: What, Oedipus? What haunts you so?
OEDIPUS: Not yet.
     Laius—how did he look? Describe him.
     Had he reached his prime?
JOCASTA: He was swarthy,   245
     and the gray had just begun to streak his temples,
     and his build . . . wasn't far from yours.
OEDIPUS: Oh no no,
     I think I've just called down a dreadful curse
     upon myself—I simply didn't know!
JOCASTA: What are you saying? I shudder to look at you.   250
OEDIPUS: I have a terrible fear the blind seer can see.
     I'll know in a moment. One thing more—
JOCASTA: Anything,
     afraid as I am—ask, I'll answer, all I can.
OEDIPUS: Did he go with a light or heavy escort,
     several men-at-arms, like a lord, a king?   255
JOCASTA: There were five in the party, a herald among them,
     and a single wagon carrying Laius.
OEDIPUS: Ai—
     now I can see it all, clear as day.
     Who told you all this at the time, Jocasta?
JOCASTA: A servant who reached home, the lone survivor.   260
OEDIPUS: So, could he still be in the palace—even now?
JOCASTA: No indeed. Soon as he returned from the scene
     and saw you on the throne with Laius dead and gone,
     he knelt and clutched my hand, pleading with me
     to send him into the hinterlands, to pasture,   265
     far as possible, out of sight of Thebes.
     I sent him away. Slave though he was,
     he'd earned that favor—and much more.
OEDIPUS: Can we bring him back, quickly?
JOCASTA: Easily. Why do you want him so?
OEDIPUS: I am afraid,   270
     Jocasta, I have said too much already.
     That man—I've got to see him.
JOCASTA: Then he'll come.
     But even I have a right, I'd like to think,
     to know what's torturing you, my lord.
OEDIPUS: And so you shall—I can hold nothing back from you,   275
     now I've reached this pitch of dark foreboding.
     Who means more to me than you? Tell me,
     whom would I turn toward but you
     as I go through all this?

     My father was Polybus, king of Corinth.   280
     My mother, a Dorian, Merope. And I was held
     the prince of the realm among the people there,

till something struck me out of nowhere,
something strange . . . worth remarking perhaps,
hardly worth the anxiety I gave it. 285
Some man at a banquet who had drunk too much
shouted out—he was far gone, mind you—
that I am not my father's son. Fighting words!
I barely restrained myself that day
but early the next I went to mother and father, 290
questioned them closely, and they were enraged
at the accusation and the fool who let it fly.
So as for my parents I was satisfied,
but still this thing kept gnawing at me,
the slander spread—I had to make my move.
                                        And so, 295
unknown to mother and father I set out for Delphi,
and the god Apollo spurned me, sent me away
denied the facts I came for,
but first he flashed before my eyes a future
great with pain, terror, disaster—I can hear him cry, 300
"You are fated to couple with your mother, you will bring
a breed of children into the light no man can bear to see—
you will kill your father, the one who gave you life!"
I heard all that and ran. I abandoned Corinth,
from that day on I gauged its landfall only 305
by the stars, running, always running
toward some place where I would never see
the shame of all those oracles come true.
And as I fled I reached that very spot
where the great king, you say, met his death. 310
Now, Jocasta, I will tell you all.
Making my way toward this triple crossroad
I began to see a herald, then a brace of colts
drawing a wagon, and mounted on the bench . . . a man,
just as you've described him, coming face-to-face, 315
and the one in the lead and the old man himself
were about to thrust me off the road—brute force—
and the one shouldering me aside, the driver,
I strike him in anger!—and the old man, watching me
coming up along his wheels—he brings down 320
his prod, two prongs straight at my head!
I paid him back with interest!
Short work, by god—with one blow of the staff
in this right hand I knock him out of his high seat,
roll him out of the wagon, sprawling headlong— 325
I killed them all—every mother's son!

Oh, but if there is any blood-tie
between Laius and this stranger . . .
what man alive more miserable than I?
More hated by the gods? *I* am the man 330
no alien, no citizen welcomes to his house,

law forbids it—not a word to me in public,
driven out of every hearth and home.
And all these curses I—no one but I
brought down these piling curses on myself!   335
And you, his wife, I've touched your body with these,
the hands that killed your husband cover you with blood.

Wasn't I born for torment? Look me in the eyes!
I am abomination—heart and soul!
I must be exiled, and even in exile   340
never see my parents, never set foot
on native ground again. Else I am doomed
to couple with my mother and cut my father down . . .
Polybus who reared me, gave me life.
                                        But why, why?
Wouldn't a man of judgment say—and wouldn't he be right—   345
some savage power has brought this down upon my head?

Oh no, not that, you pure and awesome gods,
never let me see that day! Let me slip
from the world of men, vanish without a trace
before I see myself stained with such corruption,   350
stained to the heart.
LEADER: My lord, you fill our hearts with fear.
    But at least until you question the witness,
    do take hope.
OEDIPUS: Exactly. He is my last hope—
    I am waiting for the shepherd. He is crucial.   355
JOCASTA: And once he appears, what then? Why so urgent?
OEDIPUS: I will tell you. If it turns out that his story
    matches yours, I've escaped the worst.
JOCASTA: What did I say? What struck you so?
OEDIPUS: You said *thieves*—
    he told you a whole band of them murdered Laius.   360
    So, if he still holds to the same number,
    I cannot be the killer. One can't equal many.
    But if he refers to one man, one alone,
    clearly the scales come down on me:
    I am guilty.
JOCASTA: Impossible. Trust me,   365
    I told you precisely what he said,
    and he can't retract it now;
    the whole city heard it, not just I.
    And even if he should vary his first report
    by one man more or less, still, my lord,   370
    he could never make the murder of Laius
    truly fit the prophecy. Apollo was explicit:
    my son was doomed to kill my husband . . . my son,
    poor defenseless thing, he never had a chance
    to kill his father. They destroyed him first.   375

So much for prophecy. It's neither here nor there.
From this day on, I wouldn't look right or left.
OEDIPUS: True, true. Still, that shepherd,
    someone fetch him—now!
JOCASTA: I'll send at once. But do let's go inside.   380
    I'd never displease you, least of all in this.

                              [OEDIPUS *and* JOCASTA *enter the palace.*]

CHORUS: Destiny guide me always
    Destiny find me filled with reverence
        pure in word and deed.
    Great laws tower above us, reared on high   385
    born for the brilliant vault of heaven—
        Olympian Sky their only father,
    nothing mortal, no man gave them birth,
    their memory deathless, never lost in sleep:
    within them lives a mighty god, the god does not grow old.   390

    Pride breeds the tyrant
    violent pride, gorging, crammed to bursting
        with all that is overripe and rich with ruin—
    clawing up to the heights, headlong pride
    crashes down the abyss—sheer doom!   395
        No footing helps, all foothold lost and gone.
    But the healthy strife that makes the city strong—
    I pray that god will never end that wrestling:
    god, my champion, I will never let you go.

    But if any man comes striding, high and mighty   400
        in all he says and does,
    no fear of justice, no reverence
    for the temples of the gods—
        let a rough doom tear him down,
    repay his pride, breakneck, ruinous pride!   405
    If he cannot reap his profits fairly
        cannot restrain himself from outrage—
    mad, laying hands on the holy things untouchable!

        Can such a man, so desperate, still boast
        he can save his life from the flashing bolts of god?   410
            If all such violence goes with honor now
                why join the sacred dance?

    Never again will I go reverent to Dephi,
        the inviolate heart of Earth
    or Apollo's ancient oracle at Abae   415
    or Olympia of the fires—
        unless these prophecies all come true
    for all mankind to point toward in wonder.
    King of kings, if you deserve your titles
        Zeus, remember, never forget!   420

You and your deathless, everlasting reign.

They are dying, the old oracles sent to Laius,
now our masters strike them off the rolls.
Nowhere Apollo's golden glory now—
the gods, the gods go down.   425

SCENE 3

[*Enter* JOCASTA *from the palace, carrying a suppliant's branch wound in wool.*]

JOCASTA: Lords of the realm, it occurred to me,
just now, to visit the temples of the gods,
so I have my branch in hand and incense too.

Oedipus is beside himself. Racked with anguish,
no longer a man of sense, he won't admit   5
the latest prophecies are hollow as the old—
he's at the mercy of every passing voice
if the voice tells of terror.
I urge him gently, nothing seems to help,
so I turn to you, Apollo, you are nearest.   10

[*Placing her branch on the altar, while an old herdsman enters from the side, not the
one just summoned by the king but an unexpected* MESSENGER *from Corinth.*]

I come with prayers and offerings . . . I beg you,
cleanse us, set us free of defilement!
Look at us, passengers in the grip of fear,
watching the pilot of the vessel go to pieces.

MESSENGER:

[*Approaching* JOCASTA *and the* CHORUS.]

Strangers, please, I wonder if you could lead us   15
to the palace of the king . . . I think it's Oedipus.
Better, the man himself—you know where he is?
LEADER: This is his palace, stranger. He's inside.
But here is his queen, his wife and mother
of his children.
MESSENGER: Blessings on you, noble queen,   20
queen of Oedipus crowned with all your family—
blessings on you always!
JOCASTA: And the same to you, stranger, you deserve it . . .
such a greeting. But what have you come for?
Have you brought us news?
MESSENGER: Wonderful news—   25
for the house, my lady, for your husband too.
JOCASTA: Really, what? Who sent you?
MESSENGER: Corinth.
I'll give you the message in a moment.

You'll be glad of it—how could you help it?—
though it costs a little sorrow in the bargain.   30
JOCASTA: What can it be, with such a double edge?
MESSENGER: The people there, they want to make your Oedipus
    king of Corinth, so they're saying now.
JOCASTA: Why? Isn't old Polybus still in power?
MESSENGER: No more. Death has got him in the tomb.   35
JOCASTA: What are you saying? Polybus, dead?—dead?
MESSENGER: If not,
    if I'm not telling the truth, strike me dead too.
JOCASTA:

[*To a servant.*]

Quickly, go to your master, tell him this!

You prophecies of the gods, where are you now?
This is the man that Oedipus feared for years,   40
he fled him, not to kill him—and now he's dead,
quite by chance, a normal, natural death,
not murdered by his son.
OEDIPUS:

[*Emerging from the palace.*]

                           Dearest,
what now? Why call me from the palace?
JOCASTA:

[*Bringing the* MESSENGER *closer.*]

Listen to *him,* see for yourself what all   45
those awful prophecies of god have come to.
OEDIPUS: And who is he? What can he have for me?
JOCASTA: He's from Corinth, he's come to tell you
    your father is no more—Polybus—he's dead!
OEDIPUS:

[*Wheeling on the* MESSENGER.]

What? Let me have it from your lips.
MESSENGER: Well,   50
    if that's what you want first, then here it is:
    make no mistake, Polybus is dead and gone.
OEDIPUS: How—murder? sickness?—what? what killed him?
MESSENGER: A light tip of the scales can put old bones to rest.
OEDIPUS: Sickness then—poor man, it wore him down.
MESSENGER: That,   55
    and the long count of years he'd measured out.
OEDIPUS: So!
    Jocasta, why, why look to the Prophet's hearth,
    the fires of the future? Why scan the birds
    that scream above our heads? They winged me on
    to the murder of my father, did they? That was my doom?   60

Well look, he's dead and buried, hidden under the earth,
and here I am in Thebes, I never put hand to sword—
unless some longing for me wasted him away,
then in a sense you'd say I caused his death.
But now, all those prophecies I feared—Polybus   65
packs them off to sleep with him in hell!
They're nothing, worthless.

JOCASTA: There.
     Didn't I tell you from the start?

OEDIPUS: So you did. I was lost in fear.

JOCASTA: No more, sweep it from your mind forever.   70

OEDIPUS: But my mother's bed, surely I must fear—

JOCASTA: Fear?
     What should a man fear? It's all chance,
     chance rules our lives. Not a man on earth
     can see a day ahead, groping through the dark.
     Better to live at random, best we can.   75
     And as for this marriage with your mother—
     have no fear. Many a man before you,
     in his dreams, has shared his mother's bed.
     Take such things for shadows, nothing at all—
     Live, Oedipus,   80
     as if there's no tomorrow!

OEDIPUS: Brave words,
     and you'd persuade me if mother weren't alive.
     But mother lives, so for all your reassurances
     I live in fear, I must.

JOCASTA: But your father's death,
     that, at least, is a great blessing, joy to the eyes!   85

OEDIPUS: Great, I know . . . but I fear *her*—she's still alive.

MESSENGER: Wait, who is this woman, makes you so afraid?

OEDIPUS: Merope, old man. The wife of Polybus.

MESSENGER: The queen? What's there to fear in her?

OEDIPUS: A dreadful prophecy, stranger, sent by the gods.   90

MESSENGER: Tell me, could you? Unless it's forbidden
     other ears to hear.

OEDIPUS: Not at all.
     Apollo told me once—it is my fate—
     I must make love with my own mother,
     shed my father's blood with my own hands.   95
     So for years I've given Corinth a wide berth,
     and it's been my good fortune too. But still,
     to see one's parents and look into their eyes
     is the greatest joy I know.

MESSENGER: You're afraid of that?
     That kept you out of Corinth?

OEDIPUS: My *father*, old man—   100
     so I wouldn't kill my father.

MESSENGER: So that's it.
     Well then, seeing I came with such good will, my king,
     why don't I rid you of that old worry now?

OEDIPUS: What a rich reward you'd have for that!

MESSENGER: What do you think I came for, majesty?   105
    So you'd come home and I'd be better off.

OEDIPUS: Never, I will never go near my parents.

MESSENGER: My boy, it's clear, you don't know what you're doing.

OEDIPUS: What do you mean, old man? For god's sake, explain.

MESSENGER: If you ran from *them,* always dodging home . . .   110

OEDIPUS: Always, terrified Apollo's oracle might come true—

MESSENGER: And you'd be covered with guilt, from both your parents.

OEDIPUS: That's right, old man, that fear is always with me.

MESSENGER: Don't you know? You've really nothing to fear.

OEDIPUS: But why? If I'm their son—Merope, Polybus?   115

MESSENGER: Polybus was nothing to you, that's why, not in blood.

OEDIPUS: What are you saying—Polybus was not my father?

MESSENGER: No more than I am. He and I are equals.

OEDIPUS: My father—
    how can my father equal nothing? You're nothing to me!

OEDIPUS: Neither was he, no more your father than I am.   120

OEDIPUS: Then why did he call me his son?

MESSENGER: You were a gift,
    years ago—know for a fact he took you
    from my hands.

OEDIPUS: No, from another's hands?
    Then how could he love me so? He loved me, deeply . . .

MESSENGER: True, and his early years without a child   125
    made him love you all the more.

OEDIPUS: And you, did you . . .
    buy me? find me by accident?

MESSENGER: I stumbled on you,
    down the woody flanks of Mount Cithaeron.

OEDIPUS: So close,
    what were you doing here, just passing through?

MESSENGER: Watching over my flocks, grazing them on the slopes.   130

OEDIPUS: A herdsman, were you? A vagabond, scraping for wages?

MESSENGER: Your savior too, my son, in your worst hour.

OEDIPUS: Oh—
    when you picked me up, was I in pain? What exactly?

MESSENGER: Your ankles . . . they tell the story. Look at them.

OEDIPUS: Why remind me of that, that old affliction?   135

MESSENGER: Your ankles were pinned together. I set you free.

OEDIPUS: That dreadful mark—I've had it from the cradle.

MESSENGER: And you got your name from that misfortune too,
    the name's still with you.

OEDIPUS: Dear god, who did it?—
    mother? father? Tell me.

MESSENGER: I don't know.   140
    The one who gave you to me, he'd know more.

OEDIPUS: What? You took me from someone else?
    You didn't find me yourself?

MESSENGER: No sir,
    another shepherd passed you on to me.

OEDIPUS: Who? Do you know? Describe him.   145
MESSENGER: He called himself a servant of . . .
    if I remember rightly—Laius.

    [JOCASTA *turns sharply.*]

OEDIPUS: The king of the land who ruled here long ago?
MESSENGER: That's the one. That herdsman was *his* man.
OEDIPUS: Is he still alive? Can I see him?   150
MESSENGER: They'd know best, the people of these parts.

    [OEDIPUS *and the* MESSENGER *turn to the* CHORUS.]

OEDIPUS: Does anyone know that herdsman,
    the one he mentioned? Anyone seen him
    in the fields, here in the city? Out with it!
    The time has come to reveal this once for all.   155
LEADER: I think he's the very shepherd you wanted to see,
    a moment ago. But the queen, Jocasta,
    she's the one to say.
OEDIPUS: Jocasta,
    you remember the man we just sent for?
    Is *that* the one he means?
JOCASTA: That man . . .   160
    why ask? Old shepherd, talk, empty nonsense,
    don't give it another thought, don't even think—
OEDIPUS: What—give up now, with a clue like this?
    Fail to solve the mystery of my birth?
    Not for all the world!
JOCASTA: Stop—in the name of god,   165
    if you love your own life, call off this search!
    My suffering is enough.
OEDIPUS: Courage!
    Even if my mother turns out to be a slave,
    and I a slave, three generations back,
    you would not seem common.
JOCASTA: Oh no,   170
    listen to me, I beg you, don't do this.
OEDIPUS: Listen to you? No more. I must know it all,
    must see the truth at last.
JOCASTA: No, please—
    for your sake—I want the best for you!
OEDIPUS: Your best is more than I can bear.
JOCASTA: You're doomed—   175
    may you never fathom who you are!
OEDIPUS:

    [*To a servant.*]

    Hurry, fetch me the herdsman, now!
    Leave her to glory in her royal birth.
JOCASTA: Aieeeeee—
                    man of agony—
    that is the only name I have for you,   180

that, no other—ever, ever, ever!

[*Flinging through the palace doors. A long, tense silence follows.*]

LEADER: Where's she gone, Oedipus?
  Rushing off, such wild grief . . .
  I'm afraid that from this silence
  something monstrous may come bursting forth.   185
OEDIPUS: Let it burst! Whatever will, whatever must!
  I must know my birth, no matter how common
  it may be—I must see my origins face-to-face.
  She perhaps, she with her woman's pride
  may well be mortified by my birth,   190
  but I, I count myself the son of Chance,
  the great goddess, giver of all good things—
  I'll never see myself disgraced. She is my mother!
  And the moons have marked me out, my blood-brothers,
  one moon on the wane, the next moon great with power.   195
  That is my blood, my nature—I will never betray it,
  never fail to search and learn my birth!
CHORUS: Yes—if I am a true prophet
      if I can grasp the truth,
        by the boundless skies of Olympus,   200
  at the full moon of tomorrow, Mount Cithaeron
  you will know how Oedipus glories in you—
  you, his birthplace, nurse, his mountain-mother!
  And we will sing you, dancing out your praise—
  you lift our monarch's heart!   205
      Apollo, Apollo, god of the wild cry
          may our dancing please you!
                                          Oedipus—
              son, dear child, who bore you?
  Who of the nymphs who seem to live forever
  mated with Pan, the mountain-striding Father?   210
  Who was your mother? who, some bride of Apollo
  the god who loves the pastures spreading toward the sun?
      Or was it Hermes, king of the lightning ridges?
  Or Dionysus, lord of frenzy, lord of the barren peaks—
  did he seize you in his hands, dearest of all his lucky finds?— 215
      found by the nymphs, their warm eyes dancing, gift
  to the lord who loves them dancing out his joy!

SCENE 4

  [OEDIPUS *strains to see a figure coming from the distance. Attended by palace guards,*
  an old SHEPHERD *enters slowly, reluctant to approach the king.*]

OEDIPUS: I never met the man, my friends . . . still,
  if I had to guess, I'd say that's the shepherd,
  the very one we've looked for all along.
  Brothers in old age, two of a kind,

he and our guest here. At any rate 5
the ones who bring him in are my own men,
I recognize them.

[*Turning to the* LEADER.]

But you know more than I,
you should, you've seen the man before.
LEADER: I know him, definitely. One of Laius' men,
a trusty shepherd, if there ever was one. 10
OEDIPUS: You, I ask you first, stranger,
you from Corinth—is this the one you mean?
MESSENGER: You're looking at him. He's your man.
OEDIPUS:

[*To the* SHEPHERD.]

You, old man, come over here—
look at me. Answer all my questions. 15
Did you ever serve King Laius?
SHEPHERD: So I did . . .
a slave, not bought on the block though,
born and reared in the palace.
OEDIPUS: Your duties, your kind of work?
SHEPHERD: Herding the flocks, the better part of my life. 20
OEDIPUS: Where, mostly? Where did you do your grazing?
SHEPHERD: Well,
Cithaeron sometimes, or the foothills round about.
OEDIPUS: This man—you know him? ever see him there?
SHEPHERD:

[*Evasive, glancing from the* MESSENGER *to the king.*]

Doing what?—what man do you mean?
OEDIPUS:

[*Pointing to the* MESSENGER.]

This one here—ever have dealings with him? 25
SHEPHERD: Not so I could say, but give me a chance,
my memory's bad . . .
MESSENGER: No wonder he doesn't know me, master.
But let me refresh his memory for him.
I'm sure he recalls old times we had 30
on the slopes of Mount Cithaeron;
he and I, grazing our flocks, he with two
and I with one—we both struck up together,
three whole seasons, six months at a stretch
from spring to the rising of Arcturus in the fall, 35
then with winter coming on I'd drive my herds
to my own pens, and back he'd go with his
to Laius' folds.

[*To the* SHEPHERD.]

                     Now that's how it was,
    wasn't it—yes or no?
SHEPHERD: Yes, I suppose . . .
    it's all so long ago.
MESSENGER: Come, tell me,   40
    you gave me a child back then, a boy, remember?
    A little fellow to rear, my very own.
SHEPHERD: What? Why rake up that again?
MESSENGER: Look, here he is, my fine old friend—
    the same man who was just a baby then.   45
SHEPHERD: Damn you, shut your mouth—quiet!
OEDIPUS: Don't lash out at him, old man—
    you need lashing more than he does.
SHEPHERD: Why,
    master, majesty—what have I done wrong?
OEDIPUS: You won't answer his question about the boy.   50
SHEPHERD: He's talking nonsense, wasting his breath.
OEDIPUS: So, you won't talk willingly—
    then you'll talk with pain.

[*The guards seize the* SHEPHERD.]

SHEPHERD: No, dear god, don't torture an old man!
OEDIPUS: Twist his arms back, quickly!
SHEPHERD: God help us, why?—   55
    what more do you need to know?
OEDIPUS: Did you give him that child? He's asking.
SHEPHERD: I did . . . I wish to god I'd died that day.
OEDIPUS: You've got your wish if you don't tell the truth.
SHEPHERD: The more I tell, the worse the death I'll die.
OEDIPUS: Our friend here wants to stretch things out, does he? 60

[*Motioning to his men for torture.*]

SHEPHERD: No, no, I gave it to him—I just said so.
OEDIPUS: Where did you get it? Your house? Someone else's?
SHEPHERD: It wasn't mine, no, I got it from . . . someone.
OEDIPUS: Which one of them?

[*Looking at the citizens.*]

                    Whose house?
SHEPHERD: No—   65
    god's sake, master, no more questions!
OEDIPUS: You're a dead man if I have to ask again.
SHEPHERD: Then—the child came from the house . . .
    of Laius.
OEDIPUS: A slave? or born of his own blood?
SHEPHERD: Oh, no,

I'm right at the edge, the horrible truth—I've got to say it!	70
OEDIPUS: And I'm at the edge of hearing horrors, yes, but I must hear!
SHEPHERD: All right! His son, they said it was—his son!
But the one inside, your wife,
she'd tell it best.
OEDIPUS: My wife—	75
she gave it to you?
SHEPHERD: Yes, yes, my king.
OEDIPUS: Why, what for?
SHEPHERD: To kill it.
OEDIPUS: Her own child,	80
how could she?
SHEPHERD: She was afraid—
frightening prophecies.
OEDIPUS: What?
SHEPHERD: They said—
he'd kill his parents.	85
OEDIPUS: But you gave him to this old man—why?
SHEPHERD: I pitied the little baby, master,
hoped he'd take him off to his own country,
far away, but he saved him for this, this fate.
If you are the man he says you are, believe me,	90
you were born for pain.
OEDIPUS: O god—
all come true, all burst to light!
O light—now let me look my last on you!
I stand revealed at last—
cursed in my birth, cursed in marriage,	95
cursed in the lives I cut down with these hands!

[*Rushing through the doors with a great cry. The Corinthian* MESSENGER, *the*
SHEPHERD *and attendants exit slowly to the side.*]

CHORUS: O the generations of men
the dying generations—adding the total
of all your lives I find they come to nothing . . .
does there exist, is there a man on earth	100
who seizes more joy than just a dream, a vision?
And the vision no sooner dawns than dies
blazing into oblivion.

You are my great example, you, your life
your destiny, Oedipus, man of misery—	105
I count no man blest.

You outranged all men!
Bending your bow to the breaking-point
you captured priceless glory, O dear god,
and the Sphinx came crashing down,
the virgin, claws hooked	110
like a bird of omen singing, shrieking death—
like a fortress reared in the face of death
you rose and saved our land.

From that day on we called you king
we crowned you with honors, Oedipus, towering over all— 115
mighty king of the seven gates of Thebes.

But now to hear your story—is there a man more agonized?
More wed to pain and frenzy? Not a man on earth,
the joy of your life ground down to nothing
O Oedipus, name for the ages— 120
      one and the same wide harbor served you
                    son and father both
son and father came to rest in the same bridal chamber.
How, how could the furrows your father plowed
bear you, your agony, harrowing on 125
in silence O so long?

                   But now for all your power
Time, all-seeing Time has dragged you to the light,
judged your marriage monstrous from the start—
the son and the father tangling, both one—
O child of Laius, would to god 130
      I'd never seen you, never never!
         Now I weep like a man who wails the dead
and the dirge comes pouring forth with all my heart!
I tell you the truth, you gave me life
my breath leapt up in you 135
and now you bring down night upon my eyes.

SCENE 5

[*Enter a* MESSENGER *from the palace.*]

MESSENGER: Men of Thebes, always first in honor,
    what horrors you will hear, what you will see,
    what a heavy weight of sorrow you will shoulder . . . .
    if you are true to your birth, if you still have
    some feeling for the royal house of Thebes. 5
    I tell you neither the waters of the Danube
    nor the Nile can wash this palace clean.
    Such things it hides, it soon will bring to light—
    terrible things, and none done blindly now,
    all done with a will. The pains 10
    we inflict upon ourselves hurt most of all.
LEADER: God knows we have pains enough already.
    What can you add to them?
MESSENGER: The queen is dead.
LEADER: Poor lady—how?
MESSENGER: By her own hand. But you are spared the worst, 15
    you never had to watch . . . I saw it all,
    and with all the memory that's in me
    you will learn what that poor woman suffered.

    Once she'd broken in through the gates,

dashing past us, frantic, whipped to fury,   20
ripping her hair out with both hands—
straight to her rooms she rushed, flinging herself
across the bridal-bed, doors slamming behind her—
once inside, she wailed for Laius, dead so long,
remembering how she bore his child long ago,   25
the life that rose up to destroy him, leaving
its mother to mother living creatures
with the very son she'd borne.
Oh how she wept, mourning the marriage-bed
where she let loose that double brood—monsters—   30
husband by her husband, children by her child.
                  And then—
but how she died is more than I can say. Suddenly
Oedipus burst in, screaming, he stunned us so
we couldn't watch her agony to the end,
our eyes were fixed on him. Circling   35
like a maddened beast, stalking, here, there,
crying out to us—
            Give him a sword! His wife,
no wife, his mother, where can he find the mother earth
that cropped two crops at once, himself and all his children?
He was raging—one of the dark powers pointing the way,   40
none of us mortals crowding around him, no,
with a great shattering cry—someone, something leading him on—
he hurled at the twin doors and bending the bolts back
out of their sockets, crashed through the chamber.
And there we saw the woman hanging by the neck,   45
cradled high in a woven noose, spinning,
swinging back and forth. And when he saw her,
giving a low, wrenching sob that broke our hearts,
slipping the halter from her throat, he eased her down,
in a slow embrace he laid her down, poor thing . . .   50
then, what came next, what horror we beheld!

He rips off her brooches, the long gold pins
holding her robes—and lifting them high,
looking straight up into the points,
he digs them down the sockets of his eyes, crying, "You,   55
you'll see no more the pain I suffered, all the pain I caused!
Too long you looked on the ones you never should have seen,
blind to the ones you longed to see, to know! Blind
from this hour on! Blind in the darkness—blind!"
His voice like a dirge, rising, over and over   60
raising the pins, raking them down his eyes.
And at each stroke blood spurts from the roots,
splashing his beard, a swirl of it, nerves and clots—
black hail of blood pulsing, gushing down.

These are the griefs that burst upon them both,   65
coupling man and woman. The joy they had so lately,
the fortune of their old ancestral house

was deep joy indeed. Now, in this one day,
wailing, madness and doom, death, disgrace,
all the griefs in the world that you can name,   70
all are theirs forever.
LEADER: Oh poor man, the misery—
has he any rest from pain now?

[*A voice within, in torment.*]

MESSENGER: He's shouting,
"Loose the bolts, someone, show me to all of Thebes!
My father's murderer, my mother's—"
No, I can't repeat it, it's unholy.   75
Now he'll tear himself from his native earth,
not linger, curse the house with his own curse.
But he needs strength, and a guide to lead him on.
This is sickness more than he can bear.

[*The palace doors open.*]

                                        Look,
he'll show you himself. The great doors are opening—   80
you are about to see a sight, a horror
even his mortal enemy would pity.

[*Enter* OEDIPUS, *blinded, led by a boy. He stands at the palace steps, as if surveying his
people once again.*]

CHORUS: O the terror—
        the suffering, for all the world to see,
        the worst terror that ever met my eyes.
        What madness swept over you? What god,   85
        what dark power leapt beyond all bounds,
        beyond belief, to crush your wretched life?—
        godforsaken, cursed by the gods!
        I pity you but I can't bear to look.
        I've much to ask, so much to learn,   90
        so much fascinates my eyes,
        but you . . . I shudder at the sight.
OEDIPUS: Oh, Ohh—
        the agony! I am agony—
        where am I going? where on earth?
                where does all this agony hurl me?   95
        where's my voice?—
                winging, swept away on a dark tide—
                My destiny, my dark power, what a leap you made!
CHORUS: To the depths of terror, too dark to hear, to see.
OEDIPUS: Dark, horror of darkness   100
        my darkness, drowning, swirling around me
        crashing wave on wave—unspeakable, irresistible
                headwind, fatal harbor! Oh again,
        the misery, all at once, over and over
        the stabbing daggers, stab of memory   105

raking me insane.
CHORUS: No wonder you suffer
    twice over, the pain of your wounds,
    the lasting grief of pain.
OEDIPUS: Dear friend, still here?
        Standing by me, still with a care for me,
        the blind man? Such compassion,   110
            loyal to the last. Oh it's you
        I know you're here, dark as it is
        I'd know you anywhere, your voice—
    it's yours, clearly yours.
CHORUS: Dreadful, what you've done . . .
    how could you bear it, gouging out your eyes?   115
    What superhuman power drove you on?
OEDIPUS: Apollo, friends, Apollo—
    he ordained my agonies—these, my pains on pains!
        But the hand that struck my eyes was mine,
        mine alone—no one else—   120
            I did it all myself!
    What good were eyes to me?
    Nothing I could see could bring me joy.
CHORUS: No, no, exactly as you say.
OEDIPUS: What can I ever see?
        What love, what call of the heart   125
    can touch my ears with joy? Nothing, friends.
        Take me away, far, far from Thebes,
        quickly, cast me away, my friends—
    this great murderous ruin, this man cursed to heaven,
        the man the deathless gods hate most of all!   130
CHORUS: Pitiful, you suffer so, you understand so much . . .
    I wish you had never known.
OEDIPUS: Die, die—
        whoever he was that day in the wilds
    who cut my ankles free of the ruthless pins,
        he pulled me clear of death, he saved my life   135
        for this, this kindness—
                    Curse him, kill him!
        If I'd died then, I'd never have dragged myself,
        my loved ones through such hell.
CHORUS: Oh if only . . . would to god.
OEDIPUS: I'd never have come to this,   140
        my father's murderer—never been branded
    mother's husband, all men see me now! Now,
        loathed by the gods, son of the mother I defiled
        coupling in my father's bed, spawning lives in the loins
    that spawned my wretched life. What grief can crown this grief?   145
            It's mine alone, my destiny—I am Oedipus!
CHORUS: How can I say you've chosen for the best?
    Better to die than be alive and blind.
OEDIPUS: What I did was best—don't lecture me,

no more advice. I, with *my* eyes, 150
how could I look my father in the eyes
when I go down to death? Or mother, so abused . . .
I have done such things to the two of them,
crimes too huge for hanging.
                    Worse yet,
the sight of my children, born as they were born, 155
how could I long to look into their eyes?
No, not with these eyes of mine, never.
Not this city either, her high towers,
the sacred glittering images of her gods—
I am misery! I, her best son, reared 160
as no other son of Thebes was ever reared,
I've stripped myself, I gave the command myself.
All men must cast away the great blasphemer,
the curse now brought to light by the gods,
the son of Laius—I, my father's son! 165

Now I've exposed my guilt, horrendous guilt,
could I train a level glance on you, my countrymen?
Impossible! No, if I could just block off my ears,
the springs of hearing, I would stop at nothing—
I'd wall up my loathsome body like a prison, 170
blind to the sound of life, not just the sight.
Oblivion—what a blessing . . .
for the mind to dwell a world away from pain.

O Cithaeron, why did you give me shelter?
Why didn't you take me, crush my life out on the spot? 175
I'd never have revealed my birth to all mankind.

O Polybus, Corinth, the old house of my fathers,
so I believed—what a handsome prince you raised—
under the skin, what sickness to the core.
Look at me! Born of outrage, outrage to the core. 180

O triple roads—it all comes back, the secret,
dark ravine, and the oaks closing in
where the three roads join . . .
You drank my father's blood, my own blood
spilled by my own hands—you still remember me? 185
What things you saw me do? Then I came here
and did them all once more!
                    Marriages! O marriage,
you gave me birth, and once you brought me into the world
you brought my sperm rising back, springing to light
fathers, brothers, sons—one murderous breed— 190
brides, wives, mothers. The blackest things
a man can do, I have done them all!
                    No more—
it's wrong to name what's wrong to do. Quickly,
for the love of god, hide me somewhere,

kill me, hurl me into the sea   195
where you can never look on me again.

[*Beckoning to the* CHORUS *as they shrink away.*]

                                        Closer,
it's all right. Touch the man of grief.
Do. Don't be afraid. My troubles are mine
and I am the only man alive who can sustain them.

[*Enter* CREON *from the palace, attended by palace guards.*]

LEADER: Put your requests to Creon. Here he is,   200
    just when we need him. He'll have a plan, he'll act.
    Now that he's the sole defense of the country
    in your place.
OEDIPUS: Oh no, what can I say to him?
    How can I ever hope to win his trust?
    I wronged him so, just now, in every way.   205
    You must see that—I was so wrong, so wrong.
CREON: I haven't come to mock you, Oedipus,
    or to criticize your former failings.

[*Turning to the guards.*]

                                    You there,
    have you lost all respect for human feelings?
    At least revere the Sun, the holy fire   210
    that keeps us all alive. Never expose a thing
    of guilt and holy dread so great it appalls
    the earth, the rain from heaven, the light of day!
    Get him into the halls—quickly as you can.
    Piety demands no less. Kindred alone   215
    should see a kinsman's shame. This is obscene.
OEDIPUS: Please, in god's name . . . you wipe my fears away,
    coming so generously to me, the worst of men.
    Do one thing more, for your sake, not mine.
CREON: What do you want? Why so insistent?   220
OEDIPUS: Drive me out of the land at once, far from sight,
    where I can never hear a human voice.
CREON: I'd have done that already, I promise you.
    First I wanted the god to clarify my duties.
OEDIPUS: The god? His command was clear, every word: 225
    death for the father-killer, the curse—
    he said destroy me!
CREON: So he did. Still, in such a crisis
    it's better to ask precisely what to do.
OEDIPUS: So miserable—
    you would consult the god about a man like me?   230
CREON: By all means. And this time, I assume,
    even you will obey the god's decrees.
OEDIPUS: I will,
    I will. And you, I command you—I beg you . . .

the woman inside, bury her as you see fit.
It's the only decent thing,   235
to give your own the last rites. As for me,
never condemn the city of my fathers
to house my body, not while I'm alive, no,
let me live on the mountains, on Cithaeron,
my favorite haunt, I have made it famous.   240
Mother and father marked out that rock
to be my everlasting tomb—buried alive.
Let me die there, where they tried to kill me.

Oh but this I know: no sickness can destroy me,
nothing can. I would never have been saved   245
from death—I have been saved
for something great and terrible, something strange.
Well let my destiny come and take me on its way!

About my children, Creon, the boys at least,
don't burden yourself. They're men,   250
wherever they go, they'll find the means to live.
But my two daughters, my poor helpless girls,
clustering at our table, never without me
hovering near them . . . whatever I touched,
they always had their share. Take care of them,   255
I beg you. Wait, better—permit me, would you?
Just to touch them with my hands and take
our fill of tears. Please . . . my king.
Grant it, with all your noble heart.
If I could hold them, just once, I'd think   260
I had them with me, like the early days
when I could see their eyes.

[ANTIGONE *and* ISMENE, *two small children, are led in from the palace by a nurse.*]

               What's that?
O god! Do I really hear you sobbing?—
my two children. Creon, you've pitied me?
Sent me my darling girls, my own flesh and blood!   265
Am I right?
CREON: Yes, it's my doing.
I know the joy they gave you all these years,
the joy you must feel now.
OEDIPUS: Bless you, Creon!
May god watch over you for this kindness,
better than he ever guarded me.
                  Children, where are you?   270
Here, come quickly—

[*Groping for* ANTIGONE *and* ISMENE, *who approach their father cautiously, then embrace him.*]

          Come to these hands of mine,
your brother's hands, your own father's hands

that served his once bright eyes so well—
that made them blind. Seeing nothing, children,
knowing nothing, I became your father,   275
I fathered you in the soil that gave me life.

How I weep for you—I cannot see you now . . .
just thinking of all your days to come, the bitterness,
the life that rough mankind will thrust upon you.
Where are the public gatherings you can join,   280
the banquets of the clans? Home you'll come,
in tears, cut off from the sight of it all,
the brilliant rites unfinished.
And when you reach perfection, ripe for marriage,
who will he be, my dear ones? Risking all   285
to shoulder the curse that weighs down my parents,
yes and you too—that wounds us all together.
What more misery could you want?
Your father killed his father, sowed his mother,
one, one and the selfsame womb sprang you—   290
he cropped the very roots of his existence.

Such disgrace, and you must bear it all!
Who will marry you then? Not a man on earth.
Your doom is clear: you'll wither away to nothing,
single, without a child.

[*Turning to* CREON.]

               Oh Creon,   295
you are the only father they have now . . .
we who brought them into the world
are gone, both gone at a stroke—
Don't let them go begging, abandoned,
women without men. Your own flesh and blood!   300
Never bring them down to the level of my pains.
Pity them. Look at them, so young, so vulnerable,
shorn of everything—you're their only hope.
Promise me, noble Creon, touch my hand!

[*Reaching toward* CREON, *who draws back.*]

You, little ones, if you were old enough   305
to understand, there is much I'd tell you.
Now, as it is, I'd have you say a prayer.
Pray for life, my children,
live where you are free to grow and season.
Pray god you find a better life than mine,   310
the father who begot you.
CREON: Enough.
    You've wept enough. Into the palace now.
OEDIPUS: I must, but I find it very hard.
CREON: Time is the great healer, you will see.
OEDIPUS: I am going—you know on what condition?   315

CREON: Tell me. I'm listening.

OEDIPUS: Drive me out of Thebes, in exile.

CREON: Not I. Only the gods can give you that.

OEDIPUS: Surely the gods hate me so much—

CREON: You'll get your wish at once.

OEDIPUS: You consent?   320

CREON: I try to say what I mean; it's my habit.

OEDIPUS: Then take me away. It's time.

CREON: Come along, let go of the children.

OEDIPUS: No—

don't take them away from me, not now! No no no!

[*Clutching his daughters as the guards wrench them loose and take them through the palace doors.*]

CREON: Still the king, the master of all things?   325

No more: here your power ends.

None of your power follows you through life.

[*Exit* OEDIPUS *and* CREON *to the palace.*]

[*The* CHORUS *comes forward to address the audience directly.*]

CHORUS: People of Thebes, my countrymen, look on Oedipus.

He solved the famous riddle with his brilliance,

he rose to power, a man beyond all power.

Who could behold his greatness without envy?

Now what a black sea of terror has overwhelmed him.

Now as we keep our watch and wait the final day,

count no man happy till he dies, free of pain at last.

[*Exit in procession.*]

THE RECEPTIVE READER

1. (Prologue) How much of the background or context needed to understand the play does the *exposition* provide for you? ✧ What is the role of Oedipus in the initial exchange with his people? What kind of a leader is he? What is the role of Creon in this scene? ✧ What makes the first chant of the *chorus* more than a dutiful invocation of the gods? Which gods does the chorus invoke—how does it remind you of things you know about the Greek gods?

2. (Scene 1) What picture of Oedipus as the king do you form during his long speech to the citizens who have turned to him for help? ✧ Does your picture of Oedipus change as he responds to Tiresias' ominous hint of "dreadful secrets"? What traits of his character does Oedipus show in his denunciation of Creon and in his taunts of the blind seer? ✧ What role do blindness and riddles play in the rapid trading-off of taunts between the king and the prophet? How and how well does Tiresias establish his authority? ✧ What is the reaction of the chorus to what happened in this scene? What stand does it take?

3. (Scene 2) Is Creon is this scene a worthy *antagonist* for Oedipus? How do the two men handle themselves in this scene? ✧ What role does Jocasta play in the conflict between her husband and her brother? What role does the chorus play? Are you surprised by its reactions? ✧ How does Jocasta in this scene first show her doubts about or-

acles? Does she succeed in persuading Oedipus? ✧ By the end of this scene, Oedipus has reached "a pitch of dark foreboding." How much does he already know or suspect?

4. (Scene 3) What essential pieces of the puzzle does the *messenger* in this scene provide? How does Oedipus show that he is still in the dark? ✧ Why and how does Jocasta voice her doubts about priests and oracles in this scene? When or how does Jocasta show that she already knows the truth? What are your feelings as you watch her attempts to head off the worst?

5. (Scene 4) In this climactic scene, the truth is finally revealed to Oedipus. What is ironic about the deadly game of question-and-answer played out between him and the old *shepherd*? ✧ What motives on the part of the shepherds thwarted the plans of Oedipus' parents to head off the prediction of the oracle? What makes their motivation ironic? ✧ Except for the brief summing up at the conclusion of the final scene, the chorus here pronounces its final words on the fate of Oedipus. What to it is the meaning of what has happened?

6. (Scene 5) How does Oedipus face the terrible truth? How does Oedipus meet his fate? How does he explain what he has done and what he proposes to do? Does he show any remnant of his old pride? ✧ What happens when Oedipus asks to meet his two young daughters for the last time? Does this part of the scene change your view of Oedipus? of Creon?

THE WHOLE PLAY—For Discussion or Writing

1. As you look back over the play as a whole, what is your final estimate of Oedipus? Does he have the kind of *tragic flaw* that was required by Aristotle? Is his tragic flaw pride? anger? blindness to the truth? stubborn pursuit of the "truth that kills"? What qualities does he have that might make audiences nevertheless consider him great and admirable?

2. By the time of Sophocles, the belief in *prophecy* and other tenets of traditional religion were coming under attack. How close to a modern sceptic is Jocasta? How diametrically opposed is her attitude toward the "search for truth" from that of her husband? Do you consider her a strong or a weak character?

3. One critic called Creon in this play "the man of spotless reputation who extricates himself from every risk. . . securing himself, intriguing. . . . He is a man who is cheap by an average standard, born to be second in all things." What do you think explains this estimate? Do you agree with it?

4. To what extent does the chorus in the play seem the voice of orthodox Greek religion? To what extent does it seem to reflect reactions and feelings that might be shared by modern spectators?

THE CREATIVE DIMENSION

Much research has gone into reconstructing the original staging of the Greek plays—the use of masks, the movements and gesture language of the chorus, the nature of Greek music. (Recordings of reconstructed early Greek music are available.) Your class may want to initiate a research project leading to a miniproduction of selected or adapted scenes from *Antigone* or *Oedipus Rex*. The project should attempt to give your classmates a sense of the visual and auditory effects and of the overall impact of Greek drama.

CROSS-REFERENCES—For Discussion or Writing

✧ Although *Oedipus Rex* and *Antigone* are often treated as companion plays, they were written more than ten years apart, and some readers find in them different answers to a key question: Does human fate result from fateful human choices or from the mysterious will of the gods? The translator quotes a fragment of a lost play by Sophocles: "Since the gods conceal all things divine, you will never understand them, not though you go searching to the ends of the earth." Compare and contrast the role of human free will and of the will of the gods in the two plays.

✧ One critic has observed that some of Ibsen's plays resemble *Oedipus Rex* in their basic plot. There is a kind of "retrospective analysis"; the plot is devoted to the "revelation of past mistakes." Compare the plot of *A Doll's House* and of *Oedipus Rex* from this point of view.

JUXTAPOSITIONS
The Range of Interpretation

> *The hypothesis is that . . . we live in a world shaped by previous interpretations, and a properly self-aware approach to the texts of our tradition requires the recovery of their earlier receptions—one might say that the books bear the patina of their previous readings.*
>
> EVA BRANN

For many critics, interpreting *Oedipus Rex* has been a touchstone for their vision of literature and of life. Study the following excerpts as a sampling of the range of interpretation.

MOSES HADAS
Oedipus as Hero 1967

The type of the Sophoclean hero is the large and intense and tormented character who is by no means faultless but who nevertheless achieves the status of hero. A hero, in the Greek sense, is a man who by his extraordinary career has pushed back the horizons of what is possible for humanity and is therefore deemed worthy of commemoration after his death. He is not a flawless man, but his flaws are inherent in and inseparable from the virtues which enable him to become a hero. . . .

It is always tempting to readers to look upon the *Oedipus* as a tableau of horrible crimes and their just requital: Oedipus had done lawless things and in the end received deserved punishment. So conceived, the requital seems monstrously unfair, for Oedipus had done his best to avoid the crimes and had committed them unwittingly. Actually the play is rather a glorification than a condemnation of Oedipus. Only an uncommonly good man would persist in his investigation so unflaggingly even after it had become manifest that it might be disastrous. He did indeed have flaws: He was self-righteous and hasty and suspicious of his well-wishers; but if he had not been these things he could never have gone on with his inquiry.

Though he is destroyed in the end, in a true sense he is the victor, and the conclusion is satisfying rather than disturbing to the perceptive reader. According to human standards (what Greek could know what divine standards might be?) Oedipus had behaved not only well, but extraordinarily well and had asserted the dignity of manhood. If there is a villain in the piece, it is not Oedipus but Apollo; however, Apollo cannot be a villain for he is a god, and the moral arithmetic of the gods is different from men's and inscrutable to men. When a man behaving well as a man is nevertheless tripped up by powers he cannot control or even understand, then we have tragedy. And the big man who has the mind and the energy to pioneer is most exposed.

From *The Complete Plays of Sophocles*

QUESTIONS

What does this writer mean when he says that Oedipus asserted human dignity? Do you agree that the play "is rather a glorification than a condemnation of Oedipus"? Do you agree with this editor's account of Oedipus' flaws? What is this writer's perspective on the religious element in the play?

FRANCIS FERGUSSON
Oedipus as Ritual Sacrifice   1949

[In a preceding passage, Fergusson had linked Greek tragedy generally to the form of ancient ceremonies enacting the ritual sacrifice of a seasonal god. In such rituals, found in many early cultures, the quasi-divine hero-king fights with a rival, is slain and dismembered, but then rises again with the coming of spring. Oedipus' struggle, his fall, and his final acceptance of his fate roughly parallel this pattern of death and rebirth. As the culprit who is identified as the source of pollution, Oedipus also fits the mythical figure of the scapegoat driven out of the city into the desert, carrying with it the sins and corruptions of the community, bringing about a cleansing or purgation.]

The figure of Oedipus himself fulfills all the requirements of the scapegoat, the dismembered king or god-figure. The situation in which Thebes is presented at the beginning of the play—in peril of its life; its crops, its herds, its women mysteriously infertile, signs of a mortal disease of the city, and the disfavor of the gods—is like the withering which winter brings, and calls, in the same way, for struggle, dismemberment, death, and renewal. And this tragic sequence is the substance of the play. It is enough to know that myth and ritual are close together in their genesis, two direct imitations of the perennial experience of the race.

But when one considers *Oedipus* as a ritual one understands it in ways which one cannot by thinking of it merely as a dramatization of a story, even that story. Harrison has shown that the Festival of Dionysus, based ultimately upon the yearly vegetation ceremonies, included *rites de passage* [rituals marking the passing from one stage of life to another], like that celebrating the assumption of adulthood—celebrations of the mystery of individual growth and development. At the same time, it was a prayer for the welfare of the whole city; and this welfare was understood not only as material prosperity, but also as the natural order of the family, the ancestors, the present members, and the generations still to come, and, by the same token, obedience to the gods who were jealous, each in his own province, of this natural and divinely sanctioned order and proportion.

We must suppose that Sophocles' audience (the whole population of the city) came early, prepared to spend the day in the bleachers. At their feet was the semicircular dancing-ground for the chorus, and the thrones for the priests, and the altar. Behind that was the raised platform for the principal actors, backed by the all-purpose emblematic façade, which would presently be taken to represent Oedipus' palace in Thebes. The actors were not professionals in our sense, but citizens selected for religious office, and Sophocles himself had trained them and the chorus.

. . . the element which distinguishes this theater, giving it its unique directness, is the *ritual expectancy,* which Sophocles assumed in his audience. The nearest thing we have to this ritual sense of theater is, I suppose, to be found at an Easter performance of the St. Matthew passion. We can also observe something similar in the dances and ritual mummery of the Pueblo Indians.

From *The Idea of a Theater*

QUESTIONS

What does Fergusson mean by "the ritual expectancy" that Sophocles assumed in his audience? In how many ways does this writer remind you of the religious roots and the religious dimension of Greek tragedy? How continuous or persistent is the theme of pollution and purgation as you read the play?

SIGMUND FREUD
The Oedipus Complex   1914

[Jocasta says to Oedipus in Scene 3, "Many a man before you, / in his dreams, has shared his mother's bed." Although the sceptical Jocasta dismisses such dreams as mere "shadows," modern depth psychology, or psychoanalysis, has looked in such dreams for clues to deep hidden desires and traumas of human beings. Sigmund Freud (1865–1939), in his *Interpretation of Dreams,* went beyond the surface action of the play to probe for a deeper underlying meaning that would explain the hold the play has on the human imagination. Art and literature, to the psychoanalyst, are like dreams in that much of their deeper meaning is repressed, hidden in the subconscious, acted out in disguises to protect them from condemnation by our moral selves. Seen in this light, Oedipus becomes a symbol of one of the oldest patterns in the collective experience of the human race: The son, as a very young child, depends on and responds with all his being to the overpowering mother love that makes the mother the sun of the child's universe. The father, grudging the undivided attention lavished by the mother on the child, becomes the rival for the mother's affection—and, in the Freudian mythology, a deadly enemy. Secretly, unconsciously, the son comes to wish the father dead. Since the conscious, moral, rational self condemns this parricidal desire with horror, the result is a tortured conscience, self-loathing.]

Oedipus Rex is what is known as a tragedy of destiny. Its tragic effect is said to lie in the contrast between the supreme will of the gods and the vain attempts of mankind to escape the evil that threatens them. The lesson, which, it is said, the deeply moved spectator should learn from the tragedy, is submission to the divine will and realization of his own impotence. Modern dramatists have accordingly tried to achieve a similar tragic effect by weaving the same contrast into a plot invented by themselves. But the spectators have looked on unmoved while a curse or an oracle was fulfilled in spite of all the efforts of some innocent man: later tragedies of destiny have failed in their effect.

If *Oedipus Rex* moves the modern audience no less than it did the contemporary Greek one, the explanation can only be that its effect does not lie in the contrast between destiny and human will, but is to be looked for in the particular nature of the material on which that contrast is exemplified. There must be something which makes a voice within us ready to recognize the compelling force of destiny in the *Oedipus*, while we can dismiss as merely arbitrary such dispositions as are laid down in modern tragedies of destiny. And a factor of this kind is in fact involved in the story of King Oedipus. His destiny moves us only because it might have been ours—because the oracle laid the same curse upon us before our birth as upon him. It is the fate of all of us, perhaps, to direct our first sexual impulse toward our mother and our first hatred and our first murderous wish against our father. Our dreams convince us that this is so.

Translated by James Strachey

QUESTIONS

Where in your reading (or viewing) have you encountered reflections of the Freudian triangle of mother—son—father? Can you recall examples of the deadly struggle between father and son? Can you recall examples of a strange, powerful bond between mother and son?

MICHÈLE FABIEN
I Am Jocasta   1981

[Modern readers have begun to claim that playwrights and critics, focusing on Oedipus, tend to overlook Jocasta, who from some points of view "is the most interesting character in the play." Expressing the "intellectual doubts" of Sophocles' age, she provides the only real challenge to the authority of the priests and the belief in oracles, saying "As for prophecy, I would not look right or left because of it. . . . Chance rules life." One attempt to right the balance is *Jocasta*, by the French playwright Michèle Fabien. In the following excerpt from this short play, Jocasta voices thoughts going through her mind shortly before her death.]

Who is Jocasta?

Ask! Must I too make an end?
Yes . . .
Later . . .
Wait . . .
You know, and I know too: I am here for that.

I was Queen, still young, still beautiful. Adored, worshipped.

Thebes was good to him . . .
And then I became his mother . . .

No, no!
I'm still Jocasta, your Queen, spouse of your King,
the hero who governs the city, the man who confronted
the Sphinx, and won, and delivered you . . .
And now a long wall of ice, of the forgotten past,
has cut me off from everyone who . . .
The court, the seers, the shepherds, the messengers, the chorus, their leader . . .
they too have turned to ice, but they do not see it.
For help, for love, I call out to my son, my husband, the seer,
the shepherds, the messengers, the leaders, the people of Thebes,
but my cries do not penetrate their deaf ears, saturated with horrors.
They roll their eyes in terror, only the whites show through the half-shut lids.

What is left for them to see?
Their king, their hero, their savior, is now the
incestuous son, the murderer of his father, Laius, and
their queen has become her son's wife.
Don't look away, do not avert your eyes, not you too.

Transparent because unbearable?
Easy to say!
I shall seek out Jocasta, who is nothing but her name.
Wrong! She is not far, Jocasta, she is here, very near.

My hair, so often stroked.
My cheeks, flushed with desire.
My arms, that embraced Laius so tightly.
My hands, that caressed his thighs.
My breasts, taut with desire for his body.
My womb, which bore my son's children.
My thighs, spread wide to welcome my son's body.
You see, it can be said, can't it?
I'm tired.
A wall of glacial cold and forgotten past separates me from
    the living, the unknowing.

Tell me what you expect of me.
Do you want something of me?
I know: Jocasta must kill herself. That is why she is here.
Jocasta is guilty, isn't she?
I look at myself in the mirror.
I pick up the dagger.
I shall kill the young bride of the great Laius, King of Thebes.

I shall kill the queen of Thebes.
I shall kill the mother who had Oedipus exposed.
I shall kill the Queen who made him King and father of his sisters, his brothers.
I look at myself in the mirror and I see a face
I do not know, a new body, never seen before.
I press the glittering blade against

that unknown breast.
The point grazes the material. It is unbearable.
I am blinded by a reflection in the mirror. I raise the dagger
to the neck, the mouth, the eyes.
I seek my image in the mirror. My body
grows tense, my fist tightens, it breaks the mirror.
There is blood on the shattered fragments of glass.

From *Plays by Women*

QUESTIONS

In your own reading of the play, did you tend to lose sight of Jocasta as you concentrated on Oedipus as the tragic protagonist? In this excerpt, does Jocasta become more of a human being for you than in the original play? Why or why not?

WRITING ABOUT LITERATURE

26. Tracing a Central Conflict (Focusing Your Paper)

The Writing Workshop A well-focused paper may target the central conflict in a play. Is an embattled protagonist locked in a struggle with a worthy antagonist? Is there a clash between two opposed forces or points of view? Does a central confrontation help shape the play as a whole? Here are some possibilities you might consider for a paper focused on a central conflict:

✧ For many in the audience, the heart of Ibsen's *A Doll's House* is the conflict between Torvald's paternalistic attitude toward women and Nora's need to be respected for her own decisions, right or wrong.

✧ The heart of Sophocles' *Antigone* is the conflict between Creon's insistence on loyalty to the state and Antigone's stubborn insistence on obeying the laws of the gods. In *Oedipus Rex,* you might focus on the conflict between Oedipus and fate, or between the different perspectives of Oedipus the King and Tiresias the Priest.

✧ In the plays by Arthur Miller, Lorraine Hansberry, or Tennessee Williams later in this book, you might focus on the conflict between the generations.

In working up material for your paper, you will soon want to push beyond the kind of open, exploratory note taking you might do in a journal. Early in your thinking and writing, try to bring the central conflict into focus. You can then start the purposeful note taking that will give you ample evidence to draw on as you trace basic opposites and their ramifications.

Focused Note Taking Look for details and quotations that help you line up the two sides in the central conflict. For instance, in Shakespeare's *Macbeth,* Lady Macbeth is committed to having her husband become king of Scotland through the murder of King Duncan. She early starts to prod and criticize her reluctant, hesitating partner in crime. She preaches the need for moving ahead swiftly and without scruples. (She knows that dwelling on the horror of the deed will drive them mad.)

Reading notes like the following will give you the ammunition needed to drive home the contrast between the two characters in your paper:

At the beginning of the play, the two partners seem to have a kind of tacit understanding. Lady Macbeth makes the expected Renaissance choice, to become his "dearest partner in greatness." Today, we would criticize her for not creating a life of her own, for her ruthless ethics, and for following the party line, buying into "what greatness is promised thee" (I.v.14).

The key difference between the two shows in their different way of looking at ambition. To Macbeth, "o'ervaulting ambition" gives him pause (it leaps and falls on the other side); ambition represents his "deep and dark desires." Lady Macbeth early points to his problem: He is not ruthless enough; he wants to win the prize by honest means. She perceives him as ambitious but too sensitive, too kind:

> Yet do I fear thy nature;
> It is too full o' th' milk of human kindness
> To catch the nearest way (I.v.17–19).

When he falters, she shames her husband: "Art thou afeard / To be the same in thine own act and valor / As thou art in desire?" (I.vii.39–41).

She finds she has to attend to much of the actual preparation of the deed, relieving Macbeth of petty planning details. She attends to their alibi: "I have drugged their possets, / That death and nature do contend about them, / Whether they live or die" (II.ii.6–8) and plants the tools: "I laid their daggers ready" (II.ii.11).

As Macbeth is conscience-stricken over his "deed," she keeps him focused and attends to the grisly coverup:

> Infirm of purpose!
> Give me the daggers. The sleeping and the dead
> Are but as pictures. 'Tis the eye of childhood
> That fears a painted devil. If he do bleed,
> I'll gild the faces of the grooms withal,
> For it must seem their guilt (II.ii.51–56).
>
> My hands are of your color, but I shame
> To wear a heart so white. . . .
> Retire we to our chamber.
> A little water clears us of this deed:
> How easy is it then! Your constancy
> Hath left you unattended (II.ii.63-68).

Understanding that Duncan's murder is only the beginning, Macbeth is perturbed by setbacks: "We have scorched the snake, not killed it" (III.ii.13). Lady Macbeth thinks that "things without all remedy / Should be without regard: what's done is done" (III.ii.11–12).

Clustering　**Cluster** a key character or key idea. Let associations and details branch out from a central core as they come to mind. Let your cluster help you map important associations and help you see them as part of a pattern. The following sample cluster brings into focus a range of ideas that will help you define one pole in the play of opposites in the *Macbeth* play:

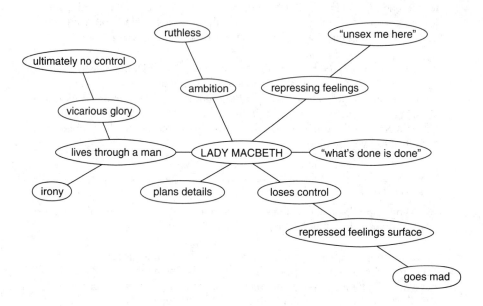

Here is the capule portrait of Lady Macbeth that grew out of this cluster:

> Early in the play, Lady Macbeth seems to be the stronger of the two partners. She eggs on her husband and plans or supervises the details of the murder. She appears ruthless and bold, driven by overriding ambition. She represses any natural feelings of remorse or pity ("Unsex me here"). But the only way she has of realizing her ambitions is through her husband. She shares vicariously in his glory, and she has no control over an independent destiny. Her statement that "what's done is done" is ironic, because what she and her husband have done will destroy them both. The fears she had repressed or pushed down rise to the surface to destroy her, and she goes mad.

Summing Up the Contrast　As your paper begins to take shape in your mind, clarify or sharpen the overall pattern, the overall strategy. Push toward a summing up; line up the conflicting positions or agendas. Sharpen the contrast so that the basic conflict comes clearly into focus:

LADY MACBETH: Lady Macbeth holds the view, much echoed in later centuries, that power goes to the strong and ruthless. Traditional values like meekness, loyalty, and pity are designed to "hold the strong in awe." They are a handicap for those who are truly ambitious. Conscience and fear of divine retribution are creations of our own guilty imaginations; they are like tales told to frighten children.

MACBETH: Macbeth is torn between ambition and his guilty conscience, "the scorpions of the mind." When he talks to the murderers, he talks as if manliness meant being strong and tough, like the strongest and swiftest predators in the animal kingdom. But at other times he talks as if being a man meant being more than an animal—honoring ties of kinship, of gratitude, of friendship. Even when he has intellectually accepted the arguments of his wife, "horrible imaginings" rise from his subconscious.

Focusing on Confrontations   Look for material that will help you highlight the central conflict. Pay special attention to scenes in which two conflicting forces or views seem to clash head-on. In a famous scene in *A Doll's House,* a climactic exchange between Torvald and Nora brings into the open Nora's challenge to the traditional definition of a woman's duty:

HELMER: You haven't thought of what people will say.
NORA: I can't consider that. All I know is that this is necessary for me.
HELMER: But this is disgraceful. Is this the way you neglect your most sacred duties?
NORA: What do you consider is my most sacred duty?
HELMER: Do I have to tell you that? Isn't it your duty to your husband and children?
NORA: I have another duty, just as sacred.
HELMER: You can't have. What duty do you mean?
NORA: My duty to myself.

Focusing on Parallels   Often supporting characters or subplots echo and reinforce the major concerns of a play. Try to work into your paper exchanges that parallel in some way the major confrontations between protagonist and antagonist. For instance, in the initial exchange in *Antigone,* the heroine tests the loyalty of her sister Ismene, who has no wish "to dishonor the laws that the gods hold in honor" but who says: "Defy the city? I have no strength for that." The sisters' disagreement anticipates the later clashes between Antigone and Creon over the demands of religious law and the conflicting demands of the state. Later, the exchange between Creon and his son Haemon again focuses on the central question: Does Creon's need for loyalty and obedience give him the right "to trample down the honor of the gods"?

Focusing on the Resolution   How is the conflict resolved? In Shakespeare's *Macbeth,* Macbeth himself seems for a time the weaker partner. But in the end, Lady Macbeth crumbles, her mind diseased by "that perilous stuff / Which weighs upon the heart." The guilt feelings she has belittled or repressed surface and drive her insane. Macbeth, by contrast, is terribly lucid at the end. He finds that by denying all human ties and feelings he has isolated himself from all human contact. Wanting to be first, he has wound up alone:

All that which should accompany old age,
As honor, love, obedience, troops of friends,
I must not look to have; but in their stead,
Curses, not loud but deep, mouth-honor, breath,
Which the poor heart would fain deny, and dare not. (5.3.25–29)

Study the following sample student paper. How well does it bring the central conflict of the play into focus? How well does it trace the conflict into its ramifications? Does the writer adopt an independent view? Does the writer succeed in showing the appeal of the play to the modern audience?

SAMPLE STUDENT PAPER

Antigone: A Contest of Wills

All ways of thinking contain their own blindnesses.
Marilyn French

In his tragedy *Antigone,* Sophocles sets up a classic conflict between two characters who are neither entirely in the right nor entirely in the wrong. Instead, both are sincere in their beliefs. Both are proud and self-righteous. The difference is that one turns out to be right in putting the law of the gods above human laws.

When Antigone's brother, Polynices, dies a traitor, King Creon orders that his body remain unburied. He wants the corpse to be "carrion for the birds and dogs to tear, / an obscenity for the citizens to behold." Creon's decree serves a double purpose: it continues to punish Polynices even after death (his soul cannot go to heaven if he is not properly buried), and it is a reminder to the citizens of Thebes that the king's will is law. Anyone who defies the king defies the state, and is therefore a traitor. From Creon's point of view, there is no more deadly peril than disobedience. Even though Creon has declared that the penalty for defying his order is death, Antigone decides that god's law supersedes Creon's edict, and she buries her brother.

The striking feature of this play is that we see two strong-willed characters locked in battle. The trait that both Antigone and Creon have in common is their stubbornness—their unshakable conviction that they are right, their inability to change their minds until it is too late. However, American readers tend to view Antigone as the "righter" of the two characters, although perhaps for somewhat different reasons than the original Greek audience. We tend to rank the voice of the individual above that of society or the state. We tend to agree with Henry David Thoreau that a person who is in the right is in a majority of one already. As a result, we are predisposed to agree with Antigone when she says, "It wasn't Zeus, not in the least, / who made this proclamation." For her, "Justice, dwelling with the gods," has more force than the edict of "a mere mortal."

On the other hand, Antigone is totally unyielding, and her tremendous faith in her own righteousness can be seen as a flaw that helps bring disaster down on her and her lover and betrothed. She is totally contemptuous of her sister Ismene, who at first opts to take the practical, reasonable course: "to obey the ones who stand in power." Ismene says,

we must be sensible. Remember we are women.
we're not born to contend with men. Then too,
we're underlings, ruled by much stronger hands.
so we must submit in this, and things still worse.

The word *submit* is not in Antigone's vocabulary; she vows to reject Ismene's help "even if you should have a change of heart."

Creon speaks up for the safety of the "ship of state," and at first the chorus seems to honor his claim. The leader of the chorus says about Antigone: "Like father, like daugher, / passionate, wild . . . / she hasn't learned to bend before adversity." Later, the chorus tells Antigone, "attacks on power never go unchecked."

However, Creon doesn't get any more sympathy from a modern audience than he received from his advisors, his family, or, finally, his subjects. To us, he really does not seem to aim at serving his people; he does not profess to serve a higher power; he only serves himself. His image as a man is at stake: "There's no room for pride, not in a slave, / not with the lord and master standing by." Several characters try to point out to Creon that he is suffering from an excess of egotism, willfulness, and pride. But he's too self-absorbed to accept any of this criticism. His son provides us with an accurate sketch of Creon's character when he observes,

Whoever thinks that he alone possesses intelligence,
the gift of eloquence, he and no one else,
and character too . . . such men, I tell you,
spread them open—you will find them empty.

This self-righteousness, coupled with Creon's refusal to acknowledge the laws of heaven, leads him down the dark path of tragedy. It takes the death of his wife and son to convince him that he has been mistaken.

In the contest of wills, it is Antigone who stays the course. In the end, Antigone remains true to her principles; she chooses to die rather than acquiesce in an unjust civil law. It is Creon who capitulates (too late to save anyone but himself). It is Creon who changes his mind and admits, "it's best to keep the established laws / to the very day we die." In the contest of wills, Antigone has perished, but her principles have prevailed.

Creon tried to coerce his subjects into being loyal by making the penalty for disobedience as severe as he could. He failed to take into account the fact that loyalty cannot be commanded into existence—or coerced into being. It must be given freely, or it can no longer be called loyalty; it becomes subjugation.

QUESTIONS

1. What is the *thesis* of this paper? Does it offer you a new or different perspective on the play? Do you agree with it, or would you take issue with it?

2. Where is the *central conflict* best summed up or described? Does the writer trace it into its ramifications? Does she look at the role of supporting characters?

3. What is the general *plan* or strategy of the paper? Is it easy or hard to outline?

4. Does the writer use sufficient *evidence*? What use does the writer make of first-hand quotation? Are any quotations especially telling or effective?

5. Does the paper leave you with any unanswered questions or loose ends?

6. Do you agree with the writer on the way a contemporary audience is likely to respond to the play?

27 SHAKESPEAREAN TRAGEDY
The Inner Conflict

All the world's a stage,
And all the men and women merely players.
They have their exits and their entrances,
And one man in his time plays many parts.
WILLIAM SHAKESPEARE, *AS YOU LIKE IT*

Shakespeare's plays are not in the rigorous and critical
sense either tragedies or comedies, but compositions of a
distinct kind—exhibiting the real state of sublunary
nature, which partakes of good and evil, joy and sorrow
. . . and expressing the course of the world, in which the
loss of one is the gain of another; in which, at the same
time, the reveller is hastening to his wine, and the
mourner burying his friend.
SAMUEL JOHNSON, *PREFACE TO SHAKESPEARE,* 1765

FOCUS ON SHAKESPEARE'S WORLD

Shakespeare's plays—including *Romeo and Juliet, As You Like It, Hamlet, Macbeth, King Lear*—belong to the heritage of educated people everywhere. In the English-speaking world, Shakespeare and the Bible were for generations twin sources of commonplaces and allusions but also of ways to think and talk about life, about God and humanity. Juliet and Romeo, Portia and Shylock from *The Merchant of Venice,* Hamlet, and Lady Macbeth are among characters peopling the imagination of theatergoers around the world.

Although the plays speak a universal language, they are rooted in the assumptions, the lore, and the politics of Shakespeare's time. His plays were part of a great flowering of the theater during the Elizabethan Age. The golden age of the English stage lasted from the 1580s to the time the Puritans closed the theaters in 1642. Several points about the contemporary setting are worth keeping in mind as you read a Shakespeare play:

✧ Shakespeare wrote when England under Queen Elizabeth I (of the house of Tudor) enjoyed a measure of prosperity, self-confidence, and national unity. Under the Tudor monarchy, England was leaving behind the fratricidal

1038

civil wars of the feudal Middle Ages. Feudalism had been a system of splintered authority. Powerful local warlords owed allegiance and military service to the king, but often, like the rebellious barons in Shakespeare's history plays, they were his rivals for power. The kings of the house of Tudor took the country into a period of strengthened central authority, relative political stability, and national pride.

The second of the Tudors, Henry VIII, had broken with the Roman Catholic church when the pope refused to grant him a divorce from the first of his six wives. Henry established himself as the head of a new independent Protestant (Anglican) Church of England. Elizabeth I, his child by his second wife Anne Boleyn, consolidated the strength of the monarchy. She was a "remarkable woman and a person of power" who skillfully evaded marriage and thus succeeded in not sharing her authority (Irene G. Dash). She was celebrated by poets as the Virgin Queen and became a symbol of a new nationalism, warding off short-lived rebellions by prominent courtiers and threats from abroad. A high point of her reign was the defeat and dispersal of the mighty Spanish invasion fleet, the Armada, in 1588.

✧ Shakespeare's first successes were history plays that dramatized the insurrections and usurpations of recent English history. The history plays show us a nation trying to emerge from the "civic broils" that pitted brother against brother, blood against blood, "Self against Self" (*Richard III* 2.4.62–64). A recurrent theme in these plays is the yearning for stable, legitimate government (legitimized by true religion and "true descent"). However, the plays are set in the feudal world: Many of the plays (including *Hamlet*) center on the quarrels of the succession. An older relative tries to head off a young heir's succession to the throne. A person with a dubious claim to the throne takes on a vulnerable incumbent. Powerful individuals challenge traditional authority, and often the rebels have good lines. In some of Shakespeare's most searing plays (including *Hamlet*), authority seems corrupt beyond redemption.

SHAKESPEARE'S STAGE

The characteristic complexity of Elizabethan plays suggests that Elizabethan audiences were more accustomed to comprehending a large cast and an intricate plot than modern drama has trained us to be.

PETER SACCIO

When in doubt, the golden rule for directors and actors alike is to shun theatrical effects, relying instead upon what Shakespeare himself described as "the proud full sail of his great verse."

MAURICE EVANS

Shakespeare himself was an actor, and the art of acting is at the very root of his whole playwrighting art.

FRANCIS FERGUSSON

Shakespeare's audiences came to the theater for a spectacle with a large cast and a sprawling plot—often with the future of a kingdom at stake, with astonishing instances of loyalty and treachery, and with moments of high drama in climactic confrontations. Often the central issue was settled in the ordeal of the final battle. The task of playwright and cast was to fill a commercial theater—"large, cheap, and popular"—several times a week (G. E. Bentley). Plays were at first performed in the courtyards of inns (which saw such popular entertainments as bearbaitings and cockfights on other occasions). They gradually moved to specially constructed wooden open-roofed theaters holding several thousand spectators. There were special seats in "galleries," or roofed balconies, for the wealthy; there was standing room in the "yard" (surrounding the stage) for those Hamlet calls the "groundlings." There were also some smaller private indoor theaters, for use especially during the winter.

Although the theater, including Shakespeare's own theatrical company, enjoyed the patronage of the court, the clergy and civil authorities suspected the stage of breeding immorality. Like dubious entertainment in our own time, the theaters were often located outside the city limits. Thus, the Globe Theater, most famous of the Elizabethan theaters, was built in 1599 on the other (south) side of the Thames River, beyond the reach of the restrictive city ordinances of London magistrates.

The repertory changed with popular taste—with some plays, as Hamlet says to the players visiting his court, performed "not above once." Others en-

A conjectural reconstruction of an Elizabethan theater. From C. Walter Hodges, *The Globe Restored*. Reprinted by permission of Oxford University Press.

joyed long runs. The plays, like Hollywood scripts, were often the result of collaboration. They were further adapted and modified by actors. Clowns especially, as Hamlet says, were apt to speak "more than was set down for them" to get cheap laughs from a "quantity of barren spectators." There were no authorized texts or definitive versions. When the plays were printed, the printer might use imperfect actors' copies. Modern editors have tried to reconstruct authentic texts of Shakespeare's plays by comparing early printings—the *quartos*—with the *folio*—texts collected and printed in 1623, seven years after the playwright's death. (The smaller quartos and the large folio are named after the size of the page.)

Modern directors have restored key features of the Elizabethan stage. Boy actors, it is true, no longer play the women's roles. But we often see Shakespeare performed, as in his time, on an open stage, with free-flowing action and no curtain coming down between acts or scenes. (These were edited in by later editors.) There may be two levels (with a balcony as in *Romeo and Juliet*). The action moves rapidly from place to place.

Some of the great successes of the Elizabethan stage show us what audiences were ready to expect and accept when Shakespeare came to London from his hometown Stratford-on-Avon:

✧ One of the first great popular successes was Thomas Kyd's *The Spanish Tragedy,* a tragedy of murder and revenge. It was first written and acted about 1585 and was still frequently put on when Shakespeare came to the big city to make his way in the theater as an actor and apprentice playwright. When Shakespeare wrote *Hamlet,* it was not the first time his audiences had seen a **revenge tragedy:** a play that starts with the ghost of the victim clamoring for revenge for a foul murder and ends with the avenger triumphing over his adversaries, taking them down with him to bloody death. Like Shakespeare's *Hamlet,* Kyd's play had a plot of **intrigue,** of plotting and counterplotting. Hamlet delights in playing cat and mouse with the king (and with the king's flunkeys). He delights in seeing "the enginer hoist with his own petar"—to see the plotter blown up by his own badly handled bomb.

✧ The most successful long-running play staged during Shakespeare's early years in London was Christopher Marlowe's *Tamburlane the Great,* first performed in 1587. It was the spectacular story of an obscure Near Eastern shepherd who by sheer force of ambition made himself emperor of the known world. Tamburlane is the **colossal protagonist,** a larger-than-life central figure dominating the stage. He is the Renaissance superman, subduing his enemies by ruthless terror. At the same time, he has whole armies and their generals crossing over to his side, dazzled by the force of his personality. Part of Tamburlane's charisma is his soaring eloquence: He threatens "the world with high astounding terms," in extended soliloquies that provide bravura passages for the actor. The play is in **blank verse**—the unrhymed iambic pentameter line that was to become the dominant medium of Shakespeare's serious plays. In the following sample passage, some lines are regular five-beat lines, with stress always on the second syllable of each foot: "UnTIL | we REACH | the RIP | est FRUIT | of ALL." Others play familiar variations on the underlying iambic beat. The next line starts with trochaic inversion, and it has an unstressed or weakly stressed second syllable in the third foot: "NATure | that FRAMED | us of | four EL | eMENTS." (Notice how the departure from the regular beat makes the key word—*nature*—seem to stand out.) As later in Shakespeare, a dozen or more lines tend to combine in a verse paragraph that develops it own soaring rhythm:

> Nature that framed us of four elements
> Warring within our breasts for regiment,
> Doth teach us all to have aspiring minds:
> Our souls whose faculties can comprehend
> The wondrous architecture of the world
> And measure every wandering planet's course,
> Still climbing after knowledge infinite,
> And always moving as the restless spheres,
> Will us to wear ourselves and never rest
> Until we reach the ripest fruit of all
> The perfect bliss and sole felicity,
> The sweet fruition of an earthly crown.

SHAKESPEARE AND THE MODERN READER

Dust has long since closed the eyes of the first arrivals, but Shakespeare's audience is living still; there have always been more than enough newcomers to fill the vacant places.
ALFRED HARBAGE

As a modern reader and theatergoer, you will want to do more than study Shakespeare as a literary monument, dutifully viewed at a distance. You will want to experience the excitement and challenge of a Shakespeare play at first hand. To do so, you will have to become used to his language and his range of reference. For instance, religion plays more of a role in the language of Shakespeare's plays than it does in the language and thinking of many moderns. Playwright and audience shared religious beliefs, spirit lore, and popular superstitions—whether believed wholeheartedly or viewed more skeptically. (Hamlet's good friend Horatio says about some of the spirit lore, "So have I heard and do in part believe it" 1.1.165.)

The Elizabethan Age was part of the European Renaissance, a time of revived interest in ancient Greek and Roman art and literature. Shakespeare is steeped in Greek legend and **mythology.** (As a young man, he wrote a long poem about Venus, the goddess of love, and her mortal lover Adonis.) The dialogue of a Shakespeare play is shot through with allusions to such mythological standbys as playful Cupid aiming his darts or arrows at lovers and "plated Mars"—the armor-plated god of war. When Hamlet asks the itinerant player to recite a favorite speech about the death of Priam, the playwright expects the audience to know at least in broad outline the story of the fall of Troy. The player then proceeds to raise a storm of passion over Hecuba's witnessing the slaying of her husband Priam, king of Troy, father of Hector. ("What's Hecuba to him, or he to Hecuba?")

The language of Shakespeare's time was in transition from medieval English (or Middle English) to modern speech:

✧ There still were special pronouns (and matching verb forms) for talking to one rather than several persons: *thou art, thou wilt, thou canst;* and also *may it please thee* and *take what is thine.* (Use of this familiar *thou* instead of the more formal *you* corresponded roughly to being on a first-name basis.) *Methinks* and *methought* were still used for *I think* and *I thought.* Many of our modern auxiliaries or helping verbs are still missing: *Ride you tonight?* for *do you ride?* and *prepare we* for *let us prepare.*

✧ Word order often differs from ours: "We will *our kingdom* give" has become "We will give *our kingdom*" in modern English. "Hamlet, thou hast *thy father* much offended" today would be "Hamlet, you have much offended *your father.*" (Objects now generally follow the complete verb.)

✧ Listeners and readers soon get used to frequently used words like *prithee* (please), *forsooth* (in truth), *anon* (presently, very soon), *aught* (anything), *ere* (before). *Would* is often used in the sense of *wish* or *want* (*Would it were true* for *I wish it were true*).

In the new edition of *Hamlet* that follows, the more usual footnotes have been replaced by marginal glosses to facilitate close reading and study of the play. These glosses give you suggested modern meanings close at hand and in the context of the line. (Where the text is obscure or imperfect, these meanings represent the educated guesses of editors and scholars.) As in other modern editions aimed at the general reader, spellings and sometimes word forms have been cautiously modernized.

THE ENIGMA OF HAMLET

> *Since* Hamlet *touches the complete alphabet of human experience, every actor feels he is born to play it. The bold extrovert will dazzle and play with the word power, the scenes of vengeance, and blast Ophelia and Gertrude off the stage. The introvert will see every line pointed at him, the outsider, the loner, the watcher, he with his one trusting friend, and a quick answer for everything lest it be a barb. The wit will play for laughs and the lunatic for madness. The romantic for ideals. So you cannot be miscast for Hamlet.*
>
> STEVEN BERKOFF

To many critics, *Hamlet* has been Shakespeare's most searching comment on life and human nature. "It is *we* who are Hamlet," said the Romantic critic William Hazlitt. Directors and actors have made the play their Mount Everest. As the actor-director Steven Berkoff says in *I Am Hamlet,* "In every actor is a Hamlet struggling to get out." Yet at the same time, *Hamlet* has proved Shakespeare's most challenging and mysterious play. A small library of critical volumes has been written on the contest of wills between Prince Hamlet and his murderous stepfather Claudius; on Hamlet's relationship with his doting mother, Queen Gertrude (who "lives by his looks"); on his harsh treatment of Ophelia (whom he tells, "I loved you once"); and on his long-delayed revenge on Claudius, the "king of shreds and patches," who killed his father and married with his mother.

Although Hamlet is often accused of inaction, the play itself is a fast-moving spectacle, with much **stage business**—encounters with a ghost, a quarrel at a graveside, a climactic duel. Many scenes have long been audience favorites: Hamlet taunts the king's talky and slow-witted counselor (and Ophelia's father) Polonius. Hamlet talks with a group of itinerant, traveling players about his love of the theater. Hamlet plays cat and mouse with the king's spies, his former schoolmates Rosencrantz and Guildenstern. However, audiences and critics rivet their attention especially on the great **soliloquies** in which Hamlet bares his soul: "To be, or not to be"; "O that this too too sullied flesh would melt."

Shakespeare does two things to wind up the play in a manner likely to have satisfied his contemporary audiences. The dying Hamlet asks his friend Horatio "to tell my story"—to clear his reputation, to clear his "wounded name" of false accusations and evil rumors. Then Hamlet casts his vote for young Fortinbras, son of the king of Norway, to be the next king. Order will be restored and continuity ensured. However, audiences and critics have not been content to let the matter rest there. They have found Hamlet a rich, complex, paradoxical character. As you read the play, keep in mind some of the questions audiences and critics have asked about Hamlet and his role in the play:

✧ How trustworthy is the ghost? Is the ghost of Hamlet's father, who spurs Hamlet on to revenge, a good or an evil spirit? Is he a "spirit of health or goblin damned"? Hamlet concludes that he is seeing and talking to an "honest ghost," and he reluctantly responds to the ghost's call for vengeance. But at least one modern critic has argued that, according to the spirit lore of Shakespeare's time, the ghost must have been an evil spirit, luring Hamlet on to damnation (as the witches did Macbeth).

✧ What explains the delay? Why does it take Hamlet so long to accomplish his revenge, his "almost blunted purpose"? Are some of the reasons Hamlet gives for delaying his revenge merely pretexts? Is he temperamentally averse to decisive action? Is he too much of an intellectual, forever debating, forever finding scruples and complications? Does he suffer from paralysis of the will, as the Romantic critics claimed?

✧ What are the true sources of Hamlet's melancholy? Is he melancholy by temperament, illustrating one of the character types of the psychology of Shakespeare's time? (According to the psychology of "humors," excess of one such humor or bodily fluid would tilt a person toward melancholy, chronic anger, or cheerfulness.)

✧ How mad is Hamlet? He feigns madness to gain time to prepare his revenge. How close is the turmoil in his soul to driving him truly mad—instead of his just pretending to be insane to disorient the king?

✧ What is Hamlet's true relationship with his mother? Why is he so obsessed with lurid images of physical intimacy between her and the uncle? What evidence is there for or against his having Oedipal feelings toward his mother? (In some modern productions, these are acted out graphically in the bedroom scene.)

WILLIAM SHAKESPEARE (1564–1616)

Hamlet   1600–1601

> *Hamlet must be the best-known of all characters in the*
> *theater of the world.*
>   BERNARD LOTT

CHARACTERS

CLAUDIUS, King of Denmark
HAMLET, nephew to the King
GERTRUDE, Queen of Denmark, mother to HAMLET
GHOST of HAMLET's father
POLONIUS, counselor to the King
LAERTES, son to POLONIUS
OPHELIA, daughter to POLONIUS
HORATIO, friend to HAMLET

And also:

VOLTEMAND
CORNELIUS
ROSENCRANTZ   } courtiers,
GUILDENSTERN
OSRIC
A gentleman
MARCELLUS
BERNARDO   } soldiers
FRANCISCO
REYNALDO, servant to POLONIUS
FORTINBRAS, Prince of Norway
PLAYERS
Two CLOWNS, gravediggers
A Norwegian CAPTAIN
English Ambassadors
Lords, Ladies, Priests, Officers, Soldiers, Sailors, Messengers, Attendants

ACT ONE

SCENE 1. Elsinore Castle. The platform of the guard.

[*Enter* BERNARDO *and* FRANCISCO, *two sentinels from opposite directions.*]

BERNARDO: Who's there?

FRANCISCO: Nay, answer me. Stand and unfold° yourself. *identify*

BERNARDO: Long live the King!

FRANCISCO: Bernardo?

BERNARDO: He. 5

FRANCISCO: You come most carefully upon your hour.° *at the exact time*

BERNARDO: 'Tis now struck twelve. Get thee to bed, Francisco.

FRANCISCO: For this relief much thanks. 'Tis bitter cold,
    And I am sick at heart.

BERNARDO: Have you had quiet guard?

FRANCISCO: Not a mouse stirring. 10

BERNARDO: Well, good night.
    If you do meet Horatio and Marcellus,
    The rivals° of my watch, bid them make haste. *partners*

[*Enter* HORATIO *and* MARCELLUS.]

FRANCISCO: I think I hear them. Stand! Who's there?

HORATIO: Friends to this ground.

MARCELLUS: And liegemen to the Dane.° *loyal Danish subjects* 15

FRANCISCO: Give you good night.

MARCELLUS: O, farewell, honest soldier.
    Who hath relieved you?

FRANCISCO: Bernardo hath my place.
    Give you good night.

[*He leaves.*]

MARCELLUS: Holla, Bernardo!

BERNARDO: Say—
    What, is Horatio there?

HORATIO: A piece of him.

BERNARDO: Welcome, Horatio. Welcome, good Marcellus. 20

MARCELLUS: What, has this thing appeared again tonight?

BERNARDO: I have seen nothing.

MARCELLUS: Horatio says 'tis but our fantasy,
    And will not let belief take hold of him
    Touching this dreaded sight, twice seen of us. 25
    Therefore I have entreated him along,
    With us to watch the minutes of this night,
    That, if again this apparition come,
    He may approve our eyes° and speak to it. *confirm what we saw*

HORATIO: Tush, tush, 'twill not appear.

BERNARDO: Sit down awhile, 30
    And let us once again assail your ears,
    That are so fortified against our story,
    What we two nights have seen.

HORATIO: Well, sit we down,
    And let us hear Bernardo speak of this.
BERNARDO: Last night of all,   35
    When yond same star that's westward from the pole
    Had made his° course to illume that part of heaven   *its*
    Where now it burns, Marcellus and myself,
    The bell then beating one—

    [*Enter* GHOST.]

MARCELLUS: Peace! break thee off! Look where it comes again!   40
BERNARDO: In the same figure,° like the King that's dead.   *looking the same as*
MARCELLUS: Thou art a scholar; speak to it, Horatio.
BERNARDO: Looks it not like the King? Mark it, Horatio.
HORATIO: Most like. It harrows me with fear and wonder.
BERNARDO: It would be spoke to.
MARCELLUS: Question it, Horatio.   45
HORATIO: What art thou that usurpest this time of night
    Together with that fair and warlike form
    In which the majesty of buried Denmark°   *the buried Danish king*
    Did sometimes march? By heaven I charge thee speak!
MARCELLUS: It is offended.
BERNARDO: See, it stalks away!   50
HORATIO: Stay! Speak, speak! I charge thee speak!

                          [GHOST *leaves.*]

MARCELLUS: 'Tis gone and will not answer.
BERNARDO: How now, Horatio? You tremble and look pale.
    Is not this something more than fantasy?
    What think you on't?°   *do you think of it* 55
HORATIO: Before my God, I might not this believe
    Without the sensible and true avouch°   *concrete testimony*
    Of mine own eyes.
MARCELLUS: Is it not like the King?
HORATIO: As thou art to thyself.
    Such was the very armor he had on   60
    When he the ambitious Norway° combated;   *(king of Norway)*
    So frowned he once when, in an angry parle,°   *parley*
    He smote the sledded Polacks° on the ice.   *Poles in sleds*
    'Tis strange.
MARCELLUS: Thus twice before, and jump° at this dead hour,   *exactly*   65
    With martial stalk hath he gone by our watch.
HORATIO: In what particular thought to work I know not;
    But, in the gross and scope of my opinion,°   *in my general opinion*
    This bodes some strange eruption° to our state.   *means some strange upheaval*
MARCELLUS: Good now, sit down and tell me, he that knows,   70
    Why this same strict and most observant watch
    So nightly toils the subject of the land,°   *makes our citizens toil*
    And why such daily cast of brazen cannon
    And foreign mart° for implements of war;   *shopping abroad*
    Why such impress° of shipwrights, whose sore task   *rushed hiring* 75
    Does not divide the Sunday from the week;

What might be toward,° that this sweaty haste   *be in store*
Doth make the night joint-laborer with the day?
Who is't that can inform me?
HORATIO: That can I.
    At least, the whisper goes so. Our last King,   80
    Whose image even but now appeared to us,
    Was, as you know, by Fortinbras of Norway,
    Thereto pricked on by a most emulate° pride,   *envious*
    Dared to the combat; in which our valiant Hamlet°   *(Hamlet senior, the dead king)*
    (For so this side of our known world esteemed him)   85
    Did slay this Fortinbras; who, by a sealed compact,°   *solemnly sealed treaty*
    Well ratified by law and heraldry,
    Did forfeit, with his life, all those his lands
    Which he stood seized of,° to the conqueror;   *which he held*
    Against the which a moiety competent°   *similar pledge*   90
    Was gaged by our King; which had° returned   *would have*
    To the inheritance of Fortinbras,
    Had he° been vanquisher, as, by the same comart°   *if he had/agreement*
    And carriage of the article designed,°   *meaning of the stipulated article*
    His fell to Hamlet. Now, sir, young Fortinbras,   95
    Of unimproved mettle° hot and full,   *untested spirit*
    Hath in the skirts° of Norway, here and there,   *outskirts*
    Sharked up° a list of lawless resolutes,°   *drummed up/adventurers*
    For food and diet to some enterprise
    That hath a stomach in't;° which is no other,   *that takes courage*   100
    As it doth well appear unto our state,
    But to recover of us, by strong hand
    And terms compulsatory,° those foresaid lands   *(threatening terms)*
    So by his father lost; and this, I take it,
    Is the main motive of our preparations,   105
    The source of this our watch, and the chief head°   *main well-spring*
    Of this post-haste and romage° in the land.   *commotion and turmoil*
BERNARDO: I think it be no other but e'en so.
    Well may it sort° that this portentous figure   *it fits well*
    Comes armed through our watch, so like the King   110
    That was and is the question° of these wars.   *cause*
HORATIO: A mote° it is to trouble the mind's eye.   *speck of dust*
    In the most high and palmy state of Rome,
    A little ere the mightiest Julius fell,°   *before Julius Caesar was killed*
    The graves stood tenantless,° and the sheeted dead   *without their occupants*   115
    Did squeak and gibber in the Roman streets;
    As stars with trains of fire,° and dews of blood,   *(meteors or comets)*
    Disasters in the sun; and the moist star°   *the moon (governing the tides)*
    Upon whose influence Neptune's empire stands
    Was sick almost to doomsday with eclipse.   120
    And even the like precurse° of fierce events,   *forerunners*
    As harbingers° preceding still the fates   *messengers*
    And prologue to the omen coming on,
    Have heaven and earth together demonstrated
    Unto our climatures° and countrymen.   *area*   125

[*Enter* GHOST *again.*]

But soft! behold! Lo, where it comes again!
I'll cross it,° though it blast me—Stay, illusion!   *cross its path*
If thou hast any sound, or use of voice,
Speak to me.
If there be any good thing to be done,   130
That may to thee do ease, and grace to me,
Speak to me.
If thou art privy to° thy country's fate,   *if you have secret knowledge of*
Which happily foreknowing may avoid,
O, speak!   135
Or if thou hast uphoarded in thy life
Extorted treasure in the womb of earth
(For which, they say, you spirits oft walk in death),

[*The cock crows.*]

Speak of it! Stay, and speak!—Stop it, Marcellus!
MARCELLUS: Shall I strike at it with my partisan?°   *weapon*   140
HORATIO: Do, if it will not stand.
BERNARDO: 'Tis here!
HORATIO: 'Tis here!
MARCELLUS: 'Tis gone!

[GHOST *leaves.*]

We do it wrong, being so majestical,
To offer it the show of violence;
For it is as the air, invulnerable,   145
And our vain blows malicious mockery.
BERNARDO: It was about to speak, when the cock crew.
HORATIO: And then it started, like a guilty thing
Upon a fearful summons. I have heard
The cock, that is the trumpet to the morn,   150
Doth with his lofty and shrill-sounding throat
Awake the god of day; and at his warning,
Whether in sea or fire, in earth or air,
The extravagant and erring spirit hies°   *hurries back*
To his confine;° and of the truth herein   *prison*   155
This present object made probation.°   *showed proof*
MARCELLUS: It faded on the crowing of the cock.
Some say that ever 'gainst that season comes
Wherein our Savior's birth is celebrated,
The bird of dawning singeth all night long;   160
And then, they say, no spirit dare stir abroad,
The nights are wholesome, then no planets strike,°   *no evil influences of planets*
No fairy takes, nor witch hath power to charm,
So hallowed° and so gracious is the time.   *sacred*
HORATIO: So have I heard and do in part believe it.   165
But look, the morn, in russet mantle clad,°   *in a reddish coat*
Walks over the dew of yon high eastern hill.

Break we our watch up;° and by my advice   *let us break up our watch*
Let us impart what we have seen tonight
Unto young Hamlet; for, upon my life,   170
This spirit, dumb to us, will speak to him.
Do you consent we shall acquaint him with it,
As needful in our loves, fitting our duty?
MARCELLUS: Let's do't, I pray; and I this morning know
Where we shall find him most conveniently.   175

[They leave.]

SCENE 2. Elsinore Castle. An audience chamber.

[*Flourish of trumpets. Enter* CLAUDIUS, *King of Denmark,* GERTRUDE
the Queen, HAMLET, POLONIUS, LAERTES *and his sister* OPHELIA, *and
attending lords.*]

KING: Though yet of Hamlet our dear brother's death
The memory be green,° and that it us befitted   *is very recent*
To bear our hearts in grief, and our whole kingdom
To be contracted in one brow of woe,
Yet so far hath discretion fought with nature   5
That we with wisest sorrow think on him
Together with remembrance of ourselves.
Therefore our sometime sister,° now our queen,   *former sister-in-law*
The imperial jointress° to this warlike state,   *partner*
Have we, as 'twere with a defeated joy,   10
With an auspicious,° and a dropping eye,   *happy*
With mirth in funeral, and with dirge in marriage,
In equal scale weighing delight and dole,°   *grief*
Taken to wife; nor have we herein barred
Your better wisdoms,° which have freely gone   *wise advice*   15
With this affair along. For all, our thanks.
Now follows, that you know, young Fortinbras,
Holding a weak supposal° of our worth,   *estimate*
Or thinking by our late dear brother's death
Our state to be disjoint° and out of frame,   *weakened*   20
Colleagued with° this dream of his advantage,   *joined to*
He hath not failed to pester us with message
Importing° the surrender of those lands   *asking for*
Lost by his father, with all bands of law,°   *due formalities*
To our most valiant brother. So much for him.   25

[*Enter* VOLTEMAND *and* CORNELIUS.]

Now for ourself and for this time of meeting.
Thus much the business is: we have here writ°   *written*
To Norway,° uncle of young Fortinbras—   *(the king of Norway)*
Who, impotent and bedrid,° scarcely hears   *bedridden*
Of this his nephew's purpose—to suppress°   *stop*   30
His further gait herein, in that the levies,°   *proceedings*
The lists, and full proportions are all made

Out of his subject;° and we here dispatch   *from among his subjects*
You, good Cornelius, and you, Voltemand,
For bearers of this greeting to old Norway,   35
Giving to you no further personal power
To business° with the King, more than the scope   *to do business*
Of these dilated articles° allow.   *detailed points*

[*Gives a paper.*]

Farewell, and let your haste commend your° duty.   *show your sense of*
CORNELIUS, VOLTEMAND: In that, and all things, will we show our duty.   40
KING: We doubt it nothing.° Heartily farewell.   *not at all*

[VOLTEMAND *and* CORNELIUS *leave.*]

And now, Laertes, what's the news with you?
You told us of some suit.° What is't, Laertes?   *request*
You cannot speak of reason to the Dane°   *(the Danish king)*
And lose your voice.° What wouldst thou beg, Laertes,   *speak in vain*   45
That shall not be my offer, not thy asking?
The head is not more native° to the heart,   *akin*
The hand more instrumental to the mouth,
Than is the throne of Denmark to thy father.
What wouldst thou have, Laertes?
LAERTES: My dread lord,   50
Your leave° and favor to return to France,   *permission*
From whence° though willingly I came to Denmark   *from where*
To show my duty in your coronation,
Yet now I must confess, that duty done,
My thoughts and wishes bend again toward France   55
And bow them to your gracious leave and pardon.°   *submit to your permission*
KING: Have you your father's leave? What says Polonius?
POLONIUS: He hath, my lord, wrung from me my slow leave°   *reluctant approval*
By laborsome petition, and at last
Upon his will I sealed my hard consent.   60
I do beseech you give him leave to go.
KING: Take thy fair hour,° Laertes. Time be thine,   *use the favorable hour*
And thy best graces spend it at thy will!
But now, my cousin Hamlet, and my son—
HAMLET [*aside*]: A little more than kin, and less than kind!°   *(a play on "one's kind" and*   65
KING: How is it that the clouds still hang on you?   *"being kind")*
HAMLET: Not so, my lord. I am too much in the sun.
QUEEN: Good Hamlet, cast thy nighted color off,
And let thine eye look like a friend on Denmark.°   *(the king of Denmark)*
Do not for ever with thy vailèd° lids   *lowered*   70
Seek for thy noble father in the dust.
Thou know'st 'tis common,° all that lives must die,   *common experience*
Passing through nature to eternity.
HAMLET: Ay, madam, it is common.
QUEEN: If it be,
Why seems it so particular with thee?   75

HAMLET: Seems, madam? Nay, it is. I know not "seems."
    'Tis not alone my inky° cloak, good mother,   *ink-black*
    Nor customary suits of solemn black,
    Nor windy suspiration° of forced breath,   *heavy sighs*
    No, nor the fruitful river in the eye,   80
    Nor the dejected havior of the visage,°   *behavior of the face*
    Together with all forms, moods, shapes of grief,
    That can denote me truly. These indeed seem,
    For they are actions that a man might play;
    But I have that within which passeth show—   85
    These but the trappings and the suits of woe.
KING: 'Tis sweet and commendable in your nature, Hamlet,
    To give these mourning duties to your father;
    But you must know, your father lost a father;
    That father lost, lost his, and the survivor bound   90
    In filial obligation for some term
    To do obsequious sorrow.° But to persever   *to show downcast grief*
    In obstinate condolement° is a course   *stubborn grieving*
    Of impious stubbornness. 'Tis unmanly grief;
    It shows a will most incorrect° to heaven,   *rebellious*   95
    A heart unfortified, a mind impatient,
    An understanding simple and unschooled;
    For what we know must be, and is as common
    As any the most vulgar° thing to sense,   *ordinary*
    Why should we in our peevish opposition   100
    Take it to heart? Fie! 'tis a fault to heaven,
    A fault against the dead, a fault to nature,
    To reason most absurd, whose common theme
    Is death of fathers, and who still° hath cried,   *which always*
    From the first corse° till he that died today,   *corpse* 105
    "This must be so." We pray you throw to earth
    This unprevailing woe, and think of us
    As of a father; for let the world take note
    You are the most immediate° to our throne,   *next in line*
    And with no less nobility of love   110
    Than that which dearest father bears his son
    Do I impart toward you. For your intent
    In going back to school in Wittenberg,
    It is most retrograde to our desire;°   *the opposite of our wish*
    And we beseech you, bend you to remain   115
    Here in the cheer and comfort of our eye,
    Our chiefest courtier, cousin, and our son.
QUEEN: Let not thy mother lose her prayers, Hamlet:
    I pray thee° stay with us, go not to Wittenberg,   *I ask you to*
HAMLET: I shall in all my best obey you, madam.   120
KING: Why, 'tis a loving and a fair reply.
    Be as ourself in Denmark. Madam, come.
    This gentle and unforced accord° of Hamlet   *consent*
    Sits smiling to my heart; in grace whereof,°   *in honor of which*
    No jocund health° that Denmark drinks today   *joyful toast* 125

But the great cannon to the clouds shall tell,
And the King's rouse the heaven shall bruit again,°   *the sky shall echo the king's celebration*
Respeaking earthly thunder. Come away.

[*Flourish of trumpets. All leave except* HAMLET.]

HAMLET: O that this too too sullied flesh would melt,
Thaw, and resolve° itself into a dew!   *dissolve*   130
Or that the Everlasting had not fixed
His canon° 'gainst self-slaughter! O God! God!   *law*
How weary, stale, flat, and unprofitable
Seem to me all the uses of this world!
Fie on't! ah, fie!° 'Tis an unweeded garden   *for shame*   135
That grows to seed; things rank and gross in nature
Possess it merely.° That it should come to this!   *have taken it over*
But two months dead—nay, not so much, not two!
So excellent a king, that was to this
Hyperion to a satyr;° so loving to my mother   *like a god compared to a being half goat*   140
That he might not beteem° the winds of heaven   *allow*
Visit her face too roughly. Heaven and earth!
Must I remember? Why, she would hang on him
As if increase of appetite had grown
By what it fed on; and yet, within a month—   145
Let me not think on't! Frailty, thy name is woman!—
A little month, or ere° those shoes were old   *before*
With which she followed my poor father's body
Like Niobe, all tears—why she, even she
(O God! a beast that wants discourse of reason°   *lacks reasoning power*   150
Would have mourned longer) married with my uncle;
My father's brother, but no more like my father
Than I to Hercules. Within a month,
Ere yet the salt of most unrighteous tears
Had left the flushing in her gallèd eyes,°   *had stopped reddening her inflamed eyes*   155
She married. O, most wicked speed, to post°   *hurry*
With such dexterity° to incestuous sheets!   *agility*
It is not, nor it cannot come to good.
But break my heart, for I must hold my tongue!

[*Enter* HORATIO, MARCELLUS, *and* BERNARDO.]

HORATIO: Hail to your lordship!
HAMLET: I am glad to see you well.   160
Horatio—or I do forget myself!
HORATIO: The same, my lord, and your poor servant ever.
HAMLET: Sir, my good friend—I'll change that name with you.
And what make you from° Wittenberg, Horatio?   *are you doing away from*
Marcellus?   165
MARCELLUS: My good lord!
HAMLET: I am very glad to see you.—[*to* BERNARDO] Good even, sir.—
But what, in faith, make you from Wittenberg?
HORATIO: A truant disposition, good my lord.
HAMLET: I would not hear your enemy say so,   170

Nor shall you do my ear that violence
To make it truster of° your own report   *to make it trust*
Against yourself. I know you are no truant.
But what is your affair in Elsinore?
We'll teach to drink deep ere° you depart.   *before*   175
HORATIO: My lord, I came to see your father's funeral.
HAMLET: I prithee do not mock me, fellow student,
   I think it was to see my mother's wedding.
HORATIO: Indeed, my lord, it followed hard upon.°   *closely after*
HAMLET: Thrift, thrift, Horatio! The funeral baked meats   180
   Did coldly furnish forth° the marriage tables.   *served as cold cuts for*
   Would I° had met my dearest foe in heaven   *I wish I had*
   Or ever° I had seen that day, Horatio!   *before*
   My father—methinks I see my father.
HORATIO: O, where, my lord?
HAMLET: In my mind's eye, Horatio.   185
HORATIO: I saw him once. He was a goodly king.
HAMLET: He was a man, take him for all in all.
   I shall not look upon his like again.
HORATIO: My lord, I think I saw him yesternight.
HAMLET: Saw? who?   190
HORATIO: My lord, the King your father.
HAMLET: The King my father?
HORATIO: Season your admiration° for a while   *control your amazement*
   With an attent° ear, till I may deliver,   *attentive*
   Upon the witness of these gentlemen,
   This marvel to you.
HAMLET: For God's love let me hear!   195
HORATIO: Two nights together had these gentlemen
   (Marcellus and Bernardo) on their watch
   In the dead vast° and middle of the night   *vast emptiness*
   Been thus encountered. A figure like your father,
   Armed at point exactly, cap-a-pe,°   *head to foot*   200
   Appears before them and with solemn march
   Goes slow and stately by them. Thrice he walked
   By their oppressed and fear-surprisèd eyes,
   Within his truncheon's length; whilst they, distilled°   *changed*
   Almost to jelly with the act of fear,   205
   Stand dumb and speak not to him. This to me
   In dreadful secrecy impart they did,°   *they told*
   And I with them the third night kept the watch;
   Where, as they had delivered,° both in time,   *reported*
   Form of the thing, each word made true and good,   210
   The apparition comes. I knew your father:
   These hands are not more like.
HAMLET: But where was this?
MARCELLUS: My lord, upon the platform where we watched.
HAMLET: Did you not speak to it?
HORATIO: My lord, I did;
   But answer made it none. Yet once methought   215
   It lifted up it head and did address

Itself to motion,° like as it would speak; *prepared to move*
But even then the morning cock crew° loud, *crowed*
And at the sound it shrunk in haste away
And vanished from our sight.
HAMLET: 'Tis very strange. 220
HORATIO: As I do live, my honored lord, 'tis true;
    And we did think it writ down in our duty
    To let you know of it.
HAMLET: Indeed, indeed, sirs, but this troubles me.
    Hold you the watch tonight?
BOTH [MARCELLUS *and* BERNARDO]: We do, my lord. 225
HAMLET: Armed, say you?
BOTH: Armed, my lord.
HAMLET: From top to toe?
BOTH: My lord, from head to foot.
HAMLET: Then saw you not his face?
HORATIO: O, yes, my lord! He wore his beaver° up. *the face cover of his helmet* 230
HAMLET: What, looked he frowningly?
HORATIO: A countenance more in sorrow than in anger.
HAMLET: Pale or red?
HORATIO: Nay, very pale.
HAMLET: And fixed this eyes upon you?
HORATIO: Most constantly.
HAMLET: I would I had° been there. *wish I could have* 235
HORATIO: It would have much amazed you.
HAMLET: Very like,° very like. Stayed it long? *very likely*
HORATIO: While one with moderate haste might tell a hundred.
BOTH: Longer, longer.
HORATIO: Not when I saw't.
HAMLET: His beard was grizzled—no? 240
HORATIO: It was, as I have seen it in his life,
    A sable silvered.° *black with silver touches*
HAMLET: I will watch tonight.
    Perchance° 'twill walk again. *perhaps*
HORATIO: I warrant it will.
HAMLET: If it assume my noble father's person,
    I'll speak to it, though hell itself should gape 245
    And bid me hold my peace.° I pray you all, *tell me to be quiet*
    If you have hitherto concealed this sight,
    Let it be tenable in your silence still;° *go on keeping it silent*
    And whatsoever else shall hap° tonight, *happen*
    Give it an understanding but no tongue.° *think but do not speak about it* 250
    I will requite° your loves. So, fare you well. *reward*
    Upon the platform, 'twixt° eleven and twelve, *between*
    I'll visit you.
ALL: Our duty to your honor.
HAMLET: Your loves, as mine to you. Farewell.

[*All but* HAMLET *leave.*]

My father's spirit—in arms? All is not well. 255
I doubt° some foul play. Would the night were come! *suspect*

Till then sit still, my soul. Foul deeds will rise,
Though all the earth overwhelm them, to men's eyes.

[*He leaves.*]

SCENE 3. Elsinore. POLONIUS' house.

[*Enter* LAERTES *and* OPHELIA.]

LAERTES: My necessaries are embarked.° Farewell.   *luggage is on board*
        And, sister, as the winds give benefit
        And convoy is assistant,° do not sleep,   *ships are available*
        But let me hear from you.
OPHELIA: Do you doubt that?
LAERTES: For Hamlet, and the trifling of his favor,   5
        Hold it a fashion, and a toy in blood;°   *think of it as a fad and whim*
        A violet in the youth of primy nature,°   *nature at springtime*
        Forward,° not permanent; sweet, not lasting;   *fleeting*
        The perfume and suppliance° of a minute;   *aroma and pastime*
        No more.
OPHELIA: No more but so?
LAERTES: Think it no more.   10
        For nature crescent° does not grow alone   *a maturing person*
        In thews and bulk, but as this temple waxes,°   *not only in body, but as it grows*
        The inward service of the mind and soul
        Grows wide withal.° Perhaps he loves you now,   *along with it*
        And now no soil nor cautel° doth besmirch   *no stain nor deceit*   15
        The virtue of his will; but you must fear,
        His greatness weighed,° his will is not his own,   *when his status is weighed*
        For he himself is subject to his birth.°   *the role he was born into*
        He may not, as unvalued persons do,
        Carve for himself, for on his choice depends   20
        The safety and health of his whole state,
        And therefore must his choice be circumscribed°   *limited*
        Unto the voice and yielding of that body
        Whereof he is the head. Then if he says he loves you,
        It fits your wisdom so far to believe it   25
        As he in his particular act and place
        May give his saying deed,° which is no further   *follow word with deed*
        Than the main voice of Denmark goes withal.°   *public opinion permits*
        Then weigh what loss your honor may sustain
        If with too credent ear you list° his songs,   *too willing ear you listen to* 30
        Or lose your heart, or your chaste treasure open
        To his unmastered importunity.°   *uncontrolled urging*
        Fear it, Ophelia, fear it, my dear sister,
        And keep you in the rear of your affection,
        Out of the shot° and danger of desire.   *out of firing range*   35
        The chariest° maid is prodigal° enough   *most careful/loose*
        If she unmask her beauty to the moon.
        Virtue itself scapes° not calumnious strokes.   *escapes*

The canker galls the infants of the spring°   *worm ruins spring flowers*
Too oft before their buttons be° disclosed,   *their buds are*   40
And in the morn and liquid dew of youth
Contagious blastments are most imminent.
Be wary then; best safety lies in fear.
Youth to itself° rebels, though none else near.   *by itself*
OPHELIA: I shall the effect of this good lesson keep   45
As watchman to my heart. But, good my brother,
Do not as some ungracious pastors° do,   *faithless priests*
Show me the steep and thorny way to heaven,
Whiles, like a puffed and reckless libertine,°   *pleasure lover*
Himself the primrose path of dalliance treads   50
And recks not his own rede.°   *disregards his own counsel*
LAERTES: O, fear me not!°   *do not worry about me*

[*Enter* POLONIUS.]

I stay too long. But here my father comes.
A double blessing is a double grace;
Occasion smiles upon a second leave.°   *leave-taking*
POLONIUS: Yet here, Leartes? Aboard, aboard, for shame!   55
The wind sits in the shoulder of your sail,°   *wind is favorable*
And you are stayed for.° There—my blessing with thee!   *waited for*
And these few precepts in thy memory
Look thou character.° Give thy thoughts no tongue,   *make sure to record*
Nor any unproportioned thought his act.°   *its action*   60
Be thou familiar,° but by no means vulgar: *mingling with all*
Those friends thou hast, and their adoption tried,°   *after testing them*
Grapple them to thy soul with hoops of steel;
But do not dull thy palm° with entertainment   *wear out your hand*
Of each new-hatched, unfledged comrade. Beware   65
Of entrance to a quarrel; but being in,
Bear't that the opposed° may beware of thee.   *act so that the opponent*
Give every man thine ear, but few thy voice;
Take each man's censure, but reserve thy judgment.
Costly thy habit as thy purse can buy,°   *buy clothes you can afford*   70
But not expressed in fancy; rich, not gaudy;
For the apparel oft proclaims the man,
And they in France of the best rank and station
Are most select and generous, chief in that.
Neither a borrower nor a lender be;   75
For loan oft loses both itself and friend,
And borrowing dulls the edge of husbandry.°   *undermines good management*
This above all: to thine own self be true,
And it must follow, as the night the day,
Thou canst not then be false to any man.   80
Farewell. My blessing season this in thee!
LAERTES: Most humbly do I take my leave, my lord.
POLONIUS: The time invites you. Go, your servants tend.°   *wait*
LAERTES: Farewell, Ophelia, and remember well
What I have said to you.

OPHELIA: 'Tis in my memory locked,   85
    And you yourself shall keep the key of it.
LAERTES: Farewell.

                      [He leaves.]

POLONIUS: What is't, Ophelia, he hath said to you?
OPHELIA: So please you, something touching the Lord Hamlet.
POLONIUS: Marry, well bethought!°   *good thinking*   90
    'Tis told me he hath very oft of late
    Given private time to you, and you yourself
    Have of your audience been most free and bounteous.°   *have been freely available*
    If it be so—as so 'tis put on me,°   *as I've been told*
    And that in way of caution—I must tell you   95
    You do not understand yourself so clearly
    As it behooves° my daughter and your honor.   *as is required of*
    What is between you? Give me up the truth.
OPHELIA: He hath, my lord, of late made many tenders°   *given many signs*
    Of his affection to me.   100
POLONIUS: Affection? Pooh! You speak like a green girl,
    Unsifted° in such perilous circumstance.   *inexperienced*
    Do you believe his tenders, as you call them?
OPHELIA: I do not know, my lord, what I should think.
POLONIUS: Marry, I will teach you! Think yourself a baby   105
    That you have taken these tenders for true pay,
    Which are not sterling.° Tender yourself more dearly,   *not true currency*
    Or (not to crack the wind of the poor phrase,
    Running it thus) you'll tender me° a fool.   *make me (or you) seem*
OPHELIA: My lord, he hath importuned me with love   110
    In honorable fashion.
POLONIUS: Ay, fashion you may call it. Go to, go to!
OPHELIA: And hath given countenance to his speech, my lord,
    With almost all the holy vows of heaven.
POLONIUS: Ay, springes to catch woodcocks!° I do know,   *traps for birds* 115
    When the blood burns, how prodigal the soul
    Lends the tongue vows. These blazes, daughter,
    Giving more light than heat, extinct° in both   *ready to go out*
    Even in their promise, as it is a-making,
    You must not take for fire. From this time   120
    Be somewhat scanter of your maiden presence.°   *make yourself scarcer*
    Set your entreatments at a higher rate
    Than a command to parley.° For Lord Hamlet,   *a mere summons to talk*
    Believe so much in him, that he is young,
    And with a larger tether may he walk   125
    Than may be given you. In few,° Ophelia,   *in short*
    Do not believe his vows; for they are brokers,
    Not of that dye which their investments° show,   *appearances*
    But mere implorators of unholy suits,°   *instigators of dishonest proposals*
    Breathing like sanctified and pious bawds,°   *pimps* 130
    The better to beguile. This is for all:
    I would not, in plain terms, from this time forth

Have you so slander any moment° leisure   *so misuse any moment's*
As to give words or talk with the Lord Hamlet.
Look to't, I charge you. Come your ways.   135
OPHELIA: I shall obey, my lord.

[*They leave.*]

SCENE 4. Elsinore Castle. The platform of the guard.

[*Enter* HAMLET, HORATIO, *and* MARCELLUS.]

HAMLET: The air bites shrewdly; it is very cold.
HORATIO: It is a nipping and an eager air.
HAMLET: What hour now?
HORATIO: I think it lacks of° twelve.   *it's not quite*
MARCELLUS: No, it is struck.
HORATIO: Indeed? I heard it not. It then draws near the season°   *near the time*   5
      Wherein the spirit held his wont to walk.°   *used to walk*

[*A flourish of trumpets, and two cannons go off.*]

      What does this mean, my lord?
HAMLET: The King doth wake tonight and takes his rouse,°   *stays up to carouse*
      Keeps wassail, and the swaggering upspring reels,°   *drinks and dances*
      And, as he drains his draughts of Rhenish° down,   *Rhine wine*   10
      The kettledrum and trumpet thus bray out
      The triumph of his pledge.
HORATIO: Is it a custom?
HAMLET: Ay, marry, is't;
      But to my mind, though I am native here
      And to the manner born, it is a custom   15
      More honored in the breach° than the observance.   *in disregarding it*
      This heavy-headed revel east and west
      Makes us traduced and taxed of° other nations;   *defamed and blamed by*
      They call us drunkards and with swinish phrase
      Soil our addition;° and indeed it takes   *stain our reputation*   20
      From our achievements, though performed at height,
      The pith and marrow of our attribute.°   *the core of our good name*
      So oft it chances in particular men
      That for some vicious mole of nature in them,
      As in their birth—wherein they are not guilty,   25
      Since nature cannot choose his origin—
      By their overgrowth of some complexion,°   *some exaggerated trait*
      Oft breaking down the pales and forts° of reason,   *defenses*
      Or by some habit that too much overleavens
      The form of plausive° manners, that these men   *acceptable*   30
      Carrying, I say, the stamp of one defect,
      Being nature's livery,° or fortune's star—   *which nature has dressed them in*
      Their virtues else (be they as pure as grace,
      As infinite as man may undergo)
      Shall in the general censure take corruption°   *in everyone's opinion be tarnished*   35
      From that particular fault. The dram° of evil   *drop*

Doth all the noble substance often dout°   *drive out*
To his own scandal.°   *its complete disgrace*

[*Enter* GHOST.]

HORATIO: Look, my lord, it comes!
HAMLET: Angels and ministers of grace defend us!
 Be thou° a spirit of health or goblin damned,   *whether you are* 40
 Bring with thee airs from heaven or blasts from hell,
 Be thy intents wicked or charitable,
 Thou com'st in such a questionable shape
 That I will speak to thee. I'll call thee Hamlet,
 King, father, royal Dane. O, answer me!   45
 Let me not burst in ignorance, but tell
 Why thy canonized° bones, hearsed in death, *sanctified and duly buried*
 Have burst their cerements;° why the sepulchre *left their burial shroud*
 Wherein we saw thee quietly inurned,
 Hath oped his° ponderous and marble jaws   *opened its* 50
 To cast thee up again. What may this mean
 That thou, dead corpse, again in complete steel,° *in full armor*
 Revisits thus the glimpses of the moon,
 Making night hideous, and we fools of nature
 So horridly to shake our disposition°   *upset our reason* 55
 With thoughts beyond the reaches of our souls?
 Say, why is this? wherefore? What should we do?

[GHOST *beckons* HAMLET.]

HORATIO: It beckons you to go away with it,
 As if it some impartment° did desire   *communication*
 To you alone.
MARCELLUS: Look with what courteous action   60
 It waves you to a more removed ground.
 But do not go with it!
HORATIO: No, by no means!
HAMLET: It will not speak. Then will I follow it.
HORATIO: Do not, my Lord!
HAMLET: Why, what should be the fear?
 I do not set my life at a pin's fee;°   *the price of a pin* 65
 And for my soul, what can it do to that,
 Being a thing immortal as itself?
 It waves me forth again. I'll follow it.
HORATIO: What if it tempt you toward the flood, my lord,
 Or to the dreadful summit of the cliff   70
 That beetles° over his base into the sea,   *juts out*
 And there assume some other, horrible form
 Which might deprive your sovereignty of reason° *overthrow your sovereign reason*
 And draw you into madness? Think of it.
 The very place puts toys of desperation,°   *desperate thoughts* 75
 Without more motive, into every brain
 That looks so many fathoms to the sea
 And hears it roar beneath.

HAMLET: It waves me still.
   Go on, I'll follow thee.
MARCELLUS: You shall not go, my lord.
HAMLET: Hold off your hands!   80
HORATIO: Be ruled, you shall not go.
HAMLET: My fate cries out
   And makes each petty artery in this body
   As hardy as the Nemean lion's nerve.°   *lion's sinews*

[GHOST *beckons.*]

   Still am I called. Unhand me, gentlemen—
   By heaven, I'll make a Ghost of him that lets° me!   *stops*   85
   I say, away!—Go on, I'll follow thee.

[GHOST *and* HAMLET *leave.*]

HORATIO: He waxes° desperate with imagination.   *grows*
MARCELLUS: Let's follow; 'tis not fit thus to obey him.
HORATIO: Have after.° To what issue will this come?   *let's go after him*
MARCELLUS: Something is rotten in the state of Denmark.   90
HORATIO: Heaven will direct it.
MARCELLUS: Nay, let's follow him.

[*They leave.*]

SCENE 5. Same. Another part of the ramparts.

[*Enter* GHOST *and* HAMLET.]

HAMLET: Wither° wilt thou lead me? Speak, I'll go no further.   *where*
GHOST: Mark me.°   *listen carefully*
HAMLET: I will.
GHOST: My hour is almost come,
   When I to sulphurous and tormenting flames
   Must render up myself.
HAMLET: Alas, poor ghost!
GHOST: Pity me not, but lend thy serious hearing   5
   To what I shall unfold.
HAMLET: Speak, I am bound to hear.
GHOST: So art thou to revenge, when thou shalt hear.
HAMLET: What?
GHOST: I am thy father's spirit,
   Doomed for a certain term to walk the night,   10
   And for the day confined to fast in fires,
   Till the foul crimes done in my days of nature
   Are burnt and purged away. But that I am forbid
   To tell the secrets of my prison house,
   I could a tale unfold whose lightest word   15
   Would harrow up thy soul, freeze thy young blood,
   Make thy two eyes, like stars, start from their spheres,
   Thy knotted and combined locks to part,

And each particular hair to stand on end
Like quills upon the fretful porpentine.°   *angry porcupine*   20
But this eternal blazon° must not be   *this news of the supernatural world*
To ears of flesh and blood. List, list, O, list!
If thou didst ever thy dear father love—
HAMLET: O God!
GHOST: Revenge his foul and most unnatural murder.   25
HAMLET: Murder?
GHOST: Murder most foul, as in the best it is;
   But this most foul, strange, and unnatural.
HAMLET: Hast me to know't, that I, with wings as swift
   As meditation or the thoughts of love,   30
   May sweep to my revenge.
      GHOST: I find thee apt;
   And duller shouldst thou be than the fat weed
   That rots itself in ease on Lethe° wharf,   *river of oblivion*
   Wouldst thou not stir° in this. Now, Hamlet, hear: *take action*
   'Tis given out that, sleeping in my orchard,   35
   A serpent stung me; so the whole ear of Denmark
   Is by a forgèd process° of my death   *false account*
   Rankly abused; but know, thou noble youth,
   The serpent that did sting thy father's life
   Now wears his crown.
HAMLET: O my prophetic soul!   40
   My uncle?
GHOST: Ay, that incestuous, that adulterate beast,
   With witchcraft of his wit, with traitorous gifts—
   O wicked wit and gifts, that have the power
   So to seduce!—won to his shameful lust   45
   The will of my most seeming-virtuous queen.
   O Hamlet, what a falling-off was there,
   From me, whose love was of that dignity
   That it went hand in hand even with the vow
   I made to her in marriage, and to decline°   *to lower herself*   50
   Upon a wretch whose natural gifts were poor
   To those of mine!
   But virtue, as it never will be moved,
   Though lewdness court it in a shape of heaven,
   So lust, though to a radiant angel linked,   55
   Will sate itself° in a celestial bed   *will grow bored*
   And prey on garbage.
   But soft! methinks I scent the morning air.
   Brief let me be. Sleeping within my orchard,
   My custom always of the afternoon,   60
   Upon my secure° hour thy uncle stole,   *thought to be safe*
   With juice of cursed hebenon° in a vial,   *poison plant*
   And in the porches of my ears did pour
   The leperous distilment,° whose effect   *deadly liquid*
   Holds such an enmity with° blood of man   *is so at war with*   65
   That swift as quicksilver it courses° through   *runs*
   The natural gates and alleys of the body,

And with a sudden vigor it doth posset°   *curdle*
And curd, like eager droppings° into milk,   *acid drops*
The thin and wholesome blood; so did it mine,   70
And a most instant tetter barked about,°   *sudden rash covered*
Most lazar-like,° with vile and loathsome crust   *like a leper*
All my smooth body.
Thus was I, sleeping, by a brother's hand
Of life, of crown, of queen, at once dispatched;   75
Cut off even in the blossoms of my sin,°   *with my sins in full flower*
Unhouseled, disappointed, unaneled,°   *without sacrament or forgiveness of sins*
No reckoning made, but sent to my account
With all my imperfections on my head.
HAMLET: O, horrible! O, horrible! most horrible!   80
GHOST: If thou hast nature in thee, bear it not.
Let not the royal bed of Denmark be
A couch for luxury° and damnèd incest.   *bed for licentiousness*
But, howsoever thou pursuest this act,
Taint not thy mind, nor let thy soul contrive   85
Against thy mother aught.° Leave her to heaven,   *anything against your mother*
And to those thorns that in her bosom lodge
To prick and sting her. Fare thee well at once,
The glowworm shows the matin° to be near   *morning*
And gins to pale his uneffectual fire.°   *begins to make it seem pale*   90
Adieu, adieu, adieu! Remember me.

[He leaves.]

HAMLET: O all you host of heaven! O earth! What else?
And shall I couple hell?° O fie! Hold, hold, my heart!   *shall I add hell*
And you, my sinews, grow not instant old,
But bear me stiffly up. Remember thee?   95
Ay, thou poor ghost, while memory holds a seat
In this distracted globe.° Remember thee?   *perturbed (globelike) head*
Yea, from the table° of my memory   *record*
I'll wipe away all trivial fond records,°   *foolish entries*
All saws° of books, all forms, all pressures past   *wise sayings*   100
That youth and observation copied there,
And thy commandment all alone shall live
Within the book and volume of my brain,
Unmixed with baser matter. Yes, by heaven!
O most pernicious woman!   105
O villain, villain, smiling, damnèd villain!
My tables, my tables!° Meet it is° I set it down   *note-keeping slates/it's right*
That one may smile, and smile, and be a villain;
At least I'm sure it may be so in Denmark.

[Writes.]

So, uncle, there you are. Now to my word: 110
It is "Adieu, adieu! Remember me."
I have sworn't.
HORATIO [*within*]: My lord, my lord!

[*Enter* HORATIO *and* MARCELLUS.]

MARCELLUS: Lord Hamlet!
HORATIO: Heaven secure him!°   *keep him safe*
HAMLET: So be it!
MARCELLUS: Illo, ho, ho, my lord!°   *(falconer's call)*   115
HAMLET: Hillo, ho, ho, boy! Come, bird, come.
MARCELLUS: How is't, my noble lord?
HORATIO: What news, my lord?
HAMLET: O, wonderful!
HORATIO: Good my lord, tell it.
HAMLET: No, you'll reveal it.
HORATIO: Not I, my lord, by heaven!
MARCELLUS: Nor I, my lord.   120
HAMLET: How say you then? Would heart of man once think it?
    But you'll be secret?
BOTH: Ay, by heaven, my lord.
HAMLET: There's never a villain dwelling in all Denmark
    But he's an arrant knave.°   *utter scoundrel*
HORATIO: There needs no ghost, my lord, come from the grave   125
    To tell us this.
HAMLET: Why, right! You are in the right!
    And so, without more circumstance° at all,   *ceremony*
    I hold it fit that we shake hands and part;
    You, as your business and desires shall point you,
    For every man hath business and desire,   130
    Such as it is; and for my own poor part,
    Look you, I'll go pray.
HORATIO: These are but wild and whirling words, my lord.
HAMLET: I am sorry they offend you, heartily;
    Yes, faith, heartily.
HORATIO: There's no offense, my lord.   135
HAMLET: Yes, by Saint Patrick, but there is, Horatio,
    And much offense too. Touching this vision here,
    It is an honest ghost,° that let me tell you.   *(not an evil spirit)*
    For° your desire to know what is between us,   *as for*
    O'ermaster't° as you may. And now, good friends,   *overcome it*   140
    As you are friends, scholars, and soldiers,
    Give° me one poor request.   *grant*
HORATIO: What is't, my lord? We will.
HAMLET: Never make known what you have seen tonight.
BOTH: My lord, we will not.
HAMLET: Nay, but swear't.
HORATIO: In faith,   145
    My lord, not I.
MARCELLUS: Nor I, my lord—in faith.
HAMLET: Upon my sword.
MARCELLUS: We have sworn, my lord, already.
HAMLET: Indeed, upon my sword, indeed.

    [GHOST *cries under the stage.*]

GHOST: Swear.

HAMLET: Aha boy, say'st thou so? Art thou there, true-penny? 150
    Come on! You hear this fellow in the cellarage.
    Consent to swear.

HORATIO: Propose the oath, my lord.

HAMLET: Never to speak of this that you have seen.
    Swear by my sword.

GHOST [*beneath*]: Swear. 155

HAMLET: Hic et ubique?° Then we'll shift our ground.   *(Latin) here and everywhere*
    Come hither, gentlemen,
    And lay your hands again upon my sword.
    Never to speak of this that you have heard:
    Swear by my sword. 160

GHOST [*beneath*]: Swear by his sword.

HAMLET: Well said, old mole! Canst work in the earth so fast?
    A worthy pioner!° Once more remove, good friends.   *miner*

HORATIO: O day and night, but this is wondrous strange!

HAMLET: And therefore as a stranger give it welcome. 165
    There are more things in heaven and earth, Horatio,
    Than are dreamt of in your philosophy.
    But come!
    Here, as before, never, so help you mercy,
    How strange or odd soever° I bear myself   *however strange or odd* 170
    (As I perchance hereafter shall think meet°   *perhaps will think it right*
    To put an antic disposition on),°   *to act very strange*
    That you, at such times seeing me, never shall,
    With arms encumbered° thus, or this head-shake,   *folded*
    Or by pronouncing of some doubtful phrase, 175
    As "Well, well, we know," or "We could, an if we would,"
    Or "If we list° to speak," or "There be, an if they might,"   *if we wanted*
    Or such ambiguous giving out, to note
    That you know aught of me—this not to do,
    So grace and mercy at your most need help you, 180
    Swear.

GHOST [*beneath*]: Swear.

[*They swear.*]

HAMLET: Rest, rest, perturbèd spirit! So, gentlemen,
    With all my love I do commend me to you;
    And what so poor a man as Hamlet is 185
    May do to express his love and friending° to you,   *friendship*
    God willing, shall not lack. Let us go in together;
    And still° your fingers on your lips, I pray.   *always*
    The time is out of joint. O cursèd spite
    That ever I was born to set it right! 190
    Nay, come, let's go together.

[*They leave.*]

THE RECEPTIVE READER

1. (Scene 1) Shakespeare treats the sighting of the ghost in carefully worked out detail. Why do you think the playwright shows us that the guards are punctual for the changing of the watch? What picture do we get of Horatio here? What are his credentials; what is his attitude? Is he superstitious? How much of contemporary spirit lore can we reconstruct from this scene? ✧ Why do you think the playwright kept Hamlet out of these first encounters with the ghost of his murdered father?

2. (Scene 2) In this scene, what first impression do you form of Hamlet as the central character and *protagonist*? What different sides of his personality do you see in his interaction with the king and queen, in his soliloquies and asides, and in his interaction with Horatio? ✧ How does Hamlet react to his friends' reports of the ghost?

3. (Scene 3) What first impressions do you form of Polonius, Laertes, and Ophelia as major *supporting characters* in the play? How do Polonius and Laertes treat Ophelia, and how does she respond?

4. (Scenes 4 and 5) What are the major elements in the ghost's indictment of Claudius and Queen Gertrude? How implicated or guilty do you think she is? ✧ In these scenes, Hamlet seems a man of fluctuating, rapidly changing moods. What are his behavior and mood when he first encounters the ghost? What is his reaction after he listens to the ghost's charges? How does his mood change when his associates rejoin him? How do you explain his irreverent behavior toward the ghost at the end of the scene? ✧ What does Hamlet say about the pretended madness that becomes a major strand in the play (and in critical studies of his character)? How does he begin to act out his "antic disposition"?

THE PERSONAL DIMENSION

Do you recognize any of the people in this play? Can you identify with or relate to any of them? Do you begin to understand their situation, their concerns, their motives?

ACT TWO

SCENE 1. Elsinore. POLONIUS' house.

[*Enter* POLONIUS *and* REYNALDO.]

POLONIUS: Give him this money and these notes, Reynaldo.
REYNALDO: I will, my lord.
POLONIUS: You shall do marvelous wisely, good Reynaldo,
　　　Before you visit him, to make inquire
　　　Of his behavior.
REYNALDO:　　　　My lord, I did intend it.　　　　　　　　　　　5
POLONIUS: Marry, well said, very well said. Look you, sir,
　　　Inquire me first what Danskers° are in Paris;　　　*Danish visitors*
　　　And how, and who, what means, and where they keep,
　　　What company, at what expense; and finding
　　　By this encompassment and drift of question°　　*roundabout questioning*　10
　　　That they do know my son, come you more nearer
　　　Than your particular demands will touch it.
　　　Take you,° as 'twere, some distant knowledge of him;　　*pretend*

As thus, "I know his father and his friends,
  And in part him." Do you mark this, Reynaldo?   15
REYNALDO: Ay, very well, my lord.
POLONIUS: "And in part, him, but," you may say, "not well.
  But if't be he I mean, he's very wild,
  Addicted so and so"; and there put on him
  What forgeries° you please; marry,° none so rank   *falsehoods/truly*   20
  As may dishonor him—take heed of that;
  But, sir, such wanton, wild, and usual slips
  As are companions noted and most known
  To youth and liberty.
REYNALDO: As gaming, my lord.
POLONIUS: Ay, or drinking, fencing, swearing, quarrelling,   25
  Drabbing.° You may go so far.   *running after loose women*
REYNALDO: My lord, that would dishonor him.
POLONIUS: Faith, no, as you may season it in the charge.°   *word it mildly*
  You must not put another scandal on him,
  That he is open to incontinency.°   *loose living*   30
  That's not my meaning. But breathe his faults so quaintly°   *carefully*
  That they may seem the taints of liberty,
  The flash and outbreak of a fiery mind,
  A savageness in unreclaimèd blood,
  Of general assault.°   *commonly befalling young people*
REYNALDO: But, my good lord—   35
POLONIUS: Wherefore should you do this?
REYNALDO: Ay, my lord,
  I would know that.
POLONIUS: Marry, sir, here's my drift,
  And I believe it is a fetch of warrant.°   *permissible ploy*
  You laying these slight sullies on my son
  As 'twere a thing a little soiled in the working,   40
  Mark you,
  Your party in converse,° him you would sound,   *conversation*
  Having ever seen in the prenominate° crimes   *before-named*
  The youth you breathe of guilty, be assured
  He closes with you in this consequence:°   *chimes in in this conclusion*   45
  "Good sir," or so, or "friend," or "gentleman"—
  According to the phrase or the addition°   *proper way to address*
  Of man and country—
REYNALDO: Very good, my lord.
POLONIUS: And then, sir, does he this—he does—What was I
  about to say? By the mass, I was about to say something!   50
  Where did I leave?
REYNALDO: At "closes in the consequence," at "friend or so,"
  and "gentleman."
POLONIUS: At "closes in the consequence"—Ay, marry!
  He closes thus: "I know the gentleman.   55
  I saw him yesterday, or the other day,
  Or then, or then, with such or such; and, as you say,
  There was he gaming; there o'ertook in 's rouse;°   *overcome in his carousing*
  There falling out at tennis"; or perchance,

"I saw him enter such a house of sale," 60
Videlicet,° a brothel, or so forth.   *namely*
See you now—
Your bait of falsehood takes this carp of truth;
And thus do we of wisdom and of reach,
With windlasses and with assays of bias,°   *approaching it sideways* 65
By indirections find directions out.
So, by my former lecture and advice,
Shall you my son. You have° me, have you not?   *understand*
REYNALDO: My lord, I have.
POLONIUS: God be wi' you, fare you well!
REYNALDO: Good my lord! 70
POLONIUS: Observe his inclination in yourself.°   *for yourself*
REYNALDO: I shall, my lord.
POLONIUS: And let him ply his music.°   *do not interfere*
REYNALDO: Well, my lord.
POLONIUS: Farewell!

[REYNALDO *leaves.*]

[*Enter* OPHELIA.]

                    How now, Ophelia? What's the matter?
OPHELIA: O my lord, my lord, I have been so affrighted!°   *frightened* 75
POLONIUS: With what, in the name of God?
OPHELIA: My lord, as I was sewing in my closet,°   *private room*
Lord Hamlet, with his doublet all unbraced,°   *jacket all loosened*
No hat upon his head, his stockings fouled,°   *twisted*
Ungartered, and down-gyvèd° to his ankle;   *coiled down* 80
Pale as his shirt, his knees knocking each other,
And with a look so piteous in purport°   *meaning*
As if he had been loosèd out of hell
To speak of horrors—he comes before me.
POLONIUS: Mad for thy love?
OPHELIA: My lord, I do not know, 85
But truly I do fear it.
POLONIUS: What said he?
OPHELIA: He took me by the wrist and held me hard;
Then goes he to the length of all his arm,
And, with his other hand thus over his brow,
He falls to such perusal° of my face   *study* 90
As° he would draw it. Long stayed he so.   *as if*
At last, a little shaking of mine arm,
And thrice his head thus waving up and down,
He raised a sigh so piteous and profound
As it did seem to shatter all his bulk 95
And end his being. That done, he lets me go,
And with his head over his shoulder turned
He seemed to find his way without his eyes,
For out of doors he went without their help
And to the last bended their light on me. 100

POLONIUS: Come, go with me. I will go seek the King.
    This is the very ecstasy° of love,   *the true madness*
    Whose violent property° fordoes itself   *quality*
    And leads the will to desperate undertakings
    As oft as any passion under heaven   105
    That does afflict our natures. I am sorry.
    What, have you given him any hard words of late?
OPHELIA: No, my good lord; but, as you did command,
    I did repel° his letters and denied   *reject*
    His access to me.
POLONIUS: That hath made him mad.   110
    I am sorry that with better heed and judgment
    I had not quoted° him. I feared he did but trifle   *observed*
    And meant to wrack° thee; but beshrew° my jealousy!   *ruin/curse*
    By heaven, it is as proper to our age
    To cast beyond ourselves in our opinions   115
    As it is common for the younger sort
    To lack discretion. Come, go we to the King.
    This must be known; which, being kept close,° might move   *if kept secret*
    More grief to hide than hate to utter love.°   *cause more grief to hide love than*
    Come.   *it would cause hate to reveal it*   120

[*They leave.*]

SCENE 2. Elsinore. A room in the Castle.

[*Flourish of trumpets. Enter* KING *and* QUEEN, ROSENCRANTZ, *and* GUILDENSTERN, *and others.*]

KING: Welcome, dear Rosencrantz and Guildenstern.
    Moreover° that we much did long to see you,   *besides*
    The need we have to use you did provoke
    Our hasty sending. Something have you heard
    Of Hamlet's transformation. So I call it,   5
    Sith° nor the exterior nor the inward man   *since*
    Resembles that it was. What it should be,
    More than his father's death, that thus hath put him
    So much from the understanding of himself,
    I cannot dream of. I entreat you both   10
    That, being of so young days° brought up with him,   *from your youngest days*
    And since so neighbored° to his youth and havior,   *so close*
    That you vouchsafe your rest° here in our court   *consent to stay*
    Some little time; so by your companies
    To draw him on to pleasures, and to gather   15
    So much as from occasion you may glean,
    Whether aught to us unknown afflicts him thus
    That, opened,° lies within our remedy.   *when known*
QUEEN: Good gentlemen, he hath much talked of you,
    And sure I am two men there are not living   20
    To whom he more adheres.° If it will please you   *feels closer*

To show us so much gentry° and good will   *courtesy*
As to expend your time with us awhile
For the supply and profit of our hope,°   *so we may gain what we hope for*
Your visitation shall receive such thanks   25
As fits a king's remembrance.
ROSENCRANTZ: Both your Majesties
Might, by the sovereign power you have of us,
Put your dread pleasures° more into command   *wishes that we must treat with awe*
Than to entreaty.°   *polite request*
GUILDSTERN: But we both obey,
And here give up ourselves, in the full bent,°   *to the fullest* 30
To lay our service freely at your feet,
To be commanded.
KING: Thanks, Rosencrantz and gentle Guildenstern.
QUEEN: Thanks, Guildenstern and gentle Rosencrantz.
And I beseech you instantly to visit   35
My too much changed son.—Go, some of you,
And bring these gentlemen where Hamlet is.
GUILDENSTERN: Heavens make our presence and our practices
Pleasant and helpful to him!
QUEEN: Ay, amen!

[ROSENCRANTZ *and* GUILDSTERN *leave, with some attendants.*]

[*Enter* POLONIUS.]

POLONIUS: The ambassadors from Norway, my good lord,   40
Are joyfully returned.
KING: Thou still hast° been the father of good news.   *you always have*
POLONIUS: Have I, my lord? Assure you, my good liege,°   *overlord*
I hold my duty as I hold my soul,
Both to my God and to my gracious king;   45
And I do think—or else this brain of mine
Hunts not the trail of policy° so sure   *statecraft*
As it hath used to do—that I have found
The very cause of Hamlet's lunacy.
KING: O, speak of that! That do I long to hear.   50
POLONIUS: Give first admittance to the ambassadors,
My news shall be the fruit° to that great feast.   *come as dessert*
KING: Thyself do grace to them, and bring them in.

[POLONIUS *leaves.*]

He tells me, my dear Gertrude, he hath found
The head and source of all your son's distemper.°   *disturbed mind* 55
QUEEN: I doubt° it is no other but the main,°   *suspect/chief cause*
His father's death and our overhasty marriage.
KING: Well, we shall sift° him.   *examine*

[*Enter* POLONIUS, VOLTEMAND, *and* CORNELIUS.]

                 Welcome, my good friends.
Say, Voltemand, what from our brother Norway?

VOLTEMAND: Most fair return of greetings and desires.   60
    Upon our first, he sent out to suppress
    His nephew's levies,° which to him appeared   *warlike preparations*
    To be a preparation 'gainst the Polack,°   *against the Poles*
    But better looked into,° he truly found   *when he looked into it*
    It was against your Highness; whereat grieved,   65
    That so his sickness, age, and impotence°   *infirmity*
    Was falsely borne in hand,° sends out arrests°   *deceived/commands*
    On Fortinbras; which he, in brief, obeys,
    Receives rebuke from Norway, and, in fine,°   *finally*
    Makes vow before his uncle never more   70
    To give the assay of arms° against your Majesty.   *make war*
    Whereon old Norway, overcome with joy,
    Gives him three thousand crowns in annual fee°   *payment*
    And his commission to employ those soldiers,
    So levied as before, against the Polack;   75
    With an entreaty, herein further shown,

    [*Gives a paper.*]

    That it might please you to give quiet pass°   *grant the right to pass*
    Through your dominions for this enterprise,
    On such regards° of safety and allowance   *with such assurances*
    As therein are set down.
KING: It likes us well;°   *we like it*   80
    And at our more considered time we'll read,
    Answer, and think upon this business.
    Meantime we thank you for your well-took labor.
    Go to your rest; at night we'll feast together.
    Most welcome home!

                [*Ambassadors leave.*]

POLONIUS: This business is well ended.   85
    My liege, and madam, to expostulate
    What majesty should be, what duty is,
    Why day is day, night night, and time is time,
    Were nothing but to waste night, day, and time.
    Therefore, since brevity is the soul of wit,°   *intelligence*   90
    And tediousness the limbs and outward flourishes,
    I will be brief. Your noble son is mad.
    Mad call I it; for, to define true madness,
    What is't but to be nothing else but mad?
    But let that go.
QUEEN: More matter,° with less art.   *substance*   95
POLONIUS: Madam, I swear I use no art at all.
    That he is mad, 'tis true: 'tis true 'tis pity;
    And pity 'tis 'tis true. A foolish figure!°   *figure of speech*
    But farewell it, for I will use no art.
    Mad let us grant him then. And now remains   100
    That we find out the cause of this effect—
    Or rather say, the cause of this defect,

For this effect defective comes by cause.
Thus it remains, and the remainder thus.
Perpend:°   *listen carefully*   105
I have a daughter (have while she is mine),
Who in her duty and obedience, mark,
Hath given me this. Now gather, and surmise.

[*Reads the letter.*]

  To the celestial, and my soul's idol, the most beautified
    Ophelia,—   110
That's an ill phrase, a vile phrase; "beautified" is a vile phrase.
But you shall hear. Thus:

[*Reads.*]

  In her excellent white bosom, these, etc.
QUEEN: Came this from Hamlet to her?
POLONIUS: Good madam, stay awhile. I will be faithful.°   *patient*   115

[*Reads.*]

  Doubt thou the stars are fire;
    Doubt that the sun doth move;
  Doubt truth to be a liar;
    But never doubt I love.

  O dear Ophelia, I am ill at these numbers;° I have not art to   *not good at verse*   120
reckon my groans; but that I love thee best, O most
best, believe it. Adieu.
      Thine evermore, most dear lady, whilst this machine°   *body*
        is to him, HAMLET.

This, in obedience, hath my daughter shown me;°   *has reported to me*   125
And more above, hath his solicitings,°   *pleas*
As they fell out by time, by means, and place,
All given to mine ear.
KING: But how hath she
  Received his love?
POLONIUS: What do you think of me?
KING: As of a man faithful and honorable.   130
POLONIUS: I would fain° prove so. But what might you think,   *gladly*
  When I had seen this hot love on the wing
  (As I perceived it, I must tell you that,
  Before my daughter told me), what might you,
  Or my dear Majesty your queen here, think,   135
  If I had played the desk or table book,°   *mere passive recorder*
  Or given my heart a winking, mute and dumb,
  Or looked upon this love with idle sight?
  What might you think? No, I went round to work
  And my young mistress thus I did bespeak:°   *lecture*   140
  "Lord Hamlet is a prince, out of thy star.°   *outside your sphere*
  This must not be." And then I precepts gave her,
  That she should lock herself from his resort,°   *company*
  Admit no messengers, receive no tokens.

Which done, she took the fruits of my advice, 145
And he, repulsed, a short tale to make,
Fell into a sadness, then into a fast,
Thence to a watch, thence into a weakness,
Thence to a lightness, and, by this declension,° *downward progression*
Into the madness wherein now he raves, 150
And all we mourn for.
KING: Do you think 'tis this?
QUEEN: It may be, very like.° *very likely*
POLONIUS: Hath there been such a time—I would fain know that—
   That I have positively said "'Tis so,"
   When it proved otherwise?
KING: Not that I know. 155
POLONIUS [*points to his head and shoulder*]: Take this from this, if this
   be otherwise.
   If circumstances lead me, I will find
   Where truth is hid, though it were hid indeed
   Within the center
KING: How may we try° it further? *check*
POLONIUS: You know sometimes he walks four hours together 160
   Here in the lobby.
QUEEN: So he does indeed.
POLONIUS: At such a time I'll loose° my daughter to him. *release*
   Be you and I behind an arras° then. *tapestry curtain*
   Mark the encounter. If he love her not,
   And be not from his reason fallen° thereon, *gone out of his mind* 165
   Let me be no assistant for a state,° *councilor of state*
   But keep a farm and carters.° *drivers of carts*
KING: We will try it.

[*Enter* HAMLET, *reading a book.*]

QUEEN: But look where sadly the poor wretch comes reading.
POLONIUS: Away, I do beseech you, both away!
   I'll board° him presently. O, give me leave. *approach* 170

[KING *and* QUEEN *leave, with attendants.*]

   How does my good Lord Hamlet?
HAMLET: Well, God-a-mercy.
POLONIUS: Do you know me, my lord?
HAMLET: Excellent well. You are a fishmonger.
POLONIUS: Not I, my lord. 175
HAMLET: Then I would you were so honest a man.
POLONIUS: Honest, my lord?
HAMLET: Ay, sir. To be honest, as this world goes, is to be one
   man picked out of ten thousand.
POLONIUS: That's very true, my lord. 180
HAMLET: For if the sun breed maggots in a dead dog, being a
   god kissing carrion—Have you a daughter?
POLONIUS: I have, my lord.
HAMLET: Let her not walk in the sun. Conception is a blessing,
   but not as your daughter may conceive. Friend, look to't. 185

POLONIUS [*aside*]: How say you by that? Still harping on my daughter. Yet he knew me not at first. He said I was a fishmonger. He is far gone, far gone! And truly in my youth I suffered much extremity for love—very near this. I'll speak to him again.—What do you read, my lord? 190

HAMLET: Words, words, words.

POLONIUS: What is the matter, my lord?

HAMLET: Between who?

POLONIUS: I mean, the matter that you read, my lord.

HAMLET: Slanders, sir; for the satirical rogue says here that old 195 men have grey beards; that their faces are wrinkled; their eyes purging° thick amber and plum-tree gum; and that *dripping* they have a plentiful lack of wit, together with most weak hams. All which, sir, though I most powerfully and potently believe, yet I hold it not honesty° to have it thus set *good manners* 200 down; for you yourself, sir, should be old as I am if, like a crab, you could go backward.

POLONIUS [*aside*]: Though this be madness, yet there is method in't.—Will you walk out of the air, my lord?

HAMLET: Into my grave? 205

POLONIUS: Indeed, that is out of the air. [*aside*] How pregnant° sometimes his replies are! a happiness that often *meaningful* madness hits on, which reason and sanity could not so prosperously be delivered of. I will leave him and suddenly contrive the means of meeting between him and my 210 daughter.—My honorable lord, I will most humbly take my leave of you.

HAMLET: You cannot, sir, take from me anything that I will more willingly part withal°—except my life, except my life, *part with* except my life. 215

[*Enter* ROSENCRANTZ *and* GUILDENSTERN.]

POLONIUS: Fare you well, my lord.

HAMLET: These tedious old fools!

POLONIUS: You go to seek the Lord Hamlet. There he is.

ROSENCRANTZ [*to* POLONIUS]: God save you, sir!

[POLONIUS *leaves.*]

GUILDENSTERN: My honored lord! 220

ROSENCRANTZ: My most dear lord!

HAMLET: My excellent good friends! How dost thou, Guildenstern? Ah, Rosencrantz! Good lads, how do ye both?

ROSENCRANTZ: As the indifferent° children of the earth. *ordinary*

GUILDENSTERN: Happy in that we are not over-happy. 225 On Fortune's cap we are not the very button.° *top*

HAMLET: Nor the soles of her shoe?

ROSENCRANTZ: Neither, my lord.

HAMLET: Then you live about her waist, or in the middle of her favors? 230

GUILDENSTERN: Faith, her privates° we. *intimate friends*

HAMLET: In the secret parts of Fortune? O, most true! she is a
strumpet. What news?

ROSENCRANTZ: None, my lord, but that the world's grown
honest. 235

HAMLET: Then is doomsday near! But your news is not true.
Let me question more in particular. What have you, my
good friends, deserved at the hands of Fortune that she
sends you to prison hither?

GUILDENSTERN: Prison, my lord? 240

HAMLET: Denmark's a prison.

ROSENCRANTZ: Then is the world one.

HAMLET: A goodly one; in which there are many confines,°   *cells*
wards, and dungeons, Denmark being one of the worst.

ROSENCRANTZ: We think not so, my lord. 245

HAMLET: Why, then 'tis none to you, for there is nothing either good or bad but thinking makes it so. To me it is a
prison.

ROSENCRANTZ: Why, then your ambition makes it one. 'Tis
too narrow for your mind. 250

HAMLET: O God, I could be bounded in a nutshell and count
myself a king of infinite space, were it not that I have bad
dreams.

GUILDENSTERN: Which dreams indeed are ambition; for the
very substance of the ambitious is merely the shadow of a 255
dream.

HAMLET: A dream itself is but a shadow.

ROSENCRANTZ: Truly, and I hold ambition of so airy and light
a quality that it is but a shadow's shadow.

HAMLET: Then are our beggars bodies, and our monarchs and 260
outstretched heroes the beggars' shadows. Shall we to the
court? for, by my fay,° I cannot reason.   *faith*

BOTH: We'll wait upon you.

HAMLET: No such matter! I will not sort° you with the rest of   *class*
my servants; for, to speak to you like an honest man, I am 265
most dreadfully attended.° But in the beaten way of   *very poorly served*
friendship, what make you at Elsinore?

ROSENCRANTZ: To visit you, my lord; no other occasion.

HAMLET: Beggar that I am, I am even poor in thanks; but I
thank you; and sure, dear friends, my thanks are too dear°   *too dear at (or by)* 270
a halfpenny. Were you not sent for? Is it your own inclin-
ing? Is it a free visitation? Come, deal justly with me.
Come, come! Nay, speak.

GUILDENSTERN: What should we say, my lord?

HAMLET: Why, anything, but to the purpose.° You were sent   *point* 275
for, and there is a kind of confession in your looks, which
your modesties have not craft enough to color.° I know   *not skill enough to disguise*
the good King and Queen have sent for you.

ROSENCRANTZ: To what end, my lord?

HAMLET: That you must teach me. But let me conjure you° by   *plead with you* 280
the rights of our fellowship, by the consonancy° of our   *harmony*
youth, by the obligation of our ever-preserved love, and

by what more dear a better proposer° could charge you *talker*
withal, be even and direct with me, whether you were sent
for or no. 285

ROSENCRANTZ [*aside to* GUILDENSTERN]: What say you?

HAMLET [*aside*]: Nay then, I have an eye of you.° If you love *I am on to you*
me, hold not off.

GUILDENSTERN: My lord, we were sent for.

HAMLET: I will tell you why, so shall my anticipation prevent 290
your discovery,° and your secrecy to the King and Queen *your giving yourself away*
moult no feather.° I have of late—but wherefore I know *not be damaged*
not—lost all my mirth, forgone all custom of exercises;° *all ordinary activities*
and indeed, it goes so heavily with my disposition that this
goodly frame, the earth, seems to me a sterile 295
promontory;° this most excellent canopy, the air, look *barren outcropping*
you, this brave overhanging firmament, this majestical roof
fretted° with golden fire—why, it appeareth no other thing *ornamented*
to me than a foul and pestilent congregation of vapors.
What a piece of work is a man! how noble in reason! how 300
infinite in faculties! in form and moving how express° and *well made*
admirable! in action how like an angel! in apprehension° *understanding*
how like a god! the beauty of the world, the paragon of
animals! And yet to me what is this quintessence° of dust? *ultimate essence*
Man delights not me—no, nor woman neither, though by 305
your smiling you seem to say so.

ROSENCRANTZ: My lord, there was no such stuff in my
thoughts.

HAMLET: Why did you laugh then, when I said "Man delights
not me"? 310

ROSENCRANTZ: To think, my lord, if you delight not in man,
what lenten entertainment° the players shall receive from *meager treatment*
you. We coted° them on the way, and hither are they com- *passed*
ing to offer you service.

HAMLET: He that plays the king shall be welcome—his Majesty 315
shall have tribute of me; the adventurous knight shall use
his foil and target;° the lover shall not sigh gratis; the hu- *sword and shield*
morous man shall end his part in peace; the clown shall
make those laugh whose lungs are tickle o' the sere;° and *quick on the trigger*
the lady shall say her mind freely, or the blank verse shall 320
halt° for't. What players are they? *stumble*

ROSENCRANTZ: Even those you were wont to° take such de- *you used to*
light in, the tragedians of the city.

HAMLET: How chances it they travel? Their residence, both in
reputation and profit, was better both ways. 325

ROSENCRANTZ: I think their inhibition° comes by the means of *their being kept out*
the late innovation.° *recent fad*

HAMLET: Do they hold the same estimation they did when I
was in the city? Are they so followed?

ROSENCRANTZ: No indeed are they not. 330

HAMLET: How comes it? Do they grow rusty?

ROSENCRANTZ: Nay, their endeavor keeps in the wonted° pace; *accustomed*

but there is, sir, an eyrie of children, little eyases,° that cry *bird's brood of shrill little hawks*
out on the top of question and are most tyrannically
clapped° for't. These are now the fashion, and so berattle *wildly applauded* 335
the common stages° (so they call them) that many wearing *put down ordinary theaters*
rapiers are afraid of goosequills° and dare scarce come *fear the playwrights pen*
thither.

HAMLET: What, are they children? Who maintains them? How
are they escoted?° Will they pursue the quality° no longer *supported/play this role* 340
than they can sing? Will they not say afterwards, if they
should grow themselves to common players (as it is most
like, if their means are no better), their writers do them
wrong to make them exclaim against their own
succession?° *future roles* 345

ROSENCRANTZ: Faith, there has been much to do on both
sides; and the nation holds it no sin to tarre them° to con- *egg them on*
troversy. There was, for a while, no money bid for argu-
ment° unless the poet and the player went to cuffs in the *for a new play*
question.° *on this topic* 350

HAMLET: Is't possible?

GUILDENSTERN: O, there has been much throwing about of
brains.

HAMLET: Do the boys carry it away?

ROSENCRANTZ: Ay, that they do, my lord—Hercules and his 355
load° too. *Hercules carrying the globe (as on the Globe theater sign)*

HAMLET: It is not very strange; for my uncle is King of Denmark, and those that would make mows° at him while my *faces*
father lived give twenty, forty, fifty, a hundred ducats
apiece for his picture in little.° 'Sblood,° there is some *miniature portrait/ by God's blood* 360
thing in this more than natural, if philosophy could find it
out.

[*Flourish of trumpets for the* PLAYERS.]

GUILDENSTERN: There are the players.

HAMLET: Gentlemen, you are welcome to Elsinore. Your
hands, come! The appurtenance° of welcome is fashion *usual expression* 365
and ceremony. Let me comply with you in this garb,° lest *treat you in this fashion*
my extent° to the players (which I tell you must show fair- *welcome*
ly outwards) should more appear like entertainment than
yours. You are welcome. But my uncle-father and aunt-
mother are deceived. 370

GUILDENSTERN: In what, my dear lord?

HAMLET: I am but mad north-north-west. When the wind is
southerly I know a hawk from a handsaw.

[*Enter* POLONIUS.]

POLONIUS: Well be with you, gentlemen!

HAMLET: Hark you, Guildenstern—and you too—at each ear a 375
hearer! That great baby you see there is not yet out of his
swaddling clouts.° *diapers*

ROSENCRANTZ: Happily he's the second time come to them; for they say an old man is twice a child.

HAMLET: I will prophesy he comes to tell me of the players. Mark it.—You say right, sir; a Monday morning; 'twas so indeed. 380

POLONIUS: My lord, I have news to tell you.

HAMLET: My lord, I have news to tell you: when Roscius was an actor in Rome— 385

POLONIUS: The actors are come hither, my lord.

HAMLET: Buzz, buzz!

POLONIUS: Upon my honor—

HAMLET: Then came each actor on his ass—

POLONIUS: The best actors in the world, either for tragedy, 390 comedy, history, pastoral, pastoral-comical, historical-pastoral, tragical-historical, tragical-comical-historical-pastoral; scene individable, or poem unlimited.° Seneca *plays classical or irregular* cannot be too heavy, nor Plautus° too light. For the law of *(Roman playwrights)* writ and the liberty, these are the only men. 395

HAMLET: O Jephthah,° judge of Israel, what a treasure hadst *(a biblical figure)* thou!

POLONIUS: What a treasure had he, my lord?

HAMLET: Why,

> One fair daughter, and no more, 400
> The which he loved passing well.

POLONIUS [*aside*]: Still on my daughter.

HAMLET: Am I not in the right, old Jephthah?

POLONIUS: If you call me Jephthah, my lord, I have a daughter that I love passing well. 405

HAMLET: Nay, that follows not.

POLONIUS: What follows then, my lord?

HAMLET: Why,

> As by lot, God wot,

and then, you know, 410

> It came to pass, as most like it was.

The first row° of the pious chanson will show you more; *stanza* for look where my abridgement° comes. *interruption*

[*Enter four or five* PLAYERS.]

You are welcome, masters; welcome, all.—I am glad to see thee well.—Welcome, good friends.—O, my old friend? 415 Why, thy face is valanced° since I saw thee last. Com'st *fringed* thou to beard me in Denmark?—What, my young lady and mistress? By'r Lady,° your ladyship is nearer to heaven *by Our lady* than when I saw you last by the altitude of a chopine.° *the length of high heels* Pray God your voice, like a piece of uncurrent gold,° be *defective coin* 420 not cracked° within the ring.—Masters, you are all wel- *do not crack (or change)* come. We'll even to't° like French falconers, fly at any- *we'll go to it*

thing we see. We'll have a speech straight. Come, give us a
taste of your quality.° Come, a passionate speech.   *talent*

1. PLAYER: What speech, my good lord?   425

HAMLET: I heard thee speak me a speech once, but it was never
acted; or if it was, not above once; for the play, I remem-
ber, pleased not the million, 'twas caviary to the general;°   *too choice for the many*
but it was (as I received it, and others, whose judgments
in such matters cried in the top of mine)° an excellent   *outweighed mine*   430
play, well digested° in the scenes, set down with as much   *arranged*
modesty as cunning.° I remember one said there were no   *moderation as skill*
sallets° in the lines to make the matter savory, nor no mat-   *coarse jokes*
ter in the phrase that might indict the author of affecta-
tion; but called it an honest method, as wholesome as   435
sweet, and by very much more handsome than fine. One
speech in it I chiefly loved. 'Twas Æneas' tale to Dido,
and thereabout of it especially where he speaks of Priam's
slaughter. If it live in your memory, begin at this line—let
me see, let me see: 440

  The rugged Pyrrhus, like the Hyrcanian beast°—   *Asian tiger*

'Tis not so; it begins with Pyrrhus:

  The rugged Pyrrhus, he whose sable arms,°   *black-hued armor*
  Black as his purpose, did the night resemble
  When he lay crouched in the ominous horse,°   *hidden in the wooden Trojan horse*   445
  Hath now this dread and black complexion smeared
  With heraldry more dismal. Head to foot
  Now is he total gules,° horridly tricked   *heraldic red*
  With blood of fathers, mothers, daughters, sons,
  Baked and impasted with the parching° streets,   *fire-parched*   450
  That lend a tyrannous and a damned light
  To their lord's murder. Roasted in wrath and fire,
  And thus oversized with coagulate gore,°   *smeared with clotted gore*
  With eyes like carbuncles,° the hellish Pyrrhus   *fiery-red stones*
  Old grandsire Priam seeks.   455

So, proceed you.

POLONIUS: Fore God, my lord, well spoken, with good accent
and good discretion.

1. PLAYER: *Anon he finds him,*
  Striking too short at Greeks. His antique sword,   460
  Rebellious to his arm, lies where it falls,
  Repugnant to command.° Unequal matched,   *refusing obedience*
  Pyrrhus at Priam drives, in rage strikes wide;
  But with the whiff and wind of his fell° sword   *deadly*
  The unnerved father falls. Then senseless Ilium,°   *the unfeeling city*   465
  Seeming to feel this blow, with flaming top°   *with a tower on fire*
  Stoops to his base,° and with a hideous crash   *crashes to its base*
  Takes prisoner° Pyrrhus' ear. For lo! his sword,   *distracts*
  Which was declining on the milky° head   *milk-white*
  Of reverend Priam, seemed in the air to stick.   470

So, as a painted tyrant, Pyrrhus stood,
And, like a neutral to° his will and matter,　　　　　　　*as if detached from*
Did nothing.
But, as we often see, against some storm,
A silence in the heavens, the rack° stand still,　　　　　*threatening clouds*　475
The bold winds speechless, and the orb below
As hush as death—anon the dreadful thunder
Doth rend the region; so, after Pyrrhus' pause,
Aroused vengeance sets him new awork;
And never did the Cyclops' hammers fall　　　　　　　　　　　　480
On Mars's armor, forged for proof eterne,°　　　　　*made to last forever*
With less remorse than Pyrrhus' bleeding sword
Now falls on Priam.
Out, out, thou strumpet Fortune! All you gods,
In general synod° take away her power;　　　　　　　　　*council*　485
Break all the spokes and fellies° from her wheel,　　　　　*outer rim*
And bowl the round nave° down the hill of heaven,　　　　　*hub*
As low as to the fiends!

POLONIUS: This is too long.

HAMLET: It shall to the barber's, with your beard.—Prithee say　490
　　on. He's for a jig or a tale of bawdry, or he sleeps.° Say on;　*or else he falls asleep*
　　come to Hecuba.

1. PLAYER: *But who, O who, had seen the mobled° queen—*　　　　*veiled*

HAMLET: "The mobled queen"?

POLONIUS: That's good! "Mobled queen" is good.　　　　　　　　495

1. PLAYER: *Run barefoot up and down, threatening the flames*
　　　　　With bisson rheum;° a clout° upon that head　　*blinding tears/rag*
　　　　　Where late the diadem stood, and for a robe,
　　　　　About her lank and all overteemed° loins,　　*worn out from childbirth*
　　　　　A blanket, in the alarm of fear caught up—　　　　　　　　500
　　　　　Who this had seen, with tongue in venom steeped
　　　　　'Gainst Fortune's state would treason have pronounced.
　　　　　But if the gods themselves did see her then,
　　　　　When she saw Pyrrhus make malicious sport
　　　　　In mincing with his sword her husband's limbs,　　　　　　505
　　　　　The instant burst of clamor that she made
　　　　　(Unless things mortal move them not at all)
　　　　　Would have made milch° the burning eyes of heaven　　*moist with the milk of tears*
　　　　　And passion in the gods.

POLONIUS: Look, whether he has not turned his color, and has　510
　　tears in his eyes. Prithee no more!

HAMLET: 'Tis well. I'll have thee speak out the rest of this
　　soon.—Good my lord, will you see the players well be-
　　stowed?° Do you hear? Let them be well used; for they are　*accommodated*
　　the abstract° and brief chronicles of the time. After your　*summary*　515
　　death you were better have a bad epitaph than their ill re-
　　port while you live.

POLONIUS: My lord, I will use them according to their desert.

HAMLET: God's bodykins, man, much better! Use every man
   after his desert, and who should scape whipping? Use   520
   them after your own honor and dignity. The less they deserve, the more merit is in your bounty.° Take them in.   *generosity*
POLONIUS: Come, sirs.
HAMLET: Follow him, friends. We'll hear a play tomorrow.

        [POLONIUS *and* PLAYERS *(except the first) leave.*]

   Dost thou hear me, old friend? Can you play "The Mur-   525
   der of Gonzago"?
1. PLAYER: Ay, my lord.
HAMLET: We'll have it tomorrow night. You could, for a need,
   study a speech of some dozen or sixteen lines which I
   would set down and insert in it, could you not?   530
1. PLAYER: Ay, my lord.
HAMLET: Very well. Follow that lord—and look you mock him
   not. [*First* PLAYER *leaves. To* ROSENCRANTZ.] My good
   friends, I'll leave you till night. You are welcome to Elsinore.   535
ROSENCRANTZ: Good my lord!
HAMLET: Ay, so, Good bye to you.

        [ROSENCRANTZ *and* GUILDENSTERN *leave.*]

        Now I am alone.
   O, what a rogue and peasant slave am I!
   Is it not monstrous that this player here,
   But in a fiction, in a dream of passion,   540
   Could force his soul so to his own conceit°   *imagination*
   That, from her working, all his visage wanned,°   *his face paled*
   Tears in his eyes, distraction in's aspect,°   *in his looks*
   A broken voice, and his whole function suiting
   With forms to his conceit? And all for nothing!   545
   For Hecuba!
   What's Hecuba to him, or he to Hecuba,
   That he should weep for her? What would he do,
   Had he the motive and the cue for passion
   That I have? He would drown the stage with tears   550
   And cleave the general ear° with horrid speech;   *split everyone's ear*
   Make mad the guilty and appal the free,°   *innocent*
   Confound the ignorant, and amaze indeed
   The very faculties of eyes and ears.
   Yet I,   555
   A dull and muddy-mettled° rascal, peak°   *weak-souled/mope*
   Like John-a-dreams, unpregnant of° my cause,   *unmoved by*
   And can say nothing! No, not for a king,
   Upon whose property and most dear life
   A damned defeat was made.° Am I a coward?   *inflicted* 560
   Who calls me villain? breaks my pate across?°   *cudgels my head*
   Plucks off my beard and blows it in my face?
   Tweaks me by the nose? gives me the lie in the throat°   *calls me a liar*

As deep as to the lungs? Who does me this, ha?
'Swounds,° I should take it! for it cannot be   *by God's wounds*   565
But I am pigeon-livered and lack gall
To make oppression bitter, or ere this°   *before now*
I should have fatted all the region kites°   *the vultures in the air*
With this slave's offal.° Bloody, bawdy, villain!   *rotting scraps*
Remorseless, treacherous, lecherous, kindless° villain!   *unnatural*   570
O, vengeance!
Why, what an ass am I! This is most brave,
That I, the son of a dear father murdered,
Prompted to my revenge by heaven and hell,
Must (like a whore) unpack my heart with words   575
And fall a-cursing like a very drab,°   *a true harlot*
A scullion!°   *kitchen wench*
Fie upon't! foh! About, my brain! I have heard
That guilty creatures, sitting at a play,
Have by the very cunning° of the scene   *ingenious arrangement*   580
Been struck so to the soul that presently
They have proclaimed their malefactions;°   *crimes*
For murder, though it have no tongue, will speak
With most miraculous organ. I'll have these players
Play something like the murder of my father   585
Before mine uncle. I'll observe his looks,
I'll tent° him to the quick; if he but blench,°   *test/turn pale*
I know my course. The spirit that I have seen
May be a devil; and the devil hath power
To assume a pleasing shape; yea, and perhaps   590
Out of my weakness and my melancholy,
As he is very potent with such spirits,°   *knows how to exploit such traits*
Abuses° me to damn me. I'll have grounds   *deceives*
More relative° than this. The play's the thing   *relevant*
Wherein I'll catch the conscience of the King.   595

[He leaves.]

THE RECEPTIVE READER

1. (Acts 1 and 2) One reviewer described the Claudius in a new production as a king "who is disturbed, dishonest, and yet an ordinary respectable and sensual stuffed-shirt politician" (Harold Clurman). What in Claudius' talk and behavior in the first two acts lives up to this billing? What image do we get of him in his dealings with Laertes, Polonius, Hamlet? How formidable an *antagonist* does he present for Hamlet?

2. (Act 2, Scene 1) Here and earlier, how silly or pompous, or how worthy of at least some respect, does Polonius seem to you? What kind of father is he for Laertes and Ophelia? How weak and submissive is Ophelia? Does she have any good lines?

3. (Act 2, Scene 2) In this scene, Hamlet starts his fencing and sparring with those in the service of the king. Is there a pattern in Hamlet's baiting of Polonius? (What makes Polonius say, "Though this be madness, yet there is method in't"?) ✧ How does Hamlet deal with Rosencrantz and Guildenstern? Of what does he accuse them? ✧ Hamlet's "I have of late" speech is seen by many as a major *thematic* passage. What are the polarities that help structure the speech? What is the keynote? How or

why could this speech be seen as central to the play as a whole? ◇ Polonius serves as *foil* in Hamlet's dealings with the players. What side of Hamlet's character does his relationship with the actors bring out? ◇ What do we learn here and in Act 3, Scene 2, indirectly about Shakespeare's views about the theater? ◇ The concluding "O what a rogue and peasant slave" *soliloquy* is prime evidence for critics debating the question of Hamlet's delay or hesitation in pursuing his revenge. What occasions this speech? What is the keynote or prevailing tone? Does it lead anywhere? ◇ How does the apparent digression of Hamlet's dealing with the players relate to the main business of the play?

ACT THREE

SCENE 1. Elsinore. A room in the Castle.

[*Enter* KING, QUEEN, POLONIUS, OPHELIA, ROSENCRANTZ, GUILDENSTERN, *and lords.*]

KING: And can you by no drift of circumstance°		*roundabout talk*
Get from him why he puts on this confusion,°		*acts in this disturbed fashion*
Grating so harshly all his days of quiet		
With turbulent and dangerous lunacy?		
ROSENCRANTZ: He does confess he feels himself distracted,		5
But from what cause he will by no means speak.		
GUILDENSTERN: Nor do we find him forward to be sounded,°		*willing to be found out*
But with a crafty madness keeps aloof		
When we would bring him on to some confession		
Of his true state.		
QUEEN: Did he receive you well?		10
ROSENCRANTZ: Most like a gentleman.		
GUILDENSTERN: But with much forcing of his disposition.°		*strained politeness*
ROSENCRANTZ: Niggard of question,° but of our demands		*asking few questions*
Most free in his reply.°		*answering freely*
QUEEN: Did you assay° him		*invite*
To any pastime?		15
ROSENCRANTZ: Madam, it so fell out that certain players		
We overraught° on the way. Of these we told him,		*overtook*
And there did seem in him a kind of joy		
To hear of it. They are here about the court,		
And, as I think, they have already order		20
This night to play before him.		
POLONIUS: 'Tis most true;		
And he beseeched me to entreat your Majesties		
To hear and see the matter.		
KING: With all my heart, and it doth much content me		
To hear him so inclined.		25
Good gentlemen, give him a further edge		
And drive his purpose on to these delights.		
ROSENCRANTZ: We shall, my lord.		

[ROSENCRANTZ *and* GUILDENSTERN *leave.*]

KING: Sweet Gertrude, leave us too;
    For we have closely sent for Hamlet hither,
    That he, as 'twere by accident, may here   30
    Affront° Ophelia.   *encounter*
    Her father and myself (lawful espials)°   *spies in a good cause*
    Will so bestow ourselves that, seeing unseen,
    We may of their encounter frankly judge
    And gather° by him, as he is behaved,   *make up our minds*   35
    If't be the affliction of his love, or no,
    That thus he suffers for.
QUEEN: I shall obey you;
    And for your part, Ophelia, I do wish
    That your good beauties be the happy cause
    Of Hamlet's wildness. So shall I hope your virtues   40
    Will bring him to his wonted way° again,   *normal state*
    To both your honors.
OPHELIA: Madam, I wish it may.

                                    [QUEEN *leaves.*]

POLONIUS: Ophelia, walk you here.—Gracious, so please you,
    We will bestow ourselves.°—[*To* OPHELIA.] Read on this book,   *take up our posts*
    That show of such an exercise may color°   *may serve as an excuse for*   45
    Your loneliness.—We are oft to blame in this,
    'Tis too much proved, that with devotion's visage°   *with the façade of religion*
    And pious action we do sugar over
    The devil himself.
KING [*aside*]:   O,'tis too true!
    How smart a lash that speech doth give my conscience!   50
    The harlot's cheek, beautied with plastering art,
    Is not more ugly to the thing that helps it
    Than is my deed to my most painted word.
    O heavy burden!
POLONIUS: I hear him coming. Let's withdraw, my lord.   55

                        [KING *and* POLONIUS *leave.*]

    [*Enter* HAMLET.]

HAMLET: To be, or not to be, that is the question:
    Whether 'tis nobler in the mind to suffer
    The slings and arrows of outrageous fortune
    Or to take arms against a sea of troubles,
    And by opposing end them.° To die—to sleep—   *end them by fighting them*   60
    No more; and by a sleep to say we end
    The heartache, and the thousand natural shocks
    That flesh is heir to. 'Tis a consummation°   *crowning end result*
    Devoutly to be wished. To die—to sleep.
    To sleep—perchance to dream: ay, there's the rub!°   *that's what stops us*   65
    For in that sleep of death what dreams may come
    When we have shuffled off this mortal coil,°   *shell*

Must give us pause. There's the respect
That makes calamity of so long life.°   *makes misery so long-lived*
For who would bear the whips and scorns of time,   70
The oppressor's wrong, the proud man's contumely,°   *contempt*
The pangs of despised love, the law's delay,
The insolence of office, and the spurns°   *abuses*
That patient merit of the unworthy takes,
When he himself might his quietus° make   *ending for good*   75
With a bare bodkin?° Who would fardels° bear,   *dagger/burdens*
To grunt and sweat under a weary life,
But that the dread of something after death—
The undiscovered country, from whose bourn°   *border*
No traveler returns—puzzles the will,   80
And makes us rather bear those ills° we have   *evils*
Than fly to others that we know not of?
Thus conscience does make cowards of us all,
And thus the native hue of resolution
Is sicklied over° with the pale cast of thought,   *made to look sick*   85
And enterprises of great pitch and moment°   *great force and impact*
With this regard° their currents turn awry   *because of this*
And lose the name of action.—Soft you now!°   *now let me be quiet*
The fair Ophelia!—Nymph, in thy orisons°   *prayers*
Be all my sins remembered.

OPHELIA: Good my lord,   90
How does your honor for this many a day?

HAMLET: I humbly thank you; well, well, well.

OPHELIA: My lord, I have remembrances of yours°   *souvenirs from you*
That I have longed long to redeliver.
I pray you, now receive them.

HAMLET: No, not I!   95
I never gave you aught.°   *anything*

OPHELIA: My honored lord, you know right well you did,
And with them words of so sweet breath composed
As made the things more rich. Their perfume lost,
Take these again; for to the noble mind   100
Rich gifts wax poor when givers prove unkind.°   *turn cheap*
There, my lord.

HAMLET: Ha, ha! Are you honest?°   *virtuous*

OPHELIA: My lord?

HAMLET: Are you fair?°   *beautiful*   105

OPHELIA: What means your lordship?

HAMLET: That if you be honest and fair, your honesty should
admit no discourse to° your beauty.   *should not talk to*

OPHELIA: Could beauty, my lord, have better commerce than
with honesty?   110

HAMLET: Ay, truly; for the power of beauty will sooner trans-
form honesty from what it is to a bawd° than the force of   *turn virtue into vice*
honesty can translate beauty into his likeness. This was
sometime a paradox, but now the time gives it proof. I did
love you once.   115

OPHELIA: Indeed, my lord, you made me believe so.

HAMLET: You should not have believed me; for virtue cannot so inoculate our old stock but we shall relish of it.° I loved you not. *so change our sinful nature that we no longer show it*

OPHELIA: I was the more deceived. 120

HAMLET: Get thee to a nunnery! Why wouldst thou be a breeder of sinners? I am myself indifferent honest,° but yet *fairly virtuous* I could accuse me of such things that it were better my mother had not borne me. I am very proud, revengeful, ambitious; with more offenses at my beck than I have 125 thoughts to put them in, imagination to give them shape, or time to act them in. What should such fellows as I do, crawling between earth and heaven? We are arrant knaves° *utter villains* all; believe none of us. Go thy ways to a nunnery. Where's your father? 130

OPHELIA: At home, my lord.

HAMLET: Let the doors be shut upon him, that he may play the fool nowhere but in's own house. Farewell.

OPHELIA: O, help him, you sweet heavens!

HAMLET: If thou dost marry, I'll give thee this plague° for thy *curse* 135 dowry: be thou as chaste as ice, as pure as snow, thou shalt not escape calumny. Get thee to a nunnery. Go, farewell. Or if thou wilt needs° marry, marry a fool; for wise men *if you absolutely want to* know well enough what monsters you make of them. To a nunnery, go; and quickly too. Farewell. 140

OPHELIA: O heavenly powers, restore him!

HAMLET: I have heard of your paintings° too, well enough. *makeup* God hath given you one face, and you make yourselves an- other. You jig, you amble, and you lisp; you nickname° *give fancy names to* God's creatures and make your wantonness your igno- 145 rance.° Go to, I'll no more on't! it hath made me mad. I *pretend you act wanton* say, we will have no more marriages. Those that are mar- *from ignorance* ried already—all but one—shall live; the rest shall keep as they are. To a nunnery, go.

[*He leaves.*]

OPHELIA: O, what a noble mind is here o'erthrown! 150
The courtier's, soldier's, scholar's, eye, tongue, sword,
The expectancy° and rose of the fair state, *hope*
The glass of fashion and the mould of form,
The observed of all observers—quite, quite down!
And I, of ladies most deject° and wretched, *dejected* 155
That sucked the honey of his music vows,
Now see that noble and most sovereign reason,
Like sweet bells jangled, out of tune and harsh;
That unmatched form and feature of blown youth° *youth in full bloom*
Blasted with ecstasy.° O, woe is me *ruined by madness* 160
To have seen what I have seen, see what I see!

[*Enter* KING *and* POLONIUS.]

KING: Love? his affections do not that way tend;
　　Nor what he spoke, though it lacked form a little,
　　Was not like madness. There's something in his soul
　　Over which his melancholy sits on brood°　　　　　　　*brooding*　165
　　And I do doubt the hatch and the disclose°　　*I fear the hatching and disclosure*
　　Will be some danger, which for to prevent,　　　*(of what was inside)*
　　I have in quick determination
　　Thus set it down: he shall with speed to England
　　For the demand of our neglected tribute.°　　*tribute due but in arrears*　170
　　Haply° the seas, and countries different,　　　　　　　*perhaps*
　　With variable objects, shall expel
　　This something°-settled matter in his heart,　　　　*somewhat*
　　Whereon his brains still beating puts him thus
　　From fashion of himself.° What think you on't?　　*beside himself*　175
POLONIUS: It shall do well. But yet do I believe
　　The origin and commencement of his grief
　　Sprung from neglected love. How now, Ophelia?
　　You need not tell us what Lord Hamlet said,
　　We heard it all. My lord, do as you please;　　　　　　　　　　180
　　But if you hold it fit, after the play
　　Let his queen mother all alone entreat him
　　To show his grief. Let her be round° with him;　　　　*open*
　　And I'll be placed, so please you, in the ear°　　*within earshot*
　　Of all their conference.° If she find him not,°　*talk/not find out about him*　185
　　To England send him; or confine him where
　　Your wisdom best shall think.
KING:　　　　　　　　　　It shall be so.
　　Madness in great ones must not unwatched go.

[They leave.]

SCENE 2. Elsinore. A hall in the Castle.

　[Enter HAMLET and three of the PLAYERS.]

HAMLET: Speak the speech, I pray you, as I pronounced it to
　　you, trippingly on the tongue. But if you mouth it, as
　　many of our players do, I had as lief° the town crier spoke　　*as soon*
　　my lines. Nor do not saw the air too much with your
　　hand, thus, but use all gently; for in the very torrent, tem-　　　　5
　　pest, and (as I may say) whirlwind of your passion, you
　　must acquire and beget a temperance that may give it
　　smoothness. O, it offends me to the soul to hear a robus-
　　tious periwig-pated° fellow tear a passion to tatters, to very　*boisterous bewigged*
　　rags, to split the ears of the groundlings, who (for the　　　　　　10
　　most part) are capable of° nothing but inexplicable dumb　　*who can take in*
　　shows° and noise. I would have such a fellow whipped for　　*mimed action*
　　overdoing Termagant. It out-herods Herod.° Pray you　*(bombastic stage characters)*
　　avoid it.
PLAYER: I warrant your honor.°　　　　　　　　　　*I promise it*　15
HAMLET: Be not too tame neither; but let your own discretion

be your tutor. Suit the action to the word, the word to the
action; with this special observance,° that you o'erstep not   *rule*
the modesty of nature: for anything so overdone is from
the purpose of playing, whose end, both at the first and   20
now, was and is, to hold, as 'twere, the mirror up to nature; to show virtue her own feature, scorn her own
image, and the very age and body of the time his form and
pressure. Now this overdone, or come tardy off,° though   *be badly done*
it make the unskilful° laugh, cannot but make the judi-   *uneducated*   25
cious grieve; the censure of the which one must in your al-
lowance° overweigh a whole theater of others. O, there be   *judgment*
players that I have seen play, and heard others praise, and
that highly (not to speak it profanely),° that, neither hav-   *speaking without offense*
ing the accent of Christians, nor the gait of Christian,   30
pagan, nor man, have so strutted and bellowed that I have
thought some of Nature's journeymen° had made men,   *day laborers*
and not made them well, they imitated humanity so
abominably.

PLAYER: I hope we have reformed that indifferently° with us,   *fairly well*   35
   sir.

HAMLET: O, reform it altogether! And let those that play your
   clowns speak no more than is set down for them. For
   there be of them that will themselves laugh, to set on
   some quantity of barren spectators to laugh too, though in   40
   the mean time some necessary question of the play be then
   to be considered. That's villainous and shows a most pitiful ambition in the fool that uses it. Go make you ready.

                        [*The* PLAYERS *leave.*]

[*Enter* POLONIUS, ROSENCRANTZ, *and* GUILDENSTERN.]

   How now, my lord? Will the King hear this piece of work?
POLONIUS: And the Queen too, and that presently.   45
HAMLET: Bid the players make haste. [POLONIUS *leaves.*] Will
   you two help to hasten them?
BOTH: We will, my lord.

                              [*Both leave.*]

HAMLET: What, ho, Horatio!

[*Enter* HORATIO.]

HORATIO: Here, sweet lord, at your service.   *you are indeed*   50
HAMLET: Horatio, thou art even° as just a man   *as I have ever met*
   As ever my conversation coped withal.°
HORATIO: O, my dear lord!
HAMLET: Nay, do not think I flatter;
   For what advancement may I hope from thee,
   That no revenue° hast but thy good spirits   *income*   55
   To feed and clothe thee? Why should the poor be flattered?
   No, let the candied tongue lick absurd pomp,
   And crook the pregnant° hinges of the knee   *bend the willing*

Where thrift may follow° fawning. Dost thou hear?   *profit may result from*
Since my dear soul was mistress of her choice   60
And could of men distinguish, her election°   *choice*
Hath sealed thee for herself.° For thou hast been   *has singled you out*
As one, in suffering all, that suffers nothing;
A man that Fortune's buffets° and rewards   *blows*
Hast taken with equal thanks; and blest are those   65
Whose blood and judgment° are so well commingled   *passion and reason*
That they are not a pipe for Fortune's finger
To sound what stop she please.° Give me that man   *(as on a flute)*
That is not passion's slave, and I will wear him
In my heart's core, ay, in my heart of heart,   70
As I do thee. Something too much of this.
There is a play tonight before the King.
One scene of it comes near the circumstance,°   *parallels the details*
Which I have told thee, of my father's death.
I prithee, when thou seest that act afoot,   75
Even with the very comment of thy soul
Observe my uncle. If his occulted° guilt   *hidden*
Do not itself unkennel in° one speech,   *reveal itself during*
It is a damnèd ghost that we have seen,
And my imaginations are as foul°   *dark and dirty*   80
As Vulcan's stithy.° Give him heedful note;   *the divine blacksmith's workshop*
For I mine eyes will rivet to his face,
And after we will both our judgments join
In censure of his seeming.°   *to judge his behavior*
HORATIO: Well, my lord.
If he steal aught the whilst this play is playing,   85
And scape detecting, I will pay the theft.°   *pay for the stolen item*

[*Flourish of trumpets. Trumpets and kettledrums play a
Danish march. Enter* KING, QUEEN, POLONIUS, OPHELIA,
ROSENCRANTZ, GUILDENSTERN, *and other lords, with the*
KING'S *guard carrying torches.*]

HAMLET: They are coming to the play: I must be idle.° Get   *play the fool*
   you a place.
KING: How fares our cousin Hamlet?
HAMLET: Excellent, in faith, of the chameleon's dish:° I eat   *food*   90
   the air, promise-crammed. You cannot feed capons so.
KING: I have nothing with this answer, Hamlet. These words
   are not mine.
HAMLET: No, nor mine now. [*to* POLONIUS] My lord, you
   played once i' the university, you say?   95
POLONIUS: That did I, my lord, and was accounted a good
   actor.
HAMLET: What did you enact?
POLONIUS: I did enact Julius Caesar; I was killed in the Capi-
   tol; Brutus killed me.   100
HAMLET: It was a brute part of him to kill so capital° a calf   *outstanding*
   there. Be the players ready?

ROSENCRANTZ: Ay, my lord. They stay upon your patience.° *await your permission*

QUEEN: Come hither, my dear Hamlet, sit by me.

HAMLET: No, good mother, here's metal more attractive.° *magnetic* 105

POLONIUS [*aside to the* KING]: O, ho! do you mark that?

HAMLET [*to* OPHELIA]: Lady, shall I lie in your lap?

OPHELIA: No, my lord.

HAMLET: I mean, my head upon your lap?

OPHELIA: Ay, my lord. 110

HAMLET: Do you think I meant country matters?° *rustic horseplay*

OPHELIA: I think nothing, my lord.

HAMLET: That's a fair thought to lie between maids' legs.

OPHELIA: What is, my lord?

HAMLET: Nothing. 115

OPHELIA: You are merry, my lord.

HAMLET: Who, I?

OPHELIA: Ay, my lord.

HAMLET: O God, your only jig-maker! What should a man do but be merry? For look you how cheerfully my mother 120 looks, and my father died within 's two hours.° *no more than two hours ago*

OPHELIA: Nay, 'tis twice two months, my lord.

HAMLET: So long? Nay then, let the devil wear black, for I'll have a suit of sables.° O heavens! die two months ago, and *of rich dark cloth and fur* not forgotten yet? Then there's hope a great man's memo- 125 ry may outlive his life half a year. But, by'r Lady, he must build churches then; or else shall he suffer not thinking on,° with the hobby-horse, whose epitaph is "For O, for *not being remembered* O, the hobby-horse is forgot!"

[*Oboes play. The dumb show enters: Enter a King and a Queen very lovingly; the Queen embracing him. She kneels, and makes show of protestation unto him. He takes her up, and declines his head upon her neck. He lays him down upon a bank of flowers. She, seeing him asleep, leaves him. Anon comes in a fellow, takes off his crown, kisses it, pours poison in the King's ears, and exits. The Queen returns, finds the King dead, and makes passionate action. The Poisoner, with some two or three Mutes, comes in again, seeming to lament with her. The dead body is carried away. The Poisoner woos the Queen with gifts; she seems loath and unwilling awhile, but in the end accepts his love.*]

[*They leave.*]

OPHELIA: What means this, my lord? 130

HAMLET: Marry, this is miching malicho;° it means mischief. *bad trouble*

OPHELIA: Belike° this show imports the argument° of the play. *probably/summarizes the action*

[*Enter* PROLOGUE.]

HAMLET: We shall know by this fellow.° The players cannot *from what he says* keep counsel; they'll tell all.

OPHELIA: Will he tell us what this show meant? 135

HAMLET: Ay, or any show that you'll show him. Be not you ashamed to show, he'll not shame to tell you what it means.

OPHELIA: You are naught,° you are naught! I'll mark° the play.   *wicked/pay attention to*
PROLOGUE: *For us, and for our tragedy,*   140
    Here stooping to your clemency,
    We beg your hearing patiently.

[*Leaves.*]

HAMLET: Is this a prologue, or the posy° of a ring?   *inscription*
OPHELIA: 'Tis brief, my lord.
HAMLET: As woman's love.   145

[*Enter two* PLAYERS *as King and Queen.*]

PLAYER KING: *Full thirty times hath Phoebus' cart gone round*
    Neptune's salt wash and Tellus' orbed ground,°   *the ocean and the round earth*
    And thirty dozen moons with borrowed sheen
    About the world have times twelve thirties been,
    Since love our hearts, and Hymen° did our hands,   *(god of marriage)*   150
    Unite comutual° in most sacred bands.   *mutually*
PLAYER QUEEN: *So many journeys may the sun and moon*
    Make us again count over ere love be done!
    But woe is me! you are so sick of late,
    So far from cheer and from your former state,   155
    That I distrust you.° Yet, though I distrust,   *I fear for you*
    Discomfort you, my lord, it nothing must;
    For women's fear and love holds quantity,°   *go together*
    In neither aught, or in extremity.°   *either nonexistent or extreme*
    Now what my love is, proof hath made you know;   160
    And as my love is sized, my fear is so.
    Where love is great, the littlest doubts are fear;
    Where little fears grow great, great love grows there.
PLAYER KING: *Faith, I must leave thee, love, and shortly too;*
    My operant° powers their functions leave to do.°   *vital/cease to do*   165
    And thou shalt live in this fair world behind,
    Honored, beloved, and haply one as kind
    For husband shalt thou—
PLAYER QUEEN: *O, confound the rest!*
    Such love must needs be treason in my breast.
    In second husband let me be accurst!   170
    None wed the second but who killed the first.
HAMLET [*aside*]: Wormwood, wormwood!°   *a bitter potion*
PLAYER QUEEN: *The instances that second marriage move°*   *the motives for marrying again*
    Are base respects of thrift,° but none of love.   *thoughts of property*
    A second time I kill my husband dead   175
    When second husband kisses me in bed.
PLAYER KING: *I do believe you think what now you speak;*
    But what we do determine oft we break.
    Purpose is but the slave to memory,
    Of violent birth, but poor validity;   180
    Which now, like fruit unripe, sticks on the tree,
    But fall unshaken when they mellow be.
    Most necessary 'tis that we forget

To pay ourselves what to ourselves is debt.
What to ourselves in passion we propose,   185
The passion ending, doth the purpose lose.
The violence of either grief or joy
Their own enactures° with themselves destroy.   *acts*
Where joy most revels, grief doth most lament;
Grief joys, joy grieves, on slender accident.   190
This world is not for aye,° nor 'tis not strange   *forever*
That even our loves should with our fortunes change;
For 'tis a question left us yet to prove,
Whether love lead fortune, or else fortune love.
The great man down, you mark his favorite flies,°   *his protégé abandons him*   195
The poor advanced makes° friends of enemies;   *when the poor succeed, they make*
And hitherto doth love on fortune tend,
For who not needs° shall never lack a friend,   *who is not in need*
And who in want a hollow friend doth try,
Directly seasons° him his enemy.   *immediately makes*   200
But, orderly to end where I begun,
Our wills and fates do so contrary run
That our devices° still are overthrown;   *plans*
Our thoughts are ours, their ends none of our own.
So think thou wilt no second husband wed;   205
But die thy thoughts° when thy first lord is dead.   *your intentions will change*

PLAYER QUEEN: *Nor earth° to me give food, nor heaven light,*   *let the earth not . . .*
Sport and repose lock from me day and night,
To desperation turn my trust and hope,
An anchor's cheer in prison be my scope,°   *let a hermit's fare be my portion*   210
Each opposite that blanks the face of joy
Meet what I would have well, and it destroy,
Both here and hence pursue me lasting strife,
If, once a widow, ever I be wife!

HAMLET: If she should break it now!   215

PLAYER KING: *'Tis deeply sworn. Sweet, leave me here awhile.*
My spirits grow dull, and fain I would beguile
The tedious day with sleep.

PLAYER QUEEN: *Sleep rock thy brain,*

[*He sleeps.*]

And never come mischance between us twain!

[*She leaves.*]

HAMLET: Madam, how like you this play?   220
QUEEN: The lady doth protest° too much, methinks.   *advertise her feelings*
HAMLET: O, but she'll keep her word.
KING: Have you heard the argument?° Is there no offense in it?   *plot*
HAMLET: No, no! They do but jest, poison in jest; no offense
    in the world.   225
KING: What do you call the play?
HAMLET: "The Mousetrap." Marry, how? Tropically.° This play   *metaphorically*
    is the image of a murder done in Vienna. Gonzago is the

duke's name: his wife, Baptista. You shall see anon. 'Tis a
knavish° piece of work; but what of that? Your Majesty,   *villainous*   230
and we that have free souls,° it touches us not. Let the   *who are innocent*
galled jade° wince; our withers are unwrung.°   *sore horse/our own necks are untouched*

[*Enter* LUCIANUS.]

This is one Lucianus, nephew to the King.
OPHELIA: You are as good as a chorus, my lord.
HAMLET: I could interpret between° you and your love, if I   *speak for*   235
could see the puppets dallying.°   *(as in a puppet show)*
OPHELIA: You are keen,° my lord, you are keen.   *sharp*
HAMLET: It would cost you a groaning to take off my edge.
OPHELIA: Still better, and worse.
HAMLET: So you must take your husbands. Begin, murderer.   240
Pox,° leave thy damnable faces, and begin! Come, the   *a plague on it*
croaking raven doth bellow for revenge.
LUCIANUS: *Thoughts black, hands apt, drugs fit, and time agreeing;*
Confederate season,° else no creature seeing;   *with the occasion conspiring*
Thou mixture rank, of midnight weeds collected,   245
With Hecate's ban thrice blasted, thrice infected,
Thy natural magic and dire property
On wholesome life usurp° immediately.   *inflict*

[*Pours the poison in his ears.*]

HAMLET: He poisons him in the garden for his estate; his
name's Gonzago. The story is extant,° and writ° in choice   *exists/written*   250
Italian. You shall see anon how the murderer gets the love
of Gonzago's wife.
OPHELIA: The King rises.
HAMLET: What, frighted with false fire?°   *gunfire without bullets*
QUEEN: How fares my lord?   255
POLONIUS: Give over° the play.   *stop*
KING: Give me some light! Away!
ALL: Lights, lights, lights!

[*All leave but* HAMLET *and* HORATIO.]

HAMLET: Why, let the strucken deer go weep,
    The hart ungallèd° play;   *uninjured deer*   260
For some must watch, while some must sleep:
    Thus runs the world away.
Would not this, sir, and a forest of feathers—if the rest of
my fortunes turn Turk° with me—with two Provincial   *take a bad turn*
roses on my razed shoes, get me a fellowship in a cry of°   *a group of*   265
players, sir?
HORATIO: Half a share.
HAMLET: A whole one I!
For thou dost know, O Damon dear,°   *(a faithful friend)*
    This realm dismantled was   270
Of Jove himself; and now reigns here
    A very, very—pajock.°   *(repulsive) peacock*

HORATIO: You might have rhymed.

HAMLET: O good Horatio, I'll take the ghost's word for a
thousand pound! Didst perceive? 275

HORATIO: Very well, my lord.

HAMLET: Upon the talk of the poisoning?

HORATIO: I did very well note him.

HAMLET: Aha! Come, some music! Come, the recorders!
For if the King like not the comedy, 280
Why then, belike he likes it not, perdy.
Come, some music!

[*Enter* ROSENCRANTZ *and* GUILDENSTERN.]

GUILDENSTERN: Good my lord, vouchsafe me a word with you.

HAMLET: Sir, a whole history.

GUILDENSTERN: The King, sir— 285

HAMLET: Ay, sir, what of him?

GUILDENSTERN: Is in his retirement,° marvellous distempered.° *private rooms/upset*

HAMLET: With drink, sir?

GUILDENSTERN: No, my lord; rather with choler.° *anger*

HAMLET: Your wisdom should show itself more richer to signi- 290
fy this to his doctor; for, for me to put him to his purgation would perhaps plunge him into far more choler.

GUILDENSTERN: Good my lord, put your discourse into some
frame, and start not so wildly from my affair.

HAMLET: I am tame, sir; pronounce. 295

GUILDENSTERN: The Queen, your mother, in most great affliction of spirit hath sent me to you.

HAMLET: You are welcome.

GUILDENSTERN: Nay, good my lord, this courtesy is not of the
right breed. If it shall please you to make me a 300
wholesome° answer, I will do your mother's command- *right kind of*
ment; if not, your pardon and my return shall be the end
of my business.

HAMLET: Sir, I cannot.

GUILDENSTERN: What, my lord? 305

HAMLET: Make you a wholesome answer; my wit's diseased.
But, sir, such answer as I can make, you shall command;
or rather, as you say, my mother. Therefore no more, but
to the matter! My mother, you say—

ROSENCRANTZ: Then thus she says: your behavior hath struck 310
her into amazement and admiration.° *wonder*

HAMLET: O wonderful son, that can so astonish a mother! But
is there no sequel at the heels of this mother's admiration?
Impart.° *let me know*

ROSENCRANTZ: She desires to speak with you in her closet° ere *private room* 315
you go to bed.

HAMLET: We shall obey, were she° ten times our mother. Have *even if she were*
you any further trade with us?

ROSENCRANTZ: My lord, you once did love me.

HAMLET: And do still, by these pickers and stealers!° *thieving hands* 320

ROSENCRANTZ: Good my lord, what is your cause of distemper? You do surely bar the door upon your own liberty,° if you deny your griefs to your friend. — *liberation from grief*

HAMLET: Sir, I lack advancement.

ROSENCRANTZ: How can that be, when you have the voice of the King himself for your succession in Denmark? — 325

HAMLET: Ay, sir, but "while the grass grows"°—the proverb is something musty. — *(". . . the horse starves")*

[*Enter the* MUSICIANS *with recorders.*]

O, the recorders! Let me see one. To withdraw with you—why do you go about to recover the wind of° me, as if you would drive me into a toil?° — *to be downwind from* / *trap* — 330

GUILDENSTERN: O my lord, if my duty be too bold, my love is too unmannerly.° — *makes me forget good manners*

HAMLET: I do not well understand that. Will you play upon this pipe?° — *recorder* — 335

GUILDENSTERN: My lord, I cannot.

HAMLET: I pray you.

GUILDENSTERN: Believe me, I cannot.

HAMLET: I do beseech you.

GUILDENSTERN: I know no touch of it, my lord. — 340

HAMLET: It is as easy as lying. Govern these ventages° with your finger and thumb, give it breath with your mouth, and it will discourse° most eloquent music. Look you, these are the stops. — *control these openings* / *make*

GUILDENSTERN: But these cannot I command to any utterance of harmony. I have not the skill. — 345

HAMLET: Why, look you now, how unworthy a thing you make of me! You would play upon me; you would seem to know my stops; you would pluck out the heart of my mystery; you would sound me from my lowest note to the top of my compass;° and there is much music, excellent voice, in this little organ,° yet cannot you make it speak. 'Sblood, do you think I am easier to be played on than a pipe? Call me what instrument you will, though you can fret° me, you cannot play upon me. — 350 — *range* / *instrument* — *annoy (pun on preparing an instrument)* — 355

[*Enter* POLONIUS.]

God bless you, sir!

POLONIUS: My lord, the Queen would° speak with you, and presently. — *wants to*

HAMLET: Do you see yonder cloud that's almost in shape of a camel? — 360

POLONIUS: By the mass, and 'tis like a camel indeed.

HAMLET: Methinks° it is like a weasel. — *I think*

POLONIUS: It is backed like a weasel.

HAMLET: Or like a whale.

POLONIUS: Very like a whale. — 365

HAMLET: Then will I come to my mother by-and-by. They fool
    me° to the top of my bent. I will come by-and-by.   *make me play the fool*
POLONIUS: I will say so.

[*He leaves.*]

HAMLET: "By-and-by" is easily said. Leave me, friends.

[*All but* HAMLET *leave.*]

'Tis now the very witching time of night,   370
When churchyards yawn, and hell itself breathes out
Contagion to this world. Now could I drink hot blood
And do such bitter business as the day
Would quake to look on. Soft! now to my mother!
O heart, lose not thy nature;° let not ever   *let me not be unnatural* 375
The soul of Nero° enter this firm bosom.   (*the bloody Roman emperor*)
Let me be cruel, not unnatural;
I will speak daggers to her, but use none.
My tongue and soul in this be hypocrites—
How in my words soever she be shent,°   *shamed* 380
To give them seals° never, my soul, consent!   *seal them with actions*

[*He leaves.*]

SCENE 3. A room in the Castle.

[*Enter* KING, ROSENCRANTZ, *and* GUILDENSTERN.]

KING: I like him not, nor stands it safe with us
    To let his madness range. Therefore prepare you;
    I your commission will forthwith dispatch,°   *right away draw up your orders*
    And he to England shall along° with you.   *shall travel*
    The terms of our estate° may not endure   *my position* 5
    Hazard° so near us as doth hourly grow   *extreme danger*
    Out of his lunacies.
GUILDENSTERN: We will ourselves provide.°   *will get ready*
    Most holy and religious fear it is
    To keep those many many bodies safe
    That live and feed upon your Majesty.   10
ROSENCRANTZ: The single and peculiar° life is bound   *private*
    With all the strength and armor of the mind
    To keep itself from noyance;° but much more   *harm*
    That spirit upon whose weal° depends and rests   *welfare*
    The lives of many. The cease of majesty°   *death of a king* 15
    Dies not alone, but like a gulf° doth draw   *whirlpool*
    What's near it with it. It is a massy wheel,
    Fixed on the summit of the highest mount,
    To whose huge spokes ten thousand lesser things
    Are mortised° and adjoined; which when it falls,   *attached* 20
    Each small annexment,° petty consequence,   *minor attachment*

Attends° the boisterous ruin. Never alone   *shares in*
Did the king sigh, but with a general groan.°   *sorrow for all the people*
KING: Arm you,° I pray you, to this speedy voyage;   *prepare yourselves*
For we will fetters put upon° this fear,   *will chain up* 25
Which now goes too free-footed.
BOTH: We will haste us.

[*They leave.*]

[*Enter* POLONIUS.]

POLONIUS: My lord, he's going to his mother's closet.
Behind the arras° I'll convey myself   *wall hanging*
To hear the process. I'll warrant she'll tax him home;°   *rebuke him sharply*
And, as you said, and wisely was it said,   30
'Tis meet° that some more audience than a mother,   *it's right*
Since nature makes them partial, should overhear
The speech, of vantage.° Fare you well, my liege.   *from a vantage point*
I'll call upon you ere you go to bed
And tell you what I know.
KING: Thanks, dear my lord.   35

[POLONIUS *leaves.*]

O, my offense is rank, it smells to heaven;
It hath the primal eldest° curse upon't,   *first and oldest*
A brother's murder! Pray can I not,
Though inclination be as sharp as will.
My stronger guilt defeats my strong intent,   40
And, like a man to double business bound,°   *who has to do two things*
I stand in pause° where I shall first begin,   *hesitate*
And both neglect. What if this cursèd hand
Were thicker than itself with brother's blood,
Is there not rain enough in the sweet heavens   45
To wash it white as snow? Whereto serves mercy
But to confront the visage of offense?°   *to battle with the face of guilt*
And what's in prayer but this twofold force,
To be forestalled ere we° come to fall,   *before we*
Or pardoned being down?° Then I'll look up;   *when we have fallen* 50
My fault is past. But, O, what form of prayer
Can serve my turn? "Forgive me my foul murder"?
That cannot be; since I am still possessed
Of those effects for which I did the murder—
My crown, mine own ambition, and my queen.   55
May one be pardoned and retain the offense?°   *the fruits of the crime*
In the corrupted currents of this world
Offense's gilded hand may shove by° justice,   *push aside*
And oft 'tis seen the wicked prize itself
Buys out the law; but 'tis not so above.   60
There is no shuffling;° there the action lies°   *no cheating/appears*
In his° true nature, and we ourselves compelled,   *its*
Even to the teeth and forehead of our faults,

To give in evidence. What then? What rests?
Try what repentance can. What can it not? 65
Yet what can it when one cannot repent?
O wretched state! O bosom black as death!
O limèd° soul, that, struggling to be free,   *trapped*
Art more engaged!° Help, angels! Make assay.   *becomes more entangled*
Bow, stubborn knees; and heart with strings of steel, 70
Be soft as sinews of the new-born babe!
All may be well.

   [*He kneels.*]
      [*Enter* HAMLET.]

HAMLET: Now might I do it pat, now he is praying;
And now I'll do't. And so he goes to heaven,
And so am I revenged. That would be scanned.°   *should be examined* 75
A villain kills my father; and for that,
I, his sole son, do this same villain send
To heaven.
Why, this is hire° and salary, not revenge!   *reward*
He took my father grossly, full of bread,°   *after a heavy meal* 80
With all his crimes broad blown,° as flush as May;   *in full bloom*
And how his audit stands, who knows save heaven?
But in our circumstance and course of thought,°   *according to common opinion*
'Tis heavy with him;° and am I then revenged,   *he is in deep trouble*
To take him in the purging° of his soul,   *cleansing* 85
When he is fit and seasoned for his passage?
No.
Up, sword, and know thou a more horrid hent.°   *be ready for more horrible use*
When he is drunk asleep; or in his rage;
Or in the incestuous pleasure of his bed; 90
At gaming, swearing, or about some act
That has no relish of salvation in't—
Then trip him, that his heels may kick at heaven,
And that his soul may be as damned and black
As hell, whereto it goes. My mother stays.°   *waits* 95
This physic° but prolongs thy sickly days.   *medicine*

                              [*He leaves.*]

KING [*rises*]: My words fly up, my thoughts remain below;
Words without thoughts never to heaven go.

                              [*He leaves.*]

SCENE 4. The QUEEN'S private chamber.

   [*Enter* QUEEN *and* POLONIUS.]

POLONIUS: He will come straight. Look you lay home to him.°   *see that you speak frankly*
Tell him his pranks have been too broad to bear with,
And that your Grace hath screened and stood between

Much heat and him. I'll silence me even here.° *I'll say no more*
Pray you be round° with him. *outspoken* 5
HAMLET [*within*]: Mother, mother, mother!
QUEEN: I'll warrant° you; fear me not. Withdraw; I *I promise*
   hear him coming.

   [POLONIUS *hides behind the arras.*]
     [*Enter* HAMLET.]

HAMLET: Now, mother, what's the matter?
QUEEN: Hamlet, thou hast thy father much offended. 10
HAMLET: Mother, you have my father much offended.
QUEEN: Come, come, you answer with an idle tongue.
HAMLET: Go, go, you question with a wicked tongue.
QUEEN: Why, how now, Hamlet?
HAMLET: What's the matter now?
QUEEN: Have you forgot me?
HAMLET: No, by the rood,° not so! *by the Cross* 15
   You are the Queen, your husband's brother's wife,
   And—would it were° not so—you are my mother. *I wish it were*
QUEEN: Nay, then I'll set those to you° that can speak. *I'll make you talk to those*
HAMLET: Come, come, and sit you down, you shall not budge!
   You go not till I set you up a glass° *mirror* 20
   Where you may see the inmost part of you.
QUEEN: What wilt thou do? Thou wilt not murder me?
   Help, help, ho!
POLONIUS [*behind the arras*]: What, ho! help, help, help!
HAMLET [*draws his sword*]: How now? a rat? Dead for a ducat,° dead! *(a gold coin)* 25

   [*Stabs through the arras and kills* POLONIUS.]

POLONIUS: O, I am slain!
QUEEN: O me, what hast thou done?
HAMLET: Nay, I know not. Is it the King?
QUEEN: O, what a rash and bloody deed is this!
HAMLET: A bloody deed—almost as bad, good mother,
   As kill a king, and marry with his brother. 30
QUEEN: As kill a king?
HAMLET: Ay, lady, 'twas my word.

   [*Pulls aside arras and sees* POLONIUS.]

Thou wretched, rash, intruding fool, farewell!
I took thee for thy better.° Take thy fortune. *mistook you for your king*
Thou find'st to be too busy is some danger.
[*to his mother*] Leave° wringing of your hands. Peace!
sit you down *stop* 35
And let me wring your heart; for so I shall
If it be made of penetrable° stuff; *that can be penetrated*
If damnèd custom have not brazed it so° *force of habit has not made it so brazen*
That it is proof and bulwark against sense.° *feeling*
QUEEN: What have I done that thou dar'st wag thy tongue 40
   In noise so rude against me?

HAMLET: Such an act
    That blurs the grace and blush of modesty;
    Calls virtue hypocrite; takes off the rose
    From the fair forehead of an innocent love,
    And sets a blister° there; makes marriage vows   *brand of shame*   45
    As false as dicers'° oaths. O, such a deed   *gamblers'*
    As from the body of contraction° plucks   *marriage contract*
    The very soul, and sweet religion makes
    A rhapsody° of words! Heaven's face doth glow;°   *garbled string/blush*
    Yea, this solidity and compound mass,°   *this solid earth*   50
    With tristful visage,° as against the doom,°   *mournful face/on the eve of doom*
    Is thought-sick at the act.
QUEEN: Ay me, what act,
    That roars so loud and thunders in the index?°   *in your listing*
HAMLET: Look here upon this picture, and on this,
    The counterfeit presentment° of two brothers.   *painted likeness*   55
    See what a grace was seated on this brow;
    Hyperion's° curls; the front of Jove himself;   *(beautiful divine being)*
    An eye like Mars,° to threaten and command;   *(god of war)*
    A station° like the herald Mercury°   *bearing/(messenger of the gods)*
    New lighted° on a heaven-kissing hill: *having just landed*   60
    A combination and a form indeed
    Where every god did seem to set his seal
    To give the world assurance of a man.
    This was your husband. Look you now what follows.
    Here is your husband, like a mildewed ear°   *an infected ear of corn*   65
    Blasting° his wholesome brother. Have you eyes?   *spreading infection to*
    Could you on this fair mountain leave to feed,
    And batten on this moor?° Ha! have you eyes?   *feed greedily on a swamp*
    You cannot call it love; for at your age
    The heyday in the blood° is tame, it's humble,   *of physical passion*   70
    And waits upon the judgment;° and what judgment   *is guided by reason*
    Would step from this to this? Sense° sure you have,   *sensations*
    Else could you not have motion; but sure that sense
    Is apoplexed;° for madness would not err,   *paralyzed*
    Nor sense to ecstasy was never so thralled°   *was never such a slave to madness*   75
    But it reserved some quantity of choice
    To serve in such a difference. What devil was't
    That thus hath cozened you at hoodman-blind?°   *cheated you at blindman's bluff*
    Eyes without feeling, feeling without sight,   *game with blindfold player)*
    Ears without hands or eyes, smelling sans° all,   *without*   80
    Or but a sickly part of one true sense
    Could not so mope.°   *blunder*
    O shame! where is thy blush? Rebellious hell,
    If thou canst mutiny in a matron's bones,
    To flaming youth let virtue be as wax   85
    And melt in her own fire. Proclaim no shame
    When the compulsive ardor gives the charge,°   *passion leads the attack*
    Since frost itself as actively doth burn,
    And reason panders will.°   *panders to desire*

QUEEN: O Hamlet, speak no more! 90
  Thou turn'st mine eyes into my very soul,
  And there I see such black and grainèd° spots   *ingrained*
  As will not leave their tinct.°   *lose their color*
HAMLET: Nay, but to live
  In the rank sweat of an enseamed° bed,   *greasy*
  Stewed in corruption, honeying and making love
  Over the nasty sty!
QUEEN: O, speak to me no more! 95
  These words like daggers enter in mine ears.
  No more, sweet Hamlet!
HAMLET: A murderer and a villain!
  A slave that is not twentieth part the tithe°   *tenth share*
  Of your precedent° lord; a vice° of kings;   *former/parody*
  A cutpurse° of the empire and the rule,   *purse snatcher* 100
  That from a shelf the precious diadem stole
  And put it in his pocket!
QUEEN: No more!

  [*Enter* GHOST.]

HAMLET: A king of shreds and patches—
  Save me and hover over me with your wings,
  You heavenly guards! What would your gracious figure? 105
QUEEN: Alas, he's mad!
HAMLET: Do you not come your tardy son to chide,
  That, lapsed° in time and passion, lets go by   *negligent*
  The important acting of your dread command?
  O, say! 110
GHOST: Do not forget. This visitation
  Is but to whet thy almost blunted purpose.
  But look, amazement on thy mother sits.
  O, step between her and her fighting soul!
  Conceit° in weakest bodies strongest works.   *imagination* 115
  Speak to her, Hamlet.
HAMLET: How is it with you, lady?
QUEEN: Alas, how is't with you,
  That you do bend your eye on vacancy,°   *vacant space*
  And with the incorporal° air do hold discourse?   *bodiless*
  Forth at your eyes your spirits wildly peep; 120
  And, as the sleeping soldiers in the alarm,
  Your bedded hairs, like life in excrements,°   *inert outgrowths*
  Start up and stand on end. O gentle son,
  Upon the heat and flame of thy distemper°   *your disturbed mind*
  Sprinkle cool patience! Whereon do you look? 125
HAMLET: On him, on him! Look you how pale he glares!
  His form and cause conjoined, preaching to stones,
  Would make them capable°—Do not look upon me,   *enable them to feel*
  Lest with this piteous action you convert
  My stern effects.° Then what I have to do   *my stern deeds* 130

Will want° true color—tears perchance for blood.   *lack*
QUEEN: To whom do you speak this?
HAMLET: Do you see nothing there?
QUEEN: Nothing at all; yet all that is I see.
HAMLET: Nor did you nothing hear?
QUEEN: No, nothing but ourselves.
HAMLET: Why, look you there! Look how it steals away!   135
    My father, in his habit° as he lived!   *garment*
    Look where he goes even now out at the portal!

                    [GHOST *leaves.*]

QUEEN: This is the very coinage of your brain.
    This bodiless creation ecstasy°   *madness*
    Is very cunning in.°   *is very good at*
HAMLET: Ecstasy?   140
    My pulse as yours doth temperately keep time
    And makes as healthful music. It is not madness
    That I have uttered. Bring me to the test,
    And I the matter will reword, which madness
    Would gambol from.° Mother, for love of grace,   *shy away from*   145
    Lay not that flattering unction° to your soul,   *soothing ointment*
    That not your trespass but my madness speaks.
    It will but skin and film° the ulcerous place,   *cover up*
    Whilst rank corruption, mining° all within,   *undermining*
    Infects unseen. Confess yourself to heaven;   150
    Repent what's past; avoid what is to come;
    And do not spread the compost on the weeds
    To make them ranker.° Forgive me this my virtue;   *grow wilder*
    For in the fatness of these pursy° times   *bloated*
    Virtue itself of vice must pardon beg—   155
    Yea, curb and woo for leave° to do him good.   *bow for permission*
QUEEN: O Hamlet, thou hast cleft° my heart in twain.   *you have split*
HAMLET: O, throw away the worser part of it,
    And live the purer with the other half.
    Good night—but go not to my uncle's bed.   160
    Assume a virtue,° if you have it not.   *pretend to be virtuous*
    That monster, custom,° who all sense doth eat   *habit*
    Of habits evil, is angel yet in this,
    That to the use of actions fair and good
    He likewise gives a frock or livery,°   *an outward appearance*   165
    That aptly is put on. Refrain tonight,
    And that shall lend a kind of easiness
    To the next abstinence; the next more easy;
    For use° almost can change the stamp of nature,   *force of habit*
    And either master the devil, or throw him out
    With wondrous potency. Once more, good night;   170
    And when you are desirous to be blest,
    I'll blessing beg of you.—For this same lord,
    I do repent; but heaven hath pleased it so,

To punish me with this, and this with me, 175
That I must be their scourge and minister.
I will bestow him,° and will answer well   *dispose of him*
The death° I gave him. So again, good night.   *for the death*
I must be cruel, only to be kind;
Thus bad begins, and worse remains behind.°   *is yet to come* 180
One word more, good lady.
QUEEN: What shall I do?
HAMLET: Not this, by no means, that I bid you do:
Let the bloat King tempt you again to bed;
Pinch wanton on your cheek; call you his mouse;
And let him, for a pair of reechy° kisses,   *reeking* 185
Or paddling in your neck with his damned fingers,
Make you to ravel all this matter out,
That I essentially am not in madness,
But mad in craft.° 'Twere good you let him know;   *on purpose*
For who that's but a queen, fair, sober, wise, 190
Would from a paddock,° from a bat, a gib,°   *toad/tomcat*
Such dear concernings hide? Who would do so?
No, in despite of sense and secrecy,
Unpeg° the basket on the house's top,   *unfasten*
Let the birds fly, and like the famous ape, 195
To try conclusions,° in the basket creep   *make an experiment*
And break your own neck down.°   *fall down (while trying to fly)*
QUEEN: Be thou assured, if words be made of breath,
And breath of life, I have no life to breathe°   *reveal*
What thou hast said to me. 200
HAMLET: I must to England; you know that?
QUEEN: Alack,°   *alas*
I had forgot! 'Tis so concluded on.°   *so decided*
HAMLET: There's letters sealed; and my two schoolfellows,
Whom I will trust as I will adders fanged,
They bear the mandate;° they must sweep my way   *carry the instructions* 205
And marshal me to knavery. Let it work;
For 'tis the sport to have the enginer°   *engineer*
Hoist with his own petar;° and 't shall go hard   *blown up by his own bomb*
But I will delve° one yard below their mines   *dig*
And blow them at the moon. O 'tis most sweet 210
When in one line two crafts directly meet.°   *two plots converge*
This man shall set me packing:
I'll lug the guts into the neighbor room.
Mother, good night. Indeed, this counsellor
Is now most still, most secret, and most grave, 215
Who was in life a foolish prating knave.
Come, sir, to draw toward an end with you.
Good night, mother.

     [*Both leave, with* HAMLET *dragging* POLONIUS.]

THE RECEPTIVE READER

1. (Scene 1) By the end of this scene, how aware is the audience of a plot of *intrigue?* How much has it seen of plotting and counterplotting on the part of two major opposed parties? ✧ The "To be, or not to be" soliloquy is usually seen as Hamlet's debating the pros and cons of suicide. (Some critics read the speech as a debate on "To act, or not to act"—whether to take decisive action against Claudius.) What are the pros and cons? Does he seem to you to be in a highly disturbed or suicidal frame of mind? How does this speech round out your understanding of Hamlet's character? ✧ In his encounter with Ophelia, why does Hamlet deny having loved her or having given her tokens of affection? What is the point of Hamlet's *satirical* commentary on beauty, marriage, and offspring? Why does he direct it at Ophelia? Does Ophelia hold her own, or is she the passive victim?

2. (Scene 2) What does Hamlet's relationship with Horatio show about his character? When Hamlet praises his friend, what are to him the ideal qualities of an admirable person? ✧ What is the tone or direction of Hamlet's running commentary during the play-within-the-play? What is the upshot of Hamlet's "mousetrap" scheme? What is Hamlet's frame of mind by the end of this scene? ✧ What is sarcastic about remarks like "We shall obey, were she ten times our mother"? What other examples of Hamlet's *sarcastic tone* can you cite?

3. (Scene 3) Does the prayer scene change your view of Claudius as the villain of the play? How?

4. (Scene 4) The killing of Polonius can be seen as a major turning point in the *plot* of the play. How and why? ✧ How does Hamlet explain his killing of Polonius? What is his reaction; how does treat the dead body? ✧ What are the major themes in Hamlet's denunciation of his mother? What picture does he paint of his dead father, of Claudius (his "father-uncle"), of his mother? Is he in full control of his senses, as he claims, or profoundly disturbed? ✧ How does Queen Gertrude act in this *climactic* scene? What do you conclude about her guilt—her implication in the murder? ✧ What does the reappearance of the ghost add to this climactic scene?

THE RANGE OF INTERPRETATION

Hamlet's role in the prayer scene has been much debated. He refuses to kill the king at prayer because in the state of repentance Claudius might be forgiven his sin, with his soul going to heaven. To make the revenge complete, Claudius should be sent to hell—killed when caught in some sinful act without a chance of repentance. Some critics have found this attitude too brutal and un-Christian to fit with their understanding of Hamlet's character. Is he more harsh and brutal in this thirst for revenge than you would expect? Or is his attitude here in keeping with his character as you understand it? Or is Hamlet perhaps using the king's praying as a pretext, as an excuse for further delaying his task? Or is the playwright perhaps signaling to the audience that Hamlet is not as admirable and virtuous as we might think—he himself is also infected by the moral corruption of his time?

ACT FOUR

SCENE 1. Elsinore. A room in the Castle.

[*Enter* KING *and* QUEEN, *with* ROSENCRANTZ *and* GUILDENSTERN.]

KING: There's matter in these sighs. These profound heaves
    You must translate; 'tis fit we understand them.
    Where is your son?
QUEEN: Bestow this place on us° a little while.   *leave us alone*

[ROSENCRANTZ *and* GUILDENSTERN *leave.*]

    Ah, mine own lord, what have I seen tonight!   5
KING: What, Gertrude? How does Hamlet?
QUEEN: Mad as the sea and wind when both contend
    Which is the mightier. In his lawless fit,
    Behind the arras hearing something stir,
    Whips out his rapier, cries "A rat, a rat!"   10
    And in this brainish apprehension° kills   *brainsick fit*
    The unseen good old man.
KING: O heavy deed!
    It had been so with us,° had we been there.   *this would have happened to me*
    His liberty is full of threats to all—
    To you yourself, to us, to every one.   15
    Alas, how shall this bloody deed be answered?
    It will be laid to us,° whose providence   *we will be blamed*
    Should have kept short, restrained, and out of haunt°   *away from people*
    This mad young man. But so much was our love
    We would not understand what was most fit,   20
    But, like the owner of a foul disease,
    To keep it from divulging,° let it feed   *from being known*
    Even on the pith° of life. Where is he gone?   *essence*
QUEEN: To draw apart the body he hath killed,
    Over whom his very madness, like some ore°   *a more valuable vein*   25
    Among a mineral of metals base,
    Shows itself pure. He weeps for what is done.
KING: O Gertrude, come away!
    The sun no sooner shall the mountains touch
    But we will ship him hence; and this vile deed   30
    We must with all our majesty and skill
    Both countenance° and excuse. Ho, Guildenstern!   *sanction*

[*Enter* ROSENCRANTZ *and* GUILDENSTERN.]

    Friends both, go join you with some further aid.
    Hamlet in madness hath Polonius slain,
    And from his mother's closet hath he dragged him.   35
    Go seek him out; speak fair,° and bring the body   *talk to him politely*
    Into the chapel. I pray you haste in this.

[ROSENCRANTZ *and* GUILDENSTERN *leave.*]

Come, Gertrude, we'll call up our wisest friends
And let them know both what we mean to do
And what's untimely done. So haply° slander   *perhaps*   40
Whose whisper over the world's diameter,
As level as the cannon to his blank,°   *straight . . . to its target*
Transports his poisoned shot—may miss our name
And hit the woundless° air.—O, come away!   *which cannot be wounded*
My soul is full of discord and dismay.   45

[*They leave.*]

SCENE 2. The same. A passage in the Castle.

[*Enter* HAMLET.]

HAMLET: Safely stowed.°   *hidden*
GENTLEMEN (*within*): Hamlet! Lord Hamlet!
HAMLET: But soft! What noise? Who calls on Hamlet? O, here
    they come.

[*Enter* ROSENCRANTZ *and* GUILDENSTERN.]

ROSENCRANTZ: What have you done, my lord, with the dead   5
    body?
HAMLET: Compounded° it with dust, whereto 'tis kin.   *mingled*
ROSENCRANTZ: Tell us where 'tis, that we may take it thence
And bear it to the chapel.
HAMLET: Do not believe it.   10
ROSENCRANTZ: Believe what?
HAMLET: That I can keep your counsel,° and not mine own.   *secret*
    Besides, to be demanded of° a sponge, what replication°   *when questioned by/answer*
    should be made by the son of a king?
ROSENCRANTZ: Take you me for a sponge, my lord?   15
HAMLET: Ay, sir, that soaks up the King's countenance,° his re-   *looks*
    wards, his authorities.° But such officers do the King best   *appointments*
    service in the end. He keeps them, like an ape, in the cor-
    ner of his jaw; first mouthed, to be last swallowed.° When   *(like saving unswallowed*
    he needs what you have gleaned, it is but squeezing you   *food in one's cheeks)*   20
    and, sponge, you shall be dry again.
ROSENCRANTZ: I understand you not, my lord.
HAMLET: I am glad of it: a knavish° speech sleeps in a foolish   *wicked*
    ear.
ROSENCRANTZ: My lord, you must tell us where the body is   25
    and go with us to the King.
HAMLET: The body is with the King, but the King is not with
    the body. The King is a thing—
GUILDENSTERN: A thing, my lord?
HAMLET: Of nothing. Bring me to him. Hide fox, and all after.   30

[*They leave.*]

SCENE 3. The same. A room as before.

[*Enter* KING.]

KING: I have sent to seek him and to find the body.
    How dangerous is it that this man goes loose!
    Yet must not we put the strong law on him.
    He's loved of the distracted multitude,°   *by the fickle crowds*
    Who like not in their judgment,° but their eyes;   *not by good judgment*   5
    And where 'tis so, the offender's scourge is weighed,°   *the penalty is questioned*
    But never the offense. To bear all° smooth and even,   *to make all seem*
    This sudden sending him away must seem
    Deliberate pause.° Diseases desperate grown   *like a well-weighed plan*
    By desperate appliance° are relieved,   *remedies*   10
    Or not at all.

[*Enter* ROSENCRANTZ.]

       How now? What hath befallen?
ROSENCRANTZ: Where the dead body is bestowed, my lord,
    We cannot get from him.
KING: But where is he?
ROSENCRANTZ: Without,° my lord; guarded, to know your pleasure.   *outside*
KING: Bring him before us.   15
ROSENCRANTZ: Ho, Guildenstern! Bring in my lord.

[*Enter* HAMLET *and* GUILDENSTERN *with attendants.*]

KING: Now, Hamlet, where's Polonius?
HAMLET: At supper.
KING: At supper? Where?
HAMLET: Not where he eats, but where he is eaten. A certain   20
    convocation of politic° worms are even at him. Your worm   *assembly of politically*
    is your only emperor for diet. We fat° all creatures else to   *minded/fatten*
    fat us, and we fat ourselves for maggots. Your fat king and
    your lean beggar is but variable service—two dishes, but
    to one table. That's the end.   25
KING: Alas, alas!
HAMLET: A man may fish with the worm that hath eat of a
    king, and eat of the fish that hath fed of that worm.
KING: What dost thou mean by this?
HAMLET: Nothing but to show you how a king may go a   30
    progress° through the guts of a beggar.   *make his way*
KING: Where is Polonius?
HAMLET: In heaven. Send thither to see. If your messenger
    find him not there, seek him in the other place yourself.
    But indeed, if you find him not within this month, you   35
    shall nose° him as you go up the stairs into the lobby.   *smell*
KING [*to attendants*]: Go seek him there.
HAMLET: He will stay till you come.

                    [*Attendants leave.*]

KING: Hamlet, this deed, for thine especial safety—
　　Which we do tender° as we dearly grieve　　　　　　　　　　　　　　*cherish*　40
　　For that which thou hast done—must send thee hence
　　With fiery quickness. Therefore prepare thyself.
　　The bark is ready and the wind at help,
　　The associates tend,° and everything is bent　　　　　*your companions are waiting*
　　For England.
HAMLET:　　　　　For England?
KING:　　　　　　　　　Ay, Hamlet.
HAMLET:　　　　　　　　　　　　Good.　　　　　　　　　　　　　　　　　　45
KING: So is it, if thou knew'st our purposes.
HAMLET: I see a cherub° that sees them. But come, for Eng-　　　*an all-knowing angel*
　　land! Farewell, dear mother.
KING: Thy° loving father, Hamlet　　　　　　　　　　　　　　　　*I am your*
HAMLET: My mother! Father and mother is man and wife; man　　　　　　　　50
　　and wife is one flesh; and so, my mother. Come, for Eng-
　　land!

　　　　　　　　　　　　　　　　　[*He leaves.*]

KING: Follow him at foot; tempt° him with speed aboard;　　　　　　　*urge*
　　Delay it not, I'll have him hence° tonight.　　　　　　　　*away from here*
　　Away! for everything is sealed and done　　　　　　　　　　　　　　55
　　That else leans on° the affair. Pray you make haste.　　　　　*relates to*

　　　　　　　　　[ROSENCRANTZ *and* GUILDENSTERN *leave.*]

　　And, England, if my love thou hold'st at aught°—　　　　*value my love at all*
　　As my great power thereof may give thee sense,°　　　*may impress it on you*
　　Since yet thy cicatrice° looks raw and red　　　　　　　　　　　*scar*
　　After the Danish sword, and thy free awe°　　　　　*you willingly out of fear*　60
　　Pays homage to us—thou mayst not coldly set°　　　　　　　*set aside*
　　Our sovereign process,° which imports at full,　　　　　　*royal command*
　　By letters congruing to° that effect,　　　　　　　　　　　*pointing to*
　　The present° death of Hamlet. Do it, England;　　　　　　　*immediate*
　　For like the hectic° in my blood he rages,　　　　　　　　*severe fever*　65
　　And thou must cure me. Till I know 'tis done,
　　However my haps,° my joys were never begun.　　　　　*whatever my fortunes*

　　　　　　　　　　　　　　　　　　[*Leaves.*]

SCENE 4. Near Elsinore Castle.

　　[*Enter* FORTINBRAS *with his army, marching across the stage.*]

FORTINBRAS: Go, Captain, from me greet the Danish king.
　　Tell him that by his license° Fortinbras　　　　　　　　　*permission*
　　Craves the conveyance° of a promised march　　　　*requests safe conduct*
　　Over° his kingdom. You know the rendezvous.　　　　　　　*through*
　　If that his Majesty would aught with us,°　　　　　　　　*wants to see us*　5
　　We shall express our duty in his eye;
　　And let him know so.

CAPTAIN: I will do't, my lord.
FORTINBRAS: Go softly on.

[*All but the* CAPTAIN *leave.*]
[*Enter* HAMLET, ROSENCRANTZ, GUILDENSTERN, *and others.*]

HAMLET: Good sir, whose powers° are these?   *forces*
CAPTAIN: They are of Norway, sir.   10
HAMLET: How purposed,° sir, I pray you?   *with what destination*
CAPTAIN: Against some part of Poland.
HAMLET: Who commands them, sir?
CAPTAIN: The nephew to old Norway, Fortinbras.
HAMLET: Goes it against the main° of Poland, sir,   *the central part*   15
    Or for some frontier?
CAPTAIN: Truly to speak, and with no addition,
    We go to gain a little patch of ground
    That hath in it no profit° but the name.   *value*
    To pay five ducats, five, I would not farm it;   20
    Nor will it yield to Norway or the Pole
    A ranker rate, should it be sold in fee.°   *a higher rate if sold outright*
HAMLET: Why, then the Polack never will defend it.
CAPTAIN: Yes, it is already garrisoned.
HAMLET: Two thousand soul and twenty thousand ducats   25
    Will not debate the question of° this straw.   *settle the argument over*
    This is the imposthume° of much wealth and peace,   *malignant growth*
    That inward breaks, and shows no cause without°   *external cause*
    Why the man dies—I humbly thank you, sir.
CAPTAIN: God be wi' you, sir.

[*He leaves.*]

ROSENCRANTZ: Will't please you go, my lord?   30
HAMLET: I'll be with you straight. Go a little before.

[*All but* HAMLET *leave.*]

    How all occasions do inform against me°   *accuse me*
    And spur my dull revenge! What is a man,
    If his chief good and market of his time
    Be but to sleep and feed? A beast, no more.   35
    Sure he that made us with such large discourse,°   *far-ranging reasoning*
    Looking before and after, gave us not
    That capability and godlike reason
    To fust° in us unused. Now, whether it be   *spoil*
    Bestial oblivion, or some craven scruple°   *beastlike apathy or*   40
    Of thinking too precisely on the event,—   *cowardly hesitation*
    A thought which, quartered,° hath but one part wisdom *when divided in four*
    And ever three parts coward—I do not know
    Why yet I live to say "This thing's to do,"
    Sith° I have cause, and will, and strength, and means   *since*   45
    To do't. Examples gross as° earth exhort me.   *as plain as*
    Witness this army of such mass and charge,°   *and cost*

Led by a delicate and tender prince,
Whose spirit, with divine ambition puffed,
Makes mouths at the invisible event,°   *makes light of the outcome*   50
Exposing what is mortal and unsure
To all that fortune, death, and danger dare,
Even for an eggshell. Rightly to be great
Is not to stir without great argument,°   *take action without a great cause*
But greatly to find quarrel in a straw   55
When honor's at the stake. How stand I then,
That have a father killed, a mother stained,
Excitements° of my reason and my blood,   *incentives*
And let all sleep, while to my shame I see
The imminent death of twenty thousand men   60
That for a fantasy and trick of fame
Go to their graves like beds, fight for a plot
Whereon the numbers cannot try the cause,°   *decide the conflict*
Which is not tomb enough and continent°   *container*
To hide the slain? O, from this time forth,   65
My thoughts be bloody, or be nothing worth!

[He leaves.]

SCENE 5. Elsinore. A room in the Castle.

[Enter QUEEN, HORATIO, *and a* GENTLEMAN.]

QUEEN: I will not speak with her.
GENTLEMAN: She is importunate,° indeed distract;°   *insistent/distracted*
    Her mood will needs be° pitied.   *must be*
QUEEN: What would she have?°   *what is her wish*
GENTLEMAN: She speaks much of her father; says she hears
    There's tricks in the world, and hems, and beats her heart;   5
    Spurns enviously° at straws; speaks things in doubt,   *strikes out angrily*
    That carry but half sense. Her speech is nothing,
    Yet the unshaped use of it doth move
    The hearers to collection;° they aim at it,   *attention*
    And botch the words up fit to their own thoughts;   10
    Which, as her winks and nods and gestures yield them,
    Indeed would make one think there might be thought,
    Though nothing sure, yet much unhappily.°   *much that is sad*
HORATIO: 'Twere good she were spoken with; for she may strew
    Dangerous conjectures in ill-breeding° minds.   *thriving on bad news*   15
QUEEN: Let her come in.

*[*GENTLEMAN *leaves.]*

    [aside] To my sick soul (as sin's true nature is)
    Each toy° seems prologue to some great amiss.   *trifle*
    So full of artless jealousy° is guilt   *clumsy suspicion*
    It spills° itself in fearing to be spilt.   *reveals*   20

[Enter OPHELIA *distracted.]*

OPHELIA: Where is the beauteous Majesty of Denmark?

QUEEN: How now, Ophelia?
OPHELIA [*sings*]:
　　How should I your true-love know
　　　　From another one?
　　By his cockle hat° and staff　　　　　　　　　*pilgrim's hat (with a cockle shell)*　　25
　　　　And his sandal shoon.°　　　　　　　　　　　　　　　　　　　*shoes*

QUEEN: Alas, sweet lady, what imports° this song?　　　　　*what is the meaning of*
OPHELIA: Say you? Nay, pray you mark.°　　　　　　　　　　　　*please listen*

　　[*sings*] *He is dead and gone, lady,*
　　　　He is dead and gone;　　　　　　　　　　　　　　　　　　　　　30
　　At his head a grass-green turf,
　　　　At his heels a stone.
　O, ho!
QUEEN: Nay, but Ophelia—
OPHELIA: Pray you mark.　　　　　　　　　　　　　　　　　　　　　　35

　　[*sings*] *White his shroud as the mountain snow—*

　　[*Enter* KING.]

QUEEN: Alas, look here, my lord!

OPHELIA [*sings*]:
　　　Larded all with° sweet flowers;　　　　　　　　　　*garnished with*
　　Which bewept to the grave did not go
　　　With true-love showers.°　　　　　　　　　　　　　*showers of tears*　40

KING: How do you, pretty lady?
OPHELIA: Well, God 'ild you!° They say the owl was a baker's　　*God shield you*
　　daughter. Lord, we know what we are, but know not what
　　we may be. God be at your table!
KING: Conceit upon° her father.　　　　　　　　　　　　　*she is thinking about*　45
OPHELIA: Pray let's have no words of this; but when they ask
　　you what it means, say you this:

　　[*sings*] *Tomorrow is Saint Valentine's day,*
　　　All in the morning betime,°　　　　　　　　　　　　　　　　*early*
　　And I a maid at your window,　　　　　　　　　　　　　　　　　　50
　　　To be your Valentine.

　　Then up he rose and donned his clothes
　　　And dupped° the chamber door,　　　　　　　　　　　　　*opened*
　　Let in the maid, that out a maid°　　　　　　　　　　　*as a virgin*
　　　Never departed more.　　　　　　　　　　　　　　　　　　　　55

KING: Pretty Ophelia!
OPHELIA: Indeed, la, without an oath, I'll make an end on't!

　　[*sings*] *By Gis° and by Saint Charity,*　　　　　　　　　　*(by Jesus)*
　　　Alack, and fie for shame!
　　Young men will do't if they come to't.　　　　　　　　　　　　　60
　　　By Cock,° they are to blame.　　　*weaker swearword for "by God"*

　　Quoth she, "Before you tumbled me,
　　　You promised me to wed."

He answers:
"So would I have done, by yonder sun, 65
    An thou hadst not° come to my bed."   *if you had not*
KING: How long hath she been thus?
OPHELIA: I hope all will be well. We must be patient; but I
    cannot choose but weep to think they would lay him in the
    cold ground. My brother shall know of it; and so I thank 70
    you for your good counsel. Come, my coach! Good night,
    ladies. Good night, sweet ladies. Good night, good night.

                          [*She leaves.*]

KING: Follow her close; give her good watch, I pray you.

                          [HORATIO *leaves.*]

O, this is the poison of deep grief; it springs
All from her father's death. O Gertrude, Gertrude, 75
When sorrows come, they come not single spies,°   *not as single advance scouts*
But in battalions! First, her father slain;
Next, your son gone, and he most violent author
Of his own just remove;° the people muddied,   *deserved exile*
Thick and unwholesome in their thoughts and whispers 80
For good Polonius' death, and we have done but greenly°   *acted unthinkingly*
In hugger-mugger to inter° him; poor Ophelia   *in secrecy and disorder to bury*
Divided from herself and her fair judgment,
Without the which we are pictures or mere beasts;
Last, and as much containing as all these, 85
Her brother is in secret come from France;
Feeds on his wonder, keeps himself in clouds,
And wants not buzzers to infect his ear°   *does not lack talebearers*
With pestilent speeches of his father's death,
Wherein necessity, of matter beggared,°   *void of true substance* 90
Will nothing stick° our person to arraign   *will not hesitate*
In ear and ear.° O my dear Gertrude, this,   *in people's ears*
Like to a murdering piece,° in many places   *a cannon with scattered shot*
Gives me superfluous death.

[*A noise outside.*]

QUEEN: Alack, what noise is this?
KING: Where are my Switzers?° Let them guard the door.   *Swiss bodyguards* 95

[*Enter a* MESSENGER.]

What is the matter?
MESSENGER: Save yourself, my lord:
The ocean, overpeering of his list,°   *rising over its borders*
Eats not the flats° with more impetuous haste   *coastal flatlands*
Than young Laertes, in a riotous head,°   *heading a mob*
Overbears your officers. The rabble call him lord; 100
And, as the world were now but to begin,
Antiquity forgot,° custom not known,   *as if tradition were forgotten*

The ratifiers and props of every word,°   *pledge*
They cry "Choose we, Laertes shall be king!"
Caps, hands, and tongues applaud it to the clouds,   105
"Laertes shall be king! Laertes king!"

[*A noise outside.*]

QUEEN: How cheerfully on the false trail they cry!
   O, this is counter,° you false Danish dogs!   *on the wrong trail*
KING: The doors are broke.°   *forced open*

[*Enter* LAERTES *with others.*]

LAERTES: Where is this king?—Sirs, stand you all without.   110
ALL: No, let's come in!
LAERTES: I pray you give me leave.
ALL: We will, we will!
LAERTES: I thank you. Keep the door.

[*His followers leave.*]

   O thou vile king,
   Give me my father!
QUEEN: Calmly, good Laertes.   115
LAERTES: That drop of blood that's calm proclaims me bastard;°   *shows I am not my father's*
   Cries cuckold to my father; brands the harlot   *true son (making the*
   Even here between the chaste unsmirched brows   *mother a whore)*
   Of my true mother.
KING: What is the cause, Laertes,
   That thy rebellion looks so giantlike?   120
   Let him go, Gertrude. Do not fear our person.°   *don't be afraid on my behalf*
   There's such divinity doth hedge° a king   *such divine sanction that protects*
   That treason can but peep to what it would,°   *at its goal*
   Acts little of his will.° Tell me, Laertes,   *acts out little of what it intends*
   Why thou art thus incensed. Let him go, Gertrude.   125
   Speak, man.
LAERTES: Where is my father?
KING: Dead.
QUEEN: But not by him!
KING: Let him demand his fill.°   *question freely*
LAERTES: How came he dead?° I'll not be juggled with: *how did he die*
   To hell, allegiance! vows, to the blackest devil!
   Conscience and grace, to the profoundest pit!   130
   I dare damnation. To this point I stand,
   That both the worlds I give to negligence,°   *write off both earth and heaven*
   Let come what comes; only I'll be revenged
   Most thoroughly for my father.
KING: Who shall stay° you?   *hinder*   135
LAERTES: My will,° not all the world.   *if I have my will*
   And for my means, I'll husband° them so well   *use*
   They shall go far with little.

KING: Good Laertes,
   If you desire to know the certainty°   *actual facts*
   Of your dear father's death, is't writ in your revenge   140
   That swoopstake° you will draw both friend and foe,   *like a reckless gambler*
   Winner and loser?
LAERTES: None but his enemies.
KING: Will you know them then?
LAERTES: To his good friends thus wide I'll open my arms
   And, like the kind life-rendering pelican,   145
   Repast them with my blood.°   *feed them with my own blood (as the*
KING: Why, now you speak   *pelican was thought to feed its young)*
   Like a good child and a true gentleman.
   That I am guiltless of your father's death,
   And am most sensibly° in grief for it,   *feelingly*
   It shall as level to your judgment appear°   *strike your reason as directly*   150
   As day does to your eye.

   [*A noise outside: "Let her come in."*]

LAERTES: How now? What noise is that?

   [*Enter* OPHELIA.]

   O heat, dry up my brains! Tears seven times salt
   Burn out the sense and virtue° of mine eye!   *faculty*
   By heaven, thy madness shall be paid by weight   155
   Till our scale turn the beam.° O rose of May!   *till the retribution outweighs the*
   Dear maid, kind sister, sweet Ophelia!   *offense on the scale*
   O heavens! is't possible a young maid's wits
   Should be as mortal as an old man's life?
   Nature is fine in love, and where 'tis fine,   160
   It sends some precious instance of itself
   After the thing it loves.

OPHELIA [*sings*]:
   They bore him barefaced on the bier
      (Hey non nony, nony, hey nony)
   And in his grave rained many a tear.   165

   Fare you well, my dove!
LAERTES: Hadst thou thy wits, and didst persuade revenge,
   it could not move thus.°   *not incite me the same way*
OPHELIA: You must sing "A-down, a-down," and you, "Call
   him a-down-a." O, how the wheel becomes it! It is the   170
   false steward, that stole his master's daughter.
LAERTES: This nothing's more than matter.°   *these ramblings have more*
                                                            meaning than sane talk
OPHELIA: There's rosemary, that's for remembrance. Pray you,
   love, remember. And there is pansies, that's for thoughts.
LAERTES: A document° in madness! Thoughts and remem-   *lesson*   175
   brance fitted.
OPHELIA: There's fennel for you, and columbines. There's rue
   for you, and here's some for me. We may call it herb of
   grace o' Sundays. O, you must wear your rue with a differ-
   ence! There's a daisy. I would give you some violets, but   180

they withered all when my father died. They say he made a
good end.

[*sings*] *For bonny sweet Robin is all my joy.*

LAERTES: Thought and affliction, passion, hell itself,
　　　She turns to favor° and to prettiness.　　　　　　　　　　*charm*　185
OPHELIA [*sings*]:
　　And will he not come again?
　　And will he not come again?
　　　　No, no, he is dead;
　　　　Go to thy deathbed;
　　He never will come again.　　　　　　　　　　　　　　　　　190

　　His beard was as white as snow,
　　All flaxen was his poll.°　　　　　　　　　　　　　　　*head*
　　　　He is gone, he is gone,
　　　　And we cast away moan.
　　God have mercy on his soul!　　　　　　　　　　　　　　　195

And of all Christian souls, I pray God. God be wi' you.

　　　　　　　　　　　　　　　　　　　　[*Leaves.*]

LAERTES: Do you see this, O God?
KING: Laertes, I must commune with your grief,°　　　*talk to you in your grief*
　　　Or you deny me right.° Go but apart,　　　　　　　*what is my right*
　　　Make choice of whom your wisest friends you will,　　　　　　200
　　　And they shall hear and judge 'twixt you and me.
　　　If by direct or by collateral° hand　　　　　　　　　　*indirect*
　　　They find us touched,° we will our kingdom give,　　　*implicated*
　　　Our crown, our life, and all that we call ours,
　　　To you in satisfaction; but if not,　　　　　　　　　　　　　205
　　　Be you content to lend your patience to us,
　　　And we shall jointly labor with your soul
　　　To give it due content.
LAERTES:　　　　　　　　　Let this be so.
　　　His means of death,° his obscure funeral—　　　　*the way he died*
　　　No trophy, sword, nor hatchment° o'er his bones,　　*coat of arms*　210
　　　No noble rite nor formal ostentation°—　　　　　　　*display*
　　　Cry to be heard, as 'twere from heaven to earth,
　　　That I must call't in question.°　　　　　　　　*must raise questions*
KING:　　　　　　　　　　　So you shall;
　　　And where the offense is let the great axe fall.
　　　I pray you go with me.　　　　　　　　　　　　　　　　　215

　　　　　　　　　　　　　　　　[*They leave.*]

SCENE 6. The same. Another room in the Castle.

　　[*Enter* HORATIO *with an* ATTENDANT.]

HORATIO: What are they that would speak° with me?　　*want to speak*
SERVANT: Sailors, sir. They say they have letters for you.

HORATIO: Let them come in.

[ATTENDANT *leaves.*]

I do not know from what part of the world
I should be greeted, if not from Lord Hamlet. 5

[*Enter* SAILORS.]

SAILOR: God bless you, sir.
HORATIO: Let him bless thee too.
SAILOR: He shall, sir, an't please him.° There's a letter for you,   *if it pleases him*
    sir—it comes from the ambassador that was bound for°   *headed for*
    England—if your name be Horatio, as I am let to know 10
    it is.
HORATIO [*reads the letter*]: *Horatio, when thou shalt have over-*
    looked this,° give these fellows some means° to the King. They   *looked this over/means of*
    have letters for him. Ere we were two days old at sea, a pirate   *access*
    of very warlike appointment° gave us chase. Finding our-   *equipment* 15
    selves too slow of sail, we put on a compelled valor, and in the
    grapple I boarded them. On the instant they got clear of our
    ship; so I alone became their prisoner. They have dealt with
    me like thieves of mercy; but they knew what they did: I am
    to do a good turn for them. Let the King have the letters I 20
    have sent, and repair thou to me° with as much speed as thou   *join me*
    wouldst fly° death. I have words to speak in thine ear will   *flee from*
    make thee dumb; yet are they much too light for the bore° of   *caliber*
    the matter. These good fellows will bring thee where I am.
    Rosencrantz and Guildenstern hold their course for Eng- 25
    land. Of them I have much to tell thee. Farewell.
                 He that thou knowest thine,° HAMLET.   *he who you know is yours*

Come, I will give you way° for these your letters,   *provide a channel*
And do it the speedier that you may direct me
To him from whom you brought them. 30

[*They leave.*]

SCENE 7. Another room in the Castle.

[*Enter* KING *and* LAERTES.]

KING: Now must your conscience my acquittance seal,°   *confirm my acquittal*
And you must put me in your heart for friend,
Sith° you have heard, and with a knowing ear,   *since*
That he which hath your noble father slain
Pursued my life.
LAERTES: It well appears. But tell me 5
Why you proceeded not against these feats°   *deeds*
So crimeful and so capital in nature,°   *so criminal and deserving death*
As by your safety, wisdom, all things else,
You mainly were stirred up.°   *were mightily impelled*
KING: O, for two special reasons,

Which may to you, perhaps, seem much unsinewed,°   *very weak*   10
But yet to me they are strong. The Queen his mother
Lives almost by his looks; and for myself—
My virtue or my plague, be it either which—
She's so conjunctive° to my life and soul   *so closely joined*
That, as the star moves not but in his sphere,   15
I could not but by her. The other motive
Why to a public count° I might not go   *accounting*
Is the great love the general gender° bear him,   *common people*
Who, dipping all his faults in their affection,
Would, like the spring that turneth wood to stone,   20
Convert his gyves° to graces; so that my arrows,   *prison chains*
Too slightly timbered° for so loud a wind,   *made of too flimsy wood*
Would have reverted to my bow again,
And not where I had aimed them.
LAERTES: And so have I a noble father lost;   25
A sister driven into desperate terms,°   *conditions*
Whose worth, if praises may go back again,°   *may go back to the past*
Stood challenger on mount of all the age°   *could challenge all rivals*
For her perfections. But my revenge will come.
KING: Break not your sleeps° for that. You must not think   *do not lose sleep*   30
That we are made of stuff so flat and dull
That we can let our beard be shook with danger,
And think it pastime. You shortly shall hear more.
I loved your father, and we love ourself,
And that, I hope, will teach you to imagine—   35

[*Enter a* MESSENGER *with letters.*]

How now? What news?
MESSENGER: Letters, my lord, from Hamlet:
This to your Majesty; this to the Queen.
KING: From Hamlet? Who brought them?
MESSENGER: Sailors, my lord, they say; I saw them not.
They were given me by Claudio; he received them   40
Of him that brought them.
KING: Laertes, you shall hear them.
Leave us.

[MESSENGER *leaves.*]

[*reads*] *High and Mighty—You shall know I am set naked°*   *stripped of everything*
on your kingdom. Tomorrow shall I beg leave to see your
kingly eyes; when I shall (first asking your pardon thereunto)   45
recount the occasion of my sudden and more strange return.
                        HAMLET.

What should this mean? Are all the rest come back?
Or is it some abuse,° and no such thing?   *deception*
LAERTES: Know you the hand?°   *handwriting*
KING: 'Tis Hamlet's character.   50
"Naked!"

And in a postscript here, he says "alone."
Can you advise me?
LAERTES: I am lost in it, my lord. But let him come!
It warms the very sickness in my heart   55
That I shall live and tell him to his teeth,
"Thus did'st thou."
KING: If it be so, Laertes
(As how should it be so? how otherwise?),
Will you be ruled by me?
LAERTES: Ay, my lord,
So you will not overrule me to a peace.   60
KING: To thine own peace. If he be now returned,
As checking at° his voyage, and that he means   *abandoning*
No more to undertake it, I will work him
To an exploit now ripe in my device,°   *now fully plotted by me*
Under the which he shall not choose but fall;   65
And for his death no wind of blame shall breathe,
But even his mother shall uncharge the practice°   *not allege wrongdoing*
And call it accident.
LAERTES: My lord, I will be ruled;
The rather, if you could devise it so
That I might be the organ.°   *instrument*
KING: It falls right.   70
You have been talked of since your travel much,
And that in Hamlet's hearing, for a quality
Wherein they say you shine. Your sum of parts°   *good qualities*
Did not together pluck such envy from him
As did that one; and that, in my regard,   75
Of the unworthiest siege.°   *of least importance*
LAERTES: What part is that, my lord?
KING: A very riband° in the cap of youth—   *a mere adornment*
Yet needful too; for youth no less becomes°   *no less fits*
The light and careless livery° that it wears   *clothing*
Than settled age his sables and his weeds,°   *its rich formal garments*   80
Importing° health and graveness.° Two months since   *showing/seriousness*
Here was a gentleman of Normandy.
I have seen myself, and served against, the French,
And they can well° on horseback; but this gallant   *do well*
Had witchcraft in it. He grew unto his seat,   85
And to such wondrous doing brought his horse
As had he been incorpsed and demi-natured°   *made one body and half of its nature*
With the brave beast. So far he topped my thought
That I, in forgery of° shapes and tricks,   *even in inventing*
Come short of what he did.
LAERTES: A Norman was't?   90
KING: A Norman.
LAERTES: Upon my life, Lamound.
KING: The very same.
LAERTES: I know him well. He is the brooch° indeed   *chief ornament*
And gem of all the nation.

KING: He made confession of you;°   *conceded your superior talent*   95
        And gave you such a masterly report
        For art and exercise in your defense,
        And for your rapier most especially,
        That he cried out 'twould be a sight indeed
        If one could match you. The scrimers° of their nation   *fencers*   100
        He swore had neither motion, guard, nor eye,
        If you opposed them. Sir, this report of his
        Did Hamlet so envenom with his envy
        That he could nothing do but wish and beg
        Your sudden coming over to play° with him.   *fence*   105
        Now, out of this—
LAERTES: What out of this, my lord?
KING: Laertes, was your father dear to you?
        Or are you like the painting of a sorrow,
        A face without a heart?
LAERTES: Why ask you this?
KING: Not that I think you did not love your father,   110
        But that I know love is begun by time,
        And that I see, in passages of proof,°   *by relevant examples*
        Time qualifies the spark and fire of it.
        There lives within the very flame of love
        A kind of wick or snuff that will abate it,°   *will put it out*   115
        And nothing is at a like goodness still;
        For goodness, growing to a plurisy,°   *malignant swelling*
        Dies in his own too-much. That we would do,
        We should do when we would;° for this "would" changes,   *when we want to*
        And hath abatements° and delays as many   *has obstacles*   120
        As there are tongues, are hands, are accidents;
        And then this "should" is like a spendthrift sigh,
        That hurts by easing. But to the quick of the ulcer!
        Hamlet comes back. What would you undertake
        To show yourself your father's son in deed   125
        More than in words?
LAERTES: To cut his throat in the church!
KING: No place indeed should murder sanctuarize;°   *give sanctuary to murder*
        Revenge should have no bounds.° But, good Laertes,   *know no boundaries*
        Will you do this? Keep close° within your chamber.   *stay inside*
        Hamlet, returned, shall know you are come home.   130
        We'll put on those shall praise° your excellence   *instigate people to praise*
        And set a double varnish on the fame
        The Frenchman gave you; bring you in fine° together   *at last*
        And wager on your heads. He, being remiss,°   *unsuspecting*
        Most generous, and free from all contriving,   135
        Will not peruse the foils;° so that with ease,   *check the weapons*
        Or with a little shuffling, you may choose
        A sword unbated,° and, in a pass of practice,°   *not blunted/treachery*
        Requite him° for your father.   *pay him back*
LAERTES: I will do't!
        And for that purpose I'll anoint my sword.   140

I bought an unction of a mountebank,°   *lotion from a quack*
So mortal° that, but dip a knife in it,   *lethal*
Where it draws blood no cataplasm° so rare,   *antidote*
Collected from all simples° that have virtue   *medicinal herbs*
Under the moon, can save the thing from death   145
That is but scratched withal.° I'll touch my point   *with it*
With this contagion,° that, if I gall° him slightly,   *poison/scratch*
It may be death.
KING: Let's further think of this,
Weigh what convenience both of time and means
May fit us to our shape. If this should fail,   150
And that our drift look° through our bad performance,   *that our plan should show*
'Twere better not assayed.° Therefore this project   *tried*
Should have a back° or second, that might hold   *backup*
If this did blast in proof.° Soft! let me see.   *fail when put to the test*
We'll make a solemn wager on your cunnings—°   *skills* 155
I have it!
When in your motion you are hot and dry—
As made your bouts more violent to that end—
And that he calls for drink, I'll have prepared him
A chalice for the nonce;° whereon but sipping,   *cup for that occasion* 160
If he by chance escape your venomed stuck,°   *thrust*
Our purpose may hold° there.—But stay, what noise?   *may still prevail*

[*Enter* QUEEN.]

How now, sweet queen?
QUEEN: One woe doth tread upon another's heel,
So fast they follow. Your sister's drowned, Laertes.   165
LAERTES: Drowned! O, where?
QUEEN: There is a willow grows aslant a brook,
That shows his hoar° leaves in the glassy stream.   *silvery-grey*
There with fantastic garlands did she come
Of crowflowers, nettles, daisies, and long purples,   170
That liberal° shepherds give a grosser° name,   *outspoken/coarser*
But our cold maids° do dead men's fingers call them.   *chaste maidens*
There on the pendent boughs° her coronet weeds   *hanging branches*
Clambering to hang, an envious sliver° broke,   *spiteful small branch*
When down her weedy trophies and herself   175
Fell in the weeping brook. Her clothes spread wide
And, mermaid-like, awhile they bore her up;
Which time she chanted snatches of old tunes,
As one incapable of° her own distress,   *unaware of*
Or like a creature native and indued°   *born there and used* 180
Unto that element; but long it could not be
Till that her garments, heavy with their drink,
Pulled the poor wretch from her melodious lay°   *song*
To muddy death.
LAERTES: Alas, then she is drowned?
QUEEN: Drowned, drowned.   185
LAERTES: Too much of water hast thou, poor Ophelia,

And therefore I forbid my tears; but yet
It is our trick;° nature her custom holds,   *natural trait*
Let shame say what it will. When these are gone,
The woman will be out.° Adieu, my lord.   *the woman in me will disappear*   190
I have a speech of fire, that fain° would blaze   *gladly*
But that this folly douts it.°   *puts it out*

[*He leaves.*]

KING: Let's follow, Gertrude.
How much I had to do to calm his rage!
Now fear I this will give it start again;
Therefore let's follow.   195

[*They leave.*]

THE RECEPTIVE READER

1. (Scenes 1–3) In these scenes, the plot thickens. What are the key developments here?

2. (Scene 4) How does Fortinbras' expedition against Poland become for Hamlet an occasion "to spur my dull revenge"? ◆ Hamlet's *soliloquy* here is key evidence for critics debating the question of Hamlet's apparent or alleged delay in executing the ghost's command. What does Hamlet say about the delay? What is the tone of the soliloquy? What is Hamlet's train of thought? What is his definition of "greatness"? What is the conclusion or upshot of the soliloquy? ◆ What role do you think this soliloquy serves in the context of the play as a whole?

3. (Scene 5) How does Ophelia's madness change the course of the play? Is it dramatically a digression or detour? How is it related to the tragic vision the play as a whole develops? ◆ Is Hamlet implicated in Ophelia's madness? How does it help make Laertes a major player in the final acts ? ◆ Critics have listened to Ophelia's disjointed talk and songs for clues to a repressed or hidden personality. What kinds of clues do you think they might have found?

4. (Scenes 6 and 7) What role does *chance* or sheer accident begin to play in the plot here? ◆ What impression do you get of Laertes as the king enlists his help in the king's plot? How does the king sway him?

THE CREATIVE DIMENSION

By the end of Act 4, some of the supporting characters—Polonius, Ophelia—have already made their exit. Rosencrantz and Guildenstern will not return from their voyage to England; we will not see them again. Assume the role of one of the supporting characters in the play. Tell the story of your involvement in the events, looking at people and events from your own limited point of view. (You might want to start your story "I, Polonius, . . ." or "I, Ophelia, . . .")

ACT FIVE

SCENE 1. Elsinore. A churchyard.

[*Enter two* CLOWNS, *with spades and pickaxes.*]

CLOWN: Is she to be buried in Christian burial that wilfully seeks her own salvation?

OTHER: I tell thee she is; therefore make her grave straight. The crowner hath sat on her,° and finds it Christian burial. °*coroner has examined her case* 5

CLOWN: How can that be, unless she drowned herself in her own defense?

OTHER: Why, 'tis found so.

CLOWN: It must be *se offendendo*;° it cannot be else. For here °*"doing violence to herself"* lies the point: if I drown myself wittingly, it argues an act; and an act hath three branches—it is to act, to do, and to 10 perform; argal,° she drowned herself wittingly. °*(garbled for* ergo, *"therefore")*

OTHER: Nay, but hear you, Goodman Delver!

CLOWN: Give me leave Here lies the water; good. Here stands the man; good. If the man go to this water and drown himself, it is, will he, nill he, he goes—mark you that. But 15 if the water come to him and drown him, he drowns not himself. Argal, he that is not guilty of his own death shortens not his own life.

OTHER: But is this law?

CLOWN: Ay, marry,° is't—crowner's quest° law. °*yes indeed/inquest* 20

OTHER: Will you have the truth on't? If this had not been a gentlewoman, she should have been buried out o' Christian burial.° °*without religious rites*

CLOWN: Why, there thou say'st! And the more pity that great folk should have countenance° in this world to drown or °*more right* 25 hang themselves more than their even-Christian.° Come, °*ordinary Christians* my spade! There is no ancient gentlemen but gardeners, ditchers, and grave-makers. They hold up° Adam's profes- °*uphold* sion.

OTHER: Was he a gentleman? 30

CLOWN: He was the first that ever bore arms.° °*(pun on arms and weapons)*

OTHER: Why, he had none.

CLOWN: What, art a heathen? How dost thou understand the Scripture? The Scripture says Adam digged. Could he dig without arms? I'll put another question to thee. If thou 35 answerest me not to the purpose,° confess thyself— °*not to the point*

OTHER: Go to!

CLOWN: What is he that builds stronger than either the mason, the shipwright, or the carpenter?

OTHER: The gallows-maker; for that frame outlives a thousand 40 tenants.

CLOWN: I like thy wit well, in good faith. The gallows does well. But how does it well? It does well to those that do ill. Now, thou dost ill to say the gallows is built stronger

than the church. Argal, the gallows may do well to thee. 45
To't again, come!

OTHER: Who builds stronger than a mason, a shipwright, or a
carpenter?

CLOWN: Ay, tell me that, and unyoke.° *quit for the day*

OTHER: Marry, now I can tell. 50

CLOWN: To't.

OTHER: Mass,° I cannot tell. *by the Holy Mass*

[*Enter* HAMLET *and* HORATIO *afar off.*]

CLOWN: Cudgel thy brains no more about it, for your dull ass° *dim-witted donkey*
will not mend his pace with beating; and when you are
asked this question next, say "a grave-maker." The houses 55
he makes lasts till doomsday. Go, get thee to Yaughan;
fetch me a stoup° of liquor. *cup*

[SECOND CLOWN *leaves.*]

[CLOWN *digs and sings.*]

In youth when I did love, did love,
Methought it was very sweet;
To contract°—*O—the time for—a—my behove,*° *to shorten/my benefit* 60
O, methought there—a—was nothing—a—meet.

HAMLET: Has this fellow no feeling of his business, that he
sings at grave-making?

HORATIO: Custom hath made it in him a property of easiness.° *habit has made it natural*

HAMLET: 'Tis e'en so. The hand of little employment hath the 65
daintier sense.° *the little-used hand*
has the more sensitive touch

CLOWN [*sings*]:

But age with his stealing steps
Hath clawed me in his clutch,
And hath shipped me intil the land,° *put me in the ground*
As if I had never been such. 70

[*Digs up a skull.*]

HAMLET: That skull had a tongue in it, and could sing once.
How the knave jowls° it to the ground, as if 'twere Cain's *hurls*
jawbone, that did the first murder! This might be the pate
of a politician, which this ass now overreaches;° one that *gets the better of*
would circumvent° God, might it not? *outwit* 75

HORATIO: It might, my lord.

HAMLET: Or of a courtier, which could say "Good morrow,
sweet lord! How dost thou, good lord?" This might be
my Lord Such-a-one, that praised my Lord Such-a-one's
horse when he meant to beg it°—might it not? *beg for it* 80

HORATIO: Ay, my lord.

HAMLET: Why, even so! and now my Lady Worm's, chapless,° *jawless*
and knocked about the mazzard° with a sexton's spade. *head*
Here's fine revolution, if we had the trick to see't. Did
these bones cost no more the breeding but to play at 85
loggets with them?° Mine ache to think on't. *to throw them around like*
sticks

CLOWN [*sings*]:
> *A pickaxe and a spade, a spade,*
> > *For and a shrouding sheet;*
> *O, a pit of clay for to be made*
> > *For such a guest is meet.* 90

[*Digs up another skull.*]

HAMLET: There's another. Why may not that be the skull of a lawyer? Where be his quiddities now, his quillets,° his cases, his tenures, and his tricks? Why does he suffer this rude knave now to knock him about the sconce° with a dirty shovel, and will not tell him of his action of battery? Hum! This fellow might be in's time a great buyer of land, with his statutes, his recognizances, his fines, his double vouchers, his recoveries. Is this the fine of his fines,° and the recovery of his recoveries, to have his fine pate full of fine dirt? Will his vouchers vouch him no more of his purchases, and double ones too, than the length and breadth of a pair of indentures?° The very conveyances of his lands will scarcely lie in this box; and must the inheritor himself have no more, ha?

quibbles and hair-splittings

head 95

the final end of his fines

100

contracts

HORATIO: Not a jot more, my lord. 105

HAMLET: Is not parchment made of sheepskins?

HORATIO: Ay, my lord, and of calveskins too.

HAMLET: They are sheep and calves which seek out assurance in that. I will speak to this fellow. Whose grave's this, sirrah? 110

CLOWN: Mine, sir.
> [*sings*] *O, a pit of clay for to be made*
> > *For such a guest is meet.°*

just right

HAMLET: I think it be thine indeed, for thou liest in't.

CLOWN: You lie out on't, sir, and therefore 'tis not yours. For my part, I do not lie in't, yet it is mine. 115

HAMLET: Thou dost lie in't, to be in't and say it is thine. 'Tis for the dead, not for the quick;° therefore thou liest.

the living

CLOWN: 'Tis a quick lie, sir; 'twill away again from me to you.

HAMLET: What man dost thou dig it for? 120

CLOWN: For no man, sir.

HAMLET: What woman then?

CLOWN: For none neither.

HAMLET: Who is to be buried in't?

CLOWN: One that was a woman, sir; but, rest her soul, she's dead. 125

HAMLET: How absolute° the knave is! We must speak by the card,° or equivocation° will undo us. By the Lord, Horatio, this three years I have taken note of it, the age is grown so picked° that the toe of the peasant comes so near the heel of the courtier he galls his kibe.°—How long hast thou been a grave-maker?

what a stickler
exactly/double meanings

has become so sophisticated 130
rubs his sore heel

CLOWN: Of all the days in the year, I came to't that day that our last king Hamlet overcame Fortinbras.

HAMLET: How long is that since? 135

CLOWN: Cannot you tell that? Every fool can tell that. It was the very day that young Hamlet was born—he that is mad, and sent into England.

HAMLET: Ay, marry, why was he sent into England?

CLOWN: Why, because he was mad. He shall recover his wits there; or, if he do not, 'tis no great matter° there. 140 *does not matter much*

HAMLET: Why?

CLOWN: 'Twill not be seen in him there. There the men are as mad as he.

HAMLET: How came he mad? 145

CLOWN: Very strangely, they say.

HAMLET: How strangely?

CLOWN: Faith, even with losing his wits.

HAMLET: Upon what ground?

CLOWN: Why, here in Denmark. I have been sexton here, man and boy, thirty years. 150

HAMLET: How long will a man lie in the earth ere° he rot? *before*

CLOWN: Faith, if he be not rotten before he die (as we have many pocky corses° now-a-days that will scarce hold the laying in)°, he will last you some eight year or nine year. A tanner° will last you nine year. *pox-riddled corpses* / *last till the burial* 155 / *leather worker (preparing hides)*

HAMLET: Why he more than another?

CLOWN: Why, sir, his hide is so tanned with his trade that he will keep out water a great while; and your water is a sore decayer of your whoreson dead body. Here's a skull now: 160 this skull hath lain in the earth three-and-twenty years.

HAMLET: Whose was it?

CLOWN: A whoreson mad fellow's it was. Whose do you think it was?

HAMLET: Nay, I know not. 165

CLOWN: A pestilence on him for a mad rogue! He poured a flagon of Rhenish° on my head once. This same skull, sir, was Yorick's skull, the King's jester. *a pitcher of wine*

HAMLET: This?

CLOWN: Even that. 170

HAMLET: Let me see. [*takes the skull*] Alas, poor Yorick! I knew him, Horatio. A fellow of infinite jest, of most excellent fancy. He hath borne me on his back a thousand times. And now how abhorred in my imagination it is! My gorge rises at it. Here hung those lips that I have kissed I know 175 not how oft. Where be your gibes° now? your gambols? *barbs* your songs? your flashes of merriment that were wont to set the table on a roar?° Not one now, to mock your own *used to make the guests roar* grinning? Quite chapfallen?° Now get you to my lady's *down in the mouth* chamber, and tell her, let her paint an inch thick, to this 180 favor° she must come. Make her laugh at that. Prithee, *look* Horatio, tell me one thing.

HORATIO: What's that, my lord?

HAMLET: Dost thou think Alexander° looked of this fashion in *(Alexander the Great)* the earth?
185

HORATIO: Even so.
HAMLET: And smelt so? Pah!

[*Puts down the skull.*]

HORATIO: Even so, my lord.
HAMLET: To what base uses we may return, Horatio! Why may
    not imagination trace the noble dust of Alexander till he   190
    find it stopping a bunghole?°   *tap hole of a barrel*
HORATIO: 'Twere to consider too curiously, to consider so.
HAMLET: No, faith, not a jot; but to follow him thither with
    modesty enough, and likelihood to lead it; as thus:
    Alexander died, Alexander was buried, Alexander retur-   195
    neth into dust; the dust is earth; of earth we make loam;
    and why of that loam (whereto he was converted) might
    they not stop a beer barrel?

> *Imperious Caesar, dead and turned to clay,*
> *Might stop a hole to keep the wind away.*   200
> *O, that that earth which kept the world in awe*
> *Should patch a wall t' expel° the winter's flaw!*   *to keep out*

But soft! but soft! aside! Here comes the King—

[*Enter* KING, QUEEN, LAERTES, *and a coffin, with priests and lords.*]

The Queen, the courtiers. Who is this they follow?
And with such maimèd rites?° This doth betoken   *minimal ceremony*   205
The corpse they follow did with desperate hand
Fordo its own life. 'Twas of some estate.°   *of fairly high rank*
Couch we awhile,° and mark.   *let us lie low*

[*Retires with* HORATIO.]

LAERTES: What ceremony else?°   *additional ceremony*
HAMLET: That is Laertes,
    A very noble youth. Mark.   210
LAERTES: What ceremony else?
PRIEST: Her obsequies° have been as far enlarged   *funeral rites*
    As we have warranty. Her death was doubtful;°   *suspicious*
    And, but that° great command oversways the order,   *except that*
    She should in ground unsanctified have lodged°   *have been buried outside the churchyard* 215
    Till the last trumpet. For° charitable prayers,   *instead of*
    Shards, flints, and pebbles should be thrown on her.
    Yet here she is allowed her virgin crants,°   *garlands*
    Her maiden strewments,° and the bringing home   *strewn flowers*
    Of bell and burial.   220
LAERTES: Must there no more be done?
PRIEST: No more be done.
    We should profane the service of the dead
    To sing a requiem and such rest to her
    As to peace-parted souls.°   *those who died at peace*
LAERTES: Lay her i' the earth,
    And from her fair and unpolluted flesh   225

May violets spring! I tell thee, churlish priest,
A ministering angel shall my sister be
When thou liest howling.°   *in hell*
HAMLET: What, the fair Ophelia?
QUEEN: Sweets to the sweet! Farewell.

[*Scatters flowers.*]

I hoped thou shouldst have been my Hamlet's wife;   230
I thought thy bride-bed to have decked,° sweet maid,   *strewn with flowers*
And not have strewed thy grave.
LAERTES: O, treble woe°   *three times woe*
Fall ten times treble on that cursèd head
Whose wicked deed thy most ingenious sense
Deprived thee of!° Hold off the earth awhile,   *deprived you of your fine mind* 235
Till I have caught° her once more in mine arms.   *taken*

[*Leaps in the grave.*]

Now pile your dust upon the quick° and dead   *the living*
Till of this flat a mountain you have made
To over top old Pelion or the skyish head
Of blue Olympus.°   *to be higher than the legendary*   240
                                                              Greek mountains
HAMLET [*advancing*]: What is he whose grief
Bears such an emphasis?° whose phrase of sorrow   *cries out so loud*
Conjures the wandering stars,° and makes them stand   *puts a spell on the planets*
Like wonder-wounded hearers? This is I,
Hamlet the Dane.

[*Leaps in after* LAERTES.]

LAERTES: The devil take thy soul!   245

[*Grappling with him.*]

HAMLET: Thou pray'st not well.
I prithee take thy fingers from my throat;
For, though I am not splenitive° and rash,   *bad-tempered*
Yet have I in me something dangerous,
Which let thy wisdom fear. Hold off thy hand!   250
KING: Pluck them asunder.
QUEEN: Hamlet, Hamlet!
ALL: Gentlemen!
HORATIO: Good my lord, be quiet.

[*Attendants part them, and they leave the grave.*]

HAMLET: Why, I will fight with him upon this theme°   *for this cause*
Until my eyelids will no longer wag.
QUEEN: O my son, what theme?   255
HAMLET: I loved Ophelia. Forty thousand brothers
Could not (with all their quantity of love)
Make up my sum. What wilt thou do for her?

KING: O, he is mad, Laertes.
QUEEN: For love of God, forbear him! 260
HAMLET: 'Swounds, show me what thou't do.
   Woo't° weep? woo't fight? woo't fast? woo't tear thyself? *will you*
   Woo't drink up eisell?° eat a crocodile? *vinegar*
   I'll do't. Dost thou come here to whine?
   To outface me with leaping in her grave? 265
   Be buried quick° with her, and so will I. *alive*
   And if thou prate of mountains, let them throw
   Millions of acres on us, till our ground,
   Singeing his pate against the burning zone,° *its top burned by the sun*
   Make Ossa° like a wart! Nay, an thou'lt mouth, *(a huge Greek mountain)* 270
   I'll rant as well as thou.
QUEEN: This is mere madness;
   And thus a while the fit will work on him.
   Anon,° as patient as the female dove *soon*
   When that her golden couplets° are disclosed, *the twin yellow hatchlings*
   His silence will sit drooping.
HAMLET: Hear you, sir! 275
   What is the reason that you use° me thus? *treat*
   I loved you ever. But it is no matter.
   Let Hercules° himself do what he may, *(legendary mighty Greek hero)*
   The cat will mew, and dog will have his day.

[He leaves.]

KING: I pray thee, good Horatio, wait upon him. 280

[HORATIO leaves.]

   [to LAERTES*]* Strengthen your patience in our° last night's speech. *remembering our*
   We'll put the matter to the present push.° *immediate test*
   Good Gertrude, set some watch° over your son. *guard*
   This grave shall have a living° monument. *lasting*
   An hour of quiet shortly shall we see; 285
   Till then in patience our proceeding be.

[They leave.]

SCENE 2. A hall in the Castle.

   [Enter HAMLET *and* HORATIO.*]*

HAMLET: So much for this, sir; now shall you see the other.
   You do remember all the circumstance?
HORATIO: Remember it, my lord!
HAMLET: Sir, in my heart there was a kind of fighting
   That would not let me sleep. Methought° I lay *I thought* 5
   Worse than the mutines in the bilboes.° Rashly— *than shackled mutineers*
   (And praised be rashness for it) let us know,
   Our indiscretion sometime serves us well
   When our deep plots do pall.° And that should learn° us *falter/teach*

There's a divinity that shapes our ends,°   *that guides our path*   10
Rough-hew them how we will—°   *no matter how roughly we*
HORATIO: That is most certain.   *sketch it out*
HAMLET: Up from my cabin,
    My sea-gown scarfed about me,° in the dark   *wrapped in sailor's gown*
    Groped I to find out them, had my desire,
    Fingered° their packet, and in fine withdrew   *stole*   15
    To mine own room again, making so bold°   *becoming so bold as*
    (My fears forgetting manners) to unseal
    Their grand commission, where I found, Horatio
    (O royal knavery!), an exact command,
    Larded° with many several sorts of reasons,   *embellished*   20
    Importing° Denmark's health, and England's too,   *related to*
    With, ho! such bugs and goblins° in my life—   *such terrible deeds*
    That, on the supervise,° no leisure bated,°   *upon the reading/allowed*
    No, not to stay° the grinding of the axe,   *to wait for*
    My head should be struck off.
HORATIO: Is't possible?   25
HAMLET: Here's the commission;° read it at more leisure.   *instructions*
    But wilt thou hear me how I did proceed?
HORATIO: I beseech you.
HAMLET: Being thus benetted round° with villainies,   *trapped*
    Ere° I could make a prologue to my brains,   *before*   30
    They had begun the play. I sat me down;
    Devised a new commission; wrote it fair.
    I once did hold it, as our statists° do,   *officials*
    A baseness to write fair, and labored much
    How to forget that learning; but, sir, now   35
    It did me yeoman's service. Wilt thou know
    The effect of what I wrote?
HORATIO: Ay, good my lord.
HAMLET: An earnest conjuration° from the King,   *plea*
    As England was his faithful tributary,°   *payer of tribute*
    As love between them like the palm might flourish,   40
    As peace should still her wheaten garland wear
    And stand a comma° 'tween their amities,°   *as a link/friendships*
    And many such-like as's of great charge,
    That, on the view and knowing of these contents,
    Without debatement further, more or less,   45
    He should the bearers° put to sudden death,   *bearers of these papers*
    Not shriving time° allowed.   *no time for confession of sins*
HORATIO: How was this sealed?
HAMLET: Why, even in that was heaven ordinant.°   *heaven took charge*
    I had my father's signet° in my purse,   *signet ring*
    Which was the model of that Danish seal;   50
    Folded the writ° up in the form of the other,   *document*
    Subscribed it, gave't the impression, placed it safely,
    The changeling° never known. Now, the next day   *substitution*
    Was our sea-fight; and what to this was sequent°   *what followed*
    Thou know'st already.   55

HORATIO: So Guildenstern and Rosencrantz go to't.
HAMLET: Why, man, they did make love to this employment.°   *pursued it eagerly*
   They are not near my conscience;° their defeat   *on my conscience*
   Does by their own insinuation grow.°   *results from their meddling*
   'Tis dangerous when the baser nature comes   60
   Between the pass and fell° incensèd points   *thrust and cruel*
   Of mighty opposites.
HORATIO: Why, what a king is this!
HAMLET: Does it not, think'st thee, stand me now upon—°   *become my task*
   He that hath killed my king, and whored my mother,
   Popped in between the election° and my hopes,   *election to the throne*   65
   Thrown out his angle° for my proper life,   *his fishhook*
   And with such cozenage°—is't not perfect conscience   *trickery*
   To quit him° with this arm? And is't not to be damned   *pay him back*
   To let this canker° of our nature come   *blight*
   In further evil?   70
HORATIO: It must be shortly known to him from England
   What is the issue of the business there.
HAMLET: It will be short; the interim is mine,
   And a man's life's no more than to say "one."
   But I am very sorry, good Horatio,   75
   That to Laertes I forgot myself;
   For by the image of my cause I see
   The portraiture of his. I'll court his favors.
   But sure the bravery° of his grief did put me   *showy display*
   Into a towering passion.
HORATIO: Peace!° Who comes here?   *quiet*   80

   [*Enter young* OSRIC, *a courtier.*]

OSRIC: Your lordship is right welcome back to Denmark.
HAMLET: I humbly thank you, sir. [*aside to* HORATIO] Dost
   know this waterfly?
HORATIO [*aside to* HAMLET]: No, my good lord.
HAMLET [*aside to* HORATIO]: Thy state is the more gracious;° for   *soul is closer to grace*   85
   'tis a vice to know him. He hath much land, and fertile.
   Let a beast be lord of beasts, and his crib° shall stand at   *trough*
   the king's mess. 'Tis a chough;° but, as I say, spacious in   *chattering bird*
   the possession of dirt.
OSRIC: Sweet lord, if your lordship were at leisure, I should   90
   impart a thing to you from his Majesty.
HAMLET: I will receive it, sir, with all diligence of spirit. Put
   your bonnet to his right use, 'tis for the head.
OSRIC: I thank your lordship, it is very hot.
HAMLET: No, believe me, 'tis very cold; the wind is northerly.   95
OSRIC: It is indifferent cold,° my lord, indeed.   *fairly cold*
HAMLET: But yet methinks it is very sultry and hot for my
   complexion.
OSRIC: Exceedingly, my lord; it is very sultry, as 'twere—I cannot tell how. But, my lord, his Majesty bade me signify to   100
   you that he has laid a great wager on your head. Sir, this is
   the matter—

HAMLET: I beseech you remember.

[HAMLET *moves him to put on his hat.*]

OSRIC: Nay, good my lord; for mine ease, in good faith. Sir, here is newly come to court Laertes; believe me, an ab- 105 solute gentleman, full of most excellent differences, of very soft society and great showing. Indeed, to speak feelingly of him, he is the card or calendar° of gentry; for you shall *guide and index* find in him the continent° of what part a gentleman would *sum* see. 110

HAMLET: Sir, his definement suffers no perdition in you;° *(Hamlet is aping Osric's* though, I know, to divide him inventorially would dozy *precious and hyper-* the arithmetic of memory, and yet but yaw neither in re- *refined diction)* spect of his quick sail. But, in the verity of extolment, I take him to be a soul of great article, and his infusion of 115 such dearth and rareness as, to make true diction of him, his semblable is his mirror, and who else would trace him, his umbrage,° nothing more. *shadow*

OSRIC: Your lordship speaks most infallibly of him.

HAMLET: The concernancy,° sir? Why do we wrap the gentle- *point* 120 man in our more rawer breath?

OSRIC: Sir?

HORATIO [*aside to* HAMLET]: Is't not possible to understand in another tongue? You will do't, sir, really.

HAMLET: What imports the nomination of° this gentleman? *why do you name* 125

OSRIC: Of Laertes?

HORATIO [*aside*]: His purse is empty already; all's golden words are spent.

HAMLET: Of him, sir.

OSRIC: I know you are not ignorant— 130

HAMLET: I would you did, sir; yet, in faith, if you did, it would not much approve me. Well, sir?

OSRIC: You are not ignorant of what excellence Laertes is—

HAMLET: I dare not confess that, lest I should compare with him in excellence; but to know a man well were to know 135 himself.

OSRIC: I mean, sir, for his weapon; but in the imputation° laid *reputation* on him by them, in his meed he's unfellowed.° *his merit is unequaled*

HAMLET: What's his weapon?

OSRIC: Rapier and dagger. 140

HAMLET: That's two of his weapons—but well.

OSRIC: The King, sir, hath wagered with him six Barbary hors- es; against the which he has impawned,° as I take it, six *staked* French rapiers and poniards,° with their assigns,° as girdle, *daggers/ with their gear* hangers,° and so. Three of the carriages, in faith, are very *carrying straps* 145 dear to fancy, very responsive to the hilts, most delicate carriages, and of very liberal conceit.° *of rich design*

HAMLET: What call you the carriages?

HORATIO [*aside to* HAMLET]: I knew you must be edified by the margent° ere you had done. *helped by notes in the mar-* 150
gin (like readers of this text)

OSRIC: The carriages, sir, are the hangers.

HAMLET: The phrase would be more germane° to the matter if *suitable*
we could carry cannon by our sides. I would it might be
hangers till then. But on! Six Barbary horses against six
French swords, their assigns, and three liberal-conceited
carriages: that's the French bet against the Danish. Why is   155
this all impawned, as you call it?

OSRIC: The King, sir, hath laid° that, in a dozen passes° be-   *has bet/bouts*
tween yourself and him, he shall not exceed you three hits;
he hath laid on twelve for nine, and it would come to im-   160
mediate trial° if your lordship would vouchsafe the   *test*
answer.°   *agree to respond*

HAMLET: How if I answer no?

OSRIC: I mean, my lord, the opposition of your person° in trial.   *appearing in person*

HAMLET: Sir, I will walk here in the hall. If it please his   165
Majesty, it is the breathing time° of day with me. Let the   *exercise time*
foils° be brought, the gentleman willing, and the King   *blunt fencing weapons*
hold his purpose,° I will win for him if I can; if not, I will   *sticks to his intention*
gain nothing but my shame and the odd hits.

OSRIC: Shall I redeliver you° even so?   *bring back your answer*   170

HAMLET: To this effect, sir, after what flourish your nature will.

OSRIC: I commend my duty to your lordship.

HAMLET: Yours, yours. [OSRIC *leaves.*] He does well to com-
mend it himself; there are no tongues else for's turn.°   *to serve his turn*

HORATIO: This lapwing runs away with the shell on his head.°   *newly hatched bird* 175

HAMLET: He did comply with his dug° before he sucked it.   *spoke politely to the nipple*
Thus has he, and many more of the same bevy that I know
the drossy° age dotes on, only got the tune of the time   *silly*
and outward habit of encounter—a kind of yeasty° collec-   *frothy*
tion, which carries them through and through the most   180
fanned and winnowed opinions; and do but blow them to
their trial°—the bubbles are out.   *if you blow on them to test*
                                                                them

[*Enter a* LORD.]

LORD: My lord, his Majesty commended him to you by° young   *sent you greetings by*
Osric, who brings back to him that you attend him in the
hall. He sends to know if your pleasure hold to play° with   *fence*   185
Laertes, or that you will take longer time.

HAMLET: I am constant to my purposes; they follow the King's
pleasure. If his fitness speaks, mine is ready; now or when-
soever, provided I be so able as now.

LORD: The King and Queen and all are coming down.   190

HAMLET: In happy time.°   *at the right time*

LORD: The Queen desires you to use some gentle entertain-
ment° to Laertes before you fall to play.   *to speak courteously*

HAMLET: She well instructs me.

[LORD *leaves.*]

HORATIO: You will lose this wager, my lord.   195

HAMLET: I do not think so. Since he went into France I have
　　been in continual practice; I shall win at the odds. But
　　thou wouldst not think how ill all's here about my heart.
　　But it is no matter.

HORATIO: Nay, good my lord— 200

HAMLET: It is but foolery, but it is such a kind of gaingiving° as *misgiving*
　　would perhaps trouble a woman.

HORATIO: If your mind dislike anything, obey it. I will forestall
　　their repair° hither and say you are not fit. *prevent their coming*

HAMLET: Not a whit, we defy augury;° there's a special provi- *let us ignore evil omens* 205
　　dence in the fall of a sparrow. If it be now, 'tis not to
　　come; if it be not to come, it will be now; if it be not now,
　　yet it will come. The readiness is all. Since no man has
　　aught of what he leaves,° what is't to leave betimes?° Let *profits from what he leaves*
　　be. *behind/early* 210

[*Enter* KING, QUEEN, LAERTES, OSRIC, *and lords, with other*
attendants with foils and daggers. A table and cups of wine on it.]

KING: Come, Hamlet, come, and take this hand from me.

[*He puts* LAERTES' *hand into* HAMLET'S.]

HAMLET: Give me your pardon, sir. I have done you wrong;
　　But pardon't, as you are a gentleman.
　　This presence° knows, *assembled company*
　　And you must needs have heard, how I am punished 215
　　With sore distraction.° What I have done *a severely disturbed mind*
　　That might your nature, honor, and exception° *disapproval*
　　Roughly awake, I here proclaim was madness.
　　Was't Hamlet wronged Laertes? Never Hamlet.
　　If Hamlet from himself be taken away, 220
　　And when he's not himself does wrong Laertes,
　　Then Hamlet does it not. Hamlet denies it.
　　Who does it, then? His madness. If't be so,
　　Hamlet is of the faction that is wronged;
　　His madness is poor Hamlet's enemy. 225
　　Sir, in this audience,
　　Let my disclaiming from a purposed evil° *any evil done on purpose*
　　Free me so far in your most generous thoughts
　　That I have shot my arrow o'er the house
　　And hurt my brother.

LAERTES: 　　　　　　　　I am satisfied in nature,° *my personal feelings* 230
　　Whose motive in this case should stir me most
　　To my revenge. But in my terms of honor
　　I stand aloof,° and will no reconcilement *I have to hold off*
　　Till by some elder masters of known honor
　　I have a voice and precedent° of peace *confirmation of precedent for making peace* 235
　　To keep my name ungored. But till that time
　　I do receive your offered love like love,
　　And will not wrong it.

HAMLET: I embrace it freely,
And will this brother's wager frankly play.°   *enter fully into the contest*
Give us the foils. Come on.
LAERTES: Come, one for me.   240
HAMLET: I'll be your foil,° Laertes. In mine ignorance   *contrast setting off something precious*
Your skill shall, like a star in the darkest night,
Stick fiery off indeed.°   *show fiery by contrast*
LAERTES: You mock me, sir.
HAMLET: No, by this hand.
KING: Give them the foils, young Osric. Cousin Hamlet,   245
You know the wager?
HAMLET: Very well, my lord.
Your Grace has laid the odds on the weaker side.
KING: I do not fear it,° I have seen you both;   *I am not worried*
But since he is bettered,° we have therefore odds.   *has improved*
LAERTES: This is too heavy; let me see another.   250
HAMLET: This likes me well. These foils have all a length?

[*They prepare to fence.*]

OSRIC: Ay, my good lord.
KING: Set me the stoups° of wine upon that table.   *cups*
If Hamlet give the first or second hit,
Or quit° in answer of the third exchange,   *hit back* 255
Let all the battlements their ordnance° fire;   *cannon*
The King shall drink to Hamlet's better breath,
And in the cup an union° shall he throw   *a pearl*
Richer than that which four successive kings
In Denmark's crown have worn. Give me the cups;   260
And let the kettle° to the trumpet speak,   *the kettledrum*
The trumpet to the cannoneer without,
The cannons to the heavens, the heaven to earth,
"Now the King drinks to Hamlet." Come, begin.
And you the judges, bear a wary eye.   265
HAMLET: Come on, sir.
LAERTES: Come, my lord.

[*They fence.*]

HAMLET: One.
LAERTES: No.
HAMLET: Judgment!
OSRIC: A hit, a very palpable hit.
LAERTES: Well, again!
KING: Stay,° give me drink. Hamlet, this pearl is thine;   *wait*
Here's to thy health.

[*Drum; trumpets sound; a cannon goes off outside.*]

Give him the cup.
HAMLET: I'll play this bout first; set it by awhile.   270
Come. [*They fight.*] Another hit. What say you?

LAERTES: A touch, a touch; I do confess.
KING: Our son shall win.
QUEEN: He's fat,° and scant of breath.   *sweaty*
    Here, Hamlet, take my napkin,° rub thy brows.   *handkerchief*
    The Queen carouses to thy fortune, Hamlet.   275
HAMLET: Good madam!
KING: Gertrude, do not drink.
QUEEN: I will, my lord; I pray you pardon me.

    [*She drinks.*]

KING [*aside*]: It is the poisoned cup; it is too late.
HAMLET: I dare not drink yet, madam; by-and-by.
QUEEN: Come, let me wipe thy face.   280
LAERTES: My lord, I'll hit him now.
KING: I do not think't.
LAERTES [*aside*]: And yet it is almost against my conscience.
HAMLET: Come for the third, Laertes! You but dally;
    I pray you pass with your best violence;
    I am afeard you make a wanton of me.°   *treat me like a child* 285
LAERTES: Say you so? Come on.

    [*They fence.*]

OSRIC: Nothing neither way.
LAERTES: Have at you now!

    [LAERTES *wounds* HAMLET; *then, in scuffling, they change rapiers,*
    and HAMLET *wounds* LAERTES.]

KING: Part them! They are incensed.°   *enraged*
HAMLET: Nay come! again!

    [*The* QUEEN *falls.*]

OSRIC: Look to the Queen there, ho!
HORATIO: They bleed on both sides. How is it, my lord?   290
OSRIC: How is't, Laertes?
LAERTES: Why, as a woodcock to mine own springe,° Osric.   *like a (decoy) bird caught in*
    I am justly killed with mine own treachery.   *my own trap*
HAMLET: How does the Queen?
KING: She swoons to see them bleed.
QUEEN: No, no! the drink, the drink! O my dear Hamlet!   295
    The drink, the drink! I am poisoned.

    [*She dies.*]

HAMLET: O villainy! Ho! let the door be locked.
    Treachery! Seek it out.

    [LAERTES *falls.*]

LAERTES: It is here, Hamlet. Hamlet, thou art slain;
    No medicine in the world can do thee good.   300

In thee there is not half an hour of life.
The treacherous instrument is in thy hand,
Unbated° and envenomed. The foul practice°   *unchecked/vicious scheme*
Hath turned itself on me. Lo, here I lie,
Never to rise again. Thy mother's poisoned.   305
I can no more. The King, the King's to blame.
HAMLET: The point envenomed too?
     Then, venom, to thy work.

     [*Hurts the* KING.]

ALL: Treason! treason!
KING: O, yet defend me, friends! I am but hurt.   310
HAMLET: Here, thou incestuous, murderous, damned Dane,
     Drink off this potion! Is thy union here?°   *is this what you meant by a pearl*
     Follow my mother.

     [KING *dies.*]

LAERTES: He is justly served.
     It is a poison tempered by° himself.   *prepared by*
     Exchange forgiveness with me, noble Hamlet.   315
     Mine and my father's death come not upon thee,°   *you are not guilty of*
     Nor thine on me!

     [*Dies.*]

HAMLET: Heaven make thee free° of it! I follow thee.   *may heaven clear you*
     I am dead, Horatio. Wretched queen, adieu!
     You that look pale and tremble at this chance,°   *mischance*   320
     That are but mutes° or audience to this act,   *silent spectators*
     Had I but time (as this fell sergeant,° Death,   *this cruel law officer*
     Is strict in his arrest) O, I could tell you—
     But let it be. Horatio, I am dead;
     Thou liv'st; report me and my cause aright   325
     To the unsatisfied.°   *those who do not know the truth*
HORATIO: Never believe it.
     I am more an antique Roman° than a Dane.   *(like a Roman believing*
     Here's yet some liquor left.   *in honorable suicide)*
HAMLET: As th'art a man,
     Give me the cup. Let go! By heaven, I'll have't.
     O good Horatio, what a wounded name   330
     (Things standing thus unknown) shall live behind me!
     If thou didst ever hold me in thy heart,
     Absent thee from felicity° awhile,   *turn your back on ultimate happiness*
     And in this harsh world draw thy breath in pain,
     To tell my story.

     [*March afar off, and sound of cannon.*]

           What warlike noise is this?   335
OSRIC: Young Fortinbras, with conquest° come from Poland,   *after his conquest*
     To the ambassadors of England gives
     This warlike volley.

HAMLET: O, I die, Horatio!
The potent poison quite overcrows° my spirit.   *overpowers (like a cock in a cockfight)*
I cannot live to hear the news from England,   340
But I do prophesy the election lights
On° Fortinbras. He has my dying voice.   *choice of a new king goes to*
So tell him, with the occurrents,° more and less,   *events*
Which have solicited°—the rest is silence.   *incited me*

[*Dies.*]

HORATIO: Now cracks a noble heart. Good night, sweet prince,   345
And flights of angels sing thee to thy rest!

[*Sound of marching outside.*]

Why does the drum come hither?

[*Enter* FORTINBRAS *and English ambassadors, with drum,
flags, and attendants.*]

FORTINBRAS: Where is this sight?
HORATIO: What is it you would see?
If aught° of woe or wonder, cease your search.   *anything*
FORTINBRAS: This quarry cries on havoc.° O proud Death,   *these bodies call out for vengeance*   350
What feast is toward° in thine eternal cell   *ahead*
That thou so many princes at a shot
So bloodily hast struck?
AMBASSADOR: The sight is dismal;
And our affairs° from England come too late.   *news of our business*
The ears are senseless° that should give us hearing   *without life*   355
To tell him his commandment is fulfilled,
That Rosencrantz and Guildenstern are dead.
Where should we have our thanks?
HORATIO: Not from his° mouth,   *(Claudius')*
Had it the ability of life to thank you.
He never gave commandment for their death.   360
But since, so jump upon this bloody question,°   *right at the moment of bloodshed*
You from the Polack wars, and you from England,
Are here arrived, give order that these bodies
High on a stage be placed to the view;
And let me speak to the yet unknowing world   365
How these things came about. So shall you hear
Of carnal, bloody, and unnatural acts;
Of accidental judgments, casual slaughters;°   *accidental killings*
Of deaths put on by cunning and forced cause;
And, in this upshot, purposes mistook°   *intentions badly carried out*   370
Fallen on the inventors' heads. All this can I
Truly deliver.
FORTINBRAS: Let us haste to hear it,
And call the noblest to the audience.
For me, with sorrow I embrace my fortune.
I have some rights of memory° in this kingdom,   *remembered claims*   375
Which now to claim my vantage° doth invite me.   *opportunity*
HORATIO: Of that I shall have also cause to speak,

And from his mouth whose voice will draw on more.
But let this same be presently performed,
Even while men's minds are wild, lest more mischance   380
On plots and errors happen.
FORTINBRAS: Let four captains
  Bear Hamlet like a soldier to the stage;°   *platform*
  For he was likely, had he been put on,°   *if he had been made king*
  To have proved most royally; and for his passage
  The soldiers' music and the rites of war   385
  Speak loudly for him.
  Take up the bodies. Such a sight as this
  Becomes the field, but here shows much amiss.
  Go, bid the soldiers shoot.

    [*They leave marching, after which cannons are fired.*]

THE RECEPTIVE READER

1. (Scene 1) The gravediggers' scene is an outstanding example of the *dark humor* Elizabethan audiences apparently expected and loved. What is the content and mode of the jests? Is the grim or macabre humor here mere comic relief or interlude, or is it related to the overall development of the play? (What kind of *foreshadowing* is going on here?) ✧ How do Laertes and Hamlet behave at Ophelia's funeral? What side of either character comes to the fore here? ✧ What stance toward Ophelia's death is adopted by the church? by the other characters? Was her death suicide?

2. (Scene 2) Hamlet's final exchanges with his *confidant* Horatio give the audience a glimpse of his frame of mind as he approaches the tragic conclusion (or *denouement*) of the play. What are his last words on life, on fate, on human nature? In Hamlet's return from the voyage, what was the role of his own initiative, and what was the role of Providence? ✧ How does Hamlet react to the death of Rosencrantz and Guildenstern? ✧ The precious Osric gives Hamlet a last opportunity to display his satirical wit. What makes Osric a prime target? ✧ In preparing for the fencing contest, Hamlet treats Laertes with extreme courtesy. How and why? How do you reconcile his behavior here with his extreme lack of courtesy in other situations? ✧ Is the ending or denouement an example of happenstance—of confused accidental happenings that make a mockery of human planning? Is the ending an example of poetic justice, with the plotters finally getting their just deserts? Is the ending a triumph of *irony*, with the plot backfiring on the plotters, and with the "enginer hoist with his own petar"?

THE CREATIVE DIMENSION

Working with a group, make plans for a *miniproduction* that would focus on a major issue in the play, throw light on one of its puzzles, or look at part of it from a new or different perspective. Help the group with developing a concept and a script. You might want to transpose a scene or scenes to a modern setting, or you might want to rewrite a scene or scenes as seen through the eyes of a minor character. (In working with Shakespeare's *Macbeth*, one group of students staged "The Trial of Macbeth"—for killing King Duncan; another staged a miniproduction called "Ms. Beth," in which Lady Macbeth had become transformed into a ruthless corporation vice president plotting to take over the job of President Duncan.)

THE WHOLE PLAY—For Discussion or Writing

1. Laertes' final verdict is "The King, the King's to blame." Does guilt in this play rest mainly on a single individual? Is Claudius a *stereotypical villain*? What are the sources or what is the root cause of evil in this play?

2. Until recently, most critics did not question the validity of the *revenge ethic* preached by the ghost (an eye for an eye; a tooth for a tooth; a life for a life). Yet critics have also puzzled endlessly over Hamlet's apparent hesitation or delay in carrying out his dead father's command. How do you explain this paradox? Is Hamlet fully committed to the (pre-Christian) tradition of revenge or not?

3. Is Hamlet temperamentally unsuited for the task assigned him by the ghost? Did Shakespeare create a character too *introspective*, sensitive, or poetic for the kind of initiative and effective action needed?

4. Is Hamlet a *tragic hero*? Does he have a tragic flaw? Does he progress toward self-realization—a fuller understanding of himself and his situation?

5. Is Hamlet's treatment of Ophelia and his mother harsh and unreasonable? Is it part of a pattern of misogyny deeply engrained in the culture he represents?

6. The English critic J. Dover Wilson has said that "there is a savage side" to Hamlet's character (shown, for instance, in his ruthless treatment of Rosencrantz and Guildenstern or of Polonius), but that it is not meant to "detract from our general sense of the nobility and greatness" of Hamlet. Do you agree?

7. Rebecca West said that "Hamlet was disgusted by his own kind." How profound or complete is Hamlet's *disillusionment* with humankind?

8. Some critics have seen poison as the master metaphor in this play. What is its role, literally and figuratively, in the play? For you, does it seem a central theme?

JUXTAPOSITIONS

The Range of Interpretation

> *Some mystery should be left in the revelation of character in a play, just as a great deal of mystery is always left in the revelation of character in life, even in one's own character to himself.*
>
> TENNESSEE WILLIAMS

Of the writing of books about *Hamlet* there is no end. Interpretations of the play have ranged over the critical spectrum. Different schools of thought focus on different dimensions of Hamlet's multifaceted, complex character. In the words of C. S. Lewis, the fact that the critics "can never leave *Hamlet* alone" is strong evidence that "we have here something of inestimable importance." The following is a brief sampling of critical perspectives on Hamlet and his role in the play. Which of these seem most attuned to your own reading of and reaction to the play?

SAMUEL TAYLOR COLERIDGE
The Romantic Hamlet 1818

[The **Romantic** poets revered Shakespeare, initiating the modern Shakespeare cult. The Romantics rejected the fashionable eighteenth-century view of Shakespeare as an untutored, uncultivated natural genius who wrote irregular, uneven plays with flashes of brilliance. To Samuel Taylor Coleridge and other Romantics, Shakespeare's work showed the creative imagination at its most sublime. Every detail in a play was subordinated to an overriding purpose that gave "organic unity" to the whole. For Coleridge and other Romantic poets and critics, that overriding purpose in *Hamlet* was to explore a temperament akin to their own. The Romantic Hamlet is the melancholy, solitary, introspective Hamlet. He is forever musing; his "powers of action have been eaten up by thought." Charles Lamb spoke of the "shy, negligent retiring Hamlet"; he said, "Nine parts of what Hamlet does are transactions between himself and his moral sense; they are the effusions of his solitary musings." Coleridge, who said, "I have a smack of Hamlet myself," frequently returned to the topic of Hamlet's character in his lecture notes and critical essays.]

In Hamlet, [Shakespeare] seems to have wished to exemplify the moral necessity of a due balance between our attention to the objects of our senses and our meditations on the working of our minds—an *equilibrium* between the real and imaginary worlds. In Hamlet, this balance is disturbed: his thoughts, and the images of his fancy, are far more vivid than his actual perceptions, and his very perceptions, instantly passing through the medium of his contemplations, acquire, as they pass, a form and a color not naturally their own. Hence, we see a great, an almost enormous, intellectual activity, and a proportionate aversion to real action. . . . This character Shakespeare places in circumstances under which it is obliged to act on the spur of the moment: Hamlet is brave and careless of death; but he vacillates from sensibility, and procrastinates from thought, and loses the power of action in the energy of resolve. Thus it is that this tragedy presents a direct contrast to that of Macbeth; the one proceeds with the utmost slowness, the other with a crowded and breathless rapidity.

The effect of the overbalance of the imaginative power is beautifully illustrated in the everlasting broodings and superfluous activities of Hamlet's mind, which, unseated from its healthy relation, is constantly occupied with the world within and abstracted from the world without—giving substance to shadows and throwing a mist over all commonplace actualities.

QUESTIONS

1. What scenes in the play best bear out the Romantic conception of the solitary, melancholy Hamlet, "sicklied o'er by the pale cast of thought"?

2. Coleridge said that Hamlet "delays action till action is of no use and dies the victim of mere circumstance and accident." Is this view borne out by your reading of the final scenes of the play?

ELMER EDGAR STOLL
The Renaissance Hamlet 1933

[**Literary history** keeps us from seeing a play from an anachronistic, too modern point of view. Literary historians ask us to look at Hamlet in the historical context of the author's time. Seen from this point of view, Hamlet is a Renaissance prince—"a lord of the Renaissance, and loves name and fame" (E. E. Stoll). In Ophelia's words, he is a courtier, a soldier, and a scholar. Fortinbras says at the end that Hamlet would have made a truly kingly ruler: "he was likely, had he been put on, / To have proved most royally." The Renaissance ideal was not a solitary, withdrawn individual but a person functioning easily and competently in society. Hamlet is a trusting friend to Horatio; he is a courteous, generous host to the wandering players; he is fully in control when playing cat and mouse with Polonius or the king's spies. Elmer Edgar Stoll tries to show that Hamlet's self-image and the image of him mirrored in the words of other characters are very different from that of the indecisive, forever hesitating Romantic Hamlet. His Renaissance Hamlet is sociable, popular, and resolute. Shakespeare's contemporary audience, according to Stoll, took the play for "a story, not of Hamlet's procrastination" but of "a prolonged and artful struggle between him and the king."]

By his tone and bearing, likewise, and a conduct that is (if we be not cavilling) irreproachable, and a reputation that is stainless, is Hamlet to be judged. Even early in the play—as, in the soliloquy "O what a rogue," he looks forward to the Mousetrap—the tone is exactly the same that we notice when he is looking forward to the fencing match:

I'll tent him to the quick; if he but blench,
I know my course.

Such accents (unless I be utterly blind to the finer shades of expression, and deaf to the differences in rhythm of verse and speech) are not meant for those of irresolution or shiftiness, apathy, or frailty. . . .

In the form and fashion of Hamlet's speech, there is no trace of uncertainty or fatuity, as there is no trace of suspiciousness or childishness, before he falls into the human devil's clutches, in Othello. And after one's ear (for are we not at the theater?) one's simple wits. In this case [the killing of Polonius], as at the fencing match and on the trip to England, and in the same way, he makes his previous words good; for he kills the man he thinks to be the king. What is plainer still, he thus makes good the words he had uttered as he withheld his hand from the fratricide [of the king at prayer] a minute or so before. Here, indeed, is the "more horrid hent"—to "trip him as his heels may kick at heaven," as he catches the murderer spying on him. And these plain and tangible things, this record of promise and fulfilment, the audience would notice, and were meant to notice; and if a few of them stopped to think that in keeping the great deed to the last he was like the heroes of all revenge tragedies they knew of, they were used to that, and would instinctively approve of it. It is both the traditional form and the natural procedure; obviously, the deed done, the tragedy is over.

From *Art and Artifice in Shakespeare*

QUESTIONS

1. Can you find and cite other passages in which Hamlet sounds determined or resolute?

2. For critics in the Romantic tradition, scenes like Hamlet's deciding not to kill the king at prayer are mere *pretexts* or excuses for continued inaction. What side do you incline to after rereading the scene?

3. Do you think both the sensitive, meditative side of Hamlet's character stressed by the Romantics and the aggressive, determined side stressed by Stoll could be parts of the same character?

ERNEST JONES
The Psychoanalytic Hamlet   1947

[**Psychoanalytic criticism** focuses on Hamlet's inner turmoil as evidence of a profoundly disturbed, "unhinged" mind. What explains his misogyny—his harsh abusive treatment of the innocent Ophelia and his hateful comments about women in general? Psychoanalysts, trained to trace severe maladjustments to the workings of sexual repression, looked for buried, unacknowledged desires as the source of Hamlet's "near madness." Ernest Jones, a British follower of Freud, developed an elaborate theory to make Hamlet fit the Freudian definition of the Oedipus complex. Jones tried to show in the play detailed evidence of the Oedipal pattern: intense jealousy and resentment directed at the mother (seen as having betrayed the son's love); hatred of the mother's husband (Claudius) as the successful rival for the mother's affection; inability to overcome the fixation on the mother and transfer love or sexual desire to a younger woman (Ophelia). Jones saw in Hamlet's idealized picture of his dead father the result of the conscious mind adopting the teachings of society. These teachings cause the overlay of dutiful respect and filial piety that covers the repressed resentment and sexual jealousy against the father still harbored in the subconscious.]

His [Hamlet's] resentment against women is still further inflamed by the hypocritical prudishness with which Ophelia follows her father and brother in seeing evil in his natural affection, an attitude which poisons his love in exactly the same way that the love of his childhood, like that of all children, must have been poisoned. He can forgive a woman neither her rejection of his sexual advances nor, still less, her alliance with another man. Most intolerable of all to him, as Bradley well remarks, is the sight of sensuality in a quarter from which he had trained himself ever since infancy vigorously to exclude it. The total reaction culminates in the bitter misogyny of his outburst against Ophelia, who is devastated at having to bear a reaction so wholly out of proportion to her own offense and has no idea that in reviling her Hamlet is really expressing his bitter resentment against his mother. The identification is further demonstrated in the course of the play by Hamlet's killing the men who stand between him and his mother and Ophelia (Claudius and Polonius). On only one occasion does he for a moment escape from the sordid implication with which his love has been impregnated and achieve a healthier attitude toward Ophelia, namely at the open grave when in remorse he breaks out at Laertes for presuming to pretend that his feeling for her could ever equal that of her lover.

The intensity of Hamlet's repulsion against women in general, and Ophelia in particular, is a measure of the powerful repression to which his sexual feelings are being subjected. The outlet for those feelings in the direction of his mother has always been firmly dammed, and now that the narrower channel in Ophelia's direction has also been closed the increase in the original direction consequent on the awakening of early memories tasks all his energy to maintain the repression. His pent up feelings find a partial vent in other directions. The petulant irascibility and explosive outbursts called forth by his vexation at the hands of Guildenstern and Rosencrantz, and especially of Polonius, are evidently to be interpreted in this way, as also is in part the burning nature of his reproaches to his mother. Indeed toward the end of his interview with his mother the thought of her misconduct expresses itself in that almost physical disgust which is so characteristic a manifestation of intensely repressed sexual feeling.

> Let the bloat king tempt you again to bed;
> Pinch wanton on your cheek; call you his mouse;
> And let him, for a pair of reechy kisses,
> Or paddling in your neck with his damned fingers,
> Make you to ravel all this matter out . . . (III.iv)
> From Introduction to *Hamlet, King of Denmark*

QUESTIONS

For you, does this excerpt throw new light on Hamlet's anger and hostility? What scenes or details from the play does Jones make you reconsider? How persuasive is Jones' explanation of Hamlet's misogyny? What are other possible explanations?

SANDRA K. FISCHER
The Feminist Hamlet: Hearing Ophelia 1990

[Some **feminist criticism** has focused on those of Shakespeare's female characters who exhibit in varying degrees "independence, self-control, and, frequently, defiance": "By creating confident, attractive, independent women whom we like, he questions the wisdom of a power structure that insists they relinquish personal freedom" (Irene G. Dash). Other feminists have focused on those of Shakespeare's women who seem defeated by a patriarchal society. The author of the following excerpt said that the two essential steps toward a feminist approach to the play were (1) to notice how much in *Hamlet* is "based on a stereotyped judgment of women as *others*," and (2) "to read female characters in as real and serious a fashion as the males—as grappling with their identities, needing outlets for their conflicts, and trying to articulate their truths" when denied full voice. In the following excerpt from a longer article, the author tries to hear one of the "quieter and less powerful voices" almost drowned out by Hamlet's assertive rhetoric.]

Ophelia's debut is with Laertes, who bids her farewell by solidifying her role as object and by squelching any effort on her part for mutual perspective and adult interchange. Polonius and Laertes, father and son, both treat her like a child who lacks self-knowledge and apprehension about the ways of the world. As Polonius speaks his truisms to Laertes, so Laertes gives his platitudinous wisdom to Ophelia, establishing a chain of cultural dissemination and control. Remarkably missing in this scene is an outside audience or any sense of commentary on the action. In contradistinction, Hamlet's entrance reveals "the privileges of the Self . . . attributed to the masculine hero. The hero is, to begin with, *concerned* with himself; the first privilege of the Self is to have an *extra* Self who comments on or is simply aware of the original one. The tragic hero explains and justifies himself, he finds fault with himself, he insists on himself, he struggles to be true to himself" (Linda Bamber). In Ophelia's discourse, these functions are completely externalized: she finds herself explained, faulted, and struggled over by rival authorities outside herself.

Ophelia's language is an index to her enforced silence and circumscribed self. With Laertes, her familiar, she is allowed mostly half-lines and questions that are codes of acquiescence without the gesture of assent. They actually invite further commands: "Do you doubt that? . . . No more but so?" (I.iii,4, 9). Her allowed discourse with Polonius is even more frightening. First, in the course of thirteen lines she breaks her promise of secrecy to Laertes by relating to her father the gist of their conversation. Moreover, her speeches here are marked by phrases of self-effacing obeisance: "So please you. . . . my lord. . . . I do not know, my lord, what I should think. . . . I shall obey, my lord" (89–135).

In his intervening scene, I.iv, Hamlet again is afforded the medium of intimate and leisurely dialogue that establishes and cements his sense of self. Here is the camaraderie of the watch and the comforting mirror of Horatio; here as well is discourse with the ghost, which is remarkably similar to soliloquy. Ophelia's link with Hamlet's mission from the ghost is to be the recipient of his first attempt at an antic disposition. The prologue to her description of his madness is in her usual tentative form—"O my lord, my lord, I have been so affrighted. . . . My lord, I do not know, / But truly I do fear it" (II.i.75,85–86). As she describes to Polonius what she has witnessed, she depicts herself throughout as the passive object of Hamlet's actions: he holds her wrist; stares at her face; shakes her arm; nods, sighs; leaves while staring at her still. To obedience, acquiescence, and obeisance is now added negative objectification. The cause of this treatment has not been Ophelia's self, but rather her absence: "No, my good lord, but as you did command, / I did repel his letters and denied / His access to me" (II.i.108–10). Ophelia's closet scene is remarkable for acting as a discursive pivot. Here the characters embarked on parallel tragic courses are alone together, yet the chance for dialogue is missed, and each begins a path toward a stunning isolation. Ophelia loses all interlocutors as Polonius objectifies her further, "loosing" her (in the sense of unlocking or offering for mating) to probe the depths of Hamlet's self. Hamlet, meanwhile, complains of his isolation, yet he is constantly allowed confrontations that permit him to shape his changing sense of identity: with Polonius, with Rosencrantz and Guildenstern, and with the Players. As Belsey notes, "since meaning is plural, to be able to speak is to be able to take part in the contest for meaning which issues in the production of new subject-positions, new determinations of what it is possible to be." These exchanges result in Hamlet's second soliloquy, beginning "Now I am alone" (II.ii.543). Yet it is Ophelia whose linguistic isolation is the most profound, and she is offered no means to vent her confusion. Her confrontation with Hamlet in III.i, with Polonius and Claudius as silent observers, is a mistimed parody of what might have ensued in the closet scene.

Both are aware of their audience. Ophelia tries her usual speech forms, half-lines, and questions, in addition to cautious and polite assertions of a changed reality, but Hamlet refuses to communicate, judging her the bait in the trap of his selfhood.

QUESTIONS

This article focuses on functions of language other than merely communicating information. What are some of these functions? What is their meaning or symbolic significance? What are striking illustrations from the play? Do they alert you to striking differences between the roles of Hamlet and Ophelia? How does this article change your thinking about sex roles or gender roles in the play?

STEVEN BERKOFF
The Experimental Hamlet 1989

[Modern **experimental theater** has often taken literary monuments down from their pedestal. Steven Berkoff is an experimental actor-director who staged a modern-dress *Hamlet* with all the actors remaining on stage all the time "as if they were witnesses at a trial." Given "the most awful battering" by the English press, the production went on to a successful two-year tour of the European continent. One feature that caused a furor among the critics was that Berkoff had the gravedigger in the graveyard sing "My old man's a dustman, he wears a dustman's hat" during his labors. In the following excerpt from his book, *I Am Hamlet* (1989), Berkoff explores a biblical parallel as "one of the many backgrounds against which the play can be viewed."]

Many of Hamlet's lines have a biblical quality to them which gives Hamlet a Messianic fervor at times. Certainly a man of great moral fiber, and one through whom we test the corruption of the times: "If thine eye offend thee, pluck it out" could be *throw away the worser part of it.* He could be a preacher advising us and exhorting us to respect the sanctity of life. Hamlet the Messiah—for so the play seems as we tour Europe with our twelve disciples, armed with our play of Christian and humanistic ethics—an adventure story carefully concealing a profound, moving philosophy. A human being is pitted against the pursy corruption of his times and sacrificed like Jesus for daring to speak and fight against it. Betrayed by Judas/Laertes.

On our last tour to Europe there was a rumor that the Messiah was about to appear. It was his time to come and someone claimed to have seen him in the east end of London! One day on the train, idly letting my mind go its own way, I discovered that in our cast or company were exactly thirteen people including myself: nine actors, one musician, and three state-managers, a magic number. Then, playing around with the idea more fully, Laertes was a Judas, Claudius a Pilate, and Polonius the Fisherman. The Ghost was a spirit of God instructing me and sending me down to do his will. Gertrude was the Virgin Mary, and Ophelia, Mary Magdalene. The players were the children that Jesus loved, and Hamlet's soliloquies were sermons to the people. Hamlet was certainly a Jesus figure—someone who must be sacrificed from time to time to remind the world when it strays from the path of virtue or excellence; as if the world throws up these "purer specimens" that it worships and adores but somehow has to destroy, since the constant light is too much, but then can mourn the loss later.

Now the strange thing is that one found reflections of this within the group. As people got into their characters they tended to sleep in them. Hamlet was betrayed by Laertes who, like Judas, was once his ally, and Horatio was always his ally in a way like John the Baptist. In any great work one sees the struggle between two forces of light and darkness, if you like, and the shades of grey between; the audience or reader is gathered somehow from his slumbers in the nether region and encouraged to climb the top and see the view. The members of the audience are almost like floating voters who wish to be inspired and delivered from themselves into a collective force. In the struggle of the forces the martyr arises who is born of the struggle and who then guides it until his eventual destruction. He is invariably destroyed since, once he is discovered, he is then "claimed"—so the same struggle that would forge Jesus would forge Hamlet. Both are in a sense shaped by the very hostility around them. They become a mold which the forces of the world try to crush.

From *I Am Hamlet*

QUESTIONS

Does the biblical parallel seem far-fetched, or is it thought provoking? What features of the play does it make you rethink or reexamine?

WRITING ABOUT LITERATURE

27. *Studying Character (Reading for Clues)*

O brave new world that has such people in it!
SHAKESPEARE, *THE TEMPEST*

The Writing Workshop The theater creates characters who often assume a life of their own, beyond the duration of the two-hour or three-hour play. As spectator or reader, you enter imaginatively into how other human beings think and feel. A play may bring into focus human motives that you may have only imperfectly understood. A play may make you wonder at the fixed ideas and maddening contradictions that make a character human.

Writing a paper about a central character or about several key characters in a play gives you a chance to sum up what you see in the mirror the play holds up to human nature. Is there a single clue or dominant trait that will help the audience understand the character? Or are there perhaps several major related traits, and do they form an understandable pattern? Can you perhaps clear up puzzling questions about one limited but important trait? Can you take a close look at apparent contradictions in the character to see if they can be resolved? No matter what the exact focus on your paper, will you help your readers understand the character's thoughts, feelings, and actions?

When you write about a central character or the key characters in a play, consider the following general guidelines:

❖ *Be a patient listener.* Be prepared to quote revealing things a character says. In the theater, as in real life, language in many ways reveals (and sometimes unwittingly betrays) people's thoughts. Look for clues to a character in what he or she says at key points—for instance, when confiding in a friend, when defiantly talking back to an adversary, or when uttering last words.

❖ *Listen to the testimony of others.* However, remember who is talking. Consider the source. (People who love and those who hate a character are likely to give conflicting accounts.) Pay special attention when a consensus develops among different supporting characters. In Sophocles' *Antigone,* Creon is convicted of stubborn unreasonable pride out of the mouth not only of the hostile prophet but also of his own son.

❖ *Pay special attention to test situations.* What happens when a character is forced to make a decision or take a stand? In the Antigone play, for instance, what happens when Ismene is forced to take a stand or when Haimon faces his father?

❖ *Look at the character's behavior in revealing incidents.* Events that are apparent digressions may provide a challenge or a test. Hamlet's encounter with the players shows something about his large-mindedness or magnanimity, his liberality. "Use them after your own honor and dignity," he tells Polonius—make sure your treatment of them reflects your own stature. Don't go strictly by what is their due, as people do who engage in petty niggling and haggling (splitting a luncheon check down to the last decimal).

❖ *Pay attention to both nonverbal and verbal language.* Look for meaning in gestures, revealing incidents, or recurrent symbols. What do we learn about the character of Oedipus from the way he treats people who bring unwelcome news? What does the frantic tarantella symbolize that Nora dances at a climactic point in the Ibsen play?

❖ *Try to understand before you judge.* When you are angry enough at a character, you may be tempted to oversimplify, to stereotype. When you intensely dislike someone, it is easy to ascribe everything the person does to one single disreputable motive. Make allowance for ambivalent feelings on the part of the author—for a mixture of admirable and less admirable traits, for a mingling of lovable and hateful features.

Be prepared to watch for clues to a character at key points in a play:

❖ Watch for preliminary *capsule descriptions* of the character as part of the **exposition.** Claudius says early in *Hamlet:* "There's something in his soul / O'er which his melancholy sits on brood."

❖ Listen to the *self-revelations* of the character in **soliloquies** and confidential **asides;** in exchanges with **confidants**—trusted friends or associates:

> Give me that man
> That is not passion's slave, and I will wear him
> In my heart's core, ay, in my heart of hearts.

✧ Listen to *climactic confrontations* that bring to the surface thoughts and feelings that until then may have been hidden under polite or cautious disguises. Hamlet had earlier said: "But break my heart, for I must hold my tongue." Now, at a **climax** or high point of the play, he is ready to indict his mother. When she reproaches him for having offended his (new) father, or stepfather, he charges her with her offense against his (real) father, her murdered husband. He reveals his righteous anger:

QUEEN: Hamlet, thou hast thy father much offended.
HAMLET: Mother, you have my father much offended.
QUEEN: Come, come, you answer with an idle tongue.
HAMLET: Go, go, you question with a wicked tongue. (3.4.10–13)

Remember especially: Try not to build generalizations about character on a single quote, a single incident. Look for what is part of a *pattern:*

✧ Look for evidence of *recurrent traits.* For instance, Hamlet's harsher side shows in his baiting of Polonius and unceremonious treatment of Polonius' corpse; his passionate extended denunciation of his mother; his coolly sending his former schoolmates Rosencrantz and Guildenstern to their deaths. ("They are not near my conscience.")

✧ Bring together relevant evidence from *different parts* of the play. What evidence can you bring together on Hamlet's true feelings about Ophelia? In spite of his harsh treatment of her, was he capable of love for her? To answer this question, you would have to look at a range of contradictory evidence. For instance, Ophelia says, looking back: "And I, of ladies most deject and wretched, / That sucked the honey of his music vows, . . . " (3.1.155–156).

Hamlet, fending her off, alternately affirms and denies his love for her:

HAMLET: I did love you once.
OPHELIA: Indeed, my lord, you made me believe so.
HAMLET: You should not have believed me; for virtue cannot so inoculate our
old stock but we shall relish of it. I loved you not. (3.1.114–119)

Hamlet aggressively vaunts his love for her at her grave, in his altercation with Laertes:

I loved Ophelia. Forty thousand brothers
Could not (with all their quantity of love)
Make up my sum. What wilt thou do for her? (5.1.256–58)

The following student paper is focused on one aspect of Hamlet's multi-faceted character.

SAMPLE STUDENT PAPER

Playing for Time

Though this be madness, yet there is method in't.

Hamlet, Prince of Denmark: "unhinged mind" or master of intrigue? That this question continues to be asked after nearly four hundred years is testimony to the intriguing complexity of Hamlet's character. Samuel Taylor Coleridge, in *The Lectures of 1811–1812* (Lecture XII), regards Hamlet as

> an admirable and consistent character, deeply acquainted with his own feelings, painting them with such wonderful power and accuracy. . . . Such a mind as Hamlet's is near akin to madness.

How near? Most of the evidence points to the conclusion that Hamlet is fully in possession of his faculties. His behavior, while sometimes erratic or unpredictable, always has a rational motive behind it. It is true that he faces tremendous pressures. He is a victim of hostile circumstance. To Horatio he exclaims,

> The time is out of joint. O cursed spite,
> That ever I was born to set it right! (I.v.189–90)

However, throughout the play, Hamlet shows himself to be a perceptive, cogent observer of human nature and of his own inner being. He sees his mother's pretended grief. He recognizes Polonius' dishonesty. He sees through the hypocritical friendliness of Rosencrantz and Guildenstern. ("You were sent for, and there is a kind of confession in your looks" II.ii.275–76.) The father's ghost reveals that he was murdered by his own brother and, although Hamlet questions the validity of the apparition, he gradually accepts the evidence of foul play. ("It is an honest ghost, that let me tell you" I.v.138.) With only a few exceptions, Hamlet conducts himself not as a madman, but as a man weighed down with the task of avenging his father's death, his own grief and anger, and his princely duties. As Laertes says to Ophelia,

> his will is not his own.
> For he himself is subject to his birth. (I.iii.17–18)

This statement speaks of obligations and knowledge beyond the grasp or experience of common humanity. Neither Hamlet nor his actions can be judged within the limited understanding that ordinary vision affords.

Hamlet himself consistently maintains that he is "mad in craft." In other words, he pretends to have an unhinged mind in order to be able to observe and thwart his enemies while confusing and disorienting them. For this purpose he warns his friends that he might see fit "to put an antic disposition on" (I.v.172). As he says later,

> I am but mad north-north-west. When the wind is southerly I know a hawk from a handsaw. (II.ii.372–73)

His mother calls the ghost who speaks to him again in her bedroom "the very coinage of your brain" ("Alas, he's mad!" III.iv.106). Hamlet answers,

> My pulse as yours doth temperately keep time
> And makes as healthful music. It is not madness
> That I have uttered. . . .
> . . . .
> Lay not that flattering unction to your soul
> That not your trespass but my madness speaks. (III.iv. 141–47)

In assessing Hamlet's condition, we should remember that most of the discussion of his mental state comes from others' perceptions of his behavior. Ophelia, describing an encounter with Hamlet, tells her father that he came before her "as if he had been loosed out of hell" (II.i.83). Polonius, prime target of Hamlet's "wild and whirling words" (I.v. 133), prides himself on having found "the very cause of Hamlet's lunacy" (II.ii.49). In Act IV, as he returns from England, Hamlet hears the gravediggers talking about "Hamlet . . . he that is mad."

Modern psychoanalysts, like the Romantic poets before them, see Hamlet as flirting with the idea of suicide ("To be, or not to be, . . ."). Even in his morbid or depressed state, however, Hamlet manages to develop a brilliant strategy. No madman could have so fine-tuned his revenge as Hamlet does when he instructs the players in how to show the utmost restraint in playing the scene that he hopes will unhinge his mother and murderous uncle. He tells the players, "in the very torrent, tempest, and (as I may say) whirlwind of your passion, you must acquire and beget a temperance that may give it smoothness" (III.ii.5–8).

Here Hamlet displays a keen grasp of situation and moment; he also invokes a treasured Renaissance ideal: temperance. Temperance is the opposite of the loss of control in a deranged mind. Hamlet shows this ideal in action as the play races toward its tragic conclusion. In the scene just before the duel between Laertes and Hamlet, both men enter into a refined, gentlemanly discourse, an amends-making, that could not have been executed by a man bereft of reason. His understanding of the harm he has done and his obvious remorse comes through when he tells Laertes,

Let my disclaiming from a purposed evil
Free me so far in your most generous thoughts
That I have shot my arrow o'er the house
And hurt my brother. (V.ii.227–30)

Considering all that Hamlet faces and endures, much of which he abides with disarming grace, it hardly seems likely he is mad. That he would have known any other outcome is also unlikely, given the treachery and duplicity surrounding him. He is an extraordinary person in extraordinary circumstances. To judge him by conventional standards is to reduce the complexity of his character and situation to a trivial stature.

QUESTIONS

What is the author's thesis? Is it clearly and strategically presented? How is it reinforced and developed—what is the general plan of the paper? Which part of the argument or what evidence is most convincing? Can you think of contrary evidence that the student writer plays down? How important is the issue treated in this paper to our interpretation of the play?

28 AMERICAN DRAMA
Living the American Dream

I am simply asking for a theater in which adults who want to live can find plays that will heighten their awareness of what living in our time involves.
ARTHUR MILLER

In my plays I want to look at life—at the commonplace of existence—as if we had just turned a corner and run into it for the first time.
CHRISTOPHER FRY

FOCUS ON MODERN AMERICAN DRAMA

The modern American theater has over the years presented theatergoers with a wide range of choices: commercial and experimental, traditional and avant-garde, Broadway and off-Broadway and off-off-Broadway. The American stage has at various times been invaded by Irish playwrights like Sean O'Casey or Brendan Behan; French playwrights like Jean-Paul Sartre or Jean Genêt; German playwrights like Bertolt Brecht; and British playwrights like Harold Pinter or Tom Stoppard. This chapter will focus on modern American drama, looking at one major strand: the tradition of realistic drama, harking back to the problem plays of Henrik Ibsen and leading to such Arthur Miller plays as *All My Sons* and *Death of a Salesman* and beyond to plays like Tennessee Williams' *The Glass Menagerie* or Lorraine Hansberry's *Raisin in the Sun*.

What makes plays in this tradition realistic? They take us close to ordinary life. In the theater, we can make believe that the events on the stage could happen to people like us—or if not, to people we might encounter in our own lives. Part of this definition of **realism** is the *ordinariness* of many of the characters. They are not people of heroic caliber. They are not likely to be outstanding—either in dedication and courage, or in grandiose plans for evil. They are likely to be the modern antihero—vacillating between bravado and cowardice, capable of pettiness and vindictiveness. Critics therefore question whether true tragedy is still possible in the modern world. Can the modern stage still present great characters worthy of our admiration? Much of the time, we may witness not the fall of the mighty but the slow slide of the lowly. (We may, however, still feel pity and fear.)

Compared with Greek or Shakespearean tragedy, a modern play often seems to scale down the single dominant character. The characters are often part of a web of human relationships. They define themselves through their interaction with others. A recurrent theme in much modern American drama is invisible walls: the environment that hems the characters in. They are caught in a web of social and family ties that may become a trap. What they can do may be in large part determined by how and where they live. Even so, characters like Miller's salesman or Hansberry's Mama—the black matriarch who is a tower of strength for her family—loom large. We find it easy to forget that they are imaginary creations, not real people.

Realism in these plays means more than the surface realism of lives in tenement buildings or once-prosperous Southern mansions, of jobs as sales reps and assistant managers and truck drivers. The plays do not stay nailed down to the prosaic facts. Modern audiences expect **psychological realism.** First of all, we usually deal with the characters' *perception* of reality—their world made up of their personal memories, prejudices, and resentments. Secondly, a character like Arthur Miller's Willy Loman in *Death of a Salesman* drifts easily from his perception of reality (such as it is) to his daydreams, grievances, obsessions, and ambitions. In the enormously successful plays of Tennessee Williams—*The Glass Menagerie, A Streetcar Named Desire, Cat on a Hot Tin Roof* among the best known—the suppressed desires and frustrations smouldering under the surface break through, distorting or derailing safe, established patterns of living and thinking.

When realism tilts toward the sordid, it is traditionally called **naturalism.** Naturalism continues the tradition of a literary movement in late-nineteenth-century Europe and America that did not shrink from looking closely at the harsh or ugly underside of life. In the second half of the twentieth century, audiences got used to plays that had characters spill their guts on the stage, with the more callous among them trampling on the feelings of the more sensitive. For instance, Harold Pinter's *Homecoming* (1967) showed American audiences the brutal candor of people in the raw, who were bullying and bragging and abusing women and for whom the outward politenesses and decencies of bourgeois society had become a hollow shell.

ARTHUR MILLER AND THE AMERICAN DREAM

I understand Willy Loman's longing for immortality. . . .
Willy's writing his name in a cake of ice on a hot day but
he wishes he were writing in stone.

ARTHUR MILLER

Arthur Miller's best-known plays—*All My Sons, Death of a Salesman, The Crucible*—are classics of the modern American stage. From its legendary first production with Lee J. Cobb to its spectacular revival with Dustin Hoffman in

Dustin Hoffman and Kate Reid as Willy and Linda Loman in *Death of a Salesman*. Courtesy Kobal Collection/Superstock.

1984, *Death of a Salesman* has been the classic probing of the American dream. Willy Loman became the archetypal disciple of the American gospel of success—of popularity, of easy money for those who know how to make the system work and are "well liked." For theatergoers around the world, Willy became the symbol of the "drummer"—the traveling salesman, carrying his sample cases in search of the next sale, traveling on a shoeshine and a smile. Willy's credo was that those who command the easy smile, the glad hand, and the corny joke shall not want.

The sad and funny, or **tragicomic,** part of Willy Loman's story is that with one part of his mind he knows better than that. While he is trying hard to believe in his own cheerful clichés, he has lucid intervals. He knows deep down that stubborn reality does not conform to his optimistic bromides. The truth is that he is falling behind in the rat race. The facts—about his age, his dwindling sales, and his alienated family; about his older son (a perennial failure) and his blowhard younger son—are catching up with him.

Willy Loman is not a great heroic figure. As another modern nonhero, T. S. Eliot's Prufrock, said of himself, he is "not Prince Hamlet, nor was meant to be." Willy is not a good husband nor a model parent nor a leader in community affairs. But Arthur Miller did not want us to think of him as a fool or buffoon. Willy struggles, whistles in the dark, masks his confusions, and ultimately goes down to defeat. He fights his battle according to his limited lights. He is a modern Everyman, with a dignity of his own.

ARTHUR MILLER (born 1915)

Arthur Miller, who has been called "essentially a moralist" and "a moral force speaking for the conscience of America," has been a force in the American theater for half a century. He was born in New York City as the son of middle-class Jewish parents. His mother taught, and his father was a garment manufacturer. Miller started to write plays at the University of Michigan, and several of his plays became American classics as stage productions, movies, or television plays. He was married for a time to Marilyn Monroe and wrote the screenplay for her movie *The Misfits* (1961). He later wrote *After the Fall* (1964), a play in which he ruminated on the breakup of their marriage. In 1991, the biggest hit of the London stage was a new play by Arthur Miller, *The Ride down Mt. Morgan.*

Miller's *Death of a Salesman* was first performed in 1949 with Elia Kazan as the director and Lee J. Cobb as Willy Loman; it ran for 742 performances. In the fifties, like other writers and artists, Miller tussled with the House Un-American Activities Committee over earlier communist ties. Senator Joe McCarthy was using the press as a media circus, ferreting out alleged reds—making professors, university presidents, and politicians tremble. Out of this experience grew Miller's *The Crucible* (1953), the play in which he used the Salem witchcraft trials as a parable for the witchhunts, purges, and censorship binges of the twentieth century.

Death of a Salesman 1949

Certain Private Conversations in Two Acts and a Requiem

CHARACTERS

WILLY LOMAN
LINDA
BIFF

HAPPY
BERNARD
THE WOMAN
CHARLEY
UNCLE BEN
HOWARD WAGNER
JENNY
STANLEY
MISS FORSYTHE
LETTA

The action takes place in WILLY LOMAN'S *house and yard and in various places he visits in the New York and Boston of today.*

Throughout the play, in the stage directions, left and right mean stage left and stage right.

ACT ONE

(AN OVERTURE)

A melody is heard, played upon a flute. It is small and fine, telling of grass and trees and the horizon. The curtain rises.

Before us is the Salesman's house. We are aware of towering, angular shapes behind it, surrounding it on all sides. Only the blue light of the sky falls upon the house and forestage; the surrounding area shows an angry glow of orange. As more light appears, we see a solid vault of apartment houses around the small, fragile-seeming home. An air of the dream clings to the place, a dream rising out of reality. The kitchen at center seems actual enough, for there is a kitchen table with three chairs, and a refrigerator. But no other fixtures are seen. At the back of the kitchen there is a draped entrance, which leads to the living room. To the right of the kitchen, on a level raised two feet, is a bedroom furnished only with a brass bedstead and a straight chair. On a shelf over the bed a silver athletic trophy stands. A window opens onto the apartment house at the side.

Behind the kitchen, on a level raised six and a half feet, is the boys' bedroom, at present barely visible. Two beds are dimly seen, and at the back of the room a dormer window. (This bedroom is above the unseen living room.) At the left a stairway curves up to it from the kitchen.

The entire setting is wholly or, in some places, partially transparent. The roof-line of the house is one-dimensional; under and over it we see the apartment buildings. Before the house lies an apron, curving beyond the forestage into the orchestra. This forward area serves as the back yard as well as the locale of all Willy's imaginings and of his city scenes. Whenever the action is in the present the actors observe the imaginary wall-lines, entering the house only through its door at the left. But in the scenes of the past these boundaries are broken, and characters enter or leave a room by stepping "through" a wall onto the forestage.

From the right, WILLY LOMAN, *the Salesman, enters, carrying two large sample cases. The flute plays on. He hears but is not aware of it. He is past sixty years of age, dressed quietly. Even as he crosses the stage to the doorway of the house, his exhaustion is apparent. He unlocks the door, comes into the kitchen, and thankfully lets his burden down, feeling the soreness of his palms. A word-sigh escapes his lips—it might be "Oh, boy, oh, boy." He closes the door, then carries his cases out into the living room, through the draped kitchen doorway.*

LINDA, *his wife, has stirred in her bed at the right. She gets out and puts on a robe, listening. Most often jovial, she has developed an iron repression of her exceptions to* WILLY'S *behavior—she more than loves him, she admires him, as though his mercurial nature, his temper, his massive dreams and little cruelties, served her only as sharp reminders of the turbulent longings within him, longings which she shares but lacks the temperament to utter and follow to their end.*

LINDA (*hearing* WILLY *outside the bedroom, calls with some trepidation*): Willy!

WILLY: It's all right. I came back.

LINDA: Why? What happened? (*slight pause*) Did something happen, Willy?

WILLY: No, nothing happened.

LINDA: You didn't smash the car, did you?

WILLY (*with casual irritation*): I said nothing happened. Didn't you hear me?

LINDA: Don't you feel well?

WILLY: I'm tired to the death. (*The flute has faded away. He sits on the bed beside her, a little numb.*) I couldn't make it. I just couldn't make it, Linda.

LINDA (*very carefully, delicately*): Where were you all day? You look terrible.

WILLY: I got as far as a little above Yonkers. I stopped for a cup of coffee. Maybe it was the coffee.

LINDA: What?

WILLY (*after a pause*): I suddenly couldn't drive any more. The car kept going off onto the shoulder, y'know?

LINDA (*helpfully*): Oh. Maybe it was the steering again. I don't think Angelo knows the Studebaker.

WILLY: No, it's me, it's me. Suddenly I realize I'm goin' sixty miles an hour and I don't remember the last five minutes. I'm—I can't seem to—keep my mind to it.

LINDA: Maybe it's your glasses. You never went for your new glasses.

WILLY: No, I see everything. I came back ten miles an hour. It took me nearly four hours from Yonkers.

LINDA (*resigned*): Well, you'll just have to take a rest, Willy, you can't continue this way.

WILLY: I just got back from Florida.

LINDA: But you didn't rest your mind. Your mind is overactive, and the mind is what counts, dear.

WILLY: I'll start out in the morning. Maybe I'll feel better in the morning. (*She is taking off his shoes.*) These goddam arch supports are killing me.

LINDA: Take an aspirin. Should I get you an aspirin? It'll soothe you.

WILLY (*with wonder*): I was driving along, you understand? And I was fine. I was even observing the scenery. You can imagine, me looking at scenery, on the road every week of my life. But it's so beautiful up there, Linda, the trees are so thick, and the sun is warm. I opened the windshield and just let the warm air bathe over me. And then all of a sudden I'm goin' off the road! I'm tellin' ya, I absolutely forgot I was driving. If I'd've gone the other way over the white line I might've killed somebody. So I went on again—and five minutes later I'm dreamin' again, and I nearly—(*He presses two fingers against his eyes.*) I have such thoughts, I have such strange thoughts.

LINDA: Willy, dear. Talk to them again. There's no reason why you can't work in New York.

WILLY: They don't need me in New York. I'm the New England man. I'm vital in New England.

LINDA: But you're sixty years old. They can't expect you to keep traveling every week.

WILLY: I'll have to send a wire to Portland. I'm supposed to see Brown and Morrison tomorrow morning at ten o'clock to show the line. Goddammit, I could sell them! (*He starts putting on his jacket.*)

LINDA (*taking the jacket from him*): Why don't you go down to the place tomorrow and tell Howard you've simply got to work in New York? You're too accommodating, dear.

WILLY: If old man Wagner was alive I'd a been in charge of New York now! That man was a prince, he was a masterful man. But that boy of his, that Howard, he don't appreciate. When I went north the first time, the Wagner Company didn't know where New England was!

LINDA: Why don't you tell those things to Howard, dear?

WILLY (*encouraged*): I will, I definitely will. Is there any cheese?

LINDA: I'll make you a sandwich.

WILLY: No, go to sleep. I'll take some milk. I'll be up right away. The boys in?

LINDA: They're sleeping. Happy took Biff on a date tonight.

WILLY (*interested*): That so?

LINDA: It was so nice to see them shaving together, one behind the other, in the bathroom. And going out together. You notice? The whole house smells of shaving lotion.

WILLY: Figure it out. Work a lifetime to pay off a house. You finally own it, and there's nobody to live in it.

LINDA: Well, dear, life is a casting off. It's always that way.

WILLY: No, no, some people—some people accomplish something. Did Biff say anything after I went this morning?

LINDA: You shouldn't have criticized him, Willy, especially after he just got off the train. You mustn't lose your temper with him.

WILLY: When the hell did I lose my temper? I simply asked him if he was making any money. Is that a criticism?

LINDA: But, dear, how could he make any money?

WILLY (*worried and angered*): There's such an undercurrent in him. He became a moody man. Did he apologize when I left this morning?

LINDA: He was crestfallen, Willy. You know how he admires you. I think if he finds himself, then you'll both be happier and not fight any more.

WILLY: How can he find himself on a farm? Is that a life? A farmhand? In the beginning, when he was young, I thought, well, a young man, it's good for him to tramp around, take a lot of different jobs. But it's more than ten years now and he has yet to make thirty-five dollars a week!

LINDA: He's finding himself, Willy.

WILLY: Not finding yourself at the age of thirty-four is a disgrace!

LINDA: Shh!

WILLY: The trouble is he's lazy, goddammit!

LINDA: Willy, please!

WILLY: Biff is a lazy bum!

LINDA: They're sleeping. Get something to eat. Go on down.

WILLY: Why did he come home? I would like to know what brought him home.

LINDA: I don't know. I think he's still lost, Willy. I think he's very lost.

WILLY: Biff Loman is lost. In the greatest country in the world a young man with such—personal attractiveness, gets lost. And such a hard worker. There's one thing about Biff—he's not lazy.

LINDA: Never.

WILLY (*with pity and resolve*): I'll see him in the morning; I'll have a nice talk with him. I'll get him a job selling. He could be big in no time. My God! Remember how they used to follow him around in high school? When he smiled at one of them their faces lit up. When he walked down the street . . . (*He loses himself in reminiscences.*)

LINDA (*trying to bring him out of it*): Willy, dear, I got a new kind of American-type cheese today. It's whipped.

WILLY: Why do you get American when I like Swiss?

LINDA: I just thought you'd like a change—

WILLY: I don't want a change! I want Swiss cheese. Why am I always being contradicted?

LINDA (*with a covering laugh*): I thought it would be a surprise.

WILLY: Why don't you open a window in here, for God's sake?

LINDA (*with infinite patience*): They're all open, dear.

WILLY: The way they boxed us in here. Bricks and windows, windows and bricks.

LINDA: We should've bought the land next door.

WILLY: The street is lined with cars. There's not a breath of fresh air in the neighborhood. The grass don't grow any more, you can't raise a carrot in the back yard. They should've had a law against apartment houses. Remember those two beautiful elm trees out there? When I and Biff hung the swing between them?

LINDA: Yeah, like being a million miles from the city.

WILLY: They should've arrested the builder for cutting those down. They massacred the neighborhood. *Lost*: More and more I think of those days, Linda. This time of year it was lilac and wisteria. And then the peonies would come out, and the daffodils. What fragrance in this room!

LINDA: Well, after all, people had to move somewhere.

WILLY: No, there's more people now.

LINDA: I don't think there's more people. I think—

WILLY: There's more people! That's what's ruining this country! Population is getting out of control. The competition is maddening! Smell the stink from that apartment house! And another one on the other side . . . How can they whip cheese?

On WILLY'S *last line*, BIFF *and* HAPPY *raise themselves up in their beds, listening.*

LINDA: Go down, try it. And be quiet.

WILLY (*turning to* LINDA, *guiltily*): You're not worried about me, are you, sweetheart?

BIFF: What's the matter?

HAPPY: Listen!

LINDA: You've got too much on the ball to worry about.

WILLY: You're my foundation and my support, Linda.

LINDA: Just try to relax, dear. You make mountains out of molehills.

WILLY: I won't fight with him any more. If he wants to go back to Texas, let him go.

LINDA: He'll find his way.

WILLY: Sure. Certain men just don't get started till later in life. Like Thomas Edison, I think. Or B.F. Goodrich. One of them was deaf. (*He starts for the bedroom doorway.*) I'll put my money on Biff.

LINDA: And Willy—if it's warm Sunday we'll drive in the country. And we'll open the windshield, and take lunch.

WILLY: No, the windshields don't open on the new cars.

LINDA: But you opened it today.

WILLY: Me? I didn't. (*He stops.*) Now isn't that peculiar! Isn't that a remarkable—(*He breaks off in amazement and fright as the flute is heard distantly.*)

LINDA: What, darling?

WILLY: That is the most remarkable thing.

LINDA: What, dear?

WILLY: I was thinking of the Chevvy. (*slight pause*) Nineteen twenty-eight . . . when I had that red Chevvy—(*breaks off*) That funny? I coulda sworn I was driving that Chevvy today.

LINDA: Well, that's nothing. Something must've reminded you.

WILLY: Remarkable. Ts. Remember those days? The way Biff used to simonize that car? The dealer refused to believe there was eighty thousand miles on it. (*He shakes his head.*) Heh! (*to* LINDA) Close your eyes, I'll be right up. (*He walks out of the bedroom.*)

HAPPY (*to* BIFF): Jesus, maybe he smashed up the car again!

LINDA (*calling after* WILLY): Be careful on the stairs, dear! The cheese is on the middle shelf! (*She turns, goes over to the bed, takes his jacket, and goes out of the bedroom.*)

Light has risen on the boys' room. Unseen, WILLY *is heard talking to himself, "Eighty thousand miles," and a little laugh.* BIFF *gets out of bed, comes downstage a bit, and stands attentively.* BIFF *is two years older than his brother* HAPPY, *well built, but in these days bears a worn air and seems less self-assured. He has succeeded less, and his dreams are stronger and less acceptable than* HAPPY'S. HAPPY *is tall, powerfully made. Sexuality is like a visible color on him, or a scent that many women have discovered. He, like his brother, is lost, but in a different way, for he has never allowed himself to turn his face toward defeat and is thus more confused and hard-skinned, although seemingly more content.*

HAPPY (*getting out of bed*): He's going to get his license taken away if he keeps that up. I'm getting nervous about him, y'know, Biff?

BIFF: His eyes are going.

HAPPY: No, I've driven with him. He sees all right. He just doesn't keep his mind on it. I drove into the city with him last week. He stops at a green light and then it turns red and he goes. (*He laughs.*)

BIFF: Maybe he's color-blind.

HAPPY: Pop? Why, he's got the finest eye for color in the business. You know that.

BIFF (*sitting down on his bed*): I'm going to sleep.

HAPPY: You're not still sour on Dad, are you, Biff?

BIFF: He's all right, I guess.

WILLY (*underneath them, in the living room*): Yes, sir, eighty thousand miles—eighty-two thousand!

BIFF: You smoking?

HAPPY (*holding out a pack of cigarettes*): Want one?

BIFF (*taking a cigarette*): I can never sleep when I smell it.

WILLY: What a simonizing job, heh!

HAPPY (*with deep sentiment*): Funny, Biff, y'know? Us sleeping in here again? The old beds. (*He pats his bed affectionately.*) All the talk that went across those two beds, huh? Our whole lives.

BIFF: Yeah. Lotta dreams and plans.

HAPPY (*with a deep and masculine laugh*): About five hundred women would like to know what was said in this room.

They share a soft laugh.

BIFF: Remember that big Betsy something—what the hell was her name—over on Bushwick Avenue?

HAPPY (*combing his hair*): With the collie dog!

BIFF: That's the one. I got you in there, remember?

HAPPY: Yeah, that was my first time—I think. Boy, there was a pig! (*They laugh, almost crudely.*) You taught me everything I know about women. Don't forget that.

BIFF: I bet you forgot how bashful you used to be. Especially with girls.

HAPPY: Oh, I still am, Biff.

BIFF: Oh, go on.

HAPPY: I just control it, that's all. I think I got less bashful and you got more so. What happened, Biff? Where's the old humor, the old confidence? (*He shakes* BIFF'S *knee.* BIFF *gets up and moves restlessly about the room.*) What's the matter?

BIFF: Why does Dad mock me all the time?

HAPPY: He's not mocking you, he—

BIFF: Everything I say there's a twist of mockery on his face. I can't get near him.

HAPPY: He just wants you to make good, that's all. I wanted to talk to you about Dad for a long time, Biff. Something's—happening to him. He—talks to himself.

BIFF: I noticed that this morning. But he always mumbled.

HAPPY: But not so noticeable. It got so embarrassing I sent him to Florida. And you know something? Most of the time he's talking to you.

BIFF: What's he say about me?

HAPPY: I can't make it out.

BIFF: What's he say about me?

HAPPY: I think the fact that you're not settled, that you're still kind of up in the air . . .

BIFF: There's one or two other things depressing him, Happy.

HAPPY: What do you mean?

BIFF: Never mind. Just don't lay it all to me.

HAPPY: But I think if you just got started—I mean—is there any future for you out there?

BIFF: I tell ya, Hap, I don't know what the future is. I don't know—what I'm supposed to want.

HAPPY: What do you mean?

BIFF: Well, I spent six or seven years after high school trying to work myself up. Shipping clerk, salesman, business of one kind or another. And it's a measly manner of existence. To get on that subway on the hot mornings in summer. To devote your whole life to keeping stock, or making phone calls, or selling or buying. To suffer fifty weeks of the year for the sake of a two-week vacation, when all you really desire is to be outdoors, with your shirt off. And always to have to get ahead of the next fella. And still—that's how you build a future.

HAPPY: Well, you really enjoy it on a farm? Are you content out there?

BIFF (*with rising agitation*): Hap, I've had twenty or thirty different kinds of jobs since I left home before the war, and it always turns out the same. I just realized it lately. In Nebraska when I herded cattle, and the Dakotas, and Arizona, and now in Texas. It's why I came home now, I guess, because I realized it. This farm I work on, it's spring there now, see? And they've got about fifteen new colts. There's nothing more inspiring or—beautiful than the sight of a mare and a new colt. And it's cool there now, see? Texas is cool now, and it's spring. And whenever spring comes to where I am, I suddenly get the feeling, my God, I'm not gettin' anywhere! What the hell am I doing, playing around with horses, twenty-eight dollars a week! I'm thirty-four years old, I oughta be makin' my future. That's when I come running home. And now, I get here, and I don't know what to do with myself. (*after a pause*) I've always made a point of not wasting my life, and every time I come back here I know that all I've done is to waste my life.

HAPPY: You're a poet, you know that, Biff? You're a—you're an idealist!

BIFF: No, I'm mixed up very bad. Maybe I oughta get married. Maybe I oughta get stuck into something. Maybe that's my trouble. I'm like a boy. I'm not married, I'm not in business, I just—I'm like a boy. Are you content, Hap? You're a success, aren't you? Are you content?

HAPPY: Hell, no!

BIFF: Why? You're making money, aren't you?

HAPPY (*moving about with energy, expressiveness*): All I can do now is wait for the merchandise manager to die. And suppose I get to be merchandise manager? He's a good friend of mine, and he just built a terrific estate on Long Island. And he lived there about two months and sold it, and now he's building another one. He can't enjoy it once it's finished. And I know that's just what I would do. I don't know what the hell I'm workin' for. Sometimes I sit in my apartment—all alone. And I think of the rent I'm paying. And it's crazy. But then, it's what I always wanted. My own apartment, a car, and plenty of women. And still, goddammit, I'm lonely.

BIFF (*with enthusiasm*): Listen, why don't you come out West with me?

HAPPY: You and I, heh?

BIFF: Sure, maybe we could buy a ranch. Raise cattle, use our muscles. Men built like we are should be working out in the open.

HAPPY (*avidly*): The Loman Brothers, heh?

BIFF (*with vast affection*): Sure, we'd be known all over the counties!

HAPPY (*enthralled*): That's what I dream about, Biff. Sometimes I want to just rip my clothes off in the middle of the store and outbox that goddam merchandise manager. I mean I can outbox, outrun, and outlift anybody in that store, and I have to take orders from those common, petty sons-of-bitches till I can't stand it any more.

BIFF: I'm tellin' you, kid, if you were with me I'd be happy out there.

HAPPY (*enthused*): See, Biff, everybody around me is so false that I'm constantly lowering my ideals . . .

BIFF: Baby, together we'd stand up for one another, we'd have someone to trust.

HAPPY: If I were around you—

BIFF: Hap, the trouble is we weren't brought up to grub for money. I don't know how to do it.

HAPPY: Neither can I!

BIFF: Then let's go!

HAPPY: The only thing is—what can you make out there?

BIFF: But look at your friend. Builds an estate and then hasn't the peace of mind to live in it.

HAPPY: Yeah, but when he walks into the store the waves part in front of him. That's fifty-two thousand dollars a year coming through the revolving door, and I got more in my pinky finger than he's got in his head.

BIFF: Yeah, but you just said—

HAPPY: I gotta show some of those pompous, self-important executives over there that Hap Loman can make the grade. I want to walk into the store the way he walks in. Then I'll go with you, Biff. We'll be together yet, I swear. But take those two we had tonight. Now weren't they gorgeous creatures?

BIFF: Yeah, yeah, most gorgeous I've had in years.

HAPPY: I get that any time I want, Biff. Whenever I feel disgusted. The only trouble is, it gets like bowling or something. I just keep knockin' them over and it doesn't mean anything. You still run around a lot?

BIFF: Naa. I'd like to find a girl—steady, somebody with substance.

HAPPY: That's what I long for.

BIFF: Go on! You'd never come home.

HAPPY: I would! Somebody with character, with resistance! Like Mom, y'know? You're gonna call me a bastard when I tell you this. That girl Charlotte I was with tonight is engaged to be married in five weeks. (*He tries on his new hat.*)

BIFF: No kiddin'!

HAPPY: Sure, the guy's in line for the vice-presidency of the store. I don't know what gets into me, maybe I just have an overdeveloped sense of competition or something, but I went and ruined her, and furthermore I can't get rid of her. And he's the third executive I've done that to. Isn't that a crummy characteristic? And to top it all, I go to their weddings! (*indignantly, but laughing*) Like I'm not supposed to take bribes. Manufacturers offer me a hundred-dollar bill now and then to throw an order their way. You know how honest I am, but it's like this girl, see. I hate myself for it. Because I don't want the girl, and, still, I take it and—I love it!

BIFF: Let's go to sleep.

HAPPY: I guess we didn't settle anything, heh?

BIFF: I just got one idea that I think I'm going to try.

HAPPY: What's that?

BIFF: Remember Bill Oliver?

HAPPY: Sure, Oliver is very big now. You want to work for him again?

BIFF: No, but when I quit he said something to me. He put his arm on my shoulder, and he said, "Biff, if you ever need anything, come to me."

HAPPY: I remember that. That sounds good.

BIFF: I think I'll go to see him. If I could get ten thousand or even seven or eight thousand dollars I could buy a beautiful ranch.

HAPPY: I bet he'd back you. 'Cause he thought highly of you, Biff. I mean, they all do. You're well liked, Biff. That's why I say to come back here, and we both have the apartment. And I'm tellin' you, Biff, any babe you want . . .

BIFF: No, with a ranch I could do the work I like and still be something. I just wonder though. I wonder if Oliver still thinks I stole that carton of basketballs.

HAPPY: Oh, he probably forgot that long ago. It's almost ten years. You're too sensitive. Anyway, he didn't really fire you.

BIFF: Well, I think he was going to. I think that's why I quit. I was never sure whether he knew or not. I know he thought the world of me, though. I was the only one he'd let lock up the place.

WILLY (*below*): You gonna wash the engine, Biff?

HAPPY: Shh!

BIFF *looks at* HAPPY, *who is gazing down, listening.* WILLY *is mumbling in the parlor.*

HAPPY: You hear that?

They listen. WILLY *laughs warmly.*

BIFF (*growing angry*): Doesn't he know Mom can hear that?

WILLY: Don't get your sweater dirty, Biff!

A look of pain crosses BIFF'S *face.*

HAPPY: Isn't that terrible? Don't leave again, will you? You'll find a job here. You gotta stick around. I don't know what to do about him, it's getting embarrassing.

WILLY: What a simonizing job!

BIFF: Mom's hearing that!

WILLY: No kiddin', Biff, you got a date? Wonderful!

HAPPY: Go on to sleep. But talk to him in the morning, will you?

BIFF (*reluctantly getting into bed*): With her in the house. Brother!

HAPPY (*getting into bed*): I wish you'd have a good talk with him.

The light on their room begins to fade.

BIFF (*to himself in bed*): That selfish, stupid . . .

HAPPY: Sh . . . Sleep, Biff.

Their light is out. Well before they have finished speaking, WILLY'S *form is dimly seen below in the darkened kitchen. He opens the refrigerator, searches in there, and takes out a bottle of milk. The apartment houses are fading out, and the entire house and surroundings become covered with leaves. Music insinuates itself as the leaves appear.*

WILLY: Just wanna be careful with those girls, Biff, that's all. Don't make any promises. No promises of any kind. Because a girl, y'know, they always believe what you tell 'em, and you're very young, Biff, you're too young to be talking seriously to girls.

Light rises on the kitchen. WILLY, *talking, shuts the refrigerator door and comes downstage to the kitchen table. He pours milk into a glass. He is totally immersed in himself, smiling faintly.*

WILLY: Too young entirely, Biff. You want to watch your schooling first. Then when you're all set, there'll be plenty of girls for a boy like you. (*He smiles broadly at a kitchen chair.*) That so? The girls pay for you? (*He laughs.*) Boy, you must really be makin' a hit.

WILLY *is gradually addressing—physically—a point offstage, speaking through the wall of the kitchen, and his voice has been rising in volume to that of a normal conversation.*

WILLY: I been wondering why you polish the car so careful. Ha! Don't leave the hubcaps, boys. Get the chamois to the hubcaps. Happy, use newspaper on the windows, it's the easiest thing. Show him how to do it, Biff! You see, Happy? Pad it up, use it like a pad. That's it, that's it, good work. You're doin' all right, Hap. (*He pauses, then nods in approbation for a few seconds, then looks upward.*) Biff, first thing we gotta do when we get time is clip that big branch over the house. Afraid it's gonna fall in a storm and hit the roof. Tell you what. We get a rope and sling her around, and then we climb up there with a couple of saws and take her down. Soon as you finish the car, boys, I wanna see ya. I got a surprise for you, boys.

BIFF (*offstage*): Whatta ya got, Dad?

WILLY: No, you finish first. Never leave a job till you're finished—remember that. (*looking toward the "big trees"*) Biff, up in Albany I saw a beautiful hammock. I think I'll buy it next trip, and we'll hang it right between those two elms. Wouldn't that be something? Just swingin' there under those branches. Boy, that would be . . .

YOUNG BIFF *and* YOUNG HAPPY *appear from the direction* WILLY *was addressing.* HAPPY *carries rags and a pail of water.* BIFF, *wearing a sweater with a block "S,"* *carries a football.*

BIFF (*pointing in the direction of the car offstage*): How's that, Pop, professional?

WILLY: Terrific. Terrific job, boys. Good work, Biff.

HAPPY: Where's the surprise, Pop?

WILLY: In the back seat of the car.

HAPPY: Boy! (*He runs off.*)

BIFF: What is it, Dad? Tell me, what'd you buy?

WILLY (*laughing, cuffs him*): Never mind, something I want you to have.

BIFF (*turns and starts off*): What is it, Hap?

HAPPY (*offstage*): It's a punching bag!

BIFF: Oh, Pop!

WILLY: It's got Gene Tunney's signature on it!

HAPPY *runs onstage with a punching bag.*

BIFF: Gee, how'd you know we wanted a punching bag?

WILLY: Well, it's the finest thing for the timing.

HAPPY (*lying down on his back and pedaling with his feet*): I'm losing weight, you notice, Pop?

WILLY (*to* HAPPY): Jumping rope is good too.

BIFF: Did you see the new football I got?

WILLY (*examining the ball*): Where'd you get a new ball?

BIFF: The coach told me to practice my passing.

WILLY: That so? And he gave you the ball, heh?

BIFF: Well, I borrowed it from the locker room. (*He laughs confidentially.*)

WILLY (*laughing with him at the theft*): I want you to return that.

HAPPY: I told you he wouldn't like it!

BIFF (*angrily*): Well, I'm bringing it back!

WILLY (*stopping the incipient argument, to* HAPPY): Sure, he's gotta practice with a regulation ball, doesn't he? (*to* BIFF) Coach'll probably congratulate you on your initiative!

BIFF: Oh, he keeps congratulating my initiative all the time, Pop.

WILLY: That's because he likes you. If somebody else took that ball there'd be an uproar. So what's the report, boys, what's the report?

BIFF: Where'd you go this time, Dad? Gee we were lonesome for you.

WILLY (*pleased, puts an arm around each boy and they come down to the apron*): Lonesome, heh?

BIFF: Missed you every minute.

WILLY: Don't say? Tell you a secret, boys. Don't breathe it to a soul. Someday I'll have my own business, and I'll never have to leave home any more.

HAPPY: Like Uncle Charley, heh?

WILLY: Bigger than Uncle Charley! Because Charley is not—liked. He's liked, but he's not—well liked.

BIFF: Where'd you go this time, Dad?

WILLY: Well, I got on the road, and I went north to Providence. Met the Mayor.

BIFF: The Mayor of Providence!

WILLY: He was sitting in the hotel lobby.

BIFF: What'd he say?

WILLY: He said, "Morning!" And I said, "You got a fine city here, Mayor." And then he had coffee with me. And then I went to Waterbury. Waterbury is a fine city. Big clock city, the famous Waterbury clock. Sold a nice bill there. And then Boston—

Boston is the cradle of the Revolution. A fine city. And a couple of other towns in Mass., and on to Portland and Bangor and straight home!

BIFF: Gee, I'd love to go with you sometime, Dad.

WILLY: Soon as summer comes.

HAPPY: Promise?

WILLY: You and Hap and I, and I'll show you all the towns. America is full of beautiful towns and fine, upstanding people. And they know me, boys, they know me up and down New England. The finest people. And when I bring you fellas up, there'll be open sesame for all of us, 'cause one thing, boys: I have friends. I can park my car in any street in New England, and the cops protect it like their own. This summer, heh?

BIFF *and* HAPPY (*together*): Yeah! You bet!

WILLY: We'll take our bathing suits.

HAPPY: We'll carry your bags, Pop!

WILLY: Oh, won't that be something! Me comin' into the Boston stores with you boys carryin' my bags. What a sensation!

BIFF *is prancing around, practicing passing the ball.*

WILLY: You nervous, Biff, about the game?

BIFF: Not if you're gonna be there.

WILLY: What do they say about you in school, now that they made you captain?

HAPPY: There's a crowd of girls behind him every time the classes change.

BIFF (*taking* WILLY'S *hand*): This Saturday, Pop, this Saturday—just for you, I'm going to break through for a touchdown.

HAPPY: You're supposed to pass.

BIFF: I'm takin' one play for Pop. You watch me, Pop, and when I take off my helmet, that means I'm breakin' out. Then you watch me crash through that line!

WILLY (*kissing* BIFF): Oh, wait'll I tell this in Boston!

BERNARD *enters in knickers. He is younger than* BIFF, *earnest and loyal, a worried boy.*

BERNARD: Biff, where are you? You're supposed to study with me today.

WILLY: Hey, looka Bernard. What're you lookin' so anemic about, Bernard?

BERNARD: He's gotta study, Uncle Willy. He's got Regents next week.

HAPPY (*tauntingly, spinning* BERNARD *around*): Let's box, Bernard!

BERNARD: Biff! (*He gets away from* HAPPY.) Listen, Biff, I heard Mr. Birnbaum say that if you don't start studyin' math he's gonna flunk you, and you won't graduate. I heard him!

WILLY: You better study with him, Biff. Go ahead now.

BERNARD: I heard him!

BIFF: Oh, Pop, you didn't see my sneakers! (*He holds up a foot for* WILLY *to look at.*)

WILLY: Hey, that's a beautiful job of printing!

BERNARD (*wiping his glasses*): Just because he printed University of Virginia on his sneakers doesn't mean they've got to graduate him, Uncle Willy!

WILLY (*angrily*): What're you talking about? With scholarships to three universities they're gonna flunk him?

BERNARD: But I heard Mr. Birnbaum say—

WILLY: Don't be a pest, Bernard! (*to his boys*) What an anemic!

BERNARD: Okay, I'm waiting for you in my house, Biff.

BERNARD *goes off. The Lomans laugh.*

WILLY: Bernard is not well liked, is he?

BIFF: He's liked, but he's not well liked.

HAPPY: That's right, Pop.

WILLY: That's just what I mean. Bernard can get the best marks in school, y'understand, but when he gets out in the business world, y'understand, you are going to be five times ahead of him. That's why I thank Almighty God you're both built like Adonises. Because the man who makes an appearance in the business world, the man who creates personal interest, is the man who gets ahead. Be liked and you will never want. You take me, for instance. I never have to wait in line to see a buyer. "Willy Loman is here!" That's all they have to know, and I go right through.

BIFF: Did you knock them dead, Pop?

WILLY: Knocked 'em cold in Providence, slaughtered 'em in Boston.

HAPPY (*on his back, pedaling again*): I'm losing weight, you notice, Pop?

LINDA *enters, as of old, a ribbon in her hair, carrying a basket of washing.*

LINDA (*with youthful energy*): Hello, dear!

WILLY: Sweetheart!

LINDA: How'd the Chevvy run?

WILLY: Chevrolet, Linda, is the greatest car ever built. (*to the boys*) Since when do you let your mother carry wash up the stairs?

BIFF: Grab hold there, boy!

HAPPY: Where to, Mom?

LINDA: Hang them up on the line. And you better go down to your friends, Biff. The cellar is full of boys. They don't know what to do with themselves.

BIFF: Ah, when Pop comes home they can wait!

WILLY (*laughing appreciatively*): You better go down and tell them what to do, Biff.

BIFF: I think I'll have them sweep out the furnace room.

WILLY: Good work, Biff.

BIFF (*He goes through wall-line of kitchen to doorway at back and calls down.*): Fellas! Everybody sweep out the furnace room! I'll be right down!

VOICES: All right! Okay, Biff.

BIFF: George and Sam and Frank, come out back! We're hangin' up the wash! Come on, Hap, on the double! (*He and* HAPPY *carry out the basket.*)

LINDA: The way they obey him!

WILLY: Well, that's training, the training. I'm tellin' you, I was sellin' thousands and thousands, but I had to come home.

LINDA: Oh, the whole block'll be at that game. Did you sell anything?

WILLY: I did five hundred gross in Providence and seven hundred gross in Boston.

LINDA: No! Wait a minute, I've got a pencil. (*She pulls pencil and paper out of her apron pocket.*) That makes your commission . . . Two hundred—my God! Two hundred and twelve dollars!

WILLY: Well, I didn't figure it yet, but . . .

LINDA: How much did you do?

WILLY: Well, I—I did—about a hundred and eighty gross in Providence. Well, no—it came to—roughly two hundred gross on the whole trip.

LINDA (*without hesitation*): Two hundred gross. That's . . . (*She figures.*)

WILLY: The trouble was that three of the stores were half closed for inventory in Boston.

Otherwise I woulda broke records.

LINDA: Well, it makes seventy dollars and some pennies. That's very good.

WILLY: What do we owe?

LINDA: Well, on the first there's sixteen dollars on the refrigerator—

WILLY: Why sixteen?

LINDA: Well, the fan belt broke, so it was a dollar eighty.

WILLY: But it's brand new.

LINDA: Well, the man said that's the way it is. Till they work themselves in, y'know.

They move through the wall-line into the kitchen.

WILLY: I hope we didn't get stuck on that machine.

LINDA: They got the biggest ads of any of them!

WILLY: I know, it's a fine machine. What else?

LINDA: Well, there's nine-sixty for the washing machine. And for the vacuum cleaner there's three and a half due on the fifteenth. Then the roof, you got twenty-one dollars remaining.

WILLY: It don't leak, does it?

LINDA: No, they did a wonderful job. Then you owe Frank for the carburetor.

WILLY: I'm not going to pay that man! That goddam Chevrolet, they ought to prohibit the manufacture of that car!

LINDA: Well, you owe him three and a half. And odds and ends, comes to around a hundred and twenty dollars by the fifteenth.

WILLY: A hundred and twenty dollars! My God, if business don't pick up I don't know what I'm gonna do!

LINDA: Well, next week you'll do better.

WILLY: Oh, I'll knock 'em dead next week. I'll go to Hartford. I'm very well liked in Hartford. You know, the trouble is, Linda, people don't seem to take to me.

They move onto the forestage.

LINDA: Oh, don't be foolish.

WILLY: I know it when I walk in. They seem to laugh at me.

LINDA: Why? Why would they laugh at you? Don't talk that way, Willy.

WILLY *moves to the edge of the stage.* LINDA *goes into the kitchen and starts to darn stockings.*

WILLY: I don't know the reason for it, but they just pass me by. I'm not noticed.

LINDA: But you're doing wonderful, dear. You're making seventy to a hundred dollars a week.

WILLY: But I gotta be at it ten, twelve hours a day. Other men—I don't know—they do it easier. I don't know why—I can't stop myself—I talk too much. A man oughta come in with a few words. One thing about Charley. He's a man of few words, and they respect him.

LINDA: You don't talk too much, you're just lively.

WILLY (*smiling*): Well, I figure, what the hell, life is short, a couple of jokes. (*to himself*) I joke too much! (*The smile goes.*)

LINDA: Why? You're—

WILLY: I'm fat. I'm very—foolish to look at, Linda. I didn't tell you, but Christmas time I happened to be calling on F. H. Stewarts, and a salesman I know, as I was going in to see the buyer I heard him say something about—walrus. And I—I cracked him right across the face. I won't take that. I simply will not take that. But they do laugh at me. I know that.

LINDA: Darling . . .

WILLY: I gotta overcome it. I know I gotta overcome it. I'm not dressing to advantage, maybe.

LINDA: Willy, darling, you're the handsomest man in the world—

WILLY: Oh, no, Linda.

LINDA: To me you are. (*slight pause*) The handsomest.

From the darkness is heard the laughter of a woman. WILLY *doesn't turn to it, but it continues through* LINDA'S *lines.*

LINDA: And the boys, Willy. Few men are idolized by their children the way you are.

Music is heard as behind a scrim, to the left of the house, THE WOMAN, *dimly seen, is dressing.*

WILLY (*with great feeling*): You're the best there is, Linda, you're a pal, you know that? On the road—on the road I want to grab you sometimes and just kiss the life outa you.

The laughter is loud now, and he moves into a brightening area at the left, where THE WOMAN *has come from behind the scrim and is standing, putting on her hat, looking into a "mirror" and laughing.*

WILLY: 'Cause I get so lonely—especially when business is bad and there's nobody to talk to. I get the feeling that I'll never sell anything again, that I won't make a living for you, or a business, a business for the boys. (*He talks through* THE WOMAN'S *subsiding laughter;* THE WOMAN *primps at the "mirror."*) There's so much I want to make for—

THE WOMAN: Me? You didn't make me, Willy. I picked you.

WILLY (*pleased*): You picked me?

THE WOMAN (*who is quite proper-looking,* WILLY'S *age*): I did. I've been sitting at that desk watching all the salesmen go by, day in, day out. But you've got such a sense of humor, and we do have such a good time together, don't we?

WILLY: Sure, sure. (*He takes her in his arms.*) Why do you have to go now?

THE WOMAN: It's two o'clock . . .

WILLY: No, come on in! (*He pulls her.*)

THE WOMAN: . . . my sisters'll be scandalized. When'll you be back?

WILLY: Oh, two weeks about. Will you come up again?

THE WOMAN: Sure thing. You do make me laugh. It's good for me. (*She squeezes his arm, kisses him.*) And I think you're a wonderful man.

WILLY: You picked me, heh?

THE WOMAN: Sure. Because you're so sweet. And such a kidder.

WILLY: Well, I'll see you next time I'm in Boston.

THE WOMAN: I'll put you right through to the buyers.

WILLY (*slapping her bottom*): Right. Well, bottoms up!

THE WOMAN (*She slaps him gently and laughs.*): You just kill me, Willy. (*He suddenly grabs her and kisses her roughly.*) You kill me. And thanks for the stockings. I love a lot of stockings. Well, good night.

WILLY: Good night. And keep your pores open!

THE WOMAN: Oh, Willy!

THE WOMAN *bursts out laughing, and* LINDA'S *laughter blends in.* THE WOMAN *disappears into the dark. Now the area at the kitchen table brightens.* LINDA *is sitting where she was at the kitchen table, but now is mending a pair of her silk stockings.*

LINDA: You are, Willy. The handsomest man. You've got no reason to feel that—
WILLY (*coming out of* THE WOMAN'S *dimming area and going over to* LINDA): I'll make it all up to you, Linda, I'll—
LINDA: There's nothing to make up, dear. You're doing fine, better than—
WILLY (*noticing her mending*): What's that?
LINDA: Just mending my stockings. They're so expensive—
WILLY (*angrily, taking them from her*): I won't have you mending stockings in this house! Now throw them out!

LINDA *puts the stockings in her pocket.*

BERNARD (*entering on the run*): Where is he? If he doesn't study!
WILLY (*moving to the forestage, with great agitation*): You'll give him the answers!
BERNARD: I do, but I can't on a Regents! That's a state exam! They're liable to arrest me!
WILLY: Where is he? I'll whip him, I'll whip him!
LINDA: And he'd better give back that football, Willy, it's not nice.
WILLY: Biff! Where is he? Why is he taking everything?
LINDA: He's too rough with the girls, Willy. All the mothers are afraid of him!
WILLY: I'll whip him!
BERNARD: He's driving the car without a license!

THE WOMAN'S *laugh is heard.*

WILLY: Shut up!
LINDA: All the mothers—
WILLY: Shut up!
BERNARD (*backing quietly away and out*): Mr. Birnbaum says he's stuck up.
WILLY: Get outa here!
BERNARD: If he doesn't buckle down he'll flunk math! (*He goes off.*)
LINDA: He's right, Willy, you've gotta—
WILLY (*exploding at her*): There's nothing the matter with him! You want him to be a worm like Bernard? He's got spirit, personality . . .

As he speaks, LINDA, *almost in tears, exits into the living room.* WILLY *is alone in the kitchen, wilting and staring. The leaves are gone. It is night again, and the apartment houses look down from behind.*

WILLY: Loaded with it. Loaded! What is he stealing? He's giving it back, isn't he? Why is he stealing? What did I tell him? I never in my life told him anything but decent things.

HAPPY *in pajamas has come down the stairs;* WILLY *suddenly becomes aware of* HAPPY'S *presence.*

HAPPY: Let's go now, come on.
WILLY (*sitting down at the kitchen table*): Huh! Why did she have to wax the floors herself? Everytime she waxes the floors she keels over. She knows that!
HAPPY: Shh! Take it easy. What brought you back tonight?
WILLY: I got an awful scare. Nearly hit a kid in Yonkers. God! Why didn't I go to Alaska

with my brother Ben that time! Ben! That man was a genius, that man was success incarnate! What a mistake! He begged me to go.

HAPPY: Well, there's no use in—

WILLY: You guys! There was a man started with the clothes on his back and ended up with diamond mines!

HAPPY: Boy, someday I'd like to know how he did it.

WILLY: What's the mystery? The man knew what he wanted and went out and got it! Walked into a jungle, and comes out, the age of twenty-one, and he's rich! The world is an oyster, but you don't crack it open on a mattress!

HAPPY: Pop, I told you I'm gonna retire you for life.

WILLY: You'll retire me for life on seventy goddam dollars a week? And your women and your car and your apartment, and you'll retire me for life! Christ's sake, I couldn't get past Yonkers today! Where are you guys, where are you? The woods are burning! I can't drive a car!

CHARLEY *has appeared in the doorway. He is a large man, slow of speech, laconic, immovable. In all he says, despite what he says, there is pity, and, now, trepidation. He has a robe over pajamas, slippers on his feet. He enters the kitchen.*

CHARLEY: Everything all right?

HAPPY: Yeah, Charley, everything's . . .

WILLY: What's the matter?

CHARLEY: I heard some noise. I thought something happened. Can't we do something about the walls? You sneeze in here, and in my house hats blow off.

HAPPY: Let's go to bed, Dad. Come on.

CHARLEY *signals to* HAPPY *to go.*

WILLY: You go ahead, I'm not tired at the moment.

HAPPY (*to* WILLY): Take it easy, huh? (*He exits.*)

WILLY: What're you doin' up?

CHARLEY (*sitting down at the kitchen table opposite* WILLY): Couldn't sleep good. I had a heartburn.

WILLY: Well, you don't know how to eat.

CHARLEY: I eat with my mouth.

WILLY: No, you're ignorant. You gotta know about vitamins and things like that.

CHARLEY: Come on, let's shoot. Tire you out a little.

WILLY (*hesitantly*): All right. You got cards?

CHARLEY (*taking a deck from his pocket*): Yeah, I got them. Some place. What is it with those vitamins?

WILLY (*dealing*): They build up your bones. Chemistry.

CHARLEY: Yeah, but there's no bones in a heartburn.

WILLY: What are you talkin' about? Do you know the first thing about it?

CHARLEY: Don't get insulted.

WILLY: Don't talk about something you don't know anything about.

They are playing. Pause.

CHARLEY: What're you doin' home?

WILLY: A little trouble with the car.

CHARLEY: Oh. (*pause*) I'd like to take a trip to California.

WILLY: Don't say.

CHARLEY: You want a job?

WILLY: I got a job, I told you that. (*after a slight pause*) What the hell are you offering me a job for?

CHARLEY: Don't get insulted.

WILLY: Don't insult me.

CHARLEY: I don't see no sense in it. You don't have to go on this way.

WILLY: I got a good job. (*slight pause*) What do you keep comin' in here for?

CHARLEY: You want me to go?

WILLY (*after a pause, withering*): I can't understand it. He's going back to Texas again. What the hell is that?

CHARLEY: Let him go.

WILLY: I got nothin' to give him, Charley, I'm clean, I'm clean.

CHARLEY: He won't starve. None a them starve. Forget about him.

WILLY: Then what have I got to remember?

CHARLEY: You take it too hard. To hell with it. When a deposit bottle is broken you don't get your nickel back.

WILLY: That's easy enough for you to say.

CHARLEY: That ain't easy for me to say.

WILLY: Did you see the ceiling I put up in the living room?

CHARLEY: Yeah, that's a piece of work. To put up a ceiling is a mystery to me. How do you do it?

WILLY: What's the difference?

CHARLEY: Well, talk about it.

WILLY: You gonna put up a ceiling?

CHARLEY: How could I put up a ceiling?

WILLY: Then what the hell are you bothering me for?

CHARLEY: You're insulted again.

WILLY: A man who can't handle tools is not a man. You're disgusting.

CHARLEY: Don't call me disgusting, Willy.

> UNCLE BEN, *carrying a valise and an umbrella, enters the forestage from around the right corner of the house. He is a stolid man, in his sixties, with a mustache and an authoritative air. He is utterly certain of his destiny, and there is an aura of far places about him. He enters exactly as* WILLY *speaks.*

WILLY: I'm getting awfully tired, Ben.

> BEN'S *music is heard.* BEN *looks around at everything.*

CHARLEY: Good, keep playing; you'll sleep better. Did you call me Ben?

> BEN *looks at his watch.*

WILLY: That's funny. For a second there you reminded me of my brother Ben.

BEN: I only have a few minutes. (*He strolls, inspecting the place.* WILLY *and* CHARLEY *continue playing.*)

CHARLEY: You never heard from him again, heh? Since that time?

WILLY: Didn't Linda tell you? Couple of weeks ago we got a letter from his wife in Africa. He died.

CHARLEY: That so.

BEN (*chuckling*): So this is Brooklyn, eh?

CHARLEY: Maybe you're in for some of his money.

WILLY: Naa, he had seven sons. There's just one opportunity I had with that man . . .

BEN: I must take a train, William. There are several properties I'm looking at in Alaska.

WILLY: Sure, sure! If I'd gone with him to Alaska that time, everything would've been totally different.

CHARLEY: Go on, you'd froze to death up there.

WILLY: What're you talking about?

BEN: Opportunity is tremendous in Alaska, William. Surprised you're not up there.

WILLY: Sure, tremendous.

CHARLEY: Heh?

WILLY: There was the only man I ever met who knew the answers.

CHARLEY: Who?

BEN: How are you all?

WILLY (*taking a pot, smiling*): Fine, fine.

CHARLEY: Pretty sharp tonight.

BEN: Is Mother living with you?

WILLY: No, she died a long time ago.

CHARLEY: Who?

BEN: That's too bad. Fine specimen of a lady, Mother.

WILLY (*to* CHARLEY): Hey?

BEN: I'd hoped to see the old girl.

CHARLEY: Who died?

BEN: Heard anything from Father, have you?

WILLY (*unnerved*): What do you mean, who died?

CHARLEY (*taking a pot*): What're you talkin' about?

BEN (*looking at his watch*): William, it's half-past eight!

WILLY (*As though to dispel his confusion he angrily stops* CHARLEY'S *hand.*): That's my build!

CHARLEY: I put the ace—

WILLY: If you don't know how to play the game I'm not gonna throw my money away on you!

CHARLEY (*rising*): It was my ace, for God's sake!

WILLY: I'm through, I'm through!

BEN: When did Mother die?

WILLY: Long ago. Since the beginning you never knew how to play cards.

CHARLEY (*picks up the cards and goes to the door*): All right! Next time I'll bring a deck with five aces.

WILLY: I don't play that kind of game!

CHARLEY (*turning to him*): You ought to be ashamed of yourself!

WILLY: Yeah?

CHARLEY: Yeah! (*He goes out.*)

WILLY (*slamming the door after him*): Ignoramus!

BEN (*as* WILLY *comes toward him through the wall-line of the kitchen*): So you're William.

WILLY (*shaking* BEN'S *hand*): Ben! I've been waiting for you so long! What's the answer? How did you do it?

BEN: Oh, there's a story in that.

LINDA *enters the forestage, as of old, carrying the wash basket.*

LINDA: Is this Ben?

BEN (*gallantly*): How do you do, my dear.

LINDA: Where've you been all these years? Willy's always wondered why you—

WILLY (*pulling* BEN *away from her impatiently*): Where is Dad? Didn't you follow him?

How did you get started?

BEN: Well, I don't know how much you remember.

WILLY: Well, I was just a baby, of course, only three or four years old—

BEN: Three years and eleven months.

WILLY: What a memory, Ben!

BEN: I have many enterprises, William, and I have never kept books.

WILLY: I remember I was sitting under the wagon in—was it Nebraska?

BEN: It was South Dakota, and I gave you a bunch of wild flowers.

WILLY: I remember you walking away down some open road.

BEN (*laughing*): I was going to find Father in Alaska.

WILLY: Where is he?

BEN: At that age I had a very faulty view of geography, William. I discovered after a few days that I was heading due south, so instead of Alaska, I ended up in Africa.

LINDA: Africa!

WILLY: The Gold Coast!

BEN: Principally diamond mines.

LINDA: Diamond mines!

BEN: Yes, my dear. But I've only a few minutes—

WILLY: No! Boys! Boys! (YOUNG BIFF *and* HAPPY *appear*.) Listen to this. This is your Uncle Ben, a great man! Tell my boys, Ben!

BEN: Why, boys, when I was seventeen I walked into the jungle, and when I was twenty-one I walked out. (*He laughs.*) And by God I was rich.

WILLY (*to the boys*): You see what I been talking about? The greatest things can happen!

BEN (*glancing at his watch*): I have an appointment in Ketchikan Tuesday week.

WILLY: No, Ben! Please tell about Dad. I want my boys to hear. I want them to know the kind of stock they spring from. All I remember is a man with a big beard, and I was in Mamma's lap, sitting around a fire, and some kind of high music.

BEN: His flute. He played the flute.

WILLY: Sure, the flute, that's right!

New music is heard, a high, rollicking tune.

BEN: Father was a very great and a very wild-hearted man. We would start in Boston, and he'd toss the whole family into the wagon, and then he'd drive the team right across the country; through Ohio, and Indiana, Michigan, Illinois, and all the Western states. And we'd stop in the towns and sell the flutes that he'd made on the way. Great inventor, Father. With one gadget he made more in a week than a man like you could make in a lifetime.

WILLY: That's just the way I'm bringing them up, Ben—rugged, well liked, all-around.

BEN: Yeah? (*to* BIFF) Hit that, boy—hard as you can. (*He pounds his stomach.*)

BIFF: Oh, no, sir!

BEN (*taking boxing stance*): Come on, get to me! (*He laughs.*)

WILLY: Go to it, Biff! Go ahead, show him!

BIFF: Okay! (*He cocks his fists and starts in.*)

LINDA (*to* WILLY): Why must he fight, dear?

BEN (*sparring with* BIFF): Good boy! Good boy!

WILLY: How's that, Ben, heh?

HAPPY: Give him the left, Biff!

LINDA: Why are you fighting?

BEN: Good boy! (*Suddenly he comes in, trips* BIFF, *and stands over him, the point of his umbrella poised over* BIFF'S *eye*.)

LINDA: Look out, Biff!

BIFF: Gee!

BEN (*patting* BIFF'S *knee*): Never fight fair with a stranger, boy. You'll never get out of the jungle that way. (*taking* LINDA'S *hand and bowing*) It was an honor and a pleasure to meet you, Linda.

LINDA (*withdrawing her hand coldly, frightened*): Have a nice—trip.

BEN (*to* WILLY): And good luck with your—what do you do?

WILLY: Selling.

BEN: Yes. Well . . . (*He raises his hand in farewell to all.*)

WILLY: No, Ben, I don't want you to think . . . (*He takes* BEN'S *arm to show him.*) It's Brooklyn, I know, but we hunt too.

BEN: Really, now.

WILLY: Oh, sure, there's snakes and rabbits and—that's why I moved out here. Why, Biff can fell any one of these trees in no time! Boys! Go right over to where they're building the apartment house and get some sand. We're gonna rebuild the entire front stoop right now! Watch this, Ben!

BIFF: Yes, sir! On the double, Hap!

HAPPY (*as he and* BIFF *run off*): I lost weight, Pop, you notice?

CHARLEY *enters in knickers, even before the boys are gone.*

CHARLEY: Listen, if they steal any more from that building the watchman'll put the cops on them!

LINDA (*to* WILLY): Don't let Biff . . .

BEN *laughs lustily.*

WILLY: You shoulda seen the lumber they brought home last week. At least a dozen six-by-tens worth all kinds a money.

CHARLEY: Listen, if that watchman—

WILLY: I gave them hell, understand. But I got a couple of fearless characters there.

CHARLEY: Willy, the jails are full of fearless characters.

BEN (*clapping* WILLY *on the back, with a laugh at* CHARLEY): And the stock exchange, friend!

WILLY (*joining in* BEN'S *laughter*): Where are the rest of your pants?

CHARLEY: My wife bought them.

WILLY: Now all you need is a golf club and you can go upstairs and go to sleep. (*to* BEN) Great athlete! Between him and his son Bernard they can't hammer a nail!

BERNARD (*rushing in*): The watchman's chasing Biff!

WILLY (*angrily*): Shut up! He's not stealing anything!

LINDA (*alarmed, hurrying off left*): Where is he? Biff, dear! (*She exits.*)

WILLY (*moving toward the left, away from* BEN): There's nothing wrong. What's the matter with you?

BEN: Nervy boy. Good!

WILLY (*laughing*): Oh, nerves of iron, that Biff!

CHARLEY: Don't know what it is. My New England man comes back and he's bleedin', they murdered him up there.

WILLY: It's contacts, Charley, I got important contacts!

CHARLEY (*sarcastically*): Glad to hear it, Willy. Come in later, we'll shoot a little casino. I'll take some of your Portland money. (*He laughs at* WILLY *and exits.*)

WILLY (*turning to* BEN): Business is bad, it's murderous. But not for me, of course.

BEN: I'll stop by on my way back to Africa.

WILLY (*longingly*): Can't you stay a few days? You're just what I need, Ben, because I—I have a fine position here, but I—well, Dad left when I was such a baby and I never had a chance to talk to him and I still feel—kind of temporary about myself.

BEN: I'll be late for my train.

They are at opposite ends of the stage.

WILLY: Ben, my boys—can't we talk? They'd go into the jaws of hell for me, see, but I—

BEN: William, you're being first-rate with your boys. Outstanding, manly chaps!

WILLY (*hanging on to his words*): Oh, Ben, that's good to hear! Because sometimes I'm afraid that I'm not teaching them the right kind of—Ben, how should I teach them?

BEN (*giving great weight to each word, and with a certain vicious audacity*): William, when I walked into the jungle, I was seventeen. When I walked out I was twenty-one. And, by God, I was rich! (*He goes off into darkness around the right corner of the house.*)

WILLY: . . . was rich! That's just the spirit I want to imbue them with! To walk into a jungle! I was right! I was right! I was right!

BEN *is gone, but* WILLY *is still speaking to him as* LINDA, *in nightgown and robe, enters the kitchen, glances around for* WILLY, *then goes to the door of the house, looks out and sees him. Comes down to his left. He looks at her.*

LINDA: Willy, dear? Willy?

WILLY: I was right!

LINDA: Did you have some cheese? (*He can't answer.*) It's very late, darling. Come to bed, heh?

WILLY (*looking straight up*): Gotta break your neck to see a star in this yard.

LINDA: You coming in?

WILLY: Whatever happened to that diamond watch fob? Remember? When Ben came from Africa that time? Didn't he give me a watch fob with a diamond in it?

LINDA: You pawned it, dear. Twelve, thirteen years ago. For Biff's radio correspondence course.

WILLY: Gee, that was a beautiful thing. I'll take a walk.

LINDA: But you're in your slippers.

WILLY (*starting to go around the house at the left*): I was right! I was! (*half to* LINDA, *as he goes, shaking his head*) What a man! There was a man worth talking to. I was right!

LINDA (*calling after* WILLY): But in your slippers, Willy!

WILLY *is almost gone when* BIFF, *in his pajamas, comes down the stairs and enters the kitchen.*

BIFF: What is he doing out there?

LINDA: Sh!

BIFF: God Almighty, Mom, how long has he been doing this?

LINDA: Don't, he'll hear you.

BIFF: What the hell is the matter with him?

LINDA: It'll pass by morning.

BIFF: Shouldn't we do anything?

LINDA: Oh, my dear, you should do a lot of things, but there's nothing to do, so go to sleep.

HAPPY *comes down the stairs and sits on the steps.*

HAPPY: I never heard him so loud, Mom.

LINDA: Well, come around more often; you'll hear him. (*She sits down at the table and mends the lining of* WILLY'S *jacket.*)

BIFF: Why didn't you ever write me about this, Mom?

LINDA: How would I write to you? For over three months you had no address.

BIFF: I was on the move. But you know I thought of you all the time. You know that, don't you, pal?

LINDA: I know, dear, I know. But he likes to have a letter. Just to know that there's still a possibility for better things.

BIFF: He's not like this all the time, is he?

LINDA: It's when you come home he's always the worst.

BIFF: When I come home?

LINDA: When you write you're coming, he's all smiles, and talks about the future, and— he's just wonderful. And then the closer you seem to come, the more shaky he gets, and then, by the time you get here, he's arguing, and he seems angry at you. I think it's just that maybe he can't bring himself to—to open up to you. Why are you so hateful to each other? Why is that?

BIFF (*evasively*): I'm not hateful, Mom.

LINDA: But you no sooner come in the door than you're fighting!

BIFF: I don't know why. I mean to change. I'm tryin', Mom, you understand?

LINDA: Are you home to stay now?

BIFF: I don't know. I want to look around, see what's doin'.

LINDA: Biff, you can't look around all your life, can you?

BIFF: I just can't take hold, Mom. I can't take hold of some kind of a life.

LINDA: Biff, a man is not a bird, to come and go with the springtime.

BIFF: Your hair . . . (*He touches her hair.*) Your hair got so gray.

LINDA: Oh, it's been gray since you were in high school. I just stopped dyeing it, that's all.

BIFF: Dye it again, will ya? I don't want my pal looking old. (*He smiles.*)

LINDA: You're such a boy! You think you can go away for a year and . . . You've got to get it into your head now that one day you'll knock on this door and there'll be strange people here—

BIFF: What are you talking about? You're not even sixty, Mom.

LINDA: But what about your father?

BIFF (*lamely*): Well, I meant him too.

HAPPY: He admires Pop.

LINDA: Biff, dear, if you don't have any feeling for him, then you can't have any feeling for me.

BIFF: Sure I can, Mom.

LINDA: No. You can't just come to see me, because I love him. (*with a threat, but only a threat, of tears*) He's the dearest man in the world to me, and I won't have anyone making him feel unwanted and low and blue. You've got to make up your mind now, darling, there's no leeway any more. Either he's your father and you pay him that respect, or else you're not to come here. I know he's not easy to get along with—nobody knows that better than me—but . . .

WILLY (*from the left, with a laugh*): Hey, hey, Biffo!

BIFF (*starting to go out after* WILLY): What the hell is the matter with him? (HAPPY *stops him.*)

LINDA: Don't—don't go near him!

BIFF: Stop making excuses for him! He always, always wiped the floor with you. Never had an ounce of respect for you.

HAPPY: He's always had respect for—

BIFF: What the hell do you know about it?

HAPPY (*surlily*): Just don't call him crazy!

BIFF: He's got no character—Charley wouldn't do this. Not in his own house—spewing out that vomit from his mind.

HAPPY: Charley never had to cope with what he's got to.

BIFF: People are worse off than Willy Loman. Believe me, I've seen them!

LINDA: Then make Charley your father, Biff. You can't do that, can you? I don't say he's a great man. Willy Loman never made a lot of money. His name was never in the paper. He's not the finest character that ever lived. But he's a human being, and a terrible thing is happening to him. So attention must be paid. He's not to be allowed to fall into his grave like an old dog. Attention, attention must be finally paid to such a person. You called him crazy—

BIFF: I didn't mean—

LINDA: No, a lot of people think he's lost his—balance. But you don't have to be very smart to know what his trouble is. The man is exhausted.

HAPPY: Sure!

LINDA: A small man can be just as exhausted as a great man. He works for a company thirty-six years this March, opens up unheard-of territories to their trademark, and now in his old age they take his salary away.

HAPPY (*indignantly*): I didn't know that, Mom.

LINDA: You never asked, my dear! Now that you get your spending money someplace else you don't trouble your mind with him.

HAPPY: But I gave you money last—

LINDA: Christmas time, fifty dollars! To fix the hot water it cost ninety-seven fifty! For five weeks he's been on straight commission, like a beginner, an unknown!

BIFF: Those ungrateful bastards!

LINDA: Are they any worse than his sons? When he brought them business, when he was young, they were glad to see him. But now his old friends, the old buyers that loved him so and always found some order to hand him in a pinch—they're all dead, retired. He used to be able to make six, seven calls a day in Boston. Now he takes his valises out of the car and puts them back and takes them out again and he's exhausted. Instead of walking he talks now. He drives seven hundred miles, and when he gets there no one knows him any more, no one welcomes him. And what goes through a man's mind, driving seven hundred miles home without having earned a cent? Why shouldn't he talk to himself? Why? When he has to go to Charley and borrow fifty dollars a week and pretend to me that it's his pay? How long can that go on? How long? You see what I'm sitting here and waiting for? And you tell me he has no character? The man who never worked a day but for your benefit? When does he get the medal for that? Is this his reward—to turn around at the age of sixty-three and find his sons, who he loved better than his life, one a philandering bum—

HAPPY: Mom!

LINDA: That's all you are, my baby! (*to* BIFF) And you! What happened to the love you had for him? You were such pals! How you used to talk to him on the phone every night! How lonely he was till he could come home to you!

BIFF: All right, Mom. I'll live here in my room, and I'll get a job. I'll keep away from him, that's all.

LINDA: No, Biff. You can't stay here and fight all the time.

BIFF: He threw me out of this house, remember that.

LINDA: Why did he do that? I never knew why.

BIFF: Because I know he's a fake and he doesn't like anybody around who knows!

LINDA: Why a fake? In what way? What do you mean?

BIFF: Just don't lay it all at my feet. It's between me and him—that's all I have to say. I'll chip in from now on. He'll settle for half my pay check. He'll be all right. I'm going to bed. (*He starts for the stairs.*)

LINDA: He won't be all right.

BIFF (*turning on the stairs, furiously*): I hate this city and I'll stay here. Now what do you want?

LINDA: He's dying, Biff.

HAPPY *turns quickly to her, shocked.*

BIFF (*after a pause*): Why is he dying?

LINDA: He's been trying to kill himself.

BIFF (*with great horror*): How?

LINDA: I live from day to day.

BIFF: What're you talking about?

LINDA: Remember I wrote you that he smashed up the car again? In February?

BIFF: Well?

LINDA: The insurance inspector came. He said that they have evidence. That all these accidents in the last year—weren't—weren't—accidents.

HAPPY: How can they tell that? That's a lie.

LINDA: It seems there's a woman . . . (*she takes a breath as*)

⎧ BIFF (*sharply but contained*): What woman?

⎩ LINDA (*simultaneously*): . . . and this woman . . .

LINDA: What?

BIFF: Nothing. Go ahead.

LINDA: What did you say?

BIFF: Nothing. I just said what woman?

HAPPY: What about her?

LINDA: Well, it seems she was walking down the road and saw his car. She says that he wasn't driving fast at all, and that he didn't skid. She says he came to that little bridge, and then deliberately smashed into the railing, and it was only the shallowness of the water that saved him.

BIFF: Oh, no, he probably just fell asleep again.

LINDA: I don't think he fell asleep.

BIFF: Why not?

LINDA: Last month . . . (*with great difficulty*) Oh, boys, it's so hard to say a thing like this! He's just a big stupid man to you, but I tell you there's more good in him than in many other people. (*She chokes, wipes her eyes.*) I was looking for a fuse. The lights blew out, and I went down the cellar. And behind the fuse box—it happened to fall out—was a length of rubber pipe—just short.

HAPPY: No kidding?

LINDA: There's a little attachment on the end of it. I knew right away. And sure enough, on the bottom of the water heater there's a new little nipple on the gas pipe.

HAPPY (*angrily*): That—jerk.

BIFF: Did you have it taken off?

LINDA: I'm—I'm ashamed to. How can I mention it to him? Every day I go down and take away that little rubber pipe. But, when he comes home, I put it back where it was. How can I insult him that way? I don't know what to do. I live from day to day, boys. I tell you, I know every thought in his mind. It sounds so old-fashioned and silly, but I tell you he put his whole life into you and you've turned your backs on him. (*She is bent over in the chair, weeping, her face in her hands.*) Biff, I swear to God! Biff, his life is in your hands!

HAPPY (*to* BIFF): How do you like that damned fool!

BIFF (*kissing her*): All right, pal, all right. It's all settled now. I've been remiss. I know that, Mom. But now I'll stay, and I swear to you, I'll apply myself. (*kneeling in front of her, in a fever of self-reproach*) It's just—you see, Mom, I don't fit in business. Not that I won't try. I'll try, and I'll make good.

HAPPY: Sure you will. The trouble with you in business was you never tried to please people.

BIFF: I know, I—

HAPPY: Like when you worked for Harrison's. Bob Harrison said you were tops, and then you go and do some damn fool thing like whistling whole songs in the elevator like a comedian.

BIFF (*against* HAPPY): So what? I like to whistle sometimes.

HAPPY: You don't raise a guy to a responsible job who whistles in the elevator!

LINDA: Well, don't argue about it now.

HAPPY: Like when you'd go off and swim in the middle of the day instead of taking the line around.

BIFF (*his resentment rising*): Well, don't you run off? You take off sometimes, don't you? On a nice summer day?

HAPPY: Yeah, but I cover myself!

LINDA: Boys!

HAPPY: If I'm going to take a fade the boss can call any number where I'm supposed to be and they'll swear to him that I just left. I'll tell you something that I hate to say, Biff, but in the business world some of them think you're crazy.

BIFF (*angered*): Screw the business world!

HAPPY: All right, screw it! Great, but cover yourself!

LINDA: Hap, Hap!

BIFF: I don't care what they think! They've laughed at Dad for years, and you know why? Because we don't belong in this nuthouse of a city! We should be mixing cement on some open plain, or—or carpenters. A carpenter is allowed to whistle!

WILLY *walks in from the entrance of the house, at left.*

WILLY: Even your grandfather was better than a carpenter. (*Pause. They watch him.*) You never grew up. Bernard does not whistle in the elevator, I assure you.

BIFF (*as though to laugh* WILLY *out of it*): Yeah, but you do, Pop.

WILLY: I never in my life whistled in an elevator! And who in the business world thinks I'm crazy?

BIFF: I didn't mean it like that, Pop. Now don't make a whole thing out of it, will ya?

WILLY: Go back to the West! Be a carpenter, a cowboy, enjoy yourself!

LINDA: Willy, he was just saying—

WILLY: I heard what he said!

HAPPY (*trying to quiet* WILLY): Hey, Pop, come on now . . .

WILLY (*continuing over* HAPPY'S *line*): They laugh at me, heh? Go to Filene's, go to the Hub, go to Slattery's, Boston. Call out the name Willy Loman and see what happens! Big shot!

BIFF: All right, Pop.

WILLY: Big!

BIFF: All right!

WILLY: Why do you always insult me?

BIFF: I didn't say a word. (*to* LINDA) Did I say a word?

LINDA: He didn't say anything, Willy.

WILLY (*going to the doorway of the living room*): All right, good night, good night.

LINDA: Willy, dear, he just decided . . .

WILLY (*to* BIFF): If you get tired hanging around tomorrow, paint the ceiling I put up in the living room.

BIFF: I'm leaving early tomorrow.

HAPPY: He's going to see Bill Oliver, Pop.

WILLY (*interestedly*): Oliver? For what?

BIFF (*with reserve, but trying, trying*): He always said he'd stake me. I'd like to go into business, so maybe I can take him up on it.

LINDA: Isn't that wonderful?

WILLY: Don't interrupt. What's wonderful about it? There's fifty men in the City of New York who'd stake him. (*to* BIFF) Sporting goods?

BIFF: I guess so. I know something about it and—

WILLY: He knows something about it! You know sporting goods better than Spalding, for God's sake! How much is he giving you?

BIFF: I don't know, I didn't even see him yet, but—

WILLY: Then what're you talkin' about?

BIFF (*getting angry*): Well, all I said was I'm gonna see him, that's all!

WILLY (*turning away*): Ah, you're counting your chickens again.

BIFF (*starting left for the stairs*): Oh, Jesus, I'm going to sleep!

WILLY (*calling after him*): Don't curse in this house!

BIFF (*turning*): Since when did you get so clean?

HAPPY (*trying to stop them*): Wait a . . .

WILLY: Don't use that language to me! I won't have it!

HAPPY (*grabbing* BIFF, *shouts*): Wait a minute! I got an idea. I got a feasible idea. Come here, Biff, let's talk this over now, let's talk some sense here. When I was down in Florida last time, I thought of a great idea to sell sporting goods. It just came back to me. You and I, Biff—we have a line, the Loman Line. We train a couple of weeks, and put on a couple of exhibitions, see?

WILLY: That's an idea!

HAPPY: Wait! We form two basketball teams, see? Two water-polo teams. We play each other. It's a million dollars' worth of publicity. Two brothers, see? The Loman Brothers. Displays in the Royal Palms—all the hotels. And banners over the ring and the basketball court: "Loman Brothers." Baby, we could sell sporting goods!

WILLY: That is a one-million-dollar idea!

LINDA: Marvelous!

BIFF: I'm in great shape as far as that's concerned.

HAPPY: And the beauty of it is, Biff, it wouldn't be like a business. We'd be out playin' ball again . . .

BIFF (*enthused*): Yeah, that's . . .

WILLY: Million-dollar . . .

HAPPY: And you wouldn't get fed up with it, Biff. It'd be the family again. There'd be the old honor, and comradeship, and if you wanted to go off for a swim or somethin'—well, you'd do it! Without some smart cooky gettin' up ahead of you!

WILLY: Lick the world! You guys together could absolutely lick the civilized world.

BIFF: I'll see Oliver tomorrow. Hap, if we could work that out . . .

LINDA: Maybe things are beginning to—

WILLY (*wildly enthused, to* LINDA): Stop interrupting! (*to* BIFF) But don't wear sport jacket and slacks when you see Oliver.

BIFF: No, I'll—

WILLY: A business suit, and talk as little as possible, and don't crack any jokes.

BIFF: He did like me. Always liked me.

LINDA: He loved you!

WILLY (*to* LINDA): Will you stop! (*to* BIFF) Walk in very serious. You are not applying for a boy's job. Money is to pass. Be quiet, fine, and serious. Everybody likes a kidder, but nobody lends him money.

HAPPY: I'll try to get some myself, Biff. I'm sure I can.

WILLY: I see great things for you kids, I think your troubles are over. But remember, start big and you'll end big. Ask for fifteen. How much you gonna ask for?

BIFF: Gee, I don't know—

WILLY: And don't say "Gee." "Gee" is a boy's word. A man walking in for fifteen thousand dollars does not say "Gee!"

BIFF: Ten, I think, would be top though.

WILLY: Don't be so modest. You always started too low. Walk in with a big laugh. Don't look worried. Start off with a couple of your good stories to lighten things up. It's not what you say, it's how you say it—because personality always wins the day.

LINDA: Oliver always thought the highest of him—

WILLY: Will you let me talk?

BIFF: Don't yell at her, Pop, will ya?

WILLY (*angrily*): I was talking, wasn't I?

BIFF: I don't like you yelling at her all the time, and I'm tellin' you, that's all.

WILLY: What're you, takin' over this house?

LINDA: Willy—

WILLY (*turning on her*): Don't take his side all the time, goddammit!

BIFF (*furiously*): Stop yelling at her!

WILLY (*suddenly pulling on his cheek, beaten down, guilt-ridden*): Give my best to Bill Oliver—he may remember me. (*He exits through the living-room doorway.*)

LINDA (*her voice subdued*): What'd you have to start that for? (BIFF *turns away.*) You see how sweet he was as soon as you talked hopefully? (*She goes over to* BIFF.) Come up and say good night to him. Don't let him go to bed that way.

HAPPY: Come on, Biff, let's buck him up.

LINDA: Please, dear. Just say good night. It takes so little to make him happy. Come. (*She goes through the living-room doorway, calling upstairs from within the living room.*) Your pajamas are hanging in the bathroom, Willy!

HAPPY (*looking toward where* LINDA *went out*): What a woman! They broke the mold when they made her. You know that, Biff?

BIFF: He's off salary. My God, working on commission!

HAPPY: Well, let's face it: he's no hot-shot selling man. Except that sometimes, you have to admit, he's a sweet personality.

BIFF (*deciding*): Lend me ten bucks, will ya? I want to buy some new ties.

HAPPY: I'll take you to a place I know. Beautiful stuff. Wear one of my striped shirts tomorrow.

BIFF: She got gray. Mom got awful old. Gee, I'm gonna go in to Oliver tomorrow and knock him for a—

HAPPY: Come on up. Tell that to Dad. Let's give him a whirl. Come on.

BIFF (*steamed up*): You know, with ten thousand bucks, boy!

HAPPY (*as they go into the living room*): That's the talk, Biff, that's the first time I've heard the old confidence out of you! (*from within the living room, fading off*) You're gonna live with me, kid, and any babe you want just say the word . . . (*The last lines are hardly heard. They are mounting the stairs to their parents' bedroom.*)

LINDA (*Entering her bedroom and addressing* WILLY, *who is in the bathroom. She is straightening the bed for him.*): Can you do anything about the shower? It drips.

WILLY (*from the bathroom*): All of a sudden everything falls to pieces! Goddam plumbing, oughta be sued, those people. I hardly finished putting it in and the thing . . . (*His words rumble off.*)

LINDA: I'm just wondering if Oliver will remember him. You think he might?

WILLY (*coming out of the bathroom in his pajamas*): Remember him? What's the matter with you, you crazy? If he'd've stayed with Oliver he'd be on top by now! Wait'll Oliver gets a look at him. You don't know the average caliber any more. The average young man today—(*He is getting into bed.*)—is got a caliber of zero. Greatest thing in the world for him was to bum around.

BIFF *and* HAPPY *enter the bedroom. Slight pause.*

WILLY (*stops short, looking at* BIFF): Glad to hear it, boy.

HAPPY: He wanted to say good night to you, sport.

WILLY (*to* BIFF): Yeah. Knock him dead, boy. What'd you want to tell me?

BIFF: Just take it easy, Pop. Good night. (*He turns to go.*)

WILLY (*unable to resist*): And if anything falls off the desk while you're talking to him— like a package or something—don't you pick it up. They have office boys for that.

LINDA: I'll make a big breakfast—

WILLY: Will you let me finish? (*to* BIFF) Tell him you were in the business in the West. Not farm work.

BIFF: All right, Dad.

LINDA: I think everything—

WILLY (*going right through her speech*): And don't undersell yourself. No less than fifteen thousand dollars.

BIFF (*unable to bear him*): Okay. Good night, Mom. (*He starts moving.*)

WILLY: Because you got a greatness in you, Biff, remember that. You got all kinds a greatness . . . (*He lies back, exhausted.* BIFF *walks out.*)

LINDA (*calling after* BIFF): Sleep well, darling!

HAPPY: I'm gonna get married, Mom. I wanted to tell you.

LINDA: Go to sleep, dear.

HAPPY (*going*): I just wanted to tell you.

WILLY: Keep up the good work. (HAPPY *exits.*) God . . . remember that Ebbets Field game? The championship of the city?

LINDA: Just rest. Should I sing to you?

WILLY: Yeah. Sing to me. (LINDA *hums a soft lullaby.*) When that team came out—he was the tallest, remember?

LINDA: Oh, yes. And in gold.

BIFF *enters the darkened kitchen, takes a cigarette, and leaves the house. He comes downstage into a golden pool of light. He smokes, staring at the night.*

WILLY: Like a young god. Hercules—something like that. And the sun, the sun all around him. Remember how he waved to me? Right up from the field, with the representatives of three colleges standing by? And the buyers I brought, and the cheers when he came out—Loman, Loman, Loman! God Almighty, he'll be great yet. A star like that, magnificent, can never really fade away!

The light on WILLY *is fading. The gas heater begins to glow through the kitchen wall, near the stairs, a blue flame beneath red coils.*

LINDA (*timidly*): Willy dear, what has he got against you?
WILLY: I'm so tired. Don't talk any more.

BIFF *slowly returns to the kitchen. He stops, stares toward the heater.*

LINDA: Will you ask Howard to let you work in New York?
WILLY: First thing in the morning. Everything'll be all right.

BIFF *reaches behind the heater and draws out a length of rubber tubing. He is horrified and turns his head toward* WILLY'S *room, still dimly lit, from which the strains of* LINDA'S *desperate but monotonous humming rise.*

WILLY (*staring through the window into the moonlight*): Gee, look at the moon moving between the buildings!

BIFF *wraps the tubing around his hand and quickly goes up the stairs.*
Curtain.

ACT TWO

Music is heard, gay and bright. The curtain rises as the music fades away. WILLY, *in shirt sleeves, is sitting at the kitchen table, sipping coffee, his hat in his lap.* LINDA *is filling his cup when she can.*

WILLY: Wonderful coffee. Meal in itself.
LINDA: Can I make you some eggs?
WILLY: No. Take a breath.
LINDA: You look so rested, dear.
WILLY: I slept like a dead one. First time in months. Imagine, sleeping till ten on a Tuesday morning. Boys left nice and early, heh?
LINDA: They were out of here by eight o'clock.
WILLY: Good work!
LINDA: It was so thrilling to see them leaving together. I can't get over the shaving lotion in this house!
WILLY (*smiling*): Mmm—
LINDA: Biff was very changed this morning. His whole attitude seemed to be hopeful. He couldn't wait to get downtown to see Oliver.
WILLY: He's heading for a change. There's no question, there simply are certain men that take longer to get—solidified. How did he dress?
LINDA: His blue suit. He's so handsome in that suit. He could be a—anything in that suit!

WILLY *gets up from the table.* LINDA *holds his jacket for him.*

WILLY: There's no question, no question at all. Gee, on the way home tonight I'd like to buy some seeds.
LINDA (*laughing*): That'd be wonderful. But not enough sun gets back there. Nothing'll grow any more.

WILLY: You wait, kid, before it's all over we're gonna get a little place out in the country, and I'll raise some vegetables, a couple of chickens. . .

LINDA: You'll do it yet, dear.

WILLY *walks out of his jacket.* LINDA *follows him.*

WILLY: And they'll get married, and come for a weekend. I'd build a little guest house. 'Cause I got so many fine tools, all I'd need would be a little lumber and some peace of mind.

LINDA (*joyfully*): I sewed the lining . . .

WILLY: I could build two guest houses, so they'd both come. Did he decide how much he's going to ask Oliver for?

LINDA (*getting him into the jacket*): He didn't mention it, but I imagine ten or fifteen thousand. You going to talk to Howard today?

WILLY: Yeah. I'll put it to him straight and simple. He'll just have to take me off the road.

LINDA: And Willy, don't forget to ask for a little advance, because we've got the insurance premium. It's the grace period now.

WILLY: That's a hundred . . . ?

LINDA: A hundred and eight, sixty-eight. Because we're a little short again.

WILLY: Why are we short?

LINDA: Well, you had the motor job on the car . . .

WILLY: That goddam Studebaker!

LINDA: And you got one more payment on the refrigerator . . .

WILLY: But it just broke again!

LINDA: Well, it's old, dear.

WILLY: I told you we should've bought a well-advertised machine. Charley bought a General Electric and it's twenty years old and it's still good, that son-of-a-bitch.

LINDA: But, Willy—

WILLY: Whoever heard of a Hastings refrigerator? Once in my life I would like to own something outright before it's broken! I'm always in a race with the junkyard! I just finished paying for the car and it's on its last legs. The refrigerator consumes belts like a goddam maniac. They time those things. They time them so when you finally paid for them, they're used up.

LINDA (*buttoning up his jacket as he unbuttons it*): All told, about two hundred dollars would carry us, dear. But that includes the last payment on the mortgage. After this payment, Willy, the house belongs to us.

WILLY: It's twenty-five years!

LINDA: Biff was nine years old when we bought it.

WILLY: Well, that's a great thing. To weather a twenty-five-year mortgage is—

LINDA: It's an accomplishment.

WILLY: All the cement, the lumber, the reconstruction I put in this house! There ain't a crack to be found in it any more.

LINDA: Well, it served its purpose.

WILLY: What purpose? Some stranger'll come along, move in, and that's that. If only Biff would take this house, and raise a family . . . (*He starts to go.*) Good-by, I'm late.

LINDA (*suddenly remembering*): Oh, I forgot! You're supposed to meet them for dinner.

WILLY: Me?

LINDA: At Frank's Chop House on Forty-eighth near Sixth Avenue.

WILLY: Is that so! How about you?

LINDA: No, just the three of you. They're gonna blow you to a big meal!

WILLY: Don't say! Who thought of that?

LINDA: Biff came to me this morning, Willy, and he said, "Tell Dad, we want to blow him to a big meal." Be there six o'clock. You and your two boys are going to have dinner.

WILLY: Gee whiz! That's really somethin'. I'm gonna knock Howard for a loop, kid. I'll get an advance, and I'll come home with a New York job. Goddammit, now I'm gonna do it!

LINDA: Oh, that's the spirit, Willy!

WILLY: I will never get behind a wheel the rest of my life!

LINDA: It's changing, Willy, I can feel it changing!

WILLY: Beyond a question. G'by, I'm late. (*He starts to go again.*)

LINDA (*calling after him as she runs to the kitchen table for a handkerchief*): You got your glasses?

WILLY (*He feels for them, then comes back in.*):—Yeah, yeah, got my glasses.

LINDA (*giving him the handkerchief*): And a handkerchief.

WILLY: Yeah, handkerchief.

LINDA: And your saccharine?

WILLY: Yeah, my saccharine.

LINDA: Be careful on the subway stairs.

> *She kisses him, and a silk stocking is seen hanging from her hand.* WILLY *notices it.*

WILLY: Will you stop mending stockings? At least while I'm in the house. It gets me nervous. I can't tell you. Please.

> LINDA *hides the stocking in her hand as she follows* WILLY *across the forestage in front of the house.*

LINDA: Remember, Frank's Chop House.

WILLY (*passing the apron*): Maybe beets would grow out there.

LINDA (*laughing*): But you tried so many times.

WILLY: Yeah. Well, don't work hard today. (*He disappears around the right corner of the house.*)

LINDA: Be careful!

> As WILLY *vanishes,* LINDA *waves to him. Suddenly the phone rings. She runs across the stage and into the kitchen and lifts it.*

LINDA: Hello? Oh, Biff! I'm so glad you called, I just . . . Yes, sure, I just told him. Yes, he'll be there for dinner at six o'clock, I didn't forget. Listen, I was just dying to tell you. You know that little rubber pipe I told you about? That he connected to the gas heater? I finally decided to go down the cellar this morning and take it away and destroy it. But it's gone! Imagine? He took it away himself, it isn't there! (*She listens.*) When? Oh, then you took it. Oh—nothing, it's just that I'd hoped he'd taken it away himself. Oh, I'm not worried, darling, because this morning he left in such high spirits, it was like the old days! I'm not afraid any more. Did Mr. Oliver see you? . . . Well, you wait there then. And make a nice impression on him, darling. Just don't perspire too much before you see him. And have a nice time with Dad. He may have big news too! . . . That's right, a New York job. And be sweet to him tonight, dear. Be loving to him. Because he's only a little boat looking for a harbor. (*She is trembling with sorrow and joy.*) Oh, that's wonderful, Biff, you'll save his life. Thanks, darling. Just put your arm around him when he comes into the restaurant. Give him a smile. That's the boy . . . Goody-by, dear . . . You got your comb? . . . That's fine. Good-by, Biff dear.

In the middle of her speech, HOWARD WAGNER, *thirty-six, wheels on a small typewriter table on which is a wire-recording machine and proceeds to plug it in. This is on the left forestage. Light slowly fades on* LINDA *as it rises on* HOWARD. HOWARD *is intent on threading the machine and only glances over his shoulder as* WILLY *appears.*

WILLY: Pst! Pst!

HOWARD: Hello, Willy, come in.

WILLY: Like to have a little talk with you, Howard.

HOWARD: Sorry to keep you waiting. I'll be with you in a minute.

WILLY: What's that, Howard?

HOWARD: Didn't you ever see one of these? Wire recorder.

WILLY: Oh. Can we talk a minute?

HOWARD: Records things. Just got delivery yesterday. Been driving me crazy, the most terrific machine I ever saw in my life. I was up all night with it.

WILLY: What do you do with it?

HOWARD: I bought it for dictation, but you can do anything with it. Listen to this. I had it home last night. Listen to what I picked up. The first one is my daughter. Get this. (*He flicks the switch and "Roll out the Barrel" is heard being whistled.*) Listen to that kid whistle.

WILLY: That is lifelike, isn't it?

HOWARD: Seven years old. Get that tone.

WILLY: Ts, ts. Like to ask a little favor if you . . .

The whistling breaks off, and the voice of HOWARD'S *daughter is heard.*

HIS DAUGHTER: "Now you, Daddy."

HOWARD: She's crazy for me! (*Again the same song is whistled.*) That's me! Ha! (*He winks.*)

WILLY: You're very good!

The whistling breaks off again. The machine runs silent for a moment.

HOWARD: Sh! Get this now, this is my son.

HIS SON: "The capital of Alabama is Montgomery; the capital of Arizona is Phoenix; the capital of Arkansas is Little Rock; the capital of California is Sacramento. . ." (*and on, and on*)

HOWARD (*holding up five fingers*): Five years old, Willy!

WILLY: He'll make an announcer some day!

HIS SON (*continuing*): "The capital . . ."

HOWARD: Get that—alphabetical order! (*The machine breaks off suddenly.*) Wait a minute. The maid kicked the plug out.

WILLY: It certainly is a—

HOWARD: Sh, for God's sake!

HIS SON: "It's nine o'clock, Bulova watch time. So I have to go to sleep."

WILLY: That really is—

HOWARD: Wait a minute! The next is my wife.

They wait.

HOWARD'S VOICE: "Go on, say something." (*pause*) "Well, you gonna talk?"

HIS WIFE: "I can't think of anything."

HOWARD'S VOICE: "Well, talk—it's turning."

HIS WIFE (*shyly, beaten*): "Hello." (*silence*) "Oh, Howard, I can't talk into this . . ."

HOWARD (*snapping the machine off*): That was my wife.

WILLY: That is a wonderful machine. Can we—

HOWARD: I tell you, Willy, I'm gonna take my camera, and my bandsaw, and all my hobbies, and out they go. This is the most fascinating relaxation I ever found.

WILLY: I think I'll get one myself.

HOWARD: Sure, they're only a hundred and a half. You can't do without it. Supposing you wanna hear Jack Benny, see? But you can't be at home at that hour. So you tell the maid to turn the radio on when Jack Benny comes on, and this automatically goes on with the radio . . .

WILLY: And when you come home you . . .

HOWARD: You can come home twelve o'clock, one o'clock, any time you like, and you get yourself a Coke and sit yourself down, throw the switch, and there's Jack Benny's program in the middle of the night!

WILLY: I'm definitely going to get one. Because lots of time I'm on the road, and I think to myself, what I must be missing on the radio!

HOWARD: Don't you have a radio in the car?

WILLY: Well, yeah, but who ever thinks of turning it on?

HOWARD: Say, aren't you supposed to be in Boston?

WILLY: That's what I want to talk to you about, Howard. You got a minute? (*He draws a chair in from the wing.*)

HOWARD: What happened? What're you doing here?

WILLY: Well . . .

HOWARD: You didn't crack up again, did you?

WILLY: Oh, no. No . . .

HOWARD: Geez, you had me worried there for a minute. What's the trouble?

WILLY: Well, tell you the truth, Howard. I've come to the decision that I'd rather not travel any more.

HOWARD: Not travel! Well, what'll you do?

WILLY: Remember, Christmas time, when you had the party here? You said you'd try to think of some spot for me here in town.

HOWARD: With us?

WILLY: Well, sure.

HOWARD: Oh, yeah, yeah. I remember. Well, I couldn't think of anything for you, Willy.

WILLY: I tell ya, Howard. The kids are all grown up, y'know. I don't need much any more. If I could take home—well, sixty-five dollars a week, I could swing it.

HOWARD: Yeah, but Willy, see I—

WILLY: I tell ya why, Howard. Speaking frankly and between the two of us, y'know— I'm just a little tired.

HOWARD: Oh, I could understand that, Willy. But you're a road man, Willy, and we do a road business. We've only got a half-dozen salesmen on the floor here.

WILLY: God knows, Howard, I never asked a favor of any man. But I was with the firm when your father used to carry you in here in his arms.

HOWARD: I know that, Willy, but—

WILLY: Your father came to me the day you were born and asked me what I thought of the name of Howard, may he rest in peace.

HOWARD: I appreciate that, Willy, but there just is no spot here for you. If I had a spot I'd slam you right in, but I just don't have a single solitary spot.

He looks for his lighter. WILLY *has picked it up and gives it to him. Pause.*

WILLY (*with increasing anger*): Howard, all I need to set my table is fifty dollars a week.

HOWARD: But where am I going to put you, kid?

WILLY: Look, it isn't a question of whether I can sell merchandise, is it?

HOWARD: No, but it's a business, kid, and everybody's gotta pull his own weight.

WILLY (*desperately*): Just let me tell you a story, Howard—

HOWARD: 'Cause you gotta admit, business is business.

WILLY (*angrily*): Business is definitely business, but just listen for a minute. You don't understand this. When I was a boy—eighteen, nineteen—I was already on the road. And there was a question in my mind as to whether selling had a future for me. Because in those days I had a yearning to go to Alaska. See, there were three gold strikes in one month in Alaska, and I felt like going out. Just for the ride, you might say.

HOWARD (*barely interested*): Don't say.

WILLY: Oh, yeah, my father lived many years in Alaska. He was an adventurous man. We've got quite a little streak of self-reliance in our family. I thought I'd go out with my older brother and try to locate him, and maybe settle in the North with the old man. And I was almost decided to go, when I met a salesman in the Parker House. His name was Dave Singleman. And he was eighty-four years old, and he'd drummed merchandise in thirty-one states. And old Dave, he'd go up to his room, y'understand, put on his green velvet slippers—I'll never forget—and pick up his phone and call the buyers, and without ever leaving his room, at the age of eighty-four, he made his living. And when I saw that, I realized that selling was the greatest career a man could want. 'Cause what could be more satisfying than to be able to go, at the age of eighty-four, into twenty or thirty different cities, and pick up a phone, and be remembered and loved and helped by so many different people? Do you know? when he died—and by the way he died the death of a salesman, in his green velvet slippers in the smoker of the New York, New Haven and Hartford, going into Boston—when he died, hundreds of salesmen and buyers were at his funeral. Things were sad on a lotta trains for months after that. (*He stands up. HOWARD has not looked at him.*) In those days there was personality in it, Howard. There was respect, and comradeship, and gratitude in it. Today, it's all cut and dried, and there's no chance for bringing friendship to bear—or personality. You see what I mean? They don't know me any more.

HOWARD (*moving away, to the right*): That's just the thing, Willy.

WILLY: If I had forty dollars a week—that's all I'd need. Forty dollars, Howard.

HOWARD: Kid, I can't take blood from a stone, I—

WILLY (*desperation is on him now*): Howard, the year Al Smith was nominated, your father came to me and—

HOWARD (*starting to go off*): I've got to see some people, kid.

WILLY (*stopping him*): I'm talking about your father! There were promises made across this desk! You mustn't tell me you've got people to see—I put thirty-four years into this firm, Howard, and now I can't pay my insurance! You can't eat the orange and throw the peel away—a man is not a piece of fruit! (*after a pause*) Now pay attention. Your father—in 1928 I had a big year. I averaged a hundred and seventy dollars a week in commissions.

HOWARD (*impatiently*): Now, Willy, you never averaged—

WILLY (*banging his hand on the desk*): I averaged a hundred and seventy dollars a week in the year of 1928! And your father came to me—or rather, I was in the office here—it was right over this desk—and he put his hand on my shoulder—

HOWARD (*getting up*): You'll have to excuse me, Willy, I gotta see some people. Pull yourself together. (*going out*) I'll be back in a little while.

On HOWARD'S *exit, the light on his chair grows very bright and strange.*

WILLY: Pull myself together! What the hell did I say to him? My God, I was yelling at him! How could I! (WILLY *breaks off, staring at the light, which occupies the chair, animating it. He approaches this chair, standing across the desk from it.*) Frank, Frank, don't you remember what you told me that time? How you put your hand on my shoulder, and Frank . . . (*he leans on the desk and as he speaks the dead man's name he accidentally switches on the recorder, and instantly*)

HOWARD'S SON: ". . . of New York is Albany. The capital of Ohio is Cincinnati, the capital of Rhode Island is . . ." (*The recitation continues.*)

WILLY (*leaping away with fright, shouting*): Ha! Howard! Howard! Howard!

HOWARD (*rushing in*): What happened?

WILLY (*pointing at the machine, which continues nasally, childishly, with the capital cities*): Shut it off! Shut it off!

HOWARD (*pulling the plug out*): Look, Willy. . .

WILLY (*pressing his hands to his eyes*): I gotta get myself some coffee. I'll get some coffee . . .

WILLY starts to walk out. HOWARD *stops him.*

HOWARD (*rolling up the cord*): Willy, look. . .

WILLY: I'll go to Boston.

HOWARD: Willy, you can't go to Boston for us.

WILLY: Why can't I go?

HOWARD: I don't want you to represent us. I've been meaning to tell you for a long time now.

WILLY: Howard, are you firing me?

HOWARD: I think you need a good long rest, Willy.

WILLY: Howard—

HOWARD: And when you feel better, come back, and we'll see if we can work something out.

WILLY: But I gotta earn money, Howard. I'm in no position to—

HOWARD: Where are your sons? Why don't your sons give you a hand?

WILLY: They're working on a very big deal.

HOWARD: This is no time for false pride, Willy. You go to your sons and you tell them that you're tired. You've got two great boys, haven't you?

WILLY: Oh, no question, no question, but in the meantime . . .

HOWARD: Then that's that, heh?

WILLY: All right, I'll go to Boston tomorrow.

HOWARD: No, no.

WILLY: I can't throw myself on my sons. I'm not a cripple!

HOWARD: Look, kid, I'm busy this morning.

WILLY (*grasping* HOWARD'S *arm*): Howard, you've got to let me go to Boston!

HOWARD (*hard, keeping himself under control*): I've got a line of people to see this morning. Sit down, take five minutes, and pull yourself together, and then go home, will ya? I need the office, Willy. (*He starts to go; turns, remembering the recorder, starts to push off the table holding the recorder.*) Oh, yeah. Whenever you can this week, stop by and drop off the samples. You'll feel better, Willy, and then come back and we'll talk. Pull yourself together, kid, there's people outside.

HOWARD *exits, pushing the table off left.* WILLY *stares into space, exhausted. Now the music is heard—*BEN'S *music—first distantly, then closer, closer. As* WILLY *speaks,* BEN *enters from the right. He carries valise and umbrella.*

WILLY: Oh, Ben, how did you do it? What is the answer? Did you wind up the Alaska deal already?

BEN: Doesn't take much time if you know what you're doing. Just a short business trip. Boarding ship in an hour. Wanted to say good-by.

WILLY: Ben, I've got to talk to you.

BEN (*glancing at his watch*): Haven't the time, William.

WILLY (*crossing the apron to* BEN): Ben, nothing's working out. I don't know what to do.

BEN: Now, look here, William. I've bought timberland in Alaska and I need a man to look after things for me.

WILLY: God, timberland! Me and my boys in those grand outdoors!

BEN: You've a new continent at your doorstep, William. Get out of these cities, they're full of talk and time payments and courts of law. Screw on your fists and you can fight for a fortune up there.

WILLY: Yes, yes! Linda, Linda!

LINDA *enters as of old, with the wash.*

LINDA: Oh, you're back?

BEN: I haven't much time.

WILLY: No, wait! Linda, he's got a proposition for me in Alaska.

LINDA: But you've got—(*to* BEN) He's got a beautiful job here.

WILLY: But in Alaska, kid, I could—

LINDA: You're doing well enough, Willy!

BEN (*to* LINDA): Enough for what, my dear?

LINDA (*frightened of* BEN *and angry at him*): Don't say those things to him! Enough to be happy right here, right now. (*to* WILLY, *while* BEN *laughs*) Why must everybody conquer the world? You're well liked, and the boys love you, and someday—(*to* BEN)—why, old man Wagner told him just the other day that if he keeps it up he'll be a member of the firm, didn't he, Willy?

WILLY: Sure, sure. I am building something with this firm, Ben, and if a man is building something he must be on the right track, mustn't he?

BEN: What are you building? Lay your hand on it. Where is it?

WILLY (*hesitantly*): That's true, Linda, there's nothing.

LINDA: Why? (*to* BEN) There's a man eighty-four years old—

WILLY: That's right, Ben, that's right. When I look at that man I say, what is there to worry about?

BEN: Bah!

WILLY: It's true, Ben. All he has to do is go into any city, pick up the phone, and he's making his living and you know why?

BEN (*picking up his valise*): I've got to go.

WILLY (*holding* BEN *back*): Look at this boy!

BIFF, *in his high school sweater, enters carrying suitcase.* HAPPY *carries* BIFF'S *shoulder guards, gold helmet, and football pants.*

WILLY: Without a penny to his name, three great universities are begging for him, and from there the sky's the limit, because it's not what you do, Ben. It's who you know and the smile on your face! It's contacts, Ben, contacts! The whole wealth of Alaska passes over the lunch table at the Commodore Hotel, and that's the wonder, the wonder of this country, that a man can end with diamonds here on the basis of being liked! (*He turns to* BIFF.) And that's why when you get out on that field today it's important. Because thousands of people will be rooting for you and loving you. (*to* BEN, *who has again begun to leave*) And Ben! when he walks into a business office his name will sound out like a bell and all the doors will open to him! I've seen it, Ben, I've seen it a thousand times! You can't feel it with your hand like timber, but it's there!

BEN: Good-by, William.

WILLY: Ben, am I right? Don't you think I'm right? I value your advice.

BEN: There's a new continent at your doorstep, William. You could walk out rich. Rich! (*He is gone.*)

WILLY: We'll do it here, Ben! You hear me? We're gonna do it here!

YOUNG BERNARD *rushes in. The gay music of the Boys is heard.*

BERNARD: Oh, gee, I was afraid you left already!

WILLY: Why? What time is it?

BERNARD: It's half-past one!

WILLY: Well, come on, everybody! Ebbets Field next stop! Where's the pennants? (*He rushes through the wall-line of the kitchen and out into the living room.*)

LINDA (*to* BIFF): Did you pack fresh underwear?

BIFF (*who has been limbering up*): I want to go!

BERNARD: Biff, I'm carrying your helmet, ain't I?

HAPPY: No, I'm carrying the helmet.

BERNARD: Oh, Biff, you promised me.

HAPPY: I'm carrying the helmet.

BERNARD: How am I going to get in the locker room?

LINDA: Let him carry the shoulder guards. (*She puts her coat and hat on in the kitchen.*)

BERNARD: Can I, Biff? 'Cause I told everybody I'm going to be in the locker room.

HAPPY: In Ebbets Field it's the clubhouse.

BERNARD: I meant the clubhouse. Biff!

HAPPY: Biff!

BIFF (*grandly, after a slight pause*): Let him carry the shoulder guards.

HAPPY (*as he gives* BERNARD *the shoulder guards*): Stay close to us now.

WILLY *rushes in with the pennants.*

WILLY (*handing them out*): Everybody wave when Biff comes out on the field. (HAPPY *and* BERNARD *run off.*) You set now, boy?

The music has died away.

BIFF: Ready to go, Pop. Every muscle is ready.

WILLY (*at the edge of the apron*): You realize what this means?

BIFF: That's right, Pop.

WILLY (*feeling* BIFF'S *muscles*): You're comin' home this afternoon captain of the All-Scholastic Championship Team of the City of New York.

BIFF: I got it, Pop. And remember, pal, when I take off my helmet, that touchdown is for you.

WILLY: Let's go! (*He is starting out, with his arms around* BIFF, *when* CHARLEY *enters, as of old, in knickers.*) I got no room for you, Charley.

CHARLEY: Room? For what?

WILLY: In the car.

CHARLEY: You goin' for a ride? I wanted to shoot some casino.

WILLY (*furiously*): Casino! (*incredulously*) Don't you realize what today is?

LINDA: Oh, he knows, Willy. He's just kidding you.

WILLY: That's nothing to kid about!

CHARLEY: No, Linda, what's goin' on?

LINDA: He's playing in Ebbets Field.

CHARLEY: Baseball in this weather?

WILLY: Don't talk to him. Come on, come on! (*He is pushing them out.*)

CHARLEY: Wait a minute, didn't you hear the news?

WILLY: What?

CHARLEY: Don't you listen to the radio? Ebbets Field just blew up.

WILLY: You go to hell! (CHARLEY *laughs. Pushing them out.*) Come on, come on! We're late.

CHARLEY (*as they go*): Knock a homer, Biff, knock a homer!

WILLY (*the last to leave, turning to* CHARLEY): I don't think that was funny, Charley. This is the greatest day of his life.

CHARLEY: Willy, when are you going to grow up?

WILLY: Yeah, heh? When this game is over, Charley, you'll be laughing out of the other side of your face. They'll be calling him another Red Grange. Twenty-five thousand a year.

CHARLEY (*kidding*): Is that so?

WILLY: Yeah, that's so.

CHARLEY: Well, then, I'm sorry, Willy. But tell me something.

WILLY: What?

CHARLEY: Who is Red Grange?

WILLY: Put up your hands. Goddam you, put up your hands!

CHARLEY, *chuckling, shakes his head and walks away, around the left corner of the stage.* WILLY *follows him. The music rises to a mocking frenzy.*

WILLY: Who the hell do you think you are, better than everybody else? You don't know everything, you big, ignorant, stupid . . . Put up your hands!

Light rises, on the right side of the forestage, on a small table in the reception room of CHARLEY'S *office. Traffic sounds are heard.* BERNARD, *now mature, sits whistling to himself. A pair of tennis rackets and an overnight bag are on the floor beside him.*

WILLY (*offstage*): What are you walking away for? Don't walk away! If you're going to say something say it to my face! I know you laugh at me behind my back. You'll laugh out of the other side of your goddam face after this game. Touchdown! Touchdown! Eighty thousand people! Touchdown! Right between the goal posts.

BERNARD *is a quiet, earnest, but self-assured young man.* WILLY'S *voice is coming from right upstage now.* BERNARD *lowers his feet off the table and listens.* JENNY, *his father's secretary, enters.*

JENNY (*distressed*): Say, Bernard, will you go out in the hall?

BERNARD: What is that noise? Who is it?

JENNY: Mr. Loman. He just got off the elevator.

BERNARD (*getting up*): Who's he arguing with?

JENNY: Nobody. There's nobody with him. I can't deal with him any more, and your father gets all upset everytime he comes. I've got a lot of typing to do, and your father's waiting to sign it. Will you see him?

WILLY (*entering*): Touchdown! Touch—(*He sees* JENNY.) Jenny, Jenny, good to see you. How're ya? Workin'? Or still honest?

JENNY: Fine. How've you been feeling?

WILLY: Not much any more, Jenny. Ha, ha! (*He is surprised to see the rackets.*)

BERNARD: Hello, Uncle Willy.

WILLY (*almost shocked*): Bernard! Well, look who's here! (*He comes quickly, guiltily, to* BERNARD *and warmly shakes his hand.*)

BERNARD: How are you? Good to see you.

WILLY: What are you doing here?

BERNARD: Oh, just stopped by to see Pop. Get off my feet till my train leaves. I'm going to Washington in a few minutes.

WILLY: Is he in?

BERNARD: Yes, he's in his office with the accountant. Sit down.

WILLY (*sitting down*): What're you going to do in Washington?

BERNARD: Oh, just a case I've got there, Willy.

WILLY: That so? (*indicating the rackets*) You going to play tennis there?

BERNARD: I'm staying with a friend who's got a court.

WILLY: Don't say. His own tennis court. Must be fine people, I bet.

BERNARD: They are, very nice. Dad tells me Biff's in town.

WILLY (*with a big smile*): Yeah, Biff's in. Working on a very big deal, Bernard.

BERNARD: What's Biff doing?

WILLY: Well, he's been doing very big things in the West. But he decided to establish himself here. Very big. We're having dinner. Did I hear your wife had a boy?

BERNARD: That's right. Our second.

WILLY: Two boys! What do you know!

BERNARD: What kind of a deal has Biff got?

WILLY: Well, Bill Oliver—very big sporting-goods man—he wants Biff very badly. Called him in from the West. Long distance, carte blanche, special deliveries. Your friends have their own private tennis court?

BERNARD: You still with the old firm, Willy?

WILLY (*after a pause*): I'm—I'm overjoyed to see how you made the grade, Bernard, overjoyed. It's an encouraging thing to see a young man really—really—Looks very good for Biff—very—(*he breaks off, then*) Bernard—(*He is so full of emotion, he breaks off again.*)

BERNARD: What is it, Willy?

WILLY (*small and alone*): What—what's the secret?

BERNARD: What secret?

WILLY: How—how did you? Why didn't he ever catch on?

BERNARD: I wouldn't know that, Willy.

WILLY (*confidentially, desperately*): You were his friend, his boyhood friend. There's something I don't understand about it. His life ended after that Ebbets Field game. From the age of seventeen nothing good ever happened to him.

BERNARD: He never trained himself for anything.

WILLY: But he did, he did. After high school he took so many correspondence courses. Radio mechanics; television; God knows what, and never made the slightest mark.

BERNARD (*taking off his glasses*): Willy, do you want to talk candidly?

WILLY (*rising, faces* BERNARD): I regard you as a very brilliant man, Bernard. I value your advice.

BERNARD: Oh, the hell with the advice, Willy. I couldn't advise you. There's just one thing I've always wanted to ask you. When he was supposed to graduate, and the math teacher flunked him—

WILLY: Oh, that son-of-a-bitch ruined his life.

BERNARD: Yeah, but, Willy, all he had to do was go to summer school and make up that subject.

WILLY: That's right, that's right.

BERNARD: Did you tell him not to go to summer school?

WILLY: Me? I begged him to go. I ordered him to go!

BERNARD: Then why wouldn't he go?

WILLY: Why? Why! Bernard, that question has been trailing me like a ghost for the last fifteen years. He flunked the subject, and laid down and died like a hammer hit him!

BERNARD: Take it easy, kid.

WILLY: Let me talk to you—I got nobody to talk to. Bernard, Bernard, was it my fault? Y'see? It keeps going around in my mind, maybe I did something to him. I got nothing to give him.

BERNARD: Don't take it so hard.

WILLY: Why did he lay down? What is the story there? You were his friend!

BERNARD: Willy, I remember, it was June, and our grades came out. And he'd flunked math.

WILLY: That son-of-a-bitch!

BERNARD: No, it wasn't right then. Biff just got very angry, I remember, and he was ready to enroll in summer school.

WILLY (*surprised*): He was?

BERNARD: He wasn't beaten by it at all. But then, Willy, he disappeared from the block for almost a month. And I got the idea that he'd gone up to New England to see you. Did he have a talk with you then?

WILLY *stares in silence.*

BERNARD: Willy?

WILLY (*with a strong edge of resentment in his voice*): Yeah, he came to Boston. What about it?

BERNARD: Well, just that when he came back—I'll never forget this, it always mystifies me. Because I'd thought so well of Biff, even though he'd always taken advantage of me. I loved him, Willy, y'know? And he came back after that month and took his sneakers—remember those sneakers with "University of Virginia" printed on them? He was so proud of those, wore them every day. And he took them down in the cellar, and burned them up in the furnace. We had a fist fight. It lasted at least half an hour. Just the two of us, punching each other down the cellar, and crying right through it. I've often thought of how strange it was that I knew he'd given up his life. What happened in Boston, Willy?

WILLY *looks at him as at an intruder.*

BERNARD: I just bring it up because you asked me.

WILLY (*angrily*): Nothing. What do you mean, "What happened?" What's that got to do with anything?

BERNARD: Well, don't get sore.

WILLY: What are you trying to do, blame it on me? If a boy lays down is that my fault?

BERNARD: Now, Willy, don't get—

WILLY: Well, don't—don't talk to me that way! What does that mean, "What happened?"

CHARLEY *enters. He is in his vest, and he carries a bottle of bourbon.*

CHARLEY: Hey, you're going to miss that train. (*He waves the bottle.*)

BERNARD: Yeah, I'm going. (*He takes the bottle.*) Thanks, Pop. (*He picks up his rackets and bag.*) Good-by, Willy, and don't worry about it. You know, "If at first you don't succeed . . ."

WILLY: Yes, I believe in that.

BERNARD: But sometimes, Willy, it's better for a man just to walk away.

WILLY: Walk away?

BERNARD: That's right.

WILLY: But if you can't walk away?

BERNARD (*after a slight pause*): I guess that's when it's tough. (*extending his hand*) Good-by, Willy.

WILLY (*shaking* BERNARD's hand): Good-by, boy.

CHARLEY (*an arm on* BERNARD's *shoulder*): How do you like this kid? Gonna argue a case in front of the Supreme Court.

BERNARD (*protesting*): Pop!

WILLY (*genuinely shocked, pained, and happy*): No! The Supreme Court!

BERNARD: I gotta run. 'By, Dad!

CHARLEY: Knock 'em dead, Bernard!

BERNARD *goes off.*

WILLY (*as* CHARLEY *takes out his wallet*): The Supreme Court! And he didn't even mention it!

CHARLEY (*counting out money on the desk*): He don't have to—he's gonna do it.

WILLY: And you never told him what to do, did you? You never took any interest in him.

CHARLEY: My salvation is that I never took any interest in anything. There's some money—fifty dollars. I got an accountant inside.

WILLY: Charley, look . . . (*with difficulty*) I got my insurance to pay. If you can manage it—I need a hundred and ten dollars.

CHARLEY *doesn't reply for a moment; merely stops moving.*

WILLY: I'd draw it from my bank but Linda would know, and I . . .

CHARLEY: Sit down, Willy.

WILLY (*moving toward the chair*): I'm keeping an account of everything, remember. I'll pay every penny back. (*He sits.*)

CHARLEY: Now listen to me, Willy.

WILLY: I want you to know I appreciate . . .

CHARLEY (*sitting down on the table*): Willy, what're you doin'? What the hell is goin' on in your head?

WILLY: Why? I'm simply . . .

CHARLEY: I offered you a job. You can make fifty dollars a week. And I won't send you on the road.

WILLY: I've got a job.

CHARLEY: Without pay? What kind of a job is a job without pay? (*He rises.*) Now, look, kid, enough is enough. I'm no genius but I know when I'm being insulted.

WILLY: Insulted!

CHARLEY: Why don't you want to work for me?

WILLY: What's the matter with you? I've got a job.

CHARLEY: Then what're you walkin' in here every week for?

WILLY (*getting up*): Well, if you don't want me to walk in here—

CHARLEY: I am offering you a job.

WILLY: I don't want your goddam job!

CHARLEY: When the hell are you going to grow up?

WILLY (*furiously*): You big ignoramus, if you say that to me again I'll rap you one! I don't care how big you are! (*He's ready to fight.*)

Pause.

CHARLEY (*kindly, going to him*): How much do you need, Willy?

WILLY: Charley, I'm strapped, I'm strapped. I don't know what to do. I was just fired.

CHARLEY: Howard fired you?

WILLY: That snotnose. Imagine that? I named him. I named him Howard.

CHARLEY: Willy, when're you gonna realize that them things don't mean anything? You named him Howard, but you can't sell that. The only thing you got in this world is what you can sell. And the funny thing is that you're a salesman, and you don't know that.

WILLY: I've always tried to think otherwise, I guess. I always felt that if a man was impressive, and well liked, that nothing—

CHARLEY: Why must everybody like you? Who liked J. P. Morgan? Was he impressive? In a Turkish bath he'd look like a butcher. But with his pockets on he was very well liked. Now listen, Willy, I know you don't like me, and nobody can say I'm in love with you, but I'll give you a job because—just for the hell of it, put it that way. Now what do you say?

WILLY: I—I just can't work for you, Charley.

CHARLEY: What're you, jealous of me?

WILLY: I can't work for you, that's all, don't ask me why.

CHARLEY (*angered, taking out more bills*): You been jealous of me all your life, you damned fool! Here, pay your insurance. (*He puts the money in* WILLY'S *hand.*)

WILLY: I'm keeping strict accounts.

CHARLEY: I've got some work to do. Take care of yourself. And pay your insurance.

WILLY (*moving to the right*): Funny, y'know? After all the highways, and the trains, and the appointments, and the years, you end up worth more dead than alive.

CHARLEY: Willy, nobody's worth nothin' dead. (*after a slight pause*) Did you hear what I said?

WILLY *stands still, dreaming.*

CHARLEY: Willy!

WILLY: Apologize to Bernard for me when you see him. I didn't mean to argue with him. He's a fine boy. They're all fine boys, and they'll end up big—all of them. Someday they'll all play tennis together. Wish me luck, Charley. He saw Bill Oliver today.

CHARLEY: Good luck.

WILLY (*on the verge of tears*): Charley, you're the only friend I got. Isn't that a remarkable thing? (*He goes out.*)

CHARLEY: Jesus!

CHARLEY *stares after him a moment and follows. All light blacks out. Suddenly raucous music is heard, and a red glow rises behind the screen at right.* STANLEY, *a young waiter, appears, carrying a table, followed by* HAPPY, *who is carrying two chairs.*

STANLEY (*putting the table down*): That's all right, Mr. Loman, I can handle it myself.

(*He turns and takes the chairs from* HAPPY *and places them at the table.*)

HAPPY (*glancing around*): Oh, this is better.

STANLEY: Sure, in the front there you're in the middle of all kinds of noise. Whenever you got a party, Mr. Loman, you just tell me and I'll put you back here. Y'know, there's a lotta people they don't like it private, because when they go out they like to see a lotta action around them because they're sick and tired to stay in the house by theirself. But I know you, you ain't from Hackensack. You know what I mean?

HAPPY (*sitting down*): So how's it coming, Stanley?

STANLEY: Ah, it's a dog's life. I only wish during the war they'd a took me in the Army. I coulda been dead by now.

HAPPY: My brother's back, Stanley.

STANLEY: Oh, he come back, heh? From the Far West.

HAPPY: Yeah, big cattle man, my brother, so treat him right. And my father's coming too.

STANLEY: Oh, your father too!

HAPPY: You got a couple of nice lobsters?

STANLEY: Hundred per cent, big.

HAPPY: I want them with the claws.

STANLEY: Don't worry, I don't give you no mice. (HAPPY *laughs.*) How about some wine? It'll put a head on the meal.

HAPPY: No. You remember, Stanley, that recipe I brought you from overseas? With the champagne in it?

STANLEY: Oh, yeah, sure. I still got it tacked up yet in the kitchen. But that'll have to cost a buck apiece anyways.

HAPPY: That's all right.

STANLEY: What'd you, hit a number or somethin'?

HAPPY: No, it's a little celebration. My brother is—I think he pulled off a big deal today. I think we're going into business together.

STANLEY: Great! That's the best for you. Because a family business, you know what I mean?—that's the best.

HAPPY: That's what I think.

STANLEY: 'Cause what's the difference? Somebody steals? It's in the family. Know what I mean? (*sotto voce*) Like this bartender here. The boss is goin' crazy what kinda leak he's got in the cash register. You put it in but it don't come out.

HAPPY (*raising his head*): Sh!

STANLEY: What?

HAPPY: You notice I wasn't lookin' right or left, was I?

STANLEY: No.

HAPPY: And my eyes are closed.

STANLEY: So what's the—?

HAPPY: Strudel's comin'.

STANLEY (*catching on, looks around*): Ah, no, there's no—

He breaks off as a furred, lavishly dressed girl enters and sits at the next table. Both follow her with their eyes.

STANLEY: Geez, how'd ya know?

HAPPY: I got radar or something. (*staring directly at her profile*) Oooooooo . . . Stanley.

STANLEY: I think that's for you, Mr. Loman.

HAPPY: Look at that mouth. Oh, God. And the binoculars.

STANLEY: Geez, you got a life, Mr. Loman.

HAPPY: Wait on her.

STANLEY (*going to the girl's table*): Would you like a menu, ma'am?

GIRL: I'm expecting someone, but I'd like a—

HAPPY: Why don't you bring her—excuse me, miss, do you mind? I sell champagne, and I'd like you to try my brand. Bring her a champagne, Stanley.

GIRL: That's awfully nice of you.

HAPPY: Don't mention it. It's all company money. (*He laughs.*)

GIRL: That's a charming product to be selling, isn't it?

HAPPY: Oh, gets to be like everything else. Selling is selling, y'know.

GIRL: I suppose.

HAPPY: You don't happen to sell, do you?

GIRL: No, I don't sell.

HAPPY: Would you object to a compliment from a stranger? You ought to be on a magazine cover.

GIRL (*looking at him a little archly*): I have been.

STANLEY *comes in with a glass of champagne.*

HAPPY: What'd I say before, Stanley? You see? She's a cover girl.

STANLEY: Oh, I could see, I could see.

HAPPY (*to the girl*): What magazine?

GIRL: Oh, a lot of them. (*She takes the drink.*) Thank you.

HAPPY: You know what they say in France, don't you? "Champagne is the drink of the complexion"—Hiya, Biff!

BIFF *has entered and sits with* HAPPY.

BIFF: Hello, kid. Sorry I'm late.

HAPPY: I just got here. Uh, Miss—?

GIRL: Forsythe.

HAPPY: Miss Forsythe, this is my brother.

BIFF: Is Dad here?

HAPPY: His name is Biff. You might've heard of him. Great football player.

GIRL: Really? What team?

HAPPY: Are you familiar with football?

GIRL: No, I'm afraid I'm not.

HAPPY: Biff is quarterback with the New York Giants.

GIRL: Well, that is nice, isn't it? (*She drinks.*)

HAPPY: Good health.

GIRL: I'm happy to meet you.

HAPPY: That's my name. Hap. It's really Harold, but at West Point they called me Happy.

GIRL (*now really impressed*): Oh, I see. How do you do? (*She turns her profile.*)

BIFF: Isn't Dad coming?

HAPPY: You want her?

BIFF: Oh, I could never make that.

HAPPY: I remember the time that idea would never come into your head. Where's the old confidence, Biff?

BIFF: I just saw Oliver—

HAPPY: Wait a minute. I've got to see that old confidence again. Do you want her? She's on call.

BIFF: Oh, no. (*He turns to look at the girl.*)

HAPPY: I'm telling you. Watch this. (*turning to the girl*) Honey? (*She turns to him.*) Are you busy?

GIRL: Well, I am . . . but I could make a phone call.

HAPPY: Do that, will you, honey? And see if you can get a friend. We'll be here for a while. Biff is one of the greatest football players in the country.

GIRL (*standing up*): Well, I'm certainly happy to meet you.

HAPPY: Come back soon.

GIRL: I'll try.

HAPPY: Don't try, honey, try hard.

The girl exits. STANLEY *follows, shaking his head in bewildered admiration.*

HAPPY: Isn't that a shame now? A beautiful girl like that? That's why I can't get married. There's not a good woman in a thousand. New York is loaded with them, kid!

BIFF: Hap, look—

HAPPY: I told you she was on call!

BIFF (*strangely unnerved*): Cut it out, will ya? I want to say something to you.

HAPPY: Did you see Oliver?

BIFF: I saw him all right. Now look, I want to tell Dad a couple of things and I want you to help me.

HAPPY: What? Is he going to back you?

BIFF: Are you crazy? You're out of your goddam head, you know that?

HAPPY: Why? What happened?

BIFF (*breathlessly*): I did a terrible thing today, Hap. It's been the strangest day I ever went through. I'm all numb, I swear.

HAPPY: You mean he wouldn't see you?

BIFF: Well, I waited six hours for him, see? All day. Kept sending my name in. Even tried to date his secretary so she'd get me to him, but no soap.

HAPPY: Because you're not showin' the old confidence, Biff. He remembered you, didn't he?

BIFF (*stopping* HAPPY *with a gesture*): Finally, about five o'clock, he comes out. Didn't remember who I was or anything. I felt like such an idiot, Hap.

HAPPY: Did you tell him my Florida idea?

BIFF: He walked away. I saw him for one minute. I got so mad I could've torn the walls down! How the hell did I ever get the idea I was a salesman there? I even believed myself that I'd been a salesman for him! And then he gave me one look and—I re- alized what a ridiculous lie my whole life has been! We've been talking in a dream for fifteen years. I was a shipping clerk.

HAPPY: What'd you do?

BIFF (*with great tension and wonder*): Well, he left, see. And the secretary went out. I was all alone in the waiting room. I don't know what came over me, Hap. The next thing I know I'm in his office—paneled walls, everything. I can't explain it. I—Hap, I took his fountain pen.

HAPPY: Geez, did he catch you?

BIFF: I ran out. I ran down all eleven flights. I ran and ran and ran.

HAPPY: That was an awful dumb—what'd you do that for?

BIFF (*agonized*): I don't know, I just—wanted to take something, I don't know. You gotta help me, Hap, I'm gonna tell Pop.

HAPPY: You crazy? What for?

BIFF: Hap, he's got to understand that I'm not the man somebody lends that kind of money to. He thinks I've been spiting him all these years and it's eating him up.

HAPPY: That's just it. You tell him something nice.

BIFF: I can't.

HAPPY: Say you got a lunch date with Oliver tomorrow.

BIFF: So what do I do tomorrow?

HAPPY: You leave the house tomorrow and come back at night and say Oliver is thinking it over. And he thinks it over for a couple of weeks, and gradually it fades away and nobody's the worse.

BIFF: But it'll go on forever!

HAPPY: Dad is never so happy as when he's looking forward to something!

WILLY *enters.*

HAPPY: Hello, scout!

WILLY: Gee, I haven't been here in years!

STANLEY *has followed* WILLY *in and sets a chair for him.* STANLEY *starts off but* HAPPY *stops him.*

HAPPY: Stanley!

STANLEY *stands by, waiting for an order.*

BIFF (*going to* WILLY *with guilt, as to an invalid*): Sit down, Pop. You want a drink?

WILLY: Sure, I don't mind.

BIFF: Let's get a load on.

WILLY: You look worried.

BIFF: N-no. (*to* STANLEY) Scotch all around. Make it doubles.

STANLEY: Doubles, right. (*He goes.*)

WILLY: You had a couple already, didn't you?

BIFF: Just a couple, yeah.

WILLY: Well, what happened, boy? (*nodding affirmatively, with a smile*) Everything go all right?

BIFF (*takes a breath, then reaches out and grasps* WILLY'S *hand*): Pal . . . (*He is smiling bravely, and* WILLY *is smiling too.*) I had an experience today.

HAPPY: Terrific, Pop.

WILLY: That so? What happened?

BIFF (*high, slightly alcoholic, above the earth*): I'm going to tell you everything from first to last. It's been a strange day. (*Silence. He looks around, composes himself as best he can, but his breath keeps breaking the rhythm of his voice.*) I had to wait quite a while for him, and—

WILLY: Oliver?

BIFF: Yeah, Oliver. All day, as a matter of cold fact. And a lot of—instances—facts, Pop, facts about my life came back to me. Who was it, Pop? Who ever said I was a salesman with Oliver?

WILLY: Well, you were.

BIFF: No, Dad, I was a shipping clerk.

WILLY: But you were practically—

BIFF (*with determination*): Dad, I don't know who said it first, but I was never a salesman for Bill Oliver.

WILLY: What're you talking about?

BIFF: Let's hold on to the facts tonight, Pop. We're not going to get anywhere bullin' around. I was a shipping clerk.

WILLY (*angrily*): All right, now listen to me—

BIFF: Why don't you let me finish?

WILLY: I'm not interested in stories about the past or any crap of that kind because the woods are burning, boys, you understand? There's a big blaze going on all around. I was fired today.

BIFF (*shocked*): How could you be?

WILLY: I was fired, and I'm looking for a little good news to tell your mother, because the woman has waited and the woman has suffered. The gist of it is that I haven't got a story left in my head, Biff. So don't give me a lecture about facts and aspects. I am not interested. Now what've you got to say to me?

STANLEY *enters with three drinks. They wait until he leaves.*

WILLY: Did you see Oliver?

BIFF: Jesus, Dad!

WILLY: You mean you didn't go up there?

HAPPY: Sure he went up there.

BIFF: I did. I—saw him. How could they fire you?

WILLY (*on the edge of his chair*): What kind of a welcome did he give you?

BIFF: He won't even let you work on commission?

WILLY: I'm out! (*driving*) So tell me, he gave you a warm welcome?

HAPPY: Sure, Pop, sure!

BIFF (*driven*): Well, it was kind of—

WILLY: I was wondering if he'd remember you. (*to* HAPPY) Imagine, man doesn't see him for ten, twelve years and gives him that kind of a welcome!

HAPPY: Damn right!

BIFF (*trying to return to the offensive*): Pop, look—

WILLY: You know why he remembered you, don't you? Because you impressed him in those days.

BIFF: Let's talk quietly and get this down to the facts, huh?

WILLY (*as though* BIFF *had been interrupting*): Well, what happened? It's great news, Biff. Did he take you into his office or'd you talk in the waiting room?

BIFF: Well, he came in, see, and—

WILLY (*with a big smile*): What'd he say? Betcha he threw his arm around you.

BIFF: Well, he kinda—

WILLY: He's a fine man. (*to* HAPPY) Very hard man to see, y'know.

HAPPY (*agreeing*): Oh, I know.

WILLY (*to* BIFF): Is that where you had the drinks?

BIFF: Yeah, he gave me a couple of—no, no!

HAPPY (*cutting in*): He told him my Florida idea.

WILLY: Don't interrupt. (*to* BIFF) How'd he react to the Florida idea?

BIFF: Dad, will you give me a minute to explain?

WILLY: I've been waiting for you to explain since I sat down here! What happened? He took you into his office and what?

BIFF: Well—I talked. And—and he listened, see.

WILLY: Famous for the way he listens, y'know. What was his answer?

BIFF: His answer was—(*He breaks off, suddenly angry.*) Dad, you're not letting me tell you what I want to tell you!

WILLY (*accusing, angered*): You didn't see him, did you?

BIFF: I did see him!

WILLY: What'd you insult him or something? You insulted him, didn't you?

BIFF: Listen, will you let me out of it, will you just let me out of it!

HAPPY: What the hell!

WILLY: Tell me what happened!

BIFF (*to* HAPPY): I can't talk to him!

> *A single trumpet note jars the ear. The light of green leaves stains the house, which holds the air of night and a dream.* YOUNG BERNARD *enters and knocks on the door of the house.*

YOUNG BERNARD (*frantically*): Mrs. Loman, Mrs. Loman!

HAPPY: Tell him what happened!

BIFF (*to* HAPPY): Shut up and leave me alone!

WILLY: No, no! You had to go and flunk math!

BIFF: What math? What're you talking about?

YOUNG BERNARD: Mrs. Loman, Mrs. Loman!

> LINDA *appears in the house, as of old.*

WILLY (*wildly*): Math, math, math!

BIFF: Take it easy, Pop!

YOUNG BERNARD: Mrs. Loman!

WILLY (*furiously*): If you hadn't flunked you'd've been set by now!

BIFF: Now, look, I'm gonna tell you what happened, and you're going to listen to me.

YOUNG BERNARD: Mrs. Loman!

BIFF: I waited six hours—

HAPPY: What the hell are you saying?

BIFF: I kept sending in my name but he wouldn't see me. So finally he . . . (*He continues unheard as light fades low on the restaurant.*)

YOUNG BERNARD: Biff flunked math!

LINDA: No!

YOUNG BERNARD: Birnbaum flunked him! They won't graduate him!

LINDA: But they have to. He's gotta go to the university. Where is he? Biff! Biff!

YOUNG BERNARD: No, he left. He went to Grand Central.

LINDA: Grand—You mean he went to Boston!

YOUNG BERNARD: Is Uncle Willy in Boston?

LINDA: Oh, maybe Willy can talk to the teacher. Oh, the poor, poor boy!

> *Light on house area snaps out.*

BIFF (*at the table, now audible, holding up a gold fountain pen*): . . . so I'm washed up with Oliver, you understand? Are you listening to me?

WILLY (*at a loss*): Yeah, sure. If you hadn't flunked—

BIFF: Flunked what? What're you talking about?

WILLY: Don't blame everything on me! I didn't flunk math—you did! What pen?

HAPPY: That was awful dumb, Biff, a pen like that is worth—

WILLY (*seeing the pen for the first time*): You took Oliver's pen?

BIFF (*weakening*): Dad, I just explained it to you.

WILLY: You stole Bill Oliver's fountain pen!

BIFF: I didn't exactly steal it! That's just what I've been explaining to you!

HAPPY: He had it in his hand and just then Oliver walked in, so he got nervous and stuck it in his pocket!

WILLY: My God, Biff!

BIFF: I never intended to do it, Dad!

OPERATOR'S VOICE: Standish Arms, good evening!

WILLY (*shouting*): I'm not in my room!

BIFF (*frightened*): Dad, what's the matter? (*He and* HAPPY *stand up.*)

OPERATOR: Ringing Mr. Loman for you!

WILLY: I'm not there, stop it!

BIFF (*horrified, gets down on one knee before* WILLY): Dad, I'll make good, I'll make good. (WILLY *tries to get to his feet.* BIFF *holds him down.*) Sit down now.

WILLY: No, you're no good, you're no good for anything.

BIFF: I am, Dad, I'll find something else, you understand? Now don't worry about anything. (*He holds up* WILLY'S *face.*) Talk to me, Dad.

OPERATOR: Mr. Loman does not answer. Shall I page him?

WILLY (*attempting to stand, as though to rush and silence the* OPERATOR): No, no, no!

HAPPY: He'll strike something, Pop.

WILLY: No, no . . .

BIFF (*desperately, standing over* WILLY): Pop, listen! Listen to me! I'm telling you something good. Oliver talked to his partner about the Florida idea. You listening? He—he talked to his partner, and he came to me . . . I'm going to be all right, you hear? Dad, listen to me, he said it was just a question of the amount!

WILLY: Then you . . . got it?

HAPPY: He's gonna be terrific, Pop!

WILLY (*trying to stand*): Then you got it, haven't you? You got it! You got it!

BIFF (*agonized, holds* WILLY *down*): No, no. Look, Pop. I'm supposed to have lunch with them tomorrow. I'm just telling you this so you'll know that I can still make an impression, Pop. And I'll make good somewhere, but I can't go tomorrow, see?

WILLY: Why not? You simply—

BIFF: But the pen, Pop!

WILLY: You give it to him and tell him it was an oversight!

HAPPY: Sure, have lunch tomorrow!

BIFF: I can't say that—

WILLY: You were doing a crossword puzzle and accidentally used his pen!

BIFF: Listen, kid, I took those balls years ago, now I walk in with his fountain pen? That clinches it, don't you see? I can't face him like that! I'll try elsewhere.

PAGE'S VOICE: Paging Mr. Loman!

WILLY: Don't you want to be anything?

BIFF: Pop, how can I go back?

WILLY: You don't want to be anything, is that what's behind it?

BIFF (*now angry at* WILLY *for not crediting his sympathy*): Don't take it that way! You think it was easy walking into that office after what I'd done to him? A team of horses couldn't have dragged me back to Bill Oliver!

WILLY: Then why'd you go?

BIFF: Why did I go? Why did I go! Look at you! Look at what's become of you!

Off left, THE WOMAN *laughs.*

WILLY: Biff, you're going to go to that lunch tomorrow, or—

BIFF: I can't go. I've got no appointment!

HAPPY: Biff, for . . . !

WILLY: Are you spiting me?

BIFF: Don't take it that way! Goddammit!

WILLY (*He strikes* BIFF *and falters away from the table*.): You rotten little louse! Are you spiting me?

THE WOMAN: Someone's at the door, Willy!

BIFF: I'm no good, can't you see what I am?

HAPPY (*separating them*): Hey, you're in a restaurant! Now cut it out, both of you! (*The girls enter.*) Hello, girls, sit down.

THE WOMAN *laughs, off left.*

MISS FORSYTHE: I guess we might as well. This is Letta.

THE WOMAN: Willy, are you going to wake up?

BIFF (*ignoring* WILLY): How're ya, miss, sit down. What do you drink?

MISS FORSYTHE: Letta might not be able to stay long.

LETTA: I gotta get up very early tomorrow. I got jury duty. I'm so excited! Were you fellows ever on a jury?

BIFF: No, but I been in front of them! (*The girls laugh.*) This is my father.

LETTA: Isn't he cute? Sit down with us, Pop.

HAPPY: Sit him down, Biff!

BIFF (*going to him*): Come on, slugger, drink us under the table. To hell with it! Come on, sit down, pal.

On BIFF'S *last insistence,* WILLY *is about to sit.*

THE WOMAN (*now urgently*): Willy, are you going to answer the door!

THE WOMAN'S *call pulls* WILLY *back. He starts right, befuddled.*

BIFF: Hey, where are you going?

WILLY: Open the door.

BIFF: The door?

WILLY: The washroom . . . the door . . . where's the door?

BIFF (*leading* WILLY *to the left*): Just go straight down.

WILLY *moves left.*

THE WOMAN: Willy, Willy, are you going to get up, get up, get up, get up?

WILLY *exits left.*

LETTA: I think it's sweet you bring your daddy along.

MISS FORSYTHE: Oh, he isn't really your father!

BIFF (*at left, turning to her resentfully*): Miss Forsythe, you've just seen a prince walk by. A fine, troubled prince. A hard-working, unappreciated prince. A pal, you understand? A good companion. Always for his boys.

LETTA: That's so sweet.

HAPPY: Well, girls, what's the program? We're wasting time. Come on, Biff. Gather round. Where would you like to go?

BIFF: Why don't you do something for him?

HAPPY: Me!

BIFF: Don't you give a damn for him, Hap?

HAPPY: What're you talking about? I'm the one who—

BIFF: I sense it, you don't give a good goddam about him. (*He takes the rolled-up hose from his pocket and puts it on the table in front of* HAPPY.) Look what I found in the cellar, for Christ's sake. How can you bear to let it go on?

HAPPY: Me? Who goes away? Who runs off and—

BIFF: Yeah, but he doesn't mean anything to you. You could help him—I can't! Don't you understand what I'm talking about? He's going to kill himself, don't you know that?

HAPPY: Don't I know it! Me!

BIFF: Hap, help him! Jesus . . . help him . . . Help me, help me, I can't bear to look at his face! (*Ready to weep, he hurries out, up right.*)

HAPPY (*starting after him*): Where are you going?

MISS FORSYTHE: What's he so mad about?

HAPPY: Come on, girls, we'll catch up with him.

MISS FORSYTHE (*as* HAPPY *pushes her out*): Say, I don't like that temper of his!

HAPPY: He's just a little overstrung, he'll be all right!

WILLY (*off left, as* THE WOMAN *laughs*): Don't answer! Don't answer!

LETTA: Don't you want to tell your father—

HAPPY: No, that's not my father. He's just a guy. Come on, we'll catch Biff, and, honey, we're going to paint this town! Stanley, where's the check! Hey, Stanley!

They exit. STANLEY *looks toward left.*

STANLEY (*calling to* HAPPY *indignantly*): Mr. Loman! Mr. Loman!

STANLEY *picks up a chair and follows them off. Knocking is heard off left.* THE WOMAN *enters, laughing.* WILLY *follows her. She is in a black slip; he is buttoning his shirt. Raw, sensuous music accompanies their speech.*

WILLY: Will you stop laughing? Will you stop?

THE WOMAN: Aren't you going to answer the door? He'll wake the whole hotel.

WILLY: I'm not expecting anybody.

THE WOMAN: Whyn't you have another drink, honey, and stop being so damn self-centered?

WILLY: I'm so lonely.

THE WOMAN: You know you ruined me, Willy? From now on, whenever you come to the office, I'll see that you go right through to the buyers. No waiting at my desk any more, Willy. You ruined me.

WILLY: That's nice of you to say that.

THE WOMAN: Gee, you are self-centered! Why so sad? You are the saddest, self-centeredest soul I ever did see-saw. (*She laughs. He kisses her.*) Come on inside, drummer boy. It's silly to be dressing in the middle of the night. (*as knocking is heard*) Aren't you going to answer the door?

WILLY: They're knocking on the wrong door.

THE WOMAN: But I felt the knocking. And he heard us talking in here. Maybe the hotel's on fire!

WILLY (*his terror rising*): It's a mistake.

THE WOMAN: Then tell him to go away!

WILLY: There's nobody there.

THE WOMAN: It's getting on my nerves, Willy. There's somebody standing out there and it's getting on my nerves!

WILLY (*pushing her away from him*): All right, stay in the bathroom here, and don't come out. I think there's a law in Massachusetts about it, so don't come out. It may be that new room clerk. He looked very mean. So don't come out. It's a mistake, there's no fire.

The knocking is heard again. He takes a few steps away from her, and she vanishes into the wing. The light follows him, and now he is facing YOUNG BIFF, *who carries a suitcase.* BIFF *steps toward him. The music is gone.*

BIFF: Why didn't you answer?

WILLY: Biff! What are you doing in Boston?

BIFF: Why didn't you answer? I've been knocking for five minutes, I called you on the phone—

WILLY: I just heard you. I was in the bathroom and had the door shut. Did anything happen home?

BIFF: Dad—I let you down.

WILLY: What do you mean?

BIFF: Dad . . .

WILLY: Biffo, what's this about? (*putting his arm around* BIFF) Come on, let's go downstairs and get you a malted.

BIFF: Dad, I flunked math.

WILLY: Not for the term?

BIFF: The term. I haven't got enough credits to graduate.

WILLY: You mean to say Bernard wouldn't give you the answers?

BIFF: He did, he tried, but I only got a sixty-one.

WILLY: And they wouldn't give you four points?

BIFF: Birnbaum refused absolutely. I begged him, Pop, but he won't give me those points. You gotta talk to him before they close the school. Because if he saw the kind of man you are, and you just talked to him in your way, I'm sure he'd come through for me. The class came right before practice, see, and I didn't go enough. Would you talk to him? He'd like you, Pop. You know the way you could talk.

WILLY: You're on. We'll drive right back.

BIFF: Oh, Dad, good work! I'm sure he'll change it for you!

WILLY: Go downstairs and tell the clerk I'm checkin' out. Go right down.

BIFF: Yes, sir! See, the reason he hates me, Pop—one day he was late for class so I got up at the blackboard and imitated him. I crossed my eyes and talked with a lithp.

WILLY (*laughing*): You did? The kids like it?

BIFF: They nearly died laughing!

WILLY: Yeah? What'd you do?

BIFF: The thquare root of thixthy twee is . . . (WILLY *bursts out laughing;* BIFF *joins him.*) And in the middle of it he walked in!

WILLY *laughs, and* THE WOMAN *joins in offstage.*

WILLY (*without hesitation*): Hurry downstairs and—

BIFF: Somebody in there?

WILLY: No, that was next door.

THE WOMAN *laughs offstage.*

BIFF: Somebody got in your bathroom!

WILLY: No, it's the next room, there's a party—

THE WOMAN (*Enters, laughing. She lisps this.*): Can I come in? There's something in the bathtub, Willy, and it's moving!

WILLY *looks at* BIFF, *who is staring open-mouthed and horrified at* THE WOMAN.

WILLY: Ah—you better go back to your room. They must be finished painting by now.

They're painting her room so I let her take a shower here. Go back, go back . . . (*He pushes her.*)

THE WOMAN (*resisting*): But I've got to get dressed, Willy, I can't—

WILLY: Get out of here! Go back, go back . . . (*suddenly striving for the ordinary*) This is Miss Francis, Biff, she's a buyer. They're painting her room. Go back, Miss Francis, go back . . .

THE WOMAN: But my clothes, I can't go out naked in the hall!

WILLY (*pushing her offstage*): Get outa here! Go back, go back!

BIFF *slowly sits down on his suitcase as the argument continues offstage.*

THE WOMAN: Where's my stockings? You promised me stockings, Willy!

WILLY: I have no stockings here!

THE WOMAN: You had two boxes of size nine sheers for me, and I want them!

WILLY: Here, for God's sake, will you get outa here!

THE WOMAN (*entering, holding a box of stockings*): I just hope there's nobody in the hall. That's all I hope. (*to* BIFF) Are you football or baseball?

BIFF: Football.

THE WOMAN (*angry, humiliated*): That's me too. G'night. (*She snatches her clothes from* WILLY, *and walks out.*)

WILLY (*after a pause*): Well, better get going. I want to get to the school first thing in the morning. Get my suits out of the closet. I'll get my valise. (BIFF *doesn't move.*) What's the matter? (BIFF *remains motionless, tears falling.*) She's a buyer. Buys for J. H. Simmons. She lives down the hall—they're painting. You don't imagine— (*He breaks off. After a pause.*) Now listen, pal, she's just a buyer. She sees merchandise in her room and they have to keep it looking just so . . . (*Pause. Assuming command.*) All right, get my suits. (BIFF *doesn't move.*) Now stop crying and do as I say. I gave you an order. Biff, I gave you an order! Is that what you do when I give you an order? How dare you cry! (*putting his arm around* BIFF) Now look, Biff, when you grow up you'll understand about these things. You mustn't—you mustn't overemphasize a thing like this. I'll see Birnbaum first thing in the morning.

BIFF: Never mind.

WILLY (*getting down beside* BIFF): Never mind! He's going to give you those points. I'll see to it.

BIFF: He wouldn't listen to you.

WILLY: He certainly will listen to me. You need those points for the U. of Virginia.

BIFF: I'm not going there.

WILLY: Heh? If I can't get him to change that mark you'll make it up in summer school. You've got all summer to—

BIFF (*his weeping breaking from him*): Dad . . .

WILLY (*infected by it*): Oh, my boy . . .

BIFF: Dad . . .

WILLY: She's nothing to me, Biff. I was lonely, I was terribly lonely.

BIFF: You—you gave her Mama's stockings! (*His tears break through and he rises to go.*)

WILLY (*grabbing for* BIFF): I gave you an order!

BIFF: Don't touch me, you—liar!

WILLY: Apologize for that!

BIFF: You fake! You phony little fake! You fake! (*Overcome, he turns quickly and weeping fully goes out with his suitcase.* WILLY *is left on the floor on his knees.*)

WILLY: I gave you an order! Biff, come back here or I'll beat you! Come back here! I'll whip you!

STANLEY *comes quickly in from the right and stands in front of* WILLY.

WILLY (*shouting at* STANLEY): I gave you an order . . .

STANLEY: Hey, let's pick it up, pick it up, Mr. Loman. (*He helps* WILLY *to his feet.*) Your boys left with the chippies. They said they'll see you home.

A second waiter watches some distance away.

WILLY: But we were supposed to have dinner together.

Music is heard, WILLY'S *theme.*

STANLEY: Can you make it?

WILLY: I'll—sure, I can make it. (*suddenly concerned about his clothes*) Do I—I look all right?

STANLEY: Sure, you look all right. (*He flicks a speck off* WILLY'S *lapel.*)

WILLY: Here—here's a dollar.

STANLEY: Oh, your son paid me. It's all right.

WILLY (*putting it in* STANLEY'S *hand*): No, take it. You're a good boy.

STANLEY: Oh, no, you don't have to . . .

WILLY: Here—here's some more, I don't need it any more. (*after a slight pause*) Tell me—is there a seed store in the neighborhood?

STANLEY: Seeds? You mean like to plant?

As WILLY *turns,* STANLEY *slips the money back into his jacket pocket.*

WILLY: Yes. Carrots, peas . . .

STANLEY: Well, there's hardware stores on Sixth Avenue, but it may be too late now.

WILLY (*anxiously*): Oh, I'd better hurry. I've got to get some seeds. (*He starts off to the right.*) I've got to get some seeds, right away. Nothing's planted. I don't have a thing in the ground.

WILLY hurries out as the light goes down. STANLEY *moves over to the right after him, watches him off. The other waiter has been staring at* WILLY.

STANLEY (*to the waiter*): Well, whatta you looking at?

The waiter picks up the chairs and moves off right. STANLEY *takes the table and follows him. The light fades on this area. There is a long pause, the sound of the flute coming over. The light gradually rises on the kitchen, which is empty.* HAPPY *appears at the door of the house, followed by* BIFF. HAPPY *is carrying a large bunch of long-stemmed roses. He enters the kitchen, looks around for* LINDA. *Not seeing her, he turns to* BIFF, *who is just outside the house door, and makes a gesture with his hands, indicating "Not here, I guess." He looks into the living room and freezes. Inside,* LINDA, *unseen, is seated,* WILLY'S *coat on her lap. She rises ominously and quietly and moves toward* HAPPY, *who backs up into the kitchen, afraid.*

HAPPY: Hey, what're you doing up? (LINDA *says nothing but moves toward him implacably.*) Where's Pop? (*He keeps backing to the right, and now* LINDA *is in full view in the doorway to the living room.*) Is he sleeping?

LINDA: Where were you?

HAPPY (*trying to laugh it off*): We met two girls, Mom, very fine types. Here, we brought you some flowers. (*offering them to her*) Put them in your room, Ma.

She knocks them to the floor at BIFF'S *feet. He has now come inside and closed the door behind him. She stares at* BIFF, *silent.*

HAPPY: Now what'd you do that for? Mom, I want you to have some flowers—

LINDA (*cutting* HAPPY *off, violently to* BIFF): Don't you care whether he lives or dies?

HAPPY (*going to the stairs*): Come upstairs, Biff.

BIFF (*with a flare of disgust, to* HAPPY): Go away from me! (*to* LINDA) What do you mean, lives or dies? Nobody's dying around here, pal.

LINDA: Get out of my sight! Get out of here!

BIFF: I wanna see the boss.

LINDA: You're not going near him!

BIFF: Where is he? (*He moves into the living room and* LINDA *follows.*)

LINDA (*shouting after* BIFF): You invite him for dinner. He looks forward to it all day— (BIFF *appears in his parents' bedroom, looks around, and exits.*)—and then you desert him there. There's no stranger you'd do that to!

HAPPY: Why? He had a swell time with us. Listen, when I—(LINDA *comes back into the kitchen.*)—desert him I hope I don't outlive the day!

LINDA: Get out of here!

HAPPY: Now look, Mom . . .

LINDA: Did you have to go to women tonight? You and your lousy rotten whores!

BIFF *reenters the kitchen.*

HAPPY: Mom, all we did was follow Biff around trying to cheer him up! (*to* BIFF) Boy, what a night you gave me!

LINDA: Get out of here, both of you, and don't come back! I don't want you tormenting him any more. Go on now, get your things together! (*to* BIFF) You can sleep in his apartment. (*She starts to pick up the flowers and stops herself.*) Pick up this stuff, I'm not your maid any more. Pick it up, you bum, you!

HAPPY *turns his back to her in refusal.* BIFF *slowly moves over and gets down on his knees, picking up the flowers.*

LINDA: You're a pair of animals! Not one, not another living soul would have had the cruelty to walk out on that man in a restaurant!

BIFF (*not looking at her*): Is that what he said?

LINDA: He didn't have to say anything. He was so humiliated he nearly limped when he came in.

HAPPY: But, Mom, he had a great time with us—

BIFF (*cutting him off violently*): Shut up!

Without another word, HAPPY *goes upstairs.*

LINDA: You! You didn't even go in to see if he was all right!

BIFF (*still on the floor in front of* LINDA, *the flowers in his hand; with self-loathing*): No. Didn't. Didn't do a damned thing. How do you like that, heh? Left him babbling in a toilet.

LINDA: You louse. You . . .

BIFF: Now you hit it on the nose! (*He gets up, throws the flowers in the wastebasket.*) The scum of the earth, and you're looking at him!

LINDA: Get out of here!

BIFF: I gotta talk to the boss, Mom. Where is he?

LINDA: You're not going near him. Get out of this house!

BIFF (*with absolute assurance, determination*): No. We're gonna have an abrupt conversation, him and me.

LINDA: You're not talking to him!

Hammering is heard from outside the house, off right. BIFF *turns toward the noise.*

LINDA (*suddenly pleading*): Will you please leave him alone?

BIFF: What's he doing out there?

LINDA: He's planting the garden!

BIFF (*quietly*): Now? Oh, my God!

> BIFF *moves outside,* LINDA *following. The light dies down on them and comes up on the center of the apron as* WILLY *walks into it. He is carrying a flashlight, a hoe, and a handful of seed packets. He raps the top of the hoe sharply to fix it firmly, and then moves to the left, measuring off the distance with his foot. He holds the flashlight to look at the seed packets, reading off the instructions. He is in the blue of night.*

WILLY: Carrots . . . quarter-inch apart. Rows . . . one-foot rows. (*He measures it off.*) One foot. (*He puts down a package and measures off.*) Beets. (*He puts down another package and measures again.*) Lettuce. (*He reads the package, puts it down.*) One foot—(*He breaks off as* BEN *appears at the right and moves slowly down to him.*) What a proposition, ts, ts. Terrific, terrific. 'Cause she's suffered, Ben, the woman has suffered. You understand me? A man can't go out the way he came in, Ben, a man has got to add up to something. You can't, you can't—(BEN *moves toward him as though to interrupt.*) You gotta consider, now. Don't answer so quick. Remember, it's a guaranteed twenty-thousand-dollar proposition. Now look, Ben, I want you to go through the ins and outs of this thing with me. I've got nobody to talk to, Ben, and the woman has suffered, you hear me?

BEN (*standing still, considering*): What's the proposition?

WILLY: It's twenty thousand dollars on the barrelhead. Guaranteed, gilt-edged, you understand?

BEN: You don't want to make a fool of yourself. They might not honor the policy.

WILLY: How can they dare refuse? Didn't I work like a coolie to meet every premium on the nose? And now they don't pay off? Impossible!

BEN: It's called a cowardly thing, William.

WILLY: Why? Does it take more guts to stand here the rest of my life ringing up a zero?

BEN (*yielding*): That's a point, William. (*He moves, thinking, turns.*) And twenty thousand—that *is* something one can feel with the hand, it is there.

WILLY (*now assured, with rising power*): Oh, Ben, that's the whole beauty of it! I see it like a diamond, shining in the dark, hard and rough, that I can pick up and touch in my hand. Not like—like an appointment! This would not be another damned-fool appointment, Ben, and it changes all the aspects. Because he thinks I'm nothing, see, and so he spites me. But the funeral—(*straightening up*) Ben, that funeral will be massive! They'll come from Maine, Massachusetts, Vermont, New Hampshire! All the old-timers with the strange license plates—that boy will be thunderstruck, Ben, because he never realized—I am known! Rhode Island, New York, New Jersey—I am known, Ben, and he'll see it with his eyes once and for all. He'll see what I am, Ben! He's in for a shock, that boy!

BEN (*coming down to the edge of the garden*): He'll call you a coward.

WILLY (*suddenly fearful*): No, that would be terrible.

BEN: Yes. And a damned fool.

WILLY: No, no, he mustn't, I won't have that! (*He is broken and desperate.*)

BEN: He'll hate you, William.

The gay music of the Boys is heard.

WILLY: Oh, Ben, how do we get back to all the great times? Used to be so full of light, and comradeship, the sleigh-riding in winter, and the ruddiness on his cheeks. And always some kind of good news coming up, always something nice coming up ahead. And never even let me carry the valises in the house, and simonizing, simonizing that little red car! Why, why can't I give him something and not have him hate me?

BEN: Let me think about it. (*He glances at his watch.*) I still have a little time. Remarkable proposition, but you've got to be sure you're not making a fool of yourself.

BEN *drifts off upstage and goes out of sight.* BIFF *comes down from the left.*

WILLY (*suddenly conscious of* BIFF, *turns and looks up at him, then begins picking up the packages of seeds in confusion*): Where the hell is that seed? (*indignantly*) You can't see nothing out here! They boxed in the whole goddam neighborhood!

BIFF: There are people all around here. Don't you realize that?

WILLY: I'm busy. Don't bother me.

BIFF (*taking the hoe from* WILLY): I'm saying good-by to you, Pop. (WILLY *looks at him, silent, unable to move.*) I'm not coming back any more.

WILLY: You're not going to see Oliver tomorrow?

BIFF: I've got no appointment, Dad.

WILLY: He put his arm around you, and you've got no appointment?

BIFF: Pop, get this now, will you? Every time I've left it's been a fight that sent me out of here. Today I realized something about myself and I tried to explain it to you and I—I think I'm just not smart enough to make any sense out of it for you. To hell with whose fault it is or anything like that. (*He takes* WILLY'S *arm.*) Let's just wrap it up, heh? Come on in, we'll tell Mom. (*He gently tries to pull* WILLY *to left.*)

WILLY (*frozen, immobile, with guilt in his voice*): No, I don't want to see her.

BIFF: Come on! (*He pulls again, and* WILLY *tries to pull away.*)

WILLY (*highly nervous*): No, no, I don't want to see her.

BIFF (*trying to look into* WILLY'S *face, as if to find the answer there*): Why don't you want to see her?

WILLY (*more harshly now*): Don't bother me, will you?

BIFF: What do you mean, you don't want to see her? You don't want them calling you yellow, do you? This isn't your fault; it's me, I'm a bum. Now come inside! (WILLY *strains to get away.*) Did you hear what I said to you?

WILLY *pulls away and quickly goes by himself into the house.* BIFF *follows.*

LINDA (*to Willy*): Did you plant, dear?

BIFF (*at the door, to* LINDA): All right, we had it out. I'm going and I'm not writing any more.

LINDA (*going to* WILLY *in the kitchen*): I think that's the best way, dear. 'Cause there's no use drawing it out, you'll just never get along.

WILLY *doesn't respond.*

BIFF: People ask where I am and what I'm doing, you don't know, and you don't care.

That way it'll be off your mind and you can start brightening up again. All right? That clears it, doesn't it? (WILLY *is silent, and* BIFF *goes to him.*) You gonna wish me luck, scout? (*He extends his hand.*) What do you say?

LINDA: Shake his hand, Willy.

WILLY (*turning to her, seething with hurt*): There's no necessity to mention the pen at all, y'know.

BIFF (*gently*): I've got no appointment, Dad.

WILLY (*erupting fiercely*): He put his arm around . . . ?

BIFF: Dad, you're never going to see what I am, so what's the use of arguing? If I strike oil I'll send you a check. Meantime forget I'm alive.

WILLY (*to* LINDA): Spite, see?

BIFF: Shake hands, Dad.

WILLY: Not my hand.

BIFF: I was hoping not to go this way.

WILLY: Well, this is the way you're going. Good-by.

BIFF *looks at him a moment, then turns sharply and goes to the stairs.*

WILLY (*stops him with*): May you rot in hell if you leave this house!

BIFF (*turning*): Exactly what is it that you want from me?

WILLY: I want you to know, on the train, in the mountains, in the valleys, wherever you go, that you cut down your life for spite!

BIFF: No, no.

WILLY: Spite, spite, is the word of your undoing! And when you're down and out, remember what did it. When you're rotting somewhere beside the railroad tracks, remember, and don't you dare blame it on me!

BIFF: I'm not blaming it on you!

WILLY: I won't take the rap for this, you hear?

HAPPY *comes down the stairs and stands on the bottom step, watching.*

BIFF: That's just what I'm telling you!

WILLY (*sinking into a chair at the table, with full accusation*): You're trying to put a knife in me—don't think I don't know what you're doing!

BIFF: All right, phony! Then let's lay it on the line. (*He whips the rubber tube out of his pocket and puts it on the table.*)

HAPPY: You crazy—

LINDA: Biff! (*She moves to grab the hose, but* BIFF *holds it down with his hand.*)

BIFF: Leave it there! Don't move it!

WILLY (*not looking at it*): What is that?

BIFF: You know goddam well what that is.

WILLY (*caged, wanting to escape*): I never saw that.

BIFF: You saw it. The mice didn't bring it into the cellar! What is this supposed to do, make a hero out of you? This supposed to make me sorry for you?

WILLY: Never heard of it.

BIFF: There'll be no pity for you, you hear it? No pity!

WILLY (*to* LINDA): You hear the spite!

BIFF: No, you're going to hear the truth—what you are and what I am!

LINDA: Stop it!

WILLY: Spite!

HAPPY (*coming down toward* BIFF): You cut it now!

BIFF (*to* HAPPY): The man don't know who we are! The man is gonna know! (*to* WILLY)

We never told the truth for ten minutes in this house!

HAPPY: We always told the truth!

BIFF (*turning on him*): You big blow, are you the assistant buyer? You're one of the two assistants to the assistant, aren't you?

HAPPY: Well, I'm practically—

BIFF: You're practically full of it! We all are! And I'm through with it. (*to* WILLY) Now hear this, Willy, this is me.

WILLY: I know you!

BIFF: You know why I had no address for three months? I stole a suit in Kansas City and I was in jail. (*to* LINDA, *who is sobbing*) Stop crying. I'm through with it.

LINDA *turns away from them, her hands covering her face.*

WILLY: I suppose that's my fault!

BIFF: I stole myself out of every good job since high school!

WILLY: And whose fault is that?

BIFF: And I never got anywhere because you blew me so full of hot air I could never stand taking orders from anybody! That's whose fault it is!

WILLY: I hear that!

LINDA: Don't, Biff!

BIFF: It's goddam time you heard that! I had to be boss big shot in two weeks, and I'm through with it!

WILLY: Then hang yourself! For spite, hang yourself!

BIFF: No! Nobody's hanging himself, Willy! I ran down eleven flights with a pen in my hand today. And suddenly I stopped, you hear me? And in the middle of that office building, do you hear this? I stopped in the middle of that building and I saw—the sky. I saw the things that I love in this world. The work and the food and time to sit and smoke. And I looked at the pen and said to myself, what the hell am I grabbing this for? Why am I trying to become what I don't want to be? What am I doing in an office, making a contemptuous, begging fool of myself, when all I want is out there, waiting for me the minute I say I know who I am! Why can't I say that, Willy? (*He tries to make* WILLY *face him, but* WILLY *pulls away and moves to the left.*)

WILLY (*with hatred, threateningly*): The door of your life is wide open!

BIFF: Pop! I'm a dime a dozen, and so are you!

WILLY (*turning on him now in an uncontrolled outburst*): I am not a dime a dozen! I am Willy Loman, and you are Biff Loman!

BIFF *starts for* WILLY, *but is blocked by* HAPPY. *In his fury,* BIFF *seems on the verge of attacking his father.*

BIFF: I am not a leader of men, Willy, and neither are you. You were never anything but a hard-working drummer who landed in the ash can like all the rest of them! I'm one dollar an hour, Willy! I tried seven states and couldn't raise it. A buck an hour! Do you gather my meaning? I'm not bringing home any prizes any more, and you're going to stop waiting for me to bring them home!

WILLY (*directly to* BIFF): You vengeful, spiteful mut!

BIFF *breaks from* HAPPY. WILLY, *in fright, starts up the stairs.* BIFF *grabs him.*

BIFF (*at the peak of his fury*): Pop, I'm nothing! I'm nothing, Pop. Can't you understand that? There's no spite in it any more. I'm just what I am, that's all.

BIFF'S fury *has spent itself, and he breaks down, sobbing, holding on to* WILLY, *who dumbly fumbles for* BIFF'S *face.*

WILLY (*astonished*): What're you doing? What're you doing? (*to* LINDA) Why is he crying?

BIFF (*crying, broken*): Will you let me go, for Christ's sake? Will you take that phony dream and burn it before something happens? (*Struggling to contain himself, he pulls away and moves to the stairs.*) I'll go in the morning. Put him—put him to bed. (*Exhausted,* BIFF *moves up the stairs to his room.*)

WILLY (*after a long pause, astonished, elevated*): Isn't that—isn't that remarkable? Biff—he likes me!

LINDA: He loves you, Willy!

HAPPY (*deeply moved*): Always did, Pop.

WILLY: Oh, Biff! (*staring wildly*) He cried! Cried to me. (*He is choking with his love, and now cries out his promise.*) That boy—that boy is going to be magnificent!

BEN *appears in the light just outside the kitchen.*

BEN: Yes, outstanding, with twenty thousand behind him.

LINDA (*sensing the racing of his mind, fearfully, carefully*): Now come to bed, Willy. It's all settled now.

WILLY (*finding it difficult not to rush out of the house*): Yes, we'll sleep. Come on. Go to sleep, Hap.

BEN: And it does take a great kind of a man to crack the jungle.

In accents of dread, BEN'S *idyllic music starts up.*

HAPPY (*his arm around* LINDA): I'm getting married, Pop, don't forget it. I'm changing everything. I'm gonna run that department before the year is up. You'll see, Mom. (*He kisses her.*)

BEN: The jungle is dark but full of diamonds, Willy.

WILLY *turns, moves, listening to* BEN.

LINDA: Be good. You're both good boys, just act that way, that's all.

HAPPY: 'Night, Pop. (*He goes upstairs.*)

LINDA (*to* WILLY): Come, dear.

BEN (*with greater force*): One must go in to fetch a diamond out.

WILLY (*to* LINDA, *as he moves slowly along the edge of the kitchen, toward the door*): I just want to get settled down, Linda. Let me sit alone for a little.

LINDA (*almost uttering her fear*): I want you upstairs.

WILLY (*taking her in his arms*): In a few minutes, Linda. I couldn't sleep right now. Go on, you look awful tired. (*He kisses her.*)

BEN: Not like an appointment at all. A diamond is rough and hard to the touch.

WILLY: Go on now. I'll be right up.

LINDA: I think this is the only way, Willy.

WILLY: Sure, it's the best thing.

BEN: Best thing!

WILLY: The only way. Everything is gonna be—go on, kid, get to bed. You look so tired.

LINDA: Come right up.

WILLY: Two minutes.

LINDA *goes into the living room, then reappears in her bedroom.* WILLY *moves just outside the kitchen door.*

WILLY: Loves me. (*wonderingly*) Always loved me. Isn't that a remarkable thing? Ben, he'll worship me for it!

BEN (*with promise*): It's dark there, but full of diamonds.

WILLY: Can you imagine that magnificence with twenty thousand dollars in his pocket?

LINDA (*calling from her room*): Willy! Come up!

WILLY (*calling into the kitchen*): Yes! Yes. Coming! It's very smart, you realize that, don't you, sweetheart? Even Ben sees it. I gotta go, baby. 'By! 'By! (*going over to* BEN, *almost dancing*) Imagine? When the mail comes he'll be ahead of Bernard again!

BEN: A perfect proposition all around.

WILLY: Did you see how he cried to me? Oh, if I could kiss him, Ben!

BEN: Time, William, time!

WILLY: Oh, Ben, I always knew one way or another we were gonna make it, Biff and I!

BEN (*looking at his watch*): The boat. We'll be late. (*He moves slowly off into the darkness.*)

WILLY (*elegiacally, turning to the house*): Now when you kick off, boy, I want a seventy-yard boot, and get right down the field under the ball, and when you hit, hit low and hit hard, because it's important, boy. (*He swings around and faces the audience.*) There's all kinds of important people in the stands, and the first thing you know . . . (*suddenly realizing he is alone*) Ben! Ben, where do I . . . ? (*He makes a sudden movement of search.*) Ben, how do I . . . ?

LINDA (*calling*): Willy, you coming up?

WILLY (*uttering a gasp of fear, whirling about as if to quiet her*): Sh! (*He turns around as if to find his way; sounds, faces, voices, seem to be swarming in upon him and he flicks at them, crying.*) Sh! Sh! (*Suddenly music, faint and high, stops him. It rises in intensity, almost to an unbearable scream. He goes up and down on his toes, and rushes off around the house.*) Shhh!

LINDA: Willy?

There is no answer. LINDA *waits.* BIFF *gets up off his bed. He is still in his clothes.* HAPPY *sits up.* BIFF *stands listening.*

LINDA (*with real fear*): Willy, answer me! Willy!

There is the sound of a car starting and moving away at full speed.

LINDA: No!

BIFF (*rushing down the stairs*): Pop!

As the car speeds off, the music crashes down in a frenzy of sound, which becomes the soft pulsation of a single cello string. BIFF *slowly returns to his bedroom. He and* HAPPY *gravely don their jackets.* LINDA *slowly walks out of her room. The music has developed into a dead march. The leaves of day are appearing over everything.* CHARLEY *and* BERNARD, *somberly dressed, appear and knock on the kitchen door.* BIFF *and* HAPPY *slowly descend the stairs to the kitchen as* CHARLEY *and* BERNARD *enter. All stop a moment when* LINDA, *in clothes of mourning, bearing a little bunch of roses, comes through the draped doorway into the kitchen. She goes to* CHARLEY *and takes his arm. Now all move toward the audience, through the wall-line of the kitchen. At the limit of the apron,* LINDA *lays down the flowers, kneels, and sits back on her heels. All stare down at the grave.*

REQUIEM

CHARLEY: It's getting dark, Linda.

LINDA *doesn't react. She stares at the grave.*

BIFF: How about it, Mom? Better get some rest, heh? They'll be closing the gate soon.

LINDA *makes no move. Pause.*

HAPPY *(deeply angered)*: He had no right to do that. There was no necessity for it. We would've helped him.

CHARLEY *(grunting)*: Hmmm.

BIFF: Come along, Mom.

LINDA: Why didn't anybody come?

CHARLEY: It was a very nice funeral.

LINDA: But where are all the people he knew? Maybe they blame him.

CHARLEY: Naa. It's a rough world, Linda. They wouldn't blame him.

LINDA: I can't understand it. At this time especially. First time in thirty-five years we were just about free and clear. He only needed a little salary. He was even finished with the dentist.

CHARLEY: No man only needs a little salary.

LINDA: I can't understand it.

BIFF: There were a lot of nice days. When he'd come home from a trip; or on Sundays, making the stoop; finishing the cellar; putting on the new porch; when he built the extra bathroom; and put up the garage. You know something, Charley, there's more of him in that front stoop than in all the sales he ever made.

CHARLEY: Yeah. He was a happy man with a batch of cement.

LINDA: He was so wonderful with his hands.

BIFF: He had the wrong dreams. All, all, wrong.

HAPPY *(almost ready to fight BIFF)*: Don't say that!

BIFF: He never knew who he was.

CHARLEY (*Stopping* HAPPY'S *movement and reply. To* BIFF.): Nobody dast blame this man. You don't understand: Willy was a salesman. And for a salesman, there is no rock bottom to the life. He don't put a bolt to a nut, he don't tell you the law or give you medicine. He's a man way out there in the blue, riding on a smile and a shoeshine. And when they start not smiling back—that's an earthquake. And then you get yourself a couple of spots on your hat, and you're finished. Nobody dast blame this man. A salesman is got to dream, boy. It comes with the territory.

BIFF: Charley, the man didn't know who he was.

HAPPY *(infuriated)*: Don't say that!

BIFF: Why don't you come with me, Happy?

HAPPY: I'm not licked that easily. I'm staying right in this city, and I'm gonna beat this racket! (*He looks at* BIFF, *his chin set.*) The Loman Brothers!

BIFF: I know who I am, kid.

HAPPY: All right, boy. I'm gonna show you and everybody else that Willy Loman did not die in vain. He had a good dream. It's the only dream you can have—to come out number-one man. He fought it out here, and this is where I'm gonna win it for him.

BIFF (*With a hopeless glance at* HAPPY, *he bends toward his mother.*): Let's go, Mom.

LINDA: I'll be with you in a minute. Go on, Charley. (*He hesitates.*) I want to, just for a minute. I never had a chance to say good-by.

CHARLEY *moves away, followed by* HAPPY. BIFF *remains a slight distance up and left of* LINDA. *She sits there, summoning herself. The flute begins, not far away, playing behind her speech.*

LINDA: Forgive me, dear. I can't cry. I don't know what it is, but I can't cry. I don't understand it. Why did you ever do that? Help me, Willy, I can't cry. It seems to me that you're just on another trip. I keep expecting you. Willy, dear, I can't cry. Why did you do it? I search and search and I search, and I can't understand it, Willy. I made the last payment on the house today. Today, dear. And there'll be nobody home. (*A sob rises in her throat.*) We're free and clear. (*sobbing more fully, released*) We're free. (BIFF *comes slowly toward her.*) We're free . . . We're free . . .

BIFF *lifts her to her feet and moves out up right with her in his arms.* LINDA *sobs quietly.* BERNARD *and* CHARLEY *come together and follow them, followed by* HAPPY. *Only the music of the flute is left on the darkening stage as over the house the hard towers of the apartment buildings rise into sharp focus, and*
The curtain falls.

THE RECEPTIVE READER

Like other classics, *Death of a Salesman* is a play that different spectators see in their own personal light. Much of your own reaction is likely to be determined by how you react to the different *characters* and their interplay in Miller's drama. How would you answer questions like the following?

1. In Willy Loman, Arthur Miller created an unforgettable character whom many readers and theatergoers know better than a close friend. How and where in the play do you come to know and understand Willy Loman? What are revealing things he says and does? ✧ There are different sides to Willy Loman. (At times, he will say in the same breath the opposite of what he just said.) What are striking contradictions in the way he talks about himself, others, business, life? Is there an explanation for some of these contradictions?

2. Who or what is to blame for Willy's disastrous relationship with Biff, his older son? How central is Biff's traumatic discovery of the father's infidelity? ✧ How are we supposed to feel about Happy, the younger brother? (How do you react to the names of the two sons?)

3. Is Uncle Ben, who went to Alaska and came back rich, just another vehicle for one of Willy's pipe dreams? (Or is he meant to be a symbol of predatory business practices destroying the environment?)

4. How does Uncle Charley serve as a *foil* for Willy? How do you think you are meant to react to him? How do you react to his sayings? (How do you react to Bernard, who serves as a foil to Biff?)

5. Linda, Willy's downtrodden wife, is loyal to Willy to the end and is one of the last people to speak up in his defense. What does she say? Why do you think some critics have taken the comments she makes on Willy Loman toward the end as the *theme* of the play? ✧ At the same time, however, Linda has been blamed for encouraging or at least tolerating Willy's "self-deceit and lies" or, alternately, for prodding and nagging him to his destruction. What is her role in Willy's life and in the play as a whole?

6. As feminist critics point out, in this play from the fifties women serve in stereotypically subordinate roles. They are housekeepers, dates, receptionists. What are striking examples? ✧ How much do the men in the play conform to familiar patterns: idolizing the mother but bragging about their conquests of the other sex, using sports

for male bonding, thinking of business as an arena in which males compete? (How much has the business environment changed—or failed to change?)

7. Freud and his disciples popularized the Oedipus situation, in which the son competes with the father for the love of the mother and—actually or symbolically—destroys his rival. Many critics have seen the relationship between Biff and his father as the core of the play. For Biff, the father who was to serve him as role model has failed him. What were Willy's dreams and hopes for his son? What defeated them? What do we learn from the flashbacks, from the mutual accusations and recriminations?

THE PERSONAL RESPONSE

✧ What to you is the verdict of the play as a whole on Willy Loman? Is Willy simply a creature of his time and of his circumstances? Was he the wrong man for his job? Was he a product and a victim of the "system"? Did he ever have a real chance to make his life take a different turn? How?

✧ In this play, do you sympathize with the younger or with the older generation?

CROSS-REFERENCES—For Discussion or Writing

Both Ibsen and Miller shone a searching light on the ethics and self-image of a middle-class business society. Are there points where their analyses converge? Does their criticism of middle-class society have a common base? On the other hand, are there important differences between Nora Helmer's nineteenth-century Europe and Willy Loman's twentieth-century America?

JUXTAPOSITIONS

Unheard Voices—Linda Loman

You're my foundation and my support, Linda.
WILLY LOMAN IN *DEATH OF A SALESMAN*

In current reexaminations of Miller's play, readers have paid special attention to the role of Linda Loman, Willy's wife. In the first of the following excerpts, a feminist critic examines gender roles in the play, looking closely at Linda Loman's second-class status yet essential role in the Loman household. Second, a critic indebted to the Marxist emphasis on economic relations and realities looks at Linda's role in the economics of Willy Loman's world. What do these critics alert you to that you might have missed in your own reading? Where do you tend to agree or disagree with them?

KAY STANTON

Women and the American Dream   1989

The Loman men are all less than they hold themselves to be, but Linda is more than she is credited to be. She is indeed the foundation that has allowed the Loman men to build themselves up, if only in dreams, and she is the support that enables them to continue despite their failures. Linda is the one element holding the façade of the family together. Yet even Miller, her creator, seems not to have fully understood her character. Linda is described in the opening stage directions as follows: "Most often jovial, she has developed an iron repression of her exceptions to Willy's behavior—she more than loves him, she admires him, as though his mercurial nature, his temper, his massive dreams and little cruelties, served her only as sharp reminders of the turbulent longings . . . which she shares but lacks the temperament to utter and follow to their end." She thus seems inferior to Willy; yet she demonstrates a level of education superior to his in terms of grammatical and mathematical ability, and she is definitely more gifted in diplomatic and psychological acumen. In her management of Willy, she embodies the American Dream ideal of the model post–World War II wife, infinitely supportive of her man. She makes no mistakes, has no flaws in wifely perfection. But the perfect American wife is not enough for American Dreamers like Willy. He has been unfaithful to her, and he rudely interrupts and silences her, even when she is merely expressing support for him. She can be the foundation of the house; he must rebuild the façade.

If the Loman house represents the Loman family, with Linda as the steady foundation and support, the façade is constructed with stolen goods. The enemy apartment buildings that so anger Willy have provided the materials that he and his sons used in such projects as rebuilding the front stoop. Linda knows that they need not have been "boxed in" by the apartment buildings; she says, "We should've bought the land next door." Possibly she had suggested the idea at the appropriate time but was ignored. But Willy prefers to transfer the blame for the diminishment of his Green World: "They should've had a law against apartment houses. Remember those two beautiful elm trees out there? . . . They should've arrested the builder for cutting those down." Of course, there is a law against stealing property, which Willy thought nothing of disobeying when he encouraged the boys to steal from the construction site, calling them "fearless characters." Laws are for lesser men to follow, not the Loman men. In the realm of the Home, Willy and his sons are associated with rebuilding through theft, and Linda is associated with cleaning, mending, and repair.

In Willy's flashback sequences, Linda habitually appears with the laundry, suggesting that it is her responsibiity to clean up the males' dirtiness, on all levels. In both past and present, she is shown mending, not only her own stockings but also Willy's jacket. Often when Linda speaks, she discusses repairs, which she oversees; she must mend the male machinery. Willy is "sold" by other salesmen or advertisements on the quality of products and fails to recognize that even the "best" breaks down from daily wear and tear—including Willy himself. Although Linda's functions of cleaning, mending, and overseeing repairs are traditionally "feminine," they are significant because they are the ones maintained when other traditionally "feminine" elements are appropriated by Willy. It is not Linda but Willy who asserts the importance of physical attractiveness, who prefers a fantasy life of glamor to the reality of daily toil, who suffers from the "empty nest syndrome," and who insists on having the most significant role in child-rearing.

Willy works hard at preventing Linda from having any substantive impact on shaping the boys' characters; he tries continually to make them his alone, just as he had implied that they had sprung from his "stock" alone. After thanking God for Adonis-like looks in his sons, Willy confesses to Linda that he himself is "not noticed," "fat," "foolish to look at," and had been called a "walrus." Evidently, the physical attractiveness, strength, and resilience of the boys derive from Linda rather than Willy, but "God," not she, is given credit. Although Linda is the continual presence in the boys' lives at home, as Mother Loman had been for Willy, Willy undermines Linda's authority when he returns from the road. In a flashback sequence, Linda disapproves of various manifestations of Biff's bad behavior and runs from the scene almost in tears after Willy refuses to support her. She represents human dignity and values: cooperative, moral, humane behavior as opposed to lawless assertion of self over all others through assumed superiority. . . . in the home, Woman through Linda as submerged element is the measure of human dignity and the accountant of worth.

From "Women and the American Dream," *Feminist Readings of Modern American Drama*, ed. June Schlueter

QUESTIONS

Where does this critic most effectively anchor her interpretation to the text of the play? In her discussion, what elements of the play assume unexpected symbolic value or significance? What are the key elements in her reevaluation of Linda's role in the play?

BEVERLY HUME
Linda Loman as "The Woman" 1985

It has never been acknowledged by critics of Miller's *Death of a Salesman* that in Linda Loman one finds traces of an intense materialism which not only estranges her from her husband, Willy, but places her in league with "the Woman" who haunts Willy's memory and, along with the ghostly Ben, helps drive him toward suicide. Linda's materialistic attitude partially exists because, as family bookkeeper, she is aware of their financial problems; but it primarily exists because of her absorption in Willy's success dream, an absorption which proves malignant, fatal.

In his stage directions, Miller characterizes Linda Loman as a woman with an "iron repression of her exceptions to Willy's behavior," as a woman who not only loves Willy, but "admires him, as though his mercurial nature, his temper, his massive dreams and little cruelties, served her only as sharp reminders of the turbulent longings within him, longings which she shares but lacks the temperament to utter and follow to their end." Linda, then, is a woman who is at once passive and possessed by intense (perhaps unconscious) longings; and in *Salesman*, her "iron repression" often combines with these longings to make her presence painful to Willy.

In the memory sequences of the play, for example, Willy frequently recalls how Linda's materialism increases his sense of failure. Just before "the Woman" first enters, Willy and Linda engage in this economic exchange:

LINDA: . . . Did you sell anything?

WILLY: I did five hundred gross in Providence and seven hundred gross in Boston.

LINDA: No! Wait a minute, I've got a pencil. (*She pulls pencil and paper out of her apron pocket.*) That makes your commission . . . Two hundred—my God! Two hundred and twelve dollars!

WILLY: Well, I didn't figure it yet, but . . .

LINDA: How much did you do?

WILLY: Well, I—I did—about a hundred and eighty gross in Providence. Well, no—it came to—roughly two hundred gross on the whole trip.

LINDA (*without hesitation*): Two hundred gross. That's . . . (*She figures.*)

WILLY: The trouble was that three of the stores were half closed for inventory in Boston. Otherwise I woulda broke records.
LINDA: Well, it makes seventy dollars and some pennies. That's very good.

First, Linda asks the tentative (and, for her, typical) question. Then, encouraged by Willy's response, she grows excited at the amount of money, but when she sees Willy falter, she retreats back to another tentative question. He fumbles, answers her question, and then, "without hesitating," she calculates (exactly) how well he's done, finally offering the patronizing sentiment, "Well, it makes seventy dollars and some pennies. That's very good." One finds Linda repeating this pattern of meekness, materialistic excitement, more meekness, pragmatic calculation, and, finally, patronizing compassion throughout the play. Indeed, it is not surprising that "the Woman" enters Willy's memory shortly after this particular dialogue—directly, in fact, after his reflection that he fears "that I'll never sell anything again, that I won't make a living for you [Linda], or a business . . . for the boys." With mocking laughter, "the Woman" disrupts Willy's understandable anxiety about failing to meet Linda's contradictory demands; "the Woman" disrupts his statement to flatter him and tell him he need not worry about failing her. And Willy responds quickly to the deception.

"The Woman" and audience know that she is lying, that she is manipulating Willy only for money (or stockings); but her manipulations strangely mirror the deceptions Linda practices on Willy, and it cannot be a coincidence that Miller early has Linda's laughter "blend" with "the woman's." For both women contribute, through their material longings, to Willy's final destruction—"the Woman" mockingly, maliciously by her betrayal of Willy before Biff; Linda unwittingly, in her repressed need to realize Willy's materialistic success dream. Like "the Woman," Linda constantly lies to Willy to build him up, constantly insists that she doesn't want anything from him (even though she does), constantly tells him that she thinks him potent, lively (even when it is clear that he is depressed).

From *Notes on Modern American Literature*

QUESTIONS

What are some of the identical elements in the play that both of these critics examine? How and why do they differ in their interpretations? What details examined by Hume make you rethink your reaction to the play? Overall, which of the two views of Linda is closer to your own? Which of the views seems to carry more weight, is more convincing?

LORRAINE HANSBERRY AND THE DREAM DEFERRED

One cannot live with sighted eyes and a feeling heart and not know and react to the miseries which afflict this world.

LORRAINE HANSBERRY

Like Arthur Miller's *Death of a Salesman*, Lorraine Hansberry's *A Raisin in the Sun* appeals to its audiences' belief in the American dream: the right of people to a decent place to live, to a fair reward for hard work, to a recognition of their worth as human beings. The two plays share other major themes, such as the worry of parents about the confusions of the young—and the rebellion of the young against the nagging of their elders. At the same time, Hansberry's play is about what it means to be black in white America. Whether to hold on to the dream or abandon it in disillusionment becomes a major issue in her play.

Lorraine Hansberry was the first African-American woman to have a play performed on Broadway (after she had raised the money for the out-of-town tryouts herself). Her *Raisin in the Sun*, a "milestone in the American theater" (Leonard Ashley), opened in New York in 1959 and ran for nineteen consecutive months. The original cast included Ruby Dee, Sidney Poitier, Claudia McNeil, and Louis Gossett; the play was later made into a movie with these same actors. The author became the youngest playwright and the first black woman to receive the New York Drama Critics' Circle Award. Her play was made into a musical in 1973 and ran for three years on Broadway; it was revived in 1988 for "American Playhouse" on television.

For a time, when more aggressive plays like Imamu Baraka's (Leroi Jones') *The Dutchman* put raw interracial tensions on the stage, *A Raisin in the Sun* seemed tame and old-fashioned. Today, with the race issue in this country largely unresolved, Hansberry's play remains a powerful study of the invisible walls that keep America's minorities from achieving their place in the sun. After watching the play in 1959, James Baldwin said "it will demand a far less guilty and constricted people than the present-day Americans to be able to assess it . . . I had never in my life seen so many black people in the theater. And the reason was that never before, in the entire history of the American theater, had so much of the truth of black people's lives been seen on the stage."

Hansberry had witnessed the struggle against racial segregation at first hand. She was eight when her family moved into affluent and segregated Hyde Park in Chicago, where she encountered the curses, spitting, and brick throwing of "hellishly hostile" white neighbors. Her family was evicted from the house; her father, a real-estate broker, worked with NAACP lawyers to carry his case all the way to the Supreme Court, which ruled in favor of the Hansberry family. Hansberry attributed her father's early death to this bitter struggle. When the Younger family in *A Raisin in the Sun* battles for the right to buy a decent house of their own choosing, the author wrote from her own bitter experience.

A Raisin in the Sun was part of the search for a new black identity and a new definition of the black role in society. Hansberry's play prophetically raised issues that were to be at the storm center of much discussion and controversy. She looked at the movement back to African roots and the challenge it presented to the traditional ideal of assimilation. She dramatized the role of the strong maternal female, or matriarch, in the black family, with the corresponding marginalization of the young black male. She shone a probing light into the workings of prejudice and tried to help people gain the spiritual strength to deal with it. She once said, "The supreme test of technical skill and creative imagination is the depth of art it requires to render the infinite varieties of the human spirit—which invariably hangs between despair and joy."

LORRAINE HANSBERRY   (1930–1965)

Born in Chicago, Hansberry had been interested in the theater and in painting since her high school years. She studied at the Chicago Art Institute and later at the University of Wisconsin and in Guadalajara, Mexico. She died young of cancer shortly after her second play, *The Sign in Sidney Brustein's Window,* opened on Broadway in 1964. After her death, her husband, Robert Nemiroff, edited and published several of her unpublished plays. In 1969, a dramatic adaptation of a biography drawing on her letters, journals, and plays was produced posthumously under the title *To Be Young, Gifted, and Black.* It became a long-running off-Broadway play and toured hundreds of college campuses.

Working as a journalist for a progressive paper, Hansberry met leading black intellectuals and artists like Paul Robeson, W. E. B. Du Bois, and Langston Hughes, and she was friends with James Baldwin, author of *Notes of a Native Son* and *The Fire Next Time.* She championed the work of the French feminist Simone de Beauvoir, author of *The Second Sex.* She quoted with admiration a speech made in 1879 by Susan B. Anthony, the early American feminist, who challenged the denial of a woman's right to vote as the denial of her "right of consent as one of the governed" and who called on "every man and woman in whose veins coursed a drop of human sympathy" to break the law that forbade offering a cup of water or a night's shelter to a fugitive slave.

A Raisin in the Sun   1959

> What happens to a dream deferred?
> Does it dry up
> Like a raisin in the sun?
> Or fester like a sore—
> And then run?
> Does it stink like rotten meat?
> Or crust and sugar over—
> Like a syrupy sweet?
>
> Maybe it just sags
> Like a heavy load.
>
> Or does it explode?
>   LANGSTON HUGHES

CHARACTERS

RUTH YOUNGER
TRAVIS YOUNGER
WALTER LEE YOUNGER (BROTHER)
BENEATHA YOUNGER
LENA YOUNGER (MAMA)
JOSEPH ASAGAI
GEORGE MURCHISON
KARL LINDNER
BOBO
MOVING MEN

The action of the play is set in Chicago's Southside, sometime between World War II and the present.

ACT ONE
SCENE 1: *Friday morning.*
SCENE 2: *The following morning.*

ACT TWO
SCENE 1: *Later, the same day.*
SCENE 2: *Friday night, a few weeks later.*
SCENE 3: *Moving day, one week later.*

ACT THREE
An hour later.

ACT ONE

SCENE 1

The YOUNGER *living room would be a comfortable and well-ordered room if it were not for a number of indestructible contradictions to this state of being. Its furnishings are typical and undistinguished and their primary feature now is that they have clearly had to accommodate the living of too many people for too many years—and they are tired. Still, we can see that at some time, a time probably no longer remembered by the family (except perhaps for* MAMA*), the furnishings of this room were actually selected with care and love and even hope—and brought to this apartment and arranged with taste and pride.*

That was a long time ago. Now the once loved pattern of the couch upholstery has to fight to show itself from under acres of crocheted doilies and couch covers which have themselves finally come to be more important than the upholstery. And here a table or a chair has been moved to disguise the worn places in the carpet; but the carpet has fought back by showing its weariness, with depressing uniformity, elsewhere on its surface.

Weariness has, in fact, won in this room. Everything has been polished, washed, sat on, used, scrubbed too often. All pretenses but living itself have long since vanished from the very atmosphere of this room.

Moreover, a section of this room, for it is not really a room unto itself, though the landlord's lease would make it seem so, slopes backward to provide a small kitchen area, where the family prepares the meals that are eaten in the living room proper, which must also serve as dining room. The single window that has been provided for these "two" rooms is located in this kitchen area. The sole natural light the family may enjoy in the course of a day is only that which fights its way through this little window.

At left, a door leads to a bedroom which is shared by MAMA *and her daughter,* BE-NEATHA. *At right, opposite, is a second room (which in the beginning of the life of this apartment was probably a breakfast room) which serves as a bedroom for* WALTER *and his wife,* RUTH.

TIME: *Sometime between World War II and the present.*
PLACE: *Chicago's Southside.*
AT RISE: *It is morning dark in the living room.* TRAVIS *is asleep on the make-down bed at center. An alarm clock sounds from within the bedroom at right, and presently* RUTH *enters from that room and closes the door behind her. She crosses sleepily toward the window. As she passes her sleeping son she reaches down and shakes him a little. At the window*

she raises the shade and a dusky Southside morning light comes in feebly. She fills a pot with water and puts it on to boil. She calls to the boy, between yawns, in a slightly muffled voice.

RUTH *is about thirty. We can see that she was a pretty girl, even exceptionally so, but now it is apparent that life has been little that she expected, and disappointment has already begun to hang in her face. In a few years, before thirty-five even, she will be known among her people as a "settled woman."*

She crosses to her son and gives him a good, final, rousing shake.

RUTH: Come on now, boy, it's seven thirty! (*Her son sits up at last, in a stupor of sleepiness.*) I say hurry up, Travis! You ain't the only person in the world got to use a bathroom! (*The child, a sturdy, handsome little boy of ten or eleven, drags himself out of the bed and almost blindly takes his towels and "today's clothes" from drawers and a closet and goes out to the bathroom, which is in an outside hall and which is shared by another family or families on the same floor.* RUTH *crosses to the bedroom door at right and opens it and calls in to her husband.*) Walter Lee! . . . It's after seven thirty! Lemme see you do some waking up in there now! (*She waits.*) You better get up from there, man! It's after seven thirty I tell you. (*She waits again.*) All right, you just go ahead and lay there and next thing you know Travis be finished and Mr. Johnson'll be in there and you'll be fussing and cussing round here like a madman! And be late too! (*She waits, at the end of patience.*) Walter Lee—it's time for you to GET UP!

She waits another second and then starts to go into the bedroom, but is apparently satisfied that her husband has begun to get up. She stops, pulls the door to, and returns to the kitchen area. She wipes her face with a moist cloth and runs her fingers through her sleep-disheveled hair in a vain effort and ties an apron around her housecoat. The bedroom door at right opens and her husband stands in the doorway in his pajamas, which are rumpled and mismated. He is a lean, intense young man in his middle thirties, inclined to quick nervous movements and erratic speech habits—and always in his voice there is a quality of indictment.

WALTER: Is he out yet?

RUTH: What you mean *out*? He ain't hardly got in there good yet.

WALTER (*wandering in, still more oriented to sleep than to a new day*): Well, what was you doing all that yelling for if I can't even get in there yet? (*stopping and thinking*) Check coming today?

RUTH: They *said* Saturday and this is just Friday and I hopes to God you ain't going to get up here first thing this morning and start talking to me 'bout no money—'cause I 'bout don't want to hear it.

WALTER: Something the matter with you this morning?

RUTH: No—I'm just sleepy as the devil. What kind of eggs you want?

WALTER: Not scrambled. (RUTH *starts to scramble eggs.*) Paper come? (RUTH *points impatiently to the rolled up* Tribune *on the table, and he gets it and spreads it out and vaguely reads the front page.*) Set off another bomb yesterday.

RUTH (*maximum indifference*): Did they?

WALTER (*looking up*): What's the matter with you?

RUTH: Ain't nothing the matter with me. And don't keep asking me that this morning.

WALTER: Ain't nobody bothering you. (*reading the news of the day absently again*) Say Colonel McCormick is sick.

RUTH (*affecting tea-party interest*): Is he now? Poor thing.

WALTER (*sighing and looking at his watch*): Oh, me. (*He waits.*) Now what is that boy

doing in that bathroom all this time? He just going to have to start getting up earlier. I can't be being late to work on account of him fooling around in there.

RUTH (*turning on him*): Oh, no he ain't going to be getting up no earlier no such
thing! It ain't his fault that he can't get to bed no earlier nights 'cause he got a
bunch of crazy good-for-nothing clowns sitting up running their mouths in what
is supposed to be his bedroom after ten o'clock at night . . .

WALTER: That's what you mad about, ain't it? The things I want to talk about with my
friends just couldn't be important in your mind, could they?

*He rises and finds a cigarette in her handbag on the table and crosses to the little
window and looks out, smoking and deeply enjoying this first one.*

RUTH (*almost matter of factly, a complaint too automatic to deserve emphasis*): Why you
always got to smoke before you eat in the morning?

WALTER (*at the window*): Just look at 'em down there . . . Running and racing to
work . . . (*he turns and faces his wife and watches her a moment at the stove, and
then, suddenly*) You look young this morning, baby.

RUTH (*indifferently*): Yeah?

WALTER: Just for a second—stirring them eggs. Just for a second it was—you looked
real young again. (*He reaches for her; she crosses away. Then, drily.*) It's gone now—
you look like yourself again!

RUTH: Man, if you don't shut up and leave me alone.

WALTER (*looking out to the street again*): First thing a man ought to learn in life is not
to make love to no colored woman first thing in the morning. You all some eeeevil
people at eight o'clock in the morning.

TRAVIS *appears in the hall doorway, almost fully dressed and quite wide awake now,
his towels and pajamas across his shoulders. He opens the door and signals for his
father to make the bathroom in a hurry.*

TRAVIS (*watching the bathroom*): Daddy, come on!

WALTER *gets his bathroom utensils and flies out to the bathroom.*

RUTH: Sit down and have your breakfast, Travis.

TRAVIS: Mama, this is Friday. (*gleefully*) Check coming tomorrow, huh?

RUTH: You get your mind off money and eat your breakfast.

TRAVIS (*eating*): This is the morning we supposed to bring the fifty cents to school.

RUTH: Well, I ain't got no fifty cents this morning.

TRAVIS: Teacher say we have to.

RUTH: I don't care what teacher say. I ain't got it. Eat your breakfast, Travis.

TRAVIS: I *am* eating.

RUTH: Hush up now and just eat!

*The boy gives her an exasperated look for her lack of understanding, and eats
grudgingly.*

TRAVIS: You think Grandmama would have it?

RUTH: No! And I want you to stop asking your grandmother for money, you hear me?

TRAVIS (*outraged*): Gaaaleee! I don't ask her, she just gimme it sometimes!

RUTH: Travis Willard Younger—I got too much on me this morning to be—

TRAVIS: Maybe Daddy—

RUTH: *Travis!*

The boy hushes abruptly. They are both quiet and tense for several seconds.

TRAVIS (*presently*): Could I maybe go carry some groceries in front of the supermarket for a little while after school then?

RUTH: Just hush, I said. (*Travis jabs his spoon into his cereal bowl viciously, and rests his head in anger upon his fists.*) If you through eating, you can get over there and make up your bed.

The boy obeys stiffly and crosses the room, almost mechanically, to the bed and more or less folds the bedding into a heap, then angrily gets his books and cap.

TRAVIS (*sulking and standing apart from her unnaturally*): I'm gone.

RUTH (*looking up from the stove to inspect him automatically*): Come here. (*He crosses to her and she studies his head.*) If you don't take this comb and fix this here head, you better! (TRAVIS *puts down his books with a great sigh of oppression, and crosses to the mirror. His mother mutters under her breath about his "stubbornness."*) 'Bout to march out of here with that head looking just like chickens slept in it! I just don't know where you get your stubborn ways . . . And get your jacket, too. Looks chilly out this morning.

TRAVIS (*with conspicuously brushed hair and jacket*): I'm gone.

RUTH: Get carfare and milk money—(*waving one finger*)—and not a single penny for no caps, you hear me?

TRAVIS (*with sullen politeness*): Yes'm.

He turns in outrage to leave. His mother watches after him as in his frustration he approaches the door almost comically. When she speaks to him, her voice has become a very gentle tease.

RUTH (*mocking; as she thinks he would say it*): Oh, Mama makes me so mad sometimes, I don't know what to do! (*She waits and continues to his back as he stands stock-still in front of the door.*) I wouldn't kiss that woman good-bye for nothing in this world this morning! (*The boy finally turns around and rolls his eyes at her, knowing the mood has changed and he is vindicated; he does not, however, move toward her yet.*) Not for nothing in this world! (*She finally laughs aloud at him and holds out her arms to him and we see that it is a way between them, very old and practiced. He crosses to her and allows her to embrace him warmly but keeps his face fixed with masculine rigidity. She holds him back from her presently and looks at him and runs her fingers over the features of his face. With utter gentleness.*) Now—whose little old angry man are you?

TRAVIS (*The masculinity and gruffness start to fade at last.*): Aw gaalee—Mama . . .

RUTH (*mimicking*): Aw—gaaaaalleeeee, Mama! (*She pushes him, with rough playfulness and finality, toward the door.*) Get on out of here or you going to be late.

TRAVIS (*in the face of love, new aggressiveness*): Mama, could I *please* go carry groceries?

RUTH: Honey, it's starting to get so cold evenings.

WALTER (*coming in from the bathroom and drawing a make-believe gun from a make-believe holster and shooting at his son*): What is it he wants to do?

RUTH: Go carry groceries after school at the supermarket.

WALTER: Well, let him go . . .

TRAVIS (*quickly, to the ally*): I *have* to—she won't gimme the fifty cents . . .

WALTER (*to his wife only*): Why not?

RUTH (*simply, and with flavor*): 'Cause we don't have it.

WALTER (*to* RUTH *only*): What you tell the boy things like that for? (*reaching down into his pants with a rather important gesture*) Here, son—

He hands the boy the coin, but his eyes are directed to his wife's. TRAVIS *takes the money happily.*

TRAVIS: Thanks, Daddy.

He starts out. RUTH *watches both of them with murder in her eyes.* WALTER *stands and stares back at her with defiance, and suddenly reaches into his pocket again on an afterthought.*

WALTER (*without even looking at his son, still staring hard at his wife*): In fact, here's another fifty cents . . . Buy yourself some fruit today—or take a taxicab to school or something!

TRAVIS: Whoopee—

He leaps up and clasps his father around the middle with his legs, and they face each other in mutual appreciation; slowly WALTER LEE *peeks around the boy to catch the violent rays from his wife's eyes and draws his head back as if shot.*

WALTER: You better get down now—and get to school, man.

TRAVIS (*at the door*): O.K. Good-bye.

He exits.

WALTER (*after him, pointing with pride*): That's *my* boy. (*She looks at him in disgust and turns back to her work.*) You know what I was thinking 'bout in the bathroom this morning?

RUTH: No.

WALTER: How come you always try to be so pleasant!

RUTH: What is there to be pleasant 'bout!

WALTER: You want to know what I was thinking 'bout in the bathroom or not!

RUTH: I know what you thinking 'bout.

WALTER (*ignoring her*): 'Bout what me and Willy Harris was talking about last night.

RUTH (*immediately—a refrain*): Willy Harris is a good-for-nothing loudmouth.

WALTER: Anybody who talks to me has got to be a good-for-nothing loudmouth, ain't he? And what you know about who is just a good-for-nothing loudmouth? Charlie Atkins was just a "good-for-nothing loudmouth" too, wasn't he! When he wanted me to go in the dry-cleaning business with him. And now—he's grossing a hundred thousand a year. A hundred thousand dollars a year! You still call *him* a loudmouth!

RUTH (*bitterly*): Oh, Walter Lee . . .

She folds her head on her arms over the table.

WALTER (*rising and coming to her and standing over her*): You tired, ain't you? Tired of everything. Me, the boy, the way we live—this beat-up hole—everything. Ain't you? (*She doesn't look up, doesn't answer.*) So tired—moaning and groaning all the time, but you wouldn't do nothing to help, would you? You couldn't be on my side that long for nothing, could you?

RUTH: Walter, please leave me alone.

WALTER: A man needs for a woman to back him up . . .

RUTH: Walter—

WALTER: Mama would listen to you. You know she listen to you more than she do me and Bennie. She think more of you. All you have to do is just sit down with her when you drinking your coffee one morning and talking 'bout things like you do and—(*He sits down beside her and demonstrates graphically what he thinks her methods and tone should be.*)—you just sip your coffee, see, and say easy like that you been thinking 'bout that deal Walter Lee is so interested in, 'bout the store and all, and sip some more coffee, like what you saying ain't really that important to you— And the next thing you know, she be listening good and asking you questions and when I come home—I can tell her the details. This ain't no fly-by-night proposition, baby. I mean we figured it out, me and Willy and Bobo.

RUTH (*with a frown*):   Bobo?

WALTER: Yeah. You see, this little liquor store we got in mind cost seventy-five thousand and we figured the initial investment on the place be 'bout thirty thousand, see. That be ten thousand each. Course, there's a couple of hundred you got to pay so's you don't spend your life just waiting for them clowns to let your license get approved—

RUTH: You mean graft?

WALTER (*frowning impatiently*):   Don't call it that. See there, that just goes to show you what women understand about the world. Baby, don't *nothing* happen for you in this world 'less you pay *somebody* off!

RUTH: Walter, leave me alone! (*she raises her head and stares at him vigorously—then says, more quietly*) Eat your eggs, they gonna be cold.

WALTER (*straightening up from her and looking off*):   That's it. There you are. Man say to his woman: I got me a dream. His woman say: Eat your eggs. (*sadly, but gaining in power*) Man say: I got to take hold of this here world, baby! And a woman will say: Eat your eggs and go to work. (*passionately now*) Man say: I got to change my life, I'm choking to death, baby! And his woman say—(*in utter anguish as he brings his fists down on his thighs*)—Your eggs is getting cold!

RUTH (*softly*):   Walter, that ain't none of our money.

WALTER (*not listening at all or even looking at her*):   This morning, I was lookin' in the mirror and thinking about it . . . I'm thirty-five years old; I been married eleven years and I got a boy who sleeps in the living room—(*very, very quietly*)—and all I got to give him is stories about how rich white people live . . .

RUTH: Eat your eggs, Walter.

WALTER (*slams the table and jumps up*):   DAMN MY EGGS—DAMN ALL THE EGGS THAT EVER WAS!

RUTH: Then go to work.

WALTER (*looking up at her*):   See—I'm trying to talk to you 'bout myself—(*shaking his head with the repetition*)—and all you can say is eat them eggs and go to work.

RUTH (*wearily*):   Honey, you never say nothing new. I listen to you every day, every night and every morning, and you never say nothing new. (*shrugging*) So you would rather *be* Mr. Arnold than be his chauffeur. So—I would *rather* be living in Buckingham Palace.

WALTER: That is just what is wrong with the colored woman in this world . . . Don't understand about building their men up and making 'em feel like they somebody. Like they can do something.

RUTH (*drily, but to hurt*):   There *are* colored men who do things.

WALTER: No thanks to the colored woman.

RUTH: Well, being a colored woman, I guess I can't help myself none.

She rises and gets the ironing board and sets it up and attacks a huge pile of rough-

dried clothes, sprinkling them in preparation for the ironing and then rolling them into tight fat balls.

WALTER (*mumbling*): We one group of men tied to a race of women with small minds!

His sister BENEATHA *enters. She is about twenty, as slim and intense as her brother. She is not as pretty as her sister-in-law, but her lean, almost intellectual face has a handsomeness of its own. She wears a bright-red flannel nightie, and her thick hair stands wildly about her head. Her speech is a mixture of many things; it is different from the rest of the family's insofar as education has permeated her sense of English— and perhaps the Midwest rather than the South has finally—at last—won out in her inflection; but not altogether, because over all of it is a soft slurring and transformed use of vowels which is the decided influence of the Southside. She passes through the room without looking at either* RUTH *or* WALTER *and goes to the outside door and looks, a little blindly, out to the bathroom. She sees that it has been lost to the Johnsons. She closes the door with a sleepy vengeance and crosses to the table and sits down a little defeated.*

BENEATHA: I am going to start timing those people.

WALTER: You should get up earlier.

BENEATHA (*Her face in her hands. She is still fighting the urge to go back to bed.*): Really—would you suggest dawn? Where's the paper?

WALTER (*pushing the paper across the table to her as he studies her almost clinically, as though he has never seen her before*): You a horrible-looking chick at this hour.

BENEATHA (*drily*): Good morning, everybody.

WALTER (*senselessly*): How is school coming?

BENEATHA (*in the same spirit*): Lovely. Lovely. And you know, biology is the greatest. (*looking up at him*) I dissected something that looked just like you yesterday.

WALTER: I just wondered if you've made up your mind and everything.

BENEATHA (*gaining in sharpness and impatience*): And what did I answer yesterday morning—and the day before that?

RUTH (*from the ironing board, like someone disinterested and old*): Don't be so nasty, Bennie.

BENEATHA (*still to her brother*): And the day before that and the day before that!

WALTER (*defensively*): I'm interested in you. Something wrong with that? Ain't many girls who decide—

WALTER *and* BENEATHA (*in unison*): —"to be a doctor."

Silence.

WALTER: Have we figured out yet just exactly how much medical school is going to cost?

RUTH: Walter Lee, why don't you leave that girl alone and get out of here to work?

BENEATHA (*exits to the bathroom and bangs on the door*): Come on out of there, please!

She comes back into the room.

WALTER (*looking at his sister intently*): You know the check is coming tomorrow.

BENEATHA (*turning on him with a sharpness all her own*): That money belongs to Mama, Walter, and it's for her to decide how she wants to use it. I don't care if she wants to buy a house or a rocket ship or just nail it up somewhere and look at it. It's hers. Not ours—*hers.*

WALTER (*bitterly*): Now ain't that fine! You just got your mother's interest at heart, ain't you, girl? You such a nice girl—but if Mama got that money she can always take a few thousand and help you through school too—can't she?

BENEATHA: I have never asked anyone around here to do anything for me!

WALTER: No! And the line between asking and just accepting when the time comes is big and wide—ain't it!

BENEATHA (*with fury*): What do you want from me, Brother—that I quit school or just drop dead, which!

WALTER: I don't want nothing but for you to stop acting holy 'round here. Me and Ruth done made some sacrifices for you—why can't you do something for the family?

RUTH: Walter, don't be dragging me in it.

WALTER: You are in it—Don't you get up and go work in somebody's kitchen for the last three years to help put clothes on her back?

RUTH: Oh, Walter—that's not fair . . .

WALTER: It ain't that nobody expects you to get on your knees and say thank you, Brother; thank you, Ruth; thank you, Mama—and thank you, Travis, for wearing the same pair of shoes for two semesters—

BENEATHA (*dropping to her knees*): Well—I *do*—all right?—thank everybody! And forgive me for ever wanting to be anything at all! (*pursuing him on her knees across the floor*) FORGIVE ME, FORGIVE ME, FORGIVE ME!

RUTH: Please stop it! Your mama'll hear you.

WALTER: Who the hell told you you had to be a doctor? If you so crazy 'bout messing 'round with sick people—then go be a nurse like other women—or just get married and be quiet .

BENEATHA: Well—you finally got it said . . . It took you three years but you finally got it said. Walter, give up; leave me alone—it's Mama's money.

WALTER: *He was my father, too!*

BENEATHA: So what? He was mine, too—and Travis' grandfather—but the insurance money belongs to Mama. Picking on me is not going to make her give it to you to invest in any liquor stores—(*underbreath, dropping into a chair*)—and I for one say, God bless Mama for that!

WALTER (*to* RUTH): See—did you hear? Did you hear!

RUTH: Honey, please go to work.

WALTER: Nobody in this house is ever going to understand me.

BENEATHA: Because you're a nut.

WALTER: Who's a nut?

BENEATHA: You—you are a nut. Thee is mad, boy.

WALTER (*looking at his wife and his sister from the door, very sadly*): The world's most backward race of people, and that's a fact.

BENEATHA (*turning slowly in her chair*): And then there are all those prophets who would lead us out of the wilderness—(WALTER *slams out of the house.*)—into the swamps!

RUTH: Bennie, why you always gotta be pickin' on your brother? Can't you be a little sweeter sometimes? (*Door opens.* WALTER *walks in. He fumbles with his cap, starts to speak, clears throat, looks everywhere but at* RUTH. *Finally.*)

WALTER (*to* RUTH): I need some money for carfare.

RUTH (*looks at him, then warms; teasing, but tenderly*): Fifty cents? (*She goes to her bag and gets money.*) Here—take a taxi!

WALTER *exits.* MAMA *enters. She is a woman in her early sixties, full-bodied and strong. She is one of those women of a certain grace and beauty who wear it so unobtrusively that it takes a while to notice. Her dark-brown face is surrounded by the total whiteness of her hair, and, being a woman who has adjusted to many things in life and overcome many more, her face is full of strength. She has, we can see, wit and faith of a kind that keep her eyes lit and full of interest and expectancy. She is, in a word, a beautiful woman. Her bearing is perhaps most like the noble bearing of the women of the Hereros of Southwest Africa—rather as if she imagines that as she walks she still bears a basket or a vessel upon her head. Her speech, on the other hand, is as careless as her carriage is precise—she is inclined to slur everything—but her voice is perhaps not so much quiet as simply soft.*

MAMA: Who that 'round here slamming doors at this hour?

She crosses through the room, goes to the window, opens it, and brings in a feeble little plant growing doggedly in a small pot on the window sill. She feels the dirt and puts it back out.

RUTH: That was Walter Lee. He and Bennie was at it again.

MAMA: My children and they tempers. Lord, if this little old plant don't get more sun than it's been getting it ain't never going to see spring again. (*She turns from the window.*) What's the matter with you this morning, Ruth? You looks right peaked. You aiming to iron all them things? Leave some for me. I'll get to 'em this afternoon. Bennie honey, it's too drafty for you to be sitting 'round half dressed. Where's your robe?

BENEATHA: In the cleaners.

MAMA: Well, go get mine and put it on.

BENEATHA: I'm not cold, Mama, honest.

MAMA: I know—but you so thin . . .

BENEATHA (*irritably*): Mama, I'm not cold.

MAMA (*seeing the make-down bed as* TRAVIS *has left it*): Lord have mercy, look at that poor bed. Bless his heart—he tries, don't he?

She moves to the bed TRAVIS *has sloppily made up.*

RUTH: No—he don't half try at all 'cause he knows you going to come along behind him and fix everything. That's just how come he don't know how to do nothing right now—you done spoiled that boy so.

MAMA (*folding bedding*): Well—he's a little boy. Ain't supposed to know 'bout housekeeping. My baby, that's what he is. What you fix for his breakfast this morning?

RUTH (*angrily*): I feed my son, Lena!

MAMA: I ain't meddling—(*underbreath; busy-bodyish*) I just noticed all last week he had cold cereal, and when it starts getting this chilly in the fall a child ought to have some hot grits or something when he goes out in the cold—

RUTH (*furious*): I gave him hot oats—is that all right!

MAMA: I ain't meddling. (*pause*) Put a lot of nice butter on it? (RUTH *shoots her an angry look and does not reply.*) He likes lots of butter.

RUTH (*exasperated*): Lena—

MAMA (*To* BENEATHA. MAMA *is inclined to wander conversationally sometimes.*): What was you and your brother fussing 'bout this morning?

BENEATHA: It's not important, Mama.

She gets up and goes to look out at the bathroom, which is apparently free, and she picks up her towels and rushes out.

MAMA: What was they fighting about?

RUTH: Now you know as well as I do.

MAMA (*shaking her head*): Brother still worrying hisself sick about that money?

RUTH: You know he is.

MAMA: You had breakfast?

RUTH: Some coffee.

MAMA: Girl, you better start eating and looking after yourself better. You almost thin as Travis.

RUTH: Lena—

MAMA: Un-hunh?

RUTH: What are you going to do with it?

MAMA: Now don't you start, child. It's too early in the morning to be talking about money. It ain't Christian.

RUTH: It's just that he got his heart set on that store—

MAMA: You mean that liquor store that Willy Harris want him to invest in?

RUTH: Yes—

MAMA: We ain't no business people, Ruth. We just plain working folks.

RUTH: Ain't nobody business people till they go into business. Walter Lee say colored people ain't never going to start getting ahead till they start gambling on some different kinds of things in the world—investments and things.

MAMA: What done got into you, girl? Walter Lee done finally sold you on investing.

RUTH: No. Mama, something is happening between Walter and me. I don't know what it is—but he needs something—something I can't give him any more. He needs this chance, Lena.

MAMA (*frowning deeply*): But liquor, honey—

RUTH: Well—like Walter say—I spec people going to always be drinking themselves some liquor.

MAMA: Well—whether they drinks it or not ain't none of my business. But whether I go into business selling it to 'em *is,* and I don't want that on my ledger this late in life. (*stopping suddenly and studying her daughter-in-law*) Ruth Younger, what's the matter with you today? You look like you could fall over right there.

RUTH: I'm tired.

MAMA: Then you better stay home from work today.

RUTH: I can't stay home. She'd be calling up the agency and screaming at them, "My girl didn't come in today—send me somebody! My girl didn't come in!" Oh, she just have a fit . . .

MAMA: Well, let her have it. I'll just call her up and say you got the flu—

RUTH (*laughing*): Why the flu?

MAMA: 'Cause it sounds respectable to 'em. Something white people get, too. They know 'bout the flu. Otherwise they think you been cut up or something when you tell 'em you sick.

RUTH: I got to go in. We need the money.

MAMA: Somebody would of thought my children done all but starved to death the way they talk about money here late. Child, we got a great big old check coming tomorrow.

RUTH (*sincerely, but also self-righteously*): Now that's your money. It ain't got nothing to do with me. We all feel like that—Walter and Bennie and me—even Travis.

MAMA (*thoughtfully, and suddenly very far away*): Ten thousand dollars—

RUTH: Sure is wonderful.

MAMA: Ten thousand dollars.

RUTH: You know what you should do, Miss Lena? You should take yourself a trip somewhere. To Europe or South America or someplace—

MAMA (*throwing up her hands at the thought*): Oh, child!

RUTH: I'm serious. Just pack up and leave! Go on away and enjoy yourself some. Forget about the family and have yourself a ball for once in your life—

MAMA (*drily*): You sound like I'm just about ready to die. Who'd go with me? What I look like wandering 'round Europe by myself?

RUTH: Shoot—these here rich white women do it all the time. They don't think nothing of packing up they suitcases and piling on one of them big steamships and— swoosh!—they gone, child.

MAMA: Something always told me I wasn't no rich white woman.

RUTH: Well—what are you going to do with it then?

MAMA: I ain't rightly decided. (*Thinking. She speaks now with emphasis.*) Some of it got to be put away for Beneatha and her schoolin'—and ain't nothing going to touch that part of it. Nothing. (*She waits several seconds, trying to make up her mind about something, and looks at* RUTH *a little tentatively before going on.*) Been thinking that we maybe could meet the notes on a little old two-story somewhere, with a yard where Travis could play in the summertime, if we use part of the insurance for a down payment and everybody kind of pitch in. I could maybe take on a little day work again, few days a week—

RUTH (*studying her mother-in-law furtively and concentrating on her ironing, anxious to encourage without seeming to*): Well, Lord knows, we've put enough rent into this here rat trap to pay for four houses by now . . .

MAMA (*looking up at the words "rat trap" and then looking around and leaning back and sighing—in a suddenly reflective mood*): "Rat trap"—yes, that's all it is. (*smiling*) I remember just as well the day me and Big Walter moved in here. Hadn't been married but two weeks and wasn't planning on living here no more than a year. (*She shakes her head at the dissolved dream.*) We was going to set away, little by little, don't you know, and buy a little place out in Morgan Park. We had even picked out the house. (*chuckling a little*) Looks right dumpy today. But Lord, child, you should know all the dreams I had 'bout buying that house and fixing it up and making me a little garden in the back—(*She waits and stops smiling.*) And didn't none of it happen.

Dropping her hands in a futile gesture.

RUTH (*keeps her head down, ironing*): Yes, life can be a barrel of disappointments, sometimes.

MAMA: Honey, Big Walter would come in here some nights back then and slump down on that couch there and just look at the rug, and look at me and look at the rug and then back at me—and I'd know he was down then . . . really down. (*After a second very long and thoughtful pause; she is seeing back to times that only she can see.*) And then, Lord, when I lost that baby—little Claude—I almost thought I was going to lose Big Walter too. Oh, that man grieved hisself! He was one man to love his children.

RUTH: Ain't nothin' can tear at you like losin' your baby.

MAMA: I guess that's how come that man finally worked hisself to death like he done. Like he was fighting his own war with this here world that took his baby from him.

RUTH: He sure was a fine man, all right. I always liked Mr. Younger.

MAMA: Crazy 'bout his children! God knows there was plenty wrong with Walter Younger—hard-headed, mean, kind of wild with women—plenty wrong with him. But he sure loved his children. Always wanted them to have something—be something. That's where Brother gets all these notions, I reckon. Big Walter used to say, he'd get right wet in the eyes sometimes, lean his head back with the water standing in his eyes and say, "Seem like God didn't see fit to give the black man nothing but dreams—but He did give us children to make them dreams seem worth while." (*She smiles.*) He could talk like that, don't you know.

RUTH: Yes, he sure could. He was a good man, Mr. Younger.

MAMA: Yes, a fine man—just couldn't never catch up with his dreams, that's all.

BENEATHA *comes in, brushing her hair and looking up to the ceiling, where the sound of a vacuum cleaner has started up.*

BENEATHA: What could be so dirty on that woman's rugs that she has to vacuum them every single day?

RUTH: I wish certain young women 'round here who I could name would take inspiration about certain rugs in a certain apartment I could also mention.

BENEATHA (*shrugging*): How much cleaning can a house need, for Christ's sakes.

MAMA (*not liking the Lord's name used thus*): Bennie!

RUTH: Just listen to her—just listen!

BENEATHA: Oh, God!

MAMA: If you use the Lord's name just one more time—

BENEATHA (*a bit of a whine*): Oh, Mama—

RUTH: Fresh—just fresh as salt, this girl!

BENEATHA (*drily*): Well—if the salt loses its savor—

MAMA: Now that will do. I just ain't going to have you 'round here reciting the scriptures in vain—you hear me?

BENEATHA: How did I manage to get on everybody's wrong side by just walking into a room?

RUTH: If you weren't so fresh—

BENEATHA: Ruth, I'm twenty years old.

MAMA: What time you be home from school today?

BENEATHA: Kind of late. (*with enthusiasm*) Madeline is going to start my guitar lessons today.

MAMA *and* RUTH *look up with the same expression.*

MAMA: Your *what* kind of lessons?

BENEATHA: Guitar.

RUTH: Oh, Father!

MAMA: How come you done taken it in your mind to learn to play the guitar?

BENEATHA: I just want to, that's all.

MAMA (*smiling*): Lord, child, don't you know what to get tired of this now—like you got tired of that little do with yourself? How long it going to be before you play-acting group you joined last year? (*looking at* RUTH) And what was it the year before that?

RUTH: The horseback-riding club for which she bought that fifty-five-dollar riding habit that's been hanging in the closet ever since!

MAMA (*to* BENEATHA): Why you got to flit so from one thing to another, baby?

BENEATHA (*sharply*): I just want to learn to play the guitar. Is there anything wrong with that?

MAMA: Ain't nobody trying to stop you. I just wonders sometimes why you has to flit so from one thing to another all the time. You ain't never done nothing with all that camera equipment you brought home—

BENEATHA: I don't flit! I—I experiment with different forms of expression—

RUTH: Like riding a horse?

BENEATHA: —People have to express themselves one way or another.

MAMA: What is it you want to express?

BENEATHA (*angrily*): Me! (MAMA *and* RUTH *look at each other and burst into raucous laughter.*) Don't worry—I don't expect you to understand.

MAMA (*to change the subject*): Who you going out with tomorrow night?

BENEATHA (*with displeasure*): George Murchison again.

MAMA (*pleased*): Oh—you getting a little sweet on him?

RUTH: You ask me, this child ain't sweet on nobody but herself—(*underbreath*) Express herself!

> *They laugh.*

BENEATHA: Oh—I like George all right, Mama. I mean I like him enough to go out with him and stuff, but—

RUTH (*for devilment*): What does *and stuff* mean?

BENEATHA: Mind your own business.

MAMA: Stop picking at her now, Ruth. (*She chuckles—then a suspicious sudden look at her daughter as she turns in her chair for emphasis.*) What DOES it mean?

BENEATHA (*wearily*): Oh, I just mean I couldn't ever really be serious about George. He's—he's so shallow.

RUTH: Shallow—what do you mean he's shallow? He's *Rich!*

MAMA: Hush, Ruth.

BENEATHA: I know he's rich. He knows he's rich, too.

RUTH: Well—what other qualities a man got to have to satisfy you, little girl?

BENEATHA: You wouldn't even begin to understand. Anybody who married Walter could not possibly understand.

MAMA (*outraged*): What kind of way is that to talk about your brother?

BENEATHA: Brother is a flip—let's face it.

MAMA (*to* RUTH, *helplessly*): What's a flip?

RUTH (*glad to add kindling*): She's saying he's crazy.

BENEATHA: Not crazy. Brother isn't really crazy yet—he—he's an elaborate neurotic.

MAMA: Hush your mouth!

BENEATHA: As for George. Well. George looks good—he's got a beautiful car and he takes me to nice places and, as my sister-in-law says, he is probably the richest boy I will ever get to know and I even like him sometimes—but if the Youngers are sitting around waiting to see if their little Bennie is going to tie up the family with the Murchisons, they are wasting their time.

RUTH: You mean you wouldn't marry George Murchison if he asked you someday? That pretty, rich thing? Honey, I knew you was odd—

BENEATHA: No I would not marry him if all I felt for him was what I feel now. Besides, George's family wouldn't really like it.

MAMA: Why not?

BENEATHA: Oh, Mama—The Murchisons are honest-to-God-real-*live*-rich colored people, and the only people in the world who are more snobbish than rich white people are rich colored people. I thought everybody knew that. I've met Mrs. Murchison. She's a scene!

MAMA: You must not dislike people 'cause they well off, honey.

BENEATHA: Why not? It makes just as much sense as disliking people 'cause they are poor, and lots of people do that.

RUTH (*A wisdom-of-the-ages manner. To* MAMA.): Well, she'll get over some of this—

BENEATHA: Get over it? What are you talking about, Ruth? Listen, I'm going to be a doctor. I'm not worried about who I'm going to marry yet—if I ever get married.

MAMA *and* RUTH: *If!*

MAMA: Now, Bennie—

BENEATHA: Oh, I probably will . . . but first I'm going to be a doctor, and George, for one, still thinks that's pretty funny. I couldn't be bothered with that. I am going to be a doctor and everybody around here better understand that!

MAMA (*kindly*): 'Course you going to be a doctor, honey, God willing.

BENEATHA (*drily*): God hasn't got a thing to do with it.

MAMA: Beneatha—that just wasn't necessary.

BENEATHA: Well—neither is God. I get sick of hearing about God.

MAMA: Beneatha!

BENEATHA: I mean it! I'm just tired of hearing about God all the time. What has He got to do with anything? Does he pay tuition?

MAMA: You 'bout to get your fresh little jaw slapped!

RUTH: That's just what she needs, all right!

BENEATHA: Why? Why can't I say what I want to around here, like everybody else?

MAMA: It don't sound nice for a young girl to say things like that—you wasn't brought up that way. Me and your father went to trouble to get you and Brother to church every Sunday.

BENEATHA: Mama, you don't understand. It's all a matter of ideas, and God is just one idea I don't accept. It's not important. I am not going out and be immoral or commit crimes because I don't believe in God. I don't even think about it. It's just that I get tired of Him getting credit for all the things the human race achieves through its own stubborn effort. There simply is no blasted God—there is only man and it is *he* who makes miracles!

MAMA *absorbs this speech, studies her daughter and rises slowly and crosses to* BENEATHA *and slaps her powerfully across the face. After, there is only silence and the daughter drops her eyes from her mother's face, and* MAMA *is very tall before her.*

MAMA: Now—you say after me, in my mother's house there is still God. (*There is a long pause and* BENEATHA *stares at the floor wordlessly.* MAMA *repeats the phrase with precision and cool emotion.*) In my mother's house there is still God.

BENEATHA: In my mother's house there is still God.

A long pause.

MAMA (*Walking away from* BENEATHA, *too disturbed for triumphant posture. Stopping and turning back to her daughter.*): There are some ideas we ain't going to have in this house. Not long as I am at the head of this family.

BENEATHA: Yes, ma'am.

MAMA *walks out of the room.*

RUTH (*almost gently, with profound understanding*): You think you a woman, Bennie— but you still a little girl. What you did was childish—so you got treated like a child.

BENEATHA: I see. (*quietly*) I also see that everybody thinks it's all right for Mama to be a tyrant. But all the tyranny in the world will never put a God in the heavens!

She picks up her books and goes out. Pause.

RUTH (*goes to* MAMA'S *door*): She said she was sorry.

MAMA (*coming out, going to her plant*): They frightens me, Ruth. My children.

RUTH: You got good children, Lena. They just a little off sometimes—but they're good.

MAMA: No—there's something come down between me and them that don't let us understand each other and I don't know what it is. One done almost lost his mind thinking 'bout money all the time and the other done commence to talk about things I can't seem to understand in no form or fashion. What is it that's changing, Ruth.

RUTH (*soothingly, older than her years*): Now . . . you taking it all too seriously. You just got strong-willed children and it takes a strong woman like you to keep 'em in hand.

MAMA (*looking at her plant and sprinkling a little water on it*): They spirited all right, my children. Got to admit they got spirit—Bennie and Walter. Like this little old plant that ain't never had enough sunshine or nothing—and look at it . . .

She has her back to RUTH, *who has had to stop ironing and lean against something and put the back of her hand to her forehead.*

RUTH (*trying to keep* MAMA *from noticing*): You . . . sure . . . loves that little old thing, don't you? . . .

MAMA: Well, I always wanted me a garden like I used to see sometimes at the back of the houses down home. This plant is close as I ever got to having one. (*She looks out of the window as she replaces the plant.*) Lord, ain't nothing as dreary as the view from this window on a dreary day, is there? Why ain't you singing this morning, Ruth? Sing that "No Ways Tired." That song always lifts me up so—(*She turns at last to see that* RUTH *has slipped quietly to the floor, in a state of semiconsciousness.*) Ruth! Ruth honey—what's the matter with you . . . Ruth!

Curtain.

SCENE 2

It is the following morning; a Saturday morning, and house cleaning is in progress at the YOUNGERS. *Furniture has been shoved hither and yon and* MAMA *is giving the kitchen-area walls a washing down.* BENEATHA, *in dungarees, with a handkerchief tied around her face, is spraying insecticide into the cracks in the walls. As they work, the radio is on and a Southside disk-jockey program is inappropriately filling the house with a rather exotic saxophone blues.* TRAVIS, *the sole idle one, is leaning on his arms, looking out of the window.*

TRAVIS: Grandmama, that stuff Bennie is using smells awful. Can I go downstairs, please?

MAMA: Did you get all them chores done already? I ain't seen you doing much.

TRAVIS: Yes'm—finished early. Where did Mama go this morning?

MAMA (*looking at* BENEATHA): She had to go on a little errand.

The phone rings. BENEATHA *runs to answer it and reaches it before* WALTER, *who has entered from bedroom.*

TRAVIS: Where?

MAMA: To tend to her business.

BENEATHA: Haylo . . . (*disappointed*) Yes, he is. (*She tosses the phone to* WALTER, *who barely catches it.*) It's Willie Harris again.

WALTER (*as privately as possible under* MAMA'S *gaze*): Hello, Willie. Did you get the papers from the lawyer? . . . No, not yet. I told you the mailman doesn't get here till ten-thirty . . . No, I'll come there . . . Yeah! Right away. (*He hangs up and goes for his coat.*)

BENEATHA: Brother, where did Ruth go?

WALTER (*as he exits*): How should I know!

TRAVIS: Aw come on, Grandma. Can I go outside?

MAMA: Oh, I guess so. You stay right in front of the house, though, and keep a good lookout for the postman.

TRAVIS: Yes'm. (*He darts into bedroom for stickball and bat, reenters, and sees* BENEATHA *on her knees spraying under sofa with behind upraised. He edges closer to the target, takes aim, and lets her have it. She screams.*) Leave them poor little cockroaches alone, they ain't bothering you none! (*He runs as she swings the spraygun at him viciously and playfully.*) Grandma! Grandma!

MAMA: Look out there, girl, before you be spilling some of that stuff on that child!

TRAVIS (*safely behind the bastion of* MAMA): That's right—look out, now! (*He exits.*)

BENEATHA (*drily*): I can't imagine that it would hurt him—it has never hurt the roaches.

MAMA: Well, little boys' hides ain't as tough as Southside roaches. You better get over there behind the bureau. I seen one marching out of there like Napoleon yesterday.

BENEATHA: There's really only one way to get rid of them, Mama—

MAMA: How?

BENEATHA: Set fire to this building! Mama, where did Ruth go?

MAMA (*looking at her with meaning*): To the doctor, I think.

BENEATHA: The doctor? What's the matter? (*They exchange glances.*) You don't think—

MAMA (*with her sense of drama*): Now I ain't saying what I think. But I ain't never been wrong 'bout a woman neither.

The phone rings.

BENEATHA (*at the phone*): Hay-lo . . . (*pause, and a moment of recognition*) Well—when did you get back! . . . And how was it? . . . Of course I've missed you—in my way . . . This morning? No . . . house cleaning and all that and Mama hates it if I let people come over when the house is like this . . . You *have?* Well, that's different . . . What is it— Oh, what the hell, come on over . . . Right, see you then. *Arrividerci.*

She hangs up.

MAMA (*who has listened vigorously, as is her habit*): Who is that you inviting over here with this house looking like this? You ain't got the pride you was born with!

BENEATHA: Asagai doesn't care how houses look, Mama—he's an intellectual.

MAMA: *Who?*

BENEATHA: Asagai—Joseph Asagai. He's an African boy I met on campus. He's been studying in Canada all summer.

MAMA: What's his name?

BENEATHA: Asagai, Joseph. Ah-sah-guy . . . He's from Nigeria.

MAMA: Oh, that's the little country that was founded by slaves way back . . .

BENEATHA: No, Mama—that's Liberia.

MAMA: I don't think I never met no African before.

BENEATHA: Well, do me a favor and don't ask him a whole lot of ignorant questions about Africans. I mean, do they wear clothes and all that—

MAMA: Well, now, I guess if you think we so ignorant 'round here maybe you shouldn't bring your friends here—

BENEATHA: It's just that people ask such crazy things. All anyone seems to know about when it comes to Africa is Tarzan—

MAMA (*indignantly*): Why should I know anything about Africa?

BENEATHA: Why do you give money at church for the missionary work?

MAMA: Well, that's to help save people.

BENEATHA: You mean save them from *heathenism*—

MAMA (*innocently*): Yes.

BENEATHA: I'm afraid they need more salvation from the British and the French.

RUTH *comes in forlornly and pulls off her coat with dejection. They both turn to look at her.*

RUTH (*dispiritedly*): Well, I guess from all the happy faces—everybody knows.

BENEATHA: You pregnant?

MAMA: Lord have mercy, I sure hope it's a little old girl. Travis ought to have a sister.

BENEATHA *and* RUTH *give her a hopeless look for this grandmotherly enthusiasm.*

BENEATHA: How far along are you?

RUTH: Two months.

BENEATHA: Did you mean to? I mean did you plan it or was it an accident?

MAMA: What do you know about planning or not planning?

BENEATHA: Oh, Mama.

RUTH (*wearily*): She's twenty years old, Lena.

BENEATHA: Did you plan it, Ruth?

RUTH: Mind your own business.

BENEATHA: It is my business—where is he going to live, on the *roof*? (*There is silence following the remark as the three women react to the sense of it.*) Gee—I didn't mean that, Ruth, honest. Gee, I don't feel like that at all. I—I think it is wonderful.

RUTH (*dully*): Wonderful.

BENEATHA: Yes—really. (*There is a sudden commotion from the street and she goes to the window to look out.*) What on earth is going on out there? These kids. (*There are, as she throws open the window, the shouts of children rising up from the street. She sticks her head out to see better and calls out.*) TRAVIS! TRAVIS! . . . WHAT ARE YOU DOING DOWN THERE? (*She sees.*) Oh Lord, they're chasing a rat!

RUTH *covers her face with hands and turns away.*

MAMA (*angrily*): Tell that youngun to get himself up here, at once!

BENEATHA: TRAVIS . . . YOU COME UPSTAIRS . . . AT ONCE!

RUTH (*her face twisted*): Chasing a rat . . .

MAMA (*looking at* RUTH, *worried*): Doctor say everything going to be all right?

RUTH (*far away*): Yes—she says everything is going to be fine . . .

MAMA (*immediately suspicious*): "She"—What doctor you went to?

RUTH *just looks at* MAMA *meaningfully and* MAMA *opens her mouth to speak as* TRAVIS *bursts in.*

TRAVIS: (*excited and full of narrative, coming directly to his mother*): Mama, you should of seen the rat . . . Big as a cat, honest! (*He shows an exaggerated size with his hands.*) Gaaleee, that rat was really cuttin' and Bubber caught him with his heel and the janitor, Mr. Barnett, got him with a stick—and then they got him in a corner and—BAM! BAM! BAM!—and he was still jumping around and bleeding like everything too—there's rat blood all over the street—

RUTH *reaches out suddenly and grabs her son without even looking at him and clamps her hand over his mouth and holds him to her.* MAMA *crosses to them rapidly and takes the boy from her.*

MAMA: You hush up now . . . talking all that terrible stuff . . . (TRAVIS *is staring at his mother with a stunned expression.* BENEATHA *comes quickly and takes him away from his grandmother and ushers him to the door.*)

BENEATHA: You go back outside and play . . . but not with any rats. (*She pushes him gently out the door with the boy straining to see what is wrong with his mother.*)

MAMA (*worriedly hovering over* RUTH): Ruth honey—what's the matter with you—you sick?

RUTH *has her fists clenched on her thighs and is fighting hard to suppress a scream that seems to be rising in her.*

BENEATHA: What's the matter with her, Mama?

MAMA (*working her fingers in* RUTH'S *shoulders to relax her*): She be all right. Women gets right depressed sometimes when they get her way. (*speaking softly, expertly, rapidly*) Now you just relax. That's right . . . just lean back, don't think 'bout nothing at all . . . nothing at all—

RUTH: I'm all right . . .

The glassy-eyed look melts and then she collapses into a fit of heavy sobbing. The bell rings.

BENEATHA: Oh, my God—that must be Asagai.

MAMA (*to* RUTH): Come on now, honey. You need to lie down and rest awhile . . . then have some nice hot food.

They exit, RUTH'S *weight on her mother-in-law.* BENEATHA, *herself profoundly disturbed, opens the door to admit a rather dramatic-looking young man with a large package.*

ASAGAI: Hello, Alaiyo—

BENEATHA (*holding the door open and regarding him with pleasure*): Hello . . . (*long pause*) Well—come in. And please excuse everything. My mother was very upset about my letting anyone come here with the place like this.

ASAGAI (*coming into the room*): You look disturbed too . . . Is something wrong?

BENEATHA (*still at the door, absently*): Yes . . . we've all got acute ghetto-itus. (*She smiles and comes toward him, finding a cigarette and sitting.*) So—sit down! No! Wait! (*She whips the spraygun off sofa where she had left it and puts the cushions back. At last perches on arm of sofa. He sits.*) So, how was Canada?

ASAGAI (*a sophisticate*): Canadian.

BENEATHA (*looking at him*): Asagai, I'm very glad you are back.

ASAGAI (*looking back at her in turn*): Are you really?

BENEATHA: Yes—very.

ASAGAI: Why?—you were quite glad when I went away. What happened?

BENEATHA: You went away.

ASAGAI: Ahhhhhhhh.

BENEATHA: Before—you wanted to be so serious before there was time.

ASAGAI: How much time must there be before one knows what one feels?

BENEATHA (*Stalling this particular conversation. Her hands pressed together, in a deliberately childish gesture.*): What did you bring me?

ASAGAI (*handing her the package*): Open it and see.

BENEATHA (*eagerly opening the package and drawing out some records and the colorful robes of a Nigerian woman*): Oh, Asagai! . . . You got them for me! . . . How beautiful . . . and the records too! (*She lifts out the robes and runs to the mirror with them and holds the drapery up in front of herself.*)

ASAGAI (*coming to her at the mirror*): I shall have to teach you how to drape it properly. (*He flings the material about her for the moment and stands back to look at her.*) Ah—Oh-pay-gay-day, oh-gbah-mu-shay. (*a Yoruba exclamation for admiration*) You wear it well . . . very well . . . mutilated hair and all.

BENEATHA (*turning suddenly*): My hair—what's wrong with my hair?

ASAGAI (*shrugging*): Were you born with it like that?

BENEATHA (*reaching up to touch it*): No . . . of course not.

She looks back to the mirror, disturbed.

ASAGAI (*smiling*): How then?

BENEATHA: You know perfectly well how . . . as crinkly as yours . . . that's how.

ASAGAI: And it is ugly to you that way?

BENEATHA (*quickly*): Oh, no—not ugly . . . (*more slowly, apologetically*) But it's so hard to manage when it's, well—raw.

ASAGAI: And so to accommodate that—you mutilate it every week?

BENEATHA: It's not mutilation!

ASAGAI (*laughing aloud at her seriousness*): Oh . . . please! I am only teasing you because you are so very serious about these things. (*He stands back from her and folds his arms across his chest as he watches her pulling at her hair and frowning in the mirror.*) Do you remember the first time you met me at school? . . . (*He laughs.*) You came up to me and you said—and I thought you were the most serious little thing I had ever seen—you said: (*He imitates her.*) "Mr. Asagai—I want very much to talk with you. About Africa. You see, Mr. Asagai, I am looking for my *identity!*"

He laughs.

BENEATHA (*turning to him, not laughing*): Yes—

Her face is quizzical, profoundly disturbed.

ASAGAI (*still teasing and reaching out and taking her face in his hands and turning her profile to him*): Well . . . it is true that this is not so much a profile of a Hollywood queen as perhaps a queen of the Nile—(*a mock dismissal of the importance of the question*) But what does it matter? Assimilationism is so popular in your country.

BENEATHA (*wheeling, passionately, sharply*): I am not an assimilationist!

ASAGAI (*The protest hangs in the room for a moment and* ASAGAI *studies her, his laughter fading.*): Such a serious one. (*There is a pause.*) So—you like the robes? You must take excellent care of them—they are from my sister's personal wardrobe.

BENEATHA (*with incredulity*): You—you sent all the way home—for me?

ASAGAI (*with charm*): For you—I would do much more . . . Well, that is what I came for. I must go.

BENEATHA: Will you call me Monday?

ASAGAI: Yes . . . We have a great deal to talk about. I mean about identity and time and all that.

BENEATHA: Time?

ASAGAI: Yes. About how much time one needs to know what one feels.

BENEATHA: You see! You never understood that there is more than one kind of feeling which can exist between a man and a woman—or, at least, there should be.

ASAGAI (*shaking his head negatively but gently*): No. Between a man and a woman there need be only one kind of feeling. I have that for you . . . Now even . . . right this moment . . .

BENEATHA: I know—and by itself—it won't do. I can find that anywhere.

ASAGAI: For a woman it should be enough.

BENEATHA: I know—because that's what it says in all the novels that men write. But it isn't. Go ahead and laugh—but I'm not interested in being someone's little episode in America or—(*with feminine vengeance*)—one of them! (ASAGAI *has burst into laughter again.*) That's funny as hell, huh!

ASAGAI: It's just that every American girl I have known has said that to me. White—black—in this you are all the same. And the same speech, too!

BENEATHA (*angrily*): Yuk, yuk, yuk!

ASAGAI: It's how you can be sure that the world's most liberated women are not liberated at all. You all talk about it too much!

MAMA *enters and is immediately all social charm because of the presence of a guest.*

BENEATHA: Oh—Mama—this is Mr. Asagai.

MAMA: How do you do?

ASAGAI (*total politeness to an elder*): How do you do, Mrs. Younger. Please forgive me for coming at such an outrageous hour on a Saturday.

MAMA: Well, you are quite welcome. I just hope you understand that our house don't always look like this. (*chatterish*) You must come again. I would love to hear all about—(*not sure of the name*)—your country. I think it's so sad the way our American Negroes don't know nothing about Africa 'cept Tarzan and all that. And all that money they pour into these churches when they ought to be helping you people over there drive out them French and Englishmen done taken away your land.

The mother flashes a slightly superior look at her daughter upon completion of the recitation.

ASAGAI (*taken aback by this sudden and acutely unrelated expression of sympathy*): Yes . . . yes . . .

MAMA (*smiling at him suddenly and relaxing and looking him over*): How many miles is it from here to where you come from?

ASAGAI: Many thousands.

MAMA (*looking at him as she would* WALTER): I bet you don't half look after yourself, being away from your mama either. I spec you better come 'round here from time to time to get yourself some decent homecooked meals . . .

ASAGAI (*moved*): Thank you. Thank you very much. (*they are all quiet, then*) Well . . . I must go. I will call you Monday, Alaiyo.

MAMA: What's that he call you?

ASAGAI: Oh—"Alaiyo." I hope you don't mind. It is what you would call a nickname, I think. It is a Yoruba word. I am a Yoruba.

MAMA (*looking at* BENEATHA): I—I thought he was from—(*uncertain*)

ASAGAI (*understanding*): Nigeria is my country. Yoruba is my tribal origin—

BENEATHA: You didn't tell us what Alaiyo means . . . for all I know, you might be calling me Little Idiot or something . . .

ASAGAI: Well . . . let me see . . . I do not know how just to explain it . . . The sense of a thing can be so different when it changes languages.

BENEATHA: You're evading.

ASAGAI: No—really it is difficult . . . (*thinking*) It means . . . it means One for Whom Bread—Food—Is Not Enough. (*He looks at her.*) Is that all right?

BENEATHA (*understanding, softly*): Thank you.

MAMA (*looking from one to the other and not understanding any of it*): Well . . . that's nice . . . You must come see us again—Mr.—

ASAGAI: Ah-sah-guy . . .

MAMA: Yes . . . Do come again.

ASAGAI: Good-bye.

> *He exits.*

MAMA (*after him*): Lord, that's a pretty thing just went out here! (*insinuatingly, to her daughter*) Yes, I guess I see why we done commence to get so interested in Africa 'round here. Missionaries my aunt Jenny!

> *She exits.*

BENEATHA: Oh, Mama! . . .

> *She picks up the Nigerian dress and holds it up to her in front of the mirror again. She sets the headdress on haphazardly and then notices her hair again and clutches at it and then replaces the headdress and frowns at herself. Then she starts to wriggle in front of the mirror as she thinks a Nigerian woman might.* TRAVIS *enters and stands regarding her.*

TRAVIS: What's the matter, girl, you cracking up?

BENEATHA: Shut up.

> *She pulls the headdress off and looks at herself in the mirror and clutches at her hair again and squinches her eyes as if trying to imagine something. Then, suddenly, she gets her raincoat and kerchief and hurriedly prepares for going out.*

MAMA (*coming back into the room*): She's resting now. Travis, baby, run next door and ask Miss Johnson to please let me have a little kitchen cleanser. This here can is empty as Jacob's kettle.

TRAVIS: I just came in.

MAMA: Do as you told. (*He exits and she looks at her daughter.*) Where you going?

BENEATHA (*halting at the door*): To become a queen of the Nile!

> *She exits in a breathless blaze of glory.* RUTH *appears in the bedroom doorway.*

MAMA: Who told you to get up?

RUTH: Ain't nothing wrong with me to be lying in no bed for. Where did Bennie go?

MAMA (*drumming her fingers*): Far as I could make out—to Egypt. (RUTH *just looks at her.*) What time is it getting to?

RUTH: Ten twenty. And the mailman going to ring that bell this morning just like he done every morning for the last umpteen years.

TRAVIS *comes in with the cleanser can.*

TRAVIS: She say to tell you that she don't have much.

MAMA (*angrily*): Lord, some people I could name sure is tight-fisted! (*directing her grandson*) Mark two cans of cleanser down on the list there. If she that hard up for kitchen cleanser, I sure don't want to forget to get her none!

RUTH: Lena—maybe the woman is just short on cleanser—

MAMA (*not listening*): Much baking powder as she done borrowed from me all these years, she could of done gone into the baking business!

The bell sounds suddenly and sharply and all three are stunned—serious and silent— mid-speech. In spite of all the other conversations and distractions of the morning, this is what they have been waiting for, even TRAVIS, *who looks helplessly from his mother to his grandmother.* RUTH *is the first to come to life again.*

RUTH (*to* TRAVIS): *Get down them steps, boy!*

TRAVIS *snaps to life and flies out to get the mail.*

MAMA (*her eyes wide, her hand to her breast*): You mean it done really come?

RUTH (*excited*): Oh, Miss Lena!

MAMA (*collecting herself*): Well . . . I don't know what we all so excited about 'round here for. We known it was coming for months.

RUTH: That's a whole lot different from having it come and being able to hold it in your hands . . . a piece of paper worth ten thousand dollars . . . (TRAVIS *bursts back into the room. He holds the envelope high above his head, like a little dancer, his face is radiant and he is breathless. He moves to his grandmother with sudden slow ceremony and puts the envelope into her hands. She accepts it, and then merely holds it and looks at it.*) Come on! Open it . . . Lord have mercy, I wish Walter Lee was here!

TRAVIS: Open it, Grandmama!

MAMA (*staring at it*): Now you all be quiet. It's just a check.

RUTH: Open it . . .

MAMA (*still staring at it*): Now don't act silly . . . We ain't never been no people to act silly 'bout no money—

RUTH (*swiftly*): We ain't never had none before—OPEN IT!

MAMA *finally makes a good strong tear and pulls out the thin blue slice of paper and inspects it closely. The boy and his mother study it raptly over* MAMA'S *shoulders.*

MAMA: Travis! (*She is counting off with doubt.*) Is that the right number of zeros?

TRAVIS: Yes'm . . . ten thousand dollars. Gaalee, Grandmama, you rich.

MAMA (*She holds the check away from her, still looking at it. Slowly her face sobers into a mask of unhappiness.*): Ten thousand dollars. (*She hands it to* RUTH.) Put it away somewhere, Ruth. (*She does not look at* RUTH; *her eyes seem to be seeing something somewhere very far off.*) Ten thousand dollars they give you. Ten thousand dollars.

TRAVIS (*to his mother, sincerely*): What's the matter with Grandmama—don't she want to be rich?

RUTH (*distractedly*): You go on out and play now, baby. (TRAVIS *exits.* MAMA *starts wiping dishes absently, humming intently to herself.* RUTH *turns to her, with kind exasperation.*) You've gone and got yourself upset.

MAMA (*not looking at her*): I spec if it wasn't for you all . . . I would just put that money away or give it to the church or something.

RUTH: Now what kind of talk is that. Mr. Younger would just be plain mad if he could hear you talking foolish like that.

MAMA (*stopping and staring off*): Yes . . . he sure would. (*sighing*) We got enough to do with that money, all right. (*She halts then, and turns and looks at her daughter-in-law hard;* RUTH *avoids her eyes and* MAMA *wipes her hands with finality and starts to speak firmly to* RUTH.) Where did you go today, girl?

RUTH: To the doctor.

MAMA (*impatiently*): Now, Ruth . . . you know better than that. Old Doctor Jones is strange enough in his way but there ain't nothing 'bout him make somebody slip and call him "she"—like you done this morning.

RUTH: Well, that's what happened—my tongue slipped.

MAMA: You went to see that woman, didn't you?

RUTH (*defensively, giving herself away*): What woman you talking about?

MAMA (*angrily*): That woman who—

WALTER *enters in great excitement.*

WALTER: Did it come?

MAMA (*quietly*): Can't you give people a Christian greeting before you start asking about money?

WALTER (*to* RUTH): Did it come? (RUTH *unfolds the check and lays it quietly before him, watching him intently with thoughts of her own.* WALTER *sits down and grasps it close and counts off the zeros.*) Ten thousand dollars—(*He turns suddenly, frantically to his mother and draws some papers out of his breast pocket.*) Mama—look. Old Willy Harris put everything on paper—

MAMA: Son—I think you ought to talk to your wife . . . I'll go on out and leave you alone if you want—

WALTER: I can talk to her later—Mama, look—

MAMA: Son—

WALTER: WILL SOMEBODY PLEASE LISTEN TO ME TODAY!

MAMA (*quietly*): I don't 'low no yellin' in this house, Walter Lee, and you know it— (WALTER *stares at them in frustration and starts to speak several times.*) And there ain't going to be no investing in no liquor stores.

WALTER: But, Mama, you ain't even looked at it.

MAMA: I don't aim to have to speak on that again.

A long pause.

WALTER: You ain't looked at it and you don't aim to have to speak on that again? You ain't even looked at it and *you* have decided—(*crumpling his papers*) Well, *you* tell that to my boy tonight when you put him to sleep on the living-room couch . . . (*turning to* MAMA *and speaking directly to her*) Yeah—and tell it to my wife, Mama, tomorrow when she has to go out of here to look after somebody else's kids. And tell it to *me*, Mama, every time we need a new pair of curtains and I have to watch *you* go out and work in somebody's kitchen. Yeah, you tell me then!

WALTER *starts out.*

RUTH: Where you going?

WALTER: I'm going out!

RUTH: Where?

WALTER: Just out of this house somewhere—

RUTH (*getting her coat*): I'll come too.

WALTER: I don't want you to come!

RUTH: I got something to talk to you about, Walter.

WALTER: That's too bad.

MAMA (*still quietly*): Walter Lee—(*She waits and he finally turns and looks at her.*) Sit down.

WALTER: I'm a grown man, Mama.

MAMA: Ain't nobody said you wasn't grown. But you still in my house and my presence. And as long as you are—you'll talk to your wife civil. Now sit down.

RUTH (*suddenly*): Oh, let him go on out and drink himself to death! He makes me sick to my stomach! (*She flings her coat against him and exits to bedroom.*)

WALTER (*violently flinging the coat after her*): And you turn mine too, baby! (*The door slams behind her.*) That was my biggest mistake—

MAMA (*still quietly*): Walter, what is the matter with you?

WALTER: Matter with me? Ain't nothing the matter with *me*!

MAMA: Yes there is. Something eating you up like a crazy man. Something more than me not giving you this money. The past few years I been watching it happen to you. You get all nervous acting and kind of wild in the eyes—(WALTER *jumps up impatiently at her words.*) I said sit there now, I'm talking to you!

WALTER: Mama—I don't need no nagging at me today.

MAMA: Seem like you getting to a place where you always tied up in some kind of knot about something. But if anybody ask you 'bout it you just yell at 'em and bust out the house and go out and drink somewheres. Walter Lee, people can't live with that. Ruth's a good, patient girl in her way—but you getting to be too much. Boy, don't make the mistake of driving that girl away from you.

WALTER: Why—what she do for me?

MAMA: She loves you.

WALTER: Mama—I'm going out. I want to go off somewhere and be by myself for a while.

MAMA: I'm sorry 'bout your liquor store, son. It just wasn't the thing for us to do. That's what I want to tell you about—

WALTER: I got to go out, Mama—

He rises.

MAMA: It's dangerous, son.

WALTER: What's dangerous?

MAMA: When a man goes outside his home to look for peace.

WALTER (*beseechingly*): Then why can't there never be no peace in this house then?

MAMA: You done found it in some other house?

WALTER: No—there ain't no woman! Why do women always think there's a woman somewhere when a man gets restless. (*picks up the check*) Do you know what this money means to me? Do you know what this money can do for us? (*puts it back*) Mama—Mama— I want so many things . . .

MAMA: Yes, son—

WALTER: I want so many things that they are driving me kind of crazy . . . . Mama—look at me.

MAMA: I'm looking at you. You a good-looking boy. You got a job, a nice wife, a fine boy and—

WALTER: A job. (*looks at her*) Mama, a job? I open and close car doors all day long. I drive a man around in his limousine and I say, "Yes, sir; no, sir; very good, sir; shall I take the Drive, sir?" Mama, that ain't no kind of job . . . that ain't nothing at all. (*very quietly*) Mama, I don't know if I can make you understand.

MAMA: Understand what, baby?

WALTER (*quietly*): Sometimes it's like I can see the future stretched out in front of me—just plain as day. The future, Mama. Hanging over there at the edge of my days. Just waiting for me—a big, looming blank space—full of *nothing*. Just waiting for *me*. But it don't have to be. (*Pause. Kneeling beside her chair.*) Mama— sometimes when I'm downtown and I pass them cool, quiet-looking restaurants where them white boys are sitting back and talking 'bout things . . . sitting there turning deals worth millions of dollars . . . sometimes I see guys don't look much older than me—

MAMA: Son—how come you talk so much 'bout money?

WALTER (*with immense passion*): Because it is life, Mama!

MAMA (*quietly*): Oh—(*very quietly*) So now it's life. Money is life. Once upon a time freedom used to be life—now it's money. I guess the world really do change . . .

WALTER: No—it was always money, Mama. We just didn't know about it.

MAMA: No . . . something has changed. (*She looks at him.*) You something new, boy. In my time we was worried about not being lynched and getting to the North if we could and how to stay alive and still have a pinch of dignity too . . . Now here come you and Beneatha—talking 'bout things we ain't never even thought about hardly, me and your daddy. You ain't satisfied or proud of nothing we done. I mean that you had a home; that we kept you out of trouble till you was grown; that you don't have to ride to work on the back of nobody's streetcar— You my children—but how different we done become.

WALTER (*A long beat. He pats her hand and gets up.*): You just don't understand, Mama, you just don't understand.

MAMA: Son—do you know your wife is expecting another baby? (WALTER *stands, stunned, and absorbs what his mother has said.*) That's what she wanted to talk to you about. (WALTER *sinks down into a chair.*) This ain't for me to be telling—but you ought to know. (*She waits.*) I think Ruth is thinking 'bout getting rid of that child.

WALTER (*slowly understanding*): No—no—Ruth wouldn't do that.

MAMA: When the world gets ugly enough—a woman will do anything for her family. *The part that's already living.*

WALTER: You don't know Ruth, Mama, if you think she would do that.

RUTH *opens the bedroom door and stands there a little limp.*

RUTH (*beaten*): Yes I would too, Walter. (*pause*) I gave her a five-dollar down payment.

There is total silence as the man stares at his wife and the mother stares at her son.

MAMA (*presently*): Well—(*tightly*) Well—son, I'm waiting to hear you say something . . . (*She waits.*) I'm waiting to hear how you be your father's son. Be the man he was . . . (*Pause. The silence shouts.*) Your wife say she going to destroy your child. And I'm waiting to hear you talk like him and say we a people who give children life, not who destroys them—(*She rises*). I'm waiting to see you stand up and look like your daddy and say we done give up one baby to poverty and that we ain't going to give up nary another one . . . I'm waiting.

WALTER: Ruth—(*He can say nothing.*)

MAMA: If you a son of mine, tell her! (WALTER *picks up his keys and his coat and walks out. She continues, bitterly.*) You . . . you are a disgrace to your father's memory. Somebody get me my hat!

Curtain.

ACT TWO

SCENE 1

TIME: *Later the same day.*

AT RISE: RUTH *is ironing again. She has the radio going. Presently* BENEATHA'S *bedroom door opens and* RUTH'S *mouth falls and she puts down the iron in fascination.*

RUTH: What have we got on tonight!

BENEATHA (*emerging grandly from the doorway so that we can see her thoroughly robed in the costume Asagai brought*): You are looking at what a well-dressed Nigerian woman wears—(*She parades for* RUTH, *her hair completely hidden by the headdress; she is coquettishly fanning herself with an ornate oriental fan, mistakenly more like Butterfly than any Nigerian that ever was.*) Isn't it beautiful? (*She promenades to the radio and, with an arrogant flourish, turns off the good loud blues that is playing.*) Enough of this assimilationist junk! (RUTH *follows her with her eyes as she goes to the phonograph and puts on a record and turns and waits ceremoniously for the music to come up. Then, with a shout—*) OCOMOGOSIAY!

RUTH *jumps. The music comes up, a lovely Nigerian melody.* BENEATHA *listens, enraptured, her eyes far away—"back to the past." She begins to dance.* RUTH *is dumfounded.*

RUTH: What kind of dance is that?
BENEATHA: A folk dance.
RUTH (*Pearl Bailey*): What kind of folks do that, honey?
BENEATHA: It's from Nigeria. It's a dance of welcome.
RUTH: Who you welcoming?
BENEATHA: The men back to the village.
RUTH: Where they been?
BENEATHA: How should I know—out hunting or something. Anyway, they are coming back now . . .
RUTH: Well, that's good.
BENEATHA (*with the record*):
   Alundi, alundi
   Alundi alunya
   Jop pu a jeepua
   Ang gu sooooooooooo

   Ai yai yae . . .
   Ayehaye—alundi . . .

WALTER *comes in during this performance; he has obviously been drinking. He leans against the door heavily and watches his sister, at first with distaste. Then his eyes look off—"back to the past"—as he lifts both his fists to the roof, screaming.*

WALTER: YEAH . . . AND ETHIOPIA STRETCH FORTH HER HANDS AGAIN! . . .

RUTH (*drily, looking at him*): Yes—and Africa sure is claiming her own tonight. (*She gives them both up and starts ironing again.*)

WALTER (*all in a drunken, dramatic shout*): Shut up! . . . I'm digging them drums . . . then drums move me! . . . (*He makes his weaving way to his wife's face and leans in close to her.*) In my *heart of hearts*—(*He thumps his chest.*)—I am much warrior!

RUTH (*without even looking up*): In your heart of hearts you are much drunkard.

WALTER (*coming away from her and starting to wander around the room, shouting*): Me and Jomo . . . (*Intently, in his sister's face. She has stopped dancing to watch him in this unknown mood.*) That's my man, Kenyatta. (*shouting and thumping his chest*) FLAMING SPEAR! HOT DAMN! (*He is suddenly in possession of an imaginary spear and actively spearing enemies all over the room.*) OCOMOGOSIAY . . .

BENEATHA (*to encourage* WALTER, *thoroughly caught up with this side of him*): OCO-MOGOSIAY, FLAMING SPEAR!

WALTER: THE LION IS WAKING . . . OWIMOWEH! (*He pulls his shirt open and leaps up on the table and gestures with his spear.*)

BENEATHA: OWIMOWEH!

WALTER (*On the table, very far gone, his eyes pure glass sheets. He sees what we cannot, that he is a leader of his people, a great chief, a descendant of Chaka, and that the hour to march has come.*): Listen, my black brothers—

BENEATHA: OCOMOGOSIAY!

WALTER: —Do you hear the waters rushing against the shores of the coastlands—

BENEATHA: OCONOGOSIAY!

WALTER: —Do you hear the screeching of the cocks in yonder hills beyond where the chiefs meet in council for the coming of the mighty war—

BENEATHA: OCOMOGOSIAY!

And now the lighting shifts subtly to suggest the world of WALTER'S *imagination, and the mood shifts from pure comedy. It is the inner* WALTER *speaking: the Southside chauffeur has assumed an unexpected majesty.*

WALTER: —Do you hear the beating of the wings of the birds flying low over the mountains and the low places of our land—

BENEATHA: OCOMOGOSIAY!

WALTER: —Do you hear the singing of the women, singing the war songs of our fathers to the babies in the great houses? Singing the sweet war songs! (*The doorbell rings.*) OH, DO YOU HEAR, MY *BLACK* BROTHERS!

BENEATHA (*completely gone*): We hear you, Flaming Spear—

RUTH *shuts off the phonograph and opens the door.* GEORGE MURCHISON *enters.*

WALTER: Telling us to prepare for the GREATNESS OF THE TIME! (*Lights back to normal. He turns and sees* GEORGE.) Black Brother!

He extends his hand for the fraternal clasp.

GEORGE: Black Brother, hell!

RUTH (*having had enough, and embarrassed for the family*): Beneatha, you got company—what's the matter with you? Walter Lee Younger, get down off that table and stop acting like a fool . . .

WALTER *comes down off the table suddenly and makes a quick exit to the bathroom.*

RUTH: He's had a little to drink . . . I don't know what her excuse is.

GEORGE (*to* BENEATHA): Look honey, we're going *to* the theatre—we're not going to be *in* it . . . so go change, huh?

BENEATHA *looks at him and slowly, ceremoniously, lifts her hands and pulls off the headdress. Her hair is close-cropped and unstraightened.* GEORGE *freezes mid-sentence and* RUTH'S *eyes all but fall out of her head.*

GEORGE: What in the name of—

RUTH (*touching* BENEATHA'S *hair*): Girl, you done lost your natural mind!? Look at your head!

GEORGE: What have you done to your head—I mean your hair!

BENEATHA: Nothing—except cut it off.

RUTH: Now that's the truth—it's what ain't been done to it! You expect this boy to go out with you with your head all nappy like that?

BENEATHA (*looking at* GEORGE): That's up to George. If he's ashamed of his heritage—

GEORGE: Oh, don't be so proud of yourself, Bennie—just because you look eccentric.

BENEATHA: How can something that's natural be eccentric?

GEORGE: That's what being eccentric means—being natural. Get dressed.

BENEATHA: I don't like that, George.

RUTH: Why must you and your brother make an argument out of everything people say?

BENEATHA: Because I hate assimilationist Negroes!

RUTH: Will somebody please tell me what assimila-who-ever means!

GEORGE: Oh, it's just a college girl's way of calling people Uncle Toms—but that isn't what it means at all.

RUTH: Well, what does it mean?

BENEATHA (*cutting* GEORGE *off and staring at him as she replies to* RUTH): It means someone who is willing to give up his own culture and submerge himself completely in the dominant, and in this case *oppressive* culture!

GEORGE: Oh, dear, dear, dear! Here we go! A lecture on the African past! On our Great West African Heritage! In one second we will hear all about the great Ashanti empires; the great Songhay civilizations; and the great sculpture of Bénin—and then some poetry in the Bantu—and the whole monologue will end with the word *heritage!* (*nastily*) Let's face it, baby, your heritage is nothing but a bunch of raggedy-assed spirituals and some grass huts!

BENEATHA: GRASS HUTS! (RUTH *crosses to her and forcibly pushes her toward the bedroom.*) See there . . . you are standing there in your splendid ignorance talking about people who were the first to smelt iron on the face of the earth! (RUTH *is pushing her through the door.*) The Ashanti were performing surgical operations when the English—(RUTH *pulls the door to, with* BENEATHA *on the other side, and smiles graciously at* GEORGE. BENEATHA *opens the door and shouts the end of the sentence defiantly at* GEORGE.)—were still tatooing themselves with blue dragons! (*She goes back inside.*)

RUTH: Have a seat, George. (*They both sit.* RUTH *folds her hands rather primly on her lap, determined to demonstrate the civilization of the family.*) Warm, ain't it? I mean for September. (*pause*) Just like they always say about Chicago weather: If it's too hot or cold for you, just wait a minute and it'll change. (*She smiles happily at this cliché of clichés.*) Everybody say it's got to do with them bombs and things they keep setting off. (*pause*) Would you like a nice cold beer?

GEORGE: No, thank you. I don't care for beer. (*He looks at his watch.*) I hope she hurries up.

RUTH: What time is the show?

GEORGE: It's an eight-thirty curtain. That's just Chicago, though. In New York standard curtain time is eight forty.

He is rather proud of this knowledge.

RUTH (*properly appreciating it*): You get to New York a lot?

GEORGE (*offhand*): Few times a year.

RUTH: Oh—that's nice. I've never been to New York.

WALTER *enters. We feel he has relieved himself, but the edge of unreality is still with him.*

WALTER: New York ain't got nothing Chicago ain't. Just a bunch of hustling people all squeezed up together—being "Eastern."

He turns his face into a screw of displeasure.

GEORGE: Oh—you've been?

WALTER: *Plenty* of times.

RUTH (*shocked at the lie*): Walter Lee Younger!

WALTER (*staring her down*): Plenty! (*pause*) What we got to drink in this house? Why don't you offer this man some refreshment. (*to* GEORGE) They don't know how to entertain people in this house, man.

GEORGE: Thank you—I don't really care for anything.

WALTER (*feeling his head; sobriety coming*): Where's Mama?

RUTH: She ain't come back yet.

WALTER (*looking* MURCHISON *over from head to toe, scrutinizing his carefully casual tweed sports jacket over cashmere V-neck sweater over soft eyelet shirt and tie, and soft slacks, finished off with white buckskin shoes*): Why all you college boys wear them faggoty-looking white shoes?

RUTH: Walter Lee!

GEORGE MURCHISON *ignores the remark.*

WALTER (*to* RUTH): Well, they look crazy as hell—white shoes, cold as it is.

RUTH (*crushed*): You have to excuse him—

WALTER: No he don't! Excuse me for what? What you always excusing me for! I'll excuse myself when I needs to be excused! (*a pause*) They look as funny as them black knee socks Beneatha wears out of here all the time.

RUTH: It's the college *style*, Walter.

WALTER: Style, hell. She looks like she got burnt legs or something!

RUTH: Oh, Walter—

WALTER (*an irritable mimic*): Oh, Walter! Oh, Walter! (*to* MURCHISON) How's your old man making out? I understand you all going to buy that big hotel on the Drive? (*He finds a beer in the refrigerator, wanders over to* MURCHISON, *sipping and wiping his lips with the back of his hand, and straddling a chair backwards to talk to the other man.*) Shrewd move. Your old man is all right, man. (*tapping his head and half winking for emphasis*) I mean he knows how to operate. I mean he thinks *big*, you know what I mean, I mean for a *home*, you know? But I think he's kind of running out of ideas now. I'd like to talk to him. Listen, man, I got some plans that could turn this city upside down. I mean think like he does. *Big*. Invest big, gamble big, hell, lose *big* if you have to, you know what I mean. It's hard to find a man on this whole Southside who understands my kind of thinking—you dig? (*He scrutinizes* MURCHISON *again, drinks his beer, squints his eyes and leans in close, confidential, man to man*.) Me and you ought to sit down and talk sometimes, man. Man, I got me some ideas . . .

MURCHISON (*with boredom*): Yeah—sometimes we'll have to do that, Walter.

WALTER (*understanding the indifference, and offended*): Yeah—well, when you get the time, man. I know you a busy little boy.

RUTH: Walter, please—

WALTER (*bitterly, hurt*): I know ain't nothing in this world as busy as you colored college boys with your fraternity pins and white shoes . . .

RUTH (*covering her face with humiliation*): Oh, Walter Lee—

WALTER: I see you all the time—with the books tucked under your arms—going to your (*British A—a mimic*) "clahsses." And for what! What the hell you learning over there? Filling up your heads—(*counting off on his fingers*)—with the sociology and the psychology—but they teaching you how to be a man? How to take over and run the world? They teaching you how to run a rubber plantation or a steel mill? Naw—just to talk proper and read books and wear them faggoty-looking white shoes . . .

GEORGE (*looking at him with distaste, a little above it all*): You're all wacked up with bitterness, man.

WALTER (*intently, almost quietly, between the teeth, glaring at the boy*): And you—ain't you bitter, man? Ain't you just about had it yet? Don't you see no stars gleaming that you can't reach out and grab? You happy?—You contented son-of-a-bitch—you happy? You got it made? Bitter? Man, I'm a volcano. Bitter? Here I am a giant—surrounded by ants! Ants who can't even understand what it is the giant is talking about.

RUTH (*passionately and suddenly*): Oh, Walter—ain't you with nobody!

WALTER (*violently*): No! 'Cause ain't nobody with me! Not even my own mother!

RUTH: Walter, that's a terrible thing to say!

BENEATHA *enters, dressed for the evening in a cocktail dress and earrings, hair natural.*

GEORGE: Well—hey—(*crosses to* BENEATHA; *thoughtful, with emphasis, since this is a reversal*) You look great!

WALTER (*seeing his sister's hair for the first time*): What's the matter with your head?

BENEATHA (*tired of the jokes now*): I cut it off, Brother.

WALTER (*coming close to inspect it and walking around her*): Well, I'll be damned. So that's what they mean by the African bush . . .

BENEATHA: Ha ha. Let's go, George.

GEORGE (*looking at her*): You know something? I like it. It's sharp. I mean it really is. (*helps her into her wrap*)

RUTH: Yes—I think so, too. (*She goes to the mirror and starts to clutch at her hair.*)

WALTER: Oh no! You leave yours alone, baby. You might turn out to have a pin-shaped head or something!

BENEATHA: See you all later.

RUTH: Have a nice time.

GEORGE: Thanks. Good night. (*Half out the door, he reopens it. To* WALTER.) Good night, Prometheus!

BENEATHA *and* GEORGE *exit.*

WALTER (*to* RUTH): Who is Prometheus?

RUTH: I don't know. Don't worry about it.

WALTER (*in fury, pointing after* GEORGE): See there—they get to a point where they can't insult you man to man—they got to go talk about something ain't nobody never heard of!

RUTH: How do you know it was an insult? (*to humor him*) Maybe Prometheus is a nice fellow.

WALTER: Prometheus! I bet there ain't even no such thing! I bet that simple-minded clown—

RUTH: Walter—

She stops what she is doing and looks at him.

WALTER (*yelling*): Don't start!

RUTH: Start what?

WALTER: Your nagging! Where was I? Who was I with? How much money did I spend?

RUTH (*plaintively*): Walter Lee—why don't we just try to talk about it . . .

WALTER (*not listening*): I been out talking with people who understand me. People who care about the things I got on my mind.

RUTH (*wearily*): I guess that means people like Willy Harris.

WALTER: Yes, people like Willy Harris.

RUTH (*with a sudden flash of impatience*): Why don't you all just hurry up and go into the banking business and stop talking about it!

WALTER: Why? You want to know why? 'Cause we all tied up in a race of people that don't know how to do nothing but moan, pray and have babies!

The line is too bitter even for him and he looks at her and sits down.

RUTH: Oh, Walter . . . (*softly*) Honey, why can't you stop fighting me?

WALTER (*without thinking*): Who's fighting you? Who even cares about you?

This line begins the retardation of his mood.

RUTH: Well—(*She waits a long time, and then with resignation starts to put away her things.*) I guess I might as well go on to bed . . . (*more or less to herself*) I don't know where we lost it . . . but we have . . . (*then, to him*) I—I'm sorry about this new baby, Walter. I guess maybe I better go on and do what I started . . . I guess I just didn't realize how bad things was with us . . . I guess I just didn't really realize—(*She starts out to the bedroom and stops.*) You want some hot milk?

WALTER: Hot milk?

RUTH: Yes—hot milk.

WALTER: Why hot milk?

RUTH: 'Cause after all that liquor you come home with you ought to have something hot in your stomach.

WALTER: I don't want no milk.

RUTH: You want some coffee then?

WALTER: No, I don't want no coffee. I don't want nothing hot to drink. (*almost plaintively*) Why you always trying to give me something to eat?

RUTH (*standing and looking at him helplessly*): What *else* can I give you, Walter Lee Younger?

She stands and looks at him and presently turns to go out again. He lifts his head and watches her going away from him in a new mood which began to emerge when he asked her "Who cares about you?"

WALTER: It's been rough, ain't it, baby? (*She hears and stops but does not turn around and he continues to her back.*) I guess between two people there ain't never as much understood as folks generally thinks there is. I mean like between me and you— (*She turns to face him.*) How we gets to the place where we scared to talk softness to each other. (*He waits, thinking hard himself.*) Why you think it got to be like that? (*He is thoughtful, almost as a child would be.*) Ruth, what is it gets into people ought to be close?

RUTH: I don't know, honey. I think about it a lot.

WALTER: On account of you and me, you mean? The way things are with us. The way something done come down between us.

RUTH: There ain't so much between us, Walter . . . Not when you come to me and try to talk to me. Try to be with me . . . a little even.

WALTER (*total honesty*): Sometimes . . . sometimes . . . I don't even know how to try.

RUTH: Walter—

WALTER: Yes?

RUTH (*coming to him, gently and with misgiving, but coming to him*): Honey . . . life don't have to be like this. I mean sometimes people can do things so that things are better . . . You remember how we used to talk when Travis was born . . . about the way we were going to live . . . the kind of house . . . (*She is stroking his head.*) Well, it's all starting to slip away from us . . .

He turns her to him and they look at each other and kiss, tenderly and hungrily. The door opens and MAMA *enters*—WALTER *breaks away and jumps up. A beat.*

WALTER: Mama, where have you been?

MAMA: My—them steps is longer than they used to be. Whew! (*She sits down and ignores him.*) How you feeling this evening, Ruth?

RUTH *shrugs, disturbed at having been interrupted and watching her husband knowingly.*

WALTER: Mama, where have you been all day?

MAMA (*still ignoring him and leaning on the table and changing to more comfortable shoes*): Where's Travis?

RUTH: I let him go out earlier and he ain't come back yet. Boy, is he going to get it!

WALTER: Mama!

MAMA (*as if she has heard him for the first time*): Yes, son?

WALTER: Where did you go this afternoon?

MAMA: I went downtown to tend to some business that I had to tend to.

WALTER: What kind of business?

MAMA: You know better than to question me like a child, Brother.

WALTER (*rising and bending over the table*): Where were you, Mama? (*bringing his fists down and shouting*) Mama, you didn't go do something with that insurance money, something crazy?

The front door opens slowly, interrupting him, and TRAVIS *peeks his head in, less than hopefully.*

TRAVIS (*to his mother*): Mama, I—

RUTH: "Mama I" nothing! You're going to get it, boy! Get on in that bedroom and get yourself ready!

TRAVIS: But I—

MAMA: Why don't you all never let the child explain hisself.

RUTH: Keep out of it now, Lena.

MAMA *clamps her lips together, and* RUTH *advances toward her son menacingly.*

RUTH: A thousand times I have told you not to go off like that—

MAMA (*holding out her arms to her grandson*): Well—at least let me tell him something. I want him to be the first one to hear . . . Come here, Travis. (*The boy obeys, gladly.*) Travis—(*She takes him by the shoulder and looks into his face.*)—you know that money we got in the mail this morning?

TRAVIS: Yes'm—

MAMA: Well—what you think your grandmama gone and done with that money?

TRAVIS: I don't know, Grandmama.

MAMA (*putting her finger on his nose for emphasis*): She went out and she bought you a house! (*The explosion comes from* WALTER *at the end of the revelation and he jumps up and turns away from all of them in a fury.* MAMA *continues, to* TRAVIS.) You glad about the house? It's going to be yours when you get to be a man.

TRAVIS: Yeah—I always wanted to live in a house.

MAMA: All right, gimme some sugar then—(TRAVIS *puts his arms around her neck as she watches her son over the boy's shoulder. Then, to* TRAVIS, *after the embrace.*) Now when you say your prayers tonight, you thank God and your grandfather—'cause it was him who give you the house—in his way.

RUTH (*taking the boy from* MAMA *and pushing him toward the bedroom*): Now you get out of here and get ready for your beating.

TRAVIS: Aw, Mama—

RUTH: Get on in there—(*closing the door behind him and turning radiantly to her mother-in-law*) So you went and did it!

MAMA (*quietly, looking at her son with pain*): Yes, I did.

RUTH (*raising both arms classically*): PRAISE GOD! (*Looks at* WALTER *a moment, who says nothing. She crosses rapidly to her husband.*) Please, honey—let me be glad . . . you be glad too. (*She has laid her hands on his shoulders, but he shakes himself free of her roughly, without turning to face her.*) Oh, Walter . . . a home . . . *a home.* (*She comes back to* MAMA.) Well—where is it? How big is it? How much it going to cost?

MAMA: Well—

RUTH: When we moving?

MAMA (*smiling at her*): First of the month.

RUTH (*throwing back her head with jubilance*): *Praise God!*

MAMA (*tentatively, still looking at her son's back turned against her and* RUTH): It's—it's a nice house too . . . (*She cannot help speaking directly to him. An imploring quality in her voice, her manner, makes her almost like a girl now.*) Three bedrooms—nice big one for you and Ruth . . . Me and Beneatha still have to share our room, but Travis have one of his own—and (*with difficulty*) I figure if the—new baby—is a boy, we could get one of them double-decker outfits . . . And there's a yard with a little patch of dirt where I could maybe get to grow me a few flowers . . . And a nice big basement . . .

RUTH: Walter honey, be glad—

MAMA (*still to his back, fingering things on the table*): 'Course I don't want to make it sound fancier than it is . . . It's just a plain little old house—but it's made good and solid—and it will be *ours*. Walter Lee—it makes a difference in a man when he can walk on floors that belong to *him* . . .

RUTH: Where is it?

MAMA (*frightened at this telling*): Well—well—it's out there in Clybourne Park—

RUTH'S *radiance fades abruptly, and* WALTER *finally turns slowly to face his mother with incredulity and hostility.*

RUTH: Where?

MAMA (*matter-of-factly*): Four o six Clybourne Street, Clybourne Park.

RUTH: Clybourne Park? Mama, there ain't no colored people living in Clybourne Park.

MAMA (*almost idiotically*): Well, I guess there's going to be some now.

WALTER (*bitterly*): So that's the peace and comfort you went out and bought for us today!

MAMA (*raising her eyes to meet his finally*): Son—I just tried to find the nicest place for the least amount of money for my family.

RUTH (*trying to recover from the shock*): Well—well—'course I ain't one never been 'fraid of no crackers, mind you—but—well, wasn't there no other houses nowhere?

MAMA: Them houses they put up for colored in them areas way out all seem to cost twice as much as other houses. I did the best I could.

RUTH (*Struck senseless with the news, in its various degrees of goodness and trouble, she sits a moment, her fists propping her chin in thought, and then she starts to rise, bringing her fists down with vigor, the radiance spreading from cheek to cheek again.*): Well— well!—All I can say is—if this is my time in life—MY TIME—to say good-bye—(*And she builds with momentum as she starts to circle the room with an exuberant, almost tearfully happy release.*)—to these Goddamned cracking walls!—(*She pounds the walls.*)—and these marching roaches!—(*She wipes at an imaginary army of marching roaches.*)—and this cramped little closet which ain't now or never was no kitchen! . . . then I say it loud and good, HALLELUJAH! AND GOOD-BYE MISERY . . . I DON'T NEVER WANT TO SEE YOUR UGLY FACE AGAIN! (*She laughs joyously, having practically destroyed the apartment, and flings her arms up and lets them come down happily, slowly, reflectively, over her abdomen, aware for the first time perhaps that the life therein pulses with happiness and not despair.*) Lena?

MAMA (*moved, watching her happiness*): Yes, honey?

RUTH (*looking off*): Is there—is there a whole lot of sunlight?

MAMA (*understanding*): Yes, child, there's a whole lot of sunlight.

Long pause.

RUTH (*collecting herself and going to the door of the room* TRAVIS *is in*): Well—I guess I better see 'bout Travis. (*to* MAMA) Lord, I sure don't feel like whipping nobody today!

She exits.

MAMA (*The mother and son are left alone now and the mother waits a long time, considering deeply, before she speaks.*): Son—you—you understand what I done, don't you? (WALTER *is silent and sullen.*) I—I just seen my family falling apart today . . . just falling to pieces in front of my eyes . . . We couldn't of gone on like we was today. We was going backwards 'stead of forwards—talking 'bout killing babies and wishing each other was dead . . . When it gets like that in life—you just got to do something different, push on out and do something bigger . . . (*She waits.*) I wish you say something, son . . . I wish you'd say how deep inside you think I done the right thing—

WALTER (*crossing slowly to his bedroom door and finally turning there and speaking measuredly*): What you need me to say you done right for? *You* the head of this family. You run our lives like you want to. It was your money and you did what you wanted with it. So what you need for me to say it was all right for? (*bitterly, to hurt her as deeply as he knows is possible*) So you butchered up a dream of mine—you—who always talking 'bout your children's dreams . . .

MAMA: Walter Lee—

He just closes the door behind him. MAMA *sits alone, thinking heavily.*

Curtain.

SCENE 2

TIME: *Friday night. A few weeks later.*

AT RISE: *Packing crates mark the intention of the family to move.* BENEATHA *and* GEORGE *come in, presumably from an evening out again.*

GEORGE: O.K. . . . O.K., whatever you say . . . (*They both sit on the couch. He tries to kiss her. She moves away.*) Look, we've had a nice evening; let's not spoil it, huh? . . .

He again turns her head and tries to nuzzle in and she turns away from him, not with distaste but with momentary lack of interest; in a mood to pursue what they were talking about.

BENEATHA: I'm *trying* to talk to you.

GEORGE: We always talk.

BENEATHA: Yes—and I love to talk.

GEORGE (*exasperated; rising*): I know it and I don't mind it sometimes . . . I want you to cut it out, see—The moody stuff, I mean. I don't like it. You're a nice-looking girl . . . all over. That's all you need, honey, forget the atmosphere. Guys aren't going to go for the atmosphere—they're going to go for what they see. Be glad for that. Drop the Garbo routine. It doesn't go with you. As for myself, I want a nice—(*groping*)—simple (*thoughtfully*)—sophisticated girl . . . not a poet—O.K.?

He starts to kiss her, she rebuffs him again and he jumps up.

BENEATHA: Why are you angry, George?

GEORGE: Because this is stupid! I don't go out with you to discuss the nature of "quiet desperation" or to hear all about your thoughts—because the world will go on thinking what it thinks regardless—

BENEATHA: Then why read books? Why go to school?

GEORGE (*with artificial patience, counting on his fingers*): It's simple. You read books— to learn facts—to get grades—to pass the course—to get a degree. That's all—it has nothing to do with thoughts.

A long pause.

BENEATHA: I see. (*He starts to sit.*) Good night, George.

GEORGE *looks at her a little oddly, and starts to exit. He meets* MAMA *coming in.*

GEORGE: Oh—hello, Mrs. Younger.

MAMA: Hello, George, how you feeling?

GEORGE: Fine—fine, how are you?

MAMA: Oh, a little tired. You know them steps can get you after a day's work. You all have a nice time tonight?

GEORGE: Yes—a fine time. A fine time.

MAMA: Well, good night.

GEORGE: Good night. (*He exits.* MAMA *closes the door behind her.*) Hello, honey. What you sitting like that for?

BENEATHA: I'm just sitting.

MAMA: Didn't you have a nice time?

BENEATHA: No.

MAMA: No? What's the matter?

BENEATHA: Mama, George is a fool—honest. (*She rises.*)

MAMA (*Hustling around unloading the packages she has entered with. She stops.*): Is he, baby?

BENEATHA: Yes.

BENEATHA *makes up* TRAVIS' *bed as she talks.*

MAMA: You sure?

BENEATHA: yes.

MAMA: Well—I guess you better not waste your time with no fools.

BENEATHA *looks up at her mother, watching her put groceries in the refrigerator. Finally she gathers up her things and starts into the bedroom. At the door she stops and looks back at her mother.*

BENEATHA: Mama—

MAMA: Yes, baby—

BENEATHA: Thank you.

MAMA: For what?

BENEATHA: For understanding me this time.

She exits quickly and the mother stands, smiling a little, looking at the place where BENEATHA *just stood.* RUTH *enters.*

RUTH: Now don't you fool with any of this stuff, Lena—

MAMA: Oh, I just thought I'd sort a few things out. Is Brother here?

RUTH: Yes.

MAMA (*with concern*): Is he—

RUTH (*reading her eyes*): Yes.

MAMA *is silent and someone knocks on the door.* MAMA *and* RUTH *exchange weary and knowing glances and* RUTH *opens it to admit the neighbor,* MRS. JOHNSON,* *who is a rather squeaky wide-eyed lady of no particular age, with a newspaper under her arm.*

---

*This character and the scene of her visit were cut from the original production and early editions of the play.

MAMA (*changing her expression to acute delight and a ringing cheerful greeting*): Oh—hello there, Johnson.

JOHNSON (*This is a woman who decided long ago to be enthusiastic about EVERYTHING in life and she is inclined to wave her wrist vigorously at the height of her exclamatory comments.*): Hello there, yourself! H'you this evening, Ruth?

RUTH (*not much of a deceptive type*): Fine, Mis' Johnson, h'you?

JOHNSON: Fine. (*reaching out quickly, playfully, and patting RUTH's stomach*) Ain't you starting to poke out none yet! (*She mugs with delight at the over-familiar remark and her eyes dart around looking at the crates and packing preparation; MAMA's face is a cold sheet of endurance.*) Oh, ain't we getting ready round here, though! Yessir! Lookathere! I'm telling you the Youngers is really getting ready to "move on up a little higher!"—Bless God!

MAMA (*a little drily, doubting the total sincerity of the Blesser*): Bless God.

JOHNSON: He's good, ain't He?

MAMA: Oh yes, He's good.

JOHNSON: I mean sometimes He works in mysterious ways . . . but He works, don't He!

MAMA (*the same*): Yes, he does.

JOHNSON: I'm just soooooo happy for y'all. And this here child—(*about RUTH*) looks like she could just pop open with happiness, don't she. Where's all the rest of the family?

MAMA: Bennie's gone to bed—

JOHNSON: Ain't no . . . (*The implication is pregnancy.*) sickness done hit you—I hope . . . ?

MAMA: No—she just tired. She was out this evening.

JOHNSON (*All is a coo, an emphatic coo.*): Aw—ain't that lovely. She still going out with the little Murchison boy?

MAMA (*drily*): Ummmm huh.

JOHNSON: That's lovely. You sure got lovely children, Younger. Me and Isaiah talks all the time 'bout what fine children you was blessed with. We sure do.

MAMA: Ruth, give Mis' Johnson a piece of sweet potato pie and some milk.

JOHNSON: Oh honey, I can't stay hardly a minute—I just dropped in to see if there was anything I could do. (*accepting the food easily*) I guess y'all seen the news what's all over the colored paper this week . . .

MAMA: No—didn't get mine yet this week.

JOHNSON (*lifting her head and blinking with the spirit of catastrophe*): You mean you ain't read 'bout them colored people that was bombed out their place out there?

RUTH *straightens with concern and takes the paper and reads it.* JOHNSON *notices her and feeds commentary.*

JOHNSON: Ain't it something how bad these here white folks is getting here in Chicago! Lord, getting so you think you right down in Mississippi! (*with a tremendous and rather insincere sense of melodrama*) 'Course I thinks it's wonderful how our folks keeps on pushing out. You hear some of these Negroes round here talking 'bout how they don't go where they ain't wanted and all that—but not me, honey! (*This is a lie.*) Wilhemenia Othella Johnson goes anywhere, any time she feels like it! (*with head movement for emphasis*) Yes I do! Why if we left it up to these here crackers, the poor niggers wouldn't have nothing—(*She clasps her hand over her mouth.*) Oh, I always forgets you don't 'low that word in your house.

MAMA (*quietly, looking at her*): No—I don't 'low it.

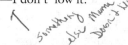

JOHNSON (*vigorously again*): Me neither! I was just telling Isaiah yesterday when he come using it in front of me—I said, "Isaiah, it's just like Mis' Younger says all the time—"

MAMA: Don't you want some more pie?

JOHNSON: No—no thank you; this was lovely. I got to get on over home and have my midnight coffee. I hear some people say it don't let them sleep but I finds I can't close my eyes right lessen I done had that laaaast cup of coffee . . . (*She waits. A beat. Undaunted.*) My Goodnight coffee, I calls it!

MAMA (*with much eye-rolling and communication between herself and* RUTH): Ruth, why don't you give Mis' Johnson some coffee.

RUTH *gives* MAMA *an unpleasant look for her kindness.*

JOHNSON (*accepting the coffee*): Where's Brother tonight?

MAMA: He's lying down.

JOHNSON: MMmmmmm, he sure gets his beauty rest, don't he? Good-looking man. Sure is a good-looking man! (*reaching out to pat* RUTH's *stomach again*) I guess that's how come we keep on having babies around here. (*She winks at* MAMA.) One thing 'bout Brother, he always know how to have a *good* time. And soooooo ambitious! I bet it was his idea y'all moving out to Clybourne Park. Lord—I bet this time next month y'all's names will have been in the papers plenty—(*holding up her hands to mark off each word of the headline she can see in front of her*) "NE-GROES INVADE CLYBOURNE PARK—BOMBED!"

MAMA (*She and* RUTH *look at the woman in amazement.*): We ain't exactly moving out there to get bombed.

JOHNSON: Oh, honey—you know I'm praying to God every day that don't nothing like that happen! But you have to think of life like it is—and these here Chicago peck-erwoods is some baaaad peckerwoods.

MAMA (*wearily*): We done thought about all that Mis' Johnson.

BENEATHA *comes out of the bedroom in her robe and passes through to the bathroom.*
MRS. JOHNSON *turns.*

JOHNSON: Hello there, Bennie!

BENEATHA (*crisply*): Hello, Mrs. Johnson.

JOHNSON: How is school?

BENEATHA (*crisply*): Fine, thank you. (*She goes out.*)

JOHNSON (*insulted*): Getting so she don't have much to say to nobody.

MAMA: The child was on her way to the bathroom.

JOHNSON: I know—but sometimes she act like ain't got time to pass the time of day with nobody ain't been to college. Oh—I ain't criticizing her none. It's just—you know how some of our young people gets when they get a little education. (MAMA *and* RUTH *say nothing, just look at her.*) Yes—well. Well, I guess I better get on home. (*unmoving*) 'Course I can understand how she must be proud and everything—being the only one in the family to make something of herself. I know just being a chauffeur ain't never satisfied Brother none. He shouldn't feel like that, though. Ain't nothing wrong with being a chauffeur.

MAMA: There's plenty wrong with it.

JOHNSON: What?

MAMA: Plenty. My husband always said being any kind of a servant wasn't a fit thing for a man to have to be. He always said a man's hands was made to make things, or to turn the earth with—not to drive nobody's car for 'em—or—(*She looks at her own hands.*) carry they slop jars. And my boy is just like him—he wasn't meant to wait on nobody.

JOHNSON (*rising, somewhat offended*): Mmmmmmmmmm. The Youngers is too much for me! (*She looks around.*) You sure one proud-acting bunch of colored folks. Well—I always thinks like Booker T. Washington said that time—"Education has spoiled many a good plow hand"—

MAMA: Is that what old Booker T. said?

JOHNSON: He sure did.

MAMA: Well, it sounds just like him. The fool.

JOHNSON (*indignantly*): Well—he was one of our great men.

MAMA: Who said so?

JOHNSON (*nonplussed*): You know, me and you ain't never agreed about some things, Lena Younger. I guess I better be going—

RUTH (*quickly*): Good night.

JOHNSON: Good night. Oh—(*thrusting it at her*) You can keep the paper! (*with a trill*) 'Night.

MAMA: Good night, Mis' Johnson.

MRS. JOHNSON *exits.*

RUTH: If ignorance was gold . . .

MAMA: Shush. Don't talk about folks behind their backs.

RUTH: You do.

MAMA: I'm old and corrupted. (BENEATHA *enters.*) You was rude to Mis' Johnson, Beneatha, and I don't like it at all.

BENEATHA (*at her door*): Mama, if there are two things we, as a people, have got to overcome, one is the Klu Klux Klan—and the other is Mrs. Johnson. (*She exits.*)

MAMA: Smart aleck.

The phone rings.

RUTH: I'll get it.

MAMA: Lord, ain't this a popular place tonight.

RUTH (*at the phone*): Hello—Just a minute. (*goes to door*) Walter, it's Mrs. Arnold. (*Waits. Goes back to the phone. Tense.*) Hello. Yes, this is his wife speaking . . . He's lying down now. Yes . . . well, he'll be in tomorrow. He's been very sick. Yes—I know we should have called, but we were so sure he'd be able to come in today. Yes—yes, I'm very sorry. Yes . . . Thank you very much. (*She hangs up.* WALTER *is standing in the doorway of the bedroom behind her.*) That was Mrs. Arnold.

WALTER (*indifferently*): Was it?

RUTH: She said if you don't come in tomorrow that they are getting a new man . . .

WALTER: Ain't that sad—ain't that crying sad.

RUTH: She said Mr. Arnold has had to take a cab for three days . . . Walter, you ain't been to work for three days! (*This is a revelation to her.*) Where you been, Walter Lee Younger? (WALTER *looks at her and starts to laugh.*) You're going to lose your job.

WALTER: That's right . . . (*He turns on the radio.*)

RUTH: Oh, Walter, and with your mother working like a dog every day—

A steamy, deep blues pours into the room.

Walter is fine but just won't go because he couldn't figrd tris way childish.

WALTER: That's sad too—Everything is sad.

MAMA: What you been doing for these three days, son?

WALTER: Mama—you don't know all the things a man what got leisure can find to do in this city . . . What's this—Friday night? Well—Wednesday I borrowed Willy Harris' car and I went for a drive . . . just me and myself and I drove and drove . . . Way out . . . way past South Chicago, and I parked the car and I sat and looked at the steel mills all day long. I just sat in the car and looked at them big black chimneys for hours. Then I drove back and I went to the Green Hat. (*pause*) And Thursday—Thursday I borrowed the car again and I got in it and I pointed it the other way and I drove the other way—for hours—way, way up to Wisconsin, and I looked at the farms. I just drove and looked at the farms. Then I drove back and I went to the Green Hat. (*pause*) And today—today I didn't get the car. Today I just walked. All over the Southside. And I looked at the Negroes and they looked at me and finally I just sat down on the curb at Thirty-ninth and South Parkway and I just sat there and watched the Negroes go by. And then I went to the Green Hat. You all sad? You all depressed? And you know where I am going right now—

RUTH *goes out quietly.*

MAMA: Oh, Big Walter, is this the harvest of our days? *[handwritten: ← The children therapy]*

WALTER: You know what I like about the Green Hat? I like this little cat they got there who blows a sax . . . He blows. He talks to me. He ain't but 'bout five feet tall and he's got a conked head and his eyes is always closed and he's all music—

MAMA (*rising and getting some papers out of her handbag*): Walter—

WALTER: And there's this other guy who plays the piano . . . and they got a sound. I mean they can work on some music . . . They got the best little combo in the world in the Green Hat . . . You can just sit there and drink and listen to them three men play and you realize that don't nothing matter worth a damn, but just being there—

MAMA: I've helped do it to you, haven't I, son? Walter I been wrong.

WALTER: Naw—you ain't never been wrong about nothing, Mama.

MAMA: Listen to me, now. I say I been wrong, son. That I been doing to you what the rest of the world been doing to you. (*She turns off the radio.*) Walter—(*She stops and he looks up slowly at her and she meets his eyes pleadingly.*) What you ain't never understood is that I ain't got nothing, don't own nothing, ain't never really wanted nothing that wasn't for you. There ain't nothing as precious to me . . . There ain't nothing worth holding on to, money, dreams, nothing else—if it means—if it means it's going to destroy my boy. (*She takes an envelope out of her handbag and puts it in front of him and he watches her without speaking or moving.*) I paid the man thirty-five hundred dollars down on the house. That leaves sixty-five hundred dollars. Monday morning I want you to take this money and take three thousand dollars and put it in a savings account for Beneatha's medical schooling. The rest you put in a checking account—with your name on it. And from now on any penny that come out of it or that go in it is for you to look after. For you to decide. (*She drops her hands a little helplessly.*) It ain't much, but it's all I got in the world and I'm putting it in your hands. I'm telling you to be the head of this family from now on like you supposed to be. *[handwritten: ← showing a lot of Trust]*

WALTER (*stares at the money*): You trust me like that, Mama?

MAMA: I ain't never stop trusting you. Like I ain't never stop loving you.

She goes out, and WALTER *sits looking at the money on the table. Finally, in a decisive gesture, he gets up, and, in mingled joy and desperation, picks up the money. At the same moment,* TRAVIS *enters for bed.*

TRAVIS: What's the matter, Daddy? You drunk?

WALTER (*sweetly, more sweetly than we have ever known him*): No, Daddy ain't drunk. Daddy ain't going to never be drunk again . . .

TRAVIS: Well, good night, Daddy.

The FATHER *has come from behind the couch and leans over, embracing his son.*

WALTER: Son, I feel like talking to you tonight.

TRAVIS: About what?

WALTER: Oh, about a lot of things. About you and what kind of man you going to be when you grow up . . . Son—son, what do you want to be when you grow up?

TRAVIS: A bus driver.

WALTER (*laughing a little*): A what? Man, that ain't nothing to want to be!

TRAVIS: Why not?

WALTER: 'Cause, man—it ain't big enough—you know what I mean.

TRAVIS: I don't know then. I can't make up my mind. Sometimes Mama asks me that too. And sometimes when I tell her I just want to be like you—she says she don't want me to be like that and sometimes she says she does . . .

WALTER (*gathering him up in his arms*): You know what, Travis? In seven years you going to be seventeen years old. And things is going to be very different with us in seven years, Travis . . . One day when you are seventeen I'll come home—home from my office downtown somewhere—

TRAVIS: You don't work in no office, Daddy.

WALTER: No—but after tonight. After what your daddy gonna do tonight, there's going to be offices—a whole lot of offices . . .

TRAVIS: What you gonna do tonight, Daddy?

WALTER: You wouldn't understand yet, son, but your daddy's gonna make a transaction . . . a business transaction that's going to change our lives . . . That's how come one day when you 'bout seventeen years old I'll come home and I'll be pretty tired, you know what I mean, after a day of conferences and secretaries getting things wrong the way they do . . . 'cause an executive's life is hell, man— (*The more he talks the farther away he gets.*) And I'll pull the car up on the driveway . . . just a plain black Chrysler, I think, with white walls—no—black tires. More elegant. Rich people don't have to be flashy . . . though I'll have to get something a little sportier for Ruth—maybe a Cadillac convertible to do her shopping in . . . And I'll come up the steps to the house and the gardener will be clipping away at the hedges and he'll say, "Good evening, Mr. Younger." And I'll say, "Hello, Jefferson, how are you this evening?" And I'll go inside and Ruth will come downstairs and meet me at the door and we'll kiss each other and she'll take my arm and we'll go up to your room to see you sitting on the floor with the catalogues of all the great schools in America around you . . . All the great schools in the world! And—and I'll say, all right son—it's your seventeenth birthday, what is it you've decided? . . . Just tell me where you want to go to school and you'll *go*. Just tell me, what it is you want to be—and you'll *be* it . . . Whatever you want to be—Yessir! (*He holds his arms open for* TRAVIS.) You just name it, son . . . (TRAVIS *leaps into them.*) and I hand you the world!

WALTER'S *voice has risen in pitch and hysterical promise and on the last line he lifts* TRAVIS *high.*

(*Blackout*)

SCENE 3

TIME: *Saturday, moving day, one week later.*

Before the curtain rises, RUTH'S *voice, a strident, dramatic church alto, cuts through the silence.*

It is, in the darkness, a triumphant surge, a penetrating statement of expectation: "Oh, Lord, I don't feel no ways tired! Children, oh, glory hallelujah!"

As the curtain rises we see that RUTH *is alone in the living room, finishing up the family's packing. It is moving day. She is nailing crates and tying cartons.* BENEATHA *enters, carrying a guitar case, and watches her exuberant sister-in-law.*

RUTH: Hey!

BENEATHA (*putting away the case*): Hi.

RUTH (*pointing at a package*): Honey—look in that package there and see what I found on sale this morning at the South Center. (RUTH *gets up and moves to the package and draws out some curtains.*) Lookahere—hand-turned hems!

BENEATHA: How do you know the window size out there?

RUTH (*who hadn't thought of that*): Oh—Well, they bound to fit something in the whole house. Anyhow, they was too good a bargain to pass up. (RUTH *slaps her head, suddenly remembering something.*) Oh, Bennie—I meant to put a special note on that carton over there. That's your mama's good china and she wants 'em to be very careful with it.

BENEATHA: I'll do it.

BENEATHA *finds a piece of paper and starts to draw large letters on it.*

RUTH: You know what I'm going to do soon as I get in that new house?

BENEATHA: What?

RUTH: Honey—I'm going to run me a tub of water up to here . . . (*with her fingers practically up to her nostrils*) And I'm going to get in it—and I am going to sit . . . and sit . . . and sit in that hot water and the first person who knocks to tell *me* to hurry up and come out—

BENEATHA: Gets shot at sunrise.

RUTH (*laughing happily*): You said it, sister! (*noticing how large* BENEATHA *is absent-mindedly making the note*) Honey, they ain't going to read that from no airplane.

BENEATHA (*laughing herself*): I guess I always think things have more emphasis if they are big, somehow.

RUTH (*looking up at her and smiling*): You and your brother seem to have that as a philosophy of life. Lord, that man—done changed so 'round here. You know— you know what we did last night? Me and Walter Lee?

BENEATHA: What?

RUTH (*smiling to herself*): We went to the movies. (*looking at* BENEATHA *to see if she understands*) We went to the movies. You know the last time me and Walter went to the movies together?

BENEATHA: No.

RUTH: Me neither. That's how long it been. (*smiling again*) But we went last night. The picture wasn't much good, but that didn't seem to matter. We went—and we held hands.

BENEATHA: Oh, Lord!

RUTH: We held hands—and you know what?

BENEATHA: What?

RUTH: When we come out of the show it was late and dark and all the stores and things was closed up . . . and it was kind of chilly and there wasn't many people on the streets . . . and we was still holding hands, me and Walter.

BENEATHA: You're killing me.

WALTER *enters with a large package. His happiness is deep in him; he cannot keep still with his new-found exuberance. He is singing and wiggling and snapping his fingers. He puts his package in a corner and puts a phonograph record, which he has brought in with him, on the record player. As the music, soulful and sensuous, comes up he dances over to* RUTH *and tries to get her to dance with him. She gives in at last to his raunchiness and in a fit of giggling allows herself to be drawn into his mood. They dip and she melts into his arms in a classic, body-melding "slow drag."*

BENEATHA (*regarding them a long time as they dance, then drawing in her breath for a deeply exaggerated comment which she does not particularly mean*): Talk about—old-dddddddddd-fashiondddddddd—Negroes!

WALTER (*stopping momentarily*): What kind of Negroes?

He says this in fun. He is not angry with her today, nor with anyone. He starts to dance with his wife again.

BENEATHA: Old-fashioned.

WALTER (*as he dances with* RUTH): You know, when these *New Negroes* have their convention—(*pointing at his sister*)—that is going to be the chairman of the Committee on Unending Agitation. (*He goes on dancing, then stops.*) Race, race, race! . . . Girl, I do believe you are the first person in the history of the entire human race to successfully brainwash yourself. (BENEATHA *breaks up and he goes on dancing. He stops again, enjoying his tease.*) Damn, even the N double A C P takes a holiday sometimes! (BENEATHA *and* RUTH *laugh. He dances with* RUTH *some more and starts to laugh and stops and pantomimes someone over an operating table.*) I can just see that chick someday looking down at some poor cat on an operating table and before she starts to slice him, she says . . . (*pulling his sleeves back maliciously*) "By the way, what are your views on civil rights down there? . . . "
He laughs at her again and starts to dance happily. The bell sounds.

BENEATHA: Sticks and stones may break my bones but . . . words will never hurt me!

BENEATHA *goes to the door and opens it as* WALTER *and* RUTH *go on with the clowning.* BENEATHA *is somewhat surprised to see a quiet-looking middle-aged white man in a business suit holding his hat and a briefcase in his hand and consulting a small piece of paper.*

MAN: Uh—how do you do, miss. I am looking for a Mrs.— (*He looks at the slip of paper.*) Mrs. Lena Younger? (*He stops short, struck dumb at the sight of the oblivious* WALTER *and* RUTH.)

BENEATHA (*smoothing her hair with slight embarrassment*): Oh—yes, that's my mother.

Excuse me. (*She closes the door and turns to quiet the other two.*) Ruth! Brother! (*Enunciating precisely but soundlessly: "There's a white man at the door!" They stop dancing,* RUTH *cuts off the phonograph,* BENEATHA *opens the door. The man casts a curious quick glance at all of them.*) Uh—come in please.

MAN (*coming in*): Thank you.

BENEATHA: My mother isn't here just now. Is it business?

MAN: Yes . . . well, of a sort.

WALTER (*freely, the Man of the House*): Have a seat. I'm Mrs. Younger's son. I look after most of her business matters.

RUTH *and* BENEATHA *exchange amused glances.*

MAN (*regarding* WALTER, *and sitting*): Well—My name is Karl Lindner . . .

WALTER (*stretching out his hand*): Walter Younger. This is my wife—(RUTH *nods politely.*)—and my sister.

LINDNER: How do you do.

WALTER (*amiably, as he sits himself easily on a chair, leaning forward on his knees with interest and looking expectantly into the newcomer's face*): What can we do for you, Mr. Lindner!

LINDNER (*some minor shuffling of the hat and briefcase on his knees*): Well—I am a representative of the Clybourne Park Improvement Association—

WALTER (*pointing*): Why don't you sit your things on the floor?

LINDNER: Oh—yes. Thank you. (*He slides the briefcase and hat under the chair.*) And as I was saying—I am from the Clybourne Park Improvement Association and we have had it brought to our attention at the last meeting that you people—or at least your mother—has bought a piece of residential property at—(*He digs for the slip of paper again.*)—four o six Clybourne Street . . .

WALTER: That's right. Care for something to drink? Ruth, get Mr. Lindner a beer.

LINDNER (*upset for some reason*): Oh—no, really. I mean thank you very much, but no thank you.

RUTH (*innocently*): Some coffee?

LINDNER: Thank you, nothing at all.

BENEATHA *is watching the man carefully.*

LINDNER: Well, I don't know how much you folks know about our organization. (*He is a gentle man; thoughtful and somewhat labored in his manner.*) It is one of these community organizations set up to look after—oh, you know, things like block upkeep and special projects and we also have what we call our New Neighbors Orientation Committee . . .

BENEATHA (*drily*): Yes—and what do they do?

LINDNER (*turning a little to her and then returning the main force to* WALTER): Well—it's what you might call a sort of welcoming committee, I guess. I mean they, we—I'm the chairman of the committee—go around and see the new people who move into the neighborhood and sort of give them the lowdown on the way we do things out in Clybourne Park.

BENEATHA (*with appreciation of the two meanings, which escape* RUTH *and* WALTER): Uh-huh.

LINDNER: And we also have the category of what the association calls—(*He looks elsewhere.*)—uh—special community problems . . .

BENEATHA: Yes—and what are some of those?

WALTER: Girl, let the man talk.

LINDNER (*with understated relief*): Thank you. I would sort of like to explain this thing in my own way. I mean I want to explain to you in a certain way.

WALTER: Go ahead.

LINDNER: Yes. Well. I'm going to try to get right to the point. I'm sure we'll all appreciate that in the long run.

BENEATHA: Yes.

WALTER: Be still now!

LINDNER: Well—

RUTH (*still innocently*): Would you like another chair—you don't look comfortable.

LINDNER (*more frustrated than annoyed*): No, thank you very much. Please. Well—to get right to the point I—(*A great breath, and he is off at last.*) I am sure you people must be aware of some of the incidents which have happened in various parts of the city when colored people have moved into certain areas—(BENEATHA *exhales heavily and starts tossing a piece of fruit up and down in the air.*) Well—because we have what I think is going to be a unique type of organization in American community life—not only do we deplore that kind of thing—but we are trying to do something about it. (BENEATHA *stops tossing and turns with a new and quizzical interest to the man.*) We feel—(*gaining confidence in his mission because of the interest in the faces of the people he is talking to*)—we feel that most of the trouble in this world, when you come right down to it—(*He hits his knee for emphasis.*)—most of the trouble exists because people just don't sit down and talk to each other.

RUTH (*nodding as she might in church, pleased with the remark*): You can say that again, mister.

LINDNER (*more encouraged by such affirmation*): That we don't try hard enough in this world to understand the other fellow's problem. The other guy's point of view.

RUTH: Now that's right.

BENEATHA *and* WALTER *merely watch and listen with genuine interest.*

LINDNER: Yes—that's the way we feel out in Clybourne Park. And that's why I was elected to come here this afternoon and talk to you people. Friendly like, you know, the way people should talk to each other and see if we couldn't find some way to work this thing out. As I say, the whole business is a matter of *caring* about the other fellow. Anybody can see that you are a nice family of folks, hard working and honest I'm sure. (BENEATHA *frowns slightly, quizzically, her head tilted regarding him.*) Today everybody knows what it means to be on the outside of *something.* And of course, there is always somebody who is out to take advantage of people who don't always understand.

WALTER: What do you mean?

LINDNER: Well—you see our community is made up of people who've worked hard as the dickens for years to build up that little community. They're not rich and fancy people; just hard-working, honest people who don't really have much but those little homes and a dream of the kind of community they want to raise their children in. Now, I don't say we are perfect and there is a lot wrong in some of the things they want. But you've got to admit that a man, right or wrong, has the right to want to have the neighborhood he lives in a certain kind of way. And at the moment the overwhelming majority of our people out there feel that people get along better, take more of a common interest in the life of the community, when they share a common background. I want you to believe me when I tell you that race prejudice simply doesn't enter into it. It is a matter of the people of

Clybourne Park believing, rightly or wrongly, as I say, that for the happiness of all concerned that our Negro families are happier when they live in their *own* communities.

BENEATHA (*with a grand and bitter gesture*): This, friends, is the Welcoming Committee!

WALTER (*dumfounded, looking at* LINDNER): Is this what you came marching all the way over here to tell us?

LINDNER: Well, now we've been having a fine conversation. I hope you'll hear me all the way through.

WALTER (*tightly*): Go ahead, man.

LINDNER: You see—in the face of all the things I have said, we are prepared to make your family a very generous offer . . .

BENEATHA: Thirty pieces and not a coin less!

WALTER: Yeah?

LINDNER (*putting on his glasses and drawing a form out of the briefcase*): Our association is prepared, through the collective effort of our people, to buy the house from you at a financial gain to your family.

RUTH: Lord have mercy, ain't this the living gall!

WALTER: All right, you through?

LINDNER: Well, I want to give you the exact terms of the financial arrangement—

WALTER: We don't want to hear no exact terms of no arrangements. I want to know if you got any more to tell us 'bout getting together?

LINDNER (*taking off his glasses*): Well—I don't suppose that you feel . . .

WALTER: Never mind how I feel—you got any more to say 'bout how people ought to sit down and talk to each other? . . . Get out of my house, man.

He turns his back and walks to the door.

LINDNER (*looking around at the hostile faces and reaching and assembling his hat and briefcase*): Well—I don't understand why you people are reacting this way. What do you think you are going to gain by moving into a neighborhood where you just aren't wanted and where some elements—well—people can get awful worked up when they feel that their whole way of life and everything they've ever worked for is threatened.

WALTER: Get out.

LINDNER (*at the door, holding a small card*): Well—I'm sorry it went like this.

WALTER: Get out.

LINDNER (*almost sadly regarding* WALTER): You just can't force people to change their hearts, son.

He turns and put his card on a table and exits. WALTER *pushes the door to with stinging hatred, and stands looking at it.* RUTH *just sits and* BENEATHA *just stands. They say nothing.* MAMA *and* TRAVIS *enter.*

MAMA: Well—this all the packing got done since I left out of here this morning. I testify before God that my children got all the energy of the *dead!* What time the moving men due?

BENEATHA: Four o'clock. You had a caller, Mama.

She is smiling, teasingly.

MAMA: Sure enough—who?

BENEATHA (*her arms folded saucily*): The Welcoming Committee.

WALTER *and* RUTH *giggle.*

MAMA (*innocently*): Who?

BENEATHA: The Welcoming Committee. They said they're sure going to be glad to see you when you get there.

WALTER (*devilishly*): Yeah, they said they can't hardly wait to see your face.

Laughter.

MAMA (*sensing their facetiousness*): What's the matter with you all?

WALTER: Ain't nothing the matter with us. We just telling you 'bout the gentleman who came to see you this afternoon. From the Clybourne Park Improvement Association.

MAMA: What he want?

RUTH (*in the same mood as* BENEATHA *and* WALTER): To welcome you, honey.

WALTER: He said they can't hardly wait. He said the one thing they don't have, that they just *dying* to have out there is a fine family of fine colored people! (*to* RUTH *and* BENEATHA) Ain't that right!

RUTH (*mockingly*): Yeah! He left his card—

BENEATHA (*handing card to* MAMA): In case.

MAMA *reads and throws it on the floor—understanding and looking off as she draws her chair up to the table on which she has put her plant and some sticks and some cord.*

MAMA: Father, give us strength. (*knowingly—and without fun*) Did he threaten us?

BENEATHA: Oh—Mama—they don't do it like that any more. He talked Brotherhood. He said everybody ought to learn how to sit down and hate each other with good Christian fellowship.

She and WALTER *shake hands to ridicule the remark.*

MAMA (*sadly*): Lord, protect us . . .

RUTH: You should hear the money those folks raised to buy the house from us. All we paid and then some.

BENEATHA: What they think we going to do—eat 'em?

RUTH: No, honey, marry 'em.

MAMA (*shaking her head*): Lord, Lord, Lord . . .

RUTH: Well—that's the way the crackers crumble. (*a beat*) Joke.

BENEATHA (*laughingly noticing what her mother is doing*): Mama, what are you doing?

MAMA: Fixing my plant so it won't get hurt none on the way . . .

BENEATHA: Mama, you going to take *that* to the new house?

MAMA: Un-huh—

BENEATHA: That raggedy-looking old thing?

MAMA (*stopping and looking at her*): It expresses ME!

RUTH (*with delight, to* BENEATHA): So there, Miss Thing!

WALTER *comes to* MAMA *suddenly and bends down behind her and squeezes her in his arms with all his strength. She is overwhelmed by the suddenness of it and, though delighted, her manner is like that of* RUTH *and* TRAVIS.

MAMA: Look out now, boy! You make me mess up my thing here!

WALTER (*His face lit, he slips down on his knees beside her, his arms still about her.*): Mama . . . you know what it means to climb up in the chariot?

MAMA (*gruffly, very happy*): Get on away from me now . . .
RUTH (*near the gift-wrapped package, trying to catch* WALTER'S *eye*): Psst—
WALTER: What the old song say, Mama . . .
RUTH: Walter—Now?

　She is pointing at the package.

WALTER (*speaking the lines, sweetly, playfully, in his mother's face*):
　　I got wings . . . you got wings . . .
　　All God's Children got wings . . .
MAMA: Boy—get out of my face and do some work . . .
WALTER:
　　When I get to heaven gonna put on my wings,
　　Gonna fly all over God's heaven . . .
BENEATHA (*teasingly, from across the room*): Everybody talking 'bout heaven ain't going there!
WALTER (*to* RUTH, *who is carrying the box across to them*): I don't know, you think we ought to give her that . . . Seems to me she ain't been very appreciative around here.
MAMA (*eying the box, which is obviously a gift*): What is that?
WALTER (*taking it from* RUTH *and putting it on the table in front of* MAMA): Well—what you all think? Should we give it to her?
RUTH: Oh—she was pretty good today.
MAMA: I'll good you—

　She turns her eyes to the box again.

BENEATHA: Open it, Mama.

　She stands up, looks at it, turns and looks at all of them, and then presses her hands together and does not open the package.

WALTER (*sweetly*): Open it, Mama. It's for you. (MAMA *looks in his eyes. It is the first present in her life without its being Christmas. Slowly she opens her package and lifts out, one by one, a brand-new sparkling set of gardening tools.* WALTER *continues, prodding.*) Ruth made up the note—read it . . .
MAMA (*picking up the card and adjusting her glasses*): "To our own Mrs. Miniver—Love from Brother, Ruth and Beneatha." Ain't that lovely . . .
TRAVIS (*tugging at his father's sleeve*): Daddy, can I give her mine now?
WALTER: All right, son. (TRAVIS *flies to get his gift.*)
MAMA: Now I don't have to use my knives and forks no more . . .
WALTER: Travis didn't want to go in with the rest of us, Mama. He got his own. (*somewhat amused*) We don't know what it is . . .
TRAVIS (*racing back in the room with a large hatbox and putting it in front of his grandmother*): Here!
MAMA: Lord have mercy, baby. You done gone and bought your grandmother a hat?
TRAVIS (*very proud*): Open it!

　She does and lifts out an elaborate, but very elaborate, wide gardening hat, and all the adults break up at the sight of it.

RUTH: Travis, honey, what is that?
TRAVIS (*who thinks it is beautiful and appropriate*): It's a gardening hat! Like the ladies always have on in the magazines when they work in their gardens.
BENEATHA (*giggling fiercely*): Travis—we were trying to make Mama Mrs. Miniver—not Scarlett O'Hara!

MAMA (*indignantly*): What's the matter with you all! This here is a beautiful hat! (*absurdly*) I always wanted me one just like it!

She pops it on her head to prove it to her grandson, and the hat is ludicrous and considerably oversized.

RUTH: Hot dog! Go, Mama!

WALTER (*doubled over with laughter*): I'm sorry, Mama—but you look like you ready to go out and chop you some cotton sure enough!

They all laugh except MAMA, *out of deference to* TRAVIS' *feelings.*

MAMA (*gathering the boy up to her*): Bless your heart—this is the prettiest hat I ever owned— (WALTER, RUTH and BENEATHA *chime in—noisily, festively and insincerely congratulating* TRAVIS *on his gift.*) What are we all standing around here for? We ain't finished packin' yet. Bennie, you ain't packed one book.

The bell rings.

BENEATHA: That couldn't be the movers . . . it's not hardly two good yet—

BENEATHA *goes into her room.* MAMA *starts for door.*

WALTER (*turning, stiffening*): Wait—wait—I'll get it.

He stands and looks at the door.

MAMA: You expecting company, son?

WALTER (*just looking at the door*): Yeah—yeah . . .

MAMA *looks at* RUTH, *and they exchange innocent and unfrightened glances.*

MAMA (*not understanding*): Well, let them in, son.

BENEATHA (*from her room*): We need some more string.

MAMA: Travis—you run to the hardware and get me some string cord.

MAMA *goes out and* WALTER *turns and looks at* RUTH. TRAVIS *goes to a dish for money.*

RUTH: Why don't you answer the door, man?

WALTER (*suddenly bounding across the floor to embrace her*): 'Cause sometimes it hard to let the future begin! (*stooping down in her face*)
  I got wings! You got wings!
  All God's children got wings!

He crosses to the door and throws it open. Standing there is a very slight little man in a not too prosperous business suit and with haunted frightened eyes and a hat pulled down tightly, brim up, around his forehead. TRAVIS *passes between the men and exits.* WALTER *leans deep in the man's face, still in his jubilance.*

  When I get to heaven gonna put on my wings,
  Gonna fly all over God's heaven . . .

The little man just stares at him.

  Heaven—

Suddenly he stops and looks past the little man into the empty hallway.

Where's Willy, man?

BOBO: He ain't with me.

WALTER (*not disturbed*): Oh—come on in. You know my wife.

BOBO (*dumbly, taking off his hat*): Yes—h'you, Miss Ruth.

RUTH (*quietly, a mood apart from her husband already, seeing* BOBO): Hello, Bobo.

WALTER: You right on time today . . . Right on time. That's the way! (*He slaps* BOBO *on his back.*) Sit down . . . lemme hear.

RUTH *stands stiffly and quietly in back of them, as though somehow she senses death, her eyes fixed on her husband.*

BOBO (*his frightened eyes on the floor, his hat in his hands*): Could I please get a drink of water, before I tell you about it, Walter Lee?

WALTER *does not take his eyes off the man.* RUTH *goes blindly to the tap and gets a glass of water and brings it to* BOBO.

WALTER: There ain't nothing wrong, is there?

BOBO: Lemme tell you—

WALTER: Man—didn't nothing go wrong?

BOBO: Lemme tell you—Walter Lee. (*looking at* RUTH *and talking to her more than to* WALTER) You know how it was. I got to tell you how it was. I mean first I got to tell you how it was all the way . . . I mean about the money I put in, Walter Lee . . .

WALTER (*with taut agitation now*): What about the money you put in?

BOBO: Well—it wasn't much as we told you—me and Willy—(*He stops.*) I'm sorry, Walter. I got a bad feeling about it. I got a real bad feeling about it . . .

WALTER: Man, what you telling me about all this for? . . . Tell me what happened in Springfield . . .

BOBO: Springfield.

RUTH (*like a dead woman*): What was supposed to happen in Springfield?

BOBO (*to her*): This deal that me and Walter went into with Willy—Me and Willy was going to go down to Springfield and spread some money 'round so's we wouldn't have to wait so long for the liquor license . . . That's what we were going to do. Everybody said that was the way you had to do, you understand, Miss Ruth?

WALTER: Man—what happened down there?

BOBO (*a pitiful man, near tears*): I'm trying to tell you, Walter.

WALTER (*screaming at him suddenly*): THEN TELL ME, GODDAMMIT . . . WHAT'S THE MATTER WITH YOU?

BOBO: Man . . . I didn't go to no Springfield, yesterday.

WALTER (*halted, life hanging in the moment*): Why not?

BOBO (*the long way, the hard way to tell*): 'Cause I didn't have no reasons to . . .

WALTER: Man, what are you talking about!

BOBO: I'm talking about the fact that when I got to the train station yesterday morning—eight o'clock like we planned . . . Man—*Willy didn't never show up.*

WALTER: Why . . . where was he . . . where is he?

BOBO: That's what I'm trying to tell you . . . I don't know . . . I waited six hours . . . I called his house . . . and I waited . . . six hours . . . I waited in that train station six hours . . . (*breaking into tears*) That was all the extra money I had in the world . . . (*looking up at* WALTER *with tears running down his face*) Man, *Willy is gone.*

WALTER: Gone, what you mean Willy is gone? Gone where? You mean he went by himself. You mean he went off to Springfield by himself—to take care of getting the license—(*turns and looks anxiously at* RUTH) You mean maybe he didn't want too many people in on the business down there? (*looks to* RUTH *again, as before*) You know Willy got his own ways. (*looks back to* BOBO) Maybe you was late yesterday and he just went on down there without you. Maybe—maybe—he's been callin' you at home tryin' to tell you what happened or something. Maybe—maybe—he just got sick. He's somewhere—he's got to be somewhere. We just got to find him—me and you got to find him. (*grabs* BOBO *senselessly by the collar and starts to shake him*) We got to!

BOBO (*in sudden angry, frightened agony*): What's the matter with you, Walter! *When a cat take off with your money he don't leave you no road maps!*

WALTER (*turning madly, as though he is looking for* WILLY *in the very room*): Willy! . . . Willy . . . don't do it . . . Please don't do it . . . Man, not with that money . . . Man, please, not with that money . . . Oh, God . . . Don't let it be true . . . (*He is wandering around, crying out for* WILLY *and looking for him or perhaps for help from God.*) Man . . . I trusted you . . . Man, I put my life in your hands . . . (*He starts to crumple down on the floor as* RUTH *just covers her face in horror.* MAMA *opens the door and comes into the room, with* BENEATHA *behind her.*) Man . . . (*He starts to pound the floor with his fists, sobbing wildly.*) THAT MONEY IS MADE OUT OF MY FATHER'S FLESH—

BOBO (*standing over him helplessly*): I'm sorry, Walter . . . (*Only* WALTER'S *sobs reply.* BOBO *puts on his hat.*) I had my life staked on this deal, too . . .

He exits.

MAMA (*to* WALTER): Son—(*She goes to him, bends down to him, talks to his bent head.*) Son . . . Is it gone? Son, I gave you sixty-five hundred dollars. Is it gone? All of it? Beneatha's money too?

WALTER (*lifting his head slowly*): Mama . . . I never . . . went to the bank at all . . .

MAMA (*not wanting to believe him*): You mean . . . your sister's school money . . . you used that too . . . Walter? . . .

WALTER: Yessss! All of it . . . It's all gone . . .

There is total silence. RUTH *stands with her face covered with her hands;* BENEATHA *leans forlornly against a wall, fingering a piece of red ribbon from the mother's gift.* MAMA *stops and looks at her son without recognition and then, quite without thinking about it, starts to beat him senselessly in the face.* BENEATHA *goes to them and stops it.*

BENEATHA: Mama!

MAMA *stops and looks at both of her children and rises slowly and wanders vaguely, aimlessly away from them.*

MAMA: I seen . . . him . . . night after night . . . come in . . . and look at that rug . . . and then look at me . . . the red showing in his eyes . . . the veins moving in his head . . . I seen him grow thin and old before he was forty . . . working and working and working like somebody's old horse . . . killing himself . . . and you—you give it all away in a day—(*She raises her arms to strike him again.*)

BENEATHA: Mama—

MAMA: Oh, God . . . (*She looks up to Him.*) Look down here—and show me the strength.

BENEATHA: Mama—

MAMA (*folding over*): Strength . . .
BENEATHA (*plaintively*): Mama . . .
MAMA: Strength!

Curtain.

ACT THREE

TIME: *An hour later.*

At curtain, there is a sullen light of gloom in the living room, gray light not unlike that which began the first scene of Act One. At left we can see WALTER *within his room, alone with himself. He is stretched out on the bed, his shirt out and open, his arms under his head. He does not smoke, he does not cry out, he merely lies there, looking up at the ceiling, much as if he were alone in the world.*

In the living room BENEATHA *sits at the table, still surrounded by the now almost ominous packing crates. She sits looking off. We feel that this is a mood struck perhaps an hour before, and it lingers now, full of the empty sound of profound disappointment. We see on a line from her brother's bedroom the sameness of their attitudes. Presently the bell rings and* BENEATHA *rises without ambition or interest in answering. It is* ASAGAI, *smiling broadly, striding into the room with energy and happy expectation and conversation.*

ASAGAI: I came over . . . I had some free time. I thought I might help with the packing. Ah, I like the look of packing crates! A household in preparation for a journey! It depresses some people . . . but for me . . . it is another feeling. Something full of the flow of life, do you understand? Movement, progress . . . It makes me think of Africa.
BENEATHA: Africa!
ASAGAI: What kind of a mood is this? Have I told you how deeply you move me?
BENEATHA: He gave away the money, Asagai . . .
ASAGAI: Who gave away what money?
BENEATHA: The insurance money. My brother gave it away.
ASAGAI: Gave it away?
BENEATHA: He made an investment! With a man even Travis wouldn't have trusted with his most worn-out marbles.
ASAGAI: And it's gone?
BENEATHA: Gone!
ASAGAI: I'm very sorry . . . And you, now?
BENEATHA: Me? . . . Me? . . . Me, I'm nothing . . . Me. When I was very small . . . We used to take our sleds out in the wintertime and the only hills we had were the ice-covered stone steps of some houses down the street. And we used to fill them in with snow and make them smooth and slide down them all day . . . and it was very dangerous, you know . . . far too steep . . . and sure enough one day a kid named Rufus came down too fast and hit the sidewalk and we saw his face just split open right there in front of us . . . And I remember standing there looking at his bloody open face thinking that was the end of Rufus. But the ambulance came and they took him to the hospital and they fixed the broken bones and they sewed it all up . . . and the next time I saw Rufus he just had a little line down the middle of his face . . . I never got over that . . .
ASAGAI: What?
BENEATHA: That that was what one person could do for another, fix him up—sew up

the problem, make him all right again. That was the most marvelous thing in the world . . . I wanted to do that. I always thought it was the one concrete thing in the world that a human being could do. Fix up the sick, you know—and make them whole again. This was truly being God . . .

ASAGAI: You wanted to be God?

BENEATHA: No—I wanted to cure. It used to be so important to me. I wanted to cure. It used to matter. I used to care. I mean about people and how their bodies hurt . . .

ASAGAI: And you've stopped caring?

BENEATHA: Yes—I think so.

ASAGAI: Why?

BENEATHA (*bitterly*): Because it doesn't seem deep enough, close enough to what ails mankind! It was a child's way of seeing things—or an idealist's.

ASAGAI: Children see things very well sometimes—and idealists even better.

BENEATHA: I know that's what you think. Because you are still where I left off. You with all your talk and dreams about Africa! You still think you can patch up the world. Cure the Great Sore of Colonialism—(*loftily, mocking it*) with the Penicillin of Independence—!

ASAGAI: Yes!

BENEATHA: Independence *and then what?* What about all the crooks and thieves and just plain idiots who will come into power and steal and plunder the same as before—only now they will be black and do it in the name of the new Independence—WHAT ABOUT THEM?!

ASAGAI: That will be the problem for another time. First we must get there.

BENEATHA: And where does it end?

ASAGAI: End? Who even spoke of an end? To life? To living?

BENEATHA: An end to misery! To stupidity! Don't you see there isn't any real progress, Asagai, there is only one large circle that we march in, around and around, each of us with our own little picture in front of us—our own little mirage that we think is the future.

ASAGAI: That is the mistake.

BENEATHA: What?

ASAGAI: What you just said—about the circle. It isn't a circle—it is simply a long line— as in geometry, you know, one that reaches into infinity. And because we cannot see the end—we also cannot see how it changes. And it is very odd but those who see the changes—who dream, who will not give up—are called idealists . . . and those who see only the circle—we call *them* the "realists"!

BENEATHA: Asagai, while I was sleeping in that bed in there, people went out and took the future right out of my hands! And nobody asked me, nobody consulted me— they just went out and changed my life!

ASAGAI: Was it your money?

BENEATHA: What?

ASAGAI: Was it your money he gave away?

BENEATHA: It belonged to all of us.

ASAGAI: But did you earn it? Would you have had it at all if your father had not died?

BENEATHA: No.

ASAGAI: Then isn't there something wrong in a house—in a world—where all dreams, good or bad, must depend on the death of a man? I never thought to see *you* like this, Alaiyo. You! Your brother made a mistake and you are grateful to him so that now you can give up the ailing human race on account of it! You talk about what good is struggle, what good is anything! Where are we all going and why are we bothering!

BENEATHA: AND YOU CANNOT ANSWER IT!

ASAGAI (*shouting over her*): *I LIVE THE ANSWER!* (*pause*) In my village at home it is the exceptional man who can even read a newspaper . . . or who ever sees a book at all. I will go home and much of what I will have to say will seem strange to the people of my village. But I will teach and work and things will happen, slowly and swiftly. At times it will seem that nothing changes at all . . . and then again the sudden dramatic events which make history leap into the future. And then quiet again. Retrogression even. Guns, murder, revolution. And I even will have moments when I wonder if the quiet was not better than all that death and hatred. But I will look about my village at the illiteracy and disease and ignorance and I will not wonder long. And perhaps . . . perhaps I will be a great man . . . I mean perhaps I will hold on to the substance of truth and find my way always with the right course . . . and perhaps for it I will be butchered in my bed some night by the servants of empire . . .

BENEATHA: *The martyr!*

ASAGAI (*He smiles.*): . . . or perhaps I shall live to be a very old man, respected and esteemed in my new nation . . . And perhaps I shall hold office and this is what I'm trying to tell you, Alaiyo: Perhaps the things I believe now for my country will be wrong and outmoded, and I will not understand and do terrible things to have things my way or merely to keep my power. Don't you see that there will be young men and women—not British soldiers then, but my own black country-men—to step out of the shadows some evening and slit my then useless throat? Don't you see they have always been there . . . that they always will be. And that such a thing as my own death will be an advance? They who might kill me even . . . actually replenish all that I was.

BENEATHA: Oh, Asagai, I know all that.

ASAGAI: Good! Then stop moaning and groaning and tell me what you plan to do.

BENEATHA: Do?

ASAGAI: I have a bit of a suggestion.

BENEATHA: What?

ASAGAI (*rather quietly for him*): That when it is all over—that you come home with me—

BENEATHA (*staring at him and crossing away with exasperation*): Oh—Asagai—at this moment you decide to be romantic!

ASAGAI (*quickly understanding the misunderstanding*): My dear, young creature of the New World—I do not mean across the city—I mean across the ocean: home—to Africa.

BENEATHA (*slowly understanding and turning to him with murmured amazement*): To Africa?

ASAGAI: Yes! . . . (*smiling and lifting his arms playfully*) Three hundred years later the African Prince rose up out of the seas and swept the maiden back across the middle passage over which her ancestors had come—

BENEATHA (*unable to play*): To—to Nigeria?

ASAGAI: Nigeria. Home. (*coming to her with genuine romantic flippancy*) I will show you our mountains and our stars; and give you cool drinks from gourds and teach you the old songs and the ways of our people—and, in time, we will pretend that—(*very softly*)—you have only been away for a day. Say that you'll come—(*He swings her around and takes her full in his arms in a kiss which proceeds to passion.*)

BENEATHA (*pulling away suddenly*): You're getting me all mixed up—

ASAGAI: Why?

BENEATHA: Too many things—too many things have happened today. I must sit down and think. I don't know what I feel about anything right this minute.

She promptly sits down and props her chin on her fist.

ASAGAI (*charmed*): All right, I shall leave you. No—don't get up. (*touching her, gently, sweetly*) Just sit awhile and think . . . Never be afraid to sit awhile and think. (*He goes to door and looks at her.*) How often I have looked at you and said, "Ah— so this is what the New World hath finally wrought . . ."

He exits. BENEATHA *sits on alone. Presently* WALTER *enters from his room and starts to rummage through things, feverishly looking for something. She looks up and turns in her seat.*

BENEATHA (*hissingly*): Yes—just look at what the New World hath wrought! . . . Just look! (*She gestures with bitter disgust.*) There he is! *Monsieur le petit bourgeois noir*—himself! There he is—Symbol of a Rising Class! Entrepreneur! Titan of the system! (WALTER *ignores her completely and continues frantically and destructively looking for something and hurling things to floor and tearing things out of their place in his search.* BENEATHA *ignores the eccentricity of his actions and goes on with the monologue of insult.*) Did you dream of yachts on Lake Michigan, Brother? Did you see yourself on that Great Day sitting down at the Conference Table, sur-rounded by all the mighty bald-headed men in America? All halted, waiting, breathless, waiting for your pronouncements on industry? Waiting for you—Chair-man of the Board! (WALTER *finds what he is looking for—a small piece of white paper—and pushes it in his pocket and puts on his coat and rushes out without ever having looked at her. She shouts after him.*) I look at you and I see the final triumph of stupidity in the world!

The door slams and she returns to just sitting again. RUTH *comes quickly out of* MAMA'S *room.*

RUTH: Who was that?

BENEATHA: Your husband.

RUTH: Where did he go?

BENEATHA: Who knows—maybe he has an appointment at U.S. Steel.

RUTH (*anxiously, with frightened eyes*): You didn't say nothing bad to him, did you?

BENEATHA: Bad? Say anything bad to him? No—I told him he was a sweet boy and full of dreams and everything is strictly peachy keen, as the ofay kids say!

MAMA *enters from her bedroom. She is lost, vague, trying to catch hold, to make some sense of her former command of the world, but it still eludes her. A sense of waste overwhelms her gait; a measure of apology rides on her shoulders. She goes to her plant, which has remained on the table, looks at it, picks it up and takes it to the window sill and sits it outside, and she stands and looks at it a long moment. Then she closes the window, straightens her body with effort and turns around to her children.*

MAMA: Well—ain't it a mess in here, though? (*a false cheerfulness, a beginning of some-thing*) I guess we all better stop moping around and get some work done. All this unpacking and everything we got to do. (RUTH *raises her head slowly in response to the sense of the line; and* BENEATHA *in similar manner turns very slowly to look at her mother.*) One of you all better call the moving people and tell 'em not to come.

RUTH: Tell 'em not to come?

MAMA: Of course, baby. Ain't no need in 'em coming all the way here and having to go back. They charges for that too. (*She sits down, fingers to her brow, thinking.*) Lord, ever since I was a little girl, I always remembers people saying, "Lena—Lena Eggleston, you aims too high all the time. You needs to slow down and see life a little more like it is. Just slow down some." That's what they always used to say down home—"Lord, that Lena Eggleston is a high-minded thing. She'll get her due one day!"

RUTH: No, Lena . . .

MAMA: Me and Big Walter just didn't never learn right.

RUTH: Lena, no! We gotta go. Bennie—tell her . . . (*She rises and crosses to* BENEATHA *with her arms outstretched.* BENEATHA *doesn't respond.*) Tell her we can still move . . . the notes ain't but a hundred and twenty-five a month. We got four grown people in this house—we can work . . .

MAMA (*to herself*): Just aimed too high all the time—

RUTH (*turning and going to* MAMA *fast—the words pouring out with urgency and desperation*): Lena—I'll work . . . I'll work twenty hours a day in all the kitchens in Chicago . . . I'll strap my baby on my back if I have to and scrub all the floors in America and wash all the sheets in America if I have to—but we got to MOVE! We got to get OUT OF HERE!!

MAMA *reaches out absently and pats* RUTH'S *hand.*

MAMA: No—I sees things differently now. Been thinking 'bout some of the things we could do to fix this place up some. I seen a second-hand bureau over on Maxwell Street just the other day that could fit right there. (*She points to where the new furniture might go.* RUTH *wanders away from her.*) Would need some new handles on it and then a little varnish and it look like something brand-new. And—we can put up them new curtains in the kitchen . . . Why this place be looking fine. Cheer us all up so that we forget trouble ever come . . . (*to* RUTH) And you could get some nice screens to put up in your room round the baby's bassinet . . . (*She looks at both of them, pleadingly.*) Sometimes you just got to know when to give up some things . . . and hold on to what you got . . .

WALTER *enters from the outside, looking spent and leaning against the door, his coat hanging from him.*

MAMA: Where you been, son?

WALTER (*breathing hard*): Made a call.

MAMA: To who, son?

WALTER: To The Man. (*He heads for his room.*)

MAMA: What man, baby?

WALTER (*stops in the door*): The Man, Mama. Don't you know who The Man is?

RUTH: Walter Lee?

WALTER: *The Man.* Like the guys in the streets say—The Man. Captain Boss—Mistuh Charley . . . Old Cap'n Please Mr. Bossman . . .

BENEATHA (*suddenly*): Lindner!

WALTER: That's right! That's good. I told him to come right over.

BENEATHA (*fiercely, understanding*): For what? What do you want to see him for!

WALTER (*looking at his sister*): We going to do business with him.

MAMA: What you talking 'bout, son?

WALTER: Talking 'bout life, Mama. You all always telling me to see life like it is. Well—

I laid in there on my back today . . . and I figured it out. Life just like it is. Who gets and who don't get. (*He sits down with his coat on and laughs.*) Mama, you know it's all divided up. Life is. Sure enough. Between the takers and the "tooken." (*He laughs.*) I've figured it out finally. (*He looks around at them.*) Yeah. Some of us always getting "tooken." (*He laughs.*) People like Willy Harris, they don't never get "tooken." And you know why the rest of us do? 'Cause we all mixed up. Mixed up bad. We get to looking 'round for the right and the wrong; and we worry about it and cry about it and stay up nights trying to figure out 'bout the wrong and the right of things all the time . . . And all the time, man, them takers is out there operating, just taking and taking. Willy Harris? Shoot— Willy Harris don't even count. He don't even count in the big scheme of things. But I'll say one thing for old Willy Harris . . . he's taught me something. He's taught me to keep my eye on what counts in this world. Yeah—(*shouting out a little*) Thanks, Willy!

RUTH: What did you call that man for, Walter Lee?

WALTER: Called him to tell him to come on over to the show. Gonna put on a show for the man. Just what he wants to see. You see, Mama, the man came here today and he told us that them people out there where you want us to move—well they so upset they willing to pay us *not* to move! (*He laughs again.*) And—and oh, Mama—you would of been proud of the way me and Ruth and Bennie acted. We told him to get out . . . Lord have mercy! We told the man to get out! Oh, we was some proud folks this afternoon, yeah. (*He lights a cigarette.*) We were still full of that old-time stuff . . .

RUTH (*coming toward him slowly*): You talking 'bout taking them people's money to keep us from moving in that house?

WALTER: I ain't just talking 'bout it, baby—I'm telling you that's what's going to happen!

BENEATHA: Oh, God! Where is the bottom! Where is the real honest-to-God bottom so he can't go any farther!

WALTER: See—that's the old stuff. You and that boy that was here today. You all want everybody to carry a flag and a spear and sing some marching songs, huh? You wanna spend your life looking into things and trying to find the right and the wrong part, huh? Yeah. You know what's going to happen to that boy someday — he'll find himself sitting in a dungeon, locked in forever—and the takers will have the key! Forget it, baby! There ain't no causes—there ain't nothing but taking in this world, and he who takes most is smartest—and it don't make a damn bit of difference *how*.

MAMA: You making something inside me cry, son. Some awful pain inside me.

WALTER: Don't cry, Mama. Understand. That white man is going to walk in that door able to write checks for more money than we ever had. It's important to him and I'm going to help him . . . I'm going to put on the show, Mama.

MAMA: Son—I come from five generations of people who was slaves and sharecrop-pers—but ain't nobody in my family never let nobody pay 'em no money that was a way of telling us we wasn't fit to walk the earth. We ain't never been that poor. (*raising her eyes and looking at him*) We ain't never been that—dead inside.

BENEATHA: Well—we are dead now. All the talk about dreams and sunlight that goes on in this house. It's all dead now.

WALTER: What's the matter with you all! I didn't make this world! It was give to me this way! Hell, yes, I want me some yachts someday! Yes, I want to hang some real pearls 'round my wife's neck. Ain't she supposed to wear no pearls? Somebody tell me—tell me, who decides which women is suppose to wear pearls in this world. I tell you I am a *man*—and I think my wife should wear some pearls in this world!

This last line hangs a good while and WALTER *begins to move about the room. The word "Man" has penetrated his consciousness; he mumbles it to himself repeatedly between strange agitated pauses as he moves about.*

MAMA: Baby, how you going to feel on the inside?

WALTER: Fine! . . . Going to feel fine . . . a man . . .

MAMA: You won't have nothing left then, Walter Lee.

WALTER (*coming to her*): I'm going to feel fine, Mama. I'm going to look that son-of-a-bitch in the eyes and say—(*He falters.*)—and say, "All right, Mr. Lindner—(*He falters even more.*)—that's *your* neighborhood out there! You got the right to keep it like you want! You got the right to have it like you want! Just write the check and—the house is yours." And—and I am going to say—(*His voice almost breaks.*) "And you—you people just put the money in my hand and you won't have to live next to this bunch of stinking niggers! . . ." (*He straightens up and moves away from his mother, walking around the room.*) And maybe—maybe I'll just get down on my black knees . . . (*He does so;* RUTH *and* BENNIE *and* MAMA *watch him in frozen horror.*) "Captain, Mistuh, Bossman—(*groveling and grinning and wringing his hands in profoundly anguished imitation of the slow-witted movie stereotype*) A-hee-hee-hee! Oh, yassuh boss! Yasssssuh! Great white—(*Voice breaking, he forces himself to go on.*)—Father, just gi' ussen de money, fo' God's sake, and we's—we's ain't gwine come out deh and dirty up yo' white folks neighborhood . . ." (*He breaks down completely.*) And I'll feel fine! Fine! FINE! (*He gets up and goes into the bedroom.*)

BENEATHA: That is not a man. That is nothing but a toothless rat.

MAMA: Yes—death done come in this here house. (*She is nodding, slowly, reflectively.*) Done come walking in my house on the lips of my children. You what supposed to be my beginning again. You—what supposed to be my harvest. (*to* BENEATHA) You—you mourning your brother?

BENEATHA: He's no brother of mine.

MAMA: What you say?

BENEATHA: I said that that individual in that room is no brother of mine.

MAMA: That's what I thought you said. You feeling like you better than he is today? (BENEATHA *does not answer.*) Yes? What you tell him a minute ago? That he wasn't a man? Yes? You give him up for me? You done wrote his epitaph too—like the rest of the world? Well, who give you the privilege?

BENEATHA: Be on my side for once! You saw what he just did, Mama! You saw him—down on his knees. Wasn't it you who taught me to despise any man who would do that? Do what he's going to do?

MAMA: Yes—I taught you that. Me and your daddy. But I thought I taught you something else too . . . I thought I taught you to love him.

BENEATHA: Love him? There is nothing left to love.

MAMA: There is *always* something left to love. And if you ain't learned that, you ain't learned nothing. (*looking at her*) Have you cried for that boy today? I don't mean for yourself and for the family 'cause we lost the money. I mean for him: what he been through and what it done to him. Child, when do you think is the time to love somebody the most? When they done good and made things easy for everybody? Well then, you ain't through learning—because that ain't the time at all. It's when he's at his lowest and can't believe in hisself 'cause the world done whipped him so! When you starts measuring somebody, measure him right, child, measure him right. Make sure you done taken into account what hills and valleys he come through before he got to wherever he is.

TRAVIS *bursts into the room at the end of the speech, leaving the door open.*

TRAVIS: Grandmama—the moving men are downstairs! The truck just pulled up.

MAMA (*turning and looking at him*): Are they, baby? They downstairs?

She sighs and sits. LINDNER *appears in the doorway. He peers in and knocks lightly, to gain attention, and comes in. All turn to look at him.*

LINDNER (*hat and briefcase in hand*): Uh-hello . . .

RUTH *crosses mechanically to the bedroom door and opens it and lets it swing open freely and slowly as the lights come up on* WALTER *within, still in his coat, sitting at the far corner of the room. He looks up and out through the room to* LINDNER.

RUTH: He's here.

A long minute passes and WALTER *slowly gets up.*

LINDNER (*coming to the table with efficiency, putting his briefcase on the table and starting to unfold papers and unscrew fountain pens*): Well, I certainly was glad to hear from you people. (WALTER *has begun the trek out of the room, slowly and awkwardly, rather like a small boy, passing the back of his sleeve across his mouth from time to time.*) Life can really be so much simpler than people let it be most of the time. Well—with whom do I negotiate? You, Mrs. Younger, or your son here? (MAMA *sits with her hands folded on her lap and her eyes closed as* WALTER *advances.* TRAVIS *goes closer to* LINDNER *and looks at the papers curiously.*) Just some official papers, sonny.

RUTH: Travis, you go downstairs—

MAMA (*opening her eyes and looking into* WALTER'S): No. Travis, you stay right here. And you make him understand what you doing, Walter Lee. You teach him good. Like Willy Harris taught you. You show where our five generations done come to. (WALTER *looks from her to the boy, who grins at him innocently.*) Go ahead, son— (*She folds her hands and closes her eyes.*) Go ahead.

WALTER (*at last crosses to* LINDNER, *who is reviewing the contract*): Well, Mr. Lindner. (BENEATHA *turns away.*) We called you—(*There is a profound, simple groping quality in his speech.*)—because, well, me and my family (*He looks around and shifts from one foot to the other.*) Well—we are very plain people . . .

LINDNER: Yes—

WALTER: I mean—I have worked as a chauffeur most of my life—and my wife here, she does domestic work in people's kitchens. So does my mother. I mean—we are plain people . . .

LINDNER: Yes, Mr. Younger—

WALTER (*really like a small boy, looking down at his shoes and then up at the man*): And—uh—well, my father, well, he was a laborer most of his life . . .

LINDNER (*absolutely confused*): Uh, yes—yes, I understand. (*He turns back to the contract.*)

WALTER (*a beat; staring at him*): And my father—(*with sudden intensity*) My father almost *beat a man to death* once because this man called him a bad name or something, you know what I mean?

LINDNER (*looking up, frozen*): No, no, I'm afraid I don't—

WALTER (*A beat. The tension hangs; then* WALTER *steps back from it.*): Yeah. Well—what I mean is that we come from people who had a lot of *pride.* I mean—we are very proud people. And that's my sister over there and she's going to be a doctor—and we are very proud—

LINDNER: Well—I am sure that is very nice, but—

WALTER: What I am telling you is that we called you over here to tell you that we are very proud and that this—(*signaling to* TRAVIS) Travis, come here. (TRAVIS *crosses and* WALTER *draws him before him facing the man.*) This is my son, and he makes the sixth generation our family in this country. And we have all thought about your offer—

LINDNER: Well, good . . . good—

WALTER: And we have decided to move into our house because my father—my father—he earned it for us brick by brick. (MAMA *has her eyes closed and is rocking back and forth as though she were in church, with her head nodding the Amen yes.*) We don't want to make no trouble for nobody or fight no causes, and we will try to be good neighbors. And that's *all* we got to say about that. (*He looks the man absolutely in the eyes.*) We don't want your money. (*He turns and walks away.*)

LINDNER (*looking around at all of them*): I take it then—that you have decided to occupy . . .

BENEATHA: That's what the man said.

LINDNER (*to* MAMA *in her reverie*): Then I would like to appeal to you, Mrs. Younger. You are older and wiser and understand things better I am sure . . .

MAMA: I am afraid you don't understand. My son said we was going to move and there ain't nothing left for me to say. (*briskly*) You know how these young folks is nowadays, mister. Can't do a thing with 'em! (*As he opens his mouth, she rises.*) Good-bye.

LINDNER (*folding up his materials*): Well—if you are that final about it . . . there is nothing left for me to say. (*He finishes, almost ignored by the family, who are concentrating on* WALTER LEE. *At the door* LINDNER *halts and looks around.*) I sure hope you people know what you're getting into.

He shakes his head and exits.

RUTH (*looking around and coming to life*): Well, for God's sake—if the moving men are here—LET'S GET THE HELL OUT OF HERE!

MAMA (*into action*): Ain't it the truth! Look at all this here mess. Ruth, put Travis' good jacket on him . . . Walter Lee, fix your tie and tuck your shirt in, you look like somebody's hoodlum! Lord have mercy, where is my plant? (*She flies to get it amid the general bustling of the family, who are deliberately trying to ignore the nobility of the past moment.*) You all start on down . . . Travis child, don't go empty-handed . . . Ruth, where did I put that box with my skillets in it? I want to be in charge of it myself . . . I'm going to make us the biggest dinner we ever ate tonight . . . Beneatha, what's the matter with them stockings? Pull them things up, girl . . .

The family starts to file out as two moving men appear and begin to carry out the heavier pieces of furniture, bumping into the family as they move about.

BENEATHA: Mama, Asagai asked me to marry him today and go to Africa—

MAMA (*in the middle of her getting-ready activity*): He did? You ain't old enough to marry nobody—(*seeing the moving men lifting one of her chairs precariously*) Darling, that ain't no bale of cotton, please handle it so we can sit in it again! I had that chair twenty-five years . . .

The movers sigh with exasperation and go on with their work.

BENEATHA (*girlishly and unreasonably trying to pursue the conversation*): To go to Africa, Mama—be a doctor in Africa . . .
MAMA (*distracted*): Yes, baby—
WALTER: *Africa!* What he want you to go to Africa for?
BENEATHA: To practice there . . .
WALTER: Girl, if you don't get all them silly ideas out your head! You better marry yourself a man with some loot . . .
BENEATHA (*angrily, precisely as in the first scene of the play*): What have you got to do with who I marry!
WALTER: Plenty. Now I think George Murchison—
BENEATHA: *George Murchison!* I wouldn't marry him if he was Adam and I was Eve!

WALTER *and* BENEATHA *go out yelling at each other vigorously and the anger is loud and real till their voices diminish.* RUTH *stands at the door and turns to* MAMA *and smiles knowingly.*

MAMA (*fixing her hat at last*): Yeah—they something all right, my children . . .
RUTH: Yeah—they're something. Let's go, Lena.
MAMA (*stalling, starting to look around at the house*): Yes—I'm coming. Ruth—
RUTH: Yes?
MAMA (*quietly, woman to woman*): He finally come into his manhood today, didn't he? Kind of like a rainbow after the rain . . .
RUTH (*biting her lip lest her own pride explode in front of* MAMA): Yes, Lena.

WALTER'S *voice calls for them raucously.*

WALTER (*off stage*): Y'all come on! These people charges by the hour, you know!
MAMA (*waving* RUTH *out vaguely*): All right, honey—go on down. I be down directly.

RUTH *hesitates, then exits.* MAMA *stands, at last alone in the living room, her plant on the table before her as the lights start to come down. She looks around at all the walls and ceilings and suddenly, despite herself, while the children call below, a great heaving thing rises in her and she puts her fist to her mouth to stifle it, takes a final desperate look, pulls her coat about her, pats her hat and goes out. The lights dim down. The door opens and she comes back in, grabs her plant, and goes out for the last time.*

Curtain.

THE RECEPTIVE READER

1. How much does the playwright steer the reader's (and the director's and actors') interpretation of the characters in the *stage directions*? Prepare a capsule portrait of one or more of the characters as she sketches them out in these introductory descriptions.

2. Mama is the family's link with the past. What does she tell the younger genera-

tion about the history of her people and the history of her family? ✧ What makes Mama the strong *central character* in the play? What for you are the crucial confrontations where her strength is tested? ✧ Some critics have questioned Hansberry's treatment of the black matriarch as stereotyped or sentimental. Does Mama seem to you overidealized? Or does she seem a believable strong character to you?

3. Would you agree that, among the characters in this play, Walter is most nearly in open rebellion against his environment and against the situation in which he finds himself? What are the sources of his hostility and rebellion? Where in the play do you most clearly see and understand his bitterness? ✧ How are Walter and his actions central to the *plot* of the play? (Some critics have asked how believable or plausible some of the key plot developments are in this play. Why or why not do you find them believable?) ✧ Do you think the author is too harsh toward or biased against Walter as the young black male in the family?

4. What is the role of Ruth in the play? Does the confrontation between Walter and his mother make her a *minor character?* What is her relationship with her mother-in-law? What is her relationship with Walter?

5. What roles do the supporting characters play? What role does Murchison play? ✧ How does the playwright sketch the rejection by Beneatha and Asagai of the "melting pot" ideal of assimilation? How does Beneatha see the future? How does Asagai? ✧ How does Beneatha provide a *foil* for Walter?

6. Always in the background of the play is the world of "the Man." What role does it have in the play as a whole? What does Mr. Lindner as its emissary reveal about the working of prejudice or of segregation?

7. Does the play have a "happy ending"? Do you consider the play as a whole optimistic, pessimistic, or neither? What vision does the play as a whole present of the future for African-Americans?

THE PERSONAL RESPONSE

Do you see yourself anywhere in this play? Is there a character with whom you closely identify? Is there a character toward whom you feel strong antagonism? (With which of the characters do you think the author identified most closely?)

THE CREATIVE DIMENSION

As an exercise in *role playing*, prepare a brief monologue in which you assume the role of one of the characters in the play. Bring the character to life for your audience by talking about yourself in this assumed role: your background, your ties with other people, your hopes and aspirations.

CROSS-REFERENCES—For Discussion or Writing

✧ In both *Death of a Salesman* and *A Raisin in the Sun,* the extended family provides the world in which much of the characters' lives is played out. Compare and contrast the web of interpersonal relations in Miller's and in Hansberry's play.

✧ Critics have asked whether Ibsen's *A Doll's House* speaks to men and women alike or whether it pits men and women against one another. Similarly, some critics have stressed Hansberry's commitment to the struggle of the black community, but it has also been fashionable to claim that Hansberry's play speaks to our "common humanity." Reexamine one of these plays (or both) to decide if you see the play as a polarizing or a unifying force.

WRITING ABOUT LITERATURE

28. The Play and the Critics (Documented Paper)

The Writing Workshop The critical reception of a major play or of a challenging new playwright makes a good topic for a research paper or library paper on a literary subject. Such a paper allows you to explore questions that fascinate people who love the theater. What makes a play a success or failure? What makes a major new playwright controversial? How receptive or wrongheaded are critics and reviewers?

Other questions that you might want to explore: Why do some plays seem major hits at the time but slowly fade from view? Why are others underrated when they first appear? What makes a play a *succès d'estime*—treated with respect (or esteem) by critics and reviewers, although audiences don't seem to warm to it? What is the reaction of critics when a prominent director or cast launches a major new production of a classic, such as a revival of an Ibsen play starring Liv Ullman—or a new production of *Death of a Salesman* with Dustin Hoffman in the title role?

Finding Promising Leads To work up material for your paper, you are likely to begin by checking in electronic or printed indexes of periodical literature for reviews and critical appraisals in the year of the original production and in the years immediately following. Sometimes, a survey article or an appraisal of the playwright published years later may prove a valuable guide to the original and later reviews. For instance, you might be investigating the critical reception of Lorraine Hansberry's *A Raisin in the Sun*. You might come up with leads like the following:

REVIEWS OF THE ORIGINAL PRODUCTION

Atkinson, Brooks. "The Theater: *Raisin in the Sun*." *New York Times* 12 Mar. 1959. Rpt. in *New York Theatre Critics' Reviews* (1959): 345.

Driver, Tom F. "Theater: *A Raisin in the Sun*." *New Republic* 13 Apr. 1959: 21.

Weales, Gerald. "Thoughts on *A Raisin in the Sun*." *Commentary* 27.6 (June 1959): 527–30.

Lewis, Theophilus. "Social Protest in *A Raisin in the Sun*." *Catholic World* 190 (Oct. 1959): 31–35.

Reviews of the 1961 Columbia Pictures motion picture in *Commonweal* 7 Apr. 1961; *Ebony* 16 (Apr. 1961): 53–56; *New Republic* 20 Mar. 1961: 19; *New York Times* 30 Mar. 1961: 24; *New Yorker* 8 Apr. 1961: 164; *Newsweek* 10 Apr. 1961: 103.

LATER ASSESSMENTS

Brown-Guillory, Elizabeth. *Their Place on the Stage: Black Women Playwrights in America*. Westport: Greenwood P, 1988.

Ashley, Leonard R. N. "Lorraine Hansberry and the Great Black Way." *Modern American Drama: The Female Canon*. Ed. June Schlueter. Cranbury, NJ: Assoc. University Presses, 1990.

Taking Notes   Exploratory reading requires the ability to look a source over quickly but also to slow down and close in when promising materials surface. Be alert for possibly useful material such as, with the Hansberry materials, evidence of the reluctance of white producers or of the compensating eagerness of others to support a black woman playwright. Make sure to copy **direct quotations** exactly, word for word. Put all the quoted material in quotation marks to show material copied verbatim. (Make sure to include the closing quotation mark to show where the quotation ends.) Include all the publishing information you will need later when you identify your sources in a documented paper. Include exact page numbers. A sample note might look like this:

RELUCTANCE OF WHITE PRODUCERS

"*To Be Young, Gifted, and Black* was originally conceived not in its present form, but as a work for the stage. As had been the case with *A Raisin in the Sun,* however (and every other black play that I have ever heard of), established producers evinced skepticism—in this case that sufficient public interest would exist in the life of a deceased playwright whose entire reputation rested on two plays."

Robert Nemiroff. Postscript. *To Be Young, Gifted and Black: Lorraine Hansberry in Her Own Words,* adapt. Robert Nemiroff (Englewoods Cliffs: Prentice, 1969), p. 263.

Distinguish clearly between **paraphrase** and direct firsthand quotation. When you paraphrase, you put someone else's ideas in your own words. You can thus highlight what seems most important to you and condense other parts. Even when you paraphrase, be sure to use quotation marks for striking phrases that you keep in the exact wording of the author. The following note might be your summing up of comments on the original casting of *Death of a Salesman* that Arthur Miller made in an article in *Theater Week* in 1991:

Miller admits he believes in typecasting, choosing the actor who looks right for the role, since no director really wants to make over an actor into something he or she isn't. But although Miller wrote the part of Willy Loman originally with a "small, feisty man" in mind, the original Willy Loman turned out to be Lee Cobb, "the closest thing in Equity to a hippo."

Your note taking becomes truly productive when you begin to follow up tentative patterns and promising connections that you discover in your reading. For instance, many reviews of the *Death of a Salesman* revival with Dustin Hoffman talked at length about the contrast between Cobb and Hoffman. (Miller made Cobb say, "I look like a walrus," but for Hoffman he changed the line back to the original "I look like a shrimp.")

Here are related notes from a review by Lloyd Roe, titled "Lost in America," in the *Atlantic* for April 1984. (Note finer points like *single quotation marks* for the phrase "common man," which appears as a quote-within-a-quote. Note the use of the *ellipsis*—three spaced periods to show an omission, or four when the periods include the period at the end of a sentence. Note the use of *square brackets* to show that material has been inserted into the original quotation.)

"Big and slow-moving, with a suffering dignity in his thick face," Cobb "gave the lie to Miller's view of Willy as a 'common man.' Cobb's pain was outsized. He was like a huge, wounded animal dying from a bullet he never heard coming, and he was as private as an animal—the real source of his agony was hidden and mute. Cobb rendered irrelevant the question of Willy's responsibility for his own defeat by making his sorrow too deep for the circumstances of his life."

"Coming to the play from a different generation and a different tradition, Hoffman, though he can't ignore Cobb, hardly labors in his shadow. Hoffman couldn't be more different from Cobb, both physically and technically, but he doesn't try for contrasts. . . . His Willy is freshly conceived—the characterization feels new, and there's a sense of discovery in it."

"Hoffman's Willy is collapsed in on himself, as if he were shrinking . . . Hoffman makes [the Willy in his forties in the flashbacks] optimistic, and then demonstrates how this never-say-die quality, originally a source for strength, is corrupted by time and hardship. Willy's self-delusions, which may impress a reader of the play as stupid or psychotic, are in Hoffman's performance the end of the optimism of his youth; they're what optimism has to become as life gets smaller."

Pushing toward a Thesis Even during your exploratory reading and note taking, you will be looking for a possible unifying thread, for a figure in the carpet. Avoid a pattern that goes from "one person said this" to "another person said something else." Look for recurrent issues; look for a note that in your materials is sounded again and again.

In reading contemporary reactions to Ibsen's plays, for instance, it is hard not to be impressed by their tendency to polarize the audience. Again and again, fervent defenders celebrated him as one of the pioneers of modern emancipated thinking. And also again and again, outraged champions of public morality targeted him as an enemy of decency and Western civilization. This recurrent pattern points toward a possible unifying **thesis:** Ibsen, in the words of an English director, "split the English theater in two." The following might be a tentative thesis:

TRIAL THESIS: Ibsen's plays were denounced as immoral by his outraged enemies and at the same time championed as ushering in a new morality.

Using a Working Outline To give direction to your reading and writing, sketch out a **working outline** as soon as you have a rough idea how your material is shaping up. At first, your plan might be very tentative. The whole point of a working outline is to help you visualize a possible pattern and to help you refine it as you go along. At an intermediate stage in the Ibsen paper, the writer's working outline might look like this:

WORKING OUTLINE: —polarizing effect of Ibsen's plays
        the "new" morality in his plays
        "the "old" morality of his contemporaries
    —the attack on Ibsen
        Scott's denunciation
        Archer's collection of criticism
    —Shaw's defense of the plays
    —Ibsen's getting back at his critics
        portrait of the moralist in his plays
        Ibsen's letters

Documenting the Paper When you draw on a range of not easily accessible sources—for instance, reviews that took initiative and perseverance to track down—you may be asked to provide full **documentation.** Documentation identifies your sources, complete with publishing information and exact page numbers. Remember that it should enable your readers to verify your sources and to get further information from them if they wish. Unless told differently by your instructor or editor, follow the style of documentation of the Modern Language Association (MLA). Use **parenthetical documentation** in the running text of your paper (mostly to provide page numbers, but also to tag author and title as needed). Then give complete information about each source in a final alphabetical listing of **Works Cited.** (This was once the **bibliography,** or "book list," but it may now include nonprint sources like videocassettes, radio and television programs, and computer software.)

Parenthetical documentation has done away with footnotes, the typist's nemesis. (Numbered explanatory notes may still follow a paper or article.) If you have said that Susan Sontag in *Against Interpretation* speaks of the "volleying back and forth of clichés" in a typical play by Ionesco, all you need is the page number or numbers in parentheses (119). However, if you have merely said that a prominent critic used that phrase, you will have to include her name, so that the reader can find the source in the Works Cited (Sontag 119). If you plan to quote another book or article by Sontag, you will have to tag the first source here, using a shortened version of the title—if possible without interfering with alphabetical ordering later (Sontag, *Against Interpretation* 119). Remember to tag author or title in parentheses only if you have not already given the information in your running text.

For classics that are available in many different editions, show act, scene, and line in arabic numerals instead of page numbers (3.2.46–49). Some prefer the traditional large and small roman numerals for act and scene (III.ii.46–49).

Here are some standard entries for your alphabetical listing of Works Cited. Remember: italics (or underlining on a typewriter) for titles of separate publications; quotation marks for titles of articles or of plays that are part of a collection. Remember to leave two spaces after periods marking off chunks of information in the entry. Remember to indent the second and following lines of each entry *five* spaces.

Primary sources: listing of a play

Wilson, August. *The Piano Lesson.* New York: Plume-NAL, 1990.
[Plume is an imprint, or special line of books, of New American Library.]

Beckett, Samuel. *Waiting for Godot: Tragicomedy in 2 Acts.* New York: Grove, 1954.
[Note italicized (underlined) subtitle.]

Shakespeare, William. *The Tragedy of Hamlet.* Ed. Edward Hubler. New York: NAL, 1963.
[Special edition of a play.]

Hubler, Edward, ed. *The Tragedy of Hamlet.* By William Shakespeare. New York: NAL, 1963.
[Editor's name first—editor's work important.]

Hansberry, Lorraine. *A Raisin in the Sun. Black Theater: A Twentieth-Century Collection of the Work of Its Best Playwrights.* Ed. Lindsay Patterson. New York: Dodd, 1971. 221–76.
[Play in a collection, with complete page numbers for the play.]

Aristophanes. *Lysistrata.* Trans. Donald Sutherland. *Classical Comedy Greek and Roman.* Ed. Robert W. Corrigan. New York: Applause, 1987. 11–68.
[Play in a collection (with page numbers); translator's name included.]

Secondary sources listing of a critical study or review

Lebowitz, Naomi. *Ibsen and the Great World.* Baton Rouge: Louisiana State UP, 1990.
[Book published by a university press.]

Goodman, Charlotte. "The Fox's Cubs: Lillian Hellman, Arthur Miller, and Tennessee Williams." *Modern American Drama: The Female Canon.* Ed. June Schlueter. New York: Associated UP, 1990. 135–39.
[Article in a collection.]

Greeley, Andrew. "Today's Morality Play: The Sitcom." *New York Times* 17 May 1987, late ed. , sec. 2: 1+.
[Newspaper article, with edition and section specified. Article starts on page 1 and continues later in the newspaper.]

Lewis, Theophilus. "Social Protest in *Raisin in the Sun.*" *Catholic World* 190 (Oct. 1959): 31–35.
[Journal article, with volume number.]

Davis, Ossie. "The Significance of Lorraine Hansberry." *Freedomways* 5.3 (Summer 1965): 396–402.
[With number of volume and issue.]

Driver, Tom F. Rev. of *A Raisin in the Sun,* by Lorraine Hansberry. *New Republic* 13 Apr. 1959: 21.
[Untitled review.]

The following is an example of a documented paper. How successful was the student author in finding contemporary sources? How well does the paper support its main points? Study the use of parenthetical documentation and the entries in the Works Cited. Are there unusual situations or entries?

SAMPLE STUDENT PAPER

The Furor over Ibsen

What did Henrik Ibsen do? According to Granville-Barker, "he split the English theater in two" (24). Indeed, "as everyone knows, the introduction of Ibsen into England was not a peaceful one. In its wake came one of those great outbursts of critical frenzy and inflamed controversy which at regular intervals enliven literary history" ("Retrospective" 199). In England, as in the rest of Europe, the public was split into two factions: those who placed Ibsen on the blacklist as "immoral," and those who saw him as the champion of a new morality. A hundred years later, Ibsen continues to stir the conscience of a later generation. In a recent study, Naomi Lebowitz quotes a leading European intellectual on "the shame that overcomes the descendant in the face of an earlier possibility that he has neglected to bring to fruition" (Theodor Adorno, qtd. in Lebowitz 2).

Ibsen's plays aroused both indignation and enthusiasm because he fought against maintaining appearances at the expense of happiness, or what he termed hypocrisy. Una Ellis-Fermor, a translator and lifelong student of Ibsen, said that he "took upon himself the task of exposing the makeshift morality of his contemporaries in private and public life":

> In *The Pillars of the Community* he examines the lie in public life, the tragic struggle of Karsten Bernick to hide his sin and preserve his reputation at the expense of another man's good name. . . . In *A Doll's House* and *Ghosts* the subject is the lie in domestic life; the first shows the destruction of a marriage by an unreal and insincere relationship between husband and wife, and the second the destruction of the lives and souls of the characters by the oppressive tyranny of convention. (Ibsen, *Three Plays* 9–11)

In *Ghosts*, a dutiful and unloving wife keeps up an elaborate façade of respectability for a profligate husband. She finds herself defeated when her cherished son returns home suffering incurably from the syphilis he has inherited from his father. According to Bernard Shaw, the play was "an uncompromising and outspoken attack on marriage as a useless sacrifice," the story of a woman who had wasted her life in manufacturing a "monstrous fabric of lies and false appearances" (86, 88).

Against the tyranny of middle-class standards, Ibsen pitted his own concept of individual integrity. He felt, according to Georg Brandes, that "the individuality of the human being is to be preserved for its own sake, not for the sake of higher powers; and since beyond all else the individual should remain free and whole, all concessions made to the world represent to Ibsen the foul fiend, the evil principle" (373). One of the main ideas fused into Ibsen's plays, according to an article in the *Encyclopaedia Britannica*, is "the supreme importance of individual character, of personality: in the development and enrichment of the individual he saw the only hope for a really cultured and enlightened society" ("Drama" 65).

A Doll's House was particularly loaded with the "first duty to oneself" theme. Nora, in the last act, wakes to the fact that she is not worthy to be a good mother and wife because she has been merely a submissive servant and foil first for her father and then for her husband; she has been so protected and guided by them that she has no individual conception of life and its complexities. Nora realized that she did not know enough about the world and her place in it to be really "a reasonable human being," and she felt a duty to become one (Ibsen, *Three Plays* 65). Her life all at once seemed so artificial and meaningless to her that she felt like a doll living in a doll's house.

Nora left her husband and children to try to gain an understanding of real life, and when she "banged the door of A Doll's House, the echo of that violence was heard across the continent" ("Drama" 600).

Ibsen wrote these plays at a time when people felt a general ferment, a "spirit of the age" or a "movement of the century" that had introduced everywhere a tendency toward change. Voices heralding the modern age referred to the "new phase into which humanity is passing" and expressed the conviction that "society must undergo a transformation or perish" (Goodwin 124, 122). But the voices resisting the clamor for "innovations" were equally strong. Their watchword was devotion to duty—toward God, country, one's family and husband. Self-denial for the sake of greater forces was the commendable action. The churches taught it was sinful to assert one's own wishes and desires. The people, especially the dominated wife with whom Ibsen frequently deals, were exhorted to live for the good of everyone but themselves. Advocates of the emancipation of women were told in the public press that "men are men and women women"; that "sex is a fact—no Act of Parliament can eliminate it"; and that "where two ride on a horse, one must needs ride behind" (Goodwin 103, 109). They were told that in women's hands "rests the keeping of a pure tone in society, of a high standard in morality, of a lofty devotion to duty in political life." If she were to enter openly into political conflict, she would "debase her sex" and "lower the ideal of womanhood amongst men" (Goodwin 103–04).

The old-fashioned moralists were shocked by the "Ibsenist" view that self-fulfillment is more important than the sanctity of marriage, one's duty to others, and even business success. According to Arthur Bingham Walkley, drama critic for the London Times, "Ibsen became a bogey to many worthy people who had never read or seen a single one of his plays." To these people, "Ibsenism was supposed vaguely to connote 'Woman's Rights,' Free Love, a new and fearful kind of wildfowl called 'Norwegian Socialism,' and generally, every manifestation of discontent with the existing order of things" (790). Clement Scott, a prominent drama critic, led such formidable opposition against Ibsen's dramas, especially A Doll's House and Ghosts, that they were actually banned for a time from English stages. "Ibsen fails," Scott says, "because he is, I suppose, an atheist, and has not realized what the great backbone of religion means to the English race." Scott continues, "He fails because his plays are nasty, dirty, impure, clever if you like, but foul to the last degree; and healthy-minded English people don't like to stand and sniff over an ash-pit" (qtd. in Granville-Barker 24).

Many of the people causing the uproar against Ibsen used similar language. William Archer, the first English translator of Ibsen, collected some of the attacks appearing in the English press when Ghosts was first produced. The play was called "disgusting," "loathsome," "gross," and "revoltingly suggestive and blasphemous." It was compared to "a dirty act done publicly" and was called "a piece to bring the stage into disrepute and dishonour with every right-thinking man and woman" (qtd. in Shaw 91–93).

Those who defended Ibsen—Shaw, Archer, Walkley—blamed his unpleasant reception in England on both his revolutionary themes and his new dramatic technique. I shall steer away from Ibsen's new dramatic technique and instead discuss the defense of Ibsenism as a new moral philosophy. Shaw himself has been called one of the men "who summon their generation to act by a new and higher standard." He made Ibsen his hero because Ibsen championed the view that Shaw made the basis for many of his own plays:

> By "morals" (or "ideals") Shaw means conventional, current standards. Because these standards are universal and inherited from the past, they often do not fit particular situations and present-day societies. Therefore good men—

like some of Ibsen's characters—often choose to act "immorally," contrary to accepted morality. (Brower 687)

To Shaw, Ibsen became the first of the two types of pioneers classified by Shaw in *The Quintessence of Ibsenism*. This type of pioneer asserts "that it is right to do something hitherto regarded as infamous." Ibsen felt that it was right to think first of building himself and secondly of building the institutions of society. To Shaw, this change explained the unkindly reception of Ibsen's new thoughts in England: "So much easier is it to declare the right wrong than the wrong right. . . . a guilty society can more readily be persuaded that any apparently innocent act is guilty than that any apparently guilty act is innocent" (23–25). Shaw seems to feel that Ibsen would have had more success telling people it was wrong to work on Monday than he would have had saying it was right to work on Sunday. Men could not accept the idea that the obligation of self-sacrifice could be removed from them—that it would be all right for them to consider a duty toward themselves first.

Shaw complained of the difficulty of finding "accurate terms" for Ibsen's new "realist morality." To Shaw, it was Ibsen's thesis that "the real slavery of today is slavery to ideals of goodness" (146–49). Ibsen had devoted himself to showing that "the spirit of man is constantly outgrowing the ideals," and the "thoughtless conformity" to them is constantly producing tragic results (152). Among those "ridden by current ideals," Ibsen's plays were bound to be denounced as immoral. But, Shaw concluded, there can be no question as to the effect likely to be produced on an individual by his conversion from the ordinary acceptance of current ideals as safe standards of conduct, to the vigilant openmindedness of Ibsen. It must at once greatly deepen the sense of moral responsibility (154).

Ibsen himself knew well and satirized in his plays the moralists who inveighed against "the undermining of family life" and the "defiance of the most solemn truths." In *Ghosts*, Pastor Manders, who represents a timid regard for convention, warns people against books that he vaguely associates with "intellectual progress"—and that he has not read. Rörlund, the schoolmaster in *The Pillars of the Community*, sums up the position of the guardians of conventional morality when he says: "Our business is to keep society pure . . . to keep out all these experimental notions that an impatient age wants to force on us" (Ibsen, *Three Plays* 27–28). Ironically, Rörlund provides a moral façade for "practical men of affairs" like the ship owner Bernick. Bernick, who talks about his "deep-rooted sense of decency," has abandoned the woman he loved in order to marry a wealthy girl and save the family business. He has abandoned to need and shame a married woman with whom he has had a secret affair. He has saved his own reputation in the community at the expense of having a younger friend blackened as a libertine and a thief. Bernick's defense of his conduct is that he lives in a community in which "a youthful indiscretion is never wiped out." The "community itself forces us into crooked ways" (97–98). But Ibsen's heroes are people who rebel against the "tyranny of custom and convention," who hold that "the spirit of truth and the spirit of freedom" are the "true pillars of the community" (116, 137).

Ibsen was not intimidated by the controversy caused by his plays. In a letter to a friend he wrote in 1881, he said: "*Ghosts* will probably cause alarm in some circles. . . . If it didn't do that, there would have been no need to write it." In a letter written a year later, he said: "That my new play would produce a howl from the camp of those 'men of stagnation' was something I was quite prepared for" (*Ghosts* 126). Shortly afterward, he summed up his faith in the future in a letter that said in part:

In time, and not before very long at that, the good people up home will get into their heads some understanding of *Ghosts*. But all those desiccated, decrepit individuals who pounced on this work, they will come in for devastating criticism in the literary histories of the future. People will be able to sniff out the nameless snipers and thugs who directed their dirty missiles at me from their ambush in Professor Goos's mouldy rag and other similar places. My book holds the future. Yon crowd that roared about it haven't even any proper contact with their own genuinely vital age. (*Ghosts* 129–30)

It was Ibsen's assertion of man's duty to himself, against the tradition of conformity to custom and convention, that was the main grounds of significant controversy over Ibsen's works. In presenting this view in his plays, as a modern critic says, "Ibsen established realism as the ruling principle of modern drama." Problems of the day had been aired on the stage before, "but nobody before Ibsen had treated them without equivocation or without stressing secondary matters while ignoring primary ones." Because he was the first, "Henrik Ibsen . . . has long held the unofficial title of 'father of the modern drama'" (Gassner vii-viii).

Works Cited

Brandes, Georg. *Creative Spirits of the Nineteenth Century.* Trans. Rasmus B. Anderson. New York: Crowell, 1923.

Brower, Reuben A. "George Bernard Shaw." *Major British Writers.* Ed. G. B. Harrison. Vol. 2. New York: Harcourt, 1959. 687. 2 vols.

"Drama." *Encyclopaedia Britannica.* 1958 ed.

Gassner, John. Introduction. *Four Great Plays by Ibsen.* By Henrik Ibsen. New York: Dutton, 1959. i–x.

Goodwin, Michael, ed. *Nineteenth-Century Opinion: An Anthology (1877–1901).* Hammondsworth, Middlesex: Penguin, 1951.

Granville-Barker, Harley. "When Ibsen Split the English Stage in Two." *Literary Digest* 28 (1928): 24–25.

Ibsen, Henrik. *Ghosts.* Trans. Kai Jurgensen and Robert Schenkkan. New York: Avon, 1965.

—. *Three Plays.* Trans. Una Ellis-Fermor. Harmondsworth, Middlesex: Penguin, 1950.

Lebowitz, Naomi. *Ibsen and the Great World.* Baton Rouge: Louisiana State UP, 1990.

"A Retrospective Eye on Ibsen." *Theatre Arts Monthly* 12 (1928): 199–211.

Shaw, Bernard. *The Quintessence of Ibsenism.* 3rd ed. New York: Hill, 1957.

Walkley, A. B. "Ibsen in England." *Living Age* 12 (1901): 790.

QUESTIONS

Does the paper succeed in drawing you into the controversy? Why or why not? What quotations do most to bring the two opposed factions to life? Does the writer do justice to both, or is one slighted? For what points does the writer choose to use extended quotations, printed as *block quotations* (indented ten spaces)? What questions remain in your mind as you read the paper?

29 COMEDY
The Gift of Laughter

Characters in a play don't always have to be bigger fools than in everyday life.

EUGÈNE IONESCO

Humor is born in dark places of the soul, masking anguish with a tilt toward absurdity.

AL MARTINEZ

My grandfather used to make home movies and edit out the joy.

ANONYMOUS

FOCUS ON COMEDY

Comedy takes us into a golden world of liberating laughter. Tragedy makes us face our limits; it brings men and women up against the boundaries of human hope and endeavor. Comedy celebrates the renewal of hope. Traditionally, it stresses what is congenial to human life; it celebrates the life-affirming forces in our world. Scholars have traced the roots of comedy to pre-Christian Easter festivals that celebrated the return of the sun after the dead of winter. They have looked for its origins in marriage festivals and fertility rites that celebrated the bonding of love and the renewal of the community. At its best, comedy preserves the spirit of holiday—of mirth, merrymaking, celebration, fiesta, festival, carnival, or revelry.

Comedy can mold the grey world of every day closer to the heart's desire. It can take us from the iron world of history to the green world of Shakespeare's mythical Forest of Arden, where lovers hang love poems on trees and live "like the old Robin Hood of England." When we become too bitter or cynical, comedy can restore our faith in good fortune, in young love, in the human capacity for generosity and sudden changes of heart.

Comedy intersects with reality when it makes us laugh at people and attitudes that stand in the way of a more humane world. It may mock eccentrics. It may satirize traits that narrow life, forces that shut off possibility. Wielding humor as a weapon, the comic playwright may use his or her gift for **satire** to do battle against stinginess, pomposity, lust, or hypocrisy. We stay in the comic realm when these forces may be threatening—but they do not become overpowering. We know that we can best them. At any rate, cleansed by laughter, we can best our own inclinations toward narrowness, intolerance, and tunnel vision.

TRAGEDY AND COMEDY

While tragedy celebrates the hero's capacity to suffer, and thereby to earn a new and deeper knowledge of himself and his universe, comedy tends to be more concerned with the fact that, for all our individual defeats, life does nonetheless continue on its merry way.

ROBERT W. CORRIGAN

The pleasures of lamenting the decline of tragedy among us have perhaps gone stale, so for a change we might lament the decline of comedy.

DONALD SUTHERLAND

Walking into the playhouse, you may see the two masks that are the traditional symbols of the theater: the weeping mask of tragedy and the laughing mask of comedy. Whenever the classical Greek influence has been strong in the theater, tragedy and comedy have been separate **genres.** However, both in ancient Greece and sometimes later, the two theatrical forms appeared on the same playbill, with shorter comic pieces following the tragic main offerings. When we avoid too rigid a separation of the two genres, we acknowledge that ideally as human beings we are capable of both tears and laughter.

Traditionally, critics have distinguished the two genres first of all by social level: Comedy takes us down from the palace steps to mingle with the populace. However, this change in social level brings with it a change in perspective. In comedy, we are likely to look at life from the point of view of the merrymaker rather than the peace officer, the sinner rather than the saint. Comedy often breaches etiquette to nose about taboo-ridden subjects; it catches us in clumsy moments with essential garments down.

In ancient Greece, the same audiences who watched with awe as the oracle of Apollo caught up with Oedipus might watch with happy laughter as the women in Aristophanes' *Lysistrata* (411 B.C.) staged a sex strike to stop their men from dragging out a senseless war. No peace, no sex! No more swaggering among the pottery or the beans and greens of the marketplace in full military regalia! "Stay away from me," they tell their husbands and lovers, "or you will never eat garlic and black beans again!" Aristophanes established the tradition of irreverence that serves as the comic antidote to solemnity and self-importance. He set a high standard for audacity in insults "against political figures; in obscenity; in mockery of gods, philosophers, and the latest literature; in hilarious spoofs of political and military science—even of economics itself" (Donald Sutherland).

The great comic genius in the tradition of separate theatrical genres is the French seventeenth-century playwright Molière. He is part of the French **neoclassical** tradition—the "new classicism" or classical revival—of the reign of Louis XIV, the Sun King. Molière observed the rules of neoclassical **decorum**—of appropriateness to time, occasion, and social class. Tragedy dignifies the concerns of people of high status. Comedy has fun with the foibles and misadventures of people like ourselves. While contemporary tragedies put on the stage noble Greeks and Romans, Molière put on the stage *The Would-Be Gentleman*—the commoner who yearned to be noble. His Monsieur Jourdain is everyone's suddenly wealthy, nouveau riche neighbor. He yearns to improve his social status and acquire culture. He brings into the neighborhood dancing masters, music teachers, fencing experts, and philosophy tutors. He looks like a stuffed canary in the latest sartorial chic. And he is fleeced by decaying aristocrats. When we laugh at Monsieur Jourdain's pretensions to culture and his aping of the aristocracy, we laugh with a playwright observing the neoclassical requirement that comedy should "sport with human follies, not with crimes" (Ben Jonson).

The alternative to tragedy and comedy as separate forms is to mix laughter and tears, as they mix in real life. Shakespeare wrote tragedies and comedies, but even a Shakespearean tragedy may have a licensed jester who tells bitter truths. (A precarious occupation: The fool says to King Lear, "I marvel what kin thou and thy daughters are: they'll have me whipped for speaking true, thou'lt have me whipped for lying, and sometimes I am whipped for holding my peace.") Shakespeare wrote other plays that represent **tragicomedy**—a mixed genre in which the tragic and the comic visions contend. The major characters in such a play may go about their business with deadly seriousness while humor has taken refuge in the tavern, the jail, or the bordello.

What makes audiences laugh? Humor may seem a marvelous gift, but critics have found it puzzling and paradoxical. It seems to serve a variety of functions, not all of them easily reconcilable:

✧ Among influential theories of humor, that of the French critic Henri Bergson intrigues people who encourage what is natural or organic in human life: We laugh at what is rigid, mechanical, unnatural. People who dance as if they were counting "one-two-three" in their heads; people who follow a too rigid regimen of diet, exercise, or hygiene (becoming health fanatics or fitness freaks); people who are totally unbending in their religious or ideological views—these are comic, to others if not to themselves.

✧ A more cynical theory holds that we laugh at shortcomings that make us feel superior to others. People who are hamstrung by their failings are no competition for us; we don't have to take them seriously, and we laugh with relief. Thus, we laugh at bumblers, clumsy lovers, waiters who drop heavily loaded trays, and foreigners who massacre the English language. Some of the most endearing comic figures of the silent screen were lovable incompetents, forever accident-prone but harmless and good-natured—no real threat to anyone.

❖ A more defensive theory looks at humor as a kind of shield or armor. It is a mask we may put on to fend off prying or pity. A character may always be wisecracking so as not to let people see the hurt inside. The playwright Wendy Wasserstein has said that "a lot of comedy is a deflection." She said about a character in one of her plays that "she is *always* funny, so as not to say what she feels."

Looking at comedy, critics early made a distinction between two different kinds of laughter. The first kind of laughter makes us respond to things that are congenial, desirable, agreeable. We laugh (or more often smile) when something delightful happens. The most basic plot of traditional comedy has young people fall in love. They then meet obstacles—greedy parents, lusting elders—but they overcome these in the end. "Opposition, frustration, malice, lust, prejudice, and greed can and do inhabit the world of comedy, but these divisive powers are always overcome and assimilated into the lovers' happy world" (Robert W. Corrigan).

The second kind of laughter is the laughter of ridicule or derision; it is often mingled with contempt. It makes us laugh *at the opposite* of what is desirable or agreeable to human nature. It makes us laugh at deformity, at people less fortunate or less educated than ourselves, at people cheated by life or their loved ones. Much here depends on **tone**—since the same subject of ridicule may be treated in an indulgent, nearly affectionate tone or in a scornful, if not hateful, way.

In **satire**, ridicule is systematically used as a weapon to fight falsehood or abuses. To the extent that we recognize ourselves in the characters satirized, we may be shamed into changing our ways. A continuing strand in the history of comedy is satire directed at one outstanding trait that makes a character eccentric, destroying the desirable balance that we find in the well-adjusted individual. At least since the plays of the Roman playwrights Plautus and Terence, audiences have laughed at the miser, the hypochondriac, or the braggart soldier. In Shakespeare's time, such characters, dominated by one obsession or fixed idea, were considered **humor characters.** Their temperament was thought to be overbalanced by one of the bodily fluids, or "humors," supposedly responsible for character traits like anger or melancholy. Molière devoted several of his best-loved comedies to these comic types: *L'Avare* (the skinflint), *Le Malade Imaginaire* (the imaginary invalid). The miser, the hypochondriac, and the malcontent—forever dissatisfied with and critical of everything—have long been **stock characters** that audiences delight in seeing on the stage again and again.

Whether a play is delightful or bitter in tone, the soul of comedy is often quick, witty dialogue. Audiences delight in the **chase of wit**, with characters trading quick pointed remarks. (Older man: "I had advanced ideas before you were born!" Younger man: "I knew it was a long time ago.") Often comic dialogue is laced with **wordplay** or verbal humor. Just as readers today love to groan at the bad puns of compulsive punsters like Herb Caen of the *San Francisco Chronicle* ("the fastest pun in the West"), Shakespeare's audiences delighted in seeing a word put through its paces in a quickly moving exchange:

DUKE [*offering money to the jester who has just finished a song*]:
  There's for thy pains.
JESTER: No pains, sir. I take pleasure in singing, sir.
DUKE: I'll pay thy pleasure then.
CLOWN: Truly, sir, and pleasure will be paid one time or another.
  Shakespeare, *Twelfth Night*

Audiences delight in **parody**, which apes and exaggerates distinctive or eccentric traits for comic effect. Shakespeare in his comedies mimicked travelers who after returning from France or Italy dropped foreign phrases into the conversation and substituted dainty foreign manners for homespun English ways. At its most visceral (closest to gut level), comedy becomes **farce**, frowned upon by critics but beloved by the multitude. Farce means pratfalls, horseplay, offensive jokes. Elderly lovers try to climb to the balcony and fall into the rain barrel; lovers surprised by a spouse with a shotgun flee in their underwear. Farce lowers inhibitions. It often affords demonstrations of the fine art of abuse, allowing us to act out vicariously our impulse to tell the boors, sponges, and bullies of this world what we really think of them. (Sigmund Freud said, "The first human being who hurled an insult instead of a stone was the founder of civilization.")

For serious students of comedy, humor is not a laughing matter. Humor can serve as a means of in-grouping and out-grouping, of establishing or confirming group identity. Comedy can confirm our sense of belonging. For satire to work, it must in some way activate shared standards of what is acceptable and what is ridiculous. (Lily Tomlin described the group experience of humor as "sharing for the sharing-impaired.") As a result, while comedy draws us into its charmed circle, it may also leave others out. We are aware of the out-grouping effect of humor when people laugh at us behind our backs—because we are white or black, tall or short, old or young, too formally or too sloppily dressed. Much ethnic humor helps the in-group put down and keep down others. Feminist critics have looked askance at the traditional female comedian—Phyllis Diller in her fright wig, Joan Rivers—who perpetuates the comic stereotypes of the goofy housewife and the shrewish spouse. They have claimed that in traditional comedy "tension is released downward, against the vulnerable" (Nancy Henley).

JUXTAPOSITIONS

The Soul of Wit

I understand your new play is full of single entendres.
  ROBERT KASS

Impropriety is the soul of wit.
  SOMERSET MAUGHAM

The following short samples of comedy are by master practitioners of the comic playwright's art. The first of these is by Oscar Wilde, an Irish playwright who was born and educated in Dublin before being transplanted to Oxford and becoming a thorn in the side of his earnest Victorian contemporaries. The second sample is a playlet by Wendy Wasserstein, a contemporary American playwright, in whose comic sketch every satirical detail counts (and hurts).

Oscar Wilde's *The Importance of Being Earnest* (1895) is a bravura piece still brilliantly performed by modern theater companies. He wrote his comedies at a time when the English under Queen Victoria had for decades been taught a code of earnest striving and moral uprightness, creating the stereotype of the "Earnest Victorians." At a time when society put the premium on serious effort, Wilde put on the stage frivolous young people busy finding excuses for trips to the country (or the city). At a time when society put a premium on respectability and the family name, one of his heroes was a young man who at birth had been abandoned in a handbag left at a railroad station. In the following scene from *The Importance of Being Earnest,* Jack Worthing is caught in a subterfuge of his own making: His excuse for sneaking away to the city is that he claims to have a younger brother there named Ernest, who needs supervision. Then, when he gets to the city, Jack pretends to be Ernest. In the following exchange with Gwendolen, the young woman he adores, Jack learns something about the importance of being Ernest and earnest.

OSCAR WILDE (1854–1900)

A Proposal of Marriage 1895
From *The Importance of Being Earnest*

CHARACTERS

GWENDOLEN FAIRFAX
JACK WORTHING, known to GWENDOLEN as Ernest
LADY BRACKNELL, GWENDOLEN's mother

SCENE: *Algernon's apartment in London*

JACK: Charming day it has been, Miss Fairfax.
GWENDOLEN: Pray don't talk to me about the weather, Mr. Worthing. Whenever people talk to me about the weather, I always feel quite certain that they mean something else. And that makes me so nervous.
JACK: I do mean something else.
GWENDOLEN: I thought so. In fact, I am never wrong.
JACK: And I would like to be allowed to take advantage of Lady Bracknell's temporary absence. . . .
GWENDOLEN: I would certainly advise you to do so. Mama has a way of coming back suddenly into a room that I have often had to speak to her about.
JACK (*nervously*): Miss Fairfax, ever since I met you I have admired you more than any girl . . . I have ever met since . . . I met you.

GWENDOLEN: Yes, I am quite aware of the fact. And I often wish that in public, at any rate, you had been more demonstrative. For me you have always had an irresistible fascination. Even before I met you I was far from indifferent to you. (*Jack looks at her in amazement.*) We live, as I hope you know, Mr. Worthing, in an age of ideals. The fact is constantly mentioned in the more expensive monthly magazines, and has reached the provincial pulpits, I am told; and my ideal has always been to love someone of the name of Ernest. There is something in that name that inspires absolute confidence. The moment Algernon first mentioned to me that he had a friend called Ernest, I knew I was destined to love you.

JACK: You really love me, Gwendolen?

GWENDOLEN: Passionately!

JACK: Darling! You don't know how happy you've made me.

GWENDOLEN: My own Ernest!

JACK: But you don't really mean to say that you couldn't love me if my name wasn't Ernest?

GWENDOLEN: But your name is Ernest.

JACK: Yes, I know it is. But supposing it was something else? Do you mean to say you couldn't love me then? Personally, darling, to speak quite candidly, I don't much care about the name of Ernest . . . I don't think the name suits me at all.

GWENDOLEN: It suits you perfectly. It is a divine name. It has a music of its own. It produces vibrations.

JACK: Well, really, Gwendolen, I must say that I think there are lots of other much nicer names. I think Jack, for instance, a charming name.

GWENDOLEN: Jack? . . . No, there is very little music in the name Jack, if any at all, indeed. It does not thrill. It produces absolutely no vibrations. . . . I have known several Jacks, and they all, without exception, were more than usually plain. Besides, Jack is a notorious domesticity for John! And I pity any woman who is married to a man called John. She would probably never be allowed to know the entrancing pleasure of a single moment's solitude. The only really safe name is Ernest.

JACK: Gwendolen, I must get christened at once—I mean we must get married at once. There is no time to be lost.

GWENDOLEN: Married, Mr. Worthing?

JACK (*astounded*): Well . . . surely. You know that I love you, and you led me to believe, Miss Fairfax, that you were not absolutely indifferent to me.

GWENDOLEN: I adore you. But you haven't proposed to me yet. Nothing has been said at all about marriage. The subject has not even been touched on.

JACK: Well . . . may I propose to you now?

GWENDOLEN: I think it would be an admirable opportunity. And to spare you any possible disappointment, Mr. Worthing, I think it only fair to tell you quite frankly beforehand that I am fully determined to accept you.

JACK: Gwendolen!

GWENDOLEN: Yes, Mr. Worthing, what have you got to say to me?

JACK: You know what I have got to say to you.

GWENDOLEN: Yes, but you don't say it.

JACK (*goes on his knees*): Gwendolen, will you marry me?

GWENDOLEN: Of course I will, darling. How long you have been about it! I am afraid you have had very little experience in how to propose.

JACK: My own one, I have never loved anyone in the world but you.

GWENDOLEN: Yes, but men often propose for practice. I know my brother Gerald does. All my girl friends tell me so. What wonderfully blue eyes you have, Ernest! I hope you will always look at me just like that, especially when there are other people present. (*Enter* LADY BRACKNELL.)

LADY BRACKNELL: Mr. Worthing! Rise, sir, from this semirecumbent posture. It is most indecorous.

GWENDOLEN: Mama! (*He tries to rise; she restrains him.*) I must beg you to retire. This is no place for you. Besides, Mr. Worthing has not quite finished yet.

LADY BRACKNELL: Finished what, may I ask?

GWENDOLEN: I am engaged to Mr. Worthing, Mama. (*They rise together.*)

LADY BRACKNELL: Pardon me, you are not engaged to anyone. When you do become engaged to someone, I, or your father, should his health permit him, will inform you of the fact. An engagement should come on a young girl as a surprise, pleasant or unpleasant, as the case may be. It is hardly a matter that she could be allowed to arrange for herself. . . . And now I have a few questions to put to you, Mr. Worthing. While I am making these inquiries, you, Gwendolen, will wait for me below in the carriage.

GWENDOLEN (*reproachfully*): Mama!

LADY BRACKNELL: In the carriage, Gwendolen! (GWENDOLEN *goes to the door. She and* JACK *blow kisses to each other behind* LADY BRACKNELL'S *back.* LADY BRACKNELL *looks vaguely about as if she could not understand what the noise was. Finally turns around.*) Gwendolen, the carriage!

GWENDOLEN: Yes, Mama. (*goes out looking back at* JACK)

LADY BRACKNELL (*sitting down*): You can take a seat, Mr. Worthing. (*looks in her pocket for notebook and pencil*)

JACK: Thank you, Lady Bracknell, I prefer standing.

LADY BRACKNELL (*pencil and notebook in hand*): I feel bound to tell you that you are not down on my list of eligible young men. However, I am quite ready to enter your name, should your answers be what a really affectionate mother requires. Do you smoke?

JACK: Well, yes, I must admit I smoke.

LADY BRACKNELL: I am glad to hear it. A man should always have an occupation of some kind. There are far too many idle men in London as it is. How old are you?

JACK: Twenty-nine.

LADY BRACKNELL: A very good age to be married at. I have always been of the opinion that a man who desires to get married should know either everything or nothing. Which do you know?

JACK (*after some hesitation*): I know nothing, Lady Bracknell.

LADY BRACKNELL: I am pleased to hear it. I do not approve of anything that tampers with natural ignorance. Ignorance is like a delicate exotic fruit; touch it and the bloom is gone. The whole theory of modern education is radically unsound. Fortunately in England, at any rate, education produces no effect whatsoever. If it did, it would prove a serious danger to the upper classes. What is your income?

JACK: Between seven and eight thousand pounds a year.

LADY BRACKNELL (*makes a note in her book*): In land or in investments?

JACK: In investments, chiefly.

LADY BRACKNELL: That is satisfactory. What between the duties expected of one during one's lifetime, and the duties exacted from one after one's death, land has ceased to be either a profit or a pleasure. It gives one position and prevents one from keeping it up. That's all that can be said about land.

JACK: I have a country house with some land, of course, attached to it, about fifteen hundred acres, I believe; but I don't depend on that for my real income. In fact, as far as I can make out, the poachers are the only people who make anything out of it.

LADY BRACKNELL: A country house! How many bedrooms? Well, that point can be cleared up afterward. You have a town house, I hope? A girl with a simple, unspoiled nature, like Gwendolen, could hardly be expected to reside in the country.

JACK: Well, I own a house in Belgrave Square.

LADY BRACKNELL: What number in Belgrave Square?

JACK: One hundred and forty nine.

LADY BRACKNELL (*shaking her head*): The unfashionable side. I thought there was something. However, that could easily be altered.

JACK: Do you mean the fashion, or the side?

LADY BRACKNELL (*sternly*): Both, if necessary, I presume. Are your parents living?

JACK: I have lost both my parents.

LADY BRACKNELL: To lose one parent, Mr. Worthing, may be regarded as a misfortune. To lose both looks like carelessness. Who was your father? He was evidently a man of some wealth. Was he born in what the Radical papers call the purple of commerce, or did he rise from the ranks of the aristocracy?

JACK: I am afraid I really don't know. The fact is, Lady Bracknell, I said I had lost my parents. It would be nearer the truth to say that my parents seem to have lost me. . . . I don't actually know who I am by birth. I was . . . well, I was found.

LADY BRACKNELL: Found!

JACK: The late Mr. Thomas Cardew, an old gentleman of a very charitable and kindly disposition, found me and gave me the name of Worthing, because he happened to have a first-class ticket for Worthing in his pocket at the time. Worthing is a place in Sussex. It is a seaside resort.

LADY BRACKNELL: Where did the charitable gentleman who had a first-class ticket for this seaside resort find you?

JACK (*gravely*): In a handbag.

LADY BRACKNELL: A handbag?

JACK (*very seriously*): Yes, Lady Bracknell. I was in a handbag—a somewhat large, black leather handbag, with handles to it—an ordinary handbag in fact.

LADY BRACKNELL: In what locality did this Mr. James, or Thomas, Cardew come across this ordinary handbag?

JACK: In the cloakroom at Victoria Station. It was given to him in mistake for his own.

LADY BRACKNELL: The cloakroom at Victoria Station?

JACK: Yes. The Brighton line.

LADY BRACKNELL: The line is immaterial. Mr. Worthing, I confess I feel somewhat bewildered by what you have just told me. To be born, or at any rate bred, in a handbag, whether it had handles or not, seems to me to display a contempt for the ordinary decencies of family life that reminds one of the worst excesses of the French Revolution. . . . As for the particular locality in which the handbag was found, a cloakroom at a railway station might serve to conceal a social indiscretion—has probably, indeed, been used for that purpose before now—but it could hardly be regarded as an assured basis for a recognized position in good society.

JACK: May I ask you then what you would advise me to do? I need hardly say I would do anything in the world to insure Gwendolen's happiness.

LADY BRACKNELL: I would strongly advise you, Mr. Worthing, to try and acquire some relations as soon as possible, and to make a definite effort to produce at any rate one parent, of either sex, before the season is quite over.

JACK: Well, I don't see how I could possibly manage to do that. I can produce the handbag at any moment. It is in my dressing room at home. I really think that should satisfy you, Lady Bracknell.

LADY BRACKNELL: Me, sir! What has it to do with me? You can hardly imagine that I and Lord Bracknell would dream of allowing our only daughter—a girl brought up with the utmost care—to marry into a cloakroom, and form an alliance with a parcel. Good morning, Mr. Worthing! (LADY BRACKNELL *sweeps out in majestic indignation.*)

THE RECEPTIVE READER

1. Does this scene generate scornful, derisive laughter or humane, happy laughter? What evidence can you cite that would point in either direction?

2. Wilde's comic characters are very different from one another, and yet they each in turn make the audience laugh. Do a capsule portrait of each of the three characters. What makes Jack Worthing comic? What is hilarious about Gwendolen? What made Lady Bracknell immortal?

3. In his time, Wilde was notorious for witty sayings that stood some cliché or platitude on its head. Can you find examples in this scene?

4. What are the targets of Wilde's satire here? How serious and how effective is it?

5. As you look in the mirror the playwright holds up to human nature in this scene, do you see a reflection of yourself or of people you know?

6. Your class may want to have an audition for a Readers' Theater presentation of this scene. What traits and abilities would you look for in candidates for the three roles?

THE PERSONAL RESPONSE

Is Wilde's humor too frivolous for our day? Is it obsolete? Do we have more important things to worry about? Are we relapsing into the earnestness of the earnest Victorians?

The second sample of comedy in this pair is Wendy Wasserstein's *Boy Meets Girl*. Wasserstein (born 1950) knows the New York City setting of this one-act play from close firsthand experience. She was born in Brooklyn, studied creative writing at CCNY (City College of New York), and has done much of her writing in a Greenwich Village apartment. (After her senior year in college, she went west to look for work writing for television and discovered that she "loathed" California.) Several of her plays were successful off Broadway; her *Heidi Chronicles* (1988) moved on to Broadway and won a Pulitzer Prize, a Tony award, and the New York Drama Critics' Circle Award. She has written screenplays for television; she published a collection called *Bachelor Girls* in 1990.

Wasserstein is a master of **parody**—of mimicking something so as to expose the traits that make it special and laughable. Her characters in this playlet are young, urban, and professional (in short, yuppies). Before she is through with them, the playwright has dissected their dating rituals, their attitudes toward their jobs, their food fetishes, their dependence on their psychiatrists or psychologists. Above all, she mimics the trendy way they talk—about places to be seen, about clothes with snob appeal, about food that is not ordinary, and about schools that are not public schools.

Compare and contrast the workings of the comic muse in the scene from Oscar Wilde's play and in the one-act play that follows. (A few local references or allusions might need explanation for the uninitiated: Sabras are literally native-born, second-generation Israelis; here, the word stands for second-generation New York yuppies. Mrs. Helmsley became a living legend when she first became obscenely rich in New York real estate and then went to jail for cheating the IRS.)

WENDY WASSERSTEIN   (born 1950)

When a production goes wrong, it is hell. . . . From the word go, from no actors are available to the director doesn't show up, to the show doesn't work and no one's laughing, to you pick up some terrible reviews—I mean, all of that is devastating. It's just terrible. It's enough to give you a sense of humor.

WENDY WASSERSTEIN

Boy Meets Girl   1990

From *Bachelor Girls*

On a spring morning in 1972, a senior at the Spence School was in Central Park, completing her science project on the reproductive cycle of flowering plants, when she saw an unmarked bus drop off twenty women in silk suits, bow ties, and sneakers on the corner of Eighty-ninth Street and Fifth Avenue. The girl took note; when she was in sixth grade, sneakers and suits had been cause for suspension.

Meanwhile, on the West Side, a middle-aged but very nice lady was on her way to Barney Greengrass, the Sturgeon King, on Eighty-ninth Street, when three cars—a Volvo, a BMW, and a Saab with M.D. plates and a "Save the Whales" bumper sticker—pulled up to Eighty-seventh Street and Amsterdam Avenue. Fifteen young men, whom the lady thought she recognized from her son's protest days at the University of Wisconsin, emerged from the cars. Before the gracious lady could offer them an Entenmann's cake, they jogged into a dilapidated brownstone and immediately began exposing brick and hanging spider plants.

And the city embraced these pioneers, who were dressed in 100-percent-natural fabric. They prospered and they multiplied. From the now infamous drop-offs grew a new breed of New Yorkers, the Professionalites. Only their ratio of men to women, three to four, has remained constant.

What follows is a Love Story in One Act and Six Scenes between two of these sabra Professionalites: Dan and Molly.

CHARACTERS

MOLLY, thirty-three years old, single, successful, and quietly desperate. Every Saturday night, MOLLY sheds her doctorate in molecular microchips and slips into a Zandra Rhodes macromini. On the weekends, MOLLY is just another girl at The Trading Post, a popular café on the Columbus Avenue strip. Just another S.S.D.B.G. (Single/Successful/Desperate/Bachelor Girl) waiting for a discriminating Root Canal Man to invite her for an unfulfilling weekend at his summer share in the Hamptons. MOLLY, a native New Yorker, has recently begun considering relocating to the Sun Belt.

DAN, a successful creative director at B.B.D. & O. advertising agency. He is thirty-two, single, and having a ball. Every night, after twelve hours of Clio Award–winning work for his clients, DAN goes to the Odeon, where he eats poached salmon on grilled kiwi fruit at a table crowded with visual artists, conceptual artists, and performing artists. And every night, after picking up the tab, DAN swears that he, too, will one day give up his job and devote himself to art.

DR. SUSAN, MOLLY'S psychiatrist

STANLEY TANNENBAUM, PH.D., DAN'S psychologist

HER MAJESTY, THE QUEEN, ruler of the Helmsley Palace

SCENE 1

One night in late August, DAN *has a yearning to talk to someone who knows Donna Karan but has moved on to Issey Miyake.* DAN *slips into The Trading Post, where the number of single women is a plague to the West Side zoning committee. It is here that he first sees* MOLLY, *seated at the bar. She is young, she is urban, she is professional. He knows immediately that* MOLLY *is the kind of new-fashioned girl he could bring home to his analyst's couch.* DAN *sits next to her.*

DAN: Hi.

MOLLY: Hi.

DAN: Do you come here often?

MOLLY: Never.

DAN: I don't either.

MOLLY: I'm waiting here for a friend. She selected this place. I think what's happening to the West Side is outrageous.

DAN: This is really an East Side singles kind of restaurant.

MOLLY: Yes, but it's here on the West Side, so we have to deal with it.

DAN: You sound like a concerned citizen.

MOLLY: Did you ever read any Kenneth Burke? In college, maybe? Lit. Crit.?

DAN (*immediately*): Oh, sure.

MOLLY : He divides people into observers, spectators, and participants. I'm here strictly as a sociological observer. I love to watch people in New York. Otherwise I would never come to a place like this.

DAN: I wouldn't either. In my spare time I write film criticism.

MOLLY (*more interested*): Oh, you're a critic! Who do you write for?

DAN: I write for myself. I keep a film criticism journal.

MOLLY: I love film. Women in film particularly interest me. My favorites are Diane Kurys, Doris Dörrie, and Lee Grant.

DAN: I love women in film too.

MOLLY (*impressed*): You're so direct and forthcoming. What do you do?

DAN: I'm a psychiatrist.

MOLLY: Individual, group, house calls?

DAN: Actually, I'm a creative director at the B.B.D. & O. advertising agency. But I think of it as psychology. Dealing with the individual's everyday dreams and desires. I'm in charge of the Scott Paper account.

MOLLY: Fascinating. I use tissues a lot. I've always wondered why.

DAN: What do *you* do?

MOLLY: I'm a systems analyst for American Express.

DAN: "Do you know me?"

MOLLY (*very straightforward*): Not very well. But I'd like to.

DAN (*looks at her intently*): Why don't we go somewhere a little less trendy to talk. I can tell these aren't your kind of people.

MOLLY: No, I don't belong here. This isn't my New York.

DAN (*helps her on with her coat*): That's a nice jacket.

MOLLY: Donna Karan. But I've moved on to Issey Miyake.

DAN (*putting on a multilayered karate jacket*): We have so much in common.

MOLLY: "It's a phenomenon." That's a quote from a song in *Gypsy.* "Small world, isn't it?" I love Stephen Sondheim.

DAN: I'm afraid I don't know much about theater. I'm a workaholic. You know, mid-thirties New York guy, longing for Real Relationship with Remarkable Woman, meanwhile finds fulfillment through his work.

MOLLY: I think I like you. But be careful, I have Fear of Intimacy.

DAN: The Bachelor Girl's Disease. I hear it's an epidemic.

MOLLY: I'm working with my shrink to get past it.

Pause as DAN *looks at her.*

DAN: I think I like you, too.

They begin to exit restaurant.

DAN: What about your girl friend?

MOLLY: Uh, ah, she told me if she wasn't here by now she wasn't coming.

DAN: Not a very reliable friend.

MOLLY: No, but she's working with her shrink to get past it.

They exit.

SCENE 2

Phil's Risotto, a risotto and cheese emporium. DAN *and* MOLLY *stroll over to the counter arm in arm. It is mid-September.*

DAN (*ordering at the counter*): We'll have lemon risotto, chanterelle risotto, spinach risotto salad, pesto tart, carrot ravioli, goat cheese, goat cheese with ash, and a half pound of American.

MOLLY (*surprised, almost disturbed*): American?

DAN: Have you ever had real American cheese? Not the stuff they sell at the supermarket, but real American. (*He gives her a piece.*) Taste this.

MOLLY (*tasting*): Oh, that's marvelous!

DAN: I've been rediscovering American food: peanut butter, grape jelly, Marshmallow Fluff, Scooter Pies, Chef Boyardee, bologna. It is unbelievable! If it's done correctly.

MOLLY (*softly*): I love you.

DAN: Excuse me?

MOLLY: I love blue. I adore Kraft blue cheese dressing.

DAN: Well, if it's done correctly.

SCENE 3

MOLLY *in the office of her psychiatrist*, DR. SUSAN. *It is October.*

MOLLY (*sneezes*): Excuse me. I'm getting a cold.

DR. SUSAN: How do you feel about that?

MOLLY: Terrible. Tissues remind me of him. He says people should live together before they get married.

DR. SUSAN: How do you feel about that?

MOLLY: Sigourney Weaver and Glenn Close are married.

DR. SUSAN: How do you feel about that?

MOLLY: Living together was for kids in the late sixties and seventies. I'm a thirty-three-year-old woman.

DR. SUSAN: How do you feel about that?

MOLLY: I need a commitment. I want a family. I don't want to take a course at the New School on how to place a personal ad. Meryl Streep has three children already.

DR. SUSAN: Why do you always compare yourself to movie stars? You're not an actress.

MOLLY: That's true. That's really true! That's an incredible insight. Maybe my mother wanted me to be an actress. I hate her.

SCENE 4

DAN *in the office of his psychologist*, STANLEY TANNENBAUM, PH.D. *It is November.*

DAN: I don't think I want to make a commitment to Molly, but I'm afraid of what she'll say.

STANLEY TANNENBAUM, PH.D.: Well, let's put Molly in this chair, and then you can answer for her.

DAN: All right. (*talking now to an empty chair*) Molly, I don't think I want to make a commitment.

DAN *gets up and sits in chair to answer as* MOLLY *would.*

DAN (*pretending he's* MOLLY): That's okay. I'm an observer. This is all a sociological investigation. Kenneth Burke divides people into spectators, partici—

DAN *runs back to his seat to answer* MOLLY.

DAN (*angry*): Who the hell is Kenneth Burke? That is so pretentious, Molly!

DAN (*as* MOLLY): Not as pretentious as keeping a journal of film criticism.

DAN (*furious*): You resent my writing! You want to swallow me up. If I live with you, I won't be here anymore. I'll lose myself.

STANLEY TANNENBAUM, PH.D.: Did you hear what you just said?

DAN: I have it. Goddamn it! I have it. Fear of Intimacy. That Bachelor Girl's Disease. Why couldn't I just get burn-out?

SCENE 5

Central Park West. The Thanksgiving Day Parade. DAN *and* MOLLY *are watching floats of Bullwinkle and Superman pass by.*

MOLLY (*overcome by the sight of the floats*): I love this parade. Gosh, I really love this parade. Reminds me of growing up here and of New York before there were Benetton shops and a Trump Organization.

DAN: I never imagined people actually grew up in New York.

MOLLY: It was different then. There were real neighborhoods. The ladies on Madison Avenue wore white gloves and ate mashed potatoes at the Kirby Allen Restaurant. Marjorie Morningstar and her family gathered for Sabbath dinners on Central Park West. All artists wore turtlenecks and played bongo drums in the Village. And every night at seven o'clock, men in top hats and tails tap-danced from Shubert Alley to the Winter Garden Theater.

DAN: Really!

MOLLY: Well, I like to think so. Now everywhere I go all the women look like me.

DAN: What's so bad about that?

MOLLY: Nothing, it's just that it's all the same. I like the idea of a flower district, a theater district, a diamond district. The whole city is being renovated into Molly district. Dan, I have to confess. I hate goat cheese.

DAN (*softly*): Me, too. But I love you.

MOLLY: Hmmmmmm?

DAN: I hate goat cheese, but I love blue. Molly, with Bullwinkle as my witness, I want to marry you. And every Thanksgiving we can bring our children here. And someday they'll tell someone they met at The Trading Post, "I love this parade, I grew up here."

MOLLY (*no longer wistful*): But will our children go to Trinity or the Ethical Culture School? They could probably learn Chinese at Trinity, but there are a lot of Wall Street parents. Ethical Culture is nice, but maybe it's too liberal, not enough attention to the classics. How 'bout Brearley? There's something to be said for an all-women's education. (*She kisses* DAN.) Dan, just think! We can raise a family of women filmmakers!!!!!

SCENE 6

The Helmsley Palace. The Grand Ballroom. An enormous wedding party. DAN *and* MOLLY *are standing under the altar before* HER MAJESTY, THE QUEEN.

QUEEN: Dan, do you take this woman to be your wife? To love, be emotionally supportive of, have good dialogue with, as well as a country home in the Hamptons, Connecticut, or possibly upper New York State?

DAN: I do.

QUEEN: Molly, do you take this man to love, and at the same time maintain your career, spend quality time with the children, and keep yourself appealing by joining the New York Health and Racquet Club?

MOLLY: I do.

QUEEN (*addressing the wedding guests*): I've known this couple for two hours. But I've stood guard at their honeymoon suite. Molly will be able to see her makeup in soft light in the bathroom mirror. Dan will be put at ease by the suit hangers that detach from the closet. And if Dan and Molly decide to get remarried someday, and return to the honeymoon suite, I will keep a note of their room number. I wouldn't sleep in a new room, why should they?

DAN (*bows*): Thank you, Your Majesty.

MOLLY (*curtsies*): Thank you, Your Majesty.

QUEEN: And now by virtue of being Queen of all the Helmsleys, I pronounce you husband and wife. Congratulations! You may kiss the bride. (DAN *kisses* MOLLY. *There are cheers and the band begins to play "Lullaby of Broadway." Five hundred men in top hats and tails begin to tap down the aisle.*)

EPILOGUE

DAN and MOLLY became bi-island (Manhattan and Long), with bi-point three children (a girl, a boy, and an au pair from Barnard), and bi-career (a shift into management for him, a cottage industry for her). As MOLLY approached middle age she began to consult crystals about her hormonal convergence and undertook frequent pilgrimages to Stonehenge. DAN continued to pursue his interest in early American comestibles, and was featured on the cover of *Just Say Cheese* magazine for his distinguished cellar of American pasteurized-cheese foods.

The fortunes of the QUEEN, however, followed a crueler path. After a long and glorious reign, she was found to be poaching, thereby violating the charter, and was forced to abdicate. Even a monarch must obey the laws of the realm. On the day she was dethroned, she received a monogrammed Cartier sympathy note from MOLLY.

> Dear Your Majesty,
> Dan and I send you our best wishes at this
> difficult time.
>
> Molly
>
> PS. Is your estate in Greenwich for sale?

MOLLY'S mother had taught her that a lady always sends a note.

Otherwise—apart from twenty years of couples therapy, his-and-her reconstructive surgery, one triple bypass, and four extramarital affairs—they lived happily ever after.

THE RECEPTIVE READER

1. Like other successful practitioners of comedy, Wasserstein has a quick eye for small but revealing *details*. As she sets the scene in her introduction, what is the significance of details like the sneakers, the make of the cars, the bumper sticker, the fabric?

2. How does Wasserstein's playlet compare with the scene by Wilde as social satire? Which of her targets do you recognize? Which of her satirical jabs are most telling?

3. In the context of the scene, what is funny about a line like "I use tissues a lot"? What are other examples of *verbal humor*?

4. What is comic about the minidramas in the psychiatrist's and the psychologist's offices?

5. Wasserstein's plays often touch on topics of concern to feminists. What is the playwright's slant on the two sexes and the relationship between them?

THE PERSONAL RESPONSE

What kind of in-grouping or out-grouping may be part of the effect of the Wilde and Wasserstein selections? Who is included in and who is left out? *At* whom are you laughing, and *with* whom? With whom do you identify, or from what perspective do you see the people in each selection?

MOLIÈRE AND THE LIMITS OF COMEDY

The austerest of us are at heart all too human.
MOLIÈRE, *THE MISANTHROPE*

Satire is moral outrage transformed into comic art.
PHILIP ROTH

Molière (1622–1673) started his career with a group of actors traveling in the provinces and became one of the best-known and best-loved names connected with the stage. His comedies—such as *The Miser, The Imaginary Invalid, The Would-Be Gentleman, The School for Wives, The Misanthrope,* and *Tartuffe*—continue in the standard repertory at the Comédie Française in Paris and at theaters around the world. Born Jean-Baptiste Poquelin (Molière was his stage name), he first knew the royal court as furnisher and attendant, following in the footsteps of his father. However, his ambition was to be an actor, and he eventually became a protégé of Louis XIV, to whose lavish taste and patronage of the arts later generations owe the palace at Versailles. Both the architecture and the theater cultivated a **neoclassical,** or classical-revival, style designed to reflect the dignity and splendor of the Sun King's reign.

Like Shakespeare, Molière was an actor-playwright with a mastery of theatrical effects and a sense of audience reactions sharpened by much firsthand experience. Like other writers with a satirical bent, he acquired a devoted following but also powerful enemies. He was accused of lampooning important persons and religion (when actually his target was religious hypocrisy). He prospered under the protection of his royal patron, but his life was embittered toward the end by an unhappy marriage to a much younger woman, the daughter of a former mistress. Very ill, he insisted on playing his part as the hypochondriac in *The Imaginary Invalid* in early performances of the play; he died after a hemorrhage during a performance.

Molière's plays run the gamut from farcical horseplay to biting satire and wistful laughter. He knew how to do broad popular humor: In *The Doctor in*

Spite of Himself (1666), a wife-beating drunkard of a husband gets his come-uppance. His much-abused wife makes him out to be a miracle-working physician—who will, however, practice his art only after he is beaten into admitting his hidden talents. At the opposite end of the comic spectrum is Molière's *The Misanthrope* (1666)—about a man whose high standards lead him to hate human nature. Although the play has its hilarious moments, much of the laughter is thoughtful laughter—and at times the play seems to turn too serious for laughter altogether.

Molière lived in an age when elegance in manners, language, and dress was more highly valued than today. A chief goal was not to seem a country bumpkin. However, in this play, elegant manners are not the unquestioned fashionable standard; instead, they are the *issue*. Alceste, the misanthropic hero of the play, lives in an upper-class society where surface politeness and flattery are carried to ridiculous extremes in public, while malicious gossip is a favorite pastime in private. He is forever aghast at the two-faced nature of the people around him. However, he is a comic character in a comic play. The play does not simply line up honest against dishonest people. Different characters in turn have good lines, and the audience is drawn into the play of point and counterpoint on the central question: whether to be honest and rude or tolerant and polite. As you read the play, ask yourself: Who in the end has the laughers on his or her side?

Try to visualize the characters in the quick pointed exchanges and confrontations in which Molière's audiences delight. Read sample passages out loud to see if you can attune your ear to the fast-moving dialogue that, although in verse, is close to the rhythms of natural speech. Although the lines are slightly longer than Shakespeare's blank verse (averaging twelve to fourteen instead of ten or eleven syllables), they move fast because of what tends to be spoken as a four-beat instead of the familiar five-beat line:

> Il est BIEN des enDROITS où la PLAINE FranCHISE
> DevienDRAIT ridiCULE et seRAIT peu perMISE.

> But to PRACTice strict CANDor, you'll HAVE to aGREE,
> Would quite OFTen be FOOLish, and PAINful to SEE.

At the same time, the lines use end rhyme, with a passage often leading up to a neatly packaged **closed couplet** that wraps up a point. Often such a couplet plays off **antitheses,** or neatly balanced opposites, like the "esteem *for all*/esteem *for none*" in the following example:

> Estéem must seléct from the cómmon rún—
> Estéem for áll is estéem *for* nóne.

A brief pointed memorable remark is called an **epigram,** and Molière's epigrammatic style makes many of his couplets especially quotable. It also allows his characters to score points and gain (often only temporary) advantage.

Molière follows the conventions of his day in having his characters speak an elevated sugary and abstract language of the emotions. The love relationships (as least what we watch of them on the stage) are all talk, and the talk is about *ardors, vows, flames, fervors,* and *amorous fires.* Even Alceste, who denounces the sugary, insincere language of bad poetry, is caught up in this elevated **euphemistic** style. (Euphemisms make things sound more beautiful and refined than they really are.) For more pointed, down-to-earth language, we need to turn to the satirical jabs and barbs, as when Célimène skewers the host who ruined a good meal by serving up his table talk as dessert.

The translation that follows uses the rapidly moving four-beat line that French audiences hear when they watch the play or listen to it on cassette. The attempt here is to reproduce for American readers what one critic has called Molière's "sprightly and dancelike dialogue." (Other translations use the five-beat iambic pentameter line, making Molière sound like a French Alexander Pope: "Esteem is founded on comparison: / To honor all men is to honor none.")

A note on the French names: The names are generally stressed on the final syllable, with the final *e* silent: Alcest(e), Philint(e), Célimèn(e), Oront(e). (The *in* and *on* are nasalized, sounding to American ears similar to *eng* and *ong*.) Arsinoé has a stressed final *e*, pronounced closer to *a* than to *ee:* Arsinoe.

MOLIÈRE   (1622–1673)

The Misanthrope   1666

TRANSLATED BY HANS P. GUTH

CHARACTERS

ALCESTE, the misanthrope
PHILINTE, until recently ALCESTE's friend
ORONTE, gentleman of rank and part-time poet
CÉLIMÈNE, loved (with certain reservations) by ALCESTE
ÉLIANTE, friend and cousin of CÉLIMÈNE
ACASTE   } men of distinction
CLITANDRE }
ARSINOÉ, reputed to be a prude
SERVANTS
AN OFFICER

ACT ONE

SCENE 1 [PHILINTE, ALCESTE]

PHILINTE: How now? What is wrong?
ALCESTE: Please leave me alone.
PHILINTE: But please do explain your abruptness of tone . . .
ALCESTE: Please leave me, I say, and shame on your head.

PHILINTE: At least you should hear me without turning red . . .

ALCESTE: I *want* to turn red, and refuse you my ear. 5

PHILINTE: I don't understand your temper, I fear,
　　And though we are friends, I must say at long last . . .

ALCESTE [*rises abruptly*]: Who, I? and your friend? That's a thing of the past.
　　Up to now, it is true, to my heart you were dear,
　　But the traits that of late in your nature appear 10
　　Make me solemnly state that our friendship has ceased.
　　From a tainted attachment you see me released.

PHILINTE: I am then, Alceste, to blame in your eyes?

ALCESTE: All standards of honor your conduct defies.
　　For what you have done, no excuse can be found. 15
　　For remorse you should weep and your tears stain the ground.
　　I see how you greet like a dear, long-lost friend
　　A man on whose every word you attend;
　　You flatter and banter and put him at ease
　　And give to his hand the most violent squeeze; 20
　　And when I inquire: Who is he? For shame!
　　You hardly so much as remember his name!
　　As he leaves, your tender affections depart;
　　His back turned, your remarks strike a chill to the heart.
　　Just heavens! What cowardly, infamous role 25
　　To degrade and betray thus one's innermost soul.
　　And if, inadvertent, I had done the same,
　　I would hang myself straight and blot out my name.

PHILINTE: Myself, I don't think the offense merits hanging,
　　And respectfully hope, despite your haranguing, 30
　　That, a merciful judge, you will grant a delay
　　And let me stay clear of the noose, if I may.

ALCESTE: Your irony, Sir, is badly misplaced.

PHILINTE: How should I repair, then, my lapses of taste?

ALCESTE: Be sincere; by a strict code of honor abide; 35
　　Let in all that you say your heart be your guide.

PHILINTE: When someone accosts me in glad-handed ease
　　I have to repay him in kind, if you please,
　　Respond as seems best to his jovial tirade
　　And pay compliments back for each compliment paid. 40

ALCESTE: No, no! I won't stand for this cowardly way
　　That with people of your persuasion bears sway,
　　And I hate from the heart the false front you describe,
　　The hollow routines of a frivolous tribe:
　　The cordial conveyors of untruths that flatter, 45
　　Obliging dispensers of valueless chatter,
　　Who warmly converse while the heart remains cool
　　And treat thus alike the sage and the fool.
　　What boots it if people receive me with zeal
　　And tenderly talk of the friendship they feel 50
　　And commend the way I talk and behave
　　And then do the same for an errant knave?
　　No, no! And no! Such a prostitute smile

Will never a true man of honor beguile.
Our friendship turns cheap if we ever intend   55
To cherish the world at large as our friend.
Esteem must select from the common run—
Esteem for all is esteem for none.
And since you adopt this vice of our age,
My affections from you I must disengage.   60
I refuse the promiscuous warmth of a soul
That denies to merit its central role.
To accept wholesale friendship I firmly decline;
Who befriends one and all is no friend of mine.

PHILINTE: But the world expects that we give to our acts   65
 The civil exterior that custom exacts.

ALCESTE: No, no! We should chastise, upon its detection,
 With merciless rigor all bogus affection.
 We should speak man to man, and strive to reveal
 In the words we pronounce the convictions we feel.   70
 The heart should ever be heard; in no case
 Should empty phrases our feelings debase.

PHILINTE: But to practice strict candor, you'll have to agree,
 Would quite often be foolish, and painful to see,
 And at times, whatever strict honor requires,   75
 We must mask the emotions the world inspires.
 Now, would it be fitting, or make people like us,
 To let one and all know just how they strike us?
 And if people merit dislike or disgrace,
 Should we tell them so openly, straight to the face?   80

ALCESTE: Yes, indeed.

PHILINTE: You would want me to tell Colette
 At her age she is foolish to play the coquette?
 That her make-up is shocking beyond belief?

ALCESTE: That's right.

PHILINTE: I would plunge vain Jacques into grief
 And call his accounts, all heard before,   85
 Of his family's glory a crashing bore?

ALCESTE: Just so.

PHILINTE: But, surely you jest.

ALCESTE: I do not.
 I refuse to spare the fool and the sot.
 My eyes are offended; the court and the town
 Are too full of the sights that compel me to frown.   90
 My mood turns black, and my anger mounts
 To hear of men's actions the daily accounts.
 I find vile flattery ever in season—
 Injustice, deceit, selfishness, treason;
 I quiver with rage, and feel strongly inclined   95
 To challenge to battle all humankind.

PHILINTE: Your high indignation is somewhat naïve
 And I smile to see you thus chafe and grieve.
 The world for you will not change its way—

And since you believe in frankness, today 100
I'll be frank myself, and thus have you know
You amuse those you meet, wherever you go;
And your fiery anger at custom's mild yoke
Has made you the butt of many a joke.
ALCESTE: Of that I am glad. That tribute I treasure. 105
It's a very good sign, and gives me great pleasure.
The men of our times are so vile to my eyes
That I would be disturbed if they thought me wise.
PHILINTE: Your displeasure at human nature is great.
ALCESTE: I've developed for it a terrible hate. 110
PHILINTE: And all poor mortals, of every station,
Must equally share in this condemnation?
But you surely admit, there are those who call . . .
ALCESTE: I make no exception. I hate them all.
For some are actively bad and do wrong, 115
And the others still suffer this poisonous throng
And treat them with none of that vigorous scorn
That vice should inspire in the virtuous-born.
Such tolerance of the most vicious sort
Extends to the scoundrel I battle in court. 120
Behind his mask the traitor shines through,
And everyone knows what the rascal can do;
His obsequious manner, so clearly contrived,
Deceives only those who have newly arrived.
It is known that this crook, who to hell should be hurled, 125
Through sleazy employment moved up in the world,
That his fortune, now grown so tall and so lush,
Causes merit to groan and virtue to blush.
Whatever opprobrious names he is called
Hardly anyone seems by his presence appalled! 130
Call him criminal, coward, rogue, and thief
And no one will register disbelief—
Yet his leer is welcomed without dismay;
Into every circle he worms his way.
The reward that should be some honest man's prize 135
Through intrigue he will snatch from under his eyes.
God help and protect us! I'm hurt to the quick
When people condone the shady and slick.
And at times the desire for being alone
Makes me yearn for a desert where man is unknown. 140
PHILINTE: O dear! Let us cease to mourn the world's plight
And see human nature in friendlier light;
As the rigorous critic its workings dissects
Let him make some allowance for venial defects.
A flexible virtue is what the world needs: 145
Strict wisdom too often due measure exceeds.
Good sense shuns extravagance even in honor
And bids us *love* virtue, not dote upon her.
A code so austere and unforgiven

Is at odds with the mores of modern living; 150
It asks too much of mere mortal man.
We must follow the times as best we can.
Only foolish presumption would start a movement
To impose on the world a scheme for improvement.
Like yours, any day my eyes notice much 155
That could have been this way or might have been such;
But in spite of what daily thus crosses my way,
I do not (as would you) ever anger display.
I simply take men as they are; unlike you,
I accustom my soul to accept what they do. 160
Philosophical calm I aim to acquire
While you must breathe forth philosophical ire.

ALCESTE: But this calm, dear Sir, who argue so well,
Will it never allow your anger to swell?
If a bosom friend to be false is shown, 165
If one schemes to despoil you of all that you own,
If one spreads ugly rumors to murder your name—
Will your equable temper stay ever the same?

PHILINTE: I regard the defects of which you've complained
As vices in human nature ingrained, 170
And am no more incensed at the cold-blooded look
Of a self-seeking person, a rogue, or a crook
Than at vultures I see in their natural shapes,
Or ferocious wolves, or malicious apes.

ALCESTE: I must then submit to be cheated and sold 175
Without that I should . . . but the views that you hold
Are so lax they leave me speechless with rage.

PHILINTE: Indeed, to speak less you would be most sage.
To discuss your opponent in public forbear
And devote to your lawsuit all possible care. 180

ALCESTE: I shall devote nothing; that much should be clear.

PHILINTE: But to argue your case, who's been asked to appear?

ALCESTE: Only Justice and Reason—no venal drudge.

PHILINTE: So you will not arrange to have lunch with the judge?

ALCESTE: No. Why? Is my case maybe doubtful or wrong? 185

PHILINTE: Not at all. But the schemer's resources are strong,
And . . .

ALCESTE: No. I am firmly resolved to stand pat.
I am right, or I'm wrong.

PHILINTE: Don't trust in that.

ALCESTE: I won't stir.

PHILINTE: But your foe is cunning; prepare
To see him maneuver and plot . . .

ALCESTE: I don't care. 190

PHILINTE: You're deceived.

ALCESTE: Maybe so. I'll do as I choose.

PHILINTE: And yet . . .

ALCESTE: I would rather be right and lose.

PHILINTE: But at least . . .

ALCESTE: No more. I shall learn through this case
    If it's true that men are criminal, base,
    Perverse, and corrupt to such a degree   195
    As to treat me unjustly for all to see.
PHILINTE: What a man!
ALCESTE: I'd prefer, no matter the cost
    To have proved my point, though the suit was lost.
PHILINTE: Ah, people would snigger and laugh with disdain
    If they could but hear you hold forth in this vein.   200
ALCESTE: The worse for the scoffers.
PHILINTE: But tell me, Alceste,
    The standard that passes your rigorous test—
    That unflinching honor to which you aspire—
    Is it found in the woman you love and admire?
    I'm astonished, for one, that although it seems   205
    You denounce mankind, its customs and schemes,
    Though you claim it is steeped in all you decry,
    You have found in its ranks what charms your eye.
    And one thing surprises me even more:
    Your remarkable choice of a girl to adore.   210
    Sincere Éliante has a weakness for you;
    Arsinoé, the prude, but waits for her cue:
    Your heart receives them with frigid reserve
    While Célimène makes it her private preserve—
    Whose malicious wit and coquettish play   215
    Are much in accord with the trends of the day.
    If you hate our age, does your lady fair
    Of your vehement censure receive her share?
    Do these faults lose their taint in a shape so sweet?
    Are you blind as a lover, or merely discreet?   220
ALCESTE: No. The love this young widow inspires me to feel
    Has not blinded my eyes to the faults you reveal.
    I am, whatever my heart objects,
    The first one to see and condemn her defects.
    But I love her regardless, as everyone sees.   225
    I confess my weakness: she knows how to please.
    I may notice in her what is worthy of blame,
    But in spite of her faults to my heart she lays claim.
    Her appeal is too strong, and my love will cast out
    These faults of the times from her heart I don't doubt.   230
PHILINTE: If in that you succeed, you'll be famed among men.—
    She returns your love, I may take it then?
ALCESTE: Of course, or else I would not be here.
PHILINTE: But if she has shown whom she clearly prefers,
    Why then do your rivals annoy you so much?   235
ALCESTE: A true loving heart can share nothing with such.
    And my coming here today is designed
    To allow me to tell her this weighs on my mind.
PHILINTE: As for me, if I yearned for love's sweet prize,
    I'd address to Éliante, her cousin, my sighs.   240

Her heart (which esteems you) is loyal and true;
Such a choice would be happy and fitting for you.
ALCESTE: You are right. And my reason agrees every day.
But then reason in love holds but little sway.
PHILINTE: I'm disturbed, and fear for the hope you show.   245

SCENE 2 [ORONTE, ALCESTE, PHILINTE]

ORONTE: When I asked for them, I was told below
That Éliante is out, and Célimène too;
But since I was told I would still find you,
I've come up to express with sincerest zeal
The enormous esteem that for you I feel.   5
I have always hoped you would in the end
Know my ardent desire to become your friend.
My heart is eager to recognize worth
And would trade for your friendship all else on this earth;
And you, I am sure without condition   10
Will accept a friend of my position.

[*During* ORONTE'S *speech,* ALCESTE *seems absent-minded and acts as if he does not
realize he is being addressed. He takes notice only when* ORONTE *says to him*]

It is you, if you please, who are thus addressed.
ALCESTE: I, Sir?
ORONTE: Yes, you. You are not distressed?
ALCESTE: Not at all. But I'm struck by surprise, I must say,
And I did not expect to be honored this way.   15
ORONTE: You should not be surprised at the love you inspire;
In your presence, the world cannot help but admire.
ALCESTE: Dear Sir . . .
ORONTE: You surpass in merit, I claim,
The bearer of many a famous name.
ALCESTE: Dear Sir . . .
ORONTE: Yes, indeed. To me you're endeared   20
As much as the finest the country has reared.
ALCESTE: Dear Sir . . .
ORONTE: I really mean every word.
Allow me to show you how deeply I'm stirred,
To clasp to my bosom a long-cherished friend
And ask you forever on me to depend.   25
Take my hand, I beg you. May I, with respect
Call you brother and friend?
ALCESTE: Dear Sir . . .
ORONTE: You object?
ALCESTE: To accept such generous praise I am loath;
And friendship requires a more gradual growth—
One surely profanes its most holy name   30
When friend and acquaintance are one and the same.
Such knots should be tied with forethought and care;

To get better acquainted we ought to prepare:
We might differ so widely in standards or taste
As to make us too late repent of our haste.   35
ORONTE: How well you just put it! How wise and true!
   Your words but increase my regard for you.
   Let us leave it to time then to strengthen our bond;
   But meanwhile I'm yours, and hope you'll respond
   By leaving to me your concerns in high places.   40
   As you know, I enjoy the King's good graces.
   He listens to me, and indeed, I must say
   Is most kind to me in every way.
   In short, I am yours with all my might;
   And because you will judge profoundly and right,   45
   I am going to show you, to strengthen our ties,
   A sonnet I've written, and as you advise
   It shall perish or see the light of day.
ALCESTE: Dear Sir, I am hardly the man to say.
   Please excuse me.
ORONTE: But why?
ALCESTE: I have the defect   50
   To be somewhat franker than people expect.
ORONTE: That is just what I want. And I would complain
   If when asked for your candid response you should feign
   Approval or pleasure, just to be kind.
ALCESTE: If such is your wish, I shall speak my mind.   55
ORONTE: "A Sonnet . . ." (it's a sonnet). "To Hope . . ." (I allude
   To hope inspired by a lady I wooed).
   "To Hope . . ." These verses aren't meant to be grand
   But tender and sweet, you will understand.
ALCESTE: We shall see.
ORONTE: "To Hope . . ." I'm afraid that the style   60
   By its awkward spots might cause you to smile,
   And I hope you will find the thoughts well phrased.
ALCESTE: We shall shortly know.
ORONTE: I was much amazed
   It took but a quarter hour, I recall.
ALCESTE: The time is not the issue at all.   65
ORONTE   [reads]: Hope, it is true, gives solace
              And beguiles a few moments with laughter,
              But Phyllis, what unhappy comfort,
              If nothing follows thereafter!
PHILINTE: Ah, how these verses charm and delight!   70
ALCESTE [aside to PHILINTE]: Can you shamelessly tolerate stuff so trite?
ORONTE: At first you were gracious to me,
              But why did you thus incline
              If it was your cruel will
              With mere hope to let me repine?   75
PHILINTE: How elegantly these phrases are turned!
ALCESTE [aside to PHILINTE]: Great God! Vile dissembler! Such stuff should be burned.
ORONTE: If such eternal waiting

Should push my zeal to extremes
To expire I calmly prepare.   80
Your concern would be unavailing:
Such desperate hope, it seems,
Dear Phyllis, makes hope despair.
PHILINTE: The close is tender and not at all lame.
ALCESTE [*aside*]: A plague on your close, in the devil's name!   85
I wish you were safely confined and enclosed!
PHILINTE: I've never heard verses so well composed.
ALCESTE [*aside*]: The nerve!
ORONTE [*to* PHILINTE]:   You flatter, and if I may say . . .
PHILINTE: I do not.
ALCESTE [*aside*]:   Yes, you do! and cheat and betray.
ORONTE [*to* ALCESTE]: But you, Sir, remember to what you agreed.   90
Tell us frankly, I pray, what your taste has decreed.
ALCESTE: Here indeed a delicate question is raised.
Creative talents desire to be praised.
But once to a person (whose name I won't mention)
I said when his verses came to my attention   95
That a man must be armed against the bite
Of the sudden passion he feels to write;
That he must control the importunate urge
In the flood of his verses his friends to submerge;
That the would-be author in quest of his goal   100
Runs the risk of playing an unfitting role.
ORONTE: Are you trying to say that the verses I read
Would have better remained . . .
ALCESTE: That's not what I said.
Him I told: frigid writing is cold-blooded crime,
And just this one fault is enough in our time   105
To lower the worthiest man in all eyes—
It is just such defects that the world decries.
ORONTE: Do you find that my verses are not for these times?
ALCESTE: That's not what I said. But, to help stop his rhymes,
I reminded him strongly that now and then   110
Such thirst for glory has spoiled able men.
ORONTE: Are my verses then bad? Do you class me with these?
ALCESTE: That's not what I said. *Him* I asked: If you please,
What brings to your eye the ominous glint,
What devil compels you to break into print?   115
The only bad authors who find us forgiving
Are unfortunate wretches who write for a living.
So take my advice: resist the temptation;
Don't expose yourself to such recrimination;
And do not exchange so rashly your claim   120
To solid repute and an honest name
For the title some publishers gladly purvey
Of a poor foolish author sans praise and sans pay.
This was what I tried to make him see.
ORONTE: Very well. You indeed are candid with me.   125

But if you were asked how my poem would rank . . .
ALCESTE: I would quietly file it, to be quite frank.
　　You have followed bad models, as authors are prone,
　　And your phrases quite lack any natural tone.
　　For what do you mean: "beguiles with laughter," 130
　　Or what about this: "Nothing follows thereafter."
　　　　[*mimics*] To expire I calmly prepare.
　　　　　Such desperate hope, it seems,
　　　　　Dear Phyllis, makes hope despair.
　　This flowery style of which people are fond 135
　　Is far from true feeling and nature's bond.
　　You are playing with words; it's quite insincere,
　　And nature knows no such affected leer.
　　The awful taste of our time gives one pause;
　　Our parents more wisely bestowed their applause, 140
　　And I prize much less what all now admire
　　Than an old-fashioned song I learned from my sire:
　　　　If the king were to say,
　　　　"Take Paris; it's thine"
　　　　And asked me to leave 145
　　　　My sweetheart behind,
　　　　I would say, "Sir King,
　　　　Not for me your bequest;
　　　　My girl I love best, heigh ho!
　　　　My girl I love best." 150
　　The rhyme is defective, the style somewhat old,
　　But surely it's better, a hundred fold,
　　Than these trivial rhymes where good sense is asleep,
　　And surely here feeling is pure and deep?
　　　　[*hums or sings sotto voce*]
　　　　If the king were to say, 155
　　　　"Take Paris; it's thine"
　　　　And asked me to leave
　　　　My sweetheart behind,
　　　　I would say, "Sir King,
　　　　Not for me your bequest; 160
　　　　My girl I love best, heigh ho!
　　　　My girl I love best."
　　Yes, such is the language that comes from the heart.
　　[*to* PHILINTE, *who is smiling*] You sophisticates laugh at its lack of art.
　　Yet I treasure these simple lines much more 165
　　Than the glittering trifles that you all adore.
ORONTE: As for me, I maintain that my verses are fine.
ALCESTE: For good cause you no doubt to this verdict incline.
　　But for other good cause, which I hope you'll respect
　　Such a flattering judgment you see me reject. 170
ORONTE: While others do praise them, I'm pleased with my lot.
ALCESTE: They know how to flatter, and I do not.
ORONTE: You pride yourself on your agile wit.
ALCESTE: To find cause for praise, I'd need plenty of it.

ORONTE: I can do quite well *without* your acclaim. 175
ALCESTE: You will have to, because I won't furnish the same.
ORONTE: What verses could you, if faced with the task,
    Produce on this theme, I should like to ask.
ALCESTE: I could, if I would, write lines just as poor,
    Though I would not expose them to view, I am sure. 180
ORONTE: You're most self-assured; your superior tone . . .
ALCESTE: Let others adore you; leave *me* alone.
ORONTE: But, my dear little man, come off your high horse.
ALCESTE: I'll stay on, my big boy, and pursue my own course.
PHILINTE [*comes between them*]: But please, my dear Sirs, that's enough for today. 185
ORONTE: I am leaving right now. I did wrong to stay.
    Please accept, dear Sir, my most humble respect.
ALCESTE: And receive, dear Sir, my regards most abject.

                                          [ORONTE *leaves.*]

SCENE 3 [PHILINTE, ALCESTE]

PHILINTE: There you have it! Be franker than men can bear
    And at once you're embroiled in a tedious affair.
    The vanity of Oronte is such . . .
ALCESTE: Don't say any more.
PHILINTE: But . . .
ALCESTE: I've had too much.
PHILINTE: But indeed . . .
ALCESTE: Please leave me.
PHILINTE: But let . . .
ALCESTE: No talk. 5
PHILINTE: But at least . . .
ALCESTE: I won't listen.
PHILINTE :   The way you balk . . .
ALCESTE: Don't follow me. Go! Stop pulling my sleeve.
PHILINTE: You are not yourself. I refuse to leave.

ACT TWO

SCENE 1 [ALCESTE, CÉLIMÈNE]

ALCESTE: You must, dear friend, give me leave to complain.
    The way you behave gives me reason for pain:
    Too often your thoughtlessness raises my gall;
    Some day we shall separate once and for all.
    I shall not deceive you with sugared pretense— 5
    I feel I'll be forced with your love to dispense,
    And in spite of all promises you would have heard
    I might not be able to honor my word.

CÉLIMÈNE: It's to quarrel with me, I note with dismay,
        That you've wanted to come and see me today.   10
ALCESTE: I don't quarrel at all. But your generous soul
        To all comers, dear Madam, presents itself whole.
        Too many suitors beleaguer your door;
        I won't share you with every officious bore.
CÉLIMÈNE: Why should I be blamed for the suitors you see?   15
        Can I stop all these people from taking to me?
        And if someone pleads for a share of my time
        Should I reach for a stick to punish his crime?
ALCESTE: A stick, my dear Madam, is not what you need
        But a heart from too facile a tenderness freed.   20
        Your charms do go with you wherever you walk,
        But those lured by your looks are egged on by your talk;
        And your kindly reception (of those I despise)
        Completes the conquest begun by your eyes.
        The radiant smile that you offer to each   25
        Gives hope to every diligent leech.
        If you were to appear more discreetly wise
        You would soon extinguish their amorous sighs.
        But at least, dear Madam, do tell in what way
        Your Clitandre so pleases and charms you, I pray.   30
        On what solid foundation of worth and of skill
        Do you build the esteem you are granting him still?
        Is his letting his graceful fingernails grow
        The cause of the signal fondness you show?
        Have you joined those victims of fashion's cant   35
        Whom the dazzling charms of his wig enchant?
        Does his dandyish garb assure him of grace?
        Does he conquer with masses of ribbon and lace?
        Has he earned by the elegant cut of his pants
        That servitude sweet that a woman grants?   40
        Have his oily smile, his falsetto voice
        Been attractive enough to determine your choice?
CÉLIMÈNE: How unjustly you censure the course I pursue!
        Why I humor the man is no secret to you;
        For he and his friends will lend me support   45
        To help win the case I have pending in court.
ALCESTE: It were better to lose, if it came to the test,
        Than to humor a rival I must detest.
CÉLIMÈNE: The whole world now attracts your jealous abuse!
ALCESTE: The whole world shares alike in your kindness profuse.   50
CÉLIMÈNE: Just that point should appease your tempestuous soul
        Since my tender regard goes to none as a whole.
        You would have juster cause for all this ado
        If I spread it less widely than now I do.
ALCESTE: But I, whom excessively jealous you call,   55
        What is mine, may I ask, that's not shared by them all?
CÉLIMÈNE: The bliss of knowing my love for you.
ALCESTE: How can I convince my heart it is true?

CÉLIMÈNE: I think if I say as much to your face
    My word should be more than enough in this case.   60
ALCESTE: But how do I know that as part of the game
    All others might not have been told the same?
CÉLIMÈNE: Your style as a lover is sweet indeed!
    And how highly you think of the life that I lead!
    Well then! just to grant you relief from your care   65
    I deny the esteem I've been rash to declare;
    Now none will deceive you but you alone.
    Good luck!
ALCESTE: Oh, if only my heart were of stone!
    If only my soul could regain its ease
    I would thank and bless the gods on my knees.   70
    I admit it freely: I ever try
    To set myself free from this terrible tie,
    But my strongest efforts are all in vain;
    For my sins, I am sure, I thus groan and complain.
CÉLIMÈNE: Your ardor, indeed, is an unequaled one.   75
ALCESTE: Yes, it is. On this point I will yield to none.
    For no one can fathom my love for you,
    And never has anyone loved as I do.
CÉLIMÈNE: Your method is startling and new, I agree,
    For it seems that you court me to quarrel with me.   80
    Your love takes the form of tantrum and whim
    And never before was passion so grim.
ALCESTE: But it is in your power to stop all my grief.
    Let us bury right now our disputes; and in brief
    Let us open our hearts, and at once let's begin. . . .   85

SCENE 2 [CÉLIMÈNE, ALCESTE, SERVANT]

CÉLIMÈNE: What is it?
SERVANT: Acaste is below.
CÉLIMÈNE: Show him in.

SCENE 3 [CÉLIMÈNE, ALCESTE]

ALCESTE: Indeed! Are we ever alone at all?
    Forever you're ready to see those who call.
    For this once, it seems you might change your routine
    And inform your Acaste you're not to be seen.
CÉLIMÈNE: And affront him by having him sent away?   5
ALCESTE: Your concern is as usual aimed the wrong way.
CÉLIMÈNE: He's a man who would never forgive me the slight
    Of my having denied myself to his sight.
ALCESTE: But why should you care about what he may feel . . .
CÉLIMÈNE: Why indeed! His good will is worth a great deal.   10
    He is one of those who—I don't know how or why—
    Count for much in the King's and the public's eye.

Their constant meddling I watch with alarm;
They do us no good, but they *can* do us harm.
And no matter what other support we may find, 15
We should never offend loud-mouthed men of his kind.
ALCESTE: Well and good. As I only too well recall
You find reasons to suffer the presence of all;
And your pretexts, albeit transparently thin . . .

SCENE 4 [ALCESTE, CÉLIMÈNE, SERVANT]

SERVANT: Clitandre has come, if you please.
CÉLIMÈNE: Show him in.
    [*to* ALCESTE, *who is leaving*] You are off?
ALCESTE: Yes indeed.
CÉLIMÈNE: Please remain.
ALCESTE: But why?
CÉLIMÈNE: Please stay.
ALCESTE: But I can't.
CÉLIMÈNE: I insist.
ALCESTE: I won't try.
    You are set for a long conversational bout.
    It's unfair to require me to sweat it out. 5
CÉLIMÈNE: I insist, I insist!
ALCESTE: I'll be bored to tears.
CÉLIMÈNE: All right, leave! You must have it your way, it appears.

SCENE 5 [ÉLIANTE, PHILINTE, ACASTE, ALCESTE, CLITANDRE, CÉLIMÈNE, SERVANT]

ÉLIANTE [*to* CÉLIMÈNE]: I have brought two distinguished friends, as you see.
    But you knew we were here.
CÉLIMÈNE: Yes, indeed. [*to* SERVANT] Chairs for three.
    [*to* ALCESTE] Still not gone?
ALCESTE: No, not yet. I shall leave on condition
    That for them or for me you announce your decision.
CÉLIMÈNE: Oh, be still.
ALCESTE: Today you'll announce who will lose. 5
CÉLIMÈNE: You are out of your mind.
ALCESTE: Not at all. You shall choose.
CÉLIMÈNE: Indeed!
ALCESTE: You'll declare to whom you belong.
CÉLIMÈNE: You are joking, I'm sure.
ALCESTE: I've been patient too long.
CLITANDRE: I have just seen Cléonte, no sage as a rule,
    In full view of the King act the absolute fool. 10
    Let us hope a kind friend will one of these days
    Point out to the man his impossible ways.
CÉLIMÈNE: It is true, his manners amaze and amuse;
    And his bumbling behavior is hard to excuse.
    And the passage of time, it is to be feared, 15
    Far from mellowing him only makes him more weird.

ACASTE: Good grief! Since we're speaking of men who appall,
　　I have just shaken off the most tiresome of all:
　　Damon, the great talker, an hour or more
　　Made me roast in the sun at my carriage door.　　　　　　　20
CÉLIMÈNE: A strange creature, who always crosses one's way
　　And though making great speeches has nothing to say!
　　His weighty pronouncements lack meaning; and hence
　　One hears all the noise but misses the sense.
ÉLIANTE [*to* PHILINTE]: Not bad for a start; in this gay little chat　　25
　　One's neighbors are treated as mice by the cat.
CLITANDRE: Timante, dear Madam, is also quite queer.
CÉLIMÈNE: The desire for importance has spoiled him, poor dear.
　　With preoccupied air he strides into view
　　And acts always most busy—with nothing to do.　　　　　　30
　　Whatever he says, he looks solemn and grave,
　　Frowns and hems fit to kill—what a way to behave!—
　　Forever butts in to confide something awful
　　(What's a scandal to him as a rule is quite lawful).
　　He makes secrets of trifles and will by and by　　　　　　35
　　Confidentially whisper "hello" and "good-by."
ACASTE: And Gerald, dear Madam?
CÉLIMÈNE:　　　　　　　　　　　　What teller of tales!
　　He has always just dined with the Prince of Wales.
　　In his talk, he frequents the great of this earth;
　　If one isn't a duchess, one has little worth.　　　　　　　40
　　He is charmed by a title, and talks without end
　　Of the horses and dogs of some blue-blooded friend.
　　The most noble and rich are "Dear Marge" and "Old Jim";
　　As if "Sir" and "Mylady" were noxious to him.
CLITANDRE: With Bélise, it is said, he gets along well.　　　　　45
CÉLIMÈNE: Oh, how lacking in wit and how tongue-tied a belle!
　　Her calls are ordeals for whose passing I pray.
　　In cold sweat one searches for something to say;
　　Her lack of the powers of communication
　　Effectively stifles all conversation.　　　　　　　　　　50
　　Her silence is solid, and, dumb as a wall,
　　She resists all clichés that the mind can recall.
　　The sun, the rain, or the wintry blast—
　　One tries hard to make their discussion last,
　　But her visit, which calls for all of one's strength,　　　　55
　　Stretches out to the most unbearable length.
　　One yawns like a person about to expire,
　　And yet like a log she stays put by the fire.
ACASTE: And what of Adraste?
CÉLIMÈNE:　　　　　　　　　　　Presumption extreme!
　　He's a person inflated with self-esteem.　　　　　　　　60
　　He forever claims virtues the world fails to see
　　And reviles for their blindness the powers that be.
　　No matter what post someone else obtains
　　He claims he was slighted and mopes and complains.

CLITANDRE: And what of Cleon, at whose house you may meet 65
    All the people who count—don't you think he is sweet?
CÉLIMÈNE: He has hired a new cook who's unusually able,
    And the people who visit him visit his table.
ÉLIANTE: He *does* provide most magnificent food.
CÉLIMÈNE: But the last course of all quite ruins the mood: 70
    The host bends one's ear as if one were deaf—
    Thus spoiling the pleasures conferred by the chef.
PHILINTE: On his uncle Damis a man can depend.
    What of him?
CÉLIMÈNE: I have always esteemed him my friend.
PHILINTE: He seems wise and enjoys universal respect. 75
CÉLIMÈNE: He tries hard to seem witty—which is a defect.
    In the absence of any genuine spark
    He labors and strains for the clever remark.
    He decided that brilliance through scorn best is shown
    And his every word turned sardonic in tone. 80
    With all that he reads, he finds fault; I believe
    He assumes that to praise is passé and naïve,
    That one proves one's wit by withering looks,
    That only a fool would *enjoy* reading books,
    And that by sophisticates he is preferred 85
    Who looks down on what pleases the common herd.
    Yes, even mere chit-chat incurs his disdain;
    One's passing remarks he finds banal and vain;
    And crossing his arms, his answers most terse,
    With infinite pity he lets one converse. 90
ACASTE: I'll be damned. That's him! That's the man to a *T!*
CLITANDRE [*to* CÉLIMÈNE]: How precisely you paint the people you see!
ALCESTE: That's it, my dear friends! Strike again! Twist the knife!
    Let everyone join; and spare no one's life.
    Yet as soon as your victim but shows his face, 95
    You hasten to offer your cordial embrace;
    And pumping his arm, you swear and protest
    How you love and prefer him to all the rest.
CLITANDRE: Why blame *us?* If these lively portraits offend
    You should aim your complaint at your charming friend. 100
ALCESTE: No, it's you that I blame. Your gleeful assent
    Draws her out and confirms her satirical bent.
    Her malicious tongue grows more agile and pert
    As you cheer whatever she's pleased to assert.
    In her acid critiques she'd be certain to pause 105
    If for once she should notice a dearth of applause.
    Those who flatter, like you, are always to blame
    For the vices that earn us dishonor and shame.
PHILINTE: But why take the side of the people we mention,
    Who fare worse when they come to *your* attention? 110
CÉLIMÈNE: Very true! How forever he must contradict!
    Where all are agreed he states views that conflict;
    He must always give voice to that obstinate pride

That at once makes him champion the opposite side.
The ideas of others are bound to displease; 115
Dissent is with him a chronic disease.
He assumes that the world would value him less
If he ever should falter and simply say "yes."
He loves contradiction as misers their pelf
And will often in fact contradict himself. 120
He will charge at his own opinions with force
If ever he hears them when others discourse.

ALCESTE: As always the scoffers applaud what you say.
You are pleased to taunt me, and well you may.

PHILINTE: However, it's true, you are quick to slap down 125
Whatever one says; and you equally frown
At whatever one showers with ample applause
And whatever one censures, though both with good cause.

ALCESTE: But men will not ever base judgments on reason:
One's anger against them is always in season. 130
To whatever profession or trade they belong,
Their praise and their censure are equally wrong.

CÉLIMÈNE: But . . .

ALCESTE: No, dear Madam, and come what may,
You amuse yourself in a blameable way;
And it's wrong to encourage in you with glee 135
Those deplorable flaws that all can see.

CLITANDRE: I don't know about that—and indeed I object
That to me, for one, she's without a defect.

ACASTE: I can see she is blessed with charm and with grace;
If she has any flaws, they don't show in her face. 140

ALCESTE: They show clearly enough. And rather than hide them
The more that I love her, the more I must chide them.
A suitor does wrong to be meek as a dove:
To chastise is truly a labor of love.
And I'd spurn any lover—as everyone ought— 145
Who'd officiously echo my every thought,
Who would always appease me, and flatter, and coo,
And praise to the skies whatever I do.

CÉLIMÈNE: In effect, if to change us but lay in your power,
We would in true love turn all sweet into sour, 150
And to show tender passion it would be quite right
To insult those we love, with all our might.

ÉLIANTE: As a rule, true love takes a different course.
From praising their choice, our lovers turn hoarse.
Their passion affects their vision, it seems, 155
And all is most fair in the girl of their dreams.
Her very defects are transformed in this game
And often assume a most flattering name.
The pale one is "white as a lily"; and yet
The swarthy one is "an attractive brunette," 160
The skinny one "slender" or "girlish of figure,"
The fat one "majestic" (the more so the bigger).

The one that is void of what stimulates passion
Is a girl whose "beauty departs from the fashion."
The tall one looks down with a goddess's face;   165
The short one looks up with most delicate grace.
The insolent one has a "noble mind";
The rogue is "vivacious"; the stupid one "kind."
The gossipy one shows "a sociable heart";
The tongue-tied one's "modesty" sets her apart.   170
And thus our lovers, their ardor extreme,
Love us not as we are but such as we seem.

ALCESTE: And yet . . .

CÉLIMÈNE: Why persist in this line of thought?
Shall we move and look at some pictures I bought?
You're not going, my friends?

CLITANDRE AND ACASTE: Oh, no. We shall stay.   175

ALCESTE [to CÉLIMÈNE]: You're terribly worried they'll leave, I must say.
[to the others] Whatever your plans, I should like you to know
That I shall remain until after you go.

ACASTE: Unless I should be in our hostess's way
It so happens, dear friend, that I have all day.   180

CLITANDRE: Except to attend on the King tonight
I don't think I've a single appointment in sight.

CÉLIMÈNE [to ALCESTE]: You're being facetious.

ALCESTE: Of those you receive
We shall find if it's me that you'd like to see leave.

SCENE 6 [ALCESTE, CÉLIMÈNE, ÉLIANTE, ACASTE, PHILINTE, CLITANDRE, SERVANT]

SERVANT: Someone asked for you, Sir, and insists you must know
What his message is before you go.

ALCESTE: Reply that I'm busy; his message can wait.

SERVANT: His uniform's splendid with tassel and plait,
And his badge shines like gold.

CÉLIMÈNE [to ALCESTE]:   You had better go see.   5
Or let him come in.

SCENE 7 [ALCESTE, CÉLIMÈNE, ÉLIANTE, ACASTE, PHILINTE, CLITANDRE, A
UNIFORMED OFFICER]

ALCESTE [to the OFFICER]: You are looking for me?

OFFICER: Let us step aside, if you will be so kind.

ALCESTE: Please speak up and inform me of what's on your mind.

OFFICER: Well, then; you will see that my summons is clear:
In front of the Marshal you'll have to appear,   5
Dear sir.

ALCESTE: Who me?

OFFICER: That's correct.

ALCESTE: To what end?

PHILINTE: It's the quarrel you had with your poet-friend.

CÉLIMÈNE [to PHILINTE]: What's that?

PHILINTE: He insulted Oronte when distraught
     By some trivial verses the latter had brought.
     If now settled, their feud won't come to a head.   10
ALCESTE: I shall not retract one word that I said.
PHILINTE: But you'll have to appear; you had better go.
ALCESTE: What is there to settle, I'd like to know?
     And shall I be made, by official constraint,
     To admire the poem that caused this complaint?   15
     On this point I have not at all changed my mind;
     It is thoroughly bad.
PHILINTE: You could try to be kind . . .
ALCESTE: I refuse to retreat. The lines were absurd.
PHILINTE: You'll express your regret and admit that you erred.
     Come along.
ALCESTE: I shall go, but no words you might waste   20
     Can make me recant
PHILINTE: We had better make haste.
ALCESTE: Unless a royal decree is proclaimed
     To make me approve of the verses I blamed,
     I'll maintain, so help me! they're void of all worth
     And that poets so bad should be wiped off the earth.   25
     [*to* CLITANDRE *and* ACASTE, *who are laughing*] The devil! What laughter, my
          friends, and what sport
     At my humble expense.
CÉLIMÈNE: Be off, and report
     Where you must.
ALCESTE: I am going there now. After that
     I'll return, so we two can finish our chat.

ACT THREE

SCENE 1 [CLITANDRE, ACASTE]

CLITANDRE: Dear Marquis, old man, you appear well at ease;
     All strive to amuse you, and none to displease.
     But tell me at once, wishful thinking aside,
     Do you have real grounds for your joy and your pride?
ACASTE: God knows, I don't see when I look at my fate   5
     The slightest occasion for grumbling or hate.
     I am rich, I am young, and descend, as you know,
     From a house whose rank is indeed far from low;
     And my family's name is such that with ease
     I could aim at whatever position I please.   10
     As for stoutness of heart—which all must admire—
     I am hardly deficient in generous fire.
     I have shown, I may say, if it comes to the test
     I can manfully shoot it out with the best.
     I have wit and good taste, so much so indeed   15

I discuss and condemn even books I don't read.
A new play makes me haunt foyer and backstage,
Where I shine in my role of critic and sage.
In a beautiful passage when actors excel
I will clap and shout bravo! to help break the spell. 20
I am clever, look handsome; my smile is heartfelt,
My teeth brilliant white, my hips strong but svelte.
In matters of dress, I can say without fear
You'd be challenged indeed to discover my peer.
That I'm highly esteemed by all you can tell: 25
The women pursue me; the King likes me well.
With such traits, I believe, dear Marquis, old man,
One can live in content one's allotted span.
CLITANDRE: Hm—but sure elsewhere of all women's applause,
Why expend your sighs here, in a hopeless cause? 30
ACASTE: I—hopeless? Well, well! I assure you I don't
Breathe passionate love if I'm sure that *she* won't.
No, a man of mean talents and meaner fame
May in anguish adore a disdainful dame,
Go down on his knees when his suit is delayed, 35
Draw on tears and on amorous sighs for aid,
And attempt to obtain through a siege long drawn out
What at first was denied the presumptuous lout,
But the man of distinction has far too much sense
To present his love free and bear all the expense. 40
No matter how dazzling a beauty may be,
I believe that, thank God! I'm as precious as she.
And if she is destined to conquer my heart,
It appears only fair that she should do her part;
And at least, to conform to the rules of fair play, 45
She had better be ready to meet me halfway.
CLITANDRE: And you think Célimène will be glad to conform?
ACASTE: I've no reason to think she departs from the norm.
CLITANDRE: To see you so wrong I'm sincerely aggrieved.
You are blind to the truth and are badly deceived. 50
ACASTE: It is true, I'm deceived, and I'm blind, as you say.
CLITANDRE: Let me ask what has bolstered your hopes, if I may.
ACASTE: I'm deceived.
CLITANDRE: What inspires this exuberant mood?
ACASTE: I am blind.
CLITANDRE: Have you proofs of how well you have wooed?
ACASTE: As I say, I'm a fool.
CLITANDRE: What did she reveal? 55
Has she told you in secret just how she may feel?
ACASTE: She maltreats me.
CLITANDRE: Be frank to a friend true and tried.
ACASTE: I'm forever repulsed.
CLITANDRE: All joking aside:
Let me know at once what mine you have struck.
ACASTE: I'm the desolate one, and you are in luck. 60

Her aversion for me is indeed without measure,
And some day I shall hang myself just for her pleasure.
CLITANDRE: Well, well. But, my friend, befall what may,
   Let us settle this matter the amiable way:
   Whoever can show certain proof on his part   65
   That he's clearly preferred in Célimène's heart,
   Let the other make way; let it be understood
   He'll remove himself from the contest for good.
ACASTE: Ah, well put! You speak with the voice of true love.
   I agree to the terms as listed above.   70
   But quiet!

SCENE 2 [CÉLIMÈNE, ACASTE, CLITANDRE]

CÉLIMÈNE: Still here?
CLITANDRE: Love forbids us to go.
CÉLIMÈNE: I think I just heard a carriage below.
   Who is it?
CLITANDRE: Who knows?

SCENE 3 [CÉLIMÈNE , ACASTE, CLITANDRE, SERVANT]

SERVANT: Arsinoé would fain
   Have a word with you.
CÉLIMÈNE: That woman again?
SERVANT: Éliante below entertains your guest.
CÉLIMÈNE: What on earth does she want? What attracted this pest?
ACASTE: She's renowned as a terrible prude, you know,   5
   And her high moral zeal . . .
CÉLIMÈNE: Yes, indeed—all for show!
   In her heart she is worldly; her greatest desire
   Is to hook some poor man, though her schemes all misfire.
   When another of numerous lovers makes light,
   She can't help turning green with sheer envious spite.   10
   That her pitiful person's ignored by the world
   Is the clue to the angry indictments she's hurled;
   And in vain with the prude's censorious speech
   Does she cover the fact she's avoided by each.
   To protect her poor person from slighting attacks   15
   She denounces as vile the appeal that she lacks;
   And yet she would welcome a lover with zest
   And has even been known to make eyes at Alceste.
   The fact that he loves me annoys her no end,
   And she feels I have stolen her predestined friend.   20
   Her jealous dislike, which she hides very ill,
   Shows in many a token of spite and ill-will;
   And where I am concerned, she turns stupid with rage.
   Her impertinent tricks would fill many a page,
   And . . .   25

SCENE 4 [ARSINOÉ, CÉLIMÈNE, CLITANDRE, ACASTE]

CÉLIMÈNE: How nice you could come! If only you knew
    How warmly I often have thought of you.
ARSINOÉ: I've come over to tell you some things you should hear.
CÉLIMÈNE: What a genuine pleasure to see you appear!

    [CLITANDRE *and* ACASTE *walk off, laughing.*]

SCENE 5 [ARSINOÉ, CÉLIMÈNE]

ARSINOÉ: Their leaving just now is most opportune.
CÉLIMÈNE: Please sit down.
ARSINOÉ: No thanks, I'll be going quite soon.
    Dear Madam, our friendship, if earnest and great,
    Must show in the things that carry most weight.
    And because no need could be more acute   5
    Than to safeguard one's honor and good repute,
    I shall mention your own reputation to you
    As a service I feel as a friend is your due;
    For among some very fine people last night
    Your person by chance did some comment incite.   10
    And your conduct, dear Madam—the splash that you make—
    Was regrettably thought to be quite a mistake.
    The crowd that seems never for long to depart,
    Your constant flirtations, the rumors they start—
    All these found their critics, by virtue inspired,   15
    And rather more strict than I could have desired.
    As you well can imagine, I felt dismayed
    And did all that I could to come to your aid.
    I protested that all your intentions were pure,
    That we all of your goodness of heart could be sure;   20
    Even so, you admit, there are things in our lives
    That are hard to excuse, though one earnestly strives;
    And I found myself forced to make the concession
    That your conduct creates a—dubious impression.
    It appears to all in unfortunate light,   25
    And one hears the unpleasantest stories recite;
    And if ever your sober judgment prevails
    You will give less occasion to bearers of tales.
    I am sure there is nothing unethical—No!
    May heaven protect me from wronging you so!   30
    But it's easy to think of one's neighbor as vicious;
    Private virtue is wasted when all are suspicious.
    Dear Madam, I know you're too just and too kind
    Not to view this advice with an equable mind,
    To ascribe it to aught but the diligent zeal   35
    Of a friend whose devotion is such as I feel.
CÉLIMÈNE: My dear Madam, I'm heartily grateful for this,
    And so far from my taking your warning amiss,
    I shall hasten to show my sincere appreciation

And in turn shall discuss with you *your* reputation. 40
Since you show your devotion by saving each word
Of the rumors about me you chance to have heard,
Let me follow your thoughtful example. I, too,
Hear such tales—I'll repeat what they say about *you*.
A few days ago, for a visit, I went 45
To a house that the very best people frequent.
They discussed what manner of life is the best,
And your name, as it happened, was dropped by a guest.
But none of those present, alas! seemed to feel
Of your noisy crusades the inherent appeal. 50
The grave airs you put on, and the tedious vein
In which of our low moral tone you complain,
The finicky taste by which you are spurred
To find vaguely suggestive an innocent word,
Your complacent belief that *you* pass each test, 55
And those looks full of pity you cast on the rest,
Your continual lectures, the faults that you find
In what's harmless and pure to the well-balanced mind—
Dear Madam, all these, if I may be so candid,
Were censured more strictly than justice demanded. 60
What's the point (so they said) of that virtuous mien
That's belied by the deeds we recall to have seen?
What's the point of appearing in church every day
When she's beating her maids and denies them their pay?
By her pious harangues she wears men to a frazzle, 65
But she's coated with rouge and is eager to dazzle.
She's the fig-leaf's best friend, and will valiantly strive
To ban nudes from the arts (though she loves them when live).
As you well can imagine, I came to your aid
And attacked the malicious charges there made; 70
But they all with one voice rejected my plea
And concluded by saying how good it would be
If you'd leave the concerns of your neighbors alone
And invest the time saved in minding your own.
One should contemplate well one's own conduct and mind 75
Before one would rashly condemn all mankind;
The full weight of a blameless life is required
So that men can by words *and* by deeds be inspired;
And in fact, it is wisest to leave inspiration
To the men who have made it their chief occupation. 80
My dear friend, I'm convinced you're too just and too kind
Not to view this advice with an equable mind,
To ascribe it to aught but the fervor and zeal
Of a friend whose devotion is such as I feel.
ARSINOÉ: Though just censure may irk an ungrateful mind, 85
I did not quite expect a reply of this kind.
I see clearly, dear friend, in your bitter tirade,
You've been hurt to the quick by the points I just made.
CÉLIMÈNE: The reverse is the truth, dear Madam, the fact is
I would make these exchanges a permanent practice. 90

We could thus destroy and make utterly perish
The delusions concerning ourselves that we cherish.
If you were of my mind, with commendable zeal
We would loyally aim to unmask and reveal,
Conscientiously gather and store for review 95
All the things we might hear, you of me, I of you.
ARSINOÉ: Ah, dear friend! Who would censure *your* innocent life?
It's in me that faults and defects are rife.
CÉLIMÈNE: Praise and blame are capricious like sunshine and rain,
And our age helps decide what we like and disdain. 100
There's a season in life for love and flirtations
And another that's fitted for prudish orations.
It is perfectly wise to subscribe to the latter
When at last one's mirror refuses to flatter.
Thus one puts a good front on defeat. I don't claim 105
That some unpleasant day I won't do just the same.
In due course, time runs out; but right now I have plenty—
It's too soon to turn prude for a woman of twenty.
ARSINOÉ: But indeed, my dear friend, how you harp on your age!
To exult in one's birthday would hardly seem sage. 110
Dear Madam, what little we differ in years
Can hardly seem reason for joy or for tears;
And I still do not see why you go to such length
To drive home an attack so deficient in strength.
CÉLIMÈNE: And I, for my part, do not see why you aim 115
Wherever you go to destroy my good name.
Why must you work off your frustrations on *me*?
Can I help it if *you* make men falter and flee?
And if *I* chance to kindle in men ardent passion,
If I'm plagued with attentions of every fashion, 120
With avowals you wish should be lavished elsewhere—
What on earth can I do to assure you your share?
In this struggle, all women are comrades-in-arms;
I do nothing to thwart the effect of your charms.
ARSINOÉ: How sad if you think that one longs night and day 125
For the amorous crowd you so proudly display!
As if people weren't able to judge with great ease
At what price one can readily garner all these.
Would you claim that the men who pursue you in shoals
Are the kind who admire our beautiful souls? 130
That they burn with the fire of honest devotion?
That the fame of your virtues explains this commotion?
Few are quite *that* naïve; and the world, though reputed
To nod, is not blind; there are women well suited
To kindle the flame of true love in men's minds 135
Who yet are not followed by males of all kinds.
From all this it is easy to draw the conclusion:
Platonic devotion remains an illusion;
And it's certain it's not our beautiful eyes
That these lovers will yearn for with amorous sighs. 140

Is this then the glory with which you're inflated?
Your triumphs indeed seem much overrated.
To vaunt your attractions you're too much inclined—
You've no cause to look down on the rest of mankind.
If one envied the conquests that fill you with pride   145
One would easily top your success if one tried
And attract, with more tangible signs of esteem,
As many pursuers as you, it would seem.
CÉLIMÈNE: I hope you will try, and report to me then
   The results of this secret of how to please men.   150
   And without . . .
ARSINOÉ: Let's break off this fruitless debate.
   It might strain both our tempers until it's too late.
   I'd have left your apartments some minutes ago
   If my carriage had only arrived below.
CÉLIMÈNE: As long as you wish please feel free to remain;   155
   Let no hurry disturb the poise you maintain.
   Not to tire you with more than politeness demands
   I shall leave you, I hope, in congenial hands.
   And our friend here, whom chance has just caused to come by,
   Will, I'm sure, entertain you much better than I.   160

SCENE 6 [ALCESTE, CÉLIMÈNE, ARSINOÉ]

CÉLIMÈNE: Alceste, I must finish a letter today
   That it would be most awkward and rude to delay.
   Please stay with our friend. My regrets most sincere
   To you, my dear Madam, for leaving you here.

SCENE 7 [ALCESTE, ARSINOÉ]

ARSINOÉ: By her wish, as you see, we'll converse while I wait,
   Dearest friend, for my carriage to come to the gate.
   I admit that of all the kindness she shows
   I'm most charmed by the pleasure this meeting bestows.
   How true that a man of moral perfection   5
   Can command of us all both respect and affection!
   Your merit, I'm sure, has some secret charm
   That is ever at work to persuade and disarm.
   I am sure if at court one were of my mind,
   To your virtue one would be a little less blind.   10
   You have cause for complaint; and I note with dismay
   How seldom due praise or reward comes your way.
ALCESTE: Comes *my* way, dear Madam? What claim could I enter?
   What service to country has made me the center
   Of public regard? And in what respect   15
   Could I justly complain at court of neglect?
ARSINOÉ: A man that is worthy of royal reward
   Need not to such eminent heights have soared;

If occasion is wanting, with virtue imbued,
He shows a potential rectitude. 20
Your merit . . .
ALCESTE: But please, leave my merit aside;
For the court wouldn't know if I cheated and lied.
What a tedious job, what a task to inherit,
To unearth one's subjects' potential merit!
ARSINOÉ: True merit, believe me, unearths itself; 25
And the world won't let yours gather dust on the shelf.
In circles the most select, to be frank,
I have heard you commended by people of rank.
ALCESTE: Ah, Madam, today one commends left and right
And praises whatever appears to one's sight. 30
When the merit of all is extolled beyond measure.
To be recognized ceases to cause one much pleasure.
My grocer was knighted, and soon, I would guess,
My chambermaid's name will appear in the press.
ARSINOÉ: Yet I wish that to give to your talents free scope 35
You would fix on some post of distinction your hope.
Though little you now seem to covet the role,
There are means of smoothing your way to this goal.
I've connections I'd use in promoting your case
Who could have you advanced at the most rapid pace. 40
ALCESTE: And then, dear Madam, what am I to do?
How little I'm suited for public view!
When first I was born, though otherwise whole,
One thing that I lacked was a courtier's soul.
I don't have whatever it takes to succeed 45
In a cold-blooded world of ambition and greed.
Being frank to a fault is a weakness of mine;
For to polish the apple I firmly decline.
And whoever is weak in this versatile art
Cannot play in this world a conspicuous part. 50
Thus removed from the public's eye, it is true,
He lacks titles and pensions him otherwise due;
But the loss of these benefits leaves me quite cool
If it saves me the trouble of playing the fool:
I escape disappointments that sour one's kindness 55
And the tedium of chatter that's empty and mindless,
The compulsion to flatter society belles
Or hear verses against which my stomach rebels.
ARSINOÉ: I see you're determined. Before I depart,
Let me touch one more subject that's close to my heart. 60
How my feelings take part in your troubled affection—
If your love could but take a propitious direction!
You deserve to fare better by far than you do,
And the person you love is unworthy of you.
ALCESTE: But whatever kind office to me you intend, 65
You recall that the person you mean is your friend?
ARSINOÉ: Yes, I do. But my conscience has suffered too long

To pass over in silence such palpable wrong.
To see you thus slighted I'm hurt and dismayed,
And I feel you should know that your love is betrayed. 70
ALCESTE: Your remarks show a very considerate trend,
And such news obliges a lover no end.
ARSINOÉ: Be she three times my friend, she is, I repeat,
Unworthy to have a true man at her feet;
And she has only lukewarm affection for you. 75
ALCESTE: It could be—since our hearts are hidden from view;
But your role, I must say, would have been much more kind
Not to plant such a thought in a lover's mind.
ARSINOÉ: If you willingly let yourself be deluded,
Your friends must be still—I regret I intruded. 80
ALCESTE: On this subject, dear Madam, it must be plain
It's one's doubts that cause one the greatest pain;
And therefore a friend should remain aloof
Until he can furnish convincing proof.
ARSINOÉ: Very well! Fair enough. On this point you shall find 85
The evidence ample and clearly defined.
I want you to see there is cause for alarm.
If you will be so kind as to give me your arm
I'll be glad to produce the proof you desire
Of the faithless heart of the one you admire— 90
And to offer instead, if thus you should choose
What could amply console you for what you will lose.

ACT FOUR

SCENE 1 [ÉLIANTE, PHILINTE]

PHILINTE: Was ever a soul so hardened in virtue
Or retraction so strained that just watching it hurt you?
No matter what argument we would invent
In his righteous disdain we made hardly a dent;
And never a quarrel so weird in its kind 5
Arose to disturb the juridical mind.
"No, Your Honor," he said, "I am glad to retract
Whatever you wish, except obvious fact.
What was my offense? And what is his complaint?
Is one's honor at stake if one's wit is but faint? 10
My opinion hurts neither his name nor his purse:
One can live like a saint and write damnable verse.
It is not his good name that is touched, I am sure:
I am glad to pronounce his motives most pure
And proclaim his merit to all who would know it; 15
He is noble of soul—but a pitiful poet.
I will praise, if you wish, his large house and expenses,
The way he rides horses and dances and fences;
But to praise his verse I politely refuse

And maintain that a person unkissed by the muse   20
Should restrain his impulse to rhyme and compose
To escape the just censure of friends and of foes."
At last, the extreme of sweetness and light
To which he would bend his pursuit of the right
Was to say in a tone of but ill-feigned ease,   25
"Dear Sir, I regret I am hard to please.
For your sake, I could wish, from the depth of my heart,
To have found you more skilled in the poet's art."
And with this much concession and saving of face
One there made them shake hands and dismissed the case.   30
ÉLIANTE: It is true that his manner departs from the norm;
   Yet I cherish his failure to bend and conform.
   That frankness and candor he prizes so much
   Has a noble and truly heroic touch.
   In our time, these his virtues are far too rare;   35
   I would wish to encounter them everywhere.
PHILINTE: The more that I know him, the more above all
   I'm surprised by the passion that holds him in thrall.
   When a man is endowed with his frame of mind,
   I don't see how his heart could to love have inclined;   40
   And I grasp even less how your cousin became
   The person who kindled this amorous flame.
ÉLIANTE: This merely confirms that love doesn't wait
   To select for itself a compatible mate;
   And what love to congenial souls is imputed   45
   In this instance at least is amply refuted.
PHILINTE: Is he loved in return, from what you can see?
ÉLIANTE: To judge in this case is not easy for me.
   How decide if she'll render his passion in kind?
   In these matters it's rare that she knows her own mind.   50
   She will love and not know it unless she is told,
   Or else *think* she's in love when her heart is quite cold.
PHILINTE: Our friend with this cousin of yours, I believe,
   Will find ample occasion to suffer and grieve.
   If I were in his place—to bare you my soul—   55
   I should fasten my eyes on a different goal,
   And with juster discernment I should take my clue
   To respond to the kindness long proffered by you.
ÉLIANTE: On this point, I won't speak with a feigned modest air:
   Above all in this matter, I want to be fair   60
   In no way would I meddle to dampen his zeal,
   But rather I share in all he must feel.
   As far as the outcome depends on my view,
   To unite them, I gladly do all I can do.
   However, if things turn from bad to still worse   65
   And his love should encounter a serious reverse,
   If another must serve to respond to his passion,
   I would hardly object in too vigorous fashion.
   The refusal that severed his previous ties
   Would not lower the man at all in my eyes.   70

PHILINTE: In my turn, I, dear Madam, from meddling desist
    To let you be patient and kind as you list.
    He himself, if he wishes it, may let you hear
    What I have on this point taken care to make clear.
    But if at long last, through their being united,   75
    Your love should be caused to remain unrequited,
    For that favor extreme I should fervently pray
    That your heart now bestows in such one-sided way.
ÉLIANTE: You are speaking in jest.
PHILINTE: I'm in earnest as never.
    At this juncture I have no desire to be clever.   80
    I am ready to offer myself to you whole,
    And I yearn for that moment with all of my soul.

SCENE 2 [ALCESTE, ÉLIANTE, PHILINTE]

ALCESTE: Ah, Madam, I hurry to you to obtain
    Redress for an evil I cannot sustain.
ÉLIANTE: What has happened? What could have excited you so?
ALCESTE: I fear I have suffered a fatal blow.
    I'd be less overwhelmed, I assure you, dear friend,   5
    If in chaos all nature had come to its end.
    All is over. . . . My love. . . . It's too awful to say.
ÉLIANTE: But please steady yourself and be calm, I pray.
ALCESTE: Just heavens! Why send us such odious vice
    In a package that seems all sugar and spice?   10
ÉLIANTE: But, dear Sir, what event . . .
ALCESTE: All is lost . . . beyond aid.
    I am hurt unto death—I am lost and betrayed!
    Célimène . . . (could such terrible news be believed?)
    Célimène is unfaithful, and I am deceived.
ÉLIANTE: And you have just support for this grave supposition?   15
PHILINTE: Perhaps this is merely a passing suspicion;
    And your jealous temper at times makes you see . . .
ALCESTE: Please be silent; you've nothing to do with me.
    [*to* ÉLIANTE] The written proof of her treacherous spite
    Is right here in my pocket in black and white.   20
    Yes, a letter she wrote to Oronte—of all men—
    Shows my shame and her guilt in the strokes of her pen.
    Oronte—whom I thought she for sure would despise,
    Who most harmless a rival appeared to my eyes!
PHILINTE: At first glance by a letter we may be misled;   25
    It may seem less conclusive when later reread.
ALCESTE: Please withhold the advice to which you are prone
    And expend your concern on affairs of your own.
ÉLIANTE: But restrain your emotions; be calm, I ask . . .
ALCESTE: It is you who will have to perform this task;   30
    It's to you that I turn in this hour of smart
    To help me set free a suffering heart.
    Help punish your faithless, ungrateful relation,
    Who rewards with betrayal a man's dedication.

Help avenge what makes weep the angels above. 35
ÉLIANTE: Avenge? But how?
ALCESTE: By accepting my love.
Accept the heart that I snatch from her hand,
And avenge thus an act that bears treason's brand.
I shall punish her by the sincere devotion,
The passionate ardor, the urgent emotion, 40
The respectful attention, and dutiful care
Which will hallow the love that for you I declare.
ÉLIANTE: I share, I am sure, in the pain that you feel
And disdain not at all the love you reveal;
But perhaps on reflection the evil might shrink 45
And your need for revenge be less clear than you think.
When one's injured by someone so full of attractions,
Quite often one's plans are not followed by actions;
One may threaten and show all the anger you feel,
Yet the verdict of guilt is reversed on appeal. 50
Indignation will pass like a shower in May—
And such quarrels of lovers one sees every day.
ALCESTE: No, Madam. No, no. Her offense is too rank.
There's no prospect of peace; I must tell her point-blank.
To abandon the course that I take would be sin; 55
I would hate myself now if I were to give in.
Here she is. My just anger revives at her sight.
I shall strongly denounce her corruption and spite,
Confound and destroy her, and offer you then
A heart disengaged from this temptress of men. 60

SCENE 3 [CÉLIMÈNE, ALCESTE]

ALCESTE [aside]: O heavens! How can I control my rage?
CÉLIMÈNE: O my dear! What is this performance you stage?
What disaster explains these mournful sighs?
And what causes this somber look in your eyes?
ALCESTE: The lowest betrayal a soul can embrace— 5
Your behavior the most disloyal and base;
An evil more rank than could ever produce
A malicious fiend or an angry Zeus.
CÉLIMÈNE: As ever, my tender and loving Alceste.
ALCESTE: Do not laugh. This is hardly the time for jest. 10
To blush and to weep you have every reason;
I have certain proofs of your horrible treason.
Here's the fruit of forebodings my mind would have curbed;
For it wasn't in vain that my heart was disturbed.
My frequent suspicions, at which you had snorted, 15
Have at last shown themselves to be amply supported;
For in spite of your skill and deceitful charm
I could read in my stars I had cause for alarm.
But please, don't assume I'll allow this crime
To go unrevenged and be mellowed by time. 20

I know well that affection cannot be constrained,
That as nature commands one is loved or disdained,
That one does not invade someone's heart by force,
That each soul in love must pursue its own course.
And thus I'd have judged it but fair enough   25
If I had at your hands had an open rebuff.
If at first you'd extinguished my passionate flame,
I would only have had my own fate to blame.
But to nourish that flame with deceitful smile
Is most treacherous and perfidious guile.   30
No punishment ever could be too severe;
I shall shrink from nothing, I make it quite clear.
Be warned, and prepare for the worst, if you're sage—
For I'm not myself; I'm distilled into rage.
The mortal blow that has pierced my defenses   35
Has made reason surrender its rule of my senses.
I abandon myself to my wrath; I warn all:
I declare I won't answer for what may befall.
CÉLIMÈNE: To what cause should this furious tirade be assigned?
   At long last, if you please, are you out of your mind?   40
ALCESTE: I was out of my mind when I suffered your face
   To entice me to court contempt and disgrace,
   When I thought that the line of your waist and your bust
   Was sufficient as proof of a heart I could trust.
CÉLIMÈNE: And what is this treason of which you complain?   45
ALCESTE: Ah, how well you dissemble, how glibly you feign!
   But to counter your wiles I am fully prepared.
   Please look at this note: here your baseness is bared.
   Behold here a proof that you cannot refute;
   Face to face with this witness you'll have to stand mute.   50
CÉLIMÈNE: Is this then the object you find so exciting?
ALCESTE: Can you bear without blushing to look at your writing?
CÉLIMÈNE: And what is there for me to blush about?
ALCESTE: Will you be then so bold as to brazen it out,
   To disown it because it's an unsigned note?   55
CÉLIMÈNE: But why should I disown a letter I wrote?
ALCESTE: And yet you can see it without any shame
   For the crime against me that its phrases proclaim?
CÉLIMÈNE: It must be admitted: You're one of a kind.
ALCESTE: You defy then a proof to convince the most blind?   60
   The regard for Oronte that you show as you write
   Should not make me indignant nor you contrite?
CÉLIMÈNE: Oronte! And who says it's to him it was sent?
ALCESTE: The people I had it from knew where it went.
   But suppose it was meant for another—What then?   65
   Should I pardon the faults revealed by your pen?
   In what way would this fact serve to lessen your shame?
CÉLIMÈNE: But suppose the address was a *woman's* name—
   Then why should you be hurt, and where is my crime?
ALCESTE: Ah, how clever! You thought of this ruse just in time!   70

I admit, this gambit I did not expect,
And you see me at once convinced and checked.
Do you mean to rely on deception so crude?
Do you think me so easy to gull and delude?
Let us see in what way, by what means you would try   75
To maintain and support such a palpable lie,
And how, for a female recipient, you fashion
The words of a note so torrid with passion.
Now twist, if you please to conform to your aims
What I'm going to read . . .
CÉLIMÈNE: I refuse to play games.   80
     I am tired of your ludicrous bullying ways
     And the arrogant temper your conduct displays.
ALCESTE: Let us not get excited—please look at this note
     And explain then the phrases I'm going to quote.
CÉLIMÈNE: No, thanks. And I'm sure that in any event   85
     I could hardly care less what you think that it meant.
ALCESTE: But please, convince me, to put me to rest,
     How this note could have been to a woman addressed.
CÉLIMÈNE: It was meant for Oronte—You were perfectly right.
     I receive his attentions with joy and delight;   90
     His talk I admire and his smile I imbibe
     And confess to whatever crimes you describe.
     Now do as you please, ignore all restraints,
     Just stop setting my teeth on edge with complaints!
ALCESTE [aside]: O God! Was more cruel a creature created?   95
     Was ever a heart so abused and berated?
     By righteous anger my fury is fed;
     I come to complain, and am nagged instead!
     Instead of abating my sorrows and fears,
     She confirms all my charges, and does so with sneers!   100
     Yet my heart is so weak I endeavor in vain
     To break loose from so galling and shameful a chain,
     To forswear in anger all further devotion
     To the unworthy object of futile emotion.
     [to CÉLIMÈNE] Perfidious woman, how always you seem   105
     To employ against me my weakness extreme,
     And exploit for your ends the prodigious excess
     Of the fatal love that for you I profess.
     Deny at least the charges I brought;
     Cease pretending you give to your guilt any thought.   110
     Just show that this note is free of all blame,
     And I'm urged by my passion to clear your name.
     Try to act the faithful lover's part
     And I'll try to believe you with all my heart.
CÉLIMÈNE: Go on, you are mad in your jealous delusions.   115
     And you do not deserve a lover's effusions.
     I would like to find out how you could have concluded
     I would stoop to deception to keep you deluded.
     Why on earth, if my heart had inclined as you say,

Would I fail to admit it the very same day? 120
Does the open assurance of tender esteem
Fail to counter suspicions as vague as a dream?
When compared with such candor, what weight do they bear?
Why insult me by even admitting they're there?
Since we stretch our good will to its utmost span 125
In deciding to own our love for a man—
Since a woman's honor, that bridle to feeling,
Is opposed to admissions so frankly revealing—
Dare the lover, for whom these risks are incurred,
Contest unpunished the oracle's word? 130
He's to blame if he's not completely consoled
By what after much struggle he's finally told.
Your suspicions well merit my high indignation,
And you've lost all your title to consideration.
It is stupid of me, and simple of mind, 135
To continue to be even partially kind;
I should save my regard for a different face
And make sure your complaints have a solid base.
ALCESTE: Ah, temptress! My weakness for you is absurd.
You deceive me, no doubt, with each sugared word. 140
But no matter, I'll have to submit to my fate;
My heart is yours to love or to hate.
I shall see in the end what you really feel
And what treason or steadfastness time will reveal.
CÉLIMÈNE: I must say that your loving defies every rule. 145
ALCESTE: But compared with my ardor all passion is cool.
In my wish to make known to all its strength
You will see I have gone to unusual length,
For I'm wishing that no one would think you fair,
That you'd suffered a fate the most meager and bare, 150
That at birth you'd been placed in the poorest condition,
Deprived of your wealth, without rank or position,
So that then by my love and most generous trust
I could start to repair a fate so unjust
And rejoice and give thanks to the powers above 155
To see you owe all to the man that you love.
CÉLIMÈNE: Your good will, I must say, takes the strangest form,
And I hope I'll be spared the chance to conform. . . .
But here is your servant, in strange disguise.

SCENE 4 [CÉLIMÈNE, ALCESTE, DUBOIS]

ALCESTE: What's this masquerade? Why these rolling eyes?
What ails you?
DUBOIS: Dear Sir . . .
ALCESTE: What's your news?
DUBOIS: I can't tell.
ALCESTE: What on earth . . .
DUBOIS: Believe me, Sir, all is not well.

ALCESTE: Why? and how?

DUBOIS: Can I talk?

ALCESTE: Yes—right now, if you please.

DUBOIS: Will nobody hear?

ALCESTE: How this fellow will tease!   5

Speak up!

DUBOIS: Well, Sir, we must beat a retreat.

ALCESTE: What's this?

DUBOIS: It is time to be quick on our feet.

ALCESTE: But why?

DUBOIS: As I say, we will have to depart.

ALCESTE: For what cause?

DUBOIS: There's no time for goodbys; we must start.

ALCESTE: But *why*, I still ask, do you talk this way?   10

DUBOIS: Because we must pack and depart today.

ALCESTE: I shall cudgel your obstinate head, you lout,

If you will not explain what all this is about.

DUBOIS: A person in black and gloomy of face

Has come to present to you at your place   15

A paper so crowded with legal "whereases"

That to read it the devil would call for his glasses.

It's to do with your lawsuit, that much I can tell,

Though to read it would baffle a fiend out of hell.

ALCESTE: What has that got to do, kindly tell without stumbling,   20

With this hurried departure of which you were mumbling?

DUBOIS: Some time later, a man—if you'll let me explain—

Who's your guest quite often in times of less strain

Arrived at your house in the greatest hurry,

And since you were gone, with an air of great worry   25

He asked me (a trust loyal service can claim)

To inform you—now wait, what *is* the man's name?

ALCESTE: Be damned to the name! What is it he said?

DUBOIS: Well, he's one of your friends—why trouble my head?

To see urgent reason for flight he professed;   30

You are threatened, he said, with immediate arrest.

ALCESTE: He did! He explained in detail, I should think?

DUBOIS: He did ask, it is true, for some paper and ink

And has written a note which, I'm sure, will declare

In all points what's behind this mysterious affair.   35

ALCESTE: Hand it over at once!

CÉLIMÈNE: What can all this mean?

ALCESTE: I don't know, but the truth shall shortly be seen.

Will it take you all day, in the devil's name?

DUBOIS [*after taking a long time to search for the note*]: On my word, I left it at home

when I came.

ALCESTE: I don't know what restrains me . . .

CÉLIMÈNE: Be calm, I pray,   40

And be off to clear up what caused this affray.

ALCESTE: My fate, it appears, whatever I do

Has vowed to prevent me from talking to you;

But permit your suitor to thwart its spite,
And return to you, Madam, before tonight.   45

ACT FIVE

SCENE 1 [ALCESTE, PHILINTE]

ALCESTE: As I stated before, I am firmly resolved.
PHILINTE: But must you, whatever the hardship involved . . .
ALCESTE: However you may insist or upbraid me,
    From what I have said you shall never dissuade me.
    This our age has become iniquity's den,   5
    And I mean to retire from the commerce of men.
    My foe saw arraigned against him and his cause
    Integrity, decency, shame, and the laws;
    The strength of my case all were quick to cite;
    I was calm in the knowledge I was in the right—   10
    And yet all my hopes bear most bitter fruit:
    I've the right on my side, but I lose my suit.
    Yes, a scoundrel, with well-known unsavory past,
    Scores a triumph that leaves honest men aghast!
    His guile thwarts good faith, and, instead of resistance,   15
    In cutting my throat he gains legal assistance!
    His crafty eye, whose mere glance corrodes,
    Overturns plainest justice and time-honored codes!
    One rewards his offense by judicial decree!
    Not content yet with what he has done to me,   20
    He refers to a book of most scurrilous type,
    Consisting of mere pornographical tripe
    That makes one regret that the laws are not tighter—
    And whispers to all that I am the writer!
    And Oronte his devious malice now shows   25
    By spreading this slander wherever he goes!
    Oronte, a man of repute and of rank
    Whom I've injured by being sincere and frank,
    Who comes to me, full of most urgent zeal,
    To read me his verses and ask what I feel;   30
    And since I respond with unblinking eye
    And refuse to deceive him by telling a lie,
    He repays me by stooping to slander, and so
    Now my would-be friend is my bitterest foe!
    And it seems that no pardon could ever be had   35
    For just once pointing out that his sonnet was bad.
    Are these the high aims that people pursue?
    Do these acts represent the things that they do?
    Here indeed good faith and a virtuous course
    And justice and honor are shown in full force.   40

Too severe are the wounds that the heart here receives;
Let us leave then this den of cutthroats and thieves;
Since you men to be wolf among wolves are proud,
I shall gladly secede from your treacherous crowd.

PHILINTE: For so rash a decision you would be to blame; 45
And all evils are not so intense as you claim.
Your foe, in spreading a lie so abject,
Has yet to produce any serious effect.
His libelous charges fall back on his head;
In the end he will suffer for what he has said. 50

ALCESTE: You think so? Such slanders are greatly in vogue:
He has license to be a most unabashed rogue;
And this caper, so far from destroying his name,
Is bound to procure him still wider acclaim.

PHILINTE: At least, it remains little heed has been paid 55
To the spiteful rumor by which you're dismayed;
And in this respect you have nothing to fear.
In your lawsuit, whose issue I'm sorry to hear,
The decree of the court should be promptly appealed.
The verdict . . .

ALCESTE: No thanks. I shall readily yield. 60
The injustice here done is such obvious fact
I refuse to allow them a chance to retract.
Too clearly it shows how right is ignored,
And in future ages it shall be abhorred
As a famous milestone, a signal mark 65
Of the evils that render our times so dark.
It is true that the cost may well bleed me white,
But it is not too high if it gives me the right
To expose and denounce the injustice of man
And to hate human nature as hard as I can. 70

PHILINTE: But consider . . .

ALCESTE: Consider your efforts as wasted.
What can sweeten the bitter defeats I have tasted?
Can you be so brash as intend to my face
To belittle man's vice and gloss over disgrace?

PHILINTE: Not at all. Your judgment agrees with mine. 75
All moves through intrigue and ulterior design.
Only schemers succeed, and it's easy to see
That man is quite other than what he should be.
But should their so patent iniquity then
Make us want to retire from the haunts of men? 80
All these human defects but give us a chance
To develop a more philosophical stance—
And this exercise shows us all at our best;
For if all were with equal integrity blessed,
And if all were as honest and just as they should, 85
Where would be the distinction of those who are good?
Their most notable mark is a temper that smothers
Their chafing resentment at wrongs done by others.
And just as a heart of virtue profound . . .

ALCESTE: How well you talk. Your speeches abound   90
    With impeccable logic and graces sublime.
    Yet, Sir, you are wasting your breath and your time,
    For my safety, my reason enjoins my retreat.
    My tongue has not learned to be smooth and discreet;
    I can't vouch for my words, since I say what I think,   95
    And the feuds I might cause make me shudder and shrink.
    I shall see Célimène, and when she arrives
    She will have to agree to my plan for our lives.
    I shall see if her passion for me is sincere;
    Her reply will at once make all doubt disappear.   100
PHILINTE: Let us go upstairs, and wait for her there.
ALCESTE: No, my soul is too restless and troubled by care.
    Please go first and leave me; and I shall remain
    Alone with the bleakness of heart that's my bane.
PHILINTE: I wish you had company less apt to chill.   105
    I shall ask Éliante to come down, if she will.

SCENE 2 [CÉLIMÈNE, ORONTE, ACASTE]

ORONTE: Yes, Madam, you'll have to decide if it's true
    That so tender a union will tie me to you.
    The assurance I want you should quickly dispense;
    For a lover is irked to be kept in suspense.
    If my passion has wakened responsive chords,   5
    Do not grudge me the pleasure the knowledge affords.
    As your proof (need for proof was never acuter)
    You must cease to acknowledge Alceste as your suitor.
    This tangible token of love I exact;
    I insist you refuse to receive him, in fact.   10
CÉLIMÈNE: But what is the reason you suddenly flout him
    After all the to-do you at first made about him?
ORONTE: I'm afraid it's not *my* turn for interrogation.
    It is *you* whose behavior needs clarification.
    You shall choose which one you prefer of us two;   15
    And once *you* are resolved, I shall shortly be too.
ALCESTE [*emerging from his corner*]: Yes, for once he is right. You will have to decide.
    By the sentence we crave we agree to abide.
    Like him, I insist you shall not stay aloof;
    For my love now demands unmistakable proof.   20
    This affair has moved far too slow from the start,
    And right now is the time to lay bare your whole heart.
ORONTE: I am sorry with passion so inopportune
    To disturb, Sir, your chance to obtain such a boon.
ALCESTE: I am sorry to share with you, jealous or not,   25
    To the slightest extent, Sir, what heart she has got.
ORONTE: If your love she to mine should turn out to prefer . . .
ALCESTE: If the least in your favor her judgment should err . . .
ORONTE: I here swear to extinguish all amorous fire.
ALCESTE: I here swear to be cured from all loving desire.   30
ORONTE: Dear Madam, be frank; it is your turn to speak.

ALCESTE: Dear Madam, deliver the verdict we seek.
ORONTE: Let us know whom you choose for your love; please begin.
ALCESTE: Put an end to suspense; may the better man win.
ORONTE: Can you question with whom you long since should have sided?   35
ALCESTE: Can it be that you falter? You seem undecided!
CÉLIMÈNE: My word! How unwelcome the choice you exact,
     And how little you show of good sense or of tact!
     I am sure of my stand on the question you raise,
     And it's not that my heart is lost in a maze.   40
     The case is too clear to perplex or confuse,
     It's no problem for me to know how to choose.
     However, it's terribly awkward, I find,
     To announce to you two a choice of this kind.
     Whenever we have something painful to broach,   45
     We should surely employ a more subtle approach.
     There are less drastic methods of communication
     Than to shout from the rooftops the heart's inclination.
     In short, there are pleasanter means to explain
     To a dutiful lover he's burning in vain.   50
ORONTE: Not at all. For frankness is just what we need.
     At this point, we should find it most welcome.
ALCESTE: Agreed.
     It's exactly this drastic effect I desire;
     Of your tactful maneuvers I easily tire.
     To please all mankind is your driving ambition;   55
     But let's have no more trifling—pronounce your decision.
     You must openly state and reveal your affection,
     Or I'll see in your silence a tacit rejection.
     I would know how to take your refusal to speak
     And would thus see confirmed premonitions most bleak.   60
ORONTE: I'm sincerely obliged to your firmness, dear Sir;
     And in what you have said I most gladly concur.

SCENE 3 [ÉLIANTE, PHILINTE, CÉLIMÈNE, ORONTE, ALCESTE]

CÉLIMÈNE: Dear cousin, I'm treated extremely ungently
     By two men who've conspired to tease and torment me.
     In turn, each insists at the top of his voice
     That at once to them both I should publish my choice,
     That I ask one of them, in effect, to his face   5
     His affection for me to subdue and erase.
     Please confess: Is it thus that such things should be done?
ÉLIANTE: To provide such advice I am hardly the one.
     You have chosen your arbiter rashly, I fear;
     I prefer that one's words should be candid and clear.   10
ORONTE: No avenue, Madam, remains for retreat.
ALCESTE: Your evasions, dear Madam, are doomed to defeat.
ORONTE: You must open your heart; you must cast the dice.
ALCESTE: And if not, your silence alone will suffice.
ORONTE: But a single word will unravel the knot.   15

ALCESTE: By your failure to speak I shall know my lot.

SCENE 4 [ARSINOÉ, CÉLIMÈNE, ÉLIANTE, ALCESTE, PHILINTE, ACASTE, CLITANDRE,
     ORONTE]

ACASTE [*to* CÉLIMÈNE]: We have come here because we both felt we should mention
     A little affair that deserves your attention.
CLITANDRE [*to* ORONTE *and* ALCESTE]: It is fortunate that we encounter you here,
     For you both are involved, as will shortly appear.
ARSINOÉ [*to* CÉLIMÈNE]: To see me, dear friend, your surprise may be keen, 5
     But these gentlemen asked me to witness this scene.
     They both came to my house to voice their complaints
     Of a trait that would weary the patience of saints.
     Your esteemed elevation of soul is a pledge
     You can *not* have committed the crime they allege. 10
     On their proofs I bestowed the most searching attention,
     And, my friendship forgetting our little—dissension,
     I accompanied them in the hope, by and large,
     To see you deny such a slanderous charge.
ACASTE: Yes, Madam, let's see with an open mind, 15
     What you say to these comments by you undersigned.
     To Clitandre, from you, this letter was sent.
CLITANDRE: And this sweet little note for Acaste was meant.
ACASTE [*to* ORONTE *and* ALCESTE]: You will find that the hand is familiar, I trust;
     For, polite as she is, I am sure that she must 20
     On many occasions have written to you.
     But to read her own words—it's no more than her due:
          "It is ironical that you should condemn my ways and allege that I never
     enjoy myself as much as when you are away. You are most unjust; and if you
     don't appear shortly to demand my pardon, I may decide never to forgive 25
     you for your offense. Hulking Tom the Count . . ."
     He ought to be here.
          "Hulking Tom the Count, who heads your list of undesirable rivals, is not
     even in the running; and since I have seen him spend three quarters of an
     hour spitting into a puddle in order to make circles in the water, he has suf- 30
     fered somewhat in my esteem. As for our little marquis . . ."
     That's me, I'm afraid.
          "As for our little marquis, who insists on holding my hand for hours on end,
     he is the most diminutive person I ever saw, and his appearance owes as
     much to his tailor as to his creator. As for my morose friend . . ." 35
     [*to* ALCESTE] Your turn, Sir.
          "As for my morose friend, I am at times amused by his abrupt and uncouth
     behavior, but as a rule he bores me to distraction. As for the maker of son-
     nets . . ."
     [*to* ORONTE] You have not been overlooked. 40
          "As for the maker of sonnets, who trembles with the urge to create and de-
     fies humankind to call him author, it is asking too much of me to make me
     listen to what he is saying; and I find his prose as boring as his verse. Please
     admit the thought into your head that I don't always enjoy myself as much
     as you think, that I miss you—more than I care to admit—at the parties to 45

which I am dragged, and that the true seasoning of life's enjoyments is the presence of those one loves."

CLITANDRE: And here is a relevant excerpt from the other:

"Your Clitandre, who seems to annoy you by his saccharine allusions, would be the last man on earth to attract my regard. He is badly mistaken to hope 50 for my love—just as you are badly mistaken to *lack* hope. To come closer to the truth, you two should trade expectations. Come to see me as often as you can, to help me alleviate the affliction of his continual presence."

Revealing bequests of a notable mind—
And a label that fits would be easy to find. 55
Enough. We are leaving. Wherever you go
We shall publish the traits that these documents show.

ACASTE: I have plenty to tell you, and if I refrain
It's because I must think you beneath my disdain.
And I'll show you that people as little as I 60
Can find solace in worthiest hearts, if they try.

SCENE 5 [CÉLIMÈNE, ÉLIANTE, ARSINOÉ, ALCESTE, ORONTE, PHILINTE]

ORONTE: So this is how you use your fangs on your betters,
After all the sweet phrases you put in *my* letters!
And your heart, which so coyly pretended to yearn,
To all the male sex is promised in turn!
I have acted the fool, but I'm tired of the role; 5
You have done me a favor in baring your soul.
I retrieve here the heart you so lightly regard,
And I'm amply revenged now that thence you are barred.
[*to* ALCESTE] I shall cease, Sir, to stand in the way of your passion;
I am sure she'll respond in most ladylike fashion. 10

SCENE 6 [CÉLIMÈNE, ÉLIANTE, ARSINOÉ, ALCESTE, PHILINTE]

ARSINOÉ [*to* CÉLIMÈNE]: Without doubt, your behavior is vicious and low;
Indignation compels me to label it so.
Was ever like course by a woman pursued?
I say nothing of others to whom you were rude.
[*points to* ALCESTE] But this man, who aspired to make you his wife, 5
A true pillar of honor and upright life,
Who worshipped you with an idolatrous zeal,
Must he bear . . .
ALCESTE: But excuse me, dear Madam, I feel
I myself should handle my own affairs.
Why thus charge yourself with superfluous cares? 10
Though so warmly you are to my side inclined,
I'll, alas! be unable to repay you in kind.
It's not *you* I shall call on with passionate voice
If I look for redress in a different choice.
ARSINOÉ: Do you think I am yearning for such a match? 15
You must feel, Sir, you are a most precious catch.
How inflated your spirit must be, and how vain,

If such are the thoughts that you entertain!
What our friend here leaves over is hardly a prize
Of a kind to be yearned for with passionate sighs.   20
Please be undeceived, and revise your pretensions.
On a woman like me you would waste your attentions.
Sigh for *her*, as before, till your love is requited;
I can't wait to behold you content and united.

SCENE 7 [CÉLIMÈNE, ÉLIANTE, ALCESTE, PHILINTE]

ALCESTE [*to* CÉLIMÈNE]: I've been silent, you see, despite what occurred.
    I have calmly stood by until all have been heard.
    Have I curbed my temper enough then today?
    May I now . . .
CÉLIMÈNE: . . . I agree with all you can say.
    You are quite in your rights to heap scorn on my action;   5
    I shall patiently bear all blame and detraction.
    I've done wrong, I admit it. Contrition and shame
    Would make my excuses seem vapid and lame.
    I have scorned the anger the others have shown;
    But my crime toward you I am ready to own.   10
    I have shown all the traits that you justly despise,
    And I know just how guilty I seem in your eyes.
    In your charge of betrayal all proofs bear you out;
    And you have every reason to hate me, no doubt.
    Go ahead, vent your ire.
ALCESTE: I wish that I could!   15
    I am forced by my love to neglect my own good.
    Though my reason decided to hate and detest,
    Would my heart be prepared to obey its request?
    [*to* ÉLIANTE *and* PHILINTE] Here you see what an unworthy passion can do.
    You have witnessed what weakness has made me go through,   20
    But the terrible truth is, you haven't seen all:
    You shall watch me play still more abjectly her thrall.
    We're too rashly called sage—that my fate will illumine;
    The austerest of us are at heart all too human.
    [*to* CÉLIMÈNE] Yes, then; I'm prepared to forgive you; and hence   25
    I shall try to excuse and forget your offense;
    I shall call it a weakness to which your young mind
    By corrupting examples was led and inclined—
    Provided you give your wholehearted consent
    To the break with mankind upon which I am bent   30
    And determine to follow me to the retreat
    Where I've sworn I shall live in seclusion complete.
    This heroic decision no doubt in all eyes
    Soon will clear you of spite and malicious lies;
    And thus cleared of a scandal that causes me pain   35
    You'll be worthy again of a love without stain.
CÉLIMÈNE: To renounce the world at my age! Must your wife
    Be buried alive far from civilized life?
ALCESTE: If your love finds its longed-for object in mine,

Why on earth should you ever for others repine? 40
Can't we find in each other contentment in plenty?
CÉLIMÈNE: Yes, but solitude frightens a woman of twenty.
I don't feel I can marshal the grandeur of soul
That would make me resolve to pursue such a goal.
If a love sealed in marriage can make you content, 45
I could muster the courage to give my consent;
And our union will . . .
ALCESTE: No! You are all I detest.
This refusal alone is far worse than the rest.
In effect, since you will not, throughout wedded life,
Let your husband be all (as *I* would my wife), 50
I here spurn and reject you. This offer you scorn
At long last makes me break the chains I have worn.

SCENE 8 [ÉLIANTE, ALCESTE, PHILINTE]

ALCESTE [*to* ÉLIANTE]: Your virtues set off your external graces;
You've got, Madam, that candor that nothing replaces.
You have long inspired admiration extreme;
But allow me to hold you thus still in esteem
And consent that my heart, bruised by scorn and defiance, 5
Should no more court the honor of closer alliance.
Too unworthy I feel; and my reason suspects
As a lover I suffer from innate defects.
Too, the courtship you merit should not be a sequel
To the wooing of one who's in no way your equal. 10
In effect . . .
ÉLIANTE: Please do what your feelings command,
Since I'm not at a loss where to grant my hand;
And here is your friend, who in case of need,
To accept such an offer has kindly agreed.
PHILINTE: Ah! That honor, dear Madam, is all that I sigh for, 15
And a prize I am eager to live and to die for.
ALCESTE: May you both find the bliss that will banish dejection
And forever preserve an untarnished affection!
For myself—deeply wronged, maligned, and betrayed—
I shall leave the abyss where all vices parade; 20
I shall search for a place remote from the crowd
Where a life full of honor is still allowed.
PHILINTE: Let us try, dear Madam, let's do all we can
To dissuade from such steps this remarkable man.

THE RECEPTIVE READER

1. Do you find yourself taking sides between Alceste and Philinte? What are the most telling points either makes? (What are especially striking epigrammatic couplets?) Is there something to be said on both sides?

2. What makes Alceste's run-in with the would-be poet an example of delightful comedy? Can you see the difference between Oronte's sonnet and Alceste's folk song?

Do you think Alceste is absolutely right—or at least partly wrongheaded? ✧ Where does Philinte stand in this exchange?

3. Alceste criticizes Célimène's delight in malicious gossip. However, they both can be very critical of others. Compare and contrast Alceste's satirical jabs at Philinte and Oronte with Célimène's attack on Arsinoé and with Célimène's satirical portraits. Are the ways the two use satire similar or basically different? ✧ Is Philinte right in saying that the people satirized by Célimène would fare worse if judged by Alceste?

4. In plays modeled on those of Molière, the hypocritical prude became a *stock character*. What makes Arsinoé a good example of the type? Would you call Célimène's treatment of Arsinoé cruel or malicious? Why or why not?

5. How would you describe Alceste's relationship with Célimène? Is he infatuated? condescending? judgmental? ✧ Is Célimène serious about Alceste? Does Alceste's love for Célimène make you question his judgment on the major issues of the play? Why or why not?

6. Molière often uses the comic device of "The worm turns"—a character at first abused or ridiculed gets a chance to strike back. How do the minor characters such as Oronte, Acaste, and Clitandre fit this pattern?

7. Critics have pointed out that the ending may disappoint audiences used to the traditional *happy ending* of comedy. Were you surprised or disappointed? ✧ What role does the final exposure of Célimène have in the play? Does it vindicate her archenemy, Arsinoé? How does Alceste react to it—does he seem to be acting in character?

8. What has been settled by the end of the play? Does the play as a whole suggest an answer to the question it raises? How would you formulate the play's unifying *theme*?

9. Molière wrote at the beginning of the Age of Reason, when common sense was invoked as the guide to the good life. In the tradition of the *comedy of manners* that he initiated, a balanced and commonsensical character often serves as the voice of reason. Who qualifies for this role in this play and why? Does Philinte ? Does Éliante?

10. It has been said that in this play Molière reaches the limits of comedy: Because of its serious overtones, the play as a whole becomes too dark or somber, verging toward the end on *tragedy*. Why or why not would you agree with this view?

11. How important are manners? Many observers have commented on the deterioration of public manners in America, with loutishness and callousness becoming the order of the day. In this respect, do Molière's characters live on a different planet? Or does the play have something relevant to say to those concerned about public manners today?

THE PERSONAL RESPONSE

The mirror that comedy holds up to us often shows us traits that are part of our own nature. Which of the traits mirrored in this play do you relate to most strongly or understand best? a gusto for malicious gossip? an inclination to brutal honesty? the tendency to compromise? jealousy of more popular or more successful rivals? an author's or artist's vanity? Show the connection between your own personality and the treatment of your chosen trait in the play.

THE CREATIVE DIMENSION

At the end of the play, Philinte asks Éliante to help him talk Alceste out of withdrawing from society. Write a scene (in prose or verse) in which one of these two characters or both present a final plea to Alceste.

CROSS-REFERENCES—For Discussion or Writing

✧ Compare and contrast Alceste with Ibsen's Nora or Sophocles' Antigone as advocates of uncompromising honesty. Are they similar in their temperaments or in their motives? Are we supposed to identify with them?

✧ Is Célimène in this play seen from a male point of view? Compare her with another major female character in a predominantly male world, such as Nora in Ibsen's *A Doll's House* or Jule in Caryl Churchill's *Objections to Sex and Violence.*

✧ What would be a definition of comedy that would fit Molière's play and the shorter examples of comedy in this chapter?

WRITING ABOUT LITERATURE

29. Responding to Verbal Humor (Focus on Language)

The Writing Workshop The dramatist's, like the poet's, medium is words. Much critical study of imaginative literature takes a close look at the writer's language. In the comedies of writers from Shakespeare and Molière to Wilde and Wasserstein, spectators delight in the verbal fireworks. They respond to wordplay and verbal humor. They delight in the spirited trading off of barbed comments and quick-witted answers, or repartee.

The following student paper takes a close look at the fast-moving language of a Shakespeare comedy reprinted in the concluding chapter of this book. Study the way the student writer identifies major varieties of verbal humor. How successful is the paper in showing the role they play in the comedy as a whole?

SAMPLE STUDENT PAPER

The Language of Comedy in *A Midsummer Night's Dream*

Love as infatuation is the foundation for the comedy of Shakespeare's *A Midsummer Night's Dream.* We laugh at the rash actions of the lovers as their affections change at a dizzy pace during an evening in the midsummer forest. We laugh at the way Puck, the mischievous sprite, manipulates the lovers. We laugh at the play the workmen perform, the "tragedy" of Pyramus and Thisby. But the humor in Shakespeare's play is derived from more than the play's plot, the characters' actions. Weaving witty responses, puns, repartee, and malapropisms through the play's plot, Shakespeare creates a humorous, clever world made of language.

This verbal universe makes us laugh and reveals the characters' personalities and social status. The group of craftsmen, for instance, represent low social standing. Thus, their verbal humor is of a "lower" form, such as vile puns and malapropisms—humorous misuse of words. Those of higher social standing—the lovers—also humorously play with words, but they do so intentionally. They make love the subject of clever remarks, often making it sound more like an intellectual game than a physical attraction or emotional bond. Shakespeare further sets apart the two types of humor by having the workmen speak in prose and the lovers speak in verse. The two groups are brought together in the final act, in which both forms of humor meet.

The lovers—Hermia, Lysander, Helena, and Demetrius—delight in the play of opposites that makes for clever, fast-moving love talk throughout the play. They play off diametrically opposed words by way of repartee—the spirited comebacks that require a quick wit. Hermia and Helena, for instance, have an exchange, in rhymed couplets, about Demetrius. He loves Hermia—and is rejected by her; he rejects Helena, who loves him.

Hermia: I frown upon him, yet he loves me still.
Helena: O that your frowns would teach my smiles such skill.
Hermia: I give him curses, yet he gives me love.
Helena: O that my prayers could such affection move.
Hermia: The more I hate, the more he follows me.
Helena: The more I love, the more he hateth me.   (I.i.194–99)

These characters are prone to punning, another form of verbal humor. In the dialogue, the same word often echoes again and again, often changing its meaning in the process. Hermia greets Helena, calling her beautiful ("fair") Helena: "God speed fair Helena: whither away?" Helena responds: "Call you me fair? That fair again unsay. / Demetrius loves your fair. O happy fair!" (I.i.180–82). This kind of playing on a repeated word becomes outright punning when Lysander attempts to snuggle up to his love, Hermia. She says, "Nay, good Lysander: for my sake, my dear, / Lie further off yet, do not lie so near." Lysander assures her that his intentions are honorable; he is not a lying, deceiving seducer: "For lying so, Hermia, I do not lie" (II.ii.43–52).

As Helena, obsessed with her love for Demetrius, follows him around, he harshly swears, "For I am sick, when I do look on thee." Helena responds, "And I am sick, when I look not on you" (II.i.212–213). This harsh repudiation of Helena by Demetrius and her unflagging devotion are examples of the lovers' extreme statements occurring throughout the play. Much of the verbal humor results from the lovers' use of extremely exaggerated love talk that parodies the love poems of Shakespeare's time.

The hyperbolical, exaggerated language is especially hilarious when a lover swears undying passion after just having totally turned around, abandoning one love for another under the mischievous Puck's spell. We laugh at Lysander when his consummate love for Hermia suddenly becomes consummate love for Helena. In ryhming couplets he dramatically swears, "I do repent / The tedious minutes I with her [Hermia] have spent. / Not Hermia but Helena I love. / Who will not change a raven for a dove?" (II.ii.111–14).

Demetrius, too, uses extreme flowery exaggeration after falling under the spell of the woods and swearing his love for the same Helena. She is perfect, a goddess. Compared with her, crystal is like mud:

Oh Helen, goddess, nymph, perfect, divine,
To what, my love, shall I compare thine eyne!
Crystal is muddy. O, how ripe in show,
Thy lips, those kissing cherries, tempting grow!   (III.ii.137–40)

Because both men have so suddenly flip-flopped their affections, Helena is certain they, along with Hermia, are playing her for a fool. She calls Hermia a "counterfeit" and a "puppet." Hermia calls Helena a "juggler" and a "cankerblossom." Lysander swears at Hermia, calling her "thou cat, thou burr" and "you dwarf!" All this name-calling releases resentment and frustration that are usually bottled up in accordance with the requirement to be polite and mature. The exchange of insults in Act 3, Scene 2 creates a manic, humorous scene, leading Puck to exclaim, "Lord what fools these mortals be!"

The other mortals upon whom Puck eavesdrops and whom he manipulates are the honest but ignorant Athenian workmen, the characters of low comedy and low social class. These men, together in the forest on the same night as the lovers, are preparing a play to perform at the royal wedding. In prose, the workmen's verbal humor mainly focuses on malapropism—humorous misuses of words. We laugh at the unintentional blunders of these characters. For example, Quince intends to praise his friend Bottom by calling him a "paragon," a model. Instead, however, Quince says "paramour," a lover, and often an illicit or adulterous one.

Bottom constantly stumbles into the same kind of ridiculous verbal errors. Usually Bottom's mistakes stem from his desire to sound sophisticated, but his limited vocabulary leads him to unintentional humorous remarks. For example, after the craftsmen agree to meet in the woods, Bottom says, "We will meet, and there we may rehearse most obscenely and courageously ." Later, instead of saying "to the same effect," he says, "to the same defect."

Often with his blunders, Bottom uses a word of opposite meaning or connotation to what he intends. Instead of "odorous [scented] savors sweet," Bottom says "odious [hateful] savors sweet." We laugh, but Bottom is not in on the joke. Also at his own expense are his puns: Like the lovers, he puns, but not intentionally or wittily. When the mischievous fairy Puck transforms Bottom's head into an ass's head, for example, he declares that his friends are making "an ass of him."

When Bottom and his entourage come together with the lovers and the royal couple at the end of the play, the low and high strands of comedy meet. Theseus, the duke, reads the description of the workmen's play:

"A tedious brief scene of young Pyramus
And his love Thisby; very tragical mirth."   (V.i.56–57)

Here the "low" comics have created an oxymoronic, self-canceling description of their play, unaware of its absurd quality. The duke shows the absurdity with a witty retort:

Merry and tragical? tedious and brief?
That is hot ice and wondrous strange snow.
How shall we find the concord of this discord?   (V.i.58–60)

Throughout the workmen's production, the aristocrats and lovers make clever punning remarks, at the expense of the "actors." When Quince errs in the prologue with punctuation blunders, Theseus says, "This fellow doth not stand upon points," which has a double meaning: Quince does not heed niceties, nor does he pay attention to punctuation in his reading. Lysander adds, "He hath rid his prologue like a rough colt; / he knows not the stop." The "stop" has two meanings: the stopping of a colt by reining it in, and the full stop, a period as a punctuation mark.

At first glance, one might assume that only the workmen are being ridiculed in this scene. Certainly they are inept and blundering, performing a play that the critic David Bevington has called "an absurdly bad play, full of lame epithets, bombastic alliteration, and bathos." But the bathos and exaggerated laments of the workmen's "lovers" sound suspiciously like the exchanges between the Athenian lovers:

O night, O night, alack, alack, alack,
I fear my Thisby's promise is forgot.
And thou O wall, O sweet, O lovely wall,
That stand'st between her father's ground and mine . . . (V.i.169–72)

Here Shakespeare invites us, the audience, to acknowledge that the exaggerated love talk invites parody. Just as the audience of Pyramus and Thisby laugh at the workmen, we laugh at *A Midsummer Night's Dream*. Who, then, may be laughing at us?

30 NEW DIRECTIONS
The Challenge to Convention

*My characters have nothing. I'm working with impotence,
ignorance, that whole zone of being that has always been
set aside by artists as something unusable—something by
definition incompatible with art.*
SAMUEL BECKETT

*I sometimes think the whole reason I like plays is so I can
ignite these lunatic climaxes when all hell breaks loose.*
TINA HOWE

FOCUS ON NEW DIRECTIONS

Much twentieth-century drama, like much modern art, has been in rebellion against convention. Audiences have come to accept, if not always welcome, experiment and innovation. Much that is now standard theatrical fare was at one time considered revolutionary, provocative, or subversive. Playwrights from Henrik Ibsen to George Bernard Shaw and Harold Pinter delighted in bourgeois baiting—they made it their business to shock the people in the good seats. Yet middle-class audiences flocked to their plays, and after initial controversy , their plays often became part of the established repertory.

Nevertheless, some major movements have been a more radical break with the past than others. One major challenge to the tradition of issue-oriented realistic plays has been the **theater of the absurd,** which surfaced in the fifties and turned many assumptions about the theater upside down. Eugène Ionesco's *The Bald Soprano* opened in Paris in 1950 to the indignant grumblings, groans, and derisive laughter of an incredulous audience. For many of them, in the words of one of its members, the play was like a "Japanese movie without subtitles." (The play has since run in Paris without interruption for as long as anyone can remember.) In 1954, Samuel Beckett, an Irish author living in Paris and writing mostly in French, wrote *Waiting for Godot,* one of the great classics of the modern stage. It is a play about two homeless people waiting for Godot—a personage who never comes and who, it appears, does not exist. One reviewer said about another play by Beckett that "it earned the con-

1360

tempt of halfwits and filled those who are capable of telling the difference between a theater and a bawdy house with a profound and somber and paradoxical joy" (Harold Hobson).

The cornerstone of the theater of the absurd has been the conviction that the "reality" acted out in most stage plays is a sham. The sense of order and purpose they project, like the ordered patterns of traditional art, is artificial; it does not mirror the world in which most people live. Most people lead disjointed lives. They don't have grand plans. They don't have major crises; they stumble from one trivial crisis to another. They don't participate in a meaningful dialogue on the issues; instead they talk as if they were on automatic pilot, with language furnishing them a sheer endless supply of ready-made sayings and banalities.

In the last few decades, another major challenge to theater as usual has been the emergence of female playwrights challenging the traditional domination of the theater by male dramatists. We witness today a major effort to redefine and broaden the traditional canon of approved plays written by predominantly male writers. Feminist critics have reassessed the work and influence of playwrights like Susan Glaspell (*Trifles*), Lillian Hellman (*The Children's Hour*, 1934), and Clare Boothe Luce (*The Women*, 1937). Feminist critics have championed the work of women like Ntozake Shange, who wrote *for colored girls who have considered suicide, when the rainbow is enuf* (performed on Broadway in 1976) and who spoke of the "struggle to become all that is forbidden by our environment, forfeited by our gender, all that we have forgotten."

Audiences are increasingly watching plays that reexamine human relationships from a woman's point of view (or, perhaps more accurately, from women's points of view). Wendy Wasserstein in her comedy *Uncommon Women and Others* (1977) explored new directions in a world in which "women's roles have become ambiguous and confusing" (Susan L. Carson). Caryl Churchill's *Top Girls* (1982) explored the obstacles outstanding women face and the price they pay for success. Tina Howe has written comedies of life in the American nuclear family (*Birth and After Birth*, 1974; *Approaching Zanzibar*, 1988). She has said that her ambition is "to get a thousand people in a dark room laughing themselves nearly to death, drenched in tears, rolling in the aisles, ambulances rushing to theater doors." But she has also said:

> As a mother, you experience moments of excruciating tenderness and love, but there is also a great savagery—family life has been over-romanticized; the savagery has not been seen enough in the theater and in the movies.

Slowly, plays from outside the white mainstream are making their way into the established canon from minority and Third World sources. Luis Valdez' *The Shrunken Head of Pancho Villa* is making its way into anthologies. In his *Los Vendidos*, white politicians shop for token representatives of minorities the way others shop for used cars. The American playwright August Wilson is making audiences rethink their stereotypes about black people. In *The Piano*

Lesson (1990), he is teaching us to listen to authentic folk dialect as the natural expression of the exuberance and humanity of his characters rather than as the badge of poverty and illiteracy. (Willie to his sister, whom he has gotten out of bed at five in the morning: "You ain't had to come down if you didn't want to. I come eighteen hundred miles to see my sister I figure she might want to get up and say hi. Other than that you can go back upstairs.")

Among Third World authors writing in English, the Nigerian playwright Wole Soyinka stands out. Intimately acquainted with the literary traditions of the West, he yet has remained rooted in and loyal to the culture of his own people. In his *Death and the King's Horseman,* he pays tribute to a tribal culture and tribal traditions that have survived centuries of colonialism and cultural myopia.

CARYL CHURCHILL: A FEMINIST PERSPECTIVE

If people can't see the values, I don't want to spell them out.

CARYL CHURCHILL

The power to act shrinks every day.

VILFREDO PARETO

Caryl Churchill is the best known, most productive, and most internationally successful of the "next wave" of feminist playwrights (Janet Brown) challenging the traditional domination of theater playbills by male dramatists. Born in 1938 in England, she spent her teenage years in Canada after her family moved to Montreal. She returned to England to attend Oxford, where she started to write plays.

In the years before her first commercial stage play was produced, Churchill wrote radio and television plays for the BBC. (She has said about her radio plays that they "focused on the awfulness of everything, rather than on the possibilities for change.") Churchill ran into censorship problems with a television play that questioned the summary justice administered by British courts to alleged terrorists of the IRA (Irish Republican Army). Her early stage plays were produced in small experimental theaters; she has experimented with the collaborative writing of plays. She once said in an interview that she loved "the stuff of the theater the way people who like to paint like paint."

Many of her plays center on feminist themes. *Vinegar Tom* (1976) dealt in stark graphic terms with the seventeenth-century persecution of "witches"— who were healing women, single women, women who had trangressed against strict Puritanical codes, or women who had aroused the lust or ill will of evil neighbors. *Top Girls* (1982), performed successfully in many European countries as well as in the United States, asked to what extent career women should feel responsible for their less aggressive and less successful sisters.

Caryl Churchill's *Objections to Sex and Violence* shows a generation in search of coherent ideas and emotional integrity. It is a play about the violence and ideological turmoil of the sixties and seventies that was spawned by the Vietnam War. The play is dramatic, but not in the sense that it dramatizes plotting and violence and manhunts (or womanhunts). Instead, the drama is in the verbal exchanges that go on like MTV—they are always on. The basic mode of the play is an almost uninterrupted playing off of contradictory commitments and points of view. Chronologically, in fact, much of the talk about revolutionary violence on the part of radically alienated young people was then still in the talking stage. Many young people were committed to nonviolence in the tradition of Mahatma Gandhi and Martin Luther King, Jr.

Critics have been frustrated by Churchill's's tendency not to pin down each character in the play clearly on the issues; they have found her way of "sidling up to her themes and giving them a nudge" both "fascinating and maddening" (W. Stephen Gilbert). In conventional ideological terms, Jule, the central character, is criticized from two sides: Her bourgeois, middle-class sister and the sister's husband both talk about the rottenness of the system. But they criticize her for her futile protest and rebellion when everyone else has made peace with things as they are. Her own husband or ex-husband, a doctrinaire communist, thinks that the random violence of bomb-throwing anarchists is just another bourgeois luxury: It is counterproductive because it does not lead to organized mass protest and revolution; it produces a violent backlash instead.

In this "morality play without a moral," one thing that keeps the ideological lines from staying tidy is the feminist assumption that the "personal is the political": The way a woman's role is defined and her opportunities are limited by gender is the most basic political fact in a woman's life. In this play, sex keeps butting in; the ideological and the sexual intersect and clash, sometimes with hilarious results.

In one way or another (and often at unexpected moments), the play touches on a range of current topics: pornography, conventional marriage, sexual harassment, drug charges, radical alienation, violence and nonviolence, sexual exploitation, unconventional marriage, alternative lifestyles. In spite of its rapidly shifting focus, the play derives its underlying thematic unity from the archetypal modern predicament: It shows us people in search of something to believe in, something to give meaning to their lives.

CARYL CHURCHILL (born 1938)

Objections to Sex and Violence   1975

[This play was written by a British playwright for British audiences. The author is a socialist in a country that has a strong socialist tradition and has had a succession of socialist (Labor Party) governments, alternating with conservative (Tory) governments like that of Margaret Thatcher. A few references might need explanation: The M1 is the major motorway or traffic artery that connects London in the south with the north of England. An MP is a member of Parliament. *Cannabis* is used in the play as legal jargon for marijuana. A few British idioms occur: People who are "remanded to custody" are locked up; the characters often use *want* in the sense of *need* ("You want a good thrashing" means "You need a good thrashing.") At the time the play was written, the capture of Eichmann by Israeli agents and his execution as a Nazi war criminal were still fresh in people's minds. He had been the stereotypical "desktop criminal," organizing the deportation of tens of thousands of Jews.]

CHARACTERS

ANNIE, mid to late twenties
JULE, a little younger than ANNIE
ARTHUR, in his fifties
MADGE, in her fifties
PHIL, mid-thirties
ERIC, younger, early twenties
MISS FORBES, about sixty
TERRY, about thirty

PLACE: *a sandy beach with rocks behind it.*
TIME: *a June day.*
ACT ONE: *Low tide.*
ACT TWO: *High tide.*

ACT ONE

Low tide. Sunny morning.
   JULE *and* ANNIE. JULE *is in a bathing suit. She has just been swimming and is wet and slightly cold.* ANNIE *is in a coat. She has just arrived.*

ANNIE: I never thought I'd find you so easily. I came on the beach more for the breath of air. Because seeing the size of the town I said at once how silly of me to come. It seemed a pity to waste the sunshine and not start with a look at the sea. Then I thought I'd get down to it and ask at every single bed and breakfast and then at least I would have done my best.
JULE: What did you come for?
ANNIE: You sent me a postcard.
JULE: I didn't say come. I was keeping in touch.
ANNIE: I read about the trouble in the paper, but when I took a train up you'd vanished. You weren't just out because I waited all day. The police said they hadn't kept you.
JULE: It's not my fault you waited all day. I can't always be where you might drop in.
ANNIE: So when I knew from the postmark you were here, I came here, that's all.
JULE: Without the others the house felt wide open. There were still two of us. But even in bed I felt a detective sergeant might walk in. They had the mattress off that afternoon. They went through every shelf and every drawer. You don't know you've got so many things. And even here I think they're still keeping an eye—I think I'm paranoid to think that but you can't be sure. They're sly buggers and they try to be thorough. There's probably one of them watching you now.

ANNIE: I only came to make sure you were all right.

JULE: They won't hurt you. You haven't done anything.

ANNIE: Nor have you, really, Jule, have you? It was more the other people in the house the paper said were remanded in custody. They wouldn't have let you out on bail.

JULE: No, it can't be serious, can it, if I'm swimming.

ANNIE: But what have you done, Jule?

JULE: You saw in the paper what the charge was.

ANNIE: You can't think "possession of cannabis" would have me running all over the country. It's the way the paper made all those arrests come in the same story as something much worse. Everybody smokes. But I'm sure the other's nothing to do with you. Newspapers usually get it wrong. I expect you can set my mind at rest. (ANNIE *waits but* JULE *doesn't say anything.* JULE *gets her towel and puts it round her shoulders.*) Your own sister's hardly going to tell. Do you feel you have to be loyal to somebody?

JULE: It was very good of you to come, Annie. I'm really grateful. You came all this way.

ANNIE: It makes an excuse for a day by the sea. I like an outing. I never get to see you in the normal way. It takes a catastrophe to get me moving.

> ARTHUR *comes in with two deckchairs and a beachbag. He starts to put up the deckchairs, trying different places to be out of the wind, and constantly glancing at* JULE.

JULE: All well your end? Still with that bloke that had the accident?

ANNIE: He's out there by the edge of the sea.

JULE: What's he doing?

ANNIE: He thought I'd better come over first and see it was all right.

JULE: Is he frightened?

ANNIE: He's very considerate, that's all it is. Shall I call him?

JULE: You're happy enough with him, are you?

ANNIE: There are things. If I had time to tell you some time. But yes I am.

JULE: You're not sorry about the divorce anyway?

ANNIE: Oh no, that was the best thing I ever—I think if I'm having a bad day, at least I'm not still married to that.

JULE: He doesn't come round and worry you? He's not someone to let it go, from when I knew him.

ANNIE: Not any more, no. There were a few bad times. I had the police one night, he cut my eye. I still haven't got over with Phil just being with someone that isn't going to hit me. He's not going to come unless I call him.

JULE: Better call him, then.

ANNIE: And you, are you with someone?

JULE: Off and on. Things shift about a bit.

ANNIE: How exactly?

JULE: Anyway, I'm not staying in a bed and breakfast so you would have had to knock on a lot of doors. I'm in a tent up on the cliff with someone.

ANNIE: You came down here together, then?

JULE: What if I met him down here on the beach?

ANNIE: Just this last few days?

JULE: I can't know him very well, can I? No, I don't.

ANNIE: Don't start getting at me, Jule, because I'm not like that anymore. It's up to you.

JULE: Call him over. Give him a wave.

ANNIE: Phil! Phil! Jule, I want you to know. I don't blame you. In a way I think I admire—of course, I don't know what it is you've done. But knowing you, I'm sure it's something I wouldn't blame—I'm sure I could understand anything you told me, Jule. I do so little myself.

JULE: Are you working?

ANNIE: Jobs always fail me, don't they?

JULE: You manage to type.

ANNIE: Oh yes, I stuck it out well this time. I was secretary to a top executive. But you know how it is. I go to pieces. They bust me down to the typing pool for a rest, they were quite concerned. That's when I should have left. But I like to feel committed. I don't know how to keep my distance. I bring my work home in my head as if it was interesting. As if I was competing like the men. You'd love the men, Jule, you'd laugh so much. You can tell the grade of a man by his car. The company provide them with different sizes so there's no mistaking who's important. Regardless of the number of passengers they have in real life. My boss had worked up to a silver grey model with overdrive. The seats are so soft it's quite hard for a girl to get out. But just lately I switched to doing cleaning. It rests your head anyway.

ARTHUR *is doing less and less with the deckchairs. Some time ago he folded one up to move it and now stands holding it, watching* JULE.

JULE: You'd be better if there was something you cared about.

ANNIE: It's not as if you'd ever stayed with a job.

JULE: But I always think you'd make a nurse or a teacher. Something where you could wear yourself out.

ANNIE: I do that whatever I do.

JULE: But over nothing.

ANNIE: Oh it's too late, Jule, to start training for any of those vocations. The boring detail's too much once your mind's mature. Things keep striking me as irrelevant. I could never settle for discipline nowadays.

JULE: Matrons.

ANNIE: There you are. Headmistresses.

JULE: Executives.

ANNIE: The money's got to be earned. I'm not involved. For some time now I've only cleaned his house.

JULE: The same one, with the grey car?

ANNIE: I drifted into it one afternoon. He knew the company was driving me mad and his wife was just then wanting a char. It was kindly meant. There was no way I could have known.

JULE: I'm not saying teaching's worthwhile. I was thinking more what you might enjoy.

ANNIE: I don't expect to enjoy work, Jule. I rely on Phil to put me out of my misery.

JULE: Where is Phil? Collecting shells, I think. Or it might be bottletops. Yes, I do remember him as very polite.

ANNIE: But, Jule, it's one thing to be fed up. Would you kill people?

JULE: Phil!

ANNIE: Jule, if you take some part in explosions. I don't know what you've done. But the passersby who just happen—and children.

JULE: Come on, let's walk up the beach and meet him. I'm getting cold, let's walk.

ANNIE: But Jule.

JULE: Children are killed in most wars.

ANNIE: Jule.

JULE: I'm not saying I've killed anyone.

They go out.

ARTHUR *takes a step or two after them, dragging the deckchair, then remembers it and stops. He leaves it and sits in the other deckchair. From inside his jacket he takes a worn pornographic magazine, from the beachbag the* Daily Express. *He hides the magazine inside the paper and reads it.* MADGE *comes in.*

MADGE: Where did you slip off to, Arthur? I might be dead.

ARTHUR *folds up the paper, leaving the magazine in it.*

ARTHUR: I was trying to get a spot out of the wind.

MADGE: I'm two minutes spending a penny and you take advantage to set off by yourself, leaving me to handle a most sinister character.

ARTHUR: What did he do, dear?

MADGE: He didn't dare to do anything because he could tell at a glance I would call the police. But he looked at me unmistakably. And followed.

ARTHUR: Where is he now? Do you want me to deal with him?

MADGE: I shook him off by pretending to go into a café. I watched him pass, through the lace curtains. It's lucky that class of degenerate person is always stupid. Because where were you all this time? Enjoying yourself by yourself on the beach.

ARTHUR *sets up the other deckchair.*

ARTHUR: I was getting a deckchair set up for you, dear.

MADGE: It's the wrong side of the rocks.

MADGE *sits in it.*

ARTHUR: The breeze is blowing straight in off the sea. You won't get shelter either side.

MADGE: This side's very chilly.

ARTHUR *sits in the other deckchair.*

ARTHUR: It was you wanted to take the holiday early. You don't like people.

MADGE: I do indeed like people. I love people.

ARTHUR: You don't love them on the same beach.

MADGE: I'm of service to people fifty weeks a year. Everybody needs a break, Arthur. It's less of a strain to take holidays off peak. And far more public spirited.

ARTHUR *unfolds the* Express *as if to read it again. We can see, though* MADGE *can't, the magazine inside.*

ARTHUR: It doesn't seem a proper holiday unless it's in August. It's not too bad this morning, mind you, there are a few swimmers.

MADGE: While I was being pursued along the front you were off gawping at young girls in no better than their underwear.

ARTHUR: Bathing suits aren't underwear. If a girl came down on the beach in her underwear—

MADGE: While I was in danger of attack. He would have stopped at nothing in an alley. Luckily there's a good crowd on the front.

ARTHUR *folds up the magazine and puts it back in his jacket.*

ARTHUR: Why don't we have a cup of tea?

MADGE: No, I'd rather wait till I'm really cold.

ARTHUR: If you will come to the seaside in June, you have to take the weather as you find it.

MADGE *gets out knitting, a sweater for* ARTHUR, *from the beachbag, and knits.*

MADGE: We could go to the Lake District. Or a coach tour of Scotland would make a change. But oh no. It has to be a beach with bathing beauties or it's not a proper holiday.

ARTHUR: Sitting in a coach all day wouldn't take me out of the furniture department the way I can trust the sea to do.

MADGE: And don't I work hard too? A local government office is no joke.

ARTHUR: Perhaps we should take our holidays apart, dear.

MADGE: We'll have none of that, thank you, Arthur.

ARTHUR: I'm going to have a cup of tea now, whether you are or not.

ARTHUR *gets a thermos flask from the beachbag.* MADGE *gets a cardigan from the beachbag and puts it on.* ARTHUR *pours himself some tea.*

Madge, did you choose an early holiday on purpose so there wouldn't be so many people swimming?

MADGE: June often has glorious weather. Flaming June.

ARTHUR: If you think that badly of me I want you to say so.

MADGE: I just long to get away from it all. It's not much to ask.

ARTHUR: I want you to have a nice holiday, Madge, I really do.

MADGE: Come on, let's have a cup of tea. I'm just a bit shaken by my experience.

ARTHUR *pours a cup of tea for* MADGE.

ARTHUR: Some girls do go too far. Remember that one last year with the red—

MADGE: I don't want to hear anything like that. We're away from television for two weeks and I hope we've left sex and violence behind. The world is a very beautiful place if you know how to see it. I come on holiday to get my eye in by gazing at nature, which I can't do surrounded by people on towels.

ARTHUR: It is distracting when they're very close.

MADGE: Holidays should be kept for the few who really work. There's no service in shops. You even take your own shoes off the shelf. I said no thank you, I'll go where a fitting expert will bring me shoes in boxes. Because I've always had trouble with my feet, haven't I, Arthur?

ARTHUR: All our married life.

From time to time ARTHUR *glances along the beach.*

MADGE: Feet are like teeth. It's important to be in the hands of a good dentist who knows your history and doesn't cause unnecessary pain. Think of your dentures. I believe we owe it to our bodies to put them into some authority's care. I don't believe in self-service. What are you looking at, Arthur?

ARTHUR: Just gazing at nature. The little children making a sandcastle.

While MADGE *talks,* ARTHUR *stands up and takes a few steps.*

MADGE: Children are said to be a blessing but some people could restrain themselves without threatening the survival of the species. Hydra simply grow little hydra like arms and they drop off, which isn't such a messy arrangement, and they can't enjoy it. But the child must be identical with the parent, which would stand in the way of progress, when I think of my mother. Arthur, where are you going?

ARTHUR: I wondered if it wasn't so breezy . . .

MADGE: Where?

ARTHUR: Further along, by those rocks.

MADGE: There are people there already.

ARTHUR: There's plenty of room.

MADGE: In bathing suits.

ARTHUR: That's what gave me the idea it might be warmer.

MADGE: Young people don't seem to feel the cold.

ARTHUR: I thought I'd just take a turn along the sand.

MADGE: Come here and let me measure your jersey.

ARTHUR: Don't make it too small this time, Madge. If you look at me you'll see I'm quite a medium-sized man.

MADGE: Take your jacket off.

ARTHUR *takes his jacket off and the magazine falls to the ground. He puts a foot on it.* MADGE *is busy with the knitting and doesn't notice.*

I do believe in progress because it must be possible to make people perfect. I've always been a believer, Arthur. I used to believe in fairies as a child. We had to clap to save Tinker Bell. Yes, yes, yes, I used to say, leaning out of my bedroom window in the dark. Bunions, cavities, we struggle as best we can. Another two inches. We have to help each other forward and that's why I resent the disappearance of service. If the wind can be trusted to have dropped I might take my cardigan off again. I'll take my shoes off and have a rest. (*She bends down to take off her shoes. She sees the magazine and picks it up.*)

ARTHUR: I struggle too. I struggle against the flesh. I have particularly strong passions, that's all it is. Saint Augustine had the same problem.

MADGE (*reading*): "He bit her nipple till she screamed with agony then plunged his foot long red hot weapon—" What shall we do with this?

ARTHUR: I can take it back to the shop and get half the money—

MADGE: We will burn it.

ARTHUR: We're very different, Madge. I've always said that. You long to merge in something mystical. But I can't always manage to dislike what I know is disgusting. I'm always very sorry afterwards. (*He tries ineffectually to light the magazine with a match.*)

MADGE: You won't do it like that. Let me. (*She tears the magazine into pieces and heaps them on the sand.*) Match. (*She tries several times to light the paper.*)

ARTHUR: It's too breezy.

MADGE: We'll dig a hole and bury it.

ARTHUR *and* MADGE *dig a hole with their hands and bury the magazine in the sand.* MADGE *pats it firmly down.*

I always hope we'll get closer on holidays. There's nothing in the nature of the sea to bring women to mind. It always makes me think of the lifeboat service.

ARTHUR: I hate women really, you know that. Young women today want to be whipped.

MADGE: They'd take it the wrong way, Arthur.

ARTHUR: You and I, Madge, do mean the same thing by right and wrong. It's just that

I have a weakness for what's wrong. But most people give those words a different meaning.

MADGE: Your weakness, Arthur, is the result of weak government.

ARTHUR: People want to be told what to do.

MADGE: They long for a strong man.

ARTHUR: Then if I saw a young girl not properly dressed I should know I could ask a policeman to take action.

MADGE: They don't take care of us as they should. Even law and order is self service. Have a go, indeed. What we want is an ideal of service and force. The armed services are at the same time the armed forces. Young men did national service as a national force. The police force is also a service. The civil service is a civil force. Public services should force the public. Then we could have a well-deserved holiday.

ARTHUR: Self-service could mean yourself using force. Hence the daily violence in the papers.

The sun goes in.

MADGE: I think I'll need my cardigan again.

ARTHUR: I do think we might try over there. Those people haven't put on cardigans. They're still in the sun.

MADGE: If you can promise me some peace, Arthur.

ARTHUR *looks down the beach the way* JULE *and* ANNIE *went out.*

ARTHUR: I've seen that young lady before.

MADGE: What do you mean? She's not the person who was on the cliff last night?

ARTHUR: Lying on the grass with her young man in full view of the public footpath and we saw—

MADGE: I was there, Arthur, it doesn't need to be put into words. Is it the one?

ARTHUR: I got a good look—I think it is.

MADGE: It's not enough having penalties for litter.

ARTHUR: Shall I give her a piece of my mind?

MADGE: We can't be responsible for what we see. The television authority is just as bad. The cliffs would have been so beautiful in the evening light.

ANNIE, JULE *and* PHIL *come in.* PHIL *has a camera.*

PHIL: I hope we're not intruding on you at a time . . . Annie said not. She insisted we come. If there's anything we can do.

ARTHUR *goes up to them.*

ARTHUR: Excuse me. Good morning.

PHIL: Good morning. Lovely day.

ARTHUR: Have you got the time?

PHIL: Just gone a quarter to twelve.

ARTHUR: Thank you. (*Pause. Then to* JULE.) I believe I saw you yesterday evening.

JULE: Me? You might have done.

Pause.

ANNIE: It's turning a bit cold.

ARTHUR (*to* JULE): Yes, you can't be too warm in that condition.

JULE: No, I'm frozen. I must go and get dressed.
ARTHUR: That's a good idea.

Pause.

PHIL: Here on holiday, are you?
ARTHUR: Yes, my wife and myself. We go for walks sometimes on the cliffs.
PHIL: It seems very pleasant here for walking.
ARTHUR: It can be.

Pause.

PHIL: I hope it keeps fine for you.
ARTHUR: Thank you very much. That's clear, I hope. A quarter to twelve. Good morning. (*He goes back to* MADGE *and helps with folding the deckchairs.*)
PHIL: You've very welcome to come and stay with us. I don't know what your plans are at all. There's a couch in the sitting-room that makes up into a bed. You may remember. If that would be any use.
JULE: No, it's kind of you.
PHIL: You've been in touch with a solicitor, I expect.
JULE: I don't need anything.
PHIL: Because I'm sure it's important to get the legal side right.
JULE: We'll do our own defense, thank you.
PHIL: Because it's rather an expert field.
JULE: We know what we're doing.
PHIL: It's quite embarrassing to make the offer but just so you know we are on hand. If and when, if and when, or not.
JULE: It's not that I'm rude. I just don't want anything.
MADGE: How did she take that?
ARTHUR: She said she was going to go and get dressed.
MADGE: And now she'll see us pointedly move away. Small victories all add up. Now where will we be snug?

MADGE *and* ARTHUR *go out with their things, except the thermos flask, which is left behind on the sand.*

ANNIE: Oh, Jule, I wish you would come to us. I hate to think of you here all alone, and the police. If you were living with us—we couldn't stop them but it might look more reliable. They wouldn't have any excuse to get suspicious. I can't believe this holiday maker in a tent's going to look after you. You did the right thing to leave the house. You don't look so connected to the crime as you would do sitting waiting at the scene of it. But if you came to us I'd feel much safer.

The sun comes out.

JULE: You don't know what you're talking about, Annie.
ANNIE: Why don't you tell me what I'm talking about? Why, if it's just a small drugs charge, does it come in a newspaper story that starts with explosions? I know the police pick up a lot of people but why was one of them you? Is it the other people in the house and you didn't know what they were up to? It may even just be them that got you into the drugs charge. You just happen to live in the same house.
PHIL: I expect the police planted it themselves. That's the impression I get in these sort of cases. Once they make up their minds for a conviction.

JULE: Police finger prints were everywhere.

PHIL: Were they, Jule? You must be sure to bring that out in your defense.

JULE: They must have been by the time they'd finished searching, mustn't they? (*She spreads her towel out on the beach and lies down on it.*)

PHIL: Why is it you and one other were let out on bail while the other two were remanded in custody?

ANNIE: The others might have previous convictions. They might even be connected with the explosions. Because the newspaper story did say "following explosions police raided houses." They're friends of hers, she's just involved by association. Even the police can tell the difference. That's why I wish you'd come home with us, Jule, to somewhere normal and have a rest. It must be a strain, you're far too white. Considering all the fresh air too. Someone's an influence on you nowadays.

PHIL *takes off his sweater and shirt and sits on the sand, but not close to* JULE.

JULE: I don't want to.

ANNIE: You've let yourself be carried away, Jule. What is it your friends have done? My own ideas are very sympathetic but putting them into practice would be wicked. It means shutting your eyes to other people. Who's told you you can do that?

PHIL: Don't upset yourself, Annie. Come and sit down in the sun. It's quite warm.

ANNIE: You make your protest with some explosive device and that's fine for you and your friends. That proves your heart's in the right place. But someone may be killed who's not interested in your ideas. I've seen pictures in the papers and I can't go along with it, Jule. You see the man's shock. He hasn't been asked does he want his arm blown off for this cause. He has his wife and children and things to do. He doesn't want to take part.

JULE: Nobody wants to take part in war. Who's asked?

ANNIE: What war? There isn't any war. Who's been telling you you're a soldier?

PHIL: Don't get yourself too excited, Annie. We don't know what your sister's done.

ANNIE: Why don't you tell us then, Jule?

After a moment ANNIE *sits down by* PHIL, *who takes her hand.*
    ERIC, *in swimming trunks, comes in at a jog, and jogs beside them on the spot. Throughout he hardly keeps still—he walks about, jogs, does exercises, push-ups, headstands. He is pale and not muscular.*

ERIC: Made some nice friends?

JULE: My sister Annie. Phil. This is George.

ERIC: Your sister?

JULE: I told her how we met each other here on the beach and I'm staying just for now up in your tent.

ERIC: Yes. Yes that's right. We just ran into each other. I've just been running now to get warm.

PHIL: It must be very cold for swimming.

ERIC: Do you mind getting cold?

PHIL: The sea's always a little cold of course. You expect that. But I do like it warmer than this.

ERIC: Most people do. You're in the majority there.

ANNIE: It's only natural.

ERIC: You think what most people believe is bound to be right?

ANNIE: Right for them. They know if they're cold or—

ERIC: So you think the majority of people know what is right for them? And for other people?

ANNIE: That depends what—

ERIC: And suppose you have two candidates and one says swimming only in the first fortnight in August and the other says swimming only in the second fortnight, which one would you vote for?

ANNIE: It wouldn't make much difference.

ERIC: And specially not to those of us who are here in June. Democracy's a wonderful thing.

ANNIE: But that's not—

ERIC: You're not going to say you don't believe in democracy?

ANNIE: I do of course, but—

ERIC: Good girl, so do I. And in those little green men in flying saucers?

ANNIE: Which little green men?

ERIC: Don't you believe in little green men?

ANNIE: No.

ERIC: I thought if you believed in democracy you must be like me and believe anything.

ANNIE: You don't believe anything.

ERIC: I do, I believe in capitalism and revolution. But wait, you say, that is two different meanings of the word believe. One meaning is you think something exists. Example, I believe in green men. The other is you think it's a good thing. Example, I believe in the prime minister. Now of my belief in capitalism and revolution, do both exist, are both a good thing, or does one exist while the other is a good thing and if so which?

ANNIE: It's hard to believe in you.

ERIC: In either sense, yes, I know it is. And what's Jule's sister doing here?

JULE: She came to see me. She's here for the day.

ERIC: How did she know you were here?

JULE: I sent her a postcard, all right? With a picture of the harbor and a postmark.

ERIC: I'm just surprised you want to go telling people where you are.

JULE: I know you're surprised, George. You'd like to see me in a false moustache. There's no secret about where I am. What's the matter?

ERIC: Nothing at all. You just make me nervous. Doesn't she make you nervous to have in the family? Discontented people like ourselves like to learn of violence on the television news. It makes us feel better as we sip our cocoa and sleep all the sounder. But we're not sure we want it in the family.

ANNIE: Of course it doesn't make us feel better.

ERIC: You're not discontented?

ANNIE: Only like everybody.

ERIC: Everybody's discontented. That's the good news. Everybody's discontented like Jule's sister. That's the bad news. What do you do?

ANNIE: I've just been cleaning somebody's house in the mornings.

ERIC: Do they treat their servants well? I bet they let you have a cup of coffee. And you?

PHIL: I work for a large electrical company which produces equipment for various industries and a wide range of domestic appliances.

ERIC: Why it's essential to have a refrigerator is they're now marketing frozen days you can pop in the freezer and live whenever you're feeling short of time. They can't get a good product image for Mondays so they sell them with Saturdays in a double pack. And with what labor do you create yourself?

PHIL: In fact I'm on sick leave at the moment. I had an accident.

ERIC: Car? Motorbike? Plane, train, hovercraft? No, don't tell me. You were just walking along and something hit you. Industrial accident or domestic? Most accidents happen in the home. Just when you feel you're safest—bang, you fall in the fire, you slip on the wet floor, you're electrocuted by your toothbrush. Let alone acts of God like Jule, who go about causing accidents.

PHIL: Industrial accident.

ERIC: Mangled in the machinery?

PHIL: I had a fall.

ERIC: Better now?

PHIL: Thank you.

ERIC: You got plenty of money out of it, I hope. You exaggerated all your symptoms.

ANNIE: The compensation hasn't been settled yet. Phil has a lot of trouble with his back. He won't be able to do the same work. And besides, the pain must be worth something. The company's insurance company say he should be better by now, they don't believe him. Let them try living with him. Pain's something you can't get round.

PHIL: They'll pay. We're taking them to court.

ERIC: British justice will see you all right. I hope you believe in British justice.

PHIL: They won't find any contributory negligence. I'll get the full amount. I won't settle.

ANNIE: It's not exactly the money so much. Phil wants them to admit his back hurts. He wants the judge to find that's so.

ERIC: He wants justice. You've both lost sleep over that back. Shareholders don't lose sleep. Top management don't lose sleep. Money doesn't pay and nor does an old man in a wig saying yes, your back does hurt. They won't care. Get Jule here to make them jump. That's more like justice. Don't you want more than you'll ever get?

PHIL: Accidents happen.

ERIC: They do, yes, they happen to miners and even people like you, but they don't happen so often in the board room.

PHIL: Our safety level is normally very high. There's no point in me losing my temper.

ERIC: Excuse me, I believe you are one of the workers of the world we're waiting for to unite. But now you can't do the same job, is your socio-economic status about to change? Do you feel a difference in your historical role? In what way is it different from a sausage roll? You don't know? Then I won't ask you to buy my lunch. You might as well have fallen to your death for all the use you're ever going to be. Backache's too good for you. *And* compensation? Greedy bugger.

JULE: You can tell him to be quiet and lie down if you want to.

PHIL: Oh no, it doesn't bother me, thanks.

ERIC: Who are you trying to placate? I'm not your father. I'm not your boss. Nor is power growing out of the barrel of my gun.

JULE: Stop jiggetting about, George.

ERIC: She's the one who should strike terror. Not me. I come down here for a peaceful holiday and find myself in bed with a terrorist. Ninety-five percent of the dead believe in violence. Do they believe it exists or do they believe it's an effective course of action?

ANNIE: But Jule hasn't caused any deaths. Does she tell you about what she's done? Can you understand her?

ERIC: I set myself limited objectives. Understand myself today. Understand the world tomorrow. Understand Jule the day after.

JULE: George, will you keep still? You get on my nerves.

ERIC: Right, I'll just be at one with nature.

ERIC *lies down abruptly.*

ANNIE: You'd be much better coming home with us.

PHIL: It's nice and sunny now for a snap and we're all here together.

PHIL *half kneels to take a picture.* ERIC *suddenly sits up and lunges at* PHIL *, knocking the camera out of his hand.* PHIL *falls over.*

ANNIE: Here, that's an expensive camera. And mind his back.

ERIC: If he can afford an expensive camera I expect he can afford another expensive camera.

ANNIE: Is your back all right, Phil? (*to* ERIC) What's the idea?

ERIC: I'm not having pictures. It wouldn't be safe for your sister.

ANNIE: Why not? Jule, what have you done that I don't know about?

JULE: Of course he can take my picture. Of course it's safe.

ERIC: It makes me nervous.

PHIL (*examining the camera*): I don't think there's much harm done.

ANNIE: You didn't have to push him over. Think of his back.

ERIC: Did I hurt your back?

PHIL: Only a little, thank you.

ERIC: What do I owe you by way of compensation? Ten p?

ANNIE: Is your back all right, Phil?

ERIC: He doesn't mind being pushed over. Accidents happen.

PHIL: Come along, I want some smiles.

PHIL *takes a picture.* ERIC *stands well out of the way.*

ERIC: This is definitely not my picture. A happy day by the sea on a day return that returns you unused at the end of the day.

ANNIE: We came by car in fact.

ERIC: I'm not a great one for the family party, Jule. (*He goes out.*)

ANNIE: Put it away, Phil, don't waste film. I don't feel like smiling. Jule's always admired people anyone else would apologize for.

PHIL: He does seem to have more energy than he knows what to do with.

JULE: I've known him use some of that energy to stay awake three nights with a friend that needed someone to stay awake with him. I don't see you doing it. He's feeling the strain lately but I've known him take other people's strains.

ANNIE: How do you mean, lately? If you've only just met him? When did you know him stay awake three nights?

JULE: By lately I mean today.

ANNIE: Jule, how did you get into all this? Have you yourself ever made a bomb? Don't bother not to answer. I know you're not going to answer.

PHIL: It seems to me there are different things. There's indiscriminate terror. That's hard for anyone in their right mind to defend. But how do we feel about assassination? Remember the prime minister of Spain, blown over the wall in his car. There's a regime where things might be different. If Hitler had had an assassin he'd be a hero. I'm not saying I'd do it myself but it is a question. And then there's destruction of property, which again I wouldn't say yes to, but an empty car isn't a human being. You may get bricks and mortar blown down and nobody hurt except by accident. Though whether they're right to risk the accident I wouldn't like to say. It's more dangerous than driving down the M1 and with less excuse. And you can't have everybody with a grievance taking a gun and going after their MP. Where would it end? Not in a democratic country.

Meanwhile the sun has gone in. JULE *takes* PHIL's *sweater and puts it on.*

JULE: How do we feel about assassination?

PHIL: As I say, I've no view. It's not something I'd ever do but then I'm not driven by the circumstances. I think I'd always resort to non-violence.

JULE: On impulse or as a principle?

PHIL: Both, you know. I'm a great believer in things sorting out. There's more good-will than people like you think. Even in high places I hope for the best.

JULE: Are you a floating voter?

PHIL: Now and then.

ANNIE: Don't talk to her, Phil, she's laughing at you.

PHIL: I can tell.

JULE: You take care of Annie anyway.

PHIL: People like you are very arrogant. Forgive me, that was rude. I've no business.

ANNIE: I could never hurt anyone. I haven't the confidence.

JULE: But why are you crying?

ANNIE: I'm not, I've given it up, same as smoking.

PHIL: She's been on edge all week. I put it down to you. Without blaming you. I just mean my diagnosis. Try breathing slowly, Annie. You can't have any effect on any-thing so why get worked up? Come on, we'd got you feeling fine. Your sister's got her own life. We can argue about the philosophy of it without getting involved personally. It's no good if ideas make you cry.

ANNIE: It's not just the ideas. It's myself.

PHIL: There's nothing wrong with you.

ANNIE: Everything I do is a mistake. If I could start again, but how far back? Before I was born.

PHIL: Don't feel you have to stay if you don't want. I can take her away to talk in a café somewhere. You may have enough troubles of your own.

JULE: Annie dear, what is it?

ANNIE: Oh no, I despise the way I fuss. I'm not sure talking does any good. Phil usual-ly massages my neck.

JULE: Is it because of me? You mustn't mind.

ANNIE: You may have been at the back of my mind when I chose that day for saying something. It was only yesterday.

PHIL: Saying to who? At work, is it, Annie?

ANNIE: What you need explaining, Jule, is how that couple look. He is the man in the grey car but more often I see him with her. They move as a unit even when they're not together. They're after the same thing, it's one style. The surface has such a polish it's hard to think of them as victims, though what they must have done to themselves to get where they are, because it's all competition in that world. They must have been attractive at the start, the bones are still there. They're well known for a striking couple. They've lived all their life for the company. It's hard not to confuse them with the product. That way they come into every home and you can't do without them.

JULE: You can always resign.

ANNIE: I always do but it comes to the same thing. I'd only have to find another job just as bad and without even dinner with Phil in the canteen. And when I finally couldn't stand it, cleaning a clean house seemed such a treat. I took my shoes off to feel the carpets and nobody said a word. She even gave me her old clothes and I made a lot out of saying no but I took them. They were better than any new clothes we've ever had and there aren't the occasions to wear them. I feel a fool in my own home in silk.

PHIL: But what is it you've said to them, Annie? Something you're sorry for?

ANNIE: What happened is I was using the hoover and she was just sitting. I hoovered all round her. Maybe she was thinking but nothing you could call work. I said, Lift your feet, and ran the machine under her suede boots. She dresses right up in case anyone comes or perhaps just for herself so she won't go down. But what goes on in her head? I wouldn't touch it. She makes her face so you can't see and then gets up to anything she likes. I might not have been there. But her feet moved. All morning I cleaned up that woman's mess. Cigar butts by the basin. Tissues on the parquet. Broken glass in the spare bed. A little party, she said, last night. That was all she said in three hours I was there, and scratched herself. I went in the kitchen and put on the dishwasher to drown her out.

PHIL: You shouldn't let her get you upset.

ANNIE: She doesn't get me, it's nothing she does, she does nothing. It's me that's upset, myself, that's all.

PHIL: Perhaps you should give them notice if they upset you. You could give them a month without putting them out.

ANNIE: Will you let me tell you? You never let me lead up how I like. At twenty-past twelve I was back in there wasting the last bit of time and she was still sitting on that sofa, and he came in. Oh, she talked then, they had quite a conversation. I dusted round the edges and never a word to me, not a nod, not good morning, not the glance you'd give a budgerigar. They feel perfectly free with me there, they joke, they touch. I would have thought seeing them there was nobody else in the room but that was me.

PHIL: Isn't it always like that, Annie?

ANNIE: That's what I'm saying, it is, always, exactly. If it was just once I could make an excuse. I could say they had a bad hangover. They went out of the room together the way they do. They go on wheels with a very expensive motor so you don't hear it. They glide together. They have profile. So once more it was time I went and I'd got almost to the front door. The smell in the hall is the kind of wax on the wood. Then he did that thing of coming up behind me. I was in no mood. I said to him, Look, I'm sick of blackmailing you all this time, it makes me feel ill. Because it does, doesn't it? Those stomach aches have all been this trouble. I said, Look, I wouldn't tell your wife. Not the abortion, not even that you ever touched me. I can't give the money back, I told him, because it's spent. But I won't have any more. And no more of him in any way ever. So that was good so far, wasn't it, and it was partly with Jule in mind because (*to* JULE) I can't see you working in that house.

PHIL: Was he offended?

ANNIE: What he said was—he might have been lying which would be a comfort, to think of him annoyed enough to lie.

PHIL: He said what?

ANNIE: It might have been made up to hurt, because he is a very intelligent man. He said she knew anyway all along. From right at the beginning, before I thought of asking him for money, right back when it started in the office down behind the desk. He told her each night. He says they agreed to give me the money as a way of giving me money because they know I'm proud and wouldn't accept—

PHIL: They may have meant it kindly, Annie.

ANNIE: Do you think I care how they meant it?

PHIL: They can't help the kind of people they are. They're very efficient at a certain job and that's all they know.

ANNIE: But I really thought I was doing something to them. I used to feel good cleaning up her shit because I thought I knew what was what and she'd got no idea. When really I was the one. That's all it is. Whatever you do to them, they can afford it, they include it, they glide. That's all it is that makes me cry.

JULE: But leave them, Annie, tell them what you think. Put a brick through their window. You don't have to take any of that. Why ever get into it? Why get involved with a man like that?

ANNIE: I keep quiet about your men.

JULE: But blackmailing him and cleaning his house, what's it about?

ANNIE: In fact Jule he reminds me of you about sex. I don't think he knows what else he could do to give himself a shock. He's got past the end of his fantasies and does things he hasn't even thought of.

JULE: I'm not afraid to do anything I want anymore, if that's what you mean.

ANNIE: You do things you don't even want to see where it gets you.

JULE: Not anymore I don't, I do what I want. How do you know what you don't like if you haven't tried?

ANNIE: What don't you like? Alsatian dogs?

JULE: No, and I don't like women much. I like men, and only very few, and usually only one at a time, and just now one more than the rest.

ANNIE: Oh, Jule, how do you concentrate? On—what is it you concentrate on? Yourself? I never carry anything right through. I'm always turning off sideways. I can't get into an extreme position. I can't even hate those two enough to do anything about them. Their rooms are full of useful things that are none of them necessary like fondue dishes and matching toilet paper and there's no good reason for getting rid of any of them but it just shouldn't be like that. The company has profit sharing and a pingpong room and its products are harmless and sometimes even helpful, and he was so efficient in bed, Jule, I didn't know myself. But what's the point? I sometimes get the feeling my arms and legs and body and head aren't all joined together. I see my hands a long way away.

PHIL: Annie, Annie, don't be upset.

JULE: But if you can't stand it, Annie, you should—

PHIL: Leave her alone, will you, leave her alone.

JULE: I can talk to her.

PHIL: You upset her, go away.

ANNIE: Don't, don't, oh don't.

JULE: You're the one upsetting her. She cries if we quarrel.

PHIL: I'm sorry if I seem to lose my temper. But please leave her alone to calm down.

JULE: Why should she calm down? There's nothing to be calm about that I can see.

ANNIE: Don't, don't.

PHIL: Annie. (*He puts his arms round her.*)

JULE: I'm going to go and get dressed before it starts to rain. (*She goes out.*)

ANNIE: I'm sorry.

PHIL: No, I'm sorry.

ANNIE: What for?

PHIL: I can't talk to your sister very well.

ANNIE: You were talking.

PHIL: No, something blocks my chest. I try to get my views into focus and they disappear the minute I squint at them. Was I like that before the accident?

ANNIE: You're no different.

PHIL: It must be what I'm like, I'm afraid.

> ARTHUR *comes in to look for the thermos flask. He finds it but stays half-hidden crouching behind the rocks to watch them.*

ANNIE: We're a pair.

PHIL: I won't let you go.

ANNIE: No, I like it when you hold me.

PHIL: It helps me breathe. I feel fine when we're alone.

ANNIE: So do I. We should come to the sea sometimes.

PHIL: We are.

ANNIE: Other times too, with no Jule. I haven't even looked at the sea till now. I'd like us to walk along the shore. Once you start watching the waves it's very interesting. I wouldn't need anything else to do all day.

PHIL: I picked you up some shells, little yellow ones.

ANNIE: It seems crazy to me now, the way I've been with those two, you know. It's over now.

PHIL: It doesn't have to be.

ANNIE: But it is.

PHIL: You've said that before.

ANNIE: But this time it is. I feel different. I hate to be tricked. I hate it if what's going on isn't what I thought.

PHIL: You're not very honest yourself.

ANNIE: I am.

PHIL: You steal things from supermarkets.

ANNIE: Ah yes, but that's just hitting back.

PHIL: I don't like it. You'd be better joining a political party.

ANNIE: You won't be the one who gets caught. You're not honest yourself. You're too quiet. We talk about what's wrong with me endlessly, we know there's lots of things wrong with me. You soak it up. You could be a professional. We've been together three years nearly and I wouldn't know what to tell someone about you. I can't imagine what you think about when I'm not with you.

PHIL: I'm the strong silent type.

ANNIE: Silent.

PHIL: I don't think very much, that's what it is. I do things or I see things. I don't think.

ANNIE: But how do you see?

PHIL: I was living for too many years secretly. You were married five years that I was alone, and I'm older than you. It's hard to lose the habit of being alone. My mother was a mistake.

ANNIE: You wouldn't rather be alone again?

PHIL: You like to hear me keep saying I'll never leave you.

ANNIE: When I think what it's like, because I know, living with someone you find you don't love, and then living with you, every day.

PHIL: Oh Annie, you're endless to me.

ANNIE: I wish it wasn't starting to rain and we weren't on a public beach.

PHIL: But it is starting to rain, isn't it. Where's my sweater?

ANNIE: Jule put it on, didn't you notice?

PHIL: That girl's a nuisance.

ANNIE *and* PHIL *go off.* ARTHUR *watches them go, then hurries off the other way. The sky has darkened. There is a loud sound of rain.*

MISS FORBES *comes in, wet with rain, looking for shelter. She is wearing a coat and carrying a handbag and several carrier bags. She shelters by the rocks and mutters to herself.*

MISS FORBES: Oh, damn you, damn you, why do you do it to me? Every time. I won't bear it. I've a right to a fine day like anyone else. Oh, you bastard, dripping down my neck, oh it's not fair. (*She mutters on inaudibly.*)

JULE *comes in, dressed.*

JULE: Annie?

JULE *also shelters by the rocks in a different place.*

MISS FORBES: There's not much shelter here.

JULE: It's only a shower.

MISS FORBES: It's no good going on anyway, is it? We'd get far more wet before we could keep dry. But it's so wet here, I don't know why I'm bothering to keep still. I'll catch a cold now and I'd only just got rid of the cold I had the whole winter, the same cold all winter without a single day's break. You might have thought it was ten different colds, but no.

JULE: I think this place is drier. Come over here.

MISS FORBES: Are you quite sure? It's going to mean crossing an open space.

JULE: As you like.

MISS FORBES: At least it can't be worse than where I am, can it. Ohhhhhh.

MISS FORBES *hurries across to* JULE.

There. There. Well, it's still not what I'd call dry. But it's very kind of you to try and save my day though I don't think I'm in the right place.

JULE: Why, where should you be?

MISS FORBES: On a beach, I've got that much right, but I think it must be the wrong one. I came here years ago and it wasn't the same. I came somewhere years ago. I forget the name. I looked on the map in the right area and this name leaped out at me but perhaps that was from something different. I could have seen it in the paper or heard it on the news. There's so much information you can't keep out.

JULE: Was it a holiday you had here?

MISS FORBES: I had a happy day here once. Or wherever it was. With a man, I need hardly say. And now and then it comes over me. Oh, I could scream but of course I can't. I blame myself, oh, I blame myself. I used to think I'd been too ugly. I accepted that because it couldn't be helped. But no, it was my hesitation that drove him away. It wasn't at all like this beach. There were golden sand dunes. Very very hot sand dunes.

JULE: You've never tried to go back to the beach till now?

MISS FORBES: I've tried, I've often tried. I miss the train. I can't get out of the door to go to the station. But I managed all that this time. I've been taking a very good new pill. Though I don't like pills, I don't trust them. They may not mean well. They won't last. But they got me onto the train and down here. But then look at the rain.

JULE: It's not so heavy now.

MISS FORBES: It's the wrong beach. There wasn't that big stretch of mud.

JULE: It's low tide.

MISS FORBES: But there should be sand dunes, not rocks and cliffs.

JULE: I think there may be some dunes in the next bay.

MISS FORBES: It's too far. I've a drawer at home of things that are impossible. Letters I can't answer, bills I can't pay, library books I can't take back. Oh my family was behind it all. There's nothing you can tell me about myself. You can deal out psychological terms like tarot cards and I'll read my fortune. I had a brother. My father was always dead in the first war. My mother lived on and on. My family burst in my flesh like shrapnel.

JULE: There's not enough rain to worry about.

JULE *comes out from the rocks. After a moment* MISS FORBES *tentatively follows.*

MISS FORBES: I was so angry last time I missed the train that I left my umbrella in the tea-room.

JULE: The wind's blowing the weather over quite fast. It won't be one thing or another.

MISS FORBES: Are you busy?

JULE: Not exactly.

MISS FORBES: You wouldn't come along with me, would you? To look for the dunes.

JULE: I really ought to find my sister.

MISS FORBES: It wouldn't come over me so much if you were there.

JULE: She'd wonder where I was.

MISS FORBES: Please, I need you to come with me.

JULE: Can't you see I don't want to.

MISS FORBES: Now I must take off my coat. I must take off my cardy. I never can get in agreement with the temperature. I bring everything I could possibly need. I'll put on my jacket. My raincoat won't go over my jacket but my jacket's not waterproof and my raincoat's not warm enough. My jacket can't go over my cardy but my cardy will go under my raincoat.

JULE: Where do you live?

MISS FORBES: Will you come and see me?

JULE: No, I just wondered.

MISS FORBES: I live in Woking. What's it to you?

JULE: You managed to get all this way.

MISS FORBES: Don't ask me things about myself unless you mean it.

JULE: Mean what?

MISS FORBES: I get so angry. I get so angry. I bite myself. I tear out tufts of my hair. And it's not my fault, it can't be.

JULE: Of course it's not.

MISS FORBES: You're nice to me, you don't want trouble. I'm a strong woman.

JULE: But do you ever hurt other people?

MISS FORBES: Only if I'm in love. That hasn't happened to me very often.

JULE: Suppose you had the material to blow something up? What would you do with it?

MISS FORBES: I'd throw it—I'd throw it—No, I'd hold it tight against myself, and there, at last.

JULE: But it's not your fault.

MISS FORBES: Oh it is, it is. I blame myself. I shouldn't have ever said no. He was very good-looking in what I recognized as a dangerous way and he had a wife. My brother would have killed him. I often think of that. And I could never stop thinking of my brother when I should have stopped thinking entirely. Even in the dunes. I blame myself. He was very gentle. But I couldn't stop thinking even in the dunes.

JULE: Perhaps he would have left you anyway.

MISS FORBES: Why have I never been loved too much? So that whatever I do the other person loves me too much and can't stop loving me whatever I do.

JULE: You want too much.

MISS FORBES: Yes, I want too much, that's what I want. You can't help.

JULE: I never thought I could.

MISS FORBES: You won't come with me up the beach because that would be boring for you.

JULE: And I have to find my sister.

MISS FORBES: You make me angry. You'll forget all about me as soon as I've gone. But I'll be stuck with hating you all afternoon, all up the beach. And if it's the wrong beach, what am I to do?

JULE: I'll come with you, just a little way.

MISS FORBES: There's no need to trouble.

JULE: Not far because—

PHIL (*off*): Jule.

JULE: Oh, here they are now. I won't come. I'm sorry.

PHIL *comes in.* MISS FORBES *waits a moment, then goes out.*

PHIL: We went into a café while it rained. I hope you don't mind. Are you very wet?

JULE : Do you want your sweater?

PHIL: Only if you've quite finished with it.

JULE: I should have said "please."

JULE *takes off his sweater, which she was wearing over her own clothes.*

Thank you. Is Annie feeling better?

PHIL: Before we go back to the café—

JULE: Yes, what?

PHIL: I wanted to say. I never told Annie.

JULE: Told her what?

PHIL: About us.

JULE: What about us?

PHIL: I'd like to pretend it didn't happen myself. It's not an episode I'm proud of. But we'd far better face up to it, Jule.

JULE: I'm not pretending. I don't think I remember.

PHIL: All right, lie. It fits with your destructive character.

JULE: Oh, I remember what you mean. At Christmas the Christmas before last, when I came to stay with Annie and you at Christmas.

PHIL: She remembers. Put it like that if you like. You're prepared to talk about it now anyway.

JULE: Nothing much happened, did it? You were drunk.

PHIL: Nothing happened except I came into your room in the night and tried to get into bed with you.

JULE: And I said piss off and you did, as far as I remember.

PHIL: Not straight away.

JULE: What happened then? We kissed each other.

PHIL: You weren't wearing a nightdress either.

JULE: I don't if it isn't cold.

PHIL: And you'd really forgotten.

JULE: I did have the impression when I saw you again that you'd always fancied me a bit but I'd forgotten what gave me the idea. It was all very passing, we were quite drunk, it was Christmas.

PHIL: I've remembered it all in great detail.

JULE: It's nothing to worry about.

PHIL: Yes it is, Jule. I love Annie. It worries me a lot that you're her sister.

JULE: I can't help that.

PHIL: I have feelings for you I'd rather not have for someone I'm likely to see again. If you'd been no relation that night, I could let it go. I see attractive women all the time. I might do something about it or I might not, but on they go, on I go, our separate ways.

JULE: But we hardly do see each other again. I don't think I've seen Annie and you once since that Christmas. I've been very tied up with the people I'm living with. My family's the last thing I bother to visit.

PHIL: But I'd like to see you.

JULE: You just said you wouldn't.

PHIL: It preys on my mind. I go over and over that night and I ask myself how I could do it. You're Annie's sister. I'm not married to Annie but it's the same, it makes you my sister. It should do. It should rule out that kind of obsession.

JULE: Of course it doesn't.

PHIL: Doesn't it for you?

JULE: Do I have to feel you're my brother? I don't at all.

PHIL: Then perhaps I should just yield.

JULE: How do you mean?

PHIL: Let my feelings take me over.

JULE: But just because you're not my brother doesn't mean I've any interest in you. It might be more interesting if you were.

PHIL: You're saying you don't want me because of Annie. You're right, of course.

JULE: No, because I don't.

PHIL: Why didn't you say so in the first place?

JULE: I did, I said piss off.

PHIL: Not at once.

JULE: A few kisses at Christmas is nothing. I'd quite like to kiss you now but I wouldn't want to go on.

PHIL: Why, what's wrong with me?

JULE: I'm involved with someone else. I couldn't be bothered.

PHIL: That one jogging about?

JULE: No, no, he's just a passing . . .

PHIL: Then what's wrong with me just passing?

JULE: You'd go on thinking about it for a year and a half. I don't want you thinking about me.

PHIL: Because of Annie?

JULE: No, because of the way you'd go on and on thinking. I'm not interested in being your guilty obsession.

PHIL: You mean, you will if I don't feel guilty?

JULE: Go away and tie a knot in it.

PHIL: No, but Jule, I could try to change the way I feel guilty. I know I worry too much. I lived alone with my mother a long time. I got the courage to say something to you about it. I never thought I would. I get a pain across my chest, here, like an iron bar. I can't lash out. You can so you don't know the problem. With you I could—

JULE: No, I don't want to. You make it sound so therapeutic.

PHIL: Yes, Jule, yes.

JULE: No, it's all so heavy. Where's the joy?

PHIL: I think the joy would come.

JULE: Not to me.

PHIL: You make me want to hurt you. It's a terrible feeling. I want to break you up on these rocks.

JULE: But you won't because you'd feel guilty. It might give you a pain in your chest. And you've already got one in your back.

PHIL: And you can jeer but that's lucky for you, isn't it. Isn't it lucky for you I'm the decent sort of person I am? You're proud of being a slut and a murderer. You—oh, you fucking fucking—oh, I hate you—

JULE: I think that's Annie coming.

PHIL: I hate you, I hate hate you.

JULE: Yes, it is Annie.

PHIL: You're saying that to distract me.

JULE: No, it is Annie if you look. (*She waves to* ANNIE *in the distance.*)

PHIL: That's lucky for you, isn't it. I can't face Annie now. This must be like a horrible dream. I forget all my dreams but sometimes when I wake up I think I must have had a horrible dream because I feel—oh, what shall I do?

JULE: Whatever you like.

PHIL: I must look like myself. I must get my face— (*He turns aside.*)

In a moment ANNIE *comes in.*

ANNIE: The café seemed so dreary now it's dry.

JULE: I'm not hungry.

ANNIE: Why don't we make a fire and get warm? There's plenty of wood on the beach if it wasn't so wet. We always used to make bonfires, didn't we, Jule?

JULE: The bigger pieces wouldn't be soaked through if we could get it started.

ANNIE: I could go and buy a packet of firelighters.

JULE: Or paraffin would do.

PHIL: You want to light a fire? I'll get you something. (*He goes out.*)

ANNIE: Look at all the oil on this bit. Will it burn better?

JULE: My feet are covered with oil. This beach is all rubbish if you look.

ANNIE: We'll clean it up with our fire.

JULE: What you are, Annie, is a girl guide.

JULE *and* ANNIE *start building up a fire, with a newspaper of* ANNIE*'s, driftwood, etc.*

ANNIE: I'm sorry, Jule, bursting out like that. I feel better now.

JULE: Did you have a good cry? What does that change? Don't cry, don't feel better, and do something about it.

ANNIE: But doing something would just make me feel better. Nothing changes.

JULE: Suppose you killed that man you work for.

ANNIE: That's one of the reasons I can't do anything. You make me think of terrible things I'd never dare. And don't even want to. It stops me thinking of sensible things that might be some use.

JULE: Yes, I'm sorry. I know I do that to you. But what you call terrible things aren't all so impossible. You think you'd stop being Annie. But I haven't become unrecognizable this last year, have I? Look at me. Listen, Annie, there are quite a few of us—

PHIL *comes back carrying a can of petrol.*

PHIL: What nonsense is your sister talking now?
ANNIE: What have you got there? Not petrol?
PHIL: I always carry a spare can in the boot to be on the safe side.
ANNIE: Yes, but you want to be very careful.

PHIL *pours some petrol into an old tin from the beach.*

JULE: So you hurt your back.
PHIL: Yes.
JULE: So you can't work.
PHIL: I might take up something different. I'd like to.
JULE: Why? Does your life seem a bit pointless?
PHIL: There are things I'm interested in.
JULE: So it's all for the best?
PHIL: I wouldn't go that far.
JULE: How long were you lying flat in hospital?
PHIL: Two months.
JULE: And you didn't feel furious and helpless?
PHIL: Only sometimes.
JULE: And Annie in the silver grey car? At about the same time?
PHIL: I'd been home a week out of hospital before she told me.
ANNIE: I couldn't tell you sooner in case it made you ill.
PHIL: It did make me ill.
ANNIE: You were very understanding about it.
PHIL: I was, yes.
ANNIE: You don't put your own feelings first. That's one of the things I love you for, Phil.
PHIL: For being a fool. For just taking everything.
ANNIE: No, for—
PHIL: A fool not to go and smash his face.
ANNIE: I'm the one who talks about violence. I get aggressive about him and you say how good he is at his job, how in some ways it's an honor, how you have to admire—
PHIL: I smile, I smile, my face is beyond me. I can't spit.
JULE: You can.
ANNIE: Jule, don't upset him, he's been ill. I'm going to try and get this lit without petrol. (*She busies herself with the fire. The newspaper burns but the wood is too damp.*)
JULE: You could change the way you feel guilty. You could get rid of that pain across your chest. You could probably get rid of that pain in your back. You could secretly do something to that executive, or another one, the function's the same, they've no faces, and only you would know, you alone, and you would know you felt quite different.
PHIL: Secretly—
JULE: Through the post—
PHIL: A letter to blow his hand—
JULE: Or in the office. You could leave something. Or in the house, where Annie can easily go.

ANNIE *gets up from the fire.*

ANNIE: No, Jule, we don't want to.

JULE: Think how they glide, Annie, all their lives. That woman knew all along about you.

ANNIE: No, Jule, that's something of my own. I mind it myself, in myself, I don't do something—

PHIL: Jule—

JULE: Phil, yes, Annie, listen, my loves. It's not your fault. It's not just what's done to you. It's because you're just things to them, like all of us are just things to them. They produce more and more useless things. And they're just things, the way things are now. And being hurt is all they notice.

PHIL: My face always smiles. I smile even more often than I'm insulted. But I can feel how I could hurt them.

JULE *squats by the fire, adding more paper, nursing a small flame.*

JULE: You smile yes to it all. You must learn to say no.

PHIL: I do say no.

JULE: You must do it then. (*She bends low over the fire.*)

ANNIE: Do what? Nothing violent?

PHIL *suddenly throws the petrol over the fire.* JULE *just manages to get out of the way as it flares up.*

How can you be so stupid, Phil? Jule, are you hurt?

PHIL: Oh to feel how I hate . . . how things blaze up . . . then you'll see the joy you're after.

JULE: Don't turn away from it, Annie.

ACT TWO

High tide. Sunny afternoon.
    JULE *in a bathing suit is lying in the sun.* ERIC *comes in. He is dressed and his long hair has been cut very short. He is carrying a child's bucket and spade.*

ERIC: Would you recognize me?

JULE: Yes, of course.

ERIC: I was hoping you'd say my own mother wouldn't know me. But then she hasn't for a long time so perhaps she would again. I must look more like I did at ten.

JULE: I never noticed your face too much in all that hair.

ERIC: Why, what's wrong with my face?

JULE: It's not so much as if you were in disguise. More as if you'd taken a disguise off. There's nowhere to hide your eyes.

ERIC: You're saying I looked like a different person before?

JULE: Slightly?

ERIC: Good, that's all. I don't need to know if it makes me ugly.

JULE: There's nothing to get in my fingers when I kiss you.

ERIC: Do you still want to now you can see my face?

JULE: It still feels like the same face.

ERIC: I'll miss you, Jule. Look, I found a nice bucket and spade nobody was making use of. (*He starts making sand pies.* JULE *idly knocks them flat.*)

JULE: Eric, have you decided yet where you're going?

ERIC: Wide open spaces.

JULE: Strangers stand out more in open spaces. Manchester's where to get lost, or Birmingham.

ERIC: I'd rather be found than hide in Birmingham.

JULE: I'm not sure what it is this trip's for.

ERIC: A new life.

JULE: Finish up your old one first.

ERIC: I want it quiet. I want to get into one of those butter ads and see the cows.

JULE: Sounds more like a holiday than a life.

ERIC: It makes a start.

JULE: But you can't be away long.

ERIC: I can't know exactly when I'll be back before I've even gone, can I?

JULE: Will you go to Wales?

ERIC: I might do.

JULE: Have you not decided or are you not saying?

ERIC: I've somewhere in mind but I like to change my mind.

JULE: You're not saying.

ERIC: Leave it alone, Jule, O.K.?

JULE: Do you think I'll be after you with tracker dogs?

ERIC: I'll just feel better, O.K., Jule, if nobody at all has any idea where I am. And stop knocking the fucking pies over.

JULE: Look, I told my sister I'd only just met you. I called you George. I lie about you without even bothering to think, as if lies are the only way to talk about you.

ERIC: Fine, keep it up.

JULE: You're feeling paranoid so I humor you. I feel I'm being watched myself sometimes, I feel I must be doing something wrong, I must be very conspicuous. I want to keep still. But if you're really planning to disappear you're humoring yourself too far.

ERIC: I don't accept I have to go back to court just because of the bail. My father can afford to lose the money.

JULE: Not because of the bail. Because of all the things we're planning to do. As soon as you came back to us, the police would pick you up then, they're not stupid. You'd just waste time.

ERIC *has stopped making pies. He starts digging a hole.*

ERIC: I don't accept I have to go back.

JULE: Of course you have to.

ERIC: If I choose to go back that's a different thing.

JULE: You'd better choose it then.

ERIC: I'd like to show them we're not so easy. We slip through their fingers. I thought I'd dye my hair.

JULE: And a false beard? and glasses? and rubber ears? and walk with a limp?

ERIC: Yes, I have got some glasses I'm meant to wear for reading.

JULE: Is there something I don't know about?

ERIC: I thought you knew everything.

JULE: Previous convictions?

ERIC: I would have boasted of them, wouldn't I?

JULE: Then why bother running away from a drug charge that isn't even what the police are after? You know that was just to get us in. They didn't find anything they wanted. The only worry we've got is Vin and Rose being kept on the grounds there may be "more serious charges," and that's just a bluff, it must be. Because what can they use? They're onto us too soon. There's nothing Vin's done. But you hardly need more than nothing for conspiracy. That's what you should be worrying about, not going on the run to make yourself interesting.

ERIC: I will if I choose.

JULE: They'll soon get you, Eric.

ERIC: Do you want them to?

ERIC *moves away.* JULE *starts making the pile of sand from the hole into a castle.*

ERIC: It's easy for Vin.

JULE: What is?

ERIC: He's been in prison.

JULE: How does that help?

ERIC: He's been living this same life since he was what? Fifteen?

JULE: It's not the same life. He used to get into fights and steal cars. He didn't see what it was about. Anything he does now is deliberate. He knows what's been done to him. He knows who his enemy is.

ERIC: Yes, there you are. That's what I mean.

JULE: Are you making your point? Are you winning your argument?

ERIC: No, listen, Jule. I know you love him. I do too, I'm not attacking him. That's not what I'm saying.

JULE: Now you've talked about what you're not saying. Now you'll talk about what you are saying.

ERIC: Vin talks. You listen by the hour. His mother, his mother, and him, age six, out on the street. Think sometimes when he's on about his father, how that all helps. He lashes out with that child's anger.

JULE: So what are you saying? He's just a psychopath?

ERIC: What it is, Jule, you're too like me. That's why you don't like to listen. We can't stand what's done to other people. Vin can't stand what's done to himself. He's not unselfish and he's stronger for it.

JULE: I can't stand what's done to me.

ERIC: Nothing bad's ever been done to you except in your head.

JULE: I've one life just like anyone.

ERIC: You and I are too well-read. All Vin finds in books is what he already knows. He can read that violence is man recreating himself and that probably is true for him. He never has been anything except through violence. When he learnt some theories he didn't have to change, he just got a better idea of himself.

JULE: So what are you saying?

ERIC: He can read, "Freedom, the power to act, shrinks every day except for the criminal in the so-called free society." Lucky him to have been a criminal first and read that afterwards. I have to make myself a criminal in order to act. It's the harder way round, that's all I'm saying.

JULE: It's not all you're saying.

ERIC: What then?

JULE: You're saying you've had enough. Just one little nudge from the police. Didn't you know they meant to frighten us? How can you let them do it?

ERIC: Jule, come on.

JULE: We won't be hearing from you again. Isn't that what it is? Your new life?

ERIC *sits down and helps with the castle.*

ERIC: Jule, all I'm saying is, I want some time. We were all only talking about what we might do. Things have suddenly started moving on. You wanted to get out of that house yourself.

JULE: Yes, but I always knew I was going back.

ERIC: Did you? Every minute of this week?

ANNIE *comes in with three ice-cream cones.*

ANNIE: I was getting an ice-cream from the van and I saw you here.

JULE: This is Peter. Brother of George.

ANNIE: Yes, I can see the family likeness. Are you twins?

ERIC: No, I'm the elder and better.

ANNIE: Are you camping on the cliffs as well?

JULE: It's the same man, Annie. He's cut his hair.

ANNIE: I liked it better long.

JULE: He's really called Eric Montgomery. He expects you to know the name from the papers. He came down to the sea with me to get away from it all but now he wants to get even further away. I'm surprised you recognized him with short hair because he's in disguise.

ERIC: I don't mind you telling your sister that. Tell her what you like.

JULE: He's a coward.

ANNIE: Have you changed your mind, Eric, about what you and Jule are doing?

ERIC: Yes. Yes, I have, now you ask. That shocks Jule.

JULE: Does the thought of what we might do make you feel guilty, Eric? Tell Annie. She'll know what you mean.

ERIC (*Though what he says is often aimed at* JULE *he addresses himself entirely to* ANNIE. *He forgets to eat the ice-cream, which melts.*): Jule doesn't have these bourgeois senti-ments. She knows only villains are nasty enough to be heroes. Nice people don't make revolutions, they count the dead. All right, if the wretched are violent who can blame them? But I think they're all in other countries. In that house where we were all living I did feel wretched enough. That house, if you'd seen it, the dark stairs, the layers of wallpaper coming off the damp, the house next door, the num-ber of people in it, the rent they paid, the work they went out to, the street they went out into with more houses of too many people, the rent they were paying, the work they were going out to, the children in the street growing up to more of the same, and the next street the same, the next same, too much ever to grasp, the children growing up to more. Waking up in the morning there was waking up to need to do something impossible. The kitchen window was stuck. We didn't clean it. I'd get up and be thinking how does anyone get through a day? Outside the window all the streets. I thought we were being suffocated. I smashed the win-dow one morning but it just made us cold. I mended it with a piece of hardboard.

JULE: But a few days by the sea in the sunshine and he's a different man.

ERIC (*still to* ANNIE): Are you very, somewhat or not at all happy? Somewhat? If not at all and you wanted to die, you wouldn't ask me to do it for you. Most people are somewhat happy, they'd say they are, I'm not going to tell them they're not. Happy just walking along, liking each other, liking their work even, some of them. Some of them don't. I know all sorts of economic arguments, I expect you've heard them yourself. Say we go on with what we've talked about. What's the most obvious difference it makes? A bit of rubble and perhaps a few people not walking along that were walking along somewhat happy.

ANNIE: You say, what you've talked about. Has it just been talk?

ERIC: Is that a relief? Because of course it would be wrong to indulge in violence. Not "of course" Annie. But Jule herself knows what's good is very simple times that are happy. We have them. Cooking a meal up on the cliffs when it's getting dark. Making love and talking after. It may be Jule and Vin is something more extreme I don't know about. Vin and me is something very extreme. But do I want it? The way Jule and I are together seems more what my life might be about. But Vin can't be happy, like that, she'll say, plenty of people can't. They're too put down to make love, they haven't time to look at the sea. Does that mean I can't ever be happy when I can be? If only it was you, Annie, I was asking. Will you come with me, Jule?

JULE: The ice-cream's melting all over your hand.

ERIC *crumples the cone in his fist and drops it on the sand.*

ERIC: Don't I get an answer?

JULE: Of course we've been happy. It shows up more compared to how things are. Like feeling most strongly for someone just when you know you won't see him again. It won't stop me doing whatever has to be done.

ANNIE: But, Jule, it is important to be happy.

ERIC: Do you think I mean happy like you? I mean what I meant before I met Vin. I mean starting with changing myself.

ANNIE: You could do with it.

JULE *starts digging a moat round the castle. Apparently aimlessly she throws the sand at* ERIC.

ERIC: Why can't I think of my life as a slow explosion into other lives, not hurting but somehow changing—

JULE: He's going to be a saint now, Annie. Why didn't he shave his head while he was about it?

ANNIE: He still doesn't make as little sense as you.

JULE: You'll explode with a fizz in a little bottle marked Poetry. Powerful men enjoy poetry. It helps them relax after dinner.

ERIC: I just want some time, Jule. I don't know. I want to be somewhere quiet and look at things. I'd like to play some music again some time.

JULE: Is there any address we can write care of? Vin might want to get in touch.

ERIC: No address.

JULE: You can always contact us if you want to.

ERIC: Will you stop throwing bloody sand?

ERIC *digs some sand towards her.* JULE *still throws hers at him.*

JULE: Do you think you're going to want to get in touch?

ERIC: I hope you think of me sometimes, Jule.

JULE: Do you want to hide from us, Eric? Would it be more peaceful for your meditations? Do you want to hide from Vin?

ERIC: Don't think too badly of me. Fuck you.

ERIC, *getting more sand thrown at him, throws more at her again.*

JULE: Of course I think badly of you. It doesn't matter. You'll stay some sort of friend, I daresay.

ERIC: It's for Vin's sake, Jule, I've got to go. You should be grateful.

JULE: What does that mean?

ERIC: It's easy for Vin.

JULE: You've said that.

ERIC: He doesn't get confused. It's sometimes hard under pressure to know what you're doing.

JULE *stops playing with the sand.*

JULE: Eric, what have you done?

ERIC: How do you mean?

JULE: We know each other. Come on.

ERIC: Come on where?

JULE: It wasn't when we were arrested?

ERIC: I didn't say a word. I'm sure I didn't let anything out they didn't know already.

JULE: What did you say?

ERIC: I said I wouldn't tell them anything.

JULE: Anything about what?

ERIC: Anything about anything.

JULE: What did they say?

ERIC: They said to go away and think about it.

JULE: Think about what?

ERIC: Whether I had anything to say. I told them I hadn't.

JULE: So you've been thinking about it?

ERIC: Of course not. I always knew I wasn't going back.

JULE: I suppose they said they'd drop the drugs charge if you could help them about Vin.

ERIC: How could I? We haven't even done anything yet. The worst they could do would be conspiracy.

JULE: What did you say?

ERIC: Nothing. What you say to pigs doesn't count. I might have given the impression I'd think about it but that was just to get them off my back.

JULE *starts to throw small stones, aiming just short of him.*

Anyone might say anything if they were pushed. But you don't keep your word. I'm not keeping my word. I'm not going back. You can't think I'd go and give evidence against the rest of you. I never for a moment dreamt I'd do that. And now I've got to move on, you see, so they won't know where I am.

JULE: What did you say?

ERIC: Stop throwing stones. It's dangerous.

JULE: What did you say?

ERIC: Nothing, Jule, I really didn't.

JULE: Why not come back then?

ERIC: I don't choose to come back. You should be grateful.

JULE: Because if you came back you know you'd talk.

ERIC: I just want to get right out of it.

JULE: Get out of it then.

ERIC *is hit by a stone.*

ERIC: You deserve whatever you get.

ERIC *picks up some stones too.*

JULE: I don't know why you let me know you cut your hair. You'd better not let me know what color you dye it.

ERIC: You wouldn't all take some revenge would you? It wouldn't be our policy. It's more Vin himself when he's angry that makes me nervous. Perhaps if you didn't mention to Vin about my hair.

> ERIC *is slowly retreating.* JULE *starts throwing large stones harder.* ERIC *dodges and goes.* JULE *throws a few more stones down the beach after him. Then she sits in the hole dug earlier by* ERIC *and starts pulling the sand of the castle over herself.*

ANNIE: You won't go to prison, will you, Jule? Because what could he tell? It sounds as if there's only been talk. Is that right?

JULE: Remember how we used to bury each other in the sand.

ANNIE: Because surely everybody talks. I'd like to know you hadn't done anything.

JULE: It doesn't mean I'm not going to.

> ANNIE *and* JULE *concentrate on burying* JULE *in the sand. When* JULE*'s arms are buried,* ANNIE *goes on covering her, piling sand on and patting it down hard.*

You used to lie on the floor and shut your eyes and scream because someone would always come and kiss you better. They may kiss you now but not better. You should listen, Annie, when it's me telling you. But that's just why you won't listen. You never wanted to play my games. You thought being older put you in charge. But my games were always better. You don't make me worry about what I'm doing. It's not something I go into. But I love the friends I'm with more than you because what we're bound up in is more important than if we always get on. Eric's really gone. And I love you more than them, Annie, and I wish you were with me bound up in it. Even Phil sees the point. Why not you?

ANNIE: It's not a good moment to ask.

JULE: Why, what is it?

ANNIE: Phil told me.

JULE: Phil told you what?

ANNIE: Everything. Unless of course he didn't.

JULE: What everything?

ANNIE: You and him. How could you just never tell me?

JULE: Annie, your man is nice enough but mad. What's he saying? He started raving to me about it too. Nothing happened.

ANNIE: You kissed him.

JULE: Annie, don't be stupid, we were drunk.

ANNIE: You were naked.

JULE: I was trying to go to sleep and he blundered in.

ANNIE: And what?

JULE: And I told him to go away. Does he say anything different?

ANNIE: It doesn't sound quite so cool as he tells it.

JULE: Sodom and Gomorrah. The Vampire. I expect he showed you where I bit his neck.

ANNIE: Did you bite his neck?

JULE: Of course I didn't.

ANNIE: Why wasn't I told?

JULE: There wasn't anything to tell.

ANNIE: If it was nothing you would have mentioned it.

JULE: It wasn't important.

ANNIE: It was to him, it was to me. It should have been to you.

JULE: I'll tell you everything another time. "Annie, your man just gave me a piercing look."

ANNIE: We all know you're the world's most liberated woman. We all know you have five men every night.

JULE: Why don't you ever pay attention? You don't care what my life's like, you never really want me to tell you. It's been quite good the four of us living together. It's been up and down. Eric was the one who was most nearly left out but we all need each other. It's Vin he loves more than me or Rose. We all love Vin most is the trouble. Rose was with him first. I admire Rose for a lot of things and one is because she never tried to stop me joining them. Perhaps she knew I'd make no real difference to her and Vin but she can't have been sure. We all got frightened sometimes by things that happened. But we wanted to find out what made us frightened. Why should there be anything frightening about four people who want to understand each other? We've laughed a lot. Eric makes it sound as if that house was some kind of mental home. He was the one who got most depressed. But we laughed a lot. We did at the beginning. We got frightened of where our politics was taking us and what we might do. But it makes sense to other people not only us. It's not so frightening when you're used to it.

ANNIE: I don't understand you.

JULE: You don't want to.

ANNIE: No, I don't want to.

JULE: I don't know what's going to happen to us. You can't think it's all for nothing. I wish you'd see it, Annie.

ANNIE: I can see living with three people, if that's what you like. Nobody minds that. I mind violence.

JULE: Everybody does.

ANNIE: Well, of course.

JULE: And they're meant to mind it.

They stay silent for a time. ANNIE *has finished burying* JULE *by now and only her head shows.*

Maybe I can go on lying here till the tide comes in over me. It's coming quite fast.

ANNIE: I was thinking that.

JULE: Thanks.

ANNIE: You don't ever expect me to hate you.

JULE: Not much, no.

ANNIE: Haven't you ever been jealous?

JULE: Yes, but with some reason. Or is it because I made Phil understand what I'm talking about?

ANNIE: There is a reason if he feels so strongly. I don't care what really happened. What matters is how he remembers it. Why is it a year and a half later I'm told and it mattered to him all that time? You're always more important than me. You climbed the tree too high and broke your arm, and I was obviously right not to climb so high, but you got the attention. You always get attention.

JULE: When Phil and you make love do you usually come?

ANNIE: Why?

JULE: I wondered.

ANNIE: Sometimes. Why?

JULE: Because I'd like you to. You look so sad most of the time.

ANNIE: I hate you, Jule, quite often. Now as well but often when you're not there, when I think of you. It would be a relief to know I was hurting you. I see why people use knives. I've thought that sometimes in the kitchen. I'd enjoy slashing your face and knowing it was too late, that I couldn't be sorry and change my mind. The blood would be pouring out, frightening us.

JULE (*laughing*): I'd better not come and stay with you, had I?

ANNIE: Laugh, then, laugh. How can you laugh?

JULE: It is funny when you keep saying how I've got to go and stay with you to be safe.

> JULE *laughs, her head lying right back on the sand.* ANNIE *suddenly throws sand over her face, covering it, and pats it down.* JULE *can't struggle properly because of the weight of sand on her arms.* ANNIE *goes.* JULE *struggles out. She spends some time getting sand out of her eyes and mouth, shaking her hair, slowly brushing sand off her body. It has clouded over and now starts to rain.* JULE *goes out slowly. It rains.*
> MISS FORBES *comes in, wet with rain.*

MISS FORBES: No, oh no, no, no, it's not fair. Why on me? Why rain on me? I won't stand it. Rain on me, then, rain on me. I don't care.

> MISS FORBES *stands crying in the rain.*
> ARTHUR *comes in, holding the newspaper over his head and carrying the deckchairs. He goes and shelters by the rocks. After a moment he decides to speak to* MISS FORBES.

ARTHUR: Excuse me.

> MISS FORBES *pays no attention.*

Excuse me, er, miss.

> *She turns.*

If you want to shelter, you can shelter here.

MISS FORBES: It's too late.

ARTHUR: Why too late?

MISS FORBES: I'm soaked already. I'm soaked to the skin. I can feel the water running down my back. I'll never get dry now whatever I do.

ARTHUR: Come on, come on, don't be upset. Come and shelter here.

> ARTHUR *comes from the rocks and ushers her to shelter.*

There, that's not so bad, is it. Perhaps there's something else upsetting you apart from the rain.

> MISS FORBES *cries harder.*

If you'd like to tell me about it. I don't expect I'd be able to do anything.

MISS FORBES: No, no. It's a private grief.

ARTHUR: It's terrible weather when you're not feeling so bright yourself.

MISS FORBES: You don't happen to know if there's any beach near here that has sand dunes?

ARTHUR: Sand dunes. No, it's all rocky as far as I've walked but I'm not an expert on the area. You could always ask at the police station.

MISS FORBES: It's not worth the bother. I never should have come. What did I hope to get from it anyway? Some sort of thrill I'd be better without. The tide coming in doesn't make it the right beach. I remember a beach with pounding surf.

ARTHUR: Excuse my asking, but would it be a romantic memory?

MISS FORBES: I suppose there's no harm in admitting that. Everyone has them.

ARTHUR: I have a few myself. As we get older we realize that some things may not happen to us again.

MISS FORBES: If only I had nothing to blame myself for.

ARTHUR: A clear conscience is what we'd all like. But you can't have that where romance is concerned.

MISS FORBES: You think I'm wrong to blame myself then?

ARTHUR: You may well be right to blame yourself. But everybody should blame him or herself. You're no different there.

MISS FORBES: That's a comforting way to look at it. Perhaps *he* blames himself.

ARTHUR: If he's worthy of you I'm sure he does.

MISS FORBES: But that makes it worse if he regrets it too. We might so easily still be together.

ARTHUR: Do I take it you're somewhat by yourself in life?

MISS FORBES: I have a brother in the north of England but we don't write.

ARTHUR: Not even a Christmas card?

MISS FORBES: Cards, yes, but without any message except the seasonal.

ARTHUR: That's very lonely. I know what it is.

MISS FORBES: Are you in the same position?

ARTHUR: I'm very much alone.

MISS FORBES: No family at all?

ARTHUR: It's not so much that.

MISS FORBES: Are you parted from them?

ARTHUR: I am in fact married, I regret to say. I mean I'm very happily married so far as it goes. I have a grown up son. But I still think I can say I know what it is to be lonely.

MISS FORBES: Not really lonely, no, you wouldn't know.

ARTHUR: It can be lonely even with two in a bed.

MISS FORBES: Not lonely. You'd hear the other breathing.

ARTHUR: Breathing. Yes. Well.

MISS FORBES: Tell me about your son.

ARTHUR: He's a fine boy, taller than me. He works in a bank and he looks beyond that. He's a member of the National Front.

MISS FORBES: Is that your politics too?

ARTHUR: I was never so whole-hearted. But he's a great one for purity. He has these high ideals for the British people. The foreigners won't do themselves any good by coming here. I'm not saying we ought not to welcome them, just that they've no place in our midst. We brought him up to an ideal of purity. We washed out his mouth a few times and then we had no more trouble. Instant obedience we taught him and it's served him in good stead in his working life. He knows how to obey in his party and therefore he knows how to command. Obey and command, two precious words, that young people today sometimes forget.

MISS FORBES: My brother has always been more of a socialist. He's a trade union man.

ARTHUR: That's not my idea at all.

MISS FORBES: Your son's a fascist.

ARTHUR: That word may not be the insult it's sometimes used as today. It's a proud word.

MISS FORBES: I mean it as an insult.

They stand there. MISS FORBES *holds out her hand but it is still raining.*

ARTHUR: Come, come, let's not quarrel about politics. Religion and politics should never be discussed at dinner and certainly not with a lady.

MISS FORBES: This isn't dinner.

ARTHUR: No, but stuck here side by side in the rain is just like a social occasion, don't you think?

MISS FORBES: I don't have very much social life.

ARTHUR: My own life's very quiet. There's an annual dinner dance that goes with my work.

MISS FORBES: I wouldn't remember how to dance.

ARTHUR: I'm sure you dance very well. You look like someone who knows how. Once you've done it it always comes back.

MISS FORBES: I used to dance.

ARTHUR: I like a dance. An old-fashioned dance where you take your partner in your arms. Not one of those dances the young do where you don't touch each other. I like the kind of dance like a last waltz cheek to cheek, don't you? Highly romantic and nobody takes offense.

MISS FORBES: I have my own memories of course.

ARTHUR: My wife disapproves of everything. I'm forced to go to shops for literature. I can't help it, it's a natural urge, it's disgusting but I can't help that. You're the same, you're no better, you dance, you've had men, you like it, you like it, you'd like it now, you want me to do it now, it's not my fault, you're making me do it, you're making me.

ARTHUR *undoes his trousers.*

Touch me, quick, touch me, touch me, touch me—

MISS FORBES *shrieks and rushes away. She trips over some rocks near the sea's edge and falls heavily.* ARTHUR *hastily does up his trousers.*

Look what you made me do. It's not my fault. It's you. It should be stopped.

ARTHUR *picks up the deckchairs and hurries off.* MISS FORBES *shrieks again. She stays lying where she is and shrieks again.*
     MADGE *comes in.*

MADGE: Whatever is it? Oh, you poor dear. Did you slip? You've fallen in a little rock pool, you're all wet. Can you get up?

MISS FORBES: My ankle—

MADGE: Have you sprained it? Let me have a look.

MISS FORBES: Ohhh.

MADGE: It isn't broken but it might be sprained. We can't be too careful. Let me help you up a little bit. You're rather heavy. I don't know if I can—oh—if you hop—

MISS FORBES: I can just put it to the ground.

MADGE: That's wonderful. That's wonderful. We're moving now. I wish my husband was here with a deckchair.

MISS FORBES: I'll sit on the ground.

MADGE: It's very wet.

MISS FORBES: I'm wet through anyway. (*She sits on the ground*.)

MADGE: The rain's stopped again, that's one blessing. Had we better take off your shoe? Is your ankle swelling? Don't cry, dear. It's the shock, I know.

MISS FORBES: It's not . . . it's not . . .

MADGE: Just sit quiet a minute.

MISS FORBES: It's not my ankle. There was a man.

MADGE: A man?

MISS FORBES: He . . . oh . . . he . . . need I say?

MADGE: No, did he really? What exactly?

MISS FORBES *whispers in* MADGE*'s ear*.

We must call the police. What did he look like? I saw a most suspicious character earlier, I expect it was him.

MISS FORBES: He looked quite a harmless little man.

MADGE: I can't possibly leave you here alone. He might come back. As soon as you're feeling well enough we must go to the police. I wish my husband was here. I was just spending a penny and when I came out it was pouring with rain and he'd folded up the deckchairs and was gone. He could run and find a policeman.

MISS FORBES: I'm not sure I want the police.

MADGE: Of course we must get the police. Think of the danger to the public prowling the beach.

MISS FORBES: I would never have screamed like that in the normal way. It was more the surprise, and slipping over.

MADGE: A terrible terrible shock.

MISS FORBES: I don't think he meant to hurt me at all. I expect he was quite frightened when I screamed.

MADGE: Always scream and hit out with a handbag or better still a sharp umbrella.

MISS FORBES: I didn't mean to make such a fuss.

MADGE: You're having a happy time by the sea and someone does that to you, you've every right to make all the fuss you like.

MISS FORBES: I wasn't having a happy time. I was crying and he made me feel better.

MADGE: Why were you crying, my poor dear? What a day for you.

MISS FORBES: I came to the sea hoping for a moment of—great—some great feeling.

MADGE: Yes, yes, that's what I come to the sea for.

MISS FORBES: It's so hard to get out of the house. I sometimes feel the top of my head will blow off. I very much want to relieve the lack of pressure round me. I felt that this place where I'd suffered . . . where I'd been so happy . . . where in memory I'd been so often . . . but this is the wrong beach in any case.

MADGE: Any beach, any beach, or a coach tour of Scotland would do you good.

MISS FORBES: Scotland?

MADGE: Hasn't Scotland ever occurred to you?

MISS FORBES: I could never do it alone.

MADGE: Perhaps you could do it with us.

MISS FORBES: I'd rather you didn't say that.

MADGE: Why ever not?

MISS FORBES: I'm quite used to being lonely, thank you.

MADGE: But what a terrible thing to be used to. I'm used to my feet hurting but that's past help. You must come to tea with us every Saturday. It's very rarely I meet anyone who cares for higher things as you do. In this day and age we must cling together. Now how's that ankle coming along?

MISS FORBES: A little better I think.

MADGE: Let's go and tell the police.

MISS FORBES: No, the poor man.

MADGE: Whatever do you mean?

MISS FORBES: He probably isn't very happy himself. He said he was lonely.

MADGE: They always say something like that to try and catch you.

MISS FORBES: I think he was lonely.

MADGE: There, there's my husband. He suddenly came out from behind those rocks. What is he doing right down there? Arthur! Arthur! Come here at once. Do you hear me? Come here quickly. We want the police.

MISS FORBES: I'm not sure we do.

MADGE: It's very unpleasant to have to put into words a horrible experience, but you must be brave, my dear, and think of the good you'll do other women. It's your duty.

ARTHUR *comes in.*

Arthur, there you are at last. This poor woman is the victim of an attack. Run for the police, Arthur.

ARTHUR: What sort of an attack?

MADGE: You don't want me to embarrass her by repeating the details. Go and get the police. A maniac is on the rampage.

MISS FORBES: I'm not sure I want to tell the police.

MADGE: Of course you do. It's the shock, Arthur, that makes her say that. Go along.

MISS FORBES: No, stop. I never should have screamed like that. It was just the surprise. I don't think he would have hurt me. He's lonely. I should have understood.

MADGE: It would be compounding a felony to keep silence. I shall inform the police if you won't. Now come along, my dear, can you walk?

MISS FORBES: Just slowly.

MADGE: Why don't we go to the café and have a nice cup of tea to help you get over the shock and Arthur can be finding a policeman.

ARTHUR: What description of your assailant shall I give the police?

MISS FORBES: Oh, he was a very tall man. Thick set and with a lot of dark hair. He was wearing a red pullover and white tennis shoes.

MADGE: That sounds like the man I saw. Very dark, and you could say thick set, I think. He wasn't wearing a red pullover. Perhaps he's changed his clothes. Unfortunately, I didn't notice his shoes. Or there may be more than one maniac at large. Nothing would surprise me. Help our friend to walk along, Arthur.

MADGE *and* ARTHUR *support* MISS FORBES *on either side and they go out.*
The sun comes out. TERRY *comes onto the beach. He is wearing a dark suit and black tie and shoes. He looks along the beach both ways.*
JULE *comes in.*

JULE: What have you come here for?

TERRY: The postcard had the necessary information.

JULE: I didn't say come.

TERRY: I don't need you to give me instructions.

JULE: You might easily not have found me. I wasn't going to come back on the beach. You would have wasted hours of your time. It's only that the sun came out again.

TERRY: Well, it did.

JULE: You don't seem very pleased to see me for someone who bothered to come.

TERRY: I took the decision not to see you again. But I resented telling you what I thought of you over and over and over in my head so I got on a train to have the satisfaction of being heard.

JULE: I can't think what it is that's upset you.

TERRY: I saw how the paper put it. I know what it means.

JULE: You've known what I think a long time. There's nothing sudden.

TERRY: I thought so this is what I've been waiting for. I knew she'd do something this stupid.

JULE: We haven't done anything yet. They're onto us too soon.

TERRY: What's the difference?

JULE: No, that's true, no difference, because we'll go on.

TERRY: The only difference is you're so inefficient you get caught before you even start. I expect you talk too much.

JULE: Have you come in some official capacity? To say the party disapproves of anarchic counter-productive individualistic violence?

TERRY: No, I came to say you're a shit.

JULE: It's the same thing because you only recognize two kinds of people, communists and shits.

TERRY: Don't pretend you're anything political. If you go on like this you'll be a murderer.

JULE: If I was it might not matter. There are far more deaths that don't worry you.

TERRY: Violence is nothing to do with revolution, it's secondary, it's incidental. There may be violence but it's not—

JULE: If you're killed in the course of incidental violence does that help you feel your dying is incidental? That must have been a great comfort in Russia at the time, knowing your death wasn't important to the revolution, just incidental.

TERRY: If, in the sweep of a huge historical movement like the working class coming into their power, there is some violence—

JULE: But there isn't too much huge historical sweep about our working class at the moment, don't you find that your problem?

TERRY: If in a revolution people get killed I accept that. But I'm not insane enough like you and Vin to think if I go out and kill someone that itself makes a revolution. Who's behind you? What mass of people? Everyone, I suppose you'll say, but they just don't know it yet.

JULE: You do look official dressed like that. Ought I to stand up?

TERRY: Even something the size of Paris in '68 didn't work because it didn't have the working class organized behind it. And what have you got? Not just no organization but no one at all.

JULE: Terry, it was nice of you to come and see me.

TERRY: Of course, if people are treated violently they react with violence, a few of them, it's surprising sometimes how few of them. One or two slaves kill one or two masters, but that's never the end of slavery. Marx ends the dream of impotent violence that you're still having. The contradictions of society—

JULE: Terry, I'm glad to see you.

TERRY: It's not the damage you do I mind most. It's stupid, it's sad, all right. What I mind is you drive people the other way, we get more law and order because of you, more power to the police, more middle of the road, more shit. All right, you can say, we'll drive them all the way to the right, make them show themselves for the fascists they are, then we can really start. I don't believe that. I can't be glad of any fascist government. I work long hours to organize. And you and Vin and your other lovely friends go out for an evening's fun smashing it up.

JULE: I hope I do. I don't want what you organize. If you ever were in power I'd be the first one out on the streets against you.

TERRY: And I'd have you arrested.

JULE: Of course you would. Tell me some time when the communist party hasn't stood in the way of revolution.

TERRY: You get angry. So what if you get angry? You've nothing to do with anything except yourselves.

JULE: You would have liked my grandmother who once told me she'd never struck a child in anger. Just coldly, you know, as a just punishment. I'd be more proud to say if I'd struck a child that I'd never done it except in anger.

TERRY: Psychopaths don't make good soldiers. It's been established that the best soldiers aren't feeling aggressive when they're fighting, they're quite calm, they do their job.

JULE: I'm sure they do, like Eichmann.

TERRY: It's a different job. That does make a difference. I may not do anything dramatic like Vin but I keep working steadily towards what will one day come about.

JULE: No, you'd never go raping and looting. You'd rape only if ordered. But if ordered, very thoroughly.

TERRY: There was a time when you would have despised someone who talks like you talk now. I can't take you and Vin seriously. He may be a threat to me but he's certainly not to the state. A long sentence is just flattery.

JULE: And what threat are you? You're out of the history books. Everybody knows nowadays there's not that to choose between what you offer and what we've got already.

TERRY: What do you offer? A little kids' gang, what do you offer? What has anything you do got to do with running a country and people living and working in it, and eating? You used to have some grasp of how things work.

JULE: It's only when things stop working that—

TERRY: Only when people stop eating.

JULE: Why should I try and explain myself to you? You won't hear a word, you never heard a word I said in three years. I don't know why you bothered to come if it's only to shout. It's nothing to do with you what I do or what I believe or anything at all about me.

TERRY: No, that's true. It's your life to waste.

JULE: So go home, will you?

TERRY: I certainly don't know why I bothered to come. I forget when I've been away from you how thick and nasty you are. I even had some idea of suggesting you came back, because I'd forgotten how much I dislike you.

JULE: Back to you?

TERRY: I'm not still suggesting it, don't worry.

JULE: Husband and wife again? All that?

TERRY: You could call it what you like. It wouldn't be the same as before. But the basis of it would be that we'd be together. Most of the time only. I was thinking of giving Liz two parents again.

JULE: Can't you manage alone?

TERRY: Yes, very well. She goes to day nursery still all day and she calls it school. She tells me bedtime stories. No, it wasn't for Liz. She's much better off without you.

JULE: Terror's always made you uneasy. You like to think things are under control. They never are and they shouldn't be. You think if you work hard enough at the little jobs, never mind what the little jobs are, everything's bound to turn out all right. If you can't quite grasp the overall strategy never mind, perhaps that's just as well since you might not agree with it, you keep marching, you keep your head down. Your Catholic mum and dad may not like your politics but they can't doubt your faith is as strong as theirs, they did a good job on you those first seven years. You try very hard to be consistent because that's part of having it under control, you read it up, you've learnt the defense of nearly every policy. If nearly everything you believe was chopped off by what your party actually do, you'd grow whole again like a starfish from one arm and a bit of your center. Why we can't live together is because we frighten each other.

TERRY: I refuse to take an interest in my character. Vin's waging a glorious liberation of himself. I've no interest in that. You've always been critical of what I'm like. If I'm full of inhibitions and fixations I haven't time to be bothered. I work all right as I am and that's what matters. If you can explain that I'm only a communist because I'm neurotic, I'm happy to stay neurotic and stay a communist. There's more important things to be put right than my mind. Afterwards perhaps I'll think about what I'm like, the time may come. And time for sitting in the sun by the sea.

JULE: You could say the same about Vin. If what's happened to him has made him what you call a psychopath that doesn't explain away what he does. It makes him able to do it.

TERRY: You can say what you like about Vin but I'm not interested.

JULE: How's your sex life these days?

TERRY: Secondary.

JULE: Like violence is secondary?

TERRY: Yes, if you like. They're both distractions from work that has to be done. Secondary and confusing.

JULE: You should pay it more attention.

TERRY: I should pay it less.

PHIL *and* ANNIE *come in.*

ANNIE: Jule. We're off now. We're going home. Though if you want to come with us we could wait while you get ready, because I saw George leaving with his tent. Terry? Is it? I didn't realize for a moment because it's so long since I saw you. I didn't know you were here.

TERRY: We both still run round after her as if she couldn't look after herself.

ANNIE: And Liz? How's Liz? Is she here?

TERRY: No, I left her with a friend. She hasn't seen Jule for a time and she's perfectly happy. I didn't want to risk upsetting her.

ANNIE: I don't think I was living with Phil when I last saw you. This is Terry. He used to be Jule's husband. Or still is.

JULE: Getting married was enough of a mistake without getting divorced as well. I don't plan to keep the state informed. It's not as if staying married means we're together. I don't recognize the marriage.

ANNIE: Jule, I'm sorry about just now. Were you all right? You once did that to me when we were children and afterwards I was sick. Phil and I should have our quarrels in private.

PHIL: Yes, I feel I should owe you an apology. I got carried away and quite confused. I exaggerated.

ANNIE: We've been for a walk along the shore and talked it over.

JULE (*to* PHIL): Now you're the person I want to show Terry. *(to* TERRY*)* He'd never work with you in the party, he's not convinced by economic arguments. But the mess of his own life convinces him. *(to* PHIL*)* Tell him what you told me about the people you work for. Tell him how you and Annie are tied up. *(to* TERRY*)* One violent action and they'll be out. *(to* PHIL*)* Tell him.

ANNIE: If you mean in a mental way, Jule, changing our attitude, we have done that I think, thanks partly to you. I won't go on working for them again. But as for this other. I don't think Phil would do anything illegal.

JULE: I don't mean mental, Annie, I mean physical. I mean illegal. Phil means that.

PHIL: I did see your point for a while there. As I say, I exaggerated all kinds of ways. About that Christmas time, and also about the couple we were telling you about, who certainly have their faults, but it isn't all exactly them to blame, it's the world we live in like it or not. I can't feel I'd be justified.

ANNIE: She can't really have thought, can she, Terry, that when Phil's back at work she'd have him setting off with an explosive carrier bag?

PHIL: It's not an action I could approve of. It wouldn't bring about what I'd like to see.

JULE: What would you like to see?

PHIL: It's hard to put into words, isn't it? The same things everybody would like to see.

ANNIE: Perhaps like you said, Jule, I should try to be something like a teacher. Something exhausting and worthwhile.

JULE: I said exhausting.

ANNIE: That sort of thing.

JULE: Terry believes in doing things that are exhausting. They give you a great impression of being worthwhile because they keep you so busy.

PHIL: Excuse me asking, if it's an impertinence, but would you be in mourning? Seeing the tie.

TERRY: Yes, that's right. I've just come from a funeral. I decided which train I was going to catch and didn't leave myself time to change.

ANNIE: Who was it, Terry? No one close I hope.

TERRY: It was my father.

PHIL: I'm very sorry. Perhaps I shouldn't have said anything.

TERRY: He's had a weak heart for some time.

ANNIE: He was a nice man.

PHIL: Once your parents have gone it brings it home to you that you're next. In my case I felt that.

TERRY: Yes, so did I.

ANNIE: Our parents have a lot of worry over Jule. You couldn't write to them, Jule, could you?

JULE: I might do.

PHIL: Well, we must be off and hope the traffic's not too heavy.

ANNIE: I feel better for some sea air. It blows away the cobwebs. Nice to see you again, Terry.

PHIL: Don't forget, Jule, anything we can do.

PHIL *and* ANNIE *go.*

TERRY: Is it much better for you with Vin? Sexually. Than me.

JULE: No.

TERRY: Why not?

JULE: I don't think he notices the other person so much.

TERRY: That sounds a bit limited.

JULE: No one's saying he's some amazing being.

TERRY: I can't think where I got the idea from then. Certainly not from meeting him.

JULE: What is better with him is what I'm like myself. I don't feel I have to try and be something I'm not.

TERRY: You don't have to with me either.

JULE: Oh but yes, you know how it was. There were things you expected a wife to be like.

TERRY: I've got over that.

JULE: I can't get over it. I can't trust you. I'm sure you'd mean to leave me room to move but you couldn't do it. I couldn't do it, it's probably my fault, I'd go back to being like I was. I'd be pretending.

TERRY: So what it comes down to is Vin is better.

JULE: Not exactly Vin. I like what we're all like. We don't crowd each other.

TERRY: So you'll stay with him.

JULE: You like to think I only believe in what I'm doing because of Vin. You think I'm some sort of gangster's moll. But I don't think his way because I love him. I love him because we think the same way.

TERRY: I'm not sure which you mean to be worse.

JULE: Even if in some ways I like you better, I can't come back and switch to your ideas.

TERRY: I had the impression you liked him better.

JULE: I wish Annie thought the same as me. I wish you did. You can't leave politics out of it yourself. You know you hate me for what I'm doing.

TERRY: But I still came to ask you to live with me again.

JULE: Thinking quite differently from you?

TERRY: There's still plenty of things we both oppose.

JULE: We'd agree to abolish the monarchy and not vote for the three major parties. But it's a bit beyond that. I want to live with the people I'm working with.

TERRY: Do you think I wouldn't find it hard too? I remember what it was like.

JULE: There you are. All our effort would go into quarrelling. We'd never get anything else done.

TERRY: Spend our lives cancelling each other out? Of course I don't want that.

JULE: I've more to do than loving another person.

TERRY: Yes, so have I.

JULE: If I can leave Liz, I can leave you.

TERRY: I know you can, you already have done.

JULE: But now and then all our lives we can meet—

ANNIE *comes back.*

ANNIE: Jule, I just came back to say goodbye. And I wish—

ANNIE *and* JULE *kiss.* ANNIE *goes.*

JULE: What's all this about your father?

TERRY: I came straight from his funeral. I couldn't come before. If you'd taken a proper look at me you might have seen.

JULE: Has he been ill long?

TERRY: He'd been having some trouble with his heart. But it happened quite suddenly the day it happened. He wasn't too good ever since Mum died.

JULE: Your mother died? When did she die?

TERRY: The end of last year.

JULE: You never told me.

TERRY: It didn't seem anything to do with you.

JULE: Was your father very lonely?

TERRY: They were close. The way it is. He's not good at getting his own dinner. He wasn't meant to get excited because of his heart. I'd go and see him and we'd make some toast because toast has always been a thing we've both liked, when I was little, and we'd talk of this and that. But after a bit we'd get embarrassed. We'd have to take the dog for a walk on the heath. Because all we wanted to talk about really was to quarrel and I wouldn't in case I gave him a heart attack and he wouldn't—perhaps less for his heart than because I was holding back. But in his mind you could always tell he never could let my communism go. I got it from him, that's what he minded most, from him talking about the thirties when I was small. He wore himself out all his life for the union and it never seemed to me to be enough. But he couldn't forgive me because of being a Catholic. He always took Stalin very much to heart, Hungary, Czechoslovakia—all my life he always had the latest newspaper cuttings that showed how badly Russia was behaving. Right up until we started being careful because of his heart.

JULE: So how did he die if you were so careful?

TERRY: There was nothing much we could talk about that wasn't upsetting. If we started on a football match we'd soon be avoiding the stadium in Chile.

JULE: You would have found things there to agree about.

TERRY: We were good at spotting ways back to our differences.

JULE: So how did he die?

TERRY: We took the dog for a walk as a distraction and it ran in the road under a car. I didn't know how to deal with this thing which was partly a mess on the road and partly a head I knew looking at me. It must have been mostly unconscious. So a vet disposed of it and so on. His heart attack was on the way home. He died luckily quicker than the dog.

JULE: Did he say anything?

TERRY: No last words to sum it all up if you mean that.

JULE: No, I meant anything.

TERRY: He hasn't got a lot of family so the funeral was quite small. I hadn't felt at all like crying till I saw his brother, who looks quite like him. I saw he wouldn't be alive for long. Or myself. Or you.

JULE: Some men never seem to cry but it never surprises you. Remember how we often couldn't sleep. Not over something that had happened to us, but we would have argued so late about why it happened and how it could have been different, that we felt right in it. We'd be really angry at whoever let it happen, even something that was over years ago. You sometimes cried.

TERRY: We've no trouble finding things we both think are wrong. It's doing something about them that comes between us.

JULE: Will you stay tonight?

TERRY: Yes. Will you come back with me?

JULE : No.

They go on sitting on the beach. The sun is shining.

THE RECEPTIVE READER

Act One

1. This play introduces a group of *characters* that interact on a beach on a summer day. Who are they, and how are they related to one another?

2. Churchill is a master at taking us gradually behind the public faces that people present to the outside world. There are sudden moments of revelation when we learn something about her characters' real histories—the way we might get to know friends or lovers when they lift their masks and take us into their confidence. What are striking examples of such revelations in this act?

3. Jule is Annie's younger sister. What is the relationship between the two sisters? What do we learn about Jule in the course of Annie's questioning of her? What do we learn about Annie? In what ways is she a foil to her sister?

4. In her notes for the play, Churchill said that the married couple (Arthur and Madge) were different on the surface but "identical" in their basic mind-sets; they represented the same basic attitude. What did she mean?

5. Eric (like the author of the play) has a quick ear for the way people talk, and he mimics and mocks the clichés and slogans of his contemporaries. What are his targets? Does he stand for anything of his own? What is his relation to the other characters?

6. What does Phil stand for in this act? How does he become the special target of Eric's satirical sallies? What is his relationship with Jule?

Act Two

7. How do you react to the interlude between Miss Forbes and Arthur? Is it farce? feminist satire? social commentary? How is it related to the rest of the play? Were you surprised by the way Miss Forbes behaved at the end of the episode?

8. How does this act clarify Eric's role in the play? How does the playwright expect you to feel about him?

9. What turn does the relationship between the two sisters take in this act? Were you surprised?

10. One of the major ideological confrontations occurs toward the end of the play between Terry and Jule. What is the crux of it? What role does the absent Vin play in it?

THE WHOLE PLAY—For Discussion or Writing

1. Feminists have charged that male playwrights cannot really enter into a woman's world; they see their female characters through male-colored glasses. In this play, is the footwear on the other foot? What here is the treatment of the male characters by a female playwright? One reviewer said that, with the possible exception of the communist husband, "each of the men makes his exit with a knife from the author quivering between the shoulder blades." Was the reviewer right?

2. What statement does the play as a whole make on terrorism as an instrument of political action? (Does it *make* a statement?)

3. In what sense is the treatment of sex and marriage in this play feminist? How is it different from what you might have expected?

THE PERSONAL RESPONSE

It is often said that American college students today are apolitical; they suffer from apathy toward political issues and shy away from political involvement. Do the discussions of politics and sexual politics in this play mean anything to you or to members of your generation?

THE CREATIVE DIMENSION

Where are you in this play? Choose a character who is some ways like you or a character with whom you can identify. Write a first-person statement (or prepare an oral presentation) in which you offer your view of the events, the people, or the world to an audience.

WOLE SOYINKA AND YORUBA CULTURE

To detract from the maximum freedom socially possible, to me, is treacherous.

WOLE SOYINKA

I discovered that you have no respect for what you do not understand.

WOLE SOYINKA, *DEATH AND THE KING'S HORSEMAN*

Wole Soyinka, from Nigeria, ranks as one of modern Africa's best-known playwrights and poets. An outspoken and politically engaged writer, he has been at the center of much controversy. He has spoken out against both colonialism and the brutal dictatorships that in some African countries succeeded independence. His failure to take sides in the Nigerian civil war caused him to spend most of the war in prison. He has said that the "truly creative writer" pursues his myth-making task "properly uninhibited by ideological winds."

Soyinka was born in western Nigeria in 1934, in the heartland of traditional Yoruba culture. His parents were converted Christians; he attended the local missionary school where his father served as headmaster. Soyinka went to England to study literature at the University of Leeds, where he became a star student of G. Wilson Knight, a celebrated Shakespearean scholar. No small part of Soyinka's education was working at odd jobs, whether as a bartender or as a teacher at a rough school. Some of his early plays were tried out at the Royal Court Theater, and he became thoroughly familiar with both the European dramatic tradition and the work of the avant-garde.

In many of Soyinka's plays, the values of traditional Yoruba culture play a central role. Religion was ever present in Yoruba life. Olorun was the supreme all-wise Creator, but many other gods played their roles in elaborate myths and ceremonies. Worship of the ancestors intertwined with homage to the gods. Spirits evil and benign animated the natural world. Ceremonies honoring the ancestors were conducted by the *egungun*, whose elaborate masks and costumes inspired awe in the beholder. A centuries-old tradition of wood carving created a wealth of sacred objects. Harvest festivals and other high ceremonial occasions established the rhythm of the year. Several of Soyinka's plays capture the mood of intense preparation for a great festival that "produces so much excitement or tension in the whole populace that everybody thinks of nothing but the great event" (Oyin Ogumba).

Although Soyinka has been a wanderer between two worlds, he has objected to the idea of the "clash of cultures" when it might seem to imply an equal contest between the alien and the more deeply rooted native culture. Perhaps more than other African writers known in the West, he has been loyal to his spiritual roots in the traditional culture. He writes about his people at times with broad humor and at times in the spirit of a solemn search for the mythical past.

Soyinka's *Death and the King's Horseman* takes you to an Africa where centuries of slave trade and European colonialism have failed to root out powerful local traditions. Colonialism has brought the English language (French or Portuguese in other parts of Africa), Christianity, and Western-style education. The key question Soyinka raises is how deeply or permanently the influence of the West has changed the spirit, the soul, of the continent.

The play takes you to Nigeria during World War II, before the end of British rule. In the play, the British colonials are foreign intruders, cut off from the native culture and only in the most superficial contact with the populations they supposedly govern, educate, or civilize. These representatives of foreign rule are mocked and mimicked by the ruled, who despise them and defy them. Caught in the middle are the collaborators, the African agents and henchmen of white rule. These imitate the language and the mannerisms of the white rulers and are taunted and abused by their compatriots.

The central crisis in the play arises when a powerful tradition is invoked upon the death of the tribal leader. The dead king's dog, his horse, and his horseman or marshal are all expected to accompany him on his journey into the beyond. The Elesin, the central character, is the horseman, who all his life has enjoyed the privileges attached to his special role. Now, what may have seemed a ceremonial role becomes a deadly serious obligation. The Elesin is reminded of his duty in solemn ceremonial exchanges with his Praise-singer, who functions as a private bard. The market women, led by Iyaloja, furnish a kind of Greek chorus, commenting on and reacting to the events. To the white colonial officials, the planned ritual sacrifice or ritual suicide seems mere superstition, and they do their best to put a stop to it. Whether the Elesin will or can live up to his destined role is the central question in the play.

WOLE SOYINKA   (born 1934)
Death and the King's Horseman   1976

CHARACTERS

PRAISE-SINGER
ELESIN, horseman of the King
IYALOJA, "mother" of the market
SIMON PILKINGS, District Officer
JANE PILKINGS, his wife
SERGEANT AMUSA
JOSEPH, houseboy to the PILKINGSES
BRIDE

H.R.H. THE PRINCE
THE RESIDENT
AIDE-DE-CAMP
OLUNDE, eldest son of ELESIN
Drummers, Women, Young Girls, Dancers at the Ball

The play should run without an interval. For rapid scene changes, one adjustable outline set is very appropriate.

ACT ONE

A passage through a market in its closing stages. The stalls are being emptied, mats folded. A few women pass through on their way home, loaded with baskets. On a cloth-stand, bolts of cloth are taken down, display pieces folded and piled on a tray. ELESIN OBA *enters along a passage before the market, pursued by his drummers and praise-singers. He is a man of enormous vitality, speaks, dances and sings with that infectious enjoyment of life which accompanies all his actions.*

PRAISE-SINGER: Elesin o! Elesin Oba! Howu! What tryst is this the cockerel goes to keep with such haste that he must leave his tail behind?

ELESIN (*slows down a bit, laughing*): A tryst where the cockerel needs no adornment.

PRAISE-SINGER: O-oh, you hear that my companions? That's the way the world goes. Because the man approaches a brand-new bride he forgets the long faithful mother of his children.

ELESIN: When the horse sniffs the stable does he not strain at the bridle? The market is the long-suffering home of my spirit and the women are packing up to go. That Esu-harassed day slipped into the stewpot while we feasted. We ate it up with the rest of the meat. I have neglected my women.

PRAISE-SINGER: We know all that. Still it's no reason for shedding your tail on this day of all days. I know the women will cover you in damask and *alari* but when the wind blows cold from behind, that's when the fowl knows his true friends.

ELESIN: Olohun-iyo!

PRAISE-SINGER: Are you sure there will be one like me on the other side?

ELESIN: Olohun-iyo!

PRAISE-SINGER: Far be it for me to belittle the dwellers of that place but, a man is either born to his art or he isn't. And I don't know for certain that you'll meet my father, so who is going to sing these deeds in accents that will pierce the deafness of the ancient ones. I have prepared my going—just tell me: Olohun-iyo, I need you on this journey and I shall be behind you.

ELESIN: You're like a jealous wife. Stay close to me, but only on this side. My fame, my honor are legacies to the living; stay behind and let the world sip its honey from your lips.

PRAISE-SINGER: Your name will be like the sweet berry a child places under his tongue to sweeten the passage of food. The world will never spit it out.

ELESIN: Come then. This market is my roost. When I come among the women I am a chicken with a hundred mothers. I become a monarch whose palace is built with tenderness and beauty.

PRAISE-SINGER: They love to spoil you but beware. The hands of women also weaken the unwary.

ELESIN: This night I'll lay my head upon their lap and go to sleep. This night I'll touch feet with their feet in a dance that is no longer of this earth. But the smell of their flesh, their sweat, the smell of indigo on their cloth, this is the last air I wish to breathe as I go to meet my great forebears.

PRAISE-SINGER: In their time the world was never tilted from its groove, it shall not be in yours.

ELESIN: The gods have said No.

PRAISE-SINGER: In their time the great wars came and went, the little wars came and went; the white slaves came and went, they took away the heart of our race, they bore away the mind and muscle of our race. The city fell and was rebuilt; the city fell and our people trudged through mountain and forest to found a new home but—Elesin Oba do you hear me?

ELESIN: I hear your voice Olohun-iyo.

PRAISE-SINGER: Our world was never wrenched from its true course.

ELESIN: The gods have said No.

PRAISE-SINGER: There is only one home to the life of a river mussel; there is only one home to the life of a tortoise; there is only one shell to the soul of man; there is only one world to the spirit of our race. If that world leaves its course and smashes on boulders of the great void, whose world will give us shelter?

ELESIN: It did not in the time of my forebears, it shall not in mine.

PRAISE-SINGER: The cockerel must not be seen without his feathers.

ELESIN: Nor will the Not-I bird be much longer without his nest.

PRAISE-SINGER *(stopped in his lyric stride)*: The Not-I bird, Elesin?

ELESIN: I said, the Not-I bird.

PRAISE-SINGER: All respect to our elders but, is there really such a bird?

ELESIN: What! Could it be that he failed to knock on your door?

PRAISE-SINGER *(smiling)*: Elesin's riddles are not merely the nut in the kernel that breaks human teeth; he also buries the kernel in hot embers and dares a man's fingers to draw it out.

ELESIN: I am sure he called on you, Olohun-iyo. Did you hide in the loft and push out the servant to tell him you were out?

ELESIN *executes a brief, half-taunting dance. The drummer moves in and draws a rhythm out of his steps.* ELESIN *dances toward the market-place as he chants the story of the Not-I bird, his voice changing dexterously to mimic his characters. He performs like a born raconteur, infecting his retinue with his humor and energy. More women arrive during his recital, including* IYALOJA.

> Death came calling.
> Who does not know his rasp of reeds?
> A twilight whisper in the leaves before
> The great araba falls? Did you hear it?
> "Not I!" swears the farmer. He snaps
> His fingers round his head, abandons
> A hard-worn harvest and begins
> A rapid dialogue with his legs.
>
> "Not I," shouts the fearless hunter, "but—
> It's getting dark, and this night-lamp
> Has leaked out all its oil. I think
> It's best to go home and resume my hunt

Another day." But now he pauses, suddenly
Lets out a wail: "Oh foolish mouth, calling
Down a curse on your own head! Your lamp
Has leaked out all its oil, has it?"
Forwards or backwards now he dare not move.
To search for leaves and make *etutu*
On that spot? Or race home to the safety
Of his hearth? Ten market-days have passed
My friends, and still he's rooted there
Rigid as the plinth of Orayan.

The mouth of the courtesan barely
Opened wide enough to take a ha'penny *robo*
When she wailed: "Not I." All dressed she was
To call upon my friend the Chief Tax Officer.
But now she sends her go-between instead:
"Tell him I'm ill: my period has come suddenly
But not—I hope—my time."

Why is the pupil crying?
His hapless head was made to taste
The knuckles of my friend the Mallam:
"If you were then reciting the Koran
Would you have ears for idle noises
Darkening the trees, you child of ill omen?"
He shuts down school before its time
Runs home and rings himself with amulets.

And take my good kinsman Ifawomi.
His hands were like a carver's, strong
And true. I saw them
Tremble like wet wings of a fowl
One day he cast his time-smoothed *opele*
Across the divination board. And all because
The suppliant looked him in the eye and asked,
"Did you hear that whisper in the leaves?"
"Not I," was his reply; "perhaps I'm growing deaf—
Good-day." And Ifa spoke no more that day
The priest locked fast his doors,
Sealed up his leaking roof—but wait!
This sudden care was not for Fawomi
But for Osanyin, courier-bird of Ifa's
Heart of wisdom. I did not know a kite
Was hovering in the sky
And Ifa now a twittering chicken in
The brood of Fawomi the Mother Hen.

Ah, but I must not forget my evening
Courier from the abundant palm, whose groan
Became Not I, as he constipated down
A wayside bush. He wonders if Elegbara
Has tricked his buttocks to discharge
Against a sacred grove. Hear him

Mutter spells to ward off penalties
For an abomination he did not intend.
If any here
Stumbles on a gourd of wine, fermenting
Near the road, and nearby hears a stream
Of spells issuing from a crouching form.
Brother to a *sigidi*, bring home my wine,
Tell my tapper I have ejected
Fear from home and farm. Assure him,
All is well.

PRAISE-SINGER: In your time we do not doubt the peace of farmstead and home, the peace of road and hearth, we do not doubt the peace of the forest.

ELESIN: There was fear in the forest too.
Not-I was lately heard even in the lair
Of beasts. The hyena cackled loud Not I,
The civet twitched his fiery tail and glared:
Not I. Not-I became the answering-name
Of the restless bird, that little one
Whom Death found nesting in the leaves
When whisper of his coming ran
Before him on the wind. Not-I
Has long abandoned home. This same dawn
I heard him twitter in the gods' abode.
Ah, companions of this living world
What a thing this is, that even those
We call immortal
Should fear to die.

IYALOJA: But you, husband of multitudes?

ELESIN: I, when that Not-I bird perched
Upon my roof, bade him seek his nest again,
Safe, without care or fear. I unrolled
My welcome mat for him to see. Not-I
Flew happily away, you'll hear his voice
No more in this lifetime—You all know
What I am.

PRAISE-SINGER: That rock which turns its open lodes
Into the path of lightning. A gay
Thoroughbred whose stride disdains
To falter though an adder reared
Suddenly in his path.

ELESIN: My rein is loosened.
I am master of my Fate. When the hour comes
Watch me dance along the narrowing path
Glazed by the soles of my great precursors.
My soul is eager. I shall not turn aside.

WOMEN: You will not delay?

ELESIN: Where the storm pleases, and when, it directs
The giants of the forest. When friendship summons
Is when the true comrade goes.

WOMEN: Nothing will hold you back?

ELESIN: Nothing. What! Has no one told you yet?

I go to keep my friend and master company.
Who says the mouth does not believe in
"No, I have chewed all that before?" I say I have.
The world is not a constant honey-pot.
Where I found little I made do with little.
Where there was plenty I gorged myself.
My master's hands and mine have always
Dipped together and, home or sacred feast,
The bowl was beaten bronze, the meats
So succulent our teeth accused us of neglect.
We shared the choicest of the season's
Harvest of yams. How my friend would read
Desire in my eyes before I knew the cause—
However rare, however precious, it was mine.

WOMEN: The town, the very land was yours.

ELESIN: The world was mine. Our joint hands
Raised houseposts of trust that withstood
The siege of envy and the termites of time.
But the twilight hour brings bats and rodents—
Shall I yield them cause to foul the rafters?

PRAISE-SINGER: Elesin Oba! Are you not that man who
Looked out of doors that stormy day
The god of luck limped by, drenched
To the very lice that held
His rags together? You took pity upon
His sores and wished him fortune.
Fortune was footloose this dawn, he replied,
Till you trapped him in a heartfelt wish
That now returns to you. Elesin Oba!
I say you are that man who
Chanced upon the calabash of honor
You thought it was palm wine and
Drained its contents to the final drop.

ELESIN: Life has an end. A life that will outlive
Fame and friendship begs another name.
What elder takes his tongue to his plate,
Licks it clean of every crumb? He will encounter
Silence when he calls on children to fulfill
The smallest errand! Life is honor.
It ends when honor ends.

WOMEN: We know you for a man of honor.

ELESIN: Stop! Enough of that!

WOMEN (*puzzled, they whisper among themselves, turning mostly to* IYALOJA): What is it? Did we say something to give offense? Have we slighted him in some way?

ELESIN: Enough of that sound I say. Let me hear no more in that vein. I've heard enough.

IYALOJA: We must have said something wrong. (*comes forward a little*) Elesin Oba, we ask forgiveness before you speak.

ELESIN: I am bitterly offended.

IYALOJA: Our unworthiness has betrayed us. All we can do is ask your forgiveness. Correct us like a kind father.

ELESIN: This day of all days . . .

IYALOJA: It does not bear thinking. If we offend you now we have mortified the gods. We offend heaven itself. Father of us all, tell us where we went astray. (*She kneels, the other women follow.*)

ELESIN: Are you not ashamed? Even a tear-veiled
             Eye preserves its function of sight.
             Because my mind was raised to horizons
             Even the boldest man lowers his gaze
             In thinking of, must my body here
             Be taken for a vagrant's?

IYALOJA: Horseman of the King, I am more baffled than ever.

PRAISE-SINGER: The strictest father unbends his brow when the child is penitent, Elesin. When time is short, we do not spend it prolonging the riddle. Their shoulders are bowed with the weight of fear lest they have marred your day beyond repair. Speak now in plain words and let us pursue the ailment to the home of remedies.

ELESIN: Words are cheap. "We know you for
             A man of honor." Well tell me, is this how
             A man of honor should be seen?
             Are these not the same clothes in which
             I came among you a full half-hour ago?

He roars with laughter and the women, relieved, rise and rush into stalls to fetch rich cloths.

WOMAN: The gods are kind. A fault soon remedied is soon forgiven. Elesin Oba, even as we match our words with deed, let your heart forgive us completely.

ELESIN: You who are breath and giver of my being
             How shall I dare refuse you forgiveness
             Even if the offense were real.

IYALOJA (*Dancing round him. Sings.*):
             He forgives us. He forgives us.
             What a fearful thing it is when
             The voyager sets forth
             But a curse remains behind.

WOMEN: For a while we truly feared
             Our hands had wrenched the world adrift
             In emptiness.

IYALOJA: Richly, richly, robe him richly
             The cloth of honor is *alari*
             Sanyan is the band of friendship
             Boa-skin makes slippers of esteem

WOMEN: For a while we truly feared
             Our hands had wrenched the world adrift
             In emptiness.

PRAISE-SINGER: He who must, must voyage forth
             The world will not roll backwards
             It is he who must, with one
             Great gesture overtake the world.

WOMEN: For a while we truly feared
             Our hands had wrenched the world
             In emptiness.

PRAISE-SINGER: The gourd you bear is not for shirking.
                The gourd is not for setting down
                At the first crossroad or wayside grove.
                Only one river may know its contents
WOMEN: We shall all meet at the great market
                We shall all meet at the great market
                He who goes early takes the best bargains
                But we shall meet, and resume our banter.

    ELESIN *stands resplendent in rich clothes, cap, shawl, etc. His sash is of a bright red* alari *cloth. The women dance round him. Suddenly, his attention is caught by an object off-stage.*

ELESIN: The world I know is good.
WOMEN: We know you'll leave it so.
ELESIN: The world I know is the bounty
          Of hives after bees have swarmed.
          No goodness teems with such open hands
          Even in the dreams of deities.
WOMEN::   And we know you'll leave it so.
ELESIN: I was born to keep it so. A hive
          Is never known to wander. An anthill
          Does not desert its roots. We cannot see
          The still great womb of the world—
          No man beholds his mother's womb—
          Yet who denies it's there? Coiled
          To the navel of the world is that
          Endless cord that links us all
          To the great origin. If I lose my way
          The trailing cord will bring me to the roots.
WOMEN: The world is in your hands.

    The earlier distraction, a beautiful young girl, comes along the passage through which ELESIN *first made his entry.*

ELESIN: I embrace it. And let me tell you, women—
          I like this farewell that the world designed,
          Unless my eyes deceive me, unless
          We are already parted, the world and I,
          And all that breeds desire is lodged
          Among our tireless ancestors. Tell me friends,
          Am I still earthed in that beloved market
          Of my youth? Or could it be my will
          Has outleapt the conscious act and I have come
          Among the great departed?
PRAISE-SINGER: Elesin-Oba why do your eyes roll like a bush rat who sees his fate like
    his father's spirit, mirrored in the eye of a snake? And all these questions! You're
    standing on the same earth you've always stood upon. This voice you hear is mine,
    Oluhun-iyo, not that of an acolyte in heaven.
ELESIN: How can that be? In all my life
          As Horseman of the King, the juiciest
          Fruit on every tree was mine. I saw,

I touched, I wooed, rarely was the answer No.
The honor of my place, the veneration I
Received in the eye of man or woman
Prospered my suit and
Played havoc with my sleeping hours.
And they tell me my eyes were a hawk
In perpetual hunger. Split an iroko tree
In two, hide a woman's beauty in its heartwood
And seal it up again—Elesin, journeying by,
Would make his camp beside that tree
Of all the shades in the forest.

PRAISE-SINGER: Who would deny your reputation, snake-on-the-loose in dark passages of the market! Bed-bug who wages war on the mat and receives the thanks of the vanquished! When caught with his bride's own sister he protested—but I was only prostrating myself to her as becomes a grateful in-law. Hunter who carries his powder-horn on the hips and fires crouching or standing! Warrior who never makes that excuse of the whining coward—but how can I go to battle without my trousers?—trouserless or shirtless it's all one to him. Oka-rearing-from-a-camou-flage-of-leaves, before he strikes the victim is already prone! Once they told him, Howu, a stallion does not feed on the grass beneath him: he replied, true, but surely he can roll on it!

WOMEN: Ba-a-a-ba O!

PRAISE-SINGER: Ah, but listen yet. You know there is the leaf-knibbling grub and there is the cola-chewing beetle; the leaf-nibbling grub lives on the leaf, the cola-chew-ing beetle lives in the colanut. Don't we know what our man feeds on when we find him cocooned in a woman's wrapper?

ELESIN: Enough, enough, you all have cause
To know me well. But, if you say this earth
Is still the same as gave birth to those songs,
Tell me who was that goddess through whose lips
I saw the ivory pebbles of Oya's river-bed.
Iyaloja, who is she? I saw her enter
Your stall; all your daughters I know well.
No, not even Ogun-of-the-farm toiling
Dawn till dusk on his tuber patch
Not even Ogun with the finest hoe he ever
Forged at the anvil could have shaped
That rise of buttocks, not though he had
The richest earth between his fingers.
Her wrapper was no disguise
For thighs whose ripples shamed the river's
Coils around the hills of Ilesi. Her eyes
Were new-laid eggs glowing in the dark.
Her skin . . .

IYALOJA: Elesin Oba . . .

ELESIN: What! Where do you all say I am?

IYALOJA: Still among the living.

ELESIN: And that radiance which so suddenly
Lit up this market I could boast
I knew so well?

IYALOJA: Has one step already in her husband's home. She is betrothed.

ELESIN (*irritated*): Why do you tell me that?

IYALOJA *falls silent. The women shuffle uneasily.*

IYALOJA: Not because we dare give you offense Elesin. Today is your day and the whole world is yours. Still, even those who leave town to make a new dwelling elsewhere like to be remembered by what they leave behind.

ELESIN: Who does not seek to be remembered?
Memory is Master of Death, the chink
In his armor of conceit. I shall leave
That which makes my going the sheerest
Dream of an afternoon. Should voyagers
Not travel light? Let the considerate traveller
Shed, of his excessive load, all
That may benefit the living.

WOMEN (*relieved*): Ah Elesin Oba, we knew you for a man of honor.

ELESIN: Then honor me. I deserve a bed of honor to lie upon.

IYALOJA: The best is yours. We know you for a man of honor. You are not one who eats and leaves nothing on his plate for children. Did you not say it yourself? Not one who blights the happiness of others for a moment's pleasure.

ELESIN: Who speaks of pleasure? O women, listen!
Pleasure palls. Our acts should have meaning.
The sap of the plantain never dries.
You have seen the young shoot swelling
Even as the parent stalk begins to wither.
Women, let my going be likened to
The twilight hour of the plantain.

WOMEN: What does he mean Iyaloja? This language is the language of our elders, we do not fully grasp it.

IYALOJA: I dare not understand you yet Elesin.

ELESIN: All you who stand before the spirit that dares
The opening of the last door of passage,
Dare to rid my going of regrets! My wish
Transcends the blotting out of thought
In one mere moment's tremor of the senses.
Do me credit. And do me honor.
I am girded for the route beyond
Burdens of waste and longing.
Then let me travel light. Let
Seed that will not serve the stomach
On the way remain behind. Let it take root
In the earth of my choice, in this earth
I leave behind.

IYALOJA (*turns to women*): The voice I hear is already touched by the waiting fingers of our departed. I dare not refuse.

WOMAN: But Iyaloja . . .

IYALOJA: The matter is no longer in our hands.

WOMAN: But she is betrothed to your own son. Tell him.

IYALOJA: My son's wish is mine. I did the asking for him, the loss can be remedied. But who will remedy the blight of closed hands on the day when all should be openness and light? Tell him, you say! You wish that I burden him with knowledge that will sour his wish and lay regrets on the last moments of his mind. You pray to him who is your intercessor to the other world—don't set this world adrift in your own time; would you rather it was my hand whose sacrilege wrenched it loose?

WOMAN: Not many men will brave the curse of a dispossessed husband.

IYALOJA: Only the curses of the departed are to be feared. The claims of one whose foot is on the threshold of their abode surpasses even the claims of blood. It is impiety even to place hindrances in their ways.

ELESIN: What do my mothers say? Shall I step
            Burdened into the unknown?

IYALOJA: Not we, but the very earth says No. The sap in the plantain does not dry. Let grain that will not feed the voyager at his passage drop here and take root as he steps beyond this earth and us. Oh you who fill the home from hearth to threshold with the voices of children, you who now bestride the hidden gulf and pause to draw the right foot across and into the resting-home of the great forebears, it is good that your loins be drained into the earth we know, that your last strength be ploughed back into the womb that gave you being.

PRAISE-SINGER: Iyaloja, mother of multitudes in the teeming market of the world, how your wisdom transfigures you!

IYALOJA (*smiling broadly, completely reconciled*): Elesin, even at the narrow end of the passage I know you will look back and sigh a last regret for the flesh that flashed past your spirit in flight. You always had a restless eye. Your choice has my blessing. (*to the women*) Take the good news to our daughter and make her ready. (*Some women go off.*)

ELESIN: Your eyes were clouded at first.

IYALOJA: Not for long. It is those who stand at the gateway of the great change to whose cry we must pay heed. And then, think of this—it makes the mind tremble. The fruit of such a union is rare. It will be neither of this world nor of the next. Nor of the one behind us. As if the timelessness of the ancestor world and the unborn have joined spirits to wring an issue of the elusive being of passage . . . Elesin!

ELESIN: I am here. What is it?

IYALOJA: Did you hear all I said just now?

ELESIN: Yes.

IYALOJA: The living must eat and drink. When the moment comes, don't turn the food to rodents' droppings in their mouth. Don't let them taste the ashes of the world when they step out at dawn to breathe the morning dew.

ELESIN: This doubt is unworthy of you Iyaloja.

IYALOJA: Eating the awusa nut is not so difficult as drinking water afterwards.

ELESIN: The waters of the bitter stream are honey to a man
            Whose tongue has savoured all.

IYALOJA: No one knows when the ants desert their home; they leave the mound intact. The swallow is never seen to peck holes in its nest when it is time to move with the season. There are always throngs of humanity behind the leave-taker. The rain should not come through the roof for them, the wind must not blow through the walls at night.

ELESIN: I refuse to take offense.

IYALOJA: You wish to travel light. Well, the earth is yours. But be sure the seed you leave in it attracts no curse.

ELESIN: You really mistake my person Iyaloja.

IYALOJA: I said nothing. Now we must go prepare your bridal chamber. Then these same hands will lay your shrouds.

ELESIN (*exasperated*): Must you be so blunt? (*recovers*) Well, weave your shrouds, but let the fingers of my bride seal my eyelids with earth and wash my body.

IYALOJA: Prepare yourself Elesin.

She gets up to leave. At that moment the women return, leading the BRIDE. ELESIN's *face glows with pleasure. He flicks the sleeves of his agbada with renewed confidence and steps forward to meet the group. As the girl kneels before* IYALOJA, *lights fade out on the scene.*

ACT TWO

The verandah of the District Officer's bungalow. A tango is playing from an old hand-cranked gramophone and, glimpsed through the wide windows and doors which open onto the forestage verandah are the shapes of SIMON PILKINGS *and his wife,* JANE, *tangoing in and out of shadows in the living-room. They are wearing what is immediately apparent as some form of fancy-dress. The dance goes on for some moments and then the figure of a "Native Administration" policeman emerges and climbs up the steps onto the verandah. He peeps through and observes the dancing couple, reacting with what is obviously a long-standing bewilderment. He stiffens suddenly, his expression changes to one of disbelief and horror. In his excitement he upsets a flowerpot and attracts the attention of the couple. They stop dancing.*

PILKINGS: Is there anyone out there?

JANE: I'll turn off the gramophone.

PILKINGS (*approaching the verandah*): I'm sure I heard something fall over. (*The constable retreats slowly, open-mouthed as* PILKINGS *approaches the verandah.*) Oh it's you Amusa. Why didn't you just knock instead of knocking things over?

AMUSA (*stammers badly and points a shaky finger at his dress*): Mista Pirinkin . . . Mista Pirinkin . . .

PILKINGS: What is the matter with you?

JANE (*emerging*): Who is it dear? Oh, Amusa . . .

PILKINGS: Yes it's Amusa, and acting most strangely.

AMUSA (*his attention now transferred to* MRS. PILKINGS): Mammadam . . . you too!

PILKINGS: What the hell is the matter with you man!

JANE: Your costume darling. Our fancy dress.

PILKINGS: Oh hell, I'd forgotten all about that. (*Lifts the face mask over his head showing his face. His wife follows suit.*)

JANE: I think you've shocked his big pagan heart bless him.

PILKINGS: Nonsense, he's a Moslem. Come on Amusa, you don't believe in all this nonsense do you? I thought you were a good Moslem.

AMUSA: Mista Pirinkin, I beg you sir, what you think you do with that dress? It belong to dead cult, not for human being.

PILKINGS: Oh, Amusa, what a let down you are. I swear by you at the club you know—thank God for Amusa, he doesn't believe in any mumbo-jumbo. And now look at you!

AMUSA: Mista Pirinkin, I beg you, take it off. Is not good for man like you to touch that cloth.

PILKINGS: Well, I've got it on. And what's more Jane and I have bet on it we're taking first prize at the ball. Now, if you can just pull yourself together and tell me what you wanted to see me about . . .

AMUSA: Sir, I cannot talk this matter to you in that dress. I no fit.

PILKINGS: What's that rubbish again?

JANE: He is dead earnest too Simon. I think you'll have to handle this delicately.

PILKINGS: Delicately my . . . ! Look here Amusa, I think this little joke has gone far enough hm? Let's have some sense. You seem to forget that you are a police officer in the service of His Majesty's Government. I order you to report your business at once or face disciplinary action.

AMUSA: Sir, it is a matter of death. How can man talk against death to person in uniform of death? Is like talking against government to person in uniform of police. Please sir, I go and come back.

PILKINGS (*roars*): Now! (AMUSA *switches his gaze to the ceiling suddenly, remains mute.*)

JANE: Oh Amusa, what is there to be scared of in the costume? You saw it confiscated last month from those *egungun* men who were creating trouble in town. You helped arrest the cult leaders yourself—if the juju didn't harm you at the time how could it possibly harm you now? And merely by looking at it?

AMUSA (*without looking down*): Madam, I arrest the ring-leaders who make trouble but me I no touch *egungun*. That *egungun* inself, I no touch. And I no abuse'am. I arrest ring-leader but I treat *egungun* with respect.

PILKINGS: It's hopeless. We'll merely end up missing the best part of the ball. When they get this way there is nothing you can do. It's simply hammering against a brick wall. Write your report or whatever it is on that pad Amusa and take yourself out of here. Come on Jane. We only upset his delicate sensibilities by remaining here.

AMUSA *waits for them to leave, then writes in the notebook, somewhat laboriously. Drumming from the direction of the town wells up.* AMUSA *listens, makes a movement as if he wants to recall* PILKINGS *but changes his mind. Completes his note and goes. A few moments later* PILKINGS *emerges, picks up the pad and reads.*

PILKINGS: Jane!

JANE (*from the bedroom*): Coming darling. Nearly ready.

PILKINGS: Never mind being ready, just listen to this.

JANE: What is it?

PILKINGS: Amusa's report. Listen. "I have to report that it come to my information that one prominent chief, namely, the Elesin Oba, is to commit death tonight as a result of native custom. Because this is criminal offense I await further instruction at charge office. Sergeant Amusa."

JANE *comes out onto the verandah while he is reading.*

JANE: Did I hear you say commit death?

PILKINGS: Obviously he means murder.

JANE: You mean a ritual murder?

PILKINGS: Must be. You think you've stamped it all out but it's always lurking under the surface somewhere.

JANE: Oh. Does it mean we are not getting to the ball at all?

PILKINGS: No-o. I'll have the man arrested. Everyone remotely involved. In any case there may be nothing to it. Just rumors.

JANE: Really? I thought you found Amusa's rumors generally reliable.

PILKINGS: That's true enough. But who knows what may have been giving him the scare lately. Look at his conduct tonight.

JANE (*laughing*): You have to admit he had his own peculiar logic. (*deepens her voice*) How can man talk against death to person in uniform of death? (*laughs*) Anyway, you can't go into the police station dressed like that.

PILKINGS: I'll send Joseph with instructions. Damn it, what a confounded nuisance!

JANE: But don't you think you should talk first to the man, Simon?

PILKINGS: Do you want to go to the ball or not?

JANE: Darling, why are you getting rattled? I was only trying to be intelligent. It seems hardly fair just to lock up a man—and a chief at that—simply on the er . . . what is that legal word again?—uncorroborated word of a sergeant.

PILKINGS: Well, that's easily decided. Joseph!

JOSEPH (*from within*): Yes master.

PILKINGS: You're quite right of course, I am getting rattled. Probably the effect of those bloody drums. Do you hear how they go on and on?

JANE: I wondered when you'd notice. Do you suppose it has something to do with this affair?

PILKINGS: Who knows? They always find an excuse for making a noise . . . (*thoughtfully*) Even so . . .

JANE: Yes Simon?

PILKINGS: It's different Jane. I don't think I've heard this particular—sound—before. Something unsettling about it.

JANE: I thought all bush drumming sounded the same.

PILKINGS: Don't tease me now Jane. This may be serious.

JANE: I'm sorry. (*Gets up and throws her arms around his neck. Kisses him. The houseboy enters, retreats and knocks.*)

PILKINGS (*wearily*): Oh, come in Joseph! I don't know where you pick up all these elephantine notions of tact. Come over here.

JOSEPH: Sir?

PILKINGS: Joseph, are you a christian or not?

JOSEPH: Yessir.

PILKINGS: Does seeing me in this outfit bother you?

JOSEPH: No sir, it has no power.

PILKINGS: Thank God for some sanity at last. Now Joseph, answer me on the honor of a christian—what is supposed to be going on in town tonight?

JOSEPH: Tonight sir? You mean that chief who is going to kill himself?

PILKINGS: What?

JANE: What do you mean, kill himself?

PILKINGS: You do mean he is going to kill somebody don't you?

JOSEPH: No master. He will not kill anybody and no one will kill him. He will simply die.

JANE: But why Joseph?

JOSEPH: It is native law and custom. The King die last month. Tonight is his burial. But before they can bury him, the Elesin must die so as to accompany him to heaven.

PILKINGS: I seem to be fated to clash more often with that man than with any of the other chiefs.

JOSEPH: He is the King's Chief Horseman.

PILKINGS (*in a resigned way*): I know.

JANE: Simon, what's the matter?

PILKINGS: It would have to be him!

JANE: Who is he?

PILKINGS: Don't you remember? He's that chief with whom I had a scrap some three or four years ago. I helped his son get to a medical school in England, remember? He fought tooth and nail to prevent it.

JANE: Oh now I remember. He was that very sensitive young man. What was his name again?

PILKINGS: Olunde. Haven't replied to his last letter come to think of it. The old pagan wanted him to stay and carry on some family tradition or the other. Honestly I couldn't understand the fuss he made. I literally had to help the boy escape from close confinement and load him onto the next boat. A most intelligent boy, really bright.

JANE: I rather thought he was much too sensitive you know. The kind of person you feel should be a poet munching rose petals in Bloomsbury.

PILKINGS: Well, he's going to make a first-class doctor. His mind is set on that. And as long as he wants my help he is welcome to it.

JANE (*after a pause*): Simon.

PILKINGS: Yes?

JANE: This boy, he was his eldest son wasn't he?

PILKINGS: I'm not sure. Who could tell with that old ram?

JANE: Do you know, Joseph?

JOSEPH: Oh yes madam. He was the eldest son. That's why Elesin cursed master good and proper. The eldest son is not supposed to travel away from the land.

JANE (*giggling*): Is that true Simon? Did he really curse you good and proper?

PILKINGS: By all accounts I should be dead by now.

JOSEPH: Oh no, master is white man. And good christian. Black man juju can't touch master.

JANE: If he was his eldest, it means that he would be the Elesin to the next king. It's a family thing isn't it Joseph?

JOSEPH: Yes madam. And if this Elesin had died before the King, his eldest son must take his place.

JANE: That would explain why the old chief was so mad you took the boy away.

PILKINGS: Well it makes me all the more happy I did.

JANE: I wonder if he knew.

PILKINGS: Who? Oh, you mean Olunde?

JANE: Yes. Was that why he was so determined to get away? I wouldn't stay if I knew I was trapped in such a horrible custom.

PILKINGS (*thoughtfully*): No, I don't think he knew. At least he gave no indication. But you couldn't really tell with him. He was rather close you know, quite unlike most of them. Didn't give much away, not even to me.

JANE: Aren't they all rather close, Simon?

PILKINGS: These natives here? Good gracious. They'll open their mouths and yap with you about their family secrets before you can stop them. Only the other day . . .

JANE: But Simon, do they really give anything away? I mean, anything that really counts. This affair for instance, we didn't know they still practiced that custom did we?

PILKINGS: Ye-e-es, I suppose you're right there. Sly, devious bastards.

JOSEPH (*stiffly*): Can I go now master? I have to clean the kitchen.

PILKINGS: What? Oh, you can go. Forgot you were still here.

JOSEPH *goes.*

JANE: Simon, you really must watch your language. Bastard isn't just a simple swear-word in these parts, you know.

PILKINGS: Look, just when did you become a social anthropologist, that's what I'd like to know.

JANE: I'm not claiming to know anything. I just happen to have overheard quarrels among the servants. That's how I know they consider it a smear.

PILKINGS: I thought the extended family system took care of all that. Elastic family, no bastards.

JANE (*shrugs*): Have it your own way.

Awkward silence. The drumming increases in volume. JANE *gets up suddenly, restless.*

That drumming Simon, do you think it might really be connected with this ritual? It's been going on all evening.

PILKINGS: Let's ask our native guide. Joseph! Just a minute Joseph. (JOSEPH *re-enters.*) What's the drumming about?

JOSEPH: I don't know master.

PILKINGS: What do you mean you don't know? It's only two years since your conversion. Don't tell me all that holy water nonsense also wiped out your tribal memory.

JOSEPH (*visibly shocked*): Master!

JANE: Now you've done it.

PILKINGS: What have I done now?

JANE: Never mind. Listen Joseph, just tell me this. Is that drumming connected with dying or anything of that nature?

JOSEPH: Madam, this is what I am trying to say: I am not sure. It sounds like the death of a great chief and then, it sounds like the wedding of a great chief. It really mix me up.

PILKINGS: Oh get back to the kitchen. A fat lot of help you are.

JOSEPH: Yes master. (*goes*)

JANE: Simon . . .

PILKINGS: Alright, alright. I'm in no mood for preaching.

JANE: It isn't my preaching you have to worry about, it's the preaching of the missionaries who preceded you here. When they make converts they really convert them. Calling holy water nonsense to our Joseph is really like insulting the Virgin Mary before a Roman Catholic. He's going to hand in his notice tomorrow you mark my word.

PILKINGS: Now you're being ridiculous.

JANE: Am I? What are you willing to bet that tomorrow we are going to be without a steward-boy? Did you see his face?

PILKINGS: I am more concerned about whether or not we will be one native chief short by tomorrow. Christ! Just listen to those drums. (*He strides up and down, undecided.*)

JANE (*getting up*): I'll change and make up some supper.

PILKINGS: What's that?

JANE: Simon, it's obvious we have to miss this ball.

PILKINGS: Nonsense. It's the first bit of real fun the European club has managed to organize for over a year, I'm damned if I'm going to miss it. And it is a rather special occasion. Doesn't happen every day.

JANE: You know this business has to be stopped Simon. And you are the only man who can do it.

PILKINGS: I don't have to stop anything. If they want to throw themselves off the top of a cliff or poison themselves for the sake of some barbaric custom what is that to me? If it were ritual murder or something like that I'd be duty-bound to do something. I can't keep an eye on all the potential suicides in this province. And as for that man—believe me it's good riddance.

JANE (*laughs*): I know you better than that Simon. You are going to have to do something to stop it—after you've finished blustering.

PILKINGS (*shouts after her*): And suppose after all it's only a wedding. I'd look a proper fool if I interrupted a chief on his honeymoon, wouldn't I? (*resumes his angry stride, slows down*) Ah well, who can tell what those chiefs actually do on their honeymoon anyway?(*He takes up the pad and scribbles rapidly on it.*) Joseph! Joseph! (*Some moments later* JOSEPH *puts in a sulky appearance.*) Did you hear me call you? Why the hell didn't you answer?

JOSEPH: I didn't hear master.

PILKINGS: You didn't hear me! How come you are here then?

JOSEPH (*stubbornly*): I didn't hear master.

PILKINGS (*controls himself with an effort*): We'll talk about it in the morning. I want you to take this note directly to Sergeant Amusa. You'll find him at the charge office. Get on your bicycle and race there with it. I expect you back in twenty minutes exactly. Twenty minutes, is that clear?

JOSEPH: Yes master. (*going*)

PILKINGS: Oh er . . . Joseph.

JOSEPH: Yes master?

PILKINGS (*between gritted teeth*): Er . . . forget what I said just now. The holy water is not nonsense. *I* was talking nonsense.

JOSEPH: Yes master. (*goes*)

JANE (*pokes her head round the door*): Have you found him?

PILKINGS: Found who?

JANE: Joseph. Weren't you shouting for him?

PILKINGS: Oh yes, he turned up finally.

JANE: You sounded desperate. What was it all about?

PILKINGS: Oh nothing. I just wanted to apologize to him. Assure him that the holy water isn't really nonsense.

JANE: Oh? And how did he take it?

PILKINGS: Who the hell gives a damn! I had a sudden vision of our Very Reverend Macfarlane drafting another letter of complaint to the Resident about my unchristian language towards his parishioners.

JANE: Oh I think he's given up on you by now.

PILKINGS: Don't be too sure. And anyway, I wanted to make sure Joseph didn't "lose" my note on the way. He looked sufficiently full of the holy crusade to do some such thing.

JANE: If you've finished exaggerating, come and have something to eat.

PILKINGS: No, put it all way. We can still get to the ball.

JANE: Simon . . .

PILKINGS: Get your costume back on. Nothing to worry about. I've instructed Amusa to arrest the man and lock him up.

JANE: But that station is hardly secure Simon. He'll soon get his friends to help him escape.

PILKINGS: A-ah, that's where I have out-thought you. I'm not having him put in the station cell. Amusa will bring him right here and lock him up in my study. And he'll stay with him till we get back. No one will dare come here to incite him to anything.

JANE: How clever of you darling. I'll get ready.

PILKINGS: Hey.

JANE: Yes darling.

PILKINGS: I have a surprise for you. I was going to keep it until we actually got to the ball.

JANE: What is it?

PILKINGS: You know the Prince is on a tour of the colonies don't you? Well, he docked in the capital only this morning but he is already at the Residency. He is going to grace the ball with his presence later tonight.

JANE: Simon! Not really.

PILKINGS: Yes he is. He's been invited to give away the prizes and he has agreed. You must admit old Engleton is the best Club Secretary we ever had. Quick off the mark that lad.

JANE: But how thrilling.

PILKINGS: The other provincials are going to be damned envious.

JANE: I wonder what he'll come as.

PILKINGS: Oh I don't know. As a coat-of-arms perhaps. Anyway it won't be anything to touch this.

JANE: Well that's lucky. If we are to be presented I won't have to start looking for a pair of gloves. It's all sewn on.

PILKINGS (*laughing*): Quite right. Trust a woman to think of that. Come on, let's get going.

JANE (*rushing off*): Won't be a second. (*stops*) Now I see why you've been so edgy all evening. I thought you weren't handling this affair with your usual brilliance—to begin with that is.

PILKINGS (*his mood is much improved*): Shut up woman and get your things on.

JANE: Alright boss, coming.

> PILKINGS *suddenly begins to hum the tango to which they were dancing before. Starts to execute a few practice steps. Lights fade.*

ACT THREE

> *A swelling, agitated hum of women's voices rises immediately in the background. The lights come on and we see the frontage of a converted cloth stall in the market. The floor leading up to the entrance is covered in rich velvets and woven cloth. The women come on stage, borne backwards by the determined progress of* SERGEANT AMUSA *and his two constables who already have their batons out and use them as pressure against the women. At the edge of the cloth-covered floor however the women take a determined stand and block all further progress of the men. They begin to tease them mercilessly.*

AMUSA: I am tell you women for last time to commot my road. I am here on official business.

WOMAN: Official business you white man's eunuch? Official business is taking place where you want to go and it's a business you wouldn't understand.

WOMAN (*makes a quick tug at the constable's baton*): That doesn't fool anyone you know. It's the one you carry under your government knickers that counts. (*She bends low as if to peep under the baggy shorts. The embarrassed constable quickly puts his knees together. The women roar.*)

WOMAN: You mean there is nothing there at all?

WOMAN: Oh there was something. You know that handbell which the whiteman uses to summon his servants . . . ?

AMUSA (*He manages to preserve some dignity throughout.*): I hope you women know that interfering with officer in execution of his duty is criminal offense.

WOMAN: Interfere? He says we're interfering with him. You foolish man we're telling you there's nothing there to interfere with.

AMUSA: I am order you now to clear the road.

WOMAN: What road? The one your father built?

WOMAN: You are a Policeman not so? Then you know what they call trespassing in court. Or—(*pointing to the cloth-lined steps*)—do you think that kind of road is built for every kind of feet.

WOMAN: Go back and tell the white man who sent you to come himself.

AMUSA: If I go I will come back with reinforcement. And we will all return carrying weapons.

WOMAN: Oh, now I understand. Before they can put on those knickers the white man first cuts off their weapons.

WOMAN: What a cheek! You mean you come here to show power to women and you don't even have a weapon.

AMUSA (*shouting above the laughter*): For the last time I warn you women to clear the road.

WOMAN: To where?

AMUSA: To that hut. I know he dey dere.

WOMAN: Who?

AMUSA: The chief who call himself Elesin Oba.

WOMAN: You ignorant man. It is not he who calls himself Elesin Oba, it is his blood that says it. As called out to his father before him and will to his son after him. And that is in spite of everything your white man can do.

WOMAN: Is it not the same ocean that washes this land and the white man's land? Tell your white man he can hide our son away as long as he likes. When the time comes for him, the same ocean will bring him back.

AMUSA: The government say dat kin' ting must stop.

WOMAN: Who will stop it? You? Tonight our husband and father will prove himself greater than the laws of strangers.

AMUSA: I tell you nobody go prove anyting tonight or anytime. Is ignorant and criminal to prove dat kin' prove.

IYALOJA (*Entering, from the hut. She is accompanied by a group of young girls who have been attending the* BRIDE.): What is it Amusa? Why do you come here to disturb the happiness of others.

AMUSA: Madame Iyaloja, I glad you come. You know me. I no like trouble but duty is duty. I am here to arrest Elesin for criminal intent. Tell these women to stop obstructing me in the performance of my duty.

IYALOJA: And you? What gives you the right to obstruct our leader of men in the performance of his duty.

AMUSA: What kin' duty be dat one Iyaloja.

IYALOJA: What kin' duty? What kin' duty does a man have to his new bride?

AMUSA (*bewildered, looks at the women and at the entrance to the hut*): Iyaloja, is it wedding you call dis kin' ting?

IYALOJA: You have wives haven't you? Whatever the white man has done to you he hasn't stopped you having wives. And if he has, at least he is married. If you don't know what a marriage is, go and ask him to tell you.

AMUSA: This no to wedding.

IYALOJA: And ask him at the same time what he would have done if anyone had come to disturb him on his wedding night.

AMUSA: Iyaloja, I say dis no to wedding.

IYALOJA: You want to look inside the bridal chamber? You want to see for yourself how a man cuts the virgin knot?

AMUSA: Madam . . .

WOMAN: Perhaps his wives are still waiting for him to learn.

AMUSA: Iyaloja, make you tell dese women make den no insult me again. If I hear dat kin' indult once more . . .

GIRL (*pushing her way through*): You will do what?

GIRL: He's out of his mind. It's our mothers you're talking to, do you know that? Not to any illiterate villager you can bully and terrorize. How dare you intrude here anyway?

GIRL: What a cheek, what impertinence!

GIRL: You've treated them too gently. Now let them see what it is to tamper with the mothers of this market.

GIRLS: Your betters dare not enter the market when the women say no!

GIRL: Haven't you learned that yet, you jester in khaki and starch?

IYALOJA: Daughters . . .

GIRL: No no Iyaloja, leave us to deal with him. He no longer knows his mother, we'll teach him.

With a sudden movement they snatch the batons of the two constables. They begin to hem them in.

GIRL: What next? We have your batons? What next? What are you going to do?

With equally swift movements they knock off their hats.

GIRL: Move if you dare. We have your hats, what will you do about it? Didn't the white man teach you to take off your hats before women?

IYALOJA: It's a wedding night. It's a night of joy for us. Peace . . .

GIRL: Not for him. Who asked him here?

GIRL: Does he dare go to the Residency without an invitation?

GIRL: Not even where the servants eat the left-overs.

GIRLS (*In turn. In an "English" accent.*): Well well it's Mister Amusa. Were you invited? (*Play-acting to one another. The older women encourage them with their titters.*)
—Your invitation card please?
—Who are you? Have we been introduced?
—And who did you say you were?
—Sorry, I didn't quite catch your name.
—May I take your hat?
—If you insist. May I take yours? (*exchanging the policeman's hats*)
—How very kind of you.
—Not at all. Won't you sit down?
—After you.
—Oh no.
—I insist.
—You're most gracious.
—And how do you find the place?
—The natives are alright.
—Friendly?
—Tractable.

—Not a teeny-weeny bit restless?
—Well, a teeny-weeny bit restless.
—One might even say, difficult?
—Indeed one might be tempted to say, difficult.
—But you do manage to cope?
—Yes indeed I do. I have a rather faithful ox called Amusa.
—He's loyal?
—Absolutely.
—Lay down his life for you what?
—Without a moment's thought.
—Had one like that once. Trust him with my life.
—Mostly of course they are liars.
—Never known a native tell the truth.
—Does it get rather close around here?
—It's mild for this time of the year.
—But the rains may still come.
—They are late this year aren't they?
—They are keeping African time.
—Ha ha ha ha
—Ha ha ha ha
—The humidity is what gets me.
—It used to be whisky.
—Ha ha ha ha
—Ha ha ha ha
—What's your handicap old chap?
—Is there racing by golly?
—Splendid golf course, you'll like it.
—I'm beginning to like it already.
—And a European club, exclusive.
—You've kept the flag flying.
—We do our best for the old country.
—It's a pleasure to serve.
—Another whisky old chap?
—You are indeed too too kind.
—Not at all sir. Where is that boy? (*with a sudden bellow*) Sergeant!
AMUSA: (*snaps to attention*): Yessir!

The women collapse with laughter.

GIRL: Take your men out of here.
AMUSA: (*Realizing the trick, he rages from loss of face.*): I'm give you warning . . .
GIRL: Alright then. Off with his knickers! (*They surge slowly forward.*)
IYALOJA: Daughters, please.
AMUSA: (*squaring himself for defense*): The first woman wey touch me . . .
IYALOJA: My children, I beg of you . . .
GIRL: Then tell him to leave this market. This is the home of our mothers. We don't
    want the eater of white left-overs at the feast their hands have prepared.
IYALOJA: You heard them Amusa. You had better go.
GIRLS: Now!
AMUSA: (*commencing his retreat*): We dey go now, but make you no say we no warn
    you.
GIRL: Now!

GIRL: Before we read the riot act—you should know all about that.

AMUSA: Make we go. (*They depart, more precipitately.*)

The women strike their palms across in the gesture of wonder.

WOMAN: Do they teach you all that at school?

WOMAN: And to think I nearly kept Apinke away from the place.

WOMAN: Did you hear them? Did you see how they mimicked the white man?

WOMAN: The voices exactly. Hey, there are wonders in this world!

IYALOJA: Well, our elders have said it: Dada may be weak, but he has a younger sibling who is truly fearless.

WOMAN: The next time the white man shows his face in this market I will set Wuraola on his tail.

A woman bursts into song and dance of euphoria—"Tani l'awa o l'ogbeja? Kayi! A l'ogbeja. Omo Kekere l'ogbeja." * *The rest of the women join in, some placing the girls on their back like infants, others dancing round them. The dance becomes general, mounting in excitement.* ELESIN *appears, in wrapper only. In his hands a white velvet cloth folded loosely as if it held some delicate object. He cries out.*

ELESIN: Oh you mothers of beautiful brides! (*The dancing stops. They turn and see him, and the object in his hands.* IYALOJA *approaches and gently takes the cloth from him.*) Take it. It is no mere virgin stain, but the union of life and the seeds of passage. My vital flow, the last from this flesh is intermingled with the promise of future life. All is prepared. Listen! (*a steady drum-beat from the distance*) Yes. It is nearly time. The King's dog has been killed. The King's favorite horse is about to follow his master. My brother chiefs know their task and perform it well. (*He listens again.*)

The BRIDE *emerges, stands shyly by the door. He turns to her.*

Our marriage is not yet wholly fulfilled. When earth and passage wed, the consummation is complete only when there are grains of earth on the eyelids of passage. Stay by me till then. My faithful drummers, do me your last service. This is where I have chosen to do my leave-taking, in this heart of life, this hive which contains the swarm of the world in its small compass. This is where I have known love and laughter away from the palace. Even the richest food cloys when eaten days on end; in the market, nothing ever cloys. Listen. (*They listen to the drums.*) They have begun to seek out the heart of the King's favorite horse. Soon it will ride in its bolt of raffia with the dog at its feet. Together they will ride on the shoulders of the King's grooms through the pulse centers of the town. They know it is here I shall await them. I have told them. (*His eyes appear to cloud. He passes his hand over them as if to clear his sight. He gives a faint smile.*) It promises well; just then I felt my spirit's eagerness. The kite makes for wide spaces and the wind creeps up behind its tail; can the kite say less than—thank you, the quicker the better? But wait a while my spirit. Wait. Wait for the coming of the courier of the King. Do you know friends, the horse is born to this one destiny, to bear the burden that is man upon its back. Except for this night, this night alone when the spotless stallion will ride in triumph on the back of man. In the time of my father I witnessed the strange sight. Perhaps tonight also I shall see it for the last time. If they arrive before the

---

*"Who says we haven't a defender? Silence! We have our defenders. Little children are our champions."

drums beat for me, I shall tell him to let the Alafin know I follow swiftly. If they come after the drums have sounded, why then, all is well for I have gone ahead. Our spirits shall fall in step along the great passage. (*He listens to the drums. He seems again to be falling into a state of semi-hypnosis; his eyes scan the sky but it is in a kind of daze. His voice is a little breathless.*) The moon has fed, a glow from its full stomach fills the sky and air, but I cannot tell where is that gateway through which I must pass. My faithful friends, let our feet touch together this last time, lead me into the other market with sounds that cover my skin with down yet make my limbs strike earth like a thoroughbred. Dear mothers, let me dance into the passage even as I have lived beneath your roofs. (*He comes down progressively among them. They make away for him, the drummers playing. His dance is one of solemn, regal motions, each gesture of the body is made with a solemn finality. The women join him, their steps a somewhat more fluid version of his. Beneath the* PRAISE-SINGER's *exhortations the women dirge "Ale le le, awo mi lo."*)

PRAISE-SINGER: Elesin Alafin, can you hear my voice?

ELESIN: Faintly, my friend, faintly.

PRAISE-SINGER: Elesin Alafin, can you hear my call?

ELESIN: Faintly my king, faintly.

PRAISE-SINGER: Is your memory sound Elesin?
Shall my voice be a blade of grass and
Tickle the armpit of the past?

ELESIN: My memory needs no prodding but
What do you wish to say to me?

PRAISE-SINGER: Only what has been spoken. Only what concerns
The dying wish of the father of all.

ELESIN: It is buried like seed-yam in my mind
This is the season of quick rains, the harvest
Is this moment due for gathering.

PRAISE-SINGER: If you cannot come, I said, swear
You'll tell my favorite horse. I shall
Ride on through the gates alone.

ELESIN: Elesin's message will be read
Only when his loyal heart no longer beats.

PRAISE-SINGER: If you cannot come Elesin, tell my dog.
I cannot stay the keeper too long
At the gate.

ELESIN: A dog does not outrun the hand
That feeds it meat. A horse that throws its rider
Slows down to a stop. Elesin Alafin
Trusts no beasts with messages between
A king and his companion.

PRAISE-SINGER: If you get lost my dog will track
The hidden path to me.

ELESIN: The seven-way crossroads confuses
Only the stranger. The Horseman of the King
Was born in the recesses of the house.

PRAISE-SINGER: I know the wickedness of men. If there is
Weight on the loose end of your sash, such weight
As no mere man can shift; if your sash is earthed
By evil minds who mean to part us at the last . . .

ELESIN: My sash is of the deep purple *alari;*
                     It is no tethering-rope. The elephant
                     Trails no tethering-rope; that king
                     Is not yet crowned who will peg an elephant—
                     Not even you my friend and King.

PRAISE-SINGER: And yet this fear will not depart from me
                     The darkness of this new abode is deep—
                     Will your human eyes suffice?

ELESIN: In a night which falls before our eyes
                     However deep, we do not miss our way.

PRAISE-SINGER: Shall I now not acknowledge I have stood
                     Where wonders met their end? The elephant deserves
                     Better than that we say "I have caught
                     A glimpse of something." If we see the tamer
                     Of the forest let us say plainly, we have seen
                     An elephant.

ELESIN (*His voice is drowsy.*):
                     I have freed myself of earth and now
                     It's getting dark. Strange voices guide my feet.

PRAISE-SINGER: The river is never so high that the eyes
                     Of a fish are covered. The night is not so dark
                     That the albino fails to find his way. A child
                     Returning homewards craves no leading by the hand.
                     Gracefully does the mask regain his grove at the end of day   . . .
                     Gracefully, Gracefully does the mask dance
                     Homeward at the end of day, gracefully . . .

ELESIN*'s trance appears to be deepening, his steps heavier.*

IYALOJA: It is the death of war that kills the valiant,
                     Death of water is how the swimmer goes
                     It is the death of markets that kills the trader
                     And death of indecision takes the idle away
                     The trade of the cutlass blunts its edge
                     And the beautiful die the death of beauty.
                     It takes an Elesin to die the death of death . . .
                     Only Elesin . . . dies the unknowable death of death . . .
                     Gracefully, gracefully does the horseman regain
                     The stables at the end of day, gracefully . . .

PRAISE-SINGER: How shall I tell what my eyes have seen? The Horseman gallops on be-
        fore the courier, how shall I tell what my eyes have seen? He says a dog may be
        confused by new scents of beings he never dreamt of, so he must precede the dog
        to heaven. He says a horse may stumble on strange boulders and be lamed, so he
        races on before the horse to heaven. It is best, he says, to trust no messenger who
        may falter at the outer gate; oh how shall I tell what my ears have heard? But do
        you hear me still Elesin, do you hear your faithful one?

ELESIN *in his motions appears to feel for a direction of sound, subtly, but he only sinks
deeper into his trance-dance.*

Elesin Alafin, I no longer sense your flesh. The drums are changing now but you
have gone far ahead of the world. It is not yet noon in heaven; let those who claim

it is begin their own journey home. So why must you rush like an impatient bride: why do you race to desert your Olohun-iyo?

ELESIN *is now sunk fully deep in his trance, there is no longer sign of any awareness of his surroundings.*

Does the deep voice of *gbedu* cover you then, like the passage of royal elephants? Those drums that brook no rivals, have they blocked the passage to your ears that my voice passes into wind, a mere leaf floating in the night? Is your flesh lightened Elesin, is that lump of earth I slid between your slippers to keep you longer slowly sifting from your feet? Are the drums on the other side now tuning skin to skin with ours in *osugbo*? Are there sounds there I cannot hear, do footsteps surround you which pound the earth like *gbedu*, roll like thunder round the dome of the world? Is the darkness gathering in your head Elesin? Is there now a streak of light at the end of the passage, a light I dare not look upon? Does it reveal whose voices we often heard, whose touches we often felt, whose wisdoms come suddenly into the mind when the wisest have shaken their heads and murmured; It cannot be done? Elesin Alafin, don't think I do not know why your lips are heavy, why your limbs are drowsy as palm oil in the cold of harmattan. I would call you back but when the elephant heads for the jungle, the tail is too small a handhold for the hunter that would pull him back. The sun that heads for the sea no longer heeds the prayers of the farmer. When the river begins to taste the salt of the ocean, we no longer know what deity to call on, the river-god or Olokun. No arrow flies back to the string, the child does not return through the same passage that gave it birth. Elesin Oba, can you hear me at all? Your eyelids are glazed like a courtesan's, is it that you see the dark groom and master of life? And will you see my father? Will you tell him that I stayed with you to the last? Will my voice ring in your ears awhile, will you remember Olohun-iyo even if the music on the other side surpasses his mortal craft? But will they know you over there? Have they eyes to gauge your worth, have they the heart to love you, will they know what thoroughbred prances towards them in caparisons of honor? If they do not Elesin, if any there cuts your yam with a small knife, or pours you wine in a small calabash, turn back and return to welcoming hands. If the world were not greater than the wishes of Olohun-iyo, I would not let you go . . .

He appears to break down. ELESIN *dances on, completely in a trance. The dirge wells up louder and stronger.* ELESIN*'s dance does not lose its elasticity but his gestures become, if possible, even more weighty. Lights fade slowly on the scene.*

ACT FOUR

A Masque. The front side of the stage is part of a wide corridor around the great hall of the Residency extending beyond vision into the rear and wings. It is redolent of the tawdry decadence of a far-flung but key imperial frontier. The couples in a variety of fancy-dress are ranged around the walls, gazing in the same direction. The guest-of-honor is about to make an appearance. A portion of the local police brass band with its white conductor is just visible. At last, the entrance of Royalty. The band plays "Rule Britannia," badly, beginning long before he is visible. The couples bow and curtsey as he passes by them. Both he and his companions are dressed in seventeenth century European costume. Following behind are the RESIDENT *and his partner similarly attired. As they gain the end of the hall where the orchestra dais begins the music comes to an end. The* PRINCE *bows to the guests. The band strikes up a Viennese waltz and the* PRINCE *formally opens the floor. Several bars later the* RESIDENT *and his companion follow suit. Others follow in appropriate pecking order. The orchestra's waltz rendition is not of the highest musical standard.*

Some time later the PRINCE *dances again into view and is settled into a corner by the* RESIDENT *who then proceeds to select couples as they dance past for introduction, sometimes threading his way through the dancers to tap the lucky couple on the shoulder. Desperate efforts from many to ensure that they are recognized in spite of, perhaps, their costume. The ritual of introductions soon takes in* PILKINGS *and his wife. The* PRINCE *is quite fascinated by their costume and they demonstrate the adaptations they have made to it, pulling down the mask to demonstrate how the* egungun *normally appears, then showing the various press-button controls they have innovated for the face flaps, the sleeves, etc. They demonstrate the dance steps and the guttural sounds made by the* egungun, *harass other dancers in the hall,* MRS. PILKINGS *playing the "restrainer" to* PILKINGS' *manic darts. Everyone is highly entertained, the Royal Party especially who lead the applause.*

At this point a liveried footman comes in with a note on a salver and is intercepted almost absent-mindedly by the RESIDENT *who takes the note and reads it. After polite coughs he succeeds in excusing the* PILKINGSES *from the* PRINCE *and takes them aside. The* PRINCE *considerately offers the* RESIDENT'S *wife his hand and dancing is resumed.*

On their way out the RESIDENT *gives an order to his* AIDE-DE-CAMP. *They come into the side corridor where the* RESIDENT *hands the note to* PILKINGS.

RESIDENT: As you see it says "emergency" on the outside. I took the liberty of opening it because His Highness was obviously enjoying the entertainment. I didn't want to interrupt unless really necessary.

PILKINGS: Yes, yes of course sir.

RESIDENT: Is it really as bad as it says? What's it all about?

PILKINGS: Some strange custom they have sir. It seems because the King is dead some important chief has to commit suicide.

RESIDENT: The King? Isn't it the same one who died nearly a month ago?

PILKINGS: Yes sir.

RESIDENT: Haven't they buried him yet?

PILKINGS: They take their time about these things sir. The pre-burial ceremonies last nearly thirty days. It seems tonight is the final night.

RESIDENT: But what has it got to do with the market women? Why are they rioting? We've waived that troublesome tax haven't we?

PILKINGS: We don't quite know that they are exactly rioting yet sir. Sergeant Amusa is sometimes prone to exaggerations.

RESIDENT: He sounds desperate enough. That comes out even in his rather quaint grammar. Where is the man anyway? I asked my aide-de-camp to bring him here.

PILKINGS: They are probably looking in the wrong verandah. I'll fetch him myself.

RESIDENT: No no you stay here. Let your wife go and look for them. Do you mind my dear . . . ?

JANE: Certainly not, your Excellency. (*goes*)

RESIDENT: You should have kept me informed Pilkings. You realize how disastrous it would have been if things had erupted while His Highness was here.

PILKINGS: I wasn't aware of the whole business until tonight sir.

RESIDENT: Nose to the ground Pilkings, nose to the ground. If we all let these little things slip past us where would the empire be eh? Tell me that. Where would we all be?

PILKINGS (*low voice*): Sleeping peacefully at home I bet.

RESIDENT: What did you say Pilkings?

PILKINGS: It won't happen again sir.

RESIDENT: It mustn't Pilkings. It mustn't. Where is that damned sergeant? I ought to get back to His Highness as quickly as possible and offer him some plausible explanation for my rather abrupt conduct. Can you think of one Pilkings?

PILKINGS: You could tell him the truth sir.

RESIDENT: I could? No no no no Pilkings, that would never do. What! Go and tell him there is a riot just two miles away from him? This is supposed to be a secure colony of His Majesty, Pilkings.

PILKINGS: Yes sir.

RESIDENT: Ah, there they are. No, these are not our native police. Are these the ringleaders of the riot?

PILKINGS: Sir, these are my police officers.

RESIDENT: Oh, I beg your pardon officers. You do look a little . . . I say, isn't there something missing in their uniform? I think they used to have some rather colorful sashes. If I remember rightly I recommended them myself in my young days in the service. A bit of color always appeals to the natives, yes, I remember putting that in my report. Well well well, where are we? Make your report man.

PILKINGS (*moves close to* AMUSA, *between his teeth*): And let's have no more superstitious nonsense from you Amusa or I'll throw you in the guardroom for a month and feed you pork!

RESIDENT: What's that? What has pork to do with it?

PILKINGS: Sir, I was just warning him to be brief. I'm sure you are most anxious to hear his report.

RESIDENT: Yes yes yes of course. Come on man, speak up. Hey, didn't we give them some colorful fez hats with all those wavy things, yes, pink tassells . . .

PILKINGS: Sir, I think if he was permitted to make his report we might find that he lost his hat in the riot.

RESIDENT: Ah yes indeed. I'd better tell His Highness that. Lost his hat in the riot, ha ha. He'll probably say well, as long as he didn't lose his head. (*chuckles to himself*) Don't forget to send me a report first thing in the morning young Pilkings.

PILKINGS: No sir.

RESIDENT: And whatever you do, don't let things get out of hand. Keep a cool head and—nose to the ground Pilkings. (*wanders off in the general direction of the hall*)

PILKINGS: Yes sir.

AIDE-DE-CAMP: Would you be needing me sir?

PILKINGS: No thanks Bob. I think His Excellency's need of you is greater than ours.

AIDE-DE-CAMP: We have a detachment of soldiers from the capital sir. They accompanied His Highness up here.

PILKINGS: I doubt if it will come to that but, thanks, I'll bear it in mind. Oh, could you send an orderly with my cloak.

AIDE-DE-CAMP: Very good sir. (*goes*)

PILKINGS: Now Sergeant.

AMUSA: Sir . . . (*Makes an effort, stops dead. Eyes to the ceiling.*)

PILKINGS: Oh, not again.

AMUSA: I cannot against death to dead cult. This dress get power of dead.

PILKINGS: Alright, let's go. You are relieved of all further duty Amusa. Report to me first thing in the morning.

JANE: Shall I come Simon?

PILKINGS: No, there's no need for that. If I can get back later I will. Otherwise get Bob to bring you home.

JANE: Be careful Simon . . . I mean, be clever.

PILKINGS: Sure I will. You two, come with me. (*As he turns to go, the clock in the Residency begins to chime.* PILKINGS *looks at his watch then turns, horror-stricken, to stare at his wife. The same thought clearly occurs to her. He swallows hard. An orderly brings his cloak.*) It's midnight. I had no idea it was that late.

JANE: But surely . . . they don't count the hours the way we do. The moon, or something . . .

PILKINGS: I am . . . not so sure.

He turns and breaks into a sudden run. The two constables follow, also at a run. AMUSA, *who has kept his eyes on the ceiling throughout waits until the last of the footsteps has faded out of hearing. He salutes suddenly, but without once looking in the direction of the woman.*

AMUSA: Goodnight madam.

JANE: Oh. (*She hesitates.*) Amusa . . . (*He goes off without seeming to have heard.*) Poor Simon . . . (*A figure emerges from the shadows, a young black man dressed in a sober western suit. He peeps into the hall, trying to make out the figures of the dancers.*) Who is that?

OLUNDE (*emerging into the light*): I didn't mean to startle you madam. I am looking for the District Officer.

JANE: Wait a minute . . . don't I know you? Yes, you are Olunde, the young man who . . .

OLUNDE: Mrs. Pilkings! How fortunate. I came here to look for your husband.

JANE: Olunde! Let's look at you. What a fine young man you've become. Grand but solemn. Good God, when did you return? Simon never said a word. But you do look well Olunde. Really!

OLUNDE: You are . . . well, you look quite well yourself Mrs. Pilkings. From what little I can see of you.

JANE: Oh this. It's caused quite a stir I assure you, and not all of it very pleasant. You are not shocked I hope?

OLUNDE: Why should I be? But don't you find it rather hot in there? Your skin must find it difficult to breathe.

JANE: Well, it is a little hot I must confess, but it's all in a good cause.

OLUNDE: What cause Mrs. Pilkings?

JANE: All this. The ball. And His Highness being here in person and all that.

OLUNDE (*mildly*): And that is the good cause for which you desecrate an ancestral mask?

JANE: Oh, so you are shocked after all. How disappointing.

OLUNDE: No I am not shocked Mrs. Pilkings. You forget that I have now spent four years among your people. I discovered that you have no respect for what you do not understand.

JANE: Oh. So you've returned with a chip on your shoulder. That's a pity Olunde. I am sorry.

An uncomfortable silence follows.

I take it then that you did not find your stay in England altogether edifying.

OLUNDE: I don't say that. I found your people quite admirable in many ways, their conduct and courage in this war for instance.

JANE: Ah yes the war. Here of course it is all rather remote. From time to time we have a black-out drill just to remind us that there is a war on. And the rare convoy passes through on its way somewhere or on maneuvers. Mind you there is the occasional bit of excitement like that ship that was blown up in the harbor.

OLUNDE: Here? Do you mean through enemy action?

JANE : Oh no, the war hasn't come that close. The captain did it himself. I don't quite understand it really. Simon tried to explain. The ship had to be blown up because it had become dangerous to the other ships, even to the city itself. Hundreds of the coastal population would have died.

OLUNDE: Maybe it was loaded with ammunition and had caught fire. Or some of those lethal gases they've been experimenting on.

JANE: Something like that. The captain blew himself up with it. Deliberately. Simon said someone had to remain on board to light the fuse.

OLUNDE: It must have been a very short fuse.

JANE (*shrugs*): I don't know much about it. Only that there was no other way to save lives. No time to devise anything else. The captain took the decision and carried it out.

OLUNDE: Yes . . . I quite believe it. I met men like that in England.

JANE: Oh just look at me! Fancy welcoming you back with such morbid news. Stale too. It was at least six months ago.

OLUNDE: I don't find it morbid at all. I find it rather inspiring. It is an affirmative commentary on life.

JANE: What is?

OLUNDE: That captain's self-sacrifice.

JANE: Nonsense. Life should never be thrown deliberately away.

OLUNDE: And the innocent people round the harbor?

JANE: Oh, how does one know? The whole thing was probably exaggerated anyway.

OLUNDE: That was a risk the captain couldn't take. But please Mrs. Pilkings, do you think you could find your husband for me? I have to talk to him.

JANE: Simon? Oh. (*as she recollects for the first time the full significance of* OLUNDE'*s presence*) Simon is . . . there is a little problem in town. He was sent for. But . . . when did you arrive? Does Simon know you're here?

OLUNDE (*suddenly earnest*): I need your help Mrs. Pilkings. I've always found you somewhat more understanding than your husband. Please find him for me and when you do, you must help me talk to him.

JANE: I'm afraid I don't quite . . . follow you. Have you seen my husband already?

OLUNDE: I went to your house. Your houseboy told me you were here. (*He smiles.*) He even told me how I would recognize you and Mr. Pilkings.

JANE: Then you must know what my husband is trying to do for you.

OLUNDE: For me?

JANE: For you. For your people. And to think he didn't even know you were coming back! But how do you happen to be here? Only this evening we were talking about you. We thought you were still four thousand miles away.

OLUNDE: I was sent a cable.

JANE: A cable? Who did? Simon? The business of your father didn't begin till tonight.

OLUNDE: A relation sent it weeks ago, and it said nothing about my father. All it said was, Our King is dead. But I knew I had to return home at once so as to bury my father. I understood that.

JANE: Well, thank God you don't have to go through that agony. Simon is going to stop it.

OLUNDE: That's why I want to see him. He's wasting his time. And since he has been so helpful to me I don't want him to incur the enmity of our people. Especially over nothing.

JANE (*sits down open-mouthed*): You . . . you Olunde!

OLUNDE: Mrs. Pilkings, I came home to bury my father. As soon as I heard the news I booked my passage home. In fact we were fortunate. We travelled in the same convoy as your Prince, so we had excellent protection.

JANE: But you don't think your father is also entitled to whatever protection is available to him?

OLUNDE: How can I make you understand? He *has* protection. No one can undertake what he does tonight without the deepest protection the mind can conceive. What can you offer him in place of his peace of mind, in place of the honor and veneration of his own people? What would you think of your Prince if he had refused to accept the risk of losing his life on this voyage? This . . . showing-the-flag tour of colonial possessions.

JANE: I see. So it isn't just medicine you studied in England.

OLUNDE: Yet another error into which your people fall. You believe that everything which appears to make sense was learned from you.

JANE: Not so fast Olunde. You have learned to argue I can tell that, but I never said you made sense. However cleverly you try to put it, it is still a barbaric custom. It is even worse—it's feudal! The king dies and a chieftain must be buried with him. How feudalistic can you get!

OLUNDE: (*Waves his hand towards the background. The* PRINCE *is dancing past again—to a different step—and all the guests are bowing and curtseying as he passes.*): And this? Even in the midst of a devastating war, look at that. What name would you give to that?

JANE: Therapy, British style. The preservation of sanity in the midst of chaos.

OLUNDE: Others would call it decadence. However, it doesn't really interest me. You white races know how to survive; I've seen proof of that. By all logical and natural laws this war should end with all the white races wiping out one another, wiping out their so-called civilization for all time and reverting to a state of primitivism the like of which has so far only existed in your imagination when you thought of us. I thought all that at the beginning. Then I slowly realized that your greatest art is the art of survival. But at least have the humility to let others survive in their own way.

JANE: Through ritual suicide?

OLUNDE: Is that worse than mass suicide? Mrs. Pilkings, what do you call what those young men are sent to do by their generals in this war? Of course you have also mastered the art of calling things by names which don't remotely describe them.

JANE: You talk! You people with your long-winded, roundabout way of making conversation.

OLUNDE: Mrs. Pilkings, whatever we do, we never suggest that a thing is the opposite of what it really is. In your newsreels I heard defeats, thorough, murderous defeats described as strategic victories. No wait, it wasn't just on your newsreels. Don't forget I was attached to hospitals all the time. Hordes of your wounded passed through those wards. I spoke to them. I spent long evenings by their bedside while they spoke terrible truths of the realities of that war. I know now how history is made.

JANE: But surely, in a war of this nature, for the morale of the nation you must expect . . .

OLUNDE: That a disaster beyond human reckoning be spoken of as a triumph? No. I mean, is there no mourning in the home of the bereaved that such blasphemy is permitted?

JANE: (*after a moment's pause*): Perhaps I can understand you now. The time we picked for you was not really one for seeing us at our best.

OLUNDE: Don't think it was just the war. Before that even started I had plenty of time to study your people. I saw nothing, finally, that gave you the right to pass judgement on other peoples and their ways. Nothing at all.

JANE (*hesitantly*): Was it the . . . color thing? I know there is some discrimination.

OLUNDE: Don't make it so simple, Mrs. Pilkings. You make it sound as if when I left, I took nothing at all with me.

JANE: Yes . . . and to tell the truth, only this evening, Simon and I agreed that we never really knew what you left with.

OLUNDE: Neither did I. But I found out over there. I am grateful to your country for that. And I will never give it up.

JANE: Olunde, please . . . promise me something. Whatever you do, don't throw away what you have started to do. You want to be a doctor. My husband and I believe you will make an excellent one, sympathetic and competent. Don't let anything make you throw away your training.

OLUNDE: (*genuinely surprised*): Of course not. What a strange idea. I intend to return and complete my training. Once the burial of my father is over.

JANE: Oh, please . . . !

OLUNDE: Listen! Come outside. You can't hear anything against that music.

JANE: What is it?

OLUNDE: The drums. Can you hear the change? Listen.

The drums come over, still distant but more distinct. There is a change of rhythm, it rises to a crescendo and then, suddenly, it is cut off. After a silence, a new beat begins, slow and resonant.

There. It's all over.

JANE: You mean he's . . .

OLUNDE: Yes Mrs. Pilkings, my father is dead. His will-power has always been enormous; I know he is dead.

JANE (*screams*): How can you be so callous! So unfeeling! You announce your father's own death like a surgeon looking down on some strange . . . stranger's body! You're just a savage like all the rest.

AIDE-DE-CAMP (*rushing out*): Mrs. Pilkings. Mrs. Pilkings. (*She breaks down, sobbing.*) Are you alright, Mrs. Pilkings?

OLUNDE: She'll be alright. (*turns to go*)

AIDE-DE-CAMP: Who are you? And who the hell asked your opinion?

OLUNDE: You're quite right, nobody. (*going*)

AIDE-DE-CAMP: What the hell! Did you hear me ask you who you were?

OLUNDE: I have business to attend to.

AIDE-DE-CAMP: I'll give you business in a moment you impudent nigger. Answer my question!

OLUNDE: I have a funeral to arrange. Excuse me. (*going*)

AIDE-DE-CAMP: I said stop! Orderly!

JANE: No, no, don't do that. I'm alright. And for heaven's sake don't act so foolishly. He's a family friend.

AIDE-DE-CAMP: Well he'd better learn to answer civil questions when he's asked them. These natives put a suit on and they get high opinions of themselves.

OLUNDE: Can I go now?

JANE : No no don't go. I must talk to you. I'm sorry about what I said.

OLUNDE: It's nothing Mrs. Pilkings. And I'm really anxious to go. I couldn't see my father before, it's forbidden for me, his heir and successor to set eyes on him from
the moment of the king's death. But now . . . I would like to touch his body
while it is still warm.

JANE: You will. I promise I shan't keep you long. Only, I couldn't possibly let you go
like that. Bob, please excuse us.

AIDE-DE-CAMP: If you're sure . . .

JANE: Of course I'm sure. Something happened to upset me just then, but I'm alright
now. Really.

The AIDE-DE-CAMP *goes, somewhat reluctantly.*

OLUNDE: I mustn't stay long.

JANE: Please, I promise not to keep you. It's just that . . . oh you saw yourself what
happens to one in this place. The Resident's man thought he was being helpful,
that's the way we all react. But I can't go in among that crowd just now and if I
stay by myself somebody will come looking for me. Please, just say something for a
few moments and then you can go. Just so I can recover myself.

OLUNDE: What do you want me to say?

JANE: Your calm acceptance for instance, can you explain that? It was so unnatural. I
don't understand that at all. I feel a need to understand all I can.

OLUNDE: But you explained it yourself. My medical training perhaps. I have seen death
too often. And the soldiers who returned from the front, they died on our hands
all the time.

JANE: No. It has to be more than that. I feel it has to do with the many things we
don't really grasp about your people. At least you can explain.

OLUNDE: All these things are part of it. And anyway, my father has been dead in my
mind for nearly a month. Ever since I learnt of the King's death. I've lived with my
bereavement so long now that I cannot think of him alive. On that journey on the
boat, I kept my mind on my duties as the one who must perform the rites over his
body. I went through it all again and again in my mind as he himself had taught
me. I didn't want to do anything wrong, something which might jeopardize the
welfare of my people.

JANE: But he had disowned you. When you left he swore publicly you were no longer
his son.

OLUNDE: I told you, he was a man of tremendous will. Sometimes that's another way
of saying stubborn. But among our people, you don't disown a child just like that.
Even if I had died before him I would still be buried like his eldest son. But it's
time for me to go.

JANE: Thank you. I feel calmer. Don't let me keep you from your duties.

OLUNDE: Goodnight Mrs. Pilkings.

JANE: Welcome home. (*She holds out her hand. As he takes it footsteps are heard approaching the drive. A short while later a woman's sobbing is also heard.*)

PILKINGS (*off*): Keep them here till I get back. (*He strides into view, reacts at the sight of*
OLUNDE *but turns to his wife.*) Thank goodness you're still here.

JANE: Simon, what happened?

PILKINGS: Later Jane, please. Is Bob still here?

JANE: Yes, I think so. I'm sure he must be.

PILKINGS: Try and get him out here as quietly as you can. Tell him it's urgent.

JANE: Of course. Oh Simon, you remember . . .

PILKINGS: Yes yes. I can see who it is. Get Bob out here. (*She runs off.*) At first I thought I was seeing a ghost.

OLUNDE: Mr. Pilkings, I appreciate what you tried to do. I want you to believe that. I can only tell you it would have been a terrible calamity if you'd succeeded.

PILKINGS (*opens his mouth several times, shuts it*): You . . . said what?

OLUNDE: A calamity for us, the entire people.

PILKINGS (*sighs*): I see. Hm.

OLUNDE: And now I must go. I must see him before he turns cold.

PILKINGS: Oh ah . . . em . . . but this is a shock to see you. I mean er thinking all this while you were in England and thanking God for that.

OLUNDE: I came on the mail boat. We travelled in the Prince's convoy.

PILKINGS: Ah yes, a-ah, hm . . . er well . . .

OLUNDE: Goodnight. I can see you are shocked by the whole business. But you must know by now there are things you cannot understand—or help.

PILKINGS: Yes. Just a minute. There are armed policemen that way and they have instructions to let no one pass. I suggest you wait a little. I'll er . . . yes, I'll give you an escort.

OLUNDE: That's very kind of you. But do you think it could be quickly arranged.

PILKINGS: Of course. In fact, yes, what I'll do is send Bob over with some men to the er . . . place. You can go with them. Here he comes now. Excuse me a minute.

AIDE-DE-CAMP: Anything wrong sir?

PILKINGS (*takes him to one side*): Listen Bob, that cellar in the disused annex of the Residency, you know, where the slaves were stored before being taken down to the coast . . .

AIDE-DE-CAMP: Oh yes, we use it as a storeroom for broken furniture.

PILKINGS: But it's still got the bars on it?

AIDE-DE-CAMP: Oh yes, they are quite intact.

PILKINGS: Get the keys please. I'll explain later. And I want a strong guard over the Residency tonight.

AIDE-DE-CAMP: We have that already. The detachment from the coast . . .

PILKINGS: No, I don't want them at the gates of the Residency. I want you to deploy them at the bottom of the hill, a long way from the main hall so they can deal with any situation long before the sound carries to the house.

AIDE-DE-CAMP: Yes of course.

PILKINGS: I don't want His Highness alarmed.

AIDE-DE-CAMP: You think the riot will spread here?

PILKINGS: It's unlikely but I don't want to take a chance. I made them believe I was going to lock the man up in my house, which was what I had planned to do in the first place. They are probably assailing it by now. I took a roundabout route here so I don't think there is any danger at all. At least not before dawn. Nobody is to leave the premises of course—the native employees I mean. They'll soon smell something is up and they can't keep their mouths shut.

AIDE-DE-CAMP: I'll give instructions at once.

PILKINGS: I'll take the prisoner down myself. Two policemen will stay with him throughout the night. Inside the cell.

AIDE-DE-CAMP: Right sir. (*salutes and goes off at the double*)

PILKINGS (*to* JANE *, who is returning*): Jane. Bob is coming back in a moment with a detachment. Until he gets back please stay with Olunde. (*He makes an extra warning gesture with his eyes.*)

OLUNDE: Please Mr. Pilkings . . .

PILKINGS: I hate to be stuffy old son, but we have a crisis on our hands. It has to do with your father's affair if you must know. And it happens also at a time when we have His Highness here. I am responsible for security so you'll simply have to do as I say. I hope that's understood. (*marches off quickly, in the direction from which he made his first appearance*)

OLUNDE: What's going on? All this can't be just because he failed to stop my father killing himself.

JANE: I honestly don't know. Could it have sparked off a riot?

OLUNDE: No. If he'd succeeded that would be more likely to start the riot. Perhaps there were other factors involved. Was there a chieftancy dispute?

JANE: None that I know of.

ELESIN (*an animal bellow from off*): Leave me alone! Is it not enough that you have covered me in shame! White man, take your hand from my body!

OLUNDE *stands frozen on the spot.* JANE *understanding at last, tries to move him.*

JANE: Let's go in. It's getting chilly out here.

PILKINGS (*off*): Carry him.

ELESIN: Give me back the name you have taken away from me you ghost from the land of the nameless!

PILKINGS: Carry him! I can't have a disturbance here. Quickly! stuff up his mouth.

JANE: Oh God! Let's go in. Please Olunde. (OLUNDE *does not move.*)

ELESIN: Take your albino's hand from me you . . .

Sounds of a struggle. His voice chokes as he is gagged.

OLUNDE (*quietly*): That was my father's voice.

JANE: Oh you poor orphan, what have you come home to?

There is a sudden explosion of rage from off-stage and powerful steps come running up the drive.

PILKINGS: You bloody fools, after him!

Immediately ELESIN, *in handcuffs, comes pounding in the direction of* JANE *and* OLUNDE *, followed some moments afterwards by* PILKINGS *and the constables.* ELESIN *confronted by the seeming statue of his son, stops dead.* OLUNDE *stares above his head into the distance. The constables try to grab him.* JANE *screams at them.*

JANE: Leave him alone! Simon, tell them to leave him alone.

PILKINGS: All right, stand aside you. (*shrugs*) Maybe just as well. It might help to calm him down.

For several moments they hold the same position. ELESIN *moves a few steps forward, almost as if he's still in doubt.*

ELESIN: Olunde? (*He moves his head, inspecting him from side to side.*) Olunde! (*He collapses slowly at* OLUNDE'*s feet.*) Oh son, don't let the sight of your father turn you blind!

OLUNDE (*he moves for the first time since he heard his voice, brings his head slowly down to look on him*): I have no father, eater of left-overs.

He walks slowly down the way his father had run. Light fades out on ELESIN *, sobbing into the ground.*

ACT FIVE

A wide iron-barred gate stretches almost the whole width of the cell in which ELESIN *is imprisoned. His wrists are encased in thick iron bracelets, chained together; he stands against the bars, looking out. Seated on the ground to one side on the outside is his recent bride, her eyes bent perpetually to the ground. Figures of the two guards can be seen deeper inside the cell, alert to every movement* ELESIN *makes.* PILKINGS *now in a police officer's uniform enters noiselessly, observes him for a while. Then he coughs ostentatiously and approaches. Leans against the bars near a corner, his back to* ELESIN. *He is obviously trying to fall in mood with him. Some moments' silence.*

PILKINGS: You seem fascinated by the moon.

ELESIN (*after a pause*): Yes, ghostly one. Your twin-brother up there engages my thoughts.

PILKINGS: It is a beautiful night.

ELESIN: Is that so?

PILKINGS: The light on the leaves, the peace of the night . . .

ELESIN: The night is not at peace, District Officer.

PILKINGS: No? I would have said it was. You know, quiet . . .

ELESIN: And does quiet mean peace for you?

PILKINGS: Well, nearly the same thing. Naturally there is a subtle difference . . .

ELESIN: The night is not at peace ghostly one. The world is not at peace. You have shattered the peace of the world for ever. There is no sleep in the world tonight.

PILKINGS: It is still a good bargain if the world should lose one night's sleep as the price of saving a man's life.

ELESIN: You did not save my life District Officer. You destroyed it.

PILKINGS: Now come on . . .

ELESIN: And not merely my life but the lives of many. The end of the night's work is not over. Neither this year nor the next will see it. If I wished you well, I would pray that you do not stay long enough on our land to see the disaster you have brought upon us.

PILKINGS: Well, I did my duty as I saw it. I have no regrets.

ELESIN: No. The regrets of life always come later.

Some moments' pause.

You are waiting for dawn white man. I hear you saying to yourself: only so many hours until dawn and then the danger is over. All I must do is keep him alive tonight. You don't quite understand it all but you know that tonight is when what ought to be must be brought about. I shall ease your mind even more, ghostly one. It is not an entire night but a moment of the night, and that moment is past. The moon was my messenger and guide. When it reached a certain gateway in the sky, it touched that moment for which my whole life has been spent in blessings. Even I do not know the gateway. I have stood here and scanned the sky for a glimpse of that door but, I cannot see it. Human eyes are useless for a search of this nature. But in the house of *osugbo*, those who keep watch through the spirit recognized the moment, they sent word to me through the voice of our sacred drums to prepare myself. I heard them and I shed all thoughts of earth. I began to follow the moon to the abode of gods . . . servant of the white king, that was when you entered my chosen place of departure on feet of desecration.

PILKINGS: I'm sorry, but we all see our duty differently.

ELESIN: I no longer blame you. You stole from me my firstborn, sent him to your country so you could turn him into something in your own image. Did you plan it all beforehand? There are moments when it seems part of a larger plan. He who must follow my footsteps is taken from me, sent across the ocean. Then, in my turn, I am stopped from fulfilling my destiny. Did you think it all out before, this plan to push our world from its course and sever the cord that links us to the great origin?

PILKINGS: You don't really believe that. Anyway, if that was my intention with your son, I appear to have failed.

ELESIN: You did not fail in the main thing ghostly one. We know the roof covers the rafters, the cloth covers blemishes; who would have known that the white skin covered our future, preventing us from seeing the death our enemies had prepared for us. The world is set adrift and its inhabitants are lost. Around them, there is nothing but emptiness.

PILKINGS: You son does not take so gloomy a view.

ELESIN: Are you dreaming now white man? Were you not present at my reunion of shame? Did you not see when the world reversed itself and the father fell before his son, asking forgiveness?

PILKINGS: That was in the heat of the moment. I spoke to him and . . . if you want to know, he wishes he could cut out his tongue for uttering the words he did.

ELESIN: No. What he said must never be unsaid. The contempt of my own son rescued something of my shame at your hands. You may have stopped me in my duty but I know now that I did give birth to a son. Once I mistrusted him for seeking the companionship of those my spirit knew as enemies of our race. Now I understand. One should seek to obtain the secrets of his enemies. He will avenge my shame, white one. His spirit will destroy you and yours.

PILKINGS: That kind of talk is hardly called for. If you don't want my consolation . . .

ELESIN: No white man, I do not want your consolation.

PILKINGS: As you wish. Your son anyway, sends his consolation. He asks your forgiveness. When I asked him not to despise you his reply was: I cannot judge him, and if I cannot judge him, I cannot despise him. He wants to come to you to say goodbye and to receive your blessing.

ELESIN: Goodbye? Is he returning to your land?

PILKINGS: Don't you think that's the most sensible thing for him to do? I advised him to leave at once, before dawn, and he agrees that is the right course of action.

ELESIN: Yes, it is best. And even if I did not think so, I have lost the father's place of honor. My voice is broken.

PILKINGS: Your son honors you. If he didn't he would not ask your blessing.

ELESIN: No. Even a thoroughbred is not without pity for the turf he strikes with his hoof. When is he coming?

PILKINGS: As soon as the town is a little quieter. I advised it.

ELESIN: Yes white man, I am sure you advised it. You advise all our lives although on the authority of what gods, I do not know.

PILKINGS (*Opens his mouth to reply, then appears to change his mind. Turns to go. Hesitates and stops again.*): Before I leave you, may I ask just one thing of you?

ELESIN: I am listening.

PILKINGS: I wish to ask you to search the quiet of your heart and tell me—do you not find great contradictions in the wisdom of your own race?

ELESIN: Make yourself clear, white one.

PILKINGS: I have lived among you long enough to learn a saying or two. One came to my mind tonight when I stepped into the market and saw what was going on. You were surrounded by those who egged you on with song and praises. I thought, are these not the same people who say: the elder grimly approaches heaven and you ask him to bear your greetings yonder; do you really think he makes the journey willingly? After that, I did not hesitate.

A pause. ELESIN *sighs. Before he can speak a sound of running feet is heard.*

JANE (*off*): Simon! Simon!
PILKINGS: What on earth. . . ! (*runs off*)

ELESIN *turns to his new wife, gazes on her for some moments.*

ELESIN: My young bride, did you hear the ghostly one? You sit and sob in your silent heart but say nothing to all this. First I blamed the white man, then I blamed my gods for deserting me. Now I feel I want to blame you for the mystery of the sapping of my will. But blame is a strange peace offering for a man to bring a world he has deeply wronged, and to its innocent dwellers. Oh little mother, I have taken countless women in my life but you were more than a desire of the flesh. I needed you as the abyss across which my body must be drawn, I filled it with earth and dropped my seed in it at the moment of preparedness for my crossing. You were the final gift of the living to their emissary to the land of the ancestors, and perhaps your warmth and youth brought new insights of this world to me and turned my feet leaden on this side of the abyss. For I confess to you, daughter, my weakness came not merely from the abomination of the white man who came violently into my fading presence, there was also a weight of longing on my earth-held limbs. I would have shaken it off, already my foot had begun to lift but then, the white ghost entered and all was defiled.

Approaching voices of PILKINGS *and his wife.*

JANE: Oh Simon, you will let her in won't you?
PILKINGS: I really wish you'd stop interfering.

They come in view. JANE *is in a dressing-gown.* PILKINGS *is holding a note to which he refers from time to time.*

JANE: Good gracious, I didn't initiate this. I was sleeping quietly, or trying to anyway, when the servant brought it. It's not my fault if one can't sleep undisturbed even in the Residency.
PILKINGS: He'd have done the same if we were sleeping at home so don't sidetrack the issue. He knows he can get round you or he wouldn't send you the petition in the first place.
JANE: Be fair Simon. After all he was thinking of your own interests. He is grateful you know, you seem to forget that. He feels he owes you something.
PILKINGS: I just wish they'd leave this man alone tonight, that's all.
JANE: Trust him Simon. He's pledged his word it will all go peacefully.
PILKINGS: Yes, and that's the other thing. I don't like being threatened.
JANE: Threatened? (*takes the note*) I didn't spot any threat.
PILKINGS: It's there. Veiled, but it's there. The only way to prevent serious rioting tomorrow—what a cheek!
JANE: I don't think he's threatening you Simon.
PILKINGS: He's picked up the idiom alright. Wouldn't surprise me if he's been mixing

with commies or anarchists over there. The phrasing sounds too good to be true. Damn! If only the Prince hadn't picked this time for his visit.

JANE: Well, even so Simon, what have you got to lose? You don't want a riot on your hands, not with the Prince here.

PILKINGS (*going up to* ELESIN): Let's see what he has to say. Chief Elesin, there is yet another person who wants to see you. As she is not a next-of-kin I don't really feel obliged to let her in. But your son sent a note with her, so it's up to you.

ELESIN: I know who that must be. So she found out your hiding-place. Well, it was not difficult. My stench of shame is so strong, it requires no hunter's dog to follow it.

PILKINGS: If you don't want to see her, just say so and I'll send her packing.

ELESIN: Why should I not want to see her? Let her come. I have no more holes in my rag of shame. All is laid bare.

PILKINGS: I'll bring her in. (*goes off*)

JANE (*hesitates, then goes to* ELESIN): Please, try and understand. Everything my husband did was for the best.

ELESIN (*He gives her a long strange stare, as if he is trying to understand who she is.*): You are the wife of the District Officer?

JANE: Yes. My name, is Jane.

ELESIN: That is my wife sitting down there. You notice how still and silent she sits? My business is with your husband.

PILKINGS *returns with* IYALOJA.

PILKINGS: Here she is. Now first I want your word of honor that you will try nothing foolish.

ELESIN: Honor? White one, did you say you wanted my word of honor?

PILKINGS: I know you to be an honorable man. Give me your word of honor you will receive nothing from her.

ELESIN: But I am sure you have searched her clothing as you would never dare touch your own mother. And there are these two lizards of yours who roll their eyes even when I scratch.

PILKINGS: And I shall be sitting on that tree trunk watching even how you blink. Just the same I want your word that you will not let her pass anything to you.

ELESIN: You have my honor already. It is locked up in that desk in which you will put away your report of this night's events. Even the honor of my people you have taken already; it is tied together with those papers of treachery which make you masters in this land.

PILKINGS: Alright. I am trying to make things easy but if you must bring in politics we'll have to do it the hard way. Madam, I want you to remain along this line and move no nearer to that cell door. Guards! (*They spring to attention.*) If she moves beyond this point, blow your whistle. Come on Jane. (*They go off.*)

IYALOJA: How boldly the lizard struts before the pigeon when it was the eagle itself he promised us he would confront.

ELESIN: I don't ask you to take pity on me Iyaloja. You have a message for me or you would not have come. Even if it is the curses of the world, I shall listen,

IYALOJA: You made so bold with the servant of the white king who took your side against death. I must tell your brother chiefs when I return how bravely you waged war against him. Especially with words.

ELESIN: I more than deserve your scorn.

IYALOJA (*with sudden anger*): I warned you, if you must leave a seed behind, be sure it is not tainted with the curses of the world. Who are you to open a new life when you dared not open the door to a new existence? I say who are you to make so bold? (*The* BRIDE *sobs and* IYALOJA *notices her. Her contempt noticeably increases as she turns back to* ELESIN.) Oh you self-vaunted stem of the plantain, how hollow it all proves. The pith is gone in the parent stem, so how will it prove with the new shoot? How will it go with that earth that bears it? Who are you to bring this abomination on us!

ELESIN: My powers deserted me. My charms, my spells, even my voice lacked strength when I made to summon the powers that would lead me over the last measure of earth into the land of the fleshless. You saw it, Iyaloja. You saw me struggle to retrieve my will from the power of the stranger whose shadow fell across the doorway and left me floundering and blundering in a maze I had never before encountered. My senses were numbed when the touch of cold iron came upon my wrists. I could do nothing to save myself.

IYALOJA: You have betrayed us. We fed your sweetmeats such as we hoped awaited you on the other side. But you said No, I must eat the world's left-overs. We said you were the hunter who brought the quarry down; to you belonged the vital portions of the game. No, you said, I am the hunter's dog and I shall eat the entrails of the game and the faeces of the hunter. We said you were the hunter returning home in triumph, a slain buffalo pressing down on his neck; you said wait, I first must turn up this cricket hole with my toes. We said yours was the doorway at which we first spy the tapper when he comes down from the tree, yours was the blessing of the twilight wine, the purl that brings night spirits out of doors to steal their portion before the light of day. We said yours was the body of wine whose burden shakes the tapper like a sudden gust on his perch. You said, No, I am content to lick the dregs from each calabash when the drinkers are done. We said, the dew on earth's surface was for you to wash your feet along the slopes of honor. You said No, I shall step in the vomit of cats and the droppings of mice; I shall fight them for the left-overs of the world.

ELESIN: Enough Iyaloja, enough.

IYALOJA: We called you leader and oh, how you led us on. What we have no intention of eating should not be held to the nose.

ELESIN: Enough, enough. My shame is heavy enough.

IYALOJA: Wait. I came with a burden.

ELESIN: You have more than discharged it.

IYALOJA: I wish I could pity you.

ELESIN: I need neither your pity nor the pity of the world. I need understanding. Even I need to understand. You were present at my defeat. You were part of the beginnings. You brought about the renewal of my tie to earth, you helped in the binding of the cord.

IYALOJA: I gave you warning. The river which fills up before our eyes does not sweep us away in its flood.

ELESIN: What were warnings beside the moist contact of living earth between my fingers? What were warnings beside the renewal of famished embers lodged eternally in the heart of man? But even that, even if it overwhelmed one with a thousand-fold temptations to linger a little while, a man could overcome it. It is when the alien hand pollutes the source of will, when a stranger force of violence shatters the mind's calm resolution, this is when a man is made to commit the awful treachery of relief, commit in his thought the unspeakable blasphemy of seeing the hand of the gods in this alien rupture of his world. I know it was this thought that killed me, sapped my powers and turned me into an infant in the hands of unnamable strangers. I made to utter my spells anew but my tongue merely rattled in my mouth. I fingered hidden charms and the contact was damp; there was no spark left to sever the life-strings that should stretch from every finger-tip. My will was squelched in the spittle of an alien race, and all because I had committed this blasphemy of thought—that there might be the hand of the gods in a stranger's intervention.

IYALOJA: Explain it how you will, I hope it brings you peace of mind. The bush-rat fled his rightful cause, reached the market and set up a lamentation. "Please save me!"—are these fitting words to hear from an ancestral mask? "There's a wild beast at my heels" is not becoming language from a hunter.

ELESIN: May the world forgive me.

IYALOJA: I came with a burden I said. It approaches the gates which are so well guarded by those jackals whose spittle will from this day on be your food and drink. But first, tell me, you who were once Elesin Oba, tell me, you who know so well the cycle of the plantain: is it the parent shoot which withers to give sap to the younger or, does your wisdom see it running the other way?

ELESIN: I don't see your meaning Iyaloja?

IYALOJA: Did I ask you for a meaning? I asked a question. Whose trunk withers to give sap to the other? The parent shoot or the younger?

ELESIN: The parent.

IYALOJA: Ah. So you do know that. There are sights in this world which say different Elesin. There are some who choose to reverse this cycle of our being. Oh you emptied bark that the world once saluted for a pith-laden being, shall I tell you what the gods have claimed of you?

In her agitation she steps beyond the line indicated by PILKINGS *and the air is rent by piercing whistles. The two* GUARDS *also leap forward and place safe-guarding hands on* ELESIN. IYALOJA *stops, astonished.* PILKINGS *comes racing in, followed by* JANE.

PILKINGS: What is it? Did they try something?

GUARD: She stepped beyond the line.

ELESIN (*in a broken voice*): Let her alone. She meant no harm.

IYALOJA: Oh Elesin, see what you've become. Once you had no need to open your mouth in explanation because evil-smelling goats, itchy of hand and foot had lost their senses. And it was a brave man indeed who dared lay hands on you because Iyaloja stepped from one side of the earth onto another. Now look at the spectacle of your life. I grieve for you.

PILKINGS: I think you'd better leave. I doubt you have done him much good by coming here. I shall make sure you are not allowed to see him again. In any case we are moving him to a different place before dawn, so don't bother to come back.

IYALOJA: We foresaw that. Hence the burden I trudged here to lay beside your gates.

PILKINGS: What was that you said?

IYALOJA: Didn't our son explain? Ask that one. He knows what it is. At least we hope the man we once knew as Elesin remembers the lesser oaths he need not break.

PILKINGS: Do you know what she is talking about?

ELESIN: Go to the gates, ghostly one. Whatever you find there, bring it to me.

IYALOJA: Not yet. It drags behind me on the slow, weary feet of women. Slow as it is Elesin, it has long overtaken you. It rides ahead of your laggard will.

PILKINGS: What is she saying now? Christ! Must your people forever speak in riddles?

ELESIN: It will come white man, it will come. Tell your men at the gates to let it through.

PILKINGS (*dubiously*): I'll have to see what it is.

IYALOJA: You will. (*passionately*) But this is one oath he cannot shirk. White one, you have a king here, a visitor from your land. We know of his presence here. Tell me, were he to die would you leave his spirit roaming restlessly on the surface of earth? Would you bury him here among those you consider less than human? In your land have you no ceremonies of the dead?

PILKINGS: Yes. But we don't make our chiefs commit suicide to keep him company.

IYALOJA: Child, I have not come to help your understanding. (*points to* ELESIN) This is the man whose weakened understanding holds us in bondage to you. But ask him if you wish. He knows the meaning of a king's passage; he was not born yesterday. He knows the peril to the race when our dead father, who goes as intermediary, waits and waits and knows he is betrayed. He knows when the narrow gate was opened and he knows it will not stay for laggards who drag their feet in dung and vomit, whose lips are reeking of the left-overs of lesser men. He knows he has condemned our king to wander in the void of evil with beings who are enemies of life.

PILKINGS: Yes er . . . but look here . . .

IYALOJA: What we ask is little enough. Let him release our King so he can ride on homewards alone. The messenger is on his way on the backs of women. Let him send word through the heart that is folded up within the bolt. It is the least of all his oaths, it is the easiest fulfilled.

The AIDE-DE-CAMP *runs in.*

PILKINGS: Bob?

AIDE-DE-CAMP: Sir, there's a group of women chanting up the hill.

PILKINGS (*rounding on* IYALOJA): If you people want trouble . . .

JANE: Simon, I think that's what Olunde referred to in his letter.

PILKINGS: He knows damned well I can't have a crowd here! Damn it, I explained the delicacy of my position to him. I think it's about time I got him out of town. Bob, send a car and two or three soldiers to bring him in. I think the sooner he takes his leave of his father and gets out the better.

IYALOJA: Save your labor white one. If it is the father of your prisoner you want, Olunde, he who until this night we knew as Elesin's son, he comes soon himself to take his leave. He has sent the women ahead, so let them in.

PILKINGS *remains undecided.*

AIDE-DE-CAMP: What do we do about the invasion? We can still stop them far from here.

PILKINGS: What do they look like?

AIDE-DE-CAMP: They're not many. And they seem quite peaceful.

PILKINGS: No men?

AIDE-DE-CAMP: Mm, two or three at the most.

JANE: Honestly, Simon, I'd trust Olunde. I don't think he'll deceive you about their intentions.

PILKINGS: He'd better not. Alright, let them in Bob. Warn them to control themselves. Then hurry Olunde here. Make sure he brings his baggage because I'm not returning him into town.

AIDE-DE-CAMP: Very good sir. (*goes*)

PILKINGS (*to* IYALOJA): I hope you understand that if anything goes wrong it will be on your head. My men have orders to shoot at the first sign of trouble.

IYALOJA: To prevent one death you will actually make other deaths? Ah, great is the wisdom of the white race. But have no fear. Your Prince will sleep peacefully. So at long last will ours. We will disturb you no further, servant of the white king. Just let Elesin fulfil his oath and we will retire home and pay homage to our King.

JANE: I believe her Simon, don't you?

PILKINGS: Maybe.

ELESIN: Have no fear ghostly one. I have a message to send my King and then you have nothing more to fear.

IYALOJA: Olunde would have done it. The chiefs asked him to speak the words but he said no, not while you lived.

ELESIN: Even from the depths to which my spirit has sunk, I find some joy that this little has been left to me.

The women enter, intoning the dirge "Ale le le" and swaying from side to side. On their shoulders is borne a longish object roughly like a cylindrical bolt, covered in cloth. They set it down on the spot where IYALOJA *had stood earlier, and form a semi-circle round it. The* PRAISE-SINGER *and* DRUMMER *stand on the inside of the semi-circle but the drum is not used at all. The* DRUMMER *intones under the* PRAISE-SINGER'*s invocations.*

PILKINGS (*as they enter*): What is *that?*

IYALOJA: The burden you have made white one, but we bring it in peace.

PILKINGS: I said *what* is it?

ELESIN: White man, you must let me out. I have a duty to perform.

PILKINGS: I most certainly will not.

ELESIN: There lies the courier of my King. Let me out so I can perform what is demanded of me.

PILKINGS: You'll do what you need to do from inside there or not at all. I've gone as far as I intend to with this business.

ELESIN: The worshipper who lights a candle in your church to bear a message to his god bows his head and speaks in a whisper to the flame. Have I not seen it ghostly one? His voice does not ring out to the world. Mine are no words for anyone's ears. They are not words even for the bearers of this load. They are words I must speak secretly, even as my father whispered them in my ears and I in the ears of my first-born. I cannot shout them to the wind and the open night-sky.

JANE: Simon . . .

PILKINGS: Don't interfere. Please!

IYALOJA: They have slain the favorite horse of the king and slain his dog. They have borne them from pulse to pulse center of the land receiving prayers for their king. But the rider has chosen to stay behind. Is it too much to ask that he speak his heart to heart of the waiting courier? (PILKINGS *turns his back on her.*) So be it. Elesin Oba, you see how even the mere leavings are denied you. (*She gestures to the* PRAISE-SINGER.)

PRAISE-SINGER: Elesin Oba! I call you by that name only this last time. Remember when I said, if you cannot come, tell my horse. (*pause*) What? I cannot hear you? I said, if you cannot come, whisper in the ears of my horse. Is your tongue severed from the roots Elesin? I can hear no response. I said, if there are boulders you cannot climb, mount my horse's back, this spotless black stallion, he'll bring you over them. (*pauses*) Elesin Oba, once you had a tongue that darted like a drummer's stick. I said, if you get lost my dog will track a path to me. My memory fails me but I think you replied: My feet have found the path, Alafin.

The dirge rises and falls.

I said at the last, if evil hands hold you back, just tell my horse there is weight on the hem of your smock. I dare not wait too long.

The dirge rises and falls.

There lies the swiftest ever messenger of a king, so set me free with the errand of your heart. There lie the head and heart of the favorite of the gods, whisper in his ears. Oh my companion, if you had followed when you should, we would not say that the horse preceded its rider. If you had followed when it was time, we would not say the dog has raced beyond and left his master behind. If you had raised your will to cut the thread of life at the summons of the drums, we would not say your mere shadow fell across the gateway and took its owner's place at the banquet. But the hunter, laden with a slain buffalo, stayed to root in the cricket's hole with his toes. What now is left? If there is a dearth of bats, the pigeon must serve us for the offering. Speak the words over your shadow which must now serve in your place.

ELESIN: I cannot approach. Take off the cloth. I shall speak my message from heart to heart of silence.

IYALOJA (*moves forward and removes the covering*): Your courier Elesin, cast your eyes on the favored companion of the King.

Rolled up in the mat, his head and feet showing at either end is the body of OLUNDE.

There lies the honor of your household and of our race. Because he could not bear to let honor fly out of doors, he stopped it with his life. The son has proved the father Elesin, and there is nothing left in your mouth to gnash but infant gums.

PRAISE-SINGER: Elesin, we placed the reins of the world in your hands yet you watched it plunge over the edge of the bitter precipice. You sat with folded arms while evil strangers tilted the world from its course and crashed it beyond the edge of emptiness—you muttered, there is little that one man can do, you left us floundering in a blind future. Your heir has taken the burden on himself. What the end will be, we are not gods to tell. But this young shoot has poured its sap into the parent stalk, and we know this is not the way of life. Our world is tumbling in the void of strangers, Elesin.

ELESIN *has stood rock-still, his knuckles taut on the bars, his eyes glued to the body of his son. The stillness seizes and paralyzes everyone, including* PILKINGS *who has turned to look. Suddenly* ELESIN *flings one arm round his neck, once, and with the loop of the chain, strangles himself in a swift, decisive pull. The guards rush forward to stop him but they are only in time to let his body down.* PILKINGS *has leapt to the door at the same time and struggles with the lock. He rushes within, fumbles with the handcuffs and unlocks them, raises the body to a sitting position while he tries to give resuscitation. The women continue their dirge, unmoved by the sudden event.*

IYALOJA: Why do you strain yourself? Why do you labor at tasks for which no one, not even the man lying there would give you thanks? He is gone at last into the passage but oh, how late it all is. His son will feast on the meat and throw him bones. The passage is clogged with droppings from the King's stallion; he will arrive all stained in dung.

PILKINGS (*in a tired voice*): Was this what you wanted?

IYALOJA: No child, it is what you brought to be, you who play with strangers' lives, who even usurp the vestments of our dead, yet believe that the stain of death will not cling to you. The gods demanded only the old expired plantain but you cut down the sap-laden shoot to feed your pride. There is your board, filled to overflowing. Feast on it. (*She screams at him suddenly, seeing that* PILKINGS *is about to close* ELESIN's *staring eyes.*) Let him alone! However sunk he was in debt he is no pauper's carrion abandoned on the road. Since when have strangers donned clothes of indigo before the bereaved cries out his loss?

She turns to the BRIDE *who has remained motionless throughout.*

Child.

The girl takes up a little earth, walks calmly into the cell and closes ELESIN's *eyes. She then pours some earth over each eyelid and comes out again.*

Now forget the dead, forget even the living. Turn your mind only to the unborn.

She goes off, accompanied by the BRIDE. *The dirge rises in volume and the women continue their sway. Lights fade to a black-out.*

THE RECEPTIVE READER

1. Soyinka's play takes us to a culture with a strong oral tradition. What is the role of proverbs or folk wisdom in the play? What are striking examples of ceremonial exchanges? Where else in the play do you see evidence of a strong oral tradition?

2. Writing about this play, Soyinka has talked about our human need for "coming to terms with death." He has talked about "humoring it," making it part of a communal experience, so as to make it more bearable for the individual. How and how much do you learn in this play about the tribal traditions concerning death and the burial of the mighty?

3. In much of the play, scenes reflecting the indigenous culture alternate with scenes in which the British colonials play out their role. What is the result of this playing off the white people's Africa against the African's Africa? What are striking ironic contrasts? How do contrasting attitudes toward the ceremonial *egungun* costume serve as a test case?

4. What is the role of the market women in the play? What is the role of Iyaloja, their leader? In the early scenes, what is their attitude toward the Elesin? How does it change? When they taunt Amusa, what is the target of their satire?

5. Some critics have discovered in the play early hints that *foreshadow* the Elesin's weakness and his later failure to live up to his mission. Do you see ominous signs of self-indulgence, of being too attached to the things of this world?

6. Olunde's return from England sets the stage for a climactic confrontation of a European and an African point of view. (What was the purpose of Olunde's return?) Olunde's European education, as Jane Pilkings says, has taught him to argue. What is the merit of his contrasting the single ceremonial suicide of local tradition with the "mass suicide" of European wars? In the same scene, the treatment of Olunde by Jane Pilkings and the aide-de-camp speaks volumes on traditional race relations. What is the scene designed to show?

7. When did you suspect what the ending would be? How is it revealed? How do you react to it?

8. One of Soyinka's plays transposed a Greek tragedy (*The Bacchae* by Euripides) to an African setting. Could the Elesin be called a tragic hero? Does he have tragic qualities? Why or why not?

THE PERSONAL RESPONSE

Some Nigerian critics have taken Soyinka to task for glorifying a "backward" custom. They have accused him of honoring a "feudal" status society where power and wealth went to a small hereditary tribal elite. Coming to his defense, one critic has claimed that Soyinka was indirectly criticizing the tradition and that the play shows him in sympathy with the Elesin's "basic human instinct for survival." What do *you* think is the playwright's relation to the tribal tradition and to the Elesin? What is your own attitude?

CROSS-REFERENCES—For Discussion or Writing

Both Soyinka's play and Sophocles' *Antigone* dramatize the paramount importance of burial customs and funeral ceremonies in a traditional society. In both, a central character faces a fateful choice; in both, secular authority interferes with the dictates of tradition; in both, minor characters act as a chorus. Compare and contrast the role of tradition in the two plays.

EXPLORATIONS

Language as Medium

> BILL MOYERS: *I was going to ask you, don't you grow weary of thinking black, writing black, being asked questions about being black?*
> AUGUST WILSON: *How could one grow weary of that? Whites don't get tired of thinking white or being who they are. I'm just who I am. You never transcend who you are. Black is not limiting. There's no idea in the world that is not contained by black life. I could write forever about the black experience in America.*

Language—our home dialect, the talk of home and neighborhood—is an integral part of who we are. Even when it is overlaid by the language of school and office, our way of talking is likely to preserve the flavor of our linguistic past. It is likely to be made human and individual by echoes of down-home speech—deplored by some, but cherished by others. In the past, when members of minority groups appeared on the stage, they often spoke a homogenized stage English. Luis Valdez' Teatro Campesino broke new ground when it had Mexican Americans repeatedly switch from English to Spanish (especially when mocking "the Man").

August Wilson is a black American playwright whose endlessly talkative and articulate characters speak black English. What features of it do you recognize? How would you react to it as a theatergoer or reader? The following excerpt is from Wilson's *The Piano Lesson*, a play first staged by the Yale Repertory Theatre in 1988.

A U G U S T   W I L S O N   (born 1945)

How Avery Got to Be Preacher   1987

From *The Piano Lesson*

BOY WILLIE: How you get to be a preacher, Avery? I might want to be a preacher one day. Have everybody call me Reverend Boy Willie.

AVERY: It come to me in a dream. God called me and told me he wanted me to be a shepherd for his flock. That's what I'm gonna call my church . . . The Good Shepherd Church of God in Christ.

DOAKER: Tell him what you told me. Tell him about the three hobos.

AVERY: Boy Willie don't want to hear all that.

LYMON: I do. Lots a people say your dreams can come true.

AVERY: Naw. You don't want to hear all that.

DOAKER: Go on. I told him you was a preacher. He didn't want to believe me. Tell him about the three hobos.

AVERY: Well, it come to me in a dream. See . . . I was sitting out in this railroad yard watching the trains go by. The train stopped and these three hobos got off. They told me they had come from Nazareth and was on their way to Jerusalem. They had three candles. They gave me one and told me to light it . . . but to be careful that it didn't go out. Next thing I knew I was standing in front of this house. Something told me to go knock on the door. This old woman opened the door and said they had been waiting on me. Then she led me into this room. It was a big room and it was full of all kinds of different people. They looked like anybody else except they all had sheep heads and was making noise like sheep make. I heard somebody call my name. I looked around and there was these same three hobos. They told me to take off my clothes and they give me a blue robe with gold thread. They washed my feet and combed my hair. Then they showed me these three doors and told me to pick one.

I went through one of them doors and that flame leapt off that candle and it seemed like my whole head caught fire. I looked around and there was four or five other men standing there with these same blue robes on. Then we heard a voice tell us to look out across this valley. We looked out and saw the valley was full of wolves. The voice told us that these sheep people that I had seen in the other room had to go over to the other side of this valley and somebody had to take them. Then I heard another voice say, "Who shall I send?" Next thing I knew I said, "Here I am. Send me." That's when I met Jesus. He say, "If you go, I'll go with you." Something told me to say, "Come on. Let's go." That's when I woke up. My head still felt like it was on fire . . . but I had a peace about myself that was hard to explain. I knew right then that I had been filled with the Holy Ghost and called to be a servant of the Lord. It took me a while before I could accept that. But then a lot of little ways God showed me that it was true. So I became a preacher.

LYMON: I see why you gonna call it the Good Shepherd Church. You dreaming about them sheep people. I can see that easy.

                                                                (Act One, Scene 1)

THE RECEPTIVE READER

1. A reviewer in the *New York Times* said about *The Piano Lesson* that "the play's real music is in the language." What did he mean?

2. In the past, regional or cultural varieties of English have often been the subject of ridicule. Do you think college audiences of your generation are ready to accept the use of language in this play ? Why or why not?

3. What role do language differences—for example, Southern speech, British accents, street language—play in American popular culture today? Do you think their role has changed over the years?

WRITING ABOUT LITERATURE

30. Branching Out (Independent Reading or Viewing)

The Writing Workshop   The test of what you have learned about drama comes when you encounter a new play or an unfamiliar classic on your own. As a theatergoer, you sooner or later have to start trusting your own judgment (if only to decide on what to spend your ticket money). What made a play like Shaffer's *Equus* or *Amadeus* a huge audience success? Why did Samuel Beckett's *Waiting for Godot* run for three hundred consecutive performances in Paris? Why was it translated into Swedish, Japanese, Yugoslavian, and many other languages and produced around the world? What did audiences see in Beth Henley's *Crimes of the Heart*—the play and the movie? What, in a few short years, has made a new black playwright like August Wilson—*Joe Turner's Come and Gone* (1988), *The Piano Lesson* (1987)—a major figure in American drama?

Consider the following guidelines when you write about your own independent reading, viewing, or playgoing:

✧ *If possible, give yourself a head start.* For instance, choose a play that was the subject of a much-discussed local production. Or choose a play that was made into a movie with a stellar cast (and perhaps with modifications and adaptations that split the critical community in half). Or decide to make first-hand acquaintance with a modern classic that you have often seen mentioned but never came to know.

✧ *Check out the critics' reactions.* You may want to turn to critics or reviewers for pointers and helpful background. You may want to let a first-rate reviewer or critic focus your attention. What have knowledgeable people said about this play? How have they reacted? What questions have the critics raised? Remember, however, not to let the critics answer all your questions for you. You are the spectator (or reader). A critic, as someone said, can no more experience the play for you than a restaurant critic can eat your dinner.

✧ *If you can, quote insiders or people in the know.* Look at comments by author, director, or actors for perspective or guidance in interpretation. Draw on their comments to give your paper the insider's touch.

✧ *Give the new and difficult the benefit of the doubt.* The easiest way to deal with something perplexing is to reject it as wrongheaded or willfully obscure. However, remember those who passed up the chance to buy for the price of a lunch the paintings by Van Gogh that now sell for a million dollars.

❖ *Push toward a central question or unifying theme.* For instance, a play from the theater of the absurd may at first sound or read like inspired nonsense. Does it perhaps actually raise serious questions about society? Does it perhaps hold the mirror up to human nature after all—even though we might not like the reflection we see? About another play, you might ask what makes it a breakthrough in our prejudice-ridden, stereotype-riddled world. In August Wilson's *The Piano Lesson,* is the play's use of down-home dialect and uneducated characters going to be offensive to educated middle-class blacks (or to white liberals who want to be politically correct)?

❖ *Anchor your impressions, conclusions, and judgments to the actual text of the play.* Make extensive use of short, apt quotation. Highlight revealing key quotes. Weave a rich tapestry of firsthand references to the play.

The following sample paper was first published in a student literary magazine. What are strong features that may have moved the editors to print the paper?

SAMPLE STUDENT PAPER

Karen Traficante

In Defense of *The American Dream*

Robert Brustein, in his attempt to discredit Edward Albee's play *The American Dream,* claimed there was an "absence of any compelling theme, commitment, or sense of life." Are these accusations true? And if so, do they classify the play as a "fumble"? Harold Clurman's review of the play in the *Nation* advised that Albee "stick closer to the facts of life so his plays may remain humanly and socially relevant." How far does Albee stray?

In order for this play to have a "compelling theme, commitment, or sense of life," a struggle or conflict is needed. But no struggle is found. There is no "man against society" here. The conventional Mommy and Daddy are relatively content with their lives. It does not matter to them that they are living conformities. There are no carrots in their family tree of apples. Mommy and Daddy are typical Jonathan apples. And they don't care. They carry their dull lives to an extreme. Everything about them points to their lack of originality. Their apartment shows no personality. The hideous gilded furniture and frames with no pictures point to their lack of individualism. Socially accepted Mrs. Barker is actually a "dreadful woman"; however, realizing that she is a professional woman and that one is expected to like such elite people, Mommy goes on and explains, "but she is chairman of our woman's club, so naturally I'm terribly fond of her." Naturally! No attempts are made to struggle against society and its conformities here either. And thus, with no struggle, no theme. But the play doesn't need a "theme." It is a parable and a parody. It makes its readers question, struggle, and laugh at the absurdity of their human freedoms. It gives its readers a theme to live by: that is, man against society, mechanization, conformity. The play is not a "fumble"; it is a successful defensive play.

Albee's characters and their lives are exaggerated examples of human mass existence and experience. But he does not deviate that far from the truth. Daniel Bell, in an article on the "Theory of Mass Society," said, "The sense of a radical dehumanization of life which has accompanied events of the past several decades has given rise to the theory of 'mass society.'" And this present mass society has lessened the possibility for "persons of achieving a sense of individual self in our mechanized society." There exists a majority of conventional Mommies and Daddies, and their dull lives are common to many. The uninventive apartment of the play is similar to some modern flats of our society: the rugs blend with the walls which in turn fuse with the upholstery which is highlighted by the paintings on the walls. Why do people tend to buy expensive pictures merely because the wood frame matches their fruitwood cocktail table and the artist's pigments match the color scheme of the room? Paintings are not a part of the furniture. They are unique expressions; they are art.

Mommy and Daddy are overjoyed with the arrival of the new "bumble." He is a "Clean-cut midwest farm boy type, almost insultingly good-looking in a typically American way. . . ." And don't most parents look for these traits in their own offspring? They not only conform, but expect their child to fit the mold as well. Mommy and Daddy's first bumble would not concede, and so he was chopped up and thrown away. Mommy and Daddy wanted only another Jonathan apple. Realistically, modern Mommies and Daddies do not chop up their undesired youth. They may, however, smother their children's individualism or simply break ties with them. Brabantio abandoned his lovely daughter Desdemona in Shakespeare's Othello. Why? Because she deviated from his hopes and from society's ideals as well. And so it is true of our modern Mommies and Daddies; unmarried pregnant daughters are banned from their homes; interracial and interreligious marriages cause conflict or rejection. So Albee is not straying far from the truth when his Mommy and Daddy throw away their stubborn bumble.

A predominant condition which exists in our world is an inability to communicate. Mommy and Daddy, though married, are essentially strangers. Their daily conversations are vacuums filled with clichés, small talk, and trivialities. Daddy avoids really talking to Mommy. He simply responds with "Have they!" or "Yes . . . yes . . .," barely recognizing what she is saying. Their marriage exists only in custom. There is no love bond established because they lack the communication necessary to understand one another and thus to love.

Mrs. Barker and Mommy also make some fruitless attempts at social intercourse. With their automatic replies, however, they miss the true substance of what seem to be urbanities: "My, what an unattractive apartment you have!" "Yes, but you don't know what a trouble it is."

Without a "compelling theme, commitment, or sense of life," Albee successfully brings his readers' attentions to the paralysis of conformity, the failure of communication, and a vision of a future world. The vision is exaggerated to the point of humor and horror. But by its existence, it points out the urgency for alterations, struggle, and reform.

QUESTIONS

What, according to this paper, accounted for the critics' hostility or lack of comprehension? What are the major points in the student writer's defense of the play? How convincing is her interpretation? How well supported is it? What are some of her most telling points? Does she make you want to see this kind of play?

Plays for Independent Reading

Edward Albee	*The American Dream, The Zoo Story*
Imamu Amiri Baraka	*The Dutchman*
Samuel Beckett	*Waiting for Godot*
Caryl Churchill	*Top Girls*
Bertolt Brecht	*Mother Courage, Galileo, The Good Woman of Setzuan*
Beth Henley	*Crimes of the Heart*
Eugène Ionesco	*The Bald Soprano, The Chairs*
David Mamet	*American Buffalo*
Sean O'Casey	*Juno and the Paycock, Red Roses for Me*
Harold Pinter	*The Homecoming, The Birthday Party*
Jean-Paul Sartre	*No Exit, Dirty Hands*
Peter Shaffer	*Equus, Amadeus*
Ntozake Shange	*for colored girls who have considered suicide, when the rainbow is enough*
Tom Stoppard	*Rosencrantz and Guildenstern Are Dead, The Real Thing*
Luis Valdez	*Zoot Suit, The Shrunken Head of Pancho Villa*
Wendy Wasserstein	*The Heidi Chronicles*
August Wilson	*Joe Turner's Come and Gone, The Piano Lesson*

31 PERSPECTIVES
Enter Critic

Just as artists seek to communicate their experience of life through the use of the raw materials and the specific means of their art, so critics, confronting the resultant creation, shed a new light on it, enhance our understanding of it, and finally end by making their own sense of life significant to their readers. At best, the critic is an artist whose point of departure is another artist's work.

HAROLD CLURMAN

FOCUS ON CRITICISM

Drama is a very public kind of literature. A successful dramatist lives with critical feedback, wanted or not. There are reviews of tryouts, reviews on opening night, reviews of a play that is having a successful run. There are critical assessments of an established play, critical reassessments on the occasion of new productions, critical assessments of a playwright's influence on others. Much drama criticism is perishable, written by newspaper reviewers scrambling to meet a deadline a few hours after they leave the theater. However, some critical assessments, like George Bernard Shaw's manifesto on Ibsenism, become classics in their own right. Some critical theories, like those that Aristotle formulated in his *Poetics,* become a code for future playwrights to honor or to break.

ARISTOTLE
On the Perfect Plot
330 B.C.

[Aristotle (384–322 B.C.), the encyclopedic philosopher of classical antiquity, wrote his *Poetics* roughly a century after the height of classical Greek drama. His discussion of tragedy is a spectacular example of a **critical theory** that was read as gospel by many and that continues to influence discussion of tragedy today. Although Aristotle developed his theories after the fact, his fol-

1457

lowers in later centuries set them up as rules for future playwrights to follow. In times of classical revival, his *Poetics* became the bible for **neoclassical** critics. The following excerpt from Aristotle's theory of tragedy includes his discussion of **hamartia,** or the tragic flaw. A few references to plays lost or little known have been omitted.]

We assume that, for the finest form of tragedy, the plot must be not simple but complex; and further, that it must imitate actions arousing fear and pity, since that is the distinctive function of this kind of imitation. It follows, therefore, that there are three forms of plot to be avoided. (1) A good man must not be seen passing from happiness to misery, or (2) a bad man from misery to happiness. The first situation is not fear-inspiring or piteous, but simply odious to us. The second is the most untragic that can be; it has not one of the requisites of tragedy; it does not appeal either to the human feeling in us, or to our pity, or to our fears. Nor, on the other hand, should (3) an extremely bad man be seen falling from happiness into misery. Such a story may arouse the human feeling in us, but it will not move us to either pity or fear; pity is occasioned by undeserved misfortune, and fear by that of one like ourselves; so that there will be nothing either piteous or fear-inspiring in the situation.

There remains, then, the intermediate kind of person, a man not pre-eminently virtuous and just, whose misfortune, however, is brought upon him not by vice and depravity but by some error of judgment (hamartia), of the number of those in the enjoyment of great reputation and prosperity; for example, Oedipus, Thyestes, and the men of note of similar families. The perfect plot, accordingly, must have a single, and not (as some tell us) a double issue; the change in the hero's fortunes must be not from misery to happiness, but on the contrary from happiness to misery; and the cause of it must lie not in any depravity, but in some great error on his part; the man himself being either such as we have described, or better, not worse, than that. Fact also confirms our theory. Though the poets began by accepting any tragic story that came to hand, in these days the finest tragedies are always on the story of some few houses, on that of Alcmeon, Oedipus, Orestes, Meleager, Tyestes, Telephus, or any others that may have been involved, as either agents or sufferers, in some deed of horror. The theoretically best tragedy, then, has a plot of this description. The critics, therefore, are wrong who blame Euripides for taking this line in his tragedies, and giving many of them an unhappy ending. It is, as we have said, the right line to take. The best proof is this: on the stage, and in the public performances, such plays, properly worked out, are seen to be the most truly tragic; and Euripides, even if his execution be faulty in every other point, is seen to be nevertheless the most tragic certainly of the dramatists.

After this comes the construction of plot which some rank first, one with a double story . . . and an opposite issue for the good and the bad characters. It is ranked as first only through the weakness of the audiences; the poets merely follow their public, writing as its wishes dictate. But the pleasure here is not that of tragedy. It belongs rather to comedy, where the bitterest enemies in the piece . . . walk off good friends at the end, with no slaying of anyone by anyone.

The tragic fear and pity may be aroused by the spectacle; but they may also be aroused by the very structure and incidents of the play—which is the better way and shows the better poet. The plot in fact should be so framed that, even without seeing the things take place, he who simply hears the account of them shall be filled with horror and pity at the incidents; which is just the effect that the mere recital of the story in *Oedipus* would have on one. To produce this same effect by means of the spectacle is less artistic, and requires extraneous aid. Those, however, who make use of the spectacle to put before us that which is merely monstrous and not productive of fear, are wholly out of touch with tragedy; not every kind of pleasure should be required of a tragedy, but only its own proper pleasure.

The tragic pleasure is that of pity and fear, and the poet has to produce it by a work of imitation; it is clear, therefore, that the causes should be included in the incidents of the story. Let us see, then, what kinds of incident strike one as horrible, or rather as piteous. In a deed of this description the parties must necessarily be either friends, or enemies, or indifferent to one another. Now when enemy does it on enemy, there is nothing to move us to pity either in his doing or in his meditating the deed, except so far as the actual pain of the sufferer is concerned; and the same is true when the parties are indifferent to one another. Whenever the tragic deed, however, is done within the family—when the murder or the like is done or meditated by brother on brother, by son on father, by mother on son, or son on mother—these are the situations the poet should seek after. The traditional stories, accordingly, must be kept as they are, for instance, the murder of Clytaemnestra by Orestes. At the same time even with these there is something left to the poet himself; it is for him to devise the right way of treating them.

Let us explain more clearly what we mean by "the right way." The deed of horror may be done by the doer knowingly and consciously, as in the old poets, and in Medea's murder of her children in Euripides. Or he may do it, but in ignorance of his relationship, and discover that afterwards, as does the Oedipus in Sophocles. . . . A third possibility is for one meditating some deadly injury to another, in ignorance of his relationship, to make the discovery in time to draw back. These exhaust the possibilities, since the deed must necessarily be either done or not done, and either knowingly or unknowingly.

The worst situation is when the character is with full knowledge on the point of doing the deed, and leaves it undone. It is odious and also (through the absence of suffering) untragic; hence it is that no one is made to act thus except in some few instances, e.g., Haemon and Creon in *Antigone*. Next after this comes the actual perpetration of the deed meditated. A better situation than that, however, is for the deed to be done in ignorance, and the relationship discovered afterwards, since there is nothing odious in it, and the discovery will serve to astound us. But the best of all is the last; what we have in *Cresphontes*, for example, where Merope, on the point of slaying her son, recognizes him in time, and in *Iphigenia*, where sister and brother are in a like position.

From *Poetics*, trans. Ingram Bywater

QUESTIONS

1. Aristotle throughout focuses on the effect a play has on the audience. How does this concern with audience reaction show in his discussion of the ideal tragic hero?

2. Does Aristotle's definition of the tragic flaw fit Antigone? Oedipus? Hamlet?

JOAN TEMPLETON

Ibsen and Feminism 1989

[The relation between **author biography** and the author's work is often speculative—hard to prove or disprove. Not so in this excerpt from a vigorously written article showing how Ibsen's *A Doll's House* is anchored in his life and times.]

Ibsen's contemporaries, the sophisticated as well as the crude, recognized *A Doll's House* as the clearest and most substantial expression of the "woman question" that had yet appeared. In Europe and America, from the 1880's on, the articles poured forth: "Der Noratypus" [The Nora Type], "Ibsen und die Frauenfragen" [Ibsen and the Women's Questions], "Ibsen et la femme," "La représentation féministe et sociale d'Ibsen," A Prophet of the New Womanhood," "Ibsen as a Pioneer of the Woman Movement." These are a small sampling of titles from scholars and journalists who agreed with their more famous contemporaries, Lou Andréas Salomé, Alla Nazimova, Georg Brandes, and August Strindberg, along with every other writer on Ibsen, whether in the important dailies and weeklies or in the highbrow and lowbrow reviews, that the theme of *A Doll's House* was the subjection of women by men.

Havelock Ellis, filled with a young man's dreams and inspired by Nora, proclaimed that she held out nothing less than "the promise of a new social order." In 1890, eleven years after Betty Hennings as Nora first slammed the shaky backdrop door in Copenhagen's Royal Theatre, he summarized what *A Doll's House* meant to the progressives of Ibsen's time:

> The great wave of emancipation which is now sweeping across the civilized world means nominally nothing more than that women should have the right to education, freedom to work, and political enfranchisement—nothing in short but the bare ordinary rights of an adult human creature in a civilized state.

Profoundly disturbing in its day, *A Doll's House* remains so still because, in James Huneker's succinct analysis, it is "the plea for woman as a human being, neither more nor less than man, which the dramatist made. . . ."

A Doll's House is a natural development of the play Ibsen had just written, the unabashedly feminist *Pillars of Society;* both plays reflect Ibsen's extremely privileged feminist education, which he shared with few other nineteenth-century male authors and which he owed to a trio of extraordinary women: Suzannah Thoresen Ibsen, his wife; Magdalen Thoresen, his colleague at the Norwegian National Theatre in Bergen, who was Suzannah's stepmother and former governess; and Camilla Wergeland Collett, Ibsen's literary colleague, valued friend, and the founder of Norwegian feminism.

Magdalen Thoresen wrote novels and plays and translated the French plays Ibsen put on as a young stage manager at the Bergen theater. She was probably the first "New Woman" he had ever met. She pitied the insolvent young writer, took him under her wing, and brought him home. She had passed her strong feminist principles on to her charge, the outspoken and irrepressible Suzannah, who adored her strong-minded stepmother and whose favorite author was George Sand [pen name of Lucile Dudevant]. The second time Ibsen met Suzannah he asked her to marry him. Hjordis, the fierce shield-maiden of *The Vikings at Helgeland,* the play of their engagement, and Svanhild, the strong-willed heroine of *Love's Comedy,* the play that followed, owe much to Suzannah Thoresen Ibsen. Later, Nora's way of speaking would remind people of Suzannah's.

The third and perhaps most important feminist in Ibsen's life was his friend Camilla Collett, one of the most active feminists in nineteenth-century Europe and founder of the modern Norwegian novel. Fifteen years before Mill's *Subjection of Women,* Collett wrote *Amtmandens Døtre* (The Governor's Daughters). Faced with the choice of a masculine *nom de plume* [pen name] or no name at all on the title page, Collett brought out her novel anonymously in two parts in 1854 and 1855, but she nonetheless became widely known as the author. Its main argument, based on the general feminist claim that women's feelings matter, is that women should have the right to educate themselves and to marry whom they please. In the world of the governor's daughters, it is masculine success that matters. Bought up to be ornaments and mothers, women marry suitable men and devote their lives to their husbands' careers and to their children. The novel, a cause célèbre, made Collett famous overnight.

Collett regularly visited the Ibsens in their years of exile in Germany, and she and Suzannah took every occasion to urge Ibsen to take up the feminist cause. They had long, lively discussions in the years preceding *A Doll's House,* when feminism had become a strong movement and the topic of the day in Scandinavia. Collett was in Munich in 1877, when Ibsen was hard at work on *Pillars of Society,* and Ibsen's biographer Koht speculates that Ibsen may have deliberately prodded her to talk about the women's movement in order to get material for his dialogue . . . .

It is foolish to apply the formalist notion that art is never sullied by argument to Ibsen's middle-period plays, written at a time when he was an outspoken and direct fighter in what he called the "mortal combat between two epochs." . . . While it is true that Ibsen never reduced life to "ideas," it is equally true that he was passionately interested in the events and ideas of his day. He was as deeply anchored in his time as any writer has been before or since.

From "The Doll House Backlash: Criticism, Feminism, and
Ibsen," PMLA 104 (Jan. 1989)

QUESTIONS

How much do you learn from this essay about the status of feminism in northern Europe a hundred years ago? How does the essay make you rethink your understanding of and your reaction to Ibsen's play? What do you learn from this essay about the relation between life and art, or between the writer's biography and literary creation?

ARTHUR MILLER
Tragedy and the Common Man 1949

[Dramatists vary greatly in how fully they articulate their own assumptions about their craft. Arthur Miller has often written eloquently about the commitments of the playwright in general and about the larger thematic implications of his own plays. Judging from the following essay, how would he have answered the question of whether Willy Loman is a tragic hero?]

In this age few tragedies are written. It has often been held that the lack is due to a paucity of heroes among us, or else that modern man has had the blood drawn out of his organs of belief by the skepticism of science, and the heroic attack on life cannot feed on an attitude of reserve and circumspection. For one reason or another, we are often held to be below tragedy—or tragedy above us. The inevitable conclusion is, of course, that the tragic mode is archaic, fit only for the very highly placed, the kings or the kingly, and where this admission is not made in so many words it is most often implied.

I believe that the common man is as apt a subject for tragedy in its highest sense as kings were. On the face of it this ought to be obvious in the light of modern psychiatry, which bases its analysis upon classific formulations, such as the Oedipus and Orestes complexes, for instance, which were enacted by royal beings, but which apply to everyone in similar emotional situations.

More simply, when the question of tragedy in art is not at issue, we never hesitate to attribute to the well-placed and the exalted the very same mental processes as the lowly. And finally, if the exaltation of tragic action were truly a property of the high-bred character alone, it is inconceivable that the mass of mankind should cherish tragedy above all other forms, let alone be capable of understanding it.

As a general rule, to which there may be exceptions unknown to me, I think the tragic feeling is evoked in us when we are in the presence of a character who is ready to lay down his life, if need be, to secure one thing—his sense of personal dignity. From Orestes to Hamlet, Medea to Macbeth, the underlying struggle is that of the individual attempting to gain his "rightful" position in his society.

Sometimes he is one who has been displaced from it, sometimes one who seeks to attain it for the first time, but the fateful wound from which the inevitable events spiral is the wound of indignity, and its dominant force is indignation. Tragedy, then, is the consequence of a man's total compulsion to evaluate himself justly.

In the sense of having been initiated by the hero himself, the tale always reveals what has been called his "tragic flaw," a failing that is not peculiar to grand or elevated characters. Nor is it necessarily a weakness. The flaw, or crack in the character, is really nothing—and need be nothing—but his inherent unwillingness to remain passive in the face of what he conceives to be a challenge to his dignity, his image of his rightful status. Only the passive, only those who accept their lot without active retaliation, are "flawless." Most of us are in that category.

But there are among us today, as there always have been, those who act against the scheme of things that degrades them, and in the process of action, everything we have accepted out of fear or insensitivity or ignorance is shaken before us and examined, and from this total onslaught by an individual against the seemingly stable cosmos surrounding us—from this total examination of the "unchangeable" environment—comes the terror and the fear that is classically associated with tragedy.

More important, from this total questioning of what has been previously unquestioned, we learn. And such a process is not beyond the common man. In revolutions around the world, these past thirty years, he has demonstrated again and again this inner dynamic of all tragedy.

Insistence upon the rank of the tragic hero, or the so-called nobility of his character, is really but a clinging to the outward forms of tragedy. If rank or nobility of character was indispensable, then it would follow that the problems of those with rank were the particular problems of tragedy. But surely the right of one monarch to capture the domain from another no longer raises our passions, nor are our concepts of justice what they were to the mind of an Elizabethan king.

The quality in such plays that does shake us, however, derives from the underlying fear of being displaced, the disaster inherent in being torn away from our chosen image of what and who we are in this world. Among us today this fear is as strong, and perhaps stronger, than it ever was. In fact, it is the common man who knows this fear best.

Now, if it is true that tragedy is the consequence of a man's total compulsion to evaluate himself justly, his destruction in the attempt posits a wrong or an evil in his environment. And this is precisely the morality of tragedy and its lesson. The discovery of the moral law, which is what the enlightenment of tragedy consists of, is not the discovery of some abstract or metaphysical quantity.

The tragic right is a condition of life, a condition in which the human personality is able to flower and realize itself. The wrong is the condition which suppresses man, perverts the flowing out of his love and creative instinct. Tragedy enlightens—and it must, in that it points the heroic finger at the enemy of man's freedom. The thrust for freedom is the quality in tragedy which exalts. The revolutionary questioning of the stable environment is what terrifies. In no way is the common man debarred from such thoughts or such actions.

Seen in this light, our lack of tragedy may be partially accounted for by the turn which modern literature has taken toward the purely psychiatric view of life, or the purely sociological. If all our miseries, our indignities, are born and bred within our minds, then all action, let alone the heroic action, is obviously impossible.

And if society alone is responsible for the cramping of our lives, then the protagonist must needs be so pure and faultless as to force us to deny his validity as a character. From neither of these views can tragedy derive, simply because neither represents a balanced concept of life. Above all else, tragedy requires the finest appreciation by the writer of cause and effect.

No tragedy can therefore come about when its author fears to question absolutely everything, when he regards any institution, habit, or custom as being either everlasting, immutable, or inevitable. In the tragic view the need of man to wholly realize himself is the only fixed star, and whatever it is that hedges his nature and lowers it is ripe for attack and examination. Which is not to say that tragedy must preach revolution.

The Greeks could probe the very heavenly origin of their ways and return to confirm the rightness of laws. And Job could face God in anger, demanding his right, and end in submission. But for a moment everything is in suspension, nothing is accepted, and in this stretching and tearing apart of the cosmos, in the very action of so doing, the character gains "size," the tragic stature which is spuriously attached to the royal or the highborn in our minds. The commonest of men may take on that stature to the extent of his willingness to throw all he has into the contest, the battle to secure his rightful place in his world.

There is a misconception of tragedy with which I have been struck in review after review, and in many conversations with writers and readers alike. It is the idea that tragedy is of necessity allied to pessimism. Even the dictionary says nothing more about the word than that it means a story with a sad or unhappy ending. This impression is so firmly fixed that I almost hesitate to claim that in truth tragedy implies more optimism in its author than does comedy, and that its final result ought to be the reinforcement of the onlooker's brightest opinion of the human animal.

For, if it is true to say that in essence the tragic hero is intent upon claiming his whole due as a personality, and if this struggle must be total and without reservation, then it automatically demonstrates the indestructible will of man to achieve his humanity.

The possibility of victory must be there in tragedy. Where pathos rules, where pathos is finally derived, a character has fought a battle he could not possibly have won. The pathetic is achieved when the protagonist is, by virtue of his witlessness, his insensitivity, or the very air he gives off, incapable of grappling with a much superior force.

Pathos truly is the mode for the pessimist. But tragedy requires a nicer balance between what is possible and what is impossible. And it is curious, although edifying, that the plays we revere, century after century, are the tragedies. In them, and in them alone, lies the belief—optimistic, if you will—in the perfectibility of man.

It is time, I think, that we who are without kings took up this bright thread of our history and followed it to the only place it can possibly lead in our time—the heart and spirit of the average man.

QUESTIONS

What, for Miller, is the most essential quality of the tragic hero or heroine? What are his arguments against the traditional view that tragedy befalls only people of high status? How does Miller redefine the *tragic flaw*? What does he mean by the "purely psychiatric" and the "purely sociological" views of life? Why are both hostile to the spirit of true tragedy? What, to Miller, is the difference between tragedy and pathos? How does he attack the common assumption that tragedy presents a pessimistic view of life?

RICHARD SCHICKEL
Rebirth of an American Dream 1984

[Drama critics, like meteorologists, must bring tidings both good and bad. In the following excerpt from a **review,** a drama critic pays tribute to a revival that some might have attended from the sense of performing a cultural duty, only to rediscover the lasting vitality of "a classic of the modern theater." Arthur Miller's *Death of a Salesman* opened on Broadway for the first time on the night of February 10, 1949. According to this reviewer, its spectacular revival in 1984, with Dustin Hoffman as Willy Loman, wiped out "the last pockets of resistance" to the enduring status of a play written with "astonishing, youthful confidence" by its then thirty-three-year-old author.]

"He's liked, but he's not—well liked."
"When I was 17 I walked into the jungle, and when I was 21 I walked out. And by God I was rich."
"He's a man way out there in the blue, riding on a smile and a shoeshine . . . A salesman is got to dream, boy. It comes with the territory."
And, above all, this: "So attention must be paid . . . . Attention, attention must be finally paid to such a person."

To hear those lines spoken from a stage now, thirty-five years after they were first heard, is to realize how deeply they have insinuated themselves into the collective unconscious of modern America. We quote them without citing their original source, in some cases without knowing what that source is. And, again, not quite consciously, many of us live our lives differently than once we might have—defining success, failure, our relationships with our children, even our notions of what constitutes a worthwhile job in new ways. That is, in part, because more than a generation gap ago Arthur Miller invented an American dreamer named Willy Loman, put him in a play called *Death of a Salesman,* and invited us to watch him and his false, almost comic, near-to-tragic dream unravel.

Such was the cautionary power of this work that one's largest fear, approaching the new, palpitatingly anticipated Broadway production of *Salesman,* starring Dustin Hoffman in a role he admitted wanting to play since he began acting, only a decade after Miller finished writing it, was that we might have learned too well the lessons Willy taught. Perhaps familiarity might have rendered him irrelevant, a figure of nostalgic curiosity, conceivably, but of vastly diminished power to engage the emotions.

That fear turns out to be entirely groundless. For Director Michael Rudman's fluid, driving production is not just a revival and a restaging, nor even a reinterpretation of the play, but a virtual reinvention of it. And Hoffman's performance as Willy is nothing short of a revelation. He has stripped away all the gloomy portents that have encrusted the character over the years and brought him down to fighting weight, a scrappy, snappy little bantam, whom the audience may, if it wishes, choose to see as a victim, but who almost never sees himself that way. Not long ago, Arthur Miller said that "Willy is foolish and even ridiculous sometimes. He tells the most transparent lies, exaggerates mercilessly, and so on. But I want you to see that the impulses behind him are not foolish at all. He cannot bear reality, and since he can't do much to change it, he keeps changing his ideas of it."

It is this Willy that Hoffman plays with the demonic ferocity that is his glory as an actor. Shifting suddenly from time present to time past and back again, the play moves along a steadily darkening arc; Hoffman bobs and weaves on that line, shadowboxing the gathering shadows, hoping to the end for a T.K.O. over reality. When the inevitable arrives, when he has lost his job, when it is clear that his sons have been ruined by his belief that success is just a matter of concealing the needle of sharp practice in a hand gloved by fraudulent gladness, his suicide is only in part dictated by despair. There is this insurance policy, and if Willy can contrive to make his demise look like an accident, then he will have achieved in death what he never could in life—a legacy for his family and, better still, that edge of the system for which he had always angled. When Hoffman makes his final exit, he actually does a little shimmy and shake, so eager is his salesman for this last but most promising road trip.

Yet exhilarating as this performance is, it does not dominate or distort Miller's vision. In fact, it frees it from the limits imposed by critics of the original production, who tended to see Willy's fate determined almost solely by capitalist economics, and by later commentators who wondered whether the salesman could be regarded as a truly tragic figure, since he was not observed to fall from the great heights demanded of such characters by the laws of Aristotelian aesthetics. From the beginning, Miller told *Time* reporter Elaine Dutka, he had seen the play as two seemingly different entities. One was "a veritable encyclopedia of information about the man," which would permit actors and audiences alike to find their own sense of what moved him. The other was a kind of free-form poem, highly condensed emotionally and verbally, "a concentration through some kind of lens of my whole awareness of life up to that point." But here again, the problem of precise clarification was left up to performers and auditors. "What it 'means,'" said Miller, "depends on where on the face of earth you are and what year it is."

He speaks from heartening experience. It has been claimed that not a night passes without *Salesman* being performed somewhere in the world, usually with success, mostly in venues where no one can possibly conceive of what America was like in 1949. For example, Miller's remarks about Willy's combative relationship with reality were contained in his advice to the players he directed last in China (an experience he has wryly, and wisely, recounted in *Salesman in Beijing*). To them he also insisted "the one red line connecting everyone in the play was a love for Willy." Even when the family are appalled by his self-delusions, they see "he is forever signaling to a future that he cannot describe and will not live to see, but he is in love with all the same."

From *Time*, April 9, 1984

QUESTIONS

According to this reviewer, what is the key to Dustin Hoffman's reinterpretation of Willy Loman? What does Schickel mean by Willy's "combative relationship with reality"? Are you surprised by the playwright's comment that the common thread connecting everyone in the play was "a love for Willy"?

WRITING ABOUT LITERATURE
31. Defining a Critical Term (Focus on Definition)

The Writing Workshop We would find it hard to talk about drama without terms like *tragedy, protagonist, tragicomedy, subplot,* or *theater of the absurd.* Such critical terms focus our attention and guide our expectations. They help us put into words important similarities and differences. They enable us to formulate our standards, to explain our preferences and aversions.

When you define an important critical term, you stake out the territory it covers. You spell out what it covers and what it fences out. In writing a definition paper, try to find a term that *needs* definition. For instance, you might focus on a term with a rich and confusing history and try to clear up basic ambiguities. Or you might zero in on a trendy term whose meaning is still fuzzy in many people's minds. Consider the following when trying to find a topic that fills a need or presents a challenge:

The History of a Term Important terms may change their meanings as they serve the agendas of different schools of critical thought. Terms that once had negative connotations may become terms of praise and vice versa. For instance, followers of the classical tradition have tended to frown on mixed genres, being suspicious of "mongrel tragicomedy" (Sir Philip Sidney). But tragicomedy has appealed to the modern temper, which welcomes irony and paradox and resists artificial oversimplification. What is it about this genre that has appealed to modern audiences?

Testing the Limits Definitions are tested when we apply them to living drama. For instance, is modern tragedy possible? Can a character like Willy Loman, who is not a prince or warlord, who never solved the riddle of the Sphinx, be a tragic hero? As for the comic muse, does Molière's *Misanthrope* turn too serious to be a true comedy?

Drawing the Line It may prove hard to draw a clear line between often-paired terms. Most definitions of comedy sooner or later contrast it with tragedy. They stress the contrast between ordinary or low-life characters and the exalted personages of the tragic muse. Or they show the difference between the marvelous arrival of good fortune in comedy and the tragic defeat of the tragic hero. What are the key differences? Where do the two genres shade over into each other?

Initiating the Reader You may want to help the reader become more knowledgeable about modern trends. Your paper might set out to define

Bertolt Brecht's epic theater; the theater of the absurd as practiced by Ionesco, Beckett, or Albee; existential drama; feminist drama as defined by leading feminist critics or written by leading feminist playwrights; the art of the mime; dramatic happenings.

In working on a definition paper, consider the following guidelines:

✧ *Be aware of traditional or conventional definitions.* Reckon with the received wisdom—what everybody knows or "what has oft been said" (Alexander Pope). Although dictionary definitions can alert you to important dimensions, you will generally do well not to quote them in your actual paper. Dictionary or encyclopedia entries tend to sound too dry and neutral to get your readers involved in the dialectic of living literature. Consider quoting a critic, a playwright, or a reviewer instead.

✧ *Pull together and spell out your own definition.* Writing a definition paper, like writing other worthwhile papers, should be a voyage of discovery. However, try to sum up somewhere in your paper what continent you have found. Often, you will want to present your overall definition as a preview or **thesis** at the end of a short introduction. For instance, let your readers know that your definition of tragedy comes in three parts. You might want to make it clear that three essential requirements, or criteria, qualify a play as a true tragedy:

CRITERION 1: A true tragedy arouses the tragic emotions of pity and fear.

CRITERION 2: The tragic hero or heroine exhibits a tragic flaw.

CRITERION 3: The play moves toward insight or self-realization.

Using an alternate strategy, you might start with a trial definition and then proceed to modify it in the light of important evidence. You will be taking your reader along *in search of* a more adequate definition. (In such an **inductive** paper—which works *toward* a general conclusion—transitions and overall direction need to be especially clear to keep the reader moving along to the destination.)

✧ *Fortify your definition against exceptions.* For instance, Molière is a master of traditional comedy, but his *Misanthrope* is on the borderline. It does not have a happy ending. It does not culminate in a marriage festival. No avaricious or lustful uncle obstructs Alceste's union with Célimène. Often a word like *generally* or *typically* can help protect you against the charge of overgeneralization. Or you can make it clear that you are talking about "true comedy" or "comedy as here defined" or "comedy in the modern vein."

✧ *Use ample supporting examples.* Bridge the gap between theory and practice. Show that your general criteria actually apply to the characters on the stage, to the things they say and do. Definitions easily remain too neat and unrealistic when they remain abstract.

✧ *Use comparison and contrast with related terms.* A term often becomes clearer as you explain what it does *not* mean. Clarify your key term by marking it off from related terms—whether near synonyms or opposites. For instance, a definition of tragedy can become more meaningful when tragedy is clearly distinguished from melodrama or from pathos—two forms that in the eyes of the critics tend to play the role of its poor relations.

Study the following sample student paper. How clear and workable is its definition of the key term?

SAMPLE STUDENT PAPER

Death of a Salesman—A Modern Tragedy?

Ever since Willy Loman trudged into his living room and set down his heavy sample satchel in the first stage production of *Death of a Salesman,* critics have been arguing whether or not Arthur Miller's creation is a tragedy. Some maintain the play is a tragedy of the ordinary person, with Willy Loman as the tragic hero. The author himself said in his "Tragedy and the Common Man" that the "common man is as apt a subject for tragedy in its highest sense as kings were." Others hold that the play does not fit the requirements of true tragedy and that Willy Loman is incapable of being a tragic hero—or indeed any other type of hero at all. Ultimately, the truth may be that Willy Loman fails to become a tragic hero, not because he is modern or because he is common, but because of basic and obvious limitations of his character.

Since Aristotle, critics have tended to agree on the first criterion of true tragedy: It should arouse the tragic emotions of pity and fear. Aristotle used the term *catharsis*—a cleansing or purgation—to describe the emotional experience of the audience. The pity the audience feels for the tragic hero is not patronizing or condescending. Instead it implies a sense of equality, a sharing of grief. The word *fear* is not restricted to fright or abject terror but implies anxious concern, awe, reverence, and apprehension.

Critics have with almost equal unanimity emphasized the second criterion: The tragic hero or heroine should have some tragic flaw that shapes the character's action and helps bring about the eventual downfall. We need to assume that the hero has free will; and we look in his or her character for a flaw that begins the chain of events leading to ruin. Some fatal blindness or weakness in an otherwise admirable person helps explain the tragic course of events.

A third criterion is less universally stressed, but it seems to do much to help the hero or heroine achieve true tragic stature. In the agony, humiliation, and suffering of defeat, the hero reaches a point of increased self-awareness. The hero or heroine is able to look back and see the steps leading to disaster. Or at least the hero or heroine shows an understanding of what is happening. Shakespeare's Macbeth, bitter and pessimistic at the end, begins to see with terrifying clarity his total isolation: "honor, love, obedience, troops of friends / I must not look to have" (5.3. 25–26). Othello, in his last words, asks the audience to remember him as one "who loved not wisely, but too well" (5.2. 344).

How do these criteria apply to Willy Loman? Miller certainly achieves the effects of pity and fear on his audience. Audiences today as much as ever can sympathize with Willy's terrifying underlying insecurity in a dog-eat-dog system. In Willy's world, as in ours, there is for many people no real safety net. Linda appeals to our sympathy when she says, "You cannot eat the fruit and throw the peel away." Her plea for "attention" is the author's plea for pity for a struggling character whom we saw in the process of going under.

Certainly, Willy possesses a tragic flaw, if not several. But this flaw is perhaps not so much a personal characteristic, a failing in an otherwise great and admirable person. It is more a burden put on him by society. Willy believed in the American dream because he was brought up to do so. He seems too gullible, too credulous. He is too much of a victim to be a great but flawed individual. Much of the play seems to illustrate pathos—the helpless suffering of someone victimized—rather than tragedy.

Willy, finally, never seems to progress toward the self-realization that should be part of true tragedy. If the play were tragic, Willy himself would realize in the last act that, as Biff says, "he had the wrong dreams. All, all, wrong." But this conception remained beyond Willy. He died dreaming another daydream, thinking of himself worth more dead than he was alive, fantasizing about the insurance money that none of his family are likely to see. He dies, as he lived, in a world of illusion, dreaming of Biff as finally a success—"Can you imagine that magnificence with twenty-thousand dollars in his pocket?"

Although Miller's play powerfully stirs the tragic emotions of pity and fear, Willy Loman lacks the stature of a tragic hero. The true tragic effect cannot be achieved without the tragic hero's bitter recognition of his true self.

QUESTIONS

How does this student writer's three-point definition of tragedy structure the paper as a whole? Do the three parts of the definition become clear and convincing? Do you agree with the way the author applies them to Miller's play? Where and why would you take issue with the student writer?

OTHER VOICES/OTHER VISIONS
Plays for Further Reading

WILLIAM SHAKESPEARE AND ROMANTIC COMEDY

Lovers and madmen have such seething brains.
Such shaping fantasies, that apprehend
More than cool reason ever comprehends.
The lunatic, the lover, and the poet,
Are of imagination all compact.
WILLIAM SHAKESPEARE,
A MIDSUMMER NIGHT'S DREAM

Shakespeare's *Midsummer Night's Dream,* the best loved of his **romantic comedies,** delights audiences by giving full range to the imagination. It roams from the spirit world of delicate, exotic beings in Oberon's fairy kingdom to the rough-hewn amateur theatricals staged by honest ignorance. In this early Shakespeare play, the magic of romance transforms the grey world of every day into a fantasy world of delightful dreams, amorous adventures, and mischievous pranks.

The common theme is love, traced through its full range of permutations. We see it at work in many contexts, ranging from airy moonlight fancies through the ardors and griefs of adolescent love to the farcical fumblings of bumpkins. On the most ethereal, fanciful level, the play takes us into the dream world of high **romance**—the magic kingdom of Oberon, king of the fairies, and Titania, his fairy queen. The moonlit forest at night is a spirit world whose inhabitants are not hemmed in by limitations of time and space (or weighed down by material bodies). Theirs is a sphere where spells and magic potions give power to make others do one's bidding. Miraculous transformations (or **metamorphoses**) are commonplace. The quasi-divine spirits are exempt from mortal inhibitions and restrictions. They delight in creating mischief and playing with human fears.

On the intermediate level, the Greek hero Theseus and the Amazon queen Hippolyta, although legendary figures, take us into the world of human desires and limitations. They provide the frame story that sets us up for a traditional **comedy of love.** Theseus has defeated and won the warlike Amazon queen, and we witness preparations for a marriage festival that set the tone of tradi-

1470

tional comedy: mirth, merriment, revelry—casting off pale melancholy. The main plot is spun around the obstacles encountered and overcome by young lovers. Egeus, the father of Hermia, is the traditional obstructing elder: He pits his tyrannical parental authority against the love of Hermia and Lysander, trying to force Hermia into an unwanted marriage with Demetrius. Demetrius in turn ignores Helena, who yearns for him in the throes of unrequited love.

On the lowest rung of the comic ladder is Peter Quince's troop of workingmen, offering their amateur production of the story of Pyramus and Thisby to their prince. In their enthusiastic but unsophisticated hands, the tragic story turns into a parody, a "lamentable comedy," as Peter Quince says. In the words of one critic, this comic play-within-a-play, or **interlude,** "epitomizes many an amateur dramatic presentation, from the choice of a work inappropriate both for the occasion and the sparse talents of the performers, right through disastrous rehearsals with lines forgotten or misread, down to a performance marred by . . . misinterpretation, unintentional bawdiness," and "actors stepping out of character to talk with the audience" (Alice Griffin).

In the play as a whole, the fanciful, the real, and the farcical intermesh. Puck, the sprite and jester, causes mischief in both the human and the fairy worlds. He gives a love potion to the wrong lover by mistake—or to the target of one of his pranks on purpose. He torments and frightens the yokels by making Bottom stumble through the woods with a human body and the head of an ass. The beings of the fairy world are not totally disembodied spirits. The queen of fairies, tricked by Puck's potion, falls in love with a half-human monster made up of the ignorant Bottom and an ass's head. Beauty and the beast inhabit the same enchanted forest.

Much of the play is in **blank verse**—the unrhymed iambic pentameter (five-beat) line. Here, as in other plays, Shakespeare's sentences may roam over half a dozen or more lines, with sentence breaks often falling in the middle of a line. Much of the solemn palaver at the court of Theseus is in blank verse. In the following sample, note the inversion (stress on first syllable) and the weaker stresses (`). These help the poet play rhythmic variations on the basic iambic (stress-on-second-syllable) pattern:

> Four dáys | will quíck | ly stéep | themsélves | in níght:
> Four níghts | will quíck ly dréam | awáy | the tíme:
> And thén | the móon, | lìke to | a síl | ver bów
> Néw-bent | in héa | ven, shàll | behóld | the níght
> Of óur | solém | nitìes.   (1.1.7–11)

However, the dialogue of the lovers and some other passages are more neatly packaged in **closed couplets**—two rhymed lines that are often more self-contained than blank verse. They sound more pat, and they seem suitable especially to the lovers' talk, because what the lovers say often seems predictable—"what they all say":

> Love looks not with the eyes, but with the MIND,
> And therefore is winged Cupid painted BLIND. (1.1.234–35)

In Shakespeare's moonlit midsummer forest, the native English folklore of elves and mischievous hobgoblins mingles with **allusions** to classical Greek myth and legend. For instance, the playwright expects us to know that the nymph Daphne was pursued by the god Apollo and was turned into a laurel tree to help her escape his unwanted attentions. We are expected to recognize allusions to the Furies, the spirits that came from hell to wreak vengeance on evildoers, and to the Fates, the three fatal sisters who spin the thread of life and whose shears cut it short.

Modern readers have traced in the play a pattern of an imaginative or spiritual journey. The subjects of Theseus move from the daylight world of his court to the magic moonlit world of the forest and then return. What do they experience during their journey? What do they learn from it? Do they return from it enlightened or more mature? Is love destructive and irrational, or is it a benign, redeeming force in our universe? What in this play is reality; what is illusion?

WILLIAM SHAKESPEARE (1564–1616)
A Midsummer Night's Dream

1594–1595

CHARACTERS

Elders and Lovers:
THESEUS, Duke of Athens
HIPPOLYTA, Queen of the Amazons, engaged to THESEUS
EGEUS, father of HERMIA
HERMIA, daughter of EGEUS, in love with LYSANDER
LYSANDER, in love with HERMIA
DEMETRIUS, also in love with HERMIA, and favored by her father
HELENA, in love with DEMETRIUS
PHILOSTRATE, Master of the Revels, in charge of court entertainments
Attendants

Spirits of the Fairy Kingdom:
OBERON, King of the fairies
TITANIA, Queen of the fairies
ROBIN GOODFELLOW, also called PUCK
PEASEBLOSSOM, COBWEB, MOTH (meaning mote or speck), and MUSTARDSEED, fairies
Other fairies

Athenian workingmen putting on the interlude (or play-within-the-play), with their roles during their performance:
PETER QUINCE, a carpenter (PROLOGUE)
NICK BOTTOM, a weaver (PYRAMUS)
FRANCIS FLUTE, a bellows-mender (THISBY)
TOM SNOUT, a tinker (WALL)
SNUG, a joiner (LION)
ROBIN STARVELING, a tailor (MOONSHINE)

[The names of the "mechanicals," or workers, echo symbols of their trades: Quince is named after quoins, or quines—wooden wedges used by carpenters. Bottom is named after the bobbin on which weavers wind yarn. Flute is named after the fluted exterior of the church organs whose bellows he mends. Snout is named after the snout, or spout, of the kettles he repairs as a tinker. Snug is named after the snug fit of the furniture he makes as a joiner. Starveling is thin and half-starved like a stereotypical tailor.]

ACT ONE

SCENE 1. The Palace of Theseus.

[*Enter* THESEUS, HIPPOLYTA, PHILOSTRATE; *with others.*]

THESEUS: Now fair Hippolyta, our nuptial° hour	*wedding*
Draws on apace:° four happy days bring in	*quickly*
Another moon: but O, methinks° how slow	*it seems to me*
This old moon wanes! she lingers° my desires,	*obstructs*
Like to a stepdame° or a dowager,°	*stepmother/rich widow*
Long withering out a young man's revenue.°	*using up his inheritance (while both wither)*
HIPPOLYTA: Four days will quickly steep themselves in night:	
Four nights will quickly dream away the time:	
And then the moon, like to a silver bow	
New-bent in heaven, shall behold the night	
Of our solemnities.°	*solemn ceremonies*
THESEUS: Go Philostrate,	
Stir up the Athenian youth to merriments,	
Awake the pert° and nimble spirit of mirth,	*lively*
Turn melancholy forth to funerals:	
The pale companion is not for our pomp.°	*not fit for our celebration*

5

10

15

[PHILOSTRATE leaves.]

Hippolyta, I wooed° thee with my sword,°	*courted/in battle*
And won thy love doing thee injuries:	
But I will wed thee in another key,°	*in different fashion*
With pomp, with triumph,° and with revelling.	*victory procession*

[*Enter* EGEUS *and his daughter* HERMIA, LYSANDER, *and* DEMETRIUS.]

EGEUS: Happy be Theseus, our renownèd duke.

THESEUS: Thanks good Egeus: what's the news with thee?

EGEUS: Full of vexation come I, with complaint
    Against my child, my daughter Hermia.
    Stand forth Demetrius. My noble lord,
    This man hath my consent to marry her.
    Stand forth Lysander. And my gracious duke,
    This man hath bewitched the bosom of my child.
    Thou, thou Lysander, thou hast given her rhymes,
    And interchanged love tokens with my child:

20

25

Thou hast by moonlight at her window sung,   30
With feigning° voice, verses of feigning love,   *deceiving, yearning ("faining")*
And stolen the impression of her fantasy°   *conned her fancy*
With bracelets of thy hair, rings, gauds,° conceits,°   *baubles/love tokens*
Knacks,° trifles, nosegays,° sweetmeats—messengers   *knickknacks/flowers*
Of strong prevailment in unhardened youth.°   *that dazzle the inexperienced*   35
With cunning hast thou filched my daughter's heart,
Turned her obedience, which is due to me,
To stubborn harshness. And my gracious duke,
Be it so she will not here before your grace
Consent to marry with Demetrius,   40
I beg the ancient privilege of Athens:
As she is mine, I may dispose of her:
Which shall be, either to this gentleman,
Or to her death, according to our law
Immediately provided° in that case.   *clearly spelled out*   45
THESEUS: What say you, Hermia? Be advised, fair maid.
    To you your father should be as a god:
    One that composed° your beauties: yea and one   *gave life to*
    To whom you are but as a form in wax
    By him imprinted, and within his power   50
    To leave the figure, or disfigure° it: *undo*
    Demetrius is a worthy gentleman.
HERMIA: So is Lysander.
THESEUS: In himself he is:
    But in this kind,° wanting° your father's voice,°   *but here/lacking/consent*
    The other must be held the worthier.   55
HERMIA: I would° my father looked but with my eyes.   *wish*
THESEUS: Rather your eyes must with his judgment look.
HERMIA: I do entreat your grace to pardon me.
    I know not by what power I am made bold,
    Nor how it may concern° my modesty,   *relate to*   60
    In such a presence,° here to plead my thoughts: *in the presence of such*
    But I beseech your grace that I may know   *high authority*
    The worst that may befall me in this case,
    If I refuse to wed Demetrius.
THESEUS: Either to die the death, or to abjure°   *give up*   65
    For ever the society of men.
    Therefore fair Hermia, question your desires,
    Know of° your youth, examine well your blood,°   *think about/passions*
    Whether, if you yield not to your father's choice,
    You can endure the livery° of a nun,   *garment*   70
    For aye° to be in shady cloister mewed,°   *forever/shut up*
    To live a barren sister all your life,
    Chanting faint hymns to the cold fruitless moon.°   *(symbol of chastity)*
    Thrice blessèd they that master so their blood,°   *control their passions so*
    To undergo such maiden pilgrimage: 75
    But earthlier happy° is the rose distilled,°   *happier in earthly fashion/made*
    Than that which, withering on the virgin thorn,   *into perfume (and used*
    Grows, lives, and dies, in single blessedness.   *for a purpose)*

HERMIA: So will I grow, so live, so die my lord,   80
　　　Ere I will yield my virgin patent° up   *privilege of virginity*
　　　Unto his lordship, whose° unwishèd yoke   *to whose*
　　　My soul consents not to give sovereignty.
THESEUS: Take time to pause, and by the next moon—
　　　The sealing day° betwixt my love and me   *day of sealing the marriage bond*
　　　For everlasting bond of fellowship—   85
　　　Upon that day either prepare to die
　　　For disobedience to your father's will,
　　　Or else to wed Demetrius, as he would,°   *as he wishes*
　　　Or on Diana's° altar to protest   *(the chaste moon goddess)*
　　　For aye, austerity and single life.°   *to swear abstinence forever*   90
DEMETRIUS: Relent, sweet Hermia, and Lysander, yield
　　　Thy crazèd title° to my certain right.   *your flawed claim*
LYSANDER: You have her father's love, Demetrius:
　　　Let me have Hermia's: do you marry him.
EGEUS: Scornful Lysander, true, he hath my love: 95
　　　And what is mine, my love shall render him.
　　　And she is mine, and all my right of her
　　　I do estate unto° Demetrius.   *I make over to*
LYSANDER: I am, my lord, as well derived° as he,   *from as good a family*
　　　As well possessed:° my love is more than his: *with as much property*   100
　　　My fortunes every way as fairly ranked
　　　(If not with vantage)° as Demetrius':   *if not above*
　　　And, which is more than all these boasts can be,
　　　I am beloved of beauteous Hermia.
　　　Why should not I then prosecute° my right?   *pursue*   105
　　　Demetrius, I'll avouch it to his head,°   *charge it to his face*
　　　Made love to Nedar's daughter, Helena,
　　　And won her soul: and she, sweet lady, dotes,
　　　Devoutly dotes, dotes in idolatry,
　　　Upon this spotted and inconstant man.   110
THESEUS: I must confess that I have heard so much,
　　　And with Demetrius thought to have spoke thereof:°   *meant to speak with him*
　　　But being over-full of self-affairs,°   *too busy with my own affairs*
　　　My mind did lose it. But Demetrius come,
　　　And come Egeus, you shall go with me: 115
　　　I have some private schooling° for you both.   *instruction*
　　　For you fair Hermia, look you arm° yourself,   *prepare*
　　　To fit your fancies° to your father's will;   *bend your desires*
　　　Or else the law of Athens yields you up
　　　(Which by no means we may extenuate)°   *which law I can in no way modify*   120
　　　To death or to a vow of single life.
　　　Come my Hippolyta, what cheer my love?
　　　Demetrius and Egeus, go along:
　　　I must employ you in some business
　　　Against our nuptial,° and confer with you   *related to our wedding*   125
　　　Of something nearly that concerns yourselves.
EGEUS: With duty and desire we follow you.
                                        [They leave.]

[LYSANDER *and* HERMIA *walk.*]

LYSANDER: How now my love? Why is your cheek so pale?
How chance the roses there do° fade so fast?   *how do the roses there happen to*
HERMIA: Belike° for want of rain, which I could well   *probably*   130
Beteem them from° the tempest of my eyes.   *shower them with*
LYSANDER: Ay me, for aught° that I could ever read,   *to judge by anything*
Could ever hear by tale or history,
The course of true love never did run smooth;
But either it was different in blood°—   *separated by social rank*   135
HERMIA: O cross! too high to be enthralled° to low.   *to be made a slave*
LYSANDER: Or else misgraffèd in respect of years°—   *mismatched in age*
HERMIA: O spite! too old to be engaged to young.
LYSANDER: Or else it stood upon the choice of friends°—   *needed relatives' approval*
HERMIA: O hell! to choose love by another's eyes.   140
LYSANDER: Or if there were a sympathy in choice,
War, death, or sickness did lay siege to it;
Making it momentary as a sound,
Swift as a shadow, short as any dream,
Brief as the lightning in the collied° night,   *coal-black*   145
That, in a spleen, unfolds° both heaven and earth;   *in a flash, reveals*
And ere° a man hath power to say "Behold,"   *before*
The jaws of darkness do devour it up:
So quick bright things come to confusion.°   *grief*
HERMIA: If then true lovers have been ever crossed,°   *always been thwarted*   150
It stands as an edict in destiny:°   *as a law of fate*
Then let us teach our trial patience,°   *learn to suffer patiently*
Because it is a customary cross,
As due to love as thoughts and dreams and sighs,
Wishes and tears; poor Fancy's followers.°   *attendants on poor Love*   155
LYSANDER: A good persuasion:° therefore hear me, Hermia: *good advice*
I have a widow aunt, a dowager,
Of great revenue,° and she hath no child: *with a large income*
From Athens is her house remote seven leagues,°   *(20 to 30 miles distant)*
And she respects me as her only son: 160
There gentle Hermia, may I marry thee,
And to that place the sharp Athenian law
Cannot pursue us. If thou lov'st me then,
Steal forth° thy father's house tomorrow night: *forth from*
And in the wood, a league without° the town,   *outside*   165
Where I did meet thee once with Helena
To do observance to a morn of May,
There will I stay for thee.°   *wait for you*
HERMIA: My good Lysander,
I swear to thee, by Cupid's strongest bow,
By his best arrow, with the golden head,°   *arrowhead implanting love*   170
By the simplicity of Venus' doves,
By that which knitteth souls and prospers loves,°   *makes love prosper*
And by that fire which burned the Carthage queen,°   *(Queen Dido, left by the Trojan*
When the false Trojan under sail was seen,   *prince Aeneas, committed*
By all the vows that ever men have broke,   *suicide by fire)*   175

(In number more than ever women spoke)
In that same place thou hast appointed me,
Tomorrow truly will I meet with thee.
LYSANDER: Keep promise love: look, here comes Helena.

[*Enter* HELENA.]

HERMIA: God speed° fair Helena: whither away?   *God's blessing on you*   180
HELENA: Call you me fair? That fair again unsay.°   *take back "beautiful"*
  Demetrius loves your fair: O happy fair!
  Your eyes are lodestars,° and your tongue's sweet air°   *guiding stars/melody*
  More tuneable° than lark to shepherd's ear,   *tuneful*
  When wheat is green, when hawthorn buds appear.   185
  Sickness is catching: O were favor so,°   *if looks were also*
  Yours would I° catch, fair Hermia, ere° I go.   *would I like to/before*
  My ear should catch your voice, my eye your eye,
  My tongue should catch your tongue's sweet melody.
  Were the world mine, Demetrius being bated,°   *with the exception of Demetrius*   190
  The rest I'd give to be to you translated.°   *be changed into you*
  O teach me how you look, and with what art
  You sway the motion of Demetrius' heart.
HERMIA: I frown upon him; yet he loves me still.
HELENA: O that your frowns would teach my smiles such skill.   195
HERMIA: I give him curses; yet he gives me love.
HELENA: O that my prayers could such affection move.
HERMIA: The more I hate, the more he follows me.
HELENA: The more I love, the more he hateth me.
HERMIA: His folly, Helena, is no fault of mine.   200
HELENA: None but your beauty;° would that fault were mine.   *only your beauty's fault*
HERMIA: Take comfort: he no more shall see my face:
  Lysander and myself will fly this place.
  Before the time I did Lysander see,
  Seemed Athens as a paradise to me: 205
  O then, what graces in my love do dwell,°   *what magic is in my love*
  That he hath turned a heaven unto a hell!
LYSANDER: Helen, to you our minds we will unfold:
  Tomorrow night, when Phoebe° doth behold   *(the moon goddess Diana)*
  Her silver visage in the watery glass,°   *mirror of the waters*   210
  Decking with liquid pearl the bladed grass
  (A time that lovers' flights doth still conceal)°   *always hides*
  Through Athens gates have we devised to steal.°   *planned to sneak out*
HERMIA: And in the wood, where often you and I
  Upon faint primrose beds were wont to° lie,   *used to*   215
  Emptying our bosoms of their counsel sweet,°   *sweet talk*
  There my Lysander and myself shall meet,
  And thence from Athens turn away our eyes,
  To seek new friends and stranger companies°   *the company of strangers*
  Farewell, sweet playfellow: pray thou for us: 220
  And good luck grant thee thy Demetrius.
  Keep word Lysander: we must starve our sight
  From lovers' food till morrow deep midnight.°   *till midnight tomorrow*

LYSANDER: I will my Hermia.

[HERMIA *leaves.*]

Helena adieu:
As you on him, Demetrius dote° on you.   *may he dote*   225

[LYSANDER *leaves.*]

HELENA: How happy some, over other some,° can be!   *compared with some others*
    Through Athens I am thought as fair as she.
    But what of that? Demetrius thinks not so:
    He will not know what all but he do know.°   *does not want to know what*
    And as he errs, doting on Hermia's eyes,   *all others know*   230
    So I,° admiring of his qualities.   *so I do also err*
    Things base and vile, holding no quantity,°   *quite out of shape*
    Love can transpose to form and dignity.°   *change to beautiful shape*
    Love looks not with the eyes, but with the mind:
    And therefore is winged Cupid painted blind.°   *painted as a blind boy*   235
    Nor hath Love's mind of any judgment taste:
    Wings, and no eyes, figure unheedy haste.°   *symbolize heedless haste*
    And therefore is Love said to be a child:
    Because in choice he is so oft beguiled.
    As waggish boys in game themselves forswear,   240
    So the boy Love is perjured everywhere.
    For ere° Demetrius looked on Hermia's eyne,°   *before/eyes*
    He hailed down oaths that he was only mine.
    And when this hail some heat from Hermia felt,
    So he dissolved, and showers of oaths did melt.   245
    I will go tell him of fair Hermia's flight:
    Then to the wood will he tomorrow night
    Pursue her: and for this intelligence,°   *information*
    If I have thanks, it is a dear expense:°   *an effort gladly invested*
    But herein mean I to enrich my pain,   250
    To have his sight thither and back again.°   *the sight of him first removed to*
                                                                            there but then back

[*She leaves.*]

SCENE 2. QUINCE's house.

[*Enter* QUINCE *the Carpenter; and* SNUG *the Joiner; and*
BOTTOM *the Weaver; and* FLUTE *the Bellows-mender; and*
SNOUT *the Tinker; and* STARVELING *the Tailor.*]

QUINCE: Is all our company here?   *name them collectively (he*
BOTTOM: You were the best to call them generally,° man by   *means individually)/list*
    man, according to the scrip.°
QUINCE: Here is the scroll of every man's name which is
    thought fit, through all Athens, to play in our inter-   5
    lude° before the duke and the duchess, on his wedding-   *short dramatic entertainment*
    day at night.

BOTTOM: First good Peter Quince, say what the play treats on, then read the names of the actors: and so grow to a point.

QUINCE: Marry,° our play is "The most lamentable comedy,° and most cruel death of Pyramus and Thisby." — *truly / (he means "tragedy")* — 10

BOTTOM: A very good piece of work I assure you, and a merry. Now good Peter Quince, call forth your actors by the scroll. Masters, spread yourselves.

QUINCE: Answer as I call you. Nick Bottom the weaver? — 15

BOTTOM: Ready: name what part I am for, and proceed.

QUINCE: You, Nick Bottom, are set down for Pyramus.

BOTTOM: What is Pyramus? A lover, or a tyrant?

QUINCE: A lover that kills himself, most gallant, for love.

BOTTOM: That will ask some tears in the true performing of it. — 20
If I do it, let the audience look to their eyes: I will move — *lament*
storms: I will condole° in some measure. To the rest—yet — *inclination Hercules*
my chief humor° is for a tyrant. I could play Ercles° rarely,
or a part to tear a cat in, to make all split.

> The raging rocks — 25
> And shivering shocks,
> Shall break the locks
> > Of prison gates,
> And Phibbus'° car — *(he means "Phoebus")*
> Shall shine from far, — 30
> And make and mar
> > The foolish Fates.

This was lofty. Now name the rest of the players. This is Ercles' vein, a tyrant's vein: a lover is more condoling.

QUINCE: Francis Flute, the bellows-mender? — 35

FLUTE: Here Peter Quince.

QUINCE: Flute, you must take Thisby on you.

FLUTE: What is Thisby? A wandering knight?

QUINCE: It is the lady that Pyramus must love.

FLUTE: Nay faith, let not me play a woman: I have a beard — 40
coming.

QUINCE: That's all one:° you shall play it in a mask, and you — *that doesn't matter*
may speak as small as you will.

BOTTOM: And° I may hide my face, let me play Thisby too: I'll — *if*
speak in a monstrous little voice; "Thisne, Thisne," "Ah — 45
Pyramus, my lover dear, thy Thisby dear, and lady dear."

QUINCE: No, no, you must play Pyramus; and Flute, you Thisby.

BOTTOM: Well, proceed.

QUINCE: Robin Starveling, the tailor?

STARVELING: Here Peter Quince. — 50

QUINCE: Robin Starveling, you must play Thisby's mother. Tom Snout, the tinker?

SNOUT: Here Peter Quince.

QUINCE: You, Pyramus' father; myself, Thisby's father; Snug the joiner, you the lion's part: and I hope here is a play fitted.° — *well joined together (as if by / a carpenter)* — 55

SNUG: Have you the lion's part written? Pray you, if it be, give it me, for I am slow of study.° — *slow to memorize*

QUINCE: You may do it extempore,° for it is nothing but roaring. — *ad lib*

BOTTOM: Let me play the lion too. I will roar, that I will do
    any man's heart good to hear me. I will roar, that I will
    make the duke say "Let him roar again: let him roar
    again." 60

QUINCE: And you should° do it too terribly, you would fright   *if you would*
    the duchess and the ladies, that they would shriek, and
    that were enough to hang us all.°   *to have us sentenced to hang* 65

ALL: That would hang us, every mother's son.

BOTTOM: I grant you, friends, if you should fright the ladies
    out of their wits, they would have no more discretion but
    to hang us, but I will aggravate my voice° so, that I will   *(he means "lighten my voice")*
    roar you as gently as any sucking dove: I will roar you and   70
    'twere° any nightingale.   *as if it were*

QUINCE: You can play no part but Pyramus, for Pyramus is a
    sweet-faced man; a proper man as one shall see in a sum-
    mer's day; a most lovely gentleman-like man: therefore
    you must needs play Pyramus.   75

BOTTOM: Well, I will undertake it. What beard were I best to
    play it in?

QUINCE: Why, what you will.

BOTTOM: I will discharge it in either your straw-color beard,
    your orange-tawny beard, your purple-in-grain beard, or   80
    your French-crown°-color beard, your perfect yellow.   *(French gold coin)*

QUINCE: Some of your French crowns have no hair at all,° and   *(heads bald from syphilis, the*
    then you will play barefaced. But, masters, here are your   *"French" disease)*
    parts, and I am to entreat you, request you, and desire you
    to con° them by tomorrow night; and meet me in the   *learn* 85
    palace wood, a mile without° the town, by moonlight;   *outside*
    there will we rehearse, for if we meet in the city, we shall
    be dogged with company, and our devices° known. In the   *plans*
    meantime, I will draw a bill of properties, such as our play
    wants.° I pray you fail me not.   *props needed for our play* 90

BOTTOM: We will and there we may rehearse most obscenely°   *(he means "seemly")*
    and courageously. Take pain, be perfect: adieu.

QUINCE: At the duke's oak we meet.

BOTTOM: Enough: hold, or cut bow-strings.°   *hold tight or cut loose*

[*They leave.*]

ACT TWO

SCENE 1. A wood near Athens.

[*Enter a* FAIRY *at one door, and* ROBIN GOODFELLOW (PUCK) *at another.*]

PUCK: How now spirit, whither° wander you?   *where to*
FAIRY: Over hill, over dale,°   *valley*
                Thorough° bush, thorough brier,   *through*
            Over park, over pale,°   *enclosure*

Thorough flood, thorough fire,   5
I do wander everywhere,
Swifter than the moon's sphere;
And I serve the Fairy Queen,
To dew her orbs upon the green.°   *rings of higher or darker grass*
The cowslips tall her pensioners° be,   *(royal) bodyguards*   10
In their gold coats, spots you see:
Those be rubies, fairy favors;°   *gifts*
In those freckles live their savors.°   *perfumes*
    I must go seek some dewdrops here,
    And hang a pearl in every cowslip's° ear.   *primrose*   15
    Farewell thou lob° of spirits; I'll be gone.   *you lout*
    Our queen and all her elves come here anon.°   *shortly*
PUCK: The king doth keep his revels here tonight.
    Take heed the queen come not within his sight.
    For Oberon is passing fell and wrath,°   *most fierce and angry*   20
    Because that she, as her attendant, hath
    A lovely boy, stolen from an Indian king.
    She never had so sweet a changeling.°   *child stolen by fairies*
    And jealous Oberon would° have the child   *wants to*
    Knight of his train, to trace° the forests wild.   *roam through*   25
    But she, perforce,° withholds the lovèd boy,   *determined*
    Crowns him with flowers, and makes him all her joy.
    And now, they never meet in grove or green,
    By fountain clear, or spangled starlight sheen,
    But they do square, that° all their elves for fear   *do quarrel, so that*   30
    Creep into acorn cups and hide them° there.   *themselves*
FAIRY : Either I mistake your shape and making quite,
    Or else you are that shrewd and knavish sprite°   *mischievous spirit*
    Called Robin Goodfellow. Are not you he
    That frights the maidens of the villagery?   35
    Skim° milk, and sometimes labor in the quern,°   *you skim/grain grinder*
    And bootless make the breathless housewife churn,°   *churn the milk without success*
    And sometime make the drink to bear no barm,°   *no foam (leaving it flat)*
    Mislead night wanderers, laughing at their harm?
    Those that Hobgoblin call you, and sweet Puck,   40
    You do their work, and they shall have good luck.
    Are not you he?
PUCK: Thou speakest aright;
    I am that merry wanderer of the night.
    I jest to Oberon, and make him smile,
    When I a fat and bean-fed horse beguile,   45
    Neighing in likeness of a filly foal;
    And sometime lurk I in a gossip's° bowl,   *old woman's*
    In very likeness of a roasted crab,°   *crabapple*
    And when she drinks, against her lips I bob,
    And on her withered dewlap° pour the ale.   *folds of skin*   50
    The wisest aunt,° telling the saddest tale,   *old woman*
    Sometime for three-foot stool mistaketh me;
    Then slip I from her bum, down topples she,

And "tailor" cries,° and falls into a cough;   *cries "hold thief!"*
And then the whole quire° hold their hips and laugh,   *company*   55
And waxen in their mirth,° and sneeze, and swear   *get more and more boisterous*
A merrier hour was never wasted° there.   *spent*
But room,° fairy: here comes Oberon.   *make room*
FAIRY : And here, my mistress. Would that he were gone.

[*Enter* OBERON, *the King of fairies, at one door with his
train of fairies; and the* QUEEN, TITANIA, *at another, with hers.*]

OBERON: Ill met° by moonlight, proud Titania.   *an unfortunate encounter*   60
QUEEN: What, jealous Oberon? Fairy, skip hence.
   I have forsworn his bed and company.
OBERON: Tarry, rash wanton. ° Am not I thy lord?   *wait, loose mischief-making woman*
QUEEN: Then I must be thy lady, but I know
   When thou has stolen away from fairyland,   65
   And in the shape of Corin° sat all day,   *(a shepherd in love)*
   Playing on pipes of corn,° and versing° love   *simple flutes/making verses of*
   To amorous Phillida. Why are thou here
   Come from the farthest steep of India?
   But that, forsooth, the bouncing Amazon,   70
   Your buskined° mistress and your warrior love,°   *booted/warlike lover*
   To Theseus must be wedded; and you come,
   To give their bed joy and prosperity.
OBERON: How canst thou thus, for shame, Titania,
   Glance at my credit° with Hippolyta,   *hint at my record*   75
   Knowing I know thy love to Theseus?
   Didst thou not lead him through the glimmering night,
   From Perigenia, whom he ravishèd?
   And make him with fair Aegles break his faith,
   With Ariadne, and Antiopa?°   *(all four women are former loves of Theseus)*   80
QUEEN: These are the forgeries of jealousy:
   And never, since the middle summer's spring,
   Met we on hill, in dale, forest, or mead°   *meadow*
   By pavèd° fountain, or by rushy brook,   *pebble-strewn*
   Or in the beachèd margent° of the sea,   *beach-lined border*   85
   To dance our ringlets° to the whistling wind,   *circle dances*
   But with thy brawls thou hast disturbed our sport.
   Therefore the winds, piping° to us in vain,   *playing music*
   As in revenge, have sucked up from the sea
   Contagious fogs, which falling in the land,   90
   Hath every pelting° river made so proud,   *petty*
   That they have overborne their continents.°   *risen over their banks*
   The ox hath therefore stretched his yoke in vain,
   The plowman lost his sweat, and the green corn
   Hath rotted ere his youth° attained a beard.   *before its young stalks*   95
   The fold° stands empty in the drownèd field,   *enclosure for sheep or cattle*
   And crows are fatted with the murrion flock.°   *fattened with carrion*
   The nine men's morris° is filled up with mud,   *area cleared for games*
   And the quaint mazes in the wanton green,°   *winding paths in the rich grass*
   For lack of tread, are undistinguishable.   100

The human mortals want their winter° here;   *miss a true winter*
No night is now with hymn or carol blest.
Therefore the moon, the governess of floods,°   *(which governs ebb and tide)*
Pale in her anger, washes all the air,°   *fills the air with moisture*
That rheumatic° diseases do abound.   *arthritic*   105
And thorough this distemperature,° we see   *because of this disturbance*
The seasons alter, hoary-headed frosts
Fall in the fresh lap of the crimson rose,
And on old Hiems' thin and icy crown,°   *on Winter's almost hairless head*
An odorous chaplet° of sweet summer buds   *sweet-smelling wreath*   110
Is, as in mockery, set. The spring, the summer,
The childing° autumn, angry winter change   *fruitful*
Their wonted liveries,° and the mazèd° world,   *usual appearance/amazed*
By their increase, now knows not which is which;
And this same progeny of evils° comes   *evil offspring*   115
From our debate, from our dissension:
We are their parents and original.°   *root cause*
OBERON: Do you amend it° then: it lies in you.   *change it all for the better*
Why should Titania cross her Oberon?
I do but beg a little changeling boy,   120
To be my henchman.°   *attendant*
QUEEN: Set your heart at rest.
The fairy land buys not° the child of me.   *all fairyland could not buy*
His mother was a votaress of my order,°   *a follower of my cult*
And in the spicèd Indian air,° by night,   *(India was famous for spices)*
Full often hath she gossiped by my side,   125
And sat with me on Neptune's yellow sands,
Marking the embarkèd traders° on the flood—   *watching the merchant ships*
When we have laughed to see the sails conceive
And grow big-bellied with° the wanton wind,   *as if pregnant with*
Which she, with pretty and with swimming gait,°   *pretending to float*   130
Following (her womb then rich with my young squire)
Would imitate, and sail upon the land,
To fetch me trifles, and return again,
As from a voyage, rich with merchandise.
But she, being mortal, of that boy did die,°   *died in childbirth*   135
And for her sake, do I rear up her boy,
And for her sake, I will not part with him.
OBERON: How long within this wood intend you stay?
QUEEN: Perchance° till after Theseus' wedding day.   *perhaps*
If you will patiently dance in our round,°   *circle dance*   140
And see our moonlight revels, go with us.
If not, shun me, and I will spare° your haunts.   *stay away from*
OBERON: Give me that boy, and I will go with thee.
QUEEN : Not for thy fairy kingdom. Fairies away
We shall chide° downright, if I longer stay.   *argue*   145

         [TITANIA *and her attendants leave.*]

OBERON: Well, go thy way. Thou shalt not from° this grove,   *not leave*
Till I torment thee for this injury.

My gentle Puck, come hither: thou rememberest,
Since once I sat upon a promontory,°   *cliff*
And heard a mermaid, on a dolphin's back,   150
Uttering such dulcet° and harmonious breath,   *sweet*
That the rude sea grew civil° at her song,   *tame*
And certain stars shot madly from their spheres,
To hear the sea maid's music.
PUCK: I remember.
OBERON: That very time, I saw (but thou couldst not)   155
Flying between the cold° moon and the earth,   *chaste*
Cupid, all armed. A certain aim he took
At a fair Vestal° thronèd by the west,   *virgin priestess (Queen Elizabeth?)*
And loosed his love-shaft smartly from his bow,
As° it should pierce a hundred thousand hearts,   *as if*   160
But I might see young Cupid's fiery shaft
Quenched in the chaste beams of the watery moon,
And the imperial votaress passed on,
In maiden meditation, fancy-free.°   *free of love's power*
Yet marked I where the bolt of Cupid fell.   165
It fell upon a little western flower,
Before, milk-white, now purple with love's wound,
And maidens call it love-in-idleness.°   *(the pansy)*
Fetch me that flower; the herb I showed thee once.
The juice of it, on sleeping eyelids laid,   170
Will make or man or woman madly dote
Upon the next live creature that it sees.
Fetch me this herb, and be thou here again
Ere the leviathan° can swim a league.   *the whale, sea monster*
PUCK: I'll put a girdle round about° the earth,   *I will circle*   175
In forty minutes.

               [*He leaves.*]

OBERON: Having once this juice,
I'll watch Titania when she is asleep,
And drop the liquor° of it in her eyes: *liquid*
The next thing then she waking looks upon,
(Be it on lion, bear, or wolf, or bull,   180
On meddling monkey, or on busy ape)
She shall pursue it, with the soul of love.
And ere I take this charm from off her sight
(As I can take it with another herb)
I'll make her render up her page° to me.   *attendant*   185
But who comes here? I am invisible,
And I will overhear their conference.

    [*Enter* DEMETRIUS, HELENA *following him.*]

DEMETRIUS: I love thee not; therefore pursue me not.
Where is Lysander and fair Hermia?
The one I'll slay; the other slayeth me.   190
Thou told'st me they were stolen unto this wood,

And here am I, and wood° within this wood, — *gone mad*
    Because I cannot meet my Hermia.
    Hence, get thee gone, and follow me no more.
HELENA: You draw me, you hard-hearted adamant,° — *diamond-hard magnetic stone* — 195
    But yet you draw not iron, for my heart
    Is true as steel. Leave you your power to draw,
    And I shall have no power to follow you.
DEMETRIUS: Do I entice you? Do I speak you fair?° — *speak kindly to you*
    Or rather do I not in plainest truth — 200
    Tell you I do not, nor I cannot love you?
HELENA: And even for that, do I love you the more:
    I am your spaniel; and Demetrius,
    The more you beat me, I will fawn on you.
    Use me but as your spaniel, spurn me, strike me, — 205
    Neglect me, lose me; only give me leave,
    Unworthy as I am, to follow you.
    What worser place can I beg in your love
    (And yet a place of high respect° with me) — *regard*
    Than to be usèd as you use your dog? — 210
DEMETRIUS: Tempt not too much the hatred of my spirit,
    For I am sick, when I do look on thee.
HELENA: And I am sick, when I look not on you.
DEMETRIUS: You do impeach° your modesty too much, — *endanger*
    To leave the city and commit yourself — 215
    Into the hands of one that loves you not,
    To trust the opportunity of night
    And the ill counsel of a desert° place — *deserted*
    With the rich worth of your virginity.
HELENA: Your virtue is my privilege.° For that — *your special powers make it right* — 220
    It is not night when I do see your face,
    Therefore I think I am not in the night.
    Nor doth this wood lack worlds of company,
    For you, in my respect,° are all the world. — *opinion*
    Then how can it be said I am alone, — 225
    When all the world is here to look on me?
DEMETRIUS: I'll run from thee and hide me in the brakes,° — *thick shrubbery*
    And leave thee to the mercy of wild beasts.
HELENA: The wildest hath not such a heart as you.
    Run when you will; the story shall be changed:° — *reversed: the nymph chases* — 230
    Apollo flies, and Daphne holds the chase; — *the god; the dove chases the*
    The dove pursues the griffin; the mild hind — *wild beast; the mild doe . . .*
    Makes speed to catch the tiger. Bootless° speed, — *useless*
    When cowardice pursues, and valor flies.
DEMETRIUS: I will not stay thy questions.° Let me go: — *wait for more argument* — 235
    Or if thou follow me, do not believe
    But I shall° do thee mischief in the wood. — *that I won't*

[DEMETRIUS *leaves.*]

HELENA: Ay, in the temple, in the town, the field,
    You do me mischief. Fie, Demetrius!

240

Your wrongs do set a scandal on my sex.°   *put women in a bad light*
We cannot fight for love, as men may do;
We should be wooed, and were not made to woo.
I'll follow thee and make a heaven of hell,
To die upon° the hand I love so well.   *die by*

[*She leaves.*]

OBERON: Fare thee well nymph. Ere he do leave this grove,   245
    Thou shalt fly° him, and he shall seek thy love.   *flee from*

[*Enter* PUCK.]

Hast thou the flower there? Welcome wanderer.
PUCK: Ay, there it is.
OBERON: I pray thee give it me.
    I know a bank where the wild thyme blows,
    Where oxlips and the nodding violet grows,   250
    Quite over-canopied with luscious woodbine,
    With sweet musk-roses, and with eglantine.°   *(names of wildflowers)*
    There sleeps Titania, sometime of the night,
    Lulled in these flowers, with dances and delight;
    And there the snake throws° her enamelled skin,   *casts off* 255
    Weed wide enough to wrap a fairy in.
    And with the juice of this, I'll streak her eyes,
    And make her full of hateful fantasies.
    Take thou some of it, and seek through this grove:
    A sweet Athenian lady is in love   260
    With a disdainful youth; anoint his eyes,
    But do it when the next thing he espies°   *sees*
    May be the lady. Thou shalt know the man
    By the Athenian garments he hath on.
    Effect it with some care, that he may prove   265
    More fond on her,° than she upon her love: *more smitten by her*
    And look thou meet me ere the first cock crow.
PUCK: Fear not my lord: your servant shall do so.

[*They leave.*]

SCENE 2. Another part of the wood.

[*Enter* TITANIA, *Queen of fairies, with her attendants.*]

QUEEN: Come, now a roundel° and a fairy song.   *circle dance*
    Then, for the third part of a minute, hence—
    Some to kill cankers° in the musk-rose buds,   *pests*
    Some war with reremice° for their leather wings,   *attack bats*
    To make my small elves coats, and some keep back   5
    The clamorous owl, that nightly hoots and wonders
    At our quaint° spirits. Sing me now asleep: *dainty*
    Then to your offices,° and let me rest.   *duties*

[*Fairies sing.*]

You spotted snakes with double tongue,
   Thorny hedgehogs be not seen,   10
Newts and blindworms° do no wrong,   *small snakelike creatures*
   Come not near our Fairy Queen.

   Philomele,° with melody,   *nightingale (in Greek myth)*
   Sing in our sweet lullaby,
Lulla, lulla, lullaby, lulla, lulla, lullaby.   15
      Never harm,
      Nor spell, nor charm,
   Come our lovely lady nigh.°   *may it not come near*
   So good night, with lullaby.

1. FAIRY: Weaving spiders come not here: 20
   Hence you long-legged spinners, hence:
Beetles black approach not near:
   Worm nor snail do no offence.

Philomele, with melody . . .

[*They repeat the refrain.* TITANIA *falls asleep.*]

2. FAIRY: Hence away! now all is well.   25
   One aloof stand sentinel.

                                             [*Fairies leave.*]
[*Enter* OBERON *and applies moisture from the flower to* TITANIA'S *eyelids.*]

OBERON: What thou seest, when thou dost wake,
   Do it for thy true love take:
   Love and languish for his sake.
   Be it ounce,° or cat,° or bear,   *lynx/wildcat*   30
   Pard,° or boar with bristled hair,   *leopard*
   In thy eye that shall appear,
   When thou wak'st, it is thy dear:
   Wake when some vile thing is near.

                                             [*He leaves.*]

[*Enter* LYSANDER *and* HERMIA.]

LYSANDER: Fair love, you faint with wandering in the wood;   35
   And to speak truth I have forgot our way.
   We'll rest us Hermia, if you think it good,
   And tarry for the comfort° of the day.   *wait for the reassuring arrival*
HERMIA: Be't so Lysander: find you out a bed,
   For I upon this bank will rest my head.   40
LYSANDER: One turf shall serve as pillow for us both,
   One heart, one bed, two bosoms, and one troth.°   *one true love*
HERMIA: Nay good Lysander: for my sake, my dear,
   Lie further off yet; do not lie so near.
LYSANDER: O take the sense, sweet, of my innocence:°   *understand my innocent meaning*   45
   Love takes° the meaning in love's conference.   *lovers understand*
   I mean that my heart unto yours is knit,

So that but one heart we can make of it:
Two bosoms interchainèd with an oath,
So then two bosoms and a single troth. 50
Then by your side no bed-room me deny,
For lying so, Hermia, I do not lie.
HERMIA: Lysander riddles very prettily.
   Now much beshrew° my manners and my pride,   *may ill befall*
   If Hermia meant to say Lysander lied. 55
   But gentle friend, for love and courtesy,
   Lie further off, in human modesty.
   Such separation as may well be said
   Becomes a virtuous bachelor and a maid,
   So far be distant, and good night, sweet friend. 60
   Thy love never alter° till thy sweet life end.   *may your love never change*
LYSANDER: Amen, amen, to that fair prayer say I,
   And then end life,° when I end loyalty.   *may my life end*
   Here is my bed: sleep give thee all his rest!
HERMIA: With half that wish, the wisher's eyes be pressed. 65

   [*They sleep.*]
      [*Enter* PUCK.]

PUCK: Through the forest have I gone,
           But Athenian found I none,
           On whose eyes I might approve°   *test*
           This flower's force in stirring love.
           Night and silence. Who is here? 70
           Weeds° of Athens he doth wear: *garments*
           This is he° (my master said)   *he who*
           Despisèd the Athenian maid:
           And here the maiden, sleeping sound,
           On the dank and dirty ground. 75
           Pretty soul, she durst not lie
           Near this lack-love, this kill-courtesy.
           Churl, upon thy eyes I throw
           All the power this charm doth owe:°   *possess*
           When thou wak'st, let love forbid 80
           Sleep his seat on thy eyelid.°   *keep sleep from your lids*
           So awake when I am gone,
           For I must now to Oberon.

                                          [*He leaves.*]
   [*Enter* DEMETRIUS *and* HELENA *running.*]

HELENA: Stay, thou kill me, sweet Demetrius.
DEMETRIUS: I charge thee: hence!° And do not haunt me thus.   *away from here* 85
HELENA: O, wilt thou darkling° leave me? Do not so.   *in the dark*
DEMETRIUS: Stay, on thy peril! I alone will go.

                              [DEMETRIUS *leaves.*]

HELENA: O, I am out of breath in this fond chase:°   *foolish love chase*
   The more my prayer, the lesser is my grace.°   *the less mercy is shown*

90

Happy is Hermia, wheresoever she lies:
For she hath blessèd and attractive eyes.
How came her eyes so bright? Not with salt tears:
If so,° my eyes are oftener washed than hers.   *if that were the cause*
No, no, I am as ugly as a bear,
For beasts that meet me run away for fear.   95
Therefore no marvel,° though Demetrius   *it's no surprise*
Do as a monster,° fly my presence thus.   *as from a monster*
What wicked and dissembling glass° of mine,   *mirror (looking glass)*
Made me compare with Hermia's sphery eyne!°   *starry eyes (set in*
But who is here? Lysander, on the ground?   *heavenly spheres)*   100
Dead, or asleep? I see no blood, no wound.
Lysander, if you live, good sir, awake.
LYSANDER [*wakes*]: And run through fire, I will for thy sweet sake.
Transparent° Helena, nature shows art°   *radiant/magic powers*
That through thy bosom makes me see thy heart.   105
Where is Demetrius? O how fit a word
Is that vile name to perish on my sword!
HELENA: Do not say so, Lysander, say not so.
What though he love your Hermia? Lord, what though?
Yet Hermia still loves you; then be content.   110
LYSANDER: Content with Hermia? No! I do repent
The tedious minutes I with her have spent.
Not Hermia, but Helena I love.
Who will not change a raven for a dove?
The will of man is by his reason swayed,   115
And reason says you are the worthier maid.
Things growing are not ripe until their season,
So I, being young, till now ripe not to reason.°   *did not reach mature understanding*
And touching now the point of human skill,°   *the height of human know-how*
Reason becomes the marshal to my will,   120
And leads me to your eyes; where I o'erlook°   *gaze upon*
Love's stories, written in love's richest book.
HELENA: Wherefore was I to this keen mockery born?
When at your hands did I deserve this scorn?
Is't not enough, is't not enough, young man,   125
That I did never, no, nor never can,
Deserve a sweet look from Demetrius' eye,
But you must flout my insufficiency?°   *mock my lack of success*
Good troth,° you do me wrong; good sooth, you do,   *in truth*
In such disdainful manner me to woo.   130
But fare you well. Perforce I must° confess,   *I am forced to*
I thought you lord of more true gentleness.°   *of a more noble spirit*
O, that a lady, of° one man refused,   *by*
Should of another, therefore be abused!

[*She leaves.*]

LYSANDER: She sees not Hermia. Hermia, sleep thou there,   135
And never mayst thou come Lysander near.
For, as a surfeit° of the sweetest things   *excessive eating*

The deepest loathing to the stomach brings,
Or as the heresies that men do leave
Are hated most of° those they did deceive,   *by*   140
So thou, my surfeit and my heresy,
Of all be hated but the most, of me;
And all my powers, address° your love and might   *apply*
To honor Helen, and to be her knight.

[*He leaves.*]

HERMIA [*wakes*]: Help me, Lysander, help me! Do thy best   145
To pluck this crawling serpent from my breast.
Ay me, for pity! What a dream was here?
Lysander, look how I do quake with fear.
Methought a serpent ate my heart away,
And you sat smiling at his cruel prey.°   *its cruel preying*   150
Lysander! What, removed?° Lysander, lord!   *gone away*
What, out of hearing, gone? No sound, no word?
Alack, where are you? Speak, and if you hear!
Speak, of all loves. I swoon almost with fear.
No? Then I well perceive you are not nigh:°   *not here*   155
Either death, or you, I'll find immediately.

[*She leaves.*]

ACT THREE

SCENE 1. The wood.

[*Enter the* CLOWNS: QUINCE, SNUG, BOTTOM, FLUTE, SNOUT,
and STARVELING.]

BOTTOM: Are we all met?
QUINCE: Pat, pat;° and here's a marvellous convenient place for   *right on time*
   our rehearsal. This green plot shall be our stage, this   *thicket/dressing room*
   hawthorn brake° our tiring-house,° and we will do it in ac-   5
   tion, as we will do it before the duke.
BOTTOM: Peter Quince?
QUINCE: What sayest thou, bully Bottom?°   *my good Bottom*
BOTTOM: There are things in this Comedy of Pyramus and
   Thisby that will never please. First, Pyramus must draw a
   sword to kill himself; which the ladies cannot abide. How   10
   answer you that?
SNOUT: By'r lakin,° a parlous° fear.   *by our lady/terrible*
STARVELING: I believe we must leave the killing out, when all is
   done.
BOTTOM: Not a whit:° I have a device° to make all well. Write   *not at all/plan*   15
   me a prologue, and let the prologue seem to say, we will
   do no harm with our swords, and that Pyramus is not
   killed indeed; and for the more better assurance, tell them

that I Pyramus am not Pyramus, but Bottom the weaver.
This will put them out of fear. 20

QUINCE: Well, we will have such a prologue, and it shall be
written in eight and six.° *in the old ballad meter (alternating 8 and 6 syllables)*

BOTTOM: No, make it two more: let it be written in eight and
eight.

SNOUT: Will not the ladies be afraid of the lion? 25

STARVELING: I fear it, I promise you.

BOTTOM: Masters, you ought to consider with yourselves, to
bring in (God shield us) a lion among ladies, is a most
dreadful thing. For there is not a more fearful wild-fowl
than your lion living; and we ought to look to't. 30

SNOUT: Therefore another prologue must tell he is not a lion.

BOTTOM: Nay, you must name his name, and half his face must
be seen through the lion's neck, and he himself must
speak through, saying thus, or to the same defect:° *(he means "effect")*
"Ladies," or "Fair ladies—I would wish you," or "I would 35
request you," or "I would entreat you, not to fear, not to
tremble: my life for yours. If you think I come hither as a
lion, it were pity of my life.° No, I am no such thing: I am *I put my life at risk*
a man as other men are." And there indeed let him name
his name, and tell them plainly he is Snug the joiner. 40

QUINCE: Well, it shall be so, but there is two hard things: that
is, to bring the moonlight into a chamber; for, you know,
Pyramus and Thisby meet by moonlight.

SNOUT: Doth the moon shine that night we play our play?

BOTTOM: A calendar, a calendar! Look in the almanac: find out 45
moonshine, find out moonshine.

QUINCE: Yes, it doth shine that night.

BOTTOM: Why, then may you leave a casement° of the great *hinged window frame*
chamber window, where we play, open; and the moon
may shine in at the casement. 50

QUINCE: Ay, or else one must come in with a bush of thorns
and a lantern,° and say he comes to disfigure,° or to pre- *(symbols of man in the moon)/(he meas "figure," "act out")*
sent, the person of Moonshine. Then, there is another
thing; we must have a wall in the great chamber; for Pyramus and Thisby, says the story, did talk through the chink 55
of a wall.

SNOUT: You can never bring in a wall. What say you, Bottom?

BOTTOM: Some man or other must present Wall: and let him
have some plaster, or some loam, or some rough-cast° *gravel plaster*
about him, to signify "Wall"; and let him hold his fingers 60
thus, and through that cranny shall Pyramus and Thisby
whisper.

QUINCE: If that may be, then all is well. Come, sit down every
mother's son, and rehearse your parts. Pyramus, you
begin. When you have spoken your speech, enter into that 65
brake, and so every one according to his cue.

  [*Enter* PUCK.]

PUCK: What hempen homespuns° have we swaggering here,   *coarsely clad bumpkins*
        So near the cradle° of the Fairy Queen?   *(where she is sleeping)*
        What, a play toward?° I'll be an auditor,°   *about to start/listener*
        An actor too perhaps, if I see cause.   70
QUINCE: Speak Pyramus. Thisby stand forth.
PYRAMUS: Thisby, the flowers of odious savors sweet—
QUINCE: "Odorous, odorous."
PYRAMUS: —odors savors sweet,
        So hath thy breath, my dearest Thisby dear.   75
        But hark, a voice: stay thou but here awhile,
        And by and by I will to thee appear.

                    [PYRAMUS *leaves.*]

PUCK: A stranger Pyramus than ever played here.

                    [*He leaves.*]

THISBY: Must I speak now?
QUINCE: Ay, marry,° must you. For you must understand he goes   *yes, indeed*   80
        but to see a noise that he heard, and is to come again.
THISBY: Most radiant Pyramus, most lily-white of hue,
        Of color like the red rose, on triumphant brier,°   *rose bush*
        Most brisky juvenal°, and eke° most lovely Jew,   *lively juvenile/also*
        As true as truest horse, that yet would never tire,   85
        I'll meet thee Pyramus, at Ninny's° tomb.   *(he means Ninus of Nineveh)*
QUINCE: "Ninus' tomb," man: why, you must not speak that
        yet. That you answer to Pyramus. You speak all your part
        at once, cues and all. Pyramus, enter; your cue is past:
        it is "never tire."   90
THISBY: O—As true as truest horse, that yet would never tire.

        [*Enter* BOTTOM *with his head changed to an ass's head, followed
        by* PUCK.]

PYRAMUS: If I were fair, Thisby°, I were only thine.   *(his script reads*
QUINCE: O monstrous! O strange! We are haunted. Pray,   *"If I were, fair Thisby"?)*
        masters! Fly, masters! Help!

                    [*They all flee.*]

PUCK: I'll follow you: I'll lead you about a round,°   *roundabout*   95
        Through bog, through bush, through brake, through brier.°   *through thicket*
        Sometime a horse I'll be, sometime a hound,   *and shrub*
        A hog, a headless bear, sometime a fire,
        And neigh, and bark, and grunt, and roar, and burn,
        Like horse, hound, hog, bear, fire, at every turn.   100

                    [*He leaves.*]

BOTTOM: Why do they run away? This is a knavery of them to
        make me afraid.

        [*Enter* SNOUT.]

SNOUT: O Bottom, thou art changed. What do I see on thee?

BOTTOM: What do you see? You see an ass-head of your own, do you?

[SNOUT *runs away.*]

[*Enter* QUINCE.]

QUINCE: Bless thee, Bottom, bless thee! Thou art translated.°   *bewitched*   105

[*He also runs away.*]

BOTTOM: I see their knavery. This is to make an ass of me, to fright me if they could: but I will not stir from this place, do what they can. I will walk up and down here, and will sing that and will sing that they shall hear I am not afraid.

[*Sings.*]

The woosel cock,° so black of hue,   *blackbird*   110
    With orange tawny bill,
The throstle, with his note so true,
    The wren, with little quill.°   *little piping voice*

TITANIA (*awakening*): What angel wakes me from my flowery bed?   115

BOTTOM [*sings*]:   The finch, the sparrow, and the lark,
    The plain-song cuckoo° gray,   *(who tells cuckolds of their unfaithful wives)*
Whose note full many a man doth mark,
    And dares not answer nay.
For indeed, who would set his wit to so foolish a bird?   120
Who would give a bird the lie,° though he cry "cuckoo"   *call it a liar*
never so?

TITANIA: I pray thee, gentle mortal, sing again.
Mine ear is much enamored of thy note:°   *music*
So is mine eye enthrallèd to° thy shape,   *enslaved to*   125
And thy fair virtue's force° perforce doth move me   *the force of your beautiful personality*
On the first view to say, to swear, I love thee.

BOTTOM: Methinks° mistress, you should have little reason for   *I think*
that. And yet, to say the truth, reason and love
keep little company together nowadays. The more   130
the pity, that some honest neighbors will not make
them friends. Nay, I can gleek° upon occasion.   *make satirical remarks*

TITANIA: Thou art as wise as thou art beautiful.

BOTTOM: Not so neither: but if I had wit enough to get out of
this wood, I have enough to serve mine own turn.   135

TITANIA: Out of this wood do not desire to go—
Thou shalt remain here, whether thou wilt or no.
I am a spirit of no common rate:°   *of no ordinary rank*
The summer still doth tend upon my state,°   *does my royal bidding*
And I do love thee; therefore go with me.   140
I'll give thee fairies to attend on thee;
And they shall fetch thee jewels from the deep,°   *ocean*
And sing, while thou on pressèd flowers dost sleep:
And I will purge thy mortal grossness so,°   *strip you of your heavy human body*

That thou shalt like an airy spirit go. 145
Peaseblossom, Cobweb, Moth, and Mustardseed!

[Enter four FAIRIES.]

PEASEBLOSSOM: Ready.
COBWEB: And I.
MOTH: And I.
MUSTARDSEED: And I.
ALL: Where shall we go?
TITANIA: Be kind and courteous to this gentleman,
Hop in his walks and gambol in his eyes,°   *dance before him* 150
Feed him with apricots and dewberries,
With purple grapes, green figs, and mulberries.
The honey bags steal from the bumblebees,
And for night tapers,° crop° their waxen thighs,   *candles / clip*
And light them at the fiery glowworm's eyes, 155
To have my love to bed and to arise;
And pluck the wings from painted butterflies,
To fan the moonbeams from his sleeping eyes.
Nod to him, elves, and do him courtesies.
PEASEBLOSSOM: Hail, mortal. 160
COBWEB: Hail.
MOTH: Hail.
MUSTARDSEED: Hail.
BOTTOM: I cry your worships mercy,° heartily; I beseech your   *I beg your honors' pardon*
worship's name. 165
COBWEB: Cobweb.
BOTTOM: I shall desire you of more acquaintance,° good Mas-   *I shall use your services*
ter Cobweb;° if I cut my finger, I shall make bold with   *(cobwebs were used as*
you. Your name, honest gentleman?   *natural bandaids)*
PEASEBLOSSOM: Peaseblossom. 170
BOTTOM: I pray you commend me to Mistress Squash,° your   *unripe pea pod*
mother, and to Master Peascod,° your father. Good Mas-   *ripe pea pod*
ter Peaseblossom, I shall desire you of more acquaintance,
too. Your name, I beseech you, sir?
MUSTARDSEED: Mustardseed. 175
BOTTOM: Good Master Mustardseed, I know your patience
well. That same cowardly giant-like ox beef° hath de-   *(beef was eaten with*
voured many a gentleman of your house. I promise you,   *mustard)*
your kindred hath made my eyes water ere now.° I desire   *(with pity or with the sharp*
you of more acquaintance, good Master Mustardseed.   *flavor?)* 180
TITANIA: Come, wait upon him; lead him to my bower.°   *enclosed leafy shelter*
The moon methinks looks with a watery eye:
And when she weeps, weeps every little flower,
Lamenting some enforcèd° chastity.   *violated*
Tie up my lover's tongue, bring him silently. 185

[They leave.]

SCENE 2. Another part of the forest.

[*Enter* OBERON, *King of fairies, alone.*]

OBERON: I wonder if Titania be awaked;
      Then what it was that next came in her eye,
      Which she must dote on in extremity.°   *love to distraction*

      [*Enter* PUCK.]

      Here comes my messenger. How now, mad spirit?
      What night-rule° now about this haunted grove?   *nighttime capers*   5
PUCK: My mistress with a monster is in love.
      Near to her close and consecrated bower,
      While she was in her dull and sleeping hour,
      A crew of patches, rude mechanicals,°   *fools (who should wear the fool's patched,*
      That work for bread upon Athenian stalls,   *motley garb), crude menials*   10
      Were met together to rehearse a play,
      Intended for great Theseus' nuptial day.
      The shallowest thickskin of that barren sort,°   *ignorant crew*
      Who Pyramus presented° in their sport,   *represented*
      Forsook° his scene and entered in a brake,°   *left/thicket*   15
      When I did him at this advantage take,
      An ass's nole° I fixèd on his head.   *noodle (head)*
      Anon° his Thisby must be answerèd,   *soon*
      And forth my mimic° comes. When they him spy,   *actor*
      As wild geese that the creeping fowler eye,°   *spot the stealthy hunter*   20
      Or russet-pated choughs,° many in sort,   *gray-headed jackdaws*
      Rising and cawing at the gun's report,
      Sever themselves and madly sweep the sky,
      So at his sight away his fellows fly;
      And at our stamp,° here over and over one falls;   *our stamping (stampeding them)*   25
      He "murder" cries, and help from Athens calls.
      Their sense thus weak, lost with their fears thus strong,
      Made senseless things begin to do them wrong.
      For briers and thorns at their apparel snatch:
      Some sleeves, some hats, from yielders° all things catch.   *from those ready*   30
      I led them on in this distracted fear,   *to yield up*
      And left sweet Pyramus translated° there: *transformed*
      When in that moment (so it came to pass)
      Titania waked, and straightway loved an ass.
OBERON: This falls out better than I could devise.   35
      But hast thou yet latched° the Athenian's eyes   *moistened*
      With the love juice, as I did bid thee do?
PUCK: I took him sleeping (that is finished too)
      And the Athenian woman by his side;
      That when he waked, of force° she must be eyed.   *necessarily*   40

      [*Enter* DEMETRIUS *and* HERMIA.]

OBERON: Stand close: this is the same Athenian.
PUCK: This is the woman, but not this the man.
DEMETRIUS: O why rebuke you him that loves you so?
      Lay breath so bitter on your bitter foe.

HERMIA: Now I but chide; but I should use thee worse, 45
    For thou, I fear, hast given me cause to curse.
    If thou hast slain Lysander in his sleep,
    Being over shoes in blood, plunge in the deep,°   *to the full depth*
    And kill me too.
    The sun was not so true unto the day, 50
    As he to me. Would he have stolen away
    From sleeping Hermia? I'll believe as soon
    This whole° earth may be bored,° and that the moon   *solid/drilled through*
    May through the center creep, and so displease
    Her brother's noontide with the Antipodes.°   *the sun at noon for those* 55
    It cannot be but thou hast murdered him.   *on the other side of the earth*
    So should a murderer look; so dead, so grim.
DEMETRIUS: So should the murdered look, and so should I,
    Pierced through the heart with your stern cruelty.
    Yet you, the murderer, look as bright, as clear, 60
    As yonder Venus in her glimmering sphere.
HERMIA: What's this to my Lysander? Where is he?
    Ah good Demetrius, wilt thou give him me?
DEMETRIUS: I had rather give his carcass to my hounds.
HERMIA: Out dog, out cur! Thou driv'st me past the bounds 65
    Of maiden's patience. Hast thou slain him then?
    Henceforth be never numbered among men.
    O, once tell true! Tell true, even for my sake:
    Durst thou have looked° upon him, being awake?   *would you have dared to look*
    And hast thou killed him sleeping? O brave touch! 70
    Could not a worm,° an adder, do so much?   *serpent*
    An adder did it: for with doubler° tongue   *more forked (and false)*
    Than thine, thou serpent, never adder stung.
DEMETRIUS: You spend your passion on a misprised mood:°   *in mistaken anger*
    I am not guilty of Lysander's blood. 75
    Nor is he dead, for aught that I can tell.
HERMIA: I pray thee, tell me then that he is well.
DEMETRIUS: And if I could, what should I get therefore?°   *in return*
HERMIA: A privilege never to see me more.
    And from thy hated presence part I so: 80
    See me no more, whether he be dead or no.

                     [*She leaves.*]

DEMETRIUS: There is no following her in this fierce vein.
    Here therefore for a while I will remain.
    So sorrow's heaviness doth heavier grow
    For° debt that bankrupt° sleep doth sorrow owe: *because of the/delayed* 85
    Which now in some slight measure it will pay,
    If for his tender here I make some stay.°   *if I wait here for payment*

    [*He lies down.*]

OBERON: What hast thou done? Thou hast mistaken quite,
           And laid the love-juice on some true-love's sight.

Of thy misprison° must perforce ensue   *mistake* 90
Some true love turned,° and not a false turned true.   *turned bad*
PUCK: Then fate overrules, that one man holding troth,°   *staying faithful*
A million fail, confounding° oath on oath.   *betraying*
OBERON: About the wood, go swifter than the wind,
And Helena of Athens look thou find.   95
All fancy-sick° she is, and pale of cheer,°   *lovesick/face*
With sighs of love that costs the fresh blood dear.°   *depletes young blood*
By some illusion see thou bring her here:
I'll charm his eyes against° she do appear.   *until*
PUCK: I go, I go, look how I go.   100
Swifter than arrow from the Tartar's bow.

[*He leaves.*]

OBERON: Flower of this purple dye,
Hit with Cupid's archery,
Sink in apple of his eye:
When his love he doth espy,°   *he sees* 105
Let her shine as gloriously
As the Venus of the sky.
When thou wak'st, if she be by,
Beg of her for remedy.

[*Enter* PUCK.]

PUCK: Captain of our fairy band,   110
Helena is here at hand,
And the youth, mistook by me,
Pleading for a lover's fee.°   *reward*
Shall we their fond° pageant see?   *foolish*
Lord, what fools these mortals be!   115
OBERON: Stand aside. The noise they make
Will cause Demetrius to awake.
PUCK: Then will two at once woo one:
That must needs be sport alone.°   *great entertainment*
And those things do best please me   120
That befall preposterously.

[*Enter* LYSANDER *and* HELENA.]

LYSANDER: Why should you think that I should woo in scorn?°   *woo to mock you*
Scorn and derision never come in tears.
Look when I vow,° I weep; and vows so born,   *swear oaths of love*
In their nativity all truth appears.°   *their tear-stained origin* 125
    makes them genuine
How can these things in me seem scorn to you,
Bearing the badge of faith to prove them true?
HELENA: You do advance° your cunning more and more.   *show*
When truth kills truth,° O devilish-holy fray!   *(a new "true love" kills the old)*
These vows are Hermia's. Will you give her o'er?°   *give her up* 130
Weigh oath with oath, and you will nothing weigh.
Your vows to her and me, put in two scales,

Will even weigh; and both as light as tales.

LYSANDER: I had no judgment, when to her I swore.

HELENA: Nor none, in my mind, now you give her o'er. 135

LYSANDER: Demetrius loves her: and he loves not you.

DEMETRIUS (*awakes*): O Helen, goddess, nymph, perfect, divine,
    To what, my love, shall I compare thine eyne!
    Crystal is muddy. O, how ripe in show,
    Thy lips, those kissing cherries, tempting grow! 140
    That pure congealèd white, high Taurus'° snow,   (*Near Eastern mountain*)
    Fanned with the eastern wind, turns to a crow,
    When thou hold'st up thy hand. O let me kiss
    This princess of pure white, this seal of bliss.

HELENA: O spite! O hell! I see you all are bent 145
    To set against me, for your merriment.
    If you were civil and knew courtesy,
    You would not do me thus much injury.
    Can you not hate me, as I know you do,
    But you must join in souls to mock me too? 150
    If you were men, as men you are in show,°   *appearance*
    You would not use a gentle lady° so;   *treat a well-born lady*
    To vow, and swear, and superpraise my parts,
    When I am sure you hate me with your hearts.
    You both are rivals, and love Hermia; 155
    And now both rivals, to mock Helena.
    A trim° exploit, a manly enterprise,   *fine*
    To conjure tears up in a poor maid's eyes
    With your derision.° None of noble sort   *mockery*
    Would so offend a virgin, and extort°   *wear down* 160
    A poor soul's patience, all to make you sport.

LYSANDER: You are unkind, Demetrius: be not so.
    For you love Hermia; this you know I know.
    And here, with all good will, with all my heart,
    In Hermia's love I yield you up my part; 165
    And yours of Helena to me bequeath,
    Whom I do love, and will do to my death.

HELENA: Never did mockers waste more idle breath.

DEMETRIUS: Lysander, keep thy Hermia; I will none.°   *none of her*
    If ever I loved her, all that love is gone. 170
    My heart to her but as guestwise sojourned,°   *stayed with her only as a guest*
    And now to Helen is it home returned,
    There to remain.

LYSANDER: Helen, it is not so.

DEMETRIUS: Disparage not the faith thou dost not know,
    Lest to thy peril thou aby it dear.°   *pay for it dearly* 175
    Look where thy love comes; yonder is thy dear.

    [*Enter* HERMIA.]

HERMIA: Dark night, that from the eye his function takes,°   *makes the eye useless*
    The ear more quick of apprehension makes.°   *gives the ear sharper hearing*
    Wherein it doth impair the seeing sense,

It pays the hearing double recompense. 180
Thou art not by mine eye, Lysander, found;
Mine ear, I thank it, brought me to thy sound.
But why unkindly didst thou leave me so?
LYSANDER: Why should he stay, whom love doth press ° to go? *force*
HERMIA: What love could press Lysander from my side? 185
LYSANDER: Lysander's love, that would not let him bide:
Fair Helena, who more engilds the night
Than all you fiery oes and eyes° of light. *o's and i's—orbs and eyes*
Why seek'st thou me? Could not this make thee know,
The hate I bore thee made me leave thee so? 190
HERMIA: You speak not as you think; it cannot be.
HELENA: Lo, she is one of this confederacy!
Now I perceive they have conjoined all three,
To fashion this false sport in spite of me.
Injurious° Hermia, most ungrateful maid, *insulting* 195
Have you conspired,° have you with these contrived *plotted*
To bait me with this foul derision?
Is all the counsel that we two have shared,
The sisters' vows, the hours that we have spent,
When we have chid° the hasty-footed time *scolded* 200
For parting us; O, is all forgot?
All schooldays' friendship, childhood innocence?
We Hermia, like two artificial° gods, *skilled in art*
Have with our needles created both one flower,
Both on one sampler, sitting on one cushion, 205
Both warbling of one song, both in one key;
As if our hands, our sides, voices, and minds
Had been incorporate. So we grew together,° *made one body*
Like to a double cherry, seeming parted,
But yet an union in partition, 210
Two lovely berries molded on one stem:
So with two seeming bodies, but one heart,
Two of the first, like coats in heraldry,° *a double coat of arms*
Due but to one, and crownèd with one crest.
And will you rent° our ancient love asunder, *tear apart* 215
To join with men in scorning your poor friend?
It is not friendly, 'tis not maidenly.
Our sex, as well as I, may chide you for it;
Though I alone do feel the injury.
HERMIA: I am amazèd at your passionate words: 220
I scorn you not. It seems that you scorn me.
HELENA: Have you not set Lysander, as in scorn,
To follow me, and praise my eyes and face?
And made your other love, Demetrius
(Who even but now did spurn me with his foot) 225
To call me goddess, nymph, divine, and rare,
Precious, celestial? Wherefore speaks he this
To her he hates? And wherefore doth Lysander
Deny your love,° so rich within his soul, *his love for you*

And tender me (forsooth)° affection, *in truth* 230
But by your setting on, by your consent?
What though I be not so in grace as you,
So hung upon with love, so fortunate,
But miserable most, to love unloved?
This you should pity, rather than despise. 235
HERMIA: I understand not what you mean by this.
HELENA: Ay, do. Persèver,° counterfeit sad looks: *persevere*
Make mouths upon° me when I turn my back: *make faces at*
Wink each at other, hold the sweet jest up.
This sport well carried, shall be chronicled.° *if well carried out, should* 240
be written up
If you have any pity, grace, or manners,
You would not make me such an argument.° *such a target*
But fare ye well. 'Tis partly my own fault,
Which death or absence soon shall remedy.
LYSANDER: Stay, gentle Helena; hear my excuse,° *defense* 245
My love, my life, my soul, fair Helena.
HELENA: O excellent!
HERMIA: Sweet, do not scorn° her so. *mock*
DEMETRIUS: If she cannot entreat,° I can compel. *succeed by entreating*
LYSANDER: Thou canst compel no more than she entreat.
Thy threats have no more strength than her weak prayers. 250
Helen, I love thee, by my life I do:
I swear by that which I will lose° for thee, *by my life, which I will risk*
To prove him false that says I love thee not.
DEMETRIUS: I say I love thee more than he can do.
LYSANDER: If thou say so, withdraw° and prove it too. *draw your sword* 255
DEMETRIUS: Quick, come.
HERMIA: Lysander, whereto tends all this?
LYSANDER: Away, you Ethiope.° *(he calls her names alluding*
to her dark hair)
DEMETRIUS: No, no, sir,
Seem to break loose: take on as you would follow,° *pretend you'll follow me*
(to a duel)
But yet come not. You are a tame man, go.
LYSANDER: Hang off, thou cat, thou burr! Vile thing, let loose,° *let go* 260
Or I will shake thee from me like a serpent.
HERMIA: Why are you grown so rude? What change is this,
Sweet love?
LYSANDER: Thy love? Out, tawny Tartar, out!
Out, loathèd medicine! O hated potion, hence!
HERMIA: Do you not jest?
HELENA: Yes, sooth;° and so do you. *truly* 265
LYSANDER: Demetrius, I will keep my word with thee.
DEMETRIUS: I would I had your bond.° For I perceive *wish I had it in writing*
A weak bond holds you. I'll not trust your word.
LYSANDER: What? Should I hurt her, strike her, kill her dead?
Although I hate her, I'll not harm her so. 270
HERMIA: What? Can you do me greater harm than hate?
Hate me, wherefore? O me, what news, my love?
Am not I Hermia? Are not you Lysander?
I am as fair now, as I was erewhile.° *a while ago*

Since night,° you loved me; yet since night, you left me.   *when night fell*   275
Why then, you left me—O, the gods forbid—
In earnest, shall I say?
LYSANDER: Ay, by my life!
And never did desire to see thee more.
Therefore be out of hope, of question, of doubt:
Be certain: nothing truer. 'Tis no jest   280
That I do hate thee, and love Helena.
HERMIA: O me, you juggler, you canker blossom,°   *worm blighting the blossom*
You thief of love! What, have you come by night,
And stolen my love's heart from him?
HELENA: Fine, in faith.
Have you no modesty, no maiden shame,   285
No touch of bashfulness? What, will you tear
Impatient answers from my gentle tongue?
Fie, fie, you counterfeit, you puppet,° you.   *little doll*
HERMIA: Puppet? why so—ay, that way goes the game.
Now I perceive that she hath made compare   290
Between our statures, she hath urged her height,°   *pointed out how tall she is*
And with her personage, her tall personage,
Her height (forsooth) she hath prevailed with him.
And are you grown so high in his esteem,
Because I am so dwarfish and so low?   295
How low am I, thou painted maypole? Speak:
How low am I? I am not yet so low,
But that my nails can reach unto thine eyes.
HELENA: I pray you, though you mock me, gentlemen,
Let her not hurt me. I was never curst;°   *ill-tempered*   300
I have no gift at all in shrewishness;°   *bad temper*
I am a right maid° for my cowardice.   *true to the stereotype*
Let her not strike me. You perhaps may think,
Because she is something lower than myself,
That I can match her.
HERMIA: Lower? Hark again.   305
HELENA: Good Hermia, do not be so bitter with me,
I evermore did love you, Hermia,
Did ever keep your counsels,° never wronged you;   *always kept your secrets*
Save that in love unto Demetrius,
I told him of your stealth° unto this wood.   *secret trip*   310
He followed you; for love I followed him.
But he hath chid me hence, and threatened me
To strike me, spurn me, nay to kill me too;
And now, so° you will let me quiet go,   *if only*
To Athens will I bear my folly back,   315
And follow you no further. Let me go.
You see how simple and how fond° I am.   *silly*
HERMIA: Why, get you gone. Who is't that hinders you?
HELENA: A foolish heart, that I leave here behind.
HERMIA: What, with Lysander?
HELENA: With Demetrius.   320

LYSANDER: Be not afraid. She shall not harm thee, Helena.

DEMETRIUS: No, sir; she shall not, though you take her part.

HELENA: O when she's angry, she is keen and shrewd.°   *sharp-tongued and hostile*

    She was a vixen when she went to school;

    And though she be but little, she is fierce.   325

HERMIA: "Little" again? nothing but "low" and "little"?

    Why will you suffer her to flout me thus?

    Let me come to her.

LYSANDER: Get you gone, you dwarf;

    You minimus,° of hindering knot-grass° made;   *tiniest thing/growth-stunting weed*

    You bead, you acorn!

DEMETRIUS: You are too officious   330

    In her behalf that scorns your services.

    Let her alone. Speak not of Helena;

    Take not her part. For if thou dost intend

    Never so little show of love to her,

    Thou shalt aby° it.   *pay for*

LYSANDER: Now she holds me not: 335

    Now follow, if thou dar'st, to try° whose right,   *test in combat*

    Of thine or mine, is most in Helena.

DEMETRIUS: Follow? Nay, I'll go with thee, cheek by jowl.

[LYSANDER *and* DEMETRIUS *leave.*]

HERMIA: You, mistress, all this coil is long of you.°   *this turmoil is because of you*

    Nay, go not back.

HELENA: I will not trust you, I,   340

    Nor longer stay in your curst company.

    Your hands than mine are quicker for a fray;

    My legs are longer though, to run away.

HERMIA: I am amazed,° and know not what to say.   *totally confused*

[*They both leave.*]

OBERON: This is thy negligence: still thou mistak'st,°   *you always blunder* 345

    Or else commit'st thy knaveries wilfully.

PUCK: Believe me, king of shadows, I mistook.°   *made an honest mistake*

    Did not you tell me I should know the man

    By the Athenian garments he had on?

    And so far blameless proves my enterprise   350

    That I've anointed an Athenian's eyes:

    And so far am I glad it so did sort,°   *worked out as such*

    As this their jangling I esteem a sport.

OBERON: Thou seest these lovers seek a place to fight;

    Hie,° therefore, Robin; overcast the night,   *make haste* 355

    The starry welkin cover thou° anon   *cover the heavens*

    With drooping fog as black as Acheron,°   *(a river bordering Hell)*

    And lead these testy° rivals so astray   *angry*

    As° one come not within another's way.   *that*

    Like to Lysander sometime frame thy tongue;°   *talk like Lysander* 360

    Then stir Demetrius up with bitter wrong;°   *insults*

    And sometime rail thou like Demetrius—

And from each other look thou lead them thus;
Till over their brows death-counterfeiting sleep
With leaden legs and batty° wings doth creep.   *batlike* 365
Then crush this herb into Lysander's eye,
Whose liquor hath this virtuous property°   *whose liquid has the power*
To take from thence all error with his might,
And make his eyeballs roll with wonted° sight.   *usual*
When they next wake, all this derision°   *frivolity* 370
Shall seem a dream, and fruitless vision,
And back to Athens shall the lovers wend,°   *go*
With league whose date° till death shall never end.   *in a union whose*
Whiles I in this affair do thee employ,   *appointed time*
I'll to my queen and beg° her Indian boy: *beg for* 375
And then I will her charmèd° eye release   *bewitched*
From monster's view, and all things shall be peace.
PUCK: My fairy lord, this must be done with haste,
For night's swift dragons cut the clouds full fast:
And yonder shines Aurora's harbinger,°   *(the morning star,* 380
At whose approach, ghosts wandering here and there   *the messenger of dawn)*
Troop home to churchyards; damnèd spirits all,
That in crossways and floods have burial,°   *(suicides buried outside churchyards)*
Already to their wormy beds are gone.
For fear lest day should look their shames upon,   385
They wilfully themselves exile from light,
And must for aye consort° with black-browed night.   *must forever keep company*
OBERON: But we are spirits of another sort.
I with the morning's love° have oft made sport,   *(the love of Aurora—or her*
And like a forester, the groves may tread   *legendary lover?)* 390
Even till the eastern gate all fiery red,
Opening on Neptune,° with fair blessèd beams,   *(god of the ocean)*
Turns into yellow gold his salt green streams.
But notwithstanding, haste, make no delay:
We may effect his business yet ere day.°   *before daybreak* 395

[*He leaves.*]

PUCK: Up and down, up and down,
     I will lead them up and down.
     I am feared in field and town.
     Goblin, lead them up and down.
Here comes one.   400

[*Enter* LYSANDER.]

LYSANDER: Where art thou, proud Demetrius? Speak thou now.
PUCK: Here villain, drawn° and ready. Where art thou?   *with sword drawn*
LYSANDER: I will be with thee straight.
PUCK: Follow me then
     To plainer° ground.   *more level*

[LYSANDER *leaves.*]

[*Enter* DEMETRIUS.]

DEMETRIUS: Lysander, speak again.
    Thou runaway, thou coward, art thou fled?   405
    Speak: in some bush? Where dost thou hide thy head?
PUCK: Thou coward, art thou bragging to the stars,
    Telling the bushes that thou look'st for wars,
    And wilt not come? Come, recreant;° come, thou child;   *faithless creature*
    I'll whip thee with a rod. He is defiled°   *dishonored*   410
    That draws a sword on thee.
DEMETRIUS: Yea, art thou there?
PUCK: Follow my voice: we'll try no manhood° here.   *will not test our manly courage*

                                                    [*They leave.*]

    [*Enter* LYSANDER.]

LYSANDER: He goes before me and still dares me on:
    When I come where he calls, then he is gone.
    The villain is much lighter-heeled than I;   415
    I followed fast, but faster he did fly,
    That fallen am I in dark uneven way,
    And here will rest me. [*lies down*] Come, thou gentle day,
    For if but once thou show me thy grey light,
    I'll find Demetrius and revenge this spite.   420

    [*Sleeps.*]
        [*Enter* PUCK, *taunting* DEMETRIUS *in the voice of* LYSANDER.]

PUCK: Ho, ho, ho! Coward, why com'st thou not?
DEMETRIUS: Abide° me, if thou dar'st, for well I wot°   *wait for/I know*
    Thou run'st before me, shifting every place,
    And dar'st not stand, nor look me in the face.
    Where art thou now?
PUCK: Come hither; I am here.   425
DEMETRIUS: Nay then thou mock'st me. Thou shalt buy this dear,°   *pay for this dearly*
    If ever I thy face by daylight see.
    Now go thy way. Faintness constraineth me
    To measure out° my length on this cold bed.   *stretch out*
    By day's approach look to be visited.   430

    [*Lies down and sleeps.*]
        [*Enter* HELENA.]

HELENA: O weary night, O long and tedious night,
                Abate° thy hours; shine comforts° from the east,   *shorten/may comforting*
        That I may back to Athens by daylight,   *rays of light shine*
                From these that my poor company detest:
        And sleep, that sometimes shuts up sorrow's eye,   435
        Steal me awhile from mine own company.

    [*Sleeps.*]

PUCK: Yet but three? Come one more,
        Two of both kinds makes up four.
        Here she comes, curst° and sad.   *cross*

Cupid is a knavish lad,   440
Thus to make poor females mad.

[*Enter* HERMIA.]

HERMIA: Never so weary, never so in woe,
          Bedabbled with the dew, and torn with briers,
          I can no further crawl, no further go:
          My legs can keep no pace with my desires.   445
          Here will I rest me till the break of day.
          Heavens shield Lysander, if they mean a fray.°   *intend to fight*

[*Lies down and sleeps.*]

PUCK: On the ground,
                    Sleep sound:
                    I'll apply   450
                    To your eye,
                Gentle lover, remedy.

[*Squeezes the love-juice on* LYSANDER's *eyelids.*]

                    When thou wak'st,
                    Thou tak'st
                    True delight   455
                    In the sight
                Of thy former lady's eye:
                And the country proverb known,
                That every man should take his own,
                In your waking shall be shown.   460
                    Jack shall have Jill
                    Naught shall go ill;
          The man shall have his mare again, and all shall be well.

[*He leaves. The others remain sleeping on the stage through the next act.*]

ACT FOUR

SCENE 1

[*Enter* TITANIA, *Queen of fairies, and* BOTTOM THE CLOWN,
and fairies, and the King, OBERON, *behind them unseen.*]

TITANIA: Come sit thee down upon this flowery bed,
          While I thy amiable cheeks do coy,°   *caress your lovely cheeks*
          And stick musk-roses in thy sleek smooth head,
          And kiss thy fair large ears, my gentle joy.
BOTTOM: Where's Peaseblossom?   5
PEASEBLOSSOM: Ready.
BOTTOM: Scratch my head, Peaseblossom. Where's Monsieur
    Cobweb?
COBWEB: Ready.

BOTTOM: Monsieur Cobweb, good monsieur, get you your   10
   weapons in your hand, and kill me a red-hipped humble-
   bee on the top of a thistle; and, good monsieur, bring me
   the honey bag. Do not fret° yourself too much in the ac-   *exert*
   tion, monsieur; and, good monsieur, have a care the honey
   bag break not, I would be loath° to have you overflowen   *I would hate*   15
   with a honey bag, signior. Where's Monsieur Mustard-
   seed?
MUSTARDSEED: Ready.
BOTTOM: Give me your neaf,° Monsieur Mustardseed. Pray   *hand*
   you leave your curtsy,° good monsieur.   *stop your ceremonious greeting*   20
MUSTARDSEED: What's your will?
BOTTOM: Nothing, good monsieur, but to help Cavalery°   *(he means "cavalier" knight)*
   Cobweb to scratch. I must to the barber's monsieur, for
   methinks I am marvellous hairy about the face. And I am
   such a tender ass, if my hair do but tickle me, I must   25
   scratch.
TITANIA: What, will thou hear some music, my sweet love?
BOTTOM: I have a reasonable good ear in music. Let's have the
   tongs and the bones.°   *(peasant music made with*
TITANIA: Or say, sweet love, what thou desirest to eat.   *clanging metal and bone*   30
                                                                       clappers)
BOTTOM: Truly, a peck of provender. I could munch your
   good dry oats. Methinks I have a great desire to a bottle°   *bundle*
   of hay. Good hay, sweet hay, hath no fellow.°   *is unmatched (as good food)*
TITANIA: I have a venturous fairy that shall seek
   The squirrel's hoard, and fetch thee new nuts.   35
BOTTOM: I had rather have a handful or two of dried peas. But
   I pray you, let none of your people stir me: I have an ex-
   position° of sleep come upon me.   *(he means "disposition")*
TITANIA: Sleep thou, and I will wind thee° in my arms.   *hold you*
   Fairies, be gone, and be all ways away.   40

                       [FAIRIES *leave.*]

So doth the woodbine the sweet honeysuckle
Gently entwist; the female ivy so
Enrings the barky fingers° of the elm.   *like a woman, it embraces*
O how I love thee! how I dote on thee!   *the bark-covered branches*

[*They sleep.*]
[*Enter* ROBIN GOODFELLOW (PUCK).]

OBERON [*advances*]: Welcome, good Robin. Seest thou this sweet sight?   45
   Her dotage° now I do begin to pity.   *infatuation*
   For meeting her of late behind the wood,
   Seeking sweet favors° for this hateful fool,   *flowery love tokens*
   I did upbraid her and fall out° with her.   *berate her and quarrel*
   For she his hairy temples then had rounded   50
   With coronet° of fresh and fragrant flowers.   *crownlike garland*
   And that same dew which sometime on the buds

Was wont to swell like round and orient pearls,°   *precious pearls from the East*
Stood now within the pretty flowerets' eyes,
Like tears that did their own disgrace bewail.   55
When I had at my pleasure taunted her,
And she in mild terms begged my patience,
I then did ask of her her changeling child,
Which straight she gave me, and her fairy sent
To bear him to my bower in fairy land.   60
And now I have the boy, I will undo
This hateful imperfection° of her eyes.   *malfunction*
And gentle Puck, take this transformèd scalp
From off the head of this Athenian swain;°   *rustic lover*
That he, awaking when the other do,   65
May all to Athens back again repair,°   *go back*
And think no more of this night's accidents,°   *happenings*
But as the fierce vexation of a dream.
But first I will release the Fairy Queen.
        Be as thou wast wont to° be: *as you used to*   70
        See, as thou wast wont to see.
        Dian's bud° o'er Cupid's flower   *flower dedicated to the chaste*
        Hath such force and blessèd power.   *goddess Diana*
Now my Titania, wake you, my sweet queen.
TITANIA: My Oberon, what visions have I seen!   75
Methought I was enamored of an ass.
OBERON There lies your love.
TITANIA: How came these things to pass?
O, how mine eyes do loathe his visage now!
OBERON: Silence awhile. Robin, take off this head.
Titania, music call, and strike more dead°   *make their senses slumber*   80
Than common sleep of all these five the sense.   *in a more deathlike sleep*
TITANIA: Music, ho music! such as charmeth sleep.
PUCK: Now, when thou wak'st, with thine own fool's eyes peep.
OBERON: Sound, music! [*music*] Come my queen, take hands with me,
And rock the ground whereon these sleepers be.   85

[*Dance.*]

Now thou and I are new in amity,
And will tomorrow midnight solemnly
Dance in Duke Theseus' house triumphantly,
And bless it to all fair prosperity.
There shall the pairs of faithful lovers be   90
Wedded, with Theseus, all in jollity.
PUCK: Fairy King, attend and mark:
        I do hear the morning lark.
OBERON: Then my queen, in silence sad,°   *in solemn silence*
        Trip we after the night's shade.   95
        We the globe can compass° soon,   *can circle the globe*
        Swifter than the wandering moon.
TITANIA: Come my lord, and in our flight,

Tell me how it came this night
That I sleeping here was found,
With these mortals on the ground.   100

[*They leave.*]
[*The sound of horns. Enter* THESEUS, HIPPOLYTA, EGEUS, *and all his train.*]

THESEUS: Go one of you, find out the forester:
For now our observation° is performed.   *observance of May Day*
And since we have the vaward° of the day,   *the vanguard (early morning)*
My love shall hear the music of my hounds.
Uncouple° in the western valley, let them go: *unleash them*   105
Dispatch,° I say, and find the forester.   *hurry*

[*An attendant hurries off.*]

We will, fair queen, up to the mountain's top,
And mark the musical confusion
Of hounds and echo in conjunction.   110
HIPPOLYTA: I was with Hercules and Cadmus° once,   *(legendary Greek monster killers)*
When in a wood of Crete they bayed° the bear,   *cornered (brought it to bay)*
With hounds of Sparta; never did I hear
Such gallant chiding.° For besides the groves,   *brave barking*
The skies, the fountains, every region near   115
Seemed all one mutual cry.° I never heard   *seemed filled by one single*
So musical a discord, such sweet thunder.   *pack of hounds*
THESEUS: My hounds are bred out of the Spartan kind:
So flewed, so sanded,° and their heads are hung   *with hanging cheeks and*
With ears that sweep away the morning dew,   *sand colored*   120
Crook-kneed, and dewlapped° like Thessalian bulls—   *with chin folds*
Slow in pursuit, but matched in mouth° like bells,   *in sound*
Each under each. A cry more tuneable°   *a pack more musical*
Was never holloa'd to,° nor cheered with horn,   *greeted by the hunters' call*
In Crete, in Sparta, nor in Thessaly.°   *(sites in Greece)*   125
Judge when you hear. But soft. What nymphs are these?
EGEUS: My lord, this is my daughter here asleep,
And this Lysander, this Demetrius is,
This Helena, old Nedar's Helena.
I wonder of their being here together.   130
THESEUS: No doubt they rose up early to observe
The rite of May, and, hearing our intent,
Came here in grace of our solemnity.°   *to honor our festivities*
But speak Egeus, is not this the day
That Hermia should give answer of her choice?   135
EGEUS: It is, my lord.
THESEUS: Go bid the huntsmen wake them with their horns.

[*Shout within and sound of horns. They all start up.*]

Good morrow, friends. Saint Valentine is past.
Begin these wood-birds° but to couple now?   *(birds supposedly began to*
LYSANDER: Pardon, my lord.   *mate on Valentine's Day)*

[*They kneel.*]

THESEUS: I pray you all, stand up.   140
    I know you two are rival enemies.
    How comes this gentle concord in the world,
    That hatred is so far from jealousy,°   *suspicion*
    To sleep by hate,° and fear no enmity?   *near a hated person*
LYSANDER: My lord, I shall reply amazedly,°   *bewildered*   145
    Half sleep, half waking. But as yet, I swear,
    I cannot truly say how I came here.
    But as I think—for truly would I speak,
    And now I do bethink me, so it is—
    I came with Hermia hither. Our intent   150
    Was to be gone from Athens, where we might,
    Without the peril of° the Athenian law—   *beyond the threat from*
EGEUS: Enough, enough, my lord: you have enough.
    I beg the law, the law, upon his head.
    They would have stolen away, they would, Demetrius,   155
    Thereby to have defeated° you and me: *defrauded*
    You of your wife, and me of my consent—
    Of my consent that she should be your wife.
DEMETRIUS: My lord, fair Helen told me of their stealth,°   *secret flight*
    Of this their purpose hither, to this wood,   160
    And I in fury hither followed them;
    Fair Helena in fancy° following me.   *driven by love*
    But my good lord, I wot not° by what power   *know not*
    (But by some power it is) my love to Hermia,
    Melted as the snow, seems to me now   165
    As the remembrance of an idle gaud,°   *worthless toy*
    Which in my childhood I did dote upon;
    And all the faith, the virtue of my heart,
    The object and the pleasure of mine eye,
    Is only Helena. To her, my lord,   170
    Was I betrothed ere I saw Hermia:
    But like a sickness,° did I loathe this food.   *as in sickness*
    But as in health, come to my natural taste,
    Now I do wish it, love it, long for it,
    And will for evermore be true to it.   175
THESEUS: Fair lovers, you are fortunately met.
    Of this discourse we more will hear anon.
    Egeus, I will overbear° your will: *overrule*
    For in the temple, by and by,° with us,   *soon*
    These couples shall eternally be knit.   180
    And for the morning now is something worn,°   *in part gone*
    Our purposed° hunting shall be set aside.   *intended*
    Away with us to Athens. Three and three,
    We'll hold a feast in great solemnity.
    Come Hippolyta.   185

[DUKE, HIPPOLYTA, EGEUS, *and lords leave.*]

DEMETRIUS: These things seem small and undistinguishable,

Like far-off mountains turnèd into clouds.
HERMIA: Methinks I see these things with parted° eye,   *unfocused*
When everything seems double.
HELENA: So methinks:
And I have found Demetrius, like a jewel,   190
Mine own, and not mine own.°   *(because the jewel might have to be*
DEMETRIUS: Are you sure   *returned to whoever lost it)*
That we are awake? It seems to me,
That yet we sleep, we dream. Do not you think
The duke was here, and bid us follow him?
HERMIA: Yea, and my father.
HELENA: And Hippolyta.   195
LYSANDER: And he did bid us follow to the temple.
DEMETRIUS: Why then, we are awake: let's follow him,
And by the way let us recount our dreams.

                              [*The lovers leave.*]

BOTTOM (*wakes*): When my cue comes, call me, and I will an-
swer. My next is "Most fair Pyramus." Hey, ho! Peter   200
Quince? Flute the bellows-mender? Snout the tinker?
Starveling? God's my life!° Stol'n hence, and left me   *God bless my life*
asleep? I have had a most rare vision. I have had a dream,
past the wit of man to say what dream it was. Man is but
an ass, if he go about to expound this dream. Methought°   *I thought*   205
I was—there is no man can tell what. Methought I was,
and methought I had—but man is but a patched fool,° if   *fool with patched*
he will offer to say what methought I had. The eye of man   *(motley) garb*
hath not heard, the ear of man hath not seen, man's hand
is not able to taste, his tongue to conceive, nor his heart   210
to report, what my dream was. I will get Peter Quince to
write a ballad of this dream: it shall be called Bottom's
Dream, because it hath no bottom; and I will sing it in the
latter end of our play, before the duke. Peradventure,° to   *perhaps*
make it the more gracious, I shall sing it at her death.°   *at the death of Thisby*   215

                              [*He leaves.*]

SCENE 2. Athens. QUINCE'S *house.*

      [*Enter* QUINCE, FLUTE, SNOUT, *and* STARVELING.]

QUINCE: Have you sent to Bottom's house? Is he come home
      yet?
STARVELING: He cannot be heard of. Out of doubt he is trans-
      ported.°   *carried off by the spirits*
FLUTE: If he come not, then the play is marred. It goes not   5
      forward, doth it?
QUINCE: It is not possible. You have not a man in all Athens
      able to discharge° Pyramus but he.   *portray*
FLUTE: No, he hath simply the best wit of any handicraft man
      in Athens.   10

QUINCE: Yea, and the best person too, and he is a very para-
mour° for a sweet voice.   *secret lover*
FLUTE: You must say "paragon." A paramour is (God bless us)
a thing of naught.°   *a wicked thing*

[*Enter* SNUG *the Joiner.*]

SNUG: Masters, the duke is coming from the temple, and there   15
is two or three lords and ladies more married. If our sport
had gone forward, we had all been made men.°   *our fortunes would have been made*
FLUTE: O sweet bully Bottom. Thus hath he lost sixpence a
day during his life: he could not have 'scaped sixpence a
day.° And the duke had not given him sixpence a day for   *a pension of sixpence*   20
playing Pyramus, I'll be hanged. He would have deserved
it. Sixpence a day in Pyramus, or nothing.

[*Enter* BOTTOM.]

BOTTOM: Where are these lads? Where are these hearts?
QUINCE: Bottom! O most courageous° day! O most happy   *(he may mean "auspicious")*
hour!   25
BOTTOM: Masters, I am to discourse° wonders; but ask me not   *speak of*
what. For if I tell you, I am not true Athenian. I will tell
you everything, right as it fell out.
QUINCE: Let us hear, sweet Bottom.
BOTTOM: Not a word of me. All that I will tell you is, that the   30
duke hath dined. Get your apparel together, good strings
to your beards, new ribbands to your pumps, meet
presently at the palace, every man look over his part; for
the short and the long is, our play is preferred.° In any   *accepted for performance*
case, let Thisby have clean linen, and let not him that plays   35
the lion pare his nails, for they shall hang out for the lion's
claws. And most dear actors, eat no onions nor garlic, for
we are to utter sweet breath; and I do not doubt but to
hear them say it is a sweet comedy. No more words: away,
go away.   40

[*They leave.*]

ACT FIVE

SCENE 1. The palace of THESEUS.

[*Enter* THESEUS, HIPPOLYTA, *and* PHILOSTRATE, *and his lords.*]

HIPPOLYTA: 'Tis strange, my Theseus, that these lovers speak of.
THESEUS: More strange than true. I never may believe
These antick fables, nor these fairy toys.°   *strange tales and trifles*
Lovers and madmen have such seething brains,
Such shaping fantasies, that apprehend°   *take in*   5
More than cool reason ever comprehends.

The lunatic, the lover, and the poet
Are of imagination all compact.°   *made of sheer imagination*
One sees more devils than vast hell can hold:
That is the madman. The lover, all as frantic,   10
Sees Helen's beauty in a brow of Egypt.°   *in a gypsy's face*
The poet's eye, in a fine frenzy rolling,
Doth glance from heaven to earth, from earth to heaven.
And as imagination bodies forth
The forms of things unknown, the poet's pen   15
Turns them to shapes, and gives to airy nothing
A local habitation and a name.
Such tricks hath strong imagination,
That if it would but apprehend some joy,
It comprehends° some bringer of that joy.   *imagines*   20
Or in the night, imagining some fear,
How easy is a bush supposed a bear.
HIPPOLYTA: But all the story of the night told over,
    And all their minds transfigured so together,
    More witnesseth than° fancy's images,   *proves it's more than*   25
    And grows to something of great constancy;°   *a very consistent story*
    But howsoever,° strange and admirable.°   *nevertheless/wonderful*

    [*Enter lovers:* LYSANDER, DEMETRIUS, HERMIA, *and* HELENA.]

THESEUS: Here come the lovers, full of joy and mirth.
    Joy, gentle friends, joy and fresh days of love
    Accompany° your hearts.   *may they accompany*
LYSANDER: More° than to us   *more of these*   30
    Wait° in your royal walks, your board, your bed.   *may they be found*
THESEUS: Come now, what masques,° what dances shall we have,   *richly costumed*
    To wear away this long age of three hours   *song-and-dance shows*
    Between our aftersupper° and bedtime?   *late snack*
    Where is our usual manager of mirth?   35
    What revels are in hand? Is there no play,
    To ease the anguish of a torturing hour?
    Call Philostrate.
PHILOSTRATE: Here, mighty Theseus.
THESEUS: Say, what abridgment° have you for this evening?   *pastime*
    What masque, what music? How shall we beguile   40
    The lazy time, if not with some delight?
PHILOSTRATE: There is a brief how many sports are ripe:°   *list of entertainments*
    Make choice of which your highness will see first.   *that are ready*

    [*Gives a paper.*]

THESEUS: "The battle with the Centaurs,° to be sung   *(creatures half human, half horse)*
    By an Athenian eunuch to the harp."   45
    We'll none of that. That have I told my love
    In glory of my kinsman Hercules.
    "The riot of the tipsy Bacchanals,°   *(frenzied followers of Bacchus*
    Tearing the Thracian singer in their rage."   *dismembering Orpheus)*
    That is an old device;° and it was played   *play*   50

When I from Thebes came last a conqueror.
"The thrice three° Muses mourning for the death   *three times three (= nine)*
Of Learning, late deceased in beggary."°   *which died as a pauper*
That is some satire keen and critical,
Not sorting with a nuptial ceremony.°   *not fitting for a wedding*   55
"A tedious brief scene of young Pyramus
And his love Thisby; very tragical mirth."
Merry and tragical? tedious and brief?
That is hot ice and wondrous strange snow.
How shall we find the concord of this discord?   60
PHILOSTRATE: A play there is, my lord, some ten words long,
  Which is as brief as I have known a play:
  But by ten words, my lord, it is too long,
  Which makes it tedious; for in all the play
  There is not one word apt, one player fitted.°   *fit for the role*   65
  And tragical, my noble lord, it is,
  For Pyramus therein doth kill himself.
  Which when I saw rehearsed, I must confess,
  Made mine eyes water; but more merry tears
  The passion° of loud laughter never shed.   *excitement*   70
THESEUS: What are they that do play it?
PHILOSTRATE: Hard-handed men, that work in Athens here,
  Which never labored in their minds till now;
  And now have toiled their unbreathed memories°   *put their untried memories*
  With this same play, against your nuptial.   *to work*   75
THESEUS: And we will hear it.
PHILOSTRATE: No, my noble lord,
  It is not for you. I have heard it over,
  And it is nothing, nothing in the world;
  Unless you can find sport in their intents,°   *good intentions*
  Extremely stretched and conned° with cruel pain,   *memorized*   80
  To do you service.
THESEUS: I will hear that play.
  For never anything can be amiss,
  When simpleness and duty tender it.°   *when honest loyalty offers it*
  Go bring them in, and take your places, ladies.

      [PHILOSTRATE *leaves.*]

HIPPOLYTA: I love not to see wretchedness overcharged,°   *wretches attempting too much*   85
  And duty in his service perishing.°   *killing itself to do its service*
THESEUS: Why, gentle sweet, you shall see no such thing.
HIPPOLYTA: He says they can do nothing in this kind.°   *of this nature*
THESEUS: The kinder we, to give them thanks for nothing.
  Our sport shall be to take what they mistake.°   *untangle what they scramble*   90
  And what poor duty cannot do, noble respect°   *a generous outlook*
  Takes it in might,° not merit.   *according to effort*
  Where I have come, great clerks have purposèd°   *scholars have prepared*
  To greet me with premeditated welcomes;
  Where I have seen them shiver and look pale,   95
  Make periods in the midst of sentences,

Throttle their practised accent in their fears,° *their well-rehearsed speech*
And in conclusion dumbly have broke off, *because of stage fright*
Not paying me a welcome. Trust me, sweet,
Out of this silence yet I picked a welcome; 100
And in the modesty of fearful duty° *of scared but loyal subjects*
I read as much as from the rattling tongue
Of saucy and audacious eloquence.
Love, therefore, and tongue-tied simplicity,
In least, speak most, to my capacity.° *are most eloquent in the fewest* 105
  words, in my opinion

[*Enter* PHILOSTRATE.]

PHILOSTRATE: So please your grace, the Prologue is addressed.° *ready*
THESEUS: Let him approach.

[*Flourish of trumpets. Enter* QUINCE *as the* PROLOGUE.]

PROLOGUE: If we offend, it is with our good will.° *(by stopping in the wrong places,*
    That you should think, we come not to offend, *Quince changes the meaning*
But with good will. To show our simple skill, *of the sentences to their opposites)* 110
    That is the true beginning of our end.
Consider then, we come but in despite.
    We do not come, as minding° to content you, *having in mind*
Our true intent is. All for your delight,
    We are not here. That you should here repent you, 115
The actors are at hand; and by their show,
You shall know all, that you are like to know.
THESEUS: This fellow doth not stand upon points.° *worry overly about points*
LYSANDER: He hath rid his prologue like a rough colt: he *of etiquette—and of*
  knows not the stop. A good moral my lord: it is not *punctuation* 120
  enough to speak; but to speak true.
HIPPOLYTA: Indeed he hath played on his prologue like a child
  on a recorder: a sound, but not in government.° *under control*
THESEUS: His speech was like a tangled chain: nothing im-
  paired,° but all disordered. Who is next? *broken* 125

[*Enter* PYRAMUS *and* THISBY, WALL, MOONSHINE, *and* LION.]

PROLOGUE: Gentles, perchance you wonder at this show,
    But wonder on, till truth make all things plain.
This man is Pyramus, if you would know;
    This beauteous lady, Thisby is certain.
This man, with lime and rough-cast,° doth present *plaster* 130
    Wall, that vile wall which did these lovers sunder;° *separate*
And through Wall's chink, poor souls, they are content
    To whisper. At the which, let no man wonder.
This man, with lantern, dog, and bush of thorn,
    Presenteth Moonshine. For if you will know, 135
By moonshine did these lovers think no scorn
    To meet at Ninus' tomb, there, there to woo.
This grisly beast (which Lion hight° by name) *is called*
The trusty Thisby, coming first by night,

Did scare away, or rather did affright; 140
And as she fled, her mantle she did fall.°   *she dropped her coat*
    Which Lion vile with bloody mouth did stain.
Anon comes Pyramus, sweet youth and tall,
    And finds his trusty Thisby's mantle slain:°   *as if she were slain*
Whereat, with blade, with bloody blameful blade, 145
    He bravely broached° his boiling bloody breast.   *stabbed (the many b-words*
And Thisby, tarrying in mulberry shade,   *mimic old-fashioned alliteration)*
    His dagger drew, and died. For all the rest,
Let Lion, Moonshine, Wall, and lovers twain,°   *the two lovers*
At large discourse,° while here they do remain.   *speak in full detail* 150
THESEUS: I wonder if the lion be° to speak.   *is going*
DEMETRIUS: No wonder, my lord: one lion may, when many asses do.

    [PROLOGUE, PYRAMUS, LION, THISBY, *and* MOONSHINE *leave.*]

WALL: In this same interlude it doth befall
    That I, one Snout by name, present a wall;
    And such a wall, as I would have you think, 155
    That had in it a crannied hole or chink,
    Through which the lovers, Pyramus and Thisby,
    Did whisper often, very secretly.
    This loam, this rough-cast, and this stone doth show
    That I am that same wall; the truth is so. 160
    And this the cranny is, right and sinister,°   *running right and left*
    Through which the fearful lovers are to whisper.
THESEUS: Would you desire lime and hair° to speak better?   *(ingredients of mortar)*
DEMETRIUS: It is the wittiest° partition that ever I heard discourse,   *most intelligent*
    my lord. 165

    [*Enter* PYRAMUS.]

THESEUS: Pyramus draws near the wall: silence.
PYRAMUS: O grim-looked night, O night with hue so black,
    O night, which ever art when day is not:
O night, O night, alack, alack, alack,
    I fear my Thisby's promise is forgot. 170
And thou O wall, O sweet, O lovely wall,
    That stand'st between her father's ground and mine,
Thou wall, O wall, O sweet and lovely wall,
    Show me thy chink, to blink through with mine eyne.°   *eyes*

    [WALL *holds up his fingers.*]

Thanks, courteous wall. Jove shield thee well for this. 175
    But what see I? No Thisby do I see.
O wicked wall, through whom I see no bliss,
    Cursed be thy stones for thus deceiving me.
THESEUS: The wall, methinks, being sensible, should curse again.°   *being alive, should*
PYRAMUS: No, in truth, sir, he should not. "Deceiving me" is   *curse back* 180
    Thisby's cue. She is to enter now, and I am to spy° her   *spot*
    through the wall. You shall see it will fall pat as I told you:
    yonder she comes.

[*Enter* THISBY.]

THISBY: O Wall, full often hast thou heard my moans,
   For parting my fair Pyramus and me.   185
  My cherry lips have often kissed thy stones;
   Thy stones with lime and hair° knit up in thee.   *(to make mortar)*
PYRAMUS: I see a voice: now will I to the chink,
  To spy an° I can hear my Thisby's face.   *to see if*
  Thisby?   190
THISBY: My love thou art, my love I think.
PYRAMUS: Think what thou wilt, I am thy lover's grace;°   *your gracious lover*
  And, like Limander,° am I trusty still.   *(he means "Leander")*
THISBY: And I like Helen, till the Fates me kill.
PYRAMUS: Not Shafalus to Procrus,° was so true.   *(he means "Cephalus and Procris,"* 195
THISBY: As Shafalus to Procrus, I to you.   *legendary lovers)*
PYRAMUS: O kiss me through the hole of this vile wall.
THISBY: I kiss the wall's hole, not your lips at all.
PYRAMUS: Wilt thou at Ninny's tomb meet me straightway?
THISBY: Tide life, tide death,° I come without delay.   *come what may—life or death* 200

     [PYRAMUS *and* THISBY *leave.*]

WALL: Thus have I, Wall, my part dischargèd so;
  And being done, thus Wall away doth go.

        [*He leaves.*]

THESEUS: Now is the mural° down between the two neighbors.   *wall*
DEMETRIUS: No remedy, my lord, when walls are so wilful to
  hear° without warning.   *eager to listen* 205
HIPPOLYTA: This is the silliest stuff that ever I heard.
THESEUS: The best in this kind are but shadows; and the worst
  are no worse, if imagination amend them.°   *helps them out*
HIPPOLYTA: It must be your imagination then, and not theirs.
THESEUS: If we imagine no worse of them than they of them-   210
  selves, they may pass for excellent men. Here come two
  noble beasts in, a man and a lion.

   [*Enter* LION *and* MOONSHINE.]

LION: You ladies, you, whose gentle hearts do fear
   The smallest monstrous mouse that creeps on floor,
  May now perchance both quake and tremble here,   215
   When lion rough in wildest rage doth roar.
  Then know that I, as Snug the joiner am
  A lion fell,° nor else no lion's dam:°   *fierce/mate*
  For if I should as lion come in strife°   *aggressively*
  Into this place, 'twere pity on my life.°   *my life would be at stake* 220
THESEUS: A very gentle° beast, and of a good conscience.   *noble*
DEMETRIUS: The very best at a beast, my lord, that ever I saw.
LYSANDER: This lion is a very fox for his valor.
THESEUS: True, and a goose for his discretion.°   *caution*

DEMETRIUS: Not so my lord: for his valor cannot carry his discretion, and the fox carries the goose. 225

THESEUS: His discretion, I am sure, cannot carry his valor; for the goose carries not the fox. It is well: leave it to his discretion, and let us listen to the moon.

MOONSHINE: This lanthorn° doth the hornèd° moon present— *lantern/crescent (with two horn-like points like a cuckolded husband)* 230

DEMETRIUS: He should have worn the horns on his head.

THESEUS: He is no crescent, and his horns are invisible within the circumference.

MOONSHINE: This lanthorn doth the hornèd moon present; Myself, the man in the moon do seem to be. 235

THESEUS: This is the greatest error of all the rest; the man should be put into the lanthorn. How is it else the man in the moon?

DEMETRIUS: He dares not come there for the candle; for you see, it is already in snuff.° *in need of trimming* 240

HIPPOLYTA: I am aweary of this moon. Would he would change.° *(like the real moon)*

THESEUS: It appears, by his small light of discretion, that he is in the wane; but yet in courtesy, in all reason, we must stay the time.° *be patient for the allowed time* 245

LYSANDER: Proceed, Moon.

MOONSHINE: All that I have to say, is to tell you that the lanthorn is the moon, I the man in the moon, this thornbush my thornbush, and this dog my dog.

DEMETRIUS: Why, all these should be in the lanthorn, for all these are in the moon. But silence: here comes Thisby. 250

[*Enter* THISBY.]

THISBY: This is old Ninny's tomb. Where is my love?
LION: Oh!

[*The* LION *roars.* THISBY *runs off.*]

DEMETRIUS: Well roared, Lion.
THESEUS: Well run, Thisby. 255
HIPPOLYTA: Well shone, Moon. Truly, the moon shines with a good grace.

[*The* LION *shakes* THISBY'S *coat.*]

THESEUS: Well moused,° Lion. *shaken, as a cat does to a mouse*
DEMETRIUS: And then came Pyramus.

[*Enter* PYRAMUS. *The* LION *leaves.*]

LYSANDER: And so the lion vanished. 260
PYRAMUS: Sweet moon, I thank thee for thy sunny beams,
    I thank thee, moon, for shining now so bright.
  For by thy gracious, golden, glittering gleams,
    I trust to take of truest Thisby sight.

But stay: O spite! 265
But mark, poor knight,
What dreadful dole° is here?   *sorrow*
Eyes, do you see!
How can it be!
O dainty duck, O dear! 270
Thy mantle good,
What, stained with blood?
Approach, ye Furies° fell!   *(fierce avenging spirits)*
O Fates!° come, come: *(sisters spinning and cutting*
Cut thread and thrum,   *the thread of fate)* 275
Quail, crush, conclude, and quell.°   *destroy, crush make an*
THESEUS: This passion, and the death of a dear friend, would go   *end, and kill*
near to° make a man look sad.   *come close to*
HIPPOLYTA: Beshrew° my heart, but I pity the man.   *wish ill to*
PYRAMUS: O wherefore, Nature, didst thou lions frame?°   *create lions* 280
Since lion vile hath here deflowered my dear.
Which is—no, no—which was the fairest dame
That lived, that loved, that liked, that looked with cheer.
Come tears, confound.°   *sweep all away*
Out sword, and wound 285
The pap° of Pyramus;   *breast*
Ay, that left pap,
Where heart doth hop.

[*Stabs himself.*]

Thus die I, thus, thus, thus.
Now am I dead, 290
Now am I fled,
My soul is in the sky.
Tongue lose thy light,
Moon take thy flight,

[MOONSHINE *leaves.*]

Now die, die, die, die, die. 295

[PYRAMUS *dies.*]

DEMETRIUS: No die, but an ace for him.° For he is but one.   *not the whole die, but only a*
LYSANDER: Less than an ace, man. For he is dead, he is   *throw of one (at dice)*
nothing.
THESEUS: With the help of a surgeon, he might yet recover,
and prove an ass.°   *(play on "ace")* 300
HIPPOLYTA: How chance Moonshine is gone before Thisby
comes back and finds her lover?

[*Enter* THISBY.]

THESEUS: She will find him by starlight. Here she comes, and   *grief*
her passion° ends the play.
HIPPOLYTA: Methinks she should not use a long one for such a 305
Pyramus; I hope she will be brief.

DEMETRIUS: A mote will turn the balance,° which Pyramus, *speck will tilt the scale*
    which Thisby, is the better: he for a man, God warrant° *protect*
    us; she for a woman, God bless us.
LYSANDER: She hath spied him already with those sweet eyes.   310
DEMETRIUS: And thus she means, videlicet°— *laments, namely*
THISBY: Asleep my love?
                    What, dead, my dove?
               O Pyramus, arise,
                     Speak, speak. Quite dumb?   315
                     Dead, dead? A tomb
               Must cover thy sweet eyes.
                     These lily lips,
                     This cherry nose,
               These yellow cowslip cheeks,   320
                     Are gone, are gone.
                     Lovers, make moan:
               His eyes were green as leeks.
                     O Sisters Three,° *(the three Fates)*
                     Come, come to me,   325
               With hands as pale as milk,
                     Lay them in gore,
                     Since you have shore° *shorn*
               With shears his thread of silk.
                     Tongue, not a word: 330
                     Come trusty sword,
               Come blade, my breast imbrue°— *cover with blood*

[*Stabs herself.*]

               And farewell, friends.
               Thus Thisby ends.
           Adieu, adieu, adieu.   335

[*She dies.*]

THESEUS: Moonshine and Lion are left to bury the dead.
DEMETRIUS: Ay, and Wall too.
BOTTOM [*starts up*]: No, I assure you, the wall is down that
    parted their fathers. Will it please you to see the Epilogue,
    or to hear a Bergomask dance° between two of our com- *(Italian peasant dance)*   340
    pany?
THESEUS: No epilogue, I pray you; for your play needs no ex-
    cuse. Never excuse: for when the players are all dead, there
    need none to be blamed. Marry, if he that writ it had
    played Pyramus and hanged himself in Thisby's garter, it   345
    would have been a fine tragedy; and so it is truly, and very
    notably discharged.° But come, your Bergomask: let your *performed*
    Epilogue alone.

[*A dance.*]

The iron tongue of midnight hath told° twelve. *the bell . . . has tolled*
Lovers, to bed, 'tis almost fairy time.   350

I fear we shall outsleep the coming morn,
As much as we this night have overwatched.
This palpable gross° play hath well beguiled   *brash and crude*
The heavy gait° of night. Sweet friends, to bed.   *slow motion*
A fortnight° hold we this solemnity,   *for two weeks*   355
In nightly revels, and new jollity.

[*They leave.*]

[*Enter* PUCK *with a broom.*]

PUCK: Now the hungry lion roars,
                     And the wolf behowls the moon;
                 Whilst the heavy plowman snores,
                     All with weary task fordone.   360
                 Now the wasted brands° do glow,   *burnt-out embers*
                     Whilst the screech owl, screeching loud,
                 Puts the wretch that lies in woe
                     In remembrance of a shroud.
                 Now it is the time of night,   365
                     That the graves, all gaping wide,
                 Every one lets forth his sprite,°   *ghost*
                     In the churchway paths to glide.
                 And we fairies, that do run
                     By the triple Hecate's° team,   (*moon goddess of three names:* 370
                 From the presence of the sun,   *Diana-Phoebe-Hecate*)
                     Following darkness like a dream,
                 Now are frolic:° not a mouse   *make merry*
                 Shall disturb this hallowed house.
                 I am sent with broom before,   375
                 To sweep the dust behind the door.°   (*he supposedly helped*
                                                               with household chores)

[*Enter King and Queen of fairies, with all their train.*]

OBERON: Through the house give glimmering light,
                     By the dead and drowsy fire,
                 Every elf and fairy sprite,
                     Hop as light as bird from brier,   380
                 And this ditty after me,
                 Sing, and dance it trippingly.
TITANIA: First rehearse your song by rote,
                 To each word a warbling note.
                 Hand in hand, with fairy grace,   385
                 Will we sing and bless this place.

[*Song and dance.*]

OBERON: Now, until the break of day,
                 Through this house each fairy stray.
                 To the best bride-bed will we,
                 Which by us shall blessèd be;   390

And the issue there create,°   *the children there created*
Ever shall be fortunate.
So shall all the couples three
Ever true in loving be;
And the blots of Nature's hand   395
Shall not in their issue stand.°   *shall not mar their offspring*
Never mole, harelip, nor scar,
Nor mark prodigious,° such as are   *frightening birthmark*
Despisèd in nativity,°   *feared in the newborn*
Shall upon their children be.   400
With this field-dew consecrate,°   *consecrated*
Every fairy take his gait,
And each several° chamber bless,   *separate*
Through this palace, with sweet peace;
And the owner of it blest,   405
Ever shall in safety rest.
Trip away; make no stay;
Meet me all by break of day.

[All but PUCK *leave.]*

PUCK: If we shadows° have offended,   *players*
Think but this and all is mended: 410
That you have but slumbered here,
While these visions did appear.
And this weak and idle° theme,   *foolish*
No more yielding but° a dream,   *producing nothing more than*
Gentles, do not reprehend.   415
If you pardon, we will mend.
And as I am an honest Puck,
If we have unearnèd luck,
Now to scape the serpent's tongue,°   *snakelike hissing of a hostile audience*
We will make amends, ere long: 420
Else the Puck a liar call.
So, good night unto you all.
Give me your hands, if we be friends;
And Robin shall restore amends.°   *do better next time*

[He leaves.]

THE RECEPTIVE READER

Act One

1. (Scene 1) How does the opening set up the *frame story* for the comedy as a whole? How does the exchange between Theseus and Hippolyta create the dominating mood? ✧ What is the dilemma facing Hermia? Are you surprised by her defiance? ✧ How do the two young men come off in this opening scene? ✧ What is the role of Helena on the merry-go-round of love? How do you think the audience relates to her?

2. (Scene 2) Much of the humor in this play is at the expense of the uneducated lower-class characters. What makes them such lovable bumblers?

Act Two

3. (Scene 1) Puck becomes a kind of mastermind in much of what happens during the play. What is his characteristic stance or attitude? Why does he have so much audience appeal? ✧ How serious is the quarrel between Oberon and Titania? How much and what kind of storytelling are woven into their exchanges? How playful or how serious is Oberon's plan for his revenge? ✧ What changes does the relationship between Demetrius and Helena ring on more usual patterns of courtship? Is her predicament sad or funny? What hope do you think there is for her?

4. (Scene 2) In these early scenes, does Titania seem a good or evil spirit? What do you think she might symbolize? ✧ What kind of couple do Hermia and Lysander make in this scene? ✧ How does Puck start the comedy of errors that will account for many of the *plot* developments in the play? ✧ Do you think the sudden transformation of Lysander would be unbelievable to a modern audience? How does Helena react to the change? How does Hermia?

Act Three

5. (Scene1) What are striking examples of the would-be actors' literal-mindedness and naiveté? What are examples of their tendency toward *malapropism*—choosing the wrong, and often the opposite, word, such as *odious* (hateful) instead of *odorous* (sweet-smelling)? ✧ What keeps Bottom's transformation from being an isolated practical joke? How does it relate to what comes before it in this scene and what comes after? How does it parallel or help tie together other plot elements? ✧ What is the mood or spirit of the love scene between the fairy queen and Bottom in the likeness of an ass? Should it be acted as gross *farce*? Does it have any symbolic or thematic overtones?

6. (Scene 2) How does this scene follow up or reiterate the *theme* of mortals at cross-purposes? (Where or how was this theme sounded earlier in the play?) ✧ How does Puck continue his mischief making in this scene? How do Oberon and Puck begin to steer the tangled relations of the lovers toward a resolution?

Act Four

7. (Scene 1) How does this scene get us as the audience ready to return to Athens and daylight from the forest of moonlight and dreams? Do Athens and daylight symbolize reality in the play? Did we leave reality behind when we entered the forest? ✧ Does Theseus seem to represent benign power, benevolent authority? Does he play a godlike role?

8. (Scenes 1 and 2) How is the playwright going to bring the three strands of the play—the fairies, the lovers with their elders, and the mechanicals—together at the end?

Act Five

9. (Scene 1) How do the "mechanicals" turn the traditional tragic story into a farce? How does their stage audience react or participate? ◇ What are the last words of the major figures—Theseus, Oberon, Puck? What light do their final comments cast on the play as a whole?

THE WHOLE PLAY—For Discussion or Writing

1. Look at the sources of conflict and misunderstanding in this play and at the way they are resolved. How much in the play can you relate to the theme of mortals at cross-purposes—but brought into harmony by the power of love?

2. Modern readers are often wary of the power of humor to hurt and to exclude. In this play, are the same people exclusively the perpetrators and others exclusively the targets of humor? Are there examples of humor cutting both ways? Are any of the characters at times the joker and at other times the butt of the joke?

THE PERSONAL RESPONSE

How silly or how real do the lovers appear to you?

THE CREATIVE DIMENSION

Two selections from this play lend themselves exceptionally well to performance as *amateur theatricals:* the rehearsal in the woods, with the transformation of Bottom, followed by his encounter with the fairy queen; and the staging of the lamentable comedy of Pyramus and Thisby at the court, with the wisecracking comments of the court audience. You and your classmates may want to stage a miniproduction of one or both for a class party or other special occasion.

THE WORLD OF TENNESSEE WILLIAMS

*I have found it easier to identify with the characters who
verge upon hysteria, who were frightened of life, who were
desperate to reach out to another person.*

TENNESSEE WILLIAMS

Much of Tennessee Williams' work shows his fascination with characters facing lonely struggles in emotionally starved environments. Much of his work has biographical roots, harking back to his own family's atmosphere of repression and anger, evoked through characterizations of psychologically vulnerable women and domineering men. Williams began writing in high school; his first short story was published when he was seventeen. During his college years, he wrote one-act plays. The year 1940 saw the production of his first full-length play. In 1945, *The Glass Menagerie* won the Drama Critics' Circle Award. It was also a spectacular commercial success, the beginning of a series of theatrical triumphs including *A Streetcar Named Desire* (1947), *The Rose Tattoo* (1950), *Cat on a Hot Tin Roof* (1955), *Suddenly Last Summer* (1958), and *The Night of the Iguana* (1961).

Williams' plays are often the result of an ongoing cycle of reworking and revision. "Typically, a Williams play starts life as a poem or short story, is revised to a one-act, then a full-length play; the play itself is changed during performance and again between performance and publication" (Brian Parker). Many of his plays were made into movies, including the classic *Streetcar* with Vivien Leigh as Blanche and Marlon Brando as Kowalski. *Cat on a Hot Tin Roof* starred Elizabeth Taylor and Paul Newman. Critics have commented on the affinity between Williams' theater and the art of the filmmaker, pointing out, for instance, his use of spotty, shadowy lighting or the use of evocative background music (such as the circus music in *Menagerie*). As Roger Boxill says, Williams "belongs to the first generation of dramatists brought up on the movies instead of on plays, as the strong influence of film on his stagecraft suggests."

In his memoirs, Williams called *The Glass Menagerie,* with its burden of guilt and cruelty, "the big one—close to the marrow of my being." This play, in which Laura retreats to the private world of her glass animals and Tom leaves while carrying with him an obsession with the past, has its roots in Williams' actual relationship with his sister, Rose, whom he felt he failed in her greatest need. He writes: "It's not very pleasant to look back on [1937] and to know that Rose knew she was going mad and to know, also, that I was not too kind to my sister." In a moment of fury, he hissed at her, "I hate the sight of your ugly old face!" He said about this experience, "This is the cruelest thing I have done in my life, I suspect, and one for which I can never properly atone." After he left home, his parents permitted the performance of a frontal lobotomy. These traumatic events left the playwright with a deep sense that love leads inevitably to loss and betrayal. Although the play is usually talked of as Tom's exorcism of a traumatic memory, it can also be seen as an obsessive reenactment.

After all, he does not really escape the family trap. . . . And when the play is seen in this way, one must recognize that, besides its gentle sadness and remorse, there is also ruthlessness in Tom's final command, "Blow out your candles, Laura—and so goodbye. . . ." For Williams, in fact, love and betrayal are always two sides of the same emotion. . . . his brutal and gentle characters do more than co-exist, they interexist, one creates the other in a vicious circle of disaster. (John Buell)

Tennessee Williams' theater typically takes his audiences to a Southern setting, made intensely real by his command of Southern speech and manners. His poetic and symbolic drama goes beyond the realistic surface of life to probe the complex psychological intermeshings of "love, pity, regret, guilt, self-lacerating ruthlessness, posing, and bravado" (Brian Parker).

TENNESSEE WILLIAMS (1911–1983)
The Glass Menagerie 1945

CHARACTERS

AMANDA WINGFIELD, the mother. A little woman of great but confused vitality clinging frantically to another time and place. Her characterization must be carefully created, not copied from type. She is not paranoiac, but her life is paranoia. There is much to admire in AMANDA, and as much to love and pity as there is to laugh at. Certainly she has endurance and a kind of heroism, and though her foolishness makes her unwittingly cruel at times, there is tenderness in her slight person.

LAURA WINGFIELD, her daughter. AMANDA, having failed to establish contact with reality, continues to live vitally in her illusions, but LAURA'S situation is even graver. A childhood illness has left her crippled, one leg slightly shorter than the other, and held in a brace. This defect need not be more than suggested on the stage. Stemming from this, LAURA'S separation increases till she is like a piece of her own glass collection, too exquisitely fragile to move from the shelf.

TOM WINGFIELD, her son, and the narrator of the play. A poet with a job in a warehouse. His nature is not remorseless, but to escape from a trap he has to act without pity.

JIM O'CONNOR, the gentleman caller. A nice, ordinary, young man.

SCENE: *An alley in St. Louis.*
PART I: *Preparation for a gentleman caller.*
PART II: *The gentleman calls.*
TIME: *Now and the past.*

AUTHOR'S PRODUCTION NOTES

Being a "memory play," The Glass Menagerie can be presented with unusual freedom of convention. Because of its considerably delicate or tenuous material, atmospheric touches and subtleties of direction play a particularly important part. Expressionism and all other unconventional techniques in drama have only one valid aim, and that is a closer approach to truth. When a play employs unconventional techniques, it is not, or certainly shouldn't be, trying to escape its responsibility of dealing with reality, or interpreting experience, but is actually or should be attempting to find a closer approach, a more penetrating and vivid expression of things as they are. The straight realistic play with its genuine frigidaire and authentic ice-cubes, its characters that speak exactly as its audience speaks, corresponds to the academic landscape and has the same virtue of a photographic likeness. Everyone should know nowadays the unimportance of the photographic in art: that truth, life, or reality is an organic thing which the poetic imagination can represent or suggest, in essence, only through transformation, through changing into other forms than those which were merely present in appearance.

These remarks are not meant as a preface only to this particular play. They have to do with a conception of a new, plastic theatre which must take the place of the exhausted theater of realistic conventions if the theatre is to resume vitality as a part of our culture.

The Screen Device: There is *only one important difference between the original and acting version of the play* and that is the *omission* in the latter of the device which I tentatively included in my *original* script. This device was the use of a screen on which were projected magic-lantern slides bearing images or titles. I do not regret the omission of this device from the present Broadway production. The extraordinary power of Miss Taylor's performance made it suitable to have the utmost simplicity in the physical production. But I think it may be interesting to some readers to see how this device was conceived. So I am putting it into the published manuscript. These images and legends, projected from behind, were cast on a section of wall between the front-room and dining-room areas, which should be indistinguishable from the rest when not in use.

The purpose of this will probably be apparent. It is to give accent to certain values in each scene. Each scene contains a particular point (or several) which is structurally the most important. In an episodic play, such as this, the basic structure or narrative line may be obscured from the audience; the effect may seem fragmentary rather than architectural. This may not be the fault of the play so much as a lack of attention in the audience. The legend or image upon the screen will strengthen the effect of what is merely allusion in the writing and allow the primary point to be made more simply and lightly than if the entire responsibility were on the spoken lines. Aside from this structural value, I think the screen will have a definite emotional appeal, less definable but just as important. An imaginative producer or director may invent many other uses for this device than those indicated in the present script. In fact the possibilities of the device seem much larger to me than the instance of this play can possibly utilize.

The Music: Another extra-literary accent in this play is provided by the use of music. A single recurring tune, "The Glass Menagerie," is used to give emotional emphasis to suitable passages. This tune is like circus music, not when you are on the grounds or in the immediate vicinity of the parade, but when you are at some distance and very likely thinking of something else. It seems under those circumstances to continue almost interminably and it weaves in and out of your preoccupied consciousness; then it is the lightest, most delicate music in the world and perhaps the saddest. It expresses the surface vivacity of life with the underlying strain of immutable and inexpressible sorrow. When you look at a piece of delicately spun glass you think of two things: how beautiful it is and how easily it can be broken. Both of those ideas should be woven into the recurring tune, which dips in and out of the play as if it were carried on a wind that changes. It serves as a thread of connection and allusion between the narrator with his separate point in time and space and the subject of his story. Between each episode it returns as reference to the emotion, nostalgia, which is the first condition of the play. It is primarily LAURA's music and therefore comes out most clearly when the play focuses upon her and the lovely fragility of glass which is her image.

The Lighting: The lighting in the play is not realistic. In keeping with the atmosphere of memory, the stage is dim. Shafts of light are focused on selected areas or actors, sometimes in contradistinction to what is the apparent center. For instance, in the quarrel scene between TOM and AMANDA, in which LAURA has no active part, the clearest pool of light is on her figure. This is also true of the supper scene, when her silent figure on the sofa should remain the visual center. The light upon LAURA should be distinct from the others, having a peculiar pristine clarity such as light used in early religious portraits of female saints or madonnas. A certain correspondence to light in religious paintings, such as El Greco's, where the figures are radiant in atmosphere that is relatively dusky, could be effectively used throughout the play. (It will also permit a more effective use of the screen.) A free, imaginative use of light can be of enormous value in giving a mobile, plastic quality to plays of a more or less static nature.

T. W.

SCENE 1

The Wingfield apartment is in the rear of the building, one of those vast hive-like conglomerations of cellular living-units that flower as warty growths in overcrowded urban centers of lower middle-class population and are symptomatic of the impulse of this largest and fundamentally enslaved section of American society to avoid fluidity and differentiation and to exist and function as one interfused mass of automatism.

The apartment faces an alley and is entered by a fire-escape, a structure whose name is a touch of accidental poetic truth, for all of these huge buildings are always burning with the slow and implacable fires of human desperation. The fire-escape is included in the set— that is, the landing of it and steps descending from it.

The scene is memory and is therefore nonrealistic. Memory takes a lot of poetic license. It omits some details; others are exaggerated, according to the emotional value of the articles it touches, for memory is seated predominantly in the heart. The interior is therefore rather dim and poetic.

At the rise of the curtain, the audience is faced with the dark, grim rear wall of the Wingfield tenement. This building, which runs parallel to the footlights, is flanked on both sides by dark, narrow alleys which run into murky canyons of tangled clotheslines, garbage cans and the sinister lattice work of neighboring fire-escapes. It is up and down these side alleys that exterior entrances and exits are made, during the play. At the end of TOM's opening commentary, the dark tenement wall slowly reveals (by means of a transparency) the interior of the ground floor Wingfield apartment.

Downstage is the living room, which also serves as a sleeping room for LAURA, the sofa unfolding to make her bed. Upstage, center, and divided by a wide arch or second proscenium with transparent faded portieres (or second curtain), is the dining room. In an old-fashioned what-not in the living room are seen scores of transparent glass animals. A blown-up photograph of the father hangs on the wall of the living room, facing the audience, to the left of the archway. It is the face of a very handsome young man in a doughboy's First World War cap. He is gallantly smiling, ineluctably smiling, as if to say, "I will be smiling forever."

The audience hears and sees the opening scene in the dining room through both the transparent fourth wall of the building and the transparent gauze portieres of the dining-room arch. It is during this revealing scene that the fourth wall slowly ascends, out of sight. This transparent exterior wall is not brought down again until the very end of the play, during TOM'S *final speech.*

The narrator is an undisguised convention of the play. He takes whatever license with dramatic convention as is convenient to his purposes.

TOM *enters dressed as a merchant sailor from alley, stage left, and strolls across the front of the stage to the fire-escape. There he stops and lights a cigarette. He addresses the audience.*

TOM: Yes, I have tricks in my pocket, I have things up my sleeve. But I am the opposite of a stage magician. He gives you illusion that has the appearance of truth. I give you truth in the pleasant disguise of illusion. To begin with, I turn back time. I reverse it to that quaint period, the thirties, when the huge middle class of America was matriculating in a school for the blind. Their eyes had failed them, or they had failed their eyes, and so they were having their fingers pressed forcibly down on the fiery Braille alphabet of a dissolving economy. In Spain there was revolution. Here there was only shouting and confusion. In Spain there was Guernica. Here there were disturbances of labor, sometimes pretty violent, in otherwise peaceful cities such as Chicago, Cleveland, Saint Louis . . . This is the social background of the play.

(*Music.*)

The play is memory. Being a memory play, it is dimly lighted, it is sentimental, it is not realistic. In memory everything seems to happen to music. That explains the fiddle in the wings. I am the narrator of the play, and also a character in it. The other characters are my mother, Amanda, my sister, Laura, and a gentleman caller who appears in the final scenes. He is the most realistic character in the play, being an emissary from a world of reality that we were somehow set apart from. But since I have a poet's weakness for symbols, I am using this character also as a symbol; he is the long delayed but always expected something that we live for. There is a fifth character in the play who doesn't appear except in this larger-than-life-size photograph over the mantel. This is our father who left us a long time ago. He was a telephone man who fell in love with long distances; he gave up his job with the telephone company and skipped the light fantastic out of town . . . The last we heard of him was a picture post-card from Mazatlan, on the Pacific coast of Mexico, containing a message of two words—"Hello—Good-bye!" and no address. I think the rest of the play will explain itself. . . .

AMANDA'S *voice becomes audible through the portieres.*
(*Legend on screen: "Où sont les neiges."*)
He divides the portieres and enters the upstage area.
AMANDA *and* LAURA *are seated at a drop-leaf table. Eating is indicated by gestures without food or utensils.* AMANDA *faces the audience.* TOM *and* LAURA *are seated in profile.*
The interior has lit up softly and through the scrim we see AMANDA *and* LAURA *seated at the table in the upstage area.*

AMANDA (*calling*): Tom?

TOM: Yes, Mother.

AMANDA: We can't say grace until you come to the table!

TOM: Coming, Mother. (*He bows slightly and withdraws, reappearing a few moments later in his place at the table.*)

AMANDA (*to her son*): Honey, don't *push* with your *fingers.* If you have to push with something, the thing to push with is a crust of bread. And chew—chew! Animals have sections in their stomachs which enable them to digest food without mastication, but human beings are supposed to chew their food before they swallow it down. Eat food leisurely, son, and really enjoy it. A well-cooked meal has lots of delicate flavors that have to be held in the mouth for appreciation. So chew your food and give your salivary glands a chance to function!

TOM *deliberately lays his imaginary fork down and pushes his chair back from the table.*

TOM: I haven't enjoyed one bite of this dinner because of your constant directions on how to eat it. It's you that make me rush through meals with your hawk-like attention to every bite I take. Sickening—spoils my appetite—all this discussion of—animals' secretion—salivary glands—mastication!

AMANDA (*lightly*): Temperament like a Metropolitan star! (*He rises and crosses downstage.*) You're not excused from the table.

TOM: I'm getting a cigarette.

AMANDA: You smoke too much.

LAURA *rises.*

LAURA: I'll bring in the blanc mange.

He remains standing with his cigarette by the portieres during the following.

AMANDA (*rising*): No, sister, no, sister—you be the lady this time and I'll be the darky.

LAURA: I'm already up.

AMANDA: Resume your seat, little sister—I want you to stay fresh and pretty—for gentlemen callers!

LAURA: I'm not expecting any gentlemen callers.

AMANDA (*Crossing out to kitchenette. Airily.*): Sometimes they come when they are least expected! Why, I remember one Sunday afternoon in Blue Mountain—(*enters kitchenette*)

TOM: I know what's coming!

LAURA: Yes. But let her tell it.

TOM: Again?

LAURA: She loves to tell it.

AMANDA *returns with bowl of dessert.*

AMANDA: One Sunday afternoon in Blue Mountain—your mother received—*seventeen!*—gentlemen callers! Why, sometimes there weren't chairs enough to accommodate them all. We had to send the nigger over to bring in folding chairs from the parish house.

TOM (*remaining at portieres*): How did you entertain those gentlemen callers?

AMANDA: I understood the art of conversation!

TOM: I bet you could talk.

AMANDA: Girls in those days *knew* how to talk, I can tell you.

TOM: Yes?

(*Image:* AMANDA *as a girl on a porch, greeting callers.*)

AMANDA: They knew how to entertain their gentlemen callers. It wasn't enough for a girl to be possessed of a pretty face and a graceful figure—although I wasn't slighted in either respect. She also needed to have a nimble wit and a tongue to meet all occasions.

TOM: What did you talk about?

AMANDA: Things of importance going on in the world! Never anything coarse or common or vulgar. (*She addresses* TOM *as though he were seated in the vacant chair at the table though he remains by portieres. He plays this scene as though he held the book.*) My callers were gentlemen—all! Among my callers were some of the most prominent young planters of the Mississippi Delta—planters and sons of planters!

TOM *motions for music and a spot of light on* AMANDA.
Her eyes lift, her face glows, her voice becomes rich and elegiac.
(*Screen legend: "Où sont les neiges."*)

There was young Champ Laughlin who later became vice-president of the Delta Planters Bank. Hadley Stevenson who was drowned in Moon Lake and left his widow one hundred and fifty thousand in Government bonds. There were the Cutrere brothers, Wesley and Bates. Bates was one of my bright particular beaux! He got in a quarrel with that wild Wainwright boy. They shot it out on the floor of Moon Lake Casino. Bates was shot through the stomach. Died in the ambulance on his way to Memphis. His widow was also well-provided for, came into eight or ten thousand acres, that's all. She married him on the rebound—never loved her—carried my picture on him the night he died! And there was that boy that every girl in the Delta had set her cap for! That beautiful, brilliant young Fitzhugh boy from Greene County!

TOM: What did he leave his widow?

AMANDA: He never married! Gracious, you talk as though all of my old admirers had turned up their toes to the daisies!

TOM: Isn't this the first you've mentioned that still survives?

AMANDA: That Fitzhugh boy went North and made a fortune—came to be known as the Wolf of Wall Street! He had the Midas touch, whatever he touched turned to gold!

And I could have been Mrs. Duncan J. Fitzhugh, mind you! But—I picked your *father!*

LAURA (*rising*): Mother, let me clear the table.

AMANDA: No, dear, you go in front and study your typewriter chart. Or practice your shorthand a little. Stay fresh and pretty!—It's almost time for our gentlemen callers to start arriving. (*She flounces girlishly toward the kitchenette.*) How many do you suppose we're going to entertain this afternoon?

TOM *throws down the paper and jumps up with a groan.*

LAURA (*alone in the dining room*): I don't believe we're going to receive any, Mother.

AMANDA (*reappearing, airily*): What? No one—not one? You must be joking! (LAURA *nervously echoes her laugh. She slips in a fugitive manner through the half-open portieres and draws them gently behind her. A shaft of very clear light is thrown on her face against the faded tapestry of the curtains.*) (*Music: "The Glass Menagerie" under faintly.*) (*lightly*) Not one gentleman caller? It can't be true! There must be a flood, there must have been a tornado!

LAURA: It isn't a flood, it's not a tornado, Mother. I'm just not popular like you were in Blue Mountain. . . . (TOM *utters another groan.* LAURA *glances at him with a faint, apologetic smile. Her voice catching a little.*) Mother's afraid I'm going to be an old maid.

(*The scene dims out with "Glass Menagerie" music.*)

SCENE 2

"Laura, Haven't You Ever Liked Some Boy?"

On the dark stage the screen is lighted with the image of blue roses.
Gradually LAURA'S *figure becomes apparent and the screen goes out.*
The music subsides.
LAURA *is seated in the delicate ivory chair at the small claw-foot table.*
She wears a dress of soft violet material for a kimono—her hair tied back from her forehead with a ribbon.
She is washing and polishing her collection of glass.
AMANDA *appears on the fire-escape steps. At the sound of her ascent,* LAURA *catches her breath, thrusts the bowl of ornaments away and seats herself stiffly before the diagram of the typewriter keyboard as though it held her spellbound.*
Something has happened to AMANDA. *It is written in her face as she climbs to the landing: a look that is grim and hopeless and a little absurd.*
She has on one of those cheap or imitation velvety-looking cloth coats with imitation fur collar. Her hat is five or six years old, one of those dreadful cloche hats that were worn in the late twenties and she is clasping an enormous black patent-leather pocketbook with nickel clasps and initials. This is her full-dress outfit, the one she usually wears to the D.A.R.
Before entering she looks through the door.
She purses her lips, opens her eyes very wide, rolls them upward and shakes her head.
Then she slowly lets herself in the door. Seeing her mother's expression LAURA *touches her lips with a nervous gesture.*

LAURA: Hello, Mother, I was— (*She makes a nervous gesture toward the chart on the wall.* AMANDA *leans against the shut door and stares at* LAURA *with a martyred look.*)

AMANDA: Deception? Deception? (*She slowly removes her hat and gloves, continuing the sweet suffering stare. She lets the hat and gloves fall on the floor—a bit of acting.*)

LAURA (*shakily*): How was the D.A.R meeting? AMANDA *slowly opens her purse and removes a dainty white handkerchief which she shakes out delicately and delicately touches to her lips and nostrils.*) Didn't you go to the D.A.R. meeting, Mother?

AMANDA (*faintly, almost inaudibly*): —No.—No. (*then more forcibly*) I did not have the strength—to go to the D.A.R. In fact, I did not have the courage! I wanted to find a hole in the ground and hide myself in it forever! (*She crosses slowly to the wall and removes the diagram of the typewriter keyboard. She holds it in front of her for a second, staring at it sweetly and sorrowfully—then bites her lips and tears it in two pieces.*)

LAURA (*faintly*): Why did you do that, Mother? (AMANDA *repeats the same procedure with the chart of the Gregg Alphabet.*) Why are you—

AMANDA: Why? Why? How old are you, Laura?

LAURA: Mother, you know my age.

AMANDA: I thought that you were an adult; it seems that I was mistaken. (*She crosses slowly to the sofa and sinks down and stares at* LAURA.)

LAURA: Please don't stare at me, Mother.

AMANDA *closes her eyes and lowers her head. Count ten.*

AMANDA: What are we going to do, what is going to become of us, what is the future?

Count ten.

LAURA: Has something happened, Mother? (AMANDA *draws a long breath and takes out the handkerchief again. Dabbing process.*) Mother, has—something happened?

AMANDA: I'll be all right in a minute, I'm just bewildered—(*count five*)—by life. . . .

LAURA: Mother, I wish that you would tell me what's happened!

AMANDA: As you know, I was supposed to be inducted into my office at the D.A.R. this afternoon. (*Image: A swarm of typewriters.*) But I stopped off at Rubicam's business college to speak to your teachers about your having a cold and ask them what progress they thought you were making down there.

LAURA: Oh. . . .

AMANDA: I went to the typing instructor and introduced myself as your mother. She didn't know who you were. Wingfield, she said. We don't have any such student enrolled at the school! I assured her she did, that you had been going to classes since early in January. "I wonder," she said, "if you could be talking about that terribly shy little girl who dropped out of school after only a few days' attendance?" "No," I said, "Laura, my daughter, has been going to school every day for the past six weeks!" "Excuse me," she said. She took the attendance book out and there was your name, unmistakably printed, and all the dates you were absent until they decided that you had dropped out of school. I still said, "No, there must have been some mistake! There must have been some mix-up in the records!" And she said, "No—I remember her perfectly now. Her hands shook so that she couldn't hit the right keys! The first time we gave a speed-test, she broke down completely—was sick at the stomach and almost had to be carried into the wash-room! After that morning she never showed up any more. We phoned the house but never got any answer—while I was working at Famous and Barr, I suppose, demonstrating those—Oh!" I felt so weak I could barely keep on my feet! I had to sit down while they got me a glass of water! Fifty dollars' tuition, all of our plans— my hopes and ambitions for you—just gone up the spout, just gone up the spout like that. (LAURA *draws a long breath and gets awkwardly to her feet. She crosses to the victrola and winds it up.*) What are you doing?

LAURA: Oh! (*She releases the handle and returns to her seat.*)

AMANDA: Laura, where have you been going when you've gone out pretending that you were going to business college?

LAURA: I've just been going out walking.

AMANDA: That's not true.

LAURA: It is. I just went walking.

AMANDA: Walking? Walking? In winter? Deliberately courting pneumonia in that light coat? Where did you walk to, Laura?

LAURA: All sorts of places—mostly in the park.

AMANDA: Even after you'd started catching that cold?

LAURA: It was the lesser of two evils, Mother. (*Image: Winter scene in the park.*) I couldn't go back up. I—threw up—on the floor!

AMANDA: From half past seven till after five every day you mean to tell me you walked around in the park, because you wanted to make me think that you were still going to Rubicam's Business College?

LAURA: It wasn't as bad as it sounds. I went inside places to get warmed up.

AMANDA: Inside where?

LAURA: I went in the art museum and the bird-houses at the Zoo. I visited the penguins every day! Sometimes I did without lunch and went to the movies. Lately I've been spending most of my afternoons in the Jewel-box, that big glass house where they raise the tropical flowers.

AMANDA: You did all this to deceive me, just for deception? (LAURA *looks down.*) Why?

LAURA: Mother, when you're disappointed, you get that awful suffering look on your face, like the picture of Jesus' mother in the museum!

AMANDA: Hush!

LAURA: I couldn't face it.

Pause. A whisper of strings.
    (*Legend: "The Crust of Humility."*)

AMANDA (*hopelessly fingering the huge pocketbook*): So what are we going to do the rest of our lives? Stay home and watch the parades go by? Amuse ourselves with the glass menagerie, darling? Eternally play those worn-out phonograph records your father left as a painful reminder of him? We won't have a business career—we've given that up because it gave us nervous indigestion! (*laughs wearily*) What is there left but dependency all our lives? I know so well what becomes of unmarried women who aren't prepared to occupy a position. I've seen such pitiful cases in the South—barely tolerated spinsters living upon the grudging patronage of sister's husband or brother's wife!—stuck away in some little mouse-trap of a room—encouraged by one in-law to visit another—little birdlike women without any nest—eating the crust of humility all their life! Is that the future that we've mapped out for ourselves? I swear it's the only alternative I can think of! It isn't a very pleasant alternative, is it? Of course—some girls *do marry.* (LAURA *twists her hands nervously.*) Haven't you ever liked some boy?

LAURA: Yes. I liked one once. (*rises*) I came across his picture a while ago.

AMANDA (*with some interest*): He gave you his picture?

LAURA: No, it's in the year-book.

AMANDA (*disappointed*): Oh—a high-school boy.

(*Screen image:* JIM *as high-school hero bearing a silver cup.*)

LAURA: Yes. His name was Jim. (LAURA *lifts the heavy annual from the claw-foot table.*) Here he is in *The Pirates of Penzance.*

AMANDA (*absently*): The what?

LAURA: The operetta the senior class put on. He had a wonderful voice and we sat across the aisle from each other Mondays, Wednesdays and Fridays in the Aud. Here he is with the silver cup for debating! See his grin?

AMANDA (*absently*): He must have had a jolly disposition.

LAURA: He used to call me—Blue Roses.

(*Image: Blue roses.*)

AMANDA: Why did he call you such a name as that?

LAURA: When I had that attack of pleurosis—he asked me what was the matter when I came back. I said pleurosis—he thought that I said Blue Roses! So that's what he always called me after that. Whenever he saw me, he'd holler, "Hello, Blue Roses!" I didn't care for the girl that he went out with. Emily Meisenbach. Emily was the best-dressed girl at Soldan. She never struck me, though, as being sincere . . . It says in the Personal Section—they're engaged. That's—six years ago! They must be married by now.

AMANDA: Girls that aren't cut out for business careers usually wind up married to some nice man. (*gets up with a spark of revival*) Sister, that's what you'll do!

LAURA *utters a startled, doubtful laugh. She reaches quickly for a piece of glass.*

LAURA: But, Mother—

AMANDA: Yes? (*crossing to photograph*)

LAURA (*in a tone of frightened apology*): I'm—crippled!

(*Image: Screen.*)

AMANDA: Nonsense! Laura, I've told you never, never to use that word. Why, you're not crippled, you just have a little defect—hardly noticeable, even! When people have some slight disadvantage like that, they cultivate other things to make up for it—develop charm—and vivacity—and—*charm!* That's all you have to do! (*She turns again to the photograph.*) One thing your father had *plenty of*—was *charm!*

TOM *motions to the fiddle in the winds.*

(*The scene fades out with music.*)

SCENE 3

(*Legend on screen: "After the Fiasco—"*)
    TOM *speaks from the fire-escape landing.*

TOM: After the fiasco at Rubicam's Business College, the idea of getting a gentleman caller for Laura began to play a more and more important part in Mother's calculations. It became an obsession. Like some archetype of the universal unconscious, the image of the gentleman caller haunted our small apartment. . . . (*Image: Young man at door with flowers.*) An evening at home rarely passed without some allusion to this image, this spectre, this hope. . . . Even when he wasn't mentioned, his presence hung in Mother's preoccupied look and in my sister's frightened, apologetic manner—hung like a sentence passed upon the Wingfields! Mother was a woman of action as well as words. She began to take logical steps in the planned direction. Late that winter and in the early spring—realizing that extra money would be needed to properly feather the nest and plume the bird—she conducted a vigorous campaign on the telephone, roping in subscribers to one of those magazines for matrons called *The Home-maker's Companion,* the type of journal that features the serialized sublimations of ladies of letters who think in terms of delicate cup-like breasts, slim, tapering waists, rich, creamy thighs, eyes like wood-smoke in autumn, fingers that soothe and caress like strains of music, bodies as powerful as Etruscan sculpture.

(*Screen image: Glamor magazine cover.*)
        AMANDA *enters with phone on long extension cord. She is spotted in the dim stage.*

AMANDA: Ida Scott? This is Amanda Wingfield! We *missed* you at the D.A.R. last Monday! I said to myself: She's probably suffering with that sinus condition! How is that sinus condition? Horrors! Heaven have mercy!—You're a Christian martyr, yes, that's what you are, a Christian martyr! Well, I just now happened to notice that your subscription to the *Companion's* about to expire! Yes, it expires with the next issue, honey!—just when that wonderful new serial by Bessie Mae Hopper is getting off to such an exciting start. Oh, honey, it's something that you can't miss! You remember how *Gone With the Wind* took everybody by storm? You simply couldn't go out if you hadn't read it. All everybody *talked* was Scarlett O'Hara. Well, this is a book that critics already compare to *Gone With the Wind*. It's the *Gone With the Wind* of the post-World War generation!—What?—Burning?—Oh, honey, don't let them burn, go take a look in the oven and I'll hold the wire! Heavens—I think she's hung up!

(*Dim out.*)
        (*Legend on screen: "You think I'm in love with continental shoemakers?"*)
        Before the stage is lighted, the violent voices of TOM *and* AMANDA *are heard. They are quarreling behind the portieres. In front of them stands* LAURA *with clenched hands and panicky expression.*
        A clear pool of light on her figure throughout this scene.

TOM: What in Christ's name am I—
AMANDA (*shrilly*): Don't you use that—
TOM: Supposed to do!
AMANDA: Expression! Not in my—
TOM: Ohhh!
AMANDA: Presence! Have you gone out of your senses?
TOM: I have, that's true, *driven* out!
AMANDA: What is the matter with you, you—big—big—IDIOT!
TOM: Look—I've got *no thing*, no single thing—
AMANDA: Lower your voice!
TOM: In my life here that I can call my own! Everything is—
AMANDA: Stop that shouting!
TOM: Yesterday you confiscated my books! You had the nerve to—
AMANDA: I took that horrible novel back to the library—yes! That hideous book by that insane Mr. Lawrence. (TOM *laughs wildly.*) I cannot control the output of diseased minds or people who cater to them—(TOM *laughs still more wildly.*) BUT I WON'T ALLOW SUCH FILTH BROUGHT INTO MY HOUSE ! No, no, no, no, no!
TOM: House, house! Who pays rent on it, who makes a slave of himself to—
AMANDA (*fairly screeching*): Don't you DARE to—
TOM: No, no, *I* mustn't say things! *I've* got to just—
AMANDA: Let me tell you—
TOM: I don't want to hear any more! (*He tears the portieres open. The upstage area is lit with a turgid smoky red glow.*)

AMANDA'S *hair is in metal curlers and she wears a very old bathrobe, much too large for her slight figure, a relic of the faithless Mr. Wingfield.*

An upright typewriter and a wild disarray of manuscripts is on the drop-leaf table. The quarrel was probably precipitated by AMANDA'S *interruption of his creative labor. A chair lying overthrown on the floor.*

Their gesticulating shadows are cast on the ceiling by the fiery glow.

AMANDA: You *will* hear more, you—

TOM: No, I won't hear more, I'm going out!

AMANDA: You come right back in—

TOM: Out, out, out! Because I'm—

AMANDA: Come back here, Tom Wingfield! I'm not through talking to you!

TOM: Oh, go—

LAURA (*desperately*):—Tom!

AMANDA: You're going to listen, and no more insolence from you! I'm at the end of my patience! (*He comes back toward her.*)

TOM: What do you think I'm at? Aren't I supposed to have any patience to reach the end of, Mother? I know, I know. It seems unimportant to you, what I'm *doing*— what I *want* to do—having a little *difference* between them! You don't think that—

AMANDA: I think you've been doing things that you're ashamed of. That's why you act like this. I don't believe that you go every night to the movies. Nobody goes to the movies night after night. Nobody in their right minds goes to the movies as often as you pretend to. People don't go to the movies at nearly midnight, and movies don't let out at two A.M. Come in stumbling. Muttering to yourself like a maniac! You get three hours' sleep and then go to work. Oh, I can picture the way you're doing down there. Moping, doping, because you're in no condition.

TOM (*wildly*): No, I'm in no condition!

AMANDA: What right have you got to jeopardize your job? Jeopardize the security of us all? How do you think we'd manage if you were—

TOM: Listen! You think I'm crazy *about* the *warehouse?* (*He bends fiercely toward her slight figure.*) You think I'm in love with the Continental Shoemakers? You think I want to spend fifty-five *years* down there in that—*celotex interior!* with— *fluorescent—tubes!* Look! I'd rather somebody picked up a crowbar and battered out my brains—than go back mornings! I *go!* Every time you come in yelling that God damn *"Rise and Shine!" "Rise and Shine!"* I say to myself, "How *lucky dead* people are!" But I get up. I *go!* For sixty-five dollars a month I give up all that I dream of doing and being *ever!* And you say self—*self's* all I ever think of. Why, listen, if self is what I thought of, Mother, I'd be where he is—GONE! (*pointing to father's picture*) As far as the system of transportation reaches! (*He starts past her. She grabs his arm.*) Don't grab at me, Mother!

AMANDA: Where are you going?

TOM: I'm going to the *movies!*

AMANDA: I don't believe that lie!

TOM (*Crouching toward her, overtowering her tiny figure. She backs away, gasping.*): I'm going to opium dens! Yes, opium dens, dens of vice and criminals' hang-outs, Mother. I've joined the Hogan gang, I'm a hired assassin, I carry a tommy-gun in a violin case! I run a string of cat-houses in the Valley! They call me Killer, Killer Wingfield, I'm leading a double-life, a simple, honest warehouse worker by day, by night a dynamic *czar* of the *underworld, Mother.* I go to gambling casinos, I spin away fortunes on the roulette table! I wear a patch over one eye and a false mustache, sometimes I put on green whiskers. On those occasions they call me—*El Diablo!* Oh, I could tell you things to make you sleepless! My enemies plan to dynamite this place. They're going to blow us all sky-high some night! I'll be glad, very happy, and so will you! You'll go up, up on a broomstick, over Blue Mountain with seventeen gentlemen callers! You ugly—babbling old—*witch.* . . . (*He goes through a series of violent, clumsy movements, seizing his overcoat, lunging to the door, pulling it fiercely open. The women watch him, aghast. His arm catches in the sleeve of the coat as he struggles to pull it on. For a moment he is pinioned by the bulky garment. With an outraged groan he tears the coat off again, splitting the shoulder of it, and hurls it across the room. It strikes against the shelf of* LAURA'S *glass collection, there is a tinkle of shattering glass.* LAURA *cries out as if wounded.*)

(*Music. Legend: "The Glass Menagerie."*)

LAURA (*shrilly*): *My glass!*—menagerie. . . . (*She covers her face and turns away.*)

But AMANDA *is still stunned and stupefied by the "ugly witch" so that she barely notices this occurrence. Now she recovers her speech.*

AMANDA (*in an awful voice*): I won't speak to you—until you apologize! (*She crosses through portieres and draws them together behind her.* TOM *is left with* LAURA. LAURA *clings weakly to the mantel with her face averted.* TOM *stares at her stupidly for a moment. Then he crosses to shelf. Drops awkwardly on his knees to collect the fallen glass, glancing at* LAURA *as if he would speak but couldn't.*)

"The Glass Menagerie" steals in as

(*The scene dims out.*)

SCENE 4

The interior is dark. Faint light in the alley.

A deep-voiced bell in a church is tolling the hour of five as the scene commences.

TOM *appears at the top of the alley. After each solemn boom of the bell in the tower, he shakes a little noise-maker or rattle as if to express the tiny spasm of man in contrast to the sustained power and dignity of the Almighty. This and the unsteadiness of his advance make it evident that he has been drinking.*

As he climbs the few steps to the fire-escape landing light steals up inside. LAURA *appears in night-dress, observing* TOM'S *empty bed in the front room.*

TOM *fishes in his pockets for door-key, removing a motley assortment of articles in the search, including a perfect shower of movie-ticket stubs and an empty bottle. At last he finds the key, but just as he is about to insert it, it slips from his fingers. He strikes a match and crouches below the door.*

TOM (*bitterly*): One crack—and it falls through!

LAURA *opens the door.*

LAURA: Tom! Tom, what are you doing?
TOM: Looking for a door-key.
LAURA: Where have you been all this time?
TOM: I have been to the movies.
LAURA: All this time at the movies?

TOM: There was a very long program. There was a Garbo picture and a Mickey Mouse and a travelogue and a newsreel and a preview of coming attractions. And there was an organ solo and a collection for the milk-fund—simultaneously—which ended up in a terrible fight between a fat lady and an usher!

LAURA (*innocently*): Did you have to stay through everything?

TOM: Of course! And, oh, I forgot! There was a big stage show! The headliner on this stage show was Malvolio the Magician. He performed wonderful tricks, many of them, such as pouring water back and forth between pitchers. First it turned to wine and then it turned to beer and then it turned to whiskey. I know it was whiskey it finally turned into because he needed somebody to come up out of the audience to help him, and I came up—both shows! It was Kentucky Straight Bourbon. A very generous fellow, he gave souvenirs. (*He pulls from his back pocket a shimmering rainbow-colored scarf.*) He gave me this. This is his magic scarf. You can have it, Laura. You wave it over a canary cage and you get a bowl of gold-fish. You wave it over the gold-fish bowl and they fly away canaries. . . . But the won-derfullest trick of all was the coffin trick. We nailed him into a coffin and he got out of the coffin without removing one nail. (*He has come inside.*) There is a trick that would come in handy for me—get me out of this 2 by 4 situation! (*flops onto bed and starts removing shoes*)

LAURA: Tom—Shhh!

TOM: What're you shushing me for?

LAURA: You'll wake up Mother.

TOM: Goody, goody! Pay 'er back for all those "Rise an' Shines."(*lies down, groaning*) You know it don't take much intelligence to get yourself into a nailed-up coffin, Laura. But who in hell ever got himself out of one without removing one nail?

As if in answer, the father's grinning photograph lights up.
    (*Scene dims out.*)
    Immediately following: The church bell is heard striking six. At the sixth stroke the alarm clock goes off in AMANDA'S *room, and after a few moments we hear her calling: "Rise and Shine! Rise and Shine! Laura, go tell your brother to rise and shine!"*

TOM (*sitting up slowly*): I'll rise—but I won't shine.

The light increases.

AMANDA: Laura, tell your brother his coffee is ready.

    LAURA *slips into front room.*

LAURA: Tom!—It's nearly seven. Don't make Mother nervous. (*He stares at her stupid-ly. Beseechingly.*) Tom, speak to Mother this morning. Make up with her, apolo-gize, speak to her!

TOM: She won't to me. It's her that started not speaking.

LAURA: If you just say you're sorry she'll start speaking.

TOM: Her not speaking—is that such a tragedy?

LAURA: Please—please!

AMANDA (*calling from kitchenette*): Laura, are you going to do what I asked you to do, or do I have to get dressed and go out myself?

LAURA: Going, going—soon as I get on my coat! (*She pulls on a shapeless felt hat with nervous, jerky movement, pleadingly glancing at* TOM. *Rushes awkwardly for coat. The coat is one of* AMANDA'S, *inaccurately made-over, the sleeves too short for* LAURA.) Butter and what else?

AMANDA (*entering upstage*): Just butter. Tell them to charge it.

LAURA: Mother, they make such faces when I do that.

AMANDA: Sticks and stones can break our bones, but the expression on Mr. Garfinkel's face won't harm us! Tell your brother his coffee is getting cold.

LAURA (*at door*): Do what I asked you, will you, will you, Tom?

He looks sullenly away.

AMANDA: Laura, go now or just don't go at all!

LAURA (*rushing out*): Going—going! (*A second later she cries out.* TOM *springs up and crosses to door.* AMANDA *rushes anxiously in.* TOM *opens the door.*)

TOM: Laura?

LAURA: I'm all right. I slipped, but I'm all right.

AMANDA (*peering anxiously after her*): If anyone breaks a leg on those fire-escape steps, the landlord ought to be sued for every cent he possesses! (*She shuts door. Remembers she isn't speaking and returns to other room.*)

As TOM *enters listlessly for his coffee, she turns her back to him and stands rigidly facing the window on the gloomy gray vault of the areaway. Its light on her face with its aged but childish features is cruelly sharp, satirical as a Daumier print.*
(Music under: "Ave Maria.")
(TOM *glances sheepishly but sullenly at her averted figure and slumps at the table. The coffee is scalding hot; he sips it and gasps and spits it back in the cup. At his gasp,* AMANDA *catches her breath and half turns. Then catches herself and turns back to window.*
TOM *blows on his coffee, glancing sidewise at his mother. She clears her throat.* TOM *clears his. He starts to rise. Sinks back down again, scratches his head, clears his throat again.* AMANDA *coughs.* TOM *raises his cup in both hands to blow on it, his eyes staring over the rim of it at his mother for several moments. Then he slowly sets the cup down and awkwardly and hesitantly rises from the chair.*

TOM (*hoarsely*): Mother. I—I apologize, Mother. (AMANDA *draws a quick, shuddering breath. Her face works grotesquely. She breaks into childlike tears.*) I'm sorry for what I said, for everything that I said, I didn't mean it.

AMANDA (*sobbingly*): My devotion has made me a witch and so I make myself hateful to my children!

TOM: No, you *don't.*

AMANDA: I worry so much, don't sleep, it makes me nervous!

TOM (*gently*): I understand that.

AMANDA: I've had to put up a solitary battle all these years. But you're my right-hand bower! Don't fall down, don't fail!

TOM (*gently*): I try, Mother.

AMANDA (*with great enthusiasm*): Try and you will SUCCEED! (*The notion makes her breathless.*) Why, you—you're just *full* of natural endowments! Both of my children—they're *unusual* children! Don't you think I know it? I'm so—*proud!* Happy and—feel I've—so much to be thankful for but—Promise me one thing, Son!

TOM: What, Mother?

AMANDA: Promise, son, you'll—never be a drunkard!

TOM (*turns to her grinning*): I will never be a drunkard, Mother.

AMANDA: That's what frightened me so, that you'd be drinking! Eat a bowl of Purina!

TOM: Just coffee, Mother.

AMANDA: Shredded wheat biscuit?

TOM: No. No, Mother, just coffee.

AMANDA: You can't put in a day's work on an empty stomach. You've got ten minutes—don't gulp! Drinking too-hot liquids makes cancer of the stomach. . . . Put cream in.

TOM: No, thank you.

AMANDA: To cool it.

TOM: No! No, thank you, I want it black.

AMANDA: I know, but it's not good for you. We have to do all that we can to build ourselves up. In these trying times we live in, all that we have to cling to is—each other. . . . That's why it's so important to— Tom, I— I sent out your sister so I could discuss something with you. If you hadn't spoken I would have spoken to you. (*sits down*)

TOM (*gently*): What is it, Mother, that you want to discuss?

AMANDA: *Laura!*

> TOM *puts his cup down slowly.*
> (*Legend on screen: "Laura."*)
> (*Music: "The Glass Menagerie."*)

TOM: —Oh.—Laura . . .

AMANDA (*touching his sleeve*): You know how Laura is. So quiet but—still water runs deep! She notices things and I think she—broods about them. (TOM *looks up.*) A few days ago I came in and she was crying.

TOM: What about?

AMANDA: You.

TOM: Me?

AMANDA: She has an idea that you're not happy here.

TOM: What gave her that idea?

AMANDA: What gives her any idea? However, you do act strangely. I—I'm not criticizing, understand *that!* I know your ambitions do not lie in the warehouse, that like everybody in the whole wide world—you've had to—make sacrifices, but—Tom— Tom—life's not easy, it calls for—Spartan endurance! There's so many things in my heart that I cannot describe to you! I've never told you but I—*loved* your father. . . .

TOM (*gently*): I know that, Mother.

AMANDA: And you—when I see you taking after his ways! Staying out late—and—well, you *had* been drinking the night you were in that—terrifying condition! Laura says that you hate the apartment and that you go out nights to get away from it! Is that true, Tom?

TOM: No. You say there's so much in your heart that you can't describe to me. That's true of me, too. There's so much in my heart that I can't describe to *you!* So let's respect each other's—

AMANDA: But, why—*why*, Tom—are you always so *restless?* Where do you *go* to, nights?

TOM: I—go to the movies.

AMANDA: Why do you go to the movies so much, Tom?

TOM: I go to the movies because—I like adventure. Adventure is something I don't have much of at work, so I go to the movies.

AMANDA: But, Tom, you go to the movies *entirely* too much!

TOM: I like a lot of adventure.

AMANDA *looks baffled, then hurt. As the familiar inquisition resumes he becomes hard and impatient again.* AMANDA *slips back into her querulous attitude toward him.*
(*Image on screen: Sailing vessel with Jolly Roger.*)

AMANDA: Most young men find adventure in their careers.

TOM: Then most young men are not employed in a warehouse.

AMANDA: The world is full of young men employed in warehouses and offices and factories.

TOM: Do all of them find adventure in their careers?

AMANDA: They do or they do without it! Not everybody has a craze for adventure.

TOM: Man is by instinct a lover, a hunter, a fighter, and none of those instincts are given much play at the warehouse!

AMANDA: Man is by instinct! Don't quote instinct to me! Instinct is something that people have got away from! It belongs to animals! Christian adults don't want it!

TOM: What do Christian adults want, then, Mother?

AMANDA: Superior things! Things of the mind and the spirit! Only animals have to satisfy instincts! Surely your aims are somewhat higher than theirs! Than monkeys—pigs—

TOM: I reckon they're not.

AMANDA: You're joking. However, that isn't what I wanted to discuss.

TOM (*rising*): I haven't much time.

AMANDA (*pushing his shoulders*): Sit down.

TOM: You want me to punch in red at the warehouse, Mother?

AMANDA: You have five minutes. I want to talk about Laura.

(*Legend: "Plans and Provisions."*)

TOM: All right! What about Laura?

AMANDA: We have to be making some plans and provisions for her. She's older than you, two years, and nothing has happened. She just drifts along doing nothing. It frightens me terribly how she just drifts along.

TOM: I guess she's the type that people call home girls.

AMANDA: There's no such type, and if there is, it's a pity! That is unless the home is hers, with a husband!

TOM: What?

AMANDA: Oh, I can see the handwriting on the wall as plain as I see the nose in front of my face! It's terrifying! More and more you remind me of your father! He was out all hours without explanation!—Then *left! Good-bye!* And me with the bag to hold. I saw that letter you got from the Merchant Marine. I know what you're dreaming of. I'm not standing here blindfolded. Very well, then. Then *do* it! But not till there's somebody to take your place.

TOM: What do you mean?

AMANDA: I mean that as soon as Laura has got somebody to take care of her, married, a home of her own, independent—why, then you'll be free to go wherever you please, on land, on sea, whichever way the wind blows you! But until that time you've got to look out for your sister. I don't say me because I'm old and don't matter! I say for your sister because she's young and dependent. I put her in business college—a dismal failure! Frightened her so it made her sick at the stomach. I took her over to the Young People's League at the church. Another fiasco. She spoke to nobody, nobody spoke to her. Now all she does is fool with those pieces of glass and play those worn-out records. What kind of a life is that for a girl to lead?

TOM: What can I do about it?

AMANDA: Overcome selfishness! Self, self, self is all that you ever think of! (Tom *springs up and crosses to get his coat. It is ugly and bulky. He pulls on a cap with earmuffs.*) Where is your muffler? Put your wool muffler on! (*He snatches it angrily from the closet and tosses it around his neck and pulls both ends tight.*) Tom! I haven't said what I had in mind to ask you.

TOM: I'm too late to—

AMANDA (*Catching his arm—very importunately. Then shyly.*): Down at the warehouse, aren't there some—nice young men?

TOM: No!

AMANDA: There *must* be—*some* . . .

TOM: Mother—

Gesture.

AMANDA: Find out one that's clean-living—doesn't drink and—ask him out for sister!

TOM: What?

AMANDA: For *sister!* To *meet!* Get *acquainted!*

TOM (*stamping to door*): Oh, my *go-osh!*

AMANDA: Will you? (*He opens door. Imploringly.*) Will you? (*He starts down.*) Will you? *Will* you, dear?

TOM (*calling back*): YES!

> AMANDA *closes the door hesitantly and with a troubled but faintly hopeful expression.* (*Screen image: Glamor magazine cover.*) *Spot* AMANDA *at phone.*

AMANDA: Ella Cartwright? This is Amanda Wingfield! How are you, honey? How is that kidney condition? (*count five*) Horrors! (*count five*) You're a Christian martyr, yes, honey, that's what you are, a Christian martyr! Well, I just now happened to notice in my little red book that your subscription to the *Companion* has just run out! I knew that you wouldn't want to miss out on the wonderful serial starting in this new issue. It's by Bessie Mae Hopper, the first thing she's written since *Honeymoon for Three.* Wasn't that a strange and interesting story? Well, this one is even lovelier, I believe. It has a sophisticated, society background. It's all about the horsey set on Long Island!

> (*Fade out.*)

SCENE 5

> (*Legend on screen: "Annunciation."*) *Fade with music.*
>
> *It is early dusk of a spring evening. Supper has just been finished in the Wingfield apartment.* AMANDA *and* LAURA *in light-colored dresses are removing dishes from the table, in the upstage area, which is shadowy, their movements formalized almost as a dance or ritual, their moving forms as pale and silent as moths.*
>
> TOM, *in white shirt and trousers, rises from the table and crosses toward the fire-escape.*

AMANDA (*as he passes her*): Son, will you do me a favor?

TOM: What?

AMANDA: Comb your hair! You look so pretty when your hair is combed! (TOM *slouches on sofa with evening paper. Enormous caption "Franco Triumphs."*) There is only one respect in which I would like you to emulate your father.

TOM: What respect is that?

AMANDA: The care he always took of his appearance. He never allowed himself to look untidy. (*He throws down the paper and crosses to fire-escape.*) Where are you going?

TOM: I'm going out to smoke.

AMANDA: You smoke too much. A pack a day at fifteen cents a pack. How much would that amount to in a month? Thirty times fifteen is how much, Tom? Figure it out and you will be astounded at what you could save. Enough to give you a night-school course in accounting at Washington U! Just think what a wonderful thing that would be for you, Son!

TOM *is unmoved by the thought.*

TOM: I'd rather smoke. (*He steps out on landing, letting the screen door slam.*)

AMANDA (*sharply*): I know! That's the tragedy of it. . . . (*Alone, she turns to look at her husband's picture.*)

(*Dance music: "All the world is waiting for the sunrise!"*)

TOM (*to the audience*): Across the alley from us was the Paradise Dance Hall. On evenings in spring the windows and doors were open and the music came outdoors. Sometimes the lights were turned out except for a large glass sphere that hung from the ceiling. It would turn slowly about and filter the dusk with delicate rainbow colors. Then the orchestra played a waltz or a tango, something that had a slow and sensuous rhythm. Couples would come outside, to the relative privacy of the alley. You could see them kissing behind ash-pits and telephone poles. This was the compensation for lives that passed like mine, without any change or adventure. Adventure and change were imminent in this year. They were waiting around the corner for all these kids. Suspended in the mist over Berchtesgaden, caught in the folds of Chamberlain's umbrella— In Spain there was Guernica! But here there was only hot swing music and liquor, dance halls, bars, and movies, and sex that hung in the gloom like a chandelier and flooded the world with brief, deceptive rainbows. . . . All the world was waiting for bombardments!

AMANDA *turns from the picture and comes outside.*

AMANDA (*sighing*): A fire-escape landing's a poor excuse for a porch. (*She spreads a newspaper on a step and sits down, gracefully and demurely as if she were settling into a swing on a Mississippi veranda.*) What are you looking at?

TOM: The moon.

AMANDA: Is there a moon this evening?

TOM: It's rising over Garfinkel's Delicatessen.

AMANDA: So it is! A little silver slipper of a moon. Have you made a wish on it yet?

TOM: Um-hum.

AMANDA: What did you wish for?

TOM: That's a secret.

AMANDA: A secret, huh? Well, I won't tell mine either. I will be just as mysterious as you.

TOM: I bet I can guess what yours is.

AMANDA: Is my head so transparent?

TOM: You're not a sphinx.

AMANDA: No, I don't have secrets. I'll tell you what I wished for on the moon. Success and happiness for my precious children! I wish for that whenever there's a moon, and when there isn't a moon, I wish for it, too.

TOM: I thought perhaps you wished for a gentleman caller.

AMANDA: Why do you say that?

TOM: Don't you remember asking me to fetch one?

AMANDA: I remember suggesting that it would be nice for your sister if you brought home some nice young man from the warehouse. I think that I've made that suggestion more than once.

TOM: Yes, you have made it repeatedly.

AMANDA: Well?

TOM: We are going to have one.

AMANDA: *What?*

TOM: A gentleman caller!

> (*The annunciation is celebrated with music.*)
> AMANDA *rises.*
> (*Image on screen: Caller with bouquet.*)

AMANDA: You mean you have asked some nice young man to come over?

TOM: Yep. I've asked him to dinner.

AMANDA: You really did?

TOM: I did!

AMANDA: You did, and did he—*accept?*

TOM: He did!

AMANDA: Well, well—well, well! That's—lovely!

TOM: I thought that you would be pleased.

AMANDA: It's definite, then?

TOM: Very definite.

AMANDA: Soon?

TOM: Very soon.

AMANDA: For heaven's sake, stop putting on and tell me some things, will you?

TOM: What things do you want me to tell you?

AMANDA: *Naturally* I would like to know when he's *coming!*

TOM: He's coming tomorrow.

AMANDA: *Tomorrow?*

TOM: Yep. Tomorrow.

AMANDA: But, Tom!

TOM: Yes, Mother?

AMANDA: Tomorrow gives me no time!

TOM: Time for what?

AMANDA: Preparations! Why didn't you phone me at once, as soon as you asked him, the minute that he accepted? Then, don't you see, I could have been getting ready!

TOM: You don't have to make any fuss.

AMANDA: Oh, Tom, Tom, Tom, of course I have to make a fuss! I want things nice, not sloppy! Not thrown together. I'll certainly have to do some fast thinking, won't I?

TOM: I don't see why you have to think at all.

AMANDA: You just don't know. We can't have a gentleman caller in a pig-sty! All my wedding silver has to be polished, the monogrammed table linen ought to be laundered! The windows have to be washed and fresh curtains put up. And how about clothes? We have to *wear* something, don't we?

TOM: Mother, this boy is no one to make a fuss over!

AMANDA: Do you realize he's the first young man we've introduced to your sister? It's terrible, dreadful, disgraceful that poor little sister has never received a single gentleman caller! Tom, come inside! (*She opens the screen door.*)

TOM: What for?

AMANDA: I want to ask you some things.

TOM: If you're going to make such a fuss, I'll call it off, I'll tell him not to come!

AMANDA: You certainly won't do anything of the kind. Nothing offends people worse than broken engagements. It simply means I'll have to work like a Turk! We won't be brilliant, but we will pass inspection. Come on inside. (TOM *follows, groaning.*) Sit down.

TOM: Any particular place you would like me to sit?

AMANDA: Thank heavens I've got that new sofa! I'm also making payments on a floor lamp I'll have sent out! And put the chintz covers on, they'll brighten things up! Of course I'd hoped to have these walls re-papered. . . . What is the young man's name?

TOM: His name is O'Connor.

AMANDA: That, of course, means fish—tomorrow is Friday! I'll have that salmon loaf— with Durkee's dressing! What does he do? He works at the warehouse?

TOM: Of course! How else would I—

AMANDA: Tom, he—doesn't drink?

TOM: Why do you ask me that?

AMANDA: Your father *did*!

TOM: Don't get started on that!

AMANDA: He *does* drink, then?

TOM: Not that I know of!

AMANDA: Make sure, be certain! The last thing I want for my daughter's a boy who drinks!

TOM: Aren't you being a little bit premature? Mr. O'Connor has not yet appeared on the scene!

AMANDA: But will tomorrow. To meet your sister, and what do I know about his character? Nothing! Old maids are better off than wives of drunkards!

TOM: Oh, my God!

AMANDA: Be still!

TOM (*leaning forward to whisper*): Lots of fellows meet girls whom they don't marry!

AMANDA: Oh, talk sensibly, Tom—and don't be sarcastic! (*She has gotten a hairbrush.*)

TOM: What are you doing?

AMANDA: I'm brushing that cow-lick down! What is this young man's position at the warehouse?

TOM (*submitting grimly to the brush and the interrogation*): This young man's position is that of a shipping clerk, Mother.

AMANDA: Sounds to me like a fairly responsible job, the sort of a job *you* would be in if you just had more *get-up*. What is his salary? Have you any idea?

TOM: I would judge it to be approximately eighty-five dollars a month.

AMANDA: Well—not princely, but—

TOM: Twenty more than I make.

AMANDA: Yes, how well I know! But for a family man, eighty-five dollars a month is not much more than you can just get by on. . . .

TOM: Yes, but Mr. O'Connor is not a family man.

AMANDA: He might be, mightn't he? Some time in the future?

TOM: I see. Plans and provisions.

AMANDA: You are the only young man that I know of who ignores the fact that the future becomes the present, the present the past, and the past turns into everlasting regret if you don't plan for it!

TOM: I will think that over and see what I can make of it.

AMANDA: Don't be supercilious with your mother! Tell me some more about this— what do you call him?

TOME: James D. O'Connor. The D. is for Delaney.

AMANDA: Irish on *both* sides! *Gracious!* And doesn't drink?

TOM: Shall I call him up and ask him right this minute?

AMANDA: The only way to find out about those things is to make discreet inquiries at the proper moment. When I was a girl in Blue Mountain and it was suspected that a young man drank, the girl whose attentions he had been receiving, if any girl *was,* would sometimes speak to the minister of his church, or rather her father would if her father was living, and sort of feel him out on the young man's character. That is the way such things are discreetly handled to keep a young woman from making a tragic mistake!

TOM: Then how did you happen to make a tragic mistake?

AMANDA: That innocent look of your father's had everyone fooled! He *smiled*—the world was *enchanted!* No girl can do worse than put herself at the mercy of a handsome appearance! I hope that Mr. O'Connor is not too good-looking.

TOM: No, he's not too good-looking. He's covered with freckles and hasn't too much of a nose.

AMANDA: He's not right-down homely, though?

TOM: Not right-down homely. Just medium homely, I'd say.

AMANDA: Character's what to look for in a man.

TOM: That's what I've always said, Mother.

AMANDA: You've never said anything of the kind and I suspect you would never give it a thought.

TOM: Don't be so suspicious of me.

AMANDA: At least I hope he's the type that's up and coming.

TOM: I think he really goes in for self-improvement.

AMANDA: What reason have you to think so?

TOM: He goes to night school.

AMANDA (*beaming*): Splendid! What does he do, I mean study?

TOM: Radio engineering and public speaking!

AMANDA: Then he has visions of being advanced in the world! Any young man who studies public speaking is aiming to have an executive job some day! And radio engineering? A thing for the future! Both of these facts are very illuminating. Those are the sort of things that a mother should know concerning any young man who comes to call on her daughter. Seriously or—not.

TOM: One little warning. He doesn't know about Laura. I didn't let on that we had dark ulterior motives. I just said, why don't you come and have dinner with us? He said okay and that was the whole conversation.

AMANDA: I bet it was! You're eloquent as an oyster. However, he'll know about Laura when he gets here. When he sees how lovely and sweet and pretty she is, he'll thank his lucky stars he was asked to dinner.

TOM: Mother, you mustn't expect too much of Laura.

AMANDA: What do you mean?

TOM: Laura seems all those things to you and me because she's ours and we love her. We don't even notice she's crippled any more.

AMANDA: Don't say crippled! You know that I never allow that word to be used!

TOM: But face facts, Mother. She is and—that's not all—

AMANDA: What do you mean "not all"?

TOM: Laura is very different from other girls.

AMANDA: I think the difference is all to her advantage.

TOM: Not quite all—in the eyes of others—strangers—she's terribly shy and lives in a world of her own and those things make her seem a little peculiar to people outside the house.

AMANDA: Don't say peculiar.

TOM: Face the facts. She is.

(*The dance-hall music changes to a tango that has a minor and somewhat ominous tone.*)

AMANDA: In what way is she peculiar—may I ask?

TOM (*gently*): She lives in a world of her own—a world of—little glass ornaments, Mother. . . . (*Gets up.* AMANDA *remains holding brush, looking at him, troubled.*) She plays old phonograph records and—that's about all—(*He glances at himself in the mirror and crosses to door.*)

AMANDA (*sharply*): Where are you going?

TOM: I'm going to the movies. (*out screen door*)

AMANDA: Not to the movies, every night to the movies! (*follows quickly to screen door*) I don't believe you always go to the movies! (*He is gone.* AMANDA *looks worriedly after him for a moment. Then vitality and optimism return and she turns from the door. Crossing to portieres.*) Laura! Laura! (LAURA *answers from kitchenette.*)

LAURA: Yes, Mother.

AMANDA: Let those dishes go and come in front! (LAURA *appears with dish towel. Gaily.*) Laura, come here and make a wish on the moon!

(*Screen image: Moon.*)

LAURA (*entering*): Moon—moon?

AMANDA: A little silver slipper of a moon. Look over your left shoulder, Laura, and make a wish! (LAURA *looks faintly puzzled as if called out of sleep.* AMANDA *seizes her shoulders and turns her at an angle by the door.*) Now! Now, darling, *wish!*

LAURA: What shall I wish for, Mother?

AMANDA (*her voice trembling and her eyes suddenly filling with tears*): Happiness! Good fortune!

(*The violin rises and the stage dims out.*)

SCENE 6

(*Image: High school hero.*)

TOM: And so the following evening I brought Jim home to dinner. I had known Jim slightly in high school. In high school Jim was a hero. He had tremendous Irish good nature and vitality with the scrubbed and polished look of white chinaware. He seemed to move in a continual spotlight. He was a star in basketball, captain of the debating club, president of the senior class and the glee club and he sang the male lead in the annual light operas. He was always running or bounding, never just walking. He seemed always at the point of defeating the law of gravity. He was shooting with such velocity through his adolescence that you would logically expect him to arrive at nothing short of the White House by the time he was thirty. But Jim apparently ran into more interference after his graduation from Soldan. His speed had definitely slowed. Six years after he left high school he was holding a job that wasn't much better than mine.

(*Image: Clerk.*)

He was the only one at the warehouse with whom I was on friendly terms. I was valuable to him as someone who could remember his former glory, who had seen him win basketball games and the silver cup in debating. He knew of my secret practice of retiring to a cabinet of the wash-room to work on poems when business was slack in the warehouse. He called me Shakespeare. And while the other boys in the warehouse regarded me with suspicious hostility, Jim took a humorous attitude toward me. Gradually his attitude affected the others, their hostility wore off and they also began to smile at me as people smile at an oddly fashioned dog who trots across their path at some distance.

I knew that Jim and Laura had known each other at Soldan, and I had heard Laura speak admiringly of his voice. I didn't know if Jim remembered her or not. In high school Laura had been as unobtrusive as Jim had been astonishing. If he did remember Laura, it was not as my sister, for when I asked him to dinner, he grinned and said, "You know, Shakespeare, I never thought of you as having folks!" He was about to discover that I did. . . .

(*Light up stage.*)
   (*Legend on screen: "The Accent of a Coming Foot."*)
   Friday evening. It is about five o'clock of a late spring evening which comes "scattering poems in the sky."
   A delicate lemony light is in the Wingfield apartment.
   AMANDA *has worked like a Turk in preparation for the gentleman caller. The results are astonishing. The new floor lamp with its rose-silk shade is in place, a colored paper lantern conceals the broken light fixture in the ceiling, new billowing white curtains are at the windows, chintz covers are on chairs and sofa, a pair of new sofa pillows make their initial appearance.*
   Open boxes and tissue paper are scattered on the floor.
   LAURA *stands in the middle with lifted arms while* AMANDA *crouches before her, adjusting the hem of the new dress, devout and ritualistic. The dress is colored and designed by memory. The arrangement of* LAURA'S *hair is changed; it is softer and more becoming. A fragile, unearthly prettiness has come out in* LAURA: *she is like a piece of translucent glass touched by light, given a momentary radiance, not actual, not lasting.*

AMANDA (*impatiently*): Why are you trembling?

LAURA: Mother, you've made me so nervous!

AMANDA: How have I made you nervous?

LAURA: By all this fuss! You make it seem so important!

AMANDA: I don't understand you, Laura. You couldn't be satisfied with just sitting home, and yet whenever I try to arrange something for you, you seem to resist it.

She gets up.

Now take a look at yourself. No, wait! Wait just a moment—I have an idea!

LAURA: What is it now?

AMANDA *produces two powder puffs which she wraps in handkerchiefs and stuffs in* LAURA'S *bosom.*

LAURA: Mother, what are you doing?

AMANDA: They call them "Gay Deceivers"!

LAURA: I won't wear them!

AMANDA: You will!

LAURA: Why should I?

AMANDA: Because, to be painfully honest, your chest is flat.

LAURA: You make it seem like we were setting a trap.

AMANDA: All pretty girls are a trap, a pretty trap, and men expect them to be. (*Legend: "A Pretty Trap."*) Now look at yourself, young lady. This is the prettiest you will ever be! I've got to fix myself now! You're going to be surprised by your mother's appearance! (*She crosses through portieres, humming gaily.*)

LAURA *moves slowly to the long mirror and stares solemnly at herself.*

A wind blows the white curtains inward in a slow, graceful motion and with a faint, sorrowful sighing.

AMANDA (*off stage*): It isn't dark enough yet. (*She turns slowly before the mirror with a troubled look.*)

(*Legend on screen: "This Is My Sister: Celebrate Her with Strings!" Music.*)

AMANDA (*laughing, off*): I'm going to show you something. I'm going to make a spectacular appearance!

LAURA: What is it, Mother?

AMANDA: Possess your soul in patience—you will see! Something I've resurrected from that old trunk! Styles haven't changed so terribly much after all. . . . (*She parts the portieres.*) Now just look at your mother! (*She wears a girlish frock of yellowed voile with a blue silk sash. She carries a bunch of jonquils—the legend of her youth is nearly revived. Feverishly.*) This is the dress in which I led the cotillion. Won the cakewalk twice at Sunset Hill, wore one spring to the Governor's ball in Jackson! See how I sashayed around the ballroom, Laura? (*She raises her skirt and does a mincing step around the room.*) I wore it on Sundays for my gentlemen callers! I had it on the day I met your father—I had malaria fever all that spring. The change of climate from East Tennessee to the Delta—weakened resistance—I had a little temperature all the time—not enough to be serious—just enough to make me restless and giddy!—Invitations poured in—parties all over the Delta!—"Stay in bed," said Mother, "you have fever!"—but I just wouldn't.—I took quinine but kept on going, going!—Evenings, dances!—Afternoons, long, long rides! Picnics—lovely!—So lovely, that country in May.—All lacy with dogwood, literally flooded with jonquils!—That was the spring I had the craze for jonquils. Jonquils became an absolute obsession. Mother said, "Honey, there's no more room for jonquils." And still I kept on bringing in more jonquils. Whenever, wherever I saw them, I'd say, "Stop! Stop! I see jonquils!" I made the young men help me gather the jonquils! It was a joke, Amanda and her jonquils! Finally there were no more vases to hold them, every available space was filled with jonquils. No vases to hold them? All right, I'll hold them myself! And then I—(*She stops in front of the picture. Music.*) met your father! Malaria fever and jonquils and then—this—boy. . . . (*She switches on the rose-colored lamp.*) I hope they get here before it starts to rain. (*She crosses upstage and places the jonquils in bowl on table.*) I gave your brother a little extra change so he and Mr. O'Connor could take the service car home.

LAURA (*with altered look*): What did you say his name was?

AMANDA: O'Connor.

LAURA: What is his first name?

AMANDA: I don't remember. Oh, yes, I do. It was—Jim!

> LAURA *sways slightly and catches hold of a chair.*
> (*Legend on screen: "Not Jim!"*)

LAURA (*faintly*): Not—Jim!

AMANDA: Yes, that was it, it was Jim! I've never known a Jim that wasn't nice!

> (*Music: Ominous.*)

LAURA: Are you sure his name is Jim O'Connor?

AMANDA: Yes. Why?

LAURA: Is he the one that Tom used to know in high school?

AMANDA: He didn't say so. I think he just got to know him at the warehouse.

LAURA: There was a Jim O'Connor we both knew in high school—(*then, with effort*) If that is the one that Tom is bringing to dinner—you'll have to excuse me, I won't come to the table.

AMANDA: What sort of nonsense is this?

LAURA: You asked me once if I'd ever liked a boy. Don't you remember I showed you this boy's picture?

AMANDA: You mean the boy you showed me in the year book?

LAURA: Yes, that boy.

AMANDA: Laura, Laura, were you in love with that boy?

LAURA: I don't know, Mother. All I know is I couldn't sit at the table if it was him!

AMANDA: It won't be him! It isn't the least bit likely. But whether it is or not, you will come to the table. You will not be excused.

LAURA: I'll have to be, Mother.

AMANDA: I don't intend to humor your silliness, Laura. I've had too much from you and your brother, both! So just sit down and compose yourself till they come. Tom has forgotten his key so you'll have to let them in, when they arrive.

LAURA (*panicky*): Oh, Mother—*you* answer the door!

AMANDA (*lightly*): I'll be in the kitchen—busy!

LAURA: Oh, Mother, please answer the door, don't make me do it!

AMANDA (*crossing into kitchenette*): I've got to fix the dressing for the salmon. Fuss, fuss—silliness!—over a gentleman caller!

> *Door swings shut.* LAURA *is left alone.*
> (*Legend: "Terror!"*)

She utters a low moan and turns off the lamp—sits stiffly on the edge of the sofa, knotting her fingers together.

(*Legend on screen: "The Opening of a Door!"*)

TOM *and* JIM *appear on the fire-escape steps and climb to landing. Hearing their approach,* LAURA *rises with a panicky gesture. She retreats to the portieres.*

The doorbell. LAURA *catches her breath and touches her throat. Low drums.*

AMANDA (*calling*): Laura, sweetheart! The door!

LAURA *stares at it without moving.*

JIM: I think we just beat the rain.

TOM: Uh-huh. (*He rings again, nervously.* JIM *whistles and fishes for a cigarette.*)

AMANDA (*very, very gaily*): Laura, that is your brother and Mr. O'Connor! Will you let them in, darling?

LAURA *crosses toward kitchenette door.*

LAURA (*breathlessly*): Mother—you go to the door!

AMANDA *steps out of kitchenette and stares furiously at* LAURA. *She points imperiously at the door.*

LAURA: Please, please!

AMANDA (*in a fierce whisper*): What is the matter with you, you silly thing?

LAURA (*desperately*): Please, you answer it, *please!*

AMANDA: I told you I wasn't going to humor you, Laura. Why have you chosen this moment to lose your mind?

LAURA: Please, please, please, you go!

AMANDA: You'll have to go to the door because I can't!

LAURA (*despairingly*): I can't either!

AMANDA: *Why?*

LAURA: I'm *sick!*

AMANDA: I'm sick, too—of your nonsense! Why can't you and your brother be normal people? Fantastic whims and behavior! (TOM *gives a long ring.*) Preposterous goings on! Can you give me one reason—(*calls out lyrically*) COMING! JUST ONE SECOND!—why you should be afraid to open a door? Now you answer it, Laura!

LAURA: Oh, oh, oh . . . (*She returns through the portieres. Darts to the victrola and winds it frantically and turns it on.*)

AMANDA: Laura Wingfield, you march right to that door!

LAURA: Yes—yes, Mother!

A faraway, scratchy rendition of "Dardanella" softens the air and gives her strength to move through it. She slips to the door and draws it cautiously open.

TOM *enters with the caller,* JIM O'CONNOR.

TOM: Laura, this is Jim. Jim, this is my sister, Laura.

JIM (*stepping inside*): I didn't know that Shakespeare had a sister!

LAURA (*retreating stiff and trembling from the door*): How—how do you do?

JIM (*heartily extending his hand*): Okay!

LAURA *touches it hesitantly with hers.*

JIM: Your hand's *cold*, Laura!

LAURA: Yes, well—I've been playing the victrola. . . .

JIM: Must have been playing classical music on it! You ought to play a little hot swing music to warm you up!

LAURA: Excuse me—I haven't finished playing the victrola. . . . (*She turns awkwardly and hurries into the front room. She pauses a second by the victrola. Then catches her breath and darts through the portieres like a frightened deer.*)

JIM (*grinning*): What was the matter?

TOM: Oh—with Laura? Laura is—terribly shy.

JIM: Shy, huh? It's unusual to meet a shy girl nowadays. I don't believe you ever mentioned you had a sister.

TOM: Well, now you know. I have one. Here is the *Post Dispatch*. You want a piece of it?

JIM: Uh-huh.

TOM: What piece? The comics?

JIM: Sports! (*glances at it*) Ole Dizzy Dean is on his bad behavior.

TOM (*disinterest*): Yeah? (*lights cigarette and crosses back to fire-escape door*)

JIM: Where are *you* going?

TOM: I'm going out on the terrace.

JIM (*goes after him*): You know, Shakespeare—I'm going to sell you a bill of goods!

TOM: What goods?

JIM: A course I'm taking.

TOM: Huh?

JIM: In public speaking! You and me, we're not the warehouse type.

TOM: Thanks—that's good news. But what has public speaking got to do with it?

JIM: It fits you for—executive positions!

TOM: Awww.

JIM: I tell you it's done a helluva lot for me.

(*Image: Executive at desk.*)

TOM: In what respect?

JIM: In every! Ask yourself what is the difference between you an' me and men in the office down front? Brains?—No!—Ability?—No! Then what? Just one little thing—

TOM: What is that one little thing?

JIM: Primarily it amounts to—social poise! Being able to square up to people and hold your own on any social level!

AMANDA (*off stage*): Tom?

TOM: Yes, Mother?

AMANDA: Is that you and Mr. O'Connor?

TOM: Yes, Mother.

AMANDA: Well, you just make yourselves comfortable in there.

TOM: Yes, Mother.

AMANDA: Ask Mr. O'Connor if he would like to wash his hands.

JIM: Aw, no—no—thank you—I took care of that at the warehouse. Tom—

TOM: Yes?

JIM: Mr. Mendoza was speaking to me about you.

TOM: Favorably?

JIM: What do you think?

TOM: Well—

JIM: You're going to be out of a job if you don't wake up.

TOM: I am waking up—

JIM: You show no signs.

TOM: The signs are interior.

(*Image on screen: The sailing vessel with Jolly Roger again.*)

TOM: I'm planning to change. (*He leans over the rail speaking with quiet exhilaration. The incandescent marquees and signs of the first-run movie houses light his face from across the alley. He looks like a voyager.*) I'm right at the point of committing myself to a future that doesn't include the warehouse and Mr. Mendoza or even a night-school course in public speaking.

JIM: What are you gassing about?

TOM: I'm tired of the movies.

JIM: Movies!

TOM: Yes, movies! Look at them—(*a wave toward the marvels of Grand Avenue*) All of those glamorous people—having adventures—hogging it all, gobbling the whole thing up! You know what happens? People go to the *movies* instead of *moving!* Hollywood characters are supposed to have all the adventures for everybody in America, while everybody in America sits in a dark room and watches them have them! Yes, until there's a war. That's when adventure becomes available to the masses! *Everyone's* dish, not only Gable's! Then the people in the dark room come out of the dark room to have some adventures themselves—Goody, goody!—It's our turn now, to go to the South Sea Island—to make a safari—to be exotic, far-off!—But I'm not patient. I don't want to wait till then. I'm tired of the *movies* and I am *about* to *move!*

JIM (*incredulously*): Move?

TOM: Yes.

JIM: When?

TOM: Soon!

JIM: Where? Where?

(*Theme three music seems to answer the question, while* TOM *thinks it over. He searches among his pockets.*)

TOM: I'm starting to boil inside. I know I seem dreamy, but inside—well, I'm boiling!—Whenever I pick up a shoe, I shudder a little thinking how short life is and what I am doing!—Whatever that means, I know it doesn't mean shoes—except as something to wear on a traveler's feet! (*finds paper*) Look—

JIM: What?

TOM: I'm a member.

JIM (*reading*): The Union of Merchant Seamen.

TOM: I paid my dues this month, instead of the light bill.

JIM: You will regret it when they turn the lights off.

TOM: I won't be here.

JIM: How about your mother?

TOM: I'm like my father. The bastard son of a bastard! See how he grins? And he's been absent going on sixteen years!

JIM: You're just talking, you drip. How does your mother feel about it?

TOM: Shhh!—Here comes Mother! Mother is not acquainted with my plans!

AMANDA (*enters portieres*): Where are you all?

TOM: On the terrace, Mother.

They start inside. She advances to them. TOM *is distinctly shocked at her appearance. Even* JIM *blinks a little. He is making his first contact with girlish Southern vivacity and in spite of the night-school course in public speaking is somewhat thrown off the beam by the unexpected outlay of social charm.*

Certain responses are attempted by JIM *but are swept aside by* AMANDA'S *gay laughter and chatter.* TOM *is embarrassed but after the first shock* JIM *reacts very warmly. Grins and chuckles, is altogether won over.*

(*Image:* AMANDA *as a girl.*)

AMANDA (*coyly smiling, shaking her girlish ringlets*): Well, well, well, so this is Mr. O'Connor. Introductions entirely unnecessary. I've heard so much about you from my boy. I finally said to him, Tom—good gracious!—why don't you bring this paragon to supper? I'd like to meet this nice young man at the warehouse!—Instead of just hearing him sing your praises so much! I don't know why my son is so stand-offish—that's not Southern behavior! Let's sit down and—I think we could stand a little more air in here! Tom, leave the door open. I felt a nice fresh breeze a moment ago. Where has it gone to? Mmm, so warm already! And not quite summer, even. We're going to burn up when summer really gets started. However, we're having—we're having a very light supper. I think light things are better fo' this time of year. The same as light clothes are. Light clothes an' light food are what warm weather calls fo'. You know our blood gets so thick during th' winter—it takes a while fo' us to *adjust* ou'selves!—when the season changes . . . It's come so quick this year. I wasn't prepared. All of a sudden—heavens! Already summer!—I ran to the trunk an' pulled out this light dress— Terribly old! Historical almost! But feels so good—so good an' co-ol, y' know. . . .

TOM: Mother—

AMANDA: Yes, honey?

TOM: How about—supper?

AMANDA: Honey, you go ask Sister if supper is ready! You know that Sister is in full charge of supper! Tell her you hungry boys are waiting for it. (*to* JIM) Have you met Laura?

JIM: She—

AMANDA: Let you in? Oh, good, you've met already! It's rare for a girl as sweet an' pretty as Laura to be domestic! But Laura is, thank heavens, not only pretty but also very domestic. I'm not at all. I never was a bit. I never could make a thing but angel-food cake. Well, in the South we had so many servants. Gone, gone, gone. All vestige of gracious living! Gone completely! I wasn't prepared for what the future brought me. All of my gentlemen callers were sons of planters and so of course I assumed that I would be married to one and raise my family on a large piece of land with plenty of servants. But man proposes—and woman accepts the proposal!—To vary that old, old saying a little bit—I married no planter! I married a man who worked for the telephone company!—That gallantly smiling gentleman over there! (*points to the picture*) A telephone man who—fell in love with long-distance!—Now he travels and I don't even know where!—But what am I going on for about my—tribulations? Tell me yours—I hope you don't have any! Tom?

TOM (*returning*): Yes, Mother?

AMANDA: Is supper nearly ready?

TOM: It looks to me like supper is on the table.

AMANDA: Let me look—(*She rises prettily and looks through portieres.*) Oh, lovely!—But where is Sister?

TOM: Laura is not feeling well and she says that she thinks she'd better not come to the table.

AMANDA: What?—Nonsense—Laura? Oh, Laura!

LAURA (*off stage, faintly*): Yes, Mother.

AMANDA: You really must come to the table. We won't be seated until you come to the table! Come in, Mr. O'Connor. You sit over there, and I'll—Laura? Laura Wingfield! You're keeping us waiting, honey! We can't say grace until you come to the table!

The back door is pushed weakly open and LAURA *comes in. She is obviously quite faint, her lips trembling, her eyes wide and staring. She moves unsteadily toward the table.*
(*Legend: "Terror!"*)
Outside a summer storm is coming abruptly. The white curtains billow inward at the windows and there is a sorrowful murmur and deep blue dusk.
LAURA *suddenly stumbles—she catches at a chair with a faint moan.*

TOM: Laura!

AMANDA: Laura! (*There is a clap of thunder.*) (*Legend: "Ah!"*) (*despairingly*) Why, Laura, you *are* sick, darling! Tom, help your sister into the living room, dear! Sit in the living room, Laura—rest on the sofa. Well! (*to the gentleman caller*) Standing over the hot stove made her ill!—I told her that it was just too warm this evening, but— (TOM *comes back in.* LAURA *is on the sofa.*) Is Laura all right now?

TOM: Yes.

AMANDA: What *is* that? Rain? A nice cool rain has come up! (*She gives the gentleman caller a frightened look.*) I think we may—have grace—now . . . (TOM *looks at her stupidly.*) Tom, honey—you say grace!

TOM: Oh . . . "For these and all thy mercies—" (*They bow their heads,* AMANDA *stealing a nervous glance at* JIM. *In the living room* LAURA, *stretched on the sofa, clenches her hand to her lips, to hold back a shuddering sob.*) God's Holy Name be praised—

(*The scene dims out.*)

SCENE 7

A Souvenir.

Half an hour later. Dinner is just being finished in the upstage area which is concealed by the drawn portieres.
As the curtain rises LAURA *is still huddled upon the sofa, her feet drawn under her, her head resting on a pale blue pillow, her eyes wide and mysteriously watchful. The new floor lamp with its shade of rose-colored silk gives a soft, becoming light to her face, bringing out the fragile, unearthly prettiness which usually escapes attention. There is a steady murmur of rain, but it is slackening and stops soon after the scene begins; the air outside becomes pale and luminous as the moon breaks out.*
A moment after the curtain rises, the lights in both rooms flicker and go out.

JIM: Hey, there, Mr. Light Bulb!

AMANDA *laughs nervously.*
(*Legend: "Suspension of a Public Service."*)

AMANDA: Where was Moses when the lights went out? Ha-ha. Do you know the answer to that one, Mr. O'Connor?

JIM: No, Ma'am, what's the answer?

AMANDA: In the dark! (JIM *laughs appreciatively.*) Everybody sit still. I'll light the candles. Isn't it lucky we have them on the table? Where's a match? Which of you gentlemen can provide a match?

JIM: Here.

AMANDA: Thank you, sir.

JIM: Not at all, Ma'am!

AMANDA: I guess the fuse has burnt out. Mr. O'Connor, can you tell a burnt-out fuse? I know I can't and Tom is a total loss when it comes to mechanics. (*Sound: Getting up: Voices recede a little to kitchenette.*) Oh, be careful you don't bump into something. We don't want our gentleman caller to break his neck. Now wouldn't that be a fine howdy-do?

JIM: Ha-ha! Where is the fuse-box?

AMANDA: Right here next to the stove. Can you see anything?

JIM: Just a minute.

AMANDA: Isn't electricity a mysterious thing? Wasn't it Benjamin Franklin who tied a key to a kite? We live in such a mysterious universe, don't we? Some people say that science clears up all the mysteries for us. In my opinion it only creates more! Have you found it yet?

JIM: No, Ma'am. All these fuses look okay to me.

AMANDA: Tom!

TOM: Yes, Mother?

AMANDA: That light bill I gave you several days ago. The one I told you we got the notices about?

(*Legend: "Ha!"*)

TOM: Oh.—Yeah.

AMANDA: You didn't neglect to pay it by any chance?

TOM: Why, I—

AMANDA: Didn't! I might have known it!

JIM: Shakespeare probably wrote a poem on that light bill, Mrs. Wingfield.

AMANDA: I might have known better than to trust him with it! There's such a high price for negligence in this world!

JIM: Maybe the poem will win a ten-dollar prize.

AMANDA: We'll just have to spend the remainder of the evening in the nineteenth century, before Mr. Edison made the Mazda lamp!

JIM: Candlelight is my favorite kind of light.

AMANDA: That shows you're romantic! But that's no excuse for Tom. Well, we got through dinner. Very considerate of them to let us get through dinner before they plunged us into everlasting darkness, wasn't it, Mr. O'Connor?

JIM: Ha-ha!

AMANDA: Tom, as a penalty for your carelessness you can help me with the dishes.

JIM: Let me give you a hand.

AMANDA: Indeed you will not!

JIM: I ought to be good for something.

AMANDA: Good for something? (*Her tone is rhapsodic.*) *You?* Why, Mr. O'Connor, nobody, *nobody's* given me this much entertainment in years—as you have!

JIM: Aw, now, Mrs. Wingfield!

AMANDA: I'm not exaggerating, not one bit! But Sister is all by her lonesome. You go keep her company in the parlor! I'll give you this lovely old candelabrum that used to be on the altar at the church of the Heavenly Rest. It was melted a little out of shape when the church burnt down. Lightning struck it one spring. Gypsy Jones was holding a revival at the time and he intimated that the church was destroyed because the Episcopalians gave card parties.

JIM: Ha-ha.

AMANDA: And how about you coaxing Sister to drink a little wine? I think it would be good for her! Can you carry both at once?

JIM: Sure. I'm Superman!

AMANDA: Now, Thomas, get into this apron!

> *The door of kitchenette swings closed on* AMANDA'S *gay laughter; the flickering light approaches the portieres.*
>
> LAURA *sits up nervously as he enters. Her speech at first is low and breathless from the almost intolerable strain of being alone with a stranger.*
>
> (*The legend: "I Don't Suppose You Remember Me at All!"*)
>
> *In her first speeches in this scene, before* JIM'S *warmth overcomes her paralyzing shyness,* LAURA'S *voice is thin and breathless as though she has just run up a steep flight of stairs.*
>
> JIM'S *attitude is gently humorous. In playing this scene it should be stressed that while the incident is apparently unimportant, it is to* LAURA *the climax of her secret life.*

JIM: Hello, there, Laura.

LAURA (*faintly*): Hello. (*She clears her throat.*)

JIM: How are you feeling now? Better?

LAURA: Yes. Yes, thank you.

JIM: This is for you. A little dandelion wine. (*He extends it toward her with extravagant gallantry.*)

LAURA: Thank you.

JIM: Drink it—but don't get drunk! (*He laughs heartily.* LAURA *takes the glass uncertainly; laughs shyly.*) Where shall I set the candles?

LAURA: Oh—oh, anywhere . . .

JIM: How about here on the floor? Any objections?

LAURA: No.

JIM: I'll spread a newspaper under to catch the drippings. I like to sit on the floor. Mind if I do?

LAURA: Oh, no.

JIM: Give me a pillow?

LAURA: What?

JIM: A pillow!

LAURA: Oh . . . (*hands him one quickly*)

JIM: How about you? Don't you like to sit on the floor?

LAURA: Oh—yes.

JIM: Why don't you, then?

LAURA: I—will.

JIM: Take a pillow! (LAURA *does. Sits on the other side of the candelabrum.* JIM *crosses his legs and smiles engagingly at her.*) I can't hardly see you sitting way over there.

LAURA: I can—see you.

JIM: I know, but that's not fair, I'm in the limelight. (LAURA *moves her pillow closer.*) Good! Now I can see you! Comfortable?

LAURA: Yes.

JIM: So am I. Comfortable as a cow! Will you have some gum?

LAURA: No, thank you.

JIM: I think that I will indulge, with your permission. (*musingly unwraps it and holds it up*) Think of the fortune made by the guy that invented the first piece of chewing gum. Amazing, huh? The Wrigley Building is one of the sights of Chicago.—I saw it summer before last when I went up to the Century of Progress. Did you take in the Century of Progress?

LAURA: No, I didn't.

JIM: Well, it was quite a wonderful exposition. What impressed me most was the Hall of Science. Gives you an idea of what the future will be in America, even more wonderful than the present time is! (*Pause. Smiling at her.*) Your brother tells me you're shy. Is that right, Laura?

LAURA: I—don't know.

JIM: I judge you to be an old-fashioned type of girl. Well, I think that's a pretty good type to be. Hope you don't think I'm being too personal—do you?

LAURA (*hastily, out of embarrassment*): I believe I *will* take a piece of gum, if you— don't mind. (*clearing her throat*) Mr. O'Connor, have you—kept up with your singing?

JIM: Singing? Me?

LAURA: Yes. I remember what a beautiful voice you had.

JIM: When did you hear me sing?

(*Voice off stage in the pause.*)

VOICE (*off stage*): O blow, ye winds, heigh-ho,
　　　　　　　A-roving I will go!
　　　　　　　I'm off to my love
　　　　　　　With a boxing glove—
　　　　　　　Ten thousand miles away!

JIM: You say you've heard me sing?

LAURA: Oh, yes! Yes, very often . . . I—don't suppose—you remember me—at all?

JIM (*smiling doubtfully*): You know I have an idea I've seen you before. I had that idea soon as you opened the door. It seemed almost like I was about to remember your name. But the name that I started to call you—wasn't a name! And so I stopped myself before I said it.

LAURA: Wasn't it—Blue Roses?

JIM (*springs up, grinning*): Blue Roses!—My gosh, yes—Blue Roses! That's what I had on my tongue when you opened the door! Isn't it funny what tricks your memory plays? I didn't connect you with high school somehow or other. But that's where it was; it was high school. I didn't even know you were Shakespeare's sister! Gosh, I'm sorry.

LAURA: I didn't expect you to. You—barely knew me!

JIM: But we did have a speaking acquaintance, huh?

LAURA: Yes, we—spoke to each other.

JIM: When did you recognize me?

LAURA: Oh, right away!

JIM: Soon as I came in the door?

LAURA: When I heard your name I thought it was probably you. I knew that Tom used to know you a little in high school. So when you came in the door—Well, then I was—sure.

JIM: Why didn't you *say* something, then?

LAURA (*breathlessly*): I didn't know what to say, I was—too surprised!

JIM: For goodness' sakes! You know, this sure is funny!

LAURA: Yes! Yes, isn't it, though . . .

JIM: Didn't we have a class in something together?

LAURA: Yes, we did.

JIM: What class was that?

LAURA: It was—singing—Chorus!

JIM: Aw!

LAURA: I sat across the aisle from you in the Aud.

JIM: Aw.

LAURA: Mondays, Wednesdays and Fridays.

JIM: Now I remember—you always came in late.

LAURA: Yes, it was so hard for me, getting upstairs. I had that brace on my leg—it clumped so loud!

JIM: I never heard any clumping.

LAURA (*wincing at the recollection*): To me it sounded like—thunder!

JIM: Well, well, well, I never even noticed.

LAURA: And everybody was seated before I came in. I had to walk in front of all those people. My seat was in the back row. I had to go clumping all the way up the aisle with everyone watching!

JIM: You shouldn't have been self-conscious.

LAURA: I know, but I was. It was always such a relief when the singing started.

JIM: Aw, yes, I've placed you now! I used to call you Blue Roses. How was it that I got started calling you that?

LAURA: I was out of school a little while with pleurosis. When I came back you asked me what was the matter. I said I had pleurosis—you thought I said Blue Roses. That's what you always called me after that!

JIM: I hope you didn't mind.

LAURA: Oh, no—I liked it. You see, I wasn't acquainted with many—people. . . .

JIM: As I remember you sort of stuck by yourself.

LAURA: I—I—never have had much luck at—making friends.

JIM: I don't see why you wouldn't.

LAURA: Well, I—started out badly.

JIM: You mean being—

LAURA: Yes, it sort of—stood between me—

JIM: You shouldn't have let it!

LAURA: I know, but it did, and—

JIM: You were shy with people!

LAURA: I tried not to be but never could—

JIM: Overcome it?

LAURA: No, I—I never could!

JIM: I guess being shy is something you have to work out of kind of gradually.

LAURA (*sorrowfully*): Yes—I guess it—

JIM: Takes time!

LAURA: Yes—

JIM: People are not so dreadful when you know them. That's what you have to remember! And everybody has problems, not just you, but practically everybody has got some problems. You think of yourself as having the only problems, as being the only one who is disappointed. But just look around you and you will see lots of people as disappointed as you are. For instance, I hoped when I was going to high school that I would be further along at this time, six years later, than I am now—You remember that wonderful write-up I had in *The Torch*?

LAURA: Yes! (*She rises and crosses to table.*)

JIM: It said I was bound to succeed in anything I went into! (LAURA *returns with the annual.*) Holy Jeez! *The Torch!* (*He accepts it reverently. They smile across it with mutual wonder.* LAURA *crouches beside him and they begin to turn through it.* LAURA'S *shyness is dissolving in his warmth.*)

LAURA: Here you are in *The Pirates of Penzance!*

JIM (*wistfully*): I sang the baritone lead in that operetta.

LAURA (*raptly*): So—*beautifully!*

JIM (*protesting*): Aw—

LAURA: Yes, yes—beautifully—beautifully!

JIM: You heard me?

LAURA: All three times!

JIM: No!

LAURA: Yes!

JIM: All three performances?

LAURA (*looking down*): Yes.

JIM: Why?

LAURA: I—wanted to ask you to—autograph my program.

JIM: Why didn't you ask me to?

LAURA: You were always surrounded by your own friends so much that I never had a chance to.

JIM: You should have just—

LAURA: Well, I—thought you might think I was—

JIM: Thought I might think you was—what?

LAURA: Oh—

JIM (*with reflective relish*): I was beleaguered by females in those days.

LAURA: You were terribly popular!

JIM: Yeah—

LAURA: You had such a—friendly way—

JIM: I was spoiled in high school.

LAURA: Everybody—liked you!

JIM: Including you?

LAURA: I—yes, I—I did, too—(*She gently closes the book in her lap.*)

JIM: Well, well, well!—Give me that program, Laura. (*She hands it to him. He signs it with a flourish.*) There you are—better late than never!

LAURA: Oh, I—what a—surprise!

JIM: My signature isn't worth very much right now. But some day—maybe—it will increase in value! Being disappointed is one thing and being discouraged is something else. I am disappointed but I am not discouraged. I'm twenty-three years old. How old are you?

LAURA: I'll be twenty-four in June.

JIM: That's not old age!

LAURA: No, but—

JIM: You finished high school?

LAURA (*with difficulty*): I didn't go back.

JIM: You mean you dropped out?

LAURA: I made bad grades in my final examinations. (*She rises and replaces the book and the program. Her voice strained.*) How is—Emily Meisenbach getting along?

JIM: Oh, that kraut-head!

LAURA: Why do you call her that?

JIM: That's what she was.

LAURA: You're not still—going with her?

JIM: I never see her.

LAURA: It said in the Personal Section that you were—engaged!

JIM: I know, but I wasn't impressed by that—propaganda!

LAURA: It wasn't—the truth?

JIM: Only in Emily's optimistic opinion!

LAURA: Oh—

(*Legend: "What Have You Done Since High School?"*)
JIM *lights a cigarette and leans indolently back on his elbows smiling at* LAURA *with a warmth and charm which lights her inwardly with altar candles. She remains by the table and turns in her hands a piece of glass to cover her tumult.*

JIM (*after several reflective puffs on a cigarette*): What have you done since high school? (*She seems not to hear him.*) Huh? (LAURA *looks up.*) I said what have you done since high school, Laura?

LAURA: Nothing much.

JIM: You must have been doing something these six long years.

LAURA: Yes.

JIM: Well, then, such as what?

LAURA: I took a business course at business college—

JIM: How did that work out?

LAURA: Well, not very—well—I had to drop out, it gave me—indigestion—

JIM *laughs gently.*

JIM: What are you doing now?

LAURA: I don't do anything—much. Oh, please don't think I sit around doing nothing! My glass collection takes up a good deal of time. Glass is something you have to take good care of.

JIM: What did you say—about glass?

LAURA: Collection I said—I have one— (*She clears her throat and turns away again, acutely shy.*)

JIM (*abruptly*): You know what I judge to be the trouble with you? Inferiority complex! Know what that is? That's what they call it when someone low-rates himself! I understand it because I had it, too. Although my case was not so aggravated as yours seems to be. I had it until I took up public speaking, developed my voice, and learned that I had an aptitude for science. Before that time I never thought of myself as being outstanding in any way whatsoever! Now I've never made a regular study of it, but I have a friend who says I can analyze people better than doctors that make a profession of it. I don't claim that to be necessarily true, but I can sure guess a person's psychology, Laura! (*takes out his gum*) Excuse me, Laura. I always take it out when the flavor is gone. I'll use this scrap of paper to wrap it in. I know how it is to get it stuck on a shoe. Yep—that's what I judge to be your principal trouble. A lack of confidence in yourself as a person. You don't have the proper amount of faith in yourself. I'm basing that fact on a number of your remarks and also on certain observations I've made. For instance that clumping you thought was so awful in high school. You say that you even dreaded to walk into class. You see what you did? You dropped out of school, you gave up an education because of a clump, which as far as I know was practically non-existent! A little physical defect is what you have. Hardly noticeable even! Magnified thousands of times by imagination! You know what my strong advice to you is? Think of yourself as *superior* in some way!

LAURA: In what way would I think?

JIM: Why, man alive, Laura! Just look about you a little. What do you see? A world full of common people! All of 'em born and all of 'em going to die! Which of them has one-tenth of your good points! Or mine! Or anyone else's, as far as that goes—Gosh! Everybody excels in some one thing. Some in many! (*unconsciously glances at himself in the mirror*) All you've got to do is discover in *what*! Take me, for instance. (*He adjusts his tie at the mirror.*) My interest happens to lie in electrodynamics. I'm taking a course in radio engineering at night school, Laura, on top of a fairly responsible job at the warehouse. I'm taking that course and studying public speaking.

LAURA: Ohhhh.

JIM: Because I believe in the future of television! (*turning back to her*) I wish to be ready to go up right along with it. Therefore I'm planning to get in on the ground floor. In fact I've already made the right connections and all that remains is for the industry itself to get under way! Full steam—(*His eyes are starry.*) *Knowledge*—Zzzzzp! *Money*—Zzzzzzp!—*Power*! That's the cycle democracy is built on! (*His attitude is convincingly dynamic.* LAURA *stares at him, even her shyness eclipsed in her absolute wonder. He suddenly grins.*) I guess you think I think a lot of myself!

LAURA: No—o-o-o, I—

JIM: Now how about you? Isn't there something you take more interest in than anything else?

LAURA: Well, I do—as I said—have my—glass collection—

A peal of girlish laughter from the kitchen.

JIM: I'm not right sure I know what you're talking about. What kind of glass is it?

LAURA: Little articles of it, they're ornaments mostly! Most of them are little animals made out of glass, the tiniest little animals in the world. Mother calls them a glass menagerie! Here's an example of one, if you'd like to see it! This one is one of the oldest. It's nearly thirteen. (*Music: "The Glass Menagerie."*) (*He stretches out his hand.*) Oh, be careful—if you breathe, it breaks!

JIM: I'd better not take it. I'm pretty clumsy with things.

LAURA: Go on, I trust you with him! (*places it in his palm*) There now—you're holding him gently! Hold him over the light, he loves the light! You see how the light shines through him?

JIM: It sure does shine!

LAURA: I shouldn't be partial, but he is my favorite one.

JIM: What kind of a thing is this one supposed to be?

LAURA: Haven't you noticed the single horn on his forehead?

JIM: A unicorn, huh?

LAURA: Mmm-hmmm!

JIM: Unicorns, aren't they extinct in the modern world?

LAURA: I know!

JIM: Poor little fellow, he must feel sort of lonesome.

LAURA (*smiling*): Well, if he does he doesn't complain about it. He stays on a shelf with some horses that don't have horns and all of them seem to get along nicely together.

JIM: How do you know?

LAURA (*lightly*): I haven't heard any arguments among them!

JIM (*grinning*): No arguments, huh? Well, that's a pretty good sign! Where shall I set him?

LAURA: Put him on the table. They all like a change of scenery once in a while!

JIM (*stretching*): Well, well, well, well—Look how big my shadow is when I stretch!

LAURA: Oh, oh, yes—it stretches across the ceiling!

JIM (*crossing to door*): I think it's stopped raining. (*opens fire-escape door*) Where does the music come from?

LAURA: From the Paradise Dance Hall across the alley.

JIM: How about cutting the rug a little, Miss Wingfield?

LAURA: Oh, I—

JIM: Or is your program filled up? Let me have a look at it. (*grasps imaginary card*) Why, every dance is taken! I'll just have to scratch some out. (*Waltz music: "La Colondrina."*) Ahhh, a waltz! (*He executes some sweeping turns by himself then holds his arms toward* LAURA.)

LAURA (*breathlessly*): I—can't dance!

JIM: There you go, that inferiority stuff!

LAURA: I've never danced in my life!

JIM: Come on, try!

LAURA: Oh, but I'd step on you!

JIM: I'm not made out of glass.

LAURA: How—how—how do we start?

JIM: Just leave it to me. You hold your arms out a little.

LAURA: Like this?

JIM: A little bit higher. Right. Now don't tighten up, that's the main thing about it—relax.

LAURA (*laughing breathlessly*): It's hard not to.

JIM: Okay.

LAURA: I'm afraid you can't budge me.

JIM: What do you bet I can't? (*He swings her into motion.*)

LAURA: Goodness, yes, you can!

JIM: Let yourself go, now, Laura, just let yourself go.

LAURA: I'm—

JIM: Come on!

LAURA: Trying!

JIM: Not so stiff—Easy does it!

LAURA: I know but I'm—

JIM: Loosen th' backbone! There now, that's a lot better.

LAURA: Am I?

JIM: Lots, lots better! (*He moves her about the room in a clumsy waltz.*)

LAURA: Oh, my!

JIM: Ha-ha!

LAURA: Oh, my goodness!

JIM: Ha-ha-ha! (*They suddenly bump into the table.* JIM *stops.*) What did we hit on?

LAURA: Table.

JIM: Did something fall off it? I think—

LAURA: Yes.

JIM: I hope that it wasn't the little glass horse with the horn!

LAURA: Yes.

JIM: Aw, aw, aw. Is it broken?

LAURA: Now it is just like all the other horses.

JIM: It's lost its—

LAURA: Horn! It doesn't matter. Maybe it's a blessing in disguise.

JIM: You'll never forgive me. I bet that that was your favorite piece of glass.

LAURA: I don't have favorites much. It's no tragedy, Freckles. Glass breaks so easily. No matter how careful you are. The traffic jars the shelves and things fall off them.

JIM: Still I'm awfully sorry that I was the cause.

LAURA (*smiling*): I'll just imagine he had an operation. The horn was removed to make him feel less—freakish! (*They both laugh.*) Now he will feel more at home with the other horses, the ones that don't have horns. . . .

JIM: Ha-ha, that's very funny! (*suddenly serious*) I'm glad to see that you have a sense of humor. You know—you're—well—very different! Surprisingly different from anyone else I know! (*His voice becomes soft and hesitant with a genuine feeling.*) Do you mind me telling you that? (LAURA *is abashed beyond speech.*) I mean it in a nice way . . . (LAURA *nods shyly, looking away.*) You make me feel sort of—I don't know how to put it! I'm usually pretty good at expressing things, but—This is something that I don't know how to say! (LAURA *touches her throat and clears it— turns the broken unicorn in her hands.*) (*even softer*) Has anyone ever told you that you were pretty? (*Pause: Music.*) (LAURA *looks up slowly, with wonder, and shakes her head.*) Well, you are! In a very different way from anyone else. And all the nicer because of the difference, too. (*His voice becomes low and husky.* LAURA *turns away, nearly faint with the novelty of her emotions.*) I wish that you were my sister. I'd teach you to have some confidence in yourself. The different people are not like other people, but being different is nothing to be ashamed of. Because other people are not such wonderful people. They're one hundred times one thousand. You're one times one! They walk all over the earth. You just stay here. They're common as—weeds, but—you—well, you're—*Blue Roses!*

(*Image on screen: Blue roses.*)
   (*Music changes.*)

LAURA: But blue is wrong for—roses . . .

JIM: It's right for you!—You're—pretty!

LAURA: In what respect am I pretty?

JIM: In all respects—believe me! Your eyes—your hair—are pretty! Your hands are pretty! (*He catches hold of her hand.*) You think I'm making this up because I'm invited to dinner and have to be nice. Oh, I could do that! I could put on an act for you, Laura, and say lots of things without being very sincere. But this time I am. I'm talking to you sincerely. I happened to notice you had this inferiority complex that keeps you from feeling comfortable with people. Somebody needs to build your confidence up and make you proud instead of shy and turning away and— blushing—Somebody—ought to—Ought to—*kiss you, Laura!* (*His hand slips slowly up her arm to her shoulder.*) (*Music swells tumultuously.*) (*He suddenly turns her about and kisses her on the lips. When he releases her,* LAURA *sinks on the sofa with a bright, dazed look.* JIM *backs away and fishes in his pocket for a cigarette.*) (*Legend on screen: "Souvenir."*) Stumble-john! (*He lights the cigarette, avoiding her look. There is a peal of girlish laughter from* AMANDA *in the kitchen.* LAURA *slowly raises and opens her hand. It still contains the little broken glass animal. She looks at it with a tender, bewildered expression.*) Stumble-john! I shouldn't have done that—That was way off the beam. You don't smoke, do you? (*She looks up, smiling, not hearing the question. He sits beside her a little gingerly. She looks at him speechlessly—waiting. He coughs decorously and moves a little farther aside as he considers the situation and senses her feelings, dimly, with perturbation.*) (*gently*) Would you—care for a—mint? (*She doesn't seem to hear him but her look grows brighter even.*) Peppermint—Life-Saver? My pocket's a regular drug store—wherever I go . . . (*He pops a mint in his mouth. Then gulps and decides to make a clean breast of it. He speaks slowly and gingerly.*) Laura, you know, if I had a sister like you, I'd do the same thing as Tom. I'd bring out fellows and—introduce her to them. The right type of boys of a type to—appreciate her. Only—well—he made a mistake about me. Maybe I've got no call to be saying this. That may not have been the idea in having me over. But what if it was? There's nothing wrong about that. The only trouble is that in my case—I'm not in a situation to—do the right thing. I can't take down your number and say I'll phone. I can't call up next week and—ask for a date. I thought I had better explain the situation in case you—misunderstood it and—hurt your feelings. . . . (*pause*) (*Slowly, very slowly,* LAURA'S *look changes, her eyes returning slowly from his to the ornament in her palm.*) (AMANDA *utters another gay laugh in the kitchen.*)

LAURA (*faintly*): You—won't—call again?

JIM: No, Laura, I can't. (*He rises from the sofa.*) As I was just explaining, I've—got strings on me. Laura, I've—been going steady! I go out all of the time with a girl named Betty. She's a home-girl like you, and Catholic, and Irish, and in a great many ways we—get along fine. I met her last summer on a moonlight boat trip up the river to Alton, on the *Majestic.* Well—right away from the start it was—love! (*Legend: Love!*) (LAURA *sways slightly forward and grips the arm of the sofa. He fails to notice, now enrapt in his own comfortable being.*) Being in love has made a new man of me! (*Leaning stiffly forward, clutching the arm of the sofa,* LAURA *struggles visibly with her storm. But* JIM *is oblivious, she is a long way off.*) The power of love is really pretty tremendous! Love is something that—changes the whole world, Laura! (*The storm abates a little and* LAURA *leans back. He notices her again.*) It happened that Betty's aunt took sick, she got a wire and had to go to Centralia. So Tom—when he asked me to dinner—I naturally just accepted the invitation, not knowing that you—that he—that I— (*He stops awkwardly.*) Huh—I'm a stumble-john! (*He flops back on the sofa.*) (*The holy candles in the altar of* LAURA'S *face have been snuffed out. There is a look of almost infinite desolation.*) (JIM *glances at her uneasily.*) I wish that you would—say something. (*She bites her lip which was trembling and then bravely smiles. She opens her hand again on the broken glass ornament. Then she gently takes his hand and raises it level with her own. She carefully places the unicorn in the palm of his hand, then pushes his fingers closed upon it.*) What are you—doing that for? You want me to have him?—Laura? (*She nods.*) What for?

LAURA: A—souvenir . . .

She rises unsteadily and crouches beside the victrola to wind it up.
   (*Legend on screen: "Things Have a Way of Turning Out So Badly!"*)
   (*Or image: "Gentleman Caller Waving Good-bye!—Gaily."*)

At this moment AMANDA *rushes brightly back in the front room. She bears a pitcher of fruit punch in an old-fashioned cut-glass pitcher and a plate of macaroons. The plate has a gold border and poppies painted on it.*

AMANDA: Well, well, well! Isn't the air delightful after the shower? I've made you children a little liquid refreshment. (*turns gaily to the gentleman caller*) Jim, do you know that song about lemonade?
"Lemonade, lemonade
Made in the shade and stirred with a spade—
Good enough for any old maid!"

JIM (*uneasily*): Ha-ha! No—I never heard it.

AMANDA: Why, Laura! You look so serious!

JIM: We were having a serious conversation.

AMANDA: Good! Now you're better acquainted!

JIM (*uncertainly*): Ha-ha! Yes.

AMANDA: You modern young people are much more serious-minded than my generation. I was so gay as a girl!

JIM: You haven't changed, Mrs. Wingfield.

AMANDA: Tonight I'm rejuvenated! The gaiety of the occasion, Mr. O'Connor! (*She tosses her head with a pearl of laughter. Spills lemonade.*) Oooo! I'm baptizing myself!

JIM: Here—let me—

AMANDA (*setting the pitcher down*): There now. I discovered we had some maraschino cherries. I dumped them in, juice and all!

JIM: You shouldn't have gone to that trouble, Mrs. Wingfield.

AMANDA: Trouble, trouble? Why, it was loads of fun! Didn't you hear me cutting up in the kitchen? I bet your ears were burning! I told Tom how outdone with him I was for keeping you to himself so long a time! He should have brought you over much, much sooner! Well, now that you've found your way, I want you to be a very frequent caller! Not just occasional but all the time. Oh, we're going to have a lot of gay times together! I see them coming! Mmm, just breathe that air! So fresh, and the moon's so pretty! I'll skip back out—I know where my place is when young folks are having a—serious conversation!

JIM: Oh, don't go out, Mrs. Wingfield. The fact of the matter is I've got to be going.

AMANDA: Going, now? You're joking! Why, it's only the shank of the evening, Mr. O'Connor!

JIM: Well, you know how it is.

AMANDA: You mean you're a young workingman and have to keep workingmen's hours. We'll let you off early tonight. But only on the condition that next time you stay later. What's the best night for you? Isn't Saturday night the best night for you workingmen?

JIM: I have a couple of time-clocks to punch, Mrs. Wingfield. One at morning, another one at night!

AMANDA: My, but you *are* ambitious! You work at night, too?

JIM: No, Ma'am, not work but—Betty! (*He crosses deliberately to pick up his hat. The band at the Paradise Dance Hall goes into a tender waltz.*)

AMANDA: Betty? Betty? Who's—Betty! (*There is an ominous cracking sound in the sky.*)

JIM: Oh, just a girl. The girl I go steady with! (*He smiles charmingly. The sky falls.*)

(*Legend: "The Sky Falls."*)

AMANDA (*a long-drawn exhalation*): Ohhhh . . . Is it a serious romance, Mr. O'Connor?

JIM: We're going to be married the second Sunday in June.

AMANDA: Ohhhh—how nice! Tom didn't mention that you were engaged to be married.

JIM: The cat's not out of the bag at the warehouse yet. You know how they are. They call you Romeo and stuff like that. (*He stops at the oval mirror to put on his hat. He carefully shapes the brim and the crown to give a discreetly dashing effect.*) It's been a wonderful evening, Mrs. Wingfield. I guess this is what they mean by Southern hospitality.

AMANDA: It really wasn't anything at all.

JIM: I hope it don't seem like I'm rushing off. But I promised Betty I'd pick her up at the Wabash depot, an' by the time I get my jalopy down there her train'll be in. Some women are pretty upset if you keep 'em waiting.

AMANDA: Yes, I know—The tyranny of women! (*extends her hand*) Good-bye, Mr. O'Connor. I wish you luck—and happiness—and success! All three of them, and so does Laura!—Don't you, Laura?

LAURA: Yes!

JIM (*taking her hand*): Good-bye, Laura. I'm certainly going to treasure that souvenir. And don't you forget the good advice I gave you. (*raises his voice to a cheery shout*) So long, Shakespeare! Thanks again, ladies—Good night!

He grins and ducks jauntily out.

　　Still bravely grimacing, AMANDA *closes the door on the gentleman caller. Then she turns back to the room with a puzzled expression. She and* LAURA *don't dare to face each other.* LAURA *crouches beside the victrola to wind it.*

AMANDA (*faintly*): Things have a way of turning out so badly. I don't believe that I would play the victrola. Well, well—well—Our gentleman caller was engaged to be married! Tom!

TOM (*from back*): Yes, Mother?

AMANDA: Come in here a minute. I want to tell you something awfully funny.

TOM (*enters with macaroon and a glass of the lemonade*): Has the gentleman caller gotten away already?

AMANDA: The gentleman caller has made an early departure. What a wonderful joke you played on us!

TOM: How do you mean?

AMANDA: You didn't mention that he was engaged to be married.

TOM: Jim? Engaged?

AMANDA: That's what he just informed us.

TOM: I'll be jiggered! I didn't know about that.

AMANDA: That seems very peculiar.

TOM: What's peculiar about it?

AMANDA: Didn't you call him your best friend down at the warehouse?

TOM: He is, but how did I know?

AMANDA: It seems extremely peculiar that you wouldn't know your best friend was going to be married!

TOM: The warehouse is where I work, not where I know things about people!

AMANDA: You don't know things anywhere! You live in a dream; you manufacture illusions! (*He crosses to door.*) Where are you going?

TOM: I'm going to the movies.

AMANDA: That's right, now that you've had us make such fools of ourselves. The effort, the preparations, all the expense! The new floor lamp, the rug, the clothes for Laura! All for what? To entertain some other girl's fiancé! Go to the movies, go! Don't think about us, a mother deserted, an unmarried sister who's crippled and has no job! Don't let anything interfere with your selfish pleasure! Just go, go, go —to the movies!

TOM: All right, I will! The more you shout about my selfishness to me the quicker I'll go, and I won't go to the movies!

AMANDA: Go, then! Then go to the moon—you selfish dreamer!

TOM *smashes his glass on the floor. He plunges out on the fire-escape, slamming the door.* LAURA *screams—cut by door.*

Dance-hall music up. TOM *goes to the rail and grips it desperately, lifting his face in the chill white moonlight penetrating the narrow abyss of the alley.*

(*Legend on screen: "And So Good-bye . . ."*)

TOM'S *closing speech is timed with the interior pantomime. The interior scene is played as though viewed through soundproof glass.* AMANDA *appears to be making a comforting speech to* LAURA *who is huddled upon the sofa. Now that we cannot hear the mother's speech, her silliness is gone and she has dignity and tragic beauty.* LAURA'S *dark hair hides her face until at the end of the speech she lifts it to smile at her mother.* AMANDA'S *gestures are slow and graceful, almost dancelike, as she comforts the daughter. At the end of her speech she glances a moment at the father's picture—then withdraws through the portieres. At close of* TOM'S *speech,* LAURA *blows out the candles, ending the play.*)

TOM: I didn't go to the moon, I went much further—for time is the longest distance between two places—Not long after that I was fired for writing a poem on the lid of a shoe-box. I left Saint Louis. I descended the steps of this fire-escape for a last time and followed, from then on, in my father's footsteps, attempting to find in motion what was lost in space—I traveled around a great deal. The cities swept about me like dead leaves, leaves that were brightly colored but torn away from the branches. I would have stopped, but I was pursued by something. It always came upon me unawares, taking me altogether by surprise. Perhaps it was a familiar bit of music. Perhaps it was only a piece of transparent glass—Perhaps I am walking along a street at night, in some strange city, before I have found companions. I pass the lighted window of a shop where perfume is sold. The window is filled with pieces of colored glass, tiny transparent bottles in delicate colors, like bits of a shattered rainbow. Then all at once my sister touches my shoulder. I turn around and look into her eyes . . . Oh, Laura, Laura, I tried to leave you behind me, but I am more faithful than I intended to be! I reach for a cigarette, I cross the street, I run into the movies or a bar, I buy a drink, I speak to the nearest stranger—anything that can blow your candles out! (LAURA *bends over the candles.*)—for nowadays the world is lit by lightning! Blow out your candles, Laura—and so good-bye. . . (*She blows the candles out.*)

(*The scene dissolves.*)

THE RECEPTIVE READER

1. In what ways do the first and the last scenes interconnect? For example, does the line "Hello—Good-bye" resurface in some way in the last scene?

2. The play of light and darkness becomes a recurrent symbolic pattern in the play. (The lights go out because Tom has not paid the electric bill; Amanda "brightens" and darkens; it is a world of "the blind"; Laura "blows the candles out.") Look for other passages that reflect not only literal darkness but the darkness of extinguished hopes.

3. Tennessee Williams crafted his plays carefully, with much connection between, and echoing of, images, phrases, symbols, and other elements. With a classmate or in a small group, trace one continuing strand that helps braid all or part of the play into a cohesive whole. Share your findings with the class.

4. Symbols are plentiful in this play. What about the typewriter? Could Laura have been taking harpsichord lessons instead of typing lessons? What is significant about the victrola? the glass animals Laura collects? the unicorn and the loss of its horn?

5. Is the playwright's portrayal of Amanda cruel?

6. If Laura's escape is her glass menagerie, what is Tom's escape? What is Amanda's? How successful are they?

7. What is the role of Laura's physical disability in the play? To what extent is it symbolic?

THE PERSONAL RESPONSE

Traditionally, critics have used the term *pathos* instead of tragedy when a central character in a play is an example of passive suffering. To you, is Laura a tragic character or merely pathetic?

BIOGRAPHIES OF POETS

MATTHEW ARNOLD (1822–1888)—English critic, educator, and poet—graduated from Oxford and became inspector of the British schools for most of his life. As a poet, Arnold was inspired by Greek tragedies, Keats, and Wordsworth. In 1857 he began to teach poetry at Oxford and to publish numerous books on literary criticism. In much of his writing, Arnold took the position of the agnostic unable to accept traditional faith, wishing to replace doctrines that had become doubtful with great literature as a source of inspiration and moral guidance. His prose writings helped define the nineteenth-century ideal of high culture, which he saw as a synthesis of Judeo-Christian ethics and the classical dedication to reason and form.

MARGARET ATWOOD (born 1939) has said, "My life really has been writing since the age of sixteen; all other decisions I made were determined by that fact." Born in Ottawa, Canada, Atwood resides in Toronto but has lived all over Canada as well as in the United States and England. She studied at the University of Toronto and Harvard, and has taught and lectured widely. In addition to two collections of short stories and seven volumes of poetry, Atwood has published six novels, including *The Edible Woman, Cat's Eye,* and a chilling portrayal of a nightmarish dystopian future, *The Handmaid's Tale,* which won a *Los Angeles Times* award for best fiction and was made into a movie.

W. H. AUDEN (1907–1973) knew science, history, politics, philosophy, psychology, art, music, and literature. As a result, his poetry "is full of knowledge and wisdom and ideas" (Kenneth Koch). Auden believed that "living is always thinking." Born in the ancient city of York, Wystan Hugh graduated from Oxford University and became an important voice for the radical criticism of established society by the Marxist left. After serving on the Loyalist side in the Spanish Civil War, he emigrated to America in 1939 and became a U.S. citizen. His first collection of poetry, *Poems,* appeared in 1930. In 1948 he won the Pulitzer Prize for his collection *The Age of Anxiety,* an expression he coined to describe the 1930s. Auden saw poetry "as a game of knowledge, a bringing to consciousness, by naming them, of emotions and their hidden relationships."

BASHO (1644–1694) was a famous Japanese writer of haiku in the seventeenth century. His simple, descriptive poems evoke emotions.

WENDELL BERRY (born 1934) is a poet, novelist, and essayist who was educated at the University of Kentucky, where he also has taught for many years. Although Berry deals primarily with Kentucky and its people, "one would be hard pressed to dismiss him as a mere regionalist. . . . his work is rooted in the land and in the values of an older America" (Jonathan Yardly). Among his many titles are *The Broken Ground* (1964), *Findings* (1969), *To What Listens* (1975), and *Clearing* (1977).

ELIZABETH BISHOP (1911–1979), who said, "There's nothing more embarrassing than being a poet," was born in Massachusetts. Only four years old when her father died, she was taken to live with her grandmother after her mother suffered a mental breakdown. After graduating from Vassar, Bishop planned to enter Cornell Medical School, but poet Marianne Moore persuaded her to become a writer. She served as a poetry consultant to the Library of Congress (1949–1950) and taught poetry writing at Harvard. She received numerous awards, including a Pulitzer Prize (1956). Bishop's poetry has been called "both precise and suggestive . . . fantastic yet fanciful" (Louis Untermeyer).

WILLIAM BLAKE (1757–1827), a forerunner of the English Romantic movement, "could transmit his basic consciousness and communicate it to somebody else after he was dead—in other words, build a time machine," said poet Allen Ginsberg. Born in London, Blake was apprenticed at the age of fourteen to an engraver; his engravings illustrated many popular books of his day as well as his own poems. He began to write his richly symbolic, mystical poetry in his youth, and with the financial assistance of his friends published his first collection of poems, *Poetical Sketches,* in 1783. However, efforts to find a publisher for his second manuscript, *Songs of Innocence,* were unsuccessful. The last twenty-five years of his life were marked by extreme poverty; it remained for later audiences to appreciate the complex symbolism of his mystical, enigmatic poetry.

LOUISE BOGAN (1897–1970), born in Livermore Falls, Maine, was educated at Boston University. She served as consultant in poetry to the Library of Congress, taught at a number of universities in the United States and Austria, and served over twenty years as a poetry critic for the *New Yorker.* Her books of poetry include *Body of This Death, Dark Summer, The Blue Estuaries,* and *Collected Poems, 1923–1953,* which won the Bollingen Prize in poetry.

ARNA BONTEMPS (1902–1973)—American poet, novelist, editor, and biographer—was born in Alexandria, Louisiana and raised in California. A 1923 graduate of Pacific Union College, Bontemps first published his poetry in *Crisis* magazine in 1924. He turned to the novel, publishing *God Sends Sunday* in 1931, *Black Thunder* in 1936, and *Drums at Dusk* in 1939. His *Story of the Negro* received the Jane Adams Children's Book Award in 1956. In *Any-*

place but Here he gathered brief biographies of outstanding black Americans. He published a much-read biography of Frederick Douglass in 1959 and an anthology of poetry written by African Americans in 1963.

KAY BOYLE (born 1903), a native of St. Paul, Minnesota, lived much of her life in France, Austria, Germany, and England. Being in Europe at the beginning of World War II led her to write three books that described the unfolding war: *Primer for Combat, Avalanche,* and *1939.* Her novel *Generation without Farewell* deals with conditions in postwar Germany. Prior to the war, Boyle published a collection of short stories in 1929 and a novel the following year. She became an English professor at San Francisco State University in 1963.

ANNE BRADSTREET (about 1612–1672) wrote the first volume of original poetry published in the British colonies of North America. She had sailed for America from her native England after marrying at the age of 16. Her father, Thomas Dudley, became a governor of the Massachusetts Bay Colony. The mother of eight children, Bradstreet wrote an autobiography entitled *Religious Experiences.*

BERTOLT BRECHT (1898–1956), a German communist poet and playwright, has enjoyed a tremendous international vogue since his death. One of his German editors has said of him that "in poetry and drama he wrote the history of our land since 1918." As a young man in a country embittered by its defeat in World War I, Brecht joined the radical left in its criticism of exploitation and imperialistic wars. When Hitler's anticommunist crusade drove him into exile, he wrote grimly prophetic poetic commentaries on his countrymen's march into catastrophe. For a time he joined other refugees from Hitler's Germany in the United States, returning to East Berlin after World War II to serve the East German communist regime as head of the famed Berliner Ensemble. Plays like *The Caucasian Chalk Circle, Galileo,* and *Mother Courage* have become classics of the modern theater.

GWENDOLYN BROOKS (born 1917) was the first African American woman to achieve widespread critical acclaim as a poet. Brooks began writing poetry as a child in Chicago and had her first poem published at age ten in a children's magazine. In high school, she saw several of her poems published in *Defender,* a Chicago newspaper. In the early 1940s she won prizes for her poetry and published her first poetry collection in 1945. The first African American woman to be so honored, Brooks won a Pulitzer Prize for poetry in 1950 for her second collection, *Annie Allen.* Other works include *The Bean Eaters* (1960), *In the Mecca* (1968), and *To Disembark* (1981). Brooks became a major force in the movement to define black identity and to foster black pride.

ELIZABETH BARRETT BROWNING (1806–1861), who wrote "grief may be joy misunderstood," had a difficult young life. Born into a well-to-do family in Durham, England, as the oldest of eleven children, Barrett Browning was reading Greek at the age of eight and writing poems that imitated her favorite authors. At fifteen she suffered a spinal injury when she fell from a pony and was a partial invalid when she met the poet Robert Browning in 1845. The two fell in love immediately, but she had to elope to escape from her obsessively jealous father. Because of her health, the couple went to live in Italy. Her most famous collection, *Sonnets from the Portuguese*, love poems written to her husband, was published in 1850.

ROBERT BROWNING (1812–1889) was born in Camberwall, England. He decided to become a poet at seventeen and after setbacks became one of the best-known and most influential poet-sages of Victorian England. He was still receiving financial support from his family when in 1845 he met and fell in love with Elizabeth Barrett, one of the leading poets of the day. *The Ring and the Book*, a series of dramatic monologues based on a seventeenth-century murder, appeared in 1869 and finally brought him popular acclaim. His metrically rough and intellectually challenging poetry secured him a following of dedicated admirers, with Browning Societies surviving to this day.

ROBERT BURNS (1759–1796)—born in a small cottage in Alloway, Scotland, to a family of poor tenant farmers—knew poverty and exploitation at first hand. He was steeped in the traditional ballads and songs of his country, and he became for the Romantic poets the type of untutored, spontaneous, original genius throwing off artificial conventions. After years of trying unsuccessfully to earn a living as a farmer, he was offered a job as an overseer in Jamaica. To pay for his passage, he published in 1786 a collection of poems and songs entitled *Poems Chiefly in the Scottish Dialect*. Because of its tremendous success, he was able to give up his Jamaica project. Like the Romantic poets after him, he was fired with generous enthusiasm for the aims of the French Revolution, envisioning a world in which the aristocracy would be swept away and brotherhood and human dignity would prevail.

ROSEMARY CATACALOS (born 1944) is a bilingual Hispanic poet whose work has been reprinted in recent anthologies stressing multicultural themes. She was born in St. Petersburg, Florida, and grew up and attended a two-year college in San Antonio, Texas. She has conducted poetry workshops in schools throughout Texas and has published more than thirty chapbooks, or pamphlets, of students' work. Her collection *Again for the First Time* received the Texas Institute of Letters Poetry Award in 1985.

LORNA DEE CERVANTES (born 1954) discovered the world of books in the homes that her mother cleaned. "We were so poor . . . We were brilliant at wishing," she wrote in her poem "To My Brother." Born in San Francisco of Mexican descent, Cervantes published her first poetry collection, *Emplumada*, in 1981. Educated at San Jose State University, she is the founder of Mango Publications, a small press that publishes books and a literary magazine.

KAWAI CHIGETSU-NI (1632–1736) was a Japanese woman writer of the seventeenth century.

LUCILLE CLIFTON (born 1936) has said, "I am a Black woman poet, and I sound like one." Born in Depew, New York, and educated at Howard University, Clifton taught at several colleges, worked as a claims clerk in the New York State Division of Employment, and was a literature assistant in the Office of Education in Washington, D.C. Her first collection of poetry, *Good Times,* was selected as one of the ten best books of 1969 by the *New York Times.* Among her awards are the University of Massachusetts Press' Juniper Prize for Poetry, an Emmy Award, and creative writing fellowships from the National Endowment for the Arts. In 1979 she was named Maryland's poet laureate.

WILLIAM COWPER (1731–1800) was bullied as a child in school. As an adult, Cowper suffered from fits of depression aggravated by his obsession with the doctrine of eternal damnation. He found comfort for a time in his association with evangelical Christians (he coauthored the *Olney Hymns* still familiar to Methodists) but struggled with mental illness to the end of his life.

STEPHEN CRANE (1871–1900), admired for his harsh realism in the tradition of American naturalism, is best known for his imaginative reenacting of the traumas of the Civil War experience in his novel *The Red Badge of Courage.* Crane was born in Newark, New Jersey, and spent most of his youth in upstate New York. After attending college for two years, he moved to New York City to become a free-lance journalist. His fame as a writer grew in the same year with the publication of *The Black Riders,* a collection of free verse. "The Open Boat," one of his two most famous short stories, appeared in 1897. The other, "The Blue Hotel," was published the year before his death of a tubercular infection at the age of twenty-nine.

COUNTEE CULLEN (1903–1946) was a moving force in the Harlem Renaissance of the 1920s and 1930s, which made the work of poets like Claude McKay, Langston Hughes, and Helene Johnson known to a large public. Cullen's poetry, traditional in form, deals memorably with the joys and sorrows of African Americans. Born and raised in New York City, Cullen graduated from New York University in 1925 and received a master's degree from Harvard the following year. His first three collections of poetry—*Color, Copper Sun,* and *The Ballad of a Brown Girl*—were published in the mid-1920s. His only novel, *One Way to Heaven,* a description of life in Harlem, appeared in 1932. A selection of his own favorite poems, *On These I Stand,* appeared a year after his death.

E. E. CUMMINGS (1894–1962) believed that "poetry is being, not doing." One of the most provocative and unconventional of modern poets, cummings was born in Cambridge, Massachusetts, and educated at Harvard. During World War I, cummings served as a volunteer ambulance driver and was held briefly as a prisoner of war. After the war he spent several years in Paris studying art. A talented painter, he often exhibited his artwork. His first volume of poetry, *Tulips and Chimneys* (1923), was both criticized and praised for its unusual use of language and punctuation, which is reflected in the unorthodox use of lowercase letters in his name. "The effect of this experimentation is not to take the meaning away but to add or emphasize a certain kind of meaning. His way of writing seems to call attention to the sense of each word, so that each word counts and is important in the poem" (Kenneth Koch).

ANN DARR (born 1920) has said, "If I could write the way I want to my writing would be a cross between that of Woody Allen and Pablo Neruda. I want the poems to be honest and alive, as immediate as I can make them." In addition to writing poetry, Darr has worked as a radio writer and actress for NBC and ABC in New York and as poet-in-residence at several universities. During World War II, she served as an air force pilot. "My dominant metaphor has been flight in all of its meanings," she said.

NORA DAUENHAUER (born 1927) is a linguist and author of instructional materials in her native language, Tlingit. A native Alaskan, Dauenhauer comes from a family of noted carvers and beadwork artists.

REUEL DENNEY (born 1913) has said, "When I learned to write, I chalked criticisms of the household on the tile entry of the house. For example, slogans taken from fairy tales such as the Little Tailor's lampoon against the castle holding him prison: 'Too much potatoes and not enuff meat.' Instead of being told that some children somewhere in the world didn't even have potatoes . . . I was praised for my literacy. This was the start of my writing, although I was not published until later, at sixteen or so." Born in New York, Denney was educated at Dartmouth. He lives in Honolulu, Hawaii, where he writes "for three to fifteen hours a week."

COUNTESS OF DIA (born about 1140) was one of the women troubadours of the Provençal courts in southern France, who provided counterpoint to the usually male-oriented tradition of courtly love.

WILLIAM DICKEY (born 1928) "is a national treasure" says critic Brown Miller, adding that "Dickey writes a rare and enviable sort of poem, truly humorous and truly serious at once." Educated at Harvard and Oxford universities, Dickey has taught at Cornell, San Francisco State, and the University of Hawaii. His award-winning work has appeared widely in periodicals such as the *New Yorker, Harper's,* and the *Atlantic.* He lives in San Francisco.

EMILY DICKINSON (1830–1886) is now considered one of the greatest American poets, but only a few of her poems were published—and those in edited and conventionalized versions—in her lifetime. After attending Amherst Academy and a year in a seminary, she spent her life and died in the same house in Amherst, Massachusetts, where she was born. In 1862, she wrote to Thomas Wentworth Higginson, editor of the *Atlantic* magazine, enclosing some poems and asking his opinion. Unable to deal with her strange, provocative poetry, he encouraged her to make her poetry more "regular." After her death, 1,775 poems were discovered in a dresser drawer in her bedroom. "She did in her poetry what she could never have done out loud," writes Louise Bernikow. "She found a voice both original and strange in which to speak with the kind of honesty that exists in no other poet of her time."

JOHN DONNE (1572–1631), English poet, preacher, and religious prose writer, was born in London. He enrolled in Oxford; after converting from Roman Catholicism to the Anglican church, he was ordained into its priesthood in 1614. In 1621 he became dean of St. Paul's Cathedral in London, a position he held as an influential and compelling preacher until his death. When he was very ill in 1623, he wrote a series of essays called *Meditations*. His early love poems were probably written before 1614; his later religious poems were published in *Poems* in 1633. In recent decades, Donne's poetry and that of other metaphysical poets of the seventeenth century have been the object of much critical discussion. His poems appeal strongly to modern readers who prefer the challenging to the conventional, the complex to the superficial, the ironic to the sentimental.

H. D. (1886–1961), pseudonym of Hilda Doolittle, took on the "prophet's mantel in poetry, anticipating the spirit of the current feminist movement by a good half century" (Tom Clark). Born in Bethlehem, Pennsylvania, H. D. attended Bryn Mawr. In 1911 she went to Europe, where she lived most of her life. She began publishing when in 1913 Ezra Pound sent some of her poems to Harriet Monroe of *Poetry* magazine. H. D. soon became known as one of the leaders of the Imagist poets. She published six poetry collections, wrote several novels, and translated Greek literature.

RICHARD EBERHART (born 1904), critically acclaimed American poet, was educated at Cambridge and worked as a tutor to the son of the king of Siam, and as a businessman, a naval officer, a cultural adviser, and a professor. His books of poetry include *Selected Poems, 1930–1965* and *Gifts of Being* (1968).

T. S. ELIOT (1888–1965) was a chief architect of modern poetic theory and one of his century's most influential poets. Born in St. Louis, Missouri, he studied at Harvard, then settled in London in 1915, becoming a British citizen thirteen years later. His poetry departed dramatically from familiar conventions and techniques, notably in "The Love Song of J. Alfred Prufrock" and the epochal *The Waste Land*, which he dedicated to Ezra Pound. Eliot's later works include *Four Quartets* (1943), his plays *Murder in the Cathedral* (1935) and *The Family Reunion* (1939), and poems for cat lovers, which inspired a triumphantly successful musical. He won the Nobel Prize for literature in 1948.

LOUISE ERDRICH (born 1954) writes about American Indian traditions in her novels *Beet Queen* and *Love Medicine,* as well as in her shorter works. Part Chippewa Indian, Erdrich is intensely involved in native American land claims and other issues concerning native Americans. Born in Little Falls, Minnesota, she spent much of her youth on the North Dakota reservation where her father taught school. She was educated at Dartmouth and Johns Hopkins. She has collaborated with her husband, Michael Dorris, on a nonfiction book, *Broken Chord,* about fetal alcohol syndrome among American Indians.

MARTIN ESPADA (born 1958) was raised in a Brooklyn housing project and became an attorney and a poet, using the "power of the word to fight against what I consider to be wrong." He won the 1991 Peterson Poetry Prize for *Rebellion Is the Circle of a Lover's Hands.*

NELLE FERTIG (born 1919) is included in current collections of work by women poets.

DONALD FINKEL (born 1929) "is one of the few Americans," says Peter Meinke, "trying to extend poetry past the internal into the external world." Much of Finkel's work has been praised by the critics for its startling images and "comic extravagance." A New York native, Finkel has taught at the University of Iowa, Washington University, and Princeton. His numerous awards include the National Book Award for his 1979 poetry collection *The Garbage Wars.* Joseph Bennet wrote in the *New York Times Book Review* that Finkel is "so gifted he does not need subjects for his poems. . . . He has, above all, the gift of wonderment."

ROBERT FROST (1874–1963), born in San Francisco, moved to New England at age ten upon his father's death, and his poetry is closely linked with rural Vermont and New Hampshire. After briefly attending Dartmouth and Harvard, Frost worked as a shoemaker, schoolteacher, editor, and farmer. Unable to make a living, he took his family to England, where his first poetry collection, *A Boy's Will,* appeared in 1913. By 1914 his reputation had become firmly established through the publication of *North of Boston,* a collection containing what were to become some of his most popular poems, including "Mending Wall" and "The Death of the Hired Man." Frost won Pulitzer Prizes for poetry in 1924, 1931, 1937, and 1943. He developed a legendary reputation as America's best-known poet; he read "The Gift Outright" at John F. Kennedy's inauguration in 1960.

FEDERICO GARCÍA LORCA (1898–1936) was killed by the Fascists during the Spanish Civil War. Born in Andalusia, in southern Spain, Lorca spent some time in New York and Cuba in his early thirties. He is best known for his play *Blood Wedding,* which was first performed in Madrid in 1933. His early poems have been compared to "strange folk or fairy tales," and his New York poems have been described as "rougher and freer and less songlike." Kenneth Koch notes that "Lorca's poetry is always wild and strange in one way or another." Lorca believed his dreamlike images reached the complex truth that direct language does not reach.

DANA GIOIA (born 1950), whose surname is pronounced *"Joy*-a," was born in Los Angeles to a cabdriver and a telephone operator. Educated at Stanford and Harvard universities, Gioia has said, "Though most of my poems use rhyme or meter, they rarely follow 'traditional' patterns. I love traditional forms, but I find them slightly dangerous. Their music can become so seductive that one loses touch with contemporary speech, which is, to my judgment, the basis for all genuine poetry."

NIKKI GIOVANNI (born 1943) believes that "a poem is a way of capturing a moment. . . . A poem's got to be a single stroke, and I make it the best I can because it's going to live." Born Yolande Cornelia Giovanni in Knoxville, Tennessee, Giovanni was the daughter of a probation officer and a social worker. In 1967, she graduated from Fisk University in Nashville and later did graduate work at both the University of Pennsylvania and Columbia University. *Black Feeling, Black Talk,* her first volume of poetry, appeared in 1968, and in 1970 she established her own publishing firm. A prolific writer, Giovanni believes that "poetry is the most mistaught subject in any school because we teach poetry by form and not by content."

JUDY GRAHN (born 1940), born in Chicago, graduated from San Francisco State University. She has published eight books of poetry, including *The Work of a Common Woman* and *The Queen of Swords,* which was performed in San Francisco. She has also published books about poetry and language, as well as a novel, *Mundane's World.* The winner of several grants and awards, Grahn founded the Women's Press Collective in 1970 and has taught writing and mythology.

ANNE HALLEY (born 1928)—the daughter of a German mother and a Jewish father, both physicians—came to America in 1938 from Germany as a refugee from Nazism. Educated at Wellesley and the University of Minnesota, Halley studied with Mary Curran and Robert Penn Warren and was influenced in her early years by the English metaphysical poets. She lives in Massachusetts, where she has taught at several colleges and edited the *Massachusetts Review* out of the University of Massachusetts. Her work centers on women's concerns, the legacies of a German-Jewish past, social issues, and problems of language.

THOMAS HARDY (1840–1928)—a major British novelist *(Tess of the D'Urbervilles, The Mayor of Casterbridge)*—produced eleven novels and three collections of stories before he finally abandoned prose for his first love, poetry, in his sixtieth year. He produced delicately bittersweet poems until he was almost ninety. Critics, thinking his power had waned, did not take his poetry seriously until he published his epic, *The Dynasts* (1904), which established his reputation as a poet. The young poet Siegfried Sassoon wrote that Hardy recorded life with "microscopic exactitude . . . and a subtle ironic sense" of the tragic in human existence: "But his despair is mitigated by tenderness and pity for his fellows. With a wistful understanding he surveys the human scene." As an octogenarian, Hardy published *Late Lyrics and Earlier* (1922); his posthumous *Winter Words in Various Moods and Metres* was arranged by him before his death. Louis Untermeyer observed that, although his syntax was often clumsy, his poetry is "as disciplined as it is original."

JEFFREY HARRISON (born 1957) believes that "poetry is the lens through which the soul looks at the world, thereby keeping the soul alive." Harrison, an Ohio native who lives in Cincinnati, is author of the poetry collection *The Singing Underneath* and a contributor to many magazines. Educated at Columbia University and the University of Iowa, Harrison has taught English in Japan and has worked as a researcher in Washington, D.C.

ROBERT HASS (born 1941) was born and raised in San Francisco and studied at St. Mary's College in Oakland and Stanford University. He has taught at the State University of New York at Buffalo, St. Mary's College, and Berkeley. His first book, *Field Guide,* won the 1973 Yale Series of Younger Poets Award; he received a MacArthur Foundation award in 1985. "Hass believes that poetry is what defines the self, and it is his ability to describe that process that is the heart" of the pleasure his work gives his readers (Anthony Libby).

ROBERT HAYDEN (1913–1980), born in Detroit, Michigan, graduated from Wayne State University in Detroit and did graduate work at the University of Michigan. He later joined the faculty of Fisk University. *Heartshape in the Dust,* his first poetry collection, appeared in 1940. His 1963 collection *A Ballad of Remembrance* received the grand prize at the World Festival of Negro Arts. Hayden called his work "a form of prayer—a prayer of illumination, perfection."

SEAMUS HEANEY (born 1939) was born to a rural Catholic family in Northern Ireland, received a B.A. from Queen's University in Belfast in 1961, and taught in secondary schools and universities. His first published book, *Death of a Naturalist,* set his reputation of being a powerful "rural poet," a label he addresses in these lines: "Between my fingers and my thumb / The squat pen rests. / I'll dig with it." Heaney's poetry is steeped in Irish lore and history and noted for its "inventive language and sharp, immediate physical imagery." More than simply portraying the Irish countryside and folklore, however, Heaney is concerned with the poet's political role, seeing poets as "both helpless witnesses and accomplices in the fratricidal battles" of Ireland.

JOHN HEAVISIDE published his poem in the *Olivetree Review,* a publication devoted to student work and published at Hunter College of the City University of New York.

GEORGE HERBERT (1593–1633), a younger son of a wealthy aristocratic English family, began writing religious verse while an undergraduate at Cambridge University. Until the death of King James in 1625, Herbert enjoyed royal favor and participated in the life of the court. Undecided for a time between the uncertain promise of a career in public office and a career as a churchman, he eventually became an Anglican priest. His collected poems were published after his death in a volume entitled *The Temple.* Like other metaphysical poets of his time, Herbert introduced into religious poetry complex imagery and intense personal emotion.

ROBERT HERRICK (1591–1674) addressed lightweight conventional poems about love to imaginary Corinnas and Julias while leading a quiet life as a country priest. Born in London, Herrick was apprenticed as a young man to his uncle, a wealthy goldsmith. Later Herrick entered Cambridge, and at some point before 1627 he was ordained an Anglican priest. Two years later the king appointed him to a rural parish in a location he hated at first but grew to love. His *Hesperion,* published in 1648, contains 1,200 poems.

A. D. HOPE (born 1907), a native of Australia, attended Sydney and Oxford universities. A teacher and lecturer as well as a poet, Alec Derwent Hope has been called "one of the two or three best poets writing in English." Hope himself has said that "poetry is principally concerned to 'express' its subject and in doing so to create an emotion which is the feeling of the poem and not the feeling of the poet." Hope is interested in philosophy, biology, and history and claims he has "no very fixed convictions on anything." His most recent collection is *Selected Poems* (1986).

GERARD MANLEY HOPKINS (1844–1889) saw none of his poems published during his lifetime. Born in London, this English poet earned a degree from Oxford in 1867, one year after he had converted to Roman Catholicism. He then entered the Society of Jesus and was ordained a Jesuit priest. Troubled by what he saw as a conflict between his life as a priest and as a poet, he had burned all his poems when he entered the Jesuit order but began to write poetry again in 1875. His complete poetic works were published nineteen years after Hopkins' death by his friend, the poet Robert Bridges. Modern poets and critics soon provided a receptive audience for its complex diction, startling imagery, and intense religious emotion. His poems defied convention and are marked by what one of his editors called "a kind of creative violence."

LADY HORIKAWA (twelfth century) was a woman poet living in Japan in the 1100s.

A. E. HOUSMAN (1859–1936), born in Worcestershire, England, failed his final examinations at Oxford in 1881. Sometime during the previous four years he had changed from lively and outgoing to strictly reserved and melancholy, a change that culminated in this bitter disappointment. Working as a clerk in the Patent Office, he pursued studies on his own and contributed numerous articles to classical journals. Eventually he was named professor of Latin at Cambridge and published *A Shropshire Lad,* his major collection of poems, in 1896.

LANGSTON HUGHES (1902–1967) was a central figure of the Harlem Renaissance of the 1920s, a movement that examined and celebrated American black life and its African heritage. Hughes focused on what it was like to be black in America, a thread that runs through his work as poet, editor, and biographer. Born in Joplin, Missouri, Hughes attended high school in Cleveland, and his first published poems appeared in the school's literary magazine. He attended New York's Columbia University for a year and graduated from Lincoln University in Pennsylvania. His first poetry collection, *The Weary Blues,* appeared in 1926. In addition to numerous collections of poetry, Hughes wrote novels, short stories, plays, radio and motion picture scripts, and nonfiction. In his frequent lecture appearances at black colleges throughout the South, Hughes encouraged others to write. He also translated into English the poetry of black writers from other parts of the world. His own poetry has been translated into many other languages.

BEN JONSON (1572–1637), called by one critic "the most scholarly of all Elizabethan playwrights," worked for a time at bricklaying, his stepfather's trade. Jonson's real love, however, was the theater, and after military service he became attached to a company of actors as player and playwright. His *Every Man in His Humour* was performed in 1598, with Shakespeare in the cast. Jonson also wrote love lyrics and songs for his many plays and masques.

MARIE LUISE KASCHNITZ (1902–1974), like many German artists and writers, was censored and driven into exile by Hitler. Born in Karlsruhe, she was honored with some of the most prestigious German literary prizes after the war. In addition to writing short stories, essays, and poetry, Kaschnitz produced several radio plays. Her reflections of an aging woman in *Tage, Tage, Jahre (Days, Days, Years)* "define the high point of her literary achievement" (Marilyn Sibley Fries).

JOHN KEATS (1795–1821) died at age twenty-six from tuberculosis and became for later generations a symbol of the sensitive artist destroyed by a harsh world. Born in London, Keats gave up studying medicine for writing when thirty-three of his poems were published. He produced some of his finest poetry in 1818 and 1819, including "La Belle Dame sans Merci" and "Ode on a Grecian Urn." Admired for the rich sensuous imagery of his poetry, Keats was passionately concerned with the relationship between emotion and knowledge, between beauty and truth. He expressed a conviction shared by many Romantic writers when he wrote, "I am certain of the heart's affections and the truth of imagination—What the imagination seizes as beauty must be truth."

MAXINE KUMIN (born 1925) was born in Philadelphia, Pennsylvania. She earned her B.A. and M.A. degrees from Radcliffe and lives on a farm in New Hampshire. She published her first collection of poetry in 1961 and won the Pulitzer Prize in 1973 for her collection of poems entitled *Up Country*. She has written a number of novels and numerous successful children's books, several in collaboration with her friend, poet Anne Sexton. She has lectured at the University of Massachusetts, Columbia, Brandeis, and Princeton. May Swenson has called Kumin's work "large-hearted, articulate, and acute."

MELVIN WALKER LA FOLLETTE (born 1930) "believes in the sensuous body of the world," wrote Richard Eberhart, adding, "He finds his feelings of the greatest richness of life in three areas . . . youth, the love of small animals," and "the devotion to the idea of saints and sainthood." La Follette was born in Evansville, Indiana. He received his B.A. in creative writing at the University of Washington. He taught for many years at colleges in California, Canada, and Oregon. He also spent time in forestry work in various parts of the Pacific Northwest.

PHILIP LARKIN (1922–1985), a native of Coventry, England, was considered by some critics to be the finest English poet of his generation. Larkin began his studies at Oxford in 1940. After graduating, he became a librarian at the University of Leicester. In 1946 he published his first poetry collection, *The North Ship,* but it wasn't until 1960, with the publication of *The Less Deceived,* that he gained critical recognition. In addition to publishing many poetry collections, he served as editor of the *Oxford Book of Twentieth Century Verse* and was a recognized expert on jazz. Larkin once said, "Form holds little interest for me. Content is everything."

JAMES LAUGHLIN (born 1914) has made the writing of love poems and light verse his principal avocation. He is also well known as publisher of New Directions Books. Laughlin was friends with William Carlos Williams and e. e. cummings, and the influence of both poets is clear in his work. City Lights Books published Laughlin's *Selected Poems, 1935–1985.*

LI-YOUNG LEE (born 1957) has said, "I believe the King James Bible to contain some of the greatest poetry in the world and I hope to own some of its glory and mystery in my own writing one day." Lee was born in Jakarta, Indonesia, to Chinese parents "who were classically educated and in the habit of reciting literally hundreds of ancient Chinese poems." His father, jailed by then-dictator Sukarno in a leper colony, escaped, and the family fled to the United States. They settled in Pennsylvania, where his father became a Presbyterian minister. His volume of poems, *Rose,* appeared in 1986.

URSULA K. LE GUIN (born 1929), the daughter of an anthropologist and a folklorist, has been called "the best living writer of fantasy and science fiction." Her novels include *The Left Hand of Darkness, The Dispossessed,* and *Always Coming Home.* In addition to adult fiction, she has published poetry, children's books, and essays about her travels and her political commitments as a strong feminist, environmentalist, and champion of the dispossessed.

DENISE LEVERTOV (born 1923) has said she grew up in "a house full of books and everyone in the family engaged in some literary activity." The family's vast library and the diverse visitors to the house—"Jewish booksellers, German theologians, Russian priests from Paris, and Viennese opera singers"—were her education. Her father, a biblical scholar and Anglican priest, harbored the lifelong hope of the unification of Judaism and Christianity. Born in Essex, England, Levertov was a civilian nurse in London during World War II, then settled in New York in 1948 with her American husband. The influence of the American poet William Carlos Williams helped her to develop "from a British Romantic with almost Victorian background to an American poet of . . . vitality."

AUDRE LORDE (born 1934) describes herself as a "black lesbian feminist warrior poet." Born in New York City of West Indian parents, Lorde attended Hunter College and Columbia. She worked as a librarian and then taught at several colleges before becoming a professor of English at Hunter College in New York City. She lives on Staten Island with her companion and her two children. Her first poetry collection, *The First Cities* (1968), chronicles the effects of racism on African Americans. A more recent work, *Zami: A New Spelling of My Name,* Lorde calls her "biomytho-graphy." In what Claudia Tate calls "stunning figurative language," Lorde "outlines the progress of her unyielding struggle for the human rights of all people."

RICHARD LOVELACE (1618–1658) was born in Kent and studied at Oxford. An ardent supporter of Charles I, he was held in London as a prisoner during the civil war between the monarchists and the Puritan rebels. When the king was executed, Lovelace lost everything; he spent the remainder of his life in poverty. Most of his poetry was not published in his lifetime, but today he is one of the best remembered of the Cavalier (royalist) poets.

EDWARD LUCIE-SMITH (born 1933) was born in Kingston, Jamaica, and educated at Oxford. He went to live in London, working as a free-lance writer, an art critic, an anthologist, and a translator.

HUGH MACDIARMID (1892–1978) "effected, almost single-handed, a literary revolution," wrote David Daiches. "He . . . destroyed one Scottish tradition and founded another." In order to identify himself with the Scots' heritage, MacDiarmid changed his name from Christopher Grieve, his English name. Setting himself the task of reviving the great Scottish poetic tradition, he wrote the much-admired lyric poetic sequence *A Drunk Man Looks at the Thistle* in 1926.

CLAUDE MCKAY (1890–1948), who wrote militant poetry attacking the racism he encountered as a black immigrant to the United States, surprised some readers by converting to Roman Catholicism in the 1940s. "To have a religion," he wrote, "is very much like falling in love with a woman. You love her for her beauty, which cannot be defined." Born in Jamaica, McKay was a published poet before coming to the United States at age twenty-three. His 1919 poem "If We Must Die" helped inaugurate the 1920s Harlem Renaissance. His writings include an autobiography entitled *A Long Way from Home,* published in 1927.

ROD MCKUEN (born 1933) built a business empire consisting of four record labels, three book publishers, two music-publishing companies, a mail-order venture, and a clothing company named "Rod McKuen Casuals." A resident of Los Angeles, he has published many collections of poetry, composed musical scores, and written more than a thousand songs.

ARCHIBALD MACLEISH (1892–1982) was for a time a leading advocate of the role of poetry in contemporary society. Born in Glencoe, Illinois, he served in World War I in 1917–1918. He graduated from Yale in 1915 and received a law degree from Harvard Law School in 1919. He grew tired of law practice and turned to study literature, reading the works of the great early moderns, T. S. Eliot and Ezra Pound. President Franklin Roosevelt appointed MacLeish librarian of Congress in 1939, and he served as assistant secretary of state during the final two years of World War II. In 1953, his *Collected Poems 1917–1952* won him his second Pulitzer. MacLeish taught at Harvard and at Amherst College.

ANDREW MARVELL (1621–1678) was known in his day for satirical commentary on political events; his poetry was not published until after his death. Today his "To His Coy Mistress" is one of the best-known poems in the English language. Twentieth-century critics rediscovered Marvell and other metaphysical poets (John Donne, George Herbert), championing their love of irony and paradox and their blend of intellectual vigor and passionate intensity. Born in Yorkshire, Marvell entered Oxford at the age of twelve. When the civil war broke out, he was appointed assistant to John Milton in the Cromwell government. After the monarchy was restored, he served in Parliament until his death.

JOHN MASEFIELD (1878–1967), a native of Herefordshire, England, was a young boy when his father, a lawyer, died. At fourteen Masefield was indentured to a merchant ship and became a wanderer for several years. Staying for a time in New York, he took odd jobs before returning to England at nineteen. After Masefield read Chaucer, he was determined to become a poet. Not until the 1911 publication of *The Everlasting Mercy* did he become famous. In addition to his poetry, he wrote more than a dozen plays, a book on Shakespeare, twelve volumes of essays, books for youths, and adventure novels.

PETER MEINKE (born 1932) was born in Brooklyn, New York. He served in the U.S. Army and received a B.A. from Hamilton College, an M.A. from the University of Michigan, and a Ph.D. from the University of Minnesota. Meinke's reviews, poems, and stories have appeared in periodicals such as the *Atlantic,* the *New Yorker,* and the *New Republic.* His collection of short stories, *The Piano Tuner,* won the 1986 Flannery O'Connor Award.

WILLIAM MEREDITH (born 1919), a native of New York City, graduated from Princeton in 1940 and served as a naval aviator during World War II. His award-winning poetry has been published in several collections, including *Ships and Other Figures, The Open Sea,* and *Earth Walk: New & Selected Poems.* He taught at Princeton and Carnegie-Mellon, and has been with Connecticut College since 1955.

EVE MERRIAM (born 1916) grew up in a suburb of Philadelphia. A 1937 graduate of the University of Pennsylvania, Merriam continued her studies at Columbia and the University of Wisconsin. In 1946 she published her first poetry collection, *Family Circle,* which received the Yale Younger Poets Prize. She wanted to share her lifelong love of words with children, so she began writing poetry designed for young people. The first of these collections appeared in 1962 under the title *There Is No Rhyme for Silver.* Other titles followed: *It Doesn't Always Have to Rhyme, Catch a Little Rhyme,* and *Independent Voices.*

W. S. MERWIN (born 1927), one of the most prolific poets and translators of his generation, was born the son of a Presbyterian minister in New York City. Educated at Princeton, Merwin was influenced by poet Robert Graves, whose son he tutored in Majorca, Spain. Merwin has translated widely from Spanish, Portuguese, Latin, French, and Russian in both conventional forms and free verse. He has received numerous fellowships and awards, including a Pulitzer Prize in 1971 for his collection *A Carrier of Ladders.* He went to live in Hawaii in 1968.

EDNA ST. VINCENT MILLAY (1892–1950) began writing poetry as a child in Camden, Maine, encouraged by her mother, who had left her father when Millay was eight years old. While a rebellious student at Vassar, Millay dared the president to expel her, and he explained that he didn't want a "banished Shelley on my doorstep." She supposedly replied, "On those terms, I think I can continue to live in this hellhole." She graduated in 1917, the same year her first book of poems was published. In 1923 she won a Pulitzer Prize for her poetry collection, *The Harp-Weaver*. In addition to over twenty volumes of verse, she published three verse plays, wrote a libretto for an opera, and translated Baudelaire. Neglected for a time by critics who thought her poetry too traditional in form and too frankly emotional, she has recently been rediscovered by feminist critics as an early champion of feminist themes.

VASSAR MILLER (born 1924) calls poetry "an act of love." Born in Houston, Miller was educated at the University of Houston. She has published several poetry collections, including *Wage War on Silence*. Afflicted with cerebral palsy from birth, Miller has dedicated herself to poetry "and has demonstrated . . . that craftsmanship, religious fervor, and personal joy and agony can produce major poetry" (Chad Walsh).

CZESLAW MILOSZ (born 1911) "deals in his poetry with the central issues of our time: the impact of history upon moral being, the search for ways to survive spiritual ruin in a ruined world" (Terrence Des Pres). Milosz, a native of Lithuania, published his first book of poetry at age twenty-one. When Poland was invaded by Germany and Soviet Russia in 1939, Milosz worked with the underground Resistance in Warsaw, writing and editing several books published secretly. After the war, Milosz became a member of the new communist government's diplomatic service but left this post in 1951 and defected to the West. He joined the faculty at the University of California at Berkeley in 1960 and won the Nobel Prize for literature in 1980.

JOHN MILTON (1608–1674) was poet deeply involved in the political and religious turmoil of his time. Born in Cheapside, London he was steeped in classical literature and wrote some of his early poems in Latin and in Italian. After graduating from Cambridge, Milton traveled the continent, returning to England shortly before the civil war. Milton was an ardent supporter of the Puritan cause. He joined in the vigorous polemics of the time and published aggressive prose tracts on subjects including censorship. After the overthrow of King Charles I, Milton became Latin secretary in charge of diplomatic correspondence under the dictator Cromwell. He escaped death as a traitor to the crown after the restoration of the monarchy, publishing his monumental religious epic *Paradise Lost* in 1667. By this time he was completely blind and living in poverty. "Lycidas," the best known of his shorter poems, appeared in 1637.

GABRIELA MISTRAL (1889–1956) adopted her pen name from the names of two poets she admired, Gabriele D'Annunzio and Frédéric Mistral. Born in Chile, Mistral wrote about her concerns for children, the social condition of Chilean workers, and the social emancipation of women. Some of her books include *Sonetos de la Muerte* (1914), *Desolación* (1922), and *Ernura and Tala* (1923). In 1945 she was awarded the Nobel Prize for literature.

N. SCOTT MOMADAY (born 1934) is a Kiowa whose writing explores the history and culture of his people. Momaday was born in Lawton, Oklahoma. He graduated from the University of New Mexico in 1958 and received master's and doctoral degrees from Stanford. He began his academic career teaching English at the University of California, Santa Barbara, in 1973. He told the story of his rediscovery of his heritage in *The Journey of Tai-me* (1968)—republished with illustrations by his father Al Momaday under the title *The Way to Rainy Mountain*. His novel *The House Made of Dawn* won a Pulitzer Prize in 1969.

OGDEN NASH (1902–1971) gave pleasure to untold readers with a steady stream of irreverent light verse. Born in Rye, New York, Nash attended Harvard and worked as a teacher, a bond salesperson, and an editor for Doubleday Publishers in New York City. Later he joined the editorial staff of the *New Yorker*. His collected poems, *I Wouldn't Have Missed It,* appeared in 1975.

THOMAS NASHE (1567–1601), the son of a minister, was born in Lowestoft, England. After graduating from Cambridge, Nashe toured France and Italy and by 1588 was a professional writer living in London. Nashe wrote pamphlets to defend the Anglican church against attacks by the Puritans. He also wrote several plays and in 1594 published an adventure novel, *The Unfortunate Traveler.*

HOWARD NEMEROV (born 1920), American poet and literary critic, was born and raised in New York City. He graduated from Harvard and served in World War II with a fighter squadron in the British Royal Air Force. He has taught at Bennington College in Vermont and George Washington University in St. Louis. Known for its clarity and simplicity, much of his poetry sings the praises of nature and the simple life.

PABLO NERUDA (1904–1973) said, "I like the lives of people who are restless and unsatisfied, whether they are artists or criminals." Neruda himself lived a restless, adventure-filled life. Born "Neftali Beltran" in a small frontier town in southern Chile, Neruda took his pseudonym at a young age out of admiration for a nineteenth century Czech writer. When Neruda was still a boy, his father, a railroad worker, was killed in a fall from a train. At nineteen, Neruda published a book called *Twenty Poems of Love and One Ode of Desperation*, which is still loved in South America. During that period, he said, "Love poems were sprouting out all over my body." In later years much of his poetry became political. He served as consulate in the Far East and Mexico and traveled widely. He became a member of the Chilean Senate, fleeing from dictatorship for a time. During his years of exile, Neruda wrote *Canto General,* which his translator, Robert Bly, called "the greatest long poem written on the American continent since *Leaves of Grass.*"

NILA NORTHSUN (born 1951) was born in Schurz, Nevada, of Shoshoni-Chippewa heritage. She coauthored *After the Drying Up of the Water* and *Diet Pepsi and Nacho Cheese*. She has written about the ironies of exchanging reservation life for city life.

SHARON OLDS (born 1942) has said, "One of the hardest tasks as a poet is to believe in oneself—or to act as if we do!" A self-described "late bloomer," Olds says she was thirty before she found her voice, her ability "to embody on the page thinking about an actual self." Born in San Francisco, Olds earned a B.A. from Stanford and a Ph.D. from Columbia. A winner of many awards, she has taught and given numerous readings at colleges and universities. Her poetry books are *Satan Says* (1980), *The Dead and the Living* (1982), *The Gold Cell* (1987), and *The Father* (1992). She writes with astonishing frankness and authentic emotion about being a child, a woman, and a mother.

MARY OLIVER (born 1935), was born in Cleveland, Ohio, and attended both Ohio State and Vassar. She worked as a secretary to the sister of poet Edna St. Vincent Millay. Her first collection of poetry, *No Voyage, and Other Poems*, appeared in 1963, then again in 1965 with nineteen additional poems. Her second collection, *The River Styx, Ohio, and Other Poems*, appeared in 1972.

WILFRED OWEN (1893–1918) wrote powerful antiwar poems during World War I—poems that are a lasting memorial and tribute to a generation destroyed in the trenches of Flanders and northern France. Owen was killed in action one week before the armistice, at age twenty-five. Born in Shropshire, England, into a devout, relatively poor family, Owen was educated at London University and enlisted in military service when England entered the war. In late 1917 he was wounded and sent to a military hospital. There he met the poet Siegfried Sassoon, who edited and published Owen's poems after Owen's death.

DOROTHY PARKER (1893–1967) has been called "the quintessential New York wit, known as much for what she said as for what she wrote." Parker often wrote bitter satire and showed empathy toward suffering. "The humorist has never been happy, anyhow," she once said. "Today he's whistling past worse graveyards to worse tunes." In addition to writing for the *New Yorker* and *Vanity Fair*, Parker wrote screenplays for Hollywood.

LINDA PASTAN (born 1932) was born in New York City and studied at Brandeis and Radcliffe. Her first poetry collection, *A Perfect Circle of Sun*, appeared in 1971. Other collections include *Five Stages of Grief* (1978), *AM/PM* (1982), *Imperfect Paradise* (1988), and *Heroes in Disguise* (1991). Poet laureate of the State of Maryland, she has been honored with fellowships from the National Endowment for the Arts. The *Washington Post* noted that Pastan "writes with a music of her own—reinforced by overtones of Yeats and Frost."

OCTAVIO PAZ (born 1914), Mexican poet and critic, won the Nobel Prize for literature in 1991. He has lectured to large audiences in the United States and served as Mexico's ambassador to India, a post from which he resigned in 1968 in protest over the bloody repression of student demonstrators before the Olympic Games in Mexico City. He has written much about the dialogue between the North American and Latin American cultures. Published collections of his poetry include *Savage Moon* (1933), *Sun Stone* (1957), and *Selected Poems* (1960).

FRANCESCO PETRARCA (1304–1374) was a humanist of the early Italian Renaissance, participating in the rediscovery of the learning and literature of classical antiquity. His *Canzoniere*, a collection of songs *(canzoni)* and sonnets, started the vogues of Petrarchan love poetry that dominated lyric poetry in Europe for centuries.

MARGE PIERCY (born 1936) was born in poverty in Detroit during the depression. She was the first in her family to go to college and "took five years to recover." She has published eight novels, including *Woman on the Edge of Time,* a science fiction work in which she experiments with a "woman's language." She has also written a play, essays, and nine volumes of poetry. Recent works include a 1988 volume of poems entitled *Available Light.* When she is not giving readings and conducting workshops throughout the country, she writes in her Cape Cod home.

CHRISTINE DE PISAN (about 1364–1430), called "France's first woman of letters" by biographer Charity Cannon Willard, lived and wrote at the end of the Middle Ages. Born in Venice, Italy, she moved to Paris, France, at age four. There her family became part of the royal court, for her father, a scientist, was employed by King Charles V. At age fifteen she married but was widowed after ten years. Her first poetry collection, published by 1402, marked the beginning of a long literary career, during which de Pisan wrote lyrical and allegorical poetry, biographies of important political figures (including Charles V), textbooks, and books about women and government. She is also known for her role in a debate over contemporary negative attitudes toward women and for her championing of women's rights.

SYLVIA PLATH (1932–1963) was born in Boston of an Austrian-born father who was an instructor at Boston University and an expert on bees. She began writing early and sold several stories and poems to *Seventeen* magazine. A 1955 summa cum laude graduate in English from Smith, Plath earned an M.A. at Cambridge as a Fulbright scholar. In 1956 she married English poet Ted Hughes. *The Colossus,* published in 1960, was her only poetry collection to appear before she committed suicide. *The Bell Jar,* a quasi-autobiographical novel, chronicles the struggles of a brilliant young woman with radical alienation from her environment and her bouts with suicidal depression. Critic David Young says Plath "lived on a knife-edge, in the presence of a tremendous attraction to death and nothingness," Since her death, her powerful and disturbing poetry has been widely discussed and anthologized.

ALEXANDER POPE (1668–1744) became an arbiter of literary taste in the age of reason. Born into the family of a prosperous London merchant, Pope's formal education was largely confined to his own home. Excluded from universities discriminating against Catholics, Pope quickly demonstrated his ability to overcome obstacles and adverse criticism. His *Essay on Criticism* (1711), a discussion in poetic form of literary taste and style, established its author's reputation. He undertook monumental translations of Homer's *Iliad* and *Odyssey* by public subscription and became financially independent in the process. *An Essay on Man,* a versified compendium of the fashionable optimistic philosophy of his age, appeared in 1733.

EZRA POUND (1885–1972) was one of the great innovators and nonconformists of early modern poetry. He championed or inspired writers like Marianne Moore, T. S. Eliot, Robert Frost, William Carlos Williams, Ernest Hemingway, and James Joyce. Pound was born in Idaho and educated at Hamilton College and the University of Pennsylvania. Associated with the imagist poets, Pound translated Chinese, Latin, Japanese, German, French, Italian, Greek, Anglo-Saxon, and Provençal (thirteenth-century French) poetry. In 1945 he was arrested for treason because of radio broadcasts in Fascist Italy during World War II. Found unfit for trial by reason of insanity, he was committed to St. Elizabeth's Hospital in Washington, D.C., where he spent over ten years. His most ambitious and complex work is *The Cantos,* a vast, richly allusive collection of poems he worked on while in a prisoner of war camp near Pisa, Italy.

LEROY V. QUINTANA (born 1944) has said, "In many ways, I'm still basically a small-town New Mexico boy carrying on the oral tradition." Born in Albuquerque, Quintana was raised by his grandparents, who told him *cuentos*—traditional Mexican folktales—and stories of life in the Old West. "I seem to be tied to a sense of the past," he said. "My work reflects the 'sense of place' evoked by New Mexico. I hope I am worthy of portraying the land and its people well." Quintana, a graduate of the University of New Mexico, won the American Book Award for poetry in 1982 for *Sangre.* His other titles include *Hijo del Pueblo: New Mexico Poems* (1976) and *The Reason People Don't Like Mexicans* (1984).

JOHN CROWE RANSOM (1888–1974), both as a poet and a critic, shared in the redirection of modern literary taste associated with the rediscovery of the metaphysical poets of the seventeenth century. Born in Pulaski, Tennessee, Ransom was educated at Vanderbilt University and Oxford, where he was a Rhodes scholar. Ransom made a name for himself as both poet and critic in the 1920s and 1930s. He taught at Vanderbilt and then at Kenyon College, where he was a faculty member for almost forty years. At Kenyon he founded and edited the *Kenyon Review.* He became a leader in what was then called the New Criticism, publishing *The World's Body* in 1938 and *The New Criticism* in 1941.

HENRY REED (born 1914), poet and playwright, was born in Birmingham, England. After earning a B.A. from the University of Birmingham in 1937, he worked as a teacher and free-lance writer. He served a stint in the British army and wrote poetry about his experience in cadet training, as well as about political events of the time. His only collection of poetry, *A Map of Verona,* appeared in 1946. Soon thereafter, he began writing radio plays, including the popular BBC "Hilda Tablet" series, a parody of British society in the 1930s.

KENNETH REXROTH (born 1905) has been a painter, essayist, radio and television performer, editor, and journalist as well as a poet. Born in Indiana, Rexroth was mostly self-educated. A guru of the Beat Generation, for many years he lived in San Francisco and has written extensively about California's High Sierra Mountains. "Some of his mountain poems are the best nature writing we have" (Hayden Carruth). Rexroth has translated from six languages and has written three volumes of critical essays.

ADRIENNE RICH (born 1929) was educated by her parents in their Baltimore, Maryland, home until fourth grade, when she entered public school. A 1951 Phi Beta Kappa graduate of Radcliffe, Rich won the Yale Younger Poets competition that same year for her collection *A Change of World.* Since then she has been awarded the prestigious Bollingen Prize and in 1974 was a cowinner with Allen Ginsberg of the National Book Award for poetry. She has published more than half a dozen books of poetry, including *Diving into the Wreck* (1973) and *The Dream of a Common Language: Poems 1974–1977.* An inspiration to feminist poets and critics, Rich collected some of her incisive, thought-provoking prose in *On Lies, Secrets, and Silence.*

RAINER MARIA RILKE (1875–1926), perhaps the most widely admired and translated of the twentieth-century German poets, was born in Prague to German-speaking parents. In 1898 he went to Russia, where he met Leo Tolstoy, author of *War and Peace.* In 1905 in France, Rilke served as secretary for the famous French sculptor Rodin, and the influence of this experience can be seen in his collection *New Poems.* When World War I broke out, Rilke moved to Switzerland, where he wrote *Sonnets to Orpheus* and the *Duino Elegies.* Critic Kenneth Koch has said of Rilke's power as a poet: "When Rilke writes about a subject, it is as if nothing were known about it, as if he started from the very beginning in order to understand deeply, for himself, the power or purpose or beauty of it."

THEODORE ROETHKE (1908–1963), grew up in Saginaw, Michigan, where his father and uncle owned a greenhouse; greenhouses would serve as prominent images in his poetry. He studied at the University of Michigan and Harvard, and he taught and coached tennis at a number of colleges. He sold his first poems for a dollar, but shortly thereafter his poetry appeared in several widely read magazines. He won a Pulitzer Prize in 1954 for *The Waking: Poems 1933–1953,* which was followed by the Bollingen Prize in 1959 for *Words for the Wind* and two National Book Awards. Abrasive in his criticism of contemporary culture and fellow poets, Roethke looked into the world of nature for sources of spiritual renewal.

CHRISTINA ROSSETTI (1830–1894), whose father had come to England as a political refugee from his native Italy, was born in London in a poor neighborhood. Rossetti had no formal education but was taught to read by her mother. From her earliest days she loved to write, and her grandfather had a number of her poems privately printed when she was twelve. Her first collection of poetry, *Goblin Market and Other Poems,* appeared in 1862.

LAURA ST. MARTIN (born 1957) has been anthologized in recent collections of contemporary American poets.

SAPPHO (about 620–550 B.C.), called "the tenth Muse" by Plato, lived on the Greek island of Lesbos, where she wrote passionate love poems addressed to younger women she may have taught. She was an aristocrat involved in controversial political activities which led to her being exiled twice. She married a rich merchant and bore a daughter. In 1073 A.D., a large collection of her verse was publicly burned by church dignitaries of Rome and Constantinople. However, some of her writing—as well as her legendary reputation—has remained intact.

ANNE SEXTON (1928–1974) encouraged writers to "put your ear close down to your soul and listen hard." Born in Newton, Massachusetts, she studied at Boston University and Brandeis. At twenty-eight, a suburban housewife, she suffered a nervous breakdown. Her therapist encouraged her to write, and she soon became a successful poet. She claimed that when she began to write she was reborn, for "suicide is the opposite of the poem." She wrote eight books of poetry; her *Live or Die* won the 1967 Pulitzer Prize. Sexton lived a troubled life, punctuated by suicide attempts and hospitalizations, until she finally took her life in 1974, mourned by fellow poets who thought of her as one of the great poetic talents of our time. "When I'm writing, I know I'm doing the thing I was born to do," she said. "I guess I listen for my melody. When it comes, I just turn . . . like a little dancer." A 1991 biography of Anne Sexton made the *New York Times* bestseller list.

WILLIAM SHAKESPEARE (1564–1616) is the foremost English dramatist of the reigns of Queen Elizabeth and King James I. Shakespeare was actor, playwright, and shareholder in a theatrical company at a time when the English stage enjoyed both royal patronage and popular support. He wrote some thirty-five plays for an audience that liked spectacle and was used to keen competition among theatrical companies and to rapid changes in dramatic fashions. A vast literature of comment, analysis, background information, and textual study has grown up around his works. His great tragedies—*Romeo and Juliet, Hamlet, Othello, King Lear, Macbeth*—probe the paradoxes of our human nature and destiny. Little is known about his life: He was born in the small town of Stratford-on-Avon, and his formal studies ended with grammar school. At eighteen he married Anne Hathaway. He retired to his hometown at the end of his career.

PERCY BYSSHE SHELLEY (1792–1822), most iconoclastic of the younger Romantic poets, was born in Sussex, England, as the eldest son of a conservative country squire. He went to Oxford but was expelled for publishing a pamphlet that advocated atheism. This was but the first of many rebellions against convention and established institutions that marked his brief life. Shelley spent most of his adult life in Italy; many of his shorter and more famous lyric poems, such as "To a Skylark" and "Ode to the West Wind," he wrote in Pisa in 1819. One of his last poems is the elegy written to mourn the death of his close friend John Keats. Shelley himself, who had written "How wonderful is Death, / Death and his brother Sleep," died in a boating accident at age thirty.

CHARLES SIMIC (born 1938) came to the United States at age eleven from his native Yugoslavia. The son of an engineer and a dress designer, Simic has published twelve poetry collections. Robert Shaw of the *New Republic* said that Simic's poems are "at once weighty and evasive, and describing them is about as easy as picking up blobs of mercury with mittens on." Many critics have commented on the enigmatic quality of Simic's poetry: "I have not yet decided," writes Diane Wakoski in *Poetry*, "whether Charles Simic is America's greatest living surrealist poet, a children's writer, a religious writer, or simple-minded. . . . his poetry is cryptic and fascinating."

GARY SOTO (born 1952), award-winning Mexican American poet, believes that "writing makes the ordinary stand out, thus enabling us to build in some kind of metaphorical meaning." Much of Soto's writing includes the ordinary events of his childhood in Fresno, California. In addition to the prose memoir *Living up the Street,* Soto has published five books of poetry, including *Home Course in Religion* (1991). An alumnus of Fresno State and the University of California, Irvine, he joined the faculty at Berkeley. Soto says that literature "reshapes experience—both real and invented—to help us see ourselves—our foibles, failures, potential, beauty, pettiness. In short, literature helps define the world for us."

WOLE SOYINKA (born 1934) is associated worldwide with the struggle for justice and freedom in Africa. Born in Nigeria of Yoruban parents, this Nobel laureate writes plays, poems, and novels. He has worked as a teacher and served as secretary general of the Union of African Writers. His plays were first performed in England while he was a student at the University of Leeds. His poetry collection titles include *Idanre and Other Poems* and *A Shuttle in the Crypt,* which contains poems written while he was imprisoned during the Nigerian civil war.

WILLIAM STAFFORD (born 1914) grew up in small towns of central Kansas, hunting, camping, and fishing in the countryside. He earned a doctorate in English from Iowa State. A member of the United Brethren, Stafford became a conscientious objector during World War II. He worked in labor camps, an experience recorded in a prose memoir, *Down in My Heart.* In 1947 his first collection of poems appeared, and the next year he joined the faculty at Lewis and Clark College in Oregon. His third poetry collection, *Traveling through the Dark,* received the National Book Award in 1963. His poems often explore commonplace events; critics note, however, that on closer examination, Stafford proves to be "a very elusive poet with a distinctive private vision that slips through our grasp when we try to identify, summarize, or paraphrase it" (David Young).

WALLACE STEVENS (1879–1955), who commanded a large loyal following among readers dedicated to the cause of poetry, believed "the poem refreshes the world." Born in Reading, Pennsylvania, Stevens attended Harvard University and New York Law School. He began practicing law in 1904 and then joined the legal department of a Connecticut insurance company, retiring as vice president of the firm. His challenging, complex poetry appeared in journals as early as 1914; his first collection, *Harmonium,* appeared in 1923. His second collection, *Ideas of Order,* appeared thirteen years later.

SIR JOHN SUCKLING (1609–1642), who has been called "the most skeptical and libertine of the Cavaliers," was born the son of the secretary of state to King James I. Suckling studied at Cambridge and then traveled throughout Europe. A courtier with a reputation of brilliant wit, Suckling wrote four plays and a number of lyric poems. He became embroiled in political intrigue; he committed suicide in 1642.

JON SWAN contributed poems to the *New Yorker* in the 1950s and 1960s. He published *Journey and Return: Poems 1960* in the Poets of Today series.

MAY SWENSON (born 1919), a child of immigrant Swedish parents, was born in Logan, Utah. After graduating from Utah State University, she came to New York City and worked as an editor. She has received many awards for her poetry, which is noted for its freshness of perspective and experimental form. Some of her poetry collection titles are *Another Animal* (1954), *Iconographs* (1970), and *Poems to Solve* (1966), a volume for children.

JONATHAN SWIFT (1667–1745), a towering figure in eighteenth-century English literature, was born in Dublin, Ireland, of English parents. His father died shortly before he was born, and his mother gave him over to the care of a nurse. He was a rebellious and angry youth who barely graduated from Trinity College in Dublin. Swift was ordained a priest of the Anglican church, although he was more interested in politics than in the church. He wrote political tracts for the Whig party and later for the Tories, becoming editor of the Tory newspaper. He castigated England's unfair treatment of Ireland and became a hero to the Irish. In 1726 he published *Gulliver's Travels,* a satirical masterpiece in an age of satire.

ALFRED, LORD TENNYSON (1809–1892), poet laureate of Victorian England, gave voice to characteristic assumptions and aspirations of his contemporaries. Born the son of a clergyman, Tennyson was educated at Cambridge. His first published poems appeared in 1830; in 1842 he published two volumes that included "Morte d'Arthur" and "Ulysses." His *In Memoriam* (1850), written after the death of a close friend, mirrored the religious doubts and earnestness of his time. His *Idylls of the King* (1859) became required reading for generations of high school students.

DYLAN THOMAS (1914–1953) called his poetry a record of his "struggle from darkness toward some measure of light." Born in Wales, Thomas had his only formal education in grammar school. When his first poetry collection appeared in 1932, he was hailed as a leading modern poet. His radio work in England and his numerous poetry readings at American college campuses made him a popular figure on both sides of the Atlantic. His passionate, visionary tone and wild flights of the imagination appealed to readers starved for mysticism and emotion. Alcoholism and lung ailments precipitated in his early death. Thomas once said that his poems, "with all their crudities, doubts, and confusions, are written for the love of man and in Praise of God, and I'd be a damn fool if they weren't."

UKIHASHI (seventeenth century) was a Japanese woman poet of the 1600s. Her work has been translated from the Japanese by Kenneth Rexroth and Ikuko Atsumi.

DAVID WAGONER (born 1926), "a master technician" (Daniel Halpern), was born in Ohio and educated at Penn State and Indiana University. An award-winning poet and novelist, Wagoner taught English at several colleges and made his home in Seattle. He has been praised for his witty and deep perceptions, as well as his "skillful manipulation of language" (Halpern).

ALICE WALKER (born 1944) has said, "All of my poems . . . are written when I have successfully pulled myself out of a completely numbing despair, and stand again in the sunlight." Born in the small town of Eatonsville, Georgia, Walker received her bachelor's degree in 1965 from Sarah Lawrence College. After graduating, she taught at several universities and worked for voter registration and welfare rights. Her novel *The Color Purple* (1982) made her the best-known black writer of her generation. In 1983, she published the essay collection *In Search of Our Mothers' Gardens.* Using language as catharsis and potential for growth is essential to Walker, who said, "No person is your friend (or kin) who demands your silence, or denies your right to grow and be perceived as fully blossomed as you were intended. Or who belittles in any fashion the gifts you labor so to bring into the world."

WALT WHITMAN (1819–1892), a giant of American and world literature, successfully created a public persona as the poet of democracy and the voice of an expansive vision of America. Son of a carpenter and farmer, he spent much of his life as a journalist in Brooklyn, Manhattan, and Long Island. In 1855, he published the first edition of *Leaves of Grass,* a milestone of nineteenth-century American literature. He celebrated the varied scene of contemporary America: the steamers and railroads and ferries, the carpenters and pilots and farmers, the cities and plains and mountains. He once said, "the United States themselves are essentially the greatest poem."

C. K. WILLIAMS (born 1936) was born in Newark, New Jersey, and was educated at Bucknell and the University of Pennsylvania. He established a program of poetry-therapy for emotionally disturbed patients at the Institute of the Pennsylvania Hospital in Philadelphia, where he also served as a group therapist in the treatment of disturbed adolescents. He has taught at Boston University, Columbia, and George Mason. He was awarded a Guggenheim Fellowship in 1974.

WILLIAM CARLOS WILLIAMS (1883–1963), writer of fiction, essays, and poetry, also had a full-time career as a physician. Born in Rutherford, New Jersey, Williams attended preparatory schools in New York and Switzerland and studied medicine at the University of Pennsylvania, where he met Ezra Pound. With Pound's encouragement, Williams began publishing poetry. Winner of many prestigious awards, including a National Book Award and a Pulitzer Prize, Williams worked in New Jersey as both a poet and a doctor until his death.

WILLIAM WORDSWORTH (1770–1850), in collaboration with his friend Samuel Taylor Coleridge, published the collection *Lyrical Ballads* in 1798. The poems in this volume and its programmatic preface broke with the poetic conventions of the eighteenth century and signaled the beginning of the English Romantic movement. Wordsworth, born in Westmoreland, was educated at Cambridge. He for a time was caught up in the revolutionary fervor of the French Revolution but became a voice of conservatism in his later years. He is best remembered for his poems that turn to the healing influence of nature as the antidote to the ills of city civilization.

SIR THOMAS WYATT (1503–1541) was the first to introduce into England Petrarch's sonnets of frustrated love, which started the sonnet vogue of the Elizabethan Age. Born in Kent, England, Wyatt was educated at Cambridge. His father was a joint constable with the father of Anne Boleyn, who was to become the second wife of Henry VIII and the mother of Elizabeth, the future queen. Wyatt was assigned his first diplomatic mission by Henry VIII in 1525 and led a busy life as a courtier and diplomat.

WILLIAM BUTLER YEATS (1865–1939) became known for poems drawing on the heritage of Irish myth and legend and developed a rich symbolic language in his later poetry. Yeats, who won the Nobel Prize for literature in 1923, is widely recognized as one of the most outstanding poets of the English-speaking world. An Irish dramatist and poet, he was born in Dublin. In the 1890s he became involved in the developing revolution against British rule in Ireland. Cofounder of the Irish Literary Theater, he wrote plays for its stage. From 1922—the year of the Proclamation of the Irish Free State—until 1928 he was a member of the Irish Senate. Poet Seamus Heaney says that "a Yeats poem gives the feeling of being empowered and thrilled."

AL YOUNG (born 1939) has said, "long before the printed word and stuffy ideas about literature turned up in my life, and certainly long before I became the willing ward of schoolteachers, I was sleeping with words." His love for language began in his childhood home in Ocean Springs, Mississippi, where "talk was musical. Clusters of people were forever talking with one another, telling stories, sharing experiences, observations, jokes, riddles, conundrums, and swapping lies." Young believes in the Kenyan proverb, "Talking with one another is loving one another." Because of his background, he "never outgrew the need for magic or the curative powers of language." Educated at the University of Michigan, Berkeley, and Stanford—where he was a Wallace E. Stegner Creative Writing Fellow—Young has worked as a free-lance musician and disc jockey, and has taught at Berkeley, Stanford, and the University of Washington. In 1982 he was named Distinguished Andrew Mellon Professor of Humanities at Rice University in Houston. In 1972 began editing with Ishmael Reed the *Yardbird Reader* and *Quilt Magazine.* Young has published four novels and two plays, in addition to four collections of poetry. Commenting on the power of poetry, Young said, "Word by word, line by line, season upon season, poetry keeps teaching me that the only time there is is now."

GLOSSARY OF LITERARY TERMS

Abstraction   A generic, broad label that describes a large category—such as happiness, freedom, or honor. See *concrete.*

Absurd, theater of the   Drama that points to the absurdity of the human condition, often employing nonrealistic, untraditional dramatic devices. "Conceived in perplexity and spiritual anguish, the theater of the absurd portrays not a series of connected incidents telling a story but a pattern of images presenting people as bewildered beings in an incomprehensible universe" (Hugh Holman).

Alexandrine   A twelve-syllable line made up of six iambic feet (iambic hexameter). Edmund Spenser used the alexandrine in his Spenserian stanza, which is composed of eight pentameter lines followed by an alexandrine. See *iamb.*

Allegory   A symbolic work in which characters, events, or settings represent moral qualities. The characters of an allegory are often *abstractions* personified. The meaning existing below the surface in an allegorical work may be religiously, morally, politically, or personally significant. Some famous allegories include Spenser's *The Faerie Queene* and Bunyan's *The Pilgrim's Progress.*

Alliteration   The repetition of the same sound at the beginning of words, as in "He Clasps the Crag with Crooked hands."

Allusion   A reference in a literary work to a historical or literary character, event, idea, or place outside the work. Allusion serves to tap indirectly into an association already existing in the reader's mind. Greek mythology has been a major source of allusion over the ages, and Biblical allusions also are frequent in English literature.

Ambiguity   A quality of certain words and phrases whereby the meaning is left unclear. Authors often use ambiguity deliberately to create multiple layers of meaning.

Anapest   Two unaccented syllables followed by an accented one, as in New RoCHELLE. The following lines from Percy Bysshe Shelley's "The Cloud" are anapestic: "Like a CHILD from the WOMB, like a GHOST from the TOMB,/ I aRISE and unBUILD it aGAIN."

Antagonist   The character or force that is the rival, opponent, or enemy of the principle character, or *protagonist,* in a work.

1599

Antithesis A playing off of opposites or a balancing of one term against another, as in the point/counterpoint statement, "Man proposes, God disposes." "Thesis" and "antithesis" in the original Greek mean "statement" and "counterstatement."

Antonym A word with the opposite or nearly the opposite meaning of another word. See *synonym*.

Apostrophe A dignified invocation to someone or something not present, often to a personified abstraction, like Liberty or Justice. Emily Dickinson employs apostrophe in her address to God: "Papa Above! / Regard a Mouse."

Archaic language Language that is no longer in common use. Unlike *obsolete language*, archaic words and phrases have survived but have an old-fashioned flavor. Used intentionally, archaisms can be useful in re-creating a past style.

Archetype An image, character, or event recurrent in the literature and life of diverse cultures, suggestive of universal patterns of experience. According to psychologist Carl Jung, archetypes link common human experiences. Jung held that within the human race exists a "collective unconscious" formed by the repeated experience of our ancestors. The collective unconscious is expressed in myths, religion, dreams, fantasies, and literature.

Assonance Repetition of similar internal vowel sounds of final syllables, as in *break/fade, mice/flight, told/woe*. See *consonance*.

Author biography criticism See *criticism*.

Autobiographical "I" The personal voice through which poets share their personal experiences and feelings. Confessional poets use the autobiographical "I" to make public their private, often painful, experiences and observations. Use of first person point of view in poetry is not always the autobiographical "I," particularly when the "I" is more a *persona* speaking, rather than the poet personally. See *confessional poetry, point of view*, and *speaker*.

Ballad A songlike, narrative poem traditionally characterized by a recurring refrain and four-line stanzas rhyming *abcb*. Anonymous folk ballads were originally sung as the record of a notable exploit or calamity. From *balar*, "to dance," ballads are created both by individual composers and through communal activity. See *literary ballad*.

Blank verse Unrhymed iambic pentameter. Commonly used for long poems, blank verse has been employed by many poets over the ages from Marlowe to Wordsworth to Frost. Shakespeare used blank verse in most of his serious plays.

Byplay An action or gesture which takes place apart from the main action of the play, as in an aside, and which can prepare the audience for future conflict.

Caesura A pause or a break within a line of verse. From the Latin for "a cutting off," a caesura can occur at almost any point in the line, as the first four lines of Andrew Marvell's "To His Coy Mistress" demonstrate:

> Had we but world enough, ‖ and time
> This coyness, lady, ‖ were no crime.

We would sit down, ‖ and think which way
To walk, ‖ and pass our long love's day.

Caricature A comic distortion exaggerating key traits to make them ridiculous. From the Italian for "exaggeration," a caricature usually focuses on personal, physical qualities. Although caricature is most often associated with drawing, it can also refer to writing.

Carpe diem Latin for "seize the day," a poetic convention urging us to make use of the passing day, to live for the moment. This theme was common in sixteenth- and seventeenth-century love lyrics, as in Robert Herrick's lines, "Gather ye rosebuds while ye may / Old Time is still a-flying; / And this same flower that smiles today, / Tomorrow will be dying."

Character The representation of a person in a play, story, novel, or poem. A character who has a one-track personality, or who represents a stereotype, is often referred to as **flat.** A character who displays a realistically complex combination of traits—including mixed emotions, conflicting motivations, and divided loyalties—is often called **round.**

Characterization The way in which an author portrays a character to the reader. Characterization can occur through author exposition about a character as well as through the character's actions, speech, and thoughts. In drama a character's thoughts can be revealed through *soliloquy.*

Chorus A group of performers in ancient Greek drama that comments on the action through word, song, and dance. The chorus often moves the action forward, links acts, and foreshadows coming events. In Elizabethan drama, a single actor sometimes plays the chorus role, reciting the prologue and epilogue and commenting between acts.

Circumlocution Indirect, roundabout phrasing, such as calling a "home" a "primary residence." A *euphemism* can be a form of circumlocution.

Cliché A term that has lost its freshness due to overuse, such as "strong as an ox," "tip of the iceberg," and "American as apple pie." Overused situations and plots in written works also can be regarded as clichés.

Climax The highest point of interest or intensity in a literary work, reached after a series of preparatory steps. The climax is usually the point in a story where the fortunes of the protagonist take an important turn.

Closure A satisfying conclusion or sense of completion at the end of a work.

Comedy A form of drama in which there is a happy ending, the protagonist's situation changes for the better, and the strength of the community is reaffirmed. **High comedy,** which appeals to the intellect, focuses on the inconsistencies and incongruities of human nature. **Low comedy** is less serious, tending more toward physical and boisterous humor. See *comedy of manners, farce,* and *romantic comedy.*

Comedy of manners A comedy that satirizes the stylized fashions and manners of sophisticated society. This type of comedy is characterized by jabs at convention and witty dialogue, or *repartee.* Some typical comedies of manners include Oliver Goldsmith's *She Stoops to Conquer,* Oscar Wilde's *The Importance of Being Earnest,* and Philip Barry's *The Philadelphia Story.* See *comedy.*

Comic relief A moment of humor in a serious work. Comic relief provides a temporary break from emotional intensity and often, paradoxically, heightens the seriousness of the story. Shakespeare, for example, employed comic relief in the gravedigger scene in *Hamlet* (Act 5, Scene 1).

Comic repetition   A character's mocking imitation of another character's remarks.

Conceit   An extended, elaborate and often far-fetched analogy. Love poems of earlier centuries often featured conceits, comparing the subject of the poem extensively and elaborately to some object, such as a rose, a garden, or a ship.

Concrete   Vivid, graphic images that appeal strongly to the senses, as opposed to generalized *abstractions.*

Concrete poetry   Poems that use the physical arrangement of words on a page to mirror meaning (for example, a poem about a bell that is bell-shaped). Concrete poetry takes advantage of the visible shapes of letters and words to create a picture.

Confessional poetry   Poetry that employs the *autobiographical "I"* as the poem's speaker for an often painful, public display of personal, private matters. Confessional poets such as Anne Sexton, John Berryman, and Sylvia Plath came into the forefront during the 1960s and 1970s. Although confessional poetry is most often associated with contemporary poets, poets over the ages, such as the ancient Greek poet Sappho, for instance, have employed confessional techniques.

Conflict   An essential element of a literary work that creates interest and suspense and leads to resolution. Four different types of conflicts are the *protagonist's* struggle against: (1) nature, (2) another person (the *antagonist*), (3) society, or (4) himself or herself (in other words, a struggle between two contradictory elements within one person).

Connotation   The associations and attitudes called up by a word, as opposed to its *denotation* or straight, literal definition. For instance, the words "aroma" and "odor" both denote a "scent," but each word has a different connotation: "aroma" connotes a rich, pleasing scent, whereas "odor" suggests something pungent and foul-smelling.

Consonance   Repetition of similar sounds in the final consonants of words, as in *torn/burn, add/read, heaven/given.* See *assonance.*

Context   The information surrounding a particular word or expression that often determines its meaning.

Conventional symbol   A symbol with familiar, agreed-upon uses. For example, a rose conventionally symbolizes love.

Counterpoint   A contrasting but parallel element or statement. See *antithesis.*

Couplet   Two rhymed lines of verse. If set aside or self-contained, the two rhymed lines are called a *closed couplet.*

Criticism   The study, analysis, and evaluation of works of art. Traditionally, literary critics employed **author biography criticism**, looking for the meaning of the work by examining the writer's background and historical milieu. The **New Critics** of the 1940s and 1950s moved away from this stress on context. Instead, they paid close attention to the intrinsic features of a work (such as imagery, symbolism, and point of view) and to how these contribute to meaning. Any such critical position focusing on the form and technique of a work is termed **formalist criticism**. In recent decades, many critics have once again widened their scope to consider the historical, personal, or sociological context of literary works.

Contemporary critics vary greatly in their approaches to literature. **Feminist criticism** examines representations of the feminine in all literature and often focuses on works written by women. **Marxist criticism** examines the political content of a work; it often examines how works either depict or contribute to the power struggle between the classes. **Language-centered criticism** looks closely at the characteristic or changing patterns of language in a work. **Reader response criticism** focuses on how the reader contributes to the meaning of a text. **Psychoanalytic criticism** traces in literary works the typical patterns of human development and consciousness first theorized by psychoanalysts such as Freud and Jung. **Myth criticism** examines the archetypal echoes and recurrent mythical allusions or themes in literary works.

Cumulative repetition See *repetition*.

Dactyl One stressed syllable followed by two unstressed syllables, as in BALtimore.

Dark humor A paradoxical humor that often uses irony to find a comic angle on catastrophe, illness, and other events that usually defeat people.

Denotation The literal definition of a word; its stripped-down meaning devoid of *connotation*.

Dénouement French for "untying," the plot's unraveling, clarification, or solution. The term implies an ingenious, satisfying outcome of the main dilemma, as well as an explanation of the minor plot complications.

Deus ex machina Latin for "god from a machine." In the ancient Greek theater a contraption lowered a god or goddess onto the stage to intervene in the action and to work a last-minute solution. Thus, the phrase refers to any device, character, or event introduced suddenly to resolve a conflict in a literary work.

Dialects The regional variations of a common language that are still mutually intelligible, although some actually border on becoming separate languages.

Dialectic The playing off of opposing forces or points of view.

Dialogue Conversation between two or more people. In a literary work, dialogue advances plot and reveals characterization and can provide relief from expository or descriptive passages. See *monologue*.

Diction The writer's choice and use of words.

Didacticism In a literary work, the presentation of ideas intended to instruct or improve the reader.

Dramatic irony Audience awareness of the meaning of words or actions unknown to one or more characters. Dramatic irony occurs when we are "in on" something that a character is not. In *Oedipus Rex* the readers or viewers know that Oedipus has killed his father and married his mother, a situation Oepidus remains unaware of until the last scene.

Dramatic monologue A lengthy first-person speech which enlightens the reader about the setting, the speaker's identity, and the dramatic situation.

Elegy A poem of mourning and lamentation. Elegies are most often sustained, formal poems with a meditative, solemn mood. Notable examples include John Milton's "Lycidas," Walt Whitman's "When Lilacs Last in the Dooryard Bloom'd," and John Berryman's "Formal Elegy."

Elizabethan Age The English literary period named after Queen Elizabeth and lasting from 1558 until 1642, the year of the closing of the theaters. This "golden age" saw such literary figures as Shakespeare develop the beginnings of modern drama and an outburst of lyric poetry. Other notable names of the period include Sidney, Spenser, Marlowe, Jonson, and Donne.

Empathy Identifying deeply with the experience, situation, feelings, or motives of another.

End rhyme A rhyme in which the last words of two or more lines of poetry rhyme with one another. See *internal rhyme*.

End-stopped line A line of poetry that ends with a period, colon, or semicolon. See *enjambment*.

Enjambment The continuation of a sentence in a poem so that it spills over from one line to the next. See *end-stopped line*.

Epic poem A long narrative poem that speaks to the listener in an elevated style and embodies the central values of a civilization. The traditional epic recorded the adventures of a hero and focused on a high point in history. Some important epics are Homer's *Iliad* and *Odyssey*, the Old English *Beowulf*, the Spanish *El Cid*, and Virgil's *Aeneid*. See *lyric poem*.

Epigram A concise, cleverly worded remark making a pointed, witty statement. From the Greek for "inscription," an epigram often contains an antithesis, as in "Man proposes, God disposes."

Epiphany A sudden flash of intuitive understanding in which the true meaning of things and events is revealed. The term was coined by James Joyce, and epiphanies appear at the end of many of his stories, including "Araby."

Euphemism From the Greek for "good saying," the substitution of an indirect statement for a direct statement, often with the intention of sounding less offensive or more refined. Examples of euphemisms are calling a "janitor" a "sanitation engineer" or calling "death" "passing away."

Existentialism A twentieth-century philosophy that denies the existence of a transcendent meaning to life and the universe and places the burden of justifying existence on individual human beings. Playwrights like Beckett, Ionesco, and Sartre helped to develop existentialism, which then influenced their drama (frequently called the *theater of the absurd*); Albert Camus called Kafka an existentialist novelist.

Explication The line-by-line explanation of a literary text. Explication differs from interpretation in that it usually refers to a literal, step-by-step scrutiny of the language of a work, as opposed to a broader, more subjective look at its overall significance.

Exposition The part of a play or story that established setting and situation and that often introduces important characters and themes.

Extended (or sustained) metaphor   A metaphor traced throughout a work.

External evidence   Evidence outside a piece of literature itself, examined in an attempt to understand a work's meaning. Characteristic themes in the author's other works or information found in the author's letters or interviews are common forms of external evidence.

Farce   An exaggerated kind of low comedy that derives its humor through broad wit, improbable situations, and rambunctious horseplay. See *comedy*.

Feminine (or double) rhyme   Two-syllable rhyme, with the first syllable stressed and the second unstressed, as in *ocean/motion, started/parted*. See *masculine rhyme*.

Feminist criticism   See *criticism*.

Figurative language   Language in which the writer means something more than what is literally stated. See *allegory, hyperbole, metaphor*, and *simile*.

Flashback   A narrative structure whereby the chronological order between two or more scenes is reversed. A flashback presents a scene which took place before the time in which the story is taking place.

Foil   A character that, by contrast, underscores or enhances the distinctive characteristics of another.

Folklore   Traditional stories reflecting the customs and beliefs of a particular culture. Folklore can include supersitions, proverbs, myths, legends, riddles, charms, spells, omens, ballads, nursery rhymes, and songs.

Folk speech   The colloquial speech particular to a certain group.

Foot   A segment of verse composed of stressed and unstressed syllables. For different types of metric feet, see *anapest, dactyl, iamb, spondee*, and *trochee*.

Foreshadowing   Hints in a literary work concerning a future development. Foreshadowing can be achieved through establishment of a certain mood or atmosphere in the setting or through more concrete means such as objects, narration, or a character's speech or traits.

Formalist criticism   See *criticism*.

Frame story   A narrative which frames the main series of events of a story, and tends to be separated either in space or time, or both, from that main story.

Free verse   Poetry with no strong, regular pattern of meter or rhyme.

Genre   From the Latin *genus* meaning "type" or "kind," a category of literature defined by form, technique, or subject matter. Fiction, poetry, and drama are the three major genres; subgenres include the novel, the short story, the lyric, the epic, tragedy, and comedy.

Ghazal   A traditional Persian (Iranian) poetry form made up of sequences of five to fifteen related couplets.

Grotesque   Literature or art characterized by bizarre, fantastic, or ominous characters or events.

Haiku   A traditional Japanese poetry form of three lines of five, seven, and five syllables each. Although haiku appears starkly simplistic, it offers serious, profound insight into a captured moment in time, often drawing on associations from nature's seasons, elements, and animals. Henry David

Thoreau, Ezra Pound, Robert Bly, and Gary Snyder are a few of the western writers who have written short pieces aimed at capturing the spirit of haiku. See *tanka*.

Half-rhymes   Words that do not rhyme but distantly sound alike.

High comedy   See *comedy*.

Hubris   The overreaching pride of humans that leads to their tragic downfall. The word *hubris* comes from the Greek for "insolence" or "outrage." A *tragic flaw* of protagonists, *hubris* makes them forget their human limitations and makes them challenge the gods. Oedipus, for example, challenged the gods by believing he could escape their prophecy.

Hyperbole   A figure of speech using extreme exaggeration. From the Greek for "excess," hyperbole is often expressed as a simile, as in "he's as strong as an ox."

Iamb   A two-syllable foot with the stress on the last syllable, as in DeTROIT. Over the centuries, iambic meter with four or five beats to the line (iambic tetrameter and iambic pentameter) has become the most common meter in English-language poetry.

Idiom   The characteristic language style of a person or group of people. From the Greek for "peculiarity," idiom can refer to a regional speech or dialect or to the specialized vocabulary or jargon of a group such as doctors, lawyers, or scientists.

Image   A literal or concrete detail that speaks to the physical senses of sight, hearing, smell, taste, or touch. See *concrete*.

Incongruity   The quality of being composed of inconsistent, discordant parts. The *metaphysical poets* focused on incongruity in their works. See *irony, paradox,* and *polarity*.

Interlude   A short humorous play or performance presented between the acts of a play.

Internal rhyme   A rhyme within a line of poetry. See *end rhyme*.

Interpretation   Moving beyond line-by-line *explication* of a text and examining its major themes in order to see its larger human significance.

Intruding author   A narrative device whereby the author, or a persona representing the author, interrupts the story and addresses the reader directly, offering asides, philosophical reflections, or comments upon the plot of the story. The reader thus becomes aware of the author's presence outside the story.

Inversion   The reversal of normal word order in a sentence or the reversal of the rhythmic stress in a poem.

Irony   An effect produced when there is a discrepancy between two levels of meaning. **Irony of situation** refers to a contrast between what we expect to happen and what really happens. **Verbal irony** refers to a deliberate contrast between what is said and what is meant. See *dramatic irony, paradox,* and *hyperbole*.

Language-centered criticism   See *criticism*.

Literary ballad   A conscious imitation of a traditional *ballad*.

Low comedy   See *comedy*.

Lyric poem   A brief, compressed poem. See *epic*.

Malaproprism   An often humorous misuse of a word. The term is derived from the character Mrs. Malaprop, in Sheridan's play *The Rivals,* who voiced such expressions as "illiterate him . . . from your memory."

Marxist criticism   See *criticism.*

Masculine (or single) rhyme   A rhyme in which the final syllables of two or more words are accented and rhyme, such as *high/sky, leave/grieve, renown/gown.* See *feminine rhyme.*

Melodrama   A play or story characterized by an overly dramatic, sensationalized romantic plot. Traditional melodramas present good and evil stock characters and have a happy ending, although tragedies that use similar techniques are also sometimes called melodramatic.

Metaphor   A comparison between two essentially unlike things. With metaphor, the speaker treats one thing as if it were another, without the use of "like" or "as," as in these Emily Dickinson lines: "Hope is the thing with feathers / That perches in the soul." See *extended metaphor, organizing metaphor,* and *simile.*

Metaphysical poets   Poets of the seventeenth century whose work is noted for its complex imagery, demanding form, and abundant use of *incongruity, paradox* and *irony.* Famous metaphysical poets include John Donne, Andrew Marvell, and George Herbert.

Meter   An underlying regular beat in a poem. **Trimeter** is meter with three stressed syllables to the line, **tetrameter** has four stressed syllables, **pentameter** has five, and **hexameter** has six.

Metonymy   A figure of speech in which a term closely related to something serves as its substitute. For instance, the word "sword" means "military career" in the line "He abandoned the sword." See *synechdoche.*

Minimalism   A contemporary style of writing that tries to eliminate all rhetoric and emotion or at least to reduce these elements to bare essentials. Minimalist writers include Anne Beattie and Raymond Carver.

Modernism   A movement of the early twentieth century against the conventions of Romantic literary representation. In their search for new modes of expression, the modernists rejected the flowery and artificial language of Victorian literature and began using techniques such as *stream of consciousness* in fiction and *free verse* in poetry. Famous modernists include James Joyce, Virginia Woolf, Ezra Pound, and T. S. Eliot.

Monologue   A speech made by one person. A monologue, since it is directed to one or more listeners, is less a private revelation of personal feelings than is a *soliloquy.*

Mood   The emotional or psychological cast of a work, generally produced by literary devices such as *tone, imagery,* and *setting.*

Morality play   A play that dramatizes personified abstractions, such as Shame, Mercy, and Conscience, in order to teach a lesson. Originating in the late fourteenth century, these *didactic* dramas lost their popularity in the *Elizabethan Age.* See *allegory.*

Myth criticism   See *criticism.*

Narrator   The person who relates the story. See *point of view, reflector,* and *speaker.*

Naturalism A literary movement in the late nineteenth and early twentieth centuries characterized by frank, unidealized portrayals of life's raw elements. Naturalism strives toward objective portrayal, often resulting in a neutral portrayal of nature and a recognition of humanity's physical and emotional needs. Some notable writers of this period include John Steinbeck, Stephen Crane, and Guy de Maupassant.

Neoclassicism The eighteenth-century revival of interest in classical Greek and Roman works. Neoclassical writers believed that sound judgment should guide and restrain the poetic imagination. They prized order, concentration, economy, logic, restrained emotion, correctness, and decorum. Notable writers of this period include Milton, Pope, and Johnson.

New critics See *criticism*.

Novel A work of narrative prose fiction, generally considerably longer and more complex than a short story, with a central character or group of characters whose experiences, actions, and feelings make up the plot.

Novella A pointed story shorter than a full-length novel but longer than a traditional short story.

Obsolete language Words and phrases that are no longer in use. See *archaic language*.

Octave An eight-line stanza.

Ode An elaborately crafted, stately poem fit for solemn subjects.

Onomatopoeia The use of a word that sounds like its meaning, such as *pop, hiss,* or *buzz.*

Open form A poetic form characterized by a lack of regular rhyme, meter, line length, or stanza form.

Oral history A cultural tradition of passing spoken stories from one generation to the next, often combining myth, history, and current events.

Organizing (or controlling) metaphor A single extended metaphor that gives shape to a poem as a whole.

Ottava rima From the Italian for "eighth rhyme," a finely crafted stanza consisting of eight iambic pentameter lines with the rhyme pattern *abababcc.*

Pantomime Acting that relies solely on gestures rather than words to communicate a story.

Paradox An apparent contradiction that, on second thought, illuminates a truth. See *incongruity, irony,* and *polarity.*

Parallelism The repetition of similar or identical structures within phrases or sentences of prose or poetry.

Paraphrase Stating someone else's ideas in your own words.

Para-rhyme See *slant rhyme.*

Parody A humorous, mocking imitation of a serious piece.

Pastoral A poetic tradition offering harried city dwellers a nostalgic vision of the idealized simplicity and leisure of country life. Pastorals were first written by the Greeks and continue to be written today. Traditional pastorals use courtly language to refer to the shepherds and the countryside. In modern terms, pastoral often means any poem about rural people and rural settings.

Pathos   A quality in literature or art that arouses pity, sympathy, tenderness, or sorrow. From the Greek for "suffering" and "passion," pathos usually applies to a helpless character who suffers passively.

Peripety   A sudden reversal of fortune for a protagonist brought on by an unexpected discovery. From the Greek for "to change suddenly."

Persona   See *speaker*.

Personification   Figurative language that endows something nonhuman with human qualities, as in "the trees whispered in the wind."

Petrarchan sonnet   See *sonnet*.

Plot   The pattern of events in a story. See *subplot*.

Poetic diction   Language more elevated and refined than ordinary speech.

Point of view   The angle from which a story is told. In **first-person** point of view, one of the characters narrates the story. In **third-person omniscient** point of view, the writer may write as an "all-seeing" author, revealing actions and mental activities of the characters. In **third-person limited** point of view, the writer reveals the actions and thoughts of only some of the characters. In **third-person objective,** the writer offers little or no comment on the action.

Polarity   The play of two opposites on a spectrum. See *incongruity, irony,* and *paradox*.

Problem play   A play that deals with a social problem or issue as confronted by the protagonist.

Prose poem   A poem written with the margins justified like prose.

Protagonist   The leading or principle figure in a work. The protagonist and the antagonist, the second most important character, are generally rivals, enemies, or foils. See *antagonist*.

Psychoanalytical criticism   See *criticism*.

Pun   A type of *word play*, sometimes on the similar sense or sound of two words and sometimes on different meanings of the same word.

Quatrain   A four-line poetic stanza.

Reader response criticism   See *criticism*.

Realism   A literary movement which lasted from roughly the mid-nineteenth century to the early twentieth century in America, England, and France. Realism is characterized by the attempt to truthfully depict the lives of ordinary men and women through the accurate description of details and psychologically realistic characters. Some famous writers of the period include Henrik Ibsen, Thomas Hardy, and Honoré de Balzac.

Recurrence   The reappearance of themes or key elements that serves to echo issues and concerns introduced earlier.

Reflector   A person through whom the reader experiences the story. Although this is often the narrator, it can also be a character within the story if important information is communicated through his or her perceptions or thoughts.

Refrain   The same line (or group of lines) repeated at intervals in a poem.

Reiteration   Purposeful, insistent repetition in poetry or prose that reinforces a basic point.

Repartee   A quick exchange of pointed, witty remarks.

Repetition Recurrence of the same word or phrase used to highlight or emphasize something in a poem or story. Poets often use purposeful cumulative repetition for a rhythmic, building effect.

Revenge tragedy A form of tragedy that traditionally begins with a ghost of a murdered victim clamoring for revenge and eventually finding a living person to carry out that revenge. Shakespeare's *Hamlet* is a famous revenge tragedy.

Rhetoric The study of the content, structure, and style of literature, with particular attention paid to the effective or persuasive use of language.

Rhyme Echo effect produced when a writer repeats the same sounds at the ends of words. See *end rhyme, feminine rhyme, half-rhyme, internal rhyme, masculine rhyme, sight rhyme, slant rhyme,* and *triple rhyme.*

Romantic comedy A type of *comedy* focusing on love as a chief element of the plot. Romantic comedies usually culminate in easy reconciliations and result in a happy ending.

Romanticism An artistic revolt of the late eighteenth and early nineteenth centuries against the traditional, formal, and orderly *Neoclassicism.* Whereas Neoclassicism stressed the "order in beauty," Romanticism stresses the "strangeness in beauty" (Walter Pater). The writers of this time dropped conventional poetic diction and forms in favor of freer forms and bolder language, and explored nature, "organic unity," mysticism, the grotesque, and emotional psychology in their art. Some famous writers of this period include Blake, Keats, and Shelley.

Sarcasm A bitter or cutting remark that moves beyond verbal irony.

Satire An ironic, witty literary work that criticizes human misconduct and ridicules stupidity, vice, and folly. Offenders are measured against an implied standard of humane behavior.

Scansion A system for charting the underlying beat, or meter, of a literary work.

Sentimentality An oversimplified, emotional quality of a literary work.

Sestet A six-line poetic stanza.

Setting The location and time in which the action of a story takes place.

Shakespearean sonnet See *sonnet.*

Sight rhyme Words that coincide in spelling but not in sound, like *come* and *home.*

Simile A comparison between two essentially unlike things, using "as" or "like" or "as if": "My love is like a red, red rose." Unlike the implied comparison of a *metaphor,* a simile says outright that something is like something else.

Slang Colloquial, informal language not acceptable for highly formal usage.

Slant (or para-) rhyme The near rhyming of words that distantly sound alike. See *assonance* and *consonance.*

Soliloquy A solo speech a character makes in a drama revealing his or her feelings and inner conflicts. During a soliloquy, a character usually stands alone on stage, talking without addressing another character. See *monologue.*

Sonnet An elaborately crafted fourteen-line poem in iambic pentameter. The

Petrarchan sonnet contains an eight-line stanza, or octave, with an *abbaabba* rhyme scheme, followed by a sestet (six-line stanza) of *cdcdee* or *cdecde*. The octave often raises a question or states a predicament or proposition that is answered in the sestet. The **Shakespearean sonnet** generally is arranged as three quatrains (four-line stanzas) and a couplet (two lines), with the typical rhyme scheme of *abab/cdcd/efef/gg*. The **Spenserian sonnet** uses three quatrains and a couplet like the Shakespearean sonnet but employs a linking rhyme scheme more similar to the Petrarchan sonnet: *abab/bcbc/cdcd/ee*. Among the famous sonneteers in England and America have been Sidney, Wordsworth, Auden, Longfellow, e. e. cummings, and John Berryman. See *sonnet sequence.*

Sonnet sequence   A group of sonnets thematically connected. One of the most famous sonnet sequences (or "cycles") is Elizabeth Barrett Browning's *Sonnets from the Portuguese,* which explores her love for Robert Browning.

Speaker   The voice speaking in a poem or story, as distinct from the author as a person. Also called "persona."

Spenserian sonnet   See *sonnet.*

Spenserian stanza   A nine-line stanza used by Edmund Spenser. It follows the rhyming pattern *ababbcbcc;* the first eight lines are pentameter and the last is an *alexandrine* (iambic with six stresses).

Spondee   A metrical foot of two stressed syllables, as in HEARTBREAK or HONG KONG.

Sprung rhythm   An irregular rhythmic pattern developed by Gerard Manley Hopkins in which stressed syllables are followed by a varying number of unstressed syllables.

Stanza   A grouping of lines that traditionally marks the completion of a metrical pattern within a poem. *Couplets, tercets, quatrains, sestets,* and *octaves* are all types of stanzas. In *free verse* or *open form* poetry, stanza breaks mark shifts in meaning or theme.

Stress   An accent that makes one syllable stand out from the others in a word or phrase.

Stream of consciousness   A narrative technique that reflects the mental world of a shifting sequence of sensations, thought, and feelings—a kaleidoscopic mix of fleeting images, bodily sensations, memories, half-finished trains of thought.

Stock character   A conventional character; a stereotype. Stock characters people literary works as the allegorical personifications in ancient morality plays to immediately recognizable characters in modern drama, such as the meddling in-laws or the studious "nerd."

Style   An author's unmistakable personal choice of words, sentence construction, diction, imagery, tone, and ideas.

Subplot   Story lines or conflicts parallel to the main plot that reinforce a work's central theme. See *plot.*

Symbol   An object or action that has acquired a meaning beyond itself. Symbols are often used to articulate the themes of a literary work. See *conventional symbol.*

Synechdoche A figure of speech that uses the part to stand for the whole, or the whole to stand for the part: "wheels" to mean "car" and "hired hands" to mean "hired people." See *metonymy*.

Synonym A word that has the same or nearly the same meaning as another word. See *antonym*.

Tanka A Japanese poetic form that, like *haiku*, fixes a moment in time, but is five lines long: three lines of five, seven, and five syllables each and two lines of seven syllables.

Tercet A three-line stanza.

Theater of the absurd See *absurd, theater of the*.

Theme A recurring, unifying subject, idea, or motif; the primary idea being explored or general statement being made by a literary work.

Thesis statement A concise, memorable statement of what a written work is attempting to prove. The thesis statement often appears toward the beginning of the work but can also appear at the end. A thesis statement can be explicit, meaning it is stated outright, or implicit, meaning the work's theme is implied.

Tone The implied attitude of a writer toward the subject, material, and reader.

Tragedy A work that dramatizes traditional stories about lethal conflicts and fateful choices. The traditional tragedy recounts the fall of heroes or persons of high degree, as in the fall of a king in Sophocles' *Oedipus Rex* and Shakespeare's *Macbeth*. See *comedy* and *revenge tragedy*.

Tragic flaw A character flaw in a tragic hero that leads to his or her downfall. This flaw can be anything from anger or self-righteousness to indecision or impatience. See *hubris*.

Tragicomedy A mixed genre in which the tragic and comedic elements contend. A tragicomedy, for instance, can employ a tragic plot but end happily, like a comedy.

Transition A link that smoothly moves the reader from one stanza, paragraph, or idea to the next.

Triple rhyme Rhyme in which the rhyming stressed syllable is followed by two unstressed syllables, as in *moralities/realities* or *meticulous/ridiculous*.

Trochee A metrical rhythm with the stress on the first syllable, as in this example from Coleridge: "TROchee|TRIPS from|LONG to|SHORT."

Understatement Lack of emphasis on the undercurrents or implications of what is being talked about. See *tone*.

Vignette A sketch or brief narrative that concisely captures a moment in time. It may be a separate whole or a portion of a larger work.

Villanelle A nineteen-line poetic form employing only two rhymes and repeating two lines at various intervals. Line 1 is repeated at lines 6, 12, and 18; line 3 at lines 9, 15, and 19. The first and third lines return as a rhymed couplet at the end. These intermeshing rhymes link five tercets rhymed *aba*. The poem ends with a quatrain rhymed *abaa*.

Word play Witty or clever use of words. See *pun*.

ACKNOWLEDGMENTS

FICTION

Chinua Achebe. "Why the Turtle's Shell Is Not Smooth" from *Things Fall Apart*. Copyright © 1959 by Chinua Achebe. Reprinted by permission of William Heinemann Limited.

Sherwood Anderson. "Paper Pills," from *Winesburg, Ohio* by Sherwood Anderson, Introduction, Malcolm Cowley. Copyright 1919 by B. W. Huebsch. Copyright 1947 by Eleanor Copenhaver Anderson. Used by permission of Viking Penguin, a division of Penguin Books USA Inc.

Toni Cade Bambara. "The Lesson." From *Gorilla, My Love* by Toni Cade Bambara. Copyright © 1972 by Toni Cade Bambara. Reprinted by permission of Random House, Inc.

Donald Barthelme. "The Balloon" from *Unspeakable Practices, Unnatural Acts*. Copyright 1968 by Donald Barthelme, reprinted with the permission of Wylie, Aitken & Stone, Inc.

Ann Beattie. "Shifting." From *Secrets and Surprises* by Ann Beattie. Copyright © 1976, 1977, 1978 by Ann Beattie. Reprinted by permission of Random House, Inc.

Ray Bradbury. "There Will Come Soft Rains." Reprinted by permission of Don Congdon Associates, Inc. Copyright 1950, renewed © 1977 by Ray Bradbury. Originally published in *Collier's* Magazine. Sara Teasdale poem "There Will Come Soft Rains" reprinted with permission of Macmillan Publishing Company from *Collected Poems of Sara Teasdale*. Copyright 1920 by Macmillan Publishing Company, renewed 1948 by Mamie T. Wheless.

Raymond Carver. "The Third Thing That Killed My Father Off" from *Furious Seasons* (in which it appeared entitled "Dummy"), copyright © 1977 by Raymond Carver. Reprinted by permission of Capra Press, Santa Barbara.

John Cheever. "The Enormous Radio." From *The Stories of John Cheever* by John Cheever. Copyright 1947 by John Cheever. Reprinted by permission of Alfred A. Knopf, Inc.

Anton Chekhov. "Vanka" by Anton Chekhov and translated by Avrahm Yarmolinsky, from *The Portable Chekhov* by Avrahm Yarmolinsky, editor. Copyright 1947, 1968 by Viking Penguin Inc. Renewed copyright © 1975 by Avrahm Yarmolinsky. Used by permission of Viking Penguin, a division of Penguin Books USA Inc.

Rick DeMarinis. Excerpt from *The Coming Triumph of the Free World* by Rick DeMarinis. Copyright © 1988 by Rick DeMarinis. Used by permission of Viking Penguin, a division of Penguin Books USA Inc.

Ralph Ellison. "Mister Toussan," *New Masses, 41* (November 4, 1941.) Reprinted by permission of the William Morris Agency, Inc.

William Faulkner. "A Rose for Emily." From *Collected Stories of William Faulkner* by William Faulkner. Copyright 1930 and renewed 1958 by William Faulkner. Reprinted by permission of Random House, Inc.

Ernst Fisher. "'The Country Doctor' and Ideology." From "Kafka-Konferenz" in *Franz Kafka aus Prager Sicht 1963* (Prague, 1965) pp. 157–168.

Gabriel García Márquez. "The Handsomest Drowned Man in the World" from *Leaf Storm and Other Stories* by Gabriel García Márquez, translated by Gregory Rabassa. English translation © 1970 by Gabriel García Márquez. Reprinted by permission of HarperCollins Publishers.

Richard Giannone. "The Mystery of Love." Excerpted from *Flannery O'Connor and the Mystery of Love* by Richard Giannone, © 1989. Reprinted by permission of the University of Illinois Press.

Ernest Hemingway. "Hills Like White Elephants." Reprinted with permission of Charles Scribner's Sons, an imprint of Macmillan Publishing Company, from *Men Without Women* by

1613

INDEX OF AUTHORS, TITLES, AND FIRST LINES

INDEX OF LITERARY AND RHETORICAL TERMS